McGRAW-HILL
ENCYCLOPEDIA OF
SCIENCE &
TECHNOLOGY

3

BIO-CHA

McGRAW-HILL
ENCYCLOPEDIA OF
SCIENCE &
TECHNOLOGY

3

BIO-CHA

10th Edition

An international reference work in twenty volumes including an index

McGraw-Hill

New York   Chicago   San Francisco   Lisbon   London   Madrid   Mexico City
Milan   New Delhi   San Juan   Seoul   Singapore   Sydney   Toronto

The **McGraw·Hill** Companies

On the front cover

Haleakala silversword (*Argyroxiphium sandwicense*), Haleakala National Park,
Maui, Hawaii. (*Photo: Mindy S. Phillips*)

Library of Congress Cataloging-in-Publication Data

McGraw-Hill encyclopedia of science & technology—10th ed.
     p.   cm.
   Includes bibliographical references and index.
   ISBN 978-0-07-144143-8 (alk. paper)
    1. Science—Encyclopedias.   2. Technology—Encyclopedias.
    I. Title: Encyclopedia of science & technology.
    II. Title: McGraw-Hill encyclopedia of science and technology.
Q121.M3   2007
503—dc22   2007006137

13-digit ISBN: 978-0-07-144143-8 (set)

10-digit ISBN: 0-07-144143-3 (set)

McGraw-Hill

*A Division of The **McGraw·Hill** Companies*

This book set was printed on acid-free paper.

*It was set in Garamond Book and Neue Helvetica Black Condensed
by Aptara, Falls Church, Virginia. The art was prepared by Aptara.
The book was printed and bound by R. R. Donnelley, Willard, Ohio.*

Organization of the Encyclopedia

The *McGraw-Hill Encyclopedia of Science & Technology* presents pertinent information in every field of modern science and technology. The 7100 articles are arranged alphabetically in the 19 text volumes. The range of article titles included in each volume is indicated on the spine and front cover (for example, volume 1 contains articles with titles starting with "Aar" up to "Ano"). Thus the reader may quickly locate an article by its title. The 20th volume contains the indexes and ancillary materials.

Broad survey articles are available for each of the disciplines covered; even readers with little prior knowledge of that discipline will find the basic concepts covered in these articles. From the survey article, the reader may proceed to more specialized articles using the cross-referencing system. These cross references are set in small capital letters for emphasis and are inserted at the relevant points in the text. For example, in a survey article such as **Digital computer**, the reader is directed to numerous other articles such as COMPUTER PERIPHERAL DEVICES, COMPUTER STORAGE TECHNOLOGY, MICROPROCESSOR, and PROGRAMMING LANGUAGES. The references may lead to subjects that have not occurred to the reader. The article **Solvent** has such diverse cross references as COORDINATION CHEMISTRY, HALOGENATED HYDROCARBON, INDUSTRIAL HEALTH AND SAFETY, and WATER POLLUTION. The cross references not only lead to articles of greater specialization but also help illuminate the context of the article and the broader connections among topics. This edition contains more than 60,000 cross references.

The pattern of proceeding from the general to the specific has been employed not only in the plan of the Encyclopedia but within the body of the articles. Each article begins with a definition of the subject, followed by sufficient background material to give a frame of reference and permit the reader to move into the detailed text of the article. Within the text are centered heads and two levels of sideheads that outline the article; they are intended to enhance understanding and can guide the user that prefers to read selectively the sections of a long article.

Alphabetization of article titles is by word, not by letter, with a comma providing a stop in occasional inverted article titles (so that subject matter can be grouped). Two examples of sequence are:

Air	**Earth, age of**
Air-cushion vehicle	**Earth, heat flow of**
Air mass	**Earth crust**
Air-traffic control	**Earth tides**
Aircraft fuel	**Earthquake**

Numerous illustrations, both line drawings and images, contribute to the utility, clarity, and interest of the text. Each illustration (as well as each table) is called out in boldface at its first mention in the text. This emphasis enables the reader to move from an illustration to the point in the text where the illustration is often discussed in detail.

To meet the needs of the Encyclopedia's broad readership, measurements are given in dual systems of units: The U.S. Customary System is used throughout the text along with equivalent measurements in the International System of Units. In particular cases, such as references to measurements in some illustrations or tables, conversion factors may be given for simplicity.

The contributor's full name appears at the end of an article section or an entire article. Each author is identified in an alphabetical Contributors list in volume 20, which cites the university, laboratory, business, or other organization with which the author is affiliated and the titles of the articles written by that contributor.

Most of the articles contain bibliographies citing useful sources. The bibliographies are placed at the ends of articles or occasionally at the ends of major sections in long articles. For additional bibliographies, the reader should refer to related articles as indicated by cross references.

Thus, the alphabetical arrangement of article titles, the text headings, the cross references, and the bibliographies permit the reader to research a particular topic by simply taking a volume from the shelf. However, the reader can also find information in the Encyclopedia by using the Analytical Index and the Topical Index in volume 20. The Analytical Index—over 500 pages in length—contains each important term, concept, and person mentioned throughout the 19 text volumes. It guides the reader to the volume numbers and page numbers concerned with a specific point. The reader wishing to consult everything in the Encyclopedia on a particular aspect of a subject will find that the Analytical Index is the best approach. A broader survey may be made through the Topical Index, which groups all article titles of the Encyclopedia under 90 general headings. For example, under "Atomic and molecular physics," 90 articles and listed, and under "Biochemistry," 147. The Topical Index thus enables the reader quickly to identify all articles in the Encyclopedia in a particular subject area.

The Study Guides in volume 20 provide highly structured outlines of major scientific disciplines and relate groups of Encyclopedia articles to each outline heading. By following a guide, the reader is led through pertinent Encyclopedia articles in a sequence that provides an overall grasp of the discipline.

A useful feature is the section "Scientific Notation" in volume 20. It clarifies usage of symbols, abbreviations, and nomenclature, and is especially valuable in making conversions between the International System, U.S. Customary, and metric measurements.

With the 10th edition, the editors are introducing a new feature to enhance the usefulness of the Encyclopedia: a companion Web site

http://MHEST.com

containing periodically updated collections of articles, graphics, and multimedia content pertaining to a timely theme, as well as selected updates of Encyclopedia articles as developments in science and technology dictate. We encourage readers to visit the site to benefit from this material.

McGRAW-HILL
ENCYCLOPEDIA OF
SCIENCE &
TECHNOLOGY

3

BIO-CHA

Bioacoustics, animal

The study of the role of sounds in the life history of animals. Almost all animals, from insects to large mammals, depend on sounds for their well-being and survival. Sounds are used by animals for a wide variety of reasons such as advertisement for mating, territory demarcation, group cohesion, prey location, infant-mother identification and contact, predator detection, alarm warning, and social communication. The field of animal bioacoustics can be subdivided into the acoustics of terrestrial animals and aquatic animals. Each field of study can be subdivided into (1) auditory capabilities and processes, (2) characteristics of sound emissions and mechanisms of sound production, and (3) the function and meaning of specific vocalizations.

Airborne and underwater acoustics. Airborne acoustics, associated with terrestrial animals, and underwater acoustics, associated with aquatic animals, have three primary differences. First, the amount of acoustic energy that is absorbed and transformed into heat is much higher in air than underwater. Acoustic transmission loss in both media has a geometric spreading loss component plus an absorption loss component. The geometric spreading loss is dependent on the propagation geometry and not the medium, whereas absorption loss is directly dependent on the medium. Absorption loss in both media increases with frequency, although it is much higher in air than underwater (**Fig. 1**). Therefore, the acoustic range of most aquatic animals is considerably larger than for terrestrial animals. Animals interested in long-range communications naturally use lower-frequency sounds. *See* SOUND ABSORPTION.

Second, airborne acoustics and underwater acoustics differ greatly in the respective values of the acoustic impedance, ρc, where ρ is the density of the medium and c is the sound velocity in that medium. The density of water is approximately 1000 times greater than that of air, and the sound velocity in

water is about 4.5 times greater than in air. Therefore, the acoustic impedance of water is approximately 3600 times greater than air. This difference in acoustic impedance has great ramifications on how sounds are produced and received in both media. For example, the middle-ear ossicular chain of terrestrial mammals serves as an impedance-matching transformer between the air in the external auditory meatus and the fluid in the cochlea, or inner ear. Such a chain is not needed for animals hearing underwater since the impedance of water is already matched to the fluid of the inner ear. The impedance difference issue becomes rather complex with regard to hearing and sound production in amphibians and pinnipeds, which must have good in-air and underwater hearing. *See* ACOUSTIC IMPEDANCE; AMPHIBIA; PINNIPEDS.

Third, between airborne acoustics and underwater acoustics there is a large pressure difference. Pressure underwater increases by 1 atmosphere for approximately every 10-m (34-ft) increase in depth. As animals in an underwater environment swim deeper, the pressure they experience will be considerably higher than at the surface and will cause the air in body cavities to compress and increase in density, which in turn affects the production and reception of

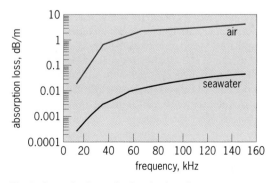

Fig. 1. Acoustic absorption loss in air and seawater as a function of frequency.

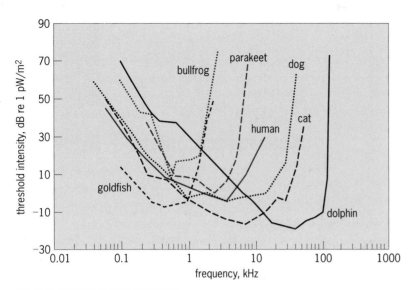

Fig. 2. Audiogram of different animals.

sounds. *See* ATMOSPHERIC ACOUSTICS; HYDROSTATICS; SOUND; UNDERWATER SOUND.

Auditory capabilities and processes. The structure and function of the ears of terrestrial mammals, including humans, are similar in nature; and although the ears of marine mammals are homologous to those of terrestrial mammals, there can be some distinct differences. For example, cetaceans do not have pinnas (external ears), and the auditory meatus in dolphins is but a fibrous tissue which is not capable of conducting sounds. Although there is a middle-ear ossicular chain, there is no direct connection between the tympanic membrane and the malleus. Sound enters into the dolphin's auditory system via the lower jaw and is probably conducted via fat channels directly into the cochlea. *See* CETACEA; EAR (VERTEBRATE).

Birds have a feather-covered auditory meatus and no pinnas. The feathers seem to minimize air turbulence and the subsequent flow noise associated with turbulent flow. The middle ear consists of a single major ossicle, the columella or stapes. The cochlea is elongated rather than curled in a shell. *See* ACOUSTIC NOISE; AVES.

Of the amphibians, the anurans, which include frogs and toads, have been studied the most. The outer and middle ears of anurans consist of a large tympanic membrane that is flush with the surface skin, and a columella which transmits sounds to the inner ear. The inner ear includes the basilar papilla and the amphibian papilla, operating independently in overlapping frequency ranges, with the amphibian papilla responding to sound from about 100 Hz to 1 kHz and the basilar papilla responding to frequencies of several hundred hertz to several kilohertz. The outer ear and middle ear of reptiles are similar to that of anurans except that the tympanic membrane may be recessed below the skin. *See* ANURA; REPTILIA.

The bodies of fishes are closely matched in impedance to water so that sounds can propagate

through the body to the three otolith organs—the sacculus, lagena, and utricle—which contain hair cells that are excited by acoustic energy. In most fishes, the sacculus is the primary auditory organ; however, in some fishes the utricle is the primary receptor of sounds. Most fishes have swim bladders that can be compressed and expanded when impinged upon by an acoustic wave, and the subsequent motions are coupled to the auditory organs. Fishes also possess lateral lines which can sense particle motions caused by low-frequency acoustic waves in the water. *See* OSTEICHTHYES; PISCES (ZOOLOGY); SWIM BLADDER.

The structure and location of ears of insects tend to vary considerably from species to species. In some, the ears are located on different appendages, while in other the ears may be located on the abdomen or on other parts of the body. *See* INSECTA.

The hearing sensitivity of animals is determined by careful laboratory psychophysical experiments in which the subjects are trained to respond to an acoustic stimulus of varying frequency and amplitude. The audiograms of some representative species of terrestrial mammals are shown in **Fig. 2**. The human audiogram is included to serve as a reference. Intensity rather than pressure of the acoustic stimulus must be used to compare the hearing sensitivity of terrestrial and aquatic animals, because of the difference in the acoustic impedances of the respective media. A unit of acoustic pressure conveys different amounts of energy in the two media. Acoustic intensity for a plane acoustic wave is defined as $p^2/\rho c$, where p is the sound pressure. Allowance must also be made for the difference in reference units, 20 micropascals for airborne acoustics and 1 μPa for underwater acoustics. Dolphins have the highest upper-frequency limit of hearing and have the most acute hearing sensitivity of all animals. Fishes tend to have a limited frequency range of hearing. The best sensitivities of the species represented in Fig. 2, except for the bullfrog, are within 20 dB of each other. *See* AUDIOMETRY; HEARING (HUMAN); PHONORECEPTION; PSYCHOACOUSTICS; PSYCHOPHYSICAL METHODS.

Sound emissions and production. Animals use a wide variety of different sounds in different frequency ranges and for different purposes. Sounds can be very short events lasting less than 100 microseconds for some echolocating dolphins or can be very long duration events lasting several hours for singing humpback whales. The sounds can be infrasonic, with frequencies below the human hearing capability, or ultrasonic, with frequencies above the human hearing range. Most terrestrial animals, including mammals, birds, amphibians, and reptiles, produce sounds that are within the human frequency range, or sonic sounds. Many aquatic animals, including fishes and marine mammals, also produce sounds that are in the sonic range; however, some marine mammals also produce sounds that can extend either beyond (ultrasonic) or below (infrasonic) the human frequency range. Dolphins can produce very high frequency echolocation sounds having frequency components up to 200 kHz. However, the animal that probably produces the highest-frequency sound is the snapping shrimp *Synalpheus parneomeris* (**Fig. 3**). The difference between the peak amplitude and the minimum amplitude in the spectrum of a snap is only 20 dB, an indication of a very broadband signal. *See* DECAPODA (CRUSTACEA); INFRASOUND; ULTRASONICS.

The mechanism of sound production in most animals is well known. Mammals and birds typically use their lungs as a source of air that is forced through a small orifice such as a larynx in mammals or a syrinx in birds. Amphibians such as frogs also use their lungs to force air through a larynx; however, the acoustic energy is coupled to an expandable air sac in the throats, which resonates to amplify sounds. For some frogs, the inflatable sac also strikes the substrate, causing seismic vibrations. Insects and crustaceans strike or rub certain appendages against other parts of their bodies. Some fishes produce sounds by inflating and compressing their swim bladder, causing vibrations in the water, while others may use the swim bladder as a resonator of sounds produced by stridulation between bony parts of their bodies.

The sound production mechanism of the odontocete, or toothed, whales baffled researchers for many years. In 1997, T. Cranford demonstrated that dolphins produce sounds with a pair of phonic lips previously called the monkey lips–dorsal bursae complex that are embedded in the nasal system. The simultaneous manipulation of these phonic lips and the production of echolocation clicks and whistles have been documented. Sperm whales probably use a similar set of phonic lips of the museau de singe, which are located in the forward portion of the animal's forehead. The exact mechanism of sound production by baleen whales is still a mystery.

Function and meaning of vocalizations. Careful studies in the field are often required in order to determine the function and meaning of specific vocalizations to conspecifics and to other species. Birds sing to mark territory and to attract potential mating partners. Some nonhuman primates use specific sounds as alarm calls indicating whether the threat is a predator bird or a mammal. Male frogs use their sound to attract females for mating. Dolphins and bats emit ultrasonic echolocation signals to detect and localize prey. Pinniped and dolphin mother-calf pairs use specific acoustic signals for identification purposes. Elephants use their infrasonic calls to maintain social contact and to coordinate family group movements. As sunset approaches in the savannahs of Africa, there is often a temperature inversion in the air mass where a layer of warm air is trapped by cooler denser air above. This inversion layer forms an acoustic duct to trap sounds and allows for good propagation of infrasonic sounds over tens of kilometers, making it possible for elephants in a family group to coordinate their movements over large distances. *See* ECHOLOCATION.

The meaning of many animal sounds still escapes

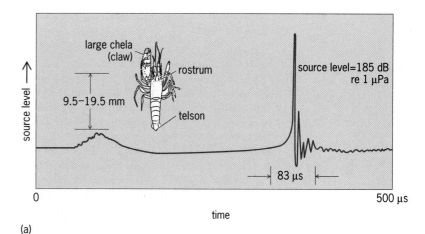

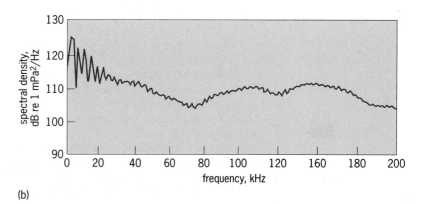

Fig. 3. Single snap of a snapping shrimp, *Synalpheus parneomeris* (shown in inset). (*a*) Waveform. Source level is sound pressure level 1 m (3.3 ft) from the source. (*b*) Spectrum.

human understanding. The infrasonic sounds of blue whales can propagate over hundreds of kilometers if trapped in a surface duct or in the deep sound channel of the ocean. Unfortunately, the aquatic environment has made it very difficult to study the behavior of blue whales and to determine how they respond to different sounds. Certain dolphins such as spinner and spotted dolphins often are found in groupings of up to several hundred animals. These dolphins may be swimming in the same direction but are spread out over hundreds of meters. Yet, some of these schools have been observed to suddenly change their course abruptly as a response to some kind of signal, probably acoustic in nature. However, the difficulty in conducting research in the ocean has made it next to impossible to determine the specific acoustic signals used in group coordination. Humpback whales have been known to "sing" for hours on end, yet there is no consensus on the role of the songs in their natural history. *See* ANIMAL COMMUNICATION.　　　　　　　　　　　Whitlow W. L. Au

Bibliography. W. W. L. Au, *The Sonar of Dolphins*, Springer-Verlag, New York, 1993; J. W. Bradbury and S. L. Vehrencamp, *Principles of Animal Communications*, Sinauer Associates, Sunderland, MA, 1998; R. R. Fay, *Hearing in Vertebrates: A Psychophysics Databook*, Hill-Fay Associates, Winnetka, IL, 1988.

Bioarcheology

The study of skeletal remains from archeological sites by biological (or physical) anthropologists. Bioarcheology differs in several ways from traditional skeletal research. Previous work focused on individual case studies (for example, individuals with identifiable diseases) or on typological analyses of cranial form, the object of which was to classify collections into racial or ethnic groups. Bioarcheology looks at populations rather than individuals, often highlighting variation within groups as much as differences between them. In addition, it considers the interaction of biology with human culture and behavior, and the effects of the latter upon skeletal morphology or form. Technological advances in computers and methodology have opened up new fields of study, such as biomechanics and paleonutrition, while revolutionizing older interests, such as biological distance studies (a measure of genetic relatedness). Finally, bioarcheology, in part because of the specialized nature of some subfields and in part because of its biocultural approach, emphasizes collaboration with other anthropologists as well as researchers in other disciplines. *See* ANTHROPOLOGY; ARCHEOLOGY.

Health. The field of bioarcheology is built in large part upon the traditional study of human disease in prehistoric remains, or paleopathology. Bioarcheologists are more interested in the effect of disease on populations, and interrelationships between disease and social systems. Only a few infectious diseases leave diagnostic lesions on the skeleton (including tuberculosis, treponemal diseases such as syphilis, and leprosy). A good deal of attention has centered on tracing the evolution of these diseases: leprosy in the Old World, syphilis (arguably) in the New World, and tuberculosis, which appears in both hemispheres. More common than these specific infections in skeletal collections are generalized indicators of health problems: osteitis or periostitis (bone infections due to a variety of agents), growth disruptions in tooth enamel (enamel hypoplasias) or bone (Harris lines), reduced growth rates (as seen in shorter bones in children than are expected for their age), and porotic hyperostosis and cribra orbitalia (bone porosity on the surface of the skull and the upper surface of the eye orbits, respectively, the result of anemia during childhood).

Infectious diseases increase in frequency in agricultural communities due to a variety of factors, including population growth, increasing sedentism, and an expansion in trade contacts with other societies. However, it would be an oversimplification to state that health always deteriorates with the advent of agriculture; for example, stored agricultural crops may alleviate seasonal fluctuations in nutritional availability. *See* DISEASE; EPIDEMIOLOGY; PATHOLOGY.

Paleonutrition. The study of prehistoric diet has been revolutionized by work on bone chemistry and isotopic variation. Essentially, this research focuses on the fact that some dietary ingredients leave a chemical or isotopic trace in bones; for example, carnivores retain less strontium than do herbivores, so that strontium can indicate the amount of meat in the diet. Carbon isotope analyses of bone also indicate when maize (corn), the main component of historical Native American diets, was introduced into North America. Such studies have also uncovered differences in the level of reliance on maize within populations based on sex and status, and between societies, which in turn have been tied to differences in general health. Other dietary components, such as marine resources, may also be determined utilizing nitrogen isotopes.

Injuries. Traumatic injuries and osteoarthritis (arthritis in the bony sections of joints) are extremely common in prehistoric populations. Although it is difficult to separate accidental trauma from that caused by interpersonal violence, bioarcheologists can identify examples of violent death in prehistory (for example, arrowpoints lodged in bone, around which there is no healing). These studies indicate that violence escalated in late prehistory in North America as societies became increasingly agricultural and population size rose. Osteoarthritis is common throughout prehistory and may be tied in part to levels of activities, although it is also caused by other factors, including injuries and infections of the joints. *See* ARTHRITIS.

Biomechanics. An area of research that has only recently become feasible through computer-aided technology is biomechanics. Like muscles, bones respond to higher-than-normal physical activities by increasing in mass, and can therefore indicate the usual level of physical exertion during life. Biomechanical studies have shown that physical activities changed as populations adopted agriculture, although the nature of the change varies in different regions of North America. In the Midwest and Deep South of the United States, activities increased when agriculture was adopted, especially in females, while the opposite is true in coastal Georgia. This variability may be linked with differences in the intensity of agricultural practices, but other activities may also be important. *See* BIOMECHANICS.

Biodistance. With more sophisticated computer technology, biodistance studies, which seek to establish genetic relationships between populations, are increasingly complex. To some extent, this means an elaboration of intricate typologies. However, biodistance studies can be used productively to answer questions about the evolution of regional societies, as well as to illuminate such practices as residence patterns.

Summary. New methods, technologies, and theoretical questions have transformed the fields of skeletal biology and paleopathology into modern bioarcheology. In spite of controversy concerning the proper treatment of human skeletal remains, bioarcheological research remains strong today. More information is contained in a single human burial than in any other archeological feature, and skeletons are the only source of data that focuses directly on individual humans. Burial information provides a long-term perspective on changes in the human condition: for instance, the evolution of diseases and the effects of societal changes such as the adoption of agriculture. Therefore, human skeletal remains are a critical part of archeological research. With the innovations mentioned above, bioarcheological studies will continue to play a vital role in the interpretation of past societies. *See* BONE; PHYSICAL ANTHROPOLOGY.

Patricia S. Bridges; Clark Spencer Larsen

Bibliography. R. L. Blakely (ed.), *Biocultural Adaptation in Prehistoric America*, 1977; M. N. Cohen and G. J. Armelagos (eds.), *Paleopathology at the Origins of Agriculture*, 1984; C. S. Larsen, *Bioarchaeology: Interpreting Behavior from the Human Skeleton*, 1997; M. L. Powell, P. S. Bridges, and A. M. W. Mires (eds.), *What Mean These Bones?: Studies in Southeastern Bioarchaeology*, 1989; R. H. Steckel and J. C. Rose (eds.), *The Backbone of History: Health and Nutrition in the Western Hemisphere*, 2002.

Bioassay

A method for the quantitation of the effects on a biological system by its exposure to a substance, as well as the quantitation of the concentration of a substance by some observable effect on a biological system. The biological material in which the effect is measured can range from subcellular components and microorganisms to groups of animals. The substance can be stimulatory, such as an ion increasing taxis behavior in certain protozoans, or inhibitory, such as an antibiotic for bacterial growth. Bioassays are most frequently used when there is a number of steps, usually poorly understood, between the substance and the behavior observed, or when the substance is a complex mixture of materials and it is not clear what the active components are. Bioassays can be replaced, in time, by either a more direct measure of concentration of the active principle, such as an analytical method (for example, mass spectrometry, high-pressure liquid chromatography, radioimmunoassay), or a more direct measurement of the effect, such as binding to a surface receptor in the case of many drugs, as the substance or its mechanism of action is better characterized.

Assays to quantitate the effects of an exposure model the effect of a substance in the real world. Complex biological responses can be estimated by laboratory culture tests, which use, for example, bacteria or cells cultured in a petri dish (usually to model an effect either on the organism of interest, such as bacteria, or on some basic cellular function); by tissue or organ culture, which isolates pieces of tissue or whole organs in a petri dish (usually to model organ function); or in whole animals (usually to model complex organismic relationships). Tests which measure direct effects on an organism, for example, inhibition of mold growth by an antimold agent in a petri dish, are frequently easier to extrapolate to real-world situations (although they are still only laboratory simulations) than are more indirect tests, such as measurement of tumor induction in rats under restricted conditions as a model for tumor induction in people. However, each assay has advantages and disadvantages, including factors such as ease, cost, and feasibility which have to be weighted in using the test. The usefulness of an assay usually improves as the relationship of concentration and effect, that is, the dose-response curve, is characterized. Although this curve can be complex, many systems have a linear range—doses between which the biological effect is a constant times the dose—generally the most useful range for quantitation.

Assays to estimate concentrations of substances usually require a simple, reproducible end point which can be quantitated easily. The more complex the biological end point measured, the greater the number of factors that can modulate the expression of the phenomenon and, therefore, the greater the amount of control and cost necessary to have a reproducible measure. Usually this type of assay is used when the dose is in the linear range, and conditions are frequently adjusted to make the response a linear one.

Ronald W. Hart; Angelo Turturro

Microorganism Assay

Use of animals for bioassay antedated use of microorganisms. However, the expansion of knowledge of microbial nutrition which occurred during the period 1936–1945 stimulated the development of microbiological assay methods as a routine tool for determining vitamins and amino acids in natural materials. These methods possessed the required precision, and were found also to be rapid, convenient, and remarkably sensitive for detecting the presence and for following the isolation of new vitamins or vitaminlike materials present in trace amounts in crude materials. Many of these substances (nicotinic acid, pantothenic acid, pantetheine, inositol, biotin, pyridoxal, pyridoxamine) were found only subsequently to be important in animal nutrition. The development of microbiological assay methods for folic acid and vitamin B_{12} was of great aid in permitting isolation of these vitamins as well. In some cases microbiological assay remains today the only rapid and specific assay available for determination of individual vitamins.

Microbiological assay has several advantages over animal assay. It requires much less time, labor, and materials to perform. It is consequently less expensive than animal assay, and in most instances is much more precise. One disadvantage of microorganisms as compared with animals as assay tools is that extraction of the vitamin from the combined forms in which most of these naturally occur is usually required to make these available to the microorganism. It is generally assumed (sometimes on insufficient grounds) that animals utilize such combined forms completely. This disadvantage of the microbiological assay as an analytical tool has proved to be an asset in that it has permitted detection, isolation, and quantitative determination of several hitherto unknown

TABLE 1. Representative methods of assay for the water-soluble vitamins

Vitamin	Test organism
p-Aminobenzoic acid	Neurospora crassa (mutant)
Biotin	Lactobacillus arabinosus
	Saccharomyces cerevisiae
Choline	Neurospora crassa (mutant)
Folic acid	Lactobacillus casei
	Streptococcus faecalis
Inositol	Saccharomyces carlsbergensis
Lipoic acid	Lactobacillus lactis
Nicotinic acid	Lactobacillus arabinosus
Pantothenic acid	Lactobacillus arabinosus
Riboflavin	Lactobacillus casei
Thiamin	Lactobacillus fermenti
	Saccharomyces cerevisiae
Vitamin B_6	
Pyridoxine + pyridoxamine + pyridoxal	Saccharomyces carlsbergensis
Pyridoxamine + pyridoxal	Streptococcus faecalis
Pyridoxal	Lactobacillus casei
Vitamin B_{12}	Lactobacillus leischmannii

combined forms of the vitamins, for example, pantotheine, folinic acid, and pyridoxamine phosphate. *See* VITAMIN.

Vitamin assay. Microorganisms are known which require one or more of all of the water-soluble vitamins except ascorbic acid. Various yeasts and lactic acid bacteria have been most widely used for assay of these substances. The latter group includes species in the genera *Lactobacillus, Streptococcus*, and *Pediococcus* (or *Leuconostoc*), and has been used more widely than any other organisms for assay of both vitamins and amino acids. Although many modifications of the originally devised methods have been published, the methodology is similar in all cases. A single procedure for the vitamin nicotinic acid (niacin) describes the general method. Suitable methods for other vitamins are referred to in **Table 1.**

1. For extraction of nicotinic acid, an accurately known weight for finely ground or homogenized sample is autoclaved for 15 min in sufficient 1 N H_2SO_4 to give an estimated nicotinic acid content of 1 microgram per milliliter of extract. The cooled mixture is adjusted to pH 6.8, diluted to an estimated nicotinic acid content of 0.1–0.2 μg/ml, and filtered.

2. The assay organism, *Lactobacillus arabinosus* 8014, is maintained by monthly transfer of stab cultures on a medium containing 1% yeast extract, 0.25% glucose, and 1.5% agar.

3. See **Table 2** for the basal medium.

4. The inoculum is prepared the day before the assay is run. A transfer is made from a stab of the stock culture into a sterile 10-ml aliquot of basal medium (single strength) supplemented with 1 μg of nicotinic acid per tube. This culture is incubated for 16–24 h at 98.6°F (37°C). The cells are centrifuged, washed with sterile water, and resuspended in 10 ml of sterile water or saline. One drop of this suspension is used to inoculate each assay tube.

5. The assay is carried out in lipless 18- by 150-mm test tubes individually supported in a metal rack. To one series of tubes, the freshly diluted standard nicotinic acid solution (0.1 μ/ml) is added as follows with duplicate tubes at each level: 0, 0.25, 0.5, 1.0, 1.5, 2.0, 2.5, 3.0, 3.5, 4.0, 4.5, and 5.0 ml. An extract of each material to be assayed, prepared as described in step 1, is similarly added in duplicate to a series of tubes in amounts estimated to supply 0.025–0.45 μg of nicotinic acid. The volume of extract added should not exceed 5 ml. All tubes are now diluted with distilled water to 5 ml; and 5 ml of the double-strength basal medium is added to each tube. The culture tubes are plugged with cotton or covered with glass or metal caps and autoclaved at 15 lb pressure (10.4 kilopascals) for 10–15 min. After cooling, each tube is inoculated with 1 drop of the inoculum suspension. The racks of tubes are incubated at 98.6°F (37°C) for 24 h, after which the turbidity of each culture tube is measured with a photoelectric colorimeter, preferably above 560 nm, where absorption of light due to color of the growth medium is minimized. The colorimeter reading is referred to a previously prepared curve relating turbidity of the cell suspension to dry cell weight. Such a curve is easily prepared by recording the optical density (OD) of serial dilutions of a heavy suspension of cells, a known aliquot of which is evaporated to dryness and weighed. A plot of optical density versus the corresponding calculated dry cell weight at each dilution gives the desired reference curve. Instead of measuring the growth response turbidimetrically, the incubation may be extended to 72 h and the acid produced in each assay tube measured by direct titration with 0.1 N NaOH.

6. In calculating results, a standard dose-response curve for nicotinic acid is prepared by plotting the average of the turbidity (recorded as optical

TABLE 2. Basal medium for determination of nicotinic acid with *Lactobacillus arabinosus*

Constituent	Amount per 100 ml of double-strength medium
Vitamin-free, acid-hydrolyzed casein	1.0 g
Glucose	2.0 g
Sodium acetate	1.2 g
L-Cystine	0.02 g
L-Tryptophan	0.02 g
Adenine	2.0 mg
Guanine	2.0 mg
Uracil	2.0 mg
Riboflavin	40 μg
Thiamin chloride	20 μg
Calcium pantothenate	20 μg
Pyridoxine	20 μg
Biotin	0.08 μg
Inorganic salts*	
Solution A	1.0 ml
Solution B	1.0 ml
pH adjusted to	6.8

*Solution A, 25 g K_2HPO_4, 25 g KH_2PO_4, water to make 250 ml solution. Solution B, 10 g $MgSO_4 \cdot 7H_2O$, 0.5 g NaCl, 0.5 g $FeSO_4 \cdot 7H_2O$, 0.5 g $MnSO_4 \cdot H_2O$, water to make 250 ml solution.

densities or, preferably, dry weight of cells produced) or titration values found at each level of the nicotinic acid standard against the amount of nicotinic acid present. The nicotinic acid content of the sample is determined by interpolating the response to known amounts of the test solution onto this standard curve. Only those values which fall on the rapidly ascending portion of the curve should be used. A typical standard curve obtained under these conditions is shown in the **illustration**.

The accuracy of the microbiological methods is usually given as ±10%. However, this limitation is set by procedural variations, and not by reproducibility of the growth response as such. Under proper conditions the reproducibility of assay results may surpass ±3%. Comparative data for the same material assayed by independent reliable methods are scarce. In evaluating an assay method, investigators have therefore relied on internal evidence, such as the ability to secure quantitative recoveries of the added test substance and also the reproducibility of assay values. In general, an assay for an essential nutrient is more accurate than one for a nutrient that is only stimulatory to growth of the test organism. *See* NIACIN.

Amino acid assay. These methods depend upon the use of microorganisms which have specific growth requirements for the individual amino acids. One microorganism may be used for the assay of several amino acids. *See* AMINO ACIDS.

The basal media used for assay of amino acids resemble those that are used for nicotinic acid (Table 2), but they contain a complete assortment of vitamins and an appropriate complete mixture of pure amino acids (save for the one to be determined) in place of the hydrolyzed casein. Procedures are then entirely similar to those described for the nicotinic acid assay, and dose-response curves similar to that of the graph are obtained for each of the amino acids.

The assay organisms useful for estimation of individual amino acids are listed in **Table 3**. L-Amino acids of demonstrated purity must be used as standards. With few exceptions, the D-isomers of the amino acids are inactive for most of the common assay organisms. The concentrations of the amino acids required to establish a standard curve are given in **Table 4**.

Peptides are widely utilized by certain microorganisms, and may, depending upon the assay conditions and the test organism, exhibit activity which is greater than, less than, or equal to that expected from their amino acid composition. In general, therefore, proteins should be hydrolyzed completely before

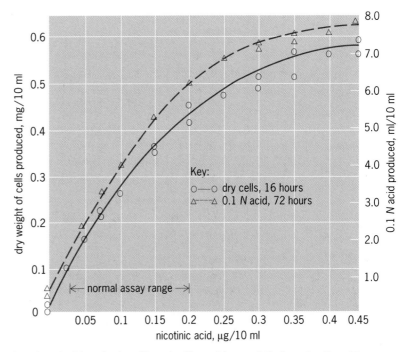

Growth and acid production of *Lactobacillus arabinosus* plotted as a function of the nicotinic acid concentration.

they are assayed microbiologically. The minimum time required for complete hydrolysis of any given protein can be determined experimentally. However, a general useful procedure for acid hydrolysis of protein samples for assay is as follows: The finely divided, weighed sample is placed in a test tube together with a 40-fold excess of $3N$ hydrochloric acid, and the tube is sealed under reduced pressure. It is autoclaved at 15 lb (10.4 kPa) pressure for 5–10 h, cooled, opened, and neutralized before assay. Tryptophan, tyrosine, and variable small amounts of other amino acids are destroyed by acid hydrolysis; modified procedures must be used to avoid this.

Antibiotic assay. Antibiotic assays depend upon the inhibition of growth of a susceptible microorganism. They are used to standardize batches of manufactured material, to test the potency of antibiotics in pharmaceutical preparations, for the estimation of antibiotics (which have been administered as chemotherapeutic agents) in body fluids, and for the detection of new antibiotics in culture filtrates of microorganisms and other source materials. The test organisms selected, in addition to being sensitive to the antibiotic being assayed, should be stable (not prone to changes in sensitivity or phase), easily

TABLE 3. Bacteria used for the determination of amino acids	
Name and strain no. (ATCC)	For determination of
Lactobacillus arabinosus 8014	Glutamic acid, leucine, isoleucine, valine, phenylalanine, tryptophan
Lactobacillus delbrückii 9595	Phenylalanine, tyrosine, serine
Leuconostoc citrovorum 8081	Alanine; could also be used for most other amino acids
Leuconostoc mesenteroides 8042	All amino acids except alanine
Streptococcus faecalis 8043	Glutamic acid, histidine, lysine, arginine, leucine, isoleucine, valine, methionine, threonine, tryptophan

TABLE 4. Concentrations of various amino acids suitable for establishing a standard curve

Amino acid (L form)	Assay range, μg/ml
Alanine	0–25
Arginine	0–20
Aspartic acid	0–20
Cystine	0–5
Glutamic acid	0–25
Glycine	0–15
Histidine	0–5
Isoleucine	0–15
Leucine	0–15
Lysine	0–20
Methionine	0–5
Phenylalanine	0–5
Proline	0–10
Serine	0–10
Threonine	0–10
Tryptophan	0–2
Tyrosine	0–10
Valine	0–15

cultivated, and preferably nonpathogenic. The method selected depends upon the intended purpose.

Dilution methods. The substance to be tested is diluted to several concentrations and placed in a series of vessels containing a suitable liquid of solid nutrient medium. Sterile technique is observed except when the incubation period is as short as 3–5 h. The vessels are inoculated with a sensitive microorganism, and after incubation the lowest concentration of the substance which will just prevent, or reduce to one-half, growth or some other easily observable function of the microorganism is ascertained.

When a solid medium is used (agar streak method), several organisms are streaked on the surface of agar plates containing various dilutions of the antibiotic. This method is less accurate than the broth dilution method, but is useful as a rapid method of determining what organisms are inhibited and the approximate degree to which they are inhibited by the antibiotic (the antibiotic spectrum).

Diffusion methods. The agar plate (cup, cylinder, or paper disk) method is the most common horizontal diffusion method in use. A petri plate (or some variation thereof) containing nutrient agar is inoculated in bulk or on the surface (by spreading an aqueous suspension of cells, or a thin layer of inoculated agar) with vegetative cells or spores of a sensitive organism, and partially dried at 98.6°F (37°C). Four or five cylinders of glass, porcelain, or stainless steel are spaced on the plate and filled with the solutions to be tested. Absorbent paper disks may be used in place of the cylinders, or depressions or holes may be made in the agar to admit the solutions. The plates are incubated for a suitable period (12–16 h at 98.6°F or 37°C for penicillin). Clear zones appear around the point of application of the test substances where the antibiotic has diffused out to prevent growth of the microorganism. The diameters of the zones are measured (with a millimeter ruler, pointed dividers or calipers, or specially designed projection devices) and are compared with the dimensions of zones produced by known concentrations of the standard antibiotic.

Turbidimetric methods. These differ from dilution methods in that the response they give is a graded instead of an all-or-none response. The growth of the test organism in a liquid nutrient medium containing various known concentrations of the antibiotic is measured photoelectrically, and a standard curve is obtained by plotting the galvanometer readings versus the corresponding concentrations of antibiotic. Turbidity measurements of test solutions set up at the same time and under the same conditions are referred to the standard curve for evaluation.

Assay in body fluids. The assay of antibiotics in body fluids presents certain difficulties. The antibiotic may be present in low concentrations, and limited amounts of the body fluid may be available; therefore, the method must be sensitive and in some cases must be conducted on a microscale. Furthermore, the antibiotic may be destroyed or its potency changed by the presence of certain constituents in normal body fluids. Likewise, the growth of the test organism may be affected either favorably or adversely by the constituents in blood or serum. In general, the difficulties may be surmounted by employing one or more of the following procedures: (1) choosing a sensitive assay organism, avoiding those which are inhibited or stimulated by constituents of body fluids to be assayed; (2) when a micromethod is indicated, choosing a test organism which will grow on the undiluted body fluid; and (3) extracting the antibiotic from interfering materials.

The accuracy of these methods depends considerably upon the skill of the operator. Reproducibility of assay values is the only criterion of accuracy which has been extensively used.

Beverly M. Guirard; Esmond E. Snell

Disinfectant testing. A disinfectant serves to prevent infection. It must successfully kill microorganisms which occur on inanimate surfaces and can produce infection. These microorganisms include bacteria, fungi, yeasts, protozoa, and viruses. A knowledge of the effectiveness of disinfectants is important in many different areas. Most manufacturers of disinfectants require regular quality-control information; consumers such as hospitals have the responsibility of protecting their patients; regulatory agencies must make sure that all commercial products meet legal standards; and research scientists need to develop new products that will be superior to those already on the market. Therefore, standardized testing methods have been developed and improved in a century of experimentation.

Since disinfectants represent different chemical species and are used under different environmental conditions to act on different microorganisms, different methods must be employed as the specific situation requires. Some tests are strictly for use in the laboratory, others simulate practical conditions in the laboratory, and still others involve testing when in use under actual conditions. To illustrate the necessity for simulated and in-use tests, a disinfectant was shown to be 20 times as effective on a ceramic tile wall as on a rubber tile wall; thus, a test unrelated to the actual surface in use would have given misleading results. The presence of organic matter is another of the many factors which may have a profound influence in reducing the activity of a disinfectant and must be taken into account in the testing process. The type of microorganism used is also very important to the results. Some disinfectants, for example, are active only on gram-positive bacteria, not on gram-negative organisms. The same organism may give different results if not treated in the same manner in laboratory culture; therefore, it is necessary to standardize the method of culture of the organism, as well as the other aspects of the test procedure. In the hopsital it may be necessary to additionally test wild species of the same organism that is used in the standard test, when such wild organisms are responsible for infection and may respond differently from the normal, standard culture grown in the laboratory.

While it would be desirable to test with a large number of different organisms and under practical conditions of use, the realistic considerations of cost and time most often dictate the use of repeatable tests performed in the laboratory with one to three organisms. Such standard tests have received many years of evaluation and improvement, and have been published under the auspices of authoritative professional organizations in the United States and Europe. There is no international set of standard tests, and the tests of different countries vary considerably from each other. In the United States the officially recognized methods are those published by the Association of Official Analytical Chemists (AOAC). Since not all microbiological testing methods are applicable to all types of disinfectants, different methods have been developed. The following briefly describes the more important AOAC methods for disinfectants.

Phenol-coefficient method. This is the oldest of the methods for testing disinfectants (dating from 1912) that is still in use. It is based upon a comparison of the disinfectant to be evaluated with a common standard, phenol. It is useful solely for chemicals which, by their type of action, are similar to phenol. It employs bacteria in liquid suspension and compares the concentration necessary for killing them in a specific time by the disinfectant and by an equal quantity

TABLE 5. Example of test by the phenol-coefficient method employing *Salmonella typhosa*[*]				
		Growth[†] in subculture tubes in		
Substance	Dilution	5 min	10 min	15 min
Disinfectant X	1:300	0	0	0
	1:325	+	0	0
	1:350	+	0	0
	1:375	+	+	0
	1:400	+	+	+
Phenol	1:90	+	0	0
	1:100	+	+	+

[*]Phenol coefficient of Disinfectant X: 350/90 = 3.9.
[†]Symbol + indicates growth, and 0 no growth.

of phenol, as determined by subculturing the bacteria in a special medium following contact with the chemical. Chemicals unlike phenol, such as mercurials and quaternary ammonium compounds, yield erroneous test results. Thus, the phenol-coefficient method is not widely in use.

An example of the phenol-coefficient method is shown in **Table 5**. The phenol coefficient is calculated by dividing the greatest dilution of the disinfectant tested which is effective in killing the bacteria in 10 min, but not in 5 min, by the greatest dilution of phenol demonstrating the same result. This test method has been shown to yield a standard deviation of ±21%.

The phenol-coefficient method is restricted to disinfectants which are miscible with water or emulsifiable in water. Test organisms specified are *Salmonella typhosa*, *Staphylococcus aureus*, and *Pseudomonas aeruginosa*. They must be cultured in a specific manner on a stipulated medium in order to have a specific resistance, as shown in **Table 6**.

It was the commonly accepted criterion that disinfectants for general use be applied at a dilution equivalent in germicidal effectiveness against *Salmonella typhosa* to 5% phenol solution. This was determined for the phenolic-based disinfectant in question by multiplying the phenol-coefficient number against *Salmonella typhosa* by 20 to obtain the number of parts of water in which one part of the disinfectant should be incorporated. This is regarded as the highest possible dilution which could be considered for practical disinfection, and is valid only if the

TABLE 6. Resistance of test cultures to phenol as required by the phenol-coefficient method				
		Growth[*] in subculture tubes in		
Organism	Dilution	5 min	10 min	15 min
Salmonella typhosa	1:90	+ or 0	+ or 0	0
	1:100	+	+	+ or 0
Staphylococcus aureus	1:60	+ or 0	+ or 0	0
	1:70	+	+	+
Pseudomonas aeruginosa	1:80	+ or 0	+ or 0	0
	1:90	+	+	+

[*]Symbol + indicates growth, and 0 no growth.

bactericidal adequacy of the solution can be confirmed by the use-dilution method.

Use-dilution method. Owing to the introduction of nonphenolic-based disinfectants, the use-dilution method is currently the test most commonly used to measure efficacy of disinfectants. This confirmation method tests effectiveness of disinfectants under semipractical conditions of use, namely on hard, nonporous surfaces where a substantial reduction of the bacterial contamination has not been achieved by prior cleaning. In the use-dilution method, the bacteria are applied to stainless steel cylinders, resulting in 1,000,000 bacteria per cylinder. Experience has shown this method to be much more reliable in indicating safe, practical dilutions for all types of disinfectants than the phenol-coefficient method, in which the bacteria are acted on in the form of suspensions. The use-dilution method simulates the action of the germicide on catheters, surgical instruments, and so forth. The steel cylinders are dipped into a 48-h culture of the bacteria and are allowed to drain and dry under set conditions. They are then immersed in dilutions of the disinfectant for 10 min at a standard temperature and transferred to subculture broth and incubated to determine whether complete kill of the test bacterium has occurred. Chemicals such as lecithin and thioglycollate are used in the subculture broth to neutralize any carry-over of disinfectant on the cylinder.

In this test the bacteria specified are *Salmonella choleraesius, Staphylococcus aureus*, and *Pseudomonas aeruginosa*. Disinfectants for hospital use or similar application require that all three bacteria be tested on three separate formulated product batches (one batch should be at least 60 days old), 60 carriers per bacterium, for a total of 540 determinations. Killing of 59 out of each set of 60 carriers or better is required.

Test for germicidal spray products. This method was developed to evaluate spray products, manual and pressurized, for disinfecting surfaces, and is adapted from the use-dilution method. It employs glass microscope slides instead of steel cylinders as the carriers for a suspension of *Salmonella choleraesius, Staphylococcus aureus, Pseudomonas aeruginosa*, and, if fungus control is claimed, spores of *Trichophyton mentagrophytes*. The inoculated slides are sprayed for 30 s and allowed 10 min contact time. Following broth culture of the treated slides and incubation, killing of all three test bacteria, as set forth for hospital disinfectants under the use-dilution method, is evidence of disinfecting action.

Germicidal and detergent sanitizer method. Public health standards require a percentage reduction of bacteria on precleaned surfaces that come in contact with food. Such surfaces could be dishes and utensils in restaurants, and dairies and other food-processing plants. The germicidal and detergent sanitizer test measures speed of kill with or without the presence of hardness in the test water. The test bacteria are *Escherichia coli* and *Staphylococcus aureus*, and are grown and diluted until a final concentration of 75,000,000 to 125,000,000 bacteria per milliliter

is achieved. One milliliter of the bacterial suspension is added to 100 ml of the sanitizer diluted to use concentration at 77°F (25°C). After 30 to 60 s, the solution is sampled and the sample plated out. Colony-forming units are counted and compared to the original bacterial count. A 99.999% reduction in 30 s meets standards set by the U.S. Public Health Service Code, with or without hard water. This test should be clearly separated from the use-dilution method. In that test, complete kill of a target pathogenic bacterium is necessary. In this sanitizer test, a percentage reduction of bacteria found in the inanimate environment is necessary.

Available chlorine equivalent concentration method. Where sanitizers that are not solely chlorine-based are used on food contact surfaces, a separate test is used to measure efficacy. This test is designed to meet the requirements of the U.S. Public Health Service Code for sanitizers: at least 50 ppm of available chlorine and a 99.999% reduction of the test bacterium. This test shows whether or not a nonchlorine sanitizer is equivalent to a standardized concentration of chlorine. The test bacteria are *Salmonella typhosa* and *Staphylococcus aureus*. The bacteria are grown for broth for 24 h. For each concentration of chlorine (50, 100, and 200 ppm), 10 ml is placed in one tube. For the sanitizer under test, three concentrations are made and 10 ml of each concentration placed in a respective single tube. Over a period of 10 time-measured increments, each tube is dosed with one drop of bacterium, and after 1 min one drop is removed and placed in fresh media. The single tube is repeatedly dosed 10 times and subcultured 10 times. The media are incubated and observed for growth/no growth. If 25 ppm of iodine, for example, shows the same pattern of no growth for 1–5-min increments, and growth for 6–10-min increments, it would be equivalent to 200 ppm of chlorine, which would show the same growth/no growth pattern.

Sporicidal test. By definition, a disinfectant kills vegetative cells but not necessarily bacterial spores, which are the most resistant forms of life. When claims are made for sporicidal action, the test is made with resistant spores of *Bacillus subtilis, Clostridium sporogenes*, and spores of other species of particular interest, such as *Bacillus anthracis* and *Clostridium tetanis*. The sporicidal test is the same as a test for assessing sterilizers. (Sterilization is the killing of all life.) Much like the use-dilution method, this is a carrier test measuring disinfection at surfaces, in this case using silk surgical suture loops and porcelain cylinders impregnated with spores which have shown standard resistance to 2.5 *N* hydrochloric acid. The spore-treated carriers are exposed to the disinfectant (which may be a liquid or gas) for selected intervals at specified temperatures. This is followed by transfer to subculture media containing neutralizing compounds to prevent carry-over of bacteriostatic action, and incubation to indicate killing or survival of the spores. In actual tests, some 720 individual carriers are tested, with no failures in the final result.

Fungicidal test. A disinfectant may be employed to kill pathogenic fungi and fungal spores, which are less resistant to chemicals than bacterial spores. The test procedure is similar to the phenol-coefficient test, but employs a suspension of spores of the dermatophyte *Trichophyton mentagrophytes*, which has been shown to demonstrate the required resistance to phenol. The highest dilution that kills spores in 10 min exposure is considered effective.

Test for swimming pool disinfectants. This is a suspension test comparing bactericidal activity of the product to that of hypochlorite (chlorine). The organisms specified are *Escherichia coli* and *Streptococcus faecalis*. The test is based on the effectiveness of a swimming pool disinfectant in killing 1,000,000 test bacteria per milliliter of water in 30 s. After increasing contact times of 0.5 to 10 min with dilutions of the product, the culture is neutralized and subcultured in fresh medium. The concentration of the disinfectant under test that gives results equivalent to those of an NaOCl solution containing 0.58–0.62 ppm available chlorine at zero time and greater than 0.4 ppm after 10 min, is considered effective. Various swimming pool additives used to enhance the action of a disinfectant can be included in the test.

Test of tuberculocidal activity. A special test is required to determine tuberculocidal activity due to both the great resistance and slow growth of pathogenic mycobacteria. This test is divided into two parts: a screening test employing the more rapidly growing *Mycobacterium smegmatis* and a confirmatory test employing *Mycobacterium tuberculosis* var. *bovis*. The culture of organisms is applied to a carrier of cylinders made of porcelain, using 10 per trial, with 10 min exposure. In the confirmatory test, each carrier with tuberculosis bacteria is transferred to a tube with serum or neutralizer, followed by subculture in three different broth media with serum. Three different media are used because each furnishes to the damaged tuberculosis organism a growth factor that can be used to repair itself if the disinfectant did not kill the organism. The tubes are incubated for 60 days and, if there is no growth, for 30 days more. The maximum dilution of the disinfectant and the test organisms in the 10 carriers which shows no growth in the subculture represents the maximum safe use-dilution for practical tuberculocidal disinfection.

Virucidal methods. There is no official standard method for testing the effect of disinfectants on viruses; however, there are unofficial methods which are accepted by the U.S. Environmental Protection Agency on an individual case basis. These methods include the suspension method where the virus is suspended with the germicide in 5% blood serum and held for 10 min; the carrier method using dried viruses on inanimate surfaces; and the disinfectant spray method. In all cases, the virus is recovered and assayed in tissue culture, in embryonated egg, or in a living animal, depending on the virus under study. The work requires qualified laboratories and highly trained personnel.

Other methods. There are many other methods for testing disinfectants and antimicrobial chemicals.

Some, for example, are practical tests for determining activity for dairy use where milk protein is an interfering substance; or tests on hospital linens and textiles, and for carpet sanitizers, where the disinfectant may be adsorbed on the fibers to reduce its activity. There are methods for testing antiseptics for use on the skin, and substances which are bacteriostatic or fungistatic, that is, which inhibit growth and reproduction but do not kill the cells. There are tests which determine the activity of chemicals to protect products such as foods, cosmetics, pharmaceuticals, paints, paper, wood, and petroleum from microbiological deterioration or destruction. There are methods which do not depend on observation of cell growth/no growth but determine microbial survival by such measurements as respiration and enzyme action.   Seymour S. Block

Animal Assay

Animals, from hydra to humans (in humans, assays are termed clinical tests), are used in many ways in a wide range of different assays, from measuring clumping in slime molds for the estimation of minuscule levels of biological compounds, to sampling umbilical blood to evaluate human drug distribution in fetuses during pregnancy. Although there have been great strides in the development of computer simulation and predictive toxicological methods, it is still presently necessary to do animal tests because biological systems are so complex that the only way to be sure about the result is to study effects in animals.

Techniques. Animal bioassays are generally direct evaluations of agent efficacy (such as the number of dead mosquitoes in a standardized cage, or mice with cured cancers), indirect evaluations of agent efficacy using some marker (for example, reducing expression of an enzyme activity associated with AIDS progression), or estimations of agent toxicity using either short-term or long-term studies (mostly for regulatory purpose). Although similar whole-animal assays are sometimes used to determine substance concentrations, such tests, because of their high cost when compared to analytical methods or tests in microorganisms, are fairly rare and are usually confined to experimental situations where the active component is being sought or is in very low concentrations. *See* PHARMACOLOGY; TOXICOLOGY.

Bioassays, whether direct or indirect, for drug efficacy (or potency) also usually evaluate toxic effects. Animals are dosed with an agent, either acutely or chronically, under specified conditions, and the end result is evaluated. Tests using indirect evaluations of efficacy or toxicity tend to be of shorter duration than direct tests. Acute action of a single dose, such as lethality resulting from injection of digitalis, or chronic action of an acute or chronic dose (for example, long-term evaluation of the efficacy and toxicity of a single dose of carcinogen or lifelong treatment with diuretics for hypertension) can be evaluated. Drug potency evaluations are relatively short-term (especially in humans), since most drugs are usually intended to be given for a limited time, while toxicity evaluations tend to be both short- and long-term. Acute effects can include vasodilation or heartbeat alterations when estimating drug potency, or weight loss and organ necrosis when estimating toxicity. Chronic action for potency can include changes in organ weight or blood composition, or for toxicity, carcinogenicity, teratogenicity, and mutational changes in the second and third generation following chemical exposure.

Although it is important to have a good experimental design in evaluating acute action, this becomes crucial in long-term tests, in part because of their cost. Some important factors can be illustrated by considering the chronic bioassay, a test to evaluate the change in tumor incidence and time-to-tumor in a rodent species as a result of chronic exposure to an agent. Issues which are constantly evaluated and debated include the number of animals used per dose, the strain and species used (although some strains are conventionally used), the maximum dose used, the number of other doses used, the dose route, the number of tissues evaluated for carcinogenicity, questions of tissue pathology, how long the assay should last (2 years is conventional), and the relevance of the test to aspects of human tumorigenesis (which the test is supposed to model). For example, the role that animal body weight has on influencing chronic bioassay sensitivity and outcome has been debated. This is especially true since the results of these assays have direct practical significance because they are presently used to set limits for human exposure to certain chemicals. This whole reevaluation process has led to basic questions, for example, about the extrapolation of data from animals given high doses to humans, especially in light of the low doses usually seen in living human subjects; and about what animal systems are proper models for humans.

Statistics. Because of the costs involved, while short-term tests tend to use large numbers of test animals, long-term animal assays are usually designed with the fewest animals possible. Another factor resulting in decreased animal numbers is concern about needless animal suffering. As a result, the tests tend to be fairly insensitive when used to model the response of a large human population. Because of this insensitivity, and biological variation between individuals and species, statistics (always a factor to consider in test analysis) assume special importance. Experimental design and data analysis are heavily influenced by statistical considerations, and special statistical techniques, such as methods for determining the effects of life-shortening and non-life-shortening tumor incidence, or determining the effect of agents on the time-to-tumor, have been developed which have subsequently been adapted for more general use (for example, factoring out the effect of life-shortening tumors on mortality in aging studies). *See* BIOMETRICS; STATISTICS.

Data management. Because of the vast amount of data generated by a large number of short-term tests, or even a single chronic bioassay, especially when good dose-response data are generated, there has arisen a need for automated systems for data acquisition and management. The costs of long-term tests has led to automation in the animal facility. An animal room without a computer terminal has become a rarity. Many short-term tests are automated, with robots doing the labor-intensive adding and mixing of solutions as well as the injection of samples into instruments for measurement. Integration of laboratory function with computers is increasing, with data being placed into databases. Extensive new data are becoming available on the Internet.

Angelo Turturro; Ronald Hart

Bibliography. G. E. Glass (ed.), *Bioassay Techniques and Environmental Chemistry*, Ann Arbor Science, Ann Arbor, MI, 1973; International Agency for Research in Cancer Working Group, Long-term and short-term screening assays for carcinogens: A critical appraisal, *IARC Monogr.* (Lyon, France), suppl. 2, 1980; *National Toxicology Program Specifications for the Conduct of Studies to Evaluate the Toxic and Carcinogenic Potential of Chemical, Biological, and Physical Agents in Laboratory Animals for the National Toxicology Program*, National Institutes for Environmental Health Sciences, Research Triangle Park, NC, 1992; R. L. Prentice, Surrogate measures in clinical trials: Definition and operational criteria, *Stat. Med.*, 8:963–974, 1989; R. Tennant and E. Zeigler, Genetic toxicology: Current status of methods of carcinogen identification, *Environ. Health Perspect.*, 100:307–315, 1993; A. Turturro et al., Body weight impact on spontaneous and agent-induced diseases in chronic bioassays, *Int. J. Toxicol.*, 17:79–100, 1998.

Biocalorimetry

The measurement of the energetics of biological processes such as biochemical reactions, association of ligands to biological macromolecules, folding of proteins into their native conformations, phase transitions in biomembranes, and enzymatic reactions, among others. Two different types of instruments have been developed to study these processes: differential scanning calorimeters and isothermal titration calorimeters.

Differential scanning calorimeters. These instruments measure the heat capacity at constant pressure of a sample as a continuous function of temperature. A typical high-sensitivity differential scanning calorimeter consists of two cells that are suspended inside an adiabatic shield (to prevent heat loss) and connected to each other through one or several thermopiles. One cell is filled with a solution containing the sample under study, and the other with a reference solution. The measurement is performed by heating both cells at a constant rate (approximately 1°C/min). When a thermally induced endothermic transition occurs in the sample cell, the temperature of this cell lags behind that of the reference cell. This phenomenon occurs because some of the applied thermal energy is utilized to induce the transition rather than to increase the temperature of the solution. This temperature difference is sensed by the thermopiles and used by a feedback circuit which adds additional energy to the sample cell in order to maintain the temperature difference equal to zero. The additional electric power applied to the sample cell is the basic signal measured by a differential scanning calorimeter. Normalization of this signal by the scanning rate and the amount of solute in the sample cell permits a determination of the heat capacity function as a function of temperature. Modern instrumentation allows for increased sensitivity and accurate measurements of protein folding and unfolding transitions with approximately 1 mg of material. *See* THERMOCHEMISTRY.

Differential scanning calorimetry is the only technique that permits a direct measurement of the thermodynamics of thermally induced transitions. Thus it plays a unique role in the determination of the forces that stabilize the native structure of proteins, nucleic acids, and other biological structures. The combination of thermodynamic information with high-resolution molecular structures obtained by x-ray crystallography or nuclear magnetic resonance provides a powerful tool for the development of rational algorithms for protein engineering and drug design. At a most fundamental level, differential scanning calorimetry is also used to study the mechanisms of protein folding, since this technique permits a characterization of the energetics of partially folded structures along the folding pathway.

Isothermal titration calorimeters. Isothermal titration calorimeters measure directly the energetics (through heat effects) associated with biochemical reactions or processes occurring at constant temperatures. Experiments are performed by titrating reactants into sample solutions containing other reactants. After each addition, the heat released or absorbed as a result of the reaction is monitored by the instrument. The difference in heat effects between the sample solution and the reference solution is equal to the heat of reaction. In a power compensation instrument, the temperature difference between the sample and reference cells is monitored to maintain the temperature difference equal to zero. Instruments can measure heat effects down to about 4 microjoules (1 microcal) of total heat, the volume of the reaction cells is about 1 milliliter, and the volume introduced by each injection usually is 5–20 microliters. *See* TITRATION.

Isothermal titration calorimeters are typically used to measure the binding of a ligand to a macromolecule (for example, proteins) or larger macromolecular assemblies (for example, multisubunit proteins and membrane receptors). Usually, a sequence of injections are administered until all of the binding sites are saturated with a specific ligand. Since the heat effect for each injection is directly proportional to the amount of ligand bound, its magnitude decreases as the fractional saturation is titrated stepwise to completion. The output of a calorimetric titration experiment is the reaction heat as a function of the total amount of ligand added. A single calorimetric titration curve can be analyzed to yield the binding enthalpy, binding entropy, and therefore the Gibbs energy of binding. Performing the titration experiment at different temperatures allows estimation of the heat capacity change that accompanies the binding reaction. *See* THERMAL ANALYSIS.

Isothermal titration calorimeters can also be used to measure enzymatic reactions and, in general, biochemical reactions that can be initiated by the mixing of two or more reagents (for example, protein denaturation by the addition of chemical denaturants or by changes in pH). In all cases, the uniqueness of calorimetry resides in its capability to measure directly and in a model-independent fashion the heat energy associated with a process. *See* CALORIMETRY.

Ernesto Freire

Bibliography. A. E. Beezer (ed.), *Biological Microcalorimetry*, 1980; W. Hemminger and G. Hohne, *Calorimetry: Fundamentals and Practice*, 1984; J. A. McLean and G. Tobin, *Animal and Human Calorimetry*, 1988.

Biochemical engineering

The application of engineering principles to conceive, design, develop, operate, and/or use processes and products based on biological and biochemical phenomena. Biochemical engineering (also known as biomolecular engineering because of the emphasis on the molecular basis of biological phenomena) influences a broad range of industries, including health care, agriculture, food, enzymes, chemicals, waste treatment, and energy, among others. Historically, biochemical engineering has been distinguished from biomedical engineering by its emphasis on biochemistry and microbiology and by the lack of a health care focus. This is no longer the case. There is increasing participation of biochemical engineers in the direct development of pharmaceuticals and other therapeutic products. Biochemical engineering has been central to the development of the biotechnology industry, given the need to generate prospective products (often using genetically engineered microorganisms and cells) on scales sufficient for testing, regulatory evaluation, and subsequent sale. *See* BIOMEDICAL ENGINEERING; BIOTECHNOLOGY.

Historical perspective. Biochemical engineering takes its roots as a discipline in the fermentation of carbohydrates to produce alcohol, typically for beverages. This practice can be traced back to before 6000 B.C. The demand for large quantities of penicillin as part of the Allies' effort during World War II brought together microbiologists, biochemists, and chemical engineers to design and construct large reactors (which came to be known as fermenters) to cultivate the antibiotic-producing microorganism. Subsequently, this combination of expertise facilitated the development of a number of industries manufacturing products ranging from chemicals (organic acids and solvents) to pharmaceuticals (antibiotics and therapeutic proteins) to foods (alcoholic beverages, sweeteners, and cheeses). The advent of genetic engineering expanded the prospects for biological products and processes as well as the role that biochemical engineers have come to play. Thus, training in this discipline has evolved from a strong emphasis on chemical engineering fundamentals with some elements of microbiology and biochemistry to a broader scope that includes molecular genetics, cell biology, pharmacology, materials science, and biophysics. *See* BIOPHYSICS; CHEMICAL ENGINEERING; GENETIC ENGINEERING; MATERIALS SCIENCE.

General principles. At the heart of biochemical engineering are the same principles that form the basis for chemical engineering, the discipline from which the engineering component is primarily derived. Whether the system is a large-scale bioreactor (a fermenter for microorganisms or a cell culture reactor for plant, insect, or mammalian cells) or a single cell, controlling the fluxes of heat, mass, and momentum between the system and its environment is central to effective operation. In fact, the biochemical engineer views a living cell as a minute but highly efficient bioreactor in which thousands of enzyme-catalyzed chemical reactions are orchestrated to serve the cell's needs to survive, reproduce, and possibly carry out a specific function in a multicellular organism. These reactions are subject to complex regulatory mechanisms that remain incompletely understood. Faced with the prospect of designing and operating a bioreactor in which billions of cells are cultivated, the biochemical engineer must often cope with overriding the intrinsic control system of the cell to produce a given substance. Thus, a biochemical engineer's task is often to promote inefficiencies in the cell's operation to produce a desired substance at higher levels than it would produce in its natural setting. This is particularly true for genetically engineered cells designed to overproduce a biochemical or protein, which may or may not be part of their normal metabolism.

Cultivation of microorganisms and cells. In the initial stages of the discipline, biochemical engineers were chiefly concerned with optimizing the growth of microorganisms under aerobic conditions, at scales of up to thousands of liters. While the scope of biochemical engineering has expanded in recent years, this remains a focus. More often, the aim is the development of an economic process to maximize production of a particular biomolecule (for example, a protein or metabolite), taking into consideration raw-material and other operating costs. The elemental constituents of biomass (carbon, nitrogen, oxygen, hydrogen, and to a lesser extent phosphorus, sulfur, mineral salts, and trace amounts of certain metals) are added to the bioreactor and consumed by the cells as they reproduce and carry out metabolic processes. Sufficient amounts of oxygen (usually supplied as sterile air) are also made available to the growing culture, usually involving mechanical agitation and gas sparging to overcome the low solubility of oxygen in aqueous media and to encourage the release of carbon dioxide formed from cellular respiratory processes. In some cases, cell morphology changes or extracellular metabolic products lead to increased viscosity of the media, thereby hindering gas-liquid mass transfer, a problem that must be addressed through specialized techniques. *See* CHEMICAL REACTOR; FERMENTATION; TRANSPORT PROCESSES.

The cultivation of anaerobic microorganisms, typically associated with fermentations in which organic acids or other solvents are produced, is usually characterized by slower growth rates and lower biomass yields; here, dissolved oxygen adversely affects microbial activity. The foremost application of anaerobic microorganisms is in waste treatment, where anaerobic digesters containing mixed communities of anaerobic microorganisms are used to reduce solids levels in industrial and municipal waste streams. *See* SEWAGE TREATMENT.

While the operation and optimization of large-scale microbial culture is still of major importance in biochemical engineering, the capability to cultivate a wide range of cell types has been developed. Biochemical engineers are often involved in the culture of cells derived from multicellular organisms, notably mammals, plants, and insects, for research purposes and to harness the unique biosynthetic capabilities of these cells. Most often, genetically engineered variants of these cell types are established for production of recombinant proteins. The ability of these cells to secrete proteins with proper glycosylation (attachment of sugar groups to proteins) and other modifications—a critical determinant of therapeutic protein quality—compensates for their slower growth, sensitivity to processing conditions (such as agitation, pH, and presence of metabolic waste products), and the need to formulate complex, defined media for their cultivation. *See* INDUSTRIAL MICROBIOLOGY.

Immobilized enzymes and cells. To harness the biocatalytic capacity of a cell or to make economic use of an enzyme needed for a particular biotransformation, immobilization of the cell or enzyme may be considered. In this case, the cells or enzymes are first produced on a large scale and then concentrated before immobilization. Next, the enzyme or cell is either attached to an inert support or embedded within a porous network or membrane. In doing so, a bioreactor can be operated such that the substrate is converted to products continuously by the immobilized biocatalyst, yielding enhanced throughput and obviating the separation of the biocatalyst from substrates and products. In some cases, living cells may be used to avoid the need for cofactor regeneration or to take advantage of a cascade of enzyme-catalyzed reactions that might be a component of the cell's metabolism. In this situation, some care must be taken to ensure cell viability, while discouraging unnecessary increases in biomass and in substrate consumption. In all cases, engineering aspects enter into the reactor design, such as the intensity of fluid agitation and the characteristic size of the insoluble support, which affect molecular transport of substrates and nutrients, as well as consideration of the material composition and structure and method of immobilization. *See* CELL (BIOLOGY); ENZYME.

Downstream processing. While the fermentation/cell culture and the associated reactor operation are central to bioprocess design, product recovery from solutions of cells and media is most often the more challenging and expensive task. Compared with the recovery of traditional chemicals, the needs for concentrating the product and ensuring its purity are often far higher for biological products, and bioseparation processes must avoid damaging conditions such as heat and the addition of denaturing solvents. Approaches used for recovering biological products include various forms of liquid chromatography (such as ion exchange, hydrophobic interaction, size exclusion, and affinity), filtration, and electrophoresis. To the extent that the biological activity of the product must be maintained, care must be taken not to damage or adversely modify the molecule of interest during recovery. In the case of pharmaceuticals, this necessitates the development of purification protocols that must be strictly followed once regulatory approval of the drug and its manufacturing process is granted. Changes to the overall process necessitate a potentially long and expensive reevaluation from regulatory agencies. Thus, the design and operation of bioseparation processes are subject to constraints not encountered in chemical separations, such that they cannot be continuously optimized. *See* ELECTROPHORESIS; LIQUID CHROMATOGRAPHY.

New directions in biochemical/biomolecular engineering. Advances in modern biology and in the health sciences have led to the creation of new areas of interest that use biochemical engineering expertise. The focus on the molecular scale has given rise to the use of biomolecular engineering as the most appropriate descriptor for this engineering discipline. Within this field, there are a number of maturing and emerging specializations. Metabolic engineering uses the tools of molecular genetics, often in conjunction with whole-genome profiling of gene expression patterns and quantitative, mathematical models of metabolic pathways and bioreactor operation, to optimize cellular function for the production of specific metabolites and proteins. Protein engineering focuses on the identification of proteins with enhanced or novel biological activity for use as biocatalysts or proteins with therapeutic value, through functional screening of randomized protein variants or rational design based on protein structure. Cell and tissue engineering involves analysis and manipulation of the intra- and intercellular mechanisms and pathways that prompt and regulate cell functional responses in the context of an individual cell or multicellular tissue, as well as the design and characterization of artificial or composite biological/synthetic materials and tissues for biomedical applications.

Biochemical/biomolecular engineers are also actively involved in development of systems and processes for bioremediation and for the detection and clearance of hazardous/lethal biological agents, development of vaccines and antibodies, and the discovery and use of cells and enzymes capable of functioning in extreme environments. Biochemical and biomolecular engineering is viewed as a critical and enabling expertise in biological and biomedical research and in the further development of the biotechnology industry.   Jason M. Haugh; Robert M. Kelly

Bibliography. J. E. Bailey and D. F. Ollis, *Biochemical Engineering Fundamentals*, 2d ed., 1986; I. B. Glowinski and G. Georgiou (eds.), *Research Opportunities in Biomolecular Engineering: The Interface between Chemical Engineering and Biology*, National Institutes of Health, Bethesda, MD, 1994; W. E. Goldstein et al. (eds.), *Biochemical Engineering VI: Annals of the New York Academy of Sciences*, vol. 589, 1990; D. A. Lauffenburger and J. J. Linderman, *Receptors: Models for Binding, Trafficking, and Signaling*, 1993; B. O. Palsson and S. N. Bhatia, *Tissue Engineering*, 2003; H. Pedersen et al. (eds.), *Biochemical Engineering VII: Annals of the New York Academy of Sciences*, vol. 665, 1992; M. L. Shuler and F. Kargi, *Bioprocess Engineering: Basic Concepts*, 2d ed., 2002; M. L. Shuler and W. A. Weigand (eds.), *Biochemical Engineering V: Annals of the New York Academy of Sciences*, vol. 506, 1987; G. N. Stephanopoulos, A. A. Aristidou, and J. Nielsen, *Metabolic Engineering: Principles and Methodologies*, 1998.

Biochemistry

The study of the substances and chemical processes which occur in living organisms. It includes the identification and quantitative determination of the substances, studies of their structure, determining how they are synthesized and degraded in organisms, and elucidating their role in the operation of the organism. Some processes of particular interest are the conversion of foods to energy, respiration, the synthesis of nucleic acids and proteins, and the regulation of the chemical activities of cells and organisms.

Substances. Carbohydrates are a class of substances which includes simple sugars such as glucose (also called dextrose) and large polysaccharides such as cellulose, a major structural material in plants, and starch, a storage form of glucose in plants. Carbohydrates are an important source of energy and structural materials in organisms, and may also be found linked to proteins in glycoproteins and linked to lipids in glycolipids. In addition, nucleic acids are composed partially of certain sugars. *See* CARBOHYDRATE; CELLULOSE.

Proteins are intimately involved in all life processes. Some function as biological catalysts called enzymes, speeding up chemical reactions which ordinarily proceed slowly at the temperatures of living organisms. Other proteins may act as carriers of material, as in the case of hemoglobin, which functions as a carrier of oxygen in many animals. Some proteins (such as collagen) act as structural material, for instance, as portions of cellular membranes and as the major component of hair, horn, skin, and feathers. Contractile proteins are involved in muscular activity and cell division. Proteins vary in size, but all are composed of essentially the same 20 amino acids; each protein molecule is composed of a definite sequence of 100 or more amino acids chemically linked one to the other. Normally, each chain of amino acids is folded into a specific three-dimensional structure. *See* AMINO ACIDS; ENZYME; PROTEIN.

There are two classes of nucleic acids, deoxyribonucleic acid (DNA) and ribonucleic acid

(RNA). The nucleic acids are large molecules composed of long chains of primarily four different nucleotides. Nucleotides are composed of sugar phosphates bonded to organic bases; they exist as small molecules in addition to providing the material for large nucleic acids. The sequential array of nucleotides is quite specific for each molecule and constitutes the form in which genetic information is stored and transferred. *See* DEOXYRIBONUCLEIC ACID (DNA); NUCLEIC ACID; RIBONUCLEIC ACID (RNA).

Lipids are a diverse group of "greasy" substances which are soluble in organic solvents but insoluble in water. Cells and tissues are composed predominantly of water, so cellular structures must be composed of materials which are insoluble in an aqueous environment. Cellular membranes are composed mainly of a class of lipids called phospholipids. The most common lipids are the fats, which serve as insoluble stores of biological fuel. Some other lipids are cholesterol and steroid hormones. *See* LIPID.

Minerals such as salts of sodium, potassium, calcium, and magnesium contribute to the ionic environment within and around cells. In addition, calcium phosphate is an important constituent of bone, and iron is a necessary part of respiratory proteins such as hemoglobin and cytochromes. Trace metals such as zinc, selenium, and molybdenum have been found to be constituents of certain enzymes. *See* CALCIUM METABOLISM; HEMOGLOBIN; PHOSPHATE METABOLISM.

Vitamins and hormones are substances which are biologically effective in small amounts. In living organisms, vitamins are converted into coenzymes, substances which collaborate with some enzymes in catalyzing reactions. Hormones are made in and secreted by endocrine glands, and they act in regulating the activities of other tissues. *See* COENZYME; ENDOCRINE SYSTEM (VERTEBRATE); HORMONE; VITAMIN.

Processes. Many of the chemical steps involved in the biological breakdown of sugars, fats, and amino acids are known. It is well established that living organisms capture the energy liberated from these reactions by forming a high-energy compound, adenosine triphosphate (ATP). In the absence of oxygen, some organisms and tissues derive ATP from an incomplete breakdown of glucose, degrading the sugar to an alcohol or an acid in the process. In the presence of oxygen, many organisms degrade glucose and other foodstuff to carbon dioxide and water, producing ATP in a process known as oxidative phosphorylation. In spite of many years of intensive investigation, the chemical reactions of oxidative phosphorylation are not well understood. *See* BIOLOGICAL OXIDATION; CARBOHYDRATE METABOLISM; LIPID METABOLISM; PROTEIN METABOLISM.

Structure and function. The relationship of the structure of enzymes to their catalytic activity is becoming increasingly clear. It is now possible to visualize atoms and groups of atoms in some enzymes by x-ray crystallography. Some enzyme-catalyzed processes can now be described in terms of the spatial arrangement of the groups on the enzyme surface and how these groups influence the reacting molecules to promote the reaction. It is also possible to explain how the catalytic activity of an enzyme may be increased or decreased by changes in the shape of the enzyme molecule, an important aspect of regulation. An important advance has been the development of an automated procedure for joining amino acids together into a predetermined sequence. This procedure permits the chemical synthesis of peptide hormones and enzymes. The use of recombinant DNA technology also makes possible the controlled biosynthesis of peptides and proteins of any amino acid sequence. This has permitted the chemical synthesis of the enzyme ribonuclease. This technology will permit the synthesis of slightly altered enzymes and will improve the understanding of the relationship between the structure and the function of enzymes. In addition, this procedure permits the synthesis of medically important polypeptides (short chains of amino acids) such as some hormones and antibiotics.

Genetic code. A subject of intensive investigation has been the explanation of genetics in molecular terms. It is now well established that genetic information is encoded in the sequence of nucleotides of DNA and that, with the exception of some viruses which utilize RNA, DNA is the ultimate repository of genetic information. The sequence of amino acids in a protein is programmed in DNA; this information is first transferred by copying the nucleotide sequence of DNA into that of messenger RNA, from which this sequence is translated into the specific sequence of amino acids of the protein. Each amino acid is specified by a sequence of three nucleotides (a triplet code); an amino acid may be specified by more than one triplet. This code has been deciphered and appears to be identical for all known organisms, thus supporting the concept of a unitary origin of life on Earth. Attempts have been made to simulate the conditions on Earth before life appeared; it has been possible to demonstrate, under these simulated conditions, the formation of substances such as sugars, amino acids, and nucleotides from the simpler substances which are presumed to have been present. *See* GENETIC CODE; MOLECULAR BIOLOGY; PREBIOTIC ORGANIC SYNTHESIS.

Disease. The biochemical basis for a number of diseases is becoming increasingly clear. This is particularly true for some genetically inherited diseases, in which the cause has been traced to the production of a defective protein. Sickle cell anemia is a particularly striking example; it is well established that the change of a single amino acid in hemoglobin has resulted in a serious abnormality in the properties of the hemoglobin molecule. *See* DISEASE.

Regulation. Increased understanding of the chemical events in biological processes has permitted the investigation of the regulation of these processes. An important concept in biological regulation is the chemical feedback circuit: the product of a series of reactions can itself influence the rates of the reactions. For example, the reactions which lead to the production of ATP proceed vigorously when the supply of ATP within the cell is low, but they slow down markedly when ATP is plentiful. These observations can be explained, in part, by the fact that ATP molecules bind to some of the enzymes involved, changing the surface features of the enzymes sufficiently to decrease their effectiveness as catalysts. While it is possible to regulate a series of reactions by controlling the activities of the catalyzing enzymes, it is also possible to regulate these reactions by changing the amounts of the enzymes; the amount of an enzyme can be controlled by modulating the synthesis of its specific messenger RNA or by modulating the translation of the information of the RNA molecule into the enzyme molecule. Another level of regulation involves the interaction of cells and tissues in multicellular organisms. For instance, endocrine glands can sense certain tissue activities and appropriately secrete hormones which control these activities. The chemical events and substances involved in cellular and tissue "communication" have become subjects of much investigation. In addition, the process of biological development is also being examined. Chemical explanations are being sought, for instance, for the orderly changes that occur in an embryo as it develops.

Biological membranes. It has been known for some time that biological membranes exhibit selective permeability; some substances cross membranes easily, others are excluded completely. Indeed, some materials are actively pumped across membranes from a region of low concentration to a region of high concentration. A particularly striking example is the case of sodium ions which are actively transported out of most cells. Detailed explanations of selective permeability and active transport are not yet available and await a better understanding of membrane structure and function. A second aspect of membrane function that has received much attention involves the transfer of information across the cellular membrane. Some hormones, for instance, influence the metabolic activities of certain tissues without entering the affected cells and are thought to act by altering the activities of certain enzymes which are located on or within the cellular membrane. *See* CELL MEMBRANES.

Photosynthesis and nitrogen fixation. Two subjects of substantial interest are the processes of photosynthesis and nitrogen fixation. In photosynthesis, the chemical reactions whereby the gas carbon dioxide is converted into carbohydrate are understood, but the reactions whereby light energy is trapped and converted into the chemical energy necessary for the synthesis of carbohydrate are unclear. The process of nitrogen fixation involves the conversion of nitrogen gas into a chemical form which can be utilized for the synthesis of numerous biologically important substances; the chemical events of this process are not fully understood. *See* NITROGEN CYCLE; PHOTOSYNTHESIS.

Methods. The development of biochemistry closely parallels developments in methods of separately and quantitatively measuring small amounts of substances and of determining the structures of substances. The following are some methods employed in biochemistry.

1. Photometry for determining the absorption or emission of light by substances. Measurements conducted with ultraviolet light, below wavelengths of 400 nanometers, or with visible light, 400 to 700 nm, generally furnish information on the concentrations of substances. Infrared measurements, involving wavelengths greater than 700 nm, furnish information on chemical structure as well.

2. Chromatography for separating dissolved substances from one another. This may involve the differential binding of some substances to solid support, the partitioning of substances between two liquid phases, or separation by molecular sieving.

3. Gas chromatography for separation of substances in the gas phase.

4. Isotope labeling for following atoms through reactions, for locating elements in tissues by isotope measurements or radiography, and for ultramicroanalyses, including activation analysis by bombardment with neutrons.

5. Ultracentrifugation for separating large molecules in solution or cell particles in suspension by their differential migration in a centrifugal field. This method is also employed for the determination of molecular weight and for the separation of large molecules which differ from one another in their densities.

6. Electrophoresis for the separation of dissolved charged molecules on the basis of differential migration in an electric field.

7. X-ray crystallography for the determination of the three-dimensional structure of molecules. The method is based on the analysis of the diffraction patterns obtained when a crystal is placed in a beam of monochromatic x-rays.

8. Mass spectrometry for the identification of substances. The substance to be analyzed is volatilized, and the individual molecules are broken into charged fragments. The mass of each charged fragment is determined by its migration in an electric field; the number and characteristics of the fragments permit the deducing of the structure of the parent compound.

9. Nuclear magnetic resonance spectroscopy for the identification of chemical groups in substances and for evaluating changes in the environment around these groups. Certain atomic nuclei, for instance the nucleus of hydrogen, oscillate at radio frequencies when subjected to a strong constant magnetic field. When radio waves of varying frequencies are passed through the solution, absorption of the radio waves is observed at frequencies at which resonance occurs. The frequency at which resonance is observed is a function of the nucleus, the group of which the nucleus is a part, and the environment around the group. *See* ACTIVATION ANALYSIS; AUTORADIOGRAPHY; CHROMATOGRAPHY; ELECTROPHORESIS; GAS CHROMATOGRAPHY; HISTORADIOGRAPHY; MASS SPECTROMETRY; RADIOCHEMISTRY; SPECTROSCOPY; ULTRACENTRIFUGE; X-RAY CRYSTALLOGRAPHY.   A. S. L. Hu

Bibliography. R. C. Bohinski, *Modern Concepts in Biochemistry*, 5th ed., 1987; T. M. Devlin, *Textbook of Biochemistry*, 4th ed., 1997; D. E. Schumm, *Essentials of Biochemistry*, 1988.

Biodegradation

The destruction of organic compounds by microorganisms. Microorganisms, particularly bacteria, are responsible for the decomposition of both natural and synthetic organic compounds in nature. Mineralization results in complete conversion of a compound to its inorganic mineral constituents [for example, carbon dioxide (CO_2; from carbon), sulfate or sulfide (from organic sulfur), nitrate or ammonium (from organic nitrogen), phosphate (from organophosphates), or chloride (from organochlorine)]. Since carbon comprises the greatest mass of organic compounds, mineralization can be considered in terms of CO_2 evolution. Radioactive carbon-14 (^{14}C) isotopes enable scientists to distinguish between mineralization arising from contaminants and soil organic matter. However, mineralization of any compound is never 100% because some of it (10–40% of the total amount degraded) is incorporated into the cell mass or products that become part of the amorphous soil organic matter, commonly referred to as humus. Thus, biodegradation comprises mineralization and conversion to innocuous products, namely biomass and humus. Primary biodegradation is more limited in scope and refers to the disappearance of the compound as a result of its biotransformation to another product. *See* HUMUS.

Enrichment culture. Compounds that are readily biodegradable are generally utilized as growth substrates by single microorganisms. Many of the components of petroleum products (and frequent ground-water contaminants), such as benzene, toluene, ethylbenzene, and xylene, are utilized by many genera of bacteria as sole carbon sources for growth and energy. Microorganisms can be isolated by a small environmental sample that is placed into a flask containing a mineral salts medium with the desired growth substrate (for example, benzene). Thus, the medium is enriched to select those microorganisms (prototrophs) able to utilize the substrate for growth and to synthesize all of their amino acids, nucleic acids, vitamins, and other cellular constituents from inorganic nutrients. Organisms that are capable of metabolizing the compound but require organic growth factors (auxotrophs) are not selected by this procedure. The addition of trace quantities of yeast extract or other growth supplements may enable selection of some auxotrophs, but a high concentration of growth supplements should be avoided as it will enrich for yeast extract utilizers instead of benzene utilizers in the example above. *See* BACTERIAL GROWTH; CULTURE.

Cometabolism and fortuitous metabolism. The process whereby compounds not utilized for growth or energy are nevertheless transformed to other products by microorganisms is referred to as cometabolism. Chlorinated aromatic hydrocarbons, such as diphenyldichloroethane (DDT) and polychlorinated biphenyls (PCBs), are among the most persistent environmental contaminants; yet they are cometabolized by several genera of bacteria, notably *Pseudomonas, Alcaligenes, Rhodococcus, Acinetobacter, Arthrobacter,* and *Corynebacterium.* Cometabolism is caused by enzymes that have very broad substrate specificity. *See* POLYCHLORINATED BIPHENYLS; PSEUDOMONAS.

Bacteria that have evolved pathways for the complete catabolism of aromatic hydrocarbons use these same enzymes to fortuitously transform many chlorinated analogs to more oxidized metabolites. However, not all enzymes in the catabolic pathway have broad specificity, so that a chlorinated product eventually accumulates. For example, bacteria that utilize biphenyl cometabolize polychlorinated biphenyls to chlorobenzoates, which are not acted upon by the enzymes that process benzoate. However, chlorobenzoates are further metabolized by other bacteria that have enzymes which act upon them. Although cometabolism of polychlorinated biphenyls in the environment is a very slow process, it can be greatly enhanced by the addition of analogous growth-promoting substrates, such as biphenyl, a process referred to as analog enrichment. *See* BACTERIAL PHYSIOLOGY AND METABOLISM; CITRIC ACID CYCLE.

Microbial consortia and catabolic genes. Recalcitrant compounds are not degraded by single microorganisms but by a consortium of different organisms. In some cases, the interactions may be loosely associated or asymbiotic (protocooperation) whereby each organism carries out a different step in the catabolic pathway, yet is not dependent upon the other. In other cases, the association may be symbiotic where both benefit (mutualism) or only one benefits (commensalism). Biodegradation of polychlorinated biphenyls in soil is an example of commensalism in which the organism carrying out the initial oxidation receives no benefit while another organism benefits from utilizing the products of cometabolism (chlorobenzoates) for growth. Mutualism normally involves cross-feeding (syntrophism) in which all members are dependent upon each other.

It was discovered in the mid-1970s that dichlorodiphenyltrichloroethane was dehalogenated anaerobically and then mineralized aerobically by different bacteria. It has been shown that polychlorintated biphenyls that are inert to aerobic oxidations (particularly those containing six or more chlorine atoms per molecule) are dehalogenated to lesser chlorinated congeners by anaerobic bacteria in sediments. Thus, the potential exists for complete biodegradation of chlorinated aromatic hydrocarbons by a sequence of anaerobic/aerobic catabolic reactions.

An alternative strategy to mineralization by microbial consortia is to combine the genes of parental strains having the complementary parts of the catabolic pathway into a single organism by recombinant deoxyribonucleic acid (DNA) technology or by natural enhanced mating of parental strains. Catabolic genes that are encoded on plasmids, which are small extrachromosomal elements, are much more readily transferred and expressed in other bacteria than genes coded on the chromosome. Genetic exchange of catabolic plasmids among indigenous bacteria occurs naturally in the environment.

Bioremediation. The use of microorganisms to remediate the environment of contaminants is referred to as bioremediation. This process is most successful in contained systems such as surface soil or ground water where nutrients, mainly inorganic nitrogen and phosphorus, are added to enhance growth of microorganisms and thereby increase the rate of biodegradation. The process has little, if any, applicability to a large open system such as a bay or lake because the nutrient level (that is, the microbial density) is too low to effect substantive biodegradation and the system's size and distribution preclude addition of nutrients. Bioremediation of oil spills on beaches and of ground water containing xylene, from leaking storage tanks can be enhanced by the addition of nitrogen (N) and phosphorus (P), which are essential macroelements of all cells.

Remediation of petroleum products from ground waters is harder to achieve than from surface soil because of the greater difficulty in distributing the nutrients throughout the zone of contamination, and because of oxygen (O_2) limitations. The latter problem is caused by the low solubility of oxygen and by the high biological oxygen demand that occurs when the organisms are present in high numbers and actively mineralizing the contaminant. Hydrogen peroxide (H_2O_2), which is completely miscible in water and rapidly decomposes to oxygen, has been added with nutrients to overcome this problem. Another approach involves a venting system whereby a stream of air is continuously introduced at injection wells at the site. This process also brings about volatilization of the contaminants, which may be metabolized by the indigenous microorganisms as they move upward through the soil. The removal of volatile organic compounds by air stripping and enhancement of biodegradation is referred to as bioventing. This process has proved to be successful in removing chlorinated organic solvents such as trichloroethylene that are major ground-water contaminants.

Fungal enzymes. Bacteria are the primary biocatalysts of organic contaminants, and no eukaryotic organism has ever been isolated that can utilize an aromatic hydrocarbon for growth. Nevertheless, fungi have superior ability to degrade lignin, the primary and most recalcitrant constituent of wood fiber. The extracellular enzymes, in the presence of oxygen, create highly oxidative radicals which break many of the carbon-carbon bonds and the aromatic ether bonds of lignin. The ligninases of *Phanerochaete chrysosporium* fortuitously oxidize many aromatic compounds, including diphenyldichloroethane, polychlorinated biphenyls, polyaromatic hydrocarbons, and trinitrotoluene.

Because this mode of biodegradation is nonspecific and does not proceed in a sequential manner as with bacterial consortia, it is less predictable, less controllable, and less likely to proceed to completion. It is also far less successful in soil than in culture because soil organic matter and other soil constituents also react with the enzyme-catalyzed radicals. Nevertheless, this obstacle has been partially overcome in land-farming operations by diluting soil with massive amounts of plant residues upon which the fungus is maintained or by adding the contaminated soil to reactors containing the fungus. *See* ENZYME; FUNGI. Dennis D. Focht

Bibliography. R. M. Atlas, *Petroleum Microbiology*, 1984; R. M. Atlas and R. Bartha, *Microbial Ecology: Fundamentals and Applications*, 4th ed., 1997; D. T. Gibson, *Microbial Degradation of Organic Compounds*, 1984; T. Leisinger et al. (eds.), *Microbial Degradation of Xenobiotic and Recalcitrant Compounds*, 1982; W. W. Mohn and J. M. Tiedje, Microbial reductive dehalogenation, *Microbiol. Rev*, 56:482–507, 1992; M. J. Pelczar, Jr., E. C. S. Chan, and N. R. Krieg, *Microbiology: Concepts and Applications*, 1993.

Biodiversity

The variety of all living things; a contraction of biological diversity. Biodiversity can be measured on many biological levels ranging from genetic diversity within a species to the variety of ecosystems on Earth, but the term most commonly refers to the number of different species in a defined area.

Global biodiversity. Recent estimates of the total number of species range from 7 to 20 million, of which only about 1.75 million species have been scientifically described. The best-studied groups include plants and vertebrates (phylum Chordata), whereas poorly described groups include fungi, nematodes, and arthropods (see **table**). Species that live in the ocean and in soils remain poorly known. For most groups of species, there is a gradient of increasing diversity from the Poles to the Equator, and the vast majority of species are concentrated in the tropical and subtropical regions.

Human activities, such as direct harvesting of species, introduction of alien species, habitat destruction, and various forms of habitat degradation (including environmental pollution), have caused dramatic losses of biodiversity. The sixth major extinction event in geologic history is well under way. Indeed, current extinction rates are estimated to be 100–1000 times higher than prehuman extinction rates. This rapid loss of species has spurred a great deal of scientific interest in the topic of biodiversity. Currently, many biologists are working to catalog and describe extant species before they are lost. In addition, much research is focused on understanding the importance of biodiversity, particularly whether high levels of biodiversity are essential for proper functioning of ecosystems.

Importance. Ethical and esthetic arguments have been offered regarding the value of biodiversity and why it is necessary to guard against its reduction. Scientists, however, focus on issues such as the biological or ecological functions of biodiversity that can be addressed with experiments rather than debates about values. Certainly, some measure of biodiversity is responsible for providing essential functions and services that directly improve human life. For example, many medicines, clothing fibers, and industrial products and the vast majority of foods are derived from naturally occurring species. In addition, species are the key working parts of natural

Numbers of extant species for selected taxanomic groups				
Kingdom	Phylum	Number of species described	Estimated number of species	Percent described
Protista		100,000	250,000	40.0
Fungi	Eumycota	80,000	1,500,000	5.3
Plantae	Bryophyta	14,000	30,000	46.7
	Tracheophyta	250,000	500,000	50.0
Animalia	Nematoda	20,000	1,000,000	2.0
	Arthropoda	1,250,000	20,000,000	5.0
	Mollusca	100,000	200,000	50.0
	Chordata	40,000	50,000	80.0

*With permission modified from G. K. Meffe and C. R. Carroll, *Principles of Conservation Biology*, Sinauer, Massachusetts, 1997.

ecosystems. They are responsible for maintenance of the gaseous composition of the atmosphere, regulation of the global climate, generation and maintenance of soils, recycling of nutrients and waste products, and biological control of pest species. Ecosystems surely would not function if all species were lost, although it is unclear just how many species are necessary for an ecosystem to function properly. Thus, the current extinction crisis has provoked many scientists to ask how many species can be lost from an ecosystem before the system is negatively affected.

Ecosystem function. Since species are the key working parts of ecosystems, biodiversity must be related to ecosystem function. Studies have assessed this relationship in ecosystem functions such as biogeochemical processes; the flow of nutrients, water, and atmospheric gases; and the processing of energy. Evidence of the importance of biodiversity for ecosystem function is derived from comparing ecosystems that differ in the number of species present. More recently, ecologists have undertaken manipulative experiments in which the number of species has been directly varied. Two notable experimental efforts include manipulations of plant diversity in a Minnesota grassland and manipulations of species and functional diversity in microbial communities. In general, these studies have demonstrated that various measures of ecosystem function such as production of biomass and nutrient uptake increase as the number of species present increases. However, some studies report no effect or even negative relationships between biodiversity and ecosystem processes.

Although some evidence supports the hypothesis that biodiversity increases or improves the overall functioning of ecosystems, the underlying mechanisms remain unclear. For example, a positive relationship between species diversity and productivity could result because including more species to increases the chance of encompassing particularly productive or fast-growing species. Alternatively, a diverse group of species may use the available resources more efficiently, since each species has slightly different requirements, resulting in higher overall growth.

It is unclear whether the number of species or the number of different functional types of species is driving these effects. This distinction is impor-

tant because if the number of species matters most, every species that is added to an ecosystem should cause an improvement in ecosystem function (**illus.** *a*). In contrast, if the diversity of functional types is more important than the number of species per se, there will be initial increases in ecosystem function as species number rises, but these effects should level off once all of the functional types are represented (illus. *b*). Indeed, a nonlinear or satiating effect of species number on ecosystem processes is frequently observed (illus. *b*), suggesting that ecosystem function may be relatively unaffected by initial losses of species but may become severely impaired after some critical number of species is lost.

Ecosystem stability. A second purported benefit of biodiversity is that more diverse ecosystems may be more stable or more predictable through time when compared to species-poor ecosystems. Stability can be defined at the community level as fewer invasions and fewer extinctions, meaning that a more stable community will contain a more stable composition of species. However, stability can also be defined at the population level as reduced fluctuations in population size, meaning that a more stable population will contain a more constant number of individuals.

The idea that biodiversity confers stability upon ecosystems has a long and controversial history. Early ecologists used several lines of reasoning to argue that diverse ecosystems are more stable than those with fewer species. First, attempts to create simple, low-diversity ecosystems in the laboratory tended to fail, with most or all of the species declining to extinction. Second, unpredictable or strongly cyclical population dynamics are often observed in animals that live at high latitudes, and high-latitude

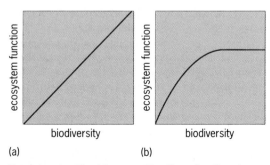

Ecosystem function (*a*) as a positive, linear function of biodiversity and (*b*) as a nonlinear, satiating function of biodiversity.

ecosystems generally include relatively few species. Finally, islands, which generally have fewer species than mainlands, tend to be more easily invaded by introduced species. In 1955, an additional argument was proposed in favor of a positive relationship between biodiversity and ecosystem stability. With more species in an ecosystem, there are more paths through which energy and nutrients can flow; therefore, in diverse ecosystems each species should be less affected by changes in the abundance of other species, leading to higher overall stability. Thus, the general consensus among early ecologists was that more diverse ecosystems should be more stable. *See* ECOSYSTEM; POPULATION ECOLOGY.

In 1973, mathematical models of many species interacting simultaneously were used to explore the relationship between biodiversity and population stability. The major outcome was that higher species diversity led to less stable population sizes of individual species. However, the apparent conflict between these modeling results and the intuitions of earlier ecologists remained unresolved for many years.

Recent studies in which the number of species has been experimentally manipulated have helped to resolve this long-standing controversy. For example, manipulations of plant diversity were used to examine not only the productivity of a grassland ecosystem but also the stability of ecosystem productivity over time. This and other studies have shown that although the abundance of individual species fluctuates more dramatically in high-diversity ecosystems, the total abundance or productivity of all species combined is actually more stable. High biodiversity decreased the stability of each species' population, lending support to mathematical modeling results, whereas the positive relationship between biodiversity and the stability of overall ecosystem productivity supports the proposals of the earlier ecologists.

Although the relationship between biodiversity and ecosystem stability is fairly clear, the mechanisms generating this pattern are not. In particular, diverse groups of species may be more stable because complementary species compensate for changes in one another's abundance. Alternatively, variation in aggregate measures such as total productivity may increase with richness due to averaging of random fluctuations in the growth of each species. Based on simple probability theory, it is expected that the more independently varying species added together, the more stable the sum of their abundances. The strength of this averaging effect depends on correlations among the species' fluctuations, but a positive relationship between biodiversity and the stability of aggregate measures of ecosystem function should usually be expected, simply due to averaging.

Clearly, biodiversity is (at least sometimes) related to both the overall rates and the stability of ecosystem functions. However, documenting a relationship between biodiversity and some measure of ecosystem function or stability does not reveal its underlying cause. Current ecological research continues to explore the mechanisms by which species diversity and functional diversity contribute to ecosystem function.

Species importance. Some species clearly play very important roles in ecosystems. In some cases, the addition or deletion of a single species can lead to dramatic changes in ecosystem functions such as productivity or nutrient uptake. For example, the introduction of a nitrogen-fixing tree species to Hawaii resulted in substantially altered productivity and nutrient dynamics in submontane forest ecosystems. Species that exert such strong control over ecosystems are termed keystone species.

It is not at all clear that most species in an ecosystem have such important effects. In other words, it may be possible to lose a number of species from an ecosystem and yet observe little overall impact on ecosystem function. This could be the case if several species that perform approximately the same function are present in the original ecosystem. The situation where multiple species play a similar role has been termed species redundancy. If species redundancy is a common phenomenon, ecosystem function should be largely independent of species diversity as long as major functional types are represented. Thus, when one species is lost from an ecosystem, some other species with a similar function may become abundant and compensate for the lost species, leaving the ecosystem as a whole relatively unaffected. Indeed, ecosystem processes often do remain stable despite large fluctuations in the abundance of the various species involved. In addition, the relationship between ecosystem function and biodiversity is often observed to be nonlinear (illus. *b*), suggesting that, at least initially, the loss of species would have little overall effect.

The term species redundancy may seem to imply that all species are not necessary for an ecosystem to function properly. However, species redundancy may be an essential feature for the long-term health of ecosystems. Just as engineers include multiple structures with redundant functions to increase overall reliability of the final structure, ecosystems with sets of functionally redundant species may have a built-in safety net that is lacking in species-poor ecosystems.

Rare species (those that occur in low abundance) may also appear to contribute relatively little to overall ecosystem functioning. However, during dramatic environmental changes, such as acidification of a lake, rare species can become very abundant, thereby compensating for reductions in other species. Even species that appear relatively unimportant because they are rare and functionally redundant with others may in fact be important in stabilizing ecosystem function during periods of rare but intense stress.

The overwhelming variety of life has captivated the human imagination for centuries, so it is surprising how much scientific uncertainty currently surrounds the role of biodiversity. Ignorance probably reflects the fact that biodiversity has been taken for granted; only over the last few decades, as biodiversity's staggering decline became more apparent, did ecologists start investigating what exactly is being lost. Most experiments provide compelling evidence that at some point the erosion of biodiversity will impair ecosystem function and stability. However, these same experiments also show that a great deal of biodiversity can typically be lost with minimal effects. The value of biodiversity may well be revealed only on huge time scales that incorporate extremely infrequent but dramatic environmental challenges. If this is the case, standard short-term experiments will be unable to document the value of many species. Clearly, any failure of short-duration, small-scale experiments to identify a function for total biodiversity or for every species should not be used as a disingenuous argument to excuse human-caused extinctions. *See* EXTINCTION (BIOLOGY).   Michelle A. Marvier

Bibliography. F. S. Chapin III et al., Ecosystem consequences of changing biodiversity, *Bioscience*, 48:45–52, 1998; M. A. Huston, *Biological Diversity: The Coexistence of Species on Changing Landscapes*, Cambridge University Press, 1994; C. G. Jones and J. H. Lawton (eds.), *Linking Species and Ecosystems*, Chapman & Hall, 1995; G. H. Orians, R. Dirzo, and J. H. Cushman (eds.), *Biodiversity and Ecosystem Processes in Tropical Forests*, Springer-Verlag, 1996.

Bioelectromagnetics

The study of the interactions of electromagnetic energy (usually referring to frequencies below those of visible light; **Fig. 1**) with biological systems.

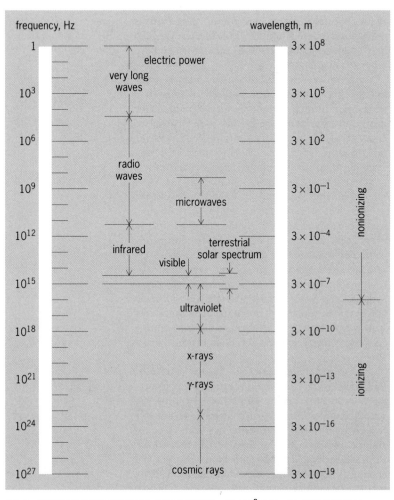

Fig. 1. Electromagnetic spectrum. Speed of light = 3 × 10⁸ m/s = frequency (Hz) × wavelength (m).

This includes both experimental and theoretical approaches to describing and explaining biological effects. Diagnostic and therapeutic uses of electromagnetic fields are also included in bioelectromagnetics.

Background. The interaction of electromagnetic fields with living organisms has intrigued both physicians and engineers since 1892 when J. A. d'Arsonval, a French physician and physicist, applied an electromagnetic field to himself and found that it produced warmth without muscle contraction. Subsequently, the use of electromagnetic energy to heat tissue became a common therapy, and in 1908 Nagelschmidt introduced the term diathermy to describe this process. During the 1930s "short-wave" diathermy (27 MHz) was in common use by physicians. World War II spurred the development of high-power microwave sources for use in radar systems. Shortly thereafter, concern over the safety of radar was voiced, leading to investigation of the biological effects of microwave radiation. Detailed study of the therapeutic potential of diathermy at microwave frequencies began after World War II as high-power equipment became available for medical and other civil applications.

Rapid growth in electronic systems for industrial, military, public service, and consumer use occurred during the 1970s and 1980s. Much of this equipment has the capability of emitting significant levels of electromagnetic radiation. The most extensive exposure to radio-frequency energy is from the thousands of transmitters authorized by the Federal Communications Commission (including commercial broadcast stations, cellular telephone transmitters, walkie-talkies, and microwave and satellite links). In addition, there are millions of unregulated citizen-band stations in use. The National Institute for Occupational Safety and Health estimates that more than 20,000,000 Americans are occupationally exposed to radio-frequency sources mainly from the heating and drying of plastics, textiles, wood products, and other manufactured goods. The use of electromagnetic fields in medicine increased as radio-frequency-induced hyperthermia was applied to cancer therapy. *See* AMATEUR RADIO.

Energy absorption. Electromagnetic energy is not absorbed uniformly across the geometric cross section of a biological organism. The total quantity of energy absorbed and the sites of maximum energy absorption depend on the frequency and polarization of the electromagnetic field, as well as on the electrical characteristics (the dielectric constant and conductivity—two properties of the tissue that control its interaction with electromagnetic radiation—which are frequency-dependent and vary with type of tissue), mass, and geometry of the absorbing object. In principle, the distribution of absorbed energy in an animal can be calculated from classical electromagnetic theory. However, the problem of energy distribution has not been solved for an object as complex as an animal. Simple calculations that assume the exposed system is of regular shape (for example, spheroidal) and of homogeneous composition allow some generalizations to be made. For an average person, maximal absorption (resonance) is predicted at

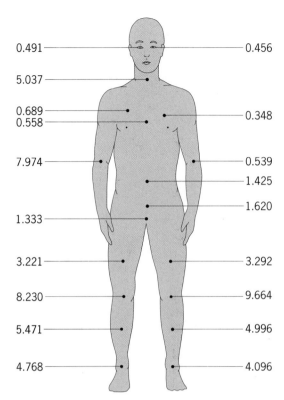

0.491 ——— 0.456

5.037 ———

0.689 ———
0.558 ———   0.348

7.974 ———   0.539

                          1.425

                          1.620

1.333 ———

3.221 ———   3.292

8.230 ———   9.664

5.471 ———   4.996

4.768 ———   4.096

Fig. 2. Distribution of energy deposited in a human being exposed to electromagnetic radiation near the resonant frequency. The numbers provide an indication of the differences in energy absorbed by different parts of the body. (After O. P. Gandhi, Dosimetry: The absorption properties of man and experimental animals, Ann. N.Y. Acad. Med., 55(11):999–1020, December 1979)

approximately 70 MHz. When a complex target, such as a human being, is considered, resonant frequencies are also found in anatomically distinct portions of the body, such as head or leg. The internal energy absorption pattern has been calculated for several simple models: semi-infinite slab, homogeneous sphere, multishell sphere, and multiblock model of a human. While none of these models actually simulates a real human being, local regions of higher-than-average levels of energy absorption have been calculated (**Fig. 2**). Development of instruments that do not interfere with the field permit measurement of partial body resonances and the pattern of energy deposition within some experimental systems. *See* ABSORPTION OF ELECTROMAGNETIC RADIATION.

Biological effects. The induction of cataracts has been associated with exposure to intense microwave fields. Although heating the lens of the eye with electromagnetic energy can cause cataracts, the threshold for cataract production is so high that, for many species, if the whole animal were exposed to the cataractogenic level of radiation, it would die before cataracts were produced.

In 1961 it was reported that people can "hear" pulsed microwaves at very low averaged power densities (50 microwatts/cm^2). It is now generally accepted that the perceived sound is caused by elastic-stress waves which are created by rapid thermal expansion of the tissue that is absorbing microwaves. The temperature elevation occurs in

10 microseconds, so that the rate of heating is about 1.8°F/s (1°C/s). However, the temperature increase is only about 0.00009°F (0.00005°C).

There are reports that microwave irradiation at very low intensities can affect behavior, the central nervous system, and the immune system, but many of these reports are controversial. Animals exposed to more intense electromagnetic fields that produce increases in body temperature of 1.8°F (1°C) or higher (thermal load equal to one to two times the animal's basal metabolic rate) demonstrate modification of trained behaviors and exhibit changes in neuroendocrine levels. Exposure of small animals to weaker fields has been shown to produce some changes in the functioning of the central nervous system and the immune system. While the mechanism is not yet known, a thermal hypothesis is not ruled out. Reports of the effect of very low-level, sinusoidally modulated electromagnetic fields on excitable cell and tissue systems have raised questions about the basic understanding of how those systems function.

Exposure of pregnant rodents to intense electromagnetic fields can result in smaller offspring, specific anatomic abnormalities, and an increase in fetal resorption. However, fields that produce significant heating of the gravid animal have been shown to be teratogenic.

Most biological effects of microwaves can be explained by the response of the animal to the conversion of electromagnetic energy into thermal energy within the animal. However, a few experiments yield results that are not readily explained by changes of temperature.

In an industrial society, an appreciation of the effects of stationary electric and magnetic fields, and of extremely low-frequency fields are important because of the ubiquitous nature of electricity. When the body is in contact with two conductors at different potentials, current flows through it. Typical adult-human thresholds for 50- or 60-Hz currents are:

Reaction	Total body current
Sensation	1 mA
"Let go"	10 mA
Fibrillation	100 mA

The "no contact" case, such as that experienced by an individual or animal under a high-tension transmission line (the field strength directly under a 765-kV line is 4–12 kV/m), has been investigated under controlled experimental conditions.

The possibility of hazard from occupational exposure to 50- or 60-Hz electric and magnetic fields has not been documented and is a subject of debate. Epidemiological studies have been undertaken to determine the health implications for workers and the general public exposed to these possible hazards. In addition, laboratory experiments have been designed to study the interactions of electric and magnetic fields with biological systems.

Some bacteria swim northward in stationary magnetic fields as weak as 0.1 gauss (the Earth's magnetic field is about 0.5 gauss at its surface). These bacteria contain iron organized into crystals of

Activation energies of molecular effects in biological systems*

Effect	Activation energy			Radiation parameters	
	kcal/mole	kJ/mole	eV	Frequency, GHz	Wavelength, μm
Thermal or brownian motion (at 30°C)	0.60	(2.50)	0.026	6.3×10^3	47.6
Ionization	230	(961)	10	2.4×10^6	0.12
Covalent bond disruption	115	(481)	5	1.21×10^6	0.25
London–van der Waals interactions	23	(96)	1	2.4×10^5	1.25
Hydrogen bond disruption	1.8–4.6	(7.5–14.2)	0.08–0.2	1.9×10^4–4.8×10^4	15.8–6.25
Proton tunneling	16.1	(67.3)	0.7	1.71×10^5	1.76
Disruption of bound water	12.9	(53.9)	0.56	1.4×10^5	2.14
Rotation of polar protein molecules	0.92–9.2	(3.8±38)	0.04–0.4	9.7×10^3–9.7×10^4	30.9–3.1
Reversible conformational changes in protein molecules	9.2	(38)	0.4	9.7×10^4	3.1
Charge transfer interaction	138–69	(577–288)	6.3	1.45×10^6–7.25×10^5	0.2–0.4
Semiconduction	23–69	(96–288)	1–3	2.4×10^5–7.25×10^5	1.2–0.41
Microwave radiation	2.7×10^{-6}	(1.12×10^{-7})	1.2×10^{-7}		10^7–10^3
	0.03	(0.12)	1.2×10^{-3}	0.03±300	

*From S. F. Cleary, Uncertainties in the evaluation or the biological effects of microwave and radiofrequency radiation, *Health Phys.*, 25:387–404, 1973.

magnetite. Magnetite is also found in the brains and Harderian glands of birds that can use local variations in the Earth's magnetic field for navigation and orientation. *See* BIOMAGNETISM; MICROWAVE; RADIATION BIOLOGY.

Mechanisms. The energy associated with a photon of radio-frequency radiation is orders of magnitude below the ionization potential of biological molecules (see **table**). Covalent bond disruption, London–van der Waals interactions, and hydrogen-bond disruption, as well as disruption of bound water or reversible conformational changes in macromolecules, all require more energy that is contained in a single microwave photon. There is a possibility that absorption of microwaves (or slightly shorter millimeter waves) may produce vibrational or torsional effects in bio-macromolecules. Thus, if radio-frequency electromagnetic fields have a specific action on molecules that alter their biological function, it will be through a route more complicated and less understood than that associated with ionizing radiation.

The most common mechanism by which electromagnetic fields interact with biological systems is by inducing motion in polar molecules. Water and other polar molecules experience a torque when an electric field is applied. In minimizing potential energy, the dipole attempts to align with the ever-changing electric field direction, resulting in oscillation. Both free and oriented (bound) water undergo dielectric relaxation in the radio-frequency region. The excitation of water, or other polar molecules, in the form of increased rotational energy is manifest as increased kinetic energy (elevation of temperature), but molecular structure is essentially unaltered if elevations are not excessive.

Alternating electromagnetic fields can cause an ordering of suspended particles or microorganisms. This effect, often called pearl-chain formation because the particles line up like a string of beads, results from a dipole-dipole interaction. Nonspherical particles may also be caused to orient either parallel or perpendicular to an applied field. These effects have been observed only at a very high field strength.

Electromagnetic energy absorbed by biological material can be converted into stress by thermal expansion. This phenomenon is caused by a rapid rise of temperature either deep within or at the surface of the material, and thus creates a time-varying thermal expansion that generates elastic stress waves in the tissue.

Medical applications. The therapeutic heating of tissue, diathermy, has been used by physicians for many years. "Short-wave" diathermy has been assigned the frequencies 13.56, 27.12, and 40.68 MHz, while microwave diathermy has been assigned 915, 2450, 5850, and 18,000 MHz. Short-wave diathermy provides deeper, more uniform heating than does diathermy at higher frequencies. *See* THERMOTHERAPY.

High-intensity radio-frequency fields have been used to produce hyperthermia in cancer patients. If a part of the body containing a tumor is heated, the difference of temperature between tumor and surrounding tissue can be increased, at times producing elevations to tumoricidal temperatures of 110–122°F (43–45°C) within the tumor while the surrounding tissue is below the critical temperature at which normal cells are killed. In addition, radio-frequency hyperthermia is often used in combination with x-ray therapy or with chemotherapy. In these cases, the tumor temperature is kept at 114–116°F (41–42°C) to enhance the effectiveness of radiation or chemotherapy.

The development of bone tissue (osteogenesis) can be stimulated electrically either with implanted electrodes or by inductive coupling through the skin. The noninvasive technique uses pulsed magnetic fields to induce voltage gradients in the bone. This therapy has been used successfully to join fractures that have not healed by other means.

Electromagnetic fields were first used for medical diagnosis in 1926 when the electrical resistance across the chest cavity was used to diagnose pulmonary edema (water in the lungs). At frequencies below 100 kHz the movement of ions through extracellular spaces provides the major contribution to conductivity through the body. Thus, fluid-filled lungs can be detected by their lower resistivity. *See* RADIOLOGY.

Another diagnostic tool, magnetic resonance imaging, uses the behavior of protons, or other nuclei, in an electromagnetic field to obtain images of organs in the body. These images are as good as, and sometimes better than, those obtained with x-ray computed tomography. Magnetic resonance imaging is especially useful when viewing the head, breast, pelvic region, or cardiovascular system. In magnetic resonance imaging, a static magnetic field is applied to align nuclear magnetic moments, which then precess about the field direction with a characteristic frequency. When a radio-frequency field is applied transverse to the direction of the magnetic field, nuclei are driven to the antiparallel state. As they return to the ground state, they radiate at their resonant frequency. The strength of the signal is proportional to the concentration density of the nuclei being studied. Other information for image analysis can be obtained from the relaxation time constants of the excited nucleus. *See* COMPUTERIZED TOMOGRAPHY; MEDICAL IMAGING.

Internally generated fields associated with nerve activity (electroencephalography) and with muscle activity (electrocardiography, magnetocardiography) are used to monitor normal body functions. There may be other uses of electric currents or fields in growth differentiation or development which have not yet been explored. *See* CARDIAC ELECTROPHYSIOLOGY; ELECTROENCEPHALOGRAPHY; ELECTROMAGNETIC RADIATION; ELECTROMYOGRAPHY.

Electric fields now play a role in biotechnology. Intense, pulsed electric fields (about 60,000 V/m) produce short-lived pores in cell membranes by causing a reversible rearrangement of the protein and lipid components. This permits the entrance of deoxyribonucleic acid (DNA) fragments or other large molecules into the cell (electroporation). The fusion of cells using electric fields (electrofusion) is easy to control and provides high yields. A weak, nonuniform alternating-current field is used to bring the cells into contact (dielectrophoresis), and then a brief, intense direct-current field is applied, causing the cell membranes to fuse.   Elliot Postow

Bibliography. S. M. Michaelson and J. C. Lin, *Biological Effects and Health Implications of Radiofrequency Radiation*, 1987; C. Polk and E. Postow, *Handbook of Biological Effects of Electromagnetic Fields*, 2d ed., 1996.

Bioelectronics

A discipline in which biotechnology and electronics are joined in at least three areas of research and development: biosensors, molecular electronics, and neuronal interfaces. Some workers in the field include so-called biochips and biocomputers in this area of carbon-based information technology. They suggest that biological molecules might be incorporated into self-structuring bioinformatic systems which display novel information processing and pattern recognition capabilities, but these applications—although technically possible—are speculative.

It is an interesting reversal of the past in that bioelectronics uses the biological sciences in the development of the physical sciences and technologies, whereas the prior direction was to use the tools of the physical sciences to investigate and advance the biological sciences, life sciences, and medicine.

Of the three disciplines—biosensors, molecular electronics, and neuronal interfaces—which collectively constitute bioelectronics the most mature is the burgeoning area of biosensors. The term biosensor is used to describe two sometimes very different classes of analytical devices—those that measure biological analytes and those that exploit biological recognition as part of the sensing mechanism—although it is the latter concept which truly captures the spirit of bioelectronics. Molecular electronics is a term coined to describe the exploitation of biological molecules in the fabrication of electronic materials with novel electronic, optical, or magnetic properties. Finally, and more speculatively, bioelectronics incorporates the development of functional neuronal interfaces which permit contiguity between neural tissue and conventional solid-state and computing technology in order to achieve applications such as aural and visual prostheses, the restoration of movement to the paralyzed, and even expansion of the human faculties of memory and intelligence. The common feature of all of this research activity is the close juxtaposition of biologically active molecules, cells, and tissues with conventional electronic systems for advanced applications in analytical science, electronic materials, device fabrication, and neural prostheses.

Biosensors. A biosensor is an analytical device that converts the concentration of an analyte in an appropriate sample into an electrical signal by means of a biological sensing element intimately connected to, or integrated into, a transducer. Biosensors differ from existing analytical technologies in several important respects. First, there is intimate contact between the biological component, whether it be an enzyme, sequence of enzymes, organelle, whole cell, tissue slice, antibody, or other receptor or

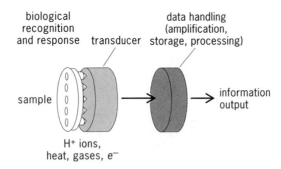

biological recognition and response

transducer

data handling (amplification, storage, processing)

sample

information output

H+ ions, heat, gases, e−

Fig. 1. Schematic representation of the essential features of a typical biosensor. (*After I. J. Higgins and C. R. Lowe, Introduction to the principles and applications of biosensors, Phil. Trans. Roy. Soc. Lond., B316:3–11, 1987*)

binding protein, and the transducer. Second, most new-generation biosensors are functionally small in size, thereby permitting small sampling volumes with minimum interruption of bodily functions following implantation, or, if used with process streams, following insertion in-line. Third, the biological material may be tailored to suit the medical or industrial needs and operate at various levels of specificity. Finally, biosensors are simple to use; they are single-step, reagentless devices which are inexpensive, disposable, and fully compatible with conventional data-processing technologies.

Figure 1 illustrates the general principle of a biosensor. Intimate contact between the biological and electrochemical systems is usually achieved by immobilization of the biosensing system on the transducer surface by physical restraint behind a polymer membrane or within a gel matrix, by chemical cross-linking with a bifunctional agent, or by direct covalent attachment. The biological system is responsible for the specific recognition of the analyte and subsequently responds with a concomitant change in a physicochemical parameter associated with the interaction. For example, if the biological interaction results in a change in pH, uptake or release of gases, ions, heat, or electrons, or a perturbation of an optical parameter proximal to the transducer, the biological signal may be converted into an electrical signal prior to being amplified, digitized, and outputted in the desired format.

Transducers. These are physicochemical devices that respond to the products of the binding or biocatalytic process. The choice of the most appropriate transducer configuration will be conditioned largely by the nature of the biocatalyst system, the secondary products to be monitored, and the potential application of the final device. The ideal transducer should display a moderately fast response time, typically 1–60 s, be amenable to the facile fabrication and miniaturization, be reliable, and should compensate for adverse environmental effects such as temperature dependency and drift. *See* TRANSDUCER.

One of the best-known transducers is the potentiometric ion-sensitive electrode which measures the accumulation of charge density at the electrode surface under equilibrium conditions. The potential of an ion-sensitive electrode is a logarithmic function of ionic activity, with a 59.2-mV change in electrode potential per tenfold change in concentration of a monovalent ion. Since the late 1970s, major improvements in electrode design and performance have been achieved, and ion-sensitive electrodes have been developed for monitoring a variety of cations, anions, metabolites, solvents, gases, mutagens, amino acids, drugs, and other analytes. This diversity has been made possible by coupling enzymes; whole plant, animal, and microbial cells; organelles; tissues; and immuno-enzymatic assay systems to conventional ion-sensitive electrodes to generate appropriate enzyme and immuno-enzyme electrodes. *See* ION-SELECTIVE MEMBRANES AND ELECTRODES.

The analyte-sensitive membranes of the ion-sensitive electrodes have been integrated with monolithic solid-state field-effect transistor (FET) technology to introduce a range of ion-selective and substrate-specific FETs. For example, an FET sensitive to penicillin has been constructed which responded to penicillin concentrations up to 50–60 millimoles in less than 30 s, displayed a lifetime of approximately 2 months, and permitted automatic compensation for temperature and ambient pH. The device comprised a matched pH-responsive ion-selective FET pair with an active gate film of cross-linked albumin-penicillinase and a reference gate film of cross-linked albumin. The enzyme present in the active gate polymer catalyzed the hydrolysis of penicillin with the concomitant release of hydrogen ion (H+) and subsequent detection in the silicon nitride (Si_2N_4) gate material. When operated in differential mode, the sensor pair was reported to be relatively free from thermal effects and from changes in the ambient pH of the analyte solution. However, the buffer capacity of the analyte was found to have a profound influence on the sensitivity, range, and linearity of the response.

Similar limitations were experienced with other enzyme-modified FET devices, such as those responsive to glucose, urea, acetylcholine, adenosine triphosphate (ATP), and lipid, with the complementary enzymes glucose oxidase, urease, acetylcholinesterase, adenosine triphosphatase (ATPase), and lipase immobilized to pH-responsive Si_3N_4 or iridium oxide (Ir_2O_3) gate materials. A co-integrated coulometric feedback system may circumvent these limitations. The electrolysis of water at a noble-metal electrode spatially positioned close to a urea-sensitive FET generates H+, which can be used to balance the uptake engendered by the enzyme activity. However, in addition to the problems encountered by immobilization of small quantities of enzyme for the determination of substrates in samples containing a high buffering capacity, the difficulty in fabricating small, well-defined immobilized enzyme membranes on the ion-selective gate of an FET is a hurdle which must also be circumvented prior to manufacturing monolithic enzyme-modified FETs. *See* TRANSISTOR.

Photoactivatable *p*-nitrophenylazides, photosensitive polyvinylalcohol with pendant stilbazolium groups as a photo-cross-linkable entrapment matrix,

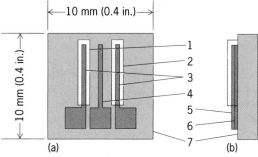

Key:

1 = polyvinyl alcohol with active
     glucose oxidase
2 = polyvinyl alcohol with inactive
     glucose oxidase
3 = anode
4 = common cathode
5 = gold layer (150 nm)
6 = chromium layer (10–30 nm)
7 = glass plate

Fig. 2. Configuration of a thin-film glucose biosensor, (*a*) **front view and** (*b*) **side view, and glucose oxidase-immobilized polyvinyl alcohol membranes. (*After T. Moriizumi, Solid state biosensors, Proceedings of International Symposium on Future Electron Devices, Tokyo, pp. 73–80, 1985*)**

and piezoelectric ink-jet devices have all been used successfully to generate active small-area enzyme membranes. For example, it has been demonstrated that it is feasible to generate monolothic multienzyme-modified FET biosensors by using photolithographically patterned, enzyme-loaded polyvinyl alcohol films, and a triple-function, silicon-on-sapphire array, with an on-chip pseudo-reference electrode for the measurement of urea, glucose, and potassium ion (K^+). Thus, despite some unresolved problems, biosensors based on integrated solid-state devices display considerable potential for miniaturization of multifunction configurations.

Amperometric devices. Also known as current-measuring devices, these offer a wider scope of applications than potentiometric techniques and are linearly dependent on analyte concentration, thereby giving a normal dynamic range and normal response to errors in the measurement of current. A solid-state hydrogen peroxide (H_2O_2) sensor has been fabricated and used in a glucose sensor. **Figure 2** shows the electrode pattern on the sensor chip; it comprises three double-layer (150-nm-thick gold, 10 to 30-nm-thick chromium) electrodes deposited on a glass substrate with a bare gold-film constituting the central common cathode. Glucose oxidase-loaded membranes were spin-coated over one of the gold-film electrodes and photopolymerized, while denatured enzyme was deposited over the other pair of electrodes. The electrodes were connected to a potentiostat which followed the difference in anode currents from the active and reference electrodes caused by the reoxidation of enzymatically generated H_2O_2 when the anodes were biased at +0.8 V; with respect to the cathode. **Figure 3** shows a typical calibration curve for

the miniaturized amperometric glucose sensor. Thin-film microsensors of this type are promising devices for H_2O_2 detection since they are widely applicable and display good sensitivity.

Solution conductance. An alternative measuring principle which is also widely applicable to biological systems is the exploitation of solution conductance. The development and operation of an accurate microelectronic conductance biosensor which operates in a differential mode by monitoring the change in conductance occasioned by the catalytic action of enzymes immobilized proximal to a planar microelectronic conductance cell of defined geometry has also been described. Each conductance device comprised a pair of serpentined and interdigitated parallel trimetallic (gold, platinum, titanium) tracks, 1000–3500 nm thick and 4000 nm wide, deposited onto an oxidized silicon surface by using standard sputter deposition processes or thermal evaporation under vacuum followed by appropriate photolithographic processes and metal etching. An enzyme-loaded cross-linked albumin membrane was cast over the interdigitated sample pair of electrodes, but not over the reference pair, so that subtraction of the amplified signals emanating from the conductimeter electronics continuously corrected for nonspecific variations in basal conductivity of the buffers and biological fluids in which measurements were being made. The output response of the differential enzyme microconductimeter with urease immobilized over the sample cell was linear up to 5 min at all urea concentrations in the range 0.1–10 millimoles. There was a linear correlation between serum urea concentrations determined with the microelectronic device and those determined by conventional procedures at a major hospital laboratory. The microelectronic enzyme conductimeter can be used with many other enzymes that create changes in solution conductance, thus providing a most useful and versatile addition to available analytical techniques.

Other measurement devices. Other on-chip measuring principles have also been exploited in the fabrication

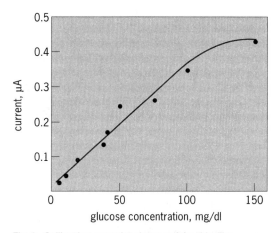

Fig. 3. Calibration curve for glucose of the thin-film biosensor at pH 7.0 and 37°C (98.6°F). (*After T. Moriizumi, Solid state biosensors, Proceedings of International Symposium on Future Electron Devices, Tokyo, pp. 73–80, 1985*)

of biosensors. For example, it has been demonstrated that two integrated-circuit temperature-sensitive devices, each composed of 3 Darlington connected *npn* transistors and a complementary metal-oxide semiconductor constant-current circuit, can be used for the differential calorimetric determination of glucose concentrations. The difference in steady-state output voltage of the enzyme-modified sensor compared to the unmodified sensor after addition of 2–100 millimoles glucose was related to the catalytically induced temperature change and thus to the glucose concentration.

Furthermore, miniature piezoelectric sensors, for example, quartz crystal and surface-acoustic-wave devices, can be used directly in aqueous solution as enzyme substrate and immunochemical sensors. Organophosphorus pesticides and parathion were detected with coatings of immobilized cholinesterase and anti-parathion antibodies respectively. Excellent reproducibilities, coating lifetimes, response times, and sensitivities were observed in the research. The most likely application of this type of biosensor technology lies in the detection of illicit drugs, of explosives in airport and post office surveillance, and of toxic pollutants.

Potential for the technology. Clearly biosensors have evolved into miniaturized, disposable, solid-state devices with the theoretical capacity to cointegrate the signal-processing and -conditioning circuitry directly on-chip and thereby obviate the requirement for traditional external instrumentation. A multifunction chip comprising an array of biologically sensitized gates deposited on a monolithic silicon chip could also incorporate sufficient signal-conditioning capability to interrogate each sensor in turn, assess the outputs, compare with a calibration standard, and release the information as the concentration of the analyte together with the date, batch code, expiration date, and operator code. However, the obstacles that remain from the commercial applications of this technology are formidable. Passivation of the sensitive electronic components to the rigors of aqueous solutions and the lability of the biologically active areas remain problems in the long-term acceptability of these devices.

Molecular electronics. Biology has many examples of organized structures on an intracellular, cellular, or intercellular level, and, at the molecular level, of complex biological analogs of conventional electronic data processing. Biological systems, in fact, perform all of the functions of interest to the modern electronics industry (sensing, input/output, memory, computation) as well as functions not yet achieved (rapid complex pattern recognition and learning). However, the lability and general prerequisite for an aqueous environment militate against the use of biological molecules as active components in nonbiological microsystems. It is more likely that the self-assembly properties of proteins will be exploited to form a template or matrix for the proper assembly of complex architectures from conventional electronic components. In addition, biological analogies

are likely to suggest the development of novel structures and algorithms to achieve functions not readily accomplished by computing devices of present-day design.

Neuronal interfaces. The term biochip is sometimes used to describe an implantable system that would enable the interconnection of nervous tissue with conventional computer devices. However, like the construction of a biosensor, the fabrication of a functioning neuronal interface or artificial synapse will require the development of appropriate reversible chemical-to-electrical transduction processes. The development of a neuronal interface is thus likely to require greater knowledge about the chemical mechanisms which govern synaptic communication. *See* NEURON.   Christopher R. Lowe

Bibliography. N. C. Foulds and C. R. Lowe, Biosensors: Current applications and future potential, *Bioessays*, 3:129–132, 1985; C. R. Lowe, Biosensors, *Trends Biotechnol.*, 2:59–65, 1984; C. R. Lowe, An introduction to the concepts and technology of biosensors, *Biosensors*, 1:3–16, 1985; A. Sibbald, Recent advances in field-effect chemical microsensors, *J. Mol. Electr.*, 2:51–83, 1986.

Bioeroding sponges

Marine sponges that are able to erode calcareous substrates such as coral, mollusk shells, and limestone, also called boring or excavating sponges. Confirmed eroders belong to the families Samidae, Thoosidae, Clionaidae, Spirastrellidae, Acarnidae, and Phloeodictyidae, which are all demosponges. The best-known species belong to the genera *Cliona*, *Pione*, and *Aka*. Species are identified by their skeletal elements, morphology, tissue characteristics, and erosion traces. *See* DEMOSPONGIAE.

Description and characteristics. Bioeroding sponges occur in three growth forms: alpha, beta, and gamma (**Fig. 1**). Sponges in alpha form live almost entirely inside the substrate and fill the cavities and tunnels they produce. They reach the surrounding water with small tubes of tissue protruding from the substrate surface, the fistules (centimeter scale; Fig. 1*a*) or papillae (millimeter scale; Fig. 1*b*). The beta form additionally covers the substrate surface with a coherent layer of tissue (Fig. 1*c*). Gamma specimens resemble noneroding sponges and can be massive or cup-shaped. They may contain remnants of calcareous matter. The growth forms are thought to represent stages during the life of some bioeroding sponges, but by far most species occur only in the alpha form.

The life inside hard substrate provides the sponge with shelter against predators and adverse conditions such as desiccation at low tide or extreme temperatures. The sponge larva settles on a suitable surface and starts to erode into the substrate. In order to grow, the sponge forms or enlarges chambers and tunnels (**Fig. 2***a*). Specialized cells with fine, thread-like extensions secrete chemicals, which dissolve

Bioeroding sponges

Growth forms of bioeroding sponges.

(a) Alpha form. Fistules of *Aka mucosa* (Phloeodictyidae) breaking through the surface of a live coral. Scale: 5 cm.

(b) Alpha form. *Cliona celata* papillae (Clionaidae). Sievelike inhalant papillae, with four open exhalant papillae in upper half of photograph. Scale: 2 cm.

(c) Beta form. *Cliona orientalis* (Clionaidae, left) competing with a free-living sponge. Yellow structures on the surface of *C. orientalis* are exhalants. Finger at low right for scale.

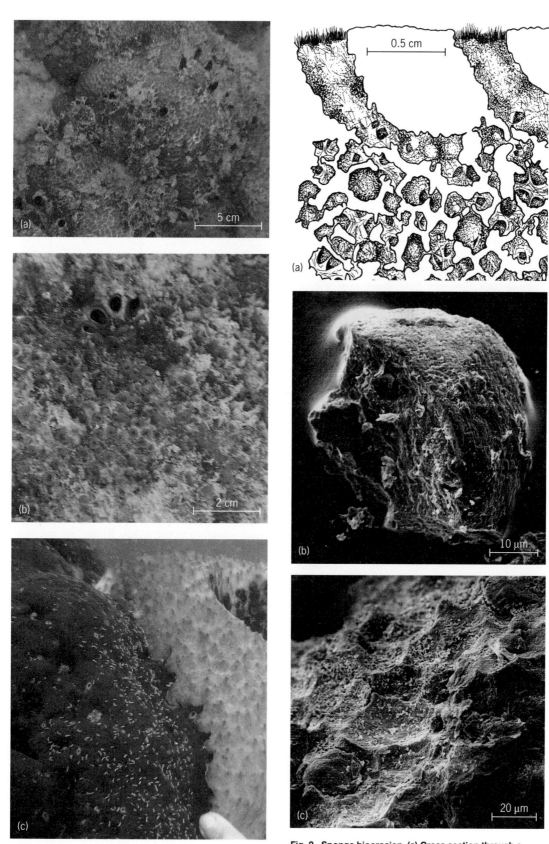

Fig. 1. Growth forms of bioeroding sponges. (*a*) Alpha form. Fistules of *Aka mucosa* (Phloeodictyidae) breaking through the surface of a live coral. (*b*) Alpha form. *Cliona celata* papillae (Clionaidae). Sievelike inhalant papillae, four open exhalant papillae in upper half of photograph. (*c*) Beta form. *Cliona orientalis* (Clionaidae, left) competing with a free-living sponge. Lighter structures on the surface of *C. orientalis* are exhalants. Finger in lower right for scale.

Fig. 2. Sponge bioerosion. (*a*) Cross section through a colony of *Cliona celata* in coral. Gray areas are bioerosion chambers filled with sponge tissue and pin-shaped skeletal elements. The latter are arranged in pallisade in the two papillae that break through the substrate surface (*drawing courtesy of Sula Blake*). (*b*) Sponge chip from *C. orientalis*. (*c*) Pitted structure of chamber walls in a clam shell eroded by *C. orientalis*. In lower left and upper right corners, sponge chips are still in the process of being cut.

2–3% of the eroded material. The sponge etches cup-shaped fissures into the material, cutting out lentil-shaped chips with a diameter of 20–100 μm (Fig. 2b). The activity of many cells results in a typical pitted structure on the walls of the eroded material (Fig. 2c). The silt-sized chips are expelled with the water that is pumped through the sponge and can contribute 30–40% of the sediments on tropical coral reefs. Erosion rates depend on environmental factors such as nutrient and light levels, currents, and substrate density.

Effects of bioerosion. Bioeroding sponges recycle calcareous materials, create new three-dimensional microhabitats in which other organisms can hide, and enhance coral dispersal by fragmentation. However, coral fragments may also be moved to environments with unfavorable conditions. In normal circumstances, coral reef growth is larger or equal to bioerosion. However, this balance may shift due to environmental disturbances such as overfishing of predators, increased nutrient levels, and the reduction of live surface cover. High levels of sponge bioerosion on coral reefs would result in an altered carbonate budget, a significant decline of three-dimensional structure provided by healthy coral; a reduction of biodiversity of organisms that need a high degree of structural diversity, including commercially used species; and the destruction of what we perceive as a beautiful reef, and consequently losses for the tourism industry. *See* REEF.

Bioeroding sponges are also destructive parasites of mollusks. Oysters in aquaculture are coated with protective paint or regularly cleaned to prevent the sponge larvae settling and developing on the shells. *See* MOLLUSCA.

Diversity and range. The guild of bioeroding sponges presently consists of about 250 valid species. The highest biodiversity of bioeroding sponges is recorded from tropical coral reefs in the Indian Ocean. Slightly fewer are known from the Atlantic and Pacific oceans and only two or three species from polar waters. The sponges mainly occur in shallow water 0–50 m (0–165 ft) deep, but have been sampled from as deep as 2030 m (6300 ft) [*Alectona mesatlantica*, Thoosidae]. The fossil record confirms the occurrence of bioeroding sponges as early as the Devonian (*Entobia devonica*, in fossil stromatoporoids and bivalves).

Christine Schönberg

Bibliography. J. N. A. Hooper and R. W. M. van Soest (eds.), *Systema Porifera: A Guide to the Classification of Sponges*, vol. 1, *Introductions and Demospongiae*, Kluwer Academic/Plenum, New York, 2002; K. Rützler and C. Rieger, Sponge burrowing: Fine structure of *Cliona lampa* penetrating calcareous substrata, *Mar. Biol.*, 21:144–162, 1973; C. H. L. Schönberg, Growth and erosion of the zooxanthellate Australian bioeroding sponge *Cliona orientalis* are enhanced in light, *Proc. 10th Int. Coral Reef Symp.*, Okinawa, Japan, in press; C. H. L. Schönberg, Substrate effects on the bioeroding demosponge *Cliona orientalis*, 1. Bioerosion rates, *PSZNI: Mar. Ecol.*, 23(4):313–326, 2002.

Biofilm

An adhesive substance, the glycocalyx, and the bacterial community which it envelops at the interface of a liquid and a surface. When a liquid is in contact with an inert surface, any bacteria within the liquid are attracted to the surface and adhere to it. In this process the bacteria produce the glycocalyx. The bacterial inhabitants within this microenvironment benefit as the biofilm concentrates nutrients from the liquid phase. However, these activities may damage the surface, impair its efficiency, or develop within the biofilm a pathogenic community that may damage the associated environment. Microbial fouling or biofouling are the terms applied to these actual or potential undesirable consequences.

Microbial fouling affects a large variety of surfaces under various conditions. Microbial biofilms may form wherever bacteria can survive; familiar examples are dental plaque and tooth decay. Dental plaque is an accumulation of bacteria, mainly streptococci, from saliva. The attachment of bacteria to the tooth is not random. Certain types of bacteria are specific to certain locations on the tooth: anaerobic bacteria are found deep within the biofilm, whereas aerobes are found near the plaque-air interface. The ability of the biofilm to concentrate nutrients is not important in this environment because the mouth itself is rich in nutrients; rather, the plaque protects the bacterial inhabitants from being transported by swallowing to a more hostile environment in the stomach. The process of tooth decay begins with the bacteria colonizing fissures in and contact points between the teeth. Dietary sucrose is utilized by the bacteria to form extracellular glucans that make up the glycocalyx and assist adhesion to the tooth. Within this microbial biofilm or plaque the metabolic by-products of the bacterial inhabitants are trapped; these include acids that destroy the tooth enamel, dentin, or cementum. *See* PERIODONTAL DISEASE; TOOTH DISORDERS.

Nature and formation. The formation of a biofilm commences with the transportation of bacteria from the liquid phase to a contiguous surface. The mechanisms involved are sedimentation, chemotaxis, Brownian motion, cell surface hydrophobicity, and fluid dynamic forces. A hypothesis explaining the process of attraction postulates that different combinations of force affect the bacteria according to their distance from the surface. Van der Waals forces operate at a distance greater than 50 nanometers from the surface and give a rapid but weak attraction; both van der Waals and electrostatic interactions occur together between 10 and 20 nm from the surface. At a distance of less than 1.5 nm from the surface, van der Waals forces, electrostatic interactions, and specific interactions occur, producing an irreversible binding between the bacteria and the surface. This binding is associated with the activation of glycogen-producing genes. Then production by the bacteria of adhesive materials, such as exopolysaccharides, that form the glycocalyx begins. Not all of the different adhesive media are known. Many factors affect the initial colonization of the surface, including surface roughness, the nature of the surface, the velocity of liquid next to the surface, and the temperature. *See* INTERMOLECULAR FORCES.

After initial attachment, the organisms grow and divide to form microcolonies within the glycocalyx. Microbial products and organic and inorganic matter are trapped within the microbial biofilm. This occurrence creates a concentration of nutrients in the biofilm. In addition, other microorganisms join and are protected within the glycocalyx. In this way, the structure of the microbial biofilm changes; as the biofilm matures, it is influenced by interrelated physical, chemical, and biological components. But the bacterial inhabitants exert the largest influence on biofilm development because they create a favorable environment and can alter the physical and chemical properties of the microbial biofilm.

Of less importance are the chemical and physical factors that influence biofilm development. Biofilm stability is promoted by the presence of calcium, magnesium, or iron, and the growth of the biofilm microorganisms is associated with the availability of nutrients. Physical factors include the volume and mass of the biofilm and the diffusion of gases, nutrients, and heat within it.

The concentration of bacteria within a microbial biofilm is associated with the concentration of nutrients to support growth. This is a useful response for survival in low-nutrient environments such as the so-called clean industrial processes, treated drinking water systems, and clear mountain streams. Microbial biofilms have been found in all such environments. In low-nutrient environments, such as an oil reservoir, studies show that bacteria adopt starvation responses, for example, they may become smaller, and that under long-term starvation regimes bacteria may produce less glycocalyx.

Microbial fouling. The process of microbial fouling involves the secretion by the biofilm inhabitants of metabolites that damage the surface or the production of organic or inorganic deposits upon the surface. The consequences of microbial fouling are (1) physical damage to the surface as a result of microbial growth and metabolite activity; (2) the reduction in the proper function of the surface because of the presence of the biofilm; and (3) the creation of a reservoir of potential pathogens within the biofilm. These consequences are not mutually exclusive. Microbial fouling in such places as drinking water, food industries, marine environments, and industrial water systems is of great concern, and it is therefore carefully monitored.

Drinking water and food industries. In these industries there is considerable concern with the potential for the microbial biofilm to act as a reservoir for potential pathogens. The presence of pathogens is often detected by sampling the bacteria in the liquid phase. This approach, however, neglects the fact that bacteria are concentrated within the biofilm, so that readings from the liquid sample may be misleading. In such cases, contamination is detected only when pathogens become detached from the mature biofilm and appear in the liquid phase.

In the water industry, biofouling is difficult to monitor and control because the supply system is made up of an extensive network of treatment plants and delivery pipes. Thus the absence of pathogens within a biofilm in one part of the system does not mean that other parts are not contaminated. The use of copper pipes in distribution does not lessen the chances of biofouling; at one time it was considered that bacteria would not grow on such materials, but later research showed that this was not the case. For example, a study of a drinking water utility showed that bacterial counts were above permitted levels. Samples of biofilms were taken as pipe scrapings from various parts of the system. While the treatment plant was found to contain bacteria within permitted levels, unacceptable levels were found in biofilms in the distribution system and along the way to the consumer. In addition, treatment by free chlorine did not control the problem because the pathogens were protected from the antimicrobial agents by the biofilms. *See* WATER SUPPLY ENGINEERING.

In the food industry the food comes into contact with a large number of surfaces during processing and packaging. This situation raises concerns regarding the prevention of contamination that are similar to those in the water supply industry. Some research has been carried out to find processes to reduce the opportunities for bacterial detachment from stainless steel or nylon; results so far, however, have been inconclusive because the type of surface and the type of bacteria studied were shown to affect the possibility of detachment. *See* FOOD MICROBIOLOGY.

Marine environments. Microbial fouling in seawater begins with the submerged surface absorbing organic material from the water before being colonized by a succession of different bacteria. The final event is confluent glycocalyx production. The biofouling is generally followed by macrofouling as various creatures are attracted to the surface to feed off the biofilm.

The fouling of hulls reduces vessel speed and increases the cost of transport. The fouling of metal marine structures may result in corrosion. Sulfate in seawater acts as an electron acceptor for sulfate-reducing bacteria. This leads to the production of sulfide, which enhances the corrosion of the surface. Antifouling paints are not always effective and may be damaging to the marine environment. Treated surfaces can be colonized within 2 weeks of submersion, and the glycocalyx may protect the biofilm inhabitants from the paint.

Industrial water systems. Water is used in industry for cleaning, as a coolant, or for a specific part of a process. The large surface areas associated with cooling systems and heat exchangers, such as radiators, give ample opportunity for biofouling, provided the water supports bacteria. This is not always so; pure water is used in the pharmaceutical industry to combat biofouling, but there is a risk of subsequent contamination.

Metal corrosion is the result of an electrochemical process whereby an anode site on the metal yields a supply of electrons that travel through the metal to a cathode site elsewhere on the surface. This process forms anodic pits and cathodic depositions on the surface. Microorganisms are attracted to and colonize a metal surface, and activity within the biofilm generates conditions that are favorable for the sulfate-reducing bacteria, anaerobic bacteria that are the principal corroding organisms. That is, aerobic microorganisms in the upper biofilm deplete oxygen, producing anaerobic conditions in the lower biofilm contiguous to the metal surface. Sulfate-reducing bacteria produce hydrogen sulfide, which is highly corrosive, but in addition the electrochemical corrosion process is intensified by the activity of sulfate-reducing bacteria. The bacteria utilize hydrogen by means of hydrogenase enzymes, and this generates the anodic reaction. In addition, within the biofilm, production of bacterial metabolites and biopolymers with differing electrical charges and composition is sufficient to develop a corrosion potential. This process of corrosion by pitting of the metal means that failure tends to occur at points on the surface. *See* CORROSION.   Hilary Lappin-Scott; J. W. Costerton

Bibliography. W. G. Characklis and P. A. Wildrer (eds.), *Structure and Function of Biofilms,* 1989; M. Fletcher and B. Capdeville (eds.), *Biofilms: Science and Technology,* vol. 223, 1992; S.P. Gorman and M. Sussman (eds.), *Microbial Biofilms: Formation and Control,* 1994; M. W. Mittleman and G. G. Geesey, *Biological Fouling of Industrial Water Systems: A Problem Solving Approach,* 1987; D. C. Savage and M. Fletcher, *Bacterial Adhesion Mechanisms and Physiological Significance,* 1985.

Biogeochemistry

The study of the cycling of chemicals between organisms and the surface environment of the Earth. The chemicals either can be taken up by organisms and used for growth and synthesis of living matter or can be processed to obtain energy. The chemical composition of plants and animals indicates which elements, known as nutrient elements, are necessary for life. The principal element composition of land plants is shown in the **table.** The most abundant nutrient elements, carbon (C), hydrogen (H), and oxygen (O), supplied by the environment in the form of carbon dioxide (CO_2) and water (H_2O), are usually present in excess. The other nutrient elements, which are also needed for growth, may sometimes be in short supply; in this case they are referred to as limiting nutrients. The two most commonly recognized limiting nutrients are nitrogen (N) and phosphorus (P).

Biogeochemistry is concerned with both the biological uptake and release of nutrients, and the transformation of the chemical state of these biologically active substances, usually by means of energy-supplying oxidation-reduction reactions, at the Earth's surface. Emphasis is on how the activities of organisms affect the chemical composition of natural waters, the atmosphere, rocks, soils, and sediments. Thus, biogeochemistry is complementary to

Elemental composition of plants*

Element	Concentration, % dry weight of tissue
Carbon	45
Oxygen	45
Hydrogen	6
Nitrogen	1.5
Potassium	1.0
Calcium	0.5
Phosphorus	0.2
Magnesium	0.2
Sulfur	0.1
Chlorine	0.01
Iron	0.01
Manganese	0.005
Zinc	0.002
Boron	0.002
Copper	0.0006
Molybdenum	0.00001

*From W. Stumm (ed.), *Global Chemical Cycles and Their Alterations by Man,* Dahlem Konferenzen, 1977.

the science of ecology, which includes a concern with how the chemical composition of the atmosphere, waters, and so forth affects life. *See* ECOLOGY; OXIDATION-REDUCTION.

The two major processes of biogeochemistry are photosynthesis and respiration. Photosynthesis involves the uptake, under the influence of sunlight, of carbon dioxide, water, and other nutrients by plants to form organic matter and oxygen. A generalized expression is shown in reaction (1), where the ex-

$$CO_2 + H_2O + (xN + yP + \cdots) \rightarrow$$
$$CH_2ON_xP_y + \cdots + O_2 \quad (1)$$

pression ($xN + yP + \cdots$) represents other nutrient elements in various chemical forms and $CH_2ON_xP_y\ldots$ represents organic matter. Respiration is the reverse of photosynthesis and involves the oxidation and breakdown of organic matter and the return of nitrogen, phosphorus, and other elements, as well as carbon dioxide and water, to the environment. *See* PHOTOSYNTHESIS; PLANT RESPIRATION.

Biogeochemistry is usually studied in terms of biogeochemical cycles of individual elements. This gives rise to expressions such as the biogeochemical cycle of carbon and the terrestrial cycle of phosphorus. Time is an important consideration in such cycles: there are short-term cycles ranging from days to centuries and long-term (geological) cycles ranging from thousands to millions of years.

There has been increasing interest in biogeochemistry because the human influence on short-term biogeochemical cycling has become evident. Perhaps the best-known example is the changes in the biogeochemical cycling of carbon due to the burning of fossil fuels and the cutting and burning of tropical rainforests. The cycles of nitrogen and phosphorus have been altered because of the use of fertilizer and the addition of wastes to lakes, rivers, estuaries, and the oceans. Acid rain, which results from the addition of sulfur and nitrogen compounds to the atmosphere by humans, affects biological systems in

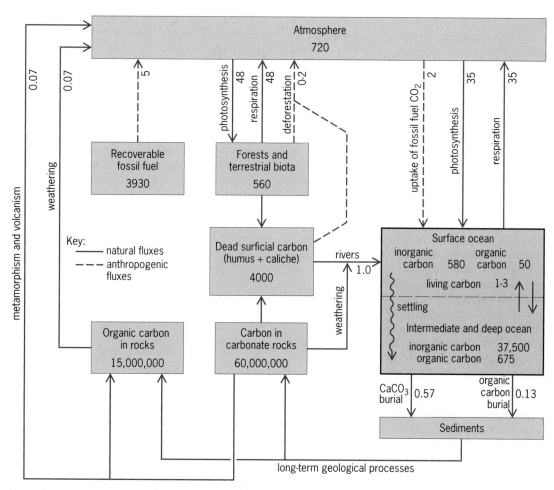

Fig. 1. Carbon cycle. Photosynthetic fluxes between the atmosphere and oceans, and the atmosphere and land, represent net primary productivity. Reservoir units, gigatons (10^{15} g) C; flux units, gigatons C/yr.

certain areas. A solid understanding of the biogeochemical cycles of the major nutrient elements is, therefore, basic to dealing with current and future problems caused by human impact on the environment. *See* HUMAN ECOLOGY.

Carbon cycle. Carbon is the basic biogeochemical element. The carbon cycle shown in **Fig. 1** provides a basis for understanding biogeochemical cycling. The atmosphere contains carbon in the form of carbon dioxide gas. There is a large annual flux of atmospheric carbon dioxide to and from forests and terrestrial biota, amounting to nearly 7% of total atmospheric carbon dioxide. This is because carbon dioxide is used by plants to produce organic matter through photosynthesis, and when the organic matter is broken down through respiration, carbon dioxide is released to the atmosphere. The concentration of atmospheric carbon dioxide shows a yearly oscillation (**Fig. 2**) because there is a strong seasonal annual cycle of photosynthesis and respiration in the Northern Hemisphere.

Photosynthesis and respiration in the carbon cycle can be represented by reaction (2), which is a sim-

plified version of reaction (1). Breakdown of organic matter via respiration is accomplished mainly by bacteria that live in soils, sediments, and natural waters. As can be seen from Fig. 1, there is a very large reservoir of terrestrial carbon in carbonate rocks, which contain calcium carbonate ($CaCO_3$), and in rocks such as shales which contain organic carbon. Major exchange of carbon between rocks and the

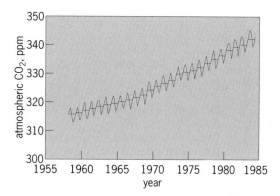

Fig. 2. Concentration of atmospheric carbon dioxide (CO_2) at Mauna Loa Observatory, Hawaii; ppm stands for parts per million volume fraction. Horizontal bars represent yearly averages. (After J. R. Trabalka, ed., *Atmospheric Carbon Dioxide and the Global Carbon Cycle*, U. S. Department of Energy, DOE/ER-0239, 1985)

$$CO_2 + H_2O \underset{\text{respiration}}{\overset{\text{photo-synthesis}}{\rightleftharpoons}} CH_2O + O_2 \qquad (2)$$

atmosphere is very slow, on the scale of thousands to millions of years, compared to exchange between plants and the atmosphere, which can even be seasonal. *See* MICROBIAL ECOLOGY; SOIL MICROBIOLOGY.

Organic carbon burial on land is not important now, but was important in the geologic past when coal deposits formed in swamps. Carbon is lost from the land by river transport of dissolved bicarbonate ion $[(HCO_3)^-]$ and of dissolved and particulate organic carbon. Overall, about two-thirds of the river load is derived from the biological cycle and from atmospheric carbon dioxide, and the rest comes from the weathering of carbonate rocks. However, the river transport of carbon (1 gigaton or 10^{15} g per year) is small compared to the amount of carbon cycled between the atmosphere and the land (48 gigatons/yr) or the atmosphere and the oceans (35 gigatons/yr). *See* CARBONIFEROUS.

The oceans taken as a whole represent a major reservoir of carbon. Carbon in the oceans occurs primarily as dissolved $(HCO_3)^-$ and to a lesser extent as dissolved carbon dioxide gas and carbonate ion $[(CO_3)^{2-}]$. The well-mixed surface ocean (the top 250 ft or 75 m) rapidly exchanges carbon dioxide with the atmosphere. However, the deep oceans are cut off from the atmosphere and mix with it on a long-term time scale of about 1000–2000 years. Most of the biological activity in the oceans occurs in the surface (or shallow) water where there is light and photosynthesis can occur. *See* MARITIME METEOROLOGY.

The main biological process in seawater is photosynthetic production of organic matter by phytoplankton. Some of this organic matter is eaten by animals, which are in turn eaten by larger animals farther up in the food chain. Almost all of the organic matter along the food chain is ultimately broken down by bacterial respiration, which occurs primarily in shallow water, and the carbon dioxide is quickly recycled to the atmosphere. However, some occurs in deeper waters which can accumulate excess dissolved carbon dioxide because of a lack of exchange with the atmosphere. Overall, of the large annual carbon flux (35 gigatons/yr) between the atmosphere and the oceans, only a small fraction (0.13 gigaton/yr) escapes destruction as organic matter that falls to the bottom and is buried in ocean sediments; part of this sedimentary organic matter is marine and part is transported by rivers from land. Most organic carbon is buried nearshore, for example, in marine deltas where the sediment deposition rate is high. *See* FOOD WEB; NEARSHORE PROCESSES; PHYTOPLANKTON; SEAWATER.

Another major biological process is the secretion of shells and other hard structures by marine organisms. Bicarbonate is removed from the water in the form of solid calcium carbonate (calcite and aragonite minerals), as shown in reaction (3).

$$Ca^{2+} + 2(HCO_3)^- \rightarrow CO_2 + H_2O + CaCO_3 \qquad (3)$$

A biogeochemical cycle of calcium and bicarbonate exists within the oceans, linking the deep and shallow water areas. Bottom dwellers in shallow water, such as corals, mollusks, and algae, provide calcium carbonate skeletal debris. Since the shallow waters are saturated with respect to calcium carbonate, this debris accumulates on the bottom and is buried, providing the minerals that form carbonate rocks such as limestone and dolomite. Calcium carbonate is also derived from the shells of organisms inhabiting surface waters of the deep ocean; these are tiny, floating plankton such as foraminiferans, pteropods, and coccoliths. Much of the calcium carbonate from this source dissolves as it sinks into the deeper ocean waters, which are undersaturated with respect to calcium carbonate. The undissolved calcium carbonate accumulates on the bottom to form deep-sea limestone. The calcium and the bicarbonate ions $[Ca^{2+}$ and $(HCO_3)^-]$ dissolved in the deep ocean water eventually are carried to surface and shallow water, where they are removed by planktonic and bottom-dwelling organisms to form their skeletons. *See* CARBONATE MINERALS; LIMESTONE.

The long-term biogeochemical carbon cycle occurs over millions of years when the calcium carbonate and organic matter that are buried in sediments are returned to the Earth's surface. There, weathering occurs which involves the reaction of oxygen with sedimentary organic matter with the release of carbon dioxide and water (analogous to respiration), and the reaction of water and carbon dioxide with carbonate rocks with the release of calcium and bicarbonate ions. This latter process is the reverse of that shown in reaction (3). *See* WEATHERING PROCESSES.

Human perturbation of carbon cycle. Fossil fuels (coal and oil) represent a large reservoir of carbon (Fig. 1). Burning of fossil fuels releases carbon dioxide to the atmosphere, and an increase in the atmospheric concentration of carbon dioxide has been observed since the mid-1950s (Fig. 2). While much of the increase is attributed to fossil fuels, deforestation by humans accompanied by the decay or burning of trees is another possible contributor to the problem.

When estimates are made of the amount of fossil fuels burned from 1959 to 1980, only about 60% of the carbon dioxide released can be accounted for in the atmospheric increase in carbon dioxide. The remaining 40% is known as excess carbon dioxide. The surface oceans are an obvious candidate for storage of most of the excess carbon dioxide by the reaction of carbon dioxide with dissolved carbonate to form bicarbonate. Because the increase in bicarbonate concentration in surface waters due to excess carbon dioxide uptake would be small, it is difficult to detect whether such a change has occurred. Greater quantities of excess carbon dioxide could be stored as bicarbonate in the deeper oceans, but this process takes a long time because of the slow rate of mixing between surface and deep oceans.

An increase in atmospheric carbon dioxide is of concern because of the greenhouse effect. The carbon dioxide traps heat in the atmosphere; notable increases in atmospheric carbon dioxide should cause an increase in the Earth's surface temperature by as much as several degrees. This temperature increase would be greater at the poles, and the effects could include melting of polar ice, a rise in sea level, and changes in rainfall distribution, with droughts in interior continental areas such as the Great Plains of the United States. *See* DROUGHT; GREENHOUSE EFFECT.

Terrestrial nitrogen cycle. Nitrogen is dominantly a biogenic element and has no important mineral forms. It is a major atmospheric constituent with a number of gaseous forms, including molecular nitrogen gas (N_2), nitrogen dioxide (NO_2), nitric oxide (NO), ammonia (NH_3), and nitrous oxide (N_2O). As an essential component of plant and animal matter, it is extensively involved in biogeochemical cycling. On a global basis, the nitrogen cycle is greatly affected by human activities.

Nitrogen gas (N_2) makes up 80% of the atmosphere by volume; however, nitrogen is unreactive in this form. In order to be available for biogeochemical cycling by organisms, nitrogen gas must be fixed, that is, combined with oxygen, carbon, or hydrogen. There are three major sources of terrestrial fixed nitrogen: biological nitrogen fixation by plants, nitrogen fertilizer application, and rain and particulate dry deposition of previously fixed nitrogen. Biological fixation occurs in plants such as legumes (peas and beans) and lichens in trees, which incorporate nitrogen from the atmosphere into their living matter; about 30% of worldwide biological fixation is due to human cultivation of these plants. Nitrogen fertilizers contain industrially fixed nitrogen as both nitrate and ammonium. *See* FERTILIZER; NITROGEN FIXATION.

Fixed nitrogen in rain is in the forms of nitrate [$(NO_3)^-$] and ammonium [$(NH_4)^+$] ions. Major sources of nitrate, which is derived from gaseous atmospheric nitrogen dioxide (and nitric oxide), include (in order of importance) combustion of fossil fuel, especially by automobiles; forest fires (mostly caused by humans); and lightning. Nitrate in rain, in addition to providing soluble fixed nitrogen for photosynthesis, contributes nitric acid (HNO_3), a major component of acid rain. Sources of ammonium, which is derived from atmospheric ammonia gas (NH_3), include animal and human wastes, soil loss from decomposition of organic matter, and fertilizer release. *See* ACID RAIN.

The basic land nitrogen cycle (**Fig. 3**) involves the photosynthetic conversion of the nitrate and ammonium ions dissolved in soil water into plant organic material. Once formed, the organic matter may be stored or broken down. Bacterial decomposition of organic matter (ammonification) produces soluble ammonium ion which can then be either taken up again in photosynthesis, released to the atmosphere as ammonia gas, or oxidized by bacteria to nitrate ion (nitrification).

Nitrate ion is also soluble, and may be used in photosynthesis. However, part of the nitrate may undergo reduction (denitrification) by soil bacteria to nitrogen gas or to nitrous oxide which are then lost to the atmosphere. Compared to the land carbon cycle, the land nitrogen cycle is considerably more complex, and because of the large input of fixed nitrogen by humans, it is possible that nitrogen is building up on land. However, this is difficult to determine since the amount of nitrogen gas recycled to

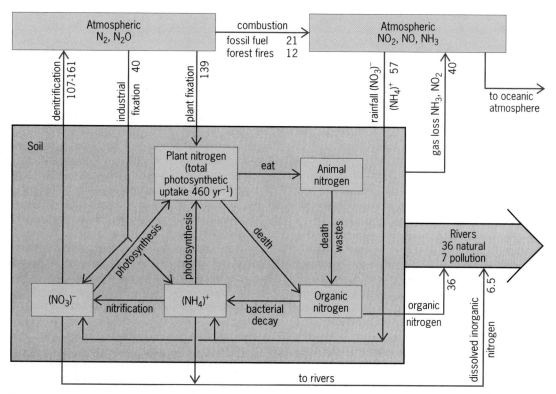

Fig. 3. Terrestrial nitrogen cycle; organic nitrogen includes both particulate and dissolved material. Flux units, teragrams (10^{12} g) N/yr.

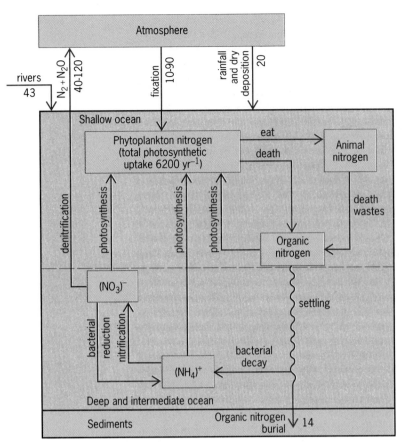

Fig. 4. Marine nitrogen cycle; organic nitrogen includes both particulate and dissolved material. Flux units, teragrams (10^{12} g) N/yr.

the atmosphere is not known and any changes in the atmospheric nitrogen concentration would be too small to detect. *See* NITROGEN CYCLE.

Oceanic nitrogen cycle. The oceans are another major site of nitrogen cycling (**Fig. 4**): the amount of nitrogen cycled biogenically, through net primary photosynthetic production, is about 13 times that on land. The main links between the terrestrial and the oceanic nitrogen cycles are the atmosphere and rivers. Nitrogen gases carried in the atmosphere eventually fall as dissolved inorganic (mainly nitrate) and organic nitrogen and particulate organic nitrogen in rain on the oceans. The flux of river nitrogen lost from the land is only about 9% of the total nitrogen recycled biogeochemically on land each year and only about 25% of the terrestrial nitrogen flux from the biosphere to the atmosphere.

River nitrogen is an important nitrogen source to the oceans; however, the greatest amount of nitrogen going into ocean surface waters comes from the upwelling of deeper waters, which are enriched in dissolved nitrate from organic recycling at depth. Dissolved nitrate is used extensively for photosynthesis by marine organisms, mainly plankton. Bacterial decomposition of the organic matter formed in photosynthesis results in the release of dissolved ammonium, some of which is used directly in photosynthesis. However, most undergoes nitrification to form nitrate, and much of the nitrate may undergo denitrification to nitrogen gas which is released to

the atmosphere. A small amount of organic-matter nitrogen is buried in ocean sediments, but this accounts for a very small amount of the nitrogen recycled each year. There are no important inorganic nitrogen minerals such as those that exist for carbon and phosphorus, and thus there is no mineral precipitation and dissolution. *See* UPWELLING.

Phosphorus cycle. Phosphorus, an important component of organic matter, is taken up and released in the form of dissolved inorganic and organic phosphate. Phosphorus differs from nitrogen and carbon in that it does not form stable atmospheric gases and therefore cannot be obtained from the atmosphere. It does form minerals, most prominently apatite (calcium phosphate), and insoluble iron (Fe) and aluminum (Al) phosphate minerals, or it is adsorbed on clay minerals. The amount of phosphorus used in photosynthesis on land is large compared to phosphorus inputs to the land (**Fig. 5**). The major sources of phosphorus are weathering of rocks containing apatite and mining of phosphate rock for fertilizer and industry. A small amount comes from precipitation and dry deposition. *See* PHOSPHATE MINERALS.

Phosphorus is lost from the land principally by river transport, which amounts to only 7% of the amount of phosphorus recycled by the terrestrial biosphere; overall, the terrestrial biosphere conserves phosphorus. Humans have greatly affected terrestrial phosphorus: deforestation and agriculture have doubled the amount of phosphorus weathering; phosphorus is added to the land as fertilizers and from industrial wastes, sewage, and detergents. Thus, about 75% of the terrestrial input is anthropogenic; in fact, phosphorus may be building up on the land.

In the oceans, phosphorus occurs predominantly as dissolved orthophosphates [PO_4^{3-}, $(HPO_4)^{2-}$ and $(H_2PO_4)^-$]. Since it follows the same cycle as do carbon and nitrogen, dissolved orthophosphate is depleted in surface ocean waters where both photosynthesis and respiration occur, and the concentration builds up in deeper water where organic matter is decomposed by bacterial respiration. The major phosphorus input to the oceans is from rivers, with about 5% coming from rain. However, 75% of the river phosphorus load is due to anthropogenic pollutants; humans have changed the ocean balance of phosphorus. Most of the dissolved oceanic orthophosphate is derived from recycled organic matter. The output of phosphorus from the ocean is predominantly biogenic: organic phosphorus is buried in sediments; a smaller amount is removed by adsorption on volcanic iron oxides. In the geologic past, there was a much greater inorganic precipitation of phosphorite (apatite) from seawater than at present, and this has resulted in the formation of huge deposits which are now mined.

Nutrients in lakes. Biogeochemical cycling of phosphorus and nitrogen in lakes follows a pattern that is similar to oceanic cycling: there is nutrient depletion in surface waters and enrichment in deeper waters. Oxygen consumption by respiration in deep water

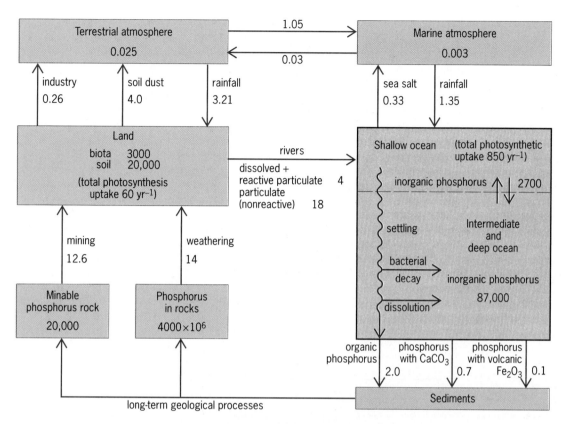

Fig. 5. Phosphorus cycle. Reservoir units, teragrams (10^{12} g) P; flux units, teragrams P/yr.

sometimes leads to extensive oxygen depletion with adverse effects on fish and other biota. In lakes, phosphorus is usually the limiting nutrient.

Many lakes have experienced greatly increased nutrient (nitrogen and phosphorus) input due to human activities. This stimulates a destructive cycle of biological activity: very high organic productivity, a greater concentration of plankton, and more photosynthesis. The result is more organic matter falling into deep water with increased depletion of oxygen and greater accumulation of organic matter on the lake bottom. This process, eutrophication, can lead to adverse water quality and even to the filling up of small lakes with organic matter. *See* EUTROPHICATION; LIMNOLOGY.

Biogeochemical sulfur cycle. A dominant flux in the global sulfur cycle (**Fig. 6**) is the release of 65–70 teragrams of sulfur per year to the atmosphere from burning of fossil fuels. Sulfur contaminants in these fuels are released to the atmosphere as sulfur dioxide (SO_2) which is rapidly converted to aerosols of sulfuric acid (H_2SO_4), the primary contributor to acid rain. Forest burning results in an additional release of sulfur dioxide. Overall, the broad range of human activities contribute 75% of sulfur released into the atmosphere. Natural sulfur sources over land are predominantly the release of reduced biogenic sulfur gases [mainly hydrogen sulfide (H_2S) and dimethyl sulfide] from marine tidal flats and inland waterlogged soils and, to much lesser extent, the release of volcanic sulfur. The atmosphere does not have an appreciable reservoir of sulfur because most

sulfur gases are rapidly returned (within days) to the land in rain and dry deposition. There is a small net flux of sulfur from the atmosphere over land to the atmosphere over the oceans.

Ocean water constitutes a large reservoir of dissolved sulfur in the form of sulfate ions [$(SO_4)^{2-}$]. Some of this sulfate is thrown into the oceanic atmosphere as sea salt from evaporated sea spray, but most of this is rapidly returned to the oceans. Another major sulfur source in the oceanic atmosphere is the release of oceanic biogenic sulfur gases (such as dimethyl sulfide) from the metabolic activities of oceanic organisms and organic matter decay. Marine organic matter contains a small amount of sulfur, but sulfur is not a limiting element in the oceans.

Another large flux in the sulfur cycle is the transport of dissolved sulfate in rivers. However, as much as 43% of this sulfur may be due to human activities, both from burning of fossil fuels and from fertilizers and industrial wastes. The weathering of sulfur minerals, such as pyrite (FeS_2) in shales, and the evaporite minerals, gypsum and anhydrite, make an important contribution to river sulfate. The major mechanism for removing sulfate from ocean water is the formation and burial of pyrite in oceanic sediments, primarily nearshore sediments. (The sulfur fluxes of sea salt and biogenic sulfur gases do not constitute net removal from the oceans since the sulfur is recycled to the oceans.)

Biogeochemical cycles and atmospheric oxygen. The main processes affecting atmospheric oxygen, as shown by reaction (2), are photosynthesis and

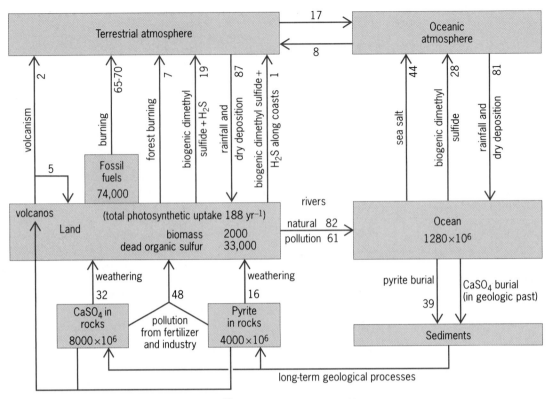

Fig. 6. Sulfur cycle. Reservoir units, teragrams (10^{12} g) S; flux units, teragrams S/yr.

respiration; however, these processes are almost perfectly balanced against one another and, thus, do not exert a simple effect on oxygen levels. Only the very small excess of photosynthesis over respiration, manifested by the burial of organic matter in sediments, is important in raising the level of oxygen. This excess is so small, and the reservoir of oxygen so large, that if the present rate of organic carbon burial were doubled, and the other rates remained constant, it would take 5–10 million years for the amount of atmospheric oxygen to double. Nevertheless, this is a relatively short time from a geological perspective. *See* ATMOSPHERE; ATMOSPHERE, EVOLUTION OF; ATMOSPHERIC CHEMISTRY; BIOSPHERE; GEOCHEMISTRY; HYDROSPHERE; MARINE SEDIMENTS.

Elizabeth K. Berner; Robert A. Berner

Bibliography. E. K. Berner and R. A. Berner, *The Global Water Cycle: Geochemistry and Environment*, 1987; R. A. Berner (ed.), Geochemical cycles of nutrient elements, *Amer. J. Sci.*, 282:401–542, 1982; C. B. Gregor et al., *Chemical Cycles in the Evolution of the Earth*, 1988; G. E. Likens, F. H. Bormann, and N. M. Johnson, *Biogeochemistry of a Forested Ecosystem*, 2d ed., 1995; J. R. Trabalka (ed.), *Atmospheric Carbon Dioxide and the Global Carbon Cycle*, U. S. Department of Energy, DOE/ER-0239, 1985.

Biogeography

A synthetic discipline that describes the distributions of living and fossil species of plants and animals across the Earth's surface as consequences of ecological and evolutionary processes. Biogeography overlaps and complements many biological disciplines, especially community ecology, systematics, paleontology, and evolutionary biology. *See* PLANT GEOGRAPHY; ZOOGEOGRAPHY.

Development. Early biogeographers were natural historians who collected data regarding the geographic locations of different species. Initial research focused on Europe. Data from Africa, Asia, and the New World were compiled as explorations of these regions by Europeans progressed. These early compilations of data on geographic distributions played a key role in C. Darwin's demonstration that species were not generated by independent events, but were derived from other species. Darwin showed that despite being designed in different ways, most organisms found together in a geographic region were closely related. For example, features of reproductive biology indicated that marsupial "moles" in Australia were more closely allied with kangaroos than with European moles, which looked superficially similar. Similar patterns, found within many different groups of plants and animals, could not be reconciled with arguments from design that assumed similarity in appearance was a basis for classifying species into natural groups. Biogeographic patterns supported Darwin's alternative view that natural groups of organisms were formed by genealogical relationships.

Based on relatively complete compilations of species within well-studied groups, such as birds and mammals, biogeographers identified six different realms within which species tend to be closely related and between which turnovers in major groups

Biogeographic realms		
Realm	Continental areas included	Examples of distinctive or endemic taxa
Palearctic	Temperate Eurasia and northern Africa	Hynobiid salamanders
Oriental	Tropical Asia	Lower apes
Ethiopian	Sub-Saharan Africa	Great apes
Australian	Australia and New Guinea	Marsupials
Nearctic	Temperate North America	Pronghorn antelope, ambystomatid salamanders
Neotropic	Subtropical Central America and South America	Hummingbirds, antbirds, marmosets

of species are observed (see **table**). The boundaries between biogeographic realms are less distinct than was initially thought, and the distribution of distinctive groups such as parrots, marsupials, and southern beeches (*Nothofagus* spp.) implies that modern-day biogeographic realms have been considerably mixed in the past. *See* ANIMAL EVOLUTION; PALEOBOTANY; PALEOECOLOGY; PALEONTOLOGY; PLANT EVOLUTION; SPECIATION.

Historical biogeography. In the 1920s, data on the distribution of certain groups of living and fossil plants and animals were used by the German meteorologist Alfred L. Wegener to argue that continents had once been connected with one another. When the physical basis for plate tectonics was discovered, a revolution in biogeography ensued. Previously, biogeographic distributions of taxa were explained by dispersal of species away from centers of origin. For example, marsupials were thought to have originated in Australia and then dispersed by some means to South America. After it was realized that continents had moved across the face of the Earth in the past, and are in fact currently moving, explanations for disjunct distributions of taxa like marsupials could be explained as the initial evolutionary radiation of a group on a continent, followed by a splitting of that continent into two or more pieces.

A key to explaining the existence of disjunct distributions within a taxon is having an estimate of the evolutionary history of that taxon. The discovery that such estimates could be obtained using phylogenetic systematics ushered in yet another revolution in biogeography. Using the methods of phylogenetic systematics, estimates of phylogenies called cladograms are obtained (**Fig. 1**). A cladogram is a bifurcating network, where nodes in the network represent hypothesized common ancestors. When the geographic distributions of different taxa are superimposed upon a cladogram, the resulting area cladogram provides an estimate of the geological history of the areas (Fig. 1). Geographic regions with shallow branches in an area cladogram are predicted to have shared a recent geological history, while those with deep branches are hypothesized to have shared a more ancient history. Thus, area cladograms generate predictions about unobservable and unique historical events that can be examined with independent geological, paleontological, or biogeographic data sets.

Ecological biogeography. Historical approaches to biogeography are well suited for developing an un-

derstanding of geographic patterns in the distribution of taxa, but they have provided relatively little insight into patterns of species diversity within and among different geographic regions. Two such patterns have stimulated a great deal of progress in developing ecological explanations for geographic patterns of species richness. The first is that the number of species increases in a regular fashion with the size of the geographic area being considered. The second is the nearly universal observation that there are more species of plants and animals in tropical regions than in temperate and polar regions.

In order to answer questions about why there are a certain number of species in a particular geographic region, biogeography has incorporated many insights from community ecology. Species number at any particular place depends on the amount of resources available there (ultimately derived from the amount of primary productivity), the number of ways those resources can be apportioned among

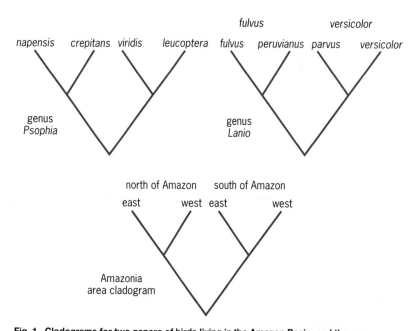

Fig. 1. Cladograms for two genera of birds living in the Amazon Basin, and the area cladogram most consistent with the data from these genera. Within each genus, taxa have disjunct, nonoverlapping distributions. *Psophia napiens* and *P. crepitans* live north of the Amazon, with *napiens* farthest west. *Psophia viridis* and *P. leucoptera* are south of the Amazon, with *leucoptera* farthest west. Two species in *Lanio* are sister taxa, with *L. fulvus* distributed north of the Amazon and *L. versicolor* south of the Amazon. Each species has two subspecies. *L. f. peruvianus* and *L. v. versicolor* are the westernmost subspecies in each case. The area cladogram implies that the Amazon marked a boundary that isolated populations of a single species in each genus on its north and south banks. Subsequently, barriers formed that isolated eastern and western populations within the northern and southern populations. (*Data from J. Cracraft, Deep-history biogeography: Retrieving the historical pattern of evolving biotas, Sys. Zool., 37:221–236,1988*)

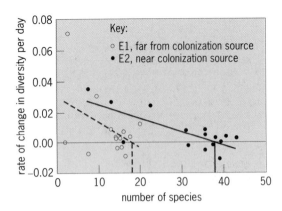

Fig. 2. Patterns of colonization by arthropod species for mangrove islands that were experimentally defaunated show colonization rates that correspond to those predicted from the equilibrium theory of island biogeography. Here, the rate of change in number of species as the islands recovered from the defaunation is plotted against the number of species on two islands. Least-squares regression lines were fitted to the rate data for each island. The equilibrium number of species is the number for which the rate of change in diversity is zero, shown here by the x-intercepts of the regression lines. The theory predicts that islands closer to a colonization source (island E2) should have a higher equilibrium diversity than islands farther from the source (island E1). This prediction is clearly substantiated by the experiment. (*Data from D. S. Simberloff and E. O. Wilson, Experimental zoogeography of islands: The colonization of empty islands, Ecology, 50:278–296, 1969*)

species, and the different kinds of ecological requirements of the species that can colonize the region. The equilibrium theory of island biogeography arose as an application of these insights to the distribution of species within a specified taxon across an island archipelago. This theory generated specific predictions about the relationships among island size and distance from a colonization source with the number and rate of turnover of species. Large islands are predicted to have higher equilibrium numbers of species than smaller islands; hence, the species area relationship can be predicted in principle from the ecological attributes of species. Experimental and observational studies have confirmed many predictions made by this theory (**Fig. 2**).

Applying the insights from the equilibrium theory of island biogeography to patterns in species diversity across continents has been much more difficult. Islands are discrete geographic features. Analogous "habitat" islands exist in some places on continents, but most terrestrial habitats are connected together within landscapes so that dispersal from one segment of habitat to another is relatively common. Populations on continents that might normally become extinct if they were located on islands (with relatively small likelihood of receiving colonists) can persist on a continent by frequent immigration from nearby populations. A consensus theory of species diversity on continents has not yet arisen, but current work on the subject indicates that the ability of organisms to disperse from one population to the next, and how this varies among species and landscapes, will be a primary component of the extension of island biogeographic theory to continents.

Aquatic organisms are exposed to unique physical and biotic conditions that make it difficult to extend ecological biogeographic theory from terrestrial to aquatic ecosystems. Fresh-water organisms inhabiting lakes can be viewed as inhabiting aquatic islands in a sea of terrestrial ecosystems, but species distributed in rivers exist within effectively linear biogeographic realms where physical flow tends to be in a single direction (such as downstream). Marine organisms often have larval dispersal strongly constrained by major oceanographic features such as directional ocean currents and gyres. Population sizes and species diversity may depend less on available local resources and more strongly on successful transportation of larvae across large distances. Such unique features of aquatic biology place unique challenges to constructing a general-theory ecological biogeography applicable to both aquatic and terrestrial biomes. *See* ECOLOGICAL COMMUNITIES; ECOLOGICAL SUCCESSION; ECOLOGY; ECOSYSTEM; ISLAND BIOGEOGRAPHY; TERRESTRIAL ECOSYSTEM.

The latitudinal gradient in species richness has generated a number of explanations, none of which has been totally satisfactory. One explanation is based on the observation that species with more temperate and polar distributions tend to have larger geographic ranges than species from tropical regions. This is not an artifact of the distribution of tropical regions on continents because similar patterns are seen in marine environments. It is thought that since species with large geographic ranges tend to withstand a wider range of physical and biotic conditions, this allows them to penetrate farther into regions with more variable climates at higher latitudes. If this were true, then species with smaller geographic ranges would tend to concentrate in tropical regions where conditions are less variable. While this might be generally true, there are many examples of species living in high-latitude regions that have small geographic regions. *See* ALTITUDINAL VEGETATION ZONES.

Modern developments. Historical biogeography and ecological biogeography have developed essentially independent of one another, involving research from entirely different groups of scientists that seldom communicate. This has traditionally hindered the development of a robust evolutionary approach to biogeography, which must necessarily incorporate both ecological and historical explanations. Consider the problem of understanding why a particular number of species inhabit a particular geographic region. The current number of species will be determined by a complex interaction of a number of factors operating at different temporal and spatial scales. Ecological factors might include the effects of climate on the spatial population dynamics across a species' ranges, spatial variation in appropriate biotic and abiotic resources, and the geographic distribution of competitors and natural enemies. Evolutionary factors might include the rate and mode of speciation and extinction, the rate of adaptive divergence, and the nature of barriers to gene flow across species' ranges. Attempts to resolve the effects of these kinds of processes must incorporate an understanding of the natural history of the species involved, estimates of phylogenetic relationships among them, and the structure of the environment across which species are arrayed.

Recent attempts to integrate the perspectives described in the previous paragraph under the rubrics of macroecology, dynamic biogeography, and areography suggest promising directions for future research. Areography was a term devised by the Argentinian plant ecologist Eduardo Rapoport in 1982 to describe his approach to studying the properties of geographic ranges of species. His approach was explicitly synthetic, and he attempted to devise quantitative models that described variation in the properties of geographic ranges within and among species. His insights were later expanded by the concept of dynamic biogeography. This approach focused not only on the static properties of geographic ranges but also on changes in ranges due to invasions, climate change, and extinction. Dynamic biogeography sought to explain how biological processes operated across a geographic range to determine spatial variation in local abundance, and how this affects the size, shape, and dynamics of the range boundary for a species. Additional insights to the explanations of biogeographic patterns were developed by showing that patterns of body size variation among species were closely related to variation in range size, average abundance, trophic level, and phylogeny. This approach, termed macroecology, emphasized that most explanations for biogeographic phenomena required a comparative approach. It was found that patterns in the variation among species implied the operation of relatively general evolutionary processes, such as nonrandom speciation and extinction.

Biogeography is entering a phase where data on the spatial patterns of abundance and distribution of species of plants and animals are being analyzed with sophisticated mathematical and technological tools. Geographic information systems and remote sensing technology have provided a way to catalog and map spatial variation in biological processes with a striking degree of detail and accuracy. These newer technologies have stimulated research on appropriate methods for modeling and analyzing biogeographic patterns. Modern techniques of spatial modeling are being applied to geographic information systems data to test mechanistic explanations for biogeographic patterns that could not have been attempted without the advent of the appropriate technology. These innovations promise to make biogeography a vital and exciting field in the future. *See* GEOGRAPHIC INFORMATION SYSTEMS.   Brian A. Maurer

Bibliography. J. H. Brown and M. V. Lomolino, *Biogeography*, Sinauer, Sunderland, MA, 1998; A. Hallam, *Outline of Phanerozoic Biogeography*, Oxford University Press, Oxford, 1994; R. H. MacArthur, *Geographical Ecology*, Harper and Row, New York, 1972; A. A. Myers and P. S. Giller, *Analytical Biogeography*, Chapman and Hall, London, 1988.

Bioinorganic chemistry

The field at the interface between biochemistry and inorganic chemistry; also known as inorganic biochemistry or metallobiochemistry. This field involves the application of the principles of inorganic chemistry to problems of biology and biochemistry. Because most biological components are organic, that is, they involve the chemistry of carbon compounds, the combination of the prefix bio- and inorganic may appear contradictory. However, organisms require a number of other elements to carry out their basic functions. Many of these elements are present as metal ions that are involved in crucial biological processes such as respiration, metabolism, cell division, muscle contraction, nerve impulse transmission, and gene regulation. The characterization of the interactions between such metal centers and biological components is the heart of bioinorganic chemistry. *See* BIOCHEMISTRY; INORGANIC CHEMISTRY.

Metal ions influence biological phenomena by interacting with organic functional groups on small and large biomolecules, forming metal complexes. From this perspective, much of bioinorganic chemistry may be considered as coordination chemistry applied to biological questions. In general, bioinorganic chemists tackle such problems by first focusing on the elucidation of the structure of the metal complex of interest and then correlating structure with function. The attainment of solutions usually requires a combination of physical, chemical, and biological approaches. Biochemistry and molecular biology are often used to provide sufficient amounts of the system for investigation. Physical approaches such as crystallography and spectroscopy are useful in defining structural properties of the metal site. Synthetic methods can be used for the design and assembly of structural, spectroscopic, and functional models of the metal site. All these approaches then converge to elucidate how such a site functions. *See* COORDINATION CHEMISTRY; CRYSTALLOGRAPHY; MOLECULAR BIOLOGY; SPECTROSCOPY.

Low-molecular-weight compounds. A number of coordination compounds found in organisms have relatively low molecular weights. Ionophores, molecules that are able to carry ions across lipid barriers, are polydentate ligands designed to bind alkali and alkaline-earth metal ions; they span membranes and serve to transport such ions across these biological barriers. Molecular receptors known as siderophores are also polydentate ligands; they have a very high affinity for iron. Bacteria and fungi use them to scavenge for this crucial element in the environment. Siderophores can thus be used as growth factors and antibiotics and for complexing excess iron in cases of iron overload. *See* CHELATION; IONOPHORE.

Other low-molecular-weight compounds are metal-containing cofactors that interact with macromolecules to promote important biological processes. Perhaps the most widely studied of the metal ligands found in biochemistry are the porphyrins; iron protoporphyrin IX (**Fig. 1**) is an example of the all-important complex in biology known as heme.

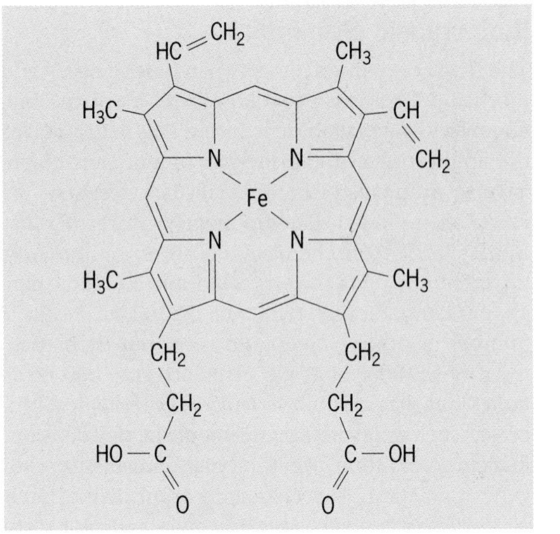

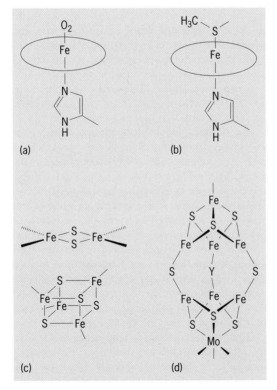

Fig. 1. Iron complex of protoporphyrin IX, or heme.

The iron (Fe) is attached to the four nitrogen (N) atoms of the porphyrin. Since iron can bind as many as six ligands, there are two other sites perpendicular to the heme plane that are available for coordination. One or both sites can be used to attach the heme to a protein via a coordinating amino acid residue. For example, in hemoglobin the iron is attached to only one protein residue. Thus the remaining coordination site opposite the protein attachment site is available for dioxygen (O_2) binding (**Fig. 2a**). This ability to bind O_2 is the basis

for the biological function of hemoglobin, which is the red substance in blood cells that transports oxygen to the tissues. Both available coordination sites in cytochrome c, however, are attached to protein residues (Fig. 2b). Cytochrome c participates in electron-transfer processes that are important in supplying energy for cellular functions. The electron-transfer function does not require the iron atom to bind exogenous ligands (like O_2); indeed, the efficiency of electron transfer is facilitated by the presence of the two protein ligands. In the preceding two examples, it can be seen that the structure of the metal site is intimately correlated with its function. *See* CYTOCHROME; ELECTRON-TRANSFER REACTION; HEMOGLOBIN; PORPHYRIN.

Chlorophyll and vitamin B_{12} are chemically related to the porphyrins. The carbon-nitrogen skeleta are similar, and a metal ion coordinates to the four nitrogen atoms of the macrocycle. Magnesium is the central metal ion in chlorophyll, which is the green pigment in plants used to convert light energy into chemical energy. Cobalt is the central metal ion in vitamin B_{12}; it is converted into coenzyme B_{12} in cells, where it participates in a variety of enzymatic reactions. *See* CHLOROPHYLL; VITAMIN B_{12}.

Another example of a metal-containing cofactor is molybdopterin, which can be extracted from a number of molybdenum (Mo)-containing enzymes that catalyze the transfer of oxygen atoms to and from substrates, for example, nitrate reductase and sulfite oxidase. When bound to the enzyme, the molybdenum is believed to be the locus of the oxo-transfer activity. *See* ENZYME.

Metalloproteins and metalloenzymes. These are metal complexes of proteins. In many cases, the metal ion is coordinated directly to functional groups on amino acid residues. In some cases, the protein contains a bound metallo-cofactor such as heme or molybdopterin. In metalloproteins with more than one metal-binding site, the metal ions may be found in clusters. Examples include ferredoxins, which contain iron-sulfur clusters (Fe_2S_2 or Fe_4S_4), and nitrogenase, which contains both Fe_4S_4 units and a novel $MoFe_7S_8$ cluster (Fig. 2c). *See* PROTEIN.

Some metalloproteins are designed for the storage and transport of the metal ions themselves—for example, ferritin and transferrin for iron and metallothionein for zinc (Zn). Others, such as the yeast protein Atx1, act as metallochaperones that aid in the insertion of the appropriate metal ion into a metalloenzyme. Still others function as transport agents. Cytochromes and ferredoxins facilitate the transfer of electrons in various metabolic processes. Hemoglobin is required for oxygen transport in humans and higher animals, while hemocyanin (containing a dicopper active site; **Fig. 3**) and hemerythrin (containing a diiron active site) perform the analogous function in crustaceans and sipunculids, respectively.

Many metalloproteins catalyze important cellular reactions and are thus more specifically called metalloenzymes. Enzymes are biological catalysts; when a metal ion is present, it is often the site at which

Fig. 2. Active sites of some metalloproteins. (*a*) Hemoglobin and (*b*) cytochrome c; ovals represent the porphyrin ring. (*c*) Ferredoxins. (*d*) Nitrogenase; the identity of the Y atom is unknown.

catalytic activity occurs. The metal ion can serve as a redox site to facilitate the oxidation or reduction of substrate. Superoxide dismutase, which removes potentially toxic superoxide by disproportionating it to O_2 and hydrogen peroxide (H_2O_2), can be found in nature as a copper-zinc enzyme, an iron enzyme, or a manganese enzyme. Cytochrome oxidase is the respiratory enzyme in mitochondria responsible for disposing of the electrons generated by mammalian metabolism; it does so by reducing O_2 to water with the help of both heme and copper centers. In contrast, the conversion of water to O_2 is carried out in the photosynthetic apparatus by manganese centers. *See* SUPEROXIDE CHEMISTRY.

Other metalloenzymes are involved in the transformation of organic molecules in cells. For example, tyrosine hydroxylase (an iron enzyme) and dopamine β-hydroxylase (a copper enzyme) carry out oxidation reactions important for the biosynthesis of neurotransmitters. Cytochrome P450 (a heme enzyme) and methane monooxygenase (a nonheme iron enzyme) hydroxylate unactivated aliphatic carbon-hydrogen (C-H) bonds in molecules such as steroids and methane; these reactions are difficult to carry out efficiently and specifically outside the biological milieu.

Alternatively, the metal center can serve as a Lewis acidic site to activate substrates for nucleophilic displacement reactions (that is, hydrolysis). Carboxypeptidase, which catalyzes the cleavage of peptide bonds, and alkaline phosphatase, which catalyzes the cleavage of phosphate ester bonds, are examples of zinc-containing hydrolytic enzymes. Metal ions have also been found to be required for the hydrolytic reactions catalyzed by some ribozymes (biological catalysts based on polyribonucleotides). *See* RIBOZYME.

Bioinorganic models. Insights into the metal sites of macromolecules can also be obtained from studies of much simpler metal complexes that can be designed to mimic some aspect of the active site structure and function. For example, a number of metal complexes can act like carboxypeptidase and hydrolyze peptide bonds. Though the metalloenzyme itself does this more efficiently, a comparison of the simpler complexes with their more complicated biochemical relatives can often provide clues to the behavior of the macromolecular catalyst. Modeling efforts have developed to the extent that a number of important metalloprotein active sites (like some of those in Fig. 2) can be synthesized independent of the protein backbone and can be studied in great detail. The greater challenge is to design models that can carry out the same reactions as those carried out by their macromolecular counterparts. Examples of functional models that have been synthesized are heme and dicopper complexes that model the reversible oxygen-binding ability of hemoglobin and hemocyanin, respectively. *See* SUPRAMOLECULAR CHEMISTRY.

Metal regulation of gene expression. Metalloproteins also play roles in gene expression. In some cases, the metal ion coordinates to several residues

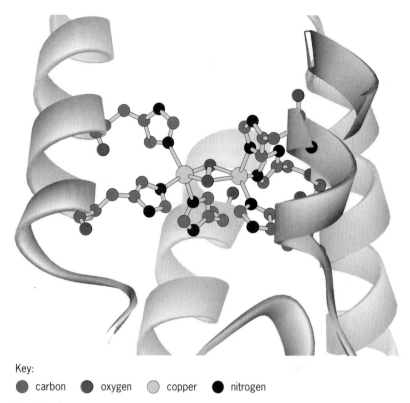

Key:

● carbon   ● oxygen   ○ copper   ● nitrogen

Fig. 3. Active site structure of oxyhemocyanin, the oxygen-bound form of hemocyanin, the oxygen carrier protein in arthropods and mollusks.

in a protein, imposing a particular structure on the polypeptide chain that enables it to interact with deoxyribonucleic acid (DNA); for example, zinc is a crucial component of the so-called zinc finger proteins that recognize and bind particular sequences of DNA and activate transcription. In other cases, the metal ion acts as a signal triggering the expression or repression of genes involved in respiration and metabolism. For example, the binding of nanomolar concentrations of mercuric ion to the merR protein activates the genetic machinery to produce enzymes responsible for the detoxification of mercury. In mammalian cells, a single protein that senses the presence of ferrous ion interacts with ferritin and transferrin receptor messenger ribonucleic acids (mRNAs) to regulate translation of the corresponding ferritin and transferrin receptor proteins. *See* DEOXYRIBONUCLEIC ACID (DNA); GENE ACTION; GENETIC CODE; RIBONUCLEIC ACID (RNA).

Metals in medicine. Metal complexes have also been found to be useful as therapeutic or diagnostic agents. Prominent among metal-based drugs is cisplatin, which is particularly effective in the treatment of testicular and ovarian cancers; second- and third-generation variants of this drug have been developed to mitigate undesirable side effects of drug treatment. Gold, gallium, and bismuth compounds are used for the treatment of rheumatoid arthritis, hypercalcemia, and peptic ulcers, respectively.

In clinical diagnosis, metal complexes can be used as imaging agents. The convenient half-life and radioemission properties of technetium-99 make its complexes very useful for a number of applications; by varying the ligands bound to the metal ion, diagnostic agents have been developed for imaging the heart, brain, and kidneys. Complexes of paramagnetic metal ions such as gadolinium(III), iron(III), and manganese(II) are also used as contrast agents to enhance images obtained from magnetic resonance imaging (MRI). *See* COORDINATION COMPLEXES; MEDICAL IMAGING; ORGANOMETALLIC COMPOUND.   Lawrence Que, Jr.

Bibliography. Bioinorganic chemistry (spec. issue), *Science*, 261:699–730, 1993; J. A. Cowan, *Inorganic Biochemistry: An Introduction*, 2d ed., 1997; S. J. Lippard and J. M. Berg, *Principles of Bioinorganic Chemistry*, 1994; J. Reedijk (ed.), *Bioinorganic Catalysis*, 2d ed., 1999; R. M. Roat-Malone, *Bioinorganic Chemistry: A Short Course*, 2002; Spec. issues, *Chem. Rev.*, 96:2237–3042, 1996, and 99:2201–2842, 1999.

Bioleaching

The use of naturally occurring microorganisms to dissolve metals from minerals. This biotechnical process, involving bacteria, archaea, fungi, and yeast, can be applied to both sulfide and nonsulfide minerals. At present, bioleaching is employed on a large commercial scale to extract metals from sulfide minerals. *See* HYDROMETALLURGY; LEACHING.

Bioleaching of Sulfide Minerals

Sulfide minerals bioleaching has its technical origins in the 1940s, when researchers discovered the acid-loving bacterium *Thiobacillus ferrooxidans* (now reclassified as *Acidithiobacillus ferrooxidans*) and found that it obtained energy for reproduction and cellular functioning by oxidizing (removing electrons from) inorganic substances, principally ferrous iron (Fe^{2+}). Subsequently, other microorganisms capable of dissolving metals were characterized and their biochemical mechanisms defined, while engineered systems to commercially exploit these organisms were developed. *See* BACTERIA; SULFIDE AND ARSENIDE MINERALS.

Principles of bioleaching. Microorganisms involved in bioleaching of sulfide minerals are chemolithotrophic: they use carbon dioxide (CO_2) from the atmosphere as their carbon source for building cellular constituents and derive energy for their existence and reproduction from inorganic materials. To obtain energy, the microorganisms oxidize iron [reaction (1)] and certain chemically reduced sulfur

$$4Fe^{2+} + O_2 + 4H^+ \longrightarrow$$

Ferrous   Oxygen   Hydrogen
ion   ions

$$4Fe^{3+} + 2H_2O \quad (1)$$

Ferric   Water
ion

compounds [reaction (2)], which are sulfur species

$$S + H_2O + 1\frac{1}{2}O_2 \longrightarrow$$

Elemental   Water   Oxygen
sulfur

$$2H^+ + SO_4^{2-} \quad (2)$$

Hydrogen   Sulfate
ions   ion

having readily removable electrons such as the sulfide ion (S^{2-}) and elemental sulfur (S).

These oxidation reactions require oxygen (O_2), so the microorganisms are aerobic. The microorganisms also need ammonium ions (NH_4^+), phosphate ions (PO_4^{3-}), and a few trace elements, such as magnesium (Mg^{2+}) and potassium (K^+). The bioleaching microorganisms are also acidophilic (acid loving), requiring the solution to be less than pH 2.5 and preferably higher than pH 1.0, created by sulfuric acid. This pH range ensures that ferrous iron (Fe^{2+}) is dissolved and readily available for oxidation. The bioleaching microorganisms tolerate very high concentrations of dissolved metals in their acidic environment (for example, 30 g/L of dissolved copper ions, Cu^{2+}). *See* OXIDATION-REDUCTION; SULFUR.

Bioleaching microorganisms can be grouped into temperature ranges at which they grow and function (see **table**). Mesophilic (middle-loving) bacteria function in the range 15–45°C (60–113°F). Moderately thermophilic (heat-loving) bacteria thrive in the range 40–65°C (104–150°F). Extremely thermophilic microorganisms, which are not bacteria but archaea (organisms that evolved from ancient Earth life forms), grow in the range 60–95°C (140–203°F). *See* ARCHAEBACTERIA.

The mechanism used by the bioleaching microorganisms to actually extract metals—such as copper, zinc, cobalt, and iron, from solid sulfide minerals—and cause these metals to dissolve has been studied and debated by scientists for decades. Free-floating microorganisms oxidize the dissolved Fe^{2+} and chemically reduced sulfur compounds. Some organisms attach to mineral surfaces using a biofilm composed of polymers that complex (bind) ferric iron (Fe^{3+}) to very high concentrations (53 g/L). The biofilm-mineral interface is the reaction zone where metal dissolution takes place. *See* BIOFILM.

Fe^{3+} is a very strong oxidizing agent that chemically attacks sulfide minerals, releasing metal ions and sulfur as either elemental sulfur (S) [reaction (3)] or other sulfur compounds such as sulfate

$$CuFeS_2 + 4Fe^{3+} \longrightarrow$$

Chalcopyrite   Ferric
ion

$$Cu^{2+} + 5Fe^{2+} + 2S \quad (3)$$

Copper   Ferrous   Elemental
ion   ion   sulfur

(SO_4^{2-}) [reaction (4)]. Having removed an electron from the metal sulfide mineral in these reactions, Fe^{3+} is chemically reduced to Fe^{2+} (gaining an electron), which is quickly oxidized by the microorganisms, regenerating the oxidizing agent for dissolution

Examples of mesophilic, moderately thermophilic, and extremely thermophilic bioleaching microorganisms, their characteristics, and natural habitats		
Temperature range	Genus and species examples and organism characteristics	Natural habitats
Mesophilic	*Acidithiobacillus ferrooxidans*: rod-shaped bacterium, approximately 0.5 μm $\times$ 1.0 μm; oxidizes ferrous iron (Fe^{2+}) and chemically reduced sulfur compounds	Acid springs; geological outcrops of rocks bearing sulfide minerals; acid mine waters; sulfide mineral rock piles exposed to the atmosphere
	Acidithiobacillus thiooxidans: rod-shaped bacterium, approximately 0.5 μm $\times$ 1.0 μm; oxidizes chemically reduced sulfur compounds	
	Leptospirillum ferrooxidans: rod-shaped bacterium, approximately 0.5 μm $\times$ 1.0 μm; oxidizes Fe^{2+} only	
Moderately thermophilic	*Sulfobacillus thermosulfidooxidans*: rod-shaped bacterium, approximately 1 μm by 2–3 μm; oxidizes Fe^{2+} and chemically reduced sulfur compounds	Acid, hot springs; volcanic areas; warm, acid mine waters; warm sulfide mineral rock piles exposed to the atmosphere
	Thiobacillus caldus: rod-shaped bacterium, approximately 1 μm $\times$ 2–3 μm; oxidizes chemically reduced sulfur compounds only	
Extremely thermophilic	*Acidianus brierleyi, Sulfolobus metallicus*; spherical-shaped archaea about 1 μm in diameter; oxidize Fe^{2+} and chemically reduced sulfur compounds	Hot, acid springs; volcanic areas

$$ZnS + Fe^{3+} + 4H_2O \longrightarrow$$

Sphalerite   Ferric ion   Water

$$Zn^{2+} + SO_4^{2-} + Fe^{2+} + 8H^+ \quad (4)$$

Zinc ion   Sulfate ion   Ferrous ion   Hydrogen ion

of the sulfide minerals [reaction (1)]. Chemically reduced sulfur compounds are also used by the microorganisms for energy [reaction (2)]. These redox (oxidation-reduction) reactions are catalyzed (accelerated) by the microorganisms [reactions (1)–(4)].

The oxidation of many mineral sulfides, including pyrite (FeS_2) by Fe^{3+}, results in acid (H^+) production, establishing the acidic environment for the microorganisms and keeping the metals dissolved for effective concentration and recovery [reaction (5)].

$$FeS_2 + 14Fe^{3+} + 8H_2O \longrightarrow$$

Pyrite   Ferric iron   Water

$$15Fe^{2+} + 2SO_4^{2-} + 16H^+ \quad (5)$$

Ferrous iron   Sulfate ion   Hydrogen ion

The oxidation of some sulfide minerals releases heat (exothermic reaction). This is an important consideration in the type(s) of microorganisms used and the design of industrial-scale bioleaching operations. *See* BACTERIAL PHYSIOLOGY AND METABOLISM.

Industrial applications of bioleaching. The first industrial bioleaching applications were in the 1950s, when several major copper producers exploited microorganisms to scavenge copper from rocks containing very low amounts of copper in the form of sulfide minerals. This practice, called copper dump leaching, is used today.

In the 1980s, the fundamental principles of bioleaching were combined with standard metallurgical and dump bioleaching practices to create heap bioleaching and stirred-tank bioleaching processes. To this day, copper dump leaching, heap bioleaching, and stirred-tank bioleaching are employed industrially at very large scales throughout the world. The drivers for commercial bioleaching are (1) significantly reduced production costs owing to lower energy requirements, lower labor costs, and lower reagent usage; (2) diminished capital costs due to simpler equipment and rapid construction; (3) increased mineral reserves, because lower grade ores can be economically treated and varied mineral types can be processed; and (4) better environmental conditions and worker safety because there are no toxic gas emissions and, in some cases, no aqueous (water-based) discharges.

Copper dump bioleaching. Many of the world-class copper deposits are very large, low-grade (typically less than 1% copper), sulfide-mineral ore bodies, which are usually mined by open-pit methods. Ore grading higher than 0.5% copper is customarily processed by smelting. The vast tonnage of material grading lower than about 0.5% cannot be treated by conventional crushing, grinding, and smelting technologies, as the processing cost exceeds the value of the copper in the rock. Instead, these materials are blasted in the mine and hauled as large rock fragments, often exceeding 1 m (3.3 ft) in size, to dumps, where piles contain millions of tons of fragmented rock and reach 60 m (200 ft) high. Dilute acidic water is applied to the top surface of the dump, resulting in the growth of naturally occurring *Acidithiobacillus ferrooxidans, Acidithiobacillus thiooxidans, Leptospirillum ferrooxidans,* and other similar microorganisms throughout the rock pile. The microorganisms oxidize certain sulfur compounds, as well as Fe^{2+} to Fe^{3+}. In turn, Fe^{3+} oxidizes copper sulfide minerals, such as chalcocite (Cu_2S), covellite (CuS), to a lesser extent chalcopyrite ($CuFeS_2$), and pyrite (FeS_2), usually associated with copper deposits. Heat is generated and the temperature increases in the dump. The hot gases rise and air for the microorganisms is pulled into the dump interior via convection from the porous sides of the rock pile. As the rock pile heats above the functional temperature (about 45°C) of the mesophilic bacteria, the moderately thermophilic microorganisms begin to grow (see table). When the temperature exceeds the upper limit (about 45°C) for the moderately thermophilic) microorganisms, they die. Insufficient studies have been done to determine whether the extremely thermophilic archaea replace the moderate thermophiles when the temperature in the dump exceeds 65°C (150°F). *See* OPEN PIT MINING; ORE AND MINERAL DEPOSITS.

Dissolved Cu^{2+}, resulting from bioleaching, is flushed from the rock pile by irrigation. The Cu^{2+}-containing solution is directed to a solvent extraction circuit, where the Cu^{2+} is stripped from the acidic water and the water is returned to the dump surface. Because less than optimal conditions exist for the microorganisms in the dump, the degradation of the sulfide minerals takes several decades. Nevertheless, dumps are a highly economical means of recovering copper, because an enormous volume of rock is processed and the production costs are low. *See* COPPER METALLURGY.

Heap bioleaching. The principles of heap bioleaching (also called bioheap leaching) are similar to dump leaching. However, heap bioleaching is done on ores with a higher copper grade or some gold content. This higher intrinsic value allows the system to be more highly engineered than dumps, resulting in greater metal recovery in less time.

Since the 1980s, heap bioleaching of the copper sulfide minerals Cu_2S and CuS has been widely practiced commercially for ores grading 1% Cu or higher. The ore is typically crushed to less than 19 mm (0.75 in.) and agglomerated (formed into a ball-shaped mass) with acidic water to bind finely ground

rock into larger rock particles, hence improving air and water distribution in the heap. Large, earthen pads are covered with plastic and two arrays of perforated plastic pipe (one for air and the second for solution collection) are placed on the plastic. The ore is stacked 6–10 m (20–33 ft) deep on top of the plastic. The heap is drip irrigated with slightly acidic water and forced air is provided through the pipes under the crushed ore. Naturally occurring microorganisms proliferate, reaching 10^6 to 10^7 (1–10 million) per gram of ore and per milliliter of solution. Temperatures in the heap generally stay within the range for mesophilic bacteria (see table). Copper extraction of 85–90% is achieved in about a year.

When gold (Au) is associated with sulfide minerals, usually FeS_2 or arsenopyrite (FeAsS), micrometer-sized gold particles are embedded within the sulfide minerals. These gold ores are not amenable to direct cyanide treatment for gold extraction. The sulfide minerals first must be oxidized to liberate the gold. Since the mid-1990s, heap bioleaching of these ores has been practiced. Gold bioheaps increase in temperature when FeS_2 with embedded gold is oxidized [reaction (5)]. Temperatures can reach 70°C (170°F) or higher. To accommodate this temperature rise, the ore is agglomerated with all three groups of microorganisms (see table), with each group becoming active as its temperature range is achieved. *See* GOLD METALLURGY.

Gold is not dissolved when FeS_2 and FeAsS are oxidized; rather, the gold particles are liberated and remain as solids. After sufficient sulfide is oxidized (which can take up to 1.5 years depending on the ore particle size and other factors), the pretreated ore is removed from the pad, neutralized with lime, and chemically leached, usually with a dilute cyanide solution to dissolve the gold. The dissolved gold is processed into bullion. Bioleaching typically results in gold recoveries of 75–85%. Without bioleaching pretreatment, the gold recovery from these same ores would be 0–30%.

Aerated, stirred-tank bioleaching. Bioleaching is also accomplished in highly engineered, aerated, continuously stirred tank reactors (CSTR). Because of the high capital and operating costs of the process, the minerals must be of high value. Therefore, ores are preprocessed to remove worthless material, increasing the concentration of the valuable metal.

Stainless-steel tanks, each as large as 1380 m^3 (364,500 gallons), are equipped with agitators that maintain the finely ground sulfide mineral concentrate in suspension and ensure that oxygen is efficiently transferred to the microorganisms. Each tank is cooled to maintain the bioleach solution at the proper temperature for the microorganisms used. The **illustration** depicts a typical CSTR bioleach industrial plant.

The mineral concentrate is added to acidified water containing NH_4^+ and PO_4^{3-} ions and fed continuously to the first tank (stage) in a series of tanks. Because conditions are optimized for the microorganisms, numbers reach 10^9 to 10^{10} (one billion to

Industrial-scale, aerated, continuously stirred tank plant for bioleaching sulfidic-refractory gold concentrate. The large tanks are the bioleach circuit for pretreating the mineral concentrate and in front of them is the circuit for extracting the gold from the bioleached solids. (*Photo courtesy of BacTech Mining Corp.*)

10 billion) organisms per ml of solution. Continuously stirred tank reactors can be operated with any of the three microbial groups by controlling the temperature. Mineral concentrates move from the first-stage reactor(s) on a continuous basis through three to four CSTRs in series until the sulfide minerals are oxidized. This usually requires about a five-day residence time across the entire bioleaching circuit.

If the metal is a base metal, such as Cu^{2+} or Zn^{2+}, it dissolves when the mineral is oxidized. The oxidized slurry exits the final reactor and undergoes solid/liquid separation, after which the solid is discarded and the liquid is processed to recover the metal. If the mineral concentrate is gold bearing, the liquid from the last-stage reactor is neutralized and stabilized for safe disposal and the solid is processed to recover the gold. Metal recoveries in CSTR bioleach circuits are in the 95–98% range.

Using extremely thermophilic archaea, CSTR bioleaching of $CuFeS_2$ has recently been commercially developed. Unlike mesophilic and moderately thermophilic microorganisms, archaea have no cell walls. Improved agitator design has been incorporated to minimize shear forces and enhance oxygen mass transfer in the hot solutions, which diminish O_2 solubility. Highly resistant construction materials are used to resist the corrosive conditions due to the high temperatures and strongly oxidizing conditions.

Bioleaching of Nonsulfide Minerals

The dissolution of metals from minerals can be accomplished using microorganisms other than the acid-loving, chemolithotrophic microorganisms. Heterotrophic bacteria, yeast, and fungi require organic carbon for growth and produce organic acids or other substances that dissolve metals. Some heterotrophic organisms use inorganic compounds, such as metal oxides, rather than oxygen as electron acceptors. *See* FUNGI; YEAST.

One example of nonsulfide mineral bioleaching is the use of fungal strains of *Aspergillus* and *Penicillium* to produce bioacids that dissolve cobalt (Co^{2+}) and nickel (Ni^{2+}) from laterite, an iron and aluminum oxide material containing nickel and other base metals. The fungi oxidize organic compounds (such as sugars) and produce citric or lactic acids, which dissolve the laterite and release the metals. *See* FUNGAL BIOTECHNOLOGY; LATERITE.

Shewanella oneidensis, a bacterium found in soils, sediments, ground water, and surface water, oxidizes organic compounds and in the absence of oxygen (anaerobic conditions) passes the electrons to iron oxyhydroxides, such as hematite (Fe_2O_3) and goethite ($FeOOH$). This reaction dissolves the mineral. Although the thrust of this research is toward bioremediation of subsurface contaminants, the same approach might be considered for bioleaching a manganese dioxide (MnO_2) ore that hosts silver. The reduction of the manganese (Mn^{4+}) by the bacterially mediated electron transfer to the solid phase MnO_2 releases manganese as Mn^{2+} and allows the silver to be extracted.

Heterotrophic bioleaching requires large quantities of organic matter, and the process design of such systems poses significant problems, because unwanted microorganisms grow even in the absence of oxygen and consume the organic matter without releasing metals. Nonsulfide mineral bioleaching is not currently economical at commercial scale because of high costs, engineering complexities, and slow rates of metal dissolution.

Future Developments

Sulfide-mineral bioleaching relies on naturally occurring microorganisms. Despite revolutionary developments in molecular biology, its application in bioleaching is currently confined to microorganism identification. During bioleaching operations, occasional toxicity problems arise from certain anions (negatively charged ions), which might be mitigated by molecular modification of the microorganisms. However, if engineered microorganisms are used, the problem of competition from naturally occurring microorganisms must be resolved.

Chalcopyrite ($CuFeS_2$) is effectively bioleached in CSTRs using extremely thermophilic archaea and finely ground mineral concentrate. However, the greatest copper resource in the world is $CuFeS_2$ that is too low grade to be economically concentrated or extracted by any method other than heap bioleaching or in-situ (extraction of the metal without physical removal of the rock from the mineral deposit) bioleaching. Although we understand the chemical conditions under which $CuFeS_2$ is effectively bioleached in CSTRs, the challenge is to technically and cost-effectively establish and maintain suitable conditions for $CuFeS_2$ bioleaching in a bioheap or in-situ leach system.

In addition, more research is needed on the bioleaching of nonsulfide minerals to enhance reaction rates, find more effective microorganisms, and develop more effective engineering designs.

Corale L. Brierley

Bibliography. C. L. Brierley and A. P. Briggs, Selection and sizing of biooxidation equipment, *Mineral Processing Plant Design, Practice and Control*, Society for Mining, Metallurgy, and Exploration, Inc., Littleton, CO, pp. 1540–1568, 2002; H. L. Ehrlich, How microbes mobilize metals in ores: A review of current understandings and proposals for further research, *Miner. Metallurg. Process.*, 19:220–224, 2002; G. J. Olson, J. A. Brierley, and C. L. Brierley, Bioleaching review part B—Progress in bioleaching: Applications of microbial processes by the minerals industries, *Appl. Microbiol. Biotechnol.*, 63:249–257, 2003; G. J. Olson and T. R. Clark, Fundamentals of metal sulfide biooxidation, *Mining Eng.*, 56:40–46, 2004; D. E. Rawlings, Heavy metal mining using microbes, *Annu. Rev. Microbiol.*, 56:65–91, 2002; T. Rohwerder et al., Bioleaching review part A—Progress in bioleaching: Fundamentals and mechanisms of bacterial metal sulfide oxidation, *Appl. Microbiol. Biotechnol.*, 63:239–248, 2003.

Biological clocks

Self-sustained circadian (approximately 24-hour) rhythms, which regulate daily activities such as sleep and wakefulness, were described as early as 1729 by the French geologist de Mairan. He placed a plant in constant darkness and noticed that leaf movements continued to occur at specific times of day despite the absence of the day-night cycle. The notion that this rhythmicity was still driven in some fashion by the Earth's rotation was resolved in the midtwentieth century when it became clear that the period of self-sustained (free-running) oscillations usually does not match that of the environmental cycle, therefore the expression "approximately 24 hours." Moreover, the free-running period varies among species and also somewhat from one individual to another. Circadian rhythmicity is often referred to as the biological clock. *See* PHOTOPERIODISM; PLANT MOVEMENTS.

Almost all organisms display circadian rhythms, indicating an evolutionary benefit, most likely facilitating adaptation to the cyclic nature of the environment. Physiological processes that occur with a circadian rhythm range from conidiation (spore production) in the bread mold, *Neurospora crassa*, and leaf movements in plants to rest-activity behavior in animals. Despite the diversity of these phenomena, the basic properties of the rhythms are the same— they synchronize to environmental cues, predominantly light, but are maintained in the absence of such cues, and they display a constant periodicity over a wide temperature range.

Circadian rhythms in humans. In humans, circadian rhythmicity is manifested in the form of sleep-wake cycles, and control of body temperature, blood pressure, heart rate, and release of many endocrine hormones (melatonin, growth hormone, cortisol, and so on). This list is by no means complete, and as more is learned about human physiology and circadian rhythms, it is increasingly apparent that temporal ordering is a fundamental aspect of physiological processes. In fact, several disorders such as asthma, stroke, and myocardial infarction also tend to occur more frequently at certain times of the day. Awareness of circadian control has led to the concept of chronotherapeutics, which advocates drug delivery timed to the host's circadian rhythms. This concept is most popular in the treatment of cancer. Circadianly timed chemotherapy (chronochemotherapy), radiation therapy, or even surgery can enhance tumor regression and reduce toxic side effects.

While the importance of circadian rhythms in the disorders mentioned above is still under investigation, their role in jet lag or other problems related to light-dark synchronization is unquestionable. Shift work, travel to a different time zone, or any other activity that results in a lack of synchrony between the body circadian clock and the environment produces disturbances not only in the sleep-wake cycle but also in other body functions. In recent years, melatonin, a hormone produced by the pineal gland, has become the drug of choice for alleviating jet-lag symptoms, but its efficacy is debatable. While melatonin can induce temporary sleepiness and also produce a small shift in the circadian clock, it does not appear to be sufficient to synchronize all circadian rhythms. As a matter of fact, the function of melatonin in humans is unknown. In seasonal mammals such as hamsters, whose reproductive cycles are driven by day length (photoperiod), melatonin serves to convey length-of-day information. Basically the production of melatonin is restricted to the dark phase and thus defines the length of the night. In nonseasonal mammals, including humans, the release of melatonin cycles in a similar manner, but the functional significance of this is unknown. *See* PINEAL GLAND.

In humans, circadian rhythms have a potential role in psychiatric disorders, particularly those that cause depression. The disorder in which involvement of circadian rhythms has been best studied is seasonal affective disorder (SAD). Patients with SAD suffer from fall-winter depression, and there is some evidence to suggest that they have deficits in circadian rhythms, including poor entrainment to light. This is supported by the fact that SAD patients respond well to light therapy. Finally, circadian rhythms tend to be disorganized in older people, the effects being especially pronounced in aged individuals with some type of dementia such as Alzheimer's disease. The underlying basis has not been elucidated.

Localization of circadian clocks. In mammals the "master clock" controlling circadian rhythms is located in the hypothalamus, within a small group of neurons called the suprachiasmatic nucleus. Lesions of the suprachiasmatic nucleus in rodents eliminate all the rhythms mentioned above such as rest-activity cycles and rhythmic hormone release. Transplantation of a fetal suprachiasmatic nucleus will restore rest-activity cycles in a lesioned host, and the periodicity of the restored rhythm corresponds to that of the donor animal. How exactly the suprachiasmatic nucleus imparts temporal information to the rest of the organism is still unknown. Available data suggest that the suprachiasmatic nucleus transmits signals in the form of humoral factors as well as neural connections. The humoral hypothesis is best supported by experiments in which a suprachiasmatic nucleus encapsulated in a porous membrane was shown to be effective in restoring activity rhythms in a lesioned host. Since hormonal rhythms are not restored by these or by regular transplants, neural connectivity must be important also, probably more so for certain outputs. It should be stressed that while coordinated clock activity presumably requires a group of cells, approximately 24-h oscillations are generated within individual suprachiasmatic nucleus cells through the action of clock genes. *See* NERVOUS SYSTEM (INVERTEBRATE); NERVOUS SYSTEM (VERTEBRATE).

For many years the suprachiasmatic nucleus was thought to be the only site of a clock in mammals. This was in contrast to several other vertebrates where clocks were known to be present in the pineal gland and the eye as well. However, it is now clear that the mammalian eye also contains an oscillator (something that generates an approximately 24-h cycle) whose activity can be assayed by measuring melatonin release in isolated retinas. Although the function of the eye clock is unknown, it is not difficult to envision a need for circadian control of visual sensitivity or some other related property. Perhaps more surprising is the accumulating evidence on circadian oscillators in other body regions.

Research done in fruit flies (*Drosophila melanogaster*) suggests that independent clocks are present in many different parts of the body. The rest-activity cycle in the fruit fly is controlled by a group of neurons in the central brain referred to as lateral neurons which are essentially the fly's suprachiasmatic nucleus. While these neurons may well constitute the master clock in flies, many other tissues also contain oscillators in that they express clock genes in a cyclic fashion even when severed from the lateral neurons. Since the identification of these oscillators is based upon the assay of molecular markers, as opposed to physiological processes, their functions are largely unknown. However, as in the case of the eye, it is easy to conceive of possible functions. For instance, the oscillator in the fly's prothoracic gland is most likely required to regulate eclosion (hatching of adult flies from pupae) which occurs predominantly at dawn and is known to be under circadian control. The oscillator in the malpighian tubule (kidney equivalent) may effect rhythmic excretion or osmoregulation.

The fruit fly study raises the tantalizing possibility that independent body clocks also occur in mammals, perhaps even humans. This idea is supported by the finding that recently identified mammalian clock genes are expressed in many tissues other than the suprachiasmatic nucleus and the retina. Several of these tissues also express molecules that are thought to serve as circadian photoreceptors. Finally, treatment of Rat-1 fibroblast cells with serum leads to the induction and subsequent cyclic expression of clock genes, again supporting the notion that oscillators can be generated outside the known clock tissues.

Genetic basis. The genetic basis of circadian rhythms was established through the identification of altered circadian patterns that were inherited. Such mutants were found first in *Drosophila* and then in *Neurospora* in the early 1970s. These two organisms, which are favored for their genetic amenability, became the systems of choice for those interested in pursuing the molecular dissection of circadian clocks. The earlier work in each of these organisms ended up focusing on a single gene that was the target of many mutations—*period* (*per*) in *Drosophila* and *frequency* (*frq*) in *Neurospora*. Both these genes are central components of the circadian clock.

The *Drosophila* and *Neurospora* studies set the stage for subsequent genetic analyses in these two systems and also in others. Mutations affecting circadian rhythms are now known in *Chlamydomonas*, *Arabidopsis thaliana*, cyanobacteria, hamsters, and mice. In addition, there is now an impetus to identify circadian abnormalities or naturally occurring variations in human populations. For instance, the difference between people that wake up and function most effectively in the early morning hours as opposed to those who prefer to sleep late into the morning may well lie in polymorphisms within clock genes.

Molecular basis. The question of how a clock is generated intrigued chronobiologists for many years. Theoreticians developed models to explain how oscillations could be generated and sustained, and these models invariably involved a feedback mechanism. It is now known that a feedback loop composed of cycling gene products that influence their own synthesis underlies overt rhythms in at least three organisms (*Drosophila*, *Neurospora*, and cyanobacteria) and most likely in a fourth (mammals). Similar feedback loops have also been found in plants, although it is not clear that they are part of the clock.

A genetic screen for new circadian rhythm mutations in *Drosophila* led to the identification of the *timeless* (*tim*) gene in the early 1990s. Like *per*, *tim*, can be mutated to yield diverse rhythm phenotypes, and loss of either gene product results in a loss of eclosion and behavioral activity rhythms. For example, the *per^s* mutation shortens the circadian period of eclosion and rest-activity rhythms to approximately 19 h, *per^l* lengthens period to approximately 29 h, and the *per^0* mutation eliminates rhythms altogether. Likewise, the *tim^0* mutation abolishes rhythms, the *tim^{SL}* mutation shortens circadian period by 0.5 h, and other lesions in *tim* can lengthen period to less than 30 h.

While the biochemical function of these genes has been difficult to assess, molecular analysis of their mode of regulation has been very informative. The two genes are coregulated and encode physically interacting and mutually dependent proteins that function in a common feedback loop (see **illus.**). The *per* and *tim* messenger ribonucleic acid (mRNA) levels cycle with a circadian rhythm, such that RNA levels are high at the end of the day or beginning of the night and low at the end of the night. The two proteins (PER and TIM) also cycle, with protein accumulation starting in the early evening and peaking in the middle of the night. As they are accumulating in the cytoplasm, PER and TIM associate to form heterodimers. This association stabilizes PER and permits nuclear entry of both proteins. Thus, while TIM does not require PER for stability, it is dependent on PER for nuclear transport. In the nucleus, either one or both proteins repress the synthesis of their own mRNAs. Turnover of the two proteins, TIM in the late night and PER in the early morning, allows RNA levels to rise once again and the cycle continues.

Advances in 1999 added three components to this feedback loop. Two of these proteins, *Clock* (CLK) and *Cycle* (CYC), are positive regulators of *per* and *tim*. Both these proteins are transcriptional activators, which means that they stimulate the production of *per* and *tim* RNA. They do so by interacting with specific deoxyribonucleic acid (DNA) sequences called E-boxes that are upstream of protein-coding regions in the *per* and *tim* genes. As might

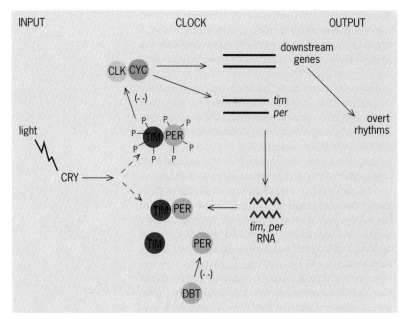

INPUT   CLOCK   OUTPUT

Model for the molecular clock with possible sites of interaction with input and output pathways. The negative signs reflect inhibitory influences of the proteins TIM and PER on CLK/CYC transcriptional activity, as well as the decrease in levels of PER monomers brought about by activity of the DBT casein kinase. While TIM levels are known to be reduced by light, negative notations are not used here because the relationship between cryptochromes (CRY) and TIM is not known.

be predicted, flies that are deficient in either CLK or CYC express very low levels of *per* and *tim* RNA as well as protein and, as a result, are arrhythmic. Since neither PER nor TIM appears to bind DNA, the current model for how they repress synthesis of their own mRNAs is based upon their interactions with CLK/CYC. Indeed, both PER and TIM bind CLK, and apparently this interaction inhibits transcriptional activation by CLK-CYC.

The third component added to the loop is a casein kinase produced by the *double-time* (*dbt*) gene. This kinase phosphorylates PER and renders it unstable in the absence of TIM. In a day-night cycle, as well as in free-running conditions, PER is increasingly phosphorylated as it accumulates, and maximally phosphorylated forms are found prior to the daily decay of the protein. Mutations in *dbt* affect period length by acclerating or delaying the rate of PER phosphorylation, which in turn affects stability of PER. Like PER, TIM is cyclically phosphorylated, but the mechanisms are not known.

In *Neurospora*, as well as in cyanobacteria, a similar transcription-based feedback loop underlies overt rhythms. However, the genes involved are very different, suggesting that clocks evolved more than once, but each time the same mechanism was used to assemble them. Thus, this type of feedback loop would appear to be the most efficient way of making a clock. Perhaps the only common feature of clocks in diverse organisms is a tendency to use proteins that contain PAS domains. PAS, named after the first three genes in which it was found (per, aryl hydrocarbon receptor nuclear translocator, single-minded), is a protein-protein interaction motif present in the PER, CLK, and CYC proteins. The *Neurospora frq* gene,

which is the *per-tim* equivalent and functions in a feedback loop, does not contain a PAS domain, but each of the *white collar 1* (*wc1*) and *white collar 2* (*wc2*) genes, that are also important for *Neurospora* rhythms, contains a single PAS repeat. Given that the *wc* proteins are required for the light response of the *frq* clock gene and other PAS-containing proteins in lower organisms are associated with photoreception, it is conceivable that PAS proteins link photoreception pathways to central clocks.

In mammals, circadian rhythms appear to use homologs of the *Drosophila* genes with some additional complexity. For instance, there are three *per* genes, all of which cycle in the suprachiasmatic nucleus. Cyclic expression of mammalian *tim* (mtim) is controversial, but it is expressed in the suprachiasmatic nucleus and in a cell culture system, mammalian TIM, together with mammalian PER, can inhibit the transcriptional activity of a CLK-BMAL1 (mammalian version of CLK-CYC) heterodimer. Thus, while a feedback loop has not been demonstrated within an intact mammal, culture studies support its existence. In vivo studies are much more difficult in mammals. *Clock* is the only mammalian gene that was isolated as a result of a forward genetic screen for circadian rhythm mutations.

Synchronization to light. Light is the predominant environmental cue that synchronizes the circadian clock. The mechanisms used by the clock to entrain to light invariably involve a change in the levels of a clock component: in *Neurospora* levels of *frq* RNA are increased in response to light, in *Drosophila* levels of TIM protein are reduced, and in mammals levels of *mPer1* mRNA are increased (the other *mPer* and *mTim* RNAs can also be induced by light, but only at certain times of night). If one accepts that these molecules are timekeepers and their levels constitute time-of-day cues, then it follows that light would act by driving the levels in a particular direction, that is, up or down. It should be mentioned that in the mammalian suprachiasmatic nucleus other signaling pathways as well as several immediate early genes (for example, *c-fos*, *c-jun*) are also induced in response to light. The relevance of these molecules to the clock is not yet understood.

An area that is of great interest is the nature of the photoreception pathway used by the clock. In flies, ocular photoreceptors are not essential for circadian entrainment, although they are probably used, and may even dominate, when present. In mammals, there is general consensus that the eyes are required. However, the conventional photoreceptor cells, rods and cones, that mediate vision are dispensable for purposes of circadian entrainment. Again, this is not to say that rods and cones are incapable of transmitting signals to the clock; rather, other cell types, which presumably contain a novel photoreceptor, can carry out this function.

The nature of the novel photoreceptor in mammals is still debatable, although considerable attention is focused on the cryptochromes. Cryptochromes (CRY) are flavin-binding molecules that belong to a family whose members include photolyases, which are DNA repair enzymes, and homologous proteins which are not photolyases and were first shown to be blue light photoreceptors in *Arabidopsis*. The latter are called cryptochromes, and it is now known that they function as circadian photoreceptors in plants and flies. In mammals, cryptochromes appear to be essential for free-running clock function, and their identity as photoreceptors remains to be proven. Expression of the cryptochromes cycles in both flies and mammals; in mammals this may be explained by their role in clock activity, but in flies it is of unknown significance. Interestingly, cryptochromes, like the clock genes, are expressed in many mammalian body tissues that, to date, are not associated with clock function.

Output signals. How the circadian clock conveys time-of-day information to the rest of the organism and produces rhythmic molecular, behavioral, and physiological outputs is a big unknown. At a molecular level, it is believed that clock genes affect output through transcriptional regulation. Thus, when PER-TIM enter the nucleus to regulate their own transcription, they presumably also regulate downstream genes that are targets of CLK/CYC. Genes that cycle under control of the clock have, in fact, been identified in several organisms, but the links between these genes and the clock or between these genes and the overt rhythm are yet to be determined.

The most direct link between clock genes and a known clock output comes from analysis of the gene encoding vasopressin, a peptide whose levels cycle in the suprachiasmatic nucleus. Suprachiasmatic nucleus vasopressin acts locally to regulate neuronal activity and is also released to other brain regions. A recent study showed that the vasopressin gene is transcriptionally regulated by the CLK, BMAL1, PER, and TIM proteins in a manner analogous to that described above for *per* and *tim*; that is, an E-box in the vasopressin promoter mediates transcriptional activation by CLK-BMAL1, and this activation is inhibited by PER-TIM. While these studies were conducted in a cell culture system, CLK-dependence of vasopressin cycling is supported by the observation that vasopressin does not cycle in CLK/CLK mutant mice.

The area of clock output is clearly going to be the focus of intense research for many years. It is likely that these studies will have relevance not only for chronobiology but also for a general understanding of physiological processes, such as sleep and hormone action, which happen to be controlled by the clock. *See* MIGRATORY BEHAVIOR; REPRODUCTIVE BEHAVIOR.   Amita Sehgal

Bibliography. J. Arendt, Complex effects of melatonin, *Therapie*, 53(5):479–488, 1998; A. R. Cashmore et al., Cryptochromes: Blue light receptors for plants and animals, *Science*, 284:760–765, 1999; J. C. Dunlap, Molecular bases for circadian clocks, *Cell*, 96:271–290, 1999; X. Jin et al., A molecular mechanism regulating rhythmic output from the suprachiasmatic circadian clock, *Cell*, 96:57–68, 1999; R. Lydic and H. A. Baghdoyan (eds.), *Handbook of Behavioral State Control, Cellular and Molecular Mechanisms*, Sec. 1: Mammalian circadian (24-hour) rhythms, CRC Press, 1999; D. Whitmore and P. Sassone-Corsi, Cryptic clues to clock function, *Nature*, 398:557–558, 1999; P. A. Wood and W. J. Hrushesky, Circadian rhythms and cancer chemotherapy, *Crit. Rev. Eukaryotic Gene Expression*, 6(4):299–343, 1996.

Biological oxidation

A biochemical reaction involving the transfer of a negatively charged electron from one organic compound to another organic compound or to oxygen. When a compound loses an electron, or is oxidized, another compound gains the electron, or is reduced. Oxidation-reduction (redox) reactions represent the main source of biological energy. Redox reactions occur simultaneously, and one does not occur without the other. The principal sources of reductants for animals are the numerous breakdown products of the major foodstuffs: carbohydrates, fats, and proteins. Energy release from these substances occurs in a stepwise series of hydrogen and electron transfers to molecular oxygen. *See* OXIDATION-REDUCTION.

Biological oxidation-reduction reactions. There are four prevalent varieties of biological redox reactions.

Direct transfer of electron. In one type of redox reaction, an electron is transferred directly from a donor to an acceptor [reaction (1)]. In this process, an elec-

$$\text{Cytochrome } c\,(\text{Fe}^{3+}) + \text{cytochrome } b\,(\text{Fe}^{2+}) \rightarrow$$
$$\text{cytochrome } c\,(\text{Fe}^{2+}) + \text{cytochrome } b\,(\text{Fe}^{3+}) \quad (1)$$

tron is removed from the ferrous iron (Fe^{2+}) of a protein called cytochrome b and is transferred to the ferric iron (Fe^{3+}) of cytochrome c. Cytochrome c is the oxidizing agent, or oxidant, and cytochrome b is the reducing agent, or reductant. The cytochromes are a family of heme proteins; the heme group is an iron-porphyrin system similar to that found in hemoglobin, the protein that gives red blood cells their color. *See* CYTOCHROME.

Electrons transferred with protons. In a second type of redox reaction, electrons are transferred with protons in a process formally equivalent to the transfer of a hydrogen atom, which is made up of two positively charged protons and two negatively charged electrons ($2\text{H}^+ + 2e^-$). The enzyme pyruvate dehydrogenase functions in this fashion. This enzyme complex contains tightly bound flavin adenine dinucleotide (FAD). Pyruvate dehydrogenase mediates reaction (2).

$$\text{Pyruvate} + \text{coenzyme A} + \text{pyruvate dehydrogenase-FAD} \rightarrow$$
$$\text{acetyl-coenzyme A} + \text{carbon dioxide}$$
$$+ \text{pyruvate dehydrogenase-FADH}_2 \quad (2)$$

Coenzyme A (for acylation) functions in the transfer of acyl [R—C(=O)—] groups, and pyruvate is a breakdown product of glucose. In reaction (2), pyruvate donates the equivalent of a hydrogen molecule to FAD, the oxidizing agent. *See* COENZYME; ENZYME.

Transfer of hydride ion. In a third type of redox reaction, a hydride ion (H:$^+$) is transferred; the hydride ion consists of a proton and two electrons and bears a negative charge. This is illustrated in the final portion of the pyruvate dehydrogenase reaction (3) where the hydride ion is transferred from

Pyruvate dehydrogenase-FADH$_2$ + NAD$^+$ →

pyruvate dehydrogenase-FAD + NADH + H$^+$ (3)

tightly bound FADH$_2$ to nicotinamide adenine dinucleotide (NAD$^+$). NAD$^+$ functions as the oxidizing agent. FAD is alternately reduced by pyruvate and reoxidized by NAD$^+$. In order for such reactions to continue, the reduced coenzyme (NADH) has to be reoxidized by another substance. NAD$^+$ and nicotinamide dinucleotide phosphate (NADP$^+$) are derivatives of the vitamin niacin. Some enzymes use NAD$^+$ as oxidant, others use NADP$^+$, and still others can use either NAD$^+$ or NADP$^+$. *See* NICOTINAMIDE ADENINE DINUCLEOTIDE (NAD$^+$); NICOTINAMIDE ADENINE DINUCLEOTIDE PHOSPHATE (NADP$^+$).

Electron transfer via direct reaction with oxygen. In a fourth type of oxidation-reduction, molecular oxygen (O$_2$) reacts directly with the reductant. This can be a monooxygenase or a dioxygenase process. In a monooxygenase reaction, one atom of O$_2$ is reduced to H$_2$O and the other is incorporated in the product [reaction (4)]. Phenylalanine, an amino acid, is

Phenylalanine + tetrahydrobiopterin + O$_2$ →

tyrosine + H$_2$O + dihydrobiopterin   (4)

oxidized to tyrosine, an amino acid that contains a hydroxyl group. The reaction is catalyzed by phenylalanine hydroxylase.

In a dioxygenase reaction, both atoms of molecular oxygen can be incorporated into an organic molecule [reaction (5)]. Both atoms of oxygen occur

Homogentisate + O$_2$ → 4-maleylacetoacetate   (5)

in 4-maleylacetoacetate. Homogentisate is a breakdown product of the amino acids phenylalanine and tyrosine.

Molecular oxygen exhibits two properties that make it a good oxidant. First, oxygen is very electronegative (second only to fluorine) and tends to attract electrons to it. Second, oxygen is electron-deficient. Each oxygen atom in the molecule lacks a complete octet of electrons. When oxygen reacts with two molecules of hydrogen, two molecules of water form, and the oxygen in water has a complete

octet of electrons [reaction (6)], which is a more

$$H \overset{\times}{\times} H + \overset{..}{:}\overset{..}{O}:\overset{..}{:}O: + H \overset{\times}{\times} H \rightarrow \overset{..}{:}\overset{\times}{O}\overset{\times}{\times}H + H\overset{\cdot}{\times}\overset{..}{O}: \quad (6)$$

stable condition. (The electrons in molecular oxygen are represented by the dots, and the electrons in molecular hydrogen are represented by x's.)

Oxidative phosphorylation. Oxidative phosphorylation is responsible for most of the adenosine triphosphate (ATP) generated in animals, plants, and many bacteria. The transfer of electrons from NADH or FADH$_2$ to oxygen sustains the synthesis of ATP from adenosine diphosphate (ADP) and inorganic phosphate (P$_i$) by oxidative phosphorylation. Oxidative phosphorylation requires an electron transport chain in a membrane, O$_2$, and an ATP synthase. *See* ADENOSINE TRIPHOSPHATE (ATP).

Mitochondrial electron transport. The components of the electron transport chain are found in the inner mitochondrial membrane of animal and plant cells. The electron transport chain consists of four independent protein complexes (I, II, III, and IV). Coenzyme Q and cytochrome *c* transport electrons between the complexes. The transfer of electrons from reductant to oxidant is energetically favorable.

NADH, which is generated by pyruvate dehydrogenase [reaction (3)] and many other processes, donates its electrons to complex I (see **illus.**). Electrons are transferred from complex I to coenzyme Q to produce coenzyme QH$_2$. The flavin dehydrogenases, such as succinate dehydrogenase (complex II), transport electrons to coenzyme Q. (Succinate dehydrogenase is one of the enzymes of the Krebs tricarboxylic acid cycle.) Coenzyme QH$_2$, in turn, donates its electrons to complex III. Cytochrome *c* carries an electron from complex III to complex IV, or cytochrome oxidase. The cytochrome oxidase reaction of complex IV accounts for more than 95% of all oxygen consumed by humans. *See* CITRIC ACID CYCLE; MITOCHONDRIA.

Proton translocation in oxidative and photosynthetic phosphorylation. The chemiosmotic theory proposed by Peter Mitchell in 1961 provides the conceptual framework for understanding the mechanism of oxidative phosphorylation. The redox reactions of electron transport provide energy for the translocation of protons (H$^+$) from the inside (matrix) of the mitochondria to the space between its inner and outer membranes. Electron transport generates and maintains an electrochemical proton concentration difference across the inner membrane. An analogous

Overview of the mitochondrial electron transport chain.

situation occurs in aerobic bacteria, in which protons are translocated from the interior to the exterior of the cell membrane. The protons return into mitochondrial matrix, or bacterial cells, through a membrane-bound ATP synthase, and this energetically downhill process drives the energetically uphill conversion of ADP and P_i to ATP. Photophosphorylation in photosynthetic cells occurs by an analogous mechanism, except that light provides the energy to generate reductants for an electron transport chain. *See* PHOTOSYNTHESIS.

Reactive oxygen species. The reaction of oxygen with a single electron results in the formation of the superoxide anion radical [reaction (7)]. Superoxide

$$O_2 + e^- \rightarrow O_2^- \qquad (7)$$

formation can occur by the spontaneous (nonenzymatic) reaction of oxygen with ferrous ion or reactive oxidation-reduction intermediates. Superoxide is a reactive substance that can cause the modification of cellular proteins, nucleic acids, and lipids in membranes, and is therefore toxic.

Superoxide dismutase is the enzyme that catalyzes the conversion of two superoxide anions and two protons to oxygen and hydrogen peroxide [reaction (8)]. Superoxide dismutase plays a pivotal role in pro-

$$2O_2^- + 2H^+ \rightarrow O_2 + H_2O_2 \qquad (8)$$

tecting cells against oxygen toxicity.

Hydrogen peroxide is a reactive substance that can modify cellular macromolecules, and it is toxic. Hydrogen peroxide is converted to oxygen and water in a process mediated by the enzyme catalase [reaction (9)].

$$H_2O_2 \rightarrow H_2O + {}^1/_2 O_2 \qquad (9)$$

A third toxic oxygen derivative is the hydroxyl free radical. The hydroxyl free radical is more reactive and toxic than superoxide and peroxide. The hydroxyl free radical (denoted by the dot) can be formed through a nonenzymatic reaction of hydrogen peroxide with ferrous iron [reaction (10)]. The

$$H_2O_2 + Fe^{2+} \rightarrow Fe^{3+} + OH^- + OH^\bullet \qquad (10)$$

hydroxyl free radical is also formed by the reaction of superoxide with hydrogen peroxide [reaction (11)].

$$H_2O_2 + O_2^- \rightarrow O_2 + OH^- + OH^\bullet \qquad (11)$$

In addition, the hydroxyl free radical can be formed by the radiolysis of water produced by cosmic rays, x-rays, and other energetic electromagnetic radiation. The hydroxyl free radical reacts with and modifies cellular macromolecules. A widespread enzyme, glutathione peroxidase, mediates the destruction of hydroxyl free radicals [reaction (12)]. Glutathione

$$2OH^\bullet + 2GSH \rightarrow 2H_2O + GSSG \qquad (12)$$

(GSH) is a peptide consisting of three amino acid residues, and its —SH group is the reductant. Moreover, a hydroxyl free radical can be destroyed by

its reaction with ascorbate (vitamin C), β-carotene (vitamin A), or vitamin E. These actions may play a role in the beneficial and protective antioxidant effects of these vitamins. *See* ANTIOXIDANT.

Robert Roskoski, Jr.

Bibliography. J. M. Berg, J. L. Tymoczko, and L. Stryer, *Biochemistry*, 5th ed., 2001; C. Mathews, K. Van Holde, and K. Ahern, *Biochemistry*, 3d ed., 2000; D. L. Nelson and M. M. Cox, *Lehninger Principles of Biochemistry*, 3d ed., 2000; D. G. Nicholls and S. J. Ferguson, *Bioenergetics 3*, 2002; R. Roskoski, *Biochemistry*, 1996.

Biological productivity

The amount and rate of production which occur in a given ecosystem over a given time period. It may apply to a single organism, a population, or entire communities and ecosystems. Productivity can be expressed in terms of dry matter produced per area per time (net production), or in terms of energy produced per area per time (gross production = respiration + heat losses + net production). In aquatic systems, productivity is often measured in volume instead of area. *See* BIOMASS.

Ecologists distinguish between primary productivity (by autotrophs) and secondary productivity (by heterotrophs). Plants have the ability to use the energy from sunlight to convert carbon dioxide and water into glucose and oxygen, producing biomass through photosynthesis. Primary productivity of a community is the rate at which biomass is produced per unit area by plants, expressed in either units of energy [joules/(m^2)(day)] or dry organic matter [kg/(m^2)(year)]. The following definitions are useful in calculating production: Gross primary production (GPP) is the total energy fixed by photosynthesis per unit time. Net primary production (NPP) is the gross production minus losses due to plant respiration per unit time, and it represents the actual new biomass that is available for consumption by heterotrophic organisms. Secondary production is the rate of production of biomass by heterotrophs (animals, microorganisms), which feed on plant products or other heterotrophs. *See* PHOTOSYNTHESIS.

Productivity is not spread evenly across the planet. For instance, although oceans cover two-thirds of Earth's surface, they account for only one-third of the Earth's productivity: it is estimated that the global terrestrial primary productivity is approximately 120×10^9 tons of dry weight per year, while the sea primary productivity is estimated at approximately 60×10^9 tons per year. Furthermore, the factors that limit productivity in the ocean differ from those limiting productivity on land, producing differences in geographic patterns of productivity in the two systems. In terrestrial ecosystems, productivity shows a latitudinal trend, with highest productivity in the tropics and decreasing progressively toward the Poles; but in the ocean there is no latitudinal trend, and the highest values of net primary production are found along coastal regions.

In the ocean, primary productivity is controlled by light and nutrient availability. Oceans do not show a gradient of productivity from the Equator to the Poles. Instead, there is a vertical productivity gradient, depending on the rate at which light decreases with depth. Primary production in the oceans is relatively low in the surface, due to excessive light, and is highest at 10–30 m (33–100 ft) depth. If light were the main factor controlling productivity in the ocean, an increasing productivity gradient should be seen in moving toward the Equator. However, some parts of the tropics and subtropics are very unproductive, while the Antarctic Ocean is one of the most productive oceanic regions. In the ocean, nutrients are often the factor limiting primary productivity. Nutrient concentration tends to be high in the deep water and low in the surface layers, where plankton lives. The highest-net-productivity areas in the ocean are found along coastal regions, where seawater mixes with nutrient-rich estuarine water, and in regions of upwelling, where nutrient-rich deep-ocean water is brought to the surface. As a consequence, in the ocean there are areas of high productivity even at high latitudes and low temperatures. The nutrients that most commonly limit productivity in the ocean are phosphorus, nitrogen, and iron. Different areas in the ocean are limited by different nutrients. An experiment in the Sargasso Sea demonstrated that nutrients are the limiting factor in this area of low productivity. If nitrogen and phosphorus but no iron were added, primary productivity barely increased. The addition of iron stimulated primary productivity but only for a short time. The addition of phosphorus, nitrogen, and iron increased productivity for prolonged periods, suggesting that although iron is the most limiting nutrient, availability of phosphorus and nitrogen in the region is also very low.

In terrestrial communities, primary productivity is correlated to actual evapotranspiration: the amount of water lost to the atmosphere by evaporation from the ground and by transpiration from the vegetation. Evapotranspiration is a measure of solar radiation, temperature, and rainfall, and primary productivity increases with actual evapotranspiration. Direct radiation from the Sun and temperature tend to increase toward the Equator. When water is not limited, photosynthetic rate increases with radiant energy and with temperature, and this translates into higher primary productivity. Other factors, such as leaf area and water-holding capacity of the soil, will affect evapotranspiration, and thus primary production. For example, in areas with no water shortage, plants will tend to have broad leaves, which will allow them to capture solar radiation and increase the circulation of air inside the leaves, where photosynthesis occurs. In these areas, primary productivity will tend to be high. In contrast, in areas where water is a limiting resource, plants will tend to have smaller leaf area to reduce water loss, reducing transpiration rate but also reducing photosynthetic rate. Finally, primary productivity in terrestrial communities can be limited by nutrients—nitrogen being the most common limiting nutrient.

To illustrate productivity at an ecosystem level,

TABLE 1. Energy flow of autotrophic and heterotrophic production and respiration in lightly grazed shortgrass prairie at Pawnee Site, Colorado, 1972*

Energetic parameters	Production, kJ/m^2	Respiration, kJ/m^2
Autotrophic activity		
Gross primary production	21,900	
Net primary production	14,455	7,445
Aboveground	2,165	5,725
Belowground	12,290	1,720
Heterotrophic activity		
Herbivory	99	242
Decomposers	2,930	9,640

*"Lightly grazed" indicated 1 steer per 10.8 hectares or per 4.32 acres over 180 years.
SOURCE: Modified from D. C. Coleman et al., Energy flow and partitioning in selected man-managed and natural ecosystems, Agroecosystems, 3:45–56, 1976.

a terrestrial ecosystem is used in **Table 1**. For a lightly grazed shortgrass prairie, the gross rate of photosynthesis was 21,900 kJ/m^2 over 180 days. After accounting for respiration losses from the plants (7450 kJ), a net production of 14,455 kJ remained. This net primary production, partitioned as above- and belowground, flows principally into the decomposition pathways. The predominant flow of energy of primary production thus goes to the decomposers (bacteria, fungi, and detritivores). Although animal heterotrophs account for only a small fraction of the total energy flow (2–4%), they may play a synergistic or catalytic role in subsequent new plant production.

Production of agroecosystems and natural systems can be compared using net ecosystem production (NPP − respiration of heterotrophs) and ecosystem metabolism (GPP/net ecosystem respiration = autotrophic + heterotrophic respiration). Production and respiration in more mature ecosystems are nearly in balance, while there is more harvestable production in an agroecosystem (production greater than respiration) [**Table 2**]. Unfortunately, there is little information for many agroecosystems concerning belowground energy costs. Much of the existing information on production refers to readily harvested fibrous material; yet there may be considerable amounts of root exudates and sloughed cells produced in addition to the fibrous roots. These exudates represent an additional "cost of doing business" for plants in either old-growth forest or annual field crops. For example, it has been estimated that perhaps 23–25% of the carbon fixed by photosynthesis in a rice crop goes to furnish root exudates for rhizosphere (root-associated) microflora active in nitrogen fixation. This is an important link between carbon-energy flow and nutrient cycling. *See* AGROECOSYSTEM.

The production and activity of certain microflora may be of considerable importance to plant growth in a wide variety of terrestrial ecosystems. Thus various beneficial root-associated fungi (mycorrhizae) may facilitate uptake of a limiting nutrient, such as

TABLE 2. Annual production and respiration [kJ/(m^2)(year)] in growth-type and more mature ecosystems*

Energetic parameters	Types of ecosytems			
	Alfalfa field (U.S.)	Young pine plantation (U.K.)	Shortgrass prairie (Table 1)	80-year deciduous forest (Tennessee)
Gross primary production (GPP)	102,190	51,095	21,900	117,165
Autotrophic respiration (R_A)	38,530	19,685	7,445	76,220
Net primary production (NPP)	63,660	31,410	14,455	40,940
Heterotrophic respiration (R_H)	12,565	19,265	9,965	38,410
Net ecosystem production (NEP = NPP$-R_H$)	51,095	12,145	4,495	2,530
Net ecosystem respiration ($R_E = R_A + R_H$)	51,095	38,950	17,410	114,635
Ecosystem metabolism (GPP/R_E)	2.00	1.31	1.26	1.02

*Systems are arranged in decreasing magnitudes of net ecosystem production.

phosphorus, permitting a doubling of harvestable shoot production of plants such as clover. However, the net carbon energy cost to the plant is quite low: approximately 1% of the total carbon allocation of the host plant. *See* MYCORRHIZAE.

It is apparent that the important aspects of biological productivity must be defined carefully. Depending on management techniques, the amount and activity of beneficial microorganisms, such as mycorrhizae, may have an importance equal to that of the crop species of interest. A holistic approach should be important to manage ecosystems using lower inputs of fossil fuels for tillage and fertilizers. *See* ECOLOGICAL ENERGETICS; ECOSYSTEM; FOOD WEB.   David C. Coleman; Ellen Gryj

Bibliography. M. Begon, J. L. Harper, and C. R. Townsend, *Ecology*, Blackwell Science, Cambridge, MA, 1996; K. Blaxter, *Energy Metabolism in Animals and Man*, Cambridge University Press, New York, 1989; R. L. Hanson, Evapotranspiration and droughts, in R. W. Paulson et al. (eds.), *National Water Summary 1988-89: Hydrological Events and Floods and Droughts*, 1991; C. J. Krebs, *Ecology*, Harper Collins, New York, 1994; S. J. McNaughton, Serengeti migratory wildebeest: Facilitation of energy flow by grazing, *Science*, 191:92-94, 1976; W. H. Schlesinger, *Biogeochemistry: An Analysis of Global Change*, Academic Press, San Diego, 1997.

Biological specificity

The orderly patterns of metabolic and developmental reactions giving rise to the unique characteristics of the individual and of its species. It is one of the most widespread and characteristic properties of living organisms. Biological specificity is most pronounced and best understood at the cellular and molecular levels of organization, where the shapes of individual molecules allow them to selectively recognize and bind to one another. The main principle which guides this recognition is termed complementarity. Just as a hand fits perfectly into a glove, molecules which are complementary have mirror-image shapes that allow them to selectively bind to each other.

This ability of complementary molecules to specifically bind to one another plays many essential roles in living systems. For example, the transmission of specific hereditary traits from parent to offspring depends upon the ability of the individual strands of a deoxyribonucleic acid (DNA) molecule to specifically generate two new strands with complementary sequences. Similarly, metabolism, which provides organisms with both the energy and chemical building blocks needed for survival, is made possible by the ability of enzymes to specifically bind to the substrates whose interconversions they catalyze. *See* DEOXYRIBONUCLEIC ACID (DNA); ENZYME; METABOLISM.

In addition to metabolism and DNA replication, many other attributes of living systems depend upon specific recognition between molecules. During embryonic development, for example, individual cells associate with each other in precise patterns to form tissues, organs, and organ systems. These ordered interactions are ultimately dependent upon the ability of individual cells to recognize and specifically bind to other cells of a similar type. The existence of such preferential cell-cell interactions can be demonstrated experimentally by isolating individual cells from two different tissues and then mixing the two populations together in a test tube. If liver cells are mixed with cartilage cells, for example, the liver cells will preferentially bind to other liver cells, while the cartilage cells will adhere to other cartilage cells. This ability of cells to selectively bind to other cells of the same type is based upon specific recognition between molecules located at the cell surface. *See* CELL ADHESION; DEVELOPMENTAL BIOLOGY.

In addition to binding to one another, cells can also interact by releasing hormones into the bloodstream. Though all of an organism's cells are exposed to hormones circulating in the bloodstream, only a small number of target cells respond to any particular hormone. This selectivity occurs because the specific receptor molecules to which hormones bind are restricted to certain cell types. Thus each hormone exerts its effects on a few selected cell types because only those cells contain the proper receptor. Specific receptors are also involved in interactions between neurotransmitters and the cells they stimulate or inhibit, between certain types of drugs and the cells they affect, and between viruses and the cells they infect. This last phenomenon has an important influence on the susceptibility of individuals to virally transmitted diseases. The reason that humans are resistant to infection by viruses which destroy bacteria, for example, is that human cells do not contain the cell-surface receptors present in bacterial cells. *See* ENDOCRINE MECHANISMS; HORMONE.

Although most examples of biological specificity are based upon interactions occurring at the molecular level, such phenomena affect many properties manifested at the level of the whole organism. The ability of individuals to defend against infectious diseases, for example, requires the production of antibody molecules which specifically bind to bacteria and viruses. The fertilization of an egg by a sperm is facilitated by specific recognition between molecules present on the surfaces of the sperm and egg cells. Finally, even communication between organisms can be mediated by specific chemical signals, called pheromones. Such chemical signals are utilized in trail marking by ants and bees, in territory marking by certain mammals, and as sexual attractants. Specific molecular interactions thus exert influences ranging from the replication of genes to the behavior of organisms. *See* CHEMICAL ECOLOGY; FERTILIZATION (ANIMAL); IMMUNOLOGY; MOLECULAR BIOLOGY; PHEROMONE.   Lewis J. Kleinsmith

Biologicals

Biological products used to induce immunity to various infectious diseases or noxious substances of biological origin. The term is usually limited to immune serums, antitoxins, vaccines, and toxoids that have the effect of providing protective substances of the same general nature that a person develops naturally from having survived an infectious disease or having experienced repeated contact with a biological poison. As a matter of governmental regulatory convenience, certain therapeutic substances which have little to do with conferring immunity have been classified as biological products primarily because they are derived from human or animal sources and are tested for safety by methods similar to those used for many biological products. *See* IMMUNITY.

Immune serums. One major class of biologicals includes the animal and human immune serums. All animals, including humans, develop protective substances in their blood plasma during recovery from many (but not all) infectious diseases or following the injection of toxins or killed bacteria and viruses. These protective substances called antibodies usually are found in the immunoglobulin fraction of the plasma and are specific since they react with and neutralize only substances identical or closely similar to those that caused them to be formed. Thus serum containing antibodies induced by injections of diphtheria toxin neutralizes diphtheria toxin, but not tetanus toxin. *See* ANTIBODY; IMMUNOGLOBULIN; SERUM.

Antibody-containing serum from another animal is useful in the treatment, modification, or prevention of certain diseases of humans when it is given by intramuscular or intravenous injection. The use of these preformed "borrowed" antibodies is called passive immunization, to distinguish it from active immunization, in which each person develops his or her own antibodies. Passive immunization has the advantage of providing immediate protection, but it is temporary because serum proteins from other animals and even from other humans are rapidly destroyed in the recipient.

Types. Serums which contain antibodies active chiefly in destroying the infecting virus or bacterium are usually called antiserums or immune serums; those containing antibodies capable of neutralizing the secreted toxins of bacteria are called antitoxins. Immune serums have been prepared to neutralize the venoms of certain poisonous snakes and black widow spiders; they are called antivenins.

Because all products used for passive immunization are immune serums, or globulin fractions from such serums, they are named to indicate the diseases that they treat or prevent, the substances that they inhibit or neutralize, the animal from which they came, and whether they are whole serums or the globulin fractions thereof. Thus there is, for example, antipertussis immune rabbit serum, measles immune globulin (human), diphtheria antitoxic globulin (horse), tetanus immune globulin (human), and anti-Rh$_0$ (D) gamma globulin (human).

Preparation. The general methods of preparation of various immune serums and antitoxins differ only in details. Horses, cows, rabbits, or humans are injected with slowly increasing amounts of either the virus, bacterium, toxin, erythrocyte, or venom as antigens against which immunity is to be developed. These agents are usually treated with chemicals to render them noninfectious or nontoxic before injection. Injections are given over several months and the animals respond by producing relatively large amounts of specific antibody against the injected material. When the antibody concentration has reached a high level in the blood, the animals are bled and the blood is allowed to clot. The liquid serum can be separated from the blood cells after the clot has contracted. This serum is usually fractionated chemically to obtain the concentrated antibody-globulin fraction free of albumin and other nonantibody fractions. The antibody-globulin fraction may be digested with enzymes to remove other extraneous components. The antibody solution is then sterilized by filtration through a bacteriaproof filter, and a small amount of preservative antibacterial chemical is added to protect the solution from bacterial contamination during administration.

Standardization. Each lot of immune serum or globulin concentrate is tested to make certain that it is sterile, free of fever-producing impurities (pyrogens), and free of accidentally introduced poisonous materials. In addition, each serum is tested to determine the antibody concentration in it. Although methods vary, depending upon the type of immune serum, potency is usually measured by determining the amount of antibody that is required to protect mice or guinea pigs from the fatal effects of a standard amount of the living infectious agent or of the corresponding toxin. When the protective dose of the unknown serum is compared to the protective dose of a standard antitoxin or reference immune serum, it is possible to calculate the relative potency in the serum or globulin concentrate that is being tested. The dosages of antitoxins are usually specified in units. The dosages of antibacterial or antiviral immune serums or globulin concentrates are usually expressed in milliliters.

Disadvantages. The use of animal immune serums for prevention of therapy in humans has certain disadvantages. The serum proteins themselves may cause the production of specific antibodies in the recipient of the immune serum, and thus the person may become allergically sensitized to the serum protein of this animal species. Therefore, a second dose of serum from the same species of animal given weeks, months, or years later may cause an acute anaphylactic reaction that may be fatal. It is advisable, particularly in cases in which serum may have been given to a patient previously, to test for hypersensitivity by injecting a tiny amount of serum into the skin of the patient. A positive reaction indicating hypersensitivity is evidenced by the rapid development of itching, inflammation, and swelling at the site of the injection. *See* ANAPHYLAXIS; HYPERSENSITIVITY.

A second and less acute type of reaction resulting from the injection of animal immune serum is so-called serum sickness. About 4–10 days after the administration of serum, the patient develops fever, urticarial (hivelike) rash, and sometimes joint pains. These reactions are not ordinarily fatal.

Many people have significant amounts of measles and poliomyelitis antibodies in their serums as a result of recovery from either the clinical diseases or inapparent infections. Therefore, the globulin concentrates from normal pooled human serums collected at random have sufficient antibody to be useful in preventing or moderating these infections in persons who have been exposed. Such human serum proteins rarely produce the allergic hypersensitivity problems that often follow the passive transfer of animal serum. Enzyme-digested globulins of human origin have the added advantage of intravenous administration.

Active immunity production. Products used to produce active immunity constitute the other large class of biological products. They contain the actual toxins, viruses, or bacteria that cause disease, but they are modified in a manner to make them safe to administer. Because the body does not distinguish between the natural toxin or infectious agent and the same material when properly modified, immunity is produced in response to injections of these materials in a manner very similar to that which occurs during the natural disease. Vaccines are suspensions of the killed or attenuated (weakened) bacteria or viruses or fractions thereof. Toxoids are solutions of the chemically altered specific bacterial toxins which cause the major damage produced by bacterial infections. Biological products producing active immunity are usually named to indicate the disease they immunize against and the kind of substance they contain: thus typhoid vaccine, diphtheria toxoid, tetanus toxoid, measles vaccine, mumps vaccine, and poliomyelitis vaccine. *See* VACCINATION.

Antigen modification. It is most important that vaccines and toxoids be altered in a way to make them safe, but not so drastically altered that they will no longer produce immunity. Certain strains of smallpox, measles, yellow fever, mumps, and polio viruses, and the tubercle bacillus have been attenuated so that, although they can still undergo limited multiplication in the body, they do not produce progressive infection or symptoms of disease. Vaccines made from these strains are called attenuated vaccines. Other viruses are rendered completely noninfectious by the addition of small amounts of formaldehyde, and bacteria may be killed with formaldehyde, phenol, or mercurial compounds. Vaccines made from these killed infectious agents are called killed vaccines. Typhoid vaccine, pertussis (whooping cough) vaccine, and Salk polio vaccine are examples of this type of product. Many bacterial toxins can be made nontoxic by incubation at 98.6°F (37°C) with small amounts of formaldehyde. These altered toxins are called toxoids and stimulate the body to produce antitoxin capable of specifically neutralizing the toxin. Diphtheria toxoid and tetanus toxoid are the two most common toxoids used to immunize humans.

Vaccine preparation. Bacterial vaccines are usually prepared by growing specially selected strains in suitable culture media, harvesting the bacteria from the media, and suspending them in saline. A killing agent is added to the bacterial suspension and is allowed to act at about 98.6°F (37°C) until no bacteria remain alive. The bacteria may be extracted or chemically fractionated to purify the immunizing antigen. The suspensions or purified antigens are then diluted with physiological saline to the desired potency. These vaccines, after testing for sterility, lack of abnormal toxicity, and immunizing potency, are ready for use.

Because viruses must be grown in the presence of living cells, these agents are inoculated into embryonated eggs, live animals, or cultures of living cells growing in bottles in the laboratory. The egg fluids, animal tissue juices, or the supernatant fluid of tissue cultures then contain the viruses. Treatment with formaldehyde destroys the infectivity of viruses, and these virus-containing solutions may be used for immunization after suitable tests to ensure safety, sterility, and potency. Live virus vaccines are made with viruses attenuated by serial passage in various species of animals or tissue cultures. They are grown in living cells and may be used for immunization after suitable tests to ensure safety, bacterial sterility, potency, and freedom from adventitious agents. Live virus vaccines may be given orally (Sabin poliomyelitis vaccine) or injected (measles vaccine). Live virus vaccines produce subclinical infections that confer a durable immunity equivalent to that which occurs following the natural disease.

Toxoids. With certain toxoids the addition of a small amount of alum, aluminum hydroxide, or aluminum phosphate precipitates the toxoid molecules and changes the solution to a suspension that is more effective when injected than the original toxoid solution. These precipitated toxoids may be given in smaller amounts to produce equal or greater immunity than that caused by the plain toxoid. Alum-precipitated diphtheria toxoid is widely used in preference to plain toxoid.

Multiple immunization. Because it is frequently expedient to immunize people simultaneously against several diseases, various immunizing agents have been combined so that they can be given in a single series of two or three doses. A combination of pertussis vaccine, diphtheria toxoid, and tetanus toxoid with alum added has become very widely used as an immunizing agent for babies. Vaccines against three types of poliomyelitis have been added to this mixture. Combinations of typhoid vaccine and tetanus toxoid and of measles and smallpox vaccines have been used.

The combination of a large number of different immunizing agents within a single immunization dosage is an exceedingly complex problem because dosage volume must be kept small and the various agents must be compatible. This has resulted in much research on purification and concentration of antigens to reduce their volumes and eliminate toxic impurities. Tetanus and diphtheria toxoids and influenza vaccine have been considerably purified, and chemical fractions of various pathogenic bacteria (pertussis and cholera vaccines) are used as immunizing agents.

Veterinary use. Because livestock and pets as well as human beings require protection from infectious diseases, there is an extensive assortment of veterinary biological products. Many of these are vaccines and toxoids prepared in the same way as are products for human use.

Blood derivatives. In addition to products for active and passive immunization, a few other substances of human or animal origin are also classed (mostly for regulatory convenience) as biological products. One group of these is normal human blood plasma and its derivatives. Whole plasma and serum albumin are used to combat hemorrhage and shock, and other fractions are used in the treatment of hemophilia and for their clotting properties. The use of anti-Rh_0 (D) gamma globulin in Rh-negative women at parturition inhibits Rh sensitization and erythroblastosis fetalis in subsequent offspring. Although they do not produce immunity to infectious diseases, these substances require testing for sterility, safety, and freedom from pyrogens as to the immune serums. *See* BLOOD GROUPS; RH INCOMPATIBILITY.

Diagnostic agents. Another group of biological products consists of a miscellany of reagents used in the diagnosis of infectious diseases. These include immune serums for the serological typing and identification of pathogenic bacteria and viruses, and various antigens for the detection of antibodies in patients' serums as a means of assisting in diagnosis. In addition to these substances used in the laboratory diagnosis of disease, certain extracts of bacteria and fungi have been prepared for injection into the skin to detect allergic hypersensitivity. In certain diseases such as tuberculosis and brucellosis, the patient usually becomes hypersensitive to certain components of the infecting organism. Extracts of these organisms injected into the skin of such a person cause inflammation, whereas no reaction occurs in a person who has not been infected. These skin tests therefore are of assistance in the diagnosis of various infectious diseases.

Allergenic products are administered to humans for the diagnosis, prevention, or treatment of allergies to various plant and animal substances. They usually are suspensions of the allergenic substance (pollens, feathers, hairs, or danders) in 50% glycerin. *See* IMMUNOLOGY.   Lee F. Schuchardt

Bibliography. E. A. Kabat, *Experimental Immunochemistry*, 1971; M. J. Pelczar, Jr., E. C. Chan, and N. R. Krieg, *Microbiology*, 5th ed., 1986; M. M. Wintrobe, *Blood, Pure and Eloquent*, 1980.

Biology

A natural science concerned with the study of all living organisms. Although living organisms share some unifying themes, such as their origin from the same basic cellular structure and their molecular basis of inheritance, they are diverse in many other aspects. The diversity of life leads to many divisions in biological science involved with studying all aspects of living organisms. The primary divisions of study in biology consist of zoology (animals), botany (plants), and protistology (one-celled organisms), and are aimed at examining such topics as origins, structure, function, reproduction, growth and development, behavior, and evolution of the different organisms. In addition, biologists consider how living organisms interact with each other and the environment on an individual as well as group basis. Therefore, within these divisions are many subdivisions such as molecular and cellular biology, microbiology (the study of microbes such as bacteria and viruses), taxonomy (the classification of organisms into special groups), physiology (the study of function of the organism at any level), immunology (the investigation of the immune system), genetics (the study of inheritance), and ecology and evolution (the study of the interaction of an organism with its environment and how that interaction changes over time).

The study of living organisms is an ongoing process that allows observation of the natural world and the acquisition of new knowledge. Biologists accomplish their studies through a process of inquiry known as the scientific method, which approaches a problem or question in a well-defined orderly sequence of steps so as to reach conclusions. The first step involves making systematic observations, either directly through the sense of sight, smell, taste, sound, or touch, or indirectly through the use of special equipment such as the microscope. Next, questions are asked regarding the observations. Then a hypothesis—a tentative explanation or educated guess—is formulated, and predictions about what will occur are made. At the core of any scientific study is testing of the hypothesis. Tests or experiments are designed so as to help substantiate or refute the basic assumptions set forth in the hypothesis. Therefore, experiments are repeated many times. Once they have been completed, data are collected and organized in the form of graphs or tables and the results are analyzed. Also, statistical tests may be performed to help determine whether the data are significant enough to support or disprove the hypothesis. Finally, conclusions are drawn that provide explanations or insights about the original problem. By employing the scientific method, biologists aim to be objective rather than subjective when interpreting the results of their experiments. Biology is not absolute: it is a science that deals with theories or relative truths. Thus, biological conclusions are always subject to change when new evidence is presented. As living organisms continue to evolve and change, the science of biology also will evolve. *See* ANIMAL; BOTANY; CELL BIOLOGY; ECOLOGY; GENETICS; IMMUNOLOGY; MICROBIOLOGY; PLANT; TAXONOMY; ZOOLOGY.   Lee Couch

Bibliography. N. A. Campbell, *Biology*, 3d ed., 1993; H. Curtis and N. S. Barnes, *Biology*, 5th ed., 1989; R. H. Saigo and B. Saigo, *Careers in Biology II*, 1988.

Bioluminescence

The emission of light by living organisms that is visible to other organisms. The enzymes and other proteins associated with bioluminescence have been developed and exploited as markers or reporters of other biochemical processes in biomedical research. Bioluminescence provides a unique tool for investigating and understanding numerous basic physiological processes, both cellular and organismic.

Luminous organisms. Although rare in terms of the total number of luminous species, bioluminescence is phylogenetically diverse, occurring in many different groups (**Table 1**). Luminescence is unknown in higher plants and in vertebrates above the fishes, and is also absent in several invertebrate phyla. In some phyla or taxa, a substantial proportion of the genera are luminous (for example, ctenophores, about 50%; cephalopods, greater than 50%; echinoderms and annelids, about 4%). Commonly, all members of a luminous genus emit light, but in some cases there are both luminous and nonluminous species.

Bioluminescence is most prevalent in the marine environment; it is greatest at midocean depths, where some daytime illumination penetrates. In these locations, bioluminescence may occur in over 95% of the individuals and 75% of the species in fish, and about 85% of the individuals and 80% of the species in shrimp and squid. A midwater luminous

TABLE 1. Major groups having luminous species	
Group	Features of luminous displays
Bacteria	Organisms glow constantly; system is autoinduced
Fungi	Mushrooms and mycelia produce constant dim glow
Dinoflagellates	Flagellated algae flash when disturbed
Coelenterates	Jellyfish, sea pansies, and comb jellies emit flashes
Annelids	Marine worms and earthworms exude luminescence
Mollusks	Squid and clams exude luminous clouds; also have photophores
Crustacea	Shrimp, copepods, ostracods; exude luminescence; also have photophores
Insects	Fireflies (beetles) emit flashes; flies (diptera) glow
Echinoderms	Brittle stars emit trains of rapid flashes
Fish	Many bony and cartilaginous fish are luminous; some use symbiotic bacteria; others are self-luminous; some have photophores

fish (*Cyclothone*) is considered to be the most abundant vertebrate on the planet. Where high densities of luminous organisms occur, their emissions can exert a significant influence on the communities and may represent an important component in the ecology, behavior, and physiology of the latter. Above and below midocean depths, luminescence decreases to less than 10% of all individuals and species; among coastal species, less than 2% are bioluminescent.

Although luminescence is prevalent in the deep sea, it is not associated especially with organisms that live in total darkness. There are no known luminous species either in deep fresh-water bodies, such as Lake Baikal, Russia, or in the darkness of terrestrial caves. Luminous dipteran insect larvae live in caves near the mouths of New Zealand, but they also occur in the undercut banks of streams, where there is considerable daytime illumination. Firefly displays of bioluminescence are among the most spectacular, but bioluminescence is rare in the terrestrial environment. Other terrestrial luminous forms include millipedes, centipedes, earthworms, and snails, but the display in these is not very bright.

Functions. The functional importance of bioluminescence and its selection in evolution are based largely on detection by another organism; the responses of that organism then favor in some way the luminous individual. In some organisms, such as the fungi, it is difficult to determine what the function of the light emission is. Both the mycelium and fruiting body emit a dim continuous light day and night, but its function is not evident.

While not metabolically essential, light emission can confer an advantage on the organism. The light can be used in diverse ways. Most of the perceived functions of bioluminescence fall into four categories: defense, offense, communication, and dispersal to enhance propagation (**Table 2**).

Defense. Several different defensive strategies are associated with bioluminescence: to frighten, to serve as a decoy, to provide camouflage, and to aid in

TABLE 2. Functions of bioluminescence		
Function	Strategy	Method and examples
Defense	Frighten or startle	Bright, brief flashes
	Decoy or divert	Glow, luminous cloud, sacrificial lure
	Camouflage	Ventral luminescence during the day, disrupting or concealing the silhouette seem from below
Offense	Frighten or startle	Bright flash may temporarily immobilize prey
	Lure	Glow to attract, then capture prey
	Enhance vision	See and capture prey
Communication	Signals for courtship and mating	Specific flashing signals; patterns of light emission are recognized by the opposite sex
Dispersal, propagation	Glow to attract feeders	Bacteria ingested by the feeder pass through the gut tract alive and are thereby dispersed

vision. Organisms may be frightened or diverted by flashes, which are typically bright and brief (0.1 s); light is emitted in this way by many organisms. A glowing object in the ocean often appears to attract feeders or predators. While a luminous organism would evidently be at risk by virtue of this attraction, an organism may create a decoy of exuded light to attract or confuse the predator, and then may slip off under the cover of darkness. This is done by luminous squid, which in the dark squirt a luminescent substance instead of ink, which would be useless in such a case. Some organisms sacrifice more than light: in scaleworms and brittle stars a part of the body may be shed and left behind as a luminescent decoy to attract the predator. In these cases the body part flashes while still intact but glows after detachment—evidence that a flash deters while a glow attracts.

A unique method for evading predation from below is to camouflage the silhouette by emitting light that matches the color and intensity of the downwelling background light. This has been called counterillumination, and it is used by many luminous marine organisms, including fish, to help escape detection.

Offense. Luminescence can aid in predation in several ways. Flashes, which are typically used defensively, can be used offensively in order to temporarily startle or blind prey. A glow can also be used offensively: it can serve as a lure, as in the angler fish. The prey organism is attracted to the light but is then captured by the organism that produced the light. Camouflage may also be used offensively, allowing the luminous predator to approach its prey undetected. Vision is certainly useful offensively: prey may be seen and captured under conditions that are otherwise dark.

Communication. The use of light for information exchange between individuals of a species occurs in several different ways. Best known is the use of flashing for courtship and mating in fireflies. There are also numerous examples in the ocean, such as the Bermuda fireworm, where mating occurs just posttwilight a few days after the full moon. The females swim in a tight circle while a male streaks from below and joins a female, with eggs and sperm being shed in the ocean in a brilliant luminous circle. Among ostracod crustaceans over shallow reefs in the Caribbean, males produce complex species-specific trains of secreted luminous material—"ladders of light"—which attract females.

Propagation. A continuous light emission serves as an attractant for feeding organisms, and saprophytic luminous bacteria typically grow on suitable substrates. After ingestion, the bacteria propagate as they pass through the gut tract and are then dispersed.

Physical and chemical mechanisms. Bioluminescence does not come from or depend on light absorbed by the organism. It derives from an enzymatically catalyzed chemiluminescence, a reaction in which the energy released is transformed into light energy. One of the reaction intermediates or products is formed in an electronically excited state, which then emits a photon. *See* CHEMILUMINESCENCE.

Chemiluminescence. Light emission due to a chemical reaction is a special case of the general phenomenon of luminescence, in which energy is specifically channeled to a molecule. Other kinds of luminescence include fluorescence and phosphorescence, in which the excited state is created by the prior absorption of light, or triboluminescence and piezoluminescence, involving crystal fracture and electric discharge, respectively. Electron bombardment, as in a television screen, also produces luminescence. The color is a characteristic of the excited molecule, irrespective of how the molecule was excited. *See* LUMINESCENCE.

Incandescence. In incandescence, excited states are produced by virtue of the thermal energy. An example is the light bulb, in which a filament is heated, and the color of the light depends on the temperature ("red hot" reflecting a lower temperature than "white hot"). *See* INCANDESCENCE; LIGHT.

Energy. The energy (E) of the photon is related to the color or frequency of the light: $E = h\nu$, where h is Planck's constant and ν the frequency. In the visible light range, E is very large in relation to most biochemical reactions. Thus, the energy released by a mole of photons (6.02×10^{23}) in visible wavelengths is about 50 kcal, which is much more than the energy from the hydrolysis of a mole of adenosine triphosphate (ATP), about 7 kcal. A visible photon is therefore able to do a lot of work (photosynthesis) or a lot of damage (mutation; photodynamic action, which can kill). Conversely, it takes a reaction which releases a large amount of energy to create a photon.

Mechanism. Chemiluminescence in solution generally requires oxygen which, in its reaction with a substrate, forms an organic peroxide. The energy from the breakdown of such peroxides, which should generate up to 100 kcal per mole, is ample to account for a product in an electronically excited state, and such reactions are typically responsible for bioluminescence.

A model of the mechanism in such chemiluminescent reactions is referred to as chemically initiated electron exchange luminescence (CIEEL). In this mechanism, peroxide breakdown involves electron transfer with chemiexcitation. It is initiated by an electron transfer from a donor species (D) to an acceptor (A), which is the peroxide bond in this case. After electron transfer the weak O-O bond cleaves to form products B and C^-. The latter is a stronger reductant than A^-, so the electron is transferred back to D with the concomitant formation of a singlet excited state D^* and emission.

It is useful to think of chemiluminescence as the reverse of a photochemical reaction. In the primary step of photosynthesis, for example, the energy of the excited state of chlorophyll (chl^*) gives rise to an electron transfer, with the consequent formation of an oxidant and reductant. Most of these redox species give rise to stable products and ultimately to CO_2 fixation. However, some species recombine and reemit a "delayed light." This is essentially the reverse of the reaction, with the formation of the singlet excited state of chlorophyll and its subsequent emission of a photon. *See* PHOTOSYNTHESIS.

Biology and biochemistry. Bioluminescence originated and evolved independently many times, and is thus not an evolutionarily conserved function. How many times this may have occurred is difficult to say, but it has been estimated that present-day luminous organisms come from as many as 30 different evolutionarily distinct origins. In the different groups of organisms, the genes and proteins involved are unrelated, and it may be confusing that the substrates and enzymes, though chemically different, are all referred to as luciferin and luciferase, respectively. To be correct and specific, each should be identified with the organism (**Table 3**). These differences are indicative of the independent evolutionary origins of the different systems.

Bacteria. Luminous bacteria typically emit a continuous light, usually blue-green. When strongly expressed, a single bacterium may emit 10^4 or 10^5 photons per second. A primary habitat where most species abound is in association with another (higher) organism, dead or alive, where growth and propagation occur. Luminous bacteria are ubiquitous in the oceans and can be isolated from most seawater samples, from the surface to depths of 1000 m (3280 ft) or more. However, they do not grow in seawater, as it is a poor growth medium; they occur there by spilling over from primary habitats.

Associations and symbiosis. The most exotic specific associations involve specialized light organs (for example, in fish and squid) in which a pure dense culture of luminous bacteria is maintained. In teleost fishes, 11 different groups carrying such bacteria are known, an exotic example being the flashlight fish. Exactly how symbioses are achieved—the initial infection, exclusion of contaminants, nutrient supply, restriction of growth but maintenance of bright light emission—is not understood. In such associations, the host receives the benefit of the light and may use it for one or more specific purposes; the bacteria in return receive a niche and nutrients. However, many fish are self-luminous, not dependent on bacteria.

Direct (nonspecific) luminous bacterial associations include parasitizations and commensals. Intestinal bacteria in marine animals, notably fish, are often luminous, and heavy pigmentation of the gastrointestinal tract is sometimes present, presumably to prevent the light from revealing to predators the location of the fish. Indeed, the light emission of fecal material, which can be quite bright, is thought to benefit the bacteria more directly, for example by attracting feeders and thereby promoting bacterial dispersion and propagation.

Terrestrial luminous bacteria are rare. The best-known are those harbored by nematodes parasitic on insects such as caterpillars. The nematode carries the bacteria as symbionts and injects them into the host along with its own fertilized eggs. The bacteria

TABLE 3. Luciferases and related proteins from four groups		
Group	Molecular weight, kDa	GenBank™
Bacteria		
Vibrio fischeri luciferase	~80 (α, 41; β, 39)	VIBLUXAB (*Vibrio fischeri*)
Vibrio fischeri YFP	~28	VIBLUXY (yellow fluorescent protein)
Photobacterium phosphoreum LUMP	~28	PHRLUMP (LUMP proteins)
Dinoflagellates		
Gonyaulax luciferase	~135	GONLUCA (*Gonyaulax polyhedra*)
Gonyaulax LBP	~75	GONLUCIFER (luciferin-binding protein)
Coelenterates		
Renilla luciferase	~25	RELLUC (*Renilla reniformis*)
Aequorea luciferase	~25	AEVAEQA (*Aequorea victoria*)
Aequorea GFP	~21	AEVGFPA (green fluorescent protein)
Firefly		
Photinus pyralis luciferase	~60	PPYLUC (*Photinus pyralis*)

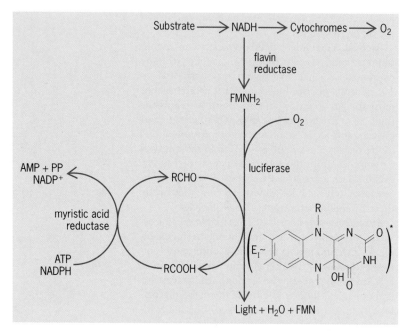

Fig. 1. **Pathways and intermediates in the bacterial luciferase reaction. Luciferase reacts with reduced flavin from the electron transport pathway using molecular oxygen to form a flavin-peroxy intermediate. In the subsequent mixed function, oxidation with long-chain aldehyde hydroxy-FMN is formed in the excited state, and light is thereby emitted. The acid and FMN products are recycled.**

grow, and the developing nematode larvae feed on them. The dead but now luminous caterpillar attracts predators, which serves to disperse the nematode offspring, along with the bacteria.

Biochemistry. The bacterial system is biochemically unique and is diagnostic for bacterial involvement in the luminescence of a higher organism, such as endosymbionts. The pathway itself (**Fig. 1**) constitutes a shunt of cellular electron transport at the level of flavin, and reduced flavin mononucleotide is the substrate (luciferin) that reacts with oxygen in the presence of bacterial luciferase to produce an intermediate peroxy flavin. This intermediate then reacts with a long-chain aldehyde (tetradecanal) to form the acid and the luciferase-bound hydroxy flavin in its excited state. The light-emitting steps have been modeled in terms of an electron exchange mechanism, and the quantum yield is estimated to be 20–30%. Although there are two substrates in this case, the flavin is the one called luciferin, since it forms, or bears, the emitter. There are enzyme systems that serve to maintain the supply of tetradecanal, and the oxidized flavin is likewise recycled (Fig. 1).

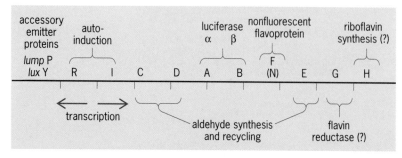

Fig. 2. **Organization of the *lux* genes in *Vibrio fischeri*.**

Antenna proteins. The biochemistry of the reaction is the same in all luminous bacteria, which typically emit light peaking at about 490 nanometers. However, in some bacterial strains the color of the light emitted by the living cell is blue- or red-shifted, even though the isolated luciferases still peak at about 490 nm. In both cases a second (antenna) protein with its own chromophore is responsible—lumazine and flavin, respectively (Table 3). A functional importance for such spectral shifts has not yet been elucidated, although strains with a blue-shifted emission occur at depths of approximately 600 m (1970 ft) in the ocean.

Luciferases. The proteins themselves are homologous heterodimeric (α-β) proteins (80 kilodaltons) in all bacterial species. They possess a single active center per dimer, mostly associated with the α subunit. Structurally, they appear to be relatively simple: no metals, disulfide bonds, prosthetic groups, or non-amino acid residues are involved. The three-dimensional x-ray crystal structure was reported in 1995, but without the flavin substrate, so the details of the active center are not yet known. However, a deep pocket on the α subunit extending to the β subunit may be the catalytic site. The two subunits fold in a very similar manner, assuming a single-domain eight-stranded motif with alternating α helices and β sheets.

The mechanism of the bacterial luciferase reaction has been studied in great detail. An interesting feature is its inherent slowness: at 20°C (68°F) about 20 s is required for a single catalytic cycle. The luciferase peroxy flavin itself has a long lifetime; at low temperatures [0° to −20°C (32° to −2°F)] it has been isolated, purified, and characterized. It can be further stabilized by aldehyde analogs such as long-chain alcohols and amines, which bind at the aldehyde site.

Genes. Lux genes cloned from several different bacterial species exhibit sequence similarities indicative of evolutionary relatedness and conservation. In *Vibrio fischeri*, the species most extensively studied, the *lux* operon has five structural and two regulatory genes (**Fig. 2**) with established functions. These include *lux* A and B that code for the α and β subunits of luciferase, and *lux* C, D, and E that code for the reductase, transferase, and synthetase components of the fatty acid reductase complex. Upstream, in the same operon, is the regulatory gene *lux* I, and immediately adjacent but transcribed in the opposite direction is *lux* R, whose product is responsible for the transcriptional activation of *lux* A through E. Other genes are also subject to this regulation, including those coding for the antenna proteins responsible for color shifting.

Regulation. Luminous bacteria are unable to regulate emission on a fast time scale (milliseconds, seconds), as in organisms that emit flashes. However, they typically control the development and expression of luminescence at both physiological and genetic levels. Physiologically, luciferase and aldehyde synthesis genes of the *lux* operon are regulated by a substance produced by the cells called autoinducer (a homoserine lactone) such that these genes are transcribed only after the substance has accumulated at a high cell density. Autoinducer is a product of the *lux* I gene and stimulates *lux* R. The mechanism has been dubbed quorum sensing, and similar mechanisms occur in other types of bacteria with different genes. The ecological implications are evident: in planktonic bacteria, a habitat where luminescence has no value, autoinducer cannot accumulate, and no luciferase synthesis occurs. However, in the confines of a light organ, high autoinducer levels are reached, and the luciferase genes are transcribed.

Transcription of the lux operon is also regulated by glucose, iron, and oxygen, each of which has ecological implications. But there is also control at the genetic level: in some species of bacteria, dark (very dim) variants arise spontaneously, and the synthesis of the luminescent system does not occur. However, the *lux* genes are not lost and revertants occur, so that under appropriate conditions, where luminescence is advantageous, luminous forms will be available to populate the appropriate habitat.

Dinoflagellates. Dinoflagellates occur ubiquitously in the oceans as planktonic forms in surface waters, and contribute substantially to the luminescent flashing commonly seen at night (especially in summer) when the water is disturbed. In phosphorescent bays (for example, in Puerto Rico and Jamaica), high densities of a single species (*Pyrodinium bahamense*) occur; this is also true in red tides, which are blooms of dinoflagellates. Many species are photosynthetic.

All luminous dinoflagellates are marine, but only about 30% of the marine species are luminous. As a group, dinoflagellates are important as symbionts, notably for contributing photosynthesis and carbon fixation in animals; but unlike bacteria, no luminous dinoflagellates are known from symbiotic niches.

Dinoflagellates are stimulated to emit light when predators (such as crustaceans) are feeding, which can startle and divert the predator, resulting in a reduced predation. The response time to stimulation (milliseconds) is certainly fast enough to have this effect. Predation on dinoflagellates may also be impeded more indirectly, since predators of the crustaceans might be alerted, thereby increasing predation on the crustaceans themselves.

Cell biology. Luminescence in dinoflagellates is emitted from many small (about 0.4 micrometer) cortical locations. The structures have been identified in *Gonyaulax polyhedra* as novel organelles, termed scintillons (flashing units). They occur as outpocketings of the cytoplasm into the cell vacuole, like a balloon, with the neck remaining connected. However, scintillons contain only dinoflagellate luciferase and luciferin (with its binding protein), other cytoplasmic components somehow being excluded. Ultrastructurally, they can be identified by immunolabeling with antibodies raised against the luminescence, proteins, and visualized by their bioluminescent flashing following stimulation, as well as by the fluorescence of luciferin.

Biochemistry. Dinoflagellate luciferin is a novel tetrapyrrole related to chlorophyll (**Fig. 3**). The luciferase is an unusual 135-kDa protein with three

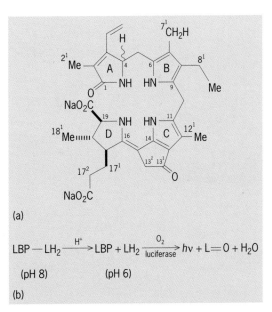

(a)

$$LBP-LH_2 \xrightarrow[\text{(pH 8)}]{H^+} LBP + LH_2 \xrightarrow[\text{luciferase}]{O_2} h\nu + L{=}O + H_2O$$

(b)

Fig. 3. Dinoflagellate luciferin (LH$_2$). (*a*) Structure of this tetrapyrrole. Oxygen addition occurs at position 13^2. (*b*) Schematic of reaction pathway. Luciferin, bound to the luciferin-binding protein (LBP) at pH 8, is released at pH 6 and is oxidized by luciferase to form an exicited state emitter (L=O*).

conserved active sites within the single molecule. The reaction involves the luciferase-catalyzed oxidation of luciferin triggered by a change of the pH from 8 to 6, which releases the luciferin from its binding protein and activates the luciferase. The flashing of dinoflagellates in vivo is postulated to result from a rapid and transient pH change in the scintillons, triggered by an action potential in the vacuolar membrane which, while sweeping over the scintillon, opens ion channels that allow protons from the acidic vacuole to enter.

Circadian clock control. Cell density and the composition of the medium have no effect on the development and expression of luminescence in dinoflagellates. However, in *G. polyhedra* and some other dinoflagellates, luminescence is regulated by day-night light-dark cycles and an internal circadian biological clock mechanism. The flashing response to mechanical stimulation is far greater during the night than during the day phase, and a dim glow exhibits a rhythm (**Fig. 4**). The regulation is due to an

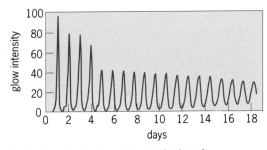

Fig. 4. Circadian rhythm of the steady glow of bioluminescence in *Gonyaulax*. The culture, grown in a 24-h light-dark cycle, was transferred to constant light on the first day. Measurements of the spontaneous light emission were made about once every hour for the subsequent 18 days. The period of the rhythm is about 25 h.

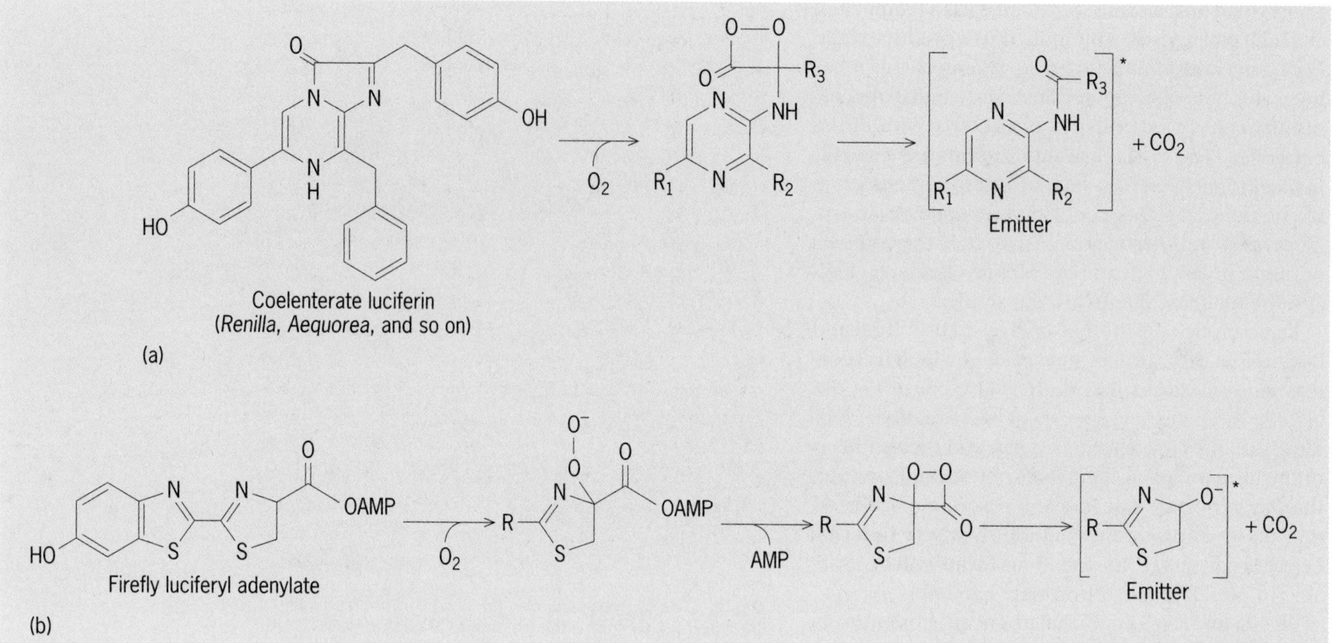

Fig. 5. Luciferin structures. (*a*) Coelenterate luciferin (coelenterazine) and its reaction with oxygen to give a postulated cyclic peroxide intermediate and then an excited emitter in the light-emitting reaction. (*b*) Firefly luciferin and the analogous intermediates in the firefly luciferase reaction.

endogenous mechanism; cultures maintained under constant conditions continue to exhibit rhythmicity for weeks, with a period that is not exactly 24 h but about one day (*circa diem*).

The nature of the circadian clock remains an enigma. In humans and other higher animals, where it regulates the sleep-wake cycle and many other physiological processes, the mechanism involves the nervous system. But it also occurs in plants and unicellular organisms, which lack neural control. In the case of *G. polyhedra*, daily changes occur in the cellular concentrations of both luciferase and luciferin and its binding protein: the proteins are synthesized and destroyed each day. Hence, the biological clock exerts control at a very basic level, by controlling gene expression.

Coelentrates and ctenophores. Luminescence is common and widely distributed in these groups. In the ctenophores (comb jellies), luminous forms make up over half of all genera, and in the coelenterates (cnidarians) it is about 6%. Luminous hydroids, siphonophores, sea pens, and jellyfish are mostly sessile or sedentary and, upon stimulation, emit flashes. Sea anemones and corals are not known to be bioluminescent.

Hydroids occur as plantlike growths, typically adhering to rocks below low tide level in the ocean. Upon touching them, there is a sparkling emission conducted along the colony; repetitive waves from the origin may occur. In luminous jellyfish (such as *Pelagia noctiluca* and *Aequorea victoria*) the bright flashing comes from photocytes along the edge of the umbrella at the base of the tentacles. *Aequorea* is the source of a photoprotein that emits light upon the addition of calcium and is widely used in research for calcium detection and measurement. The

sea pansy, *Renilla*, which occurs near shore on sandy bottoms, has also figured prominently in studies of bioluminescence.

Cell biology. Photocytes occur as specialized cells located singly or in clusters in the endoderm. They are commonly controlled by epithelial conduction in hydropolyps and siphonophores and by a colonial nerve net in anthozoans. The putative neurotransmitter involved in luminescent control in *Renilla* is adrenaline or a related catecholamine.

Biochemistry. Coelenterate luciferase has a similarity to calmodulin in its amino acid sequence. The luciferin, coelenterazine (**Fig. 5a**), possesses an imidazopyrazine skeleton. It has widespread phylogenetic distribution in nonluminous species, but whether the reason is nutritional or genetic (hence, possible evolutionary relatedness) has not yet been elucidated. In some cases (such as *Renilla*), the sulfated form of luciferin may occur as a precursor or storage form, and is convertible to active luciferin by sulfate removal with the cofactor 3'5'-diphosphadenosine. The active form may also be sequestered by a calcium-sensitive binding protein, analogous to the dinoflagellate binding protein. In this case, calcium triggers the release of luciferin and flashing.

Another type of control of the same luciferin in other cnidarians ultilizes a luciferase-peroxy luciferin intermediate poised for the completion of the reaction. The photoprotein aequorin, isolated from the jellyfish *Aequorea* (in the presence of EDTA to chelate calcium), emits light simply upon the addition of calcium, which is presumably the trigger in vivo. The luciferin and luciferase react with oxygen to form a peroxide in a calcium-free compartment (the photocyte), where it is stored. An action potential allows calcium to enter and bind to the protein, changing its conformational state and allowing the reaction to continue, but without the need for free oxygen at this stage. An enzyme-bound cyclic peroxide, a dioxetenone (Fig. 5a), is a postulated intermediate; it breaks down with the formation of an excited emitter, along with a molecule of CO_2. Early literature reported that ctenophores could emit bioluminescence without oxygen. The explanation is now evident: the animal contains the luciferase-bound peroxy-luciferin in a stored and stable state, and only calcium is needed to emit light.

Antenna proteins and GFPs. In several coelenterates the light emission in vivo occurs at a longer wavelength than in vitro, similar to that described above for bacteria. In this case the different protein with a second chromophore is called green fluorescent protein (GFP), widely used as a reporter in molecular biology. Radiationless energy transfer is believed to be involved, with emission from a chromophore whose structure is unusual; it is part of the primary structure of the protein, three residues of which are chemically modified posttranslationally to produce a fluorescence with a peak emission at about 408 nm. Different groups appear to have different GFP proteins, but the chromophores are the same.

Fireflies. Of the approximately 70,000 insect genera, only about 100 are classed as luminous. But their luminescence is impressive, especially in the fireflies and their relatives. Fireflies possess ventral light organs on posterior segments; the South American railroad worm, *Phrixothrix*, has paired green lights on the abdominal segments and red head lights; while the click and fire beetles, Pyrophorini, have both running lights (dorsal) and landing lights (ventral). The dipteran cave glow worm, in a different group and probably different biochemically, exudes beaded strings of slime from its ceiling perch, serving to entrap minute flying prey, which are attracted by the light emitted by the animal.

Function. The major function of light emission in fireflies is for communication during courtship, typically involving the emission of a flash by one sex as a signal, to which the other sex responds, usually in a species-specific pattern. The time delay between the two may be a signaling feature; for example, it is precisely 2 s in some North America species. But the flashing pattern (such as trains distinctive in duration and intensity) is also important in some cases, as is the kinetic character of the individual flash (duration; onset and decay kinetics).

Fireflies in Southeast Asia are noteworthy for their synchronous flashing. Congregations of many thousands form in trees, where the males produce an all-night-long display, with flashes every 1–4 s, dependent on species. This may serve to attract females to the tree.

Biochemistry. The firefly system was the first in which the biochemistry was characterized. It had been known before 1900 that cold water extracts could continue to emit light for several minutes or hours, and that after the complete decay of the light, emission could be restored by adding a second ex-

tract, prepared by using boiling water to extract the cells, then cooling the liquid. The enzyme luciferase was assumed to be in the cold water extract (with all the luciferin substrate being used up during the emission), whereas the enzyme was denatured by the hot water extraction, leaving some substrate intact. This was referred to as the luciferin-luciferase reaction; it was already known in the first part of the twentieth century that luciferins and luciferases from the different major groups would not cross-react, indicative of their independent evolutionary origins.

In 1947 it was discovered that bioluminescence was restored in an exhausted cold water extract simply by the addition of adenosine triphosphate (ATP). But ATP could not be the emitter, since it does not have the appropriate fluorescence, and could not provide the energy for light emission, since the energy available from ATP hydrolysis is only about 7 kcal per mole, whereas the energy of a visible photon is 50 kcal per mole. It was concluded that luciferin had not actually been used up in the cold water extract, and it was soon shown that ATP functions to form a luciferyl adenylate intermediate. This then reacts with oxygen to form a cyclic luciferyl peroxy species, which breaks down to yield CO_2 and an excited state of the carbonyl product (Fig. 5b).

The crystal structure of firefly luciferase has been determined recently, but without substrate, so the binding site is not established. The gene has been cloned and expressed in other organisms, including *Escherichia coli* and tobacco. In both cases, luciferin must be added exongenously; tobacco "lights up" when the roots are dipped in luciferin. Luciferase catalyzes both the reaction of luciferin with ATP and the subsequent steps leading to the excited product. There are some beetles in which the light from different organs is a different color, but no second emitter protein appears to be utilized. Instead, the same ATP-dependent luciferase reaction with the same luciferin occurs in the different organs, but the luciferases are slightly different, coded by different (but homologous) genes. They are presumed to differ with regard to the structure of the site that binds the excited state, which could thereby alter the emission wavelength.

Cell biology. The firefly light organ comprises a series of photocytes arranged in a rosette, positioned radially around a central tracheole, which supplies oxygen to the organ. Organelles containing luciferase have been identified with peroxisomes on the basis of immunochemical labeling.

Regulation of flashing. Although flashing is initiated by a nerve impulse that travels to the light organ, photocytes are not stimulated directly. The nerves in the light organ terminate on the tracheolar end cells, accounting for the considerable time delay between the arrival of the nerve impulse at the organ and the onset of the flash. The flash might be controlled by the availability of oxygen.

Mollusks. Snails (gastropods), clams (bivalves), and squid (cephalopods) have bioluminescent members. Squid luminous systems are numerous and diverse in both form and function, rivaling the fishes in these respects. As is also true for fishes, some squid utilize symbiotic luminous bacteria, but most are self-luminous, indicating that bioluminescence had more than one evolutionary origin even within the class.

Compound photophores have associated optical elements such as pigment screens, chromatophores, reflectors, lenses, and light guides. Many squid possess such photophores, which may be used in spawning and other interspecific displays (communication). They may emit different colors of light, and are variously located near the eyeball, on tentacles, or on the body integument, or associated with the ink sac or other viscera. In some species, luminescence intensity has been shown to be regulated in response to changes in ambient light, indicative of a camouflage function.

Along the coasts of Europe a clam, *Pholas dactylus*, inhabits compartments that it makes by boring holes into the soft rock. When irritated, these animals produce a bright cellular luminous secretion, squirted out through the siphon as a blue cloud. This luminescent animal has been known since Roman times, and the system was used in the discovery and description of the luciferin-luciferase reaction in the 1880s. The reaction involves a protein-bound chromophore, and the luciferase is a copper-containing large (greater than 300 kDa) glycoprotein. Well ensconced in its rocky enclosure, the animal presumably used the luminescence to somehow deter or thwart would-be predators.

The New Zealand pulmonate limpet, *Latia neritoides*, is the only known luminous organism that can be classed as a truly fresh-water species. It secretes a bright luminous slime (green emission, $\lambda_{max} = 535$ nm), whose function may be similar to that of the *Pholas* emission. Its luciferin is an enol formate of an aldehyde, and a "purple protein" is also required, but only in catalytic quantities, suggesting that it may be somehow involved as a recycling emitter.

Annelids. *Chaetopterus* is a marine polychaete that constructs and lives in U-shaped tubes in sandy bottoms and exudes luminescence upon stimulation to deter or thwart predators. Other annelids include the Syllidae, such as the Bermuda fireworm, and the polynoid worms, which shed their luminous scales as decoys. Extracts of the latter have been shown to emit light upon the addition of superoxide ion.

Terrestrial earthworms, some of which are quite large, over 24 in. (60 cm) in length, exude coelomic fluid from the mouth, anus, and body pores upon stimulation. This exudate contains cells that lyse to produce a luminous mucus, emitting in the blue-green region. In *Diplocardia longa* the cells responsible for emission have been isolated; luminescence in extracts involves a copper-containing luciferase (about 300 kDa), and *N*-isovaleryl-3 amino-1 propanal. The in vitro reaction requires hydrogen peroxide, not free oxygen. But the exudate from animals deprived of oxygen does not emit, but will do so after the admission of molecular oxygen to the free exudate.

Crustaceans. Cyprindinid ostracods such as *Vargla hilgendorfii* are small organisms that possess two glands with nozzles from which luciferin and luciferase are squirted into the seawater, where they react and produce a spot of light useful either as a decoy or for communication. Cypridinid luciferin is a substituted imidazopyrazine nucleus, similar to coelenterazine, which reacts with oxygen to form an intermediate cyclic peroxide, breaking down to yield carbon dioxide and an excited carbonyl. However, the cypridinid luciferase gene has no homology with the gene for the corresponding coelenterate proteins, and calcium is not involved in the cypridinid reaction. Thus, the two different luciferases reacting with similar luciferins have apparently had independent evolutionary origins, indicative of convergent evolution at the molecular level.

Blue ventrally directed luminescence is emitted by compound photophores in euphausiid shrimp. The system is unusual because both its luciferase and luciferin cross-react with the dinoflagellate system. This cross-taxon similarity indicates a possible exception to the rule that luminescence in distantly related groups had independent evolutionary origins. The shrimp might obtain luciferin nutritionally, but the explanation for the functionally similar proteins is not known, and the shrimp luciferase gene has not been cloned. One possibility is lateral gene transfer; convergent evolution is another.

Fishes. Both teleost (bony) and elasmobranch (cartilaginous) fishes have luminous species. Many coastal and deep-sea fishes culture luminous bacteria in special organs, but most are self-luminous. These include *Porichthys*, the midshipman fish, having linear arrays of photophores distributed along the lateral lines, as with buttons on a military uniform. Its luciferin and luciferase cross-react with the cypridinid ostracod crustacean system described above, and the fish apparently obtain luciferin nutritionally.

Open-sea and midwater species include sharks (elasmobranchs), which may have several thousand photophores; the gonostomatids, such as *Cyclothone*, with simple photophores; and the hatchet fishes, having compound photophores with elaborate optical accessories to direct luminescence downward, indicative of a camouflage function of the light.

Different kinds of photophores located on different parts of the fish evidently have different functions. One arrangement, known in both midwater squid and myctophids, makes use of a special photophore positioned so as to shine on the eye or a special photoreceptor. Its intensity parallels that of the other photophores, so it provides information to the animal concerning the organism's brightness, thus allowing the animal to match the intensity of its counterillumination to that of the downwelling ambient light. A different functional use is in *Neoscopelus*, where photophores on the tongue attract prey to just the right location.

Luminescence in many fish is sexually dimorphic, and the use of the light differs in male and female. Some self-luminous fish eject luminous material; in the searsid fishes this material is cellular in nature, but it is not bacterial, and its biochemical nature is not known. Such fish may also possess photophores.

Applications. The measurement of light emission is typically more sensitive than many other analytical techniques. A typical photon-counting instrument can readily detect an emission of about 10^4 photons per second, which corresponds to the transformation of 10^5 molecules per second (or 6×10^6 per minute) if the quantum yield is 10%. A substance at a concentration of 10^{-9} M could readily be detected in a single cell 10 μm in diameter by this technique.

Bioluminescence and chemiluminescence have thus come into widespread use for quantitative determinations of specific substances in biology and medicine. Luminescent tags have been developed that are as sensitive as radioactivity, and now replace radioactivity in many assays.

Analytical measurements. The biochemistry of different luciferase systems is different, so many different substances can be detected. One of the first, and still widely used, assays involves the use of firefly luciferase for the detection of ATP. Since many different enzymes use or produce ATP, their activities may be followed using this assay. With bacterial luciferase, any reaction that produces or utilizes NAD(H), NADP(H), or long-chain aldehyde either directly or indirectly, can be coupled to this lightemitting reaction. The purified photoprotein aequorin has been widely used for the detection of intracellular calcium and its changes under various experimental conditions; the protein is relatively small (about 20 kDa), is nontoxic, and may be readily injected into cells in quantities adequate to detect calcium over the range of 3×10^{-7} to 1×10^{-4} M.

The amount of oxygen required for bioluminescence in luminescent bacteria is small and therefore the reaction readily occurs. Luminous bacteria can be used as a very sensitive test for oxygen, sometimes in situations where no other method is applicable. An oxygen electrode incorporating luminous bacteria has been developed.

Reporter genes. Luciferase and antenna proteins have also been exploited as reporter genes for many different purposes. Analytically, such systems are virtually unique in that they are noninvasive and nondestructive: the relevant activity can be measured as light emission in the intact cell and in the same cell over the course of time. Examples of the use of luciferase genes are the expression of firefly and bacterial luciferases under the control of circadian promoters; and the use of coelenterate luciferase expressed transgenically to monitor calcium changes in living cells over time.

Green fluorescent protein is widely used as a reporter gene for monitoring the expression of some other gene under study, and for how the expression may differ, for example at different stages of development or as the consequence of some experimental procedure. As with the luciferases, this is done by placing the GFP gene under the control of the promoter of the gene being investigated.

Studies of bioluminescence have thus contributed to knowledge in ways not foreseen at the time of the investigations, illustrating how basic knowledge can be a powerful tool for advancing understanding in unrelated areas.　　　　J. Woodland Hastings

Bibliography. T. Baldwin et al., Structure of bacterial luciferase, *Curr. Biol.*, 5:798-809, 1995; M. Chalfie and S. Kain (eds.), *Green Fluorescent Protein: Properties, Applications and Protocols*, Wiley-Liss, New York, 1998; E. Conti, N. P. Franks, and P. Brick, Crystal structure of firefly luciferase throws light on a superfamily of adenylate-forming enzymes, *Structure*, 4:287-298, 1996; J. W. Hastings, Chemistries and colors of bioluminescent reactions: A review, *Gene*, 173:5-11, 1996; J. W. Hastings and J. G. Morin, Bioluminescence, in C. L. Prosser (ed.), *Neural and Integrative and Animal Physiology*, Wiley Interscience, New York, 1991; J. W. Hastings and D. Tu (eds.), Molecular mechanisms in bioluminescence, *Photochem. Photobiol.*, 62:599-673, 1995; J. W. Hastings, L. J. Kricka, and P. E. Stanley (eds.), *Bioluminescence and Chemiluminescence: Molecular Reporting with Photons*, Wiley, Chichester, 1997; P. J. Herring (ed.), *Bioluminescence in Action*, Academic, London, 1978; M. K. Nishiguchi, E. G. Ruby, and M. J. McFall-Ngai, Competitive dominance among strains of luminous bacteria provides an unusual form of evidence for parallel evolution in sepiolid squid-*Vibria* symbioses, *Appl. Environ. Microbiol.*, 64:3209-3213, 1998; T. Wilson and J. W. Hastings, Bioluminescence, *Annu. Rev. Cell Dev. Biol.*, 14:197-230, 1998.

Biomagnetism

The production of a magnetic field by a living object. The living object presently most studied is the human body, for two purposes: to find new techniques for medical diagnosis, and to gain information about normal physiology. Smaller organisms studied include birds, fishes, and objects as small as bacteria; many scientists believe that biomagnetics is involved in the ability of these creatures to navigate. This article deals only with the human body. *See* MIGRATORY BEHAVIOR.

Magnetic field production. The body produces magnetic fields in two main ways: by electric currents and by ferromagnetic particles. The electric currents are the ion currents generated by the muscles, nerves, and other organs. For example, the same ion current generated by heart muscle, which provides the basis for the electrocardiogram, also produces a magnetic field over the chest; and the same ion current generated by the brain, which provides the basis for the electroencephalogram, also produces a magnetic field over the head. Ferromagnetic particles are insoluble contaminants of the body; the most important of these are the ferromagnetic dust particles in the lungs, which are primarily Fe_3O_4 (magnetite). Magnetic fields can give information about the internal organs not otherwise available.

These magnetic fields are very weak, usually in the range of 10^{-14} to 10^{-9} tesla; for comparison, the Earth's field is about 10^{-4} T (1 T = 10^4 gauss, the older unit of field). The fields at the upper end of

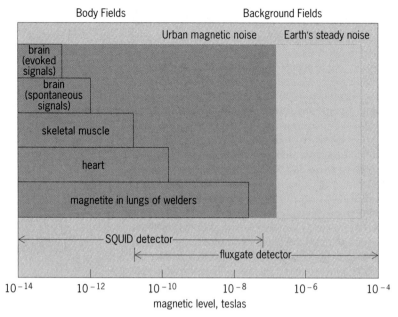

Fig. 1. Levels of the body's magnetic fields and background magnetic fields, as well as the range encompassed by the detectors.

this range, say stronger than 10^{-4} T, can be measured with a simple but sensitive magnetometer called the fluxgate; the weaker fields are measured with the extremely sensitive cryogenic magnetometer called the SQUID (superconducting quantum interference device). The levels of the body's fields are shown in **Fig. 1**. These fields, whether they are fluctuating or steady, are seen to be orders of magnitude weaker than the fluctuating or steady background fields. They can, however, be measured by using either a magnetically shielded room **(Fig. 2)** or two detectors connected in opposition so that much of

Fig. 2. Magnetic field of the brain being measured in a magnetically shielded room. The SQUID detector is in the tail of a Dewar cylinder containing liquid helium, which maintains the cryogenic temperature of the SQUID.

the background is canceled, or a combination of both methods.

The organs producing magnetic fields which are of most interest are the brain, the lungs, and the liver. These are discussed below.

Brain measurement. Theory suggests that a measurement of the brain's magnetic field, the magnetoencephalogram (MEG), could reveal new information on the brain that is not available from the electroencephalogram (EEG). In the first place, the MEG sees only the electrical sources in the head which are oriented tangentially to the skull, while the EEG sees both tangential sources and sources oriented radially. The MEG therefore sees a subgroup of the electrical sources in the brain, that is, those tangential sources not seen on the EEG because they are "swamped" by the radial sources, which dominate the EEG. Second, the MEG pattern on the head due to a tangential source is oriented perpendicularly to the EEG pattern on the head, due to the same source **(Fig. 3)**. Because of this difference, the MEG is complementary to the EEG in localizing a source in the brain, such as an epileptic focus. The EEG localizes better in one direction on the scalp (x direction in Fig. 3), while the MEG localizes better in the other direction (y directional). Third, the MEG pattern on the head is somewhat smaller than the EEG pattern (Fig. 3). This is because the skull, through which the current must pass in order to be recorded by the EEG electrodes, diffuses the current, while the MEG sees only the deep currents at the source and therefore is unaffected by the skull; without the skull, the MEG and EEG patterns would be of about equal size (although rotated by $90°$). This smaller pattern on the MEG allows it to localize better in its best (y) direction, in comparison to the EEG in its best (x) direction.

These theoretical differences have received experimental confirmation. Further, MEGs are recorded on many of the same types of electrical events seen on the EEG, including evoked responses (where the stimuli, such as periodic clicks to the ear, are controlled) and spontaneous events such as epileptic discharges. In the evoked responses and spontaneous events, new information appears to be seen in the MEG, of use in clinical diagnosis and in research of the normal brain. *See* ELECTROENCEPHALOGRAPHY.

Lung measurement. To measure ferromagnetic dust in the lungs, the dust in a subject's lungs is first magnetized by an externally applied magnetic field. Then, after the external field is removed, the remanent field of magnetized dust is measured around the torso with a fluxgate or a SQUID; this yields the amount of dust in the lungs. These measurements are made for three main reasons.

First, when Fe_3O_4 dust is inhaled through occupational exposure, a magnetic measurement of the amount of dust in the lungs provides a measure of the dust exposure in that worker. For example, a magnetic measurement of the amount of Fe_3O_4 itself is relatively harmless, but other associated dusts could be quite harmful; therefore knowledge of the presence of Fe_3O_4 is useful.

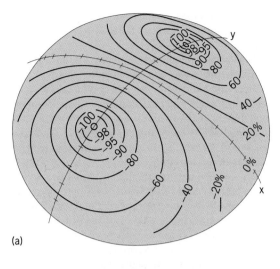

(a)

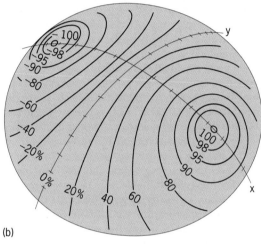

(b)

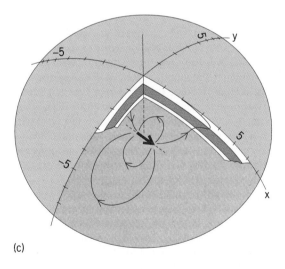

(c)

Fig. 3. Theoretical calculations showing two of the three differences between (*a*) the MEG pattern and (*b*) the EEG pattern, due to a tangential source. The theoretical calculation was performed by using a four-layer spherical model of the head. (*c*) A section of the sphere produced by computer modeling, where the electrical source (heavy arrow) produces currents (light arrows) in the conducting medium of the head. The tick marks are in centimeters on the scalp surface. The MEG and EEG patterns are shown in percent of their maximum, on the same spherical cap. The MEG pattern is seen to be rotated by 90° to that of the EEG, and is somewhat smaller.

The second reason involves the clearance of dust from the lungs. Inhaled dust is deposited either in the airways (bronchi) or in the terminal chambers (alveoli). The dust deposited in the airways is known to be cleared out by the mucociliary carpet in a matter of hours; this rate, called short-term clearance, has been accurately measured in the human lung by using short-lived radioactive dust. The dust deposited in the alveoli is cleared out much more slowly, in a matter of weeks or months. This rate, called long-term clearance, had not previously been accurately measured, because of the hazard of using long-lived radioactive dust. However, this rate can now be measured by using only Fe_3O_4, which is non-hazardous. In one study the clearance rate in smokers was compared with that in nonsmokers, and was found to be considerably slower in the smokers. This impaired clearance of carcinogenic dust may contribute to the high incidence of lung cancer in smokers.

The third reason involves the phenomenon called relaxation. This takes place when the external field, which first magnetizes the lung, is removed. The remanent field at the chest due to the particles is not steady, but decreases during the first hour to about 10% of its initial value. This is because the particles, originally aligned by the applied field, receive physiological impulses which randomly rotate them; as they become scrambled in direction, the net remanent field they create decreases in strength. The source of the impulses is now known to be motion within the macrophage cells. Measurement of the rate of relaxation is useful as a new index of internal cell function; that is, the rate of decrease of the remanent field gives information about the internal activity of the cell.

Liver measurement. Unlike the lung or the brain, the magnetic field of the liver is measured via its magnetic susceptibility. This is a third way the body produces a magnetic field. When an external magnetic field is applied to the body, each element of the body produces its own weak magnetic field in response to the applied field. The susceptibility measurement consists in determining the amount and polarity of this weak field, in the presence of the applied field; the weak field can be in the same or in the opposite direction as the applied field, and the element producing the response is called paramagnetic or diamagnetic, respectively. The liver is normally a diamagnetic organ; however, it is the main localized storage site of iron in the body, and its susceptibility depends on the amount of iron it contains within its organic molecules. In the normal liver, a few parts in 10^4 consist of iron, but this concentration may rise a hundredfold in iron-overload disease, or drop by a similar large factor in iron-deficiency disease; the iron concentration changes the liver susceptibility so that it becomes paramagnetic for iron concentrations greater than 6 parts in 10^3, which is within the overload range. While departures from normal are associated with widespread medical problems, no reliable noninvasive method has been found to assess this iron store. Thus an estimation of the iron concentration from a magnetic susceptibility measurement is of clinical value.

In SQUID measurements in a hospital, where this method is being evaluated, it was found that the iron concentration estimated from this susceptibility was in agreement with the iron concentration determined by a direct chemical analysis of liver tissue obtained in biopsy. The two estimates were in substantial agreement over a range from normal to some 30 times normal; hence, the measurement of the magnetic field of the liver, via its susceptibility, appears to be a promising technique. *See* BIOELECTROMAGNETICS.   David Cohen

Bibliography. D. Cohen, Magnetic fields of the human body, *Phys. Today*, pp. 34–43, August 1975; D. Cohen and B. N. Cuffin, Demonstration of useful differences between MEG and EEG, *Electroencephalography and Clinical Neurophysiology*, 56:38–51, 1983; J. L. Kirschvink, Birds, bees, and magnetism: A new look at the old problem of magnetoreception, *Trends Neurosci.*, 5:160–167, 1982; S. J. Williamson and L. Kaufman, Biomagnetism, *J. Magnetism Magnetic Mater.*, 22:129–201, 1981; S. Willamson et al. (eds.), *Biomagnetism: An Interdisciplinary Approach*, 1983.

Biomass

The organic materials produced by plants, such as leaves, roots, seeds, and stalks. In some cases, microbial and animal metabolic wastes are also considered biomass. The term "biomass" is intended to refer to materials that do not directly go into foods or consumer products but may have alternative industrial uses. Common sources of biomass are (1) agricultural wastes, such as corn stalks, straw, seed hulls, sugarcane leavings, bagasse, nutshells, and manure from cattle, poultry, and hogs; (2) wood materials, such as wood or bark, sawdust, timber slash, and mill scrap; (3) municipal waste, such as waste paper and yard clippings; and (4) energy crops, such as poplars, willows, switchgrass, alfalfa, prairie bluestem, corn (starch), and soybean (oil). *See* BIOLOGICAL PRODUCTIVITY.

Composition. Biomass is a complex mixture of organic materials, such as carbohydrates, fats, and proteins, along with small amounts of minerals, such as sodium, phosphorus, calcium, and iron. The main components of plant biomass are carbohydrates (approximately 75%, dry weight) and lignin (approximately 25%), which can vary with plant type. The carbohydrates are mainly cellulose or hemicellulose fibers, which impart strength to the plant structure, and lignin, which holds the fibers together. Some plants also store starch (another carbohydrate polymer) and fats as sources of energy, mainly in seeds and roots (such as corn, soybeans, and potatoes). Starch and cellulose are homopolymers (long chains of a single component) of glucose. Glucose is the main sugar used by living systems as a source of biochemical energy. Hemicellulose is a structural polymer made of sugars, such as xylose, glucose, arabinose, and mannose. Lignin is a much more complex mixture of organic materials, composed of highly cross-linked phenylpropane units with other organic components attached. Heterogeneous biomass materials, such as hemicellulose and lignin, are more difficult to decompose to make useful chemicals than homogeneous materials, such as starch and cellulose. Fats are triacylglycerides, three long-chain fatty acids (hydrocarbonlike structures) attached to a glycerol molecule. The major part of the fat molecule is fatty acids, which have a chemical structure very similar to hydrocarbons (petroleum). The general chemical structures are hydrocarbons, C_nH_{2n+2}; carbohydrates, $C_nO_nH_{2n}$; and triacylglycerides, $3(C_{n+1}H_{2n+1}O)+C_3H_5O_3$ [fatty acids plus glycerol].

Hydrocarbons are composed of only carbon and hydrogen. Upon combustion with oxygen, carbon dioxide and water are formed and thermal energy is released. The more oxygen reacted, the more energy released. Since carbohydrates already contain oxygen, their combustion releases less thermal energy than hydrocarbons. With fats, the fatty acids are usually separated from glycerol, then processed to make fuels and chemicals. Fatty acids contain nearly the same amount of energy as hydrocarbons. *See* CELLULOSE; LIGNIN.

Renewability. A major advantage of using biomass as a source of fuels or chemicals is its renewability. Utilizing sunlight energy in photosynthesis, plants metabolize atmospheric carbon dioxide to synthesize biomass. An estimated 140 billion metric tons of biomass are produced annually.

Combustion of biomass forms carbon dioxide, and plants metabolize carbon dioxide to form more biomass via photosynthesis. The overall process is an ecological cycle called the carbon cycle, since elemental carbon is recycled. From an energy viewpoint, the net effect of the carbon cycle is to convert solar energy into thermal energy that can be converted into more useful forms of energy, such as electricity and fuels (**Fig. 1**). *See* BIOGEOCHEMISTRY.

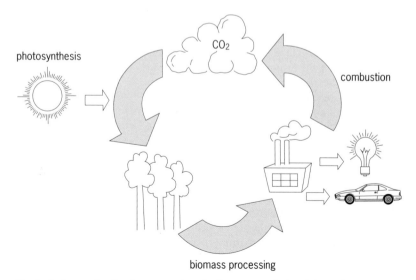

Fig. 1. Carbon cycle, showing conversion of solar energy to fuel and electricity.

Utility. Historically, humans have used biomass for energy (burning wood) and a variety of consumer products (paper, lumber, cloth). Current industrial biomass utilization is focused on the production of fuels or energy and chemical intermediates (**Fig. 2**).

Energy. Coal and petroleum have gradually replaced biomass fuels, due to higher energy content and handling convenience. Coal and petroleum were actually created from biomass deep in the earth over millions of years. However, due to the long time periods needed to form these materials, they are considered nonrenewable. With global petroleum consumption expected to peak during the next 30 years, attention has focused on developing renewable biomass energy alternatives. Increases of atmospheric carbon dioxide attributed to petroleum combustion (global warming) have also contributed to interest in renewable biomass fuels. The amount of energy available from biomass is enormous, an estimated 2.89×10^4 exajoules (1 EJ = 10^{18} J). This is approximately eight times the total annual world consumption of energy from all sources (about 3600 EJ). At present, the world population obtains about 7% of its annual energy needs from biomass. *See* COAL; PETROLEUM.

Production of electricity from biomass combustion is being explored. Approximately 9 gigawatts of electricity are currently produced in the United States, primarily from forest products. For example, California power generation companies are burning scrap wood pellets to generate "green" electricity for interested consumers. Another power company is developing 27,000 acres of fast-growing hybrid poplar trees as a fuel source to generate 25 megawatts of electricity for Minnesota homes and industries.

Major limitations of solid biomass fuels are difficulty of handling and lack of portability for mobile engines. To address these issues, research is being conducted to convert solid biomass into liquid and gaseous fuels. Both biological means (fermentation) and chemical means (pyrolysis, gasification) can be used to produce fluid biomass fuels. For example, methane gas is produced in China for local energy needs by anaerobic microbial digestion of human and animal wastes. Ethanol for automotive fuels is currently produced from starch biomass in a two-step process: starch is enzymatically hydrolyzed into glucose; then yeast is used to convert the glucose into ethanol. About 1.5 billion gallons of ethanol are produced from starch each year in the United States.

Since cellulose is available in much larger quantities than starch, it would be a preferable source of biomass for making ethanol. However, cellulosic biomass is difficult to utilize since it is tightly combined with lignin and hemicellulose. It must be physically pretreated by grinding, steam explosion, chemical pulping, or solvent extraction to make the cellulose more accessible to enzymes. Additionally, the natural enzymes that break down cellulose are less efficient than starch enzymes, so research has focused on genetically engineering cellulose enzymes to improve efficiency and reduce costs. For exam-

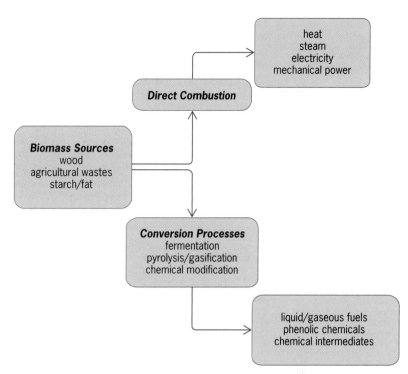

Fig. 2. Methods of converting biomass to energy, fuels, and chemicals.

ple, a facility has been built in Jennings, Louisiana, to produce 20 million gallons of ethanol per year from cellulosic biomass (sugarcane wastes and rice hulls) using novel recombinant genetic microbial technology. Another facility has been built in Middletown, New York, to recycle municipal solid wastes by recycling plastics, glass, and metal and converting cellulosic wastes into 8 million gallons of ethanol annually.

Pyrolysis and gasification. Pyrolysis involves heating biomass to high temperatures in the absence of oxygen. It rearranges the chemical bonds of lignin and hemicellulose to produce chemicals for plastics, adhesives, and resins, or short-chain hydrocarbons for fuels and chemical intermediates. Given the highly variable composition of lignins and hemicelluloses, pyrolysis biomass products are very complex mixtures. Research is focused on developing reaction conditions and catalysts that make reproducible product compositions from biomass materials.

Synthetic fuel gases (mainly methane, ethane, and small hydrocarbons) can be produced by adding hydrogen and carbon monoxide during pyrolysis. This process is called gasification and converts about 65–70% of the biomass energy content into combustible gas fuels. This fuel is used like natural gas to create electricity, is used to power vehicles, or is chemically converted to other synthetic fuels. *See* PYROLYSIS.

Biodiesel fuel. Since fatty acids from plant fats and petroleum hydrocarbons have very similar chemical structures, plant fats can also be converted into a liquid fuel similar to diesel fuel. Fatty acids obtained from soybeans or other oil-rich plants are reacted with methanol to form fatty methyl esters. Since these methyl esters have nearly equivalent energy content and similar chemical structure to petrochemical diesel fuels, they have been called biodiesel fuels. Biodiesel fuels have been demonstrated to work well in diesel engines and have reduced exhaust particulate emissions. Methyl esters have also been used as industrial cleaning solvents, in cosmetics, and for other industrial applications. *See* ALCOHOL FUEL; ETHYL ALCOHOL; GASOLINE.   Bernard Y. Tao

Bibliography. J. P. Henderson, Anaerobic digestion in rural China, *BioCycle*, 39(1):79, 1997; C. M. Kinoshita et al., *Power Generation Potential of Biomass Gasification Systems: Proceedings of the American Power Conference*, Chicago, 1996; J. Lee, Biological conversion of lignocellulosic biomass to ethanol, *J. Biotechnol.*, 56:1, 1997; R. G. Lugar and R. J. Woolsey, The new petroleum, *Foreign Affairs*, 78(1):88, 1999; L. Salisbury, Customers go for the green in power supply, *Reuter Business Rep.*, February 17, 1998.

Biome

A major community of plants and animals having similar life forms or morphological features and existing under similar environmental conditions. The biome, which may be used at the scale of entire continents, is the largest useful biological community unit. In Europe the equivalent term for biome is major life zone, and throughout the world, if only plants are considered, the term used is formation. *See* ECOLOGICAL COMMUNITIES.

Each biome may contain several different types of ecosystems. For example, the grassland biome may contain the dense tallgrass prairie with deep, rich soil, while the desert grassland has a sparse plant canopy and a thin soil. However, both ecosystems have grasses as the predominant plant life form, grazers as the principal animals, and a climate with at least one dry season. Additionally, each biome may contain several successional stages. A forest successional sequence may include grass dominants at an early stage, but some forest animals may require the grass stage for their habitat, and all successional stages constitute the climax forest biome. *See* DESERT; ECOLOGICAL SUCCESSION; ECOSYSTEM; GRASSLAND ECOSYSTEM.

Distributions of animals are more difficult to map than those of plants. The life form of vegetation reflects major features of the climate and determines the structural nature of habitats for animals. Therefore, the life form of vegetation provides a sound basis for ecologically classifying biological communities. Terrestrial biomes are usually identified by the dominant plant component, such as the temperate deciduous forest. Marine biomes are mostly named for physical features, for example, for marine upwelling, and for relative locations, such as littoral. Many biome classifications have been proposed, but a typical one might include several terrestrial biomes such as desert, tundra, grassland, savanna, coniferous forest, deciduous forest, and tropical forest. Aquatic biome examples are fresh-water lotic (streams and rivers), fresh-water lentic (lakes and ponds), and marine littoral, neritic, up-welling, coral reef, and pelagic. *See* FRESH-WATER ECOLOGY; MARINE ECOLOGY; PLANTS, LIFE FORMS OF; TERRESTRIAL ECOSYSTEM.   Paul Risser

Bibliography. M. G. Barbour, J. H. Burk, and W. D. Pitts, *Terrestrial Plant Ecology*, 3d ed., 1998; S. J. McNaughton and L. L. Wolf, *General Ecology*, 1973; P. G. Risser et al., *The True Prairie Ecosystem*, 1981; R. H. Whittaker, Classification of natural communities, *Bot. Rev.*, 28:1–239, 1962.

Biomechanics

A field that combines the disciplines of biology and engineering mechanics and utilizes the tools of physics, mathematics, and engineering to quantitatively describe the properties of biological materials. One of its basic properties is embodied in so-called constitutive laws, which fundamentally describe the properties of constituents, independent of size or geometry, and specifically how a material deforms in response to applied forces. For most inert materials, measurement of the forces and deformations is straightforward by means of commercially available devices or sensors that can be attached to a test specimen. Many materials, ranging from steel to rubber, have linear constitutive laws, with the proportionality constant (elastic modulus) between the deformation and applied forces providing a simple index to distinguish the soft rubber from the stiff steel.

Living tissues. While the same basic principles apply to living tissues, the complex composition of tissues makes obtaining constitutive laws difficult. Most tissues are too soft for the available sensors, so direct attachment not only will distort what is being measured but also will damage the tissue. Devices are needed that use optical, Doppler ultrasound, electromagnetic, and electrostatic principles to measure deformations and forces without having to touch the tissue.

All living tissues have numerous constituents, each of which may have distinctive mechanical properties. For example, elastin fibers give some tissues (such as blood vessel walls) their spring-like quality at lower loads; inextensible collagen fibers that are initially wavy and unable to bear much load become straightened to bear almost all of the higher loads; and muscle fibers contract and relax to dramatically change their properties from moment to moment. Interconnecting all these fibers are fluids, proteins, and other materials that contribute mechanical properties to the tissue.

The mechanical property of the tissue depends not only upon the inherent properties of its constituents but also upon how the constituents are arranged relative to each other. Thus, different mechanical properties occur in living tissues than in inert materials. For most living tissues, there is a nonlinear relationship between the deformations and the applied forces, obviating a simple index like the elastic modulus to describe the material. In addition, the complex arrangement of the constituents leads to material properties that possess directionality; that is, unlike most inert materials that have the same properties regardless of which direction is examined, living tissues have distinct properties dependent upon the direction examined. Finally, while most inert materials undergo small (a few percent) deformations, many living tissues and cells can deform by several hundred percent. Thus, the mathematics necessary to describe the deformations is much more complicated than with small deformations.　　Frank C. P. Yin

Cells and organs. Many functions of cells and organs are biomechanical and the understanding of these functions requires application of the principles and techniques of mechanics for analysis and quantitation. Biomechanics is a discipline that forms the basis for the understanding of biological processes such as the contraction of the heart, circulation of blood, gas exchange in the lung, peristalsis of the intestine and the ureter, load bearing by bones and cartilages, lubrication of joints, contraction of skeletal muscle, and mechanical aspects of vision and hearing. Biomechanics is also the foundation for clinical applications such as the design of orthopedic prostheses and cardiac assist devices. *See* PROSTHESIS.

The biomechanical properties and behaviors of organs and organ systems stem from the ensemble characteristics of their component cells and extracellular materials, which vary widely in structure and composition and hence in biomechanical properties. An example of this complexity is provided by the cardiovascular system, which is composed of the heart, blood vessels, and blood. *See* CARDIOVASCULAR SYSTEM.

Blood is a suspension of blood cells in plasma. The mammalian red blood cell consists of a membrane enveloping a homogeneous cytoplasm rich in hemoglobin, but it has no nucleus or organelles. While the plasma and the cytoplasm behave as fluids, the red blood cell membrane has viscoelastic properties; its elastic modulus in uniaxial deformation at a constant area is four orders of magnitude lower than that for areal deformation. This type of biomechanical property, which is unusual in nonbiological materials, is attributable to the molecular structure of the membrane: the lipid membrane has spanning proteins that are linked to the underlying spectrin network. The other blood cells (leukocytes and platelets) and the endothelial cells lining the vessel wall are more complex in composition and biomechanics; they have nuclei, organelles, and a cytoskeletal network of proteins. Furthermore, they have some capacity for active motility. *See* BLOOD; CYTOSKELETON.

Cardiac muscle and vascular smooth muscle cells have organized contractile proteins that can generate active tension in addition to passive elasticity. Muscle cells, like other cells, are surrounded by extracellular matrix, and cell-matrix interaction plays an important role in governing the biomechanical properties and functions of cardiovascular tissues and organs. The study of the overall performance of the cardiovascular system involves measurements of pressure and flow. The pressure-flow relationship results from the interaction of the biomechanical functions of the heart, blood, and vasculature. To analyze the biomechanical behavior of cells, tissues, organs, and systems, a combination of experimental measurements and theoretical modeling is necessary. *See* MUSCLE.

Other organ systems present many quantitative and qualitative differences in biomechanical properties. For example, because the cardiovascular system is composed of soft tissues whereas bone is a hard tissue, the viscoelastic coefficients and mechanical behaviors are quite different. Cartilage is intermediate in stiffness and requires a poroelastic theory to explain its behavior in lubrication of joints. In general, living systems differ from most physical systems in their nonhomogeneity, nonlinear behavior, capacity to generate active tension and motion, and ability to undergo adaptive changes and to effect repair. The biomechanical properties of the living systems are closely coupled with biochemical and metabolic activities, and they are controlled and regulated by neural and humoral mechanisms to optimize performance. While the biomechanical behaviors of cells, tissues, and organs are determined by their biochemical and molecular composition, mechanical forces can, in turn, modulate the gene expression and biochemical composition of the living system at the molecular level. Thus, a close coupling exists between biomechanics and biochemistry, and the understanding of biomechanics requires an interdisciplinary approach involving biology, medicine, and engineering. *See* BIOMEDICAL ENGINEERING.　　Shu Chien; Richard Skalak

Humans. A few examples of how mechanics is applied to human problems illustrate the scope of this field.

Forces on foot. Biomechanicists often want to know the forces that humans and animals exert on the ground when walking, running, or jumping. They use force-sensitive plates set into the floor which record the magnitude of any force that acts on them, together with its direction and the position on the plate at which it acts. **Figure 1** shows a human foot at the midpoint of a running step, the stage when the force F_g is greatest. Because the feet are off the ground for much of the stride, the force while they are on the ground rises well above body weight, to about 1900 newtons (430 pounds force) on the foot of a 700-N (158-lbf) person.

This force acts on the ball of the foot, so a force F_t is needed behind the ankle to balance the moments

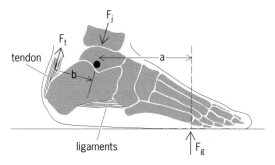

Fig. 1. Forces on a runner's foot; symbols are explained in the text.

on the foot. This is transmitted from the calf muscles through the Achilles tendon to the calcaneus (heel bone). The force F_t in the tendon can be calculated from the ground force F_g by taking moments about the ankle, as in Eq. (1). It is found to be about 4700 N

$$F_t = \frac{a}{b} F_g \qquad (1)$$

(1060 lbf, or almost a half ton) in the case here considered. Finally, a downward force F_j of about 6400 N (1440 lbf) must act at the ankle joint to balance forces F_t and F_g. *See* BONE.

That calculation illustrates the large forces that act in the human body, and leads to calculations and experiments that demonstrate a basic principle of running.

Elastic mechanisms in running. The elasticity of a bouncing ball carries energy forward from one bounce to the next. When it hits the ground it is decelerated, losing kinetic energy, which is stored as elastic strain energy in the distorted ball. Elastic recoil throws the ball back into the air, reconverting strain energy to kinetic energy. The same principle operates in running, greatly reducing the energy that has to be supplied by the metabolism of foodstuffs.

The elastic properties of tendons are investigated by stretching them in machines such as engineers use for testing metals and plastics. Tendons are moderately strong (stronger than the same thickness of rubber but less strong than nylon), and they stretch by about 8% of their length before breaking. When allowed to recoil after a smaller stretch, they return no less than 93% of the energy previously used to stretch them; the rest is lost as heat. In this respect, the tendon is a very good elastic material, as good as most rubbers.

The peak force in a runner's Achilles tendon has been calculated. By knowing the force and the dimensions and properties of the tendon, it can be calculated that it must be stretched by about 0.6 in. (15 mm); the strain energy stored in it can be found by measuring the area under a graph of the force F_t in the tendon against the length to which it is stretched. This is expressed mathematically by Eq. (2).

$$\text{Strain energy} = \int F_t \, dt \qquad (2)$$

This energy is found to be about 35 joules, which is about one-third of the kinetic energy lost and regained at each step. The elasticity of the tendon reduces the energy needed for running by about one-third.

A second elastic structure gives a further saving. The three forces shown in **Fig. 2** tend to flatten the arch of the foot. (Motion pictures of barefoot runners show the arch quite noticeably flattened at this stage of the stride.) This stretches the ligaments of the arch of the foot, which are made of material similar to tendons, storing up strain energy in them. Mechanical tests on feet that have had to be amputated for medical reasons show that this energy amounts

to some 17 J. The elasticity of the Achilles tendon and foot ligaments together reduces the metabolic energy required for running to about half of what would otherwise be needed.

Forces in leg muscles. In the example described above, the force in the Achilles tendon was easily calculated. Many other problems in biomechanics cannot be solved unambiguously, because the body is so complex. For instance, an attempt was made to estimate the forces exerted by the various muscles of the human leg during standing in various postures. The muscles do not lie in a single plane, so the problem had to be tackled in three dimensions. The human body was treated as an assembly of seven segments (two feet, two lower legs, two thighs, and a trunk). Six equations describe the equilibrium of a rigid body, so the seven segments yielded 42 simultaneous equations, 21 for each leg. These equations could have been solved to evaluate up to 21 unknown quantities, for instance, the forces exerted by 21 muscles. Unfortunately, there were 29 muscles which had to be considered in each leg, and also various ligaments and joint surfaces which exerted unknown forces. The problem could not be solved unambiguously because, with so many muscles, there were many possible solutions involving different combinations of forces in the muscles. A unique solution could be obtained only by imposing some additional criterion, for instance, by choosing the solution which minimized the total of the forces exerted by individual muscles. It is not immediately apparent whether this or any other criterion is realistic.

Further information was obtained by electromyography, a technique which is often useful in biomechanics. When a muscle is active, electrical events (action potentials) occur in it. They can be detected by means of electrodes, either metal plates attached to the skin or fine wires inserted into the muscles. The amount of electrical activity increases as the force exerted by the muscle increases, but it is unfortunately not possible to make reliable calculations of force from records of electrical activity. However, some useful information was obtained by

Fig. 2. Air flow in the wake of a slow-flying pigeon (*Columba livia*).

the following experiment. Electrodes were stuck to a person's skin, over six of the principal leg muscles. Electrical activity was recorded as the subject stood successively in various positions. The relative strengths of electrical activity in the various positions were compared to the muscle forces calculated by using various criteria. The electrical records were most easily reconciled with the estimates of force when the criterion for choosing a solution was to minimize the moments at joints which had to be resisted by ligaments. Even this elaborate technique gave some results which seem unlikely on other grounds. For instance, it indicated that one of the calf muscles (the soleus) exerted more than 6 kilonewtons (0.6 metric ton weight) in a deep crouch position. It is very doubtful whether the muscle is strong enough to do so.

Animals. The examples presented above concern the human body and use only solid mechanics. A final example will show that biomechanics deals also with animals, and uses fluid mechanics.

Formerly, biomechanicists tried to understand bird flight by using the aerodynamics that engineers apply to fixed-wing aircraft. It was realized that this approach could not give reliable estimates of the forces on a flapping wing, and they set out to observe the air movements in the wake of flying birds so that the forces could be calculated from first principles. Air movements were made visible by releasing small soap bubbles, filled with helium; this gas is lighter than air and so bubbles of a certain size have exactly the same density as the air and move with it. Birds were flown through clouds of helium-filled bubbles and multiple-flash photographs were taken, using two cameras to record the movement of the bubbles in three dimensions. *See* AERODYNAMICS.

Figure 2 shows the pattern of air flow behind a slow-flying bird. Each downstroke of the wings drives a downward puff of air that is surrounded by a vortex ring, like the smoke rings formed around puffs of air from a smoker's mouth. Only the downstroke drives air downward, and so it alone is responsible for supporting the bird's weight. In fast flight, however, air is driven downward throughout the down- and up-strokes, and the wake is not broken up into discrete vortex rings. Instead, the wings leave trailing vortices behind them, like the vortices that sometimes become visible as vapor trails behind the wing tips of aircraft. *See* BIOPHYSICS; FLIGHT.

R. McNeill Alexander

Bibliography. B. Alberts et al., *Molecular Biology of the Cell*, 3d ed., 1994; R. McN. Alexander, *Elastic Mechanisms in Animal Movement*, 1988; J. Currey, *The Mechanical Adaptations of Bones*, 1984; Y. C. Fung, *Biomechanics: Mechanical Properties of Living Tissues*, 2d ed., 1993; J. D. Murray, *Mathematical Biology*, 2d ed., 1993; R. Skalak and S. Chien, *Handbook of Bioengineering*, 1987; J. Valenta (ed.), *Biomechanics*, 1993; S. Vogel, *Life in Moving Fluids*, 2d revised ed., 1994.

Biomedical chemical engineering

The application of chemical engineering principles to the solution of medical problems due to physiological impairment. Knowledge of organic chemistry is required of all chemical engineers, and many study biochemistry and molecular biology. This training at the molecular level gives chemical engineers a unique advantage over other engineering disciplines in communication with life scientists and clinicians in medicine, since the technical language of modern medicine is based in biochemistry and molecular biology. Practical applications include the development of tissue culture systems, the construction of three-dimensional scaffolds of biodegradable polymers for cell growth in the laboratory, and the design of artificial organs. *See* BIOCHEMISTRY; MOLECULAR BIOLOGY.

Vascular biology. An example of where the interaction between biomedical chemical engineers and life scientists has been extremely beneficial is the area of vascular biology. The leading causes of death in the western world are coronary thrombosis (heart attack), stroke, and cancer. All these pathological states involve alterations in the cardiovascular system, eventually leading to cessation of blood flow to a vital organ. Understanding the complex interplay between blood flow, cell metabolism, cell adhesion, and vessel pathology leading to these diseases is possible only with an interdisciplinary approach.

The vascular system is naturally dynamic, with fluid mechanics and mass transfer closely integrated with blood and vascular cell function. Bioengineers are able to understand how local wall shear stress and strain modulate endothelial cell metabolism at the level of the gene. Tissue culture systems make it possible to control both the biochemical and mechanical environment—usually not possible in animal models (**Fig. 1**). This knowledge may help explain the

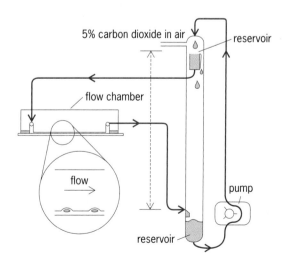

Fig. 1. Schematic of a flow loop used to study the effect of controlled flow on the metabolism of cultured endothelial cells. Cells form a monolayer on one surface of a parallel plate flow chamber that is mounted in a loop for media circulation. The flow rate is determined by the vertical distance between the upper and lower reservoirs.

focal nature of many vascular pathologies, including atherosclerosis. Understanding mechanical control of gene regulation, at the level of specific promoter elements and transcription factors involved, permits development of novel constructs for localized delivery of specific gene products in regions of high or low shear stress or strain in the vascular system. In addition, local fluid mechanics can alter receptor specificity in cell-cell and cell-matrix protein adhesion and aggregation. Knowledge of the specific molecular sequences involved in cell-cell recognition is necessary for development of targeted therapeutics, with applications in thrombosis, inflammation, cancer metastasis, and sickle cell anemia. *See* ARTERIOSCLEROSIS; TISSUE CULTURE; VASCULAR DISORDERS.

Cell transplantation therapy. Cell transplantation is explored as a means of restoring tissue function. With this approach, individual cells are harvested from a healthy section of donor tissue, isolated, expanded in culture, and implanted at the desired site of the functioning tissue. Also, cell-based therapies involve the return of genetically altered cells to the host by using gene insertion techniques.

Cell transplantation has several advantages over whole-organ transplantation. Because the isolated cell population can be expanded in the laboratory by using cell culture, only a small number of donor cells are needed to prepare an implant. Consequently, the living donor need not sacrifice an entire organ. The need for a permanent synthetic implant is eliminated through the use of natural tissue constituents, without the disruption and relocation of a whole piece of normal tissue. Isolating cells allows removal of other cell types that may be the target of immune responses, thus diminishing the rejection process. Major surgery on the recipient and donor, with its inherent risks, is avoided. Finally, the cost of the transplantation procedure can be significantly reduced.

Isolated cells cannot form new tissues and require specific environments that often include the presence of supporting material to act as a template for growth. Three-dimensional scaffolds can be used to mimic their natural counterparts, the extracellular matrices of the body. These scaffolds serve as both a physical support and an adhesive substrate for isolated parenchymal cells during cell culture and subsequent implantation. Because of the multiple functions that these materials must fill, the physical and chemical requirements are numerous. In order to accommodate a sufficient number of cells for functional replacement, a cell transplantation device must have a large surface area for cell adhesion. High porosity provides adequate space for cell seeding, growth, and production of extracellular matrices. A uniformly distributed and interconnected pore structure is important so that cells are easily distributed throughout the device and so that an organized network of tissue constituents can be formed, allowing for cell-cell communication through direct contact and via soluble factors. Also, nutrients and waste products must be transported to and from differentiated groups of cells, often in ways that maintain cell

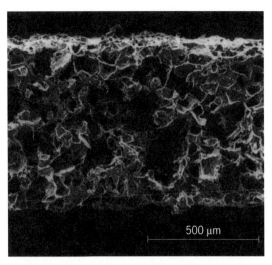

Fig. 2. Scanning electron micrograph of a biodegradable poly(L-lactic acid) foam of 91% porosity and 94-micrometer median pore diameter prepared by a particulate-leaching method which involved the casting of polymer/salt composite membranes followed by the dissolution of the salt.

polarity. In the reconstruction of structural tissues such as bone and cartilage, tissue shape is integral to function. Therefore, these scaffolds must be made of varying thickness and shape. Furthermore, because of eventual human implantation, the scaffold must be made of biocompatible materials. As the transplanted cell population grows and the cells function normally, they will begin to secrete their own extracellular matrix support. The need for an artificial support will gradually diminish; and thus if the implant is biodegradable, it will be eliminated as its function is replaced. The development of processing methods to fabricate reproducibly three-dimensional scaffolds of biodegradable polymers that will provide temporary scaffolding to transplanted cells until they secrete their own matrix components to form a completely natural tissue replacement (**Fig. 2**) will be instrumental in engineering tissues.

The study of the adhesive interactions between cells and both synthetic and biological substrates is pivotal in determining the effect of different physical and chemical factors on cell and tissue growth and function. Much biomaterials research has focused on minimizing biological fluid and tissue interactions with biomaterials in an effort to prevent either fibrous encapsulation from foreign-body reaction or clotting in blood that contacts artificial devices. Innovations utilizing the inverse approach, that of programmed extensive interaction of the material with biological tissue, is an alternative focus for biomaterials research. One concept is novel biomaterials that incorporate specific peptide sequences to enhance cell adhesion and promote differentiated cell growth by releasing growth factors, angiogenic factors, and other bioactive molecules. *See* CELL (BIOLOGY); CELL BIOLOGY; TRANSPLANTATION BIOLOGY.

Artificial organs. When the primary organ cells cannot be grown in culture to provide the critical mass required for cell transplantation and functional

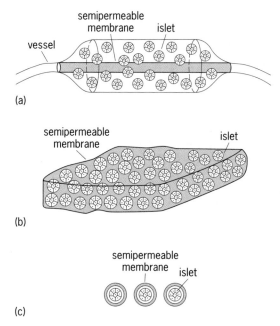

(a)

(b)

(c)

Fig. 3. Designs for islet immunoisolation devices.
(a) Intravascular devices. (b) Extravascular macrocapsules.
(c) Extrovascular microcapsules.

replacement, xenografts (tissue from other species) may be used to replace tissue function. Xenogeneic cells can be encapsulated in membranes and implanted to restore metabolic regulation and activity. These membranes are designed to isolate the cells from the body, thereby avoiding the immune responses that the foreign cells could initiate, and to allow the desired metabolites, such as insulin and glucose for pancreatic islet cells, to diffuse in and out of the membrane. Islet immunoisolation devices to replace the pancreas are classified as intravascular and extravascular (**Fig. 3**). Intravascular devices consist of a tubular membrane connected directly to the vascular system. Extravascular devices include macrocapsules and microcapsules. Macroencapsulation involves the envelopment of a large mass of cells or tissue in planar membranes, hollow fibers, or diffusion chambers. Microencapsulation involves the envelopment of single cells, islets, or a small number thereof into microspheres of diameter smaller than 1 mm. The critical issues for the development of bioartificial organs include membrane biocompatibility, diffusion limitations, device retrieval in the event of failure, and mechanical stability.

Chemical engineers have made significant contributions to the design and optimization of many commonly used devices for both short-term and long-term organ replacement. Examples include the artificial kidney for hemodialysis and the heart-lung machine employed in open-heart surgery. The artificial kidney removes waste metabolites (such as urea and creatinine) from blood across a polymeric membrane that separates the flowing blood from the dialysis fluid. The mass transport properties and biocompatibility of these membranes are crucial to the functioning of hemodialysis equipment. The heart-lung machine replaces both the pumping function

of the heart and the gas exchange function of the lung in one fairly complex device. While often life saving, both types of artificial organs only partially replace real organ function. Long-term use often leads to problems with control of blood coagulation mechanisms to avoid both excessive clotting initiated by blood contact with artificial surfaces and excessive bleeding due to platelet consumption or overuse of anticoagulants. *See* BLOOD; DIALYSIS; MEMBRANE SEPARATIONS.

Other applications include methodology for development of artificial bloods, utilizing fluorocarbon emulsions or encapsulated or polymerized hemoglobin, and controlled delivery devices for release of drugs or of specific molecules (such as insulin) missing in the body because of disease or genetic alteration. *See* BIOMEDICAL ENGINEERING; POLYMER.
                    Larry V. McIntire; Antonios G. Mikos

Bibliography. S. Bhatia, *Microfabrication in Tissue Engineering and Bioartificial Organs*, 1999; J. D. Bronzino, *Tissue Engineering and Artificial Organs*, 3d ed., 2006; J. Enderle et al., *Introduction to Biomedical Engineering*, 1999; J. A. Frangos (ed.), *Physical Forces and the Mammalian Cell*, 1992; J. K.-J. Li, *Dynamics of the Vascular System* (*Series on Bioengineering & Biomedical Engineering*, vol. 1), 2004; A. G. Mikos et al., Islet transplantation to create a bioartificial pancreas, *Biotechnol. Bioeng.*, 43:673–677, 1994; G. Vunjak-Novakovic and R. I. Freshney, *Culture of Cells for Tissue Engineering*, 2006.

Biomedical engineering

An interdisciplinary field in which the principles, laws, and techniques of engineering, physics, chemistry, and other physical sciences are applied to facilitate progress in medicine, biology, and other life sciences. Biomedical engineering encompasses both engineering science and applied engineering in order to define and solve problems in medical research and clinical medicine for the improvement of health care. Biomedical engineers must have training in anatomy, physiology, and medicine, as well as in engineering.

Biomedical engineering entails the design and development of tools and instrumentation to enhance the ability of physicians and life scientists to obtain information on physiological and biological processes, and to aid in the treatment of diseases or other abnormalities. It is also an important component in the design and development of artificial organs, limbs, and other prosthetic devices that replace missing body parts or that enhance deteriorated physiological functions. Biomedical engineering also contributes to medical and biological research aimed at learning more about the functional processes in various physiological systems. An important part of biomedical engineering research is the use of computer techniques to develop mathematical models of physiological functions and processes to expand available theoretical knowledge. *See* SIMULATION.

The impact of biomedical engineering is manifested in the many instruments and devices that surround a patient in the modern hospital and in the many sophisticated artificial organs and other prosthetic devices available. In addition, biomedical engineering contributes greatly to medical and biological research.

Instrumentation. A wide variety of instrumentation is available to the physician and surgeon to facilitate the diagnosis and treatment of diseases and other malfunctions of the body. Instrumentation has been developed to extend and improve the quality of life. A primary objective in the development of medical instrumentation is to obtain the required results with minimal invasion of the body. Invasion refers to the penetration of the skin or external integument, usually involving increased risk and trauma to the patient. A device in the stomach accessed through the throat is not invasive, in contrast to a needle penetrating the skin to withdraw blood from a vein, or a blood pressure transducer at the tip of a catheter introduced into a blood vessel. In a broader sense, exposing the body to x-radiation or radioisotopes can also be considered invasive.

Diagnostic instrumentation. Medical diagnosis requires knowledge of the condition of specified organs or systems of the body, and a vast array of instrumentation has been developed. Bioelectric potentials, that is, electrical signals generated within the body, provide a useful source of information. Much can be learned about the functioning of the heart by using electrocardiography (EKG) to measure and analyze the electrical activity of the heart. Electrocardiographic signals are used to measure heart rate and to identify certain types of abnormalities within the heart. They also serve as a means of synchronizing other measurements with cardiovascular activity. Neurological activity within the brain can be assessed by using electroencephalography (EEG) to measure and analyze the electrical activity of the brain. Muscular activity can be measured by using electromyography (EMG), which utilizes the electrical activity of muscles. These bioelectric potentials are generally obtained noninvasively, but localized measurements may require placement of electrodes at sites that require invasive procedures. Neurological measurements usually require invasive placement of electrodes within or adjacent to specific nerves or neurons. Although bioelectric potentials have been used clinically for several decades, improved electrode design and instrumentation have made these measurements more reliable and have increased their usefulness. *See* BIOPOTENTIALS AND IONIC CURRENTS; CARDIAC ELECTROPHYSIOLOGY; ELECTRODIAGNOSIS; ELECTROENCEPHALOGRAPHY.

Sounds generated within the body constitute another source of information. Notable are heart sounds corresponding to the pumping action of the heart and operation of the heart valves; and sounds generated by blood pulsating through a partially occluded vessel, used in indirect blood pressure measurements.

Electrical impedance measurements are utilized to obtain information noninvasively. Impedance plethysmography is a technique by which changes in the volume of certain segments of the body can be determined by impedance measurements. These changes are related to factors involving the mechanical activity of the heart such as cardiac output, or conditions of the circulatory system such as blood volume and flow in various regions, or to respiratory flow and other physiological functions.

Ultrasound is utilized in many types of diagnostic measurements. In most applications, periodic bursts of ultrasound are introduced into a region of the body, and echoes from various structures and organs are measured. Echocardiography is an ultrasound procedure which provides an indication of the physical movements of the walls and valves of the heart. Echoencephalography involves ultrasonic echoes from the midline of the brain to detect tumors that would shift that midline. Electronically produced images of various internal organs and body structures are obtained by using different types of ultrasonic scans. All of these measurements are performed noninvasively. *See* ECHOCARDIOGRAPHY; MEDICAL ULTRASONIC TOMOGRAPHY.

X-rays have long been utilized to visualize internal body structures, but computerized tomographic methods and other improvements have greatly increased their diagnostic potential, permitting measurements with reduced radiation exposure to the patient. Also, better contrast media have been developed to make organs or regions of interest more clearly identifiable in the x-ray image. *See* COMPUTERIZED TOMOGRAPHY; RADIOGRAPHY; RADIOLOGY.

Another imaging process is magnetic resonance, which requires excitation of the site of measurement by an alternating magnetic field in the radio-frequency range. Magnetic resonance utilizes the principle that the nuclei of certain elements resonate when excited by a given radio frequency. Different elements have different resonance characteristics for identification. Like ultrasound, the excitation required for magnetic resonance measurements has not shown any indication of harming the body. *See* MEDICAL IMAGING; NUCLEAR MAGNETIC RESONANCE (NMR).

Imaging of organs and body structures has been greatly enhanced by computerized tomography. A number of linear scans through a given cross section of the organ or body are taken from different vantage points and combined mathematically by computer to produce a cross-sectional image in which all features are clearly shown. Tomography applied to x-ray images produces computerized tomography or computerized axial tomography (CAT) scans. When radioisotopes are used, the result is called positron emission tomography (PET) or single photon emission computerized tomography (SPECT). Computerized tomography is also applied to obtain images from other types of measurements. For example, tomographic imaging from electrical impedance measurements within the body is called electrical impedance tomography (EIT).

Monitoring equipment found at the bedside of each patient in the intensive care unit of a hospital combines a number of biomedical measurement devices to perform continuous noninvasive measurements of body temperature, heart rate, blood pressure, respiration, blood gases, and other variables that indicate the condition of the patient and that alert hospital personnel to an impending emergency. Noninvasive transcutaneous sensors permit reliable measurement of blood gases, oxygenation, and other factors in the blood. Telemetry makes it possible to monitor many of these physiological variables from an ambulatory person.

There are still many clinical situations in which noninvasive measurements are unable to provide adequate data. For example, systolic and diastolic blood pressure can be measured noninvasively by using an indirect method involving occluding cuffs and detection of the sounds of blood flowing through the occlusions. However, measurement of the actual blood pressure waveform itself is often required, and a blood pressure transducer must be carried by a catheter to a specified location within the cardiovascular system. Similarly, blood flow through a major artery or region of the body can be estimated or traced qualitatively from a probe outside the body, but reliable quantitative measurements still require invasive procedures. These examples from the cardiovascular system are typical of similar problems in nearly all of the physiological systems of the body.

Therapeutic instrumentation. Instrumentation is used in many ways for the treatment of disease. Devices are available to provide control for the automated administration of medication or other substances such as insulin for diabetics. In some cases, the rate at which the substance is administered is controlled by the level of certain constituents of the blood or other body fluids. Examples of this equipment may be found in the hospital, where the medication is administered to a patient who is in bed or whose movement is otherwise restricted. Other devices are designed to be worn on the body or even implanted within the body. *See* DRUG DELIVERY SYSTEMS.

Implanted pacemakers have been available for some time, but improvements have made them more sensitive to the natural function of the heart and the demands of the body. Such pacemakers monitor the patient's electrocardiogram and other physiological data and stimulate the heart only when the natural functions become insufficient to meet demands. The size and life of the batteries powering such devices have been improved, thus reducing the need for surgery to replace pacemaker batteries. Implantable defibrillators are available for special situations in which periodic automatic defibrillation is required to maintain functionality of a heart.

Another therapeutic technique involves the application of electrical stimulation to muscles or nerves to block involuntary muscle contractions or pain. The stimulating electrodes can be implanted or can be placed on the surface of the skin, depending on the depth of the site to be stimulated.

Surgical equipment. A number of tools are available to the surgeon in the operating room in addition to the monitoring instruments. The family of electrosurgical tools uses highly concentrated electric currents to precisely cut tissue and at the same time control bleeding. Lasers, which deliver highly concentrated light energy, are also used for making incisions and for fusion of tissue, as in the reattachment of the retina in the eye. *See* SURGERY.

Clinical engineering. Responsibility for the correct installation, use, and maintenance of all medical instrumentation in the hospital is usually assigned to individuals with biomedical engineering training. This phase of biomedical engineering is termed clinical engineering, and often involves providing training for physicians, nurses, and other hospital personnel who operate the equipment. Another responsibility of the clinical engineer is to ensure that the instrumentation meets functional specifications at all times and poses no safety hazard to patients. In most hospitals, the clinical engineer supervises one or more biomedical engineering technicians in the repair and maintenance of the instrumentation.

Biomedical research. The application of engineering principles and techniques has a significant impact on medical and biological research aimed at finding cures for a large number of diseases, such as heart disease, cancer, and AIDS, and at providing the medical community with increased knowledge in almost all areas of physiology and biology. The data obtained by medical and biological research are also used to develop more realistic and sophisticated prosthetic devices, making possible better methods of control and better understanding of the natural systems that the prostheses are designed to replace.

Biomedical engineers are involved in the development of instrumentation for nearly every aspect of medical and biological research, either as a part of a team with medical professionals or independently, in such varied fields as electrophysiology, biomechanics, fluid mechanics, microcirculation, and biochemistry. A number of fields, such as cellular engineering and tissue engineering, have evolved from this work.

Physiological modeling. A significant role for biomedical engineers in research is the development of mathematical models of physiological and biological systems. A mathematical model is a set of equations that are derived from physical and chemical laws and that describe a physiological or biological function. Experimental data obtained under conditions for which the model is expected to be valid can be used to test the model, which can then be used in several ways to represent the function or process for which it was created. By utilizing computer implementation, mathematical models can be used to predict the effect of given events, such as the administration of a given drug or treatment.

Modeling can be done at various physiological levels, from the cellular or microbiological level to that of a complete living organism, and can be of various degrees of complexity, depending on which kinds of functions they are intended to represent and how much of the natural function is essential for the purpose of the model. Mechanical, neurological, neuromuscular, electrochemical, biochemical, thermal, biological, metabolic, pneumatic (pulmonary), hydraulic (cardiovascular), and behavioral (psychological) systems are among the many types of systems for which models have been developed and studied. The models involve transport, utilization, and control of mass, energy, momentum, and information within these systems. A major objective of biomedical engineering is to create models that more closely approximate the natural functions they represent and that satisfy as many of the conditions encountered in nature as possible. *See* MATHEMATICAL BIOLOGY.

Artificial organs and prosthetics. A highly important contribution of biomedical engineering is in the design and development of artificial organs and prosthetic devices which replace or enhance the function of missing, inoperative, or inadequate natural organs or body parts. Hemodialysis units, which perform the functions of the kidney, have been in use for a long time, but most are large external devices that must be connected to the patient periodically to remove wastes from the body. A major goal in this area is to develop small, self-contained, implantable artificial organs that function as well as the natural organs, which they can permanently supersede.

Artificial hips, joints, and many other body structures and devices designed to strengthen or reinforce weakened structures must be implanted and must function for the life of the patient. They must be made of biocompatible materials that will not cause infection or rejection by the body. They must be built with sufficient reliability that the need for adjustment, repair, or replacement will be minimized.

Sophisticated artificial limbs for amputees and neural prostheses to facilitate or strengthen the use of nonfunctional limbs is another area in which biomedical engineers are involved. Prosthetic limbs attempt to replicate the vital features of natural limbs with miniature electric motors acting as muscles to operate the moving parts. Control of the movements is a major challenge, especially for the arm and hand, where there is a particular need to provide dexterity for the user. Electromyographic signals from muscles remaining in the stump and elsewhere in the body are utilized where possible. However, the limitations are severe, and the ability of the user to learn to operate the device effectively poses a further problem. The problem is compounded by the need for sensory feedback from the prosthesis in order to provide smooth control. Simple on-off switching operations can be accomplished by moving a part of the body such as the shoulder, by placing a device in the mouth that can be operated by the tongue, by a puff-sip action, or by other motions within the physical capability of the patient.

Neural prostheses bypass a portion of the nervous system and provide electrical stimulation to existing muscles in situations where paralysis has interrupted the natural control pathways. The electrical stimulation can be applied either along the surface of the skin over the muscles to be stimulated or via electrodes implanted within or immediately adjacent to the muscle. Control of the muscle action when using these prostheses is even more difficult than with artificial limbs, especially if the sensory path from the muscle has also been interrupted. Some success has been achieved in providing functional electrical stimulation to specified muscles in the foot to overcome a condition called drop foot. The stimulation is controlled by a switch activated by the position of the foot at a specified portion of the walking cycle. Neural prostheses for the lower limbs have been successful in helping paralyzed patients walk to a limited degree. *See* PROSTHESIS.

Rehabilitation engineering. The goal of rehabilitation engineering is to increase the quality of life for the disabled. One major part of this field is directed toward strengthening existing but weakened motor functions through use of special devices and procedures that control exercising of the muscles involved. Another part is devoted to enabling disabled persons to function better in the world and live more normal lives.

Included in this area are devices to aid the blind and hearing-impaired. Hearing aids are available to assist persons in which the acoustical signal has weakened. Cochlear implants that bypass the hair cells and directly stimulate the auditory nerve make it possible to restore some hearing ability to many individuals. Reading machines that either produce greatly enlarged images or convert written words into sound have been developed to assist the visually impaired. All of these devices have their shortcomings, and work to create improved visual and auditory aids continues. *See* HEARING AID.

Human-factors engineering is utilized in modifying the home and workplace to accommodate the special needs of disabled persons. Improved wheelchairs and wheelchair control devices and modified automobile control mechanisms permit greater mobility for many who are unable to walk or drive a conventional vehicle. Special modifications to the control mechanisms of television sets and other devices and appliances in the home allow for use by people with disabilities. *See* BIOMECHANICS; HUMAN-FACTORS ENGINEERING; MEDICAL CONTROL SYSTEMS.

Fred J. Weibell

Bibliography. L. A. Geddes and L. E. Baker, *Principles of Applied Biomedical Instrumentation*, 3d ed., 1989; D. C. Mikulecky and A. M. Clarke (eds.), *Biomedical Engineering: Opening New Doors*, 1990; D. J. Schneck, *Engineering Principles of Physiologic Function*, 1990; R. B. Stein, P. H. Peckham, and D. B. Popovic (eds.), *Neural Prostheses: Replacing Motor Function after Disease or Disability*, 1992; J. G. Webster (ed.), *Medical Instrumentation: Applications and Design*, 3d ed., 1997; D. L. Wise (ed.), *Bioinstrumentation: Research, Developments and Applications*, 1990.

Biomedical ultrasonics

The applications to medicine and biology of sound waves that have a frequency higher than the audible spectrum. Biomedical applications of ultrasound range from cell sonicators using frequencies in the kilohertz range to ultrasonic imaging in the megahertz range. The best-known application, ultrasonic imaging, is the second most utilized diagnostic imaging modality, after x-rays. High-intensity ultrasound has been used for therapeutic applications.

Ultrasonic imaging possesses numerous advantages over other imaging modalities of similar capabilities such as x-ray computed tomography, radionuclide imaging, and magnetic resonance imaging. It uses radiation that is noninvasive to the human body at the diagnostic intensity level, produces images at a very fast rate of 30 frames per second, and can be used to yield blood flow information by applying the Doppler principle. It has been used in a variety of medical disciplines, including cardiology, obstetrics, and radiology. *See* MEDICAL IMAGING.

Notable disadvantages of ultrasound are that organs containing gases and bony structures cannot be adequately imaged, and only a limited acoustic window (space or opening between bones) is available for examination of organs such as the heart and the neonatal brain.

Ultrasound at high intensity levels has been used for hyperthermia treatment of tumors, frequently in combination with chemotherapy or radiotherapy, and for tissue ablation. *See* ONCOLOGY; THERMOTHERAPY.

Ultrasonic wave propagation. Ultrasound is a form of acoustic wave with a frequency higher than 20 kHz. Ultrasound parameters include pressure, velocity, displacement, density, and temperature. Ultrasound velocity and wavelength in water are approximately 1.48×10^5 cm/s and 0.03 cm at 5 MHz and $20°C$ ($68°F$). The sound speeds in soft biological tissues are similar to that in water.

An acoustic disturbance in a fluid propagates as a longitudinal or compressional wave, which has a displacement in the same direction as the direction of wave propagation. On the other hand, the displacement of a shear or transverse wave is perpendicular to the wave direction. The sound speeds of shear and longitudinal waves are different. Biological tissues other than bone can be treated as fluidlike media, and as such they cannot support shear-wave propagation. *See* SOUND.

Characteristic acoustic impedance. The characteristic acoustic impedance of a medium is defined as the ratio of the pressure to medium velocity. Since these quantities are analogous to the voltage and current in an electrical circuit, the acoustic impedance carries the same physical significance as the electrical impedance. For a fluid medium, the characteristic acoustic impedance Z is given by Eq. (1),

$$Z = \rho c \qquad (1)$$

where ρ is the density and c is the sound speed. The

unit of acoustic impedance, the rayl, is 1 kg/(m^2-s). The acoustic impedance of water is approximately 1.48×10^6 rayl, and the acoustic impedances of tissues are of similar magnitude. *See* ACOUSTIC IMPEDANCE.

Intensity. Analogous to the power in electrical circuits, the intensity of an acoustic wave is defined as the power carried by the wave per unit area, propagating in a medium of acoustic impedance Z. It is related to the pressure, p, by Eq. (2).

$$I(t) = \frac{p^2(t)}{Z} \qquad (2)$$

A conventional pulse-echo ultrasonic image is formed by launching an ultrasonic pulse into the body, and detecting and displaying the echoes reflected or scattered from the tissues. The pulse duration of the scanner is very short, typically less than 1 microsecond, but the period between successive pulses is relatively long, typically greater than 1 millisecond. Consequently, the instantaneous pressure when the pulse is on can be quite high, reaching a few megapascals, but the time-averaged pressure over the whole cycle is much lower. *See* SOUND PRESSURE.

Attenuation, reflection, and scattering. As an ultrasonic wave penetrates a tissue, part of the ultrasonic energy is lost through absorption of the energy by tissues and part by scattering or reflection, which diverts the energy from the incident direction whenever the wave encounters a discontinuity in acoustic properties. For a plane wave, the sound pressure decreases as a function of the propagation distance, x, exponentially, as given by Eq. (3), where $p(0)$ is

$$p(x) = p(0)e^{-\alpha x} \qquad (3)$$

the pressure at $x = 0$ and α is the attenuation coefficient in neper/cm. The attenuation coefficient in tissues has been found to be linearly proportional to frequency in the range from 1 to 30 MHz. In soft tissues it is approximately 0.03 neper/(cm-MHz). *See* SOUND ABSORPTION.

The behavior of a plane wave at a flat boundary between two media depends on the acoustic impedances of the media and on the angles of reflection and transmission of the sound wave. Most of the incident energy is reflected at the interface of two media of very different acoustic impedances. Ultrasound is not useful for imaging anatomical structures that contain air, such as lung and bones, because their acoustic impedances are very different from those of the surrounding body tissues, so that most of the ultrasound energy is reflected at these boundaries and does not penetrate them.

Echoes that result from reflection or scattering in the tissues are used by pulse-echo ultrasonic scanners to form an image. Scattering is described by a parameter called the scattering cross section, defined as the power scattered by the object when the incident beam has unit incident power per unit area. The scattering cross section of a scatterer of simple geometry, for example, a sphere, whose dimensions are much smaller than a wavelength, can be solved analytically, and is called Rayleigh scattering. At 10 MHz, the scattering cross section of a human red blood cell is approximately $1.5 \times 10^{-12} \text{cm}^2$, which is extremely small.

Doppler effect. The Doppler principle has been used to estimate blood flow in a blood vessel non-invasively. For an ultrasound beam making an angle θ relative to blood flowing at velocity V, the Doppler frequency shift f_{Dop} is related to V by Eq. (4), where f

$$f_{\text{Dop}} = \frac{2V \cos \theta}{c} f \qquad (4)$$

is the frequency of the sound. The Doppler frequencies associated with blood flow typically are in the audible range for medical ultrasound frequencies. *See* DOPPLER EFFECT.

Ultrasonic imaging. An ultrasonic image is formed from echoes returned from tissues. Although there are a number of ways of displaying the image, the B (brightness) mode is the most common. In this mode, the echo amplitude is displayed in gray scale as a function of the distance into the tissue. The center of the B-mode imaging system (**Fig. 1**) is an energy-conversion device, the ultrasonic transducer, which converts the electric signal into ultrasound and vice versa. *See* MEDICAL ULTRASONIC TOMOGRAPHY; TRANSDUCER.

Transducers. An ultrasonic transducer contains one or more elements made from a piezoelectric ceramic such as lead zirconate titanate. Depending upon how a transducer is driven, ultrasonic scanners are classified as mechanical-sector and electronic-array scanners. Electronic-array systems produce images of better quality and are faster. Mechanical-sector scanners are no longer used except for special applications. A typical array has dimensions of 1×8 cm (0.4×3.2 in.), and consists of 128

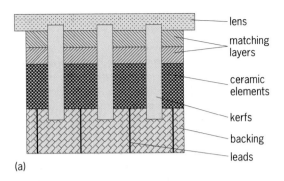
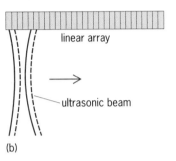

Fig. 2. Ultrasonic transducer consisting of linear array of piezoelectric elements. (*a*) Cross section of array. (*b*) Electronic focusing and sweeping of a beam by a linear sequenced array (or simply linear array). Generation of beam indicated by the solid line is followed by that indicated by the broken line.

or more small rectangular piezoelectric elements (**Fig. 2***a*). The gaps between the elements, called kerfs, are filled with an acoustic insulating material. In a linear sequenced array, or simply a linear array, a subaperture of 32 elements or more is fired simultaneously to form a beam. The beam is electronically focused and swept across the aperture surface from one end to the other (Fig. 2*b*). Electronic dynamic focusing can be achieved by appropriately controlling the timing of the signals to each individual element. In a linear phased array, the beam is also electronically steered, resulting in a pie-shaped image. Dynamic focusing can be used to better focus the beam throughout the field of view during reception or transmission. *See* PIEZOELECTRICITY.

The array may include two matching layers, a lens, and a backing material (Fig. 2*a*). The matching layers are needed to reduce the acoustic impedance mismatch between the piezoelectric ceramic and water or soft tissues. The lens is used to focus the beam to control the thickness of the image slice. The backing modifies the duration and shape of the excited acoustic pulse. A transducer consisting of only one piezoelectric element is the simplest type used in biomedical ultrasonics.

The array is excited by a pulser (Fig. 1). The returned echoes from the tissues are detected by the same transducer. Beam sweeping and position are controlled and encoded by the beam former, which may be either analog, consisting of a matrix of delay lines and amplifiers, or digital, consisting of an array of preamplifiers and analog-to-digital converters. The signal-processing chain performs functions

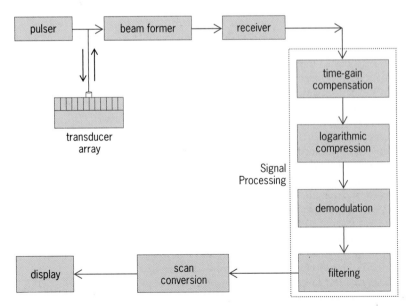

Fig. 1. Block diagram of a B-mode ultrasonic imaging system.

including time-gain compensation, signal compression, demodulation, and filtering. Time-gain compensation is used to compensate for the signal loss due to tissue attenuation and beam divergence as the beam penetrates the body. Logarithmic signal compression accentuates lower-level signals. Following signal processing, the signal may be digitized by an analog-to-digital converter. In high-end systems, analog-to-digital conversion is done in the beam former. The scan converter is a digital memory device that stores data that have been converted into a format that is displayable by a monitor. Before display, the video data may be processed again. Modern B-mode scanners can acquire images at a rate of 30 frames per second, allowing the motion of an organ to be monitored (**Fig. 3**).

The B-mode ultrasonic images exhibit a granular appearance, called a speckle pattern, which is caused by the constructive and destructive interference of the wavelets scattered by the tissue components as they arrive at the transducer surface. Ultrasound imaging is diffraction-limited because focusing can be achieved only within a limited field of view, not in the regions near and very far from the transducer. *See* SPECKLE.

Flow measurements. Two approaches have been used for ultrasonic Doppler flow measurements: continuous-wave and pulsed-wave Doppler. A probe consisting of two piezoelectric elements, one for transmitting the ultrasound signal and one for receiving the echoes returned from blood, is used in continuous-wave Doppler. The returned Doppler-shifted echoes are amplified, demodulated, and low-pass-filtered to remove the carrier frequency. The demodulated signal can be heard with a speaker or analyzed with a spectrum analyzer. Alternatively, a zero-crossing counter can be used to estimate the mean Doppler frequency.

A pulsed-wave Doppler may be used to alleviate the problem that a continuous-wave Doppler is unable to differentiate the origins of the Doppler signals produced within the ultrasound beam. Ultrasound bursts of 5–10 cycles are used, and the time of flight of the returned signal yields information about the signal's origin. *See* FLOW MEASUREMENT.

Color Doppler flow imaging. Color Doppler flow imaging scanners are capable of obtaining both B-mode images and Doppler blood flow data simultaneously in real time. The Doppler information is encoded in color. Red and blue are assigned to indicate flow toward and away from the transducer, respectively. The magnitude of the velocity is represented by the shade of the color. The color Doppler image is superimposed on the gray-scale B-mode image.

The basic concept of the color Doppler imager is similar to that of the pulsed Doppler instruments, which extract the mean Doppler-shift frequency from a sample volume. The only difference is that the color Doppler instruments are capable of estimating the mean Doppler shifts of many sample volumes along a scan line in a very short period of time, of the order of 30–50 ms. A fast algorithm has been developed to do so. It calculates the mean Doppler shift

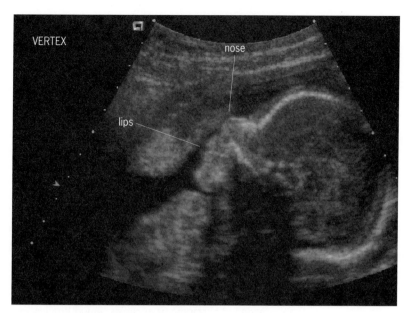

Fig. 3. B-mode image of a fetus in the uterus

and variance from the autocorrelation function of the signal, reducing significantly the processing time. If, instead of the mean Doppler shift, the power of the signal is displayed, this mode of imaging is called color Doppler power imaging. It has the advantages that (1) the data can be averaged to achieve a better signal-to-noise ratio and (2) signal distortion is no longer a problem since only the power is detected. The disadvantages are that it is more susceptible to motion artifacts and the image contains no information on flow velocity and direction.

Multidimensional arrays. The linear arrays used by current scanners are capable of dynamic focusing in only one dimension, in the azimuthal or imaging plane. Beam focusing in the elevational plane, the plane perpendicular to the imaging plane, which determines the slice thickness, must be achieved by a lens. This means that the slice thickness varies in the field of view and is the smallest only near the focus. To further improve the image quality, multidimensional arrays are necessary to control the beam in the elevational plane. The design and fabrication of such arrays have proved difficult. The technology used in microelectromechanical systems (MEMS) to miniaturize electronic components as well as novel interconnection technology may have to be incorporated in these systems.

3-D imaging and parallel processing. Three dimensional (3-D) reconstruction from multiple two-dimensional ultrasonic images can be readily achieved off-line by spatially encoding the imaging plane. Ultrasonic imaging in three dimensions in real time is feasible only with two-dimensional arrays which allow beam steering and dynamic focusing in three dimensions and parallel processing of the data. Only one acoustic pulse is propagated in the tissue at any one time in conventional ultrasonic image processing. The scanning time can be considerably shortened if several scan lines of information can be collected and processed at the same time by transmitting a broad beam.

Contrast media and harmonic imaging. Ultrasonic contrast agents have been successfully developed to enhance the image contrast of anatomic structures that contain the agents. A majority of these agents utilize microscopic encapsulated gas bubbles, which are strong scatterers because of the acoustic impedance mismatch. Moreover, the bubbles can resonate when insonified by an ultrasonic wave, and therefore the echoes from the bubbles can be further enhanced if the incident wave is tuned to the resonant frequency of the bubbles. These bubbles have a mean diameter of less than 5 micrometers and can be injected intravenously.

An important application of the gas-containing agents is in harmonic imaging and Doppler measurements, where the effect of the surrounding stationary structures on the image and results is minimized because only microbubbles resonate and emit ultrasound at harmonic frequencies. Blood flowing in a blood vessel containing the contrast agent will produce harmonic signals, but the blood vessel will not. Various types of oral contrast media which absorb or displace stomach or bowel gas for ultrasonic imaging have also been developed for better visualization of the abdominal organs.

Harmonic imaging has also been found to be useful even without a contrast agent to improve the image quality, especially in patients who are difficult to image with conventional ultrasound devices. This technique is possible because harmonic signals are produced from the nonlinear interaction of ultrasound and tissues.

Biological effects of ultrasound. Although ultrasound is known as a form of noninvasive radiation, biological effects inevitably result if its intensity is increased beyond some limit. Two types of ultrasound bioeffects can be produced: thermal and mechanical. The thermal effect results from an increase in temperature when the ultrasound energy is absorbed by the tissue, whereas the mechanical effect is caused by the generation of microscopic air bubbles or cavitation. No bioeffects have been found for ultrasound with a spatial peak temporal average intensity less than 100 mW/cm². *See* CAVITATION.

Therapeutic ultrasound. Ultrasound has been used for therapeutic purposes since high-intensity ultrasound produces biological effects. Based upon the duration and intensity level of the exposure during therapy, ultrasonic therapeutic applications can be categorized as hyperthermia and noninvasive surgery. Tissues are exposed to ultrasound of longer duration at lower intensity levels in ultrasound hyperthermia. The duration is 10–30 min at an intensity level of a few watts per square centimeter, elevating tissue temperature to 43–45°C (109–113°F). For noninvasive surgery, the duration is shorter, on the order of a few seconds, at an intensity level of a few hundred watts per square centimeter, raising the temperature in the focused region of the transducer to 70–90°C (158–194°F) within a short period of time. Cell death results immedi-

ately at this temperature. High-intensity focused ultrasound surgery has been shown to be clinically efficacious in the treatment of benign prostate hyperplasia, ocular tumor, and retinal tear. *See* ULTRASONICS.

K. Kirk Shung

Bibliography. D. H. Evans et al., *Doppler Ultrasound: Physics, Instrumentation, and Signal Processing*, 2d ed., Wiley, New York, 2000; W. N. McDicken, *Diagnostic Ultrasonics: Principles and Use of Instruments*. 3d ed., Churchill Livingstone, Edinburgh, 1991; J. A. Zagzebski, *Essentials of Ultrasound Physics*, Mosby, St. Louis, 1996.

Biometeorology

A branch of meteorology and ecology that deals with the effects of weather and climate on plants, animals, and humans.

Thermal equilibrium. The principal problem for living organisms is maintaining an acceptable thermal equilibrium with their environment. Mechanisms used to accomplish this equilibrium vary widely. Organisms have natural techniques for adapting to adverse conditions. These techniques include acclimatization, dormancy, and hibernation, or in some cases an organism can move to a more favorable environment or microenvironment. Humans often establish a favorable environment through the use of technology. *See* DORMANCY; HIBERNATION AND ESTIVATION; MICROMETEOROLOGY.

Homeotherms, that is, humans and other warm-blooded animals, maintain relatively constant body temperatures under a wide range of ambient thermal and radiative conditions through physiological and metabolic mechanisms. Poikilotherms, that is, cold-blooded animals, have a wide range in body temperature that is modified almost exclusively by behavioral responses. Plants also experience a wide range of temperatures, but because of their immobility they have less ability than animals to adapt to extreme changes in environment. *See* THERMOREGULATION.

Healthy humans, for example, maintain a body temperature of about 98.6°F (37°C). The thermal equilibrium is maintained through metabolism and through heat exchange and radiative exchange with the environment. Heat is gained by metabolism, gained or lost by radiative exchange, and generally lost by convection, conduction, and evaporation. The body surface loses heat when it radiates heat away from the body toward a colder environment, such as a cold wall or a clear sky, and gains radiative heat from the Sun or from a warm surface. Heat is exchanged directly to the air or through physical contact with a surface by conduction or convection. If the surfaces are cooler than the body temperature, heat is removed from the body, and if the surfaces are warmer, the body gains heat. Evaporation always causes a heat loss, while metabolism is always a source of heat. The amount of heat gained by metabolism is a function of the level of activity. *See* HOMEOSTASIS; METABOLISM.

TABLE 1. Insulating qualities of clothing

Environment	Sex	Garments	clo units
Tropical heat	m	Open-necked shirt, shorts, sandals	0.20
	f	Bra and panties, short-sleeved blouse, shorts, sandals	0.25
Warm summer	m	Open-necked shirt, slacks, shorts, ankle socks, shoes	0.40
	f	Bra and panties, short-sleeved blouse, light skirt, short stockings, shoes	0.30
Comfortable weather	m	Business suit, cotton underwear, long-sleeved shirt, socks, shoes	1.0
	f	Bra and panties, slip, dress, panty-hose, pumps	1.0
Cool weather	m	Business suit, light underwear, socks, shoes, light overcoat	1.5
	f	Bra and panties, stockings, slip, dress, sweater, shoes	1.5
Cold weather	m	Business suit, long underwear, woolen socks, shoes, hat, overcoat	2–2.5
	f	Warm underwear, skirt or slacks, slip, long-sleeved blouse, heavy sweater, hat, overcoat	2–2.5
		(For very cold weather, add lined gloves, fur or leather garment for both m & f)	3–3.5
Polar cold	m & f	Woolen underwear, coveralls, quilted parka with hood, fur mittens, fur-lined boots, face mask	4–4.5

Humans are physically adapted to a narrow range of temperature, with the metabolic mechanism functioning best at air temperatures around 77°F (25°C). There is a narrow range above and below this temperature where survival is possible. To regulate heat loss, warm-blooded animals developed hair, fur, and feathers. Humans invented clothing and shelter. The amount of insulation required to maintain thermal equilibrium is governed by the conditions in the atmospheric environment. There are a limited number of physiological mechanisms, controlled by the hypothalamus, that regulate body heat. In cold environments these mechanisms increase metabolic heat production, as in shivering, and lower the temperature at the skin surface by restricting blood flow. This mechanism, known as vasoconstriction, lowers the temperature at the body surface and therefore reduces the radiative heat loss. In warm environments the blood flow to the surface is increased, raising the temperature and thus increasing the radiative heat loss. In addition, evaporative cooling is enhanced by perspiration and respiration. *See* RESPIRATION.

The earliest humans had only the natural defenses available to counteract the atmospheric environment; hence their habitat was restricted to the warm climates of the tropics. The development of clothing permitted settlement of other climates. The insulating quality of clothing is measured by a unit (clo) derived from the metabolic heat losses and predicated on maintenance of skin temperature of 91.4°F (33°C). The heat flux from the body can be calculated with Eq. (1), where n = number of degrees

$$\text{Heat flux} = \frac{n}{0.18(x)} \quad (1)$$

(°C) and x = number of clo units (**Table 1**). Many animals exhibit winter fur that has significant insulating qualities (**Table 2**).

Cold stress. Clothing, shelter, and heat-producing objects can largely compensate for environmental cold, but with extensive exposure to cold, vasoconstriction in the peripheral organs can lead to chilblains and frostbite on the nose, ears, cheeks, and toes. This exposure is expressed quantitatively as a wind chill equivalent temperature that is a function of air temperature and wind speed. The wind chill

equivalent temperature is a measure of convective heat loss and describes a thermal sensation equivalent to a lower-than-ambient temperature under calm conditions, that is, for wind speeds below 4 mi/h (1.8 m/s). *See* COMFORT TEMPERATURES.

Persons exposed to extreme cold develop hypothermia, which may be irreversible when the core temperature drops below 91°F (33°C). The core temperature defines the temperature of the internal vital organs, for example, the cardiopulmonary system, in contrast to that of the peripheral organs, for example, hands or skin. On the whole, there is a clear correlation between winter death rates and temperature: the colder the winter, the more deaths occur. Research findings seem to indicate that outdoor deaths may be caused by breathing cold air, which lowers the temperature of the cardiopulmonary system to a lethal level. When the ambient temperature is 68°F (20°C), exhaled air has a temperature of about 91°F (33°C). It has a value of 73°F (23°C) when the ambient air is at 23°F (−5°C). *See* HYPOTHERMIA.

Heat stress. The combination of high temperature with high humidity leads to a very stressful thermal environment. The combination of high temperature with low humidity leads to a relatively comfortable thermal environment, but such conditions create an environment that has a very high demand for water.

Conditions of low humidity exist principally in subtropical deserts, which have the highest daytime temperatures observed at the Earth's surface. Temperatures of 86–104°F (30–40°C) are common, and occasionally even temperatures of 122°F (50°C) or higher are observed in these areas. Simultaneous rel-

TABLE 2. Insulating characteristic of winter fur of selected mammals

Species	Approximate thickness, in. (cm)	Relative insulation quality
Weasel	0.4 (1)	2
Squirrel	0.8 (2)	2.5
Rabbit	1.2 (3)	5
Dog	1.6 (4)	6
Beaver	1.6 (4)	5
Sheep	2.8 (7)	8

ative humidities are usually below 10% and rarely exceed 30% in daytime. Human and animal bodies are also exposed to strong solar radiation and and radiation reflected from the surface of the sand. This combination makes extraordinary demands on the sweat mechanism. Water losses of 1.06 quarts (1 liter) per hour are common in humans and may be even greater with exertion. Unless the water is promptly replaced by fluid intake, dehydration sets in. In humans a 2% weight loss by dehydration is slight and causes no symptoms other than thirst. If the loss rises to 6%, scanty urine and a rapid pulse accompanying a temperature rise of 3.6°F (2°C) will ensue; a greater weight loss by dehydration will cause circulatory failure and brain damage. Death occurs when the weight loss reaches 10–15% of body weight. Desert populations use the cooler night hours, with absence of incoming radiation, for travel and other activities. *See* DESERT; HUMIDITY; SOLAR RADIATION.

Animals that live in deserts are mostly nocturnal. Lizards and rodents spend the day in hollows and burrows because temperatures are 18–36°F (10–20°C) cooler than the extreme temperatures near the surface. Desert animals have also developed various mechanisms to maintain thermal equilibrium. The most water-efficient desert animal is the camel, which can store fluid in its system and survive several days without water. Camels can survive a 25% weight loss by dehydration. In other species, 10–15% weight loss is the limit.

Dehydration can occur in heated buildings during winter because the cold outside air has very little moisture, and as it infiltrates into the building the relative humidity drops drastically. Household activities such as cooking, laundering, bathing, and growing house plants add moisture, but unless humidifiers are used, water losses of occupants can be substantial. At a room temperature of 70°F (21°C) and a relative humidity of 50%, a resting individual loses about 1.06 quarts (1 liter) of water in 24 h. At a relative humidity of 30% and the same temperature, the water loss is about 1.16 quarts (1.1 liters), mostly from insensible perspiration and exhaled air.

Both outdoor and indoor comfort is governed by temperature and humidity conditions. However, there is a great variability among individuals in terms of comfort zones. Acclimatization plays a role, but in general, older persons and infants require higher temperature values for comfort. On the average, there is a spread of 2.6–9°F (2–5°C) for comfort sensations for persons living in middle or higher latitudes compared with residents of subtropical or tropical climates, where there is a narrower spread of 2–5°F (1–3°C). In the warmer climates, the absolute comfort values for individuals are 5–7°F (3–4°C) higher than for those in the cooler climates.

When humans are exposed to warm environments, the first physiological response is dilation of blood vessels, which increases the flow of blood near the skin. The next response occurs through sweating, panting, and evaporative cooling. Since individuals differ in their physiological responses to environmental stimuli, it is difficult to develop a heat stress index based solely on meteorological variables. Nevertheless, several useful indices have been developed.

Several indices describe comfort sensations as functions of ambient temperatures and humidities. These include the humiture index, the humidex, and the temperature-humidity index (THI). The THI value is computed from Eqs. (2), using wet- (T_w)

$$\text{THI} = 0.4(T_d + T_w) + 15 \quad [\text{for } T_d, T_w \text{ in } °F] \quad (2a)$$

$$\text{THI} = 0.4(T_d + T_w) + 4.78 \quad [\text{for } T_d, T_w \text{ in } °C] \quad (2b)$$

and dry-bulb (T_d) temperatures measured with a psychrometer. *See* PSYCHROMETER.

Only a few people will be comfortable when THI = 53°F (21°C) or less, and almost everyone will be uncomfortable when THI = 80°F (26.5°C). When THI exceeds 91°F (33°C), heat stroke leading to death may occur. Under exertion, even at lower THI values, panting, high pulse rate, and cardiopulmonary symptoms may develop. Indices based solely on temperature and humidity data are applicable for buildings and other confined conditions where wind and solar radiation loads are at low levels.

Since wind moves body heat away and increases the evaporation from a person, it should be accounted for in developing comfort indices describing the outdoor environment. One such index, used for many years by heating and ventilating engineers, is the effective temperature (see **illustration**). People will feel uncomfortable at effective temperatures above 81°F (27°C) or below 57°F (15°C); between 63°F (17°C) and 77°F (25°C) they will feel comfortable.

Statistics for the United States show increased mortality during summer heat waves. Older persons living in non-air-conditioned quarters are particularly afflicted. Individuals with congestive heart disease are especially endangered by heat. Victims of multiple sclerosis also find their symptoms aggravated by hot atmospheric environments.

The use of certain drugs is inadvisable during hot weather. For example, phenothiazines, which include several major tranquilizers, reduce the ability to sweat and can cause heat stroke. The use of diuretics should be restricted, and drugs used to alleviate Parkinson's disease must be avoided during hot periods. Many drugs that inhibit sweating have been banned from use in the tropics. Coffee or caffeine-containing preparations should also be avoided because they constrict the peripheral blood vessels. The use of fans, shade, and especially air conditioning can reduce the acute troubles caused by excessive heat. *See* AIR CONDITIONING.

Weather sensitivity. Both physiological and psychological responses to weather changes (meteorotropisms) are widespread and generally have their origin in some bodily impairment. Reactions to weather changes commonly occur in anomalous skin tissue such as scars and corns, changes in atmospheric moisture cause differential hygroscopic expansion and contraction between healthy and abnormal skin, leading to pain. Sufferers from rheumatoid arthritis are commonly affected by weather changes; both pain and swelling of affected joints have been noted with increased atmospheric humidity. Sudden cooling can also trigger such symptoms. Clinical tests have shown that in these individuals the heat regulatory mechanism does not function well, but the underlying cause is not understood.

Weather is a significant factor in asthma attacks. Asthma as an allergic reaction may, in rare cases, be directly provoked by sudden changes in temperature that occur after passage of a cold front. Often, however, the weather effect is indirect, and attacks are caused by airborne allergens, such as air pollutants and pollen. An even more indirect relationship exists for asthma attacks in autumn, which often seem to be related to an early outbreak of cold air. This cold air initiates home or office heating, and dormant dust or fungi from registers and radiators are convected into rooms, irritating allergic persons. *See* ALLERGY; ASTHMA.

A variety of psychological effects have also been attributed to heat. They are vaguely described as lassitude, decrease in mental and physical performance, and increased irritability. Similar reactions to weather have been described for domestic animals, particularly dogs, hence hot, humid days are sometimes known as dog days.

Many of the physiological or pathological reactions to weather in the middle and higher latitudes have been related to a typical sequence of weather events that are common in the cold season. In such a sequence there are six weather phases: (1) high pressure: clear sunny sky, light winds, cool; (2) falling pressure: few clouds, dry moderate winds, solar warming; (3) falling pressure: increasing cloudiness; (4) passage of warm front: rain (or snow in winter), rising temperatures, fresh winds, occasional fog, high humidity; (5) passage of cold front: precipitation, sharp drop in temperature, rapidly rising pressure, brisk winds; (6) high pressure, cool temperature, low humidity. A weather map can be used to show these phases with specific notations for each phase. Weather phase 4, the warm front passage, is the one most frequently related to meteorotropic symptoms. It also has an apparent relation to the frequency of industrial accidents and suicides. In schools, disciplinary infractions are higher and students' test scores are lower. In phases 4 and 5, weather elements change most rapidly, and there is an increase in cardiovascular deaths; also, phase 5 has been associated with the initiation of labor at the end of pregnancies. *See* WEATHER MAP.

There is speculation concerning biological effects of small atmospheric ions that are continuously created by cosmic radiation and by decay of natural radioactive substances. Their lifetime is very short, and they either recombine or attach themselves to larger aerosols, most of which in settled regions are air pollutants. These ions can cause allergic reactions. *See* AIR POLLUTION.

Meteorological and seasonal changes in natural illumination have a major influence on animals. Photoperiodicity is widespread. The daily cycle of illu-

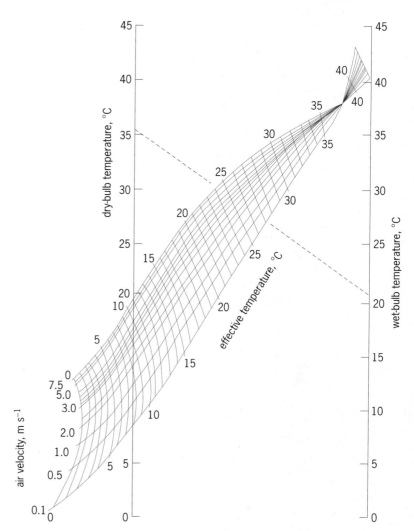

Chart of the effective temperature as a function of air velocity and wet-bulb and dry-bulb temperatures $°F = (°C × 1.8) + 32°$; 1 m s^{-1} = 0.21 mi/h.

mination triggers the feeding cycle in many species, especially birds. In insectivores the feeding cycle may result from the activities of the insects, which themselves show temperature-influenced cycles of animation. Bird migration may be initiated by light changes, but temperature changes and availability of food are also involved. In the process of migration, especially over long distances, birds have learned to take advantage of prevailing wind patterns. In humans, light deprivation, as is common in the cold weather season in higher latitudes, is suspected as a cause of depression. Exposure to high-intensity light for several hours has been found to be an effective means of treating this depression. *See* AFFECTIVE DISORDERS; MIGRATORY BEHAVIOR; PHOTOPERIODISM.

Ultraviolet radiation. The atmosphere forms a protective shield from cosmic radiation. This energetic, lethal, shortwave radiation is absorbed in the highest layers of the atmosphere and is involved in the formation of ozone. Fortunately, ozone absorbs all ultraviolet radiation less than about 290 nanometers wavelength and much of the radiation between 290 and 320 nm, known as UV-B radiation, which causes sunburn and with repeated lengthy exposure can lead to skin cancer. Solar radiation in the 320–400-

nm range, known as UV-A, is less dangerous, but it can produce sunburn. All ultraviolet radiation can produce thickening and aging of the skin. Exposure of the human eye to ultraviolet radiation, especially UV-B, can lead to cataracts and lesions of the cornea and retina. Discovery of an ozone hole over the polar regions led to widespread concern that manufactured chemicals such as the chlorofluoro-hydrocarbons are interacting with the ozone and reducing the protective ozone shield, thereby permitting increasing amounts of ultraviolet radiation to reach the Earth's surface. *See* RADIATION INJURY (BIOLOGY); ULTRAVIOLET RADIATION (BIOLOGY).

Altitude. With an increase in altitude there is a decrease in the amount of oxygen, and individuals who are accustomed to the amount of oxygen in the air near sea level may suffer from hypoxia (lack of oxygen) at higher elevations, especially upon exertion. The result may be mountain or altitude sickness. For this reason, cabins of high-flying aircraft are pressurized. However, humans and animals can become acclimatized to higher elevations through changes in the cardiopulmonary system. This acclimatization is accomplished by large increases in the oxygen-carrying red blood corpuscles and in lung alveoli. *See* HYPOXIA.

Weather and animals. Wild animals have adapted to their environment through natural selection, but domesticated animals, because of their selective breeding and confinement, are often poorly adapted. The maintenance of a proper body temperature and an acceptable water status is critical for the growth, production, and survival of animals. Production of meat, eggs, and milk by farm animals is often closely linked to weather conditions. There has been considerable research to determine the response of animals to their atmospheric environment, and to develop management practices to help minimize losses and maximize production.

Many breeds of domesticated animals are adapted to temperate climates and do not do well under hot, humid conditions. Not only does production fall under hot, humid conditions, but care must be taken to prevent death. Animals should be placed where air circulates freely, where water is readily available, and where shade is provided. In many cases, animals are kept in confined conditions where temperature, humidity, and ventilation are controlled. In other instances, they may be in partially confined conditions, or the microclimate may be beneficially modified. *See* AGRICULTURAL BUILDINGS; AGRICULTURAL SCIENCE (ANIMAL).

Adaptation and acclimatization. Humans and animals often exhibit a remarkable ability to adapt to harsh or rapidly changing environmental conditions. An obvious means of adaptation is to move to areas where environmental conditions are less severe, examples are birds and certain animals that migrate seasonally, animals that burrow into the ground, and animals that move to shade or sunshine depending on weather conditions. Animals can acclimatize to heat and cold. The acclimatization process is generally complete within 2–3 weeks of exposure to the stress-

ful conditions. For example, in hot climates heat regulation is improved by the induction of sweating at a lower internal body temperature and by the increasing of sweating rates. The acclimatization to cold climates is accomplished by increase in the metabolic rate, by improvement in the insulating properties of the skin, and by the constriction of blood vessels to reduce the flow of blood to the surface. *See* ADAPTATION (BIOLOGY); BURROWING ANIMALS.

Weather and insects. Weather plays a major role in the development and movement of insects. Winds carries some insects long distances. The primary control of body temperature by insects is accomplished through behavioral responses. They regulate their thermal balance by moving to and from the sunshine, by burrowing, by flying or gliding, or by attaching themselves to objects such as rocks or vegetation. Temperature plays a significant role in determining the rate of growth and development of insects. The timing of transitions from one stage of growth to another is determined in large measure by the thermal environment. Temperature is the most important environmental variable that influences insect development, but humidity and moisture content also play a role. *See* INSECT PHYSIOLOGY.

Weather and flora. Unlike humans and animals, plants cannot move from one location to another; therefore, they must adapt genetically to their atmospheric environment. Plants are often characteristic for their climatic zone, such as palms in the subtropics and birches or firs in regions with cold winters. Whole systems of climatic classification are based on the native floras. *See* ALTITUDINAL VEGETATION ZONES; PLANT GEOGRAPHY.

In plants, photosynthesis, respiration, and transpiration are governed by the atmospheric environment. In these processes, water is usually limiting, and so the ratio of rainfall to evapotranspiration is a governing factor in plant development. In addition, growth requires certain soil and air threshold temperatures; soil temperature and moisture regulate seed germination; and photosynthetic rates are also governed by light and temperature. *See* HYDROMETEOROLOGY; PHOTOSYNTHESIS; PLANT GROWTH; PLANT RESPIRATION.

In responding to their environment, plants experience various cycles, so that at certain levels of light and temperature, specific growth responses such as leaving, flowering, and fruit development take place. These seasonal phases can be disrupted by adverse weather conditions, such as drought and frosts. *See* COLD HARDINESS (PLANT); VERNALIZATION.

Agriculture has adopted many management practices to help modify microclimatic conditions to improve the atmospheric environment to enhance crop production. For example, irrigation is used to supplement natural precipitation; windbreaks are established to reduce mechanical damage to plants, to improve plant-water relations, and to increase plant photosynthesis; mulches are used to retard soil evaporation, thereby making more water available to plants and plastic mulches warm soils more rapidly in the spring. Numerous frost protection practices have been developed. *See* AGRICULTURAL METEOROL-OGY; ECOLOGY; IRRIGATION (AGRICULTURE); METEO-ROLOGY.   Blaine L. Blad; H. E. Landsberg

Bibliography. G. S. Campbell, *An Introduction to Environmental Biophysics*, 2d ed., 1998; G. E. Folk, *Introduction to Environmental Physiology*, 2d ed., 1974; D. M. Gates, *Biophysical Ecology*, 1980; N. J. Rosenberg, B. L. Blad, and S. B. Verma, *Micro-climate: The Biological Environment*, 1983; S. W. Tromp, *Biometeorology*, 1980.

Biometrics

The application of mathematical and statistical methods to describe and analyze data concerning the variation of biological characteristics obtained from either observation or experiment. The concept of a population and the samples derived from it are discussed in this article.

A population, or "universe," is a technical term meaning a collection of events or objects with certain characteristics. A population may be finite or infinite. It may exist in physical form or may be abstract and conceptual. Examples of a population are income of all families in the United States, height of all college males, outcome of throwing a die an infinitely large number of times, and all possible offspring of a specified type of mating. The population must be precisely identified and defined in any study.

An observation technically means recording the actual value of the characteristic of a member, or element, of the population under investigation. Such a value is an observed value. A complete recording of the values of all the members of a (finite) population is called a census, while a partial recording consisting of only a limited number of observations (for example, n) is called a sample. A sample may be large (n large) or small (n small). In most practical cases, a complete examination of a population is unattainable, and one must be satisfied with the study of a limited number of observations based on one or more samples. From any specified population, many samples can be drawn which, although from the same population, may consist of quite different observed values. These actually observed sets of values are usually referred to as data.

Random sample refers to a sample wherein each member is drawn at random from a population. At random means the complete lack of any systematic selection scheme in drawing members of the samples. In particular, members of a sample are not chosen with reference a priori to their values for each characteristic. Various mechanical devices and tables of random numbers have been prepared to facilitate random sampling. Such a sample is most important in theory and practice because long-range properties of such samples, based on the totality of all possible samples, are known and may be described by mathematical expressions.

Sample size is the number n of observations in a sample. Under a random sampling scheme, each sample would be more or less different from other similarly drawn samples. As sample sizes increase, however, the random variation from sample to sample decreases, and the sample itself resembles the population more and more. Size, therefore, is an important feature of a sample. It determines essentially the reliability or degree of resemblance between the sample and the population.

Parameter and statistics. If y is the measurement of a characteristic (height, weight, age, income, blood pressure, or some other quantitative trait) of an individual member, and there are n such values in a sample, then the value, as in Eq. (1), is called the

$$\bar{y} = (y_1 + \cdots + y_n)/n = \Sigma y/n \qquad (1)$$

arithmetic mean of the sample. The mean value of y for the entire population is denoted by $\mu = E(y)$, which is a fixed value. $E(y)$ is read as the expected value of y. It can be said that μ is a parameter of the population and $\bar{y}$ is an estimate of μ. As a general term, any value calculated from the n observations of a sample is called a statistic. The arithmetic mean illustrates simply the meaning and relationship between a population parameter and a sample statistic. If the $\bar{y}$ is calculated from n random observations, then the long-range average value of $\bar{y}$ from a large number of such samples is equal to the population mean μ. Therefore, one can state that $e(\bar{y}) = \mu$. In such a case, $\bar{y}$ is an unbiased estimate of μ. Various other parameters of a population may be defined, and the corresponding sample estimates may be constructed. Next to the mean, the most important parameter is variance.

Variance and its estimates. With each y value is associated a value $y - \mu$, known as the deviation from the mean. Population variance σ^2 is defined as the average value (expected value) of the squared deviations in the population, as shown by Eq. (2), where

$$\sigma^2 = E[(y - \mu)^2] \qquad (2)$$

E is "expectation of $\ldots$," y is a measurement of a characteristic, and μ is mean value of y. Since the magnitude of σ^2 depends on the magnitude of the deviations $y - \mu$, variance is employed as a measure of variability or dispersion of the y values about their mean. In usual cases, when the true population mean μ is unknown, the value of σ^2 may be estimated by the statistic, sample variance, as in Eq. (3).

$$s^2 = \frac{\Sigma(y - \bar{y})^2}{n - 1} \qquad (3)$$

The numerator $\Sigma(y - \bar{y})^2$ is the sum of squares of deviations from the sample mean. The estimate is so constructed that the long-range average value of s^2 from repeated random sampling is equal to the population variance σ^2; namely, $E(s^2) = \sigma^2$. Thus, s^2 is an unbiased estimate of σ^2. The square root of a variance is called the standard deviation.

Degrees of freedom. The denominator of s^2 is $n-1$. Although there are n independently observed ys in the sample, the sum of squares in the numerator is calculated from the sample mean $\bar{y}$, not from the fixed population mean μ. Thus, one constant has been fitted to the data before the deviations can be obtained. This fitting causes the loss of 1 degree of freedom for estimating the errors so that the sum of squares has only $(n-1)$ degrees of freedom. Hence, the above expression for s^2. Generally, each linear restriction on the observed values takes up one degree of freedom. The estimate of a variance is always a certain sum of squares divided by its corresponding degree of freedom.

Variance of sample mean. The sample mean varies from sample to sample, although it does not vary as such as the single ys. For random samples of n observations each, the variate $\bar{y}$ has a mean μ (as stated previously) and the variance of $\bar{y}$ is expressed by Eq. (4), or more simply as Eq. (5). The variance of $\bar{y}$ is only $1/n$ of

$$E[(\bar{y}-\mu)^2] = \sigma_{\bar{y}}^2 = \sigma^2/n \tag{4}$$

$$\sigma_{\bar{y}} = \sigma/\sqrt{n} \tag{5}$$

the variance for single values. When n is large, the sampling variance of $\bar{y}$ is small, so that the sample mean is close to the population mean.

Data presentation and description. When the amount of data is large, whether from a large sample or an entire population, it is convenient to arrange such data into tabular form to facilitate grasping the salient features of the data. This is done by collecting observations of more or less the same value into one class, and the result is a frequency table.

Frequency table. In **Table 1** the measurements of height of 400 college males are grouped into nine classes. There are 12 individuals with height between 61 and 63 in., which are one set of class limits. The width of a class, known as the class interval, is 2 in. The number of individuals in a class is called the frequency of the class. The sum of all the class frequencies is the total number of observations: $\Sigma f = n$. The fraction f/n is the relative frequency. Thus, for the 61–63 class, the relative frequency is $12/400 = 0.030$, or 3% of the total observations. Relative frequencies always add up to unity of 100%. In condensing the 400 single observations into a compact frequency table, some of the details of individual measurements are lost, but a quick recognition of the distribution of height is gained. In practical calculations, the height of the f students in a class is taken to be the midpoint of that class. The mean and standard deviation are then calculated by using Eqs. (6), (7), and (8). The standard error of the sam-

$$\bar{y} = \frac{1}{n}\Sigma fy = 67.50 \text{ in.} \tag{6}$$

$$s^2 = \frac{1}{n}\Sigma f(y-\bar{y})^2 = \frac{1}{n}(\Sigma fy^2) - \bar{y}^2 = 7.07 \text{ in.}^2 \tag{7}$$

$$s = \sqrt{7.07} = 2.66 \text{ in.} \tag{8}$$

TABLE 1. Frequency table

Class limits, in.	Midpoint, y	Frequency, f	Relative frequency, f/n
59–61	60	4	0.010
61–63	62	12	0.030
63–65	64	50	0.125
65–67	66	102	0.255
67–69	68	120	0.300
69–71	70	78	0.195
71–73	72	28	0.070
73–75	74	4	0.010
75–77	76	2	0.005
Total		400	1.000

ple mean from $n = 400$ observations is $s_{\bar{y}} = s/\sqrt{n} = 2.66/20 = 0.133$ in. In calculating s^2 in this example, n is used for simplicity instead of the correct $n - 1$, since n is large and it makes little difference whether 400 or 399 is being employed.

Histogram and frequency polygon. A frequency table may be converted into a diagram for easy visual inspection of the distribution. The diagram commonly used is a series of rectangles of equal width corresponding to the equal class intervals and height proportional to the class frequency or relative frequency. Such a series of rectangles is called a histogram (**Fig. 1**). If all individuals in a class are assumed to have the same midpoint value, these midpoints may be plotted against their corresponding frequencies. These points lie in the middle at the top of the rectangles. Two adjacent points may be connected by a straight line. The resulting series of straight lines is called a frequency polygon. If the variate, such as height, takes only certain discrete values, a bar or solid column may be erected at each value with the height

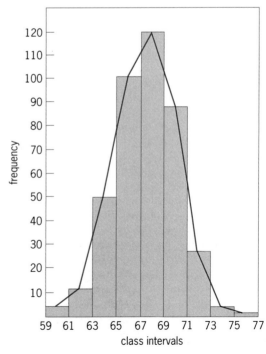

Fig. 1. Histogram and frequency polygon.

proportional to the frequency. The result is a bar graph. Even in such a case, one may still use the frequency polygon to help trace the change in frequency from class to class.

Frequency curve. Although the data are condensed into a frequency table which consists of a limited number of classes with arbitrary class limits, it is recognized that such a variate as height really changes continuously and may assume any value within a certain range. If there are a very large number of observations (theoretically, infinitely large) and the class interval becomes infinitely narrow, the frequency polygon will approach a smooth frequency curve as a limit (**Fig. 2**). Therefore, in all theoretical work dealing with a continuous variate, the distribution (height, for example) in the entire population will be described by a mathematical expression which, when plotted, will assume the shape of the frequency curve. Such a mathematical expression is called the density function. The relative frequency between two values a and b is the area under the frequency curve. This relative frequency is bounded by the ordinates $y = a$ and $y = b$.

Mode and median. The mode is the value of the variate at which the frequency is the highest, that is, the most frequently occurring value of the variate. For example, for the height of the college male students the modal value is 68 in., taken as the midpoint of the modal class 67–69 in. For a continuous distribution, the modal value is that at which the frequency curve reaches its peak. If there is one peak in the frequency curve, the distribution is said to be unimodal. If there are two peaks, the distribution is bimodal. The median is such a value in the variate that half of the observations are greater and half are smaller than it. Thus, the median height in the example is approximately 67.53 in., assuming that the 120 individuals are uniformly distributed in the 67–69 class and applying linear interpolation. Then 200 students are taller and 200 students are shorter than 67.53 in. For a continuous distribution, the vertical line erected at the median divides the entire area under the frequency curve into two equal halves. The ratio of standard deviation to mean is called the coefficient of variability (c.v.).

Normal distribution. Normal distribution refers to a symmetrical bell-shaped frequency distribution (**Fig. 3**). Many distributions in nature are approximately of the normal shape. It may be shown that if a variate y, such as height, is influenced by a large number of factors, each exerting independently a small effect on y, and if these effects are additive, the resulting distribution of y will approach the normal shape as a limit. If a large number of measurements are taken repeatedly of an object, these measurements will not be identical no matter how carefully taken, but will assume more or less varying values which are, again, normally distributed. For this reason, the normal distribution is also known as the distribution of errors. Large deviations are comparatively few, while small deviations may occur quite frequently. It is the most useful distribution in both theoretical and practical statistics, for, in many cases, a normal pop-

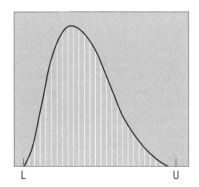

Fig. 2. Frequency curve. L and U represent the lower and upper limits of the range of values.

ulation may be assumed; and when the population is not normal, the statistics calculated from repeated random samples (sampling distribution) assume approximately the normal form. A normal distribution has two parameters: the mean μ and the variance σ^2 (or standard deviation σ). When these two values are specified, the normal curve is uniquely determined. In terms of standardized units, the mean is zero and variance is unity whatever the actual values of μ and σ^2 are. Since the normal distribution is symmetrical, mean = mode = median; the area under the normal curve between the mean μ and $\mu + \sigma$ is approximately 0.34, and so the relative frequency of the y values within the interval $\mu \pm \sigma$ is approximately 0.68, or 68%. At the y values $\mu \pm \sigma$, the curve twists from a concave to a convex one. The relative frequency within the interval $\mu \pm 1.96\sigma$ (slightly less than 2σ on either side of the mean) is 0.95, and thus, that outside the same interval is 0.05 with 0.025 under each tail. The areas or relative frequencies of the normal distribution have been tabulated in various ways, but always with the standardized unit as the independent variable.

The sample mean $\bar{y}$ from n observations is almost normally distributed, even though the y population may not be normal itself. This is true especially when the population is unimodal, and the size of the sample is moderately large. The facts that $E(\bar{y}) = \mu$ and $\sigma_{\bar{y}}^2 = \sigma^2/n$ make possible certain statements about the population mean. The normal deviate for the

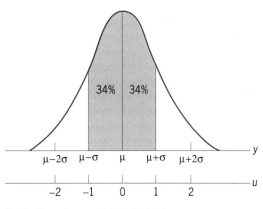

Fig. 3. Normal, symmetrical distribution.

variate $\bar{y}$ (not y) is expressed by Eq. (9). Then the

$$u = \frac{\bar{y} - \mu}{\sigma_{\bar{y}}} \qquad (9)$$

probability is 0.95 that inequality (10) holds. The inequality may be written as (11), in which the limits

$$-1.96 < \frac{\bar{y} - \mu}{\sqrt{\sigma^2/n}} < +1.96 \qquad (10)$$

$$\bar{y} - 1.96\sqrt{\sigma^2/n} < \mu < \bar{y} + 1.96\sqrt{\sigma^2/n} \qquad (11)$$

vary from sample to sample while the central item μ remains constant. In repeated sampling, these varying limits will "catch" or cover the population mean 95% of the time. This gives an interval estimate of μ. For practical calculation, s^2 may be substituted for σ^2. The values $\bar{y} \pm 1.96; \sigma^{\bar{y}}$ are called the 95% confidence limits, and the width between these two limits is called the 95% confidence interval. The 95% confidence in this example is arbitrary. Other degrees of confidence may be chosen.

Test of hypothesis. This is also known as a test of significance. Assume that $\bar{y}$ and s^2 have been calculated from a moderately large sample and that, instead of using $\bar{y}$ as an estimate of the population mean, one may want to test the hypothesis that the population mean is equal to a certain fixed value, for example, m. If m is indeed the population mean, then the normal deviate for the variate $\bar{y}$ is calculated from Eq. (12), where s^2 may be substituted for σ^2 in

$$u = \frac{\bar{y} - m}{\sqrt{\sigma^2/n}} \qquad (12)$$

practical calculations for large samples. The probability that this u value will lie between -1.96 and 1.96 is 0.95 and that it will lie outside this interval is $\alpha = 0.05$, if m is the true population mean. The rule of testing is that if $|u| > 1.96$, it is regarded as an unusual phenomenon hardly consistent with the hypothesis. In such an event, the hypothesis is abandoned and the difference $\bar{y} - m$ is said to be statistically at the $\alpha = 5\%$ significance level. Instead of the normal deviate 1.96 and the corresponding probability of 0.05, used as an example here, other significance levels may be chosen. The testing of a hypothesis results in either its acceptance or rejection. In so doing, either a type I or a type II error may be committed.

Type I and type II errors. If $|u| > 1.96$ is employed as the criterion to reject the hypothesis $\mu = m$ which happens to be true, the probability of this wrong rejection is $\alpha = 0.05$. This type of error is called the type I error. It is the error of attribution of false significance. On the other hand, the hypothesis itself may be untrue. Suppose that the true mean is M, and yet is is hypothesized that it is m. Ideally, the untrue hypothesis should be rejected. However, the distribution with mean M overlaps with the distribution with mean m, and the sample may well yield a value of u within the interval -1.96 and 1.96. In such a situation, the untrue hypothesis would not be rejected. This error is called type II error, the error

TABLE 2. Decision about hypothesis		
	Reject	Accept
Hypothesis $\mu = m$ true	Type I error	Correct conclusion
Hypothesis $\mu = m$ false	Correct conclusion	Type II error

of failure to detect significance. The probability of committing a type II error depends upon, among several other things, the value of M. The greater the difference between M and m, the less probability of committing the second type of error. The two types of errors cannot be committed at the same time. In any particular test, if significance is declared, only the risk of committing an error of type I is run; and if the hypothesis is retained, only the risk of committing an error of type II is run. With proper balancing of the two types of error in a long series of similar tests, the first kind of error is sometimes committed and the second kind of error committed other times, but one will be correct in rejecting the wrong hypothesis and accepting the right hypothesis most times. The increase of sample size can reduce both types of error (**Table 2**).

Difference between two means. Suppose that there are two independent samples of sizes s_1^2 and s_2^2. To determine if these two means can be considered significantly different, one sets up the hypothesis that the two population means are equal: $\mu_1 = \mu_2$. A hypothesis of this nature is called a null hypothesis, because it assumes the absence of differences. Now consider the new variate $d = \bar{y}_1 - \bar{y}_2$. If the null hypothesis is true, the expected value of d is shown by Eq. (13), and the variance of d is shown by Eq. (14). Hence,

$$E(\bar{y}_1) - E(\bar{y}_2) = \mu_1 - \mu_2 = 0 \qquad (13)$$

$$\sigma_d^2 = \sigma_{y1}^2 + \sigma_{y2}^2 = \frac{\sigma_1^2}{n_1} + \frac{\sigma_2^2}{n_2} \qquad (14)$$

the normal deviate for the variate d is represented by Eq. (15). The procedure of testing the significance

$$u = \frac{d}{\sqrt{\sigma_d^2}} = \frac{(\bar{y}_1 - \bar{y}_2)}{\sqrt{\sigma_1^2/n_1 + \sigma_2^2/n_2}} \qquad (15)$$

is the same as discussed previously except that the variate d is being considered and the particular hypothesis being tested is that its mean value is zero.

Student's t distribution. Since σ is unknown, s may be used in its place for large samples without introducing serious error. However, in small samples the value of s varies from sample to sample too much to be taken as a constant. Student's t is the ratio of a deviation to its varying sample s. In other words, it is a normal variate standardized in terms of the sample standard deviation. The distribution of t closely resembles that of u, being bell-shaped with zero mean, but is lower in the middle portion and higher in the two tail regions than the normal curve. The exact dispersion of the t distribution depends on the number of degrees of freedom, which is $n - 1$ for samples of size n. The areas under the t curve have been tabulated for various degrees of freedom at various significance levels.

Student's test. If the σ in a previous expression for u is replaced by the corresponding s, the resulting standardized unit is the t value, Eq. (16). To test the

$$t = \frac{(\bar{y} - m)}{\sqrt{s^2/n}} \tag{16}$$

hypothesis that the population mean is equal to m based on a sample of only $n = 14$ observations, where s^2 has 13 degrees of freedom, the absolute value of t has to be equal to or greater than 2.16 (instead of 1.96 for the u test) at the same $\alpha = 0.05$ significance level. Confidence intervals may be constructed in the same way as before, using the appropriate t value instead of the u value.

If the two population variances σ_1^2 and σ_2^2 are not equal, there is no simple method to test the significance of the difference $\bar{y}_1 - \bar{y}_2$ in comparing two sample means. If the two variances and the two sample sizes do not differ too much, it may be assumed that the population variances are equal, and a pooled estimate of the common variance from the two samples may be obtained by calculating Eq. (17). Then t can be expressed as Eq. (18), with degree of free-

$$s^2 = \frac{\Sigma(y_1 - \bar{y}_1)^2 + \Sigma(y_2 - \bar{y}_2)^2}{(n_1 - 1) + (n_2 - 1)} \tag{17}$$

$$t = \frac{(\bar{y}_1 - \bar{y}_2)}{s\sqrt{1/n_1 + 1/n_2}} \tag{18}$$

dom $= n_1 + n_2 - 2$. For example, if $n_1 = 15$ and $n_2 = 12$, so that the degree of freedom is 25, the absolute value of t has to be equal to or greater than 2.06 (instead of 1.96 for the u test) at the same $\alpha = 0.05$ significance level. In the special case where the observations of the two samples are paired, the n differences for the n pairs are then regarded as the n observations of one sample and the t value (with $n - 1$ degrees of freedom) may be calculated to test the null hypothesis that the true difference is zero. When the number of degrees of freedom is large, the t distribution becomes the u distribution.

Two-tail and one-tail tests. The examples given above for both u and t tests are two-tail tests because the significance of a difference is being tested, whether one is larger than the other or vice versa. If one is interested only in testing if $\bar{y}$ is greater than m, and uses $u = +1.645$ as the criterion, the probability of reaching a wrong rejection of the null hypothesis is $\alpha = 0.05$, which is the area under the right-hand tail of the normal curve. Testing the significance of difference in one direction only is called a one-tail test. Both types of tests are in common practice, depending upon the nature of the problem.

Analysis of variance. Analysis of variance is a method of comparing the differences between several sample means; it is a more general tool than the t test. This method is used most frequently in analyzing experimental data. Suppose there are k groups

(or k samples), and in the first group there are n_1 observations with mean $\bar{y}_1$; in the second, n_2 observations with mean $\bar{y}_2$; and so on, the total number of observations being $n_1 + \cdots + n_k = N$ with the general mean y. If the k populations from which the k samples are derived have the same variance, a pooled estimate of the common variance σ^2 from the k samples is given by Eq. (19), which has $N - k$

$$s^2 = \frac{\Sigma(y_1 - \bar{y}_1)^2 + \cdots + \Sigma(y_k - \bar{y}_k)^2}{(n_1 - 1) + \cdots + (n_k - 1)} \tag{19}$$

degrees of freedom. On the null hypothesis that the k population means are equal, another estimate of the common variance may be obtained from the k sample means by calculating the quantity shown in Eq. (20), which has $k - 1$ degrees of freedom. The

$$s_m^2 = \frac{n_1(\bar{y}_1 - \bar{y})^2 + \cdots + n_k(\bar{y}_k - \bar{y})^2}{k - 1} \tag{20}$$

sum of squares in the numerator of s^2 and s_m^2 add up to the total sum of squares for the N observations as a whole $\Sigma\Sigma(y - \bar{y})^2$; and so the degrees of freedom in the denominators are $(N - k) + (k - 1) = N - 1$. If the variates are normally distributed, the ratio of two independent estimates of the same variance has a sampling distribution known as the F or variance-ratio distribution. Thus, to test the null hypothesis that the k population means are equal, the ratio $F = s_m^2/s^2$ is calculated, and the table is consulted for the F value with $k - 1$ degrees of freedom for the numerator and $N - k$ degrees of freedom for the denominator. If the observed F is greater than the tabulated F, the null hypothesis is discarded, and the significance of the differences between the k means is assumed. When there are only two samples, the F test is equivalent to the t test, for $F = t^2$ in such a case.

Linear regression. Very frequently the variate y under investigation is influenced by another (sometimes uncontrollable) variate x. For example, the yield y of a crop may be influenced by the amount of rainfall x during the growing season. When the pairs of values (y, x) are plotted in rectangular coordinates, the points form a scatter diagram (**Fig. 4**). If these points show a linear trend, a straight line running among these points may be fitted to represent the trend. Such a line is called the linear regression line. The problem is how to draw that line other than freehand.

Method of least squares. This is a method for fitting a straight line to a series of points. For the given value $x = x_i$, the observed $y = y_i$, while the y value on the straight line is $y' = y_i'$. Then $d = y - y'$ is the vertical distance from the observed y to the y' on the straight line. The method of least squares requires that the straight line should be drawn such that $\Sigma d^2 = \Sigma(y - y')^2$ is as small as possible. The equation of the straight line is $y' = a + bx$, where a is the intercept on the y axis and b, the slope of the line, is known as the regression coefficient of y on

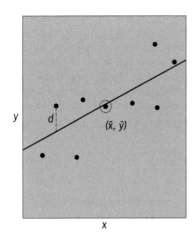

Fig. 4. Scatter diagram and linear regression.

x. The least-square solutions for a and b are derived from Eqs. (21) and (22), respectively. The regression

$$a = \bar{y} - b\bar{x} \qquad (21)$$

$$b = \frac{\Sigma(y - \bar{y})(x - \bar{x})}{\Sigma(x - \bar{x})^2} \qquad (22)$$

coefficient is in terms of the number of y units per x unit, for example 2 lb/in. This line passes through the central point $(\bar{y}, \bar{y})$.

Residual variation of y. Substituting these values of a and b in the straight-line equation, $y\prime$ is obtained. Since these $y\prime$ values are determined by the regression line, their variation is measured by $\Sigma(y\prime - \bar{y})^2$, with one degree of freedom accounted for by the variation of x. The deviation $d = y - y\prime$ from the regression line, the "residual," is regarded as the random error of y. Hence, the estimate of $\sigma^2 = \sigma^2_{y \cdot x}$ free of x influence is expressed as Eq. (23). For practical

$$s^2 = s^2_{y \cdot x} = \Sigma(y - y\prime)^2/(n-2) \qquad (23)$$

calculation, the individual $yy\prime$ values and the individual distances d need not be obtained, because of the relationship in Eq. (24).

$$\Sigma d^2 = \Sigma(y - y\prime)^2$$
$$= \Sigma(y - \bar{y})^2 - b^2\Sigma(x - \bar{x})^2 \qquad (24)$$

Significance test for b. The sampling variance of b is $\sigma^2/\Sigma(x - \bar{x})^2$. To test the hypothesis that the true regression coefficient is β, the expression shown in Eq. (25) may be calculated. This follows Student's t

$$t = \frac{b - \beta}{\sqrt{s^2/\Sigma(x - \bar{x})^2}} \qquad (25)$$

distribution with $n - 2$ degrees of freedom. To test the hypothesis that y is not linearly influenced by x, β is set equal to 0.

Analysis of covariance. This is a combined application of linear regression and an analysis of variance. Suppose that the effects of three fertilizers on corn yield y are studied. The significance of the treatment effects may be tested by the analysis of variance method. Now suppose that a complicating factor intervenes: the number of plants x, known as the concomitant variate in general, varies from plot to plot for reasons other than the treatments applied, so that the comparison of the yield between the three fertilizer groups may be partially blurred or distorted by the influence of x. To correct for the influences of x, the regression coefficient of y on x and the residual variation of y free from the influence of x are first found and then the F, or variance ratio, test is applied.

Correlation. A correlation problem considers the joint variation of two measurements, neither of which is restricted by the experimenter. Examples of correlation problems are studies of the relationship between school grades and IQ; yield and cornstalk height; and metabolism and blood pressure. Both variables are observed as they naturally occur, neither variable being set at prescribed levels. For n pairs of observed values (y, x), the quantity in Eq. (26) is defined as the correlation coefficient be-

$$r = r_{xy} = \frac{\Sigma(y - \bar{y})(x - \bar{x})}{\sqrt{\Sigma(y - \bar{y})^2 \cdot \Sigma(x - \bar{x})^2}} \qquad (26)$$

tween y and x. This value ranges from $+1$ to -1. If the points in the scatter diagram are close to a straight line, r will be close to $+1$ or -1, depending on the direction of the line. If the points are scattered without a linear trend, r will be close to zero. The r and b coefficients are related and always have the same sign. This may be expressed by Eqs. (27) and (28). The quantity $\Sigma(y - \bar{y})(x - \bar{x})/(n - 1) = s_{xy}$

$$b = r\frac{s_y}{s_x} \qquad (27)$$

$$r = b\frac{s_x}{s_y} \qquad (28)$$

is called the covariance of y and x. Thus, $r = s_{xy}/s_x s_y$ for a sample, and the population correlation is defined as $\rho = \sigma_{xy}/\sigma_x\sigma_y$. Testing the null hypothesis $\rho = 0$ is equivalent to testing $\beta = 0$, and the same t test may be used. Or, from the relation $\Sigma(y - y\prime)^2 = (1 - r^2)\Sigma(y - \bar{y})^2$, the test may be rewritten as Eq. (29). The definition of r, being symmetrical with

$$t = \frac{r}{\sqrt{(1 - r^2)/(n - 2)}} \qquad (29)$$

respect to y and x, measures the mutual association of the two variates. The interpretation of r is another problem. The existence of a significant r value does not imply a causal relationship between y and x. Both variates may be influenced by a common factor or factors omitted from consideration in this discussion.

Path coefficients. These are regression coefficients with respect to standardized variates. When y and x are standardized, the regression equation of y on x will be $y = p_{y-x}x + e$, where p_{y-x} is called the path coefficient from x to y. In this simple case, p_{y-x} is simply r_{yx}, since the latter is the standardized covariance. One application of the path method is the

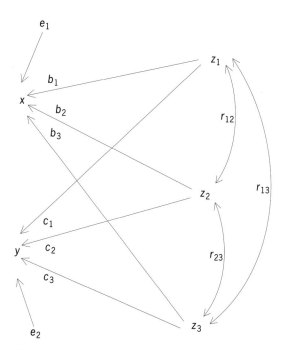

Fig. 5. Analysis of correlation of two variates, x and y, which are linear functions of the e's and z's. The b's and c's are path coefficients.

deduction of the chain property of correlation under certain simple conditions. Suppose that $y = p_1 x + e_1$ where $x = p_2 z + e_2$, the p's being path coefficients and the e's random errors. Substitution gives $y = p_1 p_2 z + e$. Hence, the path coefficient from z to y is the product of that from z to x and that from x to y. Also, $r_{yz} = r_{yx} r_{xz}$. Next, consider a standardized multiple regression equation $y = p_1 z_1 + p_2 z_2 + e$. Since every variate has unit variance, one obtains $1 = p^2_1 + p^2_2 + 2 p_1 p_2 r_{12} + \text{Var }(e)$. The term p_1 is called the coefficient of determination of z_1 on y, and so on. Another application is the analysis of correlation between two variates which are linear functions of other common variables. Suppose that in **Fig. 5**, x and y were expressed as Eqs. (30) and (31),

$$x = b_1 z_1 + b_2 z_2 + b_3 z_3 + e_1 \qquad (30)$$

$$y = c_1 z_1 + c_2 z_2 + c_3 z_3 + e_2 \qquad (31)$$

respectively, where the e's are uncorrelated with z's or among themselves, and the b's and c's are path coefficients. The total correlation can then be written as Eq. (32), where for brevity r_{12} is the correlation be-

$$\begin{aligned} r_{xy} = \text{cov}(x, y) = {}& b_1 c_1 + b_1 r_{12} c_2 + b_1 r_{13} c_3 \\ & + b_2 c_2 + b_2 r_{21} c_1 + b_2 r_{23} c_3 \\ & + b_3 c_3 + b_3 r_{31} c_1 + b_3 r_{32} c_2 \quad (32) \end{aligned}$$

tween z_1 and z_2 (cov indicates covariance). Thus the total correlation r_{yx} has been analyzed into nine components corresponding to the nine different ways x and y are connected in the diagram. A correlation line has two arrowheads and can be used in both directions. When the common causes (z_1, z_2, z_3) are uncorrelated, $r_{xy} = b_1 c_1 + b_2 c_2 + b_3 c_3$. The general theorem is that the total correlation between two variates is the sum of all paths by which they are connected. To apply the method of path coefficients in practical problems the relationship of the variates must be specified prior to the evaluation of the various paths. The path method has been highly successful in certain types of genetical problems where the causal relationship is known. *See* POPULATION GENETICS.

Binomial population and sampling. In biological and medical research, variates are frequently dealt with that fall into either of two categories, for example, alive or dead, ill or well, male or female, and, generally, with or without a certain trait. This is known as a binomial variate. A complete description of a binomial population requires only one parameter, such as the proportion P of individuals with the trait; for then the proportion of those without the trait is $Q = 1 - P$. The statistical device of handling such a variate is to let $y = 1$ for individuals with the trait, and $y = 0$ for those without it. Then the population mean is $\mu = P \times 1 + Q \times 0 = P$, and the population variance is $\sigma^2 = P(1 - \mu)^2 + Q(0 - \mu)^2 = P(1 - P) = PQ$.

If a random sample of n observations is taken from a binomial population, the observations will take the form $y = 0, 1, 1, 0, 1, 0, 0, 0, 1, \ldots$. The sample total is a, the number of ones in the sample, and the sample mean is $\bar{y} = a/n = p$. The variance of $\bar{y}$ is σ^2/n, which may be estimated by pq/n. When n is large, the sampling distribution of $\bar{y}$ is nearly normal if P is not close to zero or unity. In determining how large a sample is "large," the usual working rule is that nP and nQ should be greater than 5, so the largeness of a sample depends on both n and P. For large samples, the test of significance follows the general procedure of the normal test. For example, to test the hypothesis that the population mean is P, Eq. (33) is used.

$$u = \frac{p - P}{\sqrt{PQ/n}} \qquad (33)$$

The u test is appropriate here because the hypothesis of mean P implies the population variance PQ.

Suppose that there are two samples. The observed results are $a/n_1 = p_1$ for the first sample and $b/n_2 = p_2$ for the second. The null hypothesis $P_1 = P_2$ implies equal variance for the two populations, and the pooled estimate of the common variance is pq, where p equals the value of Eq. (34) and repre-

$$p = \frac{a + b}{n_1 + n_2} \qquad (34)$$

sents the overall proportion from the two samples. Then the null hypothesis ($P_1 = P_2$) may be tested by calculating the normal deviate, Eq. (35). On the

$$u = \frac{p_1 - p_2}{\sqrt{pq(1/n_1 + 1/n_2)}} \qquad (35)$$

other hand, if the hypothesis to be tested is $P_1 - P_2 = D$, then the u test should be modified, Eq. (36),

$$u = \frac{(p_1 - p_2) - D}{\sqrt{p_1 q_1/n_1 + p_2 q_2/n_2}} \qquad (36)$$

since the two populations with different mean values necessarily have different variances.

For small samples from a binomial population, the sampling distribution is given by the expansion of $(P + Q)^n$. The exact probabilities of obtaining certain sampling results may be thus calculated. The values of these probabilities have been extensively tabulated for various values of P and n.

Poisson distribution. If P of a binomial population is very small, then the occurrence of a member with the trait is considered a rare event. A rare event can be observed only in a very large sample. If n is so large that $nP = m$ is some finite value, then the sampling distribution is given by the expansion of e^m in powers of m, each term being divided by e^m so that the total probability is unity:

$$e^{-m} \left\{ 1, m, \frac{m^2}{2!}, \frac{m^3}{3!}, \cdots \right\}$$

Many empirical observations of natural and experimental events conform with this distribution. The mean number of events is m and its variance is also m. When m is 5 or less, the distribution is skewed, but when it is larger, it becomes more symmetrical. In some fields of application, if the observed number of events is a, $\sqrt{a}$ is taken as the standard error of the observed number.

Chi-square test. The quantity χ^2 is the sum of several independent squared normal deviates. In the analysis of frequency data, the χ^2 test is a generalization of the previous test for binomial data in two respects. (1) It extends to a multinomial population where each observation may fall into one of several classes. (2) It furnishes a comparison between several samples instead of only two. The χ^2, as a generalization of u, is analogous to F as a generalization of t.

Calculation. The calculation of χ^2 for testing the goodness of fit may be illustrated as shown in **Table 3**. According to a certain genetic theory, the breeding should yield 9/16 red, 6/16 sandy, 1/16 white. To test this theory, the number of pigs is divided into three classes in the proportions 9:6:1. Then the value of χ^2 is as shown in Eq. (37). If there

$$\chi^2 = \sum \frac{(f - f')^2}{f'}$$
$$= \frac{25}{63} + \frac{49}{42} + \frac{4}{7} = 2.135 \qquad (37)$$

are k classes, the χ^2 has $k - 1$ degrees of freedom because the total number of observations is the same for the two sets of frequencies. In this example, de-

TABLE 3. Data for χ^2 calculation

Color of pig	Observed number, f	Expected number, f'	Difference, $f - f'$
Red	58	63	−5
Sandy	49	42	7
White	5	7	−2
Total	112	112	0

TABLE 4. Contingency table

Category	Inoculated	Not inoculated	Total
Dead	a	b	$a + b$
Alive	c	d	$c + d$
Total	$a + c$ $= n_1$	$b + d$ $= n_2$	$a + b + c + d$ $= N$

grees of freedom $= 3 - 1 = 2$. If the genetic hypothesis is true, the probability that the χ^2 with two degrees of freedom should exceed 5.99 (read from χ^2 table) is 0.05. The statistical reasoning for the test of significance is the same as before. Since the χ^2 in question is smaller than 5.99, the hypothesis is retained, the observed results not being contradictory to the genetic theory. The χ^2 test is a one-tail test. It does not prove that the theory is the correct one. It is conceivable that the observed results are also consistent with some other hypothesis. However, as the class frequencies become larger, the test becomes more discriminating. When an expected class frequency is 5 or less, the χ^2 test is not applicable, and a more exact method, if available, should be employed. Several small classes may be pooled to form one larger class.

Contingency table (2 × 2). If the observed frequencies are classified dichotomously according to two different characteristics simultaneously, as exemplified by the fourfold **Table 4**, it may often be desirable to know if the two characteristics are independent of each other. If the characteristics are independent, the proportions of inoculated and not inoculated should be the same among the dead and the alive, or, stated alternatively, the proportions of dead and alive should be the same among those inoculated and those not inoculated. In such a case, the expected frequency in the inoculated dead cell should be $a' = (a + b) \times (a + c)/N$, and so on. Then $\chi^2 = (a - s')^2/a' - \cdots$ which simplifies to $\chi^2 = N(ad - bc)^2/(a + b)(c + d)(a + c)(b + d)$. Since the expected frequencies are calculated on the basis of the marginal totals, this χ^2 has only one degree of freedom. At the 0.05 significance level and for 1 degree of freedom the critical value is $\chi^2 = u^2 = (1.96)^2 = 3.84$. The χ^2 test for independence in a 2 × 2 table is equivalent to the u test for the hypothesis $P_1 = P_2$ for two binomial samples.

The test for independence may be extended to contingency tables of any size, for example m rows times k columns. The expected frequency of the cell in the third row and the second column, for example, is equal to third row total times second column total over the grand total. The χ^2 may then be calculated in the usual manner. It has $(m - 1) - (k - 1)$ degrees of freedom. For a 2 × k table, the χ^2 test is equivalent to testing the hypothesis that the means of the k binomial populations are equal.

Maximum likelihood method. There are many methods of estimating a parameter which underlies the probability of an event. The most efficient method

TABLE 5. Estimation by maximum likelihood method		
Category	Probability	Observed number of occurrences
1st trial success; no 2d trial	p	a
1st trial failure; 2d success	qp	b
1st and 2d trials failure	q^2	c
Total	1	n

of estimating is known as the maximum likelihood method, the principle of which may be illustrated by the following example.

Suppose that p is the (unknown) probability of success (and $q = 1 - p$) in a trial (for example, hitting a ball, recovery from an illness, or germination of a seed), and that the individual is allowed a second trial if the first one is a failure. The observed frequencies for the three possible outcomes are a, b, c, as shown in **Table 5**. The principle of maximum likelihood says that the value of p should be so chosen that the probability of observing such a set of frequencies is a maximum. The probability of observing such a set of occurrences (Table 5) is expressed as Eq. (38).

$$P(S) = \text{const}(p)^a (qp)^b (q^2)^c \qquad (38)$$

This expression without the constant is called "likelihood," the logarithm of which is calculated from Eqs. (39a) and (39b).

$$L = (a + b)\log p + (b + 2c)\log q \qquad (39a)$$

$$\frac{dL}{dp} = \frac{a + b}{p} - \frac{b + 2c}{q} \qquad (39b)$$

The value of p that maximizes the likelihood (and hence its logarithm L) is given by the solution of the equation $dL/dp = 0$. Solving, $\hat{p}$ gives the value shown in Eq. (40), where $T = a + 1b + 2c$ is the total

$$\hat{p} = \frac{a + b}{a + 2b + 2c} = \frac{a + b}{T} \qquad (40)$$

number of trials, of which $a + b$ are successful ones. The variance $V(\hat{p})$ is given by Eq. (41). The chief

$$\frac{1}{V(\hat{p})} = \frac{-d^2L}{dp^2} = \frac{a + b}{p^2} + \frac{b + 2c}{q^2} = \frac{T}{pq} \qquad (41)$$

drawback of this powerful method is that, in most cases, and especially when they are two or more parameters to be estimated, explicit expressions for the estimates are unobtainable, and for a solution, one must resort to iteration methods. Calculation of the variances is even more tedious.

Transformation. The four statistical tests u, t, χ^2, F are all based on the normal distribution. If the variate y is not normally distributed, often a change of scale renders the new variate $z = f(y)$ approximately normal, so that the standard tests may be employed on the new variate. Such a change of scale is called a transformation of variables. There is no rule of thumb as to how a variate scale should be changed to render it normal and to equalize the variances of two or

more samples. The following are some of the commonly used transformations.

Logarithmic. Probably the most frequently used transformation is $z = \log y$ or $\log(y + c)$. If the new variate z is normal, then y is said to be log-normal, a special name for the original distribution of y. It may be shown that if the measurement y is influenced by a large number of factors acting multiplicatively (instead of additively), then y has a log-normal distribution. A logarithmic transformation also changes the original exponential relationship with another variable into a linear one which is much easier to handle statistically.

Angular. For samples from a binomial population, the mean $y = p$ and its variance pq/n are correlated The p's of several samples cannot be averaged in the usual manner because each has a different variance. The angular transformation is to replace the proportion p by an angle θ such that $p = \sin^2 \theta$. The variance of θ depends on n only. Then the angular values can be treated by standard statistical methods. The square-root transformation accomplishes the same purpose for a Poisson distribution.

Probit. This is the normal deviate plus five $(u + 5)$ to avoid negative numbers. Suppose that $p = 12/20 = 0.65$ is the observed proportion of deaths in a group of 20 animals treated with a certain dose of drug. The assumption is that the individual lethal dose level is normally distributed. Then the area $p = 0.65$ under the left side of the normal curve is set off by an ordinate at $u = 0.385$ or a probit value 5.385. The probit transformation thus replaces a proportion (area) by its corresponding normal deviate (abscissa value) plus 5. The reason for doing this is that the mortality curve for proportions against dosage is sigmoid in shape, but the mortality curve for probits against dosage is linear. (The dosage may be replaced by log dosage, but this is not a part of the probit transformation.) Probits are widely used in toxicology, biological assay, and similar problems where response is of the all-or-none type. *See* ANALYSIS OF VARIANCE; HUMAN GENETICS; STATISTICS.   C. C. Li

Bibliography. C. C. Li, *Introduction to Experimental Statistics*, 1964; G. W. Snedecor and W. G. Cochran, *Statistical Methods*, 8th ed., 1989; R. Sokal and F. Rohlf, *Biometry: The Principles and Practice of Statistics in Biological Research*, 3d ed., 1994.

Bioorganic chemistry

The science that describes the structure, interactions, and reactions of organic compounds of biological significance at the molecular level. It represents the meeting of biochemistry, as attempts are made to describe the structure and physiology of organisms on an ever smaller scale, with organic chemistry, as attempts are made to synthesize and understand the behavior of molecules of ever-increasing size and complexity. Areas of research include enzymatic catalysis, the structure and folding of proteins, the structure and function of biological membranes, the chemistry of poly(ribonucleic acids) and poly(deoxyribonucleic acids), biosynthetic pathways, immunology, and mechanisms of drug action.

Being at the interface of two disciplines, bioorganic chemistry utilizes experimental techniques and theoretical concepts drawn from both. Important experimental techniques include organic synthesis, kinetics, structure-activity relationships, the use of model systems, methods of protein purification and manipulation, genetic mutation, cloning and overexpression (engineered enhancement of gene transcription), and the elicitation of monoclonal antibodies. Theoretical concepts important to bioorganic chemistry include thermodynamics, transition-state theory, acid-base theory, concepts of hydrophobicity and hydrophilicity, theories of stereocontrol, and theories of adaptation of organisms to selective pressures.

Enzyme catalysis. Historically, a major focus of bioorganic research has been the study of catalysis by enzymes. Enzymes are proteins that are responsible for catalyzing nearly every chemical reaction that occurs in living systems. Without enzymes, the reactions that support living organisms would occur too slowly to maintain life.

Mechanisms of rate increase. Enzymes have a dramatic ability to increase the rates at which reactions occur. Enzyme-catalyzed reactions typically proceed 10^6–10^{12} times faster than they would otherwise. Enzymes accomplish these enormous rate increases for a wide variety of reactions, despite the fact that most biological reactions occur between 0 and 38°C (32 and 100°F) and at essentially neutral pH.

One of the ways that enzymes increase the rates of bimolecular reactions is to overcome the entropic barrier associated with bringing two particles together to form one. At 25°C (77°F), the loss of entropy experienced by two molecules combining to form one transition state accounts for an energetic barrier of 10–11 kcal mol^{-1}. Overcoming this entropic barrier could increase the rate of a reaction by a factor of 10^8. Enzymes use favorable noncovalent interactions (ionic, dipole-dipole, hydrogen bonding, or hydrophobic) to bind the two reactants in proximity and in the right orientation for a reaction to occur. Thus, the reaction is said to occur intramolecularly. Although the reaction is strictly intermolecular, the entropy of the reaction is like that of an intramolecular reaction because the reaction occurs within a single molecular complex. Intramolecular reactions occur much more rapidly than similar intermolecular reactions. For example, the rate of acid-catalyzed lactonization of hydroxyacid [(**1**) in reaction (1)] is

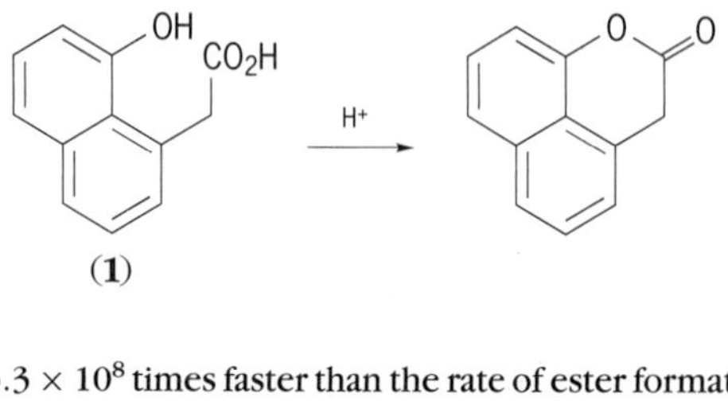

(1)

(**1**)

5.3×10^8 times faster than the rate of ester formation by phenol and acetic acid [reaction (2)].

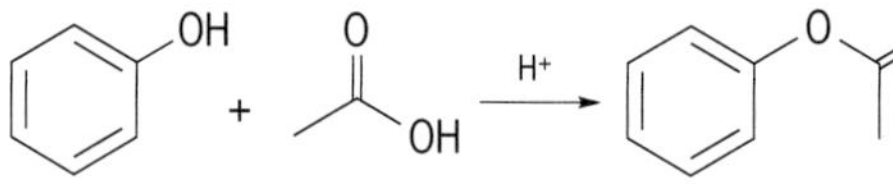

(2)

See CHEMICAL DYNAMICS.

Enzymes also catalyze reactions by facilitating proton transfers. Many of the reactions catalyzed by enzymes, such as the formation and hydrolysis of esters and amides, require the deprotonation of a nucleophile (base catalysis) or the protonation of an electrophile (acid catalysis). However, enzymes function in an aqueous environment that is thermodynamically essentially neutral. Enzymes overcome this limitation by using their own amino acid side-chain functional groups to donate or accept protons as necessary. These proton-transferring groups are called general acids and general bases, respectively. They interact with enzyme substrates so that proton transfers occur simultaneously with the cleavage or formation of bonds between heavy (nonhydrogen) atoms. Thus, no large equilibrium concentration of hydronium or hydroxide ion is required. *See* ACID AND BASE.

Intramolecular general acid catalysis by the carboxylic acid group [reaction (3)] causes acetal (**2**)

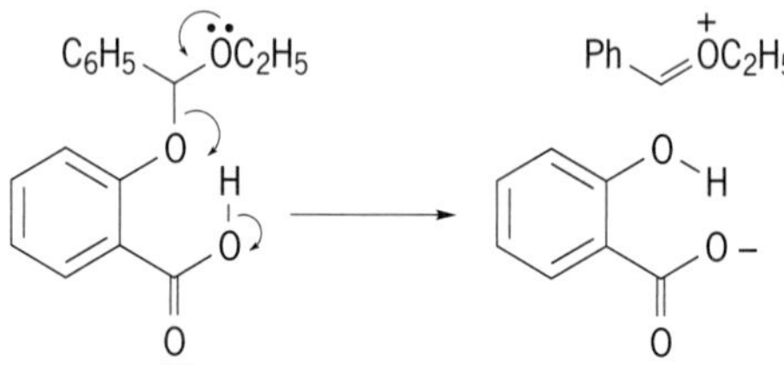

(3)

(**2**)

to hydrolyze 10^7 times faster than the related acetal [(**3**) in reaction (4)] at pH 7.0. In compound (**4**), the

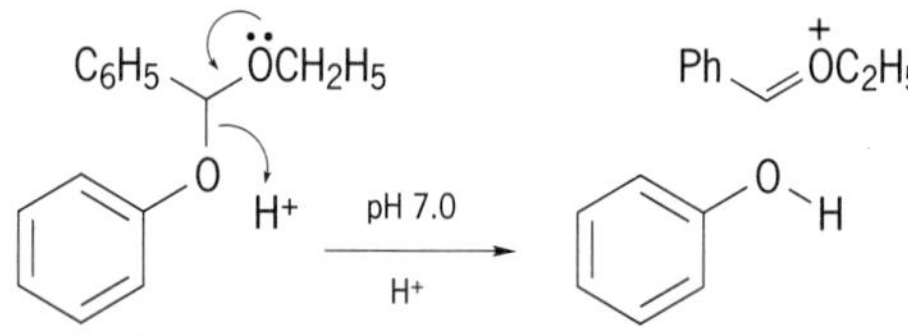

(4)

(**3**)

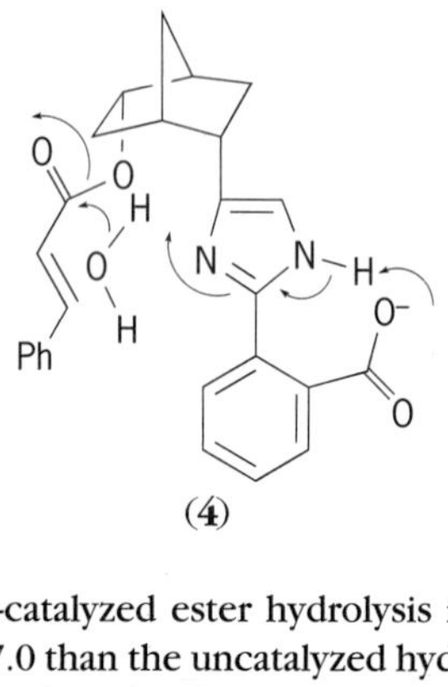

(**4**)

general base-catalyzed ester hydrolysis is 10^5 times faster at pH 7.0 than the uncatalyzed hydrolysis. The carboxylate and imidazole groups in compound (**4**) mimic the charge relay system composed of aspartate and histidine side chains in the active site of the proteolytic enzyme α-chymotrypsin.

Enzymes bind metal ions in their active sites by coordinating them to the side-chain thiol groups of cysteine or imidazole groups of histidine. The metal ions catalyze reactions by acting as Lewis acids or as sources of nucleophilic hydroxide ion. As Lewis acids, metal ions coordinate substrate molecules, making them more electrophilic or easier to deprotonate. Compound (5) is a model of the active site

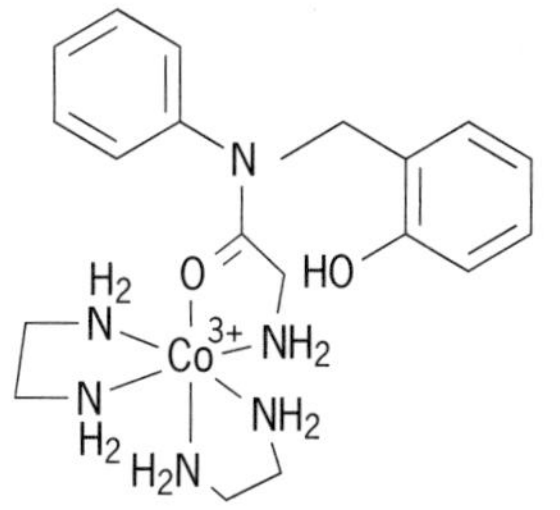

(5)

of the proteolytic enzyme, carboxypeptidase A. Electrophilic coordination of the amide carbonyl group by the cobalt(III) cation (Co^{3+}) makes the amide more susceptible to hydrolysis than it is in the absence of cobalt(III).

Metal ions can also bind water molecules to their vacant coordination sites. Metal-bound water is more acidic and thus dissociates more readily to form hydroxide ion than unbound water. Metal-bound hydroxide ion, however, is nearly as nucleophilic as free hydroxide ion. Metals thus serve to increase the local concentrations of hydroxide ion in the active sites of enzymes. In compound (6), the cobalt(III)-bound hy-

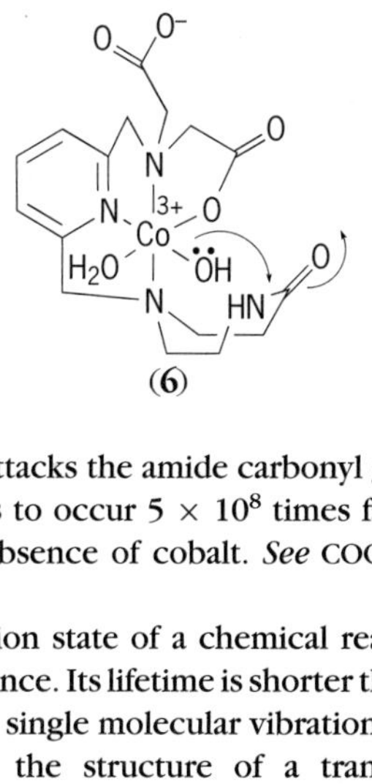

(6)

droxide ion attacks the amide carbonyl group, causing hydrolysis to occur 5×10^8 times faster than it does in the absence of cobalt. *See* COORDINATION CHEMISTRY.

The transition state of a chemical reaction has a fleeting existence. Its lifetime is shorter than the time required for a single molecular vibration ($\leq 10^{-13}$ s). Furthermore, the structure of a transition state (shape, bond lengths, extent of charge separation) always differs from that of a ground-state reactant. In solution, a transition state is always less than optimally solvated, because solvent molecules cannot reorganize quickly enough to accommodate the shape, size, and dipole moments of the transition state. Enzymes, however, may act as preorganized solvation shells for transition states. If the active site of an enzyme has just the right size, shape, and arrangement of functional groups to bind a transition state, it will automatically bind the reactants less well. Selective binding of the transition state lowers the energy of

the transition state relative to that of the reactants. Because the energy barrier between reactants and transition state is reduced, the reaction proceeds more rapidly.

Experiments with monoclonal antibodies have demonstrated that catalysis by selective binding of transition states is possible. Antibodies are proteins that can bind small molecules tightly. Unlike enzyme proteins, antibodies usually show no catalytic behavior. However, monoclonal antibodies that have been raised against ground-state molecules that "look" like transition states of reactions can act as catalysts. A monoclonal antibody raised against phosphonate ester (7) increases the rate of hydrolysis of cocaine to

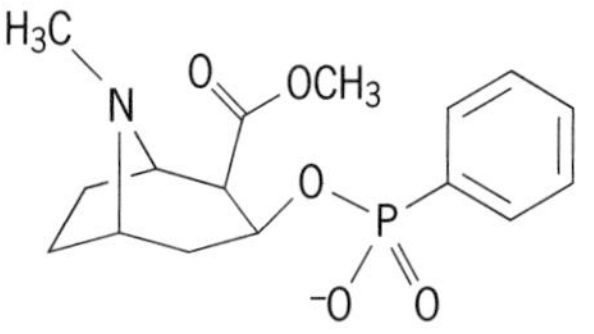

(7)

ecgonine methyl ester 540-fold. In this case, compound (7) resembles the transition state leading to the tetrahedral intermediate formed during hydrolysis of the carboxylic ester in cocaine [reaction (5)].

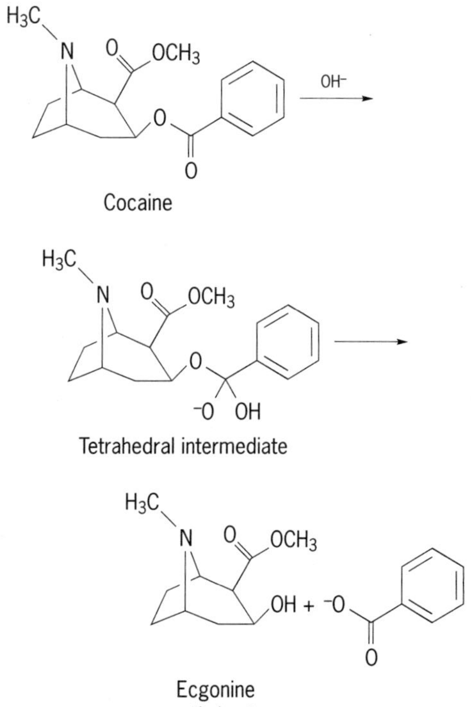

Cocaine

Tetrahedral intermediate

(5)

Ecgonine
methyl ester

The antibody that binds compound (7) tightly also binds the transition state for hydrolysis of cocaine tightly. *See* MONOCLONAL ANTIBODIES.

This example also illustrates two important features of catalytic antibodies. First, by appropriate choice of a "transition-state mimic," it is possible to create custom-designed catalysts. Second, some of these catalysts may be therapeutically useful. Because ecgonine methyl ester lacks the pharmacological activity of cocaine, the monoclonal antibody

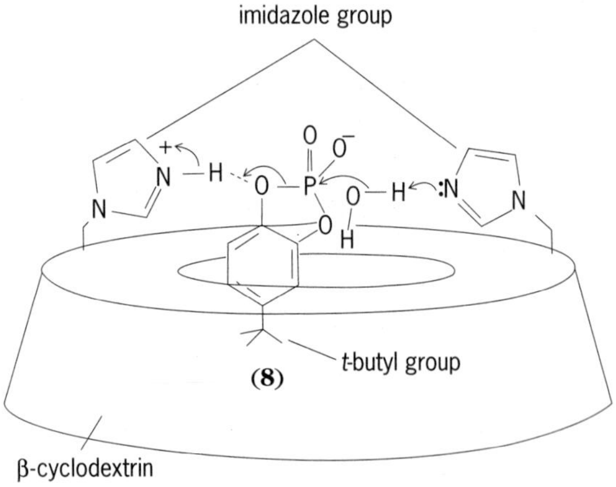

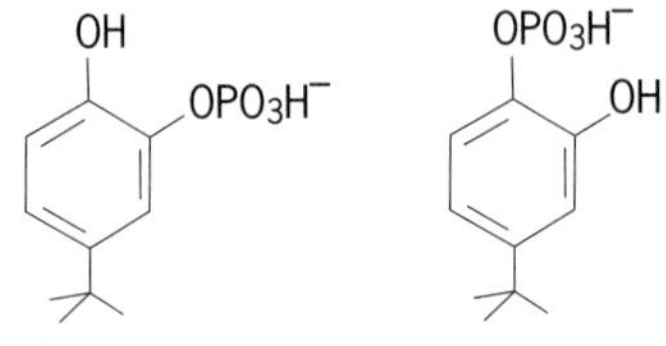

imidazole group

(8)

t-butyl group

β-cyclodextrin

(6)

(9)

Only product
formed

(10)

Not formed

catalyzing the hydrolysis of cocaine may be useful as a source of passive immunity for those who are trying to overcome addiction to cocaine.

Selectivity of enzymatic catalysis. Another property of enzymes is the tremendous selectivity with which they catalyze reactions. For example, fumarase catalyzes the addition of water across the double bond of fumaric acid to form L-malic acid. It does not catalyze the addition of nucleophiles other than water to fumaric acid, nor does it catalyze the hydration of compounds that are structurally similar to fumaric acid. The solvent-derived proton adds to the carbon-carbon double bond of fumaric acid from the face opposite to that to which the hydroxyl

group adds (the addition is diastereoselective), and the hydroxyl group adds to only one of the two enantiotopic faces of fumaric acid, forming only the L enantiomer of malic acid (the addition is enantio-selective).

Few synthetic catalysts exhibit enzymelike selectivities. However, the hydrolysis of regioselective phosphodiester (8) catalyzed by a derivatized cyclodextrin [reaction (6)] is an example of the mechanism by which selective catalysis occurs. β-Cyclodextrin (the cyclic α-1,4-linked heptamer of glucose) can be viewed as a large molecular "doughnut" with a hydrophobic interior (8). When imidazole groups are attached to the first and fourth glucose residues of β-cyclodextrin, they act as general acid and base catalysts for the hydrolysis of compound (8). This hydrolysis mimics the cleavage of the phosphodiester linkages of ribonucleic acid (RNA) by the enzyme ribonuclease (RNase). Because the t-butyl group of compound (8) first binds inside the hydrophobic cleft of the cyclodextrin, the interaction with the imidazole catalysts is regioselective, leading to the formation of compound (9), not compound (10), as the only product of hydrolysis. The key to selective catalysis is thus the binding of specific substrates in a unique orientation so that they interact selectively with functional groups appropriately positioned within the active site of the catalyst. *See* RIBONUCLEIC ACID (RNA).

Enzymes in organic synthesis. The selectivity of enzymes makes them useful as catalysts for organic synthesis. Surprisingly, enzymes are able to catalyze not only the reactions that they mediate in living systems but also similar, selective transformations of unnatural substrates. Enzyme-catalyzed reactions that have been scaled up as industrial processes include the conversion of corn starch to high-fructose corn syrup [reaction (7)], the transamidation of porcine insulin to form human insulin [reaction (8)], and the kinetic chiral resolution of glycidol [reaction (9)].

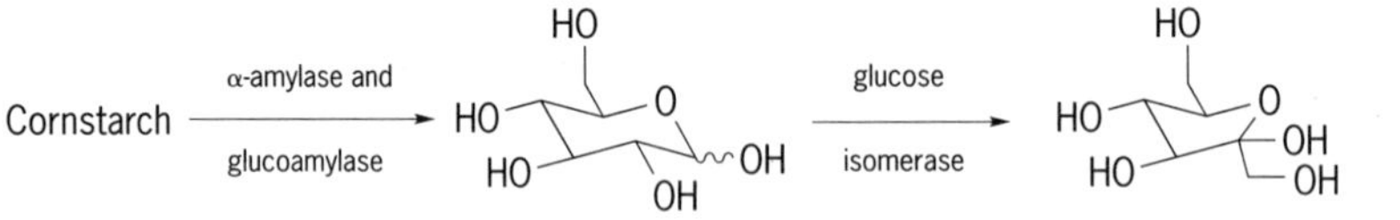

(7)

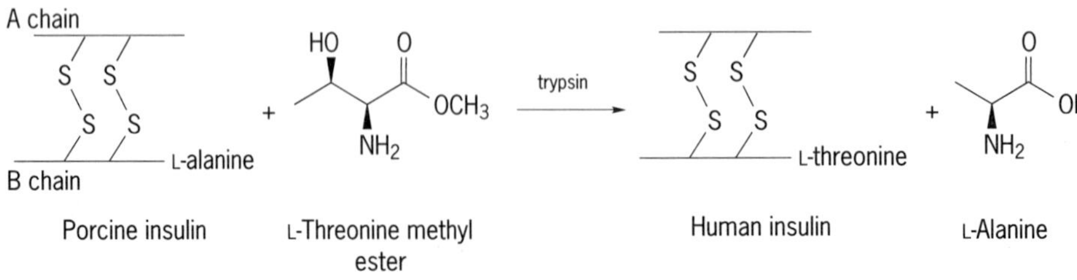

Porcine insulin

L-Threonine methyl
ester

Human insulin

L-Alanine

(8)

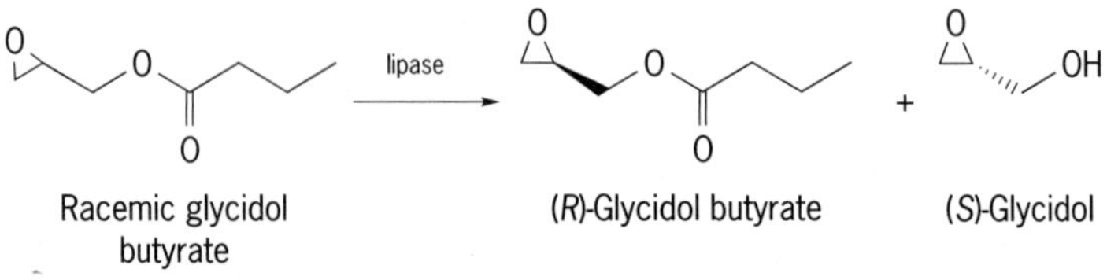

Racemic glycidol
butyrate

(R)-Glycidol butyrate

(S)-Glycidol

(9)

The first process utilizes enzymes simply to act upon their natural substrates. The latter two processes, however, require enzymes to act upon unnatural substrates that would not be encountered by the enzymes in the living system.

The application of enzymes to organic synthesis is made possible by advances in genetic cloning and overexpression, protein purification, and enzyme immobilization. Immobilization of enzymes on solid, insoluble supports or on soluble polymers allows the enzymes to be retained within flow-through reactors and to be recovered for reuse. Immobilization often has the added benefit of increasing the stability of the enzyme protein.

Enzymes can catalyze reactions in organic solvents as well as in water. Changing the solvent from water to an organic solvent often has profound effects on the equilibria of reactions. Because the solvent affects the conformation of an enzyme and thus the shape of its active site, a change in solvent may also change the substrate specificity or stereoselectivity of an enzyme.

Because of their selectivity, several enzyme-catalyzed reactions may run simultaneously in the same vessel. Thus, a reactant can undergo several reactions in series without the need for isolation of intermediates. Enzymes can be combined so as to reconstitute within a reaction vessel naturally occurring metabolic pathways or to create new, artificial metabolic pathways. Sequences of up to 12 serial reactions have been executed successfully in a single reaction vessel. *See* CATALYSIS; ENZYME; ORGANIC SYNTHESIS.

Protein folding. The biological activity of a protein, whether binding, catalytic, or structural, depends on its full three-dimensional or conformational structure. The linear sequence of amino acids that make up a protein constitutes its primary structure. Local regions of highly organized conformation (α-helices, β-pleats, β-turns, and so on) are called secondary structure. Further folding of the protein causes regions of secondary structure to associate or come into correct alignment. This action establishes the tertiary structure of the native (active) protein. Sometimes, covalent disulfide bonds between cysteine side chains help to "lock in" the correct tertiary structure.

A goal of bioorganic chemistry is to achieve an understanding of the process of protein folding. The primary structure of a protein contains all of the information necessary to determine its tertiary structure in the native state. Some proteins, after being unfolded by heat or chemical treatment, spontaneously refold into their native conformation. Others, however, do not. Some proteins may fold up as they are coming off the ribosome during synthesis into a conformation that differs from the one that they would adopt if the fully formed protein were allowed to fold. In fact, the native conformation of a protein may be only a metastable state and not its thermodynamically most stable conformation. Some experiments indicate that regions of secondary structure form spontaneously and subsequently control the formation of tertiary structure. Other experiments have shown that hydrophobic interactions between nascent α-helices facilitate helix formation. *See* RIBOSOMES.

Necessary to an understanding of protein folding is a knowledge of the factors that stabilize secondary and tertiary structures. Certain amino acids, such as alanine and valine, are known to be α-helix stabilizing. Proline promotes β-turn formation. Bonding interactions between amino acid side chains on successive turns of α-helices have been used to "crosslink" the α-helices in unnatural peptides. Both noncovalent (hydrogen bonding, ionic, or metal chelation) and covalent (disulfide or amide bond) interactions have been used. Nonpeptide prosthetic groups having rigid conformations have been incorporated into peptides and found to nucleate secondary structure formation. Attempts to stabilize tertiary structures by introduction of genetically engineered disulfide bonds have, in general, been unsuccessful. *See* AMINO ACIDS; PROTEIN.

DNA binding and cleavage. Understanding mechanisms of DNA binding and cleavage is important to understanding the activities of many antibiotics and to the development of new therapeutic agents. The design of agents that would cleave DNA selectively at specific nucleotide sequences would also benefit genetic research and molecular biology. Compounds that bind DNA usually interact with exposed nucleotide bases and often bind to either the major or the minor groove of double-stranded α-helical deoxyribonucleic acid (DNA). *See* ANTIBIOTIC; DEOXYRIBONUCLEIC ACID (DNA).

Mechanisms of drug action. A major success of bioorganic chemistry is its ability to elucidate the chemical mechanisms responsible for the biological activities of drugs. Invariably, drugs react by the same mechanisms by which other organic molecules react. An example is the mechanism of action of the enediyne antibiotics. Calicheamicin, esperamicin, and dynamicin are antitumor antibiotics that possess at their core an enediyne structure. In the case of calicheamicin (**11**), reductive or nucleophilic

(10)

cleavage of the pendant trisulfide by a reductant or nucleophile (shown as Nuc⁻ and a curved arrow) leads to a Michael addition at a bridgehead carbon. A Michael addition is the addition of a nucleophile to one end of a carbon-carbon double bond that has an electron-withdrawing double bond attached at the other end. In this case, the $C{=}O$ attached to the $C{=}C$ is the electron-withdrawing double bond.

Rehybridization of the bridgehead carbon allows the enediyne to undergo ring closure, generating a benzendiyl diradical [(**12**) in reaction (10)]. If the antibiotic is bound to DNA, the diradical can abstract a hydrogen atom from the sugar phosphate backbone, leading to DNA strand scission. Although the first enediyne antibiotic was discovered in 1987, the mechanism of enediyne cyclization to form a benzenediyl diradical was elucidated in 1972. *See* BIOCHEMISTRY; ORGANIC CHEMISTRY.

H. Keith Chenault

Bibliography. R. Breslow (ed.), International Symposium on Bioorganic Chemistry, *Ann. N.Y. Acad. Sci.*, vol. 471, 1986; R. Jaenicke, Protein folding: Local structures, domains, subunits, and assemblies, *Biochemistry*, 30:3147–3161, 1991; A. J. Kirby, Effective molarities for intramolecular reactions, *Adv. Phys. Org. Chem.*, 17:183–278, 1980; R. A. Lerner, S. J. Benkovic, and P. G. Shultz, At the crossroads of chemistry and immunology: Catalytic antibodies, *Science*, 252:659–667, 1991; J. F. Liebman and A. Greenberg (eds.), *Mechanistic Principles of Enzyme Activity*, 1988; G. M. Whitesides and C.-H. Wong, Enzymes as catalysts in synthetic organic chemistry, *Angew. Chem. Int. Ed. Engl.*, 24:617–638, 1985.

Biophysics

A hybrid science involving the overlap of physics, chemistry, and biology. A dominant aspect of biophysics is the use of the ideas and methods of physics and chemistry to study and explain the structures of living organisms and the mechanisms of life processes.

Many eminent scientists of previous generations, such as A. Volta, H. von Helmholtz, and J. L. M. Poiseuille, were really biophysicists because they made important contributions to both biology and physics. Helmholtz and his contemporaries explicitly planned to explain biological phenomena in terms of the physical sciences. Nevertheless, the recognition of biophysics as a separate field is relatively recent, having been brought about, in part, by the invention of physical tools such as the electron microscope, the ultracentrifuge, and the electronic amplifier, which greatly facilitate biophysical research. These tools are peculiarly adapted to the study of problems of great current importance to medicine, problems related to virus diseases, cancer, heart disease, and the like.

Furthermore, with the advent of the space and atomic age, new problems of survival, which involve hitherto unthought-of reactions with the physical environment, have been thrust upon humans. Study of biological processes at every level, molecular or macroscopic, continues to reveal the complex physical and chemical basis of life, demanding the development of physical thought for the special task of interpreting physical measurements on living systems. As a result, biophysics departments and research programs in many universities, which provide opportunities for study at undergraduate, graduate, and postdoctoral levels, were established, and the Biophysical Society was organized.

There are several areas within biophysics, the major ones being molecular biophysics, radiation biophysics, physiological biophysics, and mathematical or theoretical biophysics.

Molecular biophysics has to do with the study of large molecules and particles of comparable size which play important roles in biology. Favorite physical tools for such research are the electron microscope, the ultracentrifuge, and the x-ray diffraction camera. Conspicuous success has been achieved in the study of viruses and in the investigation of nucleic acid, the substance which is involved in hereditary mechanisms. *See* ELECTRON MICROSCOPE; MOLECULAR BIOLOGY; ULTRACENTRIFUGE; X-RAY DIFFRACTION.

Radiation biophysics consists of the study of the response of organisms to ionizing radiations, such as alpha particles, beta particles, gamma rays, and x-rays, and to ultraviolet light. The biological responses are death of cells and tissues, if not of whole organisms, and mutation, either somatic or genetic. Somatic mutations represent changes in nonreproductive cells and might lead to uncontrolled or cancerous growth. Genetic mutations involve changes in the germ cells which can be transmitted to future generations. *See* MUTATION; RADIATION BIOLOGY.

Physiological biophysics, called by some classical biophysics, is concerned with the use of physical mechanisms to explain the behavior and the functioning of living organisms or parts of living organisms and with the response of living organisms to physical forces. The questions of how nerve impulses are transmitted; what the mechanism of muscle contraction is; what the visual mechanism is; how one hears, tastes, smells, or feels; and why living cells are able to ingest some substances and excrete others have been studied and, in part at least, answered by physiological biophysicists. Closely related matters are the changes in normal functioning of organisms, including the human body, when the physical environment is changed. Of particular importance in the space age are the changes brought about in the human body by subjecting the individual to high accelerations.

Mathematical and theoretical biophysics deals primarily with the attempt to explain the behavior of living organisms on the basis of mathematics and physical theory. Biological processes are being examined in terms of thermodynamics, hydrodynamics, and statistical mechanics. Mathematical models are being investigated to see how closely they simulate biological processes. *See* BIOMECHANICS; BIOPOTENTIALS AND IONIC CURRENTS; BONE; MATHEMATICAL

BIOLOGY; MICROMANIPULATION; MICROSCOPE; MUS-
CLE; MUSCULAR SYSTEM; OXIMETRY; SKELETAL SYS-
TEM; SPACE BIOLOGY; THERMOREGULATION; THER-
MOTHERAPY.   Max A. Lauffer

Biopolymer

A macromolecule derived from natural sources; also
known as biological polymer. Nature has developed
effective means for efficiently preparing and utilizing
biopolymers. Some are used as structural materials,
food sources, or catalysts. Others have evolved as
entities for information storage and transfer. Familiar examples of biopolymers include polypeptides,
polysaccharides, and polymers derived from ribonucleic acid (RNA) and deoxyribonucleic acid (DNA).
Other examples include polyhydroxybutyrates, a
class of polyesters produced by certain bacteria, and
cis-1,4-polyisoprene, the major component of rubber
tree latex.

Polypeptides. Amino acids are the monomers from
which polypeptides (**1**) are derived. Only one of the

(1)

two enantiomers of amino acids, the S or levo isomer, is used to make polypeptides. Polypeptides may
be polymers of a single amino acid, but far more
commonly they are polymers of many (up to about
20) amino acids arranged in a specific sequence in
the polymer chain. This specific sequence is called
the primary structure. The side chains (R's) of the
amino acids differ in their size and charge, and their
placement in a chain determines how the chain
will interact with itself (intramolecularly) and with
other chains (intermolecularly). For example, if the
side chain is simply a hydrogen atom, a polypeptide will tend to form extended sheets (a so-called
β-pleated sheet) via intermolecular hydrogen bonding between amides. If the side chain is large, steric
interactions force hydrogen bonding intramolecularly, leading to a helix (more formally termed an
α-helix). The extended sheets and helices are examples of secondary structure, the regular, recurring
arrangement in space of the polypeptide chain in
one dimension. *See* AMINO ACIDS; HYDROGEN BOND;
STEREOCHEMISTRY.

Many polypeptides, however, fold into three-
dimensional structures through association of different parts of the chain, and this arrangement is known
as tertiary structure. Polypeptide chain folding occurs by association of oppositely charged side chains
or association of nonpolar (hydrophobic) side chains
that tend to be clustered rather than individually surrounded by polar water molecules. In many cases,
tertiary structures are held in place through the formation of covalent disulfide (—S—S—) by reaction
of a pair of thiol (—S—H) side chains.

More than one polypeptide chain can associate
through primarily noncovalent association to yield
quaternary structure. Polypeptides alone, as well
as multipolypeptide complexes or complexes with
other molecules, are known as proteins, and each has
a specific biological function. Examples of proteins
are enzymes, which are highly efficient and selective
catalysts for many chemical reactions, and collagen,
the fibrous material of skin and cartilage. *See* CATAL-
YSIS; COLLAGEN; ENZYME; PROTEIN.

Polysaccharides. In polysaccharides, sugar units,
predominantly glucose (**2**), are linked together by acetal (glycoside) bonds. Amylose is a polysaccharide
having α-1,4 linkages between repeat units (**3**). It is

(2)   (3)

a component of starch, the other component being
amylopectin, a branched version of amylose. Glycogen is another important polysaccharide and is even
more branched than amylopectin. Both starch (in
plants) and glycogen (in mammals) serve as sources
of glucose, the food used to produce adenosine
triphosphate (ATP), the energy source that promotes
many biological reactions. An interesting contrast
is provided by cellulose (**4**), which is a linear

(4)

homopolymer of glucose but with exclusively β-1,4
linkages. Cellulose is a water-insoluble, structural
polymer found in the cell walls of plants. The β-1,4
linkages encourage an extended-chain conformation
and aggregation into fibrils. The α-1,4 linkages of
glycogen, however, favor a coiled helix. Besides
these differences, cellulose cannot be metabolized
by humans, and therefore it is not a useful energy
source. However, ruminants such as cattle have
in their digestive tracts bacteria that produce the
enzymes necessary to catalyze the breakdown of
cellulose into glucose. *See* ADENOSINE TRIPHOS-
PHATE (ATP); CARBOHYDRATE; CELLULOSE; GLUCOSE;
GLYCOGEN; GLYCOSIDE; POLYSACCHARIDE; STARCH.

Polypeptide/polysaccharide hybrids. There are numerous examples of biopolymers having a polysaccharide and polypeptide in the same molecule,
usually with a polysaccharide as a side chain in a
polypeptide, or vice versa. Covalent bonds between
the polysaccharides and polypeptides are made via a

glycoside bond to side chains of the latter, which are usually serine, threonine, or asparagine. Examples are proteoglycans, which are primarily polysaccharides, and glycoproteins, which are primarily polypeptides. Proteoglycans are frequently found in connective tissue. Many of the hydroxyls of the sugars are sulfated, and hence these molecules are highly anionic (negatively charged). Several glycoproteins are known wherein the protein part of the molecule embeds itself in a cell membrane, with the polysaccharide (glyco) part projecting outward from the membrane surface. These sugar residues act as signals to the immune system that identify the type of cell with which they are associated. In this way, foreign cells are recognized, and the immune system is activated. Proteoglycans are frequently aggregated into network structures, an example of which is a bacterial cell wall. Here polysaccharide chains form a gridlike network crosslinked by short peptide segments. *See* BACTERIAL PHYSIOLOGY AND METABOLISM.

DNA and RNA. The macromolecules DNA (**5**) and RNA (**6**) are polymers of nucleotides, which com-

(**5**)　　　　(**6**)

prise a sugar, a phosphate group, and an appendage referred to as a base. The bases are either purines, such as adenine (**7**), or pyrimidines, such as thymine (**8**). Intermolecular hydrogen bonding between

(**7**)　　　　(**8**)

guanine-cytosine or adenosine-thymine pairs (called Watson-Crick base pairs) is responsible for the formation of the DNA double helix. The order of appearance of bases (primary structure) along a DNA chain translates into a set of instructions for the synthesis of a particular polypeptide. There are three-base codes associated with each amino acid. A sequence of bases representing the sequence of amino acids in a particular polypeptide is termed a gene. This information is copied in the base sequence of a special RNA molecule (messenger RNA, or mRNA) which forms the template upon which polypeptides are synthesized. The correct amino acid is brought to the correct location on mRNA via a transfer RNA (tRNA) molecule which has bases that are comple-

mentary to those on the mRNA. The correctly positioned amino acid is then linked to the polypeptide with the aid of enzymes. Without the mRNA template, amino acids would react to form polypeptides with random and hence useless sequences.

Polynucleotides of any base sequence, sometimes referred to as designer genes, can be readily prepared by automated synthesis in the laboratory and inserted into the DNA of simple organisms. The organisms with the new piece of DNA spliced into their own DNA can be easily cloned. These organisms will make the polypeptide coded by the new DNA sequence in addition to all of the others in their DNA program. By using this recombinant DNA technology, valuable polypeptides, such as hormones, as well as completely new ones, can be produced. The isolation of key proteins from a broth of many proteins represents a major challenge in the biotechnology industry. *See* DEOXYRIBONUCLEIC ACID (DNA); RIBONUCLEIC ACID (RNA).

Polyesters. Certain bacteria, when grown under conditions of limited nutrient supply, synthesize polyesters that can be broken down later and used for food and, therefore, energy. The principal class of polyesters that the bacteria produce is known as poly(β-hydroxyalkenoates), structure (**9**). The most common monomer is d-(−)-3-hydroxybutyric acid (**10**), and the resulting polymer is known as

(**9**)　　　　(**10**)

poly(3-hydroxybutyrate), or PHB (R = methyl). Commercial interest in this material stems from the fact that it is biodegradable.

Copolyesters can be readily prepared by controlling the nature of the nutrient medium. For example, d-(−)-3-hydroxybutyrate is synthesized in bacterial cells by utilizing acetate as the carbon source. However, addition of propionate results in the synthesis of a copolyester having both hydroxybutyrate and hydroxyvalerate (R = ethyl) units. The copolyesters are biodegradable and in addition have good mechanical properties, making them attractive for many applications. This approach has been extended to the synthesis of a whole series of novel copolyesters. PHB and related polymers also can be prepared in the laboratory by ring-opening polymerization of cyclic esters known as lactones. However, the purity of the biological product and the reliability of the biological "machines" make biosynthesis an attractive route. *See* BIODEGRADATION.

Polyisoprenes. The latex from rubber trees consists of tiny spheres of *cis*-1,4-polyisoprene (**11**)

(**11**)

stabilized from coagulation by a proteinaceous coating. The latex from *Gutta percha* and balata is primarily *trans*-1,4-polyisoprene (**12**). Both are polymers of the monomer isoprene (**13**).

$$+ H_2C \quad CH_3$$
$$\diagdown C = C \diagup$$
$$H \quad CH_2 +_n$$
$$(\mathbf{12})$$

$$H_2C = CH - C = CH_2$$
$$|$$
$$CH_3$$
$$(\mathbf{13})$$

The latex can be coagulated in aqueous salt solutions. The resulting material from the rubber tree is known as natural rubber and is particularly important, finding extensive use in crosslinked form as an elastomer for tires, gaskets, and other applications. Demand for natural rubber decreased after chemists discovered how to prepare high-quality *cis*-polyisoprene in the laboratory. The *trans*-isomer is a hard, semicrystalline polymer that is used for golf ball covers, and also can be easily prepared abiologically.

There seems to be no agreement as to a biological motivation for certain plants to produce polyisoprenes. Some suggestions are that polyisoprenes are nutrient sources or the waste products of metabolic processes, or that they provide protection from infection when the tree is damaged.　　Gary E. Wnek

Bibliography. A. L. Lehninger, D. L. Nelson, and M. M. Cox, *Principles of Biochemistry*, 4th ed., 2004; A. K. Mohanty et al. (eds.), *Natural Fibers, Biopolymers, and Biocomposites*, 2005; J. D. Watson et al., *Molecular Biology of the Gene*, 5th ed., 2003.

Biopotentials and ionic currents

The voltage differences which exist between separated points in living cells, tissues, organelles, and organisms are called biopotentials. Related to these biopotentials are ionic charge transfers, or currents, that give rise to much of the electrical changes occurring in nerve, muscle, and other electrically active cells. Electrophysiology is the science concerned with uncovering the structures and functions of bioelectrical systems. This study involves a search for pertinent molecular entities directly involved with or related to biological potentials and currents. According to their function, these structures are given descriptive names such as channels, carriers, ionophores, gates, and pumps. Several of these operational entities have been identified with molecular structures whose precise chemical composition and configuration are known at the atomic level.

Electrophysiology has become increasingly a major subdiscipline of biophysics, and with the advent of studies relating molecular structure to physiological activity it has leaned heavily on the methods and insights of molecular biology and biochemistry. As the methods and techniques used in electrophysiology involve sophisticated instrumentation, this endeavor has resulted in the development of a new area of biomedical engineering. Much of what is now possible technically has resulted from rapid advances in solid-state physics and in computer sciences. Many bioelectrical systems lend themselves readily to mathematical descriptions. These applied mathematical models continue to be a significant concern of mathematical biophysicists. *See* BIOCHEMISTRY; BIOMEDICAL ENGINEERING; CARDIAC ELECTROPHYSIOLOGY; MATHEMATICAL BIOLOGY.

Electric fishes developed a bioelectrical system that became one of the first biological systems studied systematically. Animal electricity was known by its effects to ancient Egyptians, who made observations of the electric catfish, *Malapterurus*, about 2600 B.C. The early Egyptians, Greeks, and Romans were fascinated by these creatures, and recommended using the electric discharges of the fishes for the treatment of such disorders as headaches and epilepsy.

While A. Galvani is usually credited with having performed in 1790 the first laboratory experiments on the stimulation to activity of a bioelectrical system, J. Swammerdam performed somewhat similar experiments in 1658, and P. van Musschenbroeck of Leyden described in the mideighteenth century the effects of the electric discharge of a Leyden jar (an early type of capacitor for storing electric charge) on his own nervous system. *See* ELECTRIC ORGAN (BIOLOGY).

Galvani performed two basic experiments. In the first he showed that electricity from any source could stimulate (or galvanize) muscle to contract even when the electricity was applied to the nerve innervating the muscle. In the second experiment he connected nerves in the spinal cord of a frog to the leg muscles through a bimetallic arc and caused the leg muscles to contract. He hypothesized that electricity in the spinal neurons passed through the metallic arc to the leg muscles, indicating that this electricity was of biological origin. He made an analogy to a Leyden jar discharged through a short circuit. Volta believed that the source of electric current in Galvani's second experiment was the bimetallic arc itself, and ran a series of experiments examining different metals, which culminated in the discovery of the electromotive force series (for metals) and the invention of the voltaic pile (or electrophorus). Volta compared his electrochemical battery with the plates in the electric organ of an electric fish. By the midnineteenth century, in his popular physics text, Ganot began his section on dynamic electricity with an introduction featuring what was then known about bioelectricity. Galvani's successors, C. Matteucci, E. Dubois-Reymond, H. L. F. von Helmholz, and Hermann, over the half-century from 1830 to 1880, extended Galvani's observations and founded the science of electrophysiology.

Resting potentials. The potential difference measured with appropriate electrodes between the interior cytoplasm and the exterior aqueous medium of the living cell is generally called the membrane potential or resting potential (E_{RP}). This potential is usually in the order of several tens of millivolts and is relatively constant or steady. The range of E_{RP} values in various striated muscle cells of animals from insects through amphibia to mammals is about -50 to -100 mV (the voltage is negative inside with respect to outside). Nerve cells show a similar range in such diverse species as squid, cuttlefish, crabs, lobsters, frogs, cats, and humans. Even in the coenocytic marine algae, *Valonia, Halicystis,* and *Nitella,* potentials up to about -140 mV are measured between the cell sap and the outside medium. Similar potentials have been recorded in single tissue-culture cells.

Steady potential differences also can be measured across various tissues, such as the frog skin and the gastric mucosa of the stomach, and often have been shown to exist between cells. These potentials are often of complex cellular origins, but it is thought that their origin is predicted from the resting potentials of the cells making up the tissues, or involve mechanisms similar in kind if not in detail to those described here. *See* CELL (BIOLOGY).

The first indication of a cellular resting potential involved the measurement of an injury or demarcation potential by employing two nonpolarizable electrodes and a galvanometer. Dubois-Reymond showed in 1848 that a potential difference existed between the cut ends of muscle fibers and the intact external surface that was bathed in saline.

However, it was not until the use of true internal electrodes that accurate measurements of cellular resting potentials were made. These measurements demanded certain requirements: the measurement should not injure the cell; the measurement should not draw any appreciable current from the cell; and the electrode (properly the salt bridge) should not contribute any large and unknown potentials of its own to the measurement. Many investigators tried a variety of intracellular electrode measurements during the 1920s and the early 1930s, but the modern approach began with the use of the giant axons radiating from the stellate ganglia of the squid *Loligo*. *See* ELECTRODE.

In the late 1930s, H. J. Curtis and K. S. Cole in the United States and A. L. Hodgkin and A. F. Huxley in England used these giant axons to make resting potential measurements by using internal recording electrodes. The giant axons were large enough (0.02–0.04 in. or 0.5–1 mm in diameter) to allow penetration well into an axon of an axial capillary tube filled with potassium chloride solution. The potential difference across the membrane was determined by connecting the capillary (salt bridge) to a reversible electrode and positioning its open end opposite an external reversible electrode. These measurements supported and confirmed much of the earlier work done with indirect techniques.

Microelectrodes. In the late 1940s Judith Graham and R. W. Gerard perfected the microelectrode, which was a glass pipet pulled out to a fine tip with an opening in the order of the wavelength of visible light. This pipet was filled with concentrated potassium chloride and was connected as a salt bridge to a reversible electrode, such as a calomel half-cell or a silver–silver chloride wire. This electrode allowed the measurement of the resting potentials of a wide variety of cells whose diameter prohibited the use of capillary electrodes. Because of its very small opening the microelectrode has a very high resistance that necessitates the use of a preamplifier with a fixed gain and high input impedance, such as obtained by using a field-effect transistor (FET) at the input. In practice the microelectrode and the external reference electrode are first placed in the medium external to the cell. Any potential difference between the two electrodes is balanced to zero, and then the microelectrode is pushed through the cell surface. If done properly, an immediate jump in potential is recorded as soon as the microelectrode makes contact with the interior of the cell. By using a calibrated chart recorder, this potential is monitored as a function of time or as a function of a set of alterations in the environment of the cell. Electrochemically, because of the similarity in the mobilities of potassium and chloride ions in aqueous solution, use of concentrated KCl solutions for salt bridges reduces to a minimum extraneous potentials due to junctions between the electrodes and media they contact.

Voltage source. Biopotentials arise from the electrochemical gradients established across cell membranes. In most animal cells, potassium ions are in greater concentration internally than externally, and sodium ions are in less concentration internally than externally. Generally, chloride ions are in less concentration inside cells than outside cells, even though there are abundant intracellular fixed negative charges. While calcium ion concentration is relatively low in body fluids external to cells, the concentration of ionized calcium internally is much lower (in the nanomolar range) than that found external to the cells. The earliest detailed explanations of the origin of the resting potential involved the application of ideas that came from electrochemistry. In 1888 and 1889 the physicist W. Nernst proposed that the potential difference measured with reversible electrodes between regions of a solution having different concentrations of the same univalent electrolyte could be explained on the basis of the ions diffusing passively toward an equilibrium (equilibration of concentration throughout the solution). Nernst considered that ions moved with a velocity proportional to the potential and the concentration gradients. The potential arose as a result of the tendency for the more mobile ion species to get ahead, even though electrostatic attraction prevented any appreciable separation of charges. The relation describing this condition is represented by Eq. (1), where E is the potential, F is the Faraday con-

$$E = \frac{U - V}{U + V} \frac{RT}{ZF} \ln \frac{C_1}{C_2} \tag{1}$$

stant [96,500 coulombs/(g)(ion)], R is the gas constant, T is the absolute temperature, Z is the valence, C_1 and C_2 are different concentrations of the electrolyte, and U and V are the aqueous mobilities of the cation (+) and the anion (−), respectively. This relation was subsequently modified by substituting activities for concentrations in order to take account of the intermolecular attractions.

A system may be set up in which two solutions of the same electrolyte at different concentrations (C_1, C_2) are separated by a membrane or barrier which allows only one ion species to permeate through it, and there is zero net current through the membrane. It is possible to derive from thermodynamics that the potential difference between the two solutions measured with reversible electrodes is given by Eq. (2),

$$E = \frac{RT}{ZF} \ln \frac{a_1}{a_2} \qquad (2)$$

where a_1 and a_2 are the ion activities of the permeant species in the respective solutions. For a membrane permeable to a single ion species and separating two solutions of a salt, this relation predicts a 58-mV potential difference for a 10-fold difference in ion activity at about room temperature. This type of potential is called a concentration potential.

By 1900 it was well recognized that living cells contained higher concentrations of potassium internally than externally, that they had lower concentrations of sodium internally than externally, and that they contained internal anions which were large and thus assumed to be impermeant. In 1902 J. Bernstein proposed that the resting potential (demarcation potential) could be explained as a potassium ion concentration potential, assuming that cell membranes are impermeable to sodium ions and that potassium ions neutralize the internal impermeant anions (Gibbs-Donnan equilibrium).

During the late 1930s and early 1940s considerable evidence was accumulated showing that the resting potential was indeed a function of the external potassium ion concentration. Curtis and Cole in 1942 showed that over a given range of concentrations the relation between changes in E_{RP} and the log of the external K^+ concentration was linear with a slope given by RT/F. However, at low external potassium concentrations, deviations from predictions derived from consideration of a simple potassium concentration potential were obtained which could not be explained by experimental error.

Actual measurements of ionic movements through cell membranes of muscle fibers by H. B. Steinbach using chemical analysis and by L. A. Heppel using tracer techniques did not support the idea that membranes are impermeable to sodium ions. In fact, it was found that radioisotopically labeled sodium ion movement through the cell membrane from inside to outside seemed to depend upon the metabolism of the cell. I. M. Glynn showed that the sodium efflux from red cells depended on the ambient glucose concentration, and Hodgkin and R. D. Keynes demonstrated in squid and *Sepia* giant axons that the sodium efflux could be blocked by a variety of metabolic inhibitors (cyanide, 2,4-dinitrophenol, and azide). Inasmuch as the impermeant internal anions could not account for the low in-

ternal sodium ion concentration (via a Gibbs-Donnan equilibrium), it was proposed that a metabolic process (sodium pump) located in the cell membrane extruded sodium from the cell interior against an electrochemical gradient.

P. C. Caldwell's experiments on the squid's giant axon in the late 1950s indicated that there was a close relation between the activity of the sodium pump and the intracellular presence of high-energy compounds, such as adenosine triphosphate (ATP) and arginine phosphate. Caldwell suggested that these compounds might be directly involved in the active transport mechanism. Evidence by R. L. Post for red cells and by Caldwell for the giant axon also suggested that there was a coupling between sodium extrusion and potassium uptake. Experiments involving internal perfusion of these axons with various phosphagens support these ideas. Convincing evidence has been presented that ATP breakdown to adenosine diphosphate and phosphorus (ADP + P) provides the immediate energy for sodium pumping in the squid giant axon. It seems that the sodium pump is a sufficient explanation to account for the high internal potassium and the low internal sodium concentrations in nerve, muscle, and red blood cells. *See* ABSORPTION (BIOLOGY); ADENOSINE TRIPHOSPHATE (ATP).

It has been suggested that the key part of the sodium pump is the enzyme adenosinetriphosphatase (ATPase). This enzyme has been found in the membranes of most animal cells. The squid axon internal dialysis experiments have provided the stoichiometry for the action of membrane ATPase in catalyzing ATP breakdown promoting sodium extrusion and potassium uptake in the axon.

The existence of measurable resting sodium and chloride permeabilities in cell membranes, however, would make less acceptable the idea that the resting potential is solely due to a pure concentration potential for potassium ion. In some respects, the resolution of this was made less difficult by the earlier introduction of the constant field equation by D. E. Goldman in 1943. Assuming that the potential gradient across the thickness of the cell membrane was linear, Goldman determined a relation for the resting ionic conductances in the membrane. This relationship under the condition of zero net current flow was expressed as Eq. (3) by Hodgkin and B. Katz, where

$$E_{RP} = \frac{-RT}{F}$$
$$\times \ln \frac{[K^+]_{in} + P_{Na}[Na^+]_{in} + P_{Cl}[Cl^-]_{out}}{[K^+]_{out} + P_{Na}[Na^+]_{out} + P_{Cl}[Cl^-]_{in}} \qquad (3)$$

the P values indicate the ionic membrane permeabilities relative to potassium ion permeability, and the brackets indicate the concentrations (more correctly, the activities) of the enclosed ions. Assuming anion impermeability (and zero net current), the relation reduces to Eq. (4). Hodgkin and P. Horowicz

$$E_{RP} = \frac{-RT}{F} \ln \frac{[K]_{in} + P_{Na}[Na]_{in}}{[K]_{out} + P_{Na}[Na]_{out}} \qquad (4)$$

were able to fit the experimentally determined curvilinear relation between E_{RP} of muscle fibers and the logarithm of external potassium ion concentration by using this equation. *See* CELL MEMBRANES.

Ionic channels. Most of the foregoing discusses systems and relationships which applied only to macroscopic conditions (many ions and large areas) and often invoked the restriction of zero net current. A zero net ionic current is a balance between equal and opposite ionic movements. In living cells there are two general types of transport processes. In the first, the transported ionic species flows down the gradient of its own electrochemical potential. In the second, there is a requirement for immediate metabolic energy. Ionic currents flowing during such active events as the nerve impulse apparently belong to the first category, even though they are ultimately dependent on energy-requiring pump systems that maintain the ionic gradients across the membrane of the living cell. This first category of bioelectrical events is associated with a class of molecules called channels, embedded in living cell membranes.

It is now known that cell membranes contain many types of transmembrane channels. Channels are protein structures that span the lipid bilayers forming the backbones of cell membranes. The cell membranes of nerve, muscle, and other tissues contain ionic channels. These ionic channels have selectivity filters in their lumens such that in the open state only certain elementary ion species are admitted to passage, with the exclusion of other ion species. Other tissue cells such as epithelial cells, endocrine gland cells, lymphocytes, and sperm cells require channel activity for their functioning. In some cases, specific channels have been implicated in diseases such as cystic fibrosis and diabetes. There is now evidence of a specialized chloride channel called the cystic fibrosis transmembrane conductance regulator (CFTR). In cystic fibrosis, epithelial cells produce abnormally thick secretions, particularly in airways to mammalian lungs. The CFTR channel is regulated by cyclic adenosine monophosphate (cAMP) and can transport many substances vital to cell function as well as chloride ions.

Nerve impulse. It is now widely accepted that a two-state ion-selective membrane channel, capable of being gated between closed and open states, is the molecular mechanism responsible for excitation in neuromuscular systems. It is also accepted that these channels are specific protein molecules capable of undergoing conformational changes in their structure that account for the observed gating properties.

There are two general types of channels, and these are classified according to the way in which they respond to stimuli. Electrically excitable channels have opening and closing rates that are dependent on the transmembrane electric field. Chemically excitable channels (usually found in synaptic membranes) are controlled by the specific binding of certain activating molecules (agonists) to receptor sites associated with the channel molecule.

The long conducting parts of nerve cells, such as axons, transmit information by trains of constant-amplitude nerve impulses, or action potentials. The information content is encoded into the frequency of impulse transmission. The generation of any one of these impulses is brought about by a sequence of movements of specific ions through an ensemble of protein molecules bridging the nerve cell membrane.

Calcium channels are involved in synaptic transmission. When a nerve impulse arrives at the end of a nerve fiber, calcium channels open in response to the change in membrane potential. These channels admit calcium ions, which act on synaptic vesicles, facilitating their fusion with the presynaptic membrane. Upon exocytosis, these vesicles release transmitter molecules, which diffuse across the synaptic cleft to depolarize the postsynaptic membrane by opening ionic channels. Transmitter activity ceases from the action of specific transmitter esterases or by reabsorption of transmitter back into vesicles in the presynaptic neuron. Calcium channels inactivate and close until another nerve impulse arrives at the presynaptic terminal. Thus biopotentials play an important role in both the regulation and the genesis of synaptic transmission at the membrane channel level. There are many neurotransmitters. Glutamate is the most prevalent transmitter in central nervous system synapses in the human brain. Acetylcholine is a common transmitter at nerve muscle junctions.

The propagation of the conducted action potential in nerve cells (**Fig. 1**) results from fast, accurately voltage-dependent permeability changes to specific ions that take place across the nerve cell membrane. In the case of the squid giant axon, the permeation of sodium ions occurs in pores in the cell membrane that have been called sodium channels. Similarly, potassium ion permeation takes place through pores called potassium channels. These channels have been identified as molecular entities with distinct operational characteristics. These membrane proteins or channels can exist in either of two states.

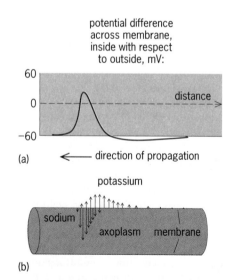

Fig. 1. Action potential in squid giant axon. (*a*) Voltage waveform. (*b*) Direction of flow of sodium and potassium ions corresponding to the action potential in *a*. The lengths of the arrows are proportional to the conductances to sodium and potassium ions. (*After W. J. Adelman, Jr., and R. J. French, The squid giant axon, Oceanus, 19(2):6–16, 1976*)

In the open state they admit ion flow, and in the closed state ion flow is prohibited. Transitions between resting, open, and closed states, or vice versa, are referred to as channel gating. It is now clear that such gating is the result of channel molecule conformational changes.

In order to describe the sequence of events that occur during an action potential, and to explain the macroscopic properties of electrically excitable membranes (such as threshold, propagation velocity, refractoriness, and anesthetic blockade), it is necessary to understand that these properties arise from the ensemble characteristics of many channels activated in some form of recruited synchrony. The most accurate measurement of these ensemble characteristics has involved voltage-clamping a reasonably large area of excitable membrane and recording the ionic current flow through thousands of parallel channels.

In 1952 Hodgkin and Huxley had described in quantitative detail the ionic currents flowing through a large area of nerve membrane containing an ensemble of many channels. From this description, they were able to reconstruct the action potential and predict many of its characteristics. *See* NERVE.

Single channels. Irwin Neher and Bert Sakmann were awarded a Nobel prize in 1991 for their development of the patch electrode and the description of the function of single channels in cells. **Figure 2** shows a glass pipette electrode sealing to the membrane of a cell such that a single channel is held in the orifice of the pipette. Ionic currents flowing through the channel can be recorded, and the membrane potential across the channel can be clamped to different values (patch clamp). With improvements in techniques such as the use of ultraclean or specially coated pipettes and use of negative pressures (reambient) inside the pipette, gigohm seals of the pipette electrode to the cell membrane could be achieved. These high-resistance seals meant that the background noise generated in the shunt resistance across the seal was reduced to a minimum (the higher the resistance, the lower the Johnson noise). This made the recording of single-channel ionic currents more distinct from background noise.

In 1980, R. Horn and J. Patlak showed that an isolated patch of membrane with its functioning membrane channels could be torn off from the cell and remain attached to the gigaseal electrode. The channel activity was the same as in the intact cell, and manipulation of internal solutions was made much easier.

Figure 3 shows records of single-channel potassium currents recorded with a patch electrode sealed to the inside of a squid giant axon. As the patch membrane was voltage-clamped, the membrane voltage and hence the voltage across the channel could be set to different values. The records clearly show that the dwell time in the conducting and nonconducting states is a function of voltage. In 1980 the results of using the patch electrode technique were published, indicating that single-channel sodium currents in muscle cells are related to macroscopic

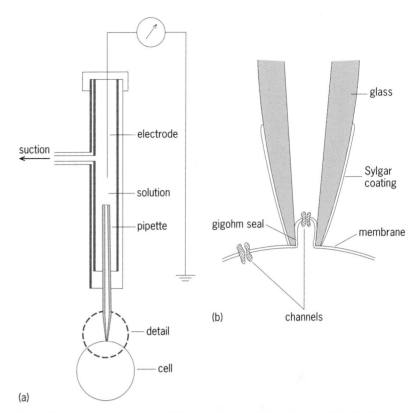

Fig. 2. Single-channel recording. (*a*) Gigaseal electrode holder, gigaseal glass pipette attached to a living cell, silver-silver chloride electrode in the test solution, and side arm for attaching tubing to produce the negative pressure required to establish the gigaseal. (*b*) Enlargement of detail in *a*. Not to scale.

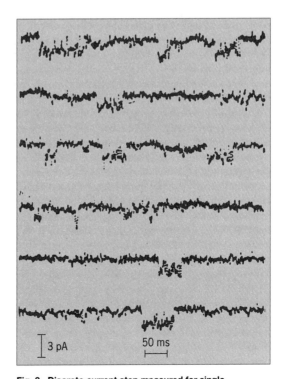

Fig. 3. Discrete current step measured for single potassium channels in the squid giant axon membrane. The upper three recordings were obtained with a −25-mV membrane potential. The lower three recordings were obtained with a −35-mV potential. The current steps are less frequent in the lower recording, indicating that the number of steps is voltage-dependent. (*After F. Conti and E. Neher, Single channel recordings of K*⁺ *currents in squid axons, Nature, 285:140–143, 1980*)

measurements of sodium currents from the cells. The response of a single sodium channel to a step in membrane potential repeated and summed many times has the same shape as the macroscopic membrane response to a single voltage clamp step, which presumably arose from the spatial summation of a set of similar unit channels. This superposition summation experiment has been taken by many investigators as the most convincing evidence that the phenomena giving rise to the nerve impulse have their origin in single-channel kinetics.

Mechanisms exist whereby specific ion channels can be opened and closed. Fluctuation between open and closed states among a population of channels determines both the magnitude and the sign of the biopotential existing across the cell membrane at any time. In general, there are two classes of channels: those that respond to the electric field across the membrane, and those that respond to chemical stimuli. Even channels that admit a specific ion can be of these two general classes, for example, voltage-activated potassium channels and acetylcholineactivated potassium channels. Acetylcholine released by vagus nerve activity has been shown to activate potassium channels in nodes and atrial muscles of the heart, which are different from the usual cardiac potassium channels. In human vascular smooth muscle cell membranes, at least four different types of potassium channels have been found (calcium-sensitive, voltage-dependent, adenosine triphosphate–sensitive, and inward rectifying channels). In 1984, B. Hille suggested that the human genome probably codes for as many as 50 different types of membrane channels.

Ionic currents flow through open channels. The ion impermeable membrane lipid bilayer acts as a dielectric separating two highly conductive salt solutions. Ionic channels have the electrical property of a conductance between these solutions. In 1939, Cole and Curtis showed that this conductance could be viewed as existing in parallel with the membrane capacitance arising from the lipid bilayer. The membrane conductance at any moment depends on the total number of channels, the type of channels, the fraction of channels found in the open state, and the unit conductances of these open channels. This unit conductance, g_{open}, is expressed in Eq. (5),

$$g_{open} = I_{open}/f(V - E_i) \qquad (5)$$

where V is the voltage across the channel, and E_i is the reversal potential for the ionic current; $f(V - E_i)$ considers that often current voltage relations are not linear and the possibility of competition among ion species for selectivity filter sites is of concern. The average conductance of a single channel fluctuating between open and closed states, g_{aver}, is given by Eq. (6), where p is the probability of finding the channel in the open state. When p is 1 the channel is open all the time; when p is zero the channel is closed all the time. For a given area of membrane containing N

$$g_{aver} = pg_{open} \qquad (6)$$

channels of the same type, the conductance is given by Eq. (7), where p may be a function of the electric

$$g = Npg_{open} \qquad (7)$$

field or of agonist binding to a channel receptor or both, depending on the type of channel.

The most common channels directly giving rise to biopotentials are those admitting mainly sodium ions, potassium ions, chloride ions, or calcium ions. These channels are named after the predominant charge carrier admitted in the open state, such as potassium channels. It is now known that there are charged amino acid groups lining the channel lumen that determine the specificity of the channel for particular ions. These selectivity filters admit only ions of the opposite charge.

For a membrane area containing a variety of ionic channels, the overall ionic conductance, G_m, is given by Eq. (8), where the subscripted conductances are

$$G_m = g_{Na} + g_K + g_{Cl} + g_{Ca} + \cdots + g_i \qquad (8)$$

the specific channel conductances. Each is described in Eq. (9). The ionic current, I, through a parallel ar-

$$g_i = N_i pg_{i,open} \qquad (9)$$

ray of channel conductances may then be readily expressed as Eq. (10). The membrane current flowing

$$\begin{aligned} I_i = {}& g_{Na}f(V - E_{Na}) + g_K f(V - E_K) \\ & + g_{Cl}f(V - E_{Cl}) + g_{Ca}f(V - E_{Cl}) \\ & + \cdots + g_i (V - E_i) \end{aligned} \qquad (10)$$

during a step change in membrane potential is given by Eq. (11), where C_m is the membrane capacity.

$$I_m = C_m(dV/dt) + I_i \qquad (11)$$

When dV/dt is zero (constant voltage), the capacity current is zero, and the membrane current is the ionic current. In principle, this is the basis for step voltage clamping. In practice, step voltage clamping requires that changes in membrane voltage be virtually instantaneous so that the capacity current settles to zero before ionic currents begin to flow.

In order to explain how channels gate from closed to open states and conversely, Hodgkin and Huxley proposed in 1952 that there were charged molecular entities responsible for the opening and closing of the ionic conductance pathways. These structures had to be charged to be able to move in response to changing electrical forces when the membrane voltage changed. Any movement of the gating structures would require a movement of charge and hence should have a detectable component of current flow across the membrane. It was not until 1973 that the existence of a gating current in squid axon sodium channels was demonstrated. By eliminating ionic charge carriers from the preparation, researchers measured a small but finite current whose characteristics had the properties of the expected gating charge movement. This was confirmed, and gating currents and their significance became a lively endeavor in membrane biophysics.

Channels appear to exist in all living excitable membranes. There are at least 10 classes of channels, and unit channels found in human muscle membranes bear a striking resemblance to those found in lower species. Many laboratories have attempted to isolate, purify, and then reconstitute biological channels into artificial lipid membranes.

The study of channel molecular structure has been extended into developmental biology. Channels develop, mature, differentiate, and are suppressed throughout the development of an organism from the initial egg cell to the mature organism. This process can be followed by electrophysiological methods (such as patch clamping) and by molecular biological methods.

Channel proteins. It has become almost routine to be able to isolate channel proteins from natural membranes and reconstitute these channels into artificial bilayer membranes formed between aqueous salt solutions. Acetylcholine receptor channels, sodium channels from the electric eel (*Electrophorus electricus*), sodium channels from mammalian brain, calcium-activated potassium channels from the sarcoplasmic reticulum of skeletal muscle, calcium channels from several sources, and potassium channels from muscle have all been isolated and reconstituted into planar bilayers.

More importantly, it has become possible to make use of gene expression to produce specific channel proteins in certain egg cells, such as eggs from the toad (*Xenopus laevis*). By obtaining the channel messenger ribonucleic acid (mRNA) from its appropriate complementary deoxyribonucleic acid (cDNA), and injecting this mRNA into an egg with proper substrates and activators, channel proteins may be synthesized in the egg and the channels reconstituted into the egg membrane.

Patch-clamping these channels has shown that they have ionic currents and closed-open transition kinetics that are similar to those measured in the original channel systems from which the cDNA was obtained. It is now possible to use genetic engineering techniques to alter the channel DNA and obtain new messengers which can be used to synthesize and incorporate in living membranes specifically altered channel proteins.

One of the major advances in the application of the techniques of molecular biology and genetic engineering to the study of channels took place in Japan in the early 1980s. Following the successful sequence of several pituitary hormones and significant active peptides such as beta lipotropin, the gene sequencing for the different subunits of the acetylcholine receptor channel was determined. From the nucleic acid sequence it was possible to determine the precise amino acid sequence of this protein. Following this success, the sequence of the sodium channel protein, of the transducer protein in visual cells which is linked to activated rhodopsin, and of the sodium-potassium adenosinetriphosphatase pro-

tein (the sodium pump molecule) was also determined.

Several neurotoxins have been shown to bind specifically to sodium channels in chick cardiac muscle cells, skeletal muscle fibers of the rat, rat brain cells, and the electric organ of the eel (*E. electricus*). By making use of these specific bindings, highly purified sodium channel protein has been obtained. The molecular weight of the polypeptide sodium channel protein ranges from 200,000 to 300,000, depending on the species. Recombinant DNA methods were used to clone DNA sequences complementary to mRNA coding for the sodium channel polypeptide of the eel electroplax. The complete amino acid sequence of this polypeptide was obtained by making use of a nucleotide sequence analysis of this cloned cDNA.

The eel electroplax sodium channel protein was shown to contain 1820 amino acid residues with a molecular weight of 208,321. Late in 1984 the nature of this primary structure of the sodium channel of the eel electroplax as based on cDNA sequencing was described. It was suggested that this primary sequence was composed of four domains of six subgroups each. A theoretical space-filling molecular model of the tertiary structure of the membrane-bound sodium channel based on the primary sequence and energy considerations was produced.

Use has been made of mRNAs derived from acetylcholine channel cDNAs in which the code for the synthesis of the channel had been changed for only one key amino acid at a time. By making use of the expression of genetically engineered altered channel proteins in *Xenopus* eggs, researchers have been able to show which specific amino acids in the acetylcholine channel protein are involved in specific channel functions. Once the expressed channels were incorporated in the oocyte membrane, these channels were patch-clamped and their characteristics were measured. This has allowed a direct correlation between the structural chemistry of the channel subunits and the biopotentials and ionic currents generated through the channels. *See* BIO-PHYSICS.   William J. Adelman, Jr.

Bibliography. K. S. Cole, *Membranes, Ions, and Impulses*, University of California Press, Berkeley, 1968; R. J. French and W. J. Adelman, Jr., Competition, saturation and inhibition: Ionic interactions shown by membrane ionic currents in nerve, muscle and bilayer systems, *Curr. Top. Membranes Transport*, 8:161–207, 1976; A. D. Grinnell, D. Armstrong, and M. B. Jackson (eds.), *Calcium and Ion Channel Modulation*, Plenum Press, New York, 1988; A. L. Hodgkin and A. F. Huxley, A quantitative description of membrane current and its application to conduction and excitation in nerve, *J. Physiol. (London)*, 117:500–544, 1952; H. Lecar, C. Morris, and B. S. Wong, Single-channel currents and the kinetics of agonist-induced gating, in D. C. Chang et al., *Structure and Function in Excitable Cells*, Plenum Press, New York, 1983; V. Milesi et al., Role of a Ca^{2+}-activated K^+ current in the maintenance of resting membrane potential of isolated human saphenous vein smooth muscle cells, *Pflugers Arch. Eur. J. Physiol.*, 437:455–461, 1999; B. Sakmann and E. Neher (eds.), *Single-Channel Recording*, 2d ed., Plenum Press, New York, 1995; E. M. Schweibert et al., CFTR is a conductance regulator as well as a chloride channel, *Physiol. Rev.*, 79 (suppl. 1):S145–S173, 1999; K. Takahashi and Y. Okamura, Ion channels and early development of neural cells, *Physiol. Rev.*, 78:307–337, 1998; H. Wheal and A. Thomson (eds.), *Excitatory Amino Acids and Synaptic Transmission*, 2d ed., Academic Press, London, 1995.

Biopyribole

A member of a chemically diverse, structurally related group of minerals that comprise substantial fractions of both the Earth's crust and upper mantle. The term was coined by Albert Johannsen in 1911 to describe collectively the rock-forming pyroxene, amphibole, and mica minerals [biopyribole is a contraction of biotite (a mica), pyroxene, and amphibole]. In addition to these common and long-recognized biopyriboles, several other members of the group have been recognized since the mid-1970s.

The pyroxene minerals contain single chains of corner-sharing silicate (SiO_4) tetrahedra (**Fig. 1a**), and the amphiboles contain double chains (Fig. 1b). Likewise, the micas and other related biopyriboles (talc, pyrophyllite, and the brittle micas) contain two-dimensionally infinite silicate sheets, which result in their characteristic sheetlike physical properties. In the pyroxenes and amphiboles, the silicate chains are articulated to strips of octahedrally coordinated cations, such as magnesium and iron; and in the sheet biopyriboles, the silicate sheets are connected by two-dimensional sheets of such cations. *See* AMPHIBOLE; MICA; PYROXENE.

In addition to the classical single-chain, double-chain, and sheet biopyriboles, several biopyriboles that contain triple silicate chains (Fig. 1c) have been discovered. These minerals had been overlooked previously due to small crystal size and similarity in physical properties to those of the more common pyriboles (pyribole is a term applied to the chain-silicate subset of the biopyribole group).

Structurally disordered types. Triple silicate chains of the type shown in Fig. 1c were first found as isolated faults in amphibole asbestos. Such triple chains, as well as quadruple, quintuple, and wider chains, occur as defects in many amphibole specimens. The intergrowth of these triple and wider chains in amphibole is a type of structural disorder. In addition, similar structural disorder occurs in some pyroxenes, where double, triple, and wider silicate chains are intergrown with the predominantly single-chain structure.

Much of the knowledge about structurally disordered biopyriboles has been obtained by the use of high-resolution transmission electron microscopy. An electron micrograph of structurally disordered anthophyllite (an amphibole) is shown in **Fig. 2**. In this electron image, the crystal is viewed parallel

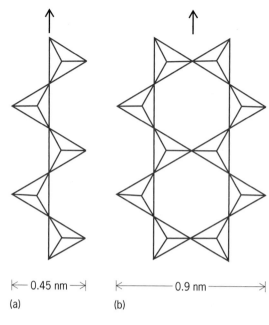

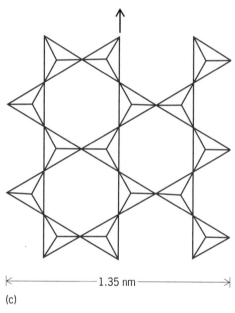

Fig. 1. Silicate-chain structures for biopyribole minerals. (*a*) Single silicate chain characteristic of pyroxenes. (*b*) Double silicate chain of amphiboles. (*c*) Triple silicate chain as found in the new biopyriboles. (*After D. R. Veblen et al., Asbestiform chain silicates: New minerals and structural groups, Science, 198:359–365, 1977*)

to the silicate chains, which define the direction of the *c* crystallographic axis. In addition to the double-chain structure characteristic of amphibole, the crystal contains slabs with triple, quadruple, and sextuple silicate chains.

Structurally ordered wide- and mixed-chain types. The wide-chain biopyribole minerals containing ordered arrays of triple silicate chains were discovered by using single-crystal x-ray diffraction methods. The minerals jimthompsonite and clinojimthompsonite consist purely of triple-silicate-chain structure. The mineral chesterite and an unnamed mineral contain both triple and double silicate chains that alternate

System	Pyroxenes, $(Mg,Fe)_2Si_2O_6$	Amphiboles, $(Mg,Fe)_7Si_8O_{22}(OH)_2$	Triple-chain silicates, $(Mg,Fe)_{10}Si_{12}O_{32}(OH)_4$	Mixed-chain silicates, $(Mg,Fe)_{17}Si_{20}O_{54}(OH)_6$
Orthorhombic	Enstatite $a = 1.82$ nm $b = 0.88$ $c = 0.52$ Pbca	Anthophyllite $a = 1.86$ nm $b = 1.81$ $c = 0.53$ Pnma	Jimthompsonite $a = 1.86$ nm $b = 2.72$ $c = 0.53$ Pbca	Chesterite $a = 1.86$ nm $b = 4.53$ $c = 0.53$ $A2_1ma$
Monoclinic	Clinoenstatite $a = 0.96$ nm $b = 0.88$ $c = 0.52$ $\beta = 108.3°$ C2/m	Cummingtonite $a = 0.95$ nm $b = 1.81$ $c = 0.53$ $\beta = 109.6°$ I2/m	Clinojimthompsonite $a = 0.99$ nm $b = 2.72$ $c = 0.53$ $\beta = 109.5°$ C2/c	Unnamed mineral $a = 0.99$ nm $b = 4.53$ $c = 0.53$ $\beta = 109.7°$ A2/m

Chemical formulas, unit-cell parameters, and space group symmetries of ferromagnesian biopyriboles*

*The space groups are for high-temperature forms.

rigorously parallel to the *b* crystallographic axis. Chesterite is the first known example of a mixed-chain silicate in that it contains two topologically distinct types of silicate chains.

The properties of some ferromagnesian pyroxenes and amphiboles are listed in the **table**, along with those of the more recently recognized wide-chain ordered pyriboles. The differences in chain width among these minerals are revealed by the lengths of the *b* crystallographic axes, which are parallel to the widths of the chains ($b \cong 0.9$ nanometer for single chains, 1.8 nm for double chains, 2.7 nm for triple chains, and 4.5 nm for alternating double and triple chains). All of the monoclinic chain silicates listed in the table possess *a* axes of approximately 1.0 nm, because their chains are stacked in an identical fashion parallel to this axis. Likewise, all of the orthorhombic minerals in the table have *a* axes of about 1.8 nm, the result of their identical stacking parallel to *a* that differs from that of the monoclinic members of the group. These relationships among unit-cell parameters are the direct result of the close structural relationships among all the biopyriboles. *See* CRYSTAL STRUCTURE.

The sequences of silicate chains in biopyriboles can be represented as follows: pyroxene [1], amphibole [2], chesterite [23], jimthompsonite [3], and mica or talc [∞]. As an example, in this notation [2] implies that double silicate chains repeat infinitely with the sequence ...222222222... in the direction of the *b* axis. Of these macroscopically occurring, ordered biopyriboles, only chesterite is a mixed-chain silicate because it is the only structure that contains more than one type of silicate chain. However, many additional ordered, mixed-chain structures have been observed with electron microscopy. These include biopyriboles with more complicated chain sequences, such as [2233], [233], [2333], [234], and [222222333333]. In addition, mixed-chain biopyriboles containing single chains have been observed, such as [1112], and the structure [12] has been synthesized at very high pressures as single crystals large enough for analysis by x-ray diffraction methods. *See* X-RAY CRYSTALLOGRAPHY.

Theoretical basis of structures. Amphibole structures consist of slabs of pyroxene (P) structure and mica or talc structure (M). These slabs alternate rigorously parallel to the (010) planes of amphibole in the sequence ... MPMPMP ..., or simply (MP). Any amphibole can thus be thought of as a 1:1 mechanical mixture of pyroxene and mica. The pyriboles containing triple silicate chains also have structures made of the same types of slabs, with the sequence (MMP) in pure triple-chain minerals such as jimthompsonite and the sequence (MPMMP) in the mixed-chain members of the group such as chesterite.

Because all of the biopyriboles consist of such mixtures of two different kinds of structural slabs, or of pure M slabs (mica) or P slabs (pyroxene), they all have stoichiometries that are collinear with the pyroxene and mica (or talc) stoichiometries. This chemical relationship is shown in **Fig. 3** for the idealized pure magnesium compositions. A group of structures that possesses this kind of structural and chemical relationship has been called a polysomatic series.

The biopyribole crystal structures are very compliant and, within the constraints of their stoichiometries, can adapt to wide variations in chemical composition, pressure, and temperature. Depending on the exact geochemical and physical conditions, the

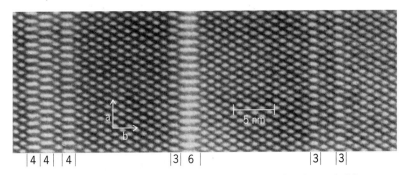

Fig. 2. Transmission electron micrograph of a structurally disordered crystal of the amphibole anthophyllite. Normal double-chain structure is unlabeled, and planar defects with triple-, quadruple-, and sextuple-chain structure are labeled 3, 4, and 6, respectively. (*From D. R. Veblen, ed., Amphiboles and Other Hydrous Pyriboles: Mineralogy, Mineral. Soc. Amer. Rev. Mineral., vol. 9a, 1981*)

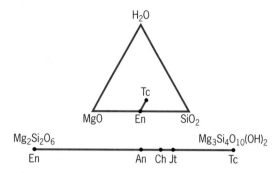

Fig. 3. Chemical compositions of ideal pure magnesium biopyriboles. En = enstatite (pyroxene), An = anthophyllite (amphibole), Ch = chesterite, Jt = jimthompsonite, and Tc = talc (sheet silicate). (*After D. R. Veblen et al., Asbestiform chain silicates: New minerals and structural groups, Science, 198:359–365, 1977*)

various naturally occurring biopyribole minerals can contain major amounts of hydrogen, lithium, oxygen, fluorine, sodium, magnesium, aluminum, silicon, chlorine, potassium, calcium, titanium, magnesium, and iron, in addition to other elements that may occur less commonly. Furthermore, compositions containing a much broader range of elements can be synthesized in the laboratory. In some biopyriboles, vacancies are also abundant on some crystallographic sites, and sites that are filled for some compositions may be vacant for others. *See* ELEMENT (CHEMISTRY).

Occurrence and stability. Pyroxenes, amphiboles, and micas of various compositions can occur in igneous, metamorphic, and sedimentary rocks. Pyroxenes are the second most abundant minerals in the Earth's crust (after feldspars) and in the upper mantle (after olivine). Amphiboles occur as at least minor constitutents in many common igneous rocks and may make up the bulk of some metamorphic rocks. The sheet-silicate biopyriboles are major phases in some sedimentary rocks such as shales, occur in many igneous rocks, can make up the bulk of some metamorphic rocks, and may even be important volatile-bearing minerals in the upper mantle. These biopyriboles clearly have fields of thermodynamic stability. *See* IGNEOUS ROCKS; METAMORPHIC ROCKS; SEDIMENTARY ROCKS.

Unlike the pyroxenes, amphiboles, and micas, the wide-chain biopyriboles do not occur as abundant minerals in a wide variety of rock types. However, some of them may be widespread in nature as components of fine-grain alteration products of pyroxenes and amphiboles and as isolated lamellae in other biopyriboles (but single crystals up to several millimeters long and a few tenths of a millimeter wide have been observed for jimthompsonite and chesterite). Also, unlike the classical biopyriboles, it is not known whether or not any of the wide-chain pyriboles possess true fields of thermodynamic stability. Possibly, they always form as a result of metastable reaction or growth processes. There has been no experimental confirmation of the stability relations of these wide-chain structures. *See* BIOTITE; SILICATE MINERALS.   David R. Veblen

Bibliography. J. Akai, Polymerization process of biopyribole in metasomatism at the Akatani ore deposit, Japan, *Contrib. Mineral. Petrol.*, 80:117–131, 1982; S. W. Bailey (ed.), Micas, *Mineral. Soc. Amer. Rev. Mineral.*, no. 13, 1984; W. A. Deer, R. A. Howie, and J. Zussman, *Rock-Forming Minerals*, 2d ed., Geological Society, London, vol. 2A, 1978, vol. 2B, 1997; B. H. Grobéty, New short-range biopyribole polysomes from the Lepontine Alps, Switzerland, *Amer. Mineral.*, 81:404–417, 1996; B. H. Grobéty, The replacement of anthophyllite by jimthompsonite: A model for hydration reactions in biopyriboles, *Contrib. Mineral. Petrol.*, 127:237–247, 1997; B. E. Leake et al., Nomenclature of amphiboles, *Amer. Mineral.*, 82:1019–1037, 1997; N. Morimoto et al., Nomenclature of pyroxenes, *Amer. Mineral.*, 73:1123–1133, 1988; C. T. Prewitt (ed.), Pyroxenes, *Mineral. Soc. Amer. Rev. Mineral.*, no. 7, 1980; M. Rieder et al., Nomenclature of the micas, *Can. Mineral.*, 36:905–912, 1998; J. B. Thompson, Jr., Biopyriboles and polysomatic series, *Amer. Mineral.*, 63:239–249, 1978; D. R. Veblen (ed.), Amphiboles and Other Hydrous Pyriboles: Mineralogy, *Mineral. Soc. Amer. Rev. Mineral.*, no. 9A, 1981; D. R. Veblen, Polysomatism and polysomatic series: A review and applications, *Amer. Mineral.*, 76:801–826, 1991; D. R. Veblen and P. H. Ribbe (eds.), Amphiboles: Petrology and Experimental Phase Relations, *Mineral. Soc. Amer. Rev. Mineral.*, vol. 9B, 1982.

Biorheology

The study of the flow and deformation of biological materials. As all living things flow and deform, biorheology is involved in the study of every aspect of biology. The behavior and fitness of living organisms depend partly on the mechanical properties of their structural materials. Humans are healthy when the rheological properties of their tissues are normal; deviations lead to illness. For example, a thinner than normal fluid in the knee joint results in pain and arthrosis, and softened or weakened bones result in fractures.

Thus, biologists are interested in biorheology from the point of view of evolution and adaptation to the environment. Physicians are interested in it in order to understand health and disease. Bioengineers devise methods to measure or to change the rheological properties of biological materials, develop mathematical descriptions of biorheology, and create new practical applications for biorheology in agriculture, industry, and medicine.

The rheological behavior of most biological materials is more complex than that of air, water, and most structural materials used in engineering. Air and water are viscous fluids; all fluids whose viscosity is similar to that of air and water are called newtonian fluids. Biological fluids such as protoplasm, blood, and synovial fluid behave differently, however, and they are called non-newtonian fluids. For example, blood behaves like a fluid when it flows, but when it stops flowing it behaves like a solid with a small but finite yield stress. When it does flow, its viscosity decreases when the shear-strain rate increases. Thus, in a tube the faster the blood flows, the less viscous it becomes. These features are non-newtonian. *See* NON-NEWTONIAN FLUID; VISCOSITY.

Most materials used in engineering construction, such as steel, aluminum, or rock, obey Hooke's law, according to which stresses are linearly proportional to strains. These materials deviate from Hooke's law only when approaching failure. Solids obeying Hooke's law are said to be Hookean. A structure made of Hookean materials behaves linearly: load and deflection are linearly proportional to each other in such a structure. Some biological materials, such as bone and wood, also obey Hooke's law in their normal state of function, but many others, such as skin, tendon, muscle, blood vessels, lung, and liver, do not. These materials, referred to as non-Hookean, become stiffer as stress increases. *See* BONE; ELASTICITY; HOOKE'S LAW; STRESS AND STRAIN.

Microbiorheology. To gain a fundamental understanding of the rheological properties of biological tissues, a modern trend is to probe deeper into the cellular and molecular aspects of the system. Since the knowledge gained is applicable at the basic level, this approach often provides important practical uses.

Mucus. The rheological properties of mucus may be determined by a high-molecular-weight glycoprotein that is covered by carbohydrate side chains. Variations of this molecule are introduced by the secretory cells of the epithelium. In the case of ciliated epithelia, the mucus forms a layer in contact with the cilia and is rheologically adjusted so as to cause optimal transport and clearance. There are reasons to think that mucus is not normally present over the ciliary epithelium and that the cilia are not normally in motion. Secretion is stimulated when loads impinge over a particular section of the epithelium. Ciliary motion is initiated by the presence of mucus and ceases when the patch of mucus has moved over and beyond the cells in question. In this view, mucociliary transport action is initiated by mechanical events. Further, it is recognized that mucus production results from concerted function of not one but several cellular types: secretory cells that produce the raw materials and other epithelial cells which are responsible for the postsecretory formation of a hydrogel. *See* EPITHELIUM.

Soft tissue. Soft tissues are often very complex in composition. A connective tissue is composed of structural proteins such as collagen and elastin, ground substances such as glycosaminoglycans, and cellular components. If the properties of individual components are known and the structure of the tissue is determined, then the mechanical properties of the tissue can be computed according to appropriate models. In practical applications, physical, chemical, and biological interventions may be introduced to influence the individual components or the structure as a whole in order to control the properties of the tissue. These studies have important applications to surgery, rehabilitation, and control of hypertrophy and resorption. *See* COLLAGEN; CONNECTIVE TISSUE.

Muscle. The rheological properties of muscles are of fundamental importance to medicine. Constitutive equations are not available, but with a constitutive equation for the active contraction of the heart muscle, a rigorous theory of cardiology could be developed. Similarly, a constitutive equation for vascular smooth muscle would allow hypertension and circulatory regulation to be analyzed. A phenomenological approach has not been very successful for these muscles. Since the advent of the sliding filament model, most researchers have focused their attention on the study of the actin and myosin molecules and cross bridges between them in order to understand the generation of force and motion. Other researchers study the collagen fibers in the muscle bundle which control the mechanical properties of the muscle when it is in a resting state, and the constitutive equation when it is contracting. The difficulty lies in the nonlinear behavior of these fibers, so that the contributions from different sources cannot be simply added. *See* MUSCLE; MUSCLE PROTEINS.

Motility of leukoytes. The interior structure of leukocytes is nonhomogeneous. Under suitable stimulation, sol-gel transformation takes place in the cell at various localities. The basic mechanism seems to be closely associated with actin molecules, that is, stress fibers, in the cells. Leukocytes and platelets contain a protein, gelsolin, which binds calcium ion (Ca^{2+}) and has powerful effects on actin: in the presence of micromolar Ca^{2+}, gelsolin severs actin filaments. Leukocyte rheology is of great importance in medicine. *See* BLOOD.

Thrombus formation and dissolution. Blood may form a thrombus in response to injury on the inner wall of a blood vessel or the presence of a cardiovascular device. This function is normally a life-saving process in that it seals up blood vessels that are injured as a result of cuts and bruises. It is, however, also implicated in atherosclerosis and stroke, and it is a major problem for successful implantation of artificial internal organs. The molecular mechanisms of thrombus formation and dissolution involve a change of blood rheology and are very complex. *See* ARTERIOSCLEROSIS; THROMBOSIS.

Cell membrane. Since a living cell contacts other cells, the importance of cell membrane biorheology is evident. The subject includes not only the elasticity, viscoelasticity, and viscoplasticity of the cell membrane but also adhesion and other interaction between membranes. *See* CELL ADHESION; CELL MEMBRANES.

Macrobiorheology. On the other end of the scale from microbiorheology are the macroscopic phenomena, such as blood flow, breathing, micturition, heartbeat, and intestinal peristalsis. Many important aspects of these phenomena depend on the rheological properties of the tissues. For example, the flow separation in arteries at points of bifurcation is a phenomenon intimately related to plaque formation in atherosclerosis. In this case the elasticity of the wall and the non-newtonian rheology of the blood have considerable influence on the separation process. Such problems are often treated in biomechanics.

Constitutive equations. In biorheology, so-called constitutive equations are used to describe the complex mechanical behavior of materials in terms of mathematics. At least three kinds of constitutive equations are needed: those describing stress-strain relationships of material in the normal state of life; those describing the transport of matter, such as water, gas, and other substances, in tissues; and those describing growth or resorption of tissues in response to long-term changes in the state of stress and strain. The third type is the most fascinating, but there is very little quantitative information available about it except for bone. The second type is very complex because living tissues are nonhomogeneous, and since mass transport in tissues is a molecular phenomenon, it is accentuated by nonhomogeneity at the cellular level. The best-known constitutive equations are therefore of the first kind. Some examples of these equations are described below.

Blood. If blood is tested in a Couette viscometer (a rotational viscometer) or a cone-plate viscometer, it is found that in a steady flow the shear stress τ is approximately related to the shear strain rate by Casson's equation (1), where the constant τ_y has the

$$\sqrt{\tau} = \sqrt{\tau_y} + \sqrt{\eta\dot{\gamma}} \qquad (1)$$

significance of a yield stress and the constant η is called Casson's coefficient. This relation reflects the deformability of blood cells in shear flow, and the ability of the red cells to stick to each other and form rouleaux (stacks of erythrocytes) when the shear gradient decreases. Equation (1) does not account for the normal stress due to shear, nor for other viscoelastic features of the blood. The mathematical description of blood viscoelasticity is quite complex, but it is important because the viscoelasticity affects flow separation of blood at points of bifurcation of the arteries or at sites of severe stenosis. Hence it is implicated in atherogenesis, and is relevant to technical problems of prosthetic heart valves and implantable artificial organs.

Red blood cells are filled with hemoglobin solution, which in normal blood is a newtonian fluid with a viscosity of about 6 centipoise. These cells are severely deformed when flowing through capillaries, but when stationary they assume the regular shape of a biconcave circular disk. Normal human red cells have an average disk diameter of about 7.8 micrometers, a maximum thickness of about 2.6 μm, a minimum thickness of 0.8 μm, and a wall (membrane) thickness of about 0.005 μm. For such a thin shell, mechanical analysis shows that the discoid shape implies that the membrane stress resultant in the cell membrane is zero in the normal condition, and that the membrane stress remains small in deformed states. Hence, a great engineering marvel is

achieved by a simple design of geometric shape: the discoid shape makes the cells flexible and unstressed in severe deformation. Strength is achieved by flexibility.

By extensive study of cell deformation in response to external loading, it has been determined that the shear modulus of elasticity of the red cell membrane is about 10,000 times smaller than the elastic modulus for the change of membrane surface area. Hence the area of the membrane does not change significantly when the cell deforms. In fact, the membrane breaks when its area is increased by approximately 5% above the normal, but the cell membrane can be stretched several hundred percent in any direction if the area is preserved.

The interior material of the white blood cells is viscoelastic, and sol-gel transformation takes place when pseudopods form. Chemotaxis of leukocytes is related to the change in rheological properties of the cellular material, and it is most likely that the formation, movement, and desolution of the vesicles and their membranes cause these rheological changes.

Blood vessels. All living tissues are pseudoelastic; that is, they are not elastic, but under periodic loading a steady-state stress-strain relationship exists which is not very sensitive to strain rate. The loading and unloading branches can be treated separately, and a pseudoelastic potential can be introduced to describe the stress-strain relationship in either loading or unloading. The pseudoelastic potential $\rho_0 W$ (where W is defined for unit mass of the vessel wall and ρ_0 is the density in the initial state) is a function of Green's strain components E_{ij}, and is the strain energy per unit initial volume. The partial derivatives of $\rho_0 W$ with respect to E_{ij} give the corresponding stresses S_{ij} (Kirchhoff stress). For arteries and veins the pseudostrain-energy functions can be expressed either in the form of a polynomial, or as an exponential function, Eq. (2), where Q is a function of the strain components shown in Eq. (3). The subscripts

$$\rho_0 W = Ce^Q \qquad (2)$$

$$Q = a_1 E_1^2 + a_2 E_2^2 + a_3 E_3^2$$
$$+ 2a_4 E_1 E_2 + 2a_5 E_2 E_3 + 2a_6 E_3 E_1 \qquad (3)$$

1, 2, 3 in Eq. (3) refer to the circumferential, longitudinal, and radial directions respectively, and E_1, E_2, E_3 are shorthand for the strain components E_{11}, E_{22}, E_{33} respectively. Cylindrical symmetry is assumed in this expression for simplicity; otherwise one should generalize the quadratic form Q to include all six strain components. If the vessel wall can be considered homogeneous, then the constants $C, a_1, \ldots, a_6$ are independent of the location in the blood vessel. If, in addition, the arterial wall material is assumed to be incompressible, then the condition of incompressibility, Eq. (4), may be introduced through a lagrangian multiplier H. A new pseudoelastic function

$$(1 + 2E_1)(1 + 2E_2)(1 + 2E_3) = 1 \qquad (4)$$

grangian multiplier H. A new pseudoelastic function

is defined by Eq. (5) so that the Kirchhoff stresses are expressed by Eq. (6). It is well known that H has

$$\rho_0 W^* = \\ Ce^Q + H[(1 + 2E_1)(1 + 2E_2)(1 + 2E_3) - 1] \quad (5)$$

$$S_i = \frac{\partial(\rho W^*)}{\partial E_i} \qquad (i = 1, 2, 3) \qquad (6)$$

the significance of a hydrostatic pressure which can assume an arbitrary value. The true value is determined by the equations of motion (or equilibrium) and boundary conditions.

Other soft tissues. The elastic behavior of many soft tissues, such as the skin, tendon, cartilage, mesentery, bladder, ureter, muscles, and taenia coli, is similar to that of the blood vessels in the sense that Eqs. (2)-(6) may be made to fit the experimental data. These materials become stiffer when stressed, and their incremental elastic moduli are almost linearly proportional to the stresses.

All of these soft tissues also have a fairly similar viscoelastic behavior. They all show hysteresis when subjected to cyclic loading and unloading but the hysteresis loop is fairly insensitive to the strain rate. Typically, in a thousandfold change in strain rate, the stress at a given strain in a loading (or unloading) process does not change by more than a factor of 2. When a tissue is stretched suddenly to a new dimension, which is then held constant, it will show the phenomenon of stress relaxation, that is, the stress gradually decreases with increasing time. The degree of relaxation depends on the tissue. In time, an extended ureter can relax off almost all the stress, whereas an artery can relax off only 20-30%, and a ligament nuchae relaxes off only a few percent. When the tissues are stressed suddenly by a step function and then the stress is kept constant, the tissue creeps; that is, its strain increases with increasing time. The degree of creep also depends on the tissue; but is usually fairly small in tendons, ligaments, skin, and arteries. These features, relaxation, creep, hysteresis, and strain-rate insensitivity, can be condensed in a mathematical formulation called the quasilinear viscoelasticity theory. It is nonlinear in elastic stress response to strain, linear in relating the stress at present to the elastic stress of the past, with a continuous relaxation spectrum.

Synovial and other body fluids. Most of these fluids, containing large molecules such as hyaluronic acid, behave rheologically in a manner similar to the blood. They are shear thinning, that is, their coefficients of viscosity decrease with increasing shear strain rate, and viscoelastic.

Mucus and saliva. Mucus is a complex mixture of water, electrolytes, glycoproteins, epithelial cells, and white blood cells. It is a viscoelastic material. When mucus is subjected to a small oscillatory deformation in a testing machine, the shear stress τ can be related to the shear strain γ by Eq. (7), where $G(i\omega)$

$$\tau = G(i\omega)\gamma \qquad (7)$$

is the complex modulus of elasticity, i is the imaginary number $\sqrt{-1}$, and ω is the circular frequency of the oscillation. The real part of $G(i\omega)$ is called the storage modulus, and the imaginary part of $G(i\omega)$ is called the loss modulus. These names are associated with the fact that if the material obeys Hooke's law, then the strain energy stored in the material is proportional to the storage modulus; whereas if the material behaves like a newtonian viscous fluid, then the energy dissipated is proportional to the loss modulus.

Saliva is also viscoelastic, in many ways similar to bronchotracheal mucus. It has been proposed that the testing of drugs to combat the common cold, which usually aim at modifying the rheological property of mucus, may well be carried out by using saliva. *See* BIOMECHANICS; RHEOLOGY.   Y. C. Fung

Bibliography. A. L. Copley and A. Silberberg (eds.), Symposia on cellular and molecular basis of mucus rheology and molecular biorheology, *Biorheology J.*, 24:535-687, 1987; E. A. Evans and R. Skalak, *Mechanics and Thermodynamics of Biomembranes*, 1980; E. Fukada and T. Azuma (eds.), Perspectives in biorheology, *Biorheology J.*, 25:1-401, 1988; Y. C. Fung, *Biomechanics: Mechanical Properties of Living Tisssues*, 2d ed., 1993; S. Oka, *Cardiovascular Hemorheology*, 1981; G. H. Pollack and H. Sugi, *Contractile Mechanisms in Muscle*, 1984.

Biosensor

An integrated device consisting of a biological recognition element and a transducer capable of detecting the biological reaction and converting it into a signal which can be processed. Ideally, the sensor should be self-contained, so that it is not necessary to add reagents to the sample matrix to obtain the desired response. There are a number of analytes (the target substances to be detected) which are measured in biological media: pH, partial pressure of carbon dioxide (pCO_2), partial pressure of oxygen (pO_2), and the ionic concentrations of sodium, potassium, calcium, and chloride. However, these sensors do not use biological recognition elements, and are considered chemical sensors. Normally, the biological recognition element is a protein or protein complex which is able to recognize a particular analyte in the presence of many other components in a complex biological matrix. Recently this definition has been expanded to include oligonucleotides. The recognition process involves a chemical or biological reaction, and the transducer must be capable of detecting not only the reaction but also its extent. An ideal sensor should yield a selective, rapid, and reliable response to the analyte, and the signal generated by the sensor should be proportional to the analyte concentration.

Biosensors are typically classified by the type of recognition element or transduction element employed. A sensor might be described as a catalytic biosensor if its recognition element comprised an enzyme or series of enzymes, a living tissue slice (vegetal or animal), or whole cells derived from microorganisms such as bacteria, fungi, or yeast. The sensor might be described as a bioaffinity sensor if the basis of its operation were a biospecific complex formation. Accordingly, the reaction of an antibody with an antigen or hapten, or the reaction of an agonist or antagonist with a receptor, could be employed. In the former case, the sensor might be called an immunosensor.

Catalytic biosensors. Historically, the first biosensor was based on the measurement of an enzyme-catalyzed reaction. This device, described by L. C. Clark and C. Lyons in 1962, involved the incorporation of glucose oxidase into a membrane. This enzyme catalyzes the highly selective oxidation of glucose by oxygen to form gluconic acid and hydrogen peroxide, as in reaction (1). The reaction rate is rendered

$$\text{Glucose} + O_2 \rightarrow \text{gluconic acid} + H_2O_2 \qquad (1)$$

dered proportional to the concentration of glucose, and it is measured by monitoring the formation of hydrogen peroxide. This is accomplished by applying a controlled potential between two electrodes. There is produced a current which is proportional to the peroxide concentration and hence to the concentration of glucose. This device is called an enzyme electrode, because an enzyme is the recognition element and the transducer an electrode. This is by far the most important biosensor, largely because it is used extensively for clinical monitoring of blood glucose in the detection and treatment of diabetes. A potential is applied between a silver and a platinum electrode, and the resulting current from the peroxide produced in the oxidase enzyme membrane is measured. A cellulose acetate membrane and a polycarbonate membrane (see **illus.**) are used to screen out species that might interfere with analyte detection. Additional so-called oxidase enzymes catalyze the oxidation of other analytes (enzyme substrates) in a manner analogous to glucose. The two most important are lactate and glutamate. Lactate is used clinically in monitoring patients following myocardial infarction, and in sports medicine to assess exercise which can delay the buildup of lactate, a source of the pain of exertion. Monitoring of glucose, lactate, and glutamate are important in the food processing industry and in aiding the control of fermentation processes in bioreactors. *See* ANALYTICAL CHEMISTRY.

Alternatively, reaction (1) can be coupled with reaction (2) [catalyzed by a second enzyme, per-

$$H_2O_2 + MBTH + DMAB \rightarrow MBTH - DMAB \text{ (blue)} \qquad (2)$$

oxidase], which generates a color to which the concentration of glucose can be related. MBTH is 3-methyl-2-benzothiazolinone hydrazone, and DMAB is 3-dimethylaminobenzoic acid. This principle forms the basis for the majority of "fingerstick" home monitoring blood glucose systems used by diabetic patients. The intensity of the color development is evaluated using a simple device which measures the light reflected off the surface where the reaction occurs.

Enzyme-based biosensors are not restricted to oxidases. A large class of enzymes known as dehydrogenases also catalyze the oxidation of analyte substrates without using oxygen. For example, a glucose dehydrogenase is used in one of the home monitoring blood glucose systems. Sometimes more than one enzyme is needed to convert the analyte into a form suitable for detection. The determination of acetylcholine, a key neurotransmitter, can be effected in two steps: the conversion of acetylcholine to choline, catalyzed by the enzyme acetylcholinesterase, followed by the oxidation of choline by oxygen using choline oxidase. Organophosphates such as Malathion (insecticide) and organophosphonates such as Sarin (nerve gas) are toxic to living organisms because they inhibit acetylcholinesterase activity. Thus this same system can be used to determine the inhibition of enzyme activity instead of substrate concentration, making it suitable for the detection of insecticides or nerve gas. Enzyme-based sensors are not restricted to oxidation-reduction reactions. Urease is used to hydrolyze urea to yield ammonia and carbon dioxide. The urea concentration can be related to the resulting pH change due to the reaction.

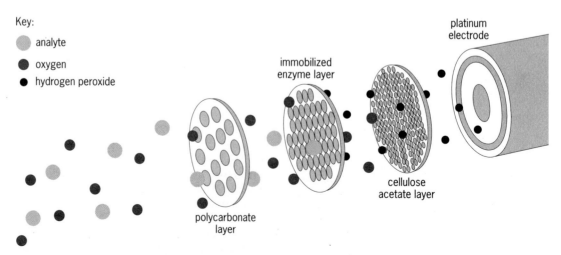

Key:
- analyte
- oxygen
- hydrogen peroxide

platinum electrode

immobilized enzyme layer

cellulose acetate layer

polycarbonate layer

Biosensor employed in a commercially available clinical glucose analyzer. (*Yellow Springs Instrument Co. Inc.*)

Tissue slices and bacterial cultures have also formed the basis for electrochemical biosensors. Because they comprise many enzymes, the reactions are complex. However, they are useful for estimating the toxicity of a sample (inhibition of activity) and for such measurements as biochemical oxygen demand (BOD), an important measure of wastewater quality.

Since enzyme-based sensors measure the rate of the enzyme-catalyzed reaction as the basis for their response, any physical measurement which yields a quantity related to this rate can be used for detection. The enzyme may be immobilized on the end of an optical fiber, and the spectroscopic properties (absorbance, fluorescence, chemiluminescence) related to the disappearance of the reactants or appearance of products of the reaction can be measured. Since biochemical reactions can be either endothermic (absorbing heat) or exothermic (giving off heat), the rate of the reaction can be measured by microcalorimetry. Miniaturized thermistor-based calorimeters, called enzyme thermistors, have been developed and widely applied, especially for bioprocess monitoring.

Affinity biosensors. The highly selective and high-affinity binding of a molecule to a receptor forms the basis for a relatively new class of biosensors. The most common bioaffinity sensors are based on an antibody (Ab) reaction with an antigen (Ag), such as a protein, peptide, or oligonucleotide, or with a hapten, which is a small organic molecule such as a drug. Accordingly, the purpose of the biosensor is to detect the extent of the binding process and relate it to the concentration of the analyte. Unfortunately, detection of binding is not simple. An increase (albeit extremely small) in the mass of the sensor can be used as the basis for detection of binding, and indeed sensors based on the quartz crystal microbalance have been developed. The antibody is immobilized on the sensor surface, and when the antibody-antigen reaction takes place, an increase in mass results, forming the basis for an immunoassay. A second approach, called surface plasmon resonance (SPR), exploits the change in refractive index of a bioaffinity coating on a gold film when binding takes place. Biospecific interaction analysis (BIA), based on this approach, has proven useful for fundamental studies of interactions between well-defined reactants in a simple matrix. Unfortunately, it shares with the microbalance the problem that any interaction with the surface can result in a change in signal, thus making the detection of binding an inherently nonspecific method.

The alternative to the above approaches is to label one of the reactants with a fluorescent tag or an enzyme which generates a product that can be detected by its fluorescence, absorbance, chemiluminescence, or electroactivity. For example, an antibody may be immobilized on an optical-fiber outer surface and reacted with a fluorescent-labeled antigen. An appropriately chosen light beam is passed down the fiber so that it couples optically with the fluorescent label on the outer surface (the evanes-

cent wave). Next, the sample containing the antigen is introduced, and it displaces the labeled antigen, causing a reduction in signal. The extent of this reduction can be related to the concentration of the antigen (analyte) in the samples. Since the evanescent wave samples only the immediate vicinity of the surface, species present in the bulk sample do not interfere. Other bioaffinity systems include deoxyribonucleic acid (DNA) hybridization and purified and reconstituted membrane receptors, including the glutamate receptor ion channel and the nicotinic acetylcholine receptor.

As in the case of the catalytic biosensors, many physical techniques can be used to detect affinity binding: microcalorimetry (thermometric enzyme-linked immunosorbent assay, or TELISA), fluorescence energy transfer, fluorescence polarization, or bioluminescence.

The quality of the results obtained from sensors based on biological recognition elements depends most heavily on their ability to react rapidly, selectively, and with high affinity. Antibodies and receptors frequently react with such high affinity that the analyte does not easily become unbound. To reuse the sensor requires a time-consuming regeneration step. Nonetheless, if this step can be automated, semicontinuous monitoring may be possible. Successful use of biosensors requires detailed understanding of their operating principles.

George S. Wilson

Bibliography. A. E. G. Cass (ed.), *Biosensors: A Practical Approach*, Oxford University Press, 1990; A. J. Cunningham, *Introduction to Bioanalytical Sensors*, John Wiley, 1998; E. A. H. Hall, *Biosensors*, Prentice Hall, 1991; A. P. F. Turner, I. Karube, and G. S. Wilson (eds.), *Biosensors: Fundamentals and Applications*, Oxford University Press, 1987.

Biosphere

The thin film of living organisms and their environments at the surface of the Earth. Included in the biosphere are all environments capable of sustaining life above, on, and beneath the Earth's surface as well as in the oceans. Consequently, the biosphere overlaps virtually the entire hydrosphere and portions of the atmosphere and outer lithosphere.

Neither the upper nor lower limits of the biosphere are sharp. Spores of microorganisms can be carried to considerable heights in the atmosphere, but these are resting stages that are not actively metabolizing. A variety of organisms inhabit the ocean depths, including the giant tubeworms and other creatures that were discovered living around hydrothermal vents. Evidence exists for the presence of bacteria in oil reservoirs at depths of about 6600 ft (2000 m) within the Earth. The bacteria are apparently metabolically active, utilizing the paraffinic hydrocarbons of the oils as an energy source. These are extreme limits to the biosphere; most of the mass of living matter and the greatest diversity of organisms are within the upper 330 ft (100 m) of the lithosphere and hydrosphere, although there are places even within this zone that are too dry or too cold to support much life. Most of the biosphere is within the zone which is reached by sunlight and where liquid water exists.

Origin. For over 50 years after Louis Pasteur disproved the theory of spontaneous generation, scientists believed that life was universal and was transplanted to other planets and solar systems by the spores of microorganisms. This is the theory of panspermia. In the 1920s the modern theory of chemical evolution of life on Earth was proposed independently by A. I. Oparin, a Soviet biochemist, and J. B. S. Haldane, a British biochemist. The basic tenet of the theory is that life arose through a series of chemical steps involving increasingly complex organic substances that had been chemically synthesized and had accumulated on the prebiotic Earth. The first organisms originated under anaerobic conditions in an atmosphere devoid of free molecular oxygen. Because they were incapable of aerobic photosynthesis, a complex process which evolved undoubtedly after life originated, the oxygen in the present atmosphere arose as a secondary addition.

The first organisms appeared probably prior to 3.5 billion years ago (Ga) and possibly earlier than 3.8 Ga. Carbon (C) isotopes provide one piece of evidence pinpointing the time of emergence of the first cells. The $^{13}C/^{12}C$ ratio of the insoluble organic carbon, or kerogen, in sedimentary rocks from Greenland extending about 3.8 Ga is within the range of reduced carbon found in all younger rocks; this is an indication that organisms, which are responsible for the isotopic fractionation of carbon, had already appeared.

These approximately 3.8-billion-year-old sedimentary rocks from the Isua region of western Greenland contain no evidence that life existed at this time other than that provided by their carbon isotopic composition. These rocks, however, demonstrate that liquid water was present and that the processes of erosion, transportation, and deposition of sediments were occurring, all indicative of conditions on the Earth conducive to life-forms. If life did exist by this time, the preceding period of chemical evolution leading up to the first cells lasted for about 0.3–0.5 billion years, or about the time span between 3.8 Ga and the cooling of the Earth's surface sufficiently to contain liquid water, an event that may have occurred within a few hundred million years of the formation of the Earth about 4.6 Ga. *See* ORGANIC EVOLUTION; PREBIOTIC ORGANIC SYNTHESIS.

The fossil record provides more direct evidence for the existence of early life-forms. The oldest known microfossils are from the early Archean Apex Chert and Towers Formation (both about 3.5 billion years old) in Western Australia. The microfossils from the Apex Chert are present in siliceous grains up to a few millimeters in diameter that were apparently eroded from an even older deposit and subsequently incorporated into the Apex Chert. This deposit contains a diverse assemblage of filamentous microfos-

sils resembling cyanobacteria that were apparently capable of oxygen-producing photosynthesis. The discovery of these fossils establishes that the early Archean biota was quite diverse, and it suggests that cyanobacterial photoautotrophs capable of oxygen production may have already existed this early in Earth history. The time required for these advanced prokaryotic organisms to evolve means that the first primitive cells must have appeared much earlier. *See* ARCHEAN; CYANOBACTERIA; FOSSIL; PROKARYOTAE.

Evolution. The changes wrought during the evolution of the biosphere had profound effects on the atmosphere, hydrosphere, and outer lithosphere.

Photosynthesis. Probably the first significant event in the evolution of the biosphere was the development of photosynthesis, a process that led to autotrophic organisms capable of synthesizing organic matter from inorganic constituents. This evolutionary advance freed the early organisms from a dependence on the coexisting abiogenic organic matter, which was being depleted by heterotrophic anaerobes. These autotrophs were anaerobic organisms similar to modern photosynthetic bacteria, and they did not release oxygen as a by-product. Some time later, probably by about 3.5 Ga with the appearance of cyanobacteria, oxygen-releasing photosynthesis, another major milestone in the development of the biosphere, evolved. *See* PHOTOSYNTHESIS.

Eukaryotes. A profound evolutionary event was the emergence of eukaryotic organisms. All early life-forms were prokaryotic, as are modern bacteria and cyanobacteria; all other organisms are eukaryotic, characterized by the presence of a nucleus and capable of reproducing by meiosis and mitosis. The origin of eukaryotic organisms was an important evolutionary event, as it represented the emergence of sexual reproduction and set the stage for the later evolution of multicellular organisms. Recent evidence, based on molecular fossils, now places the time of first appearance of eukaryotic organisms as long as 2.7 Ga. This is about 0.5–1.0 billion years before eukaryotic remains are found in the fossil record. *See* EUKARYOTAE.

Animals. The final major evolutionary advance leading to the development of the modern biosphere was the rise of multicellular animals (Metazoa). Although a diverse metazoan assemblage (the so-called Ediacaran fauna) first appeared in the fossil record in the latest Precambrian Eon about 600 million years ago (Ma), the origin and early evolutionary stages of these organisms must predate this time by a few hundred million years. Because these early metazoans had soft bodies that are not readily preserved as fossils, it may never be known precisely how and when the animal ancestors of humans evolved. Within a short span of geologic time after their first appearance, however, metazoans developed the ability to form shells of calcium carbonate and calcium phosphate, which can be easily preserved as fossils. The dramatic increase in fossils of multicellular organisms at the beginning of the Cambrian Period (about 570 Ma) is due to the preservability of their exoskeletons. Eventually, both plants and animals escaped the confines

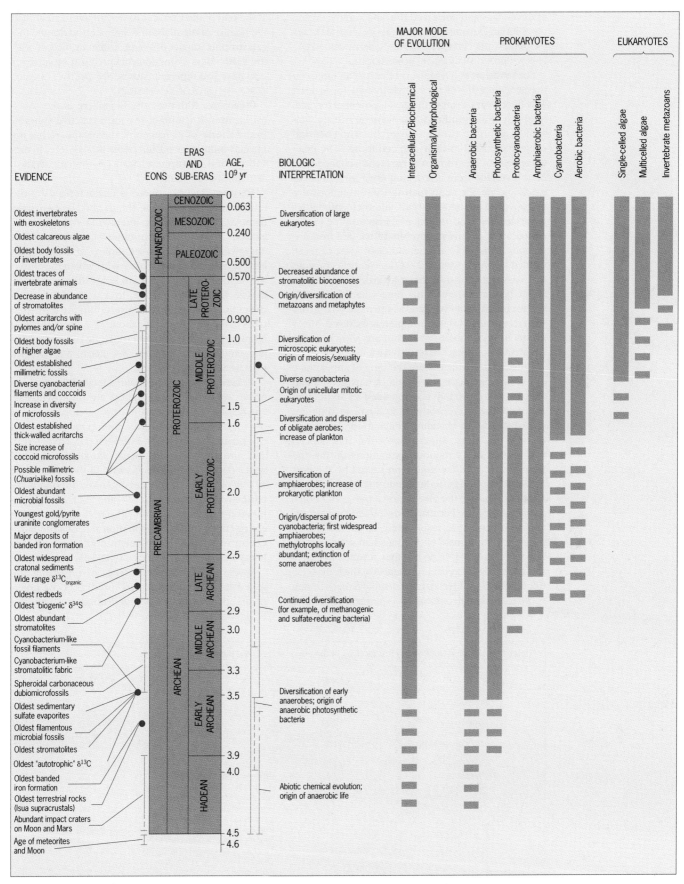

Geochronological summary of evidence relating to the origin and evolution of the earliest biosphere. (After J. W. Schopf et al., eds., Earth's Earliest Biosphere: Its Origin and Evolution, Princeton University Press, 1983)

of the oceans and colonized the land surface during the Silurian-Devonian periods (about 400 Ma). *See* CAMBRIAN; DEVONIAN; EDIACARAN BIOTA; METAZOA; PRECAMBRIAN; SILURIAN; STROMATOLITE.

Geochemical cycles. Organisms have had an effect on the geochemistry of their environment for at least 3.5 billion years. Prior to the development of oxygen-releasing photosynthesis, the Earth's surface was anoxic, all organisms were anaerobic, and chemical elements existed in their reduced forms. The gradual release of free oxygen permanently changed the Earth's surface from a reducing environment to an oxidizing one. Elements such as iron and sulfur were converted to an oxidized state, and their solubilities were changed. The oxidation of iron resulted in precipitation of extensive deposits of banded iron formations from 3.8 to 1.8 Ga, although most of these formed between 3.0 and 2.0 Ga. Scientists consider that cessation of banded iron formation deposition about 1.8 Ga represents the time when the Earth's surface became fully oxic and all the reduced iron dissolved in the oceans was completely oxidized. Major events in Precambrian evolution are shown in the **illustration.** *See* BIOGEOCHEMISTRY.

Extinctions. Virtually from the time of appearance of the first organisms, evolution of new genera and species was inevitably accompanied by extinction of others that were not able to adapt to different environments, to changing climatic conditions, or to new predators. Superimposed on this general background of continuous extinctions during the Phanerozoic Eon, the time represented by the best fossil record, are periodic occurrences of mass extinctions. During the two largest mass extinctions, at the ends of the Permian and Cretaceous periods, about 60% and 35%, respectively, of marine genera perished. Other mass extinctions had a less severe impact on the biosphere, but they resulted in extensive mortalities of genera. The cause of these mass extinctions is the subject of considerable debate among geologists and paleontologists. The mass extinction at the end of the Cretaceous Period, which included the demise of the dinosaurs, has been attributed to a catastrophic impact of a large comet or meteor with the Earth. Mass extinctions occurring at other times may have had different causes. *See* CRETACEOUS; EXTINCTION (BIOLOGY); PERMIAN.

Organisms. Although the biosphere is the smallest in mass, it is one of the most reactive spheres. In the course of its reactions, the biosphere has important influences on the outer lithosphere, hydrosphere, and atmosphere. *See* ATMOSPHERE; HYDROSPHERE; LITHOSPHERE.

Ecosystem. The biosphere is characterized by the interrelationship of living things and their environments. Communities are interacting systems of organisms tied to their environments by the transfer of energy and matter. Such a coupling of living organisms and the nonliving matter with which they interact defines an ecosystem. An ecosystem may range in size from a small pond, to a tropical forest, to the entire biosphere. Ecologists group the terrestrial parts of the biosphere into about 12 large units called biomes. Examples of biomes include tundra, desert, grassland, and boreal forest. *See* BIOME; ECOLOGICAL COMMUNITIES; ECOSYSTEM.

Metabolic processes. The major metabolic processes occurring within the biosphere are photosynthesis and respiration. Green plants, through the process of photosynthesis, form organic compounds composed essentially of carbon (C), hydrogen (H), oxygen (O), and nitrogen (N) from carbon dioxide (CO_2) and water (H_2O), and nutrients, with O_2 being released as a by-product. The O_2 and organic compounds are partially reconverted into CO_2 and H_2O through respiration by plants and animals. Driving this cycle is energy from the Sun; respiration releases the Sun's energy which has been stored by photosynthesis. *See* PHOTORESPIRATION; PHOTOSYNTHESIS.

Types. The fundamental types of organisms engaged in these activities are producers, or green plants that manufacture their food through the

Annual and seasonal Net Primary Productivity of the major units of the biosphere[*]			
	Ocean		Land
Seasonal			
April to June	10.9		15.7
July to September	13.0		18.0
October to December	12.3		11.5
January to March	11.3		11.2
Biogeographic			
Oligotrophic	11.0	Tropical rainforests	17.8
Mesotrophic	27.4	Broadleaf deciduous forests	1.5
Eutrophic	9.1	Broadleaf and needleleaf forests	3.1
Macrophytes	1.0	Needleleaf evergreen forests	3.1
		Needleleaf deciduous forests	1.4
		Savannas	16.8
		Perennial grasslands	2.4
		Broadleaf shrubs with bare soil	1.0
		Tundra	0.8
		Desert	0.5
		Cultivation	8.0
Total	48.5		56.4

[*]From satellite data. Values are in petagrams of carbon (1 Pg = 10^{15} g).
SOURCE: C. B. field et al., Primary production of the biosphere: Integrating terrestrial and oceanic components, *Science*, 281:239, 1998.

process of photosynthesis and respire part of it; consumers, or animals that feed on plants directly or on other animals by ingestion of organic matter; and decomposers, or bacteria that break down organic substances to inorganic products.

Productivity, the rate of formation of living tissue per unit area in a given time, is one of the fundamental attributes of an ecosystem. All organisms in the community are dependent on the energy obtained through gross primary productivity. The productivity of an ecosystem is determined by a number of environmental variables, particularly temperature and the availability of water and nutrients such as phosphate and nitrate. In marine environments, availability of light and nutrients is the limiting factor, while the productivity in terrestrial environments is limited by the availability of water and nutrients. The productivity of different ecosystems is given in the **table**. *See* BIOLOGICAL PRODUCTIVITY.

The portion of gross primary productivity that is not respired by green plants is the net primary productivity that is available to consumer and decomposer organisms. Organic matter and energy are passed from one organism to another along food chains. The steps, or groupings of organisms, in a chain are trophic levels. Green plants, the producers, occupy the first trophic level, followed by herbivores (primary consumers), primary carnivores, secondary carnivores, and tertiary carnivores. The number of links in a food chain is variable, but three to five levels are common. Only about 10% or less of the matter and energy is passed from one trophic level to the next because of the utilization of energy in respiration at each level. *See* FOOD WEB.

Not all ecosystems depend on photoautotrophs or green plants for their food and energy. One of the most exotic ecosystems consists of giant tubeworms, clams, and other organisms that thrive around hydrothermal vents, the jets of hot water gushing from portions of mid-oceanic ridges. These communities, discovered only in the late 1970s, are based on chemosynthetic bacteria that live inside the tubeworms. Since then, similar communities of organisms, although living in cold water, have been found near oil and gas seeps on the sea floor. *See* HYDROTHERMAL VENT; TUBEWORMS.

Living and dead organic matter that is not consumed by higher trophic levels is decomposed as dead tissue through bacterial action. Decomposers play a major role in the flow of matter and energy in ecosystems, because they are the final agents to release the photosynthetic energy from the organic compounds that they utilize. Decomposers recycle the chemical components, but not energy, back into the ecosystem. *See* POPULATION ECOLOGY.

The biomass, or the total mass of living organisms at one time in an ecosystem, may or may not correlate with productivity. In fact, the total terrestrial biomass, composed largely of tropical, temperate, and boreal forests, greatly exceeds that of the total oceanic biomass; yet their net primary productivities are nearly equal. An accurate tally of forested biomass, of importance for balancing the global carbon budget, has been lacking, however, because of the difficulty in estimating the total areas of forest cover and the average biomass per unit area for each forest type. Use of remote-sensing data from satellites will improve biomass estimates and will provide baseline measurements for determining whether any of the forested biomasses are increasing or decreasing as a consequence of human activities. *See* BIOMASS.

Human impact. Human beings are part of the biosphere, and some of their activities have an adverse impact on many ecosystems and on themselves. Ecologists are concerned that another mass extinction, caused by human activity, may be under way. As a consequence of deforestation, urban sprawl, spread of pollutants, and overharvesting, both terrestrial and marine ecosystems are being destroyed or diminished, populations are shrinking, and many species are dying out. Whales are one group of marine mammals that have been extensively hunted, leading to near extinction of some species such as the blue whales and the humpback whales. The decrease in commercial whaling since the late 1980s may enable these populations to recover, although decades will be required because whales have a low birthrate. In the United States, many organisms threatened with extinction are federally protected through the Endangered Species Act.

In addition to causing extinctions of some species, humans are expanding the habitats of other organisms, sometimes across oceanic barriers, through inadvertent transport and introduction into new regions. Cargo ships, for example, discharge their water ballast, teeming with plankton from the port of origin, into the waters of another port at a distant location, thereby introducing many new organisms into a similar habitat where they can thrive.

Humans also add toxic or harmful substances to the outer lithosphere, hydrosphere, and atmosphere. Many of these materials are eventually incorporated into or otherwise affect the biosphere, and water and air supplies in some regions are seriously fouled. The major types of environmental pollutants are sewage, trace metals, petroleum hydrocarbons, synthetic organic compounds, and gaseous emissions. *See* HAZARDOUS WASTE.

Sewage. Bulk sewage is generally disposed of satisfactorily and is normally not a problem unless it contains one or more of the other types of substances. Under certain conditions, either when the load of organic matter is at a high level or nutrients lead to eutrophication, dissolved oxygen is depleted, creating undesirable stagnation of the water. Just such an occurrence exists during the summer months off the mouth of the Mississippi River in the Gulf of Mexico, where a large volume of water near the bottom (the "dead zone") has a dissolved oxygen concentration that is too low to support shellfish and fin fish. Scientists consider the cause of the dead zone to be high productivity in the surface waters of the Gulf due to runoff of fertilizer nutrients from farms in the Mississippi River drainage basin, combined with lower dissolved oxygen concentration in the water column during warmer months. *See* EUTROPHICATION; SEWAGE TREATMENT.

Trace metals. Some metals are toxic at low concentrations, while other metals that are necessary for metabolic processes at low levels are toxic when present in high concentrations. Examples of metals known to be toxic at low concentrations are lead, mercury, cadmium, selenium, and arsenic. Industrial uses and automobile exhaust are the chief sources of these metals. Additions of these metals through human activity are, in some cases, about equal to the natural input. Great increases of metals are observed near major sources. Plants and soils near highways or lead-processing facilities contain as much as 100 times the unpolluted value of lead. Introduction of unleaded gasoline and passage of legislation requiring safer disposal practices and clean-up of contaminated land should reduce the danger from trace-metal contamination.

Petroleum hydrocarbons. Petroleum hydrocarbons from runoff, industrial and ship discharges, and oil spills pollute coastal waters and may contaminate marine organisms. Oil slicks smother marine life by preventing the diffusion of oxygen into the water or by coating the organisms with a tarry residue. Aromatic constituents of petroleum are toxic to all organisms. Large doses can be lethal, while sublethal quantities can have a variety of physiological effects, especially carcinogenicity. The hydrocarbons are lipophilic and, because they are not metabolized or excreted, tend to accumulate in fatty tissues. Even when marine life has not been subjected to massive contamination by an oil spill, the organisms may be gradually contaminated by accumulating the hydrocarbons to which they have been continuously exposed at low concentrations. Contamination of shellfish, in particular, is of concern because they are consumed in great quantities by humans. *See* WATER POLLUTION.

Synthetic organic compounds. Manufacture and use of synthetic organic compounds, such as insecticides and plasticizers, are commonplace worldwide. Many of these chemicals are chlorinated hydrocarbons, a category of substances that is known to be generally toxic to organisms. Of even greater concern is that chlorinated hydrocarbons are carcinogenic and long-term exposure to sublethal doses increases the risk of cancer. The widespread use of chlorinated hydrocarbons in industrial society leads to an increasing background of these compounds in natural waters, including drinking water.

Synthetic organic compounds and petroleum hydrocarbons are generally not metabolized or excreted by organisms. Both groups tend to be retained in the fatty tissues and passed on to other organisms in the next level of the food chain. Consequently, predators high in the food chain are exposed to much greater concentrations of toxic or carcinogenic substances through their ingested food than is present at background levels in the environment. Prior to banning its widespread use in the United States (use is still legal in many other countries), DDT was found in concentrations as high as tens of parts per million in fish-eating birds such as gulls and grebes, even though the concentration of DDT in the lower organisms of their food chain and in the bottom sediment was as low as 0.01 ppm. The high concentrations led to thinning of egg shells and decline in reproduction rate in many predator bird species, including the bald eagle. Due to the ban on DDT use in the United States, as well as other protective measures of the Endangered Species Act, the eagle population has increased and is no longer considered endangered, although the bird remains on "threatened" status. *See* ENDANGERED SPECIES; INSECTICIDE; MUTAGENS AND CARCINOGENS.

Gaseous emissions. Gaseous emissions to the atmosphere from industrial sources and automobiles represent both short-term and long-term hazards. Short-term problems include the addition of sulfurous gases leading to more acidic rainfall, the emission of nitrogen oxides which form smog, and carbon monoxide from automobile exhaust which leads to impairment of breathing in cities. *See* SMOG.

Of more long-term concern is the potential impact on global climate due to the increase in CO_2, methane, chlorofluorocarbons, and nitrous oxide in the atmosphere. These gases absorb heat radiated from the Earth—the so-called greenhouse effect—which will lead to a gradual warming of the Earth's surface and the attendant problems of shifting of climatic zones, upsetting of ecosystem balances, partial melting of polar icecaps, and possibly other unanticipated effects. Combustion of fossil fuels and deforestation are the major sources of the CO_2, the concentration of which has been increasing at the rate of about 1 part per million by volume each year since measurements began in the late 1950s. Since the early 1960s the increase in CO_2 correlates precisely with the growth of world population.

Only about one-half of the estimated annual release of CO_2 stays in the atmosphere. A portion of the other half dissolves in the ocean. The fate of the remainder, which cannot be found either in the atmosphere or in the ocean, has been the subject of considerable dispute. One view is that portions of the biosphere, largely temperate or boreal forests, are converting the balance of the CO_2 into new growth. Another view is that clearing of tropical forests adds a significant additional amount of CO_2 to the atmosphere, so that the biosphere is a net source of CO_2 rather than a possible sink for CO_2. The problem with both scenarios is that estimates of total forest biomass cannot be made accurately enough to establish whether this biomass is increasing or decreasing.

Atmospheric methane, another so-called greenhouse gas, has doubled during the last few hundred years. Methane is produced naturally by bacterial decomposition of organic matter in the absence of oxygen, with major sources being rice paddies, natural wetlands, and animal digestive tracts (termites, for example, are a significant source). Like that of CO_2, the increase in atmospheric methane may also be due to population-related environmental pressures as forests are cleared and rice paddies are expanded.

The synthetic organic compounds called chlorofluorocarbons, also known as the freons, used in aerosol sprays and refrigeration equipment, are both greenhouse gases and a threat to the Earth's ozone layer, which shields organisms from lethal ultraviolet radiation. Scientists predict that a partial depletion of the ozone layer will cause an increase in the incidence of skin cancer and a decrease in crop and seafood yields due to the increased dosage of damaging ultraviolet radiation. Concern about the potential destruction of the ozone layer has escalated with the discovery of a large hole in it centered over Antarctica. This concern led to the signing in 1987 of an international ozone protection treaty, known as the Montreal Protocol, since revised and updated three times, in which the developed countries agreed to phase out the production of chlorofluorcarbons and other chemicals that destroy ozone by the end of the twentieth century.

Nitrous oxide (N_2O), derived by nitrification and denitrification reactions in fertilized soils, sewage, and animal wastes, is another agent leading to depletion of ozone. Increasing reliance on chemical fertilizers to increase crop productivity is generating a larger N_2O flux to the atmosphere. *See* FERTILIZER.

Most, if not all, of the additions of potentially harmful substances to the environment are a result of the population growth and the technological advances of industrial society. The impact of these pollutants will be felt by future generations. Humans are conducting a global ecological experiment with uncertain consequences by altering the fragile equilibrium between the biosphere and its environment. *See* ACID RAIN; AIR POLLUTION; ATMOSPHERIC CHEMISTRY; GREENHOUSE EFFECT; HUMAN ECOLOGY.

Fate of biosphere. The survival of the biosphere depends on the continued availability of liquid water, CO_2, and sunlight. Insufficient amounts of any one of these will cause productivity to cease. Scientists estimate that lack of CO_2 will ultimately doom the biosphere on Earth. On a long-term basis, the amount of CO_2 in the atmosphere is maintained within broad but sufficient limits by input through volcanic emanations and removal by weathering of rocks. Scientists also estimate that solar luminosity is increasing, and that the Sun's luminosity when the Earth formed was about 30% lower than it is now. As the Sun's energy output continues to rise, the temperature of the Earth will increase, as will the rate of rock weathering. Consequently, atmospheric CO_2 will decline when the rate of rock weathering exceeds the rate of return of CO_2 to the atmosphere by volcanic emanations. Scientists estimate that in about 1 billion years the CO_2 concentration will be too low to support plant productivity and the biosphere on Earth will cease to exist.   Richard M. Mitterer

Bibliography. J. J. Brocks et al., Archean molecular fossils and the early rise of eukaryotes, *Science*, 285:1033-1036, 1999; R. P. Detwiler and C. Hall, Tropical forests and the global carbon cycle, *Science*, 239:42-47, 1988; C. B. Field et al., Primary production of the biosphere: Integrating terrestrial and oceanic components, *Science*, 281:237-240, 1999; D. M. Raup and G. E. Boyajian, Patterns of generic extinction in the fossil record, *Paleobiology*, 14:109-125, 1988; M. T. Rosing, ^{13}C-depleted carbon microparticles in >3700-Ma sea-floor sedimentary rocks from West Greenland, *Science*, 283:674-676, 1999; J. W. Schopf (ed.), *Major Events in the History of Life*, 1992; J. W. Schopf, Microfossils of the Early Archean Apex Chert: New evidence for the antiquity of life, *Science*, 260:640-646, 1993; J. W. Schopf et al. (eds.), *Earth's Earliest Biosphere: Its Origin and Evolution*, 1983; T. Takahashi et al., Balancing the budget: Carbon dioxide sources and sinks, and the effects of industry, *Oceanus*, 35:18-28, 1992.

Biosynthesis

The synthesis of more complex molecules from simpler ones in cells by utilizing biosynthetic pathways consisting of a series of reactions mediated by enzymes. The overall economy and survival of the cell is governed by the interplay between the energy gained from the breakdown of compounds and that supplied to biosynthetic pathways for the synthesis of compounds having a functional role, such as deoxyribonucleic acid (DNA), ribonucleic acid (RNA), and enzymes. Biosynthetic pathways (see **illus.**) give rise to two distinct classes of metabolite, primary and secondary. Primary metabolites (DNA, RNA, fatty acids, α-amino acids, chlorophyll in green plants, and so forth) are essential to the metabolic functioning of the cells. Secondary metabolites (antibiotics, antifeedants, alkaloids, pheromones, skunk scent, and so forth) aid the functioning and survival of the whole organism more generally. Unlike primary metabolites, secondary metabolites are often unique to individual organisms or classes of organisms. *See* ENZYME; METABOLISM.

The selective pressures that drive evolution have ensured a rich and diverse array of secondary metabolite structures. Despite this diversity, secondary metabolites can be grouped (for example, as terpenes or polyketides) to some extent by virtue of their origin from key biosynthetic pathways. It is often in the latter stages of these pathways that the structural diversity is introduced. All terpenes, for example, originate from the C_5 intermediate isopentenyl pyrophosphate via mevalonic acid. The mammalian steroids, such as cholesterol, derive from the C_{30} steroid lanosterol, which is constructed from six C_5 units. Alternatively, C_{10} terpenes (for example, menthol from peppermint leaves) and C_{15} terpenes (for example, juvenile hormone III from the silk worm) are derived after the condensation of two and three C_5 units, respectively, and then with further enzymatic customization in each case. *See* CHOLESTEROL; ORGANIC EVOLUTION; STEROID; TERPENE; TRITERPENE.

The polyketide pathway has its origin in fatty acid biosynthesis. Fatty acids are assembled in a similar manner in all cells by fatty acid synthase enzymes, and they are built by the condensation of C_2 fragments derived from acetyl coenzyme A (acetyl CoA).

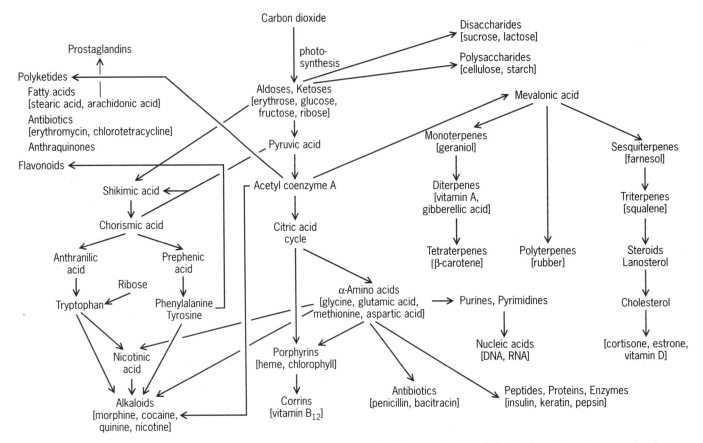

Biosynthetic relationships of some natural products. Specific examples which belong to the various classes are given in brackets.

First, acetyl CoA and malonyl-SEnz (itself derived from acetyl CoA) condense to give acetoacetyl-SEnz, an enzyme-bound C_4 intermediate (SEnz stands for S-enzyme and indicates that the acetoacetyl group is linked to the enzyme by a sulfur atom). The ketone group ($C=O$) of this intermediate is then removed by the action of three enzymes to generate a saturated C_4 fatty acid. This process repeats in a cyclical manner, adding C_2 units until the synthase releases a saturated fatty acid (such as C_{16}-palmitic acid or C_{18}-stearic acid) of optimal length for that synthase. *See* COENZYME; LIPID METABOLISM.

Secondary metabolic pathways have evolved that modify the fatty acid pathway, giving rise to many highly complex structures. The antibiotics chlorotetracycline and erythromycin-A, which are metabolites of Actinomycetes (soil bacteria), are such polyketides. Chlorotetracycline derives from the condensation of acetate units, but unlike fatty acids, all of the ketone groups are retained in the early stages, and are not removed. The result is an enzyme-bound polyketo-intermediate which can cyclize to form four fuzed aromatic rings. Further enzymatic elaborations then generate chlorotetracycline. Similarly, erythromycin-A is a structurally elaborate polyketide antibiotic. It is also biosynthesized by a pathway that has evolved from classical fatty acid biosynthesis. In this case, C_3 propionate units are condensed, in place of the C_2 acetate units in fatty acid assembly, and the cyclical processing of

fatty acid biosynthesis is modified appropriately during each cycle to generate ketones, alcohols, double bonds, and methylene ($-CH_2-$) groups along the backbone of a complex precursor "fatty acid" thioester. This thioester cyclizes to a 14-membered lactone, which is then further modified to the antibiotic.

α-Amino acids combine to generate functional peptides and proteins (for example, enzymes) and are important primary metabolites for this reason. α-Amino acids also contribute to the biosynthesis of many secondary metabolites (such as alkaloids or snake venoms). There are fungi (for example, *Penicillium chrysogenum, Cephalosporium acremonium*) in which a pathway operates from three α-amino acids to the antibiotic penicillin-N. *See* ANTIBIOTIC.

Generally, biosynthetic pathways are elucidated by isotopic labeling techniques, often termed tracer studies. This technique involves introducing an early precursor or intermediate on a pathway, enriched with an isotope at a specific atomic site, into the relevant biological system. The successful or unsuccessful incorporation of the isotope into the metabolite can then give information on true intermediates on the biosynthetic pathway. Radioactive isotopes, such as carbon-14 and hydrogen-3 (tritium), emit β particles during their radioactive decay and can thus be detected. However, it has become more common to probe the details of biosynthetic pathways with the stable isotopes of carbon-13 and hydrogen-2 (deuterium), as the location of these isotopes can be probed directly by nuclear magnetic resonance (NMR) spectroscopy. *See* BACTERIAL PHYSIOLOGY AND METABOLISM; NUCLEAR MAGNETIC RESONANCE (NMR); PHOTOSYNTHESIS; PLANT METABOLISM; RADIOACTIVE TRACER.   David O'Hagan

Bibliography. R. B. Herbert, *The Biosynthesis of Secondary Metabolites*, 2d ed., 1989; G. Zubay, *Biochemistry*, 4th ed., 1999.

Biot-Savart law

A law of physics which states that the magnetic flux density (magnetic induction) near a long, straight conductor is directly proportional to the current in the conductor and inversely proportional to the distance from the conductor. There is also a law in fluid dynamics bearing this name; it is concerned with vortex motion, and bears a close analogy to the law discussed in the present article.

The field near a straight conductor can be found by application of Ampère's law. Consider any element dl of the current-carrying conductor (see **illus.**). The contribution of this element to the flux density at point P is perpendicular to the plane of the paper and directed into the paper. *See* AMPÈRE'S LAW.

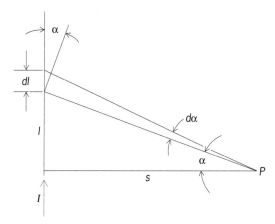

Diagram of the Biot-Savart law.

The flux density B at point P is found by summing up the contributions of all elements of the conductor from one end to the other. All these contributions are in the same direction at P, and hence the vector sum is the simple integral taken from one end of the wire to the other. The limits for the angle α are chosen to represent this sum. For a wire of any length, the lower end is represented by $\alpha = \alpha_1$ and the upper end by $\alpha = \alpha_2$. If I is the current, μ_0 the permeability of free space, and s the distance of P from the conductor, then the flux density is expressed by Eq. (1). For the special case of an infinite straight

$$B = \int dB = \frac{\mu_0 I}{4\pi s} \int_{\alpha_1}^{\alpha_2} \cos\alpha \, d\alpha$$

$$= \frac{\mu_0 I}{4\pi s}(\sin\alpha_2 - \sin\alpha_1) \qquad (1)$$

conductor, that is, one that is long in comparison to s, $\alpha_2 = 90°$ and $\alpha_1 = -90°$. Then Eq. (2) holds. This

$$B = \frac{\mu_0 I}{4\pi s}\left[\sin 90° - \sin(-90°)\right] = \frac{\mu_0 I}{4\pi s}(1+1)$$

$$\text{or} \qquad B = \frac{\mu_0 I}{2\pi s} \qquad (2)$$

relation was originally developed from experimental observations by J. Biot and F. Savart, and was named after them as the Biot-Savart law.

The magnetic flux density B near the long, straight conductor is at every point perpendicular to the plane determined by the point and the line of the conductor. Therefore, the lines of induction are circles with their centers at the conductor. Furthermore, each line of induction is a closed line. This observation concerning flux about a straight conductor may be generalized to include lines of induction due to a conductor of any shape by the statement that every line of induction forms a closed path.   Kenneth V. Manning

Bibliography. E. M. Purcell, *Electricity and Magnetism*, 2d ed., 2000; W. M. Schwartz, *Intermediate Electromagnetic Theory*, 1964; H. D. Young et al., *Sears and Zemansky's University Physics*, 10th ed., 1999.

Biotechnology

Generally, any technique that is used to make or modify the products of living organisms in order to improve plants or animals or to develop useful microorganisms. By this definition, biotechnology has actually been practiced for centuries, as exemplified by the use of yeast and bacteria in the production of various foods, such as wine, bread, and cheese. However, in modern terms, biotechnology has come to mean the use of cell and tissue culture, cell fusion, molecular biology, and in particular, recombinant deoxyribonucleic acid (DNA) technology to generate unique organisms with new traits or organisms that have the potential to produce specific products. The advances and products in the biotechnology arena have been developing at a rapid pace. Some examples of products in a number of important disciplines are described below.

Genetics. Recombinant DNA technology has opened new horizons in the study of gene function and the regulation of gene action. In particular, the ability to insert genes and their controlling nucleic acid sequences into new recipient organisms allows for the manipulation of these genes in order to examine their activity in unique environments, away from the constraints posed in their normal host. Transformed plants, animals, yeast, and bacterial genes may be examined in this way. *See* GENE.

Microbiology. Genetic transformation normally is achieved easily with microorganisms; new genetic material may be inserted into them, either into their chromosomes or into extrachromosomal elements, the plasmids. Thus, bacteria and yeast can be created to metabolize specific products or to produce new products. Concomitant technologies have been developed to scale up the production of the microorganisms to generate products, such as enzymes, carbohydrates, and proteins, in great quantity. *See* BACTERIAL GENETICS; PLASMID.

Immunology. Genetic engineering has allowed for significant advances in the understanding of the structure and mode of action of antibody molecules. Practical use of immunological techniques is pervasive in biotechnology. Notably, antibodies are used in diagnostic procedures for detecting diseases of plants and animals, and in detecting minute amounts of such materials as toxic wastes, drugs, and pesticides. The antibodies themselves are being employed to target therapeutic agents to specific cellular sites. Antibodies are bivalent molecules that bind to their target molecules at one or both of their two combining sites. Hybrid antibodies are being produced in which one of the sites contains a drug or a poison while the other site directs the antibody to its target, that is, a cancerous cell. The ability to artificially combine subunits of antibodies produced in different species also will tailor them for specific targets. Antibodies are also being developed with enzymatic properties, thereby enabling them to deactivate target molecules with which they combine in a cell. *See* ANTIBODY.

Monoclonal antibodies respond to a single antigenic site, allowing for great specificity. They have been most important in the diagnostic arena, where tests have been developed for human, plant, and animal diseases and for pregnancy and ovulation prediction. *See* MONOCLONAL ANTIBODIES.

Agriculture. Few commercial products have been marketed for use in plant agriculture, but many have been tested. Interest has centered on producing plants that are tolerant to specific herbicides. This tolerance would allow crops to be sprayed with the particular herbicide, and only the weeds would be killed, not the genetically engineered crop species. Some herbicide-tolerant crop species have been isolated by selection of tissue culture variants, but in other cases plants have been transformed with genes from bacteria that detoxify the herbicide. For example, a gene isolated from the soil bacterium *Klebsiella ozaenae* has been used to create plants that are resistant to the herbicide bromoxynil. Other strategies have been to alter plants so that they will overproduce the herbicide-sensitive biochemical target, or so that the biochemical target will be altered, thereby reducing the affinity of the herbicide for its biochemical target in the crop species. *See* HERBICIDE.

Tolerance to plant virus diseases has been induced in a number of crop species by transforming plants with portions of the viral genome, in particular the virus's coat protein and the replicase enzyme used for virus multiplication. Plants exhibiting this tolerance are available for commercial use once regulatory constraints are removed. Genes coding for protein toxins from the bacterium *Bacillus thuringiensis* have been introduced into a number

of plant species to provide insect tolerance. Potato plants tolerant to the Colorado potato beetle and cotton plants tolerant to the cotton boll worm were the first commercial products of this technology.

To enhance the quality and nutrition of foods, a number of techniques have been developed. Recombinant DNA strategies can be used to retard the softening of tomatoes so they can reach the consumer with better flavor and keeping qualities. A technique was developed to increase the starch content of the potato to enhance the quality of french fries and potato chips, including reduction of their capacity to absorb oils during processing. With both selective plant breeding and genetic engineering, oil seed rape (also known as canola or *Brassica napus*) has been produced to yield plant-based oils (oleochemicals) for the specialty chemicals industry. Such oils are used to produce amides, fatty acids, esters, and other chemical intermediates. Oils high in erucic acid are used as lubricants and as additives to automatic transmission fluid. Oil seed rape is also an important source of oil for margarine production and cooking. Genetic engineering techniques can be used to lower the proportion of saturated fat by inserting the gene for the stearoyl–acyl carrier protein desaturase enzyme gene into oil seed rape and other oil-producing crop plants. *See* FAT AND OIL (FOOD).

Biotechnology also holds great promise in the production of vaccines for use in maintaining the health of animals. However, because of the economics of the market, most emphasis has been placed on race horses and pets, such as cats and dogs. Subunit vaccines are being developed to replace live-virus or killed-whole-virus vaccines. Feline leukemia virus is an important disease, estimated to infect 1.5 million cats annually in the United States. Conventional vaccines are ineffective against the virus and may actually spread the disease. Subunit vaccines have been developed that overcome these disadvantages. Pseudorabies virus is the causal agent of an important disease affecting hogs. The conventional killed-virus vaccine gives only partial protection, and a live-virus vaccine is only slightly more effective. A genetically engineered vaccine has been developed in which the gene producing the enzyme that enables the virus to escape from nervous tissue has been deleted, thus reducing virus virulence. Another vaccine incorporates genes for pseudorabies proteins into viable vaccinia virus as a vector to immunize animals. Recombinant vaccines are being produced for many other diseases, including foot-and-mouth virus and parvovirus.

Interferons are also being tested for their use in the management of specific diseases. They show some promise in treating bovine shipping fever, a complex of respiratory infections manifested during the crowded conditions experienced by cattle when shipped. Recombinant produced bovine growth hormone has been shown to be effective in increasing the production of milk in cows and in reducing the ratio of fat to lean meat in beef cattle.

Animals may be transformed to carry genes from other species, including humans, and are being used to produce valuable drugs. This technology has been termed biopharming. For example, goats are being used to produce tissue plasminogen activator, which has been effective in dissolving blood clots. Transgenic animals have been produced that carry the acquired immune deficiency syndrome (AIDS) virus, providing a practical cost-effective experimental model system to test control measures for the disease, which infects only primates in nature.

Plant science. Plant scientists have been amazed at the ease with which plants can be transformed to enable them to express foreign genes. This field has developed very rapidly since the first transformation of a plant was reported in 1982, and a number of transformation procedures are available. Most widely used as a transformation vector is the plasmid derived from the plant pathogenic bacterium *Agrobacterium tumefaciens*. Another method involves shooting DNA-coated tungsten (or gold) particles into cells. Controlling genetic elements have been identified that allow for the insertion of genes into specific tissues or plant organs. For example, nucleic acid sequences may be targeted to the pollen grain to specifically inactivate genes involved in producing pollen, thereby allowing for the production of sterile male plants. Such a technique will be very useful in the commercial production of hybrid seeds of crop species.

Coupled with these transformation procedures has been the development of tissue culture techniques to enable the transformed cells to be regenerated into whole plants (termed totipotency). Many plant species have been regenerated, thereby facilitating the transfer of useful genes to the most important crops (rice, maize, wheat, and potatoes). Cultures of plant cells, roots, and tissues are used to produce secondary plant products, such as the anticancer drug taxol. *See* BREEDING (PLANT); TISSUE CULTURE.

Medicine. Genetic engineering has enabled the large-scale production of proteins which have great potential for treatment of heart attacks. Most promising of these new drugs is tissue plasminogen activator, which has been shown to be effective in dissolving blood clots. Active tissue plasminogen activator, a very minor constituent of human blood vessels and some other tissues, may now be produced by recombinant technology in transformed tissue culture cells or in the filamentous fungus *Aspergillus nidulans*. Another substance produced by recombinant technology that has been tested for treatment of heart attacks is urokinase.

Many human gene products, produced with genetic engineering technology, are being investigated for their potential use as commercial drugs. Cloned human growth hormone is being used for the treatment of childhood dwarfism. Epidermal growth factor is a protein that causes the replication of epidermal cells and has applications to wound healing. Interleukins produced by blood cells are being tested for treatment of specific cancers. Granulocyte macrophage colony–stimulating factor is being tested as a treatment for ovarian cancer.

Recombinant technology has been employed to produce vaccines from subunits of viruses, so that the use of either live or inactivated viruses as immunizing agents is avoided. Conventional vaccines are sometimes infectious in themselves, and most require refrigeration which makes their use in tropical countries a problem. Poliovirus vaccines involving attenuated live virus are a source of the perpetuation of the disease due to rare mutations of the virus to virulence. Recombinant technology is being used to modify the viral genome to prevent reversion. Other viruses being investigated are hepatitis B and herpes simplex, where surface antigens are being produced in yeast cells. Malaria, one of the most important parasitic diseases of humans, is another case in which biotechnology is being applied to produce a vaccine. Proteins from the causal organism, *Plasmodium* sp., are poorly immunogenic. To enhance immunogenicity, they are transferred to the attenuated bacterium *Salmonella typhimurium*, which is then used as an immunizing agent. Another strategy has been to fuse the gene for the immunological determinant to that of a hepatitis B virus protein, to express the fusion protein in yeast, and to use that chimeric protein as a vaccine. *See* VACCINATION.

Cloned genes and specific, defined nucleic acid sequences can be used as a means of diagnosing infectious diseases or in identifying individuals with the potential for genetic disease. The specific nucleic acids used as probes are normally tagged with radioisotopes, and the DNAs of candidate individuals are tested by hybridization to the labeled probe. The technique has been used to detect latent viruses such as herpes, bacteria, mycoplasmas, and plasmodia, and to identify Huntington's disease, cystic fibrosis, and Duchenne muscular dystrophy. In many cases, restriction-length polymorphisms are being utilized. When DNA is cut into small fragments by specific restriction enzymes and then is probed with specific genes or nucleic acids, differences between individuals in a population can be identified, and the relationships of specific patterns to specific diseases or traits can be determined. This technology is being used in many other useful ways, such as identifying important genes in plants and animals as an aid in breeding improved stocks, and as a forensic tool by assigning specific identity to individuals through their DNA in much the same way that fingerprints are now used. The technique is called DNA fingerprinting, and it is as reliable as conventional fingerprinting. The technique has the potential of distinguishing the DNA from one individual in a population of 10 billion. Tissue samples containing DNA left at the scene of a crime, such as bone, blood, semen, skin, hair (if it is attached to its root), saliva, and sweat, can be used in the procedure. If the amount of DNA found is too small to be useful, a new technique, the polymerase chain reaction, has been developed to amplify it to practical levels. *See* FORENSIC MEDICINE.

Gene functions can often be blocked by attacking them with complementary or antisense sequences of the same gene. This technology has been used by molecular biologists to define functions for specific genes, but it has also been shown to have a number of practical applications. In agriculture it has been used to generate male sterile plants, enabling the production of hybrid varieties more easily, and to slow the ripening of tomatoes. Most importantly, antisense technology presents the possibility of useful gene therapy. For example, the human immunodeficiency virus (considered to be the casual agent of AIDS) can be inhibited by transforming T lymphocytes with antisense nucleic acids directed against a virus enzyme, reverse transcriptase.

It is now possible to put foreign genes into cells and to target them to specific regions of the recipient genome. This presents the possibility of developing specific therapies for hereditary diseases, exemplified by sickle-cell anemia, which is caused by a defect in the β-globin gene which results in defective hemoglobin in affected individuals.

Environment. Microorganisms, either genetically engineered or selected from natural populations, are used to degrade toxic wastes in the environment. For example, polycyclic aromatic compounds, such as polychlorinated biphenyls, and petroleum products which contaminate soil and ground-water supplies may be degraded by populations of microorganisms. These technologies have the potential to solve some significant environmental problems. Waste products of industry and agriculture are being composted, with added microorganisms selected for their capacity to degrade organic materials. *See* BIODEGRADATION; GENETIC ENGINEERING; MOLECULAR BIOLOGY.

Milton Zaitlin

Bibliography. M. Butler, *Mammalian Cell Biotechnology: A Practical Approach*, 1991; P. N. Cheremisinoff and L. M. Ferrante (eds.), *Biotechnology: Current Progress*, vol. 1, 1991; J. Farrington, *Agriculture Biotechnology*, 1990; G. LeWandowski, *Biotechnology Application*, 1990; P. M. Peters, *Biotechnology: A Guide to Genetic Engineering*, 1993.

Biotelemetry

The use of telemetry methods for sending signals from a living organism over some distance to a receiver. Usually, biotelemetry is used for gathering data about the physiology, behavior, or location of the organism. Generally, the signals are carried by radio, light, or sound waves. Consequently, biotelemetry implies the absence of wires between the subject and receiver.

The basic equipment required for biotelemetry includes a transmitter, a receiver, and their antennas. The receiver usually converts the incoming signal (for example, radio frequency) to an electronic signal that can be recorded or stored (for example, in a computer), or to a sound that can be monitored by a human attendant. *See* ANTENNA (ELECTROMAGNETISM); RADIO RECEIVER; RADIO TRANSMITTER.

Generally, biotelemetry techniques are necessary in situations when wires running from a subject to a recorder would inhibit the subject's activity; when the proximity of an investigator to a subject might alter the subject's behavior; and when the movements of the subject and the duration of the monitoring make it impractical for the investigator to remain within sight of the subject. Biotelemetry is widely used in medical fields to monitor patients and research subjects, and now even to operate devices such as drug delivery systems and prosthetics. Sensors and transmitters placed on or implanted in animals are used to study physiology and behavior in the laboratory and to study the movements, behavior, and physiology of wildlife species in their natural environments.

Applications. There is tremendous diversity of applications of biotelemetry, and as new electronics technology develops, biotelemetry will be applied even more broadly.

Medicine. Biotelemetry is an important technique for biomedical research and clinical medicine. Holter monitoring, or storage telemetry, was one of the earliest applications of biotelemetry to human medicine. Holter monitoring involves transmitting a signal, such as heart rate, to a receiver on a person who is free to move about. This idea is still widely used in medicine; however, with new technology many other biotelemetry methods are used in research and during treatment.

Another example of medical telemetry is the placement of a pressure transducer on the biting surface of a tooth and radio transmission of the resulting signal to provide data about tooth contact and bruxing, that is, unconscious tooth grinding that can cause severe headaches and muscle pain. The use of pressure sensors and small transmitters permits dental researchers to monitor bruxing without disrupting the individual's behavior.

Sensors placed on muscles can detect contractions, and those data can be transmitted to a remote receiver, allowing monitoring of muscle tension. To study digestive disorders, telemetry is used to monitor the muscular contractions of the intestinal tract, the movements of gut contents, and aspects of the digestive tract environment (for example, pH). Urinary incontinence can be studied by using telemetry to monitor urethral and bladder pressure, urine flow, and the effects of drug therapy. Biotelemetry allows this to be done while the individual conducts normal daily activities.

Electrode sensors with leads to transmitters are used to study the nervous system. By using telemetry, records of the brain's activity (electroencephalograms) can be obtained from epileptics. Sometimes electroencephalograms are measured in conjunction with telemetry of muscle activity to learn when epileptics experience neural dysfunction during regular activity. Also, there has been research with biotelemetry to develop nerve stimulation, including biofeedback mechanisms for people who have suffered nerve damage. Phrenic nerve stimulation, scoliosis correction, and epilepsy control have all been investigated with the aid of biotelemetry. *See* ELECTROENCEPHALO-GRAPHY.

Furthermore, telemetry methods are employed in studies of breathing abnormalities during sleep, including sleep apnea, snoring, and sudden death syndrome. Fetal and neonatal brain patterns and heart rates can easily be monitored with telemetry, thereby circumventing restrictions to the person's movements, while facilitating nursing care.

Perhaps cardiovascular research and treatment have benefited the most from biotelemetry. Heart rate, blood flow, and blood pressure can be measured in ambulatory subjects and transmitted to a remote receiver-recorder. Telemetry also has been used to obtain data about local oxygen pressure on the surface of organs (for example, liver and myocardium) and for studies of capillary exchange (that is, oxygen supply and discharge). Biomedical research with telemetry includes measuring cardiovascular performance during the weightlessness of space flight and portable monitoring of radioactive indicators as they are dispersed through the body by the blood vessels. *See* SPACE BIOLOGY.

For applied medicine, anesthesia can be evaluated during surgery by telemetric monitoring of electroencephalograms. Fetal heart rates and the mother's uterine contractions can be monitored in preparation for child delivery. After birth, the cardiopulmonary function of neonates and premature babies can be checked with telemetry. After treatment by drug therapy or coronary surgery, telemetry is useful for monitoring cardiovascular performance so that recovery and the efficacy of the treatment can be evaluated.

Telemetry has significant potential applications for controlling drug dosages from implanted delivery systems (for example, insulin pumps), adjusting cardiac pacemakers, operating prosthetics, and assessing the function of orthopedic implants.

In sports medicine, by measuring heart rate, physiologists can assess the differences in conditioning caused by interval and continuous training regimens. Telemetry also permits monitoring of athletes during actual conditions of training and competition, so it has been applied to runners, swimmers, rowers, and others. In one study the heart rate of cyclists and the physical parameters from the bicycle wheels were simultaneously recorded by telemetry so that performance could be evaluated over the turns and hills of the race course.

Animal behavior. Just as telemetry has been used in many ways to study human subjects, it has been applied widely to animal research. To avoid disturbing animals or restricting their movements unnecessarily, telemetry has been used to record electroencephalograms, heart rates, heart muscle contractions, and respiration, even from sleeping mammals and birds (**Fig. 1**). Telemetry and video recording have been combined in research of the relationships between neural and cardiac activity and behavior. Using miniature electrodes and transmitters, ethologists have studied the influence of one

Fig. 1. Location transmitter glued to the back of a 1-oz (30-g) thrush. Such transmitters, usually used in collars for mammals, have revolutionized animal ecology studies by allowing investigators to find and identify individual animals at will. (*From L. D. Mech, Handbook of Animal Radio-Tracking, University of Minnesota Press, 1983*)

bird's song on the heart rate and behavior of a nearby bird.

Many studies of domestic animals have included techniques of biotelemetry. The performance of race horses has been monitored by using heart rate and respiratory data obtained with telemetry. In this way, the effects of different diets, different training methods, and the age or sex of the horse can be evaluated. Telemetry can help to provide information about the social behavior and energetics of livestock that is raised for food. For example, biotelemetry was used to monitor heart rate and body temperature, to learn that a breed of pigs was less disturbed and exhibited more control of body temperature when kept in pens with other pigs than when housed individually. These conditions resulted in better swine growth and productivity for farmers.

Biotelemetry has been applied in several ways to animals such as cattle that are allowed to wander over large areas in herds. Implanted temperature-sensing transmitters are used to monitor the breeding condition of female animals so that the likelihood of successful artificial insemination can be maximized. Individually coded transmitters are used to mark animals to census their presence in the herd, as well as to automatically dispense a specialized portion of food when each animal's signal is received at the feeding trough. Such techniques permit some attention to individual animals, without the effort needed to observe or capture each animal every day.

Ecology. Many species of wildlife are difficult to find and observe because they are secretive, nocturnal, wide-ranging, or move rapidly. Since the 1960s, biotelemetry has been a valuable technique for many animal ecology studies. Most commonly, a transmitter is placed on a wild animal so that biologists can track or locate it by homing toward the transmitted signal or by estimating the location by plotting the intersection of two or more bearings from the receiver toward the signal. For some purposes, after homing to a transmitter-marked animal, the biologists observe its behavior. For other studies, successive estimates of location are plotted on a map to describe movement patterns, to delineate the amount of area the animal requires, or to determine dispersal or migration paths. Ecologists can associate the vegetation or other features of the environment with the locations of the animal.

Sensors can be placed on animals' transmitters to provide data about the temperature, humidity, and air pressure around the animal. The general activity of transmitter-marked animals can be related to signal modulation caused by transmitter antenna movements or to a motion-sensing mercury switch placed inside the transmitter. Implanted sensors, or entirely implanted transmitters equipped with sensors, are used to record body temperature, heart rate, pH, and muscular activity. The depths at which eels and whales swim and penguins feed have been studied with telemetry. The temperatures around transmitters on grouse have been monitored to learn when the birds roost under the snow and emerge to fly into the treetops to eat the buds from leafless winter branches. Biologists have also used telemetry to study the responses of fish to thermal pollution caused by electrical and nuclear generating plants.

Ecologists can mark numerous animals, each with a unique frequency or coded signal, and thus keep track of many individuals simultaneously without having to observe them all at once. In this way, biotelemetry can be useful for studying the social interaction among animals, such as the seasonal gathering of adults for breeding, and the proximity and duration of parent-offspring relationships. The survival of many transmitter-marked animals can be monitored, and the dead animals can be located in order to determine the cause of death. Consequently, with the tools of biotelemetry ecologists are learning more about wildlife diseases, predator-prey relationships, and the productivity and longevity of many wildlife species.

Fig. 2. Basic receiving system for biotelemetry signals uses a portable receiver and a hand-held directional antenna. (*From L. D. Mech, Handbook of Animal Radio-Tracking, University of Minnesota Press, 1983*)

Workplace. Biotelemetry has been used to study the performance, the comfort, and the health of workers. For example, the cardiovascular strain on glassblowers has been measured, as have the changes in body temperature and heart rate of factory employees as they move among different work stations. Telemetry has been used to monitor the effects of changing air pressure on workers who descend into subway tunnels. Video recordings of workers' behavior and activity have been combined with telemetry to identify those situations that cause stress to employees. For example, changes in heart rate or oxygen uptake, monitored by telemetry, and combined with a video of eye blinking, have been used to detect stress. Also, measurements of the environment, such as humidity, ambient temperature, and gas concentrations, can be monitored at many sites, sent by telemetry to a central receiver, and ultimately combined with biotelemetry to help evaluate working conditions.

Technical aspects. Biotelemetry is used to measure biological attributes over some distance without disrupting the subject's normal behavior. Consequently, there are usually two concerns associated with the use of biotelemetry: the distance over which the signal can be received, and the size of the transmitter package. Often, both of these concerns depend on the power source for the transmitter. Generally, the greater the radiated power from the transmitter antenna, the greater the distance of reception, when all other factors remain constant. But most transmitters are powered by primary batteries using mercuric oxide, silver oxide, or lithium chemical reactions. These batteries are available in a variety of sizes, with larger sizes having more energy capacity. Larger batteries can be used to make a transmitter last longer or to produce a more powerful signal. Integrated circuits and surface mount technology allow production of very small electronic circuitry in transmitters, making batteries the largest part of the transmitter package. However, the more powerful transmitters with their larger batteries are more difficult to place on or implant in a subject without affecting the subject's behavior or energetics. *See* BATTERY.

The mere presence of a transmitter can bother subjects, thus distracting them from routine behavior. Transmitters can interfere with normal movements. The additional mass of a transmitter package increases the energy required by the subject to maintain posture and to move about. On flying or swimming subjects, externally mounted transmitters can increase drag. The placement of the transmitter can affect a subject's balance and maneuverability. External transmitters, antenna, and attachment materials can become ensnared on objects in the subject's environment. The presence of the transmitter can affect the way that other organisms behave toward the subject, and on some animals a transmitter can increase the risk of the subject being attractive to a predator. Concern about these factors has led biologists to develop and test many attachment and implant methods for different sizes of transmitters. Nevertheless, these factors limit the power, and thus the operational life and reception distance, of biotelemetry transmitters.

In addition, there are several factors related to the receiver and antennas that are important for functional aspects of biotelemetry. For instance, comparatively simple and insensitive radio receivers, like an AM/ FM transistor radio, can be used with powerful transmitters or at relatively short distances (for example, less than 30 ft or 10 m), but more sensitive receivers are capable of picking up less powerful transmitter signals or those from larger distances. Transmitting and receiving antennas also come in many designs, some more sensitive or more directional than others. As signals (radio, sound, or light) travel farther from the transmitter, they become weaker and can be detected only by the more sensitive receiving equipment.

There are many environmental factors that influence signals and consequently the reception range. Sources of signals at or on the operating frequency will cause interference that can reduce, or eliminate, reception range of target transmitters. Radio signals can be absorbed and scattered by the Earth's surface, vegetation, moisture in the air, and the subject's body. Therefore, many studies are designed to maximize the relationship between the transmitting and receiving antennas. For example, a single-element wire transmitting antenna is most efficient when positioned at an angle away from the subject's body. Also, whenever possible, the receiving antennas are raised above the ground, or vegetation, by placing them on a mast or the wing of an airplane or, for some applications, in an orbiting satellite.

Transmitter power, antenna (transmitting and receiving) design and position, receiver sensitivity, atmospheric conditions, and interference all interact to affect the quality of biotelemetry signals and the distance over which they can be detected. Radio transmitters that are small, a few millimeters in diameter (25 mm = 1 in.) and weighing less than a gram (28g = 1 oz), might transmit only 3 ft (1 m) from within a subject to a receiver in a laboratory, or less than 300 ft (100 m) from an animal's body surface to a receiver and antenna held by a wildlife biologist. Infrared light signals are usually limited to an area within a room. The radio signal from a 1-oz (30-g) transmitter around the neck of a mammal might be received over 12 mi (20 km), while the same package on the back of a flying bird could be received over 120 mi (200 km) away in an airplane. Signals from 0.4–11 lb (0.2–5 kg) transmitters are sent to satellites that are 520 mi (860 km) in space; some transmitters send sound waves more than 60 mi (100 km) through water. In some applications, signals are sent a relatively short distance to local receivers, from which they are amplified and sent much greater distances to another receiver.

Receiving systems (**Fig. 2**) can function simply to transform an incoming signal from one form (for example, radio) to another (for example, sound) or can be combined with a recording device (for example, magnetic tape recorder or paper chart recorder). Receiving systems can function to decode complex digital and modulated signals. Receivers can be combined with computing equipment to sample various frequencies at preprogrammed intervals, to sample incoming signals, to perform analyses, and to display and sort data derived from transmitted signals. *See* TELEMETERING.   Mark Roy Fuller

Bibliography. C. J. Amlaner (ed.), *Biotelemetry: Proceedings of the 10th International Symposium on Biotelemetry*, 1989 (and also earlier proceedings); C. J. Amlaner and D. W. McDonald (eds.), *A Handbook on Biotelemetry and Radio Tracking*, 1980; R. Kenward, *Wildlife Radio Tagging*, 2d ed., 2000.

Biotin

A vitamin, widespread in nature, whose deficiency causes dermatitis and other disturbances in animals and humans. It is only sparingly soluble in water (0.03 g/100 ml H_2O at 25°C or 77°F). It is stable in boiling water solutions, but can be destroyed by oxidizing agents, acids, and alkalies. Under some conditions, it can be destroyed by oxidation in the presence of rancid fats. Its structural formula is shown below.

Occurrence. Biotin's occurrence in nature is so widespread that it is difficult to prepare a natural deficient diet. Studies of egg-white injury resulted in the discovery of biotin deficiencies in animals. Raw egg white contains a protein, avidin, which combines with biotin to form an indigestible complex. The feeding of large amounts of raw egg white has been used in producing experimental biotin deficiencies. Heating of egg white denatures avidin, destroying its biotin complexing ability. Although the avidin-biotin complex is stable to intestinal enzymes, it is hydrolyzed when administered parenterally.

Bioassay. Chemical and physical methods for biotin analysis are not available. Rat and chick assays are not very good and are seldom used. Microbiological assays using yeast or *Lactobacillus arabinosus* are commonly used.

Nutritional value. Biotin deficiency in animals is associated with dermatitis, loss of hair, muscle incoordination and paralysis, and reproductive disturbances. Biotin deficiency produced in human volunteers by feeding large amounts of egg white resulted in dermatitis, nausea, depression, muscle pains, anemia, and a large increase in serum cholesterol.

Biochemistry. Biotin occurs in nature mainly in bound forms. One of these isolated from yeast, biocytin, is ϵ-N-biotinyl-L-lysine. Biocytin can replace biotin as a growth factor for many organisms. Although the metabolic role of biocytin is unknown, its structure and concentration in some materials suggest that it is more than an oddity. Biotin functions as a coenzyme in carbon dioxide fixation and decarboxylation enzymes, as illustrated by the reversible reaction: pyruvic acid + CO_2 ⇌ oxaloacetic acid. The amino acid aspartic acid can replace biotin for some microorganisms because the bacteria require aspartic acid for growth, and the oxaloacetic acid produced by biotin-containing enzymes can be converted by transamination to aspartic acid. Biotin is also involved in deamination of some amino acids: aspartic acid ⇌ NH_3 + fumaric acid. Some microorganisms require oleic acid if biotin is not supplied. Biotin may be important for oleic acid synthesis, or vice versa. Under normal conditions, biotin is synthesized to such a degree by intestinal bacteria that a dietary source is probably not necessary. Most diets contain 25–50 micrograms per day, but 2–5 times as much is excreted in the urine and feces. *See* COENZYME; VITAMIN B_{12}.   Stanley N. Gershoff

Industrial synthesis. The structure of biotin was established and the vitamin synthesized by V. du Vigneaud and coworkers in a masterpiece of technical management of a highly complicated synthesis. *meso*-Dibenzylaminosuccinic acid is reacted with phosgene to close the imidazolidone ring. The two carbocyclic groups enable closing the adjacent thiophanone ring by reduction and sulfonation. A three-carbon chain is then introduced by reaction with ethoxypropylmagnesium bromide. Upon closing a third (thiophanium) ring, resolution of the optical antipodes is possible. A malonic ester condensation providing the necessary side chain is followed by dibenzylation, saponification, and decarboxylation, giving the naturally occurring dextrorotatory biotin. *See* VITAMIN.   Roger A. Mercanton

Bibliography. K. Dakshinamurti and H. N. Bhagavan, *Biotin*, 1985.

Biotite

An iron-magnesium-rich layer silicate; it is also known as black mica. Biotite is the most abundant of the mica group of minerals. The name is derived from that of the French chemist J. Biot. The formula for the ideal end member, phlogopite, is $KMg_3AlSi_3O_{10}(OH)_2$. The more general formula is $AX_3Y_4O_{12}(Z)_2$, where A (interlayer cation) = K, Na, Ca, Ba, or vacancies; X (octahedral cations) = Li, Mg, Fe^{2+}, Fe^{3+}, Al, Ti, or vacancies; and Y (tetrahedral cation) = Fe^{3+}, Al, Si; Z = (OH), F, Cl, O^{2-}. This formula is more indicative of the wide range of compositions known for this mineral. Biotite has no commercial value, but vermiculite, an alteration product of magnesium-rich biotite, is used as insulation, as packing material, and as an ingredient for potting soils. *See* VERMICULITE.

The crystal structure of biotite is based on a sheet of octahedrally coordinated iron or magnesium ions sandwiched between two sheets of tetrahedrally coordinated silicon and aluminum ions to form a layer. The layers are bonded by interlayer alkali or alkaline-earth ions. Over 20 different polytypes have been discovered, all based on multiple layers of the basic unit which has monoclinic symmetry. The observed polytypes belong to the triclinic, monoclinic, and trigonal crystal systems. *See* CRYSTAL STRUCTURE.

The hardness of biotite ranges between 2.5 and 3 on Mohs scale, and the specific gravity between 2.7 and 3.5. The color ranges from colorless (phlogopite) through shades of brown and green to black. Oxidized and Ti-rich biotites are usually reddish brown. Iron-rich varieties of biotite have been referred to as lepidomelane, and biotites rich in both iron and aluminum are called siderophyllites. When Fe^{3+} substitutes in the tetrahedral layers for Al and Si, the orientation of the optic plane changes, and such varieties of biotite are referred to as anomites.

Biotites are found commonly in igneous and metamorphic rocks. They are the common ferromagnesian phase in most granitic rocks, and are also found in some siliceous and intermediate volcanic rocks. In basaltic rocks biotite sometimes occurs in the crystalline groundmass, and is a common late interstitial phase in gabbroic rocks. It has been recognized in samples of the Earth's mantle found as inclusions in volcanic rocks. Biotite has not been observed in lunar rocks. *See* IGNEOUS ROCKS; METAMORPHIC ROCKS.

Biotites are not stable at the surface of the Earth, as they decompose by both hydrolysis and oxidation when exposed to the Earth's atmosphere. They alter to vermiculite, chlorite, and iron oxides, and thus are uncommon in sedimentary rocks. Biotites in erupted lavas will undergo dehydrogenation, a process in which hydrogen leaves the crystal structure, and the charge balance is maintained by the conversion of Fe^{2+} to Fe^{3+} and (OH) to O^{2-}. Such crystals are known as oxybiotites.

Biotites are important constituents of metamorphic rocks such as schist and gneiss, and the first appearance of biotite is an important marker in metamorphism. Biotite persists to very high grades of metamorphism, where it reacts with quartz to form granulites made up of potassium feldspar and orthopyroxene, garnet, or cordierite, in addition to quartz and plagioclase. Under conditions of ultrametamorphism, biotite reacts with quartz, plagioclase, and alkali feldspar to form siliceous melts. Biotite is also a common gangue mineral in ore deposits. The mineral has been used as an indicator of H_2O, HF, O_2, and S_2 activities in both rock- and ore-forming processes. Its absence in lunar rocks can be attributed to the extremely low contents of H_2O and F in lunar materials. *See* METAMORPHISM; MICA; SILICATE MINERALS.   David R. Wones

Birch

A deciduous tree of the genus *Betula* which is distributed over much of North America, in Asia south to the Himalaya, and in Europe. About 40 species are known. The birches comprise the family Betulaceae in the order Fagales. The sweet birch, *B. lenta* (**illus.** *a*), the yellow birch, *B. alleghaniensis* (illus. *b*), and the paper birch, *B. papyrifera*, are

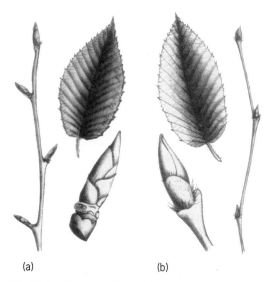

Birch twigs, leaves, and buds: (a) sweet birch (*Betula lenta*); (b) yellow birch (*B. alleghaniensis*).

all important timber trees of the eastern United States. The yellow and the paper species extend into Canada. The gray birch, *B. populifolia*, is a smaller tree of the extreme northeastern United States and adjacent Canada. Both sweet (black) and yellow birches can be recognized by the wintergreen taste of the bark of the young twigs. A flavoring similar to oil of wintergreen is obtained from the bark of the sweet birch. The paper and gray birches can be easily identified by their white bark. The bark of the paper birch peels off in thin papery sheets, a characteristic not true of the gray birch. The river birch, *B. nigra*, is a less common tree of wet soils and banks of streams and is important as an ornamental and for erosion control. The hard, strong wood of the yellow and the sweet birches is used for furniture, boxes, baskets, crates, and woodenware. The European birches, *B. pubescens* and *B. pendula*, are the counterparts of the paper and gray birches in the United States. European birches are also cultivated in America. *See* FAGALES; FOREST AND FORESTRY; TREE.

Arthur H. Graves; Kenneth P. Davis

Birefringence

The splitting which a wavefront experiences when a wave disturbance is propagated in an anisotropic material; also called double refraction. In anisotropic substances the velocity of a wave is a function of a displacement direction. Although the term birefringence could apply to tranverse elastic waves, it is usually applied only to electromagnetic waves.

In birefringent materials either the separation between neighboring atomic structural units is different in different directions, or the bonds tying such units together have different characteristics in different directions. Many crystalline materials, such as calcite, quartz, and topaz, are birefringent. Diamonds on the other hand, are isotropic and have no special effect on polarized light of different orien-

tations. Plastics composed of long-chain molecules become anisotropic when stretched or compressed. Solutions of long-chain molecules become birefringent when they flow. This first phenomenon is called photoelasticity; the second, streaming birefringence. *See* PHOTOELASTICITY.

For each propagation direction with linearly polarized electromagnetic waves, there are two principal displacement directions for which the velocity is different. These polarization directions are at right angles. The difference between the two indices of refraction is also called the birefringence. When the plane of polarization of a light beam does not coincide with one of the two principal displacement directions, the light vector will be split into components that are parallel to each direction. At the surface of such materials the angle of refraction is different for light that is polarized parallel to the two principal directions.

For additional information on befringence and birefringent materials *see* CRYSTAL OPTICS; POLARIZED LIGHT; REFRACTION OF WAVES.   Bruce H. Billings

Birth control

Methods of fertility control, including contraception, that are intended to prevent pregnancy, and means of interrupting early pregnancy. The efficacy of the various methods and consistency of use vary widely. Factors associated with degree of effectiveness include user age, income, marital status, and intention (that is, whether contraception is used to delay or to prevent pregnancy). The available methods consist of hormonal methods (including oral contraceptives, subdermal implants, and injectable formulations), sterilization, intrauterine devices, barrier and chemical methods, and fertility awareness methods.

Hormonal contraceptives. Hormonal contraception relies upon the use of various synthetic hormones that are either identical or similar in action to those normally produced within a woman's body. However, by varying the dosages and combinations of these hormones, ovulation is generally suppressed, producing temporary infertility. These contain one or both of two compounds (estrogen and progestin) similar to the hormones that regulate the menstrual cycle. Each monthly series of pills either suppresses ovulation or alters the uterine lining and the cervical mucus, or both. Oral contraceptives can help protect users against anemia, ectopic pregnancy, pelvic inflammatory disease, benign breast disease, ovarian cysts, and carcinoma of the ovary and of the endometrium. Complications include blood clots, which can cause stroke or heart attack; their occurrence, although rare, is far more likely for women over age 35 who smoke heavily or have certain preexisting health problems, for example, hypertension, than for other users. Cardiovascular risk may be lower with use of low-dose oral contraceptives. Those containing the progestins norgestimate, desogestral, or gestodene may even offer some protective effects. *See* ENDOCRINE MECHANISMS; ESTROGEN; MENSTRUATION; PROGESTERONE.

Postcoital contraception is another hormonal method. In emergency situations (for example, rape) high dosages of oral contraception can be used. One dose is given within 72 h after the episode of unprotected intercourse, and an additional dose is given 12 h later.

Subdermal implants. The subdermal implant consists of small hollow rods that are placed under the skin of a woman's upper arm and release a low, continuous dose of a progestin. It is more effective than the oral contraceptives and, because it lacks estrogens, does not pose a risk of cardiovascular complications. It is reversible, lasts for 5 years, is nearly as reliable as sterilization, and is less expensive than birth control pills. Women using this method experience more irregular bleeding than with other hormonal methods. No serious complications have been documented; however, it is essential that insertion and removal of subdermal implants be performed by a physician fully trained in this procedure.

Injectables. An injection of progestin suppresses ovulation and can be given every 3 months. It can be used by women who should not take estrogens. Women experience irregular bleeding in the first 6 months of use, often followed by cessation of menses with continuing use. It has been shown to be as safe and reliable as sterilization, yet is readily reversible.

Intrauterine devices. The main mode of action for the intrauterine device (IUD) is considered to be prevention of fertilization. Of the two commercially available IUDs in the United States, the one containing copper is designed to remain in place for 10 years; for users over the age of 25, the pregnancy rate is less than 1%. The other one releases a daily dosage of the natural hormone progesterone to suppress the uterine lining and requires annual replacement.

Use of an IUD can seriously increase the risk of pelvic infection and subsequent infertility if a user's relationship with her partner is not monogamous; thus, the IUD is not suited for women who have more than one sexual partner, or whose partner does. Other problems associated with IUD use can include cramps, increased menstrual bleeding, expulsion of the device, and, more rarely, perforation of the uterus or tubal (ectopic) pregnancy. However, since the risk of pregnancy is low among IUD users, the absolute risk of ectopic pregnancy is significantly less for users of the copper IUD than among women not using contraception.

Barrier methods. Such methods include the male condom, female intravaginal pouch, diaphragm, cervical cap, vaginal contraceptive sponge, and various chemical preparations. The condom is a sheath of thin latex (sometimes coated with spermicide) or animal tissue that covers the penis. The intravaginal pouch, also known as a female condom, is a loose-fitting vaginal liner with an external rim designed to hold it in place. The diaphragm is a shallow rubber cup with a ring rim that fits securely in the vagina to cover the cervix. The cervical cap is a smaller, thimble-shaped latex device that fits over the cervix. The diaphragm and cervical cap are used with spermicides. The vaginal contraceptive sponge is a soft, synthetic, disposable sponge that fits over the cervix and, when moistened, continuously releases spermicide. Among the chemical preparations available as vaginal contraceptives are foams, creams, jellies, and suppositories.

Fertility awareness methods. Fertility awareness methods enable a woman to estimate when she is fertile so that she can practice abstinence or use a barrier method during those times. Techniques used to determine fertility include cervical mucus observation, and body signs with temperature tracking. Such methods are often less effective for contraception.

Sterilization. Sterilization is the most commonly used method of birth control for women and men both in the United States and worldwide. It is preferred by women over the age of 30 who have had the desired number of children. Less than 1% of males who have a vasectomy or females who undergo tubal sterilization are thereafter involved in pregnancy, and so the individuals no longer need to practice a method of birth control. The procedures do not adversely affect the production of male or female hormones, so that individual sexual characteristics such as sex drive and menses usually remain unchanged.

Vasectomy is a minor male surgical procedure that occludes the vas deferens by various means (such as by cautery or suture).

In the United States, tubal sterilization in the female is an operation commonly performed through the laparoscope, a long, thin, tubular instrument with magnifying mirrors that is inserted through the navel for visualization. The instrument that performs the tubal occlusion may be either attached to the laparoscope or inserted through the lower abdomen. Clips, bands, or cautery are used to close off the fallopian tubes. Minilap, an operation to tie the tubes, may also be performed through a small incision in the lower abdomen. Serious complications such as hemorrhage or infection are very rare.

The individual needs to be sure that children are no longer wanted before opting for sterilization, because the operation should be considered as permanent. Only in a small number of instances has it been successfully reversed.

Future methods. New systems to deliver long-acting steroidal contraceptives are likely to become available. Examples of systems that are in the research stage are injectable microcapsules, vaginal rings, and transdermal patches. Vaccines that would be injected annually are also being tested. Antiprogesterone compounds, which were developed in Europe, block receptors for progesterone, a key hormone in establishing and maintaining pregnancy. *See* FERTILIZATION (ANIMAL); PREGNANCY.   Louise B. Tyrer

Bibliography. L. Corson, R. J. Derman, and L. B. Tyrer (eds.), *Fertility Control,* 2d ed., 1995.

Bismuth

The metallic element, Bi, of atomic number 83 and atomic weight 208.980 belonging in the periodic table to group 15. Bismuth is the most metallic element in this group in both physical and chemical properties. The only stable isotope is that of mass 209. It is estimated that the Earth's crust contains about 0.00002% bismuth. It occurs in nature as the free metal and in ores. The principal ore deposits are in South America. However, the primary source of bismuth in the United States is as a by-product in refining of copper and lead ores. *See* PERIODIC TABLE.

Physical and mechanical properties of bismuth		
Property	Value	Temperature
Melting point, °C	271.4	
Boiling point, °C	1559	
Heat of fusion, kcal/mole	2.60	
Heat of vaporization, kcal/mole	36.2	
Vapor pressure, mm Hg	1	917°C
	10	1067°C
	100	1257°C
Density, g/cm³	9.80	20° (solid)
	10.03	300° (liquid)
	9.91	400° (liquid)
	9.66	600° (liquid)
Mean specific heat, cal/g	0.0294	0–270°C
	0.0373	300–1000°C
Coefficient of linear expansion	$13.45 \times 10^{-6}/°C$	
Thermal conductivity, cal/(s)(cm²)(°C)	0.018	100° (solid)
	0.041	300° (liquid)
	0.037	400° (liquid)
Electrical resistivity, μohm-cm	106.5	0° (solid)
	160.2	100° (solid)
	267.0	269° (solid)
	128.9	300° (liquid)
	134.2	400° (liquid)
	145.3	600° (liquid)
Surface tension, dynes/cm	376	300°C
	370	400°C
	363	500°C
Viscosity, centipoise	1.662	300°C
	1.280	450°C
	0.996	600°C
Magnetic susceptibility, cgs units	-1.35×10^{-6}	
Crystallography	Rhombohedral, $a_0 = 0.47457$ nm	
Thermal-neutron absorption cross section, barns	0.032 ± 0.003	
Modulus of elasticity, lb/cm²	4.6×10^6	
Shear modulus, lb/cm²	1.8×10^6	
Poisson's ratio	0.33	
Hardness, Brinell	4–8	

The main use of bismuth is in the manufacture of low-melting alloys which are used in fusible elements in automatic sprinklers, special solders, safety plugs in compressed gas cylinders, and automatic shutoffs for gas and electric water-heating systems. Some bismuth alloys, which expand on freezing, are used in castings and in type metal. Another important use of bismuth is in the manufacture of pharmaceutical compounds.

Bismuth is a gray-white, lustrous, hard, brittle, coarsely crystalline metal. It is one of the few metals which expand on solidification. The thermal conductivity of bismuth is lower than that of any metal, with the exception of mercury. The **table** cites the chief physical and mechanical properties of bismuth. Bismuth is inert in dry air at room temperature, although it oxidizes slightly in moist air. It rapidly forms an oxide film at temperatures above its melting point, and it burns at red heat, forming the yellow oxide, Bi_2O_3. The metal combines directly with halogens and with sulfur, selenium, and tellurium; however, it does not combine directly with nitrogen or phosphorus. Bismuth is not attacked at ordinary temperatures by air-free water, but it is slowly oxidized at red heat by water vapor.

Almost all compounds of bismuth contain trivalent bismuth. However, bismuth can occasionally be pentavalent or monovalent. Sodium bismuthate and bismuth pentafluoride are perhaps the most important compounds of Bi(V). The former is a powerful oxidizing agent, and the latter a useful fluorinating agent for organic compounds.   Samuel J. Yosin

Bibliography. F. A. Cotton et al., *Advanced Inorganic Chemistry*, 6th ed., Wiley-Interscience, 1999; D. R. Lide, *CRC Handbook Chemistry and Physics*, 85th ed., CRC Press, 2004; D. F. Shriver and P. W. Atkins, *Inorganic Chemistry*, 3d ed., 1999.

Bison

The name for two species of the Bovidae, the cattle family, in the mammalian order Artiodactyla, found in North America and Europe. The European bison (*Bison bonasus*) is commonly known as the wisent. The American species (*B. bison*; see **illus.**), is often called buffalo but should not be confused with the African buffalo.

The American Bison Society was formed in 1905 to preserve this species. A small herd was established

North American bison (*Bison bison*).

in the Wichita Forest Reserve in Oklahoma. This herd prospered, and many specimens of this stock were sent to zoos, where they adjusted and reproduced. Another herd was established in South Dakota; it is culled annually, and the excess animals are sold at auction for food. Experimental crosses have been made with range cattle. The resulting offspring forage and survive adverse environmental conditions much better than cattle do.

Wisent. The European bison was originally abundant in the forested areas of western Europe during the late Cenozoic Era. The wisent is a browsing, woodland animal which congregates in relatively small herds. It is almost extinct in its natural range and, although a few herds exist, it is known mainly from a few hundred specimens preserved in zoological gardens and zoos. The few protected wild herds, which were maintained on the large landed estates of Poland and Lithuania prior to World War I, were killed off for food, thus reducing the numbers drastically. An intensive effort has been made to preserve the species by breeding and maintaining this animal in captivity.

After World War II a concerted effort was made to locate these scattered animals and determine their pedigree. At the present time, it is estimated that more than 400 pureblood wisents have been recorded. In an effort to maintain the animals in Europe, they had frequently been crossed with the American bison. The hybrids have been excluded from the pedigree stock lists.

Although there are differences, the wisent is closely allied to the American species. The wisent has a small head carried in a high position and a short mane, and is more graceful and less massive than the North American species. The hump is less noticeable, the legs are longer, the horns are more slender, and the body is not so shaggy. A wary animal, the wisent has poor vision and a keen sense of smell. A single calf is born after a gestation period of 39–40 weeks. Cows mature at about 4 years and bulls at about 6–8 years.

American bison. Enormous herds of the American bison existed on the Plains area of North America in western Canada and the western United States during the nineteenth century. It is estimated that there are still about 20,000 bison in Canada and the United States on preserves and national parks. These bovines are massive, with the males attaining a length of 9 ft (3 m), a height of 6 ft (2 m) at the shoulder, and a weight of up to 3000 lb (1350 kg).

These animals are herbivorous, and migrated originally when the grass or forage became scarce. The bison chews a cud, and the teeth are typically those of grazing animals with a dental formula of I 0/3 C 0/1 Pm 3/3 M 3/3 for a total of 32 teeth. The large head is held in a low position, and behind the neck region is a characteristic hump. The forequarters are shaggy with the hair more pronounced in the male than the female. The senses of smell and hearing are well developed, while vision is poor. Both the male and female have horns which are small and set far apart. The bison is unusual in having 14 pairs of ribs in contrast to the usual 13 pairs. The female comes into heat in late summer, and after a gestation period of over 9 months, a single calf is born in the spring. The maximum lifespan of the bison is about 30 years. *See* ARTIODACTYLA; BUFFALO; MAMMALIA.

Charles B. Curtin

Bit

A binary digit. In the computer, electronics, and communications fields, "bit" is generally understood as a shortened form of "binary digit." In a numerical binary system, a bit is either a 0 or 1. Bits are generally used to indicate situations that can take one of two values or one of two states, for example, on and off, true or false, or yes or no. If, by convention, 1 represents a particular state, then 0 represents the other state. For example, if 1 stands for "yes," then 0 stands for "no." *See* BOOLEAN ALGEBRA; NUMBERING SYSTEMS.

In a computer system a bit is thought of as the basic unit of memory where, by convention, only either a 0 or 1 can be stored. In a computer memory, consecutive bits are grouped to form smaller or larger "units" of memory (see **table**). Depending upon the design of the computer, units up to 64 bits long have been considered. Although there is common agreement as to the number of bits that make up a byte, for larger memory units the terminology depends entirely on the convention used by the manufacturer. In all of these units the leftmost bit is generally called

Units of computer memory	
Unit name	Number of consecutive bits
Nibble	4
Byte	8
Word or half-word	16
Double word or full-word	32

the most significant bit (msb) and the rightmost the least significant bit (lsb).

Alphanumeric representation. Bytes and larger units can be used to represent numerical quantities. In these cases the most significant bit is used to indicate the "sign" of the value being represented. By convention a 0 in the msb represents a positive quantity; a 1 represents a negative quantity. Depending on the convention used to represent these numbers, the remaining bits may then be used to represent the numerical value. In addition to numerical quantities, bytes are used to represent characters inside a computer. These characters include all letters of the English alphabet, the digits 0 through 9, and symbols such as comma, period, right and left parentheses, spaces, and tabs. Characters can be represented using the ASCII code (American Standard Code for Information Interchange) or the EBCDIC code (Extended Binary Coded Decimal Interchange Code). The latter is used by some mainframe computers. Computers are set up to handle only one of these two character codes. Generally, the internal representation of a character is different in the two codes. For instance, in ASCII the plus sign is represented by the numerical sequence 00101011, and in EBCDIC, by 01001110. *See* NUMERICAL REPRESENTATION (COMPUTERS).

Terminology. The word "bit" seems to have been coined during a meeting convened by John Von Neumann and Norbert Wiener during the winter of 1943–1944 in Princeton, New Jersey. The participants found it convenient to measure information in terms of numbers of "yes" and "no" and to call this unit of information a bit. In 1975 the International Organization for Standardization (OSI) defined a new unit, the shannon (honoring C. E. Shannon). A shannon is a unit of measure equal to the decision content of a set of two mutually exclusive events. In information theory, the word "bit" is sometimes used as a synonym for this preferred term. *See* INFORMATION THEORY.　　　　　　　　　Ramon A. Mata-Toledo

Bibliography. W. Stallings, *Computer Organization and Architecture*, 3d ed., 1993; R. White, *How Computers Work*, Ziff-Davis, 1993.

Bitumen

A term used to designate naturally occurring or pyrolytically obtained substances of dark to black color consisting almost entirely of carbon and hydrogen with very little oxygen, nitrogen, and sulfur. Bitumen may be of variable hardness and volatility, ranging from crude oil to asphaltites, and is largely soluble in carbon disulfide. *See* ASPHALT AND ASPHALTITE.
Irving A. Breger

Bivalve, rudist

An extinct group of epifaunal bivalves that constructed reefs during the late Mesozoic. The valves of rudists are coiled to cylindrical in external form, and the shapes and sizes of rudist shells are extreme relative to other members of the class Bivalvia. Rudists lived as solitary individuals or in large clusters on predominantly carbonate substrates in low to mid-paleolatitudes until their demise near or at the end of the Cretaceous. *See* BIVALVIA; MESOZOIC.

Evolution. The earliest rudists are found in rocks more than 150 million years old. Rudist ancestry can be traced to thick-shelled megalodontid bivalves through a series of comparative internal features such as ligament, dentition, and muscle supports, and through external shape of the asymmetrical valves. Rudists are animals classified in the paleontologic literature as mollusks under the superfamily Hippuritoidea. There are more than 200 genera and more than 1500 named species of rudists. *See* MOLLUSCA.

Morphology. Rudists are similar to bivalves with which they are classified, yet they evolved unique features in their epifaunal shells. Rudists and all bivalves have two calcium carbonate valves hinged together. The valves protect the heart, kidneys, and other organs vital to the biological processes of the animal. The calcium carbonate valves of rudists have distinct outer calcite and inner aragonite layers, and the animal lived inside the shell, protected by these hard, mineralized deposits. The internal part of the rudist shell is partitioned to accommodate growth, and shell layers were accreted as the animal grew. Unlike most members of the Bivalvia, size variation among rudist individuals is extreme and ranges from a few centimeters to more than 1 m (3.3 ft). The rudist animals with shells of doubly coiled morphologies tended to dwell as individuals or in small clusters, whereas the cylindrically shaped valves allowed for closer packing of individuals and construction of reefs.

Paleoecology. The substrates on which rudists dwelled consisted of silt-sized carbonate particles that shifted with bottom currents, and carbonate mud that was relatively nonmobile. Rudist larvae attached themselves to mobile grains, and the rudist animal secreted cements that adhered the shell to the substrate early in life. Immobilization of the grains was likely aided by microbial biomineralization. In all substrates, rudists grew their shells at a rate faster than the rate of sediment accumulation. In this manner, they elevated the commissure—the opening between the valves—above the substrate and kept it free from sediments entering the valves and impairing vital life functions. Although rudists lived primarily on carbonate sediments, they adapted through time to substrates that contained rock particles derived from land and from reworked submarine volcanic rocks. Within these carbonate to mixed carbonate-siliciclastic and volcaniclastic substrates, rudists lived on all parts of the shallow-water marine platforms. Rudists are known from isolated lagoons with relatively poor water circulation through reef crests and forereefs where they constructed the largest buildups in relatively higher energy surf conditions. The deepest water in which rudists lived is not known but it is shelfal, and

Fig. 1. Rudist bivalve morphology. Cluster of individual rudists showing the conical shape of the erect-growing lower valves and the operculiform shape of the upper valves. Two generations of rudists preserved as silicified specimens illustrate the bivalved nature of this group that allows for their classification within the class Bivalvia. These hippuritid rudists are from Maastrichtian strata of Puerto Rico.

shelfal in present-day measurements indicates less than 200 m (660 ft). On the platforms and shallower parts of the shelves, rudists were subjected to both calm water and hurricane-force energy conditions, as are the reefs of today. Rudists reefs were thus destroyed frequently by high-energy waves and were rebuilt during calmer conditions, resulting in thick accumulations of numerous generations of buildups. *See* PALEOECOLOGY; REEF.

Global distribution in tropical seas. Although rudists dominated the reefs through most of the Cretaceous, their numerical and ecological development can be traced through time. During the earliest Cretaceous, reefs and biotic accumulations of low relief were constructed by rudist bivalves and corals in the shallower marine waters, whereas corals, silica-secreting sponges, and microbes built biotic structures in deeper waters. By the Middle Cretaceous, about 100 million years ago, rudist bivalves diversified and dominated the shallow-water marine ecosystems both numerically and ecologically across low paleolatitudes in tropical seas. In later Cretaceous times, reefs composed of rudist bivalves were distributed east to west between the Arabian Peninsula and the Americas, and north to south from the low to mid-paleolatitudes. Westward-flowing surface currents accounted for the low- to mid-latitude distribution pattern of reefs, whereas northward surface currents accounted for northern occurrences in the European and North American regions, especially during sea-level highstands when shelfal areas were flooded. A global correspondence exists between the development of Upper Cretaceous reefs and highstands of the seas, but there is only a regional, not global, correlation between reefs and sea-level fluctuations of lesser magnitudes. Fluctuations in the levels of the seas are responsible for both fluxes in the amount of sediment spread across carbonate platforms and for the pathways of surface currents that bring larvae for settlement and subsequent colonization by reefal biota. *See* SEDIMENTATION.

Large Upper Cretaceous reefs containing rudist bivalves as the dominant constructor also contained corals, sponges, stromatoporoids, and algae in lesser numbers and as secondary ecological constituents. North of the rudist reefs in the Northern Hemisphere, corals dominated the shallow-water ecosystems, and north of the corals were bioconstructions of silicious sponges or bryozoans. In the Southern Hemisphere, corals dominated the reefs in higher paleolatitudes. A zonation in reefs by a variety of dominant organisms thus occurred along paleolatitudinal bands, suggesting a thermal and/or chemical signature to the control of the reef-building biota.

Thermal conditions of the Middle and Late Cretaceous oceans were warmer than those of today in both the high and low paleolatitudes, with warmth extending to the polar regions as evidenced by freshwater lizards in the high northern paleolatitudes. The expanded tropics, the realm of the rudist bivalves, were hot, with ocean temperatures exceeding those of today by several degrees. Thermal and salinity conditions were probably higher in the shallowest waters in comparison to the open seas. Rudists were adapted to a wide range of thermal and saline conditions, even to temperatures and salinities that were not tolerated by corals, algae, and other biota. *See* CRETACEOUS.

Extinction. From their origins in the Late Jurassic through their terminal extinction in the latest Cretaceous, rudists as a group persisted through several regional and global extinction events. The exact timing of their terminal extinction is debatable. The extinction occurred either prior to the Cretaceous-Paleogene boundary or right at the boundary. The causes of the extinction remain unclear but are attributed to the thermal and chemical conditions of the latest Cretaceous oceans, perhaps in combination with effects of the extraterrestrial impact that formed the Chicxulub crater in the Yucatan Peninsula in the Caribbean ocean. *See* EXTINCTION (BIOLOGY).

Claudia C. Johnson; Erle G. Kauffman

Bibliography. R. Hofling and R. W. Scott, Early and mid-Cretaceous buildups, in W. Kiessling, E. Flugel,

Fig. 2. Rudist reef. Ecological association of rudists in proximity. Variation in valve shapes and sizes is illustrated in this photo from the latest Cretaceous Maastrichtian stage of Jamaica.

and J. Golonka (eds.), *Phanerozoic Reef Patterns*, pp. 521–548, Soc. Sed. Geol. Spec. Publ. 72, Tulsa, 2002; C. C. Johnson, The rise and fall of rudist reefs, *Amer. Scientist*, 90:148–153, 2002; C. C. Johnson et al., Patterns and processes influencing Upper Cretaceous reefs, in W. Kiessling, E. Flugel, and J. Golonka (eds.), *Phanerozoic Reef Patterns*, pp. 549–585, Soc. Sed. Geol. Spec. Publ. 72, Tulsa, 2002; C. C. Johnson and E. G. Kauffman, Maastrichtian extinction patterns of Caribbean Province rudists, in N. MacLeod and G. Keller (eds.), *Cretaceous-Tertiary Mass Extinctions: Biotic and Environmental Changes*, W. W. Norton, New York, 1996; T. Steuber et al., Catastrophic extinction of Caribbean rudist bivalves at the Cretaceous-Tertiary boundary, *Geology*, 30:999–1002, 2002.

Bivalvia

One of the five classes in the phylum Mollusca; sometimes known as Pelecypoda. All bivalves are aquatic, living at all depths of the sea and in brackish and fresh waters. With about 25,000 living species (**Fig. 1**), Bivalvia is second to class Gastropoda (over 74,000) in molluscan species diversity. However, the total biomass of bivalves is much greater, and certain bivalve species are numerically dominant in many benthic ecosystems. The most primitive bivalves are infaunal, burrowing into soft sediments, but many families are epifaunal, attached to rocks or shells or residing on the sediment surface. Bivalves are well represented in the fossil record from the Early Paleozoic because of their calcareous shells. *See* MOLLUSCA.

Anatomy and physiology. In general, bivalves are bilaterally symmetrical and laterally compressed. They have a fleshy mantle that secretes the shell enclosing the body (**Fig. 2**). The mouth is located anteriorly in bivalves; and in the Lamellibranchiata, the largest subclass, the mouth is flanked by paired labial palps that act to sort food prior to ingestion. Sensory organs are located on the outer mantle margin that has the closest contact with the environment. Frequently these sensory organs are borne on tentacles, and they are sensitive to tactile and chemical stimuli. Certain species of scallops have highly developed light-sensing organs or "eyes" on their mantle tentacles. *See* LAMELLIBRANCHIA.

The shell consists of two valves with a noncalcified connecting ligament holding them together at a hinge plate. The shell layers consist of an outer horny periostracum (protective layer) that can be either absent or eroded in some species, a middle prismatic layer consisting of crystalline calcium carbonate, and an inner lamellar or nacreous layer. In some families such as the Mytilidae (mussels) or the Pteriidae (winged or pearl oysters), the nacreous layer can exhibit a beautiful iridescent sheen, whereas in most bivalves the inner layer is smooth but with a chalky appearance. Hinge ligament tension holds the valves in a gaping position, with valve closure effected by adductor muscles. Paired adductor muscles can be of equal size (isomyarian) such as those found in clams of the family Mactridae or Veneridae, or of unequal size as in the Mytilidae (heteromyarian); the adductor muscle also may be single as in oysters of the family Ostreidae (monomyarian). There are two muscle fiber types. Fast muscle fibers cause rapid closure of the valves, and catch fibers maintain closure for long periods of time without a great expenditure of metabolic energy. The ciliated molluscan gills, properly called ctenidia, are enlarged in the subclass Lamellibranchiata and occupy a substantial portion of the mantle cavity. The ctenidia consist of layered filaments which function primarily to pump water into the mantle cavity and to filter particulate food from the incurrent water stream. Observations using fiber-optic endoscopy in actively feeding bivalves have shown that both food and nonfood (silt) particles are trapped on mucous sheets on the ctenidia during the filter-feeding process. From the ctenidial face, trapped particles are passed ventrally to a ctenidial food groove that acts as a conveyor belt transferring the particles anteriorly to the labial palps, where they are sorted prior to ingestion. Rejected particles encased in mucus are dropped onto the mantle and eventually released as pseudofeces. There is evidence that large populations of filter-feeding bivalves can increase the clarity of natural waters by actively removing phytoplankton and other particles.

The ctenidia of bivalves of the subclass Protobranchia also serve to pump water, but they are smaller and less developed than in the lamellibranchs and do not serve to filter food particles. Protobranch bivalves are deposit feeders that gather food by extending thin muscular palp proboscides to probe soft sediments and entrap organic detrital particles. Cilia on the proboscides transfer particles to labial palps for sorting prior to ingestion. Bivalves of the subclass Septibranchia (sometimes called Anomalodesmata) have highly modified ctenidia that lack filaments. A septum divides the mantle cavity into dorsal and ventral chambers, and water is pumped by muscular contraction of the septum wall. Septibranch bivalves often feed on zooplankton or water-borne detritus particles. Their labial palps are reduced in size and do not have a sorting function. *See* PROTOBRANCHIA; SEPTIBRANCHIA.

In the protobranchs and lamellibranchs, ingested food particles pass through an esophagus to the gut, which in some species contains the crystalline style, a clear worm-shaped gelatinous worm-shaped organ that is continually rotated by cilia in a stomach pouch (style sac). The rotation of the style acts to release digestive enzymes and mix the stomach contents. Septibranch stomachs lack a crystalline style but are often stiff and chitinous to grind food particles. The bivalve stomach also contains a number of tiny sacs (digestive diverticula) that serve as sites for nutrient absorption. From the stomach, the digestive tract consists of an intestine that frequently passes through the heart of many bivalves and leads to the anus, which releases feces into the excurrent water stream. In the cases in which the bivalve intestine passes through the heart, the heart

Fig. 1. Some bivalve species. (*a*) Scallop, *Amusium pleuronectes*, Pectinidae, Philippines. (*b*) Arkshell, *Barbatia reevana*, Arcidae, Ecuador. (*c*) Mangrove oyster, *Crassostrea rhizophorae*, Ostreidae, West Indies. (*d*) Zebra mussel, *Dreissena polymorpha*, Dreissenidae, Michigan. (*e*) Freshwater clam, *Eliptio complanata*, Unionidae, Rhode Island. (*f*) Estuary clam, *Geloina coaxans*, Corbiculidae, Philippines. (*g*) Giant clam, *Hippopus hippopus*, Tridacnidae, Samoa. (*h*) Pearl oyster, *Pinctada margaritifera*, Pteriidae, Indonesia. (*i*) Spiny oyster, *Spondylus princeps*, Spondylidae, Baja California, Mexico. (*j*) Pismo clam, *Tivela stultorum*, Veneridae, California.

performs the dual function of pumping blood and passing food particles down the digestive tract.

Alternative feeding mechanisms include the direct uptake of dissolved organic molecules from seawater across the ctenidial and mantle surfaces of actively pumping animals; and in some species, symbiotic organisms in the mantle or ctenidia serve to supply nutrients. For example, in giant clams of the family

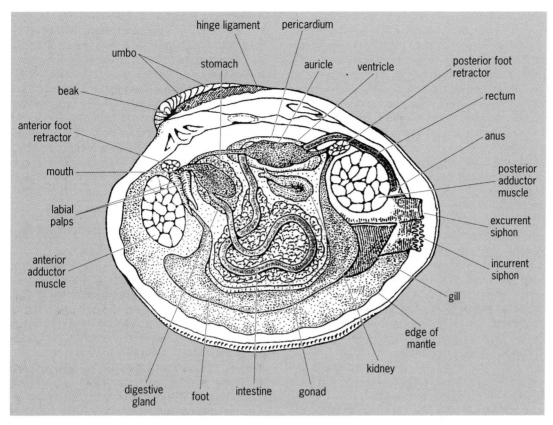

Fig. 2. Bivalve anatomy as represented by the quahog clam, *Mercenaria mercenaria*.

Tridacnidae, photosynthetically active symbiotic phytoplankton called zooxanthellae reside in the mantle tissue, allowing the clams to thrive in clear tropical waters that have little particulate food. Similarly, other bivalves in harsh sulfide-rich environments have symbiotic bacteria in their ctenidia that can chemically synthesize organic molecules that nourish the host. For example, mussels of the genus *Bathymodiolus* that reside near deep-ocean hydrothermal vents are totally dependent upon chemosynthetic symbiotic bacteria for their nutrition.

The body of bivalves is often attached to the shell by one or two paired pedal retractor muscles. Some bivalves have a foot for locomotion. If present, the foot can be extended from the shell by blood pressure and dilated to act as an external anchor while movement is effected by contraction of the retractor muscles. Some bivalves of the family Pectinidae (scallops) lack a foot, but are highly active swimmers through clapping their valves and jetting water through orifices (openings) near the hinge. Some bivalves, such as oysters and giant clams, are sedentary and lack a foot as adults.

Reproduction and development. Bivalves exhibit a wide range of reproductive strategies. Most bivalves are dioecious or have separate sexes, while others exhibit various forms of hermaphrodism. For example, as mature adults, scallops carry both eggs and sperm, while oysters exhibit protandric hermaphrodism in which they first develop as males and in subsequent years change sex to develop ovaries. Most species of bivalves shed eggs and sperm directly into the water, where fertilization occurs; in others, eggs may be held in a brood chamber, where they are fertilized by sperm in incurrent water and released as well-developed larvae into the water. Most bivalves go through several planktonic stages prior to settlement and metamorphosis to their benthic form. As a notable exception to this planktonic larval pattern, freshwater mussels of the family Unionidae produce larvae that are parasitic on fish gills.

Economic importance. A number of bivalve species are harvested for human consumption. According to the United Nations Food and Agriculture Organization, in 2003 world bivalve shellfishery landings (harvest of wild stock) were about 2.6 million metric tons with an estimated value of $2 billion. Many species of bivalves are actively farmed either for human consumption of the meats or for shell products. Worldwide production of farmed bivalves for food consumption in 2003 was 11.1 million metric tons with a value of about $10.8 billion. Most of the gem-quality pearls sold in the world originate from farmed pearl oysters of the genus *Pinctada* in Japan, Australia, and islands of the tropical Pacific. Freshwater pearls are produced from freshwater mussels in the United States, China, and Japan. Estimates of the worldwide trade in farmed pearls exceed $1.5 billion annually. Some species of bivalves are of economic concern as pest organisms or biological invaders. Historically, shipworms of the genus *Teredo* were the bane of wooden sailing ships, and they still pose problems by boring into wooden pilings and weakening piers or other coastal structures. Exotic species of bivalves intentionally or accidentally introduced into North America have caused millions of dollars worth of damage to public and commercial infrastructure. In the 1950s, Asian freshwater clams of the genus *Corbicula* spread extensively through the waterways of the Tennessee Valley, causing damage to irrigation dams and power generation facilities. In 1985, zebra mussels (genus *Dreissena*) native to the Caspian Sea area in Eurasia were discovered in Lake St. Clair between Ontario and Michigan. Planktonic zebra mussel larvae were probably transported from Europe in the ballast water of a freighter entering the Great Lakes. In less than 10 years, zebra mussels had spread throughout the Great Lakes and down the Mississippi River drainage to New Orleans. Zebra mussels have few natural enemies in North America and have caused millions of dollars worth of damage by clogging power plants, water pumping stations, and other industrial facilities. There is also evidence that the prolific zebra mussels have supplanted native North American freshwater unionid bivalves in many water bodies. *See* SHIPWORM.

Fossils. The fossil record of the Bivalvia can be traced to the Lower Cambrian *Fordilla*, which had a small, round, laterally compressed shell. The early origins of bivalves remain murky, but recent molecular analysis of molluscan DNA indicates that the Bivalvia and other molluscan classes are probably derived from an extinct conchiferan ancestor with bivalves diverging relatively late in the Cambrian. The Ordovician was a major period of bivalve speciation, but throughout the Paleozoic the molluscan Bivalvia remained second to brachiopodan bivalves in species diversity and abundance. A number of ancient molluscan bivalve families first appearing during the Paleozoic Era still have representative species, which include Nuculidae, Nuculanidae, Pteriidae, Arcidae, Pectinidae, Mytilidae, Lucinidae, and Carditidae.

During the Mesozoic Era, the brachiopods declined in importance. Various adaptations of the Bivalvia that developed during the era include active swimming by scallops, deep burrowing by many sediment-dwelling infaunal species, and extremely thick-shelled oysters. It is probable that the diverse adaptations of the Bivalvia to avoid predatory gastropods, arthropods, and fish evolving during the Mesozoic were a major factor in the replacement of the more exposed brachiopods as the dominant bivalves. The evolutionary radiation occurring during the Mesozoic includes the emergence of many species of bivalves that bore into rocks, hard corals, and wood. The emergent family Ostreidae, which includes oysters, remains to the present. The transition from the Mesozoic to Cenozoic began with the extinction of many ancient families and the emergence of several modern families. Important emergent modern families of Bivalvia during the Cenozoic Era include Chamidae, Cardiidae, Mactridae, Solenacidae, Tellinidae, Veneridae, Myidae, and Pandoridae.   Michael A. Rice

Bibliography. J. T. Carlton, Introduced marine and estuarine mollusks of North America: An end-of-the-

20th-century perspective, *J. Shellfish Res.*, 11:489–505, 1992; C. M. Cavanaugh et al., Symbiosis of methylotrophic bacteria and deep-sea mussels, *Nature*, 325:346, 1987; C. R. Fassler, Pearl farming, *World Aquacult.*, 29(1):6–13, 1998; E. Gosling, *Bivalve Molluscs: Biology, Ecology and Culture*, 2003; R. C. Moore (ed.), *Treatise on Invertebrate Paleontology*, Pt. N: *Mollusca 6*, 1969; J. A. Schneider, Bivalve systematics in the 20th century, *J. Paleontol.*, 75:1119–1127, 2001; R. K. Trench et al., Observations on the symbiosis with zooxanthellae among the Tridacnidae, *Biol. Bull.*, 161:180–198, 1981; P. R. Walne, *Culture of Bivalve Mollusks*, 1974.

Black hole

One of the end points of gravitational collapse, in which the collapsing matter fades from view, leaving only a center of gravitational attraction behind. Any other given point in space has a past and a future. A black hole is a region that has a past but no future, or at least none that is accessible to an external observer. The center of a black hole is said to be a singular region of space-time. The existence of such a singularity is predicted by the theory of general relativity. If a star of more than about 3 solar masses has completely burned its nuclear fuel, it should collapse to a black hole. The resulting object is independent of the properties of the matter that produced it and can be completely described by specifying its mass, spin, and charge. The most striking feature of this object is the existence of a surface, called the horizon, which completely encloses the collapsed matter. The horizon is an ideal one-way membrane: that is, particles and light can go inward through the surface, but none can go outward. As a result, the object is dark, that is, black, and hides from view a finite region of space (a hole). Arguments concerning the existence of black holes originally centered on the fact that there are many stars of over 3 solar masses and that there seemed to be no other outcome of collapse than the formation of a black hole. In 1971, however, some direct observational evidence was obtained for a black hole in the binary x-ray system Cygnus X-1. Since that time, black holes have been identified by similar evidence in a number of other x-ray binaries, two notable examples being A0620−00 in the Milky Way Galaxy and LMC X-3 in the Large Magellanic Cloud. There are more than 15 identified black holes, in the Milky Way Galaxy. In addition, supermassive black holes may be responsible for the large energy output of quasars and other active galactic nuclei, and there is growing evidence that black holes exist also at the center of many other galaxies, including the Milky Way Galaxy. *See* GRAVITATIONAL COLLAPSE; RELATIVITY.

Theory. Shortly after Albert Einstein formulated the general theory of relativity in 1916, the solution of the field equations corresponding to a nonrotating black hole was found. For many years this solution, called the Schwarzschild solution, was used to describe the gravitational attraction outside a spherical star. However, the interpretation of the Schwarzschild solution as a solution for a black hole was not made at the time. More than 20 years elapsed before it was shown that such a black hole could, and probably would, be formed in the gravitational collapse of a nonrotating star of sufficient mass. It was not until 1963 that the solution for a spinning black hole, the Kerr solution, was found. This was particularly important, since most stars are rotating, and the rotation rate is expected to increase when such stars collapse. Although some collapsing, rotating stars might avoid becoming black holes by ejecting matter, thereby reducing their mass, many stars will evolve to a stage of catastrophic collapse in which the formation of a black hole is the only conceivable outcome. However, unlike the case of nonrotating black holes, no one has shown that a collapsing, rotating star of sufficient mass must form a Kerr black hole. On the other hand, it has been shown that if the collapse of a star proceeds past a certain point, the star must evolve to a singularity, that is, an infinitely dense state of matter beyond which no further evolution is possible. Such singularities are found inside black holes in all known black hole solutions, but it has only been conjectured that the singularity produced in a collapse must be inside a black hole. However, the existence of such a naked singularity would have undesirable consequences, such as allowing the violation of fundamental physical laws that appeal to the conservation of mass-energy and to causality. The so-called cosmic censorship theorem is based on the conjecture that formation of a naked singularity is impossible. *See* STELLAR EVOLUTION.

Black hole solutions have also been found for the case in which the black holes have a charge, that is, an electrical as well as a gravitational influence. However, since matter on the large scale is electrically neutral, black holes with any significant charge are not expected in astronomy. Similarly, black hole solutions allow black holes to possess magnetic charge, that is, a magnetic single-pole interaction. Although some elementary-particle theories predict that there should exist particles with magnetic charge, called magnetic monopoles, sufficient experimental evidence is not yet available to confirm their existence. Even if monopoles did exist, they would play little part in the formation of black holes, and so astronomical black holes are expected to be both electrically and magnetically neutral. *See* MAGNETIC MONOPOLES.

Uniqueness theorems about black holes make it likely that at least some Kerr black holes would be formed. Uniqueness theorems address the question of how many kinds of black holes could exist and how complicated their structure could be. These theorems show that black holes must have a simple structure. In fact, the mass, spin, charge, and magnetic charge are all that are needed to specify completely a black hole. Further, any distortion of a black hole, such as is caused by a chunk of matter falling inside, is removed by a burst of radiation. Therefore, although the collapse of a rotating star would be quite complicated, it appears that the final system, the Kerr black hole, would be relatively simple and independent of the details of collapse.

The possible formation of black holes depends critically on what other end points of stellar evolution are possible. Chunks of cold matter can be stable, but their mass must be considerably less than that of the Sun. For masses on the order of a solar mass, only two stable configurations are known for cold, evolved matter. The first, the white dwarf, is supported against gravitational collapse by the same quantum forces that keep atoms from collapsing. However, these forces cannot support a star whose mass exceeds about 1.2 solar masses. (A limiting value of 1.4 solar masses was first found by S. Chandrasekhar and is known as the Chandrasekhar limit. More realistic models of white dwarfs, taking into account nuclear reactions, lower this number somewhat, but the actual value depends on the composition of the white dwarf.) The second stable configuration, the neutron star, is supported against gravitational collapse by the same forces that keep the nucleus of an atom from collapsing. There is also a maximum mass for a neutron star, estimated to be between 1 and 3 solar masses, the uncertainty being due to the poor knowledge of nuclear forces at high densities. Both white dwarfs and neutron stars have been observed, the former for many years at optical wavelengths and the latter more recently in the studies of radio pulsars and binary x-ray sources. *See* NEUTRON STAR; PULSAR; WHITE DWARF STAR.

It would appear from the theory that if a collapsing star of over 3 solar masses does not eject matter, it has no choice but to become a black hole. There are, of course, many stars with mass larger than 3 solar masses, and it is expected that a significant number of them will reach the collapse stage without having ejected sufficient matter to take them below the 3-solar-mass limit. Further, more massive stars evolve more rapidly, enhancing the rate of formation of black holes. It seems reasonable to conclude that a considerable number of black holes should exist in the universe. One major problem is that, since the black hole is dark, it is itself essentially unobservable. Fortunately, some black holes may be observable in the sense that the black hole maintains its gravitational influence on other matter, and thus it can make its presence known. This is precisely how, in a binary system in which a black hole has a massive stellar companion, some of the ejecta from the evolving massive star are accreted by the black hole and yield a distinct x-ray signature. Otherwise, the detection of a black hole would be limited to observations of the collapse of a star to a black hole, a rare occurrence in the Milky Way Galaxy and one which happens very quickly. Astronomers expect that such collapses would occur about once every thousand years in our galaxy. By continuously surveying many thousands of galaxies, one could therefore hope to detect black hole formation. This is the goal of detectors under construction to search for gravitational waves from stars collapsing and binary neutron stars merging to form black holes. *See* GRAVITATIONAL RADIATION.

Structure. For a nonrotating black hole, the radius of the horizon (Schwarzschild radius) is determined entirely by the mass. Defining R so that the surface area of the spherical horizon is $4\pi R^2$, the equation relating R to the mass M is $R = 2GM/c^2$, where G is the constant of gravity and c is the speed of light. Classical general relativity would allow M to take on all possible values, but quantum effects suggest that the lowest possible value of M is about 10^{-8} kg (2×10^{-8} lb). However, the lower-mass black holes may not be astronomically relevant, since collapsing stars with masses less than about a solar mass (2×10^{30} kg or 4×10^{30} lb) would become white dwarfs or neutron stars. It is thought that low-mass black holes could exist only if they were created at the time of the origin of the universe.

An astronomical black hole of 5 solar masses would have a radius of about 20 km (12 mi). This size is comparable to that expected for neutron stars. The density to which matter would have to be compressed in order to form such a black hole is comparable to that found in neutron stars or in the nuclei of atoms. Black holes with a mass larger than 1000 solar masses may be formed from the collapse of supermassive stars. The existence of such supermassive stars has not been proven, but supermassive stars and supermassive black holes are thought to be at the cores of quasars and active galactic nuclei. Infall of matter released by colliding stars in the dense nuclei of galaxies feeds such black holes, releasing gravitational energy as the matter falls in, and provides the energy that powers active galactic nuclei. A supermassive black hole with a mass of a few thousand solar masses would have a radius comparable to the radius of the Earth. Black holes of 10^6 to 10^9 solar masses are likely to exist in the center of some galaxies, including the Milky Way Galaxy. These could be formed either in the collapse of a supermassive star with a possible subsequent accretion of matter, or in the coalescing of a large number of black holes of more modest mass. The density required to form these very massive black holes is low, approaching that of ordinary terrestrial densities. There is now considerable evidence that black holes exist in the cores of many galaxies. *See* GALAXY, EXTERNAL; MILKY WAY GALAXY; QUASAR; SUPERMASSIVE STARS.

For nonrotating black holes, the horizon is also a surface of infinite redshift; that is, light emitted from just above the surface reaches a distant observer with a much lower frequency and energy than it had when it was emitted. As a result, an object that falls into a black hole appears to an observer to take an infinite time to reach the Schwarzschild radius, with the observed light coming from the object redshifting quickly to darkness as the approach is made. The picture would be quite different for an observer associated with the falling object. The "rider" would reach the Schwarzschild radius in a finite time, feeling nothing more unusual than gravitational tidal forces. However, once inside, the person would be

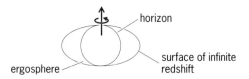

Fig. 1. The Kerr, or rotating, black hole. (*After P. C. Peters, Black holes: New horizons in gravitational theory, Amer. Sci., 62(5):575–583, 1974*)

trapped since even light which moves outward cannot escape. The theory predicts that this individual, as well as everything else within the horizon, would be crushed to infinite density within a short time.

For rotating black holes, the surface of infinite redshift lies outside the horizon except at the poles, as illustrated in **Fig. 1**. The region between the two surfaces is called the ergosphere. This region is important because it contains particle trajectories that have negative energy relative to an outside observer. Roger Penrose showed that it is possible, though perhaps unlikely astronomically, to use these trajectories to recover even more than the rest mass energy of matter sent into a rotating black hole, the extra energy coming from the slowing down of the rotation of the black hole. Others have proposed that radiation incident on a rotating black hole could be similarly amplified.

The black hole solutions of general relativity, ignoring quantum-mechanical effects as described below, are completely stable. Once massive black holes form, they will remain forever; and subsequent processes, for example, the accumulation of matter, only increase their size. Two black holes could coalesce to form a single, larger black hole, but a single black hole could not split up into two smaller ones. This irreversibility in time led researchers to consider analogies between black holes and thermal properties of ordinary matter, in which there is a similar irreversibility as matter becomes more disordered as time goes on. In 1974, Steven Hawking showed that when quantum effects are properly taken into account, a black hole should emit thermal radiation, composed of all particles and quanta of radiation that exist. This established the black hole as a thermal system, having a temperature inversely proportional to its mass. Since a radiating system loses energy and therefore loses mass, a black hole can shrink and decay if it is radiating faster than it is accumulating matter. For black holes formed from the collapse of stars, the temperature is about 10^{-7} K (2×10^{-7}°F above absolute zero, -459.67°F). Regardless of where such black holes are located, the ambient radiation incident on the black hole from other stars, and from the big bang itself, is much larger than the thermal radiation emitted by the black hole, implying that the black hole would not shrink. Even if the ambient radiation is shielded from the black hole, the time for the black hole to decay is much longer than the age of the universe, so that, in practice, black holes formed from collapse of a star are essentially as stable as they were thought to be before the Hawking radiation was predicted.

Theoretically, black holes of any mass could have been created at the beginning of the universe in the big bang. For smaller-mass black holes, the Hawking radiation process would be quite important, since the temperatures would be very high. For example, a black hole created with mass of 10^{12} kg (2×10^{12} lb), about the mass of a mountain, would have just radiated away all of its mass, assuming that no mass had been accreted in the meantime. Black holes created with a mass smaller than 10^{12} kg would have disappeared earlier, and those with a larger mass would still exist. The final stage of evaporation would be quite violent and would take place quickly. As a black hole radiates, it loses mass and its temperature rises. But a higher temperature means that it radiates and loses mass at a faster rate, raising its temperature even further. The final burst, as the black hole gives up the remainder of its mass, would be a spectacular event. The final emission would contain all radiation and particles that could exist, even those not generated by existing accelerators. At present, there is no evidence that points to the existence of black holes with small mass or to their evaporation by the Hawking radiation process.   Philip C. Peters; Joseph Silk

Observation. Observations of black holes—which, by definition, are not directly detectable—rely on indirect methods using the gravitational interaction of the black hole with its surroundings. The first successful detections were accomplished in binary x-ray systems. These systems are thought to be close binary systems composed of a massive and very dense object—a black hole or a neutron star—and a companion star. Due to strong gravitational forces, the companion star loses mass that settles down into an accretion disk around the compact object (**Fig. 2**). Frictional forces cause the matter in the disk to spiral inward and also heat up the disk, causing it to emit thermal x-rays.

A neutron star is distinguished from a black hole as the compact object by analyzing the internal motion of the binary and calculating the mass of the compact body. In the notable case of the x-ray binary system Cygnus X-1, the mass determination gives a value of about 10 solar masses, a value much larger than the maximum mass for a gravitationally stable neutron star and therefore strong evidence for the existence of a black hole in this system. About 30 candidates for black hole x-ray binaries have been detected in the Milky Way Galaxy, of which about half have secure

mass estimates that support the black hole assumption.

Another line of observational evidence for the existence of black holes is drawn from active galactic nuclei (AGNs), whose luminosities are several times larger than those of the largest nonactive galaxies. Variations on time scales of tens of hours in the luminosities of AGNs indicate a central engine whose diameter should be of the order of the product of the variation time scale and the speed of light. To generate observed AGN luminosities in a spherical volume defined by this diameter in nuclear processes like those taking place in stars, one would need such large quantities of matter that the gravitational potential energy would far exceed the nuclear energy. Therefore, the origin of the luminosity is attributed to the transformation of potential energy into radiation.

The arguments in favor of a scenario in which potential energy is released in the accretion of gas onto a supermassive black hole are twofold. First, optical and ultraviolet emission lines of AGNs show so-called Doppler broadening corresponding to velocities of 2000–10,000 km/s (1200–6000 mi/s), indicating gas moving around a massive compact region. Second, AGNs display jets that are well collimated and straight, two properties that a central engine consisting of many bodies cannot accomplish easily, favoring a single black hole as the central engine. *See* DOPPLER EFFECT.

Mass determinations of black holes in AGNs rely on measurements of the properties of the accretion disk, such as the rotational velocity of this disk at different separations from the central engine after correcting for projection effects. In the case of a Keplerian rotation around the center, as for the galaxy M87, the rotational velocity should become smaller with increasing radius, and should be proportional to the square root of the enclosed mass. The mass of the central black hole is derived to be 3×10^9 solar masses for M87. Another frequently used technique is to measure the spectrum of the accretion disk. Since the accretion disk is optically thick, radiation on its way through the disk will be scattered many times before it leaves the surface of the disk, generating a disk nearly in thermodynamic equilibrium. The spectra of such disks have the form of a black body spectrum with characteristic temperature depending on the black hole mass and the mass accretion rate onto the black hole. Typical values derived using this method find black holes with masses in the range 1×10^6 to 3×10^9 solar masses.

The majority of estimates of the masses of black holes in the centers of normal galaxies are based on techniques using stellar dynamical methods. The orbits of stars in galaxies are affected significantly only by gravitational forces exerted on them. Unlike gas in an accretion disk, stars have significant random motions. A measure of the random motions of the stars is the so-called velocity dispersion, which characterizes the distribution of the different stellar velocities. Random motions of stars contribute to their overall velocity in addition to their systemic rotational

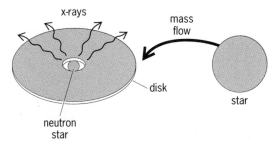

Fig. 2. Schematic diagram of a binary x-ray source. (*After P. C. Peters, Black holes: New horizons in gravitational theory, Amer. Sci., 62(5):575–583, 1974*)

velocity. Therefore, it is necessary to measure not only the rotational velocity at different radii, as in the case of a gas accretion disk; but also the velocity dispersion at different radii. As a further observational input to measure the black hole mass, the galaxy's luminosity density at different radii is needed. This is necessary because the black hole mass determination involves modeling the stellar structure in the galaxy. In practice, one assumes a model for the orbital structure of the stars in the galaxy and calculates the density of the stars at each radius from the luminosity density assuming a constant mass-to-light ratio. From the model, it is now possible to calculate the velocity dispersion from the rotational velocity and vice versa. In the case of a black hole at the center, it is not possible to use a constant mass-to-light ratio at all radii to recover the observed velocity dispersion from the observed rotational velocity of the galaxy using the model. Instead, one finds a steep increase in the mass-to-light ratio when going to small radii. Using the mass-to-light ratio, it is then possible to calculate the black hole mass. Approximately 30 black hole masses in the centers of galaxies have been obtained using this and similar techniques, and more are being calculated.

Another stellar dynamical measurement of a black hole mass is the one in the center of our Milky Way Galaxy. In this case the orbits of individual stars have been measured in the vicinity of the center over a period of more than 15 years. The orbits of the stars are Kepler ellipses, which allow calculation of the mass of the central body with high precision. The calculations reveal a black hole mass of 3×10^6 solar masses at the center of the Milky Way Galaxy; it is believed to be associated with the radio source Sagittarius A*. *See* ASTROPHYSICS, HIGH-ENERGY; BINARY STAR; X-RAY ASTRONOMY.   Sadegh Khochfar; Joseph Silk

Bibliography. J. S. Al-Khalili, *Black Holes, Wormholes and Time Machines*, 1999; M. Begelman and M. Rees, *Gravity's Fatal Attraction: Black Holes in the Universe*, 1998; S. W. Hawking, *A Brief History of Time: From the Big Bang to Black Holes*, 2d ed., 1996; J.-P. Luminet, *Black Holes*, 1992; F. Melia, *The Black Hole at the Center of Our Galaxy*, 2003; S. L. Shapiro and S. A. Teukolsky, *Black Holes, White Dwarfs, and Neutron Stars: The Physics of Compact Objects*, 1983; E. F. Taylor and J. A. Wheeler, *Exploring Black Holes: Introduction to General Relativity*, 2000; K. S. Thorne, *Black Holes and Time Warps*, 1994; R. Wald, *Space, Time, and Gravity: The Theory of the Big Bang and Black Holes*, 2d ed., 1992.

Black pepper

One of the oldest and most important of the spices. It is the dried, unripe fruit of a weak climbing vine, *Piper nigrum*, a member of the pepper family (Piperaceae), and a native of India or Indomalaysia. The fruits are small one-seeded berries which, in ripening, undergo a color change from green to red to yellow. When in the red stage, they are picked, sorted, and dried. The dry, wrinkled berries (peppercorns) are ground to make the familiar black pepper of commerce. White pepper is obtained by grinding the seed separately from the surrounding pulp. *See* PIPERALES; SPICE AND FLAVORING.

Perry D. Strausbaugh; Earl L. Core

Black Sea

A semienclosed marginal sea with an area of 420,000 km² (160,000 mi²) bounded by Turkey to the south, Georgia to the east, Russia and Ukraine to the north, and Romania and Bulgaria to the west (**Fig. 1**). The physical and chemical structure of the Black Sea is critically dependent on its hydrological balance. As a result, it is the world's largest anoxic basin. It has recently experienced numerous types of environmental stress.

The Black Sea consists of a large basin with a depth of about 2200 m (7200 ft). The continental shelf is mostly narrow except for the broad shelf in the northwest region. Fresh-water input from rivers (about 350 km³ y⁻¹; 84 mi³ y⁻¹), especially the Danube, Dniester, and Don, and precipitation (about 300 km³ y⁻¹; 72 mi³ y⁻¹) exceeds evaporation (about 350 km³ y⁻¹; 84 mi³ y⁻¹). Low-salinity surface waters are transported to the Mediterranean as a surface outflow (flux of 600 km³ y⁻¹; 144 mi³ y⁻¹). High-salinity seawater from the Mediterranean enters the Black Sea as a subsurface inflow through the Bosporus (flux of 300 km³ y⁻¹; 72 mi³ y⁻¹). This estuarine circulation (seawater inflow at depth and fresh-water outflow at the surface) results in an unusually strong vertical density gradient determined mainly by the salinity. Thus the Black Sea has a two-layered structure with a lower-salinity surface layer (0–100 m or 328 ft; volume = 42,000 km³ or 10,000 mi³; salinity = 18.5) and a higher-salinity deep layer (100–2200 m or 328–7218 ft; volume = 780,000 km³ or 187,000 mi³; salinity = 22.3).

The vertical stratification has a strong effect on the chemistry of the sea. Respiration of particulate organic carbon sinking into the deep water has used up all the dissolved oxygen. Thus, conditions favor bacterial sulfate reduction and high sulfide concentrations. As a result, the Black Sea is the world's largest anoxic basin and is commonly used as a modern analog of an environment favoring the formation of organic-rich black shales observed in the geological sedimentary record.

Circulation. Representative vertical profiles of temperature (T), salinity (S), and density (kg/m³ and σ_t) for the central, western Black Sea are shown in **Fig. 2**. There are two important factors that control these distributions: (1) The only source of high-salinity water is through the Bosporus, which has a maximum sill depth of only 35 m (115 ft). (2) The temperature of the Bosporus inflow is about 15°C (59°F); thus the only source of cold water ($T < 15$°C or 59°F) is the surface of the Black Sea. The main

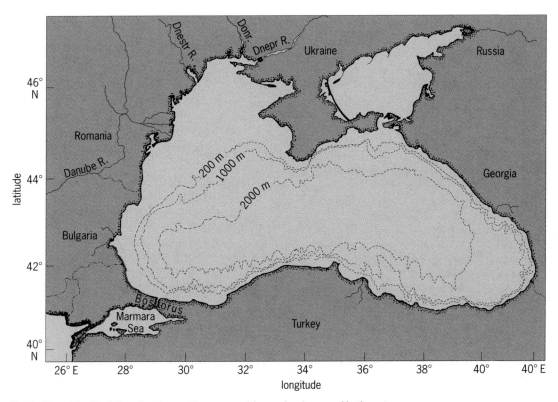

Fig. 1. Map of the Black Sea showing contiguous countries, major rivers, and bathymetry.

features in the vertical profiles are the seasonally and spatially variable surface layer, a cold intermediate layer (CIL; $T < 8°C$ or $46.4°F$) at about 50 m (164 ft) and a deep layer with slowly increasing salinity with depth. The cold intermediate layer forms annually by the convective processes associated with winter cooling of surface waters in the central gyre areas and on the northwestern shelf. It has a residence time of about one year. The deep water ($S = 22.3$) forms from an average mixture of about 1 part Bosporus inflow ($S = 35.0$) with 3.3 parts of cold intermediate layer ($S = 18.5$) which mix together on the shelf region just east of the Bosporus. This water is then injected into the deep basin. The resulting residence time of the deep layer is about 600 years. Since the residence time is the average time that a parcel of water spends beneath the surface layer of the ocean, its temperature and salinity are no longer influenced by the Sun, evaporation, or fresh-water run-off. As a result, T and S in the parcel of water can change only by mixing with other parcels.

The primarily cyclonic (counterclockwise) surface circulation results from the cyclonic nature of the wind field. The main current is the Rim Current, which flows along the edge of the continental slope completely around the basin. A series of anticyclonic eddies are confined between the coast and the Rim Current. A consequence of the surface circulation is that the isopycnal (constant-density) surfaces in the center of the Black Sea rise closer to the surface (called the doming effect). Thus the first appearance of hydrogen sulfide (H_2S), which always occurs at a density of about 1016.15 kg/m^3 ($\sigma_t = 16.15$), is

found at depths of 80–100 m (262–328 ft) in the central basin and >150–200 m (492–656 ft) along the margins.

Chemical distributions. As a consequence of the hydrologic balance and circulation, dissolved oxygen is confined to the surface layer while the deep water is anoxic. The distributions of oxygen, sulfide, nitrate, nitrite, manganese, iron, ammonia and phosphate from a density of 1015 to 1016.5 kg/m^3 ($\sigma_t = 15.0$ to 16.5) [approximately the upper 300 m or 984 ft] are shown in **Fig. 3**. The distributions are plotted versus density rather than depth, because while the depth of specific features may vary, due to the doming effect, they always occur at the same density. Anthropogenic effects have had a significant impact on many of the nutrients in the surface layer. For example, the inventory and concentration of nitrate has increased by about a factor of 5 since 1969 due to eutrophication. Dissolved silicate concentrations have decreased by 50% over the same time period due to dam construction.

In the deep anoxic layer, hydrogen sulfide increases to values over 400 μM and methane increases to over 10 μM.

At the oxic-anoxic interface, there is a suboxic zone. The suboxic zone has a thickness of about 10 to 50 m (33 to 164 ft) and is found between the oxygen-containing surface layer and the sulfide-containing deep layer. In the suboxic zone, both oxygen and sulfide have very low concentrations and no perceptible horizontal or vertical gradients. This zone appears to be a site of oxidation-reduction reactions involving species of nitrogen, manganese,

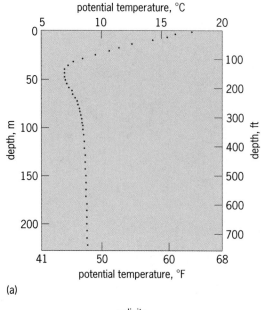

(a)

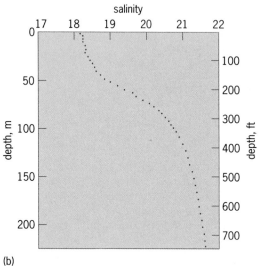

(b)

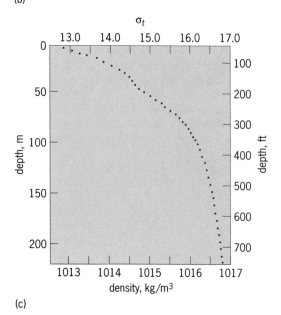

(c)

Fig. 2. Representative vertical profiles for 0–200 m (0–656 ft) of (a) temperature, (b) salinity, and (c) density (kg/m³ and σ_t).

and iron, such as reactions (1)–(4).

$$3NO_3^- + 5NH_4^+ \rightarrow 4N_2 + 9H_2O + 2H^+ \qquad (1)$$

$$2NO_3^- + 5Mn^{2+} + 4H_2O \rightarrow N_2 + 5MnO_2(s) + 8H^+ \qquad (2)$$

$$2NO_3^- + 10Fe^{2+} + 24H_2O \longrightarrow$$
$$N_2 + 10Fe(OH)_3(s) + 18H^+ \qquad (3)$$

$$2NH_4^+ + 3MnO_2(s) + 4H^+ \rightarrow N_2 + 3Mn^{2+} + 6H_2O \qquad (4)$$

Consequences of these reactions are: (1) The upward flux of sulfide appears to be oxidized by oxidized forms of manganese and iron rather than directly by oxygen. (2) The downward flux of nitrate (NO_2^- and the upward flux of ammonium (NH_4^+) are consumed at the same density level and are converted to nitrogen gas (N_2). (3) Manganese cycling between the II, III, and IV oxidation states appears to play a key catalytic role in these reactions. (4) Phosphate is adsorbed by particulate forms of manganese and iron, resulting in an intense phosphate minimum. (5) The suboxic zone reactions act as a nutrient trap preventing the upward flux of nutrients from the deep water from entering the surface layer and euphotic zone. The suboxic zone also contains high concentrations of bacteriochlorophylls and bacteriocarotenoids characteristic of the brown sulfur bacteria *Chlorobium*. Anaerobic photosynthesis, in which H_2S oxidation supports the phototrophic reduction of carbon dioxide (CO_2) to organic carbon, is also a strong possibility.

Biology. Before the 1970s the Black Sea had a highly diverse and healthy biological population. Its species composition was similar to that of the Mediterranean but with less quantity. The phytoplankton community was characterized by a large diatom bloom in May–June followed by a smaller dinoflagellate bloom. The primary zooplankton were copepods, and there were 170 species of fish, including large commercial populations of mackerel, bonito, anchovies, herring, carp, and sturgeon.

Since about 1970 there have been dramatic changes in the food web due to anthropogenic effects and invasions of new species. It is now characterized as a nonequilibrium, low-diversity, eutrophic state. The large increase in input of nitrogen due to eutrophication and decrease in silicate due to dam construction have increased the frequency of noxious algal blooms and resulted in dramatic shifts in phytoplankton from diatoms (siliceous) to coccolithophores and flagellates (nonsiliceous). The most dramatic changes have been observed in the northwestern shelf and the western coastal regions, which have the largest anthropogenic effects. The water overlying the sediments in these shallow areas frequently go anoxic due to this eutrophication. In the early 1980s the grazer community experienced major increases of previously minor indigenous species such as the omnivorous dinoflagellate *Noctilluca scintillans* and the medusa *Aurelia aurita*. The ctenophore *Mnemopsis leidyi* was imported at the end of the 1980s from the east coast of

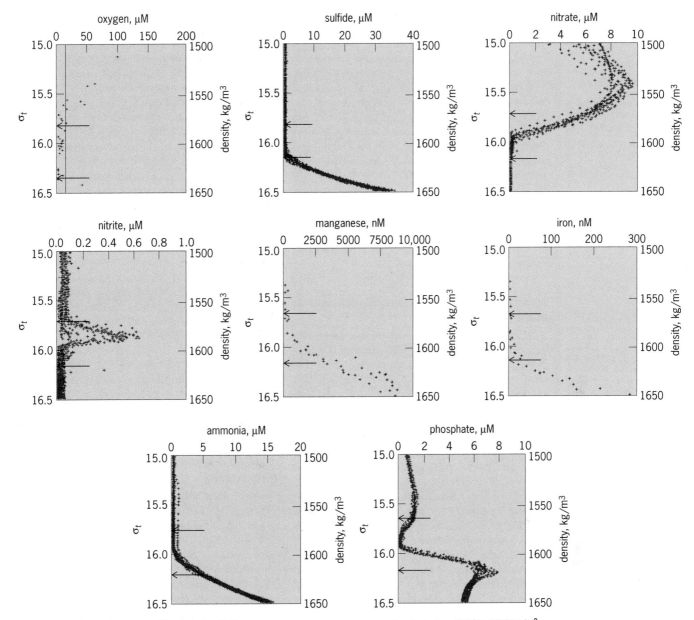

Fig. 3. Distributions of oxygen, sulfide, nitrate, nitrite, manganese, iron, ammonia, and phosphate from 1500 to 1650 kg/m³ (σ_t = 15.0 to 16.5).

the United States as ballast water in tankers and experienced an explosive unregulated growth. These changes plus overfishing resulted in a collapse of commercial fish stocks during the 1990s.

Geological history. The geological evolution of the Black Sea has been recorded in the sediments. Prior to 7800 years ago, the sediment record suggests that the Black Sea was a fresh-water lake that formed during a period of lower sea level, when the Black Sea was isolated from the Mediterranean (Unit III). At about 7800 years ago, sea level rose to the point where it began to enter the Black Sea. Water column anoxia in the deep water was initiated, and the present two-layer structure developed. The sediment record at this time is characterized by a microlaminated, organic-rich (up to 20%) sapropel (Unit II). The onset of Unit II sapropel deposition was rapid and synchronous across the basin and at all

water depths greater than 200 m (656 ft). At about 2000 years before present, the salinity distribution in the Black Sea had reached its present distribution, and since then the sediment record has been characterized by a laminated, moderately organic rich (~2%), coccolith-rich marl (Unit I). Remains of the calcium carbonate ($CaCO_3$)-secreting coccolithophorid *Emiliania huxleyi* are used to define this layer as the surface water salinity had to be at least $S = 11$ for their production. *See* EUTROPHICATION; SAPROPEL.   James W. Murray

Bibliography. M. A. Arthur and W. E. Dean, Organic-matter production and preservation and evolution of anoxia in the Holocene Black Sea, *Paleoceanography*, 13:395–411, 1998; L. Codispoti et al., Chemical variability in the Black Sea: Implications of continuous vertical profiles that penetrated the oxic/anoxic interface, *Deep-Sea Res.,*

38:S691–S710, 1991; C. Humborg et al., Effect of Danube River dam on Black Sea biogeochemistry and ecosystem structures, *Nature*, 386:385–388, 1997; J. W. Murray et al., Hydrographic properties and ventilation of the Black Sea, *Deep-Sea Res.*, 38:S663–S689, 1991; J. W. Murray et al., Oxidation-reduction environments: The suboxic zone in the Black Sea, in *Aquatic Chemistry: Interfacial and Interspecies Processes*, American Chemical Society, 1995; T. Oguz et al., Circulation in the surface and intermediate layers of the Black Sea, *Deep-Sea Res.*, 140:1597–1612, 1993; D. J. Repeta et al., Evidence for anoxygenic photosynthesis from the distribution of bacteriochlorophylls in the Black Sea, *Nature*, 342:69–72, 1989; Y. Zaitsev and V. Mamaev, *Marine Biological Diversity in the Black Sea: A Study of Change and Decline*, GEF Black Sea Environmental Programme, United Nations, 1997.

Black shale

A distinctive, fine-grained mudrock that derives its dark color from an unusually high content of organic matter, ranging from around 2% to over 50% of the weight of the rock (typical shales contain less than 1% organic matter). Most black shales can split into paper-thin sheets, and these are sometimes called paper shales. *See* SHALE.

Formation. The organic content of black shales is derived primarily from plankton and, to a lesser extent, small woody particles. Under normal deposition conditions in seas and lakes, planktonic organic matter is rapidly degraded by dissolved oxygen in the water column with little, if any, surviving to be buried. Two models explain the special conditions needed to produce organic-rich rocks. One model considers that black shales are likely to form only where the water column is stagnant such that the dissolved oxygen is rapidly consumed by decaying organic matter, producing oxygen-free (anoxic) conditions. Anoxia is considered to hinder the decay of organic matter and promote its burial. The modern-day Black Sea is an example of an anoxic basin in which organic-rich sediments are accumulating. The other model considers that areas of extremely high marine productivity, such as the upwelling zones off the coast of North and South America, are likely to produce organic-rich sediments. In these settings, the oxygen available in the water column is simply consumed by the large amount of decaying organic matter, some of which survives and is buried in the sediments. Both models involve an anoxic condition for deposition. In the former, it is due to a poor oxygen supply, whereas in the latter it is due to a large oxygen demand. *See* ANOXIC ZONES; BLACK SEA; DEPOSITIONAL SYSTEMS AND ENVIRONMENTS; MARINE SEDIMENTS; SEDIMENTOLOGY; UPWELLING.

Fossil content. The lack of oxygen in black shale depositional environments often ensures excellent fossil preservation due to the lack of scavengers and currents on the seabed or lakebed. Fossil diversity is often restricted to organisms, such as fish and am-monites, which lived above the uninhabitable seabed but sank to it after death. However, fossils of bottom-living organisms are also encountered in black shales. Their origin is controversial, although it seems likely that they colonized during brief periods with improved levels of bottom-water oxygen.

Global significance. Black shales are of unrivaled economic importance because they are sources of nearly all the world's hydrocarbons (coals are the only other significant source). During burial, alteration of organic matter releases complex hydrocarbons, which migrate and are trapped in oil and gas reservoirs. In addition, black shales are important for understanding many of the mass extinction events of the fossil record. Many of these extinctions coincided with intervals when black shale deposition was especially widespread. It appears that many marine extinctions were caused by the widespread development of stagnant (anoxic) conditions. Such conditions typify two of the largest mass extinctions of all time—the Late Devonian (365 million years ago) and the Late Permian (250 million years ago). *See* DEVONIAN; EXTINCTION (BIOLOGY); PERMIAN.   Paul B. Wignall

Bibliography. A. Hallam and P. B. Wignall, *Mass Extinctions and Their Aftermath*, Oxford University Press, 1997; B. J. Katz (ed.), *Petroleum Source Rocks*, Springer, 1995; P. B. Wignall, *Black Shales*, Oxford University Press, 1994.

Blackberry

Any of several species of the genus *Rubus* (family Rosaceae) having fruit consisting of many drupelets attached to a common fleshy, elongated core (receptacle) which is removed with the fruit. Ripe fruit is usually black or dark purple, and often sweet and flavorful. The bushy plants have perennial roots from which arise long, often thorny, biennial stems (canes) with compound leaves (see **illus.**). Many species are native to temperate regions, especially in the Northern Hemisphere, to which they are best

Blackberry fruit on a thorny, biennial cane.

adapted. They are commonly found on the edges of forests, along streams, and in clearings. Because of their thorns and prolific growth habit, blackberries are a nuisance in some areas. *See* ROSALES.

Blackberry cultivation began early in the nineteenth century, mainly in North America. Several species have been domesticated and used in the development of cultivars. Horticulturally important cultivars are separated into trailing (prostrate) types which require a trellis for support, and erect or semierect types which do not. Blackberries grow in most well-drained soils, except very sandy types, which may be too dry. Erect blackberries are more winter-hardy and grow best in cool, humid summers, whereas some trailing types, also called dewberries, can be grown in hot, dry climates if irrigated. Canes of hardy cultivars can withstand air temperatures below −20°F (−29°C) but require protection from more severe cold or drying winds. Bees are attracted to blackberry flowers and are required for good fruit production of cross-pollinated cultivars. Most blackberries are self-pollinating but still benefit from visits by bees and other pollinating insects.

Blackberries are vegetatively propagated from root suckers or root cuttings, or by burying the cane tips of trailing types, causing them to form new plants. *See* PLANT PROPAGATION; REPRODUCTION (PLANT).

Commercial blackberry production occurs mainly in the United States, but appreciable quantities are grown in the United Kingdom and in New Zealand. In commercial plantings in the United States, harvesting is often done by machines which shake the canes and catch the ripe fruit, most of which is frozen or canned for use in bakery products and yogurt or made into jelly, jam, or wine. Some fruit is hand-harvested and sold fresh. The Pacific Coast states account for about 80% of the annual North American production, with Oregon the major producer. The leading cultivars in this region are Thornless Evergreen, Marion, Olallie, and the blackberry-raspberry hybrids, Boysenberry and Loganberry. Cultivars grown in other producing regions include Cherokee, Comanche, and Dirksen Thornless (central United States), and Brazos and Humble (Texas). Blackberries, especially thornless cultivars such as Thornfree, Smoothstem, Dirksen Thornless, Black Satin, and Hull Thornless, are popular in home gardens and in "you-pick" enterprises.

Common diseases of blackberry are crown gall, a bacterial disease, and fungus diseases such as verticillium wilt, anthracnose, leaf and cane spot, double blossom (rosette), and orange rust. A prevalent viral disease (Rubus sterility) has symptoms of increased plant vigor, poor fruit set, and misshapen fruit. Although blackberries are often comparatively free of injury due to insects, canes are occasionally attacked by borers and the roots by white grubs. *See* FRUIT; PLANT PATHOLOGY.   Patrick J. Breen

Bibliography. G. M. Darrow, The cultivated raspberry and blackberry in North America: Breeding and improvement, *Amer. Hort. Mag.*, 46:202–218, 1967; J. W. Hull and F. J. Lawrence, *Growing Blackberries*, USDA Farmer's Bull. 2160, 1972; J. N. Moore, Black-berry production and cultivar situation in North America, *Fruit Varieties J.*, 34:36–42, 1980; J. S. Shoemaker, *Small Fruit Culture*, 5th ed., 1978.

Blackbody

An ideal energy radiator, which at any specified temperature emits in each part of the electromagnetic spectrum the maximum energy obtainable per unit time from any radiator due to its temperature alone. A blackbody also absorbs all the energy which falls upon it. The radiation properties of real radiators are limited by two extreme cases—a radiator which reflects all incident radiation, and a radiator which absorbs all incident radiation. Neither case is completely realized in nature. Carbon and soot are examples of radiators which, for practical purposes, absorb all radiation. Both appear black to the eye at room temperature, hence the name blackbody. Often a blackbody is also referred to as a total absorber. Such a total absorber constitutes a standard for the radiation of nonblackbodies, since Kirchhoff's law demands that the blackbody radiate the maximum amount of energy possible in any wavelength interval. For an extended discussion of blackbody radiation and Kirchhoff's law *See* GRAYBODY; HEAT RADIATION.   Heinz G. Sell; Peter J. Walsh

Blackleg

An acute, usually fatal, disease of cattle and occasionally of sheep, goats, and swine, but not humans. The infection is caused by *Clostridium chauvoei (C. feseri)*, a strictly anaerobic, spore-forming bacillus of the soil. The disease is also called symptomatic anthrax or quarter-evil. The characteristic lesions in the natural infection consist of crepitant swellings in involved muscles, which at necropsy are dark red, dark brown, or blue black. Artificial immunization is possible by use of blackleg aggressin or whole-culture bacterin. Animals surviving an attack of blackleg are permanently immune to its recurrence. *See* IMMUNITY.   Leland S. McClung

Bibliography. I. S. Ross (ed.), *Veterinary Handbook for Cattlemen*, 5th rev. ed., 1980; P. Summanen et al., *Wadsworth Anaerobic Bacteriology Manual*, 5th ed., 1993.

Blastoidea

A class of extinct Pelmatozoa in the subphylum Blastozoa which arose in the Ordovician and flourished in the Carboniferous and Permian. Blastoids did not survive the Permo-Triassic mass extinction event. Historically, two orders of the Blastoidea have been recognized: the Fissiculata with exposed hydrospire slits and the Spiraculata with concealed hydrospires. In recognition of their polyphyletic origins, the Spiraculata are now subdivided into the

Troosticrinida, Nucleocrinida, Granatocrinida, and Pentremitida. *See* PELMATOZOA.

Echinoderms, including blastoids, have very complex mesodermal skeletons with many thousands of individual ossicles. The typical blastoid had approximately 190,000 ossicles. The blastoid theca has 18 major plates (three basals, five radials, five deltoids, five lancets) which are attached to a stem typically 10 cm (4 in.) in length. A few blastoid genera were stemless, had asymmetrical thecae, and sat or lay directly on the sea floor. Although the presence of tube feet in blastoids is controversial, these animals fed by capturing food in a brachiolar filtration fan, passing it down to the ambulacra into the mouth through a system of food grooves. Waste products were eliminated from a separate anus. Each of the five ambulacra is composed of a lancet flanked by rows of side plates and outer side plates which carried a branch of the ambulacral food groove to a brachiole. A typical blastoid had approximately 100 side food grooves on each of five ambulacra, which supported one brachiole each. The vast majority of the skeletal ossicles in a blastoid theca is located in this brachiolar system (see **illustration**). *See* ECHINODERMATA.

Respiration in blastoids occurred in the hydrospires, a series of thin calcite folds underneath the ambulacra hanging into the coelom. In fissicu-

late blastoids, the hydrospires are exposed to seawater. In the other orders, the hydrospires are internal. Water entered through hydrospire pores at the lateral margins of the ambulacra, traversed the hydrospire folds, and exited through spiracles juxtaposed to the mouth. The anal opening is often contained within one spiracle, producing an anispiracle. A reproductive structure, the gonopore, has been identified in some blastoid genera. In life, the mouth and spiracles were covered by a pyramid of small ossicles.   Johnny A. Waters

Bibliography. T. W. Broadhead, *Blastozoa*, 1980; T. W. Broadhead and J. A. Waters (eds.), *Blastoidea in Echinoderms*, 1980; A. S. Horowitz and J. A. Waters, Ordinal level evolution in the Blastoidea, *Lethaia*, 26:207–213, 1993; C. R. C. Paul and A. B. Smith (eds.), *Echinoderm Phylogeny and Evolutionary Biology*, 1988.

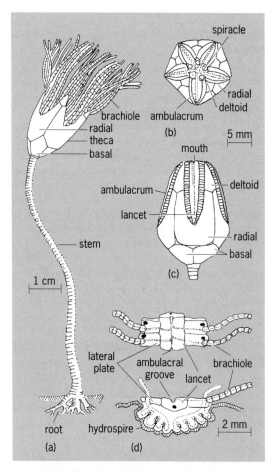

A blastoid, *Pentremites*. (*a*) Whole animal. (*b*) Adoral aspect of theca. (*c*) Lateral aspect of theca. (*d*) Details of ambulacral region in surface view and section.

Blastomycetes

A group of fungi consisting of yeasts that reproduce asexually by budding or splitting of single cells. In spite of simple morphology, these yeasts are quite diverse in terms of evolutionary origins and environmental roles. The group contains the yeasts used in baking and brewing. Some other yeasts are responsible for infections in humans and animals, while others occur on leaves or fruits. A few species are used for biological control of microbial plant pathogens. A very small number are pathogens of plants. *See* FUNGI; PLANT PATHOLOGY; YEAST.

Classification and identification. "Blastomycetes" was formerly accorded recognition as a class within a larger group consisting of all fungi reproducing asexually, the Deuteromycotina (deuteromycetes). Even at the time, it was recognized that the Blastomycetes contained fungi that were only distantly related: the Cryptococcales (belonging to ascomycetes) and the Sporobolomycetales (belonging to basidiomycetes). A later scheme divided yeasts into three classes: Saccharomycetes (for yeast-forming ascomycetes, notably *Saccharomyces*), Holobasidiomycetes, and Teliomycetes (both including other basidiomycetes in addition to yeast-forming basidiomycetes). Current practice places much less emphasis on a single classification scheme for yeasts per se, and "Blastomycetes" is seldom employed by contemporary taxonomists. Classification systems have changed rapidly with new information available from molecular-genetic techniques. However, certain characters continue to be informative. Formation of new cells via splitting (as opposed to budding) indicates the fission yeasts (such as *Schizosaccharomyces*, Schizosaccharomycetes), which are ascomycetes. The presence of reddish or orange carotenoid pigments, as in *Rhodotorula*, is evidence for affinity with basidiomycetes. An ability to produce ballistospores (spores which are "shot off" as in the "mirror yeast" *Sporobolomyces*) creates a mirror image of a colony on the lid of its petri dish. These mirror yeasts are considered basidiomycetes.

Most yeast-forming fungi are members of Saccharomycetes sensu stricto, are ascomycetes, and reproduce asexually by budding. The term "yeast" is itself without taxonomic significance, except that all yeasts are fungi. *See* ASCOMYCOTA ; BASIDIOMYCOTA; DEUTEROMYCOTINA; EUMYCOTA.

It is relatively easy to identify a microbe as a yeast because the single budding or splitting cell is large relative to bacteria. Assignment of a genus or species name has conventionally been accomplished by constructing a substrate utilization profile based on the ability to use a range of nutrient sources. Multiwell plates have a different substrate in each well, and the yeast growth in each well can be read automatically by computer and an identification returned. Several commercial systems are available. Recent molecular-genetic techniques use sequence analysis of one or more regions of DNA or RNA to identify yeasts as to genus or species.

Economic, medical, and ecological importance. *Saccharomyces cerevisiae*, the brewer's and baker's yeast, has arguably been the most important biotechnology organism in history. Other yeasts play similar but more minor roles in brewing and baking, and undesirable yeasts may impart bad flavors to juices or fermented beverages. The genera *Candida* and *Cryptococcus* contain species presenting medical problems which are especially severe in persons with compromised immune systems. Entirely different species of *Candida* and *Cryptococcus* have been used successfully for biological control of postharvest diseases of fruits. Perhaps the most important role for yeasts in the environment is their ubiquitous presence on plant surfaces, where they act as a major constraint on the growth of other microbes. *See* YEAST INFECTION.   Frank Dugan

Bibliography. J. A. Barnett, A history of research on yeasts 8: Taxonomy, *Yeast*, 21:1141–1193, 2004; J. A. Barnett, R. W. Payne, and D. Y. Yarrow, *Yeasts: Characteristics and Identification*, 3d ed., Cambridge University Press, 2000; C. P. Kurtzman and J. W. Fell (eds.), *The Yeasts: A Taxonomic Study*, 4th ed., Elsevier, 1998.

Blastulation

The formation of a segmentation cavity or blastocoele within a mass of cleaving blastomeres and rearrangement of blastomeres around this cavity in such a way as to form the type of definitive blastula characteristic of each species. The blastocoele originates as an intercellular space which sometimes arises as early as the four- or eight-cell stage. Thus blastulation is initiated during early cleavage stages, and formation of the definitive blastula is thought to terminate cleavage and to initiate gastrulation. Accordingly, cleavage and blastulation are simultaneous events which follow activation of the egg and precede the next major step in development, namely, gastrulation. Initially the diameter of the blastula is no greater than that of the activated egg; subse-

quently it increases. *See* CLEAVAGE (DEVELOPMENTAL BIOLOGY); GASTRULATION.

Blastula. The blastula is usually a hollow sphere. Its wall may be only one cell thick in many species, but in others it is several cells in thickness. In eggs which contain considerable amounts of yolk the blastocoele may be eccentric in position, that is, shifted toward the animal pole. The animal portion of its wall is always completely divided into relatively small cells, whereas the vegetative portion tends to be composed of relatively large cells and may be incompletely cellulated in certain species. The blastocoele contains a gelatinous or jellylike fluid, which originates in part as a secretion by the blastomeres and in part by passage of water through the blastomeres or intercellular material, or both, into the blastocoele.

The chemical nature of this secretion appears to vary in different species. In some it is said to be albuminous, in others to contain polysaccharides. It also contains certain salts. It possesses a viscosity which renders it visible when released from the blastocoele by puncture of the wall of the latter; however, the viscosity changes with time. The pH of this substance may be the same as that of seawater, or it may be more alkaline. It usually stains in preserved material, and stains most vividly during concentration of blastocoele fluid in those species where the blastocoele becomes reduced in size during gastrulation until it is eventually crowded out of existence. If fluid is withdrawn from the blastocoele with a hypodermic needle, the wall of the blastula crumples, but the quantity of blastocoele fluid is quickly restored to normal, as is the shape of the blastula. The volume of blastocoele fluid can also be reduced osmotically by placing blastulas in sucrose seawater, whereupon the diameter of blastulas decreases. Both of these observations indicate that blastocoele fluid exerts considerable pressure on the wall of the blastula and that the coherence of blastomeres must be considerable to resist this pressure. Cells and intercellular substance provide this structural stability, although the latter is often reinforced by an external elastic hyaline membrane. Permeability of the wall of the blastula changes during blastulation in certain species. At first it is freely permeable to all dissolved substances, but as the cells become smaller with each succeeding cleavage, permeability of the wall is reduced and the fluid in the blastocoele becomes increasingly cut off from the external environment. For example, the wall of the developing blastula of sand dollar eggs is freely permeable to large molecules such as those of sucrose up to the tenth cleavage, but thereafter this permeability is lost.

Wall of the blastula. The wall of the blastula is a mosaic of cellular areas, each of which will normally produce a certain structure during subsequent development. In other words, each area of cells in the wall of the blastula has a certain prospective fate which will be realized in normal development. In blastulas of some species the outlines of these several areas can be determined directly because the cytoplasm of cells within one area may be colored orange-yellow, that in another area light gray, and that in still another area dark gray. This is the case in the blastula of the tunicate *Styela*, but this is an exceptional situation. In most cases it is necessary to determine the prospective fate of each cellular area indirectly by marking experiments, that is, by staining cells in each area with a vital stain, determining by observation what organ or organs are formed from each stained area, and with the aid of this information, constructing a prospective fate map secondarily on the surface of the blastula. This does not mean that each of these areas would develop independently into the structure in question if isolated from other areas of the blastula. It merely means that these several cellular areas are so related to one another spatially in the blastula stage that they can be shifted subsequently in an orderly way by the morphogenetic movements of gastrulation into appropriate positions which will enable them to cooperate in the formation of tissues and organs through processes of self-differentiation or interaction or both. Thus the events of blastulation appear to be necessary prerequisites for the succeeding period in development, namely, gastrulation. The blastocoele appears to be essential in many species to provide a space into which certain of the special cellular areas of the wall of the blastula can move en masse or individually during gastrulation. *See* FATE MAPS (EMBRYOLOGY).　　　　Ray L. Watterson

Blattaria (Blattodea)

An order included in the Dictyoptera, and comprising 3500–4000 insect species, commonly known as roaches. The fossil record extends back some 400 million years, and roaches were found in abundance in the Carboniferous age. Blattaria are grouped with orders Isoptera (termites) and Mantodea (mantids) within the Dictyoptera. In fact, recent studies support the notion that termites are social roaches; Isoptera appear to be a sister group of roach species in the genus *Cryptocercus* that, like termites, digest wood with the aid of symbiotic intestinal protozoans. *See* INSECTA; ISOPTERA; ORTHOPTERA.

Characteristics. In general, cockroaches range in length from a few millimeters to 10 cm (4 in.), and have a flat oval body, a darkened cuticle, and a thoracic shield, the pronotum, which extends dorsally over the head. A pair of sensory organs, the whip-like antennae, are located on the head, and a much shorter pair of sensory organs, the cerci, are located at the end of the abdomen. Although some species are wingless, most have two pairs of wings but seldom fly. Most species are nocturnal and live in narrow crevices and under stones and debris. A few species actively burrow and others live on plants. The mouthparts are of the biting-chewing type but are relatively weak. Cockroaches are omnivorous, and a few species have adapted to the human environment, becoming household pests since they can chew foodstuffs, clothing, paper, and even plastic insulation. They also can emit a highly disagreeable order.

Adult cockroaches. (*a*) *Blaberus giganteus*. (*b*) *Cryptocercus punctulatus.*

Reproduction. Most species are sexual, although a few reproduce asexually. Eggs are typically laid in capsules (oothecae) which can be carried on the end of the abdomen. In some species the eggs hatch just as the ootheca is produced, whereas in others hatching occurs inside the female resulting in live birth. Nymphs go through several molts as they grow. The time from egg to adult varies from species to species, but can be longer than a year.

Pests. Although over 99% of species are not pests, several well-known roaches infest households. *Periplaneta americana*, the American cockroach, is a rust-colored insect 1.2–2.4 in. (30–60 mm) long. *Blatta orientalis*, the Asian cockroach, and *Blattella germanica*, the German cockroach, are smaller, darker-brown roaches which can infest houses in many parts of the world. German roaches have been found in heated buildings just a few hundred kilometers from the North Pole.

Other cockroaches. Other cockroaches of special interest are *Blaberus giganteus* (**illus.** *a*), a South American roach that can grow to 3.2 in. (80 mm); *Cryptocercus punctulatus*, a wood roach which has unicellular organisms in its gut to digest the consumed wood (illus. *b*); and *Gromphadorhina portentosa*, the Madagascar roach, which can compress its body and force air through modified spiracles (breathing pores), producing a loud hissing sound.

Use in research. Cockroaches have been claimed as vectors for numerous human diseases. There is little evidence to support this claim; however, there is evidence that they can produce allergenic reactions in humans. Because of their large size, cockroaches have proved to be very useful animals for scientific research on general problems of insect behavior, physiology, and biochemistry. *See* ALLERGY.
　　　　Darryl T. Gwynne; Charles R. Fourtner

Bibliography. D. G. Gordon, *The Compleat Cockroach: A Comprehensive Guide to the Most Despised (and Least Understood) Creatures on Earth*, Ten Speed Press, Berkeley, CA, 1996; I. Huber, E. P. Masler, and B. R. Rao, *Cockroaches as Models for Neurobiology*, CRC Press, Boca Raton, FL, 1990.

Bleaching

The process in which natural coloring matter is removed from a fiber to make it white. The process may be used on fiber, yarn, or fabric. Prior to the bleaching of a fabric, preliminary purification processes should be used. These processes remove applied encrustants (desizing) and natural encrustants (scouring or boil-off) so that the bleaching agent may act uniformly on the material free of impediment.

Bleaching is also classified as a purification process and varies with the content of the substrate or fibrous content of the material. It should not be confused with the stripping process, which is the removal of applied color.

The fabric off the loom is called gray, grey, or greige goods to distinguish it from the partially or completely finished fabric.

Desizing. This process removes sizing agents (slasher compounds) which have been added to the warp yarns (lengthwise yarns) prior to weaving to protect them against the abrasive action of loom parts during the formation of gray fabric. Cellulosics are slashed primarily with starches which may be removed with enzymes of the malt (low-temperature–resistant) or bacteriostatic (high-temperature–resistant) types and are called amylolytic enzymes. Enzymes break down or become inactive on a time basis at room temperature. This inactivation is accelerated by increasing the temperature, which decreases the time. The use of enzymes is thus a time-temperature inverse relationship activity which may accomplish the desizing process at low temperatures for lengthy times or at high temperatures in much shorter periods with equal efficiency.

Other effective agents are dilute mineral acids at high temperatures and sodium bromite in cold solution. Protein warps are sized or slashed or pretreated with proteinaceous agents such as gelatin, casein, albumin, or glue and require the use of proteolytic enzymes for their removal. Synthetics are slashed with water-soluble agents such as poly(vinyl alcohol) or sodium salts of poly(acrylic acids) which are removed by hot detergent solutions. Use of poly(vinyl alcohols) and carboxymethyl celluloses is increasing with cotton and other cellulosic fiber materials because of their biodegradable characteristics and as a means of decreasing stream pollution. They are removed by detergent solutions, as with synthetics. Elimination of the desizing operation creates insurmountable problems in subsequent processes, including bleaching.

Scouring. This process removes natural encrustants which are of a resistant nature from the fibers. In natural fibers such as cotton or linen, very resistant and water-repellent waxes are the main concern. These waxes may vary from $1/2$ to 1% by weight and require relatively severe treatment with caustic soda and other auxiliaries at high temperatures to form a wax soap (saponification); thus the waxes are emulsified prior to being rinsed or washed out. Meanwhile pectoses, proteins, and mineral matter in the order of 4–6% by weight are simultaneously removed. With protein fibers such as wool, the repellent is a natural grease. This also must be removed by emulsification with a slightly alkalinized soap or detergent, but with much lower temperature and alkaline content because of the greater susceptibility of wool to alkali damage at high temperatures as well as the greater receptivity of the grease to emulsification. Manufactured fibers, including rayons and synthetics, contain no natural encrustants but have so-called producer oils added to them as protective agents. These are self-emulsifiable oils and are removed concurrently with any sizing agent used in the desizing process, thus eliminating the need for a scour or boil-off. Conversely, if water-soluble sizes are used on manufactured fibers, desizing can be eliminated and the scour or boil-off will accomplish both simultaneously.

The equipment to be used in the process of scouring also depends upon the fiber content in the fabric. Continuous processing (the forerunner of automated processes) is utilized most extensively for cotton with kiers next in productive rate and finally smaller lots by kettles, becks, and jigs. Kettles, becks, jigs, and Hinnekin-type full-width units are used for synthetics. The Hinnekin units are used on filament rayons to prevent cracking or crease formation. Wool and wool blends with synthetics are scoured in rotary (Dolly) washers or kettles.

Continuous ranges for desizing, scouring, and peroxide bleaching of cotton dominate with the material in the rope or full-width form, based upon weight and susceptibility to irremovable wrinkle formation. These ranges consist of saturators, J boxes, and washers in sequence with no variance in feed of fabric and delivery rate of the fabric. Ranges are individual units used in sequence and synchronized in productive rates which allow this continuity of processing. The caustic saturator contains the scouring solution and is composed of caustic soda (emulsifier), sodium silicate (buffer), detergent, and a sequestrant or chelating agent to immobilize metallic salts, especially copper and iron. These two metals may create problems in bleaching and subsequent processing by degradation of the cellulose to oxycellulose. The presence of caustic soda in quantities necessary for saponification indicates that a high pH is present. This pH must be under strict control. The temperature range for this scouring is 206–214°F (96.7–101°C).

The kier is a pressurized, vertical autoclave with capacities as high as 4–5 tons (3.5–4.5 metric tons) of fabric with essentially the same reagents being used in much the same quantity but with cycles of 6–8 h. Pressure is 15 pounds per square inch gage (103 kilopascals), yielding a processing temperature of 240°F (116°C) and with continuous circulation of the solution through the mass and the unit as compared with 1–2-h cycles in the J box in the continuous unit. Care must be exercised in the kier to have uniform packing of the roped fabric to prevent channeling (free solution passage through the mass rather than seepage). Channeling and exposure to air (oxygen which develops oxycellulose) are the major side effects which may create problems in the uniform emulsification and purification of a fabric free of damage. Kiers, with the exception of the horizontal kier used for heavy goods, are limited to the processing of soft goods which are amenable to roping. Other less productive units for full-width processing of heavy cotton goods are continuous jigs and individual jigs which are not pressurized. Horizontal kiers, continuous jigs, and jigs are used to prevent the heavy-weight goods from producing irremovable wrinkles.

Subsequent developments resulted in the use of solvent scouring with trichlorethylene or perchlorethylene at the boil of the solvent. This is a continuous scour at full width and is claimed to allow 96–97% solvent recovery, which is a necessity to make it economically feasible to compete with other systems.

Scouring of wool is accomplished in rotary or Dolly washers and, therefore, is a batch process having relatively low productive rates. The pH is much lower (8.2–8.4) and the scouring solution consists of soap or deteregent built to the proper pH with soda ash. The temperature is much lower with an average of 120–130°F (49–54°C). The use of caustic soda is prohibited because of the high decomposition rate of wool when exposed to this agent, in particular at elevated temperatures. The use of sequestrants or chelating agents is recommended, especially with soaps, to prevent the formation of insoluble metallic soaps, especially on the fabric. An alternative to this process of scouring is the use of the Derby dry cleaner unit, using solvent as the extractant for the wool grease and oils. Much wool is scoured in the fibrous state, but lubricants are subsequently added and must be removed during the processing of the eventual fabric. The lubricants are self-emulsifiable, and a detergent or soap solution will readily remove them with lesser time being necessary for this scouring or washing.

Scouring or the preferential term boil-off on rayons and synthetics is readily accomplished by using detergents built with soda ash or sodium polyphosphates. The producer oils are readily emulsified, as they are produced to be self-emulsifiable. Boil-off is the term acquired from the degumming of silk, which is accomplished in a soap solution at or near boil temperatures.

Bleaching processes. The three most prominent commercial bleaching processes are the peroxide, the chlorine, and the chlorite, in that order. In home bleaching the predominant bleach is the chlorine bleach, followed by the use of peroxygen compounds such as persulfates and perborates. The latter two are recommended for minimum-care and permanent-press fabrics to preclude the yellowing of the whites and the stripping of colored fabrics, which are always potentials when chlorine bleaches are used.

Peroxide bleaching. Hydrogen perioxide is the most universal of commercial bleaches, despite its higher cost compared with chlorine. This is compensated for by the need of less time and higher productive rates. More than 85% of the commercial bleaching of cotton today is done with prepared concentrates of 27.5, 35, and 50% hydrogen peroxide being properly diluted with water to appropriate low peroxide content for use in the bleaching. The designation of strength used in bleaching is most frequently by volume rather than by percentage peroxide strength, although they are interrelated proportionally. For example, 27.5% hydrogen peroxide is 100 volume, 35% is 130 volume, and 50% is 197 volume. Volume relates to the volume of oxygen released by one volume of the designated hydrogen peroxide. Bleaching of cotton with hydrogen peroxide solution may have an average composition of 34 to 2 volume peroxide, sodium silicate as a buffer to control and maintain pH, sodium polyphosphate as a sequestrant for iron or a chelating agent for copper and iron, plus sodium hydroxide to obtain an optimum pH. There is always the danger of too rapid evolution of nascent oxygen unless the solution is carefully controlled in pH and the potential of developing oxycellulose. The degraded and brittle cellulose shows as tender areas, pinholes, and so on in the bleached cotton. The presence of iron or copper accelerates the oxygen release and oxycellulose formation; thus the need exists for agents to inhibit any action on the part of these metals. The release or control of the release of nascent oxygen is closely associated with the pH according to reaction (1). A chart indicates the optimum con-

$$H_2O_2 \rightarrow H_2O + O \qquad (1)$$

ditions which control the evolution of oxygen and thus deter oxycellulose development.

Peroxide bleaching is controlled by the accurate consideration of the following factors: concentration or volume of peroxide used, pH of the bath, temperature of the bath, and time of exposure. Time and temperature are inverse in relationship.

Production rates are also closely dependent upon the weight and construction of the fabric. Heavy-weight goods processed full width have production rates of 45–50 yd/min (36–45 m/min) continuously, whereas soft and lighter-weight fabrics which may be roped may be processed as high as 250 yd/min (225 m/min). It has become feasible with pressurized and sealed equipment to process even heavy-weight fabrics at 100 yd/min (90 m/min) continuously at 250–300°F (121–149°C).

Inasmuch as the release of nascent oxygen is controlled in an alkaline bath, it is evident that for shipping and storage an acid condition must prevail. Further precaution against breakdown of hydrogen peroxide, especially under nonacidic conditions, is exemplified by the use of brown bottles for 3% or 10-volume medicinal peroxide. Commercial shipments of concentrates are in tank cars or in large drums which are vented to release any pressure buildup within the container.

Wool. The percentage of wool bleached is much less than the percentage of cotton bleached. The wool which is bleached is processed through a peroxide system. As a result of the wool's nature and its susceptibility to alkali, especially in hot solutions, both the pH and the temperature are lower than for cellulosics with a compensating increase in time required to complete the process. This time may be shortened, however, by incorporating optical bleaches which are compatible with the peroxide. By substituting ammonia for the soda ash or tetrasodium pyrophosphate, the pH may be raised to 10 rather than the normal pH of 8-9 with a potential decrease in the peroxide time cycle. Present methods utilize batch rather than continuous systems. Precautions to be taken consist of acidification with an organic acid to a pH of 6.5-7.0 prior to the immersion of the fabric in the peroxide solution and again subsequent to the postrinsing following the bleach to reduce the alkali retention by the wool.

Wool cannot be bleached with hypochlorite since it contains amino components which cause a permanent yellowing of the fiber due to the formation of yellow chloramines. Silk also is bleached by peroxide but at a somewhat higher temperature and with a compensating shorter cycle for the bleaching. Wool and silk, being protein fibers, were initially bleached by the stoving process. This was a reduction bleach in which the uniformly wet fabric was exposed to sulfur dioxide gas in an enclosed chamber for an extensive period of time. Sulfur on burning released SO_2, which caused color reduction and bleaching. The process has been abandoned because the white obtained soon reverted to the prebleached color.

Synthetics such as polyamides, polyesters, and acrylics do not lend themselves to peroxide bleaching because of the alkalinity and the potential damage to the fibers. The chlorite bleach is used for these fibers. Manufactured fibers made from cellulose, such as viscose and Bemberg, are primarily white on production but, if necessary, peroxide bleach may be used for very short cycles, or a cold saturation followed by dwelling on the roll overnight when required. The exception is acetate rayon, whose lack of resistance is such that is cannot withstand alkalinity. Acetate, therefore, is better bleached with another peroxygen compound, peracetic acid, in an acid medium.

Hypochlorite bleaching. This bleaching process is most commonly called the chlorine bleach. This was the foremost bleaching process for cellulosics until after World War II, when the continuous peroxide system, which was restrained during the war, gained favor rapidly. Hypochlorite, however, is still the predominant agent used in household or home bleaching. The sodium rather than the calcium hypochlorite (bleaching powder) is dominant. Sodium hypochlorite may be readily made by the electrolysis of sodium chloride, but in actual plant manufacture it emanates from the bubbling of chlorine gas from pressurized tanks into dilute caustic soda or soda ash. During the process of bleaching with sodium hypochlorite in water solution, hydrolysis occurs with the production of hypochlorous acid. This is represented by reaction (2). This acid is very unstable and breaks

$$NaOCl + HOH \rightarrow HClO + NaOH \qquad (2)$$

down, releasing nascent oxygen as shown by reac-

tion (3). Excess NaOH and the pH condition con-

$$HClO \rightarrow HCl + O \qquad (3)$$

trol the nascent oxygen release and thus the ultimate whitening. Unless the controls are exercised, oxycellulose may develop as in the peroxide system. Care must also be used commercially to antichlor with acid and sulfur dioxide or sodium bisulfite to preclude later damage to the fiber caused by the retention of chlorine which will hydrolyze the cellulose. It is also good household practice to use the sodium bisulfite in an automatic washer rinse, but this care is seldom exercised. Developments have resulted in a proposal to use a continuous hot chlorine bleach commercially. This requires very strict control of conditions such as varying the concentration, time, pH, and temperature.

Chlorite bleach. The use of sodium chlorite (Textone) as a bleaching agent first emerged about 1941, subsequent to the introduction of the continuous peroxide bleach in 1939. Unlike the other bleaches, the effective bleaching agent is ClO_2, chlorine dioxide. The use of $NaClO_2$ is quite distinctive also because it is accomplished as an acid system at an optimum pH of 3.5. The temperature recommended for the bleaching is 185°F (85°C). A significant characteristic of this bleaching process is the freedom from the degradation of cellulose and, consequently, no oxycellulose is produced as is true in the peroxide and hypochlorite systems. There is objection to its use commercially because its crystals are subject to explosive tendencies under suitable conditions and the ClO_2 gas is itself an obnoxious and toxic gas. Another factor is that even stainless steel is pitted when the acid bleaching medium is present. Despite these characteristics, it is the most effective bleaching agent for synthetics and is used on cotton in a few continuous systems. In a continuous system, a pitting inhibitor, a special J box with a seal to prevent ClO_2 escape, and a siphon to remove excess $NaClO_2$ and ClO_2 are components. Some consideration has been given to the use of fiberglass and ceramic equipment with this bleach. The ClO_2 release may be represented by reaction (4).

$$5NaClO_2 + 4HCl \rightarrow 4ClO_2 + 5NaCl + 2H_2O \qquad (4)$$

Optical bleaching. There are organic compounds which are capable of absorbing waves shorter than visual waves and emitting waves within the visible range. The most notable of the short waves absorbed is the ultraviolet light present in daylight. These compounds absorb ultraviolet light which is less than 400 nanometers and emit blue light which is in the visible range of 400-700 nanometers. This emitted light will counteract the yellow on the fabric surface and by the subtractive theory of color will produce a white. The agents are also characterized as brighteners and are extensively used in household detergents. They are, however, effective only in daylight because of the ultraviolet light therein. They are also subject in varying degrees to loss of effect upon exposure to sunlight as a result of fading. Materials

Characteristics of textile bleaching				
Bleach	Fibers	pH	Temperature, °F (°C)	Time
Hypochlorite	Cellulosics	9.5–10.0	70–80 (21–27)	4–12 h
Hypochlorite	Cellulosics	10–11	180 (82)	5–10 s
Peroxide	Cellulosics	10.4–11.5	180 (82)	2–4 h
Peroxide	Cellulosics	10.4–11.5	208 or greater(98 or greater)	1–1$\frac{1}{2}$ min
Peroxide	Wool	9.0–10.0	120 (49)	2–6 h
Peroxide	Silk	9.0–10.0	160 (71)	$\frac{1}{2}$ h
Chlorite	Cellulosics and synthetics	3.5	185 (85)	$\frac{3}{4}$–1 h
Optical	Cellulosics and synthetics	5.0 or less	180 (82)	$\frac{1}{4}$–1 h
Optical	Wool	8.0–8.5	160 (71)	$\frac{1}{4}$–$\frac{1}{2}$ h
NaOCl/NaClO$_2$	Cellulosics	8.7–9.0	70–80 (21–27)	1 h
NaOCl/H$_2$O$_2$	Cellulosics	9.5/10.5	70–80/200 or greater (21–27/93 or greater)	$\frac{1}{3}$–$\frac{1}{2}$ h

treated with these optical bleaches or agents fluoresce brilliantly in an ultraviolet light source. They are often used to supplement fabrics bleached by other methods, especially the hypochlorite and peroxide systems where selectively they can be incorporated in the normal bleaching solution. This may result in the cost of the bleaching being reduced because less bleach is used or the cycle is shortened. Furthermore, losses in strength may be minimized because less oxygen bleach is used and the opticals do not affect the strength of fibers.

Combination bleaching. There are several bleaching systems which are classified as combination bleaches because two different bleaching agents are used together or in tandem. These have been projected to lower the cost, lower the degradation, or shorten the cycle as well as to preclude equipment damage in certain cases.

Solvay activated peroxide bleach. This consists of first exposing cotton to cold hypochlorite. After this fewer chemicals and less time and heat exposure are necessary than is true with peroxide alone.

Hypochlorite-chlorite bleach. This process shortens the hypochlorite bleach time, releases ClO$_2$ rather than O, and prevents equipment damage since the process takes place under alkaline conditions. No heat is necessary as is true for the chlorite bleach. The **table** summarizes conditions for this and all the other bleaching processes discussed. *See* NATURAL FIBER; OXIDIZING AGENT; TEXTILE CHEMISTRY.

John J. McDonald

Bibliography. E. R. Trotman, *Dyeing and Chemical Technology of Textile Fibers*, 6th ed., 1985; T. L. Vigo, *Textile Processing and Properties*, 1994.

Blimp

A name originally applied to nonrigid airships and usually implying small size. Early blimps contained about 100,000 ft^3 (2800 m^3) and were only a fraction of the size of the rigid airships of that period. The nonrigid pressure-type airship, however, did not stay small; each succeeding model built was substantially larger than its predecessor until ships with volumes of approximately 1,500,000 ft^3 (42,000 m^3) were operational in the U.S. Navy. With the advent of these larger sizes it appeared that the name blimp would be replaced by the more general term airship. However, the principles of construction of these ships are basically the same regardless of the size.

Main envelope. The airship envelope is a symmetrical airfoil in the form of a body of revolution, circular in cross section and elliptical along its longitudinal axis. The fabric of the main envelope or pressure hull is usually made up of two or three plies of cloth impregnated with an elastomer; at least one of these plies is placed in a bias direction with respect to the others. This tends to make the fabric more resistant to shear loads and results in a stabilized structure. The materials used for the envelope must be lightweight, extremely strong, and resistant to gas diffusion. Chronologically the fibers and elastomers used were (1) cotton and rubber, (2) cotton and neoprene, (3) Fortisan rayon and neoprene, (4) nylon and neoprene, (5) Dacron and neoprene, (6) polyester, urethane, and Tedlar laminates. Each newly developed material improved some property required of envelope structures; and these improved fabrics, along with advancements in assembly techniques, permitted the increase in size of the pressure-type airship to fulfill any possible need. *See* MANUFACTURED FIBER; POLYMER; RUBBER.

A pattern is made for each panel and gore so that, when the fabric pieces are cemented, sewed, or heat-sealed together, the envelope will have the required shape when filled with gas. The outside of the envelope is sometimes coated with aluminized paint for protection against the sunlight. In later versions an ultraviolet shield is incorporated in the top surface of the fabric.

Inside the envelope are catenary curtains (**Fig. 1**). They support the weight of the car by distributing the loads imposed by it into the envelope fabric. This suspension system can be arranged in a number of ways, depending upon the particular airship configuration (**Fig. 2**). Basically, however, they all consist of cable systems attached to the car which terminate in fabric curtains, which in turn are cemented and

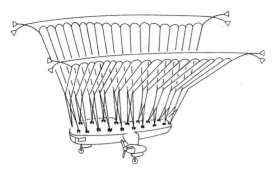

Fig. 1. Typical internal rigging of nonrigid airships.

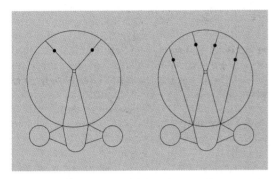

Fig. 2. Two types of internal suspension for nonrigid airship cars.

sewed or otherwise sealed to the envelope proper. The envelope also contains one or more air cells, fastened to the bottom or sides of the envelope, which are used to maintain the required pressure in the envelope without adding or valving of gas as the ship ascends or descends. These air cells are called ballonets and are usually made of a fabric much lighter in weight than that of the envelope, because they must merely retain gas tightness and do not have to withstand the normal envelope pressure.

The fabric envelopes, when not in use, can be folded or shipped or stored in a space which takes up less than 1% of the inflated volume of the envelope. This feature and the ability to erect the envelope by merely inflating it are two of the advantages of the fabric pressure-type airship over the rigid one.

Other components. The airship car is of conventional aircraft construction, earlier of a fabric-covered tubing framework but now of a metal or plastic monocoque design. Much like an airplane, it contains the crew compartments, the engines, the landing gear, and all the related instruments, controls, and fuel. A few additional accessories required for the airship car are the pressure controls, air scoops behind the propellers, valves, and the fan system necessary for maintaining the pressure in the envelope by pumping air in and out of the ballonets.

The airship tail surfaces have taken on three typical configurations, named from the placement of the surfaces on the envelope. They are the cruciform (+), the X, and the inverted Y. These tails are made up of a fixed main surface and a controllable smaller surface on the aft end. The construction consists primarily of lightweight metal structural beams covered with doped fabric. These are held to the envelope by cables which distribute the load into fabric patches cemented to the envelope proper. These surfaces are so efficiently designed that they weigh less than 0.9 lb/ ft^2 (4.4 kg/m^2) of tail area.

The nose cone, made up of metal, wood, or plastic battens, is laced to the envelope to serve the dual purpose of providing a good point of attachment for mast mooring and of adding extra rigidity to the nose, because it encounters the greatest dynamic pressure loads in flight. Sometimes the nose battens are covered to provide streamlining.

Erection for flight. The erection of a fabric pressure-type airship is a spectacular sight and takes place in a relatively short time. The envelope is spread out on the floor of the airship hangar and a net is placed over it. As gas is fed into the envelope from tank cars, each containing about 200,000 ft^3 (5700 m^3) of 99.9% pure helium compressed to 2100 lb/in.^{2} (14.5 megapascals), the net which is held down by sand bags is permitted to rise slowly, care being taken that the envelope does not slip out from under the net. Fins, nose cone, battens, air valves, and helium valves are attached, and the envelope is then allowed to rise high enough from the floor to permit rolling the car underneath. After attachment of the car, the net is removed and the airship is rigged for flight.

The strength required of the material used in the fabric pressure-type airship envelope is a function of the internal gas pressure, the distribution of the gas in the envelope, the location of the weights attached to it, and the aerodynamic and ground-handling loads imposed on the airship in flight and at the mast. One of the most important properties of the fabric pressure-type airship is its ability to accept an overload condition, which in a nonpressurized airship would result in a structural failure. In other words, if the airship envelope should encounter, for example, a gust of greater velocity than it had been designed to withstand, there would be a momentary buckle or wrinkle in the envelope with a complete structural recovery the moment the force was removed. This "forgiveness" is a special feature of the pressure-type structure utilizing a flexible material for the load-carrying members.

Applications. Up until the late 1980s, the only commercial airships operating in the United States were the Goodyear Tire and Rubber Company advertising blimps of about 150,000 ft^3 (4200 m^3). Fundamentally, they were communications platforms used for public service where airship characteristics are superior to other forms of flight.

Because of its ability to practically hover over one spot, the airship forms an excellent airborne platform for a TV camera and operator viewing major sports events such as football games, golf tournaments, or automobile or boat races. In times of emergency, it is also used to inspect the consequences of natural disasters such as floods or forest fires. Lightweight TV cameras with zoom lenses can

Typical operating blimps				
	Goodyear		Airship Industries	
Characteristic	GZ-20	GZ-22	Skyship 500	Skyship 600
Length, ft (m)	192 (58.5)	205.5 (62.6)	170.6 (52.0)	193.6 (59.0)
Width, ft (m)	46 (14.0)	47 (14.3)	45.93 (14.0)	49.86 (15.2)
Volume, ft^3 (m^3)	202,700 (5740)	247,800 (7017)	180,355 (5107)	233,100 (6600)
Height, ft (m)	57.5 (17.5)	60.2 (18.3)	61.2 (18.7)	66.6 (20.3)
Maximum speed, mi/h (km/h)	50 (80)	65 (105)	60 (97)	65 (105)
Maximum car length, ft (m)	22.75 (6.93)	34.75 (10.59)	29.44 (8.97)	37.44 (11.41)

readily pick up an overall color picture of a live happening or pinpoint a special detail.

For television operations the airship carries a pilot, a full-sized transistorized color TV camera, and a camera operator. The airship also carries monitoring equipment, encoding and microwave transmitting equipment, and an antenna. Usually the TV camera and its related equipment are operated by network personnel. Signals from the camera are monitored and corrected for picture quality and color balance before being fed to the conditioning equipment for transmission to the microwave antenna and for radiation from the airship antenna to a ground parabolic tracking antenna. These signals are then fed into a network connection or are transmitted to a station by a microwave radio system. *See* TELEVISION CAMERA; TELEVISION NETWORKS.

Another form of communication for which the airship is used is the night sign. The sign consists of a matte of multicolor incandescent lamps permanently fixed to the sides of the airship envelope. By programming the operating of these lamps, stationary or moving letters or pictures can be displayed against a night background.

Originally, these sign messages were developed by electromechanical relays. Now magnetic tapes are prepared on the ground by composing equipment. The tapes are then carried along on the flight and fed into an airborne reader, which plays the taped information back through a computer to the lamp driver circuits. The resulting message, which usually supports a civic endeavor such as a bond drive or water-saving campaign, is then readily seen by people from a substantial area of the ground. Because the airship can move quite slowly, extended news messages can be transmitted this way.

During the 1980s, several companies other than Goodyear began to produce blimps for advertising purposes, passenger operations, and even possible military missions. Typical of these was Airship Industries of England, which produces the Skyships 500 and 600, used in Europe, the United States, Australia, and Japan, primarily as advertising billboards. In 1988, Goodyear introduced the GZ-22, the largest and most advanced blimp flying at the time, featuring a unique X-configuration tail and shrouded, swivable turboprop power plants (Fig. 5). The relative characteristics of four widely used blimps are shown in the **table**.

Because of their endurance, slow flight capability,

and stability, these vehicles were also tested for possible use in patrol of national borders, control of shipping, pollution monitoring, fishery protection, and search-and-rescue operations. A boarding boat can be lowered from a particular blimp model for possible use against drug smuggling. Applications to mine countermeasures as well as airborne early warning were also studied by the military services in order to define possible use with the U.S. Navy of a much larger version with exceptional range, endurance, and payload capabilities. *See* AIRSHIP.   Robert S. Ross

Bibliography. W. E. Althoff, *Sky Ships: A History of the Airship in the United States Navy*, 1990, reissue 1998; B. Bailey and N. J. Mayer, *Military and Civil Application of Airships*, 1986; L. Gerkin, *Airships: History and Technology*, 1990; R. A. Grossnick (ed.), *Kite Balloons to Airships ... The Navy's Lighter-Than-Air Experience*, 1988; L. Payne, *Lighter Than Air: An Illustrated History of the Airship*, 1977, reprint 1991.

Bloch theorem

A theorem that specifies the form of the wave functions that characterize electron energy levels in a periodic crystal. Electrons that move in a constant potential, that is, a potential independent of the position **r**, have wave functions that are plane waves, having the form exp(i**k** · **r**). Here, **k** is the wave vector, which can assume any value, and describes an electron having momentum $\hbar$**k**. (The quantity $\hbar$ is Planck's constant divided by 2π.)

Electrons in a crystal experience a potential that has the periodicity of the crystal lattice. Lattice translations {**L**}, are the vectors (in space) that describe the relative locations of any two primitive cells (for example, molecular units). The electron's potential, $V(\mathbf{r})$, is periodic, meaning that it is unchanged by all translations of the form $\mathbf{r} \to \mathbf{r} + \mathbf{L}$.

The Bloch theorem states that wave functions that characterize electron energy levels in a periodic crystal may always be written as in the equation below,

$$\psi_n(\mathbf{k}, \mathbf{r}) = e^{i\mathbf{k}\cdot\mathbf{r}} u_n(\mathbf{k}, \mathbf{r})$$

where n is an energy-band index. Here, $u_n(\mathbf{k},\mathbf{r})$ is a function that has the same periodicity as the potential $V(\mathbf{r})$. The wave vector **k** can no longer assume any value. Instead, it is restricted to a polyhedral volume called the Brillouin zone. For example, the Brillouin zone of a cubic crystal having lattice constant a is a cube (in $\mathbf{k}$ space) having edge length $2\pi/a$. The loss in allowed $\mathbf{k}$ space is compensated by the band index n, which can have integer values from 0 to ∞. *See* BRILLOUIN ZONE.

Electrons described by a Bloch function, as above, do not have momentum $\hbar\mathbf{k}$, but their mean momentum is the same in every cell of the crystal. Thus, the Bloch theorem resolved the paradox of how an electron can travel indefinitely in a perfect crystal without being scattered randomly by the atomic potentials. The practical utility of the Bloch theorem is that $\mathbf{k}$ and n are the indices needed to enumerate electron states when equilibrium or nonequilibrium phenomena are described. *See* BAND THEORY OF SOLIDS.   Albert Overhauser

Block and tackle

Combination of a rope or other flexible material and independently rotating frictionless pulleys; the pulleys are grooved or flat wheels used to change the direction of motion or application of force of the flexible member (rope or chain) that runs on the pulleys. As in a lever, the summation of torques about the axis of rotation of the pulley equals zero for static equilibrium. Tension T in the rope is the same on both sides of the pulley. *See* LEVER.

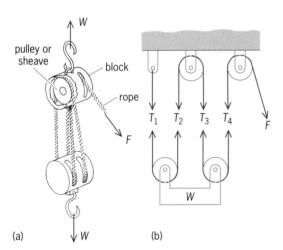

Block and tackle. (*a*) Actual view. (*b*) Schematic.

For example, in the particular block and tackle in the **illustration**, at static equilibrium, the summation of forces in any direction equals zero. Each vertical rope carries one-fourth the weight; algebraically $T_1 = T_2 = T_3 = T_4 = W/4$, and therefore the applied force F also equals one-fourth the weight W. For this case mechanical advantage MA is shown by the equation below. The block and tackle is used

$$MA = \frac{W}{F} = \frac{W}{W/4} = 4$$

where a large multiplication of the applied forces is desirable. Examples are lifting weights, sliding heavy

machinery into position, and tightening fences. *See* SIMPLE MACHINE.   Richard M. Phelan

Block diagram

A convenient graphical representation of input-output behavior of a system or subsystem, where the signal into the block represents the input and the signal out of the block represents the output. The flow of information (the signal) is unidirectional from the input to the output. A complex system, comprising several subsystems, is represented by the interconnection of blocks that represent the subsystems. The primary use of the block diagram is to portray the interrelationship of distinct parts of the system.

A block diagram consists of two basic functional units that represent system operations. The individual block symbols portray the dynamic relations between the input and output signals. The relationship between input and output signals of a subsystem is typically represented by what is known as the transfer function of the subsystem. In management science, criminal justice systems, and economic systems, a block diagram may represent a system function describing a set of activities. The second type of unit, called a summing point, is represented by a circle with arrows feeding into it. The operation that results is a linear combination of incoming signals to generate the output signal. The sign appearing alongside each input to the summing point indicates the sign of that signal as it appears in the output.

Block diagrams are widely used in all fields of engineering, management science, criminal justice, economics, and the physical sciences for the modeling and analysis of systems. In modeling a system, some parameters are first defined and equations governing system behavior are obtained. A block diagram is constructed, and the transfer function for the whole system is determined.

If a system has two or more input variables and two or more output variables, simultaneous equations for the output variables can be written. In general, when the number of inputs and outputs is large, the simultaneous equations are written in matrix form. *See* MATRIX THEORY; MULTIVARIABLE CONTROL.

Block diagrams can be used to portray nonlinear as well as linear systems, such as a cascade containing a nonlinear amplifier and a motor (see **illustration**).

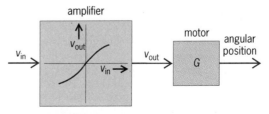

Block diagram of a motor and an amplifier with a nonlinear gain characteristic. v_{in} = input time variable, v_{out} = output time variable, G = transfer function.

If the motor is assumed to be linear, it can be represented by a transfer function. The nonlinear amplifier gain can describe only the relationship between the input time variable and the output time variable, and no transfer function exists between them. An overall transfer function relation cannot be defined for this cascade system unless the amplifier is represented by a linear gain model. *See* COMPUTER PROGRAMMING; CONTROL SYSTEMS; GAIN; NONLINEAR CONTROL THEORY; SYSTEMS ENGINEERING.   G. V. S. Raju

Bibliography. J. J. D'Azzo, C. H. Houpis, and S. N. Sheldon, *Linear Control System Analysis and Design with MATLAB*, 5th ed., 2003; J. DiStefano, A. Stubberud, and I. Williams, *Feedback and Control Systems*, 2d ed., 1990; E. Kamen, *Introduction to Signals and Systems*, 2d ed., 1989; M. Sain, Miniaturization of large criminal justice systems, *J. Interdis. Model. Simul.*, 1(2):97–122, 1978; S. M. Shinners, *Modern Control System Theory and Design*, 2d ed., 1998.

Blood

The fluid that circulates in the blood vessels of the body. Blood consists of plasma and cells floating within it. The chief components of plasma are proteins (albumin and globulins), anions (mainly chloride and bicarbonate), and cations (mainly sodium, with smaller concentrations of potassium, calcium, and magnesium). The cells are derived from extravascular sites and then enter the circulatory system. They frequently leave the blood vessels to enter the extravascular spaces, where some of them may be transformed into connective tissue cells. The fluid part of the blood is in equilibrium with the tissue fluids of the body. The circulating blood carries nutrients and oxygen to the body cells, and is thus an important means of maintaining the homeostasis of the body. It carries hormones from their sites of origin throughout the body, and is thus the transmitter of the chemical integrators of the body. Blood plasma also circulates immune bodies and contains several of the components essential for the formation of blood clots. Finally, blood transports waste products to excretory organs for elimination from the body. Because of its basic composition (cells surrounded by a matrix), development, and ability to modify into other forms of connective tissues, blood can be regarded as a special form of connective tissue. *See* CONNECTIVE TISSUE.

Formed Elements

The cells of the blood include the red blood cells and the white blood cells. In all vertebrates, except nearly all mammals, the red blood cells or corpuscles contain a nucleus and cytoplasm rich in hemoglobin. In nearly all mammals the nucleus has been extruded during the developmental stages.

Erythrocytes. In normal adult men the blood contains about 5,000,000 red blood corpuscles or erythrocytes per cubic millimeter; in normal adult women, about 4,500,000. The erythrocytes in humans are about 8 micrometers in diameter and about 2 micrometers at their thickest and have a biconcave shape. They contain hemoglobin, which imparts to them their color, and possess an envelope, which when viewed with the electron microscope appears highly structured. The hemoglobin is involved in the transport of oxygen and carbon dioxide and plays a role in maintaining a constant pH in the blood. When circulating in the blood vessels, the red blood cells are not evenly dispersed. In the narrowest vessels, the capillaries, the erythrocytes are often distorted. In certain conditions they may be densely aggregated. This is known as a sludge. The erythrocytes respond to changes in osmotic pressure of the surrounding fluid by swelling in hypotonic fluids and by shrinking irregularly in hypertonic fluids. Shrunken red blood cells are referred to as crenated cells. The average life of the mature red blood cell is surprisingly long, spanning about 120 days. *See* HEMATOLOGIC DISORDERS; HEMOGLOBIN.

Leukocytes. In humans the white blood cells in the blood are fewer in number. There are about 5000–9000/mm^3. In general, there are two varieties, agranular and granular. The agranular cells include the small, medium, and large lymphocytes and the monocyte (**Fig. 1**). The small lymphocytes are spherical, about the diameter of erthyrocytes or a little larger, and constitute about 20–25% of the white blood cells. The medium and large lymphocytes are relatively scarce. In all lymphocytes the nucleus occupies nearly the whole volume of the cell, and the cytoplasm which surrounds it forms a thin shell (**Fig. 2***a*). The cytoplasm stains deeply with basic dyes as a result of its high content of ribonucleic acid, which exists in soluble form and in larger aggregates with protein which are known as ribosomes. Ribosomes are about 18 nanometers in diameter, and are grouped in functional clusters called polysomes, which play an important role in protein synthesis. The typical monocyte is commonly as large as a large lymphocyte (12 μm), and constitutes 3–8% of the white blood cells. The nucleus is relatively small, eccentric, and oval or kidney-shaped. The cytoplasm is relatively larger in volume than that in lymphocytes and does not stain as deeply with basic dyes. *See* RIBOSOMES.

The granular white blood cells or granular leukocytes are of three varieties: neutrophil, eosinophil, and basophil. Their structure varies somewhat in different species, and the following applies to those of humans.

The neutrophils make up 65–75% of the leukocytes. They are about as large as monocytes with a highly variable nucleus, consisting of three to five lobes joined together by threads of chromatin (Fig. 2*b*). The cytoplasm contains numerous minute granules which stain with neutral dyes and eosin. In certain conditions the neutrophils leave the blood vessels and wander into the connective tissue ground substance, where they may then disintegrate, releasing their granules. These granules are rich in certain hydrolytic enzymes, which become active and take part in some phases of the defense mechanisms of

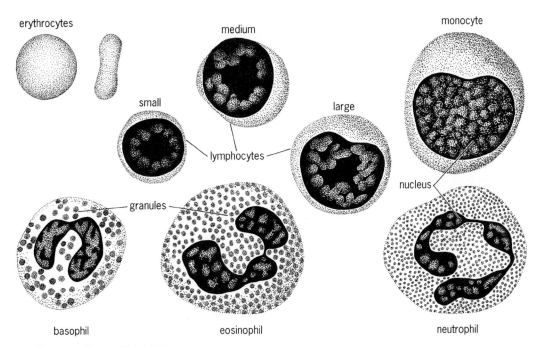

Fig. 1. **Diagrams of human blood cells.**

the body. The granules are considered to be pure lysosomes which are released from the cell during inflammation and in other conditions, thus liberating many enzymes which are important in combating infections, in cleaning up cell debris, and so on. *See* LYSOSOME.

The eosinophils (also called acidophils) are about the same size as the neutrophils but are less numerous, constituting about 1% of the leukocytes. The nucleus commonly contains but two lobes joined by a thin thread of chromatin. The granules which fill the cytoplasm are larger than those of the neutrophils and stain with acid dyes.

The basophils are about the same size as the other granular leukocytes. The nucleus may appear elongated or with one or more constrictions. The granules are moderately large, stain with basic dyes, and are water-soluble.

The functions of the leukocytes while they are circulating in the blood are not known. However, when they leave the blood vessels and enter the connective tissue, they constitute an important part of the defense mechanism and of the repair mechanism. Many of the cells are actively phagocytic and engulf debris and bacteria. Lymphocytes are of two major kinds, T cells and B cells. They are involved in the formation of antibodies and in cellular immunity. Lymphocytes develop into plasma cells, which form antibodies even more effectively than lymphocytes. The lymphocytes and plasma cells may act in conjunction with macrophages in promoting phagocytosis. In addition, lymphocytes and monocytes may develop extravascularly into macrophages (which are also phagocytic) and subsequently into fibroblasts. The fibroblasts are important in the formation of new connective tissue in

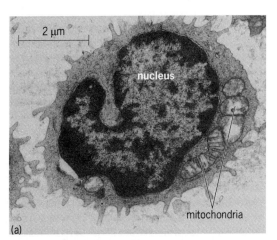

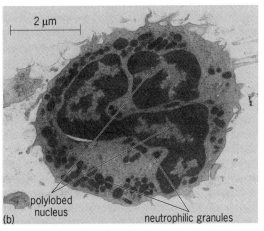

Fig. 2. **Low-power electron micrograph of (a) lymphocyte and (b) neutrophil from the blood of a calf.**

				Relative proportions of leukocytes, %*				
Vertebrate	Red blood cells, × 10^6	Blood platelets, × 10^4	Total leukocytes, × 10^3	Lympho-cytes	Mono-cytes	Neutro-phils	Eosino-phils	Baso-phils
Frog	0.2–0.7	0.34–0.39	2.4–25	24–69	2–20	17–72	6–26	1–37
Chicken	3.0–3.8 (3.3)†	1.7–5.0 (3.1)	9.3–32.3 (20)	37–90	0–1	13–49	2–14	1–7
Cat	7–10 (8.5)	15–36.5 (25.8)	8.6–27 (17.8)	10–64	1–3	31–85	1–10	0–2
Dog	5.6–6.8 (6.1)	16.5–37.8	7–11.4 (10)	9–50	1–6	42–77	0–14	0–1
White rat	5.5–10 (8)	43–48	5–25.6 (12.5)	62–75	1–6	18–36	1–4	0
Rabbit	4–6.4 (5.3)	12.6–100 (22)	5.2–12 (8)	20–90	1–4	8–50	1–3	0.5–30
Cow	5–10 (7)	10–80 (50)	4–12	45–75	2–7	15–47	2–20	0–2
Sheep	8–12 (10.8)	26.3–59.8 (40)	6.4–9.8 (8)	38–72	1–3	21–49	0–20	0.5–2
Pig	5.8–8 (6.5)	32.5–71.5 (52)	11–22 (16)	39–62	2–10	28–51	0.5–11	0.2
Horse	6.5–12.5 (9.5)	10–60 (33)	5.5–12.5 (9)	15–70	0.5–10	30–77	0–12	0–3
Elephant	2–4 (2.8)		6.4–14 (10.2)	40–60	0–5	22.50	6–15	0–1
Camel	3.8–12.6 (8.2)		12.9–27.2 (11.7)	27–65	0.1	21–56	0–19	0–1
Lion	6.9–10.9 (9.3)		8.2–19.8 (14.2)	7–37	0–2	54–97	0–6	0
Humans	4.6–6.2 (5.4)	14–44 (25)	5–9 (7)	20–25	3–8	65–75	0–1	0–0.5

*Relative proportion of leukocytes given as a range of total leukocytes per cubic millimeter of blood.
†Number of cells (average in parentheses) given as a range per cubic millimeter of blood.

regions of injury. *See* CELLULAR IMMUNOLOGY; PHAGOCYTOSIS.

Platelets. The blood platelets are small spindle-shaped or rodlike bodies about 3 μm long and occur in large numbers in circulating blood. In suitably stained specimens they consist of a granular central portion (chromomere) embedded in a homogeneous matrix (hyalomere). They change their shape rapidly on contact with injured vessels or foreign surfaces and take part in clot formation. During this process numerous fibrils of fibrin radiate from the platelets. The platelets are not to be regarded as cells and are thought to be cytoplasmic bits broken off from their cells of origin in bone marrow, the megakaryocytes.

Hematopoiesis. Some of the blood cells are terminal cells in the sense that they are fully differentiated and have little or no capacity for division. These are the erythrocytes and the granulocytes. The agranular leukocytes may develop extravascularly into other cell types (macrophages, fibroblasts, or plasma cells). All blood cells are formed in the hematopoietic organs (chiefly lymph nodes and spleen for agranular leukocytes, and red bone marrow for erythrocytes and granular lukocytes in the adult). In these organs the blood cells develop from precursor cells which themselves are thought by many to be derived eventually from the least differentiated cells of this strain, the hemocytoblast or primitive mesenchymal cell. *See* HEMATOPOIESIS.

Comparative aspects. Though blood cells occur in all vertebrates, they differ in density, in relative proportions, in morphology to some extent, and in their sites or origin (see **table**).

Although all cell types occur in all vertebrates, there are some morphological variations among the cells. The red blood cells of fish are nucleated, are ovoid or spindle-shaped, and may be larger than in any other vertebrate. They are also large in frogs, where they are somewhat less oval than in birds, and nucleated in both. Notable differences in internal structure of leukocytes are most marked in the size,

shape, and staining properties of the granular leukocytes. In the chicken the granules of the neutrophils stain like those of eosinophils and appear rodlike. In the cat the neutrophilic granules are minute, and the eosinophilic granules are rodlike. In the rabbit neutrophilic granules are rather large spheres and stain eosinophilic, while the granules of eosinophils are elongated.

In adult mammals cells of the circulating blood normally arise from bone marrow (red blood cells, granular leukocytes, and platelets), lymph nodules of spleen, lymph nodes, and other lymphoid organs (lymphocytes). But in lower animals (fishes) the connective tissue of the kidney may be important in the origin of all types of blood cells. In other fish the connective tissue of the genitalia may be the site of origin of granulocytes, and the connective tissue of the intestine may be the site of origin of lymphocytes. The liver of some amphibians may be important for the origin of blood cells.   Isidore Gersh

Plasma

Plasma is the residual fluid of blood left after removal of the cellular elements. Serum is the fluid which is obtained after blood has been allowed to clot and the clot has been removed. Serum and plasma differ only in their content of fibrinogen and several minor components which are in large part removed in the clotting process. *See* SERUM.

Plasma proteins. The major constituents of plasma and serum are proteins. The total protein concentration of human serum is approximately 7 g/ml, and most other mammals show similar levels. Birds, reptiles, amphibia, and most fishes have lower protein concentrations of approximately 3–5 g/100 ml. By various methods it can be demonstrated that serum protein is a heterogeneous mixture of a large number of constituents. Only a few are present in higher concentrations, the majority being present in trace amounts. The principal methods for demonstration of heterogeneity and for separation of defined

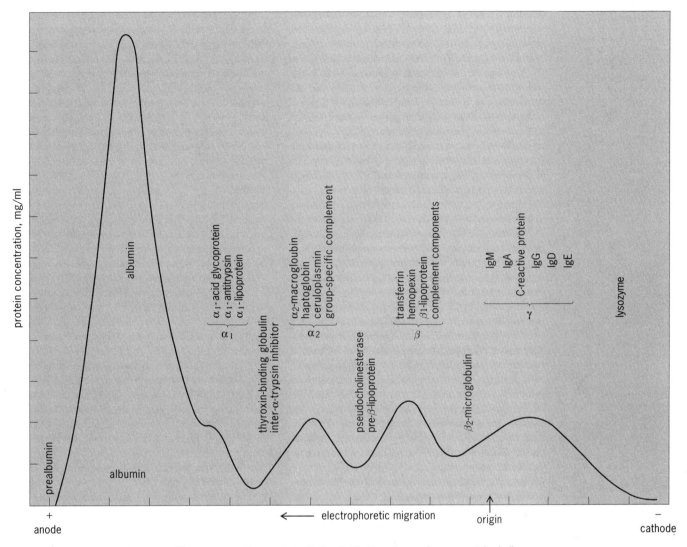

Fig. 3. Paper electrophoresis of normal human serum. Demonstrated is the distribution of several serum proteins in five major electrophoretic fractions, that is, albumin and α_1, α_2, β, and γ-globulins.

components in a high degree of purity are precipitation by various salts or organic compounds, electrophoresis, ultracentrifugation, ion-exchange chromatography, filtration on gel columns, and immunoprecipitation with antibody-containing antisera. Electrophoresis of serum in free solution or on paper strips enables separation of five major fractions called albumin and α_1, α_2, β, and γ-globulins (**Fig. 3**). Electrophoresis on starch or polyacrylamide gels and agar immunoelectrophoresis reveal the presence of more than 30 different protein components in serum. More than 60 protein components have been identified and characterized.

Albumin. This protein makes up more than one-half of the total plasma proteins and has a molecular weight of 69,000. Because of its relatively small molecular size and its high concentration, albumin contributes to 75–80% of the colloid osmotic pressure of plasma. It plays, therefore, a major role in the regulation of the intravascular volume and the fluid exchange between the vascular system and the extravascular space. In addition, albumin serves as a transport protein for various substances. It carries

small ions, such as calcium and iodine, as well as organic compounds like bilirubin.

Immunoglobulins. The immunoglobulins, which represent approximately one-sixth of the total protein, largely constitute the γ-globulin fraction. The immunoglobulins are antibodies circulating in the blood, and thus are also called humoral antibodies. They are of great importance in the organism's defense against infectious agents, as well as other foreign substances. Of the different classes of immunoglobulins that can be distinguished, the principal ones are IgG, IgM, IgA, IgD, and IgE. The molecular structure, including the amino acid sequence, of several antibodies has been elucidated, at least in part. Antibodies are formed under the stimulus of a foreign substance, the antigen, and are specifically directed against this antigen. The specificity of an antibody reaction appears to be ensured by a specific molecular structure in certain parts of the antibody molecule. In addition, inherited structural variations are recognized in molecular regions not concerned directly with the antigen-antibody reaction. Immunoglobulins are thus a complex mixture of a large number—in the order of 10,000–100,000—structurally different antibody molecules. Humoral antibodies are present in most vertebrates, apparently lacking only in certain primitive fishes. Comparative analysis of antibody structure in different species becomes increasingly important for the understanding of evolution. *See* IMMUNOGLOBULIN.

Other proteins. The lipoproteins are another class of serum proteins and make up slightly less than 10% of the total. Presumably they serve as transport proteins for lipids, such as cholesterol, cholesterol esters, and phospholipids. Three major classes can be differentiated: the α_1-, prebeta-, and β_1-lipoproteins.

A number of other serum proteins function as carriers for specific substances. These include transport proteins for metal ions such as the iron-binding protein, transferrin, and the copper-binding protein, ceruloplasmin. The thyroxin-binding globulin transports the thyroid hormone, and transcortin the steroid hormones. Hemoglobin is eliminated from the circulation by haptoglobin, and heme is bound to hemopexin.

Several serum proteins have the capacity to inhibit proteolytic enzymes, thereby protecting serum and possibly tissue proteins against enzymatic degradation. Among others, these include α_1-antitrypsin and the inter-α-trypsin inhibitor. Present in appreciable concentrations are several other glycoproteins, for instance the α_2-macroglobulin and α_1-acid glycoprotein, whose biological functions are not clearly established. A variety of enzymes are also present in plasma, in addition to an array of clotting factors.

Of considerable interest are the complement components. Complement is an important effector system in immune reactions, the target being the cell surface membranes. Its action may result in cell lysis, directed migration of cells, and preparation of damaged cells for uptake and removal by other cells, a process called phagocytosis. *See* COMPLEMENT.

On the one hand, the principal sites of synthesis appear to be the liver cells, where albumin, fibrinogen, α_1-acid glycoprotein, and others are synthesized, and on the other hand, the plasma and lymphoid cells, which are the sites of formation of immunoglobulins and several complement components.

Many plasma proteins of humans and other vertebrates are present in different molecular forms in different individuals. These structural variations are genetically determined. Thus, in addition to the well-known blood groups, there also exist inherited serum protein groups. Examples are the haptoglobins, the group-specific components, which are α_2-globulins with the capacity to bind and transport vitamin D, the different genetic groups of immunoglobulins, and variants of the enzyme pseudocholinesterase. *See* BLOOD GROUPS.

Apart from these inherited qualitative differences, genetically controlled defects of serum proteins exist, that is, the complete or almost complete absence of one or another protein. Some deficiencies are well tolerated by the affected individuals, as analbuminemia

and ahaptoglobinemia, the inherited defects for albumin and haptoglobin, respectively. Other defects, however, lead to severe diseases. Immunoglobulin defects (the most common form is agammaglobulinemia, or the lack of γ-globulin) result in increased susceptibility for bacterial infections. These individuals suffer, if left untreated, from severe and recurrent infections. Another example is the defect of the copper-binding protein ceruloplasmin in Wilson's disease, a grave inherited condition with copper deposition in brain, liver, and kidney.

Many serum proteins show changes in their concentrations during disease states. The determination of serum levels of certain proteins is, therefore, important for diagnostic purposes. The most striking abnormalities are observed in a malignant disorder of the plasma cell system called myeloma and in a disease of the lymphoid cell system known as macroglobulinemia Waldenström. The former is commonly associated with the presence of large amounts of a homogeneous protein of the IgG, IgA, IgD, or IgE class in the patient's serum. The latter is characterized by the presence of an increased homogeneous IgM (γ-macroglobulin) fraction. Other serum proteins show altered concentrations in diseases connected with inflammations, with tissue destruction, or with increased loss of proteins into the urine due to kidney damage. In many infections the so-called C-reactive protein appears in measurable quantities in serum. Damage of liver cells leads often to impairment of protein synthesis. Subsequently, serum levels of albumin and clotting factors may decrease. This results in disordered fluid regulation with accumulation of extravascular fluid, particularly in the abdomen, and in bleeding tendency. *See* CLINICAL PATHOLOGY.

Other constituents. In addition to the proteins, many other important classes of compounds circulate in the blood plasma. Most of these are smaller molecules which diffuse freely through cell membranes and are, therefore, more similarly distributed throughout all the fluids of the body and not as characteristic for plasma or serum as the proteins.

In terms of their concentration and their function, the electrolytes are most important. They are the primary factors in the regulation of the osmotic pressure of plasma, and contribute also to the control of the pH. The chief cations are sodium, potassium, calcium, and magnesium. The chief anions are chloride, bicarbonate, phosphate, sulfate, and organic acids. Sodium and chloride are present in the highest concentrations. Potassium, although present in low concentrations, is of considerable importance, and alterations of potassium metabolism may result in hypo- or hyperpotassemia. These occur in a variety of diseases, in which symptoms involve chiefly the muscles and particularly the heart muscle, with characteristic changes in the electrocardiogram. *See* PH REGULATION (BIOLOGY).

The circulating blood, the system which connects the different parts of the body, also contains the many small compounds which are transported to the sites of synthesis of larger molecules in which they are incorporated, or which are shifted as products of metabolic breakdown to the sites of their excretion from the body. Urea, uric acid, creatinine, and pyruvic acid, important organic metabolites of plasma, are significantly increased in kidney diseases and bring on the symptoms of uremia. Glucose is also an important constituent of plasma because it is a major source of energy for cells throughout the body. Nonesterified fatty acids may, in addition, serve as a source of energy. Free amino acids, the constituents of peptides and proteins, circulate in plasma. Furthermore, bilirubin, vitamin A, steroid hormones, and small peptides like angiotensin and bradykinin are among the many substances present in plasma. Many of these compounds are bound to plasma proteins while they are transported in the blood. This complex formation results generally in a reversible, temporary inactivation of the compound that is being circulated.   Hartwig Cleve

Blood Coagulation

When mammalian blood is shed, it congeals rapidly into a gelatinous clot of enmeshed fibrin threads which trap blood cells and serum. Modern theories envision a succession of reactions leading to the formation of insoluble fibrin from a soluble precursor, fibrinogen (factor I). *See* FIBRINOGEN.

Thrombin. The agent ultimately responsible for the formation of fibrin is a proteolytic enzyme, thrombin, which splits four small polypeptide fragments, the fibrinopeptides, from each molecule of fibrinogen. The remainder of the fibrinogen molecule, now called fibrin monomer, polymerizes to form insoluble fibrin, the structure of the clot. The strands of fibrin are given added strength through covalent bonds between adjacent fibrin monomers, brought about by the action of a second enzyme, the fibrin-stabilizing factor (fibrinase, factor XIII).

Thrombin does not exist as such in circulating blood but is generated during clotting from an inactive precursor, prothrombin (factor II). Under physiologic conditions thrombin is generated through one of two mechanisms, known as the extrinsic and intrinsic pathways. The extrinsic pathway comes into action when blood comes into contact with injured tissues, which provide a protein-phospholipid complex, tissue thromboplastin. The interactions of tissue thromboplastin, calcium ions, and several plasma proteins, including factor VII (formerly called proconvertin or pro-SPCA), Stuart factor (factor X), and proaccelerin (labile factor or factor V), lead to the formation of a prothrombin-converting principle which transforms prothrombin into thrombin.

Other clotting factors. Blood also clots when it touches glass or other negatively charged surfaces, through reactions described as the intrinsic pathway. The steps in the intrinsic pathway are complex and involve the participation of at least eight soluble protein factors, leading to the formation of the prothrombin-converting principle. These factors include, in the apparent order of their participation, Hageman factor (factor XII, the agent affected

by glass), Fletcher factor (a plasma prekallikrein), high-molecular-weight kininogen (Fitzgerald factor), PTA (plasma thromboplastin antecedent, factor XI), Christmas factor (plasma thromboplastin component, factor IX), anti-hemophilic factor (factor VIII), Stuart factor, proaccelerin, and prothrombin. Several of the steps in this process are dependent upon the presence in blood of calcium ions and of phospholipids, the latter derived principally from blood platelets.

The coagulation of blood can also be induced by certain snake venoms which either promote the formation of thrombin or clot fibrinogen directly, accounting in part for their toxicity. Bacterial enzymes, such as staphylcoagulase, derived from *Staphylococcus aureus*, may also induce clotting.

Liquid-state maintenance. The liquid state of the blood is maintained in the circulation by inhibitors in the blood itself and by the action of the liver and the reticuloendothelial system. It is also possible that small clots formed inadvertently within blood vessels may be dissolved by the plasma proteolytic enzyme, plasmin. *See* PLASMIN.

Platelets. Platelets, besides furnishing phospholipids for the clotting process, help to stanch the flow of blood from injured blood vessels by accumulating at the point of injury, forming a plug. Platelets participate in the phenomenon of clot retraction, in which the blood clot shrinks, expelling liquid serum. Although the function of retraction is unknown, individuals in whom this process is impaired have a bleeding tendency.

Function of clotting process. The principal function of the clotting process is to check the flow of blood from severed vessels. The clotting mechanism is also concerned with the process of thrombosis, that is, the formation of a clot (thrombus) within blood vessels. The earliest step in the intrinsic pathway, the alteration of Hageman factor by contact with glass, is intimately associated with inflammation, initiating chemical processes which lead to the liberation of small polypeptides known as kinins which induce pain, dilate and increase the permeability of small blood vessels, and promote the accumulation of leukocytes. *See* THROMBOSIS.

Hereditary defects. Hereditary deficiencies of the function of each of the protein-clotting factors have been described, notably classic hemophilia (in which antihemophilic factor is present in a nonfunctional form) and Christmas disease (the deficiency of Christmas factor), which are disorders of males and clinically indistinguishable. The various hereditary functional deficiencies are associated with a bleeding tendency with the inexplicable exception of Hageman trait, the inherited deficiency of Hageman factor, Fitzgerald trait (the inherited deficiency of high-molecular-weight kininogen), and Fletcher trait, the inherited deficiency of Fletcher factor. Acquired deficiencies of clotting factors, sometimes of great complexity, are also recognized. Therapy for bleeding due to deficiencies of clotting factors often includes the transfusion of blood plasma or fractions of plasma rich in particular substances the individual may lack. *See* HEMOPHILIA; HUMAN GENETICS.

Coagulability tests. Clinical tests of the coagulability of the blood include (1) determination of the clotting time, that is, the time elapsing until shed blood clots; (2) the prothrombin time, the time elapsing until plasma clots in the presence of tissue thromboplastin (and therefore a measure of the extrinsic pathway of clotting); (3) the partial thromboplastin time, the time elapsing until plasma clots in the presence of crude phospholipid (and therefore a measure of the intrinsic pathway of clotting); (4) the enumeration of platelets; and (5) crude quantification of clot retraction and of the various plasma protein-clotting factors. The specific diagnosis for deficiency of each of the clotting factors requires an analysis of the characteristics of the person's plasma and, in many cases, direct comparison of such plasma with that of individuals known to be deficient in the factor in question.

Role of vitamin K. Prothrombin, factor VII, Stuart factor, and Christmas factor are synthesized in the parenchymal cells of the liver in the presence of vitamin K, supplied largely by leafy vegetables and intestinal bacteria. Deficiency of vitamin K, or its inhibition by ingested coumarin compounds, impairs the synthesis of the factors and decreases the coagulability of blood. Fibrinogen and proaccelerin are also synthesized in the liver, and antihemophilic factor is synthesized at least partly in endothelial cells, but the site of synthesis of other factors is not known. *See* VITAMIN K.

Heparin. Heparin, a polysaccharide–sulfuric acid complex found particularly in the liver and lungs, impairs coagulation by interfering with the formation of the prothrombin-converting principle and with the action of thrombin; its presence in normal blood is disputed. Both coumarin and heparin are used clinically to impede coagulation in thrombotic states, including thrombophlebitis and coronary heart disease. *See* CIRCULATION; HEPARIN.   Oscar D. Ratnoff

Bibliography. P. Astrup and J. W. Severinghaus, *The History of Blood Gases, Acids and Bases*, 1986; S. Gosh, *Handbook of Blood and Blood Products*, 1988; J. M. Jandl, *Blood: Textbook of Hematology*, 2d ed., 1996; D. R. Philips and M. A. Schulman (eds.), *Biochemistry of Platelets*, 1986; S. I. Rapaport, *Introduction to Hematology*, 1987; M. M. Wintrobe, *Blood, Pure and Eloquent*, 1980.

Blood groups

Genetically determined markers on the surface of cellular blood elements (red and white blood cells, platelets). They have medical, legal, and anthropologic importance. In medicine, the matching of ABO and Rh groups of recipients and donors before blood transfusion is of paramount importance; other blood groups also can be implicated in incompatibility. Markers on white cells (histocompatibility antigens) are shared by a number of body tissue cells; these markers are important to the survival of transplanted

TABLE 1. Characteristics of blood group antibodies

Characteristic	Naturally acquired	Immune
Immunoglobulin	IgM	IgG
Sedimentation constant	19 S	7 S
Molecular weight	900–1000 kDa	150 kDa
Electrophoretic mobility	Between β and γ	γ
Bind complement	Often	Some
Placental transfer	No	Yes
Direct agglutinin	Yes	Rarely
Hemolytic in vitro	Often	Rarely
Example	Anti-A, anti-B	Rh antibodies

organs and bone marrow. In law, the recognition of identity between bloodstains found at the scene of a crime and those on clothing of a suspect has resulted in many convictions, and blood typing has served to resolve paternity disputes. From an anthropologic standpoint, some blood groups are unique to specific populations and can be a reflection of tribal origin or migration patterns. Blood groups are also valuable markers in gene linkage analysis, and their study has contributed enormously to the mapping of the human genome.

Antibodies. Antibodies are proteins made in response to exposure to blood group antigens. They can be acquired either naturally or through immunization with foreign antigen. The physical and biological properties of these two antibody types are shown in **Table 1**. Human blood can be classified into different groups based on the reactions of red blood cells with blood group antibodies. *See* ANTIBODY; ANTIGEN.

Naturally acquired antibodies. These antibodies are normally found in serum from persons whose red blood cells lack the corresponding antigen. They are of the IgM type, since IgM production is the immune response to carbohydrate antigens and they are stimulated by antigens present in the environment. Many bacteria that constitute normal intestinal flora carry blood group A- and B-like polysaccharides. In newborn infants, as the normal bacterial population of the gut is established, these organisms provide the immune stimulus for anti-A and anti-B production. Three observations support this hypothesis: (1) The serum of newborn infants does not contain naturally acquired anti-A and anti-B; these antibodies begin to appear at about age 3 months. (2) Animals raised in a germ-free environment do not acquire natural antibodies. (3) Infants treated with antibiotics from birth maintain a bacteria-free gut and do not develop anti-A and anti-B until the antibiotic treatment is stopped. Because anti-A and anti-B occur naturally, and because these antibodies can cause rapid life-threatening destruction of incompatible red blood cells, blood for transfusion is always selected to be ABO compatible with the plasma of the recipient.

Immune antibodies. Most blood group antibodies are immune in origin and do not appear in serum or plasma unless the host is exposed directly to foreign red blood cell antigens. The most common stimulating event is blood transfusion or pregnancy. Since many blood group antigens are proteins, the immune response tends to involve first the formation of IgM antibodies and then IgG.

Because of the large number of different blood group antigens, it is impossible, when selecting blood for transfusion, to avoid transfusing antigens that the recipient lacks. However, these foreign antigens can be immunogenic; a single-unit transfusion of Rh D-positive to an Rh D-negative recipient causes production of anti-D in about 85% of cases. Consequently, in addition to matching for ABO types, Rh D-negative blood is almost always given to Rh D-negative recipients. In about 3% of all transfusions, antibodies to other blood group system antigens are formed.

In pregnancy, fetal red blood cells cross the placenta and enter the maternal circulation, particularly at delivery. The fetal red blood cells may carry paternally derived antigens that are foreign to the mother and stimulate antibody production. These antibodies may affect subsequent pregnancies by destroying the fetal red blood cells and causing a disease known as erythroblastosis fetalis. *See* RH INCOMPATIBILITY.

Reactions with red blood cells. Blood group antigen–antibody interactions are detected either directly by agglutination or complement-mediated hemolysis or indirectly by use of the antiglobulin test. The stages in these tests can be summarized as follows:

Direct tests, for the detection of IgM antibodies:
1. Mix serum and red blood cells.
2. Incubate (room temperature, optional).
3. Centrifuge.
4. Examine for agglutination and hemolysis.

Indirect tests, for the detection of IgG antibodies:
1. Mix serum and red blood cells (an enhancement reagent, to promote antibody uptake, may be incorporated here).
2. Incubate (37°C).
3. Examine for agglutination and hemolysis (optional).
4. Wash to remove unbound globulins.
5. Add antihuman globulin reagent.
6. Centrifuge.
7. Examine for agglutination.
8. Confirm negative tests with IgG-coated red blood cells.

Direct reactions occur in two phases: a coating phase in which antibody attaches to corresponding antigens on red cells; and an agglutination (clumping) phase during which red blood cells come close enough together for antibody molecules to span intercellular distances and bind to adjacent red blood cells to form an agglutination lattice.

Immunoglobulin M (IgM) antibodies directly agglutinate saline-suspended red blood cells; for this reason, they have been called complete antibodies. The ability of IgM antibodies to react in this manner is a reflection of both size and valency, that is, the number of antigen-binding sites (maximum of 10) per molecule. IgM antibodies are large enough to span the distance between red blood cells in suspension. Being multivalent, they can attach to antigens on adjacent red blood cells. Many IgM antibodies, especially naturally acquired anti-A and anti-B, also cause complement-mediated lysis of red blood cells.

Immunoglobulin G (IgG) antibodies, with only two antigen-binding sites per molecule, do not regularly cause direct agglutination of saline-suspended red blood cells, although they may do so if high-molecular-weight compounds or proteins (such as polyvinylpyrrolidone or bovine albumin) are added to the reaction medium. Because an additive is required to complete the agglutination of IgG-coated red blood cells, IgG antibodies have been called incomplete antibodies. In simple terms, albumin neutralizes the effect of the negative charge on red blood cells. This negative charge serves to keep red blood cells apart in suspension. Reduction in surface charge reduces intercellular repulsion, permitting red blood cells to come close together so that antigen-binding sites on IgG molecules can attach to adjacent red blood cells. *See* IMMUNOGLOBULIN.

Antigens, genes, and blood groups. Almost 300 distinct blood group antigens have been identified on human red blood cells. Biochemical analysis has revealed that most antigen structures are either protein or lipid in nature; in some instances, blood group specificity is determined by the presence of attached carbohydrate moieties. The human A and B antigens, for example, can be either glycoprotein or glycolipid, with the same attached carbohydrate structure. With few exceptions, blood group antigens are an integral part of the cell membrane.

A number of different notations are used, and different concepts have been put forth to explain the genetics of the human blood groups. The presence of a gene in the host is normally reflected by the presence of the corresponding antigen on the red blood cells. Usually, a single locus determines antigen expression, and there are two or more forms of a gene or alleles (for example, *A* and *B*) that can occupy a locus. Each individual inherits one allele from each parent. For a given blood group, when the same allele (for example, allele *A*) is inherited from both parents, the offspring is homozygous for *A* and only the antigen structure (A) will be present on the red blood cells. When different alleles are inherited (that is, *A* and *B*), the individual is heterozygous for both *A* and *B*, and both A and B antigens will be found on the red blood cells.

In some blood group systems, two genes (loci) govern the expression of multiple blood group antigens within that system. These loci are usually closely linked, located adjacent to each other on the chromosome. Such complex loci may contain multiple alleles and are referred to as haplotypes. *See* HUMAN GENETICS.

Blood group systems. Approximately 250 red cell antigens have been assigned to 29 different blood group systems (**Table 2**). For an antigen to form a new blood group system, the antigen must be defined by a human alloantibody, it must be an inherited

TABLE 2. Human blood group systems

System name	ISBT* symbol	System number	Antigens in system†	Chromosome location‡	Gene products	CD number§
ABO	ABO	001	4	9q34.1-q34.2	A = α-N-acetylgalactos-aminyl transferase B = α-galactosyl transferase	
MNS	MNS	002	43	4q28-q31	GYPA = glycophorin A; 43-kDa single-pass glycoprotein GYPB = glycophorin B; 25-kDa single-pass glycoprotein	CD235
P	P1	003	1	22q11-qter	α-Galactosyl transferase	
Rh	RH	004	50	1p36.13-p34	RHD and RHCE, 30–32-kDa multipass polypeptides	CD240
Lutheran	LU	005	19	19q13.2	78- and 85-kDa single-pass glycoproteins	CD239
Kell	KEL	006	27	7q33	93-kDa single-pass glycoprotein	CD238
Lewis	LE	007	6	19p13.3	α-Fucosyl transferase	
Duffy	FY	008	6	1q22-q23	38.5-kDa multipass glycoprotein	CD234
Kidd	JK	009	3	18q11-q12	43-kDa multipass glycoprotein	
Diego	DI	010	21	17q12-q21	95–105-kDa multipass glycoprotein	CD233
Yt	YT	011	2	7q22	160-kDa dimeric GPI-linked glycoprotein	
Xg	XG	012	2	Xp22.33, YP11.32	22–29-kDa single-pass glycoprotein	CD99
Sciana	SC	013	5	1p36.2-p22.1	60–68-kDa glycoprotein	
Dombrock	DO	014	5	12p13.2-12p12.1	47–58-kDa GPI-linked glycoprotein	
Colton	CO	015	3	7p14	28- and 40–60-kDa multipass glycoproteins; aquaporin 1	
Landsteiner-Weiner	LW	016	3	19p13.3	37–43-kDa single-pass glycoprotein	CD242
Chido/Rogers	CH/RG	017	9	6p21.3	Glycoproteins adsorbed onto red blood cells	
Hh	H	018	1	19q13	α-Fucosyl transferase	
Kx	XK	019	1	Xp21.1	37-kDa multipass glycoprotein	CD173
Gerbich	GE	020	8	2q14-q21	GYPC = glycophorin C; 40-kDa single-pass glycoprotein. Or glycophorin D; 30-kDa single-pass glycoprotein.	CD236
Cromer	CROM	021	13	1q32	CD55; GPI-linked glycoprotein	CD55
Knops	KN	022	8	1q32	CD35; single-pass glycoprotein	CD35
Indian	IN	023	2	11p13	CD44; 80-kDa single-pass glycoprotein	CD44
Ok	OK	024	1	19pter-p13.2	CD147; 35–69-kDa glycoprotein	CD147
Raph	RAPH	025	1	11p15.5	MER2; glycoprotein	
John Milton Hagen	JMH	026	1	15q24.1	GPI-linked protein	CD108
I	I	027	1	6p24.2	N-acetylglucosaminyl transferase	
Globoside	GLOB	028	1	3q26.1	β-galactosyl transferase	
Gill	GIL	029	1	9p13.3	Aquaporin 3	

*International Society of Blood Transfusion.
†Nonglycolipid antigens on red blood cells are either single-pass/multipass proteins or glycosylphosphatidylinosityl (GPI)-linked proteins.
‡Chromosome locations of genes/loci are identified by the arm (p = short; q = long), followed by the region, then by the band within the region, in both cases numbered from the centromere; ter = end.
§CD = cluster designation.

character, the gene encoding it must have been identified and sequenced, and its chromosome location must be known. Further, the gene involved must be distinct from other blood group system genes, and not a closely linked homologue of a known blood group gene.

ABO blood group. Discovered by Karl Landsteiner in 1901, ABO was the first human blood group system to be described (**Table 3**). Three major alleles at the *ABO* locus on chromosome 9 govern the expression of A and B antigens. Gene *A* encodes for a protein (α-N-acetylgalactosaminyl transferase) that attaches a blood group–specific carbohydrate (α-N-acetyl-D-galactosamine) and confers blood group A activity to

a preformed carbohydrate structure called H antigen. Gene *B* encodes for an α-galactosyl transferase that attaches α-D-galactose and confers blood group B activity to H antigen. In both instances, some H remains unchanged. The *O* gene has no detectable product; H antigen remains unchanged and is strongly expressed on red blood cells.

These three genes account for the inheritance of four common phenotypes: A, B, AB, and O. Blood types A and O are the most common, and AB the least common. The *A* and *B* genes are codominant; that is, when the gene is present the antigen can be detected. The *O* gene is considered an amorph since its product cannot be detected. When either A or B antigens are present on red blood cells, the corresponding antibody or antibodies should not be present in the serum or plasma. In adults, when A or B or both are absent from the red blood cells, the corresponding naturally acquired antibody is present in the serum. This reciprocal relationship between antigens on the red blood cells and antibodies in the serum is known as Landsteiner's law. Other ABO phenotypes do exist but are quite rare. Further, the A blood type can be subdivided, based on strength of

TABLE 3. ABO blood group system

Blood group	RBC antigens	Possible genotypes	Plasma antibody
A	A	A/A or A/O	Anti-B
B	B	B/B or B/O	Anti-A
O	—	O/O	anti-A and anti-B
AB	A and B	A/B	—

antigen expression, with A_1 red blood cells having the most A antigen.

At the molecular level, *A* and *B* allelic complementary deoxyribonucleic acids (cDNAs) are identical except for seven nucleotide substitutions resulting in four amino acid substitutions between A and B transferases. The majority of O alleles have a single nucleotide substitution close to the N-terminal of the coding sequence that shifts the reading frame of codons and results in translation of a protein lacking A or B transferase activity.

In addition to the ABO locus, expression of A and B is influenced by *H/b* and *Se/se* genes on chromosome 19. The *H* gene–specified transferase attaches fucose to paragloboside, a red blood cell membrane glycolipid. The H antigen thus formed is the structure

---

TABLE 4. Function and disease associations of blood group antigens

Antigens	Function/disease associations
A/B	Weakened in leukemia, especially cases involving chromosome 9 translocations, and in stress-induced hemopoiesis
	Altered (A to B) in acquired-B phenomenon due to modification by bacterial enzymes, especially in patients with septicemia or lesions of the gastrointestinal tract
MNSsU	Receptor for some *Escherichia coli* and for *Plasmodium falciparum*
	Receptor for complement bacteria and viruses
	Glycosylation imparts a negative electrical charge to red blood cells
Rh	May be expressed weakly in leukemia and myeloproliferative disorders
	Common target for IgG autoantibodies causing immune hemolytic anemia
	May play a role in transport of ammonia across red blood cell membranes
Lu	Adhesion molecule, integrin
Kel	Possible endopeptidase activity
	Target antigen in 0.4% of IgG autoantibodies causing immune hemolytic anemia
	Weakly expressed on red blood cells, in some cases X-linked chronic granulomatous disease, associated with acanthocytosis
	Absence in Ko (null phenotype) associated with cardiomyopathy, hypertension
Le	Le^b antigen is receptor for *Helicobacter pylori*
Fy	70% of African-Americans are Fy(a-b-); such red blood cells are resistant to invasion by *Plasmodium vivax*
Jk	Urea transporter
Di	Synonymous with band 3 or anion exchanger (AE1), involved with HCO_3^-, Cl^- transport across red blood cell membrane
Yt	Synonymous with red blood cell membrane acetylcholinesterase
	Absent on cells deficient in glycosylphosphatidylinosityl-linked proteins (paroxysmal nocturnal hemoglobinuria III cells)
	Reduced levels in myelodysplasia associated with chromosome 7 abnormalities and in some cases of systemic lupus erythematosus
Xg	Adhesion molecule
Do	Absent on cells deficient in glycosylphosphatidylinosityl-linked proteins (paroxysmal nocturnal hemoglobinuria III cells)
Co	Synonymous with CHIP-1, water transport protein
	Absence associated with monosomy 7, congenital dyserythropoietic anemia
	Weak expression seen in some chromosome 7 rearrangements, leukemia
LW	Intercellular adhesion molecule (ICAM) that binds to leukocyte integrins
CH/RG	Synonymous with C4 (C3, C4, and C5 are components of human complement)
	Patients with inherited low levels of C4 are prone to develop autoimmue disorders (insulin-dependent diabetes, autoimmune chronic active hepatitis)
	Null genes and specific allotypes are associated with Graves' disease and rheumatoid arthritis
	C4B-deficient (Ch-negative) children have increased susceptibility to bacterial meningitis
	Rg-negative individuals are predisposed to develop systemic lupus erythematosus
H	Increased expression in hemopoietic stress
	Weakened in leukemia and on malignant tissue cells
Kx	Possible transport protein
	Essential for red blood cell membrane integrity; absence on red blood cells associated with McLeod syndrome and acanthocytosis
	Absence on granulocytes associated with X-linked chronic granulomatous disease
GE	Interact with red blood cell membrane protein 4.1
	Reduced expression associated with hereditary elliptocytosis
CROM	Inhibits assembly and accelerates decay of C3 and C5 convertases
	Absent on cells deficient in glycosylphosphatidylinosityl-linked proteins (paroxysmal nocturnal hemoglobinuria III cells)
	Null phenotype (INAB) associated with intestinal disorders
KNOPS	Synonymous with complement receptor 1 (CR1)
	Mediates phagocytosis of cells coated with C3/C4
	Possible site for invasion by babesia
IN	Adhesion molecule
Raph	Raph-negative individuals predisposed to renal failure
Ii	Altered in diseases resulting in hemopoietic stress
	Anti-I associated with cold agglutinin disease and mycoplasma pneumonia
	Anti-i associated with infectious mononucleosis and lymphoproliferative disorders
P	Synonymous with globoside, receptor for Parvovirus B19
	Target for IgG autoantibody causing paroxysmal cold hemoglobinuria
	Cytotoxic IgM and IgG3 antibodies to globoside are associated with spontaneous abortions
AnWj	Receptor for *Haemophilus influenzae*
JMH	Absent on cells deficient in glycosylphosphatidylinosityl-linked proteins (paroxysmal nocturnal hemoglobinuria III cells)
	JMH-negative phenotype associated with congenital dyserythropoietic anemia

on red blood cells that serves as the substrate for *A* and *B* gene–specified transferases described above. In rare individuals, absence of *H* (that is, homozygous *h*) results in absence of H structures on red blood cell membranes and no substrate on which *A* and *B* gene products can act. The resulting phenotype is referred to as Bombay (or O_h). The *Se* gene governs the addition of fucose to type 1 chains in the secretions (such as saliva, plasma, urine) to form water-soluble H-active structures. *Se* is present in about 80% of the population; depending on genes present at the ABO locus, the secretions of *Se* individuals will contain A or B antigens or both in addition to H antigens.

Rh blood group. Currently 50 antigens are assigned to the Rh blood group system, although D is the most important. Red blood cells that carry D are called Rh-positive; red blood cells lacking D are called Rh-negative. Other important Rh antigens are C, c, E, and e. Rh antigen expression is controlled by two adjacent homologous structural genes on chromosome 1 that are inherited as a pair or haplotype. The *RhD* gene encodes D antigen and is absent on both chromosomes of most Rh-negative subjects. The *RhCE* gene encodes CE protein. Nucleotide substitutions account for amino acid differences at two positions on the CE protein and result in the Cc and Ee polymorphisms. Point mutations or rearrangement of exons from *D* with those of *CE* appear to account for other Rh polymorphisms.

Other blood groups. Prior to the discovery of Rh, Landsteiner and Philip Levine discovered three more blood group antigens (M, N, and P1) following injection of human red blood cells into rabbits. After adsorption of the rabbit serum to remove species antibodies, anti-M and anti-N were found to agglutinate 78% and 72% of human red blood cell samples, respectively. Family studies showed that M and N were inherited as the products of alleles. Later, through use of the antiglobulin test, S and s antigens were assigned to the MN system, and now over 40 MNS system antigens have been described. Anti-P1 reacted with red blood cells from 78% of Caucasians. The *P1* gene was shown to be inherited independently from the *ABO* and *MN* loci. Human examples of antibodies to M, N, and P1 were soon discovered, but they tend not to react at body temperatures and are, therefore, not usually of concern in blood transfusion practice.

Use of the antiglobulin test led to the discovery of most other blood group antigens and systems. Many of the antibodies defining the antigens were encountered as the cause of hemolytic disease of the newborn. Since such antibodies also cause accelerated destruction of transfused incompatible red blood cells, it is necessary to test a patient's serum for unexpected antibodies prior to blood transfusions.

Antigens that do not meet the criteria for assignment to a specific blood group system have been placed into collections, based primarily on biochemical data or phenotypic association, or into a series of either high- or low-frequency antigens.

Biological role. The function of blood group antigens has been increasingly apparent. Single-pass proteins such as the LU and XG proteins are thought to serve as adhesion molecules that interact with integrins on the surface of white blood cells. Multipass proteins such as band 3, which carries the DI system antigens, are involved in the transportation of ions through the red blood cell membrane bilipid layer. GPI-linked proteins such as CROM, also known as decay accelerating factor (DAF), are involved with complement regulation on the red blood cell surface. Some blood group antigens are essential to the integrity of the red blood cell membrane, for their absence results in abnormal surface shape; for example, absence of KEL protein leads to the formation of acanthocytes, and absence of RH protein results in stomatocytosis and hemolytic anemia (**Table** 4).

Many membrane structures serve as receptors for bacteria and other microorganisms (Table 4). For example, the FY or Duffy protein is the receptor on red blood cells for invasion by *Plasmodium vivax*, the cause of benign tertian malaria. Particularly significant is the fact that Fy(a-b-) phenotype is virtually nonexistent among Caucasians but has an incidence of around 70% among African-Americans. Presumably, the Fy(a-b-) phenotype evolved as a selective advantage in areas where *P. vivax* is endemic. Similarly, the S-s-U-red blood cell phenotype in the MNS blood group system affords protection against *P. falciparum*, or malignant tertian malaria. Yet other blood group antigens can be altered in disease states; A, B, and H antigens are sometimes weakened in leukemia or may be modified by bacterial enzymes in patients with septicemia. *See* BLOOD; IMMUNOLOGY.

W. John Judd

Bibliography. G. L. Daniels, *Human Blood Groups*, 2d ed., Blackwell Science, Oxford, 2002; P. D. Issitt and D. J. Anstee, *Applied Blood Group Serology*, 4th ed., Montgomery Scientific Publications, Durham, NC, 1998; M. E. Reid and C. Lomas-Francis, *Blood Group Antigen Factsbook*, 2d ed., Academic Press, San Diego, 2003.

Blood vessels

Tubular channels for blood transport, of which there are three principal types: arteries, capillaries, and veins. Only the larger arteries and veins in the body bear distinct names.

Arteries carry blood away from the heart through a system of successively smaller vessels. The three major layers which exist in the arterial wall are the outer adventitia of connective tissue, the middle elastic or muscular layer or both, and the inner lining or endothelium of squamous cells. The proportionate thickness of these layers varies according to the size and location of the artery. In the largest arteries close to the heart, such as the aorta, elastic fibers are prominent, allowing expansion and recoil with each systolic contraction of the heart. The medium-sized arteries have a predominantly muscular wall (smooth muscle fibers) with some elastic fibers. In the smaller arterioles the middle coat is entirely muscle, and even this is gradually lost as the arterioles become smaller.

Capillaries are the smallest but most extensive blood vessels, forming a network everywhere in the body tissues. Capillary beds form a huge total surface area of thin endothelium, serving as a semipermeable membrane for passage of materials between the circulatory system and body tissues. Normally, only a small portion of a capillary bed carries blood, the remaining portion being temporarily bypassed. Such alterations allow for shifts of blood, as well as increases or decreases in volume, of a particular region or organ, and constitute one of the homeostatic mechanisms of the body. *See* HOMEOSTASIS.

Veins carry blood from the capillary beds back to the heart through increasingly larger vessels. The walls of veins and venules superficially resemble those of arteries, but with several marked differences. Veins have larger diameters and thinner walls and are more distensible than corresponding arteries; they have much fewer muscle fibers and elastic fibers in their walls. Veins differ from arteries in having valves which prevent backflow of blood. The pattern of branching of veins is less regular and less constant than that of their arterial counterparts. The larger veins and arteries contain small blood vessels (vasa vasorum) for nourishment of the walls, and are innervated by a complex system of nerves from the autonomic nervous system, which innervates the smooth muscles. Contraction of these muscles is also under control of various hormones, such as norepinephrine.

In certain locations blood vessels are modified for particular functions, as the sinusoids of the liver and the spleen and the choroid plexuses of the brain ventricles. *See* LYMPHATIC SYSTEM.   Walter Bock

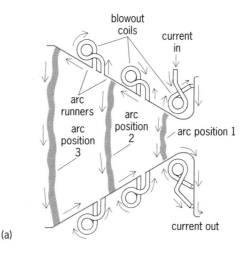

(a)

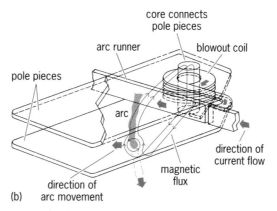

(b)

Fig. 2. Arc suppressor: (*a*) cross section and (*b*) cut-away view. As the arc progresses along the runners, it draws current through the blowout coils whose magnetic fields then drive the arc further out until it extinguishes.

Blowout coil

A coil that produces a magnetic field in an electrical switching device for the purpose of lengthening and extinguishing an electric arc formed as the contacts of the switching device part to interrupt the current. The magnetic field produced by the coil is approximately perpendicular to the arc. The interaction between the arc current and the magnetic field produces a force driving the arc in the direction perpendicular to both the magnetic flux and the arc current (**Fig. 1**).

In alternating-current circuits the arc is usually extinguished at in instant of time when the current passes through zero before reversing its direction. If, within a short time around current zero, sufficient energy can be removed from the arc, conduction will cease. The function of the blowout coil is to move the arc into a region inside a circuit interrupter, such as arc chutes in circuit breakers, where the energy removal process takes place. *See* CIRCUIT BREAKER.

In direct-current circuits there are no natural current zeros. An arc strikes when a switching device opens. Current will continue to flow as long as the voltage across the open contacts is sufficient to sustain the arc. To interrupt this dc arc, the arc must be converted to a form that, to continue, requires more than the available voltage. Thus, in a dc switching device, the function of the blowout coil is to increase the length of the arc, which increases the arc voltage, and also to move the arc into regions, inside the interrupter, where the arc voltage can be further increased.

The blowout coil is either connected in series with contacts or inserted as the arc moves along an arc runner (**Fig. 2**).   Thomas H. Lee

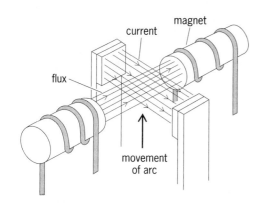

Fig. 1. Relation of directions of current, magnetic flux, and movement of arc.

Blowpipe

In glass blowing, a long straight tube on which molten glass is gathered and worked, partly by blowing into the tube. The blowpipe is spun to shape the glass object further by centrifugal force, or by a tool, in which case the blowpipe acts as a spindle for turning.

In analytical chemistry, a blowpipe is a small, tapered, and frequently curved tube that directs a jet, usually of air, into a flame to concentrate the flame onto an unknown substance. Coloration of the flame and other characteristic reactions in the reducing and in the oxidizing portions of the flame created by the blowpipe aid in identifying the substance. Such a blowpipe may be blown directly by the analyst, from a bellows, or from a pressurized line.

Frank H. Rockett

Blue straggler star

A star that is a member of a stellar association and is located at an unusual position on the association's color-magnitude diagram, above the turnoff from the main sequence.

Characteristics. A stellar cluster is observationally characterized by its color-magnitude diagram, which represents each member's luminosity plotted against its color, which in turn is related to its effective temperature. The location and structure of the various regions of a cluster's color-magnitude diagram can be made to yield crucial information on its age and chemical composition by exploiting the knowledge of the evolutionary tracks of stars with a specified range of initial masses and abundances. In order to make this method work properly, however, it is assumed that all the stars in a cluster are coeval (born at the same time), single, and isolated objects and that they are internally stable, nonrotating, nonmagnetic, and unmixed. The remarkable overall consistency between the observed color-magnitude diagrams and stellar evolutionary theory provides the most convincing evidence for the basic soundness of both the theory and the assumptions. *See* COLOR INDEX; HERTZSPRUNG-RUSSELL DIAGRAM; MAGNITUDE (ASTRONOMY).

The existence of a special group of stars known as blue stragglers represents a challenge to this tidy scenario. They were discovered by A. Sandage in 1953 in the galactic globular cluster M3 (see **illustration**). The blue stragglers are located below the horizontal branch and above the turnoff from the main sequence. They form a new sequence extending from the extrapolation of the main sequence to higher luminosities on the left to the red giant branch on the right. While the majority of the cluster members fall rather precisely on the expected isochrones for the approximately 15×10^9-year age of the cluster, the 50 or so blue stragglers in M3 are located on much younger isochrones. It seems, in other words, as if the blue stragglers somehow never made it across the gap between the main sequence and the red

giant branch as expected from stellar evolutionary theory and are, therefore, true stragglers with respect to the main body of stars in the cluster.

Occurrence. More than 3000 objects of this type have been found in practically every known type of dense stellar association, including dwarf spheroidal galaxies. They represent, therefore, a ubiquitous phenomenon. In the case of the globular clusters where this phenomenon is most pronounced, blue stragglers are found in every cluster observed so far in numbers ranging from a few dozen to a few hundred. *See* GALAXY, EXTERNAL.

In most globular clusters, they are found mainly in or very near the dense core, but in a few they have also been detected in the outer regions. This suggests that their radial distribution is bimodal with a high peak in the center decreasing in the middle and rising again in the periphery of the cluster. The total number of blue stragglers in a cluster, however, does not seem to be correlated with either the stellar density in the core or its total mass.

All indications point to these objects physically having masses consistent with their observed position above and blueward of the turnoff point of the cluster color magnitude diagram. Thus, blue stragglers in globular clusters can be clearly defined as objects having the following general range of physical parameters: temperatures between 6000 and 10,000 K, masses between 1 and 2.5 solar masses, luminosities between 3 and 30 solar luminosities, and low metal abundances consistent with the rest of the stars in the cluster.

Origin. Since such stars cannot exist in the cluster under the assumptions made above, some or all of the assumptions must be wrong. The simplest explanation of the phenomenon, of course, is violation of the coeval hypothesis; that is, the blue stragglers really are younger than the rest of the cluster members,

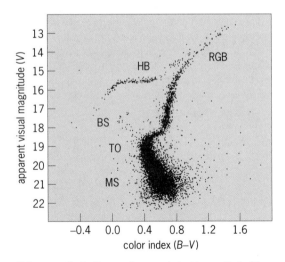

Color-magnitude diagram [apparent visual magnitude *(V)* versus color index *(B-V)*] of 10,637 stars in the galactic globular cluster M3 (NGC 5272). The important evolutionary stages are marked by MS (main sequence), TO (turn-off), RGB (red giant branch), HB (horizontal branch), and BS (blue stragglers). (*After R. Buonanno et al., High precision photometry of 10,000 stars in M3, Mem. Soc. Astron. It., 57:391-393, 1986*)

perhaps because of a recent burst of star formation. This delayed-formation scenario is possible in young open clusters and some dwarf spheroidal galaxies. However, since there is no evidence at all for recent star formation episodes in the galactic globular clusters, some other assumption must be flawed if the blue stragglers in these systems are to be explained. Three possibilities related to delayed evolution or extended lifetime in a strictly coeval ensemble have been analyzed: internal mixing that supplies new fuel from the outer layers to the core, mass transfer or merging of two low-mass stars in a binary system, or a collision between two or more unrelated stars. These last two events would lead to the formation of a relatively unevolved, more massive object only apparently younger than the rest of the cluster population. Apart from the lack of a plausible physical mixing mechanism in a single star, observations of the surface gravity and luminosities of the more massive blue stragglers seem to be inconsistent with the first hypothesis. *See* BINARY STAR.

Therefore, most astronomers in the field favor the last scenarios of the mass transfer or merging of stars in a primordial binary system and the formation of a relatively unevolved massive star by direct collision of two stars that involves a resonant 3- or 4-body encounter. The objects formed by the latter mechanism would be expected to be found in the inner denser regions where the collision probability between stars is very high, while the former mechanism would be expected to give rise preferentially to objects outside the core where primordial binaries are not so easily disrupted by encounters with neighboring objects.

All the characteristics described above can be reasonably well understood if it is assumed that both types of blue stragglers coexist in a globular cluster. The possibility of observationaly distinguishing these two populations is the subject of intense debate. The cluster-to-cluster variability in numbers of blue stragglers in the core may be the best indication available of the cluster's dynamic state, since the cluster must use its binaries to reduce the catastrophic effects of the runaway collapse that many clusters face at some point in their evolution.

By their very existence, blue stragglers sharpen the understanding of the nature of the stellar populations and their interactions in all clusters. They represent, therefore, a crucial tool in deciphering the origin and history of these objects. *See* STAR CLUSTERS; STELLAR EVOLUTION.   Francesco Paresce

Bibliography. M. B. Davies et al., Blue straggler production in globular clusters, *Mon. Not. Roy. Astron. Soc.*, 349:129–134, 2004; M. Mapelli et al., The contribution of primordial binaries to the blue straggler population in 47 Tucanae, *Astrophys. J.*, 605:29–32, 2004.

Blueberry

Several species of the genus *Vaccinium*, plant order Ericales, ranging from low-growing, almost prostrate plants to vigorous shrubs reaching a height of 12–15 ft (3.5–4.5 m). The fruit, a berry, is usually black and covered with bluish bloom, generally occurring in clusters and has numerous small seeds, a characteristic that distinguishes the blueberry from the huckleberry, which has 10 rather large, gritty seeds. Although there are blueberry species on other continents, all cultivated varieties in the United States are American in origin. *See* ERICALES.

Types. The dryland blueberry (*V. ashei*) is adapted to relatively dry soils and has been brought under cultivation in Florida and Georgia.

In the Northeast the lowbush blueberry (*V. lamarckii*) grows wild over thousands of acres of dry hillsides, where it is harvested commercially, especially in Maine, but also in other New England states, Michigan, Minnesota, and a few others. Some berries are sold fresh, but most are canned or frozen to be used for pies. In some areas the plants are burned over every 3 years to kill certain weeds and to remove the old wood, thus stimulating vigorous new growth. Lowbush blueberries are harvested with a small scoop, resembling a cranberry scoop, which combs the berries from the plants, whereas most of the highbush and dryland berries are picked by hand.

In the Northwest fruit of the evergreen blueberry (*V. ovatum*) is harvested in the wild, and tons of the leafy twigs are shipped for use as florists' greens.

The highbush blueberry, represented by *V. australe* and *V. corymbosum*, provides most of the cultivated plants. These are bushes reaching 6–8 ft (1.8–2.4 m) in height, and normally propagated by hardwood or softwood cuttings. The highbush blueberry is found in swampy land, usually on hummocks, so that its roots are not actually submerged. It does best in an acid soil, preferably sand and peat, and must have an ample water supply and good drainage. It can be grown on ordinary mineral soils if the water is properly regulated and the soil acidity is kept in the range pH 4–6. Nitrogen is utilized as ammonium rather than nitrate. The highbush blueberry has been under cultivation since 1910, when the first experiments on its culture were reported. Production in the United States is greatest in New Jersey, followed by Michigan, North Carolina, and Washington. The fruit is sold fresh, canned, and frozen. The blueberry is becoming increasingly popular in home gardens, although its cultural requirements are rather exacting. For garden culture, mulching with sawdust or other organic matter is desirable because the roots are shallow. *See* FRUIT.   J. Harold Clarke

Diseases. Blueberry diseases and their control are a major concern of commercial growers and home gardeners. Blueberries are affected by numerous diseases; however, the severity and economic importance vary from one blueberry growing region to another.

In the southeastern United States, fungal diseases such as stem canker (caused by *Botryosphaeria corticis*), stem blight (*B. dothidea*), and leaf spot (*Gloesporium minus*) are very prevalent and destructive, but are of little or no importance in the northern areas. Godronia canker, caused by the fungus *Godronia cassandrae*, is important in the northern

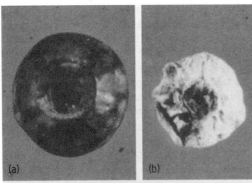

Mummy berry disease caused by the fungus *Monilinia vaccinii-corymbosi*. (a) Healthy fruit. (b) Diseased fruit. (c) Mummified fruit with spore-bearing structures called apothecia. (*Parts a and b from R. D. Milholland, Sclerotium germination and histopathology of Monilinia vaccinii-corymbosi on highbush blueberry, Phytopathology, 67:848–854, 1977; part c from R. D. Milholland, Factors affecting apothecium development of Monilinia vaccinii-corymbosi from mummified highbush blueberry fruit, Phytopathology, 64:296–300, 1974*)

regions of British Columbia, Michigan, Maine, Massachusetts, and Nova Scotia, but is not found in the south. Resistant varieties are the only means of controlling stem cankers and blights. Leaf spotting diseases can be controlled with fungicides.

Blueberry stunt is a destructive disease caused by a primitive bacterialike organism, a mycoplasma. Characteristic symptoms are small leaves, yellowing along the margins and between lateral veins, and reduced plant vigor. Viral diseases such as mosaic, shoestring, and necrotic ringspot are normally of minor importance; however, the red ringspot virus is a serious problem in New Jersey. The use of certified or virus-free plants, as well as roguing diseased bushes, is required for effective control of stunt and viral diseases.

Mummy berry, caused by the fungus *Monilinia vaccinii-corymbosi*, is one of the most widespread and devastating diseases of blueberry. The disease first appears as a blighting of new growth, and

prior to harvest the infected berries become a light cream color rather than normal blue and drop to the ground. The pathogenic cycle of the fungus is repeated the following spring when small spore-bearing structures called apothecia are produced from overwintered mummies (see **illus.**). Spores from these structures initiate primary cycles of the pathogen. In general, the rabbiteye blueberry, although severely affected by mummy berry, is more tolerant of stem cankers and root rots than highbush blueberry. The most effective control practice for mummy berry would combine the use of an eradicant ground treatment or clean cultivation and the application of protectant fungicides. Since recommended control practices vary from one region to another, it is important to consult local agricultural authorities before applying any chemicals. *See* PLANT PATHOLOGY.   Robert D. Milholland

Bibliography. T. A. Chen, Mycoplasma-like organisms in sieve tube elements of plants infected with blueberry stunt and cranberry false blossom, *Phytopathology*, 61:233–238, 1971; R. D. Milholland and G. J. Galletta, Pathogenic variation among isolates of *Botryosphaeria corticis* on blueberry, *Phytopathology*, 59:1540–1543, 1969; D. C. Ramsdell, J. W. Nelson, and R. Myers, Interaction or eradicant and protectant treatments upon the epidemiology and control of mummy berry disease of highbush blueberry, *Phytopathology*, 66:350–354, 1976; D. P. Weingartner and E. J. Klos, Etiology and symptomatology of canker and dieback diseases on highbush blueberries caused by *Godronia (Fusicoccum) cassandrae* and *Diaporthe (Phomopsis) vaccinii*, *Phytopathology*, 65:105–110, 1975.

Bluefish

A predatory and voracious species of fish that ranges throughout the tropical and temperate seas of the world, except for the eastern and central Pacific areas. A single species, *Pomatomus saltatrix* (see **illus.**), makes up the family Pomatomidae. This fish,

The bluefish (*Pomatomus saltatrix*).

also known as the skipjack, is bluish-gray with an average length of 3 ft (1 m) and weight of about 5 lb (2.25 kg). The mouth is large with sharp, strong teeth. The bluefish form schools and migrate north along the Atlantic coast, following schools of smaller fish upon which they prey. The bluefish continue to kill and destroy their prey even after feeding. About June they reach the New England coast, where the young can be found in estuaries and bays. *See* PERCIFORMES.   Charles B. Curtin

Bluegrass

Grass of genus *Poa* (also called meadowgrass), of the family Graminae (Poaceae). About 50 species are natural to the United States, and 4 are of economic importance: Kentucky bluegrass (*P. pratensis*), used in lawns and pasture; Canada bluegrass (*P. compressa*), used for erosion control; roughstalk bluegrass (*P. trivialis*), adapted for turf in cool wet shade; and annual bluegrass (*P. annua*), a weed of cool moist sites. Kentucky bluegrass was introduced from Europe to Illinois by French missionaries, and spread rapidly throughout the Midwest, thriving where mean July temperatures are below 68°F (20°C). *See* GRASS CROPS; LAWN AND TURF GRASSES.

Kentucky bluegrass (Junegrass) provides nutritious spring pasture, but tends to semidormancy and sparse pasture in summer. Replaced by other grasses for pasture, it is now valued as grass for lawns in temperate North America. Bluegrass lawn turf is planted during fall or spring from sod or seed. Seed is sown at about 2 lb/1000 ft^2 (1 kilogram/are). In fertile soil, plants spread by rhizomes to form a dense sod, favoring a soil of pH 5.8–6.8, good levels of phosphorus and nitrogen, and a mowing of not lower than 2 in. (5 cm) with a sharp blade. Fertilizer needs depend on soil, length of growing season, and whether clippings are removed or left so nutrients are recycled. Irrigation is needed in regions of low rainfall or during periods of drought.

Kentucky bluegrass is a facultative apomict, with most embryos arising from maternal tissue of the ovule instead of a fertilized egg. Chromosome numbers range from the twenties to the hundreds. As apomictic plants reproduce true from seed, single plant selections can be rapidly increased and seed sold as named varieties. Merion, the first of these varieties, was released about 1950. Seed production from Midwest pastures then moved to rogued fields in Oregon, Washington, and Idaho for production of certified varieties of bluegrass seed as a major crop. Today, many varieties are offered, selected for high seed yield, disease resistance, growth habit, and so on. Packaged lawn seed is often a blend of several bluegrass varieties, avoiding weaknesses of any single variety, or a mixture of bluegrasses with other grasses, such as red fescue or perennial ryegrass.

Several diseases that injure bluegrass include mildew in shade (caused by *Erysiphe graminis*), rusts (caused by *Puccinia* spp.), smuts (caused by *Ustilago* spp.), *Fusarium* blight, *Rhizoctonia* brown patch, and *Helminthosporium* diseases. Some 15 other fungi cause minor diseases. Disease is subject to predisposing factors such as overcast skies, short mowing, herbicide use, overfertilizing, and hot humid weather. *See* PLANT PATHOLOGY.

Insects that may reach harmful levels include moth caterpillars (such as lawn moth, cutworms), beetle grubs (such as Japanese beetle or June beetle), bugs (such as chinch bug or bluegrass bill bug), fly maggots (frit fly), and aphids. Weeds occur, especially if lawns are neglected, overwatered, or mowed too

short. The most difficult weeds to control are other grasses.   John H. Madison

Bibliography. H. T. Hartmann, W. J. Flocker, and A. M. Kofranek, *Plant Science*, 1988; J. H. Madison, *Principles of Turfgrass Culture*, 1983.

Blueschist

Regional metamorphism with the highest pressures and lowest temperatures, commonly above 5 kilobars (500 megapascals) and below 750°F (400°C). Metamorphic rocks of the relatively uncommon blueschist facies contain assemblages of minerals that record these high pressures and low temperatures. The name "blueschist" derives from the fact that at this metamorphic grade, rocks of ordinary basaltic composition are often bluish because they contain the sodium-bearing blue amphiboles glaucophane or crossite rather than the calcium-bearing green or black amphiboles actinolite or hornblende, which are developed in the more common greenschist- or amphibolite-facies metamorphism. This difference in amphiboles in metamorphosed basalts led J. P. Smith in 1906 to conclude that glaucophane-bearing metamorphosed basalts had experienced different temperature and pressure conditions from those of other metamorphic rocks. In 1939 P. Eskola proposed a glaucophane-schist facies of regional metamorphism. More recently the term "blueschist facies" has been preferred because glaucophane is not always developed in many important rock types, for example, graywacke sandstones, which may contain other minerals that are characteristic of high pressure and low temperature such as aragonite, lawsonite, and jadeite + quartz. "Blueschist facies" is more generally applicable than "glaucophane-schist facies." *See* GLAUCOPHANE.

Blueschist metamorphism developed almost exclusively in young Mesozoic and Cenozoic mountain belts. As shown in **Fig. 1**, blueschist-facies metamorphism has taken place primarily during the last 5 to 10% of geologic time, an observation of considerable importance in understanding the evolution of the Earth. During most of geologic time, high-pressure metamorphism has been dominated by high-temperature amphibolite-facies metamorphism as well as by very high-temperature granulite-facies metamorphism, the latter being uncommon during

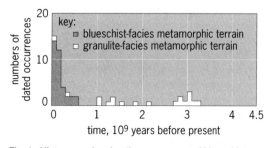

Fig. 1. Histogram showing the occurrence of blueschist-facies and granulite-facies metamorphism as a function of geologic time.

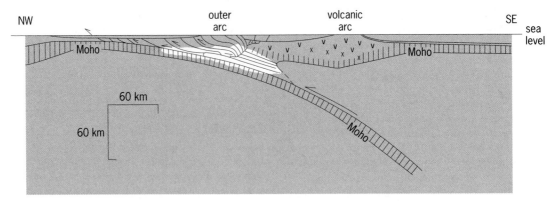

Fig. 2. Cross section of typical island arc and subduction zone with inferred region of blueschist metamorphism (white area). 1 km = 0.6 mi.

the last 5 to 10% of geologic time (Fig. 1). These phenomena are generally interpreted as being in some way an effect of the cooling of the Earth.

Mineral assemblages and physical conditions. A variety of mineral assemblages are characteristic of blueschist-facies metamorphism, depending upon the chemical composition of the rock and the actual temperature and pressure within the field of blueschist metamorphism. Detailed consideration of these assemblages and their mineral composition allows the determination of the physical conditions of metamorphism. Rocks of basaltic composition near the middle of the field of blueschist metamorphism commonly contain glaucophane + lawsonite + phengitic (silica-rich) white mica + sphene + aragonite or calcite; with increasing temperature, epidote, almandine garnet, actinolite, and rutile may appear in glaucophane-bearing assemblages; and at the very highest temperatures the sodic pyroxene omphacite or the sodic hornblende barrowisite may be present. At the lowest grades of blueschist metamorphism, blue amphibole may be missing entirely in metamorphosed basalts, with albite + pumpellyite + chlorite mineral assemblages being present. A common mineral assemblage in metamorphosed graywacke sandstone is albite + lawsonite + phengitic white mica + quartz + aragonite. At higher pressures jadeitic pyroxene or glaucophane crystallizes, and at lower pressures and temperatures pumpellyite may be present instead of lawsonite. Epidote may appear at higher temperatures. *See* EPIDOTE; GRAYWACKE.

The physical conditions of blueschist metamorphism are most easily determined from the phase relations of calcium carbonate ($CaCO_3$) and plagioclase feldspar. With increasing pressure, calcite, the trigonal polymorph of $CaCO_3$, breaks down to form aragonite, the more dense orthorhombic polymorph.

Oxygen isotope geothermometry, based on the variation in coexisting minerals of $^{18}O^{16}/O$ ratios with temperature, yields temperatures of about 570°F (300°C) for typical blueschists from western California. Higher-temperature garnet- and epidote-bearing blueschists yield temperatures of 750–930°F (400–500°C). *See* GEOLOGIC THERMOMETRY.

Tectonics. Blueschist metamorphic rocks are found almost exclusively in the young mountain belts of the circum-Pacific and Alpine-Himalayan chains. The rocks are usually metamorphosed oceanic sediments and basaltic oceanic crust. Previously continental rocks rarely exhibit blueschist metamorphism. The tectonic mechanism for blueschist metamorphism must move the rocks to depths of more than 6 to 12 mi (10 to 20 km) while maintaining relatively cool temperatures (390–750°F or 200–400°C). These temperatures are much cooler than for continental crust at those depths. Heat flow measurements above long-lived subduction zones, together with thermal models, suggest that the conditions of blueschist metamorphism exist today above subduction zones just landward of deep-sea trenches (**Fig. 2**). This tectonic setting at the time of blueschist metamorphism is independently inferred for a number of metamorphic terranes.

What is not well understood is how the blueschist metamorphic rocks return to the surface; clearly the mechanism is not simple uplift and erosion of 12–18 mi (20–30 km) of the Earth's crust. Blueschist metamorphic rocks are usually in immediate fault contact with much less metamorphosed or unmetamorphosed sediments, indicating they have been tectonically displaced relative to their surroundings since metamorphism. *See* METAMORPHIC ROCKS; METAMORPHISM; PLATE TECTONICS.   John Suppe

Bibliography. A. Miyashiro, *Metamorphism and Metamorphic Belts*, 1973; A. R. Philpotts, *Principles of Igneous and Metamorphic Petrology*, 1990; J. Suppe, *Principles of Structural Geology*, 1985.

Bluestem grass

The common generic name often applied to the genera *Andropogon*, *Dichanthium*, *Bothriochloa*, and *Schizachyrium* in the grass tribe Andropogoneae. Photosynthesis in this entire tribe follows the C_4 pathway characterized by high activity of the NADP-malic enzyme, providing adaptation to environments with high light intensities and high temperatures during the growing season. The bluestems are medium to tall, warm-season, perennial grasses with basic chromosome numbers of 9 or 10, often exhibiting polyploidy. Although asexual reproduction is common, reproduction is predominantly sexual, and ecotypic variation occurs in wide-ranging species. Prescribed burning is an important management tool, especially in subhumid and humid regions. Because of the bluestems' long season of growth, closely synchronized with decomposition rate, they usually compete successfully against cool-season grasses on soils that are low in fertility. The two most important forage species are big bluestem (*A. gerardi*) and little bluestem (*S. scoparius*). *See* CYPERALES; PHOTOSYNTHESIS.

Big bluestem. This is a tall (usually 3–6 ft or 1–2 m), deep-rooted grass with strong rhizomes; it occurs throughout the continental United States (except in the extreme western states), in southern Canada, and in northern Mexico. It is important in the true prairie, the savannas and forest openings that surround the central grassland, and even in the semiarid portion of the mixed prairie, wherever sufficient moisture compensation occurs due to subirrigation, run-in water, drifting snow, north-facing slopes, coarse-textured soil, or rock in the soil profile.

Big bluestem is one of the most palatable of all grasses when it is actively growing, but its nutritional value declines sharply with maturity. Because of its high palatability and tall growth habit, big bluestem has been reduced or eliminated by heavy grazing over much of its range. Nevertheless, it is quite grazing-resistant due to the presence of rhizomes, its large ratio of vegetative to reproductive shoots, its relatively large root-shoot ratio, and its rapid regrowth potential. Improved varieties are seeded as monocultures or in simple mixtures for warm-season grazing or hay and may be profitable for seed production, especially when grown in rows and fertilized with nitrogen. Big bluestem is used by many species of wildlife and is important as prairie chicken habitat. Along with little bluestem, it is responsible for much of the beauty of the prairies, especially late in the fall when the reddish-purple color of the foliage is fully developed.

Little bluestem. This is a medium-height bunchgrass (usually 12–24 in. or 30–60 cm, but taller in the south) which occurs in the same geographic area as big bluestem but extends farther north in the prairie provinces of Canada to the southern Yukon; it is more abundant on relatively dry sites, especially on weakly developed soils. It is an excellent grass for grazing and hay when actively growing, but nutritional value declines rapidly with maturity. Although old seedstalks are avoided, new shoots around the edge of the plant are usually grazed. When drought, heavy grazing, or fire removes the old growth, new herbage is grazed readily. Little bluestem is not very grazing-resistant because of the small ratio of vegetative to reproductive shoots and is often eliminated by heavy grazing before big bluestem. Improved varieties are available for seeding. This is the grass that provides the major aspect of the Flint Hills of Kansas and the Osage Hills of Oklahoma. *See* GRASS CROPS.

James K. Lewis

Bluetongue

An arthropod-borne disease of ruminant species. Its geographic distribution is dependent upon a susceptible ruminant population and climatic conditions that favor breeding of the primary vector, a mosquito (*Culicoides* species).

Virus. Blue tongue virus is the prototype of the *Orbivirus* genus (family Reoviridae). The viral genome exists as 10 segments of the double-stranded ribonucleic acid (RNA) that encode for seven structural and three nonstructural proteins. The viral particle has a double capsid, with the outer coat (morphologically poorly defined) being composed of two proteins. Twenty-four serotypes of blue tongue virus have been defined, and their distribution throughout the world is varied. *See* ANIMAL VIRUS.

Clinical disease. While multiple ruminant species can become infected, only sheep and deer typically display clinical blue tongue disease. Infection of sheep can result in signs ranging from subclinical to acute, with the latter being characterized by high fever, excessive salivation, nasal discharge, hyperemia (buccal and nasal mucosa, skin, coronet band), and erosions and ulcerations of mucosal surfaces in the mouth. Severity of the disease is dependent upon multiple factors, including virus strain, animal breed, and environmental conditions. Upon infection by a gnat bite, the virus apparently replicates in the local lymphatic system prior to the viral particles moving into the blood (viremia). Viral replication occurs in the endothelial cells of small vessels, resulting in narrowing of the vessel, release of proteinaceous material into the surrounding tissues, and possibly hemorrhage, with the respiratory tract, mucous membranes, cardiac and skeletal musculature, and skin being most affected. Animals experiencing acute clinical symptoms typically die from pneumonia or pulmonary failure; hemorrhage at the base of the pulmonary artery indicates the presence of a vascular lesion.

Blue tongue infection of cattle and goats is common and typically subclinical. Cattle tend to have a prolonged viremia (up to 100 days) compared with sheep (7–35 days). This extended viremia facilitates infection of numerous vectors and is thus important epidemiologically. The few reported cases of clinical blue tongue infection in cattle have been hypothesized to be the result of an allergic response. Affected cattle may develop lesions associated with mucosal surfaces in the mouth and nose, and dermatitis and thickening of skin in areas of the neck.

Blue tongue virus can also cross the placenta of pregnant animals, with the outcome being dependent upon gestational age. Infection during the first trimester may result in fetal death and resorption. As gestational age progresses, infection may result in abortion or birth of animals with hydranencephaly (a cystic brain lesion). Late-stage infection results in the birth of apparently healthy, viremic animals. While wild-type virus results in fetal disease if inoculated directly into the fetus, cell culture–adapted blue tongue virus demonstrates the greatest ability to cross the placenta. Thus, administration of attenuated blue tongue virus vaccines (the only vaccines available) to pregnant animals should be avoided.

Control. Control of blue tongue disease requires the application of vaccines and modulation of the farm environment. While blue tongue virus vaccines are available, efficacy is often incomplete and variable, in part because of the multiplicity of serotypes active throughout the world and limited cross-serotype protection. Furthermore, use of polyvalent (multiple-serotype) vaccines in the United States has been discouraged because of potential genetic reassortment between vaccine viruses and wild-type viruses, a process that could possibly lead to pathogenic variants. Relative to environment, elimination of vector breeding sites can also facilitate control of virus transmission. With the multiplicity of serotypes typically active in an endemic area, and the minimal cross-serotype protection observed, administration of vaccine in the face of an outbreak may be of limited value. *See* VACCINATION.

Because blue tongue disease is vector borne, efforts to reduce *Culicoides* breeding habitats will minimize viral transmission. Housing sheep under covered facilities will also reduce the exposure to the virus as *Culicoides* has a tendency to avoid entry into enclosed structures. Application of insect repellents may also reduce exposure. A specific treatment for blue tongue is not available; therefore, practicing good animal husbandry techniques (reducing animal stress and maintaining a warm and dry environment) and treating secondary bacterial infections with antibiotics are suggested.

Jeffrey L. Stott

Boat propulsion

The action of propelling a boat through water. A boat machinery plant consists principally of a propulsion engine, propulsor (propeller or jet pump), and driveline components. The engines are almost exclusively of the familiar internal combustion types: gasoline, diesel, or gas turbine. The gasoline engine has traditionally dominated the pleasure-boat field, while the diesel is favored for commercial and military craft. The gas turbine is comparatively rare and is found only in applications where high power from machinery of small weight and volume is essential. *See* PROPELLER (MARINE CRAFT).

Auxiliary items, such as bilge pumps, domestic water pumps and heaters, and electric generators and switchboards typically are found in the machinery plants of the larger boats. The generator (or alternator) is often driven by a belt from the propulsion engine, as in automotive practice, but is sometimes driven by a separate engine

Gasoline engines. The marine gasoline engine appears in inboard and outboard forms.

Outboard engines. The outboard engine is a unit assembly of engine, propeller, and vertical drive shaft that is usually clamped to the boat transom. It is traditionally the power plant for the smallest motor boats, or an auxiliary for rowboats and sailboats; powers as low as 1 hp are built. However, while a 50-hp (37-kW) engine driving a high-speed runabout is the most typical application, engines with power ratings as high as 300 hp (224 kW) are available. Most models use the two-stroke-cycle engine. The smaller sizes offer easy portability and adaptability to a variety of craft. The size and weight of the larger models somewhat cancel these advantages, though weight is significantly less than that of an inboard engine of the same power, and the outboard location has appeal because it frees usable space within the boat.

A cutaway view (**Fig. 1**) illustrates some of the construction features of outboard engines. The cut is taken through the engine centerline, so that pistons, flywheel, crankshaft, spark plugs, extension shaft to propeller, and gearing are visible in section. The flywheel is the cup-shaped gray component just under the top cover; the crankshaft and extension shaft run in direct line to the bevel gearing that turns the

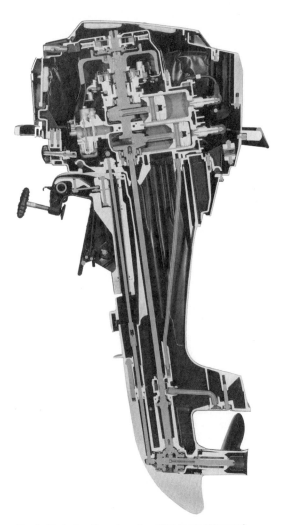

Fig. 1. Typical outboard engine. (*Kiekhaefer Mercury*)

shafting through almost 90° to the propeller. The forward-neutral-reverse actuating rod to the gearing is to the left of the shaft, and the cooling-water passage to the engine water jacket is visible to the right. Pistons, spark plugs, cylinder and crankcase walls, and part of the carburetor (left of the shaft) are shown in the figure. Engine operation is characterized by magneto ignition and by crankcase compression of the fuel-air mixture for scavenging purposes, as is typical of small two-cycle gasoline engines. Its unique marine features are principally the arrangement for mounting on the boat transom and its cooling system.

Inboard engines. The inboard form is almost exclusively adapted from one of the mass-produced automotive engines. Inboard engines are compact, light, lower in first cost than any competitor, and familiar to untrained users, and so they predominate among pleasure boats and the smaller fishing boats. **Figure 2** shows an engine of 140 hp coupled to an inboard-outboard drive unit.

Fig. 2. Typical inboard gasoline engine coupled to an inboard-outboard drive unit. (*Outboard Marine Corp.*)

Engine adaptation to marine service is largely confined to externals. The cooling system is converted to use the surrounding water, either directly in the coolant passages or indirectly via a heat exchanger. Components that might be degraded rapidly by seawater corrosion are replaced with resistant items. Risers are fitted to the exhaust manifold to prevent water from backing up into the engine.

The most important changes, however, are dictated by safety considerations. Gasoline vapor that would be swept away by the wind in automotive use is trapped around the engine by the surrounding hull envelope. This vapor is a lethal hazard, since it can ignite explosively from a stray spark or contact with the hot exhaust manifold. For this reason, the exhaust manifold must be cooled by a water jacket, the engine air intake must be covered by a backfire trap, and the carburetor and fuel system must be designed to minimize the posibility of gasoline leakage. Also, the engine compartment must be well ventilated to promote the dissipation of vapors.

Diesel engine. The diesel engine is generally higher in first cost than the gasoline engine and is somewhat heavier for the same power, but it consumes less fuel. Fuel savings make the diesel attractive if the engine is to be used more than a few hundred hours a year

Fig. 3. Jet propulsion drive unit coupled to an inboard gasoline engine. (*Berkeley Pump Co.*)

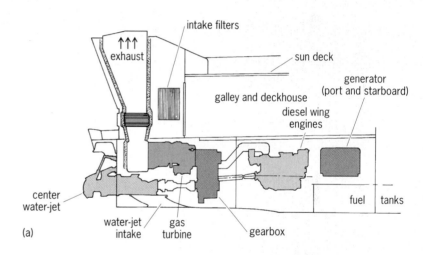

(a)

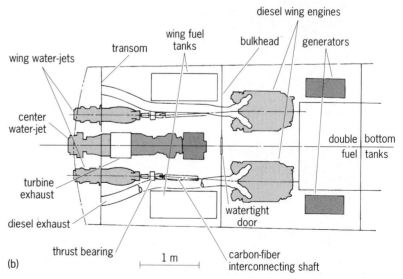

(b)

Fig. 4. Machinery layout for twin diesel engines combined with a gas turbine. (*a*) Side view. (*b*) Top view. (*Shead Design*)

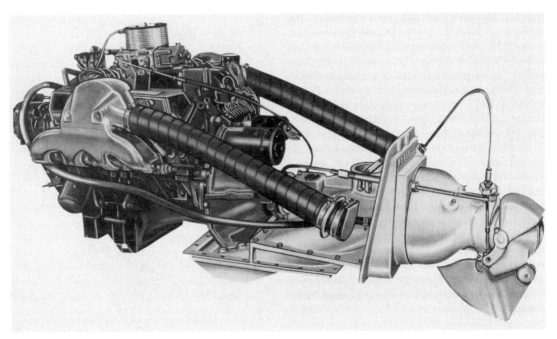

Fig. 5. Typical marine diesel engine. (*Detroit Diesel Allison, General Motors Corp.*)

or if the boat must have a long cruising range. Its principal market is thus in commercial and military craft, but some of the more compact models are used in pleasure craft.

The small-boat diesel is also almost exclusively adapted from the automotive industry, usually from a truck engine (**Fig. 3**). Both four-stroke and two-stroke models are popular. The conversion to marine use is similar to that for the gasoline engine, except that the precautions against explosion are not necessary because of the relatively high flash point of diesel fuel. *See* DIESEL ENGINE.

Gas turbine. The gas turbine engine is comparatively light and compact, making it attractive for high-speed, high-power boats. Its disadvantages are high first cost, high fuel consumption, and large exhaust and intake ducts. The last factor is due to its high rate of air consumption; the need for large volumes of air also makes it difficult, in a small vessel, to keep spray from being drawn into the engine, with consequent fouling and corrosion.

The small-craft gas turbine is typically adapted from a light-aircraft jet engine. Usually a second-stage turbine is added to the engine to drive the output shaft independently of the compressor. The combustors are modified to burn marine diesel fuel, and corrosion-resistant parts are substituted. **Figure 4** shows the propulsion machinery of a high-speed yacht. Two diesels of 1065 hp (794 kW) provide power for cruising at high speed; a single gas turbine of 4600 hp (3430 kW) provides power for sprinting at extreme speeds. *See* GAS TURBINE.

Drive systems. All of the engines usually require reduction gears to match their speeds to an efficient propeller speed. The gear boxes reduce shaft speed by factors of 1.5 up to perhaps 5, are mounted directly on the engine flywheel housing of the inboard engines, and incorporate reverse gears. A reduction

gear of this type shows at the left end of the engine in Fig. 3. Speed reduction for the outboard engine occurs in the bevel gearing in its lower unit.

Inboard-outboard drives are frequently used with inboard engines, as shown in Fig. 2. (The lighter end is mounted outboard of the vessel stern.) These units contain the reduction gears, may be turned so that a rudder is not needed, and provide a path to an underwater exhaust, all similar to the underwater portion of outboard engines.

A water-jet pump sometimes replaces the propeller. Although it tends to be less efficient than a propeller and constitutes a bulky component to be accommodated within the boat, a water-jet pump is invulnerable to damage from underwater hazards, and is safe to operate in the vicinity of swimmers. **Figure 5** shows a typical jet pump coupled to an inboard engine. This unit includes a rudder and a movable gate by which the jet is redirected for reverse thrust. *See* INTERNAL COMBUSTION ENGINE; MARINE ENGINE; MARINE MACHINERY.   John B. Woodward

Bibliography. P. Bowyer, *Diesel Boat Engines*, 1989; N. Calder, *Marine Diesel Engines: Maintenance, Troubleshooting and Repair*, 2d ed., 1991; L. Goring, *Marine Inboard Engines: Petrol and Diesel*, 1990; H. Stocker, *Marine Engines for Recreational Boats*, 1992; J. B. Woodward, *Low Speed Marine Diesel Engines*, 1981, reprint 1988.

Bog

Nutrient-poor, acid peatlands with a vegetation in which peat mosses (*Sphagnum* spp.), ericaceous dwarf shrubs, and to a lesser extent, various sedges (Cyperaceae) play a prominent role. The terms muskeg, moor, heath, and moss are used locally to indicate these sites. *See* MUSKEG.

Distribution. Bogs are most abundant in the Northern Hemisphere, especially in a broad belt including the northern part of the deciduous forest zone and the central and southern parts of the boreal forest zone. Farther south, and in drier climates farther inland, they become sporadic and restricted to specialized habitats. To the north, peatlands controlled by mineral soil water (aapa mires) replace them as the dominant wetlands.

Bogs are much less extensive in the Southern Hemisphere because there is little land in cold temperate latitudes. However, they do occur commonly on the South Island of New Zealand, in Tasmania, in southern Patagonia, and on islands in the temperate parts of the South Atlantic and South Pacific Oceans. In these Southern Hemisphere peatlands, *Sphagnum* is much less important, and Epacridaceae and Restionaceae replace the Ericaceae and Cyperaceae of the Northern Hemisphere.

Properties. Bogs have a fibric, poorly decomposed peat consisting primarily of the remains of *Sphagnum*. Decomposition is so incomplete that plant tissues, including those of mosses, are often still identifiable at a depth of more than 10 ft (3 m) and after thousands of years. Consequently, the vegetation history of bogs can be reconstructed by using time scales based on ^{14}C or other dating techniques. Well-preserved logs and bodies of animals and human beings have also been excavated from bogs. Pollen trapped and preserved in peat are commonly used to determine the vegetation history of surrounding upland areas. *See* HUMUS; PALYNOLOGY; PEAT.

Peat accumulation is the result of an excess of production over decomposition. Obviously, the very presence of bogs shows that production exceeded decay over the entire period of bog formation. However, in any given bog present production can exceed, equal, or be less than decomposition, depending on whether it is actively developing, in equilibrium, or eroding. In most bogs, production and decomposition appear to be in equilibrium at present.

Slow decay rather than high productivity causes the accumulation of peat. Decomposition of organic matter in peat bogs is slow due to the high water table, which causes the absence of oxygen in most of the peat mass, and to the low fertility of the peat. Bogs, in contrast to other peatlands, can accumulate organic matter far above the ground water table. This occurs only to any significant degree in ombrotrophic (rain-fed) bogs, the most nutrient-deficient bogs, which receive all their nutrients and water supply from the atmosphere. The level to which these bogs rise above the surroundings depends on the wetness of the climate and the size of the bog. In temperate, humid climates, the center of large bogs can be elevated more than 25 ft (8 m) above the mineral soil level in the bog border.

Permeability of peat decreases rapidly with depth, and within 1–2 ft (0.3–0.6 m) below the surface the hydraulic conductivity is so low that it can be considered impermeable for all practical purposes. As a result, almost all water movement takes place through the surface peat or over the surface. When peat accumulates above the ground water, a perched water table develops which is maintained by precipitation. In contrast to popular belief, the wetness of raised bogs is maintained by this perched water table and not by capillary water.

Types of bogs. Bogs are vegetation types as well as landforms. As vegetation types, bogs are often distinguished from fens. Bogs are ombrotrophic peatlands dependent on the atmosphere for their water and nutrient supply, whereas fens are minerotrophic peatlands influenced by water which has been in contact with the mineral soil. Hydrologically and ecologically, this is an important distinction. This restriction of the term bog to ombrotrophic peatlands is floristically a less fortunate choice because weakly minerotrophic fens have a floristic composition which is very similar to ombrotrophic peatlands and have little in common with nutrient-rich fens. The word bog is generally also used for all *Sphagnum*-dominated fens and swamps; it is used in this sense here.

As a landform, peatlands are complexes of plant communities, and all ombrotrophic peatlands include minerotrophic areas, at least in their margins. Therefore, the distinction between ombrotrophic and minerotrophic peatlands has no value here. A practical subdivision of peatlands as landforms can be based on the nature of the water which controls their development: ombrogenous, topogenous, soligenous, and limnogenous peatlands are distinguished (see **illus.**). Ombrogenous peatlands develop under the influence of rainfall and are restricted to humid, temperate climates. Topogenous peatlands develop in topographical positions with

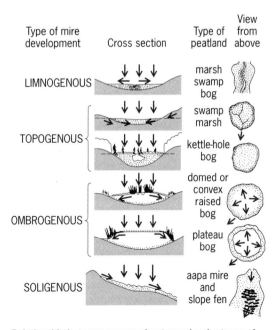

Relationship between source of water and major types of peatland development. Stippling indicates parts affected by mineral soil water; density of stippling shows relative fertility of the water. Arrows indicate source of water and major flow through peatlands. Note differences in direction of water movement.

a permanent ground-water table; they can occur under a wide range of climatic conditions but are most common in humid climates. Soligenous peatlands depend on a reliable source of minerotrophic seepage water; they are characterized by moving water, and are most common in regions with a high surplus of precipitation over evapotranspiration. Given a reliable water supply, they can also occur in warm climates. Limnogenous peatlands develop along lakes and slow-flowing streams. As landforms, bogs include all ombrogenous peatlands and some topogenous and limnogenous peatlands influenced by nutrient-poor water.

Geographic variation. Not surprisingly for a habitat which occupies such an extensive range, bogs show large geographic differences in floristic composition, surface morphology, and development. Blanket bogs, plateau bogs, domed bogs, and flat bogs represent a series of bog types with decreasing climatic humidity. Concentric patterns of pools and strings (peat dams) become more common and better developed northward. Continental bogs are often forest-covered, whereas oceanic bogs are dominated by dwarf shrub heaths and sedge lawns, with forests restricted to the bog slope if the climate is not too severe.

Uses. Bogs have long been used as a source of fuel. In Ireland and other parts of western Europe, the harvesting of peat for domestic fuel and reclamation for agriculture and forestry have affected most of the peatlands, and few undisturbed bogs are left. Other uses are for horticultural peat, air layering in greenhouses, litter for poultry and livestock, and various chemical and pharmaceutical purposes. Mechanical extraction of peat for horticultural purposes has affected large bog areas worldwide. The oil crisis stimulated an interest in peat bogs for generating electricity and gas. *See* BIOMASS; SWAMP, MARSH, AND BOG.

Antoni W. H. Damman

Bibliography. A. J. P. Gore (ed.), *Mires: Swamp, Bog, Fen and Moor*, 2 vols., 1983; H. A. P. Ingram, Size and shape in raised mire ecosystems: A geographical model, *Nature* (London), 297:300–303, 1982; K. E. Ivanov, *Water Movement in Mirelands*, 1981; P. D. Moore and D. J. Bellamy, *Peatlands*, 1974.

Bohrium

A chemical element, symbol Bh, atomic number 107. Bohrium was synthesized and identified in 1981 by using the Universal Linear Accelerator (UNILAC) of the Gesellschaft für Schwerionenforschung (GSI) at Darmstadt, West Germany, by a team led by P. Armbruster and G. Müzenberg. The reaction used to produce the element was proposed and applied in 1976 by Y. T. Oganessian and colleagues at Dubna Laboratories in Russia. A ^{209}Bi target was bombarded by a beam of ^{54}Cr projectiles.

The best technique to identify a new isotope is its genetic correlation to known isotopes through a radioactive decay chain. These decay chains are generally interrupted by spontaneous fission. In order to apply decay chain analysis, those isotopes that are most stable against spontaneous fission should be produced, that is, isotopes with odd numbers of protons and neutrons. Not only does the fission barrier govern the spontaneous fission of a species produced, but also, in the deexcitation of the virgin nucleus, fission competing with neutron emission determines the final production probability. To keep the fission losses small, a nucleus should be produced with the minimum excitation energy possible. In this regard, reactions using relatively symmetric collision partners and strongly bound closed-shell nuclei, such as ^{209}Bi and ^{208}Pb as targets and ^{48}Ca and ^{50}Ti as projectiles, are advantageous.

Six decay chains were found in the Darmstadt experiment. All the decays can be attributed to ^{262}Bh, an odd nucleus produced in a one-neutron reaction. The isotope ^{262}Bh undergoes alpha-particle decay (10.38 MeV) with a half-life of about 5 ms.

Experiments at Dubna, performed in 1983 using the 157-in. (400-cm) cyclotron, established the production of ^{262}Bh in the reaction ^{209}Bi ^{54}Cr. *See* NUCLEAR FISSION; NUCLEAR REACTION; PERIODIC TABLE; RADIOACTIVITY; TRANSURANIUM ELEMENTS.

Peter Armbruster

Bibliography. S. Hofmann, *On Beyond Uranium: Journey to the End of the Periodic Table*, 2002; G. Münzenberg et al., Identification of element 107 by alpha correlations chains, *Z. Phys.*, A300:107–108, 1981; G. Münzenberg et al., The velocity filter SHIP, a separator of unsowed heavy-ion fusion products, *Nucl. Instrum. Methods*, 161:65–82, 1979.

Boiler

A pressurized system in which water is vaporized to steam, the desired end product, by heat transferred from a source of higher temperature, usually the products of combustion from burning fuels. Steam thus generated may be used directly as a heating medium, or as the working fluid in a prime mover to convert thermal energy to mechanical work, which in turn may be converted to electrical energy. Although other fluids are sometimes used for these purposes, water is by far the most common because of its economy and suitable thermodynamic characteristics.

The physical sizes of boilers range from small portable or shop-assembled units to installations comparable to a multistory 200-ft-high (60-m) building equipped, typically, with a furnace which can burn coal at a rate of 6 tons/min (90 kg/s). In terms of steam production capacities, commercial boilers range from a few hundred pounds of steam per hour to more than 6,000,000 lb/h (750 kg/s). Pressures range from 0.5 lb/in.^{2} (3.4 kilopascals) for domestic space heating units to 5000 lb/in.^{2} (34 megapascals) for some power boilers. The latter type will deliver steam superheated to 1100±°F (593±°C) and reheated to similar values at intermediate pressures. Large units are field-assembled at the installation site but small units (frequently referred to as package boilers) are shop-assembled to minimize the overall boiler price.

Boilers operate at positive pressures and offer the hazardous potential of explosions. Pressure parts must be strong enough to withstand the generated steam pressure and must be maintained at acceptable temperatures, by transfer of heat to the fluid, to prevent loss of strength from overheating or destructive oxidation of the construction materials. The question of safety for design, construction, operation, and maintenance comes under the police power of the state and is supplemented by the requirements of the insurance underwriters. The ASME Boiler Construction Code is the prevalent document setting basic standards in most jurisdictions.

Being in the class of durable goods, boilers that receive proper care in operation and maintenance function satisfactorily for several decades. Thus the types found in service at any time represent a wide span in the stages of development in boiler technology.

The earliest boilers, used at the beginning of the industrial era, were simple vats or cylindrical vessels made of iron or copper plates riveted together and supported over a furnace fired by wood or coal. Connections were made for offtake of steam and for the replenishment of water. Evolution in design for higher pressures and capacities led to the use of steel and to the employment of tubular members in the construction to increase economically the amount of heat-transferring surface per ton of metal. The earliest improvement was the passage of hot gases through tubes submerged in the water space of the vessel, and later, arrangements of multiple water-containing tubes which were exposed on their outer surface to contact with hot gases. *See* FIRE-TUBE BOILER; WATER-TUBE BOILER.

The overall functioning of steam-generating equipment is governed by thermodynamic properties of the working fluid. By the simple addition of heat to water in a closed vessel, vapor is formed which has greater specific volume than the liquid, and can develop increase of pressure to the critical value of 3208 lb/in.^{2} absolute pressure (22.1 MPa absolute pressure). If the generated steam is discharged at a controlled rate, commensurate with the rate of heat addition, the pressure in the vessel can be maintained at any desired value, and thus be held within the limits of safety of the construction. *See* STEAM.

Addition of heat to steam, after its generation, is accompanied by increase of temperature above the saturation value. The higher heat content, or enthalpy, of superheated steam permits it to develop a higher percentage of useful work by expansion through the prime mover, with a resultant gain in efficiency of the power-generating cycle. *See* SUPERHEATER.

If the steam-generating system is maintained at pressures above the critical, by means of a high-pressure feedwater pump, water is converted to a vapor phase of high density equal to that of the water, without the formation of bubbles. Further heat addition causes superheating, with corresponding increase in temperature and enthalpy. The most advanced developments in steam-generating equipment have led to units operating above critical pressure, for example, 3600–5000 lb/in.^{2} (25–34 MPa).

Superheated steam temperature has advanced from 500±°F (260±°C) to the present practical limits of 1050–1100°F (566–593°C). Progress in boiler design and performance has been governed by the continuing development of improved materials for superheater construction having adequate strength and resistance to oxidation for service at elevated temperatures. For the high temperature ranges, complex alloy steels are used in some parts of the assembly.

Steam boilers are built in a wide variety of types and sizes utilizing the widest assortment of heat sources and fuels. *See* BOILER ECONOMIZER; BOILER FEEDWATER; BOILER FEEDWATER REGULATION; MARINE ENGINEERING; NUCLEAR POWER; STEAM-GENERATING UNIT.   Theodore Baumeister

Bibliography. E. A. Avallone and T. Baumeister III (eds.), *Marks' Standard Handbook for Mechanical Engineers*, 10th ed., 1996; M. J. Bernstein et al., *Power Boilers: A Guide to Section I of the ASME Boiler and Pressure Vessel Code*, 1998; S. C. Stultz and J. B. Kitto (eds.), *Steam: Its Generation and Use*, 41st ed., 2005.

Boiler economizer

A component of a steam-generating unit that absorbs heat from the products of combustion after they have passed through the steam-generating and superheating sections. The name, accepted through common usage, is indicative of savings in the fuel required to generate steam. *See* BOILER.

An economizer is a forced-flow, once-through, convection heat-transfer device to which feedwater is supplied at a pressure above that in the steam-generating section and at a rate corresponding to the steam output of the unit. The economizer is in effect a feedwater heater, receiving water from the boiler feed pump and delivering it at a higher temperature to the steam generator or boiler. Economizers are used instead of additional steam-generating surface because the feedwater, and consequently the heat-receiving surface, is at a temperature below that corresponding to the saturated steam temperature; thus, the economizer further lowers the flue gas temperature for additional heat recovery. *See* BOILER FEEDWATER; THERMODYNAMIC CYCLE.

Generally, steel tubes, or steel tubes fitted with externally extended surface, are used for the heat-absorbing section of the economizer; usually, the economizer is coordinated with the steam-generating section and placed within the setting of the unit.

The size of an economizer is governed by economic considerations involving the cost of fuel, the comparative cost and thermal performance of alternate steam-generating or air-heater surface, the feedwater temperature, and the desired exit gas temperature. In many cases it is economical to use both an economizer and an air heater. *See* AIR HEATER; STEAM-GENERATING UNIT.   George W. Kessler

Boiler feedwater

Water supplied to a boiler for the generation of steam. The water is heated to produce steam and acts to cool the heat-absorbing surfaces as it circulates through the boiler. The steam withdrawn from the steam drum is of high purity, and contaminants that enter with the boiler feedwater, even in small concentrations, accumulate in the boiler water.

Contaminants and impurities. Feedwater should be virtually free of impurities that are harmful to the boiler and its associated systems. Generally, natural waters are unsuitable for direct introduction into the boiler because they are contaminated from contact with the earth, the atmosphere, or other sources of pollution. The contaminants can be removed or altered by chemical treatment or other means to provide satisfactory feedwater. *See* RAW WATER; WATER TREATMENT.

The need for and type of feedwater treatment vary considerably in different plants, depending on the nature of the raw water supply and the percentage of makeup water required. The treatment of boiler feedwater is critical for steam-generating boilers operating at high pressures with high rates of heat transfer.

If not removed, the contaminants will interfere severely with boiler operation. They can cause corrosion, adversely affect boiler-water circulation or steam and water separation, or form deposits on the internal surfaces of the heat-absorbing components. Such deposits on the high-pressure parts of the boiler system result in high metal temperatures and hasten eventual failure of the parts.

Most soluble contaminants are readily removed by the blowdown of boiler water. Insoluble contaminants must be chemically treated to change their characteristics and either to ease their removal from the boiler water or to render them innocuous. *See* STEAM-GENERATING UNIT.

Components. Boiler feedwater is usually a mixture of relatively pure condensate and treated makeup water. The proportions vary with the amount of makeup water required to compensate for losses

from the system served by the boiler. In a closed power-generating steam-boiler system, losses may be less than 1% of the cycle flow. When steam is used for industrial processes, the return of part or all of the condensate may be impractical. Likewise, in forced flow, once through boilers, the water is not circulated. In these cases, impurities entering with the feedwater must either leave with the steam or be deposited within the various components or on the surfaces traversed by the steam passing through the cycle. Such units require high-purity makeup water, which is either evaporated or demineralized. *See* STEAM CONDENSER.

Processing. Processing of raw water for use as treated makeup water entails the removal or conversion of suspended and dissolved solids that could form scale or insulating deposits on the heat-transfer surfaces or that could be transported with the steam to other parts of the system. Contaminants that may be corrosive under certain conditions existing in the cycle flow must be removed or neutralized. The effectiveness of the treatment of boiler feedwater varies with the methods used and in the care taken in operation, but water can be treated to meet the most exacting requirements dictated by the plant operating conditions.

Insoluble contaminants. For most applications, it is necessary to remove all but trace quantities of the troublesome insoluble contaminants from the feedwater before it is pumped into the boiler. Hardness in the form of calcium and magnesium salts is removed from raw water before it becomes suitable as makeup feedwater. Metallic oxides, mainly those of iron and copper, are frequently removed from condensate returns by a filtering process. Residual trace amounts of these deposit-forming contaminants are inevitably present, and additional contamination may occur from the leakage of raw cooling water into the steam or hot side of heat exchangers (the turbine condenser, for example).

Calcium hardness. At lower operating pressures (below 1500 lb/in.^{2} or 10 megapascals), residual calcium hardness is treated by introducing sodium phosphate to the water. The calcium precipitates as a phosphate sludge which is removed with the boiler-water blowdown before it can deposit on the heat-transfer surfaces. At high operating pressures (above 1500 lb/in.^{2} or 10 MPa), the rate of deposition is so rapid that blowdown is ineffective. In essence, the most effective method for minimizing boiler-water deposits is to reduce the amount of deposit-forming material in the boiler feedwater.

Silica contamination. Silica, which in combination with other contaminants may form an adherent and highly insulating scale, will vaporize at significant and increasing rates if the boiler-water temperature exceeds 500°F (260°C). The concentration of silica must be held within limits by blowdown, with the maximum allowable concentration decreasing as pressure increases. Silica in vapor solution with the steam exiting from the boiler is not arrested by mechanical means. The resulting buildup of silica scale on turbine blades leads to reduced turbine output and costly outages for removal of the deposits.

Corrosion. Internal corrosion may be initiated by dissolved gases, such as oxygen and carbon dioxide, picked up by water at any point of contact with air. Accordingly, when treating feedwater, the dissolved oxygen and other gases are usually removed just before the feedwater is pumped to the boiler. Most of these gases can be removed by boiling the water in open heaters and discharging the noncondensable gases through a venting condenser. The most effective method of removal is provided by spray- or tray-type deaerating heaters arranged for countercurrent scavenging of released gases to prevent their going back into solution in the feedwater.

Care must likewise be taken to prevent corrosion of piping, heaters, and other parts of the water flow path which make up the preboiler systems. *See* CORROSION; COUNTERCURRENT TRANSFER OPERATIONS.

Corrosion prevention. Under normal operating conditions, internal corrosion of boiler steel is prevented by maintaining the boiler water in an alkaline condition. At lower operating pressures, the addition of sodium hydroxide to the boiler water will suffice to produce a pH within the range 10.5–11.5. At higher operating pressures, the presence of strong alkalies in the boiler water can cause metallic corrosion where local concentration cells become established. In addition, sodium hydroxide volatilizes at high pressure sufficiently to lead to its deposition on turbine blades, with the consequent reduction of turbine output. At higher operating pressures, modern practice seeks to maintain only a few parts per million of sodium phosphate or a volatile amine (ammonia, morpholine, or cyclohexylamine) in the water to keep the pH in the range 9.0–10.0.

Trace quantities of oxygen in the boiler water not removed by deaeration can cause corrosion and are usually scavenged chemically with hydrazine or sodium sulfite. Sodium sulfite is seldom used at pressures above 1500 lb/in.^{2} (10 MPa) because its thermal decomposition produces undesirable acidic gases. *See* BOILER.   Eugene A. Avallone

Bibliography. E. A. Avallone and T. Baumeister III (eds.), *Marks' Standard Handbook for Mechanical Engineers,* 10th ed., 2000; D. Gunn and R. Horton, *Industrial Boilers,* 1988; L. I. Pinkus, *Practical Boiler Water Treatment, Including Air Conditioning Systems,* 1962, reprint 1981; S. T. Powell, *Water Conditioning for Industry,* 1954; C. D. Schroeder, *Solutions to Boiler and Cooling Water Problems,* 1986.

Boiler feedwater regulation

Addition of water to a steam-generating unit at a rate commensurate with the removal of steam from the unit. The addition of water to a boiler requires a feedwater pump or some other device that will develop a pressure higher than that of the steam generated. Means also are required to control the rate at which water is added. *See* BOILER.

Pressurization. Reciprocating plunger pumps, driven by steam from the boiler itself, often are used for small-capacity boilers. They have simplicity and are not dependent on other sources of power. Such pumps may have single or multiple cylinders, with single- or double-acting plungers, and they can be operated at variable speeds to deliver water at a steady and controlled rate to maintain a specified water level in the steam drum of the boiler.

Pumps for high-pressure high-capacity boilers are usually of the centrifugal type, with multiple stages connected in series to develop the required feedwater pressure. They may be driven by electric motors, by auxiliary steam turbines, or directly from the main turbine shaft. When a pump is operated at constant speed, the flow of water to the economizer or boiler is controlled by regulating valves installed in the discharge piping, with a bypass around the pump to handle the excess flow from the pump.

Injectors are sometimes used to supply water to portable fire-tube boilers. The injectors utilize the energy of a jet of steam, supplied from the boiler itself, to develop a high velocity by expanding the steam through a nozzle. The kinetic energy imparted by the high-velocity steam to the entrained supply water is converted to pressure in a discharge tube which is connected to the boiler shell.

Regulation. The water level in the steam drum must be clearly indicated by an illuminated gage glass, which is required by law for reasons of safety. It is attached to a water column or vertical chamber which is connected, in turn, without obstruction, between upper and lower nozzle openings in the steam drum. In high-pressure boilers two water gages are directly connected to the steam drum, one at each end, thus eliminating the use of water columns.

Intermittent manual regulation of the feedwater flow satisfactorily maintains the steam drum water level within acceptable limits in boilers having relatively large water-storage capacity, such as shell-type or multiple drum water-tube units, but automatic control provides better regulation.

For water-tube boilers having a single steam drum of relatively small diameter, a continuous and exact regulation of the feedwater is required. Automatic single-element control devices can be used to operate the supply valve or to change pump speed in response to a change in water level.

Variations of water level in the steam drum usually are due to changes in the rate of steam generation because such changes affect the steam output, the volume of the steam below the water level, and the consequent displacement of water into or out of the drum. Changes in water level can be compensated by use of an automatic three-element control which, primarily, regulates the rate of feedwater flow to be equal to the rate of steam output, as determined by metering equipment; the control then readjusts the rate of feedwater flow to maintain the water level within the prescribed normal range. *See* BOILER FEEDWATER; STEAM-GENERATING UNIT.

George W. Kessler

Boiling

A process in which a liquid phase is converted into a vapor phase. The energy for phase change is generally supplied by the surface on which boiling occurs. Boiling differs from evaporation at predetermined vapor/gas–liquid interfaces because it also involves creation of these interfaces at discrete sites on the heated surface. Boiling is an extremely efficient process for heat removal and is utilized in various energy-conversion and heat-exchange systems and in the cooling of high-energy density components. *See* BOILER; EVAPORATION; HEAT EXCHANGER; HEAT TRANSFER.

Boiling is classified into pool and forced flow. Pool boiling refers to boiling under natural convection conditions, whereas in forced flow boiling the liquid flow over the heater surface is imposed by external means. Flow boiling is subdivided into external and internal. In external flow boiling, liquid flow occurs over heated surfaces, whereas internal flow boiling refers to flow inside tubes. Heat fluxes of 2×10^8 W/m^2, or three times the heat flux at the surface of the Sun, have been obtained in flow boiling. *See* CONVECTION (HEAT).

Pool boiling. Figure 1, a qualitative pool boiling curve, shows the dependence of the wall heat flux q on the wall superheat ΔT (the difference between the wall temperature and the liquid's saturation temperature). The plotted curve is for a horizontal surface underlying a pool of liquid at its saturation temperature (the boiling point at a given pressure). *See* BOILING POINT.

Several heat transfer regimes can be identified on the boiling curve: single-phase natural convection, partial nucleate boiling, fully developed nucleate boiling, transition boiling, and film boiling.

Boiling inception. As the heat input to the surface is increased, the first mode of heat transfer to appear in a gravitational field is natural convection (region I in Fig. 1). At a certain value of wall superheat (point A), vapor bubbles appear on the heater surface. The

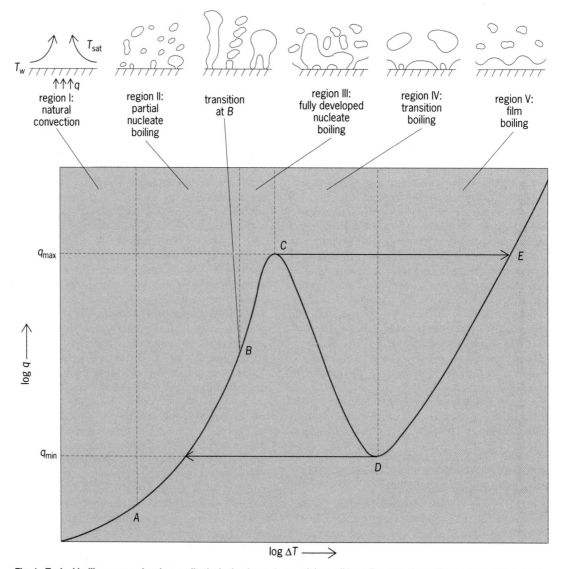

Fig. 1. Typical boiling curve, showing qualitatively the dependence of the wall heat flux q on the wall superheat ΔT, defined as the difference between the wall temperature and the saturation temperature of the liquid. Schematic drawings show the boiling process in regions I–V, and transition points A–E.

bubbles form on cavities or scratches on the surface because less surface energy is required there to form the vapor/gas–liquid interface. After inception, a bubble continues to grow until forces causing detachment exceed those holding the bubble against the wall. A complete analysis includes buoyancy, surface tension, fluid inertia, and liquid drag. *See* NUCLEATION.

Partial nucleate boiling. After inception a dramatic increase in the slope of the boiling curve is observed. In partial nucleate boiling, corresponding to region II (curve *AB*) in Fig. 1, discrete bubbles are released from randomly located active sites on the heater surface. The density of active bubble sites and the frequency of bubble release increase with wall superheat. Several parameters, such as the procedure used to prepare a surface, the wettability of the surface, the interaction between neighboring sites, and oscillations in temperature, affect the dependence of nucleation-site density on wall superheat.

Fully developed nucleate boiling. The transition (point *B* in Fig. 1) from isolated bubbles to fully developed nucleate boiling (region III) occurs when bubbles at a given site begin to merge in the vertical direction. Vapor appears to leave the heater in the form of jets. The condition of formation of jets also approximately coincides with the merger of vapor bubbles at the neighboring sites. Thus, vapor structures appear like mushrooms with several stems (**Fig. 2**). Now most of the heat transfer occurs because of evaporation at the vapor-liquid interface of the vapor stems implanted in the thermal layer adjacent to the heater surface. At present, no totally theoretical model exists for the prediction of nucleate boiling heat fluxes. However, the dependence of the heat flux on the wall superheat is given roughly by $q \propto \Delta T^{3 \text{ or } 4}$.

Maximum heat flux. The peak heat flux sets the upper limit on fully developed nucleate boiling or safe operation of equipment. For well-wetted surfaces, the upper limit on the nucleate-boiling heat flux is set by the vapor removal rate. Hydrodynamic theory based on vapor jet instability away from the heater has been successful in predicting the maximum heat flux on well-wetted surfaces. Maximum heat fluxes on partially wetted surfaces are lower than those on well-wetted walls.

Film boiling. After the occurrence of maximum heat flux, most of the surface is rapidly covered by insulating vapor, and the surface temperature rises very rapidly. When heat flux is controlled, the surface will very quickly pass through regions IV and V in Fig. 1 and stabilize at point *E*. If the temperature at *E* exceeds the melting temperature of the heater material, the heater will fail (burn out). The curve *ED* (region V) represents stable film boiling, and the system can be made to follow this curve by reducing the heat flux. In stable film boiling, the surface is totally covered by vapor film. At low wall superheats just above point *D* in Fig. 1, the radiation contribution is negligible, and film-boiling heat flux varies roughly as $q \propto \Delta T^{3/4}$.

Minimum heat flux. The heat flux at which the stable film breaks down is called the minimum heat flux. Heater surface properties and geometrical parameters affect the minimum heat flux. From purely hydrodynamic considerations involving the instability of the interface, the minimum heat flux, point *D* in Fig. 1, can be predicted by theory. The heater temperature at point *D* is often called the Leidenfrost temperature, where a liquid droplet placed on the heater will dance on the vapor cushion that forms. It is named after J. C. Leidenfrost, who observed the phenomenon in 1756.

Transition boiling. Region IV in Fig. 1 (curve *CD*), falling between nucleate and film boiling, is called transition boiling. It is a mixed mode of boiling that has features of both nucleate and film boiling. Transition boiling is very unstable, since it is accompanied by a reduction in the heat flux with an increase in the wall superheat. As a result, it is extremely difficult to obtain steady-state data in transition boiling. In general, quenching or temperature-controlled systems are used to obtain transition-boiling data. Transition boiling is the least understood mode of boiling.

Forced flow boiling. Forced flow, both external and internal, greatly changes the boiling curve in Fig. 1. External flow effects are sketched in Fig. 2. The heat flux is increased by forced convection at temperatures below boiling inception, and after that the nucleate boiling region is extended upward until a flow-enhanced higher maximum flux (corresponding to point *C*) is achieved. Forced flow boiling in tubes is used in many applications; including steam generators, nuclear reactors, and cooling of electronic components. *See* NUCLEAR REACTOR; STEAM-GENERATING UNIT.

For flow in tubes, a distinction must be made between maximum or critical heat flux under low-flow, low-heat-flux and high-flow, high-heat-flux conditions. Under low-flow conditions, the liquid film can dry out and lead to a rise in wall temperature as the heat removal rate degrades. Under high-flow conditions, the critical heat flux condition corresponds to local dry-out of the tube surface even though the

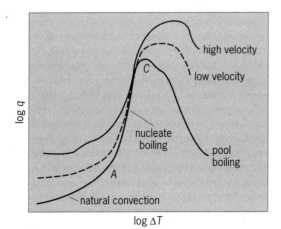

Fig. 2. Effect of external forced flow, at low and high velocity, on the boiling heat curve. The maximum heat flux is increased and the natural convection curve is shifted up due to forced convection. Locations of points *A* and *C* in Fig. 1 are indicated.

tube core is full of liquid. Upon occurrence of the critical heat flux condition, the tube surface temperature rises rapidly to a very high value, and the tube can fail if the temperature exceeds the melting temperature of the heater material. V. K. Dhir

Bibliography. Y. Cengel, *Heat Transfer*, McGraw-Hill, 1997; J. G. Collier and J. R. Thome, *Convective Boiling and Condensation*, 3d ed., Oxford University Press, 1996; F. P. Incropera and D. P. Dewitt, *Fundamentals of Heat and Mass Transfer*, 4th ed., John Wiley, 1996; L. S. Tong and Y. S. Tang, *Boiling Heat Transfer and Two-Phase Flow*, 2d ed., Taylor and Francis, 1997.

Boiling point

The boiling point of a liquid is the temperature at which the liquid and vapor phases are in equilibrium with each other at a specified pressure. Therefore, the boiling point is the temperature at which the vapor pressure of the liquid is equal to the applied pressure on the liquid. The boiling point at a pressure of 1 atmosphere is called the normal boiling point.

For a pure substance at a particular pressure P, the stable phase is the vapor phase at temperatures immediately above the boiling point and is the liquid phase at temperatures immediately below the boiling point. The liquid-vapor equilibrium line on the phase diagram of a pure substance gives the boiling point as a function of pressure. Alternatively, this line gives the vapor pressure of the liquid as a function of temperature. The vapor pressure of water is 1 atm (101.325 kilopascals) at 100°C (212°F), the normal boiling point of water. The vapor pressure of water is 3.2 kPa (0.031 atm) at 25°C (77°F), so the boiling point of water at 3.2 kPa is 25°C. The liquid-vapor equilibrium line on the phase diagram of a pure substance begins at the triple point (where solid, liquid, and vapor coexist in equilibrium) and ends at the critical point, where the densities of the liquid and vapor phases have become equal. For pressures below the triple-point pressure or above the critical-point pressure, the boiling point is meaningless. Carbon dioxide has a triple-point pressure of 5.11 atm (518 kPa), so carbon dioxide has no normal boiling point. *See* TRIPLE POINT; VAPOR PRESSURE.

The normal boiling point is high for liquids with strong intermolecular attractions and low for liquids with weak intermolecular attractions. Helium has the lowest normal boiling point, 4.2 kelvin (−268.9°C). Some other normal boiling points are 111.1 K (−162°C) for CH_4, 450°C (842°F) for $n\text{-}C_{30}H_{62}$, 1465°C (2669°F) for NaCl, and 5555°C (10031°F) for tungsten.

The rate of change of the boiling-point absolute temperature T_b of a pure substance with pressure is given by the equation below. $\Delta H_{vap,m}$ is the molar

$$\frac{dT_b}{dP} = \frac{T_b \Delta V_{vap,m}}{\Delta H_{vap,m}}$$

enthalpy (heat) of vaporization, and $\Delta V_{vap,m}$ is the molar volume change on vaporization.

The quantity $\Delta H_{vap,m}/T_b$ is $\Delta S_{vap,m}$, the molar entropy of vaporization. The molar entropy of vaporization at the normal boiling point (nbp) is given approximately by Trouton's rule: $\Delta S_{vap,m,nbp} \approx 87$ J/mol K (21 cal/mol K). Trouton's rule fails for highly polar liquids (especially hydrogen-bonded liquids). It also fails for liquids boiling at very low or very high temperatures, because the molar volume of the vapor changes with temperature and the entropy of a gas depends on its volume.

When a pure liquid is boiled at fixed pressure, the temperature remains constant until all the liquid has vaporized. When a solution is boiled at fixed pressure, the composition of the vapor usually differs from that of the liquid, and the change in liquid composition during boiling changes the boiling point. Thus the boiling process occurs over a range of temperatures for a solution. An exception is an azeotrope, which is a solution that boils entirely at a constant temperature because the vapor in equilibrium with the solution has the same composition as the solution. In fractional distillation, the variation of boiling point with composition is used to separate liquid mixtures into their components. *See* AZEOTROPIC MIXTURE; DISTILLATION; PHASE EQUILIBRIUM. Ira N. Levine

Bibliography. I. N. Levine, *Physical Chemistry*, 4th ed., 1995; J. E. Ricci, *The Phase Rule and Heterogeneous Equilibrium*, 1966.

Bolometer

A device for detecting and measuring small amounts of thermal radiation. The bolometer is a simple electric circuit, the essential element of which is a slab of material with an electrical property, most often resistance, that changes with temperature. Typical operation involves absorption of radiant energy by the slab, producing a rise in the slab's temperature and thereby a change in its resistance. The electric circuit converts the resistance change to a voltage change, which then can be amplified and observed by various, usually conventional, instruments.

Performance. The performance of a bolometer is measured in terms of its responsivity, or the electric signal generated per unit small change in incident radiation; its response time; its noise equivalent power, essentially the minimum detectable signal; and the spectral range over which the sensitive element produces a signal. Characteristics important for determining these quantities are the temperature coefficient of the sensitive element (how strongly its electrical properties change with temperature); the background electrical noise produced by the system; the thermal capacity of the element; and the thermal conductance between the element and a heat sink. These parameters can be controlled or improved by such means as encapsulating the element in a vacuum space, restricting its size, and cooling it to low temperature, such as to the boiling point of liquid helium, 4.2 K (−452.1°F), and below.

Sensitive element. The bolometer was invented in 1880 by S. P. Langley, who used a thin, blackened platinum strip as the sensitive element. Similar strips or fine wires are still used, but demands for improved performance have led to the deployment of materials with increased temperature coefficients, mainly semiconductors, such as carbon; mixed oxides of nickel, cobalt, and manganese (thermistor materials); germanium doped with gallium or indium; and indium antimonide. A class of bolometers incorporating a capacitive element uses thin films of materials with temperature-dependent electrical polarization properties. *See* SEMICONDUCTOR; THERMISTOR.

Applications. Langley used his bolometer to measure the spectral distribution of solar radiation in the infrared region. Although bolometers are useful in studying a variety of systems where detection of small amounts of heat is important, their main application is in measuring weak radiation signals in the infrared and far infrared, that is, at wavelengths from about 1 to 2000 micrometers from stars and interstellar material. *See* INFRARED ASTRONOMY; INFRARED RADIATION.

W. E. Keller

Microwave bolometers. Bolometers are also used to detect and measure microwave energy or power. A bolometer constructed for this purpose is contained in a mount that protects the usually fragile element, guides the microwave energy to the bolometer, and has connection terminals for measuring the bolometer resistance. The bolometer resistance can be measured by using direct current or low-frequency instruments. By varying the direct-current or low-frequency power, the resistance of the bolometer can be adjusted so that most of the microwave power incident upon it will be absorbed. The direct current used to measure the resistance also dissipates power in the bolometer. Therefore, when the microwave power is applied, the direct-current or low-frequency power must be reduced to keep the bolometer resistance constant. The reduction of low-frequency power is a measure of the microwave power. The ratio of the low-frequency power change to the microwave power absorbed is the effective efficiency of the bolometer mount. The ratio of the low-frequency power change to the microwave power incident upon the bolometer is called the calibration factor of the bolometer mount.

A self-adjusting current loop (see **illus.**) can be designed to adjust the current that flows through a four-terminal resistor and a four-terminal bolometer so that the bolometer resistance is the same as that of the resistor. The power dissipated in the bolometer can be calculated from the voltage measured across the resistor.

Bolometers for measurement of microwave power are usually constructed by using one of four thermal-sensitive elements, as described below.

Fine metal wires. These bolometers are called barretters. They have positive temperature coefficients of resistance, are linear and stable, and are used for the most accurate measurements. Barretters are easily burned out and therefore are not used for routine measurements. *See* BARRETTER.

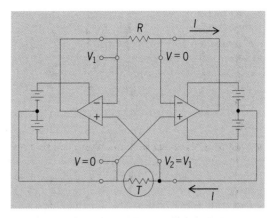

Self-adjusting current loop. The circuit adjusts currents so that the resistance of the bolometer *T* is the same as that of the resistor *R*. The circuit is shown with a semiconductor bolometer at *T*, but it can be used with a metal-type bolometer by interchanging *T* and *R*. (After N. T. Larson, A new self-balancing DC-substitution RF power meter, IEEE Trans. Instrum. Meas., 25(4):343–347, December 1976)

Semiconductor beads. These bolometers have negative temperature coefficients of resistance and are called thermistors. Thermistors are nonlinear and not as stable as barretters, but with proper techniques they can be used for accurate measurements. They are not as easily burned out as barretters and are therefore used extensively for microwave power measurements.

Thin metal films. Resistive-film bolometers are made by depositing a very thin metal film on a nonconducting substratum, and have characteristics similar to those of barretters. The microwave power dissipated in the resistance film also heats the substratum, and so these bolometers are not as sensitive or as subject to burnout as barretters. Resistive-film bolometers can be fabricated in special configurations to better fit the bolometer mount.

Ferroelectric capacitors. Thin sheets of ferroelectric material can be metallized on both sides to form a capacitor. These are called pyroelectric bolometers. The dielectric constant and the polarization of ferroelectric materials change with temperature, resulting in a change in capacity and a small current flow or voltage change. The metallized surfaces serve as electrodes and also as resistors to dissipate microwave power. Pyroelectric bolometers also may be fabricated in special shapes and have been used for pulse-power and millimeter measurements, but they are not common. *See* FERROELECTRICS; MICROWAVE POWER MEASUREMENT; PYROELECTRICITY; RADIOMETRY.

Robert C. Powell

Bibliography. R. W. Boyd, *Radiometry and the Detection of Optical Radiation*, 1983; G. H. Bryant, *Principles of Microwave Measurements*, 1988; A. E. Fantom, A. E. Bailey, and A. C. Lynch (eds.), *Radio Frequency and Microwave Power Measurement*, Institution of Electrical Engineers, 1990; F. Grum and C. J. Bartleson (eds.), *Optical Radiation Measurements*, vol. 4: W. Budde (ed.), *Physical Detectors of Optical Radiation*, 1983; N. T. Larson, A new self-balancing DC-substitution RF power meter, *IEEE*

Trans. Instrum. Meas., 25(4):343–347, December 1976; M. Ou-Yang, C.-S. Sheen, and J.-S. Shie, Parameter extraction of resistive thermal microsensors by AC electrical measurement, *IEEE Trans. Instrum. Meas.*, 47(2):403–407, April 1998.

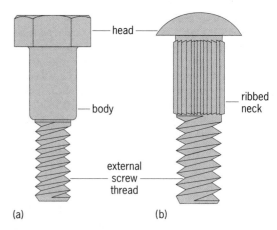

Fig. 2. Examples of bolts for interference body fits: (*a*) turned bolt and (*b*) round-head ribbed-neck bolt.

Bolt

A cylindrical fastener with an integral head on one end and an external screw thread on the other end designed to be inserted through holes in assembled parts and to mate with an internally threaded block, called a nut, which is turned to tighten or loosen the bolt. Tensioning the fastener by turning the nut differentiates a bolt from a screw, which is tightened by turning its head. *See* BOLTED JOINT; NUT (ENGINEERING).

Bolts are generally manufactured from metals, but bolts made of other materials, such as nylon, are commercially available. The properties of some bolting metals are modified by heat treatment and other means to increase yield strength. Bolt heads have various shapes to suit different applications (**Fig. 1**). Hexagon-headed bolts (hex bolts) are available in two head widths for the same body diameter—regular hex bolts and heavy hex bolts, which have wider heads. The heavy-series bolts are normally supplied with heavy nuts that are wider and thicker than regular nuts.

Manufacturing process. Modern bolt-forming processes require little machine finishing. The American National Standard requires none of the surfaces of square, hex, or heavy hex bolts to be machined except for the threads, providing that the other dimensions satisfy the Standard. Such bolts are commonly termed unfinished or rough. For the so-called finished bolts, only the undersides of the heads need to be finished; the bodies need not be machined if the forming process results in body dimensions that satisfy the Standard. Finishing of all bolt surfaces is required only for special applications. Ferrous bolts are obtainable with corrosion protection coatings such as zinc, cadmium, and organics, which are deposited on the bolts after machining.

Fits and special bolts. The holes in the assembled parts through which the bolts are inserted are usually slightly larger in diameter than the bolt body, resulting in a clearance fit. For some applications the holes are made slightly smaller than the bolt body in order to obtain an interference fit; then it is necessary to force the bolt through the holes. Bolts for force fits usually have a body diameter larger than the major diameter of the thread in order to avoid damaging the threads during installation. Two examples of such special bolts are turned bolts and ribbed bolts (**Fig. 2**). All the surfaces of the turned bolt are normally finished, with the body finished smooth. Ribbed interference-body bolts are used in structural work because the hole size is not as critical as for turned bolts. The ribs of high-strength ribbed bolts are serrated. *See* LIMITS AND FITS.

Specifications. Bolts are made in a wide range of tensile strengths. Standard specifications such as those of the American Society for Testing and Materials (ASTM), the Society of Automotive Engineers (SAE), and the International Standards Organization (ISO) identify bolts by strength, grade, or property classes.

The following information is necessary to describe a bolt: external screw thread size, thread series, class of fit, and hand of thread; length; bolt head style; reference to standard specifications or material; and coating. (The bolt length is measured from the underside of the head to the tip of the thread, except for countersunk head and other special bolts.)

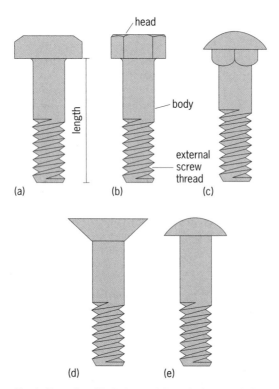

Fig. 1. Examples of bolts inserted through clearance holes: (*a*) square bolt; (*b*) hex bolt; (*c*) round-head square-neck bolt for connecting wood to metal; (*d*) countersunk bolt; and (*e*) round-head bolt.

Bolt substitutes. Straight-thread screws are sometimes substituted for bolts. The common "stove bolt" fastener is not a bolt but a slotted round-head machine screw, with a square nut. Screws are also substituted for bolts because of the wider variety of heads available on screws, some of which are designed for tightening with small portable power tools.

Uses. Various types of bolts (Figs. 1 and 2) may be used for automobile, machinery, appliance, farm implement, and structural connections. For example, low-carbon-steel unfinished bolts with hex heads (ASTM A307, Grade A) are used in machinery, and with square heads for structural steel connections. Heat-treated medium-carbon-steel finished hex-head bolts (ASTM A449) are high-strength bolts used for connections in structures as well as machinery. However, there are two kinds of high-strength bolts made specifically for structural steel connections (ASTM A325 and ASTM A490), both kinds are heavy hex structural bolts (dimensions differ slightly from those of heavy hex screws). Other kinds of bolts are medium-carbon-steel or atmospheric-corrosion-resistant-alloy-steel, quenched and tempered bolts (A325); and alloy-steel or atmospheric-corrosion-resistant-alloy-steel, quenched and tempered bolts (A490). Both the A325 and A490 bolts are designed to be tightened by torquing either the head or the nut. A hardened washer is often specified to be placed under the part being turned. *See* SCREW FASTENER; WASHER.   Charles Birnstiel

Bibliography. E. A. Avallone and T. Baumeister III (eds.), *Marks' Standard Handbook for Mechanical Engineers*, 10th ed., 2000; E. Oberg et al., *Machinery's Handbook*, 26th ed., 2000.

Bolted joint

An assembly of two or more parts fastened together by inserting bolts through matching clearance holes in the parts and engaging nuts that are then tightened to clamp the assembly. The term bolted joint also colloquially denotes a screwed joint, for which screws are inserted through clearance holes in one part and tightened into internal threads in another part by turning the screw head. *See* BOLT.

External forces on bolts. The external force acting on a bolt of a joint depends on the manner in which the joint as a whole is loaded, the geometry of the bolt pattern, and the tension induced in the bolt during installation. A bolt may be subjected to direct tension, to shear, or to simultaneous tension and shear (**Fig. 1**). Cylinder head bolts are in direct tension; bolts uniformly spaced around the periphery pass through the head as well as the flange that is integral with the cylinder wall (Fig. 1*a*). If all bolts are tightened equally and the flange and head are sufficiently rigid, all the bolts will be subjected to direct tension of equal value. The external force F applied to the bolt is due to the pressure p inside the cylinder acting on the cylinder head and to the initial tension induced in the bolt during tightening of the nut.

In a double lap joint (Fig. 1*b*), the bolts are in shear

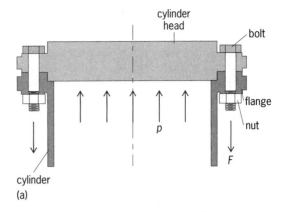

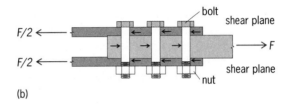

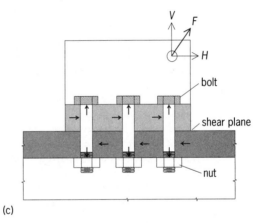

Fig. 1. Loadings on bolted joints. (*a*) Cylinder head bolts in direct tension. (*b*) Double lap joint, with bolts in double shear; small arrows represent the compressive forces applied by the plates to the bolts. (*c*) Tee bolted to a wide flange beam, with bolts in tension and shear.

at the planes between the outer and inner plates. The force F in the inner plate (due to the external loading) is equilibrated by the forces $F/2$ in the outer plates. Because each bolt passes through two shear planes, the bolts are said to be in double shear. The bolts will be subjected to different shearing forces. The two outer bolts (in the direction of loading) will be subjected to more shear than the inner bolt because of deformations of the plates. However, for design purposes the bolts are considered to be equally loaded unless the joint is long.

If the bolts are lightly tensioned (or loose), the bolt body will bear against the plates. The plates will slide with respect to each other (the joint is said to slip) until the plates bear on the bolts. Because of these bearing forces, the bolts will be subjected to bending in addition to shear. This bending is usually neglected in design. However, if the nuts on the bolts are adequately torqued, the bolts will be pretensioned and the plates will be pressed together so that the shear force will be transmitted at the interface of the outer and inner plates by friction. If the friction is adequate, the joint will not slip and the plates will not bear on the bolts. The bolts of the tee joint (Fig. 1c) are subjected to tension due to the component V of the applied external force F and also to single shear due to the component H. A force, such as F, is a vector quantity; that is, it has magnitude and line of action. It can be replaced by two orthogonal forces, known as components, according to the parallelogram law (Fig. 1c). The bolts are in single shear because they pass through only one shear plane. If the bolts are not adequately pretensioned and the joint slips, the bolts may bear on the sides of the holes because of the component H.

Bolt tension. Bolts of machinery joints that are gasketed (gaskets are soft materials used to seal joints that need to be disassembled) are tightened to minimal initial tension to avoid damaging the gasket material. However, bolts in most rigid metal-to-metal machinery joints are tightened to about 75% of the yield strength of the fastener. The bolts are tightened to high initial tension so that the bolt tension remains constant as the external tensile load (Fig. 1a and c) fluctuates, assuming that the force applied to the bolt by the external load is less than the initial tension in the bolt. In this way the bolt is not subjected to fluctuating stresses that could lead to fatigue of the bolt. Fatigue is progressive, localized damage to the bolt material caused by fluctuating stress. The damage starts with cracks that may lead to fracture after a sufficient number of stress fluctuations. The time required to fracture depends on the character, magnitude, and rate of stress fluctuation as well as the bolt metallurgy. Bolts are also tensioned at joints subjected to shear (transverse loading) so that the shear

will be transmitted between the assembled parts by friction, and the bolt body will not be subjected to shear and bending. Transverse loading of bolts is usually avoided in machinery design.

Connections of structural steel members (angles, channels, plates, and wide flanged beams) may be made with unfinished bolts of low carbon steel that are tightened with manual wrenches. Because the amount of pretension is uncertain, they are not considered pretensioned for design purposes and hence are denoted as bearing-type connections. For design, these joints are treated similarly to riveted connections, because the magnitude of the clamping force of hot-driven rivets is also variable.

High-strength structural bolts are normally tightened to a specific installation tension, which should be at least 70% of the tensile strength of the bolt. For a specific condition of the faying surface and the controlled clamping force, the force needed to cause slip of a shear joint may be computed. For certain service conditions the connection is designed such that the shear force acting on the most severely loaded fastener does not exceed that causing slip. Such joints are known as slip-critical joints.

Machinery joints. The design philosophy for bolted machinery joints (either permanent connections or those that are designed for disassembly) is that, generally, the fastener should pass through clearance holes and not be subjected to shear. Machinery joints subjected to shear are designed so that the shear is transferred between the parts by other mechanical means such as dowel pins, keys, and bearing surfaces configured into the joint. An exception is machinery mounting to structural steel (in some industries), where turned bolts in interference holes are utilized to resist shear and tension (Fig. 1c). These turned interference bolts may or may not be pretensioned. The general policy for bolt installation is to tighten

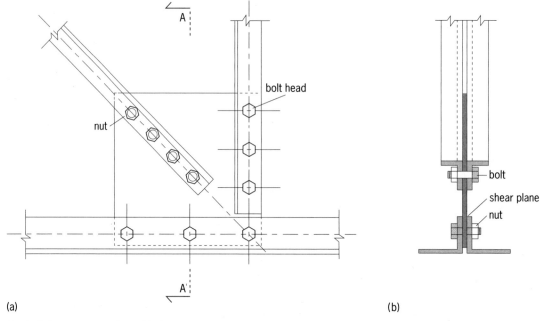

(a)   (b)

Fig. 2. Building roof truss joint. (a) High-strength bearing-type connection with all bolts in double shear. (b) Cross section A-A'.

the bolt to a specific minimum torque that is an index of the probable bolt pretension.

Structural joints. Lightly loaded beam-to-column connections in building frames are often made with unfinished bolts in clearance holes. The connections are usually configured so that the fasteners are in shear due to gravity forces. These joints are bearing-type without controlled pretension, and the connection is permitted to slip until the clearance is overcome and the bolt bodies bear against the structural steel parts.

High-strength bolts are used for connections in bridges and for building frame connections subjected to vibration and reversal of loading. The service condition is such that the connections are considered slip-critical. They are designed to transfer shear by friction, requiring controlled tensioning of the fasteners at installation.

For heavily loaded building frame joints that are not slip-critical, A325 and A490 bolts are designed as bearing-type connections. The allowable shear load per fastener is greater for the bearing-type connection than for the slip-critical connection, for the same fastener type and size. Hence, fewer bolts are required. High-strength bolts are required to be pretensioned for some bearing-type connections but need only be made snug tight for others. For example, a structural connection of a roof truss (**Fig. 2**) has high-strength bolts in double shear to transmit forces between the truss members. *See* STRUCTURAL CONNECTIONS.

High-strength bolt tightening. High-strength bolts for structural connections need to be tightened to at least 70% of their tensile strength in order to develop sufficient friction in the joint to be allowed loadings specified in building codes. The installation tensioning must be monitored. Three procedures for controlling the induced pretension for A325 and A490 bolts are the turn-of-the-nut-method, calibrated-wrench tightening, and direct-tension indicators (washers or ultrasonic transducers). For certain critical structural connections, and for special situations in machinery assembly, these three procedures are not considered sufficiently reliable, and the tension induced is monitored by measuring the bolt extension during tightening. *See* JOINT (STRUCTURES).

Charles Birnstiel

Bibliography. E. H. Gaylord and J. E. Stallmeyer, *Design of Steel Structures*, 3d ed., 2000; Industrial Fasteners Institute Staff, *Fastener Standards*, 6th ed., 1988; C. G. Salmon and J. E. Johnson, *Steel Structures: Design and Behavior*, 4th ed., 1996; J. E. Shigley and C. R. Mischke, *Mechanical Engineering Design*, 5th ed., 1989.

Boltzmann constant

A constant occurring in practically all statistical formulas and having a numerical value of 1.3807×10^{-23} joule/K. It is represented by the letter k. If the temperature T is measured from absolute zero, the quantity kT has the dimensions of an energy and is usually called the thermal energy. At 300 K (room temperature), $kT = 0.0259$ eV.

The value of the Boltzmann constant may be determined from the ideal gas law. For 1 mole of an ideal gas Eq. (1a) holds, where P is the pressure, V the

$$PV = RT \qquad (1a)$$

$$PV = NkT \qquad (1b)$$

volume, and R the universal gas constant. The value of R, 8.31 J/K mole, may be obtained from equation-of-state data. Statistical mechanics yields for the gas law Eq. (1b). Here N, the number of molecules in 1 mole, is called the Avogadro number and is equal to 6.02×10^{23} molecules/mole. Hence, comparing Eqs. (1a) and (1b), one obtains Eq. (2). Since k occurs explicitly in the distribution formula, Eq. (2),

$$k = R/N = 1.3807 \times 10^{-23} \text{ J/K} \qquad (2)$$

any quantity calculated using the Boltzmann distribution depends explicitly on k. Examples are specific heat, viscosity, conductivity, and the velocity of sound. Perhaps the most unusual relation involving k is the one between the probability of a state W and the entropy S, given by Eq. (3), which is obtained

$$S = k \ln W \qquad (3)$$

by a process of identification similar to the one just described.

Almost any relation derived on the basis of the partition function or the Bose-Einstein, Fermi-Dirac, or Boltzmann distribution contains the Boltzmann constant. *See* AVOGADRO'S NUMBER; BOLTZMANN STATISTICS; BOSE-EINSTEIN STATISTICS; FERMI-DIRAC STATISTICS; KINETIC THEORY OF MATTER; STATISTICAL MECHANICS.

Max Dresden

Boltzmann statistics

To describe a system consisting of a large number of particles in a physically useful manner, recourse must be had to so-called statistical procedures. If the mechanical laws operating in the system are those of classical mechanics, and if the system is sufficiently dilute, the resulting statistical treatment is referred to as Boltzmann or classical statistics. (Dilute in this instance means that the total volume available is much larger than the proper volume of the particles.) A gas is a typical example: The molecules interacting according to the laws of classical mechanics are the constituents of the system, and the pressure, temperature, and other parameters are the overall entities which determine the macroscopic behavior of the gas. In a case of this kind it is neither possible nor desirable to solve the complicated equations of motion of the molecules; one is not interested in the position and velocity of every molecule at any time. The purpose of the statistical description is to extract from the mechanical description just those features relevant for the determination of the macroscopic properties and to omit others.

Distribution function. The basic notion in the statistical description is that of a distribution function. Suppose a system of N molecules is contained in a volume V. The molecules are moving around, colliding with the walls and with each other. Construct the following geometrical representation of the mechanical system. Introduce a six-dimensional space (usually called the μ space), three of its coordinate axes being the spatial coordinates of the vessel x, y, z, and the other three indicating cartesian velocity components υ_x, υ_y, υ_z. A molecule at a given time, having a specified position and velocity, may be represented by a point in this six-dimensional space. The state of the gas, a system of N molecules, may be represented by a cloud of N points in this space. In the course of time, this cloud of N points moves through the μ space.

Note that the μ space is actually finite; the coordinates x, y, z of the molecules' position are bounded by the finite size of the container, and the velocities are bounded by the total energy of the system. Imagine now that the space is divided into a large number of small cells, of sizes $w_1, \ldots, w_i, \ldots$. A certain specification of the state of the gas is obtained if, at a given time t, the numbers $n_1(t), \ldots, n_i(t), \ldots$ of molecules in the cells $1, \ldots, i, \ldots$ are given. The change in the state of the system in the course of time is now determined by the behavior of the functions $n_i(t)$ as functions of time. Strictly speaking, these functions may change discontinuously in the course of time. Just how detailed the description so obtained is depends, of course, on the sizes chosen for the cells w_i. One gets the crudest possible description by having just one cell of size V in the coordinate subspace, with N particles in it all the time. A very detailed description is obtained if cells the size of a molecule are chosen. In that case even a small change in the state of the molecules will cause a profound alteration in the numbers n_i. To apply statistical methods, one must choose the cells such that on the one hand a cell size w is small compared to the macroscopic dimensions of the system, while on the other hand w must be large enough to allow a large number of molecules in one cell. That this is possible stems from the fact that the molecular dimensions (linear dimension about 10^{-8} cm) are small compared to macroscopic dimensions (typical linear dimension 10^2 cm). In this case it is possible to have about 10^{15} cells, each one of linear dimension 10^{-3}, where in each cell there is "room" for 10^{15} molecules. If the cells are thus chosen, the numbers $n_i(t)$, the occupation numbers, will be slowly changing functions of time. The distribution functions $f_i(t)$ are defined by Eq. (1).

$$n_i(t) = f_i(t)w_i \qquad (1)$$

The distribution function f_i describes the state of the gas, and f_i of course varies from cell to cell. Since a cell i is characterized by a given velocity range and position range, and since for appropriately chosen cells f should vary smoothly from cell to cell, f is often considered as a continuous function of the variables x, y, z, υ_x, υ_y, υ_z. The cell size w then can be written as $dx\,dy\,dz\,d\upsilon_x\,d\upsilon_y\,d\upsilon_z$.

In applications the continuous notation is often used; this should not obscure the fact that the cells are finite. L. Boltzmann called them physically infinitesimal.

Since a cell i determines both a position and a velocity range, one may associate an energy ϵ_i with a cell. This is the energy a single molecule possesses when it has a representative point in cell i. This assumes that, apart from instantaneous collisions, molecules exert no forces on each other. If this were not the case, the energy of a molecule would be determined by the positions of all other molecules.

Boltzmann equation; H theorem. Most of the physically interesting quantities follow from a knowledge of the distribution function; the main problem in Boltzmann statistics is to find out what this function is. It is clear that $n_i(t)$ changes in the course of time for three reasons: (1) Molecules located at the position of cell i change their positions and hence move out of cell i; (2) molecules under the influence of outside forces change their velocities and again leave the cell i; and (3) collisions between the molecules will generally cause a (discontinuous) change of the occupation numbers of the cells. Whereas the effect of (1) and (2) on the distribution function follows directly from the mechanics of the system, a separate assumption is needed to obtain the effect of collisions on the distribution function. This assumption, the collision-number assumption, asserts that the number of collisions per unit time, of type (i,j) $\rightarrow (k,l)$ [molecules from cells i and j collide to produce molecules of different velocities which belong to cells k and l], called A_{ij}^{kl}, is given by Eq. (2). Here

$$A_{ij}^{kl} = n_i n_j a_{ij}^{kl} \qquad (2)$$

a_{ij}^{kl} depends on the collision configuration and on the size and kind of the molecules but not on the occupation numbers. Furthermore, for a collision to be possible, the conservation laws of energy and momentum must be satisfied; so if $\epsilon_i' = \frac{1}{2}m\mathbf{v}_i^2$ and $\mathbf{p}_i = m\mathbf{v}_i$, then Eqs. (3a) and (3b) hold. It is possible to show

$$\epsilon_i' + \epsilon_j' = \epsilon_k' + \epsilon_l' \qquad (3a)$$

$$\mathbf{p}_i + \mathbf{p}_j = \mathbf{p}_k + \mathbf{p}_l \qquad (3b)$$

that the geometrical factor a_{ij}^{kl} has the property given by Eq. (4). Here a_{ij}^{kl} is the geometrical factor belonging to the collision which, starting from the final velocities (k and l), reproduces the initial ones (i and

$$w_i w_j a_{ij}^{kl} = w_k w_l a_{kl}^{ij} \qquad (4)$$

j). Gains and losses of the molecules in, say, cell i can now be observed. If the three factors causing gains and losses are combined, the Boltzmann equation, written as Eq. (5), is obtained. Here $\Delta_x f_i$ is the gra-

$$\frac{\partial f_i}{\partial t} + (\mathbf{v}_i \cdot \Delta_x f_i) + (\mathbf{X}_i \cdot \Delta_v f_i) = \sum_{j,k,l} a_{ij}^{kl} w_j (f_k f_l - f_i f_j)$$

$$(5)$$

dient of f with respect to the positions, $\Delta_v f_i$ refers similarly to the velocities, and $\mathbf{X}_i$ is the outside force per unit mass at cell i. This nonlinear equation determines the temporal evolution of the distribution function. Exact solutions are difficult to obtain. Yet Eq. (5) forms the basis for the kinetic discussion of most transport processes. There is one remarkable general consequence, which follows from Eq. (5). If one defines $H(t)$ as in Eq. (6), one finds by straight manipulation from Eqs. (5) and (6) that Eqs. (7) hold.

$$H(t) = \sum_i n_i \ln f_i \qquad (6)$$

$$\frac{dH}{dt} \le 0 \qquad \frac{dH}{dt} = 0 \qquad \text{if } f_i f_j = f_k f_l \qquad (7)$$

Hence H is a function which in the course of time always decreases. This result is known as the H theorem. The special distribution which is characterized by Eq. (8) has the property that collisions do not

$$f_i f_j = f_k f_l \qquad (8)$$

change the distribution in the course of time; it is an equilibrium or stationary distribution

Maxwell-Boltzmann distribution. It should be stressed that the form of the equilibrium distribution may be determined from Eq. (8), with the help of the relations given as Eqs. (3a) and (3b). For a gas which as a whole is at rest, it may be shown that the only solution to functional Eq. (8) is given by Eqs. (9a) or (9b). Here A and β are parameters, not

$$f_i = Ae^{-\beta \epsilon i} \qquad (9a)$$

$$f(\mathbf{x}, \mathbf{v}) = Ae^{(-1/2)\beta mv^2 - \beta U} \qquad (9b)$$

determined by Eq. (8), and U is the potential energy at the point x, y, z. Equations (9a) and (9b) are the Maxwell-Boltzmann distribution. Actually A and β can be determined from the fact that the number of particles and the energy of the system are specified, as in Eqs. (10a) and (10b). From Eqs. (9) and (10)

$$\sum n_i = N \qquad (10a)$$

$$\sum n_i \epsilon_i = E \qquad (10b)$$

it can be shown immediately that Eqs. (11a) and (11b) hold. Therefore β is related directed to the

$$\frac{E}{N} = \frac{3}{2\beta} \qquad (11a)$$

$$A = \frac{N}{V}\left(\frac{\beta m}{2\pi}\right)^{3/2} \qquad (11b)$$

energy per particle while A is related to β and to the number density. Other physical quantities, such as pressure, must now be calculated in terms of A and β. Comparing such calculated entities with those observed, at a certain point one identifies an entity like β (a parameter in the distribution function)

with a measured quantity, such as temperature. More precisely $\beta = 1/kT$, where k is the Boltzmann constant. This is the result of an identification. It is not a deduction. It is possible by specialization of Eq. (9b) to obtain various familiar forms of the distribution law. If $U = 0$, one finds immediately that the number of molecules whose absolute value of velocities lies between c and $c + dc$ is given approximately by Eq. (12). Equation (12) is useful in many applications.

$$4\pi V = Ae^{-(1/2)\beta mc^2}c^2 dc \qquad (12)$$

If, on the other hand, a gas is in a uniform gravitational field so that $U = -mgz$, one finds again from Eqs. (9a) and (9b) that the number of molecules at the height z (irrespective of their velocities) is given by notation (13). If one uses the fact that $\beta = 1/kT$,

$$\text{Constant} \times e^{-\beta mgz} \qquad (13)$$

then notation (13) expresses the famous barometric density formula, the density distribution of an ideal gas in a constant gravitational field.

Statistical method; fluctuations. The indiscriminate use of the collision-number assumption leads, via the H theorem, to paradoxical results. The basic conflict stems from the irreversible results that appear to emerge as a consequence of a large number of reversible fundamental processes. Although a complete detailed reconciliation between the irreversible aspects of thermodynamics as a consequence of reversible dynamics remains to be given, it is now well understood that a careful treatment of the explicit and hidden probability assumptions is the key to the understanding of the apparent conflict. It is clear, for instance, that Eq. (2) is to be understood either in an average sense (the average number of collisions is given by $\overline{n_i n_j} a_{ij}^{kl}$, where $n_i n_j$ is an average of the product) or as a probability, but not as a definite causal law. The treatment usually given actually presupposes that $n_i n_j = \overline{n_i n_j}$; that is, it neglects fluctuations. *See* CHEMICAL THERMODYNAMICS.

To introduce probability ideas in a more explicit manner, consider a distribution of N molecules over the cells w_i in μ space, as shown in notation (14). Let

$$\begin{array}{c} w_1, w_2, \ldots, w_i, \ldots \\ n_1, n_2, \ldots, n_i, \ldots \\ \epsilon_1, \epsilon_2, \ldots, \epsilon_i, \ldots \end{array} \qquad (14)$$

the total volume of the μ space be Ω. Suppose that N points are thrown into the μ space. What is the probability that just n_1 points will end up in cell 1, n_2 in cell 2, n_i in cell i, and so on? If all points in the space are equally likely (equal a priori probabilities), the probability of such an occurrence is shown in Eq. (15). One now really defines the probability of a

$$W(n_1, \ldots, n_i, \ldots) = \frac{N!}{n_1! n_2! \ldots n_i! \ldots}$$

$$\cdot \left(\frac{w_1}{\Omega}\right)^{n_1} \cdots \left(\frac{w_i}{\Omega}\right)^{n_i} \cdots \qquad (15)$$

physical state characterized by notation (14) as given

by the essentially geometric probability shown in Eq. (15). The probability of a state so defined is intimately connected with the H function. If one takes the ln of Eq. (15) and applies Stirling's approximation for $\ln n!$, one obtains Eq. (16). The H theorem,

$$\ln W = -H \qquad (16)$$

which states that H decreases in the course of time, therefore may be rephrased to state that in the course of time the system evolves toward a more probable state. Actually the H function may be related (for equilibrium states only) to the thermodynamic entropy S by Eq. (17). Here k is, again, the Boltzmann constant.

$$S = -kH \qquad (17)$$

Equations (16) and (17) together yield an important result, Eq. (18), which relates the entropy of a

$$S = k \ln W \qquad (18)$$

state to the probability of that state, sometimes called Boltzmann's relation. *See* PROBABILITY.

The state of maximum probability, that is, the set of occupation numbers $n_1, \ldots, n_i \ldots$, which maximizes Eq. (15), subject to the auxiliary conditions given in Eqs. (10a) and (10b), turns out to be given by the special distribution written as Eqs. (19a), (19b), and (19c). This again is the Maxwell-Boltzmann dis-

$$n_i = Ae^{-\beta \epsilon_i} \qquad (19a)$$

$$\sum n_i = N \qquad (19b)$$

$$\sum n_i \epsilon_i = E \qquad (19c)$$

tribution. Hence the equilibrium distribution may be thought of as the most probable state of a system. If a system is not in equilibrium, it will most likely (but not certainly) go there; if it is in equilibrium, it will most likely (but not certainly) stay there. By using such probability statements, it may be shown that the paradoxes and conflicts mentioned before may indeed be removed. The general situation is still not clear in all details, although much progress has been made, especially for simple models. A consequence of the probabilistic character of statistics is that the entities computed also possess this characteristic. For example, one cannot really speak definitively of the number of molecules hitting a section of the wall per second, but only about the probability that a given number will hit the wall, or about the average number hitting. In the same vein, the amount of momentum transferred to a unit area of the wall by the molecules per second (this, in fact, is precisely the pressure) is also to be understood as an average. This in particular means that the pressure is a fluctuating entity. In general, it may be shown that the fluctuations in a quantity Q are defined by expression (20),

$$\frac{\overline{Q^2} - (\overline{Q})^2}{(\overline{Q})^2} \cong \frac{1}{N} \qquad (20)$$

where $\overline{Q}$ = the average of Q, and N = number of particles in the systems. When the fluctuations are small, the statistical description as well as the thermodynamic concept is useful. The fluctuations in pressure may be demonstrated by observing the motion of a mirror, suspended by a fiber, in a gas. On the average, as many gas molecules will hit the back as the front of the mirror, so that the average displacement will indeed be zero. However, it is easy to imagine a situation where more momentum is transferred in one direction than in another, resulting in a deflection of the mirror. From the knowledge of the distribution function the probabilities for such occurrences may indeed be computed; the calculated and observed behavior agree very well. This clearly demonstrates the essentially statistical character of the pressure. *See* BOLTZMANN TRANSPORT EQUATION; BROWNIAN MOVEMENT; KINETIC THEORY OF MATTER; QUANTUM STATISTICS; STATISTICAL MECHANICS.　　Max Dresden

Boltzmann transport equation

An equation which is used to study the nonequilibrium behavior of a collection of particles. In a state of equilibrium a gas of particles has uniform composition and constant temperature and density. If the gas is subjected to a temperature difference or disturbed by externally applied electric, magnetic, or mechanical forces, it will be set in motion and the temperature, density, and composition may become functions of position and time; in other words, the gas moves out of equilibrium. The Boltzmann equation applies to a quantity known as the distribution function, which describes this nonequilibriium state mathematically and specifies how quickly and in what manner the state of the gas changes when the disturbing forces are varied. *See* KINETIC THEORY OF MATTER; STATISTICAL MECHANICS.

Equation (1) is the Boltzmann transport equation,

$$\frac{\partial f}{\partial t} = \left(\frac{\partial f}{\partial t}\right)_{\text{force}} + \left(\frac{\partial t}{\partial t}\right)_{\text{diff}} + \left(\frac{\partial f}{\partial t}\right)_{\text{coll}} \qquad (1)$$

where f is the unknown distribution function which, in its most general form, depends on a position vector $\mathbf{r}$, a velocity vector $\mathbf{v}$, and the time t. The quantity $\partial f/\partial t$ on the left side of Eq. (1) is the rate of change of f at fixed values of $\mathbf{r}$ and $\mathbf{v}$. The equation expresses this rate of change as the sum of three contributions: first, $(\partial f/\partial t)_{\text{force}}$ arises when the velocities of the particles change with time as a result of external driving forces; second, $(\partial f/\partial t)_{\text{diff}}$ is the effect of the diffusion of the particles from one region in space to the other; and third, $(\partial f/\partial t)_{\text{coll}}$ is the effect collisions of the particles with each other or with other kinds of particles.

The distribution function carries information about the positions and velocities of the particles at any time. The probable number of particles N at the time t within the spatial element $dx\,dy\,dz$ located at (x,y,z) and with velocities in the element $d\upsilon_x\,d\upsilon_y\,d\upsilon_z$

at the point $(v_x, v_y, v_z$ is given by Eq. (2) or, in vector notation, by Eq. (3). It is assumed that the particles

$$N = f(x, y, z, v_x, v_y, v_z, t)dxdydzdv_xdv_ydv_z \quad (2)$$

$$N = f(\mathbf{r}, \mathbf{v}, t)d^3r d^3v \quad (3)$$

are identical; a different distribution function must be used for each species if several kinds of particles are present.

Specific expressions can be found for the terms on the right side of Eq. (1). Suppose that an external force F_x acts on each particle, producing the acceleration $a_x = F_x/m$ and hence changing the velocity by $\Delta v_x = a_x \Delta t$ in the time interval Δt. If a group of particles has the velocity v_x at time t, the same particles will have the velocity $v_x + \Delta v_x$ at the later time $t + \Delta t$. Therefore the distribution functions $f(v_x, t)$ and $f(v_x + \Delta v_x, t + \Delta t)$ satisfy the equality of Eq. (4),

$$f(v_x, t) = f(v_x + \Delta v_x, t + \Delta t) \quad (4)$$

when only the effect of acceleration a_x is taken into account. Multiplying Eq. (4) by -1 and adding $f(v_x, t + \Delta t)$ to both sides yields Eq. (5).

$$f(v_x, t + \Delta t) - f(v_x, t)$$
$$= -[f(v_x + \Delta v_x, t + \Delta t) - f(v_x, t + \Delta t)] \quad (5)$$

Multiplying the left side of Eq. (5) by $1/\Delta t$ and the right side by the equal quantity $a_x/\Delta v_x$, Eq. (6) is

$$\frac{f(v_x, t + \Delta t) - f(v_x, t)}{\Delta t}$$
$$= -a_x \left[\frac{f(v_x + \Delta v_x, t + \Delta t) - f(v_x, t + \Delta t)}{\Delta v_x} \right] \quad (6)$$

obtained. In the limit as $\Delta t \to 0$, Eq. (6) becomes Eq. (7). The generalization of this result for acceleration in an arbitrary direction is then given by

$$\left(\frac{\partial f}{\partial t} \right)_{force} = -a_x \frac{\partial f}{\partial v_x} \quad (7)$$

eration in an arbitrary direction is then given by Eq. (8). The quantity $(\partial f/\partial t)_{force}$ therefore depends on

$$\left(\frac{\partial f}{\partial t} \right)_{force} = -\left[a_x \frac{\partial f}{\partial v_x} + a_y \frac{\partial f}{\partial v_y} + a_z \frac{\partial f}{\partial v_z} \right]$$
$$= -\mathbf{a} \cdot \frac{\partial f}{\partial \mathbf{v}} \quad (8)$$

both $\mathbf{a}$, the rate of change of velocity of the particles, and $\partial f/\partial \mathbf{v}$, the variation of the distribution function with velocity.

In a similar way $(\partial f/\partial t)_{diff}$ depends on both $\mathbf{v}$, the rate of change of position of the particles, and $(\partial f/\partial \mathbf{r})$, the variation of the distribution function with position. One writes $\Delta x = v_x \Delta t$ in place of $\Delta v_x = a_x \Delta t$. Then the form of Eqs. (4)–(7) is unchanged, except that v_x is replaced by x and a_x by v_x. The final expression is given by Eq. (9).

$$\left(\frac{\partial f}{\partial t} \right)_{diff} = -\left[v_x \frac{\partial f}{\partial x} + v_y \frac{\partial f}{\partial y} + v_z \frac{\partial f}{\partial z} \right]$$
$$= -\mathbf{v} \cdot \frac{\partial f}{\partial \mathbf{r}} \quad (9)$$

If Eqs. (8) and (9) are substituted into Eq. (1), one gets Eq. (10), which is the usual form of the Boltz-

$$\frac{\partial f}{\partial t} + \mathbf{a} \cdot \frac{\partial f}{\partial \mathbf{v}} + \mathbf{v} \cdot \frac{\partial f}{\partial \mathbf{r}} = \left(\frac{\partial f}{\partial t} \right)_{coll} \quad (10)$$

mann equation. Before it can be solved for f, a specific expression must be found for $(\partial f/\partial t)_{coll}$, the rate of change of $f(\mathbf{r}, \mathbf{v}, t)$ due to collisions. The calculation of $(\partial f/\partial t)_{coll}$ begins with a mathematical description of the forces acting between particles. Knowing the type of statistics obeyed by the particles (that is, Fermi-Dirac, Bose-Einstein, or Maxwell-Boltzmann), the manner in which the velocities of the particles are changed by collisions can then be determined. The term $(\partial f/\partial t)_{coll}$ is expressed as the difference between the rate of scattering from all possible velocities $\mathbf{v}'$ to the velocity $\mathbf{v}$, and the rate of scattering from $\mathbf{v}$ to all possible $\mathbf{v}'$. For example, if the particles are electrons in a metal or semiconductor and if they are scattered elastically by imperfections in the solid, it is found that $(\partial f/\partial t)_{coll}$ obeys Eq. (11),

$$\left(\frac{\partial f}{\partial t} \right)_{coll} =$$

$$\sum_{\mathbf{v}'} W_{\mathbf{v}\mathbf{v}'} f(\mathbf{r}, \mathbf{v}', t) - \sum_{\mathbf{v}'} W'_{\mathbf{v}\mathbf{v}'} f(\mathbf{r}, \mathbf{v}, t) \quad (11)$$

where $W_{\mathbf{v}\mathbf{v}'}$ is the rate of scattering of one particle from $\mathbf{v}$ to $\mathbf{v}'$ or the reverse. A basic requirement for obtaining a meaningful expression for $(\partial f/\partial t)_{coll}$ in this way is that the duration of a collision be small compared to the time between collisions. For gas of atoms or molecules this condition implies that the gas be dilute, and for electrons in a solid it implies that the concentration of imperfections must not be too high.

Discussion. The Boltzmann expression, Eq. (10), with a collision term of the form in Eq. (11), is irreversible in time in the sense that if $f(\mathbf{r}, \mathbf{v}, t)$ is a solution then $f(\mathbf{r}, -\mathbf{v}, -t)$ is not a solution. Thus if an isolated system is initially not in equilibrium, it approaches equilibrium as time advances; the time-reversed performance, in which the system departs farther from equilibrium, does not occur. The Boltzmann equation therefore admits of solutions proceeding toward equilibrium but not of time-reversed solutions departing from equilibrium. This is paradoxical because actual physical systems are reversible in time when looked at on an atomic scale. For example, in a classical system the time enters the equations of motion only in the acceleration $d^2\mathbf{r}/dt^2$, so if t is replaced by $-t$ in a solution, a new solution is obtained. If the velocities of all particles were suddenly reversed, the system would retrace its previous behavior.

An actual system does not necessarily move toward equilibrium, although it is overwhelmingly probable that it does so. From a mathematical point of view it is puzzling that one can begin with the exact equations of motion, reversible in time, and by making reasonable approximations arrive at the irreversible Boltzmann equation. The resolution of this paradox lies in the statistical nature of the Boltzmann equation. It does not describe the behavior of a single system, but the average behavior of a large number of systems. Mathematically, the irreversibility arises from the collision term, Eq. (11), where the approximation has been made that the distribution function $f(\mathbf{r},\mathbf{v},t)$ or $f(\mathbf{r},\mathbf{v}',t)$ applies to particles both immediately before and immediately after a collision.

A number of equations closely related to the Boltzmann equation are often useful for particular applications. If collisions between particles are disregarded, the right side of the Boltzmann equation, Eq. (10), is zero. The equation is then called the collisionless Boltzmann equation or Vlasov equation. This equation has been applied to a gas of charged particles, also known as a plasma. The coulomb forces between particles have such a long range that it is incorrect to consider the particles as free except when colliding. The Vlasov equation can be used by including the forces between particles in the term $\mathbf{a} \cdot (\partial f/\partial \mathbf{v})$. One takes $\mathbf{a} = q\mathbf{E}/m$, q being the charge of a particle and m the mass. The electric field $\mathbf{E}$ includes the field produced by the particles themselves, in addition to any externally produced field.

The Boltzmann equation is a starting point from which the equations of hydrodynamics, Eqs. (12a) and (12b), can be derived. The particles are now considered as a continuous fluid with density ρ and mean

$$\frac{\partial f}{\partial t} + \frac{\partial}{\partial \mathbf{r}} \cdot (\rho \mathbf{v}) = 0 \qquad (12a)$$

$$\rho \left(\frac{\partial \mathbf{v}}{\partial t} + \mathbf{v} \cdot \frac{\partial \mathbf{v}}{\partial \mathbf{r}} \right) = \mathbf{F} - \frac{\partial}{\partial \mathbf{r}} \cdot \mathbf{p} \qquad (12b)$$

sidered as a continuous fluid with density ρ and mean velocity $\mathbf{v}$. $\mathbf{F}$ is the external force per unit volume and $\mathbf{p}$ is the pressure tensor. Equation (12a) states mathematically that the mass of the fluid is conserved, while Eq. (12b) equates the rate of change of momentum of an element of fluid to the force on it. An energy conservation equation can also be derived. *See* HYDRODYNAMICS; NAVIER-STOKES EQUATIONS.

Applications. The Boltzmann equation can be used to calculate the electronic transport properties of metals and semiconductors. For example, if an electric field is applied to a solid, one must solve the Boltzmann equation for the distribution function $f(\mathbf{r},\mathbf{v},t)$ of the $\mathbf{E}$ electrons, taking the acceleration in Eq. (10) as $\mathbf{a} = q\mathbf{E}/m$ and setting $\partial f/\partial \mathbf{r} = 0$, corresponding to spatial uniformity of the electrons. If the electric field is constant, the distribution function is also constant and is displaced in velocity space in such a way that fewer electrons are moving in the direction of the field than in the opposite direction. This corresponds to a current flow in the direction of the field. The relationship between the current density $\mathbf{J}$ and the field $\mathbf{E}$ is given by Eq. (13), where

$$\mathbf{J} = \sigma \mathbf{E} \qquad (13)$$

σ, the electrical conductivity, is the final quantity of interest. *See* FREE-ELECTRON THEORY OF METALS.

With the Boltzmann equation one can also calculate the heat current flowing in a solid as the result of

a temperature difference, the constant of proportionality between the heat current per unit area and the temperature gradient being the thermal conductivity. In still more generality, both an electric field $\mathbf{E}$ and a temperature gradient $\partial T/\partial \mathbf{r}$ can be applied, where T is the temperature. Expressions are obtained for the electrical current density $\mathbf{J}$ and the heat current density $\mathbf{U}$ in the form of Eqs. (14a) and (14b). L_{11} is

$$\mathbf{J} = L_{11}\mathbf{E} + L_{12}\partial T/\partial \mathbf{r} \qquad (14a)$$

$$\mathbf{U} = L_{21}\mathbf{E} + L_{22}\partial T/\partial \mathbf{r} \qquad (14b)$$

the electrical conductivity and $-L_{22}$ the thermal conductivity. Equations (14a) and (14b) also describe thermoelectric phenomena, such as the Peltier and Seebeck effects. For example, if a thermal gradient is applied to an electrically insulated solid so that no electric current can flow ($\mathbf{J} = 0$), Eq. (14a) shows that an electric field given by Eq. (15) will appear.

$$\mathbf{E} = -(L_{12}/L_{11})(\partial T/\partial \mathbf{r}) \qquad (15)$$

The quantity (L_{12}/L_{11}) is called the Seebeck coefficient.

Finally, if a constant magnetic field $\mathbf{B}$ is also applied, the coefficients L_{ij} in Eqs. (14a) and (14b) become functions of $\mathbf{B}$. It is found that the electrical conductivity usually decreases with increasing $\mathbf{B}$, a behavior known as magnetoresistance. These equations also describe the Hall effect, the appearance of an electric field in the y direction if there is an electric current in the x direction and a magnetic field in the z direction, as well as more complex thermomagnetic phenomena, such as the Ettingshausen and Nernst effects. The conductivity σ in Eq. (13) and the L_{ij} in Eqs. (14a) and (14b) are tensor quantities in many materials. If the field $\mathbf{E}$ and the temperature gradient $\partial T/\partial \mathbf{r}$ are in a given direction, the currents $\mathbf{U}$ and $\mathbf{J}$ are not necessarily in the same direction. *See* CONDUCTION (ELECTRICITY); CONDUCTION (HEAT); GALVANOMAGNETIC EFFECTS; HALL EFFECT; MAGNETORESISTANCE; THERMOELECTRICITY; THERMOMAGNETIC EFFECTS.

Nonequilibrium properties of atomic or molecular gases such as viscosity, thermal conduction, and diffusion have been treated with the Boltzmann equation. Although many useful results, such as the independence of the viscosity of a gas on pressure, can be obtained by simple approximate methods, the Boltzmann equation must be used in order to obtain quantitatively correct results. *See* DIFFUSION; VISCOSITY.

If one proceeds from a neutral gas to a charged gas or plasma, with the electrons partially removed from the atoms, a number of new phenomena appear. As a consequence of the long-range Coulomb forces between the charges, the plasma can exhibit oscillations in which the free electrons move back and forth with respect to the relatively stationary heavy positive ions at the characteristic frequency known as the plasma frequency. This frequency is proportional to the square root of the particle density. If the propagation of electromagnetic waves through a plasma is studied, it is found that a plasma reflects an electromagnetic wave at a frequency lower than the plasma frequency, but transmits the wave at a higher frequency. This fact explains many characteristics of long-distance radio transmission, made possible by reflection of radio waves by the ionosphere, a low-density plasma surrounding the Earth at altitudes greater than 40 mi (65 km). A plasma also exhibits properties such as electrical conductivity, thermal conductivity, viscosity, and diffusion. *See* PLASMA (PHYSICS).

If a magnetic field is applied to the plasma, its motion can become complex. A type of wave known as an Alfvén wave propagates in the direction of the magnetic field with a velocity proportional to the field strength. The magnetic field lines are not straight, however, but oscillate like stretched strings as the wave passes through the plasma. Waves that propagate in a direction perpendicular to the magnetic field have quite different properties.

When the plasma moves as a fluid, it tends to carry the magnetic field lines with it. The plasma becomes partially trapped by the magnetic field in such a way that it can move easily along the magnetic field lines, but only very slowly perpendicular to them. The outstanding problem in the attainment of a controlled thermonuclear reaction is to design a magnetic field configuration that can contain an extremely hot plasma long enough to allow nuclear reactions to take place. *See* MAGNETOHYDRODYNAMICS.

Plasmas in association with magnetic fields occur in many astronomical phenomena. Many of the events occurring on the surface of the Sun, such as sunspots and flares, as well as the properties of the solar wind, a dilute plasma streaming out from the Sun in all directions, are manifestations of the motion of a plasma in a magnetic field. It is believed that a plasma streaming out from a rapidly rotating neutron star will radiate electromagnetic energy; this is a possible explanation of pulsars, stars emitting regularly pulsating radio signals that have been detected with radio telescopes.

Many properties of plasmas can be calculated by studying the motion of individual particles in electric and magnetic fields, or by using the hydrodynamic equations, Eqs. (12*a*) and (12*b*), or the Vlasov equation, together with Maxwell's equations. However, subtle properties of plasmas, such as diffusion processes and the damping of waves, can best be understood by starting with the Boltzmann equation or the closely related Fokker-Planck equation. *See* MAXWELL'S EQUATIONS.

Relaxation time. It is usually difficult to solve the Boltzmann equation, Eq. (10), for the distribution function $f(\mathbf{r},\mathbf{v},t)$ because of the complicated form of $(\partial f/\partial t)_{\text{coll}}$. This term is simplified if one makes the relaxation time approximation shown in Eq. (16),

$$\left(\frac{\partial f}{\partial t}\right)_{\text{coll}} = -\frac{f(\mathbf{r},\mathbf{v},t) - f_0(\mathbf{v})}{\tau(v)} \qquad (16)$$

where $f_0(v)$ is the equilibrium distribution function and $\pi(v)$, the relaxation time, is a characteristic time

describing the return of the distribution function to equilibrium when external forces are removed. For some systems Eq. (16) follows rigorously from Eq. (11), but in general it is an approximation. If the relaxation time approximation is not made, the Boltzmann equation usually cannot be solved exactly, and approximate techniques such as variational, perturbation, and expansion methods must be used. An important situation in which an exact solution is possible occurs if the particles exert forces on each other that vary as the inverse fifth power of the distance between them. *See* RELAXATION TIME OF ELECTRONS.

Example. As an illustration of how the Boltzmann equation can be solved, consider a spatially uniform electron gas in a metal or a semiconductor. Let the scattering of electrons be described by Eq. (16). One can calculate the electric current which flows when a small, constant electric field E_x is applied. The spatial uniformity of the electron gas implies that $\partial f/\partial \mathbf{r} = 0$; since the electric field is constant, one requires also that the distribution function be constant ($\partial f/\partial t = 0$) so that the current does not depend on time. If one writes the acceleration of the electron as $a_x = F_x - m = -eE_x - m$, where $(-e)$ is the charge and m is the mass of the electron, Eq. (10) becomes Eq. (17). The difference between f and f_0 is small;

$$\frac{-eE_x}{m}\frac{\partial f}{\partial v_x} = -\frac{f(\mathbf{v}) - f_0(\mathbf{v})}{\tau(v)} \qquad (17)$$

therefore f can be replaced by f_0 in the term containing E_x, since E_x itself is small. Thus Eq. (18) is

$$\partial f/\partial v_x \approx \partial f_0/\partial v_x = (\partial f_0/\partial v)(\partial v/\partial v_x)$$
$$= (\partial f_0/\partial v)(v_x/v) \qquad (18)$$

obtained, where $v\,(v_x^2 + v_y^2 + v_z^2)^{1/2}$ is the magnitude of the electron velocity; Eq. (17) then becomes Eq. (19). Here $f_0(\mathbf{v})$ is the equilibrium distribution

$$f(\mathbf{v}) = f_0(\mathbf{v}) + \frac{eE_x\tau}{m}\frac{v_x}{v}\frac{\partial f_0}{\partial v} \qquad (19)$$

function describing the state of the electrons in the absence of an electric field. For a high electron density, as in metals, $f_0(\mathbf{v})$ is the Fermi-Dirac distribution function given by Eq. (20), where ζ is the Fermi en-

$$f_0(\mathbf{v}) \propto \frac{1}{e^{(mv^2/2 - \zeta)/kT} + 1} \qquad (20)$$

ergy, k is the Boltzmann constant, and T is the absolute temperature. In writing $f_0(\mathbf{v})$ in the form of Eq. (20), the simplifying assumption that the energy of an electron is $mv^2/2$ has been made. If the electron density is low, as it often is in semiconductors, $f_0(\mathbf{v})$ can be approximated by the Maxwell-Boltzmann distribution given in Eq. (21). In either case $f_0(\mathbf{v})$ de-

$$f_0(\mathbf{v}) \propto e^{-mv^2/2kT} \qquad (21)$$

pends only on the magnitude and not on the direction of the velocity. *See* BOLTZMANN STATISTICS; FERMI-DIRAC STATISTICS.

Therefore $f_0(\mathbf{v})$ is centered at $\mathbf{v} = 0$ in such a way that the net flow of electrons in every direction is zero. The nonequilibrium distribution function $f(\mathbf{v})$

similar to $f_0(\mathbf{v})$, except that is shifted in the $(-v_x)$ direction in velocity space. Consequently more electrons move in the $(-x)$ direction than in the $(+x)$ direction, producing a net current flow in the $(+x)$ direction. The current density J_x is calculated from $f\mathbf{v}$ by Eq. (22), where the spatial integral is to be taken

$$J_x = -e \int v_x f(\mathbf{v}) d^3v d^3x \qquad (22)$$

over a unit volume, so that $\int d^3x = 1$. $f\mathbf{v}$ as given by Eq. (19) is substituted into Eq. (22), the term involving the equilibrium distribution function $f_0(\mathbf{v})$ by itself gives zero current, since no current flows at equilibrium. Hence one obtains Eq. (23).

$$J_x = \frac{e^2 E_x}{m} \int \frac{\tau(v)v_x^2}{v}\left(-\frac{\partial f_0}{\partial v}\right) d^3v \qquad (23)$$

If n, the density of electrons, is introduced using the equation $n = \int f_0(\mathbf{v})\, d^3v$, Eq. (23) can be written as Eq. (24), where σ is given by Eq. (25), and τ given by Eq. (26), is an average relaxation time.

$$J_x = \sigma E_x \qquad (24)$$

$$\sigma = ne^2\bar{\tau}/m \qquad (25)$$

$$\bar{\tau} = \frac{\int \tau \dfrac{v_x^2}{v}\left(-\dfrac{\partial f_0}{\partial v}\right) d^3v}{\int f_0 d^3v} \qquad (26)$$

Equation (25) is the final expression for the electrical conductivity σ.

The above treatment is applicable only if the electrons in the solid behave as if they were nearly free. In general, the wave vector $\mathbf{k}$, rather than the velocity $\mathbf{v}$, must be used as a variable in the distribution function, and the final expression for σ depends on the electronic band structure of the solid.   Ronald Fuchs

Bibliography. R. S. Brodkey and H. C. Hershey, *Transport Phenomena: A Unified Approach*, 2000; S. Chapman and T. G. Cowling, *The Mathematical Theory of Non-Uniform Gases*, 3d ed., 1970, reprint 1991; C. Cercignani, *The Boltzmann Equation and Its Applicaions*, 1988; R. O. Dendy (ed.), *Plasma Physics: An Introductory Course*, 1995.

Bond angle and distance

The angle between two bonds sharing a common atom is known as the bond angle. The distance between the nuclei of bonded atoms is known as bond distance. The geometry of a molecule can be characterized by bond angles and distances. The angle between two bonds sharing a common atom through a third bond is known as the torsional or dihedral angle (see **illus.**)

Certain pairs of atoms in a molecule are held together at distances of about 0.075–0.3 nanometer, with energies of about 150–1000 kilojoules/mol, because of a balance between electrostatic attraction

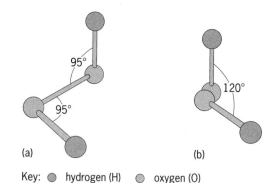

Key: ● hydrogen (H)   ● oxygen (O)

Bond angle versus torsional angle. (*a*) Two O—O—H bond angles in hydrogen peroxide (H_2O_2). (*b*) The same molecule when viewed along the O—O bond, revealing the torsional angle, that is, the angle between the two O—H bonds.

and repulsion among the electrons and nuclei, subject to the electron distributions allowed by quantum mechanics. Such interactions are called chemical bonds. *See* CHEMICAL BONDING.

Molecular properties. Bond angles and distances are important because they determine the shape and size of a molecule and therefore affect many physical properties of a substance. The shape of a molecule influences its charge distribution, often determining whether a molecule is polar or nonpolar; polar molecules exhibit stronger intermolecular attraction and thus have higher boiling points. For example, the structures of *cis* and *trans*-1,2-dichloroethylene differ only in the torsional angle about the C=C bond. The polar cis isomer has a normal boiling point (60.3°C) considerably higher than that of the nonpolar trans isomer (47.5°C). Molecular shapes also influence the packing density of molecules in solids and liquids. For example, spherical molecules pack differently from long, rod-shaped molecules. For biological molecules, the detailed shape of the molecule ultimately governs its function for example, deoxyribonucleic acid (DNA), or its specificity (for example, enzymes). *See* DEOXYRIBONUCLEIC ACID (DNA); ENZYME; MOLECULAR STRUCTURE AND SPECTRA; POLAR MOLECULE.

Bonding data. Bond angles and distances depend on the identity of the atoms bonded together and the type of chemical bonding involved. For example, carbon–hydrogen bonds are remarkably similar in length in a wide range of compounds. Bonds vary in length depending on the bond multiplicity: they are shorter for a triple bond than for a single bond (**Table 1**). Single bonds vary in length slightly, depending on whether they are adjacent to multiple bonds (**Table 2**). Bond angles vary considerably from molecule to molecule; the variation in bond angles and distances depends primarily on the electronic structures of the molecules. **Table 3** shows the variation in bond angles for a number of triatomic molecules.

The bond lengths and angles of an electronically excited molecule usually differ from the ground-state values. For example, carbon dioxide is linear in its ground state but is bent in its lowest excited state; that is, the O—C—O angle is 180° in the ground state

TABLE 1. Dependence of bond length on bond multiplicity

Bond	Molecule	Name	Length, nm*
C—C	H_3C—CH_3	Ethane	0.153
C=C	H_2C=CH_2	Ethylene	0.134
C≡C	HC≡CH	Acetylene	0.120
N—N	H_2N—NH_2	Hydrazine	0.145
N=N	N=N=O	Nitrous oxide	0.113
N≡N	N_2	Nitrogen	0.110
C—O	H_3C—OH	Methanol	0.142
C=O	H_2C=O	Formaldehyde	0.121
C≡O	CO	Carbon monoxide	0.113

*Uncertainties are ≤ 0.001 nm in bond distances and ≤ 1° in bond angles, unless otherwise stated.

TABLE 2. Variation of carbon–hydrogen bond length with neighboring carbon–carbon bond multiplicity

Molecule	C—H bond length, nm
H_3C—CH_3	0.110
H_2C=CH_2	0.108
HC≡CH	0.106

TABLE 3. Bond angles for three triatomic molecules

Molecule	Name	Angle	Value
H_2O	Water	H—O—H	105°
SO_2	Sulfur dioxide	O—S—O	119°
CO_2	Carbon dioxide	O—C—O	180°

but is $122 \pm 2°$ in the first excited state. The C=O bond distance is 0.116 nm in the ground state but is 0.125 nm in the first excited state.

Experimental determination. Much experimental effort has gone into measuring bond angles and distances, and values for individual molecules have been extensively compiled. The experimental methods can be divided into diffraction methods and spectroscopic methods.

Diffraction methods. These employ the wave properties of x-rays, electrons, and neutrons. When the wavelength of x-rays or the de Broglie wavelength of electrons or neutrons is comparable to certain interatomic distances in a sample, then the waves or particles will be diffracted through an angle determined by the ratio of the wavelength to the interatomic distance. Gases are studied with electron diffraction, while solids and liquids are studied with x-ray and neutron diffraction. See DE BROGLIE WAVELENGTH; ELECTRON DIFFRACTION; X-RAY DIFFRACTION.

Spectroscopic methods. These rely primarily on the rotational motion of molecules in the gas phase. Rotational energies are quantized and depend on the molecule's moments of inertia. These moments depend on bond distances and angles, as well as nuclear masses. Rotational transitions are observed directly in microwave absorption spectroscopy, or as rotational fine structure in infrared, visible, and ultraviolet absorption spectroscopy. For many nonpolar molecules that do not absorb microwave radiation,

the Raman effect can be employed to detect rotational or vibrational transitions. See RAMAN EFFECT; SPECTROSCOPY.

In liquids and solids, where molecules cannot rotate freely, spectroscopic structural information comes primarily from infrared and vibrational Raman spectra. Often, a comparison of the two provides qualitative symmetry information. For example, a mutual exclusion principle states that if a molecule has a center of symmetry, no vibrational mode will appear in both the infrared and Raman spectrum.

Theoretical calculation. Quantum mechanics can, in principle, be used to calculate bond lengths and angles accurately by solving the appropriate quantum-mechanical equations, although such calculations for large molecules are extremely difficult and require a great deal of computer time. A number of simple theoretical concepts have been developed that have some approximate correlation with experimentally determined bond angles and distances. One is called the electrostatic or valence-shell electron-pair repulsion model. It treats a chemical bond as a shared pair of electrons which repels other pairs associated with the same atom. An alternative model, valence-bond theory, treats a chemical bond as an overlap of electronic orbitals centered on the bonded atoms. Equivalent hybrid orbitals centered on the same atoms have a characteristic geometry. See QUANTUM CHEMISTRY; STRUCTURAL CHEMISTRY; VALENCE.   Bruce A. Garetz

Bibliography. K. Kuchitsu (ed.), *Structure Data of Free Polyatomic Molecules*, vol. 7 of Landolt-Bornstein, Group II, *Atomic and Molecular Physics*, 1995; I. Levine, *Physical Chemistry*, 4th ed., 2000; J. N. Murrell et al., *The Chemical Bond*, 2d ed., 1985; L. Pauling, *The Nature of the Chemical Bond*, 3d ed., 1960.

Bonding

A method of holding the parts of an object together with or without the aid of an adhesive such as an epoxy or a glue. Composite materials such as fiber-reinforced plastics require strong interfacial bonding between the reinforcement and the matrix. In the case of atomic or optical contact bonding, interatomic forces hold the parts together. In optical contact bonding, surface flatness and cleanliness between the mating parts determine the bonding strength, and the atoms at the surface provide the necessary forces. The number of valence electrons in the atoms of a material determines the bonding strength between the group of atoms which constitutes a molecule. In these cases the term chemical bonding is used. See ADHESIVE; CHEMICAL BONDING; COMPOSITE MATERIAL.

Wire bonding is an interconnect technique widely used in microchip manufacturing to provide electrical continuity between the metal pads of an integrated circuit chip and the electrical leads of the package housing the chip. The two common methods of wire bonding are thermocompression and ultrasonic bonding. In these, a fine aluminum or gold wire is bonded at one end to the metal pad of the integrated circuit chip, and at the other to the electrical lead of the package. There are three types of thermocompression bonds: wedge, stitch, and ball. In thermocompression bonding, a molecular metallurgical bond is formed at the two metal junctions—bond wire and IC metal pad, and bond wire and package lead metal—by applying heat and pressure without melting. In ultrasonic bonding, the molecular metallurgical bond is achieved through a combination of ultrasonic energy and pressure. The bonding operation is done under pressure to break the few surface layers of the material and form the bond between the contamination-free surfaces. Thermocompression bonding has higher throughput and speed than ultrasonic bonding. The bonding wire is usually aluminum, which does not introduce any intermetallic problems. *See* CIRCUIT (ELECTRONICS); INTEGRATED CIRCUITS.   Lakshmi Munukutla

Bone

The hard connective tissue that, together with cartilage, forms the skeleton of humans and other vertebrates. It is made of calcium phosphate crystals arranged on a protein scaffold. Bone performs a variety of functions: it has a structural and mechanical role; it protects vital organs; it provides a site for the production of blood cells; it serves as a reserve of calcium. Bone tissue is constantly renewing itself and has great capacity to respond to altered stresses and loads and to repair fractures. The formation and remodeling of bone is accomplished by the action of bone cells of the osteoblast and osteoclast lineages. The activities of these cells are directed by hormones and other molecules that circulate in the blood as well as regulators that are produced locally in the bone. There are a number of bone diseases which are the subject of vigorous research. *See* CONNECTIVE TISSUE; SKELETAL SYSTEM.

Composition and structure. There are two types of bone in the skeleton: the flat bones (for example, the bones of the skull and ribs) and the long bones (for example, the femur and the bones of the hand and feet). Although the growth and development of the two bone types are different, both types are characterized by an outer layer of dense, compact bone, known as cortical bone, and an inner spongy bone material made up of thin trabeculae, known as cancellous bone. Cortical bone consists of layers of bone (lamellae) in an orderly concentric cylindrical arrangement around tiny Haversian canals. These interconnecting canals carry the blood vessels, lymph vessels, and nerves through the bone and communicate with the periosteum and the marrow cavity. The periosteum is a thin membrane covering the outer surface of bone and consisting of layers of cells that participate in the remodeling and repair of bone. The cancellous bone is in contact with the bone marrow, in which much of the production of blood cells takes place. The interface between the cancellous bone

and the marrow is called the endosteum, and it is largely at this site that bone is removed in response to a need for increased calcium elsewhere in the body. A dramatic example is seen in the egg-laying fowl, where trabecular bone is rapidly removed to provide calcium for the egg shell and is then replaced in a cyclical manner.

Bone is formed by the laying down of osteoid (the young hyaline matrix of truebone) by osteoblasts, the bone-forming cells, and the mineralization of the osteoid by the development and deposition of crystals of calcium phosphate (in the form of hydroxyapatite) within it. It is the mineral, organized in a regular pattern on a collagen scaffold, that gives bone its stiffness. Osteoid contains largely fibers of type I collagen (a member of a large family of collagen molecules) and lesser amounts of numerous noncollagenous proteins. These proteins include osteonectin, osteopontin, bone sialoprotein, biglycan, decorin, and osteocalcin. Although the role of these proteins in bone is not well understood, it is thought that their particular combination in bone gives this tissue the unique ability to mineralize. It is clear that these proteins interact with each other and that collagen and several of the noncollagenous proteins, such as osteopontin and bone sialoprotein, can bind to specialized receptors on the surface of bone cells. This binding is important for the adhesion of the cells to the bone matrix, and it also delivers behavioral signals to the cells. *See* APATITE; COLLAGEN.

Bone cells. Bone is rich in blood vessels and nerves and thus contains the cell types associated with these structures. However, the primary cell types in bone are those that result in its formation and maintenance (osteoblasts and osteocytes) and those that are responsible for its removal (osteoclasts). Osteoblasts form from the differentiation of multipotential stromal cells that reside in the periosteum and the bone marrow. Under the appropriate stimuli, these primitive stromal cells mature to bone-forming cells at targeted sites in the skeleton. Under different stimuli, they are also capable of developing into adipocytes (fat cells), muscle cells, and chondrocytes (cartilage cells). Several developmental stages can be recognized in the differentiation of osteoblasts from their precursor cells: preosteoblasts; synthetic-phase osteoblasts that secrete the proteins that constitute osteoid; flattened lining cells that cover the endosteal surface when no bone formation or resorption is taking place; and osteocytes, which are osteoblasts that become incorporated within the bone tissue itself. Osteocytes are the most numerous cell type in bone. They reside in spaces (lacunae) within the mineralized bone, forming numerous extensions through tiny channels (cannaliculi) in the bone that connect with other osteocytes and with the cells on the endosteal surface. Osteocytes are therefore ideally placed to sense stresses and loads placed on the bone and to convey this information to the osteoblasts on the bone surface, thus enabling bone to adapt to altered mechanical loading by the formation of new bone. Osteocytes are also thought to be the cells that detect and direct the repair of microscopic damage that frequently occurs in the bone matrix due to wear and tear of the skeleton. Failure to repair the cracks and microfractures that occur in bone, or when this microdamage accumulates at a rate exceeding its repair, can cause the structural failure of the bone. This is seen, for example, in athletes where repeated loading of the bone leads to stress fractures.

A large number of molecules that regulate the formation and function of osteoblastic cells have been identified. The products of particular homeobox genes, which determine what tissue type the primitive cells will become, are especially important in the embryological development of the skeleton. Subsequently, circulating hormones, such as insulin, growth hormone, and insulinlike growth factors, combine with growth factors within the bone itself, such as transforming growth factor beta (TGFβ) and bone morphogenetic proteins (BMPs), to influence the differentiation of osteoblasts for the growth and repair of bone. During bone growth and in fracture repair, the sequential response of osteoblasts and their precursors to these influences controls each step in the cell differentiation pathway as well as the secretory activity of the mature osteoblasts.

Osteoclasts are typically large, multinucleated cells, rich in the intracellular machinery required for bone resorption. This is accomplished when the cells form a tight sealing zone by attachment of the cell membrane against the bone matrix, creating a bone-resorbing compartment. Into this space, the cell secretes acid to dissolve the bone mineral, and enzymes to digest the collagen and other proteins in the bone matrix. The removal of bone by osteoclasts is necessary to enable the repair of microscopic damage and changes in bone shape during growth and tooth eruption. Osteoclast-mediated bone resorption is also the mechanism for releasing calcium stored in bone for the maintenance of calcium levels in the blood. The level of calcium in the blood is monitored by the parathyroid gland and by the cells of the thyroid. If the level drops too low, parathyroid hormone is released to prevent the loss of calcium through the kidneys and to mobilize calcium from bone. If the blood calcium level is too high, the hormone calcitonin is released from the thyroid, which rapidly inhibits the resorptive activity of osteoclasts. Osteoclasts arise from precursor cells of the monocyte–macrophage series that are found in the bone marrow and circulate in the blood. Most agents that promote bone resorption act on osteoblastic cells, which in turn convey signals to osteoclast precursors to differentiate into mature osteoclasts. These agents include the active form of vitamin D, parathyroid hormone, interleukin-1, interleukin-6, and interelukin-11, and prostaglandins such as prostaglandin E_2. Differentiation to fully functional osteoclasts also requires close contact between osteoclast precursors and osteoblastic cells. This is due to a molecule called osteoclast differentiation factor (ODF) which is located on the surface of osteoblasts, binds to receptors on the surface of osteoclast precursor cells, and induces their progression to osteoclasts. The activity of ODF can be inhibited by a second molecule found in bone and elsewhere and termed osteoprotegerin or osteoclastogenesis-inhibitory factor (OCIF), which inhibits both the formation of osteoclasts and the activity of mature osteoclasts. Since OCIF acts as a naturally occurring ODF antagonist, it is most likely the local ODF/OCIF ratio that determines the local number and activity of osteoclasts. Thus, control of the concentrations of ODF and OCIF in various parts of the skeleton represents a possible mechanism for targeting the removal of bone to appropriate sites.

Bone formation, growth, and remodeling. The two types of bone (flat bones and long bones) are formed by different embryological means. Formation of flat bones occurs by intramembranous ossification, in which primitive mesenchymal cells differentiate directly into osteoblasts and produce bony trabeculae within a periosteal membrane. The initial nature of this bone is relatively disorganized and is termed woven bone. Later, this woven bone is remodeled and replaced by the mature lamella bone, consisting of layers of calcified matrix arranged in orderly fashion. Lamella bone has much greater strength characteristics than woven bone. Long bones are formed by intracartilaginous development in which the future bone begins as cartilage. The cartilage template is gradually replaced by bone in an orderly sequence of events starting at the center of the growing bone (the diaphysis). Cartilage remains at the ends of long bones during growth, forming a structure at each end termed the growth plate. Cartilage cells (chondrocytes) that arise in the growth plates proliferate and add to the length of the bone. This occurs during a complex series of events, with expansion away from the center of the bone to create the epiphyses, and expansion toward the center of the bone to create the metaphyses. (see **illus.**). When the bone achieves its final length in maturity, expansion from the growth plate ceases. Cartilage persists at the ends of the long bones in a specific form called articular cartilage, which provides the smooth bearing surfaces for the joints.

Bone is a dynamic tissue and is constantly being remodeled by the actions of osteoclasts and

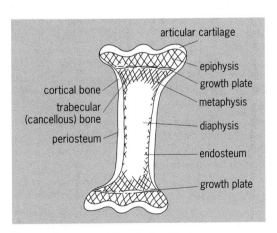

Diagramatic representation of a long bone.

osteoblasts. The removal of bone by osteoclasts occurs both on the surface of trabecular bone and within cortical bone, at random sites and at sites of microscopic damage. After bone removal, the osteoclasts either move on to new resorption sites or die; this is followed by a reversal phase where osteoblasts are attracted to the resorption site. It is thought that growth factors that are sequestered in an inactive form in the bone matrix are released and activated by the osteoclast activity and that these in turn promote fresh osteoid production by the recruited osteoblasts. The new osteoid eventually calcifies, and in this way the bone is formed and replaced in layers (lamellae), which are the result of these repeated cycles. In growing bone, the activities of bone cells is skewed toward a net increase in bone. However, in healthy mature bone there is an equilibrium between bone resorption and bone formation, due to communication between osteoblasts and osteoclasts. The nature of the signals between these two cell types is not completely understood, although, osteoclast formation and activation is directed in large part by osteoblasts. When the equilibrium between these two cell types breaks down, skeletal pathology results.

The most common bone disease is osteoporosis, in which there is a net loss of bone due to osteoclastic bone resorption that is not completely matched by new bone formation. The best-understood cause of osteoporosis is that which occurs in women due to the loss of circulating estrogen after menopause. A prolonged loss of bone in postmenopausal osteoporosis reduces bone strength, and it is the cause of a great deal of morbidity in the form of fractures, largely of the spine and femur. It is known that the frequency of this condition differs among racial groups. Exogenous estrogen, high-calcium diets, and exercise are some of the current treatments to counter the bone loss of postmenopausal osteoporosis. Another cause of osteoporotic bone loss is seen in disuse osteoporosis and in space flight. Just as bone can respond to increased loading with the production of additional bone, bone is also dependent on regular loading for its maintenance. Significant bone loss can occur during prolonged bed rest or, for example, in paraplegia and quadriplegia. Likewise, an unloading of the skeleton (due to a lack of gravitational pull) in space flight results in severe bone loss in astronauts unless the effects of gravity are simulated by special exercises and devices. *See* OSTEOPOROSIS.

Many metabolic and genetic diseases can affect the amount and quality of bone. Metabolic diseases such as diabetes, kidney disease, oversecretion of parathyroid hormone by the parathyroid glands, anorexia nervosa, and vitamin D–dependent rickets may cause osteopenias (the reduction in bone volume and bone structural quality). In addition, immunosuppressive therapy in organ transplant patients can lead to reduced bone mass. Tumors of bone and other sites can also lead to bone loss. Bone tumors include those that arise in bone and those that metastasize to bone from primary tumors in sites such as breast and prostate. Tumors can produce substances that cause the ac-

tivation of osteoclastic bone resorption, which can result in the destruction of bone and elevated levels of calcium in the blood. Two examples of genetically based diseases of bone are osteopetrosis and osteogenesis imperfecta. In the latter, mutations in the gene for type I collagen result in the production of reduced amounts of collagen or altered collagen molecules by osteoblasts, with a reduced capacity to serve as a support for bone mineral. Osteopetrosis is a rare set of conditions characterized by increased bone density due to a defect in the number or activity of osteoclasts. Other common diseases of the skeleton are diseases of the joints. Rheumatoid arthritis is an autoimmune disease characterized by inflammation of the joints and subsequent destruction of the cartilage and bone in the joints. It can be treated by management of the inflammation. The causes of osteoarthritis are less clear, but this too is characterized by the gradual destruction of the articular cartilage. When the joints become nonfunctional in these disease states, it is now common practice to surgically replace the joints with artificial prostheses. *See* CALCIUM METABOLISM; PARATHYROID GLAND; THYROID GLAND.   David M. Findlay

Bibliography. M. Favus (ed.), *Primer on the Metabolic Bone Diseases and Disorders of Mineral Metabolism*, 3d ed., Lippincott-Raven Press, Philadelphia, 1996; R. Marcus, D. Feldman, and J. Kelsey (eds.), *Osteoporosis*, Academic Press, New York, 1996; R. B. Martin and D. B. Burr (eds.), *Structure, Function, and Adaptation of Compact Bone*, Raven Press, New York, 1989.

Bone disorders

Disturbances in the structure and function of the skeletal system. The musculoskeletal system provides a rigid structural frame that permits locomotion through muscle action and aids in the functioning of the other organ systems. It also houses blood-forming marrow tissue and stores calcium, phosphorus, magnesium, and a variety of other ionic species. Bone is unique among the tissues of the body in that it responds to injury by re-forming itself identically over time, without scarring.

Trauma. Trauma to the musculoskeletal system can produce a closed or open fracture, a joint dislocation, or a sprain. The incidence of these injuries is highest among males 17–24 years of age. In the United States the annual rate of these injuries in the general population exceeds 20 million, with fractures constituting about one-fourth of the total. Fractures are manifested clinically by significant pain, swelling, and false motion, and in long-bone injuries by crepitation. Dislocation occurs more commonly in the shoulder and fingers than in any other joints. Injuries to the ligaments that maintain joint alignment are known as sprains and occur most frequently at the ankle.

The diagnosis of dislocation can frequently be made on clinical examination, but roentgenograms (x-rays) provide definitive evidence. Fractures are also diagnosed most frequently with routine roentgenograms, but special evaluation to determine the extent of the fracture or plan for surgical treatment requires computed tomography or magnetic resonance imaging. Operative treatment of long-bone fractures has become well accepted, particularly when multiple injuries are involved. Pelvic and spinal fractures are also treated with surgical correction and fixation. The traditional treatment approach of skeletal traction and casting has become less popular not only because it is more costly but also because the alternatives allow better results through earlier return to function. Even open fractures—after removal of foreign matter and damaged soft tissue and bone—are treated by internal fixation. *See* MEDICAL IMAGING; RADIOGRAPHY.

Bone healing begins with cellular proliferation and the formation of new blood vessels. These blood vessels penetrate the blood clot that fills the fracture area and provide provisional stabilization through the formation of a cartilaginous matrix. Calcification of this matrix produces a disorganized bony architecture (callus) that is larger than the original bone and provides mechanical stability at the fracture site until final internal remodeling takes place. Depending on the bone involved, this remodeling process requires weeks, months, or years for completion. Ultimately, the fracture callus is resorbed and the bone is reshaped so that it conforms to its original architecture. The extent and speed of this process depend on both mechanical stress and the age of the individual. *See* BONE.

Neoplasms. Primary neoplasms of bone and connective tissue are relatively uncommon compared with other musculoskeletal conditions; approximately 60% of all primary bone neoplasms are malignant. The most frequently occurring malignant neoplasms are multiple myeloma, osteosarcoma, chondrosarcoma, and Ewing's tumor. In young individuals the most common site of a neoplasm is the tibia or femur in the vicinity of the knee, while in older individuals the flat bones, such as the ilium and those of the axial skeleton, are frequently affected. The annual incidence of osteosarcoma, chondrosarcoma, and Ewing's tumor is 1.4–2.5 per 1 million population. Multiple myeloma, which arises from plasma cells in the bone marrow and has a higher annual incidence of 6–7 per 100,000 population, is also more prevalent among older persons. The incidence of benign bone tumors is less certain because individuals with these tumors frequently do not undergo treatment.

Benign lesions have many names and are also classified according to the type of tissue primarily affected (bone, cartilage, fibrous tissue). For example, cartilaginous tumors include the enchondroma and the exostosis, both of which may either results from hereditary factors or occur sporadically. The enchondroma is a lesion of cartilage within the bone; an exostosis is a lesion of cartilage that grows away from bone on a bony pedicle, usually near a joint. Bony lesions include the osteoblastoma and the osteoid osteoma; both of these have the histologic appearance of bone and are benign. Fibrocystic lesions include unicameral bone cysts, fibrous cortical defects, fibrous dysplasia, and giant-cell tumors. Fibrous dysplasia is a developmental lesion that often is characterized by multiply involved bones and is associated with café-au-lait spots on the skin. Unicameral bone cysts occur preferentially on the proximal humerus in adolescent children. They cause thinning of the bone and, occasionally, pathologic fractures.

Frequently, malignant tumors are identified when the individual complains of pain or swelling, or has a pathologic fracture. In contrast, many of the benign lesions are noted when routine roentgenographic examination is performed after trauma. Evaluation with various imaging techniques, including roentgenography, computed tomography, magnetic resonance imaging, and radionuclide bone scanning, is used to determine the type and extent of the tumor. If malignancy is suspected, a biopsy is performed to confirm the diagnosis. Benign tumors are treated by surgical removal and bone grafting when necessary, but malignant tumors require more aggressive treatment. If possible, the tumor is removed either by amputation or by limb salvage procedures. In the latter, the tumor and a margin of normal tissue are completely removed surgically and replaced with a prosthesis. This prosthesis, which is used to restore the associated joint or joints, is usually constructed from metal and plastic and is sometimes accompanied by bone allograft, that is, bone obtained from an unrelated donor. Chemotherapy and irradiation are used in conjunction with surgical treatment to provide additional protection against recurrence of the tumor.

Tumors arising in other organ systems, such as the gastrointestinal tract or the lungs, frequently spread to bone. These malignancies, while not bone tumors in the strict sense, affect the structural integrity of the bone and may therefore cause fractures and require treatment. In persons over 40 years of age, they occur more frequently than primary bone tumors. Because metastasis has such serious consequences, treatment of these lesions prior to fracture frequently involves radiation therapy. After fracture, treatment consists of internal fixation with the adjunct of acrylic bone cement, followed by irradiation. *See* CHEMOTHERAPY AND OTHER ANTINEOPLASTIC DRUGS; ONCOLOGY; PROSTHESIS; TUMOR.

Metabolic bone disease. Metabolic bone disease is an alteration in the normal bone metabolism. Bone structure is maintained by two types of cells: osteoclasts, responsible for removing damaged or old bone, and osteoblasts, responsible for building new bone. In various metabolic bone diseases, there are disturbances in the balance between osteoblastic and osteoclastic activity that alter the stability of skeletal structures. For example, a deficiency of vitamin C results in an inability to produce the protein matrix (osteoid) upon which bone mineral is laid by the osteoblast. Vitamin D deficiency results in an inability to mineralize the osteoid, the consequences of which are rickets in children and osteomalacia in adults. The incidence of vitamin D deficiency is quite low in developed countries, but there are various syndromes of rickets that do not respond to vitamin D. Rickets is characterized by shortness of stature and angular deformities of the weight-bearing bones. Osteomalacia is rare but can result when vitamin D is not absorbed through the gastrointestinal tract. It is associated with significant and widespread pain and tenderness of the bones and deformity of the spine and limbs. *See* ASCORBIC ACID; VITAMIN D.

Osteoporosis, the most common metabolic bone disease, occurs in a variety of diseases, including hyperparathyroidism, hyperthyroidism, hyperpituitarism, and hyperadrenocorticism. Osteoporosis in older persons can lead to fracture; thoracic vertebral bodies, the hip, and the wrist are the sites most commonly affected. While postmenopausal and senile osteoporosis results from insufficient bone production (decreased osteoblastic activity) and excessive bone destruction (increased osteoclastic activity), the precise etiology of this disorder is unknown. Hormonal factors and mechanical stress are known to play a role. *See* CALCIUM METABOLISM; OSTEOPOROSIS.

Osteomyelitis. Osteomyelitis is an infection of bone that is the result of either the blood-borne spread of an infectious agent or the secondary contamination of a fracture that has penetrated the skin. The blood-borne variety is a disease of growing bones, is more common in boys than in girls, and occurs most frequently in the end of the femur, tibia, or humerus. The bacterium *Staphylococcus aureus* is the most common causative agent; other bacteria, including the tuberculosis mycobacterium, as well as fungi also (rarely) cause osteomyelitis. The source of the infection is usually a skin lesion, although respiratory or urinary tract infections can also be a source. Acute osteomyelitis is characterized by severe bone tenderness and an unwillingness to use the limb, accompanied by loss of appetite and a fever. Osteomyelitis that results from an open fracture develops more slowly and results in a chronically draining wound, and healing of the fracture is either delayed or fails to occur at all. Treatment of either entity requires antibiotic therapy for a period of up to 6 weeks. Frequently, surgical intervention is needed to reduce an abscess and remove necrotic tissue.

Septic arthritis. Although infection of a joint can result from direct inoculation with an infectious agent, septic arthritis is most often a blood-borne condition. The incidence of this disease entity is higher in children than in adults, with the former affected primarily in the hip and elbow. As with osteomyelitis, *S. aureus* is most often responsible, while streptococci, pneumococci, and other bacteria are present less frequently. In adults, gonorrhea may be a source of joint infection. An individual with an infected joint usually experiences muscle spasm, severe tenderness and pain with the slightest movement, elevated temperature, and swelling of the joint. Immediate treatment is necessary to prevent permanent damage to the joint through the activity of enzymes generated by the infection. Surgical irrigation of the joint is frequently necessary, and optimal results are obtained if this is combined with appropriate antibiotic therapy.

Osteoarthrosis. Osteoarthrosis is a premature or excessive deterioration of the cartilage surface of a joint. This type of change occurs in all adults, but usually not to the extent that it causes symptoms. The local deterioration of the cartilage surface is associated with remodeling of the contiguous bone and subsequent secondary inflammation of the membrane lining the joint. When it reaches this stage, it is referred to as osteoarthritis (or degenerative arthritis, degenerative joint disease, or senescent arthritis).

Rheumatoid arthritis. Rheumatoid arthritis is one of a family of inflammatory polyarthritides. The condition is thought to be caused by an abnormality in the immune system in which the body produces antibodies against its own tissues. In addition to the joints, other organ systems are often involved. Nonsteroidal anti-inflammatory medications such as aspirin form the cornerstone of treatment; other drugs that may cause serious side effects are used less frequently only to control the symptoms not adequately managed by the former medications. Surgical treatment is aimed primarily at replacing the joints that have been damaged and do not respond to medication. The unpredictable exacerbations, remissions, and variable response to medication make rheumatoid arthritis difficult to treat. *See* ARTHRITIS; JOINT DISORDERS; SKELETAL SYSTEM.   Harry B. Skinner

Bibliography. J. H. Herndon, Orthopaedic surgery, *American College of Surgeons Bull.*, 74(2):18–24, 1989; T. L. Holbrook et al., *The Frequency of Occurrence, Impact, and Cost of Selected Musculoskeletal Conditions in the United States*, American Academy of Orthopedic Surgeons, 1984; D. J. McCarty (ed.), *Arthritis and Allied Conditions: A Textbook of Rheumatology*, 11th ed., 1989; R. B. Salter, *Textbook of Disorders and Injuries of the Musculoskeletal System*, 2d ed., 1983.

Bonsai

The construction of a mature, very dwarfed tree in a relatively small container. Although bonsai is formally an esoteric branch of horticulture, it is firmly based in the social, historical, and cultural ethic of Asian peoples and its introduction to Western cultures is a development of the twentieth century; indeed, Westerners had not even seen bonsai plants prior to the early decades of this century.

At the fundamental level, the word bonsai means merely "plant in a pot," and its origin can be traced back to China's Chou dynasty (900–250 B.C.), when emperors built miniaturized gardens in which soil, rocks, and plants from each province were installed as dwarfed representations of the lands held by the central government. These gardens included *punching* (potted plants within landscapes) and *shea tse ching* (plants in tubs) or, more commonly, *pun-sai* (plants in small containers). Selected species were usually those with mythic, symbolic, and esthetic significance—plum, cypress, and pines plus bamboo—or plants representing seasons of the year—peony, cherry, and maple. The introduction of Buddhism into China, with the religious stress on self-awareness and a concept of the eternal and age-lessness as exemplified by trees—concepts in keeping with tenets of Confucianism—shifted the emphasis of dwarfed potted trees from its political and esthetic aspects toward that of the construction as a representation and visual image of the eternal. The Buddhist cult of Chan (the Japanese Zen) utilized *pun-sai* as objects of contemplation to be viewed during the meditations that constituted a basic part of Chan ritual.

Up to the eleventh century A.D., China was the cultural and governmental model for most Asian cultures, and other nations sent officials, priests, and artists to China to learn the intellectual and practical skills which could be introduced into their own countries. Early Japanese visitors commented on the *pun-sai*, and some were carried back to Japan by the twelfth century. During the Kamakura period (1192–1333), a significant commerce in dwarfed plants was noted in official Japanese documents, and bonsai (a direct transliteration of *pun-sai*) were included in painting. Books and plays of the fourteenth century included bonsai as main or subsidiary themes, facilitating the diffusion of knowledge and appreciation of the plants and their significance. Bonsai in Japan received a major impetus when, in the seventeenth century, a Chinese official became disaffected with the Ming court and decamped to Japan, taking an extensive collection of plants and manuals on their construction and maintenance. A fairly complete historical record of bonsai styles, species used, and types of containers can be followed in Japanese woodblock prints dating from the sixteenth century.

In spite of the long-standing interest in bonsai in Japan and growing interest in Western nations, there have been surprisingly few controlled scientific studies related to the plants. As has long been true of most ornamental horticulture throughout the world, techniques and concepts have been passed by word of mouth or through apprenticeships, rather than having been codified and tested under controlled scientific conditions.

Esthetic aspects. There are two major aspects involved in the construction and maintenance of a bonsai plant, only one of which is susceptible to direct study. Esthetic aspects, which partake of the cultures from which the form is derived plus individual tastes, are not easily analyzed, although they undoubtedly play a more important role than do technological aspects.

Over several centuries the Japanese codified not only the plants to be used as bonsai subjects, but also the styles and sizes of the plants in their final form. In general, styles are based on observable natural growth patterns in various ecological situations. A solitary tree growing in an open field will develop a much different form than a genetically identical plant surrounded by other trees in a forest, and a tree exposed to constant winds coming from one direction will grow differently from one not so exposed. Major

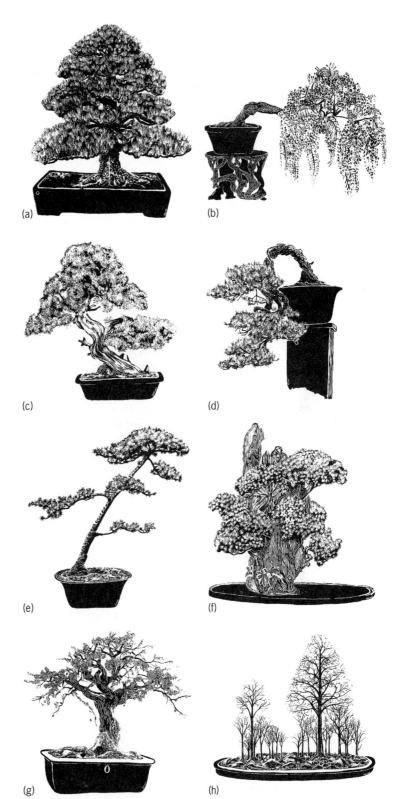

Major bonsai styles. (*a*) Formal upright (*Chokkan*); black pine. (*b*) Semicascade (*Han-Ken-gai*); wisteria. (*c*) Informal upright (*Moyogi*); juniper. (*d*) Cascade (*Kengai*); white pine. (*e*) Slanting (*Shakan*); spruce. (*f*) Rock clinging (*Ishezuke*); azalea. (*g*) Domed (*Gaito-Kengai*); plum. (*h*) Forest (*Yose-uye*); beech.

styles are shown in the **illustration**, and others have also been recognized. The rules for styles are flexible and variations are common. In Japan, some individual bonsai plants have been known as that particular plant for several centuries and are emulated and honored. Sizes, too, have been codified. Plants less than 15 cm (6 in.; pot included) are called *mame-bonsai* (hold-in-the-palm-of-one-hand), those from 15 to 30 cm (6 to 12 in.) tall are *ko-bonsai* (hold-in-one-hand), plants 30 to 60 cm (12 to 24 in.) tall are *chie-bonsai* (hold-with-two-hands), and those taller than 60 cm (24 in.) are *dai-bonsai* (two-people-needed).

The pot or container is also a matter of esthetic concern. Form, color, size, and decoration are selected to complement, enhance, or contrast with the plant. Until the eighteenth century, containers were usually Chinese antiques and correspondingly rare and expensive, but the growing enthusiasm for bonsai as both a religious form and a secular hobby caused the development of indigenous ceramic industries devoted to the manufacture of containers. These are usually clay or porcelain, high-fired and appropriately glazed, usually in earth tones of brown, blue, green, or rust. Sharp reds, purples, or other bright colors are usually avoided, although there are important exceptions.

Since, in Japan, bonsai was at first restricted to the priests and to associated nobility, monks were usually trained to make and maintain the plants. As interest rose, individuals adept at the procedures began to develop their own nurseries and to conduct classes on the technique. Some families have continued this tradition and, with formal examinations, can be designated as bonsai masters. Many have settled in Omiya, a suburb of Tokyo, where they not only keep large bonsai nurseries and teach, but also may keep precious individual plants for families who will have a plant delivered for viewing on a special holiday or for a few days when the plant is in bloom. Such viewings, mostly among the wealthy, are occasions for a tea ceremony. A national viewing and competition is held yearly under the patronage of the Emperor.

Technological aspects. To a large extent, the technology of bonsai is derived from classical horticultural procedures which are the product of long tradition firmed up with considerations of many areas of plant physiology and ecology. For optimum growth of any plant, adequate levels of water, air, nutrients, light, and temperature must be presented. Good horticultural practice is as necessary in bonsai as it is in any other aspect of gardening, although the restrictions of small containers and carefully controlled growth patterns necessitate additional care.

There are, however, some techniques which are unique to bonsai. To control and restrict top growth, nutrient levels, particularly those of nitrogen and phosphorus, require careful regulation. Most potted plants are viewed favorably when they are large and lush, while bonsai plants are admired when small, gnarled, and restrained. High levels of nitrogenous fertilizers, which facilitate rapid growth, are contraindicated, while higher P/N ratios promote woody growth with smaller leaves and better flowering. Because of small container volumes and restricted root systems, bonsai plants require a freely draining soil kept close to field capacity.

To maintain shape, not only must growth be controlled, but the branching patterns must be planned. This is done by selective pruning and by pinching out of terminal buds to release axillary buds from apical dominance. Root prunings, done at intervals as short as 2 or 3 months in some species, promote the development of a tight root ball with large numbers of young lateral roots whose ability to take up water and minerals is great.

Branch and stem position is controlled by selective pruning and by the wiring techniques developed by the Japanese in the eighteenth century. Copper wire is wound around the branch or stem, allowing the part to be moved into the desired position without cracking or breaking. Not only does the wire permit bending, but the stresses imposed by the wire and the new position induces the formation of reaction wood, xylem laid down by the cambium that fixes the branch in the new position, so that when the wire is removed, the branch remains in position. Weighting or tying is used for the same reasons. *See* PLANT GROWTH; PLANT MINERAL NUTRITION.   Richard M. Klein

Bibliography. T. Kawamota, *Saikei: Living Landscapes in Miniature*, Kodansha, Tokyo, 1967; J. Y. Naki, *Bonsai Techniques*, Bonsai Institute of California, Santa Monica, 1975; Y. Yoshimura and G. M. Halford, *The Japanese Art of Miniature Trees and Landscapes*, 1957.

Book manufacture

A series of professional operations including editing, designing, typography, platemaking, printing, and binding to transform a manuscript and its related illustrations into book form.

Books follow a distinctive technique in assembling and binding pages in sequential order and in fitting and sealing the pages into a separate cover. Those designed for relatively permanent usage are sealed into rigid or semirigid covers (called edition, case, or hardback binding; see **illustration**), and those designed for less permanent usage are sealed into paper covers (called soft or paperback binding).

The basic cell of a book's construction is called a signature or section and is composed of multiples of four pages. The folding of signatures printed on a web press is integrated with the printing units. In sheet-fed printing, folding is separate from presswork and is performed on special machines located in a book bindery.

Folding a sheet of paper once produces 4 pages, and each additional fold doubles the number of pages. A sheet folded three times yields a 16-page signature, the first page being the lowest numbered (a page number is called a folio). All right-hand pages are odd numbered, and left-hand pages are even numbered. A book of 160 pages has ten 16-page signatures, the first being folioed 1–16 and the last 145–160.

Signatures, assembled in sequence, are mechanically held together along one folded edge, called the

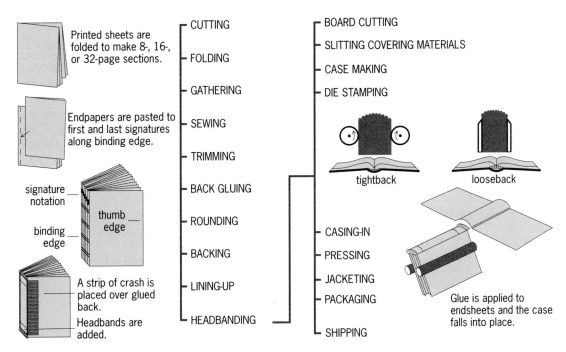

Printed sheets are folded to make 8-, 16-, or 32-page sections.

Endpapers are pasted to first and last signatures along binding edge.

signature notation

thumb edge

binding edge

A strip of crash is placed over glued back.

Headbands are added.

- CUTTING
- FOLDING
- GATHERING
- SEWING
- TRIMMING
- BACK GLUING
- ROUNDING
- BACKING
- LINING-UP
- HEADBANDING

- BOARD CUTTING
- SLITTING COVERING MATERIALS
- CASE MAKING
- DIE STAMPING

tightback   looseback

- CASING-IN
- PRESSING
- JACKETING
- PACKAGING
- SHIPPING

Glue is applied to endsheets and the case falls into place.

Steps in casebinding a book.

binding edge or spine, by continuous thread sewing through the fold of each signature; or by thread stitching through the side of the book from front to back; or by wire stapling; or by cutting off the binding-edge folds and applying a coating of strong flexible adhesive, sometimes adding an additional locking device of wide mesh textiles or stretch papers.

Purely decorative features include colorful bits of textiles added to the head and tail of the spine (called headbands) and tinted or gilded edges. One spectacular technical breakthrough was the mechanical gilding of book edges; for centuries this had been a closely guarded handicraft process.

The book cover serves to protect the pages against disintegration, to announce the title of the book, and to stimulate the visual interest of the prospective buyer. The degree of usage and permanency influences the selection of raw materials for a book cover (as in reference sets and text and library books), and visual appeal is influenced by the book's price and marketability. Permanent-type covers are made on special equipment in which the cover material and pulp-boards are assembled and joined with special adhesives. In embellishing the cover, the designer has numerous choices of special equipment and processes, such as flat ink, pigment or metal-foil stampings, embossing, silk-screening, and multicolor printing.

Preceding the final assembly of the book into its cover (called "casing in"), strong 4-page front and back end-sheets and one or more kinds of hinges (of textiles or paper) have been applied to strengthen the interlocking between book and cover (called "lining up"). The book also has acquired a concave and

convex edge and a pair of ridges or joints along the binding edge (called "backing"). These features are added by special equipment and are specifically engineered to securely lock the book into its cover and to transmit the strains of opening the book throughout the entire body instead of only to the first and last pages.

For shelf display, a book is often wrapped in a colorful, eyecatching jacket (called dust wrapper), or in a transparent synthetic if the cover is highly decorative.

Books reach their markets packaged in many different ways. Single copies are packaged and mailed directly to the consumer; sets are assembled into cartons, one set per carton; textbooks and other single titles are bulk-cartoned or skid-packed and shipped to central warehouses.

Computer-based technologies have changed the way that publishers prepare copy and printers produce books. Book manufacturing technologies that use advanced techniques include digital prepress, electronic page imposition, computer-to-print technology, digital printing, and demand-print and custom publishing services. With demand-print and custom publishing services, product literature and books are produced on demand. Information is stored in a database, and then the publishers or even the reader (if the database is maintained at point of purchase) can select chapters, pages, or articles relevant to a segment of the market and publish them in very small quantities, even a single copy. With digital technology, books are custom-made for a single need. For college courses, for example, instructors may select specific chapters from a publisher-provided digital library. The output format can be selected as well: from flexible prepunched looseleaf to high-quality patent or casebinding or in electronic form.

Book publishers and printers are on the threshold of a revolution in printing technology. Books printed by the conventional process of offset will continue to serve the needs of consumers and publishers. But decentralized multisite operations housing filmless, plateless digital presses will become more common as book publishers change from print-and-distribute to distribute-and-print, with information transmitted electronically to printing facilities or plants closer to markets. The book manufacturer takes on other functions for the publisher as well. Warehousing, inventory management, sophisticated bulk distribution, and individual fulfillment of orders of books to the consumer or reader are services offered by many book manufacturers. Printers can also be information managers for publishers, digitizing information and turning it into different media, such as electronic books in the form of CD-ROMs, on-line information services, or on-demand print products. *See* PRINTING. Gregor W. Hendricks; Thomas M. Destree

Bibliography. H. M. Fenton and F. J. Romano, *On-Demand Printing*, 1998; J. Greenfield, *ABC of Bookbinding: A Unique Glossary with Over 700 Illustrations for Collectors and Librarians*, 1998; R. M. Romano and F. J. Romano (eds.), *The GATF Encyclopedia of Graphic Communications*, 1998.

Boolean algebra

A branch of mathematics that was first developed systematically, because of its applications to logic, by the English mathematician George Boole, around 1850. Closely related are its applications to sets and probability.

Boolean algebra also underlies the theory of relations. A modern engineering application is to computer circuit design. *See* DIGITAL COMPUTER; SWITCHING THEORY.

Set-theoretic interpretation. Most basic is the use of boolean algebra to describe combinations of the subsets of a given set I of elements; its basic operations are those of taking the intersection or common part $S \cap T$ of two such subsets S and T, their union or sum $S \cup T$, and the complement S' of any one such subset S. These operations satisfy many laws, including those shown in Eqs. (1), (2), and (3).

$$S \cap S = S \quad S \cap T = T \cap S$$
$$S \cap (T \cap U) = (S \cap T) \cap U \tag{1}$$

$$S \cup S = S \quad S \cup T = T \cup S$$
$$S \cup (T \cup U) = (S \cup T) \cup U \tag{2}$$

$$S \cap (T \cup U) = (S \cap T) \cup (S \cap U)$$
$$S \cup (T \cap U) = (S \cup T) \cap (S \cup U) \tag{3}$$

If O denotes the empty set, and I is the set of all elements being considered, then the laws set forth in Eq. (4) are also fundamental. Since these laws are

$$O \cap S = O \quad O \cup S = S \quad I \cap S = S$$
$$I \cup S = I \quad S \cap S' = O \quad S \cup S' = I \tag{4}$$

fundamental, all other algebraic laws of subset combination can be deduced from them.

In applying boolean algebra to logic, Boole observed that combinations of properties under the common logical connectives *and*, *or*, and *not* also satisfy the laws specified above. These laws also hold for propositions or assertions, when combined by the same logical connectives. *See* LOGIC CIRCUITS.

Boole stressed the analogies between boolean algebra and ordinary algebra. If $S \cap T$ is regarded as playing the role of st in ordinary algebra, $S \cup T$ that of $s + t$, O of 0, I of 1, and S' as corresponding to $1 - s$, the laws listed above illustrate many such analogies. However, as first clearly shown by Marshall Stone, the proper analogy is somewhat different. Specifically, the proper boolean analog of $s + t$ is $(S' \cap T) \cup (S \cap T')$, so that the ordinary analog of $S \cup T$ is $s + t - st$. Using Stone's analogy, boolean algebra refers to boolean rings in which $s^2 = s$, a condition implying $s + s = 0$. *See* RING THEORY; SET THEORY.

Boolean algebra arises in other connections, as in the algebra of (binary) relations. Such relations ρ, σ, . . . refer to appropriate sets of elements $I, J, \ldots$. Any such ρ can be defined by describing the set of pairs (x, t), with x, in I and y, in J, that stand in the given relation—a fact symbolized $x \rho y$, just as its negation is written $x \rho' y$. Because of this set theoretic interpretation, boolean algebra obviously applies, with $x(\rho \cap \sigma)y$ meaning $x \rho y$ and $x \sigma y$, and $x(\rho \cup \sigma)y$ meaning $x \rho y$ or $x \sigma y$.

Abstract relationships. Before 1930, work on boolean algebra dealt mainly with its postulate theory, and with the generalizations obtained by abandoning one or more postulates, such as $(p')' = p$ (brouwerian logic). Since $a \cup b = (a' \cap b')'$, clearly one need consider $a \cap b$ and a' as undefined operations. In 1913 H. M. Sheffer showed one operation only $(a|b = a' \cap b')$ need be taken as undefined. In 1941 M. H. A. Newman developed a remarkable generalization which included boolean algebras and boolean rings. This generalization is based on the laws shown in Eqs. (5) and (6). From these assump-

$$a(b + c) = ab + ac$$
$$(a + b)c = ac + bc \tag{5}$$

$$a1 = 1 \quad a + 0 = 0 + a = a \quad aa' = 0$$
$$a + a' = 1 \tag{6}$$

tions, the idempotent, commutative, and associative laws (1) and (2) can be deduced.

Such studies lead naturally to the concept of an abstract boolean algebra, defined as a collection of symbols combined by operations satisfying the identities listed in formulas (1) to (4). Ordinarily, the phrase boolean algebra refers to such an abstract boolean algebra, and this convention is adopted here.

The class of finite (abstract) boolean algebras is easily described. Each such algebra has, for some nonnegative integer n, exactly 2^n elements and is algebraically equivalent (isomorphic) to the algebra of all subsets of the set of numbers 1, ... , n, under the operations of intersection, union, and complement. Furthermore, if m symbols $a_1, ... , a_m$ are combined symbolically through abstract operations $\cap$, $\cup$, and $'$ assumed to satisfy the identities of Eqs. (1) to (4), one gets a finite boolean algebra with 2^{2m} elements—the free boolean algebra with m generators.

Infinite relationships. The theory of infinite boolean algebras is much deeper; it indirectly involves the whole theory of sets. One important result is Stone's representation theorem. Let a field of sets be defined as any family of subsets of a given set I, which contains with any two sets S and T their intersection $S \cap T$, union $S \cup T$, and complements S', T'. Considered abstractly, any such field of sets obviously defines a boolean algebra. Stone's theorem asserts that, conversely, any finite or infinite abstract boolean algebra is isomorphic to a suitable field of sets. His proof is based on the concepts of ideal and prime ideal, concepts which have been intensively studied for their own sake. Because ideal theory in boolean algebra may be subsumed under the ideal theory of rings (via the correspondence between boolean algebras and boolean rings mentioned earlier), it will not be discussed here. A special property of boolean rings (algebras) is the fact that, in this case, any prime ideal is maximal.

The study of infinite boolean algebras leads naturally to the consideration of such infinite distributive laws as those in Eqs. (7a) and (7b).

$$x \cap (\cup_B y_\beta) = \cup_B(x \cap y_\beta)$$
$$x \cup (\cap_B y_\beta) = \cap_B(x \cup y_\beta) \qquad (7a)$$

$$\cap_C \left[\cup_{A_\gamma} u_{\gamma,\alpha}\right] = \cup_F \left[\cap_C u_{\gamma,\phi(\gamma)}\right]$$
$$\cup_C \left[\cap_{A_\gamma} u_{\gamma,\alpha}\right] = \cap_F \left[\cup_C u_{\gamma,\phi(\gamma)}\right] \qquad (7b)$$

For finite sets B of indices $\beta = 1, ... , n$, if $\cap_B y_\beta$ means $\cup y_1 \cdots \cup y_n$, and so on, the laws (7a) and (7b) follow by induction from (1) to (3). Also, if the symbols x, y_β, and so in (7a) and (7b) refer to subsets of a given space I, and if $\cup_B y_\beta$ and $\cap_B y_\beta$ refer to the union and intersection of all y_β in B, respectively, then (7a) and (7b) are statements of general laws of formal logic. However, they fail in most infinite boolean algebras. This is shown by the following result of Alfred Tarski: If a boolean algebra A satisfies the generalized distributive laws (7a) and (7b), then it is isomorphic with the algebra of all subsets of a suitable space I. A related result is the theorem of L. Loomis (1947) which states: Every σ-complete boolean algebra is isomorphic with a σ-field of sets under countable intersection, countable union, and complement.

In general, such completely distributive boolean algebras of subsets may be characterized by the prop-

erties of being complete and atomic. These properties may be defined roughly as the properties that (a) there exists a smallest element $\cup_B y_\beta$ containing any given set B of elements y_β and (b) any element $y > 0$ contains an atom (or point) $p > 0$, such that $p > x > 0$ has no solution (from Euclid, "A point is that which has no parts"). Condition (b) is also implied by the "descending chain condition" of ideal theory.

Other forms. Nonatomic and incomplete boolean algebras arise naturally in set theory. Thus, the algebra of measurable sets in the line or plane, ignoring sets of measure zero, is nonatomic but complete. The field of Borel sets of space is complete as regards countable families B of subsets S_β, but not for uncountable B. Analogous results hold for wide classes of other measure spaces and topological spaces, respectively. In any zero-dimensional compact space, the sets which are both open and closed (which "disconnect" the space) form a boolean algebra; a fundamental result of Stone shows that the most general boolean algebra can be obtained in this way.

Many other interesting facts about boolean algebra are known. For instance, there is an obvious duality between the properties of $\cap$ and $\cup$ in the preceding discussion. However, so many such facts have natural generalizations to the wider context of lattice theory that the modern tendency is to consider boolean algebra as it relates to such generalizations. For instance, the algebras of n-valued logic, intuitionist (brouwerian) logic, and quantum logic are not boolean algebras, but lattices of other types. The same is true of the closed sets in most topological spaces. For further information about boolean algebra *see* LATTICE (MATHEMATICS); TOPOLOGY.

Garrett Birkhoff

Bibliography. G. Birkhoff, *Lattice Theory*, 3d ed., Amer. Math. Soc. Colloq. Publ., vol. 25, 1967, reprint 1993; G. Birkhoff and S. MacLane, *A Survey of Modern Algebra*, 1997; F. M. Brown, *Boolean Reasoning*, 1990; J. D. Monk (ed.), *Handbook of Boolean Algebras*, 3 vols., 1989; Research and Education Association Staff, *The Essentials of Boolean Algebra*, rev. ed., 1993.

Boötes

The Herdsman, a constellation perhaps linked in mythology with the invention of the plow, though no specific Greek myth is associated with the name. The herdsman can be thought of holding Canes Venatici, the Hunting Dogs, and using them to drive Ursa Major, the Great Bear. The kite-shaped outline often given to the brightest stars of this northern constellation (see **illustration**) is linked to the kite's string by Arcturus, a red giant and the fourth brightest star in the sky (the second brightest in the northern sky). The arc of the Big Dipper's handle leads to Arcturus: "arc to Arcturus." *See* ARCTURUS; URSA MAJOR.

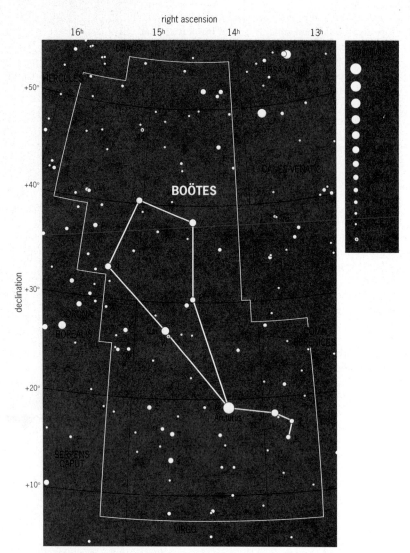

right ascension

declination

BOÖTES

Modern boundaries of the constellation Boötes, the Herdsman. The celestial equator is 0° of declination, which corresponds to celestial latitude. Right ascension corresponds to celestial longitude, with each hour of right ascension representing 15° of arc. Apparent brightness of stars is shown with dot sizes to illustrate the magnitude scale, where the brightest stars in the sky are 0th magnitude or brighter and the faintest stars that can be seen with the unaided eye at a dark site are 6th magnitude.

The modern boundaries of the 88 constellations, including this one, were defined by the International Astronomical Union in 1928. *See* CONSTELLATION.

Jay M. Pasachoff

Boracite

A borate mineral with chemical composition $Mg_3B_7O_{13}Cl$. It occurs in Germany, England, and the United States, usually in bedded sedimentary deposits of anhydrite ($CaSO_4$), gypsum ($CaSO_4 \cdot 2H_2O$), and halite (NaCl), and in potash deposits of oceanic type. The chemical composition of natural boracites varies, with Fe^{2+} or Mn^{2+} replacing part of the Mg^{2+} to yield ferroan boracite or manganoan boracite.

Boracite occurs in crystals which appear to be isometric in external form, despite the fact that the arrangement of the atoms in the crystal structure has only orthorhombic symmetry (see **illus.**).

When this natural low-temperature form is heated to 510°F (265°C), a slight readjustment of the atoms takes place internally without change in external form. The atomic symmetry of this resulting high-temperature form, which does not occur naturally, is then consistent with the external habit.

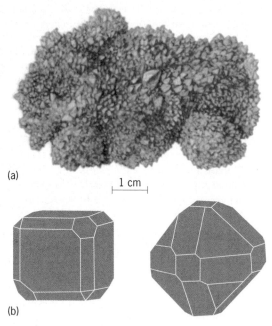

(a)

1 cm

(b)

Boracite. (*a*) Specimen from Segeberg, Germany (*specimen from Department of Geology, Bryn Mawr College*). (*b*) Crystal habits (*after C. S. Hurlbut, Jr., Dana's Manual of Mineralogy, 17th ed., Wiley, 1959*).

The hardness is 7–$7\frac{1}{2}$ on Mohs scale, and specific gravity is 2.91–2.97 for colorless crystals and 2.97–3.10 for green and ferroan types. Luster is vitreous, inclining toward adamantine. Boracite is colorless to white, inclining to gray, yellow, and green, and rarely pink (manganoan); its streak is white; and it is transparent to translucent. It is strongly piezoelectric and pyroelectric and does not cleave. *See* BORATE MINERALS.

Charles L. Christ

Borane

The general name given to any one of the binary boron hydrides of the general formula B_nH_m. Boron is the only element other than carbon that exhibits an extensive series of molecular hydrides. In contrast to the chains and rings of carbon atoms that typify carbon hydride chemistry, the structures of the boron hydrides are based on polyhedral clusters of boron atoms. These borane clusters are characterized by triangular faces, and such polyhedra are known as deltahedra. The boranes typically have a surface of *exo* B-H bonds directed radically outward from the deltahedral cluster. Deltahedra are closed if they consist entirely of triangular faces, whereas open deltahedra can also typically incorporate four-, five-, and six-membered open faces. Associated with such open faces are additional BHB bridging and/or *endo* B-H hydrogen atoms, which are held in positions approximately tangential to the cluster surface. These deltahedral cluster structures arise because assemblies of boron and hydrogen atoms have fewer electrons than bonding atomic orbitals available to hold them together. For this reason, they are sometimes described as electron-deficient. Carbon atoms have the same number of valence electrons as atomic orbitals available for bonding and can therefore form the more familiar electron-precise chains and rings of the hydrocarbons, or more electron-rich structures with active lone pairs if atoms of elements to the right of carbon in the periodic table, such as oxygen and nitrogen, are also incorporated. *See* BORON; HYDROCARBON; ORGANIC CHEMISTRY; STRUCTURAL CHEMISTRY.

The intracluster bonding framework of the boranes is typified by multicenter bonding, as there are insufficient framework electrons to provide two-electron two-center connectivity among all the atoms. In diborane, B_2H_6, the simplest borane, the two boron atoms are joined together by two BHB three-center bonds (structure **1**). There are insufficient electrons to provide the seven two-electron bonds for an ethane-like structure (**2**), although this

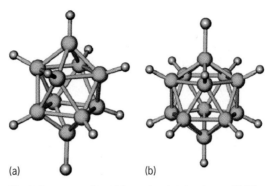

Fig. 1. Representation of the molecular structures of (*a*) the [*closo*-$B_{10}H_{10}$]$^{2-}$ dianion and (*b*) the [*closo*-$B_{12}H_{12}$]$^{2-}$ dianion. The cluster of [$B_{10}H_{10}$]$^{2-}$ is of regular bicapped-square-antiprismatic D_{4d} symmetry, and the cluster of [$B_{12}H_{12}$]$^{2-}$ is of regular icosahedral *I* symmetry.

(**1**)   (**2**)

is, in fact, the structure of the [B_2H_6]$^{2-}$ anion which, with two electrons more than neutral B_2H_6, is isoelectronic with ethane. Higher boranes incorporate additionally BBB three-center bonds. In the higher borane *nido*-decaborane, $B_{10}H_{14}$, a factorization of the bonding as in (**3**), in which circles represent

(**3**)

BH(*exo*) units, shows a typical higher-borane network of two-center bonds, three-center bonds, and partial three-center bonds. However, such renditions are simplistic, and represent a net valence-bond approximation. There is considerable multicenter delocalization in these larger clusters, best approached by molecular-orbital treatments. *See* MOLECULAR ORBITAL THEORY.

Classification. The known primary boranes fall naturally into three principal classes, the *closo* boranes, which are generally dianionic, of general formula [B_nH_n]$^{2-}$; the *nido* boranes, of general formula B_nH_{n+4}; and the *arachno* boranes, B_nH_{n+6}. These have progressively more open structures associated with a progressive increase in the number of electron pairs involved in the intracluster bonding. As an ex-

tension of the *closo-nido-arachno* sequence, *hypho* and *klado* boranes, B_nH_{n+8} and B_nH_{n+10}, can be postulated. Such structural types are not known for pure boranes, but are recognized in the carboranes, which are somewhat less electron-deficient, and in borane derivatives that incorporate electron-rich ligands. The carboranes (more rigorously, carbaboranes) are borane cluster compounds that also incorporate carbon atoms into the deltahedral clusters; they are closely related to the boranes and have the same general electronic and structural classifications. For a more detailed account of the electronic and geometric classification of boron-containing clusters *see* CARBORANE

The known single-cluster boranes are B_2H_6 (formally *nido*), *arachno*-B_4H_{10}, *nido*-B_5H_9, *arachno*-B_5H_{11}, *nido*-B_6H_{10}, *arachno*-B_6H_{12}, *nido*-B_8H_{12}, *arachno*-B_8H_{14}, *arachno*-B_9H_{15} (two isomers), and *nido*-$B_{10}H_{14}$, together with all the *closo* species [B_nH_n]$^{2-}$ from $n = 6$ through 12. The [*closo*-$B_{12}H_{12}$]$^{2-}$ ion (**Fig. 1**), with a very symmetrical icosahedral {B_{12}} configuration, is particularly stable. This closed 12-vertex configuration is, in fact, very stable, and represents an effective upper barrier to single-cluster size that is not easy to cross. Boron-based single clusters with more than 12 vertices are rare. Often, for a particular value of n, the most stable, best characterized, and best examined boranes are anions, formally obtained by deprotonation of a real or hypothetical parent neutral borane. This obviously applies to the [*closo*-B_nH_n]$^{2-}$ series, but other anions of particular stability and/or importance are [*arachno*-B_3H_8]$^-$, [*nido*-B_9H_{12}]$^-$, [*arachno*-B_9H_{14}]$^-$, [*arachno*-$B_{10}H_{14}$]$^{2-}$, and [*nido*-$B_{11}H_{14}$]$^-$. Other known borane anions include [*nido*-B_4H_9]$^-$, [*hypho*-B_5H_{12}]$^-$, and [*arachno*-B_7H_{12}]$^-$, which are mentioned because the neutral undeprotonated parent boranes have not been established. When heteroatoms are incorporated into the borane clusters as constituents to give heteroboranes, or when one-electron and two-electron substituents are attached to the boron cages, then the extent and variety of structure and chemistry, and of potential application, are increased considerably, compared to the known basic binary boron hydride species listed above.

Stability and reactivity. The boranes vary considerably in stability and reactivity. The smaller boranes spontaneously decompose to give higher boranes and hydrogen. Ultimately, an intractable hydrogen-poor boron-hydride polymeric species is formed. The smaller boranes will generally inflame spontaneously in air, whereas the larger boranes tend to be more stable. The larger borane $nido$-$B_{10}H_{14}$ is as stable in air as NaOH, and salts of the [$closo$-$B_{12}H_{12}$]$^{2-}$ dianion are indefinitely stable in air. However, these are gross generalizations, and there are many exceptions.

Syntheses. The syntheses of the boranes generally derive from the pioneering work of A. Stock and coworkers in the early 1900s. The classical route involves the thermolysis of B_2H_6, the simplest borane, which may be derived by treatment of metal borides or borohydrides with acid [reaction (1)], or by treatment of boron halides with hydridic reagents such as NaH or Li(AlH$_4$) [reaction (2)]. Thermolysis of B_2H_6

$$2M_3B_n + 6nHX \rightarrow nB_2H_6 + 6MX_n \quad (1)$$

$$2BCl_3 + 6NaH \rightarrow B_2H_6 + 6Na^+ + 6Cl^- \quad (2)$$

leads, via dihydrogen loss and a series of unstable intermediates, to the initial isolatable product $nido$-pentaborane, B_5H_9 (**Fig. 2b**), a colorless liquid with a melting point of $-47°C$ ($-52.6°F$) and a boiling point of $60°C$ ($140°F$). Subsequently, the much more stable $nido$-decaborane, $B_{10}H_{14}$ (Fig. 2c), is formed, as a colorless, volatile crystalline solid with a melting point of $99.5°C$ ($211°F$) and a boiling point of $213°C$ ($415°F$). Multiton quantities of these two substances were produced by the United States and the former Soviet Union during the Cold War, as their very high heats of combustion suggested their possible use as high-energy jet and rocket fuels. However, their combustion characteristics were far from ideal, and the problem of storing and handling the spontaneously flammable liquid B_5H_9 precluded their use as fuels. Nevertheless, the bulk of borane and carborane chemistry known to date originated largely from B_5H_9 and $B_{10}H_{14}$ as starting substrates.

These bulk sources of B_5H_9 and $B_{10}H_{14}$ no longer exist, but alternative syntheses of the important species $B_{10}H_{14}$, which is the principal entry into monocarbaborane chemistry, dicarbaborane chemistry, and most other borane and heteroborane chemistry in the 8-vertex and greater cluster-size region, are currently being developed. B_5H_9 may be prepared

in the laboratory from the [B_3H_8]$^-$ anion by reaction with BF_3 [reaction (3)], the [B_3H_8]$^-$ anion being obtained from the [BH_4]$^-$ anion by reaction with elemental iodine [reaction (4)].

$$3[B_3H_8]^- + 4BF_3 \rightarrow 2B_5H_9 + 3[BF_4]^- + 3H_2 \quad (3)$$

$$3[BH_4]^- + I_2 \rightarrow [B_3H_8]^- + 2I^- + 2H_2 \quad (4)$$

See METAL HYDRIDES.

The volatility and reactivity of B_5H_9 dictates that the study of most of its chemistry has required the use of vacuum-line techniques and a rigorously oxygen-free atmosphere. The much greater stability of $B_{10}H_{14}$ along with its consequent easier handling has generally permitted the examination of much of its chemistry under experimentally much easier conditions.

Reaction chemistry. Reactions of B_5H_9 and $B_{10}H_{14}$ are typical of general reaction behavior. In general, electrophilic substitution occurs at BH(exo) units off the open face (so-called apical positions), and nucleophilic substitution occurs at BH(exo) units around the open face. An extensive substituent chemistry is thus available, but is as yet insufficiently well refined to permit designed site-specific multiple substitution in the general case. BHB bridging hydrogen atoms are protolytically acidic; for example, $B_{10}H_{14}$ has a pK_a value in the region of 2.70, similar to that of ClH$_2$CCOOH at 2.85, giving the [$nido$-$B_{10}H_{13}$]$^-$ anion via proton loss from a bridging site. Most $nido$ and $arachno$ boranes that have BHB bridging hydrogen atoms similarly yield conjugate base anions on treatment with (non-nucleophilic) bases. Although the resulting species are still electron-deficient cluster species, the anionic sites generated can act as Lewis bases, and as such can coordinate to Lewis acid sites such as metal centers, resulting in the formation of metallaboranes. Although such species are ostensibly metal complexes with borane ligands, the metal center is generally bound very tightly. Consequently, such species are often better described as metallaborane cluster compounds in which the borane cluster has incorporated a metal center into the cluster structure.

Cluster closure along the $arachno$-$nido$-$closo$ sequence can occur by the removal of electrons from the cluster, as exemplified by the treatment of $nido$-$B_{10}H_{14}$ with amines, such as NEt$_3$, followed by thermolysis in which the [NHEt$_3$]$^+$ salt of the [$closo$-$B_{10}H_{10}$]$^{2-}$ anion is formed, along with dihydrogen [reaction (5)]. Conversely, electron addition

$$B_{10}H_{14} + 2NEt_3 \rightarrow 2[NHEt_3]^+ + [B_{10}H_{10}]^{2-} + H_2 \quad (5)$$

results in cluster opening along the $closo$-$nido$-$arachno$ sequence, as in the treatment of $nido$-$B_{10}H_{14}$ with elemental sodium in tetrahydrofuran to give the [$arachno$-$B_{10}H_{14}$]$^{2-}$ dianion by simple electron transfer. Closely related to the latter is the effective addition of electrons to the cluster by the attachment of two-electron ligands, as in the reactions of organyl phosphines, PR$_3$, with $nido$-B_8H_{12}

(a) (b) (c)

Fig. 2. Representations of the molecular structures of (a) $arachno$-B_4H_{10}; (b) $nido$-B_5H_9, and (c) $nido$-$B_{10}H_{14}$. B_4H_{10} and $B_{10}H_{14}$ have C_{2v} symmetry and B_5H_9 has C_{4v} symmetry.

to give *arachno*-$B_8H_{12}(PR_3)$ and with *nido*-B_5H_9 to give *hypho*-$B_5H_9(PR_3)_2$. An important variation of this is the reaction of *nido*-$B_{10}H_{14}$ with two two-electron ligands L to give *arachno* $B_{10}H_{12}L_2$ species with dihydrogen loss, for example, when L = SMe_2 [reaction (6)]. The *arachno* $B_{10}H_{12}L_2$ species are important intermediates in dicarborane formation from *nido*-$B_{10}H_{14}$.

$$B_{10}H_{14} + 2SMe_2 \rightarrow B_{10}H_{12}(SMe_2)_2 + H_2 \quad (6)$$

Cluster dismantling (that is, descent through a series to give lower boranes) is usually effected by stronger nucleophilic bases; for example, 10-boron *nido*-$B_{10}H_{14}$ converts to the 9-boron [*arachno*-B_9H_{14}]$^-$ anion by use of alcoholic aqueous KOH [reaction (7)]. The converse process of cluster

$$B_{10}H_{14} + 2[OH]^- + 2H_2O \rightarrow$$
$$[B_9H_{14}]^- + [B(OH)_4]^- + H_2 \quad (7)$$

Aufbau (that is, addition of vertices) is an important reaction type for the ascent of the series of boranes; for example, 10-boron *nido*-$B_{10}H_{14}$ with simple borohydride species, such as the [BH_4]$^-$ anion or neutral $BH_3(NR_3)$, will generate the 11-boron [*nido*-$B_{11}H_{14}$]$^-$ monoanion [reaction (8)] and then, under increasingly forcing conditions, the 12-boron [*closo*-$B_{12}H_{12}$]$^{2-}$ dianion [reaction (9)].

$$B_{10}H_{14} + [BH_4]^- \rightarrow [B_{11}H_{14}]^- + 2H_2 \quad (8)$$

$$B_{10}H_{14} + 2BH_3(NR_3) \rightarrow$$
$$[B_{12}H_{12}]^{2-} + 2[NHEt_3]^+ + 3H_2 \quad (9)$$

Atoms of elements other than boron can be incorporated in *Aufbau* processes, such as the incorporation of metal centers to generate metallaboranes and of sulfur to generate thiaboranes, with both falling into a general classification of heteroboranes. Many reactions are accompanied by cluster rearrangement processes. Although cluster rearrangements are difficult to recognize in pure boron-hydride chemistry, requiring site labeling for their elucidation, cluster rearrangements are established as quite common in heteroborane chemistry in which sites are effectively labeled by their occupation by the heteroatoms.

Many reaction systems incorporate two or more of the several processes defined above, such as in the reaction of *nido*-$B_{10}H_{14}$ with the polysulfide anion to give the *arachno* 10-vertex [SB_9H_{12}]$^-$ anion, an important entry into thiaborane cluster chemistry [reaction (10)].

$$B_{10}H_{14} + [S_x]^{2-} + 4H_2O \rightarrow$$
$$[SB_9H_{12}]^- + \{S_{(x-1)}\} + [B(OH)_4]^- + 3H_2 \quad (10)$$

Cluster fusion and macropolyhedral boranes. Although the cluster chemistry of boron hydrides is potentially very extensive, its widest development is inhibited by the experimental difficulty of progressing beyond the single-cluster stability barrier

of the 12-vertex icosahedron that is typified by the [*closo*-$B_{12}H_{12}$]$^{2-}$ anion. Boron-based single clusters with more than 12 vertices are rare. Although clusters can be joined by simple two-electron, two-center B—B sigma bonds—for example, in (*nido*-$B_{10}H_{13}$)$_2$, of which several isomers can be isolated in low yield from a thermolysis of *nido*-$B_{10}H_{14}$—there is difficulty in generating bigger boranes in which smaller clusters are fused together more intimately with boron atoms held in common between the two clusters, so that the multicenter bonding is contiguous across the conjunction. The development of this area is inhibited by the lack of transferable generic routes for intercluster fusion. However, the structures and chemistries of the known macropolyhedral higher boranes—$B_{12}H_{16}$, $B_{13}H_{19}$, $B_{14}H_{18}$, $B_{14}H_{20}$, $B_{15}H_{23}$, $B_{16}H_{20}$, $B_{18}H_{22}$ (two isomers), the [$B_{19}H_{22}$]$^-$ anion, and $B_{20}H_{16}$—indicate that future chemistry will be extensive, and will be rendered even more so by combining the structural features of the boranes with the extensive known types of structural features of electron-rich molecular architecture such as that of carbon-based chemistry. Of the macropolyhedral boranes, the $B_{18}H_{22}$ isomers, *n*-$B_{18}H_{22}$ and *iso*-$B_{18}H_{22}$, also known as *anti*-$B_{18}H_{22}$ and *syn*-$B_{18}H_{22}$ respectively, are the best examined (**Fig. 3**). *Anti*-$B_{18}H_{22}$ is a colorless, stable crystalline compound that may be obtained by the thermolysis of *arachno* 9-vertex $B_9H_{13}(OEt_2)$ [reaction (11)].

$$2B_9H_{13}(OEt_2) \rightarrow B_{18}H_{22} + 2OEt_2 + 2H_2 \quad (11)$$

Structurally (for example, lower schematic cluster structure diagrams in Fig. 3), the $B_{18}H_{22}$ isomers can be viewed as consisting of two *nido*-decaboranyl clusters fused together with two boron atoms held in common (for example, lower schematic cluster

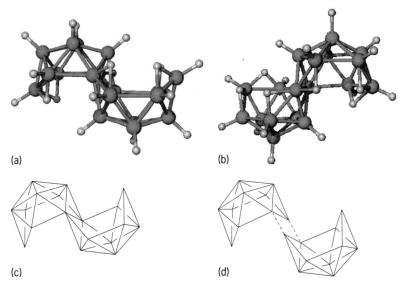

(a)   (b)

(c)   (d)

Fig. 3. Representations of the molecular structures of (*a*) *anti*-$B_{18}H_{22}$ and (*b*) *syn*-$B_{18}H_{22}$. Note the resemblance of each subcluster in each molecule to that of *nido*-$B_{10}H_{14}$ (Fig. 2*c*). Diagrams *c* and *d* illustrate for *anti*-$B_{18}H_{22}$ the manner of fusion, with two boron atoms held in common, of two *nido*-decaboranyl sub-cluster units: (*c*) a schematic representation of the boron cluster framework of *anti*-$B_{18}H_{22}$ and (*d*) a factorization of the structure into two *nido*-decaboranyl units.

structure diagrams in Fig. 3). This view is also reflected in some of their chemistry, with several, but by no means all, of their known reactions resembling those of *nido*-$B_{10}H_{14}$.

Heteroborane chemistry. The *closo/nido/arachno/* etc. geometrical and electronic principles apply to clusters that also contain atoms of elements other than boron as cluster constituents. R. Hoffman's isolobal principle for comparing molecular fragments is useful in rationalizing such heteroboranes. For example, the frontier orbitals and electron occupancy of a neutral {CH} fragment—three orbitals and two electrons—mimic those for an anionic {BH}$^-$ fragment, and so these fragments can notionally replace each other in molecular structures; that is, they are isolobal. Alternatively, cationic {CH$^+$} can be regarded as isolobal with neutral {BH}. Application of this principle generates, for example, the [*closo*-$CB_{11}H_{12}$]$^-$ monanion and neutral *closo*-$C_2B_{10}H_{12}$ from the [*closo*-$B_{12}H_{12}$]$^{2-}$ dianion. Both these carboranes are in fact well-recognized species. The same principle applies to other main-group element fragments, such as {NH} and {S}, that can be regarded as isolobal with {BH}$^{2-}$. Thus, neutral 12-vertex $HNB_{11}H_{11}$ and $SB_{11}H_{11}$ are also known analogues of the stable [*closo*-$B_{12}H_{12}$]$^{2-}$ anion. The incorporation of such heteroatoms introduces more flexibility and variety than is available to pure boron-hydride chemistry. For example, the sulfur-containing thiaboranes have enabled the extension of fused-cluster macropolyhedral architectures significantly beyond those exhibited by the boranes themselves, with the elucidation of several neutral species, [n-$S_2B_{16}H_{16}$], [*iso*-$S_2B_{16}H_{16}$], [*iso*-$S_2B_{16}H_{14}(PPh_3)$], [$S_2B_{17}H_{17}$], [$S_2B_{17}H_{17}(SMe_2)$], and [$S_2B_{18}H_{20}$], and the monoanions [$S_2B_{16}H_{15}$]$^-$, [$S_2B_{16}H_{17}$]$^-$, [*iso*-$S_2B_{16}H_{17}$]$^-$, [$SB_{17}H_{19}$]$^-$, [$S_2B_{17}H_{16}$]$^-$, [$S_2B_{17}H_{18}$]$^-$, [$S_2B_{18}H_{19}$]$^-$, and [*iso*-$S_2B_{18}H_{19}$]$^-$.

The principle of isolobal replacement also applies to the rationalization of compounds resulting from the incorporation of metal centers into the boron hydride clusters to form metallaboranes. Thus, the neutral formally octahedral iron(II) fragment {Fe(CO)$_3$} has three orbitals and two electrons available for bonding and thereby mimics a neutral {BH} fragment. The yellow low-melting [(CO)$_3$FeB$_4H_8$], isolated in low yield from the co-thermolysis of *nido*-B_5H_9 with [Fe(CO)$_5$], has a *nido* five-vertex {FeB$_4$} cluster core that overall mimics *nido*-B_5H_9. The neutral {Ru(η^6-Ar)} fragment, where Ar is an aromatic ligand such as C_6H_6 or C_6Me_6, is another {BH} mimic. In accord with this, a series of isomers of [(η^6-C_6Me_6)RuB$_9H_{13}$], all with 10-vertex {RuB$_9$} cluster structures analogous to the {B$_{10}$} unit of *nido*-$B_{10}H_{14}$, are known. The area of metallaborane chemistry is extensive. The principle of isolobal substitution is general, so that the structures of many cluster compounds that do not contain boron, particularly the carbonyls of the Fe/Ru/Os group, can be rationalized on the basis of the borane structures and the isolobal concept. *See* METAL CLUSTER COMPOUND.   John D. Kennedy

Bibliography. L. Barton, Systemisation and structures of the boron hydrides, pp. 169–206 in *New Trends in Chemistry (Topics in Current Chemistry 100)*, ed. by F. L. Boschke, Springer-Verlag, 1982; J. Bould et al., *Boron Chemistry at the Millennium* (special edition), *Inorg. Chim. Acta*, 289:95–124, 1999; M. J. Carr et al., Macropolyhedral boron-containing cluster chemistry, a metallathiaborane from $S_2B_{17}H_{17}$: Isolation and characterisation of [(PMe$_2$Ph)$_2$PtS$_2B_{16}H_{16}$], a *neo-arachno* ten-vertex cluster shape, and the constitution of the [*arachno*-$B_{10}H_{15}$]$^-$ anion, *Collect. Czechoslovak Chem. Commun.* 70:430–440, 2005; J. Casanova (ed.), *The Borane-Carborane-Carbocation Continuum*, Wiley, 1998; M. G. Davison et al. (eds.), *Contemporary Boron Chemistry*, Royal Society of Chemistry, Cambridge, 2000; N. N. Greenwood and A. Earnshaw, Boron, pp. 139–215 in *The Chemistry of the Elements*, 2d ed., Butterworth-Heineman, Oxford, 1997/1998; M. F. Hawthorne, The role of chemistry in the development of boron neutron capture therapy of cancer, *Angewandte Chem. Int. Ed.*, 32:950–984, 1993; J. D. Kennedy, The polyhedral metallaboranes, *Prog. Inorg. Chem.* 32:519–679, 1984, and 34:211–434, 1986; E. L. Muetterties (ed.), *Boron Hydride Chemistry*, Academic Press, 1975; J. Plešek, Potential applications of the boron cluster compounds, *Chem. Rev.*, 92:269–278, 1992; S. L. Shea et al., Polyhedral boron-containing cluster chemistry: Aspects of architecture beyond the icosahedron, *Pure Appl. Chem.* 75:1239–1248, 2003; A. Stock, *Hydrides of Boron and Silicon*, Cornell University Press, 1933; K. Wade, Structural and bonding patterns in cluster chemistry, *Adv. Inorg. Chem. Radiochem.*, 18:1–66, 1976; A. J. Welch et al., Beyond the icosahedron: The first 13-vertex carborane, *Angewandte Chem. Int. Ed.*, 42:225–228, 2003.

Borate minerals

A large group of minerals in which boron is chemically bonded to oxygen. Boron is a fairly rare element. However, because of its chemical character, it is very susceptible to fractionation in Earth processes and can become concentrated to a degree not found in other elements of similar abundance. Boron is symbolized B, has the atomic number 5, and has the ground-state electronic structure [He]$2s^22p^1$. The very high ionization potentials for boron mean that the total energy required to produce the B^{3+} ion is greater than the compensating structure energy of the resulting ionic solid, and hence bond formation involves covalent (rather than ionic) mechanisms. However, boron has only three electrons to contribute to covalent bonding involving four orbitals, (s, p_x, p_y, p_z). This results in boron being a strong electron-pair acceptor (that is, a strong Lewis acid) with a very high affinity for oxygen. The structural chemistry of boron and silicon (Si), when associated with oxygen (O), is quite similar. The BO_3, BO_4, and SiO_4 groups have a marked tendency to polymerize in the solid state, and this aspect of their behavior gives rise to the structural complexity of both groups. However, subtle differences in chemical bonding do give rise to differences in the character of this polymerization, particularly when H_2O is also involved. These differences result in the very different properties of the resultant minerals and their very different behavior in Earth processes. *See* BORON.

Structural classification. The boron cation is small and can occur in both triangular and tetrahedral coordination by oxygen: $(BO_3)^{3-}$ and $(BO_4)^{5-}$. Hydrogen (H) atoms readily bond to the oxygen atoms of the borate groups to form $[B(OH)_3]^0$ and $[B(OH)_4]^-$ groups or intermediate groups such as $[BO_2(OH)]^{2-}$ and $[BO_2(OH)_2]^{3-}$; all types of borate groups can be generally written as $(B\phi_3)$ or $(B\phi_4)$, where $\phi = O^{2-}$, OH^-. The borate groups readily polymerize to give great structural diversity in borate minerals. A specific structure may be characterized by the numbers of $(B\phi_3)$ triangles and $(B\phi_4)$ tetrahedra in the structure. These characteristics may be denoted by two symbols of the form $A{:}B$. A is the number of $(B\phi_3)$ and $(B\phi_4)$ groups, denoted as $A = x\triangle y\square$, where x is the number of $(B\phi_3)$ [$= \triangle$] groups and y is the number of $(B\phi_4)$ [$= \square$] groups. B is a character string that contains information on the connectivity of the polyhedra. The string is written such that adjacent $\triangle$ or $\square$ (or both) represent polyhedra that share corners, and the delimiters $<>$ indicate that the included polyhedra share corners to form a ring. The sharing of polyhedra between rings is indicated by the symbols $-$, $=$, $\equiv$, and so on, for one, two, three, or more polyhedra, respectively. For example, the *FBB* with the descriptor $2\triangle2\square{:}{<}\triangle2\square{>}{=}{<}\triangle2\square{>}$ contains two triangles and two tetrahedra. There are two three-membered rings of polyhedra, each of which contains one triangle and two tetrahedra, and the rings have two tetrahedra in common. The resulting symbol denotes the borate components and their connectivity in the crystal structure at the local level; such local clusters of polyhedra are called fundamental building blocks. These fundamental building blocks (*FBB*) link together to form the structural unit of the crystal, a strongly bonded (usually anionic) array of atoms; the structural units are then linked together by weakly bonding interstitial atoms (commonly sodium, potassium, calcium, and hydrogen in borate minerals) to form the complete crystal structure of the mineral. The structural classification of borate minerals is based on the character of the polymerization of the fundamental building blocks to form the structural unit. Polymerization may occur in 0, 1, 2, or 3 dimensions, forming structural units that are isolated polyhedra or finite clusters of polyhedra (0-dimensional polymerization), infinite chains (1-dimensional polymerization), infinite sheets (2-dimensional polymerization), and infinite frame-works (3-dimensional polymerization). In the **table** are shown the borate minerals of known structure, classified according to these principles. *See* POLYHEDRON; POLYMERIZATION.

Mixed-anion borate minerals. The $(B\phi_3)$ and $(B\phi_4)$ borate groups may combine with other geologically common oxyanions [for example, $(SO_4)^{2-}$, sulfate; $(PO_4)^{3-}$, phosphate; $(AsO_4)^{3-}$, arsenate; $(CO_3)^{2-}$, carbonate; $(SiO_4)^{4-}$, silicate; $(BeO_4)^{6-}$, beryllate] to produce mixed-anion minerals. Of these, the silicates are the most diverse (see table), and include tourmaline, a group of very common accessory minerals in a wide variety of geological environments.

Occurrence. Boron has an estimated primitive-mantle abundance of 0.6 part per million and a crustal abundance of 15 ppm. Despite this low abundance, fractionation in crustal processes results in concentration of boron to the extent that it forms an extensive array of minerals in which it is an essential constituent, and very complex deposits of borate minerals. Major concentrations of borate minerals occur in continental evaporite deposits (common in the desert regions of California and Nevada). Borate minerals are often very soluble in aqueous environments. In areas of internal drainage, saline lakes are formed, and continued evaporation leads to accumulation of large deposits of borate minerals. Borates may also occur in marine evaporites. Isolated-cluster borates (see table) are characteristic of metamorphosed boron-rich sediments and skarns. Most borosilicate minerals are characteristic of granitic-pegmatite environments, either as a pegmatite phase or as a constituent of their exocontact zone. In particular, tourmaline is the most widespread of the mixed-anion borate minerals, occurring in a wide variety of igneous, hydrothermal, and metamorphic rocks. *See* ORE AND MINERAL DEPOSITS; PEGMATITE; SALINE EVAPORITES.

Industrial uses. Despite its low crustal abundance, fractionation of boron in crustal processes leads to formation of deposits of borate minerals from which boron and (borates) can be easily extracted in large quantities. The easy availability and unique chemical properties result in boron being a major industrial material. It is widely used in soaps and washing powders. Boron combines well with silicon and other elements to form a wide variety of special-property glasses and ceramics; it also alloys with a variety of metals, producing lightweight alloys for specialty uses. Boron compounds usually have very low density; hence borates in particular are used as lightweight fillers in medicines, and also are used as insulation. The fibrous nature of some borate minerals results in their use in textile-grade fibers and lightweight fiber-strengthened materials. The mineral borax is used as a water softener and as a cleaning flux in welding and soldering. Boric acid has long been used as an antiseptic and a drying agent. Boron is also important as a constituent of inflammatory materials in fireworks and rocket fuel. Some mixed-anion borate minerals are used as gemstones. Tourmaline is of particular importance in this respect, forming pink (rubellite), blue-green (Paraiba tourmaline), green (chrome tourmaline), and pink + green (watermelon tourmaline) from a wide variety of localities. Kornerupine and sinhalite are also used

Borate minerals

Borate groups (A)	Name	Connectivity (B)	Formula
		Isolated borate-group minerals	
$1\triangle$	Fluoborite	$\triangle$	$Mg_3(BO_3)(F,OH)_3$
$1\triangle$	Painite	$\triangle$	$CaZr(BO_3)Al_9O_{15}$
$1\triangle$	Jeremejevite	$\triangle$	$Al_6(BO_3)_5F_3$
$1\triangle$	Warwickite	$\triangle$	$(Mg,Ti,Fe^{3+},Al)_2O(BO_3)$
$1\triangle$	Azoproite	$\triangle$	$(Mg,Fe^{2+})_2(Fe^{3+},Ti,Mg)O_2(BO_3)$
$1\triangle$	Bonaccordite	$\triangle$	$Ni_2Fe^{3+}O_2(BO_3)$
$1\triangle$	Fredrikssonite	$\triangle$	$Mg_2(Mn^{3+},Fe^{3+})O_2(BO_3)$
$1\triangle$	Ludwigite	$\triangle$	$Mg_2FeO_2(BO_3)$
$1\triangle$	Vonsenite	$\triangle$	$Fe_2Fe^{3+}O_2(BO_3)$
$1\triangle$	Pinakiolite	$\triangle$	$(Mg,Mn^{2+})_2(Mn^{3+},Sb^{3+})O_2(BO_3)$
$1\triangle$	Hulsite	$\triangle$	$(Fe^{2+},Mg)_2(Fe^{3+},Sn)O_2(BO_3)$
$1\triangle$	Magnesiohulsite	$\triangle$	$(Mg,Fe)_2(Fe^{3+},Sn)O_2(BO_3)$
$1\triangle$	Chestermanite	$\triangle$	$Mg_2(Fe^{3+},Mg,Al,Sb^{5+})O_2(BO_3)$
$1\triangle$	Orthopinakiolite	$\triangle$	$(Mg,Mn^{2+})_2Mn^{3+}O_2(BO_3)$
$1\triangle$	Blatterite	$\triangle$	$(Mn^{2+},Mg)_2(Mn^{3+},Sb^{3+},Fe^{3+})O_2(BO_3)$
$1\triangle$	Takéuchiite	$\triangle$	$(Mg,Mn^{2+})_2(Mn^{3+},Fe^{3+})O_2(BO_3)$
$1\triangle$	Karlite	$\triangle$	$Mg_7(OH)_4(BO_3)_4Cl$
$1\triangle$	Wightmanite	$\triangle$	$Mg_5O(OH)_5(BO_3)(H_2O)_2$
$1\triangle$	Jimboite	$\triangle$	$Mn_3(BO_3)_2$
$1\triangle$	Kotoite	$\triangle$	$Mg_3(BO_3)_2$
$1\triangle$	Nordenskioldine	$\triangle$	$CaSn(BO_3)_2$
$1\triangle$	Tusionite	$\triangle$	$MnSn(BO_3)_2$
$1\triangle$	Sassolite	$\triangle$	$[B(OH)_3]$
$1\square$	Sinhalite	$\square$	$AlMg(BO_4)$
$1\square$	Bandylite	$\square$	$Cu[B(OH)_4]Cl$
$1\square$	Teepleite	$\square$	$Na_2[B(OH)_4]Cl$
$1\square$	Frolovite	$\square$	$Ca[B(OH)_4]_2$
$1\square$	Hexahydroborite	$\square$	$Ca[B(OH)_4]_2 \cdot 2H_2O$
$1\square$	Henmilite	$\square$	$Ca_2Cu(OH)_4[B(OH)_4]_2$
		Finite-cluster borate minerals	
$2\triangle$	Suanite	$2\triangle$	$Mg_2[B_2O_5]$
$2\triangle$	Szaibelyite	$2\triangle$	$Mg_2(OH)[B_2O_4(OH)]$
$2\triangle$	Sussexite	$2\triangle$	$Mn_2(OH)[B_2O_4(OH)]$
$2\triangle$	Kurchatovite	$2\triangle$	$CaMg[B_2O_5]$
$2\square$	Pentahydroborite	$2\square$	$Ca[B_2O(OH)_6](H_2O)_2$
$2\square$	Pinnoite	$2\square$	$Mg[B_2O(OH)_6]$
$2\triangle1\square$	Ameghinite	$(2\triangle\square)$	$Na[B_3O_3(OH)_4]$
$1\triangle2\square$	Inderite	$\langle\triangle2\square\rangle$	$Mg[B_3O_3(OH)_5](H_2O)_5$
$1\triangle2\square$	Kurnakovite	$\langle\triangle2\square\rangle$	$Mg[B_3O_3(OH)_5](H_2O)_5$
$1\triangle2\square$	Inyoite	$\langle\triangle2\square\rangle$	$Ca[B_3O_3(OH)_5](H_2O)_4$
$1\triangle2\square$	Meyerhofferite	$\langle\triangle2\square\rangle$	$Ca[B_3O_3(OH)_5](H_2O)$
$1\triangle2\square$	Solongoite	$\langle\triangle2\square\rangle$	$Ca_2[B_3O_4(OH)_4]Cl$
$1\triangle2\square$	Inderborite	$\langle\triangle2\square\rangle$	$CaMg[B_3O_3(OH)_5]_2(H_2O)_6$
$3\square$	Nifontovite	$(3\square)$	$Ca_3[B_3O_3(OH)_6]_2(H_2O)_2$
$2\triangle2\square$	Hydrochlorborite	$\langle\triangle2\square\rangle\triangle$	$Ca_2[B_3O_3(OH)_4][BO(OH)_3]Cl(H_2O)_7$
$4\square$	Uralborite	$(3\square)\square$	$Ca_2[B_4O_4(OH)_8]$
$4\triangle1\square$	Sborgite	$(2\triangle\square)-(2\triangle\square)$	$Na[B_5O_6(OH)_4](H_2O)_3$
$2\triangle3\square$	Ulexite	$\langle\triangle2\square\rangle-\langle\triangle2\square\rangle$	$NaCa[B_5O_6(OH)_6](H_2O)_5$
$2\triangle2\square$	Borax	$\langle\triangle2\square\rangle=\langle\triangle2\square\rangle$	$Na_2[B_4O_5(OH)_4](H_2O)_8$
$2\triangle2\square$	Tincalconite	$\langle\triangle2\square\rangle=\langle\triangle2\square\rangle$	$Na_2[B_4O_5(OH)_4](H_2O)_3$
$2\triangle2\square$	Hungchaoite	$\langle\triangle2\square\rangle=\langle\triangle2\square\rangle$	$Mg[B_4O_5(OH)_4](H_2O)_7$
$2\triangle2\square$	Fedorovskite	$\langle\triangle2\square\rangle=\langle\triangle2\square\rangle$	$Ca_2Mg_2(OH)_4[B_4O_7(OH)_2]$
$2\triangle2\square$	Roweite	$\langle\triangle2\square\rangle=\langle\triangle2\square\rangle$	$Ca_2Mn_2(OH)_4[B_4O_7(OH)_2]$
$3\triangle3\square$	Mcallisterite	$[\phi]\langle\triangle2\square\rangle|\langle\triangle2\square\rangle|\langle\triangle2\square\rangle|$	$Mg_2[B_6O_7(OH)_6]_2(H_2O)_9$
$3\triangle3\square$	Aksaite	$[\phi]\langle\triangle2\square\rangle|\langle\triangle2\square\rangle|\langle\triangle2\square\rangle|$	$Mg[B_6O_7(OH)_6](H_2O)_2$
$3\triangle3\square$	Rivadavite	$[\phi]\langle\triangle2\square\rangle|\langle\triangle2\square\rangle|\langle\triangle2\square\rangle|$	$Na_6Mg[B_6O_7(OH)_6]_4(H_2O)_{10}$
$12\triangle3\square$	Ammonioborite	$3(\langle2\triangle\square\rangle-\langle2\triangle\square\rangle)$	$(NH_4)_3[B_{15}O_{20}(OH)_8](H_2O)_4$
		Infinite-chain borate minerals	
$1\square$	Vimsite	$\square$	$Ca[B_2O_2(OH)_4]$
$1\triangle2\square$	Colemanite	$\langle\triangle2\square\rangle$	$Ca[B_3O_4(OH)_3](H_2O)$
$1\triangle2\square$	Calciborite	$\langle\triangle2\square\rangle$	$Ca[B_2O_4]$
$1\triangle2\square$	Hydroboracite	$\langle\triangle2\square\rangle$	$CaMg[B_3O_4(OH)_3]_2(H_2O)_3$
$4\triangle1\square$	Larderellite	$(2\triangle\square)-(2\triangle\square)$	$(NH_4)[B_5O_7(OH)_2](H_2O)$
$2\triangle3\square$	Probertite	$\langle\triangle2\square\rangle-\langle\triangle2\square\rangle$	$NaCa[B_5O_7(OH)_4](H_2O)_3$
$3\triangle2\square$	Ezcurrite	$\langle\triangle2\square\rangle-(2\triangle\square)$	$Na_2[B_5O_7(OH)_3](H_2O)_2$
$3\triangle3\square$	Kaliborite	$\langle\triangle2\square\rangle-\langle\triangle2\square\rangle\triangle$	$KMg_2H[B_7O_8(OH)_5]_4(H_2O)_4$
$3\triangle4\square$	Kernite	$\langle\triangle2\square\rangle-\langle\triangle2\square\rangle-\langle\triangle2\square\rangle$	$Na_2[B_4O_6(OH)_2](H_2O)_3$
$3\triangle3\square$	Aristarainite	$[\phi]\langle\triangle2\square\rangle|\langle\triangle2\square\rangle|\langle\triangle2\square\rangle|$	$NaMg[B_6O_8(OH)_4]_2(H_2O)_4$

(cont.)

Borate minerals (*cont.*)

Borate groups (*A*)	Name	Connectivity (*B*)	Formula
Infinite-sheet borate minerals			
3△2□	Biringuccite	⟨2△□⟩–⟨△2□⟩	Na$_2$[B$_5$O$_8$(OH)](H$_2$O)
3△2□	Nasinite	⟨2△□⟩–⟨△2□⟩	Na$_2$[B$_5$O$_8$(OH)](H$_2$O)$_2$
3△2□,1△	Gowerite	⟨△2□⟩–⟨2△□⟩,△	Ca[B$_5$O$_8$(OH)][B(OH)$_3$](H$_2$O)$_3$
3△2□,1△	Veatchite	⟨△2□⟩–⟨2△□⟩,△	Sr$_2$[B$_5$O$_8$(OH)]$_2$[B(OH)$_3$](H$_2$O)
3△2□,1△	Veatchite-A	⟨△2□⟩–⟨2△□⟩,△	Sr$_2$[B$_5$O$_8$(OH)]$_2$[B(OH)$_3$](H$_2$O)
3△2□,1△	P-veatchite	⟨△2□⟩–⟨2△□⟩,△	Sr$_2$[B$_5$O$_8$(OH)]$_2$[B(OH)$_3$](H$_2$O)
3△2□,1△	Volkovskite	⟨△2□⟩–⟨2△□⟩,△	KCa$_4$[B$_5$O$_8$(OH)]$_4$[B(OH)$_3$]$_2$Cl(H$_2$O)$_4$
2△3□	Tuzlaite	⟨△2□⟩–⟨△2□⟩	NaCa[B$_5$O$_8$(OH)$_2$](H$_2$O)$_3$
3△3□	Nobleite	[φ]⟨△2□⟩|⟨△2□⟩|⟨△2□⟩|	Ca[B$_6$O$_9$(OH)$_2$](H$_2$O)$_3$
3△3□	Tunellite	[φ]⟨△2□⟩|⟨△2□⟩|⟨△2□⟩|	Sr[B$_6$O$_9$(OH)$_2$](H$_2$O)$_3$
5△3□	Strontioborite	[φ]⟨△2□⟩|⟨△2□⟩|⟨△2□⟩|2△	Sr[B$_8$O$_{11}$(OH)$_4$]
8△6□	Ginorite	[φ]⟨△2□⟩|⟨△2□⟩|⟨△2□⟩|–[φ]⟨△2□⟩|⟨△2□⟩|⟨△2□⟩|2△	Ca$_2$[B$_{14}$O$_{20}$(OH)$_6$](H$_2$O)$_5$
8△6□	Strontioginorite	[φ]⟨△2□⟩|⟨△2□⟩|⟨△2□⟩|–[φ]⟨△2□⟩|⟨△2□⟩|⟨△2□⟩|2△	Sr$_2$[B$_{14}$O$_{20}$(OH)$_6$](H$_2$O)$_5$
2△4□	Fabianite	⟨△2□⟩=⟨4□⟩=⟨△2□⟩	Ca$_2$[B$_6$O$_{10}$(OH)$_2$]
8□	Johachidolite	(6□)=⟨4□⟩	Ca$_2$Al$_2$[B$_6$O$_{14}$]
4△7□	Preobrazhenskite	□⟨△2□⟩–⟨△2□⟩–⟨△2□⟩–⟨△2□⟩□	Mg$_3$[B$_{11}$O$_{15}$(OH)$_9$]
Infinite-framework borate minerals			
3□	Metaborite	⟨3□⟩	B$_3$O$_3$(OH)$_3$
2△2□	Diomignite	⟨△2□⟩=⟨△2□⟩	Li$_2$[B$_4$O$_6$]
2△3□	Hilgardite-1A	⟨△2□⟩–⟨△2□⟩	Ca$_2$[B$_5$O$_9$]Cl(H$_2$O)
2△3□	Hilgardite-4M	⟨△2□⟩–⟨△2□⟩	Ca$_2$[B$_5$O$_9$]Cl(H$_2$O)
2△3□	Hilgardite-3A	⟨△2□⟩–⟨△2□⟩	Ca$_6$[B$_5$O$_9$]$_3$Cl$_3$(H$_2$O)$_3$
2△3□	Tyretskite-1A	⟨△2□⟩–⟨△2□⟩	Ca$_2$[B$_5$O$_9$](OH)(H$_2$O)
1△6□	Boracite (low)	[φ]⟨3□⟩|⟨3□⟩|⟨3□⟩|△	Mg$_3$[B$_3$O$_{10}$]$_2$(BO$_3$)I
1△6□	Chambersite	[φ]⟨3□⟩|⟨3□⟩|⟨3□⟩|△	Mn$_3$[B$_3$O$_{10}$]$_2$(BO$_3$)I
1△6□	Congolite	[φ]⟨3□⟩|⟨3□⟩|⟨3□⟩|△	Fe$_3$[B$_3$O$_{10}$]$_2$(BO$_3$)I
1△6□	Ericaite	[φ]⟨3□⟩|⟨3□⟩|⟨3□⟩|△	Fe$_3$[B$_3$O$_{10}$]$_2$(BO$_3$)I
1△6□	Trembathite	[φ]⟨3□⟩|⟨3□⟩|⟨3□⟩|△	Mg$_3$[B$_3$O$_{10}$]$_2$(BO$_3$)I
4□	Boracite (high)	[φ]□|□|□|□	Mg$_3$[B$_7$O$_{13}$]Cl
7△8□	Pringleite	⟨△□·⟩=⟨△2□⟩△	Ca$_9$[B$_{20}$O$_{28}$(OH)$_{18}$][B$_6$O$_6$(OH)$_6$]Cl$_4$(H$_2$O)$_{13}$
7△8□	Ruitenbergite	⟨△□·⟩=⟨△2□⟩△	Ca$_9$[B$_{20}$O$_{28}$(OH)$_{18}$][B$_6$O$_6$(OH)$_6$]Cl$_4$(H$_2$O)$_{13}$
8△8□	Penobsquisite	⟨△□·⟩=⟨△2□⟩–⟨△2□⟩	Ca$_2$Fe[B$_9$O$_{13}$(OH)$_6$]Cl(H$_2$O)$_4$
Sulfate-borates			
1□	Sulfoborite	□	Mg$_3$(OH)[B(OH)$_4$]$_2$(SO$_4$)F
2△3□	Heidornite	<△2□>–<△2□>–□	Na$_2$Ca$_3$[B$_5$O$_8$(OH)$_2$](SO$_4$)$_2$Cl
Phosphate-borates			
1□	Seamanite	□	Mn$_3$(OH)$_2$[B(OH)$_4$](PO$_4$)
1△1□	Lüneburgite	△ □	Mg$_3$(H$_2$O)$_6$[B$_2$(OH)$_6$](PO$_4$)$_2$
Arsenate-borates			
1□	Cahnite	□	Ca$_2$[B(OH)$_4$](AsO$_4$)
2△4□	Teruggite	[φ]<3□>|<△2□>–<△2□>	Ca$_4$Mg[B$_6$O$_8$(OH)$_6$]$_2$(AsO$_4$)$_2$(H$_2$O)$_{14}$
Carbonate-borates			
1△	Gaudefroyite	△	Ca$_4$Mn$_3$(O,OH)$_3$(BO$_3$)$_3$(CO$_3$)
1△	Sakhaite	△	Ca$_3$Mg(BO$_3$)(CO$_3$)(H$_2$O)
1△	Carboborite	□	Ca$_2$Mg[B(OH)$_4$]$_2$(CO$_3$)$_2$(H$_2$O)$_4$
1△	Moydite	□	(Y,REE)[B(OH)$_4$](CO$_3$)
4□	Borcarite	<4□>	Ca$_4$Mg[B$_4$O$_6$(OH)$_6$](CO$_3$)$_2$
Beryllate-borates			
1△	Berborite	△	Be$_2$(BO$_3$)(OH,F)(H$_2$O)
1△	Hambergite	△	Be$_2$(BO$_3$)(OH)
1□	Rhodizite	□	(K,Cs)Al$_4$Be$_4$(B,Be)$_{12}$O$_{28}$
Silicate-borates			
1□	Ferroaxinite	□	Ca$_2$Fe^{2+}Al$_2$BSi$_4$O$_{15}$(OH)
1□	Magnesioaxinite	□	Ca$_2$MgAl$_2$BSi$_4$O$_{15}$(OH)
1□	Manganaxinite	□	Ca$_2$Mn^{2+}Al$_2$BSi$_4$O$_{15}$(OH)
1□	Tinzenite	□	(Ca,Mn^{2+},Fe^{2+})$_3$Al$_2$BSi$_4$O$_{15}$(OH)
6□	Cappelenite-(Y)	6□	Ba(Y,Ce)$_6$Si$_3$B$_6$O$_{24}$F$_2$
2□	Danburite	2□	CaB$_2$Si$_2$O$_8$
1△	Reedmergnerite	□	NaBSi$_3$O$_8$
1□	Datolite	□	Ca$_2$B$_2$Si$_2$O$_8$(OH)$_2$
1□	Homilite	□	Ca$_2$(Fe^{2+},Mg)B$_2$Si$_2$O$_{10}$
1△	Dumortierite	△	(Al,□,Ti,Mg)Al$_6$BSi$_3$O$_{16}$(O,OH)$_2$
1△	Holtite	△	Al$_6$(Al,Ta,□)(BO$_3$)[(Si,Sb)O$_4$]$_3$(O,OH)$_3$
2△5□	Garrelsite	□<△2□>–<△2□>□	NaBa$_3$Si$_2$B$_7$O$_{16}$(OH)$_4$
1△	Grandidierite	△	(Mg,Fe^{2+})Al$_3$(BO$_3$)(SiO$_4$)O$_2$

Borate minerals (*cont.*)

Borate groups (*A*)	Name	Connectivity (*B*)	Formula
		Silicate-borates (cont.)	
2□	Hellandite	2□	$(Ca,Y)_6(Al,Fe^{3+})Si_4B_4O_{20}(OH)_4$
2□	Tadzhikite	2□	$Ca_3(Ce,Nd,La)_2(Ti,Al,Fe)B_4Si_4O_{22}$
1△4□	Howlite	2□,<△2□>	$Ca_2B_5SiO_9(OH)_5$
1□	Hyalotekite	□	$(Ba,Pb,K)_4Ca_2(B,Si)_2(Si,Be)_{10}O_{28}F$
1□	Kalborsite	□	$K_6[Al_4Si_6O_{20}][B(OH)_4]Cl$
□	Leucosphenite	□	$Na_4BaTi_2B_2Si_{10}O_{30}$
2□	Taramellite	2□	$Ba_4(Fe^{3+},Ti)_4Si_8B_2O_{27}O_2Cl_x$
2□	Titantaramellite	2□	$Ba_4(Ti,Fe^{3+})_4Si_8B_2O_{27}O_2Cl_x$
□	Nagashimalite	□	$Ba_4(V^{4+},Ti)_4Si_8B_2O_{27}(O,OH)_2Cl$
1□	Poudretteite	□	$KNa_2B_3Si_{12}O_{30}$
1□	Searlesite	□	$NaBSi_2O_5(OH)_2$
1□	Stillwellite-(Ce)	□	$(Ce,La)BSiO_5$
1△	Tourmaline	△	Group name (see the article Tourmaline)
2□	Tienshanite	2□	$Na_2BaMn^{2+}TiB_2Si_6O_{20}$
1△	Werdingite	△	$(Mg,Fe^{2+})_2Al_{14}B_4Si_4O_{37}$
2△	Wiserite	2△	$(Mn^{2+},Mg)_{14}[B_2O_5]_4(OH)_8[\{Si_xMg_{1-x}\}\{O_{1-x}(OH)_x\}_4]Cl_{2x}$
		Silicate-carbonate-borate	
1△	Harkerite	△	$Ca_{24}Mg_8Al_2(SiO_4)_8(BO_3)_6(CO_3)_{10}(H_2O)_2$

as gemstones but are far less common. *See* BORON; TOURMALINE.　　　　　　　　　　Frank C. Hawthorne

Bibliography. E. S. Grew and L. M. Anovitz (eds.), *Reviews in Mineralogy*, vol. 33: *Boron: Mineralogy, Petrology and Geochemistry*, 1996; J. D. Grice et al., Borate minerals, II. A hierarchy of structures based on the borate fundamental building block, *Can. Mineral.*, 37:731–762, 1999.

Bordetella

A genus of gram-negative bacteria which are coccobacilli and obligate aerobes, and fail to ferment carbohydrates. These bacteria are respiratory pathogens. *Bordetella pertussis*, *B. parapertussis*, and *B. bronchiseptica* share greater than 90% of their deoxyribonucleic acid (DNA) sequences and would not warrant separate species designations except that the distinctions are useful for clinical purposes. *Bordetella pertussis* is an obligate human pathogen and is the causative agent of whooping cough (pertussis). *Bordetella parapertussis* causes a milder form of disease in humans and also causes respiratory infections in sheep. *Bordetella bronchiseptica* has the broadest host range, causing disease in many mammalian species, but kennel cough in dogs and atrophic rhinitis, in which infected piglets develop deformed nasal passages, have the biggest economic impact. *Bordetella avium* is more distantly related to the other species. A pathogen of birds, it is of major economic importance to the poultry industry. *See* WHOOPING COUGH.

Infection by all four species is characterized by bacterial adherence to the ciliated cells that line the windpipe (trachea) [see **illus.**]. Proteins on the bacterial surface allow attachment to host cells. In *B. pertussis*, these proteins include filamentous hemagglutinin, pertactin, fimbriae, and BrkA. Ciliated cells infected by *B. pertussis* stop their beating and eventually die. This process is in part mediated by a factor called tracheal cytotoxin, derived from the bacterial peptidoglycan of the cell wall. Humans and other higher organisms detect and respond to peptidoglycan as a warning system for bacterial infections. The peptidoglycan of *Bordetella* is identical to that of other gram-negative bacteria. However, unlike most bacteria, *B. pertussis* releases massive amounts of peptidoglycan, causing an exaggerated immune response that is ultimately deleterious, resulting in self-induced death of the ciliated cells. *Bordetella* also produces protein toxins. The best-characterized is pertussis toxin, made only by *B. pertussis*. This toxin interferes with the mechanisms used by host cells to communicate with one another. Whooping cough symptoms attributed to pertussis toxin include altered insulin secretion, an elevated number of circulating white blood cells (primarily lymphocytes), and defects in the ability of the immune system to detect and fight infections. *Bordetella pertussis*, as well as *B. parapertussis* and *B. bronchiseptica*, produces two other toxins. The adenylate cyclase toxin can enter mammalian cells and generate cyclic adenosine monophosphate, an intracellular signaling molecule. Inappropriate production of this signaling molecule impairs the ability of the immune system to fight infections. The dermonecrotic toxin causes skin lesions following intradermal injection, but its role in disease is unclear.

Bordetella pertussis is spread by coughing and has no environmental reservoir other than infected humans. Whooping cough occurs in three stages: catarrhal, paroxysmal, and convalescent. During the initial, catarrhal phase, the bacteria damage the respiratory tract, resulting in symptoms similar to the common cold (cough, fever, and runny nose). After about a week, patients progress to the paroxysmal phase and develop the characteristic whooping cough, where prolonged expulsive coughing ends

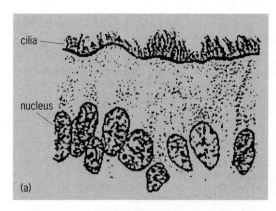

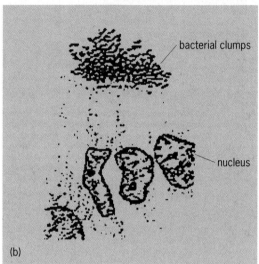

Bordetella pertussis–infected trachea. (*a*) Normal human tracheal cells; hairlike cilia project from the cell body, with the nucleus at the bottom. (*b*) Tracheal cells at autopsy from *B. pertussis*–infected child; clumps of bacteria occur between the cilia. (*After F. B. Mallory and A. A. Horner, Pertussis: The histological lesion in the respiratory tract, J. Med. Res., 134:115–123, 1912*)

with a desperate effort to inhale. The vomiting of thick mucus often follows. The symptoms can last for weeks. After a prolonged illness, patients enter the convalescent stage, and their symptoms gradually improve. Culturing the organism is difficult. Diagnosis is often based on clinical presentation, especially whooping, and is frequently delayed until the paroxysmal phase. Erythromycin is the antibiotic used most frequently to treat whooping cough. Unfortunately, antibiotic treatment improves the patient's condition only if given early, when the disease is most difficult to diagnose, and does not help after whooping has begun. This is consistent with the concept that the early symptoms of the disease result from bacterial damage to the respiratory tract and the later symptoms are due to toxins released by the bacteria. Antibiotics can eradicate the microorganisms but cannot reverse the effects of toxins, which can cause damage far from the site of bacterial growth. Antibiotics can prevent transmission and secondary infections by other microorganisms, a major cause of mortality from whooping cough in the preantibiotic era.

Vaccines have been developed for whooping cough and kennel cough. Multicomponent pertussis vaccines consisting of inactivated pertussis toxin and various combinations of filamentous hemagglutinin, pertactin, and fimbriae are now replacing the older whole-cell vaccines consisting of killed bacteria, which were suspected but not proven to cause rare but serious side effects. Vaccination programs have greatly reduced the incidence of whooping cough in affluent nations, but worldwide nearly half a million deaths occur each year, most of which are vaccine-preventable. *See* ANTIBIOTIC; DRUG RESISTANCE; MEDICAL BACTERIOLOGY; VACUUM METALLURGY.   Alison Weiss

Bibliography. J. D. Cherry, Historical review of pertussis and the classical vaccine, *J. Infect. Dis.*, 174 (suppl. 3):S259–S263, 1996; E. L. Hewlett, *Bordetella* species, *in* G. L. Mandell, J. E. Bennett, and R. Dolin (eds.), *Mandell, Douglas, and Bennett's Principles and Practice of Infectious Disease*, 4th ed., vol. 2, pp. 2078–2084, Churchill Livingstone, 1995; A. A. Weiss, The genus *Bordetella*, in A. Balows et al. (eds.), *The Prokaryotes*, 2d ed., vol. III, pp. 2530–2543, Springer-Verlag, 1991.

Boring bivalves

A variety of marine bivalve mollusks which penetrate solid substrata. They represent seven families and vary in the extent to which they are specialized, in the type of substrata they utilize, and in their method of boring. It is difficult to differentiate borers, burrowers, and nestlers because some species, such as *Hiatella arctica*, not only bore into hard limestones, calcareous sandstones, and chalks, but also burrow in peat or sand-filled crevices in hard rocks, or nestle in holdfasts of *Laminaria*. Undoubtedly the true borers evolved from burrowers via forms that were living in increasingly harder substrata.

Unlike other bivalves which use their shells as abrasive "tools," date mussels (*Lithophaga*, Mytilidae) penetrate calcareous rocks, corals, and shells by chemical means, possibly a weak carbonic acid. These borers are byssally attached and move back and forth in their burrows by alternate contractions of the anterior and posterior byssal retractor muscles. This action presses the thickened, fused, anterior mantle lobes against the end of the burrow, and when they are withdrawn they are covered with fine particles of rock which are ejected through the incurrent siphon along with the pseudofeces. Larvae of *Botula* (another small, elongate mytilid), which settle in crevices of soft rock, corals, or wood, abrade their way into the substrate by continued movement of their shells and siphons.

Rupellaria and *Petricola* (Petricolidae) are nonspecialized borers in peat, firm mud, and soft rock. *Petricola* are usually found in peat, but *Rupellaria* larvae settling in crevices of limestone and coral gradually enlarge their burrows as they grow. *Platyodon* (Myidae), closely related to the soft-shelled clam, press their valves against the walls of the burrow by engorging the mantle and then abrade the soft rock by continued movement of their unspecialized valves.

Gastrochaena and *Spengleria* (Gastrochaenidae) are specialized for boring by having a closed mantle cavity, a large pedal gape, and a truncate foot, allowing them to press the foot and shell against the burrow wall. Despite their thin, fragile shells, they drill into limestone and coral blocks by mechanical means, making flask-shaped burrows which they line posteriorly with calcareous material to ensure a snug fit around the siphons.

The Pholadacea (Pholadidae and Teredinidae) are worldwide in distribution and are highly specialized for boring into hard substrata. The family Pholodidae (common name: piddocks) is composed of 17 genera, of which 5 are restricted to wood. All species of Teredinidae are obligate wood, nut, or plant-stem borers. The major difference between these two families is the presence of accessory plates in the pholads and pallets in the teredinids. For a discussion of the latter group *see* SHIPWORM.

Most pholads are marine, living at depths ranging from intertidal to about 1000 ft (300 m), with some of the deep-sea wood borers (Xylophagainae) extend-

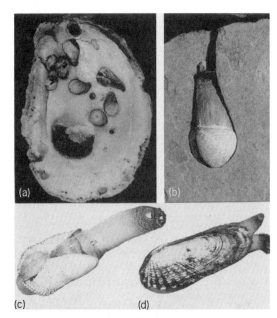

Fig. 2. Typical boring bivalves: (*a*) *Diplothyra smithii* boring in *Crassostrea virginica*; (*b*) *Penitella penita* boring in shale; (*c*) *Zirfaea crispata* removed from burrow, showing foot, anterior adductor muscle, and siphons (*from R. D. Turner, The family Pholadidae in the western Atlantic and eastern Pacific, Johnsonia, 3(33–34):1–160, 1954–1955*); (*d*) *Petricola pholadiformis* removed from burrow, showing extended siphons.

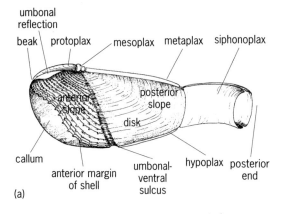

(a)

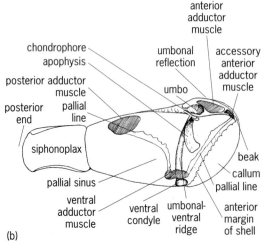

(b)

Fig. 1. A pholad shell: (*a*) external view, showing position of accessory plates and parts of the valve; (*b*) internal view, showing position of muscle and parts of the valves. (*After R. D. Turner, The family Pholadidae in the western Atlantic and eastern Pacific, Johnsonia, 3(33–34):1–160, 1954–1955*)

ing to 16,500 ft (5000 m). Specializations for boring include filelike sculpture on the shell, a large pedal gape, a truncate foot, a closed mantle cavity, the reduction of the hinge and ligament, the insertion of the anterior adductor muscle on the outside of the valves anterior to the umbos so that it works in opposition to the posterior adductor muscle, and the pivoting of the valves on a dorsoventral axis passing through the umbos and ventral condyle (**Fig. 1**). The contraction of the anterior adductor muscle brings the valves together anteriorly; the attachment of the foot anteriorly and the contraction of the pedal muscles pull the shell forward against the anterior end of the burrow; and then the forceful contraction of the posterior adductor muscle spreads the valves anteriorly and scrapes the filelike ridges against the wall of the burrow. Water jetted anteriorly from the mantle cavity flushes the burrow, and the debris is ejected from the incurrent siphon as pseudofeces. Accessory plates, developed to protect the exposed anterior adductor muscle, are unique to the Pholadidae. Additional dorsal, ventral, and siphonal plates are produced, and the pedal gape is closed with a callum when adult Martesiinae cease boring (Figs. 1 and **Fig. 2***a, b*).

Species in the genera *Zirfaea* (Fig. 2*c*) and *Barnea* hasten the recycling of submerged peat beds, and the activity of rock borers such as *Penitella* (Fig. 2*b*), *Parapholas*, *Pholas*, and *Chaceia* contribute to the breakdown of intertidal and submerged cliffs and even cement bulkheading. *Pholas dactylus* of Europe, known to penetrate schistose rock, is also famous for its luminescent properties. *Diplothyra smithii* (Fig. 2*a*) and *Penitella parva*, both shell borers, are pests of oysters and abalones respectively. The wood-boring *Martesia* are important pests of waterfront structures and may even bore into polyvinyl chloride pipes in tropical and warm temperate areas. The Xylophagainae are the most important organisms involved in recycling wood in the deep sea. This subfamily includes three genera and about 30 species. *See* MOLLUSCA.   Ruth D. Turner

Bibliography. G. L. Kennedy, *West American Cenozoic Pholadidae (Mollusca: Bivalvia)*, San Diego Soc. Nat. Hist. Mem. 8, pp. 1–128, 1974; R. C. Moore (ed.), *Treatise on Invertebrate Paleontology*, pt. N, vol. 2, 1969; R. D. Purchon, The structure and function of British Pholadidae, *Proc. Zool. Soc. London*, 124:859–911, 1955; R. D. Turner, The family Pholadidae in the western Atlantic and eastern Pacific, *Johnsonia*, 3(33–34):1–160, 1954–1955.

Physical properties of boron		
Property	Temp., °C	Value
Density		
Crystalline	25–27	2.31 g/cm^3
Amorphous	25–27	2.3 g/cm^3
Mohs hardness		
Crystalline		9.3
Melting point		2100°C
Boiling point		2500°C
Resistivity	25	1.7×10^{-6} ohm-cm
Coefficient of thermal		
expansion	20–750	8.3×10^{-6} cm/°C
Heat of combustion	25	302.0 ± 3.4 kcal/mole
Entropy		
Crystalline	25	1.403 cal/(mole)(deg)
Amorphous	25	1.564 cal/(mole)(deg)
Heat capacity		
Gas	25	4.97 cal/(mole)(deg)
Crystalline	25	2.65 cal/(mole)(deg)
Amorphous	25	2.86 cal/(mole)(deg)

Boron

A chemical element, B, atomic number 5, atomic weight 10.811, in group 13 of the periodic table. It has three valence electrons and is nonmetallic in behavior. It is classified as a metalloid and is the only nonmetallic element which has fewer than four electrons in its outer shell. The free element is prepared in crystalline or amorphous form. The crystalline form is an extremely hard, brittle solid. It is of jet-black to silvery-gray color with a metallic luster. One form of crystalline boron is bright red. The amorphous form is less dense than the crystalline and is a dark-brown to black powder. In the naturally occurring compounds, boron exists as a mixture of two stable isotopes with atomic weights of 10 and 11. *See* PERIODIC TABLE.

Many properties of boron have not been sufficiently established experimentally as a result of the questionable purity of some sources of boron, as well as of the variations in the methods and temperatures of preparation. A summary of the physical properties is shown in the **table**.

Boron and boron compounds have numerous uses in many fields, although elemental boron is employed chiefly in the metal industry. Its extreme reactivity at high temperatures, particularly with oxygen and nitrogen, makes it a suitable metallurgical degasifying agent. It is used to refine the grain of aluminum castings and to facilitate the heat treatment of malleable iron. Boron considerably increases the high-temperature strength characteristics of alloy steels. Elemental boron is used in the atomic reactor and in high-temperature technologies. The physical properties that make boron attractive as a construction material in missile and rocket technology are its low density, extreme hardness, high melting point, and remarkable tensile strength in filament form. When boron fibers are used in an epoxy (or other plastic) carrier material or matrix, the resulting composite is stronger and stiffer than steel and 25% lighter than aluminum. Refined borax, $Na_2B_4O_7 \cdot 10H_2O$, is an important ingredient of a variety of detergents, soaps, water-softening compounds, laundry starches, adhesives, toilet preparations, cosmetics, talcum powder, and glazed paper. It is also used in fireproofing, disinfecting of fruit and lumber, weed control, and insecticides, as well as in the manufacture of leather, paper, and plastics.

Boron makes up 0.001% of the Earth's crust. It is never found in the uncombined or elementary state in nature. Besides being present to the extent of a few parts per million in sea water, it occurs as a trace element in most soils and is an essential constituent of several rock-forming silicate minerals, such as tourmaline and datolite. The presence of boron in extremely small amounts seems to be necessary in nearly all forms of plant life, but in larger concentrations, it becomes quite toxic to vegetation. Only in a very limited number of localities are high concentrations of boron or large deposits of boron minerals to be found in nature; the more important of these seem to be primarily of volcanic origin. *See* BORATE MINERALS.   F. H. May; V. V. Levasheff

Bibliography. F. A. Cotton et al., *Advanced Inorganic Chemistry*, 6th ed., Wiley-Interscience, 1999; D. R. Lide, *CRC Handbook Chemistry and Physics*, 85th ed., CRC Press, 2004; J. J. Pouch and S. A. Alterovitz, *Synthesis and Properties of Boron Nitride*, 1990; K. Smith, *Organometallic Compounds of Boron*, 1985; S. E. Thomas, *Organic Synthesis: The Role of Boron and Silicon*, 1992.

Borrelia

A genus of spirochetes that have a unique genome composed of a linear chromosome and numerous linear and circular plasmids. Borreliae are motile, helical organisms with 4–30 uneven, irregular coils, and are 5–25 micrometers long and 0.2–0.5 μm wide. Their locomotory apparatus consists of 15–22 fibrils coiled around the cell body and situated between the elastic envelope and cytoplasmic membrane. Motion is forward and backward, laterally by bending and looping, and corkscrewlike. Borreliae multiply by binary fission. *See* BACTERIA.

All borreliae are arthropod-borne. Of the 24 recognized species, 21 cause relapsing fever and similar diseases in human and rodent hosts; two are responsible for infections in ruminants and horses; and the remaining one, for borreliosis in birds.

The borreliae of human relapsing fevers are transmitted by the body louse (*Pediculus humanus humanus*) or by a large variety of soft-shelled ticks of the genus *Ornithodoros*. The species *B. burgdorferi*, the etiologic agent of Lyme disease and related disorders, is transmitted by ticks of the genus *Ixodes* (*I. scapularis* and *I. pacificus* in North America, *I. ricinus* in Europe, *I. persulcatus* and other species in Asian countries). *See* RELAPSING FEVER.

Investigations into the genetic (16S rRNA) and phenotypic characterization of the Lyme disease spirochete, *B. burgdorferi*, have shown genetic differences that led to the distinction of three genomic groups designated as *B. burgdorferi* sensu stricto, *B. garinii*, and *B. afzelii*. Tick or spirochete surveys in European and Asian countries produced at least eight new species of spirochetes that appear closely related to the above-cited genomic groups.

Borrelia anserina, which causes spirochetosis in geese, ducks, turkeys, pheasants, chickens, and other birds, is propagated by ticks of the genus *Argas*. Various species of ixodid ticks are responsible for transmitting *B. theileri* among cattle, horses, and sheep. *Borrelia coriaceae*, isolated from *O. coriaceus*, is the putative cause of epizootic bovine abortion in the western United States.

Borreliae stain well with nearly all aniline dyes and can be demonstrated in tissue sections by silver impregnation techniques. Dark-field microscopy is used for rapid examination and detection of spirochetes in peripheral blood or in vector tissues. Also useful for differentiating and identifying spirochetal isolates are molecular procedures such as polyacrylamide gel electrophoresis (SDS-PAGE) of whole-cell lysates for the detection of certain outer-surface proteins (Osp), deoxyribonucleic acid (DNA) hybridization probes, plasmid profiles, restriction endonuclease patterns of total DNA, and the polymerase chain reaction (PCR). The last offers the potential for detecting a very small number of spirochetes in clinical samples as well as in infected ticks and vertebrate tissues.

SDS-PAGE of spirochetes has shown that the outer surface of the microorganisms contains numerous variable lipoproteins of which at least two (Osp A, Osp B) are abundant. The antigenic variability is well known for the relapsing fever borreliae. A switch in the major outer-surface proteins leads to recurrent spirochetemias. The ability to produce new surface antigens results from a nonreciprocal exchange of sequences between numerous silent genes and a single expression locus. The Lyme disease spirochete, *B. burgdorferi*, contains related highly variable surface proteins whose role and mechanisms of its locus needs to be defined. In addition to antigenic variations in the mammalian hosts, *B. burgdorferi* alters its surface proteins in its tick vectors.

Microaerophilic borreliae can readily be cultivated in their tick vectors or animal hosts. Kelly's medium and modifications thereof are suitable for culturing several species of relapsing fever spirochetes and the agent of Lyme disease.

Tetracyclines, penicillins, and doxycycline are the most effective antibiotics for treatment of spirochetes.

Two vaccines consisting of recombinant *B. burgdorferi* Osp A (one vaccine with, the other without adjuvant) have been evaluated in subjects of risk for Lyme disease. Both proved safe and effective in the prevention of this disease. *See* ANTIBIOTIC; MEDICAL BACTERIOLOGY.   Willy Burgdorfer; Patricia Rosa

Bose-Einstein condensation

When a gas of bosonic particles is cooled below a critical temperature, it condenses into a Bose-Einstein condensate. The condensate consists of a macroscopic number of particles, which are all in the ground state of the system. Bose-Einstein condensation (BEC) is a phase transition, which does not depend on the specific interactions between particles. It is based on the indistinguishability and wave nature of particles, both of which are at the heart of quantum mechanics.

Basic phenomenon in ideal gas. In a simplified picture, particles in a gas may be regarded as quantum-mechanical wave packets which have a spatial extent on the order of a thermal de Broglie wavelength, given by Eq. (1), where T is the temperature, m the

$$\lambda_{dB} = \left(\frac{2\pi^2 \hbar}{m k_B T} \right)^{1/2} \qquad (1)$$

mass of the particle, k_B is Boltzmann's constant, and $\hbar$ is Planck's constant divided by 2π. The wavelength λ_{dB} can be regarded as the position uncertainty associated with the thermal momentum distribution of the particles. At high temperature, λ_{dB} is small, and the probability of finding two particles within this distance of each other is extremely low. Therefore, the indistinguishability of particles is not important, and a classical description applies (namely, Boltzmann statistics). When the gas is cooled to the point where λ_{dB} is comparable to the distance between particles, the individual wavepackets start to overlap and the indistinguishability of particles becomes crucial—it is like an identity crisis for particles. For fermions, the Pauli exclusion principle prevents two particles from occupying the same quantum state; whereas for bosons, quantum statistics (in this case, Bose-Einstein statistics) dramatically increases the probability of finding several particles in the same quantum state. In the latter case, as predicted by Einstein in 1925, the system undergoes a phase transition and forms a Bose-Einstein condensate, where a macroscopic number of particles occupy the lowest-energy quantum state (**Fig. 1**). The temperature and the density of particles n at the phase transition are related by Eq. (2).

$$n\lambda_{dB}^3 = 2.612 \qquad (2)$$

Bose-Einstein condensation is a phase transition caused solely by quantum statistics, in contrast to other phase transitions (such as melting or crystallization) which depend on the interactions between particles. *See* BOLTZMANN STATISTICS; DE BROGLIE WAVELENGTH; EXCLUSION PRINCIPLE; NONRELATIVISTIC QUANTUM THEORY; PHASE TRANSITIONS; QUANTUM MECHANICS; UNCERTAINTY PRINCIPLE.

Bose-Einstein condensation can be described intuitively in the following way: When the quantum-mechanical wave functions of bosonic particles spatially overlap, the matter waves start to oscillate in concert. A coherent matter wave forms that comprises all particles in the ground state of the system. This transition from disordered to coherent matter waves can be compared to the step from incoherent light to laser light. Indeed, atom lasers based on Bose-Einstein condensation have been realized. *See* COHERENCE; LASER.

Bose-Einstein condensation occurs in thermal equilibrium. This is the way that nature maximizes entropy for a given number of atoms and a given amount of energy when the total energy is below the threshold for the phase transition to a Bose-Einstein condensate. Although the condensate itself does not contribute to the entropy, it allows the other particles to have a larger share of the total energy and thus increase the entropy.

Experimental techniques. The phenomenon of Bose-Einstein condensation is responsible for the superfluidity of helium and for the superconductivity of an electron gas, which involves Bose-condensed electron pairs. However, these phenomena happen at high density, and their understanding requires a detailed treatment of the interactions. *See* LIQUID HELIUM; SUPERCONDUCTIVITY; SUPERFLUIDITY.

The quest to realize Bose-Einstein condensation in a dilute weakly interacting gas was pursued in several directions: liquid helium diluted in vycor, a sponge-

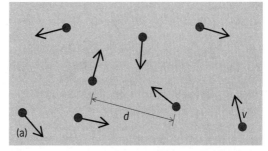

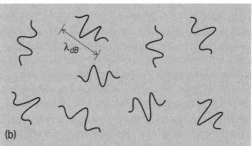

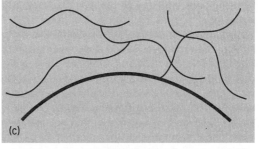

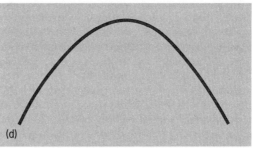

Fig. 1. Criterion for Bose-Einstein condensation in a gas of weakly interacting particles. (*a*) Gas at high temperature, treated as a system of billiard balls, with thermal velocity *v* and density d^{-3}, where *d* is the distance between particles. (*b*) Simplified quantum description of gas at low temperature, in which the particles are regarded as wave packets with a spatial extent of the order of the de Broglie wavelength, λ_{dB}. (*c*) Gas at the transition temperature for Bose-Einstein condensation, when λ_{dB} becomes comparable to *d*. The wave packets overlap and a Bose-Einstein condensate forms (in the case of bosonic particles). (*d*) Pure Bose condensate (giant matter wave), which remains as the temperature approaches absolute zero and the thermal cloud disappears. (*After D. S. Durfee and W. Ketterle, Experimental studies of Bose-Einstein condensation, Opt. Express, 2:299–313, Optical Society of America, 1998*)

like glass; excitons in semiconductors, which consist of weakly bound electron-hole pairs; and atomic gases. Most of the research activities have focused on Bose-Einstein condensation in atomic gases.

At ultralow temperatures, all atomic gases liquefy or solidify in thermal equilibrium. Keeping the gas at

Properties of a gas during successive stages of cooling to a Bose-Einstein condensate*			
Stage	Temperature	Number density of atoms, cm^{-3}	Phase-space density
Oven	500 K	10^{14}	10^{-13}
Laser cooling	50 μK	10^{11}	10^{-6}
Evaporative cooling	500 nK	10^{14}	2.612
Bose-Einstein condensate		10^{15}	10^{7}

*Numbers refer to cooling of sodium vapor in an experiment at the Massachusetts Institute of Technology. All numbers are approximate.

sufficiently low density can prevent this from occurring. Elastic collisions, which ensure thermal equilibrium of the gas, are then much more frequent than three-body collisions, which are required for the formation of molecules and other aggregates. As a result, the gaseous phase is metastable for seconds or even minutes and allows for the observation of Bose-Einstein condensation in a gas. Typical number densities of atoms between 10^{12} and $10^{15}/cm^3$ imply transition temperatures for Bose-Einstein condensation in the nanokelvin or microkelvin regime.

The realization of Bose-Einstein condensation in atomic gases required techniques to cool gases to such low temperatures, and atom traps to confine the gas at the required density and keep them away from the much warmer walls of the vacuum chamber. Most experiments use several laser-cooling techniques as precooling, then hold the atoms in a magnetic trap and cool them further by forced evaporative cooling. For atomic hydrogen, the laser-cooling step is replaced by cryogenic cooling. Evaporative cooling is done by continuously removing the high-energy tail of the thermal distribution from the trap. In a magnetic trap, this can be accomplished by flipping the atomic spins of the highest energy particles with radio-frequency radiation. Since this process reverses the magnetic force on the particles, they are expelled from the trapping region. The evaporated atoms carry away more than the average energy, which means that the temperature of the remaining atoms decreases. The high-energy tail must be constantly repopulated by collisions, thus maintaining thermal equilibrium and sustaining the cooling process. Evaporative cooling is a common phenomenon in daily life—it's how hot water cools down in a bathtub or hot coffee in a cup. In optical traps, evaporation is forced by lowering the laser power and thus the trap depth. In addition to the early observation of Bose-Einstein condensation in rubidium, sodium, lithium, and hydrogen, this condensation has now been observed also in potassium, cesium, ytterbium, chromium, metastable helium, and molecules of potassium and lithium.

In a typical cooling process (see **table**), the temperature of the gas is reduced by a factor of 10^9 though the combination of laser and evaporative cooling steps, while the density at the Bose-Einstein condensation transition is similar to the initial density in the atomic beam oven. In each step, the phase-space density, to which the ground-state population is proportional, increases by a factor of 10^6, result-ing in a total increase of phase-space density by 20 orders of magnitude.

Observation. Bose-Einstein condensation was observed by suddenly switching off the atom trap, releasing the atom cloud into a ballistic expansion. The cloud was illuminated with resonant laser light, and its shadow was imaged onto a CCD (charge-coupled-device) camera (**Fig. 2**). Such images showed the sudden appearance, near the predicted transition temperature, of a bimodal cloud consisting of a diffuse normal component and a dense core (the condensate). The condensate expanded with a kinetic energy that was much larger than the zero-point energy of the trapping potential—clear evidence for repulsive interactions between the atoms, which accelerate the ballistic expansion. *See* CHARGE-COUPLED DEVICES.

The sudden reduction of the speed of ballistic expansion has been called condensation in momentum space. However, Bose-Einstein condensation is a condensation into the lowest energy state; in an inhomogeneous trapping potential, the lowest state has the smallest spatial extent. Condensation into this state thus results in the formation of a dense core of Bose condensed atoms within a diffuse thermal cloud of atoms. This spatial structure of a Bose condensate was directly observed using dispersive imaging techniques.

Weak interactions. Bose-Einstein condensation in gases allows for a theoretical description based

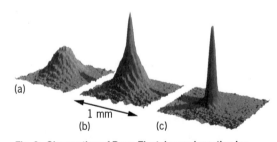

(a)

1 mm

(b)   (c)

Fig. 2. Observation of Bose-Einstein condensation by absorption imaging. Absorption is plotted in two spatial dimensions. The Bose-Einstein condensate is characterized by its slow expansion, observed after a 6-millisecond time of flight. Shown are clouds expanding (a) after cooling to just above the transition point ($T > T_c$), (b) just after the condensate appeared ($T < T_c$), and (c) after further evaporative cooling has left an almost pure condensate ($T \ll T_c$). The total number of sodium atoms at the phase transition is about 7×10^5; the temperature, T_c, at the transition point is 2 μK. (After D. S. Durfee and W. Ketterle, Experimental studies of Bose-Einstein condensation, Opt. Express, 2:299t–313, Optical Society of America, 1998)

directly on first principles because there is a clear hierarchy of length and energy scales. In a gas, the separation between atoms, $n^{-1/3}$, is much larger than the effective range of the interatomic forces (characterized by the s-wave scattering length a, typically 1–5 nanometers for alkali atoms), that is, $na^3 \ll 1$. This inequality expresses the fact that binary collisions are much more frequent than three-body collisions. It is in this limit that the theory of the weakly interacting Bose gas applies. Interactions between the Bose-condensed particles are described by a mean field energy given by Eq. (3), which is the effective

$$U_{\text{int}} = 4\pi\hbar^2 na/m \qquad (3)$$

potential energy of one particle due to the presence of the other particles in the condensate. This interaction is responsible for collective phenomena such as sound. The stability of large condensates requires repulsive interactions (positive a). For negative a, the interactions are attractive, and the condensate is unstable against collapse above a certain size.

Properties of the weakly interacting Bose gas have been studied both experimentally and theoretically. Of special interest are the collective excitations of the gas, different forms of sound (Bogoliubov, first and second sound), and the stability of vortices. *See* QUANTIZED VORTICES; QUANTUM ACOUSTICS.

When condensates were realized in a mixture of atomic hyperfine states, multicomponent condensates were observed. Their phase diagram, the spatial structure, possible metastable configurations, and properties such as miscibility and immiscibility are examples of new phenomena which have been studied. These examples show that gaseous Bose condensates are a new class of quantum fluids with properties quite different from the quantum liquids helium-3 and helium-4. Gaseous condensates provide a testing ground for aspects of many-body theories, which were developed many decades ago but never tested experimentally.

Macroscopic wave function. In an ideal gas, Bose condensed atoms all occupy the same single-particle ground-state wave function. The many-body ground-state wave function is then the product of N identical single-particle ground-state wave functions, where N is the number of condensed atoms. This single-particle wave function is therefore called the condensate wave function or macroscopic wave function. This picture is valid even when weak interactions are included. The ground-state many-body wave function is still, to a very good approximation, a product of N single-particle wave functions, which are now obtained from the solution of a nonlinear Schrödinger equation, which includes the interaction energy between atoms. The admixture of other configurations into the ground state is called quantum depletion. The theory of weakly interacting Bose gases shows that the fractional quantum depletion is given by expression (4), typically 1% or less for the

$$\frac{8}{3\pi^{1/2}}\sqrt{na^3} \qquad (4)$$

alkali condensates. This means that even for the interacting gases, with 99% accuracy, all the atoms can be regarded as having the same single-particle wave function. This is in contrast to liquid helium, in which the quantum depletion is about 90%.

The phase of the condensate and the coherence properties of its wave function are relevant for quantum fluids because the gradient of the phase is proportional to the superfluid velocity. It also determines the properties of atom lasers based on Bose-Einstein condensation. In superconductors and liquid helium, the existence of coherence and of a macroscopic wave function is impressively demonstrated through the Josephson effect. In the dilute atomic gases, the coherence has been demonstrated even more directly by interfering two Bose condensates (**Fig. 3**). The interference fringes have a spacing of 15 micrometers, a huge length for matter waves. (In contrast, the matter wavelength of atoms at room temperature is only 0.05 nm, less than the size of the atoms.)

Strongly correlated quantum gases. The study of properties of the weakly interacting Bose gas have confirmed many long-standing predictions and led to a more profound understanding of the properties of Bose-Einstein condensates. Bose-Einstein condensates display the physics of single particles occupying a macroscopic wave function, and interactions are described by a mean-field potential. More recently, researchers have used the Bose-Einstein condensate as the starting point to "engineer" other new forms of matter, which are characterized by strong interactions and strong correlations. Included are atoms in optical lattices, ultracold atoms in one-dimensional geometries, and pairing and strong interactions near Feshbach resonances.

Optical lattices are created by several optical standing waves and provide an "egg carton" potential for neutral atoms. When the depth of the optical lattice is increased, the cold gas undergoes a quantum phase transition from a superfluid to an insulator. An atom trap with very tight transverse confinement realizes a one-dimensional geometry. At low density, the atoms

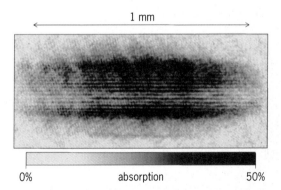

Fig. 3. Interference pattern of two expanding condensates, demonstrating the coherence of Bose-Einstein condensates. This absorption image was observed after a 40-millisecond time of flight. Interference fringes have a spacing of 15 μm. (*After D. S. Durfee and W. Ketterle, Experimental studies of Bose-Einstein condensation, Opt. Express, 2:299–313, Optical Society of America, 1998*)

are lined up like beads on a string and form a so-called Tonks gas, a gas of impenetrable bosons.

Two atoms interact most strongly when they couple resonantly to a molecular state. If the colliding atoms and the bound molecule have different spin configurations, the atoms and the molecule experience different energy shifts due to an external magnetic field (Zeeman shifts). It is possible to tune the magnetic field to a value where the bound molecular state has the same energy as the colliding atoms. This resonance is called a Feshbach resonance. Feshbach resonances have been used to create strongly interacting Bose-Einstein condensates and have triggered condensate explosions and implosions. The resonant recombination of atoms into molecules has led to the first molecular Bose-Einstein condensates. And finally, Feshbach resonances have induced the pairing of fermions in a regime of attractive interactions, where no molecular bound state exists in a vacuum. Those fermion pairs were shown to Bose-condense and to form a superfluid. A magnetic field variation across a Feshbach resonance transforms a molecular Bose-Einstein condensate into a condensate of fermion pairs, which can be regarded as tightly bound Cooper pairs and are described by an extension of the Bardeen-Cooper-Schrieffer (BCS) theory for superfluids. Feshbach resonances thus provide access to the long-sought BEC-BCS crossover from a condensate of tightly bound fermions (like molecules) to a BCS superfluid. *See* ATOMIC FERMI GAS; RESONANCE (QUANTUM MECHANICS).

Wolfgang Ketterle

Bibliography. J. R. Anglin and W. Ketterle, Bose-Einstein condensation of atomic gases, *Nature*, 416:211–218, 2002; E. A. Cornell and C. E. Wieman, The Bose-Einstein condensate, *Sci. Amer.*, pp. 40–45, March 1998; A. Griffin, D. W. Snoke, and S. Stringari (eds.), *Bose-Einstein Condensation*, Cambridge University Press, 1995; M. Inguscio, S. Stringari, and C. E. Wieman (eds.), Bose-Einstein Condensation in Atomic Gases, *Proc. Int. School Phys. Enrico Fermi*, Course CXL, IOS Press, Amsterdam, 1999; C. J. Pethick and H. Smith, *Bose-Einstein Condensation in Dilute Gases*, Cambridge University Press, 2002; L. P. Pitaevskii and S. Stringari, *Bose-Einstein Condensation*, Clarendon Press, Oxford, 2003.

Bose-Einstein statistics

The statistical description of quantum-mechanical systems in which there is no restriction on the way in which particles can be distributed over the individual energy levels. This description applies when the system has a symmetric wave function. This in turn has to be the case when the particles described are of integer spin.

Distribution probability. Suppose one describes a system by giving the number of particles n_i in an energy state ϵ_i, where the n_i are called occupation numbers and the index i labels the various states. The energy level ϵ_i is of finite width, being really a range of energies comprising, say, g_i individual (nondegenerate) quantum levels. If any arrangement of particles

over individual energy levels is allowed, one obtains for the probability of a specific distribution, Eq. (1a). In Boltzmann statistics, this same probability would be written as Eq. (1b).

$$W = \prod_i \frac{(n_i + g_i - 1)!}{n_i!(g_i - 1)!} \tag{1a}$$

$$W = \prod_i \frac{g_i^{n_i}}{n_i!} \tag{1b}$$

See BOLTZMANN STATISTICS.

The equilibrium state is defined as the most probable state of the system. To obtain it, one must maximize Eq. (1a) under the conditions given by Eqs. (2a) and (2b), which express the fact that the total number of particles N and the total energy E are fixed. One finds for the most probable distribution that Eq. (3) holds. Here, A and β are parameters to be

$$\sum n_i = N \tag{2a}$$

$$\sum \epsilon_i n_i = E \tag{2b}$$

determined from Eqs. (2a) and (2b); actually, $\beta = 1/kT$ where k is the Boltzmann constant and T is the absolute temperature.

$$n_i = \frac{g_i}{\frac{1}{A}e^{\beta \epsilon_i} - 1} \tag{3}$$

In the classical case, that is, when Boltzmann statistics is employed, the equilibrium distribution may be obtained from a specific assumption about the number of collisions of a certain kind. One assumes that the number of collisions per second in which molecules with velocities in cells i and j in phase space produce molecules with velocities in cells k and l is given by Eq. (4), where a_{ij}^{kl} is a geometrical

$$A_{ij}^{kl} = n_i n_j a_{ij}^{kl} \tag{4}$$

factor. In the Bose case, Eq. (3) may be obtained in a similar way from a collision number assumption, which is written as Eq. (5).

$$A_{ij}^{kl} = a_{ij}^{kl} n_i n_j \left(\frac{g_k + n_k}{g_k} \right) \left(\frac{g_l + n_l}{g_l} \right) \tag{5}$$

One observes the interesting fact that the number of collisions depends on the number of particles in the state to which the colliding particles are going. The more heavily populated these states are, the more likely a collision is. Quite often one defines f_i, the distribution function, by Eq. (6).

$$n_i = f_i g_i \tag{6}$$

Applications. An interesting and important result emerges when one applies Eq. (3) to a gas of photons, that is, a large number of photons in an enclosure. (Since photons have integer spin, this is legitimate.) For photons one has Eqs. (7a) and (7b), where h is

$$\epsilon = h\nu \tag{7a}$$

$$p = \frac{h\nu}{c} \tag{7b}$$

the Planck constant, v the frequency of the photon, c the velocity of light, ϵ the energy of the photon, and p the momentum of the photon. The number of photons in a given energy or frequency range is given by Eq. (8), where V is the volume of the enclosure con-

$$g = \frac{8\pi}{c^3} V v^2 \, dv \qquad (8)$$

taining the photons. Actually, for a gas of photons, Eq. (2a) is not necessary (the number of photons is not fixed), and thus the distribution function depends on just one parameter, β; A can be shown to be unity. If one also uses the fact that $\beta = 1/kT$, one obtains from Eq. (3), for the number of photons in the frequency range dv, Eq. (9). The energy den-

$$n(v) \, dv = \frac{8\pi}{c^3} V \frac{v^2 \, dv}{e^{bv/kT} - 1} \qquad (9)$$

sity (energy per unit volume) in the frequency range dv is, by Eqs. (9) and (7a), Eq. (10). Equation (10)

$$\rho(v) \, dv = \frac{8\pi b}{c^3} \frac{v^3 \, dv}{e^{bv/kT} - 1} \qquad (10)$$

is the Planck radiation formula for blackbody radiation. Thus, blackbody radiation must be considered as a photon gas, with the photons satisfying Bose-Einstein statistics. *See* HEAT RADIATION.

For material particles of mass m contained in a volume V, one may write Eq. (3) as (11), where

$$f(v_x v_y v_z) \, dv_x \, dv_y \, dv_z$$
$$= \left(\frac{m}{b}\right)^3 V \frac{dv_x \, dv_y \, dv_z}{\frac{1}{A} e^{mv^2/2kT} - 1} \qquad (11)$$

$v = \sqrt{v_x^2 + v_y^2 + v_z^2}$ is the total velocity. Equations (2a) and (2b) may now be written as integrals. If the so-called virial theorem, written as Eq. (12), is used

$$PV = {}^2/_3 E \qquad (12)$$

where P is the pressure, V the volume, and E the energy, Eqs. (2a) and (2b) yield a pair of implicit equations, which give the equation of state of an ideal Bose gas, Eqs. (13a) and (13b). Here λ^3 is defined as

$$\frac{N}{V} \lambda^3 = B_{1/2}(A) \qquad (13a)$$

$$\lambda^3 \frac{P}{kT} = B_{3/2}(A) \qquad (13b)$$

in Eq. (14) while Eq. (15) holds. In Eq. (15) Γ is the

$$\lambda^3 = \frac{b^2}{2\pi mkT} \qquad (14)$$

$$B_\rho(A) = \frac{1}{\Gamma(\rho + 1)} \int_0^\infty \frac{u^\rho \, du}{\frac{1}{A} e^u - 1} \qquad (15)$$

usual Γ function and $u = mv^2/2kT$. From Eqs. (13a) and (13b), one obtains the relation between P, V, and T by eliminating A.

Now if one develops the numerator of the integral in Eq. (15) in an infinite series, one obtains the

so-called Einstein equations, (16a) and (16b). It is

$$\frac{N}{V} = \frac{1}{\lambda^3} \sum_{l=1}^\infty \frac{A^l}{l_{3/2}} \qquad (16a)$$

$$P = \frac{kT}{\lambda^3} \sum_{l=1}^\infty \frac{A^l}{l^{5/2}} \qquad (16b)$$

easy to verify that the sums of Eqs. (16a) and (16b) diverge for $A > 1$; however, they still converge for $A = 1$. For $A = 1$, $N/V = 2.61/\lambda^3$ and $P = 1.34kT/\lambda^3$. Einstein interpreted $N/V = 2.61/\lambda^3$ as a maximum possible density. If the gas is compressed beyond this point, the superfluous particles will condense in a zero state, where they do not contribute to the density or the pressure. If the volume is decreased, this curious Bose-Einstein condensation phenomenon results, yielding the zero state which has the paradoxical properties of not contributing to the pressure, volume, or density. The particles in the zero state are coherently matched with each other, analogous to the photons in a laser beam sharing a common quantum-mechanical wave function and losing their individual identities. Many of the superfluid properties exhibited by liquid helium are believed to be manifestations of such a condensation. In 1995, Bose-Einstein condensation was first observed directly in a cloud of rubidium atoms that had been cooled to 1.7×10^{-7} K through laser cooling followed by evaporative cooling in a magnetic trap. Since then it has been observed in a number of dilute gases. *See* BOSE-EINSTEIN CONDENSATION; COHERENCE; FERMI-DIRAC STATISTICS; LASER COOLING; LIQUID HELIUM; NONRELATIVISTIC QUANTUM THEORY; PARTICLE TRAP; QUANTUM STATISTICS; STATISTICAL MECHANICS. Max Dresden

Botanical gardens

Gardens for the culture of plants collected chiefly for scientific and educational purposes. Such a garden is more properly called a botanical institution, in which the outdoor garden is but one portion of an organization including the greenhouse, the herbarium, the library, and the research laboratory. *See* HERBARIUM.

Famous botanical gardens. It was only in modern Europe, after the foundation of the great medieval universities, that botanical gardens for educational purposes began to be established in connection with the schools. The oldest gardens are those in Padua (established 1533) and at Pisa (1543). The botanical garden of the University of Leiden was begun in 1587 and the first greenhouse is said to have been constructed there in 1599. Louis XIII authorized the establishment of a royal garden in Paris "for the instruction of students"; it was opened to the public in 1640 under the name Jardin du Roy. Later the name was changed to the Museé National d'Histoire Naturelle. The Oxford University Botanic Garden, the first in Great Britain, was established in 1621. In Berlin the Botanischer Garten was established in 1646. In 1655 a garden was founded at Uppsala, Sweden, of which Carolus Linnaeus, the father of modern plant taxonomy, was director from 1742 to 1777. In Russia Peter the Great's Druggist's Garden was founded at St. Petersburg in 1713. In 1817 the Conservatoire et Jardin Botanique were established at Geneva and became one of the leading botanical centers of the world. The Royal Botanical Gardens at Kew, England, were officially opened in 1841. This institution came to be known as the botanical capital of the world.

The first of the great tropical gardens was founded at Calcutta in 1787. The original name, Royal Botanic Garden, was changed in 1947 to Indian Botanic Garden. Another great tropical garden, the Jardin Botanico of Rio de Janeiro, was founded in 1808. The great tropical botanical graden of Buitenzorg (Bogor), Java, which originated in 1817, has an area of 205 acres with an additional 150 acres in the Mountain Garden.

Gardens in North America. The first great garden of the United States was founded by Henry Shaw at St. Louis in 1859, and in now known as the Missouri Botanical Garden. The New York Botanical Garden was chartered in 1891 and the Brooklyn Botanic Garden in 1910. The Jardin Botanique of Montreal, the leading garden of Canada, was opened in 1936. *See* ARBORETUM.   Earl L. Core

Botany

That branch of biological science which embraces the study of plants and plant life. According to the specific objectives of the investigators, botanical studies may range from microscopic observations of the smallest and obscurest plants to the study of the trees of the forest. One botanist may be interested mainly in the relationships among plants and in their geographic distribution, whereas another may be primarily concerned with structure or with the study of the life processes taking place in plants.

Botany may be divided by subject matter into several specialties, such as plant anatomy, plant chemistry, plant cytology, plant ecology (including autecology and synecology), plant embryology, plant genetics, plant morphology, plant physiology, plant taxonomy, ethnobotany, and paleobotany. It may also be divided according to the group of plants being studied; for example, agrostology, the study of grasses; algology (phycology), the study of algae; bryology, the study of mosses; mycology, the study of fungi; and pteridology, the study of ferns. Bacteriology and virology are also parts of botany in a broad sense. Furthermore, a number of agricultural subjects have botany as their foundation. Among these are agronomy, floriculture, forestry, horticulture, landscape architecture, and plant breeding. *See* AGRICULTURE; AGRONOMY; BACTERIOLOGY; BREEDING (PLANT); CELL BIOLOGY; ECOLOGY; EMBRYOLOGY; FLORICULTURE; FOREST AND FORESTRY; GENETICS; LANDSCAPE ARCHITECTURE; PALEOBOTANY; PLANT ANATOMY; PLANT GROWTH; PLANT MORPHO-

GENESIS; PLANT PATHOLOGY; PLANT PHYSIOLOGY; PLANT TAXONOMY.   Arthur Cronquist

Botulism

An illness produced by the exotoxin of *Clostridium botulinum* and occasionally other clostridia, and characterized by paralysis and other neurological abnormalities. There are seven principal toxin types involved (A–G); only types A, B, E, and F have been implicated in human disease. Types C and D produce illness in birds and mammals. Strains of *C. barati* and *C. butyricum* have been found to produce toxins E and F and have been implicated in infant botulism. There is serologic cross-reactivity between *C. botulinum* and *C. sporogenes* and *C. novyi*. Botulinal toxin is among the most potent poisons known; it has a heavy chain (molecular weight about 100,000) and a light chain (about 50,000) joined by a disulfide bond. *See* ANAEROBIC INFECTION; VIRULENCE.

Mechanism of action. Botulinum neurotoxin consists of three domains with different functions: nonspecific binding, membrane translocation, and proteolysis for specific components of the neuroexocytosis apparatus. Botulinum neurotoxins act at the periphery by inducing a flaccid paralysis due to the inhibition of acetylcholine release at the neuromuscular junction. Serotypes B, F, and G toxins cleave a single peptide bond of the vesicle-associated membrane protein (VAMP) synaptobrevin. Types A and E cleave synaptosome-associated protein of 25 kilodaltons (SNAP-25) at different sites located within the carboxyl terminus. *See* ACETYLCHOLINE.

Forms. The three clinical forms are classic botulism, infant botulism, and wound botulism. Classic botulism is typically due to ingestion of preformed toxin, infant botulism involves ingestion of *C. botulinum* spores with subsequent germination and toxin production in the gastrointestinal tract, and wound botulism involves production of toxin by the organism's infecting or colonizing a wound. The incubation period is from a few hours to more than a week (but usually 1–2 days), depending primarily on the amount of toxin ingested or absorbed.

Symptoms and diagnosis. There is classically acute onset of bilateral cranial nerve impairment and subsequent symmetrical descending paralysis or weakness. Commonly noted are dysphagia (difficulty in swallowing), dry mouth, diplopia (double vision), dysarthria (a neuromuscular disorder affecting speech), and blurred vision. Nausea, vomiting, and fatigue are common as well. Ileus (impaired intestinal motility) and constipation are much more typical than diarrhea; there may also be urinary retention and dry mucous membranes. Central nervous system function and sensation remain intact, and fever does not occur in the absence of complications. Fever may even be absent in wound botulism. The diagnosis should be made clinically and confirmed by demonstrating the toxin in serum, stool, or epidemiologically implicated foods, or by recovery of the organism from the stool or wound of the patient. Toxin is identified by mouse toxicity and neutralization tests with type-specific antitoxin. *See* TOXIN.

Epidemiology. In food-borne botulism, home-canned or home-processed foods (particularly vegetables) are commonly implicated, with commercially canned foods involved infrequently. Outbreaks usually involve only one or two people, but may affect dozens. In infant botulism, honey and corn syrup have been implicated as vehicles. Therapy involves measures to rid the body of unabsorbed toxin, neutralization of unfixed toxin by antitoxin, and adequate intensive care support. *See* FOOD POISONING; MEDICAL BACTERIOLOGY; POISON.

Pharmacological agent. Ironically, botulinum toxin has been used therapeutically in a variety of situations where there is excessive contraction of local muscles: strabismus (squint), blepharospasm (spasm of the eyelid), hemifacial spasm, cervical dystonia, torticollis (a contraction of muscle causing the head to be drawn toward the contracted side), spasmodic dysphonia, spastic hypertonia of calf muscles, focal dystonia (for example, writer's cramp, musician's cramp), essential palatal tremor, detrusor-sphincter dyssynergia, achalasia (failure of the lower esophageal sphincter to relax), nonrelaxing puborectalis syndrome, facial wrinkles, some types of headache, and chronic anal fissure. Botulinum toxin can also block activation of sweat glands which are cholinergically innervated; it has been used for patients with severe hyperhidrosis (usually palmar or axillary). *See* MUSCLE.   Sydney M. Finegold

Bibliography. Centers for Disease Control, *Botulism in the United States, 1899–1977*, 1979; M. Hallett, One man's poison: Clinical applications of botulinum toxin, *New Engl. J. Med.*, 341:118–120, 1999; R. Pellizzari et al., Tetanus and botulinum neurotoxins: Mechanism of action and therapeutic uses, *Phil. Trans. Roy. Soc. Lond. B Biol. Sci.*, 354:259–268, 1999; R. L. Shapiro, C. Hatheway, and D. L. Swerdlow, Botulism in the United States: A clinical and epidemiologic review, *Ann. Intern. Med.*, 129:221–228, 1998.

Boundary-layer flow

That portion of a fluid flow, near a solid surface, where shear stresses are significant and the inviscid-flow assumption may not be used. All solid surfaces interact with a viscous fluid flow because of the no-slip condition, a physical requirement that the fluid and solid have equal velocities at their interface. Thus a fluid flow is retarded by a fixed solid surface, and a finite, slow-moving boundary layer is formed.

A requirement for the boundary layer to be thin is that the Reynolds number, Re = $\rho UL/\mu$, of the body be large, 10^3 or more, where ρ and μ are the fluid density and viscosity, respectively, U is the stream velocity, and L is the body length. Under these conditions, as first pointed out by L. Prandtl in 1904, the flow outside the boundary layer is essentially inviscid and plays the role of a driving mechanism for the layer. *See* REYNOLDS NUMBER.

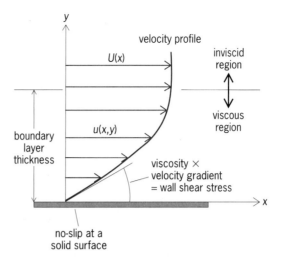

Fig. 1. Typical laminar boundary-layer velocity profile.

A typical low-speed or laminar boundary layer is shown in **Fig. 1**. Such a display of the streamwise flow vector variation near the wall is called a velocity profile. The no-slip condition requires that $u(x,0) = 0$, as shown. The velocity rises monotonically with distance y from the wall, finally merging smoothly with the outer (inviscid) stream velocity $U(x)$. At any point in the boundary layer, the fluid shear stress τ is related to the local velocity gradient by Eq. (1),

$$\tau = \mu(\partial u/\partial y) \qquad (1)$$

assuming a newtonian fluid. The value of the shear stress at the wall, τ_w, is most important, since it relates not only to the drag of the body but often also to its heat transfer. At the edge of the boundary layer, τ approaches zero asymptotically. There is no exact spot where $\tau = 0$; therefore the thickness δ of a boundary layer is usually defined arbitrarily as the point where $u = 0.99U$. *See* LAMINAR FLOW.

Boundary-layer approximations. A boundary layer is mathematically different from a general viscous flow. In a steady, two-dimensional, incompressible flow (Fig. 1), the three unknowns would be pressure $p(x,y)$, streamwise velocity $u(x,y)$, and velocity normal to the wall, $v(x, y)$. These would be solved for simultaneously from the conservation of mass and the x- and y-momentum or Navier-Stokes equations. The solution would apply throughout the entire flow field.

If, however, the viscous region is thin, the boundary-layer approximations apply in the form of Eqs. (2). Many terms may then be dropped from

$$\begin{array}{ll} v & \partial u/\partial x \quad u/\partial y \\ \partial v/\partial x \quad v/\partial y & \partial p/\partial y \cong 0 \end{array} \qquad (2)$$

the basic Navier-Stokes equations, and the resulting boundary-layer equations eliminate pressure as a variable and solve merely for u and v by extending downstream between the wall, where no-slip obtains, and the inviscid outer stream, where $U(x)$ is assumed directly related to the pressure $P(x)$ by

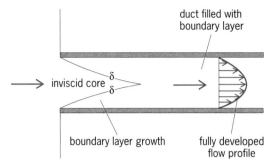

Fig. 2. Boundary-layer development in the entrance of a duct.

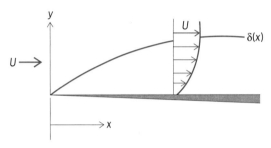

Fig. 3. Laminar boundary-layer flow past a sharp flat plate.

the Bernoulli relation (3). This is a profound mathematical simplification which permits designers to compute boundary-layer velocity, shear, temperature, and heat transfer without recourse to massive digital computer codes. *See* BERNOULLI'S THEOREM; NAVIER-STOKES EQUATION.

$$P(x) + 0.5\rho U^2(x) = \text{constant} \qquad (3)$$

Boundary layers in duct flow. When a flow enters a duct or confined region, boundary layers immediately begin to grow on the duct walls (**Fig. 2**). An inviscid core accelerates down the duct center, but soon vanishes as the boundary layers meet and fill the duct with viscous flow. Constrained by the duct walls into a no-growth condition, the velocity profile settles into a fully developed shape which is independent of the streamwise coordinate. The pressure drops linearly downstream, balanced by the mean wall-shear stress. This is a classic and simple case of boundary-layer flow which is well documented by both theory and experiment.

Flat-plate flow. A classic incompressible boundary-layer flow is a uniform stream at velocity U, moving past a sharp flat plate parallel to the stream (**Fig. 3**). In the Reynolds number range $\rho UL/\mu = 1 \times 10^3$ to 5×10^5, the flow is laminar and orderly, with no superimposed fluctuations. The boundary-layer thickness δ grows monotonically with x, and the shape of the velocity profile is independent of x when normalized, that is, u/U is a function of y/δ. The profiles are said to be similar, and they are now called Blasius profiles, after the engineer who first analyzed them in 1908.

The Blasius flat-plate flow results in closed-form algebraic formulas for such parameters as wall-

shear stress and boundary-layer thickness, given by Eqs. (4). Similar expressions can be formulated for

$$\delta \approx 5.0(\mu x/\rho U)^{1/2}$$
$$\tau_W \approx 0.332(\rho\mu U^3/x)^{1/2} \qquad (4)$$

temperature and heat-transfer parameters. These results are useful in estimating viscous effects in flow past thin bodies such as airfoils, turbine blades, and heat-exchanger plates.

Momentum and displacement thickness. As mentioned above, δ is defined arbitrarily as the point where $u = 0.99U$. This position is difficult to define experimentally. More definitive thickness measures are the two integral scales which arise from the conservation of mass and streamwise momentum. These are the displacement thickness δ^* and the momentum thickness θ, as defined in Eqs. (5). These two

$$\delta^* = \int_0^\infty (1 - u/U)dy$$
$$\theta = \int_0^\infty (u/U)(1 - u/U)dy \qquad (5)$$

terms are unambiguous and are often used to correlate data on local friction and heat transfer and on transition to turbulence of boundary layers. The displacement thickness represents the local deflection of the outer inviscid streamlines, whereas the momentum thickness is a measure of local wall-friction effects.

For flat-plate flow, if δ is given by Eq. (4), the Blasius theory predicts that $\delta^*/\delta = 0.344$ and $\theta/\delta = 0.133$.

Boundary-layer separation. The flat plate is very distinctive in that it causes no change in outer-stream velocity U. Most body shapes immersed in a stream flow, such as cylinders, airfoils, or ships, induce a variable outer stream $U(x)$ near the surface. If U increases with x, which means from Eq. (3) that pressure decreases with x, the boundary layer is said to be in a favorable gradient and remains thin and attached to the surface. If, however, velocity falls and pressure rises with x, the pressure gradient is unfavorable or adverse (**Fig. 4**). The low-velocity fluid near the wall is strongly decelerated by the rising pressure, and the wall-shear stress drops off to zero. Downstream of this zero-shear or separation point,

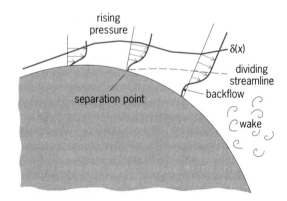

Fig. 4. Boundary-layer separation in a region of persistent rising pressure velocity.

there is backflow and the wall shear is upstream. The boundary layer thickens markedly to conserve mass, and the outer stream separates from the body, leaving a broad, low-pressure wake downstream. Flow separation may be predicted by boundary-layer theory, but the theory is not able to estimate the wake properties accurately. *See* WAKE FLOW.

In most immersed-body flows, the separation and wake occur on the rear or lee side of the body, with higher pressure and no separation on the front. The body thus experiences a large downstream pressure force called pressure drag. This happens to all blunt bodies such as spheres and cylinders and also to airfoils and turbomachinery blades if their angle of attack with respect to the oncoming stream is too large. The airfoil or blade is said to be stalled, and its performance suffers.

Instability and transition. All laminar boundary layers, if they grow thick enough and have sufficient velocity, become unstable. Slight disturbances, whether naturally occurring or imposed artificially, tend to grow in amplitude, at least in a certain frequency and wavelength range. The growth begins as a selective group of two-dimensional periodic disturbances, called Tollmien-Schlichting waves, which become three-dimensional and nonlinear downstream and eventually burst into the strong random fluctuations called turbulence. The critical parameter is the Reynolds number, usually based on boundary-layer displacement thickness, $\text{Re}_{\delta*} = \rho U \delta^*/\mu$. The process of change from laminar to turbulent flow is called transition. *See* TURBULENT FLOW.

In **Fig. 5**, the classic flat-plate flow is shown as an example. The leading-edge flow is the laminar, Blasius profile from Fig. 3. The point of first instability is at $\text{Re}_{\delta*} \approx 520$ or $\text{Re}_x \equiv \rho U x/\mu \approx 10^5$. Tollmien-Schlichting waves are formed with wavelengths of about six boundary-layer thicknesses and frequencies of approximately $0.1 U/\delta$. These waves grow, are joined by other frequencies and wavelengths, become three-dimensional, and burst into turbulence further downstream, typically at $\text{Re}_{x,\text{tr}} \approx 5 \times 10^5$. The flow downstream of this transition point is fully turbulent and remains so in almost all cases. For very smooth flows, $\text{Re}_{x,\text{tr}}$ can be as high as 5×10^6.

The transition process is affected by many parameters. The transition is delayed by favorable pressure gradients, smooth walls, and a quiet outer stream. It is hastened by adverse pressure gradients, rough walls, and a noisy freestream. The transition can be triggered abruptly by inserting an unsteady, wake-producing tripping device, such as a wire or large particle, into the boundary layer near the instability point.

The prediction of the point of first instability for various boundary-layer flows is well developed and experimentally verified. The prediction of final transition, however, is quantitatively less successful because of the many important competing parameters affecting the process.

In rare cases, a fully turbulent flow can be made to relaminarize by subjecting the boundary layer to extreme deceleration.

Turbulent boundary layers. The turbulent flow regime is characterized by random, three-dimensional fluctuations superimposed upon time-mean fluid properties, including velocity, pressure, and temperature. The fluctuations are typically 3–6% of the mean values and range in size over three orders of magnitude, from microscale movements to large eddies of size comparable to the boundary-layer thickness. They are readily measured by modern instruments such as hot wires and laser-Doppler velocimeters.

The effect of superimposing a wide spectrum of eddies on a viscous flow is to greatly increase mixing and transport of mass, momentum, and heat across the flow. Turbulent boundary layers are thicker than laminar layers and have higher heat transfer and friction. The turbulent mean-velocity profile is rather flat, with a steep gradient at the wall (Fig. 5). The edge of the boundary layer is a ragged, fluctuating interface, as shown in Fig. 5, which separates the nonturbulent outer flow from large turbulent eddies in the layer. The thickness of such a layer is defined only in the time mean, and a probe placed in the outer half of the layer would show intermittently turbulent and nonturbulent flow.

No theory for turbulent flow is based on first principles, but many successful empirical models have

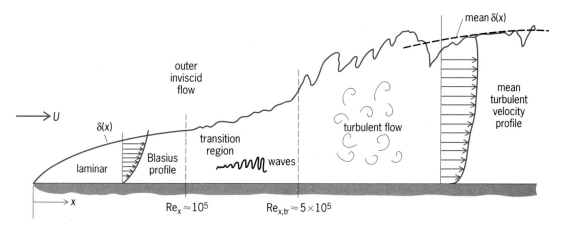

Fig. 5. Transition process in viscous flow past a sharp flat plate. The boundary-layer thickness is exaggerated. (*After F. M. White, Heat and Mass Transfer, Addison-Wesley, 1988*)

been proposed. A turbulent boundary layer may be broken into three regions: a narrow sublayer near the wall, of approximate thickness $5\mu/(\rho\tau_w)^{1/2}$, too small to be seen in Fig. 5, where eddies are damped out and molecular viscosity dominates; an intermediate layer, approximately logarithmic in shape, extending to about one-fourth of the layer thickness; and an outer wake layer, dependent on stream parameters, which rises from the log layer to merge smoothly with the stream velocity U.

The intermediate or logarithmic layer is dependent entirely on wall-related parameters and is approximated by Eq. (6). In flows with constant or

$$u/v^* \approx 2.44\log(\rho v^* y/\mu) + 5.0 \qquad (6)$$
$$v^* = (\tau_w/\rho)^{1/2}$$

falling stream pressure, the wake layer is small, and Eq. (6) can be employed to develop useful formulas for predicting turbulent boundary-layer friction and heat transfer. For example, formulas (7) result for flat-

$$\delta \approx 0.16(\mu x^6/\rho U)^{1/7}$$
$$\tau_w \approx 0.0135(\mu\rho^6 U^{13}/x)^{1/7} \qquad (7)$$

plate turbulent boundary-layer thickness and wall friction. They may be compared with their laminar-flow counterparts in Eqs. (4). For a given x, the turbulent layer is thicker and has a wall-shear stress several times larger; the wall-heat transfer is also higher.

The reason the turbulent-velocity profile in Fig. 5 is so flat is that its effective viscosity is very large. By analogy with the laminar shear-stress formula (1), an equivalent turbulent eddy viscosity may be defined to compute shear stress in a turbulent layer,

Eq. (8). The eddy viscosity is much larger than the

$$\tau_{\text{turb}} \approx \mu_{\text{turb}}(\partial u/\partial y) \qquad (8)$$

molecular viscosity μ and is not a physical property, but depends upon flow parameters such as stream velocity and wall-shear stress. For example, the logarithmic layer of Eq. (6) may be used to infer the eddy viscosity formula of Eq. (9). Many digital computer

$$\mu_{\text{turb}} \approx 0.41\rho v^* y \qquad (9)$$

codes for predicting turbulent boundary layers use eddy-viscosity correlations to complete the equations of motion. Similarly, in turbulent heat-transfer analysis, an eddy thermal conductivity is often used.

Compressible boundary layers. As the stream velocity U becomes larger, its kinetic energy, $U^2/2$, becomes comparable to stream enthalpy, $c_p T$, where c_p is the specific heat at constant pressure and T is the absolute temperature. Changes in temperature and density begin to be important, and the flow can no longer be considered incompressible. An equivalent statement is that the stream Mach number Ma_∞, defined by Eq. (10), where a is the speed of

$$\text{Ma}_\infty = U/a \qquad (10)$$

sound of the stream, becomes significant when Ma_∞ is greater than 0.5. Liquids flow at very small Mach numbers, and compressible flows are primarily gas flows. For an ideal gas of absolute temperature T, the speed of sound is given by Eq. (11), where R is the gas constant, and γ, defined by Eq. (12) where c_p

$$a = \gamma R T^{1/2} \qquad (11)$$

$$\gamma = c_p/c_v \qquad (12)$$

is the specific heat at constant pressure, is approximately 1.4 for air. If Ma_∞ is greater than 1, the flow is said to be supersonic. *See* GAS; GAS DYNAMICS; MACH NUMBER.

In a flow with supersonic stream velocity, the noslip condition is still valid, and much of the boundary-layer flow near the wall is at low speed or subsonic. The fluid enters the boundary layer and loses much of its kinetic energy, of which a small part is conducted away although most is converted into thermal energy. Thus the near-wall region of a highly compressible boundary layer is very hot, even if the wall is cold and is drawing heat away. This situation is illustrated in **Fig. 6**, comparing an incompressible and a compressible ($\text{Ma}_\infty = 2$) thermal boundary layer. The basic difference between low and high speed is the conversion of kinetic energy into higher temperatures across the entire boundary layer.

In a low-speed (incompressible) boundary layer, a cold wall simply means that the wall temperature T_w is less than the free-stream temperature T_∞. The heat flow q_w is from high toward lower temperature, that is, into the wall (Fig. 6). For a low-speed insulated

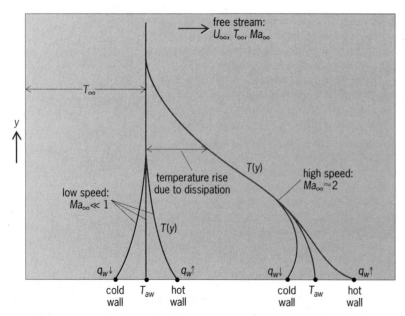

Fig. 6. Boundary-layer temperature profiles for incompressible and compressible (supersonic) stream velocities. (*After F. M. White, Heat and Mass Transfer, Addison-Wesley, 1988*)

wall, the boundary-layer temperature is uniform. For a high-speed flow, however, an insulated wall has a high surface temperature because of the viscous dissipation energy exchange in the layer. This adiabatic wall temperature T_{aw} may be estimated from Eq. (13). The parameter r is the recovery factor, in-

$$T_{aw} \approx T_{\infty} \left[1 + 0.5r \left(\gamma - 1 \right) \text{Ma}_{\infty}^2 \right] \qquad (13)$$

dicating the efficiency of energy exchange; it varies from 0.85 to 0.89 for compressible air flows. For example, if $\text{Ma}_{\infty} = 2.0$, as in Fig. 6, then $T_{aw} \approx 1.7T_{\infty}$. Equation (13) requires that temperatures be in absolute units. In such a flow, a cold wall means only that $T_w < T_{aw}$; the wall temperature itself may be considerably higher than the stream temperature, yet the fluid temperature drops off at the wall, into which heat flows.

Except for the added complexity of having to consider fluid pressure, temperature, and density as coupled variables, compressible boundary layers have similar characteristics to their low-speed counterparts. They undergo transition from laminar to turbulent flow (Fig. 5) but typically at somewhat higher Reynolds numbers. Compressible layers tend to be somewhat thicker than incompressible boundary layers, with proportionally smaller wall-shear stresses. They tend to resist flow separation (Fig. 4) slightly better than incompressible flows.

In a supersonic outer stream, shock waves can always occur. Shocks may form in the boundary layer because of obstacles in the layer or downstream, or they may be formed elsewhere and impinge upon a boundary. In either case, the pressure rises sharply behind the shock, an adverse gradient, and this tends to cause early transition to turbulence and early flow separation. Special care must be taken to design aerodynamic surfaces to accommodate or avoid shock-wave formation in transonic and supersonic flows. *See* COMPRESSIBLE FLOW; SHOCK WAVE.

Boundary-layer control. As boundary layers move downstream, they tend to grow naturally and undergo transition to turbulence. Boundary layers encountering rising pressure undergo flow separation. Both phenomena can be controlled at least partially. Airfoils and hydrofoils can be shaped to delay adverse pressure gradients and thus move separation downstream. Proper shaping can also delay transition. Wall suction removes the low-momentum fluid and delays both transition and separation. Wall blowing into the boundary layer, from downward-facing slots, delays separation but not transition. Changing the wall temperature to hotter for liquids and colder for gases delays transition. Practical systems have been designed for boundary-layer control, but they are often expensive and mechanically complex. *See* AIRFOIL; FLUID-FLOW PRINCIPLES; STREAMLINING; VISCOSITY.　　　　　　Frank M. White

Bibliography. *Illustrated Experiments in Fluid Mechanics*, NCFMF Book of Film Notes, 1972; J. A. Schetz, *Boundary Layer Analysis*, 1997; H. Schlichting, *Boundary-Layer Theory*, 8th rev. ed., 1999; F. S. Sherman, *Viscous Flow*, 1990; M. Van Dyke, *An Album of Fluid Motion*, 1982; F. M. White, *Viscous Fluid Flow*, 2d ed., 1991.

Bovine viral diarrhea

An economically important, multisystemic viral disease of cattle that is common worldwide. The causal agent is bovine viral diarrhea virus (BVDV). Cattle of all ages may be infected with this virus, and a variety of acute or chronic disease processes occur that may affect the digestive, respiratory, and reproductive systems.

The virus. Bovine viral diarrhea virus is a member of the *Pestivirus* genus within the Flaviviridae family. Pestiviruses are an antigenically related group of viruses that includes classical swine fever virus, border disease virus of sheep, and bovine viral diarrhea virus. Mature viral particles are spherical with a diameter of 40 to 60 nm. A lipid envelope surrounds a 30-nm inner shell (capsid) that contains the viral genome. The viral genome is a single, positive-stranded ribonucleic acid (RNA) that is about 12,300 nucleotides in length. The viral RNA encodes four structural and seven nonstructural proteins. The virus replicates in the cytoplasm of the host cell, eventually forming new viral particles in vesicles within the cytoplasm. The new viral particles are transported to the cell surface and released to the environment. *See* CLASSICAL SWINE FEVER; VIRUS.

Analysis of the RNA from numerous viruses collected worldwide has resulted in the identification of two genetic groups, or genotypes, of bovine viral diarrhea virus. The viral genotypes are termed type 1 and type 2. Each genotype is further divided into two or more subgenotypes such as type 1a, type 1b, etc. The subgenotypes contain viruses that are genetically most closely related. Although bovine viral diarrhea viruses are divided into two genotypes based on their nucleic acid sequence, all of the viruses are related antigenically to each other. Members of either viral genotype cause similar disease processes. In addition to two viral genotypes, there are two biotypes of bovine viral diarrhea virus that are differentiated based on their effect on infected cell cultures. Both biotypes are found in each viral genotype. The viral biotypes are termed noncytopathic or cytopathic. The noncytopathic biotype is predominant in nature and grows in cell cultures without inducing overt harmful effects. The cytopathic biotype induces morphologic changes in infected cell cultures that include formation of cytoplasmic vacuoles of variable size and number. Soon after the appearance of cytoplasmic vacuoles, the infected cell dies. The harmful effects of cytopathic bovine viral diarrhea virus in cell culture do not equate with virulence of the virus in the infected host, as the most virulent viruses for cattle are noncytopathic in cell culture. In addition to cattle, bovine viral diarrhea virus infects most even-toed ungulates, including sheep, goat, swine, deer, bison, llama, and antelope. *See* ANIMAL VIRUS.

Clinical disease. Cattle usually are infected with bovine viral diarrhea virus in the first 2 to 3 years of life. Often, infection with the virus leads to a clinically inapparent or clinically mild disease. Signs of mild disease include low-grade fever, loose stool, low white blood cell count, mild depression, transient loss of appetite, and decreased milk production. Signs of mild disease last 1 to 3 days, and recovery from disease is rapid and complete. Some viruses cause clinically severe disease that is characterized by high fever, diarrhea, very low white blood cell count, depression, dehydration, and rapid respiration. Ulceration of the mouth, esophagus, and intestine may occur. Some cattle with clinically severe disease may experience a precipitous loss of platelets from the blood followed by mild to extensive hemorrhaging. The duration of clinical signs associated with severe disease may be 4 to 7 days, and the outcome may be death. Typical outbreaks of bovine viral diarrhea are associated with high morbidity and low mortality; however, clinically severe disease may have high mortality.

Bovine viral diarrhea virus replicates in lymphoid cells and may suppress normal function of those cells. By disrupting this function, the virus compromises the ability of the infected animal to defend itself against pathogens. Thus, bovine viral diarrhea virus is often associated with respiratory and enteric disease of cattle in which multiple other agents contribute to the disease process. Bovine viral diarrhea virus readily crosses the placenta to infect the fetus and cause reproductive failure. Embryonic resorption, abortion, stillbirth, premature birth, and congenital defects of the central nervous system, eye, and musculoskeletal system occur following fetal infection. Life-long persistent viral infection may be a sequel of fetal infection with noncytopathic, but not cytopathic, virus. For persistent infection to be established, fetal infection must occur in the first 4 months of pregnancy. At birth, persistently infected calves may be weak or stunted. However, persistently infected calves also may appear healthy and vigorous. Persistently infected cattle do not mount an immune response against the virus they carry, but are capable of producing an immune response against other infectious agents.

Acute and chronic mucosal disease are rare forms of bovine viral diarrhea that occur in cattle born with a persistent infection with noncytopathic virus. The signs of acute mucosal disease are fever, low white blood cell count, profuse diarrhea that is often bloody, ulcerations throughout the digestive tract, inappetence, dehydration, and death. The course of mucosal disease is one to a few days and recovery is rare. Persistently infected cattle also may develop a chronic from of mucosal disease that is characterized by intermittent diarrhea, lameness, wasting, and death. In the chronic form, death may not occur until several months after the initial signs of disease. Both the acute and chronic forms of mucosal disease occur when persistently infected cattle become superinfected with a cytopathic bovine viral diarrhea virus. Often the cytopathic virus arises from the non-cytopathic persistent virus following a mutational event in the replication of the viral RNA. Cytopathic virus may be transmitted to persistently infected cattle from other persistently infected cattle that have mucosal disease. Also, cytopathic virus may be inoculated into a persistently infected animal through use of vaccine that contains live cytopathic virus. Mucosal disease is rare because it requires a persistently infected animal and persistent infection is relatively rare.

Pathology. Postmortem examination of cattle that have acute bovine viral diarrhea or acute mucosal disease often reveals ulcerative lesions of the mucosal surface (inner lining) of the digestive tract. Erosions and ulcerations in the mouth, esophagus, abomasum (true stomach of a ruminant), and small and large intestines are common lesions. In the intestines, ulcerations frequently are centered over submucosal lymphoid follicles. In chronic mucosal disease, there may be hair loss and thickening of the skin, usually in the neck area. Also, ulcers may be found in the skin between the claws of the hoof, around the dewclaws, or on the heel. Skin lesions often fail to heal, leading to secondary bacterial infections of the skin and occasionally hoof deformities. Some bovine viral diarrhea viruses induce thrombocytopenia (a decrease in platelets in the blood) during primary acute infection. This may lead to hemorrhages in the gums, in the sclera of the eye, and on serosal surfaces (outer surfaces) of the internal organs. The primary microscopic lesions for all forms of bovine viral diarrhea are depletion of lymphoid cells in the lymphoid follicles of the intestines. Viral antigen may be detected in lymphoid, neuronal, endocrine, skin, and bone marrow cells.

Mode of transmission. Oral or nasal exposure with virus is the primary mode of transmission of acute disease. Persistently infected cattle are efficient transmitters of virus, which is continually shed in saliva and nasal secretions. Susceptible cattle may become infected within 1 hour of contact with a persistently infected animal. Cattle afflicted with acute disease also shed virus in saliva and nasal secretions. Biting insects, veterinary instruments, or clothing contaminated with secretions or blood from an infected animal, and artificial insemination are reported to transmit disease. Because wild ruminants may be infected with bovine viral diarrhea virus, it is possible that disease may spread among farms with the movement of wildlife.

Diagnosis, treatment, and control. Clinical signs of disease and identification of mucosal ulcerations on postmortem examination support a tentative diagnosis of bovine viral diarrhea. Virus isolation in cell culture or polymerase chain reaction (PCR) using clinical specimens such as blood or nasal swabs confirm the diagnosis of acute or persistent infection with bovine viral diarrhea virus. Because most isolates of bovine viral diarrhea virus are noncytopathic in cell culture, virus isolation must be confirmed by immunohistochemistry or PCR. Antigen-capture enzyme-linked immunosorbent assays (ELISA) have proven useful for rapid detection of persistent infection using blood or skin biopsy specimens. Immunohistochemistry using monoclonal antibody specific for the virus allows rapid detection of viral antigen in frozen or fixed tissues. Serologic tests, such as viral neutralization or ELISA, that detect antibody against virus are useful for detection of past infection or for monitoring response to vaccination.

Bovine viral diarrhea is treated with supportive care. Disease is prevented or diminished in severity through vaccination. Inactivated virus and modified-live virus vaccines for bovine viral diarrhea are available for use in cattle. Typically, vaccination is first done when calves are a few months old. Vaccination is often repeated at regular intervals during the life of the animal. Identification and elimination of persistently infected cattle is an important part of any control strategy for prevention of viral spread and disease. Temporary isolation of new additions to the herd and other farm biosecurity measures, including control of movement of equipment, animals, and personnel on the farm, also are important for control of bovine viral diarrhea. *See* VACCINATION.

Steven R. Bolin

Bibliography. S. R. Bolin, Bovine viral diarrhea and mucosal disease complex, *The Merck Veterinary Manual*, 9th ed., Merck, Whitehouse Station, NJ, 2005; K. V. Brock (ed.), Bovine viral diarrhea virus: Persistence is the key, *Vet. Clin. N. Amer.: Food Anim. Prac.*, vol. 20, no. 1, 2004; D. L. Grooms, J. C. Baker, and T. R. Ames, Diseases caused by bovine viral diarrhea virus, *Large Animal Internal Medicine: Disease of Horses, Cattle, Sheep, and Goats*, 3d ed., Mosby, St. Louis, 2002; D. M. Knipe and P. M. Howley (eds.), *Fundamental Virology*, 4th ed., Lippincott, Williams & Wilkins, Philadelphia, 2001; O. M. Radostits et al., *Veterinary Medicine: A Textbook of the Diseases of Cattle, Sheep, Pigs, Goats, and Horses*, 9th ed., W. B. Saunders, London, 2000.

Boyle's law

A law of gases which states that at constant temperature the volume of a gas varies inversely with its pressure. This law, formulated by Robert Boyle (1627–1691), can also be stated thus: The product of the volume of a gas times the pressure exerted on it is a constant at a fixed temperature. The relation is approximately true for most gases, but is not followed at high pressures. The phenomenon was discovered independently by Edme Mariotte about 1650 and is known in Europe as Mariotte's law. *See* GAS; KINETIC THEORY OF MATTER.   Frank H. Rockett

Brachiopoda

A phylum of solitary, exclusively marine, coelomate, bivalved animals, with both valves symmetrical about a median longitudinal plane. Brachiopods are typically attached to the substrate by a posteriorly located cuticle-covered stalk called a pedicle. Anteriorly, a relatively large mantle cavity is always developed between the valves, and the ciliated tentacular (filamentous) feeding organ, or lophophore, is suspended within, projecting anteriorly from the anterior body wall (**Fig. 1**). The name Brachiopoda means "arm foot" and refers to the morphology and location of the lophophore.

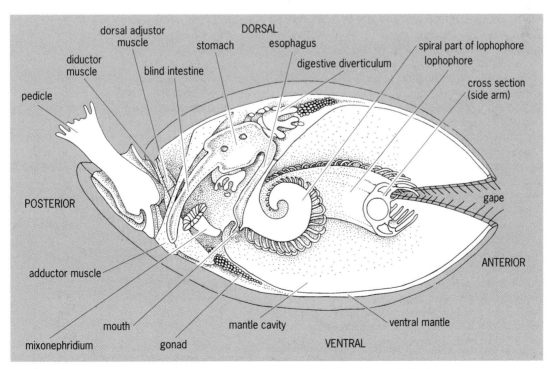

Fig. 1. Principal organs of a brachiopod as typified by *Terebratulina*. **(After R. C. Moore, ed.,** *Treatise on Invertebrate Paleontology, pt. H, Geological Society of America, Inc., and University of Kansas Press, 1965*)

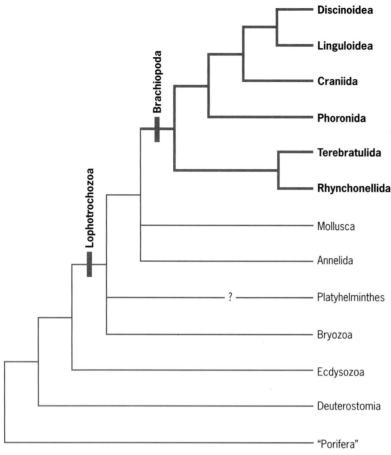

Fig. 2. Phylogenetic relationships among selected metazoans. (*Simplified from K. M. Halanych and Y. Passamaneck, Amer. Zool., 41:629–639, 2001; K. M. Halanych, Annu. Rev. Ecol. Evol. Sys., 35:229–256, 2004; and B. L. Cohen and A. Weydmann, Organisms, Diversity and Evolution, 5(4):253–273, 2005)*

This brief description serves to differentiate a brachiopod from any other animal. Within the Brachiopoda, three groups currently regarded as subphyla are recognized, each named after their most ancient living representative: Linguliformea, Craniiformea, Rhynchonelliformea. Phoroniformea are recognized by some as a fourth subphylum. The two classes (Inarticulata and Articulata), formerly distinguished by the presence or absence of articulation between the two valves of the shell, are no longer recognized as distinct taxa; rather, they appear to represent the ends of a spectrum of articulatory types, some well delineated, others less so. Rhynchonelliforms have impunctate, endopunctate, or pseudopunctate calcitic shells with a fibrous (or laminar) shell structure; most are articulated, with the valves typically hinged together by a pair of ventral teeth with complementary sockets in the dorsal valve; most have pedicles with a core of connective tissue. Craniiforms have punctate calcitic shells with a laminar (or tabular) shell structure; all lack articulation, with valves that are held together only by the soft tissue of the living animal, and all lack pedicles. Linguliforms have canaliculate organophosphatic shells with a stratiform shell structure; all lack articulation; and all have pedicles with a coelomate

core. *See* INARTICULATA; LINGULIDA; RHYNCHONELLIFORMEA.

Phylogeny and classification. Molecular sequence data from nuclear and mitochondrial genes in extant brachiopods provide strong support for brachiopods as protostomous organisms, and not deuterostomes, as some earlier morphological and developmental data seemed to suggest. These data also indicate that the Phoronida is nested within the Brachiopoda, and is not the brachiopod sister group, as previously thought. Lophophorates alone do not appear to form a clade; the Bryozoa are more distantly related within the Lophotrochozoa, a rather poorly resolved clade that also includes mollusks and annelids, among other phyla (**Fig. 2**). Only approximately 5% of named brachiopod genera (and most likely, species) are extant; most of our current understanding of brachiopod phylogeny results from a composite of molecular data from a small taxonomic sample, and morphological (and stratigraphic) data from a much larger sample of extinct fossil taxa. *See* BRYOZOA; PHORONIDA; RHYNCHONELLIFORMEA.

The phylum is currently classified as follows:

Subphylum Linguliformea
   Class Lingulata
      Order: Lingulida
         Siphonotretida
         Acrotretida
   Class Paterinata
      Order Paterinida
Subphylum Craniiformea
   Class Craniata
      Order: Craniida
         Craniopsida
         Trimerellida
Subphylum Phoroniformea (?)
Subphylum Rhynchonelliformea
   Class Chileata
      Order: Chileida
         Dictyonellida
   Class Obolellata
      Order: Obolellida
         Naukatida
   Class Kutorginata
      Order: Kutorginida
   Class Strophomenata
      Order: Strophomenida
         Billingsellida
         Orthotetida
         Productida
   Class Rhynchonellata
      Order: Protorthida
         Orthida
         Pentamerida
         Rhynchonellida
         Atrypida
         Spiriferida
         Spiriferinida
         Thecideida
         Athyridida
         Terebratulida

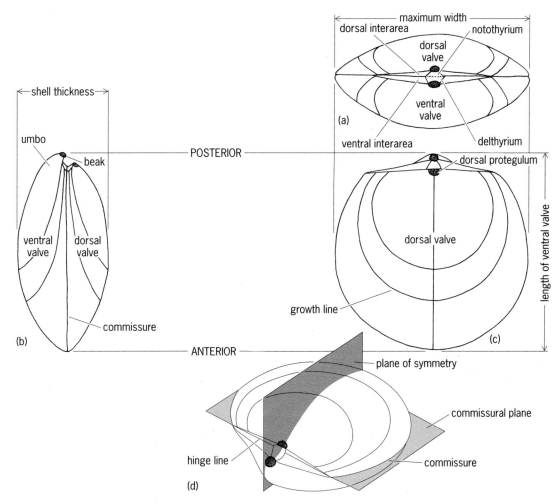

Fig. 3. Diagrammatic representation of the external features of a generalized brachiopod seen in (*a*) posterior, (*b*) left lateral, (*c*) dorsal, and (*d*) dorsolateral views. (*After R. C. Moore, ed., Treatise on Invertebrate Paleontology, pt. H, Geological Society of America, Inc., and University of Kansas Press, 1965*)

Orientation. The two brachiopod valves are currently referred to as the dorsal and ventral valves, not brachial and pedicle, because not all brachiopods possess pedicles. This body orientation distinguishes them from bivalved mollusks, which have valves on the left and right sides of the body. While topologically dorsal and ventral in adults, their developmental orientation is not entirely clear; both valves of some extant craniiforms may derive from the dorsal surface of the developing, modified trochophore larva. The pedicle either protrudes between the valves (through the delthyrium and notothyrium, which are small triangular apertures serving as pedicle openings), or (**Fig. 3**) more commonly emerges from a variably modified opening (pedicle foramen) in the ventral valve, which, in articulated forms, is the valve bearing the hinge teeth. Whatever the form of the pedicle opening, it is always at the posterior end of the animal and its enclosing shells, the opposite end being regarded as anterior. Both valves have a characteristic distribution of muscles, and any skeletal support for the lophophore is invariably developed from the dorsal valve (**Fig. 4**).

Anatomy. The pedicle is the only organ protruding outside the valves, for the remainder of the

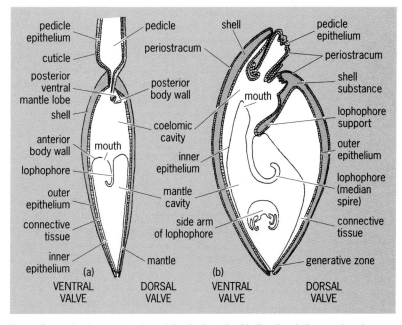

Fig. 4. Generalized representation of distribution of epithelium in relation to other tissues and organs in (*a*) lingulides and (*b*) terebratulides. (*After R. C. Moore, ed., Treatise on Invertebrate Paleontology, pt. H, Geological Society of America, Inc., and University of Kansas Press, 1965*)

animal is enclosed in the space between them. This space is divided into two unequal parts, a smaller posteriorly located body cavity and an anterior mantle cavity. The ectodermal outer epithelium underlying the shell bounding the body cavity is in a single layer; but anteriorly, laterally, and even posteriorly in most inarticulated brachiopods, it is prolonged as a pair of folds forming the ventral and dorsal mantles, from which the shells are mineralized (at the generative zones). In extant species, the two mantles approach each other and ultimately fuse along the posterior margin of rhynchonelliform brachiopods; in contrast, the mantles are invariably discrete in craniiforms and linguliforms, and are separated by a strip of body-wall inner epithelium (Fig. 4).

The body cavity contains the musculature; the alimentary canal; the mixonephridia, which are paired excretory organs also functioning as gonoducts; the reproductive organs; and the rather poorly understood circulatory and nervous systems. Except for the openings through the mixonephridia, the body cavity is enclosed, but the mantle cavity communicates freely with the sea when the valves are opened. The lophophore is a feeding and respiratory organ, typically suspended from the anterior body wall within the mantle cavity, and is always symmetrically disposed about the median plane. The lophophore consists of a ciliated, filament-bearing tube with two arms in varying configurations. The ciliary beat produces a laminar flow of water into and then out of the mantle cavity, flowing across the filaments while inside. The latter trap food particles which are carried along a groove in the lophophore to the mouth situated medially between the two arms. *See* LOPHOPHORE.

The alimentary canal of all brachiopods is broadly similar in structure, but differs in orientation in the body cavity. The mouth opens into a muscular tube, the esophagus, which continues to a stomach and intestine. In addition, there are a variable number of digestive diverticula that communicate with the stomach through narrow ducts (Fig. 1). In rhynchonelliform brachiopods, the intestine curves into a C-shape and ends blindly (with no anus) in a posteroventral location; in linguliforms, it curves into a U-shape, leaving the anus right-lateral or ventrolateral; in phoronids, it is also U-shaped, but the anus is anterodorsal; in craniiforms, the intestine is straight and does not curve or fold, leaving the anus medioposterior.

The diductor and adductor muscles that control the opening and closing of the valves are contained within the body cavity (Fig. 1), but their distribution varies among the three brachiopod subphyla. In most rhynchonelliforms, they are disposed to effect a rotation of the valves about a hinge axis located on the valves; in craniiforms and linguliforms, the hinge axis is located in the viscera between the valves; in selected linguliforms, the two valves can "scissor" past one another, allowing burrowing in a soft substrate. Adjustor muscles effect movement of the shell relative to the pedicle, and other muscles may be present that can move the lophophore slightly relative to the valves. Because of a differential rate of secretion of shell material by the epithelium at the bases of the muscles, the site of muscle attachment is commonly impressed in the valves, producing muscle scars. Rarely, the muscle scars may be elevated above the adjacent shell.

Although some small-bodied species are hermaphroditic and brood their larvae, the sexes are separate in the majority of brachiopods. The gonads, or reproductive organs, are located either within the body cavity (as in the lingulids and discinids) or more typically in slender tubelike extensions of the body cavity which project into the mantle, called the mantle canals (in craniids and rhynchonelliforms). The mantle canal pattern may be retained on the inner surface of the valves, even in fossils, by processes of differential secretion comparable with those producing the muscle scars.

Given the phylogenetic nesting of phoronids within brachiopods, the anatomy of Phoronida can be interpreted as having evolved from a brachiopod body plan; phoronid anatomy is modified largely as a reflection of the loss of the two mineralized valves. *See* PHORONIDA.

Embryology and ontogeny. Linguliforms, craniiforms, phoronids, and rhynchonelliforms share numerous aspects of embryogenesis and larval development, yet each has distinct characteristics not shared with any others (**Fig. 5**). Extant linguliforms and phoronids are planktotrophic and have likely remained so from their origin in the Cambrian (or earlier); extant craniiforms and rhynchonelliforms are lecithotrophic, and have each evolved independently from a planktotrophic ancestral state. Planktotrophic larvae remain in the water column for weeks to months, while lecithotrophic larvae remain in the water column only briefly, usually less than a week; these differences have important implications for the timing of differentiation of adult structures, and for the ability of the larvae to disperse biogeographically. Planktotrophic brachiopods develop more structures as larvae, prior to metamorphosis, and lecithotrophs develop more structures following metamorphosis, as young juveniles. Shell deposition begins at metamorphosis in all three subphyla, although mantle formation can begin during embryogenesis or, more commonly, during the larval growth period, just prior to metamorphosis.

Larvae in all three subphyla share a three-part body organization: an apical lobe, from which the lophophore differentiates in the larval stage of linguliforms and immediately following metamorphosis in craniiforms and rhynchonelliforms; a mantle lobe, from which the mantle (on which the periostracum and shells later mineralize), alimentary canal, and most of the viscera develop; and a pedicle lobe, from which the pedicle develops in linguliforms during the larval stage, and in rhynchonelliforms following settlement and metamorphosis. In rhynchonelliforms alone, the mantles are reversed after metamorphosis so that they are oriented anteriorly, partially covering what was the apical lobe of the larva, and with the original inner surface of the

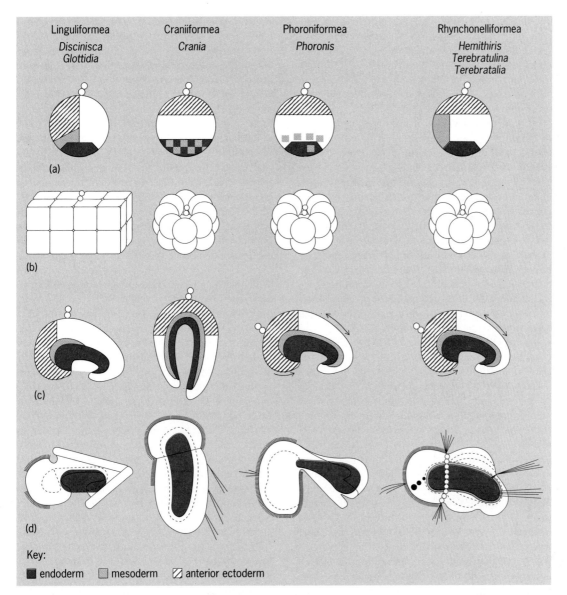

Linguliformea
Discinisca
Glottidia

Craniiformea
Crania

Phoroniformea
Phoronis

Rhynchonelliformea
Hemithiris
Terebratulina
Terebratalia

(a)

(b)

(c)

(d)

Key:

■ endoderm   ▢ mesoderm   ▨ anterior ectoderm

Fig. 5. Comparison of fate maps and selected developmental stages of the three brachiopod subphyla and Phoroniformea, considered by some to be a fourth brachiopod subphylum. (*a*) Fate maps of uncleaved eggs. (*b*) 16-cell embryos. (*c*) Late gastrula stage. (*d*) Lateral views of the early larva. (*Reprinted from G. Freeman, Developmental Biology, 261:263–287, 2003, with permission from Elsevier*)

mantle forming the outer surface of the organism. The mantles subsequently secrete the earliest, first-formed shell, the protegulum, which enlarges by terminal accretion during later shell growth. Only after metamorphosis does the rudimentary lophophore, alimentary canal, and adult musculature develop. Rhynchonelliforms and phoronids share many aspects of embryogenesis (Fig. 5*a–c*), providing further support for genetic data suggesting they evolved among brachiopods. Craniiforms do not develop pedicles or a larval pedicle lobe, but the larvae settle at their posteriormost ends, comparable to where a pedicle lobe would be located. Craniiforms do not undergo mantle reversal.

Linguliform larvae are much like miniature adults that undergo minimal morphological change at metamorphosis, having developed most of their adult features while larvae in the plankton. The two mantle

rudiments are separated from each other early in larval life, and are not fused along the posterior margin in the manner characteristic of rhynchonelliform brachiopods.

Shell morphology. The two valves are commonly of unequal size, with the ventral valve typically larger. Because the shell increases in size by increments laid down at the mantle margin, ontogenetic changes in shape are faithfully recorded by growth lines. The valves may be further ornamented by concentric folds (rugae), growth lamellae, or radially disposed ribs of various amplitude and wavelength. Numerous extinct genera are characterized by extravagant development of spines. In rhynchonelliforms, the posterior region of one or both valves is commonly differentiated from the remainder of the valve as a somewhat flattened cardinal area. The ventral area is typically further modified by the pedicle opening; among articulated brachiopods this consists of a triangular delthyrium which may be partially closed by a pseudodeltidium or a pair of deltidial plates. A corresponding triangular opening, the notothyrium, may be developed on the dorsal cardinal area. Internally, muscle scars and mantle canal impressions may be apparent, together with structures of varying complexity associated with articulation (for example, dental and socket plates) and support of the lophophore (crura, spiralia, loops). Calcite spicules are present in the mantle tissues of some extant terebratulides. Linguliform valves are less heavily mineralized and more organic-rich than rhynchelliforms. Extant craniiforms, cemented to a hard substrate, have ventral valves that are flat and extremely thin, with gently cap-shaped dorsal valves.

Shell morphology varies considerably externally in overall shape and size, relative biconvexity, and degree of ornamentation. Shell morphology also varies internally in structures involved in articulation, lophophore support, and muscle position, from order to order, among the 26 orders recognized. This extensive variation makes it difficult to succinctly characterize overall trends. *See* RHYNCHONELLIDA; TEREBRATULIDA.

Ecology and biogeography. All modern brachiopods are marine, and there is little doubt from the fossil record that brachiopods have always been confined to the sea. A few genera, however, notably the closely related linguliform brachiopods *Lingula* and *Glottidia*, can tolerate reduced salinities and may survive in environments that would be lethal to the majority of forms. Recent brachiopods occur commonly beneath the relatively shallow waters of the continental shelves, which seem to have been the most favored environment in terms of diversity and abundance, but the bathymetric range of the phylum is very large. Some modern species live intertidally and, at the other extreme, some have been dredged from depths of over 16,500 ft (5000 m).

The majority of brachiopods form part of the sessile benthos and are attached by their pedicle during postlarval life. Paleozoic brachiopods not uncommonly exhibit boreholes penetrating their shells, suggesting death by boring predation; interestingly, modern brachiopods have very few known predators, boring or otherwise, even though most are epifaunal, typically living on hard substrates. *Glottidia* and *Lingula* are exceptional in being infaunal and making burrows with the help of complex musculature connecting the two valves that lack articulation. The loss of the pedicle has occurred multiple times over the course of brachiopod evolution, by either complete suppression or atrophy early in the life of the individual. Such forms lie free on the sea floor, are attached by cementation of part or all of the ventral valve, or are anchored by spines. The geographic distribution and geological setting of some fossil species suggest that they may have been epiplanktonic, attached to floating weed, but such a mode of life is unknown in modern faunas.

Biogeographically, brachiopods today exhibit an antitropical distribution, with their highest diversity closer to the Poles than to the tropics, and higher in the Southern Hemisphere than the Northern Hemisphere. Paleobiogeographical data from the distribution of fossil species indicate that Paleozoic brachiopods exhibited a more typical latitudinal diversity gradient, with high tropical diversity, decreasing toward the polar regions, such as is observed today in the majority of marine invertebrates.

Taxonomic diversity and stratigraphic distribution. Brachiopods formed a major part of skeletonized marine faunas throughout the Paleozoic; linguliforms follow a pattern of diversity through time more or less typical for the Cambrian Evolutionary Fauna described by J. J. Sepkoski, while rhynchonelliforms typify the Paleozoic Evolutionary Fauna. The oldest undoubted brachiopods, the paterinates, occur in the Lower Cambrian Tommotian stage. Representatives of seven of the eight classes are known from the Lower Cambrian, indicating that morphological diversity was high even very early in the history of the phylum. Throughout the Cambrian, linguliforms were more abundant than rhynchonelliforms; but during the Early Ordovician radiation, rhynchonelliform diversity and abundance both increased dramatically and remained high until the end-Permian. In the late Paleozoic, a number of major brachiopod groups became extinct, and the end-Permian extinction event caused diversity to plummet. Four of the five extant orders survived this extinction event, and rediversified, although much more modestly through the Mesozoic and Cenozoic than in the Paleozoic. In the present-day oceans, approximately 120 genera are recognized, dominated by rhynchonelliforms (terebratulides and rhynchonellides in particular). *See* EXTINCTION (BIOLOGY); PATERINIDA; RHYNCHONELLIDA.   S. J. Carlson; A. J. Rowell

Bibliography. S. J. Carlson and M. R. Sandy (eds.), *Brachiopods Ancient and Modern: A Tribute to G. Arthur Cooper*, Paleontol. Soc. Pap. 7, 2001; R. L. Kaesler (ed.), *Treatise on Invertebrate Paleontology*, pt. H: *Brachiopoda* (revised), 6 vols., Geological Society of America and University of Kansas, Boulder and Lawrence, 1997–2006; M. J. S. Rudwick, *Living and Fossil Brachiopods*, Hutchinson, London, 1970.

Brain

A collection of specialized cells (neurons) in the head that regulates behavior as well as sensory and motor functions. Neurons grow long thread-like structures—an axon and a dendritic tree—from their cell bodies, which provide them with a rapid communication network throughout the body. The axon uses pulses to transmit a signal to thousands of other neurons or to muscle or gland cells. The dendritic tree uses waves of electric current to integrate the pulses from thousands of other neurons. Groups of neurons form ganglia in chains along both sides of the body axis from "head to tail." The largest of these paired groups, the brain, is in the head, where the distance receptors (nose, eyes, and ears) are located. These receptors respond to smells, sights, and sounds coming so far from the collective that the collective has time to receive the inputs, interpret them as signals, plan an action before being overtaken by circumstance, and act while monitoring and correcting its action. These are the minimal functions of a brain. The power of a brain lies not in its size but in the complexity of the connections among its functional parts. See NEURON.

Parts. The three main parts of the brain in vertebrates are the cerebrum, the cerebellum, and the brainstem that connects them with each other and with the spinal cord (**Fig. 1**). The two cerebral hemispheres are separated by a midline fissure that is bridged by a massive bundle of axons running in both directions, the corpus callosum. Each hemisphere has a core of groups of neurons (the basal ganglia); an outer shell of neurons in layers (the cerebral cortex); and massive bundles of axons for communication within the cerebrum and with the rest of the brain. These bundles are called white matter because of the waxy myelin sheaths surrounding the axons.

Basal ganglia. This component of the brain comprises three main groups. (1) The thalamus receives axons from all sensory systems and transmits information to the cortex. It also receives feedback from cortical neurons during sensory processing. (2) The striatum, comprising bundles of axons cutting through the groups of neurons, also has two-way communication with the cortex and assists in the organization of body movement. (3) The hypothalamus receives orders from the cortex and organizes the chemical systems that support body movement. One output channel is hormonal, and controls the pituitary gland (hypophysis) which in turn controls the endocrine system. The other channel is neural, comprising axons coursing through the brainstem and spinal cord to the motor neurons of the autonomic nervous system, which regulates the heart, blood vessels, lungs, gastrointestinal tract, sex organs, and skin. The autonomic and endocrine systems are largely self regulating, but they are subject to control by the cortex through the hypothalamus. See AUTONOMIC NERVOUS SYSTEM; ENDOCRINE SYSTEM (VERTEBRATE); NEUROBIOLOGY.

Cortex. This section of the brain is also called gray matter because it contains the axons, cell bodies, and dendrites of neurons but there is very little myelin. An index of the capacity of a brain is cortical surface area. In higher mammals, the cortical surface increases more rapidly than the volume during fetal development, and as a result the surface folds, taking the form of wrinkles, that is, convexities (gyri) and fissures (sulci) that vary in their details from one brain to another. However, they are sufficiently reliable to serve as landmarks on the cerebral hemisphere that it can be subdivided into lobes.

Lobes. Four lobes make up the shell of each hemisphere (**Fig. 2**), namely the frontal, parietal, temporal, and occipital lobes. Each lobe contains a motor or sensory map, which is an orderly arrangement of cortical neurons associated with muscles and sensory receptors on the body surface. The central sulcus

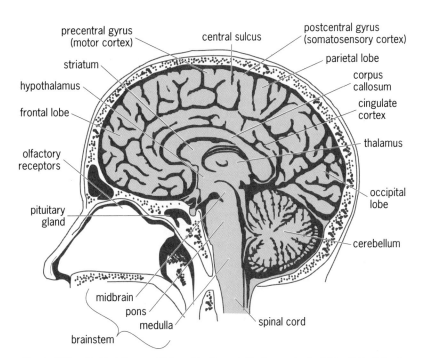

Fig. 1. Midsagittal (midline, medial) section through the human brain. (*After C. R. Noback, The Human Nervous System, 4th ed., McGraw-Hill, 1991*)

delimits the frontal and parietal lobes. The precentral gyrus contains the motor cortex whose neurons transmit signals to motor neurons in the brainstem and spinal cord which control the muscles in the feet, legs, trunk, arms, face, and tongue of the opposite side of the body, in that order from medial to lateral position between Broca's area and the tongue area of the motor cortex. The number of neurons for each section is determined by the fineness of control, not the size of the muscle; for example, the lips and tongue have larger areas than the trunk. Within the postcentral gyrus is the primary somatosensory

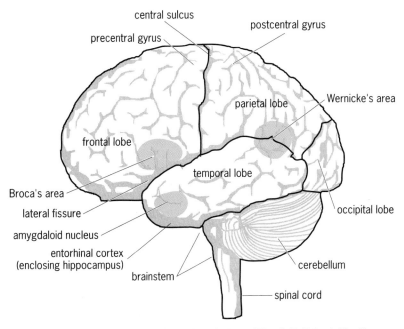

Fig. 2. Lateral surface view of the cerebral hemisphere. (*After C. R. Noback, The Human Nervous System, 4th ed., McGraw-Hill, 1991*)

cortex. Sensory receptors in the skin, muscles, and joints send messages to the somatosensory cortical cells through relays in the spinal cord and the thalamus to a map of the opposite side of the body in parallel to the map in the motor cortex. The lateral fissure separates the temporal lobe from the parietal and frontal lobes. The cortex on the inferior border of the fissure receives input relayed through the thalamus from the ears to the primary auditory cortex. The occipital lobe receives thalamic input from the eyes and functions as the primary visual cortex.

In humans, the association cortex surrounds the primary sensory and motor areas that make up a small fraction of each lobe. The occipital lobe has many specialized areas for recognizing visual patterns of color, motion, and texture. The parietal cortex has areas that support perception of the body and its surrounding personal space. Its operation is manifested by the phenomenon of phantom limb, in which the perception of a missing limb persists for an amputee. Conversely, individuals with damage to these areas suffer from sensory neglect, because parts of the body may no longer exist for them. The temporal cortex contains areas that provide recognition of faces and of rhythmic patterns, including those of speech, dance, and music. The frontal cortex provides the neural capabilities for constructing patterns of motor behavior and social behavior. It was the rapid enlargement of the frontal and temporal lobes in human evolution over the past half million years that supported the transcendence of humans over other species. This is where the capacity to create works of art, and also to anticipate pain and death is located. Insight and foresight are both lost with bilateral frontal lobe damage, leading to reduced experience of anxiety, asocial behavior, and a disregard of consequences of actions.

Motor systems. A small part of frontal lobe output goes directly to motor neurons in the brainstem and spinal cord for fine control of motor activities, such as search movements by the eyes, head, and fingers, but most goes either to the striatum from which it is relayed to the thalamus and then back to the cortex, or to the brainstem from which it is sent to the cerebellum and then through the thalamus back to the cortex. In the cerebellum, the cortical messages are integrated with sensory input predominantly from the muscles, tendons, and joints, but also from the eyes and inner ears (for balance) to provide split-second timing for rapid and complex movements. The cerebellum also has a cortex and a core of nuclei to relay input and output. Their connections, along with those in the cerebral cortex, are subject to modification with learning in the formation of a working memory (the basis for learned skills). *See* MEMORY; MOTOR SYSTEMS.

Limbic system. The cerebellum and striatum do not set goals, initiate movements, store temporal sequences of sensory input, or provide orientation to the spatial environment. These functions are performed by parts of the cortex and striatum deep in the brain that constitute another loop, the limbic system. Its main site of entry is the entorhinal cortex, which receives input from all of the sensory cortices, including the olfactory system. The input from all the sensory cortices is combined and sent to the hippocampus, where it is integrated over time. Hippocampal output returns to the entorhinal cortex, which distributes the integrated sensory information to all the sensory cortices, updates them, and prepares them to receive new sensory input. This new information also reaches the hypothalamus and part of the striatum (the amygdaloid nucleus) for regulating emotional behavior. Bilateral damage to the temporal lobe including the hippocampus results in loss of short-term memory. Damage to the amygdaloid nucleus can cause serious emotional impairment. The Papez circuit is formed by transmission from the hippocampus to the hypothalamus by the fornix, then to the thalamus, parietal lobe, and entorhinal cortex. The limbic system generates and issues goal-directed motor commands, with corollary discharge to the sensory systems that prepares them for the changes in sensory input caused by motor activity (for example, when one speaks and hears oneself, as distinct from another).

Split brain. Each hemisphere has its own limbic, Papez, cortico-thalamic, cortico-striatal, and cortico-cerebellar loops, together with sensory and motor connections. When isolated by surgically severing the callosum, each hemisphere functions independently, as though two conscious persons occupied the same skull, but with differing levels of skills in abstract reasoning and language. The right brain (spatial)–left brain (linguistic) cognitive differences are largely due to preeminent development of the speech areas in the left hemisphere in most right- and left-handed persons. Injury to Broca's area (located in the frontal lobe) and Wernicke's area (located in the temporal lobe) [Fig. 2] leads to loss of the ability, respectively, to speak (motor aphasia) or to understand speech (sensory aphasia), appearing as a loss of declarative memory for facts and words. Studies of blood flow show that brain activity during intellectual pursuits is scattered broadly over the four lobes in both hemispheres. *See* CENTRAL NERVOUS SYSTEM; HEMISPHERIC LATERALITY.   Walter J. Freeman

Bibliography. F. E. Bloom and A. Lazerson, *Brain, Mind and Behavior*, 1988; E. R. Kandel, J. H. Schwartz, and T. M. Jessell (eds.), *Essentials of Neural Science and Behavior*, Appleton & Lange, Norwalk, 1995; C. R. Noback, *The Human Nervous System*, 4th ed., 1991; H. K. Yusef, *Understanding the Brain and Its Development: A Chemical Approach*, 1992.

Brake

A machine element for applying a force to a moving surface to slow it down or bring it to rest in a controlled manner. In doing so, it converts the kinetic energy of motion into heat which is dissipated into the atmosphere. Brakes are used in motor vehicles, trains, airplanes, elevators, and other machines. Most brakes are of a friction type in which a fixed surface is brought into contact with a moving part that is to be slowed or stopped. Brakes in general connect a moving and a stationary body, whereas clutches and couplings usually connect two moving bodies. *See* AILERON; CLUTCH; COUPLING.

The limitations on the applications of brakes are similar to those of clutches, except that the service conditions are more severe because the entire energy is absorbed by slippage which is converted to heat that must be dissipated. The important thing is the rate at which energy is absorbed and heat dissipated. With friction brakes, if the temperature of the brake becomes too high, the result is a lowering of the friction force, called fading.

There are also electrical and hydrodynamic brakes. The electrical type may be electromagnetic, eddy-current, hysteresis, or magnetic-particle. The hydro-dynamic type works somewhat like a fluid coupling with one element stationary. Another type, used on electric trains, is the regenerative brake. This elec-trical machine can be used as a motor or a genera-tor. As a generator, it brakes the train and stores the generated electricity in an accumulator. Another type of brake is the air brake (flaps) on an airplane.

Friction types. Friction brakes are classified accord-ing to the kind of friction element employed and the means of applying the friction forces. *See* FRICTION.

Single-block. The simplest form of brake consists of a short block fitted to the contour of a wheel or drum and pressed against its surface by means of a lever on a fulcrum, as widely used on railroad cars. The block may have the contour lined with friction-brake material, which gives long wear and a high coefficient of friction. The fulcrum may be located with respect to the lever in a manner to aid or retard the braking torque of the block. The lever may be operated manually or by a remotely controlled force (**Fig. 1***a*).

Double-block. Two single-block brakes in symmetri-cal opposition, where the operating force on the end of one lever is the reaction of the other, make up a double-block brake (Fig. 1*b*). External thrust loads are balanced on the rim of the rotating wheel.

External-shoe. An external-shoe brake operates in the same manner as the block brake, and the designa-tion indicates the application of externally contract-ing elements. In this brake the shoes are appreciably longer, extending over a greater portion of the drum (Fig. 1*c*). This construction allows more combina-tions for special applications than the simple shoe, although assumptions of uniform pressure and con-centrated forces are no longer possible. In particu-lar, it is used on elevator installations for locking the hoisting sheave by means of a heavy spring when the electric current is off and the elevator is at rest. Self-energization is possible, as with block brakes, depending upon the arrangement of the supporting mechanism. *See* ELEVATOR.

Internal-shoe. An internal shoe has several advan-tages over an external shoe. Because the internal shoe works on the inner surface of the drum, it is protected from water and grit (Fig. 1*d*). It may be designed in a more compact package, is easily ac-

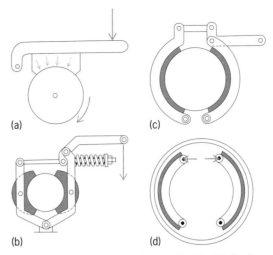

Fig. 1. Brakes. (*a*) Single-block brake. The block is fixed to the operating lever; force in the direction of the arrow applies the brake. (*b*) Double-block brake. The blocks are pivoted on their levers; force in the direction of the arrow releases the brake. (*c*) External shoe brake. Shoes are lined with friction material. (*d*) Internal shoe brake with lining.

tivated, and is effective for drives with rotations in both directions. The internal shoe is used in the auto-motive drum brake, with hydraulic piston actuation. *See* AUTOMOTIVE BRAKE.

Band. Hoists, excavating machinery, and hydraulic clutch-controlled transmissions have band brakes. They operate on the same principle as flat belts on pulleys. In the simplest band brake, one end of the belt is fastened near the drum surface, and the other end is then pulled over the drum in the direction of rotation so that a lever on a fulcrum may apply tension to the belt.

The belt may be a thin metallic strip with a fric-tion lining. The method of applying the lever on the fulcrum and attaching the belt determines the struc-tural operation of the brake. These variations make possible a sensitive differential brake, self-energizing brakes, and brakes operating with equal effective-ness in both directions. The radial force of the brake is proportional to the tension in the band. In automo-tive automatic transmissions, the bands are almost completely circular (**Fig. 2**). They are applied by

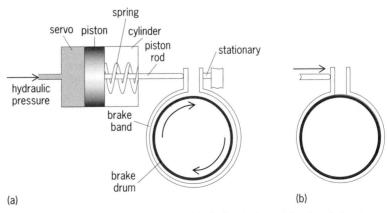

Fig. 2. Band brake around a brake drum. (*a*) Brake band released; the drum is free to rotate. (*b*) Brake applied; tightening the band stops rotation of the drum and holds it stationary. (*Automotive & Technical Writing, Charlottesville, Virginia*)

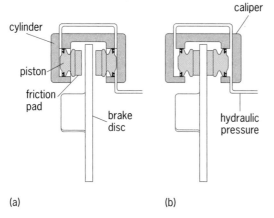

Fig. 3. Caliper disk brake. *(a)* Friction pads on either side of a disk that is free to rotate. *(b)* Brake applied, hydraulic pressure forces the pistons toward the disk to stop its rotation and hold it stationary. *(Automotive & Technical Writing, Charlottesville, Virginia)*

hydraulic pressure and released by spring force, usually aided by redirecting the hydraulic pressure.

Disk. Structurally similar to disk clutches, disk brakes have long been used on hoisting and similar apparatus. Because more energy is absorbed in prolonged braking than in clutch startup, additional heat dissipation must be provided in equivalent disk brakes. Disk brakes are used for the wheels of aircraft, where segmented rotary elements are pressed against stationary plates by hydraulic pistons. Flexibility, self-alignment, and rapid cooling are inherent in this design. Another application is the bicycle coaster brake.

The caliper disk brake (**Fig. 3**) is widely used on automotive vehicles. It consists of a rotating disk which can be gripped between two friction pads. The caliper disk brake is hydraulically operated, and the pads cover between one-sixth and one-ninth of the swept area of the disk. *See* AUTOMOTIVE BRAKE.

Actuators. A brake can be arranged so that it is normally either released or applied, a spring usually forcing it into the normal condition. A controllable external force then applies or releases the brake. This force can be, for example, mechanical through a linkage or cable to a lever, pneumatic or hydraulic through a cylinder to a piston, or electric through a solenoid to a plunger.

Air brake. Railway brakes are normally applied air brakes; if the air coupling to a car is broken, the brakes are applied automatically. To apply the brakes, the brake operator releases the compressed air that is restraining the brakes by means of a diaphragm and linkage. Over-the-road trucks and buses use air brakes. Another form of air brake consists of an annular air tube surrounding a jointed brake lining that extends completely around the outside of a brake drum. Air pressure expands the tube, pressing the lining against the drum. *See* AIR BRAKE.

Electromagnetic brake. In commonly encountered electromagnetic brakes, the actuating force is applied by an electric current through a solenoid. Direct current (dc) gives greater braking force than alternating current (ac), and is therefore used almost

exclusively; ac is rectified if used. Usually the electromagnetic force releases the brake against a compression spring, which provides braking action if the power fails, and overspeed protection when the brake is used with dc series motors.

In a towed highway vehicle, such as a boat trailer, the trailer brakes are applied by electromagnets at each wheel. When the driver operates a controller, the electromagnets are attracted to disks on the rotating wheels. This causes the electromagnets to shift through a limited arc which forces the brake shoes into contact with the drum. Further movement of the controller allows more current to flow in the electromagnets, producing stronger magnetic fields and greater braking action.   Donald L. Anglin

Bibliography. E. A. Avallone and T. Baumeister III (eds.), *Marks' Standard Handbook for Mechanical Engineers*, 10th ed., 1996; J. E. Shigley and C. R. Mischke, *Machine Design Fundamentals*, 1989.

Branch circuit

As defined by the National Electrical Code, the portion of an electrical wiring system that extends beyond the final, automatic overcurrent protective device (circuit breaker or fuse), which is recognized by the National Electrical Code for use as a branch-circuit overcurrent protector, and that terminates at the utilization equipment or outlet (such as a lighting fixture, motor, receptacle, or heater). Thermal cutouts, motor overload devices, and fuses in luminaires or plug connections, which are considered "supplementary overcurrent" devices, are not approved for branch-circuit protection and do not establish the point of origin of a branch circuit (see **illustration**).

Motor branch circuits must have conductors with current-carrying capacity at least 125% of the motor full-load current rating. Overcurrent protection must be capable of carrying the starting current of the motor. Maximum values are tabulated for

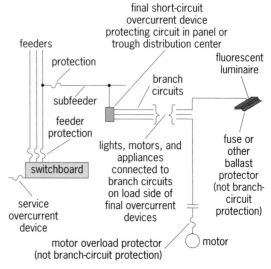

Typical electrical wiring system. Branch circuits are those portions of system beyond the final overcurrent device approved for branch-circuit protection.

various currents in the National Electrical Code. *See* ELECTRICAL CODES.

Branch circuits, other than motor branch circuits, are classified by the maximum rating of the overcurrent device. Thus a branch circuit with a 20-A circuit breaker is designated a 20-A branch circuit, even though the conductors may be capable of carrying higher current.

Individual branch circuits serving a single fixed appliance, such as a clothes dryer or a water heater, may be of any ampere rating if the overcurrent protection (fuse or circuit breaker) does not exceed 150% of the rated current of the appliance (where it is 10 A or more). For continuous loads of 3 h or longer duration, the branch circuit rating must be at least 125% of the continuous current plus the total of any noncontinuous load. Conductors supplying such loads must also have an ampacity (current-carrying capacity) equal to at least 125% of the continuous load plus any noncontinuous load.

Branch circuits serving more than one outlet or load are limited by the National Electrical Code to three types:

1. Circuits of 15 or 20 A may serve lights and appliances; the rating of one portable appliance may not exceed 80% of the circuit capacity; the total rating of fixed appliances may not exceed 50% of circuit capacity if lights or portable appliances are also supplied.

2. Circuits of 30 A may serve fixed lighting units with heavy-duty lampholders in other than dwellings or appliances in any occupancy.

3. Circuits of 40 or 50 A may serve fixed lighting with heavy-duty lampholders in other than dwellings, fixed cooking appliances, or infrared heating units.

Multiwire branch circuits consist of two or more ungrounded conductors having an identical potential difference (voltage) between each other and a grounded (neutral) conductor having an equal potential difference between it and the individual ungrounded conductors.

Conventionally the current-carrying capacity of conductors may be the same as the branch-circuit rating (for example, no. 12 conductors in a 20-A branch circuit); however, larger conductors may be required to avoid excessive voltage drop where the circuit must be run to supply remote loads. *See* WIRING.

Brian J. McPartland; J. F. McPartland

Bibliography. B. J. McPartland and J. F. McPartland, *National Electrical Code Handbook*, 25th ed., 2005; J. F. McPartland and B. J. McPartland, *The Handbook of Practical Electrical Design*, 2d ed., 2000; *National Electrical Code*, NFPA 70, 2005; H. P. Richter and H. P. Hartwell, *Practical Electrical Wiring*, 19th ed., 2005.

Branched polymer

A polymer chain having branch points that connect three or more chain segments. Examples of branched polymers include long chains having occasional and usually short branches comprising the same repeat

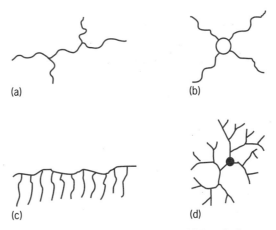

Fig. 1. Examples of branched polymers. (*a*) Branched polymer (if arms are of composition similar to backbone) or graft polymer (if compositions are different). (*b*) Star polymer. (*c*) Comb polymer. (*d*) Dendritic polymer.

units as the main chain (nominally termed a branched polymer); long chains having occasional branches comprising repeat units different from those of the main chain (termed graft copolymers); main chains having one long branch per repeat unit (referred to as comb polymers); and small core molecules with branches radiating from the core (star polymers). So-called starburst or dendritic polymers are a special class of star polymer in which the branches are multifunctional, leading to further branching with polymer growth. Star, comb, and starburst polymers, (**Fig. 1**), especially the last, represent interesting molecular structures that may lead to unusual supramolecular structures (for example, micelles and liposomes) that mimic the functions of complex biomolecules.

Classic type. A classic example of a branched polymer where the branches have the same chemical composition as the backbone is low-density polyethylene (LDPE). When ethylene is polymerized by using free-radical initiators, short branches, typically ethyl and *n*-butyl along with lesser amounts of a few other types including very long branches, are generated by a process known as chain transfer to polymer. A propagating radical at the end of a growing polyethylene chain, which is a primary alkyl radical, is capable of abstracting a backbone hydrogen atom from the polymer backbone, leading to a more stable secondary radical. The preponderance of ethyl and *n*-butyl groups is thought to be the result of intramolecular chain transfer proceeding via conformations involving six-membered ring transition states, as in the reaction below.

The short branches interfere to some degree with crystallization of the backbone and, since the chains cannot pack as efficiently, the density is lower than that of high-density polyethylene (HDPE). However, LDPE is somewhat tougher because of its greater amorphous content. The amorphous regions are above their glass transition temperature at room temperature, and the liquidlike nature of these regions provides for energy dissipation and hence toughness. Much LDPE is prepared by copolymerization of ethylene with α-olefins such as 1-hexene using organometallic initiators, a route that offers more control over branch type and concentration, and hence properties. This type is known as linear low-density polyethylene (LLDPE).

Branching can occur to some extent in the polymerization of other monomers, including vinyl acetate (radical polymerization), the base-initiated ring-opening polymerization of caprolactam, and the cationic ring-opening polymerization of ethylene-imine. Step-growth polymerizations using monomers with an average functionality greater than two can also lead to branching and, in many cases, crosslinking. An example of branching in biopolymers is the structure of amylopectin, a component of starch [monomer, structure (**1**)]; in amylopectin,

$$(1)$$

the branches on the main backbone are themselves branched [structure (**2**)]. Glycogen, the storage

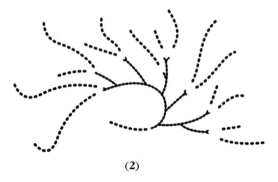

$$(2)$$

polymer of glucose in animals, is even more heavily branched than amylopectin. *See* BIOPOLYMER; GLYCOGEN; POLYOLEFIN RESINS; RING-OPENING POLYMERIZATION; STARCH.

Graft and comb. There are many examples of graft copolymers. They can be prepared by generation of a radical on a polymer backbone via ultraviolet or ionizing radiation in the presence of a monomer, or by polymerization of a monomer in the presence of a polymer with a polymerizable linkage such as a carbon-carbon double bond. An important example of the latter type is a graft copolymer of polystyrene and polybutadiene [structure (**3**)]. The resulting

$$(3)$$

material is far tougher than polystyrene itself because of the presence of small domains of rubbery polybutadiene. Graft copolymers can also be prepared by coupling polymers having reactive groups at one chain end with different polymers having functional groups on their backbones. Preformed polymers with a polymerizable end (referred to as macromonomers) can be homopolymerized to form comb polymers or can be copolymerized with a variety of monomers to yield graft copolymers. Finally, graft copolymers can be prepared by mechanically blending different polymers. Homolytic bond cleavage resulting from shearing leads to the formation of free radicals on the polymer chains, and the coupling of these onto different polymer chains results in grafting. *See* COPOLYMER; FREE RADICAL.

Star and comb. Star polymers can be prepared by a core-first or arm-first approach. In the former, initiation of polymerization occurs from a multifunctional core molecule. In the latter, polymer chains are synthesized and then coupled to a core molecule via reactive end groups. Steric considerations dictate the efficiency of the coupling process. For example, reaction of polystyryl anions with tetrachlorosilane yields a mixture of three- and four-arm star polymers along with a coupled polymer and a homopolymer. A similar reaction with the less sterically demanding polybutadienyl anion gives an almost quantitative yield of four-arm star polymer. The arms need not be homopolymers. For example, star polymers with styrene-butadiene block copolymer arms have been prepared by reaction of polybutadienyl anionic ends with reactive core molecules such as tetrachlorosilane (**Fig. 2**). Star polymers are of interest because they are smaller in size than a linear polymer of comparable molecular weight and therefore will usually have lower softening points and solution viscosities, which can facilitate processing. Comb polymers can also be prepared by using the ideas employed for the synthesis of star polymers, as well as via polymerization of macromonomers, which are polymers terminated with polymerizable groups such as vinyl and epoxy.

Starburst and dendritic. The field of branched polymers also includes starburst, or dendritic, polymers (also referred to as arborols and cascade molecules). These unique materials are characterized by a highly branched, three-dimensional structure emanating from a central, multifunctional molecule. The difference between dendritic polymers and other so-called hyperbranched polymers such as amylopectin is that in the former each monomer unit has at least one branch point, and therefore the extent of branching is extraordinarily high. The pronounced branching allows the attainment of spherical molecules that resemble micelles.

Numerous syntheses of starburst polymers have been developed. An initial example involved the addition of ammonia to methyl acrylate. The resulting triester was then reacted with a diamine such as ethylenediamine, resulting in a new triamine that was effectively the core molecule. Repetition of these steps led to the production of a starburst polymer (**Fig. 3**). This approach, in which the synthesis is begun at the center of the polymer, is termed the divergent method, and the repetitions of the reactions are referred to as generations. The number of reactions that need to be performed increases geometrically with the number of generations. The molecule will tend toward a spherical shape as the number of generations increases. The size of the molecule can be predicted from the number of generations, and indeed experimentally determined diameters (via electron microscopy and size exclusion chromatography) are in excellent agreement with predictions. Also, the surface of the molecule will have a high concentration of functional groups (amines in this case).

An alternative approach to dendrimer synthesis is the convergent method, where the synthesis is begun at the outside of the dendrimer. Here portions of what will ultimately be a dendrimer, referred to as dendrons, are synthesized and then coupled to yield the dendrimer. Use is made of series of protection or deprotection steps. One advantage of this approach is that it does not limit the type and concentration of a particular functional group at the surface of the dendrimer. It has been successfully employed to prepare a wide variety of dendrimers, including polyesters and poly(aryl ethers), as well as novel block copolymers.

Dendrimers can be viewed as nanostructural compounds that can be used as building blocks for novel supramolecular assemblies. For example, it is possible to react dendrimers bearing nucleophilic surface groups (for example, amines) with others bearing electrophilic groups to form dendrimer clusters. Dendrimers can also be reacted with functionally terminal polymers to obtain networks having junction points of very high functionality. The high concentration of surface functionality and the ability to manipulate the functionality through simple organic reactions has spurred interest in their potential use as targeted drug carriers. Indeed, it may be that applications of dendrimers will be particularly significant in biological science in view of the ability to control

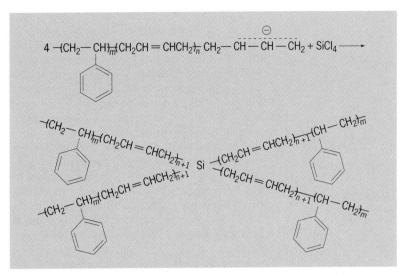

Fig. 2. Reaction for preparation of a star polymer with styrene-butadiene block copolymer arms.

Fig. 3. Steps in the synthesis of a starburst polymer. s = surface. o = interior. f_r = reactive group. f_p = protected group.

functionality and supramolecular structure. *See* MICROMOLECULAR ENGINEERING; POLYMER; POLYMERIZATION.　　　　　　　　　　　　　　Gary E. Wnek

Bibliography. N. Hadjichristidis, *Block Copolymers: Synthetic Strategies, Physical Properties, and Application*, 2002; K. Matyjaszewski and T. P. Davis (eds.), *Handbook of Radical Polymerization*, 2002; G. Odian, *Principles of Polymerization*, 4th ed., 2004.

Branchiopoda

A class of crustaceans. Formerly, four extant orders were recognized: Anostraca, Notostraca, Conchostraca, and Cladocera, the first two of which are well defined. The Conchostraca consist of two groups which, although superficially similar, differ in so many fundamental features that they have been placed in separate orders, Laevicaudata and Spinicaudata. The Cladocera are in fact a heterogeneous assemblage of organisms that have now been split into four orders: Anomopoda, Ctenopoda, Onychopoda, and Haplopoda. Although the name Cladocera has to be abandoned as a taxonomic unit, it will doubtless continue to be used as a convenient descriptive term for members of these four orders. There are also two extinct orders, Lipostraca and Kazacharthra. Branchiopods have a long history. Both the Lipostraca and Spinicaudata were differentiated by Devonian times, and their ancestors doubtless originated even earlier. *See* ANOMOPODA; ANOSTRACA; HAPLOPODA; LAEVICAUDATA; NOTOSTRACA; ONYCHOPODA; SPINICAUDATA.

Living members of the Branchiopoda range from less than 0.5 mm (0.02 in.) to (exceptionally) 100 mm (4 in.) in length. Form is exceedingly diverse. The trunk may be abbreviated and of probably as few as 5 segments (although segmentation is sometimes obscure) or elongate and of more than 40 segments. Trunk limbs range from 5 to about 70 pairs. A carapace is often present, either as a dorsal shield or as a bivalved structure; anostracans lack a carapace. The eyes were primitively paired and are sometimes stalked and sometimes sessile; in several orders they have fused to give a single median sessile eye. Members of several orders use their antennae as organs of locomotion—a retention of the similar mechanism used by the nauplius larva. Others swim by means of trunk limbs. The mandibles are usually of the crushing, rolling type; only in a few cases have biting or piercing mandibles been acquired. Other mouthparts are usually small, but important. Trunk limb structure is extremely diverse. Many-limbed orders tend to have limbs that differ from each other only in degree; the Anomopoda have limbs that differ greatly from each other in form and from species to species in relation to habits.

Most species are microphagous. Microphagous forms collect their food either by direct scraping from surfaces, which may or may not be followed by filtration, or by abstracting suspended particles by the use of complicated filtering devices. A few species are omnivores or carnivores.

Reproductive habits are diverse. Parthenogenesis is widespread, and the production of highly resistant resting eggs that can withstand freezing and drying and retain their viability for several years is highly characteristic. Almost all species live in fresh water, but a few are marine and some frequent highly saline situations. Branchiopods have a worldwide distribution. *See* CRUSTACEA.   Geoffrey Fryer

Branchiura

A subclass of the Crustacea known as the fish lice. They are ectoparasites of fresh-water and marine fish on such areas as the base of fins and the gill

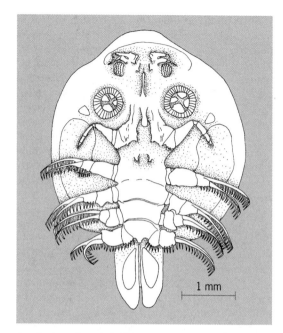

Argulus japonicus, male fish louse of the Branchiura.

chamber walls. *Argulus* (see **illus.**) is a common genus. They are a small homogeneous group, less than 100 species, with worldwide distribution, and very much alike in appearance. The disklike head and thorax (cephalothorax) is strongly flattened and bears a small unsegmented abdomen bilobed at its distal end. Larger species may exceed 1 in. (25 mm) in length.

Taxonomy. The Branchiura have often been included within the Copepoda either as the subclass Branchiura, opposed to the remainder grouped under Eucopepoda, or as the order Arguloida equivalent in rank to the Calanoida, Cyclopoida, and Harpacticoida. Though widespread acknowledgment is not yet apparent, critical appraisal of branchiuran morphology, ontogeny, and ethology has revealed several basic characteristics which have no homologs in the eucopepods. On the basis of these fundamental differences, linkage to the Copepoda is no more justified than placement within the Branchiopoda, Ostracoda, or even Cirripedia. *See* COPEPODA.

Some of the morphological characteristics distinguishing Branchiura from Copepoda include the presence of compound eyes, totally different segmentation of the swimming legs, location of the genital orifice on the thorax, absence of a spermatophore, and use of the second, third, and fourth pairs of legs in copulation. The absence of larval stages, either suppressed in the embryonic period or as a free-swimming nauplius followed by metamorphosis into the immature adult form, is noteworthy. Behavioral differences occur in the method of spawning; branchiurans attach small masses of eggs enveloped in gelatinous sheaths to stones and other firm objects on the bottom.

Morphology. The appendages, all on the cephalothorax, consist of two pairs of antennae, the mouthparts which are one pair of mandibles and two pairs of maxillae, and four pairs of swimming legs. They originate on the underside of the body near the midline and extend laterally, perpendicular to the longitudinal axis. The wafer-thin cephalothorax with its appendages appressed to the underside permits fish lice to flatten themselves against a fish's skin. The resulting highly streamlined contour serves to minimize the considerable force of frictional drag found in a dense medium like water.

Other adaptations for holding fast to a mucus-covered swimming fish include numerous spinules and strategically placed hooks on the underside of the body and utilization of specialized portions of the body as suction cups. Despite these elaborate specializations, fish lice never lose the ability to abandon a host and swim. At least some of this activity is associated with mating and spawning.

Reproduction. Breeding males seek the female which remains passively on the host. Use is made of the second to fourth pairs of swimming legs in copulation, these appendages bearing pegs and corresponding sockets arranged in a manner unique to each species. Spawning females swim from the host to find firm objects, such as stones, on which to fix the mass of eggs encased in a gelatinous sheath. Following direct embryonic development the hatching juvenile resembles the parent although the appendages do not assume an adult form until later. Sexual maturity, occurring about a month after hatching, requires at least seven molt stages and does not seem to stop growth.

Nutrition. Branchiurans feed on tissue fluids, especially blood. The mouth, located at the end of a movable proboscis, is applied to the host's skin and the rasping mandibles make the necessary wound. Fish lice usually are no threat to fish populations. In restricted areas such as hatchery ponds, however, an infestation can increase to levels that bring about high fish mortality. Treatment may require such drastic measures as drainage and cleaning before restocking can be successful. *See* CRUSTACEA.

Abraham Fleminger

Bibliography. M. F. Martin, On the morphology and classification of *Argulus* (Crustacea), *Proc. Zool. Soc. London*, 1932:771–806, 1932; O. L. Meehean, A review of the parasitic Crustacea of the genus *Argulus* in the collections of the United States National Museum, *Proc. U.S. Nat. Mus.*, 88:459–522, 1940; S. P. Parker (ed.), *Synopsis and Classification of Living Organisms*, 2 vols., 1982; C. B. Wilson, Parasitic copepods in the United States National Museum, *Proc. U.S. Nat. Mus.*, 94:529–582, 1944.

Brass

An alloy of copper and zinc. In manufacture, lump zinc is added to molten copper, and the mixture is poured either into castings ready for use or into billets for further working by rolling, extruding, forging, or a similar process. Brasses containing 75–85%

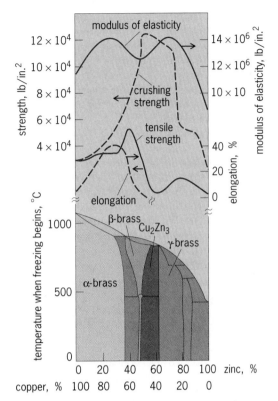

Approximate mechanical properties of cast brass in relation to alloy composition in simplified phase diagram.

copper are red-gold and malleable; those containing 60–70% are yellow and also malleable; and those containing 50% or less copper are white, brittle, and not malleable. Alpha brass contains up to 36% zinc; beta brass contains nearly equal proportions of copper and zinc. Specific brasses are designated as follows: gilding (95% copper: 5% zinc), red (85:15), low (80:20), and admiralty (70:29, with balance of tin). Naval brass is 59–62% copper with about 1% tin, less than that of lead and iron, and the remainder zinc. The nickel silvers contain 55–70% copper and the balance nickel. With small amounts of other metals, other names are used. Leaded brass is used for castings.

Addition of zinc to copper produces a material that is harder and stronger than copper, as shown in the **illustration**, yet retains the malleability, ductility, and corrosion resistance of copper. Mechanical and heat treatment greatly vary the properties of the finished product. Because brass with 64% or more copper (α-brass) forms a single solid solution, it combines high strength, ductility, and corrosion resistance. The β solid solution is harder and more brittle. With 61% zinc the compound Cu_2Zn_3 forms; it is brittle, having the lowest tensile strength of the brasses. Higher percents of zinc produce other brittle constituents.

Brass stains in moist air; however, the oxide so formed is sufficiently continuous and adherent to retard further oxidation. When brass is required to remain bright, it is either washed in nitric acid and then coated with clear lacquer, or it is regularly polished and waxed. For brightwork or other corrosion-resistant applications, α-brass is usually used. In atmospheres containing traces of ammonia, cold-worked brass or annealed brass highly stressed in tension may fail by cracking. This is called season cracking or stress corrosion cracking. Susceptibility of cold-worked brass to failure of this kind is reduced by proper annealing.

Brass is widely used in cartridge cases, plumbing fixtures, valves and pipes, screws, clocks, and musical instruments. *See* ALLOY; BRONZE; COPPER; COPPER ALLOYS; CORROSION; ZINC; ZINC ALLOYS.

Frank H. Rockett

Bibliography. R. M. Brick et al., *Structure and Properties of Engineering Materials*, 4th ed., 1977; K. G. Budinski, *Engineering Materials: Properties and Selection*, 6th ed., 1998.

Brayton cycle

A thermodynamic cycle (also variously called the Joule or complete expansion diesel cycle) consisting of two constant-pressure (isobaric) processes interspersed with two reversible adiabatic (isentropic) processes (**Fig. 1**). The ideal cycle performance, predicated on the use of perfect gases, is given by relationships (1) and (2). Thermal efficiency η_T,

$$V_3/V_2 = V_4/V_1 = T_3/T_2 = T_4/T_1 \qquad (1)$$

$$\frac{T_2}{T_1} = \frac{T_3}{T_4} = \left(\frac{V_1}{V_2}\right)^{k-1} = \left(\frac{V_4}{V_3}\right)^{k-1} = \left(\frac{p_2}{p_1}\right)^{\frac{k-1}{k}} \qquad (2)$$

the work done per unit of heat added, is given by Eq. (3). In these relationships V is the volume in

$$\eta_T = [1 - (T_1/T_2)] = \left[1 - \left(\frac{1}{r^{k-1}}\right)\right] \qquad (3)$$

cubic feet, p is the pressure in pounds per square foot, T is the absolute temperature in degrees Rankine, k is the c_p/c_v, or ratio of specific heats at constant pressure and constant volume, and r is the compression ratio, V_1/V_2.

The thermal efficiency for a given gas, air, is solely a function of the ratio of compression. This is also the case with the Otto cycle. For the diesel cycle with incomplete expansion, the thermal efficiency is lower. The overriding importance of high compression ratio for intrinsic high efficiency is clearly demonstrated by these data.

A reciprocating engine, operating on the cycle of Fig. 1, was patented in 1872 by G. B. Brayton and was the first successful gas engine built in the United States. The Brayton cycle, with its high inherent thermal efficiency, requires the maximum volume of gas flow for a given power output. The Otto and diesel cycles require much lower gas flow rates, but have the disadvantage of higher peak pressures and temperatures. These conflicting elements led to many designs, all attempting to achieve practical compromises. With a piston and cylinder mechanism the

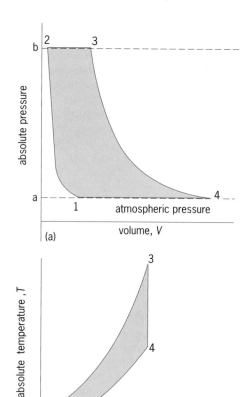

Fig. 1. Brayton cycle, air-card standard. (*a*) *p-V* cycle diagram. (*b*) *p-S* diagram. Phases: 1–2, compression; 2–3, heat addition; 3–4, expansion; and 4–1, heat abstraction.

Brayton cycle, calling for the maximum displacement per horsepower, led to proposals such as compound engines and variable-stroke mechanisms. They suffered overall disadvantages because of the low mean effective pressures. The positive displacement engine consequently preempted the field for the Otto and diesel cycles.

With the subsequent development of fluid acceleration devices for the compression and expansion of gases, the Brayton cycle found mechanisms which could economically handle the large volumes of working fluid. This is perfected today in the gas turbine power plant. The mechanism (**Fig. 2**) basically is a steady-flow device with a centrifugal or axial

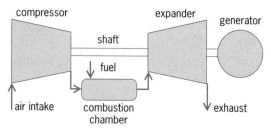

Fig. 2. Simple, open-cycle gas-turbine plant.

compressor, a combustion chamber where heat is added, and an expander-turbine element. Each of the phases of the cycle is accomplished with steady flow in its own mechanism rather than intermittently, as with the piston and cylinder mechanism of the usual Otto and diesel cycle engines. Practical gas-turbine engines have various recognized advantages and disadvantages which are evaluated by comparison with alternative engines available in the competitive marketplace. *See* AUTOMOBILE; GAS TURBINE; INTERNAL COMBUSTION ENGINE.

The net power output P_{net}, or salable power, of the gas-turbine plant (Fig. 2) can be expressed as shown by Eq. (4), where W_e is the ideal power output of

$$P_{net} = W_e \times \text{eff}_e - \frac{W_c}{\text{eff}_c} \qquad (4)$$

the expander (area b34a, Fig. 1), W_c the ideal power input to the compressor (area a12b, Fig. 1), eff_e the efficiency of expander, and eff_c the efficiency of compressor. This net power output for the ideal case, where both efficiencies are 1.0, is represented by net area (shaded) of the *p-V* cycle diagram of Fig. 1*a*. The larger the volume increase from point 2 to point 3, the greater will be the net power output for a given size of compressor. This volume increase is accomplished by utilizing the maximum possible temperature at point 3 of the cycle.

The difference in the two terms on the right-hand side of Eq. (4) is thus basically increased by the use of maximum temperatures at the inlet to the expander. These high temperatures introduce metallurgical and heat-transfer problems which must be properly solved.

The efficiency terms of Eq. (4) are of vital practical significance. If the efficiencies of the real compressor and of the real expander are low, it is entirely possible to vitiate the difference in the ideal powers W_e and W_c, so that there will be no useful output of the plant. In present practice this means that for adaptations of the Brayton cycle to acceptable and reliable gas-turbine plants, the engineering design must provide for high temperatures at the expander inlet and utilize high built-in efficiencies of the compressor and expander elements. No amount of cycle alteration, regeneration, or reheat can offset this intrinsic requirement for mechanisms which will safely operate at temperatures of about 1500°F (816°C). *See* CARNOT CYCLE; DIESEL CYCLE; OTTO CYCLE; THERMODYNAMIC CYCLE.   Theodore Baumeister

Bibliography. E. A. Avallone and T. Baumeister III (eds.), *Marks' Standard Handbook for Mechanical Engineers*, 10th ed., 1996; J. B. Jones and G. A. Hawkins, *Engineering Thermodynamics*, 1960; H. Cohen et al., *Gas Turbine Theory*, 2d ed., 1975; R. T. Harman, *Gas Turbine Engineering: Applications, Cycles, and Characteristics*, 1981; G. N. Hatsopoulos and J. H. Keenan, *Principles of General Thermodynamics*, 1965, reprint 1981; M. J. Zucrow and J. D. Hoffman, *Gas Dynamics*, vol. 1, 1976, vol. 2, 1977.

Brazil nut

A large broad-leafed evergreen tree, *Bertholettia excelsa*, that grows wild in the forests of the Amazon valley of Brazil and Bolivia. The fruit is a spherical capsule, 3–6 in. (7.5–15 cm) in diameter and weighing 2–4 lb (0.9–1.8 kg) which, when mature, consists of an outer hard indehiscent husk about $\frac{1}{2}$ in. (1.2 cm) thick enclosing an inner hard-shelled container or pod filled with about 20 rather triangular seeds or nuts. *See* LECYTHIDALES.

Although there are a few plantations in Brazil, almost the entire production is gathered from wild trees. The quantity that gets into commercial channels varies with the price paid on the world market. The nuts are gathered either by local people who live in the forest or migrants who come into the area for the harvest season. The ripened capsules fall to the ground, and because of their weight and the height of the trees are a hazard to the harvesters. The fruits are carried to the stream bank and transported in small boats to local huts, where the capsules are split open to free the nuts. These are sold to traders who ship them downstream to brokers. They are mostly exported to Europe, Canada, and the United States. About one-fourth of the crop is shelled in Brazil before export.

Brazil nuts have a high oil and protein content and require careful handling and refrigeration to prevent spoilage. The nuts are used in confectionery, baked goods, and nut mixtures. *See* NUT CROP CULTURE.

Laurence H. MacDaniels

Brazing

A group of welding processes in which coalescence is produced by heating to suitable temperatures above 450°C and by using a filler metal that must have a liquidus temperature above 450°C and below the solidus temperature of the base metal. The filler metal is distributed between the closely fitted surfaces of the joint by capillary attraction. Brazing is distinguished from soldering in that the latter employs a filler metal having a liquidus below 450°C. *See* SOLDERING.

Brazing provides advantages over other welding processes, especially because it permits joining of dissimilar metals that, because of metallurgical incompatibilities, cannot be joined by traditional fusion processes. Since base metals do not have to be melted to be joined, it does not matter that they have widely different melting points. Therefore, steel can be brazed to copper as easily as steel to steel.

Brazing also generally produces less thermally induced distortion (warping) than fusion welding does, because an entire part can be brought up to the same brazing temperature, thereby preventing the kind of localized heating that can cause distortion in welding.

Finally, and perhaps most important to the

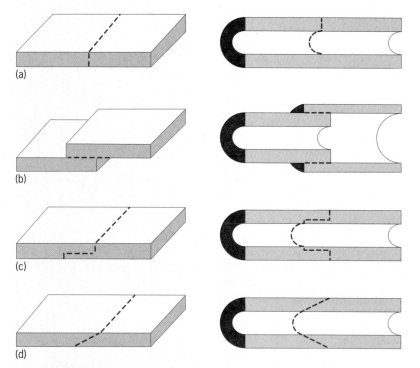

Fig. 1. Types of brazed joints, showing flat and tubular configurations. (*a*) Butt. (*b*) Lap. (*c*) Butt-lap. (*d*) Scarf.

manufacturing specialist, brazing readily lends itself to mass-production techniques.

Brazing process. The important elements of the brazing process are filler-metal flow, base-metal and filler-metal characteristics, surface preparation, joint design and clearance, temperature and time, and rate and source of heating.

A brazed joint is a heterogeneous assembly that is composed of different materials with different physical and chemical properties. In the simplest case, it consists of the base-metal parts to be joined and the added brazing filler metal. Diffusion processes, however, can change the composition and therefore the chemical and physical properties of the boundary zone formed at the interface between base metal and filler metal.

Small clearances should be used because the smaller the clearance, the easier it will be for capillarity to distribute the brazing filler metal throughout the joint area, and there will be less likelihood that voids or shrinkage cavities will form as the brazing filler metal solidifies. Small clearances and correspondingly thin filler-metal films make sound joints. The soundest joints are at least as high in tensile strength as the filler metal itself, and often higher. Clearances ranging from 0.03 to 0.08 mm are designed for the best capillary action and greatest joint strength.

Joint design. A number of factors must be considered in designing joints. First is composition and strength of the brazing filler metal. Generally, the bulk strength of the brazing filler metal is lower than that of the base metals, and so a correctly designed joint is required to obtain adequate mechanical strength. Second is capillary attraction. Because brazing depends on the principle of capillary attrac-

tion for distribution of molten brazing filler metal, joint clearance is a critical factor. Third is flux and air displacement. Not only must the filler metal be drawn into the joint, but flux and air must be displaced from it. Fourth is type of stress. In general, it is preferred that any load on a brazed joint be transmitted as shear stress rather than as tensile stress. Fifth is composition and strength of the base metals. In a joint made according to recommendations between high-strength members, the filler-metal film in the joint may actually be stronger than the base metal itself.

There are basically only two types of brazed joints, butt and lap, with all other joints being only modifications.

Butt and lap joints. The butt joint (**Fig. 1***a*) has the advantage of a single thickness at the joint. Preparation is relatively simple; however, the strength of any joint depends in part on the bonding area available. The thinnest member, therefore, dictates the maximum strength of the joint.

Strength is only one reason for the use of the lap design. Lap joints (Fig. 1*b*) can be readily designed to be self-jigging or, as in the case of tubing, self-aligning. Also, preplaced filler metal can be held in position better with such joints.

Butt-lap and scarf joints. The butt-lap joint (Fig. 1*c*) is an attempt to combine the advantage of a single thickness with maximum bonding area and strength. The scarf joint (Fig. 1*d*) represents another attempt to increase the cross-sectional area of the joint without increasing its thickness. Because the scarf joint is at an angle to the axis of tensile loading, its load-carrying capacity is similar to that of the lap joint and greater than that of the butt joint.

Joint clearance. The single most important design consideration in achieving good brazements is joint clearance—the distance between the faying surfaces to be joined. The ideal clearance for production work is frequently cited as 0.05–0.13 mm. However, some metals actually require interference fits, whereas others require clearances as great as 0.25 mm.

Selection of materials. Selection involves consideration of both the base metal and the filler metal.

Base metals. The base metal has a prime effect on joint strength. A high-strength base metal produces joints of greater strength than those made with softer base metals. In addition to the base-metal effects and the normal mechanical requirements of the base metal in the brazement, the effect of the brazing cycle on the base metal and the final joint strength must be considered. The brazing cycle by its very nature will usually anneal the cold-worked base metal, unless the brazing temperature is very low and the time at heat is very short. When it is essential to design a brazement having strength above the annealed strength of the base metals after the brazing operation, it will be necessary to specify a heat-treatable base metal.

Braze filler metals. The brazing filler metal is also known as the brazing alloy. A specific brazing filler metal cannot be chosen to produce a specific joint strength. Actually, strong joints can be brazed with almost any commercial brazing filler metal if brazing methods and joint design are done correctly.

The degree to which brazing filler metal penetrates and alloys with the base metal during brazing is referred to as diffusion. In applications requiring strong joints for high-temperature, high-stress service conditions (such as turbine rotor assemblies and jet components), it is generally good practice to specify a brazing filler metal that has high diffusion and solution properties with the base metal. When the assembly is constructed of extremely thin base metals (as in honeycomb structures and some heat exchangers), good practice generally calls for a brazing filler metal with a low-diffusion characteristic relative to the base metal.

In choosing a brazing filler metal, the first criterion is the working temperature. Very few brazing filler metals possess distinct melting points. A brazing filler metal may have to melt below the temperature at which members of the joint lose strength or above the temperature at which oxides are reduced or dissociated. Joining may have to be carried out above the solution treatment temperature of the base metal, at a structure refining temperature, or below the remelt temperature of a brazing filler metal used previously in producing a brazed subassembly.

Methods of heating. There are a variety of heating methods available for brazing. Effective capillary joining requires efficient transfer of heat from the heat source into the joint. The seven commonly used methods are torch, furnace, induction, dip, resistance, infrared, and diffusion brazing.

Torch brazing. Manual torch brazing is most frequently used for repairs, one-of-a-kind brazing jobs, and short production runs as an alternative to fusion welding. Any joint that can be reached by a torch and brought to brazing temperature can be readily brazed by this technique. The adjustment of the torch flame is important. Generally, a slightly reducing flame is desirable.

In manual torch brazing, the brazing filler metal is usually face fed in the form of wire or rod, or preplaced. To ensure uniform heating throughout the joint, an important consideration, it may be advisable to use a multiple-tip torch or more than one torch.

Torch brazing can be automated relatively easily. Usually, such systems involve multiple-station rotary indexing tables. The part is fed into a holding fixture at the first station, then indexed to one or more preheating stations, depending on the heating time required. A brazing station is next, followed by a cooling station and an ejection station (**Fig. 2**).

Furnace brazing. Furnace brazing is used extensively where the parts to be brazed can be assembled with the brazing filler metal preplaced or in the joint. There are two basic types of furnaces used for brazing: the batch and the continuous. Furnace brazing is particularly applicable for high-production brazing in which continuous-conveyor-type furnaces are used. For medium-production work, batch-type furnaces are best. When continuous-type furnaces are used, several different temperature zones may be used to provide the proper preheating, brazing, and cooling temperatures. Heating is usually produced by electrical resistance.

The parts should be self-jigging or fixtured and assembled with brazing filler metal preplaced near or in the joint. The preplaced filler metal may be in the form of wire, foil, powder, paste, slugs, or preformed shapes. Fluxing is used except when a reducing atmosphere, such as hydrogen gas, can be introduced into the furnace. Pure, dry, inert gases, such as argon and helium, are used to obtain special atmospheric properties.

A large volume of furnace brazing is performed in vacuum, which prevents oxidation and often eliminates the need for flux. Vacuum brazing has found wide application in the aerospace and nuclear fields, where reactive metals are joined or where entrapped fluxes would be intolerable.

Induction brazing. The high-frequency induction heating method for brazing is clean and rapid, lends itself to close control of temperature and location, and requires little operator skill. The heat for induction brazing is created by a rapidly alternating electric current that is induced into the workpiece by an adjacent coil. The workpiece is placed in or near a coil carrying alternating current, which induces the heating current in the desired area. Brazing filler metal is normally preplaced in the joint, and the brazing can be done in air, in an inert atmosphere, or in a vacuum. Induction brazing is well suited for mass production, and mechanized systems for moving the assemblies to and from the coils are very common.

Dip brazing. This process involves immersion of assembled parts into a suitable molten bath to effect brazing. The bath can be either molten brazing filler metal or molten chemical flux. The molten-flux method is used extensively for brazing aluminum and its alloys. The brazing filler metal is preplaced and the assembly immersed in the flux bath, which has been raised to brazing temperature. The flux bath provides excellent protection against reoxidation of the metal, which can occur quite easily with aluminum.

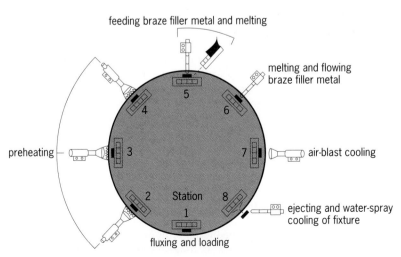

Fig. 2. Automatic eight-station torch brazing machine.

Resistance brazing. The process is most applicable to relatively simple joints in metals that have high electrical conductivity. The workpieces are heated locally, and brazing filler metal that is preplaced between the workpieces is melted by the heat obtained from resistance to the flow of electric current through the electrodes and the work. In the usual application of resistance brazing, the heating current, which is normally alternating current, is passed through the joint itself. Equipment is the same as that used for resistance welding.

Infrared brazing. The development of high-intensity quartz lamps and the availability of suitable reflectors have made infrared heat a commercially important generator for brazing. Lamps are often arranged in a toasterlike configuration, with parts traveling between two banks of lamps.

Diffusion brazing. This process is defined not by the method of heating but by the degree of mutual filler-metal solution and diffusion with the base metal resulting from the temperature used, and the time interval at heat. Temperature, time, in some cases pressure, and selection of base and filler materials are so controlled that the filler metal is partially or totally diffused into the base metal. For example, a nickel filler metal with a solidus temperature of 960°C, when partially diffused at a temperature of 1095–1150°C, will have a remelt temperature in excess of 1370°C.

Brazing environment. Fluxes, gas atmospheres, and vacuum conditions promote formation of brazed joints. They may be used to surround the work, exclude reactants, and provide active or inert protective atmospheres, thus preventing undesirable reactions during brazing.

Fluxes. The primary purpose of brazing fluxes is to promote wetting of the base metal by the brazing filler metal. The efficiency of flux activity, which is commonly referred to as wetting, can be expressed as a function of brazeability. The flux must be capable of dissolving any oxide remaining on the base metal after it has been cleaned, and also any oxide films on the liquid filler metal. To effectively protect the surfaces to be brazed, the flux must completely cover and protect them until the brazing temperature is reached. It must remain active throughout the brazing cycle.

Many chemical compounds are used in the preparation of fluxes. When a flux is heated, reactions take place between the various chemical ingredients, forming new compounds at brazing temperatures that are quite different chemically and physically from the unreacted constituents. Composition of the flux must be carefully tailored to suit all the factors of the brazing cycle.

Controlled atmospheres. The second way to control the formation of oxides during brazing and also reduce oxides present after precleaning is to surround the braze area with an appropriate controlled atmosphere. Like fluxes, controlled atmospheres are not intended to perform primary cleaning for removal of oxides, coatings, grease, oil, dirt, or other foreign materials.

In controlled-atmosphere applications postbraze cleaning is generally not necessary. Controlled atmospheres for brazing fall into three broad categories: reducing atmospheres, inert atmospheres, and vacuum conditions. They are used extensively for high-temperature brazing.

Cleaning. Cleaning of all surfaces that are involved in the formation of the desired brazed joint is necessary to achieve successful and repeatable braze joining. The presence of contaminants on one or both surfaces may result in formation of voids, restriction or misdirection of filler-metal flow, and inclusion of contaminants within the solidified braze area.

Inspection techniques. Inspection of the completed assembly or subassembly is the last step in the brazing process and is essential for ensuring satisfactory and uniform quality of the brazed unit. This operation also provides a means of evaluating the adequacy with which the prior steps in the process have been carried out with regard to ultimate integrity of the brazed joint.

The inspection methods chosen to evaluate the brazing procedure and the serviceability of the product will be largely dependent on the service requirements of the brazed assembly.

Applications. A myriad of applications of brazing occur in many fields, including automotive and aircraft designs; engines and engine components; electron tubes, vacuum equipment, and nuclear components, such as production of reliable ceramic-to-metal joints; and miscellaneous applications such as fabrication of food-service dispensers (scoops) used for ice cream and corrosion-resistant and leakproof joints in stainless steel blood-cell washers. *See* WELDING AND CUTTING OF MATERIALS.

Mel M. Schwartz

Bibliography. American Society for Metals, *Welding, Brazing, and Soldering*, vol. 6, 10th ed., 1994; American Welding Society, *Brazing Manual*, 4th ed., 1992; M. Schwartz, *Brazing for the Engineering Technologist*, 1995; M. Schwartz, *Joining Composite Materials*, 1994.

Breadboarding

Assembling an electronic circuit in the most convenient manner on a board or other flat surface, without regard for final locations of components, to prove the feasibility of the circuit and to facilitate changes when necessary. Standard breadboards for experimental work are made with mounting holes and terminals closely spaced at regular intervals, so that parts can be mounted and connected without drilling additional holes. Such breadboards are useful only for relatively simple circuits operating at audio or low radio frequencies.

Printed-circuit boards having similar patterns of punched holes, with various combinations of holes connected together by printed wiring on each side, are often used for breadboarding moderate radio frequency and digital logic circuits. *See* PRINTED CIRCUIT.

Advances in the capabilities of computer software for circuit simulation, component layout, and interconnect routing, along with "rapid prototyping" capabilities provided by a number of vendors, have made it cost-effective for circuit designers to bypass conventional breadboarding and proceed directly to the construction of printed-circuit board prototypes of their designs. For even relatively simple designs, these prototypes can be delivered much more quickly than a breadboard can be constructed. These prototypes also have most, if not all, of the board-related idiosyncrasies that would be seen in production systems, so their performance will closely approximate that to be expected from the final product. *See* CIRCUIT (ELECTRONICS); COMPUTER-AIDED CIRCUIT DESIGN; PROTOTYPE. Philip V. Lopresti; John Markus

Breadfruit

The multiple fruit of an Indo-Malaysian tree, *Artocarpus altilis*, of the mulberry family (Moraceae), now cultivated in tropical lowlands around the world (see **illus.**). Captain William Bligh was bringing

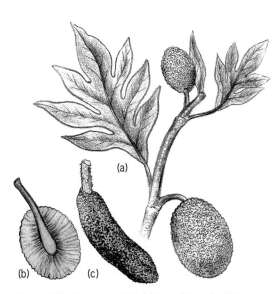

Breadfruit (*Artocarpus altilis*). (*a*) End of branch with multiple fruits. (*b*) Longitudinal section of multiple fruit. (*c*) Staminate flower cluster.

plants from Tahiti to America when the mutiny on the *Bounty* occurred. The perianth, pericarp, and receptacle are all joined in a multiple fruit having a high carbohydrate content. The fruits vary considerably in size and are often borne in small clusters. Breadfruit is a wholesome food for both humans and animals. It is eaten fresh or baked, boiled, roasted, fried, or ground up and made into bread. There are many varieties, both with and without seeds.

Earl L. Core

Breakdown potential

The potential difference at which an electrically stressed gas is tranformed from an insulator to a conductor. In an electrically stressed gas, as the voltage is increased, the free electrons present in the gas gain energy from the electric field. When the applied voltage is increased to such a level that an appreciable number of these electrons are energetically capable of ionizing the gas, the gas makes the transition from an insulator to a conductor; that is, it breaks down. The potential difference at which this transition occurs is known as the breakdown potential for the particular gaseous medium.

The breakdown potential depends on the nature, number density, and temperature of the gas; on the material, state, and geometry of the electrodes; on the type of voltage applied (steady, alternating, impulsive); and on the degree of preexisting ionization. Areas of surface roughness at the electrodes (especially the cathode) or the presence of conducting particles in the gas greatly reduces the breakdown potential because at such points the electric field is significantly enhanced, increasing the electron energies and thus gas ionization. The breakdown voltage varies considerably from one gaseous medium to another; it is very low for the rare gases, such as neon, for which a 0.394-in. (1-cm) uniform-field gap at 1 atm (101.3 kilopascals) breaks down at 0.53 kV; and very high for polyatomic, especially electronegative, gases such as sulfur hexafluoride (SF_6), for which a 0.394-in. (1-cm) uniform-field gap at 1 atm (101.3 kPa) breaks down at 88.9 kV.

The transition of a gas from an insulator to a conductor under an imposed electrical potential occurs in times ranging from milliseconds to nanoseconds, depending on the form of the applied field and the gas density. This transition depends on the behavior of electrons, ions, and photons in the gas, especially the processes which produce or deplete free electrons. Knowledge of these processes often allows prediction of the breakdown voltage of gases and the tailoring of gas mixtures which can withstand high electrical potentials for practical uses. *See* ELECTRICAL BREAKDOWN; ELECTRICAL CONDUCTION IN GASES.

Increasing the breakdown potential. Fundamental research on the microscopic physical processes which take place in an electrically stressed gas—especially those involving the interaction of slow (less than about 20 eV) electrons with atoms and molecules—has led to a better understanding of the electrical "breakdown" of gases. It has also led to the realization that an effective way of increasing the breakdown potential is to prevent the free electrons in the gas from initiating the breakdown by attaching them to gas molecules forming negative ions, which—being much heavier than the electrons—do not ionize the gas. (In such cases the breakdown potential can be defined as that value of the applied potential for which the rate of electron production by ionization is equal to the rate of electron depletion by attachment.) The ability of molecules to capture free electrons is large in the extreme low-energy range (less than about 1 eV) and decreases as the electron energy increases. For this reason, the gas itself—or an additive to it, as in a gas mixture—must be capable of reducing the energies of the free electrons and effectively scattering them into the low-energy region, where they can be captured most efficiently. Knowledge of the electron-scattering properties of gases permits selection of suitable gases for the slowing down of free electrons in dielectric gas mixtures. Combinations of two or more electron-attaching and electron-slowing-down gases have been developed in this manner which effectively control the energies and number densities of free electrons in electrically stressed gases. This approach allows the systematic identification of unitary gases (for example, sulfur hexafluoride and perfluorocarbons) and the systematic development of multicomponent gaseous dielectrics (for example, sulfur hexafluoride–nitrogen; perfluorocarbon–nitrogen; and sulfur exafluoride–perfluorocarbon–nitrogen) which are able to withstand very high potentials before breaking down and are suitable for many applications.

Applications. The systematic development of gaseous dielectrics with high dielectric strength (that is, high breakdown potential) is most significant for high-voltage technology, which has a multiplicity of gas insulation needs. Dielectric gases are widely used as insulating media in high-voltage transmission lines, circuit breakers, transformers, substations, high-voltage research apparatus, and other electrical equipment (such as Van de Graaff accelerators). In transmission lines the high-voltage conductor is held in place by solid insulators and is enclosed in a vacuum-tight pipe, the earthed electrode (often buried underground), which is filled with the insulating gas at pressures usually ranging from 1 to 10 atm (100 to 1000 kPa) depending on the voltage. The voltages in such systems can be higher than 1,000,000 V, resulting in considerable reduction of resistive losses and hence substantial energy savings. The use of compressed-gas–insulated transmission lines and other gas-insulated high-voltage electrical equipment is expected to continue increasing. *See* CIRCUIT BREAKER; DIELECTRIC MATERIALS; TRANSMISSION LINES.   L. G. Christophorou

Bibliography. L. G. Christophorou (ed.), *Gaseous Dielectrics VIII*, 1998; L. G. Christophorou, D. R. James, and R. Y. Pai, Gas breakdown and high voltage insulating gases, in *Applied Atomic Collisions*, vol. 5, pp. 87–167, 1982; E. E. Kunhardt and L. H. Luessen (eds.), *Electrical Breakdown and Discharges in Gases*, vols. 89a and 89b, NATO Advanced Science Institutes Series, 1983; J. M. Meek and J. D. Craggs (eds.), *Electrical Breakdown in Gases*, 1978.

Breast

The human mammary gland, usually well developed in the adult female but rudimentary in the male. Each adult female breast contains 15–20 separate, branching glands that radiate from the nipple. During lactation their secretions are discharged through separate openings at the base of the nipple.

In both sexes paired ridges (milk lines) develop in the 6-week-old fetus and extend from the axilla downward, converging toward the abdomen. Most portions of the milk lines regress, leaving only slight prominences in the region destined to become the breasts. During the middle part of fetal life clusters of epidermal cells grow inwardly in these areas, forming cords which develop into hollow ducts. After birth slow increase in size and branching of each primary duct occurs. Development in the male usually ends at this stage. Supernumerary nipples or breasts along the milk lines are not rare. They are of minor clinical significance because they are usually rudimentary, but may constitute a severe cosmetic or psychic problem, which is readily amenable to surgery.

In the female, hormonal changes in adolescence cause enlargement of breast tissue, but much of this is connective tissue although some glandular buds form. With the advent of full menstruation ovarian estrogenic hormones influence breast development. If pregnancy ensues, the glandular tissue reaches full development and full lactation begins shortly after birth. After cessation of lactation the breasts regress considerably and once again reflect cyclic regulation. *See* MENSTRUATION; PREGNANCY.

Occasionally the male breasts will be stimulated by estrogens, possibly of adrenal origin. Liver disease may prevent normal destruction of estrogen so that gynecomastia (enlargement of breasts in the male) results.

The breasts of infants may respond to maternal hormones during the first few days or weeks of life, but regression usually occurs spontaneously. *See* LACTATION.   Walter Bock

Breast disorders

Benign and malignant lesions of the human mammary glands. Benign breast disorders are often symptomatic and bothersome but do not have malignant potential. Malignant disorders have the potential to grow locally in the breast and spread through the bloodstream to other parts of the body.

Physiologic changes. The breast is an organ that changes in response to fluctuations in hormone levels. Physiologic changes in the breast are often confused with disease. Fibrocystic disease, chronic cystic mastitis, and mammary dysplasia are terms that have been used to describe cyclical pain, tenderness, and lumpiness in the breast. These terms are imprecise and represent the normal physiologic responses to hormonal changes in the body rather than distinct clinical entities. Cyclic breast pain can occur in response to estrogens endogenous in premenopausal women or supplemental in postmenopausal women. Diffuse, palpable irregularities or lumps in the breast are also associated with this cyclical pain. Unlike malignant masses, however, these irregularities fluctuate in size and tenderness with the menstrual cycle, and are better described as physiologic nodularity of the breast. *See* MENOPAUSE.

Benign disorders. Common benign disorders include breast masses, cysts, gynecomastia, nipple discharge, and breast infections. Breast masses or dominant lumps are different from lumpiness; they are persistent over time and are palpably distinct from the surrounding breast tissue. They can develop in any age group and should be carefully evaluated. Mammography and ultrasound can help to determine the character of the mass, depending on the age of the patient.

Dominant lumps include fibroadenomas, gross cysts, pseudolumps, and cancer. Fibroadenomas may occur in any age group but are most commonly seen in young women. They are benign tumors consisting of smooth, rounded masses that are easily palpable in the breast. The cause is unknown; however, there is evidence to support the presence of an imbalance in circulating hormone levels that might be responsible for tumor growth. Breast cysts may be difficult to identify by physical examination or mammography, but can be distinguished from solid masses by using ultrasound imaging. Treatment of a cyst involves draining it with a small needle and syringe. If the cyst completely disappears, no further treatments are required. However, if the cyst remains or recurs or the cyst fluid is bloody, further examinations are required to rule out an underlying carcinoma. *See* MAMMOGRAPHY.

Gynecomastia, a benign enlargement of the male breast which can occur at any age and in one or both breasts, is a physiologic response to hormones, drugs, or an underlying medical condition. Nipple discharge does not always indicate a pathologic process; the character of the discharge is significant. A watery bilateral discharge from multiple ducts is usually normal. A milky discharge (galactorrhea) is often physiologic but sometimes can be associated with a tumor of the pituitary gland, which secretes prolactin. Unilateral, and especially spontaneous, nipple discharge generally signifies underlying pathology. Bloody nipple discharge is of most concern. About 80% of the time, however, the underlying cause is a benign papilloma within a duct. Breast infections are a common problem seen in both lactating and nonlactating individuals. *See* LACTATION.

Proliferative breast disorders include ductal and lobular hyperplasias. It is thought that some of these disorders might represent precancerous changes since they signal an increased risk for the development of breast cancer. Women who have hyperplasia without atypical cell changes have a mildly elevated risk for the subsequent development of breast cancer when they are compared with the general population. Women with atypical hyperplasia have a risk of developing breast cancer 4.4 times that of women without identifiable risk factors. This lesion is seen in only about 4–10% of breast biopsies. It does not characteristically form lumps or show up on mammography. Other benign neoplasms of the breast include adenomas, intraductal papillomas, adenosis, and radial sclerosing lesions.

Precancer. Ductal carcinoma is a precancer. It does not have the ability to disseminate throughout the body but can progress to an invasive carcinoma if left untreated. Once discovered, this lesion can be treated with breast conservation surgery, that is, excision of the tumor with a margin of normal tissue, with or without radiation, or with total mastectomy. Lobular carcinoma, however, is a misnomer since it is not a premalignant lesion but a marker for subsequent cancer. Women with lobular carcinoma who subsequently develop cancer do so in either breast with a relative risk 5.7 times that of the general population. Treatment options include close observation with physical examination and mammography, or bilateral mastectomies.

Cancer. Breast cancer is the most common cancer in women and is the second leading cause of cancer deaths among all American women, particularly in the fifth and sixth decades of life. Almost 80% of invasive carcinomas of the breast are of ductal origin; the remainder are lobular carcinomas or other special histologic types. Invasive ductal carcinomas can be subtyped if they have one or more characteristics of a specific histologic type, including tubular, medullary, papillary, or mucinous differentiation. When a large part of the tumor is differentiated into one of these subtypes, they generally carry a more favorable prognosis.

There are no significant differences in the rates of local recurrence and survival when breast conservation surgery is combined with radiation therapy to the breast as compared with total mastectomy. Removal of axillary lymph nodes continues to be an important tool in the staging and prognosis of invasive carcinomas of the breast. If axillary lymph node metastases are detected, systemic therapy is indicated to decrease the incidence of distant metastases, and will usually decrease the risk of mortality by one-third. Combination chemotherapy is generally recommended for premenopausal women, and its use has been extended to healthy postmenopausal women. Hormonal therapy is used to treat postmenopausal women with axillary lymph node metastases and hormone receptor positive tumors. Tamoxifen (an antiestrogen) is a hormonal agent which has been shown to decrease the risk of recurrence and the development of second primary tumors in postmenopausal women. *See* CANCER (MEDICINE); CHEMOTHERAPY AND OTHER ANTINEOPLASTIC DRUGS.

Thirty percent of all women with negative lymph nodes will have developed micrometastases at the time of diagnosis and will eventually die of breast cancer. Chemotherapy or hormone therapy is therefore often recommended even for women with negative nodes. The use of chemotherapy or hormone therapy in women without axillary lymph node metastases is determined by multiple factors. The most important determinant is tumor size. Women with tumors greater than 2 cm (0.8 in.) in diameter, with negative axillary nodes, should receive systemic therapy. For individuals without axillary lymph node metastases and tumors less than 1 cm (0.4 in.) in diameter, the probability of relapse 10 years after diagnosis is less than 10%. Therefore, systemic chemotherapy is generally not recommended in this group.

Screening. Breast cancer screening is the most effective way of detecting breast cancer in its early stages. Screenings involve self-examination of the breast, physical examination, and mammography. The guidelines for when these examinations should be administered depend on the individual's age. A mammogram is the most reliable screening test for the early detection of breast cancer; mammograms are recommended every 2–3 years from age 40 to 50 and annually after age 50. As the density of the breast parenchyma changes with increasing age, mammography is better able to detect abnormalities within the breast.   Kelly K. Hunt; Susan M. Love

Bibliography. I. M. Ariel and A. C. Cahan, *Treatment of Precancerous Lesions and Early Breast Cancer: Diagnosis and Management*, 1993; J. R. Harris et al., *Breast Diseases*, 1991; D. F. Hayes (ed.), *Atlas of Breast Cancer*, 1993; F. A. Tavassoli, *Pathology of the Breast*, 2d ed., 1999; A. K. Tucker (ed.), *Textbook of Mammography*, 1993.

Breccia

A clastic rock composed of angular gravel-size fragments; the consolidated equivalent of rubble. The designation gravel-size refers to a mean particle diameter greater than 0.08 in. (2 mm), which means that 50% or more of the particles (by volume) are this size or larger. Various classifications specify different values for the degree of angularity. One system specifies angular or subangular fragments (roundness ≤0.25), whereas another restricts the term breccia to aggregates with angular fragments (roundness ≤0.10). *See* GRAVEL.

Most classifications recognize three major types of breccia: sedimentary, igneous, and cataclastic. Sedimentary breccias are characterized as exogenic, that is, formed by processes at the surface of the Earth, while igneous and cataclastic breccias are characterized as endogenic, that is, formed within the Earth. A minor exogenic type is impact breccia, which is formed by the impact of extraterrestrial bodies, such as meteorites and comets. This type is rare on Earth, but it is abundant on the Moon, Mercury, and other heavily cratered planetary bodies.

Sedimentary breccia. These breccias, referred to as sharpstone conglomerates according to one classification, are significant because the angularity of their fragments indicates either proximity to the source or transportation by a mechanism that does not cause significant rounding of the fragments. Examples of the first condition are talus breccia formed at the base of a scarp, and reef breccia deposited adjacent to a reef margin. Transport mechanisms that can preserve the angularity of clasts over significant distances include debris flows, slumps, and glacial transport, although rounded fragments may also be carried. All of these mechanisms incorporate a large proportion of fine sediment in the transporting medium, which effectively cushions interparticle collisions and in-

hibits rounding. *See* CONGLOMERATE; REEF; SEDIMENTOLOGY.

Intraformational or intraclastic breccias are an important class of sedimentary breccias. They are formed by the breakup and incorporation of sediment aggregates from within the same formation, which requires either early cementation (for example, the formation of nodules or duricrusts) or uncemented aggregates sufficiently cohesive to be transported a short distance without disaggregation. Thus, uncemented aggregates are basically limited to sediments that are rich in clay or clay-size carbonates (calcilutites). The mechanisms for formation of intraformational breccias include bank slumping or desiccation fracturing of mud in river or tidal channels, and erosion and incorporation of mud blocks in mass flows such as slumps or turbidity currents. *See* SEDIMENTARY ROCKS.

Igneous breccia. These breccias are mainly of pyroclastic origin but may also form as intrusive breccias by forceful intrusion of magma. In the latter case the operative agent is fluid pressure; in the former it is the explosive escape of gas from solidifying viscous lava. These rocks, termed pyroclastic or volcanic breccias, are distinct from agglomerates, which accumulate mainly as lava bombs solidified during flight and which are commonly rounded. *See* PYROCLASTIC ROCKS.

Cataclastic breccia. These breccias result from the fracture of rocks by tectonic or gravitational stresses. However, since many tectonic processes are at least partly gravitational, the two processes can be considered together. Tectonic breccias include fault and fold breccias, the latter formed by fracturing of brittle layers within incompetent plastic strata during folding. In one classification, landslide and slump breccias are included in the gravitational category, but here they are considered to be sedimentary, commonly intraformational. Solution or collapse breccias are a type of nontectonic gravitational breccia. They result from the creation by ground-water solution of unsupported rock masses which collapse under their own weight to form breccia   Brian Rust

Bibliography. H. Blatt, *Sedimentary Petrology*, 2d ed., 1991; W. C. Krumbein and F. J. Pettijohn, *Manual of Sedimentary Petrography*, 1938, reprint 1988; D. W. Lewis and D. M. McConchie, *Practical Sedimentology*, 2d ed., 1993.

Breeding (animal)

The application of genetic principles to improving heredity for economically important traits in domestic animals. Examples are improvement of milk production in dairy cattle, meatiness in pigs, growth rate in beef cattle, fleece weight in sheep, and egg production in chickens. Even after thousands of years of domestication, domestic animals respond readily to genetic selection. Selection permits the best parents to leave more offspring in the next generation than do genetically inferior parents. Many specialized breeds and strains have been developed for the production of meat, fiber, and milk that are adapted to different environmental and economic conditions. *See* GENETICS.

The science of animal breeding is based on genetic principles; however, the current application of these principles relies heavily on statistical knowledge. Accurate measurement of performance of individuals, such as growth rate or milk production, is essential. Use of computers has become an integral part of animal breeding research and application. Modern computers allow the application of complicated statistical procedures to large volumes of performance data to identify the best individuals to become parents of the next generation.

Methods of genetic selection. Selection is the primary tool for generating directed genetic changes in animals. Selection may be (1) concentrated on one characteristic, (2) performed independently on several traits, or (3) conducted on an index or total score which includes information on several traits. The first method is most effective in generating improvement in the one chosen primary trait, but may generate a correlated response in other traits. The second method, independent culling levels, generates greater overall improvement in total merit than the first, but is less effective for making change in the primary trait. The third method, index selection, generates maximum improvement in several traits by weighting each trait by its relative economic importance and by the phenotypic and genetic relationships among the traits. In some species, index selection has the disadvantage of delaying selection decisions until measurements, taken at different times in the life of the animals, are completed on all traits.

In general, the third method is preferable when several important heritable traits need attention. In practice, selection is likely to be a mixture of the second and third methods.

Factors influencing genetic selection progress. Heritability, the fraction of the total variation in a trait that is due to additive genetic differences, is a key parameter in making selection decisions. Traits for which environmental effects cause most of the variation are only slightly heritable. Most economically important traits are strongly to moderately influenced by environmental or management conditions. Therefore, managing animals to equalize environmental influences on them, or statistically adjusting for environmental differences among animals, is necessary to accurately choose those with the highest genetic merit for various traits.

The accuracy with which the breeding values of the animals can be determined is directly related to the improvement achieved by selection. Accuracy, in turn, depends upon the heritabilities of the traits and whether they can be measured directly upon the subjects of selection (mass selection), their parents (pedigree selection), their brothers and sisters (family selection), or their progeny (progeny testing). Mass selection is effective for traits with high heritability which are expressed before breeding age. Pedigree selection is most useful for traits such as milk production which are expressed relatively late

in life and for traits which are limited in expression to only one sex. Pedigree selection can never be highly accurate as compared with other kinds of selection because a subject can have only two parents, a maximum of four different grandparents, and so on, whereas the number of siblings or progeny can be large. For traits of medium heritability, the following sources of information are approximately equally accurate for predicting breeding values of animals: (1) one record measured on the animal itself; (2) one record on each ancestor for three previous generations; (3) one record each on five brothers or sisters where there is no environmental correlation between family members; and (4) one record each on five progeny having no environmental correlations, each from a different mate.

The intensity of genetic selection influences the rate of genetic improvement within a population of animals. As older females are removed (culled) from the breeding population, younger females (called replacements) must be added to the breeding herd in order to maintain herd size. If, for example, only the top 20% of females are chosen from the pool of potential replacements, their average level of genetic merit will be higher than instances when the top 50% of potential females are saved for replacements (this, of course, assuming that accuracy of selection is high).

The generation interval, or the length of time between the birth of the parents and the birth of the offspring which replace the parents in the breeding herd, alters the rate of genetic improvement. Typically, breeding males are replaced more frequently than breeding females, particularly in breeding programs where replacement females are generated from within the herd. One of the challenges faced by breeders of domestic animals is to attain the proper balance between rapid genetic improvement (attained by short generation intervals) and the economic sustainability of the herd (frequent purchase of breeding sires and/or replacement females costs money).

Purebred strains. Propagation of improved animal seed stocks is achieved primarily with purebred strains descended from imported or locally developed groups or breeds of animals which have been selected and interbred for a long enough period to be reasonably uniform for certain trademark characteristics, such as coat color. Each breed is promoted and sponsored by its farmer breeders organized as a purebred society. Because the number of breeding animals is finite and because breeders tend to prefer certain bloodlines and sires, some inbreeding occurs within the pure breeds, but this has not limited productivity in most breeds.

As a rule, each breed has certain easily identifiable characteristics such as coat color, size and shape of ear, and horns or polledness. Most of these breed-specific traits are encoded by one gene (or a group of linked genes), and these traits are called qualitative (or Mendelian) traits. The particular form, or allele, of each gene is almost identical among all animals within breeds that have been subjected to intense selection for many generations. Conversely, other traits are controlled by numerous genes, each with a relatively small effect, and are known as quantitative (multigenic) traits. Traits such as growth rate or milk production are influenced by many genes, as are those concerned with appetite, ability to obtain and digest food, temperament, and energy metabolism. The effects of individual alleles upon such traits are likely to be small relative to the total variation. Hence, selection for improved performance changes the frequency of any one of the numerous desired alleles only slightly, although the cumulative improvement over many generations may be large. Selection has not always been consistent for the same goal, frequently changing intensity or direction as a consequence of changing styles or economic conditions. *See* MENDELISM.

Crossbreeding. One of the main reasons for crossbreeding is to make use of the genetic phenomenon of heterosis. Heterosis is improved performance of crossbred progeny, exceeding the average performance of their parents. Most commercial pigs, sheep, and beef cattle are produced by crossbreeding.

There are two basic types of crossbreeding systems—rotational and terminal. Rotational crossbreeding systems involve the rotation of different breeds of sires for mating of the herd females, and replacement females are chosen from the offspring produced within the herd. Rotational systems commonly utilize two or three different breeds, although four breeds may also be used. Terminal crossbreeding systems involve the mating of a sire breed, most often noted for superior meat quality, with herd females noted for maternal traits such as fertility, mothering ability, and/or milk production. All offspring produced are sent to harvest; hence the adjective "terminal." The herd females may be purebreds, but typically they are crossbred because crossbred females exhibit heterosis for reproductive traits. By mating a paternal sire breed with a female that excels in maternal traits, the resultant offspring should possess a combination of outstanding genetic characteristics not found in a single breed. Breeds should be chosen which complement one another. *See* GENETICS.

New developments. There have been new discoveries in four areas that have application, or potential application, for improvement of domestic animals: quantitative genetics, reproductive physiology, molecular genetics, and immunogenetics.

Quantitative genetics. Quantitative geneticists use statistical and genetic information to improve domestic animals. Typically a statistical procedure is used to rank animals based on their estimated breeding values for traits of economic importance. The breeding values are based on records of the animals themselves and on the records of their relatives. The animals that are ranked highest are used as parents of the next generation. The recording of animal performance, ranking the animals, and mating are repeated for successive generations of selection. The use of information on relatives allows more accurate pre-

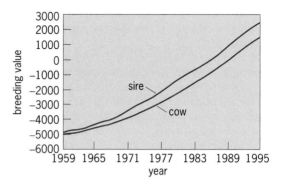

Fig. 1. Holstein average breeding value by birth year for milk. An organized breeding program in dairy cattle results in a genetic gain. The increase in breeding value of cows lags the gains made by sires; sires are more highly selected, and it takes a generation to pass the gain from a sire to offspring.

diction of the breeding values of the animals that are the subjects of selection. The statistical procedures used allow the ranking of animals across herds or flocks, provided the animals in different herds or flocks have relatives in common. This procedure allows for genetic comparisons of animals raised in different environments.

The statistical procedure called an animal model is used to compute breeding values for all dairy cattle in the United States. The well-organized breeding program in dairy cattle has resulted in a genetic gain (**Fig. 1**). In 1995–1999, the genetic trend in Holstein sires was an increase of 195.6 lb (88.9 kg) of milk, 6 lb (2.7 kg) of protein, and 5.8 lb (2.6 kg) of fat per cow per year. Breeding values are expressed relative to a base that is updated every 5 years. The actual production of Holsteins is 20,342 lb (9246 kg) per cow per year.

Reproductive physiology. The primary contribution of reproductive physiology to genetic improvement is development of techniques to increase the intensity of genetic selection and to reduce the generation interval. If genetic improvement is increasing at the same rate per generation, but generations are shorter, more genetic gain per unit of time can be attained.

The most important development of reproductive physiologists was artificial insemination, which allows extensive use of superior males. Artificial insemination allows one male to impregnate many more females than with natural mating. Artificial insemination has been used most widely in dairy cattle, where thoroughly planned young sire sampling programs are combined with carefully conducted progeny testing schemes to identify genetically superior sires whose semen is used to impregnate 70% of the dairy cows. These superior dairy sires produce many thousands of offspring. In the Holstein breed, approximately 500 sires produce enough semen to impregnate approximately 6,300,000 cows. Artificial insemination is used in all domestic animals in the United States. Its use is increasing rapidly in beef cattle, but currently less than 15% are bred artificially. The production of pork is increasingly done in large commercial operations. As a consequence, the use of artificial insemination has increased dramatically. More than 50% of sows are now artificially inseminated. In chickens, both broilers for meat and layers for eggs, artificial insemination is used for matings in the elite seedstock companies; in turkeys, nearly all matings are conducted artificially. Artificial insemination is rarely practiced in sheep, but its use is growing in the horse industry as breed association regulations are being revised to allow it.

Another significant development was embryo transplantation, which allows more extensive use of genetically superior females. Embryo transplantation is nonsurgical. Females are treated hormonally to stimulate the release of several ova at a time; subsequently the superovulated cows are inseminated. The embryos (fertilized eggs) are flushed from the female and are implanted into recipient females or frozen for later use. The usual number of embryos recovered per flush varies from none to approximately 20, with 6 being average.

A fascinating contribution made by reproductive physiologists to the field of animal breeding is the ability to produce genetically identical individuals. Identical (monozygotic) twins have been reported in virtually all domestic animals, but the frequency of naturally occurring identical twins is low. In the 1970s, attempts to produce identical twins were made by separating the individual cells of a preimplantation embryo (called blastomeres), culturing them, and subsequently transferring them to recipient females. The task was laborious, time-consuming, and inefficient. In the 1980s, the technology of embryo splitting (or bisection) was pioneered. With this technology, morula or blastocyst stage preimplantation embryos were split into halves to produce identical twins. Although this technology is well developed and is available commercially to livestock producers, an embryo may be bisected only once, limiting the number of genetically identical animals that can be produced from a single embryo to two.

After blastomere separation techniques were developed, the technology of nuclear transfer began to evolve. Most people refer to nuclear transfer methodology as cloning . The earliest form of nuclear transfer used blastomeres as the source of genetic material for cloning. Isolated blastomeres were injected into enucleated oocytes (oocytes [or eggs] whose own genetic material [chromosomes, which contain DNA] has been removed), and the blastomere–oocyte complex was subjected to pulses of electricity (electrofusion) to cause fusion of the cells and activation of cell division. The resultant "cloned" embryos were cultured in vitro until they could be transferred into recipient females. Alternatively, the cloned embryos could undergo blastomere separation and a second round of nuclear transfer, a process known as serial nuclear transplantation.

In 1997, a new method of nuclear transfer was introduced with the announcement of Dolly the sheep (**Fig. 2**). Dolly was produced via a technique known as somatic cell nuclear transfer. A somatic cell is essentially any cell of the body other than a sex cell (sperm or egg). Scientist Ian Wilmut from the Roslin Institute near Edinburgh, Scotland, led a research team that took a cell from the mammary gland of an adult sheep, cultured that cell in a specially devised medium, injected the cultured cell into an enucleated oocyte, and subjected the somatic cell-enucleated oocyte complex to electrofusion. Transfer of that embryo led to the birth of Dolly. Somatic cell nuclear transfer in some regards was very similar to nuclear transfer using blastomeres as the donor cell, but in other ways it was fundamentally different because it used a differentiated cell (from the mammary gland) rather than an undifferentiated cell (a blastomere).

Although some people oppose somatic cell nuclear transfer due to religious or ethical beliefs, there have been some issues associated with the procedure that have concerned even the most enthusiastic scientist. Some of these problems have already been overcome by changes in methodology, but other issues remain. One lingering concern is that of shortened telomeres. Telomeres are a part of the chromosome which plays an integral role in cell division. When telomeres become too short, the cell cannot divide properly and dies. The shortening of telomeres occurs naturally, and many believe this is one of the major underlying causes of aging. Many animals produced via somatic cell nuclear transfer have exhibited signs of "premature" telomere shortening.

A second remaining challenge to the efficiency of somatic cell nuclear transfer is genomic imprinting. Genomic imprinting is a phenomenon where only one allele (either the maternal or the paternal) is expressed instead of two. Researchers have identified a number of genes that ordinarily are imprinted during development, including those regulating the development of the placenta and fetal growth. There

Fig. 2. Dolly and her first-born lamb, Bonnie. (*Courtesy of the Roslin Institute*)

is abundant documentation in cloned embryos and offspring produced via somatic cell nuclear transfer technology that the genetic reprogramming of the somatic cell is not complete. Many cloned embryos exhibit either an aberrant pattern of genomic imprinting or no imprinting in some genes where it should occur. This incomplete genetic reprogramming of somatic cells leads to a major reduction in the efficiency and reliability of somatic cell nuclear transfer.

The newest approach to nuclear transfer, called chromatin transfer, is being investigated as a potential means of overcoming some of the shortcomings of the traditional somatic cell nuclear transfer approach. In this procedure, somatic cells are permeabilized to enable disassembly of nuclei in a mitotic extract, and the resultant condensed chromatin is transferred into enucleated oocytes. This is followed by electrofusion, culture, and transfer of the cloned embryo to a recipient female. Initial reports of this approach are encouraging, as survival of cloned calves to one month of age is enhanced. Whether this approach circumvents problems with telomere shortening and/or genomic imprinting remains to be seen.

Molecular genetics. Four bases (adenine, thymine, cytosine, and guanine) make the genetic code, DNA, that determines heredity. Segments of DNA that are usually several hundred bases long make up the genes that control cellular functions and, of course, the traits of economic importance. There are many thousands of genes in humans and some other species, and knowledge is increasing regarding the location of genes on the chromosomes. Knowledge of which genes control traits of economic importance would be very useful to animal breeders.

In domestic animals, polymorphisms (changes in the order of the four bases) that are discovered in the DNA may be associated with economic traits. When the polymorphisms are associated with or directly code for economic traits, they are called quantitative trait loci (QTLs). When few QTLs are known that control a portion of the variability in a trait, increasing the frequencies of favorable alleles can enhance the accuracy of selection and augment production.

One of the ways in which animal breeders use knowledge of DNA sequences is via marker-assisted selection. Marker-assisted selection is the genetic selection of animals that is assisted by the knowledge of the specific nucleotide (DNA) sequence of a QTL. Marker-assisted selection is not the selection of an animal based solely on its genetic makeup at the QTL; instead, animals are selected using a combination of "traditional" information (such as breeding values estimated from performance records) and genetic marker DNA sequence. The reason for this combined approach is to ensure that an otherwise genetically inferior animal is not selected just because it possesses a desirable DNA sequence at one QTL. In the cattle industry, commercially available DNA tests help breeders select animals for increases in milk production, in marbling (intramuscu-

lar fat that lends greater flavor and palatability), and in meat tenderness. *See* DEOXYRIBONUCLEIC ACID (DNA).

Another use of molecular genetics is to detect the genes that code for genetic defects. One example is the bovine leukocyte deficiency gene, which does not allow white blood cells to migrate out of the blood supply into the tissues to fight infection. Affected calves perish at a young age. Screening all sires that enter artificial breeding organizations (and not using sires that transmit the defect) has effectively controlled this condition. Another example is determining the DNA sequence of the prion protein gene, as this is related to a sheep's susceptibility to scrapie disease. Scrapie is a transmissible spongiform encephalopathy similar to bovine spongiform encephalopathy (or "mad cow disease"). *See* SCRAPIE.

Immunogenetics. Immunogenetics is the science of genetic control of the immune system. All domestic animals have diseases that must be controlled in order for production of food to be safe and profitable. Information is accumulating about genetic control of the immune system in domestic animals, but there is much to be learned. Study of the immune system relies heavily on molecular techniques.

There is excellent evidence in domestic and laboratory animal species demonstrating some degree of genetic control of at least a part of the immune system. A group of genes that code for disease resistance are known as the major histocompatibility complex (MHC). The MHC genes (broken into classes I, II, and III) encode for proteins displayed on cell surfaces and for a group of disease-fighting proteins known as complement. The genes play a role in resistance and susceptibility to disease. Understanding these complexes of genes is expected to offer a genetic mechanism to aid in disease control. Difference among sire progeny groups has demonstrated disease resistance in several species. It is clear that there is some degree of genetic control in diseases, and the question is how to use genetic mechanisms to improve the health of domestic animals. Natural selection over many centuries has allowed the animals that could resist a variety of diseases to survive. Breeders of domestic animals must be careful to maintain resistance to a wide variety of diseases. *See* AGRICULTURAL SCIENCE (ANIMAL); GENETIC ENGINEERING; REPRODUCTIVE SYSTEM.   C. R. Youngs; A. E. Freeman

Bibliography. D. S. Falconer, *Introduction to Quantitative Genetics*, 2d ed., 1981; E. Li, Chromatin modification and epigenetic reprogramming in mammalian development, *Nat. Rev. Genet.*, 3:662–673, 2002; M. Lynch and B. Walsh, *Genetics and Analysis of Quantitative Traits*, Sinauer Associates, Sunderland, MA, 1997; E. J. Sullivan et al., Cloned calves from chromatin remodeled in vitro, *Biol. Reprod.*, 70:146–153, 2004; X. C. Tian et al., Meat and milk composition of bovine clones, *Proc. Nat. Acad. Sci. USA*, 102:6261–6266, 2005; L. D. Van Vleck, E. J. Pollack, and E. A. B. Oltenacu, *Genetics for the Animal Sciences*, 1987.

Breeding (plant)

The application of genetic principles to the improvement of cultivated plants, with heavy dependence upon the related sciences of statistics, pathology, physiology, and biochemistry. The aim of plant breeding is to produce new and improved types of farm crops or decorative plants, to better serve the needs of the farmer, the processor, and the ultimate consumer. New varieties of cultivated plants can result only from genetic reorganization that gives rise to improvements over the existing varieties in particular characteristics or in combinations of characteristics. In consequence, plant breeding can be regarded as a branch of applied genetics, but it also makes use of the knowledge and techniques of many aspects of plant science, especially physiology and pathology. Related disciplines, like biochemistry and entomology, are also important, and the application of mathematical statistics in the design and analysis of experiments is essential. *See* GENETICS.

Scientific Method

The cornerstone of all plant breeding is selection. By selection the plant breeder means the picking out of plants with the best combinations of agricultural and quality characteristics from populations of plants with a variety of genetic constitutions. Seeds from the selected plants are used to produce the next generation, from which a further cycle of selection may be carried out if there are still differences. Much of the early development of the oldest crop plants from their wild relatives resulted from unconscious selection by the first farmers. Subsequent conscious acts of selection slowly molded crops into the forms of today. Finally, since the early years of the century, plant breeders have been able to rationalize their activities in the light of a rapidly expanding understanding of genetics and of the detailed biology of the species studies.

Conventional breeding is divided into three categories on the basis of ways in which the species are propagated. Species that reproduce sexually and that are normally propagated by seeds occupy two of these categories. First come the species that set seeds by self-pollination, that is, fertilization usually follows the germination of pollen on the stigmas of the same plant on which it was produced. The second category of species sets seeds by cross-pollination, that is, fertilization usually follows the germination of pollen on the stigmas of different plants from those on which it was produced. The third category comprises the species that are asexually propagated, that is, the commerical crop results from planting vegetative parts or by grafting. Consequently, vast areas can be occupied by genetically identical plants of a single clone that have, so to speak, been budded off from one superior individual. The procedures used in breeding differ according to the pattern of propagation of the species. While conventional methods involving crossbreeding have been used very successfully for several decades, several innovative techniques have been explored to enhance the scope, speed, and efficiency of producing new, superior cultivars. Advances have been made in extending conventional sexual crossing procedures by laboratory culture of plant organs and tissues and by somatic hybridization through protoplast fusion.

Self-pollinating species. The essential attribute of self-pollinating crop species, such as wheat, barley, oats, and many edible legumes, is that, once they are genetically pure, varieties can be maintained without change for many generations. When improvement of an existing variety is desired, it is necessary to produce genetic variation among which selection can be practiced. This is achieved by artificially hybridizing between parental varieties that may contrast with each other in possessing different desirable attributes. All members of the first hybrid (F_1) generation will be genetically identical, but plants in the second (F_2) generation and in subsequent generations will differ from each other because of the rearrangement and reassortment of the different genetic attributes of the parents. During this segregation period the breeder can exercise selection, favoring for further propagation those plants that most nearly match the breeder's ideal and discarding the remainder. In this way the genetic structure is remolded so that some generations later, given skill and good fortune, when genetic segregation ceases and the products of the cross are again true-breeding, a new and superior variety of the crop will have been produced.

This system is known as pedigree breeding, and while it is the method most commonly employed, it can be varied in several ways. For example, instead of selecting from the F_2 generation onward, a bulk population of derivatives of the F_2 may be maintained for several generations. Subsequently, when all the derivatives are essentially true-breeding, the population will consist of a mixture of forms. Selection can then be practiced, and it is assumed, given a large scale of operation, that no useful segregant will have been overlooked. By whatever method they are selected, the new potential varieties must be subjected to replicated field trials at a number of locations and over several years before they can be accepted as suitable for commercial use.

Another form of breeding that is often employed with self-pollinating species involves a procedure known as backcrossing. This is used when an existing variety is broadly satisfactory but lacks one useful and simply inherited trait that is to be found in some other variety. Hybrids are made between the two varieties, and the F_1 is crossed, or backcrossed, with the broadly satisfactory variety which is known as the recurrent parent. Among the members of the resulting first backcross (B_1) generation, selection is practiced in favor of those showing the useful trait of the nonrecurrent parent and these are again crossed with the recurrent parent. A series of six or more backcrosses will be necessary to restore the structure of the recurrent parent, which ideally should be modified only by the incorporation of the single useful attribute sought from the nonrecurrent parent.

Backcrossing has been exceedingly useful in practice and has been extensively employed in adding resistance to disease, such as rust, smut, or mildew, to established and acceptable varieties of oats, wheat, and barley. *See* PLANT PATHOLOGY.

Cross-pollinating species. Natural populations of cross-pollinating species are characterized by extreme genetic diversity. No seed parent is true-breeding, first because it was itself derived from a fertilization in which genetically different parents participated, and second because of the genetic diversity of the pollen it will have received. In dealing with cultivated plants with this breeding structure, the essential concern in seed production is to employ systems in which hybrid vigor is exploited, the range of variation in the crop is diminished, and only parents likely to give rise to superior offspring are retained.

Inbred lines. Here plant breeders have made use either of inbreeding followed by hybridization (see **illustration**) or of some form of selection. During inbreeding programs normally cross-pollinated species, such as corn, are compelled to self-pollinate by artificial means. Inbreeding is continued for a number of generations until genetically pure, truebreeding, and uniform inbred lines are produced. During the production of the inbred lines rigorous selection is practiced for general vigor and yield and disease resistance, as well as for other important characteristics. In this way desirable attributes can be maintained in the inbred lines, which are nevertheless usually of poor vigor and somewhat infertile. Their usefulness lies in the vigor, high yield, uniformity, and agronomic

merit of the hybrids produced by crossing different inbreds. Unfortunately, it is not possible from a mere inspection of inbred lines to predict the usefulness of the hybrids to which they can give rise. To estimate their values as the parents of hybrids, it is necessary to make tests of their combining ability. The test that is used depends upon the crop and on the ease with which controlled cross-pollination can be effected.

Tests may involve top crosses (inbred × variety), single crosses (inbred × inbred), or three-way crosses (inbred × single cross). Seeds produced from crosses of this kind must then be grown in carefully controlled field experiments designed to permit the statistical evaluation of the yields of a range of combinations in a range of agronomic environments like those normally encountered by the crop in agricultural use. From these tests it is possible to recognize which inbred lines are likely to be successful as parents in the development of seed stocks for commercial growing. The principal advantages from the exploitation of hybrids in crop production derive from the high yields produced by hybrid vigor, or heterosis, in certain species when particular parents are combined.

Economic considerations. The way in which inbred lines are used in seed production is dictated by the costs involved. Where the cost of producing F_1 hybrid seeds is high, as with many forage crops or with sugarbeet, superior inbreds are combined into a synthetic strain which is propagated under conditions of open pollination. The commercial crop then contains a high frequency of superior hybrids in a population that has a similar level of variability to that

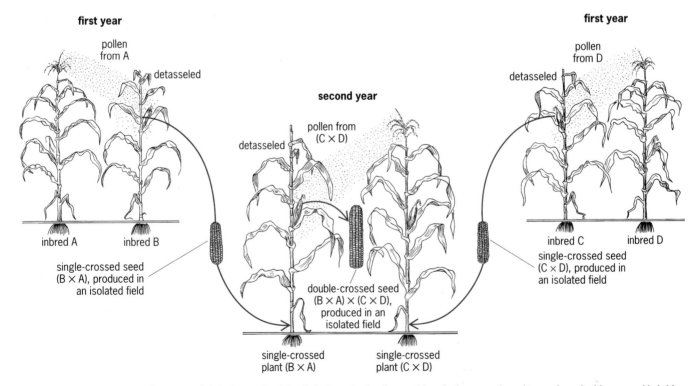

Sequence of steps in crossing inbred plants and using the resulting single-crossed seed to produce double-crossed hybrid seed. (*Crops Research Division, Agricultural Research Service, USDA*)

of an open-pollinated variety. However, because of the selection practiced in the isolation and testing of the inbreds, the level of yield is higher because of the elimination of the less productive variants.

When the cost of seed is not of major significance relative to the value of the crop produced, and where uniformity is important, F_1 hybrids from a single cross between two inbred lines are grown. Cucumbers and sweet corn are handled in this way. By contrast, when the cost of the seeds is of greater significance relative to the value of the crop, the use of single-cross hybrids is too expensive and then double-cross hybrids (single cross A × single cross B) are used, as in field corn. As an alternative to this, triple-cross hybrids can be grown, as in marrow stem kale, in the production of which six different inbred lines are used. The commerical crop is grown from seeds resulting from hybridization between two different three-way crosses.

Recurrent selection. Breeding procedures designated as recurrent selection are coming into limited use with open-pollinated species. In theory, this method visualizes a controlled approach to homozygosity, with selection and evaluation in each cycle to permit the desired stepwise changes in gene frequency. Experimental evaluation of the procedure indicates that it has real possibilities. Four types of recurrent selection have been suggested: on the basis of phenotype, for general combining ability, for specific combining ability, and reciprocal selection. The methods are similar in the procedures involved, but vary in the type of tester parent chosen, and therefore in the efficiency with which different types of gene action (additive and nonadditive) are measured. A brief description is given for the reciprocal recurrent selection.

Two open-pollinated varieties or synthetics are chosen as source material, for example, A and B. Individual selected plants in source A are self-pollinated and at the same time outcrossed to a sample of B plants. The same procedure is repeated in source B, using A as the tester parent. The two series of testcrosses are evaluated in yield trials. The following year inbred seed of those A plants demonstrated to be superior on the basis of testcross performance are intercrossed to form a new composite, which might be designated A_1. Then B_1 population would be formed in a similar manner. The intercrossing of selected strains to produce A_1 approximately restores the original level of variability or heterozygosity, but permits the fixation of certain desirable gene combinations. The process, in theory, may be continued as long as genetic variability exists. In practice, the hybrid $A_n \times B_n$ may be used commercially at any stage of the process if it is equal to, or superior to, existing commercial hybrids.

Asexually propagated crops. A very few asexually propagated crop species are sexually sterile, like the banana, but the majority have some sexual fertility. The cultivated forms of such species are usually of widely mixed parentage, and when propagated by seed, following sexual reproduction, the offspring are very variable and rarely retain the beneficial combination of characters that contributes to the success of their parents. This applies to such species as the potato, to fruit trees like apples and pears that are propagated by grafting, and to raspberries, grapes, and pineapples.

Varieties of asexually propagated crops consist of large assemblages of genetically identical plants, and there are only two ways of introducing new and improved varieties. The first is by sexual reproduction and the second is by the isolation of sports or somatic mutations. The latter method has often been used successfully with decorative plants, such as chrysanthemum, and new forms of potato have occasionally arisen in this way. When sexual reproduction is used, hybrids are produced on a large scale between existing varieties with different desirable attributes in the hope of obtaining a derivative possessing the valuable characters of both parents. In some potato-breeding programs many thousands of hybrid seedlings are examined each year. The small number that have useful arrays of characters are propagated vegetatively until sufficient numbers can be planted to allow the agronomic evaluation of the potential new variety.   Ralph Riley

Special Techniques

Breeding for new, improved varieties of crop plants is generally based on cross-pollination and hybrid production. Such breeding is limited to compatible plants, that is, plants that permit cross-pollination, fertilization of the egg cell, and development of an embryo and seedling. Compatibility lessens with increasing distance in the relationship between plants. Breeding would benefit from access to traits inherent in sexually noncompatible plants. For instance, it is desirable to breed disease resistance from mustard (*Brassica nigra*) or oil quality of Meadow foam (*Limnanthes douglasii*) into rapeseed (*B. napus*). Special techniques, collectively referred to as biotechnology, are employed to overcome incompatibility barriers. Cell biology, molecular genetics, and biological chemistry are the scientific disciplines which nurture the development of special breeding techniques.

True-to-type reproduction of plant stock is another goal of plant breeding. Traditionally it is accomplished by cuttings, tubers, and bulbs, that is, asexually. Such technique applies, for example, to propagation of sugarcane, banana, potato, or lilies. Cell technologies have been used to extend the range and efficiency of asexual plant propagation. The process is often referred to as micropropagation. *See* PLANT PROPAGATION.

Cell technologies. The regeneration of entire, fertile or mature plants from single cells excised from a source plant and cultured in a nutrient medium in an incubator constitutes the primary goal of plant cell culture. Cell development leads either to shoot and root formation or to embryo (as in seeds) and plantlet formation. Cell technologies underlie all of the following special techniques. *See* TISSUE CULTURE.

Micropropagation and cloning. Cell technologies have been applied to mass propagation of a great number of species and varieties; particularly in the realm of horticulture. Conventionally, tissues rather than single cells are excised from root, stem, petiole, or seedling and induced to regenerate plantlets. All regenerants from tissues of one source plant constitute a clone. Nutrient formulas and growth conditions are specific for cells and tissues of each plant variety. Once sufficient growth has been achieved, plantlets are acclimatized to greenhouse and field conditions on location, or via air freight close to market. The Boston fern was one of the first plants to leave micropropagation labs and arrive in stores. High-priced ornamentals (for example, orchids) have been prime targets of micropropagation. Mass propagation of nursery stock has been aided by devices for automated processing (robotics).

Micropropagation has been used to eliminate virus from contaminated stock and is being practiced in quarantine stations. This technology has also been implemented in the restoration of natural habitats (propagation of *Cypripedium*) and of species on the brink of extinction. It complements other techniques whenever seed production of prototype plants is doubtful and asexual means of propagation are called for.

Microspore or anther culture. A technique of propagation particularly useful for plant breeders is the generation of plants from cells with but one set of chromosomes, haploid cells, as occurs in the development of pollen, referred to as microspore culture. Microspores are isolated from anthers and cultured on nutrient media, or entire anthers are cultured in this manner. Given properly conditioned source plants, a high-sugar nutrient medium, and growth conditions with specific temperature regimes, embryos may form directly or subsequent to callus formation. Doubling of chromosomes that may occur spontaneously or can be induced by treatment of callus, embryos, or plantlets with colchicine leads to the formation of homozygous di-haploid plants. Such material instantly stabilizes a (new) genotype, F-1 plants, due to hybridization. *Brassica napus* (rapeseed), which responds to these techniques particularly well, enables several hundred microspores per macerated bud to develop into embryos. Anthers of certain barley varieties can yield up to 20 plantlets. Microspore culture relieves the plant breeder of several cycles of inbreeding to obtain pure lines. *See* POLLEN.

Cryopreservation. Regeneration of plants from cells and tissues opens new ways of preserving stock or germplasm. Treating pieces of tissue with cryoprotectants like sorbitol or dimethylsulfoxide followed by controlled freezing permits storage of such material in vials under low temperature ($-280°F$ or $-196°C$) for years. Thereafter the tissues may be quickly thawed in a waterbath and, upon return to nutrient media, grown to plants. Shoot tips of a variety of horticultural species and of experimental plants are being preserved in this manner. Gene resources centers around the world have adopted cryopreservation as a standard practice. *See* CRYOBIOLOGY.

In vitro fertilization. Sexual incompatibility between plants can be caused by inadequate pollen tube growth and sperm cell development. Such problems could be overcome by in vitro fertilization. Compared to animal systems, in vitro fertilization in plants is compounded by the participation of the embryo sac, accessibility of the egg cell, and complementary function of auxiliary cells. Advances have led to the isolation of viable sperm cells from pollen tubes, the regeneration of plants from embryo sacs 1 day after fertilization, the electrofusion of sperm cells with isolated egg cells, and the injection of sperm cells into the embryo sac.

Embryo rescue. The excision and culture of embryos on nutrient media under in vitro conditions has become an important technique to overcome postfertilization problems, for example, deficiencies in the development of endosperm, the tissue that stores nutrients and surrounds the embryo. The younger the embryo, the more development depends on employing ovules rather than isolated embryos. The technique is used also to overcome natural seed dormancy or to accelerate seed germination. *See* SEED.

Somaclonal variation. Cells and tissues cultured on nutrient media may undergo spontaneous changes. Frequently these changes result in declining capacity for plant regeneration over time. Also, plants regenerated from cells cultured over several months may show increasing variation in phenotype. As a result, regenerated plants may become a pool for selection of plants with desirable traits. Introduction of such plants into a breeding program requires prior demonstration of the heritability of the variant trait by analysis of the progeny of the selected regenerant. A pool of di-haploid, homozygous plants with stable regenerants obtained by culturing microspores as in the case of rapeseed is preferred by breeders.

Somatic hybridization. Enzymatic removal of walls from cells of leaves and seedlings furnishes individual naked cells, that is, protoplasts. Naked cells permit the process of cell fusion. Exposure of protoplasts to electric current or to high concentrations of poly(ethylene glycol) induces adhesion followed by fusion of cell membranes. Similarity of membrane structure throughout the plant kingdom permits the fusion of distantly related protoplasts. Fusion may lead to nuclear fusion prior to and during nuclear division, resulting in amphi-diploid somatic hybrid cells. Such fusion products may divide. Fusion products of closely related, yet sexually incompatible plants have been grown to flowering plants; the most famous example is the potato + tomato hybrid = pomato (*Solanum tuberosum* + *Lycopersicon esculentum*). These plants did not set seeds. Rapeseed (*Brassica napus*) obtained by conventional breeding has been recreated by somatic hybridization using protoplasts from *B. campestris* and *B. oleracea* Furthermore, intergeneric fertile hybrids have been obtained via protoplast fusion of various rapeseed (*Brassica*) plants with *Eruca, Sinapis,* and *Diplotaxis* species. The difference between artificial cross-pollination and fertilization is the fusion not only of nuclei but also of the cytoplasm with mitochondria and plastids of both parents. *See* PLANT CELL; SOMATIC CELL GENETICS.

DNA technologies. The development of technologies that enable the isolation of desirable genes from bacteria, plants, and animals (genes that confer herbicide resistance or tolerance to environmental stress, or encode enzymes and proteins of value to the processing industry) and the insertion of such genes into cells and tissues of target plants by direct or indirect uptake has led to the genetic transformation of plant cells. Desirable genes often are constructed to include regulatory deoxyribonucleic acid (DNA) sequences and genes which enable targeted expression, selection, and visualization of transformed cells and tissues.

Transformation technology began with the observation that nature practices this very process when crown-gall bacteria, which live in the soil, adhere to wounded tissue and release DNA with genes for hormone synthesis into neighboring nonwounded cells. The hormones subsequently drive the growth of the crown gall. In laboratories, this process is mimicked when the genes for hormones are excised from the extrachromosomal DNA of *Agrobacterium* and are replaced by desirable genes. Transformation of plant cells with this indirect method is widely used with plants which naturally respond to *Agrobacterium*, including dicotyledonous herbs and perennials, and trees like poplar. Cells and tissues of monocotyledonous plants (wheat, barley, corn, and rice) but also of conifers and a host of dicots are successfully transformed by an array of direct uptake and transformation processes, the most important of which is based on ballistic technology. Here, recombinant DNA is coated on microscopic particles of gold or tungsten, and these are introduced into cells under high velocity mediated either by gunpowder discharge or helium gas pressure. Initially, transformation success is measured by a response to products of selectable marker gene activity (such as resistance to antibiotics or pigmentation due to β-glucuronidase activity). *See* CROWN GALL; MOLECULAR BIOLOGY.

Assays for the expression of foreign genes in cells and tissues of target plants vary in technology: Southern blot analysis demonstrates the presence of the gene in a host genome; the Northern dot blot analysis, its transcription to ribonucleic acid (RNA); and the Western dot blot analysis, its translation into a gene product (protein or enzyme). The overall expression of a gene is regulated by associated genes that promote, enhance, or silence gene activity.

Transgenic plants. The regeneration of transformed plant cells and tissues results in new and novel genotypes to be assessed for transgenic phenotype. Contrary to hybrids obtained by cross-pollination, such plants are different from their parent by only one or two single, defined traits. Since the production of the first herbicide-resistant tobacco plant in 1985, transgenics of numerous species have successfully been grown and planted in field plots. Herbicide-resistant and insect pest–tolerant crops, both single-gene transgenics, have been entered into breeding programs and are close to commercialization.

Limitations to fast application of DNA technologies include the identification and isolation of useful genes, optimum combination with regulatory genes (promoters, enhancer sequences), the position of the transgene in the host genome, translation and final structure of the gene product, as well as survival of select transformed cells and refinement of nutrient and culture conditions for plant development and growth from these cells, avoiding of chimeric products. While DNA techniques generally add to or reinforce plant traits, suppression can also be valuable.

Trait changes based on the recombination of single genes represent state-of-the-art biotechnology. Multigene traits such as yield or nitrogen fixation are too complex to manipulate and transfer. Still, genes can be introduced one at a time. Rapeseed plants with genes for male sterility and fertility restoration responding to different cues have been produced, and are being assessed for hybrid seed production.

DNA-based genetic diagnostics. Traditional plant breeding is based on selection of superior plants among segregating progeny of a cross. The selection is usually based on a visible or measurable phenotype (vigor, seed color, yield and disease resistance). Using DNA markers, which cosegregate with the genes of interest, allows for greater precision in breeding assessment. Analysis of DNA restriction fragment length polymorphisms (RFLPs) has become the method of choice. It is based on a variation in length of DNA fragments obtained after treatment of a given strand of DNA with restriction enzymes and visualized by electrophoresis. Molecular markers such as RFLPs have been tagged to specific agronomic traits such as disease resistance or male sterility. Generally, they are employed to map phenotypic traits, select superior plants, reduce the transfer of unwanted traits to hybrids (linkage drag), and fingerprint cultivars prior to patent application. The RFLP assay, however, is a laborious procedure, undesirable for breeding projects with high sample throughput. The random amplification of polymorphic DNA (RAPD) assay, however, is based on the use of short sequences of nucleotides as primers for the amplification through polymerase chain reaction of randomly selected segments of the target genome. RAPD markers have assisted in mapping a variety of traits with higher cost efficiency. The polymerase chain reaction is a technique for the enzymatic amplification of specific nucleotide sequences and results in an exponential increase in copies of such sequences. Apart from facilitating RAPDs, this technology promises to assist in reconstituting the genes of extinct species such as ancestors of present-day crop plants. *See* GENETIC ENGINEERING.   Friedrich Constabel

Bibliography. A. M. R. Ferrie, C. E. Palmer, and W. A. Keller, *In Vitro Embryogenesis in Plants*, 1994; K. K. Kartha (ed.), *Cryopreservation of Plant Cells and Organs*, 1985; H. T. Stalker and J. P. Murphy, *Plant Breeding in the 1990s*, 1992; T. A. Steeves and I. M. Sussex, *Patterns in Plant Development*,

1989; I. K. Vasil (ed.), *Scale-up and Automation in Plant Propogation*, 1991; I. K. Vasil and T. A. Thorpe (eds.), *Plant Cell and Tissue Culture*, 1994.

Bremsstrahlung

In a narrow sense, the electromagnetic radiation emitted by electrons when they pass through matter. Charged particles radiate when accelerated, and in this case the electric fields of the atomic nuclei provide the force which accelerates the electrons. The continuous spectrum of x-rays from an x-ray tube is that of the bremsstrahlung; in addition, there is a characteristic x-ray spectrum due to excitation of the target atoms by the incident electron beam. The major energy loss of high-energy (relativistic) electrons (energy greater than about 10 MeV, depending somewhat upon material) occurs from the emission of bremsstrahlung, and this is the major source of gamma rays in a high-energy cosmic-ray shower. *See* COSMIC RAYS; ELECTROMAGNETIC RADIATION.

Properties. The spectrum of bremsstrahlung resulting from the collision of an electron with an atom is continuous and is roughly constant between $v = 0$ and $v = v_{max}$; v_{max} is the maximum frequency of a photon which can be emitted; that is, $hv_{max} = T$, where T is the initial kinetic energy of the electron and h is Planck's constant. The angular distribution of bremsstrahlung is roughly isotropic at low (nonrelativistic) electron energies, but is largely restricted to the forward direction at high energies. Very little bremsstrahlung is emitted at an angle much larger than $\theta_c = m_e c^2/T$ radians, where m_e is the electron mass and c is the velocity of light. Bremsstrahlung emitted at the angle θ_c is polarized with the electric vector perpendicular to the plane containing the direction of radiation and the incident electron velocity. It is difficult to observe the polarization, because it is small except near the angle θ_c. A longitudinally polarized electron (that is, one with its spin parallel to its velocity) emits circularly polarized bremsstrahlung; this effect is not sensitive to angle, and has proved useful in analysis of the longitudinal polarization of electrons emitted in beta decay.

Synchrotron radiation. In a broader sense, bremsstrahlung is the radiation emitted when any charged particle is accelerated by any force. To a great extent, as a source of photons in the ultraviolet and soft x-ray region for the investigation of atomic structure (particularly in solids), bremsstrahlung from x-ray tubes has been replaced by synchrotron radiation. Synchrotron radiation is an analog to bremsstrahlung, differing in that the force which accelerates the electron is a macroscopic (large-scale) magnetic field. Like bremsstrahlung, the synchrotron radiation spectrum is continuous and slowly varying. The main advantage of synchrotron radiation light sources is that the spectrum is accurately calculable and is uncontaminated by spectral lines from atomic transitions. In addition, they have a much higher efficiency, that is, a larger ratio of brightness to power input. This

is partly because the electrons' only loss of energy is the emission of the synchrotron radiation, but mainly because the nuclear electric fields which accelerate the electrons to produce bremsstrahlung also scatter the electrons, thus broadening the angular distribution of subsequently emitted photons. *See* SYNCHROTRON RADIATION.

Nonelectronic bremsstrahlung. Because all other charged particles are much heavier than the electron, their accelerations are generally much smaller and so their bremsstrahlung is generally much weaker. But although nonelectronic bremsstrahlung is not a useful source of photons, its observation can be a useful indicator of the accelerations undergone in a particular process. An example is proton–proton scattering; the rate of the process $p + p \rightarrow p + p + \gamma$ yields information on the *p-p* nuclear force. *See* PLASMA (PHYSICS).
Charles Goebel

Bibliography. A. Bienenstock and H. Winnick, Synchrotron-radiation research: An overview, *Phys. Today*, 36(6):48–58, 1983; W. Heitler, *The Quantum Theory of Radiation*, 3d ed., 1954; J. D. Jackson, *Classical Electrodynamics*, 3d ed., 1998; E. M. Rowe and J. H. Weaver, The uses of synchrotron radiation, *Sci. Amer.*, 236(6):32–41, 1977; Special Issue on Synchrotron Radiation, *Phys. Today*, 34(5):27–71, 1983.

Brick

A construction material usually made of clay and extruded or molded as a rectangular block. Three types of clay are used in the manufacture of bricks: surface clay, fire clay, and shale. Adobe brick is a sun-dried molded mix of clay, straw, and water, manufactured mainly in Mexico and some southern regions of the United States. *See* CLAY; CLAY, COMMERCIAL.

The first step in manufacture is crushing the clay. The clay is then ground, mixed with water, and shaped. Then the bricks are fired in a kiln at approximately 2000°F (1093°C). A modern brick manufacturing plant includes a tunnel kiln that permits a nonstop firing process. Some older plants operate beehive kilns, which require periodic firing. After manufacture, the bricks are normally packaged into a steel-strapped cube with openings for handling by a forklift; this module generally contains 500 bricks. *See* REFRACTORY.

Substances in the clay such as ferrous, magnesium, and calcium oxides impart color to the bricks during the firing process. The color may be uniform throughout the bricks, or the bricks may be manufactured with a coated face. The latter are classified as glazed, claycoat, or engobe. Engobes are coatings, also called slurries, which are applied to plastic or dry body brick units to develop the desired color and texture. Claycoat is a type of engobe that is sprayed on as a coating of liquid clay and pigments.

Clay bricks are manufactured for various applications. In the United States the specifications are determined by the American Society for Testing and Materials (ASTM).

The most commonly used brick product is known as facing brick. In the United States the standard dimensions (modular brick size) are $3^5/_8$ in. $\times$ $2^1/_4$ in. $\times$ $7^5/_8$ in. (90 mm $\times$ 57 mm $\times$ 190 mm). However, 11 other brick sizes are used for specific applications.

In addition to standard bricks, decorative bricks molded in special shapes are available in both standard and custom sizes. They are used to form certain architectural details such as water tables, arches, copings, and corners. Bricks are also used to create sculptures and murals. Michael Gurevich

Bridge

A structure built to provide ready passage over natural or artificial obstacles, or under another passageway. Bridges serve highways, railways, canals, aqueducts, utility pipelines, and pedestrian walkways. In many jurisdictions, bridges are defined as those structures spanning an arbitrary minimum distance, generally about 10-20 ft (3-6 m); shorter structures are classified as culverts or tunnels. In addition, natural formations eroded into bridgelike form are often called bridges. This article covers only bridges providing conventional transportation passageways.

The longest single span provided by a bridge—the Humber suspension bridge in England—is 4626 ft (1410 m); the longest multiple-span bridge—the Lake Pontchartrain Causeway at New Orleans, Louisiana—126,055 ft (38,422 m).

History. Bridges undoubtedly have been built since the origin of humankind, perhaps first as trees felled over waterways and later as structures of timber or stone. The art of constructing stone bridges reached a high degree of development during the Roman era, and for a thousand years or so thereafter, it continued as an empirical art rather than a science. During the nineteenth century the theories of physics and mathematics were first applied to bridges in efforts to produce structures which would be rationally and economically proportioned to take the intended loads. During the midnineteenth century, with application of wrought iron as a material for construction (in the Brittania railway bridge in England), model testing and materials testing were initiated in a scientific manner. At this time, too, and continuing nearly until the end of the century, many firms in the United States developed proprietary bridges which were competitively peddled to railroads and governmental divisions. Eventually the failures of bridges, particularly railroad bridges, because of either faulty design or skimpy construction intended to lower cost, led in the 1880s to the establishment of consulting bridge engineering as a specialized discipline of civil engineering.

Parts. Bridges generally are considered to be composed of three separate parts: substructure, superstructure, and deck. The substructure or foundation of a bridge consists of the piers and abutments which carry the superimposed load of the superstructure to the underlying soil or rock. The superstructure is that portion of a bridge lying above the piers and abutments. The deck or flooring is supported on the bridge superstructure; it carries and is in direct contact with the traffic for which passage is provided.

Types. Bridges are classified in several ways. Thus, according to the use they serve, they may be termed railway, highway, canal, aqueduct, utility pipeline, or pedestrian bridges. If they are classified by the materials of which they are constructed (principally the superstructure), they are called steel, concrete, timber, stone, or aluminum bridges. Deck bridges carry the deck on the very top of the superstructure. Through bridges carry the deck within the superstructure. The type of structural action is denoted by the application of terms such as truss, arch, suspension, stringer or girder, stayed-girder, composite construction, hybrid girder, continuous, cantilever, or orthotropic (steel deck plate), prestressed, or segmental (concrete).

The main load-carrying member or members of a bridge are almost invariably parallel to the alignment of the bridge. When the alignment of the bridge and the obstacle being bridged are not square with one another, the main structural members may not be opposite one another, and the deck may be a parallelogram in plan; in this case the bridge is said to be a skewed bridge. Otherwise, it is known as square.

Many bridges are also designed on horizontally curved alignments to conform with curved approach roadways.

The two most general classifications are the fixed and the movable. In the former, the horizontal and vertical alignments of the bridge are permanent; in the latter, either the horizontal or vertical alignment is such that it can be readily changed to permit the passage beneath the bridge of traffic, generally waterbound, which otherwise could not pass because of restricted vertical clearance. Movable bridges are sometimes called drawbridges in reference to an obsolete type of movable bridge spanning the moats of castles.

A singular type of bridge is the floating or pontoon bridge, which can be a movable bridge if it is designed so that a portion of it can be moved to permit the passage of water traffic.

The term trestle is used to describe a series of stringer or girder spans supported by braced towers or bents, and the term viaduct is used to describe a structure of many spans, often of arch construction.

Fixed Bridges

Fixed-bridge construction is selected when the vertical clearance provided beneath the bridge exceeds the clearance required by the traffic it spans. For very short spans, construction may be a solid slab or a number of beams; for longer spans, the choice may be girders or trusses. Still longer spans may dictate the use of arch construction, and if the spans are even longer, stayed-girder bridges are used. Suspension bridges are used for the longest spans.

Each of the above types of bridge is generally

designed so that the substructure, superstructure, and deck are each considered to carry only the loads directly imposed upon them. In certain types of construction, the deck and the main load-carrying superstructure members are made to participate in carrying the load in order to make the bridge more economical than ordinary stringer or girder bridges with a concrete deck. This is known as composite or hybrid construction, depending upon the type of stringers. If there is stringer or girder-type construction, with a deck partly of steel topped by an asphalt surfacing material, the bridge is known as an orthotropic bridge. When the substructure and superstructure act together, the bridge is described as being of rigid frame construction.

The longer the span of a bridge, the greater is the relative cost per unit of deck area.

The choice of type of bridge superstructure may depend not only on the obstacle to be spanned but also on the substructure. Thus, if an expensive substructure is required because of water depth or unsatisfactory foundation conditions, the selection of a longer-span superstructure may be indicated even though it may not in itself be the economical choice.

Beam bridge. Beam stringer bridges consist of a series of beams, usually of rolled steel, supporting the roadway directly on their top flanges. The beams are placed parallel to traffic and extend from abutment to abutment. When foundation conditions permit the economical construction of piers or intermediate bents, a low-cost multiple-span structure can be built. Spans of 50 ft (15 m) for railroad beam bridges and 100 ft (30 m) for highway beam bridges may be economical.

Composite I-beam bridges are beam bridges in which the concrete roadway is mechanically bonded to the I beams by means of shear connectors, which develop horizontal shear between the concrete slab and the beam. Such a connection forces a portion of the slab to act with the beam, resulting in a composite T beam. This construction yields a saving in the weight of the beams. Rolled shapes such as the channel, angle, and I, bars in serpentine form or in the form of a longitudinal helix, and steel studs are used as shear connectors. These connectors are usually welded to the flange of the steel beam and should extend at least halfway into the slab. *See* COMPOSITE BEAM.

Plate-girder bridge. Plate-girder bridges are used for longer spans than can be practically traversed with a beam bridge. In its simplest form, the plate girder consists of two flange plates welded to a web plate, the whole having the shape of an I. The railroad deck plate-girder bridge consists of two girders which support the floor system for a single track directly on their top flanges. A double-track bridge usually consists of two single-track bridges placed side by side on common abutments or piers. Through plate-girder bridges are used when clearance below the structure is limited. For railroad traffic, the floor system consists of a number of transverse floor beams which are supported by the girders just above their lower flanges. *See* PLATE GIRDER.

Box-girder bridge. Steel girders fabricated by welding four plates into a box section have been used for spans from 100 to more than 850 ft (30 to 259 m). The Rhine River crossing at Cologne, Germany, is an example of an 850-ft (259-m) span. In the United States, a 750-ft (229-m) box-girder span is used in the San Mateo–Hayward Bridge in California. Conventional floor beams and stringers can be used on box-girder bridges, but the more economical arrangement is to widen the top flange plate of the box so that it serves as the deck. When this is done, the plate is stiffened to desired rigidity by closely spaced bar stiffeners or by corrugated or honeycomb-type plates. These stiffened decks, which double as the top flange of the box girders, are termed orthotropic. The wearing surface on such bridges is usually a relatively thin layer of asphalt. Single lines of box girders with orthotropic decks can be used for two-lane bridges, but when wider decks are required, two or more box-girder bridges can be placed parallel to each other.

Curved-girder bridge. Bridges on curved roadways present special problems. Such bridges must be deck bridges. For lightly curved roadways, or when the spans are short, straight stringers or girders usually are used and are positioned under the roadway parallel to a chord of the circular arc of the roadway. When the spans are long or when the curved roadway is of short radius, girders that are curved horizontally are used. These girders parallel the curved edges of the roadway. Sometimes curved girders are chosen for esthetic considerations even when straight girders might be practical, because straight girders on curved bridges are sometimes considered unattractive.

Prior to 1961 there were only a few curved-girder bridges. Both their design and fabrication are difficult, and their erection can be troublesome. Their design involves not only the usual vertical bending forces but also torsional forces caused by the unbalanced loading of a span whose supports are offset from its center of gravity. Early in their use, design was somewhat empirical and overly conservative. However, development of reliable computer programs for curved-girder design has made the use of curved girders more practical.

In addition to individual curved girders, curved steel box girders and curved concrete box girders are used.

Truss bridge. Truss bridges, consisting of members vertically arranged in a triangular pattern, can be used when the crossing is too long to be spanned economically by simple plate girders. Where there is sufficient clearance underneath the bridge, the deck bridge is more economical than the through bridge because the trusses can be placed closer together, reducing the span of the floor beams. For multiple spans, a saving is also effected in the height of piers. *See* TRUSS.

Through-truss. A through-truss bridge is illustrated in **Fig. 1**. The top and bottom series of truss members

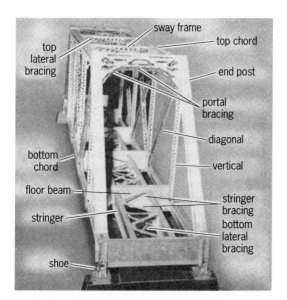

Fig. 1. Model of a through-truss railroad bridge.

length of the top chord members, reducing the cross-sectional area they require. The floor beams and the diagonals connecting the opposite ends of adjacent floor beams constitute the bottom lateral system. Although the floor system of a highway bridge can take over the function of a lateral truss, the lateral bracing must be provided to stiffen the structure during erection and to furnish wind resistance until the steel or concrete floor slab is in place.

The stringers of an open-floor railroad bridge must be braced to relieve them of bending due to lateral forces from the train. In addition, the floor beams should be provided with bracing to relieve the bending due to tractional forces.

Portal and sway bracing are systems of bracing in transverse vertical planes of a bridge. Intermediate sway frames in the plane of opposite verticals give added rigidity.

The end posts of the through-truss bridge are tied together to form a rigid frame or portal capable of transferring the end reaction of the top lateral system to the abutments. To keep the bending stresses in the end posts as small as possible and to provide a rigid portal, portal bracing should be as deep as headroom allows. Also, the end post should be braced by brackets or diagonal members.

Simple-span trusses. Common types of simple-span bridge trusses are shown in **Fig. 2.** The Pratt truss, with its various modifications (Fig. 2*a* and *b*), has tension diagonals and compression verticals. The diagonal in every other panel of a Warren truss (Fig. 2*c–e*) is in compression. The depth of short-span trusses is usually determined by the depth necessary for clearance at the portal. For long spans, it is usually economical to make the depth of the truss greater at the

parallel to the roadway are called top chords and bottom chords, respectively. The diagonals and verticals form the web system and connect the top and bottom chords. The point at which web members and a chord intersect is called a panel point. Gusset plates connect the members intersecting at a panel point.

Lateral bracing of a bridge ties the two trusses together and assures a stable and rigid structure. The top lateral bracing consists of cross struts connecting the top chords at opposite panel points and the diagonals joining the diagonally opposite ends of adjacent cross struts. It decreases the unsupported

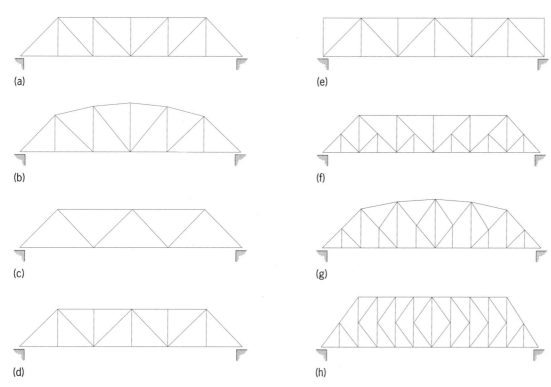

Fig. 2. Examples of simple-span trusses. (*a, b*) Pratt trusses. (*c–e*) Warren trusses. (*f–h*) Subdivided trusses.

center than at the ends. If the depth is increased in proportion to the increase in the forces tending to bend the bridge, the force in the chord members can be more nearly equalized. Figure 2b shows a curved-chord Pratt truss.

Trusses of economical proportions usually result if the ratio of depth of truss to length of span is approximately 1:5 to 1:8 and if the diagonals make angles of 45–60° with the horizontal. The panel length produced in long-span trusses when both of these factors are considered results in an uneconomical floor system. Subdivided trusses (Fig. 2f–h) are used to get reasonable length panels.

Arch bridge. In an arch bridge the main structural system supporting the deck is a curved member (or members), higher vertically at its center than its ends, acting almost entirely in compression, with this compressive load being maintained by thrust against immovable abutments. Arch bridges have been constructed of stone, brick, timber, cast iron, steel, and reinforced concrete, all of which can adequately take compressive loads. Sophistication of construction of stone masonry arch bridges reached a peak during the nineteenth century, spurred by road improvements, and the construction first of canals and then of railroads. Cast iron as a construction material was introduced at this time. *See* ARCH.

Stone masonry arch bridges are rarely constructed anymore. Almost all modern arch bridges are constructed of steel or reinforced concrete, and occasionally of timber. Also, the main structural load-carrying arch system in a modern bridge consists of a number of ribs, generally two, supporting a deck by columns, termed spandrel columns, or by suspenders, in place of the single barrel of stone masonry construction supporting the deck by walls and earth fill, termed spandrel fill. Thus the road carried by the arch no longer must be above the arch ribs, as in the stone masonry construction, but can pass

between the ribs similar to through-truss spans. The choice of arch construction depends largely on foundation conditions at the site, as they must be suitable to economically take the tremendous thrust of the arch ribs. A deck-type arch generally would be used only if the ground level was high at the site, such as at a gorge, in order to obviate long approaches. *See* REINFORCED CONCRETE; STRUCTURAL STEEL.

Arches of steel have reached a maximum span of 1700 ft (518 m) in a bridge over the New River in West Virginia, and arches of concrete a span of 1000 ft (305 m) in the Gladesville Bridge over the Parramatta River at Sydney, Australia. Spans of less than about 150 ft (46 m) generally are not economical because the cost of construction of the curved arch ribs far exceeds any advantage of an arch over other types of bridges for such short spans.

Ribs. The ribs of an arch bridge terminate at inclined faces, termed skewbacks, of the bridge abutments. While arch ribs are essentially compression members, they are also subjected to bending due to partial live loadings, expansion or contraction due to temperature changes, contraction due to shrinkage in the case of concrete ribs, and the transfer of the deck load to the rib at discrete locations. However, the geometrical shape of the vertical curve of the arch ribs is selected to fit the conditions of the site and the loadings so that ribs act mainly as compression members, and then, for the bending, to make sure that no stress exceeds the allowable. The arch ribs of concrete arch bridges are of reinforced concrete, rectangular in section, varying in depth or width from crown to abutment. The ribs of steel arch bridges may be box-shaped in section, of constant width and depth, but varying in thicknesses of steel material from crown to abutment; or, like a truss bridge with bottom and top chord sections with web members, the ribs may be of constant depth, but varying in chord section from crown to abutment. In all cases, since the ribs are compression members, they generally are braced one to the other.

Hinges. If the arch rib extends continuously from skewback to skewback, and is fixed at the skewbacks so no rotation can occur, the bridge is called a fixed arch. An example is shown in **Fig. 3**. If devices known as hinges are introduced in the arch ribs, the bridge is called a two- or three-hinged arch. The three-hinge arch has hinges at the center (or crown of the rib) and at the skewbacks, and the two-hinged arch has hinges only at the skewbacks. These hinges permit the transfer of axial compressive loads from one section of arch rib to another or to the abutments without transfer of bending moments.

The choice of the number of hinges depends on several considerations. Hinges at the skewbacks simplify the abutment design; and hinges at crown and skewbacks simplify the design of the arch rib as well as the abutment, eliminate stresses due to change in temperature, and allow the arch to tolerate minor movements of the abutments. The fixed arch is more rigid, but much more difficult to analyze, and requires the abutment to take bending loads. Arch

Fig. 3. Lewiston-Queenston Bridge over Niagara River. (*Niagara Falls Bridge Commission and Hardesty & Hanover*)

bridges have been built in all three types, and also with a single hinge at the crown.

Tied arches. While most arch bridges have abutments to take the thrust of the arch action, there are a number in which one end of the arch rib is tied to the other with a structural tension member to take the thrust of the rib. These are called tied arches. Usually these are through-arches; the tie is at about deck level and the deck is suspended from the arch rib. These spans may also be a part of another type of construction, a bridge with cantilever and anchor spans, and the tied arch suspended from the cantilever spans, known as a tied arch cantilever.

Continuous bridge. The continuous bridge is a structure supported at three or more points and capable of resisting bending and shearing forces at all sections throughout its length. The bending forces in the center of the span are reduced by the bending forces acting oppositely at the piers. Trusses, plate girders, and box girders can be made continuous. The advantages of a continuous bridge over a simple-span bridge (that is, one that does not extend beyond its two supports) are economy of material, convenience of erection (without need for falsework), and increased rigidity under traffic. Its relative economy increases with the length of span. No increase in rigidity is obtained by making more than three spans continuous. The disadvantages are its sensitivity to relative change in the levels of supporting piers, the difficulty of constructing the bridge to make it function as it is supposed to, and the occurrence of large movements at one location due to thermal changes.

Cantilever bridge. The cantilever bridge consists of two spans projecting toward each other and joined at their ends by a suspended simple span. The projecting spans are known as cantilever arms, and these, plus the suspended span, constitute the main span. The cantilever arms also extend back to shore, and the section from shore to the piers offshore is termed the anchor span (**Fig. 4a**). Trusses, plate girders, and box girders can be built as cantilever bridges.

The chief advantages of the cantilever design are the saving in material and ease of erection of the main span, both of which are due to the fact that no falsework is needed. By adding continuity of members after erection, the cantilever bridge is made to act as a continuous structure under live load. *See* CANTILEVER.

Cable-stayed bridge. A modification of the cantilever lever bridge which has come into modern use resembles a suspension bridge, and it is termed a cable-stayed bridge. It consists of girders or trusses cantilevering both ways from a central tower and supported by inclined cables attached to the tower at the top or sometimes at several levels (**Fig. 5**). Usually two such assemblies are placed end to end to provide a bridge with a long center span.

Suspension bridge. The suspension bridge is a structure consisting of either a roadway or a truss suspended from two or more cables which pass over two towers and are anchored by backstays to a firm foundation (Fig. 4b and c). If the roadway is attached directly to the cables by suspenders, the structure lacks rigidity, with the result that wind loads and moving live loads distort the cables and produce a wave motion on the roadway. When the roadway is supported by a truss which is hung from the cable, the structure is called a stiffened suspension bridge. The stiffening truss distributes the concentrated live loads over a considerable length of the cable.

Cables of the larger sizes, such as those up to 36 in. (91 cm) in diameter used for the George Washington Bridge in New York City, are assembled (or spun) in the field by using pencil-thick wires laid parallel. For smaller cables, strands of wire wound spirally in the factory are assembled into cables. Factory-made strands of parallel wires were used for the first time in 1968 for the 15-in.-diameter (38-cm) cables of the Newport Bridge in Rhode Island.

The longest bridge spans in the world are all of the suspension type. The longest main spans occur in the Humber Bridge of England (4626 ft or 1410 m), the Verrazano-Narrows Bridge in New York City (4260 ft or 1298 m; Fig. 4c), the Golden Gate Bridge in San Francisco (4200 ft or 1280 m), and the Mackinac Bridge in northern Michigan (3800 ft or 1158 m). The Akashi Strait Bridge in Japan, completed in April 1998, with the longest single span (6527 ft or 1989 m), is the world's longest suspension bridge.

Pontoon bridge. The pontoon bridge is a floating bridge supported by pontoons. The structure may be a temporary one, as for military usage, or a permanent one, if the level of the water can be carefully controlled. A pontoon bridge may be advantageous where deep water and adverse bottom conditions make piers expensive. Seattle's Lake Washington is crossed by three floating concrete bridges. Typically, the pontoons are 360 ft (110 m) long, 60 ft (18 m) wide, and 14.5 ft (4.4 m) deep. A 378-ft (115-m) pontoon is used as a floating draw span to give a clear channel opening 200 ft (61 m) wide. Adjacent pontoons are bolted together, and each is secured by a pair of anchors, one on each side. Cast-in-place reinforced concrete was used for the pontoons of the first bridge, but the later bridges are of prestressed concrete.

Concrete bridge. The bridges that have been discussed above are usually made of steel, although they may carry a concrete roadway. Increasingly, however, since the development of the prestressing method, bridges of almost every type are being constructed of concrete. Prior to the advent of prestressing, these bridges were of three types: (1) arch bridges, which were built in either short or long spans, even up to 1000 ft (305 m) for the Gladesville Bridge in Sydney, Australia; (2) slab bridges of quite short spans, which were simply reinforced concrete slabs extending from abutment to abutment; and (3) deck girder bridges, consisting of concrete slabs built integrally with a series of concrete girders placed parallel to traffic. The advent of prestressed concrete greatly extended the utility and economy of concrete for bridges, particularly by making the hollow box-girder type practicable. One of the longest such spans, 682 ft (208 m), is in a bridge over the

Fig. 4. Some major United States bridges. (*a*) Greater New Orleans cantilever bridge, across the Mississippi River (*Bethlehem Steel Co.*). (*b*) Looking from south tower during construction of Mackinac Bridge, connecting upper and lower peninsulas of Michigan (*Mackinac Bridge Authority*). (*c*) Verrazano-Narrows Bridge, New York City (*Triborough Bridge and Tunnel Authority*). (*d*) Vertical-lift span and swing bridge across Arthur Kill, between Staten Island and New Jersey. The vertical-lift bridge replaced the swing bridge, in use since 1888 (*Baltimore and Ohio Railroad Co.*).

Rhine River near Koblenz, Germany. *See* PRESTRESSED CONCRETE.

The objective in prestressing concrete is to reduce or eliminate tensile stresses in the concrete by applying a force that greatly increases internal compressive stress in the concrete member. The force is applied by stretching the reinforcing tendons, which may be either wires or bars, by means of hydraulic jacks that react against the ends of the concrete mem-

ber. Prestressing may be done to precast members, or it may be done as the concrete is being placed in the field. It may be done by either pretensioning or posttensioning. In pretensioning, the reinforcing tendons are stretched prior to the placing of the concrete. In posttensioning, the reinforcing tendons are installed in tubes so that they are isolated from the concrete while it is being placed. When the concrete hardens, the tendons are stretched by jacks reacting

Fig. 5. Sunshine Skyway Bridge in Tampa, Florida. (*Florida Department of Transportation and Figg and Muller Engineers, Inc.*)

against and compressing the concrete member.

Bridge bearings. Almost all bridges have devices known as bearings or shoes where the superstructure transfers its vertical and horizontal loads to the substructure. Exceptions can be arch bridges, rigid frame bridges, and suspension or cable-stayed bridges, where other devices or actions obviate the need of bearings. These bearings are either fixed, expansion, or sliding. All the main structural members of a single-span bridge—the stringers, girders, and trusses—have a fixed bearing at one end of the support and an expansion bearing at the other. Multiple-span bridges have a single fixed bearing and one or two expansion bearings and sliding bearings between fixed and expansion bearings on each main structural member.

The fixed bearing transfers not only vertical loads to the substructure but also the longitudinal horizontal wind or traffic tractive forces. The expansion bearing takes vertical loads but allows longitudinal movements of the end of the member it supports. These movements are caused by temperature changes and changes in the length of the span caused by loadings. Sliding bearings function similarly. All bearings accommodate rotation of the ends of the span when the span or spans deflect under loading. Also, all bearings transfer transverse wind forces from the superstructure to the substructure of the bridge.

Depending on the span of the bridge, bearings can vary from simple steel plates curved on their undersides, one of which slides, to large cast-steel devices with a rocker, or nest of cylindrical rollers at the expansion bearing.

Expansion bearings are one of the most troublesome parts of the bridge as they are exposed to deterioration from moisture and debris sifting down from expansion openings in the bridge deck. In fact, a few single- and multiple-stringer bridges have been built experimentally without bearings, depending upon the restraint of the bridge abutments and the reversed stress induced in the superstructure to substitute for allowed expansion.

Also, since the mid-1960s bearings known as elastomeric bearings have been used for spans up to about 100 ft (30 m). These are blocks of resilient synthetic rubber which deform to accommodate the expansion and rotational forces.

Movable Bridges

Modern movable bridges are either bascule, vertical lift, or swing; with few exceptions, they span waterways. They are said to be closed when they are set for the traffic they carry, and open when set to permit marine traffic to pass through the waterway they cross.

Both bascule and vertical-lift bridges operate well and reliably. Sometimes the bascule is chosen because its appearance may be pleasing and creates

Fig. 6. Stanley Stroffolino Bridge in Norwalk, Connecticut. (*Connecticut Department of Transportation and Hardesty & Hanover*)

less of a visual impact than do the towers and ropes of vertical-lift bridges.

Swing bridges are now considered almost obsolete because the center pier, on which the span rotates, occupies the portion of the waterway that is most desirable from the standpoint of mariners. However, one feature of a swing bridge, which dictates its use near airports, is that it does not encroach on flight paths as would the towers of lift bridges or the raised leaves of bascule bridges.

Bascule, swing, and lift bridges may be of either stringer, girder, or truss construction, depending upon the length of their span.

Other types of movable spans, such as the retractable, are generally obsolete.

Bascule and swing bridges provide unlimited vertical clearance in the open position, whereas the vertical clearance of a lift bridge is limited by its design.

Bascule bridge. The bascule bridge consists primarily of a cantilever span, which may be either a truss or a plate girder, extending across the channel (**Fig. 6**). This type is generally chosen for spans up to about 175 ft (53 m) for highway use. Because of the large deflection of the cantilevered leaves of the double-leaf bascule, which is excessive under railway loadings and intolerable to railroad operation, bascule spans for railway usage are exclusively single-leaf bridges with maximum spans of about 250 ft (76 m).

Bascule bridges rotate about a horizontal axis parallel with the waterway. The portion of the bridge on the land side of the axis, carrying a counterweight to ease the mechanical effort of moving the bridge, drops downward, while the forward part of the leaf opens up over the channel much like the action of a playground seesaw. Bascule bridges may be either single-leaf, where the entire leaf rotates over the waterway about a single axis on one side of the waterway, or double-leaf, where two leaves over the waterway rotate about two different axes on opposite sides of the waterway. The two leaves of double-leaf bascule bridges are locked together where they meet when the bridge is closed. If the bridge actually rotates about an axis, it is called a trunnion-type bascule. If it rolls back on a track, it is called a rolling lift span.

Vertical-lift bridge. The vertical-lift bridge has a span similar to that of a fixed bridge, and is lifted by steel ropes running over large sheaves at the tops of its towers to the counterweights, which fall as the lift span rises and rise as it falls. If the bridge is operated by machinery on each tower, it is known as a tower drive. If it is driven by machinery located on the lift span, it is known as a span drive. The 585-ft (178-m) span of the lift bridge over the Arthur Kill, an arm of New York harbor, is the longest of this type in the world (Fig. 4d). Another example of a vertical-lift bridge is shown in **Fig. 7**.

Swing bridge. Swing bridges rotate about a vertical axis on a pier, called the pivot pier, in the waterway (Fig. 4d). There are three general classes of swing bridges: the rim-bearing, the center-bearing, and the combined rim-bearing and center-bearing. A rim-bearing bridge is carried on a cylindrical girder on rollers, and a center-bearing on a single large bearing at the center of rotation. Swing bridges have been classified also as to the character of their main girders—that is, plate girder swing spans or truss swing spans.

Machinery. Almost all modern movable bridges are driven by electric motors which operate gear trains that convert the high-speed low-torque output of the motor to a low-speed high-torque output of the gear train at a pinion, acting on a rack.

Originally, movable bridges were operated by steam engines, and until recently, many still were. At least one former steam-operated bridge was operated for many years by compressed air driving the old steam engine. A very few bridges have been operated hydraulically. Some small bridges are operated by hand power. Provisions are still made on most movable bridges to operate by hand power in the event of power failure or malfunction of the bridge's electrical controls.

Machinery for early movable bridges consisted of simple custom-made components produced by the numerous small foundries, forge shops, and machine shops. Such components consisted of cast and roughcut gears of various tooth profiles, babbitt and bronze bushed bearings, custom-designed mounts for individual bearings, and common frames for the mounting of multiple bearings for open sets of reduction gears and various combination drive assemblies (**Fig. 8**). After World War II, a wide variety of standardized gear reducers, shaft bearings, and other machinery components suitable for use on bridge drives became available (**Fig. 9**). These components have generally replaced the custom-made components previously used.

Welded components have replaced cast components. Speed-reducer housings are essentially all

Fig. 7. Stratford Avenue Bridge in Bridgeport, Connecticut. (*Connecticut Department of Transportation and Hardesty & Hanover*)

Fig. 8. Exposed gear reductions on an early bascule bridge.

Fig. 9. Enclosed gear reducers on a later bascule bridge. (*Earle Gear and Machine Co.*)

welded. Even the huge sheaves for vertical-lift bridges are commonly manufactured as weldments instead of castings.

Electrical equipment. Except on the simplest small movable bridges, the electrical control of a movable bridge is so interlocked that the bridge cannot be moved until a series of prior operations have been made in correct order. Thus, on a highway bridge, first the traffic lights must be turned to red, then a set of traffic gates lowered, next the barrier gates set, and finally the locks or wedges pulled before the bridge can be moved.

The movable span generally can be completely opened or closed in from 1 to 2 min. However, the prior operations, particularly closing the bridge to traffic and making sure that the bridge is cleared of all vehicles between traffic gates, may run the cycle of operation up to 15 min or longer, depending upon the speed of passage through the span of the vessel for which the bridge has opened.

The drive systems on movable bridges have progressed from the early simpler forms of technology to the solid-state control devices permitting pushbutton operation.

Design

Bridges are designed according to the laws of physics pertaining to statics. The primary members of bridges act in tension, compression, shear, or bending, or in combinations of these. Secondary members act in the same fashion, sometimes participating in carrying the principal loads, especially if failure of any primary members should occur. Redundancy, so that failure of a single member or part of a member will not cause immediate collapse of the bridge, is now recognized as a desirable feature of design, particularly since collapse of the eyebar suspension bridge across the Ohio River at Point Pleasant, West Virginia, in 1967.

Modern design of bridges follows standards established by their principal users, the state highway or transportation departments and the railroads. In the United States, these standards are those of the American Association of State Highway and Transportation Officials and the American Railway Engineering Association, respectively. These specifications are developments of those for bridge design formulated by the early bridge engineers. While they are advisory, they are generally followed, albeit at times with modifications. Other countries have similar specifications.

The traffic load, called live load, is given in these specifications. It depends on the service to which the bridge will be subjected. The highway loadings are in terms of a simulated conventional truck or, for long spans, a uniform load with a roving concentrated load representing a line of average traffic. Railroad loadings are a simulated conventional locomotive load followed by a uniform load representing loaded freight cars. In both cases, in design, the live loads are positioned to give maximum load in the member being designed. In addition, dead load, the structure's own weight, and loads from impact, wind, temperature changes, ice, traction or braking of traffic, earthquake, and, in the case of highway bridges, pedestrians are specified. Allowable stresses and limiting deflections, too, are specified.

Other specifications followed in the design and construction of bridges include those of the American Society for Testing and Materials, the American Welding Society, and the American Institute of Steel Construction, and the construction specifications of the individual owners, and special specifications, when no other covers the situation. *See* STRUCTURAL DESIGN.

Vibration

Bridges are generally considered to be statically loaded structures under their own dead load, with dynamic loadings from the live load and from the wind.

Vibrations of bridges or individual components of a bridge occur when a resonant frequency of the bridge or a component is excited by one or more of the applied dynamic loadings. Excitation from live loads is more apt to happen on bridges carrying rail traffic than on those carrying highway traffic because of the uniform spacing of railroad cars. Excitation from wind is caused by the repeated formation of eddies or vortices as the wind travels past nonstreamlined members. Such aerodynamically induced vibrations caused the failure of the Tacoma Narrows Bridge in the state of Washington in 1941. A similar failure is recorded for a suspension bridge over the Ohio River at Wheeling, West Virginia, in 1854. In both cases, the formation of vortices built up as the torsional movements of the deck increased, ultimately leading to failure. Long, thin, H-shaped truss members have failed from similar wind-induced torsional vibrations. Wind velocities necessary to excite such vibrations need not be excessively high. The Tacoma Narrows Bridge failed under a 40 mi/h (18 m/s) wind, less than half the equivalent static wind load for which it was designed, and less than 20% of the load which would have caused structural distress.

Light lateral bracing on many spans will vibrate under the passage of live load.

Sufficient data exist on aerodynamically induced vibration to predict the possibility of its occurrence and thus modify the design when necessary to prevent serious problems.

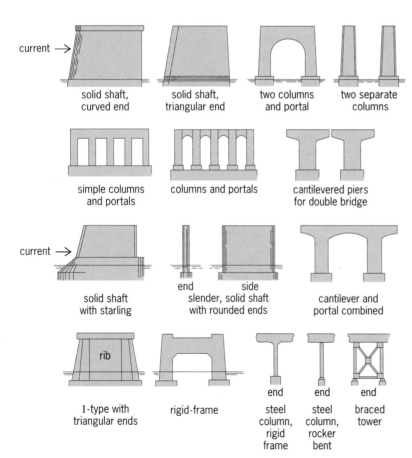

Fig. 10. General shapes of some piers for small bridges. (*After C. W. Dunham, Foundations of Structures, McGraw-Hill, 2d ed., 1962*)

current →

solid shaft, curved end   solid shaft, triangular end   two columns and portal   two separate columns

simple columns and portals   columns and portals   cantilevered piers for double bridge

current →

solid shaft with starling   end   side   slender, solid shaft with rounded ends   cantilever and portal combined

rib   I-type with triangular ends   rigid-frame   end   steel column, rigid frame   end   steel column, rocker bent   end   braced tower

Substructure

Bridge substructure consists of those elements that support the trusses, girders, stringers, floorbeams, and decks of the bridge superstructure. Piers and abutments are the primary bridge substructure elements. Other types of substructure, such as skewbacks for arch bridges, pile bents for trestles, and various forms of support wall, are also commonly used for specific applications.

The type of substructure provided for a bridge is greatly affected by the conditions of the site. Studies must be made on topography, stream currents, floating drift and ice, seismic potential, wind, and soil conditions. Forces and loads encountered in the design of substructure elements include dead load, live load, impact loads, braking forces, earth pressure, buoyancy, wind forces, centrifugal forces, earthquake loads, stream flow, and ice pressure.

Both piers and abutments are generally supported on either spread footings or pile footings. A spread footing is usually a concrete pad large enough in area to transmit all superimposed loads and forces directly to the soil on which it is founded. The size of the spread footing is related to the bearing capacity of the soil on which it rests and the external forces on the substructure which will be transmitted to the spread footing.

A pile footing is usually a large concrete block supported on piles, so that the superimposed substructure loads and forces are transmitted to the support piles through the footing. The footing piles are used primarily to transmit loads through soil formations having poor supporting properties into or onto formations that are capable of supporting the loads. Piles may be point-bearing or friction types or the two in combination, and they may be timber, steel, precast concrete, cast-in-place concrete, or prestressed concrete. They may be driven by the use of a pile driver equipped with a hammer; they may be augered, jetted or prebored, or predrilled and cast-in-place. *See* FOUNDATIONS.

Bridge piers. Bridge piers are the intermediate support systems of bridges and viaducts. They may be located in water or on dry land. When located in water, piers may be subjected to scour by current and collision by vessels. Bridge piers support the superstructure and must carry dead loads and live loads, and withstand braking forces and other induced forces peculiar to the location of the pier, such as wind, ice, earthquake, and stream flow. A major consideration in pier design is stability and the ability to support all loads without appreciable settlement.

The shape, type, and location of piers are based on many factors; the major ones are horizontal and vertical clearance requirements, subsurface conditions, architectural and esthetic considerations, political and urban planning factors, traffic, and cost.

The most common pier shapes are solid shafts, multiple columns and portal, two columns and portal, separate columns, T or hammerhead, and cantilever. There are many variations of these pier shapes, which are constructed using concrete, steel, or wood (**Fig. 10**). A pier should have sufficient horizontal area at its top to receive the superstructure bearings. Architecturally, it should give the appearance of strength; it should not look weak and flimsy, although calculations may have shown the design to be adequate.

Piers in water are sometimes faced with stone, steel, or other protective devices below the high-water line to protect the pier from scour, ice, and other floating matter. At spans over navigable waterways, the piers of the channel span are provided with resilient timber fenders and clusters of timber piles for the protection of the piers and vessels.

Abutments. The abutments of a bridge are the substructure elements that support the ends of a bridge (**Fig. 11**). Bridge abutments are generally constructed of concrete or masonry and are designed to be pleasing esthetically as well as architecturally and functionally sound. Major loads to which abutments are subjected are dead loads, live loads, braking forces, ice, wind, earthquake, stream flow, and earth pressure. The last is applied at the rear of the abutment wall.

An abutment is generally composed of a footing, a wall with a bridge seat supporting the superstructure bearings, and a backwall to retain the earth. Abutments may have wingwalls to retain the earth of the approach fill to the bridge. Proper drainage behind abutment walls is essential to avoid increasing the lateral pressure forces.

Skewbacks. A skewback is a common expression for an abutment for an arch; it is practically nothing more than an inclined footing that receives the thrust from the arch superstructure (Fig. 11).

A skewback differs from common abutments in the type and direction of forces that are applied to it. The horizontal component of an arch reaction is usually very large and exceeds the vertical component.

The large thrusts which are supported by skewbacks require good foundations. The ideal foundations are rock gorges which have strong, sound, and suitably sloping rock.

In general, a skewback for a fixed arch must provide practically no yielding. Some hinged arches, which are statically determinate structures, can sustain slight yield of the foundation. Skewbacks for these may be supported on piles or on spread footings on earth.

Caissons. A caisson is a boxlike structure, round or rectangular, which is sunk from the surface of either land or water to the desired depth as excavation proceeds inside or under it. It is an aid in making excavations for bridge piers or abutments and remains in place as part of the permanent structure.

The most common types are open caissons, which have no top or bottom. Pneumatic caissons have permanent or temporary tops and are so arranged that people can work in the compressed air trapped under the structure.

An innovation in caissons was used for the Tappan Zee Bridge, which carries the New York State Thruway across the Hudson River 13 mi (22 km) north of New York City. Here eight buoyant precast

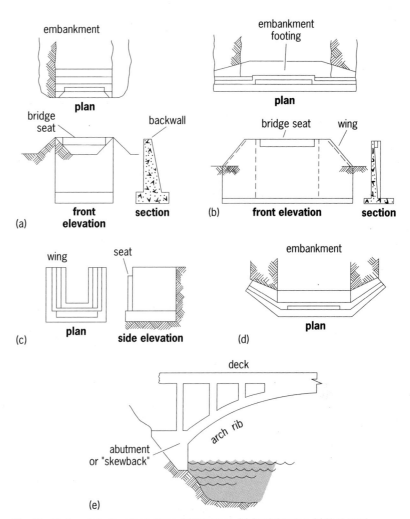

Fig. 11. Abutment designs for bridges. (*a*) Wingless. (*b*) Straight wing. (*c*) U-shaped. (*d*) Beveled wing. (*e*) Abutment for arch bridge.

concrete box caissons reduce the structure's dead load on supporting piles by 70%. The buoyant effect is maintained by keeping the boxes dewatered. Each of the two 15,000-ton (13,600-metric-ton) caissons supporting the main piers measures 100 ft (30 m) by 190 ft (58 m) and 40 ft (12 m) high.

Generally, the ultimate purpose of caisson construction is to reach a bearing stratum which will carry the load of supporting piers and abutments. *See* CAISSON FOUNDATION.

Cofferdam. A cofferdam, generally, is an enclosed temporary structure used to protect an excavation against lateral earth pressure or water pressure during construction. The material within the confines of the cofferdam is removed to allow the construction of piers and abutments below ground or water level.

In constructing cofferdams to counterbalance the upward pressure which may exist at the bottom of the caissons or cofferdams, a concrete seal, also known as tremie seal, is placed prior to dewatering. Concrete is placed in water using vertical pipes known as tremies. These pipes are continually filled with concrete. The bottom of the pipe is submerged in the plastic concrete while the concrete is poured through a funnellike top. During the pour, the tremie pipe is pounded, vibrated, and raised and lowered to increase the hydraulic head of the concrete in the tube and to cause the concrete to flow. The depth of the tremie concrete pour is a function of the upward pressure encountered after dewatering. *See* COFFERDAM.

Repair and Rehabilitation

It is imperative that bridges are structurally able to carry the traffic for which they are intended. Consequently, they must be inspected regularly for any defects which may have developed and must be appropiately repaired.

Inspection. A bridge inspection and maintenance program resulted from the 1967 collapse of the U.S. Route 35 highway bridge over the Ohio River between Ohio and West Virginia. Subsequently, a policy for the inspection of highway bridges was developed by the Federal Highway Administration. Initially the program required interim inspections of bridges every 2 years, giving priority to those built before 1935, and in-depth inspections not to exceed 5-year intervals. The first round of inspections of approximately 600,000 highway bridges found that almost half of the nation's bridges were structurally deficient or functionally obsolete.

Bridge inspection entails a close-up examination of all parts of the structure, sometimes called a tactile examination, by a team of structural engineers supervised by a licensed professional engineer. At one time inspection was made by climbing and rigging or scaffolding for access. While the early methods are still used to some extent, special automotive equipment, such as snoopers and cherry pickers, are now employed for quick and easy access below the decks.

After inspection, the condition of a bridge is rated on a sliding scale. If a bridge is rated at the low end of the scale, the bridge may be closed or a load limit established until repairs can be made. If deterioration of primary structural members is found, the bridge is rated as to its load-carrying capacity related to the load-carrying cross-sectional area, known as loss of section, found in those members.

Maintenance. Over time, bridges rust, decay, crumble, fail, grow obsolete, and become functionally inadequate. Some 400,000 bridges in the United States were built prior to 1935. They were designed for vehicles lighter than those used in the 1990s and cannot sustain heavier truck loads without extensive, expensive strengthening. Most highway bridges were designed in compliance with standards developed in the 1950s and 1960s. In the 1950s, bridges were designed to carry a 36-ton (33-metric ton) vehicle. The more recent bridges are designed for 40-ton (36-metric ton) vehicles and more, which is one of the major causes for the rapid deterioration of older bridges designed for lighter loads.

Maintenance of bridges, much of which is developed from the ongoing inspection program, is a priority function. The most common maintenance problems are deterioration of reinforced concrete decks; corrosion of steel caused by salt usage for snow and ice removal; nonfunctioning bridge bearings and drainage; deterioration of substructure elements such as piers, abutments, and walls; damage to bridges by natural causes such as floods and earthquakes; and damage by fire and allision (striking of the bridge by a vessel).

Another common maintenance issue, metal fatigue, results from unforeseen high stresses that eventually cause failure. It occurs particularly in details that are unduly restrained or that have defects. Likewise, when a crack emanating from a defect in a member or a weld (existing, accidentally induced, or developing) reaches a critical length, it will propagate through the member and may cause failure.

Bridge superstructures. An alarming aspect of the condition of bridges is that many deteriorated portions are not readily visible. Hidden problems include the deteriorated structural reinforced concrete bridge slabs covered by wearing surfaces; minute cracks in steel structures, which are possible sources of fatigue failures; and the reduction in cross section of metallic members caused by corrosion.

The major maintenance and safety problem is the deterioration of bridge decks. Three principal defects are usually encountered—cracking, scaling, and spalling. Spalling is the most serious and the most difficult to control. It is usually caused by salt solutions that permeate through small cracks and pores in the concrete and corrode the reinforcing steel, thereby weakening the bond between the steel and the concrete. The weakened deck becomes progressively more susceptible to failure under truck loading.

Repair and rehabilitation of concrete decks usually involves the removal of the deteriorated concrete. Deterioration is determined primarily by deck cores establishing the salt content in the concrete, which affects the concrete strength and the degree of corrosion in the reinforcing steel. Often it is more economical to remove and replace the entire concrete deck. Generally the life of a bridge deck under modern usage is approximately 30 years. Many bridge decks are repaired and protected with epoxy surface coatings or waterproofing materials, covered with an asphalt overlay serving as the wearing course (riding surface). Another repair method is to mill 2–3 in. (5–7.5 cm) off the existing deck and overlay the remaining deck with a high-density concrete through which salt will not penetrate.

Steel repairs of heavily corroded members usually take the form of welding or bolting reinforcing plates to substitute for the deteriorated material. Often complete replacement of the deteriorated member is warranted. Many steel bridges built prior to 1970 had obsolete structural steel details such as intersecting welds, details that have reduced fatigue life, and details that do not provide for the effects of out-of-plane deformations. Repair details for these have been developed in the United States by the Federal Highway Administration (FHWA). All new bridges are designed with these considerations, and many old bridges are being retrofitted to meet the newer standards.

Other areas of bridge superstructure repair involve bridge bearings which must allow for temperature movements, structural rotation, and seismic movements. In the United States the standards for these repairs have been developed by the FHWA and the various state departments of transportation, and they are defined in American Association of State Highway and Transportation Officials (AASHTO). Roadway bridge joints also need constant maintenance and repair. It is important that joints are frequently inspected and repaired or rehabilitated with new expansion material or devices.

Substructure. Piers and abutments are the foundations of the bridge. They may be steel or concrete. Their condition must be ascertained periodically and deterioration repaired. For concrete cracks it is possible to use epoxy inspection for the repair, or the crack can be opened to the first layer of reinforcing steel and new concrete can be bonded to the old. Similar repairs can be accomplished for spalls and other major deterioration. Scour in water piers must be repaired by rebuilding the undermined scoured area and protecting it with large stones (riprap) or a protective skirt (cofferdam). Steel substructure elements need the same degree of repair as superstructure elements. Corroded steel must be repaired through reinforcement or replaced.

E. R. Hardesty; H. W. Fischer; R. W. Christie; B. Haber

Degradation. Many factors can cause bridges to degrade and become structurally deficient and in need of repair. They include environmental factors, deicing salt, steel corrosion, vehicular damage, and special loads, such as earthquakes and wind.

Temperature changes. Two environmental factors that cause significant damage to primarily concrete components in bridges are excessive changes in temperature and freeze-thaw cycles in the presence of moisture. Such damage is aggravated if there was inadequate design for expansion and contraction due to temperature changes. In restrained members that cannot expand or contract to accommodate such changes, additional forces are developed that may cause some members to fail. Extreme temperature changes also alter the properties of some materials. Under very low temperatures, some types of steel become brittle and thus vulnerable to fatigue or repetitive load cycling from truck traffic. In concrete, freeze-thaw cycling in the presence of moisture causes cracks and spalling. Most of the degradation in concrete bridges in the northern United States is due to freeze-thaw cycling combined with corrosion of steel reinforcement.

Corrosion. Steel structures are vulnerable to corrosion, especially in prolonged moisture environments. Corrosion degrades the steel members and reduces their effective area, thus reducing their load capacity. The degree of corrosion depends on the chemical composition of steel, frequency of wetting and drying, and the location of the bridge (near salt water, near polluting plants, and so forth). Use of deicing salts on concrete pavements and bridge decks produces chemical reactions that accelerate the corrosion of reinforcing steel.

Vehicular damage. A significant cause of bridge damage is vehicular impact and fatigue from repeated truck loads. A large number of bridges are damaged by trucks driving under a bridge and hitting its girders or directly impacting other bridge members. Damage from repeated truck traffic loads is most visible in the form of potholes in the bridge deck. However, repeated truck loads also may cause cracking of steel members, especially at joints, a phenomenon known as fatigue.

Special loads. Special loads, such as seismic, wind, and snow, also may produce dramatic degradation of bridge structures. In California or other earthquake-prone regions, seismic damage to bridges has been extensive and dramatic, including the collapse of multiple bridge spans as occurred in the Cypress Freeway in Oakland during the 1989 earthquake. Earthquakes can also cause a severe loss of soil support under bridge abutments and piers, a phenomenon known as liquefaction and illustrated by the collapse of piers in the Kobe, Japan, earthquake in 1995. Wind is a special load that can damage or even collapse bridges, especially of flexible type, such as suspension bridges. Loads generated by wind pressure may produce direct damage and vibration or resonance, which results when the wind excites the bridge or sections of it to produce large oscillations. In 1940, Tacoma Narrows bridge in Washington collapsed due to such resonance. Snow is another special load on bridges. In northern regions of the United States, excessive snow and sleet can accumulate on a bridge, causing overloads and damage to the structure. This is especially true for long-span bridges in regions with heavy snowstorms. *See* EARTHQUAKE; MECHANICAL VIBRATION.

Strengthening. Some bridges need to be strengthened although they have not been damaged and are structurally sound. A bridge may need to be strengthened in order to upgrade its use for heavier truck loads. Many older bridges had been originally designed and built for truck loads of lower magnitude and number than those of today. Another cause for strengthening of bridges is to comply with current design codes. Continuous research on material behavior and effects of loads (such as earthquakes and winds) on bridges generates new knowledge, which translates into changes in codes and specifications that govern the design of bridges. Thus, older bridges may be considered structurally deficient according to new codes so that strengthening becomes necessary. The effect of new codes on the design of bridges is most evident in the earthquake regions of the United States. New data and observations collected in laboratory experimentation and actual seismic events are constantly reflected in new and improved seismic design codes. *See* SEISMIC RISK.

Strengthening techniques (concrete). The strengthening of concrete bridges is generally achieved by replacing the damaged material, incorporating additional structural members, as in external prestressing, or increasing the size and capacity of existing members.

Reinforcing bars. Reinforced concrete members are designed with compressive stresses absorbed by concrete and tensile loads taken by deformed steel bars. Concrete has very low tensile strength; thus, adding steel in the tension zones increases the load capacity of a reinforced concrete member. This strengthening method consists in relieving the stresses from the member, removing concrete cover in the area where new reinforcement will be placed, adding the new steel bars, and finally, placing new concrete. *See* REINFORCED CONCRETE.

Increasing size of members. This technique is similar to the above technique with the difference that not only is new reinforcing steel added but also the overall size of the reinforced concrete section is increased with the addition of new concrete and new steel bars.

External steel plates. Reinforced concrete members, primarily beams, may be strengthened by attaching steel plates to their external surfaces. The basic technique consists of bonding steel plates to the concrete members with epoxy resins. The purpose is to increase the effective steel reinforcement of the reinforced concrete member.

Introducing new members. A reinforced concrete bridge can be strengthened by adding new members to the structure. These new members may be reinforced concrete or steel members. An example is the addition of new girders, beams, or stringers to a bridge deck system. When this strengthening technique is used, it is important to provide adequate details so that the new member will interact effectively within the existing structure.

External prestressing. Prestressing of concrete structures is a technique not only used to strengthen existing structures but also widely used in the construction of new bridges. This technique consists of high-strength steel twisted wire (or tendons) that are tensioned and anchored to the existing concrete members. The tension in the tendons is transferred to the concrete, generating forces and stresses that counteract the effects of applied loads. Existing bridges may be strengthened with this technique by modifying the tension in existing tendons or by introducing new tendons.

Column shells and wrapping. A technique widely used to strengthen bridges in primarily seismic areas consists in externally applying a steel (or composite) shell around the perimeter of columns or piers (**Fig. 12**). Steel shells are molded around the perimeter of columns, and the resulting gap is filled with a grout material. This shell provides additional strength and confinement to the concrete columns and increases the ability of the column to undergo extensive deflections without failure. In addition to steel shells,

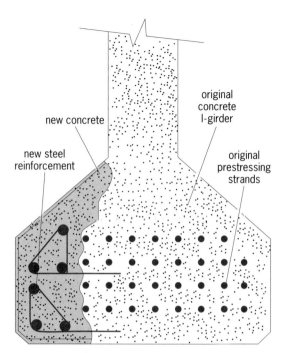

Fig. 13. Repair of a concrete I-girder by replacement of damaged concrete.

a fiber (graphite or glass)–reinforced composite can also be wet-wrapped around the column to achieve the same purpose. *See* COMPOSITE MATERIAL.

Repair techniques (concrete). Numerous repair techniques have evolved for concrete members in both bridges and buildings.

Replacement of damaged concrete. This method involves removing damaged concrete until a sound concrete surface is attained. This can be accomplished without damaging the existing steel reinforcement bars. After the damaged concrete is removed, the exposed surface is cleaned to attain an effective bonding surface, a primer is applied, and then new concrete is placed. Additional reinforcement may also be applied (**Fig. 13**).

Crack repair. Cracks that affect the structural integrity of a concrete member may be repaired by injection of materials such as cement grout (wide cracks) or epoxy resin. Cracks may both reduce the strength of elements and allow penetration of moisture to the steel bars, which will cause accelerated corrosion. Only stationary or nonpropagating cracks can be injected. Propagating cracks may require additional strengthening of the member to stop crack propagation. Crack injection with epoxy or grout does not increase the strength of the member; it may only restore its original integrity.

Corrosion of steel bars. Reinforced concrete members with excessive corrosion of the reinforcing steel bars may be repaired by removing the concrete in the affected area and restoring damaged steel. After exposing the corroded steel, the rust may be removed by sandblasting or wire-brushing. A corrosion protection coating may be applied to the reinforcement before placing the new concrete. If corrosion is too extensive, new steel reinforcement may have to be

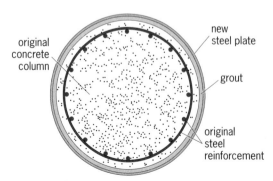

Fig. 12. Reinforcement of a circular reinforced concrete column using a steel shell.

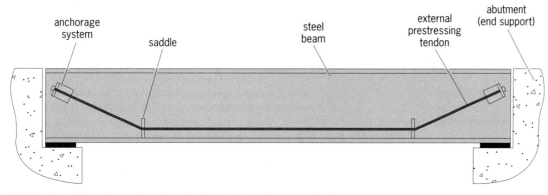

Fig. 14. Application of external prestressing force to strengthen a steel girder.

installed by either welding or mechanical attachment of new steel bars.

Strengthening techniques (steel). Steel bridges are most often strengthened by the addition of new steel members or smaller elements. Steel welding and bolting are well-developed techniques for steel connections. Thus, strengthening of steel bridges is perhaps more defined than for the concrete bridges.

External prestressing. Steel members, such as girders or truss members, can be strengthened by applying an external prestressing force (**Fig. 14**). The technique uses the same concept as described above for concrete members.

Adding supplementary members. Steel bridge structures or components can be strengthened by adding new members to the system at predetermined locations such as new girders, floor beams, or stringers. The new members are attached to the existing structure by connections that are designed to provide an effective load transfer without adversely affecting the integrity of the existing members.

Strengthening with external new plates. Steel girders or beams can be strengthened by increasing their section with the addition of plates or similar elements. An example is the addition of steel plates, usually by welding, to the flanges of an I-beam (**Fig. 15**).

Repair techniques (steel). Numerous techniques have evolved for the repair of steel bridge elements.

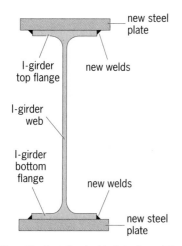

Fig. 15. Strengthening of a steel I-girder by welding new steel plates to the flanges.

Flame straightening. Steel members, such as I-girders or truss members damaged by vehicular impact, can be straightened using the flame straightening technique. Heat is applied at predetermined locations at and near the damaged region. The member is restrained and prevented from deforming in at least one direction while temperature is increased. The member is heated until permanent deformation occurs, and then the member is allowed to cool unrestrained. This will result in a permanent change of shape of the steel member. This process is repeated, if necessary, until the desired shape is attained.

Hot mechanical straightening. In this process, heat is applied to all sides of a bent member. While the member is still hot, it is straightened by applying a predetermined force. This method is used only when the heat will not adversely affect the mechanical properties of the steel.

Cold mechanical straightening. This repair method consists of straightening a bent member by applying a force without the use of heat. Cold mechanical straightening may affect the physical properties of the materials and should be used with care.

Welding. Welding of steel may be used for several types of repairs, such as crack repair, welding replacement segments into place, and addition of new plates. Special attention is required when welding members subjected to tensile loads in order to prevent the formation of cracks due to repetitive loading.

Bolting. Damaged steel members may be repaired by replacing the damaged element with a new piece of steel fastened with high-strength bolts. A combination of bolting and welding methods is sometimes effective for total repair of a member.

Partial replacement. If damage is serious, repair may be impossible, and it may be necessary to partially replace a member. This method consists of removing the damaged element and replacing it with either a welded or a bolted steel insert. This repair method may be utilized where steel members contain excessively wrinkled plates, excessive deformations and bends, tears, and large cracks.

Complete replacement. Excessively damaged members may have to be replaced entirely with a new member. Such replacement requires extensive evaluation of load redistribution while the member is being replaced.

Joseph M. Plecnik; Oscar Henriquez; Andrew Pugel

Bibliography. E. DeLong, *Landmark American Bridges*, 1993; Guidelines for Evaluation and Repair of Damaged Prestressed Concrete Bridge Members, *Nat. Coop. Highway Res. Prog. Rep.*, no. 271 and 280, 1984, 1985; G. A. Hool and W. S. Kinne, *Movable and Long Span Steel Bridges*, 1943; D. Plowden, *Bridges: The Spans of North America*, 1974; V. K. Raina, *Concrete Bridges: Inspection, Repair, Strengthening, Testing and Load Capacity Evaluation*, McGraw-Hill, 1994; S. M. Shaker and R. D. Wakefield, *Modular Steel Bridges*, 1995; J. Toneas, *Bridge Engineering*, 1995; J. A. L. Waddell, *Bridge Engineering*, 1916; C. S. Whitney, *Bridges: A Study in Their Art, Science and Evolution*, 1929.

Bridge circuit

A circuit composed of a source and four impedances that is used in the measurement of a wide range of physical quantities. The bridge circuit is useful in measuring impedances (resistors, capacitors, and inductors) and in converting signals from transducers to voltage or current signals. *See* CAPACITOR; ELECTRICAL IMPEDANCE; INDUCTOR; RESISTOR; TRANSDUCER; WHEATSTONE BRIDGE.

The bridge impedances $Z_n = |Z_n| \angle \theta_n$, where $1 \leq n \leq 4$, are shown in **Fig. 1**. (Here, phasor notation is used: $|Z_n|$ is the amplitude of the impedance Z_n, and θ_n is its phase.) They may be single impedances (resistor, capacitor, or inductor), combinations of impedances, or a transducer with varying impedance. For example, strain gages are resistive transducers whose resistance changes when they are deformed. *See* ALTERNATING-CURRENT CIRCUIT THEORY; STRAIN GAGE.

Bridge circuits are often used with transducers to convert physical quantities (temperature, force displacement, pressure) to electrical quantities (voltage and current). High-accuracy voltmeters and ammeters are relatively inexpensive, and the voltage form of a signal is usually most convenient for information display, control decisions, and data storage.

Another important advantage of the bridge circuit is that it provides greater measurement sensitivity than the transducer. When a strain gage resistance

increases from 120 to 120.10 ohms, the percentage change is small (less than 0.1%). If the same strain gage is placed in a bridge with 120-ohm resistors and a 10-V source, the output read by the meter changes from 0 to 2.082 mV. The circuit has two advantages: the percentage change may be very large (if the initial output was close to zero), and the small output voltage is more easily read. Much more precision is required of a meter to resolve small differences in larger voltages than to resolve small signals near zero.

Balance condition. The bridge circuit is balanced when the output read by the meter is zero. In this condition the voltages on both sides of the meter are identical, as shown in Eqs. (1) and (2), and the

$$V_{12} = \frac{V_S Z_2}{Z_1 + Z_2} \tag{1}$$

$$V_{34} = \frac{V_S Z_4}{Z_3 + Z_4} \tag{2}$$

equality $V_{12} = V_{34}$ implies that the output is zero and that Eqs. (3) and (4), which are known as the balance

$$|Z_1| \cdot |Z_4| = |Z_2| \cdot |Z_3| \tag{3}$$

$$\theta_1 + \theta_4 = \theta_2 + \theta_3 \tag{4}$$

condition, are satisfied. The measurement sensitivity is highest when the bridge circuit is nearly balanced, because the values read on the meter are near zero.

Measurement methods. The bridge is used in two forms. The null adjustment method requires adjustment of a calibrated impedance to balance it. In this case the meter is usually a highly sensitive current-measuring galvanometer. The null adjustment method is often used to measure impedances, with the output read from a dial attached to the adjustable impedance. The deflection method requires an accurate meter in the bridge to measure the deviation from the balance condition. Assuming the meter has good linearity, the deviation (change in $V_{12} - V_{34}$) is proportional to the quantity being measured.

Special forms. There are many special forms of the bridge circuit. When all of the impedances are resistive and the bridge is operated in direct-current mode, it is commonly called a Wheatstone bridge. Other common forms use a current source in place of the voltage source, a sinusoidal source in place of a constant (dc) source, or branch impedances which are specific combinations of single passive impedances, for example, the Hayes bridge and the Owen bridge. The bridge circuit is also used in a variety of electrical applications varying from oscillators (Wien bridge oscillator) to instrumentation amplifier circuits for extremely accurate measurements. *See* INSTRUMENTATION AMPLIFIER; OSCILLATOR; RESISTANCE MEASUREMENT.

Bridge circuits based on transformers. It is possible to replace impedances Z_1 and Z_2 in Fig. 1 with either a voltage or a current transformer to provide instead an equivalent ratio of voltage or current. The remaining two impedances (Z_3 and Z_4) then become the

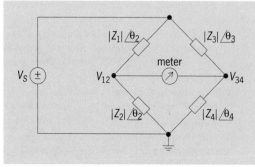

Fig. 1. Bridge circuit with source and impedances.

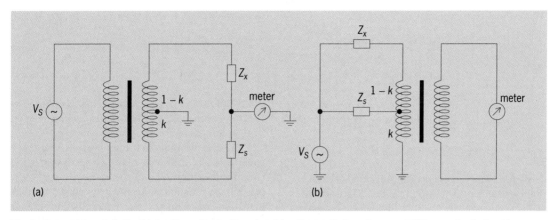

Fig. 2. Comparison of similar types of impedances based on (*a*) voltage ratio transformer and (*b*) current ratio transformer.

unknown (Z_x) and the reference (Z_s) impedances. Knowing the ratio of the voltage or current transformer and the value of Z_s then enables Z_x to be determined. The ratio of the transformer is simply given by the number of turns on the two output arms of the transformer. Although construction of the transformers is time-consuming, their voltage or current ratios can be better than a few parts-per-million accuracy, providing care is taken with the electrostatic and magnetic shielding between the primary and secondary windings of the transformer. These techniques are employed mostly by the national metrology institutes for the highest-accuracy impedance measurements.

Figure 2*a* shows a comparison of the reference impedance with the unknown impedance based on a voltage ratio transformer. The unknown impedance is then given by Eq. (5), where k is the ratio of

$$Z_x = Z_s \left(\frac{k}{1 - k} \right) \tag{5}$$

the transformer windings, and lies in the range $0 \leq k \leq 1$. Similarly, Fig. 2*b* shows the equivalent circuit for comparing the two impedances based on a current transformer. The detector is nulled when equal and opposite flux (ampere-turns) is generated in the current transformer core by the two currents flowing through the impedances. The balance equation in this case also remains identical to that given in Eq. (5). A key difference between the two circuits is the arrangement of the source and detector. In Fig. 2*a* the source is isolated from the main bridge network, whereas the null detector is connected to the junction of the two impedances. In contrast, in Fig. 2*b* the source is directly connected to the main bridge network and the null detector is isolated. Finally, it is important to note that the circuits shown in Fig. 2 operate only with alternating current. *See* TRANSFORMER.   Shakil A. Awan; Kirk D. Peterson

Bibliography. E. Barsoukov and J. R. Macdonald (eds.), *Impedance Spectroscopy: Theory, Experiment, and Applications*, 2d ed., 2005; L. K. Baxter, *Capacitive Sensors: Design and Applications*, 1997; T. G. Beckwith, R. D. Marangoni, and J. H. Lienhard

V, *Mechanical Measurements*, 6th ed., 2007; E. O. Doebelin, *Measurement Systems: Application and Design*, 5th ed., 2003; J. P. Holman, *Experimental Methods for Engineers*, 7th ed., 2000; E. J. Kennedy, *Operational Amplifier Circuits: Theory and Applications*, 1988; A. K. Walton, *Network Analysis and Practice*, 1987.

Brillouin zone

In the propagation of any type of wave motion through a crystal lattice, the frequency is a periodic function of wave vector **k**. This function may be complicated by being multivalued; that is, it may have more than one branch. Discontinuities may also occur. In order to simplify the treatment of wave motion in a crystal, a zone in **k**-space is defined which forms the fundamental periodic region, such that the frequency or energy for a **k** outside this region may be determined from one of those in it. This region is known as the Brillouin zone (sometimes called the first or the central Brillouin zone). It is usually possible to restrict attention to **k** values inside the zone. Discontinuities occur only on the boundaries. If the zone is repeated indefinitely, all **k**-space will be filled. Sometimes it is also convenient to define larger figures with similar properties which are combinations of the first zone and portions of those formed by replication. These are referred to as higher Brillouin zones.

The central Brillouin zone for a particular solid type is a solid which has the same volume as the primitive unit cell in reciprocal space, that is, the space of the reciprocal lattice vectors, and is of such a shape as to be invariant under the symmetry operations of the crystal. *See* CRYSTAL STRUCTURE; CRYSTALLOGRAPHY.

Zone construction. Let $\mathbf{a}_1$, $\mathbf{a}_2$, $\mathbf{a}_3$ be the primitive translation vectors for some crystal lattice. New vectors $\mathbf{b}_i$ with $i = 1, 2, 3$, are defined by Eq. (1), where

$$\mathbf{a}_i \cdot \mathbf{b}_j = 2\pi \delta_{ij} \tag{1}$$

δ_{ij} is unity when $i = j$, and zero for other values of i.

The vectors $\mathbf{b}_i$ are then given by Eqs. (2).

$$\mathbf{b}_1 = \frac{2\pi \mathbf{a}_2 \times \mathbf{a}_3}{\mathbf{a}_1 \cdot \mathbf{a}_2 \times \mathbf{a}_3} \quad \mathbf{b}_2 = \frac{2\pi \mathbf{a}_3 \times \mathbf{a}_1}{\mathbf{a}_1 \cdot \mathbf{a}_2 \times \mathbf{a}_3}$$
$$\mathbf{b}_3 = \frac{2\pi \mathbf{a}_1 \times \mathbf{a}_2}{\mathbf{a}_1 \cdot \mathbf{a}_2 \times \mathbf{a}_3} \tag{2}$$

Now vectors $\mathbf{K}_i$ are defined by Eq. (3), where the

$$\mathbf{K}_i = b_1 \mathbf{b}_1 + b_2 \mathbf{b}_2 + b_3 \mathbf{b}_3 \tag{3}$$

b_i's are arbitrary integers. The subscript i stands for some particular combination of the b. The end points of the vectors $\mathbf{K}_i$ form a lattice of points in reciprocal space. The vectors $\mathbf{K}_i$ have the property that plane waves of the form $e^{i\mathbf{K}_i \cdot \mathbf{r}}$ are periodic in the crystal lattice, since if some $\mathbf{r}' = \mathbf{r} + \mathbf{R}_n$ is considered, where $\mathbf{R}_n$ is a translation vector of the crystal, Eq. (4) holds.

$$e^{i\mathbf{K}_i \cdot \mathbf{r}'} = e^{i\mathbf{K}_i \cdot \mathbf{r}} e^{i\mathbf{K}_i \cdot \mathbf{R}_n} = e^{i\mathbf{K}_i \cdot \mathbf{r}} \tag{4}$$

The last step follows since $\mathbf{K}_i \cdot \mathbf{R}_n$ is an integer times 2π. Consequently, the plane waves $e^{i\mathbf{K} \cdot \mathbf{r}}$ are suitable functions for the Fourier expansion of any function which is periodic in the lattice.

Unit cells can be constructed in the reciprocal space of the lattice of the ends of the vectors $\mathbf{K}_i$, just as is done in the real crystal space. The lines connecting one point with the other lattice sites are drawn, and the planes which are the perpendicular bisectors of these lines are constructed. The smallest enclosed solid figure is the first Brillouin zone. It is the smallest unit cell in the reciprocal lattice which has the symmetry of the entire lattice. Higher Brillouin zones are also formed.

Brillouin zones for the body-centered-cubic, face-centered-cubic, and hexagonal-close-packed lattices are shown in **illus.** *a–c*.

Application to band theory. Each electron wave function in the crystal can be classified according to some $\mathbf{k}$ inside the first Brillouin zone. For if $\mathbf{k}'$ is a vector in reciprocal space whose end point lies outside the zone, then it can be written as Eq. (5), where $\mathbf{k}$

$$\mathbf{k}' = \mathbf{k} + \mathbf{K}_n \tag{5}$$

lies inside the zone and $\mathbf{K}_n$ is a reciprocal lattice vector. According to the Bloch theorem, Eq. (6a) holds.

But since $\mathbf{K}_n \cdot \mathbf{R}_j$ is an integer times 2π, Eq. (6b) is

$$\psi(\mathbf{k}', \mathbf{r} + \mathbf{R}_j) = e^{i\mathbf{k}' \cdot \mathbf{R}_j} \psi(\mathbf{k}', \mathbf{r}) \tag{6a}$$

$$e^{i\mathbf{k}' \cdot \mathbf{R}_j} = e^{i\mathbf{k} \cdot \mathbf{R}_j} e^{i\mathbf{K}_n \cdot \mathbf{R}_j} = e^{i\mathbf{k} \cdot \mathbf{R}_j} \tag{6b}$$

valid. Thus $\mathbf{k}'$ and $\mathbf{k}$ are equivalent in a certain sense. For this reason, it is possible to consider only the first zone in discussing the properties of solids.

A fundamental point in the application of Brillouin zone theory to the study of the properties of solids is that the energy $E(\mathbf{k})$ of the states ψ_k must be a continuous function of $\mathbf{k}$ inside the zone (although it will be multivalued if the reduced zone scheme is employed). Discontinuities can occur only across the faces of the zone. The number of allowed states inside each Brillouin zone can be determined as follows: The number of allowed states per unit volume in the space of the vector $\mathbf{k}$ is $1/(2\pi)^3$ for each spin per unit volume of the crystal, or $2/(2\pi)^3$ altogether. Thus, the number of states in the zone for each atom in the crystal is $2V/(2\pi)^3 N$, where N is the number of atoms of the crystal and V is the volume. A substance which has just enough electrons per atom to fill some zone may be an insulator or semiconductor. If there are not enough electrons to fill a zone, it must be a metallic conductor.

Alkali metals. These metals are body-centered cubic at high temperatures. (Sodium and lithium undergo phase transitions at low temperatures.) The volume of the zone is $2(2\pi/a)^3$, where a is the lattice constant. The number of atoms per unit volume is $2/a^3$ so that the first zone can contain two electrons per atom. However, the atoms possess only one valence electron, so that these metals are good conductors.

Noble metals. Copper, silver, and gold are face-centered cubic metals with one valence electron per atom, and again the zone can hold two electrons per atom. Thus, these also are good conductors. If noble metals were adequately described by a free electron model, the Fermi surface (the surface bounding the occupied volume of reciprocal space) would be a sphere which would approach close to the surface of the zone. It is known, however, that the free electron model is not adequate for electrons near the Fermi surface, and that the Fermi surface touches the Brillouin zone boundary near the extremities of the (111) axes.

Divalent metals. Except for barium and mercury, the divalent metals have either hexagonal close-packed or face-centered cubic structures. The zones hold two valence electrons per atom, and on the basis of simple arguments, it would be expected that these materials should be insulators. However, some of the electrons go over into the next Brillouin zone, leaving pockets of holes behind in the first zone.

Semiconductors and insulators. In diamond, silicon, and germanium, all of which have the diamond structure of two interpenetrating face-centered cubic (fcc) lattices, the Brillouin zone has the same form as for the fcc. It can hold four electrons per atom. Occupied states are separated from higher states by an energy gap, since these materials are semiconductors

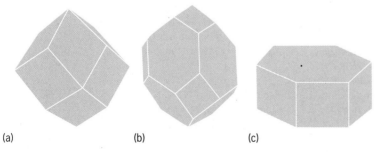

(a)   (b)   (c)

Brillouin zone for (*a*) body-centered-cubic lattice, (*b*) face-centered-cubic lattice, (*c*) hexagonal-close-packed lattice.

or insulators. Graphite, which has a hexagonal layer structure, can be regarded as a semiconductor with a vanishing energy gap. The Brillouin zone in a simple model is full at a temperature of 0 K, but there is no gap along the edges of the zone. In bismuth there is a higher Brillouin zone which holds five electrons per atom. There is a very small overlap of electrons across the faces of the zone, leading to the presence of a small number (about 10^{-5} per atom) of both electrons and holes at 0 K. *See* SEMICONDUCTOR.

Binary alloys. Many of the properties of binary alloys which form substitutional solid solutions can be explained on the hypothesis that the solute contributes its valence electrons to form a composite system whose fundamental parameter is the electron per atom ratio. The electronic structure is assumed to be essentially unaltered. Many changes of the properties, such as the lattice parameter, the concentration at which the various phases appear, and the Hall coefficient, can be explained in terms of overlap or contact of the Fermi surface with the Brillouin zone. *See* ALLOY STRUCTURES; BAND THEORY OF SOLIDS. Joseph Callaway

Bibliography. N. W. Ashcroft and N. D. Mermin, *Solid State Physics*, 2d ed., 2000; W. Hume-Rothery and R. E. Smallman, *The Structure of Metals and Alloys*, 1988; C. Kittel, *Introduction to Solid State Physics*, 7th ed., 1996; M. N. Rudden and J. Wilson, *Elements of Solid State Physics*, 2d ed., 1993.

Brittleness

The catastrophic fracture of a material or structure without a significant amount of prior extension or plastic deformation. The energy absorbed during fracture is highly dependent on whether a material or structure behaves in a brittle or ductile manner. Materials or structures that fracture in a brittle manner exhibit small amounts of plastic deformation and extension. This requires a much lower amount of energy in the fracture process compared to a material or structure that fails in a ductile manner. **Figure 1** shows the effect of a change in test temperature on the energy absorbed during the fracture of some materials, where the energy absorbed during fracture at low temperatures is significantly less than that absorbed at higher temperatures. Materials or structures in the low-temperature regime are failing via brittle fracture. Increasing the test temperature produces a significant increase in the fracture energy, where the materials behave in a much tougher manner and exhibit a more ductile fracture appearance. At intermediate temperatures, a brittle-to-ductile transition is shown. Brittleness and brittle fracture are exhibited by a number of materials, including glass, minerals, some polymers, cast iron, concrete, some refractory metals, most ceramic materials, and a number of different steels tested below their brittle-to-ductile transition temperature.

The fracture surfaces produced during brittle fracture typically exhibit characteristic features related

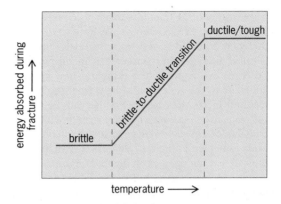

Fig. 1. Energy absorbed during fracture versus temperature. Brittle materials absorb much lower energy during fracture than ductile or tough materials. Some materials exhibit a brittle-to-ductile transition that depends on the test temperature.

to the fracture mechanisms that operate at a microscopic level. Brittle fracture that occurs in a crystalline metal (for example, iron) or alloy (for example, steel) typically occurs on a crystal plane of low atomic density, called the cleavage fracture plane. This fracture process occurs through the grains in the material, and is called transgranular cleavage fracture. This produces characteristic features that can be easily identified using a scanning electron microscope (SEM). An SEM can provide images with high resolution and high depth of field for magnifications exceeding 100,000×. An SEM image of a typical transgranular cleavage fracture surface of a steel tested at a temperature below the brittle-to-ductile transition temperature reveals some of these characteristic features (**Fig. 2**). The arrow shows the location of the suspected fracture origin, as all fracture surface features appear to radiate from this one site. Many of the features in Fig. 2 are less than 50 μm, the diameter of a human hair. The general lack of plastic deformation and elongation is reflected in the

Fig. 2. Scanning electron microscope image of a transgranular cleavage fracture surface in a steel tested at a temperature below its brittle-to-ductile transition. The arrow indicates the likely fracture initiation site.

brittle nature of the fracture surface observed at high magnification. Brittle fracture may also occur along the grain boundaries of certain materials, and this is called intergranular fracture. The fracture surface observed by eye will often exhibit a shiny appearance due to the reflection of light from the brittle features. In contrast, a material that fails in a ductile manner will exhibit a fracture surface with large amounts of elongation and plasticity. Ductile fractures examined at high magnification with an SEM typically exhibit dimples on the fracture surface and a dull gray appearance when viewed by eye. This dull gray appearance results from the diffraction of the light by the microscopic fracture features. In general, brittle fracture can be produced in susceptible materials by testing at low temperatures, at high (for example, impact) loading rates, and in the presence of stress concentrators such as notches, cracks, and defects. One example of this type of failure in a steel structure is the catastrophic fracture and sinking of the *Titanic* in 1912. *See* EMBRITTLEMENT; PLASTIC DEFORMATION OF METAL; PLASTICITY; SCANNING ELECTRON MICROSCOPE; STEEL; STRESS AND STRAIN.

John J. Lewandowski

Bibliography. *ASM Handbook*, vol. 19: *Fracture and Fatigue*, ASM International, 1996; R.W. Hertzberg, *Deformation and Fracture Mechanics of Engineering Materials*, 4th ed., Wiley, 1996; B. R. Lawn, *Fracture of Brittle Solids*, 2d ed., Cambridge University Press, 1993.

Broccoli

A cool-season biennial crucifer, *Brassica oleracea* var. *italica*, of Mediterranean origin, belonging to the plant order Papaverales. Broccoli is grown for its thick branching flower stalks which terminate in clusters of loose green flower buds (see **illus.**). Stalks and buds are cooked as a vegetable or may be processed in either canned or frozen form. Cultural practices for broccoli are similar to those used for cabbage. *See* CABBAGE; PAPAVERALES.

New varieties (cultivars) with greater disease re-

Flower buds of broccoli. (*Asgrow Seed Co., Subsidiary of the Upjohn Co.*)

sistance and higher quality are continually being developed. Broccoli is slightly tolerant of acid soils and has high requirements for boron and molybdenum. Terminal and axillary clusters are cut 80–140 days after planting. California and Texas are important broccoli-producing states.

H. John Carew

Bromegrass

A common name designating a number of grasses found in the North Temperate Zone that produce highly palatable and nutritious forage. Of these, smooth bromegrass (*Bromus inermis*) is the most important (see **illus.**). This species was introduced

Smooth bromegrass (*Bromus inermis*). (*a*) Entire plant. (*b*) Fruit. (*c*) Inflorescence.

to the United States during the 1880s from central Europe and Russia, where it is native. It proved to be well adapted to regions of cold winters and limited rainfall. Although first widely used in the eastern Great Plains and western Corn Belt regions, improved strains are now grown extensively for hay and rotation pastures north of the Mason-Dixon line, from the Plains to the Atlantic. Smooth bromegrass is a long-lived perennial, spreads by underground creeping stems, and is fairly deep rooted and drought-tolerant. Top growth is 2–4 ft (0.6–1.2 m) tall and is used for hay or pasture. Regional strains are available for Canada and the northern two-thirds of the United States. Bromegrass tolerates a wide range of soil conditions, but responds well to higher levels of fertility. Where the moisture supply is adequate, smooth bromegrass grows well in mixtures with alfalfa and red clover. The seeds of bromegrass are large, light, and chaffy, and successful planting requires special seeders. *See* CYPERALES; GRASS CROPS.

Howard B. Sprague

Bromeliales

An order of flowering plants, division Magnoliophyta (Angiospermae) in the subclass Zingiberidae of the class Liliopsida (monocotyledons). It consists of the single family Bromeliaceae, with about 45 genera and 2000 species, occurring chiefly in tropical and subtropical America. They are firm-leaved, terrestrial xerophytes (adapted structurally to live and grow with a limited water supply), or very often epiphytes (living on other plants nonparasitically), with six stamens and regular or somewhat irregular flowers that usually have septal nectaries and an inferior ovary. The order has often been associated with several related ones in a larger order, Farinosae, marked by its starchy endosperm. Spanish moss (*Tillandsia*) and the cultivated pineapple (*Ananas*) are familiar members of the Bromeliales, and many others attract attention as houseplants. *See* FLOWER; LILIOPSIDA; MAGNOLIOPHYTA; PIÑA; PINEAPPLE; PLANT KINGDOM; SECRETORY STRUCTURES (PLANT).

Arthur Cronquist; T. M. Barkley

Bromine

A chemical element, Br, atomic number 35, atomic weight 79.909, which normally exists as Br$_2$, a dark-red, low-boiling but high-density liquid of intensely irritating odor. This is the only nonmetallic element that is liquid at normal temperature and pressure. Bromine is very reactive chemically; one of the halogen group of elements, it has properties intermediate between those of chlorine and iodine. *See* HALOGEN ELEMENTS; PERIODIC TABLE.

The most stable valence states of bromine in its salts are −1 and +5, although +1, +3, and +7 are known. Within wide limits of temperature and pressure, molecules of the liquid and vapor are diatomic, Br$_2$, with a formula weight of 159.818. There are two stable isotopes (^{79}Br and ^{81}Br) that occur naturally in nearly equal proportion, so that the atomic weight is

79.909. A number of radioisotopes are also known.

The solubility of bromine in water at 20°C (68°F) is 3.38 g/100 g (3.38 oz/100 oz) solution, but its solubility is increased tremendously in the presence of its salts and in hydrobromic acid. The ability of this inorganic element to dissolve in organic solvents is of considerable importance in its reactions. The **table** summarizes the physical properties of bromine.

Although it is estimated that from 10^{15} to 10^{16} tons of bromine are contained in the Earth's crust, the element is widely distributed and found only in low concentrations in the form of its salts. The bulk of the recoverable bromine, however, is found in the hydrosphere. Sea water contains an average of 65 parts per million (ppm) of bromine. The other major sources of bromine in the United States are underground brines and salt lakes, with commercial production in Michigan, Arkansas, and California.

While many inorganic bromides have found industrial use, the organic bromides have even wider application. Because of the ease of reaction of bromine with organic compounds and the ease of its subsequent removal or replacement, organic bromides have been much studied and used as chemical intermediates. In addition, any of the bromine reactions are so clean-cut that they can be used for the study of reaction mechanisms without complication of side reactions. The ability of bromine to add into unusual places on organic molecules has added to its value as a research tool.

Bromine and its compounds have found acceptance as disinfection and sanitizing agents in swimming pools and potable water. Certain bromine-containing compounds are safer to use than the analogous chlorine compounds due to certain persistent residuals found in the chlorine-containing materials. Other bromine chemicals are used as a working fluid in gages, as hydraulic fluids, as chemical intermediates in the manufacture of organic dyes, in storage batteries, and in explosion-suppressant and fire-extinguishing systems. Bromine compounds, because of their density, also find use in the gradation

Physical properties of bromine

Property	Value
Flash point	None
Fire point	None
Freezing point, °C	−7.27
Density, 20°C	3.1226
Pounds per gallon, 25°C	25.8
Boiling point, 760 mm Hg, °C	58.8
Refractive index, 20°C	1.6083
Latent heat of fusion, cal/g	15.8
Latent heat of vaporization, cal/g, bp	44.9
Vapor density, g/liter, standard conditions (0°C, 1 atm)	7.139
Viscosity, centistokes, 20°C	0.314
Surface tension, dynes/cm, 20°C	49.5
30°C	47.3
40°C	45.2
Dielectric constant, 10^5 freq, 25°C	3.33
Compressibility, vapors, 25°C	0.998

Thermodynamic data, cal/(mole K)

	T,K	Entropy	Heat capacity
Solid	265.9	24.786	14.732
Liquid	265.9	34.290	18.579

of coal and other minerals where separations are effected by density gradients. The versatility of bromine compounds is illustrated by the commercial use of over 100 compounds that contain bromine.

Bromine is almost instantaneously injurious to the skin, and it is difficult to remove quickly enough to prevent a painful burn that heals slowly. Bromine vapor is extremely toxic, but its odor gives good warning; it is difficult to remain in an area of sufficient concentration to be permanently damaging. Bromine can be handled safely, but the recommendations of the manufacturers should be respected.

Randy C. Stauffer

Bibliography. F. A. Cotton et al., *Advanced Inorganic Chemistry*, 6th ed., Wiley-Interscience, 1999; D. Price, B. Iddon, and B. J. Wakefield (eds.), *Bromine Compounds: Chemistry and Applications*, 1988; D. F. Shriver and P. W. Atkins, *Inorganic Chemistry*, 3d ed., 1999.

Bronze

Usually an alloy of copper and tin. Bronze is used in bearings, bushings, gears, valves, and other fittings both for water and steam. Lead, zinc, silver, and other metals are added for special-purpose bronzes. Tin bronze, including statuary bronze, contains 2–20% tin; bell metal 15–25%; and speculum metal up to 33%. Gun metal contains 8–10% tin plus 2–4% zinc.

The properties of bronze depend on its composition and working. Phosphor bronze is tin bronze hardened and strengthened with traces of phosphorus; it is used for fine tubing, wire springs, and machine parts. Lead bronze may contain up to 30% lead; it is used for cast parts such as low-pressure valves and fittings. Manganese bronze with 0.5–5% manganese plus other metals, but often no tin, has high strength. Aluminum bronze also contains no tin; its mechanical properties are superior to those of tin bronze, but it is difficult to cast. Silicon bronze, with up to 3% silicon, casts well and can be worked hot or cold by rolling, forging, and similar methods. Beryllium bronze (also called beryllium copper) has about 2% beryllium and no tin. The alloy is hard and strong and can be further hardened and strengthened by precipitation hardening; it is one of the few copper alloys that responds to heat treatment, approaching three times the strength of structural steel.

Tin bronze is harder, stronger in compression, and more resistant to corrosion than the brasses. Bronze that will not be exposed to extremes of weather can be protected from corrosion by warming it to slightly over 212°F (100°C) in an oxygen atmosphere. A thin layer of oxide or patina forms to prevent further oxidation. A patina may be formed on art objects by exposure first to acid fumes and then drying as above. While still warm, the object can be further protected by a spray of wax in a solvent.

For bearings, sintered bronze is compacted from 10% tin, up to 2% graphite, and the balance by weight of copper. The aggregate is formed under pressure at a temperature below the melting point of its constituents but high enough to reduce their oxides. After forming, a bearing is repressed or sized and impregnated with oil, the pores retaining the lubricant until needed. In place of copper, alpha-bronze powder may be used; zinc may replace some of the tin. At forming temperatures below 1290°F (700°C), properties depend primarily on compacting pressure. At higher temperatures, properties depend first on temperature, although heat treatment beyond 30 min has minor influence. *See* ALLOY; ANTIFRICTION BEARING; BELL; COPPER; COPPER ALLOYS; TIN; TIN ALLOYS.

Frank H. Rockett

Brown dwarf

A starlike body whose mass is too small to sustain nuclear fusion reactions in its core. All stars, including the Sun, shine because they engage in nuclear fusion in their hot and dense cores. In the early 1960s, S. S. Kumar noted that, if they existed, stars with mass less than 8% that of the Sun would not have the high temperatures in their cores necessary to sustain nuclear fusion reactions. These objects, called brown dwarfs, would not truly be normal stars because their lack of nuclear fusion would inhibit their ability to shine. Indeed, brown dwarfs would grow dimmer as they aged. At even lower masses are the planets, such as Earth and Jupiter (which is approximately 0.1% the mass of the Sun). The distinction between planets and brown dwarfs has been debated; as of early 2006, no consensus on the scientific definition of the word "planet" had been reached. Some scientists maintained that planets ought to be distinguished from brown dwarfs by the way they form. Planets form in disks of dust and gas swirling about nascent stars, while brown dwarfs are thought to form like stars, out of the gravitational collapse of a huge cloud of gas in space. However, a basic physical distinction is that brown dwarfs are hot enough when they are young to host evanescent nuclear reactions while planets never host any fusion reactions. *See* PLANET; STAR; STELLAR EVOLUTION.

Largely because they did not know what these objects would look like, astronomers agreed in the 1970s to call them brown dwarfs. Brown is a mixture of many colors and represents the lack of agreement on the dwarf's appearance. Other proposed names include black dwarfs, infrared dwarfs, failed stars, super-Jupiters, and substellar objects.

Since the 1960s, brown dwarfs have commanded varying levels of importance in astronomical research. They have been invoked to explain the dark-matter problem of cosmology, while many astronomers believed that brown dwarfs did not exist because none had been found. In 1995, the first definitive detection of a cool brown dwarf and also the detection of three young brown dwarfs were announced. By the end of 2003, over 100 of varying ages and masses had been found, and two new spectral classes had been added to the stellar classification scheme for the first time in over 50 years. Brown dwarf research has become a mature and rich subfield of astrophysics. *See* COSMOLOGY.

Properties. Calculations by several research groups have established that the lowest-mass star (8% the mass of the Sun) will shine with a luminosity of about 10^{-4} times the luminosity of the Sun. (Luminosity here means the energy emitted per unit of time.) While young brown dwarfs can have luminosities larger than this value, they eventually cool to much smaller ranges of brilliance. These calculations also show that all brown dwarfs have essentially the same radius, about 10% that of the Sun. This is also approximately the radius of Jupiter. *See* RED DWARF STAR.

Young, hot brown dwarfs (L dwarfs). Because young brown dwarfs are hot and even more luminous than the oldest, lowest-mass stars, they are very difficult to distinguish from such stars. However, an important diagnostic exists. The fragile element lithium is transmuted in stars by high-temperature fusion reactions that are absent in most brown dwarfs' cores. Indeed, brown dwarfs below about 6% the mass of the Sun never transmute any lithium. Those between 6 and 8% the mass of the Sun transmute some or even all of the lithium because they can host the stellar nuclear fusion reactions, but only for the first 50–250 million years of their lives. All this suggests that although the youngest brown dwarfs might look identical to low-mass stars they will exhibit signs of lithium, which stars will not.

Two searches for brown dwarfs in the Pleiades, one of the youngest nearby star clusters, were undertaken in 1995. Sensitive spectroscopic observations with the Keck Telescope in Hawaii revealed for the first time the telltale features of lithium in three low-luminosity objects. These objects, the first young brown dwarfs identified, were called PPL 15, Teide 1, and Calar 3. *See* PLEIADES; TELESCOPE.

Since these discoveries, many more brown dwarfs have been identified in the Pleiades, in other star clusters, and in interstellar space. The majority of these brown dwarfs have been found due to improved astronomical imaging and spectroscopy technology, in particular, large-scale surveys of the sky in the infrared wavelengths. *See* ASTRONOMICAL SPECTROSCOPY; INFRARED ASTRONOMY.

Brown dwarfs slightly older than those found with the lithium criterion are now classified as L dwarfs, a spectral class lower in temperature than the M class, which is reserved for the lowest-temperature stars. Many examples of L dwarfs exist. The letter L has no particular significance except that, when the class was specified, L and T were among the few letters of the alphabet that were not already in use to designate classes of starlike celestial objects. The L class is generally characterized by temperatures below 1800 K (2780°F) and above 1400 K (2060°F). Spectra of L dwarfs reveal the complex chemistry present in these brown-dwarf atmospheres. Many molecules, such as chromium hydride, carbon monoxide, carbon dioxide, and water, are clearly identifiable.

L dwarfs exist in great abundance in the Milky Way Galaxy and may be twice as numerous as the number of stars. However, because they are not very massive, the population of L dwarfs in the galaxy cannot account for the "missing" or dark matter. *See* COSMOLOGY; MILKY WAY GALAXY.

Cool, old brown dwarfs (T dwarfs). In 1995, Tadashi Nakajima and coworkers at the Palomar Observatory, California Institute of Technology, discovered an object in orbit around the nearby star Gliese 229, located only 17 light-years (1.0×10^{14} mi or 1.6×10^{14} km) from the Sun (see **illus.**). With a luminosity of 6×10^{-6} that of the Sun, this object was the first unambiguous discovery of an old brown dwarf, one that had absolutely no similarity to any star. The discovery of Gliese 229B was the result of a systematic survey of nearby stars that used a camera tailored for imaging faint objects next to bright stars.

Gliese 229B has become the prototypical example of the newly invented T spectral class. Dozens of other T dwarfs have now been identified, primarily due to the work of the 2MASS infrared survey of the entire sky and spectroscopic observations

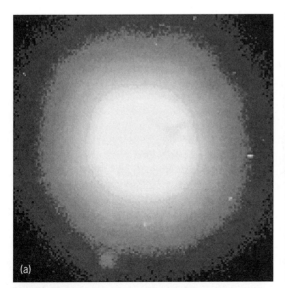

Images of the cool brown dwarf Gliese 229B. In each image, the bright primary star is at the center and the brown dwarf is the faint object near the bottom center. (*a*) Discovery image, taken with the Palomar 60-in. (1.5-m) telescope and an instrument designed to reduce the substantial glare of the nearby star. (*b*) Hubble Space Telescope image.

spearheaded by J. Davy Kirkpatrick and Adam Burgasser. The L dwarfs are believed to evolve into T dwarfs over a time span of around a billion years. The T dwarfs are distinct from the L dwarfs because they have telltale signs of methane in their spectra. The presence of methane in the atmospheres of these brown dwarfs indicates that they must be cooler than about 1200–1400 K (1700–2060°F). T dwarfs as cool as 700 K (800°F) had been identified by the end of 2003.   Ben R. Oppenheimer

Bibliography. A. Burgasser et al., The spectra of T dwarfs, *Astrophys. J.*, 564:421–451, 2002; J. Davy Kirkpatrick et al., Dwarfs cooler than "M": The definition of spectral type "L" using discoveries from the Two Micron All Sky Survey (2MASS), *Astrophys. J.*, 519:802–833, 1999; T. Nakajima et al., Discovery of a cool brown dwarf, *Nature*, 378:463–465, 1995; B. R. Oppenheimer et al., Infrared spectrum of the cool brown dwarf Gl 229B, *Science*, 270:1478–1479, 1995; R. Rebolo, M. R. Zapatero-Osorio, and E. L. Martín, Discovery of a brown dwarf in the Pleiades star cluster, *Nature*, 377:129–131, 1995.

Brownian movement

The irregular motion of a body arising from the thermal motion of the molecules of the material in which the body is immersed. Such a body will of course suffer many collisions with the molecules, which will impart energy and momentum to it. Because, however, there will be fluctuations in the magnitude and direction of the average momentum transferred, the motion of the body will appear irregular and erratic, as shown in the **illustration**.

In principle, this motion exists for any foreign body suspended in gases, liquids, or solids. To observe it, one needs first of all a macroscopically visible body; however, the mass of the body cannot be too large. If its mass is M, one can estimate the root-mean-square velocity $\overline{v}$ by the equipartition law, written as Eq. (1). Here, k is the Boltzmann constant

$$\tfrac{1}{2}M\overline{v^2} = \tfrac{3}{2}kT \tag{1}$$

$$\sqrt{\overline{v^2}} = \sqrt{\frac{3kT}{M}}$$

and T is the absolute temperature. Hence, for a large

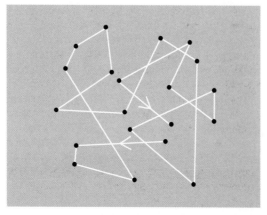

Random brownian movement of a particle.

mass, the velocity becomes small. For example, a 0.01-g mass has at 300 K a root-mean-square velocity of 3.5×10^{-6} cm/s. *See* KINETIC THEORY OF MATTER.

Mirror in a gas. A simple observable example of brownian motion is the motion of a mirror in a gas. If a mirror of moment of inertia I is suspended by a fine fiber, this mirror will execute a simple harmonic motion of natural frequency ω_0. Its mechanical equation of motion is written as Eq. (2), where θ is the angular

$$\frac{d^2\theta}{dt^2} + \omega_0^2\theta = 0 \tag{2}$$

displacement and $\omega = d\theta/dt$ the angular velocity. If this mirror is placed in the gas, the unequal forces on the two sides of it, which are due to the fluctuations in the momentum transferred by the molecules, will cause fluctuations around the harmonic oscillations. After a time, one will have equipartition of energy. For the rotational kinetic energy, one has Eq. (3a). For the rotational potential energy, one has Eq. (3b).

$$\tfrac{1}{2}I\overline{\omega^2} = \tfrac{1}{2}kT \tag{3a}$$

$$\tfrac{1}{2}I\omega_0^2\overline{\theta^2} = \tfrac{1}{2}kT \tag{3b}$$

By careful measurement, relations such as Eqs. (3a) and (3b) may be checked. Brownian motion also yields a limit for the accuracy which may be obtained in a given experiment. *See* HARMONIC MOTION.

Langevin equation. If a small particle is suspended in a liquid, its displacement x in the course of time can be observed. The displacement will of course be erratic, but one can still calculate the average displacements, or root-mean-square displacements, at any time t. It is possible to compare these experimental results with theoretical calculations. If a small body moves through a liquid, it will the usual viscous drag, $-\beta Mv$, where M is the mass, v is the velocity, and β is a numerical coefficient depending on the viscosity. For a sphere of radius R, $M\beta$ has the value given by Stokes' law: $M\beta = 6\pi R\eta$, where η is the coefficient of viscosity. In addition, a fluctuating force $MA(t)$, varying rapidly in the course of time, but of average value zero, acts on the particle. One may therefore write an equation of motion as Eq. (4).

$$\frac{dv}{dt} = -\beta v + A(t) \tag{4}$$

See VISCOSITY.

If one now multiplies Eq. (4), the Langevin equation, by x, averages over time, and applies the equipartition law, one obtains for a Stokes case Eq. (5). This result was originally derived by Albert

$$\overline{x^2} = \frac{kTt}{3\pi R\eta} \tag{5}$$

Einstein; it expresses the root-mean-square displacement explicitly in terms of observable parameters. Equation (5) has been verified with an accuracy of about 0.5%. *See* COLLOID.   Max Dresden

Bibliography. R. Durrett and H. Kesten (eds.), *Random Walks, Brownian Motion and Interacting*

Particle Systems, 2d ed., 1991; A. Einstein, *Investigations on the Theory of Brownian Movement*, 1926; D. Freedman, *Brownian Motion and Diffusion*, 1971, reprint 1983; T. Hida, *Brownian Motion*, 1980; I. Karatzas and S. E. Shreve, *Brownian Motion and Stochastic Calculus*, 2d ed., 1997; F. B. Knight (ed.), *Essentials of Brownian Motion and Diffusion*, 1981, reprint 1989; S. C. Port and C. J. Stone, *Brownian Motion and Classical Potential Theory*, 1978.

Brucellosis

An infectious, zoonotic disease of various animals and humans caused by *Brucella* species. Each species tends to preferentially infect a particular animal, but several types can infect humans. *Brucella melitensis* (preferentially infects goats and sheep), *B. suis* (infects pigs), and *B. abortus* (infects cattle) are the most common causes of human brucellosis. *Brucella melitensis* is the most virulent for humans, followed by *B. suis* and *B. abortus*. *Brucella canis* and *B. ovis*, which infect dogs and sheep respectively, rarely infect humans. Although brucellosis is found all over the world, in many countries the disease has been eradicated. The brucellae are small, gram-negative coccobacilli which are defined as facultative intracellular parasites since they are able to replicate within specialized cells of the host.

Animals. The brucellae often localize in the reproductive tract, mammary gland, and lymph node. They have a particular affinity for the pregnant uterus, leading to abortion and reduced milk production with resultant economic loss to the farmer. Males often undergo infection of the reproductive tract which is characterized by orchitis and epididymitis. Transmission of the disease may occur through the milk of infected animals, but especially through contact with aborted fetuses, afterbirth, and fluids which are very heavily contaminated with brucellae and discharged into the environment. Wildlife, including elk, feral pigs, bison, and reindeer, can become infected and can spread the disease to domestic livestock.

Humans. Brucellosis in humans is characterized by undulant fever, cold sweats, chills, muscular pain, and severe weakness. Some individuals may have recurrent bouts of the disease in which a variety of organs may be affected, sometimes resulting in death. The disease can be contracted by consuming unpasteurized milk or cheese, or via the introduction of organisms through small skin lesions or as an aerosol through the conjunctiva and the respiratory system. Treatment with tetracycline and other antibiotics is most successful if started early after symptoms occur. Development of the disease can be prevented if treatment is initiated immediately after contact with potentially infected material.

Diagnosis. Animals and humans infected with brucellae make antibodies to the bacterial component called the O-antigen. These antibodies are detected in the blood of animals and humans by a variety of serological tests; their presence indicates prior exposure. A test using milk (ring test) may also be used to diagnose the presence of the disease. The disease can also be diagnosed by culturing blood or tissue samples. However, negative culture does not mean absence of infection since numbers in small samples may be too few to be detectable.

Prevention. At present there are no effective vaccines for humans. The disease can be eliminated only by eradicating it in animals. A major source of brucellosis in humans is the consumption of *B. melitensis*-infected milk and cheese from goats. Incidence can be reduced by pasteurizing milk. Animals can be vaccinated to increase their immunity against brucellosis and therefore reduce abortions and disease transmission. Combining vaccination with the elimination of serologically positive animals can lead to disease eradication. In the past, vaccines available for cattle induced positive serological tests so that it was difficult to distinguish vaccinated animals from infected ones, complicating eradication programs. This problem has been eliminated with a new vaccine called strain RB51, which also protects swine. A vaccine, which does not avoid the serological problem, is available for goats and sheep. *See* EPIDEMIOLOGY; MEDICAL BACTERIOLOGY.

Gerhardt G. Schurig

Bibliography. G. G. Alton et al. (eds.), *Techniques for the Brucellosis Laboratory*, 1988; K. Nielsen and R. J. Duncan (eds.), *Animal Brucellosis*, 1990.

Brussels sprouts

A cool-season biennial crucifer (*Brassica oleracea* var. *gemmifera*), which is of northern European origin and belongs to the plant order Capparales. The plant is grown for its small headlike buds formed in the axils of the leaves along the plant stem (see **illus.**). These buds are eaten as a cooked vegetable.

Brussels sprouts (*Brassica oleracea* var. *gemmifera*), Jade Cross. (*Joseph Harris Co., Rochester, New York*)

Cultural practices are similar to those used for cabbage; however, monthly mean temperatures below 70°F (21°C) are necessary for firm sprouts. Brussels sprouts are moderately tolerant of acid soils and have a high requirement for boron. Popular varieties (cultivars) are Half Dwarf and Catskill; however, hybrid varieties are increasingly planted. Harvesting begins when the lower sprouts are firm and 1–2 in. (2.5–5 cm) in diameter, usually 3 months after planting. California and New York are important producing states. *See* CABBAGE; CAPPARALES. H. John Carew

Bryales

An order of the subclass Bryidae. With 11 families and perhaps 44 genera, it is defined in terms of terminal inflorescences, with rare exceptions, and perfect, double peristomes which are papillose on the outer surface. The capsules are generally inclined and more or less pear-shaped. Erect capsules are associated with reduced peristomes.

These mosses often grow in disturbed places. They are perennial and grow in tufts, with stems erect and simple or forked and often densely covered with rhizoids. The leaves are generally bordered by elongate cells and often toothed. The midrib often ends in a hairpoint. The cells, usually smooth, are not differentiated at the basal angles. The sporophytes are nearly always terminal. The setae are generally elongate, and the operculate capsules are usually symmetric but generally inclined to pendulous and commonly pyriform owing to the development of a sizable neck. The peristome is normally double, with a well-developed endostome. The 16 lanceolate teeth of the exostome are evenly tapered and papillose on the outer surface. Keeled and perforate endostome segments alternate with the teeth and arise from a generally high basal membrane. Alternating with the segments are usually one to four cilia. The calyptrae are cucullate and naked. Chromosome numbers are 5, 6, 10, 11, 12, often in polyploid series. *See* BRYIDAE; BRYOPHYTA; BRYOPSIDA.

Howard Crum

Bryidae

A subclass of the class Bryopsida. Most genera of true mosses (Bryopsida) belong in the 16 orders of the Bryidae. The most characteristic feature is the peristome consisting of one or two series of teeth, derived from parts of cells rather than whole cells, as in the Tetraphididae, Dawsoniidae, and Polytrichidae. (The Buxbaumiidae have some resemblance in peristome structure to Bryidae.) The stems may be erect and merely forked, or prostrate and freely branched, with sporophytes produced terminally or laterally, respectively. The leaves are inserted in many rows, though sometimes flattened together and appearing two-ranked, but only rarely actually in two rows. The costa may be single or double, sometimes very short, and rarely lacking. The cells are short or elongate, thin- or thick-walled, and often papillose-

roughened. The basal and especially the basal angular cells are often differentiated. The setae are generally present and elongate. The capsules dehisce by means of an operculum except in a few genera that show extreme reduction. The number of peristome teeth and segments of the inner peristome are usually 16. The spores are produced by two layers of spore mother cells; they are generally small. The calyptra may be cucullate or mitrate. *See* ARCHIDIIDAE; BRYALES; BRYOPHYTA; BRYOPSIDA; BRYOXIPHIALES; DAWSONIIDAE; DICRANALES; ENCALYPTALES; FISSIDENTALES; FUNARIALES; GRIMMIALES; HOOKERIALES; HYPNALES; ISOBRYALES; MITTENIALES; ORTHOTRICHALES; POLYTRICHIDAE; POTTIALES; SELIGERIALES; SPLACHNALES; TETRAPHIDIDAE.

Howard Crum

Bibliography. G. C. S. Clarke and J. G. Duckett, *Modern Approaches in Bryophyte Systematics*, 1979; S. P. Parker (ed.), *Synopsis and Classification of Living Organisms*, 2 vols., 1982; H. Robinson, A revised classification for the orders and families of mosses, *Phytologia*, 21:289–293, 1971; R. J. Taylor and A. E. Leviton (eds.), *The Mosses of North America*, 1980.

Bryophyta

A division that consists of some 23,000 species of small and relatively simple plants commonly known as mosses, granite mosses, peat mosses, liverworts, and hornworts (see **illus.**). The bryophytes display a distinct alternation of sexual and asexual generations; the sexual gametophyte, with a haploid chromosome number, is the more diversified. The spore-bearing, diploid sporophyte is reduced in size and structure, attached to the gametophyte, and partially or almost completely dependent on it.

Structure. The gametophytes may consist of leafy stems or flat thalli. They have no roots but are anchored to the substrate by hairlike rhizoids. Vascular tissue is at best poorly differentiated, with no lignification of cells. Growth results from the divisions of single cells (rather than meristematic tissues) located at stem tips or in notches at the margins of thalli. The sex organs are multicellular and have a jacket of sterile cells surrounding either the single egg produced in flask-shaped archegonia or the vast number of sperms produced in globose to cylindric, stalked antheridia. The sperms swim by means of two flagella. The sporophyte develops, at least during the early stages, inside a calyptra of gametophytic tissue. The sporophyte commonly consists of a capsule that produces a large number of spores, a stalklike seta, and a swollen foot anchored in the gametophyte. The seta is sometimes lacking and, in a very few thallose liverworts, the foot as well. The spores, nearly always single-celled, are dispersed in the air, except in the case of a small number of aquatics. They germinate directly or produce a juvenile stage called a protonema. *See* REPRODUCTION (PLANT).

Diversity and phylogeny. The division can be divided into five classes: Sphagnopsida (peat mosses), Andreaeopsida (granite mosses), Bryopsida (true mosses), Hepaticopsida (liverworts), and Anthocerotopsida (hornworts). The mosses have radially organized leafy gametophytes that develop from a protonema and have multicellular rhizoids with slanted crosswalls. The liverworts and hornworts are mostly flat and dorsiventrally organized and have no protonematal stage; the rhizoids are unicellular. Though obviously related, as evidenced by similar sex organs and attachment of a simplified sporophyte to a more complex and independent gametophyte, the classes differ greatly in structural detail. Swimming sperms and relative simplicity suggest an origin among the aquatic green algae, but the attachment of sporophyte to gametophyte and the frequent occurrence of trilete spores, stomata in the capsule wall, rudiments of vascular tissue of some similarity to xylem and phloem (especially in the gametophyte), protection of sex organs, and development of a sporangium that produces countless airborne spores are strong evidence for an origin on land, perhaps from a stock ancestral to the earliest vascular plants, or psilophytes. A significant difference from that group is that bryophytes never have branched sporophytes.

An outline of the Bryophyta is shown below. See separate articles on each group listed.

Class Hepaticopsida (liverworts)
  Subclass Jungermanniidae
    Order: Takakiales
        Calobryales
        Jungermanniales
        Metzgeriales
  Subclass Marchantiidae
    Order: Sphaerocarpales
        Monocleales
        Marchantiales
Class Anthocerotopsida (hornworts)
Class Sphagnopsida (peat mosses)
Class Andreaeopsida (granite mosses)
Class Bryopsida (true mosses)
  Subclass: Archidiidae
  Subclass: Bryidae
    Order: Fissidentales
        Bryoxiphiales
        Schistostegales
        Dicranales
        Pottiales
        Grimmiales
        Seligeriales
        Encalyptales
        Funariales
        Splachnales
        Bryales
        Mitteniales
        Orthotrichales
        Isobryales
        Hookeriales
        Hypnales
  Subclass: Buxbaumiidae
      Tetraphididae
      Dawsoniidae
      Polytrichidae

See PLANT EVOLUTION; PLANT KINGDOM.
Howard Crum

Bryophytes. (*a*) Moss plant, *Polytrichum juniperinum* (*General Biological Supply House*). (*b*) Male and female plants of liverwort, *Marchantia*. (*c*) Hornwort, *Anthoceros* (*Carolina Biological Supply Co.*).

Bibliography. N. S. Parihar, *An Introduction to Embryophyta*, vol. 1, 1961; P. Puri, *Bryophytes: A Broad Perspective*, 1973; D. H. S. Richardson, *The Biology of Mosses*, 1981; F. Verdoorn, *Manual of Bryology*, 1932; E. V. Watson, *The Structure and Life of Bryophytes*, 3d ed., 1971.

Bryopsida

The largest class of the division Bryophyta, the true mosses. Members of the class are best characterized by operculate capsules and a peristome that aids in the dispersal of spores, and are generally perennial. The class consists of about 14,000 species distributed in six subclasses based primarily on the structure and developmental history of the sporophyte and

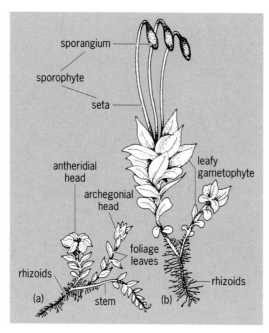

Fig. 1. True moss (*Mnium*). (*a*) Location of sex organs (male antheridia and female archegonia). (*b*) Gametophyte with attached sporophytes. (*After W. W. Robbins et al., Botany, 3d ed., 1964*)

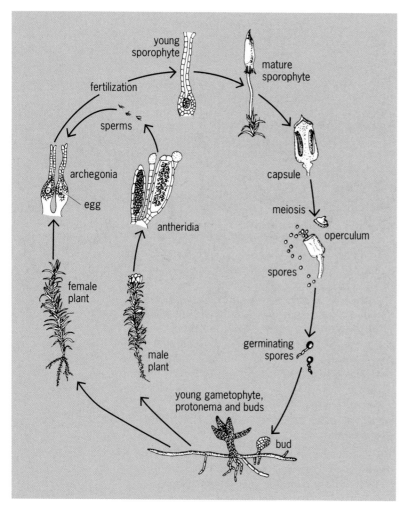

Fig. 2. Life cycle of a moss. (*After E. W. Sinnott and K. S. Wilson, Botany, 6th ed., McGraw-Hill, 1963*)

especially the peristome. The orders and families are likewise based primarily on stable sporophytic details, whereas genera and species are most often differentiated in terms of gametophytic features.

Gametophyte. The filamentous, freely branched protonema of Bryopsida gametophytes produces an abundance of leafy plants which may be erect, simple or sparsely forked, and growing in tufts and producing archegonia at the stem tips (**Fig. 1**); or, alternatively, plants may be prostrate, freely branched, growing in intertangled mats, and producing archegonia laterally. If the apical cell is used up by the formation of archegonia, growth usually continues by the formation of a new subapical branch, called an innovation. But if the terminal cell is not used up and the archegonia are produced laterally, the stems are indeterminate in growth and form numerous branches. Growth results from the activity of a single apical cell with three cutting faces, or in a few genera with two-ranked leaves the apical cell becomes, secondarily, two-faced. In large, erect-growing plants, the stems may have a central strand of vascular tissues similar to xylem and phloem but without lignification. In smaller plants, the vascular tissue is reduced or lacking. The rhizoids are multicellular, with slanted crosswalls. The inflorescences are usually enveloped in differentiated leaves, and the sex organs, of superficial origin, are often mingled with paraphyses, especially in the male inflorescence. The archegonia are flask-shaped; the antheridia are banana-shaped and stalked (**Fig. 2**). *See* PHLOEM; XYLEM.

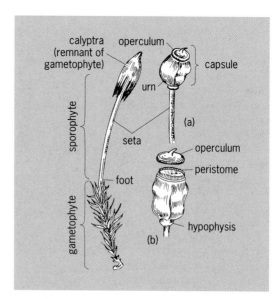

Fig. 3. Complete moss plant showing enlarged views of (*a*) tip of sporophyte with calyptra removed and (*b*) capsule (sporangium), with operculum and peristome and, beneath the capsule, the hypophysis. (*After F. W. Emerson, Basic Botany, 2d ed., Blakiston, 1954*)

Sporophyte. The long-lived sporophytes are abundantly green until maturity and largely self-supporting. They consist of foot and capsule, usually also a seta (**Fig. 3**). The capsules dehisce by means of a lidlike operculum, or rarely irregularly by rupture. Operculate capsules are provided with a single or double fringe of peristome teeth in multiples of four at the mouth. The peristome is generally derived from the amphithecium (the outer tissue of the embryonic capsule). The capsule wall is usually spongy, especially in the neck portion below the spore sac. Stomata are usually present, especially in the neck or at the junction of capsule and seta; the stomata usually have two guard cells. The spore sac is derived from the endothecium; it surrounds but does not overarch the slender columella. The calyptra may be mitrate (conic and lobed) or cucullate (slit up one side and hoodlike). The chromosome numbers are exceedingly diverse; polyploidy is common, both within species and among related ones. *See* ARCHIDIIDAE; BRYIDAE; BRYOPHYTA; BUXBAUMI-IDAE; DAWSONIIDAE; POLYTRICHIDAE; TETRAPHIDI-DAE.   Howard Crum

Bibliography. F. Cavers, The inter-relationships of the Bryophyta, *New Phytol.,* 9:81–112, 157–186, 196–234, 269–304, 341–353, 1910, and 10:1–46, 84–86, 1911; E. V. Watson, *The Structure and Life of Bryophytes,* 3d ed., 1971.

Bryopsidales

An order of the green algae (Chlorophyceae), also called Caulerpales, Codiales, or Siphonales, in which the plant body (thallus) is a coenocytic filament (tube or siphon). The filaments may be discrete with free or laterally coherent branches, or organized into a dense plexus exhibiting distinctive morphological features. Septa, which are generally infrequent and incomplete, are formed by centripetal deposition of wall material. A large, continuous central vacuole restricts the cytoplasm to a thin layer just beneath the wall. The cytoplasm contains innumerable nuclei, discoid plastids, and other organelles. Pigments are similar to those in higher plants but include two distinctive xanthophylls, siphonein and siphonaxanthin. Some genera have distinct plastids for the storage of starch. The chief constituent of the wall is frequently xylan or mannan, polysaccharides in which the monomer is xylose and mannose, respectively. Vegetative reproduction is common, usually by rhizomes or fragments. The life history, known for only a few genera, comprises either

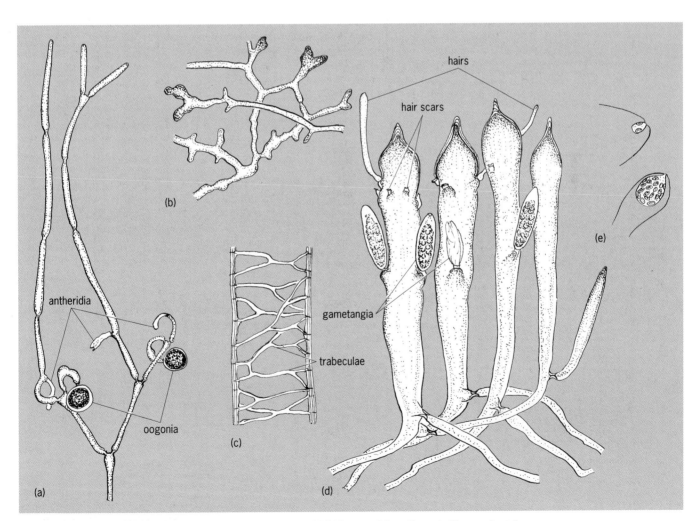

Fig. 1. Anatomical structures of selected members of Bryopsidales. (*a*) *Dichotomosiphon,* filament with oogonia and antheridia. (*b*) *Ostreobium,* filaments. (*c*) *Caulerpa,* section of filament showing trabeculae. (*d*) *Codium,* group of utricles with gametangia and hairs (or hair scars). (*e*) *Codium* gametes, male above and female below.

one somatic phase, with meiosis occurring in the production of gametes, or an alternation of strikingly dissimilar somatic phases, with meiosis occurring in the production of zoospores. Motile gametes are biflagellate, while zoospores have a subapical crown of flagella. Reproductive cells may be formed in unmodified or slightly modified portions of the filament or in special organs.

The order Bryopsidales comprises six families with about 24 genera. The Dichotomosiphonaceae, represented by a single species, *Dichotomosiphon tuberosus* (**Fig. 1***a*), occurs in fresh water, growing at the surface of pools and at depths of at least 50 ft (15 m) in lakes, where it becomes entangled in fish nets. The remaining families are marine and are most abundant and diverse in tropical and subtropical waters. *Bryopsis* (**Fig. 2***a*), an inhabitant of exposed rocky shores as well as wooden pilings in harbors, is the most commonly encountered member of the family Bryopsidaceae. The gametophyte of *Bryopsis* forms a dense tuft of profusely branched filaments, and is mosslike. The Ostreobiaceae includes a single, poorly defined genus (*Ostreobium;* Fig. 1*b*) with six species, all growing in calcareous substrates (old mollusk shells, corals, calcified red algae). *Caulerpa* (Fig. 2*b*), the only genus of the Caulerpaceae, has large filaments reinforced by strands of wall material (trabeculae; Fig. 1*c*) extending into and across the interior. The filaments may be threadlike, but usually they are coarsely cylindrical or flattened. The erect

fronds may be very similar in general appearance to other plants, such as club moss and cypress. *Caulerpa* is extremely abundant and diverse in tropical and subtropical waters and (as an exception) in temperate southern Australia. Certain species prefer a rocky substrate, while others spread over large expanses of mud or fine calcareous sand by means of rhizoids. Some species produce a toxin, caulerpicin, which may enter the food chain of the tropical Pacific.

In Udoteaceae, the basic structural unit is a dichotomously or trichotomously branched threadlike filament that is often constricted in a regular pattern. The filaments often form a dense tuft borne on a stem (or stipe), as in *Penicillus* (Neptune's shaving brush; Fig. 2*c*). The most distinctive and ecologically important genus is *Halimeda* (Fig. 2*d*), in which the thallus is an articulate series of flattened or cylindrical segments that are heavily impregnated with aragonite, a form of calcium carbonate. *Halimeda* is nearly ubiquitous in tropical and subtropical seas, and its calcified remains have contributed to the buildup of coral reefs and the infilling of atoll lagoons since the Late Cretaceous. In *Codium* (Fig. 2*e*), the only genus of the Codiaceae, the basic structural unit is similar to that in the Udoteaceae, but the filaments are intertwined to form a spongy thallus that may be crustose, spheroidal, bladelike, or dichotomously branched and up to 33 ft (10 m) long. The chloroplasts are localized in swollen segments called utricles (Fig. 1*d*), which form a palisadelike surface layer. The genus is represented in all parts of the world except the Arctic and Antarctic, but is most diverse in temperate regions. *Codium fragile* ssp. *tomentosoides* is a notorious weed, spreading rapidly in the Atlantic and Pacific by fragmentation and parthenogenesis, and damaging shellfish plantings. *See* ALGAE; CHLOROPHYCEAE.   Paul C. Silva; Richard L. Moe

Bibliography. L. Hillis-Colinvaux, Ecology and taxonomy of *Halimeda*: Primary producer of coral reefs, *Adv. Mar. Biol.,* 17:1–327, 1980; J. Ramus, *Codium*: The invader, *Discovery* (Yale Univ.), 6(2):59–68, 1971.

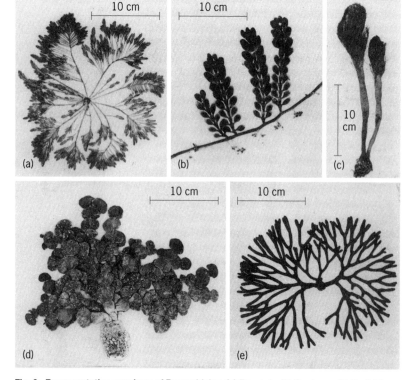

Fig. 2. Representative members of Bryopsidales. (*a*) *Bryopsis*; (*b*) *Caulerpa*; (*c*) *Penicillus*; (*d*) *Halimeda*; (*e*) *Codium*.

Bryoxiphiales

An order of the class Bryopsida in the subclass Bryidae. The order consists of a single genus and species, *Bryoxiphium norvegicum*, the sword moss. This order is characterized by a swordlike appearance owing to leaves overlapping in two rows. The shiny, rigid leaves are keeled and conduplicate-folded. The apex is long-awned at the stem tip and progressively shorter-pointed downward. The midrib bears at back a low ridge of one to four rows of cells. The leaf cells are smooth and subquadrate within, longer and narrower toward the margins. The plants are dioecious with terminal archegonia. The capsules are immersed and have an operculum but no peristome. The calyptra is cucullate, and the haploid chromosome number 14. *See* BRYIDAE; BRYOPHYTA; BRYOPSIDA. Howard Crum

Bibliography. A. Löve and D. Löve, Studies on *Bryoxiphium, Bryologist*, 56:73–94, 183–203, 1953.

Bryozoa

A phylum of sessile aquatic invertebrates (also called Polyzoa) which form colonies of zooids. Each zooid, in its basic form, has a lophophore of ciliated tentacles situated distally on an introvert, a looped gut with the mouth inside the lophophore and the anus outside, a coelomic body cavity, and (commonly) a protective exoskeleton (**Fig. 1**). The colonies are variable in size and habit (**Figs. 2 and 3**). Some are known as lace corals and others as sea mats, but the only general name is bryozoans (sea mosses).

General Characteristics

Byrozoans form colonies by asexual budding from a primary zooid, or ancestrula, formed by metamorphosis of a sexually produced larva or from some kind of resting bud. Structurally the zooids are metazoan, triploblastic, unsegmented, and bilaterally symmetrical, with a regionated fluid-filled body cavity that is considered to be a coelom. The body wall comprises epidermis underlain by a feebly developed peritoneum, between which muscle may be present. The epidermis secretes a chitinlike cuticle or gelatinous layer, and the cuticle may become calcified as a rigid exoskeleton.

Much of the zooid consists of the lophophore, alimentary canal, and associated musculature, together known as the polypide. The lophophore comprises a circle or crescent of slender, ciliated tentacles plus their supporting ridge. When spread for feeding, the tentacles form a funnel with the mouth at its vertex. During withdrawal the tentacles close, and are pulled downward from their base through the simultaneously in-rolling introvert. They then lie within the introvert, called the tentacle sheath. The open distal end of the in-rolled tentacle sheath is termed the orifice, and it may be closed simply by a sphincter muscle or by more elaborate structures.

The alimentary canal is deeply looped, and regionated into pharynx, stomach, and rectum. The limb descending from the mouth consists basically of the pharynx and stomach cardia; the central stomach and its dilatation, the cecum, form the base of the loop; and the stomach pylorus and the rectum constitute the ascending limb. The anus opens outside the lophophore. The nerve ganglion, center of a system that may be complex, lies between the mouth and the anus. There are no special excretory or respiratory organs, and no circulatory system. Colonies, but not all zooids, are hermaphrodite. Zooids are generally not more than 0.04 in. (1 mm) long.

The colony may be minute, of not more than a single feeding zooid and its immediate buds, or substantial, forming masses 3 ft (1 m) in circumference, festoons 1.5 ft (0.5 m) in length, or patches 0.67 ft^2

(0.25 m^2) in area. Commonly the colonies form incrustations not more than a few square centimeters in area, small twiggy bushes up to about 1.2 in. (3 cm) in height, or soft masses up to about 4 in. (10 cm) in the largest dimension. In many colonies much of the bulk consists of the zooid exoskeletons, termed zooecia, which may persist long after the death of the organism and account for the abundance of fossilized bryozoan remains.

Many bryozoans display polymorphism, having certain zooids adapted in particular ways to perform specialized functions, such as protection, cleaning the surface, anchoring the colony, or sheltering the embryo. The evolution of nonfeeding polymorphs is dependent upon some form of intercommunication between zooids.

All bryozoans are epibenthic, and are generally attached to firm substrata, less often anchored in or resting on sand. Most are marine, but one complete class (Phylactolaemata) is confined to fresh water. In the latter habitat, statoblasts and hibernacula, resting bodies resistant to cold and desiccation, are produced. Sexual reproduction leads either to a distinctive, planktotrophic larva, called the

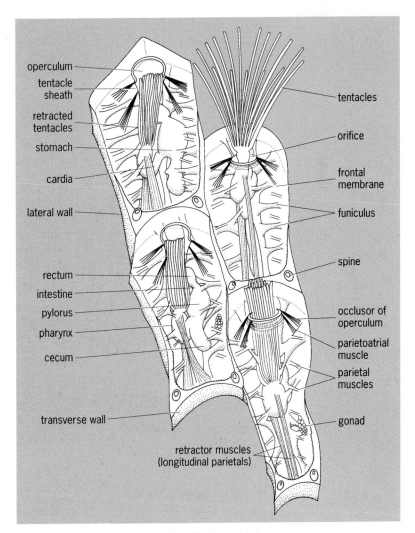

Fig. 1. Morphological features of autozooids, in frontal view.

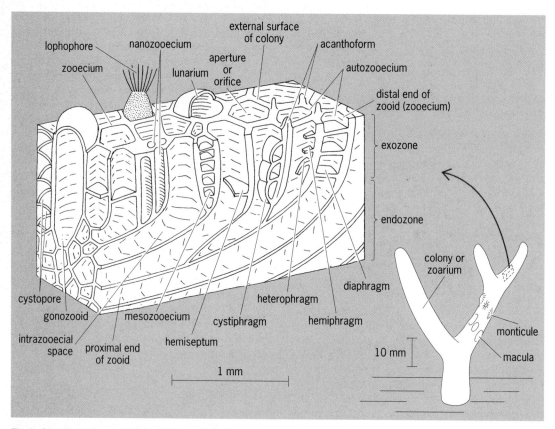

Fig. 2. Stenolaemate morphologic features, some of which are found only in living colonies and others only in fossil colonies. The enlarged oblique view is from the colony at the lower right.

cyphonautes, or more usually to a subspherical, non-feeding, short-lived type that has had no particular name until recently distinguished as "coronate," because of its extensive ciliary corona.

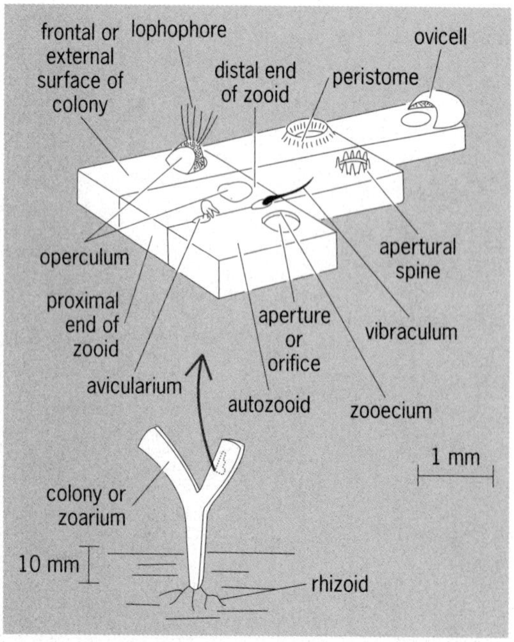

Taxonomy and classification.   Bryozoa is the name of a phylum for which Ectoprocta is generally regarded as a synonym, these names being used by zoologists according to personal preference. Entoprocta (synonym Calyssozoa) is likewise regarded as an independent phylum. A minority regard Ectoprocta and Entoprocta as subphyla within the Bryozoa, while others maintain Ectoprocta and Entoprocta as phyla but link them under Bryozoa as a name of convenience. *See* ENTOPROCTA.

The phylum contains some 20,000 described species, one-fifth of them living. These are distributed among three classes and a somewhat variable number of orders.

> Class Phylactolaemata
> Order Plumatellida
> Class Gymnolaemata
> Order: Ctenostomata
> Cheilostomata
> Class Stenolaemata
> Order: Cyclostomata
> Cystoporata
> Trepostomata
> Cryptostomata
> Hederellida

See GYMNOLAEMATA; PHYLACTOLAEMATA; STENOLAEMATA.

Until somewhat over 200 years ago bryozoans went unrecognized. When discovered they were

Fig. 3. Morphological features of gymnolaemate colony, and enlarged oblique view of block from it.

thought, with coelenterates, to be plants—a confusion that led Linnaeus to invent the term zoophyte. In 1830 J. Vaughan Thompson characterized bryozoans, separating them from other zoophytes, but at the same time ambiguously introducing a class Polyzoa. G. C. Ehrenberg's name Bryozoa followed in 1831. *See* CRYPTOSTOMATA; CTENOSTOMATA; CYCLOSTOMATA (BRYOZOA); CYSTOPORATA; HEDERELLIDA; TREPOSTOMATA.

Comparative morphologists link the Bryozoa with the Phoronida and the Brachiopoda, characterized especially by possession of a lophophore, which L. H. Hyman defined as "a tentaculated extension of the mesosome that embraces the mouth but not the anus, and has a coelomic lumen." The tentacle circlet of the Entoprocta is postanal and noncoelomic. The designation of the bryozoan lophophore as mesosomal, and its body cavity as mesocoelic, rests entirely on the interpretation of a supraoral flap of tissue, the epistome, present in phylactolaemates, as the protosome or first region of a tripartite body. In addition to the lophophore and presumed tripartite body, all three phyla have a U-shaped alimentary tract. The lophophore is crescentic in some members of all three groups. Even if the relationship is correct, however, it sheds little light on bryozoan origins. The soft-bodied Phylactolaemata have left no fossil record, but comparative anatomy suggests that they, the Stenolaemata, and the Gymnolaemata must already have been distinct by the Ordovician. The view that Bryozoa arose from entoprocts, perhaps by internal budding from the larva, seems tenuous, and implies at most no more than a similarity between larvae such as that which links Mollusca to Annelida. Certainly the immediate ancestor must have been vermiform and sedentary, for cylindrical zooids, terminal lophophores, and deeply recurved digestive tracts with the anus rather close to the mouth represent the primitive state in all classes.

Functional morphology of zooid. Zooids in all three bryozoan classes display the same ground plan: eversible lophophore, U-shaped gut, fluid-filled coelom, and deformable body wall. The lophophore is everted by increase in hydrostatic pressure caused by inflexion of the body wall; withdrawal is achieved by the direct pull of retractor muscles anchored to the wall. The flexible phylactolaemate wall incorporates circular and longitudinal muscle, and its contraction everts the lophophore. Recent work indicates that stenolaemates, as evidenced by the extant Cyclostomata, have a remarkably modified system. Throughout this class the zooid is cylindrical (often inaccurately described as tubular; only the exoskeleton is tubular). Except in the immediate vicinity of the orifice, the cuticle is calcified and totally rigid. The peritoneum, with a hypertrophied basal membrane and associated bands of circular muscle, has detached from the epidermis and lies freely as a bag, the membranous sac, anchored at some points to the body wall. The endosaccal cavity is coelomic, but the exosaccal cavity, external to the mesoderm, is not. The sac contracts to evert the lophophore; exosaccal

fluid must be displaced proximally as the polypide is eased toward the orifice.

The simplest gymnolaemates (Ctenostomata) have cylindrical zooids and deformable walls, although the musculature is extrinsic. The circular (now renamed transverse parietal) muscles lie inside the peritoneum, and the longitudinal muscles are reduced and specialized. Mechanically the system works as in Phylactolaemata. An early trend of zooidal evolution in the Gymnolaemata was toward a flat, membranous, coffinlike shape, adherent to the substratum. It seems probable that the cheilostomes arose from ctenostomes like that by calcification of the lateral walls and the differentiation of a cuticular lid, the operculum, to close the orifice. Cheilostomes of this plan, classified as the suborder Anasca, preserve a wholly or partially flexible front wall. Transverse parietal muscles, relocated to span the coelom from the rigid lateral walls to the frontal membrane, bring about its inflexion.

Natural selection in cheilostomes has favored modifications which better protect the polypide while preserving the function of the frontal membrane. Thus the frontal membrane can be underlain by a shelf, at a distance sufficient to permit inflexion; or it can be overarched by flattened spines or by a meshwork of partially fused spines. In the subclass Ascophora the membrane may be overgrown or replaced by a calcified frontal wall, but the flexible membrane either remains or is replaced more deeply by a functional equivalent. A saclike cavity or ascus, opening just behind the orifice, is created either by overgrowth of the wall or by involution from the orifice underneath the wall. Transverse parietal muscles insert on the lower face of the ascus, which is pulled down to evert the lophophore, while water to compensate for the volume change enters the ascus through its opening.

Feeding. The expanded lophophore of marine bryozoans forms an almost radially symmetrical funnel of 8–30 tentacles, although fixed or transient bilateral symmetry may occur. In gymnolaemates the base of this funnel stands free above the surface of the zooid, but in stenolaemates it lies concealed within the orificial region of the exoskeleton. The top diameter is in the range of 0.01 to 0.05 in. (0.25 to 1.25 mm). In primitive phylactolaemates 20–30 tentacles form a funnel, but in most members of this class the large lophophore comprises 100 or more tentacles disposed in a horseshoe, the lobes of which project from the adanal side.

The base of the lophophore is the most complex part of the polypide. Essentially it is a hollow epidermal annulus, with thickened basement membrane. The lumen (mesocoel) opens into the main body cavity (metacoel) by an adanal pore. The cerebral ganglion partly occludes this pore, and a nerve tract parallels the mesocoel. Radial and circular muscles open and close the mouth. The tentacles rise from the annulus as slender hollow cylinders. Their central coelom is surrounded by a thick, flanged collagenous tube, the hypertrophied basement membrane of the epidermal cells. The lumen, which opens terminally through a minute pore, is lined by peritoneum and contains frontal (that is, facing into the funnel) and abfrontal longitudinal muscles. The lateral epidermal cells bear long cilia (about 25 micrometers) and the frontal cells shorter cilia (about 15 μm). Laterofrontally is a line of static sensory cilia. The tentacles contain motor and sensory nerves.

The lateral cilia generate a water current that enters the top of the funnel and flows downward and outward between the tentacles. Particles such as bacteria and phytoplankton are separated from the water and directed at the mouth by the frontal cilia without the use of mucus. The mechanism of separation is uncertain, but a likely explanation is that particles passing out between the tentacles, perhaps sensed by the rigid laterofrontal cilia, are flicked back into the funnel by localized reversal of ciliary beat. Small particles accumulate just above the mouth; heavier particles may be projected down the funnel and directly into the partly open mouth.

Unwanted particles are rejected by closing the mouth, flicking the tentacles, closure or concerted movements of the funnel, and ejection from the pharynx (see below). A few bryozoans with large lophophores have rejection tracts leading centrifugally between the ventromedial (abanal) tentacles. Bryozoans are vigorous feeders, and it has been calculated that the lophophore of even a small zooid filters about 0.3 ml/h (and a colony may contain thousands of zooids).

Bryozoan colonies may have exhalant chimneys or set points of water outflow. The reason is clear: if the colony is large, solid, flat, and uniformly covered by tentacular funnels pumping toward its surface, the filtered water requires a means to get away. Small colonies may have a single, central chimney; large colonies may have a mamillate surface, the summit of each mamilla marking a chimney; and wholly flat colonies produce chimneys by an apparently coordinated bending away of lophophores from predetermined points. Filtered water flows toward the chimneys, through which it is expelled. Lophophores surrounding a chimney display strong bilateral symmetry, with the bordering tentacles standing tall and upright instead of curving into the chimney. A consequence of the posture is that the beat of the current-generating lateral cilia becomes centripetal to the chimney rather than being unhelpfully directed toward its base.

The pharynx is a remarkable organ. It is short, thick-walled, and situated immediately below the mouth. Its exterior is circular in section, its interior deeply furrowed. The frontal ciliation from the lophophore continues through the mouth and may cover the distal part of the pharynx: the midventral groove is ciliated, even when the rest of the pharynx is not, and its cilia beat upward, whether there is a ventromedial rejection tract or not. Between the grooves, the inwardly bulging walls are made up of vacuolated cells which incorporate intracellular myofibrils. The simultaneous contraction of all the myofibrils, acting against the fluid-filled vacuole, causes a brief convulsive dilation of the pharynx, engulfing the particles accumulated outside the mouth.

A sphincter and valve separate the pharynx from the cardia (descending arm of the stomach). In some ctenostomes, and a few other bryozoans, part of the cardia is differentiated as a gizzard, armed internally with teeth or keratinized plates, presumably for crushing the frustules of diatoms. The unmodified wall of the cardia contains secretory cells. The floor of the central stomach is ciliated, evidently to carry particles into the cecum, which is the main locus of extra- and intracellular digestion and absorption. The epithelium of the pylorus is ciliated and serves to compact the undigested remains into a revolving cord. A sphincter separates the pylorus from the rectum, which has an absorptive function and modifies the cord of reject material into fecal pellets. The pellet is moved through and expelled from the rectum by peristalsis. At summer temperatures (72°F or 22°C) the gut transit time is less than 1 h but at 43°F (6°C) it is 2 h.

Metabolic integration and colony evolution. The simplest bryozoan colonies presumably consisted of loosely interconnected, monomorphic feeding zooids. In the most ancient fossil stenolaemates, confluence of coeloms had been achieved either by means of internal pores or by the so-called double wall, in which a superficial (or hypostegal) coelom unites the colony outside the calcification. The hypostegal coelom must have been reasonably effective as a means of distributing metabolites, since the colonies of trepostomes were large by bryozoan standards, and the fenestrates evolved colony forms of considerable complexity. However, rapid growth and the proliferation of nonfeeding zooid polymorphs requires a transport system more efficient than aqueous diffusion. The funiculus provides such a system.

In living single-walled stenolaemates (cyclostomes) zooids communicate via small, open interzooidal pores. The funiculus is a small muscular strand linking the proximal end of the cecum with the base of the membranous sac at its attachment to the zooid wall. The testis is positioned where the funiculus joins the cecum. The phylactolaemate funiculus similarly is muscular, supports the testis, and links the cecum to the proximal end of the ventral body wall. More importantly, it contains a core of blastogenic tissue from which the statoblasts arise. These are the future resting buds and become richly supplied with yolk. The obvious inference is that the products of digestion are transported, perhaps to the testis but certainly to the developing statoblasts, along the funiculus. Communication between zooids in phylactolaemates is by open pores; indeed in many of them the dividing walls have almost completely broken down, so that the polypides are suspended in a communal coelom.

The adaptive radiation of zooid form has been very slight in both Cyclostomata and Phylactolaemata. Cyclostome zooids have remained as slender cylinders, while the colonies have evolved mainly in terms of the way in which the zooids are disposed.

Thus regular, alternating placement of zooid orifices is replaced by a pattern of separated short rows or fascicles, presumably to improve feeding efficiency; and erect or partially erect colonies have evolved from creeping ones. The reproductive zooids, at first clearly in series with the rest, become larger, more central, and often truly colonial by incorporating neighboring structures. Phylactolaemates have evolved larger, deeply crescentic lophophores, but the zooids have not diversified. Evolution of the colony has been toward unity by confluence of coeloms.

Primitive gymnolaemates have an organization very like that of the simpler phylactolaemates: elongate zooids connected by simple open pores, with the funiculus confined within each zooid. The radiation of stolonate ctenostomes has been facilitated by the development of a colonial, essentially nonmuscular funiculus which passes through the internal pores between zooids and along the stolons. A flux of lipid from feeding zooids into the stolonal funiculus occurs and spreads toward the growth and budding zones. The funiculus has become a colony-wide metabolic expressway.

When cheilostomes evolved from ctenostomes, they inherited the funicular system. They added mural calcification and developed complex communicating pores in the lateral walls, while retaining simple pores in the end walls. The main funicular trunks are longitudinal, passing from the proximal pores to the distal pores via the cecum, with branches to the lateral pores. The success of the Cheilostomata, in terms of species numbers, adaptive radiation, and polymorphism, is evidently the result of a high-potential module, plus the distributive efficiency of the funiculus in nourishing large numbers of specialized, nonfeeding zooids.

Nervous system. The cerebral ganglion is dorsally (adanally) situated in the lophophore base and has a diameter of 30–60 μm. It is extended circumorally as a ring or deep crescent. Apart from the fibrillar component, the anascan ganglion contains distal, central, and proximal groupings of cell bodies. The principal nerves are the following. (1) Sensory and motor lophophoral nerves. (2) Paired direct tentacle sheath nerves which unite with the first branch of the trifid nerve to form (3) the compound tentacle sheath nerves: these extend up the tentacle sheath to the superficial part of the zooid, including the sensitive region near the orifice. (4) The trifid motor nerve; of its three branches, the first, 4a, is visceral, meeting its opposite number at a small suprapharyngeal visceral ganglion; the second, 4b, innervates the paired retractor muscles of the polypide; and the third, 4c, joins the compound tentacle sheath nerve and innervates the tentacle sheath muscles, the orificial sphincter, occlusors of the operculum, and the transverse parietal muscles that deflect the frontal membrane. It will be noted that 4b and 4c innervate the antagonistic effectors in polypide withdrawal and eversion. (5) Paired parietal nerves parallel the direct tentacle sheath nerves, but pass deep to join a peripheral encircling ring which enters in turn each of the interzooidal pores. Here the parietal nerves of neighboring zooids make contact. (6) Paired visceral nerves originate in the suprapharyngeal ganglion.

Electrophysiological research has confirmed the existence of a functional colony-wide nervous system in anascans. Stimulation near the orifice results in the immediate withdrawal of all nearby expanded lophophores (while stimulation of a lophophore results only in its withdrawal).

Polymorphism. Phylactolaemates have achieved integration at the expense of zooid individuality, so that polymorphs have not evolved (unless the statoblasts are so regarded). Stenolaemates have metabolic integration dependent on diffusion gradients, and display weakly developed polymorphism. In living cyclostomes, four morphs are commonly encountered: (1) normal-feeding or autozooids; (2) empty or kenozooids of various kinds, which support colonies, make up attachment rhizoids and stolons, in-fill spaces, and project as spines; (3) female or gynozooids, also called brooding or gonozooids, that do not feed but produce ova and shelter the developing embryos; and (4) dwarf or nanozooids, containing a reduced unitentaculate polypide which sweeps and cleans the surface of the colony. All zooids which are not autozooids may be termed heterozooids.

Among gymnolaemates, which have metabolic integration via the funiculus, the ctenostomes have limited polymorphism. Apart from the autozooids, only kenozooids are commonly present, either as stolon segments or as spines attached to autozooids. The cylindrical type of zooid, whether calcified or cuticularized, has not provided the potential for extensive polymorphism. In cheilostomes, on the contrary, one sees a wide range of heterozooids, high numbers of heteromorphs per colony, and the grouping of polymorphs into functional units or cormidia (colonies within colonies). Of importance in contributing to such impressive adaptive radiation seem to be the funicular system, the retention of individualistic zooids, and the calcified, boxlike zooid with its partly membranous front and hinged, lidlike operculum closing the orifice.

Cheilostome zooid types merge with one another, but the following may usefully be recognized: (1) sterile or fertile autozooids, which may also brood embryos but do feed, at least for most of the time; (2) androzooids or nonfeeding males with reduced polypides; (3) gynozooids (gonozooids), nonfeeding females which produce ova and sometimes brood the embryo; (4) avicularia, in which the operculum is enlarged; (5) vibracula, in which the operculum is lengthened to whiplike proportions; (6) kenozooids for in-filling, or associated with attachment rootlets and stolons; (7) kenozooids in the form of spines; and (8) ooecia or brood chambers.

Avicularia appear to be zooids modified for grasping. They vary in form from something close to an autozooid, differing only in having an enlarged operculum, or mandible, to diminutive and highly modified structures. The large ones often obviously replace autozooids in the colony, and are termed vicarious; the smaller ones are attached to auto-zooids, and are termed adventitious. Often a zooid may bear several adventitious avicularia of different kinds and in a variety of positions. Abductor muscles open the mandible by pulling down the small frontal membrane just behind the hingeline, whereas larger adductors snap it shut. In its most evolved form, the bird's-head avicularium, the zooid is pedunculate and mobile. The avicularian polypide is much reduced, and is believed to fulfill a sensory role.

Some avicularia have a long slender mandible, and may be precursors of vibracula, in which the operculum has become a whiplike seta. The vibracular seta, however, is mounted on asymmetrical condyles and can be swiveled by gyrator muscles, as well as being moved through a regular arc. In some species the vibracula remove sediment from the colony surface, and in nonattached sand-living forms they also act as struts or legs.

Spines are small kenozooids of varied form. They are normally adventitious and presumably have a protective role. The arguments for regarding cheilostome spines as zooids are basically three: they are separated from their bearing autozooid by a communication pore of standard morphology; they terminate with a flat membrane, seen as homologous to a frontal membrane; and they may replace an undoubted polymorph, for example, an autozooid or avicularium. The fundamental arrangement of spines in anascans is as a marginal ring around the frontal membrane. One worker sees this as the vestige of an ancient type of budding, each spine representing what was once a free-rising series of zooids. Even when this annular pattern is modified, as in certain erect, branching anascans and in ascophorans, the basic arrangement frequently persists in the founding zooid or ancestrula. In later zooids the spines are confined to the immediate region of the orifice.

Marginal spines may be modified, as when one or a series overarches the frontal membrane. One major fossil group (with a few extant species) has a porous, protective frontal shield formed by the fusion of such spines.

Most cheilostomes brood their embryos in special external chambers of standard plan: a hoodlike upfolding from the distal/proximal boundary of two zooids, which may become partly or wholly immersed in or between these zooids. It is called an ooecium and is double-walled, with outer ectooecium and inner entooecium separated by a coelomic lumen. In some species at least, the lumen is confluent with the coelom of the bearing zooid, and the ooecium appears to be a spinous polymorph. However, its development is inconsistent, for example, commencing with paired outgrowths from the proximal zooid or with a single outgrowth from the distal zooid. It is easy to interpret the former as representing the distal pair of marginal spines, especially since these are usually otherwise lacking in ooeciferous zooids. Development from the distal zooid is more difficult to explain, although it should be noted that proximally situated spinelike zooids are not unknown in cheilostomes.

The bryozoan colony is made up from replicated zooids. The simpler polymorphs are vicarious and dispersed through the colony in an ordered or apparently random manner. With the development of adventitious polymorphs, however, a second-order unit, the cormidium, becomes recognizable. Cormidia are groupings of dissimilar polymorphs. Siphonophora (Cnidaria) provide the standard example of colonies with cormidia and it seems generally unappreciated that cheilostomes have cormidia that are at least as complex and probably better integrated. Thus an autozooid may bear spines, an ooecium, adventitious avicularia, and perhaps a vibraculum. Little is known about behavioral coordination in cormidia; much more is known about the metabolic relationships between a female zooid and its ooecium.

Reproduction and growth. Propagation by statoblasts is important in Phylactolaemata. They develop in large numbers on the funiculi, and are liberated when the colony breaks up. Statoblasts have a protective coat, often a float, and sometimes hooked spines. They are resistant to cold and desiccation and give rise to a new colony under favorable conditions. Nonphylactolaemates in fresh and brackish water may produce resting zooids or hibernacula, and many marine species overwinter as nutrient-filled stolons. Asexual reproduction by fragmentation occurs in a few marine bryozoans, and is said to be important to the free-living sand forms. Lobulation of colonies is characteristic of the more evolved phylactolaemates.

Gonads in bryozoans are associated with the peritoneum: testes on the funiculus, ovaries more often on the zooid wall. Cyclostome spermatozoa develop in tetrads, but in phylactolaemates and gymnolaemates large numbers develop around a common mass, the cytophore. In marine bryozoans (at least) they escape from the body via the mesocoel and the terminal pore in two (the dorsomedial pair) or all of the tentacles. Special male zooids with nonfeeding polypides may be localized in chimneys, thereby taking advantage of the exhalant current to disperse the spermatozoa.

The fertilized egg in phylactolaemates develops in an invagination of the body wall. When released, it is already essentially a motile zooid ready to settle and found a colony. The cyclostome gynozooid is inflated and may occupy much of the colony. Its embryo, having reached the blastula stage, lobulates a series of secondary blastulae, which may repeat the process, until the brood chamber contains 100 or more embryos. Each develops into a simple, ovoid, coronate larva which swims for a short time and then metamorphoses into a proancestrula or incomplete primary zooid. This lengthens and becomes functional.

Sexual reproduction in gymnolaemates follows one of three general patterns. (1) Small eggs are discharged into the sea via the intertentacular organ, an inflated tube situated between the dorsomedial tentacles. Fertilization takes place there. The zygote develops into a planktonic, feeding, triangular, flattened, bivalved larva or cyphonautes. This probably lives for several weeks before it settles. (2) A large, fully yolked egg is produced in the coelom, and extruded through the supraneural coelomopore (replacing the intertentacular organ) into an external brood chamber. If this is an ovicell, the embryo receives no nourishment, for its size is unchanged during development. A nonfeeding coronate larva is liberated. (3) Smallish yolky eggs are transferred to the lumen of an ovicell via the supraneural pore. The ovicell comprises the ooecium, previously described, and an internal membranous extension of the mother zooid, the inner vesicle. The fertilized egg lies between the ooecium and the inner vesicle. The vesicular epithelium, well supplied with funicular strands, hypertrophies where it is in contact with the embryo and becomes a pseudoplacenta. That food is supplied to the embryo is evidenced by its growth during development. A nonfeeding coronate larva is liberated.

The larva responds to light and other stimuli. It achieves limited dispersal and selects a settlement site. Prior to metamorphosis the larva explores a surface with special long cilia; at the moment of attachment a hollow organ, the adhesive sac, is everted, spreads as a disk, and flattens onto the surface. Metamorphosis is total and its details are complex, but the larval organization disappears and a reversed polarity emerges. (Phylactolaemate development does not include this reversal.) The ancestrular polypide differentiates from the upper wall, and colonial budding commences.

The method of budding differs between the three classes. In phylactolaemates new polypide rudiments appear, abanally to the parent, in an ordered manner which determines the branching pattern of the colony. Differentiation of cystids (the zooid walls), insofar as they are present, follows the polypides.

In stenolaemates polypide rudiments also appear first, but are adanal to the parent zooid. Since the cystids are essentially tubular, they grow around the polypide rudiments following division of the longitudinal walls. However, it is important whether these calcified walls meet or remain slightly distant from the terminal epithelium. In the latter case, coelomic confluence remains around their distal end (the double-walled structure), whereas in the former, cystids are separate once formed and communicate only through interzooidal pores.

Gymnolaemate budding is different again, and dependent from the outset on the connecting pores and funiculus. The cystid is produced first, adanally to the mother zooid, and the polypide develops within it.

The pattern of colony formation is termed astogeny. Early on, it is often characterized by sequential change in the size and morphology of the zooids; later astogeny is repetitive, with the production of virtually identical zooids, groupings of zooids, cormidia, or groups of cormidia. The continuous colony in cheilostomes arises from the apposition of repeatedly dividing lines of zooids. The walls between contiguous lines are therefore morphologically double, and the communication pores in them

have differentiated from potential zooid buds, which is one reason why they are more complex than the pores in end walls. Frontal budding, of a layer of zooids above the existing layer or layers, may also occur.

Initial formation does not complete the zooid's development. Wall thickening may continue, phases of reproductive activity come and go, while a cycle of polypide aging and renewal continues until senescence. This cycle, in which the whole polypide regresses, and is histolyzed until only a compacted, fibrous "brown body" remains, is peculiar to bryozoans. Old zooids may consist only of an accumulation of brown bodies.

Ecology. Fresh-water bryozoans are present on submerged tree roots and aquatic plants in most lakes, ponds, and rivers, especially in clear water of alkaline pH. Their presence is best confirmed by dip-netting for statoblasts at the water's edge. Most other bryozoans are marine, although some gymnolaemates inhabit brackish water. They are common in the sea, ranging from the middle shore to a depth of over 26,000 ft (8000 m), and are maximally abundant in waters of the continental shelf. Most attach to firm substrata, so that their distribution is primarily determined by the availability of support. Mud is unfavorable and so is sand unless well provided with stone, dead shells, hydroids, or large foraminiferans, as in regions of strong current, where colony densities may reach $470/\text{ft}^2$ ($5000/\text{m}^2$) of hard substrate.

Intertidal bryozoans shun the light, and are found under boulders, below overhangs, and on algae, particularly under conditions of high flow; they avoid turbid water and accumulating sediment. The seaweed dwellers are mainly fleshy ctenostomes and specially flexible cheilostomes, or are very small. Experiments with larvae have demonstrated high selectivity with regard to substrate, for example, algal species or shell surface. Settlement is influenced by texture and contour, with larvae often preferring concavities.

Colony form in bryozoans is to some extent related to habitat. Encrusting and bushy flexible species are adapted to wave exposure; brittle twiglike and foliaceous species are found deeper; some erect branching species tolerate sediment deposition. One group of tiny discoid species lives on sand in warm seas, and in one genus the colonies are so small that they live actually among the sand grains; a few species live anchored by long kenozooidal stems in mud. A number of stolonate ctenostomes bore into the substance of mollusk shells; other species are associated only with hermit crabs, and a few are commensal with shrimps or polychaete worms.

Primarily, however, bryozoans are inhabitants of shaded rock surfaces, where they compete with each other, sponges, and compound ascidians for space. They have no set size or shape, and reproductive capacity is simply a function of size. Some display adaptations, such as raised margins, long spines, or frontal budding, to resist being overgrown. When colonies meet, there is often a mutual cessation of growth, but with different species the one with larger zooids may overgrow its rival or impair its feeding efficiency. Closely related species sometimes display slightly different habitat preferences, thereby avoiding direct competition. Pendent and outgrowing colonies escape the surface competition and become better placed for feeding; they include elegant lace corals and robust fans rising 6–12 in. (15–30 cm) in height.

Bryozoans have few serious predators. Nudibranch mollusks and pycnogonids (sea spiders) specialize in feeding on zooids but are rarely destructive of entire colonies. Loxosomatids (Entoprocta) and a hydroid (*Zanclea*) are common commensals.

Life spans vary. Small algal dwellers complete their life cycle in a few months. Many species survive a year but have two overlapping generations; others are perennial, with one known to survive for 12 years.

Bryozoans may be a nuisance in colonizing ship hulls and the insides of water pipes, and one species has caused severe dermatitis in fishers. Recently some delicate kinds have been used in costume jewelry, and green-dyed clumps of dried *Bugula* are often sold as "everlasting plants."   John S. Ryland

Cystoporata

Within the Bryozoa is an extinct order, the Cystoporata, in the class Stenolaemata. Cystoporates had encrusting, mound-shaped, or basally attached, erect, calcified colonies made of sheets or branches composed of tubular feeding zooids and extrazooidal vesicular skeletal deposits.

Zooecia, the skeletal tubes delimiting the zooids, in many cystoporates are characterized by lunaria, which are thickened strips that extend up one side of each zooecium. Lunaria commonly have a different degree of transverse curvature than does the rest of the zooecium, and extend somewhat above the general surface of the colonies and arch slightly over the zooecial aperture. Polymorphic zooecia are uncommon and consist of small "space-filling" structures and, less commonly, enlarged, apparently female zooids.

Ceramoporine cystoporates are characterized by laminated wall structure, usually short zooecia, sparse diaphragms, and commonly by gaps of pores in the skeletal walls that may have served for nutrients to move between zooids. These organisms ranged from the Middle Ordovician to the Lower Devonian.

Fistuliporine cystoporates have laminated, granular, or granular-prismatic wall structure, short to long zooecia, and sparse to abundant diaphragms, and lack gaps or pores in the skeletal walls; and in many the extrazooidal vesicular skeletal deposits are replaced outwardly by continuous, dense skeletal material (stereom). Rodlike structures (acanthostyles) may occur in skeletal walls, oriented perpendicularly to the skeletal surface and projecting above the colony surface. These organisms ranged from the Lower Ordovician to the upper Permian.

Cystoporates were exclusively marine and lived in a wide variety of relatively low-energy environments on continental shelves and seas. Both subgroups had diverse growth habits, slightly greater in the fistuliporines. Erect colonies grew as two-layered sheets with zooids growing back to back (bifoliate), as narrow bifoliate branches that bifurcated to form bushes or that anastomosed to form perforated sheets, as radially symmetrical branches that could be several centimeters in diameter, and in other growth habits.

Most cystoporates, except those with narrow branches, have maculae—small, uniformly spaced areas composed of a group of zooecia or a similar-sized spot of extrazooidal skeleton. Maculae may be elevated, depressed, or surrounded by slightly enlarged zooecia that typically tilt away and have lunaria on the side closest to the maculae. Spacing, size, and disposition of zooecia around maculae suggest that they mark points where water, filtered by the surrounding zooids, flowed away from the colony surface in a focused, chimneylike flow, as seen in many living bryozoans with large surface areas.

Fossils

Fossil Bryozoa have a long geological history, from early in the Ordovician Period [500 million years ago (Ma)] to the Recent (Fig. 1). Individual fossils range in size from a few millimeters to several meters in maximum dimension. Various encrusting or erect growth forms are common, though some were free-living (Fig. 2). Representatives of the marine orders that secreted calcareous skeletons (Cryptostomata, Cyclostomata, Cystoporata, Trepostomata, and Cheilostomata) commonly are abundant in sedimentary rocks formed where benthic organisms flourished. Skeletons generally are calcite, though some are aragonite or mixed calcite and aragonite. Ctenostomata have nonmineralized skeletons, so they have been preserved only as excavations or borings in marine shells or on the undersides of other organisms that overgrew them (a preservation style termed bioimmuration). The fresh-water Phylactolaemata have gelatinous skeletons, but their tough statoblasts (dormant reproductive bodies) have been reported from sediments as old as the Jurassic (at least 150 Ma).

Fossil Bryozoa are most abundant in calcium carbonate–bearing rocks such as various limestones, calcareous shale, and calcareous siltstone, and they are especially common in some alternating thin-bedded limestones and shales. During the Ordovician, Carboniferous, and Permian periods, bryozoans were important parts of many fossil reefs, reef flanks, and other carbonate buildups in shallow (less than 100 m depth) tropical waters. Bryozoans commonly dominate and may reach very high diversities in post-Paleozoic cool-temperate carbonate deposits, indicating a shift in primary environment after the Paleozoic.

In the study of bryozoans, examination with a microscope is necessary. Although colonies of many species are large, the individual skeletons of each zooid (unit of the colony) range from less than 0.1 to about 1 mm in diameter. The smaller diameters are typical for cross sections of elongate tubes that characterize zooids in stenolaemate bryozoans, and the larger diameters are typical for the more equidimensional zooids of cheilostomes. Identification is based on numerous external and, for most stenolaemates, internal features that require study with a microscope. Adequate classification of most stenolaemate bryozoans generally requires variously oriented thin sections through the colony interior (Fig. 2).

Classification. Features of the colonial skeletons (zoaria) as well as the morphology of the individual zooidal skeletons (zooecia) are used to classify bryozoans. Many fossil bryozoans had only one type of zooid (autozooids), which apparently could feed and carry out all other necessary biological functions of the colony. Others were polymorphic, with various types of specialized zooids supplementing the autozooids. Number, types, and morphology of polymorphs is important in classification. Other characters important in classification of fossil bryozoans are wall structure, reproductive chambers, general growth habit or specific shape of colonies, and for some, surface topography of the colony.

Geological history. The earliest bryozoans (representatives of the Cryptostomata, Trepostomata, Cyclostomata, and Cystoporata) are recorded from Lower Ordovician rocks (a few fossils from the Cambrian have been assigned erroneously to the Bryozoa). In Mid-Ordovician time, diverse groups of these various bryozoan orders, including the suborder Ptilodictyoidea of the order Cryptostomata, had a broad geographic distribution (**Fig. 4**). The phylum continued to evolve rapidly, and toward the end of the Ordovician Period the Trepostomata and the ptilodictyoid Cryptostomata were dominant. The Cystoporata, Cyclostomata, and Ctenostomata were less important faunal elements of the time period.

In the Silurian, the Trepostomata and Cryptostomata were still dominant. New groups diversified in other orders, including the Fenestellina (a suborder of Cryptostomata also referred to as fenestrates), which occurred sparsely in the Late Ordovician. The cystoporates also became a more distinctive part of the bryozoan faunas. Relatively little is known about the Silurian bryozoans of many regions because the principal sedimentary rocks are dolomites and evaporites and the bryozoans are either poorly preserved or they did not inhabit these environments.

Diversity of genera and species further increased in the Devonian Period. Fenestellinid and rhabdomesine cryptostomes were very abundant, and the number of fistuliporid cystoporates increased. The trepostomes continued to be well represented by new species and genera.

The Carboniferous and Permian bryozoans were dominated by various kinds of fenestellinids, rhabdomesines, and cystoporates. The trepostomes were less numerous, and cyclostomes remained uncommon. Toward the end of the Permian Period, almost all trepostomes, cryptostomes, and cystoporates became extinct. This drastic reduction in bryozoan groups extended throughout much of the late Permian and parallels similar patterns in other Paleozoic fossil groups.

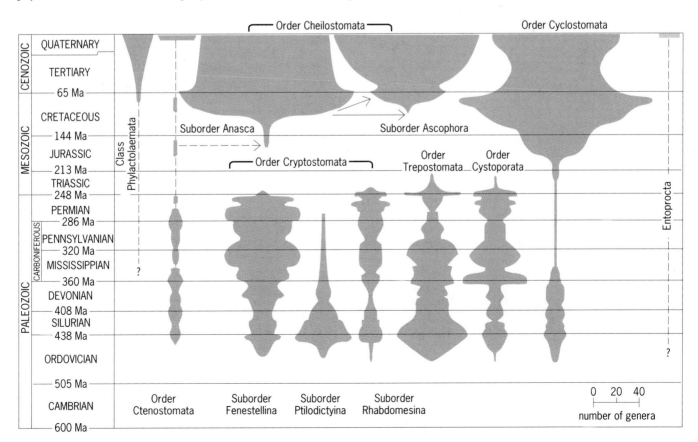

Fig. 4. Diagram of the geological distribution and abundance of Bryozoa.

Bryozoans are sparse in the Triassic Period. A few cystoporates, trepostomes, rhabdomesines, and cyclostomes occur in Triassic rocks. Representatives of the first three groups are Triassic "holdovers" from the Paleozoic fauna, and the oldest Mesozoic occurrence of cyclostomes is in Upper Triassic rocks.

The Jurassic Period witnessed a great expansion of the Cyclostomata. This order dominated bryozoan faunas until the Late Cretaceous. The Cheilostomata, initially represented by anascans, first appeared late in the Jurassic and rapidly became the dominant bryozoan group, undergoing explosive diversification during mid-Cretaceous. Many of the major cheilostome groups and major evolutionary innovations had developed before the end of the Late Cretaceous.

The cyclostomes continued to evolve a few new families during the Cenozoic Era, but their diversity was reduced by one-third at the end of the Cretaceous and the group has never rebounded. With the exception of the very beginning of the Cenozoic Era (the Danian Stage of the Paleocene Epoch), the Bryozoa of the Cenozoic Era, like the present-day fauna, were principally cheilostomes. Although cheilostome diversity was reduced by over one-fourth at the end of the Cretaceous, the group resumed rapid diversification by the Eocene Epoch (35–55 Ma). Some of the cheilostome groups, such as the cribrimorphs, which flourished in the Late Cretaceous, declined in numbers in the Cenozoic. The anascans, a dominant group in the Cretaceous, continued to maintain their importance in Cenozoic bryozoan faunas and to the present day. The ascophorans diversified especially rapidly during the Eocene, and they maintain high diversity to the present.

Bryozoans have experienced several vigorous radiations and two devastating extinction events. The first adaptive radiation occurred during the Ordovician and involved the Trepostomata and ptilodictyoid cryptostomes, and the second occurred during the Devonian and involved the fenestellinid cryptostomes, which were the dominant bryozoans during the late Paleozoic. All these stenolaemate groups, plus the rhabdomesines and cystoporates, were severely reduced by the end-Permian extinction and were completely extinct before the end of the Triassic Period. A third radiation, which involved only the cyclostome stenolaemates, occurred during the Jurassic, and the cheilostome gymnolaemates had the first of their two radiations during mid-Cretaceous. The end-Cretaceous extinction event strongly reduced the diversity of both cheilostomes and cyclostomes. The cyclostomes never recovered their Late Cretaceous diversity, but by the Eocene cheilostomes were experiencing a renewed interval of vigorous diversification and reached diversity levels higher than those of Late Cretaceous.

Evolutionary relationships. The fossil records of all orders of the class stenolaemate bryozoans (cyclostomes, cystoporates, trepostomes, and cryptostomes) begin in the Arenigian Stage (478–488 Ma) of the Lower Ordovician, and the soft-bodied gymnolaemate order Ctenostomata is represented back to the Late Ordovician Ashgillian Stage (438–448 Ma) by borings in shells. Thus, there are two problems with using the fossil record to interpret early evolutionary relationships among bryozoans. The first is that earliest representatives of the highly skeletonized stenolaemate orders appear fully differentiated and essentially simultaneously in the fossil record, so relationships among these highly mineralized groups cannot be inferred from the sequence of appearance. The other problem is that the soft-bodied ctenostomes must have had a substantially longer existence than indicated by the fossil record, because the oldest ctenostome fossils are specialized, apparently nonprimitive ctenostomes that left borings in shells. (Most ctenostomes live on surfaces of shells and other substrata and do not excavate chambers.)

Ctenostomes are widely considered to be a paraphyletic group (a group of taxa that contains the ancestar but not all of its descendants) that gave rise to the Stenolaemata during the early Paleozoic and to the cheilostome Gymnolaemata during the Jurassic. One hypothesis about the origin of the Stenolaemata concerns the method of protrusion of the tentacles of zooids to the feeding position. Ctenostomes have a completely flexible body wall. Their only defense against predators is either to remain small and cryptic or to bear allelochemicals, yet their completely flexible body wall can be easily contracted to translate fluid that pushes out the feeding apparatus (analogous with squeezing a toothpaste tube to extrude the toothpaste). Stenolaemates have rigidly calcified lateral body walls, and within the calcified tubular zooids there is a separate, mesodermal "membranous sac" that can be squeezed by transverse parietal muscles to protrude the feeding apparatus. It has been hypothesized that the stenolaemates originated when the ectodermal epithelium of a ctenostome-like ancestor secreted calcite as well as an outer organic membrane, along with separation of the muscle-bearing mesoderm from the ectoderm to form the membranous sac of the proto-stenolaemate. This condition would allow predator-resisting calcification to develop and still permit protrusion and retraction of the feeding apparatus. This evolutionary innovation apparently occurred early in the Ordovician Period, and stenolaemates rapidly diversified into several distinct types that are recognized as orders. Detailed phylogenetic analysis indicates that the Cyclostomata, as traditionally conceived, are paraphyletic and gave rise to the other, essentially Paleozoic, stenolaemate orders.

Origin of the cheilostomes is much clearer. A family of uniserial, encrusting ctenostomes with pyriform zooids is known from bioimmured (entombed while alive) representatives as old as Middle Jurassic; some Jurassic specimens have D-shaped orifices, which is normally a cheilostome rather than a ctenostome attribute. This family (arachnidiid ctenostomes) apparently gave rise to the cheilostomes. The earliest known cheilostomes were Late Jurassic, encrusting colonies of simple, uniserial to loosely pleuriserial, pyriform to elliptical feeding zooids with mineralized lateral walls.

The Phylactolaemata are probably phylogenetically most closely related to the Ctenostomata. At present all phylactolaemates live in fresh water, and their earliest fossils consist of small asexual reproductive bodies found in Jurassic fresh-water deposits. The gelatinous nonmineralized colonies in a fresh-water environment have reduced probability of preservation as fossils. The only other fresh-water bryozoans are some ctenostomes, but it is unclear whether phylactolaemates evolved from fresh-water ctenostomes or whether they originated in the oceans and later migrated into fresh water and then disappeared from the oceans.

Evolutionary paleoecology. Maximum diversity and abundance of bryozoans has historically been on middle to outer shelves and similar conditions on epeiric sea floors, inferred to be several tens of meters deep. Bryozoan-rich deposits in the Paleozoic were built up by trepostomes, cystoporates, and cryptostomes and developed in shallow equatorial to cold-temperate (midlatitude) environments. However, post-Paleozoic bryozoan-rich deposits were generated early on by cyclostomes and then by cheilostomes, and almost all formed in middle latitudes, seldom in tropical environments. This shift in pattern is probably biologically driven, rather than driven by physical or chemical changes of the world oceans. The "Mesozoic marine revolution" saw the proliferation of several groups of vigorous predators in the tropics, as well as the rise in importance in the tropics of competing organisms such as scleractinian corals and certain algae that grew much more rapidly than bryozoans. While some cheilostomes and a few cyclostomes have reached enormous sizes during the post-Paleozoic, similar large sizes were reached by Paleozoic trepostomes and cystoporates, and on average Paleozoic bryozoans, especially trepostomes and cystoporates, were larger than their post-Paleozoic relatives.

During the Paleozoic, erect growth habits became progressively more abundant; whereas during the post-Paleozoic, encrusting growth habits became progressively more abundant. These contrasting patterns have been interpreted to result in part from an increase in predation during the post-Paleozoic, because slow-growing erect bryozoans cannot as easily recover from partial predation as can encrusting forms. Among erect bryozoans during the Paleozoic and also during the post-Paleozoic, species characterized by narrow, unilaminate branches increased in importance from a trivial percentage to the most numerous. The unilaminate, narrow-branched growth habit allows food–bearing water to be processed much more efficiently than in any of the other colony morphologies, and this efficiency has been inferred to provide an adaptive advantage.

Bryozoans are competitively inferior in overgrowth interactions (so they tend to be overgrawn by other taxa) to most other encrusting organisms such as sponges, ascidians, cnidarians, and algae, and this may have been part of the reason for their relative unimportance in the post-Paleozoic tropics. Among post-Paleozoic bryozoans, cheilostomes consistently have been superior in overgrowth interactions with cyclostomes, due to multiple differences such as, on average, higher growth rates, higher colony margins, and stronger feeding currents in cheilostomes. Simultaneously, cheilostomes have evolved a larger average colony size and have undergone two vigorous stages of diversification (Late Cretaceous and, after recovery from the end-Cretaceous mass extinction, Paleogene), while cyclostomes have declined slowly from their peak diversity in Late Cretaceous and now have on average smaller colony sizes than in the Cretaceous.

The relatively small size of most bryozoan colonies and their slow growth rates, plus the general competitive inferiority of encrusting bryozoans, has relegated them to a minor role in construction of reefs and other organic buildups through geological time. There have been exceptions. During the Mid-Ordovician, encrusting bryozoans were the primary framework builders on reefs and, in many instances, erect bryozoans contributed the bulk of the skeletal debris to the reef flanks. From Silurian through Carboniferous, reef frameworks were locally predominated by bryozoans, and fenestellinid bryozoans grew abundantly on certain organic buildups during the Carboniferous and Permian. In the post-Paleozoic, multilaminar encrusting to massive cyclostome bryozoans built a few small Mesozoic reefs, and cheilostomes similarly built small reefs a few meters wide and high during the Cenozoic. Beyond these exceptions in which reefs were largely or partly built by bryozoans, bryozoans occur widely in reefs as cryptic organisms inhabiting the undersides of corals and small-scale caves.

Throughout their geological history, bryozoans have been much more common on ephemeral substrata that are available for months or years than on persistent substrata that are available for several years and longer (such as reefs). They are widespread, and diverse on brachiopod shells in Paleozoic rocks and on bivalve shells in Jurassic to Neogene deposits. Various life history strategies have evolved to utilize the relatively ephemeral, often mobile shell substrata. Short-lived colonies may live preferentially on undersurfaces of shells and develop only a few zooids before brooding embryos. In contrast, colonies of some species can effectively occupy the entire exposed shell surface and continue to live and expand time after time as the shell or small rock is overturned, so that the original substrate is buried deeply in multiple layers of bryozoan zooids of a colony that can live and function in any orientation with respect to the sea floor.

Repetitive evolution of similar colony morphologies has been the hallmark of bryozoan history. Cheilostomes have evolved unique combinations of characteristics in their successful invasion of soft substrata, where they are either free-lying or live attached by specialized zooids that resemble roots. But otherwise, similar colony morphologies have evolved convergently in many different orders. The limitations on bryozoan morphologies (including constraints on branch sizes and shapes) have been due to the basic organization of bryozoans. Zooids have always been small (almost always much less than 1 mm² in surface area), feeding bryozoans must be at the colony surface and have access to nutrient-bearing water, and the water that is drawn toward the colony surface must find a nearby outlet away from the colony after it is filtered. Paleozoic stenolaemates collectively, post-Paleozoic cyclostome stenolaemates, and cheilostome gymnolaemates have all developed similar-appearing encrusting, massive, and erect colonies. Consequently, any given bryozoan fossil commonly must be examined closely in order to place it in the correct taxonomic order.   Frank K. McKinney

Bibliography. D. P. Gordon, A. M. Smith, and J. A. Grant-Mackie (eds.), *Bryozoans in Space and Time*, 1996; P. J. Hayward, J. S. Ryland, and P. D. Taylor (eds.), *Biology and Palaeobiology of Bryozoans*, 1994; A. Herrera and J. B. C. Jackson (eds.), *Proceedings of the 11th International Bryozoology Association Conference*, 1999; F. K. McKinney and J. B. C. Jackson, *Bryozoan Evolution*, 1989; R. A. Robison (ed.), *Treatise on Invertebrate Paleontology, Part G*, rev.1983.

Buckeye

A genus, *Aesculus*, of deciduous trees or shrubs belonging to the plant order Sapindales. Buckeyes grow in North America, southeast Europe, and eastern Asia to India. The distinctive features are opposite, palmately compound leaves and a large fruit having a firm outer coat and containing usually one large seed with a conspicuous hilum. The Ohio buckeye (*A. glabra*), a small tree which may grow to a height of 30 ft (9 m), is found mainly in the Ohio valley and in the southern Appalachians. It can be recognized by the glabrous winter buds, prickly fruits 1–2 in. (2.5–5 cm) long, and compound leaves having five leaflets. *See* SAPINDALES.

Another important species, the yellow buckeye (*A. octandra*), which may reach to 90 ft (27 m), is native in the Central states, has five leaflets and smooth buds, but differs in its smooth, larger fruit, which may be 2–2½ in. (5–6 cm) long. The horse chestnut (*A. hippocastanum*), which usually has seven leaflets and resinous buds (see **illus.**), is a native of the Balkan Peninsula. It is planted throughout the United States and is a beautiful ornamental tree bearing cone-shaped flower clusters in early summer. The seeds of all species contain a bitter and narcotic principle. The wood of the native tree species is used for furniture, boxes, crates, baskets, and artificial legs. *See* FOREST AND FORESTRY; TREE.

Arthur H. Graves; Kenneth P. Davis

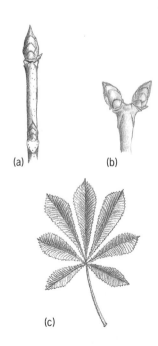

Horse chestnut (*Aesculus hippocastanum*): (a) twig, (b) buds, (c) leaf.

Buckwheat

A herbaceous, erect annual, the dry seed or grain of which is used as a source of food and feed. It is not a true cereal and is one of the very few plants, other than those of the Gramineae family, used for their starchy seed, which is processed as a meal or flour.

Buckwheat belongs to the Polygonaceae family, which also includes the common weeds dock, sorrel, knotweed, bindweed, smartweed, and climbing false buckwheat. Species of buckwheat that have been commercially grown are *Fagopyrum sagittatum* (*F. esculentum*), *F. emarginatum*, and *F. tataricum*. *See* POLYGONALES.

The plant grows to a height of 2–5 ft (0.6–1.5 m), with many broad heart-shaped leaves. It produces a single main stem which usually bears several branches, and is grooved, succulent, and smooth except for nodes (see **illus.**). Buckwheat is an indeterminate species in response to photoperiod, and produces flowers and fruits (so-called seeds) until the beginning of frost. *See* PHOTOPERIODISM.

Species differentiation. *Fagopyrum sagittatum* and *F. emarginatum* produce flowers that are densely clustered in racemes at ends of branches or on short pedicels that arise from the axils of the leaves. Individual flowers have no petals, but the calyx is composed of five petallike sepals which may be light green, white, pink, or red. Populations include plants typically of two floral types: the pin type which has flowers with long pistils and short stamens and the thrum type which has flowers with short pistils and long stamens. The pistil consists of a one-celled ovary, three-parted style with knoblike stigmas, and eight stamens. Glands (usually eight) which secrete nectar are located at the base of the ovary. Generally, self-fertilization is prevented by a heteromorphic incompatibility system, and seeds are produced only when cross-pollination occurs between the pin and thrum stylar types. The so-called seed of

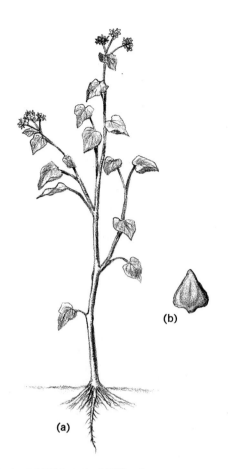

Buckwheat. (a) Mature plant. (b) Seed.

buckwheat (actually a fruit which is an achene) usually has three angles and varies in shape, size, and color. *See* FLOWER; FRUIT; SECRETORY STRUCTURES (PLANT).

Fagopyrum tataricum (commonly known as tartary buckwheat, rye buckwheat, duck wheat, or hulless) differs from the two previously described species. The leaves are narrower and arrow-shaped, and the flowers are smaller with inconspicuous greenish-white sepals. Plants are only of one flower type and are self-fertile.

Cultivation and use. Buckwheat is of minor importance as a grain crop in the United States, and is principally grown in areas of the Northeast where the weather is likely to be moist and cool. It is usually grown on land too rough or poor for other grain crops or, since it matures within 10–12 weeks, as an emergency crop where previous crops have failed. The crop is also used to smother weeds, as green manure, and as food and cover for various game birds and wildlife. Buckwheat is often used as bee pasture, and is the source of a dark, strong-flavored honey. H. G. Marshall

Processing. The production of buckwheat flour requires cleaning, grinding, and fractionation in a manner similar to that used for wheat flour. The distinctive polygonal shape of the grain kernel enables the use of sieving screens with triangular openings to facilitate separation of weed seeds and other foreign material. Sieving by size and the use of air aspira-

tion enables separation of good-quality grain. Poor-quality, low-density seed and trash are removed by air aspiration. Successive cleaning of the grain is essential for premium quality. *See* WHEAT.

Hot-water steeping or steam pretreatment of the grain may be used to improve the nutritional properties, yield, and market value of buckwheat products. Dry heating or steaming of the grain prior to drying with temperatures less than 158°F (70°C) improves the efficiency of hull removal and reduces cooking time of selected products. Hulling is accomplished by using roller mills adjusted to crack the husk with minimum damage to the kernel. This operation must be precisely controlled to avoid excessive kernel fracture. Hulls, constituting about one-fifth of the grain by weight, are separated by sieving. Buckwheat hulls provide little food value and are utilized as animal litter.

The products of dehulled buckwheat include whole groats, split kernels, middlings or farina, and flour. Whole groats, splits, and farina are obtained by selective sieving and may be utilized as breakfast cereals and porridges or as thickening agents. Dry roasting of whole groats may be employed to increase color and flavor while decreasing their preparation time. When milled as flour, buckwheat will yield 60–75% extraction. The flour is typically more coarse and more highly colored than wheat flour. Buckwheat middlings, which include the layer immediately below the hull and the germ, provide valuable animal feed stock. In the United States, buckwheat flour is used primarily in pancake mix formulations, blended with wheat, corn, rice, or oat flour. Japanese soba, a dried noodle product, is prepared from blends of buckwheat and wheat flours. *See* CEREAL; FOOD MANUFACTURING; GRAIN CROPS.

Mark A. Uebersax

Bibliography. H. G. Marshall and Y. Pomeranz, Buckwheat: Description, breeding, production, and utilization, in *Advances in Cereal Science and Technology*, vol. 5, American Association of Cereal Chemists, 1982; H. K. Wilson, *Grain Crops*, 2d ed., 1955.

Bud

An embryonic shoot containing the growing stem tip surrounded by young leaves or flowers or both, and the whole frequently enclosed by special protective leaves, the bud scales.

Position. The bud at the apex of the stem is called a terminal bud (**Fig. 1***a*). Any bud that develops on the side of a stem is a lateral bud. The lateral bud borne in the axil (angle between base of leaf and stem) of a leaf is the axillary bud (Fig. 1*a* and *d*). It develops concurrently with the leaf which subtends it, but usually such buds do not unfold and grow rapidly until the next season. Because of the inhibitory influence of the apical or other buds, many axillary buds never develop actively or may not do so for many years. These are known as latent or dormant buds. Above or beside the axillary buds, some plants regularly produce

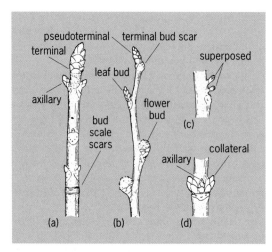

Fig. 1. Bud positions. (*a*) Terminal and axillary (buckeye). (*b*) Pseudoterminal (elm). (*c*) Superposed (butternut). (*d*) Collateral (red maple).

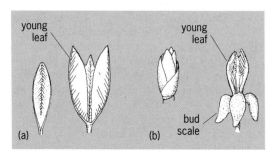

Fig. 2. Bud coverings. (*a*) Closed and open naked buds (hobblebush). (*b*) Closed and open scaly bud (hickory).

additional buds called accessory, or supernumerary, buds. Accessory buds which occur above the axillary bud are called superposed buds (Fig. 1*c*), and those beside it collateral buds (Fig. 1*d*). Under certain conditions, such as removal of terminal and auxillary buds, other buds may arise at almost any point on the stem, or even on roots or leaves. Such buds are known as adventitious buds. *See* PLANT GROWTH.

Composition. Buds that give rise to flowers only are termed flower buds (Fig. 1*b*), or in some cases, fruit buds. If a bud grows into a leafy shoot, it is called a leaf bud (Fig. 1*b*), or more accurately, a branch bud. A bud which contains both young leaves and flowers is called a mixed bud.

Covering. Buds of herbaceous plants and of some woody plants are covered by rudimentary foliage leaves only. Such buds are called naked buds (**Fig. 2*a***). In most woody plants, however, the buds

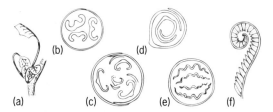

Fig. 3. Some types of vernation (prefoliation). (*a*) Conduplicate (tulip tree). (*b*) Revolute (dock). (*c*) Involute (poplar). (*d*) Convolute (cherry). (*e*) Plicate (sycamore). (*f*) Circinate (fern).

are covered with modified protective leaves in the form of scales. These buds are called scaly buds or winter buds (Fig. 2*b*). In the different species of plants, the bud scales differ markedly. They may be covered with hairs or with water-repellent secretions of resin, gum, or wax. Ordinarily when a bud opens, the scales fall off, leaving characteristic markings on the stem (bud scale scars).

Vernation. The characteristic arrangement of young leaves within the bud is known as vernation or prefoliation (**Fig. 3**). Within the buds, the leaves may be folded on the midrib, plaited, rolled, coiled, or twisted in exact order and precision, each kind of plant having its distinctive inner bud pattern. Many ferns have a coiled leaf arrangement which is known as circinate vernation. *See* LEAF; PLANT ORGANS; PLANT TAXONOMY.   Neele Ammons

Buffalo

The name for members of the family Bovidae in the mammalian order Artiodactyla. The buffalo is an Old World species and resembles the oxen in general appearance. The North American bison is often called a buffalo, but is not related to the true buffalo. The Asiatic buffalo (*Bubalus bubalis*), known as the Indian or water buffalo and also as the carabao, is found as a domestic animal in the Balkans, Asia Minor, and Egypt. These buffalo exist in the wild state in southern Asia and Borneo, where they are considered to be ferocious and dangerous. Water buffalo are stocky, heavy-built animals that are not quite 6 ft (2 m) at shoulder height. They have very short hair and the shortest, most splayed horns of any variety (see **illus.**). Like all buffalo, they have a liking for marshes, where they wallow and become caked with mud that affords protection against insects. Their wide, flattened hooves allow them to stand firmly on the soft, marshy soil. They are hardy animals, being able to resist the infections and insect-borne diseases of the country, and they can withstand cold so well that they do not need shelters. Their diet consists entirely of reeds, rushes, and other aquatic plants. Domestic herds of 200–300 animals may provide 300 pints (1400 liters) of milk a year. This milk is rich in cream and is used to make butter and yogurt. *See* MILK.

Two other Asiatic species related to, but smaller than, the water buffalo are the tamarau (*Anoa mindorensis*), which is indigenous to the Philippines, and the still smaller (40 in. or 1 m high) anoa (*A. depressicornis*), or wild dwarf buffalo, found in the Celebes.

The African buffalo, classed in the genus *Syncerus*, was very numerous until the turn of the century, when the infectious disease rinderpest caused many deaths. They are still abundant though widely hunted by the natives. There are several varieties of African buffalo, and it is thought that all may be subspecies of *S. caffer*, the Cape buffalo, which attains a height of about 5 ft (1.5 m) at the shoulder and weighs more than 1500 lb (675 kg). They live in the open country of central, eastern, and southern Africa. Mating

Herd of Indian or water buffalo (*Bubalus bubalis*).

occurs early in the year, and a single calf is born after a gestation period of 11 months. Except for its size, this animal is difficult to distinguish from the rare dwarf or forest buffalo (*S. caffer nanus*), which is less than 4 ft (1.2 m) high at the shoulder and weighs a little more than 400 lb (180 kg). It lives in marshy, forested areas of western Africa, where it is known as the bush cow. This species has not been domesticated and occurs in herds of up to 1000. *See* ARTIODACTYLA; BISON; MAMMALIA; MUSK-OX; YAK.   Charles B. Curtin

Buffers (chemistry)

Solutions selected or prepared to minimize changes in hydrogen ion concentration which would otherwise tend to occur as a result of a chemical reaction. In general, chemical buffers are systems which, once constituted, tend to resist further change due to external influences. Thus it is possible, for example, to make buffers resistant to changes in temperature, pressure, volume, redox potential, or acidity. The commonest buffer in chemical solution systems is the acid-base buffer.

Chemical reactions known or suspected to be dependent on the acidity of the solution, as well as on other variables, are frequently studied by measurements in comixture with an appropriate buffer. For example, it may be desirable to investigate how the rate of a chemical reaction depends upon the hydrogen ion activity (pH). This is accomplished by measurements in several buffer systems, each of which provides a nearly constant, different pH. Alternatively, it may be desirable to measure the effects of other variables on a pH-sensitive system, by stabilizing the pH at a convenient value with a particular buffer.

Effectiveness. Buffer action depends upon the fact that, if two or more reactions coexist in a solution, then the chemical potential of any species is common to all reactions in which it takes part, and may be defined by specification of the chemical potentials of all other species in any one of the reactions. To be effective, a buffer must be able to respond to

an increase as well as a decrease of the species to be buffered. In order to do so, it is necessary that the proton transfer step of the buffer be reversible with respect to the species involved, in the reaction to be buffered. In aqueous solution the proton transfer between most acids, their conjugate bases and water, is so rapid and reversible that the dominant direct source of protons for a chemical reaction is H_3O^+, the hydronium ion.

An acid-base buffer reaction in water is defined by reversible reaction (1), and the equilibrium constant K_a shown by Eq. (2).

$$BH^+ + H_2O \rightleftharpoons B + H_3O^+ \qquad (1)$$

$$K_a = \frac{[H_3O^+][B]}{[BH^+][H_2O]} \qquad (2)$$

In Eq. (2) the square brackets designate the activity of the species involved. In normal concentrations of buffer (0.1 mole/liter) the activity of the solvent water is essentially constant and approximately that of pure water (55.5 M). Thus the position of the equilibrium may be defined by specifying the activity of any two of the three variable species in reaction (1). Normally this is by means of the equilibrium expression shown as Eq. (3) which, upon converting to a logarithmic form, can be reduced to Eq. (4). Here f

$$[H_3O^+] = K_a \frac{[BH^+]}{[B]} \qquad (3)$$

$$pH = pK_a - \log \frac{(1-f)}{f} - \log \frac{\gamma_{BH^+}}{\gamma_B} \qquad (4)$$

is the fraction of the total buffer concentration, $(BH^+) + (B)$ existing as B, and γ is the activity coefficient relating activity a to concentration X. This relation is shown by Eq. (5). Thus a buffer pH is

$$a_x = \gamma_x(X) \qquad (5)$$

approximately defined by the dissociation constant K_a of the weak acid system and the ratio of acid to conjugate base concentrations. However, the third term in Eq. (4) indicates that the pH is dependent on the change in activity coefficients with concentration. Effects of this dependency may be eliminated in practice by providing a high and essentially invariant ionic environment in the form of an added pH-neutral strong electrolyte such as KNO_3 or NaCl.

Buffer capacity π is defined as the change in added H_3O^+ necessary to produce a given change in pH, $d[H_3O^+]/d$pH. Since the buffer comes to equilibrium with added H_3O^+, $1/\pi$ may also be defined as dpH$/df$. Inspection of Eq. (4) shows $1/\pi$ to be a minimum when $f = 1 - f$; hence a given buffer system has its highest capacity in a solution composed of equal parts BH^+ and B, and the capacity is directly proportional to the concentrations of BH^+ and B. For these reasons buffers are normally used at concentrations 10–100 times higher than the system to be controlled and, if possible, are selected so that the desired pH is approximately equal to pK_a for the buffer system. As a general rule, weak acid systems are not used to stabilize solutions whose pH is more than 2 pH units removed from pK_a, to ensure that the ratio of BH^+ to B will fall in the range 100–0.01.

Water as solvent. Buffers are particularly effective in water, because of the unusual properties of water as a solvent. Its high dielectric constant (80) tends to promote the existence of formally charged ions (ionization). Because it has both an acidic (H) and a basic (O) group, it may form bonds with ionic species leading to an organized sheath of solvent surrounding an ion (solvation). Water also tends to self-ionize to form its own conjugate acid-base system as shown by Eq. (6b), in which K_{ap} is the autoprotolysis constant. The strength of an acid (or base) in solvent water cannot be separated from reaction (6a) and

$$2H_2O \rightleftharpoons H_3O^+ + OH^- \qquad (6a)$$

$$K_{ap} = [H_3O^+][OH^-] = 10^{-14} \qquad (6b)$$

the familiar acid (or base) dissociation equilibrium reaction (1). Strong acids are those for which the K_a of Eq. (2) is very large; weak acids do not completely transfer the proton to water. The strongest acid which may exist in water is H_3O^+; the strongest base is OH^-. Thus, the maximum range of acid level which a solvent can support is governed by its own acid-base properties. In water this range is 14 pH units, or 14 orders of magnitude change in activity of H_3O^+. *See* SUPERACID.

The mechanism of buffer action may be regarded as a sequence of the proton transfer steps implied in reaction (1) coupled with reaction (6a). For example, the result of the chemical production or deliberate addition of an acid, HA, is to cause the water autoprotolysis reaction and the buffer acid reaction to respond to the change shown by reactions (7) and (8). Addition of a base would be accommodated by

$$HA + H_2O \rightleftharpoons H_3O^+ + A^- \qquad (7)$$

$$H_3O^+ + B \longrightarrow BH^+ + H_2O \qquad (8)$$

the reverse of (7) and (8). The effect of adding HA depends on the position of the equilibrium shown in reaction (7); buffer capacity π is usually defined in terms of H_3O^+ added because H_3O^+ is the strongest possible acid in aqueous solution, and would tend to create the maximum possible change in solution pH per mole of added acid. If HA is relatively weak so its degree of dissociation, in reaction (1), is small, its effective H_3O^+ addition may be calculated through Eq. (9), where C_a is the concentration of added HA.

$$[H_3O^+] \cong \sqrt{K_a C_a} \qquad (9)$$

A simple calculation using Eq. (9) shows that a given buffer solution will undergo the same change in pH for the addition of 0.1 mole/liter of a weak acid such as acetic acid ($K_a = 10^{-5}$) as for the addition of 0.01 mole/liter of strong acids such as HCl, $HClO_4$, or HNO_3.

In studies of rates of chemical reactions at constant pH, it is necessary that the proton transfer processes of the buffer acid and base and the solvent be rapid with respect to the primary reaction. The phosphate ($HPO_4^{2-}-PO_4^{3-}$) and carbonate ($HCO_3^--CO_3^{2-}$) systems, among others, sometimes give anomalous effects because this condition may not be obtained. Buffer rate effects are manifested in different reaction rates for a chemical system in two different buffers or otherwise identical ionic strength and nominal (equilibrium) pH. Later evidence seems to suggest that buffers of low-change type, for example, $NH_3-NH_4^+$, react more rapidly than high-charge types such as $HPO_4^{2-}-PO_4^{3-}$. *See* ACID AND BASE; ACID-BASE INDICATOR; IONIC EQUILIBRIUM.   A. M. Hartley

Bibliography. J. J. Cohen and J. P. Kassirer, *Acid-Base*, 1982; H. A. Laitinen, *Chemical Analysis*, 2d ed., 1975; D. D. Perrin and B. Dempsey, *Buffers for pH and Metal Ion Control*, 1979; D. A. Skoog, D. M. West, and F. J. Holler, *Fundamentals of Analytical Chemistry*, 7th ed., 1997.

Buffers (electronics)

Electronic circuits whose primary function is to connect a high-impedance source to a low-impedance load without significant attenuation or distortion of the signal. Thus, the output voltage of a buffer replicates the input voltage without loading the source. An ideal voltage buffer is an amplifier with the following properties: unity gain, $A_B = 1$; zero output impedance, $Z_{out} = 0$; and infinite input impedance, $Z_{in} = \infty$. For example, if the voltage from a high-impedance source, say a strain-gage sensor with 100 kΩ output resistance, must be processed by further circuitry with an input impedance of, say, 500 Ω, the signal will be attenuated to only $500/100,500 \approx 0.5\%$ of the sensor voltage if the two circuits are directly connected, whereas the full strain-gage voltage will be available if a buffer is used.

Operation. Buffers are generally applied in analog systems to minimize loss of signal strength due to excessive loading of output nodes (**Fig. 1a**). Two kinds of circuits are frequently used: the operational-amplifier-based buffer and the transistor follower.

Operational-amplifier-based buffer. This circuit (Fig. 1b) is based on an operational amplifier (op amp) with unity-gain feedback. The open-loop gain, $A(s)$, of the operational amplifier should be very high. To form the buffer, the amplifier is placed in a feedback loop. The buffer gain, $A_B(s)$, is then given by Eq. (1).

$$A_B(s) = \frac{V_{out}}{V_{in}} = \frac{A(s)}{1 + A(s)} \qquad (1)$$

Here, $s = j\omega$ is the Laplace transform variable, $j = \sqrt{-1}$; $\omega = 2\pi f$ is the radian frequency in radians per second (rad/s); and f is the frequency in hertz (Hz). The magnitude of A_B is approximately equal to unity, that is, $|A_B|$ approaches 1, if $|A|$ becomes very large. A common representation of the frequency dependence of the operational-amplifier gain is given

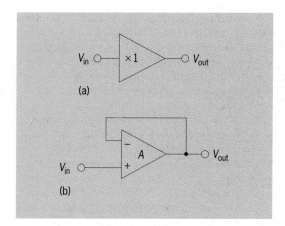

Fig. 1. Buffer circuit. (*a*) Circuit schematic symbol.
(*b*) Operational-amplifier-based circuit.

by Eq. (2), where ω_t is the operational amplifier's

$$A(s) = \frac{\omega_t}{s} \tag{2}$$

unity-gain frequency. By using this notation, Eq. (1) becomes Eq. (3), which shows that the buffer's band-

$$A_B = \frac{\omega_t}{s + \omega_t} \tag{3}$$

width is approximately equal to the unity-gain frequency of the operational amplifier, typically 1 MHz or higher.

Under the assumption that the frequency of interest is much less than ω_t, it follows from Eq. (2) that the magnitude of the operational-amplifier gain, $A(s)$, is much greater than 1. In that case, it can be shown that, because of the feedback action, the buffer's input impedance is much larger than that of the operational amplifier itself [by a factor of $A(s)$]. Similarly, the buffer's output impedance is much smaller than that of the operational amplifier [again, by a factor of $A(s)$].

The very low output impedance of operational-amplifier-based buffers assures that a load impedance, $Z_L(s)$, does not affect the buffer's gain, A_B. Also, operational-amplifier-based buffers have no systematic offset. The high-impedance input node of a buffer may in practice have to be shielded to prevent random noise from coupling into the circuit.

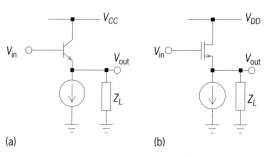

(a)   (b)

Fig. 2. Follower-type buffer circuits with load Z_L. (*a*) Bipolar emitter follower. An *npn* follower circuit is shown. V_{CC} = collector supply voltage. (*b*) Field-effect-transistor (FET) source follower. An *n*-type metal oxide semiconductor FET (MOSFET) follower circuit is shown. V_{DD} = drain supply voltage.

This shielding can be accomplished with a coaxial cable. To eliminate the capacitive loading of the source by the effective input capacitance of the cable, the shield can be driven with the output voltage of the buffer so that no voltage difference exists between the signal line and the shield. The driven shield is referred to as the guard. *See* AMPLIFIER; ELECTRICAL SHIELDING; ELECTROMAGNETIC COMPATIBILITY; OPERATIONAL AMPLIFIER.

Transistor followers. The bipolar junction transistor (BJT) emitter follower (**Fig. 2***a*) and the field-effect transistor (FET) source follower (Fig. 2*b*) are very simple but effective buffer circuits. Both consist of a single transistor and a bias-current source; they are used in applications where power consumption and circuit area must be reduced to a minimum or where specifications are not too demanding.

An important parameter for BJT operation is the current gain, β, a number of the order of 100. For large values of β, the small-signal voltage gain of the common-collector circuit or emitter follower is close to but smaller than 1. The other two parameters that are important for the buffer's operation are the input and output impedances. The input impedance is obtained approximately by multiplying the load impedance by the current gain, and the output impedance is approximately equal to the resistance at the base divided by the current gain.

The FET source follower also has an ac voltage gain that is less than 1. The output impedance is approximately the reciprocal of the transconductance of the FET transistor, g_m. The input impedance of the FET buffer is infinite, apart from a small gate capacitance.

The performance of a transistor follower circuit depends strongly on the source and load impedances, that is, on the surrounding circuitry. In fact, the transistors are so fast that the frequency response is usually determined by loading. In general, follower circuits exhibit a systematic direct-current (dc) offset equal to the base-to-emitter voltage, V_{BE}, in BJTs and equal to the gate-to-source voltage, V_{GS}, for FET. Only followers made with depletion-mode field-effect transistors can be biased with zero V_{GS} to avoid this offset. *See* EMITTER FOLLOWER; TRANSISTOR.

Other specifications. Specifications that apply to buffer circuits comprise dc and large-signal parameters on the one hand and ac and small-signal parameters on the other.

DC and large-signal parameters. Buffer circuits should have small dc offset voltages (dc outputs when no input is applied), small bias currents (to minimize the effect of high-impedance sources), large linear signal swing (to minimize distortion), and high slew rate (to handle fast transitions of the applied signals).

AC and small-signal parameters. Buffers should have a low-frequency gain of unity and wide bandwidth (to reproduce the applied signals faithfully), low phase margins (to prevent peaking and overshoots), and low equivalent input-referred noise (to have wide dynamic range). Field-effect-transistor input buffers exhibit the lowest noise for high-impedance signal sources. *See* ELECTRICAL NOISE; GAIN.

Rolf Schaumann

Bibliography. P. R. Gray and R. G. Meyer, *Analysis and Design of Analog Integrated Circuits*, 3d ed., 1993; R. Gregorian and G. C. Temes, *Analog MOS Integrated Circuits for Signal Processing*, 1986; A. S. Sedra and K. C. Smith, *Microelectronic Circuits*, 4th ed., 1997.

Buhrstone mill

A mill for grinding or pulverizing, in which a flat siliceous rock, generally of cellular quartz, rotates against a stationary stone of the same material. The Buhrstone mill is one of the oldest types of mill and, with either horizontal or vertical stones, has long been used to grind grains and hard materials. Grooves in the stones facilitate the movement of the material. Fineness of the product is controlled by the pressure between the stones and by the grinding speed. A finely ground product is achieved by slowly rotating the stone at a high pressure against the materials and its mate (see **illus.**). The capacity,

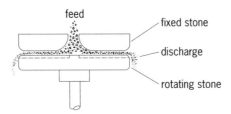

Buhrstone mill. Material moves toward outer edge of the stones where finely ground product is discharged.

or output, of a Buhrstone mill is low and its power requirements are high. The stones require frequent maintenance, even when grinding only slightly abrasive materials. *See* CRUSHING AND PULVERIZING; GRINDING MILL.

George W. Kessler

Buildings

Fixed permanent structures, more or less enclosed and designed to use as housing or shelter or to serve the needs of commerce and industry. The history of buildings is almost as old as human history. Most contemporary building techniques are possible because of materials and methods of construction that have been introduced since about 1800.

Iron and steel. With the use of cast and wrought iron early in the nineteenth century and the growth of the steel industry at the end of that century, large-scale buildings became common, and many were constructed. Notable were the Crystal Palace (London, 1851) where mass production and a demountable building were first demonstrated, the great London train sheds (Paddington Station, Victoria Station), the Eiffel Tower (Paris, 1889), and the first skyscrapers (Chicago, 1890s).

Iron and steel building components are noncombustible, and their basic strength is excellent compared to both masonry and timber of similar dimension. The strength-to-weight ratio of steel is also good. Steel is equally strong in tension and compression and possesses excellent ductility, a highly desirable quality in building design.

Contemporary applications of structural steel in building construction generally utilize rolled shapes in the form of wide flange and I beams, pipes and tubes, channels, angles, and plates. These are fabricated and erected into frameworks of beams, girders, and columns. Floors are usually concrete slabs cast on corrugated metal deck or on removable wood forms. *See* FLOOR CONSTRUCTION; STRUCTURAL STEEL.

Concrete. Another important building material, concrete, was known to builders in Roman times. Concrete is a mixture of cement, coarse and fine aggregate (usually stone and sand), and water, with other chemical admixtures sometimes introduced to impart special qualities. The material is inherently weak in tension and must be reinforced by means of steel bars embedded in and bonded to the concrete matrix. This combination of nonhomogeneous materials, called reinforced concrete, is utilized in many areas of building construction, including foundations, walls, columns, beams, floors, and roofs. *See* COLUMN; FOUNDATIONS; ROOF CONSTRUCTION; WALL CONSTRUCTION.

In its early applications in the late nineteenth century, reinforced concrete was primarily used in industrial buildings. However, because of its ability to be molded into any shape, its inherent resistance to fire and weather, and its relatively low cost, reinforced concrete has become a desirable material for all types of buildings. Construction of reinforced concrete structures is more labor intensive than steel structures because of the need to construct elaborate formwork, place the reinforcement accurately where it is required, convey the concrete materials from the mixer to the final destination, and finish and cure any exposed surfaces. Reinforced concrete structures of 40 stories and more are not uncommon. While beam and column frames are often used, reinforced concrete construction frequently involves the flat plate, a system in which the floor slab is of uniform depth with no beams projecting beneath it and with the plate supported only by columns, which may be randomly spaced rather than on a regular grid. *See* REINFORCED CONCRETE.

Concrete is subject to plastic flow (sometimes called creep) when subjected to compressive forces over a period of time. Therefore collateral building materials such as exterior walls, interior partitions, and vertical pipes and ducts must be detailed to accommodate this movement. *See* CONCRETE.

Timber. Two inventions made the use of timber extremely viable in small-scale structures: the machine-powered sawmill and the automatic nail-making machine. Previously, timbers were either hand hewed or sawed and nails were hand forged.

In North America, where large softwood forests

were plentiful, the milling of small-dimension lumber [2–3 in. (5–7.5 cm) wide by 4–12 in. (10–30 cm) deep] gave rise to the balloon frame house in the latter part of the nineteenth century. In this technique, closely space studs, joists, and rafters [no more than 24 in. (60 cm) on center] are fastened together with simple square cuts and nails. The balloon frame allowed relatively unskilled persons to erect simple frame houses. In the twentieth century, the balloon frame gave way to the platform frame, in which the studs were capped at each floor rather than running continuously for two stories (**Fig. 1**). The platform technique further simplified the framing system and compensated more uniformly for the drying shrinkage of newly milled wood with high moisture content that was often employed in construction.

Masonry. Masonry is a widely used construction technique, and perhaps the oldest building material. The three most common masonry materials are stone (quarried from natural geologic formations), brick (manufactured from clay that is exposed to high temperature in kilns), and concrete masonry units (solid or hollow blocks manufactured from carefully controlled concrete mixes). These materials are used alone or in combination, with each unit separated from the adjacent one by a bed of mortar. *See* BRICK; MORTAR; STONE AND STONE PRODUCTS.

The strength of a masonry wall depends greatly on the quality of construction. Since quality varies widely, it is desirable to introduce a relatively large factor of safety into the design. Masonry has been used in structural supporting walls built as high as 20 stories, although commonly the limit is 8–12 stories. Reinforcement can be introduced in the form of steel wires in horizontal bed joints as well as vertically in the form of rods set into grouted hollow cells of concrete masonry or in the grouted space between wythes of a brick wall. Reinforcement greatly enhances the strength of a masonry wall. *See* MASONRY.

Other materials. As new materials were developed, the technology of constructing buildings advanced, and it is anticipated that progress will continue. Newer metals include high-strength alloys of steel as well as products developed for space programs that have very high strength-to-weight ratios. Other desirable properties involve increased strength as well as resistance to corrosion, high temperature from fires, and fatigue.

Reinforced concrete with compressive strength increased from the older common range of 3000–5000 lb/in.^{2} (21–35 megapascals) up to 15,000–18,000 lb/in.^{2} (103–124 MPa) has been developed. This is of particular value in the design of columns in very tall buildings. Plastics are used in many building applications. However, these materials require improvements in strength and stiffness, long-term dimensional stability, resistance to high temperature and the degrading effects of ultraviolet radiation, and ease in being fastened and connected. Composite materials have been developed for application in buildings, and include sandwich panels in which the

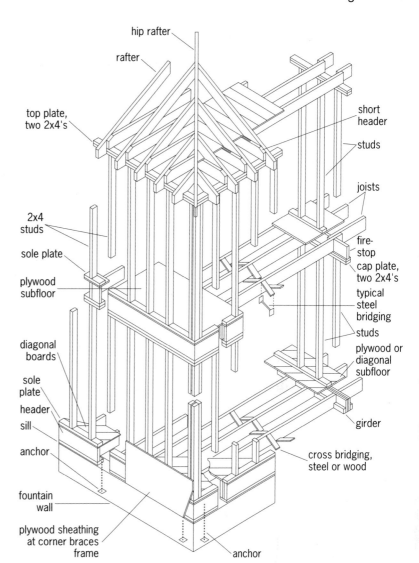

Fig. 1. Configuration of the platform frame construction. (*After C. Ramsey, Architectural Graphic Standards, 7th ed., Wiley, 1989*)

surfaces are bonded to a core. Combinations of steel and concrete (**Fig. 2**), masonry and steel reinforcement or prestress, timber and concrete, and timber and steel are in use. Other novel materials include high-performance fabric for roof coverings, structural adhesives, carbon fiber, and glass-fiber products.

These modern materials are often lighter in weight than conventional products, facilitating long-span roofs that are made of steel or alloy cables and struts, coated fabric membranes, and reinforced plastic panels. An additional benefit of lightweight structures is their ability to be prefabricated in a factory and shipped to the job site, either as panels or as completed three-dimensional modules. Materials of high strength allow the construction of taller buildings, using columns of smaller dimensions. In addition, durability can be substantially improved in basic materials that will resist corrosion and deterioration due to atmospheric conditions including pollution and acid rain, as well as in secondary materials such as sealants (at building joints and junctures of dissimilar

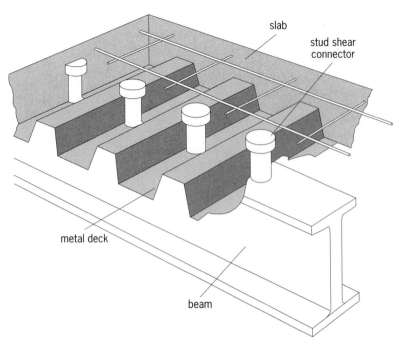

Fig. 2. Metal deck of composite design, providing a permanent form for concrete as well as a work platform. (*Nelson Studs Welding Systems*)

materials), adhesives, and connections (including bolts, screws, and nails).

Many building components are subassembled in factories prior to delivery to the job site. Wood structural members are made into glue-laminated beams using strip lumber, veneer lumber, particle board, or parallel strand lumber. Steel components include prefabricated open-web trusses and joists as well as three-dimensional space frames. Concrete components are factory precast to form hollow core planks and tee-shaped sections, often using a tech-

niques for reinforcing called prestressing, in which steel wires or strands are stretched taut in the forms prior to concrete being cast around them.

Skyscrapers. Following the invention of the high-speed safety elevator, skyscrapers were developed at the end of the nineteenth and early in the twentieth century to maximize the economic return on parcels of land in urban environments. Earlier heavy-masonry-bearing-wall buildings had walls up to 6 ft (2 m) thick at their base to support as much as 16 stories of load. These walls occupied valuable space that could otherwise be rented to tenants. This drawback provided stimulus to the development of the skeleton steel frame, in which the thin exterior cladding does not participate in the support of the building but functions as a weather enclosure and a visual expression. These external skins (curtain walls) are often constructed of light aluminum or steel supports infilled with glass or metal panels. Curtain walls may also be fabricated of masonry veneer or precast concrete panels. They are designed to resist water and wind pressure and infiltration, and they are attached to the building frame for their primary support. Curtain walls may be built up of mullions and muntins, with the glass and metal in place on the building (the so-called stick system), or may be installed as a unit, with the framing members and glazing preassembled offsite.

The major structural problem that must be considered in the design of skyscrapers is the ability of the frame to resist lateral wind loads. The building must be both strong enough to resist the applied forces and stiff enough to limit the lateral displacement or drift to amounts that are tolerable to human comfort levels and to the performance of the collateral materials such as glass, interior partitions, and ceilings. In order to meet these criteria, methods have evolved

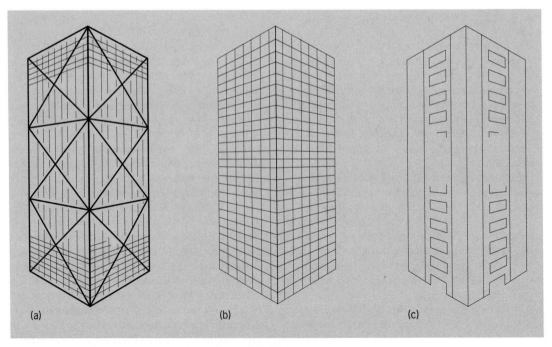

Fig. 3. Tube structural systems: (*a*) braced, (*b*) framed, and (*c*) shear wall.

since the skeleton frame was introduced. The simplest method of providing lateral rigidity is to ensure that the joints between girders and columns remain rigid, that is, their geometry remains unchanged. Thus if two members meet at a 90° angle, the design must ensure that this angle will not be changed when a load is applied. In steel frames, this requirement is accomplished by connecting the two members with adequately sized and spaced bolts, rivets, or welds. In reinforced concrete construction, the design must provide for adequately sized members and reinforcing steel that act together by virtue of the monolithic nature of the material. Rigid frame design is still the most economical method of framing buildings up to 20 stories tall. *See* STRUCTURAL ANALYSIS.

As buildings became taller than 20 stories, it was recognized that diagonal braces could be introduced between the top of one column and the bottom of an adjacent one to form a truss type of framework. The diagonals could form X's, V's, or K's and were found to be very efficient for buildings up to about 60 stories. The principle of a truss is that a series of triangles is interconnected, and these are found to be immutable shapes; that is, their geometry cannot be changed except by changing the lengths of the members. In reinforced concrete buildings, solid shear walls are used rather than diagonals. *See* TRUSS.

Special systems have been developed for constructing very tall buildings. One of the most effective is the tube system (used in the World Trade Center, New York), in which the perimeter framework of the building is composed of closely spaced columns (with small windows) and very rigid spandrel beams connected to form almost a solid tube with small penetrations. This is an efficient system because it maximizes the use of the framing material by locating it as far as possible from the center of the building, that is, at the perimeter (**Fig. 3**). Variations on the tube system include large-scale external X-bracing (as in the John Hancock Building, Chicago; **Fig. 4**) and the bundled tube (such as the Sears Tower, Chicago). In addition to these so-called passive framing systems, buildings can resist wind forces by means of tuned mass dampers. These are large weights, as much as 300–400 tons (270–360 metric tons), mounted on guided rollers or pendulums and located at the top of a skyscraper; they move counter to the direction of the wind, minimizing the deflection. The dampers are activated by the actual movement of the building, and they alter its dynamic response to wind.

Special-purpose types. Modern technology has created the need for different types of structures. Examples include aircraft maintenance hangars (the largest building in the world is the vertical assembly building at Cape Canaveral, Florida), communications and entertainment production centers, large stadiums (many of which were formerly outdoors but are now covered and climate controlled), transportation terminals, convention centers, specialized medical facilities and scientific laboratories, and high-technology manufacturing buildings. Some re-

Fig. 4. Large-scale external X-bracing as used in the John Hancock Building, Chicago. (*ESTO*)

quire long spans, others extremely stringent climate or vibration controls, and still others superclean environments.

Building services. In order for buildings to be fully functional, they must be able to provide adequate levels of comfort and service. There are many methods used to supply the services of heating and cooling. Heating may be provided by radiation, conduction, or convection. Commonly, pipes containing steam or hot water from a central boiler are installed throughout a structure and connected to radiators or convectors in each room. Alternatively, air heated in a furnace may be delivered by means of fans blowing through sheet metal or fiber-glass ducts. Fuels commonly used in boilers are oil or gas. Cooling requires that warm air inside the building pass over coils containing cold water or refrigerant that exchange the heat, so that the cooled air is delivered to the interior while the heat is conveyed to the outside. *See* AIR CONDITIONING; COMFORT HEATING.

Electrical systems are installed throughout buildings to provide lighting as well as power to operate appliances and machinery. In large buildings, high-voltage power is reduced by means of transformers to usable voltage. Elaborate distribution systems of conduits and cables, wired to circuit-breaker panels for overload protection, are installed. Signal systems for telephones, computers, and alarms are also commonly specified and built. Finally, there is plumbing service, which delivers hot and cold water and carries away wastewater as well as storm water into disposal systems such as sewers or septic systems.

Loads. Buildings are designed to resist loads due to their own weight, to environmental phenomena, and from the occupants' usage. The self-weight of a building, called dead load, is relatively easy to calculate if the composition and thickness of all of the materials are known. Included in the dead load are the building frame, walls, floors, roof, ceilings, partitions, finishes, and service equipment—that is, everything that is fixed and immovable.

Environmentally applied loads include rain, which may cause ponding, and snow and ice. Snow loads are calculated based on the weather history of the area in which the building is located. All of the loads mentioned thus far are vertical loads, but the effect of wind on a building is usually experienced as a lateral, horizontal force. Wind velocity records are kept by local weather bureaus; loads are then calculated and based on statistical probability of occurrence (usually a 50- or a 100-year return period) of peak wind speeds. These wind velocities are converted to force units, with gust loads as well as allowances for the shape of the building, its height, and exposure factored in.

Another significant load to which buildings are subjected is the force of earthquakes. The understanding of seismic activity is an emerging science. So too is the understanding of how buildings respond to seismic forces. Calculation of the probability of an earthquake occurring in any given area is based on past seismic experience as well as determination of the locations of fault lines and tectonic plates. However, it has not been possible to predict timing, location, or specific intensity of earthquakes. In fact, earthquake record-keeping, like that of snow and wind, has been effective for slightly more than 100 years, a very short period of time in the history of the Earth. Thus the models of statistical probability of the occurrence or the magnitude of an event or a storm are based on incomplete information. In many locations, building structures have been inadequately designed to meet unexpectedly large forces due to these environmental loads. *See* EARTHQUAKE.

Seismic loads, unlike most other loads except for wind, are dynamic in character rather than static. Furthermore, each seismic event produces a unique spectrum of vibrations to which a building may be subjected. The shaking of the ground causes both horizontal and vertical acceleration in a building, whose response may go through a number of vibration modes.

Engineers have devised a number of methods by which buildings can resist significant seismic loads. One is to design a maximum of energy absorption into the building by providing ductility in the frame and its connections. A second method involves an attempt to separate the superstructure of the building from ground-induced vibration—a method called base isolation. In this system, shock-absorbent mate-

rial is inserted between the foundation and the superstructure to prevent vibrations from traveling up into the building. Other principles of seismic resistance require that all parts of the building be connected, that ornamental and other nonstructural features be securely attached to the building frame, and that mechanical and electrical systems be designed to accommodate anticipated movement. *See* SEISMIC RISK.

Fire protection. The danger of fire in buildings has several aspects. Of primary importance is the assurance that all occupants can exit safely and that firefighters can perform their work with minimal danger. The second consideration involves the protection of property, the building, and its contents. In the initial planning of a building, the location, number, and size of exits must be carefully considered in relation to the anticipated occupancy and the material of construction. Where it is not possible to provide sufficient access to exit doors at ground level, fire escapes (generally steel-bar platforms and stairs) are affixed to the sides of buildings.

Sophisticated fire detection systems are available that can sense both smoke and heat. These sound audible alarms and directly contact municipal fire departments and building safety officers. In addition, the alarm may automatically shut down ventilation systems to prevent smoke from spreading, may cause elevators to return to the ground floor where they remain until the danger is passed, and may close fire doors and dampers to compartmentalize the spread of smoke or flames. Supplementing this passive detection are automatic sprinkler systems, in which water is delivered to spray heads spaced to provide complete coverage of the area to be protected. The sprinklers are activated by heat or by the alarm system. *See* AUTOMATIC SPRINKLER SYSTEM; FIRE DETECTOR; FIRE TECHNOLOGY.

Building framing system are rated for their ability to withstand fires. Actual assemblages of building materials are tested in simulated fire conditions where they are exposed to flames of a certain temperature and a water-hose stream of a specified pressure. They are then rated based on how long (generally between 1 and 4 h) they can remain intact when exposed to the design fire conditions. Structural steel rapidly loses its ability to safely support loads when its temperature exceeds $800°F$ ($427°C$). Thus steel is protected by encasing the structural members with sprayed-on mineral fibers (formerly asbestos was used), concrete, masonry, plaster, or gypsum dry wall. In one technology a thin sprayed or troweled intumescent coating turns into foam when exposed to heat; the foam then serves as an insulator for a given period of time. Wood members can be impregnated with salts (zinc chloride, ammonium sulfate, borax, or boric acid) that render the wood resistant to combustion. Reinforced concrete and masonry are naturally resistant to fire for a minimum of several hours.

Certain building materials release toxic substances when exposed to high temperature. Thus while a building structure may be safe, the occupants can be injured or killed by toxic emissions (smoke and fumes) before they have an opportunity to exit. Such materials are no longer allowed in many buildings.

In high-rise buildings the problems of fire safety are exacerbated by the inherent difficulties in avoiding a chimney stack effect for smoke and flames in elevator shafts, stairwells, ventilation shafts, and heating/cooling air ducts. Efforts are directed at compartmentalizing flames and smoke. This is often difficult to achieve, since doorways to exit stairs are frequently opened by persons fleeing the danger. These exit passages can be positively pressurized with air to deter the intrusion of smoke. Planning for evacuation of occupants without panic includes providing emergency lighting, smoke-free access routes, frequent fire drills, and positive communications during an emergency.

Building codes. The process of building is often regulated by governmental authorities through the use of building codes that have the force of law. In the United States there is no national code; rather there are regional, state, or even city building codes. Some of the more widely accepted codes are the Building Officials Conference of American (BOCA), used widely in the eastern United States; the Uniform Building Code (UBC), used in the western United States; and the Southern Building Code, used in the south. In Europe there are national codes and codes that transcend national boundaries (Eurocodes).

Codes establish classifications of buildings according to the proposed occupancy or use. Then, for any given type of construction (for example, wood, steel, or concrete), they establish minimum standards for exit and egress requirements, for height and area, and for fire resistance ratings. In addition, minimum loads are designated as well as requirements for natural light, ventilation, plumbing, and electrical services. Local codes are written to regulate zoning, stipulating items such as building type, occupancy, size, height, setbacks from property lines, and historic considerations.

Environmental concerns. The process of building raises large numbers of environmental issues. In many cases the owner must prepare an official environmental impact statement that considers the potential effect of the proposed building on traffic, air quality, sun and shadow, wind patterns, archeology, wildlife, and wetlands, as well as demands on existing utilities and services. Many building projects have had their original schemes severely altered or have been abandoned to avoid adverse effects on the environment.

One of the primary environmental concerns is energy conservation. In the initial design of a building, all systems are studied to obtain maximum efficiency. Heating and cooling are two of the largest consumers of energy, and a great deal of effort is directed toward minimizing energy consumption by techniques such as building orientation, sun shading, insulation, use of natural ventilation and outside air, recapture of waste heat, cogeneration (using waste heat to generate electricity), use of solar energy both actively and passively, and limiting heat generation from lighting. Efforts at reducing electric power consumption by designing more efficient lighting, power distribution, and machinery are also of high priority. Consumption of water and disposal of liquid and solid waste are additional concerns. Yet another aspect of energy conservation deals with the study of the quantity of embodied energy required to construct the original building. Considerations involve energy required to produce the material, transport it, and install it. *See* COGENERATION SYSTEMS; HEAT INSULATION; SOLAR HEATING AND COOLING; VENTILATION.

Planners are concerned with sustainable design and development. Included within this broad topic are not only considerations of energy conservation but also issues such as use of renewable resources, human scale, bioregionalism, and awareness of the need to nurture the planet for future inhabitants.　　　　　　　　　　　Robert Silman

Bibliography. E. Allen, *Fundamentals of Building Construction*, 3d ed., 1998; L. S. Beedle (ed.), *Second Century of the Skyscraper*, Council on Tall Buildings and Urban Habitat, 1988; C. W. Condit, *American Building*, 2d ed., 1992; M. Salvadori, *Why Buildings Stand Up*, 1992.

Bulk-handling machines

A diversified group of materials-handling machines specialized in design and construction for handling unpackaged, divided materials.

Bulk material. Solid, free-flowing materials are said to be in bulk. The handling of these unpackaged, divided materials requires that the machinery both support their weight and confine them either to a desired path of travel for continuous conveyance or within a container for handling in discrete loads. Wet or sticky materials may also be handled successfully by some of the same machines used for bulk materials. Characteristics of materials that affect the selection of equipment for bulk handling include (1) the size of component particles, (2) flowability, (3) abrasiveness, (4) corrosiveness, (5) sensitivity to contamination, and (6) general conditions such as dampness, structure, or the presence of dust or noxious fumes.

Particles range in size from those that would pass through a fine mesh screen to those that would be encountered in earth-moving and mining processes. Fine granular materials are usually designated by their mesh size, which is an indication of the smallest mesh screen through which all or a specified percent of the particles will pass. As an example, a 100-mesh screen is one in which there are 100 openings per linear inch. Where the size of the bulk material varies, it is customary to indicate the percentage of each size in each mixture.

Flowability, corrosiveness, abrasiveness, and similar terms are relative and are usually modified by adjectives to indicate the degree of the characteristic, such as "mildly" corrosive or "highly" abrasive.

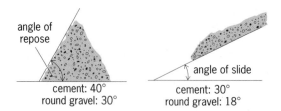

Fig. 1. Critical angles for bulk materials.

Many products are sensitive to contamination; this characteristic may be a determining factor in selecting bulk-handling equipment and its material of construction. For example, an enclosed conveyor is used to protect the material from exterior contamination; and construction from noncorrosive material, such as stainless steel, may be required to protect the handled material from interior contamination.

Consideration also must be given to the angle of repose and the angle of slide of the material (**Fig. 1**). The angle of repose is the maximum slope, expressed in degrees, which piled material will stand without sliding on itself. The angle of slide, also expressed in degrees, is the angle at which material flows freely on an inclined surface such as a chute.

Corrosiveness and other handling characteristics of materials are compiled and updated in literature provided by manufacturers of bulk-handling machines. Trade associations also publish technical bulletins on the relations of machines to jobs, applications, and operating costs. Related data are published by various governmental departments, especially the U.S. Department of Commerce.

Continuous bulk conveyor. Equipment that transports material continuously in a horizontal, inclined, or vertical direction in a predetermined path is a form of conveyor. The many different means used to convey bulk materials include gravity, belt, apron, bucket, skip hoist, flight or screw, dragline, vibrating or oscillating, and pneumatic conveyors. Wheel or roller conveyors cannot handle bulk materials.

Gravity chutes are the only unpowered conveyors used for bulk material. They permit only a downward movement of material. Variations such as chutes with steps or cleats are employed as a means of slowing product movement.

Belt conveyors of many varieties move bulk materials. Fabric belt conveyors have essentially the same operating components as those used for package service; however, these components are constructed more ruggedly to stand up under the more rigorous conditions imposed by carrying coal, gravel, chemicals, and other similar heavy bulk materials (**Fig. 2**). In the latter type, the belt runs on a bed of closely spaced rollers positioned to form a flat or troughed conveyor bed. Belts may also be made of such materials as rubber, metal, or open wire. Belt conveyors are only used within angles of 28° from horizontal. Materials feed onto belt conveyors from hoppers or from storage facilities overhead and may discharge

over the end (**Fig. 3***a*) or, if the belt is flat, by being diverted off one side. Belt conveyors can handle most materials over long distances and up and down slopes. Their advantages include low power requirements, high capacities, simplicity, and dependable operation.

An apron conveyor is a form of belt conveyor, but differs in that the carrying surface is constructed of a series of metal aprons or pans pivotally linked together to make a continuous loop. The pans, which may overlap one another, are usually attached at each end to two strands of roller chain. The chain runs on steel tracks, movement being provided by suitable chain sprockets. Turned-up edges or side wings provide a troughed carrying surface (Fig. 3*b*). As in the case of the belt conveyor, the top strand of the apron is the carrying surface. This type of conveyor is suitable for handling large quantities of bulk material under severe service conditions and can operate at speeds up to approximately 100 ft (30 m) per minute, handling up to approximately 300 tons (270 metric tons) per hour; with the addition of cleats, an apron can convey up inclines to as steep as 60°. Apron

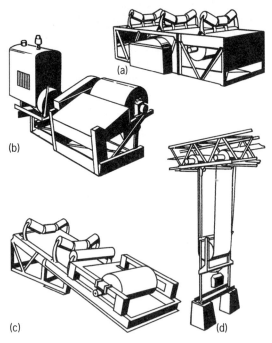

Fig. 2. Typical components of belt conveyor. (*a***) Electric motor wrap drive. (***b***) Gasoline engine head-end drive. (***c***) Screw type take-up. (***d***) Vertical gravity take-up.**

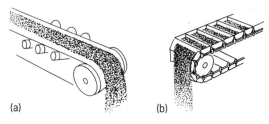

Fig. 3. Conveyors for abrasive materials, with material and conveying surface moving together. (*a***) Belt conveyor. (***b***) Apron conveyor.**

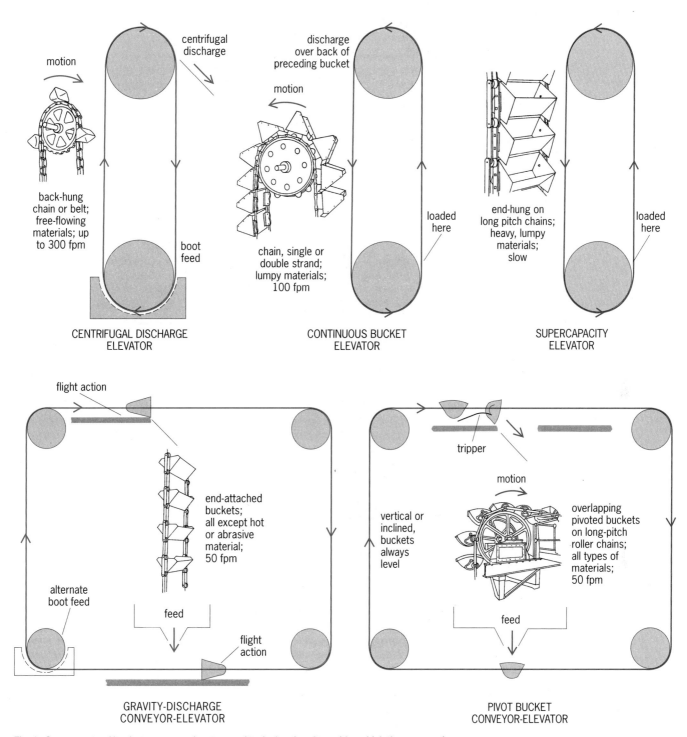

Fig. 4. Components of bucket conveyor-elevators and typical paths of travel for which they are used.

conveyors are most suitable for heavy, abrasive, or lumpy materials.

Bucket conveyors, as the name implies, are constructed of a series of buckets attached to one or two strands of chain or in some instances to a belt. These conveyors are most suitable for operating on a steep incline or vertical path, sometimes being referred to as elevating conveyors (**Fig. 4**). Bucket construction makes this type of conveyor most ideal for bulk materials such as sand or coal. Buckets are provided in a variety of shapes and are usually constructed of steel.

Flight conveyors employ flights, or bars attached to single or double strands of chain. The bars drag or push the material within an enclosed duct or trough. These are frequently referred to as drag conveyors. Although modifications of this type of conveyor are employed in a number of ways, its commonest usage is in a horizontal trough in which the lower strand of the flights actually moves the material. This type

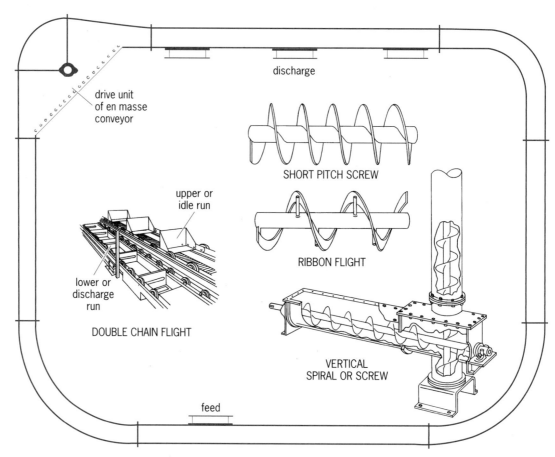

Fig. 5. Diagram of an en masse conveyor trough. The insets show some of the flight conveyors used to move bulk materials: double chain flight, and horizontal and vertical screw or spiral conveyors.

of conveyor is commonly used for moving bulk material such as coal or metal chips from machine tools (**Fig. 5**). Constant dragging action along the trough makes this type of conveyor unsuitable for materials which are extremely abrasive. Materials can be fed to the conveyor from any desired intermediate point and, by the use of gating, can be discharged at any desired point.

Dragline conveyors operate on basically the same principle as flight conveyors, as previously described. The chain, ruggedly made for this service, drags the material, such as clinkers and slag, along the bottom of a concrete trough. The dragging is done entirely by the links of the chain.

Spiral or screw conveyors rotate upon a single shaft to which are attached flights in the form of

a helical screw. When the screw turns within a stationary trough or casing, the material advances (**Fig. 6***b*). These conveyors are used primarily for bulk materials of fine and moderate sizes, and can move material on horizontal, inclined, or vertical planes (Fig. 5). The addition of bars or paddles to the flight conveyor shaft also makes it ideal for mixing or blending the materials while they are being handled. In addition, enclosed troughs may be water- or steam-jacketed for cooling, heating, drying, and so forth.

Vibrating or oscillating conveyors employ the use of a pan or trough bed, attached to a vibrator or oscillating mechanism, designed to move forward slowly and draw back quickly (Fig. 6*a*). The inertia of the material keeps the load from being carried back so that it is automatically placed in a more advanced position on the carrying surface. Adaptations of this principle are also used for moving material up spiral paths vertically. Mechanical (spring), pneumatic (vibrator), and electrical (vibrator) devices provide the oscillating motion. These conveyors can handle hot, abrasive, stringy, or irregularly shaped materials. The trough can be made leakproof or, by enclosing it, dustproof.

Pneumatic, or air, conveyors employ air as the propelling media to move materials. One implementation of this principle is the movement within an air

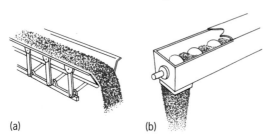

(a)   (b)

Fig. 6. Open and closed troughs. (*a*) Oscillating conveyor, with whole trough oscillating. (*b*) Screw conveyor, with helix driving material along trough.

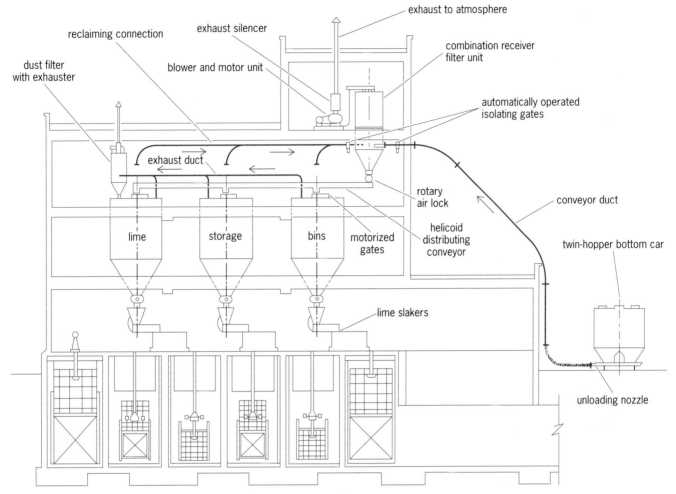

Fig. 7. Typical conveyor system, with hopper car delivering material, pneumatic lines unloading and lifting material, screw flight transferring it to bins, and gravity chutes discharging it. (*National Conveyors Co.*)

duct of cylindrical carriers, into which are placed currency, mail, and small parts for movement from one point to discharge at one of several points by use of diverters. Pneumatic pipe conveyors are widely used in industry, where they move granular materials, fine to moderate size, in original bulk form without need of internal carriers. An air compressor provides the air to move the material either by pressure or vacuum. Materials are introduced to the system by means of air locks, which are of the rotary or slide type. These locks are designed to permit the entry of the material with negligible loss of air. By means of diverted valves in the pneumatic pipe, a discharge can be effected at any one of a number of predetermined points. The small number of moving parts, the ability to move material in any direction, and the need for minimal prime plant floor space are among the advantages of this type of bulk-handling machine.

A pneumatic conveyor may form part of a conveyor system. The system comprises a network of machines, each handling the same product through its various processing stages; a single system may well employ numerous varieties of conveyors,

such as pneumatic, screw, and vibrating conveyors. **Figure 7** shows a system for handling pebble lime in a water-treatment plant. The lime is received in railroad cars or trucks, unloaded and conveyed by a pneumatic vacuum system to a receiver filter, and discharged to a screw conveyor, from which it is selectively delivered to any desired storage bin. From the bins, the lime can be delivered on demand to the slakers below.

Another adaptation of the pneumatic conveyor is to activate a gravity conveyor. Such a conveyor handles dry pulverized materials through slightly inclined chutes. Air flows through the bottom of the chute, which is usually constructed of a porous medium, fluidizing the material and causing it to flow in the manner of a liquid. An advantage of this conveyor is that there are no moving parts.

Aerial tramways and cableways employ the use of a cab or carrier suspended by a grooved wheel on an overhead cable to transport materials over long distances, particularly where the terrain is such that truck or rail transportation is impractical. They are used primarily to meet the needs of such activities as dam construction, loading ships, bringing coal to

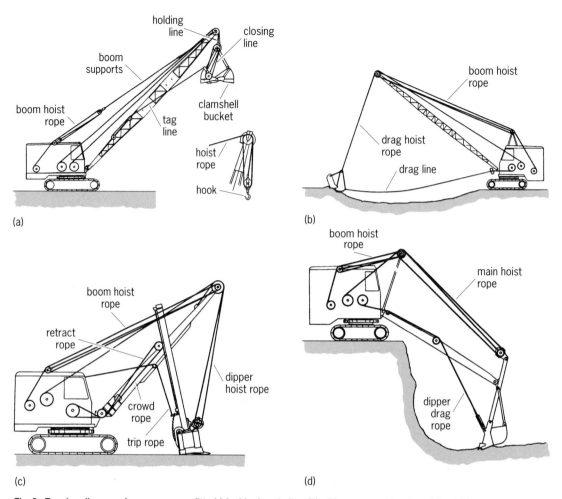

Fig. 8. Reeving diagrams for power crane fitted (*a*) with clamshell or (*b*) with scoop and for shovel fitted (*c*) with forward dipper or (*d*) with back hoe (backdigger or drag-shovel). (*United States Steel Corp.*)

and from power houses, and stock piling in open country.

Discontinuous bulk handlers. Power cranes and shovels perform many operations moving bulk materials in discrete loads. When functioning as cranes and fitted with the many below-the-hook devices available, they are used on construction jobs and in and around industrial plants. Such fittings as magnets, buckets, grabs, skullcrackers, and pile

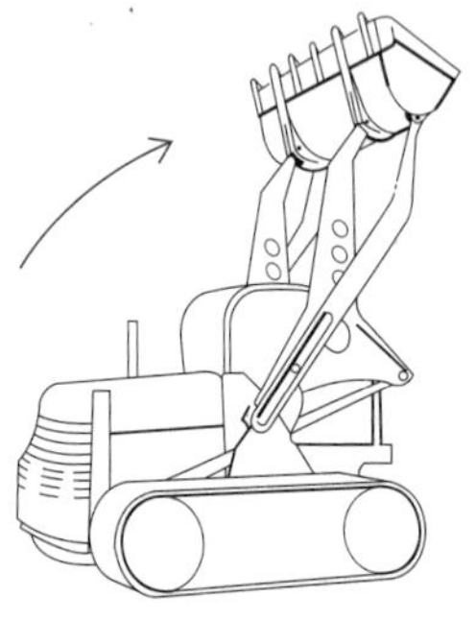

Fig. 9. Tractor fitted with shovel for up-and-over operation. (*Service Supply Corp.*)

drivers enable cranes to handle many products.

The machines of the convertible, full-revolving type are mounted on crawlers, trucks, or wheels. Specialized front-end operating equipment is required for clamshell, dragline, lifting-crane, piledriver, shovel, and hoe operations. Commercial sizes of these machines are nominally from $1/4$ to $2\frac{1}{2}$ yd^3 (0.19 to 1.9 m^3) as shovels and from $2\frac{1}{2}$ to 60 tons (2.25 to 54 metric tons).

The revolving superstructure consists of the rotating frame and the operating machinery thereon. It may be carried on a crawler mount, consisting of two continuous parallel crawler belts. A truck mount is a heavy-framed, rubber-tired carrier supported by two or more axles and having the general characteristics of a heavy-duty truck. The carrier may be controlled for road travel from a cab mounted on the carrier or located on the revolving superstructure. Machines of this type can also be secured on railroad mountings.

Six types of front-end operating equipment are standard: crane, clamshell, dragline, pile driver, shovel, and hoe. Common crane-boom equipment is used with crane, clamshell, dragline, and pile driver. The boom usually consists of two sections, between

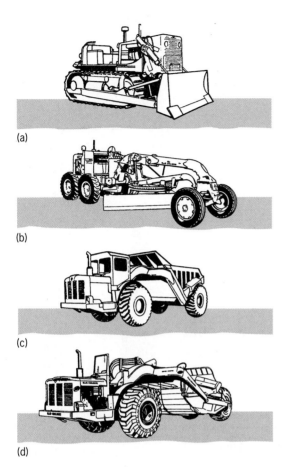

Fig. 10. Road-making machines. (*a*) Front-end shovel. (*b*) Motor grader. (*c*) Motor wagon. (*d*) Motor scraper.

which additional sections may be inserted. Shovel and hoe equipment have their distinctive mechanisms for operation (**Fig. 8**).

Scoops and shovels are used for handling bulk materials in plants and yards. Lighter models are usually wheel-mounted, while those for heavier duty are apt to be carried on tractors. Two basic types are recognized: those that load and dump only at the front or at the rear, and those with an up-and-over action which permits loading at the front end and discharging at the rear (**Fig. 9**). This last arrangement is frequently a time-saver in that it eliminates the need for maneuvering when loading wagons.

Specialized equipment for mechanized pit mining has been developed. Power cranes, shovels, and scoops are actively engaged in strip mines, quarries, and other earth-moving operations.

The rapid expansion of highway systems has led to the widespread use of road-making machines (**Fig. 10**). Some of these are modifications of equipment standard to this kind of work; others are highly specialized. Among the former are machines that have evolved by the addition of attachments to wheel and crawler tractors. Machines such as bulldozers and graders do not function as true handling equipment in that they do not pick up and transport materials but push them. On the other hand, self-loading scrapers do transport materials and are usually constructed so that they are either side- or end-dumping. Other general-purpose machines used in highway construction are trench diggers, hole diggers for utility poles, and cable-laying machines. Highly specialized equipment is used for surfacing the road with concrete or other material. *See* CONVEYOR; ELEVATING MACHINES; HOISTING MACHINES; INDUSTRIAL TRUCKS; MATERIALS-HANDLING EQUIPMENT; MONORAIL.   Arthur M. Perrin

Bibliography. S. C. Cowin (ed.), *Mechanics Applied to the Transport of Bulk Materials*, 1979; M. N. Kraus, *Pneumatic Conveying Systems for Bulk Materials*, 3d ed., 1991; F. J. Loeffler and C. R. Proctor (eds.), *Unit and Bulk Materials Handling*, 1980; J. S. Mason and A. S. Goldberg, *Bulk Solids Handling*: *An Introduction to the Practice and Technology*, 1986.

Buoy

An anchored or moored floating object, other than a lightship, intended as an aid to navigation. Buoys are the most numerous of all engineered aids to navigation, with some 20,000 in United States waters alone.

A great variety of buoys are in use. All are intended to serve as daymarks. Some buoys, particularly those at turning points in channels, are provided with lights of distinctive characteristics for location and identification at night. Some buoys are equipped with apparatus for providing distinctive sounds at intervals so they can be used as aids to navigation in fog and darkness. Some buoys are equipped with radio beacons, and some have reflectors to make them more conspicuous to radar.

Over the years, a number of different buoyage systems have been developed in various parts of the world. In an effort to reduce the differences, the International Association of Lighthouse Authorities (IALA) conducted an extensive study culminating in a recommended uniform system that has been adopted by most European, African, and Asian nations.

This system, identified as IALA system A, has one feature that has not been acceptable to most nations in the Western Hemisphere and some Asian countries. The objectionable feature is the use of red buoys to port while entering a channel from seaward. The United States and other nations were unwilling to give up their traditional "red right returning." To accommodate these nations, IALA proposed an optional system B, similar to system A but with the red buoys on the opposite side of the channel. The United States started installation of system B in 1983; with completion in 1989, the 6-year period coincides with the normal overhaul period of the buoys.

The principal features of IALA system B are shown in the **illustration**. All of these buoys are red and green. In addition, yellow buoys (with yellow lights

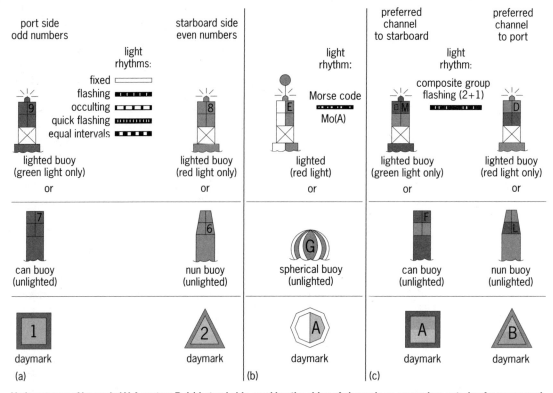

Various types of buoys in IALA system B. (*a*) Lateral aids, marking the sides of channels as seen when entering from seaward. These are marked with numbers. (*b*) Safe-water aids, marking midchannels and fairways. (*c*) Preferred-channel aids, marking bifurcations. Both safe-water and preferred-channel aids have no numbers but may be lettered. (*After U.S. Coast Guard, Modifications for a New Look in U.S. Aids to Navigation, ANSC 5N 3022, 1983*)

if such are used) are employed for ocean data acquisition systems, traffic separation schemes, dredging operations, fishnet areas, spoil grounds, military exercise zones, and anchorage areas. Orange and white buoys are used for regulatory and information markers. *See* PILOTING.   Alton B. Moody

Bibliography. N. Bowditch, *American Practical Navigator, An Epitome of Navigation, 1995 edition*, 1995; B. Clearman, *International Marine Aids to Navigation*, 2d ed., 1988; U.S. Coast Guard, *Aids to Navigation Manual*, CG-222, 1982.

Buoyancy

The resultant vertical force exerted on a body by a static fluid in which it is submerged or floating. The buoyant force F_B acts vertically upward, in opposition to the gravitational force that causes it. Its magnitude is equal to the weight of fluid displaced, and its line of action is through the centroid of the displaced volume, which is known as the center of buoyancy. With V the displaced volume of fluid and γ the specific weight of fluid (weight per unit volume), the buoyant force equation becomes $F_B = \gamma V$. The magnitude of the buoyant force must also be given by the difference of vertical components of fluid force on the lower and upper sides of the body. *See* AEROSTATICS; HYDROSTATICS.

By weighing an object when it is suspended in two different fluids of known specific weight,

the volume and weight of the solid may be determined. *See* ARCHIMEDES' PRINCIPLE.

A body floating on a static fluid has vertical stability. A small upward displacement decreases the volume of fluid displaced, hence decreasing the buoyant force and leaving an unbalanced force tending to return the body to its original position. Similarly, a small downward displacement results in a greater buoyant force, which causes an unbalanced upward force.

A body has rotational stability when a small angular displacement sets up a restoring couple that tends to return the body to its orignal position. When the center of gravity of the floating body is lower than its center of buoyancy, it will always have rotational stability. Many a floating body, such as a ship, has its center of gravity above its center of buoyancy. Whether such an object is rotationally stable depends upon the shape of the body. When it floats in equilibrium, its center of buoyancy and center of gravity are in the same vertical line. When the body is tipped, its center of buoyancy shifts to the new centroid of the displaced fluid and exerts its force vertically upward, intersecting the original line through the center of gravity and center of buoyancy at a point called the metacenter. A floating body is rotationally stable if the metacenter lies above the center of gravity. The distance of the metacenter above the center of gravity is the metacentric height and is a direct measure of the stability of the object. *See* SHIP DESIGN.
                                                    Victor L. Streeter

Burgess Shale

Part of a clay and silt sequence that accumulated at the foot of a colossal "reef" during the Cambrian explosion, a dramatic evolutionary radiation of animals beginning about 545 million years ago. Although this explosion is most obvious from the geologically abrupt appearance of skeletons, the bulk of the radiation consisted of soft-bodied animal (**Fig. 1**). The Burgess Shale fauna, located near Field in southern British Columbia, is Middle Cambrian, approximately 520 million years old.

Diversity of fauna. The Burgess Shale fauna is remarkably diverse, with about 120 genera. Its approximate composition is arthropods 37%, sponges 15%, brachiopods 4%, priapulids 5%, annelids 5%, chordates and hemichordates 5%, echinoderms 5%, cnidarians and ctenophores 2%, mollusks 3%, and "other fauna" 19%. Although arthropods are the most important group, the trilobites, normally dominant among Cambrian arthropods, are entirely overshadowed both in number of species and in absolute number of specimens by a remarkable variety of other arthropods with delicate exoskeletons. The priapulids, which today are a more or less relict group of marine worms, also show a wide diversity of anatomical form, as do the polychaete annelids. Only one species of polychaete annelids has a close parallel among the Recent assemblages.

Highlights. The Burgess Shale has revealed many other aspects of the Cambrian explosion. First, a census of the collections reveals a marine ecology that is fundamentally unchanged to the present day. Predators, long thought to be insignificant in the Cambrian, are an important component. Second, groups with a minimal fossilization potential are preserved. One example is the gelatinous and delicate ctenophores, an important pelagic group in today's oceans but practically unknown as fossils. Third, although many of the species are a product of the Cambrian explosion, rare species are clear holdovers from the primitive Ediacaran faunas of late Precambrian age. Finally, some species are of particular evolutionary importance. Most significant is the worm *Pikaia*, which is interpreted as an early chordate, and as a predecessor of fish it lies near the beginning of the evolutionary path that ultimately leads to humans.

New discoveries. More than 35 other Burgess Shale–type faunas have been recognized, and Lower Cambrian examples from Chengjiang (South China) and Sirius Passet (North Greenland) are especially significant. The diversity of Chengjiang rivals that of the Burgess Shale, and the two faunas show many parallels. Significant discoveries include a relative of *Pikaia*, known as *Cathaymyrus* (**Fig. 2**), as well as primitive vertebrates. Despite paleogeographic proximity to the Burgess Shale, the Sirius Passet fauna is less similar, but it has yielded articulated halkieriids (**Fig. 3**).

Current controversies. A number of species appear so bizarre that earlier they were interpreted as new phyla, representing extinct body plans. They are,

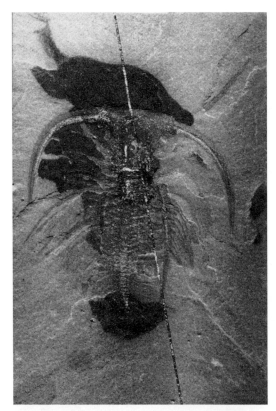

Fig. 1. *Marrella splendens*, a characteristic Burgess Shale arthropod. The head shield bears two prominent pairs of spinose extensions; also visible are various appendages that include walking legs and gills. The prominent dark areas appear to represent body contents that oozed into the newly deposited sediment. This indicates that some decay occurred before an unknown factor intervened.

however, better interpreted as belonging to stem groups. This means that the fossils possess some, but not all, of the anatomical characters that define a particular phylum. These supposedly bizarre fossils potentially allow the investigation of the assembly of a given body plan. A good example of progress in this area concerns the arthropods. Once enigmatic taxa, such as *Hallucigenia* and *Microdictyon* from the Burgess Shale and Chengjiang respectively, are now identified as primitive lobopodians, related to *Aysheaia* (also from the Burgess Shale) and the living onychophores. Such lobopodians probably

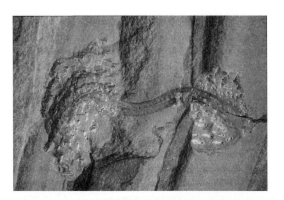

Fig. 2. *Cathaymyrus diadexus*, a primitive chordate from the Chengjiang assemblage of China. The body is eellike, and at the anterior there are a pharynx and gill slits.

Fig. 3. An articulated halkieriid, *Halkieria evangelista*, from the Sirius Passet fauna, North Greenland. The body was coated with platelike sclerites, and at either end carried a large shell.

descended from a wormlike ancestor. The succeeding stage is marked by the enigmatic anomalocaridids, which are now known to possess walking legs, either in the form of soft-bodied lobopods or sclerotized jointed appendages. From such animals it is suggested the more advanced arthropods evolved, which are exceptionally well represented in Burgess Shale–type faunas (Fig. 1). Puzzling combinations of anatomy within these various arthropods are being resolved by a series of new discoveries, as well as cladistic formulations that place these diverse faunas in a more ordered evolutionary context.

Another area of debate concerns the Burgess Shale as an exemplar of the principles of historical contingency. This view presupposes that Cambrian disparity—that is, the overall range of morphologies—was so much in excess of the present day that the whittling down was largely controlled by chance factors. Accordingly, it is argued any alternative history would have led to a radically different biosphere. Whether disparity in the Cambrian was so different from today is difficult to test. More importantly, the ubiquitous occurrence of biological convergence demonstrates that the options available to evolving life are constrained. Thus, historical con-

tingencies are of only local relevance and unlikely to determine significantly the general history of life. *See* CAMBRIAN; FOSSIL; PALEONTOLOGY.

Simon Conway Morris

Bibliography. D. E. G. Briggs, D. H. Erwin, and F. J. Collier, *The Fossils of the Burgess Shale*, 1994; J.-Y. Chen, Y.-N. Cheng, and H. van Iten (eds.), The Cambrian explosion and the fossil record, *Bull. National Mus. Nat. Sci. Taiwan*, 101:1–318, 1997; S. Conway Morris, *The Crucible of Creation: The Burgess Shale and the Rise of Animals*, 1998.

Burn

The reaction that occurs when tissue (usually skin) receives more energy (heat, chemical energy, electrical energy, or radiation) than it can absorb without injury. Factors such as the duration of contact, temperature, volume of chemical, and voltage influence the severity of the injury. The notable pathologic changes are denaturation of protein and coagulation of blood vessels. Local destruction of tissue leads to bacterial invasion and infection; loss of fluid, electrolytes, and protein; loss of temperature control; and pain. Systemic reactions include altered blood flow and temperature regulation, fluid and electrolyte imbalances, shock, infections, and catabolism. Associated problems—other illnesses (particularly cardiopulmonary), trauma, and injuries caused by inhaling carbon monoxide, smoke, and occasionally heat—may be lethal or contribute significantly to mortality and morbidity from burn injuries. *See* SKIN.

Classification. Burns are classified according to location, percentage of total body surface involved, and depth of injury (see **illus.**).

First-degree burns, for example, sunburn, are superficial burns that result in some redness, pain, and swelling. Blister formation and necrosis (tissue death) do not extend beyond the epidermis (outer layer of skin). Healing is completed in a few days, and there is no scarring.

Second-degree burns, for example, scalds, are burns that show destruction of the entire epidermis and variable portions of the dermis (inner layer of skin); blistering and swelling occur and pain is severe. The degree of scarring depends on the depth of injury to the dermis. Skin grafting may be necessary if burns are deep or if trauma or secondary infection ensues and deepens the necrosis. *See* TRANSPLANTATION BIOLOGY.

Third-degree burns, for example, flame burns, are characterized by necrosis of the epidermis and dermis, including the dermal appendages (hair follicles and sweat glands). A pearly white, tan, or brownish-black eschar ("scab") with coagulated dermal blood vessels results. After 14 to 21 days, the eschar sloughs, leaving a raw surface. Skin grafting is usually necessary.

Fourth-degree burns, for example, severe electrical injuries, involve all layers of skin, as well as the underlying fat, muscle, nerves, or bone. These injuries may require both amputation and skin grafting to heal.

Treatment. The initial step in management for a burn is to remove the injuring source from the burned patient. Attention should be directed to assessing the airway and breathing, particularly in individuals with inhalation or associated injuries. Patients with severe, extensive burns must be given large amounts of fluids and electrolytes intravenously, during the first 24 h and lesser amounts, with the addition of protein and other electrolytes, thereafter. Wound care involves removing dead tissue, preventing infection by applying antibiotics, and replacing the skin if indicated; the skin may be temporarily replaced by allografts (skin from other humans—for example, that obtained from cadavers), xenografts (skin from other species), or synthetic membranes or permanently replaced by autografts (skin from elsewhere on the patient's body). Nutritional support involves giving calories, protein, fat, and minerals by mouth and intravenously; requirements can be up to twice normal levels. Psychological support must overcome anxiety, denial, disbelief, guilt, depression, as well as fear of death, disfigurement, and disability, in order to provide coping mechanisms and enable planning for the future.

The more severe the burn or the more vulnerable the injured person (patients who are very young or very old, have other systemic diseases, or have other associated injuries are especially vulnerable), the more likely are complications. The most significant of these are systemic infections and the consequences of treating them. In addition, there may be specific or nonspecific injury to certain organs, such as Curling's ulcer (superficial ulceration of the stomach), renal damage related to inadequate fluid support, red cell or myoglobin destruction, adrenal changes, focal liver necrosis, or multiple organ failure.

Electrical burns. Electrical burns result from the amount of heat incident to the flow of a certain amount of electricity through the resistance offered by the tissues. The initial resistance is from dry skin. Large nerves and blood vessels carry electricity efficiently, but smaller blood vessels, muscle, and especially bone have higher resistance. Therefore, most electrothermal injuries consist of damage to the skin and immediately subjacent tissues, along with muscle necrosis due to the heat from bones and destruction of nutrient vessels. Deep penetration of the burn may follow large voltages. Small pitlike entrance and exit wounds may occur from arcing across adjacent flexed surfaces (for example, elbow, armpit, groin, and knee). Often the injury below a small entrance or exit wound is significantly larger and resembles tissue injured by crushing. Effects on the heart and brain are well documented and are evidenced in electric chair executions.

Chemical burns. Chemical burns result from corrosive agents that destroy tissues at the point of contact. Injury to the skin, eyes, and gastrointestinal tract are most common. The corrosives may be either acid or alkali; alkalis cause damage longer than

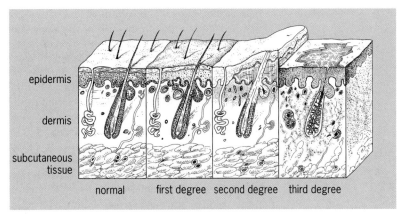

Anatomic diagram of normal and burned skin.

acids. Extremes of pH above 11.5 or below 2.5 almost always result in irreversible damage. Protein coagulation, precipitation, and actual dissolution of tissue constituents may occur. The initial treatment is to dilute and thus remove the chemical by irrigating the area copiously with water; in addition, a few chemicals, for example, hydrogen fluoride, require specific neutralization. In general, chemicals should not be neutralized on the skin. In addition to causing burns, some chemicals injure specific organs; for example, phenol and carbon tetrachloride damage the liver.

Epidemiology and prevention. Annually, 1% of the United States population is burned significantly enough to prevent participation in activities of daily living. Most burns occur in the kitchen, with scalds being the most frequent mechanism of injury; the next most frequent site of injury is the bathroom. Fire and flames cause most of the burn or inhalation injuries leading to hospital admissions and deaths. Most deaths from burns due to fire occur in the bedroom at night.

Burn prevention requires changes in behavior (conducting exit drills in the home and school, and not smoking in bed), in manufacturing (producing fire-retardant garments, fire-safe cigarettes, and lower-temperature thermostats on water heaters), in codes (requiring fire and smoke detectors, and sprinkling systems), and in laws.   Thomas L. Wachtel

Bibliography. J. A. Boswick, *The Art and Science of Burn Care*, 1987; T. L. Wachtel, Burns, *Critical Care Clinics*, vol. 1, no. 1, 1985; T. L. Wachtel, V. Kahn, and H. A. Frank, *Current Topics in Burn Care*, 1983.

Burning velocity measurement

The velocity at which the combustible gases move through a flame in the direction perpendicular to the flame surface defines the burning velocity. The term flame as used here refers to the burning of combustible gases. The process of combustion, or burning, is described as a chemical reaction of two or more substances in which a large quantity of heat is evolved. This heat is self-absorbed and goes into heating the products of combustion. Part of the light that is emitted is due to the heat of the flame, and part is due to the chemical reaction within the flame zones or thickness. It is the combustion of gases that forms the basis of a flame; and the zone in which chemical reactions occur, together with the concomitant temperature gradient, determines the location of the flame. An expression of the laminar flame speed for premixed homogeneous combustible gases has been obtained analytically, and indicates that the flame speed is proportional to the square root of the diffusivity and the reaction rate. The diffusion of heat and mass cause the flame to propagate. The reaction rate determines the temperature gradient by its effect on the thickness of the reaction zone: the slower the reaction, the thicker the zone.

A general definition of burning velocity consonant with measurement techniques cannot be formulated free from all possible objections. Ideally, if an infinite plane flame surface, considered stationary in a one-dimensional flow field, is cut perpendicularly by a stream tube, the area of the flame surface enclosed in the stream tube does not depend on how the flame is structured. The area of all parallel surfaces is the same no matter what property is chosen to define the surface, and this area is equal to the luminous surface of the flame. Where the flame surface is curved, the determination of the reference area within the flame, that is, the reaction zone, is much more difficult. For example, consider a combustible gas mixture which is supplied at a point at a steady rate and which flows radially outward in a laminar manner to a radially spherical flame. In this case the area of the surface of the combustion wave will depend on where the surface is located. Since the mass flow of the gases through the surface is constant, the flame speed will depend on the selected surface. In addition, since source flow with spherical symmetry exists, there is no constant asymptotic value for the velocity of the unburned gases. In this case, if it is assumed that the flame curvature is large compared with the flame thickness, then the burning velocity is the minimum value of the gas velocity upstream of the flame front.

Other difficulties are experimental and can arise because of the apparatus used to measure the flame speed. For example, probes cause the flow field to distort and can serve as heat sinks or catalytic surfaces for the reacting gases. In addition, where optical means are employed to measure temperature gradients in a flame, nonequilibrium effects can introduce errors in locating the reference surface for the determination of flame speed. Thus, measurement techniques that do not distort or interact with the chemistry of the flow field are preferred.

Idealized and actual flames. Experimental measurements of burning velocities have been made on both stationary and moving flames. Bunsen burners furnish a familiar example of stationary flames (**Fig. 1**). If the inner cone of a bunsen flame were a geometric cone whose base coincided with the port, the burning velocity S_u would be simply the volume of

unburned gas entering per unit time per unit area of flame cone, as shown by Eq. (1). Expressed in terms

$$S_u = \frac{\text{area of port} \times \text{average gas velocity}}{\text{area of flame cone}} \quad (1)$$

of the port radius r, cone height h, angle α which one side of the cone makes with its axis, and average gas velocity U_u, burning velocity is given by Eq. (2).

$$S_u = \frac{rU_u}{\sqrt{r^2 + h^2}} = U_u \sin \alpha \quad (2)$$

In this idealized flame, all unburned gas must have the same velocity and must flow parallel to the axis of the burner; there must be no heating of the unburned gases; and the reaction zone must be infinitely thin. Actual flames deviate appreciably from this ideal. For example, consider the following methods of observation: shadowgraph, schlieren, and interferometry. Shadowgraph measures the derivative of the gas density gradient, and it is not well defined spatially. Schlieren measures the gas density gradient which corresponds more closely to the ignition temperature and is more readily defined and preferable. Interferometry measures the density, is very sensitive, and yields complicated graphical results which are difficult to define quantitatively. The flame cone defining the front of the combustion wave is not infinitely thin, yielding different locations for the flame surface and therefore different burning velocities. *See* FLAME.

Measurement techniques. The various methods used to measure flame speeds can be grouped under the following headings: conical stationary flames; flames in tubes; soap bubble methods; constant-volume explosions in spherical vessels; flat-flame burner methods; and laser diagnostic techniques. These are briefly described below.

Bunsen burner method. Premixed gases flow up a cylindrical tube long enough to ensure fully developed laminar flow. The gas burns at the mouth of the

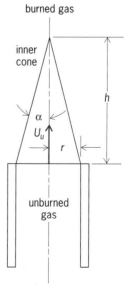

Fig. 1. Geometry of Bunsen flame.

tube, and the shape of the flame cone is recorded by photography or an equivalent method. The flame area is determined by various means of geometrical methods and the flame speed thus determined, as in Eq. (3). It is agreed that the schlieren cone is the

$$S_u = \frac{\text{volume of gas flow}}{\text{surface area of flame cone}} \qquad (3)$$

most suitable for the determination of flame speed. The cone angle is measured at the central portion of the cone in about 30% of the internal portion of the cone. Wall effects which produce flame cooling, lower reaction rates, and lower flame speeds cannot be completely eliminated.

Cylindrical tube method. In this case, a premixed gas is placed in a horizontal or vertical tube. The gas is ignited at one end, and the rate of flame propagation into the unburned gases is measured. Provided that the tube is not too short, and the energy released by the spark used for ignition is not much larger than the minimum ignition energy, the combustion wave is observed to be nearly plane and to travel at almost constant speed between 2 and 10 tube diameters from the spark. This constant speed is the empirical burning velocity. This method is approximate and suffers from errors due to wall effects, buoyancy, combustion-wave distortion, and friction.

Soap bubble method. In an effort to eliminate wall effects, two spherical methods were developed. Soap bubbles blown with homogeneous combustible gas mixtures have been used as a containing medium. Spark ignition at the center of the bubble will propagate a combustion wave at constant pressure through the mixture. The flame speed is amplified by expansion of the burned gases behind the flame front.

Measurements on such a flame are made photographically by observing the growth of the flame radius through a slit as the film moves past the slit (**Fig. 2**). If an initial volume of gas of radius r_1 burns to a final volume of radius r_2 and is measured on a film moving with a velocity S_f and a magnification factor

m, the flame speed S_s in space is given by Eq. (4),

$$S_s = m S_f \tan \alpha \qquad (4)$$

where α is the angle made with the film axis due to growth of the flame. The expansion ratio E is also a function of the burned gas density ρ_b and unburned gas density ρ_u, as expressed in Eq. (5). The mass of

$$E = \left(\frac{r_2}{r_1}\right)^3 = \frac{\rho_u}{\rho_b} \qquad (5)$$

gas entering and leaving a unit area of combustion wave per unit time is derived from Eqs. (5) and (6) and shown in Eq. (7). Afterburning, which affects the

$$S_u \rho_u = S_s \rho_b \qquad (6)$$

$$S_u = \frac{S_s \rho_b}{\rho_u} = \frac{S_s}{E} \qquad (7)$$

precision of measurement of the final radius, can be eliminated by surrounding the bubble with inert gas. The method can be used at various pressures by placing the entire apparatus inside a pressure-controlled chamber.

Closed spherical bomb method. Another technique for measuring burning velocity in which adequate control of gas composition is maintained is combustion in spherical bombs with central ignition. Since reaction occurs under constant-volume conditions in this apparatus, the calculations to find the burning velocity are much more complex.

Flat-flame burner method. The flat-flame burner method is probably the most accurate because it offers the simplest flame front and one in which the area of the shadow schlieren and visible parts are the same. A combustible gas mixture flows up a tube in which a porous plug or grid is placed at the end. The grid stabilizes the flame. If the combustion gas speed is too great, a flame cone occurs; if too slow, flashback and quenching occur. Finally the tube is shrouded by inert gas to better define the flame. This method applies to mixtures having low burning velocities and can be applied as well to low pressures.

Laser diagnostic techniques. Through the combined use of laser Raman scattering and laser Doppler velocimetry, simultaneous nonintrusive, instantaneous, and pointwise measurements of temperature, specie concentration, and velocity can be obtained in flames. The nature of this diagnostic technique is also rather complicated. *See* LASER.

Maximum burning velocity in air mixtures of most hydrocarbons under atmospheric conditions varies from 10 to 40 in./s (25 to 100 cm/s). Typical gasoline hydrocarbons have burning velocities in the range of 12–16 in./s (30–40 cm/s). *See* COMBUSTION.

Vito Agosta

Bibliography. I. Glassman, *Combination*, 1977; S. Lederman, The use of laser Raman diagnostics in flow fields and combustion, *Progress of Energy and Combustion Sciences*, vol. 3, pp. 1–34, 1977; S. Lederman, A. Celentano, and J. Glaser, Temperature, concentration and velocity in jets, flames and

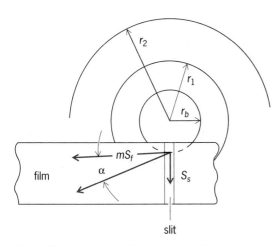

Fig. 2. Film moving past slit to record growth of flame by measurement of its radius.

shock tubes, *Phys. Fluids*, 22(6):1065–1072, 1979; H. Taylor (ed.), *Physical Measurement in Gas Dynamics*, vol. 9, 1954; L. A. Vulis, *Thermal Regimes of Combustion*, 1961; F. A. Williams, *Combustion Theory*, 2d ed., 1985.

Burrowing animals

Some terrestrial and aquatic animals are capable of excavating holes in the ground for protection from adverse environmental conditions, as well as for storing food. Burrows vary from temporary structures of simple design (for example, the nesting burrows of some birds) to more permanent underground networks that may be inhabited for several generations (for example, rabbit warrens, badger sets, fox earths, and prairie dog burrows). They vary in structure from blind burrows with a single opening to extensive systems with several openings. Some animals (for example, some species of moles) live permanently underground, and their burrows have no obvious large openings to the surface. Burrows may be shared by a number of species, and abandoned burrows may be used by other species. Animals with limbs usually excavate their burrows by using their legs, but many burrowing animals are limbless and the mechanism of progression is not always obvious.

Terrestrial burrowers. Worms, slugs, many insects, and many vertebrates live in burrows. Earthworms are important soil organisms because their burrows improve drainage and aeration, their feeding habits enhance leaf decomposition, and their droppings increase soil fertility. Earthworms burrow by contracting circular muscles in their body wall to push forward, and contracting the longitudinal muscles to widen the burrow. Termites (Isoptera) and ants (Hymenoptera) are social insects, most of which live underground. Termites are major consumers of vegetation in warm climates, and many construct extensive underground galleries extending from the mound located on the surface. The conditions in the mound are carefully regulated by the termites. Most ants are predators or scavengers, but leaf-cutter ants feed on a fungus that grows on the harvested pieces of leaf in carefully tended underground galleries. Male mole crickets (*Gryllotalpa viniae*) attract mates by singing (they rub their wings together to generate sound) in their burrows; the burrow has a double, trumpet-shaped opening which acoustically focuses the sound, thereby increasing efficiency.

Some animals bury themselves to avoid adverse conditions, abandoning the burrow when conditions improve. Lungfish, for example, inhabit seasonal rivers in Australia, Africa, and South America. They bury themselves in the mud of drying rivers, breathe with the aid of an organ resembling a lung, and become active again when the next rainy season fills the river.

Several groups of burrowing vertebrates have small limbs or, in some cases, are limbless. For example, caecilians are amphibians that resemble earthworms. Burrowing skinks show varying limb reduction. Slow worms and snakes are burrowing, limbless reptiles, though many snakes live in other habitats.

Moles are highly adapted for a permanent life underground. European moles are solitary, feed mainly on earthworms, and have shovellike front limbs and well-developed tactile and olfactory senses, but their vision is reduced. Some moles are blind. The golden mole of Namibia effectively "swims," surprisingly quickly, through the desert sand by using its front feet and its head.

Most small and medium-sized mammals (for example, shrews, mice, voles, rabbits, prairie dogs, foxes, and badgers) live in burrows, though they have few anatomical adaptations to burrowing. Small animals are more susceptible to adverse environmental conditions than large ones. Very large mammals do not burrow.

Naked mole rats (*Heterocephalus glaber*) live in East Africa in underground colonies of up to 100 individuals; a colony may have 2.5 mi (4 km) of burrows. They feed on roots and tubers. They use their large incisor teeth to excavate the burrow and scrape away the soil to widen the opening. Uniquely among mammals, mole rats show a social order similar to that of social insects: each colony has only a single breeding female and several breeding males; all others are infertile and are called helpers. Foraging and burrowing are carried out mainly by small helpers, while defensive duties are performed by large helpers.

One problem all burrow dwellers face is ventilation. Diffusion alone is insufficient for extensive burrows. In order to overcome this difficulty, prairie dogs (*Cynomys ludovicianus*) construct burrows up to 98 ft (30 m) long with two or three entrances and mounds of different shapes for each entrance. The force produced by wind creates a pressure differential between the entrances which causes air to flow through the burrow.

Aquatic burrowers. Many marine animals, including flatfish, crabs, and shrimps, take temporary refuge or live more permanently in sand or mud by burying themselves just below the surface. Aquatic sand and mud pose several problems for burrowing animals. First, the particles are usually tightly packed together, restricting movement and requiring these organisms to expend 10–1000 times as much energy to move a given distance compared to other forms of locomotion. Second, burrows readily collapse unless reinforced or consolidated. The wall of burrows may simply be consolidated with mucus, but some animals make a more permanent, substantial tube of particles stuck together with mucus. Finally, all burrowing animals must be able to create a current of water through the burrow so that they can breathe. Many animals also feed partly or wholly on particles carried in such currents.

Animals with limbs or similar appendages use them to burrow or move through sand. Crabs and shrimps use their legs. The burrowing crab (*Corystes cassivellaunus*) uses its unusually long antennae to breathe when it is buried. Interlocking setae hold the antennae together and form a tube, rather like a snorkel. The burrowing sea urchin uses spatulate spines to burrow. Many burrowing worms and mollusks have no such appendages.

Saturated sediments have two properties that such animals exploit. When an intermittent force is applied to sediments, they become liquefied (thixotropic), and when a steady force is applied they become solid (dilatant). Many burrowing animals utilize these properties to burrow in a two-stage process that is clearly demonstrated in burrowing bivalved mollusks such as clams. The shell valves open against the sediment, forming a penetration anchor. Meanwhile, the foot repeatedly extends into the sediment. The siphons (breathing tubes) then close to prevent water leakage, and adductor muscles partly close the shell. These actions have several consequences: the penetration anchor is released; water is ejected from the shell margin, excavating a cavity in the sand; blood is forced from the body into the foot, which swells to form a terminal anchor; and the elastic hinge ligament of the shell is compressed. The muscles then pull the shell downward into the cavity. Finally, stored energy in the ligament is released so that the shell reopens. This cycle is repeated several times. *See* MOLLUSCA.

The alternation of penetration and terminal anchors can be recognized in many different kinds of burrowing animals. Burrowing worms and sea anemones use circular and longitudinal muscles in the body wall to elongate or thicken the body. The liquid contents of the body cavity act as a hydrostatic skeleton, allowing the two sets of muscle to antagonize.

Lugworms (*Arenicola*) are commonly found on sandy beaches, where each inhabits a U-shaped burrow. Coiled worm casts accumulate at the rear end of the burrow, and a small depression marks the front end. The worms pump water from back to front through the burrow to produce a current that provides for respiration and feeding. The sand in front of the head acts as a filter and is enriched with planktonic food before it is swallowed and digested. The indigestible sand is then deposited as casts on the surface at regular intervals.

Nereis diversicolor is a worm found in abundance in the mud of estuaries. It also inhabits a U-shaped burrow. It has a pair of jaws and can feed either as a predator or a scavenger or by filtering. It secretes a conical net of fine mucus strands in the front part of the burrow and pumps water through the net by undulating the body within the burrow. After about 7 min of pumping, the worm moves forward in the burrow, eating the net and the trapped food particles. It then secretes another net (the whole cycle takes about 10 min). A single worm may pump over half a quart of water in an hour.

Fiddler crabs (*Uca*) are common on many tropical and subtropical muddy shores such as mangrove swamps. They are air breathing and feed when the tide is out by sieving through surface mud for food. When the tide comes in, each crab retreats to its burrow and blocks the entrance with a plug of sand.   Hugh D. Jones

Bibliography. J. Bailey, *The Life Cycle of a Crab*, 1990; M. L. Gorman and R. D. Stone, *The Natural History of Moles*, 1990; P. W. Sherman, J. U. M. Jarvis, and R. D. Alexander (eds.), *The Biology of the Naked Mole-Rat*, 1991.

Bursa

A simple sac or cavity with smooth walls and containing a clear, slightly sticky fluid interposed between two moving surfaces of the body to reduce friction. Subcutaneous bursae are found where the skin stretches around the greater curvature of a joint, as in the elbow or knee, and considerable chafing may occur; they may be single or multiple sacs. These bursae may enlarge as a result of continuous excessive irritation, as in housemaid's knee or miner's elbow. *See* BURSITIS; JOINT DISORDERS.

Synovial bursae are small closed sacs of fibrous tissue continuous with the joint cavity of a diarthrosis. They are lined with a complex membrane that secretes a clear lubricating fluid, serving to reduce friction between the opposing surfaces of the articulation.

Bursae may exist in the form of elongated sheaths surrounding tendons or ligaments, where these moving bands are in contact with another structure, such as a bone, muscle, or another tendon or ligament. Tendon sheaths are especially common where tendons bend around the ends of two bones at an articulation. *See* JOINT (ANATOMY); MUSCULAR SYSTEM; SKELETAL SYSTEM.   Walter Bock

Bursitis

Any inflammation of a bursa. Bursae are synovial pouches, positioned to minimize friction between moving parts of the body. They are cystic in appearance and are filled with fluid. More than 80 bursae have been identified on each side of the body around joints and between tendons, muscles, and ligaments. In many cases, they are continuous with or near a regular joint cavity. It is generally thought that bursae exist as normal but irregularly apparent structures, but there is some evidence that they are pathologic alterations of connective tissue produced by irritation and friction. In any case, they rarely produce symptoms unless inflammation occurs. Bursitis most often occurs near the shoulder, hip, elbow, or knee. *See* BURSA; JOINT (ANATOMY).

Inflammatory changes in bursae produce acute or chronic swelling, an increase in the fluid content, and variable degrees of pain and tenderness. Acute bursitis may be septic (caused by microorganisms) or nonseptic. Nonseptic bursitis can be further subdivided into idiopathic (of unknown cause), traumatic, and crystal-induced bursitis. Septic bursitis may result from direct penetration by microorganisms through medical instrumentation or trauma; rarely, microorganisms may reach bursae through the blood. Most cases of bursitis are nonseptic; they may result from trauma or physical stress. The fluid aspirated from an inflamed nonseptic bursa does not contain microorganisms.

In chronic bursitis, the wall of the bursa becomes thickened, shaggy, and irregular, with calcium deposits commonly being present. The fluid, which is normally clear, changes to a reddish-brown or black gritty mass as a result of repeated hemorrhages and precipitation of calcium. The treatment depends on whether the bursitis is septic or nonseptic. Septic bursitis is most commonly due to *Staphylococcus aureus* and requires prompt administration of appropriate antibiotics and repeated drainage of fluid containing pus. Nonseptic bursitis can be treated conservatively by withdrawal of fluid and administration of nonsteroidal, anti-inflammatory drugs. In nonseptic bursitis, withdrawal of the fluid can also be followed by injection of a steroid, but side effects, including chronic pain, may occur. Surgical incision and drainage are rarely necessary. Crystal-induced nonseptic bursitis is most frequently due to gout and usually responds well to drug therapy. Avoidance of trauma can help to prevent occupation-related cases of bursitis. Most cases of bursitis have a favorable prognosis. *See* CONNECTIVE TISSUE; GOUT.

Robert P. Searles

Bus

A motor vehicle for mass transit, built in various capacities and sizes, designed for carrying from 10 to 90 passengers or more on school, local, intercity, or interstate routes. In general, a bus has a long body with passengers sitting on benches or seats, while in local transit service additional passengers may be standing in the aisle. A school bus is used primarily to transport secondary school or younger students from home to school and back. Also called a coach or motor coach, the commercial bus for local transit and longer travel usually operates on a regular schedule and travels a fixed route, and each passenger pays a fare.

Motive power. Diesel engines are the principal source of motive power. Engine installation may be at the front, under the floor, at the rear (either laterally or transversely), or on the frame, according to capacity or operating specifications for the operator's unobstructed view of front entry and rear exit areas. *See* DIESEL ENGINE; INTERNAL COMBUSTION ENGINE.

In the United States, health concerns about exhaust emissions from diesel engines, especially nitrogen oxides and particulate matter, have prompted state and federal programs for retrofitting older buses with more effective emission controls, and replacing older buses with new and less polluting buses. Availability of ultralow-sulfur diesel fuel, having a sulfur content of less than 15 parts per million, allows installation of a diesel particulate-matter filter on new and in-use buses.

Some buses have a spark-ignition engine that is fueled with gasoline or natural gas, which is mostly methane. Compressed natural gas is the most common form, with far fewer buses using liquefied natural gas and propane. Natural gas is a cleaner-burning fuel that can reduce engine emissions. *See* LIQUEFIED NATURAL GAS (LNG); METHANE; PROPANE.

A battery electric bus obtains electricity from batteries stored onboard the vehicle. It is classed as a zero-emission vehicle because the bus produces zero emissions at the point of use. A hybrid electric vehicle has two onboard power sources—an internal combustion engine that provides energy conversion, and batteries or ultracapacitors that serve as energy storage devices for powering an electric motor on demand. Several transit systems have hybrid buses in service. Most are parallel hybrids in which either power source, or both, can be used to produce motive power to turn the wheels. With regenerative braking providing some recovery of the vehicle's kinetic energy, the engine can be downsized to reduce fuel consumption and exhaust emissions. Initial acceleration of a parallel hybrid bus is better than a conventional diesel-powered bus, which can outperform the hybrid bus on grades and at higher speeds. Emissions, fuel economy, and reliability of the hybrid bus are areas of continuing development.

Transit buses powered by a fuel cell have appeared in scheduled service and test programs. Some prototypes have onboard hydrogen storage, while others have an onboard reformer that converts liquid hydrocarbon fuel, such as gasoline or methanol, into hydrogen to feed the fuel cell. A liquid fuel avoids the need for expensive hydrogen-handling infrastructure at the refueling facilities. *See* FUEL CELL.

Design. Most transit buses have air brakes, air conditioning, air suspension, automatic transmission, public address system, and mobile phone for contact with the dispatcher. Location of the bus can be tracked by a global positioning system (GPS) that indicates to a control center in real time any deviation from the predetermined route. Buses for long-distance travel usually include restroom facilities. Electronic fare collection is common.

Basic bus design retains many truck components, including brake, steering, and suspension systems. Gross weight is kept at a minimum for economic operation and for maximum use of space for entry, aisle, and exit areas. Seating and safety devices must comply with federal regulations, which may require an onboard wheelchair lift or ramp. A truck-type ladder frame or integral body-and-frame construction performs the same functions as in other commercial vehicles for load-bearing capacity, rigidity, and impact resistance. *See* AUTOMOBILE; SATELLITE NAVIGATION SYSTEMS.

Body styles, seating, passenger capacity, power plant, and other equipment and passenger conveniences are available in great variety. Low boarding height and low floor height are typical of transit buses, while intercity and tour buses usually have a high floor over luggage compartments located between the axles. A double-deck bus has two separate passenger compartments, one above the other. An articulated bus is an extra-long bus (54 to 60 ft;

16.2 to 18.0 m) with two connected passenger compartments that bend at their connecting point as the bus turns. *See* MOTOR VEHICLE.   Donald L. Anglin

Bibliography. M. Ehsani, *Modern Electric, Hybrid Electric, and Fuel Cell Vehicles: Fundamentals, Theory, and Design*, 2004; R. Hodkinson and J. Fenton, *Lightweight Electric/Hybrid Vehicle Design*, 2001; International Energy Agency, *Bus Systems for the Future: Achieving Sustainable Transport Worldwide*, 2002.

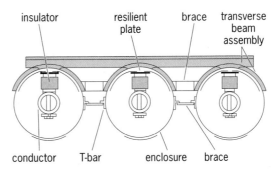

Fig. 2. **Cross section of insulated-phase bus-bar.**

Bus-bar

An aluminum or copper conductor supported by insulators that interconnects the loads and the sources of electric power in an electric power system. A typical application is the interconnection of the incoming and outgoing transmission lines and transformers at an electrical substation. Bus-bars also interconnect the generator and the main transformers in a power plant. In an industrial plant such as an aluminum smelter, large bus-bars supply several tens of thousands of amperes to the electrolytic process. A single-line diagram of a typical substation bus-bar system is shown in **Fig. 1**. The bus-bar distributes the current of the two incoming lines between the outgoing line and the transformer. In this example, bus-bar failure interrupts the load connected to the transformer and the outgoing line. In a large station, the bus-bar failure may affect thousands of customers. The reliability of a system including bus-bars can be improved by using double bus-bars, where the loads automatically switch to the operating bus-bar in case of a fault. The ring bus-bar provides two supply routes for each load, which increases the system fault tolerance. A three-phase system has three bus-bars, which collectively are called a bus. *See* ELECTRIC POWER SUBSTATION.

Types. The major types are (1) rigid bus-bars, used at low, medium, and high voltage; (2) strain bus-bars, used mainly for high voltage; (3) insulated-phase bus-bars, used at medium voltage; and (4) sulfur hexaflu-

oride (SF_6)–insulated bus-bars, used in medium- and high-voltage systems.

The rigid bus-bar is an aluminum or copper bar, which is supported by porcelain insulators. The most frequently used bar types are rectangular, U-shape, and tube. In some cases, the bus-bars are protected by a metal duct, which surrounds all three phases.

The strain bus-bar is a flexible, stranded conductor which is strung between substation metal structures and held by suspension-type insulators. Its construction is similar to that of a common transmission line.

The insulated-phase bus-bar is a rigid bar supported by insulators and covered by a grounded metal shield (**Fig. 2**). The duct is often ventilated to assure better cooling of the conductor. The main advantage of this system is the elimination of short circuits between adjacent phases.

The sulfur hexafluoride–insulated bus-bar is a rigid aluminum tube, supported by insulators and installed in a larger metal tube, which is filled with high-pressure sulfur hexafluoride gas. The high-pressure sulfur hexafluoride has very high electric flashover strength, which permits the reduction of the bus-bar size at high voltage by a factor of 10 to 20. *See* ELECTRICAL INSULATION.

Design. Bus-bars are major components of electrical systems because they distribute large amounts of energy. A bus-bar failure is a major system disturbance which should be avoided, and bus-bars are therefore designed with extreme care. The major design considerations are that the bus-bar must carry the maximum load current continuously without overheating, and the mechanical forces generated by short circuits should not cause any damage. *See* CONDUCTOR (ELECTRICITY); WIRING.   George G. Karady

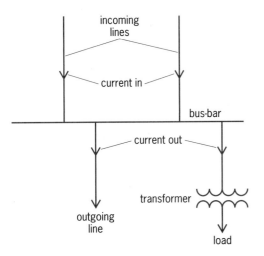

Fig. 1. **Line diagram of a substation with a single bus-bar for distribution of current.**

Bushing

A removable metal lining, usually in the form of a bearing to carry a shaft. Generally a bushing is a small bearing in the form of a cylinder and is made of soft metal or graphite-filled sintered material. Bushings are also used as cylindrical liners for holes to preserve the dimensional requirements, such as in the guide bearings in jigs and fixtures for drilling holes in machine parts. *See* CYLINDER.

James J. Ryan

Butter

A food product made by churning cream. In the United States, butter is not defined by Standard of Identity in the Food, Drug and Cosmetic Act as are most foods, but instead it was defined in 1923 by an act of Congress. Butter must contain at least 80% milk fat and may contain added salt or color. In antiquity, butter and cheese were made as a means of preserving the surplus milk for later use. *See* MILK.

Butter is a water-in-fat emulsion. Cream is a fat-in-water emulsion. Cream consists of discrete fat globules, 6–16 micrometers in size, suspended in skim milk. Fat globules have a membrane or coating consisting of natural emulsifiers, lipoproteins, fat-soluble vitamins, cholesterol, and some other materials in lesser concentrations. The membrane provides stability for the globule and protects it from attack by lipase enzymes. *See* EMULSION.

Manufacturing. In the United States and Europe, negligible amounts of farm-separated cream are produced, and little butter is made by batch churning. Thus, the handling of cream and butter has advanced technologically to improve markedly the sanitary conditions under which it is produced and the quality of the finished food that reaches the consumer.

Cream that is to be used for making butter arrives at the manufacturer's processing plant from many sources, but the major source is those dairies where whole milk is separated into skim milk and cream by centrifugal force in a separator. Skim milk in these processing plants is converted to nonfat dry milk, and the cream is sold to other users. Another source of cream is fluid milk plants, where whole milk is partially or totally separated to produce standardized whole milk, 3.25% milk fat; low-fat milks, 1 and 2% milk fat; and skim milk, no more than 0.5% milk fat. The third source of cream is the cheese industry, where incoming milk supplies may be partially separated. Also, all cheese whey is separated to recover the milk fat that was lost in making the cheese. This is known as whey cream and is somewhat inferior to the sweet cream made directly from whole milk. These two sources of cream may be combined or stored separately. *See* CHEESE.

All cream is perishable and must be handled with care to retain high quality. After separation, cream is held in stainless steel tanks and refrigerated at 39–45°F (4–7°C). The fat content of creams ranges 35–45%.

Butter manufacturers buy and transport cream from many dairy plants. In the United States, some manufacturers buy cream in 20 or more states. Cream in large tankers is delivered to a butter manufacturer and is examined on arrival for flavor and odor, followed by taking of a sample for analysis. If the cream passes the flavor and odor test, it is pumped into the butter plant and is stored in another large tank. The next step is to pasteurize the cream. This heat treatment destroys bacteria, inactivates enzymes, and gives the cream a cooked or heated flavor. Pasteurization can either be a batch process where cream is heated to a minimum of 165°F (74°C) and held at the temperature for 30 min, or continuous at 185°F (85°C) where the hold is only 15 s. *See* PASTEURIZATION.

Following pasteurization, rapid cooling promotes fat crystals on the exterior and liquid fat on the interior of the fat globules. If the cream were churned after this step, the loss of fat to the buttermilk would be high. Thus, a tempering step is used in which the cream is held at about 50°F (10°C) to allow rearrangement of the fat crystals. Then, liquid fat is on the outside of the globules to allow rapid aggregation during churning.

In the summer season, consumption of green feed by dairy cattle elevates the oleic acid content of the milk fat. This phenomenon alters the melting point so that cream during tempering must be held 3.6°F (2°C) lower in summer to minimize fat loss to buttermilk and also to allow for suitable plasticity at wrapping and packaging.

Continuous churns produce as much as 15,000 lb (6800 kg) of butter per hour. They convert cream to butter in a few minutes; with the batch churn, about 45 min is needed to produce butter, and then at least 30 min to standardize the composition and get water dispersed in tiny droplets.

Churning. In the continuous churn the entering pasteurized and tempered cream is agitated vigorously by beater bars. This causes stripping of the fat globule membrane and aggregation of the fat globules into chunks 0.2–0.4 in. (0.5–1 cm) in diameter. At this point the emulsion has been inverted. The slope of the continuous churn allows the buttermilk to drain out the rear of the churn and the butter granules to continue through the churn barrel. The next flow-through position continues the kneading process to produce butter with finely dispersed droplets of moisture. If composition or color adjustment is required, it is done in this step; also, a salt solution is added to give the finished butter 1.2–1.5% salt. As the butter continues through the last step, more kneading is done with finer bars to complete the blending process and provide for fat crystallization that will yield optimum spreadability in the finished butter. A continuous ribbon of yellow butter streams from the end of the continuous churn. Butter drops into a hopper, where it is pumped to packaging machinery.

Packaging. Butter is delivered by stainless steel pipeline to a variety of packaging machinery. A paper parchment overwrap is used on $\frac{1}{4}$- and 1-lb prints (molded portions), then a waxed cardboard overwrap. Some product is delivered to machinery that makes individual patties and wrapped pieces. For a whipped product, nitrogen gas is injected into the butter; this product is sold in tubs of many sizes both retail and wholesale. In many plants, boxes fitted with plastic bags having a capacity of 68 lb (31 kg) are filled with butter either for government purchase from approved plants or for frozen storage.

Buttermilk. This by-product of butter manufacture has many uses. The composition of buttermilk is similar to that of skim milk except that it is higher in materials found in the fat globule membrane.

Buttermilk sold in supermarkets and labeled "cultured buttermilk" has been cultured with acid and flavor-producing bacteria and may be different in composition. Buttermilk from the churn is condensed and spray-dried; in this form it is in great demand by the ice cream and bakery industries.

Composition and grading. Butter in the package has a composition close to 80.0% milk fat, 1.2–1.5% salt, 17.5–17.8% water, and 1% milk solids. If butter is salt-free, the moisture and fat contents are adjusted to a slightly higher value to compensate. Salted butter has a shelf life of 3–6 months refrigerated; salt is a preservative and is about 7–8% of the water phase. Salt-free butter must be frozen to hold it for table use; otherwise, its shelf life is only 30 days. *See* COLD STORAGE.

In the United States, all butter in commercial channels is graded by licensed inspectors from the Department of Agriculture. This evaluation is organoleptic, using the senses of sight, taste, and odor, and requires highly trained technicians working in facilities that provide adequate room and excellent control of product temperature. Top-quality butter is graded as USDA-AA. If it is slightly off in texture or flavor, it receives USDA-A grade. Unacceptable product receives no grade or is rated below grade. Robert Bradley

Butter oil. This product is made by heating butter to break the emulsion and settling or centrifuging to separate the milk serum from the fat. It may also be prepared by deemulsifying cream. Moisture is reduced to a low level by drying, the butterfat content being over 99%. Although little butter oil is produced in the United States, it is of importance in Australia and New Zealand. It is usually canned, is much more stable than butter, and does not require refrigeration. Because it is practically anhydrous, spoilage by hydrolysis and microbiological action is eliminated. Butterfat consists principally of mixed glycerides of saturated and unsaturated fatty acids in approximately the following percentages: butyric, 3.5; caproic, 1.4; caprylic, 1.7; capric, 2.6; lauric, 4.5; myristic, 14.6; palmitic, 30.2; stearic, 10.5; longer-chain saturated, 1.6; decenoic, 0.3; dodecenoic, 0.2; tetradecenoic, 1.5; hexadecenoic, 5.7; octadecenoic (oleic), 18.7; octadecadienoic (linoleic), 2.1; and longer-chain unsaturated, 0.9.

Ghee. A common food fat in India, ghee is produced from boiled buffalo milk. Its manufacture is similar to that of butter oil. It can be kept for months, or years, without refrigeration, and has a more intense flavor than butter or butter oil. Frank G. Dollear

Microbiology. Seven major groups of microorganisms may be found in dairy products: bacteria, molds, yeasts, rickettsiae, viruses, algae, and protozoa. Only the first four are significant for butter.

Public health. The almost complete conversion from farm to factory manufacture of butter has all but eliminated public health hazards. All commercial butter is produced from pasteurized cream. When properly performed, pasteurization destroys all pathogens. Postpasteurization carelessness is, therefore, the only avenue for infection.

Pathogenic organisms which could, under some circumstances, enter and exist in butter include *Staphylococcus aureus* (which produces a toxin that survives pasteurization), some genera of Enterobacteriaceae (*Proteus* and *Salmonella*), *Clostridium*, *Corynebacterium diphtheriae*, *Brucella abortus* (undulant fever), *Mycobacterium tuberculosis*, and *Coxiella burneti* (Q fever).

Defects. Proper pasteurization destroys upward of 99.9% of all ordinary organisms present in milk or cream. Microbiologically induced flavors, developed prior to pasteurization, may carry over into butter. Attempts to minimize this carryover include the use of soluble food additives (illegal in the United States on the basis of the definition of butter by an Act of Congress in 1923) which are largely removed in the buttermilk, or by vacuum treatment following pasteurization. Neither method is completely effective.

Organisms responsible for flavor defects originate from dirty utensils, water, and air (indirectly from soil or plants). The name of an organism is often indicative of the flavor it produces. Among the organisms most responsible for flavor and other defects in butter are *Pseudomonas putrifaciens*; *P. nigrifaciens*; *P. fragi* and *P. fluorescens* (hydrolytic rancidity); acid-producing types; *Streptococcus lactis* var. *maltigenes*; such yeasts as *Saccharomyces*, *Candida mycoderma*, and *Torulopsis holmii*; and the molds *Geotrichum candidum*, *Penicillium*, *Alternaria*, and *Cladosporium*. Molds are responsible for musty flavors, but they, as well as some yeasts and *Pseudomonas nigrifaciens*, may also cause color defects.

All of the *Pseudomonas* groups found in butter are psychrotrophs; that is, they grow well at refrigerator temperatures of about 42°F (5.5°C). They may cause putrid or lipolytic flavors in 5–10 days.

Factors responsible for inhibiting the development of microbiological flavor defects in butter include common salt, pH, butter structure, and storage temperatures.

Butter with 1.5% salt and 17.5% water has an overall brine concentration of 8.6%, which is inhibitory to some organisms. The growth of psychrotrophs is inhibited by a lower pH. In properly worked (mixed) butter, fat is the continuous phase and surrounds the tiny moisture droplets. Unless the water used in the manufacture of butter is contaminated, the water-droplets are overwhelmingly sterile. Also, their size is such that growth of bacteria is impossible. Only molds whose mycelia can penetrate the fat phase can reproduce. Where the interval between manufacture and sale is less than 4–6 weeks, the butter is maintained at 35–55°F (1.7–12.8°C); hence some growth of organisms may be expected to continue, but where storage is from a month to a year or more, temperatures range from 0 to −15°F (−17.8 to −26.1°C) and growth ceases. The number of living organisms may actually decrease.

Palatability development. Not all nationalities prefer butter of the same flavor intensity. Butter made from sweet pasteurized cream is bland but may

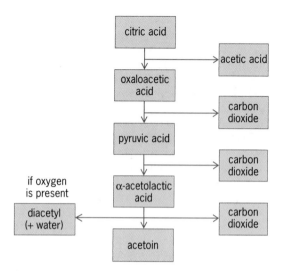

Decomposition of citric acid to diacetyl, chief component responsible for cultured butter aroma.

have a slight nutty or scalded-milk flavor. In general, Americans, Australians, and New Zealanders prefer this flavor. Europeans, Latin Americans, and some Asiatics prefer a more intense flavor. The desired flavor can be developed by the use of milk cultures of certain organisms. These cultures are referred to as starters. They may be added to the pasteurized and cooled cream at temperatures of 72°F (22.2°C) or less, or to the butter at about the time of salting. The latter practice is more economical and facilitates flavor control. The presence of citrates or citric acid is necessary for the development of diacetyl, $CH_3COCOCH_3$, recognized as the chief compound responsible for butter aroma (see **illus.**). Most unsalted butter is made by the use of starters, because they tend to inhibit the growth of psychrotrophs.

The organisms present in the starter determine how the flavor compounds develop, and their quantity and intensity. For use in buttermaking, a mixture of two or more of the following organisms is desirable: *Streptococcus lactis*, *Leuconostoc cremoris*, and *S. diacetilactis*; in recent years the last has been used alone or in combination with *S. lactis*. In some areas of Europe, *Candida krusii* (a yeast) has been tried in mixed cultures.

Starter distillates, made by steam distillation of starter cultures, are commercially available. Their advantages are economy, convenience, and uniformity. Their disadvantages are lack of delicate flavor and aroma and failure to inhibit the growth of some undesirable bacteria. Addition of lactic or other food-grade acids or of synthetic flavoring compounds could compensate for the latter disadvantage; however, such additions may not comply with the legal definition of butter.

Control. Standards and procedures for controlling the quality of butter have been developed collectively by the butter industry, dairy schools and experiment stations, the U.S. Department of Agriculture, and state regulatory agencies. By education, inspection, and the use of various tests standardized by the American Public Health Association for the mainte-

nance of quality, butter has been greatly improved since the early 1940s.

Procedures for ascertaining the numbers of psychrotrophs (as represented by *Pseudomonas putrifaciens*) and for yeasts and molds are especially important because they are, to a great extent, an indication of postpasteurization handling practices.

The introduction of stainless steel churns and the use of metal in all other equipment have eliminated many flavor problems—especially those due to yeasts and molds. The practice of all-welded pipelines and cleaning in place, when combined with the proper use of cleaners and sanitizers, likewise has been an important factor in the production of high-quality butter. *See* FOOD MANUFACTURING; FOOD MICROBIOLOGY; INDUSTRIAL MICROBIOLOGY; MICROBIOLOGY.   L. C. Thomsen

Bibliography. F. W. Bodyfelt, J. Tobias, and G. M. Trout, *The Sensory Evaluation of Dairy Products*, 1988; E. M. Foster et al., *Dairy Microbiology*, 1983; Y. H. Hui (ed.), *Dairy Science and Technology Handbook*, 3 vols., 1993; G. R. Richardson, *Standard Methods for the Examination of Dairy Products*, American Public Health Association, 16th ed., 1992; D. Swern (ed.), *Bailey's Industrial Oil and Fat Products*, vol. 1, 4th ed., 1986; N. P. Wong, *Fundamentals of Dairy Chemistry*, 3d ed., 1988.

Buxbaumiidae

A subclass of the class Bryopsida, the true mosses. It consists of a single family with four genera. The peristome shows some similarities to the double-peristome members of the subclass Bryidae, but the numerous series of teeth external to the endostomial cone are distinctive. *See* BRYIDAE.

The Buxbaumiidae is very distinctive in every way and most significantly in the structure of the peristome. The plants are small and occur especially on soil. The gametophyte is greatly reduced (*Buxbaumia*), with no stem and with leaves few

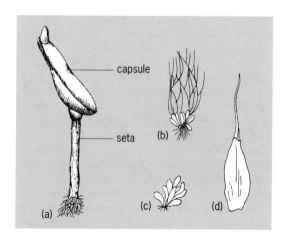

Morphological features of Buxbaumiidae. (*a*) Sporophyte of *Buxbaumia aphylla* (after W. H. Welch, *Mosses of Indiana*, Indiana Department of Conservation, 1957). *Diphyscium foliosum* (*b*) habit sketch, (*c*) leaves, and (*d*) perichaetial leaf (after H. S. Conard, *How to Know the Mosses and Liverworts*, William C. Brown, 1956).

and readily disappearing, or is better developed with well-formed leaves having a single costa and short cells. The sporophytes are terminal; the perichaetial leaves, if present, are conspicuous and exceed the capsules (see **illus.**). The capsules are disproportionately large and immersed or elevated on a seta (*Buxbaumia*). They are strongly inclined and asymmetric, tapered to a small mouth from a broad base. The operculum is small and conic. The exostome teeth of the peristome are greatly reduced in one to four series (representing several concentric series of amphithecial cells and consisting of thickenings deposited on the adjoining tangential walls between the series); the endostome consists of a tall, white, plicate cone. The calyptrae are small, conic, and naked. Chromosome numbers are 8 and 9. *See* BRYOPHYTA; BRYOPSIDA.　　　　Howard Crum

Bibliography. M. R. Crosby, *Florschuetzia*, a new genus of Buxbaumiaceae (Musci) from southern Chile, *Bryologist*, 80:149–152, 1977; A. Engler and K. Prantl, *Die natürlichen Pflanzenfamilien*, 2d ed., vol. 2, 1925.

Bytownite

A member of the plagioclase feldspar solid-solution series with a composition ranging from $Ab_{30}An_{70}$ to $Ab_{10}An_{90}$ ($Ab = NaAlSi_3O_8$ and $An = CaAl_2Si_2O_8$) [see **illus.**]. In the high-temperature form, bytownite has the high-albite structure type in which Al and

Bytownite, from Crystal Bay, Minnesota. (*Specimen from Department of Geology, Bryn Mawr College*)

Si atoms are completely disordered; that is, neither element shows a preference for any of the four distinct tetrahedral sites. During cooling, natural material changes its Al/Si distribution, tending toward an ordered state in which Al and Si concentrate in different sites which alternate with one another in all directions. Bytownite is very abundant in basic igneous rocks, where it is the first plagioclase to crystallize under plutonic conditions; it forms the cores of zoned plagioclase phenocrysts in basaltic volcanics; and it sometimes occurs in anorthosites. *See* ANORTHITE; FELDSPAR; IGNEOUS ROCKS.

Lawrence Grossman

C–H activation

The cleavage of carbon-hydrogen bonds in organic compounds, leading to subsequent functionalization to introduce useful chemical groups. For example, petroleum and natural gas, important energy resources for the modern world, are both alkanes, C_nH_{2n+2}, with many C–H bonds. One problem is to convert these alkanes to useful alcohols, $C_nH_{2n+1}OH$. This is particularly difficult because of the lack of reactivity of alkanes as indicated by their older name, paraffins (from Latin, meaning low affinity). In C–H activation, metal catalysts are often used to mediate the hydrocarbon conversion reactions. *See* ALCOHOL; ALKANE; CHEMICAL BONDING; ORGANIC CHEMISTRY.

Radical reactions. The earliest C–H activation reactions, dating from the work of H. J. H. Fenton in the late nineteenth century, used iron salts as the catalyst and hydrogen peroxide as the oxidant. These are radical-based processes involving hydrogen atom abstraction from the hydrocarbon and subsequent reaction of the radical intermediates with oxygen from the air. The role of the metal is to catalytically decompose the peroxide to provide a continuous supply of reactive radicals, such as the hydroxyl radical (OH), capable of abstracting an H atom from the hydrocarbon. The reactions tend to be unselective and very inefficient. Improved Fenton chemistry has been developed in recent years, but the selectivity is still poor unless there is only one type of C–H bond that can be attacked. Such is the case for *p*-dimethylbenzene, where the CH_3 groups have particularly weak C–H bonds and are preferentially attacked. Commercial processes use Fenton-like conditions that lead to terephthalic acid, a component of polyester materials [reaction (1)]. *See* POLYESTER RESINS.

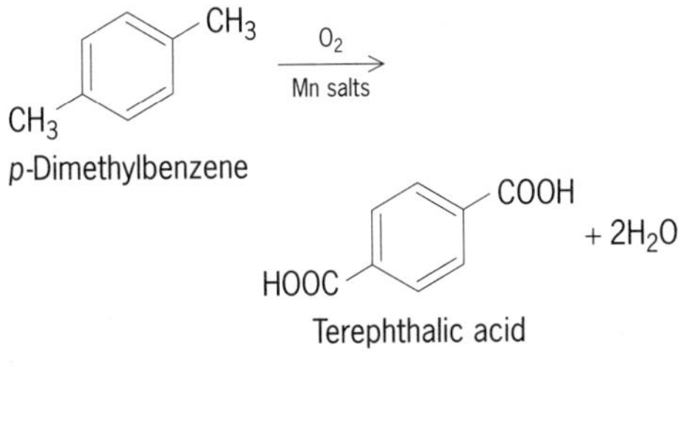

Superacid reactions. Another practically important reaction involves the rearrangement of the linear alkanes, often found in petroleum, to the more desirable branched chain isomers used in motor fuel. G. A. Olah (Nobel prize, 1994) found that this happens with very strong acids (proton sources) that abstract H^- from the hydrocarbon. These acids (superacids) can be formed by combining two acidic components. For example, HF and SbF_5 react to give the superacid $HSbF_6$, which is capable of protonating alkanes. Only a few such reactions are possible, at least on a commercial scale. These include cracking and reforming that are carried out at high temperature and are therefore unselective. *See* CRACKING; PETROLEUM PROCESSING AND REFINING; SUPERACID.

Methane-to-methanol conversion. Only certain reactions are possible using radical and superacid pathways. Additional methods are needed such as for converting natural gas, largely methane (CH_4), to methanol (CH_3OH). If realized, this would simplify the transport of natural gas from remote locations, methanol being an easily transported liquid.

The first example of this type of process was Shilov chemistry dating from 1970–1980 in the Soviet Union. In this work, Pt^{2+} salts break alkane C–H bonds under relatively mild conditions (hot aqueous solution). At first, isotopic substitution was seen (C–H → C–D), but with addition of an oxidizing agent, the desired conversion of C–H to C–OH was indeed observed. Unfortunately, the only efficient oxidant found was a very expensive platinic salt, and the rates of reaction were very slow.

R. A. Periana made the next advance by showing how a regenerable oxidant, sulfuric acid, could be

p-Dimethylbenzene

Terephthalic acid

$+ 2H_2O$ (1)

substituted for the platinic salt, and a much more efficient platinum-based catalyst (see structure) could

be substituted for the platinous salt of the original Shilov system. In this work, methane was converted to methyl bisulfate, CH_3OSO_3H, an ester from which methanol can be obtained by hydrolysis. Although a great improvement over the original system, the Periana system was still not commercially economic. In a later development, Periana saw the coupling of two methane molecules to give acetic acid, CH_3COOH, where both carbons of the product came from methane.

Alkane functionalization. A variety of ML_n fragments, consisting of a metal M and its associated ligands L_n, are capable of reaction with an alkane to give C—H bond breaking as shown in the first step of reaction (2). In principle, it should be possible to

$$CH_4 + ML_n \xrightarrow[\text{activation step}]{} \begin{matrix} CH_3 \\ \diagdown \\ H \end{matrix} ML_n \xrightarrow[\text{functionalization step}]{\frac{1}{2}O_2} CH_3OH + ML_n \quad (2)$$

follow this with a second step to give the functionalized alkane, but this has proved difficult in practice. R. G. Bergman showed as early as 1982 that $(C_5Me_5)Ir(PMe_3)$, formed photochemically, is suitable for the first reaction, for example. *See* COORDINATION CHEMISTRY; LIGAND.

Other cases are known where the first step of reaction (2) is followed by a functionalization reaction. H. Felkin, R. H. Crabtree, and A. S. Goldman showed reactions of this kind where the intermediate alkyl hydride decomposes to give alkene and free H_2 or, in the presence of a second alkene as sacrificial oxidant, alkene and hydrogenated sacrificial oxidant [reaction (3)].

$$(3)$$

Y. Saito and M. Tanaka showed that the intermediate alkyl hydride can be trapped by carbon monoxide (CO) to give aldehyde (RCHO) as final product, and J. F. Hartwig trapped the alkyl with diborane derivatives to give alkyl boronic esters [reaction (3)]. In all of these cases, C—H activation preferentially occurs at the least hindered C—H bond, leading to products that are quite different from those formed in radical and acid pathways where the most substituted

and most hindered C—H bonds are most reactive. In each case, appropriate transition-metal compounds are present and catalyze the reactions.

These do not yet form the basis of any practical process, but produce terminally functionalized products (the most desirable type) rather than the mixtures commonly found in other reactions.

Enzymes. Enzymes with iron-based reactive centers are known that catalyze alkane conversions. For example, methane monooxygenase, a bacterial enzyme, catalyzes the conversion of methane to methanol, and cytochrome P450 enzymes oxidize C—H to C—O—H in a wide variety of substrates. The mechanisms involved are not fully understood. *See* BIOINORGANIC CHEMISTRY; ENZYME.   Robert H. Crabtree

Bibliography. R. H. Crabtree, Alkane C—H activation and functionalization with homogeneous transition metal catalysts: A century of progress—a new millennium in prospect, *J. Chem. Soc. Dalton*, 17:2437–2450, 2001; W. D. Jones, Isotope effects in C—H bond activation reactions by transition metals, *Acc. Chem. Res.*, 36:140–146, 2003; B. Meunier, *Biomimetic Oxidations Catalyzed by Transition Metal Complexes*, ICP, London, 2000; M. Newcomb, P. F. Hollenberg, and M. J. Coon, Multiple mechanisms and multiple oxidants in P450-catalyzed hydroxylations, *Arch. Biochem. Biophys.*, 409:72–79, 2003; R. A. Periana et al., Catalytic, oxidative condensation of CH_4 to CH_3COOH in one step via CH activation, *Science*, 301:814–818, 2003; A. E. Shilov and G. B. Shul'pin, *Activation and Catalytic Reactions of Saturated Hydrocarbons in the Presence of Transition Metal Complexes*, Kluwer, Dordrecht, 2000.

Cabbage

A hardy, cool-season crucifer (*Brassica oleracea* var. *capitata*) of Mediterranean origin and belonging to the plant order Capparales. Cabbage is grown for its head of overlapping leaves (see **illus.**), which are generally eaten raw in salads, cooked fresh, or processed into sauerkraut. Because it normally produces seed the second year, cabbage is considered to be a biennial by most authorities. Others regard it as a perennial because it will remain vegetative unless subjected to cold weather. *See* CAPPARALES.

Chinese cabbage is a related annual of Asiatic origin. Two species are grown in the United States, pet-sai (*B. pekinensis*) and pakchoi (*B. chinensis*).

Propagation of cabbage is by seed planted in the field, or in greenhouses and outdoor beds for the production of transplants. Field spacing varies; plants are usually 8–18 in. (20–46 cm) apart in 30–36 in. (76–91 cm) rows.

Cool, moist climate favors maximum yields of firm heads. However, exposure of young plants to prolonged low temperatures favors seed-stalk formation without production of normal heads.

Varieties. Cabbage varieties (cultivars) are generally classified according to season of maturity, leaf surface (smooth, savoyed, or wrinkled), head shape

Cabbage (*Brassica oleracea* var. *capitata*). (*Joseph Harris Co., Inc., Rochester, New York*)

(flattened, round, or pointed), and color (green or red). Round, smooth-leaved, green heads are commonest. Popular varieties are Golden Acre and strains of Danish Ballhead; hybrid varieties are increasingly planted. Principal varieties of other types are Chieftain (savoy), Jersey Wakefield (pointed), Red Danish (red), and Wong Bok (Chinese cabbage). Strains of Danish Ballhead are also used for sauerkraut manufacture and for late storing. Varieties differ in their resistance to disease and in the tendency for heads to crack or split in the field.

Harvesting. Harvesting of fresh market varieties begins when the heads are hard enough to be accepted on the market, generally 60–90 days after field planting. Buyer preference for heads weighing no more than 2–3 lb (0.9–1.4 kg) has encouraged close spacing and early harvesting. In the northern states production of cabbage for winter storage has declined as the Texas and Florida winter areas have expanded production, providing green cabbage as competition on the market for the white stored heads.

Texas and Florida are important winter crop producing states; Georgia, Mississippi, and North Carolina produce large acreages in the spring; and New York, North Carolina, and Wisconsin are important for the summer and fall crops. New York and Wisconsin are the important kraut cabbage states.　　　　　　　　　　　　　H. John Carew

Diseases. About 40 diseases of cabbage and other cole crops share the worldwide distribution of these important vegetables. The most important diseases are clubroot (caused by *Plasmodiophora brassicae*), blackleg (*Phoma lingam*), yellows (*Fusarium oxysporum* f. sp. *conglutinans*), black rot (*Xanthomonas campestris*), downy mildew (*Peronospora parasitica*), and Alternaria spot (*Alternaria* sp.).

Clubroot. The clubroot organism persists in infested soils for several years. When infected, young roots are enlarged and produce masses of abnormal root tissues instead of a normal root system. Proper absorption of water and minerals from the soil is prevented, and infected plants are stunted and often wilt during the day. Moist, acid soils favor the disease. Amendments such as lime to raise the soil pH can reduce disease damage. In some countries, fungicides can control the disease. Some cultivars that are resistant to clubroot are available.

Yellows. The fungus that causes yellows can also persist in the soil for many years. The fungus infects young roots and invades the entire vascular system, causing the leaves to wilt and drop off. Xylem vessels turn brown, and the plants are severely stunted or killed. Good heads are seldom produced. Cabbage cultivars resistant to yellows are available. The letters "YR" following the cultivar name signify that it is resistant to yellows. Yellows is seldom a problem in cole crops other than cabbage.

Blackleg and black rot. Blackleg and black rot are serious diseases in seedbeds and in the field. Both pathogens may be seed-borne and can spread rapidly from plant to plant by spattering or wind-blown rain. Thus, a very small amount of disease may soon develop throughout the entire crop. Neither organism persists in the soil more than a few years. Control is achieved by crop rotation and by using pathogen-free seed. Chemical and hot water treatments can eliminate these pathogens from infested seed.

Blackleg produces grayish-brown dead areas on leaves and stems and often extends to the roots. Plants may be killed or stunted. Black rot bacteria enter leaves through hydathodes at the leaf margin and invade the plant systemically. Yellow, triangular spots appear at the leaf margin, and the vascular system turns black. Leaves are killed, and affected heads are rotted.

Downy mildew. Downy mildew is destructive on young plants and mature heads. Small, dark flecks are produced in abundance on the undersides of cotyledons and leaves and on the outer head leaves. Young seedlings are frequently killed. Fungal structures and spores may be seen as downy-white masses on the undersides of affected leaves early in the day while dew is present.

Alternaria. Alternaria leaf spot is most destructive on cabbage approaching maturity. Dark spots up to 1 in. (2.5 cm) in diameter, with concentric rings, are formed on leaves and heads. Alternaria and downy mildew can be controlled with fungicides.

Other diseases. Virus diseases sometimes affect cabbage. Symptoms include mottling, ringlike dead spots, black flecking, and stunting. Many cultivars are resistant to common viruses. Black speck, a physiological disorder, produces abundant black specks throughout the head leaves, especially after a period of storage at low temperature. *See* CAULIFLOWER; PLANT PATHOLOGY; PLANT VIRUSES AND VIROIDS.

　　　　　　　　　　　　　　　J. O. Strandberg

Bibliography. L. V. Boone et al., *Producing Farm Crops*, 4th ed., 1991; R. E. Nyvall, *Field Crop Diseases Handbook*, 1989.

Cable television system

A system that receives and processes television signals, as well as other digital forms of communications such as those related to high-speed Internet connectivity and cable telephony, from various sources and retransmits these signals through coaxial or optical-fiber (or fiber-optic) cables to subscribers' homes. The sources of the signals include broadcast transmissions, satellite-delivered programming, and local television studio productions. The facility that receives, processes, and retransmits the signals is called a headend.

Types of service. Cable television service is provided to subscribers by cable system operators that are awarded contracts or franchises by local or state governments to provide cable service to local communities. Cable television systems typically offer the customers in their franchise area four types of service options: basic service, expanded basic service, premium networks, and pay-per-view service. Modern cable systems provide a wealth of specialized programming, video-on-demand, subscription services, broadband high-speed Internet connectivity, cable telephony or voice over Internet Protocol (VoIP), and specialized interactive digital services. In exchange for being allowed to develop franchises, cable systems pay franchise fees and often set aside channels for public, educational, and governmental use, as well as providing studio and production facilities that enable community members, schools, and governments to produce and televise programs over these channels. *See* INTERNET; VOICE OVER IP.

Frequency spectrum. Compared to almost any other communications need, video requires extensive bandwidth. While telephone-quality voice transmissions require only 3 kHz of spectrum and high-fidelity sound requires about 20 kHz (double for stereo), the current United States analog video standard requires a bandwidth of 4.2 MHz. Uncompressed high-definition television requires about 30 MHz for each of the components of the color picture. Over-the-air broadcast high-definition television is limited to the same 6-MHz channel as the older analog standard, requiring complex compression algorithms. In order to carry numerous channels of programming, a separate enclosed spectrum is needed because the terrestrial broadcast frequency spectrum is too limited in bandwidth. *See* BANDWIDTH REQUIREMENTS (COMMUNICATIONS); DATA COMPRESSION.

Unlike broadcast television signals, which travel through free space, cable signals travel through coaxial cable or optical fiber, with different programs or channels traveling at different frequencies (much the same as frequency-division multiplex). In effect, the coaxial cable or optical fiber acts as a self-contained, closed, noninterfering frequency spectrum, created inside the cable by the reuse of the spectrum already in use for other purposes. Since cable television services are in an enclosed system and are not broadcast over the air, they can provide bandwidth enhancement techniques unavailable to other media providers. *See* MULTIPLEXING AND MULTIPLE ACCESS.

High-definition television (HDTV) and digital television (DTV) are two different types of service and should not be confused. High-definition television provides a sharper, larger picture using digital techniques, protocols, and algorithms. While digital television uses digital modulation techniques, it may not necessarily be of greater definition than standard analog television. Non-high-definition digital television may have several standard television programs compressed into one digital stream to be decoded at the subscriber node or set-top box. HDTV can require a greater bandwidth, depending upon compression ratios, than standard television. Likewise, DTV may also require greater bandwidth than standard television. However, DTV may have several video programs in the same spectral space, thus providing spectrum efficiency.

Transmission technology. Cable television is made possible by the technology of coaxial and optical-fiber cable and is subject to the principles of transmission-line theory. The primary disadvantage of coaxial-cable distribution systems is their relatively high loss or attenuation to television signals at the frequencies normally used in cable television systems (50–550 MHz, extending up to 1 GHz in newer systems). Amplifiers are required to overcome this signal loss, and the farther the subscriber is from the cable headend the more amplifiers are needed (**illus.** *a*). Noise and intermodulation distortions created by many cascaded amplifiers limit the practical length of any coaxial cable network. *See* COAXIAL CABLE.

Optical fiber does not have the same high attenuation or loss characteristics as coaxial cable, and optical-fiber networks can therefore be built without amplifiers (illus. *b*), or with few amplifiers for very large distribution areas. Most cable systems that use optical fibers do so in a hybrid fashion. Optical fiber is connected from the headend to some localized node or terminating location. The subscriber is then connected to the optical-fiber node by short distances of coaxial cable. The short coaxial cable subscriber connection in most cases eliminates the need for amplification, except in rare instances where one or at most two amplifiers are required. *See* COMMUNICATIONS CABLE; OPTICAL COMMUNICATIONS; OPTICAL FIBERS.

System architecture. The system design or architecture is known as a tree-and-branch design. The tree-and-branch architecture is the most efficient way to transmit a package of multiple channels of programming from a headend to all subscribers.

There is one major difference between a switched telephone network and a cable television system. Cable systems are usually built on a non-switched basis, meaning that every subscriber receives the same channels unless physically restricted by the cable television operator. Since cable television systems are not a general-purpose communications mechanism but a specialized system for transmitting numerous television channels and data

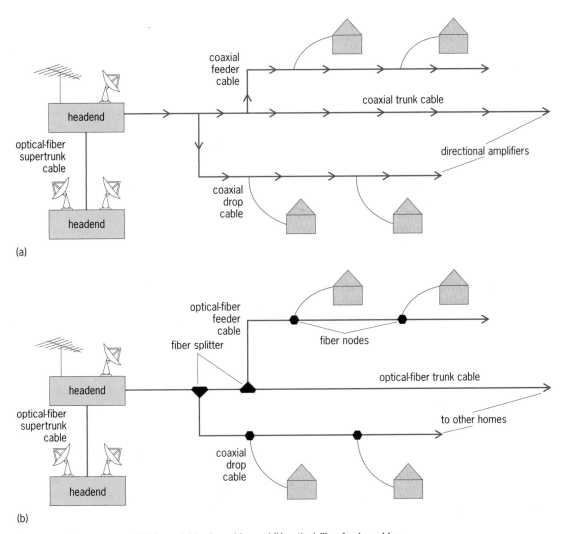

(a)

(b)

Cable television systems with (a) coaxial feeder cables and (b) optical-fiber feeder cables.

communications in a sealed spectrum, the topology can be customized for maximum efficiency. A cable television system comprises seven major parts: the headend, the fiber cable, the fiber node, the distribution (or feeder) cable in the neighborhood, the drop cable to the home, the in-home wiring, and the terminal equipment (that is, the set-top converter-descrambler). Generally, multiple-fiber strands carry the television and other communications signals from the headend to feeder or neighborhood distribution cables, and subscribers are connected through drop cables. Return or bidirectional data and voice signals, previously difficult to transmit in coaxial-only architecture, are possible with fiber cables. Multitudes of new services are possible with fiber architecture including broadband Internet connectivity, telephony services or VoIP, video on demand, interactive program guides, and video gaming.

Headend. The headend is the origination point or location where all of the cable television channels and data communications are received and assembled. Generally, the headend is centrally located in the cable television system for maximum efficiency. Multiple fibers emanate from the headend to serve many tens of thousands of subscribers.

Fiber cable. A fiber-optic cable contains a bundle of individual fiber strands (that is, individual optical conductors), a physical-strength member, and fillers, surrounded by a protective sheath. Replacing trunk cable and amplifiers, fiber-optic cables overcome most of the limitations of coaxial cable–based systems; they exhibit less attenuation per linear distance, require little or no amplification (thus reducing signal distortion), and provide greater spectral bandwidth with return or bidirectional signals on individual and dedicated fibers. Fiber strands are very small, and hundreds can be placed in the same space as one large coaxial cable.

Fiber node. A fiber node is the location in the distribution system where the fiber cable terminates and a coaxial distribution network, serving subscribers, begins. The node contains an optical receiver to convert the optical television and digital signals to radio-frequency (RF) spectrum energy for the coaxial system. Also at this node, return signals from subscriber terminals and signals related to telephony and Internet connectivity are separated from the coaxial cable for optical transmission back to the headend for processing via a separate fiber strand. A fiber node may serve 100 to 250 subscribers depending upon neighborhood densities.

Distribution cable. The fiber-optic node interfaces with the coaxial distribution cable, which delivers signals to multiple subscribers. This distribution cable runs past homes and is tapped with passive directional couplers so that multiple subscribers may be connected. One or two specialized amplifiers may be included in this cable. *See* DIRECTIONAL COUPLER.

Drop cable. A small, flexible cable is used to connect an individual subscriber to the distribution cable through a tap or directional coupler. In the subscriber's home, this flexible drop cable delivers the signal to the terminal device, cable-ready television receiver, or video cassette recorder.

Terminal device. Commonly called a set-top converter, the terminal device may perform multiple functions. A converter allows non-cable-ready consumer devices to tune to one of the multiple channels delivered by the cable television system to the subscriber. A descrambler, however, may also perform the function of a converter, but its primary purpose is to allow subscribers who have paid for premium programming channels to receive them. Addressability is another function of the terminal device, which allows the cable operator to authorize or deauthorize subscriber access levels without requiring a technician to visit the subscriber premise. The set-top box may also interconnect with game systems, and provide high-quality (stereo FM–like) audio services, interactive program guides, digital video recorders, and other services.

Advanced technology. In the past, most cable television systems were designed to maximize delivery of analog video signals in only one direction. However, the minimum transmission quality criteria of optical fibers are well above the demands of digital transmissions. Optical fiber also improves the quality of the cable television signal, primarily because few or no amplifiers are needed. In order for cable television systems to provide full-duplex data communications, the system must be built for two-way transmissions by utilizing part of the spectrum for forward or downstream transmissions and another part for the reverse. Alternatively, a second and separate cable or fiber can be used to provide the duplex transmission path.

Cable systems today are mostly constructed with hybrid fiber-coaxial architecture to provide full-duplex communications capability. Because of the great amounts of bandwidth provided by optical fiber and coaxial cable as compared with other communications media, cable systems are in a unique position to provide expanded television programming and data services, and to support advanced technologies such as video on demand, high-definition television, digital communications such as Internet connectivity, and cable telephony.

Through the promulgation of new digital standards and specifications such as DOCSIS (Digital-Over-Cable Service Interface Specification), high-speed (megabytes per second) Internet connections are possible over cable television systems. A cable modem connected to a personal computer at the subscriber's location provides Ethernet reception and transmission with a central server at the cable company's headend. This central server is in turn connected to the Internet backbone for worldwide communications. Telephony and other voice-grade services are provided in the same model as Internet connectivity, with the headend providing hub or central-office facilities. Likewise, cable telephony can be delivered via a separate modem or by using VoIP multiplexed onto the Internet cable modem. *See* CLOSED-CIRCUIT TELEVISION; DATA COMMUNICATIONS; TELEVISION.

Roger D. Pience

Bibliography. W. Ciciora et al., *Modern Cable Television Technology: Video, Voice, and Data Communication*, 2d ed., Morgan Kaufmann, 2004; D. P. Dulchinos, *Twenty First Century Television: Cable Television in the Information Age*, 1993; B. Harrell, *The Cable Television Technical Handbook*, 1985; B. E. Keiser, *Broadband Coding, Modulation, and Transmission Engineering*, 3d ed., 1998; National Cable & Telecommunications Association, Science and Technology Department, *NCTA Technical Papers*, published annually.

Cable testing (electricity)

The testing of electric circuits to determine and locate any of the following circuit conditions: (1) an open circuit, (2) a short circuit with another conductor in the same circuit, (3) a ground, which is a short circuit between a conductor and ground, (4) leakage (a high-resistance path across a portion of the circuit, to another circuit, or to ground), and (5) a cross (a short circuit or leakage between conductors of different circuits). Circuit testing for complex systems often requires extensive automatic checkout gear to determine the faults defined above as well as many quantities other than resistance. *See* OPEN CIRCUIT; SHORT CIRCUIT.

In cable testing, the first step in fault location is to identify the faulty conductor and type of fault. This is done with a continuity tester, such as a battery and flashlight bulb or buzzer (**Fig. 1**), or an ohmmeter.

Murray loop test. Useful for locating faults in relatively low-resistance circuits, the Murray loop is shown in **Fig. 2** with a ground fault in the circuit under test. A known "good" conductor is joined to the faulty conductor at a convenient point beyond the fault but at a known distance from the test

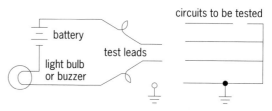

Fig. 1. Simple continuity test setup.

connection. One terminal of the test battery is grounded. The resulting Wheatstone bridge is then balanced by adjusting R_B until a null is obtained, as indicated by the detector in Fig. 2. Ratio R_A/R_B is then known. For a circuit having a uniform ratio of resistance with length, circuit resistance is directly proportional to circuit length. Therefore, the distance to the fault is determined from the procedure given by Eqs. (1)-(3). From Eq. (3) and a knowledge of

$$R_C \propto l + (l - x) \qquad R_D \propto x \qquad (1)$$

$$\frac{R_A}{R_B} = r = \frac{R_C}{R_D} = \frac{2l - x}{x} \qquad (2)$$

$$x = \frac{2l}{r - 1} \qquad (3)$$

total length l of the circuit, once ratio r has been measured, the location of the fault x is determined. If circuit resistances are not uniform with distances, as when the known faultless conductor is different in size from the faulty conductor, additional calculation taking into consideration the resistance per unit length of the conductors is necessary.

If the fault is a short circuit or a cross instead of a ground, the battery is connected to the conductor to which the short or cross has taken place (**Fig. 3**). The test circuit is then equivalent to the one used to locate a ground (Fig. 2). The bridge is balanced and the calculations carried out as before. *See* BRIDGE CIRCUIT.

Varley loop test. This is similar to the Murray loop test except for the inclusion of the adjustable resis-

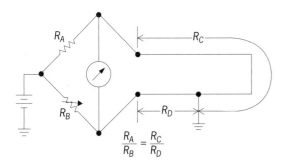

Fig. 2. Murray loop for location of ground fault.

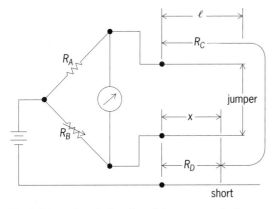

Fig. 3. Murray loop for location of short or cross fault.

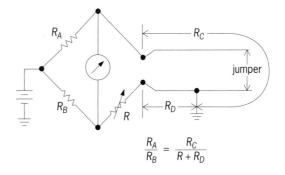

$$\frac{R_A}{R_B} = \frac{R_C}{R + R_D}$$

Fig. 4. Varley loop for location of leakage to ground.

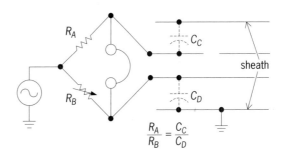

$$\frac{R_A}{R_B} = \frac{C_C}{C_D}$$

Fig. 5. Alternating-current capacitance bridge used in location of an open circuit in one conductor.

tance R. The Varley loop (**Fig. 4**) is used for fault location in high-resistance circuits.

Open circuit. An alternating-current capacitance bridge can be used for locating an open circuit as shown in **Fig. 5**. One test terminal is connected to the open conductor and the other terminal to a conductor of known continuity in the cable. All conductors associated with the test are opened at a convenient point beyond the fault but at a known distance from the test connection. An audio oscillator supplies the voltage to the bridge, which is balanced by adjusting R_B for a null as detected by the earphones. Measured ratio R_A/R_B equals the ratio of capacitances between the lines and the grounded sheath. Because each capacitance is proportional to the length of line connected to the bridge, the location of the open circuit can be determined from Eq. (4).

$$\frac{R_A}{R_B} = \frac{C_C}{C_D} \qquad (4)$$

For convenience in carrying out the tests for fault location, the fault location bridge has switches for setting up the various loop test circuits. Basically it is a bridge like other bridges used in circuit testing. *See* CIRCUIT (ELECTRICITY); OHMMETER; RESISTANCE MEASUREMENT; WHEATSTONE BRIDGE.

Charles E. Applegate

Bibliography. A. D. Helfrick and W. D. Cooper, *Electronic Instrumentation and Measurement Techniques*, 4th ed., 1990; L. Schnell (ed.), *Technology of Electrical Measurements*, 1993; L. M. Thompson, *Electrical Measurements and Calibration*, 2d ed., 1994.

Cacao

Theobroma cacao, a small tropical tree 13-19 ft (4-6 m) in height that is cultivated for the almond-shaped seeds, 0.8-1.2 in. (2-3 cm) long, which are used to make chocolate. It is a member of the tea family (Thealeae) in the order Theales. The species is native to the rainforest of the Amazon basin, and two regions of distribution in pre-Columbian times are recognized. The crop was first cultivated in Central America and northern South America, the varieties found there being known as Criollos. The second region comprises the Amazon and Orinoco basins, where the cacao populations are known as Amazonian Forastero. The second type is more commonly cultivated, particularly in Brazil, Ivory Coast, Ghana, and Nigeria, which produce 75% of the world annual output. *See* THEALES.

As a typical crop of the humid tropics, cacao is grown commercially between 15°N and 15°S, where mean annual temperatures vary from 73 to 79°F (23 to 26°C). It is generally accepted that the lower limits for successful growth are a mean monthly minimum temperature of 59°F (15°C) and an absolute minimum of 50°F (10°C). Annual rainfall in growing areas varies from 56 to 80 in. (1400 to 2000 mm).

Cultivation. Cacao can be grown in many different soils, provided they have good moisture retention and are well drained and aerated. Loose, crumbly, soft, and plastic soils facilitating root penetration are preferred. Cacao appears to have high soil fertility requirements, but can be cultivated in relatively poor soils if suitable management practices such as liming and fertilization are used.

In its natural forest habitat, cacao grows under taller trees. Traditional cultivation practices simulate such conditions by using thinned forest stands or planted shade trees. The main role of shade is to counteract unfavorable ecological factors, such as low soil fertility, wind damage, high transpiration leading to moisture stress, and increased insect attack. If all such factors can be controlled by other methods, the highest production is obtained without shade.

Cacao can be propagated by seeds or by vegetative methods (rooted cuttings or budding). The former is practically the only method used for commercial planting, with cultivars produced by hybridization. Seedlings are usually grown in shaded nurseries for 4-6 months and then transplanted to the field under temporary shade, such as that provided by banana plants. The recommended planting distance is 9 × 9 ft (3 × 3 m). The permanent shade trees are spaced at 77 ft (24 m).

Fruit and seeds. The first commercial crops are obtained in 4-5 years. In areas with even rainfall distribution, flowering may occur almost throughout the year. The flowers are borne directly on the trunk and larger branches. The fruit, an indehiscent drupe with a usually woody shell (**Fig. 1**), is red or green when unripe, and varies between 6 and 12 in. (15 and 30 cm) in length. The fruits ripen in 5-6 months and change in color to yellow or orange.

Fig. 1. Cacao (*Theobroma cacao*). (*USDA*)

The seeds, which may number up to 65 per fruit (average is 35-40), are surrounded by a mucilaginous pulp. The dry weight of the beans constitutes about one-third of the total dry weight of the pod. In most producing areas the mean annual yield varies from 660 to 1100 lb (300 to 500 kg) of dry beans per hectare, but yields of 4400-6600 lb (2000-3000 kg) may be obtained with superior cultivars and improved cultural practices. Harvesting consists of cutting the pods from the tree and opening them with a machete to remove the seeds. Following a period of 4-6 days of fermentation in heaps or "sweatboxes," the seeds (cocoa) are dried on sun-platforms or artificially until the final moisture content is about 7%.

Marketing. The produce is generally exported in the form of dry beans. The farmers' production is purchased by dealers and exported by registered exporters or government marketing boards. Sales are effected through contracts or futures markets, principally in New York and London. Growers' prices may be fixed at predetermined levels or may fluctuate according to market trends. International standards have been adopted to bring about uniformity. Accordingly, exported produce is subject to grading and treatment to avoid spoilage. The market distinguishes between bulk and fine cocoas. The latter have preferred flavor or other characteristics and receive a premium price. *See* COCOA POWDER AND CHOCOLATE.   Paulo de T. Alvim

Diseases. The most serious disease of cacao is black pod (**Fig. 2**), caused by the fungus *Phytophthora palmivora*, now recognized as having three morphological forms; two of these may be distinct species. This fungus causes great economic loss following wet weather favorable for disease development. The fungus can also attack leaves, branches, and trunks. Some control can be achieved with copper fungicides, and there is genetic material with

Fig. 2. The most widespread and most severe disease of cacao, caused by *Phytophthora palmivora*. (*Inter-American Institute of Agricultural Sciences*)

some resistance. Another pod rot, associated with the fungus *Botryodiplodia theobromae*, is occasionally a problem following wounding of pods by various vertebrates.

Witches'-broom, caused by the fungus *Crinipellis perniciosa* (formerly *Marasmius perniciosus*), occurs in tropical South America and in the West Indies. The fungus causes distorted growth of aerial plant parts, resulting in witches'-broom, and forms fruiting bodies ("mushrooms") on dead tissue. Some control is possible with sanitation and use of resistant varieties. Another New World (northwest South America, Panama, Costa Rica) disease is Monilia pod rot (watery pod rot), caused by the fungus *Monilia roreri*. Damage to pods can be severe. Control measures include removal of affected pods and use of resistant varieties. Swollen shoot, a virus disease transmitted by mealybugs, occurs only in western Africa and causes deformation of the tree and considerable economic loss. Eradication programs have been attempted. Some tolerance to the disease has been found. Other occasional problems include wilt, caused by the fungus *Ceratocystis fimbriata* and commonly spread by *Xyleborus* borers; and cushion galls, caused by a species of *Calonectria*. *See* PLANT PATHOLOGY; PLANT VIRUSES AND VIROIDS.

George A. Zentmyer

Bibliography. P. H. Gregory (ed.), *Phytophthora Disease of Cocoa*, 1974; C. A. Thorold, *Diseases of Cocoa*, 1975.

Cachexia

The severe wasting syndrome that accompanies such diseases as cancer, infection, or parasitic infestation. Occasionally, it is also observed in noninvasive conditions, such as severe cardiac failure. The causes of cachexia are only partially understood. However, it is clear that most cachexia is caused by diminished consumption of nutrients rather than by a hypermetabolic state.

Anorexia, the proximal cause of this problem, is thought to be related to the expression of endogenous factors collectively termed cytokines, some of which have now been identified. For example, tumor necrosis factor, a protein (also known as cachectin), when administered to animals for a long period of time, causes a syndrome of cachexia indistinguishable from that produced by chronic disease. Inhibitors of tumor necrosis factor activity may partially alleviate cachexia caused by experimental tumors. It is likely that other cytokines are also involved, and that together these agents cause wasting of such severity that it may lead to death in a wide variety of diseases. *See* ANOREXIA NERVOSA; CYTOKINE.

It is unclear whether cytokines suppress appetite through a direct action on satiety centers in the hypothalamus or through peripheral effects (such as effects on the bowel or other enteric structures), which then project to the central nervous system. Another clinical feature related to cachexia appears to be caused by a direct effect of cytokines (notably tumor necrosis factor and interleukin-1) on stem cells and stromal cells of the bone marrow. Tumor necrosis factor and interleukin-1 also appear to mobilize lipid through direct effects on adipocytes.

The cytokines that cause cachexia are produced mainly by cells of the immune system, especially macrophages. Synthesis is triggered by contact with molecules produced by microbial pathogens or tumor cells. Induction of synthesis depends upon both transcriptional and translational activation pathways. Rational strategies for alleviation of cachexia include eradicating the underlying infection or tumor, blocking cytokine synthesis with agents that specifically interrupt the requisite signaling pathways, or inhibiting cytokine activity with specific antibodies or other antagonists. Oral or intravenous administration of nutrients is likely to be effective if the process has not advanced to a point at which utilization of nutrients is impaired. *See* ONCOLOGY.

Bruce Beutler

Cactus

The common name for any member of the cactus family (Cactaceae). There are 120 genera with perhaps 1700 species, nearly all indigenous to America. The cacti are among the most extremely drought-resistant plants, and consequently they thrive in very arid regions. The group is characterized by a fleshy habit, presence of spines and bristles, and large, brightly colored, solitary flowers. There is a great

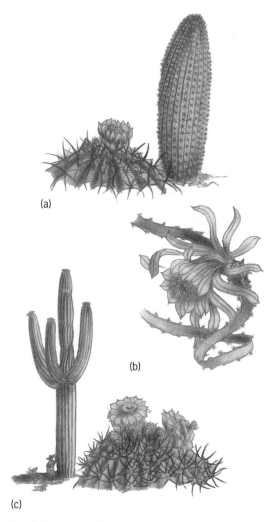

(a)

(b)

(c)

Fig. 1. Three examples of cacti. (*a*) Mule cactus, with closeup of flower, maximum height of 6 ft (2 m). (*b*) Flower of night-blooming *Cereus*, maximum height of 40 ft (12 m). (*c*) Saguaro, maximum height of 70 ft (21 m), with closeup of flower.

Fig. 2. *Mamillaria vaupellii* var. *flavispina*.

variety of body shapes and patterns, and many of the species are grown as ornamentals or oddities (**Figs. 1** and **2**). A few have edible fruits. The cochineal insect, which produces a valuable red dye, is cultivated chiefly on the cochineal cactus (*Nopalea coccinellifera*). The saguaro (*Cereus giganteus*) of Arizona and Sonora is the largest of the cacti,

attaining a height of 70 ft (21 m). *See* CARYOPHYL-LALES.   Perry D. Strausbaugh; Earl L. Core

Cacti grow in many habitats, ranging from epiphytes living on trees in dense tropical forests to large, isolated plants in deserts. In all cases, various adaptations that lead to water conservation are apparent. For example, the stems of most cacti are massive and can store large amounts of water that sustain the plants during prolonged drought. Adaptations for water conservation also occur on a metabolic level. Cacti are increasingly recognized as important crops, especially in arid and semiarid regions. Perhaps the most widespread use of cacti is as ornamentals; collectors and hobbyists worldwide cherish their shapes, attractive flowers, and ability to tolerate long periods without watering.

Cactus roots are shallow [most occur within 20 cm (8 in.) of the soil surface], which allows the plants to respond rapidly to light desert rainfalls, as only a small depth of soil needs to be wetted. Moreover, roots represent only a small fraction of a cactus plant (generally only 7–12% of the total plant dry weight), suggesting that a relatively small root surface area is necessary to supply sufficient water from the soil. A conventional way to represent the water storage capacity of a plant is the volume available for water storage divided by the area across which water can be lost to the air by transpiration. This volume-to-area ratio is high for cacti compared with the majority of plants, whose photosynthetic organs are thin flat leaves. The leaves of most cacti are ephemeral or absent, so the photosynthetic organs are the relatively massive green stems. Besides the obvious succulence of the stems of cacti, their cells are relatively large with prominent vacuoles.

Another adaptation of cacti to arid conditions is their relatively slow loss of water to the air. Cacti have a thick waxy cuticle on their stems, which acts as a waterproofing skin. Also, the pores (called stomata or stomates) in the cactus skin that are necessary for the uptake of carbon dioxide (CO_2) from the atmosphere tend to open only at night. The opening of stomata allows the vaporized water within the plant to escape to the atmosphere. Because the stem and the air temperatures are lower and the relative humidity is higher at night than during the daytime, much less water (generally 80–90% less) is lost by transpiration during the nocturnal opening of stomata by cacti compared with the daytime stomatal opening of most other plants.

The opening of stomata at night presents a problem for photosynthesis, which requires light. Specifically, photosynthesis uses atmospheric carbon dioxide and the energy of sunlight to form sugars in the chloroplasts of the chlorenchyma (the green tissue that occurs outside the whitish water-storage tissue). Open stomata are necessary for appreciable uptake of carbon dioxide, which at night for cacti is attached to the three-carbon compound phosphoenolpyruvate to form a four-carbon acid such as malic acid. During the night the acid accumulates in the large vacuoles of cactus chlorenchyma cells; during the next daytime, when the stomata have closed, carbon dioxide is released from the accumulated acid within the stems of cacti. Carbon dioxide is then fixed into sugars via photosynthesis when sunlight is available as the energy source. The opening of stomata and the increase in chlorenchyma acidity during the night followed by decarboxylation of organic acids and the formation of photosynthetic products during the daytime is known as crassulacean acid metabolism (CAM), because it was first discovered in the plant family Crassulaceae.

Crassulacean acid metabolism is crucial for the adaptation of cacti to the dry conditions characteristic of deserts. Its water-conserving attribute is also important in the increasing cultivation of cacti for their fruits and as fodder for livestock, particularly cattle. Currently just over 1 million hectares (2.5 million acres) of cacti are cultivated, mostly for the prickly pear cactus, *Opuntia ficus-indica* (the second most cultivated crassulacean acid metabolic species is pineapple, *Ananas comosus*). In particular, *O. ficus-indica* is extensively cultivated in Brazil (the leading country with over 300,000 ha) and northern Africa for fodder. In Mexico, fruit production is the main usage (about 60,000 ha); young stem segments of *O. ficus-indica* are also used in Mexico as a vegetable, termed nopalitos. Commercialization of its fruit, generally called cactus pears, requires the removal of the irritating and skin-penetrating glochids from the surface and even the application of a wax that improves appearance and prolongs shelf-life. Another use of mature stem segments of *O. ficus-indica* (and a few other cactus species), either on the plant or removed and placed in sheds, is for infestation by females of the scale insect *Dactylopius opuntiae*, which produce the brilliant red dye cochineal. Cochineal (carminic acid), 80% of which is currently produced in Peru, leads to colors ranging from yellow to purple for fabrics, foodstuffs, and even liqueurs.

Fruits termed pitayas, pitajayas, and various other names of more than 20 species of cacti are collected from the wild and sold locally throughout Latin America. These are produced by tall columnar cacti such as *Cereus peruvianus*, *Stenocereus griseus*, and *S. queretaroensis* as well as by vinelike cacti such as *Hylocereus polyrhizus*, *H. undatus*, *and Selenicereus megalanthus*. The pulp color varies from white to orange to deep purple; the seeds are small (like kiwi seeds) and readily ingested. The peels do not have the nasty glochids of *O. ficus-indica*, but certain postharvest problems such as a short shelf life require further investigation, and the market would also welcome greater year-round availability.

Cacti can grow in regions not suitable for other crops. Moreover, growth of cacti responds favorably to increasing levels of atmospheric carbon dioxide, and cacti can survive increasing atmospheric temperatures, two aspects of global climate change. Areas for cultivation of opuntias used for fodder are expanding, as are markets for fruits of many species. Indeed, because water is the principal limiting factor for agriculture in much of the world, the water-conserving qualities of cacti augur well for their increased commercialization in the future.

Park S. Nobel

Several diseases of wild cacti are known. The most conspicuous of these is probably bacterial soft rot of saguaro cacti, which is usually seen in older plants. Affected tissues appear as dark, soft lesions that usually develop a light-green border; these lesions frequently leak a dark, odorous fluid. Infected branches may fall, and the fleshy tissue of diseased plants may be destroyed in several weeks to a few months, leaving bare the woody supportive ribs (xylem elements) of the plant. Control by chemical sprays or soil drenches is not feasible. Therefore, when symptoms are first noted, rotting tissues should be removed. If the rot is limited, $1/2$ in. (13 mm) of surrounding healthy tissue should also be discarded. Immediately the cavity should be washed thoroughly with a solution of one part household bleach and nine parts water with the washing repeated in 18 to 24 h; the wound should be left open. Infections so treated frequently do not spread. Plants with numerous or large lesions should be removed and the debris thoroughly treated with the diluted bleach, or burned, or deeply buried.

The same controls apply to similarly infected organ-pipe cacti. Infected prickly-pear cacti initially have similar symptoms, but internal tissues can become so liquefied that pads bulge. The infected pad should be promptly destroyed, and the former point of attachment treated with bleach.

Recent studies in the United States have established that the soft-rot disease is caused by bacteria in the genus *Erwinia*, particularly *E. cacticida*. This species has also been isolated from rotting cacti in Australia and Mexico.

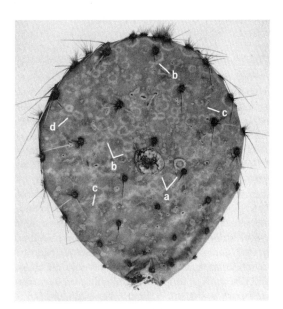

Fig. 3. Disease symptoms on prickly-pear pad: (*a*) lesions caused by *Phyllosticta concava*; (*b*) virus-induced symptoms; (*c*) injuries from penetrating cactus spines; (*d*) ring pattern caused by feeding insects. (*From S. M. Alcorn, R. L. Gilbertson, and M. R. Nelson, Some diseases of cacti in Arizona, Prog. Agr. Ariz., 27(3):3–5, 1975*)

Saguaro cacti may be toppled by heavy winds following soil-soaking rains. Roots of these plants usually have been previously weakened by the root- and wood-rotting fungus *Poria carnegieana*. Wind-thrown plants tend to be mature specimens; no control is known.

Prickly pears can be infected by other pathogens. Certain viruses cause whitish rings or irregularly shaped patterns to develop on pads (**Fig. 3**), Severely affected plants also are stunted. The light-colored lines usually are narrow. By contrast, rings caused by the feeding of sap-sucking insects have small, central green areas with broad, light-colored margins. Presumably, sap-sucking insects carry the viruses between plants, but "new," infected plants will develop if diseased pads root after their detachment from the parent plant. The fungus *Phyllosticta concava* causes the formation of generally circular, whitish to tan, depressed, dry lesions on pads; these areas usually become covered with black, slightly raised "dots." An infection may penetrate to the opposite side, where a similar lesion forms. Infected tissue can disintegrate, leaving a hole through the pad. Fungicidal sprays will minimize infections, which start in cool, rainy periods. *See* PLANT PATHOLOGY.

Stanley M. Alcorn

Bibliography. S. M. Alcorn, R. L. Gilbertson, and M. R. Nelson, Some diseases of cacti in Arizona, *Prog. Agr. Ariz.*, 27(3):3–5, 1975; S. M. Alcorn et al., Taxonomy and pathogenicity of *Erwinia cacticida* sp. nov., *Int. J. Sys. Bacteriol.*, 41(2):197–212, 1991; L. Benson, *The Cacti of the United States and Canada*, 1982; G. M. Milbrath, M. R. Nelson, and R. E. Wheeler, The distribution and electron microscopy of viruses of cacti in southern Arizona, *Phytopathology*, 63:1133–1139, 1973; Y. Mizrahi, A. Nerd, and P. S. Nobel, Cacti as crops, *Hort. Rev.*, 18:291–319, 1997; P. S. Nobel, *Remarkable Agaves and Cacti*, 1994.

Cadmium

A relatively rare chemical element, symbol Cd, atomic number 48, closely related to zinc, with which it is usually associated in nature. It is a silvery-white ductile metal with a faint bluish tinge. It is softer and more malleable than zinc, but slightly harder than tin. It has an atomic weight of 112.40 and a specific gravity of 8.65 at 20°C (68°F). Its melting point of 321°C (610°F) and boiling point of 765°C (1410°F) are lower than those of zinc. There are eight naturally occurring stable isotopes, and eleven artificial unstable radio isotopes have been reported. Cadmium is the middle member of group 12 (zinc, cadmium, and mercury) in the periodic table, and its chemical properties generally are intermediate between zinc and mercury. The cadmium ion is displaced by zinc metal in acidic sulfate solutions. Cadmium is bivalent in all its stable compounds, and its ion is colorless. *See* PERIODIC TABLE; TIN; ZINC.

Cadmium does not occur uncombined in nature, and the one true cadmium mineral, greenockite (cadmium sulfide), is not a commercial source of the metal. Almost all of the cadmium produced is obtained as a by-product of the smelting and refining of zinc ores, which usually contain 0.2–0.4% cadmium. The United States, Canada, Mexico, Australia, Belgium-Luxembourg, and the Republic of Korea are principal sources, although not all are producers.

The fumes of cadmium, its compounds, and solutions of its compounds are very toxic, and cadmium-plated articles should not be used in food, nor should cadmium-coated articles be welded or used in ovens. Nickel-cadmium batteries are the second-largest application, with pigment and chemical uses third. Sizable amounts are used in low-melting-point alloys, similar to Wood's metal, and in automatic fire sprinklers. Cadmium compounds are used in the production of cadmium phosphors. Because of its great neutron-absorbing capacity, especially the isotope 113, cadmium is used in control rods and shielding for nuclear reactors. *See* ALLOY; CADMIUM METALLURGY.

Wilber Hague

Bibliography. F. A. Cotton et al., *Advanced Inorganic Chemistry*, 6th ed., Wiley-Interscience, 1999; R. R. Lauwerys and P. Hoet, *Industrial Chemical Exposure: Guidelines for Biological Monitoring*, 3d ed., 2001; D. R. Lide, *CRC Handbook Chemistry and Physics*, 85th ed., CRC Press, 2004.

Cadmium metallurgy

Cadmium resembles zinc in its chemical properties, and its occurrence for commercial purposes is with zinc ores. A relatively rare element in the Earth's crust, cadmium ranks in abundance between mercury and silver. Most cadmium occurs in solid solution in the zinc sulfide mineral called sphalerite. Although cadmium may be recovered from some lead and copper ores, it is associated with the zinc which is also found in these ores. Although a few zinc concentrates contain as much as 1–2% cadmium, typical content ranges from 0.06 to 0.5%. Since cadmium is entirely a by-product metal, the supply available is closely aligned with zinc production, averaging about 0.4% of zinc production. *See* SPHALERITE.

Recovery methods. All cadmium recovery processes involve the dissolution of cadmium-bearing feed material (sinter fume from the sintering of zinc ores or calcines, residue from the electrolyte purification of electrolytic zinc plants or from the purification of zinc sulfate solutions in the manufacture of zinc salts and pigments, and so on) followed by various purification and cadmium displacement steps. Methods of processing can be grouped conveniently into two basic categories, electrolytic and electromotive. In the former case, cadmium is recovered by electrolyzing purified solutions; in the latter case, cadmium in the form of a metallic sponge is displaced from purified solutions by a less noble metal, zinc being used in every known commercial application, and the sponge is melted or distilled, or both.

Electrolytic recovery. In electrolytic cadmium recovery, the feed material is dissolved in spent electrolyte either from the cadmium cells or from an electrolytic zinc circuit. The leach solution is neutralized to a pH of 5.0 or above, and troublesome impurities, such as copper, are removed by adding a small amount of zinc dust. Thallium can be removed from solution by precipitating with potassium permanganate or sodium chromate. Cadmium is electrolyzed from purified solutions at cell voltages of 2.4–2.8 V. Most electrolytic cadmium plants employ a current density of 3–8 A/ft^2 (32–86 A/m^2). Extensive refining of cathode cadmium is not required to produce metal that meets market specifications. In the usual case, the cathode metal is melted under a layer of caustic at a temperature of 716–950°F (380–510°C) for 3–18 h before it is cast into commercial shapes.

Electromotive recovery. Electromotive cadmium producers recover the metal from fume produced in the sintering of zinc calcines or zinc concentrates. Most fume contains appreciable concentrations of troublesome impurities, such as arsenic. Prior to leaching, fume may be oxidized by roasting or sulfated by baking with sulfuric acid. Roasted fume is leached in sulfuric acid solution; sulfated fume is leached with water. Leach solutions are purified to remove arsenic, iron, copper, thallium, and lead. For example, a small amount of zinc dust may be added to remove copper, and the filtered solution treated with potassium permanganate to oxidize iron (which is precipitated with caustic) and remove arsenic, following which a small amount of sodium chromate may be added to precipitate lead and thallium. Cadmium sponge is precipitated from purified solutions with zinc dust (zinc is higher in the electromotive series than cadmium is, and it displaces cadmium from solutions). Most electromotive producers densify the cadmium sponge by briquetting it in a press at pressures of 3000–12,000 lb/in.^{2} (20–80 megapascals). If the cadmium sponge is sufficiently pure, metal meeting ASTM specifications may be produced by melting the compacted sponge under caustic. Less pure sponge may require retorting (distilling) to meet product cadmium specifications.

Product specifications and applications. Product specifications are set forth in the **table**. Major end uses for cadmium are in corrosion-resistant plating

Cadmium chemical requirements*	
Element	Composition, %†
Cadmium	99.90
Zinc	0.035
Copper	0.015
Lead	0.025
Tin	0.01
Silver	0.01
Antimony	0.001
Arsenic	0.003
Thallium	0.003

*ASTM designation: B 440–69.
†The minimum percentage is indicated for cadmium, the maximum percentage for the other elements.

and in cadmium compounds for use as pigments in paints, ceramics, and plastics. These two uses account for about 45% and 15%, respectively, of total cadmium production. The remainder is used in alloys, plastic stabilizers, batteries, and television picture tube phosphors. Other uses for cadmium include solar energy cells and energy storage systems.

Cadmium is a toxic element. Care must be exercised to avoid breathing or ingesting it or its compounds. *See* CADMIUM; ZINC. Robert E. Lund

Bibliography. American Society for Testing and Materials, *Annual Book of ASTM Standards*, 02.0, *Nonferrous Metals*, 1992; R. A. Burkin, *Topics in Non-Ferrous Extractive Metallurgy*, 1980; C. H. Cotterill (ed.), *AIME World Symposium on Mining and Metallurgy of Lead-Zinc*, vol. 2, 1970; C. B. Gill, *Nonferrous Extractive Metallurgy*, 1988.

Caffeine

An alkaloid, formerly synthesized by methylation of theobromine isolated from cacao, but now recovered from the solvents used in the manufacture of decaffeinated coffee. Chemically, caffeine is 1,3,7-trimethylxanthine, and has the structural formula below. It is widely used in medicine as a stimulant

for the central nervous system and as a diuretic. It occurs naturally in tea, coffee, and yerba maté, and small amounts are found in cola nuts and cacao. Caffeine crystallizes into long, white needlelike crystals that slowly lose their water of hydration to give a white solid that melts at 235–237.2°C (455–459.0°F). It sublimes without decomposition at lower temperatures. Caffeine has an intensely bitter taste, though it is neutral to litmus. *See* ALKALOID. Frank Wagner

Cage hydrocarbon

A compound that is composed of only carbon and hydrogen atoms and contains three or more rings arranged topologically so as to enclose a volume of space. In general, the "hole" within a cage hydrocarbon is too small to accommodate even a proton. The carbon frameworks of many cage hydrocarbons are quite rigid. Consequently, the geometric relationships between substituents on the cage are well defined. This quality makes these compounds exceptionally valuable for testing concepts concerning bonding, reactivity, structure-activity relationships, and structure-property relationships. *See* CHEMICAL BONDING.

Platonic solids. The carbocyclic analogs of the platonic solids that are tenable are tetrahedrane (**1**, where X = —H), cubane (**2**), and dodecahedrane (**3**). According to theory, tetrahedrane is so highly

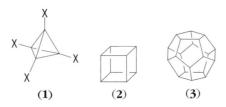

(1)   (2)   (3)

strained that it should dissociate spontaneously to two molecules of acetylene. Nevertheless, G. Maier was able to synthesize tetra-*t*-butyl tetrahedrane [**1**, X = —C(CH₃)₃] in 1978. The symmetry of the carbon skeleton of the tetrahedron permits the distances among all the bulky *t*-butyl groups [—C(CH₃)₃] to be maximized, and so their intramolecular repulsions are minimized. Cubane also requires the bond angles and bond lengths of its skeletal carbon atoms to be substantially distorted. Cubane was first prepared in 1964 by P. Eaton. Calculations suggest that octanitrocubane may be a high-density, high-energy material. Although the synthesis of dodecahedrane is difficult, independent preparations of this nearly globular cage hydrocarbon were reported in 1982 and 1987. *See* ALICYCLIC HYDROCARBON; BOND ANGLE AND DISTANCE.

Prismanes. An unsubstituted prismane has the general formula of (CH)$_n$, and the carbon atoms are located at the corners of a regular prism. Prismane (**4**), cubane, pentaprismane (**5**), and hexaprismane (**6**, unknown) are the simplest members of

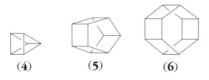

(4)   (5)   (6)

this family of cage hydrocarbons. Despite their high strain energies (which in most ring structures would facilitate ring opening), the prismanes have unusual kinetic stabilities due to the symmetry-imposed barriers that exist toward any ring opening. *See* MOLECULAR ORBITAL THEORY.

Adamantane. The monomer of the diamond carbon skeleton is adamantane (**7**, where X = —H). Al-

though this compound has been isolated from petroleum, its availability is a result of a chance observation in 1957 that tetrahydrodicyclopentadiene (**8**),

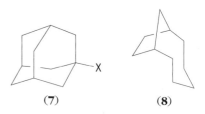

(7)   (8)

an inexpensive compound, isomerizes to adamantane in the presence of aluminum halide catalysts. Eventually, it was recognized that drugs containing adamantyl groups are fat soluble and not readily degraded in the human body. Thus, such drugs are more persistent and longer acting than formulations based on long-chain hydrocarbons. Amantadine (**7**, where X = —NH₂) was developed commercially as the first orally active antiviral drug for the prevention of respiratory illness due to influenza A2-Asian viruses. Amantadine also has been found to be clinically effective for treating the symptoms of Parkinson's disease. *See* VIRUS CHEMOPROPHYLAXIS.

The other simple diamondoid hydrocarbons, diamantane (**9**) and triamantane (**10**), can be synthe-

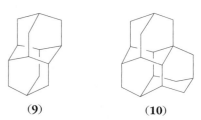

(9)   (10)

sized by the Lewis acid–catalyzed rearrangement of isomeric hydrocarbons that possess a moderate degree of strain energy. Thus, treatment of (**11**) and (**12**) with appropriate catalysts give (**9**) and (**10**), respectively.

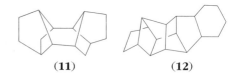

(11)   (12)

Other structures. Organic chemists have prepared a wide variety of cage hydrocarbons that do not occur in nature. Among these compounds are triasterane (**13**), iceane or wurtzitane (**14**), and pagodane (**15**). Each of these compounds is prepared by

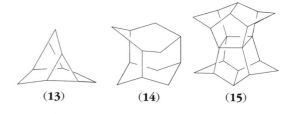

(13)   (14)   (15)

a complex multistep organic synthesis. *See* ORGANIC CHEMISTRY; ORGANIC SYNTHESIS.   Roger K. Murray, Jr.

Bibliography. G. A. Olah (ed.), *Cage Hydrocarbons*, 1990; E. Osawa and O. Yonemitsu (eds.), *Carbocyclic Cage Compounds: Chemistry and Applications*, 1992.

Caisson foundation

A permanent substructure that, while being sunk into position, permits excavation to proceed inside and also provides protection for the workers against water pressure and collapse of soil. The term caisson covers a wide range of foundation structures. Caissons may be open, pneumatic, or floating type; deep or shallow; large or small; and of circular, square, or rectangular cross section. The walls may consist of timber, temporary or permanent steel shells, or thin or massive concrete. Large caissons are used as foundations for bridge piers, deep-water wharves, and other structures. Small caissons are used singly or in groups to carry such loads as building columns. Caissons are used where they provide the most feasible method of passing obstructions, where soil cannot otherwise be kept out of the bottom or where cofferdams cannot be used. *See* BRIDGE; PILE FOUNDATION.

The bottom rim of the caisson is called the cutting edge. The edge is sharp or narrow and is made of, or faced with, structural steel. The narrowness of the edge facilitates removal of ground under the shell and reduces the resistance of the soil to descent of the caisson.

Open caisson. An open caisson is a shaft open at both ends. It is used in dry ground or in moderate amounts of water. A bottom section, having a cutting edge (**Fig. 1**), is set on the ground and soil is removed from inside while the caisson sinks by its own weight. Sections are added as excavation and sinking proceed. After excavation is completed, the hollow interior of the shaft is filled with concrete.

Open caissons are usually constructed of reinforced concrete, but if steel shells are used, concrete may also be required to provide weight. When an open caisson is to be towed into place, hollow walls or false bottoms are provided to give it buoyancy; they are removed after the caisson is in position. Open caissons can be sunk in water to practically any depth.

In deep water an open caisson is sometimes sunk by the sand-island method. A cofferdam is constructed and filled with sand to form an artificial island. The island serves as a working platform and guide for sinking the caisson. This method also avoids the necessity of transporting a fabricated shell and holding it in position.

Figure 2 shows the major types of caissons in use. Chicago caissons (open well) are formed by excavating a few feet of soil, installing short vertical pieces of wood or concrete lagging beveled to form a circle, bracing with segmental hoops, and repeating. Such caissons are used in clay that is not strong enough to carry the permanent load alone but will permit excavation for the lagging without flowing in at the

Fig. 1. Underside of open caisson for Greater New Orleans bridge over Mississippi River. (*Dravo Corp.*)

bottom. The clay is hoisted out in buckets or elevators. The bottom may be belled out. Lagging and bracing are generally left in place.

Sheeted caissons are similar to Chicago caissons, except that vertical sheeting is continuous and is driven by hand or pile-driving hammers either in advance of excavation or as it proceeds. Bracing rings are placed every few feet. Sheeting may be wood, concrete plank, or steel, and is left in place. Sheeted caissons may be round or square.

Small cylindrical caissons, 2–12 ft (0.6–3.6 m) in diameter, consist of a concrete shell or steel pipe sunk into the ground by its own or by a temporarily superimposed weight. Excavation is done by hand or mechanically, and the caisson is finally filled with concrete.

Drilled caissons are drilled holes that are filled with concrete. Rock socketing may be used at the bottom, or the bottom may be belled up to 30 ft (9 m) in diameter. The caisson may be as long as 150 ft (46 m). Cohesive soils are drilled with augers or bucket-type drills. Granular soils are drilled in the same manner with the aid of a binding agent or by rotary drills using drilling mud or water to keep the hole from caving in. Steel-shaft casings are used where needed to shut off water or keep soil out of the hole. Casings are removed before concreting, or during concreting in unstable ground.

Driven caissons are formed by driving a cylindrical steel shell with one or more pile-driving hammers. After excavation by grabs, buckets, or jetting, concrete is placed inside. The shells usually are withdrawn as the concrete rises, unless the soil is so soft or water conditions are such that they must be left in place.

Pneumatic caisson. A pneumatic caisson is like a box or cylinder in shape; but the top is closed and thus compressed air can be forced inside to keep water and soil from entering the bottom of the shaft. A pneumatic caisson is used where the soil cannot

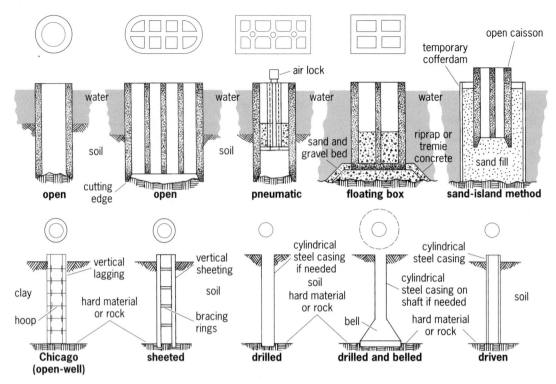

Fig. 2. Major types of caissons as they appear from top and in cross section from side.

be excavated through open shafts (for instance, where there are concrete, timbers, boulders, or masonry lying underwater) or where soil conditions are such that the upward pressure must be balanced. The air pressure must balance or slightly exceed the hydrostatic head and is increased as the caisson descends. The maximum depth is about 120 ft (37 m), corresponding to an air pressure of 52 lb/in.^{2} (360 kilopascals), which is about the limit of human endurance. Workers and materials must pass through air locks. Too rapid decompression may result in caisson disease or "bends," resulting from the expansion of bubbles of air trapped in joints, muscles, or blood. The length of time that workers can perform under pressure and the speed of decompression are regulated by law. Pneumatic caissons may be started as open caissons, then closed and air applied. They are made of reinforced concrete, which may be faced on one or both sides with steel plates. *See* DIVING.

Floating caisson. A floating or box caisson consists of an open box with sides and closed bottom, but no top. It is usually built on shore and floated to the site where it is weighted and lowered onto a bed previously prepared by divers. The caisson is then filled with sand, gravel, or concrete. This type is most suitable where there is no danger of scour. Floating caissons may be built of reinforced concrete, steel, or wood.

Small box caissons usually consist of a single cell. Large caissons are usually divided into compartments; this braces the side walls and permits more accurate control during loading and sinking. *See* FOUNDATIONS.   Robert D. Chellis

Calamine

A term that may refer to either a zinc mineral, $Zn_4Si_2O_7(OH)_2 \cdot H_2O$, which is also known as hemimorphite, or to zinc oxide, ZnO, which is used in medicinal or pharmaceutical products and in cosmetics. *See* HEMIMORPHITE; ZINC.   E. Eugene Weaver

Calanoida

An order of Copepoda that includes the larger and more abundant of the pelagic species. Some authorities consider the Calanoida an order of the subclass Copepoda. In the food cycles of the sea these copepods are the most important group of marine animals because of their overwhelming numbers, ubiquitous distribution, and position at the base of the animal food chain. *See* COPEPODA.

The anterior part of the body is cylindrical with five or six segments, and much broader than the posterior part, usually with two, three, or four segments in the female and five segments in the male. A pair of caudal rami bear short setae, often of nearly equal length. The first antennae have 20 to 25 segments and usually extend to the ends of the caudal rami or beyond. They are not for locomotion, but are stabilizers and sinking retarders, and also have an olfactory function. In the male the right first antenna is often geniculate for grasping the female. The second antennae and mandibular palps are biramous and create water currents for feeding and slow movement. These and the first and second maxillae and maxillipeds have long setae and create feeding-current

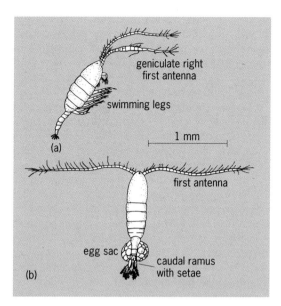

Diaptomus. **(a) Lateral view of male. (b) Dorsal view of female.**

Labels in figure: geniculate right first antenna; swimming legs; (a); 1 mm; first antenna; egg sac; caudal ramus with setae; (b)

eddies and strain small food organisms from the water. The five pairs of swimming legs are biramous, but the last pair is sometimes reduced or absent in the female, and the male's right fifth leg may be modified for grasping the female (see **illus.**). There is a small oval, dorsal thoracic heart with an anterior aortic opening, two posterior venous openings, and one ventral venous opening. A pair of excretory glands are in the second maxillae, and an oil storage sac is usually found dorsal to the digestive tract in the thorax.

In this order there are 120 or more recognized genera, some with numerous species. In the fresh-water genus *Diaptomus* about 100 species are known. However, except in surveys over very wide geographic areas, the number of species to be found in any one genus is usually less than 10 or 15.

Calanus is the most outstanding genus in boreal and arctic seas. *Calanus finmarchicus* (Gunnerus) was the first copepod to be described. It is a cold-water species, 0.12–0.24 in. (3–6 mm) long, which ranks first among North Atlantic copepods, and several researchers have claimed that, feeding at the second trophic level, it may be the world's most numerous animal species.

In biomass, the calanoids exceed all other copepod groups. In the Gulf of Maine alone the total standing crop of calanoids has been calculated at 4,000,000 tons.

Nearly all calanoids are planktonic and, as a group, occur in all parts of the oceans from the surface to abyssal depths. The geographic and bathymetric ranges of many species are, however, restricted by the nature of water currents and the chemical and physical conditions of the water. In their southernmost range the northern species are found at greater depths.

Many species live at depths of 650–1000 ft (200–300 m) during the day, but migrate upward at night and return to usual levels again at dawn. These di-

urnal migrations are doubtless in response to conditions of light, but are modified by the temperature tolerances of the species and by other factors.

In keeping with their planktonic habit, many calanoids are provided with long plumose setae and long antennae to aid in flotation. Often the body or plumes are brightly pigmented. Common colors are pink, red, green, blue, and violet. Some are mostly black or entirely hyaline. A number of species, especially of the genera *Metridia* and *Pleuromomma*, are bioluminescent, emitting flashes of phosphorescent light. *See* BIOLUMINESCENCE; ZOOPLANKTON.

Harry C. Yeatman

Bibliography. J. Green, *Biology of Crustacea*, 1961; S. M. Marshall and A. P. Orr, *The Biology of a Marine Copepod, Calanus finmarchicus (Gunnerus)*, 1955; S. P. Parker (ed.), *Synopsis and Classification of Living Organisms*, 2 vols., 1982; G. O. Sars, *Crustacea of Norway*, vol. 4, 1903; T. H. Waterman (ed.), *The Physiology of Crustacea*, 2 vols., 1960, 1961.

Calcarea

A class of the phylum Porifera, including exclusively marine sponges with a skeleton composed of spicules of calcium carbonate to which can be added a solid basal calcitic skeleton. Calcarea vary from radially symmetrical vase-shaped species, to aggregates made up of a reticulum of thin tubes, to irregular massive forms. Calcareous sponges are mostly small

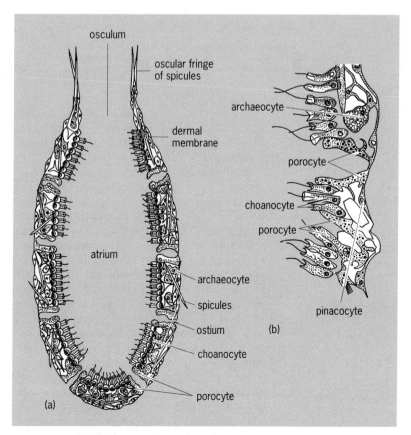

Fig. 1. Morphology of asconoid calcareous sponge. (a) Shown in longitudinal section. (b) Cross section through *Clathrina* showing cell types.

Labels in figure: osculum; oscular fringe of spicules; archaeocyte; dermal membrane; porocyte; choanocyte; porocyte; pinacocyte; atrium; archaeocyte; spicules; ostium; choanocyte; porocyte; (a); (b)

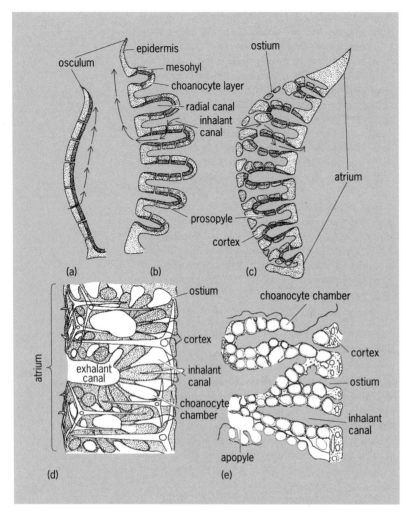

Fig. 2. Grades of construction of water-current system in Calcarea. (*a*) Asconoid type. (*b*) Syconoid type without cortex. (*c*) Syconoid type with cortex. (*d*) Intermediate or transitional stage between syconoid and leuconoid type. (*e*) Leuconoid type.

and inhabit the shallow waters of all seas, from tidal areas to depths of 660 ft (200 m), with a few species extending down to at least 13,200 ft (4000 m). *See* PORIFERA.

Morphology. The simplest calcareous sponges with an asconoid grade of construction consist of aggregates of upright tubes with unfolded walls made up of an outer epidermis of pinacocytes and an inner lining of choanocytes (**Fig. 1**). Between these layers of cells is a stratum of mesohyl including archaeocytes and spicules. Cells called porocytes, each perforated by a tubular canal, pierce the walls at intervals and allow water to enter the central cavity or atrium (**Fig. 2***a*). Water leaves by way of a terminal osculum.

A somewhat more complicated structure is seen in calcareous sponges of the syconoid grade of construction (Fig. 2*b*). Syconoid sponges are usually individual vase-shaped forms with a thick wall enclosing a large central atrium opening out through a terminal osculum. In the simplest forms the wall is pushed out at intervals into fingerlike projections, called radial canals, in which the choanocytes are localized. Water enters the radial canals directly through pores

without the intervention of special inhalant canals. In most syconoid species, however, a dermal membrane made up of pinacocytes and mesohyl forms a cortex of greater or less thickness which joins the outer ends of the radial canals. Pores or ostia pierce the dermis and open into inhalant canals which are simply the spaces between the radial canals in some cases. In forms with a thick cortex (Fig. 2*c*), the inhalant canals run a course through the cortical mesohyl before reaching the outer ends of the radial canals (choanocyte chambers).

The leuconoid grade of construction has probably evolved independently among the several lines of calcareous sponges. In those with a syconoid ancestry, the radial canals subdivide into many small choanocyte chambers which arise as outpocketings of the radial canal wall. A common intermediate stage is seen in genera in which each radial canal is subdivided into elongate choanocyte chambers grouped around a common exhalant canal (Fig. 2*d*). Several lines of calcareous sponges have apparently reached the leuconoid grade of construction during the course of evolution through the anastomosis of ascon tubes, rather than by the branching of the radial canals of a syconoid sponge (Fig. 2*e*).

Spicules. Calcareous sponge spicules are monaxonid (diactines), triradiate (triactines), or quadriradiate (tetractines) in form. Diactines, where present, tend to occur in the cortex from which they may project to form a bristly surface. In some species, diactines project around the osculum. Either triactines or tetractines or both, depending on the species, are distributed in the mesohyl, often arranged in definite patterns in relation to the cortex and internal structures. The spicules provide increased rigidity for the tube and serve as protective elements.

Calcareous spicules are secreted extracellularly in a cavity formed by several sclerocytes. Two cells participate in the formation of a diactine or each ray of a triactine and tetractine (**Fig. 3**). The groups of sclerocytes are so oriented that the individual rays

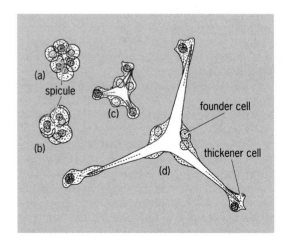

Fig. 3. Spicule formation in the calcareous sponges. (*a*–*c*) Early stages in secretion of triactine spicule, with founder and thickener cells. (*d*) Late stage of spicule formation.

fuse basally to form a triradiate or quadriradiate pattern.

Taxonomy. The monophyletic origin of calcareous sponges has been confirmed by recent molecular phylogenetic studies. Several of these studies suggest that Porifera are paraphyletic, with Calcarea appearing as a distinct phylum which would be the sister group of nonsponge metazoans. This point may be important in the knowledge of the origin of metazoans, but presently remains an open question. The Calcarea may be divided into two evolutionary lines based on morphology and development which have been recently supported by molecular phylogeny. In these two lines, corresponding to the subclasses Calcinea and Calcaronea, all the steps in increasing complexity of the aquiferous system organization and the architecture of the skeleton are present. These steps have been considered as stages in evolution, from simple forms with asconoid organization to more complex ones with leuconoid organization. Such a gradist view is now in the process of being replaced by a more phylogenetic conception, although the evolutionary pathways are presently not fully understood.

In the subclass Calcaronea, including the asconoid genus *Leucosolenia* and its syconoid and leuconoid relatives, the choanocytes have a nucleus apical in position, the triactine spicules are inequiangular, and the free-swimming larvae are amphiblastulae (**Fig. 4a**). These are larvae with an anterior hemisphere of flagellated cells and a posterior mass of nonflagellated cells. The fate of these two categories of cells is determined at an early stage of cleavage. After a short free-swimming period, the amphiblastula larva settles down on its anterior end, and gastrulation occurs by invagination of the flagellated hemisphere or by downgrowth of the nonflagellated cells. A small tubular asconoid sponge called an olynthus results, and this may retain the asconoid structure or differentiate later into a syconoid or leuconoid structure according to species. Flagellated cells become choanocytes, while nonflagellated cells are totipotent and give rise to all other cell types of the adult sponge. Calcaronea includes three orders, Leucosoleniida, Lithonida, and Baerida. In Leucosoleniida, with nine families and 42 genera, the skeleton is composed exclusively of free spicules. In Lithonida, with one family and five Recent genera, the skeleton is reinforced by linked or cemented spicules. In Baerida, with four families and nine genera, the skeleton includes microdiactines and/or dagger-shaped small tetractines and may be reinforced by a rigid basal mass of calcite. *See* CALCARONEA; LEUCOSOLENIIDA.

In the subclass Calcinea, including the asconoid genus *Clathrina* and its syconoid and leuconoid relatives, *Leucetta*, and others, the nucleus is located basally in the choanocytes, the triactine spicules are equiangular, and the free-swimming larva is a coeloblastula (Fig. 4b). In this case, cleavage results in a hollow blastula made up of a single layer of flagellated cells, with one to several nonflagellated cells at the posterior pole, some of which wander into the interior of the embryo. The larva so produced leads a short free-swimming life and then settles to the bottom, where it attaches by the anterior pole and flattens out. The cells of the larva differentiate according to their position in the metamorphosing sponge. Cells of the outer layer become pinacocytes; those of the interior become choanocytes that line the spongocoel. A young asconoid sponge or olynthus is thus formed that will develop into the adult condition. Calcinea includes two orders, Clathrinida and Murrayonida. In Clathrinida, with six families and 16 genera, the skeleton is composed exclusively of free spicules. In Murrayonida, with three Recent species classified in three families, the skeleton is reinforced either by a rigid network of calcite or by calcareous plates or spicules tracts. *See* CALCINEA; CLATHRINIDA; LEUCETTIDA.

Jean Vacelet; Willard D. Hartman

Fossils. Many fossil, and some living, sponges have a skeleton built largely of massive, nonspicular calcium carbonate; it is called a basal skeleton. Such sponges are said to be hypercalcified. Some belong to the class Calcarea, as demonstrated by the presence of typical calcarean triradiate spicules (three rays in one plane) and tetraradiate spicules (a fourth ray at right angles to the other three). Others have siliceous monaxons typical of the class Demospongea. Many have no spicules and, if fossil, cannot be assigned with certainty to a class; however, if living, they can be assigned on the basis of cell morphology. In general, basal skeletons of aragonite are found in ceractinomorph Demospongea, while basal skeletons of

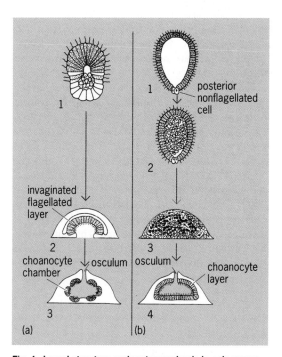

Fig. 4. Larval structure and metamorphosis in calcareous sponges. (*a*) Developmental stages characteristic of the Calcaronea: 1, amphiblastula larva; 2, newly settled larva showing metamorphosis; 3, young syconoid stage. (*b*) Developmental stages characteristic of the Calcinea: 1, coeloblastula larva; 2, solid larva; 3, newly settled larva; 4, young sponge of asconoid grade.

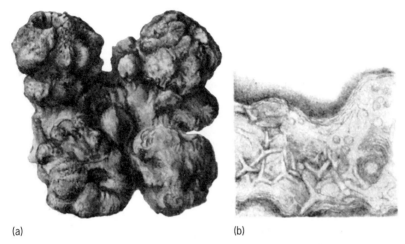

(a)   (b)

Fig. 5. *Trachysinia*, a Jurassic pharetrone with inozoan morphology. (*a*) Entire sponge. (*b*) A fiber enlarged, showing the basal skeleton with embedded triradiates and tetraradiates. (*After G. J. Hinde, 1884, and R. M. Finks and J. K. Rigby, From Treatise on Invertebrate Paleontology, courtesy of and © 2004, The Geological Society of America and The University of Kansas*)

magnesian calcite are found in Calcarea or in tetractinomorph Demospongea. *See* DEMOSPONGEA; SKELETAL SYSTEM.

All the fossil sponges of the class Calcarea belong to the subclass Calcaronea. Those with a basal skeleton are known as pharetrones. Their fossil record goes back to the Permian Period. Their morphology is either inozoan (**Fig. 5**), in which the basal skeleton is organized into a network of fibers, or sphinctozoan (**Fig. 6**), in which the basal skeleton coats the soft parts so as to form a series of perforated chambers. In both types, typical calcarean spicules—triradiates, tetraradiates, and "tuning-fork" spicules (triradiates in which two rays are subparallel)—are embedded in the basal skeleton. Forms in which the spicules are merely cemented together by calcite are known as lithonines. Their fossil record goes back to the Carboniferous Period.

There are, however, large groups of fossils of considerable abundance, often forming reefs (as do the

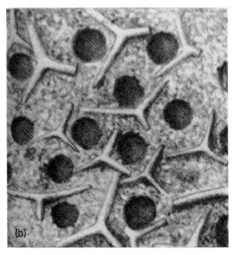

(a)

(b)

(c)

Fig. 6. *Tremacystia*, a Cretaceous pharetone with sphinctozoan morphology. (*a*) Entire sponge. (*b*) Outer surface enlarged, showing perforated basal skeleton with embedded tetraradiates (fourth ray directed inward). (*c*) Isolated tetraradiate. (*After G. J. Hinde, 1884, and R. M. Finks and J. K. Rigby, From Treatise on Invertebrate Paleontology, courtesy of and © 2004, The Geological Society of America and The University of Kansas*)

pharetrones), which have a massive calcareous skeleton but whose living relatives appear to be demosponges. These groups include species of inozoan and sphinctozoan morphology, with aragonite basal skeletons of spherulitic, penicillate, or microgranular structure, assigned to the demosponge orders Agelasida and Vaceletida, as well as some with magnesian calcite basal skeletons assigned to the demosponge order Hadromerida. They are especially abundant in the Permian and Triassic periods, and also include most of the living species called sclerosponges. They probably include as well the stromatoporoids, the chaetetids, and the favositids, formerly considered to be corals, and perhaps also the Archaeocyatha (see below). Because many of them lack spicules (when spicules are present they are siliceous monaxons), they are sometimes difficult to distinguish from pharetrones. *See* COELENTERATA; REEF; STROMATOPOROIDEA.

Another group, the Heteractinida, which is confined to the Paleozoic Era, probably belongs to the class Calcarea. Their typical spicule has six rays in one plane, sometimes with two more at right angles to the six. This type of spicule can be thought of as a double triradiate (or tetraradiate), and the interpretation is strengthened by the simultaneous occurrence of triradiates and tetraradiates (typical of Calcarea), together with the six-rayed forms, in late Paleozoic representatives of the group, such as Wewokella.

Another possibly related group is the Archeocyatha. This exclusively Cambrian group has a pharetrone-like skeleton, but the double-walled conical growth form is not a typical pharetrone shape. *See* ARCHAEOCYATHA.

Although pharetrones have existed from the Permian to the present-day, they were most abundant and diversified in the late Paleozoic and Mesozoic. The lithonines are not known before the Jurassic. *See* ECHINODERMATA.   Robert M. Finks

Bibliography. R. M. Finks and J. K. Rigby, Hypercalcified sponges, in *Treatise on Invertebrate Paleontology*, pt. E: *Porifera Revised*, vol. 3, pp. 585–764, ed. by R. L. Kaesler, 2004; W. D. Hartman, A re-examination of Bidder's classification of the Calcarea, *Sys. Zool.*, 7(3):97–110, 1958; J. N. A. Hooper and R. W. M. V. Soest, *Systema Porifera: A Guide to the Classification of Sponges*, Plenum, New York, 2002; M. Manuel et al., Phylogeny and evolution of Calcareous sponges: Monophyly of Calcinea and Calcaronea, high level of morphological homoplasy, and the primitive nature of axial symmetry, *Sys. Bio.*, 52:311–333, 2003; R. Wood, *Reef Evolution*, Oxford University Press, 1999.

Calcichordates

Primitive fossil members of the phylum Chordata with a calcite skeleton of echinoderm type. They occur in marine rocks of Cambrian to Pennsylvanian age (530–300 million years old) and, because of their skeletons, have traditionally been placed in the phylum Echinodermata. They are shown to be chordates, however, by many chordate anatomical

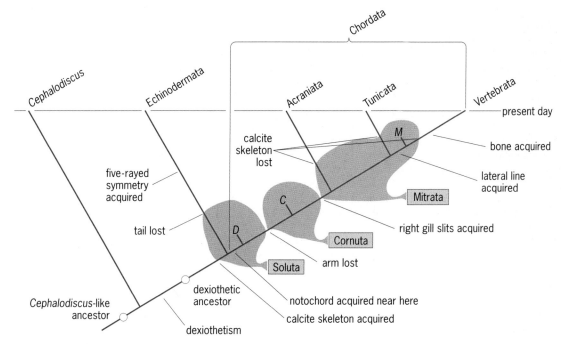

Fig. 1. Evolutionary relationships of calcichordates (Soluta, Cornuta, and Mitrata). The oldest events are at the bottom and the most recent are at the top. *D* = *Dendrocystoides*; *C* = *Cothurnocystis*; *M* = *Mitrocystites*.

features. Their calcite skeletons merely confirm an old view—that echinoderms and chordates are closely related. *See* CHORDATA; ECHINODERMATA.

There are three main groups of calcichordates—the Soluta, the Cornuta, and the Mitrata. **Figure 1** shows the relationships of these groups to each other, to the extant echinoderms and chordates, and to the recent hemichordate *Cephalodiscus*. The last is a small marine animal (**Fig. 2**) with a head shield, several pairs of arms, a trunk region with a pair of gill slits, and a locomotory stalk. *See* HEMICHORDATA.

In the common ancestry of echinoderms and chordates, a *Cephalodiscus*-like animal probably lay

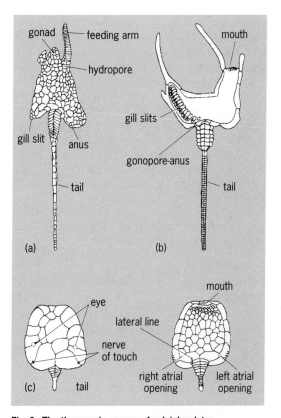

Fig. 3. The three main groups of calcichordates. (*a*) Soluta; dorsal view of *Dendrocystoides* (Ordovician, Scotland, about 440 million years old). (*b*) Cornuta; dorsal view of *Cothurnocystis* (Ordovician, Scotland, about 440 million years old). (*c*) Mitrata; dorsal and ventral views of *Mitrocystites* (Ordovician, Czechoslovakia, about 460 million years old). The atrial openings are external outlets for groups of gill slits inside the head. The lateral line is a sense organ found also in fishes.

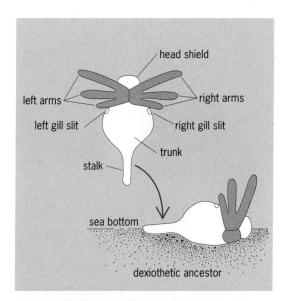

Fig. 2. The *Cephalodiscus*-like ancestor, by falling over on its right side, became the dexiothetic ancestor. This form acquired a calcite skeleton and gave rise both to the echinoderms and to the chordates.

down on its right side (dexiothetism) on the sea floor (Fig. 2). The right arms and right gill slit were lost as a result. Primitive right became ventral while primitive left became dorsal. The resulting animal, called the dexiothetic ancestor, acquired a calcite skeleton and gave rise both to the echinoderms and to the chordates.

The Soluta (**Fig. 3***a*) had an echinodermlike feeding arm and a tail homologous with the stalk of *Cephalodiscus* and with the tail of chordates. There was a gill slit at posterior left in the head, equivalent to the left gill slit of *Cephalodiscus*. The tail probably contained a notochord and would have pulled the head rearward across the sea floor, as it probably did in cornutes and mitrates also. By loss of the tail, solutes gave rise to echinoderms.

The Cornuta (Fig. 3*b*) arose from Soluta by loss of the feeding arm. Cornutes had many gill slits at left posterior in the roof of the head.

The Mitrata (Fig. 3*c*) arose from Cornuta by acquiring right gill slits. They had a complicated fishlike brain and nervous system. Right and left gill slits were inside the head. The lateral line of *Mitrocystites* is a special resemblance to vertebrates. By losing their calcite skeleton three times, mitrates gave rise to the extant groups of chordates. The phosphatic skeleton of vertebrates arose after the calcite skeleton had disappeared. *See* ANIMAL EVOLUTION.

R. P. S. Jefferies

Bibliography. A. P. Cripps, A new species of stemgroup chordate from the Upper Ordovician of Northern Ireland, *Palaeontology*, 31:1053–1077, 1988; R. P. S. Jefferies, *The Ancestry of the Vertebrates*, British Museum (Natural History), 1986; R. P. S. Jefferies, The solute *Dendrocystoides scoticus* from the Upper Ordovician of Scotland and the shared ancestry of chordates and echinoderms, *Palaeontology*, 1990; R. L. Parsley, Feeding and respiratory strategies in Stylophora, in C. R. C. Paul and A. B. Smith (eds.), *Echinoderm Phylogeny and Evolutionary Biology*, Liverpool Geological Society, 1989; G. M. Philip, Carpoids: Echinoderms or chordates?, *Biol. Rev.*, 54:439–471, 1979; G. Ubaghs, Réflexions sur la nature et la fonction de l'appendice articulé des carpoides Stylophora (Echinodermata), *Ann. Paléontol. (Invert.)*, 67:33–48, 1981.

Calcite

A mineral composed of calcium carbonate ($CaCO_3$); one of the most common and widespread minerals in the Earth's crust. Calcite may be found in a great variety of sedimentary, metamorphic, and igneous rocks. It is also an important rock-forming mineral and is the sole major constituent in limestones, marbles, and many carbonatites. Calcite in such rocks is the main source of the world's quicklime and hydrated, or slaked, lime. It is also widely used as a metallurgical flux to scavenge siliceous impurities by forming a slag in smelting furnaces. It provides the essential calcium oxide component in common glasses and cement. Limestones and marbles of lower purity may find uses as dimension stone, soil conditioners, industrial acid neutralizers, and aggregate in concrete and road building. Calcite in transparent well-formed crystals is used in certain optical instruments. *See* CARBONATITE; CRYSTAL OPTICS; LIME (INDUSTRY); LIMESTONE; STONE AND STONE PRODUCTS.

Calcite is the most stable polymorph of $CaCO_3$ under the pressure-temperature conditions existing in most of the Earth's crust. It is by far the most common polymorph to form as a result of carbon dioxide (CO_2) in the atmosphere, hydrosphere, and lithosphere, and in the upper mantle reacting with the calcium oxide (CaO) component in magmas, crustal rocks, and the oceans. Although it is commonly of high purity, calcite itself may contain other cations such as manganese, iron, magnesium, cobalt, barium, and strontium, substituting for the calcium in variable amounts. Well-developed crystals of calcite are common in cavities in limestones and basic igneous rocks. Of special interest are the large crystals of optical quality obtained from near the Eskefiord, Iceland. This material is known as Iceland spar, and single crystals several feet across have been reported. In the United States very large crystals have been mined in Taos County, New Mexico.

Crystallography. Calcite crystals may exhibit a wide variety of external forms in addition to the most common rhombohedra. Tabular, prismatic, and scalenohedral varieties are not unusual, and twinned crystals are often found (**Fig. 1**). Some fibrous varieties of calcite known as satin spar yield specimens of gem quality. Deposits in streams in calcareous regions and forming stalactites and stalagmites in limestone caves occur as masses with overall rounded forms made up of very small crystals. Travertine and onyx often consist of such material. *See* ONYX; STALACTITES AND STALAGMITES; TRAVERTINE.

Calcite has hexagonal (rhombohedral) symmetry and a structure built up of alternate layers of calcium ions (Ca^{2+}) and carbonate groups (CO_3^{2-}) stacked so that the layers lie perpendicular to the main axis of

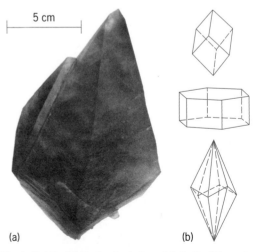

5 cm

Fig. 1. Calcite. (*a*) Scalenohedral crystal, Joplin, Missouri (*American Museum of Natural History specimens*). (*b*) Common crystal forms (*after C. S. Hurlbut, Jr., Dana's Manual of Mineralogy, 17th ed., John Wiley and Sons, 1959*).

(a)　　　　　　　　　　　　　　　(b)

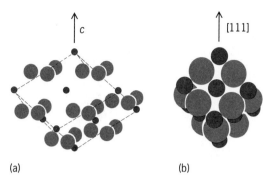

Fig. 2. Structures of (*a*) calcite and (*b*) halite. (*After K. Frye, Modern Mineralogy, Prentice-Hall, 1974*)

symmetry (**Fig. 2**). The structure may be compared with the much simpler sodium chloride structure by aligning the main symmetry axis of calcite with any of the four threefold axes in halite. If the sodium ions (Na^+) and the chloride ions (Cl^-) in the halite model are replaced by Ca^{2+} ions and CO_3^{2-} groups respectively, the selected threefold axis of halite becomes shortened to accommodate the planar CO_3^{2-} groups aligned perpendicular to it. The original halite cube is thus pulled into an obtuse rhomb to give a model of the calcite structure (Fig. 2). *See* CRYSTAL STRUCTURE.

Properties. Pure calcite is either colorless or white, but impurities can introduce a wide variety of colors; blues, pinks, yellow-browns, greens, and grays have all been reported. Hardness is 3 on Mohs scale. The specific gravity of pure calcite is 2.7102 ± 0.0002 at $68°F$ ($20°C$).

Calcite has a very low solubility in pure water (less than 0.001% at $77°F$ or $25°C$), but the solubility increases considerably with CO_2 added, as in natural systems from the atmosphere, when more bicarbonate ions and carbonic acid are formed. The solubility is also increased by falling temperature and rising total pressure. Shallow warm seas are supersaturated with calcite, while enormous quantities of calcite are dissolved in the unsaturated deep oceans.

The equilibrium amounts of certain cations that replace calcium in the calcite structure have been determined experimentally for magnesium, iron, and manganese. The amounts of each have been found to increase with temperature. At a fixed temperature the equilibrium amounts increase in the order Mg—Fe—Mn as the size of the substituting cation approaches that of calcium.

The temperature at which calcite dissociates to calcium oxide and carbon dioxide at atmospheric pressure depends on the heating rate, grain size, presence of moisture, and partial pressure of carbon dioxide. Dissociation temperatures range from $1290°F$ ($700°C$) to at least $2000°F$ ($1100°C$) [at 34 atm or 3.4 megapascals CO_2]. The equilibrium thermal dissociation temperatures have been determined experimentally, and nearly pure calcite has been melted at approximately $2440°F$ ($1340°C$) and 1000 atm (100 MPa) of carbon dioxide. Attempts to grow large single crystals of calcite of optical quality by high-temperature and high-pressure techniques have

been encouraging, although the dimensions of synthetic crystals do not yet compete with those of natural crystals. *See* HIGH-PRESSURE MINERAL SYNTHESIS.

Partly because it is available in pure, clear, well-developed crystals, calcite has played an important role in the formation of certain fundamental concepts in crystallography and mineralogy. The phenomenon of double refraction was first observed in calcite, and the discovery of the polarization of light resulted from studies of this mineral. Detailed work has shown anisotropism in most of its physical properties. *See* BIREFRINGENCE; POLARIZED LIGHT.

Robert I. Harker

Calcium carbonate relations. Calcium carbonate has a variety of polymorphs, but only calcite, aragonite, and vaterite occur in nature. Vaterite is a rare mineral and occurs as tissues of fractured shells of some gastropods, as gallstones, and as an alteration product after larnite. It probably forms under metastable conditions. The synthetic phase of vaterite has been encountered as high-temperature precipitates of calcium carbonate.

As many as five additional polymorphs not known in nature either have been encountered experimentally or have been presumed to exist. All are apparently closely related to calcite in structure and are not stable at room temperature. **Figure 3** shows the range of pressures and temperatures for which most of these phases occur; the polymorphs $CaCO_3$(II) and $CaCO_3$(III) do not possess pressure-temperature stability fields and are metastable with respect to aragonite. Two additional $CaCO_3$ polymorphs, designated as $CaCO_3$(IV) and $CaCO_3$(V), exist at temperatures above $1470°F$ ($800°C$). Phase transformations among these polymorphs appear to be rapid, and the $CaCO_3$(V) decomposes to $CaO + CO_2$ at temperatures above $1800°F$ ($1000°C$).

The aragonite–calcite transition has long been of interest to chemists and geologists. The determination of the aragonite stability field at high pressures and temperatures and the positive identification of aragonite in blueschist facies rocks in California have led petrologists to consider the utility of metamorphic aragonite as a geobarometer for blueschist facies

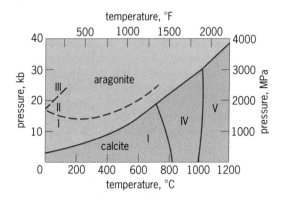

Fig. 3. Phase relations in the unary system CaCO₃. Broken lines represent metastable equilibria. Calcite polymorphs are identified as I–V. (*After R. J. Reeder, ed., Reviews in Mineralogy, vol. 11: Carbonates: Mineralogy and Chemistry, Mineralogical Society of America, 1983*)

metamorphism, and much effort has been directed to both phase relations and kinetics for the transition. The pressure-temperature slope of the equilibrium boundary for the aragonite–calcite transition changes between 660 and 930°F (350 and 500°C), as shown in Fig. 3. This change has been attributed to either a phase transition between $CaCO_3$(I) and $CaCO_3$(II) or a gradual disordering of the carbonate (CO_3) groups with increasing temperature. The presence of small amounts of strontium (Sr) in aragonite extends its stability field toward lower pressures; the opposite effect was observed for the presence of magnesium (Mg) in calcite.

Aragonite has been recognized in high-pressure metamorphic rocks such as blueschists. Its rare occurrence is attributed to rapid inversion of aragonite to calcite under shallow crustal conditions. Aragonite cannot survive in rocks in the presence of a fluid phase or in dry rocks subjected to temperatures greater than 570°F (300°C). Partial preservation of aragonite within the calcite stability field requires fast uplift rates (0.004–0.4 in./year or 0.1–10 mm/year) and temperatures of less than 250–370°F (120–190°C) along the uplift pressure-temperature-time path. The occurrence of aragonite may have been overlooked in many blueschist terranes; it does imply depths of 9–19 mi (15–30 km) for its formation. However, because the aragonite can be completely converted to calcite, the absence of aragonite does not limit the rocks to less than these depths. The common aragonite occurrence in Franciscan blueschists in California and its rarity in other blueschist terranes suggests that Franciscan metamorphism reached a lower maximum temperature (for example, 720°F or 380°C), remained dry upon uplifting, or was uplifted much more rapidly than other blueschist terranes. See ARAGONITE; BLUESCHIST; CARBONATE MINERALS.   J. G. Liou

Bibliography. C. Klein, *Manual of Mineralogy*, revised 22nd ed., 2001; R. J. Reeder (ed.), *Reviews in Mineralogy*, vol. 11: *Carbonates: Mineralogy and Chemistry*, 1983.

Calcium

A chemical element, Ca, of atomic number 20, fifth among elements and third among metals in abundance in the Earth's crust, Calcium compounds make up 3.64% of the Earth's crust. The physical properties of calcium metal are given in the table. The metal is trimorphous and is harder than sodium, but softer than aluminum. Like beryllium and aluminum, but unlike the alkali metals, it will not cause burns on the skin. It is less reactive chemically than the alkali metals and the other alkaline-earth metals. See PERIODIC TABLE.

Occurrence of calcium is very widespread; it is found in every major land area of the world. This element is essential to plant and animal life, and is present in bones, teeth, eggshell, coral, and many soils. Calcium chloride is present in sea water to the extent of 0.15%. See CARBONATE MINERALS.

Calcium metal is prepared industrially by the electrolysis of molten calcium chloride. Calcium chloride is obtained either by treatment of a carbonate ore with hydrochloric acid or as a waste product from the Solvay carbonate process. The pure metal may be machined in a lathe, threaded, sawed, extruded, drawn into wire, pressed, and hammered into plates. See ELECTROMETALLURGY.

In air, calcium forms a thin film of oxide and nitride, which protects it from further attack. At elevated temperatures, it burns in air to form largely the nitride. The commercially produced metal reacts easily with water and acids, yielding hydrogen that contains noticeable amounts of ammonia and hydrocarbons as impurities.

The metal is employed as an alloying agent for aluminum-bearing metal, as an aid in removing bismuth from lead, and as a controller for graphitic carbon in cast iron. It is also used as a deoxidizer in the manufacture of many steels, as a reducing agent in preparation of such metals as chromium, thorium, zirconium, and uranium, and as a separating material for gaseous mixtures of nitrogen and argon.

Calcium oxide, CaO, is made by the thermal decomposition of carbonate minerals in tall kilns using a continuous-feed process. The oxide is used in high-intensity arc lights (lime-lights) because of its unusual spectral features and as an industrial dehydrating agent. The metallurgical industry makes wide use of the oxide during the reduction of ferrous alloys.

Calcium hydroxide, $Ca(OH)_2$, is used in many applications where hydroxide ion is needed. During the slaking process for producing calcium hydroxide, the volume of the slaked lime [$Ca(OH)_2$] produced expands to twice that of quicklime (CaO), and because of this, it can be used for the splitting of rock or wood. Slaked lime is an excellent absorbent for carbon dioxide to produce the very insoluble carbonate. See LIME (INDUSTRY).

Calcium silicide, CaSi, an electric-furnace product made from lime, silica, and a carbonaceous reducing agent, is useful as a steel deoxidizer. Calcium carbide, CaC_2, is produced by heating a mixture of lime and carbon to 5432°F (3000°C) in an electric furnace. The compound is an acetylide which yields acetylene upon hydrolysis. Acetylene is the starting material for

Properties of calcium metal

Property	Value
Atomic number	20
Atomic weight	40.08
Isotopes (stable)	40, 42, 43, 44, 46, 48
Atomic volume, cm^3/g-atom	25.9
Crystal form	Face-centered cubic
Valence	2+
Ionic radius, nm	0.099
Electron configuration	2882
Boiling point, °C	1487(?)
Melting point, °C	810(?)
Density, g/cm³ at 20°C	1.55
Latent heat of vaporization at boiling point, kilojoules/g-atom	399

a great number of chemicals important in the organic chemicals industry.

Pure calcium carbonate exists in two crystalline forms: calcite, the hexagonal form, which possesses the property of birefringence, and aragonite, the rhombohedral form. Naturally occurring carbonates are the most abundant of the calcium minerals. Iceland spar and calcite are essentially pure carbonate forms, whereas marble is a somewhat impure and much more compact variety which, because it may be given a high polish, is much in demand as a construction stone. Although calcium carbonate is quite insoluble in water, it has considerable solubility in water containing dissolved carbon dioxide, because in these solutions it dissolves to form the bicarbonate. This fact accounts for cave formation in which limestone deposits have been leached away by the acidic ground waters. *See* CARBONATE MINERALS.

The halides of calcium include the phosphorescent fluoride, which is the most widely distributed calcium compound and which has important applications in spectroscopy. Calcium chloride has in the anhydrous form important deliquescent properties which make it useful as an industrial drying agent and as a dust quieter on roads. Calcium chloride hypochlorite (bleaching powder) is produced industrially by passing chlorine into slaked lime, and has been used as a bleaching agent and a water purifier. *See* BLEACHING; CHLORINE.

Calcium sulfate dihydrate is the mineral gypsum. It constitutes the major portion of portland cement, and has been used to help reduce soil alkalinity. A hemihydrate of calcium sulfate, produced by heating gypsum at elevated temperatures, is sold under the commercial name plaster of paris. *See* PLASTER OF PARIS.

Calcium is an invariable constituent of all plants because it is essential for their growth. It is contained both as a structural constituent and as a physiological ion. Calcium is found in all animals in the soft tissues, in tissue fluid, and in the skeletal structures. The bones of vertebrates contain calcium as calcium fluoride, as calcium carbonate, and as calcium phosphate. *See* CALCIUM METABOLISM. Reed F. Riley

Bibliography. F. A. Cotton et al., *Advanced Inorganic Chemistry*, 6th ed., Wiley-Interscience, 1999; R. Pochet et al. (eds.), *Calcium: The Molecular Basis of Calcium Action in Biology and Medicine*, 2000.

Calcium metabolism

The use and maintenance of calcium levels in the body. Calcium is essential to all forms of life. It plays fundamental roles in cell biology and signaling, in the functioning of organs and organ systems, and in the functioning of organisms. In the most complex organisms, vertebrates, calcium is a key ingredient in the skeleton. In vertebrates, about 99% of total body calcium is found in bones, in the form of a crystalline structure called hydroxylapatite. This calcium not only forms the basis of skeletal rigidity and structure but also serves as a reservoir for calcium that can be mobilized to the blood in response to specific environmental or endocrine signals. When excessive resorption of bone occurs due to inadequate calcium or vitamin D in the diet, diseases result, the symptoms of which may include misshapen skeletal structure and bones which break easily. *See* BONE; CALCIUM.

Concentration and function. The concentration of calcium in the blood is kept within narrow limits, close to 1 mM free (unbound) concentration, by a combination of factors including dietary intake, regulated deposition in and resorption from bone, and regulated excretion by the kidneys. This relatively constant extracellular calcium is required for a large variety of functions in different cells of the body. The two major functions of calcium ions are to stabilize membranes and to act as a signal inside cells. The stabilizing functions of extracellular calcium are not well understood, but likely involve interaction with acidic molecules on the cell surface. This surface-bound calcium helps to maintain the relatively low permeability of the plasma membrane to most ions; in nerve and muscle cells, it also helps to maintain control of excitability and the generation of action potentials. *See* BLOOD; CELL PERMEABILITY.

Signaling. Calcium ions also serve as intracellular signals or messengers. To understand the signaling functions of calcium ions, it is necessary first to understand the regulation and metabolism of calcium inside cells. The steady-state concentration of free calcium in the cytoplasm is around 100 nM, or 10^{-7} M, about one ten-thousandth of the extracellular concentration. This is accomplished by a combination of low plasma membrane permeability to calcium, and active extrusion across the plasma membrane by an adenosine triphosphate (ATP)–consuming calcium pump, the plasma membrane calcium ATPase. In some cells, there is also a sodium-for-calcium exchanger that can facilitate lowering of cytoplasmic calcium. Rapid, transient rises in cytoplasmic calcium can be dampened by a combination of passive and active intracellular calcium buffers. The passive buffers include calcium-binding proteins, and the active buffers are predominantly the endoplasmic reticulum and the mitochondria. The endoplasmic reticulum (and sarcoplasmic reticulum in muscle cells) accumulates calcium by means of a calcium pump similar in function to the plasma membrane calcium ATPase. This pump is called the sarcoplasmic–endoplasmic reticulum calcium ATPase, or SERCA. Mitochondria take up calcium from the cytoplasm by a process that depends on the mitochondrial membrane potential, which is strongly negative on the inside relative to the cytoplasm. This membrane potential is built from a process coupled to the respiratory chain and is utilized to drive the synthesis of ATP. The uptake of positively charged calcium ions short-circuits this membrane potential to some extent, such that calcium accumulation in mitochondria occurs at the expense of ATP production. However, the uptake of calcium into mitochondria serves as a signal to activate key enzymes involved in ATP production, so the net effect of calcium entering the mitochondria is actually to increase cellular ATP. *See* BIOPOTENTIALS AND IONIC CURRENTS; MITOCHONDRIA.

Endoplasmic reticulum. Calcium stored in the endoplasmic reticulum serves two general functions. First, it is necessary for the proper functioning of chaperone proteins, involved in regulation of protein folding and processing. When endoplasmic reticulum calcium is very low, aberrant protein folding and processing sets in motion a stress response that ultimately leads to apoptosis (cell death). Thus, apoptosis can result from either very high cytoplasmic calcium or very low endoplasmic reticulum calcium. The second major function of calcium in the endoplasmic reticulum is to serve as a rapidly mobilizable signal. When calcium rises in the cytoplasm of cells, it can bind to and regulate a variety of calcium-dependent enzymes, leading to a wide variety of cellular responses (see below). *See* ENDOPLASMIC RETICULUM; PROTEIN FOLDING.

The signal for release of calcium from the endoplasmic reticulum to the cytoplasm is conveyed inward from the cell's plasma membrane by a variety of mechanisms. In skeletal muscle, proteins in the plasma membrane interact with release channels, called ryanodine receptors, in the closely apposed sarcoplasmic reticulum membrane. Depolarization of the plasma membrane causes a conformational change in the plasma membrane proteins that is conveyed by direct protein–protein interaction to the ryanodine receptors, causing their activation and the gated release of stored calcium from the sarcoplasmic reticulum. The released calcium interacts with contractile proteins, causing shortening. This highly specialized system provides an extremely rapid signaling mechanism necessary for rapid muscle movement. In heart, and perhaps in smooth muscles and nerves, calcium ions entering the cell through plasma membrane channels (discussed below) interact with and activate closely associated ryanodine receptors, a process known as calcium-induced calcium release (CICR; see **illustration**).

In nonmuscle cells, other signaling mechanisms can induce release of endoplasmic reticulum cal-

cium. Perhaps the most pervasive mechanism involves inositol 1,4,5-trisphosphate. Neurotransmitters, growth factors, and hormones may interact with a specific class of plasma membrane receptors that are coupled to and activate a phospholipase C. The latter in turn cleaves a relatively minor membrane lipid, phosphatidylinositol 4,5-bisphosphate, into two products, diacylglycerol and inositol 1,4,5-trisphosphate (IP_3). Both of these products act as intracellular messengers; IP_3 binds to a specific

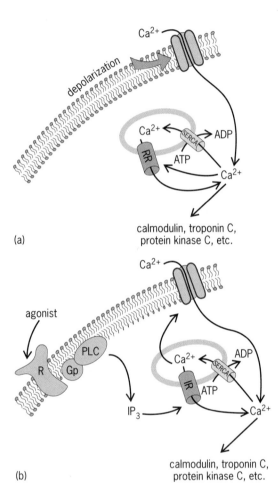

Motifs of $[Ca^{2+}]_i$ signaling. (*a*) In electrically excitable cells such as muscle and nerve cells, extracellular calcium can enter the cells when voltage-dependent calcium channels are activated by the depolarization associated with action potentials. This calcium can cause further release of intracellularly stored calcium by activating a calcium-induced calcium release mechanism associated with the ryanodine receptor calcium channel (RR). (*b*) In electrically nonexcitable cells, signaling is generally initiated when an agonist activates a surface membrane receptor (R) which, usually through a G-protein (guanine nucleotide–dependent regulatory protein, Gp), activates a phospholipase C (PLC) which degrades phosphatidylinositol 4,5-bisphosphate (PIP_2), releasing the soluble messenger, inositol 1,4,5-trisphosphate (IP_3). IP_3 activates an IP_3 receptor (IR) and thus releases calcium from the endoplasmic reticulum to the cytoplasm. The release of calcium from the organelle causes a signal to be generated which activates a plasma membrane calcium entry pathway (capacitative calcium entry). In both *a* and *b* cases, the cytoplasmic calcium signal generated activates various cellular processes by interacting with calcium-binding proteins. SERCA = sarcoplasmic–endoplasmic reticulum calcium ATPase. (*Modified from J. W. Putney, Jr., Science, 262:676–678, 1993*)

receptor on the endoplasmic reticulum. The IP_3 receptor is a calcium-permeable channel, and when IP_3 binds, the channel opens resulting in the release of stored calcium to the cytoplasm (see illustration). The other product of phosphatidylinositol 4,5-bisphosphate breakdown, diacylglycerol, acts in concert with calcium to activate a specific signaling kinase, protein kinase C. *See* CYTOPLASM.

Plasma membrane. In addition to intracellular release of calcium, there are mechanisms for permitting calcium entry to the cytoplasm across the plasma membrane. This entry occurs through calcium channels that are signaled to open in a variety of ways. In electrically excitable cells, such as nerve and muscle, there are calcium channels that open when the membrane is depolarized, as occurs during an action potential. For example, calcium entering heart cells through voltage-gated channels is essential for activation of cardiac muscle contraction (see illustration). In nonexcitable cells, as well as in many excitable cells, there are a variety of calcium-permeable channels activated by either extracellular or intracellular signals. In some cases, the channel is also the receptor for an extracellular ligand, such as acetylcholine or ATP. In other cases, the channels are activated by intracellular messengers, such as diacylglycerol, arachidonic acid, cyclic nucleotides, or even calcium itself. Perhaps the most common mode of regulation of calcium channels in nonexcitable cells involves the capacitative or store-operated channels (see illustration). These channels open when the calcium falls in the endoplasmic reticulum, thus ensuring that persistent depletion of endoplasmic reticulum stores does not occur. Calcium entering through the store-operated channels also activates physiological processes in concert with calcium released from intracellular stores. *See* CELL MEMBRANES; SIGNAL TRANSDUCTION.

The elevation of calcium in the cytoplasm, whether through one of the various mechanisms of intracellular release or through entry across the plasma membrane, signals a variety of cellular processes. These range from very rapid responses, such as muscle contraction and secretion, to more prolonged responses, such as control of glucose metabolism in the liver, to very prolonged responses, such as the control of cell proliferation and differentiation. The response pathways are initiated by calcium binding to and activating specific calcium-binding proteins. In some instances, calcium binds to and directly activates enzymes, for example protein kinase C. In the majority of instances, however, calcium binds to regulatory proteins that in turn regulate the activity of specific enzymes. An example of such a calcium-binding regulatory molecule is troponin, which dissociates from the actin–myosin complex in skeletal muscle when calcium is bound, permitting rapid muscle contraction. Perhaps the most commonly utilized intracellular calcium receptor protein is calmodulin. This protein regulates a wide variety of cellular processes, ranging from smooth muscle contraction to specific gene activation.

Excess cytoplasmic calcium and cell death. In the long term, it is necessary to maintain cellular calcium concentration at low levels because higher concentrations interfere with normal energy metabolism. Prolonged elevation of cytoplasmic calcium is generally deleterious and can eventually lead to cell death. This cell death in some circumstances can occur in a disorderly manner, leading to cell rupture and release of cellular contents. This process is called necrosis, and tends to result in secondary inflammatory responses due to the release of intracellular materials. High calcium can also induce a more ordered, physiological mode of cell death called apoptosis. When apoptosis occurs, the cell structure is dismantled by formation of smaller, membrane-delimited apoptotic bodies which are ingested by lymphocytes.

Overview. The simple chemical nature of divalent calcium ions is deceptive. No other metallic element fulfils such a myriad of significant functions in biological systems. For this reason, the fields of calcium metabolism and calcium signaling continue to be rapidly moving, providing surprises to biologists and benefits to medical science.   James W. Putney

Bibliography. E. Carafoli, *Calcium as a Cellular Regulator*, Oxford University Press, 1999; J. W. Putney, Jr., *Calcium Signaling*, CRC Press, Boca Raton, 1999; J. W. Putney, Jr., *Capacitative Calcium Entry*, Landes Biomedical, Austin, 1997.

Calculators

Desktop or, more often, portable electronic devices that are used to perform arithmetic, statistical, or other, more complex processing operations at the step-by-step direction of the user or by execution of a program (a stored sequence of processing operations) selected and initiated by the user. Models are offered with particular stored programs specialized to professional fields such as finance and science, and results are displayed in formats ranging from the still prevalent single line of alphanumeric characters to small viewing screens capable of graphical representations.

Development. Mechanical aides for performing mathematical operations have been available since at least the seventeenth century, when the slide rule was invented. The mechanical adder was introduced in 1887. Calculators in use into the 1960s were large, heavy, noisy desk- or table-top mechanical or electromechanical systems offering columns of numerical keys for selection of an operand (a number to be used in a calculation), and a manually operated lever or a small number of keys for activation of one of the few arithmetic operations of which the system was capable (**Fig. 1**). The operand was set by depression of one of the numeric keys in each of the appropriate columns. Available operand range was therefore established by the number of columns of keys provided. A decimal point location was usually fixed by the calculator, often allowing two columns to the

Fig. 1. Electromechanical calculator manufactured in the 1960s. (*Hewlett-Packard*)

right of the decimal point. Keys remained depressed until execution of the desired arithmetic operation, which was initiated by activation of the lever or crank or, if the unit was motorized, by depression of one of the operation selection keys. Electromechanical calculators offered at most a choice of the four basic arithmetic operations (addition, subtraction, multiplication, and division); many models could only add or subtract.

Improvement in calculator performance was paced by the development of components in the electronics industry. Solenoids and relays were utilized in improved designs, and a transistorized calculator, still capable of only basic arithmetic operations, was introduced in 1964. The invention of the integrated circuit in 1959 and the improvements in the performance offered by integrated circuits and in the technology employed to produce the devices have largely paced the remarkable expansion of calculator capabilities. A prototype calculator constructed of integrated circuits was completed in 1967. The first integrated circuit microprocessor was developed in 1970 for use in a Japanese calculator. The scientific pocket calculator was introduced in 1972, and the programmable scientific calculator in 1974. *See* IN-TEGRATED CIRCUITS.

Range. The capabilities of the display device employed on a calculator can establish limits to the range of operands and results that the unit can accommodate. Traditionally, electronic calculators have utilized single strings of numeric display devices. If conventional notation is used, and a polarity of the operand or result must be indicated, the allowable range is limited between a positive and a negative number with nines in all digits except the sign position. In a simple example using only whole numbers, eight display positions would provide for display of numbers from $-9,999,999$ to $+9,999,999$. Range was expanded with the introduction of scientific notation, which is now prevalent. Scientific notation uses several display positions for what is called an exponent, essentially a power of ten by which the displayed quantity must be multiplied. One position is also allowed for the sign of the exponent, with smaller numbers having less positive or more

negative exponents. The quantity $-3,256,000$ could be represented as $-3.256\ 06$ in scientific notation, where the exponent 06 corresponds to ten to the sixth power, or $1,000,000$, the number by which -3.2560 must be multiplied. Similarly, the number 0.0007517 could be represented as $7.517 - 04$, since ten to the negative fourth power is 0.0001. Depending upon the available display length, two or three digits may be allocated to the exponent. The use of scientific notation greatly expands the range of an operand or calculation result that can be represented by a linear display of a given length.

Advances in components. Current calculator designs use either a customized integrated circuit or a microprocessor and a small number of peripheral integrated circuits to perform their operations. A customized integrated circuit will accept and interpret keystrokes made by the user, perform the requested operation, and generate signals to drive the display device, providing the user an indication of the processing result. Complex mathematical processing abilities are built into some calculator integrated circuits, and some accept plug-in memory modules that extend the available processing sequences. A single line of alphanumeric readout is usually coupled with a customized calculator integrated circuit. Microprocessor-based calculators are generally more complex, more flexible, more capable, and more costly. Some accept memory modules or programs that are selected from a library to meet the particular requirements of an application and downloaded to the unit. The peripheral integrated circuits effect interfacing of the microprocessor with data and program entry and display, readout, and printout devices. *See* MICROPROCESSOR.

Displays have historically consumed the most power in calculator systems and have therefore often limited battery life. To conserve power, many calculators automatically turn their displays off after a fixed period during which no entry has been made by the operator. The large multifilament incandescent readout devices found in early calculator models were supplanted by light-emitting-diode (LED) displays that offered readout of numeric characters, some symbols such as the plus and minus sign, and a limited subset of alphabetic characters. Liquid-crystal-display (LCD) devices, however, have become the predominant calculator display. These devices require only small amounts of power and can provide very fine resolution in a display capable of representing a range of figures and symbols that extends well beyond what could be displayed on the most capable light-emitting-diode readouts. Many calculators utilizing liquid-crystal displays make use of solar cells embedded into the exposed upper surface of the units. The solar cells produce current sufficient for operation of the calculator even at room ambient light levels. *See* ELECTRONIC DISPLAY; LIGHT-EMITTING DIODE; LIQUID CRYSTALS; SOLAR CELL.

Rapid improvement of the density of semiconductor memory has also aided calculator performance.

Large amounts of random-access memory (RAM) can be built into a microprocessor or added to a calculator in the form of a single integrated circuit. Flash memory, which can be programmed and can provide nonvolatile storage between periods of calculator use, yet can be erased and reloaded with new information, facilitates either upgrading of the fixed set of processing functions performed by a model or the loading of the calculator with the specific processing programs needed for a specific application. *See* SEMICONDUCTOR MEMORIES.

Customization. Some calculator models are designed for use in specific professional fields. Most prevalent among these are calculators for business and finance and for science and engineering. A business-finance calculator may provide for determination of true value of money, interest conversions, depreciation, and other customary operations. Selection keys carry labels appropriate to those operations. Customization has more recently taken the form of the downloading of application-specific software, composed of appropriate processing subroutines, into flash memory within the calculator. Individual operations are assigned to specific keys, often function keys, with the display employed to remind the user of function key assignments (**Fig. 2**). The function keys allow the user to select processing programs that have been selected and stored in program memory. Some calculators feature a full qwerty-style keyboard and cursor key (Fig. 2), which represent additional steps away from traditional calculator design and toward the production of a complete pocket computer.

Graphing calculators. The combination of a microprocessor and a liquid-crystal display has made possible the introduction of the graphing calculator. The display is composed of a large rectangular array of liquid-crystal-display pixels (picture elements), each of which can be activated independently. A typical display (Fig. 2) has about one-fourth the pixel display capability of a conventional personal computer monitor screen, packed into a considerably smaller display area. The increased pixel density improves display resolution. This type of array supports the picturelike display of results. For example, the complex voltage waveform representing the calculated response of an electronic circuit to a specific input signal can be displayed for examination. The equation for a complex surface can be entered, and that surface can be displayed. Visual displays of this type are useful to teachers, improving the presentation made available to students, as well as to professionals using the calculator. Engineers and scientists use graphing calculators to enter a sequence of equations in standard form rather than a form dictated by the limitations of the calculator. Matrices can also be represented, and sequences of steps in calculations or in programs stored within the unit can be visually reviewed by recall to the display area.

More capable graphical units can accurately produce representations of complex results such as three-dimensional surfaces (Fig. 2). A number of cal-

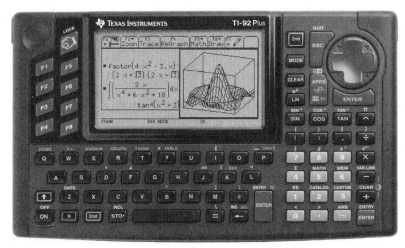

(a)

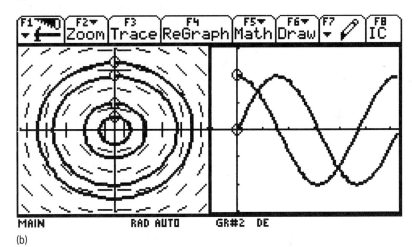

(b)

Fig. 2. Modern programmable electronic calculator. (*a*) Front of calculator, featuring liquid-crystal display, qwerty-style keyboard, cursor key, and function keys. The display is composed of 128 rows of 240 pixels each, and here shows a three-dimensional surface. Function keys allow the user to select processing programs that have been selected and stored in program memory. (*b*) Example of a display, illustrating split-screen capability. (*Texas Instruments Corporation*)

culator models support graphing in several coordinate systems (square, rectangular, polar) to improve the user's understanding and interpretation of the result. Graphing calculators are invariably described as being of the science-engineering type, although many of them are, in fact, programmable.

Prospects. The trend in design of the most capable calculators is toward a more general computer-like structure with capabilities set by the processing routines downloaded into program memory rather than by a fixed set committed to permanent memory. The routines employed in the more adaptable approach can be changed as improvements are made or as application requirements change. Connections to peripheral devices such as printers or to computers providing libraries of processing routines are becoming more prevalent. The move away from dedication of a unit to specific processing steps and toward greater dependence on downloaded routines selected to address the problem at hand is the central development of a broader trend whereby calculators are becoming devices that could more accurately be called pocket computers. *See* COMPUTER; COMPUTER PERIPHERAL DEVICES; DIGITAL COMPUTER; MATHEMATICAL SOFTWARE.　　　William W. Moyer

Bibliography. B. Slozak, *Graphing Calculator Explorations*, Addison-Wesley, 1998; D. E. Varberg and T. D. Varberg, *Algebra and Trigonometry: A Graphing Approach*, Prentice Hall, 1995.

Calculus

The branch of mathematics dealing with two fundamental operations, differentiation and integration, which are carried out on functions. The subject, as traditionally developed in college textbooks, is partly an elementary development of the purely theoretical aspects of these operations and their interrelation, partly a development of rules and formulas for applying calculus to the standard functions which arise in algebra and trigonometry (with exponentials and logarithms included), and partly a collection of applications to problems of geometry, physics, chemistry, engineering, economics, and perhaps a few other subjects.

Derivative. The fundamental concept of differential calculus is that of the derivative of a function of one variable. The classical physical prototype of this concept is that of instantaneous velocity, which is the derivative of distance as a function of time. The derivative also has a highly significant geometrical realization which depends upon the graphical representation of a function in rectangular coordinates (x, y). If y is a differentiable function of x, perhaps as x increases from x_1 to x_2, the graph of the function is a continuous curve with exactly one y for each x, and at each point the curve has a tangent line which is not parallel to the y axis. If ϕ is the angle, measured counterclockwise, from the positive x direction to the tangent (**Fig. 1**), then $\tan \phi$ is equal to the derivative of y with respect to x. (This is on the supposition that the same unit of length is used along the two axes.) This $\tan \phi$ is also called the slope of the curve.

The standard notation for the derivative of y with respect to x is dy/dx. If the functional notation $y = f(x)$ is used, the derivative is often denoted by $f'(x)$. Modern practice is to use f for the function as an abstract entity, while $f(x)$ denotes the value of f at x. Then f' denotes the derivative as a function, and $f'(x)$ is the value of f' at x. For a precise definition of the derivative *see* DIFFERENTIATION

Functions. To say that y is a function of x means that, as a consequence of some rule or definite agreement, there is a designated collection of permissible values of x (called the domain of the function) and an associated set of corresponding values of y (called the range of the function), of such a character that with each permissible value of x is paired a unique well-determined value of y. The function itself is the collection of all the pairs (x, y) which arise in this way. This collection exemplifies the rule or agree-

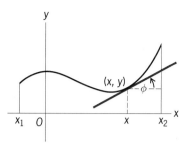

Fig. 1. Graphical representation of the derivative of *f(x)*.

ment. If f denotes the function, it is customary to write $y = f(x)$ to represent the dependence of y on x.

In calculus the domain of the function is usually composed of one or more intervals of the x axis.

Definite integral. If f is a function defined on the finite interval from x_1 to x_2 inclusive, the definite integral of f from x_1 to x_2, denoted by

$$\int_{x_1}^{x_2} f(x)\, dx$$

is defined by applying to f a rather intricate process which entails the consideration of what are called approximating sums. When the function f is subjected to certain restrictions, this process culminates in the determination of a number as the limit of the approximating sums, and this number is called the definite integral of f from x_1 to x_2. The integral is not defined unless the approximating sums do converge to a well-defined limit. A sufficient condition that this be so is that the function f be continuous.

There is a geometrical representation of the process of defining the definite integral, and it furnishes a plausible argument for the convergence of the approximating sums to a limit. Divide the interval from x_1 to x_2 into a finite number N of not necessarily equal parts. Let the lengths of these parts be $b_1, b_2, \ldots , b_N$, and let t_k be a value of x in the kth part (**Fig. 2**). Then the expression

$$f(t_1)b_1 + f(t_2)b_2 + \cdots + f(t_N)b_N$$

is called an approximating sum. In Fig. 2, where the function is continuous and the function values are all positive, each term $f(t_k)b_k$ in the approximating sum is equal to the area of a certain shaded rectangle, and the whole sum is an approximation of the

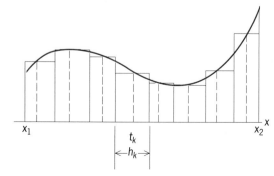

Fig. 2. The definite integral.

area between the graph of the function and the x axis, from x_1 to x_2 inclusive. The limiting process is carried on by increasing N and making the largest of the h_k's approach 0. It is then intuitively clear that the definite integral is the number which represents the exact area between the x axis and the graph. This geometrical interpretation of the integral is the basis of an important application of integral calculus, to the calculation of areas.

It would be tedious and difficult in practice to compute definite integrals by actually working out the limits of approximating sums. It is therefore fortunate that by purely mathematical reasoning it is possible to demonstrate a theorem which links derivatives and integrals and makes it possible, in many important instances, to compute definite integrals by an easier procedure. *See* INTEGRATION.

In the next paragraph are stated the two fundamental theorems of calculus. In these statements the adjective "continuous" appears. For a function $y = f(x)$ to be continuous means, roughly, that as x changes gradually, y must either change gradually, or not at all. Absolutely abrupt jumps are forbidden, and so are many more bizarre modes of irregular behavior. For a precise definition of continuity *see* DIFFERENTIATION

Fundamental theorems. For the calculation of

$$\int_{x_1}^{x_2} f(x)\,dx$$

find, if possible, a function F with continuous derivative f' such that $f'(x) = f(x)$ when $x_1 \leqq x \leqq x_2$. Then Eq. (1) can be written. This is one of the two central

$$\int_{x_1}^{x_2} f(x)\,dx = F(x_2) - F(x_1) \qquad (1)$$

theorems. The other is stated as follows: Suppose f is continuous, and consider the function F defined by Eq. (2). Then F has a derivative given by $f'(x) = f(x)$.

$$F(x) = \int_{x_1}^{x} f(t)\,dt \qquad (2)$$

Law of the mean. The most important theorem about derivatives, exclusive of those which involve integrals, is variously called "the law of the mean" and "the mean-value theorem of differential calculus." It is stated in this form: Suppose f is continuous for x from x_1 to x_2 inclusive, and suppose f has a derivative for each x between x_1 and x_2. Then there is some x of this kind for which Eq. (3) holds true. This theorem

$$f'(x) = \frac{f(x_2) - f(x_1)}{x_2 - x_1} \qquad (3)$$

enables one to prove that, if $f'(x)$ is always positive, then $f(x)$ is always zero, then $f(x)$ remains constant as x changes. The first of these results is important for applications to the investigations of graphs. The second is virtually indispensable in the proof of the fundamental theorems of calculus stated above, and in establishing the uniqueness of the solutions for

certain problems which involve antidifferentiation (the process of surmising what a function is from a knowledge of its derivative). Such problems abound in application of calculus to problems of motion.

Applications of derivatives. If y is a function of x, the derivative dy/dx is interpretable as the rate of change of y with respect to x. If y is distance and x is time, dy/dx is velocity. If y is work done by a force and x is time, dy/dx is power. Many motion problems, such as those arising in mechanics and formulated by Newton's second law, are expressible by posing an equation which a function and its derivative or derivatives must satisfy. These are called differential equations. The study of such equations is an extension and ramification of calculus. Differential equations are important in all branches of physics. They also arise in many problems of engineering and chemistry, for example, in the deformation of columns and beams, in the study of chemical reactions, and in radioactive decay. *See* DIFFERENTIAL EQUATION.

Problems of maximizing or minimizing a function usually involve derivatives. If a differentiable function f reaches a relative maximum or minimum at a point in the interior of an interval of its domain, then $f'(x)$ must be zero there. This helps in finding extreme values of f.

Applications of integrals. Integrals are used to compute areas bounded by curves in a plane. They are also used to compute other geometrical quantities, such as lengths of curves, areas of surfaces, and volumes of solids. For computing volumes and surface areas the natural tools are multiple integrals. Integrals are also used to compute quantities which occur in physics, such as center of mass, moment of inertia, work done by a variable force, and attraction due to gravitation. The concepts of first, second, and higher moments of a function, as used in statistics, are stated in terms of integrals.

Functions of several variables. To each pair (x_1, x_2) in a specified collection of number pairs, let there correspond a certain definite number y. This defines $y = f(x_1, x_2)$ as a function of two variables. Functions of three or more variables may also be considered. Differential calculus is extended to such functions through the study of partial derivatives with respect to the separate variables $x_1, x_2, \ldots$. A concept of total differential is also relevant. For details *see* PARTIAL DIFFERENTIATION

Integral calculus for functions of several variables is developed through the concept of a multiple integral. For instance, in the case of functions of two variables there is a concept of double integral. The theory of the subject deals with how the double integral is expressible in terms of two successive definite integrals of the sort occurring in calculus of functions of one variable. There is also a concept of a line integral, which is a kind of integral along a curve. There are relations between this concept, the concept of total differential, and the concept of double integral.

New developments. Calculus belongs to the branch of mathematics called analysis. One characteristic of analysis is its concern with infinite limiting processes. Current research in analysis is mostly on a level of development far beyond the elements of calculus. However, the ideas of calculus persist, though in much more generalized and abstract form, in the theory of functions and in functional analysis.

Angus E. Taylor

Bibliography. R. Courant and F. John, *Introduction to Calculus and Analysis*, vols. 1 and 2, 1965, 1974, reprint 1999; W. Kaplan, *Advanced Calculus*, 4th ed., 1991; S. Lang, *A First Course in Calculus*, 5th ed., 1986, reprint 1993; S. L. Salas and E. Hille, *Calculus: Single Variable*, 6th ed., 1990; S. K. Stein and A. Barcellos, *Calculus and Analytical Geometry*, 5th ed., 1992; E. W. Swokowski et al., *Calculus*, 6th ed., 1994; A. E. Taylor and R. W. Mann, *Advanced Calculus*, 5th ed., 1992.

Calculus of variations

An extension of the part of differential calculus which deals with maxima and minima of functions of a single variable. The functions of the calculus of variations depend in an essential way upon infinitely many independent variables. Classically these functions are usually integrals whose integrand depends on a function whose specification by any finite number of parameters is impossible. For example, let C be a smooth bounded region of a space of m variables, $x_1, x_2, \ldots, x_m$, let y be any function of some smooth class on C and its boundary into real numbers or into n-tuples of real numbers and taking specified values on the boundary, and let $f(x, y, p)$ be a smooth function of $2m + 1$ variables $x_1, x_2, \ldots, x_m, y, p_1, p_2, \ldots, p_m$. Then the integral, Eq. (1), is a function

$$J = \int \cdots \int_C f(x, y, y_x) \tag{1}$$

on the space of functions y to the real numbers, and this space of functions is infinite dimensional unless excessive restrictions are placed on it. Here y_x denotes the derivatives $\partial y / \partial x$, and throughout this article subscripts will be used to denote derivatives and occasionally where the context is clear to denote particular values.

The calculus of variations studies such functions and their maxima and minima. The limitation of the competing functions is made realistically, and with sufficient restrictions it is possible to arrive at a rewarding theory; these restrictions do not always include the fixed boundary conditions stated above.

Principal applications may be to physical systems involving flexible components or time-dependent orbits; equilibrium positions or orbits may be determined by minimizing energy or action integrals. The problems are of mathematical interest because of intrinsic difficulties (largely related to lack of topological compactness of bounded regions in spaces of infinitely many dimensions) and possibly because more progress with difficult nonlinear problems has been made here than elsewhere. *See* HAMILTON'S PRINCIPLE; LEAST-ACTION PRINCIPLE.

Theoretical basis. The classical theorems of differential calculus which are used and generalized are the following.

1. Necessary conditions for a function f of a single variable x to attain a local minimum at $x = x_0$ are $f'(x_0) = 0$ if the derivative exists at x_0 and if there are neighboring points of definition of f for arguments on each side of x_0; $f'(x_0) \geqq 0$ if the derivative exists at x_0 and if there are neighboring points of definition of f arguments larger than x_0.

2. If $f'(x_0) = 0$, if f is defined at some points neighboring x_0, and if $f''(x_0)$ exists, then a necessary condition for f to attain a local minimum at $x = x_0$ is $f''(x_0) \geqq 0$; conversely the conditions $f'(x_0) = 0$ and $f''(x_0) > 0$ guarantee a local minimum at x_0. *See* DIFFERENTIATION.

One standard technique of the calculus of variations is to derive necessary conditions for minima by restricting variations to a set of admissible variations depending smoothly on a single parameter and then to apply these theorems 1 and 2 from differential calculus.

For example, in the integral above, suppose that the function $f(x, y, p)$ is defined for all (x, y) in some region of $(m + 1)$-space and for all p, and that f and all its first and second partial derivatives are continuous in this region. Suppose that the admissible functions y are restricted to functions which have continuous second derivatives in C and which take on the required boundary values. Let $g(x)$ be such an admissible function lying in the interior of the region over which $f(x, y, p)$ is defined, and let $z(x)$ be any function with continuous second derivatives on C and taking the value 0 at all points on the boundary of C. Then for e neighboring zero, the function $y = g(x) + ez(x)$ is admissible in the problem (it has continuous second derivatives and takes the prescribed values on the boundary). Then $z(x)$ is an admissible variation. If g does indeed afford a local minimum to J and if it is specified that the functions $y = g(x) + ez(x)$ are close to g for e neighboring zero, then propositions 1 and 2 above may be applied to the function $J(e)$ of the single variable e, where $J(e)$ is the value taken by J for y defined in terms of g and z as above. Under the conditions stated, the derivative $J'(0)$ does exist, and it may be computed by differentiating under the integral sign. The result is shown in Eq. (2).

$$J'(0) = \int \cdots \int_C \left[z(x) f_y(x, g, g_x) + \sum_j z_{x,j} f_{p,j}(x, g, g_x) \right] \tag{2}$$

This expression must be zero for any admissible $z(x)$ according to proposition 1. Under the restrictions set here each term of the expression to be summed may be integrated by parts, the integration of the term with factor $z_{x,j}$ being with respect to the single variable x_j; for the formula

$$\int u \, dv = uv - \int v \, du$$

(with boundary values assigned to the term *uv*) one sets $dv = z_{x_j} dx_j$ and takes the remainder of the term as *u*. This yields, after due account is taken of the vanishing of *z* on the boundary, Eq. (3). A funda-

$$J'(0) = \int \cdots \int_C z(x)$$
$$\times \left[f_y(x, g, g_x) - \sum_j \frac{\partial}{\partial x_j} f_{p,j}(x, g, g_x) \right] \quad (3)$$

mental technique of the calculus of variations lies in exploiting the necessity of this last integral being zero independent of the admissible variation *z(x)*. The integral divided by the measure of *C* is the average over *C* of *z* times the expression in brackets, and the requirement that any function of a sufficiently wide class times a given function averages to zero is met only if the given function is itself zero. Care must be taken to assure that this fundamental condition is met—that is, that the admissible variations are sufficiently general to permit invoking this lemma. In this case the bracketed expression must be zero, and the necessary condition becomes a differential equation, the Euler equation. For the function in Eq. (4), so that Eq. (5) holds, the Euler equation is just the Laplace equation (6).

$$f(x, y, p) = p_1^2 + p_2^2 \quad (4)$$

$$J = \int \int \left[\left(\frac{\partial y}{\partial x_1} \right)^2 + \left(\frac{\partial y}{\partial x_2} \right)^2 \right] \quad (5)$$

$$\frac{\partial^2 y}{\partial x_1^2} + \frac{\partial^2 y}{\partial x_2^2} = 0 \quad (6)$$

See DIFFERENTIAL EQUATION; INTEGRATION; LAPLACE'S DIFFERENTIAL EQUATION.

Second variations are studied in a similar way, applying proposition 2 above to $J''(0)$. These give rise to conditions of Jacobi for a minimum. Generally, there are a set of conditions including Euler's condition above, a condition of Weierstrass, a condition of Legendre which may be derived from the Weierstrass condition, and the Jacobi condition, all known as necessary conditions for a minimum. These are generally set in terms of inequalities, and when the conditions are strengthened to demand strong inequalities (excluding equality) the conditions become sufficient for many interesting problems.

Multidimensional derivatives. Much of the work on the calculus of variations is devoted to meticulous detail with regard to the number of derivatives assumed to be available for various functions, particularly the competitive admissible functions *y(x)*. If too many derivatives are assumed, minima may not exist; if too few are assumed, the solution might not be sufficiently smooth to be acceptable in the light of the original statement of the problem. In an attempt to use fewer derivatives, different approaches are used depending on the number of independent variables *x*. For the multidimensional case, an approach by A. Haar leads to extended complications which are not amenable to description here. Haar introduced an additional function which has the effect of replacing the Laplace equation in the simple Dirichlet problem stated above by the Cauchy-Riemann equations. *See* COMPLEX NUMBERS AND COMPLEX VARIABLES.

Single-integral problems. For the case of single integrals, however, a lemma of du Bois–Reymond is applicable. This lemma states that a function must be a constant if the average of its product with every function of a sufficiently broad class is zero, where the class may be restricted to have average value zero. The proof takes the given function to be *u(x)* and its average over the interval to be some constant *c*, and requires that $u(x) - c$ be one of the admissible functions for comparison. This leads to a requirement that $[u(x) - c]^2$ average zero, and this means that *u(x)* is essentially *c*.

Additional illustrative material of general results obtainable will now be presented in terms of single integral problems. Here take Eq. (7) and enlarge the

$$J = \int_a^b f(x, y, y') \, dx \quad (7)$$

class of admissible curves somewhat. The precise nature of this enlargement will not be important for the moment, but assume that among the admissible curves $y = g(x)$, $a(0) \leq x \leq b(0)$ affords a minimum to *J*. Assume also that a family of curves $y = z(x, e)$, $a(e) \leq x \leq b(e)$ is admissible and that the value of $z(x, e)$ as *e* tends to zero is *g(x)*. Most particularly, however, it is desired to avoid the restriction that $z_x(x, e) \to g'(x)$, which was implied above by the variation $y = g(x) + ez(x)$. This allows variations more general than the ones above with regard to the variations of the end points of the curve, the limits of integration, and the behavior of the derivatives.

Curves of the type of $z(x, e)$ introduced here may be admitted as neighboring *y(x)* for *e* neighboring zero either by using $\max_x |z(x, e) - y(x)|$ (possibly modified by some measure of disparity between the intervals of definition) or $\int [z(x, e) - y(x)]^2$ as a measure of distance between two points in the function space. In either case, *J(e)* may be defined as the value of the integral *J* with *f* evaluated for *x*, $z(x, e)$, and $z_x(x, e)$, and it is again possible to study $J'(0)$ if it exists. However, it should be noted that there is no reason for expecting $J'(0)$ to exist in this case, for the integrand involves derivatives z_x which may not vary continuously. Actually a simple example of length shows what may happen; if *J* is a length integral, the *z* curves may be taken as zigzagging broken lines approaching a straight line segment but always making an angle of perhaps 45° with it. Then *J(e)* for any *e* not zero is $\sqrt{2}$ times *J(0)*. There is illustrated here an important property known as lower semicontinuity. Although *J(e)* is not continuous, its limit as the argument varies is never less than its value for the limiting value of the argument. This property, along with some compactness properties, suffices for all purposes of the calculus of variations, but it must be noted that it is reasonable to expect semicontinuity but not continuity in problems of the calculus of variations.

The method used before may be used to derive a formula for $J'(0)$; it is Eq. (8), where Eq. (9)

$$J'(0) = f[b_0, g(b_0), z_x(b_0, 0)]b'(0)$$
$$- f[a_0, g(a_0), z_x(a_0, 0)]a'(0) + \bar{J} \quad (8)$$

$$\bar{J} = \int_{a_0}^{b_0} \{z_e f_y[x, g, z_x(x, 0)]$$
$$+ z_{xe} f_p[x, g, z_x(x, 0)]\} \quad (9)$$

holds. This may be integrated by parts to give either Eq. (10) or Eq. (11), where H is a function of x such that Eq. (12) holds. In all these formulas $z_x(x,0)$ has

$$\bar{J} = \left\{ z_e f_p[x, g, z_x] \right\}_{a_0}^{b_0} + \int_{a_0}^{b_0} z_e \left\{ f_y - \frac{d}{dx} f_p \right\} \quad (10)$$

$$\bar{J} = \left\{ z_e H \right\}_{a_0}^{b_0} + \int_{a_0}^{b_0} z_{xe} \left\{ f_p - H \right\} \quad (11)$$

$$H' = f_y[x, g(x), g'(x)] \quad (12)$$

been retained instead of $g'(x)$ to indicate ambiguity in case of discontinuous derivatives.

End-point problems. If variations with fixed end points are admissible near g, it is possible to choose z with $z_e = 0$ at the end points, and so that a' and b' are zero for $e = 0$ and only $\bar{J}$ is left, so that $J'(0) = 0$ implies $\bar{J} = 0$. In the expression above for $\bar{J}$, Eq. (11), the first term is zero since $z_e = 0$ at the end points, the average of z_{xe} over the interval is zero, since $z_e = 0$ at both end points, and the lemma of du Bois–Reymond mentioned above may be applied. This means that the expression in curly brackets in the integrand is constant whether $f_p(x, g')$ is known to be differentiable or not. Since H is obviously differentiable if g and z have first derivatives which are continuous on each of a finite set of closed intervals covering $[a, b]$, then the whole expression is differentiable, and the Euler equation follows under these weakened conditions. Furthermore, under some conditions of regularity, it is demonstrable that the solutions of this Euler equation have two continuous derivatives, so that minimizing functions in a wide class of functions are comfortably smooth.

The same formula may be used to get conditions which must exist in a corner. It is also applicable to problems with variable end conditions. It may be applied to a special variation to get the Weierstrass condition (**Fig. 1**). These are curves with no general properties except that they vary slowly, approaching straightness at the top and conforming with the continuing curve at the bottom.

Here the lower curve $y = g(x)$ is assumed to be the extremal, and at a point $x = x_1$ on this curve a line with slope q is erected. The variations corresponding to e are taken by proceeding along g to x_1, then up the line to a point with abscissa $x_1 + e$, then along a curve of a smooth family rejoining g at a fixed point x_2, and then along g to b. The family between the line and the point of rejoining g is assumed to

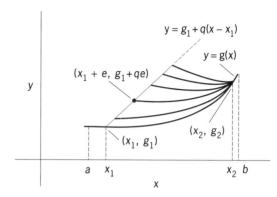

Fig. 1. Weierstrass condition. Symbols explained in text.

be smooth and to approach g with the $z_{x}(x, e)$ approaching g'. Thus the difficulty about limits of $z_x(x, 0)$ is avoided except at the point $x = x_1$. Note that the variation is defined only for nonnegative values of e, and hence the value $J'(0)$ must be nonnegative if g is a minimum, but not necessarily zero. Intelligent straightforward application of the formulas developed just above yields this condition in the form shown in Eq. (13).

$$E(x, g, g', q) = f(x, g, q) - f(x, g, q')$$
$$- (q - g')f_p(x, q, g')] \geq 0 \quad (13)$$

In problems with variable end points (which end points may, for example, be constrained to lie on prescribed curves) the end-point conditions which appear in these formulas must be taken into account. Here it is often possible to assume that $\bar{J}$ in the formula is zero, because of admissibility of sufficiently large classes of variations with fixed end points. The remaining conditions are called transversality conditions.

Alternative methods. In classical single-integral problems it is frequently possible to integrate the Euler equations into a family of curves depending on a finite set of parameters (the initial conditions, for example). However, in other cases it is not possible to do this, and a solution must be arrived at or proved to exist in more direct ways. Frequently a minimizing sequence of functions is used; that is, a set of functions y_n is chosen so that the values of J corresponding to y_n approach their greatest lower bound. If there is a convergent subsequence of these y_n and if J itself is lower semicontinuous, then a limit y to the sequence must afford a minimum to J.

Other methods of solution and of proving the existence of solutions depend on general studies of Hilbert spaces. In these studies the integrals appear as operators in Hilbert space, and they are frequently reduced to quadratic forms by some majorizing process.

Problem of Bolza. Here the admissible class of functions is restricted by differential conditions. Problems of Bolza include the classical isoperimetric problems, in which the length of the admissible curves is specified. The problem of Bolza gives rise to multiplier rules which are based on the implicit function theorem. The theorem is applied by noting that if the rank of a matrix which can be caused to arise is maximal, then the restrictions imposed on admissible curves may be retained unchanged (in particular, or more generally they may be changed arbitrarily) and the function J may still be changed arbitrarily, hence reduced. A submaximal rank for this matrix is a necessary condition for a minimum; using this result the problem of Bolza may be transformed to an ordinary problem whose integral is a linear combination of the integrand of J and functions describing the original restrictions. The coefficients of this linear combination are initially undetermined; they are called Lagrange multipliers.

Critical points. Finally, studies in the spirit of differential calculus but not restricted to local minima should be noted. Here the interest includes not only minima but all critical points (that is, all functions satisfying the Euler condition), and also other studies. It is true that classical problems in mechanics may have stable solutions corresponding to nonminimizing critical points. For sufficiently restricted problems it can be shown that the homology group of the space for which $J \leqq c$ for any c does not change as c varies until a critical level is reached; this is a level of J at which a critical point exists. The change in homology groups at critical points is related closely to the nature of the critical point. For example, in a finite-dimensional space, on a sphere the number of pits minus the number of simple passes plus the number of peaks is two; on a torus the corresponding number is zero; a pass with three grooves running down and three ridges running up from it is to be counted as two simple passes for topological reasons. This is the Morse theory. *See* TOPOLOGY.

Charles B. Tompkins

Multivariable problems. This section deals primarily with the case where the function y is vector-valued. Thus the associated Euler equation is a vector equation, or equivalently a system of real-valued equations.

There are two main cases, one where the approach through the Euler partial differential equation (PDE) has been fruitful, and one where it has been more useful to treat the problem in its original, integral form by rewriting the integral as an integral over the image set rather than the parameter domain. Most of the results discussed are for elliptic problems, but reference is made to some of the work on nonelliptic problems in the calculus of variations.

PDE approach. It will be assumed that the domain C is a bounded open subset of R^m (where R is the real numbers) with a smooth boundary and that the real-valued function f of Eq. (14) is continuous in all

$$f(x, y, p): C \times R^n \times R^{mn} \to R^1 \qquad (14)$$

its variables (though somewhat weaker assumptions are possible); as before, $J[y]$ is given by Eq. (15).

$$J[y] = \int_C f(x, y, y_x) dx \qquad (15)$$

The key ingredients for the existence of a mini-

mum of J within an admissible class of functions are as follows:

1. The integral J has the property that if a sequence of admissible functions y_i converges to an admissible function y, then $\lim \inf J[y_i]$ is no larger than $J[y]$ (this property is called sequential lower semicontinuity).

2. There exists a minimizing sequence of admissible functions which converges to an admissible function. (Typically this is arranged by requiring the set of admissible functions to have the property that any sequence has some convergent subsequence with limit in the set, which is the property of compactness.)

When these two conditions hold, the direct method can be used to find a minimizer: take any sequence y_i such that $J[y_i]$ converges toward the infimum of the possible values of J, and extract a convergent subsequence.

To have these conditions hold, it is sufficient that f be convex in the last set of variables (so that the Euler equations form a so-called strongly elliptic system of partial differential equations), that either f increases with $|y_x|$ at least as fast as $|y_x|^\alpha$ for some $\alpha > 1$ or there be some known bound given in advance on the slopes $|y_x|$ of a minimizer, and that the class of admissible functions be an appropriate Sobolev space. In particular, the class of admissible functions must allow some kinds of discontinuities, and the first derivatives of y need exist only in a "weak" sense (analogous to Schwartz's generalized functions or distributions).

This leads to the regularity problem: Are the functions obtained by this procedure indeed classical functions with enough derivatives that they are classical solutions to the Euler system of equations?

When $n = 1$ (and under the above assumption of convexity), the answer is yes. But for $n \geqq 2$, the answer is, in general, no. For example, there are integrands f satisfying all the above hypotheses such that the function $y = x/|x|$ (which is discontinuous at the origin) is the unique minimizer among functions with its boundary values.

The problem thus shifts to characterizing the set of points x such that y is not a continuously differentiable function in a neighborhood of x (that is, to characterizing the singular set of y). It has been shown that the singular set has Hausdorff dimension less than $m - 2$; it is an open question in general whether the dimension of the singular set is always less than or equal to $m - 3$. (Fractal sets can have dimensions which are not whole numbers, and the possibility of fractal singular sets has not been ruled out.) *See* FRACTALS.

One particular such case where $y = x/|x|$ is the unique minimizer is with $m = n = 3$, C the unit ball in R^3, $f(x, y, y_x) = y|x|^2$ (for this f, $J[y]$ is often called the elastic energy of the mapping y), and boundary values $y(x) = x$ for x on the boundary of the unit ball, provided the additional requirement is imposed that the image of y lies on the boundary of the unit ball. Such energy-minimizing mappings where the image is constrained to lie on a unit sphere are typical of the director fields of liquid crystals. The subject of looking for energy-minimizing mappings,

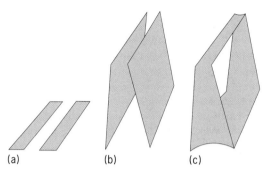

Fig. 2. Example of an area-minimizing surface that cannot be written as the graph of a single function. (*a*) Nonconvex domain C. (*b*) Minimal graph over C that is not area-minimizing. (*c*) Second surface over C that has less area. (*After F. Morgan, Geometric Measure Theory: A Beginner's Guide, Academic Press, 1988*)

or at least for mappings which are critical points of this J (called harmonic maps), is an active field of mathematics research. An example where there is no energy-minimizing mapping arises in the attempt to map a torus (an inner tube) so as to cover a sphere (a beach ball): in the limit of an energy-minimizing sequence, the torus tears apart. *See* LIQUID CRYSTALS.

The major problem with this PDE approach is that many variational problems, when formulated in this way, do not result in a strongly elliptic system of partial differential equations. For example, when a two-dimensional surface in R^3 is written as the graph of a single real-valued function y over a domain C in the plane, its area is given by Eq. (16),

$$J[y] = \int (1 + |y_x|^2)^{1/2} \, dx \qquad (16)$$

and if C is convex the above theory can be applied. But if the same surface is written parametrically, as a mapping from a parameter domain in R^2 into three-dimensional space, the area is given by integrating a different integrand, and this integrand is no longer convex in the derivatives. (For mappings of two-dimensional disks, it is possible to chose a particular parametrization so that minimizing area is equivalent to minimizing the elastic energy of the

mapping, but for higher-dimensional surfaces, for example, three-dimensional surfaces in R^4, there is no such choice of parametrization or equivalence.) Furthermore, in any dimension a typical area-minimizing surface usually cannot be written as the graph of a single function (**Fig. 2**), and thus (except for special parametrizations of some two-dimensional surfaces) the above theory simply cannot be applied. *See* PARAMETRIC EQUATION.

Geometric variational problems. For functions J such that the value of J depends only on the image surface and not on the particular parametrization chosen (as is the case for area), there is an alternative approach. Integrands F with this property are commonly (and perversely) known as parametric integrands. Since the solution to a variational problem with a parametric integrand is really a surface and not a particular parametrization of it, it has proven fruitful to translate the problem to one of integrating over the image set and not over the parameter domain. This is the point of view adopted in geometric measure theory, a subject whose modern history dates to 1960. Written in this form, the integral has the form given in Eq. (17). Here $\vec{S}(x)$ denotes the tangent plane to the

$$J = \int_{x \in S} F[x, \vec{S}(x)] \, d\sigma \qquad (17)$$

surface S at the point x on the surface, and $d\sigma$ denotes integration over the surface (specifically, with respect to Hausdorff m-dimensional measure). For example, F is just constantly 1 for all points and all tangent plane directions when J is the area functional. The integrand F is defined to be elliptic if a piece of a plane always has uniquely (and uniformly, in a certain sense) the least integral, compared to any other surface having the same boundary. If F is elliptic, then when a minimizing surface can be written as the graph of a function, the corresponding system of Euler partial differential equations is strongly elliptic.

If integration over the image set is considered, then it makes sense to speak about minimizing integrals over possible changing surface geometries. For example, surfaces with different numbers of handles or connected components can be compared. A handle is defined topologically by the operation of cutting out two disks from a surface and gluing in a cylinder. The surface in **Fig. 3***a* has no handles and more area than the surface in Fig. 3*b* with one handle, which in turn has more area than the surface in Fig. 3*c* with two handles. In Fig. 3*d, e,* and *f,* these three surfaces are deformed to show that they do have zero, one, and two handles, respectively; the cylinders (tubes) are evident in Fig. 3*e* and *f,* compared to Fig. 3*d.* An infinite sequence of handle additions results in a surface with infinitely many handles that is area-minimizing.

In this context, previously intractable problems, such as that of seeking area-minimizing surfaces with prescribed boundaries which are not graphs of functions, become elliptic and amenable to analysis. Some nonelliptic problems can also be handled. More elaborate problems can also be considered,

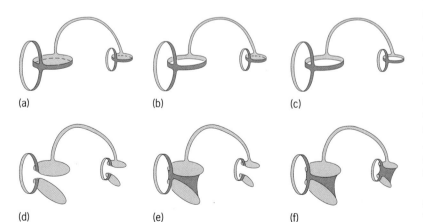

Fig. 3. Comparison of surfaces. (*a*) Surface with no handles. (*b*) Surface with one handle and less area. (*c*) Surface with two handles and still less area. (*d, e, f*) These three surfaces are deformed to show that they do have zero, one, and two handles, respectively.

such as that of finding the shape of the interface between two substances of prescribed volume filling a given knobby container with tubes running through it. The three types of surface energy per unit area—that between the two fluids as well as that between each fluid and the wall of the container—must be specified, as well as the direction and magnitude of any gravitational attractions. The object here is to minimize the sum of the gravitational energy of the bulk and the integrals of the surface energies over the relevant surfaces.

Many general results on existence, regularity, singularity structure, and computation for geometric variational problems have been developed in this context. The former questions become here questions of the existence of a minimizing surface, the existence of tangent planes to the surface and their smooth variation from point to point, and the possible structures of the surface around points where tangent planes do not exist.

There are four basic classes of surfaces considered in geometric measure theory (playing the role of admissible functions above). These four classes were created in order to solve different types of problems in the calculus of variations.

1. Integral currents are most analogous to mappings; the orientation and multiplicity (number of times a point is hit in the mapping) are included in the definition, and the boundary is defined by Stokes' theorem. An appropriately bounded set of integral currents is compact, and elliptic integrands on integral currents have the lower-semicontinuity property; thus the direct method in the calculus of variations is applicable. The singular set of an m-dimensional area-minimizing integral current is known to have dimension at most $m - 2$ [dimension $m - 7$ if the area-minimizing surface happens to lie in an $(m + 1)$-dimensional space], and there are examples which have singular sets this large. Much less is known about the possible singularities in integral currents minimizing the integral of a general elliptic integrand, except that they can be much larger. *See* STOKES' THEOREM.

2. Flat chains modulo 2 are used for unorientable surfaces like the Möbius band; in other ways, they are similar to integral currents. *See* MANIFOLD (MATHEMATICS).

3. (F,ϵ,δ)-minimal sets are useful in modeling a large variety of complicated physical surfaces, such as soap bubble clusters and soap films or the total grain-boundary structure of polycrystalline materials. Neither orientation nor multiplicity is counted for these surfaces; the defining idea is that of being close to minimizing in small balls. When F is elliptic, singularities can have dimension at most $m - 1$. (The liquid edges in soap bubble clusters form singularities of dimension 1.)

4. Varifolds are quite general (all integrands are continuous on this class of surfaces) and are useful, in particular, in the consideration of infinitesimally corrugated surfaces such as the limit of the sawtooth curves discussed above or certain boundaries of crystalline grains in materials, where the surface energy is

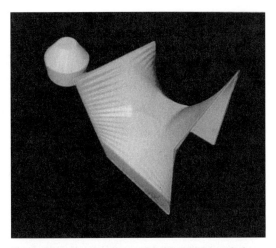

Fig. 4. Examples of surfaces minimizing the integral of a nonelliptic integrand among all bodies having the same volume (the surface at upper left) and among all surfaces having the same boundary (the saddle-shaped surface). Surfaces were computed as part of the Geometry Supercomputer Project sponsored by the National Science Foundation and the University of Minnesota.

so highly anisotropic that the integrand is not elliptic. (When varifoldlike solutions arise in the context of partial differential equations, they are often referred to as Young measures.) *See* MINIMAL SURFACES.

Computation. Research in geometric measure theory includes developing and implementing algorithms for the computation and display of surface-energy-minimizing surfaces with a variety of constraints. The integrands (surface energies) that are considered range from the constant 1 (for area-minimizing surfaces) through other elliptic integrands to integrands that are so nonelliptic that the analog of a soap bubble is a polyhedron (**Fig. 4**). A major tool in computing solutions to geometric variational problems is the Surface Evolver, a freeware program. *See* MINIMAL SURFACES.

Additional directions. Optimal design problems, where the objective is to optimize the macroscopic behavior of microscopically heterogeneous materials, can be viewed as a special type of variational problem. Typically, an optimal design problem requires minimization of a sum of energies that is not weakly lower semicontinuous; that is, the total energy of the ordinary limit of a sequence of configurations might well be higher than the limit of the total energies of the configurations themselves. Therefore, special relaxation methods are developed to find and effectively describe new types of limits to highly oscillating configurations; this is analogous to the use of varifolds. The new kinds of limits do have energies that are the limits of the energies of their sequence of oscillatory configurations, and the properties of these new types of limits are called the effective properties of the limit composite material.

Optimal structures are generally unstable. Indeed, they concentrate the resistance capacities in certain directions in order to withstand a given loading. They are thus extremely sensitive to the variation of the loadings. Furthermore, there is a great difference between two-phase and multiphase optimal structures.

Significant advances have been achieved through the use of weak convergence as a rigorous yet general language for the discussion of macroscopic behavior. There is also much interest in novel types of questions, particularly the G-closure problem. (The set of effective properties of all possible composites made from given materials is called the G-closure of the set of original properties, and the problem is to describe the G-closure for different sets of original materials.) Other areas of theoretical progress involve the introduction of new methods for bounding effective properties, and the identification of deep links between the analysis of microstructures and the multidimensional calculus of variations. This work has implications for many physical problems involving optimal design, composite materials, and coherent phase transitions. *See* COMPOSITE MATERIAL; OPTIMIZATION; PHASE TRANSITIONS.

There is at least one variational formulation for all partial differential equations, although some variational formulations are more useful than others. In the past, it has been most useful to pass from calculus of variations problems to partial differential equations, but now it is sometimes better to travel the opposite way. In particular, approximate solutions to partial differential equations involving time can sometimes be constructed via solving minimization problems over discrete time steps, and limits of such approximate solutions as the time step goes to zero can produce solutions to the equations that handle singularities in an appropriate way.   Jean E. Taylor

Bibliography. N. I. Akhiezer, *Calculus of Variations*, 1988; U. Brechtken-Menderscheid, *An Introduction to the Calculus of Variations*, 1991; A. Cherkaev and R. Kohn (eds.), *Topics in Mathematical Modelling of Composite Materials*, Birkhauser, 1997; F. Morgan, *Geometric Measure Theory: A Beginner's Guide*, 2d ed., 1995; M. Morse, *Calculus of Variations in the Large*, 8th ed., 1986, reprint 1993; E. R. Pinch, *Optimal Control and the Calculus of Variations*, 1993; F. Y. Wan, *Introduction to the Calculus of Variations and Its Applications*, 1991.

Calculus of vectors

In its simplest form, a vector is a directed line segment. Physical quantities, such as velocity, acceleration, force, and displacement, are vector quantities, or simply vectors, because they can be represented by directed line segments. The algebra of vectors was initiated principally through the works of W. R. Hamilton and H. G. Grassmann in the middle of the nineteenth century, and brought to the form presented here by the efforts of O. Heaviside and J. W. Gibbs in the late nineteenth century. Vector analysis is a tool of the mathematical physicist, because many physical laws can be expressed in vector form.

Addition of vectors. Two vectors **a** and **b** are added according to the parallelogram law (**Fig. 1**). An equivalent definition is as follows: From the end point of **a**, a vector is constructed parallel to **b**, of the same magnitude and direction as **b**. The vector from the

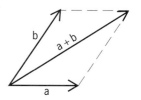

Fig. 1. Addition of two vectors.

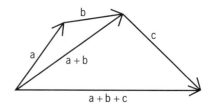

Fig. 2. Addition of three vectors.

origin of **a** to the end point of **b** yields the vector sum **s** = **a** + **b** (**Fig. 2**). Any number of vectors can be added by this rule.

Given a vector **a**, a class of vectors can be formed which are parallel to **a** but of different magnitudes. If x is a real number, the vector $x\mathbf{a}$ is defined to be parallel to **a** of magnitude $|x|$ times that of **a**. For $x > 0$, the two vectors **a** and $x\mathbf{a}$ have the same sense of direction, whereas for $x < 0$ the vector $x\mathbf{a}$ is in a reverse direction from that of **a**. The vector $-\mathbf{a}$ is the negative of the vector **a**, such that $\mathbf{a} + (-\mathbf{a}) = \mathbf{0}$, with **0** designated as the zero vector (a vector with zero magnitude). Subtraction of two vectors is defined by

$$\mathbf{a} - \mathbf{b} = \mathbf{a} + (-\mathbf{b})$$

The rules shown in notation (1), which conform

$$
\begin{aligned}
\mathbf{a} + \mathbf{b} &= \mathbf{b} + \mathbf{a} \\
(\mathbf{a} + \mathbf{b}) + \mathbf{c} &= \mathbf{a} + (\mathbf{b} + \mathbf{c}) \\
x(\mathbf{a} + \mathbf{b}) &= x\mathbf{a} + x\mathbf{b} \\
x(y\mathbf{a}) &= (xy)\mathbf{a} \\
(x + y)\mathbf{a} &= x\mathbf{a} + y\mathbf{a} \\
0 \cdot \mathbf{a} &= \mathbf{0} \\
\mathbf{a} + \mathbf{0} &= \mathbf{a} \\
\mathbf{a} + \mathbf{b} &= \mathbf{a} + \mathbf{c} \text{ implies } \mathbf{b} = \mathbf{c} \\
\mathbf{a} = \mathbf{c}, \mathbf{b} &= \mathbf{d} \text{ implies } \mathbf{a} + \mathbf{b} = \mathbf{c} + \mathbf{d}
\end{aligned}
\tag{1}
$$

$|\mathbf{a} + \mathbf{b}| \leq |\mathbf{a}| + |\mathbf{b}|$, with $|\mathbf{a}|$ = magnitude of **a**, etc.

to the rules of elementary arithmetic, can be readily deduced.

Coordinate systems. The cartesian coordinate frame of analytic geometry is very useful for yielding a description of a vector (**Fig. 3**). The unit vectors **i**, **j**, **k** lie parallel to the positive x, y, and z axes, respectively. Any vector can be written as a linear combination of **i**, **j**, **k**. From Fig. 3, it is noted that Eq. (2) holds. Furthermore, the scalars a_x, a_y, a_z are

$$\mathbf{a} = a_x\mathbf{i} + a_y\mathbf{j} + a_z\mathbf{k} \tag{2}$$

simply the projections of **a** on the x, y, and z axes, respectively, and are designated as the components of **a**. Thus, a_x is the x component of **a**, and so on.

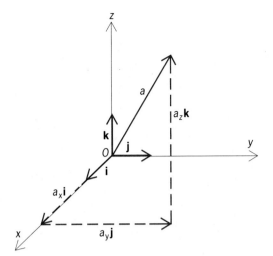

Fig. 3. Vectors in cartesian coordinate system.

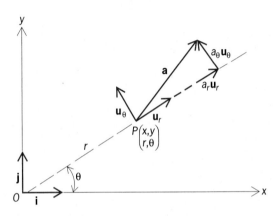

Fig. 4. Vectors in polar coordinate system.

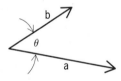

Fig. 5. Scalar product of two vectors.

If the vector **b** is described by $\mathbf{b} = b_x\mathbf{i} + b_y\mathbf{j} + b_z\mathbf{k}$, then Eq. (3) holds.

$$\alpha\mathbf{a} + \beta\mathbf{b} = (\alpha a_x + \beta b_x)\mathbf{i}$$
$$+ (\alpha a_y + \beta y_y)\mathbf{j} + (\alpha a_z + \beta b_z)\mathbf{k} \quad (3)$$

In general, the components of a vector will be functions of the space coordinates and the time. To be more specific, consider a fluid in motion. At any time t the particle which is located at the point $P(x,y,z)$ will have velocity components which depend on the coordinates x,y,z, as well as the time t. Thus, the velocity field **v** of the fluid is represented by Eq. (4). A steady-state vector field exists if the

$$\mathbf{v} = v_x(x, y, z, t)\mathbf{i} + v_y(x, y, z, t)\mathbf{j}$$
$$+ v_z(x, y, z, t)\mathbf{k} \quad (4)$$

components are time-independent. The force field of a fixed gravitating particle is of this type.

It is not necessary to describe a vector in terms of rectangular coordinates (**Fig. 4**). Let **a** be a vector in the xy plane with origin at the point $P(x,y)$. The point P can also be described in terms of polar coordinates (r,ϕ). Let $\mathbf{u}_r$, $\mathbf{u}_\phi$ be unit vectors in the directions of increasing r and θ, respectively. From Fig. 4 it follows that Eq. (5) holds

$$\mathbf{a} = a_x\mathbf{i} + a_y\mathbf{j} = a_r\mathbf{u}_r + a_\theta\mathbf{u}_\theta \quad (5)$$

with

$$a_r = a_x \cos\theta + a_y \sin\theta$$
$$a_\theta = -a_x \sin\theta + a_y \cos\theta$$

The components a_r, a_θ yield a description of the same vector **a**. Thus coordinate systems are simply a means of describing a vector. The vector is independent of the description.

Scalar or dot product of two vectors. From two vectors **a** and **b**, a scalar quantity is formed from the definition in Eq. (6), where θ is the angle between

$$\mathbf{a} \cdot \mathbf{b} = |\mathbf{a}| \cdot |\mathbf{b}| \cos\theta \quad (6)$$

the two vectors when drawn from a common origin (**Fig. 5**). It is quickly verified that Eqs. (7) hold. Here

$$\mathbf{a} \cdot \mathbf{b} = \mathbf{b} \cdot \mathbf{a}$$
$$\mathbf{a} \cdot \mathbf{a} = |\mathbf{a}|^2$$
$$(\mathbf{a} + \mathbf{b}) \cdot (\mathbf{c} + \mathbf{d}) = \mathbf{a} \cdot \mathbf{c} + \mathbf{a} \cdot \mathbf{d} + \mathbf{b} \cdot \mathbf{c} + \mathbf{b} \cdot \mathbf{d} \quad (7)$$
$$\mathbf{i} \cdot \mathbf{i} = \mathbf{j} \cdot \mathbf{j} = \mathbf{k} \cdot \mathbf{k} = 1$$
$$\mathbf{i} \cdot \mathbf{j} = \mathbf{j} \cdot \mathbf{k} = \mathbf{k} \cdot \mathbf{i} = 0$$

$\mathbf{a} \perp \mathbf{b}$ implies $\mathbf{a} \cdot \mathbf{b} = 0$, and conversely, provided $|\mathbf{a}| \cdot |\mathbf{b}| \neq 0$.

For $\mathbf{a} = a_x\mathbf{i} + a_y\mathbf{j} + a_z\mathbf{k}$, $\mathbf{b} = b_x\mathbf{i} + b_y\mathbf{j} + b_z\mathbf{k}$, it follows from Eq. (7) that Eq. (8) can be written. If

$$\mathbf{a} \cdot \mathbf{b} = a_xb_x + a_yb_y + a_zb_z \quad (8)$$

a is a force field displaced along the vector **b**, then $\mathbf{a} \cdot \mathbf{b}$ represents the work performed by this force field.

Referring to Eq. (5), let $\mathbf{b} = b_x\mathbf{i} + b_y\mathbf{j} = b_r\mathbf{u}_r + b_\theta\mathbf{u}_\theta$. Then

$$\mathbf{a} \cdot \mathbf{b} = a_xb_x + a_yb_y = a_rb_r + a_\theta b_\theta$$
$$\equiv (a_x \cos\theta + a_y \sin\theta)(b_x \cos\theta + b_y \sin\theta)$$
$$+ (-a_x \sin\theta + a_y \cos\theta)$$
$$\times (-b_x \sin\theta + b_y \cos\theta)$$

Thus the scalar product of two vectors is independent of the descriptive coordinate system as is evident from the definition of the scalar product given by Eq. (6).

Vector or cross product of two vectors. In three-dimensional space, a vector can be formed from two vectors **a** and **b** in the following manner if they are nonparallel. Let **a** and **b** have a common origin defining a plane, and let **c** be that vector perpendicular

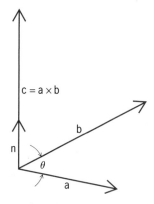

Fig. 6.   Vector product of two vectors.

to this plane of magnitude $|\mathbf{c}| = |\mathbf{a}|\,|\mathbf{b}|\sin\theta$. If $\mathbf{a}$ is rotated into $\mathbf{b}$ through the angle θ, a right-hand screw will advance in the direction of $\mathbf{c}$ (**Fig. 6**). Thus Eq. (9) can be written.

$$\mathbf{c} = \mathbf{a} \times \mathbf{b} = |\mathbf{a}|\,|\mathbf{b}|\sin\theta\,\mathbf{n} \qquad (9)$$

It follows that $\mathbf{a} \times \mathbf{b} = -(\mathbf{b} \times \mathbf{a})$, and that if $\mathbf{a}$ is parallel to $\mathbf{b}$, $\mathbf{a} \times \mathbf{b} = 0$. Conversely, if $\mathbf{a} \times \mathbf{b} = 0$, then $\mathbf{a}$ is parallel to $\mathbf{b}$ provided $|\mathbf{a}|\,|\mathbf{b}| \neq 0$.

The distributive law can be shown to hold for the vector product so that Eq. (10) holds.

$$(\mathbf{a} + \mathbf{b}) \times (\mathbf{c} + \mathbf{d})$$

$$= \mathbf{a} \times \mathbf{c} + \mathbf{a} \times \mathbf{d} + \mathbf{b} \times \mathbf{c} + \mathbf{b} \times \mathbf{d} \qquad (10)$$

It follows from

$$\mathbf{i} \times \mathbf{i} = \mathbf{j} \times \mathbf{j} = \mathbf{k} \times \mathbf{k} = 0$$

$$\mathbf{i} \times \mathbf{j} = \mathbf{k},\, \mathbf{j} \times \mathbf{k} = \mathbf{i},\, \mathbf{k} \times \mathbf{i} = \mathbf{j}$$

that for

$$\mathbf{a} = a_x\mathbf{i} + a_z\mathbf{j} + a_z\mathbf{k} \qquad \mathbf{b} = b_x\mathbf{i} + b_y\mathbf{j} + b_z\mathbf{k}$$

Eq. (11) holds. The expression in Eq. (11) is to be

$$\mathbf{a} \times \mathbf{b} = \begin{vmatrix} \mathbf{i} & \mathbf{j} & \mathbf{k} \\ a_x & a_y & a_z \\ b_x & b_y & b_z \end{vmatrix} \qquad (11)$$

expanded by the ordinary rules governing determinants.

Multiple products involving vector and scalar products can be generated. The triple scalar product $\mathbf{a} \cdot (\mathbf{b} \times \mathbf{c})$ is given by Eq. (12). It can be shown

$$\mathbf{a} \cdot (\mathbf{b} \times \mathbf{c}) = \begin{vmatrix} a_x & a_y & a_z \\ b_x & b_y & b_z \\ c_x & c_y & c_z \end{vmatrix} \qquad (12)$$

that Eq. (13) is true. Geometrically, the scalar triple

$$\mathbf{a} \cdot (\mathbf{b} \times \mathbf{c}) = (\mathbf{a} \times \mathbf{b}) \cdot \mathbf{c} \equiv (\mathbf{abc}) \qquad (13)$$

product represents the volume of a parallelepiped formed with $\mathbf{a}$, $\mathbf{b}$, $\mathbf{c}$ as coterminous sides,

$$V = |\mathbf{a} \cdot (\mathbf{b} \times \mathbf{c})|$$

Of importance in the study of rigid-body motions is the triple vector product shown in Eq. (14). From Eqs. (13) and (14) follow Eqs. (15) and (16).

$$\mathbf{a} \times (\mathbf{b} \times \mathbf{c}) = (\mathbf{a} \cdot \mathbf{c})\mathbf{b} - (\mathbf{a} \cdot \mathbf{b})\mathbf{c}$$
$$(\mathbf{a} \times \mathbf{b}) \times \mathbf{c} = (\mathbf{a} \cdot \mathbf{c})\mathbf{b} - (\mathbf{b} \cdot \mathbf{c})\mathbf{a} \qquad (14)$$

$$(\mathbf{a} \times \mathbf{b}) \cdot (\mathbf{c} \times \mathbf{d}) = (\mathbf{a} \cdot [\mathbf{b} \times (\mathbf{c} \times \mathbf{d})]$$

$$= (\mathbf{a} \cdot \mathbf{c})(\mathbf{b} \cdot \mathbf{d}) - (\mathbf{a} \cdot \mathbf{d})(\mathbf{b} \cdot \mathbf{c}) \quad (15)$$

$$(\mathbf{a} \times \mathbf{b}) \times (\mathbf{c} \times \mathbf{d}) = (\mathbf{acd})\mathbf{b} - (\mathbf{bcd})\mathbf{a}$$

$$= (\mathbf{abd})\mathbf{c} - (\mathbf{abc})\mathbf{d} \quad (16)$$

Pseudovectors. It is easy to verify that a reflection of the space coordinates given by $x' = -x$, $y' = -y$, $z' = -z$, reverses the sign of the components of a vector. Under a space reflection, however, the jcomponents of the vector $\mathbf{a} \times \mathbf{b}$ do not change sign. This is seen from Eq. (11), for if a_x, a_y, a_z are replaced by $-a_x$, $-a_y$, $-a_z$, and if $-b_x$, $-b_y$, $-b_z$ are replaced by $-b_x$, $-b_y$, $-b_z$, the components of $\mathbf{a} \times \mathbf{b}$ remain invariant. Hence, $\mathbf{a} \times \mathbf{b}$ is not a true vector and therefore is given the title pseudovector. In electricity theory the magnetic field vector $\mathbf{B}$ is a pseudovector, whereas the electric field vector is a true vector provided the electric charge is a true scalar under a reflection of axes. Pseudovectors belong properly to the domain of the tensor calculus. In general, vectors associated with rotations belong to the category of pseudovectors. In particular, the angular velocity vector associated with the motion of a rigid body is a pseudovector. *See* TENSOR ANALYSIS.

Differentiation. There are three differentiation processes that are of conceptual value in the study of vectors; the gradient of a scalar, the divergence of a vector, and the curl of a vector.

Gradient of a scalar. The vector field $\mathbf{v}$ given by Eq. (17) has the property that the components of

$$\mathbf{v} = v_1(x,y,z)\mathbf{i} + v_2(x,y,z)\mathbf{j} + v_3(x,y,z)\mathbf{k} \quad (17)$$

$\mathbf{v}$ differ at individual points $P(x,y,z)$. The differential change in the individual components of v in moving from $P(x,y,z)$ to $Q(x + dx, y + dy, z + dz)$ is given by Eq. (18). It is suggestive to define the differential

$$dv_i = \frac{\partial v_i}{\partial x}dx + \frac{\partial v_i}{\partial y}dy + \frac{\partial v_i}{\partial z}dz \qquad (18)$$
$$i = 1, 2, 3$$

of $\mathbf{v}$ by Eq. (19), because $\mathbf{i}$, $\mathbf{j}$, $\mathbf{k}$ are constant vectors (both in magnitude and direction).

$$d\mathbf{v} = dv_1\mathbf{i} + dv_2\mathbf{j} + dv_3\mathbf{k} \qquad (19)$$

If the components of a vector $\mathbf{v}$ are functions of a single parameter λ, the derivative of v with respect to λ is defined by Eq. (20).

$$\frac{d\mathbf{v}}{d\lambda} = \frac{dv_1}{d\lambda}\mathbf{i} + \frac{dv_2}{d\lambda}\mathbf{j} + \frac{dv_3}{d\lambda}\mathbf{k} \qquad (20)$$

The position vector of a particle is designated by $\mathbf{r} = x\mathbf{i} + y\mathbf{j} + z\mathbf{k}$. If the particle moves along a trajectory, the velocity and acceleration vectors associated with the motion of the particle are described by Eqs. (21).

$$\mathbf{v} = \frac{d\mathbf{r}}{dt} = \frac{dx}{dt}\mathbf{i} + \frac{dy}{dt}\mathbf{j} + \frac{dz}{dt}\mathbf{k}$$

$$\mathbf{a} = \frac{d\mathbf{v}}{dt} = \frac{d^2\mathbf{r}}{dt^2} = \frac{d^2x}{dt^2}\mathbf{i} + \frac{d^2y}{dt^2}\mathbf{j} + \frac{d^2z}{dt^2}\mathbf{k} \qquad (21)$$

The expression for the derivative of a vector described in curvilinear coordinates becomes more involved simply because the unit vectors in the curvilinear coordinate system need not remain fixed in space. Referring to Eq. (5),

$$\frac{d\mathbf{a}}{dt} = \frac{da_x}{dt}\mathbf{i} + \frac{da_y}{dt}\mathbf{j}$$
$$= \frac{da_r}{dt}\mathbf{u}_r + \frac{da_\theta}{dt}\mathbf{u}_\theta + a_r\frac{d\mathbf{u}_r}{dt} + a_\theta\frac{d\mathbf{u}_\theta}{dt}$$

From $\mathbf{u}_r = \mathbf{i}\cos\theta + \mathbf{j}\sin\theta$ and $\mathbf{u}_\theta = -\mathbf{i}\sin\theta + \mathbf{j}\cos\theta$, it follows that

$$\frac{d\mathbf{a}}{dt} = \left(\frac{da_r}{dt} - a_\theta\frac{d\theta}{dt}\right)\mathbf{u}_r + \left(\frac{da_\theta}{dt} + a_r\frac{d\theta}{dt}\right)\mathbf{u}_\theta$$

The differentiation rules shown in Eqs. (22) exist.

$$\frac{d}{d\lambda}(\mathbf{u} \cdot \mathbf{u}) \cdot \frac{d\mathbf{v}}{d\lambda} + \frac{d\mathbf{u}}{d\lambda} \cdot \mathbf{v}$$
$$\frac{d}{d\lambda}(\mathbf{u} \times \mathbf{v}) = \mathbf{u} \times \frac{d\mathbf{v}}{d\lambda} + \frac{d\mathbf{u}}{d\lambda} \times \mathbf{v} \qquad (22)$$
$$\frac{d}{d\lambda}(f\mathbf{v}) = f\frac{d\mathbf{v}}{d\lambda} + \frac{df}{d\lambda}\mathbf{v}$$

From the scalar $\phi(x,y,z)$, one can form the three partial derivatives $\partial\phi/\partial x$, $\partial\phi/\partial y$, $\partial\phi/\partial z$, from which the vector in Eq. (23) can be formed. The vector,

$$\left.\begin{array}{r}\text{gradient of } \phi \\ \text{grad } \phi \\ \text{del } \phi \equiv \nabla\phi\end{array}\right\} = \frac{\partial\phi}{\partial x}\mathbf{i} + \frac{\partial\phi}{\partial y}\mathbf{j} + \frac{\partial\phi}{\partial z}\mathbf{k} \qquad (23)$$

grad ϕ, has two important properties. Grad ϕ is a vector field normal to the surface $\phi(x,y,z) = $ constant at every point of the surface. Moreover, grad ϕ yields that unique direction such that ϕ increases at its greatest rate. If $T(x,y,z)$ is the temperature at any point in space, then ∇T at any point yields that direction for which the temperature increases most rapidly. If $\phi(x,y,z)$ represents the electrostatic potential, then $\mathbf{E} = -\nabla\phi$ yields the electric field vector.

Divergence and curl of a vector. The del operator defined by Eq. (24) plays an important role in the development of the differential vector calculus. For the vector field of Eq. (17), the divergence of v is defined by Eq. (25). The divergence of a vector is a scalar.

$$\nabla = \mathbf{i}\frac{\partial}{\partial x} + \mathbf{j}\frac{\partial}{\partial y} + \mathbf{k}\frac{\partial}{\partial z} \qquad (24)$$

$$\text{div } \mathbf{v} = \nabla \cdot \mathbf{v} = \frac{\partial v_1}{\partial x} + \frac{\partial v_2}{\partial y} + \frac{\partial v_3}{\partial z} \qquad (25)$$

If ρ is the density of a fluid and **v** the velocity field of the fluid, then div $(\rho\mathbf{v})$ represents the rate of loss of mass of fluid per unit time per unit volume.

The total loss of mass of fluid per unit time for a fixed volume V is given by the volume integral of notation (26).

$$\iiint\limits_{v} \text{div } (\rho\mathbf{v})\, dz\, dy\, dx \qquad (26)$$

In electricity theory, the divergence of the displacement vector **D** is a measure of the charge density, $\nabla \cdot \mathbf{D}$ in the development ρ.

By use of the del operator one obtains quite formally Eq. (27). The vector $\nabla \times \mathbf{v}$ is called the curl

$$\nabla \times \mathbf{v} = \begin{vmatrix} \mathbf{i} & \mathbf{j} & \mathbf{k} \\ \dfrac{\partial}{\partial x} & \dfrac{\partial}{\partial y} & \dfrac{\partial}{\partial z} \\ v_1 & v_2 & v_3 \end{vmatrix}$$

$$= \left(\frac{\partial v_3}{\partial y} - \frac{\partial v_2}{\partial z}\right)\mathbf{i} + \left(\frac{\partial v_1}{\partial z} - \frac{\partial v_3}{\partial x}\right)\mathbf{j}$$

$$+ \left(\frac{\partial v_2}{\partial x} - \frac{\partial v_1}{\partial y}\right)\mathbf{k} \qquad (27)$$

of **v** (curl **v**). Under a reflection of space coordinates, $\partial v_3/\partial y \to \partial(-v_3)/\partial(-y) = \partial v_3/y$ the curl of **v** is a pseudovector. As has been noted previously, the class of pseudovectors is associated with rotations in space; thus, it is not strange that the curl of a velocity field is closely associated with an angular velocity vector field. The velocity of a fluid at a point $Q(x + dx, y + dy, z + dz)$ near $P(x,y,z)$ can be characterized as shown in Eq. (28), where **r** is the vector from P to Q and Eq. (29) holds. Now in general, $\omega \times \mathbf{r}$ is the

$$\mathbf{v}_Q = \mathbf{v}_P + \frac{1}{2}(\nabla \times \mathbf{v})_P \times \mathbf{r} + \frac{1}{2}\nabla(\mathbf{r} \cdot \mathbf{w}) \qquad (28)$$

$$\mathbf{w} = [(\mathbf{r} \cdot \nabla)\mathbf{v}]_P = \left(x\frac{\partial\mathbf{v}}{\partial x} + y\frac{\partial\mathbf{v}}{\partial y} + z\frac{\partial\mathbf{v}}{\partial z}\right)_P \qquad (29)$$

velocity of a point due to the angular velocity ω; thus, $\nabla \times \mathbf{v} = 2\omega$. The velocity at Q is simply the sum of a translatory velocity $\mathbf{v}_P$ plus a rigid-body rotational velocity $\omega \times \mathbf{r}$, plus a nonrigid-body deformation, $\frac{1}{2}\nabla(\mathbf{r} \cdot \mathbf{w})$.

Formulas involving gradient, divergence, curl.

1. $\nabla(uv) = u\nabla v + v\nabla u$

2. $\nabla \cdot (\phi\mathbf{v}) = \phi\nabla \cdot \mathbf{v} + (\nabla\phi) \cdot \mathbf{v}$

3. $\nabla \times (\nabla\phi) = \mathbf{0}$

4. $\nabla \cdot (\nabla \times \mathbf{v}) = 0$

5. $\nabla \times (\phi\mathbf{v}) = \phi\nabla \times \mathbf{v} + (\nabla\phi) \times \mathbf{v}$

6. $\nabla \cdot (\mathbf{u} \times \mathbf{v}) = (\nabla \times \mathbf{u}) \cdot \mathbf{v} - (\nabla \times \mathbf{v}) \cdot \mathbf{u}$

7. $\nabla \times (\mathbf{u} \times \mathbf{v}) = (\mathbf{v} \cdot \nabla)\mathbf{u} - \mathbf{v}(\nabla \cdot \mathbf{u})$
   $\qquad\qquad + \mathbf{u}(\nabla \cdot \mathbf{v}) - (\mathbf{u} \cdot \nabla)\mathbf{v}$

8. $\nabla(\mathbf{u} \cdot \mathbf{v}) = \mathbf{u} \times (\nabla \times \mathbf{v}) + \mathbf{v} \times (\nabla \times \mathbf{u})$
   $\qquad\qquad + (\mathbf{u} \cdot \nabla)\mathbf{v} + (\mathbf{v} \cdot \nabla)\mathbf{u}$

9. $\nabla \times (\nabla \times \mathbf{v}) = \nabla(\nabla \cdot \mathbf{v}) - \nabla^2\mathbf{v}$

10. $d\phi = d\mathbf{r} \cdot \nabla\phi + \partial\phi/\partial t\, dt$ for $\phi = \phi(x,y,z,t)$

11. $\nabla \cdot (\nabla\phi) \equiv \nabla^2\phi = \partial^2\phi/\partial k^2 + \partial^2\phi/\partial y^2$
$= \partial^2\phi/\partial z^2$

12. If $\nabla \cdot \mathbf{f} = 0$, then $\mathbf{f} = \nabla \times \mathbf{A}$ (**A** is called the vector potential)

13. If $\nabla \times \mathbf{f} = \mathbf{0}$, then $\mathbf{f} = \nabla\phi$ (ϕ is called the scalar potential)

Integration. If a closed surface is decomposed into a large number of small surfaces, a vector field normal to the surface can be constructed, each normal element being represented by $d\sigma$. The magnitude of $d\sigma$ is the area of the surface element dS, $d\sigma = \mathbf{N}\,dS$.

If $\mathbf{f}$ is a vector field defined at every point of the surface, then notation (30) represents the total flux

$$\int\int_S \mathbf{f} \cdot d\sigma \qquad (30)$$

of $\mathbf{f}$ through the surface S. The elements $d\sigma$ point outward from the interior of S.

The divergence theorem of Gauss states that Eq. (31) is true, where R is the region enclosed by S,

$$\int\int_S \mathbf{f} \cdot d\sigma = \int\int\int_R (\nabla \cdot \mathbf{f})\,d\tau \qquad (31)$$

$d\tau$ a volume element of R. For $\mathbf{f} = \rho\mathbf{v}$, the divergence theorem states that the net loss of fluid per unit time can be accounted for by measuring the total outward flux of the vector $\rho\mathbf{v}$ through the closed surface S bounding R. *See* GAUSS' THEOREM.

The line integral of a vector field is described as follows: Let Γ be a space curve, and let $\mathbf{t}$ be the unit vector field tangent to Γ at every point of Γ in progressing from A to B, the initial and end points of the trajectory Γ.

The scalar integral in notation (32) is called the

$$\int_A^B (\mathbf{f} \cdot \mathbf{t})\,ds \qquad ((32)$$

line integral of $\mathbf{f}$ along Γ, with arc length s measured along Γ. If $\mathbf{f}$ is a force field, notation (32) represents the work performed by the force field if a unit test particle is taken from A to B along Γ.

The value of the integral of notation (32) will generally depend on the path from A to B. However, if $\mathbf{f} = \nabla\phi$, then

$$\int_A^B (\mathbf{f} \cdot \mathbf{t})\,ds = \int_A^B \nabla\phi \cdot d\mathbf{r}$$
$$= \int_A^B d\phi = \phi(B) - \phi(A)$$

and the line integral is independent of the path of integration.

The theorem of Stokes states that Eq. (33) holds,

$$\oint_\Gamma \mathbf{f} \cdot d\mathbf{r} = \int\int_S (\nabla \times \mathbf{f}) \cdot d\sigma \qquad (33)$$

where Γ is the boundary of the open surface S.

If S is a closed surface, then

$$\oiint_S (\nabla \times \mathbf{f}) \cdot d\sigma = 0$$

In electricity theory, a time-changing magnetic flux through an open surface induces a voltage in the boundary of the surface, so that

$$-\frac{\partial}{\partial t}\int\int_S \mathbf{B} \cdot d\sigma = \oint_\Gamma \mathbf{E} \cdot d\mathbf{r}$$

Applying Stokes' theorem yields one of Maxwell's equations,

$$\nabla \times \mathbf{E} = -\frac{\partial\mathbf{B}}{\partial t}$$

See OPERATOR THEORY; POTENTIALS.   Harry Lass
Bibliography. P. Baxandall and H. Liebeck, *Vector Calculus*, 1987; D. Bourne and P. C. Kendall, *Vector Analysis and Cartesian Tensors*, 3d ed., 1992; B. Davis, H. Porta, and J. J. Uhl, *Vector Calculus: Measuring in Two and Three Dimensions*, 1994; H. F. Davis and A. D. Snider, *Introduction to Vector Analysis*, 6th ed., 1991; P. C. DuChateau, *Vector Analysis*, 1993; J. E. Marsden and A. J. Tromba, *Vector Calculus*, 4th ed., 1996; E. C. Young, *Vector and Tensor Analysis*, 1992.

Caldera

A large volcanic collapse depression, typically circular to slightly elongate in shape, the dimensions of which are many times greater than any included vent (**Fig. 1**). Calderas range from a few miles to 45 mi (75 km) in diameter. A caldera may resemble a volcanic crater in form but differs genetically in that it is a collapse rather than a constructional feature. The topographic depression resulting from collapse is commonly widened by slumping of the sides along shallowly rooted faults, so that the topographic caldera wall lies outside the main structural boundary. A caldera may include vents formed by postcollapse volcanism. Its name derives from the Spanish *caldera*, meaning caldron or kettle. As originally defined, caldron referred to volcanic subsidence structures, and caldera referred only to the topographic depression formed by collapse. However, caldera is now common as a synonym for caldron, denoting both topographic and structural features of collapse. *See* PETROLOGY.

Occurrence. Calderas occur primarily in three different volcanic settings, each of which affects their shape and evolution: (1) basaltic shield cones, such as Mauna Loa and Kilauea, Hawaii; (2) stratovolcanoes, for example, Aso and Izu Oshima, Japan; and (3) volcanic centers consisting of preexisting clusters of volcanoes. These last calderas, associated with broad, large-volume andesitic-to-rhyolitic ignimbrite (or ash-flow) sheets, are generally the largest and most impressive. They are the calderas generally implied by the term, and are often referred to as ash-flow calderas. Examples include Toba

(Indonesia) and Yellowstone (Wyoming). Calderas, large and small, have formed throughout much of the Earth's history, and range in age from greater than 1 billion years to historical times. *See* IGNIMBRITE; RHYOLITE; VOLCANO.

In regions of recurrent, shallow magmatic activity, numerous calderas may be partially or entirely superimposed upon each other. For example, Toba caldera is a topographic depression comprising three large, partially superimposed calderas, each of which collapsed during a voluminous ignimbrite eruption (**Fig. 2**). The first (0.8 million years ago) and third (0.074 million years ago) accompanied collapse in the southern part of the composite depression, the second (0.05 million years ago) in the northern part.

In addition to Earth, large calderas occur on Mars, Venus, and Jupiter's moon Io. The presence of calderas on four solar system bodies indicates that the underlying mechanisms of shallow intrusion and caldera collapse are basic processes in planetary geology. *See* MAGMA.

Collapse. Collapse occurs because of withdrawal of magma from an underlying chamber, typically 2.4–3.6 mi (4–6 km) beneath the surface. The result is collapse of the roof into the chamber. Withdrawal of magma may occur either by relatively passive eruption of lavas, as for the small calderas formed on basaltic shield cones, or by catastrophic eruption of pyroclastic (fragmental) material, as accompanies formation of the largest calderas (**Fig. 3**). Eruption of small volumes (no more than 0.24 mi³ or 1 km³) of pyroclastic rock, such as has been observed in historical times, does not necessarily involve caldera collapse. Calderas typically accompany pyroclastic eruptions larger than 6–12 mi³ (25–50 km³) volume. Eruption of even larger volumes of pyroclastic material appears always to be associated with caldera collapse, because roofs of such large chambers cannot support themselves.

Calderas may form by platelike subsidence of the floor along nearly vertical annular, or ring, faults; by piecemeal collapse whereby different parts subside at different times or rates along multiple faults; by asymmetrical subsidence along incomplete ring faults or simple downsagging with no bounding faults; or by funnel-shaped collapse. From relatively young (<40 million-year-old) calderas, which preserve their broadly circular forms and annular near-surface structures, it has been inferred that large calderas form dominantly by plate subsidence. In contrast, study of older (420–470 million-year-old) and deeply eroded calderas suggests that piecemeal collapse may be a dominant mechanism, but multiple eruption and collapse events complicate their interpretation. Most calderas have transitional features, indicating that multiple mechanisms may apply. Among other factors, the collapse mechanism may depend on the thickness of the roof relative to its diameter, depth to the magma chamber, rate of eruption, and preexisting faults.

Pyroclastic eruption. Caldera-forming eruptions probably last only a few hours or days or, if intermittent, may extend over weeks or longer. Eruption of

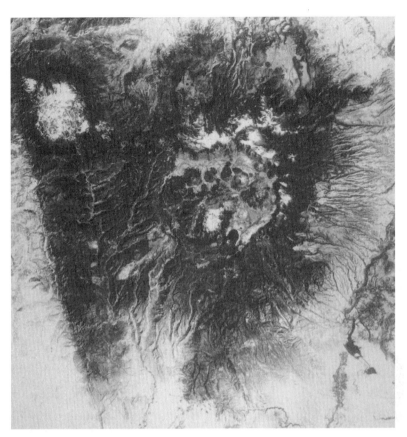

Fig. 1. Landsat Thematic Mapper image of Valles caldera in the Jemez volcanic field of New Mexico. Diameter of the topographic depression is about 13 mi (21 km). (*H. Foote, Battelle—Pacific Northwest Laboratories*)

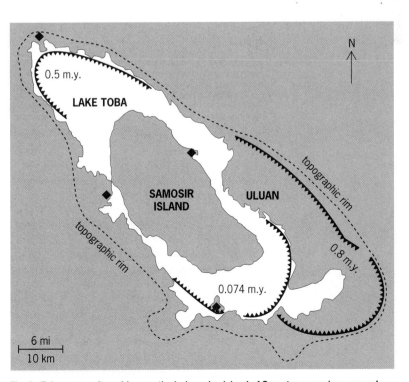

Fig. 2. Toba composite caldera on the Indonesian island of Sumatra comprises several overlapping calderas formed at different times. Spiked lines indicate major faults. Ages of the different caldera segments are indicated by m.y. (million years). Lavas were erupted at four sites (solid boxes) following the eruption 0.074 million years ago.

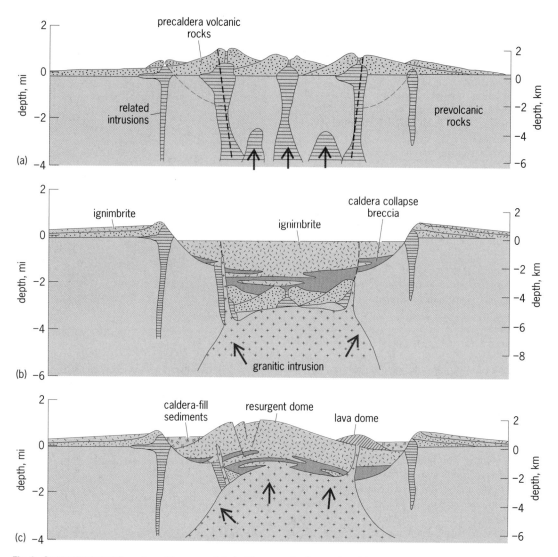

Fig. 3. Generalized evolution of a caldera associated with a pyroclastic eruption. (*a*) Precollapse volcanism. Isolated, small plutons move upward to accumulate into a single large magma chamber. Incipient ring faults are indicated by heavy broken lines, a site of subsequent caldera collapse by light broken lines. (*b*) Caldera geometry just after pyroclastic eruptions and concurrent caldera collapse. Collapse along the ring faults is followed by slumping of the oversteepened walls. (*c*) Resurgence and postcaldera deposition. A magma body has risen and intrudes intracaldera ignimbrites and breccia. Sediments and lava domes partly fill the caldera. (*After P. W. Lipman, The roots of ash flow calderas in western North America: Window into the tops of granitic batholiths, J. Geophys. Res., 89:8801–8841, 1984*)

pyroclastic material begins as gases (predominantly water) dissolved in the magma come out of solution at shallow depths. Magma is explosively fragmented into particles ranging in size from micrometers to meters. An eruption column develops, rising several miles into the atmosphere. This first and most explosive (Plinian) phase of the eruption covers the area around the vent with pumice. The Plinian phase erupts from a single conduit or from a group of closely spaced conduits. Caldera subsidence occurs during eruption, as shown by the thick wedge of ignimbrite (up to 3 mi or 5 km) within calderas (Fig. 3), and probably begins after about 20% of the total volume of associated pyroclastic material has been erupted. The thickness of intracaldera tuff (consolidated pyroclastic material) typically is much greater than that of the corresponding outflow sheets. Evidence for intermittent collapse is provided by landslide deposits, formed by the caving inward of the steep unstable walls, that interfinger

with pyroclastic rocks within the caldera, and by the presence of individual cooling units in the tuffs. *See* PYROCLASTIC ROCKS; TUFF.

As caldera subsidence proceeds and eruption becomes less explosive, the Plinian eruption column collapses. This collapse produces pyroclastic flows made of volcanic particles buoyed up and fluidized by hot gases (**Fig. 4**). These hot, ground-hugging flows can travel as far as 93 mi (150 km) outward from the vent at speeds of 330 ft/s (100 m/s). Successive collapses of the column produce multiple flow units with an aggregate thickness that may be several hundreds of feet thick near the caldera. Pyroclastic material may be erupted from multiple vents distributed around the ring fracture; vent geometry may shift during caldera subsidence. The ash and pumice of these ignimbrites are compacted, and individual particles are welded together by the intense heat (932–1112°F or 500–600°C) of the trapped gases.

Fig. 4. Pyroclastic flows from the eruption that accompanied collapse of the Crater Lake caldera in Oregon.

Postcollapse volcanism. Volcanism may resume following caldera collapse and cessation of the massive pyroclastic eruptions. This phase of activity is predominantly passive because the remaining magma is depleted in volatile components. Eruptive activity may begin shortly after caldera collapse and continue intermittently for millions of years. Eruptions may occur from vents within the caldera. Most prominent, however, are the eruptions of lava domes and flows from a series of vents along the ring fractures. These probably mark the intrusion of a ring dike, a feature exposed in some eroded calderas or in subvolcanic igneous centers such as the Mesozoic White Mountains (New Hampshire) and the Permian Oslo graben (Norway). In Valles caldera, New Mexico (Fig. 1), eight domes (up to 2300 ft or 700 m thick) and an obsidian flow were erupted along the main ring fracture from 1 million to about 50,000 years ago. *See* GRABEN; OBSIDIAN.

Resurgence. The floors of many of the largest calderas have been domed upward, resulting in a central massif or resurgent dome. A resurgent dome (Redondo Peak) is visible in the center of the Valles caldera (Fig. 1), and Samosir Island and Uluan are two sides of a single resurgent dome in Toba caldera (Fig. 2). Uplift, which probably occurs intermittently over a period of thousands of years, may exceed 0.6 mi (1 km). During resurgence, the caldera floor is forced upward so that geological units constituting the caldera fill—typically ignimbrite and landslide deposits, and possibly lake beds—have steep dips, often exceeding 45°, away from a central point or axis. Resurgence results from the continued or re-newed buoyant rise of magma after collapse. However, resurgence is not always so symmetrical, and instead it may cause broad uplift of adjacent areas of the volcanic field.

Geothermal systems. Calderas typically contain or are associated with extensive hydrothermal systems because of two factors: (1) the shallow magma chambers that underlie them provide a readily available source of heat; and (2) the floors of calderas may be extensively fractured, which condition, along with the main ring faults, allows meteoric water to penetrate deeply into the crust beneath calderas. Hydrothermal activity related to a caldera system can occur any time after magmas rise to shallow crustal levels, but it is dominant late in caldera evolution. In young calderas, such as those of the Yellowstone Plateau and Valles caldera, hydrothermal systems are still active. The spectacular geysers, hot springs, and boiling mud pots of Yellowstone National Park are part of the hydrothermal system associated with a series of three overlapping young calderas.

Magma bodies beneath large calderas cool slowly and may be important heat sources for as long as 2 million years following collapse. The hydrothermal system within Valles caldera (**Fig. 5**) is one of the best-studied systems in the world, largely because of extensive drilling to explore for potentially commercial quantities of geothermal energy. In this system, meteoric water percolates to a depth of 1.2–1.9 mi (2–3 km) in caldera-fill ignimbrites and precaldera volcanic rocks, where it is heated to temperatures of about 572°F (300°C). The heated water then rises convectively to depths of approximately 1640–1968 ft (500–600 m) before flowing laterally southwestward toward the caldera wall. A boiling interface at about 392°F (200°C) marks the upper surface of a convecting liquid-dominated system. Above this interface is a vapor-dominated zone containing steam, carbon dioxide (CO_2), hydrogen sulfide (H_2S), and other volatile components. Acid springs, mud pots, and fumaroles occur in a surface condensation zone a few feet thick. The present hydrothermal system was probably initiated about 1 million years ago, immediately after caldera collapse.

Mineralization. Many metals—including such base and precious metals as molybdenum, copper, lead, zinc, silver, gold, mercury, uranium, tungsten, and antimony—are mobile in hydrothermal circulation systems driven by the shallow intrusions which underlie and give rise to large calderas. Many economically important ore deposits in the western United Sates lie within calderas. However, the relationship of caldera collapse to mineralization is complex. Many mineral deposits are related to precaldera volcanism. Other mineral deposits are related to activity significantly after collapse (in some places by millions of years) and are simply localized by caldera structures. Deep core holes within Valles caldera indicates that mineralization is presently occurring there. *See* ORE AND MINERAL DEPOSITS.

Consequences to humans. Large pyroclastic eruptions associated with such giant (6 mi or 10 km or more in diameter) young calderas as Yellowstone, Long Valley (California), and Valles are, with the

VALLES CALDERA

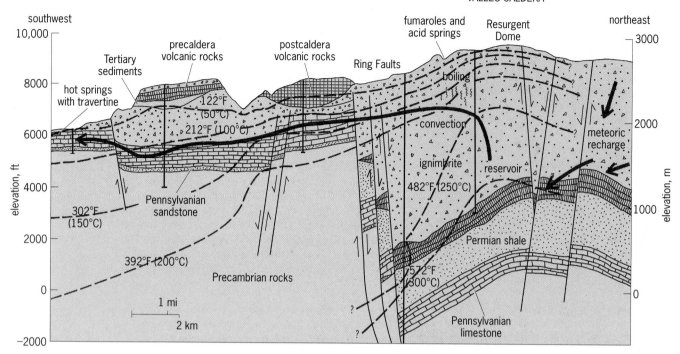

Fig. 5. Hydrothermal system beneath Valles caldera. Heavy vertical lines are drill or core holes. Heavy arrows are possible paths of thermal fluid flow. (*After F. Goff et al., The hydrothermal outflow plume of Valles caldera, New Mexico, and a comparison with other outflow plumes, J. Geophys. Res., 93:6041–6058, 1988*)

exception of impacts of large meteorites or asteroids, the most violent geological phenomena on Earth. In human terms, eruptions of this magnitude are rare, and none are yet documented in historical times.

Formation of several small calderas in the last few thousand years hints at the devastation that such giant caldera-forming eruptions could wreak. The greatest eruption of historical times was that of Tambora (Indonesia) in 1815, which created a caldera about 4 mi (6 km) in diameter. As many as 90,000 people were killed, either directly by the tephra (volcanic rock) fall and pyroclastic flows or by starvation and disease that followed. Ash fallout reached as far as 810 mi (1300 km) from the volcano; ash and sulfurous aerosols injected into the stratosphere are associated with abnormally low summer temperatures and crop failures the following year in the northeastern United States, Britain, and Europe. In approximately A.D. 260, an eruption was accompanied by formation of a caldera 5 × 7 mi (8 × 11 km) at Ilopango, devastating a wide area of central El Salvador. Thick ash flows swept as far as 28 mi (45 km) from the caldera, and ash covered much of El Salvador. Estimates of those killed or permanently displaced range from thousands to hundreds of thousands. The eruption ended Mayan society in the highlands, but migration of refugees stimulated the classic Mayan culture in lowland areas of Central America. In 1883, Krakatau (Indonesia) erupted explosively. The eruption formed a caldera some 5 mi (8 km) in diameter, the floor of which sank over 820 ft (250 m) below sea level. Displacement of the sea as it rushed to fill the void created a se-

ries of tsunamis, which killed over 36,000 people in Sumatra and Java. These examples suggest that a truly giant caldera-forming eruption could have catastrophic effect on human life both regionally and globally, with enormous economic and political consequences. *See* TSUNAMI.   W. Scott Baldridge

Bibliography. R. W. Decker and B. B. Decker, *Mountains of Fire: The Nature of Volcanoes*, Cambridge University Press, 1991; P. Francis, Giant volcanic calderas, *Sci. Amer.*, 248(6):60–70, 1983; T. Simkin and R. S. Fiske, *Krakatau 1883: The Volcanic Eruption and Its Effects*, Smithsonian Institution Press, 1983; K. Wohletz and G. Heiken, *Volcanology and Geothermal Energy*, 1989.

Calendar

A system that gives a name to each day. These day names are generally distinct, but not always. For example, the day of the week is a calendar, in a trivial sense, with infinitely many days having the same day name. The design of calendars has been driven by human needs varying over millennia, so the study of calendars is intricately bound to history, astronomy, and religion. Ancient calendars were based on simple observations of phenomena such as the waxing and waning of the Moon, the change in seasons, or the movement of heavenly bodies. Because observational methods suffer from the vagaries of weather and chance, modern calendars tend to be based solely on arithmetical rules, distanced from their motivation in nature.

Most calendars divide a year into an integral number of months and divide months into an integral number of days. However, these astronomical periods—day, month, and year—are incommensurate, so exactly how these time periods are coordinated and the accuracy with which they approximate their astronomical values are what differentiate one calendar from another. *See* DAY; EARTH ROTATION AND ORBITAL MOTION; MONTH; YEAR.

Dozens of calendars are still in use, in addition to the almost universally used Gregorian calendar. Many religious holidays and national events are determined by dates on these calendars. Many tables, algorithms, and rules of thumb for conversion of dates between calendars have been published. Solar calendars—including the Egyptian, Julian, Coptic, Ethiopic, Gregorian, and Persian—are based on the yearly solar cycle, whereas lunar calendars such as the Islamic and lunisolar calendars such as the Hebrew, Hindu, and Chinese take the monthly lunar cycle as the basic building block. Most solar calendars are divided into months, but these months are divorced from the lunar events; they are sometimes related to the movement of the Sun through the twelve signs of the zodiac.

Almost every calendar incorporates a notion of "leap" year to correct the cumulative error caused by approximating a year by an integral number of days and months. Solar calendars add a day every few years to keep up with the astronomical year.

Diurnal calendars. The simplest naming convention would be to assign an integer to each day; fixing day 1 would determine the whole calendar. The Babylonians had such a day count, as did the Maya and the Hindus. Such diurnal calendars are used by astronomers, especially those amateurs and professionals studying variable stars, who use Julian day numbers to specify dates. The Julian period, introduced in 1583 by Joseph Justus Scaliger, was originally a counting of years in a cycle of 7980 years, starting from 4713 B.C.E. (before the common era; or B.C.); nineteenth-century astronomers adapted the system into a strict counting of days backward and forward from JD0 = noon on Monday, January 1, 4713 B.C.E. (Julian) = noon on Monday, November 24, −4713 (Gregorian). A fractional part of a Julian day gives the fraction of a day beyond noon.

Computer scientists often use diurnal calendars as an intermediate device for converting from one calendar to another.

Solar calendars. The Gregorian calendar, now in common use throughout the world, is based on a 12-month year that closely approximates the Earth's solar cycle. This calendar was designed by a commission assembled by Pope Gregory XIII in the sixteenth century; the main author of the new system was the Naples astronomer Aloysius Lilius. This calendar is based on a 365-day common year divided into 12 months of lengths 31, 28, 31, 30, 31, 30, 31, 31, 30, 31, 30, and 31 days, and on 366 days in leap years, the extra day being added to make the second month 29 days long. A year is a leap year if it is divisible by 4 and is not a century year (multiple of 100) or if it

is divisible by 400. For example, 1900 is not a leap year; 2000 is a leap year. The Gregorian calendar differs from its predecessor, the Julian calendar, only in that the Julian calendar did not include the century rule for leap years—all century years were leap years.

A simpler solar calendar with a fixed year length of 365 days and no leap year rule was in use in Egypt for millennia prior to the adoption of the Julian calendar in the third century C.E. (common era), and was also used in Babylon and Persia. It served as the canonical calendar for astronomers until the sixteenth century. Each month had 30 days, and at the end of the year was an extra 5-day period, called epagomenae. Though this approximation to the tropical year results in a noticeable shift in the date of onset of the seasons, computationally such a calendar is extremely simple, and it persists in the Armenian calendar.

The Julian calendar was instituted on January 1, 709 *ab urbe condita* (from the traditional founding of Rome; about 45 B.C.E.) by Julius Caesar, with the help of the Alexandrian astronomer Sosigenes. The counting of years according to the Christian era was instituted by the Roman monk Dionysius Exiguus in the sixth century, but only became commonplace a few centuries later; Dionysius erred by a few years in his determination of the year of Jesus's birth. Dionysius did not invent the notion of "B.C."—his system started at 1. The year 1 B.C. is the year before 1 C.E. in the system introduced and popularized by the Venerable Bede around 731; the concept of zero as a number was then unknown in Europe. In this system, the number of years between January 1, x B.C.E., and January 1, y C.E., is $x + y - 1$ (not $x + y$). The use of a year 0 preceding year 1 on the Gregorian calendar is due to Jacques Cassini in 1740. *See* ZERO.

Since every fourth year on the Julian calendar was a leap year, a cycle of 4 years contained (4×365) $+ 1 = 1461$ days, giving an average length of year of 365.25 days. This is somewhat more than the mean length of the tropical year, and over the centuries the calendar slipped with respect to the seasons. By the sixteenth century, the date of the spring equinox had shifted from around March 21 to around March 11. If this error were not corrected, eventually Easter, whose date depends on that equinox, would migrate through the whole calendar year. Pope Gregory XIII instituted only a minor change in the calendar: century years not divisible by 400 would no longer be leap years. (He also improved the rules for Easter.) Thus, three out of four century years are common years, giving a cycle of 400 years containing (400×365) $+ 97 = 146,097$ days and an average year length of $146,097/400 = 365.2425$ days. He also corrected the accumulated 10-day error in the calendar by proclaiming that Thursday, October 4, 1582 C.E., the last date in the old-style (Julian) calendar, would be followed by Friday, October 15, 1582, the first day of the new-style (Gregorian) calendar. Catholic countries followed his rule, but Protestant countries resisted. Great Britain and its colonies (including the future United States) held out until 1752; Russia held out until 1918, after the Bolshevik Revolution. Different parts of what is now the United States changed over at different dates; Alaska, for example, changed only when it was purchased by the United States in 1867. Turkey did not switch to the Gregorian calendar until 1927.

An alternative to arithmetic rules to determine whether a year has 365 or 366 days is to fix the date of the new year according to some astronomical event. The Persian astronomical calendar, for example, uses the vernal (spring) equinox; the short-lived French Revolutionary calendar used the autumnal equinox.

Lunar calendars. The Islamic calendar is an example of a strictly lunar calendar, with no intercalation of months (unlike lunisolar calendars). Its independence of the solar cycle means that its months do not occur in fixed seasons but migrate through the solar year. Virtually all Moslems follow an observation-based calendar in which new moons (and hence months) are proclaimed by officials when that phase is seen. The calendar is computed, by the majority of the Moslem world, starting at sunset of Thursday, July 15, 622 C.E. (Julian), the year of Mohammed's hijra. The introduction of the calendar is often attributed to the Caliph 'Umar, in 639 C.E., but there is evidence that it was in use before his succession. Islamic astronomers developed an arithmetic approximation that is used for estimation. In it, there are 12 Islamic months, which contain, alternately, 30 or 29 days; the twelfth month contains 29 days in an ordinary year and contains 30 days in a leap year— the 2d, 5th, 7th, 10th, 13th, 16th, 18th, 21st, 24th, 26th, and 29th years of a 30-year cycle. This gives an average month of 29.5305555... days and an average year of 354 11/30 days.

Lunisolar calendars. Lunisolar calendars invariably alternate 12- and 13-month years. The so-called Metonic cycle is based on the observation that 19 solar years contain almost exactly 235 lunar months. This correspondence, named after the Athenian astronomer Meton and known much earlier to ancient Babylonian and Chinese astronomers, makes a relatively simple and accurate fixed solar/lunar calendar feasible. The $235 = (12 \times 12) + (7 \times 13)$ months in the cycle are divided into 12 years of 12 months and 7 leap years of 13 months. The 7 leap years are evenly distributed within the 19-year cycle, with gaps of 1 or 2 years between them. The Metonic cycle was used as the basis of lunisolar calendars in Mesopotamia from the fourth century B.C.E. and later in the Seleucid empire. It is (currently) accurate to within 6.5 minutes a year and is still employed in the Hebrew calendar (instituted in 359 C.E.) and for the ecclesiastical calculation of Easter (in both the Gregorian version and the Dionysian formulation of the earlier Nicaean rule). The Hebrew calendar has an average year length of 365.2468 days and month length of $29 + (13,753/25,920) \sim 29.530594$ days; the Gregorian calculation of Easter results in a mean month length of $29 + (37,405,943/70,499,183) \sim 29.530587$ days. Both these calendars may introduce a shift in the start of the year (of a day or two) for

technical purposes. (The Hebrew new year, Rosh HaShanah, for example, is not allowed to fall on the alternate days Sunday, Wednesday, and Friday; the calculated Easter full moon is not allowed to fall twice on the same Gregorian date within any one 19-year cycle.) The result is that the Hebrew calendar repeats only after 689,472 years and the ecclesiastical calendar after 5,700,000 years.

The 7-out-of-19 rule of the Metonic cycle is only one of many possibilities. Some of the older Hindu lunisolar calendars evenly distribute 66,389 leap months over 360,000 years.

Alternatively, a lunisolar calendar can follow astronomically determined patterns, as in the Chinese and Hindu, in which each month begins with a new moon, and a thirteenth month is added whenever there are 13 new moons within a solar year. The Chinese calendar has undergone numerous reforms, but since 1645 C.E. it has used astronomical calculations to fix the start of years and months. The current Hindu lunisolar calendar, based on the algorithm of the *Surya Siddhanta* (circa 1000 C.E.), employs Ptolemaic methods. The latter is distinguished by the occasional occurrence of expunged months and days.   Nachum Dershowitz; Edward M. Reingold

Bibliography. L. E. Doggett, Calendars, *Explanatory Supplement to the Astronomical Almanac*, ed. by P. K. Seidelmann, University Science Books, Mill Valley, CA, 1992; J. Meeus, *Astronomical Algorithms*, 2d ed., Willmann-Bell, Richmond, VA, 1998; E. M. Reingold and N. Dershowitz, *Calendrical Calculations: The Millennium Edition*, Cambridge University Press, Cambridge, 2000; E. G. Richards, *Mapping Time: The Calendar and Its History*, Oxford University Press, Oxford, 1998.

Calibration

The process of determining the performance parameters of an artifact, instrument, or system by comparing its performance with measurement standards. Adjustment may be part of calibration but not necessarily. It is essential that there be an unbroken traceability chain between the measurement standards being used and the appropriate national measurement standards.

All calibrations involve one or more measurement processes, which may be simple or complex. A calibration can be used to ensure that a device or system will produce results which meet or exceed some defined criteria with a specified degree of confidence. The measurement standards, the process, and the device or system being calibrated must be capable of satisfying these defined criteria.

Two concepts related to calibration are precision and accuracy. Precision refers to the minimum discernible change in the parameter being measured, while accuracy refers to the uncertainty in the measurement process.

All measurement processes used for calibration are subject to various sources of uncertainty. It is now common practice to classify them as Type A or Type B uncertainties. These approximate to the previous classification into random and systematic uncertainties, respectively. Care must be taken in classifying uncertainties. For example, a "random" component of uncertainty in one measurement may become a "systematic" component of uncertainty in another measurement in which the result of the first measurement is used as an input datum. Type A uncertainties can be estimated as a result of repeated measurements and are amenable to treatment by statistical methods. A Type B uncertainty is obtained by careful consideration of the measurement process, for example, from an estimate of the possible error in the measurement due to the effect of an influence quantity such as temperature. If the error can be calculated reliably, a correction can be made to the result. Otherwise, an estimate is made of the possible uncertainty due to this effect, and it can be incorporated into the uncertainty calculation as a Type B contribution. The two types of uncertainty can be combined by approved methods to give the total uncertainty of the measurement.

A document published by the International Organization for Standardization (ISO), *Guide to the Expression of Uncertainty in Measurement* (popularly known as *GUM*), gives the currently accepted approach to the estimation of uncertainties. Other documents give slightly simplified approaches that are consistent with the ISO standard; most of these can be downloaded from Web sites. *See* ANALYSIS OF VARIANCE; DISTRIBUTION (PROBABILITY); INSTRUMENT SCIENCE; PHYSICAL MEASUREMENT; PROBABILITY; PROBABILITY (PHYSICS); STATISTICS.   R. Gareth Jones

Bibliography. *Guide to the Expression of Uncertainty in Measurement*, 2d ed., International Organization for Standardization, Geneva, 1995.

Caliche

A soil that is mineralogically an impure limestone. Such soils are also known as duricrust, kunkar, nari, kafkalla, Omdurman lime, croute, and race. Many soil profiles in semiarid climates (that is, those characterized by a rainfall of 4–20 in. or 10–50 cm per year) contain concentrations of calcium carbonate ($CaCO_3$). This calcium carbonate is not an original feature of the soils but has been added to the C horizon during soil formation either by direct precipitation in soil pores or by replacement of preexisting material. Fossil analogs of caliche, which are widely reported in ancient sedimentary sequences, are referred to as calcrete or cornstone. *See* LIMESTONE.

Formation. The principal control on the formation of caliche is a hydrologic regime in which there is sufficient moisture to introduce calcium carbonate in solution to the soil but not enough to leach it through the system. As a result, calcium carbonate precipitates in the soil during periods of evaporation, and it will slowly increase in amount as long as the hydrologic setting remains stable. The source of the carbonate may be from the dissolution of adjacent limestones, from the hydrolysis of plagioclase and other silicates, or from carbonate loess.

Within the climatic constraints noted above, most caliche forms in river floodplains and near the surface of alluvial fans. In addition, caliche deposits may form within exposed marine and lacustrine limestones during periods of sea-level fall or lake desiccation. Caliche may also form at inert pediment (eroded rock) surfaces; in the geological record such surfaces will be seen as unconformities. In this context it is interesting that the first unconformity ever recognized as such, by James Hutton in 1787 on the Isle of Arran, western Scotland, is characterized by a development of caliche. *See* UNCONFORMITY.

The mineralogy of the host soil or rock in which a caliche develops may vary considerably; it is not essential for there to be any preexisting carbonate grains within the regolith. The most favorable medium is a clay-rich soil of limited permeability. Low permeability provides the residence time in the soil pores necessary for calcite to precipitate. *See* CALCITE; REGOLITH.

Textures. A variety of textures records the growth of the calcrete. Initially, small nodules of limestone nucleate within the soil; these nodules are usually roughly spherical but may form as elongate tubules and filaments. The latter probably form as casts around roots in the soil. Subsequently, nodules coalesce to form an increasingly solid mass of carbonate, and as a result the soil becomes increasingly rocklike. Eventually the soil profile may become plugged by a massive impermeable limestone. Above the plugged horizon a perched aquifer develops; further calcite precipitation above such a horizon may produce laminated and pisolitic deposits. Continued addition of calcite may result in the buckling and brecciation of laminae. Deoxygenated conditions may develop below the plugged zone; in the reducing environment so formed, elements held in solution in oxygenated waters may precipitate (for example, uranium). *See* OOLITE.

Microscopic fabrics in caliche are initially very fine-grained mosaics of nonferroan low-magnesian calcite crystals. However, more complicated fabrics develop as the paleosol matures. Repeated wetting and drying of the soil results in expansion and contraction of the soil; as a result nodules frequently show signs of multiple cracking. Typically these cracks have been healed because of the precipitation of coarse drusy calcite. This later calcite may be ferroan, that is, may contain some iron. Noncarbonate grains in the caliche usually show signs of intense chemical corrosion and may show signs of physical displacement by precipitating calcite crystals. During the mature stage of development, highly alkaline conditions may develop in caliches. In such conditions quartz in the soil profile may temporarily pass into solution and subsequently reprecipitate as chert, forming a silcrete. *See* CHERT; PALEOSOL.

Mature profile. When the full range of textures referred to above is developed, the caliche is regarded as a mature profile. The vertical profile of such a

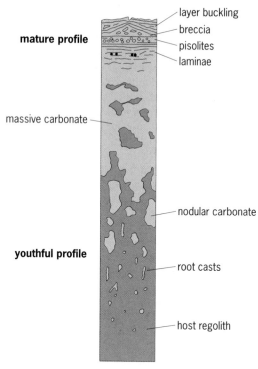

mature profile

layer buckling
breccia
pisolites
laminae

massive carbonate

youthful profile

nodular carbonate

root casts

host regolith

Typical profie through a mature caliche. The lower part of the profile is essentially a mimic of a juvenile caliche.

caliche (see **illus.**) shows a characteristic sequence passing downward from a laminated carbonate into a massive limestone, which in turn passes into increasingly more disconnected nodules. Thus the vertical profile recapitulates the growth of the caliche.

Fully mature caliche profiles may be up to 40 ft (12 m) thick, although 10–20 ft (3–6 m) is more typical. Various workers have tried to estimate the length of time required for the development of a mature caliche. Values of the order of 10,000 years are typical of such estimates. Such lengths of time imply the existence of an environment of great geomorphic stability as continued growth of the caliche requires a constant hydrologic regime. Major fluctuations of climate, variations in base level, and major pulses of tectonic activity are precluded. Environmental stability during caliche formation means that such horizons function as "time lines" in the geological record. In other words, they are important chronostratigraphic markers that permit correlation between adjacent sequences, and thus they help unravel geological history in a more rigorous fashion than would otherwise be the case. *See* SOIL.   Nowell Donovan

Bibliography. V. P. Wright (ed.), *Paleosols: Their Recognition and Interpretation*, 1986.

Caliciales

An order of the Ascolichenes. This order is characterized by an unusual apothecium. The hymenial layer originates normally, but by the time the spores are mature, the asci and paraphyses have partially disintegrated into a mass of spores and hymenial tissues

known as a mazaedium. In the family Caliciaceae the disk is borne on a short stalk 0.04–0.32 in. (1–8 mm) high, a peculiar structure that is also known in the nonlichenized Roesleriaceae. These two families are so close that some species in either one may or may not lichenize symbiotic algae. The primary thallus of the Caliciaceae is a powdery grayish or lemon-yellow crust on soil or rotten wood. There are six genera separated by spore septation and color. The family Cypheliaceae with seven genera is more typically crustose, with sessile apothecia and a more fully developed thallus. The Sphaerophoraceae are fruticose, much like *Cladonia* sp., but the thallus is solid. The apothecia are open or enclosed in a spherical chamber at the tips of branches. The largest genus, *Sphaerophorus*, is widespread in boreal zones and mountains of both hemispheres.   Mason E. Hale

Californium

A chemical element, Cf, atomic number 98, the ninth member of the actinide series of elements. Its discovery and production have been based upon artificial nuclear transmutation of radioactive isotopes of lighter elements. All isotopes of californium are radioactive, with half-lives ranging from a minute to about 1000 years. Because of its nuclear instability, californium does not exist in the Earth's crust. *See* ACTINIDE ELEMENTS; BERKELIUM; PERIODIC TABLE; RADIOACTIVITY.

The chemical properties are similar to those observed for other 3+ actinide elements: a water-soluble nitrate, sulfate, chloride, and perchlorate. Californium is precipitated as the fluoride, oxalate, or hydroxide. Ion-exchange chromatography can be used for the isolation and identification of californium in the presence of other actinide elements. Californium metal is quite volatile and can be distilled at temperatures of the order of 1100–1200°C (2010–2190°F). It is chemically reactive and appears to exist in three different crystalline modifications between room temperature and its melting point, 900°C (1600°F).

The most easily produced isotope for many purposes is ^{252}Cf, which is obtained in gram quantities in nuclear reactors and has a half-life of 2.6 years. It

1																	18
1 H	2											13	14	15	16	17	2 He
3 Li	4 Be											5 B	6 C	7 N	8 O	9 F	10 Ne
11 Na	12 Mg	3	4	5	6	7	8	9	10	11	12	13 Al	14 Si	15 P	16 S	17 Cl	18 Ar
19 K	20 Ca	21 Sc	22 Ti	23 V	24 Cr	25 Mn	26 Fe	27 Co	28 Ni	29 Cu	30 Zn	31 Ga	32 Ge	33 As	34 Se	35 Br	36 Kr
37 Rb	38 Sr	39 Y	40 Zr	41 Nb	42 Mo	43 Tc	44 Ru	45 Rh	46 Pd	47 Ag	48 Cd	49 In	50 Sn	51 Sb	52 Te	53 I	54 Xe
55 Cs	56 Ba	71 Lu	72 Hf	73 Ta	74 W	75 Re	76 Os	77 Ir	78 Pt	79 Au	80 Hg	81 Tl	82 Pb	83 Bi	84 Po	85 At	86 Rn
87 Fr	88 Ra	103 Lr	104 Rf	105 Db	106 Sg	107 Bh	108 Hs	109 Mt	110 Ds	111 Rg	112	113					

lanthanide series	57 La	58 Ce	59 Pr	60 Nd	61 Pm	62 Sm	63 Eu	64 Gd	65 Tb	66 Dy	67 Ho	68 Er	69 Tm	70 Yb

actinide series	89 Ac	90 Th	91 Pa	92 U	93 Np	94 Pu	95 Am	96 Cm	97 Bk	98 Cf	99 Es	100 Fm	101 Md	102 No

decays partially by spontaneous fission, and has been very useful for the study of fission. It has also had an important influence on the development of counters and electronic systems with applications not only in nuclear physics but in medical research as well. *See* TRANSURANIUM ELEMENTS.   Glenn T. Seaborg

Bibliography. B. B. Cunningham, Berkelium and californium, *J. Chem. Educ.*, 36:32–37, 1959; B. B. Cunningham, Chemistry of the actinide elements, *Annu. Rev. Nucl. Sci.*, 14:323–346, 1964; S. Hofmann, *On Beyond Uranium: Journey to the End of the Periodic Table*, 2002; J. J. Katz, G. T. Seaborg, and L. R. Morss (eds.), *The Chemistry of the Actinide Elements*, 2 vols., 2d ed., 1986.

Caliper

An instrument with two legs used for measuring linear dimensions. Calipers may be fixed, adjustable, or movable. Fixed calipers are used in routine inspection of standard products; adjustable calipers are used similarly but can be reset to slightly different dimensions if necessary. Movable calipers can be set to match the distance being measured. The legs may pivot about a rivet or screw in a firm-joint pair of calipers; they may pivot about a pin, being held against the pin by a spring and set in position by a knurled nut on a threaded rod; or the legs may slide either directly (caliper rule) or along a screw (micrometer caliper) relative to each other. *See* MICROMETER.

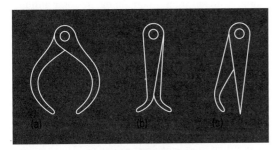

Some typical machinist's calipers. (*a*) Outside. (*b*) Inside. (*c*) Hermaphrodite. (*After R. J. Sweeney, Measurement Techniques in Mechanical Engineering, Wiley, 1953*)

The legs may be shaped to facilitate measuring outside dimensions, inside dimensions, surface dimensions as between points on a plate, or from a surface into a hole as in a keyway (see **illus.**). Other forms are adapted to special needs. *See* GAGES.   Frank H. Rockett

Callitrichales

An order of flowering plants, division Magnoliophyta (Angiospermae), in the subclass Asteridae of the class Magnoliopsida (dicotyledons). The order consists of three small families with about 50 species, most of which are aquatics or small herbs of wet places, and have much reduced vascular systems. The flowers are small and solitary in the axils of leaves or bracts. The perianth is nearly or completely absent. The pistil consists of two carpels united to form a compound, unilocular or four-chambered ovary, or sometimes the pistil appears to be of a single carpel. The Callitrichales are placed in the Asteridae largely on the basis of their embryology and phytochemistry. The ovules are anatropous and tenuinucellular and have a single integument, and the plants generally produce iridoid substances. *See* ASTERIDAE; MAGNOLIOPHYTA; MAGNOLIOPSIDA; PLANT KINGDOM.   T. M. Barkley

Calobryales

An order of liverworts. They are characterized by prostrate, simple or branched, leafless stems and erect, leafy branches of a radial organization. The order consists of a single genus, *Calobryum*, and 12 species, most of them occupying restricted ranges in apparently relic areas indicative of an ancient origin and dispersal. The order is considered primitive in comparison with the Jungermanniales, in which the leafy axis tends to be prostrate and the underleaves reduced.

The stems are thick and fleshy, with no differentiated outer layers. Rhizoids are lacking. The leaves may be small or lacking below, larger and more crowded above. They are three-ranked, with those of one rank sometimes more or less reduced. They are broad, unlobed, and entire. The cells, large and thin-walled, are often two- or three-layered at the leaf base. Slime papillae at the base of leaves secrete mucilage. The antheridia occur in axils of upper leaves or in terminal clusters subtended by three leaves; the stalk is long, four-seriate, and enlarged above. The archegonia are clustered in a terminal disk but in the absence of fertilization become lateral; the neck is long and four-seriate. The sporophyte is protected by a cylindric upgrowth of gametophytic tissue. The seta consists of numerous rows of cells, and the long-ellipsoid capsule dehisces by four valves remaining attached at the tip. The wall is unistratose below and bistratose at the apex; its cells have one or two longitudinally oriented bands. The haploid chromosome number is 9. *See* BRYOPHYTA; HEPATICOPSIDA; JUNGERMANNIALES; JUNGERMANNIIDAE.

Howard Crum

Bibliography. E. O. Campbell, The structure and development of *Calobryum gibbsiae* Steph., *Trans. Roy. Soc. N. Z.* 47:243–254; R. M. Schuster, Studies on Hepaticae, XV: Calobryales, *Nova Hedwigia*, 13:1–63, 1966.

Calomel

Mercury(I) chloride, Hg_2Cl_2, a covalent compound which is insoluble in water. The substance sublimes when heated. The formula weight is 472.086 and the specific gravity is 7.16 at 20°C (68°F). The material is a white, impalpable powder consisting of fine tetragonal crystals. Calomel is manufactured by precipitation when sodium chloride is added to a solution of mercury(I) nitrate or by direct combination of the elements.

Calomel is used in preparing insecticides and medicines. It is well known in the laboratory as the constituent of the calomel reference electrodes which are commonly used in conjunction with a glass electrode to measure pH. *See* MERCURY (ELEMENT); REFERENCE ELECTRODE.   E. Eugene Weaver

Calorimetry

The measurement of the quantity of heat energy involved in processes such as chemical reactions, changes of state, and mixing of substances, or in the determination of heat capacities of substances. The unit of energy in the International System of Units is the joule, symbolized J. Another unit still being used, but is strongly discouraged, is the calorie, symbolized cal and defined as 4.184 J. Most calorimetric measurements are made at constant pressure, and the measured change is called the enthalpy change. *See* ENTHALPY; HEAT CAPACITY.

Types of calorimeters. A calorimeter is an apparatus for measuring the quantity of heat energy released or absorbed during a process. Since there are many processes that can be studied over a wide range of temperature and pressure, a large variety of calorimeters have been developed.

Nonisothermal calorimeters. These instruments measure the temperature change that occurs during the process. An aneroid (containing no liquid) nonisothermal (temperature varying during the experiment) calorimeter is normally constructed of a material having a high thermal conductivity, such as copper, so that there is rapid temperature equilibration. It is isolated from its surroundings by a high vacuum to reduce heat leaks. This type of calorime-

ter can be used for determining the heat capacity of materials at low temperatures. Aneroid nonisothermal calorimeters have also been developed for measuring the energy of combustion for small samples of rare materials.

Another type of nonisothermal calorimeter uses a large quantity of liquid as a heat sink, so that even if there is a large amount of energy released in the process the temperature rise is not excessive. The liquid is kept at a uniform temperature by stirring, and the change in temperature can be measured accurately. In general, the size of the liquid heat sink is designed so that the temperature change is of the order of 5 K (9 °F). For measurements near room temperature, water is commonly used as the working fluid; measurements at higher temperatures use less volatile organic liquids.

With most nonisothermal calorimeters, it is necessary to relate the temperature rise to the quantity of energy released in the process. This is done by determining the calorimeter constant, which is the amount of energy required to increase the temperature of the calorimeter itself by 1 K. This value can be determined by measurement on a well-defined test system or by electrical calibration. In bomb calorimetry, for example, the calorimeter constant is usually determined from the temperature rise that occurs when a known mass of a very pure standard sample of benzoic acid is burned. Electrical calibration, however, is complex and often does not mimic the way that energy is released during the reaction.

Isothermal calorimeters. These instruments make measurements at constant temperature. The simplest example is a calorimeter containing an outer annular space filled with a liquid in equilibrium with a crystalline solid at its melting point, arranged so that any volume change will displace mercury along a capillary tube. The Bunsen ice calorimeter operates at 0 °C (32 °F) with a mixture of ice and water. Changes resulting from the process being studied cause the ice to melt or the water to freeze, and the consequent volume change is determined by measurement of the movement of the mercury meniscus in the capillary tube. While these calorimeters can yield accurate results, their operation is limited to the equilibrium temperature of the two-phase system. Other types of isothermal calorimeters use electrical energy to achieve exact balance of the heat absorption that occurs during an endothermic process. Generally, calorimeters based on this principle are more accurate than similar nonisothermal calorimeters. Many mixing and flow calorimeters operate in this mode.

Calorimeter components. All calorimeters consist of the calorimeter proper and a jacket or a bath, which is used to control the temperature of the calorimeter and the rate of heat leak to the environment. For temperatures not too far removed from room temperature, the jacket or bath contains liquid at a controlled temperature. For measurements at extreme temperatures, the jacket usually consists of a metal block containing a heater to control the temperature. With nonisothermal calorimeters, where

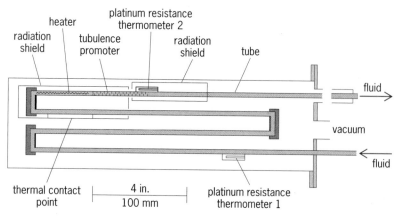

Fig. 1. High-pressure flow calorimeter for measurement of heat capacity. (*After G. Ernst, G. Maurer, and E. Wiederoh, Flow calorimeter for the accurate determination of the isobaric heat capacity at high pressures: Results for carbon dioxide, J. Chem. Thermodyn., 21:53–65, 1989*)

the jacket is kept at a constant temperature, there will be some heat leak to the jacket when the temperature of the calorimeter changes. It is necessary to correct the temperature change observed to the value it would have been if there were no leak. This is achieved by measuring the temperature of the calorimeter before and after the process and applying Newton's law of cooling. This correction can be avoided by using the technique of adiabatic (no energy loss or gain with the surroundings) calorimetry, where the temperature of the jacket is kept equal to the temperature of the calorimeter as a change occurs. This technique requires more elaborate temperature control, and its primary use is for accurate heat capacity measurements at low temperatures.

Thermometry. In calorimetric experiments, it is necessary to measure temperature differences accurately; in some cases, the temperature itself must be accurately known. Modern calorimeters use resistance thermometers to measure both temperatures and temperature differences, while thermocouples or thermistors are used to measure smaller temperature differences. A calibrated standard platinum resistance thermometer can measure temperature differences to 0.00001 °C and temperatures ranging from −260 °C to 630 °C (−436 °F to 1166 °F) with an uncertainty of ±0.001 °C. Multiple-junction thermocouples and thermistors can measure smaller temperature differences, allowing precise measurements of very small heat effects. *See* TEMPERATURE MEASUREMENT; THERMISTOR; THERMOCOUPLE; THERMOMETER.

Calorimetric measurements. Heat capacities of materials and energies of combustion are processes that are routinely measured with calorimeters. Calorimeters are also used to measure the heat involved in phase changes, for example, the change from a liquid to a solid (fusion) or from a liquid to a gas (vaporization). Calorimetry has also been applied to the measurement of the enthalpy of hydrogenation of unsaturated organic compounds, the enthalpy of dissolution of a solid in a liquid, or the enthalpy change on mixing two liquids.

Heat-capacity calorimeter. Heat capacities of gases or liquid can be determined in a flow calorimeter. Some essential features are shown in **Fig. 1**. A known mass of fluid flowing at a constant rate is pumped through the calorimeter. The inlet temperature is measured with thermometer 1. The fluid is heated with a known amount of electrical energy, and the change in temperature is observed at thermometer 2. The radiation shields reduce heat losses to the surroundings.

Enthalpy-of-vaporization calorimeter. A modern enthalpy-of-vaporization calorimeter is shown in **Fig. 2**. The material in the vaporization vessel is heated with a known amount of electrical energy, and the mass of material vaporized is determined from the change in mass of the glass collection vessel. The thermostated shields, which are maintained at the same temperature as the vaporization vessel, ensure that all the electrical energy goes to vaporize

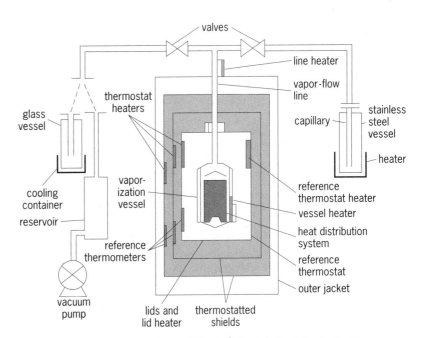

Fig. 2. Heat-of-vaporization calorimeter. (After L. Šváb et al., A calorimeter for the determination of enthalpies of vaporization at high temperatures and pressures, J. Chem. Thermodyn., 20:545–550, 1988**)**

the sample and none is lost to the surroundings. *See* CHEMICAL THERMODYNAMICS; HEAT TRANSFER; THERMOCHEMISTRY; THERMODYNAMIC PRINCIPLES.

Kenneth N. Marsh

Bibliography. K. N. Marsh and P. G. O'Hare (eds.), *IUPAC Experimental Thermodynamics*, vol. IV: *Solution Calorimetry*, 1994; J. P. McCullough and D. W. Scott (eds.), *Experimental Thermodynamics*, vol. 1: *Calorimetry of Non-Reacting Systems*, 1968; M. L. McGlashan, *Chemical Thermodynamics*, 1979; J. H. Moore and N. D. Spencer (eds.), *Encyclopedia of Chemical Physics and Physical Chemistry*, vol. 2, B1.27: *Calorimetry*, 2001; W. R. Parrish, Recent advances in calorimetry, *Fluid Phase Equil.*, 29:172–192, 1986; R. S. Porter and J. F. Johnson (eds.), *Analytical Chemistry*, vols. 2-4, 1970-1977; M. Sorai, *Comprehensive Handbook of Calorimetry and Thermal Analysis*, 2004.

Calycerales

An order of flowering plants, division Magnoliophyta (Angiospermae), in the subclass Asteridae of the class Magnoliopsida (dicotyledons). The order consists of a single family with about 60 species native to tropical America. The plants are herbs with alternate, simple leaves that do not have stipules. The flowers are borne in involucrate heads with centripetal flowering sequence. The calyx is reduced to small lobes or teeth, and the corolla consists of (4)5(6) fused lobes and is regular or somewhat irregular. The stamens are attached near the summit of the corolla tube, and the filaments are more or less connate. The pistil consists of two united carpels, which form a compound, inferior ovary wth a single, pendulous ovule. The order Calycerales is sometimes included within the Dipsacales, and the order has attracted attention because of the overall resemblance of the inflorescence to that of the Asteraceae. *See* ASTERALES; ASTERIDAE; DIPSACALES; MAGNOLIOPHYTA; MAGNOLIOPSIDA; PLANT KINGDOM.   T. M. Barkley

Cam mechanism

A mechanical linkage whose purpose is to produce, by means of a contoured cam surface, a prescribed motion of the output link of the linkage, called the follower. Cam and follower are a higher pair. *See* LINKAGE (MECHANISM).

A familiar application of a cam mechanism is in the opening and closing of valves in an automotive engine (**Fig. 1**). The cam rotates with the cam shaft,

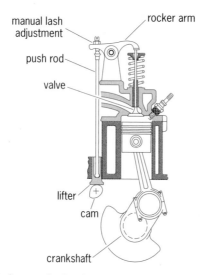

Fig. 1. Cam mechanism for opening and closing valves in automotive engine. (*Texaco, Inc.*)

usually at constant angular velocity, while the follower moves up and down as controlled by the cam surface. A cam is sometimes made in the form of a translating cam (**Fig. 2a**). Other cam mechanisms, employed in elementary mechanical analog computers, are simple memory devices, in which the position of the cam (input) determines the position of the follower (output or readout).

Although many requisite motions in machinery are accomplished by use of pin-joined mechanisms, such as four-bar linkages, a cam mechanism frequently is the only practical solution to the problem of converting the available input, usually rotating or reciprocating, to a desired output, which may be an exceedingly complex motion. No other mechanism is as versatile and as straightforward in design. However, a cam may be difficult and costly to manufacture, and it is often noisy and susceptible to wear, fatigue, and vibration.

Cams are used in many machines. They are numerous in automatic packaging, shoemaking, typesetting machines, and the like, but are often found as well in machine tools, reciprocating engines, and

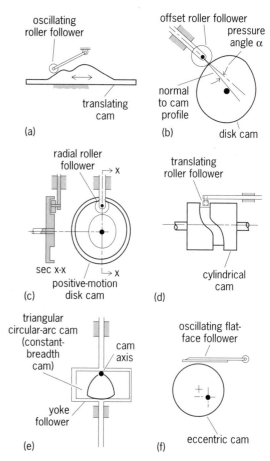

Fig. 2. Classification of cams. (*a*) Translating. (*b*) Disk. (*c*) Positive motion. (*d*) Cylindrical. (*e*) With yoke follower. (*f*) With flat-face follower.

compressors. They are occasionally used in rotating machinery.

Cams are classified as translating, disk, plate, cylindrical, or drum (Fig. 2). The link having the contoured surface that prescribes the motion of the follower is called the cam. Cams are usually made of steel, often hardened to resist wear and, for high-speed application, precisely ground.

The output link, which is maintained in contact with the cam surface, is the follower. Followers are classified by their shape as roller, flat face, and spherical face (**Fig. 3**). The point or knife-edge follower is of academic interest in developing cam profile relationships. Followers are also described by the nature of their constraints, for example, radial, in which motion is reciprocating along a radius from the cam's axis of rotation (Fig. 1); offset, in which motion is reciprocating along a line that does not intersect the axis of rotation (Fig. 2b); and oscillating, or pivoted (Fig. 2a. Three-dimensional cam-and-follower

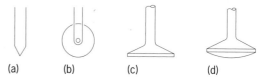

Fig. 3. Cam followers. (*a*) Knife edge. (*b*) Roller. (*c*) Flat face. (*d*) Spherical face.

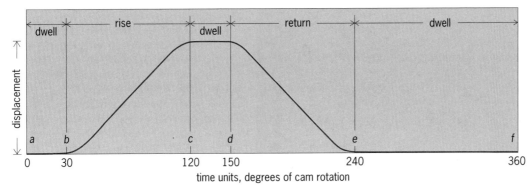

Fig. 4. Displacement-time diagram for a cam, with motion of cam follower indicated.

systems are coming into more frequent use, where the follower may travel over a lumpy surface.

Motion of cam follower. The first step in the design of a cam mechanism is the determination of the motion of the cam follower. In a packaging machine, for example, the ends of a carton may be folded by cam-operated fingers that advance at the proper times, retract as soon as the fold has been made, and then rest or dwell until the next carton is in position. The motion of the cam follower, which in turn moves the folder fingers, can be represented by a displacement-time diagram (**Fig. 4**). The time axis is usually laid off in degrees of cam rotation. The conventional meanings of follower dwell, rise, and return are indicated in the figure.

The maximum displacement of the follower and the periods of dwell are determined, more or less arbitrarily, by the designer, who has the choice of any curve to connect the dwell portions of the complete displacement-time diagram. The practical form for this curve is determined largely by the maximum acceleration that can be tolerated by the follower linkage. In addition, the pressure angle (α in Fig. 2b) must be kept fairly small, usually less than 30°, to avoid undue friction and possible jamming of the reciprocating follower in its guides. The space that is available for the cam will affect the maximum pressure angle. Usually, a small cam is preferred; yet the larger the cam can be made (which in effect physically increases the length of the time axis for the same time interval), the smaller the maximum pressure angle will be. The final form may further represent a compromise to make possible economical manufacture of the cam.

If the diagram of Fig. 4 were laid out on and cut out of steel and a knife-edge follower were constrained

to move vertically, the translating cam mechanism of **Fig. 5a** would result. The process of wrapping this translating cam around a disk (Fig. 5b), thus producing a disk cam whose follower action would be similar to that of Fig. 5a, can be visualized readily. The introduction of a roller or flat-face follower complicates the determination of the actual cam contour that will produce a desired follower displacement-time relationship; but recognition of the similarity between the displacement-time diagram and the final cam contour makes it easier to visualize the conditions that must be met to design a cam that will operate satisfactorily.

Consider the dwell-rise-dwell portion of the curve of Fig. 4. Displacement of the follower might be plotted arbitrarily as a straight line (**Fig. 6a**).

The slope $\Delta s/\Delta t$ of a displacement-time ($s-t$) curve is equal to velocity ($s/t = v$) so that velocity of the follower from A to B (dwell) will be zero, from B to C it will be constant and finite, and from C to D velocity will be zero again (Fig. 6b).

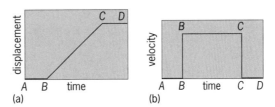

Fig. 6. Effect of (a) displacement on (b) velocity.

The slope $\Delta v//\Delta t = a$ of the velocity-time curve is correspondingly equal to acceleration. Thus, the acceleration of the follower necessary to increase velocity from zero to a finite value in zero time (B to B in Fig. 6b) is infinite. Likewise, the deceleration that occurs at C must also be infinite. The acceleration along the constant velocity line, from B to C, would be zero. Thus the curve chosen in Fig. 6a for displacement is unrealistic because of the high inertial forces that would result from abrupt changes of velocity.

Choice of acceleration curve. Therefore, a curve having a gradual transition from dwell to maximum velocity is necessary. Three such curves are plotted in **Fig. 7** and are superimposed in **Fig. 8** for comparison. The derived curves for velocity and acceleration are also plotted so comparisons may be made.

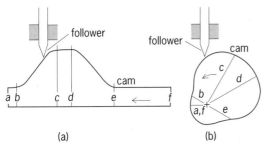

Fig. 5. Converting (a) translating cam to (b) disk cam.

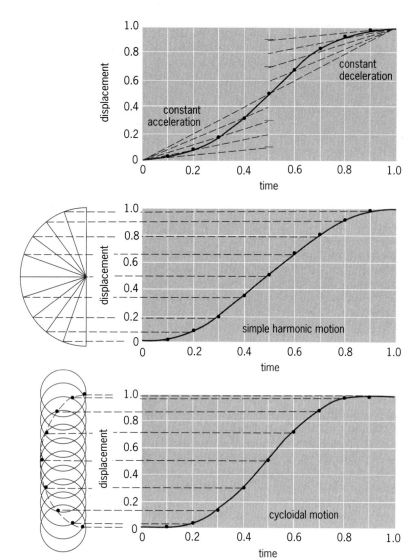

Fig. 7. Displacement-time diagrams for cam contours.

The cycloidal curve is plotted by projecting points from a cycloid whose generating circle has a diameter equal to follower displacement divided by π, as in Fig. 7. This curve has desirable acceleration characteristics, but requires that the cam face be accurately machined at the beginning and end of rise to accomplish in fact the theoretical performance.

Comparison of the three curves is shown in Fig. 8. The cycloidal curve exhibits a higher pressure angle α for a radial translating follower than the other curves, but its acceleration characteristics are much superior.

Today's extensive use of cams and the extreme demands upon them under increasing speeds of modern manufacturing have yielded still another form of cam profile, which might be called catenoidal because of its association with the catenary [the curve in which a rope or chain (catena) hangs freely]. This curve has an equation expressed primarily in terms of exponential functions ϵ^x, whose slope variation is a curve with the remarkable property that it partakes of the same general form as the original function. Hence the velocity and acceleration curves show

The constant acceleration–constant deceleration curve, in which displacement s is proportional to t^2, is desirable except for the instantaneous reversal of acceleration at the point of maximum velocity; such a reversal would cause high stresses in the mechanism. If the follower were spring-loaded, a heavy spring would be required to prevent the follower's leaving the cam face momentarily, with resulting shock to the linkage as it returned.

The simple harmonic displacement curve is plotted by projecting onto the diameter (equal to follower displacement) of a circle a point moving with constant velocity around the circle's circumference. Although maximum acceleration is higher than in the preceding curve, the abrupt changes of acceleration occur only at the beginning and end of the rise. Both of these curves have been used in cam design; both are satisfactory if speeds are low to moderate and follower mass is not large. However, serious difficulties are encountered when high speeds or heavy followers accentuate the stresses resulting from acceleration.

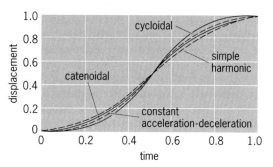

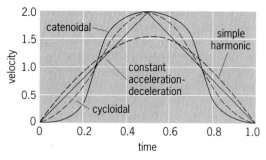

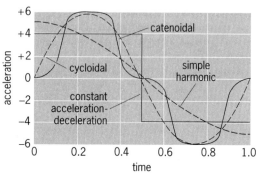

Fig. 8. Comparison of motions for three shapes of rise-return regions. Fourth motion, for catenoidal shape, also superposed. (*After G. L. Guillet and A. H. Church, Kinematics of Machines, 5th ed., Wiley, 1950*)

patterns similar to that of displacement rather than being so different, as was markedly so with the constant acceleration-deceleration profile, and less so with others. This curve (catenoidal) also is shown in the figures; it is alleged to give even smoother performance and less vibration than the cycloidal type. Its slope (jerk) will be zero four times in each cycle.

The manufacture of cam and follower from a master model is dwindling in favor of manufacture using a computer tape, which accurately directs the cutting of the surface. This procedure avoids the expensive manufacture of master cams.

In certain high-speed cam mechanisms, for example, an automotive engine valve gear, the elasticity and vibration characteristics of the follower linkage must be taken into account if faulty operation is to be avoided. The polydyne method derives its name from use of a polynomial displacement curve that suits the dynamic characteristics of the follower linkage.

Construction of cam profile. Empirically, a cam profile can be plotted to as large a scale as desired if the displacement curve and the configuration of the follower linkage are known. The method consists essentially in inverting the mechanism by fixing the cam and rotating the follower linkage about it, plotting only enough of the follower linkage to establish the successive positions of the follower face that will bear on the cam. **Figure 9** shows the method of constructing the profile for a disk cam having a radial translating roller follower whose displacement curve is given. The cam profile is faired in, being at every point tangent to the follower roller. (Accuracy is improved by using a larger scale and by plotting additional positions.)

The method of constructing a cam profile for a flat face, offset, or oscillating follower is similar to that shown in the figure. It is important, however, that the location of the point in the follower linkage whose displacement is described by the displacement-time curve be kept constantly in view while the follower linkage is plotted in various successive positions.

Analytically, a profile can be calculated to any desired accuracy and the cam profile may be shown in tabular form, giving, for example, displacement of the follower for each degree of cam rotation. If a milling cutter or grinding wheel of the same size and shape as the follower is then used to cut the cam

contour, the resulting contour will be true except for the small ridges that remain between given positions. These ridges can be removed by hand, using a file or a stone.   Douglas P. Adams

Bibliography. J. Chakraborty and S. G. Dhande, *Kinematics and Geometry of Planer and Spatial Cam Mechanisms*, 1977; F. J. Ogozalek, *Theory of Catenoidal-Pulse Motion and Its Application to High-Speed Cams*, ASME Publ. 66-Mech-45, 1966; J. E. Shigley and J. J. Uiker, *Theory of Machines and Mechanisms*, 2d ed., 1995.

Cambrian

An interval of time in Earth history (Cambrian Period) and its rock record (Cambrian System). The Cambrian Period spanned about 60 million years and began with the first appearance of marine animals with mineralized (calcium carbonate, calcium phosphate) shells. The Cambrian System includes many different kinds of marine sandstones, shales, limestones, dolomites, and volcanics. Apart from the occurrence of an alkaline playa containing deposits of trona (hydrated basic sodium carbonate) in the Officer Basin of South Australia, there is very little provable record of nonmarine Cambrian environments.

CENOZOIC	QUATERNARY	
	TERTIARY	
MESOZOIC	CRETACEOUS	
	JURASSIC	
	TRIASSIC	
PALEOZOIC	PERMIAN	
	CARBONIFEROUS	PENNSYLVANIAN
		MISSISSIPPIAN
	DEVONIAN	
	SILURIAN	
	ORDOVICIAN	
	CAMBRIAN	
PRECAMBRIAN		

The concept that great systems of rocks recorded successive periods of Earth history was developed in England in the early nineteenth century. The Cambrian, which was one of the first systems to be formally named, was proposed by the Reverend Adam Sedgwick in 1835 for a series of sedimentary rocks in Wales that seemed to constitute the oldest sediments in the British Isles. At that time, there was no real idea

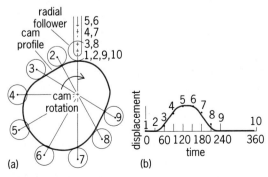

Fig. 9. Method of construction of (*a*) the cam profile for a disk cam having a radial translating roller follower, from (*b*) the displacement curve.

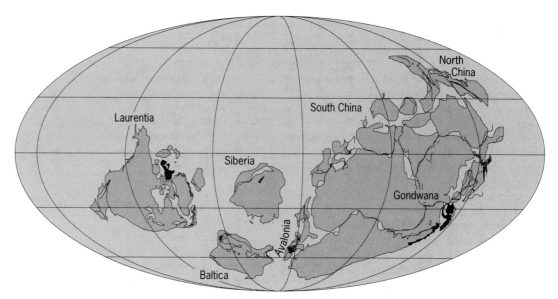

Fig. 1. Reconstruction of the Lower Cambrian world. (*After W. S. McKerrow, C. R. Scotese, and M. D. Brasier, Early Cambrian continental reconstructions. J. Geol. Soc., 149:599–606, 1992*)

of the antiquity of Cambrian rocks. They were recognized by distinctive fossils and by their geologic relations to other systems. In the early part of the twentieth century, radiometric techniques for obtaining the ages of igneous and metamorphic rocks evolved. Because of the difficulty of finding rocks that can be dated radiometrically in association with rocks, usually zircon bearing volcanic ashes, that can be dated empirically by fossils, the age in years of most Cambrian deposits is only approximate. The best present estimates suggest that Cambrian time began about 545 million years ago (Ma; earliest date close to the base of the Cambrian is 543 ± 0.2 Ma) and ended at about 485 Ma (latest date in the Upper Cambrian is 491 ± 1 Ma, but this is not terminal Cambrian). It is the longest of the Paleozoic periods and the fourth long est of the Phanerozoic periods.

Geography. Knowledge of Cambrian geography and of the dynamic aspects of evolution and history in Cambrian time is derived from rocks of this age that have been exposed by present-day erosion or penetrated by borings into the Earth's surface. Despite the antiquity of Cambrian time, a surprisingly good record of marine rocks of Cambrian age has been preserved at many localities throughout the world. Each of the different rock types contains clues about its environment of deposition that have been derived from analogy with modern marine environments. From this information, together with knowledge gained from fossils of about the same age within the Cambrian and information about the present geographic distribution of each Cambrian locality, a general picture of world geography and its changes through Cambrian time is available.

Plate tectonics. The theory of plate tectonics has provided criteria whereby ancient continental margins can be identified. By using these criteria and the spatial information about marine environments derived from study of the rocks, the Cambrian world can be resolved into at least four major continents

that were quite different from those of today (**Fig. 1**). These were (1) Laurentia, which is essentially North America, minus a narrow belt along the eastern coast from eastern Newfoundland to southern New England that belonged to a separate microcontinent, Avalonia. This microcontinent, which also included present-day England, and another microcontinent now incorporated in South Carolina were originally marginal to Gondwana; (2) Baltica, consisting of present-day northern Europe north of France and west of the Ural Mountains but excluding most of Scotland and northern Ireland, which are fragments of Laurentia; (3) Gondwana, a giant continent whose present-day fragments are Africa, South America, India, Australia, Antarctica, parts of southern Europe, the Middle East, a nd Southeast Asia; and (4) Siberia, including much of the northeastern quarter of Asia. Unfortunately, there is not enough reliable information to accurately locate these continents relative to one another on the Cambrian globe. Current Cambrian reconstructions rely on similarities of fossil faunas and on studies of magnetic polarity reversals in rock sequences through time (magnetostratigraphy). These have mostly been concentrated across the Precambrian-Cambrian boundary in Australia, Morocco, Siberia, and south China, and across the Cambrian-Ordovician boundary in Australia, North America, Kazakhstan, and north China. *See* CONTINENTAL MARGIN; CONTINENTS, EVOLUTION OF; PLATE TECTONICS.

Time divisions. For most practical purposes, rocks of Cambrian age are recognized by their content of distinctive fossils. On the basis of the successive changes in the evolutionary record of Cambrian life that have been worked out during the past century, the Cambrian System has been divided globally into three or four series, each of which has been further divided on each continent into stages, each stage consisting of several zones (**Fig. 2**). Despite the amount of work already done, precise

SERIES	STAGES	ZONES
MILLARDAN	Sunwaptan	Saukia
		Saratogia
		Taenicephalus
		Irvingella major *
	Steptoean	Elvinia
		Dunderbergia
		Prehousia
		Dicanthopyge
		Aphelaspis
		Coosella perplexa *
LINCOLNIAN	Marjuman	Crepicephalus
		Cedaria
		Bolaspidella
		Ehmaniella
		Proehmaniella basilica *
	Delamaran	Glossopleura
		Albertella
		Plagiura-Poliella
WAUCOBAN	Dyeran	Olenellus *
	Montezuman	"Nevadella"
		"Fallotaspis"
BEGADEAN	Unnamed	

Fig. 2. **North American divisions of the Cambrian System. Asterisks denote levels of major trilobite extinctions.**

intercontinental correlation of series and stage boundaries, and of zones, is still difficult, especially in the Early Cambrian due to marked faunal provinciality. Refinement of intercontinental correlation of these ancient rocks is a topic of research.

Life. The record preserved in rocks indicates that essentially all Cambrian plants and animals lived in the sea. The few places where terrestrial sediments have been preserved suggest that the land was barren of major plant life, and there are no known records of Cambrian insects or of terrestrial vertebrate animals of any kind.

Plants. The plant record consists entirely of algae, preserved either as carbonized impressions in marine black shales or as filamentous or blotchy microstructures within marine buildups of calcium carbonate, called stromatolites, produced by the actions of these organisms. Cambrian algal stromatolites were generally low domal structures, rarely more than a few meters high or wide, which were built up by the trapping or precipitation of calcium carbonate by one or more species of algae. Such structures, often composed of upwardly arched laminae, were common in regions of carbonate sedimentation in the shallow Cambrian seas. *See* STROMATOLITE.

Animals. The animal record is composed almost entirely of invertebrates that had either calcareous or phosphatic shells (**Fig. 3**). The fossils of shell-bearing

organisms include representatives of several different classes of arthropods, mollusks, echinoderms, brachiopods, and poriferans. Coelenterates, radiolarians, and agglutinated foraminiferans are extremely rare, and bryozoans are unknown from Cambrian rocks. Rare occurrences of impressions or of carbonized remains of a variety of soft-bodied organisms, including worms and a group of soft-bodied trilobites, indicate that the fossil record, particularly of arthropods, is incomplete and biased in favor of shell-bearing organisms. Some widespread fossil groups, such as Archaeocyatha, are known only from Cambrian rocks, and several extinct groups of Paleozoic organisms, such as hyolithids and conodonts, first appear in Cambrian rocks. Conodonts are thought by some specialists to have affinity with vertebrates, but others prefer to relate them to cephalochordates. Dermal plates recovered from the Late Cambrian of North America and Australia are considered to represent the earliest fish remains. *See* ARTHROPODA; CONODONT; PORIFERA.

Diversity. Although the record of marine life in the Cambrian seems rich, one of the dramatic differences between Cambrian marine rocks and those of younger periods is the low phyletic diversity of

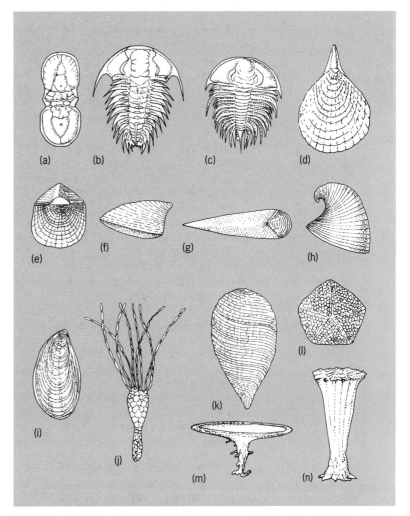

Fig. 3. **Representative Cambrian fossils:** (*a–c*) trilobites; (*d–f*) brachiopods; (*g*) hyolithid; (*h–i*) mollusks; (*j–l*) echinoderms; and (*m, n*) archaeocyathids.

most fossiliferous localities. The most diverse faunas of Cambrian age have been found along the ocean-facing margins of the shallow seas that covered large areas of the Cambrian continents. Because these margins were often involved in later geologic upheavals, their rich record of Cambrian life has been largely destroyed. Only a few localities in the world remain to provide a more accurate picture of the diversity of organisms living in Cambrian time. These are known as Konservat Lagerstätten—conservation deposits containing occurrences of extraordinary preservation, particularly of soft body parts. Globally, they are known from more than 35 localities to date if the "Orsten"-type preservation in the Swedish Alum Shale and elsewhere are considered as Lagerstätten. Orsten is an organic-rich, anthraconitic, concretionary limestone in which phosphatized cuticle-bearing organisms are exquisitely preserved in three dimensions. In Laurentia, the richest localities are in the Kinzers Formati on of southeastern Pennsylvania, the Spence Shale of northern Utah, the Wheeler Shale and Marjum Formation of western Utah, the Buen Formation of northern Greenland, and the Burgess Shale of British Columbia. The last is the largest such deposit, containing about 152 mostly monospecific genera of Middle Cambrian age. Equally spectacular is the Chengjiang fauna found at Maotianshan in Yunnan, southwest China, which contains in excess of 70 arthropod-dominated species of Early Cambrian age. However, for extremely fine morphological detail, Orsten-type preservation in the Lower Cambrian of England, the Middle Cambrian of Russia and Australia, and the Upper Cambrian of Poland and Sweden is unsurpassable.

Trilobites. The most abundant remains of organisms in Cambrian rocks are of trilobites (Fig. 3*a–c*). They are present in almost every fossiliferous Cambrian deposit and are the principal tools used to describe divisions of Cambrian time and to correlate Cambrian rocks. These marine arthropods ranged from a few millimeters to 20 in. (50 cm) in length, but most were less than 4 in. (10 cm) long. Although some groups of trilobites such as the Agnostida (Fig. 3*a*) were predominantly pelagic in habitat, most trilobites seem to have been benthic or nektobenthic and show a reasonably close correlation with bottom environments. For this reason, there are distinct regional differences in the Cambrian trilobite faunas of the shallow seas of different parts of the Cambrian world. *See* TRILOBITA.

Brachiopods. The next most abundant Cambrian fossils are brachiopods (Fig. 3*d–f*). These bivalved animals were often gregarious and lived on the sediment surface or on the surfaces of other organisms. Brachiopods with phosphatic shells, referred to the Acrotretida (Fig. 3*f*), are particularly abundant in many limestones and can be recovered in nearly perfect condition by dissolving these limestones in acetic or formic acids. Upper Cambrian limestones from Texas, Oklahoma, and the Rocky Mountains yield excellent silicified shells of formerly calcareous brachiopods when they are dissolved in dilute hydrochloric acid. *See* BRACHIOPODA.

Archaeocyathids. Limestones of Early Cambrian age may contain large reeflike structures formed by an association of algae and an extinct phylum of invertebrates called Archaeocyatha (Fig. 3*m* and *n*). Typical archeocyathids grew conical or cylindrical shells with two walls separated by elaborate radial partitions. The walls often have characteristic patterns of perforations. *See* ARCHAEOCYATHA.

Mollusks and echinoderms. The Cambrian record of mollusks and echinoderms is characterized by many strange-looking forms (Fig. 3*g–l*). Some lived for only short periods of time and left no clear descendants. Representatives of these phyla, such as cephalopods, clams, and true crinoids, which are abundant in younger rocks, are rare in Cambrian rocks; but rostroconch mollusks are known from the Early, Middle, and Late Cambrian at various times in Laurentia, Australia, Siberia, north China, and Korea. Snails, however, are found throughout the Cambrian. Discoveries of primitive clams have been made in Early Cambrian beds, but they are apparently absent from the later record of life for tens of millions of years until post-Cambrian time. *See* ECHINODERMATA; MOLLUSCA.

Corals. Except for rare jellyfish impressions, the Coelenterata were thought to be unrepresented in Cambrian rocks. Corals have now been discovered in early Middle Cambrian rocks in Australia. However, like clams, they are not seen again as fossils until Middle Ordovician time, many tens of millions of years later. *See* CNIDARIA.

Extinction. The stratigraphic record of Cambrian life in Laurentia (North America) shows perhaps five major extinctions of most of the organisms living in the shallow seas. These extinction events form the boundaries of evolutionary units called biomeres (Fig. 2). Their cause, and their presence in the Cambrian records of other continents, is under investigation. At least one of these extinction events, that at the Marjuman-Steptoean boundary, coincides with a large positive carbon isotope anomaly in Laurentia, Australia, south China, and Kazakhstan. However, perhaps it was these periodic disasters that prevented clear continuity in the evolutionary records of many groups and which led, particularly, to the discontinuous records of the echinoderms, corals, and mollusks. *See* ANIMAL EVOLUTION; EXTINCTION (BIOLOGY).

Faunal origin. One major unsolved problem is the origin of the entire Cambrian fauna. Animal life was already quite diverse before Cambrian time. The earliest Cambrian beds contain representatives of more than 20 distinctly different invertebrate groups. All of these have calcified shells, but none of the Precambrian organisms have any evidence of shells. There is still no clear evidence to determine whether shells evolved in response to predation or to environmental stress, or as the result of some change in oceanic or atmospheric chemistry. *See* PRECAMBRIAN.

History. At the beginning of Cambrian time, the continents were largely exposed, much as they are now. Following some still-unexplained event, the seas were suddenly populated by a rich fauna of shell-bearing invertebrates after 3 billion years of supporting only simple plants and perhaps 100 million years with shell-less invertebrates. *See* PRECAMBRIAN.

Belts of volcanic islands comparable to those of the western Pacific Ocean today fringed eastern Laurentia, the Australian and western Antarctic margins of Gondwana, and southern Siberia. These belts suggest that crustal plates analogous to those of the present day were in motion at that time. Thick evaporites in Siberia and the Middle Eastern and Indian parts of Gondwana suggest regions of warm temperature and high evaporation rate. Absence of significant development of limestones around Baltica suggest that it was a cool region, probably at high latitudes. Near the continental margins of eastern and western Laurentia, on and around Siberia, and on the western Antarctic, eastern Australian, northwestern African, and southern European margins of Gondwana, archaeocyathid bioherms developed and flourished. By the end of Early Cambrian time, archaeocyathids had become extinct, and shell-bearing organisms capable of building bioherms did not reappear until Middle Ordovician time, at least 45 million years later.

Volcanism and evaporitic conditions continued into the Middle Cambrian in Siberia and parts of Gondwana, and evaporites of this age are also known from northern Canada. However, a dramatic change took place in the southern European and northwestern African parts of Gondwana. Carbonate sedimentation virtually ceased throughout that region as those parts of Gondwana reached areas of cooler water and probably higher latitudes. Sea level was rising over much of the world throughout Middle Cambrian time, flooding the interiors of most continents.

In the Late Cambrian, parts of western Baltica and eastern Laurentia began to show signs of crustal deformation suggesting that Iapetus, the ocean between Laurentia, Gondwana, and Baltica, was beginning to close. Crustal deformation was also taking place in southern Siberia, eastern Australia, and western Antarctica. In the broad, shallow seas over all of the continents except Baltica and the southern European and northwestern African parts of Gondwana, extensive areas of carbonate sediments developed. At least five times in the shallow seas covering Laurentia, large parts of the animal populations became extinct and had to be replenished from the oceanic regions. The last of these extinction events marks the end of Cambrian time in Laurentia.

Throughout Cambrian time, terrestrial landscapes were stark and barren. Life in the sea was primitive and struggling for existence. Only in post-Cambrian time did the shallow marine environment stabilize and marine life really flourish. Only then did vertebrates evolve and plants and animals invade the land.   Allison R. Palmer; John H. Shergold

Bibliography. C. H. Holland (ed.), *Cambrian of the British Isles, Norden and Spitzbergen*, 1974; C. H. Holland (ed.), *Cambrian of the New World*, 1971; C. H. Holland (ed.), *Lower Paleozoic of the Middle East, Eastern and Southern Africa, and Antarctica*, 1981; W. S. McKerrow, C. R. Scotese, and M. D. Brasier, Early continental reconstructions, *J. Geol. Soc.*, 149:559–606, 1992; M. A. McMenamin and D. L. McMenamin, *The Emergence of Animals: The Cambrian Breakthrough*, 1990; A. R. Palmer, A proposed nomenclature for stages and series for the Cambrian of Laurentia, *Can. J. Earth Sci.*, 35(4):323–328, 1998; A. R. Palmer, Search for the Cambrian world, *Amer. Sci.*, 62:216–224, 1974; R. A. Robison and C. Tiechert (eds.), *Treatise on Invertebrate Paleontology*, pt. A: *Biogeography*, 1979; J. A. Secord, *Controversy in Victorian Geology: The Cambrian-Silurian Dispute*, 1986; H. B. Whittington, *The Burgess Shale*, 1985.

Camel

The name given to two species of mammals which are members of the family Camelidae in the order Artiodactyla. These are the bactrian camel (*Camelus bactrianus*) and the Arabian or dromedary camel (*C. dromedarius*). Both species are domesticated, but a few wild herds of bactrian camels are still in existence in the Gobi desert.

The legs of these animals are long and slender and terminate in two toes. The neck and head are elongate, and there is a cleft upper lip. The upper jaw has both canines and incisors, and the dental formula is I 1/3 C 1/1 Pm 3/3 M 3/3 for a total of 36 teeth. These animals do not have a gall bladder and the stomach has three divisions. The period of gestation is about 1 year and the female breeds every second year, producing one young (colt).

Bactrian camel. The bactrian camel (see **illus.**) is stronger and more heavily built than the dromedary and is more suitable as a pack animal. The long, shaggy hair allows it to withstand the cold climate of its range in central Asia. There are two humps of fatty tissue, one over the shoulders and the other atop the hindquarters. The shoulder height, excluding the hump, is about 6 ft (2 m). This animal is economically important to the region as it provides milk, meat, and leather for the nomads.

Bactrian camel (*Camelus bactrianus*). (*Brent Huffman/Ultimate Ungulate Images*)

Arabian camel. The Arabian camel is taller than the bactrian and has a single hump of fatty tissue, which can be used as a food reserve. There are two varieties of this species found in the desert. One is the baggage camel, used as a beast of burden, which can average 40 mi (65 km) a day carrying a load of about 400 lb (180 kg). The other type is the more slightly built racing camel, which can travel up to 100 mi (160 km) a day, but with a very light load. This species is well suited to desert life with its broad feet, adapted to walking on sand, its ability to close its nostrils completely, and its double row of interlocking eyelashes.

Adaptations. These two species are able to interbreed. They have a most important physiological adapation in their ability to conserve water. Camels do not store water but conserve it, since the body is well insulated by fur and has a temperature range of over 12°F (7°C) before it perspires sufficiently to prevent a further rise. The body temperature is about 93°F (34°C) in the morning and may rise to 106°F (41°C) during daytime activity before water is expended in any appreciable quantity. The camel can lose over 40% of its body water without fear of dehydration. However, although able to survive for long periods without water, it may drink as much as 15 gal (57 liters) when water is available. *See* ARTIODACTYLA.   Charles B. Curtin

Camel's hair

A fine hair known to the American consumer chiefly in the form of high-quality coat fabrics. This textile fiber is obtained from the two-humped bactrian camel, which is native to all parts of Asia. The protective hair covering of the camel is a nonconductor of both heat and cold, also water repellent. In the spring the year's growth of hair, which hangs from the camel in matted strands and tufts, falls off in clumps. This growth, plus the masses of hair shed throughout the year, is the chief source of supply. The camel is sometimes plucked to obtain the down or underhair.

Camel's-hair fabrics are ideal for comfort, particularly when used for overcoating, as they are especially warm and light in weight. Camel's hair is characterized by strength, luster, and smoothness. The best quality is expensive. It is often mixed with wool to improve the quality of the wool fabric. The price of such a mixed cloth is much less than that of a 100% camel's-hair fabric.

In the textile industry camel's hair is divided into three grades. Grade 1 is the soft and silky light-tan underhair. This is short staple or noil of 1–5 in. (2.5–12.5 cm) but is the choicest quality. This was once the only true camel's hair used in the manufacture of apparel. Grade 2 is the intermediate growth, consisting partly of short hairs and partly of coarse outer hairs. Grade 3 consists entirely of coarse outer hairs measuring up to 15 in. (27.5 cm) in length and varying in color from brownish-black to reddish brown. This grade has no value for apparel manufacture; it is suitable only for cordage and for low-quality rugs.

See ALPACA; CAMEL; CASHMERE; LLAMA; MOHAIR; NATURAL FIBER; VICUNA; WOOL.   M. David Potter

Cameo

A type of carved gemstone in which the background is cut away to leave the subject in relief. Often cameos are cut from stones in which the coloring is layered, resulting in a figure of one color and a background of another. The term cameo, when used without qualification, is usually reserved for those cut from a gem mineral, although they are known also as stone cameos. The commonly encountered cameo cut from shell is properly called a shell cameo.

Most cameos are cut from onyx or agate, but many other varieties of quartz, such as tiger's-eye, bloodstone, sard, carnelian, and amethyst, are used; other materials used include beryl, malachite, hematite, labrodorite, and moonstone. *See* GEM; INTAGLIO (GEMOLOGY).   Richard T. Liddicoat, Jr.

Camera

A device for forming and recording images; the basic tool of photography. In its simplest form, a camera is a lighttight box in which an image is formed through a pinhole or lens at one end onto a light-sensitive material at the opposite end. Most cameras contain an aperture and shutter for controlling the amount of light reaching the light-sensitive material (exposure). The recording material may be a photosensitive silver halide emulsion film, an electronic device such as a charge-coupled device (CCD) or complementary metal-oxide semiconductor (CMOS) sensor, or some other photosensitive material designed for a specific purpose. *See* CHARGE-COUPLED DEVICES.

Types. The camera was originally a lighttight chamber in which observers saw and sometimes traced the image projected by a pinhole and later by a simple biconvex lens (camera obscura); the first portable model using a lens (camera lucida) was introduced in the mid-1600s. Since the first photographic camera was built by Nicephore Niepce in 1826, many different types have been devised. They can be distinguished by function, application, film size, or format. Distinctions are also based on type of viewfinder and body construction.

Cameras for still photography include box, point-and-shoot, view-and-press, roll-film, 35mm, instant-picture, stereo, underwater, and panoramic. Some categories overlap. Still video and digital cameras use electronic sensors instead of film, and store the image in solid-state memory or on magnetic media or optical disks. Motion picture or cine cameras record movement at regular intervals in a series of frames which are later projected onto a screen to create an illusion of movement. Television and video cameras record movement electronically for broadcast and storage on magnetic media or optical disks. Camcorders are video cameras that contain both the image sensor and recording media in a single unit.

Box and simple cameras. These cameras have no (or very few) adjustments and are generally easy to use. They do not require focusing; called focus-free, universal, or fixed-focus, they have a lens with a small aperture. This design maximizes the range of distances from the subject over which sharp images can be formed. This range is called the depth of field. The focus is preset to produce the greatest depth of field, known as the hyperfocal distance. *See* GEOMETRICAL OPTICS; LENS (OPTICS).

Simple cameras rely on the wide latitude (the range of exposure which yields acceptable negatives) of modern photographic films and in particular films of color-negative emulsions. Most have a single shutter speed of 1/30 to 1/125 s and a single aperture, although a limited selection of settings such as indoors, outdoors, or sunny and cloudy may be provided. A film advance mechanism that prevents double exposure and a basic aiming device are usually present. Many cameras can trigger a flash device (**Fig. 1**).

Disposable cameras (also known as recyclable or single-use) are simple cameras that come loaded with film and are not reused.

Many cameras have few controls and are as simple to operate as the box cameras, but they have automatic electronic adjustment of the lens opening and shutter speed to produce the correct exposure. These cameras may have a switch to set the film speed, according to the International Standard Organization (ISO), and are often limited to two settings, ISO 100 and ISO 400.

Simple cameras rely on compromises for focus and exposure control. Although they can produce good photographs under average conditions, much better results can be obtained over a wider range of conditions with adjustable focus and exposure.

Zone focusing cameras are similar to the simple cameras described above, except that the focus can be set within limits. Focus settings may exist for close-up, portrait, group portrait, and landscape.

Point-and-shoot cameras. Some cameras operate as box or simple cameras but with automatic electronic adjustments for producing good pictures. These cameras set exposure control automatically. The focus may be fixed or subject to automatic electronic adjustment. These cameras often feature drop-in or automatic film loading and built-in flash. Some have user overrides, which enable the photographer to choose manual settings in extreme situations, such as strong spot or backlighting.

Although the lens is fixed, many models have dual (switchable) focal length or continuously variable focal length (zoom lenses).

Folding cameras. Except for instant-picture cameras, few folding cameras are now being made; a collapsible bellows between the back and the lens permits compact folding for carrying. Folding cameras have been made for most film sizes, especially the larger ones. Some modern cameras use a collapsible or retractable lens which is stored in the camera body when not in use.

View cameras. These large cameras were originally designed for landscapes or views but are equally

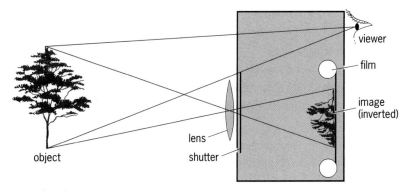

Fig. 1. Simple camera.

useful in commercial studio photography. A flexible bellows is attached to front and rear panels that swing on a rigid base. The front panel holds the lens mounted on a board. The rear panel usually contains a ground-glass plate that can be replaced by a film holder. View cameras can be folded for transport; the bellows is primarily functional, connecting the lens board to the film holder, while allowing great freedom of movement between them. These cameras offer a wide range of positions for correcting perspective and controlling the image distortion that results when the subject and film plane are not parallel. Studio or stand cameras used for portraiture are similar in construction, but they may have more limited movements.

Instant-picture cameras. Introduced in 1948 by Edwin Land, these cameras directly produce a print. The development chemicals are contained within the film package in a pod, which is broken by rollers upon ejection of the print from the camera. Instant-picture cameras must be comparatively large, since the full-size image is used. Instant-picture-type backs are made for other cameras, particularly medium- and large-format view cameras, to produce fast proofs to check lighting and composition before making an exposure on conventional film.

Motion picture cameras. Commonly called movie or cine cameras, they photograph moving objects in a series of images for sequential playback to create an illusion of movement. They differ from still cameras principally in the need to advance the film rapidly during the brief time that the shutter closes between frames. Rates of 18 to 24 frames per second are common, with other rates for special purposes such as time-lapse or high-speed photography. The format is usually specified by the width of the film: 8mm and Super 8 (8mm film with slightly larger image and different sprocketing) cameras are amateur formats, popular for home movies; 16mm cameras are used for news, scientific, and some theatrical films; and 35- and 70mm cameras are used primarily for theatrical films. *See* CINEMATOGRAPHY.

Digital or electronic cameras. Photographic technology associated with electronic or digital photography is essentially concerned with using an electronic sensor array instead of film. The optical part of the camera is unchanged as well as the need to keep non-image-forming light away from the photosensitive medium during the making of an exposure. The fact that photoelectronic recording methods are becoming prevalent also has meant that shuttering can sometimes be accomplished electronically.

The impact of the digital "revolution" is that cameras [point-and-shoot, single-lens reflex (SLR), and medium and large format] are now available with a digital method for capturing and storing images, essentially replacing photographic emulsions.

When records are needed fast, the digital camera can deliver images almost immediately that can be transmitted and distributed to locations worldwide. For the researcher, engineer, and technician, the big advantage is the immediacy of results and the fact that photography can be promptly repeated if not of suitable quality. Digital files, however, can be easily manipulated in a computer, which raises ethical questions.

The resolution of digital systems, some being cameras in their own right while others are simply accessories that can be attached to existing cameras, is close to that of film (especially smaller-size film) and is of suitable quality for many purposes.

Digital or electronic cameras are available in about as many varieties as standard film-type cameras, whether still or motion picture. Large-format cameras are only available as scanning camera backs which are best used with stationary subjects since they capture the whole image by moving one or more linear arrays of photosensors gradually from one side of the image gate to the other. Two-dimensional array cameras permit instantaneous recording of the whole scene and are thus suitable for imaging objects in motion.

A significant problem associated with digital records is the storage capacity requirement both in the camera and for archiving purposes. Film is an excellent and low-cost information storage medium, albeit somewhat susceptible to change over time due to environmental conditions. For the foreseeable future, the digital and film systems will coexist and photographers will be able to decide on the best system for a given application. The future promises development of more hybrid solutions rather than complete elimination of photographic emulsions. The question of sustainable commercial production of specialized silver-halide emulsions is a factor that will determine the ultimate impact of the digital process on traditional processes.

Reflex cameras. Reflex cameras use mirrors to reflect the object scene onto a viewing (and often focusing) screen. The mirror erects the inverted image, making viewing easier, although motion left and right is still reversed in the finder. A camera that uses this mirror with a pair of matched lenses (one for viewing and focusing, the other for picture taking) is called a twin-lens reflex. In such a camera, the two lenses are coupled and the mirror and focusing screen are placed so that a sharp image on the focusing screen corresponds to a sharp image on the film plane (**Fig. 2**).

To eliminate parallax, various methods of viewing through the lens have been used. A beam splitter may be placed behind the lens, channeling part of the image to the viewfinder and part to the film.

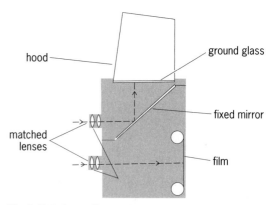

Fig. 2. Twin-lens reflex camera.

This arrangement reduces the efficiency of both the focusing and picture taking. A mirror placed directly behind the lens can reflect the image from it directly to the viewing screen. By removing the mirror from the light path during the exposure, the film receives the full intensity of the image.

The single-lens reflex camera uses the same lens with the aid of a mirror for viewing and photographing (**Fig. 3**). Since picture taking and viewing use the same lens, the single-lens reflex has the advantage that the viewfinder always shows the precise scene to be recorded by the film. In some single-lens reflexes, particularly larger ones, the mirror must be reset manually after exposure, usually by using the film advance lever. Most single-lens reflexes employ an instant-return mirror, which is virtually always in the viewing position but flips out of the way before the exposure. A pentaprism (or a group of mirrors called a Porro prism) may be used between the focusing screen and viewfinder eyepiece to restore proper left-right motion while viewing an image oriented like the subject. This makes it easy to aim the camera and follow moving subjects. Various focusing aids may be present on the built-in focusing screen, including a central split image which is brought into alignment at the point of focus. Some single-lens reflex cameras allow for a change of focusing screen for various purposes.

Autofocusing single-lens reflexes. The semisilvered mirror found in some metering cameras can be used to channel the light to a charge-coupled-device array sensor for detecting focus. The camera electronics can then be used to focus the lens. This type of autofocusing single-lens reflex is widely used by amateurs and some professional photographers and

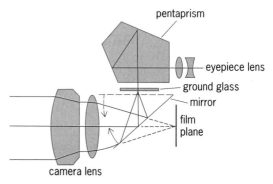

Fig. 3. Single-lens reflex camera.

is a leading feature of current 35mm camera design.

Like the focusing screen, the sensor array must be at the same distance from the mirror as the film plane. The array may detect the intensity maximum or compare two beams to check focus. The result of the measurement may be relayed to the operator via a display in the viewfinder indicating "focus" or "out of focus" or the direction to turn the lens to achieve focus.

The camera itself may focus the lens by using a motor and connecting shaft or by controlling a motor built into the lens.

Other types. Many cameras have been devised for specific purposes. Wide-field or panoramic cameras take extreme wide-angle views, some up to a full 360 degrees. This can be useful in photographing landscapes or large groups of people. In extreme wide-angle photography, some cameras swing the lens during exposure in synchronization with the shutter.

Underwater cameras must be watertight up to a pressure of several atmospheres. Some are specialized in design, although many are conventional cameras placed in a watertight container with linkages to the exterior for control of focus and exposure. *See* UNDERWATER PHOTOGRAPHY.

Aerial cameras may use special mounts to counteract vibration. They may also move the film during exposure to compensate for aircraft motion relative to the ground. These cameras can be used for reconnaissance, mapping, or scientific surveys. *See* AERIAL PHOTOGRAPH.

Stereo cameras have multiple lenses for taking pictures in pairs. When these pictures are viewed simultaneously, each with a different eye, the original three-dimensional depth is created.

Many cameras have been devised for scientific studies. Medical cameras can photograph inside the human body. Streak and slit cameras record images for time-motion studies. Holographic cameras record diffraction patterns instead of real images for reconstruction of three-dimensional subjects. Lenses adapted to ultraviolet or infrared rather than visible light are used with film of corresponding sensitivity. Cameras aboard space satellites gave the first view of the Earth from space and of the dark side of the Moon. *See* HOLOGRAPHY; REMOTE SENSING.

Viewfinders and focusing aids. The image is viewed most accurately on the film plane. The operator places a ground-glass plate at the film plane and adjusts the camera position and lens focus until the desired image appears sharp (and inverted) on the glass, which is replaced by the film in a holder for exposure. This time-consuming process is impractical for many applications, particularly if the subject is moving.

Most cameras, other than large-format view cameras that use a ground glass at the focal plane for composition and focusing, are equipped with an auxiliary framing device called a viewfinder. These viewfinders vary in complexity from open wire-frame devices that, when looked through from a given distance, provide an indication of the approximate field of view reproduced by the camera lens at the film plane, to complex systems that predict more accurately what will be recorded by the camera at the moment of exposure.

In some viewfinders there is also incorporated the ability to focus the lens at some preselected subject detail. In the most complex viewfinder and focusing mechanisms, the focusing of the lens is achieved automatically.

Viewfinders of simple cameras may consist of only a plastic or metal frame that is held up to the eye to approximate the angle of view of the camera lens. In more advanced cameras, one may find a lens or a group of lenses that compensates for the magnification or reduction of the picture-taking lens. Since viewfinders and photographic lenses on a camera are often separate, they do not see the subject exactly from the same position, and this difference in view between the two is called parallax.

Although parallax is not usually a problem when subjects are located at relatively large distances from the camera, when photographing at close range certain parts of a subject that appear in the viewfinder may be cut off in the final photograph.

A major advantage of SLR (single-lens reflex) or DSLR (digital single-lens reflex) cameras, as well as modern "point and shoot" digital cameras that preview the image on an active display such as an LCD screen, is that they do not suffer from parallax because they use the same lens for both viewing and making the photograph. Such cameras also allow the photographer to easily and accurately focus on desired parts of the subject.

Cameras are focused either by changing the distance between lens and film or by moving specific elements within a complex lens, often by turning the outer lens barrel. Some cameras are focused by turning the lens barrel until a pointer is aligned with a point on a scale that represents the distance from the camera to the subject. A rangefinder may be placed on the camera which uses a split image to determine the object's distance. When a lever or dial on the rangefinder is adjusted until the two images coincide, the distance can be read from a scale on the rangefinder. Some cameras connect the rangefinder to the lens via a cam, so that turning the lens adjusts the rangefinder to bring both to a focus at the same point; these are called rangefinder-coupled cameras. *See* RANGEFINDER (OPTICS).

Electronic rangefinding devices built into the camera may be used instead of the optical type. These may measure object distance by timing the reflection of a sound wave emanating from the camera (sonar), or by projecting an infrared beam from a small window on the camera and locating the beam by rotating a mirror behind a second window. By knowing the angle of the mirror and the distance between the mirror and the infrared emitter, the subject distance is electronically calculated by trigonometry. The lens is automatically set to the proper focus or focus zone.

Viewfinders of electronic and video cameras may be simple optical finders like those found in point-and-shoot cameras, but most use electronic viewfinders. Since the electronic sensor at the film plane relays the image information to an electronic recording device, this image can be relayed simultaneously to a small television monitor. This is usually a miniature liquid-crystal display (LCD) viewed through a magnifying eyepiece.

Exposure control. To produce a photograph or electronic image, the camera must match the image brightness to the sensitivity of the receiving medium or device. When that medium is photographic film, sensitivity is reported as ISO film speed, with each doubling of speed indicating an increase of one photographic stop of sensitivity; that is, one smaller aperture, half the shutter speed, or half the subject illumination would be required to expose the image properly. Electronic sensors may be rated with an equivalent ISO. Image intensity is usually controlled by an iris diaphragm serving as the lens aperture. The ratio of the lens focal length to this aperture is called the *f*/stop. Although technically a function of the lens, in some designs the aperture is located inside the camera. Many cameras can control the aperture in the lens, keeping it at the widest possible setting for bright viewing and focusing of single-lens reflexes and closing the aperture to the proper setting during exposure.

Shutters. The shutter controls exactly when and for how long the light is admitted to the image-forming material. This can be simply a cap that is removed and then replaced over a pinhole; or a metal flap, or a group of such blades (leaf shutter), that swings aside behind the lens to create the exposure; or a slit that moves across the film plane during the exposure (focal-plane shutter). Shutters can provide exposures ranging from several seconds to small fractions of a second. Speeds up to 1/500 s are common for leaf shutters, with focal-plane shutters routinely producing exposures as short as 1/1000 s, and some reaching 1/10,000 s.

Exposure meters. To determine the optimal shutter speed and aperture combination for the film or image sensor, it is necessary to determine the brightness of the scene being recorded. A photosensitive device such as a cadmium sulfide cell or silicon photodiode is often employed to measure illumination. Originally a separate device, the light meter was used to determine *f*/stop and shutter speed combinations for proper exposures. Today this device is often built into the camera, although it only can measure the light reflected from the subject. In some cameras, particularly 35mm point-and-shoot cameras, the cell is placed on the front behind a small lens element designed to approximate the angle of view of the photographic lens. On the most basic cameras, this shows when light is sufficient to take a picture with the recording medium of given sensitivity and the available range of shutter speeds and apertures. Some cameras automatically adjust aperture and shutter speed to obtain the proper exposure as shown by the cell. Other cameras, particularly single-lens reflexes, have an indicator in the viewfinder to show when the shutter speed–aperture combination will give proper exposure. *See* PHOTOCONDUCTIVE CELL; PHOTOELECTRIC DEVICES.

Like viewing, metering through the photographic lens has proved effective and is widely used. Some single-lens reflex cameras have photocells in the mirror box which look forward through the lens and are aimed at the subject. Others use similar cells to measure the intensity of the image (or parts thereof) formed on the focusing screen. Since the image changes with the angle of view provided by the lens, the angle of the metering is proportional to lens coverage and changes with changes of focal length.

Sometimes a semisilvered mirror is used as the instant return mirror. This mirror acts as a beam splitter, allowing a small portion of the light to pass through it to the metering device while reflecting most of the light to the focusing screen. Some cameras have cells facing toward the film plane to monitor the exposure directly from the film. Some cells are intended to measure electronic flash exposures, which are so short that they can be measured only during the actual exposure.

Metering cells may not measure the entire subject evenly. Those that do so, even approximately, are called averaging meters. Meters that concentrate their sensitivity on the center of the frame (where the main subject is often placed) are called center-weighted systems. Some systems measure only a small central portion, in so-called spot metering. Some cameras use more than one metering system. *See* EXPOSURE METER.

Automatic modes. Still cameras control the combination of shutter speed and *f*/stop used for each exposure. (Motion picture and video cameras usually offer less control of shutter speed, which must be higher than the frame rates.) Many combinations of shutter speed and aperture yield the same exposure at the image plane. Different selections produce different photographic results: higher shutter speeds freeze action or reduce blurring caused by camera motion during exposure; smaller apertures yield greater depth of field. The photographer may want the camera to select either setting or both settings automatically.

A camera selecting both shutter speed and aperture is said to be in a programmed autoexposure mode. Some cameras offer a choice of exposure programs, either automatically selected by the camera according to lens focal length, or operator-selected with a preference for greater depth of field or higher shutter speeds.

Some cameras allow the photographer to choose shutter speed or *f*/stop and automatically make the corresponding setting. When the operator sets only the shutter speed, the camera is set to shutter-priority autoexposure. Multimode cameras allow the photographer to select among autoexposure options, often including full manual control, in which the operator sets both *f*/stop and shutter speed.

So-called multimode cameras offer a choice of automated exposure modes. This versatility is especially prominent in 35mm single-lens reflexes. Some cameras offer variations of the basic autoexposure options. Some have autoexposure modes in which the photographer, instead of selecting the actual shutter speed, selects the minimum shutter speed acceptable, and the camera acts as if it were in a special program mode if there is enough light for a higher shutter speed.

Automatic multipattern metering. By dividing the scene into sections, the camera can often automatically set the best exposure in situations where a conventional, single photocell might err, as with a subject lit in silhouette or a strong spotlight. Several variations exist, but all measure the light in the center of the subject and in one or more adjoining areas. By comparing combinations of specific values and checking illumination differences in adjoining sections (and sometimes considering the subject's position and distance from the autofocusing system), the best estimate for proper exposure setting is made electronically.

Auxiliary equipment. Many cameras accommodate a variety of lenses. Those with focal lengths close to the diagonal of the camera format are considered normal lenses, and prints made with them and viewed from the proper viewing distance produce a sensation of perspective that matches well that seen by the unaided eye when examining the original scene. Lenses with shorter focal lengths are wide-angle and may give coverage up to 100°. Telephoto lenses have focal lengths longer than the format diagonal. The narrow angle of view increases the image magnification, allowing photography of small details at greater distances.

A telephoto lens is a photographic lens system specially designed to give a large image of a distant object in a camera of relatively short focal length. A telephoto lens generally consists of a positive lens system and a negative lens system, separated by a considerable distance. If color correction is desired, each of the partial systems must be color-corrected. It is usually not easy to correct distortion in a teleobjective, but occasionally it has been achieved. *See* FOCAL LENGTH; LENS (OPTICS).

Zoom lenses are made of a system of lenses in which two or more parts are moved with respect to each other to obtain a continuously variable focal length and hence magnification, while the image is kept in the same image plane.

If the diaphragm is opened at the same time so that its linear opening increases with the focal length, it is possible to keep the relative aperture of the whole system constant while the focal length varies. In any case, the system must be constructed so that the errors do not vary too much in the shifting. Thus the designer must strive for a design in which the image errors are small, at least for the beginning and end positions of the zooming procedure, and do not become too large for intermediate positions.

In general, a complicated cam is needed to control the motions of the parts of the system. However, it is possible to simplify the mechanism if the focal plane is not kept precisely constant but only required to coincide exactly with a given plane for several focal lengths while approximately coinciding for others. Such a system is called an optically compensated varifocal system.

Some early variable-focal-length lenses contained 15 or more separated elements, but this number has been reduced to as few as four. The zoom ratio (the ratio of maximum to minimum power) is in general 3:1, but it has been possible in some designs to increase the range to 4:1 or even more. Moving sets of achromatic prisms are sometimes used to achieve the zooming effect.

A flash unit produces a brief burst of bright light to allow photography under dim illumination. The camera must open the shutter fully during the brightest portion of the flash. An electronic flash can have various durations. Some cameras, particularly single-lens reflexes, can measure the subject through the lens and then control the flash via a special contact. *See* STROBOSCOPIC PHOTOGRAPHY.

Tripod stands hold cameras steady, giving sharp pictures at longer shutter speeds than are possible with hand-held cameras. Winders and motor drives allow still cameras to take short sequences at rates from one to almost six frames per second.

Special backs used on some cameras imprint digital information on or between the negatives. Accessories can fire the cameras automatically at specified intervals (intervalometers) or for specific events (remote triggers). Some backs can even change the film in midroll. *See* PHOTOGRAPHY.

Andrew Davidhazy; Lawrence R. White

Bibliography. J. Ciaglia, *Introduction to Digital Photography*, 2d ed., 2005; R. Jacobson et al., *Manual of Photography: Photographic and Digital Imaging*, 9th ed., 2000; S. F. Ray, *Applied Photographic Optics*, 3d ed., 2002.

Camerata

An extinct subclass of stalked Crinoidea; a class of the phylum Echinodermata. The Camerata include more than 235 genera confined to the Paleozoic Era, ranging from the Early Ordovician to the Late Permian. Camerate crinoids were one of the four major subclasses of Paleozoic crinoids. Others include the Cladida, Flexibilia, and Disparida. *See* CRINOIDEA; ECHINODERMATA; GEOLOGIC TIME SCALE.

General morphology. Stalked crinoids were elevated above the sea floor by a column with an attachment structure called the holdfast. Camerate crinoids are characterized by a rigid, boxlike calyx composed of many polygonal plates. The lower arm plates (fixed brachials) were solidly incorporated into the upper portion of the theca, and these fixed arm plates were separated by small interradial plates (see **illustration**). The free arms were articulated to the uppermost fixed arm plate, and all except the more primitive Ordovician forms had free arms with biserial brachials, that is, brachials composed of two articulating columns of arm plates. Camerates are also distinctive because the oral part of the calyx is roofed over, covering the mouth and proximal food grooves. Many camerate crinoids had a long, slender, solid anal tube with a terminal anal opening. More derived, younger forms commonly have fewer plates fixed into the calyx, and in extreme instances the free arms may attach directly to radial plates. The morphology of these derived camerates is convergent toward the morphology of cladid crinoids.

Two clades exist among the Camerata: dicyclic forms (order Diplobathrida; more than 60 genera)

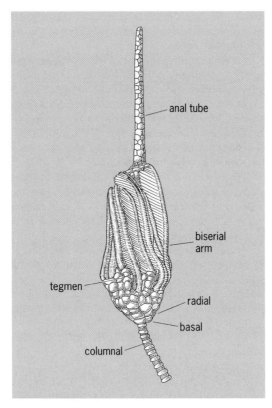

Thylacocrinus, a Devonian dicyclic camerate crinoid.

and monocyclic forms (order Monobathrida; more than 175 genera). The lower portion of the dicyclic calyx is composed, from bottom to top, of infrabasal plates, basal plates, and radial plates, whereas the monocyclic calyx has only basal plates and radial plates.

History. The origin of the camerate crinoids is a matter of current debate, with the oldest forms being from the Early Ordovician. Camerate crinoids were especially dominant forms from the Silurian through the Mississippian, where they were very abundant in various shallow, tropical environments (reefs and broad platforms) that deposited limestones. Diplobathrid camerate crinoids became extinct during the middle Mississippian, and monobathrid camerates became extinct during the Late Permian. *See* MISSISSIPPIAN.   N. Gary Lane; William I. Ausich

Bibliography. H. Hess et al., *Fossil Crinoids*, Cambridge University Press, 2002; R. C. Moore and C. Teichert (eds.), *Treatise on Invertebrate Paleontology*, Part T: *Echinodermata 2*, vols. 1 and 2, 1978.

Campanulales

An order of flowering plants, division Magnoliophyta in the subclass Asteridae of the class Magnoliopsida (dicotyledons). It consists of 7 families and about 2500 species. The order is distinguished in this subclass by its chiefly herbaceous habit, alternate leaves, inferior ovary, and stamens which are free from the corolla or attached at the base of the tube. About 2000 of the species belong to the single family Campanulaceae. This family and two others in the order have a specialized pollen presentation mechanism. The anthers converge or unite around the young style, which grows up through the anther tube and pushes out the pollen. Several familiar ornamentals, including the Canterbury bell (*Campanula medium*) and the cardinal flower (*Lobelia cardinalis*), belong to the Campanulaceae. *See* ASTERIDAE; MAGNOLIOPHYTA; MAGNOLIOPSIDA; ORNAMENTAL PLANTS; PLANT KINGDOM.

Arthur Cronquist; T. M. Barkley

Camphor

A bicyclic, saturated terpene ketone. It exists in the optically active dextro and levo forms, and as the racemic mixture of the two forms. All of these melt within a degree of 178°C (352°F). The principal form is *dextro*-camphor, which occurs in the wood and leaves of the camphor tree (*Cinnamomum camphora*). Taiwan is the chief source of natural camphor which is distilled from the wood of this tree. Camphor is also synthesized commercially on a large scale from pinene which yields mainly the racemic variety. The structural formula of the molecule is shown below.

Camphor has a characteristic odor; it crystallizes in thin plates and sublimes readily at ordinary temperatures.

Camphor has use in liniments and as a mild rubefacient, analgesic, and antipruritic. It has a local action on the gastrointestinal tract, producing a feeling of warmth and comfort in the stomach. It is also used in photographic film and as a plasticizer in the manufacture of plastics. *See* KETONE; PINE TERPENE; TERPENE.

Everett L. Saul

Bibliography. T. W. Solomons, *Organic Chemistry*, 5th ed., 1991.

Camphor tree

The plant *Cinnamomum camphora*, a member of the laurel family (Lauraceae) and a native of China, Japan, and Taiwan (see **illus.**). The tree grows to a height of 40 ft (12 m), is dense-topped, and has shiny, dark, evergreen leaves. It is widely planted as an ornamental tree. All parts of the tree contain camphor, as essential oil which is obtained from the finely ground wood and leaves by distillation with steam. The crude camphor crystallizes on the surface of the still. After it is removed and refined, it is the commercial gum camphor, which is used medicinally, in

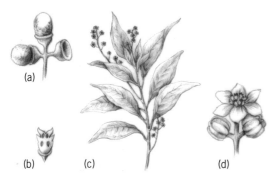

Camphor tree (*Cinnamomum camphora*). (*a*) Fruits. (*b*) Stamen. (*c*) Branch. (*d*) Flower.

perfumes and in the manufacture of celluloid and nitrocellulose compounds. *See* CAMPHOR; MAGNOLIALES. Perry D. Strausbaugh; Earl L. Core

Camptostromatoidea

A small class of primitive echinoderms (subphylum Echinozoa) known from the single species *Camptostroma roddyi* based on about 200 specimens from the Early Cambrian (*Bonnia-Olenellus* Zone) in southeastern Pennsylvania. *Camptostroma* was originally described as a hydrozoan or jellyfish, but it was recognized as an echinoderm and the new class Camptostromatoidea was set up for it. *Camptostroma* has been reinterpreted as an early edrioasteroid, and as a "stem echinoderm" ancestral to several other groups including edrioasteroids. Because of *Camptostroma*'s puzzling morphology, different reconstructions of it have been made (see **illus.**). It has a conical or domal theca or body with a nearly circular outline, divided into a pleated lower theca with larger and smaller overlapping plates, and a domed upper theca made up of large plates with

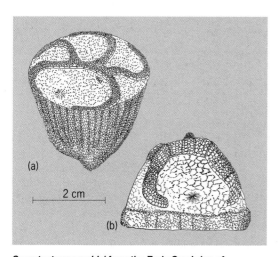

Camptostroma roddyi from the Early Cambrian of Pennsylvania. (*a*) Reconstructed oblique side view showing theca with conical lower part inferred to have been partly buried in the sea floor (*after C. R. C. Paul and A. B. Smith, Biol. Rev., 59:451, 1984*). (*b*) Reconstructed side view showing domed theca with flat lower surface inferred to have been attached to the sea floor or to objects on it (*after K. Derstler, Ph.D. dissertation, University of California, Davis, p. 120, 1985*).

pores on their margins surrounded by numerous smaller plates. The upper theca bears five straight to curved ambulacra protected by numerous cover plates and radiating from the central mouth, and a small anal pyramid at one edge. *Camptostroma* probably had the lower theca either embedded in the soft sediment or attached to objects lying on the sea floor, making it a stationary or attached, low-level suspension feeder using tube feet in the ambulacra to capture small food particles drifting by the theca. The unusual thecal plating is the main feature separating *Camptostroma* from later Edrioasteroidea, which it otherwise resembles, but this genus may also have been ancestral to other classes such as the Eocrinoidea. *See* ECHINODERMATA; ECHINOZOA; EDRIOASTEROIDEA. James Sprinkle

Bibliography. K. Derstler, Ph.D. dissertation, University of California, Davis, 1985; J. W. Durham, *J. Paleontol.*, 40:1216–1220, 1966; C. R. C. Paul and A. B. Smith, *Biol. Rev.*, 59:443–481, 1984.

Canal

An artificial open channel usually used to convey water or vessels from one point to another. Canals are generally classified according to use as irrigation, power, flood-control, drainage, or navigation canals or channels. All but the last type are regarded as water conveyance canals.

Canals may be lined or unlined. Linings may consist of plain or reinforced concrete, cement mortar, asphalt, brick, stone, buried synthetic membranes, or compacted earth materials. Linings serve to reduce water losses by seepage or percolation through pervious foundations or embankments and to lessen the cost of weed control. Concrete and other hard-surface linings also permit higher water velocities and, therefore, steeper gradients and smaller cross sections, which may reduce costs and the amount of right-of-way required.

Water conveyance canals. The character of material along the bottom and sides of a canal must be considered in determining whether lining is required. The velocity in an irrigation canal must be sufficiently low to avoid erosion of the canal banks and bottom, and it must be high enough to prevent deposition of silt: Velocities of 1.5–3.5 ft/s (0.46–1.1 m/s) are normally used for earth canals, and about 7 ft/s (2 m/s) is the usual maximum for concrete-lined irrigation canals. The velocity depends on canal slope, boundary roughness, and proportions of the cross-sectional area. Canal capacity Q in ft³/s may be expressed by the formula $Q = AV$, where A is the cross-sectional area in square feet, and V is the average velocity in ft/s.

Most irrigation canals are trapezoidal in cross section. Their side slopes are generally either 1.5:1 or 2:1 (horizontal to vertical) depending on the type of soil, but flatter slopes are used in unstable materials. Side slopes of concrete-lined irrigation canals are generally 1.25:1 or 1.5:1. They occasionally may be as high as 2:1, as for example in the San Luis Canal

Fig. 1. Segment of the San Luis irrigation canal in California. A major waterway in the western United States, it is 103 mi (165 km) long, 200 ft (60 m) wide, and 36 ft (11 m) deep. (*U.S. Bureau of Reclamation and State of California*)

(**Fig. 1**). Freeboard, or the vertical distance between maximum water surface and top of canal bank, generally ranges from 1 ft (0.3 m) for small earth laterals to 4 ft (1.2 m) for earth canals. Freeboard for concrete-lined canals ranges from 0.5 to 3.5 ft (0.15 to 1.1 m) to the top of the lining, depending on capacity.

Irrigation canal intakes usually consist of a headworks and a river control structure with some form of intake gates to regulate the quantity of water admitted or stop the flow into the canal. Frequently, when the canal diverts from a stream that transports considerable sediment, the intake may be designed to keep out as much sediment as possible. This is accomplished by (1) locating the canal intake on the stream where the bed load is the smallest; (2) using weirs that divert water from the less silty upper layers of the flowing stream called skimming weirs; or (3) interposing basins in which much of the sand and silt are deposited before the water enters the canal. The deposited material is removed from these settling or desilting basins by occasional sluicing or dredging.

Irrigation canals usually require check structures in them to regulate the elevation of the water on the upstream side and wasteways as a safety device to carry off surplus water. The checks hold back the water in case of a break in the canal banks and retard the flow when the canal is being emptied to prevent a sudden evacuation and resulting uplift in the lining or sloughing of saturated banks. Hard-surfaced linings are frequently protected from uplift by automatic relief valves placed in the bottom and sides of the canal. *See* IRRIGATION (AGRICULTURE).

Although generally similar to irrigation canals in design, power, flood-control, and drainage canals or channels have special requirements. Power canals are placed on minimum grade to conserve head for power development; hence velocities are usually low. Rectangular wooden, concrete, or steel flumes

Fig. 2. Walter F. George Lock, Dam and Powerhouse on the Chattahoochee River, Alabama-Georgia boundary. The lock chamber can be seen at right center of the photograph. (*U.S. Army Corps of Engineers*)

with high ratio of depth to width are often used for this purpose. Because power canals are subject to sudden changes in flow, overflow wasteways are usually provided as well as ample freeboard.

Banks of flood-control channels constructed in earth are lined with grass or rock riprap for protection against erosion by flood flows. Grass protection is used for velocities from about 3 to 8 ft/s (0.9 to 2.4 m/s), and riprap for velocities of 8 to 18 ft/s (2.4 to 5.5 m/s). Either rectangular or trapezoidal concrete-lined channels are used for velocities exceeding 18 ft/s (5.5 m/s), although in some cases concrete lining is used for lower velocities to reduce the size of channel.

Drainage canals are deeply excavated to facilitate the drainage of surrounding land. They usually have a minimum grade and small depths of water flow.

Navigation canals and canalized rivers. Navigation canals are artificial inland waterways for boats, barges, or ships. A canalized river is one that has been made navigable by construction of one or more weirs or overflow dams (**Fig. 2**) to impound river flow, thereby providing navigable depths. Locks may be built in navigation canals and canalized rivers to enable vessels to move to higher or lower water levels.

Navigation canals are often built along portions of canalized rivers or located so as to connect two such rivers. They are adapted to the topography by a series of level reaches connected by locks. Sea-level navigation canals, connecting two tidal bodies of water, are excavated sufficiently deep to preclude the need for locks, if the tidal flow permits.

The dimensions of a navigation canal are determined primarily by the size, and to some extent by the speed, of the vessels that are to use it. Depth must be sufficient to assure bottom clearance under all operating conditions, and ordinarily the width allows vessels to pass each other safely. The canal cross section is usually trapezoidal, with side slopes ranging from 1.5:1 to 3:1 or flatter, depending on the stability of the bank material. Sections cut in rock may have vertical or near-vertical sides. Earth banks of some navigation canals are protected against erosion from wave action by placing rock riprap or similar protection near the water surface. *See* INLAND WATERWAYS TRANSPORTATION.

Locks. A lock (Fig. 2) is a chamber equipped with gates at both upstream and downstream ends. Water impounded in the chamber is used to raise or lower a vessel from one elevation to another. The lock chamber is filled and emptied by means of filling and emptying valves and a culvert system usually located in the walls and bottom of the lock.

After a vessel enters the lock chamber, the afterward gates are closed and the water level is lowered (if the vessel is headed downstream) by operation of the emptying valve, or raised (if the vessel is headed upstream) by operation of the filling valve. When the water level in the chamber reaches the water level forward of the vessel, the forward set of gates is opened and the vessel leaves the lock.

Maximum lift of a lock is the vertical distance from the normal pool upstream of the lock to the low-

water surface downstream of the lock. Low lifts simplify design problems, but generally in developing a major waterway it will be more economical to use fewer higher-lift locks. Lock lifts vary from a few feet in tidal canals to over 100 ft (30 m) in major rivers, such as the Columbia and Snake. Lock widths vary from 56 to 110 ft (17 to 33 m) and usable lengths vary from 400 to 1200 ft (120 to 370 m), except that smaller locks are used when all the traffic consists of small craft.

On some canalized rivers having low-lift locks, dams contain movable sections which are lowered during periods of moderate or high flow to permit the unobstructed passage of vessels and barges over the dam. The locks are used in these rivers only during periods of low flow when the movable sections of the dams are closed to create sufficient depth of water for navigation. *See* OPEN CHANNEL.

Corps of Engineers; Bureau of Reclamation

Bibliography. A. J. Chadwick and J. C. Morfett, *Hydraulics in Civil and Environmental Engineering*, 3d ed., 1998; H. W. King and E. F. Brater, *Handbook of Hydraulics*, 7th ed., 1996; J. K. Vennard and R. L. Street, *Elementary Fluid Mechanics*, 7th ed., 1995.

Cancer (constellation)

The Crab, a northern zodiacal constellation, visible in winter evenings (see **illustration**). It is the source of the terrestrial name Tropic of Cancer, for the parallel

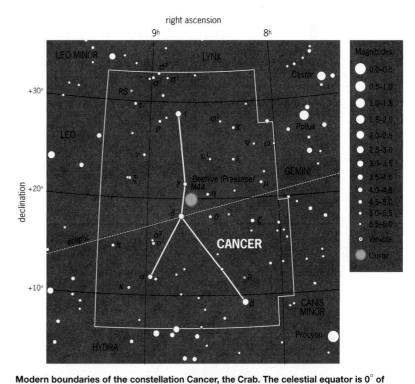

Modern boundaries of the constellation Cancer, the Crab. The celestial equator is 0° of declination, which corresponds to celestial latitude. Right ascension corresponds to celestial longitude, with each hour of right ascension representing 15° of arc. Apparent brightness of stars is shown with dot sizes to illustrate the magnitude scale, where the brightest stars in the sky are 0th magnitude or brighter and the faintest stars that can be seen with the unaided eye at a dark site are 6th magnitude. (*Wil Tirion*)

of latitude, about $23\frac{1}{2}°$ north of the Equator, where the Sun is 90° overhead at noon on the day of the summer solstice in the Northern Hemisphere (about June 21). The summer solstice used to occur when the Sun was in Cancer, but because of the precession of the equinoxes this point has moved to near the modern boundary between Gemini and Taurus (just within Taurus since 1875). *See* GEMINI; PRECESSION OF EQUINOXES; TAURUS; TROPIC OF CANCER; ZODIAC.

Though Cancer has no bright stars, it boasts of an open cluster of stars, Praesepe, the Beehive Cluster, visible to the eye as a hazy spot. In his 1610 book, *Sidereus Nuncius* (The Starry Message), Galileo reported how his newly invented telescope discovered that the haze was really a cluster of stars. *See* STAR CLUSTERS.

The modern boundaries of this and the other 87 constellations were defined by the International Astronomical Union in 1928. *See* CONSTELLATION.

Jay M. Pasachoff

Cancer (medicine)

The common name for a malignant neoplasm or tumor. Neoplasms are new growths and can be divided into benign and malignant types, although in some instances the distinction is unclear. The most important differentiating feature is that a malignant tumor will invade surrounding structures and metastasize (spread) to distant sites whereas a benign tumor will not. Other distinctions between benign and malignant growth include the following: malignancies but not benign types are composed of highly atypical cells; malignancies tend to show more rapid growth than benign neoplasms, and are composed, in part, of cells showing frequent mitotic activity; and malignant tumors tend to grow progressively without self-limitation. *See* MITOSIS; TUMOR.

Malignant neoplasms that arise from cells of mesenchymal origin (for example, bone muscle, connective tissue) are called sarcomas. Those that develop from epithelial cells and tissues (for example, skin, mucosal membranes, and glandular tissues) are termed carcinomas. Carcinomas usually metastasize initially by way of lymphatic channels, whereas sarcomas spread to distant organs through the bloodstream.

Etiology. The cause of most types of human cancers is unknown. However, a number of factors are thought to be operative in the development of some malignant neoplasms. Genetic factors are thought to be causally related to some human malignancies such as lung cancer in that the incidence of cancer among persons with a positive family history of cancer may be three times as high as in those who do not have a family history. A number of different neoplasms are known to be genetically related and may be due to damage or changes in chromosome structure. These include such neoplasms as retinoblastoma (an eye tumor), pheochromocy-

toma and medullary thyroid carcinoma (adrenal and thyroid neoplasms), and several types of neoplasms that occur in people who have genetically caused immune deficiency syndromes; in these individuals there is a marked increase in lymphoma (cancer of the lymph glands). *See* IMMUNOLOGICAL DEFICIENCY; LYMPHOMA.

Radiation in various forms is thought to be responsible for up to 3% of all cancers. Persons who receive radiation therapy for some other type of malignant neoplasm, or who are exposed to ionizing radiation from atomic blasts or accidents, have an increase in leukemia. Also, people who receive radiation to the neck have a higher incidence of thyroid carcinoma. Electromagnetic radiation from the Sun (solar radiation) is associated with a higher incidence of many types of skin cancer, including malignant melanoma. There has been a distinct and growing concern about naturally occurring radon gas, from the decay of radioactive rocks in the Earth's crust, concentrated in certain areas of the world such as the Redding Prong in the northeastern United States. Radon gas has been stated to cause up to 10% of all lung cancers, a finding that would be consistent with studies showing that certain types of lung cancer are increased in uranium miners. *See* LEUKEMIA; RADIATION BIOLOGY.

In the United States the carcinogens in tobacco account for up to one-third of all cancer deaths in men and 5–10% in women. The increasing incidence and death rate from cancer of the lung in women is alarming, and is directly related to the increasing prevalence of cigarette smoking by women. There is absolutely no doubt that the single most important action that could be taken to reduce the incidence of cancer in the United States would be to markedly reduce or to eliminate cigarette smoking. Cigarette smoking and the heavy consumption of ethyl alcohol appear to act synergistically in the development of oral, esophageal, and gastric cancers.

There are several carcinogens to which people are exposed occupationally that result in the development of cancer, although the mechanisms by which they cause neoplasms are sometimes poorly understood. For example, arsenic is associated with lung, skin, and liver cancer; asbestos causes mesotheliomas (cancer of the pleural, peritoneal, and pericardial cavities); benzene causes leukemia; and vinyl chloride causes angiosarcomas (tumors of blood vessels) of the liver. *See* MUTAGENS AND CARCINOGENS.

Certain drugs and hormones have been found to cause certain types of neoplasms. Postmenopausal women taking estrogen hormones have a much higher incidence of endometrial cancer (cancer of the lining of the uterine cavity). Alkylating agents that are used in the treatment of a variety of cancers have been shown to cause acute leukemia. Persons who receive organ transplants and are treated with immunosuppressive drugs, such as azathioprine, have an increased incidence of cancer of the lymphoid cells (lymphomas). *See* IMMUNOSUPPRESSION.

The role of diet and nutrition in the development of malignant tumors is controversial and still under investigation. Some epidemiologic studies have shown that certain diets, such as those high in saturated fats, are associated with an increased incidence of certain types of neoplasm, such as colon cancer. Vitamin A–containing compounds have also been shown epidemiologically to prevent some cancers, including lung cancers. In addition, some substances, such as nitrites, used to cure such foods as bacon, are causally associated with gastrointestinal cancers.

The role of viruses in the development of human cancers is being studied. A type of lymphoma that occurs primarily in southern Japan is known to be caused by a retrovirus referred to as human T-cell lymphoma and leukemia virus type I (HTLV-I). Epstein-Barr virus, a deoxyribonucleic acid (DNA) virus of the herpes family, is closely associated with African Burkitt's lymphoma and a tumor of the nasopharynx (nasopharyngeal carcinoma). There is an increased incidence of cancer of liver cells in people who are infected with hepatitis B virus. Whether hepatitis B virus directly causes the tumor or is one of many factors in the development of this type of tumor is uncertain. Certain strains of human papilloma virus (HPV) are thought to cause some cases of uterine cervical carcinoma. *See* EPSTEIN-BARR VIRUS; HERPES; RETROVIRUS; TUMOR VIRUSES.

It is generally accepted that the neoplastic condition is caused by alterations in genetic mechanisms involved in cellular differentiation. In malignant cells, normal cellular processes are bypassed due to the actions of a select group of genes called oncogenes which regulate cellular activities. A group of these highly conserved genes exist in normal cells and are called proto-oncogenes. These genes appear to be important in regulating cellular growth during embryonic development. Although these genes were originally identified in oncogenic retroviruses, proto-oncogenes have been found in normal tissue and also have been identified in a variety of human cancers. Increased amounts of these proto-oncogenes have been seen in small-cell undifferentiated cancer of the lung, colon cancer, breast cancer, and lymphomas. Since proto-oncogenes seem to be important in embryonic growth, it is not surprising that in the process of carcinogenesis these genes can be expressed and can lead to the proliferation of malignant cells. It is thought that in carcinogenesis these proto-oncogenes become unmasked or changed during the breakage or translocation of chromosomes. These genes that were previously suppressed in the cell then become functional, and in some instances lead to the excessive production of growth factors which could be important in the neoplastic state. *See* ONCOGENES.

Incidence. The incidence of malignancies varies with regard to race, geographical location, sex, age, hereditary factors, and socioeconomic status. In certain parts of Africa, for example, liver cancer is the most common malignant neoplasm, whereas in the United States lung cancer in men and breast cancer in women are the most common neoplasms. There has been a marked rise in the incidence of lung cancer in both men and women due to cigarette smoking, whereas most other common tumors, such as cancer of the colon and stomach, have remained stable or even decreased.

Signs, symptoms, and staging. The physical changes that cancer produces in the body vary considerably, depending on the type of tumor, location, rate of growth, and whether it has metastasized. The American Cancer Society has widely publicized cancer's seven warning signals: (1) a change in bowel or bladder habits; (2) a sore that does not heal; (3) unusual bleeding or discharge; (4) a thickening or lump in the breast or elsewhere; (5) indigestion or difficulty in swallowing; (6) an obvious change in a wart or mole; and (7) a nagging cough or hoarseness.

In current medical practice, most cancers are staged according to tumor size, metastases to lymph nodes, and distant metastases. This type of staging is useful in determining the most effective therapy and the prognosis.

Treatment. The progression, or lack thereof, of a given cancer is highly variable and depends on the type of neoplasm and the response to treatment. Treatment modalities include surgery, chemotherapy, radiation therapy, hormonal manipulation, and immunotherapy. In general, each type of cancer is treated very specifically, and often a combination of the various modalities is used, for example, surgery preceded or followed by radiation therapy. The response to treatment depends on the type of tumor, its size, and whether it has spread. *See* CHEMOTHERAPY AND OTHER ANTINEOPLASTIC DRUGS; IMMUNOTHERAPY; ONCOLOGY; RADIOGRAPHY.

Samuel P. Hammar

Bibliography. V. T. DeVita, Jr., et al., *Cancer: Principles and Practices of Oncology*, 5th ed., 1997; V. T. DeVita, Jr., et al. (eds.), *Important Advances in Oncology*, 1996; J. F. Holland and E. Frei, *Cancer Medicine*, 4th ed., 1999.

Cancrinite

A family of minerals, related to the scapolite family, characteristically occurring in basic rocks such as nepheline syenites and sodalite syenites. A typical specimen is shown in the **illustration**. Cancrinite is hexagonal, $a = 1.28$, $c = 0.52$ nanometers respectively, space group $P6_3$, and is based on a three-dimensional linkage of $[AlO_4]$ and $[SiO_4]$ tetrahedra. Four-, six-, and twelve-membered aluminosilicate rings can be discerned in the structure. Large anions such as $[SO_4]^{2-}$ and $[CO_3]^{2-}$ occur in the hexagonal channels of the structure. The cancrinite member is white, yellow, greenish, or reddish. It has perfect prismatic cleavage, hardness is 5–6 on Mohs scale, and the specific gravity is 2.45.

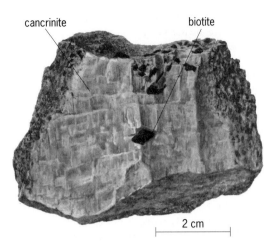

Cancrinite with biotite in nepheline syenite rock, Bigwood Township, Ontario, Canada. (*Specimen from Department of Geology, Bryn Mawr College*)

Compositionally, four members of the cancrinite family are:

Cancrinite	$Na_6Ca_2[AlSiO_4]_6(CO_3)(OH)_2$
Vishnevite	$Na_6Ca_2[AlSiO_4]_6(SO_4)(OH)_2$
Haüyne	$K_2Na_4Ca_2[AlSiO_4]_6(SO_4)(OH)_2$
Afghanite	$Na_6Ca_2[AlSiO_4]_4(SO_4)(OH)Cl$

The cancrinite structure has been proposed as a possible crystalline storage site for nuclear wastes, in particular the gases. Cancrinite can be derived from reaction of far more common nepheline with calcite.

Localities include the Fen area, southern Norway; the Kola Peninsula, Soviet Union; Bancroft, Ontario, Canada; and Litchfield, Maine. *See* FELDSPATHOID; SILICATE MINERALS.   Paul B. Moore

Candlepower

Luminous intensity expressed in candelas. The term refers only to the intensity in a particular direction and by itself does not give an indication of the total light emitted. The candlepower in a given direction from a light source is equal to the illumination in footcandles falling on a surface normal to that direction, multiplied by the square of the distance from the light source in feet. The candlepower is also equal to the illumination of metercandles (lux) multiplied by the square of the distance in meters.

The apparent candlepower is the candlepower of a point source which will produce the same illumination at a given distance as produced by a given light source.

The mean horizontal candlepower is the average candlepower of a light source in the horizontal plane passing through the luminous center of the light source.

The mean spherical candlepower is the average candlepower in all directions from a light source as a center. Since there is a total solid angle of 4π (steradians) emanating from a point, the mean spherical candlepower is equal to the total luminous flux (in lumens) of a light source divided by 4π (steradians). *See* LUMINOUS INTENSITY; PHOTOMETRY.   Russell C. Putnam

Canine distemper

A fatal viral disease of dogs and other carnivores, with a worldwide distribution. Canine distemper virus has a wide host range; most terrestrial carnivores are susceptible to natural canine distemper virus infection. All animals in the families Canidae (for example, dog, dingo, fox, coyote, wolf, jackal), Mustelidae (for example, weasel, ferret, mink, skunk, badger, stoat, marten, otter), and Procyonidae (for example, kinkajou, coati, bassariscus, raccoon, panda) may succumb to canine distemper virus infection. Members of other Carnivora families, including domestic cats and swine, may become subclinically infected. The virus has also been isolated from large cats (lions, tigers, leopards) that have died in zoological parks in North America, from wild lions in the Serengeti National Park (Tanzania), and from wild javelinas (collared peccaries). *See* CARNIVORA.

Etiologic agent. Canine distemper virus is classified as a morbillivirus within the Paramyxoviridae family, closely related to measles virus and rinderpest virus of cattle and the phocine (seal) and dolphin distemper virus. The virus is enveloped with a negative-sense ribonucleic acid and consists of six structural proteins: the nucleoprotein and two enzymes in the nucleocapsid, the membrane protein on the inside, and the hemagglutinating and fusion proteins on the outside of the lipoprotein envelope. *See* ANIMAL VIRUS; PARAMYXOVIRUS.

Transmission. Canine distemper is enzootic worldwide. Aerosol transmission in respiratory secretions is the main route of transmission. Virus shedding begins approximately 7 days after the initial infection. Acutely infected dogs and other carnivores shed virus in all body excretions, regardless of whether they show clinical signs or not.

Canine distemper virus affects susceptible dogs of all ages, but puppies are most vulnerable when their maternal antibodies are lost. Dogs that completely recover from canine distemper virus infection are immune for years and probably for life. They do not shed the virus and they are not persistently infected. Outside the host, canine distemper virus becomes inactivated rapidly, and all of the available common disinfectants are effective against it.

Disease signs. Great variations occur in the duration and severity of canine distemper, which may range from no visible signs to severe disease, often with central nervous system involvement, with approximately 50% mortality in dogs.

The first fever 3–6 days after infection may pass unnoticed; the second peak (several days later and intermittent thereafter) is usually associated with nasal and ocular discharge, depression, and anorexia. A low lymphocyte count is always present during the early stages of infection. Gastrointestinal and respiratory signs may follow, often enhanced by secondary infection.

Many infected dogs develop central nervous system disorders following systemic disease. Depending on the virus strain, the signs may be more related to acute gray matter disease or subacute white matter disease. Seizures and muscle spasms accompanied by depression predominate in gray matter disease; lack of muscle coordination, partial paralysis, and muscle tremors occur in white matter disease. Brain and spinal inflammation and cervical rigidity may be seen in both. Inflammation of the optic nerve and retinal lesions in dogs with canine distemper virus are not uncommon. Hardening of the foot pads (hyperkeratosis) and nose is produced by some virus strains. In growing dogs, loss of enamel from the teeth after canine distemper virus infection is common. Old dog encephalitis, a rare disease of middle-aged or older dogs caused by canine distemper virus, is characterized by progressive deterioration and is ultimately fatal. Postvaccinal encephalitis may develop 1–2 weeks after vaccination and usually causes behavioral changes, seizures, and blindness; but this condition is rare.

Pathology. Atrophy of the thymus gland and hardening of lung tissue are the main lesions. Discharges of mucus and pus from the nose and eyes, diarrhea, hardening of nose and foot pads, and skin pustules may be present. Depletion of lymphocytes in lymphoid tissues, interstitial pneumonia, and intracytoplasmic inclusion bodies in epithelium of the respiratory, alimentary, and urinary tracts are characteristic. In the central nervous system, the degeneration of neurons is typical, but not always present. Intracytoplasmic and intranuclear bodies can be found, predominantly in astrocytes and neurons.

Dogs with old dog encephalitis have extensive infiltration of the surrounding vessels by lymphocytes in the central nervous system, degeneration of neurons, and minimal depletion of myelin. Postvaccinal encephalitis causes lesions predominantly in the brainstem.

Treatment. A specific antiviral drug having an effect on canine distemper virus in dogs is not presently available. Treatment of canine distemper, therefore, is nonspecific and supportive. Antibiotic therapy is recommended because of the common occurrence of secondary bacterial infections of the respiratory and alimentary tracts. Administration of fluids and electrolytes may be the most important therapy for canine distemper because diseased dogs with diarrhea are often dehydrated.

Treatment of neurologic forms of canine distemper is usually not very successful. Sedatives and anticonvulsants may temporarily relieve clinical signs, but they do not have a healing effect. When central nervous system disorders are progressive and dogs become recumbent, euthanasia is usually prescribed. Some dogs with central nervous system disorders, however, recover quite well, and residual signs such as muscle spasms or inflammation of the optic nerve can improve with time.

Vaccination and control. Immunization by controlled vaccination is the only effective approach to canine distemper prophylaxis. Active immunization with modified-live virus vaccines induces long-lasting immunity and keeps the disease in dogs under control. With a few exceptions, modified-live canine distemper virus vaccines are derived from either egg and avian cell or canine cell culture adaptations. Both methods of adaptation produce vaccines that are very effective in inducing an immunity that lasts for at least 1 year and probably for several years in most dogs. Any modified-live canine distemper virus vaccine may be fatal for certain wildlife and zoo animals (such as red pandas or black-footed ferrets). Inactivated virus vaccines must be used in some species, but they are not commercially available in the United States.

Heterotypic (measles) virus vaccination has been the best approach to overcome maternal antibody interference with immunization. As with inactivated canine distemper virus vaccines, measles virus induces a limited immunity that can protect dogs against canine distemper virus disease but not against canine distemper virus infection. A combination of attenuated measles virus and canine distemper virus is still commonly used in 6–10-week-old pups. It offers the advantage of complete protection in the absence of, and partial protection in the presence of, maternal antibody. In addition, measles virus antibody titers induced by vaccination usually are below a level that would interfere with measles virus vaccination in the next generation when used in 6–10-week-old pups.

A vaccination schedule for pups against canine distemper should include a combined modified-live measle virus–canine distemper virus vaccination at 6–8 weeks of age. Two additional canine distemper virus vaccinations at 3–4-week intervals should be given. Annual booster inoculations are recommended because some dogs lose antibody titers in that time period. Pups deprived of colostrum (the first milk from the mammary gland) should not be vaccinated with modified-live canine distemper virus before they are 3–4 weeks of age. Modified-live canine distemper virus can be fatal in unprotected younger pups, as it can be in some wild or zoo animals.

Besides immunization, strict isolation of dogs with canine distemper appears to be the most important step in controlling the disease. The virus is shed in all body excretions during the acute systemic disease, and direct dog-to-dog contact appears to be the main route of viral spread. Dogs with subacute canine distemper encephalitis still may infect susceptible contact dogs. Disinfection of the environment can be accomplished with commonly used products because the enveloped virus is rapidly destroyed outside the host.   M. J. G. Appel; B. A. Summers

Bibliography. C. E. Green (ed.), *Canine Distemper in Infectious Diseases of the Dog and Cat*, 1990; M. Horzinek (ed.), *Virus Infections of Vertebrates*, 1987.

Canine parvovirus infection

Severe enteritis caused by a small nonenveloped single-stranded deoxyribonucleic acid (DNA) virus that is resistant to inactivation and remains infectious in the environment for 5–7 months. First observed in dogs in 1976, canine parvovirus may have originated by mutation of a closely related parvovirus of cats or wildlife. The original virus was designated as canine parvovirus, type 2 (CPV-2); however, since its discovery the virus has undergone two minor genetic alterations, designated CPV-2a and CPV-2b. These alterations may have enabled the virus to adapt to its new host, replicate, and spread more effectively.

Epidemiology. Canine parvovirus is transmitted between dogs by the fecal-oral route. The incubation period is 3–7 days. Virus is first shed in the feces on day 3, and shedding continues for an additional 10 days. Chronically infected dogs that shed virus intermittently are rare. Most naturally occurring infections in dogs are subclinical or result in mild signs of the disease. Dogs with subclinical infections play an important role in the spread of the disease by shedding large amounts of virus into the environment. This shedding, along with the ability of the virus to persist in the environment, contributes to the endemicity of the disease. The development of disease following infection ranges from 20 to 90%, and mortality between 0 to 50%.

Pathogenesis. Only mitotically active cells, such as those of the intestine, lymphoid system, bone marrow, and fetal tissues, support replication of the canine parvovirus. After ingestion, the virus replicates in the regional lymphoid tissues of the oropharynx, spreading to other lymphoid tissues, bone marrow, and intestinal epithelial cells by way of the blood. Viral replication in the lymphoid tissue and bone marrow leads to necrosis of the lymphoid cells and a decrease in circulating white blood cells. Viral replication in the germinal epithelium of the intestinal glands of the jejunum and ileum leads to blunting and fusing of the intestinal villi. Diarrhea results from disruption of the normal absorptive and digestive processes. In severe cases, hemorrhaging into the intestine occurs. Secondary bacterial infections occur in severely affected animals.

Diagnosis and treatment. Severe enteritis is commonly observed in dogs 6–20 weeks of age. Initial signs include depression, anorexia, and lethargy, followed by fever, abdominal pain, vomiting, and diarrhea. Blood may be found in both the vomitus and stool. Dehydration, hypothermia, and weakness develop if the vomiting and diarrhea are severe. Signs are more severe in pups that are undernourished, stressed, or concurrently infected with other organisms. Diagnosis is based on history, clinical signs, vaccination status, physical exam, and laboratory tests. The white blood cell count is usually low. Detection of virus in the feces provides a definitive diagnosis. The bowel lumen is often empty, but on occasion there may be watery or hemorrhagic intestinal matter.

The goal of treatment is to support the animal until the infection runs its course. There are no specific antiviral therapies available. The intensity of treatment depends on the severity of signs. Dehydrated pups require intensive intravenous fluid therapy. Antimicrobial drugs are useful because of the risk of secondary bacterial infections, and antiemetic drugs help control vomiting and nausea. Good nursing care is essential. All food and water should be withheld until the pup is no longer vomiting, and the pup should be kept warm, clean, and dry. Because of the infectious nature of the disease, pups should be isolated from other dogs.

Prevention. Canine parvovirus infection in pups is prevented by minimizing exposure and by vaccination. Keeping pups isolated from other dogs until completion of the vaccination series is optimal. If strict isolation is not possible, limiting the exposure of pups to areas where large numbers of dogs congregate is useful. Immunity to canine parvovirus infection can be either passive or active. Passive immunity results from absorption of maternal antibodies following ingestion of colostrum; active immunity develops following natural infection or vaccination. The maternal antibodies protect the pup from natural infection, with the duration of protection dependent on the quantity of immunoglobulins absorbed. Inactivated and modified-live forms of the canine parvovirus vaccine are available. Vaccines that include a modified-live attenuated canine parvovirus strain are preferred because immunity develops more rapidly and is of longer duration. Pups are vaccinated at 2–3-week intervals starting at 6–8 weeks of age and continuing to 16–20 weeks of age. The immune response following vaccination depends on the amount of maternal antibodies present. High levels of antibodies block the immune response to vaccination. This period of nonresponsiveness may extend up to 16–20 weeks of age. *See* ANIMAL VIRUS; IMMUNITY; VACCINATION.   Michael J. Coyne

Bibliography. M. S. Leib (ed.), *Gasteroenterology: The 1990's*, 1993; P. Tijssen (ed.), *Handbook of Parvoviruses*, 1989; C. Vella and S. W. Ketteridge, *Canine Parvovirus: A New Pathogen*, 1991.

Canis Major

The Great Dog, a southern constellation at the feet of Orion (see **illustration**). It contains Sirius, at magnitude −1.4 the brightest star in the sky. Sirius is known as the Dog Star. Its heliacal rising—its first visibility at dawn during the year—came at a time that indicated that the annual, agriculturally useful Nile floods would soon begin. Its name led to the phrase "the dog days of summer." Sirius is prominent in the winter evening sky. Its faint white-dwarf companion is difficult to detect in its glare, even using the required telescope. *See* SIRIUS.

In Greek mythology, this Big Dog could be a dog of Orion but could also be a dog of Helen, which allowed Paris to abduct her easily. *See* ORION.

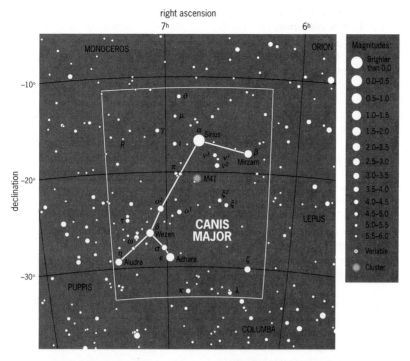

Modern boundaries of the constellation Canis Major, the Great Dog. The celestial equator is 0° of declination, which corresponds to celestial latitude. Right ascension corresponds to celestial longitude, with each hour of right ascension representing 15° of arc. Apparent brightness of stars is shown with dot sizes to illustrate the magnitude scale, where the brightest stars in the sky are 0th magnitude or brighter and the faintest stars that can be seen with the unaided eye at a dark site are 6th magnitude. (*Wil Tirion*)

The modern boundaries of the 88 constellations, including this one, were defined by the International Astronomical Union in 1928. *See* CONSTELLATION.

Jay M. Pasachoff

Canonical coordinates and transformations

Classical mechanics is the study of the positions and motions of particles or extended bodies. Initially the description used the coordinates and velocities of the objects under consideration and applied Newton's laws to describe their motions. Later the Lagrangian formulation was used to relate the positions, velocities, and resulting accelerations through an action principle. In the Lagrangian method, the velocities are considered as the time derivatives of the positions, and the equations of motion are determined by varying possible paths of the system holding the end points of the variation constant. A more general method is the Hamiltonian formulation, which considers the positions and momenta of the objects in the system under consideration as independent quantities. For the Hamiltonian variation, the momenta and the positions are varied independently subject to a constraint of the relation between the velocities and the momenta.

The Hamiltonian formulation allows the use of any system of coordinates that meet certain conditions. The advantage is that these coordinates can even be a mixture of the original positions and momenta. This freedom can often offer deeper insight into the physics of the system under consideration.

The disadvantage is that there are certain restrictions on the possible choice of the new coordinates and momenta. Coordinates that meet these restrictions are named canonical coordinates. The allowed transformations from one set of canonical coordinates to another set are termed canonical transformations. In cases where the energy of the system is conserved, the Hamiltonian is the energy of the system. *See* HAMILTON'S EQUATIONS OF MOTION; LAGRANGE'S EQUATIONS; LAGRANGIAN FUNCTION.

General principles. To be more explicit, we can consider a system of n particles. If we use Newton's laws and the Lagrangian method, the nonrelativistic Lagrangian formulation of mechanics of a system of $3n$ degrees of freedom (x_i) produces $3n$ equations involving, in general, the positions, velocities, and accelerations of the objects in the system under consideration. The momentum, formally called the conjugate momentum (p_i), is defined as equal to the derivative of the Lagrangian with respect to the velocity. In contrast, the Hamiltonian method treats the momenta as independent quantities. The variation is taken of a quantity termed the Hamiltonian, usually denoted by H, which is a function of the independent coordinates q_i and independent momenta p_i. The Hamiltonian is given by Eq. (1), where L is the

$$H = \sum_i p_i \dot{q} - L(q, \dot{q}, t) \qquad (1)$$

Lagrangian and subscripts on the q's in the Lagrangian are suppressed for simplicity. This produces $6n$ equations, which involve only the coordinates and their momenta. The problem has been reduced from a set of $3n$ second-order equations to a set of $6n$ first-order equations involving the coordinates, the momenta, the first derivatives of the momenta, and possibly time. The set of coordinates and momenta (q_i, p_i) are called canonical coordinates. Canonical transformations are transformations that maintain these definitions. The transformations can mix the original coordinates and momenta into new coordinates and momenta. The methods can be extended to a noncovariant formulation of relativistic mechanics.

Presumably "canonical" is used in the sense of designating a simple general set of standard equations. It appears that the term was introduced by C. G. Jacobi in 1837, but in a slightly different sense. Although the term rapidly gained common usage, the reason for its introduction apparently remained obscure even to contemporaries. Possibly there is an intended or unintended analogy to religious canons.

A straightforward application of the Hamiltonian formulation usually does not materially decrease the effort needed to solve a mechanics problem. The advantages are not in its use as a calculational tool but in the insight it affords to the formal structure of mechanics. Since the momenta and coordinates are treated equally, we may consider the motion of a physical system as a path in a $6n$-dimensional Cartesian space, called the phase space, which has $6n$ independent coordinates that describe the positions and momenta of each of the n particles that constitute the system. We can make invertible coordinate transformations that mix the old p_i's and q_i's into a new set of coordinates and momenta (Q_i, P_i); that is, the new coordinates can be expressed by Eqs. (2).

$$Q_i = Q_i(q_j, p_j, t)$$
$$P_i = P_i(q_j, p_j, t) \tag{2}$$

For Hamiltonian mechanics, only those transformations can be of interest that maintain the canonical nature of the new coordinates. This requirement can be satisfied only if there exists some function, $K(Q, P, t)$, such that the equations of motion in the new set of coordinates are of the Hamiltonian form given by Eqs. (3). That is, Eqs. (4) are satisfied,

$$\dot{q} = \frac{\partial H}{\partial p_i} \qquad \dot{p} = -\frac{\partial H}{\partial q_i} \tag{3}$$

$$\dot{Q} = \frac{\partial K}{\partial P_i} \qquad \dot{P} = -\frac{\partial K}{\partial Q_i} \tag{4}$$

where K is the Hamiltonian in the new coordinate system.

Hamilton's principle is satisfied for both the old coordinates and the new coordinates provided that Eq. (5) holds, where H is the original Hamiltonian.

$$\lambda \left(\sum_i p_i \dot{q} - H \right) = \sum_i P_i \dot{Q} - K + \frac{dF}{dt} \tag{5}$$

The quantity F, called the generating function of the transformation, is a function of both the new and old phase-space coordinates and possibly time, with continuous second derivatives. The constant λ corresponds to a scale transformation. (A simple example of a scale transformation would be a change in units from p and q to P and Q such as a change from centimeters to meters. Such a transformation is termed a point transformation of phase space.) It is possible for a canonical transformation to affect only some of the coordinates and momenta, leaving the others unchanged.

Canonical transformations form a group. The generator of two successive transformations is the sum of the generators in the appropriate order. *See* GROUP THEORY.

There are only four basic canonical generating functions. They are given by Eqs. (6), where the sub-

$$F = F_1(q, Q, t)$$
$$F = F_2(q, P, t) - \sum_i Q_i P_i$$
$$F = F_3(p, Q, t) + \sum_i q_i p_i \tag{6}$$
$$F = F_4(p, P, t) + \sum_i (q_i p_i - Q_i P_i)$$

scripts on the q's, p's, Q's, and P's in functions F_1 to F_4 are suppressed for simplicity. The extra terms are needed to preserve the canonical nature of the transformations. Any other generating function can be expressed as a linear combination of the basic ones.

No other coordinate transformations can preserve the canonical nature of the new coordinates. The main problem in analyzing a physical system is in determining which generating function F_i provides useful insight. Sometimes the transformation is obvious; other times trial and error are used. Some well-known and useful examples of generating functions will be discussed.

Examples. The generating function of Eq. (7) generates the transformations of Eqs. (8). For the

$$F = F_4(p_i, P_i, t) + \sum_i (p_i q_i - Q_i P_i) \tag{7}$$

$$q_i = -\frac{\partial F_{i4}}{\partial p_i} \qquad Q_i = \frac{\partial F_{i4}}{\partial P_i} \tag{8}$$

trivial special case of $F_4 = \sum_i p_i P_i$, the resulting coordinates are $Q_i = p_i$ and $P_i = -q_i$. Therefore, this canonical transformation interchanges the coordinates and the momenta.

The harmonic oscillator in one dimension provides another example. The Hamiltonian can be written as Eq. (9). This Hamiltonian is a sum of squares

$$H = \frac{1}{2m}(p^2 + m^2 \omega^2 q^2) \tag{9}$$

of the coordinate and the momentum. We can use a generating function to eliminate the coordinate with a canonical transformation of the form (10),

$$p = f(P)\cos Q \qquad q = \frac{f(P)}{m\omega}\sin Q \tag{10}$$

which gives Eq. (11). A generating function of

$$K = H = \frac{f^2(P)}{2m} \qquad (11)$$

form (12) produces the transformation of Eqs. (13),

$$F_1 = \frac{m\omega q^2}{2} \cot (Q) \qquad (12)$$

$$q = \sqrt{\frac{2P}{m\omega}} \sin Q$$

$$p = \sqrt{2Pm\omega} \cos Q \qquad (13)$$

so $f(p) = \sqrt{2m\omega P}$ and $H = \omega P$. Hence,

$$\dot{Q} = \frac{\partial H}{\partial P} = \omega \qquad Q = \omega t + \alpha$$

where α is a constant, so the usual solution for the harmonic oscillator is obtained. A coordinate that can be removed from the Hamiltonian by a canonical transformation is said to be a cyclic coordinate since it oscillates in time. This exercise may seem like "cracking a peanut with a sledge hammer," but it shows how cyclic coordinates can be extracted by canonical transformations. *See* ACTION; HAMILTON-JACOBI THEORY; HARMONIC OSCILLATOR.

Some applications. In addition to Hamiltonian-Jacobi theory and action angle variables, infinitesimal canonical transformations were used in the development of the original mathematics of quantum mechanics.

The generating function given by Eq. (14) uses

$$F(q, P, t) = \sum_j q_j P_j + \varepsilon X(q_i, P_i) \qquad (14)$$

the form F_2. Here, ε is a small displacement in time whose square can be neglected, and the subscripts in F are suppressed for simplicity. This function generates an infinitesimal canonical transformation given by Eqs. (15). The δq_i and the δp_i are thus small, and

$$\delta q_j = Q_j - q_j = \varepsilon \frac{\partial X}{\partial P_j}$$

$$\delta p_j = P_j - p_j = -\varepsilon \frac{\partial X}{\partial q_j} \qquad (15)$$

the P_i can be replaced by p_i in the function X. Thus, X generates an infinitesimal displacement in the system variables q_i and p_i. Such quantities are termed dynamical variables. For example, if X is the z component of linear momentum of a particle, it generates an infinitesimal displacement in the z direction. Likewise, a component of angular momentum generates an infinitesimal rotation, and the Hamiltonian generates a change corresponding to an infinitesimal time displacement, ε.

Poisson brackets. If $Y(q_i, p_i, t)$ is another dynamical variable, distinct from the dynamical variable, $X(q_i, p_i, t)$ introduced above, then we can consider the change in Y, δY, under the transformation X.

Equation (16) is obtained where (Y, X) is known as

$$\delta Y = \sum_j \left(\frac{\partial Y}{\partial q_j} \delta q_j + \frac{\partial Y}{\partial p_j} p_j \right)$$

$$= \sum_{j=\varepsilon} \left(\frac{\partial Y}{\partial q_j} \frac{\partial X}{\partial p_j} - \frac{\partial X}{\partial q_j} \frac{\partial Y}{\partial p_j} \right)_0 = \varepsilon(Y, X) \qquad (16)$$

the Poisson bracket of two dynamical variables Y and X. Clearly $(X, Y) = -(Y, X)$; that is, the bracket is antisymmetric.

If one of the dynamical variables is chosen to be the Hamiltonian, the Poisson bracket of any other dynamical variable is given by Eq. (17). If a dynam-

$$(X, H) = \sum_{j=1}^{f} \left(\frac{\partial X}{\partial q_j} \frac{\partial H}{\partial p_j} - \frac{\partial H}{\partial q_j} \frac{\partial X}{\partial p_j} \right)$$

$$= \frac{dX}{dt} - \frac{\partial X}{\partial t} \qquad (17)$$

ical variable does not explicitly depend upon time, its Poisson bracket with the Hamiltonian is its time derivative. If the Poisson bracket of a dynamical variable with the Hamiltonian vanishes, the dynamical variable is a constant of the motion, and it follows directly that the Hamiltonian is invariant under the infinitesimal transformation generated by that dynamical variable. This relation connects the symmetry of a system directly with the constants of motion of the system. *See* CONSERVATION LAWS (PHYSICS); SYMMETRY LAWS (PHYSICS).

Transition to quantum theory. Quantum mechanics is related to classical mechanics through the identification of the quantum commutator of two variables with $ih/(2\pi)$ times the Poisson bracket of the classically analogous dynamical variables, if they exist, where h is Planck's constant. This is one reason for the great importance of Poisson brackets. Thus, for example, classically the angular momentum components j_x, j_y, and j_z satisfy the Poisson bracket relation (18), and so on. The corresponding opera-

$$(j_x, j_y) = j_z \qquad (18)$$

tors in quantum mechanics obey the commutation relation (19), where the notation [,] is used to distin-

$$j_x j_y - j_y j_x = \frac{ih}{2\pi} j_z = [j_x, j_y] \qquad (19)$$

guish between classical variables and quantum operators. *See* ANGULAR MOMENTUM; NONRELATIVISTIC QUANTUM THEORY.　　　John L. Safko; Philip Stehle

Bibliography. T. L. Chow, *Classical Mechanics*, 1995; H. Goldstein, C. P. Poole, Jr., and J. L. Safko, *Classical Mechanics*, 3d ed., 2002; I. Percival and D. Richards, *Introduction to Dynamics*, 1982.

Cantaloupe

In the United States the name applied to muskmelon cultivars belonging to *Cucumis melo* var. *reticulatus* of the family Cucurbitaceae. *See* VIOLALES.

Cantaloupes (*Cucumis melo*).

Description. The fruits weigh 2.4 lb (1.1 kg) and are round to oval; the surface is netted and has shallow vein tracts (see **illus.**). At maturity the skin color changes from dark green or gray to light gray or yellow. The flesh is usually salmon-colored, but it may vary from green to deep salmon-orange. When mature the melon is sweet, averages 6–8% sugar, and has a distinct aroma and flavor. The flesh is high in potassium and vitamin C, and when deep orange, rich in vitamin A. The vines usually bear andromonoecious flowers which are pollinated by bees, and the fruit generally separates from the stem when mature. Melons harvested at less than full-slip maturity do not achieve their full potential for sugar content, flavor, texture, and aroma. *See* ASCORBIC ACID; VITAMIN A.

The use of the name cantaloupe to indicate these medium-sized, netted melons with green and yellow-green rinds has become firmly established in the United States. However, this is a misnomer, and the name cantaloupe should be restricted to cultivars of *C. melo* var. *cantalupensis*. The fruits of this group are rough and scaly, with deep vein tracts and a hard rind. Cultivars of the variety *cantalupensis* are grown in Europe and Asia, but seldom in the United States.

Cantaloupe culture in the United States began with the introduction of the Netted Gem cultivar by the Burpee Seed Company in 1881.

Cultivation and production. Cantaloupes require a frost-free season of about 95 days to mature. Average temperatures of 70°F (21°C) are favorable for the production of high-quality melons. Most of the United States production is on irrigated land in the arid and semiarid Southwest because of favorable temperatures and lack of rain during the growing season. California grows approximately 51% of the United States acreage, followed by Texas with 22% and Arizona with 13%. Most of the California production is in the summer in the Sacramento and San Joaquin valleys, while Texas produces in the spring. High harvest and transportation costs tend to make cantaloupes a luxury product on the eastern markets. *See* MUSKMELON. Oscar A. Lorenz

Diseases. Cantaloupe plants can be infected with bacterial wilt, angular leaf spot, downy mildew, scab, and cucumber mosaic. In addition, there are other fungal and viral diseases which can greatly reduce plant vigor and fruit quantity or quality.

Fungal diseases. Anthracnose may be the most destructive of all diseases affecting cantaloupe. All plant parts, excluding the roots, are susceptible to the pathogen *Colletotrichum lagenarium*. Lesions may coalesce to kill entire leaves, stems and runners. Depressed spots are formed on the fruits and, when wet conditions persist, are covered with a mass of pink spores. Spores easily spread to uninfected plants by splashing rain or are carried by cucumber beetles. The fungus has as many as seven races which are capable of infecting different cultivars. The disease can be controlled by using resistant varieties, although breeding for disease resistance in cantaloupes has lagged behind that in cucumbers and watermelons. Control can be achieved by crop rotation, proper drainage, and fungicides such as the dithiocarbamates.

Powdery mildew is a destructive disease caused by either *Spaerotheca fulginea* or *Erysiphe cichoracearum*. These fungi form a fuzzy white growth on the fruit, stem, or leaf. Tissue covered by the fungus for extended periods of time may be killed. Overwintering structures are tiny black fruiting bodies. Infection is most likely to occur when humidity is high and temperatures are moderately high. Powdery mildew is controlled by dusting plants with Karathane or sulfur. Resistant cultivars derived from P.M.R. 45, Georgia 47, Honey Ball 306, and Homegarden can also be planted.

Fusarium wilt, caused by *Fusarium oxysporum* f. *melonis*, is a particular problem in the northern states from Maine to Minnesota. The fungus either causes damping-off in young seedlings or a root rot and stem blight in older plants. Badly affected plant stems crack open, and the plants desiccate. The pathogen lives in old plant debris and as propagules in the soil. Hence crop rotation is not an effective control measure. The only worthwhile means of control is to plant resistant varieties, such as Honey Dew, Golden Gopher, Iroquois, Delicious 51, and Harvest Queen.

Viral diseases. Muskmelon mosaic and squash mosaic cause serious crop losses from time to time. Muskmelon mosaic virus is seed- and aphid-transmitted. Leaves develop a mottling and may be distorted in shape. Fruit production is greatly decreased. Squash mosaic virus is seed-transmitted and causes symptoms similar to those caused by muskmelon mosaic virus. Both virus diseases can be controlled by using certified disease-free seed and by eliminating wild cucurbit weeds from nearby locations. *See* PLANT VIRUSES AND VIROIDS.

Frank L. Caruso

Bibliography. R. A. Seelig, *Cantaloupes*, United Fresh Fruit and Vegetable Association, 1973; T. W. Whitaker and G. N. Davis, *Cucurbits*, 1961.

Cantilever

A linear structural member supported both transversely and rotationally at one end only; the other end of the member is free to deflect and rotate. Cantilevers are common throughout nature and engineered structures; examples are a bird's wing, an airplane wing, a roof overhang, and a balcony. *See* WING.

Horizontal axis. If the main axis of the member is horizontal and the member is loaded with a downward gravity load, the member will support the load by forming a structural couple, with the upper portion of the member being in tension and the lower portion being in compression. This is the principle on which the design of a horizontal cantilever truss is based. When a horizontal cantilever truss is under a gravity load, the top member is in tension and the bottom member is in compression. If there are no external horizontal forces, the internal forces in the top and bottom members must be equal. Because these internal forces are separated by a distance, they can resist moments and rotation. The resisting moment is defined as a couple, that is, two equal and opposite forces separated by a distance. The translation force of the cantilever (defined as the shear) is resisted by the diagonals in a truss or the web of a wide flange beam. *See* TRUSS.

For a cantilever to function, it must be counterbalanced at its one support against rotation. This requirement is simply achieved in the design of a playground seesaw, with its double-balanced cantilever, or of a chemical balance. This principle of counterbalancing the cantilever is part of the basic design of a crane, such as a tower crane (see **illus.**). More commonly, horizontal cantilevers are resisted by being continuous with a backup span that is supported at both ends. This design is common for cantilever bridges; the largest of the cantilever bridges is an 1800-ft (540-m) railroad bridge in Quebec, Canada. Cantilever bridges are simpler to erect since they can be built out from their supports. All swing bridges or drawbridges are cantilevers. *See* BRIDGE.

Vertical axis. Cantilevers also occur with the member's main axis being vertical. Vertical cantilevers primarily resist lateral wind loads and horizontal

loads created by earthquakes. Common vertical cantilevers are chimneys, stacks, masts, flagpoles, lampposts, and railings or fences. Trees are the largest vertical cantilevers found in nature.

All skyscrapers are vertical cantilevers. One common system to provide the strength to resist lateral loads acting on the skyscraper is the use of a truss (known as bracing), which cantilevers out from the foundation in the walls of the core of the building that encloses the elevators and the stairs. In apartment buildings and hotels, vertical walls that separate different living units (demising walls or shear walls) cantilever out of the foundation to resist lateral loads. *See* BUILDINGS; SHEAR.

Applications. Some of the largest cantilevers are used in the roofs of airplane hangars. The reason is that typically at one edge of an airplane hangar there is a sliding door that can be removed; thus it cannot provide support to the roof's edge. Cantilevers of up to 300 ft (90 m) have been used to enclose 747 airplanes. It has become common practice to include cantilevers in the design of theaters and stadiums, where an unobstructed view is desired, balconies and tiers are supported in the back and cantilevered out toward the stage or playing field so that the audience has column-free viewing. *See* BEAM; ROOF CONSTRUCTION.　　　　I. Paul Lew

Bibliography. M. Salvadori, *Structure in Architecture*, 1986; M. Salvadori, *Why Buildings Stand Up*, 1994.

Capability maturity modeling

A method of gathering best practices for various work processes into coherent groupings to facilitate quality and process improvement. Capability Maturity Models® (CMM®) represent a relatively recent step in the evolution of process improvement techniques that enable organizations to repeatedly produce high-quality, complex, software-intensive systems faster and within expected costs. The foundations of this work include approaches to improved quality developed by W. Edwards Deming, Joseph Juran, Walter A. Shewart, and Philip B. Crosby, particularly Crosby's quality management maturity grid.

Model structure. Capability Maturity Models are designed to describe discrete levels of improvement within process areas, measured against specific goals and generic goals. A process area is a group of related practices that are performed collectively to achieve a set of objectives. There are typically 15 to 25 process areas represented in a model. Examples of process areas include requirements development, validation, configuration management, and project planning. Each process area has specific goals that describe what must be achieved to satisfy the purpose of the process area. Each specific goal has specific practices that describe the activities expected to result in achievement of the goal. For example, some specific goals of the project planning process area involve

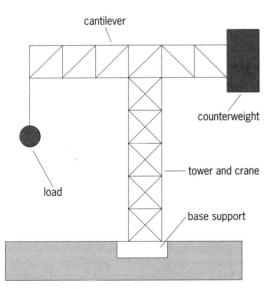

Cantilever configuration in the form of a tower support crane.

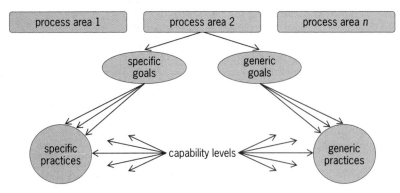

Fig. 1. Capability Maturity Models: the continuous representation.

establishing estimates, developing a project plan, and obtaining commitment to the plan. The specific practices related to the "establish estimates" goal involve estimating the scope of the project, establishing estimates of project attributes, defining the project life cycle, and determining estimates of effort and cost. Although process areas depict behavior that should be exhibited in any organization, practices must be interpreted using in-depth knowledge of the model, the organization, the business environment, and the other specific circumstances involved.

Generic goals apply to all process areas. Achievement of each of these goals in a process area signifies whether the implementation and institutionalization of each process area is effective, repeatable, and lasting. Each generic goal, in turn, has associated generic practices. For example, the generic goal "institutionalize a quantitatively managed process" has two generic practices, "establish quality objectives" and "stabilize subprocess performance."

A Capability Maturity Model does not prejudge which processes are right for any organization or project. Instead, it establishes minimal criteria that processes must meet to be considered capable. A capable process is defined, documented, practiced, supported, maintained, controlled, verified, validated, measured, and able to be improved. Also, the model should allow interpretation and modification as needed to suit an organization's size or business objectives.

Representations. Capability Maturity Models have been architected in two representations, continuous and staged. These representations provide alternative approaches to process improvement that take advantage of the familiarity of users with either approach. The representations contain the same essential content but are organized differently.

The continuous representation is based on capability within a given process area—the range of expected results that can be achieved by following a process. A low-capability process is improvised and highly dependent on current practitioners; results are difficult to predict, and product functionality and quality are typically compromised to meet schedules. A high-capability process is well controlled, defined, continually improving, supported by measurement, and is a basis for disciplined use of technology.

The continuous representation provides organizations with the flexibility to choose which processes to emphasize for improvement and how much to improve each process. Process improvement is measured using six capability levels: (0) incomplete, (1) performed, (2) managed, (3) defined, (4) quantitatively managed, and (5) optimizing. These capability levels relate to the achievement of specific and generic goals of a process area. For example, an organization can reach capability level 2 of a process area when the specific and generic goals up through capability level 2 are achieved for the process area.

The continuous representation enables selection of the order of process improvement that best meets the organization's business objectives and that most mitigates risk. **Figure 1** illustrates the structure of continuous representation.

The staged representation is based on organizational maturity—the combined capabilities of a set of related processes. Thus, in a highly mature organization, the set of organizational processes, taken as a whole, are of higher capability. Organizational improvement is measured in five maturity levels: (1) initial, (2) managed, (3) defined, (4) quantitatively managed, and (5) optimizing. The maturity levels comprise well-defined evolutionary plateaus on the path to becoming a mature organization. **Figure 2** provides a brief definition of each maturity level.

The staged representation has a recommended order for approaching process improvement, beginning with basic management practices and progressing along a proven path. The Capability Maturity Model for Software (SW-CMM) and People Capability Maturity Model (P-CMM) use this structure. **Figure 3** illustrates the structure of the staged representation.

Generic practices are often grouped by common features in the staged representation. "Commitment to perform" describes practices that relate to creating management policies and securing sponsorship.

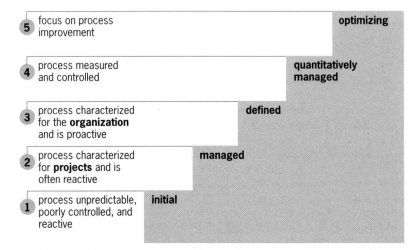

Fig. 2. Organizational maturity levels.

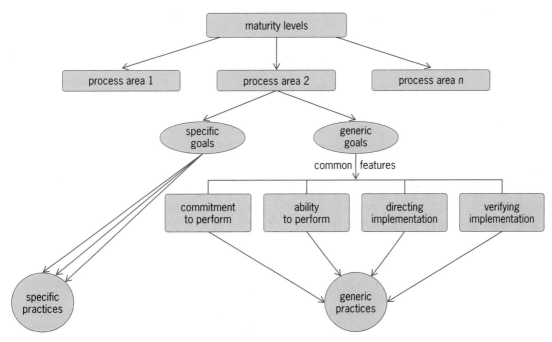

Fig. 3. Capability Maturity Models: the staged representation.

"Ability to perform" characterizes practices related to establishing and maintaining plans, resources, assigned responsibility and authority, and training. "Directing implementation" comprises measurement, control, and performance practices. "Verifying implementation" comprises practices that ensure implementation and compliance. [In the most recent version of Capability Maturity Model Integration (CMMI), discussed below, the grouping of generic practices has been deleted to reduce differences between the staged and continuous representations.]

Model evolution. In 1987, the U.S. Air Force asked Carnegie Mellon University's Software Engineering Institute to identify key practices that a contractor had to perform to deliver software-intensive systems reliably. By 1991, this tracking of practices had matured into the Capability Maturity Model for Software (SW-CMM). The success of this model for one discipline led to similar efforts for other elements of the product development community. Interest in such models for systems engineering process improvement led to two models produced in 1994. These were the Software Engineering CMM (SE-CMM), created by the Enterprise Process Improvement Collaboration (EPIC), and the Systems Engineering Capability and Assessment Method (SECAM), created by the International Council on Systems Engineering (INCOSE). These two models were successfully merged into Electronic Industries Alliance (EIA) Interim Standard 731 (EIA/IS 731) in 1998 as a result of a collaborative effort of EIA, EPIC, and INCOSE. In 1996, a sister model to cover key practices in software acquisition was created, the Software Acquisition Capability Maturity Model (SA-CMM). Concerns about preserving and enhancing the capabilities of developmental engineering staff led to the creation

of the People Capability Maturity Model (P-CMM) in 1997.

In 1997, work was underway at the Software Engineering Institute to produce an update to the SW-CMM, and also to produce a model that would capture concurrent engineering practices in an Integrated Product Development CMM (IPD-CMM). The Institute's sponsor, the U.S. Department of Defense, determined that these efforts should be merged into an integrated model, to be called Capability Maturity Model Integration (CMMI®). The feasibility of integrating a diverse set of maturity models had been demonstrated earlier that year by the Federal Aviation Administration (FAA), which had developed an integrated capability maturity model (FAA-iCMM V1.0). Due to the widespread focus on integrated product and process development (IPPD) by the Department of Defense and industry, it was decided that the initial focus of the CMMI effort would be integration of systems engineering, software engineering, and IPPD. A subsequent CMMI version added guidance for supplier sourcing. **Figure** 4 depicts the evolution of the CMMI models.

CMMs in use. Several Capability Maturity Models are now in widespread use, with some having achieved the status of de facto or recognized international standard, for the assessment and improvement of such areas as software engineering and acquisition practices, work force development practices, and systems security practices, among others.

SW-CMM. The Capability Maturity Model for Software is used for judging the maturity of the software processes of an organization and for identifying the key practices that are required to increase the maturity of these processes. Used worldwide, the SW-CMM became a de facto standard for assessing and improving software processes. As a result of the

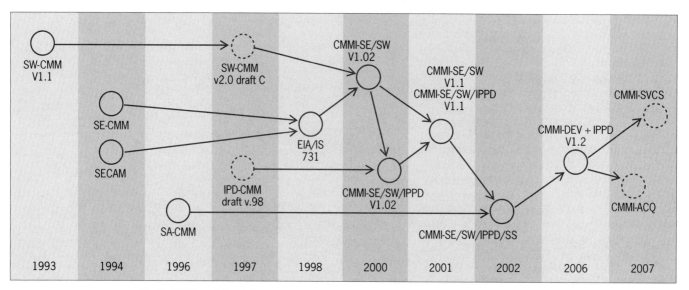

Fig. 4. CMMI model evolution.

creation of CMMI as an evolutionary improvement, appraisals against the SW-CMM are no longer supported by the Software Engineering Institute.

SA-CMM. The Software Acquisition Capability Model (SA-CMM) is used for benchmarking and improving the software acquisition process. The model follows the same architecture as the SW-CMM, but with an emphasis on acquisition issues and the needs of individuals and groups who are planning and managing software acquisition efforts. For example, unique key process areas address contractor tracking and oversight, transition to support, and acquisition risk management. Because of the move to the modernized CMMI approach, a CMMI version for acquisition is currently being developed to modernize and extend this model.

P-CMM. The People Capability Maturity Model is a framework that helps organizations successfully address people issues. Based on the best current practices in fields such as human resources, knowledge management, and organizational development, the P-CMM helps organizations characterize the maturity of their work-force practices, establish a program of continuous work-force development, set priorities for improvement actions, integrate work-force development with process improvement, and establish a culture of excellence. Its five maturity levels establish successive foundations for continuously improving individual competencies, developing effective teams, motivating improved performance, and shaping the work force that the organization needs to accomplish its future business plans. By following the maturity framework, an organization can avoid introducing work-force practices that its employees are unprepared to implement effectively.

SSE-CMM. The Systems Security Engineering Capability Maturity Model (SSE-CMM) describes the essential characteristics of an organization's security engineering process that must exist to ensure good security engineering. It is an emerging international standard (ISO/IEC 21827). The model highlights the relationship between security engineering and systems engineering. It provides a way to measure and improve capability in applying security engineering principles and to address capability-based assurance. Unique process areas include administering security controls; assessing impact, security risk, threat, and vulnerability; and verifying and validating security.

FAA-iCMM. The Federal Aviation Administration developed the FAA-iCMM to increase the efficiency and effectiveness of process improvement by providing a single reference model that integrates engineering, management, and acquisition processes used in developing, managing, acquiring, and maintaining systems. The FAA-iCMM integrates all features and practices of three that were being used separately in the FAA: the SE-CMM (V1.1), the SA-CMM (V1.01), and the SW-CMM (V1.1). A subsequent version (V2.0) has sought to integrate CMMI themes as well as concepts from the quality management standard ISO 9001:2000, which is familiar in the manufacturing domain.

CMMI. CMMI models include a common set of process areas that form the core of a model framework that integrates process improvement guidance for engineering development and integrated product and process development. In addition to the engineering development version, work is underway to produce synergistic variants to cover systems acquisition and the provision of technical services. The resulting Capability Maturity Models may be adapted to an organization's mission and business objectives. The CMMI Product Suite reduces the redundancy and complexity that can result from the use of multiple CMMs, thus improving the efficiency of and return on investment of process improvement. *See* ENGINEERING DESIGN; REENGINEERING; SOFTWARE ENGINEERING; SYSTEM DESIGN EVALUATION; SYSTEMS ENGINEERING; SYSTEMS INTEGRATION.   Mike Phillips

Bibliography. D. Ahern, A. Clouse, and R. Turner, *CMMI® Distilled: A Practical Introduction to*

Integrated Process Improvement, 2d ed., Addison-Wesley, Boston, 2003; M. Chrissis, M. Konrad, and S. Shrum, *CMMI®: Guidelines for Process Integration and Product Improvement*, Addison-Wesley, Boston, 2003; P. B. Crosby, *The Eternally Successful Organization: The Art of Corporate Wellness*, Mentor Books, 1992; P. B. Crosby, *Quality Is Free*, McGraw-Hill, New York, 1979; J. M. Juran and A. B. Godfrey (eds.), *Juran's Quality Handbook*, 5th ed., McGraw-Hill, New York, 1999; Software Engineering Institute, Carnegie Mellon University, *The Capability Maturity Model®: Guidelines for Improving the Software Process*, ed. by M. C. Paulk et al., Addison-Wesley, Boston, 1995.

Capacitance

The ratio of the charge q on one of the plates of a capacitor (there being an equal and opposite charge on the other plate) to the potential difference v between the plates; that is, capacitance (formerly called capacity) is $C = q/v$.

In general, a capacitor, often historically called a condenser, consists of two metal plates insulated from each other by a dielectric. The capacitance of a capacitor depends on the geometry of the plates and the kind of dielectric used since these factors determine the charge which can be put on the plates by a unit potential difference existing between the plates. *See* DIELECTRIC MATERIALS.

For a capacitor of fixed geometry and with constant properties of the dielectric between its plates, C is a constant independent of q or v, since as v changes, q changes with it in the same proportion. This statement assumes that the dielectric strength is not exceeded and thus that dielectric breakdown does not occur. (If it does occur, the device is no longer a capacitor.) If either the geometry or dielectric properties, or both, of a capacitor change with time, C will change with time.

In an ideal capacitor, no conduction current flows between the plates. A real capacitor of good quality is the circuit equivalent of an ideal capacitor with a very high resistance in parallel or, in alternating-current (ac) circuits, of an ideal capacitor with a low resistance in series.

Properties of capacitors. One classification system for capacitors follows from the physical state of their dielectrics. For a discussion based on this classification, *see* CAPACITOR.

Charging and discharging. These processes can occur for capacitors while the potential difference across the capacitor is changing if C is fixed; that is, q increases if v increases and q decreases if v decreases. If C and v both change with time, the rate of change of q with time is given by Eq. (1). Since the current

$$\frac{dq}{dt} = C\frac{dv}{dt} + v\frac{dC}{dt} \qquad (1)$$

i flowing in the wires leading to the capacitor plates is equal to dq/dt, Eq. (1) gives i in the wires. In many cases, C is constant so $i = C\, dv/dt$.

Energy of charged capacitor. This energy W_c is given by the formula $W_c = vq/2$, and is equal to the work the source must do in placing the charge on the capacitor. It is, in turn, the work the capacitor will do when it discharges.

Geometrical types. The geometry of a capacitor may take any one of several forms. The most common type is the parallel-plate capacitor whose capacitance C in farads is given in the ideal case by Eq. (2),

$$C = \frac{A\epsilon_r\epsilon_0}{d} \qquad (2)$$

where A is the area in square meters of one of the plates, d is the distance in meters between the plates, ϵ_0 is the permittivity of empty space with the numerical value 8.85×10^{-12} farad/m, and ϵ_r is the relative permittivity of the dielectric material between the plates. The value of ϵ_r is unity for empty space and almost unity for gases. For other dielectric materials, ϵ_r ranges in value from one to several hundred. In order for Eq. (2) to give a good value of C for an actual capacitor, d must be very small compared to the linear dimensions of either plate. *See* PERMITTIVITY.

Each plate of a parallel-plate capacitor may be made up of many thin sheets of metal connected electrically with a corresponding number of thin sheets of metal making up the other plate. The sheets of metal and their intervening layers of dielectric are chosen and stacked in such a way that A will be large

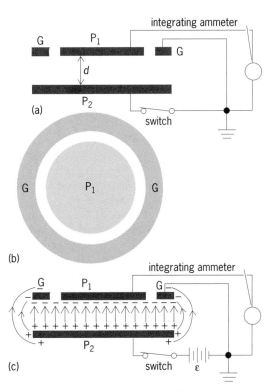

Fig. 1. Parallel-plate capacitor P_1, P_2 with guard ring GG. Spacing between guard ring and plate is exaggerated. (a) Cross section with all parts of capacitor at ground potential. (b) Top view showing plate P_1 surrounded by guard ring. (c) Cross section of capacitor charged from battery whose electromotive force is ⊴.

and d small without making the whole capacitor too bulky. The result is appreciable capacitance in a reasonable volume.

The cylindrical capacitor, as the name implies, is made of two concentric metal cylinders, each of length l in meters, with a dielectric filling the space between the cylinders. If r_2 and r_1 are the radii in meters of the outer and inner cylinders, respectively, and l is very large compared to $r_2 - r_1$, the capacitance C in farads is given by Eq. (3), where ϵ_r is

$$C = \frac{2\pi\epsilon_r\epsilon_0 l}{ln\,(r_2/r_1)} \qquad (3)$$

the relative dielectric constant of the dielectric and $\ln\,(r_2/r_1)$ indicates the natural logarithm of the ratio r_2/r_1.

Guard ring. This is often used with a standard parallel-plate capacitor, as shown in **Fig. 1**, in order that Eq. (2) shall more accurately represent its capacitance. It is the fringing of the electric lines of force which makes Eq. (2) inaccurate for an actual capacitor and, as shown in Fig. 2, the fringing is nearly all at the outside edge of the guard ring, and thus is not associated with the charge Q which is put onto plate P_1 while the capacitor is being charged. It is the charge Q that determines the integrated current flowing during the charging process. Then Eq. (2) gives the correct value of C that is needed to relate Q to the potential difference E across the plates by the equation $Q = CE$. Thus, with C known from Eq. (2) and E, known from a voltmeter measurement, Q may be computed and the integrating ammeter calibrated. An instrument called a ballistic galvanometer, which is now largely of only historical interest, constitutes an integrating ammeter. This illustrates one use of a standard capacitor having a guard ring. *See* GAL-VANOMETER. Ralph P. Winch

Types of capacitor. One classification of capacitors comes from the physical state of their dielectrics, which may be gas (or vacuum), liquid, solid, or a combination of these. Each of these classifications may be subdivided according to the specific dielectric used. Capacitors may be further classified by their ability to be used in alternating-current (ac) or direct-current (dc) circuits with various current levels.

Capacitors are also classified as fixed, adjustable, or variable. The capacitance of fixed capacitors remains unchanged, except for small variations caused by temperature fluctuations. The capacitance of adjustable capacitors may be set at any one of several discrete values. The capacitance of variable capacitors may be adjusted continuously and set at any value between minimum and maximum limits fixed by construction. Trimmer capacitors are relatively small variable capacitors used in parallel with larger variable or fixed capacitors to permit exact adjustment of the capacitance of the parallel combination.

Air, gas, and vacuum types. Made in both fixed and variable types, these capacitors are constructed with flat parallel metallic plates (or cylindrical concen-

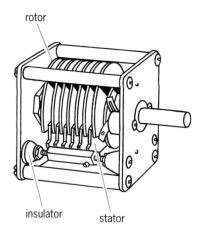

Fig. 2. Variable air capacitor.

tric metallic plates) with air, gas, or vacuum as the dielectric between plates. Alternate plates are connected, with one or both sets supported by means of a solid insulating material such as glass, quartz, ceramic, or plastic. **Figure 2** shows a variable air capacitor. Gas capacitors are similarly built but are enclosed in a leakproof case. If the gas capacitor is variable, the shaft supporting the movable plates, or rotor, is brought out through a pressure-tight insulated seal. Vacuum capacitors are of concentric-cylindrical construction and are enclosed in highly evacuated glass envelopes.

The purpose of a high vacuum, or a gas under pressure, is to increase the voltage breakdown value for a given plate spacing. For high-voltage applications, when increasing the spacing between plates is undesirable, the breakdown voltage of air capacitors may be increased by rounding the edges of the plates. Air, gas, and vacuum capacitors are used in high-frequency circuits. Fixed and variable air capacitors incorporating special design are used as standards in electrical measurements. *See* CAPACITANCE MEASUREMENT; ELECTRICAL UNITS AND STANDARDS.

Solid-dielectric types. These capacitors use one of several dieletrics such as a ceramic, mica, glass, or plastic film. Alternate plates of metal, or metallic foil, are stacked with the dielectric, or the dielectric may be metal-plated on both sides. Some of the more popular dielectric materials are listed in **Table 1**, along

TABLE 1. Dielectric materials used in capacitors

Dielectric material	Relative permittivity (ϵ_r)	Power factor, %
Vacuum or air	1	0
Kraft paper	4.0–6.5	3
Polyester	3.0	0.5
Polypropylene	2.2	0.01
Polystyrene	2.5	0.05
Glass	6.7	0.06
Mica	6–8	0.02
Aluminum oxide	10.0	5–10
Tantalum oxide	11.0	5–10
Barium titanate	10.60	0.2–2.5

with their relative permittivities and power factors. *See* DIELECTRIC MATERIALS; POWER FACTOR.

Plastic-film types. These capacitors use dielectrics such as polypropylene, polyester, polycarbonate, or polysulfone with a relative permittivity ranging from 2.2 to 3.2. This plastic film may be used alone or in combination with Kraft paper. The dielectric thicknesses range from 0.06 to over 0.8 mil (1.5 to over 20 micrometers). The most common electrodes are aluminum or zinc vacuum-deposited on the film, although aluminum foil is also used. These types generally utilize wound-roll construction (**Fig. 3**). *See* POLYESTER RESINS; POLYOLEFIN RESINS; POLYSULFONE RESINS.

Plastic-film capacitors may be constructed in a dry roll for dc and low-voltage ac applications. For ac applications above about 250 V, the capacitor winding is usually impregnated with a dielectric fluid to avoid degradation of the dielectric due to partial discharges.

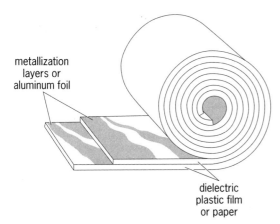

Fig. 3. **Wound-roll construction of plastic film and paper capacitors.**

Mica types. These capacitors use thin rectangular sheets of mica as the dielectric. The relative permittivity of mica is in the range of 6–8. The electrodes are either thin sheets of metal foil stacked alternately with the mica sheets, or thin deposits of silver applied directly to the surface of the mica sheets. Mica capacitors are used chiefly in radio-frequency applications. They have a low dielectric loss at very high frequencies, good temperature, frequency, and aging characteristics, and low power factor, but have a low ratio of capacitance to volume or to mass. They are made with dc voltage ratings from a few hundred to many thousands of volts and with radio-frequency current ratings up to about 50 A. *See* MICA.

Paper types. A dielectric of Kraft paper usually impregnated with mineral oil, or ester, is used in paper capacitors. Paper and plastic-film capacitors (Fig. 3) are constructed by stacking, or forming into a roll, alternate layers of foil and dielectric. Paper capacitors are gradually being replaced by metallized polypropylene and polyester films with lower cost, smaller size, and lower power factor. *See* PAPER.

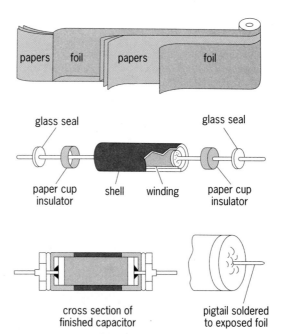

Fig. 4. **Ceramic capacitor constructed in chip form, showing cutaway of finished chip.**

Ceramic types. The monolithic ceramic capacitor consists of dielectric layers interleaved with electrode layers; the assembly is then compressed and sintered to form a solid monolithic block (**Fig. 4**). The dielectric layer may be as thin as 0.8 mil (20 μm), and as many as 40–50 layers may be interleaved. The most common dielectric material is barium titanate. The electrodes are composed of materials such as a silver-palladium mixture. The end termination is usually composed of several layers of silver-palladium, nickel, and tin. These capacitors may be constructed in radial, axial, or chip form. The chip construction is especially popular for surface mounting on electronic circuits. The chips have a typical size of $1/8$ in. $\times$ $1/6$ in. $\times$ $1/16$ in. (3.2 mm $\times$ 1.6 mm $\times$ 0.65 mm). These capacitors have the ability to withstand the 450°F (230°C) reflow solder and 540°F (280°C) wave solder mounting temperatures. *See* CERAMICS.

Electrolytic types. A large capacitance-to-volume ratio and a low cost per microfarad of capacitance are chief advantages of electrolytic capacitors. These use aluminum or tantalum plates (**Fig. 5**). A paste electrolyte is placed between the plates, and a dc forming voltage is applied. A current flows and by a process of electrolysis builds up a molecule-thin layer of oxide bubbles on the positive plate. This serves

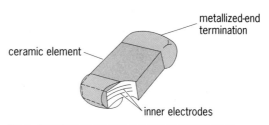

Fig. 5. **Tantalum electrolytic capacitor showing cross section. (*General Electric Co.*)**

TABLE 2. Major types of capacitors*

Type	Capacitance	Voltage (working voltage, dc), V	Applications
Monolithic ceramics	1 pF–2.2 µF	50–200	Ultrahigh frequency, rf coupling, computers
Disk and tube ceramics	1 pF–1 µF	50–1000	General, very high frequency
Paper	0.001–1 µF	200–1600	Motors, power supplies
Film			
Polypropylene	0.0001–0.47 µF	400–1600	Television vertical circuits, rf circuits
Polyester	0.001–4.7 µF	50–600	Entertainment electronics
Polystyrene	0.001–1 µF	100–200	General, high stability
Polycarbonate	0.01–18 µF	50–200	General
Metallized polypropylene	4–60 µF	400†	Alternating-current motors
Metallized polyester	0.001–22 µF	100–1000	Coupling, rf filtering
Electrolytic			
Aluminum	1 100,00 µF	5–500	Power supplies, filters
Tantalum	0.1–2200 µF	3–150	Small space requirement, low leakage
Gold	0.022–10 F	2.5–5.5	Memory backup
Nonpolarized (either aluminum or tantalum)	0.47–1000 µF	10–200	Loudspeaker crossovers
Mica	330 pF–0.05 µF	50–1000	High frequency
Silver-mica	5–820 pF	50–500	High frequency
Variable			
Ceramic	1–5 to 16–100 pF	200	Radio, television, communications
Film	0.8–5 to 1.2–30 pF	50	Oscillators, antenna, rf circuits
Air	10–365 pF	50	Broadcast receiver
Teflon	0.25–1.5 pF	2000	Very high frequency, ultrahigh frequency

*After A. Mottershead, *Electricity and Electronics*, Prentice Hall, 1990.
†Alternating-current voltage at 60 Hz.

as the dieletric. The rest of the electrolyte and the other plate make up the negative electrode (**Fig. 6a**). Such a device is said to be polarized and must be connected in a circuit with the proper polarity. To ensure proper connection, the polarization of the capacitor is clearly marked by polarity signs for the axial type (Fig. 6b) or by a longer lead for the positive side in the radial type (Fig. 6c). Polarized capacitors can be used only in circuits in which the dc component of voltage across the capacitors exceeds the crest value of the ac ripple.

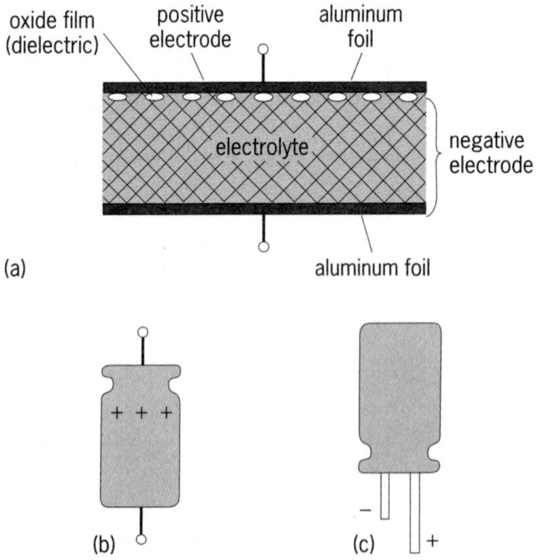

Another type of electrolytic capacitor utilizes compressed tantalum powder and the baking of manganese oxide (MnO_2) as an electrolyte. These capacitors may be constructed with either radial, axial, or chip configurations.

Nonpolarized electrolytic capacitors can be constructed for use in ac circuits. In effect, they are two polarized capacitors placed in series with their polarities reversed.

Table 2 provides a summary of the major types of discrete capacitors and some of their applications.

Thick-film types. These capacitors are made by means of successive screen-printing and firing processes in the fabrication of certain types of microcircuits used in electronic computers and other electronic systems. They are formed, together with their connecting conductors and associated thick-film resistors, upon a ceramic substrate. Their characteristics and the materials are similar to those of ceramic capacitors. *See* PRINTED CIRCUIT.

Thin-film types. Thin-film dielectrics are deposited on ceramic and integrated-circuit substrates and then metallized with aluminum to form capacitive components. These are usually single-layer capacitors. The most common dielectrics are silicon nitride and silicon dioxide. Thin-film dieletrics may be deposited by plasma deposition or sputtering. *See* INTEGRATED CIRCUITS; SPUTTERING.   Allen Mottershead

Body capacitance. When a part of the human body, say the hand, is brought near a high-impedance network, the body serves as one plate of a capacitor and the adjacent part of the network as the other plate. This situation is the equivalent of a

Fig. 6. Construction and polarity markings of aluminum electrolytic capacitor. (a) Cross section. (b Polarization markings for tabular capacitor with axial leads. (c) Polarization markings for capacitor with radial leads. (After A. Mottershead, Electricity and Electronics, Prentice Hall, 1990)

capacitor of very low capacitance, in parallel between that part of the network and its surroundings, since the human body is usually a conductor at the potential of its surroundings. This capacitance is known as body capacitance and enters as a part of the distributed capacitance of the network. A high-impedance network must be well shielded in order to eliminate the variable and undesirable effects of body capacitance.   Ralph P. Winch

Bibliography. W. J. Duffin, *Electricity and Magnetism*, 4th ed., 1990; D. Halliday, R. Resnick, and K. S. Krane, *Physics*, 5th ed., 2002; A. Mottershead, *Introduction to Electricity and Electronics*, 3d ed., 1990; W. F. Mullin, *ABC's of Capacitors*, 3d ed., 1978; E. M. Purcell, *Electricity and Magnetism*, 2d ed., 1985; H. D. Young and R. A. Freedman, *Sears and Zemansky's University Physics with Modern Physics*, 11th ed., 2003.

Capacitance measurement

The measurement of the ratio of the charge induced on a conductor to the difference in potential between it and a neighboring conductor which induces the charge. In a multiconductor system there are capacitances between each pair of conductors. In general, these capacitances are functions of the total geometry, that is, the location of all of the conducting and dielectric bodies. When, as is usually true, only the capacitance between two conductors is of interest, the presence of other conductors is an undesirable complication. It is then customary to distinguish between two-terminal and three-terminal capacitors and capacitance measurements. In a two-terminal capacitor, either one of the conductors of primary interest surrounds the other (in which case the capacitance between them is independent of the location of other bodies except in the vicinity of the terminals); or the somewhat indefinite contributions of other conductors to the capacitance of interest are accepted.

A three-terminal capacitor consists of two active electrodes surrounded by a third, or shield, conductor. The direct capacitance between the two active electrodes is the capacitance of interest, and, when shielded leads are used, it is independent of the location of all other conductors except the shield. Only certain of the measuring methods to be described are suitable for three-terminal capacitors. For greater accuracy or measurement at higher frequencies, four terminal-pair terminations described below are desirable.

Every physically realizable capacitor when being charged, as in ac use, has associated energy loss in the dielectric and in the metal electrodes. At a single frequency these are indistinguishable, and the capacitor may be represented by an equivalent circuit comprising either a parallel or series combination of pure capacitance and pure resistance. The measurement of capacitance, then, in general involves the simultaneous measurement of, or allowance for, an associated resistive element. *See* PERMITTIVITY.

Most capacitance measurements involve simply a comparison of the capacitor to be measured with a capacitor of known value. This should ideally be a reference standard whose capacitance has been established by an unbroken chain of measurements to the standards of a national metrology institute, which have been realized in terms of fundamental constants of nature. Methods that permit comparison of nearly equally valued capacitors by simple substitution of one for the other at the same point in a circuit are frequently possible and almost always preferable. *See* ELECTRICAL UNITS AND STANDARDS.

Properties of standard capacitors. The most stable capacitors available have a fused quartz dielectric and a value of 10 picofarads. The dielectric is a quartz disk about 2.8 in. (70 mm) in diameter and 0.4 in. (10 mm) thick. Gold film electrodes are formed on the two faces of the disk by sputtering gold onto the fused quartz surfaces, and a guard electrode is similarly deposited onto the circumferential surface. Because fused quartz has a temperature coefficient of permittivity of about 10 parts per million per kelvin (5 parts per million per degree Fahrenheit) it is essential to measure its temperature accurately, and to do this a resistance thermometer is wound around the disk. The unit is hermetically sealed in a container which can be put in an oil-bath or other constant-temperature enclosure. *See* SPUTTERING.

Other standard capacitors with values up to 1 nanofarad can be made with parallel-plate or cylindrical electrodes; they are hermetically sealed and evacuated or filled with dry gas. Capacitors of larger value have a solid dielectric, such as mica or polystyrene or other plastic film, and are less constant in value over time. *See* CAPACITOR.

A three-terminal arrangement is usual for standard capacitors; that is, they have a screening case with a separate connection. A three-terminal capacitor can be measured satisfactorily if the screen can be maintained at the potential of one of the capacitor terminals, but at high frequencies—above about 100 kHz—it becomes increasingly difficult to satisfy this condition, and a two-terminal capacitor may be advantageous. The disadvantage of a two-terminal capacitor is the uncertainty arising from the fringing field of its terminals, which may be a few tenths of a picofarad; however, a change in capacitance will be precise if the fringing field is unaltered. For example, the difference in the value of two capacitors with identical terminal arrangements can be measured accurately even if their individual capacitances cannot be determined with high accuracy. This remark applies even to capacitors with precision coaxial connectors for use up to a few gigahertz. Such capacitors have a series inductance of only a few nanohenries, and they, together with transmission lines of accurately known dimensions, provide the standards for high-frequency measurements. *See* INDUCTANCE; TRANSMISSION LINES.

At the other end of the frequency range, measurements are required on capacitors up to 1 farad in value at frequencies around 100 Hz. The stability of these capacitors is such that the standards used in their measurement need have an accuracy of no better than 0.01% and are often considerably worse. For this range, the standards comprise a capacitor combined with transformers for the input and associated output connections. A single capacitor, which may be a 1-microfarad mica dielectric capacitor, and multitapped input and output transformers can provide values between 1 μF and 1 F. A better performance is obtained if plastic-film capacitors of value larger than 1 μF are used and a transformer designed to give the optimum properties provides each value of the capacitance.

Frequency-dependence of capacitors. The effective value of a capacitor C_e—that is, that which corresponds to the reactance measured at its terminals—is affected by three factors. First, series inductance l apparently increases the actual capacitance C, according to Eq. (1), where ω is the angular fre-

$$C_e = \frac{C}{1 - \omega^2 l C} \qquad (1)$$

quency. Second, the properties of the dielectric in a capacitor with a solid dielectric separating the electrodes usually cause a reduction in capacitance as the frequency is raised. Third, mechanical displacement of the electrodes caused by the electric forces between them may alter the capacitance in a voltage- or frequency-dependent manner; this effect should be detectable only in air or gas dielectric capacitors, and can be quite appreciable in high-voltage capacitors. In capacitance standards provided with separate current and potential terminals, the mutual inductance between current and potential leads can also alter the effective value of a capacitor, unless the geometrical layout of the leads is arranged to minimize this effect.

The series inductance can be calculated from a measurement of the self-resonant frequency f_0 of the capacitor with its terminals connected together by a link producing only a small calculable additional inductance. The total inductance of the capacitor and link circuit is $1/[(2\pi f_0)^2 C]$.

The effect of dielectric permittivity variation is measured by ultimate reference to an air or gas dielectric capacitor whose plates have clean metal surfaces.

The electric forces between the electrodes of standard capacitors produce capacitance changes that are usually too small to be significant, except when the highest accuracy is required at more than a single applied voltage or at a frequency near that of a mechanical resonance.

Distributed capacitance of an inductor. An inductor is a particularly impure circuit component. In addition to the series resistance of the winding, distributed capacitance is always present from turn to turn and layer to layer, making the effective inductance a function of frequency. It is customary to assume that the effect of the distributed capacitance in an inductance coil may be represented by a single capacitor connected between the coil terminals. In some cases the value of this equivalent capacitor may be obtained by a determination of the self-resonant frequency of the coil; however, as a result of the distributed nature of both the inductance and the capacitance, the coil may exhibit several resonance modes, and a self-resonance determination is then ambiguous.

A procedure that usually surmounts this difficulty is that of determining the resonant frequency for several settings of a variable capacitor connected in parallel with the coil. A plot of the capacitance of the observed auxiliary capacitor against the reciprocal of the square of the corresponding resonant frequency and extrapolated to infinite frequency then gives a value for the lumped equivalent of the distributed capacitance. These measurements are now made much more conveniently by using a commercial impedance-measuring instrument (a bridge or an impedance analyzer) whose source frequency can be varied either manually or automatically. Connection to the instrument is now most often made by using a four-terminal-pair configuration, via an adapter if necessary.

AC bridge comparison methods. When capacitors must be compared with high accuracy, bridge methods must be adopted. *See* BRIDGE CIRCUIT; WHEATSTONE BRIDGE.

Bridges based on a resistance ratio. These are Wheatstone-bridge configurations in which the potential division of the capacitor being measured and either a parallel combination of a standard loss-free capacitor C_s and a conductance G_s (**Fig. 1***a*) or a series combination of C_s and a resistor R_s (Fig. 1*b*) is equated, when the detector is nulled, to the ratio of potentials across resistors R_1 and R_2. More commonly now, the reference potential division is that of a variable-ratio autotransformer known as an inductive voltage divider (IVD). *See* INDUCTIVE VOLTAGE DIVIDER.

If both the standard and unknown capacitor are represented by their parallel equivalent circuits (Fig. 1*a*), equality of potential division leads to Eqs. (2) and (3) for the unknown capacitance C_x

$$C_x = C_s \frac{R_1}{R_2} \qquad (2)$$

$$G_x = G_s \frac{R_1}{R_2} \qquad (3)$$

and conductance G_x; while, for their series equivalent circuits (Fig. 1*b*), this equality leads to Eqs. (4) and (5) for C_x and the unknown resistance R_x.

$$C_x = C_s \frac{R_1}{R_2} \qquad (4)$$

$$R_x = R_s \frac{R_2}{R_1} \qquad (5)$$

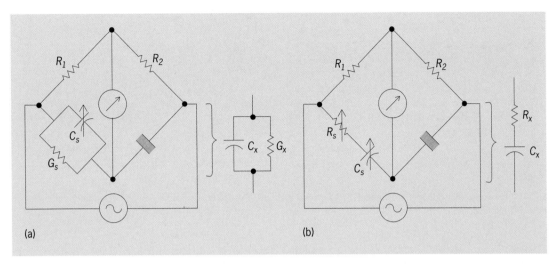

Fig. 1. Resistance-ratio bridges, in which two adjacent arms are resistors. (*a*) Parallel arrangement. (*b*) Series arrangement.

Schering bridge. This bridge yields a measurement of the equivalent series-circuit representation of a capacitor (**Fig. 2**). The equations of balance are written as (6) and (7). As with any balanced bridge net-

$$C_x = C_s \frac{R_1}{R_2} \qquad (6)$$

$$R_x = R_2 \frac{C_1}{C_s} \qquad (7)$$

work, the positions of source and detector may be interchanged without affecting the balance condition. This change may be done to gain an advantage in, for example, sensitivity to the balance condition or the voltage rating of some component.

Wagner branch. The resistance-ratio and Schering bridges are useful for two-terminal capacitance measurements. Their use may be extended to three-terminal measurements and extended in accuracy and range by the introduction of shielding and the addition of the Wagner branch which maintains a shield at the potential of the terminals connected to the detector (**Fig. 3**).

Balance is effected by the convergent procedure of alternately adjusting the main bridge arms with

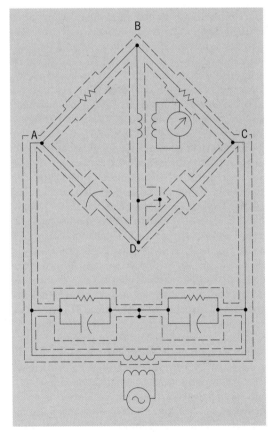

Fig. 3. Shielded resistance ratio-arm bridge with a Wagner branch for three-terminal measurements. With the switch open, capacitances to the shield at A and C shunt the Wagner arms. At balance, capacitances to the shield at B and D carry no current.

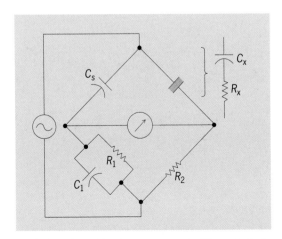

Fig. 2. Schering bridge for measurement of the equivalent series-circuit representation of a capacitor.

the switch open and adjusting the Wagner branch elements with the switch closed. The final balance is obtained with the switch open. Capacitances to the shield at two opposite corners (A and C) of the bridge then shunt the Wagner arms and do not affect the balance of the main bridge. Capacitances to the shield at the other two corners (B and D) carry no current at balance and therefore cannot introduce error either.

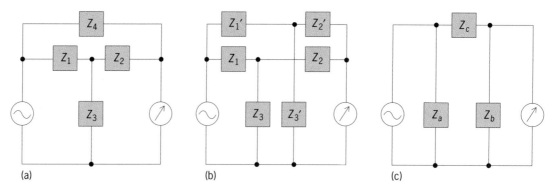

Fig. 4. T networks. (*a*) Bridged-T. (*b*) Parallel-T. (*c*) Equivalent circuit. Balance is achieved by varying network components untill the equivalent impedance Z_c is infinite.

Bridged-T and parallel-T networks. These complex bridges possess a significant advantage over four-arm bridges for medium-accuracy radio-frequency measurements of capacitance because the source and detector have a common point of connection. (**Fig. 4**). Use of the Y-delta network transformation permits reduction of either the bridged-T (Fig. 4*a*) or the parallel-T (Fig. 4*b*) to an equivalent circuit (Fig. 4*c*). Balance, or null indication of the detector, is achieved by variation of the network components until the equivalent impedance Z_c linking the source and the detector is infinite. *See* Y-DELTA TRANSFORMATIONS.

Time-constant methods. If a direct voltage is suddenly applied to the series combination of a resistor and an initially discharged capacitor, the charge and the voltage on the capacitor increase exponentially toward their full magnitudes with a time constant equal in seconds to the product of the resistance in ohms and the capacitance in farads. Similarly, when a charged capacitor is discharged through a resistor, the charge and the voltage decay with the same time constant. Various methods are available for the measurement of capacitance by measurement of the time constant of charge or discharge through a known resistor. *See* TIME CONSTANT.

In one such method the time required for the output voltage of an operational amplifier having a capacitor as a feedback component to increase to a value equal to the step-function input voltage applied through a resistor to its input is determined by an electronic voltage-comparison circuit and timer. With the assumption of ideal characteristics for the amplifier, such as infinite gain without feedback, infinite input impedance, and zero output impedance, the measured time interval is equal to the product of the values of the known resistance and the capacitance being measured. *See* OPERATIONAL AMPLIFIER.

Thompson-Lampard capacitor. The values of capacitors of similar shapes but different sizes are proportional to size; that is, a single length dimension governs their values. A. M. Thompson and D. G. Lampard showed how this principle could be applied to make a precise and practical calculable capacitor. Such capacitors require only a single length to be measured

accurately, and this is readily accomplished by optical interferometry. Their design provides the standard for the unit of capacitance defined in the International System of Units (SI).

Thompson and Lampard's theorem relates to a capacitor which, in its simple form, comprises four equal electrodes of parallel round bars arranged with their axes at the corners of a square and with small gaps between adjacent bars (**Fig. 5**). The cross-capacitances (C_A and C_B) between the two diagonally opposite electrodes per unit length of the infinite system in vacuum is given by Eq. (8). Here,

$$\exp\left(\frac{-\pi C_A}{\varepsilon_0}\right) + \exp\left(\frac{-\pi C_B}{\varepsilon_0}\right) = 1 \qquad (8)$$

the permittivity of vacuum $\varepsilon_0 = 8.8541878$ pF/m. If the two cross-capacitances are identical, each cross-

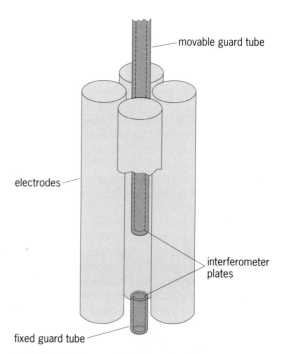

movable guard tube

electrodes

interferometer plates

fixed guard tube

Fig. 5. Calculable capacitor with an interferometer for length measurement. Surrounding shields are omitted.

capacitance is given by Eq. (9). If the two cross-

$$C_0 = 1.95354902 \text{ pF/m} \qquad (9)$$

capacitances are not quite equal and differ by ΔC, the mean capacitance is given approximately by Eq. (10).

$$C = C_0[1 + 0.0866(\Delta C/C)^2] \qquad (10)$$

Shields around the assembly and at the ends of the capacitor connected to a Wagner branch eliminate from a measurement all capacitances except the required internal ones. The capacitor is in an evacuated enclosure to avoid uncertainties arising from the relative permittivity and the refractive index of air.

If a conducting bar or tube connected to the shield is inserted into the central space between the electrodes, with only a small gap between the bar and the electrodes, the cross-capacitance is zero. Therefore, with a short, fixed tube inserted at one end, a long tube that can be moved axially at the other alters the active length of the capacitor. The change of length is measured interferometrically using reflectors mounted at the inner ends of the fixed and movable tubes. The consequent change in mean capacitance is then calculated from Eq. (10). There is a minimum separation of the tubes—about three times the space between opposing electrodes—below which the capacitance change with length becomes significantly nonlinear.

A practical cross-capacitor departs slightly from the ideal geometry in a number of ways, and consequently the accuracy is limited to about 1×10^{-8} pF; if the working range of the capacitor is 0.5 pF (equivalent to a change of length of 10 in. or 25 cm), the overall accuracy on this account is 2 parts in 10^8. The repeatability is appreciably better.

Four-terminal-pair definition. Four-terminal-pair definition of impedance standards arose from the need to measure them with sub-part-per-million accuracy. All electric and magnetic fields associated with an impedance standard must be completely defined, and the standard must be provided with separate pairs of current and potential terminals, as in the familiar four-terminal dc resistance standards. The solution is to enclose the impedance in a complete shield and to treat this shield also as a four-terminal impedance. When connected by coaxial cables to a coaxial measuring system in which the currents through the outer shield conductors of the cables and the currents through the inner conductors going to the impedance are equal and opposite (both currents being zero in the potential cables), all electric and magnetic fields are reproducibly confined within the shield. The voltage to be measured is that generated between the inner and outer coaxial terminations of the cable on one side (the "high" or H side) of the impedance, and the current is that emerging from the inner conductor of the termination at the other side (the "low" or L side). This current is closely equal to the current

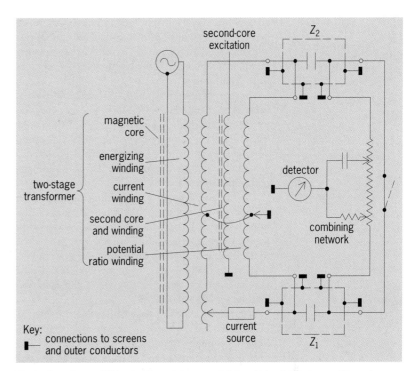

Fig. 6. Transformer bridge for the precise comparison of two similar types of impedances Z_1 and Z_2. Screens and outer conductors of the coaxial connections have been omitted for clarity, but connections to them are shown as black rectangles.

returning via the outer conductor of the same termination. There is one further condition, that the voltage between the inner and outer conductors of the second low coaxial termination should be zero. The second high coaxial termination has a source of current connected across it in order to make the measurement. The magnitude of this current is not relevant to the measured value of an impedance defined in this way since this impedance is the voltage-to-current ratio. One consequence is that the small four-terminal impedance of the outer screen is added to that of the enclosed impedance and thus becomes a part of this seemingly elaborate but complete four-terminal-pair definition.

The defining conditions can be departed from provided that the value measured is demonstrably not thereby altered. Small corrections to account for the finite impedance of the potential- and current-measuring cables are independent of the value of the impedance being measured and are negligible for all but the most accurate measurements or those at the highest frequencies.

Calibration of standard capacitors. The Thompson-Lampard capacitor provides the starting point for the calibration of standard capacitors, which are compared in 1:10 ratios by using an accurately calibrated transformer in a coaxial alternating-current bridge. A four-terminal-pair bridge based on a voltage ratio transformer for comparing capacitance standards is illustrated in **Fig. 6.**

Every mesh of the bridge network has a current equalizer which ensures that equal currents of opposite sign flow in the inner and the outer conductors of every coaxial connection. By using this coaxial equalized-current technique, the circuitry neither emits significant electromagnetic fields nor responds to external ones. Therefore, the measurements are unaffected by the layout of the conductors or by interference.

The transformer is of the two-stage type; that is, there is an energizing winding on the first core followed by a winding which supplies the current to the impedances to be compared, and finally, a second core and overall winding, which provides a precise potential ratio for comparing the two four-terminal-pair impedances. *See* INSTRUMENT TRANSFORMER.

The bridge is balanced by injecting a small known voltage into the potential circuit of one of the impedances. Adjustment of the combining network for the detector is also required. For this, the switch in the conductor joining the output current connections of the two impedances is opened, the detector is rebalanced by adjusting the combining network, and the switch is closed.

Commercial impedance-measuring instruments. As discussed above, manual bridge systems can make highly accurate impedance measurements, but are time-consuming to operate and have limited frequency range. In contrast, modern automatic inductance-capacitance-resistance (LCR) and impedance analyzer instruments have become commercially available that are claimed to offer moderate accuracies, operate at millisecond speeds, and cover a wider frequency range. In these precision instruments, an attempt is also made to implement the Cutkosky four-terminal-pair (4TP) definition given by Eq. (11). The subscripts refer to the ports of a four-

$$Z_{4TP} = \frac{V_2}{I_4}\bigg|_{I_2=I_3=V_3=V_4=0} \qquad (11)$$

terminal-pair impedance standard or device under test (DUT), as shown in **Fig. 7**. The definition of Z_{4TP} given by Eq. (11) is also illustrated in Fig. 7, as well as the notation commonly used on instruments for current (high = H_c and low = L_c) and potential (high = H_p and low = L_p) port identification. The advantage of four-terminal-pair impedance measurements (as opposed to two-terminal or three-

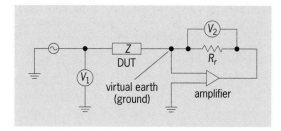

Fig. 8. Autobalancing bridge method employed in modern analyzers for measuring the four-terminal-pair impedance of a device under test (DUT). The outer shield conductors have been omitted for simplicity.

terminal) is that they remove the influence of contact impedances between the cables and the impedance being measured, as well as minimizing the effects of stray capacitance and mutual inductance between cables, assuming current-equalized networks.

The impedance measurement and frequency range of operation of some of the latest precision four-terminal-pair impedance analyzer instruments is typically 1 mΩ to 1 GΩ and few tens of hertz to 100 MHz, respectively. In addition to the alternating-current voltage that these instruments use for impedance measurements (maximum usually 1 V_{rms}), they can provide up to 40 V direct-current bias voltage for various applications. The claimed measurement uncertainty varies depending on the impedance being measured and the test frequency, but typically increases from 0.1 to 10% at the extremes of their impedance capability or at the higher frequencies. The application of such instruments is wide-ranging, from electrical and electronic component and material evaluation to chemical and biological process measurements, in a number of industries (aerospace, biomedical, research and development, and telecommunications).

Most impedance-measuring instruments (which are derivatives of the earlier models) now employ the autobalancing bridge (ABB) method, in which high-input impedance amplifiers and feedback techniques are used to create a virtual Earth (ground) at the low-potential port of the instrument (**Fig. 8**). The instruments usually connect in one of four range resistors (R_r) across which a voltage (V_2) is detected to determine the current flow through the impedance being measured. Often an assumption is made that the direct-current value of these range resistors is the same as their high-frequency value, but this is not entirely true for accurate measurements. In addition, over broad impedance and frequency ranges the defining conditions (Fig. 7) are not implemented to the required level. Several other limitations are also present in the autobalancing bridge method, such as shunt capacitance loading at the high- and low-potential ports, sufficiently high input impedance of the two voltage detectors (V_1 and V_2) over a broad frequency range, and equality of the currents in the inner and shield conductors. Even to achieve the modest accuracy claimed for modern precision impedance-measuring instruments,

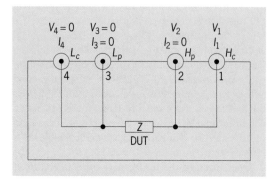

Fig. 7. Four-terminal-pair impedance component or device under test (DUT) and its complete definition, equivalent to that given in Eq. (11).

significant demand is placed on the very latest electronic passive and active components. For measurements at frequencies higher than 100 MHz, two-port, 50-Ω, matched-impedance or vector network analyzers are normally employed to at least 65 GHz. *See* MICROWAVE IMPEDANCE MEASUREMENTS; MICROWAVE MEASUREMENTS; RADIO-FREQUENCY IMPEDANCE MEASUREMENTS.

For quality-control applications where pass/fail measurements must be performed on passive components relatively quickly, instrument manufacturers supply a number of cable probes and adaptors. One combination of extension cables and connection commonly supplied is known as Kelvin clips, in which the four coaxial cables are connected to the four-terminal-pair impedance analyzer at one end, and at the other end two crocodile clips with independently insulated jaws are provided for connection to a two-terminal component. This configuration essentially converts the four terminal-pair connection at the impedance analyzer to a four-terminal connection scheme at the crocodile clips. The advantage of the Kelvin clips is that the two surfaces of each crocodile clip form the current and potential connections at the passive impedance component, with one clip being the energization side and the other the detection. The Kelvin clip scheme is also employed in various four-terminal-pair to four-terminal adaptors for repeatable measurement of surface-mount (or chip) passive components.

At the other end of the performance range, there are numerous low-accuracy two-terminal handheld LCR meters. These typically operate at one or two fixed frequencies (120 Hz and 1 kHz being the most common) and measure a wide range of inductance-capacitance-resistance values as well as the loss factor, but offer at best a 1% uncertainty. *See* CAPACITANCE; ELECTRICAL MEASUREMENTS.

Bryan P. Kibble; F. Ralph Kotter; G. H. Rayner;
Shakil A. Awan

Bibliography. D. Buchla and W. Mclachlan, *Electronic Instrumentation and Measurement*, 1992; W. J. Duffin, *Electricity and Magnetism*, 4th ed., 1990; B. Hague and T. R. Foord (ed.), *Alternating Current Bridge Methods*, 6th ed., 1971; P. Horowitz and W. Hill, *The Art of Electronics*, 2d ed., 1989; B. P. Kibble and G. H. Rayner, *Coaxial A. C. Bridges*, 1984; R. Morrison, *Grounding and Shielding Techniques in Instrumentation*, 4th ed., 1998; L. Schnell, *Technology of Electrical Measurements*, 1993.

Capacitance multiplication

The generation of a capacitance which is some multiple of that of an actual capacitor. Capacitance multiplication circuits have an input impedance which is capacitive and which is proportional to that of an actual capacitor appearing somewhere in the circuit. In most applications, capacitance multiplication circuits are used to generate an equivalent input capacitance which is much larger than that of the actual capacitor. One scenario where capacitance multiplication might prove useful is where a physical capacitor of a required capacitance may be too large, too expensive, or unavailable. A second is where the capacitor must be reasonably large and capable of handling bidirectional signals, thus precluding the direct use of widely available electrolytic capacitors and hence making practical the utilization of a much smaller nonelectrolytic capacitor in a capacitance multiplication circuit. *See* CAPACITANCE.

Capacitance multiplication circuits are often made from operational amplifiers and resistors along with the capacitor that is to be scaled, although transistors and other active devices can also be used. Capacitance multiplication circuits are closely related to classes of circuits termed generalized immittance converters and negative impedance converters. Generalized immittance converters are used to generate an equivalent input impedance that is proportional to products or quotients of specific impedances that appear in the circuit. Generalized immittance converters are often used for capacitance multiplication. Related applications of generalized immittance converters are synthetic inductance simulation and negative-resistance generation. Negative-impedance converters are also used for the generation of negative impedances. *See* ELECTRICAL IMPEDANCE; IMMITTANCE; INDUCTANCE; NEGATIVE-RESISTANCE CIRCUITS; OPERATIONAL AMPLIFIER.

A generalized immittance converter circuit is shown in **illus.** *a*. The input impedance Z_{in} of this circuit is given by Eq. (1). If the impedances

$$Z_{in} = \frac{Z_1 Z_3 Z_5}{Z_2 Z_4} \qquad (1)$$

Z_1–Z_4 are resistors and Z_5 is a capacitor, the capacitance multiplication circuit of illus. *b* is obtained. The equivalent impedance of this circuit is that of a capacitor of value C_{eq} given by Eq. (2). The resis-

$$C_{eq} = \frac{CR_2 R_4}{R_1 R_3} \qquad (2)$$

tor ratio $(R_2 R_4)/(R_1 R_3)$ determines the capacitance multiplication factor. A second capacitance multiplication circuit based upon the Miller effect is shown in illus. *c*. The equivalent capacitance of this circuit is given by Eq. (3).

$$C_{eq} = C\left(1 + \frac{R_2}{R_1}\right) \qquad (3)$$

Capacitance multiplication circuits have some practical limitations. For example, the input impedance of the circuits of illus. *b* and *c* will remain capacitive only provided the operational amplifiers are operating linearly. This requirement places some restrictions on how capacitance multiplication circuits can be used. For example, the output voltage swing, the output current, and the slew rate of the operational amplifier all have hard limits imposed by the design of the operational amplifier itself, and these limits must not be violated at either internal

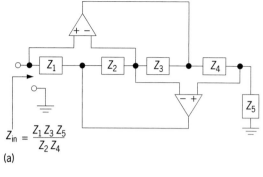

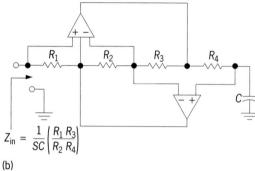

$$Z_{in} = \frac{Z_1 Z_3 Z_5}{Z_2 Z_4}$$

(a)

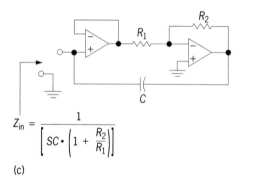

$$Z_{in} = \frac{1}{SC}\left|\frac{R_1 R_3}{R_2 R_4}\right|$$

(b)

$$Z_{in} = \frac{1}{\left[SC \cdot \left(1 + \dfrac{R_2}{R_1}\right)\right]}$$

(c)

Impedance-generation circuits. (a) Generalized immittance converter. (b) Capacitance multiplier based on generalized immittance converter. (c) Miller capacitance multiplier. Input impedance Z_{in} is given in Laplace transform notation; S is the Laplace transform variable.

or external nodes of the capacitance multiplication circuits. The bandwidth of the operational amplifier is also limited. These limits on the operational amplifier restrict the magnitude and frequency of signals that can be placed on capacitance multiplication circuits, as well as how fast these capacitors can be discharged. Although violation of these limits is usually nondestructive (provided the input voltage does not exceed the maximum allowed for the operational amplifier), violations will result in significant signal distortion. These limitations become increasingly problematic when realizing very large capacitors or when using large capacitance multiplication factors. Other capacitance multiplication circuits beyond those shown in the illustration are available which offer varying trade-offs between capacitance multiplication, signal swing, frequency response, and complexity.   Randall L. Geiger

Bibliography. L. T. Bruton, *RC-Active Circuits, Theory and Design*, 1980; A. Sedra and K. Smith, *Microelectronic Circuits*, 4th ed., 1997; F. W. Stephenson (ed.), *RC Active Filter Design Handbook*, 1985.

Capparales

An order of flowering plants (Angiospermae) of approximately 15 families of dicotyledons with over 4000 species. In molecular phylogenetic classifications, it is placed near Malvales, Myrtales, and Sapindales. *See* MALVALES; MYRTALES; PLANT KINGDOM; SAPINDALES.

The mustard family, Brassicaceae (Cruciferae), with about 3000 species, and the caper family, Capparaceae, with about 800 species, form the core of the order. An additional 200 or so species are treated in 13 families, including Caricaceae (papaya), Limnanthaceae (meadowfoam), Resedaceae (mignonette), and Tropaeolaceae (garden nasturtium). The plants are diverse in vegetative habit and in floral and fruit morphology. However, they commonly possess myrosin cells, containing the enzyme myrosinase, and produce mustard oil glucosides (glucosinolates), the breakdown products of which are the pungent compounds of radish, wasabi, horseradish, and capers. Primitive members of the order have five-parted flowers, but the core families have four-parted flowers. Common vegetables such as broccoli, brussels sprouts, cabbage, kale, radish, rutabaga, turnip, and water cress belong to the Brassicaceae. Capparales are also important sources of seed oils, from Brassicaceae (*Brassica*) and Moringaceae (*Moringa*), and of several ornamentals, such as candytuft (*Iberis*) and sweet alyssum (*Lobularia*) in Brassicaceae, spider flower (*Cleome*) in Capparaceae, mignonette (*Reseda*) in Resedaceae, and garden nasturtium (*Tropaeolum*) in Tropaeolaceae. *See* BROCCOLI; BRUSSELS SPROUTS; CABBAGE; CAULIFLOWER; COLLARD; CRESS; HORSERADISH; KALE; KOHLRABI; MUSTARD; ORNAMENTAL PLANTS; RADISH; RAPE; RUTABAGA; TURNIP.   James E. Rodman

Capricornus

The Sea Goat, a southern zodiacal constellation (see **illustration**). It is the source of the terrestrial name Tropic of Capricorn, for the parallel of latitude, about $23\frac{1}{2}°$ south of the Equator, where the Sun is overhead at noon on the day of the winter solstice in the Northern Hemisphere (the summer solstice in the Southern Hemisphere, about December 22). The winter solstice used to occur when the Sun was in Capricornus, but because of the precession of the equinoxes this point has moved to Sagittarius. *See* PRECESSION OF EQUINOXES; SAGITTARIUS; TROPIC OF CAPRICORN; ZODIAC.

Capricornus has no bright stars. In the early star atlases, it was drawn as a goat with a fish's tail. In Greek mythology, the god Pan, posing as a goat, dived into a river to escape from a demon. In his panic, he changed only his rear half. He surfaced and saved

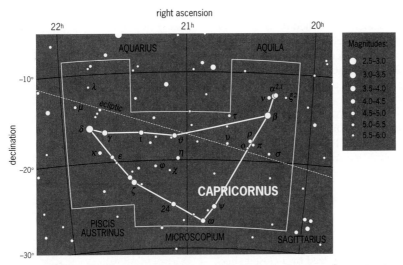

right ascension

Modern boundaries of the constellation Capricornus, the Sea Goat. The celestial equator is 0° of declination, which corresponds to celestial latitude. Right ascension corresponds to celestial longitude, with each hour of right ascension representing 15° of arc. Apparent brightness of stars is shown with dot sizes to illustrate the magnitude scale, where the brightest stars in the sky are 0th magnitude or brighter and the faintest stars that can be seen with the unaided eye at a dark site are 6th magnitude. (*Wil Tirion*)

Zeus, who had been injured and who rewarded the chimera by placing it in the heavens.

The modern boundaries of the 88 constellations, including this one, were defined by the International Astronomical Union in 1928. *See* CONSTELLATION.

Jay M. Pasachoff

Caprimulgiformes

An order of crepuscular (active during predawn or twilight hours) or mainly nocturnal birds collectively known as the goatsuckers. The group is apparently most closely related to the owls (Strigiformes) and is found worldwide, mainly in the tropics and warm temperate regions. Species breeding in the Arctic and cooler temperate regions are migratory. *See* STRIGIFORMES.

Classification. The order Caprimulgiformes is divided into the suborder Steatornithes, containing the single family Steatornithidae (oilbirds; 1 species; northern South America); and the suborder Caprimulgi, including the families Podargidae (frogmouths; 13 species; tropics, India to Australasia), Aegothelidae (owlet-frogmouths; 8 species; tropics, Australasia), Nyctibiidae (potoos; 6 species; Neotropics), and Caprimulgidae (nightjars or goatsuckers; 77 species; worldwide). The largest family, Caprimulgidae is usually divided into two subfamilies, the Caprimulginae (nightjars; worldwide) and the Chordeilinae (nighthawks; New World).

Fossil record. The goatsuckers have a poor fossil record, but some interesting forms are known from the early Tertiary well outside the current range of the different families. Specimens assigned to the oilbirds, the frogmouths, and the owlet-frogmouths have been reported from the Eocene of France.

Characteristics. The goatsuckers are primarily insectivorous, although the large frogmouths also feed on small vertebrates; the oilbird is unique in feed-

ing on fruits, especially of palms. Most goatsuckers have a huge, generally weak mouth with a flexible lower jaw that can expand widely and is surrounded by long, stout bristles; it makes an effective trap for insects caught in flight. Frogmouths and owlet-frogmouths have strong jaws.

The wings are well developed, but the feet are weak and serve mainly for perching. The plumage is soft and fluffy, and is mottled and barred brown and gray, serving as excellent cryptic protective coloration. Tree-dwelling forms, especially frogmouths and potoos, sit quietly on a tree with their body, neck, and head stretched; with their plumage matching the tree bark, the individuals look like a broken branch. White patches may exist on the wings, tail, and throat, which are visible only in flight. Some species have greatly elongated tail feathers, and a few have very elongated primary feathers forming pennants from their wings.

Goatsuckers are generally solitary but may migrate in loose flocks (nighthawks). Most species are highly vocal, using calls to attract mates and defend territories. The English names of a number of species, such as the whippoorwill and chuck-will's-widow, are based on their calls. The Caprimulgidae nest on the ground, but all other members of the Caprimulgi nest in trees; the clutch is from one to five eggs. Young are downy and remain in the nest until they are able to fly.

A few species are known to hibernate. Poorwills in the deserts of the southwestern United States hibernate in rock holes for several months at a time, often returning to the same hole in successive winters. Their body temperature falls from a normal 104–105°F (40–41°C) to 64–66°F (18–19°C).

Oilbirds. The peculiar South American oilbirds are colonial nesters, placing their nest of seeds and droppings on ledges deep in caves. Paired adults remain together throughout the year, roosting on their breeding ledge. The young become very fat, reaching twice the weight of the adults; they were once harvested in large numbers and boiled down for cooking oil. Oilbirds have excellent night vision, but inside their often totally dark caves they find their way by using echolocation based on pulses of sound of about 7000 Hz, which are audible to the human ear. *See* AVES; ECHOLOCATION.   Walter J. Bock

Bibliography. N. Cleere, *Nightjars: A Guide to the Nightjars, Nighthawks and Their Relatives*, Yale University Press, 1998; D. T. Holyoak, *Nightjars and Their Allies*, Oxford University Press, 2001.

Captorhinida

A moderately coherent group of primitive reptiles constituting an order of the subclass Anapsida. Most members are characterized by a closed cheek (temporal) region. The order is divided into four suborders: Captorhinomorpha, Millerosauria, Procolophonia, and Pareiasauria. Except for the Procolophonia, which continue into the Late Triassic, Captorhinida are confined to the Permo-Carboniferous. They lived in lowlands, where they were associated with amphibians and synapsid reptiles. Some of the smaller animals of the Captorhinomorpha and the Millerosauria fed primarily on insects and small vertebrates, but the larger genera were exclusively herbivorous. Along with the caseid pelycosaurs, they were the dominant consumers of vegetation in the middle Permian ecosystems.

At one time the Captorhinida were joined with the Diadectomorpha and Seymouriamorpha to form the order Cotylosauria (stem reptiles). This assemblage, now known to include both reptiles and amphibians, has been dropped because it is polyphyletic and also because it has carried many different meanings.

The Captorhinomorpha are the most diversified of the Captorhinida; the best-known genus is *Captorhinus* of the early Permian (**illus.** *a*). It was preceded, however, by more primitive genera from the upper Carboniferous and very early Permian and succeeded by specialized genera during the later portions of the Permian. *Captorhinus* and its successors were notable in the possession of multiple rows of teeth on the jaws and palates, related to increasingly herbivorous diets. The captorhinomorph evolutionary radiation culminated in a large, massive genus, *Moradisaurus*, from the upper Permian of Niger, Africa; it measured about 6 ft (2 m) in length.

Millerosaurs are poorly known small reptiles from the middle Permian of South Africa. Unlike most Captorhinida, they developed partially to fully open cheek regions. They have been considered to be close relatives of the lizards, but currently are thought to be merely a somewhat specialized branch of the Captorhinida.

Procolophonia were small to medium-sized animals with generalized skeletons and specialized skulls. Skulls of some of the Late Triassic procolophons such as *Hypsognathus* were set with sharp, bony projections somewhat reminiscent of those in living horned lizards. The teeth of pro-

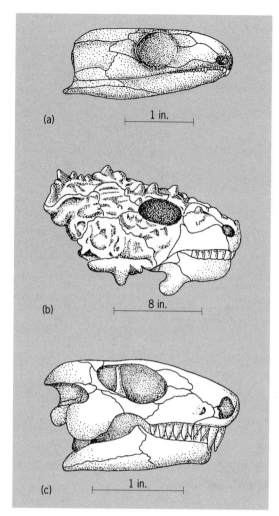

Captorhinid skulls. (*a*) *Captorhinus*. (*b*) *Pareiasaurus*. (*c*) *Procolophon*.

colophons were arrayed in single rows and were rather blunt, suggesting a herbivorous diet.

Pareiasaurs were the giants of the Captorhinida, rivaled only by *Moradisaurus*. They ranged up to about 6 ft (2 m) in length and were characterized by broad vertebrae, heavy limbs, and massive feet. Pareiasaurs were prominent herbivores during the middle and late Permian of Eurasia and Africa, where their skeletons occasionally occur in profusion in deposits formed in ancient waterholes. During the late Permian their role as primary consumers was gradually taken over by evolving herbivorous therapsids. *See* ANAPSIDA; REPTILIA; SYNAPSIDA; THERAPSIDA.   Everett C. Olson

Bibliography. C. L. Carroll, *Vertebrate Paleontology and Evolution*, 1987; A. S. Romer, *Osteology of the Reptiles*, 1956, reprint 1997.

Carat

The unit of weight now used for all gemstones except pearls. It is also called the metric carat (m.c.). By international agreement, the carat weight is set at 200 milligrams (0.00704 oz). Pearls are weighed in grains, a unit of weight equal to 50 mg (0.0018 oz), or $^1/_4$ carat.

Despite the great value of many of the gemstones weighed against a unit called the carat, the weight differed from country to country until early in the twentieth century. Although most of the weights to which the name was applied were near 205 mg (0.00722 oz), the range was from less than 190 to over 210 mg (less than 0.00669 to over 0.00739 oz). The 200-mg (0.00704-oz) carat was proposed in 1907 in Paris. This weight slowly gained acceptance, and by 1914 most of the important nations in the gem trade had accepted the metric carat as the legal standard for gemstones.

The word carat comes from the Greek word for the locust tree that is common in the Mediterranean area. This tree produces seeds that are fairly uniform in weight, averaging about 205 mg (0.00722 oz) each. As a result, locust seeds came to be used for gem weight comparisons.

The application of the term carat as a unit of weight must not be confused with the term karat used to indicate fineness or purity of the gold in which gems are mounted. *See* GEM.

Richard T. Liddicoat, Jr.

Caraway

An important spice from the fruits of the perennial herb *Carum carvi*, of the family Apiaceae. A native of Europe and western Asia, it is now cultivated in many temperate areas of both hemispheres. The small, brown, slightly curved fruits are used in perfumery, cookery, confectionery, in medicine, and for flavoring beverages. *See* APIALES; SPICE AND FLAVORING.

Perry D. Strausbaugh; Earl L. Core

Carbohydrate

A term applied to a group of substances which include the sugars, starches, and cellulose, along with many other related substances. This group of compounds is vital in the lives of plants and animals, both as structural elements and in the maintenance of functional activity. Plants are unique in that they have the power to synthesize carbohydrates from carbon dioxide and water in the presence of the green pigment chlorophyll through the energy derived from sunlight, by the process of photosynthesis. This process is responsible not only for the existence of plants but for the maintenance of animal life as well, since animals obtain their entire food supply directly or indirectly from the carbohydrates of plants. *See* PHOTOSYNTHESIS.

The carbohydrates as a group are comparable in importance with the proteins and fats. Cane or beet sugar, D-glucose, D-fructose, starch, and cellulose may be cited as typical representatives. A number of members of this group are of great industrial importance. Among undertakings dependent on carbohydrate materials are the cotton industry, explosives manufacture, brewing, and manufacture of alcohol.

The term carbohydrate originated in the belief that naturally occurring compounds of this class, for example, D-glucose ($C_6H_{12}O_6$), sucrose ($C_{12}H_{22}O_{11}$), and cellulose ($C_6H_{10}O_5$)$_n$, could be represented formally as hydrates of carbon, that is, $C_x(H_2O)_y$. Later it became evident that this definition for carbohydrates was not a satisfactory one. New substances were discovered whose properties clearly indicated that they had the characteristics of sugars and belonged in the carbohydrate class, but which nevertheless showed a deviation from the required hydrogen-to-oxygen ratio. Examples of these are the important deoxy sugars, D-deoxyribose, L-fucose, and L-rhamnose, the uronic acids, and such compounds as ascorbic acid (vitamin C). The retention of the term carbohydrate is therefore a matter of convenience rather than of exact definition. A carbohydrate is usually defined as either a polyhydroxy aldehyde (aldose) or ketone (ketose), or as a substance which yields one of these compounds on hydrolysis. However, included within this class of compounds are substances also containing nitrogen and sulfur.

The properties of many carbohydrates differ enormously from one substance to another. The sugars, such as D-glucose or sucrose, are easily soluble, sweet-tasting and crystalline; the starches are colloidal and paste-forming; and cellulose is completely insoluble. Yet chemical analysis shows that they have a common basis; the starches and cellulose may be degraded by different methods to the same crystalline sugar, D-glucose.

Classification. The carbohydrates usually are classified into three main groups according to complexity: monosaccharides, oligosaccharides, and polysaccharides.

Monosaccharides. These simple sugars consist of a single carbohydrate unit which cannot be hydrolyzed into simpler substances. These are characterized, according to their length of carbon chain, as trioses ($C_3H_6O_3$), tetroses ($C_4H_8O_4$), pentoses ($C_5H_{10}O_5$), hexoses ($C_6H_{12}O_6$), heptoses ($C_7H_{14}O_7$), and so on. A monosaccharide may be an aldose or a ketose, depending on the type of carbonyl group (C=O) present. This system gives rise to such names as aldotriose, aldotetrose, aldopentose, and aldohexose for the aldose forms and by such names as ketopentoses and ketohexoses when the ketone group is present. More recently the tendency is to indicate the presence of a ketone group by the ending "ulose" in names such as pentuloses and heptuloses. *See* MONOSACCHARIDE.

Oligosaccharides. These compound sugars are condensation products of two to five molecules of simple sugars and are subclassified into disaccharides, trisaccharides, tetrasaccharides, and pentasaccharides, according to the number of monosaccharide molecules yielded upon hydrolysis.

The sugars which include the monosaccharides and oligosaccharides are mostly crystalline compounds. The monosaccharides and disaccharides have a sweet taste. Products obtained from hydrolysis of higher molecular weight polysaccharides and consisting of compound sugars that contain as many as nine monosaccharide units are also termed oligosaccharides. However, these higher members are not crystalline compounds. The disaccharides and other groups of oligosaccharides are subclassified into reducing and nonreducing sugars, depending on whether or not the sugar has a functional carbonyl group. In a nonreducing oligosaccharide, the carbonyl groups of the constituent monosaccharide units are involved in glycosidic linkage. The compound sugars are in reality sugarlike polysaccharides, but the prefix "poly" is reserved for carbohydrates which consist of large aggregates of monosaccharide units. *See* OLIGOSACCHARIDE.

Polysaccharides. These comprise a heterogeneous group of compounds which represent large aggregates of monosaccharide units, joined through glycosidic bonds. They are tasteless, nonreducing, amorphous substances that yield a large and indefinite number of monosaccharide units on hydrolysis. Their molecular weight is usually very high, and many of them, like starch or glycogen, have molecular weights of several million. They form colloidal solutions, but some polysaccharides, of which cellulose is an example, are completely insoluble in water. On account of their heterogeneity they are difficult to classify. One common system of classification is based primarily upon the class of monosaccharide yielded on hydrolysis. Thus a polysaccharide that yields hexose monosaccharides on hydrolysis is called hexoglycan, $(C_6H_{10}O_5)_n$, where n represents the number of monosaccharide units present. A polysaccharide yielding a pentose sugar is called pentoglycan, $(C_5H_8O_4)_n$. Each major class is further subdivided according to the particular hexose or pentose produced. Thus, a polysaccharide composed of the hexose sugar D-glucose is called glucan; those composed of the pentose sugars D-xylose and L-arabinose are called xylan and araban, respectively.

Some polysaccharides, however, yield both hexose and pentose sugars on hydrolysis and are classified as mixed hexosans and pentosans; others, in addition to hexoses and pentoses, frequently on acid hydrolysis yield the uronic acids, D-glucuronic, D-galacturonic, or D-mannuronic acid. Such polysaccharides are often called polyuronides. *See* POLYSACCHARIDE.

Reducing and nonreducing sugars. The sugars are also classified into two general groups, the reducing and nonreducing. The reducing sugars are distinguished by the fact that because of their free, or potentially free, aldehyde or ketone groups they possess the property of readily reducing alkaline solutions of many metallic salts, such as those of copper, silver, bismuth, mercury, and iron. The most widely used reagent for this purpose is Fehling's solution, in which the oxidizing agent is the cupric tartrate ion, formed in a strongly alkaline solution of copper sulfate and a salt of tartaric acid. The nonreducing sugars do not exhibit this property. The reducing sugars constitute by far the larger group. The monosaccha-

rides and many of their derivatives reduce Fehling's solution. Most of the disaccharides, including maltose, lactose, and the rarer sugars cellobiose, gentiobiose, melibiose, and turanose, are also reducing sugars. The best-known nonreducing sugar is the disaccharide sucrose. Among other nonreducing sugars are the disaccharide trehalose, the trisaccharides raffinose and melezitose, the tetrasaccharide stachyose, and the pentasaccharide verbascose.

The alkali in the Fehling solution, or other such reagents used for the determination of reducing sugars, causes considerable decomposition of the sugar molecule into reactive fragments which may also reduce the metal ions. Thus, while the total reduction for a given sugar may be constant under carefully controlled conditions and can therefore be used for quantitative purposes, it is impossible to write a balanced equation for the reaction in terms of the simple oxidation of the sugar and reduction of the metal ion.

Analysis. This involves separation of the carbohydrate mixtures, identification of the individual carbohydrates, and estimation of their quantities.

Separation and identification. Sugars, in most cases, occur in living tissues as mixtures. Before a sugar can be identified, it must be isolated in pure form, preferably as a crystalline substance. The pure crystalline compound is readily identified by its melting point, optical rotation, and x-ray diffraction pattern. Preparation of certain crystalline derivatives facilitates isolation and identification of reducing sugars. The phenylhydrazone and phenylosazone derivatives of these sugars are especially useful, chiefly because of their ease of preparation. The phenylosatriazoles, benzimidazoles, and diothioacetal acetates are more advantageous for the purpose of identification.

Application of chromatographic technique provides a useful and rapid method for the separation and identification of sugars. The great advantage of this process lies in the fact that it can be applied to minute amounts as well as to relatively large quantities. For micro amounts chromatography on filter paper is used. The mixed sugar solution is applied as a spot on the narrow edge of a strip of filter paper. The sugars are then separated by using a mixture of water and a partially immiscible organic solvent, such as *n*-butanol or phenol. The paper is then dried and sprayed with coloring reagents, such as *p*-anisidine hydrochloride or aniline hydrogen phthalate, which show the location of the individual sugars. For separation of larger quantities of material, column chromatography is used. In this method the proper choice of solvents and absorbents is important. The solvent is passed through a column containing powdered cellulose, silicic acid, alumina, clay, carbon, or other adsorbent by gravity, suction, or pressure. After sufficient development to form the different zones, the products may be eluted from the column in successive batches. *See* CHROMATOGRAPHY.

Color tests. There are a number of color tests which are helpful in the identification of carbohydrates.

These tests are based on the condensation of various aromatic amines or phenolic substances with the degradation products of sugars. The Molisch test is used for the general detection of carbohydrates. In this test a purple color is produced when the solution containing carbohydrate is treated with strong sulfuric acid in the presence of α-naphthol. In the Tauber test pentose sugars produce a cherry-red color when heated with a solution of benzidine in glacial acetic acid. Another test for pentoses and uronic acids is based on the fact that a violet-red color develops when these sugars are treated with hydrochloric acid and phloroglucinol. Seliwanoff's test is used for ketoses, which give a red color with resorcinol in hydrochloric acid. The Tollens naphthoresorcinol and the Dische carbazole tests are used for the detection of the uronic acids, D-glucuronic acid, D-galacturonic acid, and D-mannuronic acid. The polysaccharide, starch, produces a blue color when treated with a dilute solution of iodine in potassium iodide, while glycogen gives a reddish-brown color with this reagent.

Paper chromatography and color tests only indicate the probable presence of a particular carbohydrate. For unequivocal proof it is necessary to resort to isolation procedures.

Estimation. The reducing properties of aldoses and ketoses are most frequently utilized for the quantitative analysis of these sugars. A nonreducing sugar such as sucrose or raffinose, or a polysaccharide such as starch, must be first hydrolyzed with acid or with an appropriate enzyme to its constituent reducing monosaccharide units before it is analyzed. Upon heating the reducing sugars with Fehling's solution, containing copper sulfate, tartrate ion, and sodium hydroxide, a brick-red color develops, a result of the formation and precipitation of cuprous oxide.

The quantity of the cuprous oxide precipitate is a measure of the amount of reducing sugar present. Several modifications of this reaction have been used for the quantitative determination of reducing sugars. The estimation of sugar by the Benedict method involves the determination of the reduced cuprous ions colorimetrically after treatment with phosphomolybdic acid. In the Somogyi-Shaffer-Hartmann method, the sugar is estimated by iodometric titration of reduced copper. Several other quantitative methods for the determination of sugars are based on the reduction of ferricyanide ions in an alkaline solution. These reactions can be applied to micro quantities of sugars. There are also spectrophotometric methods, devised by Dische, which are based on light absorption by the reaction products resulting from treatment of sugars with carbazole or cysteine-carbazole in sulfuric acid. Sugars can be accurately identified and determined by their specific optical rotations, provided they are available in sufficient quantities and no other interfering optically active material is present. *See* ALDEHYDE; TITRATION.

Stereoisomerism. The sugars consist of chains of carbon atoms which are united to one another at a tetrahedral angle of 109°28′. A carbon atom to which are attached four different groups is called asymmetric. A sugar, or any other compound containing one or more asymmetric carbon atoms, possesses optical activity; that is, it rotates the plane of polarized light to the right or left. The specific rotation of a substance possessing optical activity is the rotation expressed in angular degrees which is afforded by 1 gram of substance dissolved in 1 milliliter of water in a tube 1 decimeter in length. It is usually given for the sodium D line at a definite temperature, for example, 20°C (68°F), and is designated by $[\alpha]_D^{20}$. *See* OPTICAL ACTIVITY.

The triose glycerose, or glyceraldehyde, has one asymmetric carbon atom and therefore exists in two optically active forms, one dextrorotatory and the other levorotatory (**Fig. 1**).

The D and L forms of glycerose are related to each other as the right hand is to the left hand, being similar, but not identical. One may not be superposed upon the other. If one model is held before a mirror, the image in the mirror corresponds to the arrangement of the other model. The two compounds whose molecules are mirror images of each other are called optical antipodes or enantiomorphs.

It is difficult to represent stereochemically the more complex sugars having several asymmetric carbon atoms. An examination of the formula for an aldohexose (**Fig. 2**) reveals that it contains four different asymmetric carbon atoms; that is, each of the atoms marked with an asterisk, at positions 2, 3, 4,

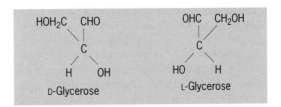

Fig. 1. Spatial arrangement of the groups around the asymmetric carbons of the two isomers of glycerose.

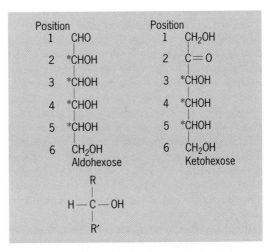

Fig. 2. Structural formulas showing asymmetric carbons (asterisk) for an aldohexose and a ketohexose. Detail of carbon at position 2 in aldohexose is shown, where R = CHO and R′ = everything below carbon atom 2.

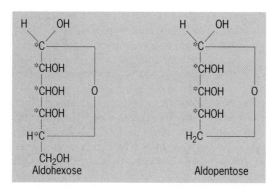

Fig. 3. Structural formulas for ring forms of an aldohexose and an aldopentose. Asymmetric carbons are marked by an asterisk.

and 5, carries four different groups or atoms. The ketohexose contains three asymmetric carbon atoms, at 3, 4, and 5 (Fig. 2).

As the number of asymmetric carbon atoms in the sugar molecule increases, from the trioses to the higher monosaccharides, the number of stereoisomers increases in accordance with the van't Hoff formula 2^n where n represents the number of asymmetric carbon atoms.

Thus the possible number of stereoisomers of an aldohexose, such as glucose or galactose, when written in open-chain form, is 2^4 or 16 (eight enantiomorphous pairs). In the ketose sugars, there is one less asymmetric center than in the aldoses of equal chain length; therefore the number of isomers is reduced by a factor of 2. The possible number of stereoisomers of a ketohexose, exemplified by fructose or sorbose, is 2^3 or 8 (four enantiomorphous pairs). Eight stereoisomers, consisting of four pairs of enantiomorphs, are possible for an aldopentose like xylose or arabinose. If, as seen in **Fig. 3**, the formulas of these sugars are represented in ring form, the first carbon atom in the monosaccharide chain becomes asymmetric because of formation of a cyclic hemiacetal with a new OH group and another center of asymmetry at carbon atom 1. The possible isomers for a cyclic aldohexose therefore become 2^5 or 32, and for an aldopentose 2^4 or 16.

The spatial arrangement of the groups around the asymmetric carbon atom of the dextrorotatory form of glyceraldehyde (glycerose) is arbitrarily called the D configuration, while that of the levorotatory form is called the L configuration. This connotation of the D and L refers to spatial configuration only and is not an indication of the direction of rotation of the plane of polarized light by the sugar. The reference carbon atom regarding D or L configuration is, for sugars containing more than one asymmetric carbon atom, the asymmetric carbon atom farthest removed from the active (that is, the aldehyde or ketone) end of the molecule and adjacent to the terminal group (**Fig. 4**).

Rosanoff, who introduced this criterion for designating the D and L form of sugars, regarded all sugars of the D series as built up, in theory, from D-glycerose, and those of the L series from L-glycerose. Although not accomplished in practice throughout the series,

such a process is rendered possible without interfering with the original asymmetric carbon atom by the stepwise addition of the repeating unit CHOH through the Kiliani cyanohydrin synthesis. It must be emphasized that Rosanoff's representation of the D and L forms of sugar is merely a convention and has no relation to their direction of rotation. If it is desired to indicate the direction of rotation of the compound, the symbols (+), meaning dextrorotatory, and (−), meaning levorotatory, are used. Thus a dextrorotatory sugar with the D configuration is indicated by the symbol D(+), while a levorotatory sugar of the same configuration is represented by D(−). **Figure 5** shows the relationship of D-glycerose to the D-trioses, D-tetroses, D-pentoses, and D-hexoses.

Formulation. Thus far the monosaccharides have been considered as open-chain compounds, designated by projection formulas. The projection formula, introduced by Emil Fischer, is based on the convention that tetrahedrons, representing individual asymmetric carbons of a sugar, viewed as though supported by their carbon to carbon bonds with the hydrogen and hydroxyl groups extending outward, are projected upon the depicting plane. This formula is quite convenient, because the relationship between various sugars is easily demonstrated. Its numbering begins at the terminal position associated with the carbonyl group; in ketoses the carbonyl group is in carbon atom 2 position. When Greek letters are used, as in the older literature, the carbon next to the CHO group is called the α-carbon atom.

Although an aldohexose such as D-glucose or an aldopentose such as D-xylose exhibits many of the properties of common aldehydes, its reactivity, when compared with acyclic hydroxyaldehydes such as glycolic aldehyde or glyceraldehyde, is not as great as would be expected if the sugar possessed the simple aldehydic projection formula (**Fig. 6**). Furthermore, the cyanohydrin reaction proceeds with difficulty, and sugars fail to give the Schiff test for aldehydes. Thus, the straight-chain aldehydic projection formula does not represent the essential features of the sugar molecules, particularly their tendency to form five- and six-membered rings. In reality, because of the tetrahedral angles between bonds of the carbon atoms, the chain tends to form a ring. Thus, the ends of a six-carbon chain approach each other as shown in **Fig. 7**, permitting a reaction between the carbonyl group and a hydroxyl on the fourth or fifth carbon atom and forming a hemiacetal.

The reaction is analogous to the formation of hemiacetals from simple aldehydes and alcohols. Admixture of an aldehyde and an alcohol produces first a

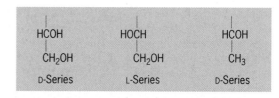

Fig. 4. Spatial configurations of D and L series showing reference carbon attached to the terminal group.

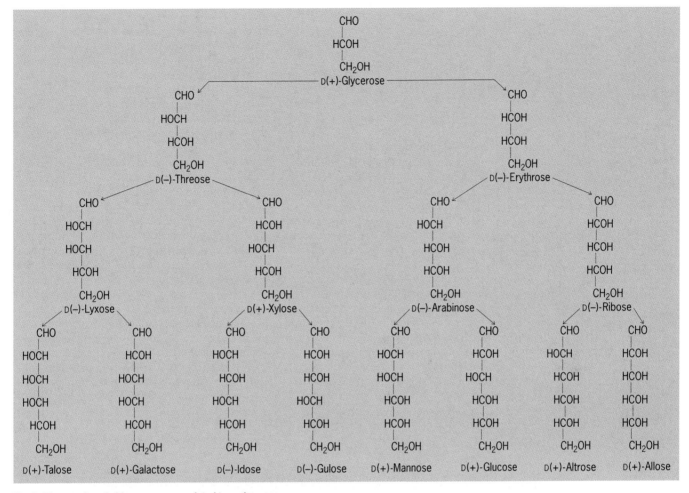

Fig. 5. The D-series of aldose sugars as related to D-glycerose.

hemiacetal. Long standing in an excess of alcohol in the presence of an acid catalyst converts the hemiacetal into a complete acetal, as shown below.

$$RCHO + ROH \underset{rapid}{\overset{H^+}{\rightleftharpoons}} RCH\begin{matrix} OH \\ \\ OR \end{matrix} \underset{slow}{\overset{ROH + H^+}{\rightleftharpoons}}$$

$$RCH\begin{matrix} OR \\ \\ OR \end{matrix} + H_2O$$

Such a reaction occurs not only with aldose but also with ketose sugars. Formation of a hemiacetal in

Fig. 6. Projection formula for the aldohexose D-glucose.

Fig. 7. Six-carbon chain forming hemiacetal ring.

a hexose monosaccharide from a reaction between carbon atom 1 and the OH group of carbon atom 6 is not likely, because this would produce a strained seven-membered ring. Six- and five-membered rings are more easily formed because there is very little distortion of the bond angles. Rings of four carbon atoms or less do not form easily.

There is abundant evidence that sugars actually exist as cyclic compounds. Most decisive proof is furnished by the phenomenon of mutarotation, by the existence of two isomeric methylglycosides, and by Haworth's methylation experiments, in which he was unable to demonstrate open-chain structure.

In the older literature the six-membered ring structure of the aldohexoses in which the first carbon

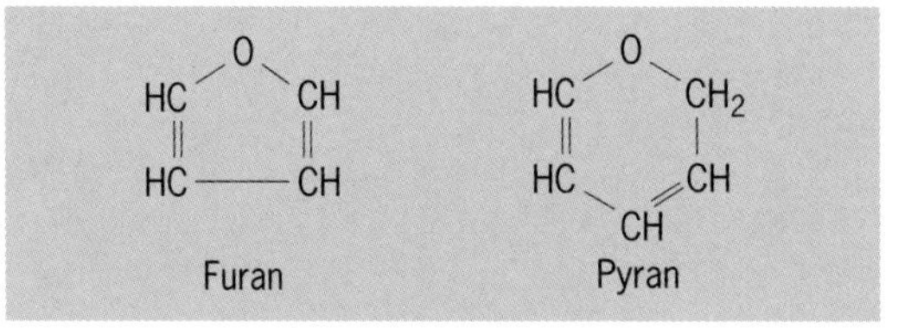

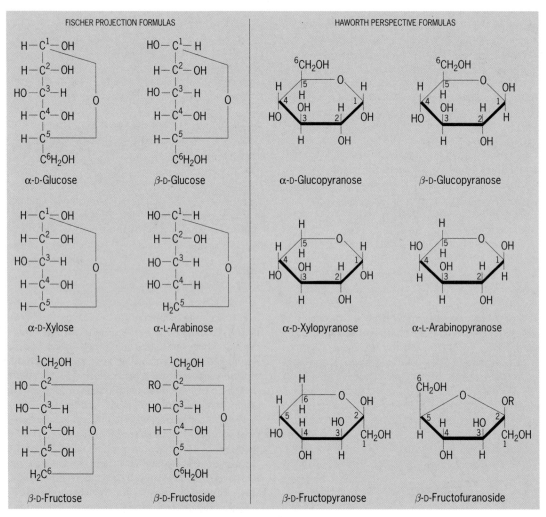

Fig. 8. Structural formulas for furan and pyran.

atom is linked to the fifth carbon atom through an oxygen atom had been named amylene oxide or δ-oxide configuration. The five-membered rings in which carbon atom 1 is linked to carbon atom 4 had been termed butylene oxide or γ-oxide configuration. In 1927 W. N. Haworth suggested that the five-atom ring sugars should be regarded as derived from furan and the six-atom ring configuration from pyran (**Fig. 8**).

Thus a sugar containing a γ-oxide or 1,4-oxide ring is called a furanose sugar, and if it is present as a glycoside, it is described as a furanoside. It must be noted, however, that unsubstituted furanose sugars have never been isolated, although they do exist in small proportion in solution. Although the 1,4 ring is stable and the 1,5 ring is relatively unstable in the sugar lactones, the reverse is true for the sugars and

glycosides. Furanose structures are therefore found either in substituted sugars such as 2,3,5,6-O-methyl-D-glucose, where there is no free hydroxyl on carbon atom 5, or more commonly, when the monosaccharide (D-fructose or L-arabinose) is a constituent of complex sugars, the oligosaccharides or polysaccharides. Similarly the names pyranose and pyranoside are applied to the sugars and sugar derivatives having the six-membered, δ-oxide, or 1,5 rings. *See* GLYCOSIDE.

In the Haworth perspective formulas, carbon atoms 1–5 and the ring oxygen are represented in a single plane projecting from the plane of the paper on which it is written. The valences of the carbon atoms not involved in ring formation are situated above or below the plane of the ring. The thickened lines at the bottom of the ring formulas represent the sides of the hexagon nearest to the observer.

When the carbon atoms in the ring are numbered clockwise, as in α-D-glycopyranose, the groups that are written on the right-hand side in the projection formula are represented as projecting below the plane of the ring, and the corresponding groups on the left-hand side are projecting above. However, there is a discrepancy in the relative positions of the substituent groups on carbon atom 5 in that the H

Fig. 9. Fischer projection formulas and Haworth perspective formulas.

atom appears in the perspective formula below instead of above the plane of the ring. This apparent anomaly is the result of torsion required to effect ring closure. In forming a ring from the straight-chain aldehydic form, the fifth carbon atom must be rotated so that the oxygen atom in the OH group on this carbon atom is brought into the plane of the first five carbon atoms. Consequently, the H atom attached to carbon atom 5 is now shifted to the other side of the chain, because this carbon atom has been rotated through more than a 90° angle.

The projection and perspective formulas for the α- and β-isomers of D-glucose and for α-D-xylose, α-L-arabinose, and β-D-fructose are shown in **Fig. 9**.

Since free D-fructose primarily exists in the pyranose configuration, the furanose ring structure of this sugar is shown with the active hydrogen of the potential reducing group substituted. The substituent R may be a D-glucopyranosyl unit as in the disaccharide, sucrose, or a chain of other fructofuranosyl units as in the polysaccharide, inulin.

Mutarotation. Two forms of glucose are known. The α-form is obtained by dissolving the sugar, D-glucose, in water and allowing it to crystallize through evaporation of the solvent. The β form is obtained by crystallizing D-glucose from pyridine or acetic acid. The products are not merely different crystallographic forms of the same substance, because they have different properties when dissolved. At 20°C (68°F) a freshly prepared solution of α-D-glucose has a specific rotation, $[\alpha]_D^{20}$, of +113°, and a freshly prepared aqueous solution of β-D-glucose at the same temperature has a specific rotation of +19°. Upon standing, both solutions gradually change in rotatory power. The optical rotation of the α-D form decreases and that of the β-D form increases until they reach the same equilibrium value of $[\alpha]_D$ + 52.5°, which corresponds to a mixture of 37% α and 63% β. This phenomenon of change in its optical property is called mutarotation. It is displayed not only with glucose but with all crystalline sugars that have a free or potentially free aldehyde or ketone group in the molecule. To account for the existence of two structures, it is assumed that the monosaccharides exist in the form of cyclic hemiacetals rather than in open-chain form (**Fig. 10**).

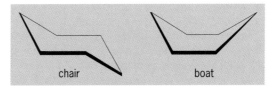

Fig. 11. Conformations of a cyclohexane.

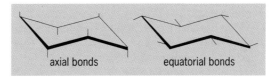

Fig. 12. Geometrical arrangements of carbon-hydrogen bonds on the chair form of a cyclohexane.

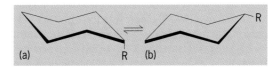

Fig. 13. Interconversion of (a) axial and (b) equatorial positions for R group of a cyclohexane derivative.

The process of mutarotation is due to the labile nature of the hemiacetal linkage and the interconversion of the α and β forms through the acyclic aldehyde form which exists in solution to a very small extent (about 0.1%). Mutarotation is catalyzed by both acid and base, with the base being by far more effective.

The α- and β-sugars are stereoisomeric, but they are not mirror images. They are known as anomers, differing from each other only in the positions of the atoms or groups attached to the terminal asymmetric carbon atom.

To avoid confusion in the matter of new isomers or anomers, a convention was proposed by C. Hudson which is generally accepted. This states that for pairs of α and β isomers of the D series, the one with the higher rotation in the positive sense shall be called the α form, whereas the isomer with the lower rotation is designated as β. The reverse holds good for the L series, the enantiomorph of α-D-glucose being α-L-glucose with a lower specific rotation of $[\alpha]_D$ − 113° than β-L-glucose, $[\alpha]_D$ − 19°. In the α-anomer of D-glucose the OH group that is attached to the aldehydic carbon atom and the OH group that is on the adjacent carbon atom are on the same side of the ring (cis position). In the β form these hydroxyl groups are on opposite sides of the hemiacetal ring (trans position).

Sugar conformations. Although the Haworth formulas are an improvement over the Fischer formulas, they still represent an oversimplification of the true configuration of the monosaccharides in space. While the five-membered furanose ring of a sugar is almost planar, a strainless six-membered pyranose ring is not. A nonplanar arrangement of the molecule must be adopted to maintain the normal valency angles in the pyranose ring. The term "conformations" was coined for the various arrangements of

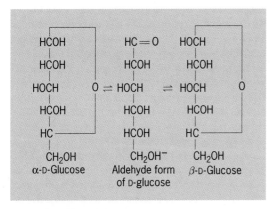

Fig. 10. Possibilities during mutarotation of D-glucose.

atoms in space that can arise by rotation about single bonds.

Since the only difference between a pyranose ring of a monosaccharide and that of a cyclohexane is the presence of an oxygen in the ring of the former compound, there is a close similarity between the molecular geometries of the two types of rings. The concepts developed for the cyclohexane ring can, therefore, be applied to the sugars containing the pyranose rings.

Results obtained by several investigators show that arrangements of cyclohexane which are free from angle strain are either of the "chair" conformation or the "boat" conformation (**Fig. 11**).

Examination of the chair form of cyclohexane shows that its carbon-hydrogen bonds can be divided into two geometrically different types. Six of them are perpendicular to the plane of the ring and are termed axial (a) bonds, while the other six radiate out from the ring and are termed equatorial (e) bonds (**Fig. 12**). Because of the staggered arrangements of the hydrogen atoms, the chair conformation (which minimizes repulsions between them) has a lower energy content and is thus more stable than the boat form. Consequently, cyclohexane and most of its derivatives tend to assume the chair conformation.

In cyclohexane derivatives, the group R is axial in one conformation but is readily convertible into the equatorial position (**Fig. 13**).

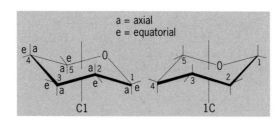

Fig. 14. Interchangeable conformations of a pyranose sugar, designated as C1 and 1C.

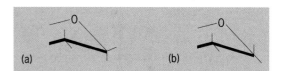

Fig. 16. Glycosidic carbon links in the C1 conformation must be as in *a*, not *b*.

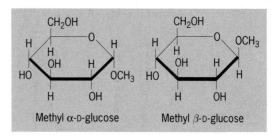

Fig. 17. Formulas for α and β forms of methyl D-glucose.

Similarly, pyranose sugars can exist in two interchangeable conformations, designated by R. E. Reeves as C1 and 1C (**Fig. 14**).

The greatest nonbonded interactions in a sugar are due to the hydroxyl groups. In considering preferred conformational stability for any sugar, conformations with large axial substituents should be avoided. In the absence of large polar interactions in the pyranose series, that chair conformation in which the largest number of the bulky groups are in equatorial position is the most stable one. In this connection it should be noted that the CH_2OH group is bulkier than the hydroxyl.

The relationship between the Haworth formulas and the two chair forms for the pyranose sugars is shown in **Fig. 15**. In each of the pyranose sugars in the illustration there are fewer axial hydroxyl groups and fewer repulsive interactions in the C1 conformation, which is the preferred form.

In conformational formulas, direction of bonds is determined by the tetrahedral valencies of the carbon atoms (**Fig. 16**).

The application of conformational analysis in carbohydrate chemistry is useful in many cases in predicting relative rates of reactions and the extent to which some reactions will proceed. As an example, the greater proportion of β-D-glucose (in which all hydroxyls are equatorial) in the equilibrium mixture compared with α-D-glucose (in which all hydroxyls are equatorial) in the equilibrium mixture compared with α-D-glucose (which has an axial hydroxyl at carbon atom 1) can be explained. Similarly, the equilibrium between α-D-galactose 1-phosphate (axial hydroxyl at carbon atom 4 in C1 conformation) and α-D-glucose 1-phosphate, which has an equatorial hydroxyl at C = 4, resulting in smaller nonbonded interactions, favors the glucose derivative.

Methyl glucosides. When a solution of glucose in cold methanol is treated with dry hydrogen chloride as catalyst, an acetal is formed. Such a compound formed from glucose is called a glucoside (**Fig. 17**); if the sugar galactose were used, the acetal would be called a galactoside. Methyl glucoside

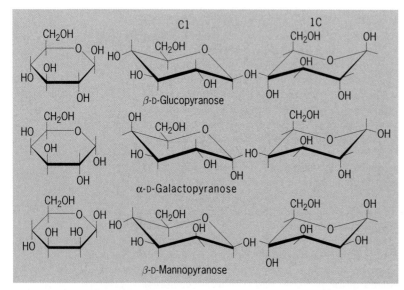

Fig. 15. Relationship between Haworth formula and chair forms for pyranose sugars.

is perhaps the simplest example of a large group of substances in which the hydroxyl of the hemiacetal group at carbon atom 1 of an aldose monosaccharide has been condensed with the hydroxyl group of an alcohol.

In aqueous solution D-glucose exists chiefly as D-glucopyranose. However, a small proportion of this sugar exists in the furanose as well as in the open-chain aldehyde forms, the last in a minute amount. Since the furanose structure reacts more rapidly to form the glucoside than does the pyranose configuration of the sugar, a considerable amount of labile methylglucofuranoside is formed in the first few hours. On prolonged standing or heating, the more stable methyl α-D-glucopyranoside and methyl β-D-glucopyranoside appear. Thus it is evident that when glucose is treated with methanolic hydrochloric acid, the yield of methylglucoside of a particular configuration has little bearing on the structure of the original sugar; that is, the structure of the glucoside may or may not correspond to the structure of the crystalline sugar. However, a relationship in this case can be established through hydrolysis of a methylglucoside. When pure methyl α-D-glucoside is hydrolyzed, the subsequent mutarotation of the hydrolysis product is found to be in the same direction as that of pure α-D-glucopyranose. It is therefore concluded that α-D-glucose and α-D-glucoside have the same configuration about the first carbon atom.

The α- and β-methylglucosides are crystalline compounds. They may be separated by fractional crystallization or through the agency of enzymes. The enzymes maltase and emulsin act selectively upon the two glucosides, the former hydrolyzing the α form only and the latter acting upon the anomeric β compound. The specific rotation of methyl α-D-glucopyranoside is $+159°$, while that of methyl β-D-glucopyranoside is $-33°$. *See* BIOCHEMISTRY.

William Z. Hassid

Bibliography. G. D. Aspinall, *Carbohydrate Chemistry*, 1976; V. Ginsburg, *Biology of Carbohydrates*, 1981; W. W. Pigman, *The Carbohydrates: Chemistry and Biochemistry*, 2d ed., 1981; J. Staněk et al., *The Monosaccharides*, 1964; J. Staněk, M. Černý, and J. Pacák, *The Oligosaccharides*, 1965.

Carbohydrate metabolism

The fields of biochemistry and physiology deal with the breakdown and synthesis of simple sugars, oligosaccharides, and polysaccharides, and with the transport of sugars across cell membranes and tissues. The breakdown or dissimilation of simple sugars, particularly glucose, is one of the principal sources of energy for living organisms. The dissimilation may be anaerobic, as in fermentations, or aerobic, that is, respiratory. In both types of metabolism, the breakdown is accompanied by the formation of energy-rich bonds, chiefly the pyrophosphate bond of the coenzyme adenosine triphosphate (ATP), which serves as a coupling agent between different metabolic processes. In higher animals, glucose is the carbohydrate constituent of blood, which carries it to the tissues of the body. In higher plants, the disaccharide sucrose is often stored and transported by the tissues. Certain polysaccharides, especially starch and glycogen, are stored as endogenous food reserves in the cells of plants, animals, and microorganisms. Others, such as cellulose, chitin, and bacterial polysaccharides, serve as structural components of cell walls. As constituents of plant and animal tissues, various carbohydrates become available to those organisms which depend on other living or dead organisms for their source of nutrients. Hence, all naturally occurring carbohydrates can be dissimilated by some animals or microorganisms. *See* ADENOSINE TRIPHOSPHATE (ATP); CARBOHYDRATE; CELLULOSE; GLYCOGEN; STARCH.

Dietary carbohydrates. Certain carbohydrates cannot be used as nutrients by humans. For example, the polysaccharide cellulose, which is one of the main constituents of plants, cannot be digested by humans or other mammals and is a useful food only for those, such as the ruminants, that harbor cellulose-decomposing microorganisms in their digestive tracts. The principal dietary carbohydrates available to humans are the simple sugars glucose and fructose, the disaccharides sucrose and lactose, and the polysaccharides glycogen and starch. Lactose is the carbohydrate constituent of milk and hence one of the main sources of food during infancy. The disaccharides and polysaccharides that cannot be absorbed directly from the intestine are first digested and hydrolyzed by enzymes secreted into the alimentary canal. The nature of these enzymes, which are known as glycosidases, will be discussed later. *See* LACTOSE.

Intestinal absorption and transport. The simple sugars, of which glucose is the major component, reach the intestine or are produced there through the digestion of oligosaccharides. They are absorbed by the intestinal mucosa and transported across the tissue into the bloodstream. This process involves the accumulation of sugar against a concentration gradient and requires active metabolism of the mucosal tissue as a source of energy. The sugars are absorbed from the blood by the liver and are stored there as glycogen. The liver glycogen serves as a constant source of glucose in the bloodstream. The mechanisms of transport of sugars across cell membranes and tissues are not yet understood, but they appear to be highly specific for different sugars and to depend on enzymelike components of the cells.

Dissimilation of simple sugars. The degradation of monosaccharides may follow one of several types of metabolic pathways. In the phosphorylative pathways, the sugar is first converted to a phosphate ester (phosphorylated) in a reaction with ATP. The phosphorylated sugar is then split into smaller units, either before or after oxidation. In the nonphosphorylative pathways, the sugar is usually oxidized to the corresponding aldonic acid. This may subsequently be broken down either with or without phosphorylation of the intermediate products. Among the principal intermediates in carbohydrate metabolism are glyceraldehyde-3-phosphate and pyruvic acid. The end products of metabolism depend on the organism and, to some extent, on the environmental conditions. Besides cell material that is formed through various biosynthetic reactions, the products may include carbon dioxide (CO_2), alcohols, organic acids, and hydrogen gas. In the so-called complete oxidations, CO_2 is the only excreted end product. In incomplete oxidations, characteristic of the vinegar bacteria and of certain fungi, oxidized end products such as gluconic, ketogluconic, citric, or fumaric acids may accumulate. Organic end products are invariably found in fermentations, since fermentative metabolism requires the reduction as well as the oxidation of some of the products of intermediary metabolism. The energy available from the complete oxidation of 1 mole of glucose with molecular oxygen is approximately 688,000 cal (2.98 megajoules), while that which can be derived from fermentation is very much less; for example, alcoholic fermentation yields about 58,000 cal (243,000 joules). In aerobic metabolism, a great deal of the available energy is harnessed for the needs of the organism as energy-rich bonds primarily in ATP through the process known as oxidative phosphorylation. In fermentation, a much smaller amount of ATP is produced. Hence, the amount of biosynthesis and mechanical work that an organism can do at the expense of a given amount of sugar is many times greater in respiration than in fermentation. *See* FERMENTATION.

Glycolysis. The principal phosphorylative pathway involved in fermentations is known as the glycolytic, hexose diphosphate, or Embden-Meyerhof pathway (see **illus.**). This sequence of reactions is the basis of the lactic acid fermentation of mammalian muscle and of the alcoholic fermentation of yeast. Its main features may be summarized as follows:

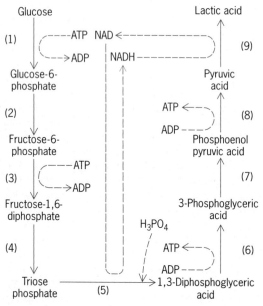

Glycolysis in lactic acid fermentation.

1. Glucose is phosphorylated to yield glucose-6-phosphate by the enzyme hexokinase with the conversion of a molecule of ATP to adenosine diphosphate (ADP).

2. Glucose-6-phosphate is epimerized to fructose-6-phosphate by phosphoglucoisomerase.

3. Fructose-6-phosphate is phosphorylated with ATP to yield fructose-1,6-diphosphate. This reaction is catalyzed by phosphofructokinase.

4. Fructose-1,6-diphosphate is split to two molecules of triose phosphate (dihydroxyacetone phosphate and glyceraldehyde phosphate) by aldolase.

5. Both molecules of triose phosphate, which are interconverted by triose phosphate isomerase, are oxidized to 1,3-diphosphoglyceric acid by triose phosphate dehydrogenase. Inorganic phosphate is esterified in this reaction, and the coenzyme nicotin amide adenine dinucleotide NAD becomes reduced to NADH.

6. 1,3-Diphosphoglyceric acid reacts with ADP to yield ATP and 3-phosphoglyceric acid in the presence of phosphoglycerate kinase.

7. 3-Phosphoglyceric acid is converted to 2-phosphoglyceric acid by phosphoglyceric acid mutase, and the product is dehydrated to phosphoenolpyruvic acid by enolase.

8. In a reaction catalyzed by pyruvic kinase, phosphoenolpyruvic acid reacts with ADP to give pyruvic acid and ATP.

9. Pyruvic acid is converted to the various end products of metabolism. In the lactic acid fermentation, it is reduced to lactic acid with the simultaneous reoxidation of NADH, which had been formed in step 5, to NAD. In alcoholic fermentation, pyruvic acid is decarboxylated to yield CO_2 and acetaldehyde, and the latter compound is reduced to alcohol with NADH.

For every molecule of glucose fermented through the glycolytic sequence, two molecules of ATP are used for phosphorylation (steps 1 and 3), while four are produced (steps 6 and 8). Thus, fermentation results in the net gain of two energy-rich phosphate bonds as ATP at the expense of inorganic phosphate esterified in step 5. The excess ATP is converted back to ADP and inorganic phosphate through coupled reactions useful to the organism, such as the mechanical work done by the contraction of muscle or biosynthetic reactions associated with growth. *See* ADENOSINE DIPHOSPHATE (ADP); NICOTINAMIDE ADENINE DINUCLEOTIDE (NAD).

Oxidative mechanisms. The oxidative or respiratory metabolism of sugars differs in several respects from fermentative dissimilation. First, the oxidative steps, that is, the reoxidation of NADH, are linked to the reduction of molecular oxygen. Second, the pyruvic acid produced through glycolytic or other mechanisms is further oxidized, usually to CO_2 and H_2O. Third, in most aerobic organisms, alternative pathways either supplement or completely replace the glycolytic sequence of reactions for the oxidation of sugars. Where pyruvic acid appears as a metabolic intermediate, it is generally oxidatively decarboxylated to yield CO_2 and the two-carbon acetyl fragment which combines with coenzyme A. The acetyl group is then further oxidized via the Krebs cycle. *See* CITRIC ACID CYCLE.

The principal alternative pathways by which sugars are dissimilated involve the oxidation of glucose-6-phosphate to the lactone of 6-phosphogluconic acid and are known as the hexose monophosphate pathways. In the best-known hexose monophosphate pathway, 6-phosphogluconic acid is formed from its lactone by hydrolysis and is oxidatively decarboxylated to yield CO_2 and the five-carbon sugar, ribulose-5-phosphate. Ribulose-5-phosphate is then converted to glucose-6-phosphate through a series of reactions in which phosphorylated sugars containing three, four, five, six, and seven carbon atoms are formed as intermediates. The principal enzymes involved in these transformations are transaldolase, transketolase, and epimerases. Since the glucose-6-phosphate that is produced from ribulose-5-phosphate is oxidized by the same sequence of reactions, the cyclic operation of this mechanism results in complete oxidation of glucose. Some of the enzymatic steps involved in this pathway provide the pentoses necessary for the synthesis of nucleotides and participate in the photosynthesis of green plants.

Simple sugars other than glucose. The metabolism of simple sugars other than glucose usually involves the conversion of the sugar to one of the intermediates of the phosphorylative pathways described for glucose metabolism. For example, fructose may be phosphorylated to fructose-6-phosphate, which can then be degraded via the glycolytic pathway or converted to glucose-6-phosphate and oxidized through the hexose monophosphate pathway. Similarly, mannose may be phosphorylated to mannose-6-phosphate, which is then transformed to fructose-6-phosphate by phosphomannose isomerase. Alternatively, in some bacteria, mannose is epimerized to fructose before phosphorylation. The principal mechanism for galactose metabolism requires the phosphorylation of the sugar to galactose-1-phosphate and the conversion of this ester to glucose-1-phosphate through the mediation of uridine diphosphoglucose. Glucose-1-phosphate is then converted to glucose-6-phosphate by phosphoglucomutase. The pentoses may be metabolized via their phosphate esters, which are converted to glucose-6-phosphate as described in the discussion of the hexose monophosphate pathway. *See* URIDINE DIPHOSPHOGLUCOSE (UDPG).

Disaccharides and polysaccharides. The dissimilation and biosynthesis of the oligosaccharides are effected through the enzymatic cleavage or formation of glycosidic bonds between simple monosaccharide constituents of the complex carbohydrates. The principal types of enzyme which split or synthesize glycosidic bonds are the hydrolases or glycosidases, phosphorylases, and transglycosylases. The enzymes are generally highly specific with respect to the glycosidic portion, or moiety, and the type of linkage of the substrates which they attack. For example, the glycosidic moiety may be glucosidic or galactosidic

and the linkage may be α or β. The essential function of all three types of enzymes is the transfer of the glycosyl moiety of the substrate, which may be designated as the glycosyl donor, to an appropriate glycosyl acceptor, with the liberation of the aglycone. The different types of enzymes generally require different types of acceptors for the transfer reactions, but some enzymes can use a variety of acceptors and can act in more than one capacity. For example, an enzyme can act as a phosphorylase, transglycosylase, or hydrolase for the same substrate.

Hydrolytic cleavage is an essentially irreversible process and hence is used mostly in dissimilative metabolism. Phosphorylases and transglycosylases, on the other hand, may function in biosynthesis as well as the degradation of oligosaccharides.

The glycosidases or hydrolytic enzymes use preferentially the hydroxyl ion of water as the glycosyl acceptor. The aglycone is liberated after combining with the remaining hydrogen ion.

Lactases, for example, are β-galactosidases, and they combine the β-galactosyl portion of the disaccharide lactose with hydroxyl ion of water to yield galactose, liberating glucose. These enzymes can also hydrolyze methyl- or phenyl-β-galactosides with the formation of galactose and methanol or phenol, respectively.

Maltases are α-glucosidases which can hydrolyze maltose to two molecules of glucose.

Sucrases or invertases are enzymes which hydrolyze sucrose to yield glucose and fructose. The typical yeast invertase is a β-fructosidase, specific for the β-fructosyl portion of sucrose. The sucrase found in the human intestinal mucosa, on the other hand, is an α-glucosidase.

Amylases or diastases are enzymes which hydrolyze (digest) starch. The α-amylases, such as the human salivary and pancreatic amylases, split starch to smaller polysaccharide units, known as dextrins, and the disaccharide maltose. The β-amylase of malt, on the other hand, produces maltose as the main product of hydrolysis.

The phosphorylases catalyze the reversible phosphorolysis of certain disaccharides, polysaccharides, and nucleosides by transferring the glycosyl moieties to inorganic phosphate. The breakdown of glycogen and starch by the enzymes known as amylophosphorylases is an example of biologically important phosphorolytic reactions. α-D-Glucose-1-phosphate, which is the product of this process, can be metabolized after conversion to glucose-6-phosphate. Starch and glycogen can be synthesized from glucose-1-phosphate by the reverse reaction. The polysaccharide chain acts as either donor or acceptor for glucosyl groups, inorganic phosphate being the alternative acceptor. The reversible synthesis of sucrose, sucrose phosphate, and cellulose from uridine diphosphoglucose is similar to the phosphorolytic reactions, with the uridine compound serving as glucosyl donor.

The transglycosylases interconvert various disaccharides and polysaccharides by the transfer of glycosyl groups. For instance, dextrins can be synthesized from maltose in a reversible reaction catalyzed by the bacterial enzyme, amylomaltase:

$$n\mathrm{C}_{12}\mathrm{H}_{22}\mathrm{O}_{11} \rightleftharpoons (\mathrm{C}_6\mathrm{H}_{10}\mathrm{O}_5)_{11} + n\mathrm{C}_6\mathrm{H}_{12}\mathrm{O}_6$$

Maltose   Dextrin   Glucose

Many glucosidases have marked transglycosylase activity. *See* BIOCHEMISTRY.   Michael Doudoroff

Carbon

A chemical element, C, with an atomic number of 6 and an atomic weight of 12.01115. Carbon is unique in chemistry because it forms a vast number of compounds, larger than the sum total of all other elements combined. By far the largest group of these compounds are those composed of carbon and hydrogen. It has been estimated that there are at least 1,000,000 known organic compounds, and this number is increasing rapidly each year. Although the classification is not rigorous, carbon forms another series of compounds, classified as inorganic, comprising a much smaller number than the organic compounds. *See* ORGANIC CHEMISTRY; PERIODIC TABLE.

1																	18
1 H	2											13	14	15	16	17	2 He
3 Li	4 Be											5 B	6 C	7 N	8 O	9 F	10 Ne
11 Na	12 Mg	3	4	5	6	7	8	9	10	11	12	13 Al	14 Si	15 P	16 S	17 Cl	18 Ar
19 K	20 Ca	21 Sc	22 Ti	23 V	24 Cr	25 Mn	26 Fe	27 Co	28 Ni	29 Cu	30 Zn	31 Ga	32 Ge	33 As	34 Se	35 Br	36 Kr
37 Rb	38 Sr	39 Y	40 Zr	41 Nb	42 Mo	43 Tc	44 Ru	45 Rh	46 Pd	47 Ag	48 Cd	49 In	50 Sn	51 Sb	52 Te	53 I	54 Xe
55 Cs	56 Ba	71 Lu	72 Hf	73 Ta	74 W	75 Re	76 Os	77 Ir	78 Pt	79 Au	80 Hg	81 Tl	82 Pb	83 Bi	84 Po	85 At	86 Rn
87 Fr	88 Ra	103 Lr	104 Rf	105 Db	106 Sg	107 Bh	108 Hs	109 Mt	110 Ds	111 Rg	112	113					

lanthanide series	57 La	58 Ce	59 Pr	60 Nd	61 Pm	62 Sm	63 Eu	64 Gd	65 Tb	66 Dy	67 Ho	68 Er	69 Tm	70 Yb
actinide series	89 Ac	90 Th	91 Pa	92 U	93 Np	94 Pu	95 Am	96 Cm	97 Bk	98 Cf	99 Es	100 Fm	101 Md	102 No

Elemental carbon exists in two well-defined crystalline allotropic forms, diamond and graphite. Other forms, which are poorly developed in crystallinity, are charcoal, coke, and carbon black. Chemically pure carbon is prepared by the thermal decomposition of sugar (sucrose) in the absence of air. The physical and chemical properties of carbon are dependent on the crystal structure of the element. The density varies from 2.25 g/cm^3 (1.30 oz/in.^{3}) for graphite to 3.51 g/cm^3 (2.03 oz/in.^{3}) for diamond. For graphite, the melting point is 3500°C (6332°F) and the extrapolated boiling point is 4830°C (8726°F). Elemental carbon is a fairly inert substance. It is insoluble in water, dilute acids and bases, and organic solvents. At elevated temperatures, it combines with oxygen to form carbon monoxide or carbon dioxide. With hot oxidizing agents, such as nitric acid and potassium nitrate, mellitic acid, $\mathrm{C}_6(\mathrm{CO}_2\mathrm{H})_6$, is obtained. Of the halogens, only fluorine reacts with elemental carbon. A number of metals combine with the element at elevated temperatures to form carbides.

Vaporizing a graphite target with an intense laser creates a nonequilibrium plasma of hot isolated carbon atoms and carbon dimers that, upon rapid cooling, coalesce into pure-carbon cage molecules. The most abundant and most stable of these molecules contain 60 carbon atoms in a highly spherical arrangement. This molecule, C_{60}, was named buckminsterfullerene, or buckyball for short, by its discoverers (in honor of R. Buckminster Fuller). This discovery initiated the field of fullerenes, the name given to this entire class of pure-carbon cage molecules. If one-half of the C_{60} molecule is removed and an extra belt of hexagons is inserted, the molecule will be extended. Successive additions of such belts of hexagons will lead to a tubular structure, a carbon nanotube. Carbon nanotubes were first experimentally observed in high-resolution transmission electron microscopy studies of fullerene by-products. The nonequilibrium synthesis methods previously described for fullerenes are also quite efficient at nanotube production. Depending on the synthesis conditions (such as type of catalyst used), nanotubes with different geometries are produced. Some are multiwalled, where many tubes are arranged coaxially and fit perfectly one inside the other; others are single walled. *See* CARBON NANOTUBES FULLERENE.

Carbon forms three gaseous compounds with oxygen: carbon monoxide, CO; carbon dioxide, CO_2; and carbon suboxide, $\mathrm{C}_3\mathrm{O}_2$. The first two oxides are the more important from an industrial standpoint. Carbon forms compounds with the halogens which have the general formula CX_4, where X is fluorine, chlorine, bromine, or iodine. At room temperature, carbon tetrafluoride is a gas, carbon tetrachloride is a liquid, and the other two compounds are solids. Mixed carbon tetrahalides are also known. Perhaps the most important of them is dichlorodifluoromethane, $\mathrm{CCl}_2\mathrm{F}_2$, commonly called Freon. *See* CARBON DIOXIDE; HALOGENATED HYDROCARBON.

Carbon and its compounds are found widely distributed in nature. It is estimated that carbon makes up 0.032% of the Earth's crust. Free carbon is found in large deposits as coal, an amorphous form of the element which contains additional complex carbon-hydrogen-nitrogen compounds. Pure crystalline carbon is found as graphite and as diamonds.

Extensive amounts of carbon are found in the form of its compounds. In the atmosphere, carbon is present in amounts of up to 0.03% by volume as carbon dioxide. Various minerals such as limestone, dolomite, marble, and chalk all contain carbon in the form of carbonate. All plant and animal life is composed of complex organic compounds containing carbon combined with hydrogen, oxygen, nitrogen, and other elements. The remains of past plant and animal life are found as deposits of petroleum, asphalt, and bitumen. Deposits of natural gas contain compounds that are composed of carbon and hydrogen. *See* CARBONATE MINERALS.

The free element has many uses, ranging from ornamental applications of the diamond in jewelry to the black-colored pigment of carbon black in automobile tires and printing inks. Another form of carbon, graphite, is used for high-temperature crucibles, arc-light and dry-cell electrodes, lead pencils, and as a lubricant. Charcoal, an amorphous form of carbon, is used as an absorbent for gases and as a decolorizing agent. *See* CARBON BLACK; CHARCOAL; DIAMOND; GRAPHITE.

The compounds of carbon find many uses. Carbon dioxide is used for the carbonation of beverages, for fire extinguishers, and in the solid state as a refrigerant. Carbon monoxide finds use as a reducing agent for many metallurgical processes. Carbon tetrachloride and carbon disulfide are important solvents for industrial uses. Freon is used in refrigeration devices. Calcium carbide is used to prepare acetylene, which is used for the welding and cutting of metals as well as for the preparation of other organic compounds. Other metal carbides find important uses as refractories and metal cutters.   E. Eugene Weaver

Bibliography. M. S. Dresselhaus et al., *Science of Fullerenes and Carbon Nanotubes: Their Properties and Applications*, 1996; *Kirk-Othmer Encyclopedia of Chemical Technology*, vol. 4, 4th ed., 1992; R. T. Morrison et al., *Organic Chemistry*, 6th ed, 1992; P. A. Thrower, *Chemistry and Physics of Carbon*, vol. 24, 1993.

Carbon black

An amorphous form of carbon produced commercially by thermal or oxidative decomposition of hydrocarbons, It is used principally in rubber goods, pigments, and printer's ink.

Because of the irregular arrangement of its carbon atoms, the physical properties of carbon black differ from the graphite and diamond forms of carbon. The surface area of blacks used for rubber reinforcement ranges 3100–46000 ft^2/oz (10–150 m^2/g) when determined by nitrogen adsorption, and the ultimate black particle has an average diameter of 20 to 300 nanometers. Pigment-grade blacks have surface areas of 150,000 ft^2/oz (300–500 m^2/g). Loose carbon black has a density of 2–3 lb/ft^3 (0.032–0.048 g/cm^3), but it is usually compressed for bag shipment or pelleted for bulk shipment in hopper cars.

Principal noncarbon components of carbon black are oxygen, hydrogen, and sulfur. Oxygen and hydrogen are combined chemically with carbon on the surface of the particle. The ratio of hydrogen to oxygen varies with the manufacturing process. In contact (channel) blacks, oxygen content is 2–5% while hydrogen amounts to about 0.5%; in furnace blacks the oxygen content of the black depends on that of the hydrocarbon feed.

Manufacturing processes may be classed as contact, furnace, or thermal. In the channel (contact) process, natural gas is burned with insufficient air for complete combustion. The smoky flame from individual burners impinges on a cool channel iron, and carbon black deposited on the channel is removed by a scraper blade. The yield of channel black is dependent upon the composition of the gas and the grade of black produced. Yield of black decreases as the heating value of the natural gas decreases. Of the three grades of black produced—easy (EPC), medium (MPC), or hard (HPC) processing channel—the yield of EPC is lowest and averages about 1.3 lb/1000 ft^3 (21 kg/1000 m^3) of natural gas.

In the furnace process, the hydrocarbon and air are fed into a reactor. Combustion of part of the hydrocarbon raises the temperature to 2000–3000°F (1100–1700°C), causing decomposition of the unburned hydrocarbon to carbon black. A water spray quickly cools the hot reaction products, and the finely divided black is recovered by cyclones and bag filters. Natural gas was the principal feed to the furnace process until 1943, when a furnace process utilizing heavy petroleum oils was introduced. The oil black produced was superior for reinforcing synthetic rubber, and oil furnace blacks now constitute the major type of carbon black produced. Yield of carbon black from the furnace process depends on feed stock used and type of black produced, ranging from 2 to 16 lb per 1000 ft^3 (32–260 kg/1000 m^3) of natural gas and 2.5 to 6 lb per gallon (0.3–0.7 kg/liter) of oil.

The oil furnace process can produce a variety of blacks specifically designed for use with various types of rubbers. For many years particle size was used as an approximate guide for black quality, the finer-particle blacks generally showing better abrasion resistance in performance tests. However, the physicochemical nature of the black surface, or "structure," became increasingly important. Structure affects the ease of compounding and modulus, stiffness, and extrusion properties of the rubber black mixture. Another development was the production of channel black substitutes from oil furnace blacks.

In the thermal process, natural gas is decomposed to carbon and hydrogen by heated refractories. Because this decomposition cools the refractories rapidly, it must be periodically interrupted to reheat the refractories. In one variant of this process employing acetylene as the feed, heat is liberated during the decomposition of acetylene. Acetylene black is distinguished by unusually high electric conductivity, and it is used in the manufacture of dry cells.

Over 90% of the production of carbon black in the United States is used by the rubber industry; hence, carbon black and rubber technology are interrelated. It is not an inert filler but enhances and reinforces various properties of rubber. Carbon black may be dispersed in rubber latex (masterbatch process) to produce, after coagulation, an intimate solid mixture of black and rubber, ready for fabrication of rubber goods.

Prior to 1940, channel black accounted for nearly 90% of domestic carbon black production; the last plant producing channel black closed in September 1976. This dramatic shift from contact to oil furnace processes was the result of the rapid price increase of natural gas along with the superior performance of oil blacks in tire manufacture. *See* DIAMOND; GRAPHITE; RUBBER; TIRE.   Carl J. Helmers

Carbon dioxide

A colorless, odorless, tasteless gas, formula CO_2, about 1.5 times as heavy as air. The specific volume at atmospheric pressure (100 kilopascals) and 70°F (21°C) is 8.74 ft³/lb (0.546 m³/kg). Under normal conditions, it is stable, inert, and nontoxic.

The decay (slow oxidation) of all organic materials produces CO_2. The burning of hydrocarbon fuels also produces CO_2. Fresh air contains approximately 0.033% CO_2 by volume. In the respiratory action (breathing) of all animals and humans, CO_2 is exhaled. *See* RESPIRATORY SYSTEM.

Carbon dioxide gas may be liquefied or solidified. For example, if the gas is compressed to 300 pounds per square inch gage (psig; 2 megapascals) and cooled to 0°F (−18°C) it becomes a liquid; or it may be liquefied at 70°F (21°C) by being compressed to 838 psig (5.78 MPa). Above the critical temperature of 87.9°F (31.1°C), CO_2 exists only as a gas, regardless of the pressure applied.

If liquid CO_2 is cooled to −69.9°F (−56.6°C) the pressure drops to 60.4 psig (417 kPa), and dry ice snow is formed. This condition of pressure and temperature is known as the triple point of CO_2, at which all three phases, solid, liquid, and gas, may exist in equilibrium with one another. Carbon dioxide cannot exist as a liquid below the triple-point temperature and pressure. If the pressure on dry-ice snow is reduced to atmospheric, its temperature drops to −109.3°F (−78.5°C). As solid CO_2 absorbs heat from its surroundings, it transforms directly to a gas (sublimes), hence the name dry ice. In still air, a film of gaseous CO_2 surrounds the dry ice, and the sublimation temperature is −109.3°F (−78.5°C); but in a vacuum or in rapidly moving air in which the CO_2 gas film is stripped away, the sublimation temperature drops to −130°F (−90°C) or lower.

Carbon dioxide is obtained commercially from four sources: gas wells, fermentation, combustion of carbonaceous fuels, and as a by-product of chemical processing.

Applications. Carbon dioxide may be used as a refrigerant, inerting medium, chemical reactant, neutralizing agent for alkalies, and pressurizing agent.

Refrigeration. Solid CO_2 has a greater refrigeration effect than water ice; the latent heat of sublimation of dry ice is 253.8 Btu/lb (595.0 kilojoules/kg), whereas the latent heat of fusion of water ice is 143.4 Btu/lb (336.2 kilojoules/kg). Furthermore, it is much colder than water ice and sublimes to a gas as it absorbs heat. Solid CO_2 may be furnished to the user in pressed blocks weighting 50–60 lb (23–27 kg) each, or as extruded pellets. It may also be made as snow at the point of use by expanding liquid CO_2 to atmospheric pressure; upon release to the atmosphere, liquid CO_2 at a pressure of 285 psig (1.97 MPa) produces about 47% dry ice snow and 53% gas by weight. However, of the total refrigerating effect originally available in the liquid, 85% remains in the ice and 15% in the vapor when the liquid CO_2 is warmed to 0°F (−18°C).

Dry ice blocks and pellets are used to chill, firm, and freeze meats, vegetables, and other perishable foods for preservation during transport. Dry ice snow produced from the expansion of liquid CO_2 may be applied directly to the surface of foods in a freezing chamber or tunnel, or it may be deposited on the contents of a container. Refrigeration may be achieved in trucks and other transport modes by vaporization of either solid or liquid CO_2. *See* DRY ICE.

Liquid CO_2 is injected into pneumatic conveyor systems to cool the contents during transport. Such items as flour, sugar, plastics, and core sand are quickly chilled by the dry ice snow and cold gas produced in the pneumatic line as liquid CO_2 is introduced through a thermostatically controlled orifice.

In low-temperature testing of aircraft and electronic parts to meet military or manufacturing specifications at −65°F (−54°C) and below, liquid CO_2 is expanded through an orifice to form dry-ice snow, which is either blown directly on the part or circulated in a test chamber; solid CO_2 is used in certain kinds of testing.

Carbon dioxide liquid injected into a hollow plastic shape while it is still in the mold reduces the temperature of the internal surface and, in turn, decreases the time required for the plastic to become sufficiently hardened to be self-supporting, allowing the part to be removed from the mold more quickly. Thus blow-molding equipment can operate on a shorter cycle time, and production can be speeded up.

Carbon dioxide liquid or ice may be used to advantage for removing the flash (mold marks) from molded rubber parts. This is done in an insulated tumbling barrel in which the mechanical action easily removes the flash that has been embrittled by contact with solid CO_2.

Carbon dioxide snow is added directly to choppers and mixers used in the preparation of hamburger, sausage, and prepared meat products such as bologna. The quick chilling reduces meat temperature rapidly, retarding bacterial growth.

Carbon dioxide is used to stiffen shortening for homogeneous blending with the dry ingredients used in piecrust mixes; to chill spices, chemicals, sugar, and rubber during high-speed grinding; and to prevent softening of thermoplastic materials during pulverizing.

Inerting. Carbon dioxide does not react with oxygen, nor does it normally function as an oxidizing agent. At high temperatures, it dissociates into carbon monoxide and oxygen (about 1% at 2800°F or 1538°C).

Liquid CO_2 is an effective fire-extinguishing agent because it rapidly reduces the temperature of burning materials below the ignition point, and the gas, being heavy and inert, displaces air, usually the source of oxygen, and blankets the flames. It is particularly effective in extinguishing fires when water cannot be used, for example, in oil and electrical fires. *See* FIRE EXTINGUISHER.

Oil tankers, barges, storage vessels, and pipelines are quickly and safely inerted with CO_2 to allow welding and other repairs. In the automatic electric–tungsten–inert gas welding of steel using a filler wire, CO_2 is used to blanket the arc, thus preventing oxidation of the molten metal. *See* WELDING AND CUTTING OF MATERIALS.

Carbon dioxide is useful in many other applications in which an inert gas is required to prevent oxidation, as in packaging foodstuffs, spray-drying eggs and other solids, blanketing paint ingredients during manufacture to prevent the formation of "skin," and protecting grain and other bulk foods stored in silos.

Chemical applications. The largest single market for CO_2 for chemical purposes is in the preparation of carbonated beverages, in which the weak carbonic acid formed by the CO_2 acts as a taste enhancer and preservative. Other uses include the hardening of foundry cores in the core box by the reaction of CO_2 with the sand binder, the neutralization of excess alkalinity in water or industrial wastes, the manufacture of salicylic acid for aspirin, the production of pure carbonates and bicarbonates, as an intermediate in the preparation of titanium dioxide, and the stimulation of oil and gas wells.

Pressure medium. Life rafts and life preservers are packaged to include small CO_2 cartridges which permit rapid inflation upon operation of a quick-opening valve. Carbon dioxide in a cartridge is used as the propellent in certain pistols. It is also used as a propellent in pressure packaging, for example, in aerosol cans, and in many instances can replace fluorinated hydrocarbons at a fraction of the cost.

Manufacture. Most CO_2 is obtained as a by-product from steam-hydrocarbon reformers used in the production of ammonia, gasoline, and other chemicals; other sources include fermentation, deep gas wells, and direct production from carbonaceous fuels. Whatever the source, the crude CO_2 (containing at least 90% CO_2) is compressed in either two or three stages, cooled, purified, condensed to the liquid phase, and placed in insulated storage vessels. Commercial liquid CO_2 is usually stored at a pressure of 225–325 psig (1.55–2.2 MPa) and is maintained in this range by refrigeration. When the liquid is placed into high-pressure cylinders and stored at ambient temperature, however, the pressure in the liquid rises to 1071 psig (7.385 MPa) when the temperature is 87.8°F (31.0°C) [the initial point], or higher, if the cylinder is completely filled with liquid.

Distribution. Carbon dioxide is distributed in three ways: in high-pressure uninsulated steel cylinders; as a low-pressure liquid in insulated truck trailers or rail tank cars; and as dry ice in insulated boxes, trucks, or boxcars.

The size of the high-pressure cylinders is limited because of the weight involved. Most commercial cylinders contain either 20 or 50 lb (9 or 23 kg) of CO_2 and are designed to deliver CO_2 gas, which can be reduced to the pressure required by the user through the action of a pressure regulator. However, some cylinders are equipped with a tube that reaches to the bottom of the cylinder and siphons liquid CO_2 to the outlet, provided the temperature of the contents is below the critical temperature (87.9°F or 31.1°C).

Truck trailer capacity is restricted by laws which govern the gross vehicle weight. Up to 20 tons (18 metric tons) of liquid CO_2 may be shipped in an insulated trailer. Suppliers of CO_2 provide their customers with storage vessels varying in capacity from 4 to 150 tons (3.6 to 135 metric tons).

When CO_2 is manufactured and transported as dry ice, losses occur because of sublimation. By storing the dry ice in a well-insulated container, losses may be kept within economical limits.

Solid CO_2 can be converted to the liquid form by placing it in a heavy-walled steel vessel known as a converter. After the vessel is sealed, it is allowed to warm to room temperature. As the temperature of the CO_2 rises past the triple point, it is converted to liquid. J. S. Lindsey

Bibliography. American Society of Heating, Refrigerating, and Air-Conditioning Engineers, *ASHRAE Handbook of Fundamentals*, 1993; W. C. Clark, *Carbon Dioxide Review*, 1982; J. Wisniewski and R. N. Sampson (eds.), *Terrestrial Carbon Fluxes: Quantification of Sinks and Sources of CO_2*, 1993; A. S. Young, *Carbon Dioxide*, 1993.

Carbon nanotubes

Molecular-scale tubes of graphitic carbon with outstanding properties. They are among the stiffest and strongest fibers known, and have remarkable electronic properties and many other unique characteristics. They have attracted huge academic and industrial interest, with thousands of papers on nanotubes being published every year. Commercial applications have been rather slow to develop, primarily because of the high production costs of the best-quality nanotubes.

History. Interest in carbon nanotubes is a direct consequence of the synthesis of buckminsterfullerene, C_{60}, and other fullerenes in 1985. The discovery that carbon could form stable, ordered structures other than graphite and diamond stimulated researchers worldwide to look for other new forms of carbon. The search was given new impetus in 1990 when it was shown that C_{60} could be produced in a simple arc-evaporation apparatus readily available in all laboratories. Using such an evaporator, the Japanese scientist Sumio Iijima discovered fullerene-related carbon nanotubes in 1991. The tubes contained at least two layers, often many more, and ranged in outer diameter from about 3 to 30 nanometers. They were invariably closed at both

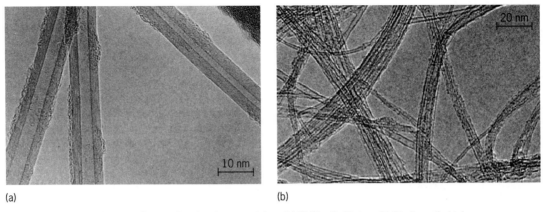

Fig. 1. Transmission electron micrographs of carbon nanotubes. (*a*) Multiwalled tubes. (*b*) Single-walled tubes.

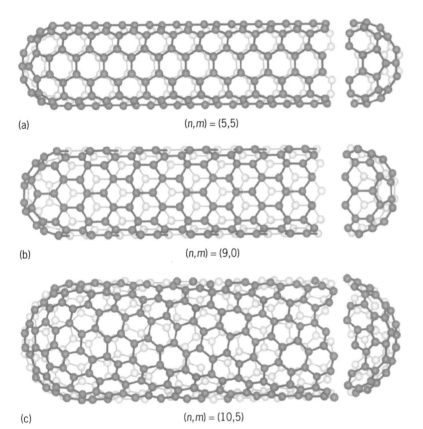

(a) $(n,m) = (5,5)$

(b) $(n,m) = (9,0)$

(c) $(n,m) = (10,5)$

Fig. 2. Nanotube structures of (*a*) armchair, (*b*) zigzag, and (*c*) chiral configurations.

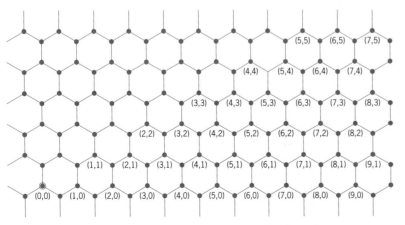

Fig. 3. Graphene sheet with carbon atoms labeled using the (*n, m*) notation.

ends. A transmission electron micrograph of some multiwalled nanotubes is shown in **Fig. 1***a*. In 1993, a new class of carbon nanotube was discovered, with just a single layer. These single-walled nanotubes are generally narrower than the multiwalled tubes, with diameters typically in the range 1–2 nm. Figure 1*b* shows some typical single-walled tubes. *See* CARBON; DIAMOND; FULLERENE; GRAPHITE.

It was soon established that these new fibers had a range of exceptional properties, and this sparked an explosion of research into carbon nanotubes. However, nanoscale tubes of carbon, produced catalytically, had been known for many years before Iijima's discovery. The main reason why these early tubes did not excite wide interest is that they were structurally rather imperfect, so they did not have particularly interesting properties.

Structure. The bonding in carbon nanotubes is sp^2, with each atom joined to three neighbors, as in graphite. The tubes can therefore be considered as rolled-up graphene sheets. (Graphene is an individual graphite layer.) There are three distinct ways in which a graphene sheet can be rolled into a tube, as shown in **Fig. 2**. The first two ways, known as armchair and zigzag, have a high degree of symmetry. The third class of tube, which in practice is the most common, is known as chiral, meaning that it can exist in two mirror-related forms. The structure of a nanotube can be specified by a vector, (n,m), which defines how the graphene sheet is rolled up. This can be understood with reference to **Fig. 3**. To produce a nanotube with the indices (6,3), say, the sheet is rolled up so that the atom labeled (0,0) is superimposed on the one labeled (6,3). It can be seen from the figure that $m = 0$ for all zigzag tubes while $n = m$ for all armchair tubes.

Synthesis. The arc-evaporation method, which produces the best-quality nanotubes, involves passing a current of about 50 amps between two graphite electrodes in an atmosphere of helium. This causes the graphite to vaporize, some of it condensing on the walls of the reaction vessel and some of it on the cathode. It is the deposit on the cathode which contains the carbon nanotubes. Single-walled nanotubes are produced when cobalt and nickel, or some other metal, is added to the anode.

It has been known since the 1950s, if not earlier, that carbon nanotubes can also be made by passing a carbon-containing gas, such as a hydrocarbon, over a catalyst. The catalyst consists of nano-sized particles of metal, usually iron, cobalt, or nickel. These particles catalyze the breakdown of the gaseous molecules into carbon, and a tube then begins to grow with a metal particle at the tip. In 1996 it was shown that single-walled nanotubes could also be produced catalytically. The perfection of carbon nanotubes produced in this way has generally been poorer than those made by arc-evaporation, but great improvements in the technique have been made. The big advantage of catalytic synthesis over arc-evaporation is that it can be scaled up for volume production. *See* CATALYSIS.

The third important method for making carbon nanotubes involves using a powerful laser to vaporize a metal-graphite target. This can be used to produce single-walled tubes at high yield.

Properties. The strength of the sp^2 carbon-carbon bonds gives carbon nanotubes amazing mechanical properties. The stiffness of a material is measured in terms of Young's modulus, the rate of change of stress with applied strain. The Young's modulus of the best nanotubes can be as high as 1000 GPa, which is approximately 5× higher than steel. The tensile strength, or breaking strain, of nanotubes can be up to 63 GPa, around 50× higher than steel. These properties, coupled with the lightness of carbon nanotubes, give them great potential in applications, such as in aerospace engineering. It has even been suggested that nanotubes could be used in the "space elevator," an Earth-to-space cable first proposed by Arthur C. Clarke. *See* STRESS AND STRAIN; YOUNG'S MODULUS.

The electronic properties of carbon nanotubes are also extraordinary. A notable fact is that nanotubes can be metallic or semiconducting depending on their structure. Thus, some nanotubes have conductivities higher than that of copper, while others behave more like silicon. There is great interest in the possibility of constructing nanoscale electronic devices from nanotubes, and some progress is being made. However, in order to construct a useful device we would need to arrange many thousands of nanotubes in a defined pattern, and we do not yet have that degree of control. *See* SEMICONDUCTOR.

Carbon nanotubes are already being used in several areas of technology. These include flat-panel displays, scanning probe microscopes, and sensing devices. The unique properties of carbon nanotubes will undoubtedly lead to many more applications. *See* NANOTECHNOLOGY.   Peter J. F. Harris

Bibliography. P. M. Ajayan, Nanotubes from carbon, *Chem. Rev.*, 99:1787–1799, 1999; P. G. Collins and P. Avouris, Nanotubes for electronics, *Sci. Amer.*, 283:38–45, December 2000; M. S. Dresselhaus, G. Dresselhaus, and P. Avouris (eds.), *Carbon Nanotubes: Synthesis, Structure, Properties and Applications*, Springer-Verlag, 2001; P. J. F. Harris, *Carbon Nanotubes and Related Structures: New Materials for the Twenty-first Century*, Cambridge University Press, 1999; M. Meyyappan, *Carbon Nanotubes: Science and Applications*, CRC Press, 2004; B. I. Yakobson and R. E. Smalley, Fullerene nanotubes: $C_{1,000,000}$ and beyond, *Amer. Scientist*, 85:324–337, 1997.

Carbon-nitrogen-oxygen cycles

A group of nuclear reactions that involve the interaction of protons (nuclei of hydrogen atoms, designated by ^1H) with carbon, nitrogen, and oxygen nuclei. The cycle involving only isotopes of carbon and nitrogen is well known as the carbon-nitrogen (CN) cycle. These cycles are thought to be the main source of energy in main-sequence stars with mass 40% or more in excess of that of the Sun. Completion of any one of the cycles results in consumption of four protons ($4\ ^1H$) and the production of a helium (^4He) nucleus plus two positrons (e^+) and two neutrinos (ν). The two positrons are annihilated with two electrons (e^-), and the total energy release is 26.73 MeV. Approximately 1.7 MeV is released as neutrino energy and is not available as thermal energy in the star. The energy $E = 26.73$ MeV arises from the mass difference between four hydrogen atoms and the helium atom, and is calculated from the Einstein mass-energy equation $E = \Delta mc^2$, where Δm is the mass difference and c^2 is the square of the velocity of light. Completion of a chain can be thought of as conversion of four hydrogen atoms into a helium atom. Because the nuclear fuel that is consumed in these processes is hydrogen, they are referred to as hydrogen-burning processes by means of the carbon-nitrogen-oxygen (CNO) cycles. *See* SOLAR NEUTRINOS.

Carbon-nitrogen cycle. The original carbon-nitrogen cycle was suggested independently by H. A. Bethe and C. F. von Weiszäcker in 1938 as the source of energy in stars. In the first reaction of the carbon-nitrogen cycle, a carbon nucleus of mass 12 captures a proton, forming a nitrogen nucleus of mass 13 and releasing a photon of energy, 1.943 MeV. This may be written: $^{12}C + {}^1H \rightarrow {}^{13}N + \gamma$, or $^{12}C(p,\gamma)^{13}N$. The nucleus ^{13}N is unstable and decays by emitting a positron (e^+) and a neutrino (ν). In reaction form, $^{13}N \rightarrow {}^{13}C + e^+ + \nu$ or $^{13}N(e^+\nu)^{13}C$. The cycle continues through ^{14}N, ^{15}O, and ^{15}N by the reactions and decays shown in $^{12}C(p,\gamma)^{13}N(e^+\nu)^{13}$

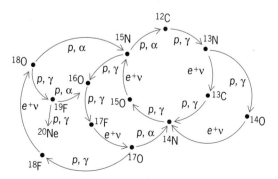

Carbon-nitrogen-oxygen cycles. (*After J. Audouze, ed., CNO Isotopes in Astrophysics, D. Reidel, 1977*)

TABLE 1. Energies involved in the carbon-nitrogen cycle, in MeV

Reaction	Q	Q (thermal)	E_ν^{max}
$^{12}C + {}^1H \rightarrow {}^{13}N + \gamma$	1.943	1.943	
$^{13}N \rightarrow {}^{13}C + e^+ + \nu$	2.221	1.51	1.199
$^{13}C + {}^1H \rightarrow {}^{14}N + \gamma$	7.551	7.551	
$^{14}N + {}^1H \rightarrow {}^{15}O + \gamma$	7.297	7.297	
$^{15}O \rightarrow {}^{15}N + e^+ + \nu$	2.753	1.75	1.731
$^{15}N + {}^1H \rightarrow {}^{12}C + {}^4He$	4.966	4.966	

$C(p,\gamma)^{14}N(p,\gamma)^{15}O(e^+\nu)^{15}N(p,\alpha)^{12}C$. These reactions form the second cycle from the right in the **illustration**. The reaction $^{15}N(p,\alpha)^{12}C$ represents emission of an alpha particle (^{4}He nucleus) when ^{15}N captures a proton and this cycle returns to ^{12}C. Because of the cycling, the total number of carbon, nitrogen, and oxygen nuclei remains constant, so these nuclei act as catalysts in the production of a helium nucleus plus two positrons and two neutrinos with the release of energy. The positrons that are created annihilate with free electrons rapidly after creation, so the energy used in their creation is returned to the energy fund. Synthesis of some of the rare carbon, nitrogen, and oxygen isotopes is accomplished through hydrogen burning by means of the carbon-nitrogen-oxygen cycles.

Table 1 shows the energy release, Q, and the average release of thermal energy, Q (thermal), in each reaction of the cycle, as well as the maximum neutrino energy E_ν^{max} in the two reactions in which a neutrino is produced.

A standard model for the Sun has been developed by J. N. Bahcall and colleagues to determine the flux of solar neutrinos that should be coming to the Earth. In this model, the site of maximum hydrogen burning is just outside the central core of the Sun. At a distance of 0.0511 solar radius from the center, chosen to lie in the most active part of that site for hydrogen burning in the proton-proton chains, the temperature is 14×10^6 K, the density is $\rho = 112$ g/cm^3 (112 times the density of water), and the mass fraction of hydrogen is $X(^1H) = 0.483$. The reaction rates, R, calculated for the carbon-nitrogen cycle reactions at that temperature, are shown in **Table 2**. Small corrections for screening of the Coulomb field between nuclei by electrons have been neglected. Taking into account the mass fraction of hydrogen and the density at the site, the number of reactions per nucleus per second is given by $\lambda = \rho RX(^1H)/1.0078$. By inverting λ, the mean lifetimes, τ, of the carbon, nitrogen, and oxygen nuclei are obtained; these are shown in the last column of Table 2 in years. The fraction of energy from CNO cycles in the Sun is calculated to be only 1.5%; the remaining 98.5% of the energy is from hydrogen burning in the proton-proton chains.

CNO bicycle. Nuclear research in the 1950s led to the addition of a second cycle to the processes of hydrogen burning by the CNO cycles. Laboratory research has shown that in a very small number of proton captures by ^{15}N a photon is emitted with the formation of an oxygen nucleus of mass 16, leading to reactions which may cycle back to ^{14}N by $^{15}N(p,\gamma)^{16}O(p,\gamma)^{17}F(e^+\nu)^{17}O(p,\alpha)^{14}N$. The pair of cycles consisting of this cycle and the carbon-nitrogen cycle, that forms the main cycle and the first cycle to the left of it in the illustration, is called the carbon-nitrogen-oxygen bicycle. The rate of the $^{12}N(p,\alpha)^{12}C$ reaction is of the order of 10^3 times that of the $^{15}N(p,\gamma)^{16}O$ reaction at most temperatures expected in stellar interiors.

Other CNO cycles. In research since 1960, it has become apparent that many possible branches among the nuclei must be included in any analysis of hydrogen burning by carbon, nitrogen, and oxygen nuclei. For example, if the unstable nucleus ^{13}N to capture a proton before it decays in its mean lifetime of 862 s, a third cycle can occur through $^{13}N(p,\gamma)^{14}O(e^+\nu)^{14}N$. This cycle is displayed in the illustration by the branch on the right-hand side of the main carbon-nitrogen cycle and is known as the fast or the hot carbon-nitrogen cycle. The other possible branches leading to additional cycles shown in the diagram are due to competition between (p,γ) and (p,α) reactions. The added reactions are $^{17}O(p,\alpha)^{18}F(e^+\nu)^{18}O(p,\alpha)^{15}N$ and $^{18}O(p,\alpha)^{19}F(p,\alpha)^{16}O$. The reaction $^{19}F(p,\gamma)^{20}Ne$ shown in the illustration leads out of the carbon, nitrogen, and oxygen nuclei and hence away from CNO cycles.

There are two additional branches that may occur if the unstable fluorine nuclei (^{17}F and ^{18}F) capture protons before they can decay. *See* NUCLEAR FUSION; NUCLEAR REACTION; NUCLEOSYNTHESIS; PROTON-PROTON CHAIN; STELLAR EVOLUTION.

Georgeanne R. Caughlan

TABLE 2. Reaction rates and mean lifetimes for carbon-nitrogen cycle in the Sun

Reaction	R, s^{-1}/(mole)(cm^3)*	λ, s^{-1}	τ, years
$^{12}C + {}^1H \rightarrow {}^{13}N + \gamma$	8.19×10^{-17}	4.40×10^{-15}	7.20×10^6
$^{13}N \rightarrow {}^{13}C + e^+ + \nu$		1.16×10^{-3}	2.73×10^{-5}
$^{13}C + {}^1H \rightarrow {}^{14}N + \gamma$	2.83×10^{-16}	1.52×10^{-14}	2.08×10^6
$^{14}N + {}^1H \rightarrow {}^{15}O + \gamma$	2.94×10^{-19}	1.58×10^{-17}	2.01×10^9
$^{15}O \rightarrow {}^{15}N + e^+ + \nu$		5.68×10^{-3}	5.58×10^{-6}
$^{15}N + {}^1H \rightarrow {}^{12}C + {}^4He$	7.27×10^{-15}	3.91×10^{-13}	8.11×10^4

*From G. R. Caughlan and W. A. Fowler, Thermonuclear reaction rates, V, *Atom. Nucl. Data Tables*, vol. 40, 1988.

Bibliography. J. N. Bahcall et al., Standard solar models and the uncertainties in predicted capture rates of solar neutrinos, *Rev. Mod. Phys.*, 54:767–799, 1982; G. R. Caughlan and W. A. Fowler, Thermonuclear reaction rates, V, *Atom. Nucl. Data Tables*, vol. 40, 1988; M. J. Harris et al., Thermonuclear reaction rates, III, *Annu. Rev. Astron. Astrophys.*, 21:165–176, 1983.

Carbon star

Any star whose spectrum shows a higher abundance of carbon than of oxygen. The carbon enhancements are easily recognizable from strong spectral absorption bands of carbon in molecular forms such as C_2, CN, and CH. Many types of carbon star are known, covering a wide variety of masses, temperatures, abundances, and luminosities. The cool red appearance, high luminosity, and intrinsic variability of bright carbon stars show that they are giant stars.

Most stars with masses between 0.6 and 5 times the mass of the Sun must pass through a carbon-star phase. Stars like the Sun, called dwarf stars, derive their energy from nuclear fusion of hydrogen to produce helium. As a star evolves and its core supply of hydrogen disappears, it can begin to burn helium into carbon, becoming a giant star. Not all giant stars dredge up from the core a sufficient quantity of newly produced carbon to change the appearance of the visible stellar surface. Asymptotic giant branch (AGB) stars are further evolved stars where nuclear burning of helium surrounds a dense carbon-oxygen core. The helium shell burning causes large temperature gradients and convection, which efficiently dredge up the processed, carbon-rich material toward the stellar surface. *See* NUCLEOSYNTHESIS.

Asymptotic giant branch carbon stars expel much of their carbon-rich envelopes as a wind. During a single year of its mass-losing phase, a carbon star may expel up to 10^{-5} of a solar mass, about 3 Earth masses, of carbon-rich material. This material may form cool envelopes of ejected circumstellar dust that dim and redden its appearance. The expelled stellar envelopes eventually mix with the surrounding interstellar environment, so that much of the carbon throughout the Milky Way Galaxy comes from mass-losing carbon stars. Still, carbon stars are not common for two reasons. First, most stars have not yet reached the asymptotic giant branch phase of their evolution. Second, that phase of a star is short compared to the lifetime of a dwarf, so it is rare to see a star in its carbon-rich phase.

Since carbon is produced and brought to the surface only in giant stars, the more recent discovery of dwarf carbon stars at first appeared to contradict basic stellar evolution theory. However, matter expelled from asymptotic giant branch stars in binary star systems may fall onto and enhance the carbon abundance of a dwarf companion star. Since dwarf carbon stars are much fainter, only a few are yet known. The long lifetimes of dwarfs, however, all but ensure that many more currently exist than do carbon giants.

The R and N classification ranks carbon stars by their colors and spectral features. The N stars are in general cooler and show much stronger molecular bands. Spectral subclasses 0 through 8 represent decreasing temperature. CH stars are warm carbon giants with an intense CH molecular band. Both R and CH stars, while giants, also have luminosities too low to be asymptotic giant branch stars. Since CH stars are apparently all binaries, they may be former dwarf carbon stars that have themselves evolved into giants. However, the R stars occur in binary systems only as often as normal (oxygen-rich) red giants, so the origin of their enhanced carbon abundance remains a mystery. *See* BINARY STAR; DWARF STAR; GIANT STAR; STAR; STELLAR EVOLUTION.

Paul J. Green

Bibliography. C. Jaschek and M. Jaschek, *The Classification of Stars*, Cambridge University Press, corrected reprint, 1990; J. B. Kaler, *The Little Book of Stars*, Copernicus Books, New York, 2001; R. Kippenhahn and J. Steinberg (translator), *100 Billion Suns: The Birth, Life, and Death of the Stars*, reprint, Princeton University, 1993; S. J. Shawl, K. M. Ashman, and B. Hufnagle, *Discovering Astronomy*, 5th ed., Kendall/Hunt, Dubique, Iowa, 2006.

Carbonate minerals

The mineral species containing the CO_3^{2-} unit as an essential structural and chemical component. Members are distinguished by chemical composition (type of metal cation and in some cases other anion present) and crystal structure. More than 200 varieties of carbonate minerals are known, but only a small number occur in abundance. Calcite ($CaCO_3$) and dolomite [$CaMg(CO_3)_2$] are the most common species, occurring as the principal mineral components in limestone and Mg-rich limestone sedimentary rocks. Carbonate minerals exhibit limited stability at high temperature unless high carbon dioxide (CO_2) pressure exists, which explains their occurrence dominantly in environments near the Earth's surface and in sedimentary rocks. However, important occurrences in metamorphic rocks include marble and hydrothermal deposits, with only rare occurrences in carbonatite and kimberlite igneous rocks. *See* CARBON DIOXIDE; CARBONATITE; CALCITE; DOLOMITE; IGNEOUS ROCKS; KIMBERLITE; LIMESTONE; MARBLE; METAMORPHIC ROCKS; SEDIMENTARY ROCKS.

Main groups and other varieties. Calcite ($CaCO_3$) is the most common carbonate mineral, notably occurring as the primary mineral constituent of limestone. Other members of the calcite group include magnesite ($MgCO_3$), rhodochrosite ($MnCO_3$), siderite ($FeCO_3$), sphaerocobaltite ($CoCO_3$), gaspeite ($NiCO_3$), smithsonite ($ZnCO_3$), and otavite ($CdCO_3$). These minerals share the same rhombohedral crystal structure and the general formula ACO_3, where A refers to a divalent metal cation, which balances the charge of the $CO_3{}^{2-}$ anionic unit. *See* MAGNESITE; RHODOCHROSITE; SIDERITE; SMITHSONITE.

The aragonite group also has the general formula ACO_3 but possesses an orthorhombic crystal structure. In addition to aragonite ($CaCO_3$), which is abundant in modern marine sediments, other members of this group include strontianite ($SrCO_3$), witherite ($BaCO_3$), and cerussite ($PbCO_3$). *See* ARAGONITE; CERUSSITE; STRONTIANITE; WITHERITE.

A second important group of rhombohedral carbonates takes its name from its most abundant member, dolomite [$CaMg(CO_3)_2$], which is the primary constituent of Mg-rich limestone rock known also as dolomite, although some authors favor the term dolostone. With the general formula $AB(CO_3)_2$, members of this group contain two divalent metal cations (A and B) in a structure similar to that of calcite but in which the A and B cations are separated into alternating layers. Other members of this group include ankerite [$Ca(Fe,Mg)(CO_3)_2$], kutnahorite [$CaMn(CO_3)_2$], and the rare minrecordite [$CaZn(CO_3)_2$]. Other carbonate minerals with the $AB(CO_3)_2$ formula are known but their structures differ slightly from that of dolomite, with examples being norsethite [$BaMg(CO_3)_2$] and paralstonite [$CaBa(CO_3)_2$]. The mineral huntite [$Mg_3Ca(CO_3)_4$], known as a weathering product of dolomite or magnesite rocks, is rhombohedral and contains two metal cations but in a different ratio than in dolomite. *See* ANKERITE.

Some carbonate minerals that crystallize from water solutions remain hydrated, such as nesquehonite ($MgCO_3 \cdot 3H_2O$) and natron ($Na_2CO_3 \cdot 10H_2O$). Others may contain hydroxyl ion (OH^-), as do malachite [$Cu_2CO_3(OH)_2$] and hydrozincite [$Zn_5(CO_3)_2(OH)_6$]. Species containing the bicarbonate unit ($HCO_3{}^-$) form the group known as acid carbonates, with nahcolite ($NaHCO_3$) being the best-known example. Of the many less common or rare carbonate minerals not described here, some contain other anion units such as sulfate ($SO_4{}^{2-}$), phosphate ($PO_4{}^{3-}$), borate ($BO_3{}^{3-}$), chloride (Cl^-), or fluoride (F^-) in different proportions, combined with a variety of metal cations and existing in numerous complex structures. There are many examples of carbonate minerals containing uranium (U) or members of the rare-earth element group owing to the strong affinity of these metals for the $CO_3{}^{2-}$ anion when present in water solutions. *See* MALACHITE; RARE-EARTH MINERALS.

Structure and properties. The $CO_3{}^{2-}$ molecular group resembles an equilateral triangle with an oxygen atom at each corner and the carbon atom at the center, bonding only to the three oxygens. Metal cations form bonds with the oxygen atoms in different configurations, resulting in a variety of crystal structures. In the calcite group (ACO_3), the divalent metal cation is bonded to six oxygen atoms, each belonging to a separate CO_3 group (**Fig. 1a**). The molar volumes and densities of members of this group differ owing to the different sizes of the metal cations. The crystal structure is rhombohedral (trigonal system) in which layers of CO_3 groups alternate with layers of metal cations perpendicular to the main symmetry axis. Symmetrically arranged planes of weak bonding cause a perfect cleavage (or fracture), giving a distinctive rhombohedral shape often seen in larger specimens of calcite (**Fig. 2**). Clear, colorless crystals of calcite are known as Iceland spar, after the location of an early discovery of high-quality specimens. Optically, rhombohedral carbonates exhibit high birefringence, and Iceland spar played an early role in understanding the polarization of light and remains useful for demonstrating the optical property double refraction (Fig. 2). Localities in Mexico, Brazil, and Russia provide most of the Iceland spar available today. *See* BIREFRINGENCE; CRYSTAL; CRYSTAL OPTICS; CRYSTAL STRUCTURE; CRYSTALLOGRAPHY.

Members of the aragonite group (ACO_3) have an orthorhombic crystal structure in which the divalent metal cation is bonded to nine oxygen atoms. Layers of divalent metal cations alternate with layers of offset CO_3 groups (Fig. 1b). This arrangement results in a more dense packing of atoms than in the calcite structure, as demonstrated by its greater density: 2.94 g/cm³ for aragonite versus 2.71 g/cm³ for calcite. A characteristic structural feature commonly observed in aragonite is twinning, where different regions of the crystal are misoriented as mirror images. This may cause crystals to display a

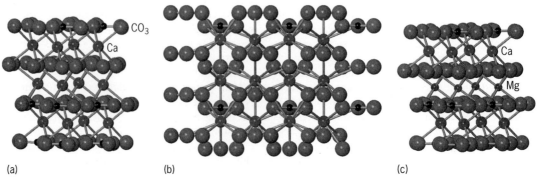

Fig. 1. Crystal structures of (*a*) calcite, (*b*) aragonite, and (*c*) dolomite.

Fig. 2. Rhombohedral cleavage crystal of calcite (Iceland spar), showing the optical property known as double refraction.

pseudohexagonal symmetry that is readily identified in larger specimens (**Fig. 3**). *See* TWINNING (CRYSTALLOGRAPHY).

It is noteworthy that only $CaCO_3$ occurs in both the calcite and aragonite structural forms (as well as a third form called vaterite), a property known as polymorphism. The preference for a metal carbonate to form in either the calcite or the aragonite structure can be attributed to the size of the divalent metal. Mg, Mn, Fe, Co, Ni, Zn, and Cd have radii smaller than Ca, and occur exclusively in the rhombohedral calcite structure. In contrast, Sr, Ba, and Pb have radii larger than Ca, and occur only in the orthorhombic aragonite structure. The larger size of the metal cation in this latter group favors the greater number of bonds to oxygen atoms as found in the aragonite structure. The size of the Ca atom allows $CaCO_3$ to exist in both structure types. *See* POLYMORPHISM (CRYSTALLOGRAPHY).

The crystal structure of the dolomite group is based on that of the calcite group but differs by the segregation of the two divalent metal cations into separate, alternating layers (Fig. 1c), referred to as cation ordering. In the mineral dolomite [$CaMg(CO_3)_2$], the layer repeat has the sequence $Ca-CO_3-Mg-CO_3-Ca$. The dolomite structure is rhombohedral; hence, members can be confused with the calcite group based on appearance, but the true symmetry is lower than that of calcite. The cation ordering necessary to form the dolomite structure is related to the difference in size between the two divalent metal cations. For example, the Ca atom is nearly 40% larger than Mg. This difference favors their ordering into separate layers, as in dolomite. By comparison, divalent iron (Fe^{2+}) is only 8% larger than Mg, and these cations show no tendency to order

into separate layers, and there is no $FeMg(CO_3)_2$ member of the dolomite group.

Carbonate minerals may be clear, translucent, or opaque and exhibit a wide variety of colors, usually reflecting the presence of minor impurities or inclusions. Some carbonate minerals display a characteristic color due to the dominance of a particular metal cation, with notable examples including the bright pink color of rhodochrosite ($MnCO_3$), the deep blue color of azurite [$Cu_3(CO_3)_2(OH)_2$], and the green of malachite [$Cu_2CO_3(OH)_2$], all of which are considered semiprecious stones. Calcite is particularly noted for exhibiting a rich variety of crystal morphologies and colors. Certain varieties of dolomite exhibit a distinctive curvature of its crystal faces. Most carbonate minerals have relatively low hardness on the Mohs scale (2.5–4.5) and rhombohedral varieties cleave readily. Many carbonate minerals dissolve in strong acids, releasing carbon dioxide. This serves as the basis for a common diagnostic test of some varieties in which several drops of a strong acid cause effervescence. *See* AZURITE.

Composition and phase relations. Significant compositional variability is observed for many carbonate minerals. Among members of the calcite group, the tendency to form solid solutions depends mostly on the respective sizes of the metal cations. The small difference in size between Fe^{2+} and Mg allows complete substitution for one another on

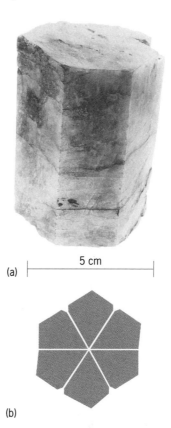

(a)

(b)

Fig. 3. Aragonite. (a) Pseudohexagonal twinning in specimen from Girgenti, Sicily (*American Museum of Natural History specimen*). (b) Arrangement of twins (*after C. Klein, Dana's Manual of Mineralogy, 21st ed., Wiley, 1993*).

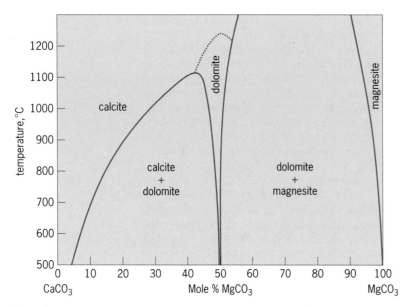

Fig. 4. Temperature-composition phase diagram for the system CaCO₃-MgCO₃. *(After J. R. Goldsmith and H. C. Heard, Subsolidus phase relations in the system CaCO₃-MgCO₃, J. Geol., 69:45–74, 1961)*

formation of the cation-ordered phase of dolomite at a composition intermediate between $CaCO_3$ and $MgCO_3$. These relationships are best seen in the phase diagram for the $CaCO_3$-$MgCO_3$ system, which also shows that increasing temperature favors solid solubility (**Fig. 4**). Despite unfavorable energetics, Mg substitution is common in calcite that forms in low-temperature environments, including in the shell material of some marine organisms, such as sea urchins. Limited cation substitution occurs among members of the aragonite group, although most aragonite contains minor Sr and strontianite ($SrCO_3$) generally contains some Ca. *See* SOLID SOLUTION.

Substitution among members of the dolomite group is more restricted, with the most important example being Fe^{2+} substitution for Mg in dolomite [$CaMg(CO_3)_2$] to form ankerite [$Ca(Fe,Mg)(CO_3)_2$]. Fe^{2+} is found to substitute up to a maximum of ~70% of the Mg sites, and the pure $CaFe(CO_3)_2$ member of the dolomite group is unknown in nature (**Fig. 5**). A distinction is usually made between species having less than 20% Fe substitution, referred to as ferroan dolomite, and those with greater Fe, called ankerite. Other cations, notably Mn, may substitute in dolomite and ankerite. Some examples of dolomite exhibit imperfect cation order and minor variation in Ca/Mg composition, typically an enrichment of Ca by up to 10%. These examples are less stable than ideal, well-ordered dolomite, and their occurrence is largely restricted to sedimentary conditions.

On heating to sufficiently high temperature, carbonate minerals decompose, giving off CO_2 gas and forming a metal oxide or a mixed solid. For calcite, this can be expressed as reaction (1). The

$$CaCO_3(s) \Leftrightarrow CaO(s) + CO_2(g) \qquad (1)$$

temperature at which decarbonation occurs varies with mineral composition and CO_2 pressure, among other factors. At ambient pressure in air, calcite and magnesite begin to decompose at approximately 700 and 500°C (1300 and 930°F), respectively. Decomposition of these minerals can be prevented up to much higher temperature only when the CO_2 pressure is increased significantly. Consequently, carbonate minerals generally persist under high-temperature conditions only when sufficiently deep in the crust that the high confining pressure prevents decomposition. In the presence of other minerals, carbonates may react at much lower temperature during metamorphism, releasing CO_2. Hydrous carbonate minerals decompose at relatively low temperature, restricting their occurrence to sedimentary deposits. On heating dolomite under sufficient CO_2 pressure to prevent decomposition, the cation ordering begins to decrease at approximately 900°C (1650°F) and vanishes completely by 1200°C (2200°F), at which point the structure is like that of the calcite group. *See* META-MORPHISM.

the same site, as illustrated by the complete solid solution between $FeCO_3$ (siderite) and $MgCO_3$ (magnesite). Extensive solid solutions exist for the end-member pairs $MgCO_3$-$FeCO_3$, $MgCO_3$-$MnCO_3$, and $FeCO_3$-$MnCO_3$. A greater difference in metal cation size results in limited formation of solid solutions between the end-member pairs $CaCO_3$-$FeCO_3$, $CaCO_3$-$MnCO_3$, and $CaCO_3$-$MgCO_3$. As noted above, the large difference in size between Ca and Mg allows the

The $CaCO_3$ polymorphs calcite and aragonite are both common, whereas vaterite is rare, transforming

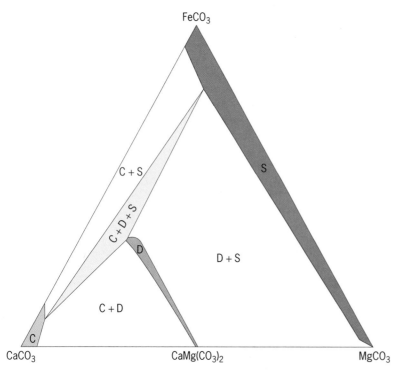

Fig. 5. Ternary phase diagram for the CaCO₃-MgCO₃-FeCO₃ system at 450°C (840°F). Solid solution phases are denoted: C = calcite; D = dolomite; S = siderite-magnesite. *(After P. E. Rosenberg, Subsolidus relations in the system CaCO₃-MgCO₃-FeCO₃ between 350 and 550°C, Amer. Mineral., 52:787–796, 1967)*

to calcite over periods as short as hours. At the temperature and pressure conditions found near the Earth's surface, calcite is the stable form, relative to aragonite. Consequently, aragonite transforms to calcite with time, which explains the occurrence of aragonite predominantly in recent sediments. Under sedimentary conditions, this transformation occurs only in the presence of water by dissolution of aragonite, followed by precipitation of calcite. Aragonite may persist for long periods of geologic time if isolated from water. Aragonite becomes more stable than calcite only at high pressure [approximately 3500 bars (350 MPa) at 25°C (77°F) and 7000 bars (700 MPa) at 300°C (570°F)], consistent with its greater density, and can be found in metamorphic rocks subjected to high pressure (**Fig. 6**). At high temperature and pressure, other structural forms of $CaCO_3$ have been produced experimentally but are not observed in nature (Fig. 6). Dolomite and magnesite have also been observed to undergo transformations to different structural forms at high pressure.

Solubility of carbonate minerals in water varies significantly depending on the acidity, the amount of dissolved carbon dioxide, and the total concentration of other dissolved ions. In general, carbonates tend to have solubilities greater than most silicate and oxide minerals but substantially less than the solubilities of common salts, such as NaCl (halite). Carbonate minerals are unusual in exhibiting a decrease in solubility with increasing temperature, a relationship called retrograde solubility. Under most conditions, this solubility behavior is attributable to a combination of factors, including the heat released during dissolution and the temperature influence on the solubility of carbon dioxide and dissolved carbonate species. *See* HALITE; OXIDE AND HYDROXIDE MINERALS; SILICATE MINERALS.

Occurrences and formation. Calcite and dolomite account for over 95% of the total abundance of carbonate minerals, primarily as constituents of sedimentary rocks (principally limestone and dolomite) but also as minor constituents in sandstone and shale, and in modern sediments. The tendency of carbon dioxide to dissolve in water, hydrate, and dissociate to form bicarbonate and carbonate species provides a source for crystallization of carbonate minerals, as illustrated for calcium carbonate [reaction (2)].

$$CO_2(g) + H_2O \Leftrightarrow H^+ + HCO_3^-$$
$$\downarrow \qquad\qquad (2)$$
$$Ca^{2+} + HCO_3^- \Leftrightarrow CaCO_3(s) + H^+$$

Significant sources of dissolved bicarbonate in water are derived from reactions involving the weathering of rocks. Crystallization of calcium carbonate may occur by purely inorganic reactions or through the biologic activity of organisms, a process known as biomineralization. In seawater, organisms such as bivalves, gastropods, and marine plankton, called foraminifera, crystallize hard exoskeletons or shells composed of calcite or aragonite. This biomineralization accounts for most of the formation of

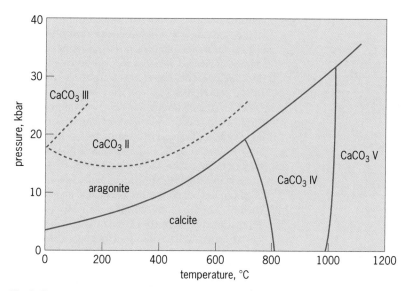

Fig. 6. Pressure-temperature phase diagram for the $CaCO_3$ system. Dashed lines refer to metastable equilibria. (*After W. D. Carlson, The calcite-aragonite equilibrium: effects of Sr substitution and anion orientational disorder, Amer. Mineral., 65:1252–1262, 1980*)

$CaCO_3$ in the oceans, despite the fact that shallow seawater is oversaturated with respect to $CaCO_3$. Accumulation of the hard skeletal remains of dead organisms represents one of the principal sources of calcium carbonate in limestone, which is formed after burial and cementation. The successive transfer of carbon dioxide gas to seawater as dissolved carbonate, its removal through biomineralization, followed by formation of limestone are fundamental processes in the global carbon cycle, which is linked to climate change over time. Carbonate minerals have also played an historic role in climate studies. Much of our present knowledge about global climate change has been derived from the carbon and oxygen isotopic compositions of marine calcium carbonate fossils. The isotopic ratios acquired during formation of the carbonate shells are sensitive to temperature. *See* BIOGEOCHEMISTRY; CLIMATOLOGY; GLOBAL CLIMATE CHANGE; WEATHERING PROCESSES.

Seawater is also oversaturated with respect to dolomite [$CaMg(CO_3)_2$], yet no significant crystallization is known, either inorganically or through biomineralization. The abundance of dolomite in sedimentary rocks, yet the lack of any significant dolomite formation in seawater, has been a source of controversy. The formation of most dolomite in sedimentary rock is thought to result from alteration of calcium carbonate sediments or limestone by Mg-containing water solutions.

Calcite also commonly occurs in soils from arid and semiarid climates, where evaporation favors the accumulation of calcium carbonate, sometimes in dense layers referred to as calcrete or caliche. Where rainfall is abundant, solution of carbonate minerals in limestone or dolomite may produce cave systems. Loss of CO_2 gas from calcium carbonate-rich water solutions in caves causes crystallization of principally calcite and aragonite, often in unusual deposits referred to generally as speleothem and including forms known as stalagmite and stalactite, soda straws, flowstone, and cave pearls. Calcite may also precipitate from springs, especially hot springs, as layered, massive, formations called travertine. *See* CALICHE; CAVE; STALACTITES AND STALAGMITES; TRAVERTINE.

Calcite and dolomite, and less commonly other carbonates, occur in marble (metamorphosed limestone) and as minor constituents of other metamorphic rocks. Aragonite is found in rare circumstances in metamorphic rocks, where its presence along with other high-pressure minerals is regarded as important evidence for pressures in excess of 5000–7000 bars (500–700 MPa), corresponding to depths greater than 10–15 mi (16–24 km) in the Earth's crust. Well-formed specimens of calcite and dolomite, in which the largest individual crystals may exceed 1 m in size, are generally hydrothermal in origin, typically forming along fractures or in cavities in rocks through which hot-water solutions flow. Carbonate minerals are commonly associated with the formation of ore bodies, often during late stages when circulating hot fluids result in their hydrothermal crystallization. Carbonate minerals also form as alteration products of primary ore minerals, with the resulting carbonate in some instances being an important ore mineral, such as malachite. *See* HYDROTHERMAL ORE DEPOSITS.

Although generally uncommon in igneous rocks, carbonates are the dominant mineral components of the relatively rare carbonatite rocks, and are found in kimberlite rocks, which are host to diamonds. The origin of carbonate magma remains enigmatic, with evidence supporting both a primary mantle source and separation from a parent melt, called liquid immiscibility. *See* DIAMOND; MAGMA.

Iron- and magnesium-rich carbonate minerals have been documented in meteorite fragments thought to have originated on Mars, but their origin remains uncertain.

Uses. Calcite finds widespread application as a filler, binder, or coloring agent in pharmaceuticals, paper, plastic and composite materials, foodstuffs, and paints. It is widely used in chemical processing and in wastewater treatment. Both natural and precipitated forms of calcium carbonate are used as calcium supplements and antacids. Calcite, as limestone, has long been used as an essential reaction ingredient in the production of steel. Calcite and dolomite, as crushed or pulverized limestone, find extensive use in roadway construction, agriculture, and lawn care. Limestone and marble are used as building stone, tile, or facing, and serve as the material in numerous monuments and statues. Calcium carbonate, after heating to produce lime (CaO), is an important raw material in the manufacturing of glass and portland cement.   Richard J. Reeder

Bibliography. L. L. Y. Chang, R. A. Howie, and J. Zussman, *Rock-Forming Minerals*, vol. 5B: *Non-Silicates: Sulfates, Carbonates, Phosphates, Halides*, 2d ed., Geological Society, London, 1996; J. W. Morse and F. T. Mackenzie, *Geochemistry of Sedimentary Carbonates*. Elsevier, 1990; R. J. Reeder (ed.), *Carbonates: Mineralogy and Chemistry, Reviews in Mineralogy*, vol. 11, Mineralogical Society of America, 1983.

Carbonatite

An igneous rock in which carbonate minerals make up at least half the volume. Individual occurrences of carbonatite are not numerous (about 330 have been recognized) and generally are small, but they are widely distributed. Carbonatites are scientifically important because they reveal clues concerning the composition and thermal history of the Earth's mantle. Economically, carbonatites provide important mines for some mineral commodities and are virtually the only sources of a few. *See* CARBONATE MINERALS.

Mineralogy. The carbonate minerals that dominate the carbonatites are, in order of decreasing abundance, calcite, dolomite, ankerite, and rarely siderite and magnesite. Sodium- and potassium-rich carbonate minerals have been confirmed in igneous rocks at only one locality, the active volcano Oldoinyo Lengai in Tanzania (**Fig. 1**). Noncarbonate minerals that typify carbonatites are apatite, magnetite, phlogopite or biotite, clinopyroxene, amphibole, monticellite, perovskite, and rarely olivine or melilite. Secondary minerals, produced by alteration of primary magmatic minerals, include barite, alkali feldspar, quartz, fluorite, hematite, rutile, pyrite, and chlorite. Minerals that are important in some carbonatites because they carry niobium, rare-earth elements, and other metals in concentrations high enough for profitable extraction are pyrochlore, bastnaesite, monazite, baddeleyite, and bornite.

Styles of occurrence. Carbonatites occur in a variety of forms, both intrusive and volcanic. Lava flows are small and rare, but pyroclastic carbonatites are numerous as thick near-vent accumulations (tuff cones) and thin but widespread airfall and surge deposits. Some pyroclastic carbonatites are especially significant, because they preserve the forms of quenched droplets of carbonate-rich liquid and

Fig. 1. Carbonatite lava from Oldoinyo Lengai volcano, Tanzania; thin section between crossed polarizers. Longest dimension of the field of view is 2.5 mm.

also record the mineral assemblages that are nearly always erased in intrusive rocks by low-temperature alteration. Carbonatite airfall tuffs are paleontologically important, because they tend to be fine grained and rapidly become lithified, preserving delicate organic structures. The hominid footprints at Laetoli, Tanzania, and remarkably detailed molds of plants and caterpillars are examples. *See* TUFF.

Most intrusive carbonatites form arrays of dikes that may be parallel, radiating, or concentric and arcuate. More irregular intrusive bodies are also known, but all are small compared to those of silicate-rich igneous rocks; the largest known carbonatite body, at Sokli in Finland, has a surface area of only 20 km^2 (8 mi^2). Carbonate-rich magmas appear to have had low viscosities, but some were emplaced with explosive violence because of their high gas content. A few carbonatites extend for several kilometers along fault surfaces; they may have been older igneous bodies that were caught up in the fault displacement and acted as cold but weak ductile lubricant between the rock masses; or they may have been injected as magma. Except for the absence of large homogeneous plutons, carbonatites form the full array of igneous rock styles that are shown by silicate-rich igneous rocks. *See* MAGMA; PLUTON.

Associated rocks. Carbonatites usually have been found with low-silica, high-alkali igneous rocks, typically melilitites, nephelinites, tephrites, and phonolites. The silicate and carbonate rocks are intimately mixed in many intrusive complexes, and the carbonatites are among the youngest and generally least abundant of rock types in any complex. Carbonatites that are unaccompanied by other igneous rocks have been recognized. Examples are at Fort Portal, Uganda; Kaluwe, Zaire; and Sarfartoq, Greenland.

Geographic distribution. Carbonatites are widely scattered (**Fig. 2**). About half of all carbonatite oc-

currences so far recognized are in Africa. The only occurrences known on oceanic crust are in the Canary and Cape Verde islands; however, carbonatite associated with deep-water marine sediments occurs under the Semail ophiolite in the United Arab Emirates. These occurrences suggest that carbonatites might actually be common on and within oceanic crust but are usually buried or destroyed by subduction. *See* OPHIOLITE.

Chemical compositions. Carbonatites, compared to the inferred composition of the Earth's mantle and to other igneous rocks, are greatly enriched in niobium, rare-earth elements, barium, strontium, phosphorus, and fluorine, and they are relatively depleted in silicon, aluminum, iron, magnesium, nickel, titanium, sodium, potassium, and chlorine. These extreme differences are attributed to strong fractionation between carbonate liquid on the one hand and silicate and oxide solid phases on the other during separation of the carbonate liquid from its source. Strontium and neodymium isotope ratios indicate that the sources of carbonatites are geologically old, inhomogeneous, and variably depleted in the radioactive parent elements rubidium and samarium.

Genesis of carbonate-rich magma. For more than two centuries, it has been known that calcite decomposes to lime (calcium oxide; CaO) and carbon dioxide (CO_2) when exposed to high temperature at atmospheric pressure. Furthermore, at high pressure calcium carbonate ($CaCO_3$) liquid is stable only at temperatures far higher than are reasonably expected in the Earth's crust. It was therefore difficult for geologists to imagine liquid carbonate being stable at or near the Earth's surface. In 1960 it was demonstrated experimentally that the addition of water (H_2O) to the system CaO-CO_2 at high pressure will stabilize a carbonate liquid at temperatures expectable in the Earth's crust. Also in 1960, the

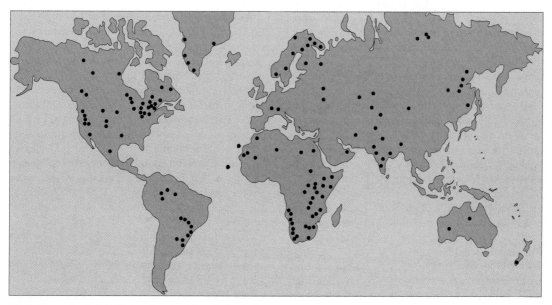

Fig. 2. Generalized distribution of carbonatites. Individual spots represent clusters of occurrences.

volcano Oldoinyo Lengai in Tanzania erupted carbonate-rich ash and subsequently carbonatite lava. Geologic mapping has confirmed that most carbonatites occur in small volumes associated with mantle-derived, high-alkali, low-silica igneous rocks. *See* CALCITE.

There are three possible origins (not mutually exclusive) for carbonatite magmas: (1) they are "primary" liquids, arriving directly from their mantle sources without change during ascent; (2) they are products of fractional crystallization from carbonate-bearing silicate magmas (if silicate minerals crystallize early from the magma, carbonate concentration should build up in the remaining liquid); or (3) they are products of immiscible separation of carbonate-rich and silicate-rich liquids (the properties of highly ionic carbonate liquid are so different from those of silicate liquid that, during cooling, carbonate-bearing silicate magma separates into two liquids, one containing nearly all the carbonate, the other nearly all the silicate).

The first origin is favored by evidence from altered mantle xenoliths (rock fragments enclosed by an unrelated igneous rock) carried to the surface by basalts, nephelinites, and kimberlites; these altered fragments demonstrate that carbonatite liquid has percolated through the mantle. A primary liquid origin is also supported by the presence in carbonatites, rarely, of magnesium- and chromium-rich spinels typical of mantle rocks, and by the absence, in some carbonatite occurrences, of associated silicate rocks that could represent parents or siblings of the carbonatites. The lack of mantle xenoliths in carbonatites is evidence against primary liquid, but the low density and low viscosity of carbonatite liquid may permit such dense fragments to settle out quickly. *See* SPINEL; XENOLITH.

The second and third origins are favored by the small volume of carbonatite relative to silicate rocks in most occurrences, and by the lateness of carbonatites in intrusive and eruptive sequences; but they are opposed by differences in isotopic ratios between carbonatite and silicate rocks in some occurrences (neither fractional crystallization nor immiscible liquid separation should change the isotopic ratios). The second origin is also opposed by experimental results indicating that silicates and carbonates crystallize simultaneously through a large temperature interval, preventing buildup of carbonate in the remaining liquid. The third origin is supported by experiments demonstrating that during cooling a carbonate-bearing silicate liquid can split into carbonate-rich and silicate-rich liquids, and by the natural occurrence of "rock emulsions" consisting of blobs of one composition enclosed in the other. On balance, the evidence is still inconclusive, and possibly any of the three mechanisms of origin can operate at different times and places.

Criteria for recognition. It is not easy to discriminate carbonatites from thoroughly recrystallized and metamorphosed marbles or from vein fillings deposited by dilute, low-temperature aqueous solutions. Because calcite has very low strength and easily deforms by plastic flow, carbonate-rich rocks can intrude their more brittle surroundings and thus imitate magmatic rocks. Furthermore, because marbles and recrystallized carbonatites converge toward the same textures and mineral assemblages, carbonatites can be misidentified as metamorphosed sedimentary rocks. The strongest indications of igneous origin for a carbonate-rich rock are considered to be quenched carbonate-rich liquid in the form of droplets or bubble walls, association with nepheline- or melilite- bearing rocks, presence of strontium-rich calcite, presence of pyrochlore and other minerals that are rich in niobium or rare-earth elements, and presence of apatite that has higher concentrations of rare-earth elements and silicon than apatite from other rock types. *See* APATITE; NIOBIUM; RARE-EARTH ELEMENTS.

Economic significance. Carbonatites yield a variety of mineral commodities, including phosphate, lime, niobium, rare-earth elements, anatase, fluorite, and copper. Agricultural phosphate for fertilizer is the most valuable single product from carbonatites; most is obtained from apatite in lateritic soils that have developed by tropical weathering of carbonatites, dissolving the carbonates and thereby concentrating the less soluble apatite. Lime for agriculture and for cement manufacture is obtained from carbonatites in regions where limestones are lacking.

The carbonatites at Bayan Obo, China, and Mountain Pass, California, dominate the world suppliers of rare-earth elements, but many other carbonatites contain unexploited reserves. Tropical weathering at several carbonatites in Brazil has produced economically important concentrations of anatase (TiO_2) from decomposition of perovskite ($CaTiO_3$). Other carbonatites are locally important sources for some commodities; for example, Amba Dongar, India, provides fluorite, and Phalaborwa, South Africa, is a major producer of copper, with zirconium, gold, silver, platinum group elements, and uranium as by-products.

Tectonic significance. Ultramafic xenoliths from lithospheric mantle commonly show textures and mineral assemblages that indicate modification of the original rock. This alteration typically results in strong enrichment in light rare-earth elements, uranium, thorium, and lead, but much less enrichment in titanium, zirconium, niobium, and strontium. These changes are commonly attributed to interaction of lithospheric mantle with an invading carbonate-rich magma. The wide geographic dispersal of these altered xenoliths suggests that carbonate-rich liquid has been more common in the upper mantle than the low abundance of carbonatites in the upper crust would suggest. According to the testimony of these samples, carbonatite magma, ascending through lithospheric mantle, commonly is trapped before it can invade the crust. In addition to the factors that can stop the rise of any magma (heat loss, increase of solidus temperature with decrease in pressure, decrease in density and increase in strength of wall rock), carbonatite magma can be halted by reaction with wall rock to form calcium and magnesium silicates plus CO_2, and by less oxidizing conditions to reduce carbonate to elemental carbon (graphite or diamond) or to methane. Both of these changes subtract dissolved CO_2 from the magma, causing crystallization. *See* DIAMOND; EARTH INTERIOR; GRAPHITE.

In some regions carbonatite magmatism has recurred after intervals of 100 million years, suggesting that carbonate-rich liquids can be regenerated by a small degree of partial fusion of locally and repeatedly carbonated mantle. This possibility, in turn, suggests that carbonate in the mantle is replenished by recycling of sedimentary carbonate. *See* SUBDUCTION ZONES.

Carbonatites are not restricted to a single tectonic regime. They occur in oceanic and continental crust and have formed in compressional fold belts and stable cratons as well as regions of crustal extension. Rather than indicating the stress field in the shallow crust in which they were emplaced, carbonatites are useful in modeling the long-term thermal and chemical development of the mantle. *See* IGNEOUS ROCKS.

Daniel S. Barker

Bibliography. K. Bell (ed.), *Carbonatites: Genesis and Evolution*, Unwin-Hyman, Boston, 1989; R. H. Mitchell (ed.), *Undersaturated Alkaline Rocks: Mineralogy, Petrogenesis, and Economic Potential*, Short Course Vol. 24, Mineralogical Association of Canada, Winnipeg, 1996; A. R. Woolley, *Alkaline Rocks and Carbonatites of the World*, pt. 1: *North and South America*, British Museum (Natural History), London, 1987.

Carboniferous

The fifth period of the Paleozoic Era. The Carboniferous Period spanned from about 355 million years to about 295 million years ago. The rocks that formed during this time interval are known as the Carboniferous System; they include a wide variety of sedimentary, igneous, and metamorphic rocks. Sedimentary rocks in the lower portion of the Carboniferous are typically carbonates, such as limestones and dolostones, and locally some evaporites. The upper portions of the system are usually composed of cyclically repeated successions of sandstones, coals, shales, and thin limestones. *See* SEDIMENTARY ROCKS.

The economic importance of the Carboniferous is evident in its name, which refers to coal, the important energy source that fueled the industrialization of northwestern Europe in the early 1800s and led to the Carboniferous being one of the first geologic systems to be studied in detail. Carboniferous coals formed in coastal and fluvial environments in many parts of the world. Petroleum, another important energy resource, accumulated in many Carboniferous marine carbonate sediments, particularly near shelf margins adjacent to basinal black shale source rocks. In many regions the cyclical history of deposition and exposure has enhanced the permeability and porosity of the shelfal rocks to make them excellent petroleum reservoirs. The limestones of the Lower Carboniferous are extensively quarried and used for building stone, especially in northwestern Europe and the central and eastern United States. *See* COAL; PETROLEUM.

The base of the Carboniferous is placed at the first appearance of the conodont *Siphonodella sulcata*, a fossil that marks a widely recognized biozone in most marine sedimentary rocks. The reference locality for this base is an outcrop in Belgium. The top of the Carboniferous is placed at the first appearance of the conodont *Streptognathus isolatus* a few meters below the first appearance of the Permian fusulinacean foraminiferal zone of *Sphaeroschwagerina fusiformis*. The reference locality is in the southern Ural region in Kazakhstan. The equivalent biozone is at the base of *Pseudoschwagerina* in North America. *See* CONODONT; FUSULINACEA.

Subdivisions. The term Carboniferous Order was originally applied by W. D. Conybeare and J. Phillips in 1822 to rocks in the British Isles that included the Old Red Sandstone, Mountain Limestone, Millstone Grit, and Coal Measures (**Fig. 1**). Later, after the Old Red Sandstone was recognized as being a continental facies of the Devonian System, the Mountain Limestone became the Lower Carboniferous and the Millstone Grit and Coal Measures were combined to be the Upper Carboniferous. In North America, the Coal Measures were readily recognized (as Upper Carboniferous), and the underlying, mainly noncoaly beds were initially called Subcarboniferous.

In 1891, the U.S. Geological Survey introduced the terms Pennsylvanian Series for the Coal Measures and Mississippian Series for the Subcarboniferous. In 1906 T. C. Chamberlain and R. D. Salisbury raised the Mississippian and Pennsylvanian to the rank of

CENOZOIC	QUATERNARY	
	TERTIARY	
MESOZOIC	CRETACEOUS	
	JURASSIC	
	TRIASSIC	
PALEOZOIC	PERMIAN	
	CARBONIFEROUS	PENNSYLVANIAN
		MISSISSIPPIAN
	DEVONIAN	
	SILURIAN	
	ORDOVICIAN	
	CAMBRIAN	
PRECAMBRIAN		

Conybeare and Phillips, 1822 (Great Britain)	Northwestern Europe, mid-1800s		Chamberlain and Salisbury, 1906 (North America)	Soviet Union, 1920s–1970s		Current usage	
Magnesian Limestone	Permian		Permian	Permian		Permian	
CARBONIFEROUS Coal Measures	**CARBONIFEROUS** Upper		Pennsylvanian System	**CARBONIFEROUS** Upper	**CARBONIFEROUS** Pennsylvanian Subsystem		
Millstone Grit				Middle			
Mountain Limestone	Lower		Mississippian System	Lower	Mississippian Subsystem		
Old Red Sandstone	Devonian		Devonian	Devonian		Devonian	

Fig. 1. Development of stratigraphic nomenclature for the Carboniferous.

systems (Fig. 1), noting that they were separated by a major unconformity and were quite different lithologically in both North American and in Europe. This nomenclature was extensively adopted in North America but not in other parts of the world. *See* MISSISSIPPIAN; PENNSYLVANIAN.

A third means of subdividing the Carboniferous was developed during the 1920s and 1930s on the Russian Platform, the western slopes of the Urals, and the greater Donetz Basin areas of Ukrainia where a three part subdivision is recognized. On the platform, the limestone succession of the Lower Carboniferous is widely recognized and is separated by a major unconformity and a hiatus from the overlying Upper Carboniferous. On the platform margins and slopes and toward the center of the Donetz Basin, additional sediments progressively filled the hiatus, so that a complete sedimentary record is available for study in a marine facies. Within the upper portion of the Carboniferous, a second regional unconformity of considerable duration is documented on the Russian Platform between the Moscovian and Kasimovian stages (Fig. 1); and as a result, the Russian Carboniferous was subdivided into three series (Fig. 1). The boundary between the Middle and Upper Carboniferous on the Russian Platform is approximately the same as the boundary between the Middle and Upper Pennsylvanian in the North American midcontinent region.

The International Subcommission on Carboniferous Stratigraphy reached general agreement in the 1970s and 1980s that the Carboniferous would be divided into two parts: a Lower Carboniferous Mississippian Subsystem and an Upper Carboniferous Pennsylvanian Subsystem.

The two Carboniferous subsystems are subdivided into a number of series and stages (**Fig. 2**) that are variously identified in different parts of the world, based on biostratigraphic evidence using evolutionary successions in fossils or overlapping assemblage zones. Many fossil groups have been studied in order to establish consistent worldwide zonations; they have included foraminifers, corals, ammonoid cephalopods, brachiopods, bryozoans, sponges, bivalves, crinoids, radiolarians, conodonts, and plants. To a large extent the distribution of each of these fossil groups was determined by climate, temperature, and other environmental and ecological conditions, evolutionary adaptations, and paleobiogeographic opportunities for dispersal. As the Carboniferous progressed, changes in each of these factors caused biotic redistributions and dispersals and, at other times, restrictions in distribution and strongly provincial biotic associations. These biogeographic differences have made detailed correlations between some regions more difficult, and as a result, there remains strong preferences for regional series and stage names. *See* INDEX FOSSIL; STRATIGRAPHY.

Paleogeography and lithology. Perhaps the strongest of the many ecological factors that controlled biotic distributions were the paleogeographic changes within the Carboniferous that were brought about by the initial assembling of the supercontinent Pangaea and the associated mountain-building activities, which greatly modified climate, ocean currents, and seaways. In the Early Carboniferous (**Fig. 3a**), a nearly continuous equatorial seaway permitted extensive tropical and subtropical carbonate sedimentation on the shelves and platforms in North America, northern and southern Europe, Kazakhstan, North and South China, and the northern shores of the protocontinent Gondwana (such as northern Africa).

The gradual collision of northern Gondwana

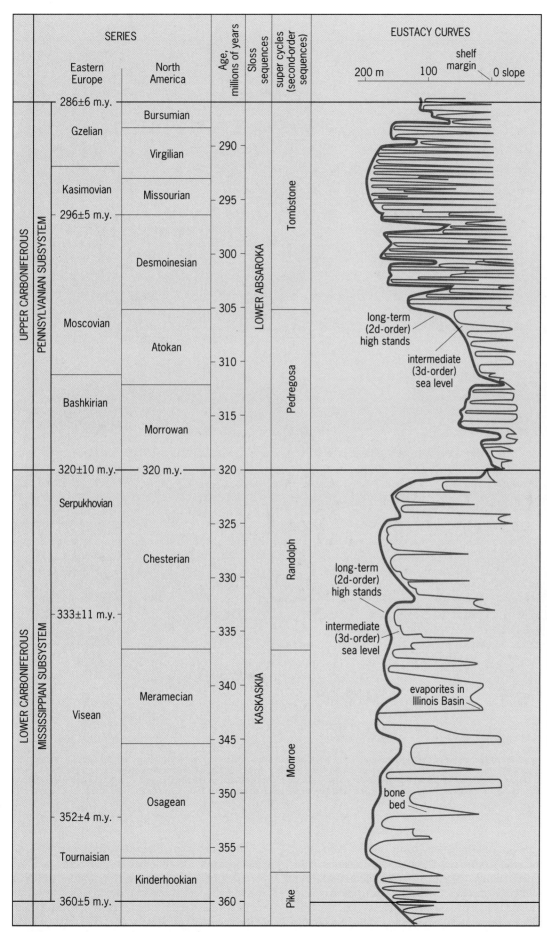

Fig. 2. Curves outlining the fluctuations of sea level during the Carboniferous. The Mississippian sea-level curve is typical of times when glaciation was not a major factor in controlling sea levels, and the Pennsylvanian sea-level curve is characteristic of extensive and protracted glaciation in the Early Pennsylvanian followed by repeated glaciation and nonglaciation events in the Middle and Upper Pennsylvanian. The time scale is estimated based on a few reliable radiometric ages for the interval. 1 m = 3.3 ft. *(After C. A. Ross and J. R. P. Ross, Late Paleozoic sea level and depositional sequences and biostratigraphic zonation of late Paleozoic depositional sequences, Cushman Found. Foraminiferal Res. Spec. Publ., no. 24, 1987)*

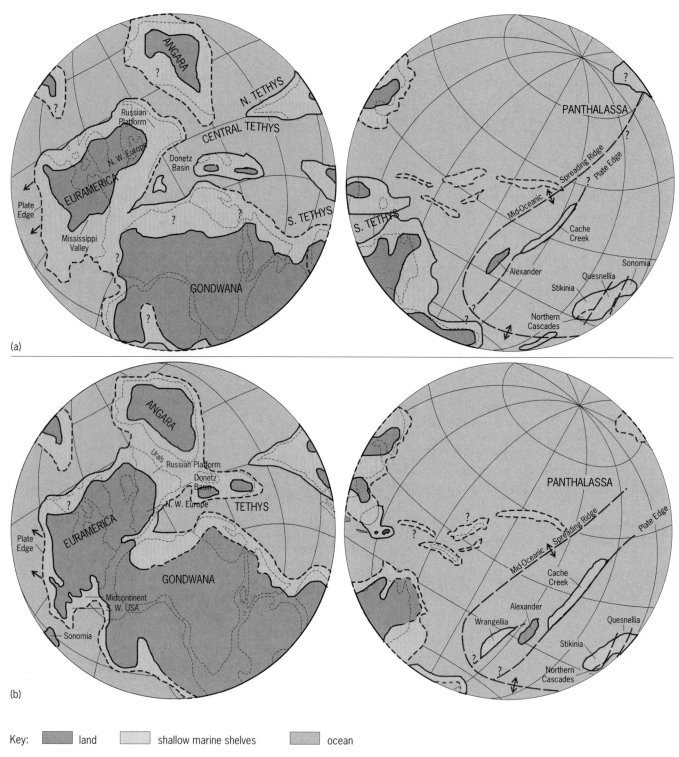

Key: ▨ land   ▨ shallow marine shelves   ▨ ocean

Fig. 3. Paleogeography of the Carboniferous. (*a*) Early Carboniferous (Mississippian) Tournaisian and Visean epochs, with a major east–west equatorial seaway between Euramerica and Gondwana. (*b*) Late Carboniferous (Pennsylvanian) Moscovian (or Desmoinesian) epochs with the east–west seaway closed by the collision of Euramerica and Gondwana and the resulting Ouchita–Appalachian–Hercynian orogeny and land barrier between the western Tethys and eastern Panthalassa oceans.

against northern Europe–North America (also called Euramerica or Laurussia) started the formation of the supercontinent of Pangaea. By the middle of the Carboniferous, this process divided the tropical equatorial seaway into two isolated segments (Fig. 3*b*). One, which represented the beginning of the Paleotethys faunal region, lay to the east of Pangaea as a large arcuate ocean with a number of small island arcs and oceanic plateaus. This warm-water ocean with vast west-flowing equatorial currents resulted in warm-water currents being directed both north and south of their normal latitudes.

The other segment of the former equatorial seaway lay to the west of Pangaea and faced a relatively large, deep Panthalassa Ocean basin, which had considerably fewer island arcs and ocean plateaus. This edge of Pangaea was not bathed by warm-water currents; it was the site of cold-water upwelling and cool-water currents from both the Northern and Southern hemispheres. When these reached equatorial areas they began to warm, and they formed the beginnings of the westward-flowing equatorial currents. As a consequence, the paleolatitudinal extent of carbonate platforms on the western margin of Pangaea was less than in the Paleotethys region. *See* CONTINENTAL DRIFT; CONTINENTS, EVOLUTION OF; PALEOGEOGRAPHY; PLATE TECTONICS.

Orogeny. The collision of Gondwana with North America–northern Europe, in addition to changing the patterns of equatorial ocean currents, created the long chain of mountains that made up the Ouachita-Appalachian-Hercynian orogenic belt. This complex set of mountains also is evident in the sedimentary patterns of clastic rocks, such as conglomerates, river and shoreline sandstones, and coals and other nonmarine clastic deposits, as well as in thick turbidite successions in several foredeep marine basins that formed along the front of the advancing orogenic thrust belts. Although this chain of mountains was mainly within the tropics and subtropics, it became very elevated, perhaps similar to the present-day Himalaya ranges; it disrupted terrestrial climates to a similar degree. *See* OROGENY.

Glaciation. An additional ramification of the formation of Pangaea was the beginning of very extensive glaciation in the Southern Hemisphere polar and high-latitude regions of the supercontinent. Glacial deposits are also known from smaller continental fragments that were at high paleolatitudes in the Northern Hemisphere. The cause for this great increase in ice accumulation is not entirely known. It may be that the diversion of warm-water currents into more southerly (and northerly) latitudes increased precipitation (as snow). Perhaps the mountain heights of the newly formed orogenic belts disrupted general atmospheric circulation from the tropics into high latitudes. Solar radiation possibly was reduced a few percent to initiate these more extensive glacial conditions. Or other, still unknown factors may be the primary causes. In any case, the Earth's climate cooled, tropical carbonate-producing areas became restricted toward the Equator, and eustatic sea-level fluctuations became prominent in the sedimentary record. *See* GLACIAL EPOCH.

Sea-level changes. The sedimentary record of sea-level changes is well documented from the beginning of the latest Mississippian through the Pennsylvanian and into the Permian. These are cyclical sediments in which the succession of depositional facies is regularly repeated by each sea-level fluctuation. As a result, these depositional sequences have great lateral extent and continuity. Because local depositional conditions depended on many other, often unique circumstances, the sedimentary patterns have considerable lateral variation (**Fig. 4**). For example, the

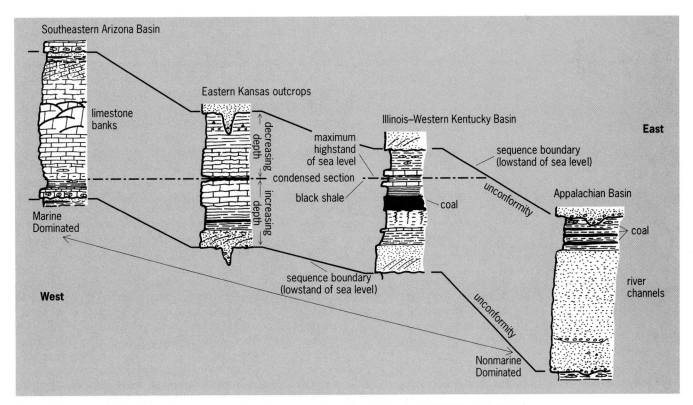

Fig. 4. Typical shelf sedimentary patterns in upper Carboniferous depositional sequences. The broken line represents the condensed section that forms during maximum sea-level highstands when sedimentation rates are low. The prominent unconformities at the base of depositional sequences in Appalachian Basin areas having well-developed fluvial beds become progressively less pronounced westward in marine-dominated successions.

cyclical sediments near the Appalachian orogenic belt contain vast amounts of clastic debris, such as sands, silts, and gravels, which were transported and deposited in rivers, lakes, deltas, and coastal features. Many of these cycles are nonmarine or only marginally marine, and many are viewed as being more strongly influenced by changes in tectonic activity and climate. The suggestion is that the amount of clastic material was supplied mainly by erosion, and sedimentation responded to wet and dry climatic cycles and only indirectly to sea-level fluctuations. In marine-dominated sequences, supratidal carbonates commonly passed upward into thin, fluvial and eolian beds that were usually reworked as debris into the succeeding basal marine transgressive beds. *See* DEPOSITIONAL SYSTEMS AND ENVIRONMENTS.

Farther west (Fig. 4) at greater distances from the Appalachian orogenic belt, as in Ohio, many of these clastic-rich cyclic sediments intertongue with marine sediments, and the influence of sea-level fluctuations becomes increasingly evident. The Illinois-Kentucky basin has about equal representation of marine deposits and fluvial channels and delta deposits. Western Missouri and eastern Kansas were far enough away from the large influx of clastic materials to have predominantly marine sediments and minor amounts of nonmarine, mostly silt and fine sand clastics. Carbonate sedimentation dominated farther from sources of clastic sediments. Oceanic plateaus in the Paleotethys and Panthalassa ocean basins, which lacked influxes of clastic materials, have cyclical sediments that are entirely in various carbonate facies that reflect differences in water depth.

The fluctuations in sea level during the Carboniferous reflect different rates of sea-level change, different durations, and different magnitudes. Minor sea-level fluctuations of a meter or two (3–6 ft) with cyclicities of 20,000–40,000 years and intermediate fluctuations of 4–6 m (13–20 ft) with cyclicities of about 100,000 years may be preserved. More easily recognized are fluctuations of about 400,000 years–1 million years, which have amplitudes of 60–200 m (200–660 ft) [Fig. 2]. Late in the Mississippian and early in the Pennsylvanian, for an interval of approximately 15–20 million years, sea-level high-stands were consistently low and infrequently reached higher than the continental shelf margins (Fig. 4), a condition that was not repeated until quite late in the Permian Period. *See* CONTINENTAL MARGIN.

The sea-level fluctuations resulted in large areas of the cratonic shelves being frequently exposed to long intervals of weathering, erosion, and diagenesis. The effects of these exposure-related events suggest that within the Carboniferous climates were not uniform and different types of paleosols (fossil soil profiles) formed under a variety of pedogenic processes. These paleosols reflect changes in world climate as well as the continued northward motion of continents across latitudinal climatic belts as a result of plate tectonics and sea-floor spreading. *See* PALEO-

CLIMATOLOGY; SEDIMENTOLOGY; WEATHERING PROCESSES.

Life. During the Carboniferous, life evolved to exploit fully the numerous marine and nonmarine aquatic environments and terrestrial and aerial habitats. Single-cell protozoan foraminifers evolved new abilities to construct layered, calcareous walls and internally complex tests. These single-celled organisms diversified into nearly all shallow-water, carbonate-producing environments from the intertidal, lagoon, shelf, shelf margin, and upper parts (within the photic zone) of the shelf slope. Ammonoid cephalopods, from their first appearance in the later part of the Devonian, diversified rapidly during the Early Carboniferous, and their occurrences were used to establish one of the earliest biostratigraphic zonation schemes for the Lower Carboniferous. Brachiopods, bryozoans, conodonts, crinoids, and corals were also widespread and locally important parts of the marine faunas. The Tournaisian and Visean shallow tropical seas abounded in blastoid echinoderms; however, these creatures became nearly extinct and were geographically restricted to a small area in the eastern Panthalassa Ocean after the Early Pennsylvanian (Morrowan). Conodonts were widespread in deeper-water deposits.

Insects have remarkable evolutionary histories during the Carboniferous. They adapted to flight and dispersed into many terrestrial and fresh-water habitats. Carboniferous insects include many unusual orders, such as one with three pairs of wings (although it is not clear that the foremost pair functioned directly in propulsion). By the Late Pennsylvanian, many large cockroachlike orders were present and also several huge dragonflylike groups, some of which reached wingspans of 90 cm (3 ft). Carboniferous insects included representatives of five Paleoptera orders (mayflies and dragonflylike orders) and at least six orthopterid (cockroachlike) orders. Insects are commonly preserved in coal swamp deposits and display the amazing diversity of life within these swamps. *See* INSECTA.

Vertebrates also evolved rapidly. Although acanthodian fish declined from their Devonian peak, sharklike fishes and primitive bony fishes adapted well to the expanded environments and the new ecological food chains of the Carboniferous. Some sharklike groups invaded fresh-water habitats, where they were associated with coal swamp deposits. For the bony fish (ray-finned fish and air-breathing choanate fishes with lobed fins), the Late Devonian and Carboniferous was a time of considerable evolutionary diversity and ecological expansion, with many lineages independently adapting to both freshwater and marine conditions. Lungfish are one of the fresh-water choanate lineages which evolved adaptations for survival in temporarily dry lakes and rivers. Near the Devonian-Carboniferous boundary, a lineage from the choanate fish had evolved into the first amphibians. *See* VERTEBRATA.

Carboniferous amphibians evolved rapidly in several directions. The earliest were the labyrinthodont embolomeres, which had labyrinthodont teeth and were mainly aquatic. Another significant labyrinthodont group was the rhachitomes, which originated in the Early Carboniferous and became abundant, commonly reaching about 1 m (3 ft) or more; they were widespread in terrestrial habitats during the Late Carboniferous and Permian. Some of the Carboniferous amphibians reverted to totally aquatic habitats, such as the lepospondyls, which lost their bony vertebrae and limbs, had large flattened broad heads, and were snakelike in appearance. Ancestors of the present-day anurans (frogs), urodeles (salamanders), and caecilians (apodans) probably date from the later part of the Carboniferous, but their record as fossils is meager. *See* AMPHIBIA.

Primitive reptiles evolved from one of the embolomere amphibian lineages during the Late Carboniferous. They formed the basal stock from which all other reptiles have evolved including the earliest mammallike reptiles in the Late Carboniferous. During the Late Carboniferous, early reptiles coexisted with several advanced amphibian groups which shared at least some, but probably not all, of their reptilelike characters. *See* REPTILIA.

Terrestrial plants also showed major diversification of habitats and the evolution of important new lineages during the Carboniferous. Initially, Early Carboniferous plants were predominantly a continuation of latest Devonian groups; however, they were distinguished in part by their large sizes with many arborescent lycopods and large articulates, and pteridosperms (seed ferns) and ferns became increasingly abundant and varied. By the Late Carboniferous, extensive swamps formed along the broad, nearly flat coastal areas; and these coal-forming environments tended to move laterally across the coastal plain areas as the sea level repeatedly rose. Other coal-forming marshes were common in the floodplains and channel fills of the broad rivers of upper delta distributary systems. During the Late Carboniferous, primitive conifers appeared and included araucarias, which became common in some, probably drier ecological habitats. One of the features of Late Carboniferous plant paleogeographic distributions is the recognition of a southern, high-latitude Gondwanan floral province, the *Glossopteris* province, and a northern high-latitude Anagaran floral province, which were cool adapted. These provinces contrasted with an extensive equatorial belt of much greater plant diversity. *See* PALEOBOTANY; PALEOZOIC.

C. A. Ross; June R. P. Ross

Bibliography. R. H. Dott, Jr., and D. R. Prothero, *Evolution of the Earth*, 5th ed., 1994; H. L. Levin, *The Earth Through Time*, 4th ed., 1994; A. L. Palmer (general ed.), Decade of North American Geology (DNAG) Project, *The Geology of North America*, Geological Society of America, 1986–1994; R. C. Moore et al., The Kansas Rock Column, *State Geol. Surv. Kans. Bull.*, no. 89, 1951; C. A. Ross and J. R. P. Ross, Late Paleozoic Sea Levels and Depositional Sequences and Biostratigraphic Zonation of Late Paleozoic Depositional Sequences, *Cushman Found. Foram. Res. Spec. Publ.*, no. 24, 1987; J. W. Skehan et al., The Mississippian and Pennsylvanian (Carboniferous) Systems in the United States, *USGS Prof. Pap.*, no. 1110-A–DD, pp. A1–DD16, 1979; R. H. Wagner, C. F. Winkler Prins, and L. F. Granados (eds.), *The Carboniferous of the World* (M. C. Diaz, general ed.), Instituto Geologico y Minero de Espana, Madrid, and Nationaal Natuurhistorisch Museum, Leiden, Parts I, II, III, IUGS Publ. 16, 20, 33, 1983, 1985, 1996; H. R. Wanless and C. R. Wright, Paleoenvironmental Maps of Pennsylvanian Rocks, Illinois Basin and Northern Midcontinent Region, *Geol. Soc. Amer. Publ.*, no. MC-23, 1978.

Carbonyl

A functional group found in organic compounds in which a carbon atom is doubly bonded to an oxygen atom

$$\begin{array}{c} X \\ \diagdown \\ C=O \\ \diagup \\ Y \end{array}$$

Depending upon the nature of the other groups attached to carbon, the most common compounds containing the carbonyl group are aldehydes (X and Y = H; X = H, Y = alkyl or aryl), ketones (X and Y = alkyl or aryl), carboxylic acids (X = OH, Y = H, alkyl, or aryl), esters (X = O-alkyl or aryl; Y = H, alkyl, or aryl), and amides (X = N—H, N-alkyl, or N-aryl; Y = H, alkyl, or aryl). Other compounds that contain the carbonyl group are acid halides, acid anhydrides, lactones, and lactams. *See* ACID ANHYDRIDE; ACID HALIDE; ALDEHYDE; AMIDE; ESTER; KETONE; LACTONE.

The direct introduction of the carbonyl group (carbonylation) has been accomplished by the reaction of alkenes with a mixture of carbon monoxide and hydrogen (synthesis gas) in the presence of metal carbonyls, of which the cobalt derivatives are the most important. This industrially important process, known as the oxo process, is shown in the reaction below. It is a principal commercial source of straight-chain aldehydes.

$$RCH=CH_2 + CO + H_2 \xrightarrow{CO_2(CO)_8} RH_2C-CH_2CH\overset{\displaystyle O}{\overset{\displaystyle \|}{}}$$

Another mode of direct introduction is by the action of Grignard reagents with carbon dioxide, which produces carboxylic acids. Formally, this reaction is analogous to the fixation of carbon dioxide in plants to produce glucose and fructose and ultimately starch and cellulose. *See* CARBOXYLIC ACID; GRIGNARD REACTION.

Indirectly, the carbonyl group can be introduced by the oxidation of primary and secondary alcohols, the former a source of aldehydes and carboxylic acids, and the latter of ketones. The hydrolysis of organic cyanides is another source of carboxylic acids.

The presence of a carbonyl group in a molecule often leads to highly desirable properties of taste and odor. Thus a large number of flavoring and perfume components are carbonyl compounds. Familiar examples are oil of spearmint, oil of peppermint, oil of cloves, oil of vanilla, and camphor. *See* ESSENTIAL OILS.

Most of the important materials of nature, including fats and oils, steroids, proteins, many carbohydrates, and other such familiar compounds as caffeine, aspirin, and pencillin, contain the carbonyl group. *See* ASPIRIN; CAFFEINE; CARBOHYDRATE; FAT AND OIL; PROTEIN; STEROID.

Synthetic fibers such as nylon and Dacron, acrylic plastics and latexes, and many adhesives and paper finishes are polymeric materials containing carbonyl groups, principally of the amide and ester type. *See* MANUFACTURED FIBER; POLYMER.

All the compounds containing this functional group are referred to in a general way as carbonyl compounds. It is important, however, to distinguish these compounds from a large group formed from metals and carbon monoxide, which are known as metal carbonyls. In these latter compounds, there is only one group attached to the carbon in addition to the oxygen, and the carbon atom is viewed as triply bonded to the oxygen. *See* METAL CARBONYL.

Jeremiah P. Freeman

Bibliography. R. T. Morrison and R. N. Boyd, *Organic Chemistry*, 7th ed., 2000; S. E. Patai and Z. Rappoport, *Chemistry of Enones and Related Compounds*, 1989; M. B. Smith and J. March, *March's Advanced Organic Chemistry: Reactions, Mechanisms, and Structure*, 5th ed., 2001.

Carborane

A cluster compound containing both carbon (C) and boron (B) atoms as well as hydrogen (H) atoms external to the framework of the cluster. A cluster compound is one with insufficient electrons to allow for classical two-center two-electron bonds between all adjacent atoms. Sometimes the term carborane is used as a synonym for *closo*-1,2-$C_2B_{10}H_{12}$, commonly referred to as *ortho*-carborane. Carboranes are of interest because of their nonclassical bonding, their relatively high thermal stability, and their ability, when containing the ^{10}B isotope, to capture neutrons efficiently. *See* BORANE.

Structure. The structures of carboranes are based upon a series of three-dimensional, cagelike geometric shapes possessing triangulated faces; such shapes are termed delta polyhedra. The structure for any given carborane may be predicted by determining the framework electrons, by determining the number of electrons involved in bonding the boron and carbon atoms of the cluster framework together, and by using Wade's rule. Wade's rule states that a cluster containing n framework electrons will be derived from a delta polyhedron containing $(n-2)/2$

vertices, the parent cluster. Once this parent cluster has been determined, the geometry of the cluster framework may be predicted by clipping off vertices from the parent cluster until a polyhedron whose number of vertices is equivalent to the sum of boron and carbon atoms in the cluster framework is obtained.

Carboranes are placed, according to their structure, into several classifications. The most common classifications are closo (closed), nido (nestlike), and arachno (cobweb). If a carborane's framework structure is that of a closed delta polyhedron, the carborane is said to be a *closo*-carborane. If a carborane's framework structure is that of a closed delta polyhedron minus one or two vertices, the carborane is said to be a *nido*- or *arachno*-carborane, respectively.

The carborane *nido*-$C_2B_4H_8$ can be used as an example for predicting the structure of a carborane. The first step is to sum all the electrons for the compound: the eight valence electrons of the two carbon atoms (four each), the 12 valence electrons of the four boron atoms (three each), and the eight valence electrons of the eight hydrogen atoms (one each). There is then a total of 28 valence electrons contained in *nido*-$C_2B_4H_8$. In the second step, the number of framework electrons is calculated, assuming that each carbon atom and each boron atom contains one bond to a hydrogen atom that is directed away from the center of the cluster, that is, a terminal hydrogen atom. For *nido*-$C_2B_4H_8$, six terminal hydrogen atoms are assumed. Then, since terminal hydrogen atoms are not involved in holding the cluster framework together, for each terminal hydrogen two electrons (the number of electrons involved in the bond between carbon or boron and the terminal hydrogen) are subtracted from the total number of valence electrons to obtain the number of cluster framework electrons—16 framework electrons for *nido*-$C_2B_4H_8$. Third, the number of vertices in the parent cluster can then be calculated by using Wade's formula, where $n = 16$, and the number of vertices $= (16 - 2)/2 = 7$. Therefore, the structure of *nido*-$C_2B_4H_8$ is derived from a seven-vertex delta polyhedron (**Fig. 1**: seven vertices, closo column). However, since the sum of carbon and boron atoms in the cluster framework is only six, one of the vertices of the seven-vertex delta polyhedron must be removed. The result is a framework structure containing a plane of five atoms capped by one atom, a pentagonal pyramid (Fig. 1: six vertices, nido column). The nonterminal hydrogen atoms are then distributed as bridging hydrogen atoms between boron atoms about the open face that resulted from the removal of the vertex from the parent cluster. The structures of other carboranes may be predicted in a similar manner.

Isomers. Since the framework structures of carboranes are based upon multivertex polyhedra, it might be expected that isomers exist in which the arrangement of the carbon and boron atoms within the cluster framework varies. Indeed, this type of isomerism is commonly observed. For carboranes containing two carbon atoms in the framework structure, dicarbon carboranes, the isomer with adjacent carbon atoms is frequently the one initially synthesized, although it is rarely, if ever, the thermodynamically preferred isomer. Typically, the thermodynamically preferred isomer in dicarbon carboranes is the one in which the carbon atoms have moved as far apart within the cluster as possible. Three isomers of *closo*-$C_2B_{10}H_{12}$ result from moving the carbons farther apart from one another (**Fig. 2**). *See* MOLECULAR ISOMERISM.

Numbering. The rules for numbering carboranes can be quite complicated; however, following is a brief explanation of the numbering employed here. The numbers directly preceding the carbon atoms in a formula indicate the numbers assigned to those carbon atoms. For example, in the formula *closo*-1,2-$C_2B_{10}H_{12}$ the 1 and 2 indicate that the carbon atoms have been assigned as atoms 1 and 2. A functional group immediately following a number in a formula indicates that the functional group is bound to the atom assigned that number. For example, in the formula *closo*-1-R-2-R'-1,2-$C_2B_{10}H_{10}$ the 1 preceding the functional group R indicates that it is bound to carbon 1, while the 2 preceding the functional group R' indicates that it is bound to carbon 2. *See* STRUCTURAL CHEMISTRY.

Bonding. The bonding within a carborane can be thought of in terms of localized atomic orbitals forming both classical two-center two-electron bonds and nonclassical three-center two-electron bonds. Each vertex boron and carbon atom can be thought of as being sp^3 hybridized, with three of these hybrid orbitals of each vertex atom employed in framework bonding (**Fig. 3**). Employing this simple approach, the bonding within carboranes can be represented by employing resonance structures. For example, *nido*-$C_2B_4H_8$ exhibits three resonance structures (**Fig. 4**). The existence of resonance structures implies a delocalization of electron density throughout the cluster framework. Indeed, carboranes exhibit a high degree of electron density delocalization, and their bonding can be described more accurately by employing molecular orbital theory. *See* CHEMICAL BONDING; DELOCALIZATION; MOLECULAR ORBITAL THEORY; RESONANCE (MOLECULAR STRUCTURE).

Preparation. The typical synthesis of a carborane involves the reaction of a boron hydride cluster, containing only boron and hydrogen, with an alkyne. The resulting carborane contains two carbon atoms in its skeletal structure, a dicarbon carborane. The dicarbon carboranes, because of their relative ease of preparation, have been the most widely studied group of carboranes. In particular, *closo*-1,2-$C_2B_{10}H_{12}$, the most readily available carborane, has been extensively studied. Other common groups of carboranes include the monocarbon and tetracarbon carboranes. In order to illustrate the general synthetic routes to carboranes, the synthesis of several common mono-, di-, and tetracarbon carboranes are described below. *See* ALKYNE.

Monocarbon carboranes. There are two common routes to the monocarbon carboranes. One in-

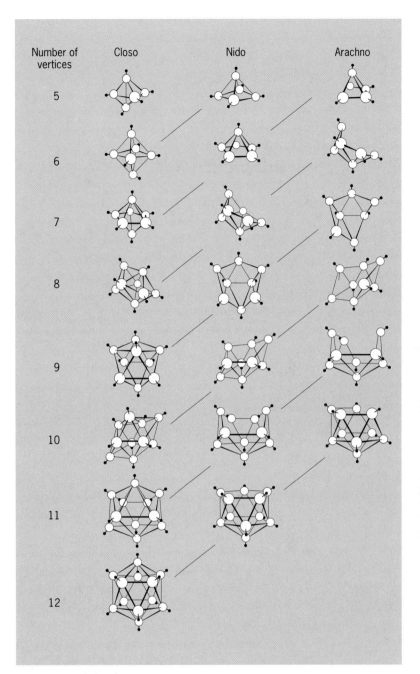

Fig. 1. Parent clusters from which carborane structures are determined. The diagonal lines define series of related closo, nido, and arachno structures.

volves the incorporation of the carbon atom of $[B_{10}H_{13}CN]^{2-}$ into the skeletal structure [reaction (1)], and the other involves the degradation of [*nido*-7,9-$C_2B_{10}H_{13}$]$^-$ [reactions (2) and (3)].

$$B_{10}H_{14} + 2NaCN \xrightarrow{-HCN} Na_2B_{10}H_{13}CN \xrightarrow{H^+}$$

$$B_{10}C(NH_3)H_{12} \xrightarrow[2.\ H_2O]{(CH_3)_2SO_4 \quad 1.\ Na} [CB_{10}H_{13}]^- \quad (1)$$

$$[C_2B_{10}H_{13}]^- \xrightarrow[N(CH_3)_3]{C_4H_8O_{(aq)}}$$

$$9\text{-}CH_3\text{-}8\text{-}(CH_3)_3N\text{-}arachno\text{-}6\text{-}CB_9H_{12} \xrightarrow[K_2CO_3]{(CH_3)_2CO}$$

$$9\text{-}CH_3\text{-}8\text{-}(CH_3)_3N\text{-}nido\text{-}6\text{-}CB_9H_{10} \quad (2)$$

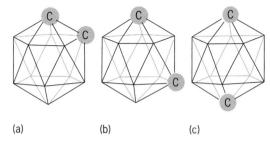

Fig. 2. Skeletal structures of the (*a*) 1,2-, (*b*) 1,7-, and (*c*) 1,12-isomers of $C_2B_{10}H_{12}$.

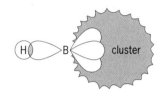

Fig. 3. Vertex boron atom with the three *sp*^{3} orbitals that it employs in cluster bonding. The BH unit contributes three orbitals and only two electrons to the bonding that holds the cluster together (framework bonding).

$$[C_2B_{10}H_{13}]^- \xrightarrow[(CH_3)_2S]{H_3O^+} \xrightarrow{[BH_4]^-} [CB_9H_{12}]^- \quad (3)$$

Dicarbon carboranes. The most common carboranes are the 12-vertex carboranes, *closo*-1,2-$C_2B_{10}H_{12}$ and its carbon-substituted derivatives. They are readily prepared by the reaction of acteylene or substituted alkynes with compounds of the form $B_{10}H_{12}L_2$ [where L = CH_3CN or $(CH_3CH_2)_2S$]. Such adducts are readily obtained by the reaction of the appropriate Lewis base with decaborane (14), $B_{10}H_{14}$ [reaction (4)]. Yields of the *closo*-12-vertex carboranes

$$B_{10}H_{14} + 2L \xrightarrow{-H_2}$$
$$B_{10}H_{12}L_2 \xrightarrow{RC\equiv CR'} 1\text{-}R\text{-}2\text{-}R'\text{-}1,2\text{-}C_2B_{10}H_{10} \quad (4)$$

depend upon the substituents R and R′ of the alkyne. With R=R′=H, the yield is typically about 60%. The substituents R and R′ can be any number of functional groups, including acetoxy, alkoxy, alkyl, aryl, carboranyl, dimethylaminomethyl, halomethyl, and

olefin. In all these syntheses, the 1,2-isomers of the corresponding carboranes are obtained.

Another readily prepared class of dicarbon carboranes are the 10-vertex carboranes, *nido*-$C_2B_8H_{12}$ and *closo*-$C_2B_8H_{10}$ and their carbon-substituted derivatives. A convenient method for the preparation of carbon-substituted derivatives, *nido*-5,6-R,R′-5,6-$C_2B_8H_{10}$, is the reaction of the appropriately substituted alkyne with $B_9H_{13} \cdot O(C_2H_5)_2$ as in reaction (5). The reaction proceeds with the

$$B_9H_{13} \cdot O(C_2H_5)_2 \xrightarrow[-B(CR=CR'H)_3]{4\,RC\equiv CR'}$$
$$\textit{nido-}5,6\text{-}R,R'\text{-}5,6\text{-}C_2B_8H_{10} \quad (5)$$

displacement of the $(C_2H_5)_2O$ and the abstraction (removal) of a BH_3 unit, by excess alkyne, from $B_9H_{13} \cdot O(C_2H_5)_2$. The unsubstituted *nido*-5,6-$C_2B_8H_{12}$ is most readily prepared by the aqueous iron(III) chloride oxidation of $[\textit{nido-}7,8\text{-}C_2B_9H_{12}]^-$. The *nido*-5,6-$C_2B_8H_{12}$ obtained by this procedure can then, if desired, be converted to *closo*-1,10-$C_2B_8H_{10}$ by vacuum pyrolysis at 525°C (977°F).

The *nido*-six-vertex carboranes, *nido*-2,3-R_2-2,3-$C_2B_4H_6$, further serve to exemplify the preparation of dicarbon carboranes. This class of carboranes is readily prepared by the reaction of pentaborane with triethylamine and the appropriate alkyne. Carboranes with the functional groups CH_3, C_2H_5, C_3H_7, or $Si(CH_3)_3$ are readily prepared via this method.

Tetracarbon carboranes. The tetracarbon carboranes are unusual in that their structures are not that of a regular delta polyhedron. Instead they are 12-vertex clusters that possess two square and 16 triangular faces (**Fig. 5**). The carboranes 2,3,7,8-R_4-2,3,7,8-$C_4B_8H_8$ are prepared by the oxidative fusion of two 2,3-R_2-2,3-$C_2B_4H_4$ fragments from the metallacarboranes $[R_2C_2B_4H_4]_2FeH_2$, where R = CH_3, C_2H_5, C_3H_7. These tetracarbon carboranes have cluster framework structures (Fig. 5).

Chemistry. The chemistry of *closo*-1,2-$C_2B_{10}H_{12}$ and carboranes derived from it provides a reasonable representation of the entire class of carboranes. The most commonly exploited reaction of *closo*-1,2-$C_2B_{10}H_{12}$ is the deprotonation (removal of hydrogen) of its carbon atoms by a lithium alkyl group. Depending on the stoichiometry of the lithium alkyl employed, either one or both of the carbon atoms may

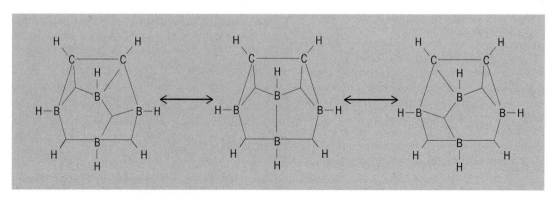

Fig. 4. Three resonance structures of *nido*-$C_2B_4H_8$.

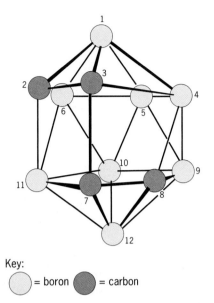

Key:

○ = boron   ● = carbon

Fig. 5. Skeletal structures of the tetracarbon carboranes, $R_4C_4B_8H_8$.

be deprotonated [reactions (6) and (7), where BuLi is

$$1,2\text{-}C_2B_{10}H_{12} + BuLi \longrightarrow$$

$$1\text{-}Li\text{-}1,2\text{-}C_2B_{10}H_{11} + butane \quad (6)$$

$$1,2\text{-}C_2B_{10}H_{12} + BuLi \longrightarrow$$

$$1,2\text{-}Li_2\text{-}1,2\text{-}C_2B_{10}H_{10} + 2\,butane \quad (7)$$

the lithium alkyl]. The resulting lithiated carboranes can then be employed as nucleophiles in a variety of organic reactions.

Closo-1,2-$C_2B_{10}H_{12}$ is thermally robust, that is, not easily degraded by heat, and is isomerized to *closo*-1,7-$C_2B_{10}H_{12}$ upon heating to $450°C$ ($842°F$) under an atmosphere of nitrogen or argon. Even upon heating to $500°C$ ($932°F$) under an atmosphere of nitrogen or argon, no decomposition is observed. However, upon heating to $600°C$ ($1112°F$), significant decomposition occurs and rearrangement to *closo*-1,12-$C_2B_{10}H_{12}$ is observed, the *closo*-1,12-$C_2B_{10}H_{12}$ being obtained in low yield. These 12-vertex carboranes are very resistant to degradation by acid. However, both *closo*-1,2-$C_2B_{10}H_{12}$ and *closo*-1,7-$C_2B_{10}H_{12}$ are degraded by strong bases such as methoxide, resulting in the removal of a BH vertex that is adjacent to both carbon atoms. This base degradation results in the formation of the isomeric [*nido*-7,8-$C_2B_9H_{12}$]$^-$ and [*nido*-7,9-$C_2B_9H_{12}$]$^-$ anions from the 1,2- and 1,7-isomers, respectively (**Fig. 6a,b**).

The two-electron reduction of a *closo*-carborane results in an opening of the cluster framework and the formation of a *nido*-carborane. This type of reductive opening of a cluster is observed when *closo*-1,2-$C_2B_{10}H_{12}$ reacts with sodium metal in solution to form [*nido*-$C_2B_{10}H_{12}$]$^{2-}$ [Fig. 6c].

One unique feature of carboranes is the ability of those with open faces to incorporate a wide variety of atomic groups into vertex positions. Anions of such carboranes are readily capped by a variety of atomic groups representing many of the elements of the periodic table. Additionally, an atom may be sandwiched between two *nido*-carborane anions; such structures are known as sandwich compounds (Fig. 6d).   Thomas D. Getman

Bibliography. J. Casanova, *The Borane, Carborane, Carbocation Continuum*, 1998; R. N. Grimes, *Carboranes*, 1970; J. Plesek, Potential applications of the boron cluster compounds, *Chem. Rev.*, 92:269–278, 1992; B. Stibr, Carboranes other than $C_2B_{10}H_{12}$, *Chem. Rev.*, 92:225–250, 1992; R. E. Williams, The polyborane, carborane, carbocation continuum: Architectural patterns, *Chem. Rev.*, 92:177–207, 1992.

Carboxylic acid

One of a large family of organic substances widely distributed in nature, and characterized by the presence of one or more carboxyl groups (—COOH). These groups typically yield protons in aqueous solution. *See* ACID AND BASE.

In the type formula, R(CXY)$_n$COOH, symbols R, X, and Y can be hydrogen, saturated, or unsaturated groups, carboxyl, alicyclic, or aromatic groups, halogens, or other substituents, and n may vary from zero (formic acid, HCOOH) to more than 100, provided that the normal carbon covalence of four is maintained.

Nomenclature and general properties. According to the International Union of Pure and Applied Chemistry, an acid is named by its relation to the parent hydrocarbon, but in common practice trivial names are used often to indicate the origin of the substance. Thus HCOOH, formic acid (from Latin *formica*, ant), is properly methanoic acid, and $CH_3(CH_2)_7COOH$, pelargonic acid, from the leaves of *Pelargonium roseum*, is nonanoic acid. Substituents are located numerically on the carbon chain, counting the carboxylic carbon as 1, but an older, common method uses Greek letters, beginning with the carbon

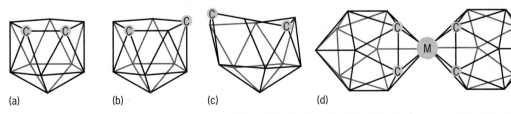

(a)   (b)   (c)   (d)

Fig. 6. Skeletal structures. (a) [*nido*-7,8-$C_2B_9H_{12}$]$^-$. (b) [*nido*-7,9-$C_2B_9H_{12}$]$^-$. (c) [*nido*-$C_2B_{10}H_{12}$]$^{2-}$ anions. (d) ($C_2B_9H_{11}$)$_2$M^{N-4} complexes, where N = oxidation state of the metal.

adjacent to the carboxyl. The following exemplifies both systems:

$$\underset{6}{CH_2}OH\underset{5}{CH_2}\underset{4}{CHBr}\underset{3}{CHBr}\underset{2}{CH_2}\underset{1}{COOH}$$
$$\overset{\epsilon}{}\overset{\delta}{}\overset{\gamma}{}\overset{\beta}{}\overset{\alpha}{}$$

is 3,4-dibromo-6-hydroxyhexanoic acid, or β,γ-dibromo-ϵ-hydroxycaproic acid. *See* ORGANIC CHEMISTRY.

Physical and chemical properties of carboxylic acids are represented, grossly, by the resultant of the various chemical groupings present in the molecule. A short-chain aliphatic acid, wherein the carboxyl is dominant, is a pungent, corrosive, water-soluble liquid of abnormally high boiling point (because of molecular association), with specific gravity close to 1 (higher for formic and acetic acids). With increasing molecular weight, the hydrocarbon grouping overbalances the carboxyl; sharpness of odor diminishes, boiling and melting points rise, the specific gravity falls toward that of the parent hydrocarbon, and the water-solubility decreases. Thus the typical high-molecular-weight saturated acid is a bland, wax-like solid.

Ionization and acidity. Ionization occurs on exposure to a proton acceptor (base, in the Brønsted-Lowry sense); in water the opposing equations shown in reaction (1) describe the fundamental equi-

$$R(CXY)_nCOOH + H_2O \rightleftharpoons R(CXY)_nCOO^- + H_3O^+ \qquad (1)$$

librium encountered with any feebly ionized, or weak, acid. Hydration of the proton to form H_3O^+ is virtually complete; thus, the process of ionization is analogous to that of neutralization, the degree to which ionization proceeds varying directly with the basicity of the solvent (proton acceptor), and inversely with the O-H bond strength of the carboxylic hydroxyl group.

The above equilibrium leads to the dissociation constant K_a defined as reaction (2), wherein the square brackets signify concentration, measured in

$$K_a = \frac{[H_3O^+][R(CXY)_nCOO^-]}{[R(CXY)_nCOOH]} \qquad (2)$$

moles per liter of solution. With simple, saturated acids, wherein X and Y are hydrogen, the value of K_a is always small (acetic acid, 1.75×10^{-5}), which means that simple organic acids are only slightly ionized in aqueous solution. However, the degree of dissociation is sensitive to electronegative (electron-attracting) substituents, particularly when located on the α- or 2-carbon (for example, K_a for trichloroacetic acid, 1.3×10^{-1}). *See* IONIC EQUILIBRIUM.

Table 1 presents a list of 30 saturated, monocarboxylic acids, together with their important constants and main sources.

Structure and properties. The un-ionized carboxyl group has been shown via many classical studies to have the structure

in which carbon 2 is doubly bonded to oxygen 1 and singly bonded to oxygen 2. Geometrical considerations lead to the conclusions that distance

$$\underset{2}{C}=\underset{1}{O}$$

should be shorter than

$$\underset{2}{C}-\underset{2}{O}$$

and the angle

$$\underset{1}{C}-\underset{2}{C}=\underset{1}{O}$$

should be greater than angle

$$\underset{1}{C}-\underset{2}{C}-\underset{2}{O}$$

This is confirmed by measurements on crystalline acids, although the fact that the single bond

$$\underset{2}{C}-\underset{2}{O}$$

never reaches the normal length (about 0.144 nm) means that some resonance is involved between the two forms

In the ionized state, however, the two resonating forms of the anion are electronically equivalent,

and the actual structure of the carboxylate ion is a stable hybrid of these.. *See* RESONANCE (MOLECULAR STRUCTURE).

In the free state (solid, liquid, or gas), the lower acids tend to exist as dimers, in which two molecules are associated through relatively weak hydrogen bonds (energy about 5 kcal/mole):

The hydrogen bonds (indicated by dotted valences) account for the abnormally high boiling points of the smaller acids. With longer-chain acids (from C_8) there is a tendency toward polymorphism, ascribable to hydrogen bonding of the following type:

As determined by x-ray diffraction studies, the carboxyl and terminal methyl groups of acids containing an odd number of carbons are on the same side of

TABLE 1. Saturated monocarboxylic acids

Name	Formula	Main source*	Melting point, °C (°F)	Boiling point, °C (°F)
Formic	HCOOH	S	8.4 (47.1)	100.5 (212.9)
Acetic	CH_3COOH	S and fermentation	16.7 (62.1)	118.1 (244.6)
Propionic	CH_3CH_2COOH	S	−22.0 (−7.6)	141.0 (285.8)
Butyric	$CH_3(CH_2)_2COOH$	F, S, and ferm.	−4.7 (23.5)	164.1 (327.4)
Valeric	$CH_3(CH_2)_3COOH$	S and *Valeriana officinalls*	−34.5 (−30.1)	186.4 (367.5)
Isovaleric	$(CH_3)_2CHCH_2COOH$	F and S	−29.3 (−20.7)	176.5 (349.7)
Caproic	$CH_3(CH_2)_4COOH$	F and S and by-product in butyric fermentation	−1.5 (29.3)	205.8 (442.4)
Heptanoic	$CH_3(CH_2)_5COOH$	S from heptaldehyde	−7.5 (18.5)	223.0 (433.4)
Caprylic	$CH_3(CH_2)_6COOH$	F and S; goat's butter	16.3 (61.3)	239.7 (463.5)
Pelargonic	$CH_3(CH_2)_7COOH$	S; oxidation of oleic and *Pelargonium roseum*	12.5 (54.5)	255.6 (492.1)
Capric	$CH_3(CH_2)_8COOH$	F; coconut; palm kernel oils	31.5 (88.7)	268.7 (515.7)
Undecylic	$CH_3(CH_2)_9COOH$	S; reduction of undecenoic acid	29.3 (84.7)	228 (442)/21 kPa
Lauric	$CH_3(CH_2)_{10}COOH$	F; coconut and laurel oils	44.1 (111.4)	225 (437)/13 kPa
Tridecylic	$CH_3(CH_2)_{11}COOH$	S	41.0 (105.8)	236 (457)/13 kPa
Myristic	$CH_3(CH_2)_{12}COOH$	F; nutmeg oil	58.0 (136.4)	250 (482)/13 kPa
Pentadecylic	$CH_3(CH_2)_{13}COOH$	S	54.0 (129.2)	257 (495)/13 kPa
Palmitic	$CH_3(CH_2)_{14}COOH$	F; palm and olive oils	62.8 (145.0)	271.5 (520.7)/13 kPa
Margaric	$CH_3(CH_2)_{15}COOH$	S	59.9 (139.8)	227 (441)/13 kPa
Stearic	$CH_3(CH_2)_{16}COOH$	F; tallow and reduction of oleic acid	69.9 (157.8)	291 (556)/15 kPa
Nonadecylic	$CH_3(CH_2)_{17}COOH$	S	66.5 (151.7)	298 (568)/13 kPa
Arachidic	$CH_3(CH_2)_{18}COOH$	F; peanut oil	77.0 (170.6)	205 (401)/130 Pa
Heneicosanoic	$CH_3(CH_2)_{19}COOH$	S	75.2 (167.4)	
Behenic	$CH_3(CH_2)_{20}COOH$	F; reduction of erucic acid	80.2 (176.3)	306 (583)/8 kPa
Tricosanoic	$CH_3(CH_2)_{21}COOH$	S	79.1 (174.4)	
Lignoceric	$CH_3(CH_2)_{22}COOH$	F; *Adenanthera pavonina* seed; beechwood tar; rotten oak	84.2 (183.6)	
Pentacosanoic	$CH_3(CH_2)_{23}COOH$	S	83.0 (181.4)	
Cerotic	$CH_3(CH_2)_{24}COOH$	Beeswax; carnauba wax	87.7 (189.9)	
Heptacosanoic	$CH_3(CH_2)_{25}COOH$	S	87.6 (189.7)	
Montanic	$CH_3(CH_2)_{26}COOH$	Montan wax from lignite	90.9 (195.6)	
Nonacosanoic	$CH_3(CH_2)_{27}COOH$	S	90.3 (194.5)	
Melissic	$CH_3(CH_2)_{28}COOH$	Beeswax	93.6 (200.5)	

*S stands for synthetic, meaning that the acid is manufactured commercially by one or more methods. F stands for fats; the fatty acids comprise a group of carboxylic acids, both saturated and unsaturated, which may be obtained by hydrolysis of animal or vegetable fats and oils.

the molecule; with acids containing an even number of carbons, these groups are on opposite sides, permitting closer packing in the crystal lattice and consequent increased van der Waals forces. Thus, the melting point of any even-numbered acid lies above that of the preceding and following odd-numbered acid.

Structural variations. These are of two types: those not involving the carboxyl group, and those involving the carboxyl, leading to the acid derivatives.

In the first type are such distinctive classes as branched-chain acids, for example, pivalic acid, $(CH_3)_3CCOOH$; alicyclic acids, for example, cyclopropane carboxylic acid,

halogenated acids, fluoro, chloro, or bromo, rarely, iodo; hydroxy acids; dicarboxylic and polycarboxylic acids; aromatic acids; β-keto acids or amino acids. *See* AMINO ACIDS; BENZOIC ACID; LACTAM; LACTONE; PROTEIN; TARTARIC ACID.

An important class of acids contains unsaturated

groups, for example, acrylic acid ($CH_2{=}CHCOOH$). Acids of this type are unstable and polymerize readily; hence they and their esters are much studied. *See* POLYACRYLATE RESIN.

Among the variations involving the carboxyl group are found many important classes of substances, derived from acids by suitable substitution within the carboxylic group. Thus, replacement of the hydroxyl group with alkoxyl gives esters; replacement of OH by halogen forms acid halides; substitution of OH by amino (NH_2) group gives amides; intermolecular dehydration of two acids generates the anhydride structure

and the hydrolysis of long-chain esters by alkali hydroxides forms soaps. *See* ACID ANHYDRIDE; ACID HALIDE; ACYLATION; AMIDE; DETERGENT; ESTER; FAT AND OIL; SOAP; UREA; WAX, ANIMAL AND VEGETABLE.

Table 2 lists some important dicarboxylic acids, aromatic acids, and unsaturated acids, together with their important physical constants.

Table 2. Dicarboxylic, aromatic, and unsaturated acids

Name	Formula*	Melting point, °C (°F)*	Boiling point, °C (°F)*
Dicarboxylic acids			
Oxalic	HOOC—COOH	189.5 (373.1) (dec)	
Malonic	$CH_2(COOH)_2$	135 (275) (dec)	
Succinic	$(CH_2)_2(COOH)_2$	185–187 (365–369)	235 (455)
Glutaric	$(CH_2)_3(COOH)_2$	98.0 (208)	302–304 (576–579)
Adipic	$(CH_2)_4(COOH)_2$	152 (306)	337.5 (639.5)
Pimelic	$(CH_2)_5(COOH)_2$	105–107 (221–225) (subl)	272 (522) at 13 kPa
Suberic	$(CH_2)_6(COOH)_2$	142 (288)	279 (534) at 13 kPa
Azelaic	$(CH_2)_7(COOH)_2$	106.5 (223.7)	286 (547) at 13 kPa
Sebacic	$(CH_2)_8(COOH)_2$	134 (273)	295 (563) at 13 kPa
Aromatic acids			
Benzoic	C_6H_5COOH	121.7 (251.1)	249 (480)
o-Toluic	*o*-$CH_3C_6H_4COOH$	104 (219)	259 (498) at 100 kPa
m-Toluic	*m*-$CH_3C_6H_4COOH$	111 (232)	263 (505)
p-Toluic	*p*-$CH_3C_6H_4COOH$	180 (356)	275 (527)
o-Ethylbenzoic	*o*-$C_2H_5C_6H_4COOH$	68 (154)	259 (498) at 100 kPa
m-Ethylbenzoic	*m*-$C_2H_5C_6H_4COOH$	47 (117)	
p-Ethylbenzoic	*p*-$C_2H_5C_6H_4COOH$	113 (235)	
o-Fluorobenzoic	*o*-FC_6H_4COOH	122 (252)	
m-Fluorobenzoic	*m*-FC_6H_4COOH	124 (255)	
p-Fluorobenzoic	*p*-FC_6H_4COOH	182–184 (360–363)	
o-Chlorobenzoic	*o*-ClC_6H_4COOH	140.2 (284.4)	
m-Chlorobenzoic	*m*-ClC_6H_4COOH	154.3 (309.7)	
p-Chlorobenzoic	*p*-ClC_6H_4COOH	239.7 (463.5)	Subl
o-Bromobenzoic	*o*-BrC_6H_4COOH	148–150 (298–302)	Subl
m-Bromobenzoic	*m*-BrC_6H_4COOH	154–155 (309–311)	
p-Bromobenzoic	*p*-BrC_6H_4COOH	251–253 (484–487)	
o-Iodobenzoic	*o*-IC_6H_4COOH	162 (324)	
o-Iodobenzoic	*o*-IC_6H_4COOH	162 (324)	
m-Iodobenzoic	*m*-IC_6H_4COOH	187 (367)	Subl
p-Iodobenzoic	*p*-IC_6H_4COOH	270 (518)	Subl
Salicylic	*o*-HOC_6H_4COOH	158.3 (316.9)	211 (412) at 2.7 kPa
m-Hydroxybenzoic	*m*-HOC_6H_4COOH	201 (394)	
p-Hydroxybenzoic	*p*-HOC_6H_4COOH	215 (419)	
Gallic	3,4,5-$(HO)_3C_6H_4COOH$	235 (455) (dec)	
Anthranilic	*o*-$H_2NC_6H_4COOH$	144–145 (291–293)	Subl
m-Anthranilic	*m*-$H_2NC_6H_4COOH$	173–174 (343–345)	
p-Anthranilic	*p*-$H_2NC_6H_4COOH$	187–188 (369–370)	
α-Naphthoic	α-$C_{10}H_7COOH$	160–161 (320–322)	300 (572)
β-Naphthoic	β-$C_{10}H_7COOH$	184 (363)	>300 (572)
Unsaturated acids			
Acrylic	$CH_2{=}CH—COOH$	14 (57)	141
Crotonic (trans)	$CH_3CH{=}CHCOOH$	71.6 (161)	185
i-Crotonic (cis)		15.5 (59.9)	
Mesaconic (trans)	$HOOC{=}CHCOOH$ (with CH_3)	202 (396)	250 (482) (dec)
Citraconic (cis)		91 (196)	
Tiglic (trans)	$CH_3CH{=}CCOOH$ (with CH_3)	64 (147)	198 (388)
Angelic (cis)		45 (133)	185 (365)
Cinnamic (trans)	$C_6H_5CH{=}CHCOOH$	133 (271)	300 (572)
Allocinnamic (cis)		68 (154)	125 (257) at 2.4 kPa
Fumaric (trans)	$HOOCCH{=}CHCOOH$	287 (549)	
Maleic (cis)		130 (266)	
Elaidic (trans)	$CH_3(CH_2)_7CH{=}HOOC(CH_2)_7CH$	44 (111)	288 (550) at 13 kPa
Oleic (cis)		13 (55)	288 (550) at 13 kPa

*dec = decomposes, subl = sublimes.

Reactions and uses. Acids are used in large quantities in the production of esters, acid halides, acid amides, and acid anhydrides. Decarboxylation of acids to form hydrocarbons containing one less carbon is accomplished by pyrolyzing the sodium or barium salt with soda lime. If the potassium salt is electrolyzed at a platinum anode (Kolbe electrolysis), the hydrocarbon RCH_2CH_2R is produced by the acid $RCH_2COO^-K^+$. Ethylenic and acetylenic acids containing unsaturation α,β to the carboxyl are easily decarboxylated by heat. Aromatic acids, such as benzoic and toluic, are frequently used as sources of hydrocarbons; the decarboxylation is effected by treating the acid in boiling quinoline with a copper powder catalyst.

Many acids obtained by acid hydrolysis of fats or waxes are reduced to the corresponding alcohols, for example, lauric acid to lauryl alcohol. The reaction is carried out in the laboratory by means of lithium aluminum hydride; the industrial procedure utilizes hydrogen at elevated temperatures, over a mixed catalyst of the oxides of copper and chromium.

Acids find use in the manufacture of soaps and detergents, in thickening lubricating greases (stearate soaps), in modifying rigidity in plastics, in compounding buffing bricks and abrasives, and in the manufacture of crayons, dictaphone cylinders, and phonograph records. The solvent action of acids finds use in manufacture of carbon paper, inks, and in the compounding of synthetic and natural rubber. Because of the stability of saturated fatty acids toward oxidation, these are often used as solvents for carrying out oxidation reactions upon the sensitive compounds.   Evans B. Reid

Carburetor

The device that controls the power output and fuel feed of internal combustion spark-ignition engines generally used for automotive, aircraft, and auxiliary services. Its duties include control of the engine power by the air throttle; metering, delivery, and mixing of fuel in the airstream; and graduating the fuel-air ratio according to engine requirements in starting, idling, and load and altitude changes. The fuel is usually gasoline or similar liquid hydrocarbon compounds, although some engines with a carburetor may also operate on a gaseous fuel such as propane or compressed natural gas. A carburetor may be classified as having either a fixed venturi, in which the diameter of the air opening ahead of the throttle valve remains constant, or a variable venturi, which changes area to meet the changing demand. *See* AUTOMOBILE; ENGINE; FUEL SYSTEM; VENTURI TUBE.

Engine air charge. A simple updraft carburetor with a fixed venturi illustrates basic carburetor action (**Fig. 1**). Intake air charge, at full or reduced atmospheric pressure as controlled by the throttle, is drawn into the cylinder by the downward motion of the piston to mix with the unscavenged exhaust remaining in the cylinder from the previous combustion. The total air-charge weight per unit time is approximately proportional to the square root of its pressure drop in the carburetor venturi (with a square-root correction, direct for change in air pressure, and inverse for change in air absolute temperature). Also, each individual cylinder air-charge volume follows the intake pressure minus about one-sixth the exhaust pressure, so that the intake

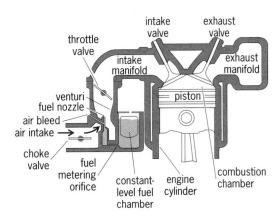

Fig. 1. Elements that basically determine air and fuel charges received by the engine through the carburetor.

manifold pressure and temperature are often taken as an approximate indication of the engine torque; this factor multiplied by the engine speed is similarly taken as a measure of the engine power output. Any given fixed part-throttle opening gives higher intake manifold pressure, increased individual-cylinder air charge, and greater engine torque, as the engine speed is decreased. *See* TORQUE.

A cylinder is most completely filled with the fuel-air mixture when no other cylinder is drawing in through the same intake passage at the same time. For high speed, best power is usually obtained with multiple carburetor and intake passages. However, on an engine so equipped, it is often difficult to throttle all the cylinders equally. *See* VOLUMETRIC EFFICIENCY.

Fuel charge. The fuel is usually metered through a calibrated orifice, or jet, at a differential pressure derived from the pressure drop in a venturi in the intake air passage. Since this fuel flow also follows the square root of its differential pressure, the fuel and air rates tend to be accurately parallel, particularly if a small bleed of air is fed into the fuel delivery or spray nozzle to overcome the retarding effect of surface tension.

Fuel-air requirements. For normal steady speed, the limits of consistent ignition lie between 0.055 and 0.09 fuel-air by weight (**Fig. 2**). Richer mixtures (more fuel) give higher power, apparently cooler combustion, and less detonation. Leaner mixtures (less fuel) give better fuel economy. *See* COMBUSTION; COMBUSTION CHAMBER.

A narrowly controlled rich mixture is required for idling because low charge densities and relatively high contamination with residual exhaust gas make combustion conditions unfavorable. Individual adjustments may be provided both for the idling fuel feed and for the throttle closure stop to keep the engine running at minimum speed. Slight intake or exhaust valve leaks can make smooth idling impossible.

Cold-engine operation. Engine fuels are a mixture of components varying in volatility, usually selected so that they evaporate completely in the intake manifold at ordinary operating temperatures at the reduced pressures of part throttle, but not at full throttle. For starting at low temperatures and for the first

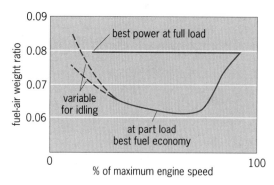

Fig. 2. **Fuel-air ratios required for engine operation.**

few ignitions with cylinder walls cold, a great increase in fuel feed is momentarily required since only the most volatile part of the fuel can vaporize and burn. *See* GASOLINE.

The higher metering suction necessary to give the excess fuel feed required for cold starting may be created by a manually or automatically operated choke valve. Partial closure of this valve also yields the moderate enrichment needed during warmup. An additional linkage is generally supplied on automotive carburetors so that pressing the accelerator pedal all the way down will open the choke valve and permit return to normal fuel feed.

Automotive carburetion. An automotive engine performs through a wider range of loads and speeds than most prime movers. Furthermore, its transient response to changes of load is highly important. For these reasons, the functions of an automotive carburetor are complex. The multiple main and boost venturi structure is used to increase the fuel metering force for a given air delivery; also, it yields better metering regulation at the higher air velocities.

Idling system. To obtain adequate metering forces at low air speeds and small throttle openings, the fuel passes through the main metering jet and is bypassed to an idle metering jet. Then the fuel mixes with air bled in through the idle air bleed, and this fuel and air are delivered to an idle port in the high suction at the edge of the throttle valve. Some graduation of fuel feed from low to high idling speed is obtained as the throttle valve edge passes across the idle port, which may include multiple delivery holes.

Because of increased piston and other friction with a cold engine, a greater throttle opening as well as more fuel is required for idle at that time. The choke valve is usually interconnected so that, in its partly closed or cold-engine position, the minimum-throttle area is increased.

Power enrichment. The richer fuel feeds necessary for best power are customarily obtained by varying the area of the main metering jet, using a valve responsive to intake manifold pressure beyond the throttle. At light loads the lowered manifold pressure draws the enrichment valve down. A rise in manifold pressure resulting either from a drop in engine speed or added throttle opening will allow the plunger spring to open the metering jet further. An approximation of this function is obtained in some carburetors by mechanical linkage between the enrichment valve and the throttle valve. On most carbureted automotive engines with a catalytic converter, the enrichment valve is computer controlled to help maintain stoichiometry.

Transitional requirements. Proper regulation under change of throttle is a major problem in obtaining good carburetor action. Any lag in evaporation of the fuel when the throttle is opened tends to give a momentary delay in power response, which is usually compensated by an accelerator pump. The pump gives a quick squirt of fuel as the throttle is opened. The apparent willingness of the engine to respond to the accelerator pedal is largely determined by how accurately the accelerator pump discharge is proportioned to the existing engine temperature and to the volatility of the fuel.

A converse transitional problem is associated with sudden closing of the throttle, when wet fuel is present on the intake manifold walls. The sudden drop in pressure causes the liquid to flash into vapor, resulting in a temporarily overrich condition in the cylinder, with subsequent misfiring and incompletely burned combustion products in the exhaust. Better manifold heating helps, as does injection of fuel at cylinder intake ports. *See* FUEL INJECTION.

Aircraft carburetion. Early aviation carburetors followed automobile carburetor practice, but in the 1940s the pressure or injection type came into use. These incorporated the following advantages:

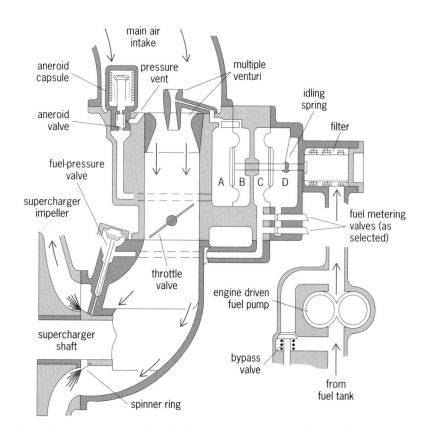

Fig. 3. **Schematic diagram of an aircraft injection-type or pressure-type carburetor.**

(1) The whole metering system is kept under pressure, to prevent formation of bubbles and disturbances to the metering under the reduced pressures at higher altitudes. (2) The fuel spray can be delivered into a heated part of the intake system so that ice formation resulting from fuel evaporation becomes impossible. (3) Correction of the metering function under changes of altitude and temperature is automatically provided. (4) The closed system avoids disturbance of the fuel metering, or leakage from vents, during vigorous maneuvers of the airplane.

In the most commonly used form, the metering function of the automobile carburetor is retained. The fuel metering differential (**Fig. 3**) is derived from the multiple venturi air differential by the system of opposed synthetic-rubber diaphragms. The idling spring adds a small positive increment to provide the required rich idle fuel flow.

The fuel pressure in the carburetor is held to a desired value above the surrounding atmosphere by the fuel-pressure valve and its regulating diaphragm and spring. Beyond the pressure valve the fuel may be led to a spinner ring which has multiple discharge orifices. The ring is mounted on, and rotates with, the supercharger shaft. On other installations, the fuel, after metering, is taken to an injection pump which divides the charge equally and delivers a portion at much higher pressure to the interior of each engine cylinder on its intake stroke.

Pressure from the engine-driven fuel pump, as regulated by its bypass valve, must be adequate to maintain flow through the system at the highest powers, but beyond this it does not affect the fuel metering. Fuel-air ratio, as desired for light or full load or as selected by the pilot, is controlled by one or more metering valves which collectively determine the flow area between the two fuel-metering chambers. A variety of combinations have been used, but all are directed toward the regulation illustrated in Fig. 2.

Correction of the fuel-air ratio at increased altitude or temperature is accomplished by differentials. A small fixed-size depression vent is provided between the innermost multiple venturi chamber and the venturi communication channel, while a large pressure vent between the main air intake and the chamber is varied by the aneroid valve. This valve is connected to the aneroid capsule, a metallic bellows filled with inert gas and extended by a spring. As the airplane gains altitude, or as the temperature of the entering air rises, the capsule extends to reduce the area of the entering air vent to the innermost chamber. This action reduces the differential between the multiple venturi chambers at a rate determined by the profile and adjustment of the aneroid valve.

Deviations from the form that provides power enrichment by varying the main metering orifice have been used on smaller aircraft engines. Similar construction has also been used to regulate fuel feed by the parameters of engine speed and intake manifold pressure. This operation is commonly called speed-density metering.

Carburetor icing. There are two reasons for condensation of atmospheric moisture and formation of ice in the intake system. First, at partly closed throttle, the adiabatic pressure drop across the throttle orifice generates a temperature drop. When atmospheric humidity is high, ice sometimes partly clogs the throttle orifice, requiring further throttle opening to keep the engine running for a short period after starting and before the engine heat has had time to build up. With carburetors having a fuel discharge at the throttle edge, the addition of water-soluble antifreeze to the fuel may reduce such icing tendency.

The other source of temperature drop in the intake system is the evaporation of fuel. Ice tends to form wherever fuel spray impinges upon an unheated surface. Such icing was formerly encountered frequently in aircraft operation and was dealt with by heating the intake air, which reduced the engine power and sometimes caused detonation. The problem was largely eliminated by use of the fuel-injection system. *See* FUEL INJECTION.   Donald L. Anglin

Bibliography.   W. H. Crouse and D. L. Anglin, *Automotive Engines*, 1995; J. B. Heywood, *Internal Combustion Engine Fundamentals*, 1988.

Cardamon

A spice from the plant *Elettaria cardamomum* (Zingiberaceae), a perennial herb 6–12 ft (1.8–3.6 m) tall and native to India. The small, light-colored seeds, borne in capsules, have a delicate flavor. An important spice in the Orient for centuries, they are used in curries, cakes, pickles, and in general cooking, as well as in medicine. In India the seeds are a favorite masticatory. *See* SPICE AND FLAVORING; ZINGIBERALES.   Perry D. Strausbaugh; Earl L. Core

Cardiac electrophysiology

The science of the electrical activity of the heart. The heartbeat results from the development and organized control of cardiac excitability, including ionic current flow across the cardiac membrane, within and between cells, and throughout the body, which in turn allows the orderly contraction of heart muscle and the efficient pumping of blood. Alterations in these determinants of normal cardiac excitability may lead to abnormalities in the rhythm of the heart (arrhythmias or dysrhythmias) and in the propagation of electrical impulses throughout the heart (conduction defects). Cellular electrophysiologic events lead to the establishment of extracellular potentials on the surface of the body. Electrocardiographic, vectorcardiographic, and other recording systems are used to determine the orientation and magnitude of that extracellular potential. The normal heart produces characteristic sequences of extracellular potentials that may be altered by disease.

Cellular electrophysiology. Cardiac excitability depends on the interaction among the determinants of the resting potential and both the active and passive cellular properties, which can be considered elements in an electrophysiologic matrix. The inside and outside of a cardiac cell are connected by channels that run through a membrane consisting of a lipid bilayer. Electrochemical gradients are established across the membrane in which the ionic activities differ inside and outside the cell. The extracellular activity of sodium ions (Na^+) and calcium ions (Ca^{2+}) exceeds the intracellular activity, which causes an inward leak; the reverse is true for potassium ion (K^+) activity. Energy-requiring pumps and other exchange mechanisms maintain the distribution of the ionic activities across the membrane. The unequal distribution of each ion species charge across the semipermeable membrane is well described by the Nernst equation, which determines the potential required to oppose the activity gradient and is termed the equilibrium potential (E_{ion}). *See* BIOPOTENTIALS AND IONIC CURRENTS; CELL PERMEABILITY.

Active cellular properties relate to the opening and closing of channels that carry ionic currents, which, in turn, are responsible for rapid depolarization and for both the slow and rapid phases of repolarization. The channels are selectively permeable to different ionic species and are controlled by gates that open and close as a function of voltage, time, or, sometimes, binding by a hormone, drug, or other ligand. The current flow of an ionic species (i_{ion}) depends on the driving force (the difference between the transmembrane voltage, V_m, and the ion's equilibrium potential, E_{ion}) and the membrane conductance (g_{ion}), that is, the ease with which ions pass through the channels. In other words, $i_{ion} = g_{ion}(E_{ion} - V_m)$. Conductance ($g$) is the reciprocal of resistance (R).

Some tissues—such as those in the atria, the Purkinje fibers of the specialized infranodal conduction system, and the ventricles—depend on the inrush of sodium ion current (i_{Na^+}) to produce the phase of rapid depolarization, phase 0. The kinetics of the channel, the inrush of sodium ion current, and the maximum rate of rise of voltage ($\dot{V}_{max}$) during phase 0 are rapid. Thus, these tissues are often called fast-response tissues. Much of what is known about cardiac electrophysiology has been determined by using microelectrodes that are inserted through the cell membrane into the interior of the cell, thus allowing the recording and perturbation of transmembrane voltages (**Fig. 1**). The resting potential (V_r) and subthreshold conductance (before excitation) in fast-response tissues are determined primarily by potassium conductance (g_K). As the cell is depolarized from a resting potential of about −90 millivolts to about −60 mV, a point often termed the threshold voltage (V_{th}), the response becomes regenerative and out of proportion to the stimulus. This regenerative response is called the action potential.

The membrane potential in fast-response tissues depends on a strictly controlled balance between de-

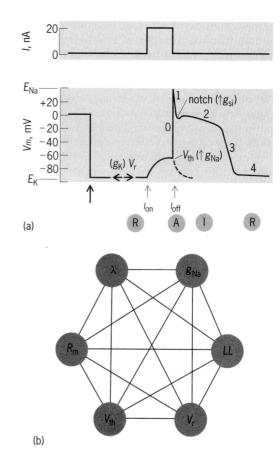

(a)

(b)

Fig. 1. Cellular electrophysiology. (*a*) Oscilloscopic representations of current (*I*) and the transmembrane voltage V_m. When the microelectrode is in the extracellular space, V_m is 0. With impalement of the tissue, V_m falls from 0 to −95 mV (colored vertical arrow) which is the resting potential (V_r). With physiologic extracellular K^+ activities, V_r approximates the potassium equilibrium potential (E_K). Depolarizing current (I_{on}) causes V_m to become more positive and to approach V_{th} for regenerative phase 0 depolarization. If the liminal length requirements are not met, V_m decays exponentially (broken line following I_{off}) because of passive membrane resistive-capacitative properties. Membrane conductances for both resting membrane and subthreshold voltage range are determined primarily by membrane potassium conductance (g_K). If liminal length requirements are met, an action potential results, and the overshoot approaches the equilibrium potential for sodium (E_{Na}). States of the sodium channel are indicated by R (resting), A (open or activated), and I (inactivated). The phases of the action potential are shown, as are the conductances of particular importance to each phase (g_K, g_{Na}, g_{si}). (*b*) Simple matrix of selected active and passive cellular properties that determine cardiac excitability. The determinants depicted include the resting potential (V_r), threshold voltage (V_{th}), sodium conductance (g_{Na}), membrane resistance (R_m), the length constant (λ), and, as a measure of overall excitability, the liminal length (*LL*). Note that each has its own determinants, but other determinants are also important, so that the scheme is multidimensional and more complex than illustrated.

polarizing inward currents, which help maintain the action potential plateau, and repolarizing outward currents, which favor a return to the resting potential. Phase 1 depends on the inactivation of sodium conductance and, in Purkinje fibers, perhaps on the activation of the positive dynamic current, which may be a calcium-activated potassium ion current. Events during phase 2, the plateau phase, are complex. The reduced transmembrane current opens the channel for the mixed calcium ion–sodium ion, or "slow inward," current (i_{si}), which helps maintain the plateau. An inward sodium current, the "window" current, is distinct from that active during phase 0 and helps maintain the plateau. At the transmembrane voltage of the plateau, potassium ion conductance decreases in the outward direction but increases in the inward direction, and thus repolarization is more difficult; this process is called inward rectification. That mechanism helps maintain the plateau. The delayed rectifier potassium current has a slow, rapid, and ultrarapid component termed, respectively, i_{Ks}, i_{Kr}, and i_{Kur}. This rectification mechanism helps maintain the plateau.

Phase 3 repolarization has also been termed the rapid repolarization phase. During phase 3, a rapid return to resting potential results from inactivation of the slow inward current, reversal of the process of inward rectification, and activation of repolarizing outward potassium currents. During this phase, enough of the sodium system is normally reactivated so that another action potential can be electrically induced. Sodium channels may exist in several states: the resting state (R) predominates in normally polarized tissues; the activated state (A) occurs transiently with opening of the sodium channel; and the inactivated state (I) dominates at more positive transmembrane conductance, such as during the plateau or in tissues that have been depolarized because of injury.

Other tissues, such as the sinoatrial (SA) and atrioventricular (AV) nodes, depend on a slow inward current of mixed calcium and sodium ions for phase 0 depolarization. They have been termed slow-response tissues because the current flows through a kinetically slow channel distinct from the channel that controls sodium. Because the channel preferentially carries calcium ions, it is often called the calcium current. Phase 0 in the sinoatrial and atrioventricular nodes normally depends on a slow inward current, and depolarized fast-response tissues may switch over to action potentials dependent on slow inward current. Slow-response tissues have a resting potential of about -60 mV, a transmembrane voltage at which the sodium system is virtually inactivated. The slow channel is voltage-dependent and has resting, active, and inactivated phases. The phase of inactivation depends on both voltage and time and extends into electrical diastole, a characteristic that limits the number of impulses that can transverse the atrioventricular node in atrial fibrillation and flutter.

The cardiac cell has a low-resistance myoplasm surrounded by a membrane that has both capacitive elements and a high resistance; it is analogous to a telegraph cable with a low-resistance core and high-resistance insulation. Cells are connected and communicate with each other through gap junctions, which normally have a low resistance to ionic flow. With injury, gap junction resistance may increase and cells may uncouple—actions mediated by changes in pH and intracellular calcium activity. Membrane insulation is imperfect, and so current leaks out, resulting in a drop in available current for the longitudinal flow of ions through the myoplasm and the gap junctions.

Liminal length. Liminal length is the amount of tissue that must be raised above threshold so that the inward depolarizing current from one region is sufficiently greater than the repolarizing influences of the adjacent tissues to permit regenerative depolarization of neighboring tissues. The liminal length is directly proportional to the charge developed by the active cellular properties and inversely proportional to the membrane capacitance and the length constant. If the liminal length requirements of an element are fulfilled, that element will influence its neighboring element. If the electrotonic influence from the first membrane element is sufficient to bring its adjacent membrane element up to threshold (or, more properly, to fulfill its liminal length requirements), regenerative depolarization and an action potential are produced in the second element. If the electrotonic influence is insufficient, the current continues to decay exponentially. Clearly, cardiac excitability depends both on the current strength created by active cellular properties and on the "sink" of the tissue's cable properties. Each membrane element that fulfills its liminal length requirement will bring about regenerative depolarization, and an action potential will propagate one unit further. Impulse propagation, then, depends on both active and passive cellular properties. Conduction velocity is much more rapid in fast-response, as compared to slow-response, tissues.

Excitation-contraction coupling. Excitation-contraction coupling in heart tissue is complex. A rise in intracellular calcium ions is required to activate the proteins responsible for myocardial contraction. The slow inward current seems to trigger and modulate the release of calcium ions from the sarcoplasmic reticulum and other intracellular storage sites and to be involved in replenishing calcium ions in those stores. Sodium current, resultant changes in intracellular sodium activity, and sodium ion–calcium ion exchange, which influences the intracellular milieu, also affect contractility.

Automaticity. True spontaneous or automatic activity arises in the absence of direct external causes. Such automaticity may be physiological, as in the sinoatrial node and the lower escape pacemakers, or pathological, as in states of accelerated, depressed, or abnormal pacemaker function. Yet another type is triggered automaticity, in which nondriven action potentials are initiated by one or more driven action potentials. Normally, the sinoatrial node is the predominant cardiac pacemaker and controls the overall heart rhythm. Pacemaker activity is the product of a changing balance between positive inward currents, which favor depolarization, and positive outward currents, which favor repolarization. The depolarization current of importance is slow inward current, although a second inward current may also play a role. A slowly decaying outward potassium current may also be involved in causing pacemaker activity. *See* HEART (VERTEBRATE); MUSCLE.

Channelopathies. Abnormalities of the function of ion channels may be inherited or acquired. Mutations can occur in the encoding genes of ion channels, which affect the gating (opening and closing) of the channel proteins. The long QT syndrome (LQTS), for example, is the phenotypic description of a clinical disorder characterized by prolongation of the QT interval on the electrocardiogram (see below) associated with a certain type of heart rhythm disturbance termed polymorphic ventricular tachycardia, most commonly torsades de pointes, or "twisting of points." The genetic basis for this syndrome was suggested by the association of LQTS with the Romano-Ward syndrome, an isolated autosomal dominant expression, and by the Jervell and Lang-Nielsen syndromes, an autosomal recessive form associated with congenital deafness. The LQTS can be inherited, but it also can be acquired in response to disease, injury, certain medications, metabolic disorders, or other causes. At the time of writing, mutations in seven genes have been identified and have been designated LQT1 through LQT7, with LQT1, 2, and 3 accounting for some 90% of congenital LQTS. LQT1 involves gene *KVLQT1* (also called *KCNQ1*) located on chromosome 11 and results in suppression of the outward-rectifying potassium current (i_{Ks}). This potassium current normally enhances repolarization, so its suppression will prolong the duration of the action potential, which in turn prolongs the duration of the QT interval. LQT2 involves the *HERG* or *KCNH2* gene on chromosome 7, which affects the rapidly acting component of the outward-rectifying potassium current, i_{Kr}, which also prolongs the action potential and, therefore, the QT interval. LQT3 is caused by a mutation in the sodium channel gene (*SCN5A*) located on chromosome 3, which impairs sodium channel inactivation so that the membrane remains depolarized through leakage of depolarizing sodium current into the cell. This prolongs the QT interval and promotes membrane instability. The other LQT syndromes have other mechanisms, and there are differing mutations within LQT groupings. Other channelopathies include some family groupings of atrial fibrillation, short QT syndrome, familial sick sinus syndrome, catecholaminergic polymorphic ventricular tachycardia, familial Wolff-Parkinson-White syndrome, Brugada syndrome, and progressive cardiac conduction defect of the Lenegre type.

Recording extracellular potentials. A dipole consists of two separated, equal but opposite charges. Positive charges flow along force lines from the positive pole to the negative pole, creating current and, perpendicular to the current flow, an electrical field. The separation of charge across the cell membrane discussed above can be considered to be a dipole layer. The changes in transmembrane voltages during depolarization, repolarization, and impulse propagation alter the polarity of the dipole layer in the activated region. The separation of charge between activated and quiescent tissues results in a boundary between surface dipoles. The dipoles are the source of extracellular current flow across the boundary and throughout the surrounding volume conductor of the human thorax; the distribution of the potential in the electrical field is at right angles to the current flow and is detected electrocardiographically.

The magnitude of the recorded extracellular potential is determined by the size and relationship of the boundary to the recording electrode, by the transmembrane voltage gradient across the boundary, and by a conductivity term. The conductivity term incorporates intercellular conductivity, which is determined largely by gap junctions, and extracellular conductivity, which incorporates the characteristics of the volume conductor of the thorax, skin, fat, muscle, mediastinal structures, electrode paste, and the electrode itself. Dipoles have magnitude and direction and, therefore, can be represented by spatial vectors. Multiple vectors may be summed and expressed as a single equivalent vector, which may be translated to a common origin. In classic physiology, the heart has been considered a single dipole current source, represented by a single equivalent spatial vector that is fixed in position but is allowed to vary in magnitude and direction during the cardiac cycle. More complex multidipole models have also been proposed.

An equivalent spatial vector may be projected onto a plane or, as with the electrocardiograph, onto a lead axis system. Leads detect potential differences between two or more sites. The Einthoven reference system uses bipolar leads that compare left arm and right arm, with the left arm being positive (lead I), as well as the right arm and left leg (lead II) and the left arm and left leg (lead III), with the left leg being positive. Unipolar leads compare an exploring electrode against two or three standard limb leads (Goldberger augmented limb leads and Wilson precordial leads, respectively). The spatial vector, then, can be projected onto a hexaxial lead system (Einthoven and Goldberger leads) that defines the frontal plane (superior, inferior, left, and right) and a precordial lead system (Wilson leads) that approximates a horizontal plane (anterior, posterior, left, and right). Other lead systems provide a more orthogonal, that is, less distorted, three-dimensional axis system. The Frank vectorcardiographic system, for example, uses an X lead (left, right) similar to standard lead I, a Y lead (inferior, superior) similar to the augmented left foot lead, and a Z lead (posterior, anterior) similar to an inverted second unipolar chest lead (V_2).

In electrocardiography the potential in a given lead system is displayed against time, usually with 12 separate leads: I, II, III, augmented right arm (aVR), augmented left arm (aVL), augmented left foot (aVF), and six unipolar chest leads, designated V_1 through V_6. In vectorcardiography the spatial orientation of successive vectors is displayed for the frontal, horizontal, or sagittal plane. The vectorcardiographic loop is formed by the instantaneous plot of one orthogonal lead against another, with the time frame indicated by an interruption in the inscribed loop every 2.0 or 2.5 ms.

Body surface mapping based on recordings made at many sites has been used because each recording

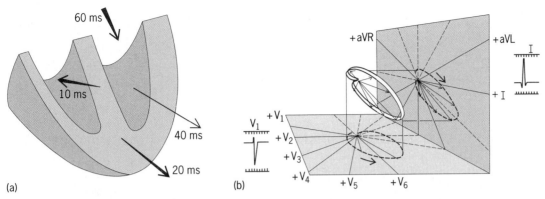

Fig. 2. Spatial vectors after onset of ventricular depolarization. (*a*) Ventricular activation at 10, 20, and 40 milliseconds. At 10 ms the subendocardial Purkinje system is depolarized, and ventricular vectorial forces are balanced except for left septal depolarization; the resultant spatial vector normally has a rightward, anterior, and superior orientation. The 20-ms vector results from activation of the septum and apex and has a leftward, anterior, and inferior orientation. The 40-ms vector arises from depolarization of the inferior and lateral walls of the left ventricle, with lesser contributions from the septum and right ventricle, and has a leftward, posterior, and inferior orientation. At 60 ms the inferior posterolateral and basal walls of the left ventricle are activated, and the spatial vector has a leftward, inferior, and even more posterior orientation. (*b*) The spatial vectors of ventricular depolarization translated in space with a common origin. The spatial QRS loop depicted is projected onto the frontal plane of the hexaxial reference system consisting of Einthoven and Goldberger leads and onto the horizontal plane created by unipolar Wilson leads. The projected loop is interrupted every 2.5 ms. The scalar recordings are shown in leads I and V$_1$. By convention, when the spatial vector approaches the positive terminal of the lead, the scalar recording is positive, and when directed away from the positive terminal of the lead, negative. (*After M. F. Arnsdorf, Electrocardiography, American Physiological Society, 1978*)

has both redundant and unique information, and computer analysis can extract the unique information. Signal averaging in the time domain and with Fourier analysis yields data that are not available with the standard electrocardiographic and vectorcardiographic approaches.

Extracellular potential measurements. The sinoatrial node is the normal pacemaker of the heart. Its mass is small, and therefore it does not appear on surface electrocardiograms. The sinoatrial nodal potential, however, initiates the activation of the atria. Atrial depolarization appears as the P wave on the electrocardiogram. Conduction from the atria to the ventricles normally takes place through the atrioventricular node and is quite slow. The impulse emerges from the atrioventricular node, penetrates the bundle of His and bundle branches, and enters the terminal Purkinje network. Because the tissue mass of the atrioventricular node, His bundle, bundle branches, and terminal Purkinje network is too small to produce a signal strong enough to be recorded at the body surface, the P wave is followed by an isoelectric interval.

The wavefront enters the ventricular muscle from the Purkinje network. The QRS complex results from depolarization of the large mass of ventricular muscle. It is followed by the T wave, the rapid phase of ventricular repolarization. U waves, which sometimes are recorded, may reflect repolarization of the terminal Purkinje system. The interval from atrial activation to the beginning of ventricular depolarization is known as the PR interval, and the isoelectric segment is the PR segment. The ST segment is inscribed during the plateau phase of ventricular action potential repolarization, which follows QRS depolarization, and it may be abnormal in disease states. The QT interval represents the entire depolarization and repolarization process of the ventricle.

Vectorcardiography records P, QRS, and T loops in a frontal, sagittal, and transverse or horizontal plane. Time intervals are represented by interruptions in the recording. The spatial vectors in **Fig. 2** point in the direction of the net potential.

The electrocardiograph and vectorcardiograph are sensitive to abnormal sequences of depolarization such as bundle branch block and preexcitation. They often are useful in detecting increase in myocardial mass, such as atrial and ventricular enlargement. They can detect ischemia and myocardial infarction and often suggest myocardial or pericardial disease, electrolyte disturbance, and drug effects.

The heartbeat is controlled primarily by the sinoatrial node, which is normally the fastest pacemaker. A marked slowing or failure of the sinus node or a conduction defect that prevents an impulse initiated by the sinus node from reaching all of the heart usually leads to the appearance of a lower escape pacemaker to assume control of the heart. Such escape pacemakers, which have intrinsic rates slower than that found in the normal sinoatrial node, may arise in the atrium, the junction (the His bundle and the region of the atrioventricular node adjacent to it), the subjunction (fascicles and bundle branches), and the terminal Purkinje fibers. The so-called idioventricular escape rhythm probably originates in the terminal Purkinje fibers rather than in the ventricle, although pathological pacemakers may arise in the ventricular tissue. Time-dependent inward and outward currents are involved in lower pacemaker function. Abnormalities in automaticity and in impulse propagation may lead to cardiac rhythm disturbances, but electrocardiography is very useful in evaluating the rhythm and conduction of the heart. Normal electrocardiograms and vectorcardiograms are shown in **Fig. 3**.

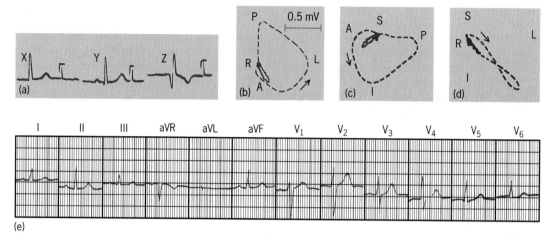

Fig. 3. Normal electrocardiograms and vectorcardiograms. (*a*) Normal orthogonal X, Y, and Z leads that are used to construct the vectorcardiogram (VCG). The X lead defines a left-right lead with the positive terminal on the left; the Y lead defines a superior-inferior lead with the positive terminal inferiority; and the Z lead defines an anterior-posterior lead with the positive terminal posteriorly. (*b–d*) Normal P, QRS, and T vectorcardiographic loops. The beam is interrupted every 2.5 ms, and the direction of inscription is indicated. Orientation in the vectorcardiograph is as follows: A, anterior; P, posterior; L, left; R, right; S, superior; I, inferior. (*b*) The horizontal plane has a left-hand (X lead) and anterior-posterior (Z lead) orientation; (*c*) the sagittal plane has a superior-inferior (Y lead) and anterior-posterior (Z lead) orientation; and (*d*) the frontal plane has a left-right (X lead) and superior-inferior (Y lead) orientation. The P loop is very small, the QRS loop is the large dominant inscription, and the T loop is the intermediate-size inscription. The P and T loops are magnified for analysis. (*e*) Normal 12-lead electrocardiogram. Note the similarity between the electrocardiographic and the orthogonal vectorcardiographic recordings: left-right (I, X), inferior-superior (aVF, Y), and the mirror image of V₁ with anterior positivity and Z with posterior positivity.

At times, pacemaker catheters are inserted into the cavities of the heart to stimulate the myocardium, provoking cardiac arrhythmias, and to record extracellular potentials. Intracavitary recordings can record small potentials from the sinoatrial node, His bundle, bundle branches, and terminal Purkinje fibers. Multiple intracavitary recording catheters permit the identification and mechanisms of reentrant arrhythmias and the localization of anomalous connections between the atria and ventricles, such as those that occur in preexcitation. An example of an intracavitary recording is shown in **Fig. 4**.

Body surface mapping and signal averaging techniques show promise for detecting abnormal potentials that indicate myocardial disease. Some studies suggest that the presence of such abnormal potentials may allow identification of the individual at risk for serious rhythm disturbances and sudden death. *See* BIOPHYSICS; CARDIOVASCULAR SYSTEM; VASCULAR DISORDERS.

Arrhythmogenesis. Heart rhythm disturbances result most commonly from reentry, but may also result from enhanced excitability, increased automaticity, and triggered activity. Reentry can be defined as the reexcitation of previously activated tissue by a continuously propagated electrical impulse. The model, such as that in **Fig. 5**, usually involves an area of slow conduction and unidirectional block. In this model of a Purkinje network, the impulse would normally travel from the central Purkinje fiber (1) down the two branches (2, 3) and activate the ventricular muscle (4) [Fig. 5*a*]. As a result of ischemia or injury, a segment with unidirectional block and slow retrograde conduction is established in one limb of the Purkinje fiber (3) [Fig. 5*b*]. The impulse descending from the central Purkinje is blocked proximally

by the area of unidirectional block, travels normally through the other branch (2), enters the ventricular muscle (4), and reenters the depressed limb (3) distally. The impulse conducts slowly through the depressed segment and, if the tissue at the bifurcation and in limb (2) has regained its excitability, it can be reexcited (reentered), once more reaching the ventricular muscle through limb (2). The

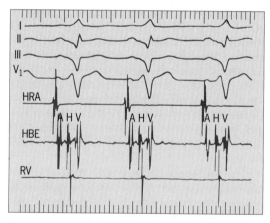

Fig. 4. Body surface and intracavitary electrocardiographic recordings. The electrocardiogram body surface leads I, II, III, and V₁ are shown in the four traces at the top. A catheter with recording electrodes was advanced through the femoral vein, the inferior vena cava, the right atrium, and right ventricle. Recordings were made in the high right atrium (HRA), in the area of the tricuspid valve (HBE, His bundle electrogram), and the right ventricle (RV). Note that the HBE records the atrial (A), His bundle (H), and ventricular (V) depolarization. The ventricular electrogram in the HBE is primarily due to left ventricular depolarization, is delayed because of a conduction block in the left bundle branch, and occurs after the right ventricular depolarization. (*Courtesy of Dr. Thomas Bump, University of Chicago*)

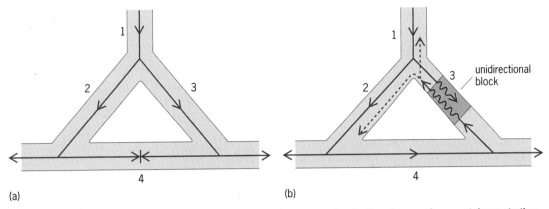

(a)   (b)

Fig. 5. Model of a Purkinje network. (*a*) Normal propagation. (*b*) Reentrant circuit with a depressed segment demonstrating slow conduction and unidirectional block.

reentry may be a single beat, or it may be sustained. The success or failure of reentry depends on the length of the functionally isolated depressed segment, the integrity of cell-cell communication through gap junctions, the conduction velocity, and the ionic mechanisms of depolarization and repolarization both within the depressed segment and the normal tissue that is to be reactivated, and the refractoriness of the previously excited tissue. These pathways may be anatomic or functional and may exist anywhere in the heart. The reentrant circuits may be large (macroreentry)—as in atrial flutter, atrioventricular nodal reentrant tachycardia, atrioventricular tachycardia that utilizes an accessory pathway, and ventricular—or they may be very small (microreentry) as in atrial and ventricular fibrillation.

Normal automaticity may be enhanced as with sinus tachycardia, or abnormal foci of spontaneously depolarizing tissue may result from ischemia, autonomic surges, electrolyte imbalance, hypoxia, or drugs, resulting in atrial, junctional, and ventricular tachycardias.

Unusual oscillatory activity may be triggered by normal or abnormal activation. As mentioned above, the long QT syndrome is characterized by prolongation of the action potential, which is manifested by QT interval prolongation on the surface electrocardiogram. The prolongation of the action potential allows more time for inward calcium current to flow, which, in turn, may load the cell with calcium and lead to the development of oscillatory afterpotentials. These afterpotentials likely are the cause of the polymorphic ventricular tachycardia called torsades de pointes. At times, tissue may demonstrate increased excitability as a result of disease or external influences.

Clinical cardiac electrophysiology. Patients may receive permanent electronic pacemakers because of slow heart rates, which often cause dizziness, lightheadedness, poor exercise tolerance, and sometimes loss of consciousness. The slow rate may result from a slowing of the normal sinus rhythm with the failure of lower spontaneous pacemakers to appear, or from a conduction defect in which the normal input of the sinus node to the ventricles is interrupted due to block, usually in the AV node, His bundle, or

bundle branches. The electronics in these artificial pacemakers has become quite sophisticated in that most can record and pace from the atrium or ventricles, can recognize slow and sometimes fast rates, and can switch from one mode of pacing to another depending on the arrhythmia or conduction abnormality that is encountered. Some pacemakers can synchronize the depolarization of the two ventricles when one is activated before the other as may occur in bundle branch block, and such cardiac resynchronization therapy has proven effective in the treatment of heart failure in some patients.

By permitting the recording of intracavitary electrical potentials, intracardiac catheters can be used to identify the mechanisms of an arrhythmia. Moreover, radio-frequency (RF) energy, which is low-voltage high-frequency electrical energy, can be delivered from the tip of a catheter to the endocardial (inside) surface of the heart to "burn" and scar the site at which an arrhythmia is arising or to interrupt a reentrant pathway. This type of RF ablation has revolutionized the treatment of macroreentrant arrhythmias such as atrial flutter, atrial tachycardias, AV nodal reentrant tachycardia, AV reentrant tachycardia using accessory pathways, conduction of atrial arrhythmias through accessory pathways, ventricular tachycardia, and other rhythms. Progress is also being made in the ablation of atrial fibrillation.

Sudden cardiac death usually results from ventricular fibrillation (VF) that sometimes is heralded by the appearance of ventricular tachycardia (VT). The external application of direct-current (DC) energy has been used since 1962 to cardiovert atrial fibrillation, atrial flutter, ventricular tachycardia, ventricular fibrillation, and other tachyarrhythmias to a normal rhythm. Electronic miniaturization and modern computer technology have allowed the development of the implantable cardioverter-defibrillator (ICD), which consists of sensing electrodes, defibrillation electrodes, and a pulse generator. The modern ICD can recognize an arrhythmia, attempt to convert a reentrant rhythm such as ventricular tachycardia to a normal rhythm by pacing, or, if necessary, defibrillate the heart as may be required with a refractory ventricular tachycardia or with ventricular

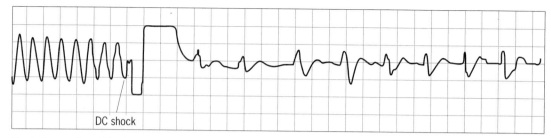

Fig. 6. Appropriate delivery of a DC shock by an implantable defibrillator. (*Courtesy of Dr. Bradley Knight, University of Chicago*)

fibrillation. An example is shown in **Fig. 6** in which a very rapid ventricular rhythm (ventricular flutter) is recognized, a DC shock is delivered, and the rhythm is converted to a normal sinus rhythm with a wide QRS complex. Current ICD lead systems are usually placed transvenously through an axillary, subclavian, or cephalic vein. The ICD has become the first line of defense in protecting the patient with heart disease from sudden cardiac death due to ventricular fibrillation.   Morton Arnsdorf

Bibliography. M. F. Arnsdorf, *Electrocardiography: I. Fundamental Theory,* and *II. Applied Theory,* 1978; M. F. Arnsdorf and J. C. Makielski, Excitability and impulse propagation, in *Physiology and Pathophysiology of the Heart,* 4thd ed., ed. by N. Sperelakis, 2000; B. Hille, *Ion Channels of Excitable Membranes,* 3d ed., 2001; M. E. Josephson, *Clinical Cardiac Electrophysiology: Techniques and Interpretations,* 3d ed., 2001; F. Lehmann-Horn and K. Jurkatt-Rott (eds.), *Channelopathies,* 2000; P. W. Macfarlane and T. D. V. Lawrie (eds.), *Comprehensive Electrocardiography,* 3 vols., 1989; D. Zipes and J. Jalife (eds.), *Cardiac Electrophysiology: From Cell to Bedside,* 4th ed., 2004.

Cardinal points

The four intersections of the horizon with the meridian and with the prime vertical circle, or simply prime vertical, the intersections with the meridian being designated north and south, and the intersections with the prime vertical being designated east and west (see **illus.**). The cardinal points are 90° apart; they lie in a plane with each other and correspond to the cardinal regions of the heavens. The four intermediate points, northeast, southeast, northwest, and southwest, are the collateral points. *See* ASTRONOMICAL COORDINATE SYSTEMS.

Frank H. Rockett

Cardioid

A heart-shaped curve generated by a point of a circle that rolls (without slipping) on a fixed circle of the same diameter. In point-wise construction of the curve, let O be a fixed point of a circle C of diameter a, and Q a variable point of C. Lay off distance a along the secant OQ, in both directions from Q. The locus of the two points thus obtained is a cardioid (see **illus.**). If a rectangular coordinate system

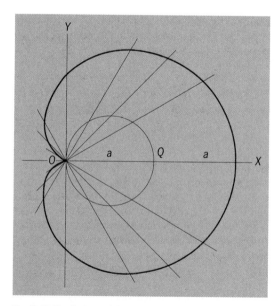

Cardioid. Symbols explained in text.

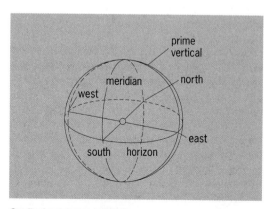

Cardinal points around horizon.

is chosen with O for origin initially and y axis tangent to C at O, the cardioid has the equation $(x^2 + y^2 - ax)^2 = a^2(x^2 + y^2)$. The equation expressed in polar coordinates is $\rho = a(1 + \cos\theta)$. The cardioid's area is $3/2\pi a^2$, or six times the area of C, and its length is $8a$. *See* ANALYTIC GEOMETRY.   Leonard M. Blumenthal

Cardiovascular system

Those structures, such as the heart, or pumping mechanism, and the arteries, veins, and capillaries, which provide channels for the flow of blood. The cardiovascular system is sometimes called the blood-vascular system. The circulatory system includes both the cardiovascular and lymphatic systems; the latter consists of lymph channels (lymphatics), nodes, and fluid lymph which finally empties into the bloodstream. This article discusses the cardiovascular system under the following major headings: comparative anatomy, comparative embryology, functional development of the heart, human fetal circulation at term, postnatal circulation, and comparative physiology. *See* BLOOD; LYMPHATIC SYSTEM.

Comparative Anatomy

All vertebrates feature a closed system of branched vessels, a ventral heart, and a basic pattern of organization that ranges from the single system in most fishes to the double system in land forms.

Heart. The hearts of vertebrates differ from those of animals in the lower phyla in their ventral rather than dorsal location. Blood is pumped anteriorly through arteries and forced to the dorsal side. The greater part then courses posteriorly through arteries which terminate in capillaries in various parts of the body. The blood returns to the heart through veins. *See* HEART (VERTEBRATE).

Phylogeny. In lower vertebrates the heart is located far forward in the body, but there is a gradual backward shifting as the vertebrate scale is ascended. The heart lies in a pericardial cavity which is surrounded by an investing membrane, the pericardium. The pericardial cavity is a portion of the coelom which has been separated from the remainder of the body cavity. In elasmobranchs, the separation is incomplete and the two portions of the coelom are connected by a pericardio-peritoneal canal. A thin serous membrane, the epicardium, covers the surface of the heart. It is continuous with the lining of the pericardial cavity.

The heart is primarily a pulsating tube, the lining (endocardium) of which is derived from fusion of two vitelline veins. Its muscular wall (myocardium) and the epicardium originate from surrounding splanchnic mesoderm. It becomes divided into chambers called atria and ventricles. In addition, two accessory chambers, called the sinus venosus and conus arteriosus, respectively, may be present. Cyclostomes and most fishes have two-chambered hearts with one atrium and one ventricle. A sinus venosus connects with the atrium and a conus arteriosus leads from the ventricle. Dipnoans and amphibians have three-chambered hearts with two atria and one ventricle. The three-chambered heart of most reptiles is similar to that of amphibians, but an incomplete partition appears in the ventricle. In crocodiles and alligators this becomes complete, forming a four-chambered heart with two atria and two ventricles. Birds and mammals have four-

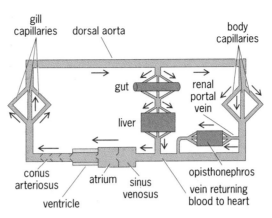

Fig. 1. Single type of circulatory system. (*After C. K. Weichert, Anatomy of the Chordates, 3d ed., McGraw-Hill, 1965***)**

chambered hearts. Valves are present to regulate the direction of blood flow.

Circulation in the heart. Vertebrates with two-chambered hearts have the single type of circulation (**Fig. 1**) in which only unoxygenated blood passes through the heart, which pumps it to the gills for aeration. The double type of circulation (**Fig. 2**) exists in three- and four-chambered hearts through which pass two streams of blood, one oxygenated and the other unoxygenated or partly oxygenated. Even in three-chambered hearts these streams do not mix to any appreciable extent. Partitioning of the heart has been associated in evolution with development of pulmonary circulation accompanying the appearance of lungs.

The conus arteriosus no longer exists as such in adults of higher forms; it is split into trunks leading to the aorta and lungs, respectively.

In those forms having two-chambered hearts unoxygenated blood from all parts of the body is collected by the sinus venosus which joins the atrium. In the three-chambered hearts of dipnoans and amphibians the sinus venosus has shifted its position and joins the right atrium. A large sinus venosus is present in certain reptiles, but in most it is very small or is

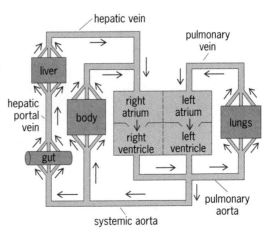

Fig. 2. Double type of circulatory system in a vertebrate having a four-chambered heart (ventral view). (*After C. K. Weichert, Anatomy of the Chordates, 3d ed., McGraw-Hill, 1965***)**

lacking. Birds and mammals possess a sinus venosus only during early embryonic development. In vertebrates having three- or four-chambered hearts, un-oxygenated blood is returned to the heart through the sinus venosus or directly to the right atrium, as the case may be.

Arterial system. Although the arterial systems of various adult vertebrates appear to be very different in arrangement, a study of development reveals that all systems are built upon the same fundamental plan.

Ventral and dorsal aortas. In lower vertebrates the conus arteriosus leads forward to a ventral aorta. During early development this vessel divides anteriorly into two aortic arches which course dorsally in the mandibular region. These continue posteriorly as the paired dorsal aortas. Additional pairs of aortic arches then appear, forming connections between ventral and dorsal aortas on each side. They appear in sequence in an anteroposterior direction, each coursing through the tissues between adjacent pharyngeal pouches. The typical number of aortic arches to form in vertebrates is six pairs (**Fig. 3a**), although there are certain discrepancies among lower forms. The paired dorsal aortas unite posterior to the pharyngeal region to form a single vessel. This single dorsal aorta continues posteriorly into the tail as the caudal artery.

Various paired and unpaired arteries arise along the length of the dorsal aorta to supply all structures of the body posterior to the pharyngeal region. Anterior continuations of the ventral aorta and the anterior remnants of the paired dorsal aortas supply the head and anterior branchial regions. Although the vessels arising from the dorsal aorta are fairly uniform throughout the vertebrate series, the aortic arches undergo profound modifications. The changes are similar in members of a given class.

Blood, pumped anteriorly by the heart, passes to the aortic arches. These vessels then carry the blood to the dorsal aorta or aortas from which it goes either anteriorly to the head or posteriorly to the remainder of the body.

Aortic arches. Changes in the aortic arch region constitute the chief differences in the arterial systems of the separate vertebrate classes. A progressive reduction in the number of aortic arches occurs as the evolutionary scale is ascended. In cyclostomes and in most fishes, in which gills are used in respiration, the aortic arches break up into afferent and efferent portions connected by numerous gill capillaries in which blood is oxygenated.

The changes in this region involve primarily a routing of the blood through certain preferred aortic arches with a consequent atrophy or disappearance

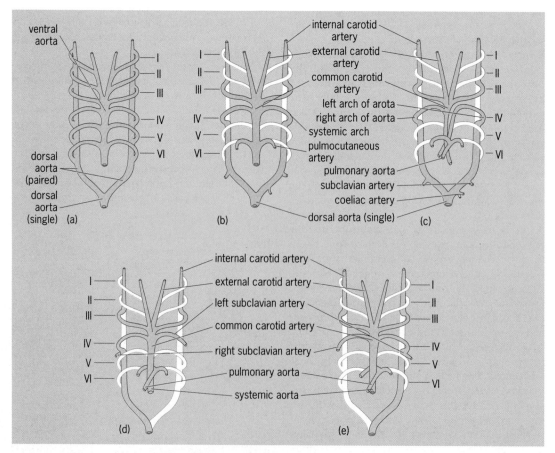

Fig. 3. Modifications of aortic arches in vertebrates, ventral views. (a) Typical condition in vertebrate embryos. Six pairs of arches connect dorsal and ventral aortas. (b) In anuran amphibians. (c) In reptiles. Ventral aorta has split into three vessels, right and left systemic trunks and a pulmonary trunk or aorta. (d) In birds. (e) In mammals. (*After C. K. Weichert, Anatomy of the Chordates, 3d ed., McGraw-Hill, 1965*)

of those which are no longer used, and a splitting of the conus arteriosus and ventral aorta, particularly in reptiles, birds, and mammals, in such a manner that systemic and pulmonary trunks are established (Fig. 3*b–e*). The systemic trunk, coming from the left ventricle (or left side of the ventricle), distributes oxygenated (or partially oxygenated) blood to the body in general. The pulmonary trunk, coming from the right ventricle (or right side of the ventricle), carries blood to the lungs. Oxygenated blood returns through veins from the lungs to the left atrium. Vessels which carry blood from the heart to the lungs and back constitute the pulmonary circulation. Branches of the sixth pair of aortic arches give rise to the pulmonary arteries.

Coronary arteries, supplying the tissues of the heart itself, arise as branches of certain aortic arches or of the systemic trunk near the point where it emerges from the heart.

Somatic arteries. The arteries supplying the body proper are usually paired structures which clearly show evidences of segmental arrangement (metamerism). They spring from the dorsolateral regions of the dorsal aorta. Fusion of two or more segmental arteries may take place, obscuring the fundamental metameric arrangement. *See* METAMERES.

Visceral arteries. Arteries supplying the viscera are of two kinds, paired and unpaired. The paired arteries, usually restricted to certain regions, are segmentally arranged. They supply structures derived from the part of the embryo from which the urogenital organs and their ducts arise.

Unpaired visceral arteries supply the spleen and digestive tract. There are usually three such vessels in vertebrates. The celiac artery supplies the stomach, spleen, pancreas, liver, and duodenum; the superior mesenteric artery supplies most of the intestine and a portion of the pancreas; and the inferior mesenteric artery goes to the posterior part of the large intestine and rectum. Variations from this condition are accounted for by fusions or separations.

Venous system. A comparison of veins in the various vertebrate groups shows that they too are arranged according to the same fundamental plan and that the variations encountered form a logical sequence as the vertebrate scale is ascended. In its development the venous system of higher forms passes through certain stages common to the embryos of lower forms.

Sinus venosus. The accessory chamber present in the hearts of lower vertebrates through which blood from all over the body is returned to the heart is the sinus venosus.

In cyclostomes and fishes the sinus venosus typically receives a pair of common cardinal veins, or ducts of Cuvier, formed by the union of anterior and posterior cardinals, a pair of small inferior jugular veins from the ventrolateral part of the head, and a pair of hepatic veins coming from the liver. In lower fishes a lateral abdominal vein also joins each duct of Cuvier. Each lateral abdominal vein receives a subclavian vein from the pectoral fin and an iliac

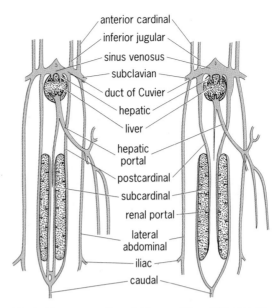

Fig. 4. Changes over the primitive condition which occur in the venous system of lower fishes, ventral view. (*After C. K. Weichert, Anatomy of the Chordates, 3d ed., McGraw-Hill, 1965*)

vein from the pelvic appendage (**Fig. 4**). In some fishes the inferior jugular veins are lacking; in others they have fused. Teleost fishes lack lateral abdominal veins; rather, the subclavians enter the common cardinals. In the dipnoan *Epiceratodus*, the lateral abdominal veins fuse to form a single anterior abdominal vein which joins the sinus venosus directly.

The sinus venosus in amphibians is conspicuous. The ducts of Cuvier have consolidated to form two precaval veins, each of which, in addition to the usual vessels, receives a large musculocutaneous vein from the skin and body wall before joining the sinus venosus. A postcava, derived partly from the sinus venosus and partly from the vitelline veins, joins the sinus venosus posteriorly.

A large sinus venosus is present in turtles; in most reptiles, however, it has been greatly reduced and much of it may be incorporated within the wall of the right atrium. In such reptiles and in adult birds and mammals which lack a sinus venosus, precaval and postcaval veins enter the right atrium directly. Valves that are present where veins enter the right atrium represent vestiges of the sinus venosus.

Cardinal veins. Anterior cardinal, or jugular, veins are prominent in cyclostomes and fishes. In amphibians, reptiles, birds, and mammals they receive internal and external tributaries before joining the precaval veins. In some mammals a single precava is present, an anastomosis having developed between the two original vessels.

Postcardinal veins, which originally course along the lateral borders of the kidneys, at first carry blood away from the kidneys. In fishes they separate into anterior and posterior portions. The posterior sections terminate in the kidneys to become the renal portal veins. The anterior sections connect with a new pair of vessels, the subcardinals, which appear along the medial borders of the kidneys. These now carry blood from the kidneys to the heart. In caudate amphibians and a few salientians the condition is similar to that of fishes, but in most salientians the anterior portions of the postcardinals disappear, and the blood from the kidneys reaches the sinus venosus by way of the postcava. In reptiles and birds the renal portal veins have lost most of their significance, and in mammals they disappear entirely. A remnant of the anterior end of the right postcardinal of mammals becomes the azygos vein, a branch of the right precava which drains the intercostal muscles.

Abdominal veins. The lateral abdominal veins of amphibians and reptiles, like those of the lungfish *Epiceratodus*, have fused to form a single anterior abdominal vein. Instead of entering the sinus venosus, however, it joins the hepatic portal vein. In reptiles, birds, and mammals the lateral abdominal veins are represented during embryonic life by allantoic or umbilical veins which lose their direct connections with the sinus venosus when the liver develops. In adult birds the anterior abdominal vein may possibly be represented by the coccygeomesenteric vein or the epigastric vein. It disappears entirely in all mammals, with the exception of the echidnas.

Portal systems. A portal system is a system of veins that breaks up into a capillary network before the blood which courses through it is returned to the heart. All vertebrates have a hepatic portal system in which blood collected from the digestive tract and spleen passes through capillaries (sinusoids) in the liver before reaching the heart. The embryonic vitelline (subintestinal) vessels are represented in adults by the hepatic portal vein and its tributaries. The renal portal system of lower vertebrates has already been mentioned. Another small but important portal system is found associated with the blood vessels draining the pituitary gland. *See* LIVER.

Miscellaneous. Coronary veins draining the tissues of the heart enter the sinus venosus in lower forms or the right atrium in higher vertebrates. Pulmonary veins, found in amphibians, reptiles, birds, and mammals, first appear in the dipnoan fishes, where their function is to drain the swim bladder. They enter the left atrium. *See* RESPIRATORY SYSTEM; SWIM BLADDER.

Charles K. Weichert

Comparative Embryology

The cardiovascular system in vertebrates arises from the splanchnic mesoderm, with the first blood and vessels formed in the wall of the yolk sac.

Heart. The heart of each species attains its characteristic morphology through an orderly series of changes which begin in early embryonic life. Although the details of development differ for different animals, there are a number of basic principles which apply to all species. Emphasis will be placed on the general principles first, and species characteristics will be noted subsequently.

The prospective heart rudiment, that is, the tissue which eventually differentiates into the heart, can be located by experimental procedures (exploration, transplantation, vital dyes, and autoradiographs) before morphological differentiation is observable. The

rudiment consists of bilateral areas of splanchnic mesoderm located near the blastopore in the early amphibian gastrulae and near the pharyngeal arches just prior to initial morphological differentiation. *See* AUTORADIOGRAPHY.

The heart field, the mesoderm with potency for heart development, is more extensive than the prospective rudiment which normally forms the organ. For example, a normal heart can develop in amphibians after complete removal of a visibly differentiated primordium. This results from migration of mesoderm from the periphery of the field to the region of extirpation.

The heart field, like the prospective rudiment, is bilateral. The potency for cardiac development is greatest at the center of the field and least at the periphery. The limits of the fields have been determined precisely in chick embryos by studies on the fates of small areas transplanted to the chorioallantoic membrane. *See* FATE MAPS (EMBRYOLOGY).

Induction. The prospective rudiment in amphibian embryos becomes destined (determined) for heart development at the time of gastrulation through an inductive effect exerted by tissue adjacent to the blastopore. Endoderm has a further inductive role on the heart-forming mesoderm at the neurula stage, as evidenced by lack of heart development following extirpation of the endoderm. *See* EMBRYONIC INDUCTION.

Determination and self-differentiation. The prospective rudiment is determined early, as outlined above. This is tested by transplantation to abnormal positions and by explantation as in tissue culture. The rudiment is described as self-differentiating when it attains the ability to develop in a foreign environment.

Polarity. Polarity or axial determination occurs at different times for the different axes. For example, when the anteroposterior axis is changed by 180° in neurula-stage amphibians, the heart develops with reversed morphology and beat. When the early rudiment is rotated around the long axis, altering only the dorsoventral and ventrolateral axes, the heart develops normally.

Totipotency. The ability of part of an organ rudiment to develop the whole organ is called totipotency. Experiments on amphibians, birds, and mammals show that either of the bilateral rudiments is capable of developing a complete organ. Furthermore, a whole organ may form from less than one-half; that is, several hearts can form from one rudiment.

Tubular heart formation. The heart is usually described as tubular during its early morphological differentiation, although it is saccular in shape in most species.

Mesenchymal cells arising from the splanchnic mesoderm of the heart rudiment differentiate into endocardium continuous with the subintestinal blood capillaries. The endocardial channels are bilateral at first; they eventually fuse into a single median tubular endocardium (**Fig. 5***a* and *b*).

The ventral portion of the splanchnic mesoderm of each bilateral heart rudiment thickens and differentiates into epimyocardium around the

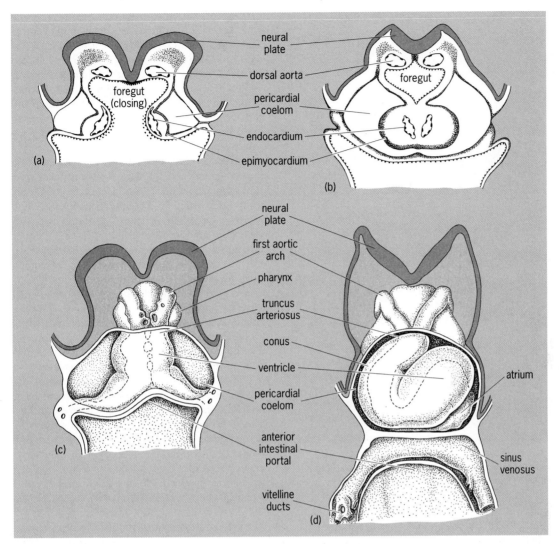

Fig. 5. Stages in development of the human heart. The organ is depicted as translucent, with the endocardium (broken lines) visible through the myocardium. (*a*) Cross section from a four-somite embryo. (*b*) Cross section at seven somites. (*c*) Ventral view at four somites. (*d*) Ventral view at thirteen somites.

endocardium (Fig. 5). A space between endocardium and myocardium during early development is filled with homogeneous material known as cardiac jelly. It is eventually replaced by connective tissue uniting the endocardium and myocardium.

The space between the splanchnic and somatic mesoderm of the heart rudiment becomes the pericardial cavity, and a part of the somatic mesoderm differentiates into parietal pericardium.

The bilateral portions of the tubular heart approach the midline and unite to form a single tubular or saccular heart (Fig. 5). Fusion progresses in a cephalocaudal direction. Likewise, structural and functional differentiation of the chambers progresses cephalocaudally. These chambers, beginning with the most caudal one, are the sinus venosus, atrium, ventricle, and bulbus cordis (conus). The sinus venosus receives the blood from the veins; the bulbus empties into the truncus arteriosus and thence into the aortic arches.

The amount of morphological differentiation seen in the bilateral heart rudiments when they reach the midventral region of the body differs for different species. For example, the bilateral rudiments of the amphibian heart are only slightly differentiated at this time, whereas those of birds and mammals show considerable differentiation prior to union in the midline (Fig. 5*a* and *c*). This is because the heart of birds and mammals develops relatively early, while the mesoderm is spread out over the yolk sac. The two sides cannot come together until the head end of the body grows and folds off from the yolk sac. An early development of the circulatory system is particularly important in mammalian embryos since they have very little yolk and come to depend very early upon metabolic exchange with the mother through a placental circulation. It is significant that the heart is the first organ to function.

Cardiac loop and regional development. The tubular heart is attached by its vascular trunks and by a continuity of visceral pericardium with the serous portion of the parietal pericardium at its venous and arterial ends. It is attached by a dorsal pericardium for only a brief period.

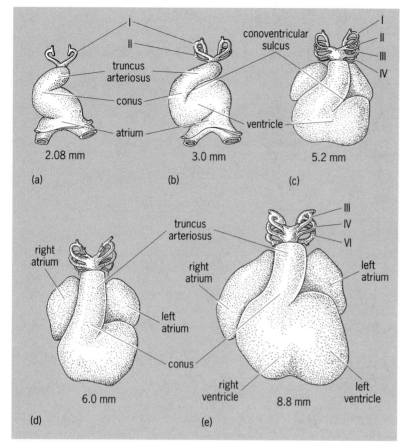

Fig. 6. Ventral views (*a-e*) of the human embryonic heart, showing the bending of the cardiac tube and the establishment of its regional divisions. The roman numerals I to VI indicate the aortic arches of corresponding numbers. (*After T. C. Kramer, Amer. J. Anat., 71(3):343–370, 1942*)

The heart becomes curved primarily due to its rapid growth. The heart increases in length so much faster than the cavity in which it lies that it first makes a U-shaped bend to the right and is then twisted into a loop. This moves the venous end cephalically and the arterial end caudally until the entering and exiting vessels approximate the same level in mammals (**Figs. 6e** and **7f**).

With the formation of the cardiac loop during the fifth week of human gestation, the primary regional divisions become clearly recognizable (Fig. 6). This is a result of the curvature and of different intrinsic growth rates in different regions. Blood flow also plays a part in the regional differentiation.

The sinus venosus is the thin-walled most caudal chamber into which the great veins enter (Fig. 7c). The atrial region is established by transverse dilation of the heart just cephalic to the sinus venosus, and the ventricle is formed by the bent midportion of the original cardiac tube (Figs. 5, 6, and 7). Between the atrium and ventricle, the heart remains relatively undilated to form the atrioventricular canal. The conus is distinguishable as a separate region prior to its later incorporation into the right ventricle. The most cephalic part of the cardiac tube undergoes the least change in appearance, persisting as the truncus arteriosus connecting the conoventricular region to the aortic arches (Figs. 5 and 6).

Studies on amphibians, birds, and mammals show that initial cardiac contractions begin in the ventricular region. The heart at this time is just slightly less developed than that illustrated in Fig. 6 for a human embryo 0.08 in. (2 mm) long (beginning of fourth week of development). With further cardiac differentiation in a cephalocaudal direction, the atrium and sinus venosus acquire the ability to contract, each with a successively higher intrinsic rate which dominates its predecessor.

Innervation of the heart occurs subsequent to the time when the sinus differentiates and takes over the pacemaker function. The fact that the embryonic heart pulsates rhythmically and carries on circulation prior to innervation indicates the beat is myogenic rather than neurogenic in origin.

The myocardium shows cytological differentiation relatively early. Electron micrographs of developing heart muscle cells show randomly oriented myofilaments (actin and myosin) prior to the time when striations appear due to the alignment of the filaments in register in myofibrils. A compact, well-oriented arrangement of myofibrils, each composed of many myofilaments, occurs earlier in the ventricle than in the atrium. The sinus venosus (shown in **Fig. 8** for the tadpole heart just prior to the time of innervation) retains an irregular arrangement in adult amphibians. In mammals, where the sinus venosus becomes incorporated into the right atrium, the sinoatrial node is composed of cells which have sparse randomly oriented myofibrils, like those which are found in the amphibian sinus venosus. The irregular arrangement is one of the characteristics of pacemaker cells. *See* HEART (INVERTEBRATE); MUSCLE.

Formation of definitive heart. The morphological changes which occur in the heart while it differentiates from a tubular structure to its definitive adult form vary for different classes and species of vertebrates in correlation with different functional requirements. The changes in elasmobranch fishes are few and simple. The heart retains all its primitive chambers in sequence (sinus, atrium, ventricle, and conus) and each chamber remains unpartitioned.

In adult amphibians the heart attains an external form and curvature beyond that illustrated in Fig. 5 for a mammalian embryo, but it retains the chambers in sequence. In urodele amphibians there is a partial division of the atrium into right and left sides; in anuran amphibians the atrial division is complete, but other parts remain undivided.

The heart of reptiles has the atrium divided completely into right and left chambers while the ventricle is divided only partially.

In birds and mammals the sinus venosus is incorporated into the right atrium, which is divided completely from the left atrium; the primitive ventricle is completely divided into right and left chambers; the conus is incorporated into the right ventricle; and the truncus arteriosus is divided into right and left sides to form the roots and proximal portions of the pulmonary artery and aorta.

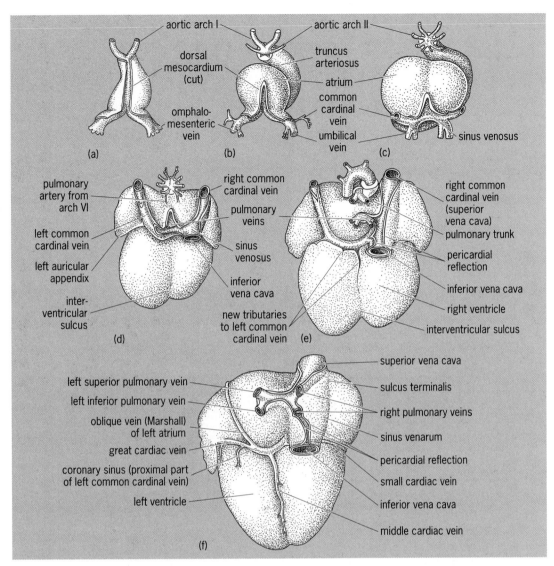

Fig. 7. Six stages in development of the heart, in dorsal aspect to show changing relations of the sinus venosus and great veins entering the heart. (*a*) 2$\frac{1}{2}$ weeks (8–10 somites). (*b*) 3 weeks (12–14 somites). (*c*) 3$\frac{1}{2}$ weeks (17–19 somites). (*d*) 5 weeks (6–8 mm or 0.24–0.31 in., crown-rump). (*e*) 8 weeks (about 25 mm or 1 in.). (*f*) 11 weeks (about 60 mm or 2 in.). (*After B. M. Patten, Human Embryology, 3d ed., Blakiston–McGraw-Hill, 1968*)

The fusion of the sinus venosus with the right atrium is somewhat more complete in most mammals than in birds. In mammals specialized tissues develop in certain areas of the original sinus region to form the sinoatrial and atrioventricular nodes. The sinoatrial node, located near the entrance of the superior vena cava, serves as the cardiac pacemaker.

Complete division of the heart into right and left sides, that is, a complete separation of respiratory and systemic circulations, is achieved only in birds and mammals. This supplies a higher arterial pressure on the systemic side and distributes oxygenated blood to the tissues more rapidly than in animals with partial separation (reptiles and amphibians) or those with no separation (fishes).

Partitioning of mammalian heart. The division of the heart into right and left sides has been studied in detail in humans and in a number of other mammals. The following account applies primarily to the human heart, but the general plan of partitioning is similar in other mammals. It should be noted that the partitioning of the embryonic heart involves more than its structural division into parts. The process is beset by striking functional exigencies. Cardiac partitioning in the human embryo does not begin until about the fifth week of development, 0.2 in. (6 mm) long, when the heart (Fig. 6*d*) is already maintaining a circulation essential for embryonic life. All of the complex changes in partitioning must be made without interruption of the blood supply to any part of the growing embryo. Starting with a stage when the blood is flowing through it in an undivided stream, the heart, by the time of birth, must become converted into an elaborately valved, four-chambered organ, pumping from its right side a pulmonary stream which is returned to its left side to be pumped out again over the aorta as the systemic bloodstream. Moreover, at the end of gestation, the vascular mechanism must be prepared for air breathing. At the moment of birth the lungs, their blood

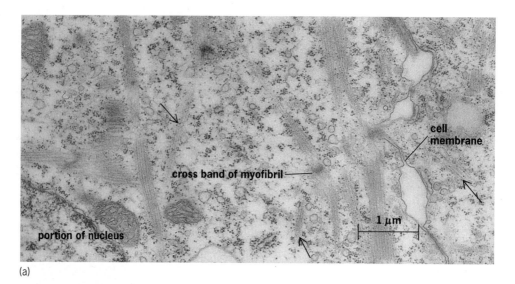

(a)

(b)

Fig. 8. Electron micrographs of cardiac muscle at different stages of development. (*a*) Section of sinus venosus from the heart of a tadpole just before the feeding stage. (*b*) Section of ventricle of adult frog. Note that the tadpole sinus has irregularly arranged myofilaments (at arrows) and poor alignment of filaments into myofibrils with only a few cross bands.

vessels, and the right ventricle (which pumps the pulmonary circuit) must be ready to take over from the placenta the entire responsibility of oxygenating the blood.

The systemic part of the circulation must also be prepared. During intrauterine life the left side of the heart receives less blood from the pulmonary veins than the right side receives from the vena cavae. Immediately after birth the left ventricle is called on to do more work than the right ventricle. It must pump sufficient blood through the myriad peripheral vessels of the systemic circulation to care for the metabolism and continued growth of all parts of the body. These are just some of the striking functional situations which the growing heart must encounter before it can attain its adult condition.

Division of atrium and ventricles. Almost from their earliest appearance, the atrium and ventricle show external indication of their impending division into right and left sides. A distinct median furrow appears at the apex of the ventricle (Figs. 7*d* and *e* and 6*c–e*). The atrium meanwhile bulges out on either side of the midline (Fig. 7). Its bilobed configuration is emphasized by the manner in which the truncus arteriosus compresses it mid-ventrally (Fig. 6*c–e*). These superficial features suggest the more important internal changes.

As the wall of the ventricle increases in thickness, it develops internally a meshwork of interlacing muscular bands, the trabeculae carneae. Opposite the external furrow these muscular bands become consolidated as a partition which projects from the apex of the ventricle toward the atrium. This is the interventricular septum (**Fig. 9**).

Meanwhile, two conspicuous masses of the loosely organized mesenchyme called endocardial cushion tissue develop in the walls of the narrowed portion of the heart between the atrium and ventricle. One of these endocardial cushions of the atrioventricular canal is formed in its dorsal wall (**Fig. 10***b*). A similar one is formed opposite it on the ventral wall. When these two masses meet, they divide the atrioventricular canal into right and left channels (**Fig. 11**).

Septum primum. Concurrently, a median partition appears in the cephalic wall of the atrium. Because another closely related partition will form adjacent to it later, this is called the first interatrial septum or septum primum. It is composed of a thin layer of young cardiac muscle covered by endothelium. It is crescent-shaped, with its concavity directed toward the ventricle. The apices of the crescent extend to the atrioventricular canal where they merge, respectively, with its dorsal and ventral endocardial cushions (Fig. 10). This leaves the atria separated from each other except for a diminishing opening called the interatrial foramen primum (Fig. 10*b*).

While these changes have been occurring, the sinus venosus has been shifted out of the midline so that it opens into the atrium to the right of the interatrial septum (Fig. 7). The heart is now in a critical stage of development. Its original simple tubular form has been altered so that the four chambers characteristic of the adult heart are clearly suggested. Partitioning of the heart into right and left sides is well under way, but there are still open communications from the right to the left side in both atrium and ventricle. If partitioning were completed now, the left side of the heart would be left almost literally dry, because the sinus venosus, into which systemic, portal, and placental currents all enter, opens on the right of the interatrial septum. Not until much later do the lungs and their vessels develop sufficiently to return any considerable volume of blood to the left atrium. The partitions in the ventricle and in the atrioventricular canal do progress rapidly to completion (Figs. 10, 11, and **Fig. 12**), but an interesting series of events takes place in the interatrial septal complex which assures that an adequate supply of blood will reach the left atrium and thence the left ventricle.

In the sixth week, just when the septum primum is about to fuse with the endocardial cushions of the atrioventricular canal, thus closing the interatrial foramen primum, a new opening is established. The more cephalic part of the septum primum becomes perforated, at first by multiple small holes. These soon coalesce to form the interatrial foramen secundum, thus keeping a route open from the right to the left atrium (Fig. 11).

Septum secundum. During the seventh week the second interatrial partition makes its appearance just to the right of the first. Like the septum primum, the septum secundum is crescent-shaped. The concavity of its crescent is, however, differently oriented. Whereas the open part of the septum primum is directed toward the atrioventricular canal, the open part of the septum secundum is directed toward the lower part of the sinus entrance which later becomes the opening of the inferior vena cava into the right

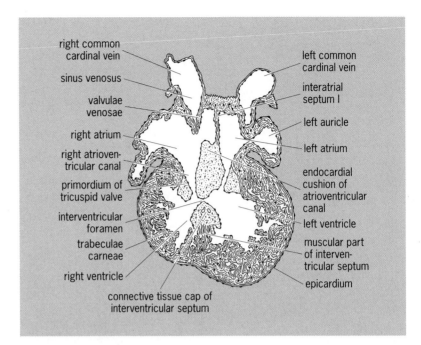

Fig. 9. Section through heart of a 9.4-mm (0.37-in.) pig embryo. Stage of development corresponds to that in a human embryo of the sixth week. (*After B. M. Patten, Foundations of Embryology, 2d ed., McGraw-Hill, 1965*)

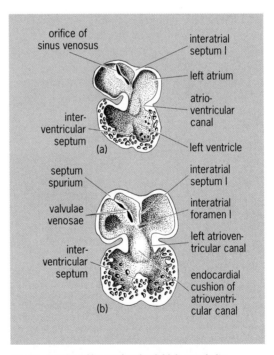

Fig. 10. Interior of heart showing initial steps in its partitioning. (*a*) Cardiac septa in human embryos early in fifth week, showing primary relations of interatrial septum primum. Based on original reconstruction of heart of a 3.7-mm (0.15-in.) pig embryo and on Tandler's reconstructions of corresponding stages of the human heart. (*b*) Cardiac septa in human embryos of sixth week. Note restriction of interatrial foramen primum by growth of interatrial septum primum. Based on original reconstructions of the heart of 6-mm (0.24-in.) pig embryo, on Born's reconstructions of rabbit heart, and Tandler's reconstructions of corresponding stages of the human heart. (*After B. M. Patten, Human Embryology, 3d ed., Blakiston–McGraw-Hill, 1968*)

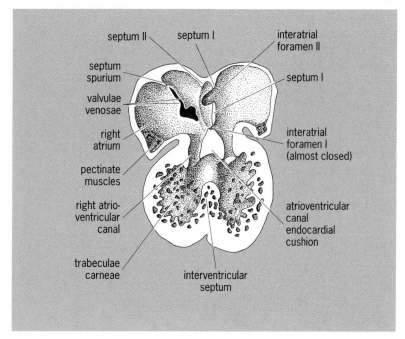

Fig. 11. Interior of heart showing start of interatrial septum secundum and appearance of interatrial foramen secundum in septum primum. Based on original reconstructions of the hearts of pig embryos and on Tandler's reconstructions of the heart of human embryos of the seventh week. (*After B. M. Patten, Human Embryology, 3d ed., Blakiston–McGraw-Hill, 1968*)

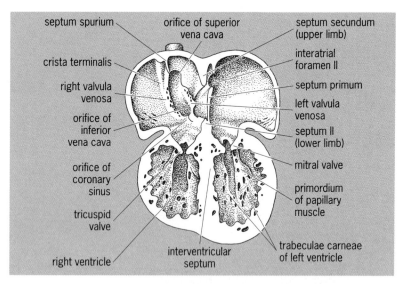

Fig. 12. Heart of third-month human embryo. Resorption has begun in valvulae venosae and septum spurium as indicated by many small perforations in their margins. Left venous valve is coming to lie against and fuse with septum secundum; it usually leaves no recognizable traces in the adult, but occasionally delicate lacelike remains can be seen adhering to septum secundum, and more rarely, extending a short distance onto the valvula foraminis ovalis. (*After B. M. Patten, Foundations of Embryology, 2d ed., McGraw-Hill, 1964*)

atrium (Figs. 11 and 12). This difference in the direction of growth in the two interatrial septa is of vital functional significance because it means that as the septum secundum grows, the opening remaining in it is carried out of line with the interatrial foramen secundum in the septum primum (Fig. 12). The opening in the septum secundum, although it becomes relatively smaller as develop-

ment progresses, will not be completely closed but will remain as the foramen ovale.

The flaplike persisting portion of the septum primum overlying the foramen ovale constitutes an efficient valvular mechanism between the two atria. When the atria are filling, some of the blood returning by way of the great veins can pass freely through the foramen ovale merely by pushing aside the flap of the septum primum. When the atria start to contract, pressure of the blood within the left atrium forces the septum primum against the septum secundum, effectively closing the foramen ovale against return flow into the right atrium. Without some such mechanism to afford a fair share of blood to the left atrium, the fetal left ventricle would receive a low blood volume, and as a result its muscular wall would not develop adequately to carry its postnatal pumping load. The strength of cardiac muscle and other muscles in the body depends on the work the muscle is called upon to do.

Division of the truncus. While these changes are going on in the main part of the heart, the truncus arteriosus is being divided into two separate channels. This process starts where the truncus joins the ventral roots of the aortic arches. Continuing toward the ventricle, the division is effected by the formation of longitudinal ridges of plastic young connective tissue of the same type as that making up the endocardial cushions of the atrioventricular canal. These ridges, called truncus ridges, bulge progressively further into the lumen of the truncus arteriosus and finally meet to separate it into aortic and pulmonary channels (**Figs. 13** and **14**). The semilunar valves of the aorta and the pulmonary trunk develop as local specializations of these truncus ridges. Toward the ventricles from the site of formation of the semilunar valves, the ridges are continued into the conus of the ventricles (**Fig. 15**). The truncoconal ridges follow a spiral course through the truncus and extend down

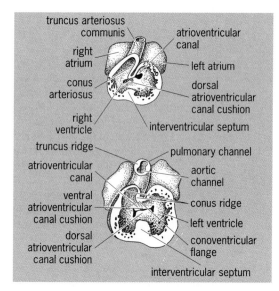

Fig. 13. Dissections of developing hearts in frontal aspect to show relations of importance in establishing aortic and pulmonary outlets. (*After T. C. Kramer, Amer. J. Anat., 71(3):343–370, 1942*)

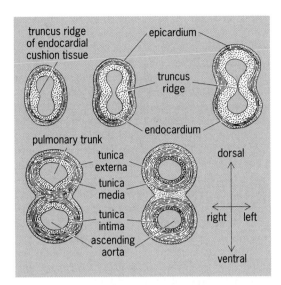

Fig. 14. Partitioning of the truncus arteriosus to form the ascending aorta and the pulmonary trunk. (*After S. E. Gould, Pathology of the Heart, Charles C. Thomas, 1953*)

into the ventricles, where they meet and become continuous with the margins of the interventricular septum. This reduces the relative size of the interventricular foramen but does not close it completely. Its final closure is brought about by a mass of endocardial cushion tissue from three sources. Bordering the interventricular foramen ventrocaudally is the interventricular septum, the crest of which, above its main muscular portion, is made up of endocardial cushion tissue (Fig. 9).

Toward the atrioventricular canal lie the masses of endocardial cushion tissue which were responsible for its partitioning (Fig. 15). In the conus outlet are the ridges that were just considered. From all three of these adjacent areas, endocardial cushion tissue encroaches on the opening. About the end of the seventh week, the interventricular fora-

men is completely plugged with a loose mass of this young, readily molded connective tissue. Later this mass differentiates into the membranous portion of the interventricular septum and the septal cusps of the atrioventricular valves. When the interventricular septum has thus been completed, the right ventricle leads into the pulmonary trunk and the left leads into the ascending aorta. With this condition established, the heart is completely divided into right and left sides except for the interatrial valve at the foramen ovale which must remain open throughout fetal life until after birth, when the lungs attain their full functional capacity and the entire volume of the pulmonary stream passes through them to be returned to the left atrium.

Ductus arteriosus. This leaves only one of the functional exigencies of heart development still to be accounted for. If, during early fetal life and before the lungs are well developed, the vessels to the lungs were the only exit from the right side of the heart, the right ventricle would not have an outlet adequate to develop its pumping power. It is only late in fetal life that the lungs and their vessels develop to a degree which prepares them for assuming their postnatal activity, and the power of the heart muscle can be built up only gradually by continued functional activity. This situation is met by the ductus arteriosus, leading from the pulmonary trunk to the aorta. Throughout fetal life any blood from the right ventricle that cannot be accepted within the pulmonary circuit is shunted by way of the ductus into the descending aorta. Thus the right ventricle is able to develop its muscular walls by pumping throughout prenatal life its full share of the cardiac load.

The foregoing account of cardiac partitioning applies particularly to the human. There are some notable exceptions in cardiac development in the opossum, a mammal in which the young are born in a primitive stage and continue their development for several weeks in the mother's pouch. This species

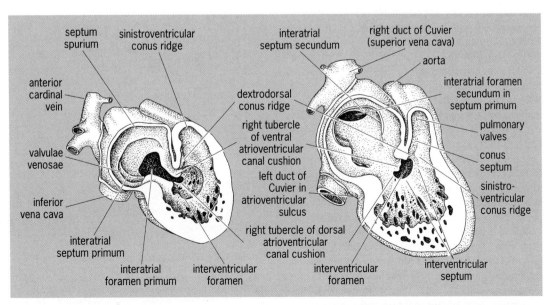

Fig. 15. Lateral dissections showing the relations of the various septa in the developing heart. (*After B. M. Patten, Human Embryology, 3d ed., Blakiston–McGraw-Hill, 1968*)

does not have a secondary interatrial septum or a fossa ovalis. The primary septum has multiple perforations, a few of which persist until birth. The sinus venosus remains in a more primitive stage, clearly defined from the right atrium. The left superior vena cava also persists, opening into the sinus portion of the atrium by way of the coronary sinus.

The rabbit also maintains a more primitive arrangement of the vessels and a more evident sinus region much like the opossum.

Embryogenesis of blood vessels. The endothelial lining of the earliest embryonic vessels arises from mesenchyme, with differentiation occurring first in the wall of the trophoblast and only slightly later in the body stalk and yolk sac. The mesenchymal cells with potency to form endothelium are designated as angioblasts.

According to one view (angioblastic theory), the vessels within the body of the embryo arise by migration of angioblasts from the body stalk and yolk sac. According to the local origin theory, the main intraembryonic vessels, such as the aorta, arise by in situ differentiation from vasoformative mesenchymal cells. Most experimental evidence favors the latter view.

After the main embryonic vessels have arisen, new vessels arise by vascular sprouts from preexisting vessels. Regeneration of endothelium of new vessels following injury in adult life is likewise dependent upon outgrowth from preexisting endothelium.

Angiogenesis. The earliest observable differentiation of endothelium occurs in blood islands of the trophoblast, body stalk, and yolk sac. Each island consists of mesenchymal cell clusters in which the central cells differentiate into blood corpuscles and the peripheral cells elongate and transform into endothelium. Growth and union of the isolated vascular spaces give a plexus of primitive vascular channels. Endothelium of the main vessels of the body of the embryo differentiates also but without relationship to blood islands.

Circulatory system morphogenesis. The earliest vessels are anastomosing, thin-walled tubes (capillaries) lined only by endothelium. In the course of differentiation, some of the capillaries enlarge to form arteries and veins, some remain as capillaries, and some fall into disuse and atrophy. It seems well established that the amount rather than the rate of blood flow through any given portion of a capillary plexus determines whether a vessel merely persists as a capillary enlarges to form an artery or vein. In a similar manner, alterations in vascular pathways occur after the capillary plexus stage of differentiation. For example, arteries atrophy when their blood flow is diverted to newly formed vessels.

Formation of ventral aorta. The aorta arises from bilateral primordia continuous with the bilateral cardiac primordia. The bilateral rudiments quickly fuse to form a common truncus arteriosus continuous with the bulbus cordis. By formation and fusion of two longitudinal ridges along the inner surface of the distal portion of the bulbus, the primitive aortic bulb is split into a pulmonary trunk and an ascending aorta.

The latter is relatively short in mammals. It connects with the dorsal aorta by means of aortic arches which vary at different embryonic stages, and the final pattern differs in different species.

Formation of aortic arches. In mammalian embryos there are usually six pairs of arches, but these do not all function simultaneously. Furthermore, the fifth pair is very rudimentary. The arch which follows the questionable fifth one is usually called the pulmonary arch because it becomes a part of the pulmonary arterial system.

The first pair of aortic arches forms in human embryos at the beginning of the fourth week, and the remaining pairs develop in sequence during the fourth week. Transformations (**Fig. 16**) occupy the fifth to seventh weeks.

The first and second pairs become dysfunctional and atrophy as the third and fourth pairs enlarge, and form more direct pathways from the ventral to the dorsal aortas. Following atrophy of portions of the dorsal aortas between levels of the third and fourth arches, the third arches and cephalic portions of the dorsal aortas remain as paired primitive internal carotid arteries. After the external carotid grows out from the third arch, the proximal portion is known as the common carotid.

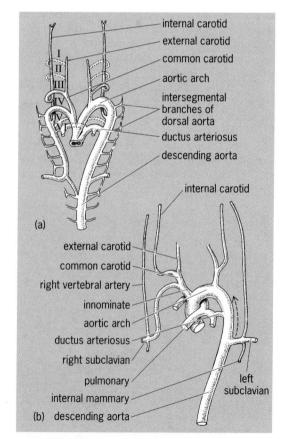

Fig. 16. Transformations of human aortic arches, ventral view. (*a*) Diagram of early stage of transformation when first, second, and fifth pairs of vessels (broken lines) have degenerated. (*b*) Adult derivatives. Diagram, from fetus, shows left subclavian arising from caudal part of arch, but shifts to a higher position at a later stage, indicated by arrow. Ductus arteriosus normally atrophies after birth.

The fate of the fourth arches differs for different classes of vertebrates. In mammals the left fourth arch persists as the arch of the aorta, whereas the right fourth arch forms a portion of the innominate artery and the proximal portion of the subclavian artery (Fig. 16). In birds the condition is the reverse, with the arch of the aorta forming on the left. In reptiles and amphibians both fourth arches retain their connection with the dorsal aorta.

Formation of dorsal aorta. The dorsal aorta arises from bilateral primordia which persist as the paired internal carotids cephalically (Fig. 16) and fuse caudally to form the descending aorta.

The aorta has dorsal, lateral, and ventral branches which are arranged serially. There are about 30 pairs of dorsal branches, which are also known as intersegmental arteries because they occur between successive body segments. Each of the intersegmental arteries divides into dorsal and ventral rami; the dorsal rami give rise to the spinal and vertebral arteries and the ventral rami form the intercostals and lumbars. The lateral aortic branches are not segmentally arranged. They form the renal, suprarenal, inferior phrenic, and internal spermatic or ovarian arteries. The ventral aortic branches develop as paired vitelline arteries to the yolk sac. They fuse when the paired aortas fuse. Later, they are reduced until they occur only at three levels, forming the celiac, superior mesenteric, and inferior mesenteric arteries.

Arteries of the extremities. Vascularization of the extremities illustrates the growth of given pathways within a plexus of vessels. At first, each extremity has a blood supply from several lateral aortic branches. Then, one lateral branch enlarges and the others fall into disuse. In the arm the main stem is the brachial artery which is a continuation from the subclavian. The extension of the brachial into the arm progresses by differential growth of pathways of a capillary plexus. At one stage, the brachial continues by the interosseous to the vessels of the hand. Later, when the median artery arises as a brachial branch and annexes the vessels of the hand, the interosseous becomes less prominent. At a still later stage, the ulnar and radial arteries develop as brachial branches and become the main vessels of the forearm.

The first axial vessel of the leg is known as the sciatic artery. Later, it is superseded by the femoral artery which is a continuation of the external iliac, a branch of the common iliac. After the femoral joins and annexes portions of the sciatic, the proximal portion of the sciatic persists merely as the inferior gluteal, whereas the distal part of the sciatic becomes the popliteal artery in continuity with the femoral.

Primitive venous system. In the early embryo there are three sets of paired veins of particular significance: vitellines carrying blood from the yolk sac to the heart, umbilicals from the placenta, and cardinals from the head and body.

Changes in vitelline veins. Changes in these vessels are correlated with the developing liver in the sense that there is a mutual intergrowth between cords of hepatic cells and endothelial sprouts from the vitelline veins. Thus the vitelline veins are interrupted by liver sinusoids. By enlargement of some of the sinusoids, a direct channel is formed between the left umbilical vein and the proximal portion of the right vitelline (the future hepatic); the channel is known as the ductus venosus.

Caudal to the liver, the right and left vitelline veins become united by three cross anastomoses. By growth of some parts and atrophy of other parts of this system, the S-shaped portal vein arises.

The segment of the right vitelline between the liver and the heart becomes the hepatic vein; the left vitelline of this level disappears.

Changes in umbilical veins. During its growth, the liver encroaches on the umbilical veins until all the umbilical blood enters the liver. Then the entire right umbilical vein atrophies, leaving the left vein which empties into the ductus venosus. The left umbilical vein and the ductus venosus persist as important vessels until birth; then they atrophy and become the ligamentum teres and the ligamentum venosum, respectively.

Plan of the cardinal veins. Paired precardinal veins from the head join paired postcardinals from the body at the level of the heart to form the common cardinals (ducts of Cuvier). During development, parts of the postcardinals are replaced and superseded by subcardinals and supracardinals. The major veins of the body arise through transformation of the cardinal system.

Changes in precardinals, common cardinals. The precardinal of each side is composed of a primary head vein and the precardinal proper extending from the head to the common cardinal. The head vein drains anterior, median, and lateral plexuses over the brain. The rostral portion of the head vein becomes the cavernous sinus; portions of the anterior plexus enlarge to become the superior sagittal sinus; and a dorsal connection between the middle and posterior plexuses becomes the transverse sinus. The main precardinal stem of each side becomes the internal jugular vein as far caudal as the level of a shunt from the left to the right precardinal (**Fig. 17**). The shunt itself becomes the left brachiocephalic (left innominate), and the left precardinal caudal to the shunt remains as the relatively small first intercostal.

The right common cardinal with the right precardinal up to the point of intercardinal anastomosis forms the superior vena cava. The left common cardinal of humans persists as the small oblique vein of the left atrium. As a congenital anomaly, it may remain as a left superior vena cava. In some mammals and in the lower vertebrates, two superior venae cavae (left and right) occur normally.

Postcardinal system transformations. Postcardinals develop primarily as vessels of the mesonephroi and their fate in different species varies with that of the mesonephroi. In *Petromyzon* the postcardinal of each side remains, as in the embryo; in elasmobranchs the plan is modified by a renal portal system; and in humans and some other mammals the postcardinals become altered, as shown in Fig. 17.

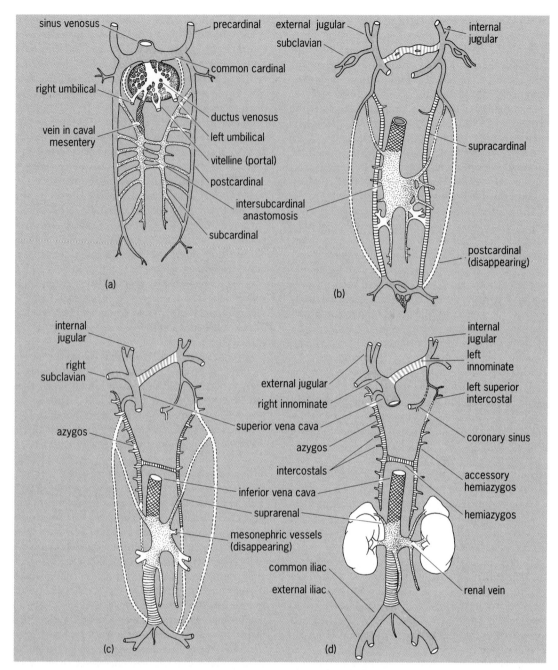

Fig. 17. Transformations of primitive veins of human embryo, ventral view. (*a*) At 5½ weeks. (*b*) At 7 weeks. (*c*) At 8 weeks. (*d*) At term. In *a*, proximal portions of umbilicals (broken lines) have atrophied. Remainder of the right umbilical atrophies later. Vitellines (omphalomesenterics) have been interrupted by liver sinusoids. Right proximal vitelline has enlarged and will become the hepatic. Caudal portions of vitellines are transforming into the portal vein. A connection from hepatic to subcardinals via ventral mesentery will form hepatic segment of inferior vena cava. Vessels associated with liver are omitted from *b*, *c*, and *d*.

This transformation is related to the development of subcardinal veins ventral to the mesonephroi, and supracardinals dorsomedial to the postcardinals. Parts of each of these systems contribute to the formation of the inferior vena cava (Fig. 17).

Veins of the extremities. These develop by channels within capillary plexuses, as already described for the arteries. Each extremity of an early embryo develops a peripheral or border vein. In the upper extremity the border vein persists on the ulnar side as the subclavian, axillary, and basilic veins; in the lower extremity the border vein persists on the fibular side.

Pulmonary veins. These develop from pulmonary plexuses. At one stage of development, all branches combine to open by a single stem into the left atrium. By growth of the atrium, more of the pulmonary vessel is drawn into the atrial wall until there are four pulmonary vein openings into the atrium, two from each lung. W. M. Copenhaver

Functional Development of Heart

The heart begins to beat before all its parts have been formed. The character of the heartbeat changes with the sequential formation of the regions of the heart.

The heart arises by the fusion of bilateral primordia which converge from positions on opposite sides of the embryo. In the human embryo virtually the entire development of the heart and major blood vessels occurs between the third and eighth weeks of embryonic life. In the chick embryo, one of the principal objects of experimental analysis, the bilateral primordia begin to fuse in the seven-somite stage. The first beats can be recorded in the embryo of nine somites, where the first cross striations also occur.

Contractions of the heart. The first contractions occur along the right side of the developing ventricle, the first part of the heart to form. The beat is at first slow but rhythmical and gradually involves the whole wall of the ventricle. The first contractions may be described as rhythmic but intermittent, that is, rhythmic contractions interrupted by rest periods. Next is added the atrium, which begins to contract at a higher rate than that of the ventricle, stepping up the rate of the entire heart, because the part of the tube with the highest rate of contraction sets the pace for the heart as a whole. At this time the blood is set in motion. The sinus venosus begins to contract somewhat later; again, its inclusion steps up the heartbeat. Contractions begin before any of the nerve fibers (which in their development grow out from the central nervous system), reach the heart and before the specialized system for conducting impulses in the heart is established. The nervous system secondarily assumes the regulation of the rate of the pulsations originating in the myocardium, retarding and accelerating functions being by the vagus and cervical sympathetic fibers, respectively.

Heart-forming areas. The first pulsations of the heart are foreshadowed by the localization of the heart-forming cells to well-demarcated regions of the embryo in the head-process stage, about 10 h earlier. **Figure 18** shows the position of the heart-forming areas as demonstrated by experimental tests of the histogenetic capacity of isolated fragments of

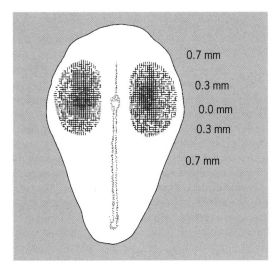

Fig. 18. Heart-forming areas in a head-process stage chick blastoderm. Numerals show distances from level of primitive pit. (*After M. E. Rawles, The heart-forming areas of the early chick blastoderm, Physiol. Zool., 16:22–42, University of Chicago Press, 1943*)

the early embryo. Although cardiac muscle arises from the mesoderm, it is impossible to state whether it develops independently in the chick or whether interactions between the mesoderm and endoderm are required. Such an inductive interaction appears to be required for normal development of the heart in the salamander embryo.

Contractile proteins. The question has been raised as to what extent the early localization of heart-forming cells reflects the early differentiation of specificity in chemical composition or metabolism. It has also been questioned whether the heart-forming areas differ chemically from adjacent regions of the embryo. Immunochemical techniques employing as tools specific antiheart sera reveal that the early embryo contains macromolecules identical with or closely related to those of the adult heart, a conclusion that is supported by the additional finding that when early embryos are cultured in a medium containing antiheart serum the development of the heart is differentially suppressed. Similar techniques show time of origin and pattern of localization of the cardiac contractile proteins, myosin and actin.

Synthesis of contractile proteins. The synthesis of cardiac myosin is initiated during the formation of the mesoderm, the protein being detected first during the movement of prospective mesodermal cells through the primitive streak. As these formative movements are terminated, myosin is distributed widely in the ectoderm and mesoderm, but cannot be detected in the endoderm. At the head-process stage, cardiac myosin is restricted to the heart-forming regions of the embryo where, at the same time, the synthesis of cardiac actin is initiated. It is impossible at the present time to say whether the myosin first detected is adult myosin, or a complete myosin molecule closely related to but not identical with the adult protein, a situation that exists in the sequential formation of fetal and adult hemoglobin molecules. It is postulated that, in the formation of cardiac muscle, the contractile proteins are synthesized and subsequently aggregated to form fibrils. Although this hypothesis of stepwise organization agrees with the limited information available on the development of the fine structure of heart muscle, a note of caution must be expressed, because in skeletal muscle myosin has been detected simultaneously with the formation of the first simple muscle fibrils, and not before. *See* HEMATOPOIESIS.

Action of inhibitors. In further studies of the biochemical differentiation of the heart-forming areas, it has been found that the metabolic pathways operating in the development of the brain and heart differ markedly. When early chick embryos are cultured in vitro on a medium containing traces of the metabolic inhibitor antimycin A, the development of the regions destined to form muscle is inhibited almost completely, whereas the developing brain and spinal cord remain intact. The heart is more sensitive than other mesodermal tissues. Another compound, sodium fluoride, also inhibits development of the heart. The inhibition of the embryo produced by sodium fluoride follows a clear-cut, reproducible pattern, in which the initial sites of inhibition are the heart-forming regions. At succeeding stages in the establishment of the heart, the locations of the cells destroyed by sodium fluoride reflect the sites of highest ability to form pulsatile heart and the area of greatest capacity for the synthesis of actin and myosin. Thus the primary forces operating in the formation of the heart must be sought at the very outset of development.   James D. Ebert

Human Fetal Circulation at Term

The circulation in the mammalian fetus at term must be thoroughly understood as a basis for the consideration of postnatal circulatory changes, because the very mechanisms which ensure intracardiac balance during prenatal life maintain a balanced cardiac load during the changes to the postnatal basis. In this discussion of the fetal circulation at term, the basic conditions presented are essentially applicable to all the higher mammals. Reference to ages and to other specific details are, however, based on the conditions in humans.

By the last trimester of pregnancy all the major blood vessels have been developed in essentially their adult pattern, and all the steps in the partitioning of the embryonic heart are leading progressively closer to the final adult condition, in which the heart is a four-chambered organ completely divided into right and left sides. However, from the nature of its living conditions it is not possible for the fetus in utero to attain fully the adult type of circulation. The plan of the divided circulation of postnatal life is predicated on lung breathing. After birth the right side of the heart receives the blood returning from a circuit of the body and pumps it to the lungs, where it is relieved of carbon dioxide and acquires a fresh supply of oxygen. The left side of the heart then receives the blood that has just been aerated in the lungs and pumps it through ramifying channels to all the tissues of the body. In the last part of intrauterine life the lungs and their blood vessels are fully formed and ready to function, but they cannot actually try out their functional competence until after birth. Nevertheless, in the first minutes of its postnatal life a fetus must successfully change from an existence submerged in the amniotic fluid to air breathing with its hitherto untested lungs. Moreover, this abrupt change must be accomplished without the sudden overloading of any part of the cardiac pump.

It is in the light of these functional exigencies that the fetal circulation at term must be considered. Of primary importance is the fact that at no time during the prenatal life are the atria completely separated from each other. This permits the left atrium to receive a contribution of blood from the inferior vena cava by a transseptal flow which compensates for the relatively small amount of blood entering the left atrium directly by way of the pulmonary circuit. The routes and the relative amounts of this interatrial shunt are different at different ages. Very early in development, before the lungs have grown to any great extent, the pulmonary return is negligible and

the flow from the right atrium through the interatrial ostium primum constitutes practically the entire intake of the left atrium (**Fig. 19***b*). After the ostium primum has been closed and while the lungs are but little developed, flow through the interatrial ostium secundum must provide for the major part of the blood entering the left atrium (Fig. 19*d*). During the latter part of fetal life the foramen ovale in the septum secundum becomes the transseptal route for blood (Fig. 19*e* and *f*).

Intracardiac circulatory balance. The precise manner in which this balancing transseptal flow occurs in a fetus at term and where and to what extent the various bloodstreams are mixed has long been a controversial subject. By a synthesis of the most significant of the anatomical evidence with the newer experimental evidence, the course followed by the blood in passing through the heart may be summarized as follows. The inferior caval entrance is so directed with reference to the foramen ovale that a considerable portion of its stream passes directly into the left atrium (**Figs. 20** and **21**). Careful measurements have shown, however, that the interatrial communication through the foramen ovale is considerably smaller than the inferior caval inlet. This implies that the portion of the inferior caval stream which could not pass through this opening into the left atrium must eddy back and mix with the rest of the blood entering the right atrium. Angiocardiographic studies confirm this inference.

Prenatal pulmonary circulation. As the lungs grow and the pulmonary circulation increases in volume relatively less of the left atrial intake comes by way of the foramen ovale and relatively more from the vessels of the growing lungs. However, the circulation of the lungs, although increased as compared with earlier stages, has been shown by angiocardiographic studies to be much less in volume than the caliber of the pulmonary vessels would lead one to expect. Until the lungs are inflated, there are evidently factors, either vasomotor or mechanical or both, which restrict flow through the smaller pulmonary vessels. Therefore, even in the terminal months of pregnancy, a considerable right-left flow must still be maintained through the foramen ovale in order to keep the left atrial intake equal to that of the right.

Balancing ventricular output. The balanced atrial intake thus maintained implies a balanced ventricular intake, and this in turn implies the necessity of a balanced ventricular output. Although not in the heart itself, there is, in the closely associated great vessels, a mechanism which affords an adequate outlet from the right ventricle during the period when the pulmonary circuit is developing. When the pulmonary arteries are formed as downgrowths from the sixth pair of aortic arches, the right sixth arch soon loses its original connection with the dorsal aorta. On the left, however, a portion of the sixth arch persists as the ductus arteriosus connecting the pulmonary artery with the dorsal aorta (Fig. 21). This vessel remains open throughout fetal life and acts as a shunt, carrying over to the aorta whatever blood the pulmonary vessels at any particular phase of their development

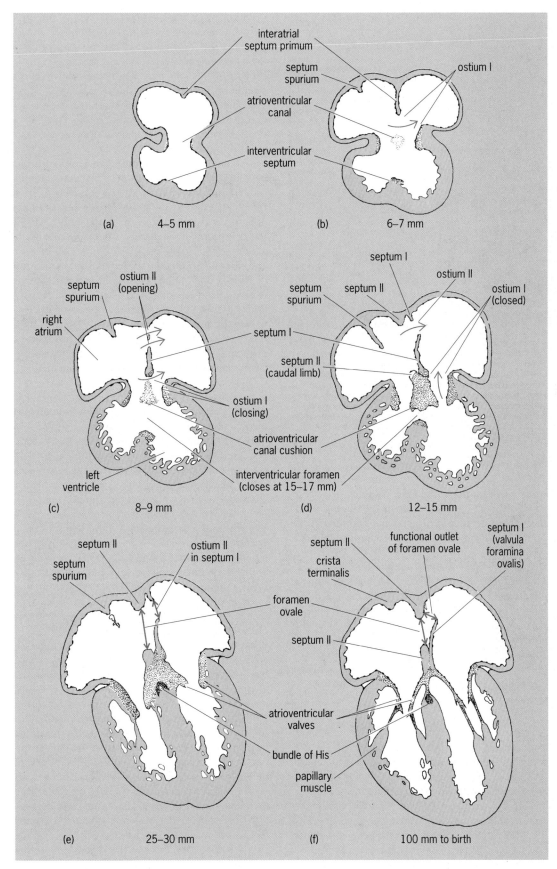

Fig. 19. Sectional plan (*a–f*) of the embryonic heart in frontal plane, showing progress of partitioning in the human embryo. The endocardial cushion tissue is indicated by stippled areas, the muscle by gray areas, and the epicardium by solid black outline. Parts *b* and *c* show the location of endocardial cushions of the atrioventricular canal before they have grown sufficiently to fuse in the plane of the diagram. (*After B. M. Patten, Developmental defects at the foramen ovale, Amer. J. Pathol., 14(2)135–161, 1938*)

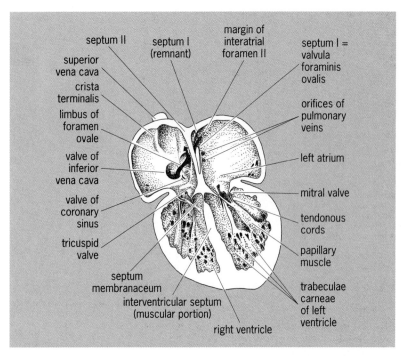

Fig. 20. Interrelations of septum primum and septum secundum during latter part of fetal life. Lower part of septum primum is situated to act as a one-way valve at the foramen ovale in septum secundum. Split arrow indicates the way a considerable part of blood from inferior vena cava passes through foramen ovale to the left atrium while remainder eddies back into the right atrium to mingle with the blood being returned by way of the superior vena cava. (*After B. M. Patten, Foundations of Embryology, 2d ed., McGraw-Hill, 1964*)

Pulmonary circuit and ductus. In much of the older literature, great emphasis was placed on what happened at the foramen ovale. It is now known that these changes are secondary and that the events of primary significance occur in connection with the pulmonary circuit and the ductus arteriosus. In the section on fetal circulation at term, the importance of the ductus arteriosus as an exercising channel for the right ventricle was emphasized. From the standpoint of postnatal circulatory changes, the reciprocal relation between flow through the ductus and flow through the lungs becomes the center of interest. As the lungs increase in size, relatively more of the blood leaving the right ventricle by way of the pulmonary trunk goes to the lungs, and relatively less goes through the ductus arteriosus to the dorsal aorta.

By the end of gestation the pulmonary vessels must be large enough to handle a blood volume adequate to care for oxygenating the blood. Injection preparations of fetuses clearly show that the vascular channels in the lungs are of generous size for this function well before birth. However, such postmortem material does not show that before birth these large vessels are not carrying the blood volume their size would suggest.

Prenatal pulmonary blood flow. The brilliant work of C. Wegelius and J. Lind, utilizing angiocardiographic methods on living fetuses, has shown that the flow of blood through the pulmonary circuit is actually restricted to a volume much below the potential capacity of the vessels. How much of this is the result of mechanical factors, such as the unexpanded condition of the lungs, and how much it depends upon differential vasoconstriction of the smaller vessels within the lungs remains to be determined. It is clear, however, that pulmonary channels of the requisite size have been formed and are ready to increase their blood flow radically and promptly with the beginning of respiration. Within a short time after birth, under the stimulus of functional activity, the lungs are able to take all the blood from the right side of the heart.

Abandonment and closure of ductus. When the lungs accept all the blood entering the pulmonary trunk, blood flow through the ductus arteriosus ceases. Following its functional abandonment, the ductus arteriosus is gradually occluded by an overgrowth of its intimal tissue. This process in the wall of the ductus is as characteristic and regular a feature of the development of the circulatory system as the formation of the cardiac septa. Its earliest phases begin to be recognizable in the fetus as the time of birth approaches, and postnatally the process continues at an accelerated rate, to terminate in complete anatomical occlusion of the lumen of the ductus some 6–8 weeks after birth.

Postnatal readjustment of the circulation cannot, however, wait on this protracted structural closure. Following birth there appears to be an immediate reduction in the bore of the ductus as a result of its muscular contraction. This is accompanied by a reduced flow of blood through it. This reduction in the

are not prepared to receive from the right ventricle. The ductus arteriosus can therefore be called the exercising channel of the right ventricle because it allows the right ventricle to do its full share of work throughout development and thus be prepared to pump its full quota of blood through the lungs at birth.

Thus by means of intake and output shunts there is maintained, throughout prenatal development, an effective right-left balance in the pumping load of the heart. The importance of this for the attainment of normal cardiac structure is forcefully shown by the abnormalities that appear when the balancing mechanisms are in any way disturbed. The importance of these same mechanisms in accomplishing postnatal circulatory changes is discussed in the following section.

Human Postnatal Circulation

The changes in circulation following birth involve some of the most dramatic and fascinating biological processes. One of the most impressive phenomena in embryology is the perfect preparedness for these changes which has been built into the very architecture of the circulatory system during its development. The shunt at the ductus arteriosus, which has been one of the factors in balancing ventricular output throughout intrauterine development, and the valvular mechanism at the foramen ovale, which has been balancing atrial intakes, are perfectly adapted to prevent any abrupt unbalancing of cardiac load as a result of postnatal changes in circulatory routes.

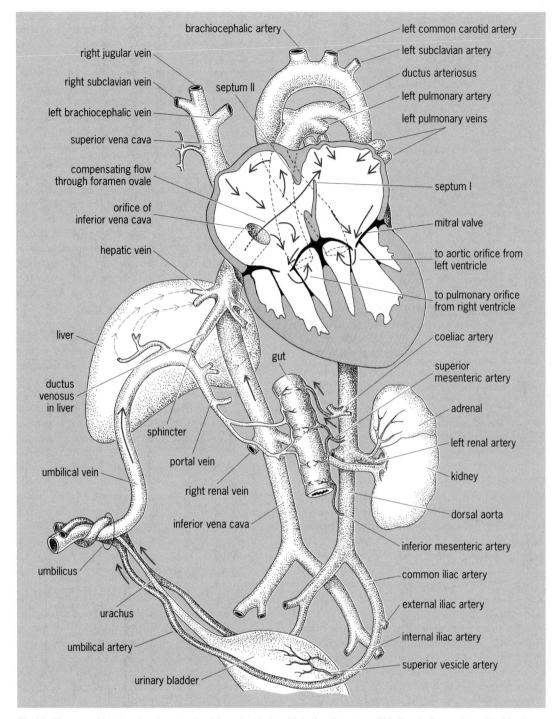

Fig. 21. Diagram of heart and major vessels of fetus just before birth. Small arrows within liver indicate alternative blood routes by way of hepatic sinusoids. (*After B. M. Patten, Human Embryology, 3d ed., McGraw-Hill, 1968*)

shunt from the pulmonary circuit to the aorta, acting together with the lowering of resistance in the vascular bed of the lungs which accompanies their newly assumed respiratory activity, aids in raising the pulmonary circulation promptly to full functional level. At the same time, the functional closure of the ductus arteriosus paves the way for the ultimate anatomical obliteration of its lumen by the active growth of its intimal connective tissue.

Closure of foramen ovale. The results of increased pulmonary circulation with the concomitant increase in the direct intake of the left atrium are manifested secondarily at the foramen ovale. Following birth, as the pulmonary return increases, compensatory blood flow from the right atrium to the left decreases correspondingly, and shortly ceases altogether. In other words, when equalization of atrial intakes has occurred, the compensating one-way valve at the foramen ovale falls into disuse and the foramen may be regarded as functionally closed. The abandonment of the shunt at the foramen ovale is indicated anatomically by a progressive reduction in the looseness

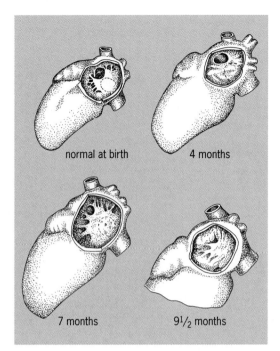

normal at birth

4 months

7 months

9½ months

Fig. 22. Hearts with left atrium opened to show gross changes in relations of valvula during period in which foramen ovale closes anatomically. (*After B. M. Patten, The closure of the foramen ovale, Amer. J. Anat., 48:19–44, 1931*)

of the valvula foraminis ovalis and the consequent diminution of the interatrial communication to a progressively narrower slit between the valvula and the septum.

Anatomical obliteration of the foramen ovale slowly follows its functional abandonment (**Fig. 22**). There is a highly variable interval of 3–9 months following birth before the septum primum fuses with the septum secundum to seal the foramen ovale. This delay is, however, of no functional import because as long as the pulmonary circuit is normal and pressure in the left atrium equals or exceeds that in the right, the orifice between them is functionally inoperative. It is not uncommon to find the fusion of these two septa incomplete in the hearts of individuals who have, as far as circulatory disturbances are concerned, lived uneventfully to maturity. Such a condition can be characterized as probe patency of the foramen ovale. When, in such hearts, a probe is inserted under the margin of the fossa ovalis and pushed toward the left atrium, the probe is prying behind the no longer used, but still unfastened, interatrial door.

Physiological aspects of transition. Much yet remains to be learned concerning the more precise physiology of the fetal circulation and concerning the interaction of various factors during the transition from intrauterine to postnatal conditions. Nevertheless, it is quite apparent that the changes in the circulation which occur following birth involve no revolutionary disturbances of the load carried by different parts of the heart. The fact that the pulmonary vessels are already so well developed before birth means that the changes which must occur following birth have been thoroughly prepared for, and the compensatory mechanisms at the foramen ovale and the ductus arteriosus which have been functioning throughout fetal life are entirely competent to effect the final postnatal reroutings of the circulation with a minimum of functional disturbance. The change from living in water to living in air is crowded into a few crucial moments that in phylogeny must have been spread over eons of transitional amphibious existence. Bradley M. Patten

Comparative Physiology

Comparative physiology describes the structure and operation of the circulation in living animals, and enquires as to how or why the circulatory system may have evolved. Comparing the circulatory system in different animal groups leads to an understanding of general principles and also to various applications of those principles, adapting animals to a wide range of habitats. The circulatory system in all vertebrates has multiple functions, but all functions are involved in regulating the internal environment of the animal (promoting homeostasis).

General physiology of circulation. In all vertebrates the circulatory system consists of a central pump, the heart, which drives a liquid transport medium, the blood, continuously around a closed system of tubes, the vascular system. The arterial portion of this system is divided into larger elastic and smaller resistance vessels (arterioles) which distribute blood to specialized regions or organs (such as muscles, gut, and lungs) where transfer of nutrients, oxygen, or waste products takes place across the walls of a fine network of microscopic capillaries. Blood from the capillaries passes through the venules (small venous vessels) into the main veins and returns to the heart (**Fig. 23**). The arterioles, venules, and capillaries make up the microcirculation, which is arguably the most important role of the vertebrate circulatory system from a functional point of view.

Blood flow in the circulation occurs from regions of high to regions of low fluid energy (or down an energy gradient). The total fluid energy consists of "pressure" energy (created by the heart) and energy contained in the blood due to its motion (kinetic energy). The latter component is small (1 to 2% of the pressure energy in main arteries) and is usually ignored. Hence, the term "pressure" has become synonymous with the total fluid energy. However, this is not always the case as pressures usually recorded in the circulation are transmural pressures; that is, pressure across the wall of the vessel.

The transmural pressure can be very misleading if it is taken as representing the energy for flow. For example, in a recumbent person, transmural pressure in the foot arteries is 1.7 lb in.$^{-2}$ or 12 kilopascals, but in an erect person, the column of fluid between the heart and foot is subjected to the gravitational force, which means the column bears down on the foot arteries with a pressure equivalent to its height (4 ft or 1.2 m), and adds to the pressure created by the pump. Due to this hydrostatic effect, transmural pressure in the foot may be 2.4 lb in.$^{-2}$ or 24 kPa.

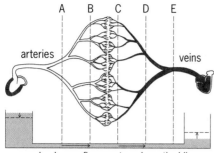

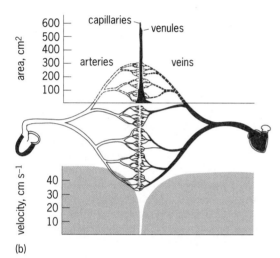

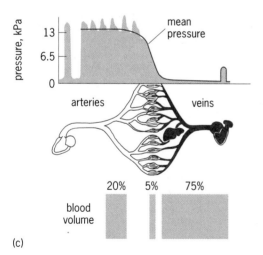

Fig. 23. Systemic circulatory system in a dog (13 kg or 28.7 lb). (*a*) Representation of the aborization of the system. All vessels of the same caliber are arranged vertically (at A, B, C, and so on). (*b*) Increase in cross-sectional area of the various segments. The velocity of blood flow (cm · s⁻¹) is inversely proportional to the cross-sectional area of the tubes through which it flows. (*c*) Pulsatile and mean pressures in the various vascular segments. At the extreme left is a representation of left ventricular pressure, while right ventricular pressure is shown at the extreme right. The boxes show the proportion of blood volume (approximately 85% of total blood volume) in the systemic arteries (including the heart), capillaries, and veins (the pulmonary circulation has about 10–15% of the total blood volume). (*After R. F. Rushmer, Cardiovascular Dynamics, W. B. Saunders, 1961*)

However, this hydrostatic effect is also added to the veins so the energy gradient for flow through the vascular beds remains unchanged. In other words, in a closed circulation, flow cannot be maintained by differences in fluid level (hydrostatic pressure). Flow occurs as a result of difference in total fluid energy between two points in the circulation; if these points are at the same fluid level (central arteries and veins), then the energy difference can be measured in terms of pressure.

Energy is dissipated unevenly around the circulation, the major portion being expended to force blood through the arterial resistance vessels (Fig. 23, energy shown as pressure). Even so, loss of energy is not altogether due to friction between the vessel wall and blood but rather to overcoming the internal friction (or viscosity) of the blood. In the circulation, blood flow is usually streamlined or laminar. If blood, flowing in a vessel, is imagined as made up of a series of thin concentric tubes (or laminae), the layer of fluid next to the wall is stationary while that in the center flows fastest. Therefore, successive layers of blood slide past one another, and friction between these layers of fluid dissipates mechanical energy as heat.

The relation between mean pressures (energy) and flows in the body circulation (equally applicable in general principle to the pulmonary circulation) is shown in Fig. 23. At every division of a blood vessel the cross-sectional area of the branches always exceeds that of the parent vessel (with two branches by a factor of 1.2 to 1.3), so there is a tremendous increase in area as the capillaries are approached (Fig. 23*b*). In a closed circulation what goes in at one end must come out the other, so the total blood flow through each region must be the same, but the rate of flow will be inversely proportional to the cross-sectional area of any given region (Fig. 23*a* and *b*). Since the cross-sectional area of the veins is not much greater than that of the arteries, venous flow rates are high (Fig. 23*b*). On the other hand, mean pressure in the circulation falls from the arteries to the veins. The major pressure drop in the circulation occurs across the arterial resistance vessels which lead to the capillaries (Fig. 23*c*). Consequently, venous pressure is low, despite high blood flow rates, and this explains why blood does not spurt out when one severs a vein. The majority of the total blood volume is stored in the venous vessels (Fig. 23*c*).

Microcirculation. The microcirculation consists of arterial (arterioles) and venous (venules) resistance vessels on either side of the capillaries. The arterioles and venules constitute the pre- and postcapillary resistances respectively. A capillary is a single layer of endothelial cells enclosed by a basement membrane. Blood flow through the capillary is low (at rest, less than 1 mm · s⁻¹) and is controlled by the opening and closing activity of a short muscular region of blood vessel at the capillary entrance (precapillary sphincter). The total number of capillaries, and therefore their surface area for exchange of materials with the cells, is enormous. The systemic (or body) circulation of humans has billion capillaries with a surface area of 10,800 ft^2 (1000 m^2). In the pulmonary (or lung) circuit there are billion capillaries with a combined surface area of 650 ft^2 (60 m^2). Lipid-soluble substances, including oxygen and carbon dioxide, and some water cross the capillary cell walls, whereas most water and all water-soluble substances are exchanged through pores either within or between the cells.

The structure of capillaries is dictated by their function in the organ supplied and falls into three main types which are basically similar in all vertebrates. Fenestrated capillaries have holes through the cells permitting large and rapid exchange of solvent and solutes; the pores may be closed by a delicate membrane. This type of capillary is found in kidney, intestine, and glands. Discontinuous capillaries have large gaps between the cells of the wall, and are found where macromolecules or even red blood cells are exchanged, as in bone marrow, liver, and spleen. Continuous capillaries have an apparently continuous layer of cells and occur in muscle, lungs, and central nervous system. However, there are small-diameter pores between the cells in all tissues except the brain. The brain capillaries of all vertebrates, except those of lampreys and hagfishes, appear to present an extremely effective barrier to the transport of materials across their walls. In conjunction with the astrocytes, modified nonnervous brain cells which invest the brain capillaries, they form an effective blood-brain barrier. Metabolites must cross the blood-brain barrier by specialized carrier systems or active transport, and this explains the abundance of mitochondria in the brain capillaries. Neurons are more sensitive than most cells to an imbalance in their environment, and homeostasis of the neuronal environment is the function of the blood-brain barrier.

Capillaries are generally about the diameter of the red blood cells (RBCs) which flow through them. Hence, in some amphibians (RBC diameter, 80 micrometers) the capillaries are far larger than, for example, in the mouse deer (RBC diameter, 1.5 micrometers). This relation between size of the RBC and capillary means that blood cells move through capillaries one at a time acting as a moving plug, sweeping unstirred fluid layers away from the capillary wall and facilitating exchange across the wall by diffusion, by reducing the diffusion distance. This is referred to as bolus flow.

Pressure and flow. The pulsatility of pressure and flow allied to the anomalous viscosity of blood greatly complicates any attempt to describe mathematically the relationship between pressure and flow in large arteries. However, in arterial resistance vessels both pressure and flow pulsations are dissipated so that a condition of steady pressure and flow is approached in the microcirculation. In large vessels, blood viscosity is high (some four times that of water) and, due to the presence of RBCs, appears to change with flow velocity (anomalous properties). In small vessels (less than 200 μm diameter) the apparent viscosity falls and, in capillaries, appears constant and similar to that of water (Fähraeus-Lindqvist effect).

Given conditions of steady pressure, flow, and viscosity, the relation between pressure and flow in the microcirculation can be described by the Hagen-Poiseuille law, Eq. (1), where Q = flow per unit time,

$$\dot{Q} = \frac{\pi r^4 \cdot [P_1 - P_2]}{8\eta L} \tag{1}$$

r = radius of the vessel, $P_1 - P_2$ = pressure difference between the upstream and downstream ends of a pipe of length L, and η = blood viscosity. An important relationship emerging from the Hagen-Poiseuille law is that flow varies with the radius of the vessel raised to the fourth power. Thus, if r is halved (by constriction of a blood vessel), then flow through that vessel will be reduced to one-sixteenth [$1/2^4$ = $1/6$] of that existing formerly for the same pressure difference.

Hagen-Poiseuille's law is often rewritten in a simplified form, Eq. (2) [where R = resistance =

$$\dot{Q} = \frac{P_1 - P_2}{R} \tag{2}$$

$8\eta L/\pi r^4$], as a direct analog of Ohm's law describing the relation between electric current, voltage and resistance. This "Ohmic" relation is frequently applied to the whole circulation (not just the microcirculation) to determine total peripheral resistance (TPR) when Q = cardiac output (volume per unit time), P_1 = mean arterial pressure (kPa), and P_2 = mean venous pressure (kPa). TPR is generally expressed in peripheral resistance units (PRU; kPa $\cdot$ ml^{-1} $\cdot$ unit time^{-1}). To simplify comparisons between animals of vastly different sizes (or even between individual vascular beds in the same animal), cardiac output is usually expressed on a unit weight basis yielding PRU per unit weight (see **table**).

Since flow per unit time (ml $\cdot$ min^{-1}) through the vascular system is the same at any two points, capillary pressure (P_c) may be calculated from arterial (P_a) and venous (P_v) pressure by application of the Hagen-Poiseuille law, yielding Eq. (3), where R_a and

$$P_c = \frac{P_a \cdot (R_v/R_a) + P_v}{1 + (R_v/R_a)} \tag{3}$$

R_v are the pre- and postcapillary resistances. Since it is the ratio of these resistances which determines capillary pressure, capillary pressure is largely independent of arterial blood pressure over a wide range. For instance, an R_a/R_v ratio of 5:1 gives P_c = 1.875 kPa when P_a = 10 kPa and P_v = 0.25 kPa. Now if P_a rose to 15 kPa, an adjustment of the ratio to 8:1 would leave P_c unchanged.

Measured capillary pressures are in the range of 1.33 to 4 kPa. This raises the question of why the single layer of cells in the capillary is not disrupted by these high internal pressures. The answer is contained in Laplace's law. This law describes how the wall tension (T) which opposes the distending force of the blood pressure (P) is critically dependent on the radius of the vessel, for Eq. (4). Hence, wall

$$P = \frac{T}{r} \tag{4}$$

Some cardiovascular variables in selected vertebrates*

Species name (common name)	Conditions	Body mass and temp.	Heart rate, beats · min^{-1}	Cardiac output, ml · min^{-1} · 100 g^{-1}	Mean arterial pressure, kPa	Mean pulmonary pressure, kPa	Peripheral resistance of body (PRU$_{100}$), kPa · ml^{-1} · min^{-1} · 100 g^{-1}	Peripheral resistance of gas exchanger (PRU$_{100}$), kPa · ml^{-1} · min^{-1} · 100 g^{-1}
Salmo gairdneri (rainbow trout)	Unrestrained, rest	1.25 kg, 10°C	38	1.76	4[†]	5.06[‡]	2.26	0.6
	Unrestrained, exercise		51	5.26	4.8[†]	8[‡]	0.9	0.6
Xenopus laevis (clawed toad)	Restrained, rest, breathing	0.1 kg, 20°C	45	11	3.74	2.8	0.57	0.43[§]
	Restrained, rest, not breathing		40	6.4	4	3.7	0.56	3.2[§]
Pseudemys scripta (red-eared turtle)	Unrestrained, rest, breathing	1.25 kg, 21°C	23	5.7	3.74	2.4	1.73	0.65
	Unrestrained, rest, not breathing		11	2.65	2.8	2.0	1.94	1.73
Anas platyrhynchos (white pekin duck)	Restrained, anesthetized	2.5 kg, 41°C	219	22	19	2.0	0.87	0.1
	Diving, unanesthetized		30	2	18	1.67	8.33	0.17
Homo sapiens (human)	Unrestrained, rest	70 kg, 37°C	72	8	12	1.75	1.5	0.2
	Maximum exercise		193	33	14.5	2.4	0.44	0.07

*In fish the gills are in series with the body circulation, so the resistances were calculated by using the pressure difference between the ventral and dorsal aorta and the dorsal aorta and veins, respectively. In fish, amphibians, and reptiles the heart is undivided and cardiac output is the total amount of blood pumped per unit time, whereas in birds and mammals cardiac output is the output of only one ventricle or half the output of the whole heart. In all cases, central venous pressures were assumed to be insignificant, except during diving in ducks when both pulmonary and central venous pressure rise to 1.3 kPa.
[†]Dorsal aorta.
[‡]Ventral aorta.
[§]Includes skin.

tension in a capillary in a human is 1/10,000 of that in the aorta, even though the pressure within is one-fifth of that in the aorta. Not surprisingly the aortic wall is 10,000 times thicker than the capillary wall.

Fluid exchange across capillaries. Water is exchanged both across the wall of the capillary and through pores. It is driven out by the blood pressure in the vessel, which is much higher than the pressure in the fluid between cells. In fact, the extracellular fluid pressure is frequently subatmospheric (negative). The venules (small veins), as well as capillaries, are apparently involved in this exchange because the venules are also highly permeable to water. The pressure which filters water out of the capillary (filtration pressure) is opposed by the colloid osmotic pressure (COP) of the blood; COP tends to pull water back into the blood vessel. The COP difference between the blood and the fluid between the cells (interstitial fluid) is almost entirely due to a higher concentration of relatively impermeable proteins in blood plasma; it is equivalent to a pressure of 1.3 to 4 kPa depending on the animal.

At the arterial end of the capillary there is usually a net loss of water because the blood pressure is higher than COP. As water leaves, the blood is concentrated, and its COP increases. This increase in COP, coupled with the fall in blood pressure along the capillary, causes fluid absorption at the venous end. In a human perhaps 21 quarts (20 liters) of fluid is filtered from the body capillaries each day, excluding kidney filtration. Of this filtrate, 17–19 quarts (16–18 liters) are reabsorbed, and the remainder returns to the blood by the lymphatic system. When filtration and absorption are more or less in balance, a Starling equilibrium is said to exist (named after E. H. Starling). However, the degree of equilibrium in individual tissues may vary; some may be exclusively involved in filtration, and others in absorption due to the independent regulation of capillary blood pressure in different tissues.

Obviously, capillary fluid exchange must be regulated if the volume of the blood is to be controlled. The vital importance of this control is seen when animals, such as humans, assume an erect posture. A column of fluid stretching from the heart to the feet applies an additional pressure of 12 kPa to the capillary pressure. This results in a pressure across the capillary wall (transmural pressure) of perhaps 16 kPa. This pressure is added to both arterial and venous sides of the circulation so the pressure gradient for flow across the vascular bed remains unchanged (except that flow resistance may drop because the vessels expand a bit due to the high transmural pressures). However, capillary pressure now greatly exceeds COP, and fluid should be filtered throughout the microcirculation. In fact, this is prevented by a marked reduction in the permeability of the microcirculation due, it is thought, to precapillary sphincters closing off capillaries and thereby reducing the surface area for capillary exchange.

In the brain of erect animals, the hydrostatic effect due to standing is reversed. The blood column must be lifted against gravity from the heart. Thus, in the head of an erect human, there is a negative hydrostatic pressure of 5 kPa, whereas in the giraffe it is 20 kPa. Consequently, a positive capillary pressure, even at the arterial end of the microvasculature, can only be achieved by a high arterial blood pressure. This is the explanation for the extremely high arterial blood pressure in the giraffe. However, at the venous end of the microcirculation, pressures could still be negative, causing veins to collapse. Even though the brain is enclosed within a rigid box, which would tend to prevent blood vessel collapse, many veins are tethered to surrounding skeletal structures to ensure that they remain open.

Control. Microvascular activity is coupled to local tissue function through intrinsic mechanisms which are independent of control by the nervous or hormonal systems. The arterioles, metarterioles, and precapillary sphincters are muscular vessels in which muscle fibers contract spontaneously (myogenic activity), keeping these vessels in a state of partial constriction (basal vascular tone). Increases in blood pressure stretch the vessels, causing an increase in myogenic activity in the vascular smooth muscle and a return toward their original diameter. Any tendency for vessels to close completely is prevented by the accumulation of vasodilator metabolites in the tissues as flow is reduced. Decreases in oxygen and increases in carbon dioxide, both in the blood and tissues, cause muscle relaxation and an increase in vessel diameter (vasodilation). However, in the lung circuit, low oxygen causes blood vessel diameter to decrease (vasoconstriction). This reversal of blood vessel response is related to the lung's role as a supplier, rather than user, of oxygen and has important consequences for distributing blood to areas of the lung where oxygen is available.

The arterioles and metarterioles are also subject to remote control by the nervous system. They are innervated by vasodilator and vasoconstrictor nerve fibers which modulate and sometimes dominate local control systems. In contrast, the precapillary sphincters lack innervation and can only be affected by local or blood-borne excitatory or inhibitory influences.

The endothelial (inner) layer of cells of the blood vessels makes an important contribution to regulation of resistance to flow. Physical stimuli such as stretch, flow, and pressure as well as hormonal influences cause the release of contracting and relaxing factors from the endothelial cells, which affect adjacent smooth muscle. These endothelium-dependent regulatory mechanisms integrate blood vessel responses, and may explain regional differences in responses of vascular beds to the same hormone. The most well-known relaxing factor is nitric oxide (NO), produced from L—arginine, which very rapidly loses its potency in the circulation. Contracting factors include peptides, such as endothelin and prostaglandin which remain active for a considerably longer period of time.

The efficacy of the local control system as an unaided regulator of blood supply to the tissues is remarkable. For example, blood flow to the brain can be maintained constant despite induced arterial blood pressure changes from 8 to 18 kPa. Such control, in the absence of nerves or blood-borne factors, is referred to as autoregulation.

Heart. The heart is a pump imparting propulsive energy to the blood. Primitively, the heart is a tubular structure equipped with valves to prevent backflow. In more advanced animals it is differentiated into receiving and storage chambers (sinus venosus and atrium) and pumping chambers (ventricle and conus arteriosus). During evolution, these chambers have become folded upon one another; some were incorporated into others, and some subdivided. Sharks and rays have all four chambers, whereas in birds and mammals, the sinus venosus is incorporated into the right atrium and the conus arteriosus into the outflow tract of the ventricle. In birds and mammals the two remaining chambers (atrium and ventricle) are subdivided to form two parallel circulations, one supplying the body and the other the lungs.

In all vertebrates the heart is enclosed in a double-layered membranous pericardium; a liquid-filled space separates the layers. The inner layer of the pericardium is applied to the ventricular surface. In elasmobranchs, the outer layer of the pericardium is extremely thick and is attached to surrounding skeletal structures. As a result, ventricular contraction creates a subatmospheric pressure within the pericardium which tends to stretch the thin-walled atrium so that it fills with blood by aspiration.

Cardiac cycle. In all vertebrates the period of one heartbeat, or cardiac cycle, can be divided into four phases (**Fig. 24***a* and *b*).

1. *Filling phase:* the inflow valves are open and the outflow valves shut. Ventricular pressure at the start of this phase is low and falling; when it falls below that in the atrium, the atrioventricular valves open and blood flows rapidly into the ventricle. Flow into the ventricle is driven by the energy contained in venous blood. As ventricular pressure rises, flow slows, and atrial contraction "tops up" the ventricle. The end of the ventricular relaxation phase (diastole) is marked by the start of ventricular contraction (systole) which increases ventricular pressure and shuts the atrioventricular valves.

2. *Isovolumetric contraction (contraction without a change in volume):* both inlet and outlet valves are shut. The ventricular muscle contracts, developing tension, and the pressure of the contained blood increases. In hearts with large and rapid pressure generation the free edges of the atrioventricular valves have guy ropes (chordae tendineae), attached to papillary muscles of the ventricular wall; these prevent the valves being turned inside out.

3. *Ejection phase:* the rising ventricular pressure exceeds that in the arteries and the outlet valves

open; the inlet valves remain closed. Blood is ejected rapidly, but pressure continues to rise in both ventricle and outflow tract until peak systolic pressure is reached. About two-thirds through this phase, ventricular contraction stops and pressure falls; when it falls below arterial pressure, the outflow valves shut, causing a disturbance in the arterial pressure pulse (incisura or dichrotic notch). The amount of blood pumped in this phase, by a single ventricle, is the stroke volume (ml), while cardiac output (ml · min^{-1}) is the product of stroke volume and heart rate (beats · min^{-1}). Backflow of blood is not necessary to shut the outflow valves. When the valve opens during blood ejection, vortices are created between the valve cusp (free edges of the valve) and the aortic wall, and the pressure distribution associated with these vortices deflects the cusps toward apposition (closure) as outflow from the ventricle decelerates. Leonardo da Vinci is credited with first describing the role of vortices in valve closure more than 100 years before W. Harvey's discovery of the circulation. Some lower vertebrates have an extra contractile chamber (conus arteriosus) on the ventricular outflow tract; the conus shuts the outflow valves when it contracts.

4. *Isovolumetric relaxation:* inflow and outflow valves shut and pressure falls rapidly as the ventricular muscle relaxes. Subatmospheric pressure can occur in this phase due to "elastic recoil" of the walls of the ventricle.

The plot of ventricular pressure against volume describes a closed loop circling counterclockwise with respect to time (Fig. 24c). The area enclosed by the loop is a measure of the work done by the ventricle in ejecting blood. Since pressures in the lung circuit of birds and mammals (see table) are lower than those in the body circulation, the work required to circulate the blood to the lungs is much less.

The ventricles are not divided in amphibians and noncrocodilian reptiles. Since both the lung and body circulations are connected to the same pressure source, flow in each circuit is inversely proportional to the resistance of that circuit. In amphibians such as frogs and toads, during periods of breath holding (apnea) blood can be circulated away from the lung circuit and sent to the body by increasing pulmonary flow resistance (**Fig. 25**). Hence, unlike the situation in avian and mammalian hearts, flows in lung and body circuits can be independent of one another. However, in incompletely divided hearts peak pressures during cardiac contraction have to be the same in both lung and body circuits because they are connected to the same pressure source. The peak pressure must be low; otherwise plasma will filter out of the lung capillaries into the lung and the animal will drown. Only when the heart is completely divided can pressures in lung and body circuits be independent of one another (high pressure in the body, low pressure in the lung), but the price to be paid is that flows in each circuit must now be exquisitely balanced.

Varanid reptiles (for example, monitor lizards), however, show clear pressure separation between

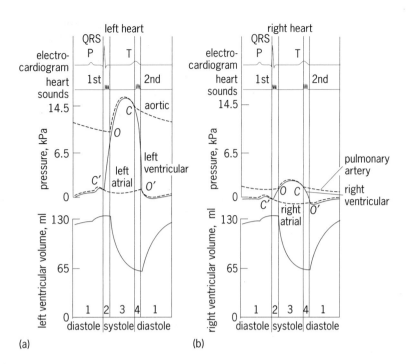

(a) (b)

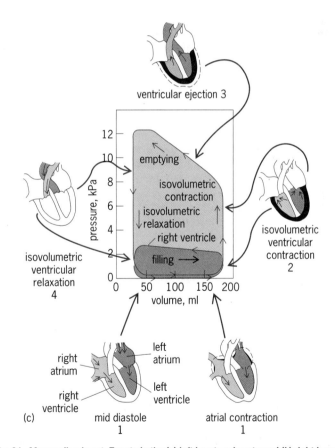

(c)

Fig. 24. Mammalian heart. Events in the (*a*) left heart and aorta and (*b*) right heart and pulmonary arteries during a cardiac cycle. In *a*: At *C'* the atrioventricular valve closes; at *O'* it opens. At *O* the aortic valve opens; at *C* it closes. In *b*: At *C'* the atrioventricular valve closes; at *O'* it opens. At *O* the pulmonary valve opens; at *C* it closes (*after A. J. Vander et al., Human Physiology, McGraw-Hill, 1975*). (c) Pressure-volume loops for the right and left ventricles. The area enclosed by the loop is a measure of the work done by the heart in ejecting blood. Diagrammatic representations of the heart during one cardiac cycle surround the loops and are linked by arrows with their appropriate position (in time) on the loop. The contracting portions of the heart are shown in black. The numbers (1 to 4) under each heart diagram refer to the phases of the cardiac cycle in *a* and *b* (*after R. Eckert and D. J. Randall, Animal Physiology, W. H. Freeman, 1978*)

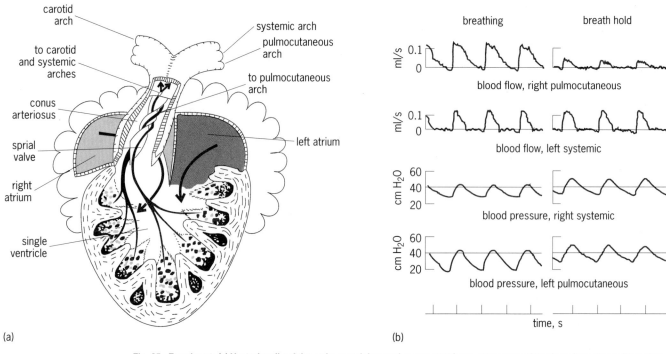

Fig. 25. Frog heart. (*a*) Ventral walls of the atria, ventricles, and conus arteriosus are removed to show flow streamlines that account for selective distribution of oxygenated blood to the head and body via the carotid and systemic arteries, and deoxygenated blood to the lungs via the pulmocutaneous arteries. (*b*) Blood pressures and flows in the blood vessels supplying the lungs (pulmocutaneous) and body (systemic) during a period of breathing and during a breath hold in the anuran amphibian *Xenopus laevis*. (*After P. S. Davies, Perspectives in Experimental Biology, vol. 1, Pergamon Press, 1976*)

lung (low pressure) and body circuits (high pressure), yet the varanid ventricle is morphologically undivided. This extraordinary triumph of physiology over morphology is achieved by partitioning the ventricular cavity during the contraction and relaxation phases. An interventricular partition formed by the atrioventricular valves divides the ventricle during diastole, whereas a musclar ridge within the ventricle divides it at a different site during systole. Crocodilians also have a high-pressure body and low-pressure lung circulation. The heart is completely divided by an interventricular septum, but the left aorta, supplying the body, arises along with the pulmonary artery from the right ventricle. Furthermore, the left and right aortas are joined just outside the heart by a hole in their common wall (foramen of Panizza) and again by a connection behind the heart. Hence, in the crocodilians a unique situation exists, because it is possible for venous blood to be transferred away from the lung circulation and sent back to the body through the left aorta so that both flows and pressures are independent of one another.

In birds and mammals the heart is completely divided, and the flows in both lung and body circuits must be matched. This matching of flows is largely achieved by nervous control although an automatic mechanism, referred to as Starling's law of the heart, could play a role. Starling's law (which also applies to the hearts of lower vertebrates) states that the energy of contraction of ventricular muscle is a function of the length of the muscle fiber. Thus, if in a particular beat a ventricle is filled to a greater extent than the previous one, the next contraction would be more

vigorous and a greater volume of blood (stroke volume) would be ejected. So, if there is an increase in pumping by the right heart, a few beats later more blood will return to the left heart and increase its filling, so its output will rise, maintaining a balance between flows in the two circuits without intervention of any nervous or humoral (blood-borne) control mechanisms.

Pacemaker. The cardiac rhythm is myogenic in all vertebrates, the heartbeat being initiated in a specialized group of muscle cells which form the pacemaker. From the pacemaker, a wave of electrical excitation passes across the heart, activating the contractile process in cardiac muscle. This wave of excitation may pass across the muscle tissue itself or along specialized conducting pathways (Purkinje fibers, which are modified muscle cells; **Fig. 26**). Pacemaker cells are different from other cardiac cells in that the electrical charge across their cell membranes spontaneously and repetitively declines (depolarization). These repeated depolarizations are called pacemaker potentials. They reach a threshold, after a depolarization of some 15 mV, and an action potential is generated (a sudden reversal of the membrane electrical charge). The action potential is propagated from cell to cell, initiating muscle contraction (Fig. 26). The cycle then repeats. An unusual feature of the cardiac action potential is its long duration, compared, for instance, with the action potential in skeletal muscle. If a muscle action potential is short, then further action potentials and contractions can be generated before the muscle relaxes. Consequently, in skeletal muscle a sequence

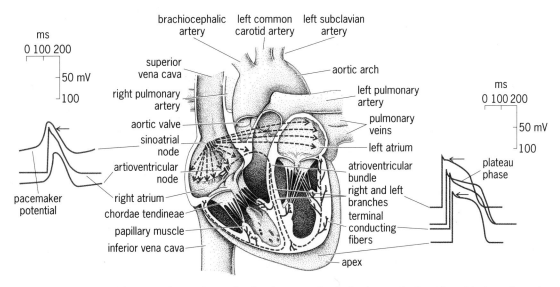

Fig. 26. Anterior view of the opened human heart, showing the pacemaker in the sinus node, the atrioventricular node, and the specialized conduction pathways of the ventricle. Intracellular action potential shapes were recorded at identified sites of the heart during one cardiac cycle. The arrows link the action potentials to the site. Time and voltage calibrations are shown at the left and right. Zero transmembrane voltage is indicated on some of the action potentials by the arrowhead. (*After J. E. Crouch, Functional Human Anatomy, Lea and Febinger, 1978*)

of contractions may sum. However, in the heart the shortest possible interval between two action potentials is still longer than the relaxation time of cardiac muscle. Thus, the sustained contractions (tetanus) characteristic of skeletal muscle, and due to the fusion of individual waves of contraction, cannot occur in cardiac muscle. Tetanus in cardiac muscle would, of course, be maladaptive.

The sum of the electrical events occurring during the synchronous activity of all the cardiac cells can be detected as a series of small voltage changes at points all over the body (Fig. 24*a* and *b*). The record of small voltage changes is the electrocardiogram; it exhibits waves associated with atrial depolarization (P-wave), ventricular depolarization (QRS complex), and repolarization (T-wave) [Fig. 24*a* and *b*].

In all vertebrate hearts there is a hierarchy of pacemakers. This is reflected in embryonic development where the ventricle is formed and begins beating before the other parts of the heart have differentiated. The ventricular pacemaker sets a slow rate and is superseded by pacemakers, first in the atrium, and ultimately in the sinus venosus. In fish and frogs heart rate is set by the pacemaker in the sinus venosus because it beats fastest and drives the other pacemakers. In birds and mammals the sinus venous is incorporated into the right atrium, and the pacemaker zone is called the sinoatrial node (Fig. 26). The wave of excitation crosses the atrium (in some mammals specialized conducting pathways have been described) at a rate of up to 1 m · s^{-1}, but it can only cross to the ventricle through the atrioventricular node. In the atrioventricular node, the rate of conduction slows to 0.05–0.1 m · s^{-1}, allowing time for the atrium to complete its contraction before the ventricle is activated. From the atrioventricular node the wave of excitation is propagated rapidly (0.05–2.5 m · s^{-1}). In birds and mammals propagation takes

place through specialized conducting fibers called, in mammals, the right and left bundles of His. Lower vertebrates lack specialized conducting fibers and even a discrete atrioventricular node; in noncrocodilian reptiles there is an almost complete ring of junctional tissue between the atria and ventricle.

In all except the lowest vertebrates the pacemaker region receives innervation both from excitatory (sympathetic) and depressor (parasympathetic) nerves. The sympathetic nerves liberate catecholamines which increase the rate of spontaneous depolarization, and therefore heart rate. The parasympathetic nerves liberate acetylcholine which stabilizes the membrane potential and decreases the rate of spontaneous depolarization, so heart rate falls. The extent to which these nerves innervate cardiac muscle or other structures, such as the atrioventricular node, is variable. However, when muscle innervation is dense, catecholamines increase the force of contraction (positive inotropic effect) while acetylcholine decreases it (negative inotropic effect).

The effects of chemicals released by nerves are due to the activation of receptors on the cardiac cell which are specific for that particular chemical. For noradrenaline and adrenaline the receptors are called α and β receptors, respectively. Adrenaline and noradrenaline increase in the circulation in response to stress and stimulate the heart. In many vertebrates, however, the effects are different from those caused by nerves. For instance, circulating adrenaline is unable to reach the same receptors which are activated neurally because the nerve ending is so closely attached to the cardiac cell. Receptors stimulated by nerves have different effects on pacemaker potentials from those accessed from the circulation.

Arteries. The arteries are the connecting tubes between the heart and the microcirculatory vessels.

They are largest and most distensible just outside the heart. The arteries decrease in diameter and flexibility at every bifurcation, so the arterial tree is said to display both geometric and elastic taper. The vessels within the thorax are extremely distensible due to a much higher proportion of rubbery (elastin) to stiff (collagen) fibers in their walls. In nonthoracic arteries collagen dominates the wall composition, but its proportion remains constant as the vessels get stiffer and stiffer with their approach to the periphery.

During the ejection phase of the cardiac cycle much of the blood is temporarily stored in the central arteries as these become distended by the pressure rise. This blood is fed into the peripheral circulation, by the rebound of the stretched elastic walls, throughout diastole. Consequently, a highly pulsatile input is transformed into a more even outflow (**Fig. 27***a*). However, in a large number of an-

imals (such as humans, dogs, and ducks) this is not the case with the pressure pulse. The pressure pulse is amplified in the peripheral vessels (peaking), and both the size and rate of rise of the pulse wave is greater than in the more central vessels (Fig. 27*a*). On the other hand, small high-frequency components such as the incisura disappear from the peripheral pulse as they are damped out (Fig. 27*a*).

The pressure pulse wave travels through the arteries at a velocity which depends on the viscosity of the fluid and distensibility of the vessel. In humans it picks up speed, from $3 \text{ m} \cdot \text{s}^{-1}$ centrally, to 5–$10 \text{ m} \cdot \text{s}^{-1}$ in peripheral arteries. At every discontinuity in the arterial tree (regions of geometric and elastic taper and, more importantly, the terminal vascular beds) the incident wave will be reflected toward the heart. At any major reflecting sites, such as the terminal vascular beds, the incident wave and the reflected wave will be almost in phase and will sum so that the pressure pulse increases in size (Fig. 27*a*). If the heart is positioned one-quarter of a wavelength back from the major reflecting sites (wavelength is the pulse velocity divided by the cycle length), the incident wave will have passed here one-quarter wavelength before (with respect to the reflecting sites) and the reflected wave will arrive here one-quarter wavelength later (with respect to the reflecting sites) so the two waves will be out of phase, by half a wavelength, and will cancel one another out. Hence, the pressure pulsations in central arteries will be reduced by wave reflection (Fig. 27*a*). In mammals about 30% of cardiac power is invested in pulsatile pressure and subsequent flow, so by reducing the pressure pulsations just outside the heart, energy can be saved. Peaking occurs only if the transit time is a significant proportion of the cardiac cycle. In humans mean pulse wave velocity is around 5–$6 \text{ m} \cdot \text{s}^{-1}$ at a cardiac interval of 1 s, so the transit time is about a quarter of the cardiac cycle (quarter wavelength) and, as described above, pulse amplification occurs. However, arteriosclerotic individuals (be they ducks, dogs, or humans) do not show peaking of the pressure pulse since the pulse wave velocity in the "hardened" arteries is extremely fast and transit time through the circulation is greatly reduced. This lack of pulse wave amplification may contribute to the deleterious effects of this condition on the heart. In frogs mean pulse wave velocity is around $3 \text{ m} \cdot \text{s}^{-1}$ at a cardiac interval of 1 s, so the transit time is about 50 ms, and the shape of the peripheral pulse in frogs is, except for damping of fast components (incisura), identical in shape to that in central arteries.

As blood is pumped through the circulation, energy is dissipated and mean pressure drops (Fig. 27*a*). Mean pressure is a steady pressure obtained by integrating the pressure pulse over one or several cardiac cycles and is somewhat lower than the arithmetic mean of systolic and diastolic pressures. When peaking occurs, the pressure pulse gets bigger but much narrower (Fig. 27*a*), and mean pressure is still lower in the peripheral arteries compared with the central arteries. Therefore, the flow occurs down the mean pressure gradient.

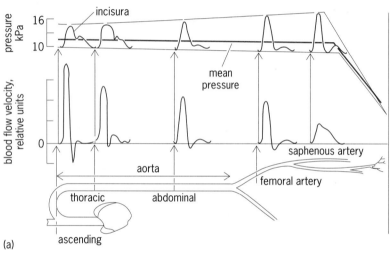

(a)

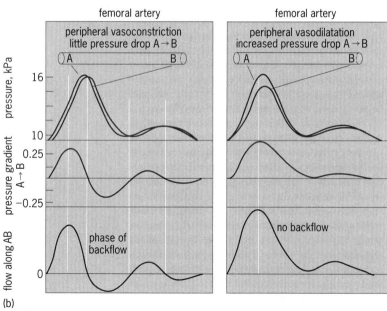

(b)

Fig. 27. Arterial circulation. (*a***) Comparison of the behavior of the pressure and flow velocity pulses from the ascending aorta until the saphenous artery. (***b***) The propagation of the pulse wave along an artery, with deduction of the pressure gradient and the phasic flow. (***After B. Folkow and E. Neil, Circulation, Oxford University Press, 1971***)**

Unfortunately, an analysis in terms of steady pressures and flows tells little about the shapes of the pressure and flow pulses. Why does flow reverse at certain portions of the cardiac cycle? The reason is that the pulsatile pressure gradient reverses in those phases (Fig. 27b). The pressure pulse travels through the arterial tree with a velocity from 3 to 10 m · s⁻¹. If pressure is recorded at two sites in a vessel that are a small distance apart, then as the wave passes the upstream point, pressure will exceed that downstream and forward flow will occur (Fig. 27b). When the wave moves on and passes the downstream point, pressure there will exceed the pressure upstream and the flow will reverse (Fig. 27b). In fact, it is the pressure difference between the upstream and downstream points (the pressure gradient) which oscillates about a mean and is closely linked to the flow velocity (Fig. 27b).

Arterial blood pressure is controlled, at least in the short term, through the agency of arterial baroreceptors. Baroreceptors are specialized nerve endings located in the walls of major vessels; they are stimulated when the wall is expanded by the blood pressure. They have been found in the aortic arch and carotid sinus of mammals, the aortic arch of birds, and the carotid labyrinth of amphibians. Claims have been made for their existence in fishes. Blood pressure is controlled using the negative feedback principle. A rise in blood pressure stimulates baroreceptors which send electrical messages (action potentials) to the brain where they are directed to regions involved in control and adjustment of heart rate, stroke volume, and resistance in the peripheral blood vessels. In response to a rise in blood pressure, heart rate, stroke volume, and peripheral resistance are reduced. Input from mechanically stimulated receptors in the heart and lungs, and from chemoreceptors (measuring blood oxygen and carbon dioxide) in the vascular system and brain, are also involved in regulating the circulatory system.

Venous system. From the capillaries the blood passes through venules to successively larger veins and returns to the heart. Aside from being conduits for returning blood to the heart, the major function of the venous system is as a storage site for blood (Fig. 23). Veins are thin-walled, although the larger ones have a muscular coat, and are distended by small changes in pressure across their walls (transmural pressure). A pressure rise causes the veins to change from an elliptical cross-sectional profile to one that is nearly circular, greatly increasing blood storage while reducing flow resistance. Contraction of the muscles in the walls of the larger veins (venomotor activity) reverses the effects of increases in transmural pressure. Venoconstriction is under the control of the sympathetic nervous system.

In larger veins, valves appear as intimal folds and ensure that flow moves only in one direction. In humans some veins such as the vena cava, hepatic, pulmonary, and cerebral veins lack valves, a feature shared with the major veins running the length of the body in fishes. In elasmobranchs, these long veins have a unique structure; they are invested with such a thick connective tissue sheath that they are virtually incompressible tubes. Elasmobranch fishes and some seals also have a muscular venous sphincter located between the liver and heart which regulates venous return when venous pressure rises during exercise (elasmobranch) or diving (seal).

In most animals the majority of the venous reservoir is placed level with or above the heart (even in giraffes). However, in erect animals (primarily humans) the majority of the venous reservoir is below the heart. Consequently, due to the hydrostatic effect (as described above), transmural pressure will increase in veins below the heart and will decrease in those above. Hence, when the animal is upright, leg veins distend and head veins may collapse. This hydrostatic effect has no "direct" effect on flow (aside from the fact that flow resistance will fall as vessels distend or increase if they collapse) since it is added to both arterial and venous sides of the circulation.

Venous return is caused by the forward push of the blood generated by the heart and transmitted in the form of a positive pressure across the capillaries (vis à tergo). In the pulmonary circulation and, on the body side in some lower vertebrates, the arterial pressure pulse may be transmitted across the capillaries. Even when these pulsations are damped out, venous pressure pulsations occur in central veins as heart movements are transmitted "backward" to these veins. In some animals venous return is promoted by a suction force (vis à fronte) due to subatmospheric pressures in the cardiac cavities caused either by a negative intrapericardial pressure stretching the atrium, as in elasmobranchs, or, in animals lacking a rigid pericardium, to "elastic recoil" of the ventricles, or atrial volume changes associated with ventricular relaxation. When veins with valves run through blocks of skeletal muscle, contraction of these muscles squeezes blood toward the heart (muscle pump).

The muscle pump works in all vertebrates; in some fishes, even the arteries within the muscle mass have valves to ensure unidirectional flow of blood. In animals that have a diaphragm, inspiration aids venous return; since pressure within the thorax is at subatmospheric level, the transmural pressure of intrathoracic veins increases, and they expand. At the same time, abdominal pressure rises, so the transmural pressure in extrathoracic veins will decrease and they will be compressed, thus forcing blood toward the heart. Hence, at the diaphragm a sharp drop in venous pressure occurs which is referred to as a vascular waterfall.   David R. Jones

Bibliography. C. R. Austin and R. V. Short, *Embryonic and Fetal Development*, 1983; H. S. Badeer, *Cardiovascular Physiology*, 1983; R. W. Blake (ed.), *Efficiency and Economy in Animal Physiology*, 1991; W. W. Nichols and M. F. Rourke, *McDonald's Blood Flow in Arteries*, 4th ed., 1997; C. L. Prosser, *Comparative Animal Physiology*, 4th ed., 1991; A. S. Romer and T. S. Parsons, *The Vertebrate Body*, 6th ed., 1986.

Caribou

A ruminant, *Rangifer tarandus*, of the deer family, Cervidae. Reindeer inhabit the Arctic region and have a circumpolar distribution. They have been domesticated for centuries and are economically important to the Laplanders, who use them as draft animals as well as for their skins, flesh, and milk. The Laplanders are nomadic people who migrate during the summer months with their herds from one feeding ground to another.

Reindeer do not display sexual dimorphism; both sexes have antlers and are brown with yellow-white areas on the neck and chest.

Both sexes have antlers (see **illus.**), a characteristic peculiar to this deer species. Although their senses of sight and hearing are not sharp, their sense of smell is quite keen. Reindeer are well adapted for life in the Arctic; the hooves are round and broad, giving the animal stable footing in snow and on ice. In the wild, they are the most migratory of all deer, traveling in large herds in search of lichens as a food source during the winter months. The rutting season begins during the autumn migrations; fawns are born during the spring. *See* ARTIODACTYLA; DEER; MIGRATORY BEHAVIOR; MOOSE.

Charles B. Curtin

Carnauba wax

Product exuded from the leaves of the wax palm, *Copernicia cerifera* (Palmae), a native of Brazil and other regions in tropical South America. The wax accumulates on the surface of the leaves; these are cut from the trees and dried, whereupon the layer of wax becomes loose and is easily removed by flailing. It is the hardest, highest-melting natural wax and is used in making candles, shoe polish, high-luster wax, varnishes, phonograph records, and surface coating of automobiles. *See* ARECALES; WAX, ANIMAL AND VEGETABLE.

Earl L. Core

Carnivora

One of the larger orders of placental mammals, including fossil and living dogs, raccoons, pandas, bears, weasels, skunks, badgers, otters, mongooses, civets, cats, hyenas, seals, walruses, and many extinct groups organized into 12 families, with about 112 living genera and more than twice as many extinct genera. The primary adaptation in this order was for predation on other vertebrates and invertebrates. A few carnivorans (for example, bear and panda) have secondarily become largely or entirely herbivorous, but even then the ancestral adaptations for predation are still clearly evident in the structure of the teeth and jaws. The Carnivora have been highly successful animals since their first appearance in the early Paleocene. During the early Tertiary they shared the predatory mode of life with carnivorous members of some other placental orders, particularly the Deltatheridia, to the extent that few other mammals succeeded in invading this adaptive zone. *See* CREODONTA.

Structural adaptations. Meat-eating adaptations involving the teeth and jaws appeared early in the history of Carnivora. The dentition is sharply divided into three functional units. The incisors act as a tool for nipping and delicate prehension, and the large interlocking upper and lower canines for heavy piercing and tearing during the killing of prey. The cheek teeth are divided into premolars (for heavy prehension) and molars (for slicing and grinding), which may be variously modified depending on the specific adaptation. A diagnostic feature of the Carnivora is the enlargement of the last (fourth) upper premolar and the first lower molar to form longitudinally aligned opposed shearing blades. This important pair of teeth are termed the carnassials. Primitively, the dental formula was that common to all early placentals, but in most carnivores there is often loss of anterior premolars and posterior molars, with the strictly carnivorous forms, such as cats, reducing the number of cheek teeth the most (**Fig. 1**). *See* DENTITION.

In all carnivorans the jaw articulation is arranged in such a manner that movement is limited to vertical

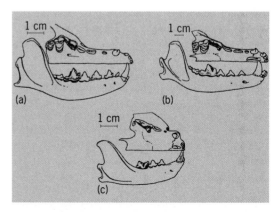

Fig. 1. Upper and lower dentition of the right side representing the superfamilies of Carnivora, carnassials shaded. (*a*) Miacoidea, *Miacis*, Eocene. (*b*) Canoidea, *Canis*, Recent. (*c*) Feloidea, *Felis*, Recent.

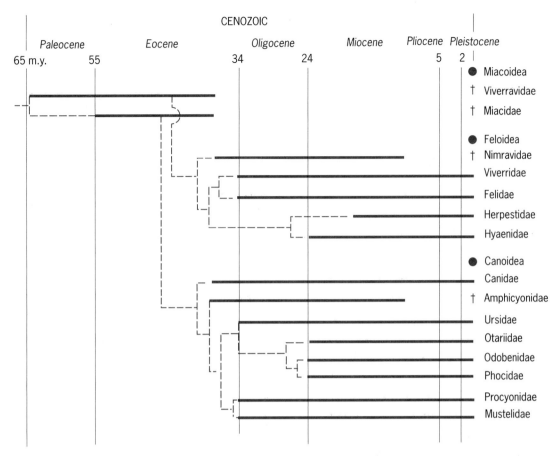

Fig. 2. Phylogenetic relationships and geologic ranges of the carnivoran families. The heavy lines indicate known geologic ranges, and the broken lines indicate predicted ranges inferred from phylogenetic relationships. Daggers indicate extinct families.

hinge motions and transverse sliding. The temporal muscle dominates the jaw musculature, forming at least one-half of the total mass of the jaw muscles. Cursorial adaptations of the limbs appeared early in carnivore history and have always been characteristic of the order. In all modern carnivorans the brain is large and the cerebral hemispheres are highly developed; evolution of the brain seems to have proceeded at an accelerated pace during the latter half of the Cenozoic.

Phylogeny. The history of the Carnivora is relatively well documented despite the fact that fossils are rarely abundant. The earliest records are early Paleocene, but the earliest well-represented material comes from the middle Paleocene of North America. During the Paleocene and Eocene the stem-carnivorans, or miacoids, underwent considerable diversification in both the Old and New worlds. These animals were small- to medium-sized, usually with the full eutherian dental formula, and the fourth upper premolars and first lower molars were developed as carnassials. The feet were plantigrade or subdigitigrade with separate scaphoid and lunar bones in the wrist. The middle-ear region lacked a completely ossified cover or bulla, although the bony tympanic ring was present. The internal carotid artery was primitively three-branched (median, promontory, and stapedial branches).

At the end of Eocene and beginning of Oligocene time throughout the Northern Hemisphere, a dramatic change took place within the Carnivora—the appearance of primitive representatives of modern carnivoran families (**Fig. 2**). These animals had more cursorial limbs than their miacoid predecessors, with fused scaphoid and lunar bones, and completely ossified bullae, and the internal carotid was reduced to a two-branched (median and promontory) or single (median) vessel. Commonly the dentition showed reduction or loss of anterior premolars and posterior molars. There is little doubt that the miacoids are the progenitors of the earliest members of the modern carnivoran families, but analysis of available fossil evidence has allowed only limited determination of the exact lineages.

A second adaptive radiation of the Carnivora was initiated by these primitive members of the living families. Eventually this radiation brought about the extinction of contemporary carnivores, the Creodonta (family Hyaenodontidae did persist into late Miocene in the Old World tropics). During this second adaptive radiation of the Carnivora, a wider variety of ecologic niches was exploited than is shown by the fossil record of the early Cenozoic radiation. Striking among these are the development of crushing dentitions for omnivorous diets, loss of teeth for ant and termite feeding, hypertrophy of both premolars and molars for bone crushing, and most spectacularly the total modifications of skeleton and soft parts for aquatic existence in the open ocean.

Taxonomy. Historically, the order Carnivora has been divided into suborders Creodonta, Fissipeda, and Pinnipedia. Research on early Cenozoic fossils casts serious doubt on the affinity of the creodonts with the remainder of the Carnivora; they appear to be a convergent group of eutherians, some of which occupied the same adaptive zone as the Fissipeda. They are now placed in their own order, Creodonta. Furthermore, the Fissipeda and Pinnipedia do not denote a primary subdivision of the Carnivora as historically conceived. Although the living pelagic carnivorans and fossil allies (Pinnipedia) do seem to form a natural (that is, monophyletic) group, they originate from carnivorans embedded within the fissiped group. Such a twofold subdivision of the order Carnivora no longer expresses knowledge of the group's phylogeny. A threefold subdivision of the order has long been practiced, and the following superfamilies seem a better expression of the phylogenetic relationships: Miacoidea, Canoidea, and Feloidea. *See* ARCHAIC UNGULATE; EUTHERIA.

Miacoidea. The basic features of these ancestral carnivorans are mentioned above. Two families, the Miacidae and the Viverravidae, are often recognized. These animals occur in early Paleocene through late Eocene deposits in North America. In Europe they are known only from the Eocene. They have not been recognized in Africa. Members of the Viverravidae occur earliest in the fossil record. They have reduced dentitions that suggest special affinity with the Feloidea. The miacids include forms that resemble the Canoidea, and some may eventually be recognized as members of canoid families.

Canoidea. This group of doglike carnivorans first appears in the late Eocene of North America and Eurasia. They possess an auditory bulla, formed from both the entotympanic and ectotympanic (tympanic ring), that primitively lacks an internal septum. The Canoidea consists of seven living families: Canidae (dogs and their allies), Procyonidae (raccoons and their allies), Ursidae (bears and their allies), Mustelidae (weasels and their allies), and the pinniped families, Otariidae (sea lions), Odobenidae (walruses), and Phocidae (seals). All the terrestrial families appear in the fossil record during the Oligocene, and there seems little doubt that they are a closely related group. The pinniped families appear to be related to an extinct group that lies within the Ursidae. The fossil record reveals an eighth canoid family, the Amphicyonidae, that lies near the base of the canoid phyletic tree. This group, which included giant predators in the Miocene, persisted into the late Miocene of Eurasia. *See* BADGER; BEAR; COATI; DOGS; FERRET; FISHER; MARTEN; MINK; OTTER; PANDA; PINNIPEDS; RACCOON; SKUNK; WEASEL; WOLVERINE.

Feloidea. The catlike carnivorans also first appear in the late Eocene or early Oligocene in both the Old and New worlds. Four living families are currently recognized: Viverridae (civets) Herpestidae (mon-

gooses), Hyaenidae (hyenas and aardwolf), and Felidae (cats and saber-toothed cats). Nearly all the fossil and living members of these families possess an auditory bulla divided by a septum formed at the junction of the entotympanic and ectotympanic bones. An exception is the living African palm civet (*Nandinia*) in which only the ectotympanic is fully ossified and the entotympanic is cartilaginous or poorly ossified. In addition, *Nandinia* appears to represent the primitive condition of the bulla in feloids. The herpestids and hyaenids appear in early to medial Miocene time and may be the youngest terrestrial carnivoran families to arise. Members of extinct family of feloids, the Nimravidae, often assigned to the Felidae, retained their primitive cranial features although possessing felid teeth and skeletons. Representatives of this group appeared first in the late Eocene of North America, and by the Oligocene the nimravids were distributed across the continents of the Northern Hemisphere. All nimravid species have bladelike upper canine teeth, and in some, such as the late Cenozoic saber-toothed felids, the canines are greatly lengthened. Saberlike upper canines also evolved in other orders of carnivorous mammals such as the Credonta (family Hyaenodontidae) and the Marsupialia (family Borhyaenidae), and at least twice within the Carnivora (families Nimravidae and Felidae), providing a striking case of convergence in a specialized feeding mechanism. *See* CAT; CIVET; HYENA; MAMMALIA; MONGOOSE.   Richard H. Tedford

---

Carnot cycle

A hypothetical thermodynamic cycle originated by Sadi Carnot and used as a standard of comparison for actual cycles. The Carnot cycle shows that, even under ideal conditions, a heat engine cannot convert all the heat energy supplied to it into mechanical energy; some of the heat energy must be rejected. In a Carnot cycle, an engine accepts heat energy from a high-temperature source, or hot body, converts part of the received energy into mechanical (or electrical) work, and rejects the remainder to a low-temperature sink, or cold body. The greater the temperature difference between the source and sink, the greater the efficiency of the heat engine.

The Carnot cycle (**Fig. 1**) consists first of an isentropic compression, then an isothermal heat addition, followed by an isothermal expansion, and concludes with an isentropic heat rejection process. In short, the processes are compression, addition of heat, expansion, and rejection of heat, all in a qualified and definite manner.

Processes. The air-standard engine, in which air alone constitutes the working medium, illustrates the Carnot cycle. A cylinder of air has perfectly insulated walls and a frictionless piston. The top of the cylinder, called the cylinder head, can either be covered with a thermal insulator, or, if the insulation is removed, can serve as a heat transfer surface for heating or cooling the cylinder contents.

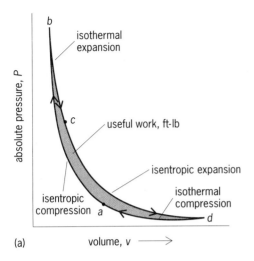

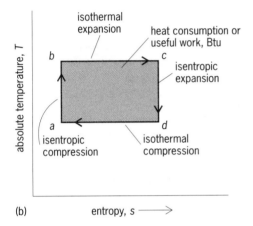

Fig. 1. Carnot cycle for air. (*a*) Pressure-volume diagram. (*b*) Temperature-entropy diagram.

Initially, the piston is somewhere between the top and the bottom of the engine's stroke, and the air is at some corresponding intermediate pressure but at low temperature. Insulation covers the cylinder head. By employing mechanical work from the surroundings, the system undergoes a reversible adiabatic, or an isentropic, compression. With no heat transfer, this compression process raises both the pressure and the temperature of the air, and is shown as the path *a-b* on Fig. 1.

After the isentropic compression carries the piston to the top of its stroke, the piston is ready to reverse its direction and start down. The second process is one of constant-temperature heat addition. The insulation is removed from the cylinder head, and a heat source, or hot body, applied that is so large that any heat flow from it will not affect its temperature. The hot body is at a temperature just barely higher than that of the gas it is to heat. The temperature gradient is so small it is considered reversible; that is, if the temperature changed slightly the heat might flow in the other direction, from the gas into the hot body. In the heat addition process, enough heat flows from the hot body into the gas to maintain the temperature of the gas while it slowly expands and does useful work on the surroundings. All the heat is added to the work-

ing substance at this constant top temperature of the cycle. This second process is shown as *b-c* on Fig. 1.

Part way down the cylinder, the piston is stopped; the hot body is removed from the cylinder head, and an insulating cover is put in its place. Then the third process of the cycle begins; it is a frictionless expansion, devoid of heat transfer, and carries the piston to the bottom of its travel. This isentropic expansion reduces both the pressure and the temperature to the bottom values of the cycle. For comparable piston motion, this isentropic expansion drops the pressure to a greater extent than the isothermal process would do. The path *c-d* on Fig. 1 represents this third process, and is steeper on the *P-v* plane than process *b-c*.

The last process is the return of the piston to the same position in the cylinder as at the start. This last process is an isothermal compression and simultaneous rejection of heat to a cold body which has replaced the insulation on the cylinder head. Again, the cold body is so large that heat flow to it does not change its temperature, and its temperature is only infinitesimally lower than that of the gas in the system. Thus, the heat rejected during the cycle flows from the system at a constant low-temperature level. The path *d-a* on Fig. 1 shows this last process.

The net effect of the cycle is that heat is added at a constant high temperature, somewhat less heat is rejected at a constant low temperature, and the algebraic sum of these heat quantities is equal to the work done by the cycle.

Figure 1 shows a Carnot cycle when air is used as the working substance. The *P-v* diagram for this cycle changes somewhat when a vapor or a liquid is used, or when a phase change occurs during the cycle, but the *T-s* diagram always remains a rectangle regardless of phase changes or of working substances employed.

It is significant that this cycle is always a rectangle on the *T-s* plane, independent of substances used, for Carnot was thus able to show that neither pressure, volume, nor any other factor except temperature could affect the thermal efficiency of his cycle. Raising the hot-body temperature raises the upper boundary of the rectangular figure, increases the area, and thereby increases the work done and the efficiency, because this area represents the net work output of the cycle. Similarly, lowering the cold-body temperature increases the area, the work done, and the efficiency. In practice, nature establishes the temperature of the coldest body available, such as the temperature of ambient air or river water, and the bottom line of the rectangle cannot circumvent this natural limit.

The thermal efficiency of the Carnot cycle is solely a function of the temperature at which heat is added (phase *b-c*) and the temperature at which heat is rejected (phase *d-a*) [Fig. 1]. The rectangular area of the *T-s* diagram represents the work done in the cycle so that thermal efficiency, which is the ratio of work done to the heat added, equals $(T_{hot} - T_{cold})T_{hot}$. For

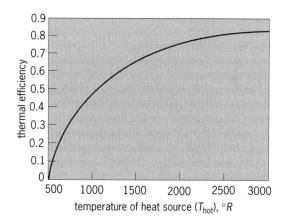

Fig. 2. Thermal efficiency of the Carnot cycle with heat-rejection temperature T_{cold} equal to 500°R (278 K).

the case of atmospheric temperature for the heat sink ($T_{cold} = 500°$R), the thermal efficiency, as a function of the temperature of the heat source, T_{hot}, is shown in **Fig. 2**.

Carnot cycle with steam. If steam is used in a Carnot cycle, it can be handled by the following flow arrangement. Let saturated dry steam at 500°F (260°C) flow to the throttle of a perfect turbine where it expands isentropically down to a pressure corresponding to a saturation temperature of the cold body. The exhausted steam from the turbine, which is no longer dry, but contains several percent moisture, is led to a heat exchanger called a condenser. In this device there is a constant-pressure, constant-temperature, heat-rejection process during which more of the steam with a particular predetermined amount of condensed liquid is then handled by an ideal compression device. The isentropically compressed mixture may emerge from the compressor as completely saturated liquid at the saturation pressure corresponding to the hot-body temperature. The cycle is closed by the hot body's evaporating the liquid to dry saturated vapor ready to flow to the turbine.

The cycle is depicted in **Fig. 3** by *c-d* as the isentropic expansion in the turbine; *d-a* is the constant-temperature condensation and heat rejection to the cold body; *a-b* is the isentropic compression; and *b-c* is the constant-temperature boiling by heat transferred from the hot body. *See* STEAM ENGINE.

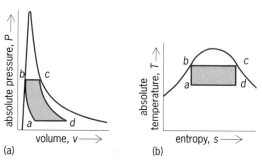

(a)   (b)

Fig. 3. Carnot cycle with steam. (a) Pressure-volume diagram. (b) Temperature-entropy diagram.

Carnot cycle with radiant energy. Because a Carnot cycle can be carried out with any arbitrary system, it has been analyzed when the working substance was considered to be a batch of radiant energy in an evacuated cylinder. If the system boundaries are perfectly reflecting thermal insulators, the enclosed radiant energy will be reflected and re-reflected with no loss of radiant energy and no change of wavelength.

The electromagnetic theory of radiation asserts that the radiant energy applies pressure P to the cylinder walls. This radiation pressure is equal to $u/3$, where u represents the radiant energy density, or the amount of radiant energy per unit volume.

The piston moves so that the cylinder boundaries expand, and additional radiant energy is supplied to the system so that the temperature remains constant. Then, cutting off any further supply of radiant energy, the system undergoes a further infinitesimal expansion with its associated pressure drop and temperature drop. The third process is an isothermal compression at the low-temperature level, accompanied by some rejection of radiant energy. One last process closes the cycle with a reversible compression that raises the temperature to the original level. The assumption is made throughout this analysis that energy density is a function of temperature alone. Thus, because this last compression process increases the energy density, it raises the temperature.

A record of all energy quantities in this radiant-energy Carnot cycle indicates that energy density u is proportional to the fourth power of the absolute temperature. Consequently the total rate of emission of radiant energy from the surface of a blackbody is also proportional to the fourth power of its absolute temperature, thereby using a Carnot cycle to provide a relationship by theoretical analysis, the same relationship which had previously been determined experimentally and labeled as Stefan's law.

Conversion of heat to electricity. Several physical phenomena convert heat energy directly into electrical energy. The extent of this direct conversion of heat to electricity is limited by the temperature levels between which the process operates. The ideal efficiency of such direct-conversion thermoelectric cycles equals the efficiency of a Carnot cycle that operates between the same temperature limits of heat source and heat sink. However, the conversion efficiency obtained in practice is only a small fraction of the ideal efficiency at the present stage of development.

The most widely known physical arrangement for direct thermoelectric generation is the thermocouple, which produces an electromotive force, or voltage, when one junction of two dissimilar conductors is heated while the other junction is kept cool. Thermocouples made of metals are inefficient converters of heat energy to electric energy, because metals that have good electrical conductivity unfortunately have equally good thermal conductivity, which permits heat loss by conduction from the hot to the cold junction. In contrast, thermocouples made of semiconductors offer the prospect of operation at high temperatures and with high temperature gradients, because semiconductors are good electrical conductors but poor heat conductors. Semiconductor thermocouples may have as large a junction potential as the metal couples do. *See* THERMOCOUPLE.

Thermionic emission is another phenomenon that permits the partial conversion of heat energy directly into electrical energy. Externally applied heat imparts kinetic energy to electrons, liberating them from a surface. The density of the emission current is a function of the absolute temperature and work function of the emitter material.

For many years thermionic emission received little attention as a source of power because of its very low conversion efficiency. However, interest was stimulated by development of a contact potential thermionic emission cell. In this device, current flows between the surfaces of two materials which have different work functions. These materials are held at different temperatures, and the gap between the electrode surfaces is filled with gas at low pressure. *See* THERMIONIC EMISSION.

Such direct-conversion techniques show promise of becoming small-scale, if unconventional, power sources. Although these techniques ideally can convert heat to electrical energy with the efficiency of a Carnot cycle operating between the same temperature levels, laboratory devices do not surpass about 8% efficiency, which is just a fraction of the ideal performance.

Reversed Carnot cycle. A Carnot cycle consists entirely of reversible processes; thus it can theoretically operate to withdraw heat from a cold body and to discharge that heat to a hot body. To do so, the cycle requires work input from its surroundings. The heat equivalent of this work input is also discharged to the hot body.

Just as the Carnot cycle provides the highest efficiency for a power cycle operating between two fixed temperatures, so does the reversed Carnot cycle provide the best coefficient of performance for a device pumping heat from a low temperature to a higher one. This coefficient of performance is defined as the ratio of the quantity of heat pumped to the amount of work required, or it equals $T_{hot}(T_{hot} - T_{cold})$ for a warming machine, and $T_{cold}(T_{hot} - T_{cold})$ for a cooling machine, where all temperatures are in degrees absolute. This is one of the few engineering indices with numerical values greater than unity. *See* HEAT PUMP; REFRIGERATION CYCLE.

Practical limitations. Good as the ideal Carnot cycle may be, there are serious difficulties that emerge when one wishes to make an actual Carnot engine. The method of heat transfer through the cylinder head either limits the operation of the engine to very low speeds, or requires an engine with a huge bore and small stroke. Moreover, the material of the cylinder head is subjected to the full top temperature of the cycle, imposing a metallurgical upper limit on the cycle's temperature. *See* HEAT TRANSFER.

A practical solution to the heat transfer difficulties which beset the Carnot cycle is to burn a fuel in the air inside the engine cylinder. The result is an internal combustion engine that consumes and replaces its working substance while undergoing a periodic sequence of processes.

The working substance in such an internal combustion engine can attain very high temperatures, far above the melting point of the metal of the cylinder walls, because succeeding lower-temperature processes will keep the metal parts adequately cool. Thus, as the contents change temperature rapidly between wide extremes, the metal walls hover near a median temperature. The fuel-air mixture can be ignited by a spark, or by the rise in temperature from the compression stroke. *See* DIESEL CYCLE; DIESEL ENGINE; INTERNAL COMBUSTION ENGINE; OTTO CYCLE.

Even so, the necessarily high peak pressures and temperatures limit the practical thermal efficiency that an actual engine can achieve. The same theoretical efficiency can be obtained from a cycle consisting of two isobaric processes interspersed by two isentropic processes. The isobaric process requires that the cycle handle large volumes of low−pressure gas, which can best be done in a rotating turbine. *See* BRAYTON CYCLE; GAS TURBINE.

Although the Carnot cycle is independent of the working substance, and hence is applicable to a vapor cycle, the difficulty of efficiently compressing a vapor-liquid mixture renders the cycle impractical. In a steam power plant the sequence of states assumed by the working substance is (1) condensate and feedwater are compressed and pumped into the boiler, (2) heat is added to the water first at constantly increasing temperature and then at constant pressure and temperature, (3) the steam expands in the engine, and (4) the cycle is completed by a constant-temperature heat-rejection process which condenses the exhausted steam. *See* VAPOR CYCLE.

By comparison to the Carnot cycle, in which heat is added only at the highest temperature, this steam cycle with heat added over a range of temperatures is necessarily less efficient than is theoretically possible. An analysis of engine operations in terms of thermodynamic cycles indicates what efficiencies can be expected and how the operations should be modified to increase engine performance, such as high compression ratios for reciprocating internal combustion engines and high steam temperatures for steam engines. *See* POWER PLANT; THERMODYNAMIC CYCLE; THERMODYNAMIC PRINCIPLES.

Theodore Baumeister

Bibliography. E. A. Avallone and T. Baumeister III (eds.), *Marks' Standard Handbook for Mechanical Engineers*, 10th ed., 1996; K. E. Bett et al., *Thermodynamics for Chemical Engineers*, 1975; T. D. Eastop and A. McConkey, *Applied Thermodynamics for Engineering Technologists*, 5th ed., 1993; D. P. Tassios, *Applied Chemical Engineering Thermodynamics*, 1993; M. W. Zemansky and R. Dittman, *Heat and Thermodynamics*, 7th ed., 1996.

Carotenoid

Any of a class of yellow, orange, red, and purple pigments that are widely distributed in nature, including vegetables, fruits, insects, fishes, and birds. Most of these pigments are carotenoids, which are generally fat-soluble unless they are complexed with proteins. In plants, carotenoids are usually located in quantity in the grana of chloroplasts in the form of carotenoprotein complexes. Carotenoprotein complexes give blue, green, purple, red, or other colors to the outer surfaces or eggs of crustaceans, such as the lobster and crab. Echinoderms, nudibranch mollusks, and other invertebrate animals also contain carotenoproteins. Some coral coelenterates exhibit purple, pink, orange, or other colors due to carotenoids in the calcareous skeletal material. Cooked or denatured lobster, crab, and shrimp show the modified colors of their carotenoproteins.

Colors exhibited by carotenoid pigments are due to the absorption of quanta of visible wavelength light by the conjugated double-bond network of carotenoids. The absorption of a light quantum by the carotenoid molecule promotes an electron (π electron) of the double-bond system to a higher-energy orbital.

Astaxanthin is the carotenoid component of crustacyanin, a carotenoprotein that determines the color of the lobster shells. The native α-crustacyanin of fresh lobster maximally absorbs light of 632-nanometer wavelength whereas the denatured pigment protein of boiled lobster shows an absorption maximum at 540 nanometers, exhibiting dark green and orange-pink colors, respectively. These color changes are apparently due to an alteration of the interactions among the carotenoid molecules or between the carotenoid and protein moieties upon heat denaturation of the crustacyanin.

The total carotenoid production in nature is estimated at about 110,000,000 tons (100,000,000 metric tons) a year. The widespread occurrence of carotenoids in nature suggests that the distribution pattern of carotenoid pigments may be valuable in chemotaxonomic analyses. Patterns of evolution of algal groups have indeed been proposed on the basis of carotenoid pigmentation patterns. *See* PIGMENTATION.

Chemical structure and classification. The general structure of carotenoids is that of aliphatic and aliphatic-alicyclic polyenes, with a few aromatic-type polyenes (**Fig. 1**). Most carotenoid pigments are tetraterpenes with a 40-carbon (C_{40}) skeleton, traditionally regarded as results from the conjugation of eight isoprene units. C_{30}, C_{45}, and C_{50} carotenoids are also known in nature. Carotenes such as α-, β-, γ-, and δ-carotene are C_{40} carotenoids containing 11 or fewer conjugated carbon-carbon double bonds. Oxygenated carotenoids with hydroxyl, epoxy, ether, aldehyde, ketone, or acid groups are generally called xanthophylls. Carotenoids may exist in either cis or trans isomeric forms, with the latter being more stable than the former. The cis-trans isomerization may

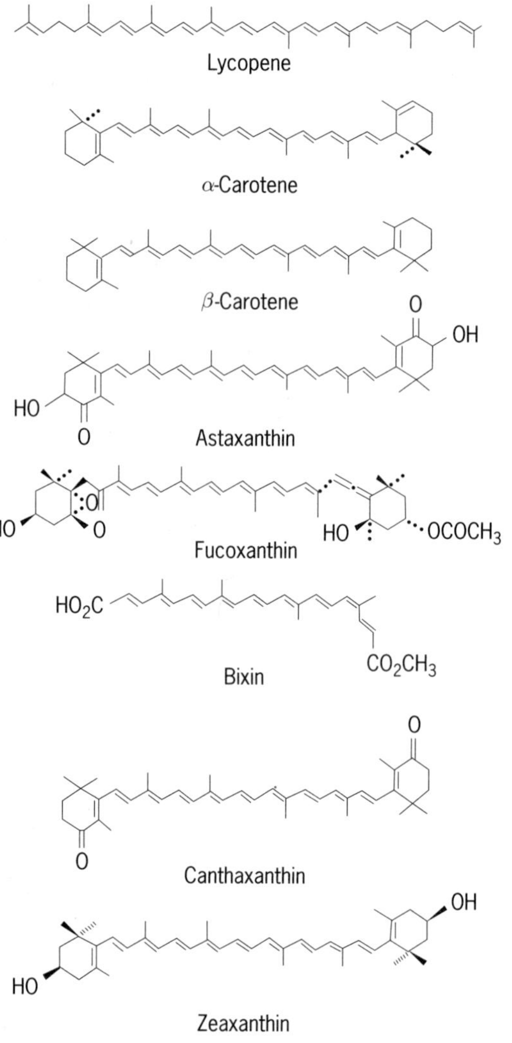

Fig. 1. Chemical structures of typical carotenoids.

be catalyzed by iodine, and blue light of 450-nm wavelength may also induce the isomerization (photoisomerization). *See* PHOTOCHEMISTRY.

More than 400 carotenoids of known structure are recognized, and the number is still on the rise.

Isolation and characterization. A rough separation of carotenes and xanthophylls (oxygen-containing carotenoids) can be achieved by partitioning a crude extract of pigment mixture between two immiscible solvents, petroleum ether or *n*-hexane and aqueous methanol (90%). Petroleum ether or *n*-hexane dissolves carotenes preferentially (epiphasic fraction), whereas aqueous methanol dissolves xanthophylls with two or more hydroxyl groups (hypophasic fraction). Monohydroxy carotenoids tend to be distributed equally between both phases.

Chromatographic methods are most effective and popular for isolation and purification of carotenoids. These include column chromatography, thin-layer chromatography, and high-pressure liquid chromatography, among others. Both column and thin-layer chromatography are based on the differential adsorption of various carotenoids to adsorbents.

Adsorbents chosen for the column method depend on the polarity of the carotenoids to be separated. For example, sucrose powder and magnesium silicate are used for separating strongly polar carotenoids, whereas carotenes are readily separated on an activated alumina column, by eluting them from the column stepwise, with a solvent mixture of increasing polarity. Thin-layer chromatography utilizes adsorbents such as silica gel, alumina, or sucrose, developed with mixtures of organic solvents. Thin-layer chromatography on cellulose layers as the stationary phase can also be used for separating different carotenoids on the basis of their partitioning between the stationary phase and the mobile phase (for example, acetone-methanol-water). Thin-layer chromatographic separation is usually more satisfactory for carotenoids than is column chromatography. **Figure 2** shows an example of the thin-layer chromatographic separation of five representative carotenoids. High-pressure liquid chromatography yields the highest resolution in separating carotenoids for identification and preparative purposes. Stereochemical isomers including cis-trans and enantiomeric isomers can be separated by high-pressure liquid chromatography. For characterization of carotenoids, various chemical and modern physical techniques such as spectroscopic and x-ray crystallographic determinations have been widely used. *See* CHROMATOGRAPHY.

Since carotenoids are blue light–absorbing pigments, absorption spectroscopy is routinely employed for the characterization of carotenoids with

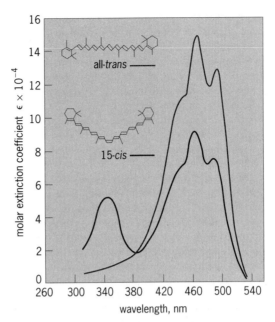

Fig. 3. Absorption spectra of all-trans carotene and 15,15′-mono-*cis*-β-carotene.

regard to the degree of conjugation and geometric isomerism. **Figure 3** illustrates spectral changes of β-carotene upon isomerization of the central carbon-carbon double bond. The near-ultraviolet peak gains its absorptivity, as the electronic system of β-carotene changes from a fully linear all-trans to a bent cis form. In contrast to linear polyenes, cyclic polyenes such as porphyrins exhibit a much stronger near-ultraviolet absorption band (Soret band) than a visible light band. Thus isomerization of fucoxanthin to isofucoxanthin by alkali can be followed spectrophotometrically at the near-ultraviolet band. Alkali also facilitates oxidation of certain carotenoids; for example, astaxanthin is oxidized to astacene. Acids also cause chemical changes in carotenoids; certain acids also form Lewis acid–carotenoid complexes.

Biosynthesis. The carbon skeletons of carotenoids are derived from the starting material, acetic acid, via a biosynthetic route similar to those of rubber and steroid syntheses. The biosynthetic pathway involves enzymatic reactions, such as hydrogenation, condensation, and dehydrogenation, followed finally by conjugation of the carbon-carbon double bonds forming the carotenoid π-electron system. Some xanthophylls are derived from β-carotene. **Figure 4** shows a simplified scheme for the biosynthesis of carotenoids.

The biosynthesis of carotenoids can be regulated by a number of exogenously added compounds. Some amines and compounds containing ammonium groups inhibit carotenoid biosynthesis in fungi and higher plants. On the other hand, many others stimulate carotenoid biosynthesis. A classic example of a compound that stimulates carotenoid biosynthesis is β-ionone, which is the ring structure occurring in β-carotene (Fig. 1). It is known that β-ionone

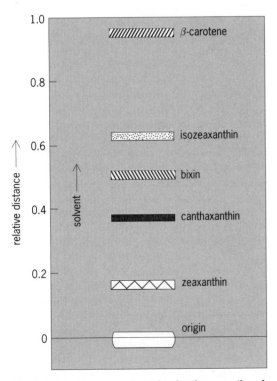

Fig. 2. Thin-layer chromatogram showing the separation of carotenoids. The adsorbent is silica gel, and the developing solvent consists of three parts *n*-hexane and seven parts ether.

itself is not incorporated into the carotenoid structure during the biosynthesis of β-ionone-containing carotenoids. It is known too that the regulation of the carotenoid biosynthesis is rather specific with respect to different geometric carotenoid isomers; thus, compounds such as diethyl alkylamines stimulate the formation of all-trans carotenes. Specifically, diethyl octylamine and diethyl nonylamine greatly enhance the biosynthesis of the cyclic carotenes, α-, β-, and δ-carotenes, along with the noncyclic pigment lycopene (Fig. 1).

The substituted benzylamines, such as *N*-benzylphenylamines and *N*-benzyl 2-naphthalene methylamine, induce the accumulation of cis-carotenoids in certain plant fruits, for example, grapefruit.

There are two major regulatory modes of action for these bioregulators in trans-carotenoid biosynthesis. One mode of action includes the inhibition of the enzyme cyclase in the formation of the monocyclic δ-carotene and the bicyclic β-carotene (Fig. 4), as shown in the scheme where X indicates a blocked pathway. The other includes activation or transcriptional induction of a gene regulating the synthesis of specific enzymes required for the biosynthetic pathway of carotenoid pigments.

The mode of action of the bioregulators for the biosynthesis of cis-carotenoids is less clear. The cyclases are not inhibited by the cis-regulators. Thus, the most likely mode of action of these regulators appears to be gene activation that results in biosynthesis of cis-carotenoids at the expense of all-trans carotenoid biosynthesis.

β-Carotene serves as a major precursor to various oxygen-containing carotenoids called xanthophylls. For example, in lobster and crab the biosynthetic pathway from β-carotene to astaxanthin (Fig. 1 and 4) involves several intermediates, as outlined in **Fig. 5**. Zeaxanthin has also been proposed as a precursor to astaxanthin in lobster.

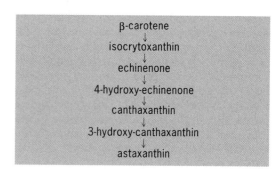

Fig. 5. Biosynthesis of astaxanthin from β-carotene in lobster and crab.

Biosynthesis of carotenoids can be enhanced by light. For example, blue light stimulates the formation of carotenoids in the fungi *Fusarium*, *Phycomyces*, and *Neurospora*. *Fusarium* synthesizes very little quantity of carotenoids in the dark, but blue light markedly stimulates the biosynthesis of carotenoids, including β-carotene and neurosporaxanthin. Blue light does so by regulating the expression of genes for the enzymes or regulatory proteins involved in the biosynthesis of carotenoids, and by photoinducing the production of certain factors used for the biosynthetic pathway of carotenoids. In addition, blue light stimulates the biosynthesis of carotenoids in algae, bacteria, and possibly in certain crustaceans and higher plants, such as angiosperms.

Red light also enhances the biosynthesis of carotenoids in higher plants; the pigment protein phytochrome acts as the red-light receptor. The red-light effect may be coupled to the blue-light effect in enhancing the biosynthetic formation of carotenoids in higher plants.

Function. The biochemical function of carotenoids is still largely unknown, although there are several biochemical functions in which the role of carotenoids is well understood. These include carotenoids in the photosynthetic apparatus of green plants, algae, and photosynthetic bacteria, where carotenoids function as a blue-light–harvesting pigment (antenna or accessory pigment) for photosynthesis. Thus carotenoids make it possible for photosynthetic organisms more fully to utilize the solar energy in the visible spectral region. Although the mechanism for the transfer of absorbed solar energy from carotenoid to chlorophyll is yet to be elucidated, it appears that carotenoid structures involving interactions of carotenoid-carotenoid as well as carotenoid-chlorophyll aggregate pairs are essential for the efficient energy transfer. This feature has been elucidated for the blue-light–harvesting carotenoid-chlorophyll protein complexes of marine dinoflagellates. **Figure 6** shows two sets of peridinin pairs (dimer) which stabilize the excited state of peridinin produced by light absorption, thus enhancing the probability of energy transfer from the carotenoid to chlorophyll. Without such interactions through exciton coupling between the two excited states of the peridinin dimer, each individual peridinin

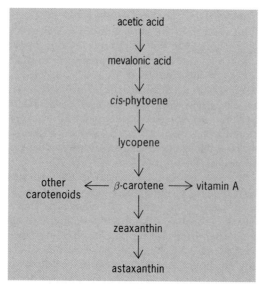

Fig. 4. Biosynthesis of carotenoids.

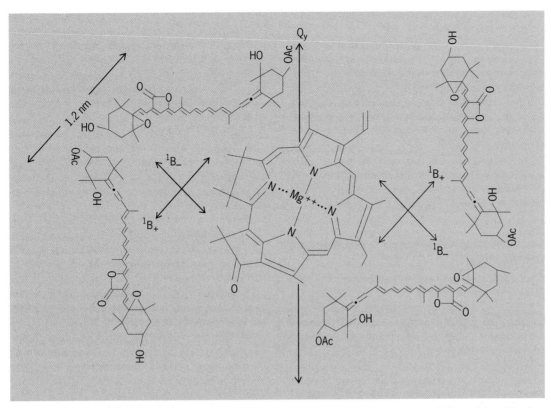

Fig. 6. A possible arrangement of four peridinin molecules (in two sets of dimer) around the chlorophyll *a* molecule. The Q_y axis of chlorophyll *a* represents the direction of fluorescence emission. B_+ and B_- represent two exciton states resulting from dimeric interactions between the peridinin molecules. Energy transfer takes place from the B_+ state to the chlorophyll molecule.

molecule does not possess a long enough lifetime for the energy transfer to chlorophyll to take place. *See* CHLOROPHYLL; PHOTOSYNTHESIS.

In addition to the light-harvesting function of carotenoids for photosynthesis, it is possible that carotenoid acts as an electron donor to the reactive chlorophyll (so-called P680), resulting in the formation of a carotenoid cation radical which may participate as an intermediate in the oxygen-evolving reaction of photosynthesis. However, this possibility remains to be studied.

Many algae, including dinoflagellates, utilize similar carotenoprotein pigments as the photoreceptor for phototaxis (swimming toward or away from blue light) and photophobic response (light-avoiding behavior). Apparently carotenoproteins in these systems serve as the antenna pigment and transfer the absorbed energy to the primary photoreceptor, probably chlorophyll, of the photosynthetic machinery which may control flagellum motion of algae in response to blue light by providing the necessary source of energy for the transduction network.

Another function of carotenoids is to protect biological systems such as the photosynthetic apparatus from photodynamic damage. Thus, plants lacking carotenoids are readily damaged by light. Certain herbicides kill weeds by blocking the biosynthesis of carotenoids so that the weed's photosynthetic apparatus is unprotected from photodynamic damage. Protection from photodynamic damage is achieved by quenching the powerful photodynamic oxidizing agent, singlet oxygen, produced as an undesirable by-product of the exposure of pigmented organisms to light. Carotenoids also protect plants from photodynamic damage by quenching the so-called triplet-state chlorophyll (where two of the π electrons in chlorophyll have their magnetic moments in parallel) in the photosynthetic apparatus.

Carotenoids are synthesized concomitantly with other photosynthetic membrane constituents for photosynthesis in the alga *Euglena*. This simultaneous synthesis appears to ensure that the membrane being assembled for the photosynthetic apparatus is stabilized by carotenoids and protected from photodynamic damage. However, this is not the case in higher plants where assembling of the photosynthetic apparatus takes place before the biosynthesis of carotenoids.

There may be many other functions of carotenoids as yet unknown. For example, it is possible that carotenoids, as important flower-petal pigments, may function in attracting insect pollinators.

Usage. Certain carotenoids are metabolized in biological systems, and some of them possess nutritional value. In particular, β-carotene is widely used as the vitamin A precursor, since it is metabolically oxidized to retinol (vitamin A) in animals, except cats. It is also used as an effective sunscreen agent in erythropoietic protoporphyria. Carotenoids, as well as a derivative, vitamin A, exhibit antitumor activity, for example, against ultraviolet-radiation–induced skin tumors. *See* VITAMIN A.

Perhaps the most important industrial application of carotenoids, including β-carotene and lycopene, which are rich in carrot and tomato, respectively, is in safe coloration of foods, as exemplified in the coloring and fortification of margarine and poultry feedstuff. *See* FOOD MANUFACTURING. Pill-Soon Song

Bibliography. G. Britton and T. W. Goodwin (eds.), *Carotenoid Chemistry and Biochemistry*, 1982; O. Isler (ed.), *Carotenoids*, 1971; H. Senger (ed.), *Blue Light Responses: Phenomena and Occurrence in Plants and Microorganisms*, 1987; P. S. Song, *Trends Biochem. Sci.*, pp. 25–27, February 1978.

Carotid body

A special sensory organ (glomus caroticum) located in the angle of the branching of the common carotid artery into the external and internal carotid arteries (see **illus.**). The human carotid body is an ovoid organ approximately 0.2 in. (5 mm) long, embedded in the outer connective tissue (adventitia) of the blood vessel. The carotid body is called a chemoreceptor because it is sensitive to oxygen and carbon dioxide in the blood. There is evidence that suggests that the carotid body is also sensitive to changes in blood pressure, blood flow, and blood osmolarity (salt content). *See* CHEMORECEPTION.

Histology. The carotid bodies are highly vascular structures composed of cords or lobules of epithelioid cells. The glomus cells, which constitute the principal cell type in the carotid body, contain numerous cytoplasmic vesicles or granules that are known to contain special transmitter substances called catecholamines. Stored together with these catecholamines are putative transmitter substances called neuropeptides that may modulate the action of the catecholamine neurotransmitter. The carotid

body also contains supporting cells, which are less abundant than glomus cells, do not contain vesicles, and partially envelop glomus cells and adjacent nerve fibers in their attenuated processes.

The glomus cells are richly innervated by sensory nerve fibers derived from the ninth cranial (glossopharyngeal) nerve, and to a lesser extent by the ganglioglomerular nerve from the superior cervical ganglion. The nerve fibers enter the carotid body and travel between and around the lobules of glomus cells, forming an interstitial plexus. Small unmyelinated nerve fibers from this plexus ultimately end on the glomus cells in a variety of synaptic configurations.

The embryology of the carotid body is controversial; experiments in birds, however, suggest that all of the cells are derived from a specialized portion of the neuroectoderm (neural crest), and there is little reason to suspect a different origin for the mammalian carotid body. The neural crest also gives rise to the adrenal medulla, whose cells closely resemble those of the carotid body. The adrenal medullary cells, however, secrete the hormones epinephrine (adrenaline) and norepinephrine (noradrenaline), whereas glomus cells release primarily dopamine and norepinephrine as neurotransmitters. *See* ADRENAL GLAND; EPINEPHRINE.

Physiology. The 1930s marked an epoch in carotid body research. It was demonstrated at that time that the carotid body and similar glomus tissue accumulations associated with the aortic arch (aortic bodies) possessed chemoreceptor properties. It was found that blood low in oxygen (hypoxemia) or high in carbon dioxide (hypercapnia) stimulated an increase in respiration and a secondary increase in heart rate and blood pressure. The increase in respiration observed after carotid body stimulation provides for an increase in the oxygenation of the red blood cells (erythrocytes). Likewise, secondary reflexes originating from the lungs cause an increase in heart rate that results in a greater blood flow from the heart to the lungs and, ultimately, the whole body. These important reflexes protect the organism from conditions of hypoxia (low tissue oxygen) such as may be experienced at high altitudes, during exercise, or during various cardiopulmonary disease states. *See* AORTIC BODY.

Although much is known about reflexes initiated by the carotid body, it is still not known how the chemical information derived from the blood is converted into electrical signals that are then transmitted to the cardiopulmonary brain centers. Current hypotheses center on the glomus cell as the immediate chemosensor which responds to stimuli by triggering nerve impulses in the sensory nerve endings. Alternatively, some studies suggest that both glomus cells and sensory nerve endings have chemosensory properties and that these elements coparticipate in the chemoresponse. Experiments to differentiate between these two possibilities are difficult to design. Moreover, different cellular elements within the carotid body may respond to different stimuli, thereby complicating the transduction

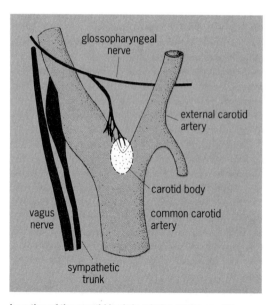

Location of the carotid body in relation to the carotid arteries.

mechanisms that normally are operative. Regardless of how chemoreception occurs, the carotid body is uniquely suited for the task of "sampling" the arterial blood. Because of its high vascularity and small size, the carotid body has one of the highest blood flow rates of any tissue in the body.

Pathological and physiological changes. Tumors of the carotid body are termed chemodectomas and are similar histologically to tumors of the adrenal medulla (pheochromocytomas) that secrete catecholamines. Carotid body tumors usually are benign, asymptomatic, and slow-growing. Individuals living at high altitudes have larger carotid bodies, and a higher incidence of carotid body tumors, although compared to all neoplasms the incidence is low. Finally, there is some evidence that the carotid body may be involved in sudden infant death syndrome (SIDS) or "crib death." It is still not known, however, whether SIDS arises from a peripheral (such as the carotid body) or from a central (such as brainstem) defect in respiratory integration. *See* CARDIOVASCULAR SYSTEM; SUDDEN INFANT DEATH SYNDROME (SIDS).   John T. Hansen

Bibliography. *Handbook of Physiology*, sec. 3: *The Respiratory System*, vol. 3: *Control of Breathing*, ed. by A. P. Fishman, 1986.

Carp

The common name for a number of cypriniform fishes of the family Cyprinidae. The carp originated in China, where for centuries it was raised for food. It was imported into the United States from Europe, where it also has been raised for years as a source of food.

Two varieties or forms of carp occur in nature (see **illus.**), but are commoner in captivity in breeding

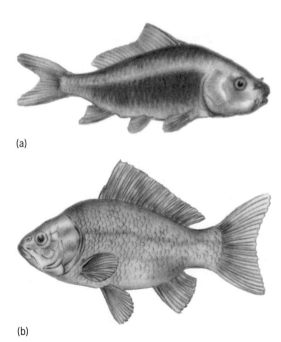

(a)

(b)

Two varieties of carp: (a) the carp (Cyprinus carpio) and (b) the goldfish (Crassius auratus).

ponds. These are the mirror carp, which has a few large scales, and the leather carp, which has no scales. In America the carp has invaded many natural bodies of water, where it has destroyed the weeds which are part of the natural breeding places of native fishes.

The carp (*Cyprinus carpio*) is a member of the Cyprinidae and is closely related to the goldfish (*Crassius auratus*). The silver carp (*Hypopthalmichthys*) is an Asiatic species in which the fourth gill arch is modified to form the helical organ, which is an accessory feeding structure. Fine, particulate food that escapes the gill rakers is entrapped in the mucus of the helical organ and passed into the stomach. The carp has pharyngeal teeth and a suckerlike mouth. A very long dorsal fin is preceded by a strong spine. The swim bladder of the carp is associated with a group of small bones at the anterior end, the Weberian ossicles. This structural modification enables the carp to perceive sound quite well. *See* ACTINOPTERYGII; CYPRINIFORMES; SWIM BLADDER.   Charles B. Curtin

Carpal tunnel syndrome

A condition caused by the thickening of ligaments and tendon sheaths at the wrist, with consequent compression of the median nerve at the palm. Affected individuals report numbness, tingling, and pain in the hand; the discomfort often becomes worse at night or after use of the hand. A physical examination of the injured hand during the early stages of the syndrome often reveals no abnormality. With more severe nerve compression, the individual experiences sensory loss over some or all of the digits innervated by the median nerve (thumb, index finger, middle finger, and ring finger) and weakness of thumb movement.

Assessment. Electrodiagnostic testing is important for an accurate diagnosis. The electromyographer uses sensory fibers to measure the nerve conduction velocity from the finger or the palm to the wrist and the motor conduction velocity from the wrist to the thumb muscles. Approximately half the individuals with carpal tunnel syndrome have abnormalities of the opposite median nerve. Electrodiagnostic values of these individuals therefore need to be compared with reference values obtained from normal subjects and with ulnar or radial nerve values. No other test has a higher diagnostic accuracy for individuals who have a final diagnosis of carpal tunnel syndrome, but to make a final diagnosis clinical data, including the individual's response to treatment, must be obtained.

False positive and false negative results are illustrated by the high rate of abnormalities in the opposite, nonsymptomatic hands of individuals with carpal tunnel syndrome. As testing becomes more complex and sophisticated, it becomes increasingly likely that results beyond the normal range (false positive) will be generated. The number of individuals with false negative results should be below 8%.

Thermography shows clear abnormalities in carpal tunnel syndrome, but an abnormal thermogram is found in many other conditions in which the pattern of blood flow to the hand is altered. Computed tomography and magnetic resonance imaging have not been widely used for carpal tunnel syndrome and have no role in management at this time.

Prevalence. Carpal tunnel syndrome is common. One study reported that 125 individuals per 100,000 were affected from 1976 to 1980. Another study estimated that 515 of every 100,000 patients sought medical attention for carpal tunnel syndrome in 1988; the syndrome in half of these patients was thought to be occupational in origin.

The incidence of carpal tunnel syndrome is greater among electronic-parts assemblers, frozen-food processors, musicians, and dental hygienists. Highly repetitive wrist movements, use of vibrating tools, awkward wrist positions, and movements involving great force seem to be correlated with the disorder. Awkward and repetitive wrist motions occur in many office tasks, such as typing and word processing. In some occupations, such as shellfish packing, the incidence is more than 200 times higher than in the baseline data. The highest reported incidence in an industrial setting, based on the numbers of carpal tunnel syndrome–based releases, was 15% among a group of meatpackers.

Carpal tunnel syndrome probably accounts for a minority of the cases of overuse syndrome (cumulative trauma syndrome), which is a common problem in occupational settings. Overuse syndrome symptoms include muscle pain, tendinitis, fibrositis (inflammation of connective tissue in a joint region), and epicondylitis (inflammation of the eminence on the condyle of a bone). Although the causative relationship between the two disorders has not been conclusively proven, the incidence of both carpal tunnel syndrome and overuse syndrome appears to increase in tandem in individuals who are at risk.

Pathophysiology. Under normal circumstances, the pressure within the tissues of a limb is 7–8 mmHg. In carpal tunnel syndrome, the pressure is often 30 mmHg, approaching the level at which nerve dysfunction occurs. With wrist flexion or extension, pressures may increase to 90 mmHg or more.

The increase in pressure within the carpal canal is usually caused by nonspecific inflammation of flexor tendon sheaths. Diabetes, pregnancy, rheumatoid arthritis, and hypothyroidism are the most common medical conditions associated with carpal tunnel syndrome. Amyloidosis, acromegaly, and mycobacterial infections are rare causes. A reduction in the flow of blood to the nerve can account for the intermittent tingling that occurs at night or with wrist flexion. *See* AMYLOIDOSIS; ARTHRITIS; DIABETES; THYROID GLAND DISORDERS.

Treatment. Nonsurgical treatment includes avoidance of the use of the wrist, use of a splint to keep the wrist in a neutral position, and anti-inflammatory medications. These treatments are especially useful in individuals with an acute flare-up and in those with minimal and intermittent symptoms. Conservative nonsurgical treatment will not succeed for individuals over the age of 50, for those who have had the syndrome for more than 10 months, and for those with constant tingling.

Surgical treatment may be used if conservative approaches fail. The procedure is usually done on an outpatient basis with prognoses of good to excellent in 80% of the cases. Although 40% of the individuals regain normal function, the condition of 5% may worsen. Most individuals return to an office job within a week of surgery, but it may be 4–6 months before carpenters, construction workers, or athletes are able to return to work. Many individuals with work-related carpal tunnel syndrome should consider changing jobs.

Surprisingly little information is available regarding the redesign of workstations and its effect on the reversal of symptoms or the prevention of carpal tunnel syndrome. Ergonomic redesign is widely practiced, but rarely described in medical terms.   David M. Dawson

Bibliography. D. M. Dawson, M. Hallett, and L. H. Millender, *Entrapment Neuropathies*, 3d ed., 1999; R. B. Rosenbaum and J. L. Ochoa, *Carpal Tunnel Syndrome and Other Disorders of the Median Nerve*, 1993.

Carpoids

The common name for four extinct classes of primitive echinoderms that have a flattened theca or body lacking radial symmetry. These enigmatic fossils were originally classified together in the class Carpoidea, but more recent echinoderm researchers have assigned them to four separate classes in the subphylum Homalozoa: the Stylophora (or Calcichordates), Homoiostelea, Homostelea, and Ctenocystoidea. These four classes include about 50 genera that range from the Early or Middle Cambrian to the Late Carboniferous.

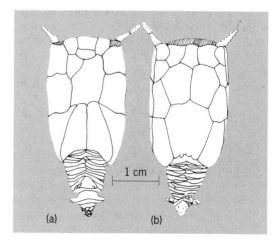

Enoploura popei, a stylophoran carpoid from the Late Ordovician of Ohio. (*a*) Concave lower side and (*b*) convex upper side of the plated theca showing part of the attached, tapering appendage used for locomotion and feeding at the bottom.

Carpoids have a flattened theca that varies from asymmetrical to nearly bilaterally symmetrical (see **illus.**) and is made up of sutured, multiporous, single-crystal, calcite plates like those found in other echinoderms. Three of the classes have a long plated appendage attached to the theca that was used for locomotion and, in the Stylophora, also for feeding. The mouth was either on the anterior margin of the theca with ambulacral grooves leading to it or at the base of the feeding appendage; the anal pyramid was usually on the opposite thecal margin or nearby at a thecal corner. Carpoids were apparently mobile, bottom-living or shallow-burrowing, detritus or suspension feeders, sifting out small food particles from the top layer of soft sediment or from the surrounding seawater. Because of the distinctive skeletons, most researchers consider carpoids as true echinoderms, although they seem only distantly related to other fossil and living echinoderms that have well-developed pentameral symmetry. *See* ECHINODERMATA; HOMALOZOA.   James Sprinkle

Bibliography. R. C. Moore (ed.), *Treatise on Invertebrate Paleontology*, pt. S, 1968.

Carrageenan

A polysaccharide that is a major constituent of the cell walls of certain red algae (Rhodophyceae), especially members of the families Gigartinaceae, Hypneaceae, Phyllophoraceae, and Solieriaceae. Extracted for its suspending, emulsifying, stabilizing, and gelling properties, it is one of three algal polysaccharides of major economic importance, the others being agar and alginate. *See* AGAR; ALGINATE.

Carrageenans form a family of linear (unbranched) sulfated polysaccharides in which the basic repeating units are exclusively D-galactose, or D-galactose and 3,6-anhydro-D-galactose, linked alternately α-1,3- and β-1,4-. Different types of carrageenans, which are designated by Greek letters, are found in different species and sometimes in different somatic phases of the same species or in different regions of the same plant. The κ- and ι-carrageenans are soluble in hot water but not cold, and gel upon cooling in the presence of potassium ion. The λ-, ϵ-, and π-carrageenans are soluble in hot water or cold, forming a viscous solution but not a gel.

Carrageenan is prepared by boiling the dried algae in slightly alkaline water. The hot solution is filtered and poured into isopropyl alcohol, which causes the carrageenan to precipitate. The product is purified, dried, ground, and packaged as a powder.

The main sources of carrageenan are *Chondrus crispus* (Gigartinaceae) from the Maritime Provinces of Canada and various species of *Eucheuma* (Solieriaceae) from the Philippines. *Chondrus*, popularly called Irish moss, is harvested from naturally occurring intertidal stands, while *Eucheuma* is successfully grown in mariculture on nets and lines.

About 80% of the refined carrageenan is used in food processing, with the dairy industry being the chief consumer. The remainder is used in the cosmetic, pharmaceutical, printing, and textile industries. *See* RHODOPHYCEAE.

Paul C. Silva; Richard L. Moe

Carrier (communications)

A periodic waveform upon which an information-bearing signal is impressed. This process is known as modulation and comprises a variety of forms such as amplitude, phase, and frequency modulation. The most common type of carrier is the sinusoidal carrier (**illus.** *a*), but in reality, any periodic waveform followed by a band-pass filter can serve as a carrier.

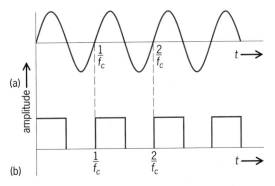

Carriers. (*a*) Sinusoidal carrier. (*b*) Square-wave carrier.

The validity of the last statement can be verified by considering a periodic function $c(t)$, and assuming that it is desired to have a message $m(t)$ double-sideband (DSB)-modulate a carrier. Since the function $c(t)$ is periodic, it can be expanded in a Fourier series of the form given by Eq. (1), where the $\{c_n\}$

$$c(t) = \sum_{n=-\infty}^{\infty} c_n e^{j2\pi n f_c t} \tag{1}$$

are the coefficients of the Fourier series, and f_c is the carrier frequency, chosen so that it exceeds W, the bandwidth of the message $m(t)$. This results in the waveform given by Eq. (2). The Fourier transform

$$m(t)c(t) = \sum_{n=-\infty}^{\infty} c_n m(t) e^{j2\pi n f_c t} \tag{2}$$

of this waveform is given by Eq. (3), where $M(\omega)$

$$F(\omega) = \sum_{n=-\infty}^{\infty} c_n M(\omega - n\omega_c) \tag{3}$$

is the Fourier transform of $m(t)$, and $\omega_c = 2\pi f_c$. If this signal is now put through a band-pass filter with center frequency f_c and bandwidth $2W$, a waveform proportional to $m(t)\cos\omega_c t$ results (that is, a double-sideband signal has been generated). *See* FOURIER SERIES AND TRANSFORMS.

A periodic waveform that is very simple to generate is a square wave composed of ones and zeros of equal duration. This allows the multiplication function inherent in the modulation process represented by the function $m(t)c(t)$ to be replaced by an on-off switch. Indeed, such a modulator is commonly known as a switching modulator, and results in a periodic square wave (illus. *b*).

At times, it is convenient to use subcarriers in addition to the main carrier. Such a situation arises when frequency-division multiplexing (FDM) is used. A set of, say, *N* information-bearing waveforms individually modulate their own subcarrier, whereby the spacing of the subcarriers is chosen so that it results in (virtually) no spectral overlap of the resulting *N* spectra. This composite baseband waveform then modulates the main carrier in preparation for transmission over the channel. For voice communications, the modulation on the subcarriers is often single-sideband (SSB), whereas typically the modulation on the carrier itself is frequency-modulation. *See* AMPLITUDE MODULATION; FREQUENCY MODULATION; MODULATION; MULTIPLEXING AND MULTIPLE ACCESS; SINGLE SIDEBAND.   Laurence B. Milstein

Carrot

A biennial umbellifer (*Daucus carota*) of Asiatic and Mediterranean origin belonging to the plant order Umbellales. The carrot is grown for its edible roots which are eaten raw or cooked (**Fig. 1**). *See* APIALES.

Cultivation and harvesting. Propagation is by seed planted directly in the field. Spacing varies; plants are usually planted $1/2$–2 in. (1.2–5 cm) apart in rows of 18–24 in. (45–60 cm). Temperature and soil moisture affect root color and shape; 60–70°F (15–21°C) is optimum for high yields of long, deep-colored roots.

Exposure of the young carrot plants to prolonged cold weather (40–50°F, or 4–10°C, for 15 or more days) favors seed-stalk formation. Misshapen roots commonly result from nematodes, aster yellows disease, or compacted soils. Most commercial plantings are weeded chemically.

Varieties (cultivars) are classified according to length of root (long or short or stump-rooted) and use (fresh market or processing). Popular varieties for fresh market are Imperator and Gold Pak; for processing, Red Cored Chantenay and Royal Chantenay are often chosen.

Harvesting of carrots for fresh market begins when the roots are $3/4$–2 in. (1.8–5 cm) in diameter, usually 60 to 90 days after planting. Harvesting by machine is common. Marketing in bunches is declining; most carrots are sold in plastic bags with the foliage removed. Carrots for canning generally have shorter roots and are grown to a larger diameter.

Texas, California, and Arizona are three important carrot-producing states. *See* NEMATA.   H. John Carew

Diseases. Carrots are affected in the field by two important leaf spot diseases and by aster yellows. In storage and transit, the roots are attacked by several kinds of rot-inducing organisms.

Carrot leaf spots are caused by the fungi *Cercospora carotae* and *Alternaria dauci*. Cercospora blight occurs on young leaves and Alternaria blight on older leaves. These fungi overwinter in debris of the previous crop. During the growing season, repeated disease cycles are caused by airborne spores.

Fig. 1. Carrots. (*Asgrow Co., Subsidiary of the Upjohn Co.*)

In humid weather, both diseases increase rapidly, and severe defoliation results. Control of these leaf spots is achieved by repeated application of a suitable fungicide.

Aster yellows is caused by a mycoplasmalike organism that can infect many weed and crop hosts. Leafhoppers, principally *Macrosteles fascifrons*, are the insect vectors. Aster yellows causes the development of many adventitious chlorotic shoots to give a witches'-broom condition. These malformed and bushy tops eventually turn bronze or reddish. Roots are also malformed and produce numerous woolly secondary roots (**Fig. 2**) and tough woody tissue in the carrot. Control of aster yellows is by control of

Fig. 2. Carrot yellows. (*Courtesy of Arden Sherf, College of Agriculture, Cornell University*)

the leafhopper vectors. Spraying with an approved insecticide should begin early in the season as vectors begin to migrate from nearby diseased weeds into carrot fields.

Rots of carrots in storage or transit are caused by several different bacteria or fungi. The classic rot is bacterial soft rot caused by *Erwinia carotovora*. This bacterium is a wound parasite and enters the carrot through openings at the crown, insect wounds, or harvest bruises. At temperatures about 40°F (4°C), the rot advances rapidly. Diseased tissues become soft and slimy and have a putrid odor. Control of soft rot requires careful handling during harvest and packing in order to reduce bruising. Storage temperature should be just above freezing, and relative humidity below 90%. *See* PLANT PATHOLOGY.

Thomas H. Barksdale

Bibliography. L. V. Boone et al., *Producing Farm Crops*, 4th ed., 1991; T. W. Whitaker et al., *Carrot Production in the United States*, U.S. Department of Agriculture, Agr. Handb. 375, 1970.

Cartilage

A firm, resilient connective tissue of vertebrates and some invertebrates. Isolated pieces act as a skeleton to provide support and anchor muscles, or cartilage is with bone to contribute its resilience and interstitial growth to bony skeletal functions. Cartilage comprises a firm extracellular matrix synthesized by large, ovoid cells (chondrocytes) located in holes called lacunae. The matrix elements are water bound by the high negative charge of extended proteoglycan (protein-polysaccharide) molecules, and a network of fine collagen fibrils. The elements furnish mechanical stability, give, and tensile strength, but allow the diffusion of nutrients and waste to keep the cells alive. Generally, blood vessels reach only to the perichondrium of fibrous connective tissue, wrapping around the cartilage and attaching it to other tissues. *See* BONE; COLLAGEN.

Cartilage is modified in several ways. In elastic cartilage, the chondrocytes add elastic fibers to the matrix to increase resilience, as in cartilages supporting the Eustachian tube, mammalian external ear, and parts of the larynx. Where cartilage joins bones tightly at certain joints with limited mobility, for example, at the pubic symphysis and between vertebrae, the matrix of fibrocartilage contains prominent collagen fibers and has less proteoglycan than the typical hyaline variety. Hyaline cartilage, named for its glassy translucence, is the major support in the airway; and throughout the embryo, pieces of it develop as a cartilaginous precursor to the bony skeleton, except in the face and upper skull.

The primitive cartilaginous skeleton undergoes another modification, by locally calcifying its matrix. At sites of calcification, invading cells destroy the cartilage and mostly replace it by bone, leaving permanent hyaline cartilage only at the joint or articular surfaces, in some ribs, and, until maturity, at growth plates set back from the joints and perpendicular to

the long axis of limb bones. The precarious physiological balance between chondrocytes and matrix materials in the heavily loaded articular cartilage breaks down in old age or in inflamed joints. *See* ARTHRITIS; CONNECTIVE TISSUE; JOINT (ANATOMY); SKELETAL SYSTEM.   William A. Beresford

Bibliography. B. K. Hall (ed.), *Cartilage*, 3 vols., 1983.

Cartography

The techniques concerned with constructing maps from geographic information. Maps are spatial representations of the environment. Typically, maps take graphic form, appearing on computer screens or printed on paper, but they may also take tactile or auditory forms for the visually impaired. Other representations such as digital files of locational coordinates or even mental images of the environment are also sometimes considered to be maps, or virtual maps.

Maps and uses. Because the environment is complex and everchanging, the variety of maps and map uses is unlimited. For instance, maps are indispensable tools for navigating over land, sea, or air. Maps are effective both in exploiting natural resources and in protecting them. They are used to investigate geographic phenomena, including environmental pollution, climate change, even the spread of diseases and the distribution of social phenomena such as poverty and illiteracy. In addition, maps can be used to communicate insights derived from geographic research through publication in periodicals and books and through distribution over computer networks and broadcast media. Every private business, government agency, and academic discipline whose products, services, or objects of study are geographically dispersed benefits from detailed, up-to-date maps. Unfortunately, appropriate maps often are unavailable.

Map scale and geographic detail. Maps often include insufficient or excessive detail for the task at hand. The amount of usable detail on a map varies with its scale, because human visual acuity and the resolution of printing and imaging devices are limited. Maps that depict extensive areas in relatively small spaces are called small-scale maps. For example, on a 1-ft-wide (30-cm) map of the world, on which the ratio of map distance to ground distance is approximately 1:125,000,000, very little perceptible detail can be preserved. As the scale of a map increases, so may the level of geographic detail it represents. Geographic features selected to appear on small-scale maps must be exaggerated in size and simplified in shape so as to be recognizable by the map user. These map generalization operations constitute an intriguing field of research by cartographers attempting to formalize, and ultimately to automate, the map creation process.

Reference maps. Topographic maps record the positions and elevations of physical characteristics of the landscape. They serve as locational dictionaries

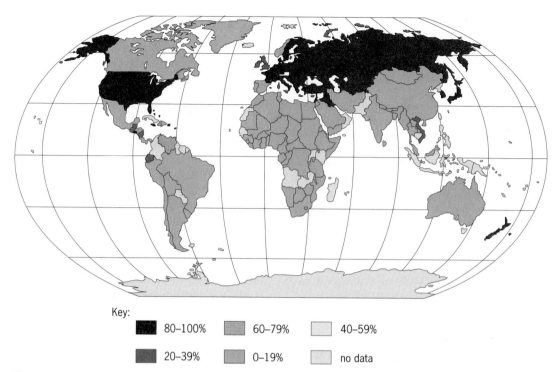

Key:

■	80–100%	60–79%	40–59%
	20–39%	0–19%	no data

Fig. 1. Large-scale topographic mapping, percent area coverage area at 1:1000 to 1:36,680 showing the uneven spatial distribution of map coverage. (*After United Nations, World Cartography, vol. 20, 1990*)

for many endeavors, including environmental planning, resource management, and recreation. The 1:24,000 scale United States Geological Survey (USGS) series covers the continental United States with approximately 57,000 map sheets and depicts 17 categories of physiographic and cultural features with more than 130 distinct graphic symbols. The enormous costs involved in compiling, producing, and revising a topographic map series account for the fact that only about 15% of Earth's surface is topographically mapped at a scale of 1:25,000 or larger (**Fig. 1**). *See* TOPOGRAPHIC SURVEYING AND MAPPING.

Thematic maps. Another problem with available maps is that they often fail to include a feature of particular interest. Maps that emphasize one or a few related geographic phenomena in the service of a specific purpose are called thematic maps. An example is a thematic map that reveals the uneven distribution of topographic map coverage around the world (Fig. 1). Thematic maps are powerful alternatives to text, tables, and graphs for visualizing potentially meaningful patterns in geographic information. Although the production of large-scale topographic map series requires the resources of large private or government agencies, individuals and small organizations with access to relatively inexpensive personal computers, mapping software, and databases can afford to produce thematic maps in support of business, scientific, political, and creative endeavors.

Constructing geographic information. Maps are composed of two kinds of geographic information: attribute data and locational data. Attribute data are

quantitative or qualitative measures of characteristics of the landscape, such as terrain elevation, land use, or population density. Locations of features on the Earth's surface are specified by use of coordinate systems; among these, the most common is the geographical coordinate system of latitudes and longitudes.

Geographical coordinates describe positions on the spherical Earth. These must be transformed to positions on a two-dimensional plane before they can be depicted on a printed sheet or a computer screen. Hundreds of map projections—mathematical transformations between spherical and planar coordinates—have been devised, but no map projection can represent the spherical Earth in two dimensions without distorting spatial relationships among features on Earth's surface in some way. One specialized body of knowledge that cartographers bring to science is the ability to specify map projections that preserve the subset of geometric characteristics that are most important for particular mapping applications.

Prior to World War II, locational data were compiled mainly by field surveys. Aerial surveillance techniques developed for the war effort were then adapted for use in civilian mapmaking. The scale distortions inherent in aerial photographs can be corrected by photogrammetric methods, yielding planimetrically correct projections on which all locations appear to be viewed simultaneously from directly above. Rectified aerial photographs (orthophotos) can be used either as bases for topographic mapping or directly as base maps. *See* AERIAL PHOTOGRAPH; LATITUDE AND LONGITUDE; PHOTOGRAMMETRY.

Influence of computing technology. Periodically, cartographic practice has been transformed by new technologies. Few have had such a profound effect as the development of computer-based mapping techniques. While printed paper maps still constitute the richest store of geographic information, cartography has become as much a digital as a paper-based enterprise. With more and more geographic data available in digital form, the computer has changed the very idea of a map from a static caricature of the environment to a dynamic interface for generating and testing hypotheses about complex environmental and social processes.

Digital geographic data. There are two major approaches to encoding geographic data for computer processing. One, commonly called raster encoding, involves sampling attribute values at some regular interval across the landscape. Imagery scanned from Earth-observing satellites works this way, recording surface reflectance values for grid cells (pixels) from 80 to 30 m (250 to 100 ft) or less in resolution. Digital elevation models are matrices of terrain elevations derived from satellite imagery or sampled from topographic maps (**Fig. 2**).

A second method, known as vector encoding, involves digitizing outlines of landscape features that are homogeneous with regard to some attribute, such as a river, a watershed, a road, or a state boundary. Vector encoding is more expensive than raster encoding, but it is more flexible for many applications. One U.S. government data-base, for example, includes street descriptions and address ranges for 345 metropolitan areas by which U.S. census statistics can be matched and precisely mapped. The U.S. government's Digital Chart of the World vector data-base includes 16 distinct feature layers, including coastlines, rivers, roads, political boundaries, and 1000-ft (300-m) terrain elevation contours for the entire world at 1:1,000,000 scale.

Although the raster and vector approaches for digital encoding predominate, these have been implemented in dozens of idiosyncratic data formats designed to suit individual mapping agencies and computer vendors. Incompatible formats have impeded data sharing and have resulted in expensive redundancies in database construction. A committee of United States academic and government cartographers specified a Spatial Data Transfer Standard to improve cooperation and data sharing among federal government agencies. The development of international data standards is needed. *See* COMPUTER GRAPHICS.

Constructing geographic understanding. Geographic illiteracy is thought to put afflicted societies at a disadvantage in an increasingly integrated international economy. Access to geographic information is a necessary but insufficient condition for constructing geographic understanding. Access to analytical expertise is required to learn from the available information.

Geographic information systems. Guiding much of the research and development efforts of academic cartographers is the concept of automated geography—an amalgam of computer databases and procedures by which analysts might model, simulate, and ideally predict the behavior of physical and social systems on the landscape. Concurrently, increasing social concern for environmental protection stimulates a market for computerized geographic information systems (GIS) that combine mapping capabilities with techniques in quantitative spatial analysis. Many of the analytical procedures in these

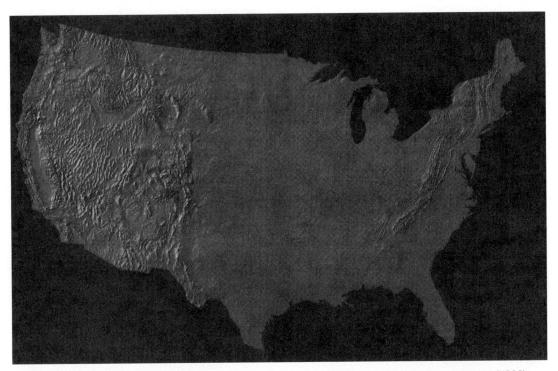

Fig. 2. Computer rendering of the topography of the 48 contiguous United States based on 12 million elevations. (USGS)

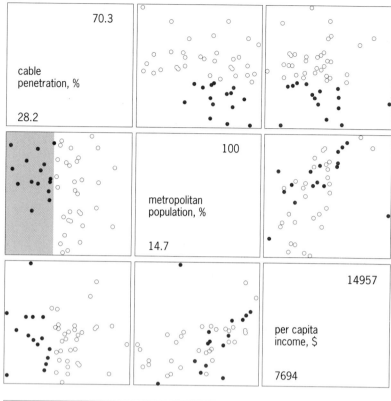

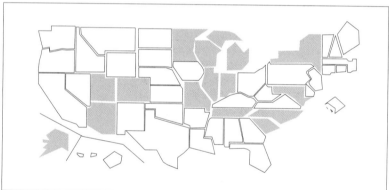

Fig. 3. Three geographic data variables related in a scatterplot matrix and linked to a map. Locations of observations selected in a scatterplot are automatically highlighted on the map. (*From M. Monmonier, Geographic brushing: Enhancing exploratory analysis of the scatterplot matrix, Geog. Anal., 21(1):81–84, 1989*)

largest research project—the search for objective guidelines, based on psychological research, to optimize map communication. Map design issues that have garnered the most attention include classification techniques for grouping attribute data into discernible map categories and logical systems for choosing appropriate graphic symbols for representing different types of attribute data.

Interactive cartography. Although many broadly applicable map design principles have been established, the goal of specifying an optimal map for a particular task is less compelling than it once was. Instead, there is interest in the potential of providing map users with multiple, modifiable representations via dynamic media such as CD-ROM, computer networks, and interactive television. Even as computer graphics technologies and numerical models provide ever more realistic environmental simulations, innovative, highly abstract display methods are being developed and tested to help analysts discover meaningful patterns in multivariate geographic data sets (**Fig. 3**). Maps, graphs, diagrams, movies, text, and sound can be incorporated in multimedia software applications that enable users to navigate through vast electronic archives of geographic information. Interactive computer graphics are eliminating the distinction between the mapmaker and the map user. Modern cartography's challenge is to provide access to geographic information and to cartographic expertise through well-designed user interfaces. *See* LAND-USE PLANNING; MAP DESIGN; MAP PROJECTIONS.

David DiBiase

Bibliography. G. L. Gaile and C. J. Willmott, *Geography in America at the Dawn of the 21st Century*, 2004; J. Makower (ed.), *The Map Catalog: Every Kind of Map and Chart on Earth and Even Some Above It*, 3d ed., 1992; P. C. Muehrcke, *Map Use: Reading, Analysis and Interpretation*, 4th ed., 2001; D. Wood, *The Power of Maps*, 1992.

systems—such as calculations of distances, areas, and volumes; of terrain surface slope and aspect; defining buffer regions surrounding landscape features; and generating maps of new features formed by the intersection of several related map layers—have been codified by cartographers. Some cartographers have investigated the potential of computerized expert systems that may be used to assist nonspecialists in performing quantitative geographic analyses. *See* EXPERT SYSTEMS; GEOGRAPHIC INFORMATION SYSTEMS.

Cartographic communication. With few exceptions, the outcomes of analyses performed with geographic information systems are maps. Just as careless or biased quantitative analyses result in erroneous conclusions, so can unskilled map designs mislead users, and even the analysts themselves. Concern for the integrity of thematic maps motivated cartography's

Caryophyllales

An order of flowering plants, division Magnoliophyta (Angiospermae), in the core eudicots. The order consists of 26 families and about 12,500 species. The order has been expanded from the traditional concept of 12 families (core Caryophyllales), which are characterized by P-type sieve-tube plastids, the presence of betalains (except in Caryophyllaceae) instead of anthocyanins, and frequent occurrence of succulent habit. The four largest families of core Caryophyllales are Aizoaceae (about 2500 species), Amaranthaceae (about 2300 species), Cactaceae (about 2000 species), and Caryophyllaceae (about 2000 species). The expanded order is more difficult to define on the basis of morphology, but anomalous secondary growth, multicellular glands (trichomes), ellagic acid, and naphthaquinones occur frequently. Many representatives grow in marginal environments such as saltmarshes and deserts.

Polygonaceae (about 1000 species) are among the additional families in the expanded order, many of the others being small, little-known groups. Aizoaceae are unarmed leaf succulents, chiefly African, with numerous tepals (divisions of the perianth) and stamens. Cactaceae are American stem succulents, mostly spiny with no leaves, again with numerous tepals and stamens. Amaranthaceae have reduced flowers, usually with a single ovule. Polygonaceae usually have prominent stipules united to form a scarious bract or ocrea, unusual vascular structure, and swollen nodes. Droseraceae are carnivorous, and capture insects by fly-paper or spring-trap mechanisms. Members of Caryophyllales include carnation (*Dianthus caryophyllus*) in Caryophyllaceae, rhubarb (*Rheum × cultorum*) in Polygonaceae, sundews (*Drosera* spp.) and Venus flytrap (*Dionaea muscipula*) in Droseraceae, and jojoba (*Simmondsia chinensis*) in Simmondsiaceae. *See* BEET; MAGNOLIOPHYTA; MAGNOLIOPSIDA; PLANT KINGDOM; SPINACH; SUGARBEET.

Michael F. Fay; Mark W. Chase

Caryophyllidae

A relatively small subclass of the class Magnoliopsida (dicotyledons) of the division Magnoliophyta (Angiospermae), the flowering plants, consisting of 3 orders, 14 families, and about 11,000 species. They have mostly trinucleate pollen and ovules with two integuments (bitegmic) and a nucellus that is more than one cell thick (crassinucellate). Also, the ovules are often distorted by unequal growth so that the micropyle is brought near the funiculus and the chalazal end (campylotropous), or half inverted so the funiculus is attached near the middle (amphitropous) and these are usually borne on a free-central or basal placenta.

Most of these plants contain betalain pigments instead of anthocyanins, and the seeds very often have a perisperm. Most of the families and species of the subclass belong to the order Caryophyllales. The other orders (Plumbaginales and Polygonales) have only a single family each. *See* CARYOPHYLLALES; MAGNOLIOPHYTA; MAGNOLIOPSIDA; PLANT KINGDOM; PLUMBAGINALES; POLYGONALES.

Arthur Cronquist; T. M. Barkley

Cascode amplifier

An amplifier stage consisting of a common-emitter transistor cascaded with a common-base transistor (see **illus.**). The common-emitter–common-base (CE-CB) transistor pair constitutes a multiple active device which essentially corresponds to a common-emitter stage with improved high-frequency performance. In monolithic integrated-circuit design the use of such active compound devices is much more economical than in discrete designs. A similar compound device is the common-collector–common-emitter connection (CC-CE), also known as the Darlington pair. *See* INTEGRATED CIRCUITS.

The cascode connection is especially useful in

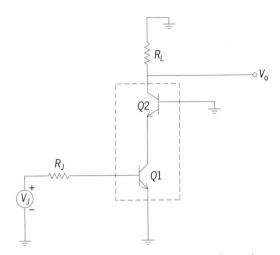

Cascode amplifier. Broken lines enclose a transistor pair consisting of a common-emitter transistor Q1 and a common-base transistor Q2.

wideband amplifier design as well as the design of high-frequency tuned amplifier stages. The improvement in high-frequency performance is due to the impedance mismatch between the output of the common-emitter stage and the input of the common-base stage. Thus the influence of the Miller effect on the first (common-emitter) transistor is minimal even when the load resistance of the amplifier, R_L, is large, because the load resistance of the first transistor is no longer R_L but the much lower input resistance of the second transistor. Furthermore, since the second transistor is in the common-base configuration, it does not suffer from the Miller effect. This effect limits the frequency response of a common-emitter stage by essentially multiplying the base-to-collector junction capacitance by the voltage gain and making it appear much larger at the input of the stage between base and emitter.

Another important characteristic of the cascode connection is the higher isolation between its input and output than for a single common-emitter stage, because the reverse transmission across the compound device stage is much smaller than for the common-emitter stage. In effect, the second (common-base) transistor acts as an impedance transformer. This isolation effect makes the cascode configuration particularly attractive for the design of high-frequency tuned amplifier stages where the parasitic cross-coupling between the input and the output circuits can make the amplifier alignment very difficult. *See* AMPLIFIER; TRANSISTOR.

Christos C. Halkias

Bibliography. A. S. Sedra and K. C. Smith, *Microelectronic Circuits*, 4th ed., 1997.

Casein

The principal protein fraction of cows' milk. It accounts for about 80% of the protein content and is present in concentrations of 2.5–3.2%. The term casein, derived from the Latin word for cheese, *caseus*, was introduced into the scientific literature early in the nineteenth century to describe the primary protein of milk. Casein is a mixed complex of phosphoproteins existing in milk as colloidally dispersed micelles 50 to 600 nanometers in diameter. The variable-sized micelles are assembled from spherical subunits of nearly uniform diameter (10 to 20 nm), containing 25–30 casein molecules, and from small amounts of calcium phosphate which, together with serum ionic calcium, plays a significant role in micellar structure. Critical to the stability and size distribution of the micellar state is a calcium-insensitive phosphoprotein component which functions as a so-called protective colloid to the system. When hydrolyzed by rennin (chymosin) as in the cheese-making process, it loses its hydrophilic, carboxy-terminal segment, predisposing the altered micellar system to the aggregation activity of calcium ions and subsequent clot formation. *See* COLLOID; MICELLE.

Caseins can be separated from the whey proteins of cows' milk by gel filtration, high-speed centrifugation, salting-out with appropriate concentrations of neutral salts, acid precipitation at pH 4.3–4.6, and coagulation with rennet (or other proteolytic enzymes), and as a coprecipitate with whey proteins. The first three methods yield preparations in essentially their native micellar state, but are impractical for commercial exploitation. Thus, commercial caseins are produced by methods more amenable to industrial practices (see **illus**).

Acid casein. Fat-free, separated milk (skim milk) is cultured with lactic acid–producing organisms, namely *Streptococcus lactic* or *S. cremoris*, until it clots at pH 4.3–4.6 (isoelectric pH of the casein complex). The clot is broken and heated to about 122°F (50°C) to expel whey, thoroughly washed, pressed, ground, dried, and milled. Alternatively, food-grade HCl or H_2SO_4 is added slowly to agitated skim milk at 86–95°F (30–35°C). The temperature is raised to 111–115°F (44–46°C) to enhance precipitation of the casein, which is collected and processed. Acid caseins are designated according to the acid utilized in their production, such as lactic casein, HCl casein, or H_2SO_4 casein. Acid caseins are insoluble and possess low ash content (see **table**).

Rennet casein. When rennet is added to skim milk, colloidal casein is destabilized and forms a gel. Sufficient rennet and $CaCl_2$ is added to skim milk at about

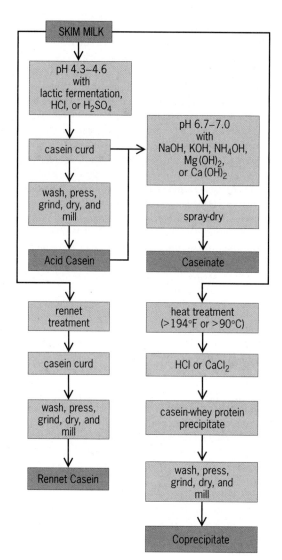

Flow chart of production of commercial casein products from skim milk.

86°F (30°C) to yield a coagulum in 20 to 30 min. Agitation is initiated following the onset of coagulation to reduce the particle size to optimize processing. After raising the temperature to 131–149°F (55–65°C) to expel whey, the curd is collected and processed. Rennet casein is frequently referred to as *para*-calcium caseinate. It is insoluble and contains a relatively high ash content consisting largely of calcium phosphate (see table). *See* RENNIN.

Approximate composition of commercial casein products, in percent					
Component	Sodium caseinate	Calcium caseinate	Acid casein	Rennet casein	Coprecipitate
Protein	94	93.5	95	89	89–94
Ash (max.)	4.0	4.5	2.2	7.5	4.5
Sodium	1.3	0.05	0.1	0.02	—
Calcium	0.1	1.5	0.08	3.0	—
Phosphorus	0.8	0.8	0.9	1.5	—
Lactose (max.)	0.2	0.2	0.2	—	1.5
Fat (max.)	1.5	1.5	1.5	1.5	1.5
Moisture (max.)	4.0	4.0	10.0	12.0	5.0
pH	6.6	6.8	—	7.0	6.8

Coprecipitates. In the production of casein isolates, only 80% of the milk protein is recovered, since undenatured whey proteins are soluble at pH 4.6 and are unaffected by rennet. Efforts to increase protein recovery and improve the nutritional quality and functionality of isolates led to the development of coprecipitates. Skim milk is heated to more than 194°F (90°C) to denature the whey proteins and induce protein-protein interactions. Either HCl or $CaCl_2$ is added to induce precipitation of the protein complex, which varies in ash content according to the amount of $CaCl_2$ and HCl employed (see table). $CaCl_2$-induced coprecipitates are usually dispersed with polyphosphate salts prior to drying.

Caseinates. Many applications for casein isolates require that they be water-soluble or dispersable. This is achieved by the slow addition of a suitable alkali to the wet curd of an acid casein, being careful not to exceed a pH of 6.7-7.0. Protein concentrations of about 20% are spray-dried. Although sodium caseinate is most commonly used in the food industry, caseinates containing cations of K, NH_4, Mg, and Ca are produced.

The early production of casein isolates was stimulated by their application in industrial products such as paper, glue, paint, and plastics. These applications have been replaced by petroleum-based polymers. Thus the emphasis has shifted to their utilization in food systems, where they add enhanced nutritional and functional characteristics. They are widely used in the formulation of comminuted meat products, coffee whitener, processed cereal products, bakery products, and cheese analogs. *See* CHEESE; FOOD MANUFACTURING; MILK.   J. Robert Brunner

Bibliography. P. F. Fox (ed.), *Developments in Dairy Chemistry*, vol. 1: *Proteins*, 1982; N. P. Wong, *Fundamentals of Dairy Chemistry*, 3d ed., 1988.

Cashew

A medium-sized (20-30 ft or 6-9 m high), spreading evergreen tree (*Anacardium occidentale*) native to Brazil, but now grown widely in the tropics for its edible nuts and the resinous oil contained in the shells. Cashews belong to the family Anacardiaceae in the order Sapindales. The fruit consists of a fleshy, red or yellow, pear-shaped receptacle, termed the apple, 2-3$^1/_2$ in. (5-8.7 cm) long at the distal end of which is borne a hard-shelled, kidney-shaped ovary or nut about 1$^1/_2$ in. (3.7 cm) long. The shell of this nut is about $^1/_8$-in. (3-mm) thick and consists of a smooth, relatively thin outer layer (exocarp) and an inner hard layer (endocarp). Between these layers is a porous layer (mesocarp), which is filled with a caustic black liquid that blisters the skin and makes the processing of the nut difficult. *See* SAPINDALES.

Although cashew trees are spread throughout the tropics, commercial production is centered in India, which handles 90% of the world trade. The trees, mostly seedlings, grow on wastelands with a minimum of care, reach full bearing at 8 years of age, and

may continue for 25 years or more. Usually the fruits fall from the trees when mature and are gathered by local labor; the nuts are separated from the apples by hand. Some of the apples are marketed locally but most are wasted.

Processing the nuts is a difficult operation because of the caustic liquid in the shells. The nuts are dried in the sun, cleaned, moistened, and kept for 12 h in heaps or silos to soften the shells. They are then roasted at 350-400°F (176-204°C). In the roasting process the cashew shell liquid is released and collected as a by-product. The kernels are extracted from the shells, heated to remove the enclosing membrane (testa), graded, and packed in tin cans for export.

Shelled cashew nuts, plus cashew shell liquid, are second only to jute in India's exports. More than half of these go to the United States; Europe and Russia are heavy importers also. *See* JUTE.

Cashew nut kernels are eaten as nuts and used extensively in the confectionery and baking trade. The cashew shell liquid is a valuable by-product, containing 90% anacardic acid and 10% cardol, and is used in the varnish and plastic industries.

The cashew apples are too astringent for eating without being processed, but when processed may be used for jams, chutney, pickles, and wine. In India much attention is being given to extending and improving the cashew industry. *See* NUT CROP CULTURE.   Laurence H. MacDaniels

Cashmere

The natural fiber obtained from the Cashmere goat, native to the Himalayan region of China and India. The fleece of this goat has long, straight, coarse outer hair of little value; but the small quantity of underhair, or down, is made into luxuriously soft woollike yarns with a characteristic highly napped finish. This fine cashmere fiber is obtained by frequent combings during the shedding season. A microscopic examination reveals that cashmere is a much finer fiber than mohair or wool fiber obtained from sheep. The scales being less distinct and farther apart, the fiber appears to be made of telescoped sections.

Cashmere first became familiar in the beautiful soft, light cashmere shawls for which India has been famous. Today, it is used for such garments as sweaters, sports jackets, and overcoats. Cashmere is soft, lighter in weight than wool, and quite warm; but because of its soft, delicate texture, cashmere is not as durable as wool. *See* ALPACA; CAMEL'S HAIR; LLAMA; MOHAIR; NATURAL FIBER; VICUNA; WOOL.
                                      M. David Potter

Cassava

The plant *Manihot esculenta* (family Euphorbiaceae), also called manioc. It is one of the 10 most important food plants, and the most important

Tuberous roots from a single cassava plant.

starchy root or tuber of the tropics. It originated in Central or South America, possibly Brazil, and was domesticated and widely distributed well before the time of Columbus. Subsequent distribution has established cassava as a major crop in eastern and western Africa, in India, and in Indonesia. Brazil continues to be the largest producer. *See* GERANIALES.

Description and cultivation. The cassava plant is a slightly woody, perennial shrub reaching 10 ft (3 m) in height. The leaves are deeply palmately lobed; the flowers are inconspicuous, and the prominent capsules are three-seeded and explosive at maturity. The roots (see **illus.**) are enlarged by the deposition of starch and constitute the principal source of food from the plant. Normal yields are about 10 lb (4.5 kg) per plant. The leaves are also eaten (after cooking), and are noteworthy for their high protein content. The plant is propagated from mature stems which are planted without special treatment. Tuberization occurs gradually; about 10 or 12 months from planting to harvest is normal. Cassava can be grown for 2 or more years, however, and thus is a food that can be used at any season. Once it is harvested, however, the roots deteriorate within a few days.

Use and food value. The chief use of cassava is as a boiled vegetable. It is also a source of flour, called farinha in Brazil and gari in western Africa, and of toasted starch granules, the familiar tapioca. It can be processed into macaroni and a ricelike food. In the form of dried chips, cassava root is an important animal feed in the international market and is used extensively in Europe. In spite of its popularity, however, cassava root is a poor food. Its protein content is extremely low, and its consumption as a staple food is associated with the protein deficiency disease kwashiorkor. In addition, all parts of the plant contain glucosides of hydrocyanic acid, substances which on decomposition yield the poisonous hydrocyanic acid (HCN, prussic acid). Chronic diseases including goiter are common in regions where cassava is a staple food.   Franklin W. Martin

Diseases. Much of the older literature implies that cassava diseases are of minor importance, but this is not the case. Numerous diseases caused by fungi, bacteria, viruses, and nematodes affect cassava. The most important cassava disease in Africa is African common cassava mosaic, which possibly also occurs in Asia. The causal agent is a virus transmitted by whiteflies. Most plants in Africa are infected, and losses of 30–80% are reported. Some lines with resistance are available, but losses can also be minimized where disease-free planting material can be produced.

Cassava bacterial blight, caused by *Xanthomonas manihotis*, is distributed worldwide and is perhaps the most devastating disease on a worldwide basis. Disease-free planting material and resistant varieties are control measures. The four species of *Cercospora* that induce leaf spots are widespread and cause significant losses. Some varieties resistant to Cercospora leaf spots occur, and wider spacing to reduce humidity can also reduce disease severity. Other important foliar diseases are superelongation (caused by *Sphaceloma manihoticola*), Phoma leaf spot, cassava rust (caused by *Uromyces* spp.), anthracnose (caused by *Colletotrichum* spp.), and cassava ash (caused by *Oidium manihotis*). Stem pathogens (*Glomerella* spp. and *Botryodiplodia* spp.) and root rot pathogens (*Phytophthora* spp. and *Pythium* spp.) may be destructive in some areas. *See* PLANT PATHOLOGY.

H. David Thurston

Bibliography. T. Brekelbaum, A. Bellotti, and J. C. Lozano (eds.), *Proceedings of the Cassava Protection Workshop*, CIAT, Cali, Colombia, 1977; J. H. Cock, *Cassava*, 1984; J. H. Cock, *Cassava: New Potential for a Neglected Crop*, 1985; W. O. Jones, *Manioc in Africa*, 1959; J. C. Lozano and R. H. Booth, Diseases of cassava (*Manihot esculenta* Crantz), *Pest Articles and New Summaries*, 20:30–54, 1974; H. D. Thurston, *Tropical Plant Disease*, American Phytopathological Society, 1984.

Cassiopeia

A constellation named for the queen of Ethiopia, who, in Greek mythology, claimed to be more beautiful than the Nereids, daughters of the sea god, Poseidon. Poseidon sent a sea monster, Cetus, in revenge, and Cassiopeia's daughter Andromeda was sacrificed to appease the monster. (In some versions of the myth, Cassiopeia boasted of Andromeda's beauty.) However, Andromeda was rescued by Perseus. The constellations named after these figures are adjacent in the sky. *See* ANDROMEDA; PERSEUS.

The celestial atlas by Bayer (1603) shows Cassiopeia as a queen in a big chair. To the side of the chair in the atlas is the bright star seen as a supernova by Tycho Brahe in 1572. In the sky, Cassiopeia is a prominent W of bright stars in the northern Milky Way (see **illustration**). It is circumpolar, never setting, from midnorthern latitudes. *See* SUPERNOVA.

The modern boundaries of the 88 constellations,

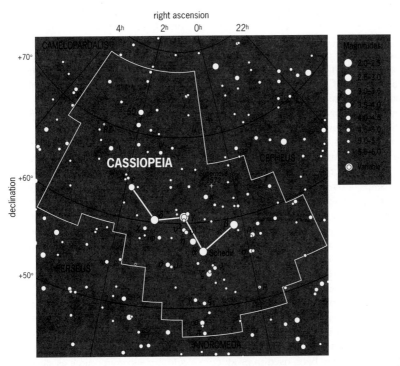

right ascension

declination

CASSIOPEIA

Modern boundaries of the constellation Cassiopeia, mythological queen of Ethiopia. The celestial equator is 0° of declination, which corresponds to celestial latitude. Right ascension corresponds to celestial longitude, with each hour of right ascension representing 15° of arc. Apparent brightness of stars is shown with dot sizes to illustrate the magnitude scale, where the brightest stars in the sky are 0th magnitude or brighter and the faintest stars that can be seen with the unaided eye at a dark site are 6th magnitude. (*Wil Tirion*)

including this one, were defined by the International Astronomical Union in 1928. *See* CONSTELLATION.

Jay M. Pasachoff

Cassiterite

A mineral having the composition SnO_2. Cassiterite is the principal ore of tin. Its crystals are of the tetragonal rutile structure type, usually in prisms terminated by dipyramids. Twins with a characteristic notch called visor tin are common. Cassiterite is usually massive granular, but may be in radiating fibrous aggregates with reniform shapes (wood tin). The hardness is 6–7 (Mohs scale), and the specific gravity is 6.8–7.1 (unusually high for a nonmetallic mineral). The luster is adamantine to submetallic. Pure tin oxide is white, but cassiterite is usually yellow, brown, or black because of the presence of iron.

Cassiterite is genetically associated with granitic rocks and pegmatites and may be present as a primary constituent. More commonly it is found in quartz veins in or near such rocks associated with tourmaline, topaz, and wolframite. Cassiterite is most abundantly found as stream tin (rolled pebbles in placer deposits). Early production of tin came from cassiterite mined at Cornwall, England, but at present, the world's supply comes mostly from placer or residual deposits in the Malay States, Indonesia, Zaire, and Nigeria. It is also mined in Bolivia. *See* TIN.

Cornelius S. Hurlbut, Jr.

Cast iron

A generic term describing a family of iron alloys containing 1.8–4.5% carbon. Cast iron usually is made into specified shapes, called castings, for direct use or for processing by machining, heat treating, or assembly. In special cases it may be forged or rolled moderately. Generally, it is unsuitable for drawing into rods or wire, although to a limited extent it has been continuously cast into rods and shapes from a liquid bath or swaged from bars into smaller-dimensional units. Silicon usually is present in amounts up to 3%, but special compositions are made containing up to 6% (Silal) and up to 12% (Duriron).

Cast iron of the above composition range is often made into blocks or rough shapes and called pig iron. It is an intermediate form of cast iron used for remelting into iron castings. Pig iron usually is produced from iron ore and coke smelted into liquid iron in the blast furnace. This liquid iron may be poured into sand molds of specific design which, when cleaned and trimmed, become ingot molds for steel manufacture. In these instances the cast iron may be referred to as direct metal, indicating its production in the blast furnace without the intermediate remelting in the cupola furnace of the foundry, which is common practice in the manufacture of iron castings.

Classification. Cast iron may be purchased in several commercial grades called gray iron, chilled iron, mottled iron, white iron, malleable iron, ductile iron, spheroidal graphite iron, nodular iron, and austenitic cast iron.

Originally, cast iron was graded by examination of fracture characteristics of the surfaces produced when a sample was broken; its true composition was unknown. This method of grading first was applied to pig iron, which was classified similarly as white, mottled, or gray. The color of the fracture governed the classification of the product until about 1888, when extensive work by W. J. Keep revealed that the silicon content in a large measure determined the character of the fracture. Further work clarified the relationships between composition, microstructure, and fracture characteristics, and gradually the importance of the examination of fractures receded until the present time, when it is used only to classify the products generally. The chemistry of cast iron today is quite well known, and gray, white, and mottled iron can be selected on the basis of composition charts which mark the areas of their occurrence.

Further developments in cast irons have adapted heat-treatment processes to produce special properties that permit classification of special grades of gray, malleable, and white cast irons. Also, metals such as cerium and magnesium have been used to produce the spheroidal graphite structures which are characteristic of ductile irons.

Properties and uses. Gray iron is an iron-base material within the broad composition limits mentioned above. Of its total carbon content, more than one-half is in the form of graphite flakes. It is the presence of the graphite flakes which produce a gray color in a fresh fracture. The remaining carbon is dissolved in the metal and is called combined carbon. It may be present in amounts ranging from 0.05 to 1.20%. Gray iron is the mainstay of iron foundry production. Its application covers practically all engineering fields involving construction, machinery, engines, power, transport, mining, and many daily uses, such as stove parts, pots and pans, and hardware.

Mottled iron solidifies as a mixture of white and gray irons. The fracture is a mottled mixture of white and gray areas. The fracture may contain as few as 10% white areas in a gray background or the reverse, namely, 10% gray areas in a white background. Mottled irons are useful for abrasion- or erosion-resisting services, where their composite structure provides a hard surface with some ability to deform. The high frictional resistance of its surface is occasionally utilized.

Chilled iron has all but disappeared as a descriptive term. It was applied to cast iron which was poured into a metal mold or chill. Frequently, a gray iron would be processed in this manner, and if the cooling rate was rapid enough, a white-iron casting or a surface zone of white iron on the casting would develop, backed by the less rapidly cooled gray iron inside. Since glass molds, for example, are often made by casting one of their surfaces against a chill, such castings would be called chilled iron. Unfortunately, the term spread to the part-white, part-gray types of cast iron and more inaccurately to a solid white iron which had been cast in a chill.

White iron is an iron-base material within the broad composition limits mentioned above whose total carbon content is in the combined form. It therefore contains little or no graphite. A fresh fracture is white (ground-glass white). Its characteristic structure usually is obtained by lowering the carbon content or the silicon content or both, so that the graphitizing power of the composition is subdued.

Malleable cast iron is made as a white-iron casting within the narrower composition range that the term implies. Annealing produces a tough, bendable, and machinable cast iron. During the anneal, all or most of the carbon is precipitated in ragged nodules of graphite. The end product is available in a number of grades that vary in strength, hardness, and toughness. Malleable iron is used widely in the transportation, valve, fitting, and hardware industries for innumerable small parts.

Ductile iron (also called spheroidal graphite iron or nodular iron) is a product of high carbon and high silicon content in which most of the carbon has been coagulated into spheres during processing in the liquid state. During processing, an ingredient such as magnesium or cerium is added, followed by another substance such as silicon, calcium, or combinations of these ingredients. The resulting product acquires the structure of steel peppered with spheres of graphite. Its strength closely approaches that of steel, and it may be heat-treated to develop a ductility exceeding that of malleable cast iron. Its properties make it useful for a great many engineering applications requiring strength and toughness levels which previously were beyond the reach of iron foundry products.

Austenitic cast irons are available in the gray-iron and ductile-iron classifications. When gray or ductile iron is alloyed with substantial amounts of nickel, manganese, silicon, or other elements to alter the basic crystalline structure from magnetic alpha iron to nonmagnetic gamma iron, the resulting product becomes austenitic cast iron. These irons generally offer better corrosion- and heat-resistance than the low-alloy irons. *See* ALLOY; HEAT TREATMENT (METALLURGY); IRON; IRON ALLOYS; METAL CASTING; STEEL; WROUGHT IRON.   James S. Vanick

Bibliography. H. T. Angus, *Cast Iron: Physical and Engineering Properties*, 2d ed., 1978; E. Dorazil, *High Strength Austempered Ductile Cast Iron*, 1991; H. Fredriksson and M. Milert (eds.), *Physical Metallurgy of Cast Iron: Materials Research Society Symposia Proceedings*, 1985; Metallurgical Society of the American Institute of Mining, Metallurgical and Petroleum Engineers, *History of Iron and Steelmaking in the United States*, 1961; L. H. Van Vlack, *Elements of Materials Science and Engineering*, 6th ed., 1989.

Castor plant

A plant, *Ricinus communis*, belonging to the spurge family (Euphorbiaceae). Castor varies greatly in height and in color of foliage, stems, and seeds and also in size and oil content of the seeds. The palmately lobed leaves are borne more or less alternately. The main stem is terminated by a raceme (primary). After appearance of the primary raceme, branches on the main stem are each in turn terminated by a raceme. Growth continues sequentially as long as the plant lives, with branches arising from recently terminated branches. Thus a plant can have racemes in all stages of development from mature to prebloom. Mature racemes mostly have 10 to 70 capsules, each capsule containing three seeds. In frost-free areas castor can attain heights of 9 to 11 m (30 to 36 ft). Castor seeds are poisonous and also contain allergens.

Distribution is in the warmer regions of the world, the plant often growing in waste places. The castor oil plant has been of utilitarian value since antiquity. Oil from the seeds is among the world's oldest nonfood products in commerce. Castor oil contains about 85% ricinoleic acid, used in making industrial products such as alkyde resins for surface coatings, blown oil used in plasticizers, cracked oil for production of synthetic perfumes, nylon, sebacic acid, synthetic detergents, drying oils, and special lubricating oils.

Farmers usually grow castors on less productive land. Culture usually is not mechanized. However, plant breeders in the United States developed types (nonshattering capsules, dwarfs, and F_1 hybrids similar to hybrid corn) suitable for completely mechanized production; concurrently, engineers developed harvesting machinery. Production in the United States, mostly in west Texas, peaked in 1968 but declined to nil because of larger economic return from food and fiber crops. Brazil is the world's largest producer and exporter of castor seed and oil.   Leroy H. Zimmerman

Bibliography. E. A. Weiss, *Castor, Sesame and Safflower*, 1971.

Casuarinales

An order of flowering plants, division Magnoliophyta (Angiospermae), in the subclass Hamamelidae of the class Magnoliopsida (dicotyledons). The order consists of a single family (Casuarinaceae) and genus (*Casuarina*), with about 50 species. Native to the southwestern Pacific region, especially Australia, they are sometimes called Australian pine. They are trees with much reduced flowers and green twigs that bear whorls of scalelike, much reduced leaves. Some species are grown as street trees in tropical and subtropical regions. *See* HAMAMELIDAE; MAGNOLIOPHYTA; MAGNOLIOPSIDA; PLANT KINGDOM.   Arthur Cronquist

Cat

The term applied to any member of the mammalian family Felidae. Commonly, the term is restricted to the domestic cat and those felids that resemble it in size, shape, and habits. Those that are larger in size are referred to as the big cats.

All members of the cat family have a round head, are digitigrade (walk on their toes), have retractile claws (with the exception of the cheetah), and have 30 teeth with the dental formula I 3/3 C 1/1 Pm 3/3 M 1/1. All species are carnivorous.

Domestic cats. The origin of domestic cats is unknown, but it is established that they have been associated with humans for many centuries. Remains of the cat have been found with artifacts and remains of cave people, but it is generally conceded that these were not domesticated species. It has been suggested that domestic cats are descended from Old World wildcats such as the caffer cat (*Felis lybica*), an African species. However, there is no evidence for this belief, although it is known that wild and domestic species interbreed. Domestic cats are generally characterized by long, thin tails, straight ears, and short hair of a variety of colorations. These are the so-called alley cats and are mixed breeds. The pure breeds, however, are notable exceptions to this general description. There is a long-haired race, apparently developed in Persia, which is represented by the Persian and the Angora. The Abyssinian breed, in contrast to the common domestic cat, is characterized by being ruddy brown in color and having a longer face and ears. Each short hair is ticked or grizzled in appearance because of its alternate dark and light banding. This is known as an agouti condition.

There are at least two tailless breeds, of which the best known is the Manx from the Isle of Man. It has a boneless tuft of hair instead of a tail. The other tailless variety is found in Japan, and there is a question as to whether the Manx was a mutation or was imported. One of the most popular breeds is the Siamese cat, an animal with great independence and individuality. Its eyes are deep blue, it has a long, kinky tail, and its fur is short and cream to buff in color.

Most cats have two periods of heat each year. After a gestation period of about 8 weeks, a litter of about five kittens is born in April and August. They are helpless, blind, and entirely dependent upon the mother after birth. The kittens are protected by the female since the male will sometimes attack them. Scientific breeding of cats is difficult, since the cat is a vagabond by nature and interbreeding usually occurs in time, making it difficult to keep races pure.

Wildcats. In addition to cats such as the lynx, bobcat, serval, ocelot, puma, leopard, lion, tiger, jaguar, and cheetah, there are a few lesser known forms that are of interest to the biologist and naturalist. Among these are the Scottish wildcat and the caracal. The Scottish wildcat resembles the domestic species but is more heavily built. It has become virtually extinct, except for the small numbers in the Scottish Highlands. It is a nocturnal animal and is both ferocious and untamable. This cat is regarded as a separate subspecies of the European wildcat (*F. sylvestris*). The long-legged caracal (*Caracal caracal*) is built better for running than are other cats. It is found in the deserts of North Africa and western Asia, where it hunts and kills many types of animals. It resembles a lynx in having ear tufts but is more closely related to the serval.

Lynx. There are a number of species of cats known by this name. The Canadian lynx (*Lynx canadensis*) is the largest North American lynx. It is found in pine-forested areas of Canada and the northern United States, where it feeds upon rabbits, mice, and birds, and during the winter on the remains of animals left by other scavengers. This animal has become relatively rare as a result of land settlement. It is a stout-bodied cat about the size of a cocker spaniel. It is trapped for its fur, and the flesh is reputed to be edible. Usually two cubs are born each year, and the gestation period is about 10 weeks. The maximum weight of the adult is about 30 lb (13 kg), and the life-span is about 10 years.

The European lynx (*L. lynx*) ranges throughout the large forested areas of northern and central Europe. Unlike the Canadian lynx, it will leave the forest to attack sheep and goats when food is scarce. *Lynx pardellus* is known as the Spanish lynx and is the smallest of the species. It is found in the Pyrenees, on the French side of the ranges. *Lynx rufus*, known as the bobcat, bay lynx, or wildcat, is very similar to the Canadian lynx but is smaller, and its ears are not conspicuously tufted. It ranges over the eastern United States from Maine to Georgia and has been divided into a number of subspecies. It is fierce and feeds on mammals and birds.

Lynx differ from other felids in having 28 instead of 30 teeth; an upper premolar is absent.

Serval. Found in the scrub grass regions south of the Sahara desert, this cat (*Leptailurus serval*) usually feeds on birds and small mammals. Being fawn colored with black spots, it blends with the landscape. It is one of the fastest-running felids and can leap up to 6 ft (2 m) to catch a flying bird.

Ocelot. This species (*F. pardalis*) is arboreal and feeds on monkeys and birds in the forested regions of South America, its native habitat. Smaller and more ornamental than the jaguar, it is known as the painted leopard. The head and back are golden and the flanks are silvery, and there are rows of somewhat metallic spots on the body with stripes on the head and neck. Near habitations this cat will feed on domestic and farmyard animals. The adult, which is almost 3 ft (0.9 m) long, can be easily trained when captured young and is apparently harmless to humans.

Puma. This member of the cat family, also known as the cougar or mountain lion, is found in various habitats in the Americas and nowhere else. The puma (*F. concolor*) has been described as resembling a small, short-legged lioness because of its uniform color. It is a good climber and is nocturnally active in its hunting. It has been theorized that the puma aided the extinction of the horse in the Americas before the discovery of these continents. The male may weigh as much as 200 lb (90 kg) and have a length of about 7 ft (2 m), and the female is nearly as large. The male is not adverse to eating the young.

Jaguar. This cat (*F. onca*) is indigenous to Central and South America, where it is found along the banks of forested rivers and in marshy areas. Remaining hidden during the day, it is a nocturnal hunter, a strong swimmer, the largest cat, and a fierce carnivore. The jaguar has been called the leopard of the New World, and its pelts are commercially important.

Cheetah. This is a peculiar animal in that it has some doglike characteristics although it is included in the cat family. Its claws are nonretractile, its legs are long, and it does not climb. A single species, *Acinonyx jubatus*, occurs from northern Africa to Asia as far south as India. This animal is doubtless the fastest animal in running over short distances. It hunts in small groups and attacks such animals as gazelles and antelopes.

Leopard. This species ranges throughout Africa and Asia and is regarded as the most athletic member of the cat family, being equally adept at climbing, swimming, jumping, and running. *Felis pardus* is the only species of true leopard; however, *Uncia uncia*, the snow leopard or ounce, also is called a leopard. This latter species occurs in the Himalayas of central Asia at high altitudes. The leopard has a more extensive distribution than any other species of Felidae. These animals hunt ceaselessly and have been known to eat humans. They can be tamed in captivity when young, but few are tamed since they cannot be trusted.

Lion. *Felis leo* was a common animal in the Near East, and its range extended into Europe during prehistoric times. In historical times it was recorded as continuing to inhabit the Balkan Peninsula. It has come to be restricted in its distribution as a result of the advances of humans. It is still abundant in the savanna areas between Senegal and East Africa, where there is much herbivorous fauna to prey upon. It is not found in deserts or thickly forested regions. The lion may weigh as much as 550 lb (248 kg) and reach a height of 3 ft (0.9 m) and a length of $6\frac{1}{2}$ ft (1.9 m). It is the largest African carnivore. There is one litter of 2–4 young per year after a gestation period of about 15 weeks. The life-span may be as long as 40 years. The lion hunts at night and is silent while approaching its prey in order to surprise it. Various races of this species have been described, such as Cape, Masai, Somali, and Indian lions, but they show few differences in color and size.

Tiger. The tiger is represented by a single species, *F. tigris* (see **illus.**). It inhabits the forests of Asia,

Tiger (*Felis tigris*).

Sumatra, Java, and southern Siberia. As a consequence of the wide climatic and geographical distribution of tigers, they show a wide range of coloration and size, and a number of varieties are recognized. After a gestation period of 3 months, two or three cubs are born helpless and blind. There is one litter every second year, and usually only one cub of each litter survives. Tigers breed in captivity, and crosses between the lion and tigress (the liger) and between the tiger and lioness (the tigron) have been obtained. The tiger takes any food available and, like many members of the cat family, returns to the kill until it is consumed. *See* CARNIVORA.   Charles B. Curtin

Cat scratch disease

Cat scratch disease in humans is typically a benign, subacute regional disease of the lymph nodes (lymphadenopathy) resulting from dermal inoculation of the causative agent. This agent has been demonstrated to be *Bartonella* (formerly *Rochalimaea*) *henselae*, a bacterium that has been isolated from immunocompromised patients with bacillary angiomatosis, a distinctive and potentially deadly vascular proliferative host response in skin, bone, or other organs associated with the presence of clumps of bacteria.

Although cat scratch disease was first described in France in 1950, the causative bacterial agent remained obscure until 1992, when *B. henselae* was implicated by serologic studies. In 1993 and 1994, major progress was made in the epidemiology of cat scratch disease. The domestic cat is the major reservoir of *B. henselae*, and the cat flea, *Ctenocephalides felis*, is the main vector of transmission from cat to cat. *Bartonella clarridgeiae* has been isolated from domestic cats, and at least two human cases of cat scratch disease have been associated with this bacterium. Recently, a new bacterium, *B. koehlerae*, has also been isolated from the blood of domestic cats.

Etiology. The cause of cat scratch disease has long been in question. It was initially considered a virus, then a gram-negative bacterium, and only recently was the specific agent confirmed. In 1983 a bacillus was identified by Warthin-Starry (silver deposition) staining of lymph node biopsies from 39 patients with cat scratch disease. In 1988 a pleomorphic, gram-negative bacterium was isolated from the lymph node of an infected individual, and was named *Afipia felis*. Its isolation was difficult, and only a few strains were ever isolated. In addition, serology was not highly specific, and it was difficult to standardize. For some years, *A. felis* was considered to be the most probable agent causing cat scratch disease. However, in the 1990s evidence clearly implicated *B. henselae* as the causative agent.

Bartonella henselae is morphologically very similar to *A. felis* when examined by Warthin-Starry staining, which may explain the previous confusion. Serological studies and isolation of the organism from lymph nodes of probable cat scratch disease cases substantiate the major role played by *B. henselae* in the etiology of the disease. *Bartonella henselae* is a small, curved gram-negative rod which exhibits a twitching motility. Optimal growth on solid media is obtained by use of rabbit blood agar and incubation at $95°F$ ($35°C$) in 5% carbon dioxide (CO_2). *Bartonella clarridgeiae* possesses flagella, which are absent in *B. henselae*.

Epidemiology. There were an estimated 22,000 individuals with cat scratch disease in the United States in 1992, and 2000 of these required hospitalization. Cat scratch disease occurs in immunocompetent patients of all ages, with 55–80% being less than 20 years of age. However, cases are more often reported among children and teenagers than adults (45–50% of infected individuals are less than 15 years old). Cat scratch disease is considered the most common cause of chronic benign adenopathy in children and young adults, but it can easily be confused with neoplastic conditions. More than 90% of cases have a history of contact with cats, and 57–83% recall being scratched by a cat. Incidence varies by season; most cases occur in the fall and winter. More cases are observed in males than females.

A 1993 epidemiological study reported that infected individuals were more likely than healthy cat-owning control subjects to have at least one kitten 12 months of age or younger, to have been scratched or bitten by a kitten, and to have at least one kitten with fleas. Of 45 individuals observed, 38 (84%) had antibodies to *B. henselae* compared to 4 of 112 control subjects (3%). Interestingly, 39 of 48 (81%) of the cats of infected individuals also had antibodies to *B. henselae*, as compared with 11 of 29 control cats (38%).

Bartonella henselae antibodies have been found to be common in cats. Geographical variations in seroprevalence were also observed, with 60% of cats seropositive in the Southeast of the United States, but with very low positivity levels in the Midwest, Alaska, and the Rocky Mountains. The presence of bacteria in the blood (bacteremia) is also very common in cats, up to 50% in warm and humid areas of North America, Australia, and the Philippines, and the range is 10–15% in pet cats in most of western Europe and in Australia. Bacteremia can last several months to a few years in cats, but very high bacteremia levels usually do not last more than 4–6 weeks. Cats can be co-infected with *B. henselae* and *B. clarridgeiae* and with various *B. henselae* types.

Clinical signs. In humans, 1–3 weeks may elapse between the scratch (or bite) and the appearance of clinical signs. In 50% of the cases, a small skin lesion, often resembling an insect bite, appears at the inoculation site (usually on the hand or forearm) and evolves from a pimple (papule) to a skin blister to partially healed ulcers. These lesions resolve within a few days to a few weeks. Inflammation of lymph nodes develops approximately 3 weeks after exposure, is generally unilateral, and commonly appears in the epitrochlear, axillary, or cervical lymph nodes.

Swelling of the lymph node is usually painful and persists for several weeks or months. In 25% of the cases, a discharge of pus occurs. A large majority of the cases show signs of systemic infection, such as fever, chills, malaise, anorexia, or headaches. In general, the disease is benign and heals spontaneously without aftereffects. Atypical manifestations of cat scratch disease occur in 5–9% of the cases. The most common is Parinaud's oculoglandular syndrome (enlargement of the lymph node around the eye and conjunctivitis); but also encephalitis, degenerative bone lesions, and thrombocytopenic purpura (a bleeding disorder due to decreased platelet levels) may occur. Usually, complete recovery occurs with few sequelae. The histological findings characteristically include stellate caseating granulomas, micro abscesses, and follicular hyperplasia. Warthin-Starry staining may reveal bacilli.

No major clinical signs of cat scratch disease have been reported in cats, although enlargement of the lymph nodes caused by a cat scratch disease–like organism has been reported. Fever, lymphadenopathy, moderate neurological symptoms, and reproductive disorders have been reported in experimentally infected cats.

Diagnosis. For years, the diagnosis was based on clinical criteria, exposure to a cat, failure to isolate other bacteria, or histologic examination of biopsies of lymph nodes. A skin test was also developed. However, the skin test antigen, prepared from pasteurized pus from lymph nodes of patients with cat scratch disease, was not standardized, and concerns were raised about the safety of such a product. Since 1992, serological tests and techniques to isolate the organism from human specimens have been developed. Additionally, the polymerase chain reaction is being used to confirm infection by *Bartonella*. At present, diagnosis is mainly based on a serological titer of 1 to 64 ratio or greater (or a fourfold titer increase between an early and late serum samples) using an indirect immunofluorescence test and a history of cat scratch or bite.

In cats, the organism is isolated from blood samples. The samples are collected in pediatric lysis-centrifugation or EDTA tubes. EDTA tubes are frozen at $-70°C$ for a few days to several weeks before plating. After centrifugation, the pellet is resuspended in inoculation media and plated onto 5% rabbit blood agar.

Treatment. Most individuals with cat scratch disease experience mild illness and require minimal treatment. Usually antimicrobial therapy is not necessary since spontaneous resolution is common. In severe forms, antibiotics such as ciprofloxacin, rifampin, or gentamicin have been recommended. Use of oral azithromycin for 5 days has shown significant clinical benefit in typical cat scratch disease. Erythromycin (500 mg four times a day) and doxycycline are effective antibiotics in the treatment of bacillary angiomatosis and may be recommended in immunodeficient persons suffering from cat scratch disease. Rifampin is recommended as a second drug in combination with either erythromycin or doxycycline for severely ill patients.   Bruno B. Chomel

Bibliography. B. B. Chomel et al., Experimental transmission of *Bartonella henselae* by the cat flea, *J. Clin. Microbiol.*, 34:1952–1956, 1996; M. J. Dolan et al., Syndrome of *Rochalimaea henselae* adenitis suggesting cat scratch disease, *Ann. Intern. Med.*, 118:331–336, 1993; C. K. English et al., Cat scratch disease: Isolation and culture of the bacterial agent, *J. Amer. Med. Ass.*, 259:1347–1352; J. E. Koehler, C. A. Glaser, and J. W. Tappero, *Rochalimaea henselae* infection: A new zoonosis with the domestic cat as reservoir, *J. Amer. Med. Ass.*, 271:531–535, 1994; D. L. Kordick et al., *Bartonella clarridgeiae*, a newly recognized zoonotic pathogen causing inoculation papules, fever, and lymphadenopathy (cat scratch disease), *J. Clin. Microbiol.*, 35:1813–1818, 1997; R. L. Regnery, M. Martin, and J. G. Olson, Naturally occurring "*Rochalimaea henselae*" infection in domestic cat, *Lancet*, 340:557–558, 1992; K. M. Zangwill et al., Cat scratch disease in Connecticut: Epidemiology, risk factors, and evaluation of a new diagnostic test, *N. Engl. J. Med.*, 329:8–13, 1993.

Cataclysmic variable

A type of close binary star system containing a cool star transferring material to its hotter, high-density, degenerate white dwarf companion. The mass transfer results in a large range of observed variability, including cataclysmic events called outbursts, which can increase the brightness of the systems by 2–10 magnitudes (a logarithmic scale with each magnitude being a factor of 2.5 in brightness) from quiescence, equivalent to a factor of 6–10,000 times in intensity. The specific behavior of each system and the extent and cause of the variability are related to whether the transferred material accumulates in an accretion disk surrounding the white dwarf, or whether it flows in a ballistic stream directly from the cool star to the white dwarf surface. Which of these processes will occur depends on the magnetic field strength of the white dwarf and the separation of the two stars in the binary, properties which are determined during the formation of the system (see **illustration**). *See* MAGNITUDE (ASTRONOMY).

Accretion disk systems. If the white dwarf magnetic field is under 100 tesla (1 megagauss), an accretion disk will form and extend close to the white dwarf surface, while a hot spot will form where the mass stream from the cool star hits the disk (illus. *a*). Systems in which the mass transfer occurs in this way constitute the most common type among the roughly 1500 known cataclysmic variables. They can be further classified as novae, dwarf novae, and novalike systems. These categories probably represent different phases of evolution of similar systems, and each is determined by the current mass-transfer rate.

Novae are the most spectacular cataclysmic variables, with 7–10-magnitude (factor of 630–10,000 times) outbursts caused by thermonuclear runaways triggered when a critical mass of hydrogen builds up in the atmosphere of the white dwarf. Usually this occurs every few thousand years, although a handful of novae with high-mass white dwarfs and mostly

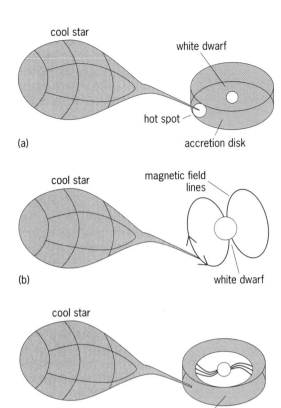

(a)

(b)

(c)

Visualizations of the components of cataclysmic variables. The components are not drawn strictly to scale, for ease of viewing. (a) Accretion disk system, the most common type. The shape of the cool star is distorted due to the gravitational influence of its close companion. (b) AM Herculis, or polar system. (c) DQ Herculis, or intermediate polar system.

giant cool stars recur on time scales of tens of years. There are typically 20 novae per year in a galaxy such as the Milky Way. Large amounts of mass ejection (1/10,000 the mass of the Sun) during the outburst and subsequent expansion of the shell and dust formation, as the nova returns to its quiescent state in months or years, can produce distinctive spectra and light curves for novae. *See* NOVA.

Dwarf novae have much smaller outbursts of 2–5 magnitudes or a factor of 6–100 times (a small number may be as large as 9 magnitudes or a factor of 4000), and they recur much more frequently, on time scales of weeks or months. Their light curves and theoretical models indicate that their outbursts are probably due to accretion disk instabilities, resulting in increased accretion onto the white dwarf when the disk reaches a critical density. The dwarf novae have a wide range of subtypes, ranging from U Gem or SS Cyg types (named after the variable stars U Geminorum and SS Cygni) with orbital periods greater than 3 h, large mass-transfer rates, and long outburst time scales, to the SU UMa types (named after SU Ursae Majoris, the prototype) with orbital periods under 2 h. These short-period systems can be further divided into the ones with medium mass-transfer rates, lowest-outburst amplitudes, and shortest recurrence times (V1159 Ori types, after V1159

Orionis) and those with very low transfer rates, very high outburst amplitudes, and very long recurrence times (WZ Sge types, after WZ Sagittae).

Novalike systems have the highest mass-transfer rates, so that their disks dominate the light output of the system and do not undergo the instability of outbursts. However, for little-understood reasons, the mass transfer may shut down at sporadic times and cause low states of brightness (VY Sc1 types, after VY Sculptoris). Systems with no recorded outbursts are often put into this novalike category until an outburst event occurs.

Magnetic systems. At very high magnetic fields, over 1000 T (10 MG), and small separations (short orbital periods), the mass-transfer stream follows the magnetic field lines of the white dwarf to the white dwarf surface (illus. *b*). This type of magnetic cataclysmic variable is termed an AM Her star (after its prototype, AM Herculis) or as a polar (after its accretion mode). The approximately 80 known polars were primarily discovered by x-ray satellites due to their large x-ray emission, caused by an accretion shock (producing hard x-rays) as the material is channeled to the magnetic pole of the white dwarf and by the subsequent heating of the white dwarf surface (producing soft x-rays). The large field strength locks the spin of the white dwarf to that of the orbit. *See* X-RAY ASTRONOMY; X-RAY TELESCOPE.

For magnetic fields of 100–1000 T (1–10 MG) and larger separations, the material will form an outer accretion disk ring and then flow from its inner edge to the white dwarf following the magnetic field lines (illus. *c*). The 22 known systems that exhibit this behavior are termed DQ Her stars (after DQ Herculis) or intermediate polars (IPs). In this situation, the accretion is more like a curtain of material raining on the magnetic pole, causing primarily hard x-rays, and the white dwarf spin is not locked, so that a signature pulse of light is detected on a time scale (minutes) shorter than the orbital period (hours).

Large-scale ground-based surveys such as the Sloan Digital Sky Survey and the Hamburg Quasar Survey have contributed to the numbers of known polars and intermediate polars. In addition, space surveys of globular clusters accomplished with the *Hubble Space Telescope* have proposed many more candidates that need confirmation. *See* HUBBLE SPACE TELESCOPE; SLOAN DIGITAL SKY SURVEY; STAR CLUSTERS.

Evolution. As most stars are members of multiple systems, the binarity of cataclysmic variables is not unusual. What sets them apart is that at some stage in their life they have a normal low-mass star existing close enough to an evolved white dwarf companion that mass transfer will occur. The evolutionary path is thought to originate with a wide binary with one star having a mass of about 1–10 times that of the Sun. During the course of its normal evolution, this star becomes a giant, engulfing the companion, which then spirals into a closer orbit due to friction, as the giant star becomes a dense, degenerate white dwarf. About 1% of these binaries will eventually evolve into a cataclysmic variable with an orbital period of several hours. As angular momentum losses continue to shrink the orbit, it evolves to a system with an orbital period near 80 min. At that point, the cool star becomes degenerate, and further loss of mass causes the orbital period to increase again. Evolution calculations show that for the lifetime of the Milky Way Galaxy most cataclysmic variables should be faint systems that have evolved past the orbital period minimum. However, selection effects result in the preferential discovery of the longer-period systems undergoing the highest accretion. In addition, strong magnetic fields may change the time scales and angular momentum losses at different stages of evolution.

During the course of evolution as cataclysmic variables, systems may cycle between nova eruptions (on long time scales), dwarf novae, novalikes, and in-between states of no mass transfer, as nova eruptions and magnetic cycles on the cool star affect the mass-transfer flow. For orbital periods of 2–3 h, the mass transfer may cease, creating a gap in the distribution of orbital periods. About 20 systems are known with extremely short orbital periods (20–50 min), which have helium white dwarfs and degenerate companions.

At late stages of evolution, only the white dwarfs will be visible in systems with faint degenerate companions. These white dwarfs will have had long cooling times, although measured temperatures of white dwarfs in cataclysmic variables show that they are generally hotter than their single counterparts, probably due to accretion heating. Perhaps the most interesting end point of evolution for a cataclysmic variable is the possibility that a system with a white dwarf near 1.4 times the mass of the Sun (the Chandrasekhar limit) will accrete enough matter to undergo a supernova event and collapse to a neutron star. If this does not disrupt the binary, it will then be known as a low-mass x-ray binary. *See* BINARY STAR; NEUTRON STAR; STELLAR EVOLUTION; SUPERNOVA; VARIABLE STAR; WHITE DWARF STAR.   Paula Szkody

Bibliography. R. Downes et al., A catalog and atlas of cataclysmic variables, *J. Astron. Data*, vol. 11, 2005; J.-M. Hameury and J.-P. Lasota (eds.), *The Astrophysics of Cataclysmic Variables and Related Objects*, Astron. Soc. Pacific Conf. Ser. no. 330, 2005; B. Warner, *Cataclysmic Variable Stars*, Cambridge University Press, 1995; D. T. Wickramasinghe and L. Ferrario, Magnetism in isolated and binary white dwarfs, *Publ. Astron. Soc. Pacific*, 112:873–924, 2000.

Catalysis

The phenomenon in which a relatively small amount of foreign material, called a catalyst, augments the rate of a chemical reaction without itself being consumed. A catalyst is material, and not light or heat. It increases a reaction rate. *See* ANTIOXIDANT; INHIBITOR (CHEMISTRY).

If the reaction $A + B \rightarrow D$ occurs very slowly but is catalyzed by some catalyst (Cat), the addition of Cat

must open new channels for the reaction. In a very simple case [reactions (1)], the two propagation processes, which are fast compared to the uncatalyzed

$$
\left.\begin{array}{l}
A + Cat \longrightarrow ACat \\
ACat + B \longrightarrow D + Cat
\end{array}\right\} \text{ Chain propagation}
$$
$$
A + B \longrightarrow D \qquad \text{Overall reaction} \tag{1}
$$

reactions, $A + B \rightarrow D$, provide the new channel for the reaction. The catalyst reacts in the first step, but is regenerated in the second step to commence a new cycle. A catalytic reaction is thus a kind of chain reaction.

An example that occurs naturally in the stratosphere is the catalytic destruction of odd oxygen (oxone, O_3, and oxygen atoms, O) by nitric oxide (NO) [reactions (2)].

$$
\left.\begin{array}{l}
O_3 + NO \longrightarrow O_2 + NO_2 \\
O + NO_2 \longrightarrow O_2 + NO
\end{array}\right\} \text{ Chain propagation}
$$
$$
O_3 + O \longrightarrow 2O_2 \qquad \text{Overall reaction} \tag{2}
$$

See CHAIN REACTION (CHEMISTRY).

If a reaction is in chemical equilibrium under some fixed conditions, the addition of a catalyst cannot change the position of equilibrium without violating the second law of thermodynamics. Therefore, if a catalyst augments the rate of $A + B \rightarrow D$, it must also augment the reverse rate, $D \rightarrow A + B$. *See* CHEMICAL THERMODYNAMICS.

Categories. Catalysis is conventionally divided into three categories: homogeneous, heterogeneous, and enzyme. Heterogeneous catalysis plays a dominant role in chemical processes in the petroleum, petrochemical, and chemical industries. Homogeneous catalysis is important in the petrochemical and chemical industries. Enzyme catalysis plays a key role in all metabolic processes and in some industries, such as the fermentation industry. The mechanisms of these categories involve chemical interaction between the catalyst and one or more reactants. In phase-transfer catalysis the interaction is physical. Electrocatalysis and photocatalysis are more specialized forms of catalysis.

Homogeneous. In homogeneous catalysis, reactants, products, and catalyst are all present molecularly in one phase, usually liquid. Examples are the odd-oxygen reaction [reaction (2)], the hydrogenation of 1-hexene in a hydrocarbon solvent catalyzed by dissolved $[(C_6H_5)_3P]_3RhH$ [reaction (3)] and the hydrolysis of an ester catalyzed by acid [reaction (4)].

$$
H_2C = CHCH_2CH_2CH_2CH_3 + H_2 \longrightarrow
$$
$$
CH_3CH_2CH_2CH_2CH_2CH_3 \tag{3}
$$
$$
CH_3COOC_2H_5 + H_2O \xrightarrow{H^+} CH_3COOH + HOC_2H_5 \tag{4}
$$

See HOMOGENEOUS CATALYSIS.

Heterogeneous. In heterogeneous catalysis, the catalyst is in a separate phase. Usually the reactants and products are in gaseous or liquid phases and the catalyst is a solid. The catalytic reaction occurs on the surface of the solid. Examples are the dehydration and the dehydrogenation of isopropyl alcohol [reactions (5) and (6)]. Reaction (5) can be affected by

$$CH_3CHOHCH_3 \longrightarrow$$
$$CH_3HC{=}CH_2 + H_2O \quad \text{Dehydration} \quad (5)$$

$$CH_3CHOHCH_3 \longrightarrow$$
$$CH_3COCH_3 + H_2 \quad \text{Dehydrogenation} \quad (6)$$

passing the vapors of the alcohol over alumina at about 300°C (570°F), and reaction (6) over copper at 200°C (390°F). It is estimated that one-quarter to one-third of all manufactured goods involve a catalytic antibody. *See* HETEROGENEOUS CATALYSIS.

Enzyme. Transformations of matter in living organisms occur by an elaborate sequence of reactions, most of which are catalyzed by biocatalysts called enzymes. Enzymes are proteins and therefore of colloidal dimensions. Although studies of interrelations between homogeneous catalysis and heterogeneous catalysis have been developing, enzyme catalysis remains a rather separate area in the nature of the catalyst in the type of reactions catalyzed and in the reaction conditions. *See* ENZYME.

Phase transfer. In phase-transfer catalysis the two reactants start in separate phases: a salt as a solid or dissolved in water, and a water-insoluble organic compound as a liquid or dissolved in a nonpolar solvent such as benzene. Mere agitation of the two phases will usually lead to little reaction. However, addition of a suitable phase-transfer catalyst such as an onium salt or a crown ether will considerably augment the rate, ordinarily by carrying the anion into the organic phase, where it is relatively unsolvated and therefore reactive. Such catalytic reactions are run in batch reactors with catalyst at the 1–3% level. Thus, the turnover number (a value related to the number of sets of molecules that react) is about 50 in typical phase-transfer catalysis. For example, an alkyl halide (RX) dissolved in benzene agitated with aqueous potassium cyanide (KCN) forms RCN + KX in the presence of tetrabutyl ammonium chloride as a catalyst. *See* PHASE-TRANSFER CATALYSIS.

Electrocatalysis. Electrochemical processes ordinarily involve an overpotential (overvoltage). Electrocatalysis aims at reducing the overpotential with consequent increase in rate and often of selectivity. The catalytic action may be innate to the electrode (for example, platinum electrodes in a hydrocarbon reaction where dissociative adsorption is involved); it may result from derivatization of the electrode (for example, by a porphyrin); or it may be indirect [for example, the electrochemical hydrogenolysis of halobenzene (RX) with added anthracene (Ar); reactions (7)].

$$Ar + e \rightleftharpoons AR^- \cdot \xrightarrow{RX} R \cdot + X^- + Ar$$
$$R \cdot + e \rightleftharpoons R^- \xrightarrow{H_2O} RH + OH^- \qquad (7)$$

It is possible to modify the activity of an electrode by the electrochemical deposition of an ion that acts as a promoter or inhibitor of the electrode for a reaction that occurs in the absence of an applied potential. This is not called electrocatalysis but nonfaradaic modification of catalytic activity. *See* OVERVOLTAGE.

Photocatalysis. Photocatalysis is a rather vague term, and in some cases it represents a nonstandard usage of catalysis. Photocatalysis should not be used to describe the use of photons for catalyst preparation; for example, the photoreduction of metal ions to form or deposit colloidal metal particles on a support is not photocatalysis. An appropriate usage is given in the following example. Water is irradiated with light of $\nu = 320$ nanometers. No light is adsorbed so nothing happens. Fine particles of titanium dioxide are now suspended in the water. Light is adsorbed and hydrogen and oxygen are evolved. It is demonstrated that the titanium dioxide is not consumed; that is, it may be recovered and reused in this reaction. This sequence is called photocatalysis. However, some chemists would distinguish this kind of catalysis, where the photon is one of the reactants, from a normal endothermic, catalytic reaction operated isothermally with heat supplied from the surroundings. The distinction is thermodynamic. In the latter case, energy is required in a First Law sense (conservation of energy), but the equilibrium of the reaction is not affected—the normal expectation of catalysis and a corollary of the definition of catalysis. Photocatalysis allows a reaction that would not occur spontaneously, for example, the dissociation of water into hydrogen and oxygen at room temperature and pressure.

Selectivity. In most cases, a given set of reactants could react in two or more ways, as exemplified by reactions (5) and (6). The degree to which just one of the possible reactions is favored over the other is called selectivity. The fraction of reactants that react by a specific path, for example, reaction (5), is called the selectivity by that path, and it will vary from catalyst to catalyst. Selectivity is a key property of a catalyst in any practical application of the catalyst.

Turnover. The number of sets of molecules that react consequent to the presence of a catalytic site (heterogeneous or enzyme catalysis) or molecule of catalyst (homogeneous catalysis), the turnover number is substantially greater than unity and may be very large. The turnover frequency is the number of sets of molecules that react per site or catalyst molecule per second. It must be greater than one or the reaction is stoichiometric, not catalytic.

Catalyst life. In practical applications, catalyst life, that is, the time or number of turnovers before the reaction rate becomes uselessly low, is important. It will be reduced by the presence of molecules that adsorb at (react with) and block the active site (poisons). *See* ADSORPTION.

Robert L. Burwell, Jr.; Gary L. Haller

Bibliography. B. C. Gates, *Catalytic Chemistry*, 1992; H. Gerischer and W. Vielstich, *Electrocatalysis*, in *Handbook of Heterogeneous Catalysis*, vol. 3, ed. by G. Ertl, H. Knözinger, and J. Weitkamp, 1997; E. Pelizzetti and N. Serpone (eds.), *Photocatalysis: Fundamentals and Applications*, 1990.

Catalytic antibody

A type of large protein naturally produced by the immune system with the capability of initiating diverse chemical reactions similarly to enzymes. Catalytic antibodies are elicited against small molecules that are bound to carrier proteins and contain a specific binding site. In their native form, they are constructed of two pairs of polypeptide chains that differ in length and are connected to each other by disulfide bridges. Various antibody molecules share a common structure (**Fig. 1**), but they differ in the N-terminal regions of antibody light and heavy chains which are responsible for antigen recognition. These regions vary greatly in the sequence and number of their constituent amino acids and therefore provide an enormous diversity of antigen-binding domains. *See* ANTIBODY; ANTIGEN; ANTIGEN-ANTIBODY REACTION; ENZYME; IMMUNITY; PROTEIN.

Description. In principle, catalysis is achieved by lowering the free energy of activation for a chemical reaction. Therefore, the catalyst has to bind the transition state more tightly then either the reactant or the product. If an antibody could be elicited against a transition state, it would have the potential to catalyze this chemical reaction. *See* CATALYSIS.

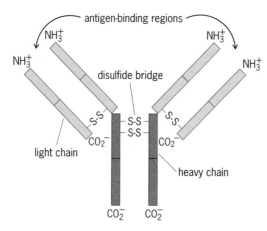

Fig. 1. Schematic structure of an antibody molecule. The protein consists of two heavy chains and two light chains.

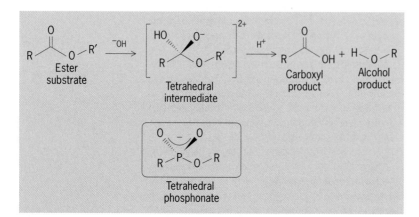

Fig. 2. Early highlights of the first antibody-catalyzed reaction of ester hydrolysis. Stable tetrahedral phosphonate was used as the transition-state analog.

Catalytic antibodies are produced according to standard monoclonal technology. Stable transition-state analogs (haptens) are synthesized and coupled to two carrier proteins. One such conjugate is used for mouse immunization, and the second for screening purposes. The carrier proteins trigger strong immune responses, and specific antibodies which bind only to the hapten are selected and screened for catalysis. *See* MONOCLONAL ANTIBODIES.

Catalytic antibodies were first reported in 1986 independently by Richard Lerner and Peter Schultz. Both used antibodies that were elicited against tetrahedral phosphonate as transition-state analog to catalyze hydrolysis reactions of aryl esters and carbonates (**Fig. 2**).

Since then, several hundred different examples of catalytic antibodies have been reported from various research groups, including highly enantioselective, disfavored, and nonenzymatic reactions. However, the transition-state analog immunization strategy produced antibodies that were highly specific for their substrates, and therefore only a very limited number of compounds could be used for antibody reactions.

A major breakthrough has been achieved with the development of a new immunization concept. Instead of immunizing against transition-state analogs, immunization is done with a highly reactive compound in order to create a chemical reaction during the binding of the antigen to the antibody. The same reaction becomes part of the mechanism of the catalytic event. In other words, the antibodies are elicited against a chemical reaction. This strategy is termed reactive immunization. *See* REACTIVE INTERMEDIATES.

1,3-Diketone was used as a trap for an amino lysine residue in an antibody active site (**Fig. 3**). Two antibodies which contained the desired lysine were found to mimic type I aldolases very efficiently. Type I aldolases are enzymes that catalyze reversible aldol reactions through the intermediacy of enamine formation with an enzyme amino group:

$$R-CH=O + R'CH_2C=OR'' \rightleftharpoons$$
$$R-CHOH-CHR'-C=OR''$$

For the first time, a catalytic antibody was capable of accepting a very broad range of substrates. Furthermore, in most cases, the antibody's reactions were highly enantioselective and could be performed easily on a preparative scale. The synthetic advantages of these unique antibodies were clearly demonstrated, and include organic enantioselective synthesis of natural products and preparation of both enantiomers of a variety of aldol products. The surprising success of this aldolase catalyst made it the first commercially available catalytic antibody. *See* ORGANIC SYNTHESIS; STEREOCHEMISTRY.

Synthetic achievements. The early skepticism of the synthetic capability of catalytic antibodies has rapidly diffused. The first large-scale reaction with a catalytic antibody was reported in 1994, in which the synthesis of 1.4 g of enantiomerically pure

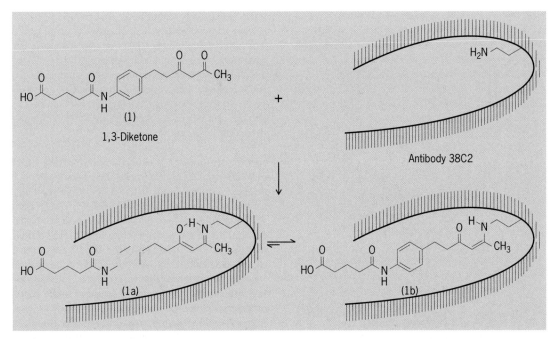

Fig. 3. Mechanism of trapping the essential ε-amino group of a lysine residue in the antibody's binding pocket by using the 1,3-diketone hapten.

enol ether was achieved. Just a year later, the first total synthesis of a natural product using a catalytic antibody was reported. Aldolase antibody 38C2 has accomplished several important achievements in organic synthetic chemistry. It started with enantioselective synthesis of the important synthetic block, the Wieland-Miescher ketone, and followed with the enantioselective total synthesis of 10 different brevicomins (sex pheromones of the bark beetle). A total synthesis of the sex pheromone frontalin was reported shortly after. *See* PHEROMONE.

The most stimulating achievement in the synthesis of a natural product by an antibody catalyst has been accomplished by the total synthesis of Epothilone, in which an important chiral synthon was prepared using antibody 38C2 to resolve 18 g of racemic mixture to 9 g of enantiomerically pure compound. Furthermore, the antibody was shown to perform aldol addition reactions very efficiently with unprotected hydroxyacetone as a donor. This is remarkable in that no other catalyst, chemical or biological, is capable of using hydroxyacetone as a donor substrate for the aldol reaction. The advantage of this reaction was elegantly demonstrated in the short total synthesis of the biologically important sugar 1-deoxy-L-xylulose.

Medical potential. The intriguing concept of using catalytic antibodies as therapeutic agents became more appealing when it was shown that most of the amino acids in a mouse antibody molecule could be replaced with human sequences and thereby

make the antibody molecule compatible for in vivo treatment in humans. This strategy has been exploited within the application of prodrug activation by a catalytic antibody.

In principle, a catalytic antibody can be designed to modify a prodrug into an active drug. Several groups reported prodrug activation by antibody catalysis. All of them used phosphonate hapten as tetrahedral transition-state analog for the hydrolytic reaction which released the free drug.

The aldolase antibody 38C2 has a major advantage regarding prodrug activation. Since it has the capability to accept a broad variety of substrates, the antibody may potentially activate any prodrug. A general prodrug chemistry was developed to take advantage of the broad scope and mechanism of catalytic antibody 38C2. The drug masking/activation concept was based on a sequential retro-aldol-retro-Michael reaction catalyzed by antibody 38C2 (**Fig. 4**).

This reaction is not known to be catalyzed by any other enzyme and has a very low background; that is, the reaction is very slow in the absence of the catalyst. This chemistry was applied to the anticancer drugs doxorubicin and camptothecin. Weakly or nontoxic concentrations of their corresponding prodrugs can be activated by therapeutically relevant concentrations of antibody 38C2 to kill colon and prostate cancer cell lines. To further test the therapeutic relevance of this model system, it was shown that antibody 38C2 remained catalytically

Fig. 4. Prodrug activation via a tandem retro-aldol-retro-Michael reaction. X stands for heteroatoms N, O, or S (nitrogen, oxygen, or sulfur).

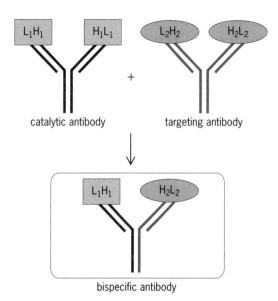

Fig. 5. Generation of bispecific antibody originating from a catalytic antibody and a targeting antibody.

active over weeks after intravenous injection into mice. Based on these findings, it is possible that the system described here has the potential to become a key tool in selective chemotherapy. *See* CHEMOTHERAPY.

The development of strategies that provide for selective chemotherapy presents significant multidisciplinary challenges. Selective chemotherapy, in the case of cancer, might be based on the enzymatic activation of a prodrug at the tumor site. The enzymatic activity must be directed to the site with a targeting

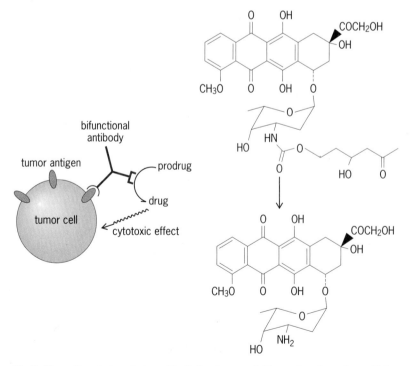

Fig. 6. Chemotherapy targeted specifically to a tumor cell. The prodrug is prodoxorubicin, which is transformed to the active drug doxorubicin by the catalytic arm of the bifunctional antibody. The other arm binds to an antigen on a tumor cell.

molecule, usually an antibody, that recognizes a cell surface molecule selectively expressed at the tumor site. Since a single molecule of enzyme catalyzes the activation of many molecules of prodrug, a localized and high drug concentration may be maintained at the tumor site. This concept of antibody-directed enzyme prodrug therapy (ADEPT) holds promise as a general and selective chemotherapeutic strategy if several criteria can be met.

A number of antigens that are expressed on the surface of tumor cells or in their supporting blood vessels (vasculature) have been shown to be effective targets for antibody-mediated cancer therapy. Thus, for the most part, the targeting antibody component of this strategy is not limiting. By contrast, the requirements of the enzyme component and complementary prodrug chemistries for ADEPT are difficult to achieve. First of all, selective prodrug activation requires the catalysis of a reaction that must not be accomplished by endogenous enzymes in the blood or normal tissue of the patient. Enzymes of non-human origin that meet these needs are, however, likely to be highly immunogenic, a fact that makes repeated administration impossible. Finally, the chemistry used to convert a drug into a prodrug should be versatile enough to allow for the modification of many drug classes while not interfering with the operation of the enzyme so that a single enzyme could be used for the activation of a multiplicity of prodrugs.

Outlook. The limitations of the ADEPT complex encourage scientists to suggest that the enzyme component for ADEPT might be replaced by a catalytic antibody. The potential of catalytic antibodies for ADEPT are indeed compelling; both catalysis of reactions not catalyzed by human enzymes and minimal immunogenicity through antibody humanization are feasible. Combining these features, the ADEPT conjugate translates into a bispecific antibody consisting of targeting and catalytic arms (**Fig. 5**). Two parent antibodies are combined in a manner such that each antibody contributes one light chain and one heavy chain. The bispecific construct contains two different binding regions. One originates from the targeting antibody and can bind specifically to antigens which are expressed on tumor cells, and the other originates from a catalytic antibody and is used to activate a prodrug.

A bispecific antibody could be used for selective chemotherapy (**Fig. 6**). This possible future treatment can consist of two steps. First, a dose of the bispecific antibody can be administered, and the targeting arm can locate and attach to specific antigens on tumor cell surface. Excess of the antibody can be cleared after a limited time from the patient's blood, preventing nonspecific prodrug activation. Second, several doses of prodrug can be administered on suitable time gaps. The prodrug can reach the tumor site through the blood circulation and can be activated by the catalytic arm very close to the tumor cell. The damage to noncancer cells should be therefore minimized, and the free drug can specifically target cancer cells.

Catalytic antibodies are useful synthetic tools in enantioselective synthesis and also play an important role in performing organic reactions with unprotected chemical functionalities. However, the most promising use for them is probably in the medicinal field. The previously described strategy of targeting cancer with selective chemotherapy is highly encouraging.   Richard A. Lerner; Doron Shabat

Bibliography. G. M. Blackburn et al., Passive and catalytic antibodies and drug delivery, *Pure Appl. Chem.*, 76(5):983–989, 2004; T. Hoffmann et al., Aldolase antibodies of remarkable scope, *J. Amer. Chem. Soc.*, 120:2768–2779, 1998; B. List et al., A catalytic enantioselective route to hydroxy-substituted quaternary carbon centers: Resolution of tertiary aldols with a catalytic antibody, *J. Amer. Chem. Soc.*, 121:7283–7291, 1999; B. List et al., Enantioselective total synthesis of some brevicomins using aldolase antibody 38C2, *Chem. Eur. J.*, 4(5):881–885, 1998; H. Miyashita et al., Prodrug activation via catalytic antibodies, *Proc. Nat. Acad. Sci. USA*, 90(11):5337–5340, 1993; P. G. Schultz and R. A. Lerner, From molecular diversity to catalysis: Lessons from the immune system, *Science*, 269(5232):1835–1842, 1995; D. Shabat et al., Multiple event activation of a generic prodrug trigger by antibody catalysis, *Proc. Nat. Acad. Sci. USA*, 96:6925–6930, 1999; S. C. Sinha, C. F. Barbas III, and R. A. Lerner, The antibody catalysis route to the total synthesis of epothilones, *Proc. Nat. Acad. Sci. USA*, 95:14603–14608, 1998; J. Wagner, R. A. Lerner, and C. F. Barbas III, Efficient aldolase catalytic antibodies that use the enamine mechanism of natural enzymes, *Science*, 270(5243):1797–1800, 1995.

Catalytic converter

An aftertreatment device used for pollutant removal from automotive exhaust. Since the 1975 model year, increasingly stringent government regulations for the allowable emission levels of carbon monoxide (CO), hydrocarbons (HC), and oxides of nitrogen (NO_x) have resulted in the use of catalytic converters on most passenger vehicles sold in the United States. The task of the catalytic converter is to promote chemical reactions for the conversion of these pollutants to carbon dioxide, water, and nitrogen.

By definition a catalyst is an agent which promotes the rates at which chemical reactions occur, without affecting the final equilibrium as dictated by thermodynamics, but which itself remains unchanged. For automotive exhaust applications, the pollutant removal reactions are the oxidation of carbon monoxide and hydrocarbons and the reduction of nitrogen oxides. Metals, base and noble, are the catalytic agents most often employed for this task. Small quantities of these metals, when present in a highly dispersed form (often as individual atoms), provide sites upon which the reactant molecules may interact and the reaction proceed.

In addition to the active metal, the converter contains a support component whose functions include yielding structural integrity to the device, providing a large surface area for metal dispersion, and promoting intimate contact between the exhaust gas and the catalyst. Two types of supports are used: pellets and monoliths. The pelleted converter consists of a packed bed of small, porous, ceramic spheres whose outer shell is impregnated with the active metal. The monolith is a honeycomb structure consisting of a large number of channels parallel to the direction of exhaust gas flow. The active metals reside in a thin layer of high-surface-area ceramic (usually γ-alumina) placed on the walls of the honeycomb. In either system the support is contained in a stainless steel can installed in the exhaust system ahead of the muffler.

Two types of catalyst systems, oxidation and three-way, are found in automotive applications. Oxidation catalysts remove only CO and HC, leaving NO_x unchanged. An air pump is often used to add air to the engine exhaust upstream of the catalyst, thus ensuring an oxidizing atmosphere. Platinum and palladium are generally used as the active metals in oxidation catalysts. Three-way catalysts are capable of removing all three pollutants simultaneously, provided that the catalyst is maintained in a "chemically correct" environment that is neither overly oxidizing or reducing. To achieve this requires that the engine air-fuel ratio always be at, or very near, stoichiometry under all vehicle operating conditions. Feedback air-fuel ratio control systems are often used to satisfy this requirement. Platinum, palladium, and rhodium are the metals most often used in three-way catalysts. In addition, base metals are frequently added to improve the ability of the catalyst to withstand small, transient perturbations in air-fuel ratio. In both oxidation and three-way catalyst systems, the production of undesirable reaction products, such as sulfates and ammonia, must be avoided.

Maintaining effective catalytic function over long periods of vehicle operation is often a major problem. Catalytic activity will deteriorate due to two causes, poisoning of the active sites by contaminants, such as lead and phosphorus, and exposure to excessively high temperatures. Catalyst overtemperature is often associated with engine malfunctions such as excessively rich operation or a large amount of cylinder misfire. To achieve efficient emission control, it is thus paramount that catalyst-equipped vehicles be operated only with lead-free fuel and that proper engine maintenance procedures be followed. In such cases catalytic converters have proved to be a very effective means for reducing emissions without sacrificing fuel economy. *See* AUTOMOTIVE ENGINE; CATALYSIS.   Norman Otto

Cataract

Any clouding or opacity of the crystalline lens of the eye. Cataracts vary markedly in degree of density and may be due to many causes, but the majority are associated with aging. Cataracts are the single leading cause of blindness in the world.

Types of cataracts: (*a*) traumatic "star-shaped," (*b*) senile "cuneiform," and (*c*) senile "morgagnian."

The lens consists of fibers arranged in regular layers, similar to the structure of an onion. It is composed of three distinct parts: an elastic capsule, the epithelium from which the lens fibers originate, and the lens substance which is plastic and capable (below the age of 40) of altering shape according to the condition of the capsule. The average diameter of the lens is 0.36 in. (9 mm), and it has a greater radius of convexity on its posterior surface. This lens is supported by the suspensory ligament and lies between the back of the iris and the anterior base of the vitreous, which is the jelly that fills the space behind the lens and in front of the retina. The lens has no blood supply, so it cannot be inflamed, but it is easily affected by metabolic changes. The essential biochemical change in a cataractous lens is the coagulation of its protein.

Senile cataract occurs with aging and is by far the most common type. Progressively blurred vision is the only symptom. There are a number of other varieties (congenital, metabolic, secondary, or traumatic; see **illus.**) and causes (such as a reaction to certain drugs or irradiation). Cataracts may also be associated with systemic diseases such as hypoparathyroidism, myotonic dystrophy, atopic dermatitis, galactosemia, and Lowe's, Werner's, and Down syndromes.

At present the treatment for cataracts, when they are sufficiently advanced to impair the vision, is surgical removal. When a cataract is surgically removed, the crystalline lens of the eye is removed much as a lens would be removed from a camera. Cataract surgery may be performed in one of three ways: (1) Intracapsular extraction: the lens, enclosed in its complete capsule, is entirely removed through a large 0.48–0.56-in. (12–14-mm) incision in the eye; this remains the most successful and common method of cataract removal in the United States. (2) Extracapsular cataract extraction: the capsule is opened, and the lens contents are removed; the posterior capsule is left intact, while the anterior capsule is partially or totally removed. (3) Ultrasound cataract surgery or phacoemulsification: an ultrasonic needle is introduced into the lens, and the lens is emulsified, fragmented, or broken up and sucked out through a small (0.12-in. or 3-mm) opening in the eye; this is a form of extracapsular cataract extraction since the anterior capsule is opened and removed along with the contents, leaving the posterior capsule intact.

In order to restore normal vision after surgery, any of a number of methods may be followed. Cataract glasses may be prescribed. Contact lenses may be fitted, but these have not been too successful in elderly cataract patients because of their inability to handle lenses. However, since soft contact lenses have been approved for extended wear, they can be left in the eye for weeks or even months, thus obviating the need for handling. Intraocular lenses made of the plastic polymethylmethacrylate can be inserted into the eye to replace the cataractous lens. There are numerous types of intraocular lenses. Their theoretical advantages include permanent placement and less distortion and magnification. Some of the disadvantages include the increased difficulty of the cataract operation, an increased incidence of operative and postoperative complications, and the inability to easily remove a lens of incorrect power. *See* EYE (VERTEBRATE). Jack Hartstein

Bibliography. O. R. Caldwell (ed.), *Cataracts*, 1988; E. L. Greve (ed.), *Surgical Management of Coexisting Glaucoma and Cataract*, 1987; J. Schulman (ed.), *Cataracts*, 1993; R. W. Young, *Age-Related Cataract*, 1990.

Catastrophe theory

A theory of mathematical structure in which smooth continuous inputs lead to discontinuous responses. Water suddenly boils, ice melts, a building crashes to the ground, or the earth unexpectedly buckles and quakes. The French mathematician René Thom conceived and developed an eclectic collection of ideas into catastrophe theory. His idea was to establish a new basis for a more mathematical approach to biology. Connotations of disaster are misleading, since Thom's intention was to emphasize sudden, abrupt changes.

Advanced areas of modern mathematics, including algebraic geometry, differential topology, and dynamical system theory, contributed to the creation of catastrophe theory. A complete mathematical theory exists for the elementary catastrophes, which can be written as the gradient of an energylike function. The physical, chemical, and engineering applications are less developed, although many are known in optics, laser theory, thermodynamics, elasticity, and chemical reaction theory. The Thom classification theorem gives exactly seven elementary catastrophes. Although a theory of generalized catastrophes exists, which extends the theory beyond gradient systems, it is not nearly as well developed mathematically or physically as that of elementary catastrophes. It does include remarkable examples of chaos (or stochastic behavior) in the solutions to nonlinear deterministic equations. These solutions include strange attractors and omega explosions among the examples of non-elementary catastrophes. *See* GEOMETRY; PERIOD DOUBLING; TOPOLOGY.

Two important aspects of catastrophe theory are frequently overlooked or misconstrued. First, as it is a rigorous mathematical theory, the characteristic catastrophe features can be proved. These features include jumps in the response; hysteresis or a path dependence in the response, representing a storage of energy for some paths; divergence, where a small path change produces a large response change (as if a source or sink were crossed); and type changes in the response, where a smooth response occurs on one path that becomes discontinuous along a nearby path.

Second, all of these features are topological, so that they are independent of the coordinates used to describe the potential. They are, therefore, qualitative features of the solutions. Some critics have concluded that because these aspects were qualitative, they could not be quantitative. This is contradicted by the solid and growing body of quantitative studies in catastrophe theory. (Problems in quantum optics, thermodynamics, and scattering theory have all been clarified by catastrophe theory.)

Definitions. The object V whose possible behavior is to be classified is a smooth, real function, having the general form given by Eq. (1), the set of real numbers, or, equivalently, Eq. (2). The r real variables

$$V : R^r \times R^n \mapsto R \qquad (1)$$

$$V_{a_1,a_2,\ldots,a_r}(x_1,\ldots,x_n) = V a_1,\ldots,a_r(x_1,\ldots,x_n) \qquad (2)$$

a_1, a_2, $\ldots$, a_r are called the control parameters; the n variables x_1, $\ldots$, x_n are the variables; and V is the response function. In mechanics, V represents a potential energy surface, and the control parameters are coupling constants, that is, the strengths of various terms in the expression for the potential energy. For a two-dimensional potential function, $V_{abc}(x_1,x_2)$, the response is the height of hills and valleys in a perpendicular x_3 direction. If a ball (with negligible inertia) is rolled onto this surface, it will roll into the lowest possible position. This lowers its potential energy to a local minimum. This is a simple example of a critical point. *See* ENERGY; PARAMETER; POTENTIALS.

In general, the critical points of $V_{a1},\ldots,_{ar}(x_1,\ldots,x_n)$ are the set of all points $P_i = (x_{1i},x_{2i},\ldots,x_{ni})$ for which Eq. (3) is satisfied, and may be maxima,

$$\left(\frac{\partial V_{a_1,\ldots,a_r}}{\partial x_j}\right)\bigg|_{P_i} = 0 \qquad (3)$$

minima, or inflection points. The hessian matrix **H** of the function $V_{a2},\ldots,_{ar}$ is the $n \times n$ matrix with ijth element given by Eq. (4). A point x_0 is called structurally stable if it is a critical point and satisfies inequality (5).

$$b_{ij} = \frac{\partial^2 V_{a_1,\ldots,a_r}}{\partial x_i \partial x_j} \qquad (4)$$

$$\det (H)_{x_0} \neq 0 \qquad (5)$$

If S is a space of points with boundary ∂S, its codimension is dimension (S) – dimension (∂S). Two subspaces V_1, V_2 of S are transverse if dimension (V_1) + dimension (V_2) = dimension (S). The Morse lemma and splitting lemma allow the number of variables considered to be reduced. The codimension is the number of variables which must be studied.

Thom classification theorem. Consider an r-parameter family of smooth real functions $V : R^r \times R^n \to R$, for any value of n and any value of $r \leq 5$. The Thom

classification theorem states that either the family is structurally stable, and is equivalent about any point to noncritical or a nondegenerate critical point (these are not catastrophes); or it is structurally unstable and is equivalent to one of the seven elementary catastrophes: (1) the fold; (2) the cusp; (3) the swallowtail; (4) the butterfly; (5) the elliptic umbecile; (6) the hyperbolic umbecile; or (7) the parabolic umbecile. If the number of parameters is finite and greater than five, complicated combinations of these seven catastrophes can occur. If r is made very large, the elementary class of catastrophes is not complete. Catastrophe geometry becomes increasingly complicated both as n increases and as the numbers of possible catastrophes increase.

One-variable cusp catastrophe. A simple example of a catastrophe is the one-variable cusp catastrophe. The response function for this catastrophe, $V_{ab}(x)$, is given by Eq. (6). A sketch of Eq. (6) for $x = x_0$, a

$$V_{ab}(x) = {}^1/_4 x^4 + {}^1/_2 a x^2 + b x \qquad (6)$$

critical point, is given in **Fig. 1**. Since the value of the critical point x_0 depends on the control parameters, a and b, in a complicated fashion, it follows that V_{ab}, evaluated at $x = x_0$, is a complicated nonlinear function of a and b. This is plotted in Fig. 1. Assuming that V_{ab} is a potential energy surface, a ball placed on the surface in Fig. 1 will roll downhill toward the right. The curves A, B, and C indicate three possible paths and, in **Fig. 2**, points 1 to 10 are labeled on these curves. Suppose further that points (1,3,5) and points (2,4,10) all have the same potential energy. This example will be used to illustrate each of the characteristic features of elementary catastrophes. It is the dependence of the response upon control parameters which is under study.

The curves A, B, and C of Fig. 1 are redrawn in Fig. 2. To see the jumps in response, consider a ball set in motion from point 5 on curve C. It will roll past point 6, and at point 7 it will fall to point 9

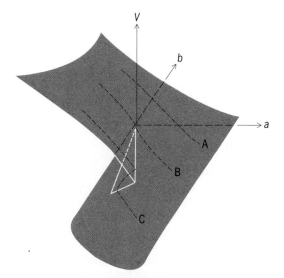

Fig. 1. Cusp catastrophe surface for the response function V_{ab} as a function of (a,b) at a critical point. Paths A, B, and C are labeled.

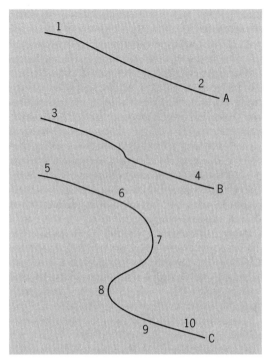

Fig. 2. Paths A, B, and C from Fig. 1, with points 1–10 marked. The response function V_{ab} has the same values at (1,3,5) and at (2,4,10).

ferroelectrics is accurately described by the butterfly catastrophe. The conclusion is that catastrophe theory has an important role to play in phase transition physics even if it is not the whole story. *See* FERROELECTRICS; PHASE TRANSITIONS.

In ecology, sharp boundaries are often important. A predator may eliminate some competing species from an area; a parasite may eliminate the food supply of another. An explanation can be obtained from curve C in Fig. 2. Along the segment 5 to 6, the conditions assure the dominance of species A. Point 7 is a catastrophe point. The segment 8-9-10 is a region where another species, species B, dominates. This simple model is, of course, nonunique. Any other model whose solution is approximately such a polynomial is an equally good candidate. Thus, some collaboration from ecology is required to determine the correct response function, but the model can help in finding this. After several successful iterations of this kind, the surviving models have a sound basis. *See* ECOLOGY.

Status. There have been vigorous controversies, as some scientists have argued that catastrophe theory is unmathematical and scientifically empty, and that some applications are foolish. The first two claims are simply false. The first objection was based

(**Fig.** 3*a*). In addition, it is impossible to go from point 10 to point 5 along curve C.

To exhibit the hysteresis effect (Fig. 3*b*), first roll a ball from point 2 to point 1 on curve A; from there to point 3 on curve B. Then roll it from point 3 to point 4 and back to the starting point 2. The area enclosed in the figure is a hysteresis effect and is quite similar to hysteresis in magnetism. *See* HYSTERESIS.

The divergence effect can be understood by considering a small counterclockwise circular path about the (*a, b*) origin. A ball which rolls in this path will see the hill at negative *b* as a source of energy. The ball will act as if it had received a divergence of potential (that is, a nonconservative force) on each trip.

To see the change in type of path, simply consider the difference in paths A and C. If the scale of the *b* control parameter is such that these paths are very "near" one another, then a small change in the *bx* term can dramatically change the path from a smooth and continuous path A to a discontinuous path C.

Applications. Many physical problems involve some or all of the four nonlinear effects just described. Phase transitions include many aspects which are surprisingly similar to these four. The jump in the latent heat at a liquid-vapor phase transition is very similar to the jump shown in Fig. 3*a*. However, the cusp catastrophe given in Eq. (6) is quite definite. It contains no cx^3 term, as such effects are transformed away by coordinate transformations in obtaining the generic form. Unfortunately, careful experiments and their analysis show that the liquid-vapor phase transition is not any of the elementary catastrophes. On the other hand, the hysteresis of

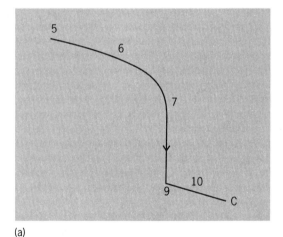

(a)

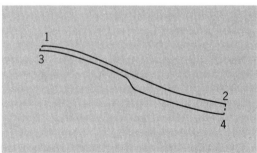

(b)

Fig. 3. Paths that exhibit features of catastrophe theory. (a) Path on curve C showing a jump in the response function. (b) Path using curves A and B which shows hysteresis. No change in potential energy V_{ab} is required to go from 1 to 3 or from 2 to 4. The area enclosed between curves is proportional to an energy stored from the overall process.

on the articles which were explicitly written to popularize the subject, while conveniently ignoring the scholarly articles which contained the mathematical proofs and examples. The second objection was based upon a very careless search of the literature; articles by many mathematicians meet the highest scientific standards. The third criticism is partially correct. Attempts to use simple models on drunkenness, prison disorders, and social problems are questionable. Even in these cases, however, the criticism seems harsh.

Catastrophe theory is an important tool for the physical sciences. If Thom's vision is correct, it may be even more important for biology and the social sciences. Brian DeFacio

Bibliography. M. V. Berry, *Adv. Phys.*, 25:1–26, 1976; R. Gilmore, *Catastrophe Theory for Engineers and Scientists*, 1982, reprint 1999; T. Poston and I. Stewart, *Catastrophe Theory and Its Applications*, 1978; H. T. Sussmann, *Synthesis*, 31:229–270, 1975; R. Thom, *Structural Stability and Morphogenesis*, 1975; E. C. Zeeman, Catastrophe theory, *Sci. Amer.*, 234(4):65–83, April 1976; E. C. Zeeman, *Catastrophe Theory: Selected Papers (1972–1977)*, 1977.

Catenanes

Catenanes are compounds that are made of interlocking macrocycles. The interlocking rings are said to be mechanically rather than chemically bound. Catenanes are named according to the number of interlocking rings. The simplest catenane, containing two interlocking rings, is called [2]-catenane (structure **1**). The most common catenanes consist of a linear arrangement of interlocking rings, so [2]-catenane is the first member of this series. Next is [3]-catenane (**2**). Linear catenanes containing up to

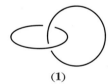

(1)

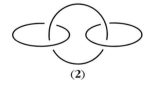

(2)

five rings are known, for example, olympiadane (**3**).

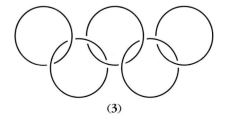

(3)

Catenanes involving necklace arrangements of bead-like rings have also been synthesized: [5]-catenane (**4**) represents the topology of this series. [7]-Catenane (**5**) combines linear and necklace topolo-

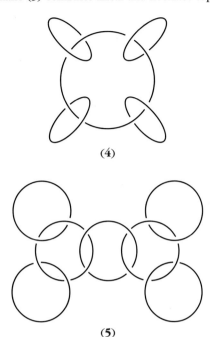

(4)

(5)

gies; it is the highest-order molecular catenane isolated so far. In fact, catenanes need not be made of simple macrocycles only. Macrobicycles or higher-order macrocycles may be involved too. Examples of catenanes constructed from such molecules are [4]-catenane (**6**), which is based on a macrobicyclic

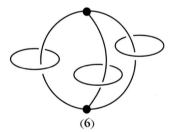

(6)

backbone, each lobe being interlocked with a macrocycle, and three-dimensionally interlocked catenane (**7**), where two macrobicycles are mutually inter-

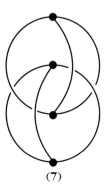

(7)

locked. A remarkable class of catenanes, from the

topological viewpoint, are the multiply interlocked catenanes. The first member of this series is the doubly interlocked [2]-catenane (**8**), made of inter-

(8)

woven macrocycles. It is topologically more complex than [2]-catenane (1), since the projection of the molecule on the plane has four crossing points whereas that of [2]-catenane has only two crossing points.

Many other catenane topologies can be envisaged. An exciting target is the so-called Borromean rings (**9**), a figure used by a famous Italian family as a sym-

(9)

bol of solidarity. There are three interlocked rings, yet any two rings are independent of each other; it is the third ring that fastens the system. Another target is the figure-eight [2]-catenane (**10**).

(10)

Occurrence. Molecular catenanes are compounds of synthetic origin. However, natural deoxyribonucleic acid (DNA) macromolecules were shown to assemble, in certain conditions, into catenated structures, which were studied by electron microscopy.

Synthesis. The rings of the catenanes may be purely organic macrocycles or metallomacrocycles, that is, macrocycles including transition-metal ions in their bond sequences. Actually, the chemical nature of the ring is dictated by the method of synthesis. Basically, three methods have been developed for the synthesis of catenanes (**Fig. 1**): statistical, directed, and template syntheses.

Statistical synthesis. Statistical synthesis relies on the probability that a macrocycle can be threaded onto a molecular string to afford an intermediate that will undergo the cyclization reaction (Fig. 1*a*). Convincing approaches to the statistical method used the trick of stabilizing the threaded complex by stoppering the extremities of the string with bulky groups: a so-called rotaxane species is obtained (Fig. 1*b*). Subsequently, conventional macrocycle synthesis is used to prepare the catenane, which is obtained after removal of the stoppers. This method produced the first hydrocarbon catenane, made of interlocked $(CH_2)_{28}$ and $(CH_2)_{46}$ macrocycles.

Directed synthesis. Directed synthesis uses a catechol-based acetal incorporated in a macrocycle (Fig. 1*c*). Two pendent arms, as precursors to the second macrocycle, are anchored perpendicularly to the plane of the first macrocycle. Their functionalized extremities are compelled to react with a complementary function localized inside the first macrocycle, so that the construction of the second macrocycle is directed to take place inside the first one. The last key step is the cleavage of the bonds linking the two macrocyclic sequences of atoms. This multistep synthetic method was used to prepare [2]- and [3]-catenanes.

Template syntheses. Template synthesis methods are highly directed and economical in terms of numbers of steps. In these methods, metal cations or molecules gather and preorganize reactive molecular fragments in a spatially controlled manner, so that the desired structure will be obtained preferentially over many others. In the first method, the transition-metal-templated synthesis of catenanes, the metal [generally Cu(I)] gathers a macrocycle incorporating a chelating subunit and a linear fragment made up of the complementary chelate such that both components are more or less at right angles to each other (Fig. 1*d*). Cyclization of the linear fragment affords the metallocatenane, or catenate. Removal of the metal template by competitive complexation provides the catenane as a free ligand, or catenand. In the one-step alternative strategy, two open-chain chelates are assembled orthogonally at a metal center. A double cyclization reaction provides the catenate in one step. The transition-metal-templated synthesis of catenanes is very flexible in terms of chemical functionality; for example, catenands containing pendent metalloporphyrins have been synthesized. The yield of catenane formation depends on the cyclization reaction used; excellent yields were observed for cyclization methods based on the ring-closing metathesis reaction.

Fig. 1. Synthetic routes to catenanes. (*a*) Statistical; f and g are complementary functions that react to close the ring. (*b*) Statistical, using a rotaxane intermediate; f and g are complementary functions that react to anchor the stoppers; i and h are complementary functions that react to form the second, interlocked ring. (*c*) Directed. (*d*) Transition-metal-templated; the thick ring portions represent the coordination sites, and the black disk is the metal; f and g are complementary functions that react to close the second, interlocked ring. (*e*) Templated by aromatic π-stacking interactions; the open rectangles are electron-rich, and the filled rectangles are electron-poor, aromatic groups; f and g are complementary functions that react to form the electron-deficient macrocycle.

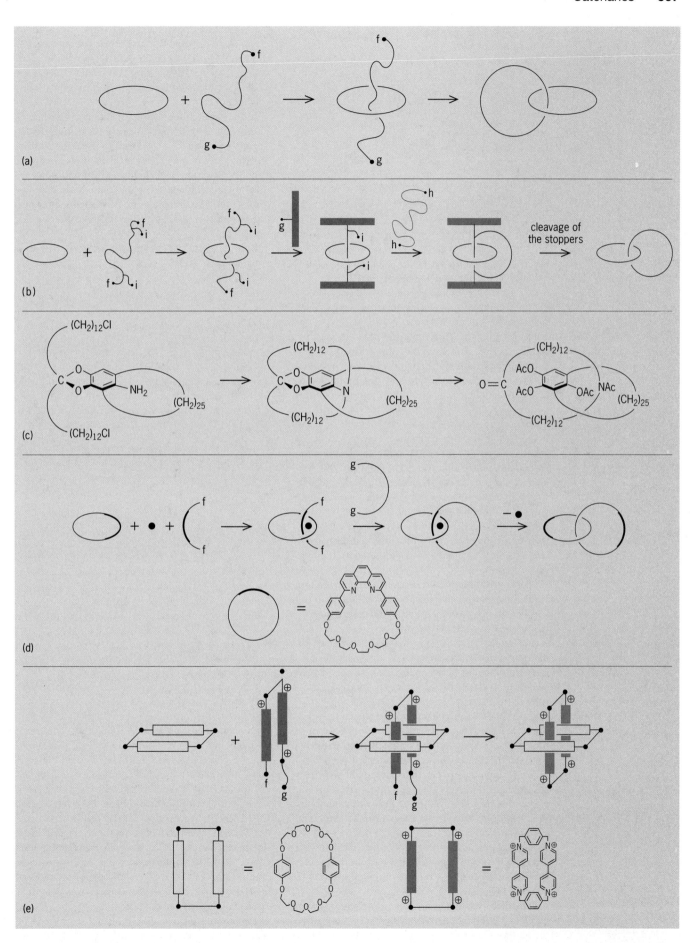

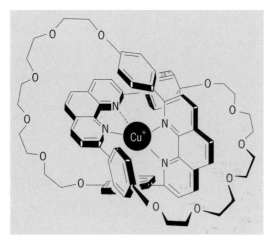

Fig. 2. Molecular structure of the copper(I) [2]-catenate of Fig. 1d, from an x-ray crystal structure analysis.

Other template syntheses involve template effects based on noncovalent bonds like van der Waals or aromatic π-stacking interactions, and hydrogen bonds. For example, the formation of a catenane based on π-stacking interactions between an electron-rich macrocycle and the precursor to an electron-deficient macrocycle; these interactions control the threading of the macrocycle onto the linear intermediate (Fig. 1e). Then cyclization can occur, affording the catenane. The principle of template methods involving molecular rather than metal templates is that, very schematically, one preformed macrocycle acts as a receptor for a molecular fragment of the other macrocycle. Moreover, in some cases the receptor macrocycle need not be made prior to the final cyclization step; self-assembly effects come into play. This was observed, in particular, in the case of catenanes assembled with the help of hydrogen bonds.

Characterization. Catenanes are characterized and studied like normal molecules, in solution or in the solid state, using routinely employed techniques, including elemental analysis, nuclear magnetic resonance (NMR) spectroscopy, mass spectrometry, osmometry, and single-crystal x-ray analysis. Because of the interactions between the macrocycles, which are compelled to stay in proximity, the NMR spectrum of the catenane species differs from the sum of the spectra of the individual, separated macrocycles. The fast atom bombardment (FAB) mass spectra of the catenanes show typical fragmentation patterns. For example, in the case of a [2]-catenane there is no ionized fragment between that of the mass of the parent catenane and that of the individual macrocycles, which are therefore the first observed fragments. This feature is considered a signature of catenated species. However, an x-ray crystal structure analysis, when possible, is the only technique that allows a direct view of the actual topology of the molecule, such as the molecular structure of the copper(I) [2]-catenate (**Fig. 2**).

Properties. Catenanes are new molecules as compared to the separated macrocycles. Some colligative properties, that is, macroscopic properties resulting from the fact that chemical compounds are molec-

ular assemblies, have been measured. For example, it was demonstrated that the molar volume of a [2]-catenane was slightly larger than the sum of the molar volumes of the separated macrocycles. This unexpected result could be rationalized by considering solvent effects.

In addition to their topology, catenanes may show interesting stereochemical properties; interlocking of rings can lead to novel kinds of stereoisomerism. Topologically chiral catenanes are molecules whose chirality cannot be inverted by continuous deformation, unlike geometrically chiral molecules. Topologically chiral [2]-catenanes can be made by interlocking oriented rings (**11**) or by double interlocking

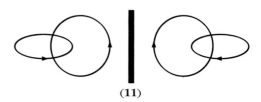

(11)

of nonoriented rings (8). They have been resolved by high-pressure liquid chromatography on optically active stationary phases. Isomerism produced by different relative orientations of nonsymmetrical rings (translational isomerism) has been described (**12–14**). Interestingly, these orientations can be

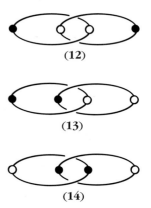

(12)

(13)

(14)

controlled by the redox state of the metal in certain metallocatenates.

Catenands, that is, coordinating catenanes, have very specific properties. As ligands, they complex first-row transition metals with high binding constants and enhanced kinetic stability, as compared to analogous open-chain chelates. This generalized macrocyclic effect has been described as the catenand effect. Most catenands synthesized and studied are tetradentate ligands that complex metals with a tetrahedral coordination sphere, like Li(I), Co(II), Cu(I), Zn(II), Ag(I), and Cd(II), but catenates of Cu(II), Ni(II), and Fe(II) have also been studied. In addition, catenands stabilize low-valent transitionmetal cations like Ni(I), and they are one of the strongest complexants of Cu(I). Catenands also show unusual acid-base properties, being stronger bases than their open-chain chelate analogues.

Applications. Applications of catenanes are a research field in its infancy, and therefore they are more or less speculative. Promising approaches include incorporation of catenane structures into polymeric species to endow the polymers with peculiar rheological properties, because of the mechanical linking; and use of catenanes as elements of molecular machines—for example, the mechanical link of catenanes could be used for making a primitive rotary motor at the molecular level. *See* ALICYCLIC HYDROCARBON; ANALYTICAL CHEMISTRY; AROMATIC HYDROCARBON; MACROCYCLIC COMPOUND; PHYSICAL ORGANIC CHEMISTRY; STEREOCHEMISTRY.   Jean-Claude Chambron;

C. O. Dietrich-Buchecker; J.-P. Sauvage

Bibliography. D. B. Amabilino and J. F. Stoddart, Interlocked and intertwined structures and superstructures, *Chem. Rev.*, 95:2725–2828, 1995; J.-C. Chambron, C. O. Dietrich-Buchecker, and J.-P. Sauvage, Transition metals as assembling and templating species: Synthesis of catenanes and molecular knots, in J.-M. Lehn (ed.), *Comprehensive Supramolecular Chemistry*, vol. 9, pp. 43–83, 1996; C. O. Dietrich-Buchecker and J.-P. Sauvage, Interlocking of molecular threads: From the statistical approach to the templated synthesis of catenands, *Chem. Rev.*, 87:795–810, 1987; M. Fujita, Self-assembled macrocycles, cages and catenanes containing transition metals in their backbone, in J.-M. Lehn (ed.), *Comprehensive Supramolecular Chemistry*, vol. 9, pp. 253–282, 1996; R. Jäger and F. Vögtle, A new synthetic strategy towards molecules with mechanical bonds: Non-ionic template synthesis of amide-linked catenanes and rotaxanes, *Angew. Chem. Int. Ed. Engl.*, 36:930–944, 1997; G. Schill, *Catenanes, Rotaxanes and Knots*, 1971.

Catenary

The curve formed by an ideal heavy uniform string hanging freely from two points of support. The lowest point A (**Fig. 1**) is the vertex. The portion AP is an equilibrium under the horizontal tension H at A, the tension F directed along the tangent at P, and the weight W of AP. If the weight of the string is w per unit length and s is the arc AP, $W = ws$; and from the force triangle, $\tan \psi = ws/H = s/c$, where $c = H/w$, is called the parameter of the catenary. Thus the catenary has the differential equation

$$dy/dx = s/c$$

The horizontal line at a distance c below the vertex A is the directrix of the catenary. With the x axis as directrix and the y axis through the vertex, the integration of the equation above yields

$$y = c \cosh \frac{x}{c} \qquad s = c \sinh \frac{x}{c}$$

for the ordinate and arc of the catenary. All catenaries are geometrically similar to the hyperbolic cosine curve, $y = \cosh x$. These equations show that $g^2 = s^2 + c^2$, and from the differential equation,

$$s = c \tan \psi \qquad y = c \sec \psi$$

The radius of curvature of the catenary at P is the

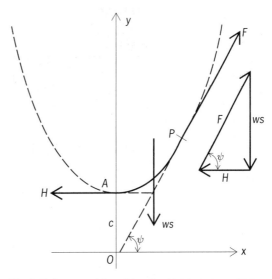

Fig. 1. Catenary and force triangle which keeps a portion of the string in equilibrium.

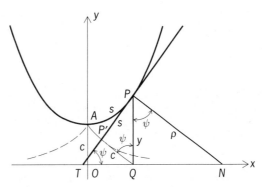

Fig. 2. Relation of catenary to the tractrix which is its involute.

length of the normal cut off by the x axis:

$$\rho = ds/d\psi = c \sec^2 \psi = y \sec \psi = PN$$

The tension at P,

$$F = H \sec \psi = wc \sec \psi = wy$$

varies as the height above the directrix.

In **Fig. 2** the tangent PT is tangent to a circle of radius c about Q, the foot of the ordinate; and since $\tan \psi = s/c$, $P'P = s =$ arc AP. Thus arc AP unwraps on the segment $P'P$. The locus of P' is a curve whose tangent $P'Q$ has the constant length c, namely a tractrix; hence the tractrix is an involute of the catenary. *See* TRACTRIX.

The surface generated by revolving a catenary about its directrix is a minimal surface, the catenoid. The catenary is an extremal for the problem of finding a curve joining two given points so that the surface generated by revolving it about a given line has minimum area. *See* HYPERBOLIC FUNCTION.

Louis Brand

Bibliography. P. A. Laurent, A. LeMehaute, and L. L. Schumaker (eds.), *Curves and Surfaces*, 1991; D. H. von Seggern (ed.), *Handbook of Mathematical Curves and Surfaces*, 2d ed. 1992.

Cathode-ray tube

An electron tube in which a beam of electrons can be focused to a small cross section and varied in position and intensity on a display surface. In common usage, the term cathode-ray tube (CRT) is usually reserved for devices in which the display surface is cathodoluminescent under electron bombardment, and the output information is presented in the form of a pattern of light. The character of this pattern is related to, and controlled by, one or more electrical signals applied to the cathode-ray tube as input information. *See* CATHODOLUMINESCENCE; ELECTRON TUBE.

The cathode-ray tube is the archetypal electronic device of the twentieth century, first serving as a valuable research tool in the early experiments in modern physics and electronics, and then during World War II in radar displays on ships, on land, and in the air. In midcentury the cathode-ray tube made possible the development of television and then later the personal computer. In the late 1990s the all-electronic cinema was demonstrated using a motion picture projector incorporating a cathode-ray tube and a liquid-crystal light valve.

Hundreds of millions of cathode-ray tubes were in service at the end of the twentieth century, and tens of thousands more were manufactured daily. These tubes were commonplace in television sets, computers, homes, hospitals, banks, airplanes, and weapons of war. Even so, the cathode-ray tube is being supplanted in many of its traditional uses by flat-panel electronic devices. This trend is expected to continue until, except for perhaps a few specialized applications, the cathode-ray tube will be primarily of historical interest.

These flat-panel devices, for example liquid-crystal, plasma, and field-emission displays, are digital in nature. Their display surfaces are structured into tiny areas, called pixels, which are individually addressed by the supporting electronics. By comparison, the cathode-ray tube is an analog device, often much bulkier and heavier, and a little out of place in what is fast becoming a digital world. *See* ELECTRONIC DISPLAY; FLAT-PANEL DISPLAY DEVICE; LIQUID CRYSTALS.

Development. The technology of the cathode-ray tube was both a product of certain late-nineteenth-century experiments which led to modern physics and an indispensable element in the conduct of such experiments. In particular, the discovery of x-rays in 1895 by William Roentgen and the discovery of the electron in 1897 by J. J. Thompson resulted from experiments in which early cathode-ray devices were involved. *See* ELECTRON; X-RAYS.

While experiments with cathode rays within partial vacuum devices had been conducted by various scientists for at least the previous 200 years, Ferdinand Braun is credited with inventing in 1897 a "cathode-ray indicator tube" from which all modern cathode-ray tubes are derived. Braun's interest in the cathode-ray tube was primarily as a device for the study of phenomena related to electricity. The cathode-ray tube was well suited to this use because of its ability to provide a visual indication of alternating electric currents at low frequencies. Oscillography was thus a natural first application for the new device. To this day, the cathode-ray oscilloscope continues to be an indispensable tool in nearly all fields of electronics.

Early experimenters in television who were attempting to develop electronic scanning realized the potential usefulness of the cathode-ray tube as a television display device. In the 1920s V. K. Zworykin developed a cathode-ray tube which was improved in ways which made it particularly suitable for the display of television images. This tube, the kinescope, first demonstrated in 1929, was the forerunner of the monochrome television picture tubes which were produced commercially in the late 1940s and the 1950s. Modifications to the kinescope, including the addition of a shadow mask, led to the commercial introduction of the color picture tube in 1953. *See* PICTURE TUBE; TELEVISION.

During the 1930s, it had become apparent that the cathode-ray tube would make an excellent display device for use with the new radar technology. Many of the early television pioneers were recruited into the effort to complete the development of radar for use in World War II. *See* RADAR.

In the 1970s the cathode-ray tube became established as a widely used device for the display of computer output information. Modifications have been made to television picture tubes, both monochrome and color, to improve characteristics which are of importance to observers of computer output information. Cathode-ray tubes specialized for this use are called data display tubes. Their use has grown rapidly because of the popularity of personal computers. *See* COMPUTER; MICROCOMPUTER.

Basic elements. In the following description of a typical cathode-ray tube, emphasis is given to those features which are common to most of the tubes now produced. Some variations in construction and function from this basic cathode-ray-tube configuration are described later in the article.

The three elements of the basic cathode-ray tube are the envelope, the electron gun, and the phosphor screen (**Fig. 1**).

Envelope. The envelope is usually made of glass, although ceramic envelopes and metal envelopes have been used. The envelope is typically funnel-shaped.

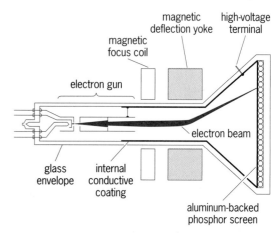

Fig. 1. Elements of a cathode-ray tube.

The small opening is terminated by the stem, a disk of glass through which pass metal leads that apply voltages to the several elements of the electron gun. A tubulation that passes through the stem is used to evacuate the air from the tube during manufacture, and is then sealed off. The electron gun is mounted within the neck portion of the envelope and is connected to the leads coming through the stem. The neck is often made sufficiently narrow to allow positioning of deflection and focusing components outside it.

The large end of the funnel is closed by a faceplate, on the inside of which the phosphor screen is deposited. The faceplate is made of high-quality clear glass in order to provide an undistorted view of the display on the phosphor screen.

Electron gun. The electron gun consists of an electrical element called a heater, a thermionic cathode, and an assemblage of cylinders, caps, and apertures which are all held in the proper orientation by devices such as glass beads, ceramic rods, and spacers.

The cathode is a source of electrons when maintained at about $1750°F$ $(1100 K)$ by thermal radiation from the heater. The heater requires from 0.5 to 5 W of input power, depending on its design. Electrons emitted by the cathode are formed into a beam, and controlled in intensity by other elements of the electron gun. Depending on the design and application of the cathode-ray tube, the current of the electron beam will have an instantaneous peak value from 0.5 to 5000 microamperes. Means are provided, either within the electron gun itself or externally, to focus the electron beam to a small cross section at its intersection with the phosphor screen and to deflect it to various locations on the screen. *See* CHARGED PARTICLE OPTICS; ELECTRON EMISSION.

A monochrome cathode-ray tube is designed to display information in a single color, usually white, although green, orange, and other colors are used. A color cathode-ray tube, such as a color picture tube, is designed to display information in a full range of colors. In most cases, monochrome cathode-ray tubes employ a single electron gun. Nearly all color picture tubes employ the shadow-mask principle and use three electron guns.

The deflection path of the electron beam on the phosphor screen depends on the intended use of the cathode-ray tube. In oscillography, a horizontal trace is swept across the phosphor screen, with vertical excursions of the beam which coincide with variations in the strength of some electrical signal. In television, a raster of closely spaced horizontal lines is scanned on the phosphor screen by the electron beam, which is intensity-modulated to produce a visible picture. Radar makes use of a variety of specialized electron-beam scanning patterns to present information to an observer. It is also a common practice to apply scan-conversion techniques to the radar signals so that they may be displayed by using a television raster scan.

In the display of computer output information, two general approaches to beam deflection are used: The raster-scan technique may be identical in format to that used for television or may utilize a greater number of scanning lines for increased definition. The random-scan technique involves computer control to direct the electron beam to locations which may be anywhere on the tube face.

Phosphor screen. The phosphor screen consists of a layer of luminescent material coated on the inner surface of the glass faceplate. Typically, the luminescent material is in the form of particles whose size is from 1 to 100 micrometers, depending upon the design and intended use of the cathode-ray tube. Monochrome cathode-ray tubes generally use a single layer of a homogeneous luminescent material. Color cathode-ray tubes typically utilize a composite screen made up of separate red-, green-, and blue-emitting luminous materials. *See* LUMINESCENCE; PHOSPHORESCENCE.

Design considerations. There are certain concerns which must be dealt with in the design of all types of cathode-ray tubes.

Safety. Foremost is the matter of safety. While cathode-ray tubes now in use generally can be considered safe, when employed as intended by their manufacturer, there are potential health hazards which must be considered in the design both of the cathode-ray tubes and of the equipment incorporating them. For example, as discussed below, it is frequently desirable to operate cathode-ray tubes at high voltages and currents, for example, tens of kilovolts and hundreds to thousands of microamperes. Consequently, there are possible hazards of electrical shock, x-radiation, and high temperatures. Designers of cathode-ray tubes and equipment using the tubes are generally quite aware of these possible hazards and are able to effectively utilize designs without undue risk to health and safety.

Vacuum maintenance. Another general concern is the absolute necessity of maintaining a high vacuum within the envelope of the cathode-ray tube so that the electron beam can travel unimpeded from the electron gun to the phosphor screen. Also, it is frequently not possible for the various electrodes within the cathode-ray tube to withstand electrical breakdown except under high vacuum. Cathode-ray tubes are exhausted by vacuum pumps for periods of up to several hours before being tipped off (permanently sealed at the exhaust tubulation). Cathode-ray tubes are typically raised to temperatures of a few hundred degrees Celsius during exhaust in order to outgas the internal parts. Internal pressure in a cathode-ray tube at tip-off is typically in the range of 10^{-4} to 10^{-8} torr (10^{-2} to 10^{-6} pascal), the desired value being determined by the design and intended use of the cathode-ray tube.

With very few exceptions, commercial cathode-ray tubes are never again vacuum-pumped after tip-off, and are expected to maintain an acceptable high level of vacuum. Leaks through the vacuum envelope are extremely rare; those problems which do arise are generally from the outgassing of internal parts. In order to assist in maintaining a high internal vacuum throughout many years of storage and use, it is now a universal practice to include within the cathode-ray tube one or more small devices called getters. Getters, through chemical action, absorb residual gas molecules within an envelope, and will continue to do so usually for several years.

Voltage control. Another general concern is the need to have several different voltages applied to structures within the cathode-ray-tube envelope. These voltages must be individually passed through the vacuum envelope, either through the stem leads or through metal buttons or pins sealed into the envelope. Frequently, an electrical cable carrying voltages as high as 50 kV will be encapsulated to a button terminal on the outside of the cathode-ray tube. Inside the cathode-ray tube, it is important that all envelope surfaces, as well as all electrode structures, be set at definite, known electric potentials. For this reason, conductive coatings which include materials such as graphite, iron oxide, stannous chloride, or evaporated aluminum are applied to nearly all interior envelope surfaces. This is one of the functions of the aluminum coating on the back of the phosphor screen. By these means, the path of the electron beam is fully established and controlled.

Performance. Two major considerations in cathode-ray-tube design are the choice of the overall operating voltage, that is, the potential difference between the cathode and the phosphor screen, and the electron-beam current to the phosphor screen. The product of the overall operating voltage (called the screen voltage) and the average value of the screen current gives the power input to the phosphor screen. For example, a cathode-ray tube operating at a screen voltage of 20 kV and screen current of 500 μA has 10 W of input power. A small fraction of this power, typically 10 to 20%, is converted into visible light by the phosphor. Less than 1% of the input power is converted into x-radiation, nearly all of which is absorbed within the glass walls of the envelope. The remainder of the input power is dissipated in the faceplate as heat. Most cathode-ray tubes operate at power levels such that this heat is allowed to radiate away or otherwise be removed by conduction and convection. Tubes which operate at very high voltages and currents, such as projection tubes, sometimes require special means, such as cooling fans, to remove heat from the faceplate.

The choice of operating screen voltage and current can have considerable effect on the design and construction of the cathode-ray-tube envelope, electron gun, and phosphor screen. It is important to consider the tradeoffs involved in making these choices. The higher the screen voltage, the greater the level of performance which can be obtained from the cathode-ray tube. The performance characteristics most directly affected by choice of screen voltage and current are screen brightness and resolution. While higher values of screen voltage will improve both brightness and resolution, higher values of screen current will improve brightness but degrade resolution performance. For any particular cathode-ray-tube design, the upper level of screen current which can be utilized is set by the allowable level of resolution degradation. On the other hand, the upper limit of screen voltage that can be utilized is set by (1) the capability of the internal tube elements, as well as the glass wall of the envelope, to withstand high potential gradients without electrical breakdown; (2) the practical problems involved in generating a very high voltage and delivering it to the cathode-ray-tube high-voltage terminal; (3) added power requirements for the deflection drive circuits; and (4) additional precautions necessary to ensure safe operation at high voltages as far as electrical and x-radiation safety are concerned.

A great deal of the design effort for any cathode-ray tube goes into obtaining the maximum attainable brightness and resolution at a selected screen voltage and current. The required brightness and resolution vary greatly, depending on the intended use of the cathode-ray tube (**Table 1**).

Envelopes. Cathode-ray-tube envelopes have been made from metal, ceramic, and glass materials. Glass is now used more than any other material, because it has the most desirable combination of mechanical, electrical, and optical properties. A variety of specialized glasses have been developed for use in cathode-ray tubes. *See* GLASS.

Electrical resistance. An important characteristic of glass for cathode-ray tubes is its electrical resistance. Early oscilloscope cathode-ray tubes, operating at voltages from 500 to 2000 V, were made by using a soda-lime-silica combination similar to that used in windows and bottles. This glass was found to be useless at higher voltages because of low electrical resistance. *See* ELECTRICAL RESISTANCE.

X-ray absorption. A second important characteristic is produced any time that electrons traveling at high speed strike a stationary target. The amount of x-radiation produced is proportional to the square of the energy of the electron and to the first power of the atomic number of the constituents of the target

TABLE 1. Characteristics of cathode-ray tubes					
Type of cathode-ray tube	Screen voltage, kV	Screen current, μA	Brightness, footlamberts (candelas/m^2)	Resolution expressed as spot size, in. (mm)	Typical application
Oscilloscope	5	100	40 (137)	0.050 (1.3)	Oscilloscope
Photorecording	15	5	3 (10)	0.001 (0.025)	Phototypesetter
Picture tube (monochrome)	20	300	100 (340)	0.015 (0.4)	Television or data display
Picture tube (color; 3 guns)	30	400	100 (340)	0.020 (0.5)	Television or data display
Projection	45	2000	10,000 (34,000)	0.004 (0.1)	Data display

material. The target material is that of the phosphor screen, the faceplate, and shadow mask, if one is present. The amount of x-radiation generated within the cathode-ray tube can be substantial at higher voltages. Manufacturers and users of cathode-ray tubes depend on the material of the envelope to absorb nearly all of this radiation. Absorption of x-radiation within the envelope depends on the thickness of the envelope and its composition, and is given by Eq. (1),

$$I = I_0 e^{-\mu t} \tag{1}$$

where I is the intensity of x-radiation at the outside surface of the cathode-ray tube; I_0 is the intensity of x-radiation at the inside surface of the cathode-ray tube; μ is the linear x-ray absorption coefficient of the particular type of glass used (usually expressed in units of 1/cm); and t is the thickness of glass (usually expressed in centimeters). *See* X-RAYS.

Optical properties. A third important characteristic for glass used in cathode-ray tubes is the optical properties of the faceplate glass. These properties vary widely, depending on the design and intended use of the cathode-ray tube. The best cathode-ray-tube faceplates have optical characteristics and quality equivalent to those of the finest photographic lenses. Cathode-ray-tube faceplates may be clear or may have intentionally reduced optical transmission in order to improve the contrast of the display. Special-purpose cathode-ray tubes have been built with fiber-optic faceplates which make possible direct-contact exposure of photosensitive film and paper.

Shapes and sizes. **Figure 2** shows a variety of cathode-ray tubes having different shapes and sizes.

Cathode-ray-tube envelopes are generally round or are rectangular with a 3 × 4 product aspect ratio, although numerous other shapes have been built. Extremes in sizes of cathode-ray tubes are exhibited by 1-in.-diameter (2.5-cm) and 36-in.-diameter (91-cm) round cathode-ray tubes.

Another parameter characterizing the shape of a cathode-ray tube envelope is its deflection angle. The deflection angle is related roughly to the angular dimension of the opening of the funnel. Cathode-ray tubes with deflection angles from 15 to 110° have been built.

Electron gun. The electron gun and its associated neck components generate the electron beam and direct it toward the phosphor screen. This assembly may conveniently be broken down into three separate systems: the electron emission system, the focusing system, and the deflection system.

Emission systems. An emission system may consist of the cathode with its associated heater, a control grid, also called grid #1, and an accelerating grid (**Fig. 3**).

The voltage applied to the accelerating grid sets up a field which penetrates the opening in the control grid and determines the magnitude of the space-charge–limited current drawn from the cathode. As the control grid is made more negative in potential, the penetration of the accelerating field and, consequently, the beam current are reduced.

The electrostatic field in the emission system of an electron gun is so shaped by the geometry of the several elements that electrons perpendicularly leaving the cathode enter trajectories which carry them across the axis of the system in the vicinity

Fig. 2. Typical cathode-ray tubes.

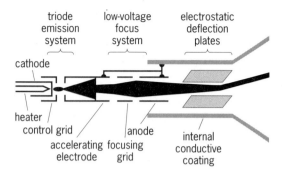

Fig. 3. Simplified electron gun with triode emission system, electrostatic focus, and electrostatic deflection.

of the control-grid–accelerator-grid space. The location at which the electrons cross the axis is called the crossover point and represents the minimum beam cross section in the vicinity of the cathode surface. Beyond this point, beam electrons enter the field-free drift space within the cylindrical electrode attached to the accelerating grid and travel along straight diverging trajectories toward the focusing system. *See* ELECTRON MOTION IN VACUUM.

A key parameter for the emission system of an electron gun is the cutoff voltage, that voltage between the control grid and the cathode which is just necessary to extinguish the flow of electrons from the cathode. Depending on a particular design, this value may lie between −15 and −150 V, the grid being at a negative voltage with respect to the cathode.

The control grid can be modulated by a video signal, or otherwise varied in voltage between cutoff and zero volts, in order to produce a desired level of beam current. The total current from the cathode (known as the Child-Langmuir current) is given by Eq. (2), where I is the actual cathode current in mi-

$$I = KV_d^3 V_c^{-3/2} \qquad (2)$$

croamperes, K is a constant whose value typically is in the range of 3 to 5, V_d is the grid drive which is equal to the difference between the actual voltage on the control grid and the cutoff voltage, and V_c is the cutoff voltage. Absolute values are used for both V_d and V_c.

Emission-system operation, as described above, in which the cathode is grounded and the control grid is modulated, is termed grid drive. Another mode of operation is cathode drive, in which grid #1 is grounded and the cathode is modulated. The formula for cathode current in the cathode-drive mode is more complicated than that given above for the grid-drive mode.

Often, a circular baffle termed a limiting aperture is introduced in the path of the electron beam. The limiting aperture intercepts the outer portions of the beam and prevents their reaching the phosphor screen, thus improving the resolution of the display. The portion of the beam intercepted may be from 0 to 98%, depending on the design and intended use of the cathode-ray tube. For this reason, the electron-beam current reaching the phosphor screen may

be a small fraction of the current emitted by the cathode.

An emission system consisting of a cathode, a control grid, and an accelerating grid is termed a triode emission system. A tetrode emission system (**Fig. 4**) has an additional electrode, called grid #2, inserted between the control grid and the accelerating grid. A primary purpose of grid #2 is to electrically isolate the emission system from the focusing system and the high-voltage portion of the envelope, so that changes in focusing or anode voltage will not affect cutoff and drive voltages. Grid #2 is typically operated within a range of 150 to 1500 V positive with respect to the cathode, depending on the design of the electron gun. Grid #2 may be adjusted in voltage to select a desired cutoff voltage. Increasing the grid #2 voltage will raise the magnitude of the cutoff voltage, and vice versa.

The element within the cathode-ray tube set at the highest voltage to which the electron beam is subjected prior to its deflection is termed the anode, or sometimes the ultor. Except in the special case of cathode-ray tubes which utilize postdeflection acceleration, the anode is the element at the highest positive direct-current voltage in the cathode-ray tube and is the element to which the aluminum backing of the phosphor screen is connected. In many cathode-ray tubes, the anode will function as the emission-system accelerating electrode.

Focusing systems. The two basic types of focusing used in cathode-ray tubes, magnetic and electrostatic, have been extensively used in many different cathode-ray-tube designs with fully acceptable performance. Electrostatic focus has the advantage of being generally less costly and easier to implement for most applications. In certain applications where resolution at high beam current is required, there is usually a performance advantage in using magnetic focus.

1. *Magnetic focusing.* In magnetic focusing systems, a short focus coil is fitted externally to the neck of the envelope of the cathode-ray tube. The coil is arranged so that magnetic flux lines flow within the neck parallel to the direction of travel of the electron beam. The focus coil is positioned toward the phosphor screen from the anode portion of the electron gun, so that focusing will take place in a region

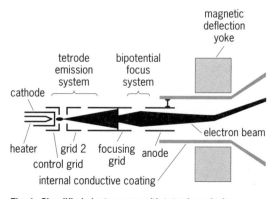

Fig. 4. Simplified electron gun with tetrode emission system, electrostatic focus, and magnetic deflection.

free from electrostatic potential gradients. Current through the focus coil is adjusted to bring the electron beam to a sharp focus on the phosphor screen. Many designs will require dynamic changes in the focus current to maintain sharp focus as the electron beam is deflected to various positions on the tube face. *See* MAGNETIC LENS.

2. *Electrostatic focusing*. In electrostatic focusing systems, an electrostatic lens is formed between two or more electrodes within the neck of the tube. Many different electrode arrangements which will give satisfactory focus are in use. Two frequently encountered arrangements are the bipotential lens (Fig. 4) and the unipotential focus lens (Fig. 3). These lenses are often used with tetrode emission systems, where the presence of grid #2 serves to prevent variations in focus voltage from altering the emission-system cutoff voltage. The bipotential lens requires an additional electrode, the focus electrode, inserted between grid #2 and the anode. The focus electrode operates at an intermediate voltage between that of grid #2 and the anode. Typically, this voltage is in the range of 20 to 40% of the anode voltage, depending on lens design, and is adjusted in value for optimum focus. In the bipotential lens, the main focusing action takes place in the region between the focus electrode and the anode.

In the unipotential lens, the anode is split into two separate cylinders and an additional electrode, the focus electrode, is inserted into the gap between them. This focus electrode operates at a potential which is only about 25% that of the anode. The unipotential lens generally will provide superior focus quality at high electron beam currents.

Some newer designs for electrostatic focusing lens involve the introduction of several focusing electrodes stacked together, each operating at a slightly different voltage. *See* ELECTRON LENS; ELECTROSTATIC LENS.

Deflection systems. Two basic types of deflection are electrostatic deflection and magnetic deflection. In principle, either types of deflection can be used for any application, although each has advantages which have led to its being favored for certain classes of use.

1. *Electrostatic deflection*. With electrostatic deflection, it is possible to very quickly deflect the beam from one location to any other location on the screen. Operation is possible over a wide frequency range. The band pass of an electrostatic deflection system is limited in a practical sense by the amount of power the equipment designer can justifiably expend in achieving adequate display brightness and size. Laboratory oscilloscopes designed around conventional cathode-ray tubes and having useful band pass to the order of 50 MHz are readily obtained.

In the electrostatic-deflection electron gun shown in Fig. 3, the deflecting system consists of a single pair of parallel electrodes mounted symmetrically about the axis of the gun. The electron beam entering and traversing the space between the electrodes does so at a constant axial velocity corresponding to the average potential of the electrodes. This potential is usually adjusted to be essentially that of the anode.

Signals to be applied to the deflecting electrodes are first passed through a paraphrase amplifier in which two components equal in voltage but opposite in polarity are generated. These two components can be applied to the opposing deflecting electrodes without affecting the average potential in the space between them. Under the influence of the applied deflection signals, an electric field is set up between the electrodes. This field imparts an acceleration to the electron beam which is perpendicular to the direction of the constant beam velocity. In the space between the electrodes, therefore, the beam travels in a parabolic path. After leaving this transverse field, the beam continues to the phosphor screen on a straight path tangent to the parabola. The assumption is made that no postdeflection acceleration is present. If the signals applied to the electrodes vary linearly with time, a straight line is traced out upon the phosphor screen. In a practical tube, a second pair of deflecting electrodes is mounted farther along the gun axis at right angles to the first. These electrodes provide a second independent axis of deflection, orthogonal to the first.

The deflection produced by a pair of parallel electrodes is given by Eq. (3), where y is the deflection

$$y = \frac{LbV_d}{2aV} \qquad (3)$$

observed at the phosphor screen in any linear units, L is the distance from the axial midpoint of the electrodes to the phosphor screen in the same linear units, b is the deflecting-electrode length in the same linear units, a is the deflecting-electrode spacing in the same linear units, V_d is the potential difference between electrodes in volts, and V is the beam acceleration potential in volts.

2. *Magnetic deflection*. Magnetic deflection systems generally require more time, perhaps tens of microseconds, to deflect the electron beam from one location on the screen to another. This is because a change in position requires a change in the value of the current through an inductive coil. Magnetic deflection systems do have an important advantage in that they can deflect the beam through a much wider deflection angle with less distortion in the shape of the cross section of the beam than is possible with electrostatic deflection. Also, with high anode voltages of 20–30 kV, the current required for magnetic deflection yokes can readily be provided; whereas the high dynamic voltages which would be required for electrostatic deflection plates, on the order of 3–4 kV peak to peak, cannot easily and economically be achieved. For these reasons, cathode-ray tubes employing magnetic deflection are widely used, particularly in television, radar, and data display.

An elementary magnetic deflection system takes the form of a pair of coils, each wound on a rectangular form, positioned externally to the cathode-ray tube with major planes parallel to beam direction on opposite sides of the neck. The magnetic field lines are thus perpendicular to the axis of the electron gun mounted therein. On entering this field, the beam electrons encounter forces which impart to them acceleration perpendicular to their velocity. If the flux density is uniform, the path followed by the electrons is circular and lies in a plane perpendicular to the lines of flux. On leaving the deflection field, the beam travels in a straight-line path tangent to the circle just described. The deflection given an electron beam which traverses a field of uniform flux density limited to the space between two planes perpendicular to the initial direction of the beam motion (that is, the tube axis) is given approximately by Eq. (4), where y is the deflection observed at the

$$y \approx \frac{LbB}{3.37\sqrt{V}} \qquad (4)$$

phosphor screen in centimeters (1 in. = 2.54 cm), L is the distance from the axial midpoint of the magnetic field to the phosphor screen in centimeters, b is the axial extent of the magnetic field in centimeters, B is the flux density in gauss (1 tesla = 10^4 gauss), and V is the beam acceleration potential in volts. By an appropriate arrangement of the windings of a magnetic-deflection coil pair, more commonly called a deflecting yoke, it is possible to obtain useful total deflection angles up to 110°.

Phosphor screen. This element converts electrical energy to visible radiation. Materials known as phosphors are said to be luminescent; that is, they are able to emit light at temperatures substantially below those which produce incandescence. A phosphor which is excited to luminescence by electron bombardment is described as cathodoluminescent. In the case of phosphors for cathode-ray tubes, luminescence invariably persists after cessation of excitation. Luminescence which continues for more than 10^{-8} s

after excitation is removed is called phosphorescence. Luminescence which is coincident in time with excitation is known as fluorescence.

A wide variety of materials display the property of cathodoluminescence. Phosphors used in commercially fabricated cathode-ray tubes are generally inorganic, nonmetallic, crystalline materials. Many phosphors now make use of materials which incorporate transition elements, such as yttrium, and the lanthanoid metals: lanthanum, cerium, europium, gadolinium, and terbium. Phosphors made from materials using these elements are known for their high luminous output, purity of color, and stability.

Some of these materials will emit radiation in the pure state. Most, however, display practical luminescence only when activated by an impurity (**Table 2**). These impurities, deliberately introduced in amounts ranging from 1 part in 100,000 to 1 part in 100, play a profound role in determining the efficiency, color, and persistence of the emission obtained from a given phosphor. **Figure 5** shows the spectral emission density curves which plot relative radiant energy versus wavelength for certain of these phosphor screens.

One of the criteria by which a phosphor material is judged is its ability to convert electrical energy to useful radiation. In many cases, cathode-ray-tube screens are intended to be viewed by human observers. It is appropriate, therefore, to speak in terms of visible flux output. The luminous efficiencies of practically all commercially significant phosphors are within the range 5–50 lumens per watt of exciting power. Light output increases with increasing bombarding-current density, eventually exhibiting evidence of saturation at current-density levels

---

TABLE 2. Characteristics of some phosphor screens used in cathode-ray tubes

WTDS* designation	Previous EIA† designation	Base material (activator)	Color of luminous emission‡	Persistence classification§	Typical application
BE	P11	Zinc sulfide (silver)	Blue	Medium short	Photorecording
BH	P47	Yttrium silicate (cerium)	Purplish blue	Very short	Flying-spot scanner
BM	P55	Zinc sulfide (silver)	Blue	Medium short	Projection, large screen
GH	P31	Zinc sulfide (copper)	Green	Medium short	Data display, oscillography
GJ	P1	Zinc orthosilicate (manganese)	Yellowish green	Medium	Projection, oscillography
GM	P7	Zinc sulfide (silver) on top of zinc cadmium sulfide (copper)	Yellowish green	Long	Radar
GY	P43	Gadolinium oxysulfide (terbium)	Yellowish green	Medium	Data display
KA	P20	Zinc cadmium sulfide (silver)	Yellow green	Medium	Storage tubes
KG	P46	Yttrium aluminate (cerium)	Yellow green	Very short	Flying-spot scanner
KH	P48	Yttrium aluminate (cerium) and yttrium silicate (cerium)	Yellow green	Very short	Flying-spot scanner
KJ	P53	Yttrium aluminum garnet (terbium)	Yellowish green	Medium	Data display
RF	P56	Yttrium oxide (europium)	Red	Medium	Projection, large screen
WB	P45	Yttrium oxysulfide (terbium)	White	Medium	Projection, large screen
WW	P4	Zinc sulfide (silver) and zinc cadmium sulfide (silver)	White	Medium short	Monochrome television, data display
		Zinc sulfide (silver)	Blue	Medium short	Color television, data display
X	P22¶	Zinc cadmium sulfide (silver)	Green	Medium short	
		Yttrium oxysulfide (europium)	Red	Medium short	

*World Wide Type Designation System. Designation administered by the Electronic Industries Association.
†Electronic Industries Association.
‡Color shown is that of phosphorescence, that is, the color after cessation of phosphor excitation.
§Persistence categories are based upon time for radiant output to drop to 10% of initial level following interruption of excitation: very long, 1 s or more; long, 100 ms to 1 s; medium, 1 ms to 100 ms; medium short, 10 μs to 1 ms; short, 1 μs to 10 μs; very short, less than 1 μs.
¶Composite structured screen used in conjunction with shadow mask for full color display. The materials shown are one example of several sets of materials used for this screen.

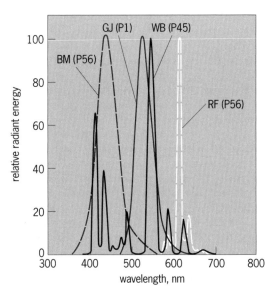

Fig. 5. Spectral emission density curves for phosphor screens.

which are characteristic of particular phosphors. For some phosphors, saturation effects are quite evident at the 10 μA/cm^2 level. Others display relatively undiminished luminous efficiencies at levels of several hundred microamperes per square centimeter.

The color of the emission from a phosphor is governed both by the base material and by the activator. The spectral-energy distributions of most phosphors are fairly broad, although colors of high saturation are readily obtained. Phosphors made from materials incorporating rare-earth and related elements are noted for having spectral-energy distributions in which the radiant energy is concentrated into very narrow emission bands at just a few wavelengths.

As is evident from Table 2, a wide range of colors is available; the tube designer is restricted in this matter only insofar as particular efficiencies and persistences must be achieved simultaneously with a given color.

A great majority of cathode-ray-tube screens now being produced are aluminized. The side of the phosphor screen facing the electron gun is coated with a thin electron-transparent film of aluminum by vacuum-deposition techniques. This process not only stabilizes the phosphor potential at the applied acceleration voltage, but also provides an increased light output because of the mirror effect of the highly reflective layer, which redirects radiation that could otherwise be lost in the interior of the envelope.

The fineness of detail in an image presented on a phosphor screen is limited to some extent by the granular nature of the screen. Both particle size and layer thickness affect performance. Phosphor screens intended for very high-resolution cathode-ray tubes employ thin layers of phosphor with particles as fine as 1 μm in size.

Varieties of tubes. A wide variety of available envelopes, electron guns, and phosphor screens have been combined in different ways to fashion cathode-ray tubes specialized to meet the needs of a host of different applications. For example, cathode-ray tubes intended for use in oscilloscopes used electrostatic deflection electron guns in order to meet the need for high-speed deflection of random waveforms. Cathode-ray tubes for World War II radar displays used a phosphor material which would persist for several seconds (GM/P7 in Table 2) in order to keep the radar image visible until the slowly rotating antenna returned to refresh the image.

When computer data processing with ample memory for image storage became readily available, such highly specialized cathode-ray-tube designs were no longer required. Instead, the basic monochrome and color cathode-ray tubes originally conceived and developed for broadcast television have now adapted for general use for the display of all types of pictorial information.

It is convenient to divide the varieties of cathode-ray tubes into three categories: direct view, projection, and photorecording.

Direct view. A large class of applications for cathode-ray tubes involves either the presentation on the cathode-ray-tube screen of an actual picture with a full black and white halftone range or with full color, such as is required for television, or the presentation of a computer-generated display which may consist of alphanumerics, graphics, or a variety of pictorial subjects. Tubes for the direct viewing of such presentations are required to have large display sizes, high brightness, high resolution, and in many cases a full halftone range and full color capability.

Cathode-ray tubes for these presentations have always employed magnetic deflection and generally electrostatic-focus electron guns operating at high voltages from 15 to 36 kV. Envelopes for television cathode-ray tubes have traditionally been rectangular, of 3 × 4 aspect ratio for standard television and 9 × 16 aspect ratio for high-definition digital television. Popular usable screen diagonals have been 10 to 36 in. (25 to 91 cm). Deflection angles have ranged from 10 to 110°.

Cathode-ray tubes for computer-generated data-display applications are very similar to television picture tubes but may use other rectangular or square display formats. The need for uniformity of resolution in the display, particularly from the center of the picture to the edge, is even more acute for tubes intended for data display than it is for tubes intended for television only. Particular attention is paid to this need in the design of cathode-ray tubes for data-display applications.

One special class of direct view applications comprises displays for use in automobiles, airplanes, boats, and military vehicles of all types. While cathode-ray tubes for such applications are similar to those described above, they tend to be smaller and brighter, and they must be quite rugged.

Projection tubes. Projection tubes are not intended to be directly viewed. The display on the phosphor screen is projected by using an optical system, such as a lens, onto large screens. Screen sizes vary widely, the largest being those in theaters and sports arenas that are equipped for projection television.

Cathode-ray tubes for projection applications are usually of the general type described above but generally are optimized for extremely high brightness and resolution capability. Projection cathode-ray tubes generally have a largest phosphor screen dimension of 3 to 8 in. (7.5 to 20 cm). This smaller size is compatible with available high-efficiency optical systems. Projection cathode-ray tubes generally operate at higher voltages than direct-view tubes. Tubes which can be operated at voltages as high as 80 kV have been built.

Projection tubes for very large projection screens, up to 32 ft (9.8 m) wide and more, are used in conjunction with liquid-crystal devices which function as image light amplifiers. The image on the projection tube is projected onto the back surface of the liquid-crystal device, and is then transferred to the front, mirrorlike surface of the device. Light from a powerful arc lamp is reflected from this front surface, projecting the image onto the projection screen. This technique allows the projection tube design to be optimized for best resolution, with a relatively low brightness requirement. Motion picture projectors using cathode-ray tubes and following this approach were used in the 1990s for the first public demonstration of all-electronic cinema.

On a different scale, projection tubes used in avionics helmet-mounted displays make use of infinity optics to project images directly onto the retina of the aviators. Such cathode-ray tubes must be very small, light, low-voltage, low-power devices.

Photorecording. Another class of cathode-ray tubes which are not intended for direct viewing by human observers comprises photorecording tubes. The applications for these tubes require that the phosphor screen display be projected by an optical system, such as a lens, onto a photosensitive medium, such as photographic film. Applications include electronic phototypesetting and the storage of computer output information on microfilm. Photorecording cathode-ray tubes are required to have extremely high resolution capability, to be extremely stable over long periods of time, and to have accurate and precise display geometry. A photorecording display may have 50 times the information content of a typical broadcast television picture. *See* PRINTING.

Photorecording tubes usually employ magnetic deflection and may utilize either magnetic or electrostatic focus. They operate at anode voltages in the range 10 to 20 kV. Many photorecording cathode-ray tubes use envelopes with 3- or 5-in. (7.5- or 12.5-cm) round faceplates of optical quality. Displays on these faceplates are projected through a lens onto the photosensitive medium. Other photorecording tubes have faceplates made from fiber-optic plates which, in use, are in direct contact with the photosensitive medium. *See* OPTICAL FIBERS.

A special cathode-ray tube which is closely related to the photorecording tube is the flying-spot scanner. The flying-spot-scanner display consists of a spot of light moving across the phosphor screen to scan a raster such as that used in television. This raster is blank and includes no video modulation other than retrace blanking. In a typical application, the raster will be projected through a lens onto a slide transparency. The light passing through the transparency is picked up by one or more photomultiplier tubes. The pictorial content of the transparency in this way is made available as a video signal, provided by the photomultiplier, which can then be displayed on a television monitor.

A special group of phosphor screens having extremely short persistence, on the order of 150 nanoseconds, has been developed for use with flying-spot scanners. These are identified in Table 2. Short persistence is necessary to avoid severe distortion of the video signal.

Competing technologies. Considering the length of time that the cathode-ray tube has been in use, and the number of uses to which it has been put, it must be considered one of the most successful electronic devices ever conceived. There are, nonetheless, certain drawbacks inherent in the use of the cathode-ray tube: (1) it must have a certain size and weight to provide a vacuum-tight enclosure and sufficient room internally for generation and deflection of the electron beam; (2) it has a long but finite lifetime, limited by degradation processes associated with the high temperatures at which the heater and cathode are operated; and (3) it is essentially an analog device which must be interfaced with other electronic devices, most of which are now exclusively digital.

Display technologies not involving the use of cathode-ray tubes have been under development for many years. The more promising make use of plasma or gas discharge, electroluminescent, and liquid-crystal devices. These devices are increasingly gaining acceptance in data display applications which previously used cathode-ray tubes.

Norman W. Patrick

Bibliography. P. A. Keller, *The Cathode-Ray Tube: Technology, History, and Applications*, 1992; S. Sherr, *Electronic Displays*, 2d ed., 1993; J. Whitaker, *Electronic Displays: Technology, Design, and Applications*, 1994.

Cathode rays

The name given to the electrons originating at the cathodes of gaseous discharge devices. The term has now been extended to include low-pressure devices such as cathode-ray tubes. Furthermore, cathode rays are now used to designate electron beams originating from thermionic cathodes, whereas the term was formerly applied only to cold-cathode devices. *See* CATHODE-RAY TUBE.

The basis for the nomenclature is purely historical. The first outward evidence was flourescence from the glass walls of cold-cathode discharge tubes. This fluorescence appeared as the pressure was reduced to the region where the mean free path became greater than the tube dimensions. At these pressures, the gas in the tube no longer emitted an appreciable amount of light. It was ascertained that the wall fluorescence had its origin in rays of particles coming from the cathode. Furthermore, it was demonstrated that these particles traveled in approximately straight lines. If an object was interposed between the cathode and the wall, the fluorescence disappeared in the optically shadowed region of the wall. In 1897 J. J. Thomson was able to show, using electric and magnetic fields, that the particles were negatively charged. In his experimental arrangement, he eliminated all but a very narrow beam of these rays. By producing an electrostatic deflection of the beam and then counteracting this with a magnetic deflection, he was able to determine the charge-mass ratio e/m. This was found to be the same as that of the electron, and resulted in the identification of these particles. *See* ELECTRON.

Thomson's measurements also form the basis for modern beta-particle spectroscopy. In this case e/m is known, so that either an electric or magnetic field may be used to determine the energy of the electrons which emanate from various radioactive materials, such as beta particles. *See* BETA PARTICLES; ELECTRICAL CONDUCTION IN GASES; ELECTRON EMISSION; PARTICLE ACCELERATOR; X-RAYS.   Glenn H. Miller

Bibliography. J. W. Rohlf, *Modern Physics from Alpha to the Z^0*, 1994; T. R. Sandin, *Essentials of Modern Physics*, 1989; J. Taylor and C. Zafaritos, *Modern Physics for Scientists and Engineers*, 1991.

Cathodoluminescence

A luminescence resulting from the bombardment of a substance with an electron (cathode-ray) beam. The principal applications of cathodoluminescence are in television, computer, radar, and oscilloscope displays. In these a thin layer of luminescent powder (phosphor) is evenly deposited on the transparent glass faceplate of a cathode-ray tube. After undergoing acceleration, focusing, and deflection by various electrodes in the tube, the electron beam originating in the cathode impinges on the phosphor. The resulting emission of light is observed through the glass faceplate, that is, from the unbombarded side of the phosphor coating. *See* CATHODE-RAY TUBE.

The luminescence of most phosphors comes from a few sites (activator centers) occupied by selected chemical impurities which have been incorporated into the matrix or host solid. The interaction of cathode rays with the phosphor involves a collective excitation of all the atoms of the host rather than a selective excitation of the luminescent centers, a condition that allows the dissipation of beam energy by competing nonluminescent processes. An appreciable energy loss occurs as soon as the primary cathode-ray beam strikes the phosphor; 25–35% of the electrons are immediately reflected (backscattered) due to coulombic repulsion. The electrons that actually penetrate the phosphor give rise to a combination of several processes that can be described only qualitatively. Some x-rays are produced, but in the main the high-energy electron beam ionizes the solid, producing a plasma of many lower-

energy (secondary) electrons. These electrons are multiply scattered, successively losing more and more energy to the solid by various nonradiative paths. Although the bombarded phosphor is in the complex excited condition described above, a small part of the excitation energy is transferred by various mechanisms to the activator centers, causing them to luminesce. Because of the complex mode of interaction of cathode rays with phosphors, the energy efficiency of light production by cathodoluminescence is lower than the best efficiencies obtainable with photoluminescence. Conversion efficiencies of currently used display phosphors are between 2 and 23%.

The brightness B of a phosphor under cathode-ray excitation depends on the accelerating voltage V and the current density j. Many phosphors exhibit a dead voltage V_0 below which they show diminished output, presumably due to radiationless dissipation of the energy by poison centers, which are present only at the surface where this low voltage excitation occurs. Above V_0, the brightness is proportional to $(V - V_0)^q$, where q is between 1 and 3. At a given voltage, the brightness initially varies linearly with the current density, and then may increase more slowly with increasing j (saturation). The blue-emitting zinc sulfide (ZnS) and green-emitting zinc-cadmium sulfide [(Zn,Cd)S] phosphors used in color television exhibit this saturation effect, as well as a color shift and shorter afterglow at high current density, but the red-emitting europium-activated phosphor and other rare earth–activated phosphors do not. Linearity at high current density is an important requirement for phosphors to be used in projection television or aircraft pilot displays.

The blue and green phosphors for television are broadband emitters with dominant wavelengths of 464 and 556 nanometers, respectively; the red europium-activated yttrium oxysulfide phosphor is a line emitter at 605 nm. Their luminous efficiencies are 7.5, 65, and 17 lumens per input watt, respectively, and all have persistences of less than 10^{-4} s to reduce the smearing of fast-moving objects in television pictures. For easy viewing of slowly scanned radar screens, on the other hand, phosphors with persistences of up to 0.55 are used.

The activators in zinc sulfide and zinc-cadmium sulfide are parts-per-million traces of donor-acceptor pairs of impurities, chlorine and silver in the former and aluminum and copper in the latter. Luminescence in these phosphors is produced when electrons trapped at donors recombine with holes trapped at acceptors. The broad emission band is a complex of emissions of slightly different wavelengths from pairs having a variety of separations in the host lattice. This mechanism can also explain phosphor saturation, shortened persistence, and color shifts in the sulfides at high current density. In the rare earth–activated phosphor, the emitting center Eu^{3+} is present at a concentration of 4 mole %. The deep-lying atomic orbits of Eu^{3+} are not appreciably affected by interaction with the other constituent atoms of the phosphor, and the red light therefore appears in a very narrow range of wavelengths. *See* HOLE STATES IN SOLIDS; SEMICONDUCTOR.

An important requirement for a good cathodoluminescent phosphor is the possession of good secondary electron emission properties; otherwise, it charges up negatively and reduces the effective potential of the bombarding beam. In most cases the secondary electron emission coefficient *R* is less than 1, and the screen must be coated with a film of aluminum to provide conductance to the power supply in order to prevent charge buildup. The film provides two additional benefits. Its action as an optical mirror nearly doubles the display brightness, and it shields the phosphor from bombardment by residual gas ions that remain or are generated in the tube (ion burn). The phosphor host crystal structure can be disrupted by ion bombardment, and to a lesser extent by prolonged electron bombardment, creating absorbing centers (discoloration), poison centers, and other lattice defects which can reduce the efficiency of the luminescence. *See* LUMINESCENCE; SECONDARY EMISSION.

Herbert N. Hersh; James H. Schulman

Cauliflower

A cool-season biennial crucifer (*Brassica oleracea* var. *botrytis*) of Mediterranean origin. Cauliflower belongs to the plant order Capparales. It is grown for its white head or curd, a tight mass of flower stalks, which terminates the main stem (see **illus.**).

Head of cauliflower. (*Burpee Seeds*)

Cauliflower is commonly cooked fresh as a vegetable; to a lesser extent, it is frozen or pickled and consumed as a relish. Cultural practices are similar to those used for cabbage; however, cauliflower is more sensitive to unfavorable environment. Strains of the variety (cultivar) Snowball are most popular; purple-headed varieties are less common. Cauliflower is slightly tolerant of acid soils and has high requirements for boron and molybdenum. A cool, moist climate favors high quality. Harvest is generally

3–4 months after planting. California and New York are important cauliflower-producing states. *See* CABBAGE; CAPPARALES.

H. John Carew

Causality

In physics, the requirement that interactions in any space-time region can influence the evolution of the system only at subsequent times; that is, past events are causes of future events, and future events can never be the causes of events in the past. Causality thus depends on time orientability, the possibility of distinguishing past from future. Not all spacetimes are orientable.

Causality and determinism. The laws of a deterministic theory (for example, classical mechanics) are such that the state of a closed system (for example, the positions and momenta of particles in the system) at one instant determines the state of that system at any future time. Deterministic causality does not necessarily imply practical predictability. It was long implicitly assumed that slight differences in initial conditions would not lead to rapid divergence of later behavior, so that predictability was a consequence of determinism. Behavior in which two particles starting at slightly different positions and velocities diverge rapidly is called chaotic. Such behavior is ubiquitous in nature, and can lead to the practical impossibility of prediction of future states despite the deterministic character of the physical laws. *See* CHAOS.

Quantum mechanics is deterministic in the sense that, given the state of a system at one instant, it is possible to calculate later states. However, the situation differs from that in classical mechanics in two fundamental respects. First, conjugate variables, for example, position x and momentum p, cannot be simultaneously determined with complete precision, the relation between their indeterminacies being $\Delta x \, \Delta p \geq \hbar$, where $\hbar$ is Planck's constant divided by 2π. Second, the state variable ψ gives only probabilities that a given eigenstate will be found after the performance of a measurement, and such probabilities are also all that is calculable about a later state ψ' by the deterministic prediction. Despite its probabilistic character, the quantum state still evolves deterministically. However, which eigenvalue (say, of position) will actually be found in a measurement is unpredictable. *See* DETERMINISM; EIGENVALUE (QUANTUM MECHANICS); NONRELATIVISTIC QUANTUM THEORY; QUANTUM MECHANICS; QUANTUM THEORY OF MEASUREMENT; UNCERTAINTY PRINCIPLE.

Causal structure of spacetimes. Nonrelativistic mechanics assumes that causal action can be propagated instantaneously, and thus that an absolute simultaneity is definable. This is not true in special relativity. While the state of a system can still be understood in terms of the positions and momenta of its particles, time order, as well as temporal and spatial length, becomes relative to the observer's frame, and there is no possible choice of simultaneous events in the universe that is the same in all reference frames. Only space-time intervals in a fused "spacetime" are invariant with respect to choice of reference frame. The theory of special relativity thus rejects the possibility of instantaneous causal action. Instead, the existence of a maximum velocity of signal transmission determines which events can causally influence others and which cannot. *See* SPACE-TIME.

The investigation of a spacetime with regard to which events can causally influence (signal) other regions and which cannot is known as the study of the causal structure of the spacetime. Thus, in the Minkowski spacetime of special relativity, an event E can causally affect another E' if and only if there is a timelike curve which joins E and E', and E' lies in the future of E. Such a curve is contained within the future light cone of E and connects E and E'. The light-cone surface is generated by null geodesics representing the velocity of light. One of the two halves of the light cone intersecting at the "present" is specified as the future, the other as the past. Paths lying within the light cone are timelike, those in the past region (or the present) being capable of influencing later events. Curves joining E with events outside the light cone are called spacelike. Their traversal requires velocities greater than that of light, and thus events which are spacelike-related cannot causally influence one another.

Closed causal curves. Different spacetimes, for example, those allowed by general relativity, are distinguished by their different causal structures. Because general relativity admits distinct spacetime metrics at adjacent points, the future directions of light cones can vary over short distances. (Light cones at adjacent points tilt with respect to one another.) Under these circumstances, it is possible for a continuous sequence of tilted cones to result in a timelike curve intersecting itself, producing a closed curve. An event on such a curve, however, both precedes and succeeds itself, and can be both its own cause and effect. Some solutions of the general relativistic field equations, for example, Gödel and Taub-Nut spacetimes, contain such closed causal curves.

However, many physicists hold that the existence of such curves is unphysical, and seek criteria to exclude them. Among the many such conditions that have been extensively discussed are the following. The causality condition excludes closed nonspacelike (that is, null or timelike) curves. Strong causality further excludes "almost closed" causal curves, wherein a nonspacelike curve returns more than once to the same infinitesimal neighborhood. Need for yet a further condition arises from the possibility that, in a quantum theory of gravity, the uncertainty principle would prevent the metric from having an exact value at every point, leading to the possibility that small variations in the metric would generate closed timelike curves. The condition of causal stability prevents such occurrences by defining a neighborhood of a point in which there are no closed timelike curves. Causal stability is the strongest condition excluding causal anomalies: violations of weaker conditions necessarily violate causal stability.

If a spacetime is causally stable, the topology of its manifold follows from the causal structure, as do the differentiable and the conformal structures. Clearly a study of the causal structure gives deep insight into the characteristics of a spacetime.

In contrast, there are also many physicists who do not consider solutions of the equations of general relativity which contain closed causal curves to be unphysical, pointing out that, in the past, possibilities treated as unphysical have frequently turned out to be physically significant. For this reason (among others), they hold that solutions with closed causal curves should be taken seriously, and should be included among, for example, the possible histories of the universe in path-integral calculations in quantum theories of gravity.

Other causality violations. Violations of conventional causality could (hypothetically) arise in ways other than through closed causal curves. For example, the possibility has been considered that tachyons, faster-than-light particles, might exist. This is tantamount to the speculation that the past (or present) could be influenced by future events through the transmission of tachyons. Existence of such particles is generally rejected on both experimental and theoretical grounds. Causality violation would also result if there were more than one dimension of time, as there are of space. Such assignments are therefore usually excluded in theories of quantum gravity. *See* QUANTUM GRAVITATION; RELATIVITY; TACHYON.

Dudley Shapere

Bibliography. R. Geroch and G. Horowitz, Global structure of spacetimes, in S. Hawking and W. Israel, *General Relativity,* 1979; S. Hawking and G. Ellis, *The Large-Scale structure of Space-Time,* 1973; P. S. Joshi, *Global Aspects in Gravitation and Cosmology,* 1993; R. Torretti, *Relativity and Geometry,* 1983; R. Wald, *General Relativity,* 1984.

Cave

A natural cavity located underground or in the side of a hill or cliff, generally of a size to admit a human. Caves occur in all types of rocks and topographic situations. They may be formed by many different erosion processes. The most important are created by ground waters that dissolve the common soluble rocks—limestone, dolomite, gypsum, and salt. Limestone caves are the most frequent, longest, and deepest. Lava-tube caves, sea caves created by wave action, and caves caused by piping in unconsolidated rocks are the other important types. The science of caves is known as speleology. *See* DOLOMITE; GYPSUM; HALITE; LIMESTONE.

Dissolution caves. The principal processes of aqueous dissolution are simple molecular dissociation for salt (NaCl, and other water-soluble salts) and gypsum ($CaSO_4 \cdot 2H_2O$), and bicarbonate solution for limestone ($CaCO_3 + H_2O + CO_2 = Ca^{2+} + 2HCO_3$) and dolomite ($CaMg \cdot 2HCO_3$). Dissociation of salt proceeds until an equilibrium concentration of 360 g/liter is achieved in standard conditions; that is, there is very rapid creation and destruction, with the consequence that salt caves survive only in arid regions and are rarely longer than 1 km (0.6 mi). Gypsum solutions equilibrate at about 2.4 g/liter, allowing enterable caves to develop in tens to hundreds of years where there is abundant water and groundwater hydraulic gradients are steep. Limestone (calcite) and dolomite solutions normally equilibrate at 0.1–0.3 g/liter; such caves require 10^3–10^6 years to be initiated and then enlarged for human entry, but then may also survive for many millions of years. *See* CALCITE; GROUND-WATER HYDROLOGY.

Limestone and dolomite dissolution is augmented or accelerated at certain locations by addition of carbon dioxide (CO_2) or hydrogen sulfide (H_2S) [oxidizing to sulfuric acid (H_2SO_4)] from deep crustal sources, and along sea coasts where mixing of fresh and salt water enhances the solubility. Microbiological processes (nanobacteria producing CO_2) may also be important. Condensation corrosion by carbonic acid (H_2CO_3) or H_2SO_4 can be significant where periodic high humidity combines with excess release of CO_2 or H_2S in some coastal or arid-zone caves.

Types. Dissolution caves have been classified by their plan morphology (see **table**). In most regions the caves are formed by meteoric water recharging through karst depressions, creating systems that are combinations of the fracture and bedding plane types. Significant karst caves from intergranular dissolution are uncommon, as are caves created by diffusion beneath porous but insoluble sandstones. Spongeworks and rudimentary networks are associated mostly with coastal mixing-zone dissolution in young (late Tertiary–Quaternary) limestones. Hypogene (ascending, deeper crustal) waters sometimes create a single-stem, treelike cave in their rise to the surface. More often they ramify into networks of fissures and rooms; the greatest known examples have invaded filled paleokarst cavities of different kinds. *See* KARST TOPOGRAPHY.

There are four principal varieties of common meteoric water caves (see **illus.**). Where densities of penetrable fissures are low or stratal dips are steep, the cave system may consist largely of a single deep (phreatic zone) loop beneath a water table that was lowered, then stabilized, by expansion of the cave (illus. *a*). Where fissure frequency is high or

Table of dissolution caves				
Type of Recharge				
via karst depressions		diffuse		hypogenic
sinkholes (limited discharge fluctuation)	sinking streams (great discharge fluctuation)	through sandstone	into porous soluble rock	dissolution by acids of deep-seated source or by cooling of thermal water
branchworks (usually several levels) and single passages	single passages and crude branchworks, usually with the following features superimposed:	most caves enlarged further by recharge from other sources	most caves formed by mixing at depth	
Fractures: angular passages	fissures, irregular networks	fissures, networks	isolated fissures and rudimentary networks	networks, single passages, fissures
Bedding partings: curvilinear passages	anastomoses, anastomotic mazes	profile: sandstone — shaft and canyon complexes, interstratal solution	spongework	ramiform caves, rare single-passage and anastomotic caves
Intergranular: rudimentary branchwork	spongework	profile: sandstone — rudimentary spongework	spongework	ramiform and spongework caves

Type of Presolutional Porosity (row grouping: Fractures, Bedding partings, Intergranular)

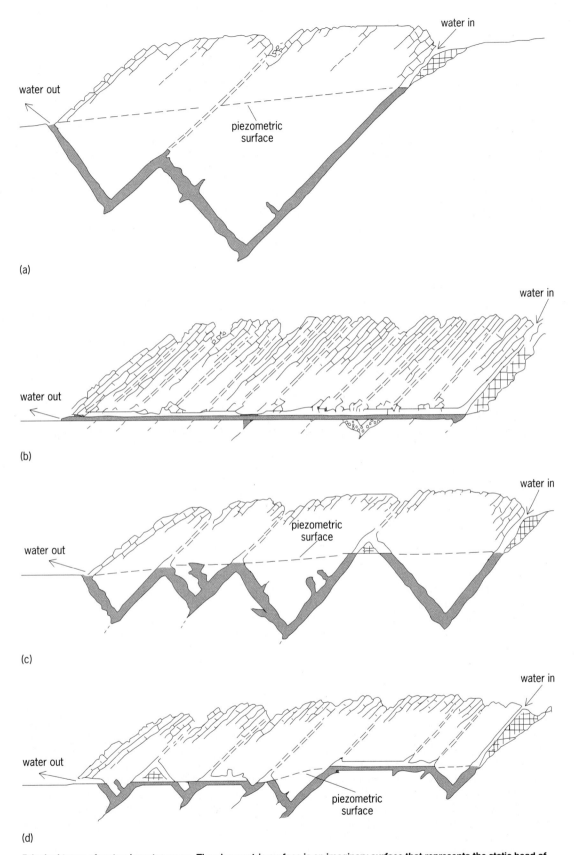

(a)

(b)

(c)

(d)

Principal types of meteoric water caves. The piezometric surface is an imaginary surface that represents the static head of ground water and is defined by the level to which the water will rise. (*a*) Bathyphreatic cave. (*b*) Ideal water-table cave. (*c*) Phreatic cave with multiple loops. (*d*) Cave with mixture of phreatic and water-table-leveled components. The letters represent the distribution (density) of major penetrable fissures in which the cave will develop. As fissure density increases, the vertical amplitude of looping in the cave diminishes. (*From D. C. Ford and P. W. Williams, Karst Geomorphology and Hydrology, Routledge, Chapman and Hall, 1989*)

there is significant intergranular porosity, or where strata are nearly flat lying, a subhorizontal, water-table passage may collect waters from higher (vadose zone) feeder galleries that were drained by the early enlargement of the cave (illus. *b*). There are two intermediate types (illus. *c*, *d*). Most of the larger cave systems that are known also display multiple phases (levels) in their development.

In the United States, Mammoth Cave National Park, Kentucky, provides excellent examples of meteoric water caves. Jewel Cave and Wind Cave, South Dakota, are superb examples of thermal water caves. Carlsbad Caverns, New Mexico, are outstanding for sulfur corrosion and magnificent speleothems.

Passages. In cross section (as they are seen by visitors), meteoric water passages display three basic shapes, alone or in combination. Phreatic passages are created below a water table, where pressure flow applies. Their ideal shape is circular (that is, minimum-friction cross section, as in a domestic pipe), but more often there is an ellipse extended along the host fissure. Vadose passages develop in the aerated zone where gravity flow prevails; shapes are varieties of entrenched canyons interspersed with fluted shafts, and there may be widening at the base to undercut the walls. In breakdown passages, parts or all of the walls or ceilings are collapsed into blocks or rubble. Breakdown is caused by loss of buoyant support upon draining, by vadose stream undercutting, by tributary waters descending through roofs, as well as other processes. Most large underground rooms are developed by progressive breakdown.

Shapes in hypogene and mixing-zone caves are phreatic, but with a greater frequency of deep, rounded dissolution alcoves (pockets) than is common in meteoric water caves. Fissure passages taper rapidly in some hydrogen sulfide caves. A swiss-cheese texture is often reported in the walls of mixing-zone caves.

Large systems. The longest known cave system is Mammoth Cave, Kentucky, a meteoric water cave in near-horizontal strata; more than 500 km (300 mi) of interconnected passages have been mapped. Phreatic tubes, vadose, and breakdown rooms are all common in this system, which has evolved through at least four phases at successively lower spring levels. Other caves exceeding 100 km (60 mi) include hypogene mazes such as Jewel Cave and Wind Cave, South Dakota, which are in limestone and dolomite, and Optimists' and Ozernaya, Ukraine, which are contained in a thin gypsum formation. Exploration in the Americas, western Europe, China, and southeastern Asia is revealing many more meteoric caves around or approaching the 100-km (60-mi) mark. Flooded (still phreatic) caves have been explored to lengths of 8 km (5 mi) in Australia, Europe, and Florida. The deepest known caves occur in high mountain areas such as the Alps, Pyrenees, Caucasus, and southern Mexico: Reseau Bernard (France) is 1590 m (5170 ft) deep, and there are at least 20 others exceeding 1000 m (3300 ft). Underwater, great springs at Mante (Mexico) and Vaucluse (France) have been explored by divers to depths of 250 m (825 ft) and 315 m (1040 ft) respectively; the latter was investigated with a remotely controlled submersible. The greatest room is in Lubang Nasib Bagus Cave, Sarawak: it measures 720 m (2400 ft), long, 400 m (1300 ft) wide, and 70 m (230 ft) high and has a volume of approximately 20,000,000 m^3 (700,000,000 ft^3). It is far larger than any space built by humans.

Cave deposits. Caves are important sediment traps, preserving evidences of past erosional, botanic, and other phases that may be obliterated aboveground. Clastic sediments include breakdown, weathering earths, water-laid gravels, sands, silts and clays, wind-borne dust, colluvium, beach deposits, and even tills injected from glaciers. Organic materials of every kind can be trapped in them. The finer-grained deposits may also contain good paleomagnetic records. *See* EROSION; PALEOMAGNETISM; WEATHERING PROCESSES.

Chemical deposits are very important. More than 100 different minerals are known to precipitate in caves. Most abundant and significant are stalactites, stalagmites, and flowstones of calcite. These may be dated with uranium series methods, thus establishing minimum ages for the host caves. They contain paleomagnetic records. Their oxygen and carbon isotope ratios and trapped organic materials may record long-term changes of climate and vegetation aboveground that can be dated with great precision. As a consequence, cave deposits are proving to be among the most valuable paleoenvironmental records preserved on the continents. *See* STALACTITES AND STALAGMITES.

All kinds of faunal remains are found in cave deposits, including human artifacts and bones. Most known sites of early *Homo sapiens, H. neanderthalensis*, and *H. erectus* are caves. Cave fauna specially adapted to the permanent darkness of underground are termed troglodytes. They include many species of fishes, insects, and crustaceans. Eyeless animals are common. *See* FOSSIL HUMANS.

Derek C. Ford

Bibliography. W. Dreybrodt, *Processes in Karst Systems: Physics, Chemistry and Geology*, 1988; D. C. Ford et al., Uranium series dating of the draining of an aquifer: The example of Wind Cave, Black Hills, S. D., *Bull. Geol. Soc. Amer.*, 105:241–250, 1993; D. C. Ford and P. W. Williams, *Karst Geomorphology and Hydrology*, 1989; C. A. Hill and P. Forti, *Cave Minerals of the World*, 2d ed., 1997; A. N. Palmer, Origin and morphology of limestone caves, *Bull. Geol. Soc. Amer.*, 103:1–21, 1991; W. B. White, *Geomorphology and Hydrology of Karst Terrains*, 1988; I. J. Winograd et al., Continuous 500,000 year climate record from vein calcite in Devils Hole, Nevada, *Science*, 258:255–260, 1992.

Cavies

Rodents comprising the family Caviidae, which includes the guinea pig, rock cavies, mountain cavies, capybara, salt-desert cavy, and mara. All members of the group are indigenous to South America and

The guinea pig (*Cavia aperea*).

comprise 15 species in six genera. Cavies have either rounded bodies with large heads and short ears and limbs, or rabbitlike bodies with long limbs and moderately long ears. They have 20 teeth with short incisors and a dental formula of I 1/1 C 0/0 Pm 1/1 M 3/3.

The guinea pig (*Cavia aperea*) originated in Peru, where there is still a wild stock. The domestic form (*C. porcellus*) [see **illus.**] has been produced by selective breeding and is a valuable laboratory animal with a life-span of 3–5 years. They are stocky animals; adults measure 8–12 in. (20–30 cm) in length and weigh less than 2 lb (0.9 kg). There are two or three litters each year with two to six young born after a gestation period of 2 months. The young cavies can see at birth and are fairly independent of the mother. These animals are docile, are easily reared in captivity, and make excellent pets.

The guinea pig has been used as an experimental animal in numerous studies. Geneticists have studied coat color and hair length and type, and have carried out numerous studies on the effects of inbreeding. Mating behavior in the guinea pig has been thoroughly studied by ethologists; in fact, it is probably the best-known insofar as mating behavior is concerned. Immunological studies using this animal are continually conducted.

A large cavy which is closely related to the guinea pig is the mara or Patagonian cavy (*Dolichotis patagonum*). It resembles a large hare, being 1 ft (0.3 m) high and having a length of 2–3 ft (0.6–0.9 m). It is a burrowing, herbivorous animal that lives in small colonies in drier areas of Argentina and Patagonia. The mara is active during the day, and is quite swift as it runs and leaps. Two litters of usually three offspring each are born in the burrows each year. The salt-desert cavy (*Pediolagus salinicola*) is a smaller species found in the salt deserts of southern Argentina.

The largest of all rodents is the capybara or carpincho (*Hydrochoerus hydrochaeris*). It grows to the size of a small pig, about 4 ft (1.2 m) long and 120 lb (54 kg). It is essentially an aquatic animal which lives in small groups along the banks of lakes and streams in tropical South America. It is a vegetarian, is easily tamed, and breeds well in captivity. The female produces one litter each year after a gestation period of 4 months with from three to eight self-sufficient young; domestication increases fertility. The life-span of the animal is about 10 years. *See* RODENTIA. Charles B. Curtin

Cavitation

The formation of vapor- or gas-filled cavities in liquids. If understood in this broad sense, cavitation includes the familiar phenomenon of bubble formation when water is brought to a boil under constant pressure and the effervescence of champagne wines and carbonated soft drinks due to the diffusion of dissolved gases. In engineering terminology, the term cavitation is used in a narrower sense, namely, to describe the formation of vapor-filled cavities in the interior or on the solid boundaries created by a localized pressure reduction produced by the dynamic action of a liquid system without change in ambient temperature. Cavitation in the engineering sense is characterized by an explosive growth and occurs at suitable combinations of low pressure and high speed in pipelines; in hydraulic machines such as turbines, pumps, and propellers; on submerged hydrofoils; behind blunt submerged bodies; and in the cores of vortical structures. This type of cavitation has great practical significance because it restricts the speed at which hydraulic machines may be operated and, when severe, lowers efficiency, produces noise and vibrations, and causes rapid erosion of the boundary surfaces, even though these surfaces consist of concrete, cast iron, bronze, or other hard and normally durable material.

Acoustic cavitation occurs whenever a liquid is subjected to sufficiently intense sound or ultrasound (that is, sound with frequencies of roughly 20 kHz to 10 MHz). When sound passes through a liquid, it consists of expansion (negative-pressure) waves and compression (positive-pressure) waves. If the intensity of the sound field is high enough, it can cause the formation, growth, and rapid recompression of vapor bubbles in the liquid. The implosive bubble collapse generates localized heating, a pressure pulse, and associated high-energy chemistry. *See* SOUND; ULTRASONICS.

Bernoulli's principle. As mentioned, cavitation occurs when the pressure in a liquid is reduced to a critical value. For the present, it will be assumed that this critical value is the vapor pressure p_v of the liquid. For clean, fresh water at 70°F (21°C), p_v has a value of about 52 lb/ft^2 (2.5 kilopascals); hence, when a liquid is moving with velocity V over a body at ordinary temperature and the pressure on the body surface is reduced to or near 52 lb/ft^2 (2.5 kPa), cavitation may be expected to occur. The condition for the onset of cavitation is therefore given by relation (1), where

$$p_m \leq p_v \tag{1}$$

p_m is the minimum pressure at any point on the surface of a moving body and p_v is the vapor pressure of the liquid at the prevailing temperature. Inversely, the condition for avoidance of cavitation is given by relation (2).

$$p_m > p_v \tag{2}$$

See VAPOR PRESSURE.

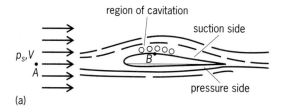

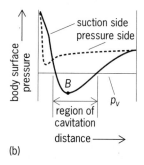

(a)

(b)

Fig. 1. Flow around a hydrofoil in a frictionless, incompressible fluid. (*a*) Cross section of flow. At point *A*, p_s = absolute static pressure, *V* = velocity of undisturbed flow. (*b*) Variation of body surface pressure along the two sides of the hydrofoil. p_v = vapor pressure of fluid.

A more practical relation than (2) is obtained when the pressure p_m is expressed in terms of easily measurable reference values. This can be done by use of Bernoulli's principle. According to this principle, the sum of pressure head and velocity head in a frictionless incompressible medium remains constant along a streamline. This may be understood by considering a hydrofoil in a stream flowing from left to right with constant velocity *V* (**Fig. 1**). Writing Bernoulli's equation for two points *A* and *B* lying on the same streamline, where the local pressure is minimum at point *B*, yields Eq. (3), where p_m = absolute local

$$p_m = p_s - \frac{\rho}{2}V^2\left[\left(\frac{v}{V}\right)^2 - 1\right] \qquad (3)$$

pressure at point *B*, *v* = velocity at point *B*, *V* = velocity of undisturbed flow at point *A*, p_s = absolute static pressure at point *A*, and ρ = density of liquid. The term in the square brackets is independent of the absolute speed *V*, because *v* changes proportionally to *V*. It follows that for a constant value of p_s the pressure p_m may be reduced to the vapor pressure p_v, to zero, or even to negative values by increasing the speed *V*. Negative values for p_m have been obtained in carefully conducted laboratory tests, proving that a pure liquid, such as clean air-free water, may sustain tension. However, in most practical cases, negative values are not obtained; instead, the flow is disrupted when cavities are formed. Combining (2) and (3), the condition for avoidance of cavitation becomes relation (4).

$$\frac{p_s - p_v}{(\rho/2)V^2} > \left[\left(\frac{v}{V}\right)^2 - 1\right] \qquad (4)$$

See BERNOULLI'S THEOREM.

Cavitation number. The term on the left of inequality (4) contains easily measurable values and is usually denoted by σ, which is called the cavitation number. The magnitude of the term on the right can be calculated for simple bodies, but for more complex configurations it cannot be calculated and must be obtained by experiment. Denoting this value by σ_c, the condition for avoidance of cavitation has the form of relation (5).

$$\sigma = \frac{p_s - p_v}{(\rho/2)V^2} > \sigma_c \qquad (5)$$

The cavitation number σ is used for flow through pipes, flow around submerged bodies, and in the design of marine propellers. In pump and hydraulic turbine work, slightly different expressions are used. The simplest one is the expression first introduced by D. Thoma which has form of relation (6), where

$$\sigma_T = \frac{H_{sv}}{H} > (\sigma_T)_c \qquad (6)$$

H_{sv} is the net positive suction head at the pump inlet, or just below the turbine runner, and *H* is the total head under which the turbine or pump operates. The value of $(\sigma_T)_c$, like the value of σ_c, is a fixed number for a given design of pump or turbine which in general must be found by experiment.

Experiments to determine σ_c and $(\sigma_T)_c$ are usually made on models geometrically similar to, but smaller than, the prototype installations. This has the advantage of less cost and more precise control of the experiments and permits correction of undesirable characteristics of a design before the prototype machine is actually constructed. For instance, should it be found in a model test that a given propeller design cavitates heavily at the design operating value, different combinations of diameter and pitch, revolutions, blade width and outline, or section shape may be tried to eliminate or alleviate the observed cavitation. The same procedure is followed in the case of pumps and turbines.

The term scale effect is given to any deviations from the elementary similarity relations linking cavitation number to geometric and kinematic conditions. The many factors producing scale effects can be divided into two types: those which affect the minimum pressure in the liquid flow, and those which cause the cavitation pressure to be different from the equilibrium vapor pressure. *See* DYNAMIC SIMILARITY.

Types. It has been found convenient to differentiate between a type of cavitation in which small bubbles suddenly appear on the solid boundary, grow in extent, and disappear, and another type in which cavities form on the boundary and remain attached as long as the conditions that led to their formation remain unaltered. The former type is known as bubble or traveling cavitation (**Fig. 2***a*) and the latter as sheet or attached cavitation (Fig. 2*b*). Tip vortex cavitation (Fig. 2*b*) occurs in the low-pressure center of a vortex formed at the tip of a lifting blade.

Physical causes. Both experiments and calculations show that with ordinary flowing water

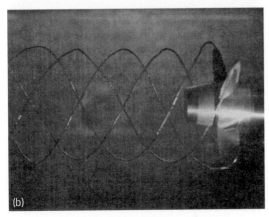

Fig. 2. Examples of cavitation on screw propellers in water tunnels. (*a*) Bubble or traveling cavitation (*U.S. Navy*). (*b*) Sheet and tip vortex cavitation (*Applied Research Laboratory, Pennsylvania State University*)

cavitation commences as the pressure approaches or reaches the vapor pressure, because of impurities in the water. These impurities, called cavitation nuclei, cause weak spots in the liquid and thus prevent it from supporting higher tensions. The various forms of cavitation nuclei are classified in two general groups, stream nuclei and surface nuclei. Stream nuclei exist in the liquid in such forms as inorganic or organic particulates or microbubbles. Surface nuclei originate at the surface of the fluid boundary by means of cracks and crevices in the boundary. Several techniques to measure stream nuclei have been standardized, and two significantly different approaches have developed. One is to measure the particulate or microbubble distribution by utilizing acoustical (wave-velocity, tone-attenuation), electrical (Coulter counter), or optical (photography, holography, laser light-scattering) techniques. The other approach measures a cavitation event rate for a liquid under various tensions (measured by a head-form venturi tube) and establishes a cavitation susceptibility.

The exact mechanism of bubble growth is generally described by mathematical relationships which depend upon the cavitation nuclei. Cavitation commences when these nuclei enter a low-pressure region where the equilibrium between the various forces acting on the nuclei surface cannot be established. As a result, bubbles appear at discrete spots in low-pressure regions, grow quickly to relatively large size, and suddenly collapse as they are swept into regions of higher pressure.

Effects. It was mentioned initially that cavitation produces noise, and, when severe, lowers the efficiency of a machine, and causes rapid erosion of boundary surfaces. The destructive effect of cavitation on solid surfaces may be explained as follows. When cavitation bubbles form in a low-pressure region, the growth is explosive, with high bubble wall velocity. The growth time interval is too short for much air or gas to come out of solution, so that the bubbles are filled primarily with vapor. On subsequent collapse in the high-pressure region, the liquid particles rush toward the center of the bubble virtually unimpeded and form a very high velocity jet. Impingement of this jet and the resulting pressure wave on a solid boundary cause very high impulsive forces. It is estimated that the surface stress caused by the impingement is of the order of 1000 atm (100 megapascals), which is sufficiently high to cause fatigue failure of the material in a relatively short time. Some investigators hold that the explosive formation of the bubbles, intercrystalline electrolytic action, and the collapse of the bubbles all are factors contributing to the observed destruction.   Michael L. Billet

Supercavitating propellers. The limitation on ship speed caused by loss of thrust when cavitation is severe has been overcome by a radical departure from conventional propeller designs. In this new design (**Fig. 3**), cavitation on the backs of the blades (forward side) is induced by special blade sections at relatively low forward speed so that, when revolutions and engine power are increased, the whole back of each blade becomes enveloped by a sheet of cavitation. When this is completed, further increase in thrust at still higher engine power and revolutions per minute is obtained by the increase in positive pressure on the blade face (rear side); erosion is avoided because the collapse of the cavitation bubbles occurs some distance behind the trailing edges of the blades. The blade sections are usually wedge-shaped with a sharp leading edge to initiate cavitation at this point, a blunt trailing edge, and a concave face. The supercavitating propeller is no replacement for the conventional propeller,

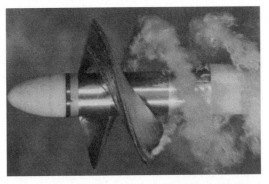

Fig. 3. Supercavitating propeller in water tunnel. (*U.S. Navy*)

being suitable only for very high ship and engine speeds.

In 1968 the supercavitating propeller was applied in two experimental hydrofoil boats: the *Denison* constructed for the U.S. Maritime Administration and another constructed for the Royal Canadian Navy. Probably it has also been used on patrol boats of various navies, but no performance data have been published. In the known installations the propellers functioned as anticipated, but some difficulties have been encountered in finding materials for these propellers strong enough to withstand the very high blade stresses. *See* PROPELLER (MARINE CRAFT).

Jacques B. Hadler

Sonochemistry. The chemical and biological effects of ultrasound were first reported by A. L. Loomis in the 1930s. With the advent of inexpensive and reliable sources of ultrasound, there has been a resurgence of interest in the chemical applications of ultrasound. Ultrasound has been found to enhance a very wide range of chemical reactions, and there has been special interest in organometallic reactions. It has been used to increase rates and yields for both stoichiometric and catalytic reactions, both in homogeneous liquids and in liquid–solid heterogeneous systems.

Since ultrasound has acoustic wavelengths of roughly 0.15–75 mm, clearly no direct coupling of the acoustic field with chemical species on a molecular level can account for sonochemistry. Instead, the chemical effects of ultrasound derive from several different physical mechanisms, depending on the nature of the system. The most important of these is cavitation. The dynamics of cavity growth and collapse are strikingly dependent on local environment, and cavitation in a homogeneous liquid should be considered separately from cavitation near a solid interface.

In homogeneous media, the generally accepted sonochemical mechanism involves pyrolysis by a localized hot spot due to the adiabatic heating which is produced by the implosive collapse of a bubble during cavitation. A measurement of the temperature generated during this implosive collapse established that the effective temperature in the gas-phase reaction zone is about 8900°F (5200 K) with pressures of hundreds of atmospheres (tens of megapascals).

When a liquid–solid interface is subjected to ultrasound, cavitation still occurs, but with major changes in the nature of the bubble collapse. No longer do cavities implode spherically. Instead, a markedly asymmetric collapse occurs, which generates a jet of liquid directed at the surface, just as in propeller-induced cavitation. The jet velocities are greater than 300 ft/s (100 m/s). The origin of this jet formation is essentially a shaped-charge effect. The impingement of this jet creates a localized erosion responsible for surface pitting and ultrasonic cleaning. Enhanced chemical reactivity of solid surfaces is associated with these processes. The cavitational erosion generates unpassivated, highly reactive surfaces; causes short-lived high temperatures and pressures at the surface; produces surface defects and deforma-

tions; creates high-velocity interparticle collisions; increases the surface area of friable solid supports; and ejects material in unknown form into solution. Finally, the local turbulent flow associated with acoustic streaming improves mass transport between the liquid phase and the surface, thus increasing observed reaction rates. In general, all of these effects are likely to occur simultaneously. *See* SEMICONDUCTOR.

Kenneth S. Suslick

Bibliography. C. E. Brennen, *Cavitation and Bubble Dynamics*, 1995; F. G. Hammitt, *Cavitation and Multiphase Flow Phenomena*, 1980; K. S. Suslick (ed.), *Ultrasound: Its Chemical, Physical and Biological Effects*, 1988; J. P. Tullis, *Hydraulics of Pipelines: Pumps, Valves, Cavitation and Transients*, 1989; F. R. Young, *Cavitation*, 2000.

Cavity resonator

An enclosure capable of resounding or resonating and thereby intensifying sound tones or electromagnetic waves. Resonance is the phenomenon which results when the frequency of the impressed driving force is the same as the natural vibration of the cavity. Vibrating rods, the tuning fork, musical instrument strings, radio and television channel tuners, and so forth, constitute resonating systems as well. The cavity resonator enclosure has a volume which stores energy oscillating between one form and another. In the case of sound, the oscillation is between displacement and velocity of particles. In the case of electromagnetic waves, the energy oscillates between the magnetic and the electric fields. *See* MUSICAL INSTRUMENTS; TUNING FORK; VIBRATION.

Sound-resonant pipes. Cavity pipes are used as resonators in musical instruments such as pipe organs and flutes to increase their sonority. The frequency of resonance is determined (to a degree of approximation) by the length of the pipe, by the velocity of sound at the ambient temperature and pressure, by the intensity of the driving force, and by the condition at the ends of the pipe: closed or open. The resulting frequency is related to multiples of quarter-wavelengths or half-wavelengths (depending on the end conditions) contained in the length of pipe. The driving force, if sufficiently strong, can force oscillations to occur at overtone frequencies which are higher multiples of the lowest or fundamental frequency, as well as at the fundamental. **Figure 1** illustrates simple cavity resonators for sound for a pipe open at one end and closed at the other. Other resonators have both ends open or both ends closed, with a small hole through which the driving force is introduced. For the case of both ends open as well as for the case of both ends closed, the resonant frequencies are those frequencies for which the pipe length is a whole number of half-wavelengths. *See* ACOUSTIC RESONATOR; SOUND.

Microwave-resonant cavities. At very high radio frequencies, losses due to radiation can be eliminated and resistive losses can be minimized by using closed resonant cavities instead of lumped-circuit

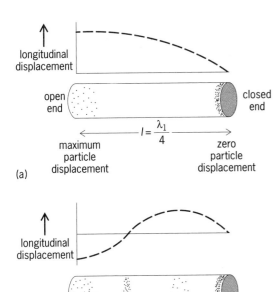

Fig. 1. Closed-end sound pipe resonating (*a*) at the fundamental frequency f_1 (the first harmonic) with wavelength λ_1, and (*b*) at an overtone, $f_3 \approx 3f_1$ (the third harmonic), with wavelength λ_3.

resonators. A cavity resonator stores both magnetic and electric fields, the energy oscillating between the two, losing energy only to the conducting walls if a perfect dielectric fills the space. The resonant frequency of the cavity is determined by the shape of the cavity and the mode, or allowable field distribution, of the electromagnetic energy that the cavity contains. Microwave transmission devices use such cavities. *See* KLYSTRON; MAGNETRON.

The usual cavities consist of closed sections of cylindrical or rectangular waveguides, or of hollow spheres or other symmetrical shapes. The choice of the shape is determined by the ease of fabrication or by the cavity's application. In the case of the cylindrical cavity resonator, the resonant frequency f_0 is computed from Eq. (1):

$$f_0 = \frac{c}{2L}\left[1 + \left(\frac{2L}{K_{nl}a}\right)^2\right]^{1/2} \quad (1)$$

where a = radius

L = cavity length

c = velocity of light

K_{nl} = lth root of $J'_n(K) = 0$ for transverse electric (TE) modes

K_{nl} = lth root of $J_n(K) = 0$ for transverse magnetic (TM) modes (J_n is the nth order Bessel function and J'_n is its derivative)

If one of the end walls of the cavity is adjustable, the cavity can act as a wavemeter; that is, the resonance frequency can change as L is adjusted. **Figure 2** illustrates how this can be done. *See* MAGNETRON; WAVELENGTH MEASUREMENT.

For the case of a rectangular cavity, the resonance frequency is determined by Eq. (2), where a, b, and

$$f_0 = \frac{c}{2}\left[\left(\frac{m}{a}\right)^2 + \left(\frac{n}{b}\right)^2 + \left(\frac{p}{d}\right)^2\right]^{1/2} \quad (2)$$

d are dimensions of the cavity and m, n, and p are integers (or zero in certain cases) as determined by the mode of the enclosed fields. *See* MICROWAVE; WAVEGUIDE.

Coupling. Coupling to cavities may be accomplished by (1) introduction of a conducting probe or antenna oriented so it coincides with the direction of the electron field; (2) introduction of a conducting loop with plane normal to the magnetic field; (3) placement of a hole or iris between the cavity and a driving waveguide, the iris being placed so that a field component in the cavity mode has a common direction with one in the waveguide or other cavity; and (4) introduction of a pulsating electron beam passing through a small gap into the cavity and in the direction of the electric field of the cavity. The first three coupling methods are illustrated in Fig. 2*b*.

Quality factor. A good measure of the quality of a typical cavity resonator is expressed by the amount of stored energy as compared with the energy lost to the imperfectly conducting walls (and if present, to the imperfect dielectric of the cavity region).

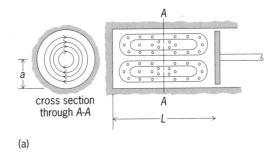

(a)

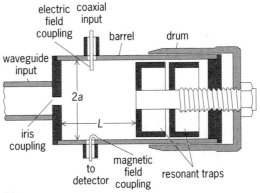

(b)

Fig. 2. Wavemeters. (*a*) Wavemeter consisting of cylindrical cavity with an adjustable end-wall, resonating in the TE_{011} mode. The free-space wavelength λ_0 corresponding to the resonant frequency f_0 is given by $\lambda_0 = 2L[1 + (2L/1.64a)]^{-1/2}$. (*b*) Practical wavemeter for the TE_{111} mode.

More precisely defined, the quality factor is represented by Eq. (3). The formula for any particular

$$Q = \frac{2\pi f_0 \times (\text{energy stored})}{\text{average power loss}}$$

$$= \frac{\pi (\text{energy stored})}{\text{energy loss per half cycle}} \quad (3)$$

cavity configuration operating in a particular mode is derived by calculating the energy stored (either in the magnetic field or in the electric field), determining the losses due to the currents flowing on the imperfect conducting walls, and substituting in Eq. (3) for Q. The formula then contains the dimensions of the cavity relevant to the mode of the field configuration and an expression for the surface resistance of the conducting walls.

If a resonant cavity which has a quality factor Q is coupled to an external load which has a factor denoted by Q_e, the combination of the two leads to a loaded quality factor Q_L, which is related to the others by Eq. (4).

$$1/Q_L = 1/Q_e + 1/Q \quad (4)$$

The Q can be measured by using two basic techniques. The first is to monitor the field intensity E as the frequency of the driving force is increased and decreased off the resonance of the cavity.

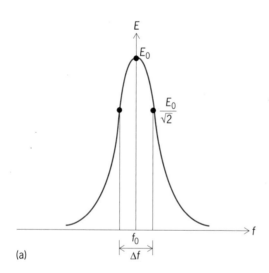

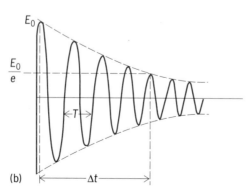

Fig. 3. Determination of the Q of a cavity resonator by (a) measuring the bandwidth and (b) measuring the damping rate of the oscillations.

Figure 3a shows the response of such a detuning. The two points representing a drop in field intensity to 0.707 or $1/\sqrt{2}$ of its peak value (half-power points) also represent the bandwidth, or Δf. Under this condition, it can be shown that Q is given by Eq. (5).

$$Q = \frac{f_0}{\Delta f} \quad (5)$$

Another approach is to make use of the damping properties which indicate the rate at which oscillations would decay if the driving source were removed. For this method the fields E decay as given in Eq. (6), where E_0 is the initial field and $e = 2.718\ldots$.

$$E = E_0 e^{-(\pi f_0/Q)t} \quad (6)$$

Consequently, if, as shown in Fig. 3b, a measure of the time taken for the field to drop to $(1/e)$th of its initial value is denoted as Δt, then Q is given by Eq. (7), and, since $1/f_0$ is the period of the oscillation T_0, then Eq. (8) is valid.

$$Q = \pi f_0 \Delta t \quad (7)$$

$$Q = \pi \Delta t / T_0 = \pi \times (\text{number of cycles in } \Delta t) \quad (8)$$

See Q (ELECTRICITY); RESONANCE (ALTERNATING-CURRENT CIRCUITS).

Optical cavity resonators. As the frequency of oscillation of the electromagnetic waves gets higher and well beyond the microwave range, the microwave cavity resonators described above become impractical. For lasers, with operation in the visible range, the infrared, or ultraviolet, the corresponding wavelengths are of the order of micrometers. The resonant cavity would have to be extremely small. If one was constructed with dimensions of millimeters, then the resonances of the possible modes of operation would be extremely close together and it would be impractical to separate them. Removing the sides of a closed cavity eliminates a large number of modes which in the absence of walls would radiate and thus be damped out. It has been shown that proper shaping and placing of the ends does support low-loss modes. Parallel plane mirrors is one system. Another consists of curved mirrors facing each other. Combinations of curved-planar mirrors, confocal mirrors, concentric mirrors, and spherical mirror configurations also constitute optical resonators. The objective in each design is to stabilize (contain) low-loss modes. *See* LASER.

The system of parallel plane reflectors has been used in interferometry and is referred to as a Fabry-Pérot resonator or etalon. *See* INTERFEROMETRY.

Optical resonators have also been made using loops of low-loss optical fibers, and in integrated optical circuits. *See* INTEGRATED OPTICS; OPTICAL FIBERS; RESONANCE (ACOUSTICS AND MECHANICS).

Diogenes J. Angelakos

Bibliography. R. E. Collin, *Foundations for Microwave Engineering*, 2d ed., 2000; J. D. Krause and K. R. Carver, *Electromagnetics*, 4th ed., 1992; M. I. Skolnik, *Radar Handbook*, 2d ed., 1990.

Cayley-Klein parameters

A set of four numbers used to specify the orientation of a body, or equivalently, the rotation R which produces that orientation, starting from some reference orientation. They can be expressed in terms of the Euler angles ψ, θ, and ϕ, as in Eqs. (1).

$$\alpha = \cos\frac{\theta}{2}e^{-i(\psi-\phi)/2} \quad \beta = -i\sin\frac{\theta}{2}e^{i(\psi-\phi)/2}$$
$$\gamma = -i\sin\frac{\theta}{2}e^{-i(\psi-\phi)/2} \quad \delta = \cos\frac{\theta}{2}e^{i(\psi-\phi)/2} \tag{1}$$

Often the set δ, $-\beta$, $-\gamma$, α is used with slightly different properties from those given here. The four complex numbers contain eight real numbers and satisfy relations in Eqs. (2), where the bar denotes

$$\delta = \overline{\alpha} \quad \gamma = -\beta$$
$$\alpha\delta - \beta\gamma = \alpha\overline{\alpha} + \beta\overline{\beta} = 1 \tag{2}$$

complex conjugate. These constitute five real conditions, leaving three independent parameters as required. *See* EULER ANGLES.

The Cayley-Klein parameters combine in a simple way under compound rotations when they are arranged in the square matrix array shown in (3).

$$\begin{pmatrix} \alpha & \beta \\ \gamma & \delta \end{pmatrix} \tag{3}$$

If α, β, γ, δ correspond to the rotation R_1 and α', β', γ', δ' to R_2, then the paramters α'', β'', γ'', δ'' of the rotation R_2R_1 (R_1 first, then R_2) are found by matrix multiplication. Thus Eq. (4) holds.

$$\begin{pmatrix} \alpha'' & \beta'' \\ \gamma'' & \delta'' \end{pmatrix} = \begin{pmatrix} \alpha' & \beta' \\ \gamma' & \delta' \end{pmatrix}\begin{pmatrix} \alpha & \beta \\ \gamma & \delta \end{pmatrix} \tag{4}$$

A rotation $R(\psi, \theta, \phi)$ can be produced by three successive rotations. The corresponding decomposition of the parameter matrix is given by Eq. (5).

$$\begin{pmatrix} \alpha & \beta \\ \gamma & \delta \end{pmatrix} =$$
$$\begin{pmatrix} e^{-i\phi/2} & 0 \\ 0 & e^{i\phi/2} \end{pmatrix}\begin{pmatrix} \cos\frac{\theta}{2} & -i\sin\frac{\theta}{2} \\ -i\sin\frac{\theta}{2} & \cos\frac{\theta}{2} \end{pmatrix}\begin{pmatrix} e^{-i\psi/2} & 0 \\ 0 & e^{i\psi/2} \end{pmatrix} \tag{5}$$

Although these parameters have been used to simplify somewhat the mathematic of spinning top motion, their main use is in quantum mechanics. There they are related to the Pauli spin matrices and represent the change in the spin state of an electron or other particle of half-integer spin under the space rotation $R(\psi, \theta, \phi)$. *See* MATRIX THEORY; SPIN (QUANTUM MECHANICS).   Bernard Goodman

Bibliography. H. Goldstein, C. P. Poole, and J. L. Safko, *Classical Mechanics*, 3d ed., 2002; L. Shepley and R. Matzner, *Classical Mechanics*, 1991.

Caytoniales

A group of Mesozoic plants first recognized in 1925. The remains consist of palmately compound leaves with 3–6 lanceolate leaflets previously known as *Sagenopteris phillipsi*, pinnately branched microsporophylls (named *Caytonanthus arberi*) that bore winged pollen in four-chambered microsporangia, and fruit-bearing inflorescences, *Caytonia* (with two species), which bore a dozen or more globular, short-stalked fruits in subopposite rows. Each fruit was 0.2 in. (5 mm) or less in diameter. Near the attachment stalk at the lower part of the fruit was a small transverse lip beneath which was a minute depression marking the place where a small opening formed at pollination time. This opening admitted the pollen into the interior, where small orthotropous ovules were attached to the surface. The inflorescence thus resembled a simply pinnate frond, of which the individual pinnules were curved so as to enclose the seeds. When first discovered, it was believed that the flap served as a stigmatic surface to receive the pollen in a manner similar to the stigma of a modern flower. Later it was found that the pollen actually entered the young fruit through the small opening and germinated on the nucellus of the ovule after the manner in gymnosperms (Pinopsida). The Caytoniales appear related to the pteridosperms. They range from the Triassic to the Cretaceous. *See* PALEOBOTANY.

   Chester A. Arnold

Cedar

Any of a large number of evergreen trees having fragrant wood of great durability. Arborvitae is sometimes called northern white cedar. *Chamaecyparis thyoides* is the botanical name of the southern white cedar, which may grow to 75 ft (22 m). It is characterized by small, spherical cones with peltate, seed-bearing scales fitted together to form a little ball, and by small scalelike evergreen leaves (**illus.** *a*). It grows only in swamps near the eastern coast of North America, where it is also known as Atlantic white cedar. The wood is soft, fragrant, and durable in the soil and is used for boxes, crates, small boats, tanks, woodenware, poles, and shingles. *See* ARBORVITAE; PINALES.

The Port Orford cedar (*C. lawsoniana*), also known as Lawson cypress, grows to 180 ft (54 m), has spherical cones larger than those of the eastern species, and is native to southwestern Oregon and northwestern California. It is the principal wood for storage battery separators, but is also used for venetian blinds and construction purposes. It is an ornamental tree which is sometimes used in shelter belts.

Alaska cedar (*C. nootkatensis*), found from Oregon to Alaska, grows to 120 ft (36 m), and has larger spherical cones which are nearly $1/2$ in. (0.6 cm) in diameter. The wood is used for interior finish, cabinetwork, small boats, and furniture. It is also grown as an ornamental tree.

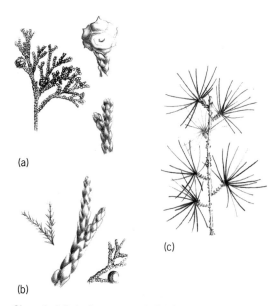

Characteristic leaf arrangements for three cedar species:
(a) **Southern white cedar (***Chamaecyparis thyoides***),**
(b) **eastern red cedar (***Juniperus virginiana***), and (c) Atlas cedar (***Cedrus atlantica***).**

Incense cedar (*Libocedrus decurrens*), a beautifully formed tree which grows to 135 ft (41 m), is found from Oregon to western Nevada and Lower California. The cones, $^3/_4$-1 in. (1.8-2.5 cm) long, resemble those of arborvitae. Incense cedar is one of the chief woods for pencils, and is also used for venetian blinds, rough construction, and fence posts and as an ornamental and shade tree.

Eastern red cedar (*Juniperus virginiana*), which may reach a height of 90 ft (27 m), is distributed over the eastern United States and adjacent Canada. Its leaves, evergreen and scalelike, occur in four rows lengthwise on the branchlets, giving a four-sided appearance (illus. *b*). On young trees or on vigorous shoots the leaves are needlelike, sometimes in threes. The fruit is spherical, berrylike, about $^1/_2$ in. (0.6 cm) in diameter, and borne on the female tree. Male trees bear only stamens. The very fragrant wood is durable in the soil and is used for fence posts, chests, wardrobes, flooring, and pencils. Cedarwood oil is used in medicine and perfumes.

Cedar of Lebanon (*Cedrus libani*) and Atlas cedar (*C. atlantica*) resemble the larch, but the leaves are evergreen and the cones are much larger and erect on the branches. The cedar of Lebanon, a native of Asia Minor, has cones 3-4 in. (7.5-10 cm) long and $1^1/_2$-$2^1/_2$ (4.3-6.8 cm) in diameter, and is sometimes cultivated in the United States. The Atlas cedar is hardier, and the variety *glauca* is popular as an ornamental (illus. *c*). See LARCH.

The deodar cedar (*Cedrus deodara*), a beautiful tree with large leaves and drooping branches, is a native of India, and although not hardy in the northern United States, it is widely cultivated in the Southeast and in California.

The cigarbox cedar (*Cedrela odorata*), also known as the West Indian cedar, belongs to the mahogany family, is a broad-leaved tree with pinnate,

deciduous leaves and is related to the *Ailanthus* and sumac. The wood is very durable and fragrant and is valued in the West Indies for the manufacture of cabinets, furniture, and canoes. It seldom grows well in the northern United States. *See* FOREST AND FORESTRY; TREE.   Arthur H. Graves; Kenneth P. Davis

Celastrales

An order of flowering plants, division Magnoliophyta (Angiospermae), in the subclass Rosidae of the class Magnoliopsida (dicotyledons). The order consists of 11 families and more than 2000 species, with the families Celastraceae (about 800 species), Aquifoliaceae (about 400 species), Icacinaceae (about 400 species), and Hippocrateaceae (about 300 species) forming the core of the group. The order is marked by its simple leaves and regular flowers, varying from hypogynous (those with the perianth and stamens attached directly to the receptacle, beneath the ovary) to perigynous (those with the perianth and stamens united at the base into a hypanthium distinct from the ovary) and with a single set of stamens which alternate with the petals. Nearly all of the species are woody

American holly (*Ilex opaca***), a characteristic member of the family Aquifoliaceae in the order Celastrales. The spiny leaves are typical of several species of holly, but not of the whole family or order. (***Photograph by Eric J. Hosking, from National Audubon Society***)**

plants. Various species of holly (*Ilex,* family Aquifoliaceae; see **illus.**) and *Euonymus* (Celastraceae) are often cultivated. *See* HOLLY; MAGNOLIOPHYTA; MAGNOLIOPSIDA; PLANT KINGDOM; ROSIDAE.
          Arthur Cronquist; T. M. Barkley

Celery

A biennial umbellifer (*Apium graveolens* var. *dulce*) of Mediterranean origin and belonging to the plant order Apiales. Celery is grown for its petioles or leafstalks, which are most commonly eaten as a salad but occasionally cooked as a vegetable (see **illus.**). Celeriac or knob celery (*A. graveolens* var. *rapaceum*) is

Celery (*Apium graveolens* var. *dulce*). (*Joseph Harris Co., Inc., Rochester, New York*)

grown for its enlarged rootlike stem and is commonly eaten as a cooked vegetable in Europe.

Propagation of celery is by seed planted in the field or sown in greenhouses or outdoor beds for the production of transplants. Field spacing varies; plants are generally grown 6–10 in. (15–25 cm) apart in 18–36-in. (0.4–0.9-m) rows. Celery requires a long growing season, cool weather, and unusually abundant soil moisture. It has a high requirement for boron; a deficiency results in "cracked stem." Exposure to prolonged cold weather (39–48°F or 4–9°C for 10–30 days) favors "bolting" or seed-stalk formation.

Varieties (cultivars) are classified primarily according to their color, green or yellow (self-blanching). The most popular green variety is Utah, of which a large number of strains are grown, such as Summer Pascal and Utah 52–70H. The acreage of yellow celery has been declining. Pink and red varieties are grown in England.

Harvesting begins generally when the plants are fully grown but before the petioles become pithy, usually 3–4 months after field planting. In periods of high prices, earlier harvesting is often practiced.

California, Florida, and Michigan are important producing states. *See* APIALES.　　　H. John Carew

Celery seedlings are often severely damaged by a variety of soil-inhabiting fungi that cause "damping-off" diseases in seedbeds. Extensive chemical fumigation treatments are commonly used to reduce seedbed losses. Some diseases caused by fungi such as *Fusarium oxysporum* f. sp. *apii* and *Septoria apii* can lead to early plant losses in the seedbed, but they usually damage plants after transplanting in the field. The crown, roots, and petioles are rotted and killed. Basal stalk rot and pink rot are other important fungal diseases in this group.

Foliar diseases caused by both fungi and bacteria reduce quality and affect the appearance of the harvested product. In most celery production areas, pesticides are routinely applied to protect the foliage from infection and damage. Common foliar diseases are caused by the fungi *Cercospora apii* and *Septoria apii*, leading to the early and late blight diseases, respectively. Bacterial leaf blight commonly damages celery foliage in seedbeds and in the field. Virus dis-

eases cause sporadic losses. Cucumber mosaic and western celery mosaic viruses are commonly encountered.

Celery exhibits several physiological disorders traceable to mineral deficiencies or imbalances. Among the most common and important disorders are blackheart, due to calcium deficiency, and cracked stem due to boron deficiency. *See* PLANT PATHOLOGY; PLANT VIRUSES AND VIROIDS.

J. O. Strandberg

Bibliography. G. N. Agrios, *Plant Pathology*, 4th ed., 1997; A. F. Sherf and A. A. MacNab, *Vegetable Diseases and Their Control*, 2d ed., 1986.

Celestial mechanics

The field of dynamics as applied to celestial bodies moving under their mutual gravitational influence in systems with few bodies. It usually describes and predicts motions in the solar system, both of natural bodies such as planets, satellites, asteroids, and comets, and of artificial bodies such as space probes. It can also be applied to small stellar systems.

Newton's laws. Isaac Newton's law of universal gravitation is the foundation of most of the field. It states that the force produced by one particle upon another is attractive along the line connecting the bodies, is proportional to the product of the masses of the bodies, and is inversely proportional to the square of the distance between the bodies. The constant of proportionality is G, the universal constant of gravitation. Newton's second law of motion then says that the acceleration experienced by a body is equal to the force on that body divided by its mass. *See* FORCE; KINETICS (CLASSICAL MECHANICS); NEWTON'S LAWS OF MOTION.

Two-body problem. The simplest and only exactly solvable problem in celestial mechanics is that of one particle moving about another. Since any body with spherical symmetry looks gravitationally like a point mass from the outside, the results from this problem may be used to describe approximately the relative motion of two finite bodies, such as a planet around the Sun or a satellite around a planet. The principal results from this problem had already been recognized empirically by Johannes Kepler and are embodied in his three laws of planetary motion. Usually the motion of the smaller body (the secondary) is described relative to the larger one (the primary). This relative motion is confined to a plane, and the path traced is a conic section such that the primary occupies one focus. If the bodies are gravitationally bound, the conic is an ellipse. The longest segment connecting opposite points on the ellipse is called the major axis, and half this length is called the semimajor axis a (see **illustration**). The departure of the ellipse from a circle is called the eccentricity e, which is usually quite small for planetary orbits. The tilt of the plane from some reference plane is called the inclination, and for the solar system that reference plane is the plane of the Earth's orbit, known as the ecliptic plane. Planetary inclinations are also usually

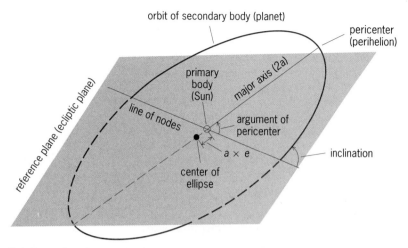

Relative motion of one body about another when the bodies are gravitationally bound. Parameters used to describe the motion are shown. (Terms used to describe the motion of a planet about the Sun are given in parentheses.) e = eccentricity.

quite small. The line of intersection of the plane of motion with the reference plane is called the line of nodes. The point on the orbit closest to the primary, which is at one end of the major axis, is called the pericenter (specifically for planetary orbits, the perihelion), and its angular distance from the node is called the argument of pericenter. The time at which the secondary passes through the pericenter is called the epoch of pericenter. A seventh parameter is the period of revolution, and the cube of the semimajor axis divided by the square of the period is proportional to the sum of the two masses. Since a planetary mass is small compared to that of the Sun, this ratio is essentially constant for the planets; this is Kepler's third law, also known as the harmonic law. *See* EL-LIPSE.

A second result applies whenever the forces are directed along the line connecting the two bodies. Angular momentum is conserved, which causes the line connecting the two bodies to sweep out equal areas in equal times, a result stated in Kepler's second law. This results in the relative velocity in the orbit being inversely proportional to the square root of the separation. Ellipses are not the only type of relative motion permitted, and the type of conic depends on the total energy in the orbit. If there is just enough energy for the bodies to escape from each other, the relative orbit is a parabola. If there is more than enough energy for escape, such that some relative velocity would still remain, the orbit is a hyperbola. A hyperbola would also describe the relative motion of two independent bodies encountering each other, as in the case of two stars within the galaxy. *See* CONIC SECTION; ESCAPE VELOCITY; ORBITAL MOTION; PLANET.

Orbit determination. One of the major operational problems of celestial mechanics is that of determining the orbit of a body in the solar system from observations of its position, or distance plus line-of-sight velocity, at various times. The objective is to determine the numerical values of the parameters characterizing the orbit, known as orbital elements. It is usually first assumed that the motion is that of a

two-body system and that the mass of the body is negligible. Thus, six elements must be determined. Each observation consists of two values at each time. Since six numbers are needed to solve for six other ones, a minimum of three observations is required. Usually there are more than three observations, which means a unique solution is not possible, but best values must be estimated in some statistical sense.

The problem is made difficult because observations are being made from the surface of the Earth, and hence parameters easily described by the two-body problem are not observed. The location of the point of observation with respect to the Sun must be accurately known, and this is often the limiting factor in orbit determination. In many cases, it is the improvement in knowledge of the orbit of the Earth that is the most useful result of a set of observations. *See* EARTH ROTATION AND ORBITAL MOTION.

Ephemeris generation. Once the orbit is known, the future locations of the object can be predicted. A table of predicted positions is called an ephemeris, and the generation of such a table is relatively straightforward. Usually, further observations are then obtained and checked for discrepancies, which in turn leads to improved values for the elements in a continually repeated cycle. *See* EPHEMERIS.

Space flight and ballistics. Another important problem is determining the proper orbit to get from one point at one time to another point at another time. This may involve getting from one body to another (space flight) or from one point to another on the same body (ballistics). For space flight, the approach is to consider several two-body problems and then patch them together. For instance, for interplanetary flight, there is an initial hyperbolic orbit with respect to one planet, an elliptic orbit with respect to the Sun for the most part, and a final hyperbolic orbit with respect to the other planet. For economy, an orbit with as little energy change as possible is desired. This dictates an elliptic heliocentric orbit that is just tangent to one planetary orbit at one extreme and just tangent to the other orbit at the other extreme. Such an orbit is known as a Hohmann transfer orbit, and it is unique for each pair of planets. The period of the orbit is known, and the tangent points are at opposite ends of the major axis. Therefore, the launch time is dictated by the relative locations of the planets. Since in practice there is a little room for adjustment, there usually is a period of time, known as the launch window, during which a launch is possible. *See* SPACE NAVIGATION AND GUIDANCE; SPACE PROBE.

The ballistic problem requires determining an Earth-centered elliptic orbit that will connect launch and target points. The actual path will be that part of the ellipse above the Earth's surface. Usually the two points are at least approximately at the same distance from the center of the Earth, but the Earth rotates. This requires a cyclic procedure of estimating travel time, allowing for the shift in target location during that time, improving the orbit, and so on. *See* BALLIS-TICS.

Binary stars. An astronomical application of the two-body problem is the relative motion of components of a binary star. It was realized in the eighteenth century that this motion obeys the same laws as the solar system, which established the case for the universality of the law of gravitation. In this application, there is the advantage of being on the outside looking in, but there is no information on separation in the line of sight. The same techniques of orbit determination can be applied in usually simplified form, but since the masses are not known, period must be treated as a seventh independent parameter. This leads to the primary astronomical interest in these objects, because if the orbit is known, the masses can be determined, and this is the only presently known way to determine directly these important stellar data. *See* BINARY STAR.

Restricted three-body problem. Only slightly increased in complexity is this problem of the motion of a massless particle moving in the gravitational field of two bodies moving around each other in two-body motion. The simplest version of this problem is called planar circular, which means the particle moves in the plane of revolution of the two bodies which are themselves in circular orbits. This can be applied to objects like a spacecraft going from the Earth to the Moon or asteroids under the influence of the Sun and Jupiter. This problem has no general solution; the analytic and numerical study of the problem is concerned with stability, periodic orbits, and topology of solutions. There are five specific solutions—the fixed points or libration points. If the massless particle is placed at any of these points with zero velocity in the coordinate system rotating with the primaries, it will remain at that point in the rotating system. Three of these points are located along the line connecting the primaries, one between them and one outside of each; these are known as the linear points. Their exact distances from the primaries depend on the ratio of the masses of the primaries.

The other two points form equilateral triangles with the primaries, one ahead and one behind as they revolve. Unlike the linear points, these triangular points can be stable, in that a slight displacement of the massless particle away from the point will not produce unbounded motion but rather an oscillation (called a libration) about the point. The requirement for this is that the primaries' mass ratio must be below about 0.04. This is indeed true for the Sun-Jupiter system, and there are asteroids, known as the Trojans, librating about both triangular points in this system. It is also true for the Earth-Moon systems but the presence of the Sun makes matters more complicated. However, it is possible to keep the particle reasonably close to one of these lagrangian or L points for extended periods of time if initial conditions are chosen properly. *See* TROJAN ASTEROIDS.

Perturbations. If there are three or more bodies, all of which have mass and therefore all of which influence each other, the problem becomes almost hopeless. The degree of complexity is essentially independent of the number of bodies, so the problem is called the n-body problem. This is usually studied by purely numerical means, but in two extreme cases some analytical progress can be made. One is when the number of bodies, n, becomes so large that statistical approaches are possible; this leads into the dynamics of star clusters and galaxies and out of the field of celestial mechanics. The other is when relative geometries or masses are such that the situation becomes a series of two-body problems with small coupling influences, or perturbations. These perturbations can be treated in some approximate way, such as series expansions or iterative solutions. *See* GALAXY, EXTERNAL; MILKY WAY GALAXY; STAR CLUSTERS.

The major efforts in these perturbation studies have been the development of general theories of motion. These are elaborate mathematical approximate solutions which almost invariably involve series expansions in some small parameter of the problem. These can be solutions for slow variations of the elements that are fixed in the two-body problem, or they can be for slow divergence from the coordinates that would result from the two-body problem, or a mixture of the two. The numerical parameters are carried as literal expressions as far as possible, but before application, actual numerical values must be estimated. This usually involves a first estimate from two-body results, then similar ephemeris generation, comparison with observations, improved estimates of the parameters, and so on.

There are two classical areas of general perturbation theory. One is the development of lunar theory, the representation of the motion of the Moon about the Earth, under the influence of rather strong perturbations from the Sun. The small parameter is the period of the Moon (a month) compared to the period of the Earth (a year), and the motion of the Earth-Moon system about the Sun is considered known. This parameter is not really very small, producing slow rates of convergence and thus expressions with thousands of terms. *See* MOON.

The other major development has been planetary theory, the description of the motion of planets (either major or minor) about the Sun, under the influence of (other) major planets. The small parameter is the mass of the perturbing planet or planets compared with the Sun, but series expansions involving powers of ratios of mutual distances are also required. These ratios can become quite large (for Neptune and Pluto, it can become unity), again producing slow convergence. Furthermore, there are many planets, which add more terms to the resulting expressions. However, the biggest complication is resonances, a situation realized when the revolution periods of two planets are related by small integers. (The most famous of these is the great inequality of Jupiter-Saturn, produced by five of Jupiter's almost-12-year periods being almost exactly the same as two of Saturn's almost-30-year periods). Fortunately, these perturbations are long-period, large-amplitude, and sensitive to the perturbing mass, making them useful for planetary mass determinations.

The use of the general theory is now giving way to that of the special or numerical theory. The full equations of motion are solved on computers in approximated numerical form to simulate the motions of the bodies and produce tables of coordinates as functions of time. Again, ephemerides must be generated and compared to observations to establish the best numerical values of the starting conditions. In addition, the extrapolatory value of these theories is more uncertain than that of analytic ones, because of the approximations inherent in the numerical solutions. *See* PERTURBATION (ASTRONOMY).

Oblateness and tides. Another set of perturbations from two-body theory arises from the finite sizes of the actual bodies. Because of rotation during the time of formation, no body is completely spherically symmetric, but rather possesses at least a small bulge around its equator. This bulge will cause slow changes in the orientation of the orbit of any object circling the oblate body. It will also cause the orbiter to pull asymmetrically on the oblate body and change its orientation in space. These slow changes in orientation are collectively referred to as precession. *See* PRECESSION OF EQUINOXES.

If a body of finite size is under the influence of another one, the parts closer to the perturber will feel a stronger pull and the parts farther away will feel a weaker pull. If the body is not infinitely rigid, this will result in a deformation known as tides. If it has a liquid or gaseous surface and is rotating, the tidal bulges will be carried at least part way around the body, but will reach a point at which the horizontal tidal forces compensate frictional drag and an equilibrium is reached. This drag will change the rotation rate of the body, at the same time releasing energy from the system, and the asymmetric bulge will perturb the orbit of the circling body to change its period and distance. The end result in one extreme is that the system will evolve until rotation and revolution rates are equal. Many planetary satellites are thus locked into synchronous rotation with their planets, and the Earth-Moon system is evolving to a time when both the day and the month will be equal to about 47 of our present days. However, solar tides will carry Earth rotation past the synchronous state, and the lunar distance will start to decrease again. Eventually the opposite extreme situation will arise, when the tidal forces on the Moon will exceed the cohesive ones and the Moon will break up. The limit on how closely a body can approach another one without breaking up is known as Roche's limit. Its exact value depends on the nature of the bodies involved, but it is usually around $2^{1}/_{2}$ times the radius of the larger body. *See* ROCHE LIMIT; SATURN; TIDE.

Unseen companions. The most complex situation is where there is a perturbation but no visible perturber. Unexplained variations can exist in observed orbits that can be due only to bodies not yet seen and therefore not yet modeled. Such was the case for Uranus after its discovery, and ultimately Neptune was discovered. Such is the case for both Uranus and Neptune, and while Pluto has been discovered, its mass is much too low to be responsible for the observed perturbations. A comparable situation can arise for a star, in which a wobble is seen in its motion across the sky, due to an unseen companion. Such detections have led to the discovery of many faint, substellar objects and may even result in the location of extrasolar planets. Since 1995, over 100 extrasolar planets have been discovered by using Doppler spectroscopy to observe variations in the radial motions of their parent stars. *See* ASTROMETRY; EXTRASOLAR PLANETS; NEPTUNE.

Post-newtonian theories. The newtonian law of universal gravitation has been remarkably successful in explaining most astronomical dynamical phenomena. However, there have been some discrepancies, the most glaring being a small unexplainable motion in the perihelion of Mercury. For a time, a planet interior to Mercury ("Vulcan") was suspected, but the problem was resolved by Einstein's theory of general relativity. Philosophically, gravitation is quite different in the two theories, but the mathematical description of motion in general relativity shows that Newton's simple relationship is "almost" correct. The errors depend on such quantities as the square of the object's velocity compared to the square of the speed of light, which make them virtually undetectable for astronomical bodies (with the exception of Mercury). These effects are, however, easily detectable in spacecraft trajectories, and thus now have to be routinely considered. Post-Einstein theories of gravitation have also been proposed, but there is no observational support for them and thus no observational need to adopt a more complex theory. *See* GRAVITATION; RELATIVITY.   Robert S. Harrington

Bibliography. R. R. Bate, D. D. Mueller, and J. E. White, *Fundamentals of Astrodynamics*, 1971; G. Beutler, *Methods of Celestial Mechanics*, 2 vols., 2005; J. M. Danby, *Fundamentals of Celestial Mechanics*, 2d ed., 1988; V. Szebehely and H. Mark, *Adventures in Celestial Mechanics*, 2d ed., 1998; M. Valtonen and H. Karttunen, *The Three-Body Problem*, 2006.

Celestial navigation

Navigation with the aid of celestial bodies, primarily for determination of position when landmarks are not available. In celestial navigation, position is not determined relative to the objects observed, as in navigation by piloting, but in relation to the points on the Earth having certain celestial bodies directly overhead.

Celestial bodies are also used for determination of horizontal direction on the Earth, and for regulating time, which is of primary importance in celestial navigation because of the changing positions of celestial bodies in the sky as the Earth rotates daily on its axis.

The navigator is concerned less with the actual motions of celestial bodies than with their apparent motions as viewed from the Earth. The heavens are pictured as a hollow celestial sphere of infinite radius, with the Earth as its center and the various celestial bodies on its inner surface. The navigator visualizes this sphere as rotating on its axis once in about 23 h 56 min—one sidereal day. The stars are then back where they were when the period started.

Bodies closer to the Earth appear to change position at a different rate than do those at a distance. The Sun appears to make a complete revolution among the stars once a year, as the Earth makes one revolution in its orbit. The apparent motion is along a great circle called the ecliptic, which is inclined nearly 23.5° to the plane of the Equator of the Earth. All of the planets stay within 8° of the ecliptic, in a band called the zodiac. Within this band they appear to move among the stars. The Moon, too, stays within the zodiac as it revolves around the Earth—or more properly as the Earth and Moon revolve around their common center of mass—once each lunar month. *See* EARTH ROTATION AND ORBITAL MOTION.

Body selection and identification. The navigator uses a limited number of celestial bodies—the Sun, Moon, 4 planets, and perhaps 20–30 stars. Although 173 stars are listed in the *Nautical Almanac*, and 57 of these are listed in the *Air Almanac* and on the daily pages of the *Nautical Almanac*, the majority of them are normally not used unless the navigator's favorite ones are unavailable. Some of the navigational stars are not seen at the latitudes traveled by many navigators. *See* ALMANAC.

With relatively few bodies in use and little change in star positions from one evening to the next, identification is seldom a problem. A tentative selection is often made in advance by means of some form of star finder. When set for the latitude of the observer and the time and date of observation, this device provides a graphical indication of the approximate altitude and azimuth of each star shown. The relative positions of other bodies can be plotted by the user. Star finders, tables, and star charts may be used to identify bodies observed before identification.

Celestial equator coordinate system. Several systems of coordinates are available to identify points on the celestial sphere. The celestial equator system of coordinates is an extension of the equatorial system commonly used on the Earth. The intersection of the plane of the terrestrial Equator, extended, with the celestial sphere is a great circle called the celestial equator. The Earth's axis, extended, intersects the celestial sphere at the north and south celestial poles. Small circles parallel to the celestial equator, similar to parallels of latitude on the Earth, are called parallels of declination. Each of these connects points of equal declination, the celestial coordinate similar to latitude on the Earth.

Great circles through the celestial poles, similar to meridians on the Earth, are called celestial meridians if they are considered to remain fixed in relation to terrestrial meridians, and hour circles if considered to remain fixed on the rotating celestial sphere.

Several different quantities on the celestial sphere are analogous to those of longitude on the Earth. Greenwich hour angle is measured westward from the Greenwich celestial meridian, through 360°. Local hour angle is similarly measured from the celestial meridian of the observer. Meridian angle is measured eastward and westward from the local

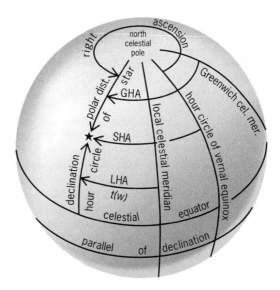

Fig. 1. Celestial equator system of coordinates. GHA is Greenwich hour angle, SHA is sidereal hour angle, LHA is local hour angle, and *t* is meridian angle (shown here as westerly).

meridian, through 180°. Sidereal hour angle is measured westward from the hour circle of the veneral equinox, the point at which the Sun crosses the celestial equator on its northward travel in spring, through 360°. Right ascension is measured eastward from the hour circle of the vernal equinox, usually in hours, minutes, and seconds, from 0 through 24 h. The various relationships of the celestial equator system are shown in **Fig. 1**.

With the exception of right ascension, all of these quantities are customarily stated to a precision of one minute of arc by the air navigator, and to one-tenth of a minute of arc by the marine navigator. The celestial equator system is used in the almanacs for indicating positions of celestial bodies at various times. *See* ASTRONOMICAL COORDINATE SYSTEMS.

Horizon system of coordinates. The navigator also uses the horizon system of coordinates, which is similar to the celestial equator system. The primary great circle is the horizon of the observer. The pole vertically overhead is the zenith, and the opposite pole is the nadir. Small circles parallel to the horizon are called parallels of altitude, each connecting all points having the same altitude. Angular distance downward from the zenith is called zenith distance. Great circles through the zenith and nadir are vertical circles. The prime vertical circle passes through the east and west points of the horizon. Azimuth is measured clockwise around the horizon, from 000° (it is generally expressed in three figures) at the north point, to 360°. Azimuth angle is measured eastward and westward to 180°, starting from north in the Northern Hemisphere, and from south in the Southern Hemisphere. Thus, it starts directly below the elevated pole, the celestial pole above the horizon. The relationships of the horizon system are shown in **Fig. 2**. The navigator uses the horizon system because it offers the most practical references for the origin of his or her measurements.

Fig. 2. Horizon system of coordinates.

Altitude and zenith distance are customarily stated by the air navigator to a precision of one minute of arc, and azimuth and azimuth angle to a precision of one degree; the marine navigator states them to one-tenth of a minute and one-tenth of a degree, respectively.

Two similar systems based upon the ecliptic and the galactic equator are used by astronomers, but not by navigators.

Position determination. Position determination in celestial navigation is primarily a matter of converting one set of coordinates to the other. This is done by solution of a spherical triangle called the navigational triangle.

The concept of the spherical navigational triangle is graphically shown in **Fig. 3**, a diagram on the plane of the celestial meridian. The celestial meridian passes through the zenith of the observer, and is therefore a vertical circle of the horizon system. Elements of both systems are shown in Fig. 3, indicating that an approximate solution can be made graphically.

The vertices of the navigational triangle are the elevated pole (P_n), the zenith (Z), and the celestial body (M). The angles at the vertices are, respectively, the meridian angle (t), the azimuth angle (Z), and the parallactic angle (X). The sides of the triangle are the codeclination of the zenith or the colatitude (colat) of the observer, the coaltitude or zenith distance (z) of the body, and the codeclination or polar distance (p) of the body.

A navigational triangle is solved, usually by computation, and compared with an observed altitude to obtain a line of position by a procedure known as sight reduction.

Observed altitude. To establish a celestial line of position, the navigator observes the altitude of a celestial body, noting the time of observation. Observation is made by a sextant, so named because early instruments had an arc of one-sixth of a circle. By means of the double reflecting principle, the altitude of the body is double the amount of arc used. Similar instru-

ments were called octants, quintants, and quadrants, depending upon the length of the arc. Today, all such instruments, regardless of length of the arc, are generally called sextants.

The marine sextant uses the visible horizon as the horizontal reference. An air sextant has an artificial, built-in horizontal reference based upon a bubble or occasionally a pendulum or gyroscope. The sextant altitude, however measured, is subject to certain errors, for which corrections are applied. *See* SEXTANT.

When a marine sextant is used, observations can be made only when both the horizon and one or more celestial bodies are visible. This requirement generally eliminates the period between the end of evening twilight and the beginning of morning twilight. The navigational stars and planets are therefore usually observable only during twilight. Air navigation is not subject to this limitation, star and planet observations being available all night.

In selecting bodies for observation, the navigator considers difference in azimuth, magnitude (brightness of the body), altitude (avoiding both extremes), and sometimes other factors. If speed is of particular concern, the navigator selects a body nearly ahead or astern to provide a speed line. A body near the ship's beam provides a course line. One north or south provides a latitude line, while one east or west provides a longitude line. One perpendicular to a shoreline provides an indication of distance offshore.

Many navigators prefer to observe three bodies differing in azimuth by about 120°, or four bodies differing by 90°, and preferably at about the same altitude. In this way any constant error in the altitudes is eliminated.

Sight reduction. The process of deriving from an observation the information needed for establishing a line of position is called sight reduction. A great variety of methods have been devised. That now in general use is called the Marcq St.-Hilaire method,

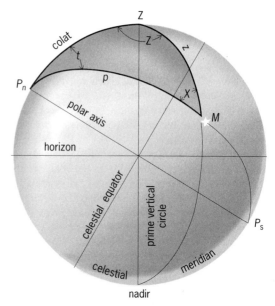

Fig. 3. Navigational triangle.

after the French naval officer who proposed it in 1875, and is described as follows.

Having obtained the body's corrected sextant altitude, called the observed altitude, the navigator uses the almanac to obtain the Greenwich hour angle and declination of the body. The navigator converts the former to local hour angle or meridian angle for an assumed position in the vicinity of actual position. With these two quantities and the latitude of the assumed position, the navigator solves the navigational triangle for altitude and azimuth.

Each altitude of a given celestial body at any one instant defines a circle having the geographical position of the body (the point on the Earth at which the body is momentarily vertically overhead) as the center, and the zenith distance as the radius. The difference between the computed altitude for the assumed position and the observed altitude at the actual position of the observer, called the altitude difference or altitude intercept, is the difference in radii of the circles of equal altitude through the two positions.

This difference is measured along an azimuth line through the assumed position, each minute of altitude difference being considered one nautical mile. A perpendicular through the point so located is considered a part of the circle of equal altitude through the position of the observer. This is the line of position sought. The intersection of two or more nonparallel lines of position adjusted to a common time defines a fix (or running fix if the elapsed time between observations is more than a few minutes) locating the position of the observer at the time of observation. Although two lines of position are sufficient for a fix, most navigators prefer to observe three or more to provide a check and to decrease somewhat the probable error of the fix.

Sometimes, however, the navigational triangle is solved in reverse, starting with altitude, assumed latitude, and declination, and solving for meridian angle. This is then compared with Greenwich hour angle at the time of observation to determine the longitude at which the line of position crosses the assumed latitude. An American, Capt. Charles H. Sumner, used this method in his discovery in 1837 of the celestial line of position. Others used one point, found by this so-called time sight method, and the azimuth of the celestial body to establish a line of position.

Special short-cut methods have been used for a body observed on or near the celestial meridian and for Polaris. Since simple methods of sight reduction have become widely used, the popularity of such special methods has decreased.

A large number of methods have been devised for solution of the navigational triangle. The most widely accepted have been mathematical, but a great many graphical and mechanical solutions have been proposed. Many of these methods are discussed in U.S. Defense Mapping Agency Hydrographic Topographic Center Publication 9, *American Practical Navigator*, originally by N. Bowditch. Most American navigators and many of other nationalities now use one of two methods, both published by

the U.S. Defense Mapping Agency Hydrographic Topographic Center. Publication 229, *Sight Reduction Tables for Marine and Air Navigation*, is intended for use with the *Nautical Almanac* for marine navigation and with the *Air Almanac* for air navigation. Editions of both of these sets of tables are also published in certain other countries.

With the emergence of electronic computers and hand-held calculators, sight reduction has been performed increasingly with limited use or elimination of tables. The extent to which a computer replaces tables depends upon the capability of the available computer and the preference of the navigator. The principal use of a nonprogrammable hand-held calculator is to perform simple arithmetical calculations such as addition, subtraction, and interpolation, with respect to both the almanac and slight reduction tables. If a programmable calculator with stored programs is available, the complete sight reduction process can be performed without the aid of tables, and if suitable data are available, even the ephemerides of celestial bodies can be computed, eliminating the need for an almanac in the usual form. An *Almanac for Computers*, providing the essential data, is published by the U.S. Naval Observatory. In the most sophisticated systems, a central computer combines sight reduction data with outputs of electronic positioning systems, perhaps including those associated with navigational satellites, and dead-reckoning data to provide continuous readout of the current most probable position. *See* CALCULATORS.

Time relationships. Time is repeatedly mentioned as an important element of a celestial observation because the Earth rotates at the approximate rate of 1 minute of arc each 4 s of time. An error of 1 s in the timing of an observation might introduce an error in the line of position of as much as one-quarter of a mile. Time directly affects longitude determination, but not latitude. The long search for a method of ascertaining longitude at sea was finally solved two centuries ago by the invention of the marine chronometer, a timepiece with a nearly steady rate.

Several different kinds of time are used by the navigator. A timepiece, which keeps watch time, usually has a small watch error. When this is applied to watch time, the result is usually zone time. This is familiar to most people as standard time (such as Pacific Standard Time) or, when clocks are set an hour ahead, as daylight saving time (such as Central Daylight Saving Time). At sea the zones may be set by each vessel or aircraft, but they are generally 15° wide, centered on the meridians exactly divisible by 15°.

When zone time is increased or decreased by 1 h per 15° longitude (the amount of the zone description, for example, +7 for Mountain Standard Time), Greenwich mean time is obtained. This is the time used in the almanacs.

Local mean time differs from zone time by the difference in longitude between the meridian of the observer and the zone meridian, at the rate of 4 min of time for each degree of longitude, the meridian to the eastward having the later time. Local mean time is used in tables indicating time of sunrise, sunset, moonrise, moonset, and beginning and ending of twilight.

All forms of mean time are based upon apparent motions of a fictitious mean sun which provides an essentially uniform time. Apparent time, based upon the apparent (visible) Sun, may differ from mean time by a maximum of nearly $16\frac{1}{2}$ min. Apparent time, plus or minus 12 h, indicates the actual position of the Sun with respect to the celestial meridian. At local apparent noon the Sun is on the celestial meridian, and the local apparent time is 1200. (Navigators customarily state time in four digits without punctuation, from 0000 at the start of a day to 2400 at the end of a day.)

Sidereal time, based upon motion of the stars, is used (indirectly in many cases) with a star finder or a star chart.

The custom of setting navigational timepieces to Greenwich mean time is growing, particularly among air navigators. This time is used almost invariably in polar regions.

Time signals are broadcast from a number of stations throughout the world to permit checking of standard timepieces. Marine chronometers are not reset by the user, an accurate record being kept of chronometer time, chronometer error, and chronometer rate. *See* TIME.

Day's work. A typical day's work of a marine navigator at sea, when using celestial navigation, is as follows:

1. Plot of dead reckoning.

2. Morning twilight observations for a fix.

3. Report of 0800 position to the commanding officer.

4. Morning sun line and compass check.

5. Winding of chronometers and determination of error and rate.

6. Noon sun line, advance of morning sun line for running fix, and report of 1200 position to the commanding officer.

7. Afternoon sun line and compass check.

8. Determination of time of sunset and preparation of a list of bodies available for observation during evening twilight.

9. Evening twilight observations for a fix.

10. Report of 2000 position to the commanding officer.

11. Determination of time of beginning of morning twilight, time of sunrise, and preparation of a list of bodies available for observation during morning twilight.

12. Time of moonrise and moonset.

Electronic applications, however, have gradually changed the pattern of celestial navigation in at least three important respects: (1) by providing noncelestial position information at sea, (2) by providing devices for automatic observation and sight reduction, and (3) by extending use of celestial navigation to all weather conditions at all times of day or night, by the use of electronic star trackers and of radio astronomy. *See* DEAD RECKONING; NAVIGA-

TION; PILOTING; POLAR NAVIGATION; RADIO ASTRONOMY. Alton B Moody

Bibliography. T. J. Cutler, *Dutton's Nautical Navigation*, 15th ed., 2003; W. B. Paulk, *Basic and Intermediate Celestial Navigation*, 1989; H. Schlereth, *Progressive Celestial Navigation*, 1996; U.S. Defense Mapping Agency Hydrographic Topographic Center, *American Practical Navigator* (2 vols., Publ. 9), *Sight Reduction Tables for Marine and Air Navigation* (6 vols., Publ. 229), published periodically; U.S. Naval Observatory, *Air Almanac*, *Almanac for Computers*, and *Nautical Almanac*.

Celestial reference system

A system for specifying coordinates for locating celestial objects. The International Celestial Reference System (ICRS) was adopted by the International Astronomical Union in 1994 as the new fundamental reference system. The ICRS is defined from a Barycentric Celestial Reference System, where "barycentric" means that the system is based on the center of mass of the solar system bodies, and a Geocentric Celestial Reference System, where "geocentric" means that the system is based on the center of the Earth. The systems are established based on specified gravitational potentials for the two origins. Their orientations are the same, and a standard set of equations, known as the Lorentz transformation, can be used to change from one to the other. Though the fiducial point (orientation of the x axis) of the new reference system is arbitrary, it has been chosen to agree with the dynamical equinox of the preexisting system of moving (dynamical) solar system objects adopted for the beginning of the year 2000, known as J2000.0, as closely as its accuracy allows. *See* LORENTZ TRANSFORMATIONS.

International Celestial Reference Frame. The International Celestial Reference System is realized by the International Celestial Reference Frame (ICRF), which is determined from the positions of approximately 400 extragalactic radio sources observed with very long baseline interferometry (VLBI). These sources are very distant, so they do not have any apparent proper motions (motions across the sky), but they can have structure that changes with time, so their individual positions have some very small uncertainty. The resulting reference frame is accurate to about 0.2 milliarcsecond or 10^{-9} radian. The International Celestial Reference Frame is a fixed, epochless frame, not changing as the epoch (such as 2000.0) changes. It replaces the historical use of fundamental star catalogs, such as the FK4 and FK5, which were based on optical observations of nearby bright stars. The standard frames, the transformations between them, and all the constants and motions involved are part of the International Celestial Reference System. The time scales, which are specified for the reference frames and origins involved, are also a part of the system. These standard values are subject to ongoing improvements based on an increasing number of highly accurate observations. *See* RADIO ASTRONOMY; RADIO TELE-SCOPE; STAR.

Moving reference frames. While the International Celestial Reference Frame is fixed, most observations are made from the Earth, which has many kinematic motions. Thus, a moving reference frame must be established. In the past the determination of this moving reference frame has been based on the dynamical motions of the solar system objects. Thus, the moving equatorial and ecliptic planes determined the equinox, with the celestial equator defined by the Earth's Equator and the ecliptic corresponding to the Earth's orbit around the Sun. With the newly defined fixed reference frame, which is independent of the equinox, it is no longer necessary to use the equinox as the fiducial point for the moving reference frame. Therefore, a new nonrotating origin has been introduced, called the Celestial Intermediate Origin. Also, a new precession-nutation model, IAU 2000A, has been adopted, and from it a Celestial Intermediate Pole is determined. There is a choice of using a moving reference frame that is based on either the equinox or the Celestial Intermediate Origin. *See* ECLIPTIC; EQUINOX.

The new precession-nutation model includes geodesic precession and nutation (which are small corrections related to a relativistic effect), but it does not include free core nutation (that is, nutation coming from unrestrained motions in the Earth's core), which cannot be predicted accurately. With the determinations of subdaily periodic motions, it has been decided to restrict nutation terms to periods greater than 2 days. All shorter-period terms are included in polar motion. For accuracies limited to a milliarcsecond, standard theories can be used, but for better accuracies, values based on current observations available from the International Earth Rotation Service (IERS) must be used. Currently the observational determinations of nutation are more accurate than can be achieved by theoretical models based on a nonrigid Earth. *See* EARTH ROTATION AND ORBITAL MOTION; NUTATION (ASTRONOMY AND MECHANICS); PRECESSION OF EQUINOXES; RELATIVITY.

Optical catalogs. The new reference frame is directly observable at radio frequencies, but optically the sources are generally fainter than 18th magnitude. The *Hipparcos Catalogue*, determined from observations by that astrometric satellite of the early 1990s, provides an optical catalog on the International Celestial Reference Frame with accuracies of about 10–20 milliarcseconds at the present epoch. New catalogs—such as the *Tycho 2* (based on lower-accuracy observations from *Hipparcos*), the *USNO* (*U.S. Naval Observatory*) *CCD Astrographic Catalog* (*UCAC*), where charge-coupled devices (CCDs) are the electronic detectors used, and *USNO B2.0*—increase the density of objects in the optical reference frame and extend it to 21st magnitude on the International Celestial Reference Frame, including fainter stars than had been previously usable. New observations and planetary ephemerides are being made directly in the International Celestial Refer-

ence Frame. Observational data determine additional standard frames, such as the solar system dynamical frame and the frames for other wavelengths of the electromagnetic spectrum. *See* ASTRONOMICAL CATALOGS; EPHEMERIS; PARALLAX (ASTRONOMY).

Observations. Continuing observations of the radio sources by VLBI are required to maintain the positional accuracies and to detect possible changes in the structures, and hence the positions, of the sources of radiation. Global Positioning System (GPS) observations can be made continuously by many receivers worldwide, so short-period (less than 1 day) Earth orientation motions can be determined. The positional observations of the sources also determine precession, nutation, and orientation of the Earth. Observations of optical sources are required to maintain the accuracy of optical catalogs, which lose accuracy due to the uncertainties of the stars' proper motions. Lunar laser ranging observations currently can be made at centimeter accuracy to determine the lunar orbit, lunar librations, Earth orientation, precession, and nutation. *See* MOON; SATELLITE NAVIGATION SYSTEMS.

Terrestrial reference frame. An International Terrestrial Reference System (ITRS) has been adopted by the International Geophysical Union. It is realized by the International Terrestrial Reference Frame (ITRF), consisting of coordinates on the surface of the Earth. These positions are specified in terms of the Terrestrial Intermediate Origin and are subject to the variations due to geophysical effects, such as plate tectonics and tidal effects. In order to analyze and use observational data from the surface of the Earth, it is necessary to include all the effects that cause differences between the celestial and terrestrial reference frames. The angle between the Celestial Intermediate Origin and the Terrestrial Intermediate Origin is the Earth Rotation Angle, while the angle between the equinox and the Terrestrial Intermediate Origin is sidereal time. The transformation between the International Celestial Reference Frame and the International Terrestrial Reference Frame includes precession, nutation, polar motion, and the real Earth rotation given by the time system known as UT1. *See* ASTROMETRY; EARTH TIDES; GEODESY; PLATE TECTONICS; TIME.

P. K. Seidelmann

Bibliography. International Earth Rotation Service, *IERS Conventions*, 2003, 2004; P. K. Seidelmann (ed.), *Explanatory Supplement to the Astronomical Almanac*, 1992.

Celestial sphere

An imaginary sphere of infinite radius centered either on an observer or at the center of the Earth. We imagine that the stars and planets are attached to the inside surface of the celestial sphere. Standing outside on a clear moonless night far from city lights, it is easy to imagine that one is at the center of such a sphere and that the stars and planets are attached to its inside surface.

Celestial poles, celestial equator, and ecliptic. Extending the Earth's axis of rotation in both directions until it "touches" the celestial sphere determines two points, the north celestial pole and the south celestial pole. Similarly, projecting the Earth's equator onto the celestial sphere determines the celestial equator. As the Earth revolves around the Sun each year, we see the Sun seeming to travel across the celestial sphere. As it does, it traces out an imaginary great circle, the ecliptic. (It may help to remember that the stars are still in the sky in the daytime; the Sun is so bright that the stars cannot be seen, but they are still there.) The plane determined by the Earth's equator is tilted with respect to the plane determined by the ecliptic, so the Sun is north of the equator for 6 months of each year and south of the equator for the other 6 months. The ecliptic and the equator cross at two points, the vernal equinox and the autumnal equinox. The vernal equinox is the point where the Sun crosses the equator on its way north each year, marking the first day of spring in the Northern Hemisphere (see **illustration**). *See* ECLIPTIC; EQUATOR; EQUINOX; NORTH POLE; SOUTH POLE.

Coordinate systems. Because the distances to the stars and planets are so great, two different observers see the same star in the same direction and thus the star can be thought of as being at a specific "position" on the sphere. Using the two poles, the equator, and the ecliptic, it is straightforward to establish a coordinate system that makes it possible to determine the position of any object in the sky. The system is similar to the system of latitudes and longitudes used for the locations of objects on the surface of the Earth. Right ascension (abbreviated RA or with the Greek letter α) is analogous to longitude. Declination (abbreviated Dec or with the Greek letter δ) is analogous to latitude. *See* LATITUDE AND LONGITUDE.

As with longitude on the Earth, it is necessary to choose a "zero" point for right ascension. On Earth we use a meridian—a great semicircle drawn from one pole to the other, perpendicular to the equator—passing through Greenwich, England. On the celestial sphere we use the meridian that passes through the vernal equinox. Every point on this prime meridian has a right ascension of zero. Right ascension is measured in hours and minutes, ranging from 0 hours, 0 minutes to 23 hours, 59.999... minutes. Hours are used rather than degrees because the entire sphere seems to rotate once per day. Each hour of right ascension corresponds to $15°$. Right ascension increases toward the east; that is, if one star is slightly east of another, the first star will have a larger right ascension than the second—unless they are on opposite sides of the prime meridian. *See* MERIDIAN.

Declinations are measured north and south of the equator with angles between $0°$ and $90°$, measured in degrees and minutes. Northern declinations are considered positive; southern declinations negative.

The brightest star, Sirius, is at RA 6 hours 45.146′ and Dec $-16°$ 43.049′ (see illustration). The star Betelgeuse is at RA 5 hours 55.172′ and Dec $+7°$ 24.424′. *See* ASTRONOMICAL COORDINATE SYSTEMS.

Motions of celestial objects. The positions of the objects on the celestial sphere are not fixed. The Sun, Moon, and planets are in constant motion relative to the Earth and thus their positions on the celestial sphere change constantly. The same is true of the stars, but to a much lesser extent. The stars are all in motion relative to one another; as a result, their positions on the celestial sphere change all the time. However, the stars are extremely far away so these changes are very small and need to be taken into consideration only when extremely accurate positioning of a telescope is required or to discuss how a star's position has changed over a long period of time. *See* MOON; PLANET; STAR.

Precession of the equinoxes. As the Earth rotates, it also wobbles. It completes one slow wobble every 26,000 years. As a result of this wobble, the vernal equinox slides along the ecliptic, making a full trip around every 26,000 years. This phenomenon is known as the precession of the equinoxes. In addition to the changes mentioned earlier, the right ascension and declination of every object in the sky changes constantly due to precession. The numbers given above for Sirius and Betelgeuse are for the first day of the year 2000. The difference between the right ascension and declination for a star on any nearby date and the values for 2000 is tiny, but that difference does matter when a telescope or other astronomical instrument is being used at high power. *See* PRECESSION OF EQUINOXES.

Celestial sphere. The arrows indicate the right ascension (RA) and declination (Dec) of Sirius. (*Wil Tirion*)

Distances. The stars are immensely distant compared to the distances to the Sun, Moon, and planets. The galaxies are immensely distant compared to the distances to the stars we see with the unaided eye. The notion of an imaginary celestial sphere is of little use when we want to talk about the actual structure of our universe.   Samuel E. Rhoads

Bibliography. A. Fraknow, D. Morrison, and S. Wolff, *Voyages Through the Universe*, Brooks/Cole, 3d ed., 2006; D. H. Levy, *Skywatching, A Nature Company Guide*, The Nature Company, 1994; G. Lovi and W. Tirion, *Men, Monsters and the Modern Universe*, Willmann-Bell, 1989; J. M. Pasachoff, *Astronomy: From the Earth to the Universe*, Saunders College Publishing, 6th ed., 2002; J. M. Pasachoff, *Field Guide to the Stars and Planets*, 4th ed., Houghton-Mifflin, 2000; J. M. Pasachoff and A. Filippenko, *The Cosmos: Astronomy in the New Millennium*, Brooks/Cole, 3d ed., 2007; H. A. Rey, *The Stars: A New Way To See Them*, Houghton Mifflin, rebound by Sagebrush, 2002; I. Ridpath (ed.), *Norton's Star Atlas and Reference Handbook*, 20th ed., Pi Press, 2004.

Celestite

A mineral with the chemical composition $SrSO_4$. Celestite occurs commonly in colorless to sky-blue, orthorhombic, tabular crystals. Fracture is uneven and luster is vitreous. Hardness is 3–3.5 on Mohs scale and specific gravity is 3.97. It fuses readily to a white pearl. It is only slowly soluble in hot concentrated acids or alkali carbonate solutions. The strontium present in celestite imparts a characteristic crimson color to the flame.

Celestite occurs in association with gypsum, anhydrite, salt beds, limestone, and dolomite. Large

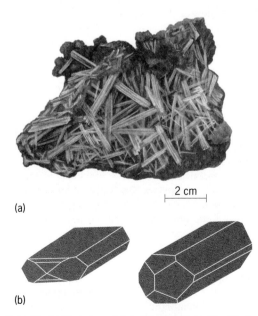

2 cm

(a)

(b)

Celestite. (*a*) Bladed crystals in limestone from Clay Center, Ohio (*specimen from Department of Geology, Bryn Mawr College*). (*b*) Crystal habits (*after C. S. Hurlbut, Jr., Dana's Manual of Mineralogy, 17th ed., Wiley, 1959*).

crystals are found in vugs or cavities of limestone (see **illus.**). It is deposited directly from seawater, by groundwater, or from hydrothermal solutions. Celestite is the major source of strontium. The principal use of strontium is in tracer bullets and in various red flares used by the armed forces. Minor applications of strontium compounds are in ceramics, depilatories, and medicine. Although celestite deposits occur in Arizona and California, domestic production of celestite has been small and sporadic. Much of the strontium demand is satisfied by imported ores from England and Mexico. *See* STRONTIUM.   Edward C. T. Chao

Cell (biology)

Cells can be separated into prokaryotic and eukaryotic categories. Eukaryotic cells contain a nucleus. They comprise protists (single-celled organisms), fungi, plants, and animals, and are generally 5–100 micrometers in linear dimension. Prokaryotic cells contain no nucleus, are relatively small (1–10 μm in diameter), and have a simple internal structure (**Fig. 1**). They include two classes of bacteria: eubacteria (including photosynthetic organisms, or cyanobacteria), which are common bacteria inhabiting soil, water, and larger organisms; and archaebacteria, which grow under unusual conditions. The archaebacteria include methanogens, which live in anaerobic conditions and reduce carbon dioxide (CO_2) to methane (swamp gas); halophiles, which thrive under extremely high salt conditions; and sulfur bacteria, which grow in hot (80°C; 176°F) sulfur springs where the pH is extremely acidic. *See* EUKARYOTAE.

Eubacteria. All eubacteria have an inner (plasma) membrane which serves as a semipermeable barrier allowing small nonpolar and polar molecules such as oxygen, carbon dioxide, and glycerol to diffuse across (down their concentration gradients), but does not allow the diffusion of larger polar molecules (sugars, amino acids, and so on) or inorganic ions such as Na^+, K^+, Cl^-, Ca^{2+} (sodium, potassium, chlorine, calcium) [Fig. 1]. The plasma membrane, which is a lipid bilayer, utilizes transmembrane transporter and channel proteins to facilitate the movement of these molecules. Eubacteria can be further separated into two classes based on their ability to retain the dye crystal violet. Gram-positive cells retain the dye; their cell surface includes the inner plasma membrane and a cell wall composed of multiple layers of peptidoglycan (Fig. 1*b*). Gram-negative bacteria (Fig. 1*a*) are surrounded by two membranes: the inner (plasma) membrane and an outer membrane that allows the passage of molecules of less than 1000 molecular weight through porin protein channels. Between the inner and outer membranes is the peptidoglycan-rich cell wall and the periplasmic space. *See* CELL MEMBRANES.

Eubacteria contain a single circular double-stranded molecule of deoxyribonucleic acid (DNA), or a single chromosome. As prokaryotic cells lack

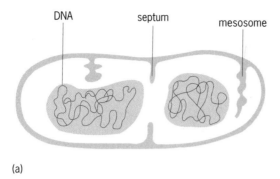

DNA   septum   mesosome

(a)

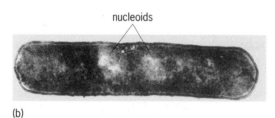

nucleoids

(b)

Fig. 1. Bacterial cell structure. (a) Artist's rendition of a gram-negative eubacterial cell (*modified from H. Lodish et al., Molecular Cell Biology, 3d ed., Scientific American, New York, 1995*). (b) Electron micrograph of a gram-positive eubacterium, *Bacillus licheniformis* (*courtesy of S. R. Goodman*).

a nucleus, this genomic DNA resides in a central region of the cell (Fig. 1*b*) called the nucleoid. *Escherichia coli*, a common gram-negative eubacteria, contains 0.4 picogram of DNA in its genome, or 4×10^6 base pairs. Bacterial replication requires accurate duplication of this chromosomal DNA, with both copies attaching by cross-wall formation to the plasma membrane, allowing the formation of two identical daughter cells by binary fission. The bacterial genome contains all the necessary information to maintain the structure and function of the cell. The processing of this information occurs in two steps. First the DNA is transcribed to form ribonucleic acid (RNA) by the enzyme RNA polymerase. Before this messenger RNA (mRNA) is completely transcribed, there is attachment of a 70S ribosome. The ribosome translates the mRNA into protein by reading three nucleotides (codon) at a time that encode a specific amino acid. The amino acids are added via specific transfer RNA (tRNA) molecules containing anticodon regions which base-pair with the mRNA codon. *Escherichia coli*, for example, contains about 30,000 cytoplasmic ribosomes and produces as much as 2000 distinct mRNAs and, therefore, protein subunits.

Many bacteria are able to move from place to place, or are motile. Their motility is based on a helical flagellum composed of interwoven protein called flagellin. The flagellum is attached to the cell surface through a basal body, and propels the bacteria through an aqueous environment by rotating like the propeller on a motor boat. The motor is reversible, allowing the bacteria to move toward chemoattractants and away from chemorepellants.

Eukaryotic cells. The smallest objects that can be visualized by the modern light microscope are ap-

proximately 0.5 μm wide. In a light microscopic view of a eukaryotic cell, a plasma membrane can be seen which defines the outer boundaries of the cell, surrounding the cell's protoplasm or contents. The protoplasm includes the nucleus, where the eukaryotic cell's DNA is compartmentalized away from the remaining contents of the cell (the cytoplasm). Therefore, the protoplasm includes the nucleus and the cytoplasm. In addition to the nucleus, the cytoplasm contains other organelles (Fig. 2*b*). The eukaryotic cell's organelles include the nucleus, mitochondria, endoplasmic reticulum, Golgi apparatus, lysosomes, peroxisomes, cytoskeleton, and plasma membrane (**Fig. 2***a*). The organelles occupy approximately half the total volume of the cytoplasm. The remaining compartment of cytoplasm (minus organelles) is referred to as the cytosol or cytoplasmic ground substance. Eukaryotic cells also differ from prokaryotic cells in having a cytoskeleton that gives the cell its shape, its capacity to move, and its ability to transport organelles and vesicles from one part of the cell cytoplasm to another. The cytoskeleton is composed of microfilaments (7–8 nanometers in diameter), intermediate filaments (10 nm), microtubules (25 nm), and a spectrin-based membrane skeleton. Eukaryotic cells are generally larger than prokaryotic cells and therefore require a cytoskeleton and membrane skeleton to maintain their shape, which is related to their functions.

The development of multicellular organisms required that cells closely related by ancestry become differentiated from one another—some developing certain features, others developing different traits. While different cells within a human tissue (such as nervous tissue) are radically different from each other, they have descended from the same fertilized egg. In most cases (one exception is human erythrocytes), cells retain all of the genetic material contained in the precursor fertilized egg. Differentiation or specialization of cells depends on gene expression. Eukaryotic cells contain a large amount of DNA (about a thousandfold more than bacterial cells), only approximately 1% of which encodes protein. The remaining DNA is structural (involved in DNA packaging) or regulatory (helping to switch on and off genes). Therefore, whether a cell becomes a muscle fiber or a neuron depends on the expression of muscle-specific genes or neuron-specific genes (although both are present).

Plasma membrane. The plasma membrane serves as a selective permeability barrier between a cell's environment and cytoplasm. The fundamental structure of plasma membranes (as well as organelle membranes) is the lipid bilayer, formed due to the tendency of amphipathic phospholipids to bury their hydrophobic fatty acid tails away from water. Human and animal cell plasma membranes contain a varied composition of phospholipids, cholesterol, and glycolipids. Cholesterol intercalates itself perpendicular to the membrane surface between the phospholipids. Glycolipids are primarily found in the noncytoplasmic leaflet of the bilayer. While lipids determine the bilayer structure, membrane proteins are

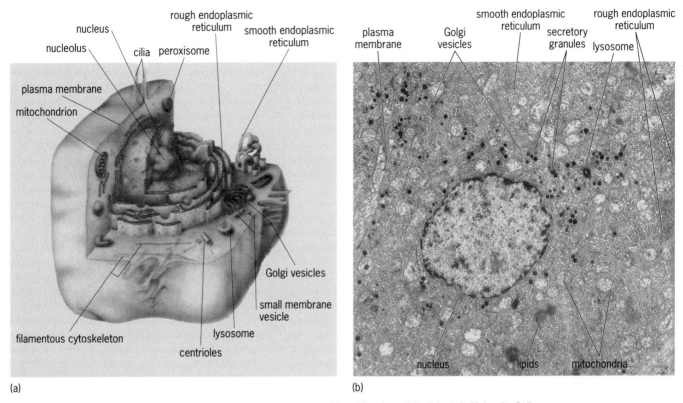

Fig. 2. Animal cell structure. (*a*) Artist's rendition of a eukaryotic animal cell (*modified from H. Lodish et al., Molecular Cell Biology, 3d ed., Scientific American, New York, 1995*). (*b*) Electron micrograph of a bovine large luteal cell (*courtesy of Dr. Phillip Fields*).

primarily responsible for membrane function. Membrane proteins can be divided into two categories: integral proteins that are embedded in the hydrophobic core of the bilayer, and peripheral proteins that are attached noncovalently to the hydrophilic membrane surfaces. Integral membrane proteins can be subdivided into transmembrane proteins that have a single alpha helix transversing the hydrophobic core of the bilayer (single-pass transmembrane proteins); multipass transmembrane proteins (transporters and channels are of this type); or proteins that are covalently linked to a fatty acid chain or phospholipid which is embedded. Both the lipids and proteins of the plasma membrane are asymmetrically distributed across the bilayer. This means that the lipid and protein in the extracellular leaflet (E face) are distinct from the protoplasmic leaflet (P face). Plasma membranes are fluid. The protein and lipids of the plasma membrane are capable of lateral movement and rotation around a central axis, but they are not capable of rapid flip-flop from one leaflet to the other. Therefore, the asymmetry of the plasma membrane protein and lipid, important to the differing functions on either side of the bilayer, is maintained over the lifespan of the cell. The lateral mobility of some transmembrane proteins is limited by their interaction with peripheral proteins on the extracellular or cytoplasmic surface of the plasma membrane. This creates a membrane topography where selected membrane domains can have differing protein and lipid composition and function.

Cytoskeleton. The cytoskeleton is involved in establishing cell shape, polarity, and motility, and in directing the movement of organelles within the cell. The cytoskeleton includes microfilaments, microtubules, intermediate filaments, and the two-dimensional membrane skeleton that lines the cytoplasmic surface of cell membranes. Microfilaments contain filamentous actin (F-actin) which is formed by the adenosine triphosphate (ATP)–dependent polymerization of globular actin (G-actin) monomers. Actin microfilaments have a polarity. They have a plus end where polymerization of additional G-actin monomers occurs at a faster rate than at the minus end of the filament. The plus end of the actin filaments associates with membranes and the Z-disk of muscle sarcomeres. Myosin is a fibrous protein which forms 15-nm-thick filaments in muscle and nonmuscle cells. In the presence of ATP, myosin head groups interact with actin microfilaments, causing contraction in muscle and nonmuscle cells (for example, contractile ring, stress fibers, adhesion belts). In addition to a contractile role, actin microfilaments have a structural role in epithelial cells, where they form the core of the fingerlike projections called microvilli. Each microvillus contains 20–30 bundled actin filaments with their plus ends contacting the tip of the microvillus, and their minus ends down in the terminal web region, attached via nonerythroid spectrin and myosin II to other actin bundles and intermediate filaments. Gel-sol transformation within the cytoplasm of human and animal cells is controlled by the length of actin filaments and the extent of microfilament crosslinking. Those actin-binding proteins which shorten actin filaments cause solation, while those which crosslink F-actin or lead to lengthening of the actin filament cause gelation. The membrane skeleton on the cytoplasmic surface of all eukaryotic cell membranes contains a fibrous protein called spectrin which crosslinks short actin protofilaments into a two-dimensional meshwork. This spectrin membrane skeleton stabilizes the bilayer, gives shape to the membrane, and controls the lateral mobility of some transmembrane proteins.

Microtubules are hollow tubes (25 nm in diameter) which are composed of alpha, beta tubulin dimers. The tubulin dimers interact head to tail to form protofilaments, and 13 protofilaments form the wall of the microtubule. Microtubules have a polarity, with polymerization occuring faster at the plus end. In vivo and in vitro microtubules undergo dynamic instability, and grow and shrink rapidly. Whether a microtubule is growing or shrinking is determined by the rate of guanosine triphosphate (GTP) hydrolysis versus the rate of tubulin dimer addition. If GTP hydrolysis is occurring faster than tubulin addition, then the microtubule will shrink; if tubulin addition is faster, then the microtubule will grow. Within a nondividing cell, microtubules grow from a single structure near the nucleus, called a centrosome or microtubule organizing center. The microtubule organizing center contains a pair of centrioles surrounded by pericentriolar material, and a microtubule is capped at its minus end by the pericentriolar material. During mitosis, the centrioles within the microtubule organizing center duplicate and form the spindle poles. The mitotic spindle is polar, with the spindle microtubule minus end facing the spindle pole. Microtubules within interphase and mitotic cells are very dynamic. However, other cellular microtubules are stable, such as the microtubules found in neuronal axons and dendrites and those found in axonemes of cilia and flagella. Several factors contribute to the stability of microtubules: posttranslational acetylation of lysine residues or removal of the C-terminal tyrosine of tubulin, microtubule associated proteins (MAPs), or minus-end capping proteins. Microtubules serve as tracks on which organelles and vesicles are transported through the cytoplasm. Two proteins called kinesin and cytoplasmic dynein have the ability to move organelles toward the plus and minus ends of microtubules, respectively. These proteins are translocating adenosine triphosphatases (ATPases), and appear to be responsible for most of the cytoplasmic movement of organelles. Cilia and flagella are extensions of the cell surface which are responsible for movement, and both have a very similar internal structure. Cilia move particulate matter across the apical surface of epithelial sheets; a flagellum forms the tail of the sperm and is responsible for its ability to swim. Both types of movement are based on an internal microtubule-based structure called an axoneme, and require ATP hydrolysis as a source of energy. The axoneme has a characteristic (9+2) pattern, with 9 outer microtubule doublets (A and B subfibers) and 2 inner singlet microtubules. The movement of cilia and flagella is based on an ATPase named dynein which is attached along the length of each A subfiber in the outer doublets. In the presence of ATP, the dynein heads reach out and attach to the B subfiber on an adjacent doublet and pull it toward the tip of the cilia or flagella. Bending rather than sliding results, because the outer doublets are attached to each other by a flexible protein called nexin. The axonemal microtubules are nucleated by basal bodies which have the same structure as centrioles. Basal bodies and centrioles are small cylinders with nine outer triplet microtubules at a 45° angle from the radius of the cylinder.

Intermediate filaments are 10 nm in diameter and play structural roles within cells. Intermediate filaments within muscle cells link the Z-disks of adjacent myofibrils together. Intermediate filaments within neurons (neurofilaments) serve as a structural support for axons and dendrites, and the intermediate filaments of epithelial cells interconnect spot desmosomes, thereby stabilizing epithelial sheets. Intermediate filaments in human and animal cells are made up of cell-type-specific proteins. The intermediate filament subunits are fibrous, and almost all subunits are incorporated into the ropelike intermediate filament in a process that does not require ATP or GTP hydrolysis. The resulting intermediate filaments have no polarity. This heterogeneous group of proteins can all form intermediate filaments of similar dimension because of a common 310-amino-acid alpha-helical region that forms the core of the intermediate filament.

Nucleus. One of the most prominent organelles within a eukaryotic cell is the nucleus. The nuclear compartment is separated from the rest of the cell by a specialized membrane complex built from two distinct lipid bilayers, referred to as the nuclear envelope. However, the interior of the nucleus maintains contact with the cells cytoplasm via nuclear pores. These structures form holes or channels in the nuclear envelope that are responsible for the selective uptake of nuclear components and release of components destined for the cell cytoplasm. Attached to the nuclear pore complex and the inner surface of the nuclear membrane is a fibrous protein network built from the intermediate-filament proteins known as nuclear lamins A, B, and C. This nuclear lamina participates in the breakdown and reformation of the nuclear boundary during mitosis and, in combination with a fibrous complex of proteins referred to as the nuclear matrix, is responsible for maintaining the structure of the nucleus. The primary function of the nucleus is to house the genetic apparatus of the cell; this genetic machinery is composed of DNA (arranged in linear units called chromosomes), RNA, and proteins. Nuclear proteins aid in the performance of nuclear functions and include polypeptides that have a direct role in the regulation of gene function and those that give structure to the genetic material. The complex of DNA and structural proteins is known as chromatin, which can be either highly compacted (heterochromatin) or dispersed (euchromatin) within the nucleus. A specialized region within the nucleus that is visible in interphase cells is the nucleolus, which functions in the production and assembly of ribosomal subunits. *See* CELL NUCLEUS.

Gene expression. The biochemical and phenotypical properties of a cell are defined by the proteins expressed within the cell. The expression of a protein involves a complex pathway that transfers information from the DNA within the nucleus to the protein-synthetic machinery within the cytoplasm. The first step of this pathway is the synthesis of an RNA molecule from the DNA template by the process known as transcription. All cells in an organism contain a complete complement of genetic material; however, only a selected portion is synthesized into RNA. Thus, the transcription process is highly regulated within each cell. In eukaryotes, RNAs are synthesized from units referred to as genes which contain the information needed to specify a protein sequence stored in three-nucleotide "words" called codons. The informational content of a gene is not necessarily contiguous in that some noncoding DNA may be found interrupting the sequences which form the functional RNA found in the cell's cytoplasm. These noninformational segments are transcribed and removed from the primary transcript in the nucleus, with the informational or exon segments of the RNA joined together by a process called splicing. Once the functional RNA is formed, it is transported to the cytoplasm via the nuclear pores. Upon exiting the nucleus, a mature RNA can be translated into a polypeptide sequence. The amount of protein that is made from an RNA can be regulated by the level of RNA available to the translational machinery or by the ability of the machinery to select specific RNAs for translation. Some proteins are not able to perform their function upon translation and are subjected to modification following translation. In summary, the transfer of information from DNA to a protein capable of performing a function within the cell involves several steps, each of which is subject to regulation. It is the composite of all the individual steps that determines the final level of expression of any given gene product. *See* DEOXYRIBONUCLEIC ACID (DNA); GENE.

Protein synthesis from mRNA occurs within the cytoplasm of eukaryotic cells, catalyzed by RNA and protein containing 80S particles called ribosomes. Proteins to be secreted or inserted into the plasma membrane, endoplasmic reticulum membrane, Golgi membrane, or lysosomal membrane are synthesized on ribosomes attached to the endoplasmic reticulum membrane. Proteins which will reside within the cytosol, some mitochondrial proteins, and peripheral membrane proteins are synthesized on free (not endoplasmic reticulum–associated) ribosomes. There is no difference between endoplasmic reticulum–associated and free ribosomes. Their position is determined by the sequence of the protein being synthesized.

Endoplasmic reticulum. The endoplasmic reticulum is composed of membrane-enclosed flattened sacs or cisternae. The enclosed compartment is called the lumen. The endoplasmic reticulum is morphologically separated into rough (RER) and smooth (SER). RER is studded with ribosomes and SER is not. RER is the site of protein synthesis, while lipids are synthesized in both RER and SER. In the case of proteins which will be synthesized in the RER, an N-terminal signal sequence causes the protein and ribosome to be bound to a signal recognition particle. The signal recognition particle and bound signal sequence and ribosome are attached to the endoplasmic reticulum through a docking protein called the signal recognition particle receptor. Then the signal peptide threads its way through a channel protein into the endoplasmic reticulum lumen, and protein synthesis continues until the nascent protein is complete and located within the lumen. If the protein is soluble, the signal sequence is cleaved, releasing the protein into the lumen. If the protein is a transmembrane integral protein, its topography across the bilayer is determined by carefully placed start and stop transfer signals (hydrophobic stretches of amino acids). Glycosylation of secretory and membrane proteins begins within the lumen of the endoplasmic reticulum and then is completed within the Golgi apparatus. Membrane lipids are also synthesized in the endoplasmic reticulum, and then they are moved to target organelles by transport vesicles or phospholipid exchange proteins. The synthesis of phospholipids occurs on the cytoplasmic leaflet of the endoplasmic reticulum (usually SER); some are moved to the luminal leaflet by specific phospholipid translocating enzymes called flippases. In this manner, membrane asymmetry is established by the specific flipping of phospholipids across the endoplasmic reticulum bilayer. Since the flippases are present at low concentration in the plasma membrane, Golgi membrane, or lysosomal membrane, the asymmetry created in the endoplasmic reticulum remains unaltered. The phospholipids synthesized in the endoplasmic reticulum are transferred to the plasma membrane, Golgi membrane, and lysosomal membrane by the budding-off of endoplasmic reticulum vesicles which travel to and fuse with the membrane of the target organelle. Mitochondria and peroxisomes receive most of their phospholipid via phospholipid exchange proteins which carry phospholipids from the endoplasmic reticulum cytoplasmic leaflet to these organelles. *See* ENDOPLASMIC RETICULUM.

Golgi apparatus. The final posttranslational modifications of proteins and glycolipids occur within a series of flattened membranous sacs called the Golgi apparatus. Vesicles which bud from the endoplasmic reticulum fuse with a specialized region of the cis Golgi compartment called the cis Golgi network. A series of posttranslational modifications occur first in the cis compartment, then in order in the medial, trans, and trans Golgi network compartments. In each case the membrane transfer occurs by the blebbing of coated vesicles from one compartment and their fusion with the next. In the trans Golgi network, proteins and lipids are sorted into transport vesicles destined for lysosomes, the plasma membrane, or secretion. The targeting of proteins to lysosomes requires mannose phosphorylation within the cis Golgi, and then concentration by a mannose 6-phosphate receptor in the trans Golgi network. Vesicles which bleb from the trans Golgi network carry the targeted proteins to one of several locations, including the lysosomes. *See* GOLGI APPARATUS.

Lysosomes. Lysosomes are membrane-bound organelles with a luminal pH of 5.0, filled with acid hydrolyses. Lysosomes are responsible for degrading materials brought into the cell by endocytosis or phagocytosis, or autophagocytosis of spent cellular material. *See* LYSOSOME.

Endocytosis and exocytosis. Movement of proteins to the plasma membrane or those destined for secretion occurs via secretory vesicles that also bleb off the trans Golgi network. These vesicles either travel directly to the plasma membrane and fuse, releasing their contents (constitutive pathway), or wait for a specific signal (usually elevated Ca^{2+}) before completing the secretion pathway (regulated pathway). The surface area of most plasma membranes does not increase due to the exocytosis that is described above, because membrane is being retrieved by the process of endocytosis. Endocytosis can be separated into pinocytosis (cell drinking) and phagocytosis (cell eating). Pinocytosis can be further subdivided into fluid-phase endocytosis and receptor-mediated endocytosis. In the former there is no concentration of small molecules being internalized, while the latter concentrates the ligand because of the presence of specific receptors within the internalized membrane. Much of the endocytosis occurs at membrane domains called coated pits, which internalize to form coated vesicles. The coat is largely composed of a protein called clathrin. Upon endocytosis or phagocytosis, the internalized endocytic vesicles or phagosomes, respectively, fuse with endosomes or lysosomes, leading to hydrolysis of the ingested molecules or particles. The resulting molecules can be released from the lysosomes into the cytoplasm for utilization. The membrane-associated receptors in receptor-mediated endocytosis are either recycled to the plasma membrane for reutilization or digested within the lysosomes.

Mitochondrion. The mitochondrion contains a double membrane: the outer membrane which contains a channel-forming protein named porin, and an inner membrane which contains multiple infolds called cristae. The porin channel allows molecules of less than 10,000 molecular weight free passage between the cytoplasm and the intermembrane space. The inner membrane, which contains the protein complexes responsible for electron transport and oxidative phosphorylation, is folded into numerous cristae that increase the surface area per volume of this membrane. The transfer of electrons from nicotinamide adenine dinucleotide (NADH) or flavin adenine dinucleotide ($FADH_2$) down the electron transfer chain to oxygen causes protons to be pumped out of the mitochondrial matrix into the intermembrane space. The resulting proton motive force drives the conversion of ADP plus inorganic orthophosphate (P_i) to ATP by the enzyme ATP synthetase. The matrix contains the mitochondrion's double-stranded DNA, which encodes 13 mitochondrial proteins. Therefore, the mitochondrion must import the vast majority of its protein from the cytosol. Proteins synthesized on free ribosomes are targeted to the mitochondria by an N terminal amphipathic, positively charged signal peptide, and they enter into the mitochondria through contact sites between the inner and outer membranes. The signal peptide is cleaved, and the remainder of the protein is unfolded and then enters the matrix. Targeting of proteins to the inner membrane, outer membrane, and intermembrane space is determined by specifically positioned start and stop transfer signals similar to endoplasmic reticulum import.

Peroxisomes. Peroxisomes import all of their proteins from the cytosol. In the case of the peroxisome, the targeting signal is three amino acids at the C terminus of the newly synthesized protein. Within the peroxisome, hydrogen atoms are removed from organic substrates and hydrogen peroxide is formed. The enzyme catalase can then utilize the hydrogen peroxide to oxidize substrates such as alcohols, formaldehydes, and formic acid in detoxifying reactions.

Cell division. Cell growth and division occur in an orderly, highly regulated, progressive series of events called the cell cycle. Advancement of cells through the cell cycle is driven by a small family of intracellular proteins, principal of which are the cyclins and a 34,000-molecular-weight protein, kinase. The cell cycle culminates in mitosis, a process that results in the production of two genetically identical diploid daughter cells. The chromosome separation events of mitosis occur as a result of the workings of the mitotic spindle apparatus, while the process of cytoplasmic division, or cytokinesis, is directed by the contractile ring. Unlike mitosis, meiosis produces nonidentical haploid cells. Meiosis, which occurs only in gonadal tissues, results in the production of either sperm or oocytes. By the process of fertilization, a new diploid is produced. Progression of cells through the cell cycle in multicellular organisms also can be affected by cell-cell interactions. This occurs when one cell secretes a growth factor that either stimulates or suppresses cell division in neighboring cells. Although cellular proliferation is tightly regulated in multicellular organisms, cells occasionally escape from these regulatory controls with resulting formation of cancerous tumors. Molecular analyses of the DNA in tumor cells have resulted in the identification of the mutated genes that allow for the onset of a cancer. The protein products of these genes, called protooncogenes and tumor suppressor genes, appear to play key roles in the regulation of cell growth in humans.

Cell adhesion. Tissues are formed by the interactions of cells with other cells and the extracellular matrix. Cell-cell interactions can occur either by adherence of neighboring cells at distinct organized regions called junctions or by the binding of randomly scattered cell surface molecules to surface molecules on adjacent cells. Cell junctions can be classified according to function, with the integrity of most types of junctional complexes being dependent upon the presence of extracellular Ca^{2+}. Tight junctions form at the apical surfaces of cells and inhibit the leakage of ions and molecules from one side of an epithelial sheet to the other side, while gap junctions play a crucial role in cell-cell communication. The anchoring junctions share a common molecular organization which allows for the cytoskeleton of one cell to be attached to the cytoskeleton of neighboring cells. This provides tissues, particularly epithelia, with great strength. The desmosome, a type of anchoring junction that acts like a spot weld to hold cells together, interacts with intermediate filaments, while adherens junctions, which are anchoring junctions that allow for cell adhesion and cellular locomotion, utilize microfilaments. The extracellular matrix also is important for tissue formation. Glycosaminoglycans and proteoglycans form a hydrated gel that is the ground substance of the extracellular matrix. The ground substance is embedded with structural proteins such as collagen, which provides tensile strength to the extracellular matrix, and elastin, which is responsible for the resilient nature of the extracellular matrix. The molecules of the extracellular matrix are attached to one another and to the cells which are embedded in the matrix by interactions with adhesive glycoproteins. Adhesive glycoproteins, such as fibronectin, are the glue that holds connective tissues together. A specialized form of extracellular matrix called the basal lamina underlies all epithelia. *See* CELL ADHESION.

Signal transduction. To coordinate cellular activities in multicellular organisms, complex mechanisms of cell-cell communication needed to evolve. A variety of different types of signaling molecules are used by cells, and several different signaling pathways are utilized. In neuronal transmission, electrical signals are converted to chemical signals at synapses. The target cells, either other neurons or muscle cells, then convert the chemical signal back to an electrical signal and respond in an appropriate manner. Cells also can signal target cells at great distances by secreting signaling molecules, or hormones, directly into the bloodstream. Steroid hormones are lipid-soluble molecules that cross the plasma membrane and bind to intracellular receptors. The activated steroid hormone receptors then bind specifically to DNA sequences and directly regulate the transcription of adjacent gene sequences. Most hormones that are secreted by endocrine cells are water-soluble molecules that bind to specific receptors located on the surface of the target cells. The activated receptors are transmembrane proteins that are able to relay the extracellular signal across the plasma membrane to the cytoplasm. This is achieved by the cytoplasmic domain of the activated receptor

molecule, which binds to and either activates or represses the activity of a cytoplasmic G-protein. Specific G-proteins then interact with target enzymes located on the inner surface of the plasma membrane to regulate the activity of these proteins. One of these enzymes, adenylate cyclase, is responsible for converting ATP to complementary adenosine monophosphate (cAMP). cAMP then sets off a reaction cascade inside cells by allosterically regulating certain molecules, thereby completing the signal transduction pathway. A second enzyme on the cell surface that is activated by G-proteins is phospholipase C. Phospholipase C cleaves a membrane lipid, phosphatidyl inositol 4,5-bisphosphate (PIP_2), into inositol 1,4,5-trisphosphate (IP_3) and diacylglycerol. IP_3 triggers the release of Ca^{2+} ions from intracellular storage sites, and the Ca^{2+} ions then bind to and activate calcium-binding proteins such as calmodulin. Diacylglycerol, however, activates protein kinase C, completing the signal transduction pathway in the cell.

Cell motility. The ability of eukaryotic cells to move through a substrate requires cytoskeletal proteins, which generate propulsion, and constant remodeling of the membrane by endocytosis and exocytosis. The stages in cell movement are the polarization of the cell and identification of a leading edge, extension of a lamellipodium or ruffled edge in the direction of movement, and breakdown of attachment with the extracellular matrix. Sometimes a cell moves toward or away from a particular chemical signal (chemotaxis). This occurs because the chemical binds to receptors on the surface of the motile cell, increasing intracellular Ca^{2+} at the leading edge. The role of Ca^{2+} in creating a motoring force is not clear, but it may act through Ca^{2+}-dependent severing proteins to cleave actin filaments both within the leading-edge membrane skeleton and in the cell cortex. The result would be a solation of the cytoplasm in the direction of motion, a membrane capable of being extended by exocytosis, and a stabilization of the extension by the rapid polymerization of actin in a direction parallel to the leading-edge lamellipodium. The migratory cell is then steered as a result of the microtubule organizing center and Golgi apparatus being realigned along an axis between the nucleus and leading edge. The Golgi apparatus produces the secretory vesicles which fuse with the leading edge of the plasma membrane, and these vesicles are transported to the leading edge by microtubule-based translocation. Membrane from the old leading edge then ruffles back toward the trailing end of the cell. During the process of cell migration, the motile cell must make and break interactions with the extracellular matrix in a traction-producing process. *See* CELL MOTILITY.

Plant cell. Outside their plasma membrane, plant cells have an extremely rigid cell wall. This cell wall is composed of cellulose and other polymers and is distinct in composition from the cell walls found in fungi or bacterial cells. The plant cell wall expands during cell growth, and a new cell wall partition is created between the two daughter cells during cell

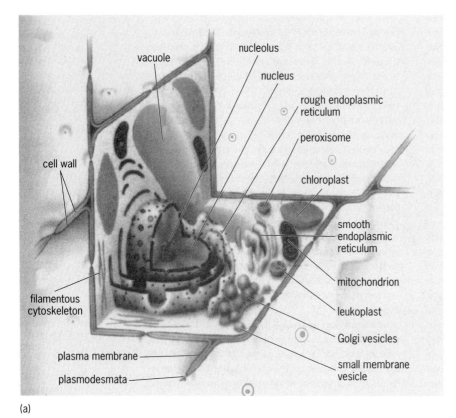

(a)

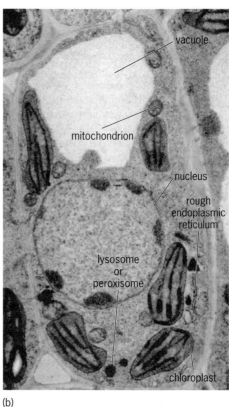

(b)

Fig. 3. Plant cell structure. (a) Artist's rendition of a typical plant cell (*modified from H. Lodish et al., Molecular Cell Biology, 3d ed., Scientific American, New York, 1999*). (b) Electron micrograph of a plant cell (*Electronmicroscopy Core Lab, Interdisciplinary Center for Biological Research, University of Florida*).

division. Similar cell walls are not observed in animal cells (**Fig. 3**).

Most plant cells contain membrane-encapsulated vacuoles as major components of their cytoplasm. These vacuoles contain water, sucrose, ions, nitrogen-containing compounds formed by nitrogen fixation, and waste products. The amount of osmotic particles within the vacuoles is much higher than in the cytosol or extracellular fluid. The encapsulating membrane is permeable to water but impermeable to the molecules within the vacuole. Therefore, water rushes into the vacuole, the vacuole expands, and a hydrostatic pressure or turgor is created within the cell. This turgor is resisted by the cellulose-containing cell wall, but as the cell wall stretches the plant grows. *See* PLANT CELL.

Chloroplasts are the other major organelle in plant cells that is not found in other eukaryotic cells. Like mitochondria, they are constantly in motion within the cytoplasm. One of the pigments found in chloroplasts is chlorophyll, which is the molecule that absorbs light and gives the green coloration to the chloroplast. Chloroplasts, like mitochondria, have an outer and inner membrane. Within the matrix of the chloroplast there is an intricate internal membrane system. The internal membranes are made up of flattened interconnected vesicles that take on a disc-like structure (thylakoid vesicles). The thylakoid vesicles are stacked to form structures called grana, which are separated by a space called the stroma. Within the stroma, carbon dioxide (CO_2) fixation occurs,

in which carbon dioxide is converted to various intermediates during the production of sugars. Chlorophyll is found within the thylakoid vesicles; it absorbs light and, with the involvement of other pigments and enzymes, generates ATP during photosynthesis. Like mitochondria, chloroplasts contain their own double-stranded circular DNA sufficient to encode a few essential proteins. Therefore, most chloroplast proteins must be imported from the cytosol following synthesis on free ribosomes.

Steven R. Goodman

Bibliography. B. Alberts et al., *Molecular Biology of the Cell*, 3d ed., 1994; S. R. Goodman, *Medical Cell Biology*, 2d ed., 1998; H. Lodish et al., *Molecular Cell Biology*, 3d ed., 1995; A. G. Moat and J. W. Foster, *Microbial Physiology*, 3d ed., 1995.

Cell, spectral analysis of

Living cells contain various substances, the concentrations and biological activity of which can be investigated by observing the spectrum of light passed through the cells. Such investigations take advantage of the fact that many substances absorb light in an individually characteristic manner. Thus, the spectrum of light passed through a green leaf has two black bands where red and blue light should appear. The absorption of red and blue light is characteristic of the chlorophylls, the photosynthetic pigments. Today, investigations of cells by optical methods go far beyond the routine analysis of brightly colored pigments that are found widespread and in high concentration, for example, hemoglobin and chlorophyll. Such methods allow the investigation of light-absorbing molecules within the cell whose concentration is 1000 times smaller that that of hemoglobin or of chlorophyll. *See* CHLOROPHYLL; HEMOGLOBIN.

Because the color of biological molecules changes when they undergo chemical reactions, such reactions in the cell can be monitored by spectral analyses. These analyses can be used to monitor reactions occurring in times ranging from 10^{-15} s to minutes. In some cases, the spectral properties can also indicate the environment of the biological molecules in the cell, that is, whether they are rigidly held or free to move and how they react with one another within the cell.

Useful kinds of spectra. Different parts of the spectrum provide different information about molecules in cells.

Infrared spectra (700–5000 nanometers) give information about the structure of molecules; all molecules absorb in the infrared in a characteristic manner.

Visible light spectra (400–700 nm) give information concerning those relatively few biological molecules that absorb light in this region. These molecules thus can be specifically studied in a cell that may contain tens of thousands of other types of molecules.

Ultraviolet spectra (200–400 nm) give information on those molecules that absorb light in this region. Such spectra are not very useful when working with living cells or other light-scattering samples.

Fluorescence and phosphorescence spectra are produced by light emission. When some molecules absorb light in the ultraviolet and visible spectral regions, they can be energized into various electronic excited states. In many instances, the energy of the excited states is dissipated rapidly as heat, and the molecule returns to its original ground state. However, the appropriate excited state can also be dissipated relatively slowly by emitting light at wavelengths slightly longer than that of the excitation light. The emitted light can take one of two forms: fluorescence, which occurs rapidly after excitation and lasts 10^{-9} to 10^{-6} s; and phosphorescence, which has a longer decay time and wavelength range than fluorescence and lasts on the order of 10^{-6} to 10^2 s. Relatively few molecules emit light after absorption.

Light scattering is of two types. When light is scattered without changing wavelength (elastic scattering), the scattering reveals the size and shape of molecules. Another type of scattering is called Raman scattering. In this case, molecules alter the light by slightly shifting the wavelength in a manner that is very specific for the particular molecule. *See* RAMAN EFFECT; SCATTERING OF ELECTROMAGNETIC RADIATION.

Magnetic resonance spectroscopy techniques frequently can resolve components of cells that cannot be visualized by optical methods. *See* ELECTROMAGNETIC RADIATION; MAGNETIC RESONANCE.

Intracellular substances. Spectral analysis by optical methods is limited to those substances which show characteristic peaks, or maxima, of absorption when light absorption is plotted as a function of light wavelength. Whether or not a given substance can be detected depends on the intensity of absorption relative to other substances present at a given absorption maximum. The molecular extinction coefficient quantitatively describes the light absorption of a given substance at a given wavelength. The dependence of absorption A on extinction coefficient ϵ, concentration c, and optical path l is expressed as Beer's law, $A = 10 \exp(-\epsilon \cdot C \cdot l)$. This dependence imposes limitations on the application of optical methods to the study of living cells; only those substances with a high extinction coefficient can be investigated successfully.

Hemoproteins. There are a variety of substances present within living cells, but the number of those of biological interest which also possess a useful extinction coefficient is limited; often these substances are pigments. A large group of biologically interesting pigments belongs to the class known as hemoproteins. Included in this group are the hemoglobins, myoglobins, catalase, peroxidase, and the cytochromes, a large family of hemoproteins that are universally present in all cells. Reduced hemoproteins are characterized by well-defined absorption maxima in the visible spectrum, while the spectra of oxidized hemoproteins are quite different. The absorption spectrum of each hemoprotein is characteristic and individual to that hemoprotein only, a property that gives a considerable degree of specificity to the optical study of these components in cells. Among the hemoproteins, the cytochromes are of particular interest because of the intimate role they play in various processes, for example, in cellular respiration and in photosynthesis. From the cytochrome spectra obtained from an investigation of cells, the ratio of oxidized to reduced forms (the oxidation state) can be determined. The oxidation state of the cytochromes, in turn, depends on the conditions under which the cell is placed. Given any steady-state condition, the oxidation state of each cytochrome component in the cell will reach a definite value, a value which can be determined by spectral analysis. *See* CYTOCHROME.

Flavoproteins and pyridine nucleotides. Other substances of biological interest that are found in cells and that can be studied optically include flavoproteins, a family of proteins that occur abundantly in nature, and the pyridine nucleotides. As in the hemoproteins, the spectral properties of flavoproteins and pyridine nucleotides depend on their oxidation state. Flavoproteins in their oxidized state absorb light in the yellow portion of the visible spectrum and fluoresce strongly in the green; light absorption and fluoresence is quenched when these proteins are reduced. Reduced pyridine nucleotides, NADH and NADPH, show strong light absorption in the blue portion of the spectrum and also fluoresce strongly at longer wavelengths, also in the blue. In the oxidized forms NAD^+ and $NADP^+$, the molecules do

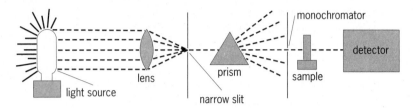

Fig. 1. Basic components used for spectral analysis.

not absorb light or fluoresce. Because of the strong fluorescence, it is often most convenient to study these components by fluorescent techniques.

Iron-sulfur clusters. There is a large group of proteins, the iron-sulfur proteins, which are of considerable biological importance. These substances, referred to individually as iron-sulfur clusters, do not have the properties that can be characterized by optical spectroscopy. However, they can be studied in considerable detail by magnetic resonance spectroscopy, a technique where the spectrum involves magnetic fields and light in the microwave spectral region. This technique is also used to study the position of protein complexes relative to one another in biological membranes.

Subcellular structures. The living cell is a highly organized biological unit. Within the cell there are a variety of structures, each one of which carries out specific functions. The necessary interactions between the subcellular structures that must provide for the normal processes of cell functions and metabolism are not yet well understood. Examples of the well-organized subcellular structures are the mitochondria, where the respiratory processes of the cell are localized, microsomes, peroxisomes, and chloroplasts. In many instances, the study of suspensions of cells, for example, yeast and algal cells, has been reasonably fruitful. However, because of light-scattering problems and the limited numbers of single cells available, it is extraordinarily difficult to study specific processes within a single cell. Rather, it has proven much more profitable to investigate suspensions of subcellular organelles which can be isolated in a reasonably undamaged state, for example, mitochondria and chloroplasts. Such suspensions, prepared by destroying the cell structure, contain a variety of substances suitable for optical, fluorescent, and magnetic resonance analysis and in sufficient concentration to allow precise and quantitative study. Suspensions of mitochondria and chloroplasts have been used extensively in the development of the understanding of cellular respiration and of photosynthesis. *See* CELL (BIOLOGY); CELL PLASTIDS; MITOCHONDRIA.

It is characteristic of biological processes that various proteins, enzymes, and coenzymes react with one another in cycles or sequences. In the processes of cellular respiration, there is a sequence of reactions which involve pyridine nucleotides, flavoproteins, iron-sulfur clusters, and cytochromes in processes involving energy transfer and oxygen consumption. Similarly, photosynthesis involves chlorophylls and accessory pigments, cytochromes,

pyridine-nucleotides, and iron-sulfur clusters. It is particularly important to discover which components are included in various biological processes and the order in which they react with one another; spectral analysis provides the methods for such investigations.

Methods. Any spectral analysis, regardless of its application, utilizes the components in **Fig. 1.** These components consist of a light source from which the light is focused by means of a lens on a narrow slit. The narrow beam of light is then resolved into its component wavelengths by means of a prism or a grating. Lasers have been used as a source of monochromatic light. A narrow band of such light is isolated by means of a second narrow slit and passes through the sample onto an appropriate detector. The signal produced on activation of the detector may be amplified and displayed or recorded on a suitable device. Instruments for measuring light absorption at varying wavelengths utilize the above basic components and are suitable for the study of clear solutions—solutions that do not impose any restrictions, other than those of Beer's law, on the amount of light passing through them.

The spectral analysis of living cells and of subcellular organelles is complicated because some suspensions of particulate matter scatter light and thus limit the amount of light that can pass through them. Suspensions of biological material scatter light by refraction and reflection, and the problem is intensified by changes in the state of the particulate matter in the suspension—such as changes of size with time: swelling and shrinking. Problems of light scattering are magnified by monochromatic light, where high light intensities are difficult to obtain. The most important problem is the impossibility of observing spectra of specific light-absorbing species. Problems of light scattering can be avoided in various ways, for example, by using a low-dispersion spectroscope or a dual-wavelength spectrophotometer.

Microspectroscope. Much of early understanding of blood and muscle pigments and of cellular respiration was obtained through the use of the microspectroscope (**Fig. 2**). Basically, this instrument is a hand spectroscope that uses the human eye as the detector. Within a narrow but biologically interesting spectral region, the human eye is capable of sharp delineation between light and dark; hence, absorption bands can be observed with a considerable degree of accuracy. This instrument is now regarded as a museum piece, but many investigators still find that it is useful for quick observations.

Spectrophotometers. Special photoelectric devices have almost completely replaced visual spectroscopy for examination of light-scattering samples.

The split-beam spectrophotometer measures the difference in absorption between two nearly identical biological suspensions. Monochromatic light is passed alternately through the two samples by means of a vibrating mirror and onto a light detector. If the suspensions under study are identical except for their oxidation state, light scattering will be the same in both, and the light detector will measure only the

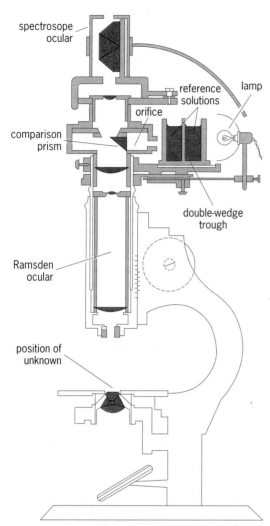

Fig. 2. Microspectroscope used by an observer to view the spectra of the specimen and reference solution simultaneously. (*After D. Keilin and Y. L. Wang, Haemoglobin of Gastrophilus larvae, Biochem. J., 40(5,6):855–866, 1946*)

Temperature studies. The light-absorbing properties of many pigments important to the economy of living cells are altered at low temperatures. Not only is there a marked sharpening of the absorption bands at low temperature, but also a considerably increased absorbancy because of increased path length due to reflections from interfaces on the ice surfaces. Thus, the use of low temperatures, 77 K and below, increases the sensitivity and specificity of detection. The effects of low temperature are illustrated in **Fig. 4** in a suspension of yeast cells, measured at 77°F (25°C) and at 77 K (−196°C). Different path lengths were used at each temperature; hence, the increased absorbancy at low temperature is not shown. The 77 K spectrum clearly shows the sharp delineation of absorbing components that can be realized at that temperature. Note that there is a shift of absorption maxima toward shorter wavelengths at 77 K.

Microspectrophotometer. Spectrophotometers, utilizing the principles discussed above but including a microscope for the localization of the object under study, have also been developed. Such microspectrophotometers are capable of carrying out spectral analyses within the dimensions of a single cell.

Ultraviolet studies. Such studies are difficult to carry out with intact cells and tissues, light-scattering problems increase with decreasing wavelengths, and there are too many substances with low extinction coefficients and overlapping absorbancies in this spectral region. Pertinent information is most easily obtained by using clear extracts of cells and tissues. Extracts can be prepared that contain nucleic acids, amino acids, various metabolites, and quinones, for example, the ubiquinones.

Infrared studies and Raman spectra. Both of these reflect the vibrational structure of the molecule. Water absorbs in the infrared region, so most infrared studies are done on concentrated solutions in order to increase the signal over that of water. Infrared studies are particularly useful for monitoring protein conformation and the structure of lipids in membranes.

difference in light adsorption between the two samples. The result is an oxidized-minus-reduced difference spectrum and will give the absorption maxima between the reduced and oxidized redox components present in the sample. Such a spectrophotometer is capable of scanning difference spectra in the visible and near-ultraviolet regions (**Fig. 3**).

The dual-wavelength spectrophotometer uses two sources of monochromatic light that are passed through a single light-scattering sample, again by means of a vibrating mirror. If one light beam is set at a known absorption maximum and the other at wavelength where there is no absorption change between the oxidized and reduced species, the photoelectric circuit will measure the true absorption difference between these two wavelengths and will reject almost completely changes of light transmission that are independent of wavelength. With such a device, one can measure rates of oxidation or reduction of redox components. As with the split-beam spectrophotometer, difference spectra of redox components of biological samples can be scanned.

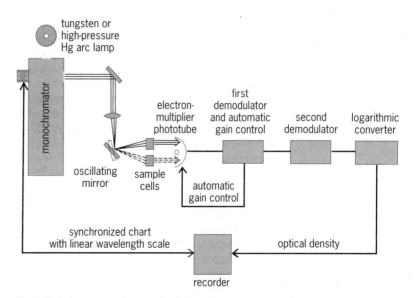

Fig. 3. Split-beam recording spectrophotometer.

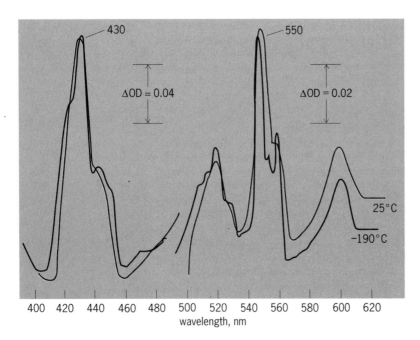

Fig. 4. Spectra, by difference, of the pigments present in suspensions of yeast cells. These spectra show the changes in absorbency plotted as a function of wavelength. ΔOD is optical density increment.

Raman spectra are relatively weak, but very useful for studying the heme proteins, where they can help determine the structure of the heme.

Fluorescence and phosphorescence. Fluorescence is widely used as an analytical tool for the investigation of cells. Similar to the spectrophotometer, a spectrofluorimeter consists of a light source from which the light is made monochromatic by a prism or grating. Instead of measuring how much light is absorbed, however, the light that is emitted from the sample is measured. The light is emitted at higher wavelengths than those of the absorbed light, and it is measured at right angles relative to the exciting light by passing it through a second monochromator. In the absorption instrument the difference in intensity between two light beams is measured. In the fluorescence spectrofluorimeter the absolute value of light intensity is measured. Because single photons of light can be measured with modern equipment, fluorescence can measure very low concentrations of molecules. However, the technique is limited to only those molecules which fluoresce.

Fluorescence measurements are especially adaptable for investigating the environment of molecules. The rotational motion of a molecule depends upon its size and viscosity. These can be measured by fluorescence polarization. In this technique the molecule is excited with polarized light. If the molecule moves in the time scale of the fluorescent excited state (1–100 nanoseconds), the emitted light will be partially depolarized, the amount of depolarization depending upon the molecular rotation. This technique has been used to determine molecular size and the viscosity of the environment around cells.

Phosphorescence can be used in much the same way as fluorescence, but molecular oxygen interferes with the phosphorescence light intensity. By measuring phosphorescence intensity or lifetime, the concentration of oxygen within the cells can be determined. *See* FLUORESCENCE; PHOSPHORESCENCE.

Measurement of cell component interaction. The reactions of the cell occur very specifically, for example, if A→B→C, the scheme A→C→B will never occur. Spectral analysis is very useful for finding the order and rate of reactions of cell components. A common method for carrying out such experiments is to initiate the reactions with a strong light signal, usually from a laser, and then to follow the reactions by measuring the absorption of the components with a weaker light. This method has been used to study photosynthesis, where reactions occur in as fast as 1 picosecond (10^{-12} s).

Walter D. Bonner, Jr.; Jane M. Vanderkooi

Bibliography. C. R. Cantor and P. R. Schimmel, *Biophysical Chemistry II: Techniques for the Study of Biological Structure and Function*, 1980; S. P. Colowick and N. O. Kaplan (eds.), *Special Techniques for the Enzymologist*, vol. 4 of *Methods in Enzymology*, 1957; D. C. Youvan and B. L. Marrs, Molecular mechanisms of photosynthesis, *Sci. Amer.*, 256(6):42–49, 1987.

Cell adhesion

The process whereby cells interact and attach to other cells or to inanimate surfaces. Cell adhesion is mediated by cell surface proteins and associated macromolecules. It forms the physical basis of multicellularity, morphogenesis and embryonic development, tissue integrity, host–pathogen interactions, immune system function, and the ecological integration of microbial communities. In addition to attaching cells to one another, cell adhesion systems act to coordinate a wide range of cellular behaviors. In animal cells, sites of adhesion serve to organize the system of intracellular protein filaments, known as the cytoskeleton, responsible for cell shape and movement. Adhesive interactions are critical for juxtacrine signaling, by which neighboring cells communicate. Juxtacrine signals regulate gene expression and cell behavior and determine whether a cell survives, divides, differentiates, or undergoes programmed cell death (apoptosis).

Cell–Cell Interactions in Microorganisms

Although it is common to think of microorganisms, for example bacteria and yeasts, as isolated individuals, more often these organisms live within complex communities known as biofilms.

Biofilms. Within a biofilm, cells are embedded in an extracellular matrix that they themselves secrete. Within this matrix the organisms interact in complex ways. Their properties, for example their susceptibility to antibiotics as well as their metabolic requirements, are often dramatically different from those of the same organism living in isolation (monoculture). In fact, only a small percentage of known microorganisms can be grown in laboratory monoculture; most are dependent upon interactions with their neighbors. Within a biofilm, organisms cooperate, compete, and prey upon one another. Many microbially derived antibiotics have their evolutionary origins in such ecological interactions. Biofilms form rapidly on wet surfaces, as in the overnight appearance of plaque on teeth. The formation of biofilms is of great practical significance for any system in which microorganisms can colonize surfaces. *See* ANTIBIOTIC; BIOFILM; CORROSION.

Adhesins. The adhesion of microorganisms to the cells of higher plants and animals is a critical prerequisite for causing disease. Such interactions are mediated by molecules, generally cell-surface proteins, known generically as adhesins (**Fig. 1**). Adhesins interact specifically with host cell surface proteins and glycolipids, which serve as pathogen receptors. The true functions of these "receptors" have nothing to do with pathogenesis: the receptors have simply been exploited by the pathogen. In some cases, the pathogen itself can synthesize and secrete its own receptor, which is taken up by host cells and then displayed on the cell surface (Fig. 1c). Once a pathogen adheres to a target cell, either it can modify the behavior of the cell (for example, *Yersinia pseudotuberculosis*) or, in cases such as *Listeria monocytogenes*, it can actually invade the cell and live within the cytoplasm. *See* LISTERIOSIS; PATHOGEN; YERSINIA.

Cell–Cell Interactions in Multicellular Organisms

Cell-cell interactions become more elaborate in true multicellular organisms such as plants and animals. These interactions play a critical role in processes such as embryonic development and the maintenance of tissue integrity, in which they have been studied extensively. In most cases, plant cells are rigidly constrained by a specialized extracellular matrix, the cell wall, which limits cell–cell movement. Dynamic adhesive interactions do occur, however, during the process of fertilization. In animal cells, adhesion is more dynamic and very highly specialized. The regulation of cell adhesion is central to morphogenesis (the process by which cells rearrange to form tissues and organs), the development of the nervous system and the specialized connections that underlie coordinated movement, memory, and cognition, and the functioning of the immune system. Aberrations in cell adhesion mechanisms underlie metastatic processes associated with cancer progression. *See* ANIMAL MORPHOGENESIS; CANCER (MEDICINE); FERTILIZATION; PLANT MORPHOGENESIS.

Origins of cell–cell adhesion. The origins of cell-cell adhesion are closely associated with the origins of true multicellularity. There are a number of protozoa, such as the choanoflagellates, that can exist in either unicellular or multicellular colonial forms. Based on the morphological similarities in cell structure, and now supported by molecular phylogenetic data, it appears that choanoflagellates are close evolutionary relatives to the animals. In true metazoans, such as the sponges (Porifera), hydra, corals, and jellyfish (Cnidaria), the number of distinct cell types

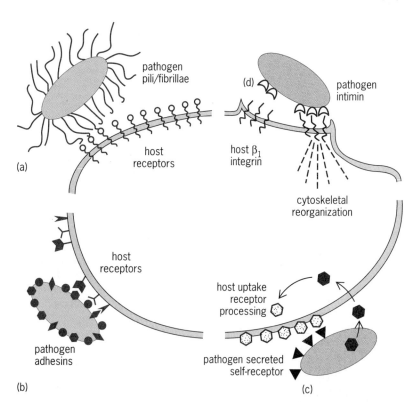

Fig. 1. Adhesive interactions between pathogen and host are central to the process of infection. Were it not for their ability to adhere to host cells, most pathogenic fungi, bacteria, and viruses would be rapidly removed from host-cell surfaces. By specifically adhering to host-cell surface molecules, a pathogen can target itself to a hospitable environment. Such adhesive interactions involve a number of mechanisms, including (*a*) fibrous pili or fibrillae, (*b*) adhesin-type carbohydrate binding proteins, or (*d*) intimins, which bind to surface integrins. In some cases, (*c*) the pathogen itself secretes its own receptor, which is taken up by the target cell; this self-receptor is then placed on the host cell surface, where it mediates pathogen adhesion. (*Adapted from T. M. Wizemann, J. E. Adamou, and S. Langermann, Adhesins as targets for vaccine development, Emerg. Infect. Dis., 5(3), 1999; http://www.cdc.gov/ncidod/eid/vol5no3/wizeman.htm*)

increases as does the repertoire of possible cell–cell interactions. These interactions, between cells and between cells and extracellular matrix, are mediated by specific membrane proteins and accessory factors. *See* CELL (BIOLOGY); CELL DIFFERENTIATION; CHOANOFLAGELLIDA.

Cell-surface adhesion proteins. Adhesion is mediated either directly by macromolecules embedded in the plasma membrane or indirectly through molecules deposited on the cell surface. In animal cells, a number of distinct protein families mediate cell-cell and cell-extracellular matrix interactions (see **table**).

Cadherins. Among the best-studied protein families are the cadherins. These proteins share a common structural motif, the cadherin domain (**Fig. 2**). A classical cadherin contains an extracellular domain composed of five linked cadherin domains, a transmembrane domain, and a "cytoplasmic" domain. Cadherins of the same type interact in a homotypic (like-to-like) manner through their extracellular domains. Different cell types synthesize different types of classical cadherins, which enables them to adhere to cells of the same type. The family of membrane proteins that contains cadherin domains is large: over 100 such genes encoding these proteins have been identified in humans. These cadherin

Some major cell adhesion proteins of animals		
Protein name	Known function	Details
Cadherins	Cell–cell adhesion	Typically homotypic
Protocadherins	Cell–cell adhesion	Synaptic adhesion
Selectins	Cell–cell adhesion	Interactions between lymphocytes and capillary cells
Ig-family adhesion molecules	Cell–cell adhesion	Diverse developmental events
Integrins	Cell-matrix interactions	Heterodimeric
Notch	Juxtacrine signaling	Transcellular signaling
T-cell receptor/MHC	Juxtacrine signaling	Transcellular signaling
Fas/Fas ligand	Juxtacrine signaling	Regulation of apoptosis

family proteins perform a wide range of adhesive and signaling functions. *See* CELL MEMBRANES; GENE; PROTEIN.

The intracellular domain of a classical cadherin protein interacts with cytoplasmic proteins known as catenins. Catenins mediate the binding of cytoskeletal polymers to the site of cell–cell adhesion, an adherence junction. They also regulate the stability of cadherin proteins. In vertebrate cells there are two generic types of cadherin-mediated cell–cell junctions: adherens junctions, which link to actin filaments, and desmosomes (macula adherens), which anchor intermediate filaments. Variants of these junctions are involved in linking the cells of the heart, skin, and vasculature together. Coordinated changes in adhesion junction–associated cytoskeletal systems are responsible for changes in the morphology of tissue sheets. Defects in either the cytoskeletal system or the adherence junction are associated with cellular fragility diseases, such as epidermolysis bullosum simplex.

Protocadherins. In addition to the classical cadherins, there is a family of cadherin-domain proteins, the protocadherins, that can be distinguished based upon gene organization. Many of these protocadherin genes are organized in a conventional manner, whereas others are more complex. The genes for the mammalian α and γ protocadherins consist of 14–22 regions (exons), each of which encodes a distinct extracellular and transmembrane domain; there is also a set of three exons that encodes a common cytoplas-

mic domain. Differential RNA splicing (a process by which different messenger RNA molecules are produced from a single gene transcript by splicing together different sets of exon regions) is used to generate a diverse set of protocadherin proteins from a single gene. Currently it is thought that this molecular diversity may be used to establish and maintain specific cell–cell contacts within the developing nervous system.

Selectins. Selectins are another class of membrane proteins associated with the invasion of white blood cells (lymphocytes) into sites of infection. The overall structure of the selectins is similar to that of the cadherins. Their extracellular domain consists of a series of repeating motifs that ends in a "carbohydrate recognition," or lectin, domain. As lymphocytes pass through the bloodstream, they interact weakly with carbohydrates associated with the surface of endothelial cells, which line blood vessels. However, in regions of cell damage, inflammatory signals transmitted by soluble proteins known as cytokines are released by the damaged or infected cell and lead to modifications in the surface of nearby capillary endothelial cells. In regions of cytokine signaling, lymphocytes (which normally move through the capillary) interact with selectins, causing them to adhere to and roll along the capillary's inner surface. Interactions with selectins together with other signaling/adhesion molecules lead lymphocytes to strongly adhere to, and then migrate between, the endothelial cells, moving out of the bloodstream

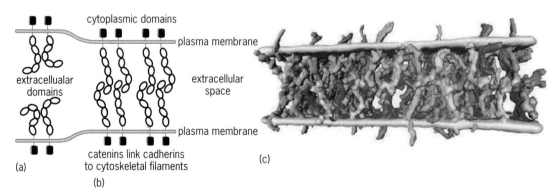

Fig. 2. Cadherins mediate homotypic (like-to-like) adhesion. (*a***) Cadherin proteins project outward from the cell surface. (***b***) When two cells come together, the opposing extracellular domains of the cadherins interact. This interaction is then stabilized through interactions with the cytoskeleton mediated by catenin proteins. Various electron microscopy techniques have been used to generate a more exact description of the adhesive interactions. (***c***) A section of the extracellular portion of a desmosome is modeled; the extracellular domains of individual cadherin molecules are indicated by various shades. (***Reprinted with permission from W. He, P. Cowin, and D. L. Stokes, Untangling desmosomal knots with electron tomography, Science, 302:109–113, 2003. Copyright © American Association for the Advancement of Science***)**

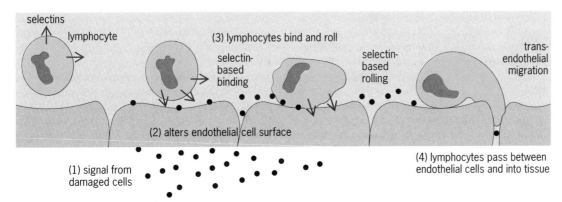

Fig. 3. Regulation of adhesion within the immune system. Normally, white blood cells (lymphocytes) migrate throughout the body via the bloodstream. However, in regions of infection or cell damage, signals from the infected cells lead to changes in the capillary endothelial cells that enable lymphocytes to adhere to the capillary surface via their selectins. The lymphocytes roll along the capillary surface and then migrate between the endothelial cells and into the tissue, where they can protect against the spread of infectious agents such as bacteria and viruses.

and into the damaged tissue (**Fig. 3**). *See* BLOOD; CYTOKINE; INFLAMMATION; LECTINS.

Immunoglobulin superfamily adhesion proteins. A third major group of cell adhesion proteins are built from a structural domain that is also found in immunoglobulin (antibody) molecules. These Ig-domain adhesion proteins can mediate either homotypic or heterotypic adhesive interactions. The genes that encode these proteins are complex, and a large number of variants can be generated from each through a process of differential splicing.

Types of cell adherence junctions. In addition to the adherens junctions and desmosomes (**Fig. 4a**), there are other distinct types of cell–cell junctions.

Hemidesmosomes. Hemidesmosomes mediate interactions with extracellular matrix fibers (Fig. 4c). Like desmosomes, they anchor intermediate filaments to the plasma membrane and act to mechanically strengthen tissues.

Tight junctions. Tight junctions (zonula occludens) are typically formed between epithelial and endothelial cells (Fig. 4a). Composed of strands of membrane proteins, tight junctions act to block the movement of extracellular fluids and molecules through the spaces between cells. The disruption of tight junction integrity has been linked to multiple sclerosis and other pathogenic conditions.

Gap junctions. Gap junctions, on the other hand, act to mediate the movement of small molecules directly from the cytoplasm of one cell to that of its neighbor (Fig. 4b). Gap junctions form when two cells are so closely opposed to one another that connexin hex-

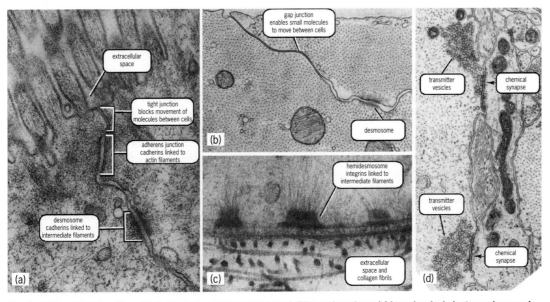

Fig. 4. Gap and tight junctions. Cell are connected by a number of different junctions. (*a*) In a classical electron micrograph of rat intestinal epithelia, the cells are linked by a complex of tight junctions, adherens junctions, desmosomes, and gap junctions (not shown). Tight junctions block molecular diffusion between cells, whereas adherens junctions and desmosomes anchor cytoskeletal systems. (*b*) Gap junctions are particularly prominent in cells that are electrically coupled to one another, such as these heart cells. (*c*) Cell layers are attached to extracellular matrix components through hemidesmosomes which anchor intermediate filaments in this electron micrograph of salamander skin. (*d*) An electron micrograph of lamprey nervous tissue showing typical neuronal synapses, which are modified adherence junctions specialized to facilitate neurotransmitter release by vesicle fusion and receptor. (*Reprinted with permission from D. W. Fawcett, The Cell, 2d ed., W. B. Saunders, 1981. Copyright © Elsevier Inc.*)

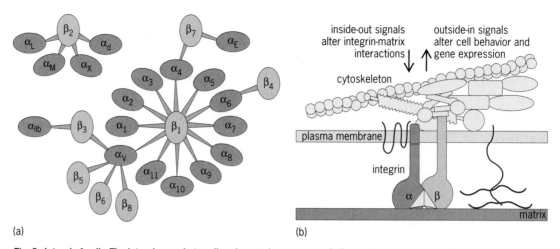

Fig. 5. Integrin family. The integrins are heterodimeric proteins, composed of α and β polypeptides. (*a*) Certain subunits are found in specific pairs; for example, the β_1 polypeptide can form functional heterodimers with many different α-type polypeptides, whereas the β_4 polypeptide is known to pair only with α_6. (*b*) The integrins are membrane proteins—their extracellular domain interacts with components of the extracellular matrix, while their intracellular domain interacts with the components of the cytoskeleton and signaling systems. Different integrin pairs have different binding affinities for matrix and intracellular molecules. The binding of an integrin can lead to a specific signal within the cell (outside-in signaling) that can alter cytoskeletal organization, cellular behavior, and gene expression. Similarly, changes within the cell (inside-out signaling) can alter the binding of the integrin to matrix components. (*Part a courtesy of T. J. Kunicki. Part b adapted with permission from R. O. Hynes and Q. Zhao, The evolution of cell adhesion, J. Cell Biol., 150:F89–F96, 2000. © The Rockefeller University Press.*)

amers on one cell can interact with connexin hexamers on the other. Together they form a transcellular protein, a connexon. Before they interact, the connexin hexamers are closed; but once they bind to one another, they form a pore that allows the direct diffusion of small molecules (less than $\sim$1000 daltons) between cells. This type of junction is used by some neurons to pass electrical information directly from cell to cell, and by cardiac muscle cells to coordinate contractile activity. At an electrical synapse, the depolarization of a presynaptic cell can directly depolarize, and thereby activate or otherwise alter, the postsynaptic cell.

Chemical synapses. At chemical synapses (Fig. 4*d*), there are no gap junctions. Instead, the pre- and postsynaptic cells are tightly adherent, but there is a clear separation between the two cell membranes. The signal between the cell involves the secretion of neurotransmitter from the presynaptic cell and its reception by proteins located in the membrane of the postsynaptic cell. The presynaptic cell can be identified by the concentration of vesicles, which contain neurotransmitter.

Cell–extracellular matrix interactions: integrins. Integrins are heterodimeric membrane proteins composed of an α-integrin and a β-integrin polypeptides (**Fig. 5***a*). Integrins mediate interactions primarily with extracellular molecules, although cell–cell adhesive functions for these proteins have also been reported. Different integrin subunit pairs have different patterns of binding specificity. The cytoplasmic domains of integrins often interact with the cytoskeleton. For example, the α_6, β_4 integrin is associated with hemidesmosomes. Disruption of these junctions is associated with the autoimmune skin disease pemphigus. Most other integrins interact with the actin cytoskeleton.

Outside-in and inside-out signaling. Cell adhesion systems can be regulated in two general ways. The binding of the extracellular domain of an adhesion molecule to a specific target molecule (ligand) can alter the structure of the cytoplasmic domain, leading to changes within the adherent cell. This is a specific form of allosteric regulation known as outside-in signaling (Fig. 5*b*). It enables cells to "know" with which types of cells and extracellular molecules they are associated. Conversely, changes within the adherent cell can lead to changes in the extracellular domain of the adhesion protein, such that the molecule no longer binds effectively to its ligands. This inside-out signaling enables cells to disconnect from their neighbors and plays a critical role in the remodeling of tissues during embryonic development and during cancer progression.

Juxtacrine signaling. There are many ways that cells can communicate with one another. By adhering to one another, signals can be directed to only a signal target cell; this type of signaling is known as juxtacrine signaling. It is most obvious in the synaptic connections that link neurons into networks capable of processing complex inputs. Juxtacrine signaling is, however, widespread within metazoans.

Notch signaling. A phylogenetically conserved juxtacrine signaling system is the Notch system (**Fig. 6***a*). Notch proteins, located on the cell surface, can bind to Notch ligand proteins located on the surface of adjacent cells—something that can occur only if the two cells are very close to one another (that is, juxtaposed). The binding of Notch to its ligand activates a protein complex containing the presenilin and γ-secretase. (Mutations in presenilin have been linked to a specific form of early-onset Alzheimer's disease.) The activated presenilin/secretase complex makes a specific cut in the

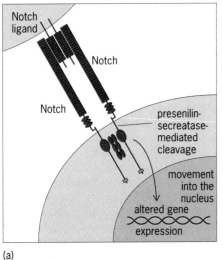
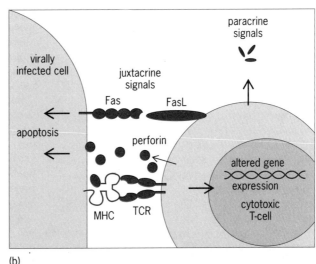

(a)   (b)

Fig. 6. Juxtacrine signaling. As two cells come close to one another, there is an opportunity for interactions between their surface components. This type of juxtacrine signaling plays critical roles during development and in the adult. (*a*) In Notch signaling, the binding of Notch to its ligand on a adjacent cell activates the proteolytic cleavage of the Notch polypeptide. The released cytoplasmic domain then moves into the nucleus where it alters gene expression and, therefore, cellular behavior and fate. (*b*) An example of immune system juxtacrine signaling. A virally infected cells displays virally derived peptides on its surface, complexed to a major histocompatibility complex (MHC) protein. A T-cell with the appropriate T-cell receptor (TCR) on its surface will recognize the infected cell, and this will initiate changes within the T-cell leading to the release of cytotoxic molecules (perforins in this example) that will lead to the apoptotic death of the infected cell. A second juxtacrine signaling event is facilitated by the MHC–TCR interaction; the surface molecule Fas binds the Fas ligand (Fas L), which induces apoptosis in the virally infected cell.

Notch protein, releasing the protein's cytoplasmic domain, which then moves into the cell nucleus and alters the expression of target genes. *See* ALZHEIMER'S DISEASE.

T-cell receptors/MHC. Juxtacrine signaling is particularly important within the immune system, in which cell surface receptors are used to recognize specific cell types and thereby target signals to these cells (Fig. 6*b*). For example, cytotoxic T-cells recognize virally infected cells through an adhesive interaction between their surface T-cell receptors (TCRs) and major histocompatibility complex (MHC) protein molecules on the infected cell surface. This interaction produces outside-in signaling in the T-cell that leads it to secrete perforins; these proteins generate pores in the target cell and lead to its death. The tight apposition of T-cell and target cell also enables the Fas protein on the target cell to bind to its ligand, FasL, on the T-cell. This interaction triggers an apoptotic (programmed cell death) reaction in the target cell. *See* APOPTOSIS; CYTOLYSIS; HISTO-COMPATIBILITY.

Morphogenesis and the regulation of adhesion. Dramatic changes in cell–cell interactions are associated with developmental events such as gastrulation, which leads to the formation of the three germ layers (ectoderm, mesoderm, and endoderm); neurulation, by which the neural plate folds to form the neural tube, which goes on to become the brain and spinal cord; neural crest formation, by which cells separate from neuroepithelium and migrate away to eventually form much of the craniofacial skeleton and the peripheral nervous system; and organogenesis, by which cells interact to form the various organs, such as the liver, kidney, and heart. In each case, cells must

make and break appropriate adhesive interactions.

The signals that instruct cells to maintain or remodel their adhesive properties are complex and depend upon gene and protein activity. Both are influenced by surrounding cells and molecules. The interplay of inside-out and outside-in signaling, together with changes in gene expression, can maintain a cell in stable association with its neighbors or lead it to disconnect. *See* DEVELOPMENTAL BIOLOGY; DEVELOPMENTAL GENETICS; EMBRYOGENESIS; EMBRYONIC INDUCTION.

Study methods. There are several methods used to study cellular adhesion.

Reassociation of dissociated cells. A common approach is to examine the reassociation of dissociated cells (**Fig. 7**). The normal structure of many cell adhesion proteins depends upon the presence of Ca^{2+} ions; removing Ca^{2+} through the use of chelators can lead to the dissociation of tissues into isolated cells. More often, the links between cells are more stable, and the proteins responsible must be digested to release individual cells. This is done using proteases, protein catalysts (enzymes) that degrade proteins. With proteases, it is generally necessary to allow the cells to recover. During this recovery period, the cell replaces membrane proteins damaged by the protease treatment.

To allow reassociation, a suspension of cells is shaken so that only cells that strongly adhere are able to establish stable junctions to one another. This leads to the formation of clumps of cells. The speed at which these cellular aggregates form is a measure of the strength of the adhesion between cells. If cells of different types are present in the suspension, they will form either separate aggregates or aggregates in

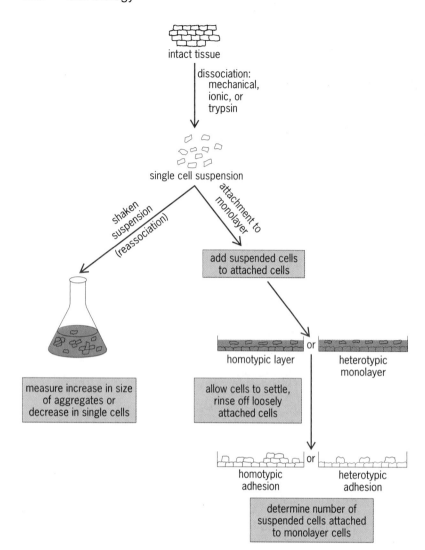

intact tissue

dissociation: mechanical, ionic, or trypsin

single cell suspension

shaken suspension (reassociation)

attachment to monolayer

add suspended cells to attached cells

homotypic layer   or   heterotypic monolayer

measure increase in size of aggregates or decrease in single cells

allow cells to settle, rinse off loosely attached cells

homotypic adhesion   or   heterotypic adhesion

determine number of suspended cells attached to monolayer cells

Fig. 7. Methods used to study reassociation of dissociated cells.

which the different cell types are segregated from one another within a single aggregate.

A related technique by which to study cell adhesion involves a preestablished layer of cells, a monolayer, grown on a tissue culture dish. Dissociated cells are added to the culture plate, and after various lengths of time the surface is washed to remove loosely adherent cells. The number of cells that remain attached to the monolayer provides a measure of adherence.

Antibody generation. Another method to study the role of a particular adhesion protein in a specific process is to generate antibodies directed against the extracellular domain of the protein. Some of these antibodies, when applied to a cell, will bind to the protein and interfere with interactions required for adhesion. Most antibody molecules are multivalent, which enables them to mediate adhesive interactions. It is, however, simple to cleave antibody molecules using specific proteases and so produce monovalent antibody fragments. Known as Fab fragments, these molecules retain their binding specificity but do not themselves promote adhesion. If a

Fab fragment that binds to a specific cell adhesion molecule blocks cell–cell aggregation, this is taken as direct evidence for the involvement of the target molecule in the adhesion process.

Genetically engineered mutant proteins. More recently, the use of genetically engineered mutant versions of various cell adhesion proteins have been used to study cell-cell and cell–matrix interactions. For example, the DNA sequence encoding a classical cadherin can be manipulated so that a new, modified version is constructed that encodes the extracellular domain and a membrane anchor, but not the cytoplasmic domain. Since the formation of a normal adhesion junction depends upon the cytoplasmic domain, this "dominant-negative"-acting polypeptide will disrupt the normal process of adhesion junction formation. *See* ANTIBODY; GENETIC ENGINEERING; MONOCLONAL ANTIBODIES; MUTATION.

Michael W. Klymkowsky

Bibliography. B. Alberts et al., *Molecular Biology of the Cell*, 4th ed., 2003; N. King, C. T. Hittinger, and S. B. Carroll, Evolution of key cell signaling and adhesion protein families predates animal origins, *Science*, 301:361–363, 2003; J. C. McKenzie and R. M. Klein, *Basic Concepts in Cell Biology and Histology*, McGraw-Hill, 2000.

Cell biology

The study of the activities, functions, properties, and structures of cells. Cells were discovered in the middle of the seventeenth century after the microscope was invented. In the following two centuries, with steadily improved microscopes, cells were studied in a wide variety of plants, animals, and microorganisms, leading to the discovery of the cell nucleus and several other major cell parts. By the 1830s biologists recognized that all organisms are composed of cells, a realization that is now known as the Cell Doctrine. The Cell Doctrine constitutes the first major tenet upon which the contemporary science of cell biology is founded. By the late 1800s biologists had established that cells do not arise de novo, but come only by cell division, that is, division of a preexisting cell into two daughter cells. This is the second major tenet upon which the modern study of cells is based. *See* CELL DIVISION; MICROSCOPE.

By the end of the nineteenth century chromosomes had been discovered, and biologists had described mitosis—the distribution at cell division of chromosomes to daughter cells. Subsequent studies showed that the chromosomes contain genes and that mitosis distributes a copy of every chromosome and hence every gene to each daughter cell during cell division. This established the basis of cell heredity and ultimately the basis of heredity in multicellular organisms. *See* CHROMOSOME; MITOSIS.

Microscope studies established that some kinds of organisms are composed of a single cell and some, such as plants and animals, are made up of many cells—usually many billions. Unicellular organisms are the bacteria, protozoa, some fungi, and some algae. All other organisms are multicellular. An adult human, for example, consists of about 200 cell types that collectively amount to more than 10^{14} cells. Microscope studies revealed that all organisms fall into two major groups, the prokaryotes and the eukaryotes. In prokaryotes, the genetic material is not segregated by a membranous envelope into a distinct nucleus. Prokaryotes are the bacteria, of which there are many thousands of species. Eukaryotes are organisms whose cells possess a nucleus that is clearly defined by an enveloping double membrane. Eukaryotes are the protozoa, fungi, algae, plants, and animals; some are unicellular and some are multicellular. The number of species is unknown, but exceeds 10 million. *See* EUKARYOTAE; PROKARYOTAE.

All modern research recognizes that in both unicellular and multicellular organisms the cell is the fundamental unit, housing the genetic material and the biochemical organization that account for the existence of life. Many millions of different species of cells, showing tremendous diversity in structure and metabolic capabilities, exist on Earth. Cells as different as a bacterium, an ameba, a plant leaf cell, and a human liver cell appear to be so unrelated in structure and life-style that they might seem to have little in common; however, the study of cells has shown that the similarities among these diverse cell types are more profound than the differences. These studies have established a modern set of tenets that bring unity to the study of many diverse cell types. These tenets are: (1) All cells store information in genes made of deoxyribonucleic acid (DNA). (2) The genetic code used in the genes is the same in all species of cells. (3) All cells decode the genes in their DNA by a ribonucleic acid (RNA) system that translates genetic information into proteins. (4) All cells synthesize proteins by using a structure called the ribosome. (5) Proteins govern the activities, functions, and structures in all cells. (6) All cells need energy to operate; they all use the molecule adenosine triphosphate (ATP) as the currency for transfer of energy from energy sources to energy needs. (7) All cells are enclosed by a plasma membrane composed of lipid and protein molecules. *See* CELL MEMBRANES; GENETICS; RIBOSOMES.

In the twentieth century the study of cells, which had been dominated for more than 200 years by microscopy, has been enormously expanded with many other experimental methods. The breaking open of a large mass of cells and the separation of released cell parts into pure fractions led to the discovery of functions contributed by different structures and organelles. For example, mitochondria were shown to be organelles that carry out energy metabolism and supply the entire cell with the energy-rich molecule adenosine triphosphate, and the thousands of small RNA-protein particles in the cell cytoplasm, called ribosomes, were discovered to be factories that carry out protein synthesis. This work was greatly accelerated after World War II by the availability of radioactive isotopes, which were used to identify and trace biochemical activities of various cell parts. *See* MITOCHONDRIA.

Beginning in the 1950s, the application of the electron microscope, with its great power of magnification, led to discoveries about cell structures, especially the endoplasmic reticulum, mitochondria and chloroplasts, the nuclear envelope, chromosomes, nucleoli, lysosomes, the Golgi complex of membranes, peroxisomes, centrioles, cilia, flagella, the cell membrane, the cytoskeleton, and cell walls. *See* CELL ORGANIZATION; ELECTRON MICROSCOPE.

Contemporary research in cell biology is concerned with many problems of cell operation and behavior. Cell reproduction is of special concern because it is essential for the survival of all unicellular and multicellular forms of life. Cell reproduction is the means by which a single cell, the fertilized egg, can give rise to the trillions of cells in an adult multicellular organism. Disrupted control of cell reproduction, resulting in accumulation of disorganized masses of functionally useless cells, is the essence of cancer. Indeed, all diseases ultimately result from the death or misfunctioning of one or another group of cells in a plant or animal. The study of cells pervades all areas of medical research and medical treatment. Great advances were made during the 1980s in learning how cells of the immune system combat infection, and the nature of their failure to resist the acquired immune deficiency syndrome (AIDS) virus. *See* ACQUIRED IMMUNE DEFICIENCY SYNDROME (AIDS); CANCER (MEDICINE); CELL SENESCENCE.

The development of methods to grow plant and animal cells in culture has provided new ways to study cells free of the experimental complications encountered with intact plants and animals. Cell culture has greatly facilitated analysis of abnormal cells, including transformation of normal cells into cancer cells. Cultured cells are also used extensively to study cell differentiation, cell aging, cell movement, and many other cell functions. *See* TISSUE CULTURE.

In parallel with cell biology, the fields of genetics, biochemistry, and molecular biology have likewise greatly expanded. As knowledge and understanding have increased, these fields have overlapped and fused more and more with one another, resulting in a unified multidisciplinary approach to the study of life. This confluence will increasingly facilitate research on the cellular basis of life and provide expanded opportunities for the study of many areas in medicine, genetic engineering, agriculture, evolution, and higher functions of the vertebrate brain. *See* BIOCHEMISTRY; CELL (BIOLOGY); GENETIC ENGINEERING; MOLECULAR BIOLOGY.   David M. Prescott

Bibliography. B. Alberts et al., *Molecular Biology of the Cell*, 3d ed., 1994; W. M. Becker, *The World of the Cell*, 4th ed., 2000; J. Darnell et al., *Molecular Cell Biology*, 1986; D. Fawcett, *The Cell*, 2d ed., 1981; L. J. Kleinsmith and V. M. Kish, *Principles of Cell Biology*, 1988; D. M. Prescott, *Cells: Principles of Molecular Structure and Function*, 1988.

Cell constancy

The condition in which the entire body of an adult animal or plant consists of a fixed number of cells that is the same in all members of the species. This phenomenon is also called eutely. The largest group of animals exhibiting eutely are the nematode worms, one of the largest of all animal phyla, and of great medical and agricultural importance as parasites of plants, animals, and humans. A plant that exhibits eutely is usually called a coenobium. Many species of semimicroscopic aquatic green algae exist as coenobia, such as the common *Volvox* and *Pandorina*.

Numerical limitation occurs in certain organs and organ systems, notably the brain and muscles of annelid worms, mollusks, and vertebrates. This is essentially a localized eutely. A related but different phenomenon, observed for many animal cells when cultured, is that normal cells divide some specific number of times and then stop dividing. Thus the life-span, as measured by number of cell cycles, is limited; for many human cell types this is about 50 cell generations.

Investigations on cell constancy and limitation center on three areas. One is the investigation of the factors that limit cell proliferation; this is related to the general problems of growth and differentiation as well as to cancer. A second active area of interest is the use of animals such as mollusks and nematodes in neurophysiological research because they possess nerve centers with a fixed and very small number of cells. Analysis of these simple nervous systems, it is anticipated, will permit better understanding of the organization and functioning of nervous systems, even those of much greater complexity. The third area is muscle development in meat animals such as chickens, beef cattle, and swine. The work on muscle in cattle was stimulated by the discovery of "doublemuscled" cattle in which many but not all of the muscles are abnormally enlarged. The muscle hypertrophy in these cattle is due to a single, semidominant gene which has several additional effects, including reduced head size and amount of fatty tissue.

Limiting factors. The factors that sharply limit cell proliferation are unknown. It is clear, however, that in both plants and animals a fundamental distinction exists between growth by cell proliferation and growth by cell enlargement. It is significant in this connection that heavy metals, which will form mercaptides with the sulfhydryl groups of the cell, will block cell division but not cell enlargement. It is also true that the formation of a coenobium in a plant bears a certain resemblance to the cleavage of an egg in an animal. In both cases, a single large cell undergoes a rapid series of mitoses, resulting in a group of many small cells. It is conceivable that in both cases the final slowdown of cell division is due to an exhaustion of the readily available supply of nucleic acids and other constituents required for the rapid formation of new chromosomes.

Although plausible, such a theory gives little insight into why in one case the cells can continue to divide at a slow pace while in the other they must wait until the initial large size is again reached. The work of G. Fankhauser on salamanders has shown that unknown factors correlated with overall size of the animal are somehow important. If these animals are made polyploid so that they have an extra set of chromosomes in every cell, the individual cells are much larger than normal. Nevertheless, the size of the adults remains close to normal. This is because in every tissue, from the brain to the mucous glands of the skin, there has occurred a reduction in cells to compensate exactly for their large size.

The cause or causes of the limit on the number of possible cell divisions in culture for vertebrate cells are unknown. One current theory is that the cumulative effects of thermal, chemical, and background radiation on the cell's deoxyribonucleic acid (DNA) result in a cell which cannot divide. However, why this always occurs after some specific number of cell divisions is hard to explain by this random damage theory. An alternative hypothesis is that cell senescence and the inability to divide are genetically programmed developmental events.

Animals. In rotifers, where cell constancy was first intensively investigated, the number of nuclei in every organ and tissue can be counted exactly. In the common species *Epiphanes* (*Hydatina*) *senta*, which has been studied by several workers, there are 958 nuclei in every individual. The skin and associated structures have 301, the pharynx 167, and the digestive tract 76, of which 15 constitute the esophagus, 35 the stomach, 12 the gastric glands, and 14 the intestine. The urogenital system consists of 43 cells, the general musculature 120, and the nervous system 247, of which 183 are in the brain and 4 in the retrocerebral organ. A. F. Shull, in an investigation of a large number of individuals of this species, found almost no deviations. The presence of 6 nuclei in each gastric gland and of 8 in the vitellarium is common to many species of rotifers.

"An outstanding anatomical feature of nematodes," according to L. H. Hyman, "is their cell constancy." This fact has been confirmed by several workers on various species, including the wellknown *Ascaris, Turbatrix aceti* (vinegar eel), and *Rhabditis*. In *Turbatrix* there are 251 nerve cells, 1 excretory cell, 18 cells in the midgut, 64 in the body-wall musculature, 59 in the pharynx, 5 in the esophagus, and so on. Since cell division comes to an end before the birth of the worm, all subsequent growth is by cell enlargement. The gonads are exceptions because they produce new eggs or sperms continuously throughout the reproductive life of the individual.

In annelids and vertebrates, cell proliferation is more or less continuous throughout life only in those tissues that are subject to wear. Thus, in adults, cell division may be found in the germinative zones of the skin, hair, finger and toe nails, the lining of the alimentary canal, and especially in the blood cellforming tissues. The muscles and nervous system, however, appear to undergo no cell division after early embryonic or fetal stages. In both earthworms and mammals, including humans, it has been demonstrated that the number of muscle nuclei and muscle fibers, but not fibrils, is fixed early and does not increase with subsequent growth. An earthworm hatches from its egg cocoon with the adult number of muscle fibers and nuclei. A human fetus, aboutbreak 5 in. (13 cm) from crown to rump, has as many muscle fibers and nuclei as an adult. It has been shown that the number of glomeruli in each kidney of a rat or human, and therefore presumably of any mammal, is fixed before birth, and that the subsequent growth of the glomeruli, either normally or resulting from compensatory hypertrophy after unilateral nephrectomy, is due entirely to the enlargement of cells already present. The same holds true for the cells of the ciliated nephrostomes of earthworms.

Plants. Coenobia, that is, adult individuals composed of a fixed and predictable number of cells, are characteristic of the species of green algae belonging to the species of *Volvox* in the order Volvocales, and to the species of *Hydrodictyon* and *Scenedesmus* in the order Chlorococcales. In these forms the number of cells in an adult ranges from 4 to 8 in certain species of *Gonium*, 32 to 64 in *Pandorina*, and from 500 (probably 512) to 60,000 (probably 65,536) in *Volvox*. During asexual reproduction in these species, either every cell or, in the larger forms, certain cells undergo a rapid series of cell divisions. This results in the formation of a miniature replica of the adult, as far as cell number is concerned, within every single cell which has so divided. Thus a very small, young volvox has as many cells as a large, mature one. The minute, new individuals are released from the parent cell by the breakdown of the old cell wall. It will be noted that the number of cell generations is always small. Thirty-two is 2^5, which means only 5 cell generations, 512 is 2^9, and even 65,536 is only 2^{16}, which means only 16 cell generations to make the largest volvox.   Gairdner B. Moment

Bibliography. B. C. Edgar, Nematodes, *"Elegans Workshops" Worm Breeder's Gazette*, vols. 1 and 2, University of California, Santa Cruz, 1977; D. F. Goldspink, *Development and Specialization of Skeletal Muscle*, 1981; L. Hayflick, Cell biology of human aging, *Sci. Amer.*, 242(1):58–66, 1980; L. H. Hyman, *The Invertebrates*, vol. 3, 1951; T. L. Lawrence (ed.), *Growth in Animals*, 1980.

Cell cycle

The succession of events that culminates in the asexual reproduction of a cell; also known as cell division cycle. In a typical cell cycle, the parent cell doubles its volume, mass, and complement of chromosomes, then sorts its doubled contents to opposite sides of the cell, and finally divides in half to yield two genetically identical offspring. Implicit in the term cycle is the idea that division brings the double-sized parent cell back to its original size and chromosome number, and ready to begin another cell cycle. This idea fits well with the behavior of many unicellular organisms, but for multicellular organisms the daugh-

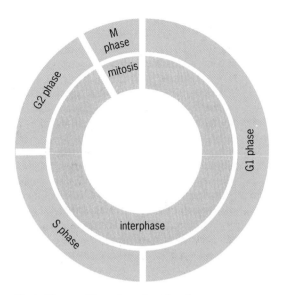

Fig. 1. Phases of the eukaryotic cell cycle.

ter cells may differ from their parent cell and from each other in terms of size, shape, and differentiation state.

The time required for completion of a eukaryotic cell cycle varies enormously from cell to cell. Embryonic cells that do not need to grow between divisions can complete a cell cycle in as little as 8 min, whereas cycling times of 10–24 h are typical of the most rapidly dividing somatic cells. Many somatic cells divide much less frequently; liver cells divide about once a year, and mature neurons never divide. Such cells may be thought of as temporarily or permanently withdrawing from the cell cycle.

Eukaryotic phases. The cell cycle is divided into two main parts: interphase and mitosis (**Fig. 1**). During interphase, the cell grows and replicates its chromosomes. Interphase accounts for all but an hour or two of a 24-h cell cycle, and is subdivided into three phases: gap phase 1 (G1), synthesis (S), and gap phase 2 (G2). Interphase is followed by mitosis (nuclear division), and cytokinesis (cell division). This relatively brief part of the cell cycle includes some of the most dramatic events in cell biology. *See* MITOSIS.

G1 phase. Gap phase 1 begins at the completion of mitosis and cytokinesis and lasts until the beginning of S phase. This phase is generally the longest of the four cell cycle phases and is quite variable in length. During this phase, the cell chooses either to replicate its deoxyribonucleic acid (DNA) or to exit the cell cycle and enter a quiescent state (the G0 phase). Late in the G1 phase, the cell becomes committed to replicating its DNA. In mammalian cells, the time at which this commitment occurs is called the restriction point.

S phase. Replication of the chromosomes is restricted to one specific portion of interphase, called S phase (DNA synthesis phase), which typically lasts about 6 h. In mammalian cells, the start of S phase—the actual initiation of DNA synthesis—takes place several hours after the cell has committed to carrying out DNA synthesis. During S phase, each chromosome replicates exactly once to form a pair of physically linked sister chromatids. In animal cells, a pair of centrioles is also duplicated during S phase. *See* CHROMOSOME; GENETICS.

G2 phase. The portion of interphase that follows S phase is called gap phase 2. Some cells can exit the cell cycle from G2 phase, just as they can from G1 phase.

M phase. M phase includes the overlapping processes of mitosis and cytokinesis. Mitosis is divided into five stages: prophase, prometaphase, metaphase, anaphase, and telophase. During prophase, the chromosomes condense and the football-shaped mitotic spindle begins to form. Prometaphase begins when the nuclear envelope abruptly disappears and the chromosomes begin to migrate toward the spindle's midline. When the chromosomes reach the midline, the cell is said to be in metaphase. Metaphase ends and anaphase begins when the sister chromatids abruptly separate from each other and move toward the spindle poles. During telophase, the nuclear envelope reforms around each set of chromosomes, the chromosomes decondense, and mitosis is completed. Cytokinesis usually begins during anaphase and ends at a point after the completion of mitosis. At the end of cytokinesis, the parent cell has formed its two G1 phase progeny and the cell is ready to repeat the cycle.

Control of cell cycle. The network of proteins that regulate DNA synthesis (G1/S), mitotic entry (G1/M), and mitotic exit (the transition from mitotic metaphase to anaphase and then out of mitosis) appears to be well conserved throughout eukaryotic evolution. At the heart of these cell cycle transitions is the periodic activation and inactivation of cyclin-dependent protein kinases. In addition, in multicellular eukaryotes, pathways regulating entry into and exit from the cell cycle entrain these central cyclin-dependent kinases to extrinsic signals.

Cell cycle entry. In multicellular eukaryotes, most cells spend most of their time in the quiescent G0 state. In response to peptide growth factors, cells initiate a signal transduction cascade that culminates in entry into G1 phase. Components of these mitogenic signaling pathways include receptor tyrosine kinases [such as the epidermal growth factor (EGF) receptor], small G-proteins (such as Ras), and signal-relaying protein kinases (such as MAP kinase). Mitogenic signaling culminates in the activation of at least two waves of gene transcription, leading to the synthesis of a G1 cyclin protein (cyclin D) and neutralization of the retinoblastoma tumor suppressor protein (pRb).

Many components of these mitogenic signaling pathways are capable of causing malignant transformation when overexpressed or inappropriately activated. The cancer-causing forms of these proteins are termed oncoproteins, and their genes are termed oncogenes; the corresponding normal forms from which oncogenes and oncoproteins are derived are termed proto-oncoproteins and proto-oncogenes. Conversely, several tumor suppressor genes (genes that can promote malignant transformation when inactivated) have now been shown to encode proteins that oppose mitogenic signaling proteins (for example, the retinoblastoma protein and the PTEN phosphatase). These discoveries underscore the idea that when the biochemical machinery that controls normal cell growth goes awry, cancer may result. *See* ONCOGENES.

Much less is known about how cells are induced to exit the cell cycle and enter the quiescent G0 state.

Mitotic control. When interphase cells are artificially fused with cells in mitosis, the interphase cells' nuclei rapidly enter mitosis. This discovery indicates that some dominant mitosis-inducing factor is present in M-phase cells. Studies on frog oocytes and eggs, unusually large cells that are naturally arrested in G2 phase (oocytes) or meiotic M phase (eggs), underscore this point: when oocytes are microinjected with cytoplasm from eggs, the oocytes enter M phase, a process termed oocyte maturation. The factor responsible, maturation promoting factor (MPF), is present and active during both meiotic M phase and mitotic M phase, and can be found in M-phase cells from evolutionarily distant organisms. This suggests that MPF is the universal M-phase trigger. The ease of obtaining large quantities of M-phase frog eggs meant that the identification of MPF could be approached biochemically.

Other crucial insights into M-phase control came from studies of growth regulation in the yeast *Schizosaccharomyces pombe*. Mutations in genes that regulate M-phase onset of *S. pombe* give rise to organisms that are too long or too short. Once such a mutant strain is isolated, the gene responsible for its altered size can be identified by molecular genetic methods. Two genes identified through this approach were $cdc2^+$ and $cdc13^+$. Genes related to $cdc2^+$ and $cdc13^+$ were found in a variety of other eukaryotes, suggesting that they encoded universal regulators of M-phase onset. *See* MOLECULAR BIOLOGY; MUTATION.

Ultimately it was realized that the biochemical studies of M-phase regulation in frog oocytes and the genetic studies of M-phase regulation in *S. pombe* had succeeded in identifying the same M-phase regulators. MPF proved to be a complex of the *Xenopus* homologs of *S. pombe* $cdc2^+$ and $cdc13^+$ (the Cdc13 protein is more usually called a B-type cyclin, because it rises and falls in abundance during the cell cycle). The fact that two very different approaches and two evolutionarily distant organisms had converged upon the same M-phase regulators underscored the importance and universality of the regulators.

The Cdc2/cyclin B complex is essential for initiation of all M phases in all organisms. The complex functions as a protein kinase—an enzyme that adds a phosphate group to specific amino acid residues in target proteins. The catalytic subunit of the complex is Cdc2; cyclin B is necessary for the activation of Cdc2 and is responsible for localizing the complex to the nucleus at the onset of M phase. The nuclear lamin proteins are Cdc2 target proteins, which

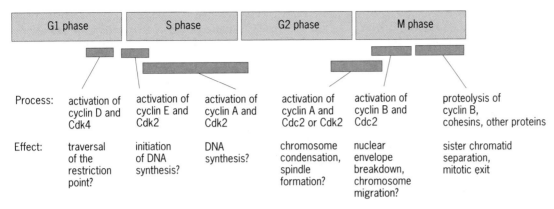

Fig. 2. Behavior of various Cdk/cyclin complexes and their cellular events.

form a scaffolding that supports the nuclear envelope. The Cdc2/cyclin B complex can phosphorylate lamins, causing the lamin network to disassemble. This disassembly allows the nuclear envelope to break down into small vesicles, which will coalesce and reassemble during telophase after cyclin B has been degraded and the lamins have been dephosphorylated. Other likely targets of Cdc2/cyclin B complex include histone proteins, whose phosphorylation may contribute to chromosome condensation, and a number of regulatory proteins.

At the onset of anaphase, a protein complex termed the anaphase-promoting complex (APC) becomes activated, bringing about the proteolytic destruction of several key mitotic regulators. One critical APC target is cyclin B; its destruction is required for mitotic exit. APC also directly or indirectly causes the destruction of other proteins (securins, cohesins) that keep the pairs of sister chromatids attached to each other and keep the cell in metaphase. As was the case with MPF, the rapid progress in the understanding of APC function and the appreciation of its universality were made possible through a combination of genetic studies (in the budding yeast *Saccharomyces cerevisiae*) and biochemical studies (mostly in frog egg extracts).

G1- and S-phase control. The other cell cycle transitions, for example, the commitment to DNA synthesis that occurs in G1 phase, and the initiation of DNA synthesis at the start of S phase, are also triggered by activation of heterodimeric protein kinases consisting of Cdc2-like catalytic subunits (termed Cdks, for cyclin-dependent kinases) and cyclin-like regulatory subunits. At least nine Cdc2-like catalytic subunits (Cdc2/Cdk1 and Cdk2–9) and at least eleven classes of cyclins (cyclins A through J and cyclin T) have now been identified in animal cells. A subset of these proteins have been implicated in cell cycle regulation (Cdc2, Cdk2, Cdk4, Cdk6; cyclins A, B, D, E). Thus, the entire cell cycle may be driven by the sequential activation and inactivation of Cdk/cyclin complexes (**Fig. 2**).   James E. Ferrell

Bibliography. A. Murray and T. Hunt, *The Cell Cycle: An Introduction*, 1993; A. W. Murray and M. W. Kirschner, What controls the cell cycle?, *Sci. Amer.*, 264:56–63, 1991.

Cell differentiation

The mechanism by which cells in a multicellular organism become specialized to perform specific functions in a variety of tissues and organs. The life cycle of a higher organism begins with a unicellular stage, the fertilized egg, and becomes more complex as the individual grows and takes on its characteristic form. The life cycle of a unicellular organism permits temporary change in shape and chemical composition. Only a multicellular organism can afford irreversibly differentiated cells.

Differentiated cells. The stable differentiated state is a consequence of multicellularity. A complex organism maintains its characteristic form and identity because populations of specialized cell types remain assembled in a certain pattern. Thus several kinds of cells make up a tissue, and different tissues build organs. The variable assortment of about 200 cell types allows for an almost infinite variety of distinct organisms.

Epithelia, sheets of cells of specific structure and function, cover the outer surface of the vertebrate body and line the lungs, gut, and vascular system. The stable form of a vertebrate is due to its rigid skeleton built from bone and cartilage, forming cells to which the skeletal muscles adhere. All other organs, such as liver and pancreas, are embedded in connective tissue that is derived from fibroblast cells which secrete large amounts of soft matrix material. *See* CONNECTIVE TISSUE; EPITHELIUM.

Some cells, like nerve cells, are so specialized that they need divide no longer in order to maintain a complex network. Their finite number decreases even during embryonic development. Other cell types are constantly worn out and must be replaced; for example, fibroblasts and pancreas cells simply divide as needed, proving that the differentiated state of cells is heritable, as the daughter cells remember and carry out the same special functions. The renewal of terminally differentiated cells that are unable to divide anymore, such as skin and blood cells, is carried out by stem cells. They are immortal and choose, as they double, whether to remain a stem cell or to embark on a path of terminal differentiation. Most stem cells are unipotent because they give rise to a single differentiated cell type. However, all cell types of the blood are derived from a single blood-forming stem cell, a pluripotent stem cell. A fertilized egg is a totipotent stem cell giving rise to all other cell types that make up an individual organism. *See* BLOOD.

Process of differentiation. Specialized cells are the product of differentiation. The process can be understood only from a historical perspective, and the best place to start is the fertilized egg. Different kinds of cell behavior can be observed during embryogenesis: cells double, change in shape, and attach at and migrate to various sites within the embryo without any obvious signs of differentiation. Cleavage is a rapid series of cell cycles during which the large egg cell is divided into a ball of small cells that line the primitive body cavity as a single layer of embryonic cells. This blastula stage is followed by gastrulation, a complex coordinated cellular migration which not only shapes the embryo but segregates the single-cell layer of the blastula into the three germ layers: endoderm, mesoderm, ectoderm. They give rise to specific cell types; for example, skin and nerves from the ectoderm, the digestive tract from the endoderm, and muscle and connective tissue from the mesoderm. *See* BLASTULATION; CLEAVAGE (DEVELOPMENTAL BIOLOGY); EMBRYOGENESIS; GASTRULATION.

Descriptive embryology has contributed elaborate body plans, but cannot explain the development of various organisms. Experimental embryologists originally concluded that all organisms can be placed in two categories. They found that either the developmental system represented by an egg acts as a fixed mosaic, or it can regulate and, for example, give rise to four complete mice from the cells produced after the first cleavage divisions. In a philosophical context, the terms preformation and epigenesis describe the two opposite kinds of development, the former claiming that an organism is physically preformed inside the egg, the latter proposing that the organism is newly created in each generation. *See* DEVELOPMENTAL BIOLOGY; EMBRYOLOGY.

Cell determination. An explanation of the two egg types by the timing of a single developmental change came from another experiment. A piece from a salamander blastula, which would have become an eye according to the body plan, was transplanted into the region destined to develop into the gut of another blastula. The implant adapted to the new environment and became part of the gut rather than an eye. A short time later, after gastrulation, the transplant resulted in the development of an eye inside the gut. This experiment holds a key to the cell differentiation process. It reveals a critical event, cell determination, which leads to the fixation of a particular developmental pathway. Before that time the embryo regulates; thereafter it has become a mosaic. Once a cell is committed to function in a specific capacity, it will not forget it, irrespective of environment. Thus, the change brought about by determination affects the internal character of a cell and results in a self-propagating change. The egg cell combines all capacities to build organisms as complex as humans, but it

can do so only if its potential is first segregated and divided into groups of stem cells with lesser developmental capacities. Two counteracting tendencies describe the developmental process: as embryonic cells lose their developmental potential, they gain specific characteristics which permit sophisticated division of labor in multicellular organisms. *See* EMBRYONIC DIFFERENTIATION.

Cell differentiation is the realization of the determined state, and since different cell types share the same genes, the central concept, if not dogma, of developmental biology is the theory of differential gene expression. This means that a myoblast becomes a muscle cell because genes responsible for muscle-specific structures, such as the contractile apparatus, are selectively activated. Conversely, muscle-specific genes remain inactive in other cell types. Molecular biologists have accumulated good evidence for selective gene expression in differentiated cells. Specific gene products, such as hemoglobin in red blood cells, have been labeled luxury molecules, because they are not essential for the lives of a cell but are required for the diversification of multicellular organisms. However, the processes of cell determination and differentiation are not accompanied by an overall increase in the number of genes that are expressed during embryonic development. To the contrary, many genes that are active in early embryos become inactivated by the time a cell becomes differentiated. It seems that the loss of developmental capacity is accompanied, or may be the consequence of, massive inactivation of genes of unknown functions. *See* GENE.

The determined state is very stable and inherited over many cell generations, but it is not irreversible. Transdetermination occurs occasionally and alters the developmental course of cells. There are some mutations that cause a similar shift of the developmental pathway. Perhaps the respective genes are "master genes" which control a whole set of cell-type-specific genes that evoke the production of the "luxury" molecules in differentiated cells. About 200 of such regulatory genes would be required to determine all existing cell types. If, however, embryonic cells could be determined by a set of regulatory genes in either "on" or "off" position, eight genes would suffice to program all different cell types ($2^8 = 256$). It can be concluded that these control genes are active in determined cells, which makes them different from those that are not determined. Consequently, committed cells must possess some less obvious luxury molecules yet to be discovered. They are distinct from undetermined cells, although not so grossly altered as the differentiated cells that are their progeny. Cell divisions occur during the transition from cell determination to differentiation. Frequently, a special kind of cell cycle, called the quantal cell cycle, is required, following which the differentiated state becomes obvious by the massive production of the cell-type-specific luxury molecules. *See* CELL CYCLE.

Embryonic induction. Another experiment has shed some light on the determination process. Implantation of that piece from the blastula, which would normally come to lie under the prospective neural tissue after gastrulation, into another blastula turns the host embryo into a monster with two complete nervous systems. This experiment defines embryonic induction. Induction works even with killed inducing cells. This result opened the search for the still elusive inducer substance. Furthermore, the capacity of induction can be traced back through earlier stages into the egg. These observations are consistent with the concept of cytoplasmic localization. It is assumed that cytoplasmic determinants are produced during the process of oogenesis and become deposited in certain areas in the egg. This concept is a modern version of the classical preformation theory. *See* OOGENESIS.

There are two ways to explain embryonic induction: either the inducer instructs the reacting tissue to become determined and, later on, differentiated, or the reacting tissue is multipotential and selects one developmental pathway over one of several others. In the first case, instruction can be viewed as a transfer of information in the form of specific protein or nucleic acid molecules. In the second case, the inducer plays a more permissive role, allowing the reacting tissue to decide what to do next. Consequently, the inducer need not confer information and may just provide a cue, like a change in ion concentration. There is evidence for unspecific cueing in the early embryogenesis of the most complex organisms, the mammals. After a few cleavage divisions, the young embryo forms the blastocyst, which consists of an outer layer of cells with a few cells inside. Any cell that happens to be inside the blastocyst takes part in building the embryo, while outside cells do not. This is germane to the inside-out concept, indicating that the cellular environment can provide cues as to the course of cell determination in the absence of localized cytoplasmic determinants. *See* EMBRYONIC INDUCTION.

Cellular nonequivalence. The shaping of an embryo is an essential routine of the developmental program. While embryonic induction leads to cell determination and differentiation, it is a complex patterning process that eventually puts different cell types into their proper territory. For example, a leg and an arm are quite distinct, although they are built from the very same cell types; but they are arranged in different patterns. More than one cell must collaborate to construct body parts, such as a segment or a wing of an insect. This process is initiated among a few founder cells in response to unknown cytoplasmic controls for which terms such as morphogenetic field, gradient, and centers have been applied.

According to the unifying position information hypothesis, embryonic cells secrete substances, perhaps an activator and an inhibitor, that generate a stable dynamic gradient of either diffusible molecules or a macromolecular extracellular network. These cells not only receive information with respect to their position, but are able to interpret that information. Interpretation is the crucial component of this hypothesis. One can assume that receptor molecules at the cell surface measure the size of the supracellular position information signal, and can postulate that they interpret different increments of that signal according to a preset behavior pattern. In the famous "French flag model," a sheet of cells with the potential to become blue, white, or red turn red at a low value, blue at a high value, and white at a medium value of the position signal. An important implication of the position information concept is that cells remember their position value. Consequently, cells of the same differentiated state can be different: they are nonequivalent. As with determination and differentiation, cellular nonequivalence is a self-perpetuating change in character. It may distinguish each cell from all other cells and allow it to home-in during the animated puzzle of embryogenesis and to stay put in a precise location. There is a class of developmental mutants, in which cells of a certain territory, called a compartment, collectively change their course of development and, for example, form a leg instead of an antenna at the head of the fruit fly *Drosophila melanogaster*. A combinational activity pattern of a few selector genes could provide for a mechanism to interpret different positive values.

It is conceivable that a single position information mechanism operates in all organisms during embryogenesis and later permits determined cells to display overt differentiation at the correct place. Together with genetic information that generates biological materials, position information could arrange these materials inside a cell to maintain a specific subcellular organization, or could operate between cells to create multicellular organisms of distinct forms.

Cellular change. In order to accurately describe a specific organism, one must know which cell types are arranged in what pattern. From a developmental perspective three different components describe the system from which a body plan emerges: cellular determination, differentiation, and nonequivalence. The developmental process proceeds according to the timing and interactions of these three kinds of cellular self-perpetuating change. Therefore, it is impossible to project a body plan into an egg cell and thus reveal the blueprint of a particular organism. The remarkable biological change initiated upon fertilization of an egg is perhaps better described as the product of the developmental program.

Molecular biology has unraveled in almost complete detail how genetic information in nucleic acids programs the linear array of amino acids in proteins. Some model systems (for example, bacteriophages and subcellular particles, such as ribosomes) need little if any additional information to assemble predictably into highly complex and functional structures by self-organization. These particles are almost exclusively programmed in the genome, but they are not alive. Even dissociated specialized cells of an adult organism can self-organize to some extent by the processes of sorting-out and differential adhesion. However, a cell is never reformed from its parts; each cell comes from a cell. Over 90% of its genome does not code for any known product. Even most known genes are made up of a mosaic of coding stretches of deoxyribonucleic acid (DNA), exons, and introns that are seemingly devoid of genetic sense. The genome is less stable than originally thought. Subtle rearrangements (by transposons) or differential ribonucleic acid (RNA) splicing may be the source for unprogrammed but essential biological change during embryonic development. In addition, the biomembrane, which is never the result of self-assembly, could store information in a two-dimensional network at its inner face to communicate with the cytoplasm, and at its outer face to respond to signals from the environment. To date, the developmental program, if it exists, has remained elusive. *See* BACTERIOPHAGE; DEOXYRIBONUCLEIC ACID (DNA); EXON; INTRON; MOLECULAR BIOLOGY; NUCLEIC ACID; PROTEIN; RIBONUCLEIC ACID (RNA); RIBOSOMES; TRANSPOSONS.

By comparing the differentiation process of cells to evolution, interesting new insights may be gained. The mechanism of cell differentiation and the establishment of nonequivalence are formally equal to speciation. Although it is hard to imagine how random change in embryonic cells will lead to complex organisms, such as humans, the developmental options of the germ cell are limited. The limitations are the linear patterns of genes, which hold the memory for their successful propagation over evolutionary time, and the constraints posed by the protoplasmic environment and its system of chemical interactions. Extinctions are common in the fossil record and, by analogy, also occur during embryogenesis. For example, the big egg cell, the totipotent stem cell, disappears after a few cleavage divisions and must be reorganized during oogenesis in the adult organism; and all neuroblasts, the precursors of terminally differentiated nerve cells, become extinct before birth. Cell death even becomes a formative tool as the human fingers are carved out from a paddlelike appendage, and the tail of a tadpole is destroyed in building the frog. Eventually the whole organism is survived only by its germ cells and the genes contained in them.

Origins. A living unit must reproduce faster than it is destroyed or taken over by other replicators. It seems that one kind of replicator made of nucleic acid and protein survived all other attempts at forming life, because all life on Earth uses the same genetic code. The most primitive cell was formed when a membrane kept the necessary building blocks close to the replicator. Prokaryotic organisms, such as bacteria and blue-green algae, may be descendants of the first cell. The eukaryotic cell achieved a higher degree of division of labor by segregating and enlarging the genome in the nuclear envelope, and by acquiring organelles, perhaps through ingestion and maintaining other primitive cells in a state of symbiosis. Flagellates may resemble that state which permitted a thousandfold increase in size. All unicellular organisms compete with each other for resources. The third step, following replicator and cell formation, is characterized by specialization of all functions assembled in the eukaryotic cell through cellular differentiation and positioning. Thus multicellularity and cell differentiation, and the switch from competitive to altruistic cellular behavior, are closely related. *See* GENETIC CODE; PREBIOTIC ORGANIC SYNTHESIS.

Some specialized functions in extant organisms may provide information as to how cell differentiation originated. Even the simplest bacterium segregates genetic material into one gene set which controls the routine processes of life, and a small additional genome, a plasmid, that permits shuttling of genetic material within and between cells, a prerequisite for sexuality. *See* BACTERIAL GENETICS.

The ciliates are the most advanced single-celled organisms. They have two nuclei, a micronucleus and a macronucleus. The micronucleus functions in gene replication and sexual recombination; its genes cannot be copied into RNA. Growth and division are controlled by the macronucleus, in which a portion of the genome is segregated, amplified, and transcribed. Ciliates display a highly organized cell surface as the result of intracellular patterning. The positioning of arrays of cilia is to some degree self-perpetuating and independent of the genome. *See* CILIOPHORA.

The switch from competitive to altruistic cell behavior happens in the life cycle of cellular slime molds. They live as individual cells while they have sufficient food. Following starvation, about 10,000 individuals aggregate into a tissuelike structure which forms a fruiting body. In this process many individuals die and allow the survival of others to propagate the genes. Formation of these fruiting bodies is a model case of cellular positioning, reversible differentiation, and altruistic cellular behavior. *See* CELL ADHESION.

A stable association of identical cells has occurred in some algae, which form a sphere from identical individuals that resemble a blastula. Plants may have arisen from algal colonies, and the high degree of regeneration in plants could indicate that cells of a plant tissue have never given up the pluripotent state. *See* ALGAE.

The plasmodial slime molds provide a model of developmental organization beyond unicellularity. These organisms can live as minute competing amebas. Under proper conditions a single cell turns into a large mass of protoplasm. Its new developmental feature is the uncoupling of nuclear divisions from cell divisions. A plasmodium is born, a giant cell which can grow to over a foot in diameter and contains billions of nuclei. In some plasmodial slime molds, cellular transformation into a multinucleated system is coupled to sexual cell differentiation and cell fusion. The life cycle continues with a patterning process in which the giant cell is divided into smaller units of about a million nuclei. Each unit undergoes morphogenesis which results in a fruiting body. During this process most nuclei become eliminated. The surviving nuclei end up in the head of the fruiting body, where each is surrounded by a portion of cytoplasm and a proper cell membrane. Thus, this organism demonstrates major events of embryogenesis, which turn a fertilized egg into a complex organism: growth, patterning, determination, cell differentiation, and morphogenesis. It is a simple model system for two reasons: the transition from the unicellular to the multicellular state occurs in the absence of the still elusive maternal programming during oogenesis, and the giant cell and the building of the fruiting body display, in mutually exclusive fashion, either growth or differentiation. One cannot distinguish whether the plasmodial slime mold represents an evolutionary dead end or whether the animals are its descendants. Once multicellularity is established, all kinds of fungi, plants, and animals can evolve by utilizing the opportunities of specialization to optimize division of labor by differentiated cells, and the constraints posed by the history of their ancestors. *See* CELL (BIOLOGY); CELL SENESCENCE.   Helmut Sauer

Bibliography. B. Alberts et al., *Molecular Biology of the Cell*, 3d ed., 1994; J. T. Bonner (ed.), *Evolution and Development* 1982; F. Jacob, *The Logic of Life*, reissued 1982; G. Karp and N. J. Berrill, *Development*, 2d ed. 1981; N. Maclean, *The Differentiation of Cells: Genetics—Principles and Perspectives* (a series of texts), 1977; R. A. Raff and T. C. Kaufman, *Embryos, Genes, and Evolution*, 1983.

Cell division

The division of a cell into daughter cells that receive identical copies of its genetic material. The cell cycle comprises the period between the formation of a cell as a progeny of division and its own subsequent division into two daughter cells. The cell cycle falls into two parts. A relatively long interphase represents the time during which the cell engages in synthetic activities and reproduces its components, even though there is no visible change. The relatively short period of mitosis provides an interlude during which the actual process of visible division into two daughter cells is accomplished.

Cell cycle. Prokaryotic and eukaryotic cells differ markedly in the coordination of deoxyribonucleic acid (DNA) synthesis and in the subsequent equal partitioning of DNA during cell division. In prokaryotes the cell cycle consists of successive periods of DNA replication and of cell division where a cell wall forms and divides the cell in two, with no visible condensation and decondensation of DNA. Eukaryotes from yeast to humans have similar cell division phases, termed G1, S, G2, and M phases. After each division there is a time gap (G1 phase) before the synthesis of DNA begins. The cell is metabolically active during this part of the cycle in which proteins and DNA precursors are made. The period of DNA synthesis (S phase) involves the replication of chromosomal DNA, and is followed by another time gap (G2 phase), after which mitosis (M phase) occurs. Interphase is the time that elapses between one M phase and the next. It is composed of successive G1, S, and G2 phases and normally comprises 90% or more of the total cell cycle time. The cell cycle varies from tissue to tissue and during development. Sea urchin blastomeres, for instance, replicate their DNA at the end of mitosis in telophase of the preceding division, thus eliminating the G1 phase entirely.

The products of the series of mitotic divisions that generate the entire organism are called somatic cells. During embryonic development, most of the somatic cells are proceeding through the cell cycle. In the adult organism, however, many cells are terminally differentiated or no longer divide; they remain in a perpetual interphase. These cells are sometimes said to be quiescent or in G0 phase. *See* CELL CYCLE; DEOXYRIBONUCLEIC ACID (DNA).

Mitotic stages. The mitotic or M phase of the cell cycle involves the separation of replicated nuclei into two identical daughter nuclei. Mitosis is divided into six distinct stages: prophase, prometaphase (or late prophase), metaphase, anaphase, telophase, and cytokinesis (see **illus.**). The length of time that a cell takes to complete mitosis varies in different organisms. In rapidly proliferating cells of higher eukaryotes, M phases generally occur only once every 16–24 h, and each M phase itself lasts only 1–2 h.

Prophase. Prior to mitosis, in the S phase of the cell cycle chromosomal DNA replicates, and each chromosome divides into two sister chromatids. At the onset of prophase, these sister chromatids condense while remaining attached at a specific sequence of DNA necessary for chromosome separation called the centromere. At this point, the condensed chromosomes become visible by light microscopy. In interphase, the centrosome also divides, giving rise to two sets of centrioles. The centrioles, which are made from microtubules, also duplicate during interphase and begin to move to opposite sides of the nucleus to form separate poles. As these centrioles move apart, the microtubules disassemble. The new microtubules or asters, which will become intimately involved in the movement of the chromosomes during mitosis, begin to radiate from the centriole pairs in all directions to form the mitotic spindle. The number of microtubules making up the mitotic spindle varies depending on the organism. The microtubules that connect at the center of the chromatid pairs are called kinetochore microtubules; others, called polar microtubules, will extend to the opposite pole. Astral microtubules radiate from the centriole pair outside the mitotic spindle. *See* CENTRIOLE; CENTROSOME.

Prometaphase. Prometaphase, or late prophase, begins with the breakdown of the nuclear membrane. At this point, the kinetochore microtubules interact with the chromosomes to form protein complexes at their centromeres. This association between the microtubules and proteins of the chromatids makes up the structure of the mitotic spindle. The microtubules that extend past the sister chromatids to each pole are stabilized through cross-linking of microtubule binding proteins. These microtubules are also protected from disassembly by the constant formation of new microtubules from tubulin molecules in the fluid portion of the cytoplasm (cytosol). The stabilization of these microtubules is necessary for mitosis, as shown by the effect of the drug colchicine which blocks the assembly of microtubules and makes cells unable to complete mitosis.

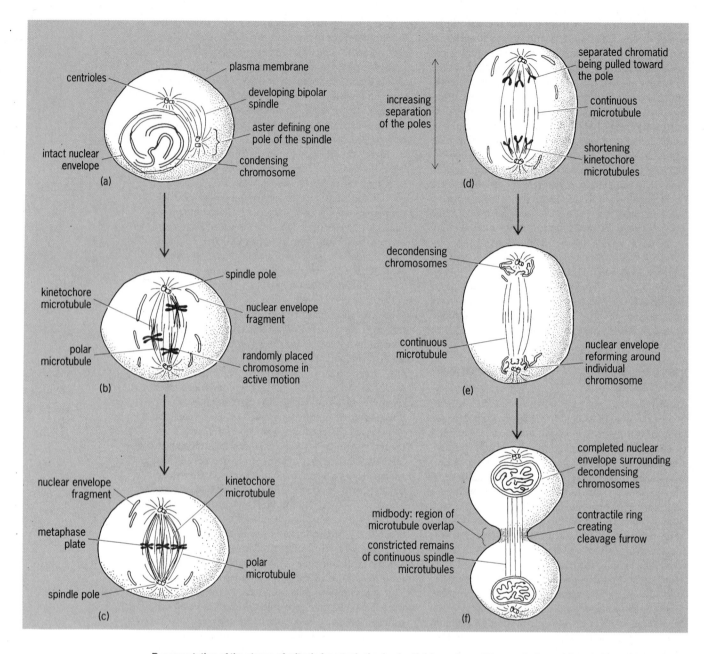

Representation of the stages of mitosis for a typical animal cell: (*a*) prophase; (*b*) prometaphase; (*c*) metaphase; (*d*) anaphase; (*e*) early telophase; (*f*) late telophase.

Metaphase. At metaphase, the kinetochore microtubules align their chromosomes in one plane called the metaphase plate, half way between the spindle poles, with one kinetochore facing each pole. Each sister chromatid is now perpendicular to the opposite poles. The metaphase stage of mitosis is the longest, lasting up to 30 min in mammalian cells. The kinetochore microtubules align the sister chromatids by holding them in tension with the two opposite poles. This tension seems to be necessary for the correct movement of the chromatids in the next stage.

Anaphase. The sister chromatids are triggered to separate and migrate to opposite spindle poles, and assemble there to form the nucleus of a new cell. Anaphase is separated into two stages. During anaphase A, a sister chromatid pair separates at the kinetochore and is guided to an opposite pole as the kinetochore microtubules begin to shorten at a rate of 1 micrometer per minute. This separation occurs simultaneously for all the chromatids. As the chromatids reach the poles, the microtubules begin to disassemble. During anaphase B, the disassembling polar microtubules begin to elongate so that the two poles of the spindle move farther apart.

Telophase. The end stage of mitosis, termed telophase, begins with the arrival of the sister chromatids at each separate pole. As the kinetochore microtubules disappear, the polar microtubules continue to elongate. A new nuclear envelope begins to form around each group of sister chromatids. The chromatin which has been condensed throughout mitosis expands, and nucleoli appear. After this stage, the cell enters cytokinesis. *See* CELL NUCLEUS.

Cytokinesis. Cytokinesis begins during anaphase and ends the mitotic process. The cytoplasm divides by a process known as cleavage to give rise to two separate daughter cells. The forces required for cleavage are generated through actin-myosin interactions, which pull the plasma membrane down a furrow, a puckering of the plasma membrane. The cleavage furrow forms around the equator of the parent cell so that the two daughter cells produced are of approximately equal size and have similar properties.

Induction of mitosis. The alternation between interphase and M phase is controlled by periodic changes in the activity of maturation promoting factor. This factor in amphibian eggs is present only in M-phase cytoplasm, and its activity is regulated by phosphorylations. Activity of maturation promoting factor depends on two protein species associated in equimolar amounts in purified preparations. The first component is the protein kinase catalytic subunit $p34^{cdc2}$. The second component is a 62-kilodalton protein which must be synthesized at each metaphase-anaphase transition in mitosis. Because of this cyclical behavior, this protein was identified as cyclin B; it is the maturation promoting factor activator protein. There is a delay in an organism between the time after which protein synthesis is no longer required and the time when $p34^{cdc2}$ kinase activation occurs. The suggestion is that cyclin B accumulation required for maturation promoting factor activation is not the only factor involved in the activation process.

Disruption. The order of the cell cycle is ensured by dependent relationships, the initiation of late events depending upon the completion of preceding ones. Such dependence can be circumvented by pharmacological intervention, such as the induction of premature chromosome condensation by caffeine, blockade of mitosis, and inhibition of microtubule formation by colcemid, or inhibition of cytokinesis by cytochalasin B. Mutations, which are more specific than inhibitions, can also detect molecules involved in cell division. Mutants and inhibitors aid in the identification of control mechanisms in cell division, named checkpoints, that govern mitotic entry and exit. *See* MITOSIS; MUTATION.

Khandan Keyormarsi; Nuala O'Leary; Arthur B. Pardee

Bibliography. N. Akkas (ed.), *Biomechanics of Cell Division*, 1987; B. Alberts et al., *Molecular Biology of the Cell*, 3d ed., 1999; R. Baserga, *The Biology of Cell Reproduction*, 1985; J. S. Hyams and B. R. Brinkley (eds.), *Mitosis*, 1989; J. D. Watson et al., *Recombinant DNA*, 1992.

Cell lineage

A type of embryological study in which the history of individual blastomeres (cells formed during division of the zygote) or meristem cells is traced to their ultimate differentiation into tissues and organs.

Animals. The question of how the animal genome can be regulated to produce the various cell types found in the larval and adult organism is a central concern in developmental biology. A possible approach to this problem would involve tracing the structural fates of the descendants of each of a population of progenitor cells, and then trying to determine which gene products are required for particular steps in the process of cell differentiation. The cleaving embryos of a limited number of invertebrates, such as some flatworms, annelids, mollusks, and ascidians, are suitable for such studies because they show stereotyped cleavage patterns and asymmetries in size and arrangement of the blastomeres. Studies of this sort have been of limited interest because the large number of cells produced make it impossible to follow clones beyond the establishment of the germ layers. *See* CLEAVAGE (DEVELOPMENTAL BIOLOGY).

Cell lineages are also studied by marking cells in developing tissues and then observing the pattern of marked descendants in the adult structure. X-ray-induced alteration of cellular phenotype is the most powerful method of studying cell lineages in the imaginal development of insects. The x-rays cause a calculable number of chromosome crossing-over events which mark the affected cells by altered phenotype, such as different color or bristle configuration. The spatial pattern of cells with altered phenotype is then observed in the adult and, in ideal cases, represents the progeny of one founder cell. *See* FATE MAPS (EMBRYOLOGY).

Some of the most promising cell lineage studies are conducted on a nematode worm, *Caenorhabditis elegans*, which is a small (1 mm or 0.04 in. in length), nearly transparent worm that lives in soil. Adults are either males or hermaphrodites; the hermaphrodites contain 959 somatic nuclei. The origin of each somatic cell can be traced back to a single blastomere, and the clonal history of each cell has been determined (see **illus.**). A detailed genetic map for the 80,000 kilobase genome has been worked out. The short (3 days) generation time makes it possible to follow the effects of defined mutations upon the differentiation of specific cells. The relative roles of genetic programs as opposed to extrinsic signals can be assessed, for example, by destroying a particular cell during a defined stage of development and observing the effect on the differentiation of surrounding cells. The techniques of molecular genetics, particularly insertion and deletion of specified stretches of deoxyribonucleic acid (DNA) at specific chromosomal sites in *C. elegans*, should be particularly useful in determining the role of regulatory genes whose product may not be a structural or enzymatic protein. Because each stage of the differentiation of a particular cell can be described, the effects of alteration of the activity of any gene on the differentiation or interaction with surrounding cells can be precisely delineated. *See* DEVELOPMENTAL GENETICS; INVERTEBRATE EMBRYOLOGY; OVUM.

Spencer J. Berry

Plants. Cell lineage analysis in plants, as in animals, involves tracing the origin of particular cells in the adult body back to their progenitor cells. The

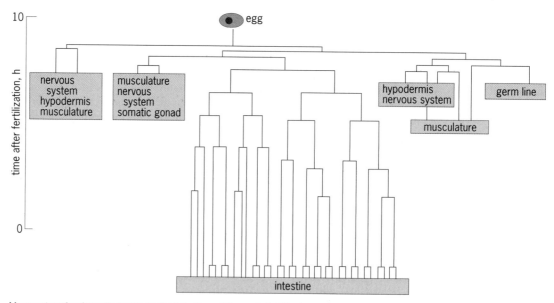

Lineage tree for the cells that form the intestine of *Caenorhabditis elegans.*

adult body of a typical plant consists primarily of leaves, stems, and roots. Cells arise continuously during plant life from specialized dividing cell populations called meristems. A shoot apical meristem produces the leaves and stem, and a root apical meristem produces root tissue. The shoot apical meristem will also produce specialized structures, such as cones, flowers, thorns, tendrils, and so on. Because plant cells do not move during development, and in many cases the plane of cell division is constant, lines of cells, called cell files, all derive from a single meristem cell at the base of the file. Cell files are particularly obvious in root tissue of ferns and higher plants. Although the organization of cells in plants follows regular patterns, the fate of individual cells is not as rigidly determined as cell fates are in animals. In plants, anatomical position determines a cell's typical fate, but if the pattern is disrupted by injury, for example, cells can differentiate into a variety of cell types. *See* APICAL MERISTEM.

Study of chimeras. Cell lineage can be examined in a more sophisticated manner by examining individual organs, such as leaves, to determine how many cells form a leaf and how these cells are oriented to one another as the organ forms. Exact cell lineages are most readily followed by using a color marker, such as chlorophyll-deficient cells which are white. Plant developmental biologists have used naturally occurring green-white chimeric plants, such as variegated ivy, or chimeras have been created by mutation. A common practice is to x-irradiate seeds that are heterozygous for one or more color loci (+ for color, − for albino) to create some meristem cells in which the chromosome arm carrying the (+) allele is lost from the cell, leaving only the (−) allele. This (−) cell and all of its progeny will be albino. *See* CHIMERA.

By using such mutated stocks, the contribution of the albino cell lineage to individual organs can be determined. Two types of observations are made. The first is the apparent cell number. If a leaf is 90% green and 10% albino, the simplest explanation is that the leaf was originally composed of 10 cells: 9 normal green ones and 1 mutant albino one. Thus the apparent cell number of the leaf is 10, indicating that 10 cells in the shoot apical meristem contributed to the leaf's formation. The second observation is the extent of the defect. If the albino sector is found in only a single leaf, this suggests that the meristem is very large and that the albino cell, and by inference all other cells in the meristem, typically contributes to only a single leaf on the plant. More often, albino sectors will be found on a number of leaves, indicating that meristem cells contribute to many different leaves. In some cases in which the plant has opposite leaves, all of the leaves on one side may be completely green while those on the opposite side all have an albino sector. Such an observation suggests that there are two groups of cells in the meristem, each producing leaves exclusively on one side of the stem.

Lineage in growing leaves. To gain further information about the pattern of cell division within an organ such as a leaf, experimentalists have x-irradiated leaves as they are growing. The earlier the mutations are induced, the larger the resulting sectors, because early in development the leaf is composed of few cells, each of which will give rise to a substantial fraction of the final leaf. Mutations induced late in development, when the leaf has thousands of cells, result in sectors that are tiny dots or streaks on the leaf. Such tiny sectors are used to determine where cell divisions are occurring in the leaf late in its development; areas lacking any dots or streaks have their final cell number, so no mutant cell lineages are visible.

Cell lineage analysis is a powerful tool for the study of plant development. By simple rules of observation and analysis, a great deal can be learned about the structure and activity of the meristems and about the timing and pattern of cell division in the developing organs. *See* PLANT GROWTH; PLANT MORPHOGENESIS.

Virginia Walbot

Bibliography. B. Alberts et al., *The Molecular Biology of the Cell*, 3d ed., 1999; E. H. Davidson, *Gene Activity in Early Development*, 2d ed., 1976; A. Garcia-Bellido, P. A. Lawrence, and G. Morata, Compartments in animal development, *Sci. Amer.*, 1979; P. Grant, *Biology of Developing Systems*, 1978; M. M. Johri and E. H. Coe, Jr., Clonal analysis of corn plant development, *Develop. Biol.*, 97:154–172, 1983; C. Kenyon, The nematode *Caenorhabditis elegans, Science*, 240:1448–1453, 1988; N. Le Douarin (ed.), *Cell Lineage, Stem Cells and Cell Differentiation*, 1979; W. F. Loomis, *Developmental Biology*, 1986; S. Subtelny and I. M. Sussex (eds.), *The Clonal Basis of Development*, 1978; K. M. Wilbur (ed.), *The Mollusca*, vol. 3, 1983.

Cell membranes

Cells maintain their content separate and distinct from the external environment by a semifluid lipid bilayer that prevents the free exchange of most biological molecules and acts as a barrier between the inside and the outside of a cell. Prokaryotic cells contain only one such membrane, the plasma membrane that delineates the border of the cell. Eukaryotic cells, in addition to the plasma membrane, contain a multitude of internal membranes that define distinct intracellular organelles. The role of the plasma membrane and the internal membranes is analogous—all prevent the free exchange of molecules between the inside and the outside of the enclosed compartment, thus allowing the generation and maintenance of specialized microenvironments within each membrane-enclosed space. *See* CELL (BIOLOGY); CELL ORGANIZATION.

Membrane structure and composition. All biological membranes are approximately 7.5–10 nm thick and have a characteristic "railroad tracks" appearance when viewed in thin sections with the electron microscope, with two dark layers of the track, each approximately 2.5 nm thick, separated by a lighter layer, also approximately 2.5 nm (**Fig. 1***a*). This appearance is due to the heavy staining of the charged head groups and the poor staining of the fatty acyl chains (long chains of C-H bonds ending in a —COOH group) of phospholipids, the predominant lipid component of membranes. All membranes are made up of two phospholipid layers in a tail-to-tail arrangement with the charged head groups on the outside and the acyl chains on the inside (Fig. 1*b*). This basic bilayer organization was shown to exist in all examined membranes, indicating that the fundamental structure of all biological membranes is constant, despite differences in their composition and function.

All membranes are made up of lipid and protein, with the ratios varying from approximately 80% lipid (in the myelin membrane) to less than 30%

lipid (in the mitochondrial membrane). All lipid constituents of the membrane are amphipathic; that is, each molecule has a hydrophilic (polar) and a hydrophobic (nonpolar) region. The structure of the membrane is intrinsically defined by this property, since amphipathic molecules spontaneously orient themselves with their hydrophobic cores to the interior and the polar groups to the exterior; by attempting to shield their hydrophobic domains, amphipathic lipids form sealed membrane "balloons" in an aqueous environment.

Proteins are the primary determinants of membrane function. They are found embedded within

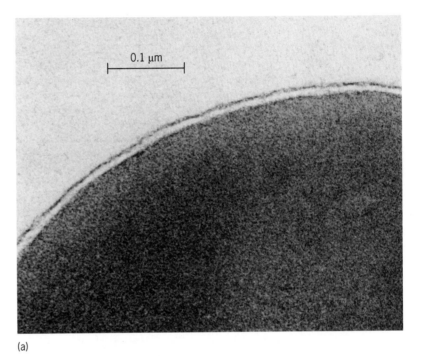

(a)

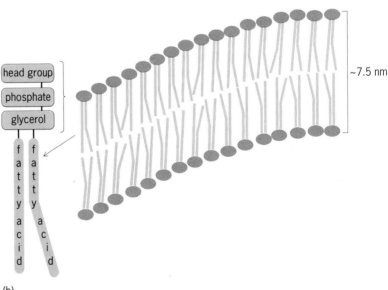

(b)

Fig. 1. Bilayer structure of biological membranes. (*a***) Electron micrograph of a thin section of a human red blood cell, showing the "railroad tracks" appearance of the plasma membrane (***from J. D. Robertson, Cell membranes, McGraw-Hill Encyclopedia of Science & Technology, 9th ed., 2002***). (***b***) Schematic diagram of the bilayer organization of phospholipids within the membrane.**

the hydrophobic core of the lipid bilayer or attached to the hydrophilic membrane surface. The protein composition of membranes varies extensively. Many membrane proteins required for basic housekeeping functions are found in all cells, whereas more esoteric proteins are expressed in a restricted manner and are found only in cells specialized to perform specific functions.

Membrane lipids. The major membrane lipids are the phospholipids, the glycolipids, and the sterols (**Fig. 2**). The relative ratios of different lipids vary in different membranes, but usually phospholipids are the major constituent (50-90% of total lipids), followed by glycolipids (5-20%) and cholesterol (0-10%). *See* LIPID.

Phospholipids are based on a glycerol backbone and contain two fatty acyl chains linked to a glycerol esterified to a phosphate that is in turn esterified to a head group such as choline (to make phosphatidylcholine, PC), serine (PS), ethanolamine (PE), or inositol (PI). However, phospholipids can also be based on sphingosine (a single fatty acyl chain linked to a serine). The size of the fatty acyl chains of membrane phospholipids varies but is usually between 14 and 24 carbons in length. The level of saturated (single) to unsaturated (double) bonds also varies depending on the membrane, and acyl chains within a single phospholipid exhibit different levels of unsaturation. *See* PHOSPHOLIPID.

Glycolipids are often based on a glycerol framework and contain two acyl chains attached to a glycerol bound to a sugar chain; these are predominantly found in plants and in bacteria. However, in animal cells the backbone of glycolipids is sphingosine. When the amino group of the serine moiety of sphingosine is linked to a second acyl chain, a ceramide is produced. Ceramide can be further modified by the attachment of a phosphate group esterified to choline to produce sphingomyelin. Alternatively, ceramide can be modified by the addition of a single sugar (galactose) to generate cerebroside, or by the addition of branched sugar chains (composed of glucose, galactose, glucosamine, and sialic acid) to form gangliosides. The complex head groups of gangliosides define their function, and the family has more than 60 different members. *See* GLYCOLIPID.

As for sterols, cholesterol is the main sterol found in animal membranes, whereas various phytosterols predominate in plants. Sterols are rare or absent in prokaryotes. Sterols have the structure of four planar rings and are thus relatively rigid, flattened structures. They orient in the membrane with the small hydrophilic hydroxyl group on the outside and the hydrophobic steroid rings buried within the membrane. *See* CHOLESTEROL.

Membrane proteins. Proteins are responsible for most of the specialized membrane functions by acting, for example, as selective transport portals, signal

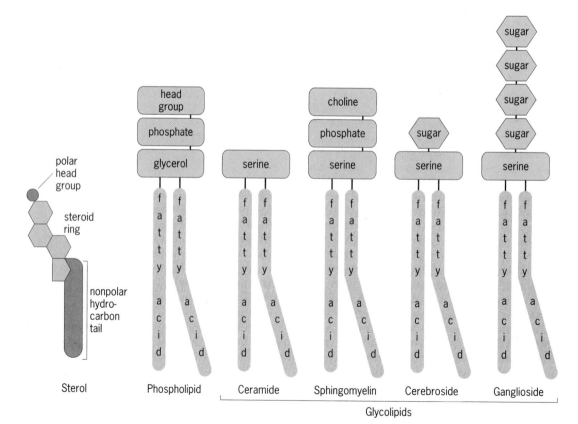

Fig. 2. Structure and arrangement of lipids within membranes. The schematic represents major membrane lipids. The head group of a phospholipid can be choline (phosphatidylcholine, PC), serine (PS), inositol (PI), or ethanolamine (PE). The sugar residue on cerebroside is galactose, and the sugar chains on gangliosides are made up of varying amounts and arrangements of glucose, galactose, *N*-acetylgalactosamine, and sialic acid. The fatty acyl chains can vary in length and in the number and position of double bonds.

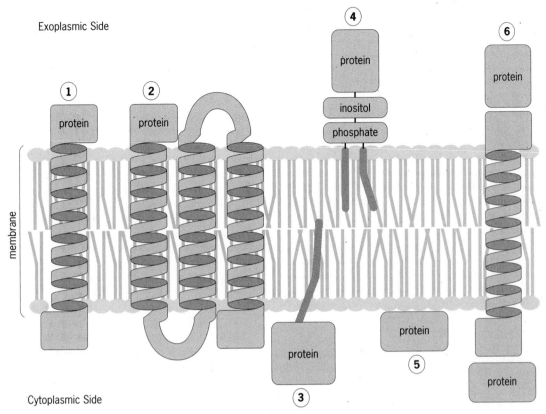

Fig. 3. Structure and arrangement of proteins within membranes. The asymmetric arrangement of various types of membrane proteins is shown in respect to the bilayer: (1) Integral single-span protein: the protein can be arranged with the N-terminus facing the exoplasmic side (type I protein) or with the N-terminus facing the cytoplasmic side (type II protein). (2) Integral multispan protein: multiple segments of the protein can span the bilayer creating cytoplasmic and exoplasmic loops. (3) Lipid-anchored protein: the protein can be attached to a myristyl, palmityl, prenyl, farnesyl, or geranylgeranyl chain. (4) GPI-linked protein. (5) Peripherally associated protein interacting with lipids. (6) Peripherally associated protein interacting with an integral membrane protein. The protein can be associated with the exoplasmic or cytoplasmic side of the membrane.

receptors and transducers, matrix attachment and cell-cell contact mediators, identity determinants, and enzymes.

Proteins that have one or more segments of their polypeptide chain threaded through the membrane with the remainder of the chain sticking out on either side of the membrane are called integral membrane proteins or transmembrane proteins (**Fig. 3**). In the majority of studied transmembrane proteins, the part that spans the membrane is either α-helical or is arranged in multiple β-strands, forming a barrel-shaped structure. The predicted length of an α-helix necessary to span the bilayer is 3.75 nm, and this usually corresponds to approximately 22 amino acids.

Other proteins are associated with the membrane by being covalently bound to specialized lipid molecules (lipid-anchored proteins), or by interacting noncovalently with transmembrane proteins (peripheral proteins). Lipid-anchored proteins that are found attached to the cytoplasmic aspect of cellular membranes are usually attached to a myristyl-, palmityl-, prenyl-, farnesyl-, or geranyl-carbohydrate moiety buried within the bilayer. In contrast, lipid-anchored proteins that are found within the lumen of secretory organelles are attached to a complex glycosylated phospholipid, glycosylphosphatidylinositol (GPI). The addition of the GPI tail occurs within the lumen of the endoplasmic reticulum after the protein is translocated there, and all GPI-linked proteins face the lumenal or the external leaflet of the membrane. Peripheral membrane proteins are usually associated through direct electrostatic interactions with the polar head groups of lipids, or by binding to integral membrane proteins. See PROTEIN.

Membrane fluidity. Membranes are fluid at ambient temperatures. They allow the free axial rotation of all components, and free flow within the plane of the bilayer is observed for lipids and for unrestricted proteins consistent with the fluid mosaic model of membrane structure, in which components are free to diffuse within the two-dimensional plane of the membrane.

Lipid molecules define the fluidity of a membrane. Lipids undergo phase transition, from a relatively rigid gel-like state at low temperature to a fluid state at high temperature. Differences in the length and the saturation of the acyl chains define how tightly the molecules can pack into the bilayer and thereby influence fluidity of the membrane. In general, lipids with short or unsaturated fatty acyl chains do not pack very tightly and undergo phase transition (are more fluid) at lower temperatures than those with long or polyunsaturated chains that can pack more tightly.

A typical lipid molecule changes places with its neighbor approximately 10^7 times per second and diffuses several micrometers per second at 37°C (98.6°F). This means that a single lipid molecule can traverse the length of a typical eukaryotic cell in approximately 5–10 s. However, the movement of lipids within the plane of the bilayer is restricted to only one leaflet, and lipids do not normally flip-flop from one side to the other. Depending on the type of cell, 30–90% of integral proteins in the plasma membrane and intracellular membranes are mobile. The mobility of membrane proteins within the lipid bilayer is significantly (approximately a hundredfold) lower than that of lipids. Protein movement is important since key cellular events, such as receptor clustering and capping and cell-cell and cell-matrix attachment, depend on the mobility of transmembrane proteins. Most transmembrane proteins are restricted by linkage to cytoskeletal components, thus tethering membranes to cytoskeletal systems.

Membrane asymmetry. Since membranes separate two compartments, each leaflet of the bilayer faces a distinct environment. For the plasma membrane, the inner (or cytoplasmic) leaflet is exposed to the cytosol while the outer (or exoplasmic) leaflet faces the extracellular space; for intracellular membranes, the cytoplasmic leaflet is exposed to the cytosol while the exoplasmic leaflet faces the inside (the lumen) of the organelle.

Membranes are asymmetric, due to differences in lipid composition between the cytoplasmic and the exoplasmic leaflet. Since lipids do not ordinarily flip-flop across the bilayer, the differential distribution is maintained throughout the life of the membrane. Lipids with neutral or negative head groups (such as PE, PS, and PI) are found preferentially facing the cytosol, whereas PC (which contains a positively charged head group) is preferentially within the exoplasmic leaflet. The fatty acyl chains in the exoplasmic leaflet tend to have longer, more saturated carbon chains than those in the cytoplasmic leaflet. Glycolipids are found exclusively in the exoplasmic leaflet since sugar addition occurs within the lumen of the endoplasmic reticulum and the Golgi apparatus. Similarly, cholesterol is predominantly located in the exoplasmic leaflet and, due to its planar structure, increases the relative "thickness" of that leaflet. Sterols are most abundant in the plasma membrane, where they increase the rigidity and the mechanical stability of the membrane.

Membrane asymmetry is also evident in the protein arrangement within the bilayer, since only a particular transmembrane orientation, which is determined by the primary sequence of the protein, is possible. Protein asymmetry is essential since it is responsible for the directionality of transport and signaling processes, the sidedness of enzymatic reactions, and the surface exposure of specific protein sequences required for recognition and adhesion of cells; protein asymmetry underlies all other protein-mediated membrane processes as well.

Membrane functions. The fundamental function of all membranes is to serve as barriers that enable cells to maintain a different composition between two aqueous compartments, and this function is due to the lipid components of the membrane. However, lipids can also play additional roles. For example, PI is involved in a signaling cascade mediating the transmission of signals from hormone receptors to influence transcription of specific genes; cholesterol is involved in the synthesis of low-density lipoprotein particles (LDLs), which are utilized in mammals to transport cholesterol from the liver to other tissues; gangliosides have been shown to define the A, B, and O blood groups; and sphingomyelin is required to surround and insulate neuronal axons, allowing neuronal transmission.

A myriad of membrane proteins mediate various additional membrane functions, among them the selective transport of molecules, reception and transduction of signals, and energy conversions. Membranes are impermeant to charged molecules such as ions, amino acids, and adenosine triphosphate (ATP) and to all large molecules such as sugars and peptides. Such compounds are transported across membranes by protein pumps that move compounds against a concentration gradient, channels that transport down concentration gradients, or transporters that move compounds down or against a concentration gradient. The fundamental importance of membrane transport systems is exemplified by the transport of neurotransmitters into synaptic vesicles that subsequently mediate neuronal transmission and the transport of calcium ions into the sarcoplasmic reticulum allowing subsequent muscle contraction. *See* BIOPOTENTIALS AND IONIC CURRENTS; CELL POLARITY (BIOLOGY); SYNAPTIC TRANSMISSION.

One of the most important functions of membranes is in signal reception and relay. Extracellular signaling molecules such as growth factors, antigens, hormones, and neurotransmitters bind to extracellular portions of integral membrane receptors. Binding results in receptor stimulation, such that the cytoplasmic portion of the receptor is activated to mediate signaling events inside the cell. In all cases, the binding of a specific ligand to the outside of the receptor will ultimately result in the activation of particular signaling cascades, resulting in changes in cell morphology, locomotion, differentiation, gene expression, and so on. For example, signaling through the nerve growth factor receptor is required for neuronal survival and development and is essential for restoring innervation in wounded skin or muscle. *See* SIGNAL TRANSDUCTION.

Membranes are also intimately involved in energy generation and conversion reactions, without which eukaryotic life would be impossible. Within mitochondria, proteins that are embedded in the mitochondrial inner membrane and make up the electron-transport chain utilize the energy generated by oxidative reactions to create a transmembrane electrochemical gradient, which ultimately is used to generate ATP. Within chloroplasts, the thylakoid membrane contains protein complexes that capture electrons after chlorophyll is excited by sunlight and other protein complexes involved in electron transport processes that ultimately result in ATP synthesis. Both ATP-producing processes are fundamentally dependent on the differential in ionic concentrations generated and maintained across the impermeant inner mitochondrial or thylakoid membrane. *See* ENERGY METABOLISM; MITOCHONDRIA; PHOTOSYNTHESIS.

Membrane biogenesis. Nearly all membrane lipid is synthesized by integral endoplasmic reticulum proteins with their catalytic domains protruding from the endoplasmic reticulum membrane into the cytosol. Thus, the synthesis of lipids occurs within an aqueous cytosolic environment. The substrates for the synthesis, for example fatty acids, are maintained in the cytosol by being esterified to acyl carrier proteins (ACPs), thereby sheltering their hydrophobicity. The first step in phospholipid synthesis involves the movement of two fatty acids from the ACP to a soluble glycerol 3-phosphate to generate phosphatidic acid (PA), which is inserted into the cytoplasmic leaflet of the endoplasmic reticulum bilayer. Phosphatidic acid is then modified by the removal of the phosphate to form diacylglycerol, which is subsequently utilized to make various phospholipids by adding specific head groups. The newly made

lipids rapidly diffuse within the cytoplasmic leaflet of the endoplasmic reticulum membrane and are apparently rapidly equilibrated between the two membrane leaflets by the action of an enzyme called a scramblase. As a result, the different types of phospholipids are equally distributed within the two endoplasmic reticulum membrane leaflets. The newly synthesized lipids are transferred by vesicle budding and fusion to membranes of distal components of the secretory patway, that is, the Golgi apparatus, lysosomes, secretory granules, and the plasma membrane. The highly asymmetric distribution of phospholipids in the two leaflets of the plasma membrane results from the action of flippases that transfer lipids containing free amino groups—phosphatidylserine and phosphatidylethanolamine—from the leaflet facing the cell exterior to the one facing the cytoplasm. Gangliosides and sphingomyelin are synthesized in the Golgi apparatus from ceramide brought from the endoplasmic reticulum and are located exclusively in the lumenal, or exoplasmic, leaflet as a consequence of their synthesis by enzymes exposed on the surface of that leaflet.

All integral and GPI-linked membrane proteins are synthesized by multicomponent synthetic

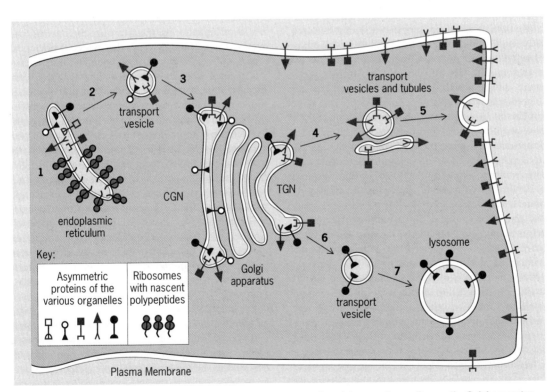

Fig. 4. Biogenesis of membranes. The membranes of the distal organelles of the secretory pathway—the Golgi apparatus, lysosomes, secretory granules, and the plasma membrane—are derived from the endoplasmic reticulum membrane by a process of vesicular transport, in which vesicles containing both lipids and proteins bud off from one compartment and fuse with a receiving compartment. Transmembrane proteins are synthesized in the endoplasmic reticulum (1) by ribosomes attached to the cytoplasmic face of the endoplasmic reticulum membrane and inserted into the membrane during the course of their synthesis. Each protein achieves in the endoplasmic reticulum a characteristic asymmetric disposition relative to the bilayer, which is maintained in recipient membranes as the protein is transported via vesicles between compartments. Some proteins are retained in the endoplasmic reticulum, and others are incorporated into transport vesicles (2) to be delivered (3) to the cis region of the Golgi apparatus (CGN). The proteins move through the Golgi apparatus by mechanisms that are not definitively established, with some remaining as residents in particular cisternae of this polarized organelle. Proteins that reach the farthest region of the Golgi apparatus, known as the trans-Golgi network (TGN), are then sorted (4, 6) into transport vesicles or tubules that bring them to the plasma membrane (5), developing lysosomes (7), or secretory granules (not shown).

machineries associated with the cytosolic side of the endoplasmic reticulum membrane. The membrane insertion of such proteins occurs while the protein is being synthesized (cotranslationally). Depending on its primary sequence, the protein will either span the membrane once or multiple times, or will acquire a GPI anchor. Proteins associated with the cytosolic side of the membrane are synthesized within the cytosol, some are modified by the attachment of lipid anchors, and all associate with the membrane after their synthesis is complete (posttranslationally). *See* ENDOPLASMIC RETICULUM.

New membrane for all secretory and endocytic organelles originates in the endoplasmic reticulum. From the endoplasmic reticulum, the newly synthesized lipid and protein components are transported by being incorporated into membrane vesicles, first to the Golgi apparatus, then from the Golgi to the plasma membrane, endosomes, lysosomes, or secretory granules. In some cases, proteins delivered from the Golgi to the plasma membrane are internalized and then delivered to endosomes or lysosomes (**Fig. 4**). Some lipids and proteins will be "left behind" in each compartment, whereas others will continue to be moved via vesicular traffic to their final destination. *See* GOLGI APPARATUS.

In contrast, organelles such as peroxisomes, mitochondria, and plastids do not receive endoplasmic reticulum–derived membranes. They maintain and enlarge their membranes by directly incorporating lipid molecules that are delivered by phospholipid transfer proteins. The transfer proteins extract a specific type of phospholipid from a membrane, diffuse within the cytosol, and then transfer the phospholipid into another membrane. Exchange appears to be concentration-dependent, and phospholipid is transported from phospholipid-rich (endoplasmic reticulum) membranes to phospholipid-poor (peroxisomal or mitochondrial) membranes. The exchange involves the transfer of phospholipid between the cytoplasmic leaflets of the two membranes, and it has been postulated that peroxisomal and mitochondrial flippases move the newly acquired phospholipid to the lumenal leaflet. Similarly, proteins are imported into peroxisomes, mitochondria, and plastids directly from the cytosol. Specific amino acid sequences in mitochondrial and plastid proteins define whether the protein will be integrated into the outer or the inner membrane and whether it will face the cytoplasmic, intermembrane, or internal compartment of these organelles. *See* CELL PLASTIDS; MITOCHONDRIA; PEROXISOME.

Membrane disease. Most membrane diseases are caused by defects in membrane proteins. One of the most studied diseases is cystic fibrosis, caused by mutations in a plasma membrane channel transporting Na^+ and Cl^- ions in epithelial cells. The most common mutation changes a single amino acid within the protein, and this leads to premature degradation and results in the absence of functional channels at the plasma membrane. As a consequence, the electrolyte homeostasis is altered in affected epithelia, leading to clinical manifestations of cystic fibrosis and ultimately death. *See* PANCREAS DISORDERS.

Elizabeth Sztul

Bibliography. B. Alberts et al., *Molecular Biology of the Cell*, 4th ed., Garland Publishing, 2002; W. R. Bishop and R. M. Bell, Assembly of phospholipids into cellular membranes: Biosynthesis, transmembrane movement, and intracellular translocation, *Annu. Rev. Cell Biol.*, 4:580–611, 1988; R. B. Gennis, *Biomembranes: Molecular Structure and Function*, Springer, New York, 1989; L. E. Henderson and S. Oroszlam, Fatty acylation of proteins, *Annu. Rev. Cell Biol.*, 4:612–648, 1988; H. Lodish, *Molecular Cell Biology*, W. H. Freeman, 2000; D. E. Vance and J. Vance (eds.), *Biochemistry of Lipids, Lipoproteins, and Membranes*, Elsevier, 1996; G. van Meer, Lipid traffic in animal cells, *Annu. Rev. Cell Biol.*, 5:247–276, 1989; K. W. A. Wirtz, Phospholipid transfer proteins, *Annu. Rev. Biochem.*, 60:73–99, 1991.

Cell metabolism

The sum of chemical reactions which transpire within cells. The cell is a self-contained chemical factory which interacts with its environment. This factory is unique in that it is a structure which moves, manufactures products for its own use and for the use of other factories, takes in from the outside that which it needs and discards that which it does not, and has the property of producing factories identical to itself from its own substance. The cell performs chemical, osmotic, mechanical, and electrical work, for which it needs energy. Plant cells obtain energy from sunlight; using light energy, they convert simple compounds such as carbon dioxide and various nitrogen, phosphate, and sulfur compounds into more complex materials. The energy in light is thus "stored" as chemical substances, mostly carbohydrates, within plant cells. Animal cells cannot use sunlight directly, and they obtain their energy by breaking down the stored chemical compounds of plant cells. Bacterial cells obtain their energy in various ways, but again mostly by the degradation of some of the simple compounds in their environment. *See* BACTERIAL PHYSIOLOGY AND METABOLISM; PHOTOSYNTHESIS; PLANT METABOLISM.

Dynamic state. The chemical atoms of the biological world are relatively few in number, being mostly carbon, hydrogen, oxygen, nitrogen, phosphorus, sulfur, iron, magnesium, and minute amounts of others. These atoms are grouped together into biological molecules, the most prevalent being proteins, carbohydrates, fats, and nucleic acids. These latter differ greatly among themselves in their chemistry and their functions. Their characteristics are given elsewhere, but they all have one thing in common: They are being continually broken down or degraded and being resynthesized by the cell. Thus, a feature of the cell is continuous metabolism of its chemical constituents.

Furthermore, cells have definite structures, and even the chemical constituents of these structures are being constantly renewed. This continuing turnover has been called the dynamic state of cellular constituents. For example, an animal cell takes in carbohydrate molecules, breaks down some of them to obtain the energy which is necessary to replace the chemical molecules that are being turned over, while another fraction of these molecules is integrated into the substance of the cell or its extracellular coverings. The energy obtained is, of course, also used for all the purposes mentioned above. Another way of stating it is that the cell is constantly striving to maintain an organized structure, a structure which has many functions, not the least of which is to duplicate itself, in the face of an environment which is continuously striving to degrade that structure into a random mixture of chemical molecules.

Chemical specificity. All the large molecules of the cell have rather specific functions: Carbohydrates, fats, and proteins constitute the structures of the cells; these, particularly the former two, are also used for food, or energy, depots; the nucleic acids are the structures involved in the continuity of cell types from generation to generation. All these large molecules are really variegated polymers of smaller molecules. These smaller molecules interact with one another in chemical reactions which are catalyzed at cellular temperature by biological protein catalysts called enzymes. These chemical reactions involve the breakdown of molecules, the condensing of one molecule to another to form a larger one, and the reforming of a third compound from parts of two constituents.

All these reactions are very specific, being catalyzed by specific enzymes, each enzyme being a specific protein, having a singular structure and performing a singular function, only reacting with its own specified substrate or substrates. At present, about a thousand chemical reactions are known which occur within cells; thus, about a thousand specific enzymes are known, some having been purified to crystalline form. See CARBOHYDRATE METABOLISM; ENZYME; LIPID METABOLISM; NUCLEIC ACID; PROTEIN METABOLISM.

Metabolic pathways. By studying how these enzymes operate and what substrates they attack, the biochemist has learned in general, and in many cases in specific, how fats, carbohydrates, proteins, and nucleic acids are synthesized and degraded in cells. Mainly through the use of radioactive tracer atoms, the pathways of many chemical compounds within the cell have been realized. For example, it is known what part of the carbohydrate molecule is used for energy production, what part is used in fat storage, and what parts end up in proteins and nucleic acids. Via the vast array of enzymatic reactions which go on inside cells, the substances which a cell "eats" or brings in are completely changed, becoming transformed into cell substance. This changeover, these syntheses of specific cell substances, need energy for accomplishment.

Energy source. As mentioned, this energy comes from the breakdown of various foodstuffs, a burning up of substrate, an oxidation; but unlike mechanical machines in which energy is given off as heat, the cell has evolved an energy coin. This coin is a chemical compound called adenosine triphosphate (ATP); it is synthesized enzymatically by the cell in a number of reactions in which various compounds coming from foodstuffs are oxidized, and thus the energy gained as a result of this oxidation is not lost as heat but stored in ATP. Subsequently, all cellular reactions which require synthesis of cell-specific substances use this ATP as a source of energy for these syntheses. For example, fats are composed mainly of carbon, oxygen, and hydrogen; when fats are used as foodstuff by the cell, the compounds are degraded, oxygen and hydrogen end up in the form of water and carbon in the form of carbon dioxide, and overall energy is gained in the form of ATP. When fats have to be synthesized by the cell, this ATP is used as an energy source to recombine small chemical molecules containing these atoms into certain kinds of fats. But since the cell needs to synthesize other molecules as well, these same carbon atoms, for example, are also found (via synthetic reactions) in carbohydrates, proteins, and nucleic acids. In this way the molecules, of which these atoms are a part, are being constantly replaced. See ADENOSINE TRIPHOSPHATE (ATP).

Control and continuity. Remarkably, even with these constant replacements going on, the cell never loses its own distinctive structure and function. The reason is that the ordering of the cell resides in a code of nucleic acids, which directs the syntheses of specific enzymes designed to do specific tasks; when these enzymes, being proteins and being also replaced like the other molecules of the cell, are degraded and have to be resynthesized, they are made again in exactly the same way as before. In this way continuity is ensured. See DEOXYRIBONUCLEIC ACID (DNA); GENETICS; RIBONUCLEIC ACID (RNA).

Metabolic differentiation in cells. To accomplish the many tasks outlined above, the cell is compartmentalized into distinctive functioning structures. The production of usable energy in the form of ATP takes place in plant and animal cells in membranous structures called mitochondria. Even in bacteria, which are about the size of mitochondria, these events occur on the membrane surrounding the bacterium. In plants the capture of light energy and the production of ATP therefrom takes place in structures called chloroplasts. Proteins, including enzyme proteins, are sythesized by tiny particles called ribosomes. The synthesis of carbohydrates in plants occurs within chloroplasts, while the synthesis of fatty acids in animal cells occurs in mitochondria. The structures involved in the continuity of cell structure and function, in the heredity of the cell, are the nucleic acid–containing chromosomes of the nucleus. In addition, cells have a variety of other structures, not as important as those above, but which nevertheless have distinctive functional tasks, such as storage granules, secretory granules, and lytic granules.

See CELL PLASTIDS; CHROMOSOME; MITOCHONDRIA; RIBOSOMES.

Control mechanisms. Finally, although a great deal is known of the metabolism of a large variety of compounds, their degradation and syntheses, and the interaction between chemical substances, little is known of how these multitudinous reactions are regulated within the cell to effect growth, particular size, and division into daughter cells having the same structure and functioning characteristics as those of the parent cells. It is known that enzymatic reaction activities within cells are strictly governed so that in quite a few cases knowledge has been gained of how a cell shuts off the synthesis of a compound of which it has enough, or speeds up the syntheses of those in short supply. It is all done by an enzyme so constructed that the compound which it synthesizes, say, can interact with this enzyme to inhibit further activity of the enzyme; thus not too much of the compound is formed at any one time. In the cells of a multicellular organism, cells interact with cells, their metabolism being geared among themselves, and this gearing, or regulation, probably occurs via the action of intercellular messengers or hormones. *See* HORMONE.

In summary, almost the sole justification for cell metabolism is the functioning of a vehicle whose major task is to reproduce as precise a replica of itself as possible. The efficiency of this metabolism has been maximized with this goal in view. *See* CELL (BIOLOGY).
Philip Siekevitz

Bibliography. T. A. Subramanian (ed.), *Cell Metabolism: Growth and Environment*, 2 vols., 1986; G. R. Welch and J. S. Clegg (eds.), *The Organization of Cell Metabolism*, 1987.

Cell motility

The movement of cells, changes in cell shape including cell division, and the movement of materials within cells. Many free-living protozoa are capable of movement, as are sperm and ameboid cells of higher organisms. Coordinated movement of cells occurs during embryogenesis, wound healing, and muscle contraction in higher organisms. Cell division is observed in all organisms and is a requirement for reproduction, growth, and development. Many cells also undergo structural changes as they differentiate, such as the outgrowth of axonal and dendritic processes during nerve cell differentiation. A more subtle form of cell motility involves the active transport of membranous organelles within the cytoplasm. This form of movement is required for proper organization of the cytoplasmic contents, and the redistribution of metabolites, hormones, and other materials within the cell.

Molecules responsible for movement. There are two basic molecular systems responsible for producing a variety of forms of movement in a wide range of cell types: one system involves filamentous polymers of the globular protein actin; the other involves hol-low, tube-shaped polymers of the globular protein tubulin, known as microtubules (see **illus.**). Associated with both actin filaments and microtubules are accessory enzymes that convert the chemical energy stored in adenosine triphosphate (ATP) into mechanical energy. Other proteins are responsible for regulating the arrangement, assembly, and organization of actin filaments and microtubules within the cell.

Actin and myosin. Muscle contraction represents one of the most extensively studied forms of cell movement, and it is from muscle that much basic knowledge of actin-based movement has been derived. Striated muscle cells found in skeletal muscle and heart muscle contain highly organized arrays of actin filaments interdigitating with filaments of the protein myosin. Myosin has an enzymatic activity that catalyzes the breakdown of ATP to adenosine diphosphate (ADP) and phosphate. The released energy is used to produce force against the actin filaments, which results in sliding between the actin and myosin filaments. *See* MUSCLE PROTEINS.

These proteins have by now been found in virtually all cell types. The actin and myosin filaments are less highly organized in smooth muscle and nonmuscle cells than in striated muscle; however, they act by the same force-producing mechanism.

Microtubules, dynein, and kinesin. Microtubules were initially described as components of eukaryotic cilia and flagella. Like actin filaments, microtubules have by now been found within the cytoplasm of almost all eukaryotic cells.

Two different molecules, dynein and kinesin, have been identified as enzymes that break down ATP to ADP and phosphate to produce force along microtubules. Dynein is a large enzyme complex that was initially identified in cilia and flagella. It has also been found associated with cytoplasmic microtubules. Kinesin is a force-producing enzyme that was initially found in microtubules prepared from neuronal cells. It is now also known to be widespread.

Despite the basic similarity in how the three force-producing enzymes (myosin, dynein, and kinesin) work, they differ from each other in structure and enzymatic properties and there is no evidence that they are evolutionarily related. Kinesin and dynein differ from each other in another important way: they produce force in opposite directions along microtubules. This suggests that they play complementary roles in the cell. As yet, no enzyme has been identified that produces force along actin filaments in the direction opposite to myosin.

Molecular and genetic analysis of a variety of organisms has revealed a remarkable diversity of kinesin- and myosin-related proteins in cells. The parts of these molecules responsible for producing force are closely related to the corresponding parts of kinesin and myosin. However, the remainder of the kinesin- and myosin-related molecules are structurally diverse. This pattern suggests that the kinesin- and myosin-related proteins attach to different structures within the cell, each individual protein being responsible for a specific type of movement. Multiple forms of dynein have also been identified. The members of the dynein family of proteins are much more closely interrelated than are the members of the myosin and kinesin families. The dyneins fall into two classes: a cytoplasmic dynein and several ciliary and flagellar dyneins. Novel tubulin- and actin-related proteins have been identified. With the exception of γ-tubulin, the functions of these proteins are as yet poorly understood.

Actin and microtubule assembly and organization. Another factor involved in cellular and intracellular movement is the assembly and rearrangement of actin and tubulin polymers. Actin filaments in muscle and microtubules in cilia and flagella are relatively stable structures. However, in other situations, both polymers are in equilibrium with their subunits. Thus the cell can make rapid and reversible changes in the number and organization of polymers.

Actin and microtubule assembly is often initiated at specific sites by specialized structures in the cell. In typical cultured eukaryotic cells, microtubules assemble outward from a centrosome. The centrosome is a complex structure that contains one or two centrioles (composed of a complex array of short microtubules) surrounded by diffusely organized proteinaceous material containing the novel protein γ-tubulin, which may serve to initiate microtubule growth. During the interphase portion of the cell cycle, the microtubules are seen to emanate radially from a single centrosome. During cell division the centrosome splits, and two overlapping radial arrays of microtubules appear. These arrays are subsequently remodeled to form the mitotic spindle. Differentiated cells exhibit a variety of microtubule arrangements consistent with the specific functional requirements of these cells. For example, neuronal cells are filled with parallel microtubules that are required for process formation and also serve as tracks along which materials are transported. Microtubules span epithelial cells and are involved in transport between the two surfaces of the epithelial cell layer. Microtubules form a circular band around blood platelets and are required for maintaining the discoid shapes of these cells. *See* CELL CYCLE; CENTROSOME.

Actin often assembles from sites associated with membranes. These sites may be diffuse or well defined, such as the cytoplasmic face of intercellular junctions. A variety of proteins that may be involved in organizing the actin filaments are localized at these sites, but the precise arrangement of these proteins and their role in initiating the assembly of actin are not fully understood.

Other factors affect the assembly of actin filaments and microtubules. Energy is required for polymerization. In the case of actin filaments, energy is supplied by the breakdown of ATP to ADP and phosphate as actin subunits add to the end of the growing filament. In the case of microtubules, energy is supplied by the breakdown of guanosine triphosphate (GTP) to guanosine diphosphate (GDP) and phosphate. Microtubule assembly is inhibited by calcium, but it is

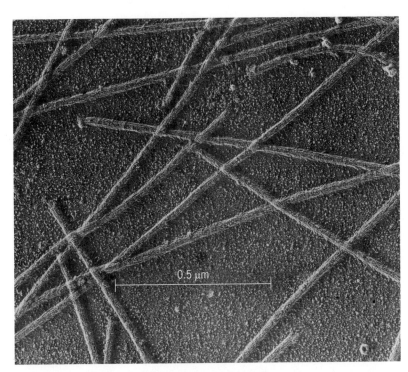

Electron micrograph of microtubules purified from calf brain cytoplasm. Rows of tubulin subunits along the microtubule axis can be discerned by close inspection. (*Courtesy of John Aghajanian*)

not certain whether this mechanism is actually used to regulate assembly in the cell.

Microtubules contain a variety of associated proteins (microtubule associated proteins, or MAPs) that have the general property of enhancing the rate and extent of polymerization. Several of these proteins appear as elongated fibrous projections on the microtubule surface, and may be involved in organizing the microtubules into parallel arrays in the cytoplasm.

A functionally diverse group of proteins affects actin assembly and organization. Profilin and thymosin $\beta 4$ regulate assembly by binding to free actin subunits and controlling their availability for polymerization. Gelsolin and severin are examples of proteins responsible for breaking actin filaments. Other proteins cross-link actin filaments; some, such as filamin and alpha actinin, produce random gels; and others, such as fascin, produce regularly packed bundles.

The organization of myosin may also be controlled in smooth muscle and nonmuscle cells by the activity of a protein kinase, an enzyme that adds a phosphate group to myosin. In the test tube, this reaction switches on the enzymatic activity of the myosin and causes it to form filaments. The protein kinase is under the control of calcium, which also turns on the severing activity of gelsolin and, in nonmuscle cells, inhibits the cross-linking activity of alpha actinin. These combined effects may be important in the solation and mobilization of gelled cytoplasm.

Actin-based cell movement. Actin is involved in a wide variety of movements in many cell types.

Ameboid movement. Ameboid movement occurs in a number of free-living amebas, in slime molds, which are colonial amebas, and in a variety of cells of higher organisms, such as white blood cells. Many of these cells are chemotactic, that is, they move toward or away from food, hormonal stimuli, and other factors. This indicates that, despite the lack of a distinct shape, these cells are capable of coordinated movement. In ameboid cells, the actin and myosin filaments are much less organized than in muscle, and may act as a contractile gel. The actin filaments are randomly arranged, and force production occurs in all directions, unlike muscle where it occurs only along the axis of the muscle fiber. The cytoplasm of the ameboid cell contains relatively rigid as well as fluid regions, which respectively reflect the cross-linked and free states of the actin filaments. Movement of the cell occurs by the extension of pseudopodia (false feet), which appears as the oozing of fluid cytoplasm through the zone of gelled cytoplasm surrounding the cell.

Other forms of locomotion. Other forms of movement also use actin and myosin to provide the motive force. The best characterized of these movements is that shown by mammalian cells, commonly fibroblasts and epithelial cells, grown in culture in plastic petri dishes. Unlike ameboid cells, these cells become very flat, and their cytoplasm shows some evidence of organized actin-containing structures. Most prominent are stress fibers, which are long cables of parallel actin filaments spanning the cells. The stress fibers also contain myosin and other proteins known to interact with actin. This suggests that they may act like myofibrils, the organized arrays of actin and myosin filaments in muscle cells, serving to produce force across the entire cell. However, experiments designed to test this possibility have generally shown that stress fibers do not really serve in force production. They may, instead, act as structural struts or simply represent by-products of the constant reshuffling of actin filaments during movement.

Cultured fibroblasts and epithelial cells, like ameboid cells, show evidence of fluid regions of cytoplasm involved in the forward migration of the cell. At the leading edge of the cell, a lamellipodium of clearer, fluid cytoplasm is usually seen, which extends at relatively rapid rates much like an ameboid pseudopodium. New sites of adhesion to the substratum are produced as the leading edge of the cell moves forward. In time, the trailing portion of the cell is released from the substratum, and contracts to join the leading portion of the cell, resulting in net movement.

Similar lamellipodial extension is observed in other forms of cell movement and may be a very general phenomenon. For example, the migration of sheets of epithelial cells that occurs in wound healing and during embryonic development may occur by a concerted extension of the leading edge of a row of cells. Neuronal cells, which produce extremely elongated axonal and dendritic processes, have a growth cone at their leading edge. The growth cone has the appearance and the actin organization of a leading lamellipodium, and seems to extend by a similar mechanism.

Actin filaments may have a relatively simple organization within lamellipodia. The filaments appear to be attached to the leading edge of the lamellipodium and extend in parallel array into the cytoplasm. These filaments may assemble by intercalation of actin subunits at the membrane. In this case, actin assembly alone, without the need for myosin, could be responsible for movement. Clear evidence that actin assembly can be responsible for movement has come from work with sperm of the sea cucumber. When the sperm contacts an egg, a long acrosomal process composed of actin filaments emerges from the head of the sperm within a few seconds and penetrates the vitelline membrane. There is no myosin in the process. Instead, it is the rapid assembly of actin that acts as the motive force for elongation of the process.

Another form of actin-based intracellular movement is cyclosis or cytoplasmic streaming. It occurs in varying patterns in a variety of plant and algal cells, as well as in the cells of a number of protozoa and the acellular slime molds. In some cases, as in the acellular slime molds, the bulk back-and-forth movement of cytoplasm appears to result from the contraction of gelled actin in the cell cortex. In walled cells, like those of plants and algae, arrays of parallel actin filaments near the cell surface are thought to be involved in propelling the cytoplasm in a continuous, circulating stream. Myosin may be involved in force production, but it is not known how force is exerted on the fluid cytoplasm to induce bulk flow.

Cytokinesis. Cell division consists of two processes: mitosis, which is responsible for chromosome separation, and cytokinesis, which divides the other contents of the cell. Mitosis is a microtubule-based process. Cytokinesis in animal cells involves the formation of a contractile ring of actin filaments. During cell division the ring constricts, as a result of the force-producing action of myosin. Ultimately, the cell is completely separated into two progeny cells. Plant cells contain a rigid cell wall, and cytokinesis occurs by a different mechanism. *See* MITOSIS.

Microtubule-based movement. Microtubules are also involved in a variety of forms of movement.

Ciliary and flagellar movement. Many eukaryotic cells bear cilia or flagella. Unlike the flagella of bacteria, eukaryotic cilia and flagella consist of a bundle of microtubules. The arrangement of microtubules is the same in cilia and flagella, and consists of nine laterally fused pairs of microtubules surrounding a central pair of unfused microtubules. This complex structure, known as the axoneme, whiplashes back and forth at very rapid rates. In the case of free-living cells, including a variety of ciliated and flagellated protozoa and most eukaryotic sperm cells, this movement propels the cell through the surrounding medium. Cilia also coat the surface of many types of epithelial cell layer in eukaryotic organisms (for example, the lining of the lung) and serve to transport the surrounding medium across the cell layer.

The basic mechanism underlying ciliary and flagellar movement is well understood. The enzyme dynein, using ATP as fuel, causes the microtubules to slide against each other. Because other proteins in the cilium or flagellum bind the microtubules together, little net movement of the microtubules relative to each other is possible. Instead, the microtubule bundle bends, much as a bimetallic strip bends in response to changes in temperature. How the elaborate bending movements of the entire structure are coordinated is not yet well understood. *See* CILIA AND FLAGELLA.

Organelle traffic. Many, perhaps all, membrane-bound organelles move about within the cell. This movement occurs in two directions, outward toward the cell membrane and inward toward the nucleus. The outward movement is part of the process of secretion, the export of materials manufactured within the cell. The inward movement represents the processing of materials that have been taken up by endocytosis and pinocytosis, such as peptide hormones that have acted on the cell surface and serum proteins destined for degradation. These movements occur in virtually all cells. In neurons, they are referred to as anterograde (outward) and retrograde (inward) axonal transport, and are responsible for supplying new materials and removing used components from the axon, which has a very limited biosynthetic capability. *See* ENDOCYTOSIS.

The oppositely directed movements of the membrane-bound organelles are thought to be due to the activities of kinesin and dynein, which produce force in opposite directions along microtubules. The tubulin subunits within a microtubule are arranged in a head-to-tail manner, and the microtubule, therefore, has a built-in polarity. The two ends of the microtubule are designated as plus (+) and minus (−). In typical cultured mammalian cells, the plus ends of the microtubules are anchored in the centrosome located on the surface of the nucleus. The plus ends of the microtubules are disposed toward the cell surface. In axons, most of the microtubules are oriented with their minus ends near the nucleus and the plus ends toward the axon terminus where the synapse is located.

Evidence suggests that kinesin and cytoplasmic dynein are attached to the surface of organelles and are responsible for transporting the organelles along microtubules. Based on what is known about the orientation of the microtubules, a simple model for the mechanism of bidirectional organelle traffic is that kinesin is responsible for organelle transport from the nucleus toward the cell surface, or toward the end of the axon, while cytoplasmic dynein is responsible for movement in the opposite, inbound, direction.

Mitosis. All eukaryotic cells reproduce by replication of their deoxyribonucleic acid (DNA) and subsequent separation of the duplicated chromosomes. The process of dividing the genetic material is referred to as karyokinesis or mitosis.

Cell division begins by the condensation of chromatin in the nucleus, followed by the breakdown of the nuclear envelope. The centrosome, the organizing center for microtubules in the interphase cell, duplicates, resulting in two radial arrays of microtubules. The overlapping microtubules interact to form a barrel- or spindle-shaped structure termed the mitotic spindle, also known as the mitotic apparatus. The chromosomes gather at the middle of the spindle, at which time they are found attached to the ends of microtubules. The chromosomal attachment site for microtubules is known as the kinetochore, which is located along a constricted region of the chromosome known as the centromere. *See* CELL DIVISION.

Chromosome movement generally occurs in two stages referred to as anaphase A and B. During anaphase A, the chromosomes move toward the poles of the spindle. During anaphase B, the entire spindle elongates, causing further separation of the chromosomes. During both processes, different classes of microtubules within the spindle shorten or lengthen. It is not known whether this behavior is a cause or a consequence of chromosome movement. Kinesin-related proteins and cytoplasmic dynein are involved in chromosome movement. CHO-1, a kinesin-related protein, has been found associated with microtubules in the middle of the mitotic spindle. It is believed to produce spindle elongation by causing microtubules to slide against one another. Other kinesin-related proteins have been found at the kinetochore, as has cytoplasmic dynein, and may pull on the ends of microtubules at their point of attachment to the kinetochore and draw the chromosome toward the spindle pole. *See* CHROMOSOME.

Other motile proteins. It appears that many forms of movement can be explained by actin and myosin or by microtubules and their associated proteins dynein and kinesin. However, other motile mechanisms certainly exist.

Many bacteria possess flagella. These are very fine helical hairs, unlike the more substantial flagella and cilia of eukaryotic cells. Another important difference is that the bacterial flagella rotate about their axis and propel the bacterium by a corkscrewlike mechanism, unlike the bending and whiplashing movements of eukaryotic cilia and flagella. Bacterial flagella are hollow filamentous polymers, like microtubules, but are composed of the protein flagellin, which has no apparent relationship to tubulin. The flagella are attached at their base to a rotary motor structure in the bacterial cell membrane. *See* BACTERIA.

Other forms of bacteria glide over solid substrata by using an excreted slime for propulsion; the mechanism of gliding is not understood. Gliding motility is also seen in a number of algae and blue-green algae.

The sperm cells of roundworms differ from other types of sperm cells in that they lack flagella and exhibit a form of ameboid movement. These cells, however, contain neither actin, which is involved in ameboid movement in other ameboid cells, nor tubulin. Movement may be produced by insertion of lipid in the forward region of the plasma membrane and rearward flow of the membrane.

A contractile protein, spasmin, has been identified in *Vorticella* and related ciliated protozoa. Spasmin is organized into a long, thick fiber within the stalk portion of the organism. In response to calcium, the fiber undergoes a rapid, drastic contraction. It is not known whether spasmin exists in other organisms. *See* CELL (BIOLOGY).

Relationship to disease. Understanding how cells move increases the ability to control abnormal cell behavior, such as the increased level of cell division responsible for cancer and the migration of cancer cells from their site of origin in the body. Errors in chromosome segregation are also known to be responsible for Down syndrome, and are prevalent during the progression of neoplastic tumors.

Because the normal functioning of cells is so dependent on proteins that compose and regulate microtubules and actin filaments, defects in these proteins are expected to have severe effects on cell viability. An example of a microtubule defect has been identified in Alzheimer's disease: a microtubule-associated protein (termed tau) is found to be a prominent component of abnormal neurofibrillary tangles seen in affected nerve cells. However, it remains unknown whether the defect involving tau is part of the cause of the disease or represents one of its effects. *See* ALZHEIMER'S DISEASE; CANCER (MEDICINE); DOWN SYNDROME.   Richard Vallee

Bibliography. M. De Brabander and J. G. De Mey (eds.), *Microtubules and Microtubule Inhibitors: Nineteen Eighty-Five*, 1987; J. A. De Grado, *Microtubule Proteins*, 1989; P. Dustin, *Microtubules*, 1984.

Cell nucleus

The largest of the membrane-bounded organelles which characterize eukaryotic cells; it is thought of as the control center since it contains the bulk of the cell's genetic information in the form of deoxyribonucleic acid (DNA). The nucleus has two major functions: (1) It is the site of synthesis of ribonucleic acid (RNA), which in turn directs the formation of the protein molecules on which all life depends; and (2) in any cell preparing for division, the nucleus precisely duplicates its DNA for later distribution to cell progeny. The discovery of the nucleus dates back to 1710, when the Dutch microscopist Antonie van Leeuwenhoek noted a centrally located "clear" area in living blood cells of birds and amphibians. However, it was not until 1831 that the British botanist Robert Brown first used the term nucleus and provided a precise morphological description. *See* DEOXYRIBONUCLEIC ACID (DNA); EUKARYOTAE; PROKARYOTAE.

Structure. The diameter of nuclei ranges from 1 micrometer in intracellular parasites and yeast cells to several millimeters in some insect sperm. Spherical or ellipsoidal nuclei are found in most cell types, al-

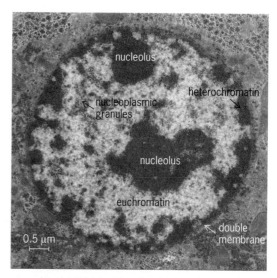

Fig. 1. Transmission electron micrograph of a thin section of a rat liver cell nucleus.

though occasionally spindle-shaped, lobulated, disc-shaped, or cup-shaped nuclei may be observed. Although nuclear size and shape are somewhat consistent features of a particular cell type, these features are more variable in cancer cells. In addition, tumor cell nuclei are characterized by indentation, furrowing, elongation, and budding.

The nucleus is bounded by a double membrane and contains several major components: chromatin, which is composed of DNA and chromosomal proteins; the nucleolus, which is the site of ribosomal RNA (rRNA) synthesis; and nucleoplasmic fibrils and granules, some of which are involved in the processing and transport of messenger RNA out of the nucleus (**Fig. 1**). The constituents of the nucleus are contained within a framework referred to as the nuclear matrix.

Nuclear envelope. The contents of the nucleus are spatially separated from the cytoplasm by a double-membrane-bounded structure called the nuclear envelope. The two membranes are both approximately 10 nanometers thick, and they are separated by a gap of 20–40 nm, known as the perinuclear space. The outer nuclear membrane is continuous with the endoplasmic reticulum and is often studded with ribosomes involved in protein synthesis.

At periodic intervals, the inner and outer membranes appear to be fused together, forming nuclear pores, averaging 120 nm in diameter. A typical mammalian cell contains 3000–4000 pores in its nuclear envelope. Each pore is composed of a nuclear pore complex measuring approximately 80 nm (inside diameter) with an estimated 9-nm open channel. The mass of each mammalian nuclear pore complex has been estimated at about 125×10^6 daltons and is composed of approximately 50 different proteins. The pores allow for the passage of molecules into and out of the nucleus. All nuclear pores appear to be functionally identical in that they can carry out both import and export. The central channel of the nuclear pore complex is thought to be involved in active transport, and eight peripheral channels, each approximately 10 nm in diameter, are proposed to function in passive exchange of small molecules as well as perhaps serving as an anchoring site for interphase chromatin. Small macromolecules below 50 kDa can diffuse through the nuclear pore complex, whereas larger macromolecules are transported via a signal-mediated process that may occur via a series of association-dissociation reactions. Targeting signals that are encoded in a protein and direct its nuclear import are called nuclear localization signals (NLS), and signals that direct nuclear export are termed nuclear export signals (NES); many different signals have been identified that function in association with different proteins. Recently, a nuclear export signal has been identified that directly interacts with transfer RNA. The largest-diameter complex that can be transported through the nuclear pore complex is estimated to be about 0.26 μm. *See* RIBOSOMES.

Internal and adjacent to the inner membrane of the nuclear envelope is an electron opaque layer termed the nuclear lamina. In most mammalian cells, the lamina is about 10 nm thick and is composed of three major polypeptides, lamins A (70 kilodaltons), B (68 kDa), and C (60 kDa), which are present in equal amounts in the interphase nucleus. Lamins possess all the major structural properties that have been described for intermediate filament polypeptides at the levels both of protomers and of assembled filaments. The lamins are thought to function in regulating nuclear envelope structure and anchoring interphase chromatin at the nuclear periphery. It has also been suggested that the lamins act as a substrate for the formation of DNA replication complexes, or regulate DNA condensation or formation of nuclear matrix elements which are required for efficient replication to occur. *See* CELL MEMBRANES.

Chromatin and chromosomes. Deoxyribonucleic acid is present in the nucleus as a DNA-protein complex referred to as chromatin. The DNA that is present in a typical human cell is composed of 3 billion base pairs of nucleotide sequence. The DNA is highly compacted, approximately 200,000-fold. If it were stretched out in a linear manner, it would extend for 6.6 ft (2 m). This DNA encodes for the estimated 50–100,000 genes which are present in each human cell. However, a significant portion of the genome does not contain any protein coding information, and it is unclear what role this DNA plays in cellular function.

Classes of chromatin. Eukaryotic chromatin has been divided into two classes, heterochromatin and euchromatin, based on its state of condensation during interphase. Heterochromatin is condensed during interphase and is therefore generally considered to be transcriptionally inactive. It is commonly located in an irregular band around the nuclear periphery (Fig. 1) and around the nucleolus as well as in patches throughout the nucleoplasm. The amount of heterochromatin present in the nucleus varies with transcriptional activity; little heterochromatin is present in transcriptionally active cancer cells whereas the nuclei of orthochromatic erythroblasts and mature spermatozoa, both transcriptionally inactive, are practically filled with condensed chromatin. In an average eukaryotic cell, approximately 90% of the chromatin is transcriptionally inactive at any given time, but all of the inactive chromatin may not be in a condensed state. However, the 10% of the chromatin that is transcriptionally active is always in the form of decondensed euchromatin.

Transcription. The process by which a segment of cellular DNA makes a copy of itself in the form of RNA is referred to as transcription. Transcription can be divided into three systems, each using a different set of enzymes and some similar as well as different factors which function to produce different classes of RNA molecules. The three systems are referred to as RNA polymerase I, II, and III. RNA polymerase I is specifically involved in transcribing ribosomal RNAs, which are components of ribosomes and are involved in the process of protein synthesis. RNA polymerase II is primarily involved in transcribing messenger RNAs which act as the template for the production of specific cellular proteins. A majority of the RNAs that are made by RNA polymerase II must be processed prior to their transport from the nucleus into the cytoplasm. This processing, referred to as splicing, involves the removal of noncoding regions (introns) which interrupt the protein coding sequence (exons) present in the transcribed RNA molecule. RNA polymerase III is primarily involved in the production of transfer RNAs, which are involved in directing specific amino acids, the building blocks of proteins, to the ribosomes, where the amino acids become incorporated in a sequence-dependent manner into the newly synthesized protein. The production of RNA molecules may be thought of as the major function of the nucleus, and the process is highly regulated, with some RNAs being transcribed at specific times during the cell cycle. *See* EXON; INTRON; RIBONUCLEIC ACID (RNA).

Replication. A second nuclear function equally important to transcription is the process of DNA replication. Because many cells in the human body are continuously dividing, it is essential to their function for each of the daughter cells to obtain a complete copy of the cell's DNA. Replication of DNA takes place only once during the cell cycle in a period referred to as the synthesis phase or S phase. As is the case for transcription, a specific series of enzymes and factors are responsible for the accurate replication of cellular DNA. *See* CELL CYCLE; CHROMOSOME.

Nucleolus. The nucleolus is a subnuclear organelle within which ribosomal genes and their products are naturally sequestered from the rest of the genome and nucleoplasm. Ribosomal gene transcription, ribosomal RNA processing, and preribosomal particle formation all occur within this highly specialized region of the nucleus. Nuclei may contain one or more nucleoli, and generally cancer cells have multiple nucleoli. Although the nucleolus is not bounded by a membrane, specific proteins have been localized to discrete functional regions within this structure and a nucleolar localization signal has been identified. Ultrastructurally, the nucleolus may be regarded as being composed of four organizational areas: a dense fibrillar region, fibrillar center or centers, a granular region, and nucleolar vacuoles. The nucleolus is usually surrounded by a shell of perinucleolar chromatin which is connected with regions of intranucleolar chromatin and is continuous with the fibrillar centers.

The cellular DNA that encodes for ribosomal RNA of higher eukaryotes occurs in multiple copies and is organized in tandem repeats which are separated from each other by nontranscribed spacer regions of DNA. Human cells contain approximately 250 copies of ribosomal DNA, and the length of a single ribosomal DNA repeat unit is 44,000 base pairs. The periphery of the nucleolar fibrillar centers are the sites that most likely represent the nucleolar regions where ribosomal DNA transcription occurs. The dense fibrillar component probably represents elongating RNA transcripts and precursor molecules. Finally, the granular region represents the site of assembling and processing mature ribosomal subunits.

Nuclear matrix. The nuclear components are present within specific macromolecular nuclear domains (**Fig. 2**). The large number of molecules present within the nucleoplasm and the high degree of efficiency with which vital nuclear functions take place suggest a high degree of nuclear organization. The concept of a nuclear matrix or nuclear scaffold seems to satisfy this role. By definition, the nuclear matrix is the residual structure left after the majority of DNA, nuclear proteins, and nuclear phospholipid are extracted from the nucleus. Numerous nuclear functions, including transcription, RNA processing, and DNA replication, are thought to take place in association with the nuclear matrix. *See* CELL (BIOLOGY); MOLECULAR BIOLOGY.   David L. Spector

Bibliography. P. S. Agutter, *Between Nucleus and Cytoplasm*, 1990; B. Alberts et al. (eds.), *Molecular Biology of the Cell*, 3d ed., 1994; H. Hillman, *The Living Cell*, 1991; D. L. Spector, Macromolecular domains within the cell nucleus, *Annu. Rev. Cell Biol.*, 9:265–315, 1993.

Cell organization

Cells are divided into several compartments, each with a characteristic structure, biochemical composition, and function (**Fig. 1**). These compartments are called organelles. They are delimited by membranes composed of phospholipid bilayers and various proteins specialized for each type of organelle. All eukaryotic cells have a nucleus surrounded by a nuclear envelope, and a plasma membrane that borders the whole cell. Most eukaryotic cells also have endoplasmic reticulum, a Golgi apparatus, lysosomes, mitochondria, and peroxisomes. Plant cells have chloroplasts for photosynthesis in addition to the organelles that they share with animal cells. These organelles are suspended in a gel-like cytoplasmic matrix composed of three types of protein polymers called actin filaments, microtubules, and intermediate filaments. In addition to holding the cell together, the actin filaments and microtubules act as tracks for several different types of motor proteins that are responsible for cell motility and organelle movements within the cytoplasm.

A major challenge in the field of cell biology is to learn how each organelle and the cytoplasmic matrix are assembled and distributed in the cytoplasm. This process is complex, since cells consist of more than 2000 different types of protein molecules together with a large number of lipids, polysaccharides, and nucleic acids, including both deoxyribonucleic acid (DNA) and many different types of ribonucleic acid (RNA). *See* NUCLEIC ACID.

The cell must possess enough information to specify which molecules are to be associated in a specific compartment, to route the appropriate groups of molecules to their compartments, and then to position each type of component appropriately in the cell. As a result of intense research on each of these topics beginning in the 1960s and continuing to the present, a number of specific chemical reactions that contribute to organizing cells are now recognized; even more important, a small number of general principles that explain these complex processes of life can be appreciated.

Principles of assembly. The following principles account for many of the processes that result in the assembly and organization of cells.

Normal cells regulate the production and degradation of all of their constituent molecules so that the right balance of molecules is present at any given time. The genes stored in nuclear DNA are duplicated precisely once per cell cycle. The supply of each of thousands of proteins is usually regulated at the level

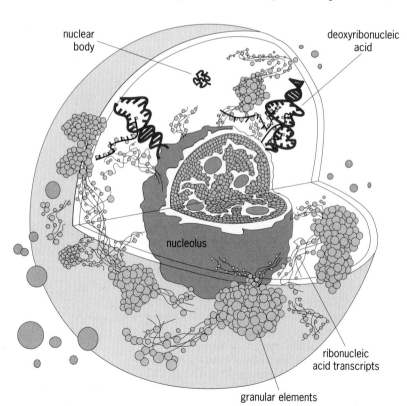

Fig. 2. Three-dimensional organization of the mammalian cell nucleus.

nuclear body

deoxyribonucleic acid

nucleolus

ribonucleic acid transcripts

granular elements

of the genes at the time of biosynthesis and by the rate of degradation. These proteins serve as enzymes that determine the rate of synthesis of themselves as well as of other cellular components such as nucleic acids, carbohydrates, and lipids. Each of these processes is regulated by molecular feedback loops to assure the proper levels of each cellular constituent. *See* CELL CYCLE; CELL METABOLISM.

A large majority of cellular components are generated by the self-assembly of their constituent molecules. Self-assembly means that the information required for molecules to bind together in the proper orientation is contained in the molecules themselves. In other words, no outside information is required. Although the amino acid sequence of each protein not only specifies its three dimensional structure and its interactions along assembly pathways, cells often use proteins called chaperones to guide the process, particularly to avoid incorrect folding events that might lead to irreversible aggregation.

Some examples of self-assembly include the binding of histones to DNA, the formation of lipid bilayers from phospholipids, and the polymerization of actin molecules into filaments. The molecules are usually brought together by diffusion. The energy required to hold them together derives from the exclusion of water from their complementary surfaces as well as from the formation of ionic bonds and hydrogen bonds. The variety of molecular structures found in proteins allows each type to self-assemble specifically, only with their correct partner molecules.

After biosynthesis, proteins and nucleic acids are routed to their proper cellular compartment by specific recognition signals consisting of parts of the molecule or, in the case of some proteins, by sugar side chains. These signals are recognized by compartment-specific receptors that guide the molecules to the correct compartment. For example, proteins destined for lysosomes have a specific sugar side chain added in the Golgi apparatus that guides them to lysosomes. Similarly, proteins destined for the nucleus all contain short sequences of amino acids that target the proteins for uptake by the nucleus. These so-called nuclear recognition sequences bind to receptor proteins that move through nuclear pores, channels through the nuclear envelope that connect the nucleus with the cytoplasm.

Most molecules move to their correct compartment by the process of diffusion down concentration gradients, but objects as large as organelles require transport systems composed of microtubules or actin filaments together with specific motor proteins to position them correctly in the cytoplasm. For example, a protein molecule destined to be part of a mitochondrion will diffuse from the site of biosynthesis through the cytoplasm to a mitochondrion, where it will bind to a receptor that guides its incorporation into the mitochondrion. On the other hand, the mitochondrion itself is too large to diffuse through the network of protein fibers in the cytoplasmic matrix, and so it must be pulled through the matrix by a motor protein that moves along microtubules to the correct place in the cell.

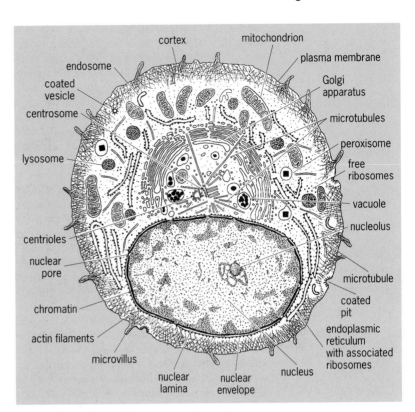

Fig. 1. Section through an animal cell showing the major components visible by electron microscopy. To simplify, a few important components, including intermediate filaments, have been omitted.

Some cellular components, such as ribosomes and the filaments of the cytoplasmic matrix, assemble afresh from their constituent molecules, but all organelles composed of membranes form only by the growth and division of preexisting organelles. The reason that these organelles require precursors is that biological membranes composed of phospholipids can grow only by expansion of preexisting bilayers. As a consequence, organelles such as mitochondria and the endoplasmic reticulum are inherited maternally starting from the egg and expanding into every cell in the body by continued growth and partition into both daughter cells at every cell division. Other membrane-bound organelles, such as lysosomes, form from vesicles that bud off the Golgi apparatus.

Many of the individual self-assembly reactions required for normal cell growth can be reproduced in the test tube, but the cell is the only place known where the entire range of reactions, including biosynthesis, targeting, and assembly, can go to completion. Thus, cells are such a special environment that the chain of life has required an unbroken lineage of cells stretching from all living cells back through their ancestors to the earliest forms of life. This requirement for cellular continuity explains why extinction is an irreversible process. *See* EXTINCTION (BIOLOGY).

Organization and assembly of organelles. All cellular organelles arise by the assembly of their components, either from constituent molecules or from preexisting structures.

Nucleus. The nucleus is a protected environment within the cell where the genes are stored in the form of specific sequences of bases in large DNA molecules. Many genes are linked together end-to-end in one giant DNA molecule. Interaction with proteins called histones coils up each of these linear DNA molecules into more compact units called chromosomes, which can fit inside the nucleus. The DNA is replicated once during each cell cycle and supplied with sufficient histones and other accessory proteins to duplicate each chromosome. Between mitotic events, the chromosomes are not distinct from each other and are called chromatin (Fig. 1). *See* CELL NUCLEUS; CHROMOSOME; GENE.

The nucleus is separated from the cytoplasm by the nuclear envelope, a specialized part of the endoplasmic reticulum consisting of two membranes and penetrated by tiny diaphragms called nuclear pores. All traffic into and out of the nucleus passes through nuclear pores. Traffic moving into the nucleus includes all of the proteins found in the nucleus and the proteins required to form ribosomes. Traffic moving out includes messenger RNA and ribosomal subunits assembled in the nucleolus. The integrity of the nuclear envelope is maintained by a network of intermediate filaments composed of protein subunits called lamins (Fig. 1) that are associated with the inner surface of the envelope. Lamins form links between the nuclear pores and between the membrane and the chromatin.

During mitosis, the replicated chromosomes must partition equally between the two daughter cells, a process that requires the disassembly and reassembly of the nuclear envelope. At the outset of mitosis, phosphate groups are added to the nuclear lamins by an enzyme called a mitotic kinase. This modification causes lamin intermediate filaments to break up into their protein subunits. The nuclear envelope membrane then fragments into small vesicles, releasing the chromosomes into the cytoplasm, where the mitotic apparatus divides them between the daughter cells. At the end of mitosis, the chromosomes cluster so close to each other that they exclude soluble macromolecules. The lamins lose their extra phosphates, and together with associated vesicles of nuclear envelope membranes they repolymerize on the surface of the condensed chromosomes. When these vesicles fuse to form a continuous nuclear envelope, virtually no cytoplasmic macromolecules are included in the nucleus. Remarkably, the entire cycle of chromosome condensation, nuclear envelope breakdown, and nuclear envelope reformation can now be carried out in the test tube. A single process, the phosphorylation and dephosphorylation of the lamins, provides the biochemical cue for this complex process. *See* MITOSIS.

Protein synthesis by ribosomes. The sequence of nucleotides in each gene determines the sequence of nucleotides in messenger RNAs and other RNAs. The nucleotide sequence of a messenger RNA specifies the sequence of amino acids in a protein as it is synthesized by RNA-protein assembly called a ribo-some. Ribosomes are giant macromolecular assemblies consisting of one large and one small subunit that are assembled in the nucleolus from more than 50 different proteins and 3 RNA molecules. As the ribosome reads the messenger RNA, transfer RNAs deliver the correct amino acid to the end of the growing polypeptide. The RNA component of the large ribosome subunit catalyzes the formation of the peptide bond between each amino acid in the protein. *See* PROTEIN; RIBOSOMES.

Endoplasmic reticulum. The endoplasmic reticulum is an extensive, membrane-bounded intracellular compartment specialized for the synthesis of lipids and proteins. The membrane forms by expansion of preexisting endoplasmic reticulum. Proteins inserted into the lipid bilayer itself synthesize the phospholipids that constitute the lipid bilayer. The proteins destined for insertion into membranes, or for lysosomes, or for secretion carry signal sequences of amino acids. As ribosomes synthesize these proteins, the signal sequence interacts with an adapter called a signal recognition particle, which links the ribosome producing the protein to a receptor protein of the endoplasmic reticulum. As the protein grows in length, a protein pore guides the protein into or across the lipid bilayer of the endoplasmic reticulum. Other zip codes retain particular proteins in the lipid bilayer or in the lumen of the endoplasmic reticulum; other zip codes direct proteins on to various parts of the cell. *See* ENDOPLASMIC RETICULUM.

Microtubules play an important role in distributing the endoplasmic reticulum within the cell. Motor proteins bind to the membrane and by moving along microtubules can pull the endoplasmic reticulum into a branching network that spreads throughout the cytoplasm.

Golgi apparatus. These stacks of flattened membrane-bounded sacks (Fig. 1) are responsible for adding sugars to proteins and for sorting membranes and secretory proteins. Complexes of cytoplasmic proteins interact with membrane proteins to pinch vesicles from the endoplasmic reticulum. These vesicles fuse with the Golgi apparatus, transferring lipids, proteins in the lumen, and membrane proteins from the endoplasmic reticulum to the Golgi apparatus. Proteins and lipids pass selectively through the compartments of the Golgi apparatus where they are modified by the covalent attachment of sugar polymers. The Golgi apparatus is characteristically located in the middle of the cell near the centrosome by the action of motor proteins that move the membranes along microtubules toward the centrosome. *See* GOLGI APPARATUS.

Plasma membrane. The components of the cell membrane (Fig. 1) are originally formed in the endoplasmic reticulum, where both the phospholipids and proteins are synthesized. The proteins are inserted into the bilayer and then transported from the endoplasmic reticulum through the Golgi apparatus via small vesicles to the plasma membrane. Remarkably the signals and receptors along this pathway are selective enough to allow plasma membrane proteins to move to their target, with the total exclusion of proteins that belong in the other membrane compartments.

Many of the components of the plasma membrane are not permanent residents there; instead, proteins that serve as receptors for extracellular molecules, including nutrients and some hormones, are taken into the cell by specializations called coated pits (Fig. 1) and can recycle in small vesicles from the plasma membrane to internal compartments called endosomes and back to the cell surface from one to hundreds of times before they are degraded. Much larger particles, such as bacteria, are taken in by the related process of phagocytosis and also delivered to lysosomes for degradation. *See* CELL MEMBRANES; ENDOCYTOSIS; PHAGOCYTOSIS.

Lysosomes. The degradative enzymes found in lysosomes are synthesized by ribosomes attached to the endoplasmic reticulum so that they pass into the lumen of the endoplasmic reticulum. From there they pass to the Golgi apparatus, where an enzyme recognizes surface features and add a special sugar called mannose-6-phosphate. This sugar is the signal for protein receptors to bind lysosomal proteins and to guide them from the Golgi apparatus to the lumen of lysosomes, as cargo in small vesicles that bud from the Golgi apparatus and fuse with forming lysosomes. *See* LYSOSOME.

Mitochondria. Mitochondria arose in an early eukaryote that engulfed a proteobacterium. The two cells established a symbiotic relationship with the proteobacterium providing enzymes to derive energy from the breakdown of lipids and the capacity for synthesis of ATP by oxidative phosphorylation. Over tens of millions of years, most of the proteobacterial genes moved to the nucleus of the host, so now nuclear genes encode most mitochondrial proteins and RNAs. Mitochondria retained a small genome, ribosomes, and messenger RNAs that produce a few special proteins.

Although mitochondria are membrane-bound organelles (Fig. 1), they form in a fundamentally different way from the other organelles since the constituent proteins do not come through the endoplasmic reticulum-Golgi pathway. Most of the proteins are synthesized on free ribosomes located in the cytoplasm. From there they diffuse to the mitochondria. Mitochondrial proteins have an identifying sequence of amino acids that reacts with receptors on the surface of mitochondria. Subsequently they are actively transported across the mitochondrial membranes into the lumen or are inserted into the membranes. A minority of the mitochondrial proteins are synthesized inside the mitochondria themselves. *See* MITOCHONDRIA.

Peroxisomes. As with mitochondria, the constituent proteins are synthesized on free ribosomes and then incorporated into the membranes and lumen of the peroxisome. Enzymes in the lumen of peroxisomes catalyze a variety of oxidation reactions. *See* PEROXISOME.

Chloroplasts. Chloroplasts arose during a singular event that resulted in a cyanobacterium becoming a symbiont in a eukaryotic cell that founded the lineages including algae and plants. The cyanobacterium brought the capacity for photosynthesis by providing the proteins required for both photosystem I and photosystem II. As in the case of mitochondria, over time most bacterial genes moved to the nucleus but chloroplasts retained a small genome and the capacity to make a number of their own proteins. Most of the proteins are made in the cytoplasm and imported as in mitochondria and peroxisomes. *See* CELL PLASTIDS; PHOTOSYNTHESIS.

Cytoskeleton. Assembly of the cytoskeleton represents a somewhat different problem for the cell than any of the examples considered above since the three types of protein polymers making up the cytoskeleton change their form relatively rapidly during the life of the cell. Consequently, information is required not only to guide assembly, but also to remodel these systems on a time scale of seconds to minutes. Since the actin filaments, intermediate filaments, and microtubules are composed of different proteins and each has distinctive functions and dynamics, they will be considered separately. *See* CYTOSKELETON.

1. Actin filaments. Actin filaments (**Fig. 2***a*) occur in all eukaryotic cells, being a fundamental structural component as well as linear tracks for movements of myosin motors. In muscle, actin filaments and myosin filaments form a highly specialized contractile system designed for forceful, rapid, one-dimensional contractions. In other cells, actin filaments and myosins are responsible for pinching daughter cells in two during cytokinesis, for some cell shape changes and for movements of some membrane bound organelles (particularly in plants and fungi). *See* CYTOKINESIS; MUSCLE PROTEINS.

Actin is a globular protein that polymerizes into long filaments composed of a double-helical array of actin subunits. Formation of these filaments is a classical example of self-assembly, but the process is tightly controlled in cells by more than 50 regulatory proteins. Some actin-binding proteins bind actin monomers and influence the number available for polymerization. Others bind to an end of actin

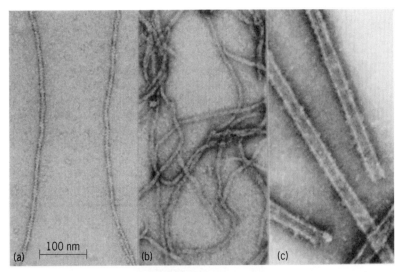

Fig. 2. Electron micrographs of the three cytoskeletal polymers: (*a*) actin filaments, (*b*) intermediate filaments, and (*c*) microtubules.

filaments. These can help initiate polymerization but allow growth in only one direction. Some can cut actin filaments into two fragments. Others cross-link actin filaments into random networks or parallel bundles. These networks form relatively rigid gels in the cortical cytoplasm of cells (Fig. 1). Actin filaments anchored to the plasma membrane reinforce the surface of the cell. Tightly packed bundles of actin filaments with closely applied plasma membrane project from the surface of many cells (like fingers in a glove). These filopodia or microvilli (Fig. 1) increase the surface area of the plasma membrane and participate in sensing the environment. Some cells have bundles of actin filaments attached at their ends to the inside of the plasma membrane. These "stress fibers" reinforce cells that are under mechanical stress such as the cells that line large arteries.

This actin filament system is dynamic, as shown by the way that a cell can change shape as it moves. Such movements require the reorganization of both the cortical network and actin filament bundles. Some of these changes are caused by myosin-mediated contractions such as the contraction of the cleavage furrow during cytokinesis. Other changes, such as the extension of the cortical cytoplasm to form a new pseudopod, depend on the assembly of new actin filaments. External signals such as chemotactic molecules can influence both actin filament organization and the direction of motility. *See* CELL MOTILITY.

About 20 families of myosin molecules are responsible for actin-based movements. In every case the energy for the movements is provided by the hydrolysis of adenosine triphosphate (ATP). Myosin II, the type originally found in muscle, forms filaments that can pull two actin filaments past each other. Other myosins interact with membranes, which they transport along actin filaments. Several types of regulation are known, including phosphorylation of the myosin and calcium-sensitive regulatory proteins bound to the actin filaments. *See* MUSCLE.

2. *Intermediate filaments.* These filaments (Fig. 2b) act as intracellular tendons in higher eukaryotic cells that are subjected to substantial physical stresses such as muscle cells and epithelial cells like skin. The various types of intermediate filaments are composed of a family of protein subunits all related to the keratin molecules found in hair. Some intermediate filaments are attached to the plasma membrane at specializations called desmosomes, while others surround the nucleus. Since intermediate filaments are inextensible (try stretching a hair), they help the cell from being over stretched. Intermediate filaments rearrange during mitosis and cell movements. Mutations in the genes for the intermediate filaments cause a variety of human diseases. Defects in keratin cause blistering of skin, while mutations in the proteins of the nuclear lamina can even cause premature aging.

3. *Microtubules.* Microtubules (Fig. 2c) are rigid polymers that form a number of structures, including the mitotic apparatus, an interphase cytoplasmic array radiating from the centrosome (Fig. 1), and

the supporting axoneme of cilia and flagella. Microtubules get their name from the cylindrical arrangement of tubulin subunits in the polymer. Their rigidity make microtubules the only cytoskeletal polymer that can resist compressive forces. Microtubules provide the internal support for asymmetrical cell processes (such as cilia) and to maintain asymmetrical cell shapes. A simplifying feature of microtubule organization in cells is that virtually all microtubules have the same polarity relative to the centrosome; the rapidly growing end is peripheral. As with actin filament polymerization, microtubule polymerization is a self-assembly process modulated by microtubule-associated proteins. Some of these proteins stabilize or destabilize microtubules. Some associate with the growing end of microtubules. Others cross-link microtubules to intermediate filaments and actin filaments, unifying the cytoskeleton into a single mechanical structure. *See* CILIA AND FLAGELLA.

Microtubules are tracks for rapid movements of membrane-bound vesicles and larger organelles, including mitochondria and the endoplasmic reticulum. In this way the microtubule system is an important determinant of cellular organization. These movements are powered by motor proteins that hydrolyze ATP to provide the energy for the motion. A family of kinesin motors generally move particles toward the peripheral end of the microtubules, while another family of motors called dynein move particles toward the cell center. Together these motors form a two-way transport system in the cell that is particularly well developed in the axons and dendrites of nerve cells, where vesicles can move more than 1 m in a few days' time.

The site and direction of microtubule assembly is determined by the centrosome (or by basal bodies in the case of cilia and flagella). Remarkably, microtubules radiating into the cytoplasm are not particularly stable, but individually undergo spontaneous fluctuations in length by the alternate loss and reassembly of thousands of tubulin subunits at their peripheral ends. These fluctuations in length called dynamic instability are important in the formation of the mitotic spindle and allow microtubules to probe all parts of the cytoplasm. *See* CELL (BIOLOGY); CYTOPLASM.   Thomas Pollard

Bibliography. B. Alberts et al., *Molecular Biology of the Cell*, 4d ed., 2002; H. Lodish et al., *Molecular Cell Biology*, 5th ed., 2004; T. Pollard and W. Earnshaw, *Cell Biology*, 2002.

Cell plastids

Specialized structures found in plant cells, diverse in distribution, size, shape, composition, structure, function, and mode of development.

Types. A number of different types is recognized. Chloroplasts occur in the green parts of plants and are responsible for the green coloration, for they contain the chlorophyll pigments. These pigments, along with certain others, absorb the light energy that drives the processes of photosynthesis, by which sugars, starch, and other organic materials are synthesized. Amyloplasts, nearly or entirely colorless, are packed with starch grains and occur in cells of storage tissue. Proteoplasts are less common and contain crystalline, fibrillar, or amorphous masses of protein, sometimes along with starch grains. In chromoplasts the green pigment is masked or replaced by others, notably carotenoids, as in the cells of carrot roots and many flowers and fruits. *See* CAROTENOID; CHLOROPHYLL; STARCH.

Occurrence. Plastids lie in the cytoplasm of the cell (**Fig. 1**), normally unattached to other structures but surrounded by a special extension of the nuclear envelope in some algae. There may be from a single plastid to many thousand plastids per cell. A mesophyll cell in a leaf contains up to about 50 chloroplasts. Some specialized cells lose their plastids at maturity. Plastids do not occur in the fungi.

Size and shape. The greatest diversity of chloroplast size and shape is found among genera and species of algae, as exemplified by branched and unbranched ribbons 100 micrometers or more in length, flat plates, and cup-shaped or stellate bodies. In some algae and in most other plants, chloroplasts are spherical or lens- or disk-shaped, with the major axis measuring 4–7 μm. *See* ALGAE.

Composition. A chloroplast in a spinach leaf has a dry weight of about 2×10^{-11} g, of which some 70% is protein (about half of this is soluble and half is membrane-bound), slightly more than 20% is lipid, and up to 7% is nucleic acid. Inorganic constituents include calcium, magnesium (largely in chlorophyll molecules), iron (partly in the proteins ferredoxin and cytochrome), manganese, and copper. Of the lipid approximately 21% is chlorophyll (100), 3% is carotenoid (22), 3% is plastoquinone and other quinonoid compounds (22), 9% is phospholipid (50), 44% is glycolipid (mainly mono- and di-galactosyl glycerides) (23), 2% is sterol (25), 0.5% is prenol (3), and 17% is as yet unidentified. Figures in parentheses are estimates of the numbers of molecules relative to 100 molecules of chlorophyll.

Structure. All types of plastids have one structural feature in common, a double envelope consisting of two concentric sheets of membrane. The outer of these is in contact with the cytoplasmic ground sub-

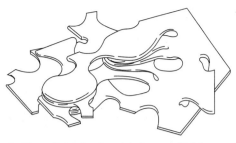

Fig. 2. **Three-dimensional model of grana with intergranal connections. (*After W. Wehrmeyer, Planta, 63:13–30, 1964*)**

stance; the inner with the plastid matrix, or stroma. They are separated by a narrow space of about 10 nanometers.

Another system of membranes generally occupies the main body of the plastid. This internal membrane system is especially well developed in chloroplasts, where the unit of construction is known as a thylakoid. In its simplest form this is a sac such as would be obtained if a balloon-shaped, membrane-limited sphere were to be flattened until the internal space was not much thicker than the membrane itself. It is usual, however, for thylakoids to be lobed, branched, or fenestrated. **Figures 2** and **3** show how disk-shaped lobes stack on top of one another to form grana. A granum may have 2–100 layers in it, and there may be more than 50 grana in a chloroplast. It is thought that all the grana are interconnected (**Fig. 4**) and that junctions with the inner layer of the chloroplast envelope are also present. As with their shape and pigmentation, algal chloroplasts are very diverse as regards the architecture of the thylakoids, and often do not possess grana. *See* CELL MEMBRANES.

Functions. The surface area of thylakoids is very large in relation to the volume of the chloroplast. This is functionally significant, for chlorophyll molecules and other components of the light-reaction systems of photosynthesis are associated with these membranes. Techniques such as shadow casting, negative staining, freeze etching, and small-angle x-ray scattering have revealed the presence of subunits within and on the surface of the thylakoid membrane itself. One such unit has been identified as a photophosphorylase enzyme involved in the final stages of the production of adenosine triphosphate by photosynthetic phosphorylation. Others have not yet had specific functions assigned to them, but since the membranes can be fractionated to yield particles that carry out one or the other of the two light reactions, it may well be that photosynthetic units of function are being visualized. Such units might be based on lipoprotein particles, with chlorophyll and other molecules associated with them.

Utilization of the products of light reactions in the actual fixation of carbon dioxide occurs not in the membranes but in the stroma, or ground substance, of the chloroplast. Here reside the enzymes of the Calvin carbon-reduction cycle, including as a major protein component of green tissues the enzyme ribulose diphosphate carboxylase (carboxydismutase). This large molecule, more than 10 nm in diameter, catalyzes the formation of phosphoglyceric

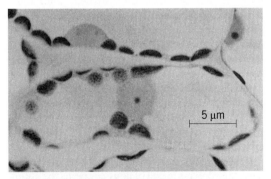

Fig. 1. **Light microscope view of part of *Hypochaeris radicata* leaf, showing chloroplasts sectioned in a variety of planes and displaying internal grana.**

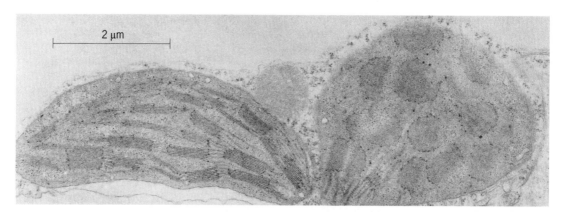

Fig. 3. Electron microscope view of two oat leaf chloroplasts, one showing successive layers of grana in side view, and the other showing grana in face view (disk shape of constituent thylakoid lobes are seen).

acid from ribulose diphosphate (the acceptor molecule) and carbon dioxide. It is, like many other molecular species in the cell, restricted to chloroplasts.

A chloroplast is much more than a device for carrying out photosynthesis. It can use light energy for uptake and exchange of ions and to drive conformational changes. The stroma contains the elements of a protein-synthesizing system—as much deoxyribonucleic acid (DNA) as a small bacterium, various types of ribonucleic acid (RNA), distinctive ri-

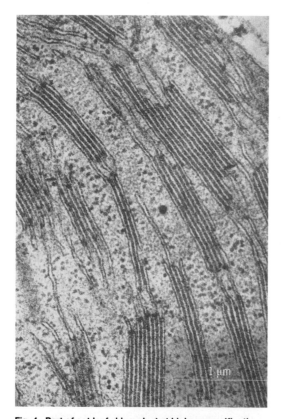

Fig. 4. Part of oat leaf chloroplast at higher magnification. Grana are seen in side view, revealing profiles of membranes. Thylakoids that interconnect grana are shown, with components of stroma, or ground substance, in which thylakoids lie. The dense granules are chloroplast ribosomes.

bosomes, and polyribosomes. There is evidence to indicate that much of the protein synthesis of a leaf takes place within the chloroplasts. *See* DEOXYRIBONUCLEIC ACID (DNA); PHOTOSYNTHESIS; PROTEIN; RIBONUCLEIC ACID (RNA); RIBOSOMES.

Mode of development. In algae, mosses, and ferns mature chloroplasts can divide. In cells of flowering plants divisions occur at a much earlier stage of development. Young, undifferentiated cells near the growing points of the plant, the meristems, contain precursor bodies called proplastids (**Fig. 5**), which apparently can divide and multiply. The proplastids only start to develop into one or other of the categories of plastid when the cell that contains them itself starts to differentiate. The ability of amyloplasts to give rise to chloroplasts (for example, when a potato tuber turns green), of chloroplasts to senesce into chromoplasts, and of chromoplasts to "re-green" to give chloroplasts, demonstrates that, although the different types normally develop from proplastids, interconvertibility is not completely lost.

A complex morphogenetic pathway leads from the proplastid to the chloroplast. Precursor molecules are synthesized; some are incorporated into the thylakoids, and the extending thylakoid surface gradually gives rise to interconnected grana. In general, light is required for this process. In darkness a precursor of chlorophyll, protochlorophyll, accumulates and the membranes assume a surprisingly different form, the unit of which is a branched tubule some 20–25 nm in diameter. These tubes interconnect to form semicrystalline lattices based on tetrahedral or cubic arrangements. The lattices, or prolamellar bodies, are up to 3 μm across and contain a relatively large surface area of membrane. When the plant is illuminated, the tubular membranes rearrange and the normal arrangement of interconnected grana develops. Since prolamellar bodies occur in etiolated plants, the plastids that contain them are known as etioplasts.

Morphogenetic autonomy. One of the most challenging problems in cell biology concerns the autonomy of organelles, such as the plastids. Chloroplasts, for instance, have their own DNA, DNA-polymerase,

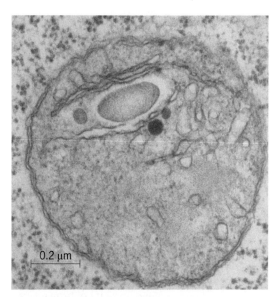

Fig. 5. Proplastid in cell of broad bean root tip. Double membranous envelope is shown and rudimentary nature of internal membrane system is obvious.

and RNA-polymerase; can make proteins; and, significantly, can mutate. All this suggests a measure of independence. It is known, however, that some nuclear genes can influence the production of molecules that are normally found only in chloroplasts, so their autonomy cannot be complete. It remains to be seen whether they control and regulate their own morphogenetic processes.   Brian E. S. Gunning

Bibliography. C. J. Avers, *Molecular Cell Biology*, 2d ed., 1986; R. J. Ellis (ed.), *Chloroplast Biogenesis*, 1985; L. Goldstein and D. M. Prescott (eds.), *Cell Biology: A Comprehensive Treatise*, vol. 4, 1980; L. J. Kliensmith and V. M. Kish, *Principles of Cell Biology*, 1987; J. J. Lee and J. F. Fredrick (eds.), *Endocytobiology III*, 1987; W. Waymouth (ed.), *Modern Cell Biology*, vol. 5: *Molecular Mechanisms in the Regulation of Cell Behavior*, 1987.

Cell polarity (biology)

The highly organized condition in most cells that is characterized by a distinct apical-basal axis with an asymmetric distribution of cytoplasmic organelles. This phenomenon of polarization is critical for living organisms to function. For example, cells in secretory organs such as the gall bladder generally secrete only at one end where secretory vesicles are localized. Another example would be a cell in the intestinal wall that must collect nutrients on the side near the lumen and transport them through the cell to the opposite end, where they can be delivered to the blood supply for transport to the rest of the body. Clearly, this cell must exhibit a polarized distribution of membrane proteins so that those necessary for sugar uptake are concentrated in the membrane facing the lumen and those needed to move the sugar out of the cell are located at the opposite side.

Most organisms begin life as a rather symmetrical, spherical, single cell called an egg. During early development this egg divides many times and forms an embryo, which exhibits much more intricate patterns (such as the polarized intestine) than were initially expressed by the egg. Determining how the embryo controls the development of such patterns has been an area of active research, and there is evidence that the plasma (outer) membrane can influence the development of cell polarity by driving ionic currents through the cell which, in turn, can influence the polarization process by generating ion concentration gradients within the cell or voltage gradients between cells. *See* DEVELOPMENTAL BIOLOGY.

Plant eggs. By far the strongest cases for a direct role of membrane-generated ion currents and concentration gradients in cell polarization are found in plant eggs which exhibit no preformed growth axis. Among the most useful have been the eggs of the brown algae *Fucus* and *Pelvetia*, common seaweeds found in the intertidal zone on both the Atlantic and Pacific coasts. The eggs develop by first secreting wall-softening and wall-building enzymes at one end. They then pump in potassium and chloride ions, and water follows these ions into the eggs to generate a large turgor pressure of about 5 atm (500 kilopascals). The eggs bulge (germinate) in the region where the wall has been softened by the secreted enzymes, thereby producing a structure that will develop into the rhizoid or holdfast. This is the first morphologically obvious axis of polarity. The establishment of the axis of secretion, and thus the morphological polarity, can be influenced by a variety of environmental factors, including unilateral light or unilateral chemical influences from nearby eggs or plants. The response to unilateral light is to germinate on the dark side; this is useful since the rhizoid outgrowth will form the holdfast for the plant and should form opposite the Sun so the plant can be anchored to a rock. Since the light receptors are located in the plasma membrane, it is not surprising that this membrane plays a key role in the signal transduction.

Transcellular ionic currents. The earliest indicator of the polarization process is the movement of ions through the egg via pores in the plasma membrane. These ionic currents crossing the plasma membrane can be detected by using a technique called the vibrating probe which measures small voltage gradients in the fluid just outside the egg. As early as 30 min after fertilization, these currents can be found entering the dark hemisphere of a unilaterally illuminated egg. The early spatial current pattern is unstable and shifts position, often with more than one inward current region. However, the current enters mainly on the side where germination will occur, and is usually largest at the prospective cortical clearing region where the rhizoid forms. The current pattern observed during the 2-h period prior to germination is more stable and looks like the pattern on the right side in **Fig. 1**. The site of inward current always predicts the germination site, even when the axis is reversed by light-direction reversal. The most likely hypothesis is that light receptors in the cell's plasma membrane control the distribution of open ion channels so that current enters the dark end.

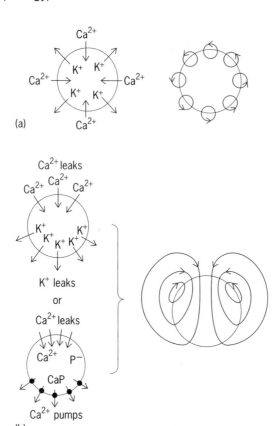

Fig. 1. Possible distribution of ion channels and pumps in a cell's plasma membrane with the resulting current pattern. (*a*) A uniform distribution of calcium (Ca^{2+}) and potassium (K$^+$) channels will result in many highly localized current loops. (*b*) Separation of the Ca^{2+} and K$^+$ channels (above) or Ca^{2+} channels and pumps (below) will result in the transcellular ion current pattern shown on the right.

In order to understand how such a transcellular current might be influencing the polarization process, it is important to determine which ions are carrying the current. By varying the composition of the artificial seawaters in which these measurements were made, it was determined that calcium ion (Ca^{2+}) influx was responsible for a small fraction of the current with chloride ion (Cl$^-$) efflux as the most likely carrier of the bulk of it. This calcium ion component was directly measured by following the movement of radioactive calcium ion through the egg. Therefore, one consequence of the transcellular ionic current in this egg is the generation of a calcium ion flux through the cell, which has been shown to generate a gradient in the intracellular concentration of calcium ion, [Ca^{2+}]$_i$. This gradient appears to play the primary role in polarizing the egg.

Calcium ion gradients. It is known that a central component of the polarization mechanism in the egg of a brown alga involves a cytoplasmic gradient in [Ca^{2+}]$_i$. This hypothesis is supported by the three criteria required for physiological significance: (1) An endogenous [Ca^{2+}]$_i$ gradient exists in the egg (although measured long after polarization); (2) modifying the direction of this gradient during polarization changes the orientation of the axis of polarization; and (3) inhibiting the gradient prevents polarization.

The gradient was detected in germinated zygotes by using calcium ion–sensitive microelectrodes, and a 10-fold higher [Ca^{2+}]$_i$ was detected in the tip region than in the subtip region of the rhizoid. A calcium ion gradient was imposed on unpolarized eggs by placing them near a fixed source of calcium ion ionophore in the dark. A majority of the eggs then germinated on the hemisphere facing the ionophore, where the influx of calcium ion is expected to be the greatest. Finally, the magnitude of the gradient can be greatly reduced by injecting the cell with a molecule that can rapidly shuttle calcium ions from regions of high concentration to regions of low concentration. Such a molecule was used to show that polarization could be blocked for weeks while the cell remained viable and even divided. This is the strongest evidence yet that a gradient in [Ca^{2+}]$_i$ is required for cell polarization.

Ionic currents and intracellular ion concentration gradients are not a unique property of brown algae, but have been detected in many other cell types as well. In fact, ionic currents have been detected in nearly every plant and animal cell and tissue investigated with the vibrating probe technique (**Fig. 2**). The transcellular current pattern is usually closely correlated with the axis of polarity. It would therefore appear that most cells do not have a uniform distribution of ion channels and pumps (Fig. 1*a*) but segregate channel types to varying degrees (Fig. 1*b*). *See* BIOPOTENTIALS AND IONIC CURRENTS.

Animal cells. A wide variety of animal systems have been investigated with the vibrating probe, and the best example of the use of ionic currents in maintaining the polarized state comes from the developing egg of the moth *Hyalophora cecropia*. This egg is connected to seven other cells called nurse cells which produce important molecules that are transported into the egg. This transport is polarized since most proteins will move from the nurse cells into the egg but will not move from the egg back to the nurse cells. It was demonstrated that a voltage difference of about 5 millivolts exists between the nurse cells and oocyte in the follicle of the silk moth. The only way that such a voltage gradient can be maintained in the conductive cytoplasm is by a steady current flow. Thus, the plasma membranes of these cells must be driving a steady current along the cytoplasmic bridge between the cells to generate the observed voltage gradient. Moreover, there is strong evidence from the behavior of microinjected proteins that intercellular electrophoresis is involved as a protein segregation mechanism here. The polarity of protein transport across the bridge connecting these two cell types can be reversed by reversing the endogenous electrical field with this bridge.

While it is not too surprising that proteins could be electrophoresed along an intercellular bridge by an imposed field, even more compelling evidence that electrophoresis is involved in this transport has been found. The polarity of movement of given protein across the bridge is dependent only on its net electric charge. Most cellular proteins are negatively charged and so would be driven from the nurse cells into the

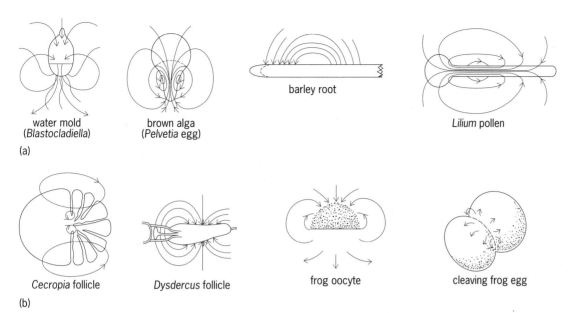

water mold
(*Blastocladiella*)

brown alga
(*Pelvetia* egg)

barley root

Lilium pollen

(a)

Cecropia follicle

Dysdercus follicle

frog oocyte

cleaving frog egg

(b)

Fig. 2. Transcellular ion current patterns measured in (*a*) plant cells and (*b*) animal cells.

oocyte by the voltage gradient along the cytoplasmic bridge. Lysozyme is a basic protein with a net positive charge, and when it is injected into either the nurse cells or the oocyte, it is found to move only in the opposite direction, from the oocyte to the nurse cells. However, when the net charge on this protein is reversed by methylcarboxylation, its transport direction was reversed, and it was observed only to move from nurse cells to oocyte. In further support for the electrophoresis mechanism, neutral proteins with no net electric charge move in both directions across the bridge. Thus, in the cecropia follicle, the polarity of protein transport, which is a critical component of the oocyte's polarity, is determined by the electrical field across the intercellular bridge. The cecropia follicle is the best example in which transcellular currents play an active, causal role in polarized transport. *See* CELL (BIOLOGY).   Richard Nuccitelli

Bibliography. C. Brownlee and J. W. Wood, A gradient of cytoplasmic free calcium in growing rhizoid cells of *Fucus serratus, Nature*, 320:624–626, 1986; L. F. Jaffe and R. Nuccitelli, An ultrasensitive vibrating probe for measuring steady extracellular currents, *J. Cell Biol.*, 63:614–628, 1974; J. R. McIntosh (ed.), *Modern Cell Biology*, vol. 2, 1983; R. Nuccitelli, Ooplasmic segregation and secretion in the *Pelvetia* egg is accompanied by a membrane-generated electrical current, *Dev. Biol.*, 62:13–33, 1978; R. I. Woodruff and W. H. Telfer, Electrophoresis of proteins in intercellular bridges, *Nature*, 286:84–86, 1980.

Cell senescence

The limited capacity of all normal human and other animal cells to reproduce and function. The gradual decline in normal physiological function of the cells is referred to as aging or senescence. The aging process ends with the death of individual cells and then, generally, the whole animal. Aging occurs in all animals, except those that do not reach a fixed body size such as some tortoises and sharks, sturgeon, and several other kinds of fishes. These animals die as the result of accidents or disease, but losses in normal physiological function do not seem to occur. Examples of cells that do not age are those composing the germ plasm (sex cells) and many kinds of cancer cells. These cells are presumed to be immortal.

Normal cells. In the mid-1960s it was found that, contrary to the prevailing belief, normal human cells cultured in the laboratory do have a limited capacity to function and to divide. This phenomenon was interpreted as aging at the cellular level. These observations have been extended to include the cells of all other animals tested. *See* TISSUE CULTURE.

Prior to this finding, it was believed that all cultured cells were potentially immortal. If that were true, aging in animals would be the result of events that occur at organizational levels higher than individual cells. That is, age changes would be attributed to nongenetic events occurring outside cells, such as changes in the substances that bind cells into tissues, externally caused injuries to cells, hormone effects, and other interactions between tissues and organs. Now that it is known that normal human and other animals cells have a limited capacity to divide and function, there is a general belief that cell senescence must be attributed to intracellular events. These events, which would play a major role in senescence or aging, are thought to occur in the deoxyribonucleic acid (DNA) and other information-containing molecules.

Studies have shown that when normal human fibroblasts, derived from human embryos, are grown in laboratory culture, they can undergo only about 50 population doublings (**Fig. 1**). Fibroblasts are found in virtually all tissues, and besides lending structural

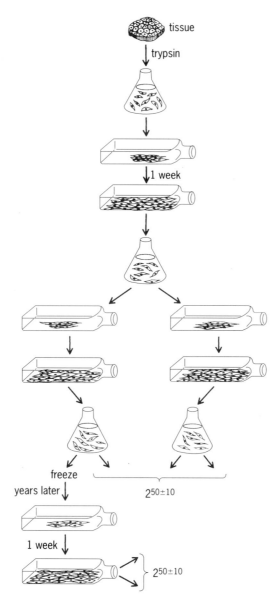

Fig. 1. Culture of normal human cells. The tissue is broken down into individual cells with the digestive enzyme trypsin. The cells are then separated from the trypsin and placed into a flat bottle, where they multiply until they cover the floor of the culture vessel. When they stop multiplying, the cells are divided into equal numbers and placed into two culture vessels. The process is repeated every few days after the cells have covered the available surface area. Each subcultivation results in one population doubling. *(After L. Hayflick, The cell biology of human aging, Sci. Amer., 242(1):58–66, 1980)*

support, they produce collagen and other proteins that bind cells into tissues. The maximum number of doublings attainable was inversely proportional to donor age: fibroblasts from older people were found to undergo fewer doublings than those derived from younger donors.

Cultured fibroblasts derived from different animal species seem to undergo a number of population doublings that are directly proportional to the species lifespan (**Fig. 2**).

Nondividing cells. Fibroblasts have a greater capacity to divide in laboratory cultures than any other nor-

mal cell type. Nevertheless, since all normal human and other animal cells have a finite capacity to divide or to function, nondividing cells, such as neurons or muscle cells, also age. The loss of function in brain neurons may indeed play a greater role in age changes than do changes in any other cell type.

When normal human embryonic cells are frozen at a particular population doubling, they "remember" at what doubling level they were frozen and, when thawed, continue to divide until the total of 50 is reached. It has been shown that the frozen cells' memory is accurate over a period of at least 22 years.

Normal human and other animal cells are mortal not only when they are grown in laboratory cultures but even when normal tissues are grafted into laboratory animals. When the laboratory animal grows old, the graft can be removed and placed on a younger host animal. This serial animal-to-animal transfer, which is analogous to cell transfers in laboratory cultures, also reveals the finitude in division capacity and function of normal cells.

Changes in senescent cells. Prior to the death of cultured normal human cells, they incur well over 100 changes that herald their approaching demise. These changes occur in lipid content and synthesis; carbohydrate utilization; protein content, synthesis, and breakdown; ribonucleic acid (RNA) and DNA content, synthesis, and turnover; enzyme activity and synthesis; cell-cycle kinetics; morphology; ultrastructure; cell architecture; and incorporation and stimulation. Of great importance is that many of these age changes seen in cultures at the cell level are also observed in humans as they age.

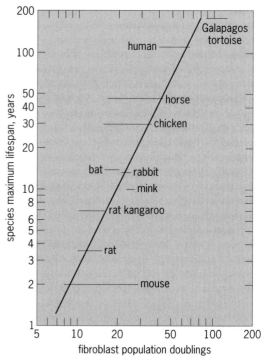

Fig. 2. Fibroblasts from the young of 10 different species multiply in culture roughly proportionate to the maximum lifespan for that species.

Immortality. Although cultured normal human and other animal cells are mortal, they can be converted to a state of immortality. The conversion can be produced in human cells by the SV40 virus and in other animal cells by other viruses, chemicals, and irradiation. This conversion from mortality to immortality is called transformation, and is characterized by the acquisition of many profound abnormal cell properties, including changes in chromosome number and form, ability of the cells to grow unattached to a solid surface, and the property of immortality. These changes, and many more, are characteristic of most cancer cells. *See* CANCER (MEDICINE); CELL (BIOLOGY); MUTATION; ONCOLOGY; TUMOR VIRUSES.

Leonard Hayflick

Bibliography. A. Comfort, *The Biology of Senescence,* 1979; C. Finch and L. Hayflick (eds.), *Handbook of the Biology of Aging,* 1977; L. Hayflick, The cell biology of aging, *Bioscience,* 25:629–636, 1975; L. Hayflick, The cell biology of human aging, *Sci. Amer.,* 242(1):58–66, 1980; L. Hayflick and P. S. Moorhead, The serial cultivation of human diploid cell strains, *Exp. Cell Res.,* 25:585–621, 1961; A. Rosenfeld, *Prolongevity,* 1976.

Cell-surface ionization

All living cells suspended in aqueous salt solutions at neutral pH values possess a negative charge. The charge is due to the dissociation of ionogenic, or charged, groups (carboxyl, amino, and others) in the cell surface. Studies of the charge carried by bacteria give information regarding the nature of the components in their surfaces; these studies have been used to measure the frequency distribution of bacterial variants in a mixed population and can assist in the selection of material for vaccine production. The occurrence and nature of tumor cells and the selection of yeasts for brewing have been studied electrophoretically. *See* BIOLOGICALS.

Electrophoretic mobility. When an electric field is applied between electrodes placed in a cell suspension, the cells migrate, generally toward the positive electrode. This migration can be observed under a microscope in a microelectrophoresis apparatus (see **illus.**). The electrophoretic mobility $\bar{v}$ (velocity per unit field strength) is measured by timing cells across a fixed distance in the observation chamber under a known field strength. In this method the mobility of individual cells of varying shape and size can be measured with minimal cellular disorganization. Migration occurs because charged groups and ions adsorbed on the surface produce a nonuniform distribution of ions in solution at the cell-liquid interface. This distribution is generally expressed in terms of the ζ potential (volts), which may be calculated from the mobility, $\zeta = 4\pi\eta\bar{v}v/D$, where η and D are the viscosity and dielectric constants, respectively, of the medium. The surface charge density in electrostatic units per square centimeter can be calculated from ζ.

Variation of charge. Factors which may affect the charge of cell surfaces are of three types: (1) biological factors—in bacterial and yeast cells, such things as sex, strain, age, growth conditions, presence of capsules or fimbriae, antibiotic resistance, virulence, and toxicity; in mammalian cells, such things as species, type of tissue, normal or pathological conditions, and the like; (2) nature of suspension medium, that is, ionic strength, pH, presence of dyes, drugs, or surface-active agents in the medium; and (3) chemical or enzymatic treatment of the surface. It is often possible to correlate alteration of charge with changes in the nature or number of ionogenic groups in the surface and hence with a particular biological property. Such a correlation is justified only if the variation of charge is measured in media of constant physical properties. An absolute value of the charge under standard conditions of test is without value; the charge carried by particles with ionogenic and nonionogenic surfaces under the same conditions may be identical. However, variations of charge with changes in the nature of the medium are completely different. With living cells, lowering the pH of the medium at constant ionic strength in general produces a lowering of the negative value of the ζ potential; at low pH value, charge reversal may occur. This change results from the decreased dissociation of acidic groups which may be characterized from the dissociation constant pK of the surface. Simultaneously there is an increased ionization of basic groups. At extreme pH values surface and possibly cellular disorganization must be investigated. When the salt concentration of the suspension medium is increased, biological and nonionogenic surfaces behave similarly. The charge-density concentration curve is a typical Langmuir adsorption isotherm, indicating adsorption of anions from solution. *See* ADSORPTION.

Ionogenic groups can be characterized by the binding properties of a series of cations. Their order of effectiveness in reversing the charge of the

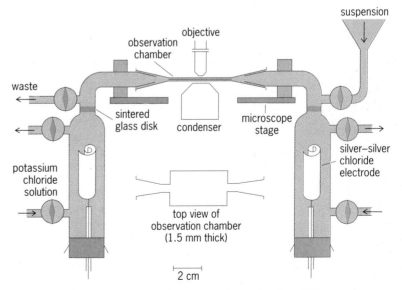

Microelectrophoresis apparatus used to measure electrophoretic mobility.

particles is known as a charge-reversal spectrum. The spectra for various cells can be compared with spectra of model systems with known ionogenic surface groups. Alteration of charge in the presence of anionic surface-active agents can reveal the presence of lipid in the surface. Mild chemical treatment to inactivate specific groups, for example, diazomethane for carboryl, results in marked changes of charge. Enzymatic treatments, for example, using the enzyme trypsin, may produce changes in the charge. *See* ENZYME; LIPID; PROTEIN.

Bacteria. Most strains show slight, if any, variation of charge density during growth. Any drastic alteration of charge always occurs during the period of active cell division, returning to the normal value during the stationary phase, as in hemolytic streptococci. Little alteration of charge generally results from changes in nutrition. Growth in the presence of some drugs, for example, *Aerobacter aerogenes* in crystal violet, results in the formation of a resistant strain with different charge characteristics. The pK values of the surfaces of *Escherichia coli* (2.9) and *A. aerogenes* (3.0), obtained from ζ-pH studies, are the same as those for a large number of polysaccharides, strongly suggesting that carboxyl and not phosphatidic groups (pK = 1.8) are present on the cell surface. Charge-reversal spectra lead to the same general conclusions. Treatment of *E. coli* K12 in aqueous suspension at pH 4.5 with gaseous diazomethane results in an 80% decrease of charge when measured at pH 7.0. Assuming that all the surface carboxyl groups have been esterified, the number of such groups is about 8×10^5 per cell. Spores of *Bacillus subtilis* treated with *p*-toluene sulfonyl chloride in aqueous suspension show a 25% increase in negative charge; this is attributed to the blocking of amino groups.

Teichoic acid, on the surface of cells of *Staphylococcus aureus* in the pH range 4–5, undergoes a change of configuration resulting in a pH-mobility curve which passes through a maximum at pH 4.5. Strains which are resistant to Methicill give a normal curve with no maximum. Cells of *Streptococcus pyogenes* which are resistant to Tetracycline possess larger amounts of surface lipid, as detected by changes of mobility in the presence of surface-active agents, than do sensitive strains.

Yeasts. In suspensions of pH greater than 2.3, yeast cells carry a negative charge. Various strains of *Saccharomyces cerevisiae* and *S. carlsbergensis* have such low charges that ion binding is small, the composition of the wall determining the charge. In some strains the charge is due to combined phosphate in the cell wall and in others to protein. The nature of the growth medium has a pronounced effect on the charge.

Blood cells. The major components on the erythrocyte surface are phospholipid in nature; protein and cholesterol may also be present near the surface. Of sheep blood cells, lymphocytes exhibit an isoelectric point at pH 2.5 (that pH at which there is a zero charge) in contrast to erythrocytes and polymorphonuclear leukocytes, which are damaged at low pH values. Charge-reversal spectra and chemical treatments of aldehyde-treated blood cells indicate that the predominant groups are carboxyl from sialic acid on erythrocytes, carboxyl on polymorphonuclear leukocytes, and both phosphate and amine on lymphocytes and platelets. *See* BACTERIA; BIOPHYSICS; BLOOD; COLLOID; ELECTROKINETIC PHENOMENA; STREAMING POTENTIAL; YEAST.

Arthur M. James

Bibliography. M. Blank, *Surface Chemistry of Biological Systems*, 1970; W. Hoppe, *Biophysics*, 1983.

Cell walls (plant)

The cell wall is the layer of material secreted by the plant cell outside its plasma membrane. All plants have cell walls that are generally very similar in chemical composition, organization, and development. The walls of the Chlorophyta (green algae) show characteristics virtually identical to those of flowering plants, another indication that flowering plants are derived evolutionarily from this division of algae. The wall serves as the first point of entry of materials into cells, functions in the movement of water throughout the plant, and is one of the major mechanical strengthening factors. In addition, the wall must be sufficiently flexible and plastic to withstand mechanical stresses while still permitting the growth of the cell. *See* CELL MEMBRANES.

Cell plate and middle lamella. The plant primary wall is initiated during the process of cell division. After chromosomes line up along the metaphase plate and begin to be pulled apart toward the poles of the cells by the spindle fibers (the anaphase portion of mitosis), a cell plate or phragmoplast can be observed at the equator of the dividing cell. Vesicles apparently derived from the dictyosomes line up on both sides of the equator to form the proteinaceous cell plate. Elements of the endoplasmic reticulum fuse with the cell plate, marking the location of

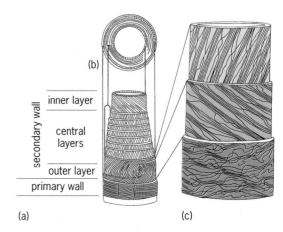

Fig. 1. Wall in a cotton fiber. (*a*) Telescoped segment and (*b*) transverse section showing spatial relation of layers and orientation of microfibrils. (*c*) Primary wall has reticulate microfibrillar structure; the outer layer of the secondary wall combines reticulate and parallel orientation of microfibrils, and the first central layer of the secondary wall has a predominantly parallel microfibrillar structure. (*After K. Esau, Plant Anatomy, 2d ed., Wiley, 1965*)

plasmodesmatal pores and pits which will eventually provide the intercellular connections between adjacent cells. The cell plate forms the matrix within which the middle lamella and primary walls are formed. The middle lamella is composed of pectic substances which are polymers of neutral (arabinogalactans) and acidic (galacturonorhamnans) pectins plus smaller amounts of other sugars, including L-fucose, D-xylose, and D-galactose. The bulk of pectic substances are long chains of α-D-galacturonic acid, with side chains composed of other sugars; the exact chemical composition and organization of pectins are still unclear. Pectins can form reversible gels or viscid solutions in water. As the middle lamella, pectic substances are usually in the water-insoluble gel state, possibly because they are esterified with calcium or magnesium ions. Such gels can be solubilized and extracted from plants. Some tissues, notably those of mature apple and citrus fruits which have high concentrations of pectins, have been extracted and purified, and their pectins have been used as gelling agents in jams, jellies, and some industrial products. The middle lamella provides some of the observed plasticity and extensibility of cell walls during cell growth, and it has also been suggested that pectins are capable of hydrogen-bonding to the cellulose that forms the plant cell primary wall.

Primary wall. Simultaneously with the middle lamella, the primary cell wall begins to form, usually before the end of telophase. During the early stages in cell wall formation, the cellulose wall is isotropic without any ordered orientation, but as cell walls continue to develop in area and in thickness and the cell grows to mature size, the walls become anisotropic or highly ordered (**Fig. 1**).

Biosynthesis and chemistry of cellulose. Cellulose, like starch, is basically a polymer of glucose, a six-carbon monosaccharide, although the biosynthetic route for cellulose synthesis differs from that of starch. The polyglucose chain of starch is derived by enzymatically regulated condensation of uridine diphosphate glucose (UDPG) or adenine diphosphate glucose (ADPG). However, the monomers that form cellulose are guanosine diphosphate glucose (GDPG) with the resulting polymer being a β-(1–4) glucoside rather than the α-(1–4) polymer characteristic of amylose. In both polymers, the terminal glucose residue can unfold into its open-chain configuration, exposing the aldehyde group that has reducing power.

Each chain of cellulose may be as long as 8000 to 12,000 glucose monomers, or up to 4 micrometers long. These are arranged linearly, with no side branching. Cellulose chains are aggregated into bundles of approximately 40 chains each, the cellulose micelles, which are held together by hydrogen bonds between the hydrogen atom of a hydroxyl group of one glucose residue and an oxygen atom of another glucose residue which is adjacent to the first glucose. Although the strength of individual hydrogen bonds is rather weak, there may be so many of them joining adjacent chains that total bonding in a micelle is quite high. There is good, albeit incomplete, evidence that

all of the chains in the same micelle bundle are directionally oriented, with the reducing groups at the same end of the micelle; and there is some fairly conclusive evidence from the x-ray diffraction patterns of cellulose that the glucose units of one chain are displaced by one-half the length of a glucose monomer, so that there are two hydrogen bonds connecting adjacent monomers. The micelle thus is a very regular, quasicrystalline structure (**Fig. 2**).

Whether isotropic or anisotropic, the micelles themselves are embedded in a matrix of other polysaccharides, the hemicelluloses. Insofar as is known, hemicelluloses are produced by the dictyosomes and associated vesicles and are moved through the cytoplasm and the plasmalemma to enter into the structure of the primary wall. In addition to glucose, seven monosaccharides are involved in hemicellulose composition. About a quarter of this monosaccharide complex is arabinose, with 10–15% each of galactose, galacturonic acid, and xylose plus smaller percentages of rhamnose, fucose, and mannose. These monosaccharides may form unispecific polymers composed of a single monomer or may be complexes containing two or more monomers. In the primary plant cell wall, these polysaccharides are covalently bonded. One model (**Fig. 3**) suggests

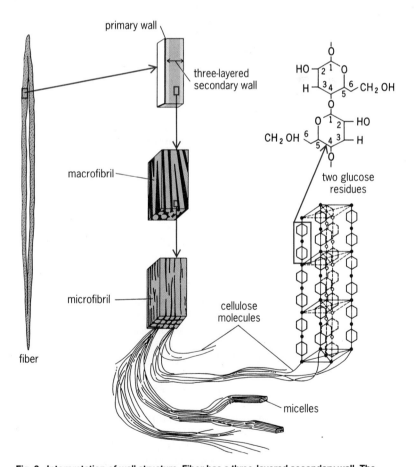

Fig. 2. Interpretation of wall structure. Fiber has a three-layered secondary wall. The macrofibrils consist of numerous microfibrils of cellulose interspersed by microporosities containing noncellulosic wall materials. Microfibrils consist of bundles of cellulose molecules, partly arranged into micelles. Micelles are crystalline because of regular spacing of glucose residues which are connected by β-1,4-glucosidic bonds. (*After K. Esau, Plant Anatomy, 2d ed., Wiley, 1965*)

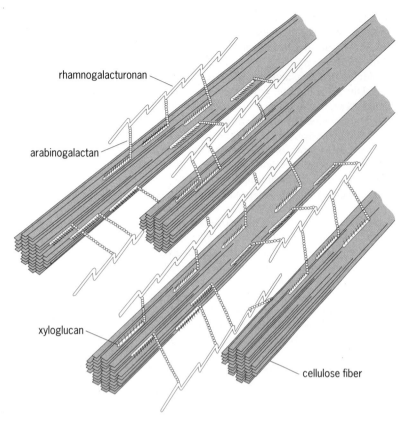

rhamnogalacturonan

arabinogalactan

xyloglucan

cellulose fiber

Fig. 3. Model of the cell wall showing cellulosic wall organization. (*After P. Albersheim, The wall growing plant cells, Sci. Amer., 232(4):80–95, April 1975*)

that each of the cellulose micelles is completely coated with a monomolecular layer of xyloglucan, with the glucose units of the xyloglucan lying parallel to the long axis of the micelle and hydrogen-bonded to glucose residues in the cellulose. Radiating at right angles from the coated micelle are arabinogalactan polymers, which are then covalently linked to rhamnogalactan polymers which run parallel to the cellulose micelle. Thus, hemicellulose serves to bind the micelle into a fairly rigid unit which retains a good deal of flexibility.

Micelles, in bundles of variable number, are bound together into the cellulose microfibril, a unit sufficiently large to be seen under the electron microscope; these, in turn, are bound together into macrofibrils which are observable under the light microscope. *See* CELLULOSE.

Organization of primary wall. During the formation of the primary wall, at locations predetermined by attachments of endoplasmic reticulum to the middle lamella, cellulose microfibrillar deposition is minimal, leaving a thin place in the primary wall which forms the plasmodesmatal connections. Running through these pores are fine strands of protoplasm, the plasmodesmata proper, which contain a tube of endoplasmic reticulum–like material. The plasmodesmata provide a cytoplasmic connection between adjacent cells. Such connections are found among all the living cells of a plant, a fact which has led to the concept that all plant cells are so interconnected that the entire plant is a cytosymplast or single unit.

In the formation of the primary cell wall, there

may be several discrete depositions of cellulose, with changes in the orientation of the micro- and macrofibrils with successive depositions. There has been some equivocation as to whether the added cellulosic fibrils are inserted among those already part of the wall (intussusception) or whether the new fibrils are laid down inside the older portions of the primary wall as a discrete layer or lamella (apposition). Most of the available evidence suggests that apposition is the only method of increasing the thickness of the wall. This can be readily seen in the formation of both primary and secondary walls in the cotton fiber, the hairs attached to the seed coat which are the starting material for cotton thread (Fig. 1).

Secondary wall. Although there are differences in nomenclature and terminology, secondary walls of plant cells are defined as those laid down after the primary wall has stopped increasing in surface area, essentially at that time when the plant cell has reached mature size. This is particularly true of those cells that, at maturity, have irreversibly differentiated into specialized cells, some of which are destined to lose their cytoplasm and become functional only as dead cells. These include xylem vessels and tracheids, and sclereids (the stone or grit cells of pear fruits). In those xylem cells differentiated from parenchyma cells to form the primary vascular xylem, secondary wall thickenings may not occur uniformly over the surface of the wall but may be in the form of bands, spirals, or reticulate thickenings.

The secondary wall of most plants seems to have the same chemical structure and physical orientation of fibrils and hemicelluloses as do primary walls. While there may be little orientation of fibrils in young primary walls, the secondary walls are composed of fibrils that are highly ordered. In general, there are three layers or lamellae of fibrils. Two of these, usually the inner and outer layers, tend to be thin and birefringent, and the middle layer tends to be thicker and less birefringent. One of the differences between the larger xylem vessels and tracheids of spring wood and the smaller xylem cells of summer wood is the thickness of the middle layer of cellulose fibrils. Part of the difference in birefringence, on the other hand, seems to be due to the reduced anisotropy of the middle secondary wall layer.

Since successive layers of cellulose fibrils are laid down inside one another, with the youngest layer closest to the plasmalemma, the lumen of the cell which contains the protoplast becomes reduced in size and, in some cells, may virtually disappear.

In most secondary walls, and particularly those of the xylem, the fibrillar structure of the primary as well as the secondary walls may become impregnated with more substances, the most prominent of these being lignin. The chemical nature and biological role of lignin is of considerable interest because of the use of wood in the lumber and pulpwood-paper industries. Lignins are polymers of complex phenolic substances (phenylpropanoid C_6-C_3 compounds), and exact composition of the polymer may be species-specific. Certainly the lignins of the softwoods (conifers) and those of hardwoods (broad-leaved trees) are chemically distinguishable based on both chemical and physical properties and on the ratios of the various phenolic monomers composing the polymer. As the secondary walls develop, lignins may be deposited either from the inside layer toward the outermost or the reverse. The primary roles of the lignins include their ability to render walls mechanically strong, rigid, and—at least to some extent—water-impermeable. It has been suggested that lignins may also serve to make wood less subject to microbially caused decay.

Depending on the species, other compounds may form part of the secondary walls of plant cells. In some of the algae, notably the diatoms and phylogenetically related classes in the division Chrysophyta, mature cell walls may consist almost entirely of silica compounds. Although silica is usually not a major component in the walls of vascular plants, grasses and sedges have walls with significant amounts of silica, and the use of the scouring rush (*Equisetum* spp.) was based in part of the silica content of the walls of stem cells. In some algae and in a few flowering plants (including *Ficus*), deposition of calcium carbonate into both primary and secondary walls has been found. In many plants, an ill-characterized compound called callose is found; it is particularly prominent in the end or sieve plates of phloem cells, where it surrounds the sieve pores. Callose may vary in amount with the developmental stage of the plant, with the seasons, and as a result of trauma.

Although frequently not considered to be a structural component of plant cell walls, water is an important constituent. A good deal of the movement of water through a tissue system occurs not by the movement of water into and out of successive and adjacent cells, but through the intercellular spaces between cells and through the primary and secondary walls. Many plant physiologists consider the walls and intercellular spaces to be the apparent free space that permits the movement of water and dissolved substances at rates considerably in excess of that possible were all water to move from cell to cell.

Other components of cell walls have received relatively little attention from chemists and developmental physiologists, although they play important roles in the economy of the plant and may, in some instances, be of commercial value. Walls of red and brown algae contain polymers such as algin, agar, and carrageenan, which form rigid gels used as substrates for growing microorganisms and as thickening and stabilizing agents in ice cream and industrial products. Cutins, waxes, and suberins are lipoidal materials that serve to waterproof cells in whose walls they are deposited. Cutin, found as the outermost layer of the outside wall of epidermal cells, is the primary barrier of the plant, serving to prevent the leaching of cell constituents and functioning as a protective layer to prevent invasion of the plant by microorganisms. Cutins also serve to lessen water loss from leaves and stems. Suberins are prominent components of the walls of cork and bark cells

and of the casparian strip of root endodermal cells. Both are polymers of fatty acids. Waxes may also be found on epidermal layers of leaves and fruit. They are usually small polymers and are responsible for the "bloom" which, in apples, allows the fruit to be polished. Waxes can be removed from plants and used in shoe polish and other applications. *See* WAX, ANIMAL AND VEGETABLE.

Pits. As the primary wall develops, areas of the wall surrounding the plasmodesmatal intercellular connections tend to be thinner than the rest of the wall and are called primary pit fields. In some cells, primary pit fields may be deeply depressed as cellulose microfibrillar layers accumulate and the rest of the primary wall becomes thicker. Pit fields are almost always paired, with the pit field of one cell oriented exactly opposite to that of the adjacent cell. Many cells have large numbers of primary pit fields.

In plant secondary walls, pits are readily distinguishable from the rest of the wall because the layers of secondary wall materials are completely interrupted at the pit with only thin coverings, if any, of primary wall. In mature cells with well-developed secondary walls, the pits may be simple or, as seen in the bordered pits common in xylem vessels, tracheids, and fibers, they may be structurally very complex. *See* XYLEM.

In bordered pits, the developing secondary wall arches over the pit to form a thickened rim (the border), enclosing a pit chamber which may be open and continuous with the cell lumen (**Fig. 4**). In conifers, the primary walls in the center become thickened (the torus), while on the edges (the margo) they become thinner as hemicelluloses are digested away. It has been suggested, primarily but not exclusively on anatomical grounds, that bordered pits in xylem may serve as valves to control the rate of water flow between the adjacent cells bearing the pair of pits. Depending on the species, bordered pits may be very complex.

Cell elongation and enlargement. In vascular plants, cells grow in length, thickness, or both, primarily by

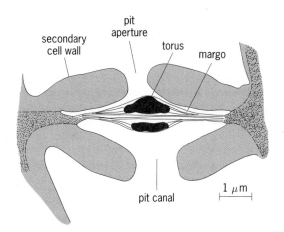

Fig. 4. Cross section through a bordered pit of a transfusion tracheid from a needle of *Pinus sylvestris*, showing the pit membrane. (*After E. G. Cutter, Plant Anatomy: Experiment and Interpretation, pt. 1, Addison-Wesley, 1969*)

the uptake of water into their vacuoles. The initiation and maintenance of growth is dependent not only upon the availability of water and the concentrations of auxins and other growth-regulating compounds that control cell enlargements, but on characteristics of the cell wall. Even in primary walls the cellulosic components and the matrix in which the fibrils are embedded form a fairly rigid structure, and for growth to occur there must be loosening of the fibrillar matrix. Furthermore, the effects of indoleacetic acid (IAA) on cell elongation are expressed within a minute or even less following presentation of auxin, indicating that the necessary loosening must occur quite rapidly. Any comprehensive theory must also account for the fact that, as a cell elongates, its wall does not become thinner, nor is new wall material deposited only at the ends of the cell. The new wall fibrils are deposited fairly uniformly over the entire surface of the cell. See AUXIN.

On the manifold questions relating to cell elongation and enlargement, the question of the deposition of new cellulose fibrils appears to be the most amenable to answer. Most, if not all, of the fibrillar material is deposited by apposition on the inner portion of the walls adjacent in the middle lamella. Intussusception, if it occurs at all, is a minor factor in new wall deposition during growth. Little attention has been directed toward understanding the possible changes in the middle lamella. Clearly, if the cell is to continue to grow, with increases in surface area of the wall, the middle lamella must either increase proportionally or be drastically thinned; no unequivocal data are available on this point.

Since cell wall area is accompanied by appositional deposition of fibrils, the fibrils existing prior to the period of growth must slide past one another. It has been suggested that this occurs by the enzymatic breaking of bonds that occur between the cross-linked fibrils with almost immediate reformation of these bonds at new sites, but no information has been provided on the chemical nature of the bonds affected or the polymers involved. Other investigators have postulated that the bond breaking and reforming may be due to changes in the proton concentration caused by application of auxin. This "acid growth theory" suggests that IAA stimulates an adenosine triphosphatase/adenosine triphosphate (ATPase/ATP) reaction, providing the energy for the mutual exchange of potassium ions and protons across the plasmalemma, and that this may be the mechanism for breaking the bonds linking fibrils together. See PLANT CELL; PLANT GROWTH.

Richard M. Klein

Bibliography. J. D. Mauseth, *Plant Anatomy*, 1988; R. D. Preston, *The Physical Biology of Plant Cell Walls*, 1974.

Cellophane

A clear, flexible film made from cellulose. It first appeared commercially in the United States in 1924, and it revolutionized the packaging industry, which had been using opaque waxed paper or glassine as wrapping materials. Cellophane was also the first transparent mending tape. By 1960, petrochemical-based polymers (polyolefins) such as polyethylene had surpassed cellophane for use as a packaging film. Nevertheless, 50,000 tons (45,000 metric tons) of cellophane are used in the United States each year for packaging because cellophane gives a material that is stiffer and more easily imprinted than are polyolefin films. See CELLULOSE.

Manufacture. Cellophane is manufactured in a process that is very similar to that for rayon. Special wood pulp, known as dissolving pulp, which is white like cotton and contains 92–98% cellulose, is treated with strong alkali in a process known as mercerization, a treatment used in processing cotton for textiles. The mercerized pulp is aged for several days. See TEXTILE CHEMISTRY.

The aged, shredded pulp is then treated with carbon disulfide, which reacts with the cellulose and dissolves it to form a viscous, orange solution of cellulose xanthate known as viscose. Rayon fibers are formed by forcing the viscose through a small hole into an acid bath that regenerates the original cellulose while carbon disulfide is given off. To make cellophane, the viscose passes through a long slot into a bath of ammonium sulfate which causes it to coagulate. The coagulated viscose is then put into an acidic bath that returns the cellulose to its original, insoluble form. The cellophane is now clear. See MANUFACTURED FIBER.

The cellophane is then treated in a glycerol bath and dried. The glycerol acts like a plasticizer, making the dry cellophane less brittle. The cellophane may be coated with nitrocellulose or wax to make it impermeable to water vapor; it is coated with polyethylene or other materials to make it heat sealable for automated wrapping machines. Cellophane is typically 0.03 mm (0.001 in.) thick, is available in widths to 132 cm (52 in.), and can be made to be heat sealable from 82 to 177°C (180 to 350°F). See POLYMER.

Uses. Cellophane is used for packaging snacks, cookies, baked goods, candy, and tobacco products. Cellophane can be cast into a ring-shaped structure to be used as sausage casings (wiener), but paper with hemp fiber is used in large sausages. Cellophane enjoys many specialized uses based on its ability to let small molecules pass through it while retaining larger molecules, although some materials are replacing cellophane for these uses. It has been used in kidney dialysis machines, battery separators for silver-zinc cells, and semipermeable membranes. It is also used in denture compression molding. See WOOD CHEMICALS; WOOD PRODUCTS.

Christopher J. Biermann

Bibliography. C. J. Biermann, *Essentials of Pulping and Papermaking*, 1993; *Kirk-Othmer Encyclopedia of Chemical Technology*, 4th ed., vol. 5, 1992; A. P. Peck, Cellophane is born, Sci. Amer., 158: 274–275, May 1938; E. Sjöström, *Wood Chemistry: Fundamentals and Applications*, 2d ed., 1993.

Cellular automata

A cellular automaton is a hypothetical computer constructed of a regular array of cells that interact with neighboring cells according to a set of simple rules. Though conceptually simple, cellular automata can produce complex and surprising behavior. To computer scientists and mathematicians, cellular automata are of great interest from a theoretical perspective, forming one of the fundamental abstractions (along with Turing machines, finite-state automata, and so on) that are a basic model for all of computing. They are also an example of evolutionary computation, a set of computing techniques that are based on nature's laws of evolution and are important in the related field of artificial life, which involves interest in virtual (computer-based) life forms. To cellular automata hobbyists, they are a dynamic art form that often produces interesting results. *See* AUTOMATA THEORY; COMPUTER; EVOLUTIONARY COMPUTATION.

The word automaton comes to us from Greek through Latin, meaning something with the ability to act spontaneously. A cellular automaton is essentially a mathematical abstraction, such as a set or a function, but not a physical machine and not really alive. Nevertheless, when cellular automata are animated, either manually or through the graphical user interface of a computer program, they give a clear sense of complex animated behavior that makes them clearly lifelike. To computer scientists, the word automaton has a more technical meaning, that of a formal mathematical representation of computation.

Conventions and rules. A basic cellular automaton consists of a one- or two-dimensional array of cells, each of which can be in one of two states (black or white). The cells react to each other in a linear (two neighbors), orthogonal (four neighbors), or fully connected (eight neighbors, including the diagonals) fashion, based upon a set of rules that govern the cellular automaton (**Fig. 1**). The cells are synchronous, reacting in unison to their neighbors. During one reaction cycle, the cells assess their neighbors (two, four, or eight) and then reset their respective values in accordance with the universal rules. Over a series of reaction cycles, the cells can collectively exhibit complex, lifelike behavior.

Cellular automata gained prominence among mathematicians, both professional and amateur, with the publication in 1970 of Martin Gardner's *Scientific American* column "The fantastic combinations of John Conway's new solitaire game 'life.'" John Horton Conway, a mathematician at the University of Cambridge at the time, was well known for his contributions to theoretical mathematics and for his interest in recreational mathematics. Conway's "Game of Life" rules established an environment for the evolution of patterns (or populations, from an artificial life perspective) in cellular automata.

A typical set of rules for a cellular automaton comes from the original Game of Life. The rules refer to states of "death" and "life," which are represented by two alternative colors in the cells. These rules assume a cellular array with full connections (eight per cell):

1. If a live cell is surrounded by zero or one live neighbor, it dies from loneliness.

2. If a live cell is surrounded by four or more neighbors, it dies from overcrowding.

3. If a dead cell is surrounded by three neighbors, it comes back to life.

Additional rules are usually included to describe how the edge cells react, since they have fewer connections than the center cells. The cells are "seeded" initially by making a few of them live. Then, over a period of cycles, interesting behavior emerges from the collective. **Figure 2** shows a pattern over four cycles of evolution in a fully connected cellular automaton.

Cells can also be arranged into three-, four-, and higher-dimensional configurations, which can be theoretically interesting, though nearly impossible to visualize and therefore less interesting from a recreational perspective. Other rule sets are possible, including variations on the number of cells associated with loneliness, birth, death, and random variations (mutations). Cells may also have more than two coloring options, giving them the ability to generate colorful graphics.

The classical "Life" rules described above were developed through experimentation with the following goals in mind.

1. There should be no initial pattern for which there is a simple proof that the population can grow without limit.

2. There should be initial patterns that apparently do grow without limit.

3. There should be simple initial patterns that grow and change for a considerable period of time before coming to an end in three possible ways: fading away completely (from overcrowding or becoming too sparse), settling into a stable configuration that remains unchanged thereafter, or entering an oscillating phase in which the patterns repeat an endless cycle of two or more periods.

As a result, populations from the Game of Life exhibit behavior that is surprising and interesting and the underlying mathematics become interesting as well. Conway initially offered a conjecture that unrestricted growth was impossible under the standard Life rules. His supposition was that every possible seed pattern would eventually die, reach a static

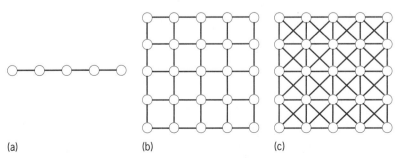

Fig. 1. Cellular automata connections: (*a*) linear, (*b*) orthogonal, and (c) full.

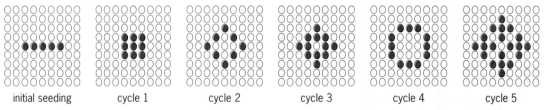

initial seeding   cycle 1   cycle 2   cycle 3   cycle 4   cycle 5

Fig. 2. Cellular automata in action.

state, or enter a permanent oscillation. He posed a reward of $50 for the first challenger to prove otherwise. The first of such patterns was found within a few months, and Conway's conjecture was disproved.

Self-replicating automata. Though Conway is credited as the originator of the Game of Life and is responsible for much of the recreational interest in cellular automata, John von Neumann, famous for his contributions to computer science and mathematics, first proposed cellular automata in 1943 as part of his research into self-replicating machines. As a young mathematician and professor, von Neumann made significant contributions in applied mathematics in a variety of fields, including game theory, fluid dynamics, and the development of the atomic bomb. During World War II, von Neumann became interested in computing and in formal models of computing in particular. He began to develop a comprehensive theory of organisms and machines, including their structure, organization, use of information, control, and language. With his automata theory, he aimed to develop a unified logical model that would explain both the organization of a computer and the operation of the human central nervous system. His theory also incorporated questions of complexity, reproduction, and self-repair. *See* CYBERNETICS; GAME THEORY.

As part of his attempt to model self-replicating automata, von Neumann developed several models of self-reproduction, both continuous and discrete, including one based on cellular automata. His self-reproducing cellular automaton formed a powerful universal computational model that could also reproduce itself within an infinite cellular automata space. In this model, the cells were arranged in an orthogonal lattice and operated on a uniform program of 29 rules. As a result of this development, von Neumann also showed that a computer structured as a cellular automaton was as powerful as any other computer and equivalent in power to the most well known model of computation, the Turing machine. Von Neumann died relatively young and was unable to complete his automata theory, but the work that he did complete was summarized and published by Arthur Burks.

Applications. Scientists in fields other than computer science have also discovered applications of cellular automata to their own research. For example, cellular automata have been used to investigate solutions to problems such as fluid dynamics, text data-compression algorithms, computational approaches to various problems in economics, tracking location of terminals in mobile computing

networks, analyzing complex chemical reactions, modeling fundamental physics, and simulating the mechanics of a landslide. *See* ALGORITHM.

The above examples suggest only some of the many different ways in which cellular automata are being used to investigate problems in natural science, social science, mathematics, and computing. There are virtually no fields of modern science in which cellular automata have not been used or proposed to solve outstanding problems. One group even suggests that the best explanation of reality is that the universe is in fact one large collection of cellular automata. In any case, there is no apparent limit to the growing scientific interest in cellular automata and their potential importance to scientific discovery.   Ralph F. Grove, Jr.

Bibliography. M. Gardner, The fantastic combinations of John Conway's new solitaire game "life," *Sci. Amer.*, 223:120–123, 1970; M. Gardner, *Wheels, Life, and Other Mathematical Amusements*, W. H. Freeman, 1983; A. Ilachinski, *Cellular Automata: A Discrete Universe*, World Scientific, 2001; T. Toffoli and N. Margolus, *Cellular Automata Machines*, MIT Press, 1987; S. Wolfram, *A New Kind of Science*, Wolfram Media, 2002.

Cellular immunology

The field concerning the interactions among cells and molecules of the immune system, and how such interactions contribute to the recognition and elimination of pathogens. Humans (and vertebrates in general) possess a range of nonspecific mechanical and biochemical defenses against routinely encountered bacteria, parasites, viruses, and fungi. The skin, for example, is an effective physical barrier to infection. Basic chemical defenses are also present in blood, saliva, and tears, and on mucous membranes. These defenses are nonspecific in that they may be effective against a broad array of organisms. Nonspecific or innate defense mechanisms offer only limited protection against pathogenic organisms, which can proliferate rapidly and overwhelm these first-line defenses. True protection stems from the host's ability to mount responses targeted to specific organisms, and to retain a form of "memory" that results in a rapid, efficient response to a given organism upon a repeat encounter. This more formal sense of immunity, termed adaptive immunity, depends upon the coordinated activities of cells and molecules of the immune system.

Cells involved. Several types of cells play a role in protecting the body from infection, and they are found primarily in the blood and lymph. Specific immune responses mainly involve the activities of T-lymphocytes and B-lymphocytes, two types of white blood cells. A response is initiated when a pathogen triggers the activity of one or both of the two major types of T cells: CD4$^+$ cells, also known as helper T cells (T$_H$); and CD8$^+$ cells, also known as cytotoxic T-lymphocytes (CTL) [see **illus.**].

When CD4$^+$ T cells are triggered, they release factors called cytokines, which in turn stimulate B-lymphocytes to make and secrete antibodies. Cytokines, principally the interleukins and interferons, are much like hormones, but they are secreted by individual cells rather than by organized tissues or glands. Cytokines play a significant role in many aspects of immune function and regulation, acting not only on B cells but also on T cells, macrophages, and other cells (thereby helping the immune response). Antibodies are molecules that are capable of binding to specific molecular structures found on microbes, and play a critical role in eliminating pathogens. Pathogen-bound antibodies can initiate a complement cascade (a series of reactions by serum proteins that burst and kill a microbe); they also serve as adapter molecules that facilitate the ingestion and destruction of microbes by phagocytic cells, such as macrophages. *See* ANTIBODY; COMPLEMENT; PHAGOCYTOSIS.

When CD8$^+$ T cells are triggered, they release factors that kill a cell harboring an infectious agent, and they also release cytokines. Virus-infected cells commonly are the targets of cytotoxic T-lymphocytes, since viruses need to get inside a cell in order to reproduce.

Antigen recognition. The immune system must detect a pathogen before a response can be made. This phase of the response is shown in the interaction between a T cell and an antigen-presenting cell (APC) [see illus.]. An antigen is a molecule, or portion of a molecule, that is recognized by a T-cell receptor (TCR) or antibody molecule. The cell surface molecules involved in antigen recognition by T cells are the T-cell receptor and class I or class II molecules of the major histocompatibility complex (MHC). Each T cell expresses a unique T-cell receptor that will interact specifically with a limited set of antigens. The antigens recognized by T-cell receptors are short peptides bound to MHC molecules. In addition to the T-cell receptor, the CD8 and CD4 molecules on the surface of T cells interact with class I and class II molecules, respectively, and define the MHC restriction of a given T cell; a circulating T cell expresses either CD8 or CD4, and it is poised to recognize peptides presented either by class I or by class II molecules. These co-receptor molecules do not engage in antigen recognition per se but help to stabilize the T cell–antigen-presenting cell interaction.

Antigen presentation. When a microbe enters or is ingested by a cell, some of the microbe's proteins are broken down by a process called proteolysis, just as cellular proteins are in the normal course of metabolism. Upon proteolysis, small fragments of protein, termed peptides, are generated. Class I and class II MHC molecules have a

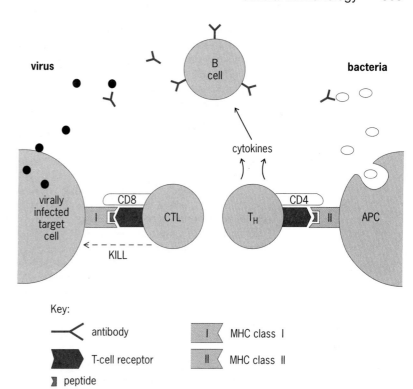

Key processes in a specific immune response.

grooved structure in their membrane-distal portions that can accommodate a short peptide generated by this process. MHC molecules are highly polymorphic (exist as many inherited varieties), and differences in this grooved domain determine the peptide-binding preferences exhibited by class I or class II molecules of a given type. A peptide that is bound to an MHC molecule forms an MHC-peptide complex, which is transported to the cell surface and displayed to roaming T cells. Most of these peptides derive from the body's own proteins, and do not elicit an immune response. T cells with receptors capable of recognizing self-peptides either are eliminated during their development in the thymus or are "trained" to ignore such peptides. However, when an infectious agent is present, some MHC-peptide complexes feature a pathogen-derived peptide. This peptide "message" alerts T cells (only those having a T-cell receptor capable of reading the particular message) to the presence of a microorganism. *See* THYMUS GLAND; TRANSPLANTATION BIOLOGY.

MHC molecules. Although class I and class II MHC molecules are structurally similar, they differ in the means by which they acquire peptides and in their patterns of cellular expression. Class I molecules can be expressed on nearly every cell type in the body, and their acquisition of peptides is optimized for the capture of peptides derived from proteins synthesized within the cell. This scheme is well suited to the presentation of virus-derived peptides, since viruses can enter many different types of cells, where they take over the biosynthetic machinery in order to produce their own proteins and replicate. Class I–peptide complexes alert CD8$^+$ T cells that a given cell is infected, and mark it for destruction.

Class II molecules, in contrast, are expressed on a

limited variety of cell types: lymphoid cells, dendritic cells, macrophages, and endothelium. Their expression on other cell types is inducible by gamma interferon. Peptide acquisition by class II molecules is biased toward the capture of peptides derived from extracellular sources, brought into the cell by phagocytosis and receptor-mediated uptake. Most bacteria thrive extracellularly, and viruses spend a portion of their cycle outside the cell. Cells presenting antigenic class II–peptide complexes generally are not marked for destruction, but stimulate CD4$^+$ cells to promote responses (such as antibody production) geared toward the elimination of extracellular pathogens. *See* HISTOCOMPATIBILITY.

Co-stimulation. Antigen recognition, as mediated by the T-cell receptor–MHC–peptide interaction, is necessary, but generally it is not sufficient for the initiation of an immune response. Several other molecular interactions occur between molecules on the T-cell surface and those on the antigen-presenting cells. Among these is the CD28-B7 interaction, which currently is understood to provide a critical costimulatory signal in the initiation of a T-cell response. CD28 and B7 molecules reside on the T-cell and antigen-presenting-cell surfaces, respectively. B7 represents a family of molecules: B7-1 (CD80) and B7-2 (CD86) are two members of this family that are ligands for the CD28 molecule. B7 molecules typically are expressed on cells referred to as professional antigen-presenting cells, such as activated dendritic cells and macrophages.

The co-stimulation provided by these additional interactions drives the production of cytokines by T cells and induces their proliferation. Because B7 molecule expression largely is restricted to professional antigen-presenting cells, this requirement for a second signal (antigen provides the first signal) can ensure that the immune response is not misdirected. Typically, T cells receive both signals from an antigen-presenting cell only in the context of an inflammatory reaction, initiated in part by innate defense mechanisms triggered by a pathogen. This context dependence is an important means for preventing T cells from reacting in a hair-trigger fashion to the presence of harmless foreign proteins (such as dietary proteins) or against self-proteins in cases where tolerance may be incomplete. *See* AUTOIMMUNITY.

Memory. Once an immune response has been initiated, T cells and B cells proliferate and become mature responder cells. These cells do not have the same requirement for co-stimulation once a response is under way; a mature cytotoxic T-lymphocyte, for example, can kill an infected cell if the cell simply presents the appropriate peptide. As pathogen elimination nears completion, many of the T and B cells involved in the response die. However, a subset of cells remain as memory cells, which can be quickly called into action if the same pathogen is encountered on a future occasion. The mechanisms that signal some cells to become memory cells and remain until needed are not well understood at present. However, it is this anamnestic feature of the immune response that gives humans the familiar experience of having a single nonrecurring instance of

childhood diseases such as mumps and chicken pox. Although there may be reexposure to the pathogens causing those illnesses, the primed immune system can deal with a repeat threat so efficiently that it goes largely unnoticed. *See* ACQUIRED IMMUNOLOGICAL TOLERANCE; CELLULAR IMMUNOLOGY; CYTOKINE; IMMUNITY; IMMUNOLOGY.   Douglas J. Loftus

Bibliography. E. A. Greenfield, K. H. Nguyen, and V. K. Kuchroo, CD28/B7 costimulation: A review, *Crit. Rev. Immunol.*, 18:389–418, 1998; C. A. Janeway et al., *Immunobiology: The Immune System in Health and Disease*, 4th ed., 1999.

Cellulose

A linear polymer of $(1 \rightarrow 4)$-linked β-D-glucopyranosyl units, and the most abundant of all naturally occurring substances. Cellulose constitutes approximately a third of all vegetable matter and thus it exists in far greater quantity than any other polysaccharide. It occurs as a principal structural component of the cell walls of mosses and seaweeds (25–30%), annual plants (25–35%), and trees (40–50%); cotton fiber contains 98% cellulose along with 1% protein, 0.65% pectic substance, and 0.15% mineral matter. Cellulose also is produced by some microorganisms, in a few cases reaching amounts of 20–30%. *See* CELL WALLS (PLANT).

Source. Cellulose for chemical modification, particularly for derivatization, is often obtained from cotton linters by boiling them with 1% sodium hydroxide solution. High-quality cellulose may be obtained from bast fibers such as flax (80–90% cellulose), hemp (65–75%), jute (60–70%), and ramie (85%). Cellulose fibers used for paper, for cardboard, or for conversion to film and synthetic fiber are obtained from wood pulp.

Structure. While cellulose is a uniform, linear polymer of a β-D-glucopyranosyl units linked $(1 \rightarrow 4)$, the β-D-glucosidic bond causes alternate units to be positioned as shown in the **illustration**, so that the molecule is essentially a polymer of the disaccharide, cellobiose, actually the cellobiosyl unit. The molecule has a nonreducing end and an aldehyde end, although at times the latter may be oxidized to a carboxyl group. Chain length varies with previous treatment, but native cellulose molecules have 7000 to 15,000 units, which are termed degrees of polymerization. *See* POLYMER.

Cellulose is the principal structural component of plants. The structural strength and integrity of plant cell walls that support even giant trees is due to the ease with which cellulose molecules fit together and bond intermolecularly, with secondary forces, over long lengths. This crystallization is due, for the most part, to hydrogen bonds such as that between the C3 hydroxyl of one chain and the C6 hydroxyl of a neighboring chain. Crystallinity may account for 60–70% of the cellulose in wood pulp and 70–80% in cotton. Rayon regenerated from pulp may redevelop 45% crystallinity. Cellulose in the cell wall is mainly in threadlike fibers, composed of smaller fibrils. These provide the reinforcing material with noncrystalline molecules running from one crystallite to another, providing elasticity in conjunction with that of hemicellulose and other filler material of the cell wall. *See* HEMICELLULOSE; HYDROGEN BOND.

Various crystalline forms of cellulose exist with the native form known as cellulose I. The unit cell is monoclinic with three unequal sides and one non-90° angle. Chains are skewed 180° along the chain axis. Strong alkali alters the polymorph to cellulose II, providing greater hydrogen bonding and a more stable, lower-energy, structure. Some covalent bonding occurs between cellulose and with the lignin of the cell wall and of the middle lamella, but mainly these molecules are free and can be extracted with reagents such as a strong alkaline solution.

Pulp. Commercial cellulose is obtained from woods by pulping procedures designed to remove lignin, hemicelluloses, gums, waxes, and other natural noncellulose constituents. Most commercial wood pulp is consumed in paper manufacture, but pulps of high α-cellulose content (90% or greater for rayon and at least 98% for cellulose ester, mainly acetate, manufacture) are considered good chemical cellulose, or dissolving-grade cellulose. α-Cellulose is that which is not soluble in 17.5% sodium hydroxide solution. Though cellulose is resistant to degradation during the pulping operation, it is partially degraded to lower molecular weights. Pulping is accomplished by mechanical or chemical means, or a combination of the two. Mechanical pulps contain the same constituents as the original wood, but fewer water-soluble substances. These pulps have shorter fibers than do chemical pulps and produce weaker paper. If steam is used to produce a thermomechanical pulp, the fibers are less degraded.

The kraft (sulfate) method is the most common chemical pulping method used in the United States, accounting for 70% of pulp production; pulp yield is 40–45%. In this process, wood chips, $^5/_8$–1 in. (1.5–2.5 cm) long by $^1/_4$ in. (0.6 cm) thick, are cooked to a maximum temperature of 334–347°F (168–175°C) for 2–6 h with a solution of sodium hydroxide and sodium sulfide, present in a ratio of 3:1. Other processes used are the sulfite and alkaline. Less than 10% of the pulp made in the United States is produced by the sulfite process. Chemical methods have become focused on improved yield, reduced environmental problems associated with sulfur chemicals, and production of high-strength fibers. Modern processes add anthraquinone to a soda (alkaline) cook, introduce soda-oxygen cooking, or use organic solvent extraction. Combinations of mechanical and chemical pulping tend to produce higher yields of high-strength fibers. *See* PAPER; WOOD CHEMICALS.

Dissolving pulp of 95–98% α-cellulose is used for viscous rayon, cellulose nonwoven materials, and cellulose derivatives. These pulps are made by alkaline washing of sulfite or sulfate pulps or by mild acid hydrolysis of chips followed by kraft pulping and bleaching to give low pulp yields of 29–35%. *See* TEXTILE CHEMISTRY.

Derivatives. Commercial derivatives are ethers that, among other properties, provide water solubility and esters which, in high degrees of substitution, provide organic solubility needed for spinning cellulose into fibers or molding it into shaped objects. One inorganic ester, the nitrate, made by reacting cellulose in a mixture of nitric and sulfuric acids, is used at high derivation as cellulose trinitrate gunpowder. Cellulose trinitrate has a degree of substitution (DS; the average number of hydroxyls substituted per glucose residue) of three. Formerly, it was used at a lower degree of substitution as a lacquer and film former. *See* ESTER; ETHER; MANUFACTURED FIBER.

Commercial ethers are carboxymethyl, methyl, hydroxyethyl, or hydroxypropyl. Mixed ethers are also made that contain methyl and hydroxyethyl or hydroxypropyl groups. All are soluble in water or mild alkaline solution. Solubility is conferred on the linear cellulose molecule by the substituent groups, which provide frequent bumps on the regular cellulose chains. This restricts them from associating when sections of chains meet in solution, thus preventing close association of chains that would lead to partial crystallization and insolubilization. Since these rather inflexible chains are still quite long with degrees of polymerization of 150–250, they sweep out large spherical volumes as they gyrate, and they collide frequently to absorb energy, producing highly viscous solutions. Such derivatives have degrees of substitution of 0.1–2.5. They are used to thicken solutions and to act as suspending agents and sometimes as mild emulsifiers.

Carboxymethylcellulose has a negative charge due to ionization of the carboxyl group, giving the molecule some emulsifying character. This derivative is used in washing powders; the molecules bind slightly to cotton fabrics, giving the cloth a negative charge that prevents negative soil particles from redepositing on the cloth.

Cellulose acetate is the principal commercial ester. Reaction is usually conducted in a mixture of acetic anhydride, acetic acid, and sulfuric acid as the catalyst to produce a degree of substitution of about 2.4, resulting in a product soluble in acetone. This has applications as a quick-drying adhesive, for film formation, or for use in cigarette filters. If propionic acid or its anhydride is used in the esterification reaction, a mixed ester is produced that forms a shock-resistant plastic useful for football helmets, telephones, and other objects that need to withstand shock. A fully acetylated cellulose (degree of substitution = 3) is used for making high-strength products, acetate rayon, and textile tow. This acetate can be made by acetylation of cellulose in dichloromethane

Positioning of units in cellulose structure.

with acetic anhydride and perchloric acid catalyst.

Degradation. Because cellulose molecules bind together so strongly, they are quite resistant to hydrolysis by acids and even cellulytic enzymes, although the free molecules or amorphous regions are hydrolyzed as easily as other polysaccharides. The end product is D-glucose; if it could be produced cheaply from cellulose, it would allow wood to be used as a source of fermentation alcohol. Hot 12% hydrochloric acid converts hemicelluloses mainly to furfural and cellulose to hydroxmethylfurfural. Unless cellulose molecules are oxidized, they are resistant to alkaline solutions, because like other polysaccharides the aldehyde functions of the D-glucopyranosyl units are tied up as acetal linkages that are resistant to alkaline cleavage.

Cellulose undergoes oxidation by numerous oxidants such as peroxides and hypochlorite. Dinitrogen tetraoxide specifically converts the hydroxymethyl group at C6 of each D-glucopyranosyl unit to a carboxyl or uronic acid. Most oxidations are catalyzed by metal ions. Therefore, iron salts allow oxidation of cotton textiles, causing yellow spots and eventually holes.

Cellulose is hydrolyzed slowly by cellulase enzymes produced by bacteria and fungi. *See* POLYSACCHARIDE. David G. Barkalow; Roy L. Whistler

Bibliography. J. P. Casey (ed.), *Pulp and Paper Chemistry and Chemical Technology*, vol. 1, 3d ed., 1980; J. F. Kennedy et al. (eds.), *Cellulose and Its Derivatives: Chemistry, Biochemistry and Applications*, 1985; T. P. Nevell and S. H. Zeronian (eds.), *Cellulose Chemistry and Its Applications*, 1985; C. E. Shuerch (ed.), *Cellulose and Wood: Chemistry and Technology*, 1989; E. Sjostrom, *Wood Chemistry: Fundamentals and Applications*, 1993; R. A. Young and R. M. Rowell (eds.), *Cellulose Structure, Modification and Hydrolysis*, 1986.

Cement

A material, usually finely divided, that when mixed with water forms a paste, and when molded sets into a solid mass. The term cement is sometimes used to refer to organic compounds used for adhering or for fastening materials, but these are more correctly known as adhesives. *See* ADHESIVE; ADHESIVE BONDING.

In the fields of architecture, engineering, and construction, the term portland cement is applied to most of the hydraulic cements used for concrete, mortars, and grouts. This article discusses portland cement and other special construction cements.

Portland cement sets and hardens by reacting chemically with water. In concrete, it combines with water and aggregates (sand and gravel, crushed stone, or other granular material) to form a stone-like mass. In grouts and mortars, cement is mixed with water and fine aggregates (sand) or fine granular materials. *See* CLAY, COMMERCIAL; CONCRETE; MORTAR.

Production. Portland cement is ground from nodules, which can vary in dimension from dust to fist-sized chunks, known as clinker. Cement clinker is the product of a high-temperature process. Manufacturing entails introduction of finely ground raw materials—mineral sources of calcium oxide, silica, alumina, and iron oxide—into a horizontally sloping rotary kiln. Raw materials are ground to a fineness to pass a 75-micrometer (200-mesh) screen in order to react within the kiln's residence time.

Materials are introduced either in powdered form, known as the dry process, or in slurry form, known as the wet process. Less energy is required to produce cement in the dry process; energy conservation efforts have led to the phasing-out of wet-process systems. Kiln systems differ, but generally materials are funneled through three major zones: drying and preheating, 70–1650°F (20–900°C), in which water is evaporated and calcination occurs; calcining, 1100–1650°F (600–900°C), where carbon dioxide is driven off but lime needed for subsequent reactions remains; and sintering or burning, 2200–2700°F (1200–1480°C), in which calcium oxide reacts with silica to form calcium silicates.

The intense heat yields clinker, whose principal chemical compounds are tricalcium silicate, dicalcium silicate, tricalcium aluminate, and tetracalcium aluminoferrite. Raw-material sources can vary according to local availability, but generally bear lime, iron, silica, alumina, and magnesia. Sources of these materials include limestone, clay, shale, and slag. Cement clinker is ground to extreme fineness in rotary steel-ball mills. Approximately 85–95% of cement particles are smaller than 45 micrometers. Small amounts of gypsum are interground with clinker to control set time.

Calcium silicates constitute about 75% of the weight of cement. When mixed with water, they form calcium hydroxide and calcium silicate hydrate or tobermorite gel. Hydrated cement contains about 25% calcium hydroxide and 50% tobermorite gel. The latter is primarily responsible for the strength and other properties of hydrated cement.

Standards. Under its C 150 classification, the American Society for Testing and Materials (ASTM) designates five basic types of portland cement. Type I is a general-purpose cement suitable for all uses where special properties are not required. Type II is used for resistance to moderate sulfate exposures. Type III is high-early-strength cement. Type IV is used where the rate and amount of heat generated from hydration must be minimized. Type V is used for resistance to severe sulfate exposure.

Types I, II, and III are also produced in air-entraining varieties. Air entrainment (incorporation of tiny air bubbles) is employed to maintain workability and cohesiveness in the fresh concrete mix and provide durability in the hardened product in climates where the material is subject to cycles of freezing and thawing. The microscopic air bubbles in the mix act as pressure-relief valves during freeze cycles. Air entrainment in a concrete mix can be achieved by using the three air-entraining portland cements (types IA, IIA, IIIA) or admixtures, which impart special properties to fresh or hardened concrete.

Adjustments in the physical and chemical compositions allow for tailoring portland cements and other hydraulic cements to special applications. Blended hydraulic cements are produced with portland cements and materials that by themselves might not possess binding characteristics.

Special varieties. Special cements are produced for mortars and architectural or engineering applications: white portland cement, masonry cement, and oil-well cement, expansive cement, and plastic cement.

In addition to acting as the key ingredient in concrete, mortars, and grouts, portland cements are specified for soil-cement and roller-compacted concrete, used in pavements and in dams, and other water resource structures, and as reagents for stabilization and solidification of organic and inorganic wastes.   Don Marsh

Bibliography. S. H. Kosmatka and W. C. Panarese, *Design and Control of Concrete Mixtures*, 13th ed., 1988; Portland Cement Association, *A New Stone Age: The Making of Portland Cement and Concrete*, 1992.

Cenozoic

Cenozoic (Cainozoic) is the youngest and the shortest of the three Phanerozoic geological eras. It represents the geological time (and rocks deposited during that time) extending from the end of the Mesozoic Era to the present day.

The geological concept of the Cenozoic, as the youngest era of the Phanerozoic, was introduced by J. Phillips in 1941. He considered it to be a unit equivalent to the Tertiary, a term that was still in use from G. Arduino's classification of Primary, Secondary, and Tertiary rocks, introduced in Italy in 1759. Arduino based his subdivision on physical attributes, such as

CENOZOIC	QUATERNARY
	TERTIARY
MESOZOIC	CRETACEOUS
	JURASSIC
	TRIASSIC
PALEOZOIC	PERMIAN
	CARBONIFEROUS — PENNSYLVANIAN / MISSISSIPPIAN
	DEVONIAN
	SILURIAN
	ORDOVICIAN
	CAMBRIAN
	PRECAMBRIAN

older magmatic and metamorphic rocks as Primary; limestone, marl, and clay with fossils as Secondary; and youngest, fossil-rich rocks as Tertiary. This classification is now largely obsolete, with the exception of the term Tertiary that is still in use in a modified sense. A. Brogninart first modified the concept of *Tertiaire* in 1810, applying it to the strata deposited above the Cretaceous chalk in the Paris Basin. The term Quaternary (the second and younger period of the Cenozoic) was introduced by M. Morlot in 1854. *See* QUATERNARY; TERTIARY.

Modern time scales include all of the past 65 million years of geological history in the Cenozoic Era. The distinction of the Cenozoic Era from older eras has been traditionally based on the occurrence of fossils showing affinities to modern organisms, and not on any particular lithostratigraphic criteria. *See* INDEX FOSSIL; PALEONTOLOGY.

Subdivisions. Traditional classifications subdivide the Cenozoic Era into two periods (Tertiary and Quaternary) and seven epochs (from oldest to youngest): Paleocene, Eocene, Oligocene, Miocene, Pliocene, Pleistocene, and Holocene. The older five epochs, which together constitute the Tertiary Period, span the time interval from 65 to 1.8 million years before present. The Tertiary is often separated into two subperiods, the Paleogene (Paleocene through Oligocene epochs, also collectively called the Nummulitic in older European literature) and the Neogene (Miocene and Pliocene epochs). These subperiods were introduced by M. Hornes in 1853. The Quaternary Period, which encompasses only the last 1.8 million years, includes the two youngest epochs (Pleistocene and Holocene). Holocene is also often referred to as the Recent, from the old Lyellian classification. Recent stratigraphic opinions are leaning toward abandoning the use of Tertiary and Quaternary (which are seen as the unnecessary holdovers from obsolete classifications) and in favor of retaining Paleogene and Neogene as the prime subdivisions of Cenozoic. *See* EOCENE; HOLOCENE; MIOCENE; OLIGOCENE; PALEOCENE; PLEISTOCENE; PLIOCENE.

Tectonics. Many of the tectonic events (mountain-building episodes or orogenies, changes in the rates of sea-floor spreading, or tectonic plate convergences) that began in the Mesozoic continued into the Cenozoic. The Laramide orogeny that uplifted the Rocky Mountains in North America, which began as early as Late Jurassic, continued into the Cretaceous and early Cenozoic time. In its post-Cretaceous phase the orogeny comprised a series of diastrophic movements that deformed the crust until some 50 million years ago, when it ended abruptly. The Alpine orogeny, which created much of the Alps, also began in the Mesozoic, but it was most intense in the Cenozoic when European and African plates converged at an increased pace. *See* CRETACEOUS; JURASSIC; MESOZOIC; OROGENY.

In the Pacific Ocean the most significant tectonic event in the Cenozoic may have been the progressive consumption of the East Pacific Rise at the Cordilleran Subduction Zone and the concomitant development of the San Andreas Fault System some

30 million years ago. *See* CORDILLERAN BELT; FAULT AND FAULT STRUCTURES; SUBDUCTION ZONES.

In the intracontinental region of the Tethys between Europe and Africa, the Cenozoic tectonic history is one of successive fragmentation and collision of minor plates and eventual convergence of the African and European plates. Africa's motion was counterclockwise relative to Europe, which began sometime in the early Mesozoic. By mid-Cenozoic, however, the motion between the two plates was largely convergent. The convergence caused a complex series of events that closed the Tethys Seaway between the two continents. In the late Cenozoic (Pliocene) the final collision of the Arabian plate with the Asian plate along Iran produced the Zagros Mountains, and partially or completely isolated the Caspian and Black seas. *See* CONTINENTAL DRIFT.

In the Indian Ocean, perhaps the most significant event during the Cenozoic was rapid movement of the Indian plate northward and its collision with Asia. India had already broken loose from the eastern Gondwana in the late Cretaceous, but around 80 million years ago its motion accelerated, and then increased further in the early Cenozoic. This movement, however, slowed down considerably around 50 million years ago when the Indian plate plowed into the Asian mainland. The first encounter of the two plates caused the initial uplift of the Himalayas. The major phase of the Himalayan orogeny, however, extends from the Miocene to the Pleistocene, when much of the high Himalayas were raised and the Tibetan Plateau was fully uplifted. The encounter also caused major reorganization of the crust both north and south of the collision zone. In the Indian Ocean the plates were reorganized, and spreading was initiated on the Central Indian Ridge system. The collision had important repercussions for the Asian mainland as well. Over 1500 km (900 mi) of crustal shortening has occurred since the collision began. The effects of diastrophism associated with this event extend some 3000 km (1800 mi) northeast of the Himalayas. This includes major strike-slip faults in China and Mongolia, which may account for a major portion of the crustal shortening, which continues to the present day. The present convergence between the Indian and Asian plates is at the rate of about 0.5 cm (0.2 in.) per year.

Another major long-term affect of the tectonic uplift of Tibetan Plateau, which is dated to have been significant by 40 million years ago, may have been the initiation of the general global cooling trend that followed this event. The uplifted plateau may have initiated a stronger deflection of the atmospheric jet stream, strengthening of the summer monsoon, and increased rainfall and weathering in the Himalayas. Increased weathering and dissolution of carbonate rock results in greater carbon dioxide (CO_2) drawdown from the atmosphere. The decreased partial pressure of carbon dioxide (pCO_2) levels may have ultimately led to the Earth entering into a renewed glacial phase.

The convergence between India and Asia and between Africa and Europe in the mid-Cenozoic destroyed the ancestral Tethys Seaway, leaving behind smaller remnants that include the Mediterranean, Black, and Caspian seas. *See* PLATE TECTONICS.

Oceans and climate. The modern circulation and vertical structure of the oceans and the predominantly glacial mode that the Earth is in at present was initiated in the mid-Cenozoic time. The early Cenozoic was a period of transition between the predominantly thermospheric circulation of the Mesozoic and the thermohaline circulation that developed in the mid-Cenozoic. By the mid-Cenozoic the higher latitudes had begun to cool down, especially in the Southern Hemisphere due to the geographic isolation of Antarctica, leading to steeper latitudinal thermal gradients and accentuation of seasonality. The refrigeration of the polar regions gave rise to the cold high-latitude water that sank to form cold bottom water. The development of the psychrosphere (cold deeper layer of the ocean) and the onset of thermohaline circulation are considered to be the most significant events of Cenozoic ocean history, which ushered the Earth into its modern glacial-interglacial cyclic mode.

The overall history of the Cenozoic oceans is marked by a long-term withdrawal of the seas from epicontinental and coastal oceans and the accretion of ice on the polar regions. The ice buildup may have been partly favored by the more poleward position of the landmasses and the eventual thermal isolation of the Antarctic continent.

In the early Paleogene, for the first time a deep connection between the North and South Atlantic was developed to allow deeper water penetration into the southern basin that intermittently led to extensive erosion on the ocean floor. However, the most likely source area for deep waters in the early Cenozoic was still in the temperate and low-latitude shelves. Farther north, in the Norwegian Sea area there is magnetic evidence of initiation of sea-floor spreading in the late Paleocene. By the middle Eocene, this area may have become a site for the formation of cold bottom waters. Erosional events on the sea floor indicate that North Atlantic Deep Water may have begun to flow southward at approximately the same time as the initial subsidence of the Greenland-Faeroe Ridge below sea level in the late Eocene. Later on, in the Miocene, the ridge subsided more actively, resulting in greater outflow of higher-salinity water to intermediate and abyssal depths of the Central Atlantic. Evidence also points to vigorous bottom waters in the late Eocene, which increased in intensity through Oligocene and Miocene time.

The most prominent feature of the surface circulation in the early Cenozoic was the westward flowing circumglobal Tethys Current, which dominated the oceanic scene in the tropical latitudes. As the Indian plate approached the Asian mainland in the early Cenozoic, it progressively restricted the flow of Tethys Current to its north. In the middle Eocene, when the general drop in global sea level and the first encounter of the Indian plate with Asia reduced the northern passage, the main flow moved to the west of the Indian plate. By Oligocene time the westward flow in the Tethys had become intermittent and severely restricted to a narrow western passage. The Tethyan passage had essentially closed by the dawn of the Neogene.

A paleogeographic event of major import for the overall Cenozoic oceanic patterns was the breaching of the straits between Antarctica and South America at the Drake Passage in the Oligocene. This event led to the development of the circum-Antarctic Current, eventual thermal isolation of Antarctica, and further enhancement of the ice cap on the continent by mid-Oligocene. Winter ice accumulation on the Arctic, which lacks a continent in the polar position, may have also begun by the Oligocene. The increased sequestration of water on ice caps may be responsible for a major global sea-level drop in the mid-Oligocene evidenced along most of the world's continental margins. By late Oligocene time the global surface circulation patterns had essentially evolved the major features of the modern oceans. *See* PALEOCEANOGRAPHY; PALEOGEOGRAPHY.

All climatic indicators point to a general warming trend through the Paleocene, culminating in a period of peak global temperatures at the close of Paleocene. The warm climates continued into the early Eocene interval. The latitudinal and vertical thermal gradients in the late Paleocene–early Eocene were low, and mean surface temperature was around $10°C$ ($50°F$) in the higher latitudes and $20°C$ ($70°F$) in the tropics. Terrestrial flora and fauna also corroborate the peak warming of this interval. For example, the Arctic island of Ellesmere has yielded a rich warm-blooded vertebrate fauna that indicates a range of temperature between 10 and $20°C$ (50 and $70°F$).

Studies have revealed a prominent carbon-isotopic shift in global carbonate reservoir that coincides with the latest Paleocene peak warming. This has been ascribed to the breakdown of deposits of methane hydrates on continental margins and catastrophic release of methane into the water and atmosphere due to rapid warming of the bottom waters. In the latest Paleocene, bottom water temperature increased rapidly (in less than 10,000 years) by as much as $4°C$ ($7.2°F$), with a coincident prominent enrichment of ^{12}C isotope of the global carbon reservoir. The isotopic changes are accompanied by important biotic changes in the oceanic microfauna and are synchronous in the oceans and on land. This rapid and prominent isotopic shift cannot be explained by increased volcanic emissions of carbon dioxide, changes in oceanic circulation, or terrestrial and marine productivity alone. Increased flux of methane from gas-hydrate sources into the ocean-atmosphere system and its subsequent oxidation to carbon dioxide is held responsible for this isotopic excursion in the inorganic carbon reservoir. High-resolution data support the gas-hydrate connection to latest Paleocene abrupt climate change. Evidence from two widely separated sites from the low- and high-latitude Atlantic Ocean indicates multiple injections of methane with global consequences during the relatively short interval at the end of the Paleocene.

The Eocene time is also characterized by higher global sea levels and increased oceanic productivity and carbonate deposition on the shelves and banks. The climate became more extreme in the late Eocene and through the Oligocene, when the latitudinal contrast increased due to development of ice in the polar regions. Himalayan uplift that produced the obstruction of the Tibetan Plateau in the path of the jet stream in the late Eocene may have been an important contributory factor to the cooling trend of the mid and late Cenozoic. Vertical thermal gradients also steepened once the cold bottom waters outflow began from the higher latitudes.

The late Cenozoic is characterized by further accentuation of the oceanographic and climatic patterns that were initiated in the early Cenozoic. By Miocene time the Tethyan connection between the Indian Ocean and the Mediterranean Sea had been broken. This event modified the circulation patterns in the North Atlantic and the Mediterranean, which for the first time began to resemble their modern analogs. Neogene climatic proxies (such as stable isotopes in cores and glacial records on land) show evidence of considerable climatic fluctuations. Six major climatic deterioration events have been identified in the Miocene-Pliocene record. These events were also associated with enhanced surface circulation, bottom erosion, and aridity on land over North Africa. The cooler early Miocene climates were followed by a climatic optimum in mid-Miocene, to be in turn followed by a significant deterioration in climate, which has been ascribed to a major enlargement of the ice sheets on Antarctica.

In the late Miocene, the Mediterranean suffered a salinity crisis following a sea-level fall and the isolation of the basin. The growth of ice caps in the Miocene eventually led to the fall of sea level below the depth of Gibraltar Sill, isolating the Mediterranean Basin. The lack of connection to the open Atlantic and excess evaporation led to high salinities and deposition of voluminous quantities of evaporites in a relatively short time. The Mediterranean was reconnected to the Atlantic in the early Pliocene, allowing cold deep waters to suddenly spill over the subsided Gibraltar Sill. The Black Sea was also converted into an alkaline lake during the salinity crisis when the Mediterranean inflow was cut off. The early Pliocene reconnection with the Mediterranean was once again followed by isolation of the Black Sea, this time as a fresh-water lake. These conditions lasted into the Quaternary, when the reconnection to the Mediterranean was established through the Bosporus Straits around 7000 years ago, ushering in the present-day conditions. *See* SALINE EVAPORITES.

Another important threshold event of the late Cenozoic was the closing of the connection between the Central Atlantic and Pacific oceans at the Isthmus of Panama. The connection was operative until the mid-Pliocene, when tectonic events led to its closure some 3 million years ago. The closure most likely led to more vigorous Gulf Stream flow due to deflected energy, displacing the stream northward to its present-day position. The modern circulation patterns in the Caribbean also date back to this event. Another major climatic-oceanographic event of the Cenozoic was the development of an extensive ice cap on the Arctic. Although there is some evidence of ice cover in the Arctic since the Oligocene, evidence of a significant amount of ice accumulation is only as old as mid-Pliocene, some 3 million years ago, coincident with the closing of the Panama isthmus. The deflection of the Gulf Stream northward due to the latter event may have provided the excess moisture needed for this accumulation.

The Quaternary climatic history is one of repeated alternations between glacial and interglacial periods. At least five major glacial cycles have been identified in the Quaternary of northwestern Europe. The most recent glacial event occurred between 30,000 and 18,000 years ago when much of North America and northern Europe was covered with extensive ice sheets. The late Pliocene and Pleistocene glacial cyclicity led to repeated falls in global sea level as a result of sequestration of water as ice sheets in higher latitudes during the glacial intervals. For example, the sea level is estimated to have risen some 110 m (360 ft) since the end of the last glacial maximum. As a by-product of these repeated drops in sea level and movement of the shorelines toward the basins, large deltas developed at the mouths of the world's major drainage systems during the Quaternary. These bodies of sand and silt constitute ideal reservoirs for hydrocarbon accumulation. *See* DELTA; PALEOCLIMATOLOGY.

Life. At the end of the Cretaceous a major extinction event had decimated marine biota and only a few species survived into the Cenozoic. The recovery, however, was relatively rapid. During the Paleocene through middle Eocene interval, the overall global sea-level rise enlarged the ecospace for marine organisms, and an associated climatic optimum led to increased speciation through the Paleocene, culminating in high marine diversities during the early and middle Eocene. Limestone-building coral reefs were also widespread in the tropical-temperate climatic belt of the early Cenozoic, and the tropical Tethyan margins were typified by expansive distribution of the larger foraminifera known as *Nummulites* (giving the Paleogene its informal name of the Nummulitic period). *See* NUMMULITES.

The late Eocene saw a rapid decline in diversities of marine phyto- and zooplankton due to a global withdrawal of the seas from the continental margins and the ensuing deterioration in climate. Marine diversities reached a new low in the mid-Oligocene, when the sea level was at its lowest, having gone through a major withdrawal of seas from the continental margins. The climates associated with low seas were extreme and much less conducive to biotic diversification. The late Oligocene and Neogene as a whole constitute an interval characterized by increasing partitioning of ecological niches into tropical, temperate, and higher-latitude climatic belts, and greater differentiation of marine fauna and flora.

The terminal Cretaceous event had also decimated the terrestrial biota. Dinosaurs, which had dominated the Mesozoic scene, became extinct. Only a few small shrewlike mammalian species survived into the Paleocene. In the absence of dinosaurian competition, mammals evolved and spread rapidly to become dominant in the Cenozoic. The evolution of grasses in the early Eocene and the wide distribution of grasslands thereafter may have been catalytic in the diversification of browsing mammals. Marsupials and insectivores as well as rodents (which first appeared in the Eocene) diversified rapidly, as did primates, carnivores, and ungulates. The ancestral horse first appeared in the early Eocene in North America, where its lineage evolved into the modern genus *Equus*, only to disappear from the continent in the late Pleistocene. A complete evolution of the horse can be followed in North America during the Cenozoic. Increase in overall size, reduction in the number of toes, and increasing complexity of grinding surface of the molars over time are some of the obvious trends. Hominoid evolution began during the Miocene in Africa. Modern hominids are known to have branched off from the hominoids some 5 million years ago. Over the next 4.5 million years the hominids went through several evolutionary stages to finally evolve into archaic *Homo sapiens* about 1 million years ago. Truly modern *Homo sapiens* do not enter the scene until around 100 thousand years ago. *See* DINOSAURIA; FOSSIL HUMANS; MAMMALIA; ORGANIC EVOLUTION.   Bilal U. Haq

Bibliography. B. U. Haq and F. W. B van Eysinga, *Geological Time Table*, Elsevier, Amsterdam 1998; K. J. Hsü (ed.), *Mesozoic and Cenozoic Oceans*, 1986; C. Pomerol, *The Cenozoic Era: Tertiary and Quaternary*, 1982; M. E. Raymo and W. F. Ruddiman, Tectonic forcing of late Cenozoic climate, *Nature*, 359:117–122, 1992.

Centaurus

The Centaur, a southern constellation in the Milky Way (see **illustration**). It is not visible from mid-northern latitudes, but observers in the Southern Hemisphere see two bright stars, Alpha Centauri (Rigel Kentaurus) and Beta Centauri (Hadar), marking the feet of the Centaur, one of the mythological Greek creatures who are half human and half horse. Centaurus honors the wise centaur Chiron, who educated Achilles and Hercules and who was elevated to the heavens by Zeus when he died. In 800 B.C., in the era when this myth was probably told, the constellation was almost completely visible from latitudes up to 40°N. Because of the precession of the equinoxes, only the upper half of the constellation is ever above the horizon at that latitude today. Other myths identify Chiron with the constellation Sagittarius. *See* PRECESSION OF EQUINOXES; SAGITTARIUS.

Rigel Kent, as it is often called, is the third brightest star in the sky; only Sirius and Canopus are brighter.

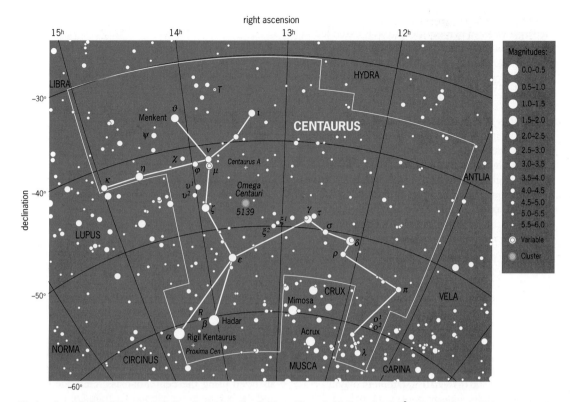

right ascension

Modern boundaries of the constellation Centaurus, the Centaur. The celestial equator is 0° of declination, which corresponds to celestial latitude. Right ascension corresponds to celestial longitude, with each hour of right ascension representing 15° of arc. Apparent brightness of stars is shown with dot sizes to illustrate the magnitude scale, where the brightest stars in the sky are 0th magnitude or brighter and the faintest stars that can be seen with the unaided eye at a dark site are 6th magnitude. (*Wil Tirion*)

Alpha and Beta Centauri together point at the Southern Cross, the constellation Crux. They are thus often called the Southern Pointers, analogously to the Pointers at the end of the Big Dipper's bowl. *See* CRUX; URSA MAJOR.

The Alpha Centauri multiple star system is the closest star system to our own solar system. A faint red-dwarf companion star, known as Proxima Centauri, is marginally closer to us, making it the closest star to the Sun. *See* ALPHA CENTAURI.

A notable globular cluster, Omega Centauri got its name when it was originally mistaken for a star. The radio source Centaurus A turns out to be a giant active galaxy, emitting strongly also in the x-ray part of the spectrum. *See* RADIO ASTRONOMY; STAR CLUSTERS.

The modern boundaries of the 88 constellations, including this one, were defined by the International Astronomical Union in 1928. *See* CONSTELLATION.

Jay M. Pasachoff

Center of gravity

A fixed point in a material body through which the resultant force of gravitational attraction acts. The resultant of all forces or attractions produced by the Earth's gravity on a body constitutes its weight. This weight is considered to be concentrated at the center of gravity in mechanical studies of a rigid body.

The location of the center of gravity for a body remains fixed in relation to the body regardless of the orientation of the body. If supported at the center of gravity, a body would remain balanced in its initial position. Coordinates, as for an aircraft, are conveniently chosen with origin at the center of gravity. *See* GRAVITY; RESULTANT OF FORCES.   Nelson S. Fisk

Center of mass

That point of a material object or a system of objects that moves as if all the external forces were acting on the entire mass of the object or the system of objects concentrated at that point. The motion of a material object or a system of objects can be described in terms of the translational motion of the center of mass and the rotational motion about the center of mass. *See* ROTATIONAL MOTION; RIGID-BODY DYNAMICS.

Location. The location of the center of mass x_{CM} for a system of two particles of mass m_1 and m_2 located at positions x_1 and x_2 along the x axis is given by Eq. (1).

$$x_{CM} = \frac{m_1 x_1 + m_2 x_2}{m_1 + m_2} \qquad (1)$$

If the two masses are equal, the center of mass lies midway between them in accord with Eq. (1). If their masses are unequal, the center of mass lies closer to the larger mass. When this definition is extended to i particles in three dimensions, the center of mass is given by Eq. (2),

$$\mathbf{r}_{CM} = \frac{\sum_i m_i \mathbf{r}_i}{M} \qquad (2)$$

where M is the total mass of the system, $\mathbf{r}_i$ is the position vector of the ith particle, and m_i is the mass of that particle.

Relation to forces and momenta. The translational motion of an object or a system of particles behaves as if the sum of the external forces acting on the individual particles can be considered a single force $\mathbf{F}$ that acts on the total mass concentrated at $\mathbf{r}_{CM}$. That is, the motion may be described by Eq. (3).

$$M\frac{d^2\mathbf{r}_{CM}}{dt^2} = \mathbf{F} \qquad (3)$$

Similarly, the product of the total mass times the velocity of the center of mass gives the total linear momentum of the system, $\mathbf{P}$, as in Eq. (4).

$$\mathbf{P} = M\frac{d\mathbf{r}_{CM}}{dt} \qquad (4)$$

Equations (3) and (4) lead to a statement of conservation of linear momentum: If the total external force is zero, the total linear momentum of a system is conserved. In this case, conserved means that a quantity is constant. In addition, the total linear momentum remains constant when the total external force is zero. *See* MOMENTUM.

Description of elastic collisions. The description of the elastic collision of two particles may be simplified by choosing a frame of reference that moves with the center of mass of the two-particle system. In that frame, the center of mass is at rest, the total momentum of the two particles is zero, and the particles are seen to be approaching the center of mass with momenta that are equal in magnitude and opposite in direction. After colliding, to conserve momentum, the particles recoil, moving in opposite directions along a line that makes an angle Θ with the initial line of motion (**Fig. 1**). The angle Θ is the scattering angle in

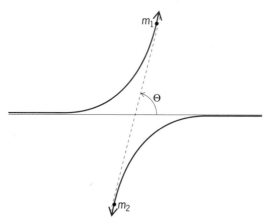

Fig. 1. Collision of two particles as seen from a frame of reference at rest with respect to the center of mass.

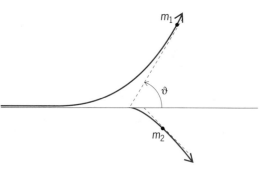

Fig. 2. Collision of two particles as seen from the frame of reference of the laboratory in which one of the particles is initially at rest.

the center-of-mass reference frame. The scattering is assumed to be axially symmetric so that no azimuthal angle need be introduced. The magnitudes of the particles' velocities must be unchanged in order that the kinetic energy is conserved, a requirement for an elastic collision. *See* COLLISION (PHYSICS).

Now consider the situation in which an incoming particle collides elastically with a particle at rest with respect to the laboratory. The collision may still be analyzed using the center-of-mass reference frame, and the results in the laboratory frame of reference may be obtained by a coordinate transformation.

For a collision between an incoming particle m_1 and a target particle m_2 initially at rest, the scattering angle ϑ measured in the laboratory is the angle between the final and incident directions of the scattered particle in laboratory coordinates (**Fig. 2**). The angle ϑ depends on the angle Θ in the center-of-mass frame and on the ratio of the two masses m_1/m_2 through the relationship in Eq. (5).

$$\tan \vartheta = \frac{\sin \Theta}{\cos \Theta + (m_1/m_2)} \qquad (5)$$

For the special situation where $m_1 \ll m_2$, the two scattering angles become approximately the same.

Edwin R. Jones

Bibliography. H. Goldstein, C. Poole, and J. Safko, *Classical Mechanics*, 3d ed., Addison-Wesley, Boston, 2002; E. R. Jones and R. L. Childers, *Contemporary College Physics 2001 Update*, 3d ed., McGraw-Hill, New York, 2001; J. B. Marion and S. T. Thornton, *Classical Dynamics of Particles and Systems*, 5th ed., Brooks Cole, Belmont, CA, 2004; C. P. Poole, Jr., *The Physics Handbook: Fundamentals and Key Equations*, Wiley, New York, 1998; K. R. Symon, *Mechanics*, 3d ed., Addison-Wesley, Boston, 1971.

Center of pressure

The center of pressure for an object is defined as the point at which the resultant surface pressure force may act and produce the same moment (torque) as the actual distributed pressure force on the object. The center of pressure is a very useful concept for simplifying the effects of fluid forces acting on a solid object. *See* TORQUE.

In the case of a flat surfaces, the center of pressure will lie on the surface. Examples include the hydrostatic pressure force acting on a dam (**Fig. 1**) or the aerodynamic loading of an aircraft wing section (**Fig. 2**). In neither case is the atmospheric pressure included since it acts equally around all sides and contributes nothing to the net force or moment on the object. The placement of a balancing force equal and opposite to the resultant pressure force at the center of pressure will establish equilibrium of the body. *See* AERODYNAMIC FORCE; EQUILIBRIUM OF FORCES.

For curved plane surfaces the center of pressure may lie off the surface, but it still correctly indicates the point at which a balancing force may be placed. For example, a circular-arc water gate (**Fig. 3**) may be balanced by a single force located at the center of gate curvature.

Axisymmetric bodies moving through a fluid have a center of pressure that lies along the central axis but near or even forward of the nose (**Fig. 4**). However, flight without tumbling requires that the center of pressure lie behind the center of gravity. The feathers on the tail of an arrow increase stability by moving the center pressure rearward. Stability may be further improved by adding weight to the nose, which moves the center of gravity forward.

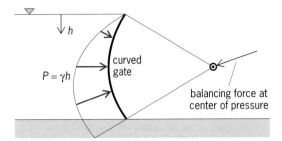

Fig. 3. Hydrostatic force on a circular-arc water gate. The pressure distribution is indicated by the arrows and their envelope. h = depth beneath surface of water, P = pressure, γ = weight density of water.

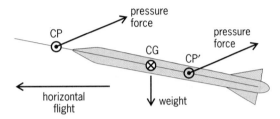

Fig. 4. Projectile in flight. The center of gravity is located at CG. The center of pressure without fins is located at CP and flight is unstable. The center of pressure with fins is located at CP' and flight is stable.

In the case of objects submerged in a motionless liquid, pressure increases with depth. The center of pressure lies at the centroid of the object's volume and is referred to as the center of buoyancy. Stability is achieved when the center of gravity of the object is below the center of pressure. The center of pressure for an object floating on a liquid surface is located at the centroid of the displaced liquid. *See* BUOYANCY; CENTER OF GRAVITY; CENTROIDS (MATHEMATICS); RESULTANT OF FORCES.   A. Gordon L. Holloway

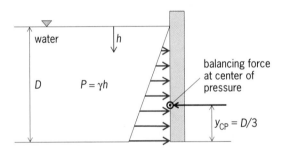

Fig. 1. Hydrostatic pressure force on a dam. The center of pressure is located at the centroid of the triangular pressure distribution indicated by arrows. h = depth beneath surface of water, D = total depth of water, P = pressure, γ = weight density of water ($\gamma = \rho g$, where ρ = mass density of water and g = acceleration of gravity); and y_{CP} = height of center of pressure above base of dam.

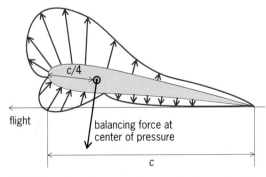

Fig. 2. Aerodynamic pressure force on a wing section. The pressure distribution is indicated by the arrows and their envelope. The center of pressure for the wing section is also referred to as the aerodynamic center of airfoil section. c = chord of airfoil.

Central force

A force whose line of action is always directed toward a fixed point. The central force may attract or repel. The point toward or from which the force acts is called the center of force. If the central force attracts a material particle, the path of the particle is a curve concave toward the center of force; if the central force repels the particle, its orbit is convex to the center of force. Undisturbed orbital motion under the influence of a central force satisfies Kepler's law of areas. *See* CELESTIAL MECHANICS.

Raynor L. Duncombe

Central nervous system

That portion of the nervous system composed of the brain and spinal cord. The brain is enclosed in the skull, and the spinal cord within the spinal canal of the vertebral column. The brain and spinal cord are intimately covered by membranes called meninges and bathed in an extracellular fluid called cerebrospinal fluid. Approximately 90% of the cells of the central nervous sytem are glial cells which support, both physically and metabolically, the other 10% of the cells, which are the nerve cells or neurons. Although the glial cells are much more numerous than neurons, the glial cells are also much smaller and do not directly participate in the propagation and integration of information. *See* MENINGES; NEURON.

Functionally similar groups of neurons are clustered together in so-called nuclei of the central nervous system. When groups of neurons are organized in layers (called laminae) on the outer surface of the brain, the group is called a cortex, such as the cerebral cortex and cerebellar cortex. The long processes (axons) of neurons course in the central nervous sytem in functional groups called tracts. Since many of the axons have a layer of shiny fat (myelin) surrounding them, they appear white and are called the white matter of the central nervous system. The nuclei and cortex of the central nervous system have little myelin in them, appear gray, and are called the gray matter of the central nervous system. The complex of gray and white matter forms the organizational pattern of the central nervous systems of all vertebrates. *See* BRAIN; NERVOUS SYSTEM (VERTEBRATE); SPINAL CORD.   Douglas B. Webster

Centrifugal force

A fictitious or pseudo outward force on a particle rotating about an axis which by Newton's third law is equal and opposite to the centripetal force. Like all such action-reaction pairs of forces, they are equal and opposite but do not act on the same body and so do not cancel each other. Consider a mass M tied by a string of length R to a pin at the center of a smooth horizontal table and whirling around the pin with an angular velocity of ω radians per second. The mass rotates in a circular path because of the centripetal force, $F_c = M\omega^2 R$, exerted on it by the string. The reaction force exerted by the rotating mass M, the so-called centrifugal force, is $M\omega^2 R$ in a direction away from the center of rotation. *See* CENTRIPETAL FORCE.

From another point of view, consider an experimenter in a windowless, circular laboratory that is rotating smoothly about a centrally located vertical axis. No object remains at rest on a smooth surface; all such objects move outward toward the wall of the laboratory as though an outward, centrifugal force were acting. To the experimenter partaking in the rotation, in a rotating frame of reference, the centrifugal force is real. An outside observer would realize that the inward force which the experimenter in the rotating laboratory must exert to keep the object at rest does not keep it at rest, but furnishes the centripetal force required to keep the object moving in a circular path. The concept of an outward, centrifugal force explains the action of a centrifuge. *See* CENTRIFUGATION.   C. E. Howe; R. J. Stephenson

Centrifugal pump

A machine for moving fluid by accelerating it radially outward. More fluid is moved by centrifugal pumps than by all other types combined. The smooth, essentially pulsationless flow from centrifugal pumps, their adaptability to large capacities, easy control, and low cost make them preferable for most purposes. Exceptions are those in which a relatively high pressure is required at a small capacity, or in which the viscosity of the fluid is too great for reasonable efficiency. *See* CENTRIFUGAL FORCE.

Centrifugal pumps consist basically of one or more rotating impellers in a stationary casing which guides the fluid to and from the impeller or from one impeller to the next in the case of multistage pumps. Impellers may be single suction or double suction (**Fig. 1**). Additional essential parts of all centrifugal pumps are (1) wearing surfaces or rings, which make a close-clearance running joint between the impeller and the casing to minimize the backflow of fluid from the discharge to the suction; (2) the shaft, which

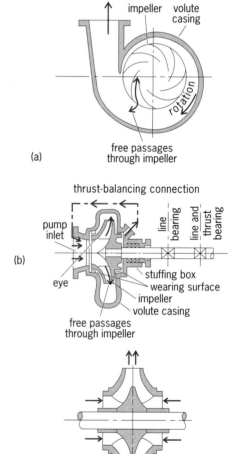

Fig. 1. Views of centrifugal pumps. (*a*) Section across the axis of a single-suction volute pump. (*b*) Section along the axis of a single-suction volute pump. (*c*) Double-suction impeller.

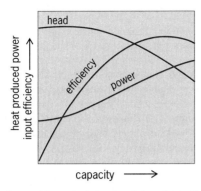

Fig. 2. Some of the typical characteristics of centrifugal pump at constant speed of rotation.

supports and drives the impeller; and (3) the stuffing box or seal, which prevents leakage between shaft and casing.

Characteristics. The rotating impeller imparts pressure and kinetic energy to the fluid pumped. A collection chamber in the casing converts much of the kinetic energy into head or pressure energy before the fluid leaves the pump. A free passage exists at all times through the impeller between the discharge and inlet side of the pump. Rotation of the impeller is required to prevent backflow or draining of fluid from the pump. Because of this, only special forms of centrifugal pumps are self-priming. Most types must be filled with liquid or primed, before they are started.

Every centrifugal pump has its characteristic curve, which is the relation between capacity or rate of flow and pressure or head against which it will pump (**Fig. 2**). At zero pressure difference, maximum capacity is obtained, but without useful work. As resistance to flow external to the pump increases, capacity decreases until, at a high pressure, flow ceases entirely. This is called shut-off head and again no useful work is done. Between these extremes, capacity and head vary in a fixed relationship at constant rpm. Input power generally increases from a minimum at shut-off to a maximum at a capacity considerably greater than that at which best efficiency is realized. The operating design point is set as close as practical to the point of best efficiency. Operation at higher or lower speed results in a change in the characteristic curves, with capacity varying directly with the speed, and head varying as the square of speed. Since the power required is proportional to the product of the head and capacity, it varies as the cube of the speed. These relations are essentially constant as long as viscosity of the fluid is low enough to be negligible.

Centrifugal impeller (and casing) forms vary with the relation of desired head and capacity at a practical rotating speed. Impellers and pumps are commonly classified as centrifugal, mixed-flow, and axial-flow or propeller (**Fig. 3**). There is a continuous change from the centrifugal impeller to the axial-flow impeller. For maximum practical head at small capacity, the impeller has a large diameter and a narrow waterway

with vanes curved only in the plane of rotation. As the desired capacity is increased relative to the head, the diameter of the impeller is reduced, the width of the waterway is increased, and the vanes are given a compound curvature. For higher capacities and less head, the mixed-flow impeller is used. It discharges at an angle approximately midway between radial and axial. For maximum capacity and minimum head, the axial-flow or propeller-type impeller is used.

Capacity. Specific speed is used to identify the place occupied by an impeller in this range of form or type. The narrow, purely radial discharge impeller is at the low end of the specific speed scale while the axial-flow impeller is at the high end. The highest pump efficiency is obtainable at a specific speed of approximately 2000 when the capacity is expressed in gallons per minute (gpm), or 94 when the capacity is expressed in cubic feet per second (cfs). Specific speed $N_s = NQ^{1/2}H^{-3/4}$ where N is rpm, H is head in feet, and Q is capacity in gpm or cfs.

Since the highest efficiency is obtained at a medium specific speed, theoretically an optimum speed of rotation may be calculated for any head and capacity. Such a selection must be adjusted for practical considerations. Because most pumps are driven directly by electric motors, available motor speeds govern operating speeds to a large extent. For small capacities, a lower specific speed is usually necessary. The low limit is set by casting limitations for long vanes and extremely narrow impellers, by the hydraulic losses from flow through the small passages, and by the friction of a large disk rotating in the fluid. At the other end of the scale, for large capacities and low heads, high specific speed is necessary to keep the driver speed as high as practical. In large pumps the head per stage may be limited by mechanical considerations. At common motor speeds, single-stage pumps are limited

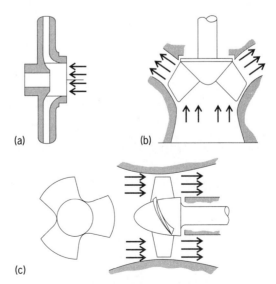

Fig. 3. Common classification of impellers. (*a*) Centrifugal for low speed. (*b*) Mixed-flow for intermediate speed. (*c*) Axial-flow or propeller for high speed.

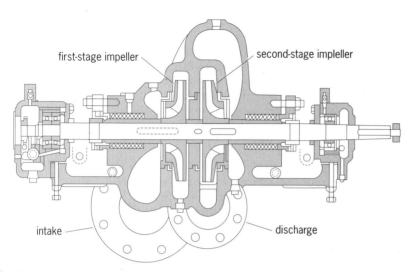

Fig. 4. Two-stage horizontally split casing pump.

first-stage impeller   second-stage impeller

intake   discharge

called cavitation. Higher operating speeds require higher suction pressure over the vapor pressure, spoken of as a net positive suction head. *See* CAVITATION.

Multistage pumps. When the required head exceeds that practical for a single-stage pump, several stages are employed. **Figure** 4 shows a typical two-stage pump with single-suction impellers mounted back to back to obtain an approximate balance of the hydraulic thrust developed by pressure acting on the greater area of the back side of the impeller. A modern high-pressure multistage centrifugal pump enclosed in a forged steel barrel with all the single-suction impellers facing in the same direction is shown in **Fig. 5**. In this design axial thrust is balanced by a rotating disk mounted at the high-pressure end of the pump. Leak-off from this balancing device, which is piped back to suction pressure, serves also to reduce, practically to suction pressure, the load on the stuffing box packing or seal at this end of the pump. Pumps of this type are built with 4 to 10 or more stages, depending on the speed, pressure, and capacity desired.

Another type of multistage pump is the vertical turbine or deep-well pump. The details of design and the choice of an impeller of relatively high specific speed are the result of a drastic limitation of the outside diameter required to fit inside drilled-well casings. Pumps of this type are built with as many as 20 or 30 stages for high lifts from relatively small-diameter wells. Pumps with this same arrangement are built with a closed-bottom cylindrical housing with the inlet connected near the top of the housing, for applications at moderate head and limited net positive suction head. The cylindrical housing, or can, is then located in a pit or dry well with suction

to heads of about 600 ft (180 m) per stage. However, at higher speeds heads up to about 2000 ft (600 m) per stage have been attained in multistage boiler feed pumps.

Cavitation limits also play a major part in limiting the operating speed and head per stage for any specified condition. High speeds of rotation require high velocities at the entrance to the impeller. Since the static pressure in a closed stream of fluid drops as velocity is increased, there is a limiting velocity at which the absolute pressure approaches the vapor pressure of the fluid. Beyond this, partial vaporization occurs and the subsequent collapse of these pockets of vapor causes noise, vibration, and ultimately destruction of the surrounding walls. This form of vaporization in a moving stream of fluid is

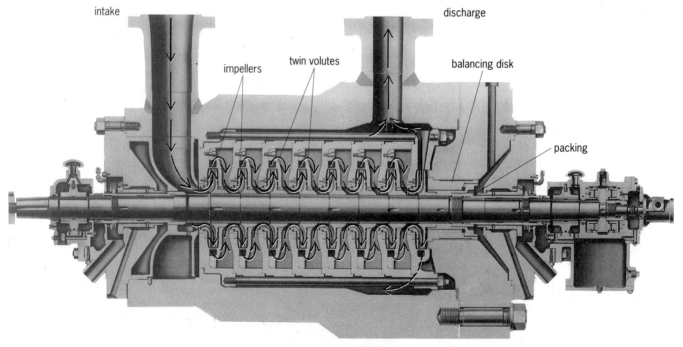

intake   discharge

impellers   twin volutes   balancing disk

packing

Fig. 5. High-pressure multistage centrifugal boiler-feed pump.

and discharge connections near ground or floor level. *See* PUMP; PUMPING MACHINERY.   Elliott F. Wright

Bibliography. J. W. Dufour and W. Nelson (eds.), *Centrifugal Pump Sourcebook*, 1992; I. J. Karassik and W. C. Krutzch, *Pump Handbook*, 3d ed., 2000; V. S. Lobanoff and R. R. Ross, *Centrifugal Pumps*, 1992; A. J. Stepanoff, *Centrifugal and Axial Flow Pumps: Theory, Design and Application*, 2d ed., 1957, reprint 1993.

Centrifugation

A mechanical method of separating immiscible liquids or solids from liquids by the application of centrifugal force. This force can be very great, and separations which proceed slowly by gravity can be speeded up enormously in centrifugal equipment.

When an object is made to move in a circular path, its direction must constantly be changed. To accomplish this, a force must be applied acting inward toward the center of rotation; otherwise the object would continue on a straight path. An equal and opposite force, the centrifugal force, acts in an outward direction on the rotating elements.

The magnitude of the centrifugal force exerted on an element depends on its angular velocity and its distance from the center of rotation. Centrifugal acceleration is usually compared with the gravitational acceleration at the Earth's surface, and centrifugal force is expressed as a relative force F_R, expressed in multiples of the force of gravity, or G's. Relative centrifugal force is given by Eq. (1), where D is

$$F_R = 5.59 \times 10^{-4} n^2 D = 0.204 V^2 / D \qquad (1)$$

the diameter of the circular path, in meters; n is the rotational speed, in rpm; and V is the peripheral speed of an element around the circle of rotation, in meters per second. In a centrifugal machine, the force varies radially from zero at the rotational axis to a maximum where D equals the inside diameter of the bowl or chamber. *See* CENTRIFUGAL FORCE.

Laboratory centrifuges are used for testing, control, and research. Industrial centrifuges find application in such diverse areas as sugar refining, chemical manufacture, dewatering diesel and jet fuel, and municipal waste treatment; they handle large amounts of material, yet require little space.

Stationary equipment: cyclones and nozzles. Centrifugal force is generated inside stationary equipment by introducing a high-velocity fluid stream tangentially into a cylindrical-conical chamber, forming a vortex of considerable intensity. Cyclone separators based on this principle remove liquid drops or solid particles from gases, down to 1 or 2 micrometers in diameter. Smaller units, called liquid cyclones, separate solid particles from liquids. The high velocity required at the inlet of a liquid cyclone is obtained with standard pumps. Units 4 to 12 in. (100 to 300 mm) in diameter make crude separations of large, heavy solid particles from liquids with a pres-

Comparison of bowl diameter and centrifugal force

Type of centrifuge	Bowl or basket diameter, in. (mm)	Rotational speed, rpm	Centrifugal force, multiples of gravity
Ultracentrifuge	0.2 (6)	230,000	177,000
Laboratory tubular	1.8 (45)	32,000	25,800
Industrial tubular	4 (100)	14,300	11,400
Disk	12 (300)	4,800	3,800
	18 (450)	3,200	2,600
Batch	30 (750)	1,900	1,500
	47 (1200)	1,200	970

sure drop across the cyclone of about 30–60 lb/in.^{2} (200–400 kilonewtons/m^2). More difficult separations may be done in banks of smaller units called hydroclones, each 0.4 in. (10 mm) in diameter, which can concentrate or remove 2–5-μm particles with a pressure drop of some 100 lb/in.^{2} (700 kN/m^2).

In the separation nozzle process for uranium enrichment, a dilute mixture of gaseous uranium hexafluoride (UF$_6$) and hydrogen is caused to flow at high velocity in a curved path of very small radius of curvature (about 0.004 in. or 0.1 mm). The high centrifugal force tends to concentrate the heavier ^{238}U near the outer wall. The issuing stream is divided in two and sent through a long series of similar nozzles to achieve the desired degree of separation.

Rotating equipment: centrifuges. Much higher centrifugal forces than in stationary equipment are generated in a mechanically driven bowl or basket, usually of metal, turning inside a stationary casing. Rotating a cylinder at high speed induces a considerable tensile stress in the cylinder wall; for a thin-walled cylinder, this self-stress is given by Eq. (2),

$$S_s = 2.74 \times 10^{-3} n^2 D^2 \rho_m \qquad (2)$$

where S_s is the stress, in N/m^2, and ρ_m is the density of the material of the wall, in kg/m^3. This limits the centrifugal force which can be generated in a unit of a given size and material of construction. Dividing Eq. (1) by Eq. (2) and rearranging gives Eq. (3). Thus

$$F_R = 0.20 S_s / D \rho_m \qquad (3)$$

if S_s is fixed at the maximum stress allowable in the material, the maximum relative centrifugal force varies inversely with cylinder diameter. Very high forces, therefore, can be developed only in very small centrifuges. The **table** shows forces generated in various types and sizes of centrifuges at a typical peripheral speed of 246 ft/s (75 m/s).

Centrifuges

There are two major types of centrifuges: sedimenters and filters. Either type may be operated batchwise, with intermittent removal of the separated phase; semibatchwise, with essentially continuous removal of the liquid and intermittent removal of the solids; or continuously, with steady uninterrupted removal of both liquid and solids. Special sedimenting gas centrifuges find application in uranium enrichment.

Sedimenting centrifuges. A sedimenting centrifuge contains a solid-wall cylinder or cone rotating about a horizontal or vertical axis. An annular layer of liquid, of fixed thickness, is held against the wall by centrifugal force; because this force is so large compared with that of gravity, the liquid surface is essentially parallel with the axis of rotation regardless of the orientation of the unit. Heavy phases "sink" outwardly from the center, and less dense phases "rise" inwardly. Heavy solid particles collect on the wall and must be periodically or continuously removed.

The sedimentation velocity of fine particles in a centrifuge is given by the form of Stokes' law shown in Eq. (4), where u is the setting velocity, n the rota-

$$u = \frac{2\pi^2 n^2 D_p^2 \rho r}{9\mu} \qquad (4)$$

tional speed, D_p the particle diameter, ρ the particle density, r the radial distance from the axis of rotation, and μ the fluid viscosity. The setting velocity of small low-density particles, to which Stokes' law applies, increases directly with the relative centrifugal force. That of large heavy particles, to which Stokes' law does not apply, increases less rapidly with an increase in centrifugal force.

Sedimenting centrifuges are divided into small, high-speed machines, which generate very high centrifugal forces, and large, comparatively slow-speed machines, which handle large amounts of material. Each group is further subdivided into liquid-liquid separators or decanters, clarifiers, sludge separators, and classifiers. Special machines partially separate gas mixtures for isotope enrichment.

Separators. Bottle centrifuges are batch laboratory centrifuges for research, analysis, or very small-scale production. The mixture to be separated is poured into bottles or test tubes which are placed in a rotor head and spun for a known length of time. An ultracentrifuge is a research unit which generates extremely high centrifugal forces inside a rotor around 0.2 in. (6 mm) in diameter (see table); sedimentation of extremely fine particles or macromolecules may be observed through a microscope and a transparent window in the rotor. *See* ULTRACENTRIFUGE.

Bowls in high-speed centrifuges for industrial use rotate about a vertical axis; liquid feed enters at or near the bottom of the bowl and escapes from the top. Stability considerations dictate one of two preferred bowl shapes: tall narrow cylinders or squat cylinders with a conical top. Tubular centrifuges typify the first design. Industrial models are 4 in. (100 mm) in diameter and 30 in. (750 mm) long and process 1.5 to 10 gal/min (0.3 to 2.5 m³/h) of liquid. They serve as centrifugal decanters and as clarifiers to remove very small amounts of solids from liquids. A maximum of about 11 lb (5 kg) settled solids may accumulate in the bowl before the machine must be stopped and cleaned.

The bowl in a disk centrifuge (**Fig. 1**) is typically 8 to 16 in. (200 to 400 mm) in diameter and con-

tains a large number of closely spaced "disks" which are actually truncated cones stacked one above the other and perforated to form passages for the liquid. The disks shorten the distance that a particle or drop must travel before being separated, compared with the distance in a tubular unit. Despite the somewhat lower centrifugal force, therefore, disk centrifuges are effective separators, especially for emulsion concentration. As shown in Fig. 1, feed enters the top of the machine and flows outward into the bowl near the bottom; separated liquids are removed through outlets at the top, while solids collect in the bowl. Large units can process 660 gal/min (150 m³/h) or more and retain 110 to 130 lb (50 to 60 kg) of settled solids before cleaning becomes necessary.

Clarifiers. In a self-discharging separator, the settled solids are removed in more or less concentrated form through openings in the bowl wall. The bowl in a nozzle-discharge centrifuge is usually conical at the bottom as well as at the top. Where the bowl diameter is a maximum, 2 to 12 nozzles, lined with abrasive-resistant material, allow a slurry to issue continuously from the periphery of the bowl. Part of the slurry may be recycled to the bottom of the bowl to build up the solids concentration. Some nozzle machines are three-way separators, discharging two clarified liquids and a solids suspension. In a valve-discharge centrifuge, the peripheral openings are circumferential slits, covered most of the time by a piston. Periodically the piston is lowered by hydraulic or mechanical action, and concentrated solids are forcefully ejected, with some liquid, into the casing.

Sludge separators. In a sludge separator the continuous removal of solids as concentrated sludge requires that settled solids be moved mechanically out of the liquid and allowed to drain while subjected to centrifugal force. This is done in a scroll-conveyor centrifuge (**Fig. 2**), in which a cylindrical bowl with a conical end section rotates about a horizontal axis. Feed enters through a stationary central pipe and sprays outward into a pond or annular layer of liquid inside the bowl. Clarified liquid escapes through overflow ports in the cover plate on the large end

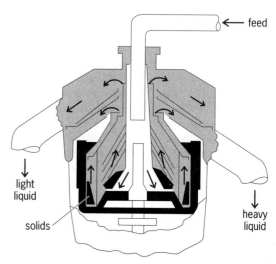

Fig. 1. Cutaway view of disk centrifuge bowl.

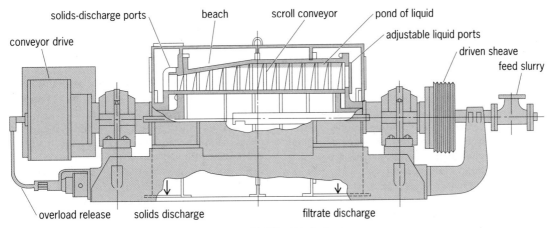

Fig. 2. Cylindrical-conical helical-conveyor centrifuge. (*Bird Machine Co.*)

of the bowl; the position of these ports fixes the depth of the pond. Solids settle under centrifugal force to the inner wall of the bowl, where a helical or scroll conveyor, turning slightly slower than the bowl, moves the solids out of the pond and up the slanting beach to discharge openings in the small end of the cone. Wash liquid may be sprayed on the solids as they travel up the beach. In some designs, feed enters near the large end of the bowl and liquid and solids travel in the same direction, with clarified liquid removed by skimmer pipes; this is effective in concentrating fine low-density solid particles encountered in sewage sludge treatment. Industrial sludge separators range in diameter from 16 to 55 in. (400 to 1400 mm), and separate from 1.1 to 2.2 tons/h (1 to 2 metric tons/h) of solids in a small machine to as much as 110 tons/h (100 metric tons/h) in a large one.

Classifiers. Classification is the sorting of solid particles in a fluid stream into two or more fractions according to particle size. Centrifugal classifiers are used when particles are too fine for separations by gravity. Scroll-conveyor centrifuges find application in large-scale wet grinding operations using ball mills, for example, separating acceptably fine particles from the oversize ones which are returned to the mill for regrinding. High-speed tubular centrifuges remove particles of grit from ultrafine cosmetics, dyes, and pigments.

Gas centrifuges. High-speed centrifuges are extensively used for uranium enrichment, partially separating ^{235}U from ^{238}U. They operate on gaseous uranium hexafluoride at moderate temperatures. The centrifugal force tends to compress the gas into a region near the bowl wall, while thermal motion tends to distribute the molecules uniformly throughout the available volume. Since thermal motion has a greater effect on light molecules than on heavy ones, a concentration gradient is established, with a higher concentration of the heavier molecules near the wall. The theoretical separation factor α is given by Eq. (5), where M_A and M_B are the molecular weights

$$\alpha = \exp \frac{(M_A - M_B)V^2}{2RTg_c} \qquad (5)$$

of the heavy and light components, respectively; V is the peripheral velocity; R is the gas constant; T is the absolute temperature; and g_c is the Newton's-law conversion factor. Since α depends on the difference between the molecular weights of the isotopes and not on their ratio, gas centrifuges have much higher separation factors than do gas diffusion units.

Gas centrifuges operate at very high speeds, for the separative capacity of a given unit depends on the fourth power of the peripheral velocity. In the typical machine shown in **Fig. 3**, a tubular rotor perhaps 8 in. (200 mm) in diameter rotates in an evacuated casing with a peripheral velocity of more

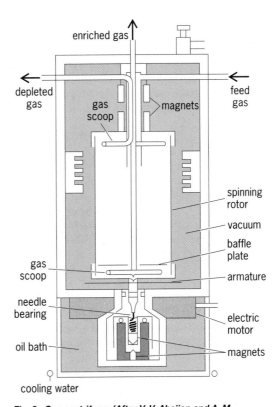

Fig. 3. Gas centrifuge. (*After V. V. Abajian and A. M. Fishman, Supplying enriched uranium, Phys. Today, 26(8):23–29, 1973*)

than 660 ft/s (200 m/s), about three times that in conventional industrial centrifuges. The centrifugal force at the bowl wall is more than 40,000 G. Feed gas enters the top near the axis of rotation; enriched gas is collected by a gas scoop near the bottom of the bowl, and depleted gas by a scoop near the bottom. Because of the high separation factor, relatively few centrifuges need be connected in series to achieve a substantial change in the concentration of ^{235}U. Productive capacities are low, however, and thousands of machines operating in parallel are needed for practical rates of throughput.

Filtering centrifugals. Centrifuges which separate by filtration are known as centrifugals or centrifugal filters. Solids and liquid are introduced into a rotating basket; after the liquid has been removed through the basket wall, the retained cake of solids is washed, spun dry, and removed. Centrifugals operate batchwise or continuously; various types differ primarily in the length of the cycle times and in the way in which solids are removed from the basket.

In large batch centrifugals, up to 47 in. (1200 mm) in basket diameter, the basket turns about a vertical axis. A solid cake 2-6 in. (50-150 mm) thick is formed, washed, spun (often at a higher speed), and then cut out of the basket, now turning very slowly, with a traveling knife. Discharged solids fall through openings in the basket floor; discharged liquid, or centrate, is removed from the casing. In some machines the cycle steps are fully automated. Free-draining crystals are separated quasicontinuously in short-cycle automatic horizontal-axis machines with baskets 20-40 in. (500-1000 mm) in diameter; solids are cut out every 45-150 s at full basket speed by a heavy-duty knife. Truly continuous filtering units for the large crystals are typified by the pusher centrifugal (**Fig. 4**), in which the solid cake, 1 to 3 in. (25 to 75 mm) thick, is moved over the inner surface of the perforated basket by a reciprocating piston. Each forward piston stroke moves the crystals an inch or so toward the basket lip; on the return stroke, a space

is opened on the filtering surface on which more solids can be deposited. When crystals reach the basket lip, they fly outward into the casing. Filtrate and any wash liquid sprayed on the crystals during their travel leave the casing through separate outlets. Multistage pusher centrifugals are used when the solids cannot be pushed the fairly long distances required in the single-stage unit shown in Fig. 4.

A filtering centrifuge operates on the same principle as the spinner in a household washing machine. The basket wall is perforated and lined with a filter medium such as a cloth or a fine screen; liquid passes through the wall, impelled by centrifugal force, leaving behind a cake of solids on the filter medium. The filtration rate increases with the centrifugal force and with the permeability of the solid cake. Some compressible solids do not filter well in a centrifugal because the particles deform under centrifugal force and the permeability of the cake is greatly reduced. The amount of liquid adhering to the solids after they have been spun also depends on the centrifugal force applied; in general, it is substantially less in the cake from other types of filtration devices. *See* ME-CHANICAL SEPARATION TECHNIQUES.   Julian C. Smith

Biological Applications

Biologists have long been interested in the effects of high centrifugal forces on cells, developing embryos, and protozoa. These studies have yielded valuable information on the properties of cells, such as surface tension, relative viscosity of the cytoplasm, and the spatial and functional interrelationship of cell organelles when redistributed in intact cells. The last finding led to the discovery that in a variety of invertebrate egg cells any disturbance of the intracellular organization of the cytoplasm will severely affect future development. *See* DEVELOPMENTAL BIOLOGY.

Another interest, partly in relation to the space program, has been the physiological effects of centrifugal forces on intact organisms, including humans. These forces are identical with the high gravitational forces astronauts must face on leaving and reentering the Earth's atmosphere. Such studies have been useful to determine the maximum forces that a person can tolerate and to develop equipment to offset the drastic effects. *See* AEROSPACE MEDICINE.

Thus the centrifuge has been applied to the whole gamut of biological systems, from humans to cells to subcellular organelles to biological molecules. It is routinely used in hospitals and clinics to collect blood cells, bacteria, and viruses, but its prime importance in biology is to isolate and determine the biological properties and functions of subcellular organelles and large molecules.

Cellular studies. During the first half of the twentieth century those interested in cell biology were generally segregated into two separate disciplines, cell biology and biochemistry. Cell biologists studied sections of tissues that had been subjected to various fixatives and then stained. From these studies evolved the identification of cell structures, but since these organelles had been rendered inactive by fixation, their function could only be guessed.

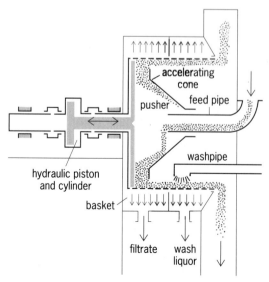

Fig. 4. Pusher-type centrifugal.

accelerating cone

pusher

feed pipe

hydraulic piston and cylinder

washpipe

basket

filtrate   wash liquor

The biochemists viewed living systems as an enzymatic and metabolite "soup." They thoroughly ground up tissues and by primarily chemical procedures isolated enzymes and substrates. Again, however, no attempts were made to correlate the discovered metabolic-enzyme pathways with their location in intact cells. *See* CELL BIOLOGY; CELL METABOLISM; CYTOCHEMISTRY.

The modern technique for the isolation of cell parts was first introduced by R. Bensley and N. L. Hoerr in 1934, when they disrupted guinea pig liver cells and isolated mitochondria. A. Claude soon saw the importance of this technique, and from 1938 to 1946 extended the findings of Bensley and Hoerr by isolating two fractions, a "large granule" fraction, which was mitochondria, and a fraction of submicroscopic granules, which he called microsomes. From these beginnings additional pioneering investigators developed the centrifugal techniques of cell fractionation now commonly used.

Differential centrifugation. A tissue, such as the liver, or a population of cells, is broken up in one of several ways. The most common method is mechanical disruption, by grinding the tissue in a test tube with a glass or Teflon pestle (tissue grinder) or with a high-speed mixer such as a Waring blender. To be certain that the cellular particles retain their structure and function, much care is taken not to destroy them by overvigorous cell disruption, and to place the disrupted cell material, or homogenate, into a sucrose and salt solution that is isotonic and as close as possible to the natural conditions inside the intact cell.

The homogenate is then centrifuged in a medium at various centrifugal forces to separate the cellular organelles from each other. Organelles that differ in density, size, or shape sediment at different rates in a field of centrifugal force. Centrifugation simply magnifies the force of gravitational acceleration, which is normally constant, 392 in./s^2 (980 cm/s^2), and accounts for the weight of objects on Earth. Spinning a particle at high speeds produces a force on it proportional to the mass of the particle, the rotational speed or angular velocity in going in circles, and the distance from the axis or point of rotation to the particle. This is stated in Eq. (6), where G is the

$$G = \omega^2 r \qquad (6)$$

gravitational acceleration, ω is the angular velocity, and r is the distance from the point of rotation to the particle. The angular velocity can be determined by knowing the rotor speed according to Eq. (7). It

$$\omega = \frac{2\pi(\text{rpm})}{60} \qquad (7)$$

is thus possible to calculate the relative centrifugal force G, knowing the revolution per minute (rpm) and the radius r of the centrifuge, using Eq. (8).

$$G = \frac{4\pi^2(\text{rpm})^2 r}{3600} = 1.11 \times 10^{-5}(\text{rpm})^2 r \qquad (8)$$

The rate at which a particle sediments in a cen-

trifugal field is proportional to the centrifugal force, but also is dependent on the density and viscosity of the medium through which it is passing. This relationship is shown by Eq. (9), which states that t

$$t = \frac{9}{2} \frac{\eta}{\omega^2 r^2 (d_p - d_m)} \cdot 2.3 \log \frac{R_{\max}}{R_{\min}} \qquad (9)$$

is the time in which a fairly spherical particle of radius r and density d_p travels from the top of the centrifuge tube, $R_{\min}$, to the bottom of the tube, $R_{\max}$, in a medium having a known viscosity η and density d_m. This makes it possible to determine the time needed to centrifuge to the base of a tube a population of relatively homogenous particles from a larger population of particles of widely varying size and density, such as occurs in a cell homogenate.

This was the basis for the first techniques developed for cell fractionation, and is called differential centrifugation. These procedures have now been standardized. Tissue, such as liver, is homogenized at 32°F (0°C) in a sucrose solution (0.22–45 M) containing both a buffer to stabilize the pH and a salt, usually magnesium chloride. The homogenate is then centrifuged at 600 G for 10 min, also at 32°F (0°C). The sediment, which is forced to the bottom of the centrifuge tube, forms a solid pellet, and the overlying solution, or supernatant, is now removed and placed in another centrifuge tube. Called the nuclear fraction, the sedimented pellet consists mainly of nuclei which are the largest and densest organelles present in cells. The supernatant is centrifuged at a higher speed to attain a higher centrifugal force, 10,000 G, for 15 min. Another group of particles, the mitochondria, now sediment. This process can then be repeated, using higher centrifugal forces, to obtain the lysosome and microsome fractions from each succeeding supernatant medium. Finally, the supernatant, following centrifugation at forces of 100,000 G for one hour or longer, is essentially nonparticulate and is called the soluble fraction, containing enzymes and other small-molecular-weight substances that are not associated with any cell organelles. *See* CELL (BIOLOGY).

Density gradient method. Since there was a great deal of cross-contamination of particles among the various fractions, modifications soon developed to improve the separation of the cell organelles into purer fractions. The chief improvement involved the formation of a density gradient in the medium through which the particles migrate by altering the concentration of the sucrose or the salt. The gradient is so formed that the density is least at the top of the tube and is greatest at the bottom. A tissue homogenate is placed on top of a density gradient, and in the presence of centrifugal force each particle sediments to a specific zone of the gradient with an equivalent density to that of the particle. In this way zones, or bands, of the various cell organelles are formed with a minimum of contamination of other particles of differing size and density. A number of variations of the density gradient centrifugation method have been developed to further refine the quality of separation of particles of similar size and shape but of slightly different density.

Another technique has enabled large volumes of material to undergo separation by a continuous flow system, in which homogenate is continually being added to a centrifugal field while the displaced material, which is essentially nonparticulate supernatant, is being discarded. Large quantities of particulate material may thus be accumulated.

Although biochemists had used centrifuges previously, with the advent of these methods cell biologists began to look at both the chemical nature and the morphology or structures of the isolated particles. In this way function could be correlated with structure and various metabolic processes could be localized in intact cells. It was established that the mitochondria were the centers for oxidative phosphorylation involved in the synthesis of adenosine triphosphate (ATP). The crude "microsome" fraction was found to consist of membranes and associated particles called ribosomes. Biochemical procedures had shown that nearly all protein synthesis occurred in the microsome fraction. By separating the membranes from the ribosomes by mild detergent treatment, the ribosome fraction retained protein synthetic activity. Several years later, ultracareful homogenization of developing red blood cells (reticulocytes) showed the ribosomes usually were aggregated and held together by a strand of ribonucleic acid (RNA). This has led to the polysome concept, in which the strand of RNA is messenger RNA (mRNA), which contains the genetic information that is obtained from the nucleus to make specific proteins. *See* RIBONUCLEIC ACID (RNA); RIBOSOMES.

A new particle was also discovered by centrifugation procedures, the lysosomes. These particles sediment very close to the mitochondria, but by careful manipulation they were separated. Lysosomes perform many of the digestive functions of the cell and contain many hydrolytic enzymes. *See* LYSOSOME; MITOCHONDRIA.

By these centrifugal procedures, then, it has been possible to isolate cell components, determine their composition and their metabolic activity, and examine the components to discover what they look like in order to find the most comparable structures in intact cells.

Molecular studies. Another valuable avenue of research and discovery opened by density gradient centrifugation techniques has been to find and isolate the large macromolecules that are involved in the various metabolic events of the cell, particularly for the nucleic acids. A complete description is not possible, but key examples may be given. There are slight but definite differences in the density of deoxyribonucleic acid (DNA) of various species isolated and centrifuged in cesium chloride gradients. This centrifugation depends of the base composition of DNA (ratio of adenine and thymine to cytosine and guanine). *See* NUCLEIC ACID.

Isotopic labeling combined with density gradient centrifugation has proved extremely useful to define

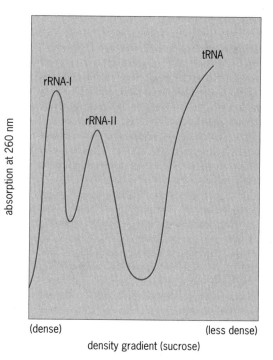

Fig. 5. Sedimentation profile showing ribosomal and transfer ribonucleic acid.

the nature and role of the various RNAs in protein synthesis. A sedimentation "profile" is illustrated in **Fig. 5**, showing the presence of the two species of RNA found in ribosomes (rRNA-I and rRNA-II) and transfer RNA (tRNA). It is known that there is a third type of RNA, messenger mRNA, that is involved with protein synthesis. It is rapidly synthesized and is rather unstable. This synthesis characteristic can be used to advantage by rapidly exposing cells or a tissue to a precursor molecule of RNA labeled with an isotope such as ^{32}P or ^{14}C. After this brief exposure the cells are homogenized and the RNA extracted and centrifuged in a density gradient centrifuge. Fractions are removed drop by drop and analyzed for the presence of RNA by ultraviolet light, which is absorbed at 260 nanometer wavelength, and for

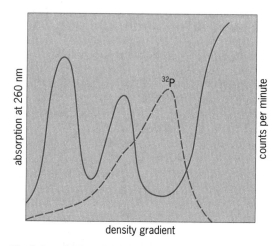

Fig. 6. Localization of radioactivity for RNA labeled with ^{32}P. Sedimentation profile of Fig. 5 is shown.

radioactivity. **Figure 6** illustrates that most of the radioactivity is localized between the tRNA and rRNA-II peaks, and composes a small portion of the total RNA of the cell. *See* PROTEIN.

A final distinction in centrifugation methodology may be made. If the contents of the centrifuge are to be analyzed after the centrifuge stops, as shown in Figs. 5 and 6, the procedure is called preparative; if the sample is examined optically during centrifugation, the procedure is called analytical. This last method is particularly important to determine the sedimentation coefficient and the molecular weight of the molecules under investigation. *See* MOLECULAR BIOLOGY.

W. Auclair

Bibliography. D. Green (ed.), *Perry's Chemical Engineer's Handbook*, 7th ed., 1991; W. L. McCabe, J. C. Smith, and P. Harriott, *Unit Operations of Chemical Engineering*, 5th ed., 1993; D. Rickwood (ed.), *Centrifugation*, 2d ed., 1984; D. Rickwood (ed.), *Preparative Centrifugation: A Practical Approach*, 1993; R. W. Rousseau, *Handbook of Separation Process Technology*, 1987.

Centriole

A morphologically complex cellular organelle at the focus of centrosomes in animal cells and some lower plant cells. Prokaryotes, some lower animal cells, higher plant cells, and a few exceptional higher animal cells do not have centrioles in their centrosomes. Centrioles typically are not found singly; the centrosome of higher animal cells contains a pair of centrioles (together called the diplosome), arranged at right angles to each other and separated by a distance ranging from 250 nanometers to several micrometers. *See* CENTROSOME.

Structure and composition. Centrioles are typically 300–700 nm in length and 250 nm in diameter. Although they can be detected by the light microscope, an electron microscope is required to resolve their substructure. At the electron microscopic level, a centriole consists of a hollow cylinder of nine triplet microtubules in a pinwheel arrangement (see **illus.**). Within each triplet, one microtubule (the A tubule) is a complete microtubule, while the others (the B and C tubules) share a portion of their wall with the adjacent tubule. In some cells these nine triplet microtubules are embedded in a densely staining cylindrical matrix that is spatially distinct from the pericentriolar material of the centrosome. Structures found in the lumen or core of the centriole include linkers between the triplets, granules, fibers, a cartwheel structure at one end of the centriole, and sometimes a small vesicle.

Centrioles have a close structural similarity to basal bodies, which organize the axoneme of cilia and flagella. In many types of mammalian somatic cells, the older of the two centrioles in the centrosome can act as a basal body during the interphase portion of the cell cycle. In such cases, tapered projections, called basal feet, are often observed on the external surface

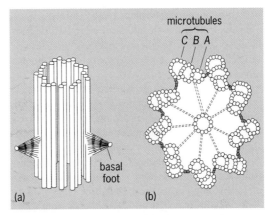

Diagrams of centriole showing (*a*) arrangement of microtubules and (*b*) cross section of proximal end, with nine triplet microtubules (A, B, and C) and central cartwheel structure.

of the centriole that is acting as the basal body. Microtubules are attached to the globular tips of the basal feet and may serve to anchor this centriole in the cell.

The centriole is a polar organelle, having a proximal end and a distal end relative to the cell center. When a centriole acts as a basal body, the ciliary or flagellar axoneme is nucleated from the distal end of the centriole. Daughter centrioles are formed perpendicular to the proximal end of the parent centriole. Within the centriole, the cartwheel structure is located at the proximal end.

The molecular composition of the centriole is poorly understood because it has not been possible to isolate enough centrioles in a sufficiently pure form to conduct biochemical analyses. The microtubule protein, tubulin, is a major constituent of centrioles; however, the identities of the proteins that make up the rest of the centriole are not known. Centrioles probably contain ribonucleic acid (RNA), but it is not known if this RNA is specific to the centriole or only represents cytoplasmic RNAs that happen to reside there. A centriole-specific role for this RNA, if any, has yet to be demonstrated.

Microtubules. During interphase the centrosome nucleates the array of cytoplasmic microtubules; later in the cell cycle the centrosome duplicates, and the daughter centrosomes form the poles of the mitotic (or meiotic) spindle. The terms "centriole" and "centrosome" are sometimes erroneously used interchangeably; centrioles are not the centrosome itself, but a part of it. The centrosome of higher animal cells has at its center a pair of centrioles, arranged at right angles to each other and separated by 250 nm or less. Spindle microtubules are nucleated by gamma tubulin containing ring complexes within the pericentriolar material, an amorphous cloud of densely staining material surrounding the centriole pair. Centrioles do not nucleate spindle microtubules. In some cells the pericentriolar material surrounds primarily the older of the two centrioles; the younger (daughter) centriole acquires pericentriolar material only later in the cell cycle when it separates from its mother and assembles its own daughter centriole.

Distribution and replication. During interphase the centriole pair and associated pericentriolar material lie closely apposed to the nuclear envelope or sometimes lie within a small indentation in the nuclear envelope.

Late in the G1 (first gap) phase of the cell cycle, the two centrioles separate slightly from each other and lose their orthogonal arrangement. When the cell initiates deoxyribonucleic acid (DNA) synthesis, short daughter centrioles (called procentrioles) are assembled at right angles to and separated slightly from the proximal ends of both mature centrioles. It is not known how daughter centrioles are formed in this way. The finding that cells from which centrioles are microsurgically removed cannot reassemble centrioles suggests that daughter centriole formation normally requires a specific organizing activity provided by the mother centriole. The procentrioles later elongate during the S (DNA synthesis) and G2 (second gap) phases of the cell cycle, reaching their mature length during mitosis or the following G1 phase. At a variable time in the G2 phase of the cell cycle, the centrosome as a whole splits, with a mother-daughter pair of centrioles distributed to each daughter centrosome. During mitosis, a pair of centrioles is found at the focus of both spindle poles. *See* CELL CYCLE; MITOSIS.

Functions. The only clearly demonstrated role for the centriole is to organize the axoneme of the primary cilium in cells having this structure, and the flagellar axoneme in sperm cells. Other possible functions for centrioles are a matter of debate. Some authorities assert that when present in the centrosome, centrioles contain activities that serve to organize the centrosome, determine the number of centrosomes in a cell, and control the doubling of the centrosome as a whole before mitosis. Evidence comes from observations that the introduction of extra centrioles into cell leads to the formation of extra centrosomes. Also, the ability of a centrosome to double between divisions is correlated with the number of centrioles that it contains.

Others believe that centrioles have no role in the formation and doubling of the centrosomes but are associated with the centrosomes only to ensure the equal distribution of basal bodies during cell division. This view is supported by the observation that all higher plant cells, most protozoa and algae and fungi, and a few animal cells form functional centrosomes without recognizable centrioles. At a minimum, the nine-triplet-microtubule aspect of the centriole is probably not required for centrosome formation or doubling. In principle, the nonmicrotubule components of the centriole might play important roles in centrosome doubling, but this has not yet been proved directly. *See* CELL (BIOLOGY); CELL DIVISION.   Greenfield Sluder

Bibliography. M. Carroll, *Organelles*, 1989; H. Hermann, *Cell Biology*, 1990; J. L. Hiatt et al., *Cell Biology-Histology*, 1993; K. Miller (ed.), *Advances in Cell Biology*, 1989; C. Widnell, *Essentials of Cell Biology*, 1990.

Centripetal force

The inward force required to keep a particle or an object moving in a circular path. It can be shown that a particle moving in a circular path has an acceleration toward the center of the circle along a radius. *See* ACCELERATION.

This radial acceleration, called the centripetal acceleration, is such that, if a particle has a linear or tangential velocity v when moving in a circular path of radius R, the centripetal acceleration is v^2/R. If the particle undergoing the centripetal acceleration has a mass M, then by Newton's second law of motion the centripetal force F_C is in the direction of the acceleration. This is expressed by Eq. (1), where ω

$$F_C = Mv^2/R = MR\omega^2 \qquad (1)$$

is the constant angular velocity and is equal to v/R. From the laws of motion given by Isaac Newton in his treatise *The Principia*, it follows that the natural motion of an object is one with constant speed in a straight line, and that a force is necessary if the object is to depart from this type of motion. Whenever an object moves in a curve, a centripetal force is necessary. In circular motion the tangential speed is constant but is changing direction at the constant rate of ω, so the centripetal force along the radius is the only force involved.

For example, a small heavy object tied by a cord of length R, with the other end of the cord held in the hand, can be whirled in a horizontal circular path. The person holding the cord has to exert an inward pull, the centripetal force, to maintain this circular motion (**Fig. 1**). When turning a corner in a car, the centripetal force necessary for the turn is provided by the frictional force between the road and the wheels. If the road is banked, then a component of the weight of the car can supply the necessary centripetal force. For a given angle of banking and radius of turn it is necessary to maintain a certain

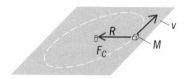

Fig. 1. Diagram of centripetal force in circular motion.

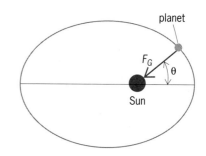

Fig. 2. Planet moving in an ellipse about the Sun.

speed, if the component of weight is to exactly provide the necessary centripetal force. *See* CENTRIFUGAL FORCE.

As another example (**Fig. 2**), consider the motion of the Earth or other planet about the Sun. The planets move in elliptical paths about the Sun. This motion is maintained by the gravitational attraction of the planet and Sun. In this case the radial distance between planet and Sun changes during the motion, so that the gravitational force is not in general equal to the centripetal force. If F_G is the gravitational force of attraction between the planet and Sun and R the distance between them, then Eq. (2) holds, where

$$F_G = M(a_R - R\omega^2) = M[d^2R/dt^2 - R(d\theta/dt)^2]   (2)$$

M is the mass of the planet, $a_R = d^2R/dt^2$ is the acceleration along the radial distance R, and $d\theta/dt$ is the instantaneous angular velocity. Since the path of a planet about the Sun is elliptical rather than circular, another force, beside the centripetal one, is required. *See* ORBITAL MOTION.   R. J. Stephenson

Bibliography. F. Bueche, *Principles of Physics*, 6th ed., 1994; D. Halliday, R. Resnick, and K. Krane, *Physics*, 5th ed., 2002; F. Miller, Jr., D. Schroeer, and R. W. Stanley, *College Physics*, 6th ed., 1989; H. D. Young, et al., *Sears and Zemansky's University Physics*, 10th ed., 2000.

Centrode

The path traced by the instantaneous center of a plane figure when it undergoes plane motion. If a plane rigid body is constrained to move in its own plane but is otherwise free to undergo an arbitrary translational and rotational motion, it is found that at any instant there exists a point, called the instantaneous center, about which the body is rotating. The path that this instantaneous center traces out in space as the motion unfolds is called the space centrode. The path that it would trace out in a coordinate system which is rigidly attached to the body is called the body centrode. The motion may therefore be specified, when the two centrodes are given, by allowing one curve to roll without slipping along the other. *See* FOUR-BAR LINKAGE; RIGID-BODY DYNAMICS.   Herbert C. Corben; Bernard Goodman

Centrohelida

An order of the Heliozoia. There is a central cell mass from which thin stiff arms radiate. The arms are supported internally by arrays of microtubules which terminate internally on a central granule, the centroplast, and the nucleus has an eccentric position. In the majority of species, the body is coated with a layer of siliceous spines or spicules and measures from 20 to 50 micrometers. These organisms are found in fresh-water and marine habitats, feeding on other protozoa, which adhere to the arms after colliding with them. In addition to about five genera

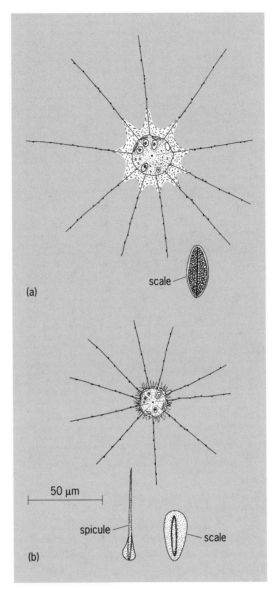

Centrohelida. (a) *Raphidiophrys ambigua*. (b) *Acanthocystis erinaceoides*.

which certainly are closely related (of which *Acanthocystis* and *Raphidiophrys* are among the most widely represented; see **illus.**), the group contains a variety of other Heliozoia of uncertain affinities. *See* ACTINOPODEA; HELIOZOIA; PROTOZOA; SARCODINA.
David J. Patterson

Bibliography. J. J. Lee, S. H. Hutner, and E. C. Bovee, *Illustrated Guide to the Protozoa*, Society of Protozoologists, 1984.

Centroids (mathematics)

Points positioned identically with the centers of gravity of corresponding homogenous thin plates or thin wires. Centroids are involved in the analysis of certain problems of mechanics, for example, the phenomenon of bending.

Centroids by integration. The centroid of plane area A is point C (**Fig. 1**). Coordinates $\bar{x}$ and $\bar{y}$ of C as

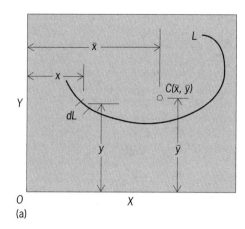

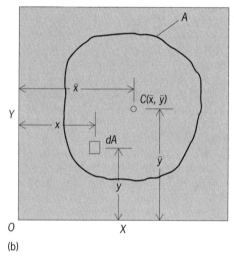

Fig. 1. Notation of integral equations for centroids.
(a) Centroid of line. (b) Centroid of area.

referred to the indicated X and Y coordinate axes are given by Eqs. (1). Similarly, the centroidal coordinates of plane curve L are given by Eqs. (2). In

$$\bar{x} = \frac{\int x\, dA}{\int dA} \qquad \bar{y} = \frac{\int y\, dA}{\int dA} \qquad (1)$$

$$\bar{x} = \frac{\int x\, dL}{\int dL} \qquad \bar{y} = \frac{\int y\, dL}{\int dL} \qquad (2)$$

these equations x and y are the coordinate locations of infinitesimal area element dA and infinitesimal line element dL, respectively.

Centroids by summation. Whether or not the above integrals can be evaluated, approximate values of $\bar{x}$ and $\bar{y}$ may be determined by summation (**Fig. 2**). To this end, area A is divided as shown into n finite elements whose areas $\Delta A_1, \ldots, \Delta A_n$ contain center points $P_1, \ldots, P_n$. Coordinates $\bar{x}, \bar{y}$ of the centroid of area A are then approximately given by Eqs. (3).

$$\bar{x} = \frac{x_1 \Delta A_1 + \cdots + x_n \Delta A_n}{\Delta A_1 + \cdots + \Delta A_n}$$

$$\bar{y} = \frac{y_1 \Delta A_1 + \cdots + y_n \Delta A_n}{\Delta A_1 + \cdots + \Delta A_n} \qquad (3)$$

In analogous fashion, equations for the centroid coordinates of a planar line L are, in summation, given

as Eqs. (4). Accuracy of the method increases as the

$$\bar{x} = \frac{\sum\limits_{i=1}^{n} x_i \Delta L_i}{\sum\limits_{i=1}^{n} \Delta L_i} \qquad \bar{y} = \frac{\sum\limits_{i=1}^{n} y_i \Delta L_i}{\sum\limits_{i=1}^{n} \Delta L_i} \qquad (4)$$

number of elements increases.

Principle of symmetry. The centroid of a geometrical figure (line, area, or volume) is at a point on a line or in a plane of symmetry of the figure.

A plane figure is symmetrical about a straight line if the figure may be decomposed into pairs of equal elements so that each pair is in reflected position about a point on the line. If every such pair is reflected in the same point, it is the point of symmetry of the figure.

Lines LL are lines of symmetry (and contain the centroids) of both the perimeter and area of the outlined shapes (**Fig. 3**). Point C is the point of symmetry (and the centroid) of the figure (**Fig. 4**).

Surface and volume of revolution. By the following theorems stated by Pappus of Alexandria (Greek mathematician, third century) a knowledge of the

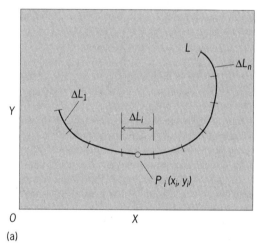

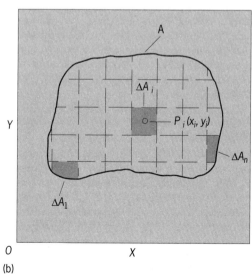

Fig. 2. Determination of centroids by summation.
(a) Centroid of line. (b) Centroid of area.

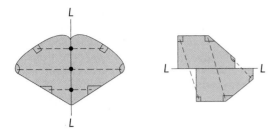

Fig. 3. Plane areas symmetric about a line.

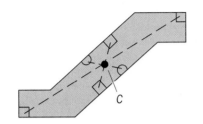

Fig. 4. Plane area symmetric about a point.

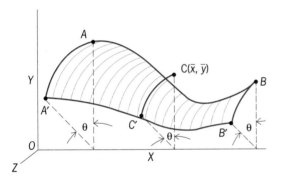

Fig. 5. Use of the centroid of a line to find area of a face of revolution, according to Pappus' theorem.

centroids of plane curves and plane areas may be employed to determine, respectively, surface areas of revolution and volumes of revolution.

Pappus' theorem of surface area is that the area of a surface generated by rotating a plane curve about a nonintersecting line in its plane is the product of the length of the curve and the arc length traveled by its centroid. Area S of the surface (indicated by shaded lines in **Fig. 5**) generated by rotating plane curve AB of length L an amount θ radians about the X axis from position AB in OXY to position $A'B'$ is $S = \bar{y}\theta L$, where $\bar{y}$ is the centroidal coordinate of curve AB referred to the OXY coordinate plane, and $\bar{y}\theta = CC'$ is the arc length traveled by its centroid.

Pappus' theorem of volume is that the volume of a solid generated by rotating a plane area about a non-intersecting line in its plane is the product of the area and the arc length traveled by its centroid. *See* CENTER OF GRAVITY; MOMENT OF INERTIA.   Nelson S. Fisk

Centrosome

An organelle located in the cytoplasm of all animal cells and many plants, fungi, and protozoa, that controls the polymerization, position, and polar orientation of many of the cell's microtubules throughout the cell cycle. There is usually one centrosome per cell, located near the cell's center; it doubles during interphase, so there are two when the cell divides. At the onset of mitosis, each centrosome increases the number of microtubules it initiates. These mitotic microtubules are more labile and generally shorter than their interphase counterparts, and as they rapidly grow and shrink they probe the space around the centrosome that initiated them. When the nuclear envelope disperses, the microtubules extend from the centrosome into the former nucleoplasm where the chromosomes have already condensed. Some of these microtubules attach to the chromosomes, while others interact with microtubules produced by the sister centrosome, forming a mitotic spindle that organizes and segregates the chromosomes. During anaphase, sister centrosomes are forced apart as the spindle elongates, allowing each daughter cell to receive one centrosome to organize its microtubules in the next cell generation. *See* CELL CYCLE; CELL MOTILITY.

Morphology and organization. There is no simple morphological description of a centrosome because its shape differs widely between organisms. The centrosomes of animal cells usually contain a pair of perpendicular centrioles (**Fig. 1**), including a parent centriole formed in an earlier cell generation and a daughter centriole formed during the most recent interphase. Centrioles can serve as basal bodies for the initiation of a cilium or flagellum in the cells that make them. They appear to be essential for the formation of these motile appendages, so centriole inheritance by both daughters at cell division is analogous to the transmission of a gene. *See* CILIA AND FLAGELLA.

The organization of a centrosome is partly dependent on centrioles when they are present. The microtubule initiation that defines the centrosome

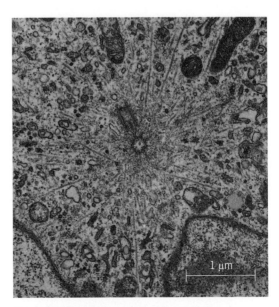

Fig. 1. Centrosome of a mammalian cell. Many microtubules radiate from the cloud of pericentriolar material which surrounds one of the two centrioles. (*Courtesy of Kent McDonald*)

is accomplished by a matrix that surrounds and is attached to the parent centriole; this matrix is often called pericentriolar material. In many cases, the pericentriolar material forms an almost spherical halo around the parent centriole, and the array of microtubules that forms is radially symmetric. In other cases, the pericentriolar material is highly structured and includes cone-shaped projections from the parent centriole (basal feet) or cross-striated fibers that extend from one end of the centriole (striated rootlets). Many of these appendages can initiate microtubules and should be regarded as a part of the centrosome. *See* CENTRIOLE; CYTOSKELETON.

In many lower eukaryotes there are no centrioles, but centrosomes still serve as both the principal organizer of interphase microtubules and as poles for the mitotic spindle (**Fig. 2**). In these centrosomes, the microtubule-initiating material is usually asymmetrically disposed, leading to the initiation of microtubule arrays without radial symmetry. Cells of higher plants lack visible centrosomes, yet they contain microtubules in both interphase and mitosis. During interphase, microtubule initiation is accomplished by cytoplasmic specializations that lie just beneath the plasma membrane at the corners and edges of the cells. During mitosis, microtubules form from two juxtanuclear regions that function similarly to centrosomes but lack a structurally defined microtubule organizing center. The cells of plants that form flagellated sperm also lack organized centrosomes, except in the sperm mother cells. The latter cells contain a more structured organelle associated with the spindle microtubules. The daughters of these cells produce even more structured centrosomes that eventually form many centrioles, each of which serves as a basal body for the formation of a sperm flagellum.

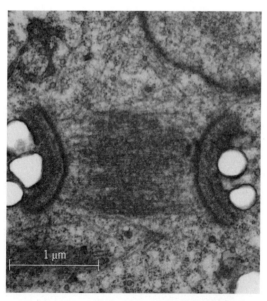

Fig. 2. Developing mitotic spindle in the alga *Stephanopyxis turris*. Microtubules are asymmetrically distributed around each centrosome (spindle pole). *(Courtesy of Kent McDonald)*

Chemistry. Centrosomes have been isolated from several lower eukaryotes, from embryos of *Drosophila*, and from mammalian cells. Biochemical descriptions of these fractions have now identified numerous centrosome components, but most of these components are unique to the cells from which they were isolated. Legitimate generalizations about the functions of centrosome components are still rare. One essentially universal centrosome component is γ-tubulin, a trace isoform of tubulin that is almost entirely confined to the centrosome. This protein may play a key role in initiating the polymerization of α- and β-tubulin. Mutations of or neutralizing antibodies to γ-tubulin and some other centrosome components prevent microtubule initiation or block cell cycle progression, implicating them in centrosome function. There are many candidates for proteins that might help to organize the centrosome and hold γ-tubulin in place, because several antigens have been localized to the pericentriolar material by using either antibodies raised against centrosome components or sera from humans with autoimmune disorders. *See* ANTIBODY; ANTIGEN.

Centrosome action is regulated as a function of time in the cell cycle. The increase in microtubule number that occurs prior to mitosis is correlated with a significant increase in the extent of phosphorylation of several centrosomal proteins. The protein kinase $p34^{cdc2}$, which helps to regulate the cell cycle, is concentrated at the centrosome, together with cyclin-B, a positive regulator of this kinase. Indirect evidence suggests that the changes in centrosome phosphorylation do not result simply from $p34^{cdc2}$, but from other kinases, some of which are regulated by $p34^{cdc2}$. Moreover, one of the regulatory subunits of cyclic adenosine monophosphate (cAMP)–dependent protein kinase is bound to a high-molecular-weight centrosome component, suggesting that additional kinases may also contribute to the regulation of centrosome activity. Phosphatases too have been localized to the centrosome.

Structural regulation. Biological reasons for centrosome regulation can be found not only in the importance of microtubules for interphase cell shape and for mitosis but also in the ways that centrosome behavior is modified in differentiative divisions during the development of metazoa. Developmental distinctions between daughter cells are often made at cell divisions that produce daughters of different size. Such divisions result from the asymmetric position of the cleavage furrow, which correlates with asymmetry in the mitotic asters, which in turn correlates with different activities at the two mitotic centrosomes. For example, when blastomeres cleave asymmetrically, the spindle's asters are of different size and shape. When oocytes go through meiosis and throw off polar bodies, one centrosome is usually attached to the cell cortex, while the other is not. *See* CELL (BIOLOGY); MITOSIS.   J. Richard McIntosh

Bibliography. D. M. Glover and J. W. Raff, The centrosome, *Sci. Amer.*, 268:62–68, 1993; V. I. Kalnins (ed.), *The Centrosome*, 1992.

Cephalaspidomorpha

The subclass of Agnatha that includes the jawless vertebrates with a single median nostril, as opposed to the subclass Pteraspidomorpha, in which there are paired nostrils. The Cephalaspidomorpha includes the orders Osteostraci, Galeaspida, Petromyzontida, and Anaspida. *See* ANASPIDA; JAWLESS VERTEBRATES; OSTEOSTRACI; PETROMYZONTIDA; PTERASPIDOMORPHA.
                                    Robert H. Denison

Cephalobaenida

One of two orders in the class Pentastomida of the phylum Arthropoda. This order includes primitive pentastomids with six-legged larvae. The hooks are simple, lacking a fulcrum, and disposed in trapeziform pattern, with the anterior pair internal to the posterior pair. The mouth is anterior to the hooks. In both sexes the genital pores are located anteriorly on the abdomen. There is no cirrus sac; the cirrus is short and united with the gubernaculum. In the female the uterus is straight or saccate.

There are two families, Raillietiellidae and Reighardiidae. The Raillietiellidae contains two genera: *Raillietiella*, with 19 species arranged in five groups; and *Cephalobaena*, with a single species. *Cephalobaena* has equal hooks at the ends of retractile, fingerlike appendages, the parapodia. The posterior end of the body is bifid. In *Raillietiella* the body is elongate with rounded ends, and there are lobes at the bases of the hooks. The anterior pair of hooks is the smaller. These animals are parasitic: adult stages occur in the lungs of lizards and snakes, and larval stages are encysted in reptiles, toads, and possibly insects. The life cycle is not well known and may be direct. The family Reighardiidae contains the single genus *Reighardia*, with one species, which infests the air passages of gulls and terns. The posterior end of this species is rounded, without lobes. The cuticula is covered with minute spines, and the hooks are small and equal. Proboscis and parapodia are lacking. *See* PENTASTOMIDA.   Horace W. Stunkard

Cephalocarida

A group of tiny marine crustaceans (body length 2.0–4.0 mm or 0.08–0.16 in.), discovered in 1954. Initially, cephalocarids were thought to be a living representation of what the primordial crustacean looked like. In recent years, that view has changed, with the Branchiopoda currently postulated to represent the most primitive of extant major crustacean taxa. In the classification of J. W. Martin and G. E. Davis (2001), the Branchiopoda are basal, whereas the Cephalocarida are positioned between the Remipedia and Maxillopoda, suggesting a more advanced evolutionary position for the class. Nonetheless, in their discussion of "most primitive," Martin and Davis acknowledge that the question is still unresolved. At present, the Cephalocarida comprise ten species, assigned to five genera in one family. They have been found in flocculent surface deposits of mud or silty sand, from the intertidal zone down to depths of 5000 ft (1500 m), on the shores of all continents except Europe. Population densities up to an average of 16 individuals/ft² (177/m²) have been recorded. *See* BRACHIOPODA; CRUSTACEA.

Species. The best-known species is *Hutchinsoniella macracantha*, from the east coast of North and South America, about 0.12–0.16 in. (3–4 mm) long, with a shovel-shaped head and a slender, very flexible body that is not covered by a carapace (**Fig. 1**). Species in the other four genera are similar, differing principally in the modifications of the

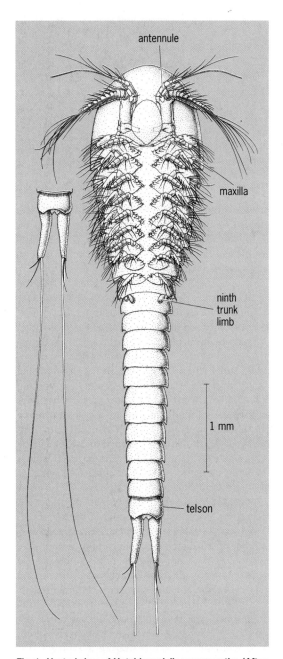

Fig. 1. Ventral view of *Hutchinsoniella macracantha*. (*After H. L. Sanders, The Cephalocarida: Functional morphology: Larval development, comparative external anatomy, Mem. Conn. Acad. Arts Sci., 15:1–80, 1963*)

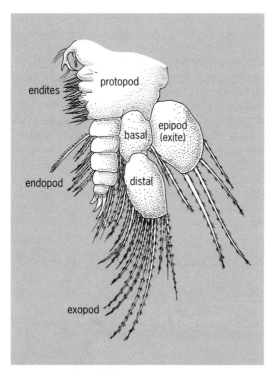

Fig. 2. *Lightiella* fourth thoracopod. (*After P. A. McLaughlin, Comparative Morphology of Recent Crustacea, W. H. Freeman, 1980*)

posterior four thoracopods, presumably as enhancements to reproductive functions. In *Lightiella*, the eighth thoracopods are entirely absent, whereas they are present but lack endopods in the other genera. In *Sandersiella* and *Hamptonellus*, the exites of the sixth thoracopods are highly modified, while the distal claw of each seventh thoracopod in *Hutchinsoniella* is bluntly rounded. These appendages show little modification in *Chiltonella*. Of the more anterior pairs of thoracopods, all are flexible but stiffened by internal turgor; each has a flattened basal protopod bearing several medial endites, a distal leglike endopod, and a distal paddle-shaped exopod; and an epipodite (or pseudepipodite) projects from the base of the exopod (**Fig. 2**). In the ventral nerve cord there is a partial coalescence of the ganglia in the head, but in the trunk a separate pair of ganglia is present in each somite. The heart extends through the limb-bearing trunk somites, in each of which it has one pair of ostia.

Morphology. Until the discoveries of the crustacean and crustacean-like fossils of the Cambrian Orsten and the Burgess and Chengjiang faunas, a number of attributes of cephalocarid morphology suggested a basic primitiveness. These included the serial homology of trunk appendages, the ventral nervous system, the uniramous, multisegmented antennules, the biramous antennae with both rami multisegmented, the large, flattened pleura on all the limb-bearing somites, and the telson freely articulated with the trunk and bearing a caudal furca. Even cephalocarid development, initially considered primitive in having a nauplius stage (**Fig. 3**) followed by a series of regular additions of body somites, has

been shown by developmental stages in Orsten taxa actually to be apomorphic. A relatively slight metamorphosis occurs at the thirteenth molt, when the antennae, mandibles, and maxillules suddenly acquire their adult form.

Cephalocarids are nonswimming, bottom-creeping, nonselective deposit feeders. Distal claws on the endopods of the thoracopods scratch up particles that are passed into the median ventral food groove and moved forward to the mouth by metachronal beating of the thoracopods. The digestive system of cephalocarids has been examined in detail only in *Hutchinsoniella* and has been found in gross morphology to be consistent with other non-malacostracan crustaceans. It consists of a cuticular esophagus and rectum separated by an endodermal midgut with cephalic diverticula. However, *Hutchinsoniella* is unique in possessing many longitudinal muscles inside the circular muscles of the anterior midgut that change to only a few outside the circular muscles in the posterior midgut. Similarly, the gross morphology of the nervous system of *Hutchinsoniella* conforms to other crustaceans, but it also has elements of uniqueness. Most significant is the total absence of eyes and the organ of Bellonci, and with these the absence of brain centers associated with these sensory attributes. The most conspicuous elements of the cephalocarid "brain" are the olfactory lobes and the "mushroom body complex" (corpora pedunculata). The size and complexity of these olfactory lobes are unique for non-malacostracan crustaceans. Likewise,

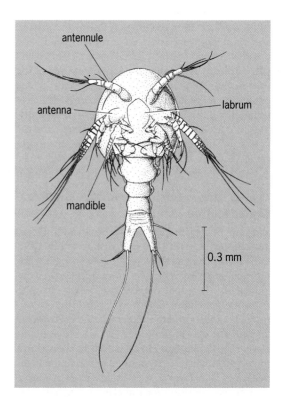

Fig. 3. Stage 1 nauplius larva of *Hutchinsoniella*. (*After H. L. Sanders, The Cephalocarida: Functional morphology, larval development, comparative external anatomy, Mem. Conn. Acad. Arts Sci., 15:1–80, 1963*)

non-malacostracans are thought to lack "mushroom bodies," and those found in *Hutchinsoniella* are distinct from those of malacostracans. *See* FEEDING MECHANISMS (INVERTEBRATE).

Reproduction. Cephalocarids are simultaneous hermaphrodites, with eggs and sperm that ripen at the same time. It is presumed that fertilization must include some form of copulation, but this has never been documented; thus self-fertilization cannot be ruled out. The sperm are not mobile and no indication of spermatophore development has been observed. The paired ovaries are located entirely in the maxillary somite, each adjacent to a tubule of the maxillary gland. The oviducts, beginning at the posteromedial margin of each ovary, extend posteriorly through the thorax and most of the trunk, then loop forward at trunk somite 18 and continue anteriorly to the sixth thoracic somite where they join the vasa deferentia. The sausage-shaped, paired testes occupy space dorsal to the gut from approximately the seventh thoracic somite to the third trunk somite. The testes have an anterior transverse connection from which the paired vasa deferentia descend to join the oviducts. The pairs of oviduct/vas deferens, each as a compact unit, then proceed to the gonopores located on the protopods of the sixth thoracopods. Each gonopore is blocked by a muscular operculum. These opercula, which are hinged laterally, can be pulled aside by the action of a set of muscles that originate in each protopod and insert centrally on the operculum. The extruded egg is attached to the knoblike tip of the very reduced ninth thoracopod by cement formed in a gland in the ninth somite. No more than two eggs are brooded at a time, and the length of time required for embryonic development makes it unlikely that individuals have more than a few broods each season. The actual extrusion and attachment of the egg has not been witnessed, but brooding embryos are always oriented the same way, with the anterior end of the cephalon directed posteriorly and its ventral surface pointed downward.

Phylogeny. The discovery of this presumably primitive class gave rise to speculation that cephalocarids stood close to the ancestral stem of the Crustacea. However, with the more recent discovery of another, and perhaps even more primitive, class, the Remipedia, this hypothesis was challenged. The exceptional morphological details described for some of the three-dimensionally preserved, phosphatized Cambrian Orsten fauna have demonstrated that a number of characters previously thought to be primitive in both the Cephalocarida and Remipedia were misinterpreted. Similarly, as more information has been gathered about the Cephalocarida, a substantial number of their attributes are now acknowledged as being unquestionably advanced. These include the lack of limbs on the last 11 trunk somites. The heart does not extend through these limbless somites. The mandibles of the adult have lost all parts distal to the coxa, and the adult maxillules are also somewhat reduced. The eighth trunk limbs are reduced or absent,

and the ninth trunk limbs are greatly reduced. The reproductive system also is unique and unlike those of other Crustacea.

Additionally, although the cephalocarid digestive system and nervous system, as exemplified by *Hutchinsonella macracantha*, are comparable in their gross morphology to that of other crustaceans, they deviate in certain elements. The suggestion made by several carcinologists that cephalocarids are simply highly specialized progenetic paedomorphs may in fact be an accurate assessment.

John H. Lochhead; Patsy McLaughlin

Bibliography. R. Elofsson and R. R. Hessler, Central nervous system of *Hutchinsoniella macracantha* (Cephalocarida), *J. Crust. Biol.*, 10(3):423–439, 1990; R. Elofsson, R. R. Hessler, and A. Y. Hessler, Digestive system of the cephalocarid *Hutchinsoniella macracantha*, *J. Crust. Biol.*, 12(4):571–591, 1992; R. R. Hessler, R. Elofsson, and A. Y. Hessler, Reproductive system of *Hutchinsoniella macracantha* (Cephalocarida), *J. Crust. Biol.*, 15(3):493–552, 1995; R. R. Hessler and Y. Wakabara, *Hampsonellus brasiliensis* n. gen., n. sp., a cephalocarid from Brazil, *J. Crust. Biol.*, 20(3):550–558, 2000; J. W. Martin and G. E. Davis, An updated classification of the Recent Crustacea, *Nat. Hist. Mus. Los Angeles County Sci. Ser.*, 39:1–124, 2001; R. F. Schram and C. H. J. Hof, Fossils and the interrelationships of major crustacean groups, in G. D. Edgecombe (ed.), *Arthropod Fossils and Phylogeny*, pp. 233–302, Columbia University Press, New York, 1998; D. Walossek, The Upper Cambrian *Rehbachiella* and the phylogeny of the Branchiopoda and Crustacea, *Fossils Strata*, 32:1–202, 1993.

Cephalochordata

A subphylum of the phylum Chordata comprising the lancelets, including *Branchiostoma* (amphioxus). They are also known as the Leptocardii. Lancelets are small fishlike animals, not exceeding 3.2 in. (80 mm) in length. They burrow in sand on the ocean bed or in estuaries in tropical and temperate regions throughout the world. Only two genera are recognized, *Branchiostoma* with 23 species and *Asymmetron* with 6 species.

Morphology. The structure of the lancelet is based on the same fundamental plan as all other chordates, but there is neither head nor paired fins (see **illus.**). The skeletal rod of the back, or notochord, extends the entire length of the body. The animal is thus pointed at both ends, a feature to which the name amphioxus refers, and lanceolate in form, hence the name lancelet. The mouth lies at the base of an oral hood fringed with sensory projections or cirri and opens into a capacious pharynx occupying over half the length of the body. The body wall in the pharyngeal region is perforated on each side by a large number of elongated gill slits. This delicate branchial basket is protected by two folds of tissues, the metapleural folds, which grow down on either side of the body and, joining midventrally, form a sac into which

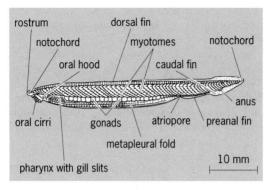

European lancelet (*Branchiostoma lanceolatum*). (*After J. E. Webb, Proc. Zool. Soc. London, 127:131, 1956*)

the gill slits open. The cavity of this sac is called the atrium and opens to the exterior through a posterior atriopore. The circulatory system resembles that of a fish, but there is no heart and the blood is colorless. The excretory system is quite unlike that of higher chordates and consists of nephridia situated above the pharynx with ciliated cells similar to those of the Platyhelminthes and the annelid worms. Lancelets are either male or female. The gonads are segmentally arranged pouches arising from the metapleural folds and discharging into the atrium.

Nutrition. Feeding in lancelets is by a ciliary or filter-feeding mechanism. Water is taken in through the mouth, passed through the gill slits into the atrium, and thence out through the atriopore. The water current is maintained by the beating of cilia on the gill bars. Microorganisms and organic debris on which the animal feeds are strained off by the gill bars onto a mucous string, the endostyle, and transported by cilia back to the intestine for digestion.

Life history. The adults burrow in rather coarse sand or shell gravel and usually lie with the mouth open at the surface of the sand. They select by trial and error sands of high permeability with rounded grains coated with microorganisms and free from organic decay. The selection of the optimum sand deposit available results in the congregation of large numbers of lancelets in small areas for spawning. The egg develops into a larvae not unlike the adult except that it is asymmetrical with a long elliptical mouth on the left side of the body and a single series of gills on the right. At first the larva is bottom-living, but later becomes planktonic. Metamorphosis to the symmetrical adult form takes place after about 11–12 weeks of life. The young adult sinks to the bottom and swims actively until a suitable sand in which it can burrow and remain undisturbed is found. Some species complete the life cycle in a year and death evidently occurs after spawning, but others may live 3 or 4 years and spawn annually. In some species metamorphosis occurs late and comparatively large larvae with 20–30 gills are formed. At one time specimens of this type were placed in a separate genus, *Amphioxides*, but these are now generally regarded as larvae of either *Branchiostoma* or *Asymmetron*.

Importance. The importance of lancelets lies chiefly in their being one of the most primitive chor-

dates. However, lancelets are eaten by the Chinese and there are lancelet fisheries at Amoy. Lancelets are also being used as indicator organisms to assist in tracing the pattern of ocean currents on which their distribution appears to depend. *See* CHORDATA.

J. E. Webb

Bibliography. S. P. Parker (ed.), *Synopsis and Classification of Living Organisms*, 2 vols., 1982; J. E. Webb and M. B. Hill, The ecology of Lagos Lagoon, pts. 3 and 4, *Phil. Trans. Roy. Soc. London B*, 241(683):334–391, 1958; C. K. Weichert, *Anatomy of the Chordates*, 4th ed., 1970; J. Z. Young, *The Life of Vertebrates*, 3d ed., 1981.

Cephalopoda

A class in the phylum Mollusca that is exclusively marine and contains the extant members—squids, cuttlefishes, octopuses, and the chambered nautiluses—and the fossil taxa—ammonoids, nautiloids, and belemnoids. The earliest known cephalopod fossils date to roughly 500 million years ago from the Upper Cambrian of northeast China. Fossilized external shells of the extinct subclass Ammonoidea and the nearly extinct subclass Nautiloidea are interpreted as indicating that these animals were shallow-living and slow-moving. Despite the thousands of species of such shelled cephalopods that have been recognized, all are extinct except for six species in two surviving genera, *Nautilus* and *Allonautilus*. Other living cephalopods, all predators in the subclass Coleoidea with internal shells, number over 725 species, with many more likely to be recognized. *See* MOLLUSCA.

General characteristics. Living cephalopods are bilaterally symmetric predatory mollusks that typically have conspicuous, laterally oriented eyes. Most have 8–10 appendages (8 arms and 2 tentacles) around the mouth; species of nautilus have over 90 arms. The appendages are lined with one to several rows of suckers or hooks, although the arms of nautilus lack conspicuous armature. Paired chitinous jaws, similar to an upside-down parrot's beak, with large muscles form the spherical buccal mass that contains the mouth and a tonguelike, toothed radula (a character that, in part, defines the Mollusca). The highly developed brain is positioned between the eyes where it is the center of the extensive, proliferated nervous system. The shell, which was external in most fossil cephalopods, as it is in modern species of nautilus, has become in all other living forms internal, highly modified, reduced, or absent. Paired fins that emerge from the side of the body in most coleoid cephalopods aid locomotion. The main thrust of primary movement is generated by jet propulsion in which water that is drawn into the sides of the mantle cavity is forcibly expelled through the nozzlelike funnel.

Classification. Among mollusks, cephalopods are thought to be most closely related to the class Gastropoda, although each group has had a very long and distinct evolutionary history. The earliest fossils are

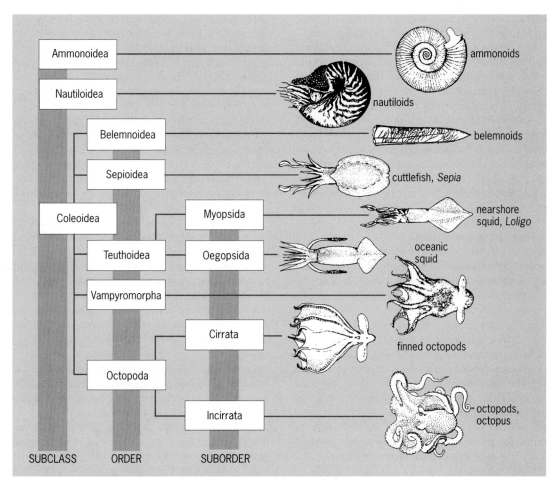

Classification and morphology (body form) of major groups of the class Cephalopoda.

external shells recognized as those of cephalopods by internal septa thought to relate to buoyancy control. The **illustration** shows the taxonomic hierarchy to the level of suborder in the extant coleoid cephalopods, with a representative figure of each taxon. *See* GASTROPODA.

Morphological characters that form the basis of fossil cephalopod classification are those associated with shells. Characters that form the basis of coleoid cephalopod classification, taxa that lack external shells, include the presence or absence of a cornealike membrane over the eye that separates nearshore or myopsid squids from oceanic or oegopsid squids. Although squids share general characters, the more than 20 families are diagnosed by a combination of the kind and arrangement of hooks or suckers on the arms and tentacles, shape of the cartilaginous connections between the mantle and funnel, and the presence or absence of tentacles at maturity. Cuttlefishes are recognized by their characteristic cuttlebone.

Among octopods, the presence or absence of fins separates the two suborders. Among finned or cirrate octopods, fin size and the shape of the supporting structure that underlies the fins provide taxonomic identification. Within-group distinctions among the finless or incirrate octopods include the arrangement of the suckers, relative arm lengths and web sec-

tor depths, skin color and texture, and copulatory organ features. Most modern cephalopod diversity lies within the three nearshore genera *Loligo*, *Sepia*, and *Octopus*.

Phylogenetic relationships among cephalopods are poorly resolved. The octopods are recognized as the sister group to the vampyromorphs, as both groups share characters that are otherwise unique in the cephalopods. Relationships within the squids and between them and the cuttlefish remain poorly understood, with several enigmatic groups complicating the issues.

Habitat. Cephalopods live in most marine habitats, from the intertidal zone to depths of over 16,500 ft (5000 m). Each extant cephalopod group tends to share ecological distribution. Chambered nautiluses are restricted to tropical and subtropical waters of the Indo-West Pacific, where they live associated with vertical reef faces from near-surface to 1600 ft (480 m) deep. Squids typically spend their lives swimming; nearshore squids typically occur on continental shelves and oceanic squids in open water. Cuttlefishes tend to occur in shallow water where they rest on the ocean floor, but they actively swim while hunting. Most octopod species are bottom-dwelling animals that occur in virtually all benthic habitats. In shallow water, octopuses tend to associate with shelters, which they either find or excavate if in heavily sedimented areas. Lesser-known groups of octopods are pelagic at various ocean depths. Cirrate or finned octopus that live at 660 ft (200 m) and deeper were once thought to spend most of their time in the water column; seafloor observations show that they may also occur on the bottom at depths of 660 to 16,500 ft (200 to 5000 m). The only species in the order Vampyromorpha occurs at midwater depths of 1650–3960 ft (500–1200 m) worldwide. Most cephalopods are thought not to tolerate brackish water, although the myopsid squid *Lolliguncula brevis* is known to enter water with salinities as low as 8.5 parts per thousand, much more dilute than the normal ocean salinity of 35 parts per thousand.

Brain and nervous system. Cephalopods are characterized by their ability to change their behavior based on past experience, which requires memory and is consistent with learning. Their eyes are extraordinarily well developed as are their multilobed brains, which by some measures (ratio of brain to body weight) exceed those of most fishes and reptiles. Diffuse ganglionated nerve cords in the arms of octopuses and mantles of squids further indicate that their advanced nervous system approaches that of some birds and mammals. Since cephalopods are direct competitors with and frequent prey of marine fishes, some experts argue that fishes have generated selective pressure resulting in the rapid evolution of skin color and texture, predator detection abilities, and eyes of modern cephalopods. *See* NERVOUS SYSTEM (INVERTEBRATE).

Eye structure. Cephalopods—with the exception of species of nautilus that have pinhole eyes and one species of finned octopod that has reduced eyes—have large eyes that are very similar to those of vertebrates. Two features demonstrate that the structures evolved in convergence. First, to focus the eye on nearby subjects, cephalopods change the shape of the eyeball rather than the thickness of the lens, as do vertebrates. Second, in cephalopods the photosensitive cells point toward the lens, allowing the nerves that connect them to the brain to exit directly out of the back of the eye. In vertebrates, the photosensitive cells point backward, toward the retina, so they detect light that bounces off the retina; their nerves must extend into and their common optic nerve must exit out of the eyeball, creating a blind spot. Because cephalopod eyes are better engineered, they have uninterrupted vision. *See* EYE (INVERTEBRATE); EYE (VERTEBRATE).

Respiration, circulation, and excretion. Cephalopods extract oxygen from the water using gills that are fully contained within the muscular mantle. The gills lie on the side of the mantle cavity between the mantle wall and the viscera, where they are immediately exposed to water as it is drawn inside the mantle. The skin may act as an additional surface for gas exchange. The gills extend most of the length of the mantle in squids. In some cirrate octopods, however, the gills are reduced—rather than two attachments, a single one creates a semicircular gill. *See* GILL (ANATOMY).

Gas exchange, oxygen uptake and release of carbon dioxide from the bloodstream, is somewhat limited in cephalopods because their copper-based oxygen-carrying blood pigment, hemocyanin, is not highly effective in binding oxygen. The nearly closed circulatory system is pressurized by right and left branchial hearts that force deoxygenated blood through their respective gills and a medially situated systematic heart that pumps oxygenated blood through the rest of the body. The elastic nature of the arteries and veins is considered by some to contribute significantly to blood circulation. The same ability to contract also allows the blood vessels to stop blood loss in the event of an injury.

Nitrogenous waste is excreted in the form of ammonia, with several organs involved. The renal sacs, branchial heart appendages, digestive duct appendages, and even the gills contribute, with the branchial heart appendages being the site of ultrafiltration. The intestine and rectum prepare and expel indigestible material eaten with food from the body. The renal sacs are unusual in harboring minute wormlike members of the Dicyemida, which are only known from these organs of cephalopods. Ingested material that resists breakdown is passed through the intestine to be released from the viscera by the rectum, at the base of the nozzlelike funnel. A vigorous exhalation flushes it from the mantle.

Food, feeding, and digestion. Cephalopods are predators that feed on a variety of invertebrates, fishes, and even each other. The relatively sluggish nautiluses feed primarily on slow-moving prey such as reed shrimps, and even scavenge castoff shells of molted spiny lobsters. Cuttlefishes prey on shrimps, crabs, and small fishes, while squids eat fishes, pelagic crustaceans, and other cephalopods. Benthic octopuses prey mostly on clams, snails, and crabs. Prey capture is treated in Coleoidea.

Salivary glands secrete enzymes that begin digestion, and in octopuses contain toxins that subdue their prey. The digestive tract begins with the buccal mass that forms a mobile muscular sphere containing the chitinous beak that holds or bites off chunks of prey. The toothed radula working as a rasp moves these bits into the esophagus. Because the esophagus passes through the brain, prey morsels need to be fairly small and lack hard points. Digestion occurs primarily in the stomach where prey bits mix with digestive juices from the salivary glands, the digestive gland (the analog of the vertebrate liver and a lot more), and its appendages. The cecum is where digestion is completed; absorption of food also occurs in this organ and in the digestive gland and its appendages. Indigestible waste is moved through the system to the rectum, where it is released from the anus at the base of the funnel. It leaves the mantle cavity with water expelled during respiratory or in jetting contractions of the mantle (body).

Size, age, and growth. Cephalopods efficiently incorporate their food into their bodies, allowing very rapid growth rates. Many species of small cuttlefishes, bobtail squids, and octopuses reach reproductive maturity in less than a year, while larger forms hatch in the summer, overwinter, and spawn at 12–14 months of age. The life spans of giant species of octopuses and squids are not known but are estimated to be 5 years or less. The smallest adult cephalopods are the Indian Ocean sepioid *Idiosepius pygamaea* at 0.2–0.8 in. (6–22 mm) body length, the Caribbean myopsid *Pickfordiateuthis pulchella* at 0.8 in. (22 mm), and the octopuses *Octopus micropyrsus* from California at 0.4–1.4 in. (10–35 mm) and *O. nanus* from the Red Sea at 0.5–1 in. (12–26 mm). The true giant squids of the family Architeuthidae are the largest invertebrates in the world, with a total length (tip of tail to tip of outstretched tentacles) of nearly 64 ft (20 m), a body length of 13–16 ft (4–5 m), and a weight of up to 1 ton. Most *Architeuthis* specimens are 32–38 ft (10–12 m) total length, 6–10 ft (2–3 m) body length, and about 450–660 lb (200–300 kg). The largest octopus, *Enteroctopus dofleini*, can have an arm span of 32 ft (10 m).

Defense. Because most cephalopods are unprotected by hard coverings, they are the prey of many other animals. Cephalopods have a myriad of defenses, most of which rely on escaping detection. To this end, they have become masters of camouflage and escape.

Chromatophore organs allow the skin of cephalopods to change color to match the background or mimic less desirable targets for predation. In addition, musculature in the skin can erect papillae, flaps, and knobs to match the background and break up the outline of the body. Many midwater oceanic squids have photophores on their ventral surface that match the intensity of light from above, thus reducing the conspicuousness of their silhouettes. Most cephalopods have an ink sac, from which blobs of dark ink are ejected to form a "decoy" for a pursuing predator. The two components of the ink, mucus and pigment, protect the cephalopod because when the predator bites the ink decoy, the ink temporarily blinds it and the mucus clouds its chemoreceptors, allowing the cephalopod to escape undetected. Jet propulsion, which despite its energy-intensive nature allows both rapid movement and extraordinarily high maneuverability, also contributes to cephalopod defenses. Benthic octopuses typically take refuge in shelters or dens that provide protection from predators. Some octopuses excavate holes in areas of soft sediment in which to hide. Squids occur in schools that may provide safety in numbers. Cuttlefish rest on the bottom and often cover their dorsal surface with a coat of sediment that effectively camouflages them. *See* CHROMATOPHORE; COLEOIDEA; PHOTOPHORE GLAND; PROTECTIVE COLORATION.

Locomotion. Cephalopods have perfected jet propulsion for many modes of locomotion, from hovering motionless, to normal cruising, to extremely rapid escape swimming. Water is drawn into the mantle cavity through openings on the sides and ventral mantle when the muscular mantle (body) expands. In squids and cuttlefish, the mantle opening can be closed by cartilaginous thickenings to ensure

that contraction drives all water out of the mantle through the narrow funnel, propelling the cephalopod tail-first through the water. A complex of nerves controls this action, the most notable of which is the giant axon. Because nerve impulses travel faster in larger nerves, the giant axon allows the impulse that starts the contraction of the mantle to reach the dead-end part of the mantle first. As the wave of contraction moves forward toward the funnel, it moves the largest possible volume of water out to generate the most possible force, moving the squid as efficiently as possible. The giant axon of cephalopods, the largest single nerve fiber in the animal kingdom, was used as a model for neurobiology to increase our understanding of how nerves function. Although the fins of sepioids, teuthoids, and cirrate octopods are conspicuous, they primarily serve as rudders and stabilizers, providing only limited locomotory power.

Benthic octopuses normally move by walking or scuttling on their arms; when hunting they use each arm to explore the substrate. Most species, however, will use jet propulsion when threatened or if they are anxious to get somewhere. The use of buoyancy devices—such as the cuttlebone of cuttlefish (*Sepia*), gas chambers in other shells (species of nautilus, *Spirula*), low-density ions, especially of ammonium in special body reservoirs (Cranchiidae) or even in the body tissues (Histioteuthidae, Architeuthidae), and large amounts of oils in the liver (Bathyteuthidae)—reduces the energy required when these cephalopods are swimming.

Reproduction. Cephalopods have separate sexes and internal fertilization. Copulation in some species (such as nearshore squids) occurs at spawning, that is, when the eggs are released; in other taxa (octopods), sperm can be stored for periods of at least several months. Females produce eggs inside their (single) ovary. When the eggs mature, they are released through the paired oviducts to be inseminated by sperm from the male. Eggs may be encased in individual capsules (most octopods, sepioids, some oceanic squids), or may be enveloped in a gelatinous matrix and shaped into fingerlike clusters (nearshore squids) or formed into sausage- or ball-shaped masses that drift in the open ocean (some oegopsids). The fragile "shell" of the epipelagic argonauts (*Argonauta*) is actually secreted by the female's arms to hold her eggs during incubation. In one midwater pelagic octopod, the eggs develop entirely within the female's long, convoluted oviducts.

Males produce sperm in their single testis; it moves through a series of organs where it is packaged into cylinders (spermatophores) that the males store. The fluid inside the spermatophore is of comparatively high salinity. When the spermatophore is exposed to normal seawater, osmosis drives water inside it. The resultant increase in internal pressure forces the spermatophore to open and eject its sperm. A male transfers spermatophores to females either with a specially modified arm, the hectocotylus, or in those squids that lack a modified arm by a penis, which is normally contained inside the mantle. Sperm in octopods is stored in glands in the oviduct, but in cephalopods without sperm storage organs, spermatophores may be injected into the female's mantle muscles, around the neck, under the eyes, or around the mouth, depending on the species. In these species, sperm is mixed with eggs as the female prepares the egg cluster.

Although most cephalopods leave their eggs to develop on their own, females of incirrate (finless) octopods care for their eggs during development, as does at least one species of oceanic squid. Egg development proceeds over a few weeks to a few months depending on the egg size and the temperature at which they develop. In deep-sea octopuses that produce very large (over 50 mm or 2 in. long) eggs, development may take years. Most hatchlings emerge from the eggs as planktonic "larvae" that, as they grow, slowly take on the adult form of their species; in some species hatchlings look like miniature adults.

Ecology. Cephalopods are important marine predators that kill and eat most marine animal taxa. They, in turn, are important prey to animals able to capture them. Because cephalopod beaks resist digestion, analysis of gut contents can identify cephalopods eaten by large predators. They are important components in the diets of toothed whales (sperm whales, dolphins), pinnipeds (seals, sea lions), pelagic birds (petrels, albatrosses), and predatory fishes (tunas, billfishes, groupers). In one case, North Atlantic pilot whales were found to prey almost exclusively on one species of squid, *Illex illecebrosus*, that aggregates for spawning in the summer. As cephalopods grow, they become less vulnerable to smaller predators, but they also become more attractive to larger predators.

Squids tend to form schools of individuals of the same size. The similar size of squids within a given school has been suggested to be due to the elimination of any smaller-than-average individuals by cannibalism. Octopuses tend to be solitary, with individuals coming together for copulation or cannibalism (the two are not exclusive, as females can cannibalize their suitors). Observational studies of a limited number of octopus species suggest that in part their high growth rates relate to the amount of time they spend resting, which is typically interrupted only by bouts of feeding.   Janet Voight; Clyde F. E. Roper

Fossils. Modern representatives of the Cephalopoda are dominated in numbers by forms without a calcareous skeleton (such as *Octopus*) or by those taxa with only a reduced or rudimentary internal skeleton (most squids). Only a small minority of forms, such as the externally shelled *Nautilus* and *Argonauta*, the internally shelled cuttlefish (*Sepia*), and the squid *Spirula*, possess significant skeletal hard parts.

Fossil record. The fossil record, however, suggests that the typical morphologies of the world's cephalopodan fauna were quite different in the past. During the Paleozoic and Mesozoic eras (from about 560 to 65 million years ago), the majority of cephalo-pod fossils came from species with external shells, similar to that produced today by *Nautilus*. Although fossils of the subclass Coleoidea (to which squids and octopus are today assigned) are known, and in some deposits can even be extremely common, it appears that they represented only a small fraction of Paleozoic and Mesozoic diversity. Even accounting for their lesser chance of incorporation into the fossil record because of their reduced internal skeletons, it appears that the coleoids were never as abundant as the groups bearing external shells during the Paleozoic and Mesozoic eras. Over 15,000 Paleozoic- and Mesozoic-aged species belonging to the subclasses Nautiloidea and Ammonoidea are now known to science. In contrast, the modern-day cephalopod fauna, dominated by the squids and octopuses, has only several hundred species described to date, and appears to be very different from the typical cephalopod faunas characteristic of the Paleozoic and Mesozoic oceans. Most evidence suggests that the modern fauna is composed of taxa which have evolved only after the end-Mesozoic extinction of most externally shelled forms. *See* MESOZOIC; PALEOZOIC.

Chambered shell. Much of what is known and inferred about the habits of the ancient cephalopods comes from study of the small number of extant forms still possessing the external shells characteristic of the Paleozoic and Mesozoic cephalopod faunas. For this reason the modern-day *Nautilus* has been the subject of much research, for it represents the last living, externally shelled cephalopod. (Although *Argonaut*, a very specialized pelagic octopus, also has an external shell, this shell is produced by females only and serves as a specialized brooding organ for developing eggs.) The *Nautilus* shell has the dual purpose of lending protection to the vulnerable soft parts and serving as a buoyancy device. The rear of the shell contains numerous compartments partitioned by calcareous walls or septa; each chamber contains a central tube within which is a strand of living flesh communicating with the rear of the soft parts. This strand, called the siphuncle, is instrumental in achieving overall neutral buoyancy of the entire animal by removing a seawater-like liquid from each chamber. Although the modern *Nautilus* shows soft-part specializations which may be adaptations to its typical deep-water existence in front of coral reefs (and hence atypical of most extinct species, which appear to have lived in water depths and environments different from those typical of *Nautilus*), the nautilus shell shows close similarity with the shells of all fossil nautiloids and their closely allied descendants, the ammonoids.

In both nautiloids and ammonoids, the soft parts rest in a large space at the front of the shell. The shell enlarges through new calcification along its aperture. New chambers are produced at the back of the soft parts and are originally filled with the seawater-like liquid. This liquid is removed via the siphuncle (a tabular extension of the mantle passing through all chambers to the apex of a shelled cephalopod) by an osmotic process at a rate that balances the density increases brought about by the production of new shell and tissue growth. After completion of a new chamber, the soft parts of the nautiloid or ammonoid move forward in the shell, creating a space behind the body for another chamber. All fossil cephalopods reached a final mature size and hence ceased shell growth.

With this cessation of shell growth, new chamber formation no longer became necessary. The buoyancy function of the chambered shell portion changed from one primarily dedicated to offsetting density increase due to shell and tissue growth, to one concerned with making small buoyancy compensations in response to slight, nongrowth weight changes, such as weight increases brought about by windfall feeding, or concerned with producing weight reduction, which could occur if shell material was broken off during predatory attacks on the nautiloid or ammonoid. There is reason to believe that buoyancy change was not used to power any sort of movement vertically through the water column. At least in the modern *Nautilus* (and by inference in the fossil nautiloids and ammonoids as well), the process of buoyancy change appears too slow to aid in any type of active locomotion brought about by rapid weight gain or loss.

Origins. The evolution of the chambered cephalopod shell, with its neutral buoyancy capability, dates back to the Cambrian Period; the shell was the central adaptation leading to the origin of the cephalopods from their snail-like molluscan ancestors. The earliest cephalopods are assigned to the subclass Nautiloidea. The first of these, known from Late Cambrian rocks in China, were small (less than 1 ft or 0.3 m long) and bore straight to slightly curved shells. By Ordovician time, however, adaptive radiations among the ancestral nautiloid stocks gave rise to a wide variety of shell shapes and sizes, including giants at least 10 ft (3 m) long. The subclass Ammonoidea arose from nautiloid ancestors in the Devonian Period, and can be differentiated from the nautiloids in details of shell morphology, especially relating to the complexity and position of the septa and siphuncle. It was also during the Devonian Period that the earliest internally shelled forms assignable to the Coleoidea appeared. *See* CAMBRIAN; DEVONIAN; ORDOVICIAN.

Evolutionary radiations and extinctions. The early Paleozoic nautiloids predated the first-known fishes and hence may have been among the earliest large predators in the sea. The subsequent evolutionary history of the nautiloids and their ammonoid descendants was one of successive waves of rapid evolutionary radiations. These externally shelled forms, however, were also very susceptible to extinction, especially during the rare intervals of mass extinction which occasionally occurred during the Paleozoic and Mesozoic eras. Following a period of extinction, a new fauna of nautiloids and ammonoids would rapidly evolve. This characteristic pattern of rapid speciation rates and high extinction rates tends to make most species chronologically short-ranging and hence useful in subdividing strata through biostratigraphy. Ammonoids are among the most useful known fossils for subdividing the stratigraphic record into small, chronological units.

The modern-day cephalopod fauna originated only after one of the most spectacular of the mass extinctions, occurring at the end of the Cretaceous Period. At this time, about 65 million years ago, a still-flourishing ammonoid fauna was totally destroyed; most nautiloids also died out as well. Although the record of Cenozoic cephalopod fossils is spotty, it appears that much of the cephalopod fauna as it is known today evolved only after the demise of the externally shelled forms. Thus, much as in the case of mammals and dinosaurs, the so-called modern fauna (the coleoid cephalopods) inherited the seas not because they were inherently superior to the ancient shelled nautiloids and ammonoids, but because they found themselves in an ocean emptied by mass extinction. *See* CENOZOIC; EXTINCTION (BIOLOGY).   Janet Voight; Peter D. Ward

Bibliography. W. Arkell et al., *Treatise on Invertebrate Paleontology*, pt. L, 1996; M. R. Clarke and E. R. Trueman (eds.), *The Mollusca*, vol. 11: *Form and Function*, 1988; M. R. Clarke and E. R. Trueman (eds.), *The Mollusca*, vol. 12: *Paleontology and Neontology of Cephalopods*, 1988; U. Lehmann, *The Ammonites: Their Life and Their World*, 1981; R. T. Hanlon and J. B. Messenger, *Cephalopod Behaviour*, Cambridge University Press, 1996; K. N. Nesis, *Cephalopods of the World*, T. F. H. Publications, Neptune City, NJ, 1987; M. Norman, *Cephalopods: A World Guide*, Conch Books, Hackenheim, Germany, 2000; P. Ward, *The Natural History of Nautilus*, Allen and Unwin. London, 1987.

Cephalosporins

A group of antibiotics that are effective in eradicating streptococcal, pneumococcal, staphylococcal, *Klebsiella*, *Neisseria*, enteric gram-negative rod bacteria that produce pulmonary, skin and soft tissue, bone and joint, endocardial, surgical, urinary, and bacteremic infections. They have been used most often in a preventive or prophylactic fashion at the time of various surgical procedures. The pharmacology of the early cephalosporins was such that the agents had to be administered by vein in frequent intervals in serious infections. This problem was overcome since most of the newer agents have much longer half-lives. All the third-generation cephalosporins penetrate well into tissues, and antibacterially active levels in various body fluids (pleural, peritoneal, synovial, biliary) and tissues such as bone are excellent. The toxic potential of the agents, considering their broad antibacterial spectrum, has been minor. Toxicities which are seen are those of bleeding due to vitamin K depletion.

There are many areas in which cephalosporins have been used, particularly respiratory, oral, abdominal, urinary tract, bone, gynecological, and neurological infections, and in septicemia. Roles in skin and soft tissue infections have been advocated for the drugs, but the agents still are a second choice and the investigational agents offer most for the uncommon multiresistant bacterial infection. *See* ANTIBIOTIC.   Harold Neu

Bibliography. H. C. Neu, *J. Antimicrob. Chemother.*, 6(Suppl.A):1–11, 1980.

Cepheids

A class of highly luminous yellow stars that vary periodically in brightness. Approximately one out of a thousand of the intrinsically brightest stars in any galaxy, like the Milky Way Galaxy, is a classical Cepheid variable. Among the 6000 apparently brightest stars visible to the unaided human eye in the night sky, more than a dozen are Cepheids (including Delta Cephei, the prototype; Beta Doradus in the south; and Polaris, the Pole Star). Cepheids have the same yellow color as the Sun (and hence, similar surface temperatures), but they have larger radii and therefore are intrinsically 1000 to over 100,000 times more luminous. Named for their naked-eye prototype Delta Cephei, the Cepheids are very well understood, and have repeatedly proved to be immensely important to many aspects of modern astronomy. Not only are Cepheids bright (supergiant) stars, so that they can be seen over large distances, but also they are at a particular stage in their evolution such that they are unstable to periodic oscillations. Motion of their surface manifests itself as regular changes in the apparent luminosity with time and so they can be easily identified. *See* POLARIS; SUPERGIANT STAR.

Distance indicators. The importance of Cepheids to astronomy comes both in their application to practical problems of distance determination (within the Milky Way Galaxy itself, and far beyond) and in their acting as critical tests of both stellar evolution and pulsation theory. From theoretical considerations, the period of oscillation and the intrinsic luminosity of a Cepheid can be understood in terms of the star's internal structure, mass, radius, and temperature. From observations it is known that the luminosity is closely predicted by the period of oscillation, a relation known as the period-luminosity relation, discovered by Henrietta Leavitt in 1912. This relation provides a powerful tool for estimating distances, since the period can be determined without prior knowledge of the distance. Using the period to predict how bright a given star would appear at various distances, it is possible to calculate the distance of a Cepheid from the observer, given its apparent luminosity. Knowledge of the intrinsic luminosity, surface temperature, and period of oscillation enable theorists to place Cepheids into their grid of evolutionary models from which ages and masses of these pulsating stars can be derived. Similarly, computer models can be constructed to match the oscillation behavior of real Cepheids, thereby predicting the mass, temperature, and internal structure needed to maintain such an instability.

In the 1920s, Edwin Hubble conclusively ended the debate as to whether other galaxies existed in addition to the Milky Way when he discovered Cepheids in nebulae now considered to make up the Local Group of galaxies. Among them were M31 and M33, situated at distances now known to be about 700 kiloparsecs (2.3×10^6 light-years). Hubble went on to show that the distances of galaxies correlated with their apparent recession velocities, consistent with an expanding universe. Cepheids have continued to play an extremely important role in measuring distances to galaxies. *See* GALAXY, EXTERNAL; HUBBLE CONSTANT; LOCAL GROUP.

Variability. Cepheids are generally identified by the distinctive and periodic optical variations in their light output. The time period over which a complete cycle is executed ranges from a few days to a few hundred days. Most Cepheids show an abrupt rise in their luminosity followed by a slower decline (**Fig. 1**), although some special varieties have a more symmetric (and generally lower-amplitude) light curve.

Light variability alone is ambiguous to interpret, but the analysis of the spectroscopic properties of a star, including the time variation of the radial velocities of Cepheids, ultimately led to the identification of the mechanism behind the changing light. The total light variation is the result of temperature changes in the stellar atmosphere, induced by, and combined with, an inward and outward motion of the surface of the star. Depending on the particular star, these excursions range from a few percent up to 10% of the mean radius of the Cepheid. The resulting velocities associated with the pulsation are observed to be in the range 10–70 km/s (6–43 mi/s).

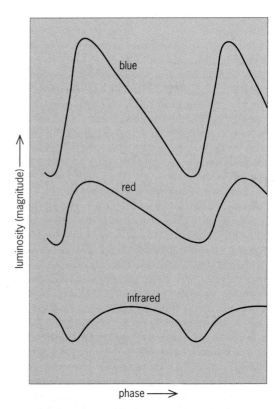

Fig. 1. Changes in Cepheid light curves as a function of wavelength.

Measurements of the color variation, interpreted as surface temperature variations, suggest that the surface temperature is changing by a few hundred kelvins during the pulsation cycle. The surface temperature changes the surface brightness and, especially at visible wavelengths, this is the primary cause of the large observed periodic light variation of a Cepheid. *See* ASTRONOMICAL SPECTROSCOPY; VARIABLE STAR.

The theory of stellar pulsation has been worked out in considerable detail, and confirmed in large measure by both linear and nonlinear computer modeling. The second helium ionization layer is now known to be the main driver of pulsation in Cepheid variables. If slightly perturbed in temperature, this zone can either add considerable energy to the flow of radiation from the center of the star, by recombining and releasing the ionization energy, or it can extract energy from the flow by ionizing new material. This situation is unstable to slight perturbations in temperature because there is an opportunity for a cycling between these two states of ionization to occur. Energy is siphoned from the flow to ionize the material. The increased number of particles (the newly liberated electrons) contribute added pressure, forcing outward the layers above. The outward motion takes the layer to cooler temperatures, which then trigger a recombination of the previously liberated electrons back onto the helium nuclei. The stored energy is released back into the flow. The pressure falls and the layer collapses. The temperature in the layer increases again, and the cycle repeats. This is a so-called heat engine, and it drives the Cepheid variability.

The interesting question remains as to what limits the variability of stars at higher and lower temperatures. If this ionization layer occurs at a point in the atmosphere where the weight of material above it is so large that it dominates the small perturbation caused by the change of state, little effect will be seen at the surface. If the same ionization layer occurs (at the same temperature) very far out in the atmosphere, there may be too little material to make any impact on the remaining atmosphere. However, at a particular placement the ionization layers can in principle impact the stability of a sizable portion of the outer layers of the star. The narrow temperature range over which the ionization layer and the mass of the atmosphere above that layer resonate with each other sets some of the fundamental limits on what observers see as the Cepheid instability strip. Although temperature is the primary cause for setting off the instability from the high-temperature side, it is generally thought that the cool-temperature limit on the strip is primarily set by the onset of convection in the atmosphere. Unfortunately, present understanding of convection is still rudimentary and details have yet to be modeled.

Types. There are several types of Cepheids. The most important distinction is between the young, high-mass classical Cepheids and their old, low-mass counterparts, the W Virginis stars. The latter belong to the population II component of the Milky Way Galaxy, and are now evolving through a completely different stage of stellar evolution than the classical Cepheids. Because their surface temperatures are virtually identical at this stage of evolution, both types of stars are subject to the same instability that allows the pulsations to occur; however, because the stars are of significantly different mass, their radii and intrinsic luminosities are quite different even for the same observed period. This ambiguity led to immense confusion early in the twentieth century, and ultimately accounted for an incorrect estimate by Hubble of the size of the universe.

Evolution. Classical Cepheids are relatively high-mass stars, 3–30 times more massive than the Sun. However, unlike the Sun, they have already exhausted the supply of hydrogen fuel in their cores and have commenced burning helium. Helium ignition occurs at a significantly higher temperature than hydrogen burning and ultimately leads the star to higher luminosities, at cooler surface temperatures and significantly larger radii. During this evolution of the star core, and the subsequent restructuring of the outer envelope and surrounding atmosphere, the supergiant star passes through a region of temperature and radius where stars are unstable to small perturbations of their atmosphere. This instability strip is narrowly defined in temperature but extends over a wide range of luminosities.

Population I stars enter the instability strip as classical Cepheids when their surface temperatures are in the 5000–7000 K range; the lower-luminosity, higher-temperature extension of the instability strip is occupied by stars called Delta Scuti variables, whose temperatures are in the 7000–8000 K range. Population II stars also pass through similar instabilities. In the low-mass, low-luminosity range are found the RR Lyrae variables (once called cluster Cepheids because of their frequent and close association with globular star clusters). RR Lyrae variables have periods in the range of 0.5–1 day. At higher luminosities are the W Virginis stars with periods up to 20 days. *See* STELLAR ROTATION.

Light curves. From an observational point of view Cepheids are known to change their light curve characteristics as a function of the wavelength at which they are observed (Fig. 1). In the green, blue, and ultraviolet wavelengths the light curves are quite asymmetric, showing a rapid rise followed by a slow, linear decline, to give a sawtooth shape. The amplitude of the variation is a declining function of wavelength, with the ultraviolet amplitudes being upward of 2 magnitudes and visual amplitudes for the same variable dropping by a factor of 2 in comparison. In the red and infrared, the amplitudes continue to decline but less rapidly than in the blue. Moreover, the shape of the light curve changes dramatically, converging on a more symmetric shape reminiscent of a cycloid rather than a sawtooth, and the maximum moves to later phases.

This change can be understood as follows. In the green and blue the dominant physics giving rise to the variability is the change in surface brightness (dominated by temperature variations). In the

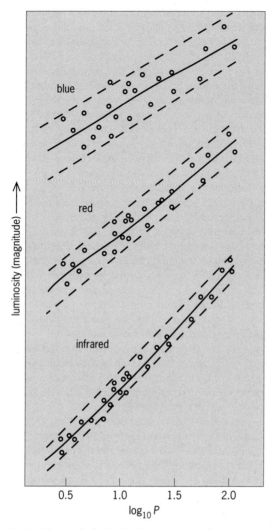

Fig. 2. Changes in the Cepheid period-luminosity relation with wavelength. Luminosity is plotted as a function of the logarithm of the period *P*, in days. In the blue the period-luminosity relation has significant scatter and its rise in luminosity with increasing period is relatively shallow. The scatter decreases with increased wavelength, while the slope of the period-luminosity relation increases toward the red and infrared.

important role in the change of brightness of the Cepheids, the temperature-induced width of the period-luminosity relation at a fixed period is expected to decrease; this is, in fact, precisely what is observed (**Fig. 2**). Observing Cepheids at infrared wavelengths leads to an increase in accuracy in distance determinations since the dispersion (scatter) in the period-luminosity relation is decreased.

There are two other significant advantages to observing at redder wavelengths. First, the effects of extinction due to dust are reduced [by a factor of 10 when going from blue (450 nanometers) to K-band (2.2 micrometers) observations]. Finally, the effects of scattering and absorption due to the presence of metals in the atmospheres of the Cepheids are most severe at bluer wavelengths. *See* INTERSTELLAR EXTINCTION.

Distance measurements. With the aid of the Hubble Space Telescope, Cepheids have been found in galaxies as far away as the Virgo cluster, more than 20 times farther away than the Andromeda galaxy, M31, in the Local Group. At these distances, the general expansion of the universe begins to dominate the radial velocities of the galaxies. (For nearby galaxies, the motions of galaxies can be perturbed by the interaction with neighbors, or motions due to bulk flows can be a significant component of the observed velocity.) Cepheids currently provide the most accurate zero point for the calibration of other (secondary) distance methods (for example, bright supernovae) which extend the range of distance measurements by over a factor of 10. At such distances, the observed velocities are representative of the overall expansion of the universe. *See* COSMOLOGY; STAR; UNIVERSE; VARIABLE STAR.   Barry F. Madore; Wendy L. Freedman

Bibliography. A. N. Cox, Cepheid masses from observations and pulsation theory, *Astrophys. J.*, 229: 212–222, 1979; M. W. Feast and A. R. Walker, The Cepheid distance scale, *Annu. Rev. Astron. Astrophys.*, 25:345–375, 1987; W. L. Freedman, The expansion rate and size of the universe, in D. H. Levy (ed.), *Scientific American Book of the Cosmos*, pp. 377–384, Scientific American, 2000; W. L. Freedman et al., Final results from the *Hubble Space Telescope* Key Project to measure the Hubble constant, *Astrophys J.*, 553:47–72, 2001; G. Jacoby et al., A critical review of selected techniques for measuring extragalactic distances, *Publ. Astron. Soc. Pacif.*, 104:599–662, 1992; B. F. Madore and W. L. Freedman, The Cepheid distance scale, *Publ. Astron. Soc. Pacif.*, 103:933–957, 1991.

infrared the variability primarily reflects the geometric change in the surface area of the star, being driven by the relatively small radius variations. The physics is such that temperature variations change the surface brightness far more dramatically in the blue than they do in the infrared. Analysis of the radial velocity curves for Cepheids predicts both the shape and amplitude of the radius-area variations; these correspond to what is indeed observed in the infrared. *See* LIGHT CURVES.

Period-luminosity relation. For the same physical reasons described above, the period-luminosity relations change as a function of wavelength. The width of the period-luminosity relation is a reflection of the color width of the instability strip. At a particular period, intrinsically bluer (hotter, therefore higher-surface-brightness) stars are brighter. Cooler, redder stars are intrinsically fainter. At longer wavelengths, where temperature variations play a decreasingly

Ceramics

Inorganic, nonmetallic materials processed or consolidated at high temperature. This definition includes a wide range of materials known as advanced ceramics and is much broader than the common dictionary definition, which includes only pottery, tile, porcelain, and so forth. The classes of materials generally considered to be ceramics are oxides, nitrides, borides, carbides, silicides, and sulfides. Intermetallic compounds such as aluminides and beryllides are also considered ceramics, as are phosphides, antimonides, and arsenides. *See* INTERMETALLIC COMPOUNDS.

Ceramic materials can be subdivided into traditional and advanced ceramics. Traditional ceramics include clay-base materials such as brick, tile, sanitary ware, dinnerware, clay pipe, and electrical porcelain. Common-usage glass, cement, abrasives, and refractories are also important classes of traditional ceramics.

Advanced materials technology is often cited as an enabling technology, enabling engineers to design and build advanced systems for applications in fields such as aerospace, automotive, and electronics. Advanced ceramics are tailored to have premium properties through application of advanced materials science and technology to control composition and internal structure. Examples of advanced ceramic materials are silicon nitride, silicon carbide, toughened zirconia, zirconia-toughened alumina, aluminum nitride, lead magnesium niobate, lead lanthanum zirconate titanate, silicon-carbide-whisker–reinforced alumina, carbon-fiber–reinforced glass ceramic, silicon-carbide-fiber–reinforced silicon carbide, and high-temperature superconductors. Advanced ceramics can be viewed as a class of the broader field of advanced materials, which can be divided into ceramics, metals, polymers, composites, and electronic materials. There is considerable overlap among these classes of materials. *See* CERMET; COMPOSITE MATERIAL; GLASS; POLYMER.

Advanced ceramics can be subdivided into structural and electronic ceramics based on primary function or application. Optical and magnetic materials are usually included in the electronic classification. Structural applications include engine components, cutting tools, bearings, valves, wear- and corrosion-resistant parts, heat exchangers, fibers and whiskers, and biological implants. The electronic-magnetic-optic functions include electronic substrates, electronic packages, capacitors, transducers, magnets, waveguides, lamp envelopes, displays, sensors, and ceramic superconductors. Thermal insulation, membranes, and filters are important advanced ceramic product areas that do not fit well into either the structural or the electronic class of advanced ceramics.

Fabrication Processes

A wide variety of processes are used to fabricate ceramics. The process chosen for a particular product is based on the material, shape complexity, property requirements, and cost. Ceramic fabrication processes can be divided into four generic categories: powder, vapor, chemical, and melt processes.

Powder processes. Traditional clay-base ceramics and most refractories are fabricated by powder processes, as are the majority of advanced ceramics. Powder processing involves a number of sequential steps. These are preparation of the starting powders, forming the desired shape (green forming), re-moval of water and organics, heating with or without application of pressure to densify the powder, and finishing.

Powder preparation. The starting powders for traditional ceramics are predominantly clays and other natural minerals which have been processed to achieve the purity and particle size desired. The methods of mining, crushing, and milling are similar to those operations in other industries. The starting powders for advanced ceramics are high-purity specialty chemicals. These powders have many similarities to high-quality inorganic pigments. Powder preparation is a critical step in the fabrication of advanced ceramics, since high-quality advanced ceramics require high-purity, submicrometer powders with controlled physical characteristics such as particle size. The availability of high-quality, low-cost powders with reproducible characteristics is a critical requirement for use of advanced ceramic materials in many emerging applications. *See* CRUSHING AND PULVERIZING; GRINDING MILL.

Advanced ceramic powders are produced by a number of processes, including precipitation, calcination, and vapor-phase processes. The primary process is chemical precipitation, followed by calcination (heating) to remove water and other volatiles and to achieve the desired crystallinity and physical characteristics. After calcination, powders are ground, usually in ball mills, to break the bonds between individual crystallites formed by diffusion during calcination, thus producing a powder with a submicrometer particle size. In addition to conventional precipitation, a number of other precipitation processes can be used, including precipitation under pressure (hydrothermal) and simultaneous precipitation of more than one cation (coprecipitation). Hydrothermal precipitation can produce mixed cation precipitates and can precipitate oxides directly, whereas conventional precipitation usually produces hydroxides or salts which must be calcined to form oxides. Coprecipitation is used for many advanced multication powders to obtain more intimate mixing of the cations than can be achieved by mixing oxides or salts of the individual cations, as discussed below under calcination. Because of the intimate mixing produced by coprecipitation, the calcination temperature required to produce the desired crystalline phase in the powder is usually lower than for calcination of mixtures of individual oxides. *See* PRECIPITATION (CHEMISTRY).

Calcination is involved in the production of most advanced ceramic powders. For precipitated powders, a subsequent calcination step is usually required, as described above. Many multi-cation powders, such as an oxide which contains nickel, zinc, and iron [$(Ni,Zn)Fe_2O_4$], are formed by calcining mixtures of the individual oxides or salts of the cations. Many nonoxide powders can also be produced by some form of calcination. Most silicon carbide (SiC) is produced by high-temperature reaction of a mixture of sand (silicon dioxide; SiO_2) and carbon powders. Silicon nitride (Si_3N_4) powder can be produced by reacting a mixture of SiO_2 and carbon at high temperature in a nitrogen atmosphere or by reacting silicon metal powder with nitrogen at high temperatures.

Powders for most advanced ceramics can also be produced by vapor-phase reaction. In this process, reactant gases are mixed and heated to nucleate and grow particles from the gas phase. A number of different heat sources for the reaction can be used, such as a direct-current or induction-coupled plasma, a laser, or a furnace.

Green forming. The ceramic fabrication step in which powders are formed into useful shapes is called green forming. A wide variety of processes are used for green forming. The process chosen is based on the material being fabricated, the shape desired, the property requirements, and the production cost. Green-forming processes include casting, extrusion, jiggering, die pressing, isostatic pressing, tape casting, and injection molding. Some form of treatment of the starting powders is usually required for green forming, and the treatment depends on the green-forming process and the material. Green-forming processes for clay-base ceramics usually take advantage of the plastic behavior of clay–water mixtures. Organic plasticizers are often added to achieve the desired plasticity if clay is not one of the starting powders.

Slip casting is a green-forming process in which the starting powders are suspended in water to form a slip. Green shapes are formed by pouring the slip into porous molds made of plaster of paris or another suitable material. The capillary action of the porous mold draws water from the slip and forms a solid layer on the inside of the mold. When the desired part thickness has been obtained, the excess slip is poured out of the mold (**Fig. 1**). The part is partially dried in the mold to cause it to shrink away from the mold and develop adequate rigidity for handling. This process is an economical way to form complex shapes and is used for hollow objects such as artware and sanitary ware. Slip preparation is critical to slip casting and requires optimization among a number of factors, including viscosity, solids contents, slip stability, casting rate, drying rate, and drying shrinkage. One of the critical factors in developing a slip is controlling the degree of deflocculation. This involves an understanding of the surface chemistry of the particles in the slip. *See* PORCELAIN; POTTERY.

Pressure casting has begun to replace conventional slip casting. In pressure casting, a pressure is applied to the slip to supplement or replace the capillary action of the porous mold. The advantages of pressure casting over conventional slip casting are higher casting rate, ability to automate the process, and extension of the useful application of slip casting to colloidal nonclay powders.

Extrusion is a process in which a stiff plastic mass is forced through a die that has the desired cross section of the object to be formed. The extruded column is then cut to the desired length. Secondary shaping processes are often used to further shape the extruded object. Extrusion is the primary pro-

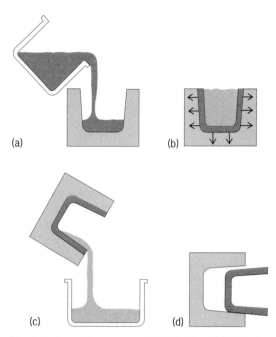

Fig. 1. Drain-casting process. (*a*) Mold being filled with slip. (*b*) Mold extracting liquid, forming compact along mold walls. (*c*) Excess slip being drained. (*d*) Casting removed after partial drying. (*After D. W. Richerson, Modern Ceramic Engineering, Marcel Dekker, 1982*)

cess used to fabricate structural clay products such as building brick and clay sewer pipe. The starting materials for these products are primarily clays that have been ground into a powder and blended with 10–15% water to form a stiff mud, which is extruded. Other products which are formed by extrusion include thermocouple insulation tubes and catalyst supports for automotive emission control. In general, any material with a constant cross section can be formed by extrusion. *See* EXTRUSION.

Jiggering is a mechanization of the hand-throwing process used by potters. It consists of molding one side of a piece by placing a slab of plastic material (usually cut from an extruded log) on a porous plaster of paris mold, placing the mold and plastic slab on a rotating head, and forming the other side of the object by forcing a template of the desired contour against the plastic slab. Dinner plates are usually formed by this process, and the powder used for this product is a mixture of clays, potter's flint, and feldspar. *See* CLAY; CLAY, COMMERCIAL; FELDSPAR.

Powder pressing is a process in which a powder containing 0–5% water is green-formed by compaction under pressure. This process is used for a wide variety of traditional and advanced ceramic products, including floor and wall tile, some refractories, spark plug insulators, and many electronic ceramics. In general, if the shape permits, powder pressing is used for green forming. There are two basic types of powder pressing, die pressing and isostatic pressing. In die pressing, which is limited to relatively simple shapes, a steel or tungsten carbide die consisting of a die cavity and internal punches is used. Powder is placed in the die cavity, and force is applied through the punches to compact the powder

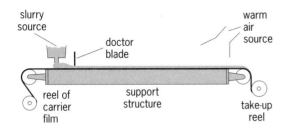

Fig. 2. Schematic diagram of doctor-blade tape casting process. (*After D. W. Richerson, Modern Ceramic Engineering, Marcel Dekker, 1982*)

into the desired shape. Isostatic pressing is used to extend green forming by powder compaction into more complex shapes. For example, spark plug insulators are pressed isostatically by placing the powder around a central mandrel pin in a flexible mold which is compressed by using a pressure vessel to apply fluid pressure to the outside of the mold. The pressed blank is then ground on an automatic grinder to form the green part to the desired dimensions and contours. Most powders used for powder pressing are wet-blended to the desired composition, which includes organic binders and lubricants, and spray-dried so that they flow. *See* ELECTRICAL INSULATION.

In tape casting or the doctor-blade process, a powder slurry is drawn under a dam (doctor blade) to form a thin layer on a moving plastic belt (**Fig. 2**). This is the primary process for forming ceramic substrates for integrated electronic circuits. An organic liquid is used as the medium for the slurry to facilitate rapid removal by subsequent evaporation to form the green tape. *See* INTEGRATED CIRCUITS.

Injection molding is a process in which a plastic blend of ceramic powder and organic materials is extruded into a steel mold to form a green shape. The process is similar to injection molding of filled plastics. However, for ceramics the organic substance must be removed so that the powder shape can be densified. Injection molding is used for forming complex shapes. Thread guides and turbocharger rotors are two ceramic products that are formed by this process.

Removal of water and organics. After green forming, a drying or organic removal step is usually required before proceeding to the densification step. The process required depends on the green-forming process and the ceramic material being fabricated. For injection-molded parts, the organic (binder) removal step is especially critical, while drying is critical for slip-cast or extruded parts.

Densification. In the densification, step the porous powder shape is converted into a dense part. The three primary processes used for final densification are sintering, hot pressing, and hot isostatic pressing. Sintering is often referred to as firing or vitrification, especially for traditional ceramics. Sintering involves heating a porous powder shape to a temperature sufficient to activate various thermal processes that lead to densification of the part. The two

general mechanisms of densification during sintering are liquid-phase sintering and solid-state sintering. The driving force for sintering is reduction of the free surface energy. Most traditional ceramics are densified by liquid-phase sintering, as are alumina spark plug insulators. Materials such as dinnerware, sanitary ware, and electrical porcelain contain finely ground feldspar as one of the starting materials. When the part is heated, the feldspar melts and forms a viscous liquid which promotes densification by viscous flow. In many other ceramics, liquid phases are formed by chemical reaction between the individual starting materials. In many advanced ceramics, solid-state sintering is the predominant sintering mechanism. Solid-state sintering occurs by solid-state diffusion processes, and high-surface-area powders, generally below 1 micrometer in diameter, are especially critical to sintering by this process. *See* SINTERING.

Hot pressing is a process in which pressure is applied to a powder or powder compact in a die at elevated temperature (**Fig. 3**). The pressure enhances the thermal processes involved in sintering and often activates new processes. Dies are generally made of graphite. Materials that cannot be densified by sintering without pressure can be densified by using hot pressing. Hot pressing can also be used to produce materials with special properties, such as cutting-tool inserts. The principal disadvantages of hot pressing are cost and a limitation on the shapes that can be fabricated.

Hot isostatic pressing (HIP) is similar to isostatic compaction of powders, except that the compaction process is carried out at elevated temperatures. The equipment consists of a cold-wall autoclave with an internal furnace. Gas, typically argon, is used as the pressurizing fluid in place of the water or oil used for cold isostatic compaction of powders. Hermetically sealed metal or glass enclosures (known as cans) are used to encase the powder compact and act as the barrier to transfer the gas pressure to an isostatic

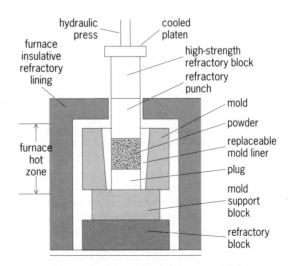

Fig. 3. Schematic diagram showing the essential elements of a hot press. (*After D. W. Richerson, Modern Ceramic Engineering, Marcel Dekker, 1982*)

compaction force on the powder compact. Hot isostatic pressing is also used to further densify materials that have been sintered to eliminate continuous or interconnected porosity. This process is referred to as post-HIP, and a can is not required since the part acts as its own can. The primary advantages of hot isostatic pressing over hot pressing are the ability to densify more complex shapes and the ability to apply higher pressures to densify a wide range of materials. *See* POWDER METALLURGY.

Finishing. After densification, many ceramic products require some finishing to achieve the required dimensional tolerance or surface finish. Since ceramics generally have high hardness, the conventional machining used for finishing metals cannot be used. Diamond cutting, grinding, and core drilling are the most common finishing techniques, but ultrasonic cutting and laser drilling and cutting are frequently used. Electric discharge machining is used if the electrical conductivity of the material is high enough.

Vapor processes. The primary vapor processes used to fabricate ceramics are chemical vapor deposition and sputtering. Vapor processes have been finding an increasing number of applications. Chemical vapor deposition involves bringing gases containing the atoms to make up the ceramic into contact with a heated surface, where the gases react to form a coating. This process is used to apply ceramic coatings to metal and tungsten carbide cutting tools as well as to apply a wide variety of other coatings for wear, electronic, and corrosion applications. Chemical vapor deposition can also be used to form monolithic ceramics by building up thick coatings. A form of chemical vapor deposition known as chemical vapor infiltration has been developed to infiltrate and coat the surfaces of fibers in woven preforms. The coating on individual fibers leads to densification of the preform to produce ceramic-ceramic composites such as silicon carbide-fiber–reinforced silicon carbide that are being developed for applications in high-temperature aerospace engines. *See* HIGH-TEMPERATURE MATERIALS; VAPOR DEPOSITION.

Several variations of sputtering and other vacuum coating processes can be used to form coatings of ceramic materials. The most common process is reactive sputtering, used to form coatings such as titanium nitride on tool steel. This process involves vaporizing titanium from a titanium target by use of a magnetron that accelerates ions such as argon against the target in order to vaporize titanium atoms, which deposit on a substrate maintained at a fixed temperature in a low-pressure plasma containing nitrogen. The titanium and nitrogen react on the substrate (such as a cutting tool) to form a titanium nitride coating. *See* MAGNETRON; SPUTTERING.

Chemical processes. A number of different chemical processes are used to fabricate advanced ceramics. The chemical vapor deposition process described above as a vapor process is also a chemical process. Two other chemical processes finding increasing application in advanced ceramics are poly-

mer pyrolysis and sol-gel technology.

Polymer pyrolysis. This involves the controlled heating of organometallic compounds to break down the organic molecules and remove the organic radicals. The residue is a ceramic material, and the starting organometallics are known as precursors. With appropriate selection of the precursor, a wide variety of oxide and nonoxide ceramics can be formed. The process is similar to the fabrication of carbon fibers or of the matrix in carbon-carbon composites by controlled pyrolysis of pitch. Silicon carbide fibers can be manufactured by using organometallic precursors such as polycarbosilane. Similar precursors can be used to incorporate a ceramic matrix in a woven preform of silicon carbide fibers to produce silicon carbide-fiber–reinforced silicon carbide composites. *See* CERMET.

Sol-gel technology. In addition to its use as a process for manufacturing advanced ceramic powders, sol-gel technology is used to fabricate advanced ceramics. This process involves the formation of a suspension of colloidal particles (sol) which is converted to a gel by chemical treatment. The gel is then dried and sintered to form a ceramic product. The overall process in which dense materials are fabricated directly from the preformed gel without going through a powder stage is known as the sol-gel monolith process. As a result of the fine pore size of the dried gel, the sintering temperatures are lower than those required for similar materials formed from powders. Many ceramic fibers are manufactured by the sol-gel monolith process, and the process is beginning to find many other applications in advanced ceramics in biomedical, electronic, and other fields. *See* COLLOID; GEL.

Melt processes. These are used to manufacture glass, to fuse-cast refractories for use in furnace linings, and to grow single crystals. *See* REFRACTORY.

Thermal spraying can also be classified as a melt process. In this process, a plasma-spray gun is used to apply ceramic (or metal) coatings by melting and spraying powders onto a substrate. Powder particles are entrained in a gas stream in which a plasma is formed to melt (or soften) the particles as they are accelerated onto the substrate surface. For materials with lower melting points, a flame-spray gun can be used. In this process, an oxygen-acetylene flame is used in place of a plasma, and the feed material can be a powder or a rod of the material to be deposited. Ceramic coatings applied by plasma spraying are used for corrosion protection in applications such as aircraft engine parts and for wear resistance in applications such as on rotating shafts in seals and slide bearings.

Applications. The selection of materials for engineering applications is based on performance requirements and cost, as well as other factors.

The general advantages of advanced structural ceramics over metals and polymers are high-temperature strength, wear resistance, and chemical stability, in addition to the enabling functions the ceramics can perform. Typical properties for some engineering ceramics are shown in the **table**.

Typical properties for some ceramic materials

Property	Aluminum oxide	Silicon nitride	Silicon carbide	Partially stabilized zirconia
Density, g/cm^3	3.9	3.2	3.1	5.7
Flexure strength, MPa	350	850	450	790
Modulus of elasticity, GPa	407	310	400	205
Fracture toughness (K_{IC}), $MPa\cdot m^{1/2}$	5	5	4	12
Thermal conductivity, W/mK	34	33	110	3
Mean coefficient of thermal expansion ($\times 10^{-6}/°C$)	7.7	2.6	4.4	10.2

High-temperature strength. This property of advanced ceramics is important in many potential applications, especially in components for the hot sections of engines and heat exchangers. The maximum use temperature for superalloys is 1800°F (1000°C). The only metals usable above this temperature are refractory metals that lack the oxidation resistance required for high-temperature applications in an oxidizing environment. Silicon nitride and silicon carbide have adequate oxidation resistance to be used in air up to 2600 and 2700°F (1400 and 1500°C), respectively. They also have adequate strength for many applications at these temperatures, although many silicon nitride materials are limited to use at lower temperatures because of additives that are used to aid in their fabrication. Many ceramic materials have higher melting points than silicon carbide and silicon nitride but lack adequate oxidation resistance for use at high temperatures. The other factor, which is usually critical for advanced ceramics in high-temperature applications, is thermal-shock fracture resistance. The thermal-shock fracture resistance under steady-state heat transfer is proportional to

$$\frac{\text{Strength}}{\text{Elastic modulus}} \times \frac{\text{thermal conductivity}}{\text{thermal expansion}}$$

Under highly transient conditions, the thermal conductivity is not a factor. Most engineering applications fall between the two extremes of steady-state and highly transient conditions. Comparison of the data in the table shows why silicon nitride and silicon carbide are far superior to alumina and zirconia for high-temperature applications where temperature gradients are expected. Two lower-temperature examples of an application involving thermal stress are ceramic stovetops and cookware. These materials have a thermal expansion near zero; therefore, stresses from thermal gradients are very low.

Wear resistance. Another important requirement for applications of materials is resistance to failure under impact loading. While metals generally exhibit ductible behavior, ceramic materials generally exhibit brittle failure; they are much more susceptible to failure due to high local stresses from impact loading. The toughness values in the table indicate the high toughness of partially stabilized zirconia relative to the other materials shown. In the same units, glass has a toughness of less than 1. The utilitarian fracture resistance of partially stabilized zirconia under impact loading is quite different from that of glass

and even of silicon nitride. For example, a hammer made from partially stabilized zirconia can be used to drive nails without chipping, and a partially stabilized zirconia shovel was dropped onto concrete from a height of three stories without breaking. In addition to partially stabilized zirconia, other materials such as alumina can be toughened by adding zirconia particles of the correct size and composition. Ceramic whisker- and fiber-reinforced ceramics possessing high toughness have also been developed. These advances have opened additional engineering applications for advanced ceramics.

In general, ceramic materials have a much higher hardness than metals, a property that leads to high wear resistance. Valve guides and cam followers for advanced engines, sandblast nozzles, grinding media, thread guides, cutting tools, pump parts, and extrusion dies are all applications for ceramics that result from their wear resistance. *See* WEAR.

Chemical stability. Ceramic materials also have better corrosion resistance than metals or polymers, particularly in erosive wear applications. This leads to applications in valves, pumps, and pipe linings for chemical, petrochemical, and other industries. *See* CORROSION.

For electronics, advanced ceramic materials have been developed which have piezoelectric, electro-optic, pyroelectric, and many other first- and second-order effects, and thus many special electronic, optical, or magnetic properties; this allows the ceramics to be tailored for specific advanced systems, a distinct advantage. *See* PIEZOELECTRICITY.

Enabling functions. Many of the applications of advanced ceramics are based on the enabling functions they can perform in advanced systems such as automotive engines, aerospace hardware, and electronics. For example, in advanced automotive engines, silicon nitride rotors enable the design of a turbocharger with a more rapid response to the accelerator, because the density of silicon nitride is lower than that of competitive metals, and its high-temperature strength, oxidation resistance, and resistance to thermal stress are good. The incentive to develop and apply advanced ceramics often lies with the manufacturer of a system, if the value added is sufficient to justify the required investment.

The enabling function of advanced ceramics is most apparent in high-temperature superconductors. In January 1986, J. G. Bednorz and K. A. Müller discovered superconductivity in lanthanum barium copper oxide and, in April 1986, announced their finding that it occurred at temperatures as high as

35 K ($-405°$F). Also, in February 1986, a group including C.-W. Chu and M. K. Wu discovered superconductivity in yttrium barium copper oxide up to 92 K ($-294°$F). Subsequent developments have resulted in higher-temperature ceramic superconductors. These events have generated a massive research and development effort around the world. The reason for the interest in this class of superconductors is its strong potential enabling functions, many of which may not yet be conceived. *See* SUPERCONDUCTIVITY.

The primary disadvantages of most advanced ceramics are in the areas of reliability, reproducibility, and cost. Major advances in reliability are being made through development of tougher materials such as partially stabilized zirconia and ceramic whiskers; and reinforced ceramics such as silicon-carbide-whisker-reinforced alumina used for cutting tools, and silicon-carbide-fiber-reinforced silicon carbide for high-temperature engine applications. Reproducibility is being improved by developments in manufacturing technology. Cost is expected to drop as materials science, manufacturing technology, and engineering design with ceramics are further developed.

The major applications for advanced ceramics are in electronics and include substrates for electronic circuits, electronic packages, capacitors, magnetic components, piezoelectric components, electronic sensors, and integrated optic components. Advanced ceramics are also finding many applications where wear resistance and corrosion resistance are critical, such as extrusion dies and pump components. Advanced ceramic components have been introduced into automotive and other engines, and these applications are expected to grow. Automotive engine applications include turbocharger rotors, valves, valve guides, valve seats and other valve-train components, fuel-injector nozzles, exhaust-port inserts, and advanced diesel engine components. Automotive gas turbines whose hot section consists wholly of advanced ceramic components are under development, and advanced ceramic composites are expected to play a major role in the engine for the aerospace plane as well as other aerospace systems. In the machine tool industry, advanced ceramic cutting tools have increased productivity up to tenfold over metal and carbide tools, and advanced ceramic bearings are being applied where high loads and high rigidity are needed. In communications, glass fiber-optic cable has revolutionized the electronic transmission of voice and data. *See* AUTOMOTIVE ENGINE.

Advanced ceramics will continue to play key enabling functions in a wide variety of advanced systems, and traditional ceramics will continue to fill important needs in consumer, building, and industrial products.   Dale E. Niesz

Bibliography. M. W. Barsoum, *Fundamentals of Ceramics*, 2002; W. D. Kingery, H. K. Bowen, and D. R. Uhlmann, *Introduction to Ceramics*, 2d ed., 1976; D. W. Richerson, *Modern Ceramic Engineering*, 3d ed., 2005; S. Saito, *Fine Ceramics*, 1987.

Cerargyrite

A mineral with composition AgCl (see **illus.**). Its structure is that of the isometric NaCl type, but well-formed cubic crystals are rare. The hardness is 2.5

Cerargyrite crystals from Leadville, Colorado. (*Specimen from Department of Geology, Bryn Mawr College*)

on Mohs scale and specific gravity 5.5. Cerargyrite is colorless to pearl-gray but darkens to violet-brown on exposure to light. It is perfectly sectile and can be cut with a knife like horn; hence the name horn silver. Bromyrite, AgBr, is physically indistinguishable from cerargyrite and the two minerals form a complete series. Both minerals are secondary ores of silver and occur in the oxidized zone of silver deposits. *See* HALITE; SILVER.   Cornelius S. Hurlbut, Jr.

Ceratophyllales

An order of flowering plants (angiosperms) previously thought to be related closely to the waterlilies because one genus of the latter, *Cabomba* (Nymphaeaceae), has similarly highly dissected leaves. Studies of deoxyribonucleic acid (DNA) sequences have revealed that the single genus of the order, *Ceratophyllum* (Ceratophyllaceae), has no close relationship to any other extant group of flowering plants. It is an old, highly specialized plant, modified for a fresh-water aquatic habitat. Fossil fruits attributed to it are more than 120 million years old, which makes it the oldest extant angiosperm genus. The plants are submersed, rootless aquatics with highly dissected, branching leaves; they have reduced, separately sexed, petalless flowers. There are probably only six species distributed throughout fresh-water systems worldwide. *See* FLOWER; FOSSIL SEEDS AND FRUITS; MAGNOLIOPHYTA; PLANT EVOLUTION.   Mark W. Chase

Cereal

Any member of the grass family (Gramineae) which produces edible grains usable as food by humans and livestock. Common cereals are rice, wheat, barley, oats, maize (corn), sorghum, rye, and certain millets. Triticale is cereal derived from crossing wheat and rye and then doubling the number of chromosomes in the hybrid. Occasionally, grains from other grasses (for example, teff) are used for food. Cereals are summer or winter annuals. Corn, rice, and wheat are the most important cereals. Today, as in ancient times, cereals provide more food for human consumption than any other crops. *See* BARLEY; CORN; CYPERALES; OATS; SORGHUM; RICE; RYE; WHEAT.

Cereal grains have many natural advantages as foods. They are nutritious. One kind or another can be grown almost anywhere on Earth. The grains are not bulky and therefore can be shipped inexpensively for long distances and stored for long periods of time. They are readily processed to give highly refined raw foods.

Preference for a cereal depends on the form and flavor of the food made from it, the amount of nourishment and contribution to health, its cost, its availability, and the food habits of a people.

Food products. Four general groups of foods are prepared from the cereal grains. (1) Baked products, made from flour or meal, include pan breads, loaf breads, pastries, pancakes, flatbreads, cookies, and cakes. (2) Milled grain products, made by removing the bran and usually the germ (or embryo of the seed), include polished rice, farina, wheat flour, cornmeal, hominy, corn grits, pearled barley, bulgur (from wheat), semolina (for macaroni products), prepared breakfast cereals, and soup, gravy, and other thickenings. (3) Beverages are made from fermented grain products (distilled or undistilled) and from boiled, roasted grains. Beverages, such as beer and whiskey, made from cereals are as old as recorded history. (4) Whole-grain products include rolled oats, brown rice, popcorn, shredded and puffed grains, breakfast foods, and home-ground meals made from wheat, corn, sorghum, or one of the other cereals. *See* DISTILLED SPIRITS.

Breeding. The long evolutionary development of the cereals has resulted in a wide array of genetic types. These and new mutants have been used to breed varieties that differ in adaptation, productivity, resistance to disease and insect pests, physical properties, composition, and nutrients.

Nutritional value. All cereal grains have high energy value, mainly from the starch fraction but also from the fat and protein. In general, the cereals are low in protein content, although oats and certain millets are exceptions. High-protein genetic types have been found, and, from their use in breeding, new varieties have been developed that possess a higher percentage of protein. Likewise, a better balance has been found among the amino acids in the protein in some lines of corn, barley, and sorghum, and research with wheat is promising. Also, the nature of the starchy fraction can be altered to give products with different physical properties. *See* GRAIN CROPS; GRASS CROPS; NUTRITION.   Louis P. Reitz

Cerebral palsy

A collection of syndromes (not a disease) of non-progressive motor dysfunction arising from abnormal development of or damage to the brain, either prenatally, at birth, or postnatally. Most cases of cerebral palsy develop in utero. Premature birth is associated with an increased risk of cerebral palsy, with the lowest birth weights carrying the highest risk. A maximum of 15% of cases are related to birth injury or perinatal oxygen deprivation. *See* PREGNANCY DISORDERS.

Although the brain damage in cerebral palsy is nonprogressive and thus deterioration does not occur, the neurological manifestations of cerebral palsy may change with neurological maturation. The precise form of cerebral palsy rarely can be characterized prior to 6 months of age; often it cannot be characterized until the individual is 2 years old. Cerebral palsy is only rarely familial. Its incidence is stable at 0.1–0.3% of live births.

Forms of handicap. Cerebral palsy is classified by the form and distribution of the motor handicap as spasticity, dyskinesia, ataxia, and hypotonia. These four forms have considerable overlap. Spasticity, seen in 75% of cases, presents a clinical picture of muscle stiffness, weakness, and imbalance of muscle tone. Common findings are contractures of joints, resulting in shortened heel cords and thus in toe walking. Tightness of the adductor muscles in the thigh may result in a scissors gait. Painful dislocation of the hip is a common problem associated with severe spasticity. Severe involvement of the brainstem may result in difficulty speaking clearly or impair feeding. Dyskinetic syndromes (athetosis or dystonia) occur in 20% of cases. Both are characterized by a severe lack of voluntary muscle control. Athetosis is characterized by slow, writhing, involuntary movements occasionally combined with quick, distal, involuntary movements (chorea). Dystonia is characterized by more or less constant muscle stiffness. Dyskinetic syndromes show no symptoms during sleep and are aggravated by emotional tension. Unclear speech (dysarthria) can be quite severe. Ataxic syndromes, characterized by impaired coordination without altered motor tone, are uncommon. A fourth syndrome, characterized by severely decreased motor tone, is called atonic cerebral palsy.

Distribution of the altered motor tone is of great importance in predicting the degree of handicap, especially in the spastic forms. (1) Hemiplegia refers to involvement of one side of the body only. (2) Paraplegia refers to involvement of both legs with no involvement of the arms and hands. These two forms constitute about 50% of the spastic cases. Individuals with them can usually walk, and 80% have normal intelligence. Most of these individuals can become independent in society. (3) Spastic quadriplegia implies equal involvement of all four extremities; individuals frequently are severely retarded and have a small head (microcephalic). (4) Diplegia refers to involvement of the legs and lesser involvement of the arms and hands. It should probably be regarded as living a transitional form between paraplegia and quadriplegia and as having an intermediate prognosis.

A specific cerebral palsy syndrome due to severe neonatal jaundice is manifested by athetosis, deafness, and deficient upward gaze. Advances in obstetric and pediatric care have made this form uncommon. Other problems associated with cerebral palsy include mental retardation, seen in about 50% of cases. Epilepsy occurs in 25% of cases; it is treated with anticonvulsant drugs. *See* SEIZURE DISORDERS.

Treatment. Treatment of cerebral palsy is aimed at maximizing lifetime independence within the limitations of the individual's handicap. Appropriate education, in a normal class when feasible, is critical. Even the most severely affected individual can profit from training in self-care and communication skills. Common treatment modalities include physical and occupational therapy to prevent contractures and facilitate optimal motor control. Speech therapy is used to improve feeding technique and communication skills. Although these therapies are used, their long-term value has not been proven. Surgical procedures to correct contractures and improve muscle balance are valuable in the spastic syndromes. Surgical and pharmacological approaches to reducing spasticity and dyskinesia remain largely experimental.   Hart de Coudres Peterson

Bibliography. E. Blair and F. J. Stanley, Intrapartum asphyxia: A rare cause of cerebral palsy, *J. Pediat.*, 112:515–519, 1988; H. Galjaard et al. (eds.), *Early Detection and Management of Cerebral Palsy*, 1987; K. B. Nelson and J. H. Ellenberg, The asymptomatic newborn and risk of cerebral palsy, *Amer. J. Dis. Child.*, 141:1333–1335, 1987; K. B. Nelson and J. Ellenberg, Obstetric complications as risk factors for cerebral palsy or seizure disorders, *J. Amer. Med. Ass.*, 251:1983–1984, 1985; F. Stanley and E. Alberman, *The Epidemiology of the Cerebral Palsies*, 1991.

Cerenkov radiation

Light emitted by a high-speed charged particle when the particle passes through a transparent, nonconducting, solid material at a speed greater than the speed of light in the material. The blue glow observed in the water of a nuclear reactor, close to the active fuel elements, is radiation of this kind. The emission of Cerenkov radiation is analogous to the emission of a shock wave by a projectile moving faster than sound, since in both cases the velocity of the object passing through the medium exceeds the velocity of the resulting wave disturbance in the medium. This radiation, first predicted by P. A. Cerenkov in 1934 and later substantiated theoretically by I. Frank and I. Tamm, is used as a signal for the indication of high-speed particles and as a means for measuring their energy in devices known as Cerenkov counters. *See* SHOCK WAVE.

Direction of emission. Cerenkov radiation is emitted at a fixed angle θ to the direction of motion of the particle, such that $\cos \theta = c/nv$, where v is the speed of the particle, c is the speed of light in vacuum, and n is the index of refraction of the medium.

The light forms a cone of angle θ around the direction of motion. If this angle can be measured, and n is known for the medium, the speed of the particle can be determined. The light consists of all frequencies for which n is large enough to give a real value of $\cos \theta$ in the preceding equation.

Cerenkov counters. Particle detectors which utilize Cerenkov radiation are called Cerenkov counters. They are important in the detection of particles with speeds approaching that of light, such as those produced in large accelerators and in cosmic rays, and are used with photomultiplier tubes to amplify the Cerenkov radiation. These counters can emit pulses with widths of about 10^{-10} s, and are therefore useful in time-of-flight measurements when very short times must be measured. They can also give direct information on the velocity of the passing particle. *See* PARTICLE DETECTOR; PHOTOMULTIPLIER.

Dielectrics such as glass, water, or clear plastic may be used in Cerenkov counters. Choice of the material depends on the velocity of the particles to be measured, since the values of n are different for the materials cited. By using two Cerenkov counters in coincidence, one after the other, with proper choice of dielectric, the combination will be sensitive to a given velocity range of particles. *See* DIELECTRIC MATERIALS.

The counters may be classified as nonfocusing or focusing. In the former type, the dielectric is surrounded by a light-reflecting substance except at the point where the photomultiplier is attached, and no use is made of the directional properties of the light emitted. In a focusing counter, lenses and mirrors may be used to select light emitted at a given angle and thus to give information on the velocity of the particle.

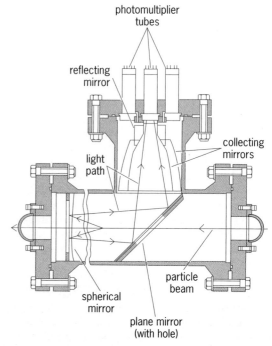

Fig. 1. Differential gas Cerenkov counter.

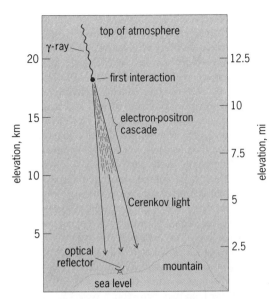

Fig. 2. Schematic view of air shower initiated by a very high energy gamma ray.

Cerenkov counters may be used as proportional counters, since the number of photons emitted in the light beam can be calculated as a function of the properties of the material, the frequency interval of the light measured, and the angle θ. Thus the number of photons which make up a certain size of pulse gives information on the velocity of the particle.

Gas, notably carbon dioxide (CO_2; **Fig. 1**), may also be used as the dielectric in Cerenkov counters. In such counters the intensity of light emitted is much smaller than in solid or liquid dielectric counters, but the velocity required to produce a count is much higher because of the low index of refraction of gas.   William B. Fretter

Cerenkov gamma-ray astronomy. The properties of Cerenkov radiation have been exploited in the development of a branch of gamma-ray astronomy that covers the energy range of about 10^5–10^8 MeV. A high-energy gamma ray from a source external to the Earth creates in the atmosphere a cascade of secondary electrons and positrons (**Fig. 2**). This cascade is generated by the interplay of two processes: electron-positron pair production from gamma rays, and gamma-ray emission as the electrons and positrons are accelerated by the electric fields of nuclei in the atmosphere (bremsstrahlung). For a primary gamma ray having an energy of 10^{12} eV (1 teraelectronvolt), as many as 1000 or more electrons and positrons will contribute to the cascade. The combined Cerenkov light of the cascade is beamed to the ground over an area a few hundred meters in diameter and marks the arrival direction of the initiating gamma ray to about $1°$. On a clear, dark night this radiation may be detected as a pulse of light lasting a few nanoseconds, by using an optical reflector (**Fig. 3**). *See* BREMSSTRAHLUNG; ELECTRON-POSITRON PAIR PRODUCTION.

This technique offers a means to study regions of the universe where charged particles are accelerated to extreme relativistic energies. Such regions involve highly magnetized, rapidly spinning neutron stars; supernova remnants; and active galactic nuclei. These same motivations drive the satellite observations of the EGRET instrument of the *Compton*

Fig. 3. The 34-ft (10-m) optical reflector at the Harvard-Smithsonian's Whipple Observatory near Tucson, Arizona.

Gamma-Ray Observatory at lower gamma-ray energies (up to about 10^4 MeV). *See* GAMMA-RAY ASTRONOMY.

The idea of using the atmosphere as an essential component of a very high energy gamma-ray detector dates from the 1960s. However, the development of the field was hindered for several decades by the enormous background to any possible gamma-ray signal that arises from cosmic-ray-induced air showers. Such showers are hundreds of times more numerous (within a $1°$ field of view) than the showers from even the strongest gamma-ray source. However, the technique remains attractive since it appears to be the only viable technique for gamma-ray astronomy in this energy range. *See* COSMIC RAYS.

Rapid development of the field dates from the late 1980s and follows the recognition that cosmic-ray air showers differ substantially from gamma-ray air showers. In order to distinguish between them, it is necessary to image each individual air shower. The imaging is accomplished through the use of an array of fast photomultipliers, operating in the focal plane of the gamma-ray telescope. Comparison of observed image parameters for each shower with the image expected for a gamma-ray shower results in rejection of more than 99% of background cosmic-ray showers, while more than 50% of gamma-ray showers are retained.

A number of imaging Cerenkov telescopes are in operation with, in most cases, focal-plane imaging detectors consisting of more than 100 pixels. By 1998, seven sources had been reliably observed with good signal-to-noise ratios.

Spin-powered neutron stars. Three of these sources are associated with spin-powered neutron stars, the Crab pulsar, Vela pulsar, and PSR B1706-44, all located within the Milky Way Galaxy less than 7000 light-years from the Earth. Unlike earlier detections, however, there is no evidence for pulsations at the spin periods of the neutron stars. (This behavior is in contrast to observations at lower gamma-ray energies from the EGRET instrument, in which the gamma-rays are dominantly pulsed.) For these sources the unpulsed gamma rays are presumably associated with a surrounding nebula. For the Crab, the nebula is clearly observed, but for the other two objects there is some ambiguity concerning the presence of any nebulae.

The observations of the Crab Nebula at teraelectronvolt energies combined with observations at lower gamma-ray energies generally support a theoretical model of the high-energy emission process in which the highest-energy radiation is due to Compton scattering between extremely relativistic electrons, with energies up to about 10^{16} eV, and lower-energy photons in the nebula. In this picture, the lower-energy photons have been created by the relativistic electrons themselves as they spiral in the magnetic field of the nebula. The underlying power for all of this high-energy activity is the rotation of a rapidly spinning neutron star (spin period 33 milliseconds) which itself is the remnant of the relatively recent supernova explosion in the year 1054.

See COMPTON EFFECT; CRAB NEBULA; NEUTRON STAR; PULSAR; SUPERNOVA.

Shell-type supernova remnants. Another of the very high energy gamma-ray sources is a shell-type supernova remnant associated with a historical supernova of the year 1006. Shell-type supernova remnants are suspected to be the dominant source of cosmic rays with energies less than about 10^{14} eV. The shock waves that occur at shell boundaries accelerate cosmic rays confined by magnetic fields near the shocks to these energies. Although SN 1006 is a shell-type supernova, it does not meet expectations. The teraelectronvolt gamma rays appear to arise principally from electrons rather than the protons and heavier nuclei that make up the bulk of the cosmic rays, since the location of the teraelectronvolt gamma-rays generally coincides with the location of nonthermal x-ray emission attributed to relativistic electrons.

Observations of other shell-type supernova remnants have failed to detect any very high energy gamma-ray emission with, in some cases, upper limits that are slightly below theoretical expectations. If the common view of the origins of cosmic rays is correct, the next generation of imaging Cerenkov detectors should easily detect the nearer shell-type remnants and map their teraelectronvolt photon emission.

Active galactic nuclei. The remaining sources seen by atmospheric Cerenkov telescopes are all extragalactic objects associated with active galactic nuclei: Markarian 421, Markarian 501, and 1ES 2344 + 514. Active galactic nuclei in general are thought to be powered by supermassive black holes (10^6–10^9 solar masses) accreting material from a surrounding disk of gas. In many cases, a jet of relativistic material and radiation is formed perpendicular to the accretion disk. In the case of the objects seen at teraelectronvolt energies, and at 100 MeV–1 GeV energies as well, the jets are apparently directed toward the Earth, so that individual gamma rays are boosted in energy and the apparent luminosity of the sources is enhanced by several orders of magnitude. Active galactic nuclei with jets aligned near to the line of sight to the Earth are called blazars. *See* BLACK HOLE.

Variations at very short time scales have been observed in the emission of the blazars. The gamma-ray flux from Markarian 421, for example, has been observed to rise and fall by a factor of 2 within 15 min. Because of the large collection area associated with Cerenkov telescopes (Fig. 2), they have the ability to probe for flux variations on a time scale unobtainable by any other detector operating above a few megaelectronvolts. The observations of Markarian 421 show the the teraelectronvolt gamma-ray emission is best characterized by succession of rapid flares with a baseline level below the sensitivity limit of the detector, consistent with little steady emission.

When the spectrum obtained at teraelectronvolt energies is combined with lower-energy spectra, a consistent picture emerges in which the teraelectronvolt photons are due to Compton scattering of radiation from a population which is dominantly relativistic electrons. However, many questions remain, and alternative scenarios in which the dominant particle species are protons are possible. The fact that gamma rays up to energies of 10^{12} eV are observed suggests that this type of source is a copious producer of high-energy cosmic rays. Their contribution to the observed cosmic ray flux at Earth has yet to be assessed. *See* ASTROPHYSICS, HIGH-ENERGY; GALAXY, EXTERNAL.   Richard C. Lamb

Bibliography. F. A. Aharonian and C. W. Akerlof, Gamma-ray astronomy with imaging atmospheric Cerenkov telescopes, *Annu. Rev. Nucl. Part. Sci.*, 47:273–314, 1997; R. Ong, Very high energy gamma-ray astronomy, *Phys. Rep.*, 305:93–202, 1998.

Ceres

The largest asteroid in the "main belt" of asteroids between Mars and Jupiter, and the first such object to be discovered.

Discovery. The reason for the apparent gap devoid of planets between Mars and Jupiter was a matter of speculation since Johannes Kepler's time. In the latter part of the eighteenth century, the Titius-Bode law (an empirical law for the spacing of planetary distances from the Sun) suggested that there should be a planet in the gap. The Titius-Bode law seemingly was supported by the location of Uranus discovered by William Herschel in 1781, intensifying the search for the "missing planet" in the region between Mars and Jupiter. On January 1, 1801, Giuseppe Piazzi serendipitously discovered the first minor planet: Ceres. At the time, it was believed to be a planet; only after the discovery in the next few years of more such objects and progress in estimating their sizes was it clear that they were much smaller than planets, and Herschel suggested that these objects be called "asteroids" rather than "planets." Today, the term "minor planets" is used to describe asteroids in the main belt as well as other small solar system bodies such as Kuiper Belt objects and near-Earth objects. *See* KUIPER BELT; PLANET; URANUS.

Properties. Ceres is a G-type asteroid; these asteroids are very dark and have a nonvolatile chemical composition similar to the Sun. Ceres orbits the Sun with a 4.4-year period, a semimajor axis of 2.7 AU (astronomical unit, the mean distance from the Sun to the Earth; 1 AU = 149,597,871 km = 92,955,807 mi), and an eccentricity of 0.097. It has a rotational period of 9.075 hours, and is a prograde rotator (that is, the direction of its rotation is in the same sense as that of the Earth and of the direction of revolution of the planets around the Sun).

Ceres has a visual geometric albedo of about 0.10, and has a red color (meaning that it tends to reflect light more strongly at longer wavelengths) from the visible part of the spectrum through much of the ultraviolet. The brightness of an asteroid is a function of how much light it reflects due to its size and albedo. Although Ceres is the largest asteroid, it is not the brightest. Its absolute magnitude of $H = 3.32$ makes it somewhat fainter than Vesta, which is brighter because it is more reflective. (Vesta's albedo

is about four times greater than that of Ceres.) The absolute magnitude of an asteroid (H) is defined differently from that of a star for practicality; H is defined as the magnitude an object would have if it were 1 AU from the Sun and 1 AU from the Earth, at zero phase angle (fully illuminated, as with a full moon). This alignment is a physical impossibility but is useful as a definition.

With a mass of about 9.5×10^{20} kg (2.1×10^{21} lb, or about 0.00016 that of the Earth), Ceres contains about 25% of the combined mass of all the main-belt asteroids (that is, not including objects in the Kuiper Belt). That mass and the measured diameter of roughly 950 km (590 mi) implies a density around 2.1 g/cm^3, roughly twice the density of water.

Ceres, like Vesta, Pallas, and other large asteroids, is a surviving protoplanet from the era of accretion in the inner solar system. It, like Vesta, is thought to have retained its primitive physical state due to the presence of water that, although causing some aqueous alteration, prevented it from melting like Vesta. Consequently, Ceres may well have the oldest intact surface in the inner solar system.

Hubble Space Telescope observations. The *Hubble Space Telescope* has observed Ceres several times, and an image from one observation is shown in the **illustration**. These observations were key in identifying the first large feature on Ceres, informally named "Piazzi" in honor of the discoverer of Ceres.

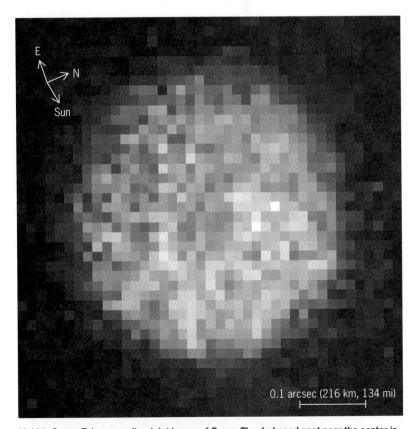

Hubble Space Telescope ultraviolet image of Ceres. The darkened spot near the center is the Piazzi feature. Arrows show the direction of the Sun, to provide an idea of the direction of illumination, and the North-East orientation of the image. However, the Sun is actually nearly behind the head of the reader looking at the image, so the arrow showing its direction should be pointing out of the page and a little down to the right. (*Southwest Research Institute, NASA*)

The Piazzi feature is roughly circular with a diameter of about 250 km (150 mi). However, it is not known whether this feature is a crater, an albedo "spot," or another effect.

Hubble observations also were used to analyze the internal structure of Ceres. Those observations showed that Ceres has a shape and smoothness indicative of a gravitationally relaxed object. Its shape is significantly less flattened than that expected for a homogeneous object, but is consistent with a central mass concentration indicative of differentiation. Possible interior configurations include water-ice-rich mantles over a rocky core. *See* ASTEROID; HUBBLE SPACE TELESCOPE.

Dawn mission. Ceres is the target of the National Aeronautics and Space Administration's Discovery mission *Dawn*, which was scheduled to launch in 2007 to orbit and study Vesta and Ceres (in 2010–2012 and 2015, respectively). The mission's goal is to characterize the conditions and processes of the solar system's earliest epoch by investigating in detail these two of the largest protoplanets that have remained intact since their formations. *See* ASTEROID; SPACE PROBE.
                                                        Joel Parker

Bibliography. J. Cunningham, *The First Asteroid: Ceres 1801–2001*, Historical Studies in Asteroid Research, vol. 1, Star Lab Press, 2001; J. W. Parker et al., Analysis of the first disk-resolved images of Ceres from ultraviolet observations with the *Hubble Space Telescope, Astron. J.*, 123:549–557, 2002; P. C. Thomas et al., Differentiation of the asteroid Ceres as revealed by its shape, *Nature*, 437:224–226, 2005.

Ceriantharia

An order of the Zoantharia, typified by *Cerianthus*, which lives in sandy marine substrata (**illus.** *a* and *b*). The animal is enclosed in a sheath formed by mucus secreted from gland cells of the column ectoderm, in which discharged nematocysts, sand grains, and other foreign objects are embedded.

The polyp is a muscular, skeletonless, elongated, cylindrical body with a smooth wall. Long, slender, unbranching, freely retractile tentacles are arranged in two cycles and consist of smaller labial and larger marginal ones. A siphonoglyph termed the hyposulculus is present and a pedal disk is lacking.

The mesenteric arrangement is most characteristic (illus. *c*). Mesenteries are arranged bilaterally in couples, not in pairs, forming a single cycle. All are complete. The three most dorsal couples or directives appear first, and then the other two appear at both sides of the directives. Additional metacnemic couples are added to the ventral intermesenteric space and are arranged in quartets with regard to length. The longitudinal muscles are weakly developed in the ventral faces of the mesenteries, whose free edges bear filaments and acontialike threads or acontioids that seem to have an adhesive function.

Pelagic larvae (illus. *d–f*) known as *Arachnactis, Cerianthula, Ovactis, Anactinia*, and others always pass through the cerinula stage with three couples of the protocnemes. Life cycles have not been fully investigated. *See* HEXACORALLIA.
                                                        Kenji Atoda

Ceriantharia. (a) *Cerianthus solitarius*. (b) *Pachycerianthus multiplicatus*. (c) Mesenteric arrangement. (d) *Cerianthula spinifer* larva. (e) *Ovactis aequatorialis* larva. (f) *Anactinia pelagica* larva.

Cerium

A chemical element, Ce, atomic number 58, atomic weight 140.12. It is the most abundant metallic element of the rare-earth group in the periodic table. The naturally occurring element is made up of the isotopes ^{136}Ce, ^{138}Ce, ^{140}Ce, and ^{142}Ce. A radioactive α-emitter, ^{142}Ce has a half-life of 5×10^{15} years. Cerium occurs mixed with other rare earths in many minerals, particularly monazite and blastnasite, and is found among the products of the fission of uranium, thorium, and plutonium. *See* PERIODIC TABLE.

Although the common valence of cerium is 3, it also forms a series of quadrivalent compounds and is the only rare earth which occurs as a quadrivalent ion in aqueous solution. Although it can be separated from the other rare earths in high purity by ion-exchange methods, it is usually separated chemically by taking advantage of its quadrivalent state.

Frank H. Spedding

Bibliography. F. A. Cotton et al., *Advanced Inorganic Chemistry*, 6th ed., Wiley-Interscience, 1999; K. A. Gschneidner Jr., J.-C. Bünzli, and V. K. Pecharsky (eds.), *Handbook on the Physics and Chemistry of Rare Earths*, 2005.

Cermet

A group of composite materials consisting of an intimate mixture of ceramic and metallic components.

Fabrication. Cermets can be fabricated by mixing the finely divided components in the form of powders or fibers, compacting the components under pressure, and sintering the compact to produce physical properties not found solely in either of the components. Cermets can also be fabricated by internal oxidation of dilute solutions of a base metal and a more noble metal. When heated under oxidizing conditions, the oxygen diffuses into the alloy to form a base metal oxide in a matrix of the more noble metal. *See* CORROSION; POWDER METALLURGY.

Components. Ceramic components may be metallic oxides, carbides, borides, silicides, nitrides, or mixtures of these compounds; the metallic components include a wide variety of metals whose selection depends on the application of the respective cermet. Some of the component materials are shown in the **table**.

Interactions. The reactions taking place between the metallic and ceramic components during fabrication of cermets may be briefly classified and described as follows: (1) Heterogeneous mixtures with no chemical reaction between the components, characterized by a mechanical interlocking of the components without formation of a new phase, no penetration of the metallic component into the ceramic component, and vice versa, and no alteration of either component (example, MgO–Ni). (2) Surface reaction resulting in the formation of a new phase as an interfacial layer that is not soluble in the component materials. The thickness of this layer depends on the diffusion rate, temperature, and time of the reaction (example, Al_2O_3–Be). (3) Complete reaction between the components, resulting in the formation of a solid solution characterized by a polyatomic structure of the ceramic and the metallic component (example, TiC–Ni). (4) Penetration along grain boundaries without the formation of interfacial layers (example, Al_2O_3–Mo). *See* DIFFUSION; PHASE EQUILIBRIUM.

Bonding behavior. One important factor in the selection of metallic and ceramic components in cermets is their bonding behavior. Bonding may be by surface interaction or by bulk interaction. In cermets of the oxide-metal type, for example, investigators differentiate among three forms of surface interaction: macrowetting, solid wetting, and wetting assisted by direct lattice fit.

Combinations. One distinguishes basically between four different combinations of metal and ceramic components: (1) the formation of continuous interlocking phases of the metallic and ceramic components, (2) the dispersion of the metallic component in the ceramic matrix, (3) the dispersion of the ceramic component in the metallic matrix, and (4) the interaction between the metallic and ceramic components.

Characteristics. The combination of metallic and ceramic components can result in cermets characterized by increased strength and hardness, higher temperature resistance, improved wear resistance, and better resistance to corrosion, each characteristic depending on the variables involved in composition and processing. In general, these materials should be corrosion resistant, have high-temperature strength, temperature (thermal) shock resistance, and a certain ductility.

The yield strength σ of a cermet depends on the component materials, the volume fraction f of the dispersed phase, the particle diameter d of the dispersed material, and the mean spacing λ between particles. These variables are related by Eqs. (1) and (2), where A and B are material constants.

$$\lambda = \frac{2d}{3f}(1-f) \qquad (1)$$

$$\sigma = -A \log \lambda + B \qquad (2)$$

Applications. Friction parts as well as cutting and drilling tools have been successfully made from cermets for many years. Certain nuclear reactor fuel elements, such as dispersion-type elements, are also made as cermets.

Fiber reinforcement. Fiber-reinforced cermets consist either of a metallic matrix reinforced by ceramic fibers (for high-temperature strength) or a ceramic matrix with metallic fibers inserted (for better heat conductivity). The term fiber refers to a multicrystalline material approximately 0.5–2.5 micrometers (0.02–0.1 mil) in diameter. Whiskers which can be used instead of fibers are short single crystals

Representative components of cermets		
Class	Ceramic	Metal addition
Oxides	Al_2O_3	Al, Be, Co, Co-Cr, Fe, stainless steel
	Cr_2O_3	Cr
	MgO	Al, Be, Co, Fe, Mg
	SiO_2	Cr, Si
	ZrO_2	Zr
	UO_2	Zr, Al, stainless steel
Carbides	SiC	Ag, Si, Co, Cr
	TiC	Mo, W, Fe, Ni, Co, Inconel, Hastelloy, stainless steel, Vitallium
	WC	Co
	Cr_3C_2	Ni, Si
Borides	Cr_3B_2	Ni
	TiB_2	Fe, Ni, Co
	ZrB_2	Ni
Silicides	$MoSi_2$	Ni, Co, Pt, Fe, Cr
Nitrides	TiN	Ni

approximately 1–10 μm in diameter. Combinations of powders and fibers can be made with short or continuous fibers, randomly dispersed or aligned (oriented). Special materials with directional properties can be made by insertion of aligned fibers.

Bulk interactions. Two different forms of bulk interaction between metals and ceramics can be distinguished; solid solution and formation of chemical compounds. Usually solid-solution bonding involves the addition, or formation, within the cermet of a small amount of the appropriate ceramic form of the metal constituent; examples of the type of phase involved are provided by the systems Al_2O_3–Cr_2O_3 and NiO–MgO for oxides, and TaC–TiC and NbC–ZrC for carbides. The systems form continuous series of solid solutions, but there are also many suitable systems in which solid solution occurs over a limited range only.

Formation of a compound in a bonding phase can best be shown by the examples of spinels, having the generalized formula RO · R'_2O_3, where R could, for example, stand for Ni^{2+}, Mg^{2+}, Fe^{2+}, or Co^{2+}, and R′ for Al^{3+}, Cr^{3+}, or Fe^{3+}. Much study has been made of the system Al_2O_3–Fe, without achieving the combination of properties required for the high-temperature engineering applications in view. *See* COMPOSITE MATERIAL; METAL MATRIX COMPOSITE.   Henry H. Hausner

Bibliography. J. Pask and A. Evans (eds.), *Surfaces and Interfaces in Ceramic and Ceramic-Metal Systems*, 1981; P. Naylor, *Introduction to Metal Ceramic Technology*, 1992; G. S. Upadhyaya (ed.), *Sintered Metal-Ceramic Composites*, 1985.

Cerussite

A common mineral in the upper oxidized zone of ore deposits containing galena (PbS). It is usually associated with anglesite, smithsonite, malachite, and other secondary minerals. Normally cerussite is close in composition to $PbCO_3$ with only minor amounts of zinc (Zn) and strontium (Sr) in place of lead (Pb). *See* ANGLESITE; MALACHITE; SMITHSONITE.

Cerussite has the aragonite-type structure with $a = 5.180$Å, $b = 8.492$Å, $c = 6.134$Å, $Z = 4$, and space group Pmcn. The average C-O bond length is 1.27 Å and O-C-O bond angle is 121.3°, which are distinct in comparison with those in alkaline earth carbonates of the aragonite-type structure. The average Pb-O bond length is 2.69Å. *See* ARAGONITE.

This mineral is biaxial and optically negative with $\alpha = 1.803$, $\beta = 2.074$, $\gamma = 2.076$, and $2V_\alpha = 9°$. Birefringence is extreme (0.273) and is structurally dependent. The mineral is usually white or gray, and often brown or black. It exhibits luminescence of considerable intensity with a broad emission band centered at 470 nanometers. The hardness of cerussite is between 3 and $3^1/_2$ on the Moh's scale, and its specific gravity is 6.55, which is a distinguishing feature of cerussite in comparison with other carbonate minerals of the aragonite-type structure. *See* BIREFRINGENCE; HARDNESS SCALES; LUMINESCENCE; SPECIFIC GRAVITY.

Cerussite decomposes to $PbCO_3 \cdot 2PbO$ at about 200°C (392°F) and CO_2 pressure lower then 1 atm (14.7 lb/in.²). At medium pressures (~1 atm), two intermediates, $PbCO_3 \cdot PbO$ and $PbCO_3 \cdot 2PbO$, were formed at 300°C and 400°C (572°F and 752°F), respectively. Cerussite decomposes to PbO via three intermediates, $2PbCO_3 \cdot PbO$, $PbCO_3 \cdot PbO$, and $PbCO_3 \cdot 2PbO$, at pressures higher than 4 atm (58.8 lb/in.²).

Cerussite generally occurs in crystal aggregates with a varied habit. Twins are common, in reticulated formations (networks), in starlike groups, or in sixling formations.   Luke L. Y. Chang

Bibliography. L. Chang, R. A. Howie, and J. Zussman, *Rock-Forming Minerals*, vol. 5B: *Non-silicates*, 2d ed., Longman, 1996.

Cesium

A chemical element, Cs, with an atomic number of 55 and an atomic weight of 132.905, the heaviest of the alkali metals in group 1 of the periodic table (except for francium, the radioactive member of the alkali metal family). Cesium is a soft, light, very low-melting metal. It is the most reactive of the alkali metals and indeed is the most electropositive and the most reactive of all the elements.

Cesium reacts vigorously with oxygen to form a mixture of oxides. In moist air, the heat of oxidation may be sufficient to melt and ignite the metal. Cesium does not appear to react with nitrogen to form a nitride, but does react with hydrogen at high temperatures to form a fairly stable hydride. Cesium reacts violently with water and even with ice at temperatures as low as −116°C (−177°F). Cesium reacts with the halogens, ammonia, and carbon monoxide. In general, cesium undergoes some of the same type of reactions with organic compounds as do the other alkali metals, but it is much more reactive. *See* SODIUM.

The physical properties of cesium metal are summarized in the **table**.

Cesium is not very abundant in the Earth's crust, there being only 7 parts per million (ppm) present. Like lithium and rubidium, cesium is found as a constituent of complex minerals and not in relatively pure halide form as are sodium and potassium.

Physical properties of cesium metal		
Property	Temp., °C	Valve
Density	20	1.9 g/cm³
Melting point	28.5	
Boiling point	705	
Heat of fusion	28.5	3.8 cal/g
Heat of vaporization	705	146 cal/g
Viscosity	100	4.75 millipoises
Vapor pressure	278	1 mm
	635	400 mm
Thermal conductivity	28.5	0.044 cal/(s)(cm²)(°C)
Heat capacity	28.5	0.06 cal/(g)(°C)
Electrical resistivity	30	36.6 microhm−cm

Indeed, lithium, rubidium, and cesium frequently occur together in lepidolite ores, such as those from Rhodesia.

Cesium metal is used in photoelectric cells, spectrographic instruments, scintillation counters, radio tubes, military infrared signaling lamps, and various optical and detecting devices.

Cesium compounds are used in glass and ceramic production, as absorbents in carbon dioxide purification plants, as components of getters in radio tubes, and in microchemistry. Cesium salts have been used medicinally as antishock agents after administration of arsenic drugs. The isotope cesium-137 is supplanting cobalt-60 in the treatment of cancer. *See* ALKALI METALS.   Marshall Sittig

Bibliography. F. A. Cotton et al., *Advanced Inorganic Chemistry*, 6th ed., Wiley-Interscience, 1999; W. A. Hart et al., *The Chemistry of Lithium Sodium, Potassium, Rubidium, Cesium, and Francium*, 1975; D. R. Lide, *CRC Handbook Chemistry and Physics*, 85th ed., CRC Press, 2004.

Cestida

An order of the phylum Ctenophora (comb jellies) containing two monospecific genera, *Cestum* and *Velamen*, which have an unusual morphology. The transparent bodies of cestids are flattened in the tentacular plane and greatly elongated in the stomodeal plane so that they have the shape of a belt or ribbon (hence the specific name *Cestum veneris*, "Venus' girdle"; see **illus.**). The mouth is at the midpoint of the length. Individuals of *Cestum* may be more than 39 in. (1 m) long, and of *Velamen* about 8 in. (20 cm). Brown or yellow pigment spots sometimes occur on the tips of the body. If disturbed, Cestids, like other ctenophores, produce brilliant bioluminescence along their meridional canals. They occur worldwide in tropical and subtropical waters; *C. veneris* is one of the most common species in the oceanic Atlantic. The extreme fragility of their bodies makes cestids difficult to collect and maintain, and living specimens have been seen by few biologists.

Because of the great lateral elongation of the body, the subtentacular comb rows are reduced to a few ctenes, but the substomodeal rows run along the entire aboral edge of the body. The beating of the comb rows propels the cestid slowly forward like a wing, with the oral edge leading. Two main tentacles arise on either side of the central stomodeum and lie in a groove along the oral edge; numerous fine side branches (tentilla) from these tentacles trail back over the flat sides of the body. The prey, mainly small crustaceans, are captured when they contact the body surface and stick to the tentilla. Contraction of the tentilla moves the prey into the oral groove, which transports it by ciliary action to the mouth. This feeding mechanism allows cestids to catch prey ranging from about 100 micrometers to several millimeters in size. It is energetically efficient, and fishing is continuous, without interruptions to transfer or handle prey. Cestids are also capable of rapid undulatory swimming along their long axis, mainly as an escape response to disturbance. They are frequently parasitized by hyperiid amphipods; predators on cestids include medusae, the ctenophore *Beroë*, and various fishes.

Like other ctenophores, cestids are simultaneous hermaphrodites, with ovaries and testes located along the meridional canals. Very little is known about the timing of their reproduction. Fertilized eggs develop first into typical cydippid larvae but soon begin to elongate and take on the typical cestid form. *See* CTENOPHORA.   Laurence P. Madin

Bibliography. G. R. Harbison, L. P. Madin, and N. R. Swanberg, On the natural history and distribution of oceanic ctenophores, *Deep-sea Res.*, 25:233–256, 1978; F. W. Harrison and J. A. Westfall (eds.), *Microscopic Anatomy of Invertebrates*, vol. 2, 2000; S. P. Parker (ed.), *Synopsis and Classification of Living Organisms*, 1982.

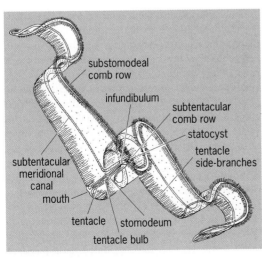

Structure of *Cestum veneris*.

Cestoda

A class of the phylum Platyhelminthes commonly referred to as tapeworms. All members are endoparasites, usually in the digestive tract of vertebrates. The class has been subdivided as follows:

Class Cestoda
   Subclass Cestodaria
      Order: Amphilinidea
            Gyrocotylidea
   Subclass Eucestoda
      Order: Proteocephaloidea
            Tetraphyllidea
            Lecanicephaloidea
            Trypanorhyncha
            Diphyllidea
            Pseudophyllidea
            Cyclophyllidea
            Nippotaeniidea

See separate articles on each group listed.

Morphology and life history. In size the tapeworms range from less than 0.04 in. (1 mm) to several feet in length. The class is differentially characterized by the presence of a cuticle rather than a cellular epidermis and by the total absence of a mouth and digestive tract. External cilia are never present, although the cuticle usually bears minute projections ranging from 0.1 to 1.0 micrometer in diameter. In most species of the class the body is divided into proglottids, each proglottid containing one or two hermaphroditic reproductive systems (**illus.** *a*). The anterior end is usually modified into a holdfast organ, bearing suckers or sucking grooves, and frequently armed with hooks. Early embryonic development occurs in the parental body, usually in a uterus, to a hook-bearing stage, the oncosphere (illus. *b*). The oncosphere leaves the parental body through a uterine pore or by liberation of the terminal segment from the main body of the worm. Further development of the worm always occurs within the body of a host, most often an invertebrate, which commonly ingests the larval form. Growth of the larval worm, frequently with differentiation of the holdfast organ, occurs in this host; in some species asexual reproduction by budding occurs. Further larval growth and development of the holdfast may require a second host. Development of the sexual phase from the larva occurs in another host. Growth with strobila-

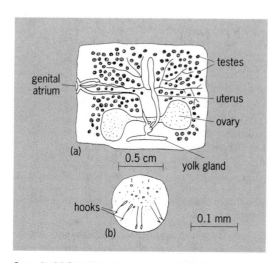

Cestoda. (*a*) Sexually mature segment of *Taenia*. (*b*) Oncosphere of a cyclophyllidean tapeworm.

tion and development of reproductive systems follow, the worm usually staying in the digestive tract. *See* PSEUDOPHYLLIDEA.

Nutrition. Food materials are presumed to be absorbed through the external surface. It has been shown that tapeworms have catalytic mechanisms for the active transport into the body of simple sugars and amino acids. Elaboration of digestive enzymes has not been demonstrated. The chemical composition of these worms is unique in that polysaccharide and fat represent a much larger proportion of the dry weight than does protein. *See* PLATYHELMINTHES.

Clark P. Read

Bibliography. A. C. Chandler and C. P. Read, *Introduction to Parasitology*, 10th ed., 1961; L. H. Hyman, *The Invertebrates*, vol. 2, 1951; E. R. Noble and G. A. Noble, *Parasitology: The Biology of Animal Parasites*, 5th ed., 1982; S. P. Parker (ed.), *Synopsis and Classification of Living Organisms*, 2 vols., 1982; R. A. Wardle and J. A. McLeod, *The Zoology of Tapeworms*, 1952.

Cetacea

A mammalian order comprising approximately 90 living species of whales, dolphins, and porpoises and their fossil relatives. Like all other mammals but unlike all fish, cetaceans nurse their young with milk produced by the mother, are endothermic (warm-blooded), breathe air, have a lower jaw that consists of a single bony element (the dentary), and have three small bones (hammer, anvil, and stirrup) subserving sound transmission within the ear.

Unlike most mammals, living cetaceans are aquatic animals that cannot live on land. They have streamlined bodies (**Fig. 1**), with the nasal opening (blowhole) on top of the head. Their forelimbs are modified into flippers, they lack external hindlimbs, and their tail forms a flat horizontal fluke. Modern cetaceans lack hair except for whiskers in the young of some species. Many of these features are common in aquatic vertebrates, and they have evolved convergently as adaptations for life in water.

Brain and sense organs. The brain of cetaceans is large and highly developed. In fact, until humans came on the scene about 2 million years ago, cetaceans had the highest brain size to body size ratio of any mammal. Cetaceans are thought to be very intelligent. The cetacean sense of smell is nearly or totally absent. In most species the nerve that carries olfactory information to the brain is absent, which is very unusual among mammals. The eyes of most species are well developed, although some species of river dolphins are nearly blind. The ear is the most important sense organ. Toothed whales (Odontoceti) echolocate, emitting high-frequency sounds and using the echoes to determine shapes and distances in their surroundings. Odontocetes do not emit sounds with their voice box (larynx) like other mammals, but have modified nasal passages through which bursts of air are forced. These sounds pass through the tissues of the head and reach a fatty organ on the forehead called the melon. The melon focuses sounds and allows a cetacean to direct its beam of echolocating calls. The sound-receiving organ of odontocetes is also highly specialized. The ear-opening of most cetaceans is minuscule; the head area that is most sound-sensitive in the dolphin is the back of the lower jaw. Sounds are transmitted from this area to the ear by means of a specialized pad of fat connecting the two structures. Mysticetes (baleen whales) do not echolocate; rather, they produce low-frequency sounds with their larynx. These sounds can travel through the ocean for hundreds of miles and are used for communication. *See* ECHOLO-CATION.

Feeding. The two extant suborders of cetaceans, odontocetes and mysticetes, have different dietary specializations. Most odontocetes have simple, pronglike teeth which are used to grab and hold, but not chew, large prey items. Prey includes a variety of fish of all sizes, crustaceans, and squid and other mollusks. Some of the larger odontocetes, such as the killer whale (*Orcinus orca*), eat large prey, including sea lions and dolphins. A pod of killer whales will also hunt together, attacking much larger prey such as gray whales. Most odontocetes are active hunters that chase their prey, although some ambush their prey.

Modern mysticetes do not have teeth and are filter feeders, straining water filled with clouds of marine organisms (krill) through a network of baleen. Baleen is a keratinlike substance that hangs down in plates from the upper jaws of the whale. For example, humpback whales (*Megaptera novaeangliae*) take a mouthful of water and squeeze it with their tongue through the baleen sieve. The water passes through, but any suspended food items (such as plankton and small fish) are caught and subsequently swallowed. Mysticetes employ a variety of krill-concentrating behaviors, such as releasing bursts of air bubbles among schools of krill and swimming in formations to encircle the prey.

Locomotion. All modern cetaceans swim by swinging their horizontal tail fluke through the water, while their forelimbs are used for steering and navigating. The flippers of modern cetaceans resemble flat oars, although the bones for five fingers are present internally. The dorsal fin stabilizes the body during swimming and is not supported by a bony skeleton. The tail fluke is supported only by a column of vertebrae. The body of cetaceans is streamlined and contributes to efficient locomotion. The neck of modern cetaceans is short, and individual vertebrae are often fused. Under the skin of cetaceans is a layer of blubber, a fatty tissue that serves to insulate the animal and affects its buoyancy and streamlining. *See* ADIPOSE TISSUE.

Sustained swimming speeds of large whales (gray whale, *Eschrichtius robustus*; sperm whale, *Physeter macrocephalus*) are around 5 mi/h (8 km/h). During flight (such as when a sperm whale is harpooned), speeds of 25 mi/h (40 km/h) can be maintained for an hour. Feeding whales swim slowly, ap-

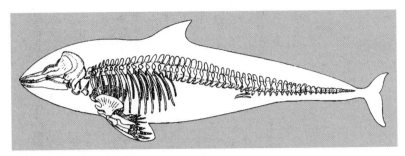

Fig. 1. Skeleton of a porpoise, highly specialized for an aquatic life. (*After Guide to the Hall of Biology of Mammals, Amer. Mus. Nat. Hist. Guide Leafl. Ser. 76, 1933*)

proximately 1–3 mi/h (2–5 km/h). Some species are capable of diving to great depths [commonly more than 5000 ft (1500 m) in the sperm whale], yet all cetaceans must come to the surface to breathe. Whales have a number of adaptations for diving and staying underwater for long periods of time. They exhale before they dive, allowing them to submerge faster. They store oxygen in the muscle (myoglobin) and not in the lungs or blood (hemoglobin) and change circulation patterns of blood to save oxygen. Their chests can easily collapse under increasing pressure (with depth) without causing permanent damage. After surfacing from a dive, whales remain at the surface for an extended period to replenish oxygen stores. *See* DIVING ANIMALS; HEMOGLOBIN.

Life history and social structure. A variety of social structures are found among cetaceans. Most marine dolphins live in schools that may contain dozens of animals, sometimes composed of multiple species. These large aggregations may increase the ability to detect large predators, such as killer whales. They also engage in cooperative hunting. Dolphin societies are loose aggregations, males and females mate multiple times with different partners, and the two parents are often not part of the same group. Bottlenosed dolphin (*Tursiops truncatus*) females have an offspring every 3–6 years; the young stays with the mother for several years. Female offspring often remain with the maternal groups, whereas males wander. These dolphins may reach 50 years of age in the wild.

Herds of sperm whales consist of related females and juveniles. Clusters of young males form bachelor groups, and adult males, much larger than the females, are solitary. During the mating season, a male temporarily dominates one of the harems, but may be easily dislodged from this position by another male. Humpback whales (mysticetes) spend the summers feeding at high latitudes but live in temperate or tropical latitudes during the winter. Here, males form large clusters around single females and engage in elaborate courting behaviors, such as special swimming displays and singing. There is also much fighting among males. Right whales (Balaenidae, also mysticetes) ram into each other with their heads, which are studded with hard, sharp layers of barnacles that may cause bloody gashes in their opponent. Many baleen whales form mating pairs that last one summer. Copulation in humpback whales occurs belly to

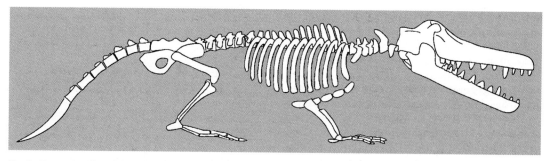

Fig. 2. Reconstruction of *Ambulocetus natans*. (*From J. G. M. Thewissen et al., Courier Forschungs-Institut Senckenberg, 1996*)

belly, while swimming vertically and surfacing. The gestation time is one year, and they may have an offspring every other year. Calving for most whales is done in shallow water; whale calves are born tail-first and are helped to the surface by the mother and other females. Humpback calves can swim in less than an hour after birth. Humpbacks are sexually mature after 8 years and live up to 50 years. Male baleen whales are usually smaller than females.

Distribution. Cetaceans are found in all oceans and seas. Some species are restricted to coastal environments (such as bottlenosed dolphins), whereas others live only in the open sea (such as sperm whales). Some species live in all seas and oceans of the world (such as killer whales). Many mysticetes and sperm whales are migratory. A number of dolphin species have left the sea and live permanently in rivers (such as the Indus, Ganges, Yellow, Amazon, and La Plata). Some river dolphins are among the most unusual modern cetaceans; they are excellent echolocators as demonstrated by their ability to navigate in muddy waters.

Systematics and evolution. Cetaceans originated from a four-footed terrestrial ancestor. This predecessor, a mesonychian, may have resembled a wolf or a hyena and lived approximately 55 million years ago. The closest living relatives of cetaceans are probably the artiodactyls (even-toed ungulates). The most primitive whales, the pakicetids, are known only from India and Pakistan; they were not sea animals, but probably lived in rivers and lakes and were no larger than a wolf. The most primitive marine whale is *Ambulocetus natans* (**Fig. 2**). A nearly complete skeleton is known for this species, and it resembles a crocodile with a long snout and eyes on top of the head. *Ambulocetus* had well-developed forelimbs and large hindlimbs; it did not have a tail fluke or flippers. Large whales first appeared around 40 million years ago; *Basilosaurus* had a long [maybe 50-ft (15-m)] snakelike body, and is known from Africa, North America, and Pakistan. Whales dating back 37 million years or more are often collectively called archaeocetes. They are primitive in that they still had teeth resembling those of land mammals, did

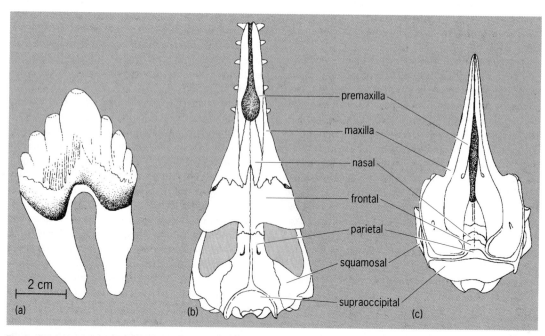

Fig. 3. Cetacean fossils. (*a*) Left upper premolar. (*b*) Skull of *Prozeuglodon stromeri* from early Oligocene of Egypt. (*c*) Skull of *Dephinodon dividum* from the middle Miocene of Maryland.

not echolocate, and had hindlimbs. Cetaceans more recent than 37 million years ago are included in the two modern suborders: Odontoceti (toothed whales, including dolphins and porpoises) and Mysticeti (baleen whales). *See* ARTIODACTYLA.

Primitive odontocetes have teeth that resemble those of sharks to some extent; some of these whales are called squalodontids (*Squalodon* is a genus of sharks; **Fig. 3**). Overall, many early odontocetes resembled dolphins. Even primitive odontocetes appear to have been echolocators. Modern odontocetes are diverse, ranging from the enormous sperm whales [up to 20 m (66 ft) long and 52,000 kg (114,500 lb)] to the tiny porpoises [Phocaenidae, smallest around 9 kg (20 lb), length 1.5 m (5 ft)]. Dolphins (Delphinidae, which includes the killer whale), porpoises (Phocaenidae), and fresh-water dolphins (Iniidae, Pontoporidae, Platanistidae) are the smallest odontocetes. Among the most unusual odontocetes is the extinct *Odobenocetops*, a whale with the face of a walrus, that probably dug for mollusks in the seas of Peru in the Pliocene. *Odobenocetops* had one tooth that was greatly enlarged and tusk-shaped. It is related to the extant narwals, which live in the Arctic. Male narwals have a straight tusk that is longer than the body. The oldest mysticetes (baleen whales) still had teeth, but these were lost early in their evolution. The largest animal ever to live on Earth is the blue whale (*Balaenoptera musculus*), a baleen whale that is 25 m (82 ft) long and weighs 130,000 km (286,340 lb). Other examples of mysticetes are humpback whales, right whales, gray whales, and minke whales. *See* MAMMALIA.   J. G. M. Thewissen

Bibliography. R. F. Fordyce and L. G. Barnes, The evolutionary history of whales and dolphins, *Annu. Rev. Earth Planet. Sci.*, 22:419–455, 1994; S. M. Minasian, K. C. Balcomb, and L. Foster, *The World's Whales: The Complete Illustrated Guide*, Smithsonian Books, 1984.

Cetane number

A number, usually between 30 and 60, that indicates the ability of a diesel engine fuel to ignite quickly after being injected into the cylinder. The higher the cetane number, the more easily the fuel can be ignited. In high-speed diesel engines, a fuel with a long ignition delay tends to produce rough operation. *See* COMBUSTION CHAMBER.

Automotive diesel engines use grades 1-D and 2-D of diesel fuel. Both grades have a minimum cetane number of 40. Low- and medium-speed diesel engines use grade 4-D, which has a minimum cetane number of 30.

To determine cetane number of a fuel sample, a specially designed diesel engine is operated under specified conditions with the given fuel. The fuel is injected into the engine cylinder each cycle at 13° before top center. The compression ratio is adjusted until ignition takes place at top center (13° delay). Without changing the compression ratio, the engine is next operated on blends of cetane (*n*-hexadecane), a short-delay fuel, and heptamethylnonane, which has a long delay. When a blend is found that also has a 13° delay under these conditions, the cetane number of the fuel sample may be calculated from the quantity of cetane required in the blend. *See* DIESEL ENGINE; DIESEL FUEL.   Donald Anglin

Bibliography. American Society for Testing and Materials, *Test Methods for Rating Motor, Diesel, and Aviation Fuels*, vol. 05.04, annually.

Cetomimiformes

An order of oceanic, mostly deep-water fishes that are structurally diverse and rare; most of the 41 species are known from one or a few specimens. Thus, their scientific study has been hindered, the anatomy is imperfectly known, and the relationships are in dispute. Five of the 10 families and 11 of the 21 genera currently placed in the order have been described since World War II. There is no fossil record.

Morphology and phylogeny. Cetomimiforms are all soft-rayed fishes. In most the mouth is large. Many are naked but a few have scales that are thin and deciduous or form an irregular mosaic; a few have the skin spinulose. Pelvic fins may be abdominal, thoracic, or jugular in position or, commonly, absent. In most forms the single dorsal and anal fins are placed rather well back and are opposed; an adipose fin is present in only one species. Studies now under way suggest that some kinds represent early developmental stages of other fishes, whereas some are the product of degenerative evolution in the deep seas. Cetomimiformes are probably polyphyletic and, when better known, the order may be dismembered and abandoned. The relationships of the constituent groups should be sought in the orders Beryciformes, Lampridiformes, and Salmoniformes.

Taxonomy. Because of the diversity, the five currently recognized suborders may be mentioned separately. Best known are the Cetomimoidei or whalefishes, also known as Cetunculi, a group of 3 families and 15 rare species of small, red or black deep-sea fishes with whale-shaped bodies and enormous mouths; they are bioluminescent. The Ateleopoidei (or Chondrobrachii) consist of 1 family, 3 genera, and 11 species of elongate fishes, the largest over half a meter, in which the long anal fin is continuous with the caudal and there is no dorsal fin. The Mirapinnatoidei (or Miripinnati) are tiny, perhaps larval fishes, all recently described. Three families, 4 genera, and 5 species are included. The Giganturoidei, with 2 families, 3 genera, and 6 species, are small mesopelagic fishes with large mouths and strong teeth; some have telescopic eyes. The Megalomycteroidei, or mosaic-scaled fishes, consist of 1 family, 4 genera, and 4 rare species of small, elongate deep-sea fishes with degenerate eyes and irregularly disposed scales. *See* ACTINOPTERYGII; OSTEICHTHYES; TELEOSTEI.   Reeve M. Bailey

Chabazite

A mineral belonging to the zeolite family of silicates. It commonly occurs in well-crystallized groupings of crystals with external rhombohedral symmetry (point group $\bar{3}2/m$) with nearly cubic angles. This well-developed external form suggests an internal structure compatible with space group $R\,\bar{3}m$; however, one structure refinement suggests lower symmetry (triclinic) with space group $P\,\bar{1}$. In addition to recognizing the distinct rhombohedral habit of chabazite crystals, the following physical properties are significant: hardness (on the Mohs hardness scale) in the range 4–5; light colors ranging from white to yellow, pink, and red; vitreous luster; and transparent to translucent in transmitted light. It is distinguished from calcite by a poorer rhombohedral cleavage and lack of effervescent reaction with dilute hydrochloric acid (HCl). *See* CRYSTAL STRUCTURE.

The ideal composition is $Ca_2Al_2Si_4O_{12} \cdot 6H_2O$ (where Ca = calcium, Al = aluminum, Si = silicon, O = oxygen, H_2O = water), but there is considerable chemical substitution of Ca by sodium (Na) and potassium (K), as well as (Na,K)Si for CaAl. The internal structure of chabazite consists of a framework linkage of (AlO_4) and (SiO_4) tetrahedra, with large cagelike openings bounded by rings of tetrahedra. The cages are connected to each other by open structural channels that allow for the diffusion of molecules through the structure of a size comparable to that of the diameter of the channels (about 0.39 nanometer in diameter). For example, argon (0.384 nm in diameter) is quickly absorbed by the chabazite structure, but *iso*-butane (0.56 nm in diameter) cannot enter the structure. In this manner, chabazite can be used as a sieve on a molecular level. *See* MOLECULAR SIEVE.

Chabazite is found, commonly with other zeolites, lining cavities in basalts as a result of low-temperature hydrothermal activity. Most of the fine chabazite crystal specimens that are exhibited in museums were found in large crystal-lined vugs in basalts. Notable localities are the Faroe Islands; the Giant's Causeway, Ireland; Seiser Alpe, Trentino, Italy; Aussig, Bohemia, former Czechoslovakia; Oberstein, Germany; and India. In the United States chabazite has been found at West Paterson, New Jersey, and Goble Station, Oregon. *See* ZEOLITE.

Cornelis Klein

Bibliography. G. Gottardi and E. Galli, *Natural Zeolites*, 1985; C. Klein and C. S. Hurlbut, Jr., *Manual of Mineralogy*, 21st ed., 1993.

Chaetodermomorpha

Burrowing, vermiform (wormlike) mollusks in the group Aplacophora. Chaetodermomorpha (also known as Caudofoveata) are covered by a cuticular integument bearing sclerites (spicules) and are recognizable by the presence of a sensory cuticular oral shield, lack of a foot, and presence of paired gills in a posterior mantle cavity. Chaetoderms (see **illustration**) range in size from less than 0.08 in. (2 mm) to more than 2.8 in. (70 mm) and are found from shelf depths to hadal depths over 23,100 ft (7000 m). There are four families with 14 genera and 128 species worldwide. Chaetoderm species are numerically dominant in certain deep-sea localities. *See* DEEP-SEA FAUNA.

General morphology. Sclerites are aragonitic and sculptured by lengthwise ridges and grooves. They are overlapping, either held flat or slightly-to-perpendicularly raised in relation to the body. The underlying epidermis secretes both cuticle and sclerites, as well as functioning for excretion through specialized papillae. Beneath the epidermis lie circular muscles, two sets of diagonal muscles, and four sets of heavy longitudinal muscle bands, the placement of which defines body shape.

Burrowing is slow, brought about by pushing the anterior end through the sediment by means of hydrostatic pressure; the longitudinal muscles then contract to bring the rest of the body forward.

Digestion. The radula is cuticular and nonrasping with two mirror-image teeth per row on a divided radular membrane, or it is specialized either as a rasping organ with distichous teeth on a unipartite membrane or as grasping pincers with two small distal denticles on a large cone. Food is entirely organic, either detritus or prey organisms, such as foraminiferans. The digestive system consists of a pharynx supplied with salivary glands, sometimes an esophagus, a stomach from which opens a blind digestive gland, and an intestine that runs from the stomach to the mantle cavity. Some families have a gastric shield at the posterior end of the stomach against which turns a mucoid rod.

Respiration, circulation, and nervous system. The paired mantle cavity gills are typical for mollusks, of aspidobranch pattern with afferent and efferent vessels. A ventricle and paired auricles lie in the pericardium. The only blood vessel is the dorsal aorta, which runs anteriorly to the head; otherwise blood moves through open sinuses of the hemocoel. Paired ventral and lateral nerve cords arise from a bilobed cerebral ganglion and run posteriorly, connected by cross-commissures; the lateral cords join above the rectum as a large ganglion, which gives off a nerve to a chemoreceptory dorsal sensory organ.

Reproduction. The gonads are paired or fused and lie in the posterior part of the body; they empty into the pericardium, which in turn empties into paired U-shaped gametoducts. The latter are without elaboration and open separately into the cloaca. Sexes are separate. Embryological development is through nonfeeding larvae.

Phylogeny. The relationship of the Chaetodermomorpha to the other aplacophoran taxon Neomeniomorpha (Solenogastres) remains unresolved, as does their phylogenetic position in the Mollusca.

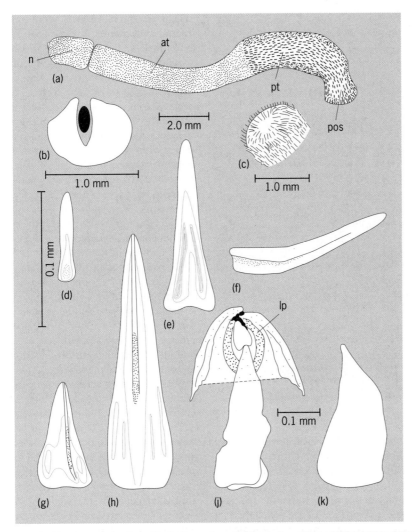

Chaetoderma argenteum Heath, occurring from Alaska to southern California from 330 to 1980 ft (100 to 600 m) depth.
(*a*) Specimen from Santa Maria Basin (USNM). (*b*) Oral shield of presumed syntype of *C. montereyensis* (MCZ). (*c*) Posterium of specimen *a*. (*d–h*) Spicules of specimen *b*, (*d*) from neck, (*e, f*) anterior trunk at constriction, (*g*) posterior region of anterior trunk, and (*h*) midposterior trunk. (*j, k*) Radula of specimen *a*, (*j*) frontal view and (*k*) lateral view of cone, frontal to right. (*From A. H. Scheltema in Taxonomic Atlas of the Benthic Fauna of the Santa Maria Basin and the Western Santa Barbara Channel, vol. 8, pt. a, The Mollusca, Santa Barbara Museum of Natural History, 1998*)

They are unknown as fossils. *See* APLACOPHORA; MOLLUSCA; NEOMENIOMORPHA.   Amelie H. Scheltema

Bibliography. L. v. Salvini-Plawen, Mollusca Caudofoveata, *Marine Invertebrates of Scandinavia*, vol. 4, 1975; A. H. Scheltema, Aplacophora as progenetic aculiferans and the coelomate origin of mollusks as the sister taxon of Sipuncula, *Biol. Bull. (Woods Hole)*, 184:57–78, 1993; A. H. Scheltema, Comparative morphology of the radulae and alimentary tracts in the Aplacophora, *Malacologia*, 20:361–383, 1981; A. H. Scheltema, Reproduction and rapid growth in a deep-sea aplacophoran mollusc, *Prochaetoderma yongei, Mar. Ecol., Prog. Ser.*, 37:171–180, 1987; A. H. Scheltema, in *Taxonomic Atlas of the Benthic Fauna of the Santa Maria Basin and the Western Santa Barbara Channel*, vol. 8, *Mollusca*, pt. 1, Santa Barbara Museum of Natural History, 1998; A. H. Scheltema and D. L. Ivanov, Prochaetodermatidae of the eastern Atlantic Ocean and Mediterranean Sea, *J. Moll. Stud.*, 66:313–362, 2000; A. H. Scheltema and D. L. Ivanov, Use of birefringence to characterize Aplacophora sclerites, *The Veliger*, 47:153–160, 2004; E. R. Trueman and M. R. Clarke (eds.), *The Mollusca*, vol. 10: *Evolution*, 1985.

Chaetognatha

A phylum of abundant planktonic arrowworms. As adults they range in size from 0.2 to 4 in. (5 to 100 mm). Their bodies are tubular and transparent, and divided into three portions: head, trunk, and tail (**illus.** *a*). The head possesses one or two rows of minute teeth anterior to the mouth and usually 7–10 larger chaetae, or seizing jaws, on each side of the head. One or two pairs of lateral fins and a caudal fin are present. In mature individuals a pair of seminal vesicles protrudes from the sides of the tail segment just forward of the caudal fin.

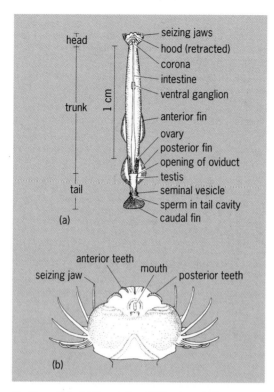

Sagitta enflata. (*a*) Dorsal view. (*b*) Head, ventral.

Nine genera and about 42 species are recognized by some specialists. Most species belong to the genus *Sagitta*, which can be recognized by the presence of two pairs of teeth (illus. *b*) and two pairs of lateral fins. Important diagnostic features for species include the shape and position of the seminal vesicles and the number and arrangement of the anterior teeth.

Morphology. The body is covered by a thin hood of epidermis. When drawn forward, the hood covers the teeth and jaws and streamlines the anterior end of the body. Two small, dark eyes are found on the dorsal side of the head. Behind the eyes, and forming an irregular loop on the epidermis, is a structure called a corona ciliata, which is visible only when stained.

The nervous system consists of a dorsal ganglion, or brain, from which nerves lead to various portions of the head and body. A pair of nerves extends posteriorly from the brain and joins the prominent ventral ganglion which lies just beneath the epidermis.

The head musculature is quite complex, but the trunk has only six longitudinal bands of muscle, which restrict the body to simple lateral movements. Arrowworms are unable to constrict their bodies. Swimming is accomplished by rapid but brief movements of the caudal fin, followed by a quiet period. They do not appear to swim much, but drift passively most of the time.

The digestive system is simple. A mouth opens ventrally in the center of the head. A short esophagus leads to a straight intestine, which begins just behind the head and terminates in an anus opening ventrally at the septum separating the trunk and tail segments. The intestine is supported by dorsal and ventral mesenteries. A large coelom surrounds the intestine.

All chaetognaths are hermaphroditic. The ovaries are tubular and lie in the trunk segment just ahead of the septum dividing the trunk from the tail. The eggs in the ovaries increase in size at maturity, only a small fraction of the eggs maturing and being spawned at one time. Alongside the ovary is an oviduct, and contained within the oviduct is a narrow sperm duct. Fertilization is internal. The fertilized eggs are spawned free in the ocean, and the young chaetognaths hatch in some instances within 48 h. There is no larval stage.

The testes are situated in either side of the tail segment. As the sperm mature, they break away and often circulate in the tail cavity. From time to time some pass through short ducts leading from inside the tail cavity to the seminal vesicles. Small quantities of sperm are stored in the ducts prior to discharge.

Natural history. Chaetognaths are cosmopolitan forms which live not only at the surface but also at great depths; however, no one species is found in all latitudes and at all depths. One of the Arctic species, *Eukrohnia hamata*, may extend to the Antarctic by way of deep water across the tropics. A few species are neritic and are not found normally beyond the continental shelf.

Their food consists principally of copepods and other small planktonic crustaceans; however, they are very predacious and will even eat small fish larvae and other chaetognaths on rare occasions. The suggestion has been made that they feed on plants as well as animals, but this needs more supporting evidence. They seize their food with their pointed jaws and, aided by the teeth, push it into their mouths. Small crustacean larvae eaten one day appear to be digested by the next.

Along the Atlantic Coast of the United States they are most abundant over the continental shelf. Numbers of five or more per cubic meter of water are common along the coast; farther offshore only a fraction of this number is normally encountered. When very abundant, they may exceed 2.8/ft^3 (100/m^3); however, this is unusual and often includes many young specimens.

Studies have shown them to be useful as indicator organisms. Certain species appear to be associated with characteristic types or masses of water, and when this water is displaced into an adjacent water mass, the chaetognaths may be used as temporary evidence for such displacement.

Their abundance and cosmopolitan distribution in marine waters, their little-known life history, their importance in the food chain both as predators and prey, and their value as indicator organisms invite further study. *See* SEAWATER FERTILITY.   E. Lowe Pierce

Bibliography. S. P. Parker (ed.), *Synopsis and Classification of Living Organisms*, 2 vols., 1982; E. L. Pierce, The Chaetognatha over the continental shelf of North Carolina with attention to their relation to the hydrography of the area, *J. Mar. Res.*, 12(1):75–92, 1953; T. Tokioka, Chaetognaths of the

Indo-Pacific, *Anat. Zool. Jap.*, 25(1,2):307–316, 1952; R. von Ritter-Zahony, *Revision der Chaetognathen*, Deutsche Südpolar-Expedition 1901–1903, Bd. 13, Zool. 5, Heft 1, 1911.

Chaetonotida

An order of the phylum Gastrotricha. Members have Y-shaped pharyngeal lumina. *Neodasys* is a marine and macrodasyid-like form that reaches 0.8 mm (0.03 in.) in length and has front, side, and rear adhesive tubes. Others seldom exceed 0.3 mm (0.01 in.); they have only two rear adhesive tubes borne on a posterior furca, or none at all. Members of the family Xenotrichulidae have locomotor cilia grouped into cirri; all three genera are marine (**illus.** *a*).

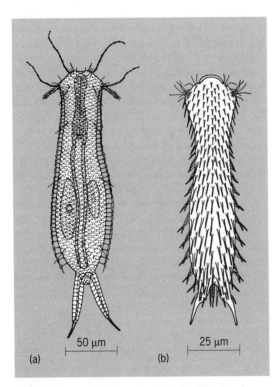

Marine gastrotrichs of the order Chaetonotida; dorsal views. (*a*) *Xenotrichula* (courtesy of W. D. Hummon). (*b*) *Chaetonotus* (after W. D. Hummon, Intertidal marine Gastrotricha from Colombia, *Bull. Mar. Sci.*, 24:396–408, 1974).

The family Chaetonotidae comprises half of all gastrotrichs: *Musellifer* and *Halichaetonotus* are marine; *Polymerurus* is fresh-water; *Aspidiophorus*, *Chaetonotus* (illus. *b*), *Heterolepidoderma*, *Ichthydium*, and *Lepidodermella* have species in each habitat. *Musellifer* lives in mud; all others inhabit sands of streams, beaches, or offshore banks, or live in the surface detritus of ponds or lake bottoms. The other seven genera, in four families, are all fresh-water and either are rare or tend toward a semiplanktonic life, especially *Neogossea* and *Stylochaeta*.

Several chaetonotids are easily kept in aquatic microcosms, and a few, such as *L. squamata*, are readily cultured in pond water on wheat grains. *See* GASTROTRICHA.

William D. Hummon

Chain drive

A flexible device of connected links used to transmit power. A drive consists of an endless chain which meshes with sprockets located on the shaft of a driving source, such as an electric motor/reducer, and a driven source, such as the head shaft of a belt conveyor.

Chains have been used for more than 2000 years. However, the modern contribution of the chain to industrialization began in 1873 with the development of a cast detachable chain. It was a simple cast-metal chain composed of identical links which could be coupled together by hand. This chain so greatly improved the performance of power takeoff drives for farm implements that mechanization became a practical reality. The first development after the success of the cast detachable chain was the cast pintle chain with a closed barrel design and steel pins. Other cast chain designs and variations evolved until an all-steel chain was developed.

Chain types. The new development, now called the roller chain (**Fig. 1**), found uses in the early 1900s on bicycles and other forms of conveyances. Constantly refined and improved, today's roller chain meets the demands of heavy-duty oil well drilling equipment, high-production agricultural machinery (**Fig. 2**), construction machinery, and similar

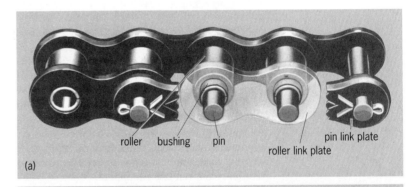

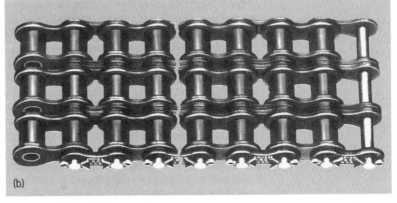

Fig. 1. Roller chains. (*a*) Single-strand. (*b*) Triple-strand.

Fig. 2. Roller chain drive. (*FMC Corp.*)

Fig. 3. Engineering steel chain drive. (*Rexnord Inc.*)

equipment. It also meets the precise timing requirements of lighter-duty equipment such as printing, packaging, and vending equipment.

Another type of chain also evolved, called the engineering steel chain (**Fig. 3**). In a broad sense, the early designs of the engineering steel chain were a blend of the other two, the cast and the roller chain. The drive chains in the engineering steel chain category are usually identified by their offset/crank-link sidebar design. Generally, larger pitch sizes as compared to the roller chain and higher-strength chains characterize this group. A third group used for chain drives is the inverted-tooth (silent) chains (**Fig. 4**). A familiar application is their use as automotive timing chains in automobile engines.

Advantage. The use of chains for power transmission rather than another device, such as V-belts or a direct coupling to the power source, is usually based

on the cost effectiveness and economy of chains and sprockets. Chains and sprockets offer the following advantages: large speed ratios; sufficient elasticity to absorb reasonable shocks; a constant speed ratio between the driving and driven shaft; long life without excessive maintenance; mechanical understandability regarding installation and functionality; coupling and uncoupling with simple tools; and a simple means to get power from its source to the location where needed. *See* BELT DRIVE.

Drive design. The design of a chain drive consists primarily of the selection of the chain and sprocket sizes. It also includes the determination of chain length, center distance, method of lubrication, and in some cases the arrangement of chain casings and idlers. Chain and sprocket selection is based on the horsepower and type of drive; the speeds and sizes of the shafting; and the surrounding conditions. A properly selected chain, following prescribed chain manufacturers' and the American Chain Association's techniques, is usually based on 15,000 hours of operation without breakage of components, considering chain wear not to exceed that which can be accommodated by the sprockets. Generally, chains are considered worn out when the roller chain exceeds approximately 3% elongation, the engineered steel chain exceeds approximately 5% elongation, and the inverted-tooth (silent) chain exhibits malfunction characteristics. To achieve the rated 15,000-h life, the environment must be clean and the chain lubricated as recommended by the manufacturer for the speed, the horsepower capacity, and the number of teeth on the smaller sprocket.

Chain and sprocket design. The particular design of the sideplate/sidebar/crank-link, pin, bushing, and roller of chains used in chain drives has been standardized to a substantial degree. The dimensional parameters regarding pitch, pin, bushing, roller, and side-plate sizes have been standardized. Interference

Fig. 4. Inverted tooth/silent chain drive.

ANSI and ISO standards for drive chains			
Chain description	ANSI standard number	ISO standard number	Title
Roller chain	B29.1	R606	(ANSI) Transmission Roller Chains and Sprocket Teeth (ISO) Short-pitch Transmission Roller Chain
Inverted-tooth (silent) chain	B29.2	—	(ANSI) Inverted-tooth (silent) Chains and Sprocket Teeth (ISO) No standard available
Engineering steel chain	B29.10	ISO3512	(ANSI) Heavy-duty Offset Sidebar Power Transmission Roller Chains and Sprocket Teeth (ISO) Heavy-duty Crank-Link Transmission Chains

between parts is usually controlled by the manufacturer, as is hardness of the chain parts, which determine the life of the chain. The selection of materials and heat treatments to obtain desired hardnesses are selected by manufacturers, but generally certain minimum hardnesses are required to meet minimum ultimate strength or breaking load criteria.

A sprocket is a wheel with teeth shaped to mesh with the chain. The sprocket tooth form, when properly selected, assures the success of the chain drive. Space limitations often determine the chain length and the number of teeth on the sprocket. Usually more than one combination of chain type, chain size, and number of sprocket teeth will satisfy a requirement. The final determination is based on economics and availability.

Lubrication. Lubrication of chains reduces joint wear as the links flex onto and off the sprockets. Lubricated bearing surfaces, that is, the chain joints, can carry high loads without galling. Chain capacity or horsepower ratings are determined for operation in a clean environment with proper lubrication. Lubrication extends the wear life of chains and sprockets operating in any environment, no matter how dirty or abrasive. Chains should not be greased. A nondetergent petroleum-base oil is recommended. For operation at high speeds, oil stream–force feed lubrication is required for cooling. An oil bath is effective at intermediate speeds, and manual lubrication is acceptable at slow speeds. *See* LUBRICANT; WEAR.

ANSI and ISO standards. The American National Standards Institute has established a committee for the standardization of transmission chains and sprockets. Also, the International Standards Organization has established a committee to promulgate international standards for chains and chain wheels for power transmission and conveyors. The **table** identifies those standards which apply to drive chains. Typically, the standards identify those characteristics of a chain which ensure that one manufacturer's chain will couple with another and that the minimum ultimate strength or breaking load characteristics have been established for each chain. The ANSI standard includes a supplemental section with horsepower rating tables and selection information. *See* CONVEYOR.   Victor D. Petershack

Bibliography. American Chain Association, *Chains for Power Transmission and Material Handling*, 1982.

Chain reaction (chemistry)

A chemical reaction in which many molecules undergo chemical reaction after one molecule becomes activated. In ordinary chemical reactions, every molecule that reacts must first become activated by collision with other rapidly moving molecules. The number of these violent collisions per second is so small that the reaction is slow. Once a chain reaction is started, it is not necessary to wait for more collisions with activated molecules to accelerate the reaction, which now proceeds spontaneously.

Photochemical reactions. A typical chain reaction is the photochemical reaction between hydrogen and chlorine as described by reactions (1).

$$
\begin{aligned}
Cl_2 + light &\rightarrow Cl + Cl \\
Cl + H_2 &\rightarrow HCl + H \\
H + Cl_2 &\rightarrow HCl + Cl \\
Cl + H_2 &\rightarrow HCl + H
\end{aligned}
\tag{1}
$$

The light absorbed by a chlorine molecule dissociates the molecule into chlorine atoms; these in turn react rapidly with hydrogen molecules to give hydrogen chloride and hydrogen atoms. The hydrogen atoms react with chlorine molecules to give hydrogen chloride and chlorine atoms. The chlorine atoms react further with hydrogen and continue the chain until some other reaction uses up the free atoms of chlorine or hydrogen. The chain-stopping reaction may be the reaction between two chlorine atoms to give chlorine molecules, or between two hydrogen atoms to give hydrogen molecules. Again the atoms may collide with the walls of the containing vessel, or they may react with some impurity which is present in the vessel only as a trace.

The length of the chain, that is, the number of molecules reacting per molecule activated, is determined by the relative rates of the competing reactions, namely, the chain-propagating reaction and the chain-stopping reactions. In the chain reaction just described, 10^6 molecules of hydrogen chloride may be formed by the photodissociation of 1 chlorine molecule.

In photochemical chain reactions, the length of the chain can be determined by measuring the number of photons of light absorbed, that is, the number of molecules activated, and dividing by the number of molecules which react chemically. *See* PHOTOCHEMISTRY.

Thermal reactions. In thermal reactions, the length of the chain may sometimes be estimated from a knowledge of the intermediate steps and the kinetics involved. The presence of a chain reaction can often be proved by adding a trace of an inhibitor, such as nitric oxide. If the reaction is slowed down greatly by a very small amount of a substance which reacts with the chain-propagating units, the reaction involves a chain. While the inhibitor is being consumed in this way, the reaction is slow. After an induction period, the inhibitor is consumed and the rapid chain reaction then takes place.

Chain reactions are erratic and are reproduced with difficulty in different laboratories because they depend so much on the presence and concentration of accidental impurities which act as inhibitors.

In many chemical reactions, particularly organic reactions at elevated temperatures, the chains are carried by free radicals which are very reactive fragments of molecules that have unshared electrons, such as $\cdot CH_3$, $\cdot C_2H_5$, $\cdot H$, and $\cdot OH$. The thermal decomposition of propane is a typical free-radical chain which follows reactions (2). One molecule

$$
\begin{aligned}
C_3H_8 &\rightarrow \cdot CH_3 + \cdot C_2H_5 \\
\cdot CH_3 + C_3H_8 &\rightarrow CH_4 + C_3H_7 \\
\cdot C_3H_7 &\rightarrow \cdot CH_3 + C_2H_4 \\
\cdot CH_3 + C_3H_8 &\rightarrow CH_4 + \cdot C_3H_7
\end{aligned}
\quad (2)
$$

of propane is decomposed into free radicals, $\cdot CH_3$ and $\cdot C_2H_5$, which then react with more propane to give the product methane and a free radical, $\cdot C_3H_7$, which decomposes into $\cdot CH_3$ and the product ethylene. The $\cdot CH_3$ reacts with more propane and continues the chain. The chain is terminated by collision of the free radicals with the wall or with each other, in reactions such as (3). Thus it is possible

$$
\cdot CH_3 + \cdot C_3H_7 \rightarrow C_4H_{10} \quad (3)
$$

to obtain products of higher molecular weight as well as products of lower molecular weight. The finding of these higher-molecular-weight products supports the theory of free-radical formation and chain reactions.

Certain oxidations in the gas phase are known to be chain reactions. The carbon knock which occurs at times in internal combustion engines is caused by a too-rapid combustion rate caused by chain reactions. This chain reaction is reduced by adding tetraethyl-lead which acts as an inhibitor.

The polymerization of styrene to give polystyrene and the polymerization of other organic materials to give industrial plastics involve chain reactions. The spoilage of foods, the precipitation of insoluble gums in gasoline, and the deterioration of certain plastics in sunlight involve chain reactions, which can be minimized with inhibitors. *See* ANTIOXIDANT; CATALYSIS; CHAIN REACTION (PHYSICS); CHEMICAL DYNAMICS; INHIBITOR (CHEMISTRY).　　Farrington Daniels

Bibliography. J. H. Espenson, *Chemical Kinetics and Reaction Mechanisms*, 2d ed., 1995; H. Eyring et al., *Basic Chemical Kinetics*, 1980; K. J. Laidler, *Reaction Kinetics*, 2 vols., 1963; J. I. Steinfeld, J. Francisco, and W. Hase, *Chemical Kinetics and Dynamics*, 2d ed., 1998.

Chain reaction (physics)

A succession of generation after generation of acts of division (called fission) of certain heavy nuclei. The fission process releases about 200 MeV (3.2×10^{-4} erg $= 3.2 \times 10^{-11}$ joule) in the form of energetic particles including two or three neutrons. Some of the neutrons from one generation are captured by fissile species (^{233}U, ^{235}U, ^{239}Pu) to cause the fissions of the next generations. The process is employed in nuclear reactors and nuclear explosive devices. *See* NUCLEAR FISSION.

The ratio of the number of fissions in one generation to the number in the previous generation is the multiplication factor k. The value of k can range from less than 1 to less than 2, and depends upon the type and amount of fissile material, the rate of neutron absorption in nonfissile material, the rate at which neutrons leak out of the system, and the average energy of the neutrons in the system. When $k = 1$, the fission rate remains constant and the system is said to be critical. When $k > 1$, the system is supercritical and the fission rate increases. *See* REACTOR PHYSICS.

A typical water-cooled power reactor contains an array of uranium rods (about 3% ^{235}U) surrounded by water. The uranium in the form of UO_2 is sealed into zirconium alloy tubes. The water removes the heat and also slows down (moderates) the neutrons by elastic collision with hydrogen nuclei. The slow neutrons have a much higher probability of causing fission in ^{235}U than faster (more energetic) neutrons do. In a fast reactor, no light nuclei are present in the system and the average neutron velocity is much higher. In such systems it is possible to use the excess neutrons to convert ^{238}U to ^{239}U. Then ^{239}U undergoes radioactive decay into ^{239}Pu, which is a fissile material capable of sustaining the chain reaction. If more than one ^{239}Pu atom is provided for each ^{235}U consumed, the system is said to breed (that is, make more fissile fuel than it consumes). In the breeder reactor, the isotope ^{238}U (which makes up 99.3% of natural uranium) becomes the fuel. This increases the energy yield from uranium deposits by more than a factor of 60 over a typical water-moderated reactor, which mostly employs the isotope ^{235}U as fuel.

A majority of power reactors use water as both the moderator and the coolant. However, a limited number of reactors use heavy water instead of light water. The advantage of this system is that it is possible to use natural uranium as a fuel so that no uranium enrichment is needed. Some other power reactors are gas-cooled by either helium or carbon dioxide and are moderated with graphite. *See* NUCLEAR REACTOR.　　Norman C. Rasmussen

Bibliography. H. A. Enge and R. P. Redwine, *Introduction to Nuclear Physics*, 2d ed., 1995; S. Glasstone and A. Sesonske, *Nuclear Reactor*

Engineering, 2 vols., 4th ed., 1993; K. S. Ram, *Basic Nuclear Engineering*, 1990.

Chalcanthite

A mineral with the chemical composition $CuSO_4 \cdot 5H_2O$. Chalcanthite commonly occurs in blue to greenish-blue triclinic crystals or in massive fibrous veins or stalactites (see **illus.**). Fracture is conchoidal and luster is vitreous. Hardness is 2.5 on Mohs scale and specific gravity is 2.28. It has a nauseating taste and is readily soluble in water. It dehydrates in dry air to a greenish-white powder.

(a)

2cm

(b)

Chalcanthite. (*a*) Crystals associated with quartz, Clifton, Arizona (*specimen from Department of Geology, Bryn Mawr College*). (*b*) Crystal habit (*after L. G. Berry and B. Mason, Mineralogy, W. H. Freeman, 1959*).

Chalcanthite is a secondary mineral associated with gypsum, melanterite, brochantite, and other sulfate minerals found in copper or iron sulfide deposits. It is also found in mine workings.

Although deposits of commercial size occur in arid areas, chalcanthite is generally not an important source of copper ore. Its occurrence is widespread in the western United States. *See* COPPER.

Edward C. T. Chao

Chalcedony

A fine-grained fibrous variety of quartz, silicon dioxide. The individual fibers that compose the mineral aggregate usually are visible only under the microscope. Subvarieties of chalcedony recognized on the basis of color differences (induced by impurities), some valued since ancient times as semiprecious gem materials, include carnelian (translu-

cent, deep flesh red to clear red in color), sard (orange-brown to reddish brown), and chrysoprase (apple green). Chalcedony sometimes contains dendritic enclosures resembling plants or trees. Major kinds of impurities that give color to chalcedony are iron oxides (carnelian and sard), nickel (chrysoprase), and manganese. *See* GEM; QUARTZ.

Chalcedony occurs as crusts with a rounded, mammillary, or botryoidal surface and as a major constituent of nodular and bedded cherts. The hardness is 6.5–7 on Mohs scale. The specific gravity is 2.57–2.64. The ultrafine structure of chalcedony has been deduced from x-ray diffraction and electron microscopy to consist of a network of microcrystalline quartz with many micropores. The amount of amorphous silica, if any, is less than 10%. The yellowish color and anomalously low indices of refraction commonly observed under a transmitted light microscope result from scattering of light from the micropores. Paleozoic and older chalcedony is usually more coarsely crystallized than younger examples, grain growth of microcrystalline quartz being a result of time.

Crusts of chalcedony generally are composed of fairly distinct layers concentric to the surface. Agate is a common and important type of chalcedony in which successive layers differ markedly in color and degree of translucency. In the most common kind of agate the layers are curved and concentric to the shape of the cavity in which the material formed. The successive layers of chalcedony and agate usually differ in permeability to solutions, and much colored agate sold commercially is artificially pigmented by dyes or inorganic chemical compounds. *See* AGATE.

Raymond Siever

Bibliography. C. Frondel, *Dana's System of Mineralogy*, vol. 3: *Silica Minerals*, 1962.

Chalk

The term "chalk" is sometimes used in a broad sense for any soft, friable, or weathered fine-grained limestone; however the term is mostly restricted to pelagic (biogenic) limestones. Chalk is a uniformly fine-grained, typically light-colored marine limestone primarily composed of the remains of calcareous nannofossils and microfossils. These minute pelagic organisms (see **illus.**) live in surface and near-surface oceanic waters and include coccolithophores (algae) and planktic foraminifers (Protozoa). Larger fossil constituents (such as bivalves, pteropods, echinoids, or ammonites) may be present, but only in subordinate amounts. The dominant pelagic skeletal remains are composed of low-magnesium calcite and, after death, settle slowly to the ocean floor, accumulating where the sea floor lies at a depth of less than about 4 km or 13,000 ft (the carbonate is redissolved at greater depths). Typical chalk sedimentation rates are 30 m (100 ft) per million years, so chalk accumulation is also dependent on the exclusion of diluting materials such as reefal detritus or terrigenous debris (clay, silt, or sand) transported from land areas

Typical chalk coccoliths, with small grain size and porous fabric. The sample is from late Oligocene chalk from the east side of Halton-Rockall Basin, North Atlantic Ocean.

by rivers. Chalks therefore form mainly in isolated outer shelf or deeper-water settings that are far from land areas. *See* CALCITE; LIMESTONE.

Because coccolithophores and planktic foraminifers did not exist prior to the Jurassic Period (about 150 million years ago), all true chalks are Jurassic or younger. Only 50 million years later (by Late Cretaceous time), chalks had become the single most volumetrically important type of limestone, a status they still retain. Most of those chalks are confined to ocean basins and so are poorly studied. The best-known chalks, such as those from the coastal cliffs of southern England (including the white cliffs of Dover), the Gulf Coast of the United States (Austin or Selma Limestones), and the U.S. Western Interior (Niobrara and Greenhorn Limestones), were deposited outside ocean basins on broad continental shelves during a worldwide sea-level high stand in Late Cretaceous time. *See* CRETACEOUS.

The small size of coccoliths and their constituent crystals means that chalks are extremely fine-grained deposits, typically with average crystal sizes of 1 micrometer or less. Because low-magnesium calcite is the least soluble form of calcium carbonate in near-surface settings, true nannofossil chalks also normally remain porous and friable. The unique combination of light color, compositional purity, softness, and fine texture led to many of the early uses of chalk for writing on blackboards or for marking athletic fields. Chalks are also widely used in the manufacture of portland cement, as lime for fertilizers, and in powders, abrasives, and coatings. More recently, chalks have become major targets for hydrocarbon exploration, especially in the Norwegian and Danish sectors of the North Sea, the southern Persian Gulf region, and U.S. Gulf Coast. Chalks lose porosity mainly through the effects of pressure-related mechanical and chemical dissolution and reprecipitation of calcium carbonate during progressive burial. Where allowed to continue unchecked, such alteration eventually leads to nearly complete porosity loss by about 3.8 km (12,000 ft) of burial. The presence of anomalously high pore-fluid pressures in basins such as the

North Sea or the early introduction of hydrocarbons can inhibit or prevent such pressure-related alteration and allow preservation of prolific oil fields in chalk reservoirs, even at depths in excess of 3 km (10,000 ft). P. A. Scholle

Bibliography. American Geophysical Union, *Short Course in Geology*, no. 4; R. S. Boynton, *Chemistry and Technology of Lime and Limestone*, 2d ed., John Wiley, 1980; H. G. Reading (ed.), *Sedimentary Environments and Facies*, 3d ed., 1994; J. P. Riley and R. Chester (eds.), *Treatise on Chemical Oceanography*, vol. 5, pp. 265–388, 1976; P. A. Scholle, Chalk diagenesis and its relation to petroleum exploration: Oil from chalks, a modern miracle?, *Amer. Ass. Petrol. Geol. Bull.*, 61(7):982–1009, 1977; P. A. Scholle, D. G. Bebout, and C. H. Moore (eds.), Carbonate depositional environments, *Amer. Ass. Petrol. Geo. Mem.*, no. 33, 1983; P. A. Scholle, N. P. James, and J. F. Read (eds.), *Carbonate Sedimentation and Petrology*, 1989.

Chameleon

The name for about 80 species of small-to-medium-sized lizards that comprise the family Chamaeleontidae and occur mainly in Africa and Madagascar. The American chameleons (*Anolis*) belong to a different family of lizards, the Iguanidae. This reptile is insectivorous and beneficial to humans. It commonly is found on vegetation, especially the green parts.

Chamaeleo chamaeleon is the most common species and is a typical example of the group. Its body is flattened from side to side; it has a long, prehensile tail; and both the forelimbs and hindlimbs have two digits that oppose the other three (see **illus.**). These feet and the tail make the chameleon well adapted for its arboreal habitat. The eyes are large and can move independently of each other in all directions. The tongue is also prehensile, being extensible for a great distance, about the length of the animal itself, and is a highly efficient organ for capturing insects. The head of the chameleon is triangular in profile and has a pointed crest.

Chameleons are noted for their ability to change color. Color changes appear to be related to

Calumma brevicornis; short-horned chameleon. (*Photo courtesy of Gerald and Buff Corsi, © California Academy of Science*)

environmental temperatures as well as other external stimuli. When the temperature is high or the animal excited, the chameleon is green in color. When the temperature is cool or the animal unmolested, it is gray in color. There are cells in the skin that contain chromatophores, pigment granules of various colors. These black, red, or yellow pigments are contained in stellate, or star-shaped, color cells. Under nervous stimulation the cell branches expand and the pigments diffuse into these areas and become visible, creating a change in skin color. Contraction of the cells causes the pigment to concentrate and appear as indefinite spots of color. The ability to change color is protective, so that the animal can blend into its surroundings.

The chameleon is oviparous. The female digs out a hollow in the ground for a nest where several dozen eggs are laid and then covered with soil. The period of incubation varies inversely with the temperature and may be as short as 4 months or as long as 10 months. Parental care of the young has not been observed.

The armored chameleon (*Leandria perarmata*), known from one specimen in Madagascar, is a highly developed representative of a group of chameleons having one or more horns on the snout instead of a crest on the head. The body has a row of spines along either side as well as a crest of spines along the back. There is a bony hood on the nape of the neck and a serrated crest down to the eye level. One species, *C. bitaeniatus*, found in the mountainous areas of eastern Africa, is ovoviviparous, and the female produces eggs that are incubated and hatched within her body. After a period of development about six young are born. *See* CHROMATOPHORE; PROTECTIVE COLORATION; REPTILIA; SQUAMATA.   Charles B. Curtin

Chamois

One of several species of mammals included in the tribe Rupicaprini of the family Bovidae. The group is heterogeneous in form, but all are intermediate in characteristics between the goats and antelopes. The chamois is the only European species of the group and is indigenous to the mountainous areas, especially the Alps. About nine races are recognized, based on their geographical range. The chamois is, however, becoming rare.

The chamois (*Rupicapra rupicapra*) lives in small herds of both sexes in numbers from 10 to 50. The female leaves the herd after the rutting season for a sheltered area, and after a gestation period of about 20 weeks gives birth to a single young in the spring. The offspring are active almost immediately and begin to forage when 10 days old. They are sexually mature at 3 years of age and the average life-span is about 10 years. The adult is almost 3 ft high and weighs about 90 lb (40 kg) maximum. Both sexes bear horns which are set close together on the forehead, project almost at right angles, and are straight except for the sharp curve backward at the top (see **illus.**). These animals have 32 teeth and the dental formula is I 0/3 C 0/1 Pm 3/3 M 3/3. A soft, pliable

Alpine chamois (*Rupicapra rupicapra*). (*Brent Huffman/ Ultimate Ungulate Images*)

leather, known as chamois cloth, is obtained from the skin of this animal. *See* DENTITION.

The goral, serow, and Rocky Mountain goat are included in the same tribe of bovids as the chamois. Both the goral (genus *Naemorhedus*) and serow (genus *Capricornis*) are found in Asia. The goral lives in small herds in the Himalayas, existing on the sparse vegetation found on the rocky slopes. It is about 2 ft (0.6 m) high and has short horns. A single young is born in the early summer after a gestation period of 6 months. The male of the Rocky Mountain goat (*Oreamnos americanus*) is larger than the female, weighing between 200 and 300 lb (90 and 135 kg) and standing over 3 ft (1 m) high. Both sexes are covered with thick, long white hair and have horns and beards. These animals are vegetarians, feeding on moss, lichens, and other vegetation of the area. In the early spring the female bears one or two young, which are quite active soon after birth. *See* ANTELOPE; MAMMALIA.   Charles B. Curtin

Chandra X-ray Observatory

A powerful x-ray telescope in orbit around the Earth. Built by the National Aeronautics and Space Administration, it was launched and deployed by space shuttle *Columbia* on July 23, 1999. Named after the Indian-American astronomer Subrahmanyan Chandrasekhar, *Chandra* is unique because of its sensitivity and its extremely high precision mirrors. These features have made possible significant advances in astronomy—especially in relation to the life cycles of stars, the role of supermassive black holes in the

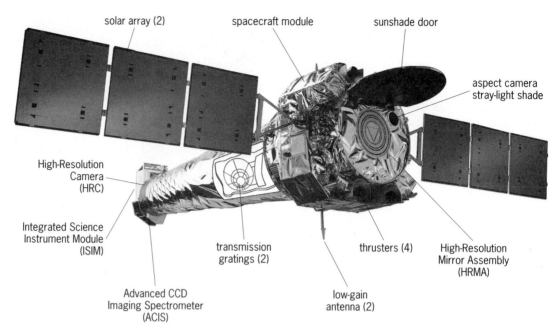

solar array (2)

spacecraft module

sunshade door

aspect camera
stray-light shade

High-Resolution
Camera
(HRC)

Integrated Science
Instrument Module
(ISIM)

transmission
gratings (2)

thrusters (4)

High-Resolution
Mirror Assembly
(HRMA)

Advanced CCD
Imaging Spectrometer
(ACIS)

low-gain
antenna (2)

Fig. 1. *Chandra X-ray Observatory* **spacecraft.**

evolution of galaxies, and the study of dark matter and dark energy.

X-rays: another form of light. Light is electromagnetic radiation and can take on many forms. Radio waves, microwaves, infrared, visible, ultraviolet, x-ray, and gamma radiation are different forms of light. Each type of light is characterized by a range of wavelengths, with radio wavelengths being the longest and gamma rays the shortest. *See* ELECTROMAGNETIC RADIATION; LIGHT.

When charged particles collide—or undergo sudden changes in their motion—they produce bundles of energy called photons that fly away from the collision at the speed of light. In fact they are light, or electromagnetic radiation. Since electrons have the smallest mass of any known type of charged particle, they are accelerated more easily. According to the laws of electrodynamics, more acceleration means more radiation, so electrons produce most of the photons in the universe. *See* ELECTRON; PHOTON.

The energy of the photon tells what form of light it is. Radio waves are composed of low-energy photons. Optical photons—the only photons perceived by the human eye—are a million times more energetic than the typical radio photon. The energies of x-ray photons range from hundreds to thousands of times higher than that of optical photons. *See* X-RAYS.

The photons collected by x-ray telescopes reveal the hot spots in the universe—regions where particles have been energized or raised to high temperatures by gigantic explosions or intense gravitational fields. X-ray astronomy has revealed that such conditions exist in a remarkable variety of places, ranging from the vast spaces between galaxies to the bizarre, collapsed worlds of neutron stars and black holes.

Description. The *Chandra X-ray Observatory* (**Fig. 1**) has three major parts: (1) the x-ray telescope,

whose mirrors focus x-rays from celestial objects; (2) the science instruments which record the x-rays so that x-ray images can be produced and analyzed; and (3) the spacecraft, which provides the environment necessary for the telescope and the instruments to work.

Mirrors and focusing. The mirrors are at the heart of the telescope and are what makes *Chandra* special. They are the smoothest mirrors ever produced—if the continental United States were relatively as smooth as *Chandra*'s mirrors, the highest mountain would be less than 13 cm (5 in.) tall.

Although x-rays are a form of light, they do not reflect off mirrors in the same way that visible light does. Because of their high energy, x-ray photons penetrate into a mirror in much the same way that bullets slam into a wall. Likewise, just as bullets ricochet when they hit a wall at a grazing angle, so will x-rays ricochet off mirrors. *See* X-RAY OPTICS.

These properties mean that mirrors built to reflect x-rays look very different from those in optical telescopes. X-ray mirrors have to be precisely shaped and aligned nearly parallel to incoming x-ray photons, so the mirrors resemble barrels in contrast to the dish shape of optical telescopes. They can be nested one inside the other, like Russian dolls, to increase their collecting area. *Chandra* has four nested pairs of mirrors, the largest being about 1.2 m (4 ft) in diameter (**Fig. 2**).

The *Chandra X-ray Observatory* combines the mirrors with four science instruments to record the x-rays from astronomical sources. The incoming x-rays are focused by the mirrors to a tiny spot (about half as wide as a human hair) on the focal plane, about 10 m (30 ft) away. The focal-plane science instruments—or cameras, the Advanced CCD Imaging Spectrometer (ACIS) and the High-Resolution Camera (HRC)—are well matched to capture the

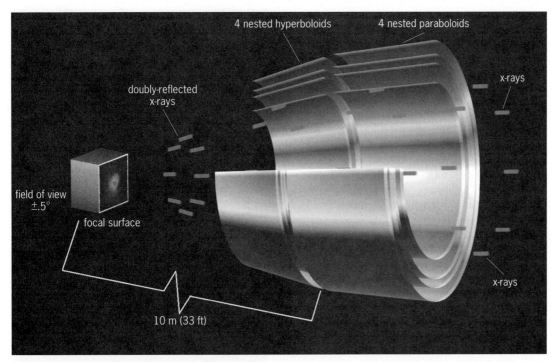

Fig. 2. Schematic diagram of *Chandra*'s grazing-incidence x-ray mirror. Mirror elements are 0.8 m (2.6 ft) long and 0.6–1.2 m (2–4 ft) in diameter. (*NASA/CXC/SAO*)

sharp images formed by the mirrors and to provide information about the incoming x-rays: their number, position, energy, and time of arrival. The close matches of the imaging capability of the instruments and the focusing power of the mirrors enables *Chandra* to make images that reveal detail as small as one-half second of arc. This resolution is equivalent to the ability to read a stop sign at a distance of 20 km (12 mi).

Science instruments. The Advanced CCD Imaging Spectrometer is an array of charge-coupled devices (CCDs), which are sophisticated versions of the crude CCDs used in camcorders. This instrument is especially useful because it can make x-ray images and at the same time measure the energy of each incoming x-ray. It is the instrument of choice for studying temperature variations across x-ray sources such as vast clouds of hot gas in intergalactic space, or chemical variations across clouds left by supernova explosions. The High Resolution Camera is especially useful for making high-quality images and measuring the time variations in x-ray sources. *See* ASTRONOMICAL IMAGING; CHARGE-COUPLED DEVICES.

Two additional science instruments, the transmission grating spectrometers, provide detailed information about the specific energy of the incoming x-rays. These spectrometers are circular gratings that can be swung into position just behind the mirrors, where they redirect (diffract) the x-rays by an amount that depends on their energies. The positions of the x-rays are measured by the focal-plane cameras, so the exact energy of the x-rays can be determined. This enables the temperature, ionization, and chemical composition of the gas around a black

hole, for example, to be determined. *See* DIFFRACTION GRATING.

Environment. Because the Earth's atmosphere absorbs cosmic x-rays, x-ray observatories must be placed high above the Earth's surface. This means that the ultraprecise mirrors and detectors, together with the sophisticated electronics that conveys the information back to Earth, must be able to withstand the rigors of a rocket launch and operate in the hostile environment of space.

Orbit. *Chandra* has an unusual, elliptical orbit that takes the spacecraft more than a third of the way to the Moon before returning to its closest approach to Earth of about 16,000 km (10,000 mi). The time to complete an orbit is 64 hours 18 minutes. The spacecraft spends 85% of its orbit above the belts of charged particles that surround the Earth and interfere with observations. Uninterrupted observations as long as 55 h are possible, and the overall percentage of useful observing time is much greater than for the low Earth orbit of a few hundred miles used by most satellites.

Control and data retrieval. The observatory is controlled by commands transmitted from the Operations Control Center in Cambridge, Massachusetts. A preplanned sequence of observations is uplinked to *Chandra* and stored in the onboard computer for later execution. Data collected by observations with *Chandra* are stored on a recorder for later transmission to the ground every 8 h during regularly scheduled Deep Space Network contacts. The data are transmitted to the Jet Propulsion Laboratory in Pasadena, California, and then to Operations Control at the *Chandra* X-ray Center in Cambridge for processing and analysis by scientists.

See SPACE COMMUNICATIONS; SPACECRAFT GROUND INSTRUMENTATION.

Major scientific achievements. *Chandra*'s unique abilities have made possible significant advances in several areas of astrophysics.

Evolution of stars. Chandra gives astronomers a unique window for viewing the drama of stellar evolution, from the formation of stars in dense clouds of dust and gas to their demise, either quietly as white dwarfs or violently as supernovae.

A *Chandra* observation of a rich cluster of young stars in the Orion Nebula showed that young Sun-like stars produce violent x-ray outbursts that are much more frequent and energetic than anything observed today from the 4.6×10^9-year-old Sun. This could have implications for understanding the conditions under which the solar system evolved. *See* ORION NEBULA; SOLAR SYSTEM; STELLAR EVOLUTION.

Stars much more massive than the Sun end their lives with a supernova explosion, one of the most energetic events in the universe. The explosion ejects material rich in the heavy elements necessary for planets and life—carbon, nitrogen, oxygen, silicon, and iron. As this stellar debris plows into surrounding gas and dust, it generates tremendous shock waves that heat gas to millions of degrees. *Chandra* images and spectra have allowed scientists to trace these shock waves and to study the amount and distribution of heavy elements expelled in the explosion (**Colorplate 1**). *See* SHOCK WAVE; SUPERNOVA.

Superbubbles of hot gas thousands of light-years across can be created by the cumulative effect of hundreds of supernovae. *Chandra* observations of the Antennae Galaxies show that superbubbles disperse heavy elements over vast distances (**Colorplate 2**).

Many supernovae leave behind a neutron star—a dense, whirling ball of neutrons that is as massive as the Sun, yet only 20 km (12 mi) in diameter. *Chandra* images have revealed spectacular rings and jets of high-energy particles created by rapidly rotating neutron stars (**Fig. 3**). *See* CRAB NEBULA; NEUTRON STAR; PULSAR.

Black hole discoveries. Chandra observations have revealed the presence of many previously undetected stellar black holes in the Milky Way Galaxy and in nearby galaxies, including a possible new class of intermediate-mass black holes (**Colorplate 3**). *See* MILKY WAY GALAXY.

On a larger scale, *Chandra* has shown that there are many more active supermassive black holes in the centers of galaxies than previously thought. At the center of a pair of colliding galaxies, *Chandra* found evidence for two supermassive black holes orbiting each other (**Colorplate 4**). In a few hundred million years, these huge black holes will merge to form an even larger black hole.

Chandra images have revealed startling evidence for the repetitive and far-reaching explosive activity associated with supermassive black holes. Jets several hundred thousand light-years in length have been traced back to central supermassive black holes. A *Chandra* observation of the Perseus galaxy cluster has revealed wavelike features that appear to

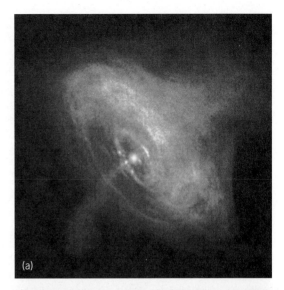

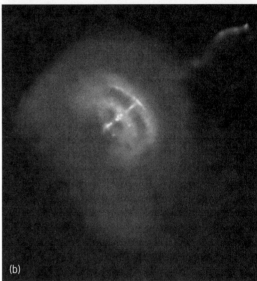

Fig. 3. *Chandra* images of x-rays from the vicinity of rapidly rotating neutron stars. (*a*) Crab Nebula, the remnant of a supernova that was seen in 1054 (*NASA/CXC/SAO*). (*b*) Vela pulsar. A jet of high-energy particles is emerging toward the upper right (*NASA/CXC/PSU/G. Pavlov et al.*).

be sound waves produced by jetlike explosive events occurring in the vicinity of a supermassive black hole in Perseus A, the huge galaxy at the center of the cluster. In another cluster, *Chandra* found evidence for what may be the most energetic explosion ever detected. These massive explosions may be part of a cosmic feedback cycle in which the black hole regulates its own growth and the growth of the galaxy in which it resides. *See* BLACK HOLE; GALAXY, EXTERNAL.

Galaxy clusters, dark matter, and the cosmic web. A large cluster of galaxies contains hundreds to thousands of galaxies immersed in an enormous cloud of multimillion-degree hot gas held together by dark matter. Such galaxy clusters are the largest gravitationally bound systems in the universe. The intergalactic hot gas clouds in clusters are detected as x-ray sources and can extend over a region several million light-years in diameter.

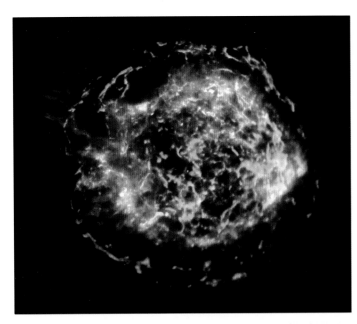

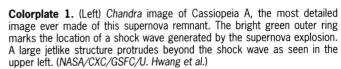

Colorplate 1. (Left) *Chandra* image of Cassiopeia A, the most detailed image ever made of this supernova remnant. The bright green outer ring marks the location of a shock wave generated by the supernova explosion. A large jetlike structure protrudes beyond the shock wave as seen in the upper left. (*NASA/CXC/GSFC/U. Hwang et al.*)

Colorplate 2. (Middle left) *Chandra* image of the Antennae Galaxies. Spectacular loops of hot gas are seen spreading out from the southern part of the Antennae into intergalactic space. Also shown are huge clouds of multimillion-degree gas and bright pointlike sources due to neutron stars and black holes. The image is color-coded so that low-, medium-, and high-energy x-rays appear as red, green, and blue, respectively. (*NASA/CXC/SAO/ G. Fabbiano et al.*)

Colorplate 3. (Bottom) A 400 by 900 light-year mosaic of several *Chandra* images of the central region of the Milky Way Galaxy, revealing hundreds of white dwarf stars, neutron stars, and black holes bathed in an incandescent-fog of multimillion-degree gas. The supermassive black hole at the center of the Galaxy is located inside the bright white patch in the center of the image. The colors indicate x-ray energy bands—red (low), green (medium), and blue (high). (*NASA/Umass/D. Wang et al.*)

Colorplate 4. (Middle right) *Chandra* image of NGC 6240, a butterfly-shaped galaxy that is the product of the collision of two smaller galaxies, revealing that the central region of the galaxy contains not one but two active giant black holes. (*NASA/CXC/MPE/S. Komossa et al.*)

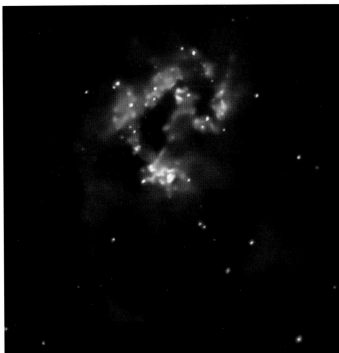

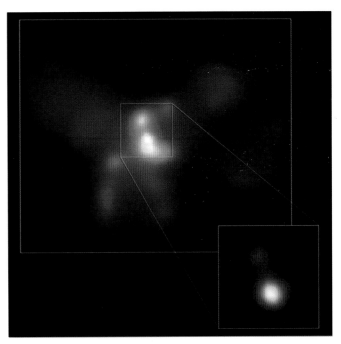

The hot gas in a galaxy cluster is in equilibrium with the gravitational pull of all the mass in the cluster. X-ray studies of numerous clusters have shown that 70 to 90% of the mass of a typical cluster consists of dark matter—hypothetical particles left over from the dense early universe that interact with each other and normal matter only through gravity. The favored type of dark matter particle is cold dark matter, which gets its name from the assumption that dark matter particles were moving slowly when galaxies and galaxy clusters began to form. *See* DARK MATTER.

While an explanation for the source of dark matter is still lacking, an effect that is even more enigmatic has been discovered. Astronomers have observed that the visible light from a certain type of supernova of well-known properties is fainter than expected in distant galaxies. The best explanation is that these supernovae are more distant than originally thought, which implies that the expansion of the universe must be accelerating. *Chandra's* measurements of the dark matter content of clusters of galaxies have provided independent evidence for this remarkable result. The data are consistent with a model in which the expansion of the universe was first decelerating until about 6×10^9 years ago and then began to accelerate. *See* ACCELERATING UNIVERSE.

Cosmic acceleration can be explained if the space between galaxies is filled with a mysterious dark energy. The existence of dark energy and its peculiar properties require either a modification of Albert Einstein's theory of general relativity or a major revision of some other area of fundamental physics. *See* DARK ENERGY.

Assuming that dark energy is responsible for cosmic acceleration, the *Chandra* results, the supernova observations, and the observations of the cosmic microwave background radiation taken together indicate that dark energy makes up about 75% of the energy density of the universe, dark matter about 21%, and visible matter about 4%. *See* COSMIC BACKGROUND RADIATION; COSMOLOGY; UNIVERSE; X-RAY ASTRONOMY; X-RAY TELESCOPE.   Wallace Tucker

Bibliography. E. M. Schlegel, *The Restless Universe*, Oxford University Press, 2002; K. S. Thorne, *Black Holes and Time Warps*, W. W. Norton, 1994; W. Tucker and K. Tucker, *Revealing the Universe: The Making of the Chandra X-ray Observatory*, Harvard University Press, 2001; K. Weaver, *The Violent Universe: Joyrides through the X-ray Cosmos*, Johns Hopkins University Press, 2005.

Channel electron multiplier

A single-particle detector which in its basic form (**Fig. 1**) consists of a hollow tube (channel) of either glass or ceramic material with a semiconducting inner surface. The detector responds to one or more primary electron impact events at its entrance (input) by producing, in a cascade multiplication process, a charge pulse of typically 10^4–10^8 electrons at its exit (output). Because particles other than electrons can impact at the entrance of the channel

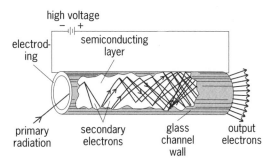

Fig. 1. Cutaway view of a straight, single-channel electron multiplier, showing the cascade of secondary electrons resulting from the initial, primary radiation event, which produces an output charge pulse. (*After J. L. Wiza, Microchannel plate detectors, Nucl. Instrum. Meth., 162:587–601, 1979*)

electron multiplier to produce a secondary electron, which is then subsequently multiplied in a cascade, the channel electron multiplier can be used to detect charged particles other than electrons (such as ions or positrons), neutral particles with internal energy (such as metastable excited atoms), and photons as well. As a result, this relatively simple, reliable, and easily applied device is employed in a wide variety of charged-particle and photon spectrometers and related analytical instruments, such as residual gas analyzers, mass spectrometers, and spectrometers used in secondary ion mass spectrometry (SIMS), electron spectroscopy for chemical analysis (ESCA), and Auger electron spectroscopy. *See* AUGER EFFECT; ELECTRON SPECTROSCOPY; MASS SPECTROMETRY; SECONDARY ION MASS SPECTROMETRY (SIMS); SPECTROSCOPY.

Photon detection. To directly detect photons, the photon energy must exceed the work function of the multiplier surface. Most channel electron multipliers require energies exceeding 5–10 eV for moderately efficient single-photon detection, limiting direct use to vacuum-ultraviolet wavelengths and shorter. Detection of longer-wavelength, lower-energy photons can be accomplished by the addition of a suitable photoelectron-emitting surface (photocathode) near the channel electron multiplier input, with an electric field to sweep liberated photoelectrons into the channel electron multiplier. *See* OPTICAL DETECTORS; PHOTOEMISSION; PHOTOMULTIPLIER; PHOTOTUBE.

Cascade multiplication. The cascade multiplication process at the heart of the channel electron multiplier's operation results from the secondary emission properties and high resistance (typically $10^9 \, \Omega$) of the inner channel surface. For multiplication to occur, there must be a high probability (expressed as a high secondary emission coefficient) that an electron impacting the surface will liberate more than one secondary electron, each of which is then accelerated toward the output to impact the surface and produce even more secondaries. In operation, it is necessary to apply a high voltage of the order of 1–4 kV between the input and output of the channel, thereby producing an electric field within the

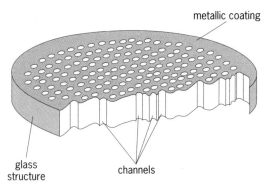

metallic coating

glass
structure

channels

Fig. 2. Cutaway of a microchannel plate, or channel electron multiplier array, not to scale. Metallic coatings on both sides of the plate serve as input and output electrodes. (*After J. L. Wiza, Microchannel plate detectors, Nucl. Instrum. Meth., 162:587–601, 1979*)

channel that accelerates secondary electrons to an energy sufficient to guarantee a high secondary emission coefficient. An electron impact energy of the order of 300 eV is generally required. High surface resistivity limits the current required from the high-voltage power supply to a few microamperes. *See* SECONDARY EMISSION.

Ion feedback. The large flux of electrons produced near the exit of a channel electron multiplier leads to a relatively high probability of electron impact ionization of residual gas molecules in the channel. The resulting ions are accelerated by the internal field toward the input, where they can impact the surface to liberate electrons that are then multiplied in the usual fashion. This is a potentially unstable condition called ion feedback and can lead to spurious outputs almost completely unrelated to real inputs. Several techniques are employed to reduce or eliminate ion feedback. Operating the channel electron multiplier in high vacuum (pressure less than 10^{-3} pascal or

10^{-5} torr) controls ion feedback by reducing residual gas density in the channel. Lowering the channel voltage limits the channel gain and hence the electron flux, thereby lowering the ionization rate. Finally, by introducing curvature in the channel, the distance that an ion can travel toward the input can be limited; since most ions are produced near the exit, limiting this distance also limits the multiplication gain and thus the amplitude of spurious ion feedback signals. Virtually all commercially available channel electron multiplier devices employ channel curvature to control ion feedback.

Configuration. A typical single channel electron multiplier will have a channel radius of 0.04 in. (1 mm) and a length of 4 in. (10 cm). The channel is often formed into a spiral or helix to conserve space and to control ion feedback. It is common to find the entrance flared into a funnel shape to increase the surface area sensitive to the primary event.

Microchannel plate. A related device is the channel electron multiplier array, often called a microchannel plate (**Fig. 2**). The channel electron multiplier array is usually a disk-shaped device with a diameter between 1 and 4 in. (2.5 and 10 cm) and a thickness of a fraction of a millimeter, and consists of millions of miniature channel electron multiplier devices arranged with channel axes perpendicular to the face of the disk. In one widely used version, the individual channels have a diameter of about 12 micrometers and are spaced at 15-μm intervals. Channel electron multiplier arrays find application as image intensifiers in night vision devices and are employed to add either large detection area or imaging capabilities, or both, to charged-particle detectors and spectrometers. Ion feedback in channel electron multiplier arrays is often controlled by using two or more arrays in succession and arranging the channel axes at an angle to the axes of the disks, so that the individual channels in successive arrays form a chevron or herringbone pattern with those in previous stages.

Position-sensitive detector. The microscopic channels in a channel electron multiplier array allow the position coordinates of an input primary event (such as a charged particle or photon) to be approximately preserved during the cascade multiplication process. This position sensitivity makes the microchannel plate amplifier a useful imaging device, with position or imaging resolution equal to a few channel spacings in a typical chevronned multiplate device. A microchannel plate with a means of reading out the coordinates of the detected output charge pulse is often called a position-sensitive detector. Several methods of position readout are commonly employed. In the image tube method, the output charge pulses strike a phosphor coating. The "image" of the event distribution at the amplifier input is converted into a visible light image, suitable for processing with conventional video devices [such as a charge-coupled-device (CCD) camera or a vidicon] and techniques. *See* CHARGE-COUPLED DEVICES; TELEVISION CAMERA TUBE.

In the discrete multiple-anode method, the output charge pulse is collected on one or more of

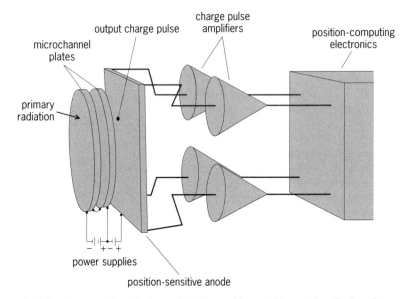

microchannel
plates

output charge pulse

charge pulse
amplifiers

position-computing
electronics

primary
radiation

power supplies

position-sensitive anode

Fig. 3. Position-sensitive detector system. The position-sensitive anode collects a charge "cloud" produced by the microchannel plate amplifier in response to primary radiation. In the charge-division method, shown here, the position of the primary event is calculated from the relative sizes of the charge pulses that subsequently migrate to the corners of the anode.

an array of conducting anodes, with the identity of the active anodes, possibly in a digitally encoded form, then determining the event position. The frequently used charge-division method employs collection of the output pulse on a resistive anode, which is terminated either at two opposite edges (for one-dimensional readout) or at four corners (for two-dimensional readout) [**Fig. 3**]. The relative fractions of the total output charge pulse of a single input event, collected at the two or four terminals, can then be used to determine the event position coordinates using relatively straightforward electronic or computing techniques. A less common time-division method uses the distributed resistance and capacitance of a resistive anode in proximity to the rear surface of the exit microchannel plate (and other possible nearby structures), and the event-position-dependent time delay thereby introduced into the peaking time of the collected charge pulses, to determine event coordinates. *See* IMAGE TUBE (ASTRONOMY); LIGHT AMPLIFIER; PARTICLE DETECTOR.   Stuart B. Elston

Bibliography. M. Lampton, The microchannel image intensifier, *Sci. Amer.*, 245(5):62–71, November 1981; J. H. Moore, C. C. Davis, and M. A. Coplan, *Building Scientific Apparatus: A Practical Guide to Design and Construction*, 2d ed., 1989.

Channeling in solids

The steering of positively charged energetic particles between atomic rows or planes of a crystalline solid. The particles can be positive ions, protons, positrons, or muons. If the angle between the direction of the particle and a particular axis or plane in the crystal is within a small predictable limit (typically a few degrees or less), then the gradually changing electrostatic repulsion between the particle and each successive atomic nucleus of the crystal produces a smooth steering through the crystal lattice (**Fig. 1**). Thus, the trajectory of the channeled particle is restricted to the open spaces between atomic rows and planes of a crystal (**Fig. 2**). *See* CRYSTAL STRUCTURE.

An obvious consequence of this steered motion is that it prevents violent collisions of the particles with atoms on the lattice sites. Hence, as compared with a randomly directed beam of particles, the channeled beam loses energy more slowly, penetrates

Fig. 2. Model of a cubic crystal lattice. (*a*) Model viewed along a ⟨100⟩ axis. The open (square) spaces are the ⟨100⟩ axial channels. (*b*) The same model viewed along a randomly chosen direction roughly 20° away from a ⟨100⟩ axis.

more deeply, creates much less damage to the crystal along its track, and is prevented from participating in all close-encounter processes (nuclear reactions, Rutherford scattering, and so forth) with lattice atoms. *See* NUCLEAR REACTION; SCATTERING EXPERIMENTS (NUCLEI).

A related channeling phenomenon is the channeling of energetic electrons or other negative particles. In this case, the particles are attracted to the positively charged atomic nuclei, so that the probability of violent collisions with atoms on lattice sites is enhanced rather than being prevented, and the particles are steered along the rows or planes of nuclei rather than between them.

Blocking. A closely related phenomenon is called blocking. In this case, the energetic positive particles originate from atomic sites within the crystal lattice by means of fission, alpha-particle decay, or by wide-angle scattering of a nonchanneled external beam in a very close encounter with a lattice atom. Those

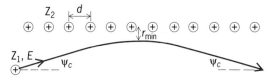

Fig. 1. Typical trajectory of a channeled ion (nuclear charge Z_1, energy E), illustrating the gentle steering caused by electrostatic repulsion from the regularly spaced nuclei of a crystal (nuclear charge Z_2, spacing d), so that the ion approaches no closer to the nuclei than r_{min}. The transverse angle ψ_c with respect to the channel axis remains almost constant as the ion penetrates through the crystal lattice.

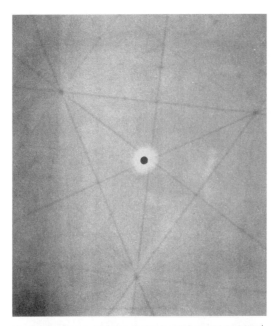

Fig. 3. Blocking pattern produced by a beam of 1-MeV He⁺ ions after backscattering from a germanium crystal onto a cellulose nitrate film 6 in. (15 cm) away. The large central spot is the hole in the film through which the incident beam reached the crystal. The intricate pattern of thin dark lines (that is, unbombarded regions of film) corresponds to the network of atomic planes along which backscattered particles are absent due to blocking. The wider spots at the intersection of several planes correspond to blocking along the major crystal axes.

particles emitted almost parallel to an atomic row or plane will be deflected away from the row by a steering process similar to that shown in Fig. 1. Consequently, no particles emerge from the crystal within a certain critical blocking angle of each major crystallographic direction. A piece of film placed some distance from the crystal provides a simple technique for recording blocking patterns (**Fig. 3**). Theoretical considerations show that the same principle is involved in blocking as in channeling; hence, both phenomena exhibit an identical dependence on particle energy, nuclear charge, lattice spacing, and so forth. *See* NUCLEAR FISSION; RADIOACTIVITY.

Development. Channeling effects were predicted by J. Stark in 1912. However, despite the evident simplicity of the channeling phenomenon, firm experimental evidence for its existence was not recognized until the early 1960s, when it was observed that energetic heavy ions sometimes penetrated to unexpectedly large depths in polycrystalline aluminum and tungsten. In 1962, it was shown by computer simulation that these deep penetrations were probably due to particles being channeled along the open directions in some correctly oriented microcrystals. Single-crystal experiments in several laboratories subsequently confirmed that such channeling was indeed an extremely general phenomenon, occurring for all charged nuclear particles (atomic nuclei, positrons, muons, and so forth) over an energy range from a few electronvolts up to hundreds of gigaelectronvolts. At about the same time, a comprehensive theoretical framework for predicting the

behavior of channeled trajectories was developed, which led not only to an understanding of the channeling phenomenon but also to its widespread application in many other fields.

Applications. Applications of channeling include the location of foreign atoms in a crystal, the study of crystal surface structure, and the measurement of nuclear lifetimes.

Location of foreign atoms. The location of foreign (solute) atoms in a crystal is one of the simplest channeling applications. It is accomplished by measuring the yields of Rutherford back-scattered particles, characteristic x-rays, or nuclear reaction products produced by the interaction of channeled particles with the solute atoms. Such yields are enhanced for solute atoms that are displaced into channels of the crystal. Thus the solute atom sites can be identified by a triangulation technique, illustrated in **Fig. 4** for a two-dimensional model of a cubic lattice. Numbers in angle brackets ⟨ ⟩ identify the different kinds of crystal axes, whereas numbers in square brackets identify specific directions within a given kind. The shaded areas are shadowed by rows of host atoms (○) in the [10] and [11] channels. As shown by the table in Fig. 4, three possible sites for a foreign atom (●, **x**, and ☐) are readily distinguished by comparing the channeling behavior along the ⟨10⟩- and ⟨11⟩-type directions. Channeled ions do not have close-encounter interactions with solute atoms in substitutional positions (●), since these are completely shadowed by atomic rows in both ⟨10⟩- and ⟨11⟩-type channels. The **x** interstitial positions (halfway along the sides of the until cells) are 50% shadowed in both the [10] and [01] channels, but lie in the center of the [11] and [1$\bar{1}$] channels. The ☐ interstitial positions (in the center of the square unit cell) are completely

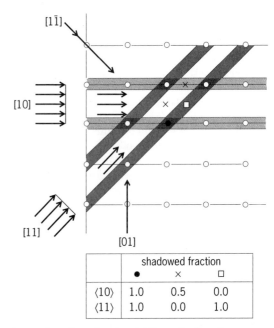

	shadowed fraction		
	●	×	☐
⟨10⟩	1.0	0.5	0.0
⟨11⟩	1.0	0.0	1.0

Fig. 4. Two-dimensional model illustrating how the channeling effect may be used to locate foreign atoms in a crystal. (*After J. N. Mundy et al., eds., Methods of Experimental Physics, vol. 21, Solid State: Nuclear Methods, Academic Press, 1983*)

shadowed in both ⟨11⟩-type channels, but lie in the center of ⟨10⟩-type channels. *See* CRYSTAL DEFECTS.

This method has been used to determine the lattice positions of solute atoms that have been introduced into crystals by a variety of means (for example, by melting, diffusion, or ion implantation). For example, channeling measurements show that furnace or laser heating of silicon that has been implanted with energetic boron, arsenic, or other electrically active atoms causes these atoms to move onto normal (substitutional) lattice sites, sometimes to concentrations far in excess of solubility limits. These measurements also are used to determine the amount of lattice damage (created by the ion implantation) which remains after the heating. These and similar applications have proved extremely useful in the development of semiconductor devices. *See* ION IMPLANTATION; LASER-SOLID INTERACTIONS.

When energetic particles strike a crystal, atoms can be ejected from normal lattice sites, leaving vacant lattice sites (vacancies). Solute atoms can trap these vacancies, creating unique geometric configurations, such as the tetravacancy–solute-atom complex (**Fig. 5**). In this complex, the solute atom (for example, a tin atom in aluminum) becomes displaced from a normal lattice site into the tetrahedral interstitial site, surrounded by four lattice vacancies at equal distance. Such a solute atom lies in the center of ⟨100⟩ channels, is halfway to the center of ⟨110⟩ channels, and is completely shadowed in ⟨111⟩ channels. Thus, its position is easily identified by channeling measurements along these three axial channels. These vacancy–solute-atom complexes are very stable thermally, and probably form nucleation centers for the creation of even larger vacancy clusters (voids) in irradiated materials. *See* RADIATION DAMAGE TO MATERIALS.

Study of surface structure. In a similar way, channeling techniques are used to study the structure of crystal surfaces. Because of the asymmetric forces between atoms on the surface of a crystal, the surface plane of atoms is often reconstructed (that is, it has a different atomic structure from that of the bulk); also, it may be relaxed inward or outward. In **Fig. 6**, a method for measuring an outward relaxation of the surface plane of atoms by the channeling technique

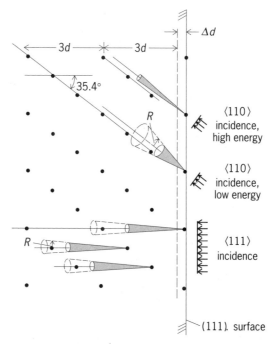

Fig. 6. Atomic configuration near the surface of a Pt(111) crystal, illustrating the use of channeling to investigate Δ*d*, the surface relaxation. *R* = radius of shadow cone cast by surface atom; *d* = bulk (111) planar spacing. (*After J. A. Davies et al., Measurement of surface relaxation by MeV ion backscattering and channeling, Phys. Lett., 54A:239–240, North Holland, 1975*)

is shown. A beam of ions directed perpendicular to the (111) surface (⟨111⟩ incidence) "sees" only one atom per row of atoms. However, because of the outward displacement of the surface atoms, a beam of ions incident along a nonperpendicular (for example, ⟨110⟩) axis "sees" two atoms per row at high ion energies (at which each surface atom casts a small shadow cone), and one atom per row at low ion energies (giving a large shadow cone). Information on surface relaxations (Δ*d*) as small as 2×10^{-12} m and also on the vibrational amplitudes of the surface plane of atoms can be obtained by such studies. *See* LATTICE VIBRATIONS; SURFACE PHYSICS.

In addition, premelting at surfaces can be investigated. Channeling studies of the surface of lead near the melting point have shown that a thin surface layer becomes molten at a lower temperature than that of the bulk material. Such studies will contribute to an understanding of melting, which remains one of the more poorly understood physical phenomena.

Measurement of nuclear lifetimes. A different type of-break application is the measurement of extremely short nuclear lifetimes. Nevertheless, the same basic principles of atom location are involved; namely, the ability, by means of channeling or blocking, to pinpoint accurately the location of a nucleus (relative to the crystal lattice) at the instant that it is struck by or emits an energetic positive particle. Suppose that a lattice nucleus under external beam bombardment captures a beam particle to form a compound nucleus, recoiling with known velocity from its lattice site, and that this nucleus subsequently decays by emitting an energetic positive particle (proton,

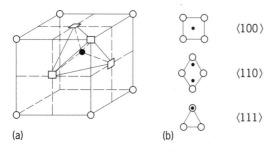

(a)   (b)

Key: ● solute atom   □ vacancies   ○ host atoms

Fig. 5. Tetravacancy–solute-atom complex. (*a*) Perspective view. (*b*) Projection of the solute atom into ⟨100⟩-, ⟨110⟩-, and ⟨111⟩-type axial channels. (*After J. N. Mundy et al., eds., Methods of Experimental Physics, vol. 21, Solid State: Nuclear Methods, Academic Press, 1983*)

alpha particle, fission fragment, and so forth). From the resulting blocking pattern of these emitted particles, the recoil distance before emission and hence the nuclear lifetime can be accurately determined. In this way, lifetimes as short as 10^{-18} s are directly observable.   John A. Davies; M. L. Swanson

Bibliography. L. C. Feldman, J. W. Mayer, and S. Thomas Picraux, *Materials Analysis by Ion Channeling*, 1982; J. N. Mundy et al. (eds.), *Methods of Experimental Physics*, vol. 21, *Solid State: Nuclear Methods*, 1983; E. Uggerhoj and A. Zucker (eds.), *Channeling and Other Penetration Phenomena*, 1989.

Chaos

System behavior that depends so sensitively on the system's precise initial conditions that it is, in effect, unpredictable and cannot be distinguished from a random process, even though it is deterministic in a mathematical sense. This article begins with a discussion of the notions of order, chaos, and noise as they occur in deterministic dynamical systems, the relation of chaos and periodicity, and the concept of an attractor. Applications of chaos to atmospheric prediction, weather, climate, electronic circuits, astronomy, acoustics, and atoms are then discussed.

Throughout history, sequentially using magic, religion, and science, people have sought to perceive order and meaning in a seemingly chaotic and meaningless world. This quest for order reached its ultimate goal in the seventeenth century when newtonian dynamics provided an ordered, deterministic view of the entire universe epitomized in P. S. de Laplace's statement, "We ought then to regard the present state of the universe as the effect of its preceding state and as the cause of its succeeding state." In everday life, the predictable swing of a long, massive pendulum or the regular motion of the Sun, Moon, and planets provides reassurance of a mechanistic newtonian order in the world.

But if the determinism of Laplace and Newton is totally accepted, it is difficult to explain the unpredictability of a gambling game or, more generally, the unpredictably random behavior observed in many newtonian systems. Commonplace examples of such behavior include smoke that first rises in a smooth, streamlined column from a cigarette, only to abruptly burst into wildly erratic turbulent flow (**Fig. 1**); and the unpredictable phenomena of the weather. *See* FLUID FLOW; TURBULENT FLOW.

At a more technical level, flaws in the newtonian view had become apparent by about 1900, leading J. H. Poincaré to remark, "Determinism is a fantasy due to Laplace," and J. C. Maxwell to assert, "The true logic of this world is the calculus of probabilities." The problem is that many newtonian systems exhibit behavior which is so exquisitely sensitive to the precise initial state or to even the slightest outside perturbation that, humanly speaking, determinism becomes a physically meaningless though mathematically valid concept. But even more is true.

Fig. 1. Transition from order to chaos (turbulence) in a rising column of cigarette smoke. The initial smooth streamline flow represents order, while the erratic flow represents chaos.

Many deterministic newtonian-system orbits are so erratic that they cannot be distinguished from a random process even though they are strictly determinate, mathematically speaking. Indeed, in the totality of newtonian-system orbits, erratic unpredictable randomness is overwhelmingly the most common behavior. *See* CELESTIAL MECHANICS; CLASSICAL MECHANICS; DETERMINISM; STOCHASTIC PROCESS.

Examples. These notions will be illustrated through three simple mapping systems which retain many features of general dynamical systems but are not encumbered by extraneous detail.

Highly ordered motion. An example of highly ordered motion is the discrete mapping of points around a circle of unit circumference in which each point is carried one-fifth way around the circle upon each iteration. After n iterations, a point initially at angular position θ_0 has been carried to position θ_n given by Eq. (1),

$$\theta_n = (0.2)n + \theta_0 \qquad (1)$$

where the angle θ has been normalized so that $\theta + 1 = \theta$. This mapping is obviously determinate since each θ_0 uniquely determines an "orbit" of θ_n iterates. The "motion" here is also highly ordered because, from Eq. (1), all orbits are periodic with $\theta_{n+5} = \theta_n$, because the entire circle of points is mapped as a rigid body upon each iteration, and because the angle of rotation is the precisely computable, terminating rational number, $1/5 = 0.2$. Moreover, except for a displacement around the circle, all orbits are identical. This mapping system is thus fully ordered, strictly deterministic, and totally dull. In more general terms, the monotony of the streamline flow in Fig. 1 may be contrasted with the greater variety of behavior of the turbulent flow. Ordered motion while comfortingly simple is also rigidly constrained motion in which all or almost all capricious options have been discarded.

Ordered motion. A less constrained but still ordered motion is generated by the mapping which rigidly rotates the whole circle of points through the larger angle upon each iteration. Here the result of n iterations is given by Eq. (2), where again

$$\theta_n = (\sqrt{2})n + \theta_0 \qquad (2)$$

$\theta + 1 = \theta$. Like the mapping of Eq. (1), except for a displacement around the circle, all orbits are identical. However, here there is one exciting difference. Because the angle of rotation α is now irrational, the θ_n iterates of each θ_0 in Eq. (2) spread out uniformly around the circle, almost as if their positions were selected from a uniform random distribution. In fact, it is possible to rigorously prove for Eq. (2) that Eq. (3) is satisfied, where f is any reasonable

$$\lim_{N \to \infty} \left(\frac{1}{N}\right) \sum_{n=0}^{N} f(\theta_n) = \int_0^1 f(\theta)\, d\theta \qquad (3)$$

well-behaved function. Equation (3), a version of the ergodic theorem, is merely a sophisticated way to assert that all θ values occur with equal frequency and that the mapping of Eq. (2) therefore passes one test for randomness. However, this slight randomness in the mathematically deterministic Eq. (2) has appeared only because a sacrifice has been tacitly made for it. Indeed, the introduction of an irrational angle of rotation into Eq. (2) which yields a uniform θ distribution simultaneously also renders Eq. (2) not fully determinate from the physical viewpoint. Specifically, humans can never compute the precise decimal representation for $\sqrt{2}$. Thus, if ϵ is the error in the determination of $\sqrt{2}$, then the error $\Delta(n)$ in θ_n will be at least $\Delta(n) = n\epsilon$. Since this error clearly grows without bound with iteration number n, physical determinism in Eq. (2) is completely lost when the error $\Delta(n)$ is about unity. Nonetheless, physical determinism over human time scales can be maintained, provided the error ϵ in the determination of $\sqrt{2}$ is sufficiently small.

It is now possible to proceed through a sequence of maps which become more "random" and less "physically determinate." For them, the error $\Delta(n)$ in each θ_n would grow as some polynomial in n, but the notions of order and physical determinism could still be maintained, at least over human time scales, by using humanly available accuracy. The great divide occurs when the error growth becomes exponential, yielding mathematically determinate systems which pass every test for randomness. Here the mapping equations require such massive input of data strings in order to maintain accuracy that, informationally speaking, they are not computing or determining the solution but rather merely copying out the solution being given to them. This case will be illustrated with a final example.

Chaotic motion. If the points on the circle of unit circumference move according to the "multiplicative" mapping equation (4), where $\theta + 1 = \theta$ as before,

$$\theta_n = 2^n \theta_0 \qquad (4)$$

then orbits starting with slightly differing θ_0 values clearly separate exponentially with iteration number n. In consequence, Eq. (4) exhibits that extreme sensitivity of final state to precise initial state characteristic of all chaotic systems; indeed, Eq. (4) is perhaps the simplest system which can serve as a paradigm for chaos.

However, Eq. (4) is no less mathematically deterministic than are Eqs. (1) and (2), since a θ_n set exists and is unique for each given θ_0. The θ_n iterates of Eq. (4) can nevertheless be unpredictably random and nondeterministic, as can be seen by considering the consequences for determinism of the exponentially separating orbits in Eq. (4). For example, if the spatial angle θ_0 is known to an accuracy of 10^{-31}, far beyond the accuracy available to contemporary science, even then, after only 100 iterations, the error in θ_{100} is of order unity, and the last vestige of determinism in Eq. (4) has been lost.

This issue may be further clarified by computing a full set of θ_n iterates of Eq. (4), each having an accuracy of at least 2^{-1}, that is, at least one-binary-digit accuracy. If 2^{-m} is the accuracy of θ_0 required to compute a given θ_n, then Eq. (5) must be satisfied. Thus

$$2^{-1} = 2^n 2^{-m} \qquad (5)$$

$m = n + 1$ or, for large n, $m \cong n$. Now the situation becomes clear. In order to ensure n informational bits of solution output, one per θ_n iterate, it is necessary to include a total of $m = n$ informational bits into the binary representation of θ_0. Equation (4) is thus seen to be merely a "copy" algorithm rather than a "deterministic" one. Alternatively stated, Eq. (4) is merely a fixed "language translation" algorithm which translates a "German" θ_0 into an "English" θ_n sequence.

Even greater insight into these matters can be obtained by writing the θ_0 of Eq. (4) in binary notation as a digit string of zeros and ones; typically it might be given by Eq. (6). Then, each iterate θ_n specified by

$$\theta_0 = 0.11101100000100\ldots \qquad (6)$$

Eq. (4) may be obtained by merely moving the "decimal" in Eq. (6) n places to the right and dropping the integer part. Now, the string of zeros and ones in Eq. (6) may be regarded as specifying a coin-toss sequence. Moreover, the set of all binary θ_0 sequences is in a one-to-one correspondence (essentially) with the set of all possible random coin-toss sequences. Consequently, almost all binary θ_0 sequences pass every humanly computable test for randomness. In short, they are random. A straightforward derivation then proves that almost all θ_0 yield random θ_n sequences despite that fact that Eq. (4) is mathematically deterministic.

Equation (4) is mathematically deterministic provided that θ_0 is given or somehow determined mathematically; however, in Eq. (4), randomness arises precisely because the infinite digit string for θ_0 is, in general, as random as a coin toss and therefore not computable by any finite algorithm. Moreover, and equally important, the exponentially sensitive dependence of final state upon initial state in Eq. (4) transforms randomness of the θ_0 digit string into randomness of the θ_n sequence. Indeed, the θ_n sequences of Eqs. (1) and (2) lack full randomness only because they lack this sensitive dependence upon initial state.

Equation (4), as mentioned above, is the epitome of chaos just as Eq. (1) is the epitome of order. In addition, Eq. (4) exhibits that richness of behavior inherent to all chaotic systems: everything that can happen does happen. In Eq. (4), for example, the full orbit is known once the θ_0 digit string of Eq. (6) is known. But here all digit strings are possible and, in fact, each digit string actually occurs for some θ_0. Thus, chaos results in richness of opportunity rather than meaninglessness.   Joseph Ford

Noise. So far, the discussion has focused on the internal dynamics of a hypothetical system. In many applications, external effects also have an impact on behavior of a system. Then, Eq. (7), which summa-

$$\theta_n = F(n, \theta_0) \tag{7}$$

rizes the governing equations for θ_n as a function F of n and θ_0, in the forms of Eqs. (1), (2), and (4), might be written as Eq. (8), in which ε_n represents

$$\theta_n = F(n, \theta_0) + \varepsilon_n \tag{8}$$

the external effect. When it is random and unpredictable, ε_n is usually called noise. Such an external effect causes at least part of θ_n to be random and unpredictable as well.

In summary, chaos is the apparently unpredictable behavior of a nonlinear deterministic system, while noise is an apparently random effect impinging on the system from an external source. The noise may be purely random or the chaotic behavior of another system.

Unpredictable behavior of a deterministic system may thus arise from internally generated chaos, from random forces imposed on the system, or from a combination of both. With real systems, it may be difficult or impossible to distinguish the two phenomena. *See* ACOUSTIC NOISE; ELECTRICAL NOISE.
                                        John A. Dutton

Systems in the real world. The use of deterministic, ordered mathematical models to describe behavior of systems in the real world is so familiar that only chaos need be discussed. One example of chaos is the evolution of life on Earth. Were this evolution deterministic, the governing laws of evolution would have had built into them anticipation of every natural crisis which has occurred over the centuries plus anticipation of every possible ecological niche throughout all time. Nature, however, economizes and uses the richness of opportunity available through chaos. Random mutations provide choices sufficient to meet almost any crisis, and natural se-

lection chooses the proper one. *See* ORGANIC EVOLUTION.

Another example concerns the problem that the human body faces in defending against all possible invaders. Again, nature appears to choose chaos as the most economical solution. Loosely speaking, when a hostile bacterium or virus enters the body, defense strategies are generated at random until a feedback loop indicates that the correct strategy has been found. A great challenge is to mimic nature and to find new and useful ways to harness chaos. *See* IMMUNITY.

Another matter for consideration is the problem of predicting the weather or the world economy. Both these systems have much in common with Eq. (4), although their governing equations are certainly more complicated. Nonetheless, like a θ_n sequence of Eq. (4), the weather and the economy are chaotic and can be predicted more or less precisely only on a very short time scale. By recognizing the chaotic nature of the weather and the economy, it may eventually be possible to accurately determine the probability distribution of allowed events in the future given the present. At that point it may be asserted with mathematical precision that, for example, there is a 90% chance of rain 2 months from today. Much work in chaos theory seeks to determine the relevant probability distributions for chaotic systems. *See* WEATHER FORECASTING AND PREDICTION.

Finally, many physical systems exhibit a transition from order to chaos, as exhibited in Fig. 1, and much work studies the various routes to chaos. Examples include fibrillation of the heart and attacks of epilepsy, manic-depression, and schizophrenia. Physiologists are striving to understand chaos in these systems sufficiently well that these human maladies can be eliminated. *See* PERIOD DOUBLING.
                                        Joseph Ford

Chaos and periodicity. In systems where the number of possible states, none of which closely resembles any other one, is limited, approximate repetitions of earlier states must eventually occur. If such a system is not chaotic, the history following a near repetition of a state will nearly repeat the history following the original occurrence, so that near repetitions will continue to occur at regular intervals, and the system will vary periodically. If, then, a system of this sort is observed not to vary periodically, it must be chaotic. Absence of periodicity often affords the means by which chaos is most easily recognized, and it has sometimes served in place of sensitive dependence as a definition of chaos. For example, a pendulum in a well-behaved clock does not swing chaotically; a flag in a moderate steady breeze may flap chaotically.

Many real systems exhibit nonperiodic variations superposed on periodic oscillations. The periodic components of these variations are entirely predictable and, like the diurnal and seasonal variations of the Earth's weather, are often externally forced. In such systems, which are also considered chaotic, two rather similar states will eventually evolve into states differing as much as states chosen from a long sequence, at similar phases of the periodic oscillations but otherwise randomly.

Attractors. Real-world systems generally entail some dissipative processes, and some external forcing that prevents them from coming to a standstill, like the clockwork that keeps a pendulum swinging or the wind that keeps a flag flapping. For such systems the set of states that can occur or be approximated again and again, after transient effects have subsided, is far more restricted than it would be if neither dissipation nor forcing were present; it is most drastically restricted when the system is not chaotic. This set of states is called the attractor of the system. Especially for simple systems, attractors are commonly represented by plane or multidimensional graphs in which each point represents a distinct state, the coordinates of the point equaling the values of some or all of the variables. For a chaotic system the graph is an infinite complex of curves or other manifolds, with finite gaps between any pair of manifolds, and the attractor is called a strange attractor. Edward N. Lorenz

Lorenz butterfly. A celebrated mathematical model exhibiting chaotic behavior was developed by E. Lorenz in the early 1960s. Seeking to understand limitations on the accuracy of weather prediction, Lorenz studied a mathematical model with just 12 differential equations representing atmospheric flow and, by calculating solutions to the equations with a digital computer, discovered that some of them were chaotic—they exhibited sensitive dependence on initial conditions. Failing to find an even simpler model of temporally dependent atmospheric flow that would clarify the mathematical origins of the chaos, Lorenz turned to two-dimensional convection in a vertical plane as modeled by a system of three differential equations that also exhibited chaotic solutions. Lorenz's 1963 article on the mathematical properties of this model became a classic in the numerical study of chaos. It provided an explicit example of chaotic behavior in a system derived from hydrodynamics, and thus seemed to dash hopes that computers would enable accurate large-scale atmospheric prediction for forecast periods of weeks or months. Indeed, Lorenz observed that an implication of his results was that the flap of a butterfly's wings could change the course of the weather a continent away.

Lorenz model and equations. The flow of a fluid heated below and cooled above, known as Rayleigh-Bernard convection, depends on the external temperature difference ΔT maintained on the two bounding surfaces. For small differences, the flow will be a slow regular overturning, while for large temperature gradients it will be intense and turbulent. The ordinary differential equations governing the amplitudes of the representation, X, Y, and Z, are calculated with Fourier techniques from the governing partial differential equations (9). Here, X' is the rate of change

$$X' = \sigma(Y - X) \qquad (9a)$$

$$Y' = -XZ + rX - Y \qquad (9b)$$

$$Z' = XY - bZ \qquad (9c)$$

of X $(dX(t)/dt)$, and the quantities Y' and Z' are similarly defined. All variables are dimensionless, with a Prandtl number σ, an aspect ratio b, and the Rayleigh number r proportional to ΔT. The nonlinear XY and XZ terms are the source of mathematical intractability and chaotic solutions.

The stationary solutions describing steady flow are readily found by setting the rates of change, X', Y', and Z', all equal to zero. The stationary point at the origin $X = Y = Z = 0$ is always a solution, and is stable only for $r < 1$. A pair of additional stationary points appears for $r > 1$ at $X = Y = \pm$, $Z = r - 1$. For small values of r, solutions spiral rapidly into one of these two points. For $r > 13.96$, solutions with initial points near one of these stable points cross over and spiral into the other point and some isolated chaotic solutions appear. When r exceeds the critical value 24.74, all three stationary points are unstable and chaotic flow is observed for almost all initial conditions.

But even then, the flow is dissipative [as a consequence of the last terms in each of Eqs. (9)] and has the critical property that a volume V of initial points (that is, a three-dimensional set) is mapped asymptotically as time increases to a set of zero volume (a set of dimension less than three). To see this, observe that in Eq. (10) the volume of an initial set of points with volume V_0 is shown in Eq. (11). Thus,

$$\frac{1}{V}\frac{dV}{dt} = \frac{\partial X'}{\partial X} + \frac{\partial Y'}{\partial Y} + \frac{\partial Z'}{\partial Z} = -(\sigma + 1 + b) \quad (10)$$

$$V = V_0 e^{-(\sigma+1+b)t} \to 0 \quad \text{as} \quad t \to \infty \qquad (11)$$

the initial volumes are mapped to sets of dimension less than volumes. But from a mathematical theorem, the attractor must be of dimension greater than two if the solutions are to be more complex than periodic orbits.

Chaotic attractor. Solving the nonlinear convection equations (9) with a computer, Lorenz compared solution trajectories in (X, Y, Z) space with those emanating from nearby initial points and discovered that, after a time, they separate from each other when r is large enough. Indeed, for the convection model described here, he found that if the Rayleigh number r exceeds the value 24.74, then the separation occurred eventually, no matter how close the initial points were. Furthermore, through numerical simulation Lorenz discovered that all solution trajectories in (X, Y, Z) space, regardless of their initial point, are attracted to a thin, curved structure where they are then trapped. This Lorenz attractor has two lobes resembling the wings of a butterfly and is called the Lorenz butterfly (**Fig. 2**).

Such attractors are identified as strange because their structure is vastly more complex than the stationary points or periodic orbits that constitute all of the mathematically possible attractors on a two-dimensional surface. The Lorenz attractor may be represented as a collection of nearly parallel sheets connected at the origin. Evolving trajectories can pass by each other on adjacent sheets without actually intersecting. The attractor can be described as resembling a Cantor set, and with advanced methods its fractal dimension can be determined as 2.06 (where a plane would be of dimension 2).

As a solution trajectory approaches the chaotic attractor, it will first circle one of the paired stationary points a number of times and then pass near the origin on the way to circle the other stationary point in the pair for one or more times. The trajectory thus continues to oscillate between the two stationary points, circling away from each one for a number of times before switching to the other one.

This phenomenon leads to a separation of solutions that forecloses the possibility of extended predictability of chaotic systems. As two solutions with nearby initial points approach the attractor, they circle, and oscillate between, the two paired stationary points for a while, staying fairly close together and tracing out a similar trajectory. But then, one solution will continue to circle one stationary point while the other will move across the origin to orbit the other stationary point. From then on, the time history of the solutions will be different and the limit of numerical predictability has been exceeded (**Fig. 3**).

Stretching, tearing, and folding. The mechanism creating chaos in the Lorenz and other chaotic models is a combination of stretching, tearing, and folding mandated by the interaction of nonlinearity and the energy constraints on the flow. In the case of the Lorenz model, it can be shown that a quadratic form in X, Y, Z is constrained and that the flow is confined to a three-dimensional ellipsoid. But because of nonlinearity, the trajectories emanating from a small volume of initial points will diverge from each other and be stretched out into a sheetlike image expanding in two dimensions and contracting in one, thus satisfying the condition that initial volumes map to sets with zero volume as time increases. The images of the initial points are stretched farther and farther apart and are torn when they split to circle different stationary points. Nevertheless, the expanding

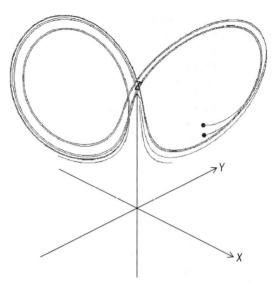

Fig. 3. Separation of solutions on the Lorenz attractor. The two trajectories starting from the nearby initial points indicated by the balls in the right lobe of the attractor stay together for several circuits around both lobes and then separate as they pass over the origin, with one proceeding around the left lobe, the other around the right. (*M. Takatsuka, GeoVISTA Center, Department of Geography, Pennsylvania State University*)

image surface must eventually fold to stay within the boundaries prescribed by the energy constraint, mixing up the originally nearby trajectories.

Butterflies and computers. Although the existence of chaotic behavior has been inferred for nearly a century, the detailed exploration of chaos has been made possible by numerical simulation with digital computers. Indeed, even today there is no way other than numerical simulation to determine whether the solutions to a given nonlinear differential system will exhibit chaotic properties for a specific range of its parameters. And thus chaos and computers go together, with computers essential to reveal the properties of chaotic systems.

As exemplified by the Lorenz butterfly, the mathematical structures of chaotic attractors are often elegant and sometimes haunting. But there is the other Lorenz butterfly, too—the one whose wings might change the course of weather events. The manifestations of that hypothetical butterfly appear in reality as differences in observed and actual states of the atmosphere and as inaccuracies inevitably introduced in trying to model an entire atmosphere in a finite computer model. The butterflies are thus in the observations and in the computer models of any chaotic system. Taking account of the effect of these virtual butterfly wings is a key challenge in the development of improved numerical methods of atmospheric prediction.   John A. Dutton

Some mathematical foundations in physics. To the uninitiated a gulf appears to exist between the ways that mathematicians and physicists study chaos. A primary difference between their modeling methods can be shown to result from the choice of size for a time-step (increment, Δt) in the integration of a system's equation of motion. Physicists generally

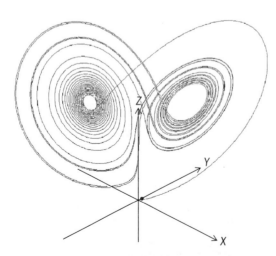

Fig. 2. Three-dimensional visualization of the Lorenz butterfly as traced out by the trajectory of the original simulation reported by Lorenz in 1963 ($\sigma = 10$, $b = 8/3$, $r = 28$) with initial conditions (X, Y, Z) = (0, 1, 0). The integration was performed with a fourth-order Runge-Kutta scheme. (*M. Takatsuka, GeoVISTA Center, Department of Geography, Pennsylvania State University*)

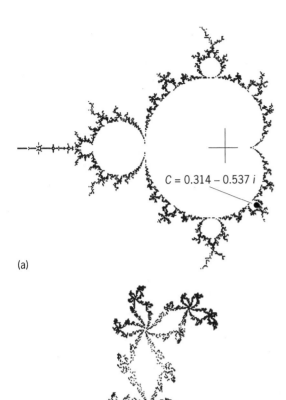

$C = 0.314 - 0.537\,i$

(a)

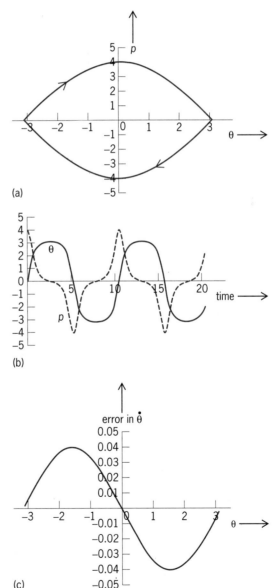

ple, the Hamiltonian of Eqs. (12) for the pendulum

$$H(p, \theta) = \frac{p^2}{2} - c\cos\theta$$

$$\dot{p} = -\frac{\partial H}{\partial \theta} = -c\sin\theta \qquad (12)$$

$$\dot{\theta} = \frac{\partial H}{\partial p} = p$$

(obtained from considerations of the total energy of the system), in which some constants that are usually included in this expression have been set equal to unity, to leave the single adjustable parameter c. Here, $\dot{p} = dp/dt$ and $\dot{\theta} = d\theta/dt$, and the two time derivatives in Eqs. (12) are called Hamilton's canonical equations of motion. Taking the time derivative of $\dot{\theta}$ gives the familiar equation of motion for the

(a)

(b)

(c)

Fig. 5. Representations of pendulum motion corresponding to a periodic variation in angular position θ whose amplitude is just less than π radians (180°). (a) Phase-space representation (plot of momentum p versus θ). (b) Time plots of θ and of $p = \dot{\theta}$. (c) Error in $\dot{\theta}$ from use of the Euler algorithm with $\Delta t = 0.01$.

(b)

Fig. 4. Examples of fractal (self-similar) sets. (a) The Mandelbrot set in the complex plane, with origin indicated by the cross. A single point in the complex plane (in this case $C = 0.314 - 0.537\,i$, where $i = \sqrt{-1}$) generates (b) an associated Julia set.

prefer to describe a system in terms of state variables (such as displacement of a pendulum θ and its momentum p) that vary continuously with time t (that is, $\Delta t \to 0$); whereas mathematicians prefer to work with "maps," which involve the repeated application of one or more recursive equations to a set of one or more variables.

The maps known as Julia sets (**Fig. 4**) and studied by Benoit Mandelbrot are among the best-known examples of fractals, which have the property of self-similarity under a change of scale. Maps of this type are generated by iteration of the equation of $Z_{n+1} = Z_n^2 + C$, where C is a complex-number constant, with $Z_0 = C$. The set of points C in the complex plane for which the associated Julia set is bounded is called the Mandelbrot set (Fig. 4), and its boundary is also a fractal. (Details of the methodology are available from Web sites.) *See* COMPLEX NUMBERS AND COMPLEX VARIABLES; FRACTAL.

Hamilton's equations and maps. A connection between phase-space representations and their associated maps, which also exhibit self-similarity for chaotic systems, is realized by applying the methods of Hamiltonian mechanics when generating the differential equations of motion. Consider, for exam-

pendulum; that is, $d\dot{\theta}/dt = \ddot{\theta} = \dot{p} = -c \sin \theta$, yielding $\ddot{\theta} + c \sin \theta = 0$. *See* HAMILTON'S EQUATIONS OF MOTION; PENDULUM.

Transition from a "physics view" to a "math view" involves the use of approximations in finite-difference form, which cause the canonical equations to take on the form of Eqs. (13). Thus θ and

$$p_{n+1} = p_n - c \sin \theta_n \Delta t$$
$$\theta_{n+1} = \theta_n + p_{n+1} \Delta t \tag{13}$$

p can be estimated for any value of n (corresponding to time $n \Delta t$) once the initial conditions at $n = 0$ have been specified. To describe the pendulum's behavior according to Eqs. (13), the graphical representation commonly employed is that which is referred to as phase space. For this low-dimensional case, it is simply a plot of p versus θ, an example of which is shown in **Fig. 5a**. For a more complicated (higher-dimensional) system, such as the Lorenz butterfly, discussed above, a third variable is necessary.

For purpose of comparison, Fig. 5b shows the temporal variations of θ and p. Such time plots are less useful than phase plots when the motion is chaotic, as opposed to the highly nonlinear, yet nonchaotic case of Fig. 5. Chaotic motion can be generated by adding to Eq. (13) both a damping term proportional to p and a driving force. This case is characterized by the fractal nature of a plot called the Poincaré section, which is obtained by "strobing" the graph of p versus θ. In other words, instead of continuously graphing p versus θ, one "turns on the graph" at one point per period of the driving force.

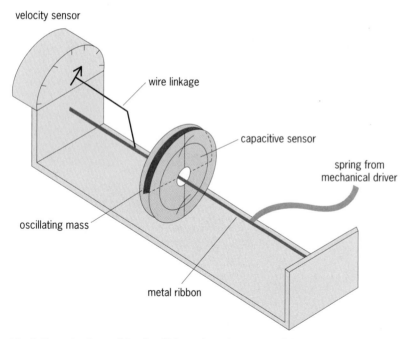

Fig. 6. Example of a pendulum in which gravity and a torsional ribbon act in opposition. The oscillating mass is a thin semicircular metal plate that is rigidly attached to the ribbon at its midpoint. The ribbon is fixed at each end but twists where the mass is attached, and torsional oscillations in the ribbon are excited by the spring. The oscillating mass is sandwiched between two stationary circular metal plates with center holes through which the ribbon passes, and together the three plates form a fully differential capacitive sensor to measure the angular position of the mass. The velocity sensor is a galvanometer operating in "reverse," and the wire linkage drives this galvanometer.

velocity sensor

wire linkage

capacitive sensor

spring from mechanical driver

oscillating mass

metal ribbon

Figure 5c shows that the numerical integration algorithm due to Euler, discussed below, is not acceptable for the treatment of these problems. The maximum size of the error increases as Δt is made larger than the indicated value of 0.01.

Iteration and numerical integration subtlety. In Eqs. (13) the update order is important, and for the position update it is also important to observe that the iteration subscript on p is not n but $n + 1$. The importance of this choice becomes clear by noting Eq. (14) for

$$\ddot{\theta}(t) \approx [\theta(2\Delta t + t) - 2\theta(\Delta t + t) + \theta(t)]/\Delta t^2$$
$$= -c \sin \theta(t') \tag{14}$$

the approximation of $\theta(t)$, in which there are two choices for the time t'. The choice $t' = t$ is equivalent to Euler's method of numerical integration, which is unstable. The instability gives rise to errors such as those discussed above in Fig. 5. On the other hand, the choice $t' = \Delta t + t$, corresponding to p_{n+1} is equivalent to the "leap-frog" method. It is stable because of the symmetry that it brings to Eq. (14), and it is increasingly used instead of more sophisticated integration algorithms, such as fourth-order Runge-Kutta.

In addition to numerical simulation of chaotic pendulum motion, it is possible to remotely control actual hardware by means of an online interactive chaotic pendulum.

Examples in two dimensions. Meaningful characteristics of the pendulum result from setting $\Delta t = 1$ in Eqs. (13), yielding Eqs. (15), a circumstance that is

$$p_{n+1} = p_n - c \sin \theta_n$$
$$\theta_{n+1} = \theta_n + p_{n+1} \tag{15}$$

surprising to some physicists. The resulting map is called the Chirikov or standard map. Its importance derives largely from the status of the pendulum as an archetype of chaos.

A similar map is obtained from consideration of a torsion-gravity pendulum, illustrated in **Fig. 6**. In the absence of torsional restoration, the oscillating mass would rest beneath the ribbon, whereas in the absence of gravity it would rest above the ribbon.

For this system, the Hamiltonian and associated canonical equations are given by Eqs. (16). Depend-

$$H(p, \theta) = \frac{p^2}{2} + \frac{\theta^2}{2} + b \cos \theta$$
$$\dot{p} = -\frac{\partial H}{\partial \theta} = -\theta + b \sin \theta \tag{16}$$
$$\dot{\theta} = \frac{\partial H}{\partial p} = p$$

ing on the size of its single adjustable parameter b, Eqs. (16) relate to three important oscillator types: (1) the harmonic oscillator for $b \ll 1$, (2) the Duffing oscillator for $1 < b < 1.5$, and (3) the superconducting quantum interference device (SQUID) for large values of b. [Involving a "double-well" potential energy function, the Duffing oscillator was first studied in 1918 by the engineer Georg Duffing. Its chaotic motion is confined in phase space without having to

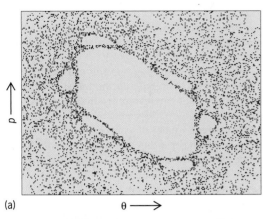

(a)

$\theta \longrightarrow$

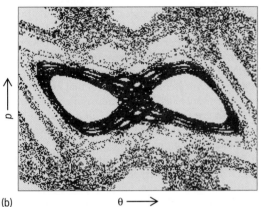

(b)

$\theta \longrightarrow$

Fig. 7. Fractal geometry attractors generated by computer.
(a) Attractor generated using the Chirikov map defined by Eqs. (15), with $c = 1.6$ and initial values $p_0 = \theta_0 = 2$.
(b) Attractor generated using the torsion-gravity pendulum map defined by Eqs. (17), with $b = 1.6$ and $p_0 = \theta_0 = 0.1$. In both plots there are periodic boundary conditions on both p and θ ($\pm\pi$).

use the periodic boundary conditions (modulo 2π) required of the pendulum. Chaotic motion of a pendulum requires motion past the vertical, which is impossible for a bob supported by a string; this in turn involves "winding" through multiple rotations.] *See* SQUID.

Approximation of canonical equations (16) in finite-difference form and setting $\Delta t = 1$ gives Eqs. (17). Examples of self-similar fractal structures

$$p_{n+1} = p_n - \theta_n + b \sin \theta_n$$
$$\theta_{n+1} = \theta_n + p_{n+1} \tag{17}$$

generated by the two-dimensional maps defined by Eqs. (15) and Eqs. (17) are provided in **Fig. 7**.

Examples in one dimension. A one-dimensional map known as the logistic equation and defined by Eq. (18) is better known to mathematicians than the

$$x_{n+1} = c x_n (1 - x_n) \tag{18}$$

previous two-dimensional maps. Its period-doubling route to chaos is illustrated by **Fig. 8a**. To generate this map, initial values for c and x were chosen at $c = 2.8$ and $x = 0.65$. For each value of c, four iterations were performed to allow convergence to any limit cycle that might exist for that value of c. (When a

nonchaotic limit cycle is reached after the settling of transients, points generated by the iterative equation or equations are repetitive. The number of steps n before the sequence repeats designates the order of the limit cycle. In a physical system such as a pendulum, steady-state motion corresponding to a limit cycle manifests itself in the Poincaré section as a set of phase-space points whose total number is n, assuming one point per cycle of the driving force. Denoting the drive frequency by f, the limit-cycle system response is at f/n, that is, a subharmonic of order n.) The value of x following the fourth iteration was subsequently plotted versus the parameter c, and c was then incremented by 0.0001 and the process repeated until the maximum value of 4 was reached. For $c < 3$, there is a single (stable) value for x. For $c = 3.2$ as an example, the previous singlet has branched into two values; that is, bifurcation has occurred. At $c = 3.5$, the consequence of an additional bifurcation can be observed, so that "two begets four," this is part of the "period-doubling route" to chaos that finally results in the vicinity of $c = 3.57$. *See* PERIOD DOUBLING.

Figure 8b was generated with an entirely different one-dimensional map that is concerned with solving Johannes Kepler's transcendental equation (19) for

$$E = M + \varepsilon \sin E \tag{19}$$

the position of a planet according to specified time

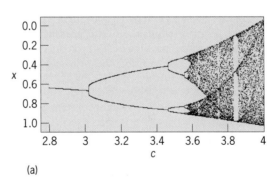

(a)

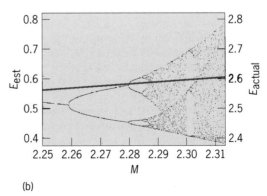

(b)

Fig. 8. Examples of the period-doubling route to chaos for two vastly different iterative expressions. (a) The logistic map, defined by Eq. (18). (b) The Chebyshev root-finding algorithm applied to Kepler's equation, defined by Eqs. (20) and (21) with eccentricity $\varepsilon = 0.55$. The colored line gives the actual value of E (referenced to the right-hand scale, E_{actual}), to which the iteration quickly converges when the starting value of E is located within the known region of convergence. The spurious output from the algorithm is referenced to the left-hand scale (E_{est}).

in orbit. The eccentric anomaly E (giving the angular position of the planet) is obtained for a given value of the mean anomaly M (proportional to the time) for a specified eccentricity ε. The root-finding technique shown in Fig. 8b for solving Eq. (19) is that of an "improved" Newton method known as the Chebyshev algorithm, which accounts for the curvature as well as the slope of the function under study. The Chebyshev algorithm is defined by Eq. (20), where,

$$E_{n+1} = E_n - (f/f')[1 + \tfrac{1}{2}(f/f')(f''/f')] \qquad (20)$$

in the case of its application to Eq. (19), f, f', and f'' are defined by Eqs. (21).

$$f = E_n - M - \varepsilon \sin E_n$$
$$f' = 1 - \varepsilon \cos E_n \qquad (21)$$
$$f'' = \varepsilon \sin E_n$$

When the starting value of E is located within the known region of convergence, the iteration converges quickly to the proper single-valued solution shown by the colored line in Fig. 8b, referenced to the right-hand scale. The parameter choices shown do not produce this convergence and result instead in the indicated spurious (nonphysical) doubling route to chaos. A noteworthy characteristic of both cases in Fig. 8 is the nonchaotic solution that appears as an "island" in the midst of chaos (period-3 limit cycle, $c = 3.832$ for Fig. 8a). *See* KEPLER'S EQUATION.

Feigenbaum constant. As the parameter c is increased in the logistic map given by Eq. (18), there is a progressive series of bifurcations (after transients are permitted to settle following each step in c). A fundamental constant emerges from this progression and was discovered by Mitchell Feigenbaum. Designating by c_n the points at which a period-2^n cycle appears, it can be shown that the Feigenbaum constant is given by Eq. (22).

$$\delta = \lim_{n \to \infty} \frac{c_{n+1} - c_n}{c_{n+2} - c_{n+1}} = 4.6692 \ldots \qquad (22)$$
$$n = 1, 2, \ldots$$

Claim for the universality of the constant δ in Eq. (22) is supported by the graph of Fig. 8b. The points where period-2^n cycles in M_n occur have not been carefully estimated; however, it appears that the Feigenbaum constant could also be generated from this map. The first three values of $M_1 = 2.25896$, $M_2 = 2.27903$, and $M_3 = 2.28368$ yield $\delta_{\text{1st est., Chebyshev}} = 4.32$; whereas the first three values from the logistic map yield $\delta_{\text{1st est., logistic}} = 4.23$.

Randall D. Peters

Atmospheric prediction. Contemporary large-scale weather prediction takes advantage of computer simulation of atmospheric behavior as modeled by a set of nonlinear partial differential equations describing the flow of the atmosphere and its thermodynamic properties. There are two sources of error: (1) the observations of the state of the atmosphere at the start of the prediction cycle may not be representative or accurate; (2) the equations do not represent all aspects of atmospheric behavior accurately. On the basis of experience with simpler nonlinear sys-

tems, one might expect that such errors in a nonlinear system would produce chaotic departure of the computer predictions from what actually transpires in the atmosphere.

Indeed, the computer models can be used to study the effect of errors in the initial conditions. When predictions are computed from slightly different initial atmospheric states, they resemble those of the Lorenz model of convection: the solutions remain similar for a time and then begin to depart from each other until eventually they are uncorrelated. Studies show that initial errors in model-scale phenomena double in about two days, but that the models demonstrate some predictive skill for large-scale features for a week or more. The considerable improvements in numerical weather prediction in the past three decades can be attributed to improved atmospheric observations, to increased model resolution made possible by increasing computer power, and to improvements in the formulation of the models and the smaller-scale processes that must be represented statistically. Such improvements push the effect of errors farther into the future, delaying but not eliminating the eventual effects of chaos and the inevitable loss of predictability.

Now a new strategy for improving numerical prediction takes advantage of increasing computer power to predict the accuracy of the forecast itself. Rather than computing a single forecast at increased resolution, the major numerical prediction centers compute a number of predictions, each starting from a set of initial conditions slightly perturbed from those observed. Thus an ensemble of forecasts is computed, suggesting confidence when and where the forecasts in the ensemble agree and suggesting uncertainty when and where they vary significantly.

This approach leads to an even more sophisticated strategy: Determine from the ensemble of forecasts where special observations might be taken to reduce uncertainty and then schedule satellite observations or dispatch piloted or remotely piloted aircraft to obtain special observations to reduce the uncertainty. Such an approach may have favorable benefit to cost ratios in the case of severe weather. Indeed, it has been employed for more than 50 years by sending aircraft to take observations in hurricanes or typhoons that might threaten inhabited regions.

John A. Dutton

Climate. Climate is sometimes identified with the set of all states of the climate system—the system consisting of the atmosphere and the upper portions of the underlying ocean and land surfaces—that may reasonably be expected to occur. It is thus identifiable with the attractor of the climate system. This system is dissipative and is forced by solar heating, and it is almost certainly chaotic; although it is not feasible to examine the actual climate system directly for sensitive dependence, mathematical models of the system, including some used in operational weather forecasting, invariably indicate sensitive dependence, while such features as migratory storms that cross the oceans and continents are not observed to occur in any periodic sequence.

Chaos can enrich the variety of weather patterns that make up the climate. Even though the weather has been observed for centuries, it is reasonable to expect something that is not known to have happened before—a record high or low temperature at some location, or a record rainfall that produces a record flood. Without chaos the weather would vary periodically, and records would simply be tied rather than broken.

Changes in external forcing will change the behavior of the climate system, thereby producing a new attractor, and hence a climatic change. Furthermore, if the state of the system normally fluctuates within one portion of the attractor for a long time and then enters into another portion, the transition will be perceived as an additional climatic change, perhaps indistinguishable from one externally produced. It is therefore sometimes preferable to identify the present climate with the portion of the attractor within which the state is presently fluctuating, thereby allowing for internally produced climatic changes.

Regardless of any chaotic weather variations occurring within the tenure of one climate, it is possible that the variations of the climate itself are chaotic. If this is so, only the periodic components of distant climatic changes can be predicted. Mathematical models of climate have not reached the degree of perfection needed to confirm or reject such a hypothesis, and recourse to observations is indicated. Where weather observations are absent or insufficient, proxy data, such as records of tree rings or oxygen isotope ratios, which are supposed to vary with climatic elements such as temperature, can be useful. There are indications of periodic variations with superposed nonperiodic variations; it is the latter that may be unpredictable. Some of the periodic variations appear to be associated with predictable changes in the Earth's orbital parameters. Some nonperiodic variations may result from irregular external forcing—perhaps nonperiodic volcanic activity. Others may be internally produced, and chaotic. *See* CLIMATIC PREDICTION; CLIMATOLOGY; DENDROCHRONOLOGY.

Since climate variations are unpredictable by deterministic means for periods of decades or centuries in advance, prediction efforts must focus on the statistical characteristics of the climate and its variations as determined by both observations and computer simulations. One possibility lies in identifying a climate attractor that is a multidimensional analog of the attractor for the Lorenz convection model described above. If such an attractor was found, and if the present climate could be located on the attractor, then it might be possible to infer statistical properties expected for the climate over a range of periods into the future. As computer power and capability increase, another possible approach might involve developing statistics from ensembles of computer climate simulations, as described above for weather prediction, that would give an indication of the confidence to be placed in various expectations about climate variations.

To use computer simulation in studying climate variations, it is necessary that the climate variations observed in such models resemble those of the actual climate. To achieve that, the climate simulation models must include realistic representations of atmospheric interactions with the ocean, the land surface, and the biosphere. The longer the period of interest, the more important such interactions presumably are, leading to the conclusion that realistic study of longer-term climate variations requires integrated simulations of the entire Earth system.　　　　　　　Edward N. Lorenz; John A. Dutton

Electronic circuits. Chaos is a ubiquitous phenomenon which is a subset of the dynamical behavior of nonlinear systems. In an electronic context, a nonlinear system is one where the output is not simply proportional to the input, and the response to a collection of excitations is not simply the sum of the individual responses to each excitation taken separately. This criterion embraces a large subset of electronic systems, including those in which there is multiple-valued behavior. Many chaotic systems observed in other disciplines are modeled well by electronic circuits. The dynamics are then susceptible to experimental analysis in a way that would be difficult in the source discipline. *See* NONLINEAR PHYSICS.

It is also possible to use electronic chaotic circuits for the direct experimental study of some arcane phenomena suggested by the rigorous mathematical analysis of nonlinear dynamical systems. Many such investigations have been reported. Intermittencies can be observed, trapping and long-lived chaotic transients are easily demonstrated, extensive catalogs of coexisting attractors can be found empirically, and synchronization and entrainment of chaotic systems can be explored, with applications to secure communications.

In analog electronic circuits, chaos can be found in overload situations, where a linear circuit is driven beyond the capacity of its power supply; in switch-mode power supplies, where energy-efficient control is achieved by using dependent switches in association with a linear circuit; and in resonant circuits which are nonlinear. These resonant circuits divide into a group wherein the natural frequency is amplitude dependent (modeled by Duffing-like equations) and also a group which contain amplitude-dependent damping, modeled by Van der Pol–like equations. *See* DIFFERENTIAL EQUATION; ELECTRONIC POWER SUPPLY.

Categories of electrical chaotic system include purely electronic; electromechanical, in which the mechanical element is nonlinear whereas the coupled electronic circuit is linear (for example, ultrasonic cleaners); and control systems generally, in which either or both the control circuit and the system being controlled are nonlinear. There is an important class of chaotic system comprising coupled oscillators; a stable oscillator necessarily has a limit cycle and is therefore nonlinear. Two such oscillators (when coupled) may pull in and out of lock in a chaotic manner.

Analyses of chaos in continuous systems using a digital computer are sometimes grossly in error owing to the extreme sensitivity to initial conditions. However, all real electronic systems are described by continuous variables plus unavoidable added noise. Real digital systems are modeled as accurately as their analog equivalents when the number of distinguishable states is greater than the number of distinguishable levels in an analog version containing unavoidable noise. Digital filters containing registers which overflow exhibit chaos. Chaos is also found in systems containing phase detectors, owing to the ambiguity in phase angle modulo $360°$, for similar reasons. *See* DIGITAL FILTER; PHASE-LOCKED LOOPS.

Chaos is found also in digital systems having more than one autonomous timing element or clock; it is therefore endemic in asynchronous parallel computation. Chaos is suspected to occur in computer networks, at the physical data level. *See* CONCURRENT PROCESSING.

Chaos in circuits is modeled reasonably well by circuit simulation packages that deal with nonlinearities in the device models by solving the dynamical equations by using numerical integration. However, the class of originally linear circuit analysis software packages that handle nonlinear circuits by methods such as harmonic balance fail completely to model chaotic dynamics. David J. Jefferies

Astronomy. The methods of nonlinear dynamics have been applied to a large number of problems in astronomy. In particular, it is clear that chaos has played an important role in determining the dynamical structure and evolution of the solar system.

The Kirkwood gaps in the asteroid belt are now thought to be chaotic regions of space from which asteroids have been removed by the nonlinear gravitational perturbations of Jupiter. An asteroid in such a region can undergo large changes in its orbital elements which can cause it to become planet-crossing; the asteroid will eventually be removed from the region by a close approach to the planet. The existence of prominent gaps at the 1/3, 1/2, and 2/5 Jovian orbit-orbit resonances is consistent with the large chaotic regions which have been discovered at these locations by full numerical integrations and the use of algebraic mappings. The 2/3 resonance is associated with the stable Hilda group of asteroids and a much smaller chaotic zone. *See* ASTEROID.

Chaos has also been used to explain the delivery of one chondrite class of meteorites from the asteroid belt to the Earth. The 1/3 Kirkwood gap at 2.5 astronomical units has been identified as the source region for these meteorites, and studies of the dynamical behavior of asteroid collision fragments at the resonance show that perturbations by the outer planets can cause the orbits to become chaotic and achieve the high eccentricities necessary to become Earth-crossing. The time scales for this process are consistent with the ages of these chondrites determined by the length of time they have been exposed to the cosmic-ray environment of the solar system. *See* METEORITE.

The Saturnian satellite Hyperion exhibits chaotic behavior in its spin motion. Most natural satellites are locked in a 1/1 spin-orbit resonance where, as a result of tidal evolution, the orbital period of the satellite is equal to its spin period. However, Hype-

rion is distinctly nonspherical, and it has a large orbital eccentricity which is fixed by its 4/3 orbit-orbit resonance with the satellite Titan. As a result, Hyperion is in a chaotic spin state, with its rotational period changing constantly. Additional instabilities imply that its pole position may also have a chaotic behavior and that Hyperion is, in fact, tumbling. *See* SATURN.

The semimajor axis of a natural satellite can change significantly over the age of the solar system because of the tide that it raises on the parent planet. Consequently Kepler's third law implies that pairs of satellites can evolve into and out of resonance. This is an example of a dissipative dynamical system, since energy is lost in the form of tidal friction. Nonlinear dynamical studies have proved useful in determining the orbital histories of the satellite systems of the outer planets.

An 850-million-year numerical integration of the orbit of Pluto has shown some evidence of chaotic motion, although the chaos is unlikely to disrupt Pluto's stable 3/2 resonance with Neptune over the lifetime of the solar system. Long-term numerical integrations have been used to investigate the stability of the solar system over time scales comparable with a significant fraction of its age. Results show that the planets' orbits are chaotic, although there are no dramatic changes over several billion years. In this case the existence of chaos implies that a small error in the measurement of a planet's position will propagate exponentially such that its orbital location cannot be calculated for arbitrary times in the future. The evolution of a planetary orbit is connected with the evolution of the orientation of its spin axis (obliquity). In the case of Mars the obliquity varies chaotically from $0°$ to $60°$, and this has important implications for climate change on the planet. *See* MARS; PLUTO; SOLAR SYSTEM.

Chaos has also helped solve problems in other branches of astronomy, including galactic dynamics and studies of stellar oscillations, and the number of applications of chaos to astronomy is expected to increase. Carl D. Murray

Acoustics. Chaos physics has shed new light on the old problem of noise, a term which has its origin in acoustics. Noise had been thought to be the outcome of interacting processes for which a deterministic formulation and description is no longer feasible because the number of such processes is extremely large. However, chaos physics has shown that noise can be present in systems with only a few interacting processes, for which a deterministic formulation can easily be written down explicitly. An example of such a system is a driven nonlinear oscillator, for example, an electric circuit consisting of only a resistor, an inductance, and a varactor diode (as the necessary nonlinear element) in series, driven by a sinusoidally varying voltage.

A chaotic (irregular, never repeating) sound wave can be produced when the chaotic voltage across this diode is fed to a loudspeaker. But systems of this kind are not considered to be genuine acoustically chaotic systems. Genuine acoustic chaos is found in ultrasonics, thermoacoustics, musical acoustics, speech, and hearing. In ultrasonics it arises in the breakdown of liquids exposed to high-intensity sound, a phenomenon called acoustic cavitation. At too high an acoustic intensity the liquid ruptures to form bubbles or cavities (almost empty bubbles). They vibrate in the sound field that originally generated them, and emit sound. The total sound output of the cavities at high sound input (of a pure tone) leads to noise with a broadband spectrum. *See* CAVITATION.

A single sound frequency is thus transformed into an almost infinite number of neighboring sound frequencies. To study this transformation, an experiment has been conceived in which the sound output is monitored as the sound intensity is raised by digitizing the output of a hydrophone and storing the samples in a memory. Power spectra calculated from the stored data give the frequency content of the sound output. A period-doubling route to chaos is observed (**Fig. 9**). When the excitation level is raised, spectral lines appear exactly between the old lines by period doubling (frequency halving) until a broadband spectrum (chaos) is reached. Thus, acoustic cavitation has been identified as a chaotic system.

Because the cavities set into oscillation are the source of sound generation, their motion should become chaotic along with the sound output. Holographic observations of acoustically driven bubbles showed that they undergo period doubling to chaos in step with the acoustic output from the liquid. **Figure 10** shows two series of images reconstructed from high-speed holograms taken at 23,100 holograms per second. The black objects on the speckle background are the cavitation bubbles that undergo period-doubling oscillations to chaos.

Sound can be generated by heat—a fact known to glass blowers. When a gas-filled tube, closed at one end and open at the other, is heated at the closed end, the gas column starts to vibrate. Alternatively the open end may be cooled. When this self-excited oscillation is disturbed by another sound wave, the interaction may lead to chaotic sound waves.

In musical acoustics, signs of chaos are observed in string instruments, woodwind instruments (recorder, clarinet), the trumpet, and gongs (vibrated shells). Musicians, however, try to avoid the occurrence of bifurcations when playing their instruments. An example is the so-called wolf note that tends to appear in playing the cello. It is a quasiperiodic oscillation with two incommensurate frequencies that stem from the string and the bridge resonance. Oscillations of this type are also observed in woodwind instruments, there called multiphonics. Subharmonic sounds and chaos have also been found, for example, in the clarinet. *See* MUSICAL ACOUSTICS.

The human speech-production process is intrinsically nonlinear. To produce voice sounds the vocal cords are set into nonlinear vibration through the air flow between them. The fundamental frequency, the pitch, is determined by the length, mass, and tension of the vocal cords. There is no doubt from present knowledge of nonlinear oscillatory systems that the vocal cord system, and thus the human speech-production system, is susceptible to chaotic sound production. *See* SPEECH.

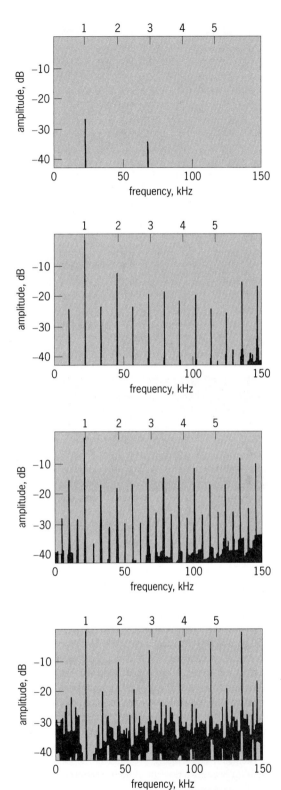

Fig. 9. Power spectra of acoustic cavitation noise at four different excitation levels, showing the successive filling of the spectrum by period doubling (frequency halving) when the sound input intensity is raised. Numbers at tops of the graphs indicate multiples of input frequency (harmonics).

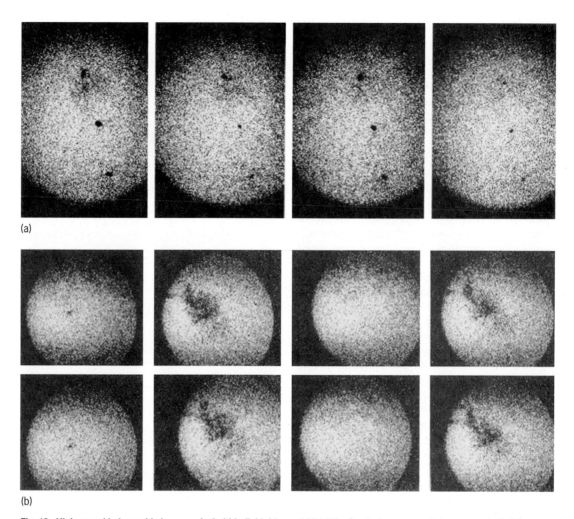

(a)

(b)

Fig. 10. High-speed holographic images of a bubble field driven at 23.1 kHz. One hologram was taken per period of the driving sound field. The bubble field oscillates as a whole periodically with the indicated period. (*a*) Period 2. (*b*) Period 8, at higher sound intensity.

The ear is a very complex sound receiver with remarkable properties, for instance in frequency selectivity. They stem from nonlinearities and active filtering with feedback, that is, filtering with amplification of sound. Such systems may become unstable and start to oscillate themselves. The ear thus also acts as a sound emitter rather than a pure receiver. This may happen in reponse to a sound wave or spontaneously, a phenomenon called objective tinnitus. Many people suffer from this property of the ear, as they hear the emitted sound. *See* HEARING (HUMAN); HEARING IMPAIRMENT.   Werner Lauterborn

Atoms. A challenging problem is the behavior of quantal systems whose nonlinear, nonintegrable classical counterparts involve irregular (chaotic) trajectories, a subject commonly called quantum chaos. Because basic atomic structure is determined by the Coulomb electrostatic force, accurate quantal, semiclassical, or classical numerical calculations are possible. High-resolution atomic spectra, and how they are influenced by externally applied fields that rival the intraatomic Coulomb force binding a weakly bound atomic electron, can be recorded by using lasers or other sources and compared with theory.

In atomic three-body systems such as the helium atom, understanding and classifying the classical orbits, most of which are chaotic, is challenging enough. Quantizing them is a problem that has defied many researchers since the beginning of quantum theory early in the twentieth century. Thus, it is notable that the semiclassical quantization of the helium atom (in states with zero total angular momentum) has been accomplished.

Most atomic studies of quantum chaos have involved a weakly bound electron in the hydrogen atom (principal quantum number $n_0 \gg 1$) exposed to a strong, externally applied force F_{ext} that may be static or time varying. For $F_{ext} = 0$, the nonrelativistic, classical trajectories are regular, keplerian ellipses with angular frequency w_{at} for bounded motion and hyperbolas for unbounded motion; the corresponding quantal spectrum consists of the discrete (Bohr) levels with total energy E proportional to n_0^{-2} for $E < 0$ and a continuum of levels for $E > 0$. (Rydberg atoms, which have one of their electrons highly excited and approximate hydrogen, are also used.) *See* RYDBERG ATOM.

Static external fields. Hydrogen in a static magnetic field (B) is the most studied example. The linear (in B) paramagnetic interaction leads to regular classical dynamics and to the Zeeman effect of textbook quantum mechanics. As B increases, however, the nonlinear (quadratic in B) diamagnetic interaction becomes dominant, and irregular (chaotic) electron trajectories begin to appear in classical numerical computations. Experimental studies of the photoabsorption spectrum of hydrogen atoms and of helium, lithium, or other Rydberg atoms (via laser-driven transitions from low-lying quantal states to strongly perturbed states near $E = 0$) revealed a complicated quantal spectrum whose changing statistical properties reflect the onset of classically chaotic trajectories. Series of sharp spectral features observed with lithium Rydberg atoms for magnetic field strengths and energies where the classical (hydrogenic) orbits are all chaotic were well reproduced by quantal numerical calculations for hydrogen. Use of scaled energy spectroscopy, which exploits scaling relations derived for the classical dynamics of the hydrogen atom in the magnetic field and applies whether or not the electron's motion is chaotic, simplifies comparisons with semiclassical theory if the photoabsorption spectrum is recorded with both the laser photon energy and B being varied such that the scaled energy remains constant. Unstable classical periodic orbits (or even just orbits that close on themselves near the nucleus) of ever longer period, which proliferate at bifurcations specified by the theory of hamiltonian dynamics, were shown to correspond in a direct way with important spectral features observed with finite resolution. *See* DIAMAGNETISM; PARAMAGNETISM; ZEEMAN EFFECT.

Examples of even more complicated situations for which classical scaling relationships have also been exploited are highly excited hydrogen or hydrogen-like Rydberg atoms in the presence of either crossed or parallel electric and magnetic fields. Photoabsorption spectra up to and beyond $E = 0$ (well into the domain of classical chaos) have been recorded experimentally and compared with results of classical, semiclassical, and quantal theory.

Time-varying external fields. For an $F_{\text{ext}}(t)$ produced by a microwave electric field with angular frequency ω and amplitude F, exchange of energy between it and the atom can lead to deexcitation to lower bound states or excitation to higher bound states or the $E > 0$ continuum (that is, ionization). (Ionization can require net absorption of many tens or even hundreds of microwave photons, which signals a very high order quantal multiphoton process.) The nature of the dynamics depends strongly on two ratios, the scaled frequency, $\omega/\omega_{\text{at}} = n_0^3\omega$, and the scaled amplitude, $F_{\text{at}} = n_0^4 F$, where F_{at} is the Coulomb electric field for the Bohr (circular) orbit for initial state n_0. If the (scaled) threshold fields $n_0^4 F$ (10%) that produced an ionization probability of 10% after the atoms were exposed to about 300 microwave field oscillations are measured and their dependence on $n_0^3\omega$ is graphed (**Fig. 11**), locally higher thresholds show up as bumps near some rational-fraction values (for example, 1/2, 1/1, and 2/1). These peaks were successfully explained via the stabilizing influence

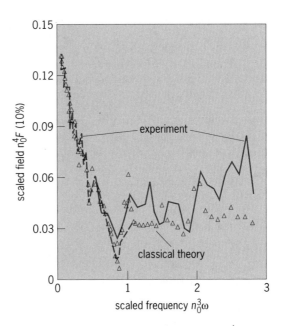

Fig. 11. Dependence of the scaled threshold field $n_0^4 F$ (10%) that produces an ionization probability of 10% after weakly bound hydrogen atoms are exposed to about 300 microwave field oscillations, on the scaled frequency $n_0^3\omega$.

of classical, nonlinear trapping resonances. At one extreme, as $n_0^3\omega \to 0$, the measured threshold fields approach, as expected, the value $n_0^4 F_0 \simeq 0.13$ for a static field. As $n_0^3\omega$ rises to near 1, classical, numerical Monte Carlo calculations (Fig. 11) that simulated the experiment reproduce the experimental curve (as do quantal calculations), but there are important, local exceptions. For example, a bump near $n_0^3\omega = 1.3$ is a quantal effect caused by the stabilizing influence of a (scarred) so-called separatrix state. (Broadband noise added to the driving field to decrease its coherence was shown to be a new spectroscopic technique for finding such states experimentally.) When $n_0^3\omega \gtrsim 2$, however, the systematic rise of experimental thresholds above those of classical calculations confirmed a prediction of quantum theory and numerical calculations that quantal interference effects would tend to suppress the effects of classical chaos for high-scaled frequencies. *See* ATOMIC STRUCTURE AND SPECTRA; MONTE CARLO METHOD; NONRELATIVISTIC QUANTUM THEORY.   Peter M. Koch

Bibliography. K. T. Alligood, T. D. Sauer, and J. A. Yorke, *Chaos: An Introduction to Dynamical Systems*, Springer-Verlag, 1996; J. R. Buchler and H. E. Kandrup (eds.), *Stochastic Processes in Astrophysics*, 1993; G. Casati and B. Chirikov (eds.), *Quantum Chaos: Between Order and Disorder*, 1995; L. O. Chua and M. Hasler (eds.), Special issues on chaos in nonlinear electronic circuits, *IEEE Trans. Circ. Sys.*, vol. CAS-40, no. 10 and 11 in CAS-I and no. 10 in CAS-II, 1993; F. Diacu and P. Holmes, *Celestial Encounters: The Origins of Chaos and Stability*, Princeton University Press, 1996; M. C. Gutzwiller, *Chaos in Classical and Quantum Mechanics*, 1990; R. C. Hilborn, *Chaos and Nonlinear Dynamics: An Introduction for Scientists and Engineers*, 2d ed.,

2000; W. Lauterborn and J. Holzfuss, Acoustic chaos, *Int. J. Bifurcations Chaos*, 1:13-26, 1991; E. N. Lorenz, Deterministic nonperiodic flow, *J. Atm. Sci.*, 20:130-141, 1963; E. N. Lorenz, *The Essence of Chaos*, University of Washington Press, 1993; B. B. Mandelbrot, *The Fractal Geometry of Nature*, W. H. Freeman, New York, 1977; T. Mullin (ed.), *The Nature of Chaos*, 1993; E. Ott, *Chaos in Dynamical Systems*, 2d ed., 2002; H.-D. Peitgen, H. Jürgens, and D. Saupe, *Chaos and Fractals: New Frontiers of Science*, 2d ed., Springer-Verlag, 2004; R. Peters, Chaotic pendulum based on torsion and gravity in opposition, *Amer. J. Phys.*, 63(12):1128-1136, 1995; I. Peterson, *Newton's Clock: Chaos in the Solar System*, W. H. Freeman, 1993; D. Ruelle, *Chance and Chaos*, Princeton University Press, 1991; M. Schroeder, *Fractals, Chaos, and Power Laws*, 1991.

Chaparral

A vegetation formation characterized by woody plants of low stature (3-9 ft or 1-3 m tall), impenetrable because of tough, rigid, interlacing branches, with small, simple, waxy, evergreen, thick leaves. The term refers to evergreen oak, Spanish *chapparo*, and therefore is uniquely southwestern North American. This type of vegetation has its center in California and occurs continuously over wide areas of mountainous to sloping topography. The Old World Mediterranean equivalent is called maquis or macchie, with nomenclatural and ecological variants in the countries ranging from Spain to the Balkans. Physiognomically similar vegetation occurs also in South Africa, Chile, and southwestern Australia in areas of Mediterranean climates, that is, with very warm, dry summers and maximum precipitation during the cool season.

The floras of these five areas with Mediterranean climates are altogether different, however, so only the assumption of close correlation between form and function in plants allows extrapolation of vegetation studies from one area to another.

California types. In western North America a number of kinds of so-called chaparral must be distinguished. In southern California the coastal sage formation consists of shrubs which are gray in color and low in stature, with soft, brittle wood; the formation contains *Artemisia californica*, shrubby species of *Salvia*, *Eriogonum fasciculatum* (typical form), and others. In the humid mountains of California, logged and burned coniferous forests have been replaced by a montane chaparral of the widespread western *Arctostaphylos patula* and *Ceanothus velutinus* plus the West Coast *Prunus emarginata*, the New Mexico-Californian-Cascade *Ceanothus integerrimus*, and the Californian endemics *Chamaebatia foliolosa*, *Castanopsis sempervirens*, *Quercus vacciniifolia*, and *Ceanothus cordulatus* (the last three at higher altitudes). North from Mexico along the Rocky Mountains to Denver and north to Cache Valley in the Wasatch Mountains is a de-ciduous chaparral characterized by *Q. gambelii*. In northern California and southwestern Oregon and in the Tehachapi and adjacent mountains of southern California is an analogous vegetation type characterized by *Q. garryana* ssp. *breweri*.

The true chaparral of California, however, is different from the above. Its characteristic species include *Adenostema fasciculatum*, *Ceanothus cuneatus*, *Q. dumosa*, *Heteromeles arbutifolia*, *Rhamnus californica*, *R. crocea*, and *Cercocarpus betuloides*, plus a host of endemic species of *Arctostaphylos* and *Ceanothus* and other Californian endemics, both shrubby and herbaceous. These plants determine the formation's physiognomy. It is a dense, uniform-appearing, evergreen, shrubby cover with sclerophyllous leaves and deep-penetrating roots.

Plant life forms. Although the shrub life form is dominant, a variety of life forms is represented in chaparral. A floristic spectrum of Raunkiaer's life forms from an area of serpentine chaparral in Napa County, California, containing 67 species of vascular plants had 4% phanerophytes, 18% nanophanerophytes, 12% chamaephytes, 27% hemicryptophytes, 18% geophytes, and 21% therophytes. Comparable data from other chaparral regions show lower nanophanerophyte and geophyte percentages and a higher therophyte percentage. *See* PLANTS, LIFE FORMS OF.

Geographic variations. The Californian type of chaparral formation runs south from the Rogue River valley of southern Oregon through the lower California mountains, west of the crest of the Sierra Nevada, below the *Pinus ponderosa* belt, to northern lower California. In Oregon *Ceanothus cuneatus* and *Arctostaphylos viscida* are characteristic; *Adenostema fasciculatum*, for example, drops out north of Shasta County, California. In this northern area summer thunderstorms occur. Another variation is evident in Arizona. Again, such Californian plants as *Adenostema fasciculatum* and *Heteromeles arbutifolia* drop out as the climate changes from winter precipitation to a bimodal occurrence of rain with a maximum in summer. The Arizona chaparral is characterized by *Q. turbinella*, *Arctostaphylos pungens*, *Rhus trilobata*, and *Ceanothus greggii*, which are all more or less desert species in California.

Ecology. There is extreme floristic diversity, and therefore presumably also ecological diversity, within the vegetation commonly called chaparral. Since the basic floristic study of the formation has not yet been done, it is extremely difficult to extrapolate ecological or experimental physiological data from one area of chaparral to another.

Climate. Ecologically, chaparral occurs in a climate which is hot and dry in summer, cool but not much below freezing in winter, with little or no snow, and with winter precipitation which is excessive and leaches the soil of nutrients. The need for water and its supply are exactly out of phase. Figures describing chaparral climates are variable. Temperatures may be maritime as at coastal San Diego or continental as at Ash Mountain at 1750 ft (530 m) elevation on the west slope of the Sierra Nevada. Amplitudes of mean monthly temperatures at these stations are 46.2 and 69.4°F (7.9 and 20.8°C). Means are 60.6 and 63.5°F (15.9 and 17.5°C). Need for water potential evapotranspiration is 31.4 and 39.0 in. (785 and 974 mm) per year. Annual precipitations are 10 and 28 in. (250 and 700 mm) at these stations, with Redding, located at the northern end of the Sacramento Valley, having 38 in. (950 mm). Actual water use varies much less, being 10 in. (250 mm) at San Diego, 15.2 in. (380 mm) at Ash Mountain, and 16 in. (400 mm) at Redding. The differences between these figures and annual precipitation are runoff. In Oregon chaparral areas, need for water is less, about 28 in. (700 mm) per year, corresponding to the lower temperatures. However, actual water use is higher than in California, being 18.8-20.0 in. (470-500 mm) per year. In Arizona chaparral, runoffs are nil, and figures for actual water use are somewhat higher than in California, 14-20 in. (350-500 mm) per year.

A fair conclusion is that chaparral grows under no unique climate. It may, of course, still be differentiated from surrounding vegetation by climatic parameters. Its prevalence on south slopes, whereas some kind of woodland or forest occupies adjacent north slopes, is clear evidence of control by local climates.

Water relations. So far as water relations are concerned, the shrubs of the chaparral presumably transpire continuously during the dry summer since they are evergreen. They photosynthesize below the wilting point, and their roots penetrate very deeply (recorded to 28 ft or 8.5 m) as well as widely (ratio of root to crown spread 2 to 4). At great depths in the fractured rock, water may be perennially available although the soil itself is reduced to the permanent wilting point each summer. Some of the xeromorphic features of the plants may be related to low nitrogen supply, as has been found for ericaceous plants of acid bogs. *See* PLANT-WATER RELATIONS.

Soils. Chaparral soils are generally rocky, often shallow, or of extreme chemistry such as those derived from serpentine, and always low in fertility. In the very precipitous southern Californian mountains, soil erosion rates may be 0.04 in. (1 mm) per year over large watershed areas. The runoff figures mentioned above also contribute to low soil fertility through their leaching effects. The result is low available nitrogen. Quantitative data which would allow a nitrogen balance to be drawn up are lacking, although data do show that a single crop of *Ceanothus leucodermis* can double soil nitrogen contents. *See* SOIL.

Succession. Successionally chaparral is various. *Quercus durata* on serpentine, to which it is limited, may be a continuing type. On deep soils at higher foothill elevations, chaparral is often replaced by *Q. kelloggii*; on the still deeper soils at lower elevations, it may have replaced *Q. douglasii*. *Pinus sabiniana* comes up through dense chaparral stands, but it seems to affect the shrubs little. *Pinus halepensis* occupies a similar ecological position in the Mediterranean maquis. Fire often thickens a stand of chaparral since many of its species are crown sprouters; in other species seed germination is stimulated by fire. Careful management of deer or sheep grazing can keep burned chaparral areas open. Under natural conditions *Eriodictyon californicum* is successional to chaparral after fires, if replacement of the original shrubs does not follow directly by sprouting or seedings. *See* ECOLOGICAL SUCCESSION.   Jack Major

Characiformes

An order of teleost fishes sharing the superorder Ostariophysi, series Otophysi, with the Cypriniformes (minnows, carps, and suckers), Siluriformes (catfishes), and Gymnotiformes (knife fishes). *See* CYPRINIFORMES; OSTARIOPHYSI; SILURIFORMES; TELEOSTEI.

Characteristics. The Characiformes are distinguished by the following characters: usually an adipose fin (only one of 18 families totally without an adipose fin; several families and genera with and without); teeth in jaws usually well-developed; pharyngeal teeth usually present but usually not specialized as in cypriniforms; upper jaw usually nonprotractile or, if movable, not protrusible as in most cyprinids; virtually all species have scales, with some being ctenoid or ctenoid-like (with a serrated margin) as opposed to the usual cycloid scales (with annual growth rings); barbels (slender, tactile processes near the mouth) are absent; usually three postcleithra; pelvic fins and pelvic girdle are minute in some species; and adult sizes range from only 13 mm (0.5 in.) to 1.4 m (4.6 ft).

Diversity and habitat. The Characiformes comprise 18 families, about 270 genera, and no less than 1675 species, all of which are limited to freshwaters in Africa (209 species) and in the New World from the southwestern United States (one species, Mexican tetra, *Astyanax mexicanus*), Mexico (eight species), and Central and South America (the remainder of the species).

Classification. The classification of the Characiformes has changed significantly since the mid-1980s. The current consensus classification for the order is as follows.

Suborder Citharinoidei. There are 20 genera and about 98 species. Features distinguishing the Citharinoidei from all other characiforms are bicuspid teeth in the jaws; second and third postcleithra fused; ascending process of premaxilla absent; and virtually all species with ctenoid scales. This suborder is endemic to Africa.

Family Distichodontidae. The family comprises 17 genera and 90 species. There are two distinct forms (see **illustration**). In one, the members have a nonprotractile upper jaw and are micropredators and herbivores, and the body shape varies from deep to moderately deep. The other group has an elongate body and movable jaws, and is carnivorous, feeding on fishes or the fins of fishes. Maximum length is about 83 cm (32.7 in.).

Family Citharinidae. There are 3 genera and 8 species. The body is deep, the dorsal and anal fins are

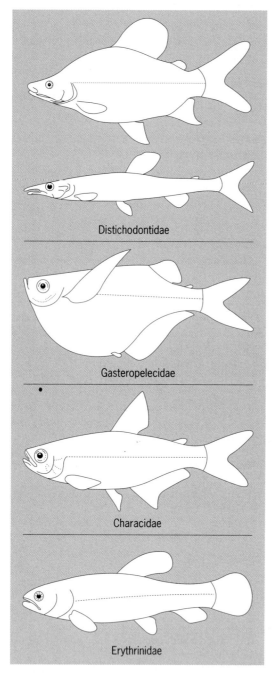

Four families of Characiformes. (*From J. S. Nelson, Fishes of the World, 2006, Wiley, New York*)

from all other characiforms, except one genus, *Anodus*, in the family Hemiodontidae. Curimatidae occurs from southern Costa Rica to northern Argentina. Maximum length is 32 cm (12.6 in.), usually much less.

Family Prochilodontidae. The family includes 3 genera and 21 species. The mouth is protractile; the lips are enlarged, forming a sucking disc; and the jaws have numerous small teeth. Most species are herbivores or detritivores (organisms that consume dead organic matter), and some swim in an oblique head-down position. This family and the next two families are commonly called headstanders. The range is primarily in the northern half of South America. Maximum length is 74 cm (29 in.).

Family Anostomidae. The Anostomidae have 12 genera and 137 species. The mouth is small and nonprotractile; the premaxilla is enlarged and excludes the maxillae from the gape; the body is usually elongate; and the anal fin is short. The range is Central and South America. Maximum total length is about 88 cm (34.6 in.).

Family Chilodontidae. There are 2 genera and 7 species. The premaxilla is relatively small and the maxillae much enlarged. The range is northern South America. Maximum total length is 18 cm (7 in.).

Family Crenuchidae. The Crenuchidae has 12 genera and 74 species. The frontal bones have paired foramina posterodorsally to the orbits, which are enlarged in the subfamily Crenuchinae. Most of the species (10 genera and 71 species) are in the subfamily Characidiinae; in the largest genus, *Characidium*, are species that have the ability to climb waterfalls by using their paired fins to cling to the underside of rocks. The family inhabits eastern Panama and South America. Maximum total length is under 110 mm (4.3 in.), with the smallest species being only 57 mm (2.2 in.).

Family Hemiodontidae. The family comprises 5 genera and about 28 described species. Members are fast swimmers with a subcylindrical to fusiform body, adipose eyelids, teeth absent on the lower jaw of adults, and typically with a round spot on the side of the body and a stripe on the lower lobe of the caudal fin. Hemiodontids range from northern South America to the Paraná-Paraguay Basin. Maximum total length is about 33 cm (13 in.).

Family Alestiidae. There are 18 genera and 110 species in the family. Many species superficially resemble clupeids, being predominantly silvery. The body varies from deep to moderately slender; the mouth varies from terminal to superior; and many species have a large black spot at the base of the caudal fin. The family, endemic to Africa, is commonly known as African tetras. The maximum length of the small tetras is no more than 21 mm (8.3 in.), whereas the giant tigerfish (*Hydrocynus goliath*), a formidable fish with jaws armed with very large saberlike teeth, attains a length up to 1.4 m (4.6 ft).

Family Gasteropelecidae. Gasteropelicids comprise 3 genera and 9 species. This small family (both in number and size) is known as freshwater hatchetfishes because of the deep and strongly compressed

relatively long, and the maxilla is quite small and lacks teeth. Maximum length is 84 cm (33 in.).

Suborder Characoidei. The following families are contained in the suborder.

Family Parodontidae. This family comprises 3 genera and about 21 described species. It is characterized by a ventral mouth with greatly enlarged, highly mobile premaxillae and teeth modified for scraping algae off rocks. It inhabits mountain streams of eastern Panama and most of South America. Most species are less than 15 cm (6 in.) in length.

Family Curimatidae. There are 8 genera and 95 species. The absence of jaw teeth distinguishes this family

body in the shape of a half disk (see illustration). An adipose fin is present in the larger species but absent in the smaller species; the pelvic fins and associated girdle are minute; the elongate pectoral fins are provided with greatly enlarged musculature and corresponding skeletal support. These fishes are capable of jumping relatively high out of the water and making short flights by using their heavily muscled pectoral fins. Commercially collected for the aquarium trade, hatchetfishes are found in Panama and all countries of South America except Chile. Maximum total length ranges from about 23 to 76 mm (0.9 to 3 in.).

Family Characidae. With 165 genera and not less than 962 species, this family is by far the largest and most diverse of characiform fishes. It presents uncertainties regarding the taxonomic affinities of numerous genera. Many genera are monotypic, whereas several genera have numerous species (such as *Astyanax* with 86 species and *Hyphessobrycon* with 97). Some characins resemble shads and herrings (Clupeidae), minnows (Cyprinidae), and darters (Percidae) (see illustration). Included in the family are popular aquarium fishes (such as neon tetras), food fishes (such as *Brycon*), and the infamous piranhas (*Serrasalmus*). Characins range from southwestern Texas, through Mexico, and into Central and South America; elsewhere they are introduced. Maximum adult length varies from less than 30 mm (1.2 in.) to over 100 cm (39 in.).

Family Acestrorhynchidae. One genus and 15 species constitute this family. Members have an elongate pikelike body covered with small scales. They are found mostly in the Orinoco and Amazon basins of South America. Maximum total length is about 44 cm (17.3 in.).

Family Cynodontidae. There are 5 genera and 14 species. The mouth is oblique and the jaws bear large canine teeth, which in some species are saberlike. The family is endemic to South America. Maximum length is about 65 cm (25.6 in.).

Family Erythrinidae. There are 3 genera and 14 species. The family is characterized by a cylindrically shaped body (similar to that of the bowfin, Amiidae) (see illustration); relatively large mouth, the gape extending beyond the anterior margin of the eye; numerous palatine teeth, as well as sharp conical teeth in the jaws; no adipose fin; and a round caudal fin. It is endemic to South America, and some species can breathe air and move overland between ponds. Maximum length is about 1.0 m (3.3 ft.).

Family Lebiasinidae. The family comprises 7 genera and 61 species. The mouth is small and superior, the gape not reaching the eye; the adipose fin is present or absent; and in some species the upper lobe of the caudal fin is longer than the lower. The family occurs in Costa Rica, Panama, and South America.

Family Ctenoluciidae. There are 2 genera and 7 species. Members are called pike-characins because they resemble Northern Hemisphere pikes (Esocidae) in having an elongate body, large terminal mouth, jaws equipped with numerous small teeth and a single row of recurved teeth posteriorly in each jaw, and the anal and dorsal fins set far back on the body. Pike-characins are carnivorous, feeding primarily on fishes. They occur in Panama and South America. Maximum length of smallest species is 23 cm (9 in.); largest is 68 cm (27 in.).

Family Hepsetidae. The single species, *Hepsetus odoe*, is called the African pike. It has a pikelike body shape and a large mouth and jaws with small pointed teeth as well as a few large canine teeth; it lays its eggs in a nest of floating foam. These characteristics readily distinguish this monotypic family from other African characiforms. It is endemic to tropical Africa. Maximum length is 30 cm (11.8 in.).   Herbert Boschung

Bibliography.   P. A. Buckup, Relationships of the Characidiinae (Teleostei, Ostariophysi) and phylogeny of characiform fishes, pp. 123–144 in L. R. Malabarba et al. (eds.), *Phylogeny and Classification of Neotropical Fishes*, Edipucrs, Porto Alegre, Brazil, 1998; J. S. Nelson, *Fishes of the World*, 4th ed., Wiley, New York, 2006; R. P. Vari, Higher level phylogenetic concepts within Characiformes (Ostariophysi), a historical review, pp. 111–122 in L. R. Malabarba et al. (eds.), *Phylogeny and Classification of Neotropical Fishes*, Edipucrs, Porto Alegre, Brazil, 1998.

Character recognition

The process of converting scanned images of machine-printed or handwritten text (numerals, letters, and symbols) into a computer-processable format; also known as optical character recognition (OCR).

Systems. A typical OCR system (**Fig. 1**) contains three logical components: an image scanner, OCR software and hardware, and an output interface. The image scanner optically captures text images to be recognized. Text images are processed with OCR software and hardware. The process involves three operations: document analysis (extracting individual character images), recognizing these images (based on shape), and contextual processing (either to correct misclassifications made by the recognition algorithm or to limit recognition choices). The output interface is responsible for communication of OCR system results to the outside world.

Image scanner. Four basic building blocks form functional image scanners: a detector (and associated electronics), an illumination source, a scan lens, and a document transport. The document transport places the document in the scanning field, the light source floods the object with illumination, and the lens forms the object's image on the detector. The detector consists of an array of elements, each of which converts incident light into a charge or analog signal. These analog signals are then converted into an image. Scanning is performed by the detector and the motion of the text object with respect to the detector. After an image is captured, the document transport removes the document from the scanning field.

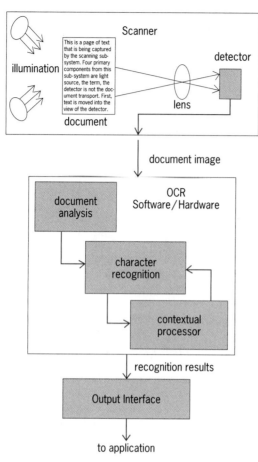

Fig. 1. General structure of an optical character recognition (OCR) system.

Over the years, advances in scanner technology made available higher resolution, often in the range of 300–400 pixels per inch (ppi). Recognition methods that use features (as opposed to template matching) use resolutions of at least 200 ppi and careful consideration of the gray scale. Lower resolutions and simple thresholding (that is, discrimination based only on whether the darkness of a pixel exceeds a certain threshold) tend to break thin lines or fill gaps, thus invalidating features.

Software and hardware. The software-hardware system that recognizes characters from a registered image can be divided into three operational steps: document analysis, character recognition, and contextual processing.

1. *Document analysis.* In this process, text is extracted from the document image. Reliable character segmentation and recognition depend upon both original document quality and registered image quality. Processes that attempt to compensate for poor-quality originals or poor-quality scanning include image enhancement, underline removal, and noise removal. Image enhancement methods emphasize discrimination between characters and objects that are not characters. Underline removal erases printed guidelines and other lines which may touch characters and interfere with character recognition. Noise

removal erases portions of the image that are not part of characters. *See* IMAGE PROCESSING.

Prior to character recognition, it is necessary to isolate individual characters from the text image. Many OCR systems use connected components for this process. For those connected components that represent multiple or partial characters, more sophisticated algorithms are used. In low-quality or nonuniform text images, these sophisticated algorithms may not correctly extract characters, and thus recognition errors may occur. Recognition of unconstrained handwritten text can be very difficult because characters cannot be reliably isolated, especially when the text is cursive handwriting.

2. *Character-recognition algorithms.* Two essential components in a character-recognition algorithm are the feature extractor and the classifier. Feature analysis determines the descriptors, or feature set, used to describe all characters. Given a character image, the feature extractor derives the features that the character possesses. The derived features are then used as input to the character classifier.

Template matching, or matrix matching, is one of the most common classification methods. In template matching, individual image pixels are used as features. Classification is performed by comparing an input character image with a set of templates (or prototypes) from each character class. Each comparison results in a similarity measure between the input character and the template. One measure increases the amount of similarity when a pixel in the observed character is identical to the same pixel in the template image. If the pixels differ, the measure of similarity may be decreased. After all templates have been compared with the observed character image, the character's identity is assigned as the identity of the most similar template.

Template matching is a trainable process because template characters may be changed. In many commercial systems, programmable read-only memories (PROMs) store templates containing single fonts. To retrain the algorithm, the current PROMs are replaced with PROMs that contain images of a new font. Thus, if a suitable PROM exists for a font, template matching can be trained to recognize that font. The similarity measure of template matching may also be modified, but commercial OCR systems typically do not allow this modification. *See* COMPUTER STORAGE TECHNOLOGY; SEMICONDUCTOR MEMORIES.

Structural classification methods utilize structural features and decision rules to classify characters. Structural features may be defined in terms of character strokes, character holes, or other character attributes such as concavities. For instance, the letter P may be described as a vertical stroke with a hole attached on the upper right side. For a character image input, the structural features are extracted and a rule-based system is applied to classify the character. Structural methods are also trainable, but construction of a good feature set and a good rule base can be time consuming.

Many character recognizers are based on mathematical formalisms that minimize a measure of misclassification. These recognizers may use pixel-based features or structural features. Some examples are discriminant-function classifiers, bayesian classifiers, artificial neural networks, and template matchers. Discriminant-function classifiers use hypersurfaces to separate the featural descriptions of characters from different semantic classes and, in the process, reduce the mean-squared error. Bayesian methods seek to minimize the loss function associated with misclassification through the use of probability theory. Artificial neural networks, which are closer to theories of human perception, employ mathematical minimization techniques. Both discriminant functions and artificial neural networks are used in commercial OCR systems. *See* BAYESIAN STATISTICS; NEURAL NETWORK.

Character misclassifications stem from two main sources: poor-quality character images and poor discriminatory ability. Poor document quality, image scanning, and preprocessing can all degrade performance by yielding poor-quality characters. However, the character recognition method may not have been trained for a proper response on the character causing the error. This type of error source is difficult to overcome because the recognition method may have limitations and all possible character images cannot possibly be considered in training the classifier. Recognition rates for machine-printed characters can reach over 99%, but handwritten character recognition rates are typically lower because every person writes differently. This random nature often results in misclassifications.

3. *Contextual processing.* Contextual information can be used in recognition. The number of word choices for a given field can be limited by knowing the content of another field. For example, in recognizing the street name in an address, the street name choices can be limited to a lexicon by first correctly recognizing the postal code. Alternatively, the result of recognition can be postprocessed to correct the recognition errors. One method used to postprocess character recognition results is to apply a spelling checker to verify word spelling. Similarly, other postprocessing methods use lexicons to verify word results, or recognition results may be verified interactively with the user.

4. *Nonroman character recognition.* There are 26 different scripts in use that are other than roman. Some have had little work done on their recognition, for example, Kannada, while a significant amount of work has been done on others, for example, Japanese. In addition to alphanumerals, Japanese text uses Kanji characters (Chinese ideographs) and Kana (Japanese syllables). Therefore, it is considerably more difficult to recognize Japanese text because of the size of the character set (usually more than 3300 characters) and the complexity and similarity of the Kanji character structures. Low data quality is an additional problem in all OCRs. A Japanese OCR is usually composed of two individual classifiers (preclassifier and secondary classifier) in a cascade structure. The preclassifier first performs a fast coarse classification to reduce the character set to a short candidate list (usually containing no more than 100 candidates). The secondary classifier then uses more complex features to determine which candidate in the list has the closest match to the test pattern.

Output interface. The output interface allows character recognition results to be electronically transferred into the domain that uses the results. For example, many commercial systems allow recognition results to be placed directly into spread sheets, databases, and word processors. Other commercial systems use recognition results directly in further automated processing and, when the processing is complete, the recognition results are discarded. The output interface, while simple, is vital to the success of OCR systems because it communicates results to the outside world. *See* DATABASE MANAGEMENT SYSTEM; WORD PROCESSING.

Applications. Commercial OCR systems can largely be grouped into two categories: task-specific readers and general-purpose page readers. A task-specific reader handles only specific document types. Some of the most common task-specific readers read bank checks, letter mail, or credit-card slips. These readers usually utilize custom-made image-lift hardware that captures only a few predefined document regions. For example, a bank-check reader may scan just the courtesy-amount field (where the amount of the check is written numerically) and a postal OCR system may scan just the address block on a mail piece. Such systems emphasize high throughput rates and low error rates. Applications such as letter-mail reading have throughput rates of 12 letters per second with error rates less than 2%. The character recognizer in many task-specific readers is able to recognize both handwritten and machine-printed text.

General-purpose page readers are designed to handle a broader range of documents such as business letters, technical writings, and newspapers. These systems capture an image of a document page and separate the page into text regions and nontext regions. Nontext regions such as graphics and line drawings are often saved separately from the text and associated recognition results. Text regions are segmented into lines, words, and characters, and the characters are passed to the recognizer. Recognition results are output in a format that can be postprocessed by application software. Most of these page readers can read machine-written text, but only a few can read hand-printed alphanumerics.

Task-specific readers. Task-specific readers are used primarily for high-volume applications that require high system throughput. Since high throughput rates are desired, handling only the fields of interest helps reduce time constraints. Since similar documents possess similar size and layout structure, it is straightforward for the image scanner to focus on those fields where the desired information lies. This approach can considerably reduce the image-processing and text-recognition time. Application areas to which task-specific readers have been applied include assigning postal codes to letter mail, reading data entered in forms such as tax forms, automatic accounting procedures used in processing utility bills, verification of account numbers and courtesy amounts on bank checks, automatic accounting of airline passenger tickets, and automatic validation of passports.

1. *Address readers.* The address reader in a postal mail sorter locates the destination address block on a mail piece and reads the postal code in this block. In the United States, additional fields in the address block are read with high confidence, the system may generate a 9-digit ZIP code for the piece. This ZIP code is then used to generate a bar code which is sprayed on the envelope (**Fig. 2**).

The multiline optical character reader (MLOCR) used by the U.S. Postal Service locates the address block on a mail piece, reads the whole address, identifies the 9-digit ZIP code, generates a 9-digit bar code, and sorts the mail to the correct stacker. The character classifier recognizes up to 400 fonts, and the system can process up to 45,000 mail pieces per hour.

2. *Form readers.* A form-reading system needs to discriminate between preprinted form instructions and filled-in data. The system is first trained with a blank form. The system registers those areas on the form where the data should be printed. During the form-recognition phase, the system uses the spatial information obtained from training to scan the regions that should be filled with data. Some readers read hand-printed data as well as various machine-written text. They can read data on a form without being confused with the form instructions. Some systems can process forms at a rate of 5800 per hour.

3. *Bill-processing systems.* In general, a bill-processing system is used to read payment slips, utility bills, and inventory documents. The system focuses on certain regions on a document where the expected information is located, such as the account number and payment value.

4. *Check readers.* A check reader captures check images and recognizes courtesy amounts and account information on the checks. Some readers also recognize the legal amounts (written alphabetically) on checks and use the information in both fields to cross-check the recognition results. An operator can correct misclassified characters by cross-validating the recognition results with the check image that appears on a system console.

5. *Airline ticket readers.* In order to claim revenue from an airline passenger ticket, an airline needs to have three records matched: the reservation record, the travel-agent record, and the passenger ticket. However, it is impossible to match all three records for every ticket sold. Current methods, which use manual random sampling of tickets, are far from accurate in claiming the maximal amount of revenue. Several airlines use a passenger-revenue accounting system to account accurately for passenger revenues. The system reads the ticket number on a passenger ticket and matches it with the one in the airline reservation database. It scans up to 260,000 tickets per day and achieves a sorting rate of 17 tickets per second.

6. *Passport readers.* An automated passport reader is used to speed passengers returning to the United States through custom inspections. The reader reads a traveler's name, date of birth, and passport number on the passport and checks these against the database records that contain information on fugitive felons and smugglers.

General-purpose page readers. The two general categories are high-end page readers and low-end page readers. High-end page readers are more advanced in recognition capability and have higher data throughput. A low-end page reader usually does not come with a scanner, and it is compatible with many flatbed scanners. Low-end page readers are used mostly in office environments with desktop workstations, which are less demanding in system throughput. Since they are designed to handle a broader range of documents, a sacrifice of recognition accuracy is

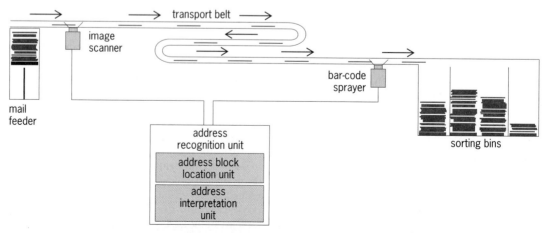

Fig. 2. Architecture of a postal address reading and sorting system.

necessary. Some commercial OCR software allows users to adapt the recognition engine to customer data for improving recognition accuracy. Some high-performance readers can detect type faces (such as boldface and italic) and output the formatted ASCII text in the corresponding style. *See* COMPUTER; COMPUTER VISION.   Sargur N. Srihari; Stephen W. Lam

Bibliography. J. Cohen, *Automatic Identification and Data Collection Systems*, 1995; M. Ogg and H. Ogg, *Optical Character Recognition: A Librarian's Guide*, 1992; J. C. Reimel, *Image Processing and Optical Character Recognition: How They Work and How to Implement Them*, 1993; G. Searfoss, *Jis-Kanji Character Recognition Method*, 1994; S. N. Srihari, High-performance reading machines, *Proc. IEEE*, 80:1120–1132, 1992; P. S. Wang (ed.), *Character and Handwriting Recognition: Expanding Frontiers*, 1990.

Characteristic curve

A graphical display depicting complex nonlinear relationships in electronic circuits. A typical use is to show voltage-current relationships in semiconductor devices. Device amplification capabilities, for example, are exhibited by a characteristic plot which traces output current versus output voltage with a third controlling variable as a parameter. This control variable could be the base current of a bipolar junction transistor (BJT) or the gate-to-source voltage of a metal-oxide-semiconductor (MOS) transistor.

The properties of this display can be illustrated by an idealized version of a characteristic curve for an enhancement-mode MOS transistor (see **illus.**). Here, drain current (i_d) is plotted versus drain-to-source voltage (v_{DS}) for each of several values of gate-to-source voltage (v_{GS}) exceeding the device threshold voltage (V_t). The transistor does not conduct if the gate-to-source voltage is below the threshold voltage. The characteristic illustrates how the transistor operating modes depend on its applied voltages, with the transistor gate-to-source voltage having a much larger, highly nonlinear effect on the drain current than does the drain-to-source voltage.

A small increase in drain current with drain-to-source voltage is caused by a phenomenon of semiconductor physics called channel length modulation. To a first-order approximation, this effect can be modeled as a linear resistor (r_a) connected between the device drain and source. The intersection point (V_a) of the projection of the line with the voltage axis is sometimes called the early voltage, a term borrowed from bipolar junction transistor theory. The inverse of V_a is called the channel-length modulation parameter (λ).

Other characteristics often included in transistor data sheets are displays of current gain versus bias current, gain versus frequency, and input and output impedances versus frequency. Less commonly, other graphical nonlinear relationships, such as the variation of thermocouple voltage with temperature or the dependence of electrical motor torque with current, also are known as characteristic curves.

In the past, characteristic curves were used as tools in the graphical solution of nonlinear circuit equations that are followed by relationships of this type. In current practice, this analysis is performed using computer packages for circuit simulation. Designers still use characteristic curves from data sheets, however, to evaluate relative performance capabilities when selecting devices, and to provide the information needed for a preliminary

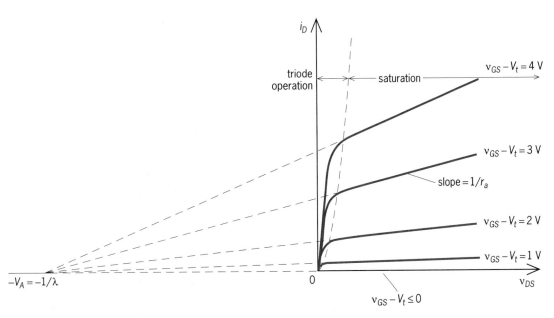

Idealized metal-oxide-semiconductor (MOS) transistor characteristic curve. The increase in drain current with drain-to-source voltage is exaggerated for clarity. (*After A. S. Sedra and K. C. Smith, Microelectronic Circuits, 4th ed., Oxford, 1998*)

pencil-and-paper circuit design. *See* AMPLIFIER; ELECTRICAL MODEL; TRANSISTOR.   Philip V. Lopresti

Bibliography. R. T. Howe and C. Sodini, *Microelectronics: An Integrated Approach*, Prentice Hall, 1997; A. S. Sedra and K. C. Smith, *Microelectronic Circuits*, 4th ed., Oxford, 1998.

Charadriiformes

A large, diverse, worldwide order of shore and aquatic birds found from dry plains to the open ocean, and from the tropics to the high latitudes. Charadriiformes may be closely related to the pigeons (Columbiformes) on the one side and to the cranes, rails, and their allies (Gruiformes) on the other. The sandgrouse, here included in the Columbiformes, are sometimes placed in the Charadriiformes. Some workers place the flamingos (Phoenicopteriformes) and the ibises (Threskionithidae; Ciconiiformes) in this order, but these decisions are highly controversial. *See* CICONIIFORMES; COLUMBIFORMES; GRUIFORMES; PHOENICOPTERIFORMES.

Classification. The order is arranged into 3 suborders and 17 families as follows:

Order Charadriiformes
  Suborder Charadrii
    Superfamily Jacanoidea
      Family: Jacanidae (jacansas or lily-walkers;
        8 species; pantropical)
        Rostratulidae (painted snipe;
        2 species; Old World tropics)
    Superfamily Charadrioidea
      Family: Graculavidae (Cretaceous of
        New Jersey)
        Haematopodidae (oyster catchers;
        7 species; worldwide, coastal)
        Charadriidae (plovers and lapwings;
        64 species; worldwide)
        Scolopacidae (sandpipers, curlews,
        phalaropes, and snipe; 86 species;
        worldwide)
        Recurvirostridae (stilts and avocets;
        10 species; worldwide)
        Dromadidae (crab plovers; 1 species;
        coast of the Arabian peninsula)
        Burhinidae (thick-knees; 9 species;
        worldwide, except North America)
        Glareolidae (pratincoles; 16 species;
        Old World)
    Superfamily Chionidoidea
      Family: Thinocoridae (seed snipe; 4 species;
        Andes of South America)
        Chionidae (sheath-bills; 2 species;
        southern tip of South America)
  Suborder Lari
    Family: Stercorariidae (skuas; 5 species;
        worldwide, oceanic)
      Laridae (gulls and terns; 88 species;
        worldwide)
      Rynchopidae (skimmers; 3 species;
        pantropical and North America)

  Suborder Alcae
    Family Alcidae (auks, murres, and
        puffins; 23 species; northern
        oceans)

Several of these families, such as the Charadriidae (plovers), Scolopacidae (sandpipers), and Laridae (gulls and terns), are divided into two or more subfamilies. Some workers place the Australian plains-wanderer (Pedionomidae) in this order, but this is still controversial and the group is here included in the Gruiformes. Some workers also place the Presbyornithidae (Eocene of North and South America) in the Charadriiformes, but they are here considered to be Anseriformes. *See* ANSERIFORMES.

Fossil record. Being shore and water birds, the charadriiforms have a long and generally good fossil record, including some of the earliest fossils that are definitely assigned to a living order. The Graculavidae are Cretaceous birds from New Jersey whose affinities to Recent families have not been established, but they may be ancestral to a diversity of orders. A number of other presumably charadriiform fossils are known from the Cretaceous, but their relationships are still uncertain. The larids and alcids have good fossil records, but most of the other families are represented by scattered remains and several are unrepresented as fossils. This lack arises presumably because of the fragile nature of the skeleton of most members of the order.

Suborders. The three suborders of charadiiforms are quite different groups.

Charadrii. The Charadrii are the typical shorebirds, usually found in marshy areas and along shores, but some are in dry areas; a few, the phalaropes, are mainly aquatic. They can run and fly well. Most live in flocks, although most breed solitarily in nests on the ground. Male ruffs (*Philomachus pugnax*; Europe) are much larger than females and court communally, in leks (gathering places for courtship), with females coming to the leks and choosing particular males. The crab plovers nest colonially in tunnels dug into sand banks. Young charadrii are downy and leave the nest on hatching. The phalaropes (Scolopacidae: Phalaropodinae) [see **illustration**], painted snipes, and jacanas show sex reversal, with the females being larger than the males, usually more brightly

Phalaropus fulicaria, the red phalarope. (© *California Academy of Sciences; photographers Gerald and Buff Corsi*)

colored, and assuming the lead in courtship; the males incubate and assume most of the care of the young. Most feed on insects and other small animals; the seed snipes are mainly vegetarian. The bills of many species are highly specialized for food capture, with the most bizarre being that of the wry-billed plover (*Anarhynchus frontalis*) of New Zealand, in which the bill tip bends sharply to the right for probing under stones for insects. Many species breed in the Arctic or cool temperate regions and migrate long distances in large flocks. Some species have long transoceanic migrations, for example, the bristle-thighed curlew (*Numenius tahitiensis*), which flies from Alaska to Hawaii and then to Tahiti and surrounding islands. Many shorebirds were, or still are, of economic importance as game birds. The numbers of many species have been greatly reduced because of overhunting or loss of habitat, mainly migration and wintering grounds. A few species, for example, the Eskimo curlew (*Numenius borealis*), are severely threatened or extinct. *See* ENDANGERED SPECIES; SEXUAL DIMORPHISM.

Lari. The Lari include the skuas, gulls, terns, and skimmers, predominantly aquatic birds that find their food by flying over the water. They are long-winged, excellent fliers with short legs, but they also can walk well. The feet are webbed. Most species breed in large colonies, laying up to four eggs, and the downy young remain in or near the nest until they can fly. Most species can swim on the water surface, although terns do so less often. A few oceanic terns lack waterproof plumage and never alight on the water, sleeping on the wing. Although many species are marine, most are found near the coast and are not truly oceanic. Skimmers have an elongated, knifelike lower jaw with which they skim the surface of the water for fish. Many species breed in the Arctic and cold temperate regions and migrate. The Arctic tern has the longest known migratory flight, up to 22,000 mi (36,000 km) per year. Skuas are highly predatory, as well as robbing other birds of their food; they have the distinction of having been seen closer to both Poles than any other birds.

Alcae. The Alcae include only the alcids, which are true marine, swimming and diving birds found only in the Northern Hemisphere. They are mainly black and white, and have webbed feet and reduced wings. Alcids are excellent divers and swim underwater by using their wings, which are reduced to rather stiff, paddlelike structures. They have a quick, buzzy flight used mainly to reach their nesting sites. Alcids feed on fish and other aquatic animals. They usually breed in large colonies, on rocky ledges, on the ground, or in burrows. However, one species of auklets, the marbled murrelet (*Brachyramphus marmorotus*), breeds in large trees, placing the nest on large branches in trees of old forests. The young are downy, and in some species leave the nest before they are fully grown. The great auk of the North Atlantic, the "penguin" of a number of writers, was the largest known species and was flightless; it is now extinct. *See* AVES.   Walter J. Bock

Bibliography. J. del Hoyo et al. (eds.), Order Charadriiformes, *Handbook of the Birds of the World*, vol. 3, pp. 276–722, Lynx Edicions, 1996; P. Hayman, J. Marchant, and T. Prater, *Shorebirds*, Houghton Mifflin, 1986; E. A. Johnsgard, *The Plovers, Sandpipers and Snipes of the World*, University of Nebraska Press, 1981.

Charcoal

A porous solid product containing 85–98% carbon produced by heating carbonaceous materials such as cellulose, wood, peat, and coals of bituminous or lower rank at 930–1110°F (500–600°C) in the absence of air. Chars or charcoals are rendered more porous and more efficient for sorption by heating in air, carbon dioxide, or steam at 1650°F (900°C) for a brief period. The surface area of activated char produced by this technique is about 800,000 ft^2/oz (1000 m^2/g). Chars from cellulose or wood are soft and friable. They are used chiefly for decolorizing solutions of sugar and other foodstuffs and for removing objectionable tastes and odors from water. Chars from nutshells and coal are dense, hard carbons. They are used in gas masks and in chemical manufacturing for many mixture separations. Another use is for the tertiary treatment of wastewater. Residual organic matter is adsorbed effectively to improve the water quality.

The sorptive properties of chars are the result of their very large internal surface. The selectivity of the sorption can be modified by mixing additives to the char, and by controlling the partial pressure or concentration of components, the temperature of the mixture, and (in liquids) the acidity or polar environment. *See* ACTIVATED CARBON; ADSORPTION; CARBON; COKE; DESTRUCTIVE DISTILLATION; PYROLYSIS; WOOD CHEMICALS.   Joseph H. Field

Charge-coupled devices

Semiconductor devices wherein minority charge is stored in a spatially defined depletion region (potential well) at the surface of a semiconductor, and is moved about the surface by transferring this charge to similar adjacent wells. The formation of the potential well is controlled by the manipulation of voltage applied to surface electrodes. Since a potential well represents a nonequilibrium state, it will fill with minority charge from normal thermal generation. Thus a charge-coupled device (CCD) must be continuously clocked or refreshed to maintain its usefulness. In general, the potential wells are strung together as shift registers. Charge is injected or generated at various input ports and then transferred to an output detector. By appropriate design to minimize the dispersive effects that are associated with the charge-transfer process, well-defined charge packets can be moved over relatively long distances through thousands of transfers.

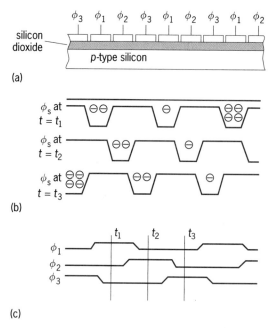

(a)

(b)

(c)

Fig. 1. Operation of three-phase charge-coupled shift register. (a) Cross section of register through channel. (b) Profile of surface potential ϕ_s for three different clock time intervals t_1, t_2, and t_3. (c) Voltage waveforms ϕ_1, ϕ_2, and ϕ_3 for the three-phase clocks.

Control of charge motion. There are several methods of controlling the charge motion, all of which rely upon providing a lower potential for the charge in the desired direction. When an electrode is placed in proximity to a semiconductor surface, the electrode's potential can control the near-surface potential within the semiconductor. The basis for this control is the same as for metal-oxide-semiconductor (MOS) transistor action. If closely spaced electrodes are at different voltages, they will form potential wells of different depths. Free charge will move from the region of higher potential to the one of lower potential. In one arrangement, a charge packet can be moved to the right by alternating the voltage on three electrodes in proper phase **(Fig. 1)**. In another scheme, an asymmetry built into a well can direct the charge in a given direction **(Fig. 2)**. Asymmetries of this type are easily created by using implanted ion layers or varying dielectric thickness. The three-phase structure shown in Fig. 1 has the ability to reverse the charge direction by a change in electrical phase.

Transfer efficiency. An important property of a charge-coupled device is its ability to transfer almost all of the charge from one well to the next. Without this feature, charge packets would be quickly distorted and lose their identity. This ability to transfer charge is measured as transfer efficiency, which must be very good for the structure to be useful in long registers. Values greater than 99.9% per transfer are not uncommon. This means that only 10% of the original charge is lost after 100 transfers.

Several mechanisms influence the transfer of charge from one well to the next **(Fig. 3)**. Initial self-induced drift acts to separate the charge. This re-

pulsion of like charge is the dominant transfer mechanism for large signals, and is effective for the first 99% or so of the charge. Near the edge of the transfer electrode the potential gradient creates a field which sweeps the charge onward. Thermal diffusion accounts for the transfer of the remaining charge.

Electron traps. It would appear that, given sufficient time, almost all of the charge could be transferred. Two other mechanisms are at work to counter this. Within the silicon and at its surface are sites that can act as electron traps. This is especially true at the surface, where numerous surface states exist. These traps collect charge when exposed to a large charge packet and then slowly release it during later cycles of small charge packets. By stringing a large number of empty charge packets together, the traps can be emptied completely. When the first packet containing charge arrives, it could be completely consumed, recharging the traps.

Other than process steps that minimize the trap density, there are two methods to alleviate the severity of this problem. The first is never to allow a series of completely empty charge packets to occur. Instead of an empty charge packet, a minimum charge quantity is always present. This charge, called a fat zero, can be 10–20% of the well capacity. Under some conditions, this can reduce the trapping effects to tolerable levels. The second approach is to use a channel for the charge whose potential minimum does not occur at the surface. This is called a buried channel device, as opposed to a surface channel device. Since the charge is located within the bulk silicon below the surface, it is not exposed to the surface-state traps. Bulk traps remain, but because of their low density they are almost insignificant.

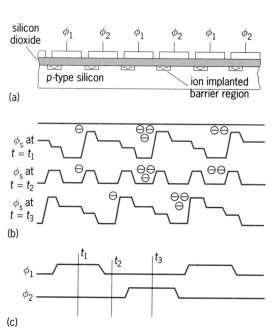

(a)

(b)

(c)

Fig. 2. Operation of two-phase charge-coupled shift register. (a) Cross section of register through channel. (b) Profile of surface potential ϕ_s for three different clock time intervals t_1, t_2, and t_3. (c) Voltage waveforms ϕ_1 and ϕ_2 for the two-phase clocks.

The process to shift the channel potential minimum below the surface can be either an ion-implant layer or an epitaxy layer combined with an implant layer. Because the charge is further removed from the surface control electrode, the maximum charge density has been reduced by a factor of 2 to 3. For the same reason, the fringing fields are greater and charge transfer can be much faster. The charge also moves with bulk mobility rather than the lower surface mobility, further enhancing performance. Fractional charge losses of as low as 5×10^{-5} at clock frequencies greater than 100 MHz have been reported for buried-channel charge-coupled-device structures. This means that such a structure could transfer 10^6 electrons from one well to another in less than 10 ns, leaving fewer than 50 electrons behind. *See* ION IMPLANTATION.

Localized potential minima. In addition to electron-trapping sites, there is another reason that charge can be left behind. Where the two adjacent surface electrodes come together, there is necessarily a gap. This gap is usually quite small, and sometimes may even be covered by one of the electrodes. However, the gap represents a region of poorly controlled surface potential. It is possible, under some conditions, for the transition from one potential well to the next to have perturbations in it. These perturbations, or glitches, can trap charge. They represent a localized minipotential well within the larger one. Charge trapped by the glitch will be left behind after a transfer. If the glitch remained filled, continued clocking of the structure would not represent a problem. However, the size of the glitch may change, depending upon electrode clock amplitude. Also, charge is released over the glitch as thermionic emission over a barrier potential. Thus a glitch can be emptied by a series of empty charge packets to trap the next packet-containing charge. Many times, glitches occur at input or output ports without detriment to the structure's operation, since their effect may be small. However, if a glitch occurs within the repetitive register, the multiplication effect can have a serious impact on overall performance.

Lifetime. A second important property of a charge-coupled-device register is its lifetime. When the surface electrode is clocked high, the potential within the semiconductor also increases. Majority charge is swept away, leaving behind a depletion layer. If the potential is taken sufficiently high, the surface goes into deep depletion until an inversion layer is formed and adequate minority charge collected to satisfy the field requirements. The time it takes for minority charge to fill the well is the measure of well lifetime. The major sources of unwanted charge are the following: thermal diffusion of substrate minority charge to the edge of the depletion region, where it is collected in the well; electron-hole pair generation within the depletion region; and the emission of minority charge by traps. Surface-channel charge-coupled devices usually have a better lifetime, since surface-state trap emission is suppressed and the depletion regions are usually smaller.

Input and output ports. Once adequate transfer efficiency and sufficient lifetime have been achieved, input and output ports must be established. The port structure of a charge-coupled device depends upon its application. Analog registers require linear inputs and outputs with good dynamic range.

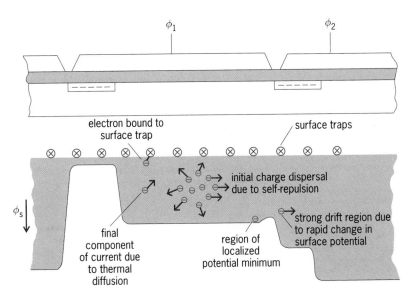

Fig. 3. Mechanisms determining charge-transfer rate. The three terms contributing to charge transfer include self-induced drift, channel drift fields, and thermal diffusion. Charge is left behind due to electron traps and localized potential minima.

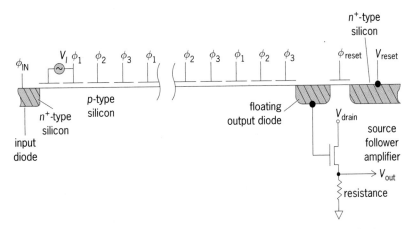

Fig. 4. Charge-coupled register showing analog input and output ports. A source follower output is shown.

Digital registers require precisely metered and detected ones and zeros. Imaging devices use photoemission at the register sites as input with analog-output amplifiers.

The most common input structure relies upon a diode as a source of minority charge (**Fig. 4**). Whenever the diode potential drops below the threshold potential of the adjacent gate, an inversion layer is formed beneath the gate. By pulsing the diode potential low or the adjacent gate potential high, charge can be injected into the register. To prevent the charge from returning to the diode, the next gate in the register immediately collects it. The amount of charge injected can be controlled by adjusting the channel potential difference between the first two gates.

A common output circuit allows the output diode to be reset at the start of each cycle to the reset level (Fig. 4). During the second part of the cycle, charge from the charge-coupled device register is dumped on the floating diode, causing its voltage to change. The diode is connected to a gate which can be used in an amplifier configuration. For digital applications, the output goes to a regenerative circuit with sufficient gain to produce full-level signals at the output.   Mark R. Guidry

Signal processing. Many of the early applications of charge-coupled-device technology were in signal processing. Most of those applications utilized a charge-coupled-device shift register as an analog delay line. In this configuration, an analog input signal was sampled and a packet of charge proportional to its amplitude was created and shifted into the register. After transferring through the register, the charge was converted back into voltage form at the output. The amount of delay was proportional to both the number of shift register elements and the clocking frequency. The charge-coupled-device analog delay line was used in various functions, including analog memory, time base correction, and analog filtering. However, as digital memory and digital signal processing technologies have advanced, the use of charge-coupled devices in signal processing has decreased.

Image sensors. The most significant current application of the charge-coupled-device concept is as an imaging device. Charge-coupled-device image sensors utilize the fact that silicon is sensitive to light. In fact, silicon is sensitive to wavelengths from about 400 to 1100 nanometers (from ultraviolet to near-infrared). When light photons penetrate the silicon surface, hole-electron pairs are created in the silicon. The number of hole-electron pairs created is a function of wavelength (photon energy), intensity (number of photons), and duration (length of time exposed to light).

In a charge-coupled-device image sensor, the light is focused upon an array of picture elements (pixels). These pixels collect the electrons as they are created. The number of electrons collected in each pixel is representative of the light intensity projected onto the sensor at that point. Periodically, the charges from all of the pixels are read out, and the image can then be reconstructed from the intensity and pixel location data.

There are two primary categories of image sensors. Linear image sensors have the pixels aligned along a central axis. Area image sensors have the pixels arranged in a rectangular (rows × columns) array pattern. Linear image sensors require relative motion between the sensor and the object being scanned. The relative motion is precisely known so that, as the object is scanned one line at a time, it can then be reconstructed one line at a time. Area image sensors do not require this motion.

Linear image sensors. The typical linear image sensor consists of a linear array of pixels (to collect the light-generated charge) with two output shift registers (one on each side) to transport the charge to the output circuit. After a set amount of time (the integration time), all of the photogenerated charge is transferred out of the pixels and into the appropriate output shift register. While the pixels begin to collect charge for the next line, the two output shift registers transfer the present line out to the output circuits.

Because the sensor must be moved relative to its target, early applications were in copiers and facsimile machines, in which either the target or the sensor was moved in a direction perpendicular to the axis of the linear array. As the speeds of linear image sensors increased into the 20–60-MHz range, charge-coupled devices were used to scan objects moving at a continuous high speed. Industrial and food inspection systems were developed to improve the quality of product by detection of defects on the line. The U.S. Postal Service now uses linear image sensors to quickly scan addresses on letters. A specialized high-speed application of the charge-coupled device is in telecine machines, which scan movie film and convert the film into a television format, allowing television stations to broadcast movies.

New applications were also created as the resolution of charge-coupled devices increased to 6000 pixels or more. Graphics arts scanners can scan photographs at higher resolution than the film used to create the photograph. High resolution is also critical for remote sensing and aerial reconnaissance. Charge-coupled-device cameras have been placed in orbit aboard satellites for remote sensing of large regions of the Earth to assist in land use management. In aerial reconnaissance applications, charge-coupled-device cameras scan the ground below while the airplane travels at a fixed speed. *See* REMOTE SENSING.

Area image sensors. The area image sensor does not require relative motion between sensor and object because the pixels are arranged in a two-dimensional array. Area image sensors have a variety of architectures, but in general they all have an array of pixels (arranged in rows and columns) and vertical shift registers to transfer the charge in parallel to the output shift register, which transports each line out serially to the output circuit.

Early area image sensors were designed to be used in simple, closed-circuit television and scientific applications. However, as the quality and resolution of area image sensors increased, they began to be used throughout the television industry. Compared to conventional vidicon-tube-based equipment, charge-coupled-device cameras benefit from reduced size and power consumption, greater ruggedness and reliability, and lower cost. Virtually all camcorders and most television cameras are now based on charge-coupled devices. Charge-coupled-device cameras are also used in surveillance and inspection systems of all kinds and are ideal for robotics applications. Video conferencing and video telephones use lower-resolution versions of these cameras. *See* COMPUTER VISION; TELEVISION CAMERA; TELEVISION CAMERA TUBE; VIDEOTELEPHONY.

The resolution of area image sensors has become equivalent to photographic film, enabling the development of digital photography. Digital imaging provides several benefits. Costly film and toxic film-developing chemicals are eliminated. Images are obtained immediately and can easily be enhanced through software. Image storage and transmission is faster and easier. Cameras with very large, very high resolution area image sensors provide professional photographers better final pictures than are obtainable with conventional film, while lower-resolution, lower-cost, digital charge-coupled-device cameras are available to consumers. *See* CAMERA.

A miniaturized charge-coupled-device camera allows a dentist to see inside a patient's mouth or a physician to see inside a patient's body. Charge-coupled-device area imagers are also used in intraoral dental x-ray systems. These imagers replace the x-ray film that is normally placed within the patient's mouth. The imager is connected to an adjacent computer where the image is immediately displayed. Since silicon-based charge-coupled devices do not image x-rays well, a layer of scintillating material is deposited or placed in front of the sensor. This material has a special phosphor that emits green light when exposed to x-ray energy. The charge-coupled device then "sees" this green image. The charge-coupled device/scintillator combination is more sensitive than standard x-ray film, allowing the dentist to reduce the x-ray exposure of the patient while still producing a superior image.

Charge-coupled-device-based systems with very large area image sensors have been introduced in mammography, to image x-rays of the human breast. Software is being developed to interpret the images and increase the accuracy of diagnosis.

Astronomers have long used charge-coupled device area image sensor cameras mounted on very high power telescopes. By synchronizing the motion of the telescope with the Earth's rotation, the camera can "stare" at one spot in space for hours at a time. The long integration times allow distant objects to be imaged that are otherwise invisible. To keep the sensor from being saturated with thermally generated charge, these cameras typically cool the charge-coupled-device chip down to -50 to $-100°C$ (-58 to $-148°F$). *See* ASTRONOMICAL PHOTOGRAPHY; INTEGRATED CIRCUITS; SEMICONDUCTOR.

Steven Onishi

Bibliography. G. C. Horst, *CCD Arrays, Cameras and Displays*, JCD Publishing, Winter Park, FL, and SPIE Optical Engineering Press, Bellingham, WA, 1996; A. J. P. Theuwissen, *Solid State Imaging with Charge-Coupled Devices*, Kluwer Academic, 1995.

Charge-density wave

A possible ground state of a metal in which the conduction-electron charge density is sinusoidally modulated in space. The periodicity of this extra modulation is unrelated to the lattice periodicity. Instead, it is determined by the dimension of the conduction-electron Fermi surface in momentum space.

Description. The conduction-electron charge density $\rho_0(\vec{r})$ would ordinarily exhibit a dependence on position $\vec{r}$ having the same spatial periodicity as that of the positive-ion lattice. A metal with a charge-density wave (CDW) has an additional charge modulation described by Eq. (1). The fractional ampli-

$$\rho(\vec{r}) = \rho_0(\vec{r})[1 + f \cos(\vec{Q} \cdot \vec{r} + \phi)] \qquad (1)$$

tude of the charge-density wave is f and typically has a value of approximately 0.1. The wave vector $\vec{Q}$ of the charge-density wave is determined by the conduction-electron Fermi surface. In a simple metal, having a spherical surface of radius p_F in momentum space, the magnitude of $\vec{Q}$ is approximately the value in Eq. (2), where h is Planck's constant.

$$Q \approx \frac{4\pi p_F}{h} \qquad (2)$$

Although the wavelength of a charge-density wave is comparable to the spacing between lattice planes, their ratio is not a rational number. The charge-density wave is then said to be incommensurate. In such a case, the total energy of the metal is independent of the phase ϕ in Eq. (1). *See* FERMI SURFACE.

Origin. In a quasi-one-dimensional metal, for which conduction electrons are mobile in one direction only, a charge-density wave can be caused by a Peierls instability. This mechanism involves interaction between the electrons and a periodic lattice distortion having a wave vector Q parallel to the conduction axis. The linear-chain metal niobium triselenide ($NbSe_3$) is prototypical, and exhibits nonlinear conduction phenomena arising from electrically induced dynamic variations of the phase ϕ in Eq. (1).

For isotropic metals, and quasi-two-dimensional metals, Coulomb interactions between electrons are the cause of a charge-density wave instability. The exchange energy, an effect of the Pauli exclusion principle, and the correlation energy, an effect of electron-electron scattering, both act to stabilize a charge-density wave. However, the electrostatic energy attributable to the charge modulation in Eq. (1) would suppress a charge-density wave were it not for a compensating charge response of the positive-ion lattice. *See* EXCHANGE INTERACTION; EXCLUSION PRINCIPLE.

Lattice distortion. Suppose that $\vec{u}(\vec{r})$ is the displacement of a positive ion from its lattice site at $\vec{r}$. Then a wavelike displacement given by Eq. (3) will generate a positive-ion charge density that almost cancels the electronic charge modulation of Eq. (1). A typical value of the displacement amplitude A is about 1% of the lattice constant. Ion-ion repulsive interactions must be small in order to permit such a distortion. Consequently, charge-density waves are more likely to occur in metals having small elastic moduli.

$$\vec{u}(\vec{r}) = \vec{A} \sin (\vec{Q} \cdot \vec{r} + \phi) \qquad (3)$$

Detection. The unambiguous signature of a charge-density wave is the observation of two satellites, on opposite sides of each Bragg reflection, in a single-crystal diffraction experiment, employing either x-rays, neutrons, or electrons. The satellites are caused by the periodic lattice displacement, Eq. (3). Charge-density waves were first seen by electron diffraction in layered metals like tantalum disulfide (TaS$_2$) and tantalum diselenide (TaSe$_2$), which have three charge-density waves. At reduced temperature, transitions from incommensurate to commensurate $\vec{Q}$'s are observed. The length of a charge-density wave in the latter case is then an integral multiple of some lattice periodicity. The charge-density wave in the elemental metal potassium has been observed by neutron diffraction. The wavelength of the charge-density wave in this case is 1.5% larger than the spacing between close-packed atomic planes. *See* ELECTRON DIFFRACTION; NEUTRON DIFFRACTION; X-RAY DIFFRACTION.

Fermi surface effects. If simple metals like sodium and potassium did not have a charge-density-wave structure, their conduction-electron Fermi surface would be almost a perfect sphere. Many electronic conduction phenomena would then be isotropic, and the low-temperature magnetoresistance would be essentially zero. The presence of a charge-density wave leads to a dramatic contradiction of such expectations. Conduction-electron dynamics will be modified by the presence of a new potential having the periodicity of Eq. (1). The Fermi surface will distort and become multiply connected. In high magnetic fields some electrons will travel in open orbits rather than in closed, cyclotron orbits. The low-temperature magnetoresistance will then exhibit sharp resonances as the magnetic field is rotated relative to the crystal axes. Such phenomena have been observed in sodium and potassium and have been explained with charge-density-wave theory. *See* MAGNETORESISTANCE.

$\vec{Q}$-domains. Generally, the $\vec{Q}$ direction will not be the same throughout an entire sample of, for example, a cubic crystal having a single charge-density wave. There will be a domain structure analogous to magnetic domains in a ferromagnet. The $\vec{Q}$ direction will (of course) prefer some specific axis described by direction cosines α, β, γ. In a cubic crystal there would be 24 equivalent axes and, therefore, 24 $\vec{Q}$-domain types. As a consequence, some physical properties of a sample will depend markedly on the orientation distribution of its $\vec{Q}$-domains. For example, the low-temperature resistivity of a potassium wire might be several times larger if its $\vec{Q}$-domains are oriented parallel to the wire, than the value obtained if the domains were oriented perpendicular. Since $\vec{Q}$-domain distribution can be altered by stress-induced domain regrowth, some physical properties will vary significantly from experiment to experiment, even on the same sample. Such behavior is observed in alkali metals. Techniques for the control of $\vec{Q}$-domain orientation have not yet been developed. *See* DOMAIN (ELECTRICITY AND MAGNETISM); ELECTRICAL RESISTIVITY.

Phasons. The energy decrease caused by the existence of an incommensurate charge-density wave is independent of the phase ϕ, Eq. (1). It follows that there are new low-frequency excitations which can be described by a slowly varying phase modulation of the charge-density wave, as represented approximately in Eq. (4). Quantized excitations of this type

$$\phi \to \phi(\vec{r}, t) = a(\vec{q}) \sin [\vec{q} \cdot \vec{r} - \omega(\vec{q})t] \qquad (4)$$

are called phasons. They exist only for small $\vec{q}$, $\vec{q} \vec{Q}$; and their frequency $\omega(\vec{q})$ approaches zero linearly with q.

A number of physical phenomena caused by phasons have been observed. Phasons give rise to a low-temperature anomaly in the heat capacity. The charge-density waves in lanthanum digerminide (LaGe$_2$) were first suspected from its anomalous heat capacity. The phason spectral density of potassium has been directly observed in point-contact spectroscopy. Phasons reduce the intensity of charge-density-wave diffraction satellites with increasing temperature and contribute a diffuse-scattering cloud which surrounds each satellite. The phason velocity in tantalum disulfide has been determined from measurements of the phason diffuse scattering. Conduction electrons are strongly scattered by phasons, and such processes modify the temperature dependence of the resistivity at low temperature. *See* BAND THEORY OF SOLIDS; CRYSTAL STRUCTURE; SPIN-DENSITY WAVE.   Albert W. Overhauser

Bibliography. F. Bassani et al. (eds.), *Highlights of Condensed-Matter Theory*, Proceedings of the International School of Physics "Enrico Fermi", Course 89, Varenna on Lake Como, 1983; T. Butz (ed.), *Nuclear Spectroscopy on Charge Density Wave Systems*, 1992; L. P. Gor'kov and G. Grüner (eds.), *Charge Density Waves in Solids*, 1990; G. Grüner, The dynamics of charge density waves, *Rev. Mod. Phys.*, 60:1129–1181, 1988.

Charge symmetry

The rule that the interchange of opposite members of a multiplet of subatomic particles in a system or process does not affect any property of the system or the outcome of the process.

Examples. A multiplet is a group of subatomic particles that are (nearly) identical except that each member of the multiplet carries a different amount of electrical charge. The simplest example is the two-member multiplet consisting of the proton and neutron. Both are called nucleons, and both are the building blocks of the atomic nucleus. They have the same spin ($\frac{1}{2}\hbar$, where $\hbar$ is Planck's constant divided by 2π) and nearly the same mass, but the proton carries one unit of positive electrical charge while the neutron has no charge. It is the proton's charge that attracts and binds negatively charged electrons to make atoms. Many other multiplets have been found in the particles created in accelerators. These include the pion with three charge states (π^+, π^0, π^-) and the delta with four (Δ^{++}, Δ^+, Δ^0, Δ^-). *See* BARYON; MESON; NEUTRON; NUCLEON; PROTON.

The mathematical framework that best describes the behavior of particles within a multiplet mirrors the framework for spin, with the value of the isospin being ($N - 1)/2$, where the number of multiplet members is N. If a process or property is the same for all members of the multiplet, that property obeys isospin (I-spin) symmetry. Charge symmetry is a special case in which the property is the same when opposite members of the multiplet are swapped. *See* I-SPIN; SPIN (QUANTUM MECHANICS).

For the nucleon, charge symmetry requires that swapping neutrons and protons in a nucleus or a subatomic reaction has no physical effect. Thus, charge symmetry would predict that the triton (nucleus made of one proton and two neutrons) would have the same spin and mass as the helium-3 (^{3}He) nucleus (two protons and one neutron). This rule has proven useful in the classification of subatomic particles and the states of the atomic nucleus. In addition, if there is a reaction among subatomic particles that can proceed through different members of a multiplet, the relative rates of these reactions are related by the mathematical rules that govern isospin. *See* ELEMENTARY PARTICLE; NUCLEAR STRUCTURE; SYMMETRY LAWS (PHYSICS).

Charge symmetry breaking. The predictions of the charge symmetry rule are not exactly obeyed. Neutrons have more mass than protons by 0.14%. Such small deviations are called charge symmetry breaking. They arise from two causes:

1. The change in electric force effects that accompanies the swap of a multiplet member with one electrical charge for another with a different charge. While the strong force between nucleons binds together the nucleus and dominates nuclear properties, the electrical force of repulsion between similar charges makes the force between two protons more repulsive than the force between two neutrons.

2. The heavier mass of the down quark compared to the up quark. Thus, the neutron (composed of two down quarks and one up quark) is heavier than the proton (two up quarks and one down quark).

By measuring the small deviations in nuclear properties and reactions that are a result of charge symmetry breaking, scientists hope to untangle these two causes and measure the size of the quark mass difference effect.

Consequences of charge symmetry breaking. The small mass difference between the neutron and the proton makes it possible for the neutron to decay into a proton, an electron, and an antineutrino while the proton is stable. Left by itself, the neutron will decay with a half-life of about 10 min. The neutron

can survive for a long time only if it is bound into a stable nucleus or is a part of a massive object such as a neutron star. In these situations, there is not enough available energy to create the decay products. *See* NEUTRON STAR.

The stability of the proton compared to the neutron led to the abundance of hydrogen (the atom made of a single proton and electron) after the universe was formed in the big bang. This makes possible the process of fusion that powers the Sun and stars. It leads to the formation of water and the many chemicals that are essential for life on Earth. *See* BIG BANG THEORY.

Effects that measure charge symmetry breaking. With the discovery of charmed particles in 1975, it was confirmed that protons and neutrons, as well as many other subatomic particles, were composed of a new kind of particles called quarks. Because quarks are permanently confined inside the nucleons and other particles, their masses cannot be directly measured. For this information, we must rely on experiments that are sensitive to some effect caused by the quark mass in combination with theoretical models that relate the mass to the effect. Measurements of charge symmetry breaking can provide information on the mass difference between the up and down quarks. *See* CHARM; QUARKS.

The mass difference between the neutron and the proton (1.2933317 ± 0.0000005 MeV/c^2, where c is the speed of light) is one such piece of information that is known to great precision. Another piece of information is the scattering length, a measure of the strength of the force between two nucleons when they collide at low speeds. After the effects of the electric force are subtracted using theory, the proton-proton length (-17.3 ± 0.4 femtometer, where the negative value indicates attraction) still differs from the neutron-neutron length (-18.8 ± 0.3 fm), an indication of charge symmetry breaking. The neutron-proton length of -23.77 ± 0.09 fm differs by an even larger amount due to the electric effects of charge independence breaking. If all three lengths had been the same, this property would have obeyed isospin symmetry. *See* SCATTERING EXPERIMENTS (NUCLEI).

At its longest ranges, the strong force that binds nucleons can be described by the exchange between nucleons of short-lived subatomic particles called mesons. Charge symmetry breaking may cause mesons that are otherwise similar but belong to different multiplets with different isospin values to mix. This allows, for example, a ρ meson (isospin = 1) to transform in flight into an ω meson (isospin = 0). Other mixings may occur (pion into η or η' meson) but have not yet been precisely measured.

The scattering of neutrons and protons from each other at speeds generated in accelerators depends on the orientation of their spin axes during the collision. A small difference of 0.6% in the scattering probability appears in the comparison of neutron versus proton spin effects, a difference attributed to charge symmetry breaking.

Effective field theories. The model connecting such experimental results with the underlying quark properties is chiral effective field theory. First developed by Steven Weinberg, this model tracks nucleons and pions within a framework that obeys the rules of quark interactions. This model points to experiments in which the pion scatters from nucleons as the best place to obtain information on the difference between the up and down quark masses. This has led to two observations of charge symmetry breaking in experiments that produce electrically neutral pions, both of which reported results in 2003. *See* QUANTUM FIELD THEORY.

Neutron-proton fusion with pion production. An experiment conducted by Allena Opper, Elie Korkmaz, and their colleagues measured the rates at which the fusion of a neutron and proton gave rise to a deuteron (the neutron-proton nuclear bound state) and a pion emerging at different angles. A difference in the rates at forward and backward angles, as shown in the **illustration**, is a signature of charge symmetry breaking. *See* DEUTERON.

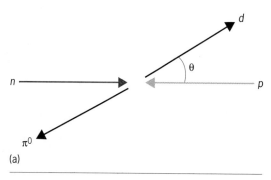

swap $n \leftrightarrow p$

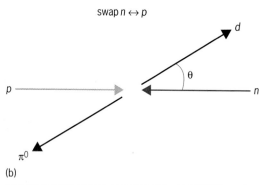

turn over

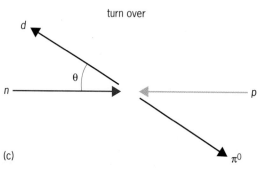

Views of the reaction that brings together a neutron and a proton to form a deuteron and an electrically neutral pion. (a) The neutron n and proton p come together from the left and right, creating a deuteron d and an uncharged pion π^0. The deuteron comes out at an angle θ. (b) The same process with the neutron and proton swapped. (c) The same process as b but turned around so that the neutron and proton again come from the left and right as in a. Then the deuteron emerges to the left instead of the right.

The illustration shows three views of the reaction. In illus. *a*, the neutron and proton enter from the left and right, producing a deuteron and pion that go out back-to-back; the scattering angle is θ. Charge symmetry requires the same reaction rate if the neutron and proton are swapped (illus. *b*). When this picture is turned around (illus. *c*) to place the proton and neutron as they were in illus. *a*, then θ is on the left instead of the right. So charge symmetry requires that just as many deuterons should go to the left as to the right at the same angle θ. Using a magnetic spectrometer located at the TRIUMF cyclotron laboratory in Vancouver, British Columbia, the experimental team was able to measure a small "fore-aft" asymmetry in this reaction rate equal to $0.17 \pm 0.10\%$, the amount of charge symmetry breaking in this process. *See* PARTICLE ACCELERATOR.

Deuteron-deuteron fusion with pion production. In this experiment, conducted by Edward Stephenson, Andrew Bacher, and their colleagues at the Indiana University Cyclotron Facility, an electron-cooled storage ring was used to bring two deuterons together to make a helium-4 (^{4}He) nucleus and a pion. In this case, swapping neutrons and protons in either the deuteron or ^{4}He nucleus changes nothing as these nuclei are self-conjugate (members of multiplets with only a single member and isospin equal to 0). But the pion is part of a multiplet having three members (π^+, π^0, and π^-) and an isospin value of 1. So this reaction is forbidden to occur to the extent that the amount of isospin before and after the reaction must remain the same. Using a very sensitive magnetic channel for ^{4}He and lead-glass Cerenkov detectors to see the light from the decay of the pion, the team was able to observe this reaction for the first time. The rate is very small; only 1 out of 10^{10} collisions between two deuterons resulted in the production of ^{4}He and a pion. *See* CERENKOV RADIATION.

Interpretation of results. The interpretation of these results is underway. In each case, all indirect mechanisms for breaking charge symmetry must be included along with the quark mass difference and electromagnetic effects. These include meson mixing, as described above. In addition, there may be states in either the deuteron or the ^{4}He nucleus that do not maintain a single value of isospin and would allow these symmetry-breaking effects to appear. The importance of such mechanisms is not well known, and will have to be determined self-consistently among all of the results of charge symmetry breaking. It is likely that such a determination will emerge and yield a better insight into the properties of the quarks inside the proton and neutron.

Edward J. Stephenson

Bibliography. A. G≤rdestig et al., Survey of charge symmetry breaking operators for $dd \rightarrow \alpha\pi^0$, *Phys. Rev. C*, 69:044606, 2004; G. A. Miller, B. M. K. Nefkens, and I. Šlaus, Charge symmetry, quarks and mesons, *Phys. Rep.*, 194:1–116, 1990; G. A. Miller and W. T. H. van Oers, Charge independence and charge symmetry, in W. C. Haxton and E. M. Henley (eds.), *Symmetries and Fundamental Interactions in Nuclei*, pp. 127–168, World Scientific, Singapore,

1995; A. K. Opper et al., Charge symmetry breaking in $np \rightarrow d\pi^0$, *Phys. Rev. Lett.*, 91:212302, 2003; E. J. Stephenson et al., Observation of the charge symmetry breaking $d + d \rightarrow {}^4\text{He} + \pi^0$ reaction near threshold, *Phys. Rev. Lett.*, 91:142302, 2003; U. van Kolck, J. A. Niskanen, and G. A. Miller, Charge symmetry violation in $pn \rightarrow d\pi^0$ and chiral effective field theory, *Phys. Lett. B*, 493:65–72, 2000.

Charged particle beams

Unidirectional streams of charged particles traveling at high velocities. Charged particles can be accelerated to high velocities by electromagnetic fields. They are then able to travel through matter (termed an absorber), interacting with it, losing energy, and causing various effects important in many applications. The velocities under consideration in this article exceed 100,000 m/s (about 60 mi/s or 200,000 mi/h), equivalent to an energy of 100 eV for a proton, and can approach the speed of light c (about 3×10^8 m/s or 6.7×10^8 mi/h). Examples of charged particles are electrons, positrons, protons, antiprotons, alpha particles, and any ions (atoms

with one or several electrons removed or added). In addition, some particles are produced artificially and may be short-lived (pions, muons).

Excluded from consideration are particles of, for example, cosmic dust (micrometeorites), which are clumps of thousands or millions of atoms. *See* COSMIC RAYS; ELECTRONVOLT; ELEMENTARY PARTICLE; PARTICLE ACCELERATOR.

Particle properties. Fast charged particles are described in terms of the following properties (values for some particles are given in **Table 1**):

Charge, z, in multiples of the electron charge $e = 1.6022 \times 10^{-19}$ coulomb. At small velocities the charge may be less than the charge of the nucleus because electrons may be present in some of the atomic shells.

Rest mass, M; usually the energy equivalent Mc^2 (in MeV) is given.

Rest mass, m, of electron; $mc^2 = 0.51104$ MeV.

Mass in atomic mass units, u; $A_m = Mc^2/931.481$ MeV.

Kinetic energy, T, in MeV.

Velocity, v, in cm/s or m/s.

$\beta = v/c$; $c = 299,792,458$ m/s = speed of light.

TABLE 1. Properties of charged particles*

Ion	z	Lifetime, ns	Mass 10^{-24} g	u	MeV
Electron[†]	−1	Stable	0.910956	0.548593	511.004
Muon	1	2198.3	0.188357	0.113432	105.6598
Pion	1	26.04	0.248823	0.149846	139.578
Kaon	1	12.35	0.880322	0.530147	493.82
Sigma[+]	1	0.081	2.120318	1.276895	1189.40
Sigma[−]	−1	0.164	2.134436	1.285398	1197.32
		Mass excess,[‡] MeV			
1N	0	8.0714	1.674920	1.0086652	939.553
1H	1	7.2890	1.672614	1.0072766	938.259
2H	1	13.1359	3.343569	2.0135536	1875.587
3H	1	14.9500	5.007334	3.0155011	2808.883
3He	2	14.9313	5.006390	3.0149325	2808.353
4He	2	2.4248	6.644626	4.0015059	3727.328
6Li	3	14.0884	9.985570	6.0134789	5601.443
7Li	3	14.9073	11.647561	7.0143581	6533.743
7Be	4	15.7689	11.648186	7.0147345	6534.093
9Be	4	11.3505	14.961372	9.0099911	8392.637
10B	5	12.0552	16.622243	10.0101958	9324.309
11B	5	8.6677	18.276741	11.0065623	10252.406
12C	6	0	19.920910	11.9967084	11174.708
13C	6	3.1246	21.587011	13.0000629	12109.314
14C	6	3.0198	23.247356	13.9999504	13040.691
14N	7	2.8637	23.246166	13.9992342	13040.024
15N	7	.1004	24.901771	14.9962676	13968.741
16O	8	−4.7365	26.552769	15.9905263	14894.875
17O	8	−.8077	28.220304	16.9947441	15830.285
18O	8	−.7824	29.880881	17.9947713	16761.791
19F	9	−1.4860	31.539247	18.9934674	17692.058
20Ne	10	−7.0415	33.188963	19.9869546	18617.472
21Ne	10	−5.7299	34.851833	20.9883627	19550.265
22Ne	10	−8.0249	36.508273	21.9858989	20479.451

*From *American Institute of Physics Handbook*, 3d ed., McGraw-Hill, 1972.
[†]Electron masses to be divided by 1000.
[‡]Mass excess given for neutral atoms; it is used to calculate nuclear reaction Q values.

For absorbers, the information needed is:

Atomic number, Z (number of protons in nucleus).
Average atomic weight, A (usually in g/mole, but numerically equal to mass in u).
Absorber thickness, x, in cm or g/cm^2.
Physical state (solid, liquid, gas, plasma).

See ATOMIC MASS UNIT; ENERGY; FUNDAMENTAL CONSTANTS; MASS.

Relation of velocity and energy. For small velocities ($\beta <$ 0.2), the approximation $T = \frac{1}{2} Mc^2\beta^2$ is accurate to 3%. The expressions $\beta^2 = \zeta(\zeta + 2)/(\zeta + 1)^2$, and $T = Mc^2[(1/\sqrt{1 - \beta^2}), - 1]$, with $\zeta = T/Mc^2$, are correct for all velocities. For $\zeta > 100$, the expression $\beta^2 = 1 - (1/\kappa^2)$, with $\kappa = \zeta + 1$, is more suitable to provide accurate values. *See* RELATIVISTIC MECHANICS.

Range. If a parallel beam of monoenergetic particles (that is, a beam in which all particles have exactly the same kinetic energy T) enters an absorber with a flat and smooth surface, it is found that all the particles (with the exception of electrons) travel along almost straight lines, slow down at approximately the same rate, and stop at approximately the same distance x from the surface (**Fig. 1**). The average distance traveled by the particles is called the mean range $R(T)$.

Energy loss and straggling. If the same beam travels through a thin absorber, it will emerge from it with a reduced average energy $\langle T_1 \rangle$ (**Table 2**). The difference between T and $\langle T_1 \rangle$ is called the average energy loss $\Delta = T - \langle T_1 \rangle$. Owing to the randomness of the number of collisions experienced by each particle, the range and the reduced energy fluctuate around the average values. This fluctuation is called straggling of energy loss or of range. (The shape of the

TABLE 2. Calculated reduced average energy at various depths in copper of protons with $T = 144$ MeV*

x/mm	T_1/MeV
1	141
5	127
10	107
15	85
20	57

*From *American Institute of Physics Handbook*, 3d ed., McGraw-Hill, 1972.

curve in Fig. 1 for $x > 22$ mm is determined by range straggling.)

Charge state. At high velocities, an ion usually has the full charge ze of the nucleus. As soon as v drops below the velocity $u_K \cong zc/137$ of the K shell electrons, electrons in the absorber will be attracted into K-shell orbits, thus reducing the total charge of the ion to a value $z^* = z - 1$ or $z - 2$. As the velocity drops further, more and more electrons will be attached to the ion; but since some of these electrons will be lost or gained as successive collisions take place, z^* must be considered as an average value which changes with v (**Fig. 2**). *See* ELECTRON CONFIGURATION.

Interactions. In traveling through matter, charged particles interact with nuclei, producing nuclear reactions and elastic and inelastic collisions with the electrons (electronic collisions) and with entire atoms of the absorber (atomic collisions). Usually, in its travel through matter a charged particle makes few or no nuclear reactions or inelastic nuclear collisions, but many electronic and atomic collisions. The average distance between successive collisions is called the mean free path, λ. In solids, it is of the order of 10 cm (4 in.) for nuclear reactions. It ranges from the diameter of the atoms (about 10^{-10} m) to about 10^{-7} m for electronic collisions. The mean free path, λ, depends on the properties of the particle and, most importantly, on its velocity.

Nuclear interactions. In nuclear reactions [for example, $Be(d,n)B$] the incident particle is removed from the beam. Therefore, a reduction in the fluence (number of particles in the beam per cm^2) will be observed. [The decrease in the number of particles in Fig. 1 for x less than about 22 mm (0.88 in.) is due to nuclear interactions.] Such an attenuation can be described by Eq. (1), where $e = 2.71828 \ldots$, $N_0 =$

$$\frac{N}{N_0} = e^{-x\Sigma} = e^{-x/\lambda} \tag{1}$$

initial particle fluence at $x = 0$, $N =$ particle fluence at x, and $\Sigma =$ probability for an interaction to take place per centimeter of absorber. The mean free path is $\lambda = 1/\sigma$; Σ is equal to $n\sigma$, where $\sigma =$ cross section per atom for nuclear reactions in square centimeters, and $n =$ number of atoms per cubic centimeter of absorber material. *See* ATTENUATION; E (MATHEMATICS); NUCLEAR CHEMISTRY; NUCLEAR REACTION; SCATTERING EXPERIMENTS (NUCLEI).

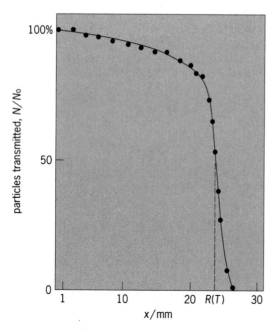

Fig. 1. Transmission curve for protons with kinetic energy $T = 144$ MeV through copper. (*After L. Koschmieder, Zur Energiebestimmung von Protonen aus Reichweitemessungen, Z. Naturforsch., 19a:1414–1416, 1964*)

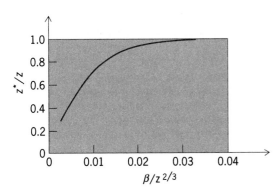

Fig. 2. Average charge z* of a particle of velocity v = βc. (After American Institute of Physics Handbook, 2d ed., McGraw-Hill, 1963)

A rough estimate of the cross section for particles with $T/A_m > 10$ MeV can be obtained from Eq. (2).

$$\sigma = 5 \times 10^{-26} \text{ cm}^2 \, (A_m^{1/3} + A^{1/3})^2 \quad (2)$$

For thin absorbers, $N/N_0 \cong 1 - x/\lambda + \cdots$.

An important nuclear interaction is Coulomb (or Rutherford) scattering: because both the incident particles and the nuclei of the absorber atoms have electric charge with values ze and Ze, respectively, a change in the direction of motion of the particles will take place during the passage of the particles near the nuclei. The total cross section for this process is only slightly less than the cross-sectional area of the total atom. Usually, though, the angular deflection is much less than 0.01°, and only multiple scattering, the compounding of collisions with many atoms, will cause noticeable total deflections. If an observation of a very fine beam of particles were made along the direction of motion, the scattering events would be seen as small lateral displacements in random directions, and the final lateral displacement would be their vector sum. Although very few particles experience no deflection, the most probable location of the particles is still on the original line of the beam.

Bremsstrahlung. If a charged particle is accelerated, it can emit photons called bremsstrahlung. This process is of great importance for electrons as well as for heavy ions with $T \gg Mc^2$. It is used extensively for the production of x-rays in radiology. Electrons circulating in storage rings emit large numbers of photons with energies (100–1000 eV) not readily available from other sources. *See* ACCELERATION; BREMSSTRAHLUNG; SYNCHROTRON RADIATION.

Atomic collisions. At low velocities it may be convenient to consider separately collisions in which most of the energy loss is given as kinetic energy to a target atom. Usually, electronic excitation, electron rearrangements, and possibly ionization accompany this process. The term nuclear collision is used by some scientists. No simple quantitative description of atomic collisions is available. *See* SCATTERING EXPERIMENTS (ATOMS AND MOLECULES).

Electronic collisions. The interaction and energy transfer (**Fig. 3**) between the charged particle and the electrons are caused by the Coulomb force. In gen-

eral, except in tenuous plasmas, electrons are bound. In gases, all electrons are bound to individual atoms or molecules in well-defined orbits. For these isolated molecules (henceforth, atoms will be included with molecules), electrons can be moved into other bound orbits (excitation) requiring a well-defined energy ϵ_2. Another possibility is the complete removal of the electron from the atom (ionization), requiring an energy $\epsilon \geq I$, where I is the ionization energy for the particular electron. The secondary electron, which is called a delta electron, will have kinetic energy $K = \epsilon - I$. In both processes, the charged particle will lose energy; the energy loss is ϵ_e or ϵ, respectively. Also, it will be deflected very slightly. However, the change in direction is so small that it does not show in Fig. 3; the larger deflection caused by Rutherford scattering at point *a* is visible. *See* ATOMIC STRUCTURE AND SPECTRA; DELTA ELECTRONS; EXCITED STATE.

In liquids and solids, only the inner electrons are associated with a specific nucleus (in aluminum metal the K- and L-shell electrons). Excitation and ionization processes for these electrons are very similar to those in free molecules. The outer electrons are either associated with several neighboring nuclei (nonconducting materials) or, in metals (in Al, the three M-shell electrons), form a plasmalike cloud. Collective or plasma excitations ($\epsilon \cong 20$ eV) take place with high probability, but direct ionization ($\epsilon \gg 20$ eV) also occurs. Because of the requirements of momentum conservation, the maximum energy loss which can occur is given by $\epsilon_M \simeq 2mv^2 = 2mc^2\beta^2$ for particles heavier than electrons. *See* SOLID-STATE CHEMISTRY.

The probability for energy losses ϵ by the incident particle is described by the energy loss spectrum $w(\epsilon)$. Theoretical values have been calculated by H. Bethe. An energy loss spectrum for heavy charged particles in adenine ($C_5N_5H_5$) is shown in **Fig. 4**. The structure between 3 and 30 eV relates to the outer electrons. Similar structures have been observed for many solids (including metals). Excitation and ionization of the K-shell of C (above 280 eV) and N (above 400 eV) cause further structure. The average energy

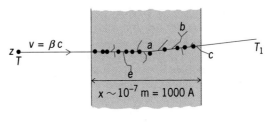

Fig. 3. Energy loss by heavy charged particle. No details shown for energy losses of secondary electrons (delta electrons). Rutherford scattering at point a. At point b, delta electron experiences collision that results in tertiary delta electron. At c, delta electron escapes from absorber.

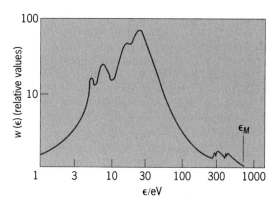

Fig. 4. Schematic single-collision spectrum $w(\epsilon)$ for heavy charged particles in adenine ($C_5N_5H_5$).

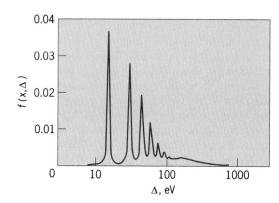

Fig. 5. Calculated straggling curve $f(x, \Delta)$ for 20-MeV protons incident on Al absorber of thickness 5.8×10^{-8} m. Spikes represent multiples of the "plasma loss" at 15 eV. (*After H. Bichsel and R. Saxon, Comparison of calculational methods for straggling in thin absorbers, Phys. Rev., A11:1286–1296, 1975*)

loss per collision is defined by Eq. (3).

$$\langle \epsilon \rangle = \int \epsilon w(\epsilon)\, d\epsilon \bigg/ \int w(\epsilon)\, d\epsilon \qquad (3)$$

Statistics of energy loss. The total energy loss δ of a particle traveling through matter is the sum of the energy losses ϵ_i in each collision: $\delta = \Sigma \epsilon_i = \epsilon_1 + \epsilon_2 + \epsilon_3 + \epsilon_4 + \cdots \epsilon_v$, where v collisions have occurred, each with a probability given by $w(\epsilon)$ [Fig. 4]. If a large number of particles are observed, they will experience on the average $q = \langle v \rangle$ collisions (q is not an integer), and an average energy loss $\Delta = \langle \delta \rangle = q\langle \epsilon \rangle$, as long as collisions are uncorrelated with another. The number of collisions is distributed according to a Poisson distribution; the fraction $P(v)$ of particles having experienced exactly v collisions is given by Eq. (4). The distribution func-

$$P(v) = \frac{q^v}{v!}e^{-q} \qquad (4)$$

tion for energy losses is called a straggling function $f(\Delta,x)$. Examples are given in **Figs. 5** and **6**. For fairly thick absorbers, $f(\Delta,x)$ is approximately a gaussian distribution of width proportional to $\sqrt{x}$. See DISTRIBUTION (PROBABILITY).

In many applications, the details of energy loss are not important, and a knowledge of the mean or average energy loss Δ is sufficient. If the total collision cross section per atom $w_t = \int w(\epsilon)d\epsilon$ is known (w_t in cm^2), the mean number of collisions is given by $q = xnw_t$, and the mean energy loss by Eq. (5). The quantity stopping power S thus is defined by Eq. (6),

$$\Delta = xn\langle \epsilon \rangle w_t \equiv xS \qquad (5)$$

$$S \equiv n\langle \epsilon \rangle w_t \qquad (6)$$

in MeV/cm. Since knowledge of w_t and $\langle \epsilon \rangle$ is not extensive, S is frequently determined in experimental measurements in which a beam passes through an absorber, and S is calculated from Eq. (7).

$$S = \lim_{x \to 0} \frac{\Delta}{x} = \lim_{x \to 0} \frac{T - \langle T_1 \rangle}{x} \qquad (7)$$

Equation (5) is valid only if x is much smaller than the mean range, $R(T)$; otherwise, S varies significantly as the particle loses energy in the absorber. If x is not small, the following procedure can be used to obtain $\langle T_1 \rangle$, provided that $R(T)$ has been tabulated: Find $R(T)$ in the range table, calculate $y = R(T) - x$, and then find the energy T_1 corresponding to y in the range table.

Stopping power. The stopping power is a function of the velocity v of the incident particle, its effective charge z^*, and the absorber material. **Figure 7** shows $S(T)$ for heavy ions of various elements in aluminum. S is expressed in MeV cm^2/g. This can be converted to MeV/cm by the formula $S(\text{MeV/cm}) = \rho S(\text{MeV cm}^2/\text{g})$, where ρ is the density of absorber material in g/cm^3. Atomic collisions dominate in region I. For region III, S can be calculated by using the theoretical Bethe expression, Eq. (8), where

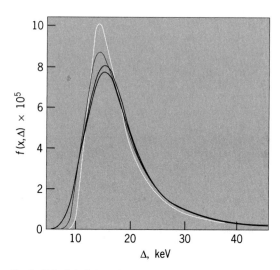

Fig. 6. Calculated straggling curve $f(x, \Delta)$ for 20-MeV protons incident on Al absorber of thickness 3.71×10^{-6} m. Various theoretical calculations are presented. (*After H. Bichsel and R. Saxon, Comparison of calculational methods for straggling in thin absorbers, Phys. Rev., A11:1286–1296, 1975*)

I_A = average excitation energy of absorber (approx-

$$S = \frac{0.30708}{\beta^2} \frac{Z}{A} \left[\ln \frac{2mc^2\beta^2}{I_A(1-\beta^2)} - \beta^2 - \frac{C}{\beta^2} - d(\beta) \right]$$

$$\cdot (z^*)^2 [1 + G(z^*, \beta)] \text{ MeV cm}^2/\text{g} \quad (8)$$

imately $Z \times 10^{-5}$ MeV); C = shell correction constant; $d(\beta)$ = density correction, important for $T > Mc^2$; and $G(z^*, \beta)$ = correction due to the second Born approximation, important only for $\beta^2 < 0.01$. *See* PERTURBATION (QUANTUM MECHANICS).

A simpler approximate expression valid to about 10% for $z \leq 10$ in the same region is given by Eq. (9).

$$S = \frac{2.6z^2}{\beta^{1.66}Z^{.25}} \text{ MeV cm}^2/\text{g} \quad (9)$$

$$0.1 < \beta < 0.88$$

Range. A good approximation to the mean range $R(T)$ can be calculated from S using Eq. (10).

$$R(T) = \int_0^T \frac{d\tau}{S(\tau)} \quad (10)$$

Usually, a numerical integration is performed to obtain R from a table of S or the Bethe formula. An approximation formula is Eq. (11). The range of validity

$$R = r \cdot \beta^s \cdot \frac{Z^{.25}}{z^2} \quad (11)$$

$$z \leq 10$$

for this range formula is given in **Table 3**.

Channeling. In absorbers consisting of a single crystal, it has been found that the energy loss will be reduced if the direction of the particle beam coincides with certain preferred alignments of the crystal. It is believed that the particles travel through "open spaces" in the crystal, thus suffering a succession of collisions with relatively small energy losses and angular deflections, and tending to stay in the preferred direction (channel). Thus, even if the total number of collisions q were unchanged, the average energy loss per collision (ϵ) would be reduced, and the total energy loss Δ would be less. *See* CHANNELING IN SOLIDS.

Ionization. The secondary electrons of energies K produced in ionizing electronic collisions will travel through the absorber and will also suffer various collisions, producing further energetic electrons, and so on. This process continues until the electrons have energy $K < I$. It has been found experimentally that the total average number j of ions produced in this

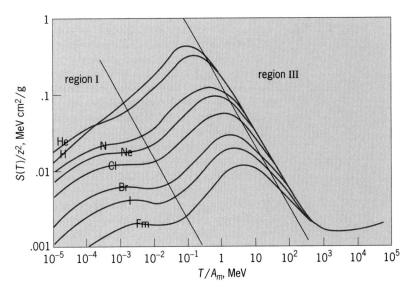

Fig. 7. $S(T)$ for heavy ions in Al. (*After L. C. Northcliffe and R. F. Schilling, Range and stopping power tables for heavy ions, Nucl. Data Tables, A7:233, 1970*)

way (in the distance x) is proportional to the energy Δ lost by the particle: $j = \Delta/\omega$.

The constant of proportionality ω introduced in this definition has values between 20 and 45 eV for gases, about 3.6 eV for silicon, and 2.96 eV for germanium. It is almost, but not exactly, independent of particle energy and type. If particles lose all their energy in the material, the total ionization J is related to the kinetic energy T: $J = T/W$. The relation between W and ω is $T/W = \int dT/\omega$. $W = \omega$ only if ω is exactly independent of energy.

The ionization j along the path of a single particle increases with the distance traveled, approximately at the same rate as S. For a beam of particles, straggling also influences the total ionization at a given location. The function obtained from the combination (actually the convolution) of both effects is the Bragg curve.

Electrons. Although the interactions discussed earlier all occur for electrons, there are some major differences between electron beams and beams of heavier particles. In general, the path of an electron will be a zigzag. Angular deflections in the collisions will frequently be large. Electron beams therefore tend to spread out laterally, and the number of primary electrons in the beam at a depth x in the absorber decreases rapidly.

Since it is not possible to distinguish individual electrons, it is customary in a collision between two electrons to consider the one emerging with the higher energy as the primary electron. The maximum energy loss in a collision therefore is $mv^2/\sqrt{4}$ (for $T \ll mc^2$). The stopping power expression therefore is somewhat different for electrons. *See* BETA PARTICLES.

Biological effects. In general, for the same dose (the energy deposited per gram along the beam line) heavy charged particles will produce, because of their higher local ionization, larger biological effects than electrons (which frequently are produced by

TABLE 3. Range of validity of range formula			
Range of kinetic energy T, MeV	Range of β	r, g/cm²	s
$10 \leq T < 90$	$0.145 < \beta < 0.4$	0.116	1.84
$90 < T < 400$	$0.4 < \beta < 0.7$	0.275	2.33
$400 < T < 1000$	$0.7 < \beta < 0.88$	0.532	3.34

x-rays). *See* NUCLEAR RADIATION (BIOLOGY); RADIATION BIOLOGY; RADIATION INJURY (BIOLOGY).

Observation. The most direct method of observing a beam of charged particles is to observe the electric current that they form (any flow of electric charges is an electric current). In all accelerators (such as cyclotrons, Van de Graaff generators, linear accelerators, and x-ray tubes) the beam current is measured as a primary monitor of the proper operation of the machine. It is not possible to identify the type of particles with current measurements (except for their electric charge). *See* PARTICLE DETECTOR.

Devices using ionization. If an electric field E is applied to an absorber irradiated with charged particles, the ions and electrons produced will travel in the direction $\mathbf{E}$, and the resulting ionization current can be measured (electronic amplification usually is needed). If an oscilloscope is available, the ionization J associated with a single particle can be observed, and the energy (or energy loss) of the particle can be calculated from $T = JW$. Semiconductor detectors (chiefly silicon and germanium) are used extensively for this purpose, but gas-filled ionization chambers have also been used. Cloud chambers and bubble chambers use this principle, but individual ions or clumps of ionization are observed visually. Proportional counters, spark chambers, and Geiger-Müller tubes also operate on the same principle; but in the latter two only the presence of a particle is indicated, and J is not related to T. *See* ELECTRIC FIELD; GEIGER-MÜLLER COUNTER; IONIZATION CHAMBER.

Devices using excitation. The excited state of energy ϵ_e produced in excitation can decay with the emission of light (luminescence or scintillation). Early observations of radioactivity were made with this method (using ZnS screens and visual observation, usually with microscopes), and the method is used extensively with luminescent dials (for example, on wristwatches). The light emitted usually is detected and amplified with photomultipliers. Again, the energy T can be measured. Scintillators used are NaI(Tl), CsI, anthracene, stilbene, and various solids and liquids. *See* LUMINESCENCE; PHOTOMULTIPLIER; SCINTILLATION COUNTER.

A more indirect use of excitations and ionizations is in "chemical" devices (such as photographic emulsions, $FeSO_4$ solutions, and thermoluminescence). *See* PHOTOGRAPHIC MATERIALS; THERMOLUMINESCENCE.

Applications. Electron beams are used in the preservation of food. In medicine, electron beams are used extensively to produce x-rays for both diagnostic and therapeutic (cancer irradiation) purposes. Also, in radiation therapy, deuteron beams incident on Be and ^{3}H targets are used to produce beams of fast neutrons, which in turn produce fast protons, alpha particles, and carbon, nitrogen, and oxygen ions in the irradiated tissue. Energetic pion (about 100 MeV), proton (about 200 MeV), alpha (about 1000 MeV), and heavier ion beams can possibly be used for cancer therapy. The existence of a Bragg peak for these particles promises improvements

in the dose distribution within the human body. *See* RADIOLOGY.

The well-defined range of heavy ions permits their implantation at given depths in solids (this is useful in the production of integrated circuits). Radiation damage studies are performed with charged particles in relation to development work for nuclear fission and fusion reactors. *See* ION IMPLANTATION; RADIATION DAMAGE TO MATERIALS.

Charged particle beams are used in many methods of chemical and solid-state analysis. Nuclear activation analysis can be performed with heavy ions. *See* ACTIVATION ANALYSIS; ELECTRON DIFFRACTION; ELECTRON SPECTROSCOPY; SECONDARY ION MASS SPECTROMETRY (SIMS).

Isotopes can be produced with fast charged ions. *See* BOHRIUM; DUBNIUM; HASSIUM; LAWRENCIUM; MEITNERIUM; MENDELEVIUM; NOBELIUM; NUCLEAR CHEMISTRY; RADIOISOTOPE; RUTHERFORDIUM; SEABORGIUM; TRANSURANIUM ELEMENTS.

Hans Bichsel

Radioactive secondary beams. Beams of nuclei with lifetimes as short as 10^{-6} s are used for studies in nuclear physics, astrophysics, biology, and materials science. Nuclear beams (or heavy-ion beams) are usually produced by accelerating naturally available stable isotopes. However, radioactive nuclei, most of which do not occur naturally on Earth, must be produced as required in nuclear reactions by using various accelerated beams. Because these radioactive nuclei are produced by the nuclear reactions of primary beams, they are called secondary particles and beams of such nuclei are called radioactive secondary beams. *See* RADIOACTIVITY.

Two methods can be used to produce radioactive beams; the methods differ in the way in which the ions of radioactive nuclei are extracted. The so-called isotope separator on line (ISOL) is used to select product nuclei. In this method, nuclei are extracted from a production target by thermal diffusion and then ionized and accelerated to a low energy (approximately 50 keV). The extracted ions are then selected in an isotope separator that consists of magnetic and electrostatic elements; the selected beam is then accelerated to the desired energy. The second method does not use an ion source but rather collects directly the recoil products from the production of nuclear reaction. A recoil mass separator is used to select the desired product. In many cases, these recoil products can be used directly in experiments. *See* ION SOURCES; MASS SPECTROSCOPE.

The recoil separator method has several advantages when applied to the separation of nuclei produced in heavy–ion induced reactions. In such reactions, the velocity of the center-of-mass system is large and product nuclei are emitted in a small-angle forward cone. In particular, nuclei that are produced by projectile fragmentation are emitted in the direction of the primary beam with almost the beam velocity.

For production and separation of radioactive nuclei, a heavy projectile of energy higher than a few hundred megaelectronvolts per nucleon results in high collection efficiency. For an experiment that requires good momentum resolution, the separated, secondary beam may be injected into a storage-cooler ring in which the radioactive nuclei are cooled to have a relative momentum broadening less than 10^{-3}. Such a cooler ring can also be used to decelerate or to accelerate the radioactive beam for experiments at various energies.

Radioactive secondary beams have made possible the study of the structure of nuclei far from stability. As an example, the sizes of neutron dripline nuclei such as lithium-11 (^{11}Li) and beryllium-14 (^{14}Be) were determined only after beams of these nuclei become available. Furthermore, the internal motion of nucleons inside a radioactive nucleus can be studied in reactions involving the radioactive nucleus as a projectile. Another important application occurs in the study of nuclear reactions of importance in hot stars and in supernovae. Such reactions, involving radioactive nuclei, are crucial for understanding nucleosynthesis in the universe. *See* EXOTIC NUCLEI; NUCLEAR STRUCTURE; NUCLEOSYNTHESIS.   Isao Tanihata

Bibliography. *American Institute of Physics Handbook*, 3d ed., 1972; F. H. Attix, *Introduction to Radiological Physics and Radiation Dosimetry*, 1986; R. D. Evans, *The Atomic Nucleus*, 1955, reprint 1982; K. R. Kase et al. (eds.), *The Dosimetry of Ionizing Radiation*, 3 vols., 1985, 1987, 1990; G. F. Knoll, *Radiation Detection and Measurement*, 3d ed., 1999.

Charged particle optics

The branch of physics concerned with the motion of charged particles under the influence of electric and magnetic fields.

Acceleration of charged particles. A positively charged particle that moves in an electric field experiences a force in the direction of this field. If the particle falls in the field from a potential of U volts to a potential zero, its energy gain, measured in electronvolts, is equal to the product of U and the particle's charge. For example, if a singly and a doubly charged particle are accelerated by a potential drop of 100 V, the two particles will gain energies of 100 eV and 200 eV, respectively. If both particles were initially at rest, they would have final velocities proportional to the square root of K/m, where K is the energy increase and m is the mass of the particle. This relation describes the velocities of energetic particles accurately as long as these velocities are small compared to the velocity of light $c \approx 300,000$ km/s (186,000 mi/s), a speed that cannot be exceeded by any particle. *See* ELECTRIC FIELD; ELECTROSTATICS.

If an ensemble of ions of equal energies but of different masses is accelerated simultaneously, the ion masses can be determined from their arrival times after a certain flight distance. Such time-of-flight mass spectrometers have successfully been used, for instance, to investigate the masses of large molecular ions, up to and beyond 350,000 atomic mass units. *See* TIME-OF-FLIGHT SPECTROMETERS.

Deflection of charged particles. If a homogeneous electric field is established between two parallel-plate electrodes at different potentials, a charged particle in the space between the electrodes will experience a force in the direction perpendicular to them. If initially the particle moved parallel to the electrodes, it will be deflected by the electric force and move along a parabolic trajectory. Magnetic fields also deflect charged particles. In contrast to electrostatic fields, however, magnetic fields change only the direction of a particle trajectory and not the magnitude of the particle velocity. A charged particle that moves perpendicular to the field lines of a homogeneous magnetic field moves through a circular path (**Fig. 1**) whose radius is determined from the balance between the centrifugal force along this circle and the magnetic force.

Charged particles that enter a magnetic field thus move along circles whose radii increase with the products of their velocities and their mass-to-charge ratios, m/q. If initially all particles start at the same potential U and are accelerated to the potential zero, they will move along radii that are proportional to the square root of $U(m/q)$. Thus, particles of different mass-to-charge ratios can be separated in a magnetic sector field (Fig. 1).

In the plane of deflection, charged particles that diverge from a point in some source are focused back to a point of the image (Fig. 1). In the perpendicular direction, however, the particles remain divergent. A straight line that connects the source and the image also passes through the center of curvature of the trajectory of the reference particle. The images of particles of different mass-to-charge ratios all lie in a plane that is usually inclined with respect to the particle beam.

A sector-field mass analyzer can be used to determine the masses of atomic or molecular ions in a cloud of such ions. Such systems can also be used to purify a beam of ions that are to be implanted in semiconductors in order to fabricate high-performance

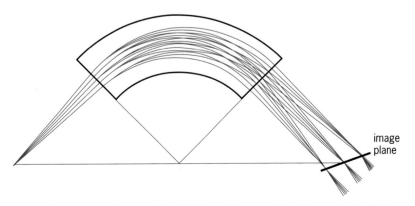

Fig. 1. Sector magnet that separates charged particles according to the products of their velocities and their mass-to-charge ratios. The straight line that connects the particle source and the image of the middle ion bundle also passes through the center of curvature of the corresponding central trajectory.

image plane

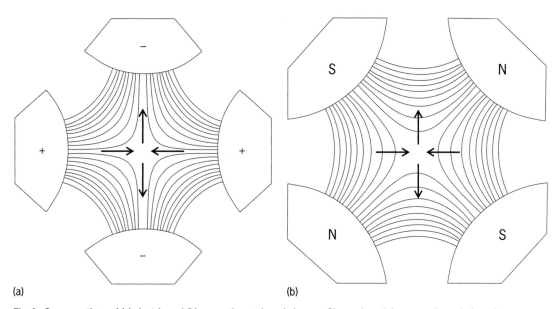

(a)   (b)

Fig. 2. Cross sections of *(a)* electric and *(b)* magnetic quadrupole lenses. Charged particles move through these lenses perpendicular to plane of drawing. Electric and magnetic field lines are shown. Arrows indicate directions of forces that drive charged particles toward or away from the optic axis. In both lenses, focusing occurs in the horizontal direction, while there is defocusing in the vertical direction.

transistors and diodes. Finally, such magnetic sector fields are found in large numbers in all types of particle accelerators. *See* ION IMPLANTATION; MASS SPECTROSCOPE.

Axially symmetric lenses. An Einzel lens consists of three cylindrical tubes, the middle one of which is at a higher potential than the outer two. Positively charged particles entering such a device are first decelerated and then accelerated back to their initial energies. Since the decelerations and accelerations are perpendicular to the eqipotential surfaces, the particles experience forces that drive them toward the optic axis in some regions and away from it in others. However, the focusing actions are always stronger than the defocusing actions since they occur in regions in which the particles are moving more slowly, that is, in the center regions. Defocusing lenses cannot be built in this fashion unless potential-defining metal grids distort the equipotential surfaces. This statement also holds for axially symmetric lenses in which the potential on the center electrode has been chosen such that the charged particles are not decelerated but accelerated while passing through the lens. *See* ELECTROSTATIC LENS.

Axially symmetric magnetic lenses have also been constructed. Such lenses, also called solenoids, consist mainly of a coil of wire through which an electric current is passed. The charged particles are then constrained to move more or less parallel to the axis of such a coil. Steel tubes with rotationally symmetric geometries can be used to surround the coil to increase the magnetic field strength. *See* MAGNETIC LENS; SOLENOID (ELECTRICITY).

Axially symmetric electric and magnetic lenses are used extensively to focus low-energy particle beams. Particularly important applications are in television tubes and in electron microscopes.

See CATHODE-RAY TUBE; ELECTRON MICROSCOPE; PICTURE TUBE.

Quadrupole lenses. By passing charged particles through electrode or pole-face arrangements (**Fig. 2**), a particle beam can also be focused toward the optic axis. In such quadrupole lenses the electric or the magnetic field strengths, and therefore the forces that drive the charged particles toward or away from the optic axis, increase linearly with the distance from the axis. This is the main property of the lens. In quadrupoles the focusing occurs in one direction only, while there is a defocusing action in the perpendicular direction. Focusing in both directions thus requires a combination of at least two quadrupole lenses. In quadrupole lenses the particle trajectories are bent toward the optic axis by the main field, while in axially symmetric lenses such a focusing action is achieved by the much weaker fringing fields. Quadrupole lens systems thus have much stronger focusing abilities than other types of lenses, and smaller field strengths can be used to focus more rigid particle beams.

While quadrupole lenses are found in systems in which low-energy particle beams must be focused, for instance, in mass spectrometers, such lenses have become indispensable for high-energy beams. Consequently, quadrupole lenses, especially magnetic ones, are found in many types of particle accelerators used in research in, for example, nuclear and solid-state physics, as well as in cancer irradiation treatment facilities. *See* CHARGED PARTICLE BEAMS; ELECTRON LENS; ELECTRON MOTION IN VACUUM; PARTICLE ACCELERATOR.   Hermann Wollnik

Bibliography. D. A. Dewolf, *Basics of Electron Optics*, 1990; P. W. Hawkes and E. Kasper, *Principles of Electron Optics*, vols. 1 and 2, 1989, vol. 3, 1994; H. Wollnik, *Optics of Charged Particles*, 1987.

Charles' law

A thermodynamic law, also known as Gay-Lussac's law, which states that at constant pressure the volume of a fixed mass or quantity of gas varies directly with the absolute temperature. Conversely, at constant volume the gas pressure varies directly with the absolute temperature. J. A. Charles and J. L. Gay-Lussac independently discovered the relation for an ideal gas. The relation is a useful and close approximation. *See* GAS; KINETIC THEORY OF MATTER.   Frank H. Rockett

Charm

A term used in elementary particle physics to describe a class of elementary particles.

Theory. Ordinary atoms of matter consist of a nucleus composed of neutrons and protons and surrounded by electrons. Over the years, however, a host of other particles with unexpected properties have been found, associated with both electrons (leptons) and protons (hadrons).

Leptons. The electron has as companions the mu meson (μ) and the tau meson (τ), approximately 200 times and 3700 times as heavy as the electron, respectively. These particles are similar to the electron in all respects except mass. In addition, there exist at least two distinctive neutrinos, one associated with the electron, v_e, and another with the mu meson, v_μ. In all, there are five or six fundamental, distinct, structureless leptons. *See* LEPTON.

Hadrons. A similar but more complex situation exists with respect to the hadrons. These particles number in the hundreds, and unlike the leptons they cannot be thought of as fundamental. In fact, they can all be explained as composites of more fundamental constitutents, called quarks. It is the quarks which now seem as fundamental as the leptons, and the number of quark types has also increased as new and unexpected particles have been experimentally uncovered. The originally simple situation of having an up quark (u; charge $+2/3$) and a down quark (d; charge $-1/3$) has evolved as several more varieties or flavors have had to be added. These are the strange quark (s; charge $-1/3$), with the additional property or quantum number of strangeness ($S = -1$), to account for the unexpected characteristics of a family of strange particles; the charm quark (c; charge $+2/3$), possessing charm ($C = +1$) and no strangeness, to explain the discovery of the J/ψ particles, massive states three times heavier than the proton; and a fifth quark (b; charge $-1/3$) to explain the existence of the even more massive upsilon (Υ) particles. *See* HADRON; *J*/PSI PARTICLE; QUARKS.

The quarks and leptons discovered so far appear to form a symmetric array (see **table**). Both the leptons and quarks come in pairs, although the anticipated partner (t) of the b quark has not yet been found.

Observations. The members of the family of particles associated with charm fall into two classes:

Fundamental constituents of matter		
Family of particles	Charge	Particles
Leptons	0	v_e, v_μ, v_τ
	−1	e, μ, τ
Quarks	+²⁄₃	u, c, (t)*
	−¹⁄₃	d, s, b

those with hidden charm, where the states are a combination of charm and anticharm quarks ($c\bar{c}$), charmonium; and those where the charm property is clearly evident, such as the D^+ ($c\bar{d}$) meson and Λ_c^+ (cud) baryon.

Charmonium. In the charmonium family, six or seven states with various masses and decay modes have been identified. Although a detailed understanding of all these experimentally measured properties has not yet been achieved, everything seems to be in qualitative agreement with theoretical expectations.

Bare charm states. There are several identified bare charm states, including the D ($c\bar{d}$) mesons in both the $J^P = 0^-$ and $J^P = 1^+$ categories (where J is spin, and P is parity), and the Σ_c^{2+} (cuu) and Λ_c^+ (cud) charmed baryons. Information about the lifetimes of these states has been derived from experiments utilizing the high resolution of emulsions to measure the finite distance traveled by charmed particles. The lifetimes of the Λ_c^+ and D^0 have been determined to be on the order of 10^{-13} s with that of the D^+ about a factor of 7 longer. These values are in good agreement with theoretical expectations.

The Λ_c^+ charmed baryon has been observed to be produced in a variety of interactions, including neutrino-proton, proton-proton, electron-positron, and neutrino-neon reactions. A large number of decay modes have been observed, including Kp, $Kp\pi$, $\Lambda\pi$, $\Lambda\pi\pi$, and $Kp\pi\pi$.

Prospects. Although reasonable progress has been made in the study of charmed states, only a handful of states has been observed. Just as the basic SU(3) symmetry arose from a study of the numerous hadron strange and nonstrange resonances, the complete understanding of charm awaits the uncovering of additional states. *See* ELEMENTARY PARTICLE.

Nicholas P. Samios

Bibliography. H. Fritzsch, *Elementary Particles: Building Blocks of Matter*, 2005; I. S. Hughes, *Elementary Particles*, 3d ed., 1991; G. Kane, *Modern Elementary Particle Physics*, 2d ed., 1993; R. F. Schwitters, Fundamental particles with charm, *Sci. Amer.*, 237(4):56–70, 1977; M. Ye and T. Huang, *Charm Physics*, 1988.

Charophyceae

A group of branched, filamentous green algae, commonly known as the stoneworts, brittleworts, or muskgrasses, that occur mostly in fresh- or brackish-water habitats. They are important as significant components of the aquatic flora in some locales, providing food for waterfowl and protection for fish and other aquatic fauna; as excellent model systems for cell biological research; and as a unique group of green algae thought to be more closely related to the land plants.

Morphology. Charophytes are multicellular, branched, macroscopic filaments from a few inches to several feet in length. Colorless rhizoidal filaments anchor the plants to lake bottoms and other substrates. The main filaments are organized into short nodes forming whorls of branches, and much longer (up to 6 in. or 15 cm) internodal cells. The general morphology varies with environmental conditions such as depth of the water, light levels, and amount of wave action. Reproductive structures occur at the nodes and consist of egg cell–containing structures, the nucules, and sperm cell–containing structures called globules. The biflagellated sperm cells are produced in antheridial filaments within the globules. In many charophytes, calicium carbonate (lime) is secreted on the cell walls, hence the name stoneworts or brittleworts. In some charophytes, the simple structure of nodal and intermodal cells is complicated by corticating elements that cover the cells of the main axis.

Taxonomy and phylogeny. Based on the morphology of the vegetative filaments and the reproductive structures, six extant genera are recognized: *Chara, Nitella, Tolypella, Nitellopsis, Lamprothamnium,* and *Lychnothamnus.* At the species level there is significant disagreement with regard to the importance and interpretation of morphological features, life cycles, and biogeography, especially for *Chara.* Hence, there is no agreement on how many valid species exist, but the maximum number of living species is probably fewer than 100. Among the special features that support the suggestion that the charophytes are closely related to the land plants are the morphologically complicated reproductive structures, the ultrastructure of the sperm cells, and the type of cell division. Some of these features have led some scientists to include other genera of green algae in this group known as the Charophyceae. Deoxyribonucleic acid (DNA) sequencing indicates that the charophytes are a distinct natural group that should be recognized at some taxonomic level (for example, as an order, Charales, or as a class, Charophyceae).

Life history. The charophytes are haploid organisms. The fusion of the sperm and egg cell produces a diploid resistant zygote which, after dormancy, undergoes meiosis to produce a new haploid generation. Thus, there is no alternation of generations. Asexual zoospores are not produced, but plants can reproduce vegetatively as the rhizoidal filaments spread and develop new plants. *See* REPRODUCTION (PLANT).

Fossils. Because the fertilized egg cells produce resistant, calcified zygotes, fossils (known as gyrogonites) provide a record of these organisms extending back to the Devonian Period (approximately 360–408 million years ago). Many genera that once existed are now extinct. *See* ALGAE; CHLOROPHYCOTA; PALEOBOTANY.   Russell L. Chapman

Bibliography. H. C. Bold and M. J. Wynne, *Introduction to the Algae: Structure and Reproduction,* 2d ed., 1985; A. Sze, *A Biology of the Algae,* 3d ed., 1997.